TIME
ALMANAC
2008

POWERED BY

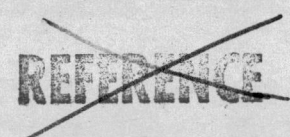

ENCYCLOPÆDIA
Britannica

www.britannica.com

Jacob E. Safra, Chairman of the Board
Jorge Aguilar-Cauz, President

Chicago · London · New Delhi · Paris · Seoul · Sydney · Taipei · Tokyo

ENCYCLOPÆDIA BRITANNICA, INC.

BLT 11/20/07 $12.99

Business

Arts, Entertainment, & Leisure

Sport

Year in Review

One Day in Iraq

by Michael Duffy, Brian Bennet, and Mark Kukis, TIME

As of Independence Day 2007, more than 3,500 Americans had died in Iraq since the war began in 2003. That's two per day, a rate that has increased with the "surge" of 30,000 US troops into Baghdad that began early in 2006. The number of US casualties increased since the buildup began, as Pres. George W. Bush predicted they would. So has the frequency of grievous single days when multiple service members were killed. One such day was 16 April 2007: six Americans died in Iraq on that day. Here are the stories of five of them.

THE BROTHER WHO DIDN'T COME HOME
Scherry, Daniel
Age 20. Lance corporal, US Marine Corps. 1st Battalion, 2nd Marine Regiment, 2nd Marine Division, 2nd Marine Expeditionary Force
Nonhostile accident, Anbar province

Leaving home in Rocky River OH was hard for Daniel Scherry. His mother and two sisters were in tears when his Marine Corps recruiter, Staff Sgt. Eric Evans, went to pick him up for basic training in the spring of 2006. Soon Scherry was crying too. "His sisters were his world," says Evans. Their names, Kacie and Lauren, were tattooed on the inside of his arms. To console Scherry, Evans told the young Marine the recruiter would be there for the sisters while he was away.

Scherry's mother Marianne had tried to talk him out of joining the Marines, at least until he finished college. In 2004, when the Marines were assaulting Fallujah and suffering heavy casualties, she showed the newspaper to her only son. Look, she said, they are so young—just 19 and 20—and they're dying. But Scherry replied that the Marines who died there must have been proud to do so for their country. "He looked at the Marines as being the best, and that's what he wanted to be—the best," says Marianne. "He knew it was the hardest boot camp. He knew it was the toughest training. That's what he wanted. He wanted to push himself."

Scherry's mentor in the Marines was Evans. He felt closer to Scherry ~~...~~ ~~...~~ Evans, who ~~...~~rry than to other recruits he had signed up; he reminded Evans of himself as an eager young recruit. Evans talked with Scherry for a long time that first night, assuring him he was embarking on a noble calling. And Evans stayed in touch with Scherry as he went through training, offering congratulations when Scherry became a mortarman, the same job Evans held when he first joined the Marine Corps.

Scherry was deployed to Anbar province in March 2007. He died after only about a month there. The Marines who broke the news to his mother said there had been an accident. Scherry had been riding in the turret of a Humvee when he reached to get a low-hanging wire out of the way. Electric current killed him.

In the days after Scherry's death, Marianne asked the Marines who had come to her house if they could please send Evans, who had never helped a family grieve before. Scherry is the first of Evans' recruits to die in Iraq. "You find yourself lying awake at night looking for some magical words that can help the family ease their pain, and there are no magical words to be had," says Evans. "You can't bring their son back for them."

A MARINE FATHER'S LAMENT
De La Torre, Jesse
Age 29. Lance corporal, US Marine Corps. 2nd Battalion, 7th Marine Regiment, 1st Marine Division, 1st Marine Expeditionary Force
Hostile fire, Anbar province

Aureliano De La Torre didn't want his son Jesse to join the Marines. "It was his own idea," Aureliano says. "I didn't agree, but there was nothing I could do." As the wars in Iraq and Afghanistan unfolded, Jesse grew determined to get involved as he mulled his future and the state of the world from his hometown of Aurora IL. He told his father that someone had to do something to stop al-Qaeda.

Jesse was a gifted saxophone player; until he joined the military, jazz had been one of his main passions. But he always seemed in search of a larger purpose. When he was about 12, he asked his father to take him to a nondenominational Bible-study group. Jesse had found it on his own and wanted to go because he was curious about religion. For two years father and son went together to Bible discussions, where Jesse was easily the youngest person. Jesse's initial curiosity grew into a deeply felt sense of spirituality that stayed with him throughout his life. He carried a Bible to school.

After graduating from high school in 1998, Jesse put jazz aside and pursued computer engineering in community-college classes in Aurora, where he also worked at an insurance company. But he abandoned the college path in 2005 to enlist in the Marines. The decision took his family by surprise. ~~In~~~~...~~ther only after ~~...~~ ~~...~~rice. Jesse told his father only after he had arrived in California for training. Soon after, Jesse left for Iraq, where word from him came rarely.

Jesse went home over Christmas in 2006 for two weeks of leave. About five weeks after returning to duty in Anbar province, he sent his father a short message saying he was OK. Aureliano never heard from his son again. At 10 AM on 16 April, four Marines arrived at his house. When Aureliano asked if they were there about his son, the Marines didn't speak, but after a moment, they explained: Jesse had died in Iraq about seven hours earlier, killed by hostile fire.

"Our lives will never be the same," says Aureliano, whose grief is colored by the anger he feels over losing a son to a war he does not support. "Now that my son is gone, there is a vacancy in Iraq. Maybe the president would like to send one of his daughters over there to continue to fight in Jesse's place."

"HE WANTED TO FIGHT"

Blue, Shaun
Age 25. 1st lieutenant, US Marine Corps. 2nd Battalion, 7th Marine Regiment, 1st Marine Division, 1st Marine Expeditionary Force
Hostile fire, Anbar province

Before he left for Iraq, Shaun Blue never talked about the war with his friends. He didn't need to. "We all knew where each other stood," says Mike Bell, a fellow Marine who attended the University of Southern California with Blue. They were juniors when the war began. "All of us wanted to go. All of us wanted to be there."

Blue had considered dropping out of college to enlist in the Marines rather than finishing school and entering as an officer. He was a voracious reader, a philosophy major whose interests ranged from hard sciences to Roman architecture. (His mother says he asked for a copy of *Moby Dick* as a Christmas present in second grade.) In college he was as serious about conditioning his body as he was his mind. He played pickup basketball in some of LA's toughest neighborhoods. Once, late at night, after drinking beer with Bell, Blue told Bell he was going for a run. He donned a flak jacket for added weight and ran the darkened LA streets alone for hours, finally returning to the house shortly before dawn.

Blue set off for his first deployment to Iraq on 4 Jul 2005. He joined the Marine campaign in Anbar province, leading a platoon in the Fallujah area. Even in the desert reaches of Iraq, Blue found ways to call Bell and his younger sister Amy Blue, who was living in Ireland at the time. "Those phone calls from him were the highlights of my days," says Amy. "Hearing him across all those miles, it was like he was right there with me." He was killed halfway through a second tour in Anbar, while riding in the passenger seat of a Humvee that was hit by a roadside bomb. "Twenty-five years is so short," his sister says, "but I am very lucky that I could call him a brother and a true best friend for that long."

"He wanted to fight," says Bell of his fallen friend. "He really, really did. He couldn't wait."

A KNACK FOR WATCHING OUT FOR OTHERS

Genevie, Aaron
Age 22. Private first class, US Army. 1st Squadron, 4th Cavalry Regiment, 4th Infantry Brigade Combat Team, 1st Infantry Division
IED blast, Baghdad

As a gunner in a scout unit, Aaron Genevie often rode through Baghdad popped up out of the top of his Humvee, manning a belt-fed automatic machine gun. Gunners are the eyes and ears of the driver, constantly scanning the horizon for threats. In Baghdad's congested streets, they are also traffic cops—waving cars out of the way, shouting at drivers who get too close. That's what Genevie was doing the day he died, telling his driver to maneuver around an Iraqi national-police checkpoint when a roadside bomb went off and killed him instantly.

A scout in the 1st Infantry Division of Fort Riley KS, Genevie had to fight to get into the army. Military doctors told him he couldn't enlist with his history of asthma and shoulder problems. But Genevie knew he could handle the training. He videotaped himself doing rigorous 20-minute workouts to show that he wouldn't slow down his unit. He even drafted a letter to President Bush asking him to intervene. Genevie

never sent it, as the army eventually let him in. His mother Patricia found the letter among his things a few days after he died.

Like many other parents of service members, she had tried her best to persuade him not to join. "You don't want to go over there," she remembers telling him. Genevie idolized his mother. He listed her as his "biggest inspiration" in his 2003 senior yearbook. But joining the military was one thing he had to do on his own, with or without his mother's blessing. Before he left for basic training, Patricia remembers telling him, "I support you 100%."

His mother has tried to make sense of Genevie's death by holding tight to the notion that he was watching over his fellow soldiers in his last moments. It was a familiar role. "He was real big on Superman," she says. Genevie tattooed a red and gold S on his chest. When his parents separated a few years ago, Genevie stayed with his mom and "took over the fatherly role," she recalls, helping them work through their problems and get back together. That's why, when he died, she wanted him to be buried in Arlington National Cemetery. "That's where heroes go," she says. "He was my hero."

A NEW FAMILY'S LIFE CUT SHORT

De Leon, Mario
Age 26. Sergeant, US Army. 1st Battalion, 18th Regiment, 2nd Brigade Combat Team, 1st Infantry Division
Sniper fire, Baghdad

When Mario De Leon returned home to the rolling hills of Petaluma CA for the last time, dozens of well-wishers, firefighters, and police officers lined the streets and stood on overpasses to see the black hearse go by. A group of teenage girls held a sign that read WE LOVE YOU. For De Leon's mother Barbara, the show of respect was in part a salve for an old wound. De Leon's father had served two tours in Vietnam. When he returned to the US, "they treated him like crap," she says. The motorcades and hand-painted signs that honored Mario's death were in stark contrast to the reprehensible way returning soldiers were treated in the last unpopular war. "America is trying to make up for that," she says.

Mario was shy when it came to praise and gratitude. Strangers stopped him and said thank you, but he didn't know how to react. Barbara had worried that she would lose him to gangs and drugs in high school. But he cleaned up and enlisted in the army after graduation. It wasn't long before De Leon was shouldering a heavy SAW (squad automatic weapon) gun on his broad 1.9-m (6-ft 2-in) frame through the rugged passes of Afghanistan.

When he finished his tour in 2002, he left the army and used the GI Bill to enroll at a local junior college. That's where he charmed his wife Erika with his handsome face, his goofy grin and a boyish obsession with *ThunderCats* cartoons and *X-Men* comic books. But by 2006, with a new baby boy named Keoni in the house, he decided to reenlist. He hoped a career in the military would provide a stable income for his family. He arrived in Baghdad in October 2007 and was promoted to sergeant and squad leader.

Two weeks later, Mario De Leon came into an enemy sniper's sights in Baghdad while leading a patrol. His squad fights on without him. "I wish to hell," Barbara says, "they'd get them home."

The Virtual World of Online Gaming

by Michael Ray

Virtual worlds generated billions of real dollars in 2006–07 as millions of players around the world fought, bought, crafted, and sold in a variety of online environments. The most populous, Blizzard Entertainment's *World of Warcraft,* drew seven million subscribers (with more than five million in China alone). This total represented more than half of the massively multiplayer online game (MMOG) community in 2006, and it brought in more than $1 billion in retail sales and subscription fees for Blizzard. MMOGs differed from traditional PC games in a number of important ways. First, Internet connectivity was a prerequisite for all MMOGs, as the games could be played only after one logged in to the server that hosted the game world (popular MMOGs required dozens of such servers to accommodate their larger player bases). Second, the social aspect of interacting with thousands of players worldwide frequently overshadowed the game content itself. A 2006 study found that almost a third of female players and nearly 10% of male players had dated someone they met in a game. Third, most MMOGs operated on a subscription basis, charging a monthly fee in addition to the initial purchase price of the game software. Some companies offered frequent downloadable "patches" of new game content to make these monthly fees more palatable to players, while others offered their games free of charge to players who were willing to tolerate a stream of in-game advertisements.

Though *World of Warcraft* and other MMOGs utilized the advanced graphics and high-end processing power typical of the current generation of PC games, online gaming had its roots in some of the earliest computing technologies. By the late 1970s, many universities in the US were linked by ARPANET, a precursor to the Internet. The structure of ARPANET allowed users to connect their computers to a central mainframe and interact in what was close to real time. In 1980 ARPANET was linked to the University of Essex, Colchester, England, where two undergraduate students had written a text-based fantasy adventure game that they called MUD, or "multiuser dungeon." When the first outside users connected to MUD through ARPANET, online gaming was born. Soon other programmers expanded on the original MUD design, adding graphic flourishes, chat functions, and player groups (or guilds). These basic features, as well as the fantasy setting, carried over into the next generation of online games, which were the first true MMOGs.

The first wave of MMOGs included such games as *Ultima Online* (debuted in 1997), the South Korean blockbuster *Lineage* (1998), and Sony's *EverQuest*

(1999). Growth for these early games was relatively slow but steady with the exception of *Lineage,* the explosive popularity of which was mainly due to the early and widespread availability of high-speed Internet connections in South Korea. This popularity did not come without a price, however. A number of Korean players died of exhaustion after marathon gaming sessions, and a 2005 South Korean government survey showed that more than half a million Koreans suffered from "Internet addiction." Game companies funded dozens of private counseling centers for addicted gamers in an effort to forestall legislation, such as that passed by China in 2005, that would force designers to impose in-game penalties for players who spent more than three consecutive hours online.

By the time *World of Warcraft* debuted in November 2004, the global gaming market was ready for a change. With the notable exceptions of *EVE Online,* a game of interstellar corporate intrigue, and the superhero-themed *City of Heroes,* the market was saturated with "swords and sorcery" fare. *World of Warcraft*'s attention to humor and team play and its shallow learning curve brought in millions of casual gamers who had never before tried an MMOG. This widespread success brought its own challenges for Blizzard, however, when the company temporarily suspended the account of a transsexual player over freedom of speech issues. While that incident seemed to have been the result of a terrible miscommunication on Blizzard's part, it did open a dialogue on the nature of online worlds. Were they like private clubs, where the management could restrict both membership and speech? Or did they fall under the scope of a public accommodation, where discrimination was expressly prohibited by US law?

> *Many groups were eager to target one of the fastest-growing communities on the Internet— Second Life's population topped 8 million in July 2007, and its numbers were increasing by some 10,000 a day.*

Another issue that game publishers had to face was the rise of secondary economies outside their game worlds. *Ultima Online* designers were the first to observe this phenomenon at work when a castle in their game world sold for several thousand dollars on the online auction site eBay. This was the beginning of a market valued at more than $1 billion in 2006. Players spent hours earning in-game wealth, hunting for rare weapons, and gaining power and prestige for their characters so that the fruits of their virtual labors could be exchanged for real cash. The buyer and seller would agree on a purchase price; the funds would be transferred electronically; and the two would then meet in the game world to complete the transaction. Some Chinese companies turned this into serious business, employing hundreds of "gold farmers," who played the game in an effort to hoard resources that would be sold to players in South

Korea or the United States. Most MMOG companies sought to control this behavior by banning the accounts of suspected gold farmers (Blizzard closed 18,000 such accounts in October–December 2005). Sony co-opted the secondary market when it launched Station Exchange, a service designed to facilitate the buying and selling of virtual goods in its EverQuest games. Thus far, however, Linden Lab was the only company to design a game around a virtual economy. That game was Second Life.

In many ways similar to The Sims, the top-selling PC game of all time, Second Life was less a game and more a virtual world. Though The Sims Online was a relative failure when it launched in late 2002, Second Life became a runaway success. The difference was in the economic models adopted by the two games. Whereas The Sims Online was criticized for its lack of any clear goals for players, Second Life offered players the opportunity to use the game world and their own talents to make as much money as they possibly could. For a monthly subscription fee, players received an allowance of Lindens (the in-game currency) that officially exchanged with US

dollars at a rate of approximately 250:1. Players could then purchase in-game items, customize those items by using 3D-imaging software, and resell them at a profit. For some, crafting items and managing virtual real estate in Second Life became a "first life" business. A German couple, acting through their in-game persona Anshe Chung, earned almost $200,000 in 2006 by developing and marketing property within Second Life. Many groups were eager to target one of the fastest-growing communities on the Internet—Second Life's population topped 8 million in July 2007, and its numbers were increasing by some 10,000 a day. Starwood Hotels built a resort on a virtual desert island; BBC Radio 1 created a concert venue for online music festivals; Sweden opened a virtual embassy; and Virginia politician Mark Warner conducted a town-hall interview with a Second Life reporter. The city of Vancouver established a police department complete with custom uniforms and badges, as a recruiting tool for its technology-related crimes unit. As the game became more like reality, some players joked that they were in need of a "third life."

Michael Ray is a freelance writer and a Research Editor at Encyclopædia Britannica.

The US 2006 Midterm Elections

by David C. Beckwith

In a stinging rebuke to Pres. George W. Bush and his party, voters swung decisively to Democrats in 2006 US congressional and state elections. The Republicans' 12-year control of Congress was abruptly ended, and recent GOP gains in state legislatures and governorships were reversed in a nationwide Democratic surge. On the federal level, Democrats captured 31 new seats in the US House of Representatives, for a prospective 233–202 advantage in the new Congress. More surprisingly, Democrats effectively gained 6 US Senate seats, turning a 55–45 deficit into narrow 51–49 control. That meant that a divided government (one party controlling the executive branch, the other the legislative branch), mandated by US voters for 26 of the past 38 years, would return again in 2007. A series of serious ethical controversies bedeviled the Republican majority during the year, allowing Democrats to decry "a culture of corruption" in Washington. Investigations of officials who dealt with convicted GOP lobbyist Jack Abramoff led indirectly to the resignation of Tom DeLay, a senior Texas congressman, and a taint on several other Republicans. GOP problems ran even deeper, however. In 1994, when Republicans captured the US House after 40 years in the minority, they relied on a "Contract with America" that promised 10 specific reforms. One was a curb on earmarking, spending on projects pushed by an indi-

> 66 *The Republicans' 12-year control of Congress was abruptly ended, and recent GOP gains in state legislatures and governorships were reversed in a nationwide Democratic surge.* 99

vidual congressman, usually at the behest of a lobbyist who reciprocated with campaign contributions. By 2006, however, many of the reforms had been eroded, and earmarking was back with a vengeance. A second-rank GOP legislator was imprisoned in March for trading earmarks for bribes, and in September a six-term representative, Bob Ney of Ohio, admitted to criminal acts associated with bribes and gift giving. Later that month Mark Foley, another senior Republican, was forced to resign after publication of sexually suggestive e-mails he had written to former House pages. Although some Democrats were accused of ethical improprieties as well, the year's multiple ethics charges only intensified voter demand for change. Sen. George Allen of Virginia, a potential 2008 Republican presidential candidate, used the term macaca (the definition of which was variously a monkey, a town in South Africa, or a racial slur against African immigrants) when referring to a Democratic campaign worker of Indian descent who was recording campaign-rally remarks for Internet use. Allen urged followers to "give a welcome to macaca, here." Though he later apologized, Allen lost a close reelection battle. Public dissatisfaction with the war in Iraq topped 65% by year's end, negating President Bush's efforts to assist individual Republican candidates in their reelection bids and spilling into Democratic politics as well. Sen. Joe Lieberman of Connecticut, his party's 2000 vice presidential nominee and Bush's strongest Democratic ally in the war on terrorism, lost his August primary to an antiwar opponent. He won reelection as an independent in November only with substantial Republican support. In contrast to 1994, the out-of-power party did not publish a clear, detailed alternate blueprint for the future, in part because of internal Democratic divisions over key issues.

Democrats did promise early action on several bills, including ones to raise the minimum wage and void recent tax concessions to unpopular oil companies. Democrats mainly concentrated on criticizing numerous Republican missteps in Iraq and in their management of Congress. The strategy worked, but the direction that the Democrats would take was anything but clear.

David C. Beckwith is a freelance writer.

Outsourcing War—The Surge in Private Military Firms
by Peter Saracino

The conflict in Iraq focused renewed attention on the role played by private military firms (PMFs) in modern war. In 2006 more than 60 firms employing 20,000 armed personnel were estimated to be operating in Iraq, which made PMFs the second largest foreign military contingent, after the United States. These firms conduct vital security duties, ranging from escorting convoys of freight to protecting key facilities and leaders. The industry even has its own lobby group, the Private Security Company Association of Iraq, with nearly 50 international corporate members. PMFs have also attracted unwanted attention, however, including allegations that contractors working in 2003 as military interrogators and translators at the notorious Abu Ghraib prison in Iraq were involved in the abuse of prisoners. In March 2006 a jury found the PMF Custer Battles guilty of having defrauded the US government of millions of dollars for work done while under contract in Iraq.

> *In 2006 more than 60 firms employing 20,000 armed personnel were estimated to be operating in Iraq, which made private military firms the second largest foreign military contingent, after the United States.*

wrong, however, to conclude that PMFs are newcomers to warfare. Prior to the 19th century, it was common for states to contract for military services, including combat. The word *soldier* itself is derived from the Latin *solidus,* meaning a gold coin. During the 3rd century BC, Alexander the Great employed mercenary forces to help conquer Asia, and Britain hired German soldiers called Hessians to fight the colonists during the American Revolution (1775–83). In the 17th and 18th centuries, the British East India Company and its Danish, Dutch, and French rivals all had private armies to help defend their government-sanctioned business interests in Asia.

EFFECTS ON MILITARY
The growth of the modern privatized military industry has had an effect on the armed forces that they were intended to assist. With PMFs offering daily wages of up to $1,000 to attract highly trained staff, there has been an exodus of soldiers from many special forces. Britain's Special Air Service, the US Army's Special Forces, and the Canadian Army's Joint Task Force 2 have all acknowledged problems retaining personnel and are offering special bonuses and pay increases in an effort to compete with lucrative wages in the private sector.

When a military organization has no organic capability, it becomes dependent on private industry to provide it. In 2000, for example, the Canadian navy had no logistics ships, and the government contracted a shipping company to take 580 vehicles and 390 sea containers full of equipment back to Canada following the completion of NATO operations in Kosovo. Owing to a dispute over unpaid bills, the ship loitered in international waters for two weeks until Canadian military personnel boarded the ship and forced it to dock in a Canadian port.

Despite these problems, PMFs are now called upon to deliver services previously considered the domain of military personnel. Kellogg, Brown & Root (KBR) runs the only permanent US base in Africa (Camp Lemonier in Djibouti, at the mouth of the Red Sea). KBR has more than 700 employees who do laundry,

THE EVOLUTION OF PMFs
The term *PMF*—also *private security company* and *military services provider*—is a catch-all expression that includes traditional security firms employing armed guards, companies shipping defense matériel, consultants offering advice on strategy, and military trainers. Unlike traditional defense industries, PMFs operate in combat zones and other areas where violence may be imminent. States, private industry, and humanitarian aid agencies all employ the services of PMFs.

The modern PMF is a product of the end of the Cold War; in the early 1990s many countries slashed defense budgets following the demise of the Soviet Union. This coincided with the growing trend of governments to outsource services to private industry. As a consequence armed forces were left to carry out their missions with fewer ships, aircraft, and personnel, leaving more support and rear-area functions (e.g., repairing tanks, training pilots, and preparing meals) to be outsourced to contractors. It would be

clean buildings, and prepare meals for 1,500 military personnel. PMFs have even been employed by governments to handle domestic emergencies, such as the initial response to Hurricane Katrina in New Orleans in 2005.

Since the 11 Sep 2001 attacks in the US, the war on terrorism has provided new opportunities for PMFs. Spy agencies now use PMFs to collect and analyze intelligence from around the world. At times contractors have outnumbered employees at the CIA's offices in both Iraq and Pakistan.

LEGAL ISSUES

International humanitarian law (which includes the Geneva Conventions) applies to every person in a war zone, even though the status of PMFs is not specifically defined. Hence PMF employees are considered civilians and must not be targeted for attack unless they form part of the armed forces of a state. If these employees participate directly in hostilities, however, they lose this legal protection. Furthermore, PMF employees participating directly in hostilities are not entitled to protection as prisoners of war under the Geneva Conventions, and they can be tried as "unlawful combatants" (in other words, as mercenaries). The distinction between combatants and civilians who are merely defending themselves becomes complicated when PMF staff wear military clothing and carry government-issued or privately owned weapons. According to the International Committee of the Red Cross, when a state outsources military functions to a PMF, the state remains legally responsible for the firm's acts.

Another legal problem is that PMF employees are usually exempt from the military laws that govern how troops behave in a conflict. Although soldiers from several coalition members in Iraq have been convicted of crimes against civilians, for example, not a single military contractor has been charged with a crime there since the US-led invasion in March 2003.

Although most states publish statistics on the numbers of their military casualties, the fate of PMF personnel goes largely unreported in the news media. With few exceptions—such as the horrific public display of murdered contractors in the Iraqi city of Fallujah in March 2004—there has been little news coverage of the nearly 650 civilian contractors working for the US government who were reportedly killed in Iraq between March 2003 and September 2006. Safety is another area of concern, especially when the responsibility for the safety of PMF employees working in war zones is undefined. The families of four employees who were killed in Colombia in 2003 when two surveillance aircraft crashed are suing California Microwave Systems, a subsidiary of Northrop Grumman, for negligence. Colombian guerrillas held three more employees as hostages. California Microwave Systems had been contracted by the US government to conduct dangerous aerial reconnaissance missions as part of the war on Colombia's cocaine industry.

Although some countries prohibit their citizens from joining the armed forces of a foreign country at war, very few prevent them from joining foreign PMFs. In 2006 the South African Parliament introduced legislation to prevent any of its citizens from participating in a foreign conflict. The bill had its genesis in the 2004 coup attempt against the president of Equatorial Guinea. Mark Thatcher, the son of former British prime minister Margaret Thatcher and a resident of South Africa at the time, helped fund the PMF allegedly hired to conduct the coup, and it in turn hired 70 South Africans to do the fighting.

Globally, the use of PMFs has grown dramatically since the 1990–91 Gulf War, when there was an estimated one contractor for every 50 military personnel involved. By the time of the Iraq invasion in 2003, the ratio had grown to one in 10. With PMFs operating on nearly every continent and generating an estimated $100 billion in revenue annually, they are certain to remain important actors in military affairs for the foreseeable future.

Peter Saracino is a freelance defense journalist.

Chronology, July 2006–June 2007

A day-by-day listing of important and interesting events, adapted from
Britannica Book of the Year. *See also Disasters.*

July 2006

1 Jul The presidency of the European Union rotates from Austria's chancellor, Wolfgang Schüssel, to the prime minister of Finland, Matti Vanhanen.

▸ With the start of the World Bank's fiscal year, the International Development Association debt of 19 of the world's poorest countries is canceled.

2 Jul The presidential election in Mexico results in a razor-thin margin between leftist Andrés Manuel López Obrador and conservative Felipe Calderón that is too close to call.

3 Jul A bomb kills seven people near a military checkpoint in Trincomalee, Sri Lanka.

▸ US federal prosecutors report that a recently discharged army private has been arrested and will be charged with having raped a woman in Iraq and having killed her and three members of her family.

4 Jul Robert Fico takes office as prime minister of Slovakia.

5 Jul In oil trading in the US, the price reaches a record high of $75.40 per barrel, passing the previous mark set on 21 April.

▸ North Korea test-fires a number of missiles over the Sea of Japan/East Sea, including an intercontinental ballistic missile, which evidently fails.

6 Jul Election officials in Mexico declare Felipe Calderón the winner of the presidential election.

7 Jul Kazimierz Marcinkiewicz resigns as prime minister of Poland.

▸ The World Conservation Union announces that the West African black rhinoceros is thought to be extinct.

8 Jul As Israeli troops pull out of northern Gaza, Palestinian Prime Minister Ismail Haniya calls for a truce.

▸ The General Synod of the Church of England for the first time agrees to allow women to serve as bishops.

▸ Frenchwoman Amélie Mauresmo takes the All-England (Wimbledon) women's tennis championship; the following day Roger Federer of Switzerland wins the men's title.

9 Jul In Berlin, Italy defeats France in a penalty shootout to win the World Cup in association football (soccer).

▸ The day after a car bomb in front of a Shi'ite mosque kills at least 12 people, gunmen rampage through a Sunni neighborhood in Baghdad, pulling people from cars and homes and killing them.

10 Jul José Ramos-Horta is inaugurated as prime minister of East Timor.

11 Jul During the evening rush hour, seven trains carrying commuters from Mumbai (Bombay) to suburbs are bombed within a few minutes, and an eighth bomb goes off at a train station; some 200 people are killed.

▸ Indonesia's legislature passes a law intended to grant significant autonomy to Aceh province in accordance with the terms of a peace agreement.

12 Jul Hezbollah fires two rockets into northern Israel and in an attack over the border kills three Israeli soldiers and captures two others, which prompts Israel to make air attacks against Hezbollah bases and bridges in southern Lebanon and send in ground forces.

13 Jul Israel attacks Beirut's airport and establishes a naval blockade of its port, while Hezbollah continues rocket attacks against Israel; Lebanon says 53 of its civilians have been killed.

▸ The Baku–Tbilisi–Ceyhan pipeline, which carries oil from the Caspian Sea to the Mediterranean, is officially opened.

14 Jul Israeli planes bomb Hezbollah's headquarters in Beirut as Hezbollah continues to shell northern Israel.

▸ In a match-fixing scandal, the governing body of Italian association football (soccer) metes out penalties to a number of top teams.

15 Jul Meeting in Russia, US Pres. George W. Bush and Russian Pres. Vladimir Putin are unable to reach an agreement that would allow Russia to join the World Trade Organization.

16 Jul A large missile launched by Hezbollah strikes a railroad maintenance building in Haifa, Israel, killing 8 people; Israel responds by bombing Beirut and southern Lebanon, killing at least 45 people.

17 Jul Gunmen open fire in a crowded Shi'ite market area in Mahmudiyah, Iraq, killing at least 48 people.

▸ The space shuttle *Discovery* safely returns to Earth after a successful 13-day mission.

18 Jul A suicide car bomber lures day laborers with the offer of work and then detonates his weapon, killing at least 53, in Kufah, Iraq.

19 Jul Lebanese Prime Minister Fouad Siniora calls a meeting of foreign diplomats seeking help in dealing with Israeli attacks against Hezbollah in the country.

> **QUOTE OF THE MONTH**
>
> *The country has been torn to shreds.... Is this the price we pay for aspiring to build our democratic institutions?*
>
> —Lebanese Prime Minister Fouad Siniora, at a meeting of foreign diplomats over the crisis between Israel and Lebanon, 19 July

▸ For the first time in his administration, US Pres. George W. Bush exercises his right to veto legislation passed by Congress; the bill he vetoes is one that would expand research into possible medical uses of embryonic stem cells.

20 Jul US Marines enter Beirut to help evacuate American citizens from the beleaguered country.

▸ It is reported that Ethiopian troops have entered Baidoa, Somalia, where the interim government is based, after fundamentalist Muslim militias approached within 35 km (22 mi) of the city.

21 Jul A government spokesman announces that King Bhumibol Adulyadej of Thailand has approved a plan to hold a general election in the country on 15 October; the election held on 2 April was invalidated.

22 Jul Israel sends ground forces into southern Lebanon, and its airplanes bomb television and cell phone towers, while Hezbollah rockets continue to rain on northern Israel.

23 Jul A suicide bomber at a market in Baghdad kills at least 35 people, while a car bomb outside the courthouse in Kirkuk, Iraq, kills at least 22; 11 other bodies are found in the Tigris River.

▸ After an astounding comeback in which he made up in the Alps the eight minutes that he had fallen behind, American cyclist Floyd Landis wins the Tour de France.

▸ Tiger Woods wins the British Open golf tournament.

24 Jul Pascal Lamy, director general of the World Trade Organization, formally suspends the Doha Round of trade talks.

25 Jul Israel announces that it intends to occupy a strip of southern Lebanon until an international force that can take control has been convened; an Israeli air strike hits a UN observation post in Lebanon, killing four unarmed UN observers.

26 Jul A meeting between the US and European and Arab countries fails to agree on a plan to stop the fighting in the Middle East; in continuing fighting 9 Israeli soldiers, at least 23 Gaza Palestinians, and dozens of Lebanese people are killed.

27 Jul In Moscow, Russian Pres. Vladimir Putin and Venezuelan Pres. Hugo Chávez announce an agreement to allow Venezuela to import military technology, including fighter jets and helicopters, from Russia.

▸ Cyclist Floyd Landis is suspended when a test taken after his comeback to win Stage 17 and, ultimately, the Tour de France shows an abnormally high level of testosterone.

28 Jul The new UN Human Rights Committee issues a report calling on the US to close its secret prisons and to allow Red Cross access to all the prisoners it has detained in connection with the war on terrorism.

29 Jul The US Department of Defense extends for a period of up to four months the tours of duty of 4,000 troops who had been scheduled to leave Iraq in the next few weeks.

30 Jul Legislative and presidential elections are held in the Democratic Republic of the Congo; they are the first multiparty elections in the country in 46 years.

▸ Israeli bombing of Qana, Lebanon, causes the collapse of an apartment building that kills nearly 60 civilians; hours later Israel agrees to suspend air strikes for 48 hours.

31 Jul Pres. Fidel Castro of Cuba announces that while he recovers from surgery, he is temporarily turning power over to his brother, Defense Minister Raúl Castro.

▸ Just 12 hours after having agreed to a 48-hour cessation of the air war on Lebanon, Israel resumes air strikes.

▸ The UN Security Council passes Resolution 1696 (2006), which demands a verifiable cessation of uranium enrichment by Iran.

August 2006

1 Aug A roadside bomb near Tikrit, Iraq, kills 23 Iraqi soldiers on a bus transferring them from Mosul to Baghdad, and in Baghdad a suicide car bomb near a bank kills 10 people; a total of at least 44 people are killed in attacks in the country.

2 Aug Forces of the Sri Lankan government and the Liberation Tigers of Tamil Eelam continue fighting after several days of conflict over an irrigation channel; at least 49 people are killed.

3 Aug In Panjwai, Afghanistan, near Kandahar, a suicide car bomber kills at least 21 people at a bazaar; 7 NATO soldiers are killed in the area in other attacks.

4 Aug Four bridges along the main north-south highway north of Beirut are destroyed by Israeli shelling, and more than 30 people are killed; Hezbollah continues to shell Israel, killing 4.

5 Aug The Pro Football Hall of Fame in Canton OH inducts quarterbacks Troy Aikman and Warren Moon, linebacker Harry Carson, tackle Rayfield Wright, defensive lineman Reggie White, and coach John Madden.

6 Aug Hezbollah rockets kill 12 Israeli reservists and 3 civilians in northern Israel as Israel continues its assault on Lebanon.

▸ At the Buick Open golf tournament, Tiger Woods wins his 50th Professional Golfers' Association of America Tour title; also, American Sherri Steinhauer wins the women's British Open golf tournament.

7 Aug Somalia's transitional government in Baidoa dissolves the cabinet; several cabinet members had quit in recent weeks.

8 Aug In Baghdad three bombs near the Interior Ministry kill 9 people, two bombs in a market claim 10 lives, and gunmen robbing a bank kill 5 others.

▸ Roger Goodell is elected commissioner of the National Football League.

9 Aug Israel's cabinet approves a plan to deploy thousands of ground troops to move farther and more quickly into Lebanon in order to push Hezbollah rocket launchers farther away from Israel.

10 Aug British authorities say that they have arrested 24 men who planned to blow up airplanes heading to the US by using liquid explosives that they intended to carry on board and mix into lethal explosives during the flight; governments of both the UK and the US immediately ban all liquids in carry-on luggage.

▸ A suicide bomber's weapons detonate as he is being frisked at a checkpoint outside the Shrine of Ali, an important Shiʿite pilgrimage site, in Najaf, Iraq; at least 35 people are killed.

11 Aug The UN Security Council unanimously adopts a resolution calling for hostilities between Israel and Lebanon to stop, peacekeeping troops to go to southern Lebanon, and armed groups—meaning Hezbollah—to be disarmed.

12 Aug Fighting in Lebanon between Hezbollah and Israeli troops intensifies as Lebanon approves the UN cease-fire resolution; the following day Israel also accepts the cease-fire.

13 Aug Five bombings that occur in two waves kill at least 63 people in a Shiʿite neighborhood of Baghdad.

14 Aug A cease-fire between Israel and Hezbollah goes into effect as tens of thousands of people return to their homes in southern Lebanon, and Sheikh Hassan Nasrallah, Hezbollah's leader, declares victory.

▸ The Liberation Tigers of Tamil Eelam say that Sri Lankan government forces bombed a school compound, killing 61 girls.

15 Aug A US federal judge rules that insurance companies do not have to pay victims of Hurricane Katrina for damage from flooding associated with wind damage but do have to pay for wind damage associated with flooding.

16 Aug An American teacher and apparent pedophile, John M. Karr, is arrested in Thailand for the unsolved murder of child beauty queen JonBenet

Ramsey, who was killed at the age of six in 1996; charges are later dropped when DNA evidence excludes him as a suspect.

17 Aug A US federal judge rules that the National Security Agency's warrantless wiretapping program is unconstitutional and should be shut down; it continues, however, pending an appeal.

18 Aug The Lebanese army enters southern Lebanon, reaching the border with Israel for the first time in nearly 40 years.

19 Aug New Zealand defeats Australia to win the Rugby Union Tri-Nations title.

20 Aug As thousands of pilgrims wend their way through Baghdad to a Shi'ite shrine, snipers and mortar fire from Sunni neighborhoods kill 20 people and injure 300.

▶ Tiger Woods wins the Professional Golfers' Association of America championship.

21 Aug A bomb in a crowded Moscow market kills at least 10 people.

▶ Tuheitia Paki is crowned king of the Maori in New Zealand.

22 Aug The UN sends peacekeepers to Kinshasa, the capital of the Democratic Republic of the Congo, and brokers a cease-fire after three days of deadly violence has left at least 15 people dead.

23 Aug The port of Mogadishu, Somalia, is opened for the first time in more than 11 years; the city's international airport, closed for the past decade, had reopened a month previously.

▶ In Vienna, Natascha Kampusch, who was kidnapped in 1998 at the age of 10, escapes her captor and tells police she has been kept locked in a cellar under a garage for eight years.

24 Aug The International Astronomical Union decides on a definition of planets that classifies Pluto, Ceres, and Eris as dwarf planets.

25 Aug The UN Security Council votes to establish a new peacekeeping force for East Timor.

26 Aug The leaders of the Lord's Resistance Army, a rebel militia in Uganda, announce that they will lay down their arms and end their war after signing a peace treaty with the Ugandan government in Juba, Sudan.

27 Aug A suicide car bomb goes off in the parking lot of *Al-Sabah*, Iraq's main newspaper, killing two people; 50 more people are killed in various acts of violence throughout the country.

▶ The Emmy Awards are presented in Los Angeles.

28 Aug A gun battle between the Mahdi Army, the militia of radical Shi'ite cleric Muqtada al-Sadr, and the Iraqi army in Al-Diwaniyah, Iraq, leaves at least 20 combatants and 8 civilians dead; in Baghdad a car bomb outside the Interior Ministry kills 13.

▶ A bomb kills three people in the resort town of Antalya, Turkey; the previous day three bombs had gone off in Marmaris, another tourist town, injuring 21 people.

29 Aug Oaxaca, Mexico, is shut down by a general strike to protest violence as representatives of striking teachers and civic groups who seek the removal of the state's governor fail to reach an agreement in talks with state officials and federal mediators.

30 Aug In Al-Hillah, Iraq, a bicycle rigged with explosives kills at least 12 people at an army recruiting center; later, in a market in Baghdad, a bomb in a vendor's cart kills at least 24 people; the death toll throughout the country for the day is 65.

31 Aug A deadline set by Western countries for Iran to stop its enrichment of uranium passes with no action from Iran.

▶ In the province of Yala in Thailand, bombs triggered by signals from cell phones explode nearly simultaneously in 22 banks; only one person is killed.

QUOTE OF THE MONTH

" *I may go down in history as the guy who killed Pluto.* "

—Michael Brown, the astronomer whose discovery of 2003 UB-313 (Eris) prompted the International Astronomical Union's decision on the definition of a planet that excludes both Pluto and Xena, 24 August

September 2006

1 Sep A US Department of Defense assessment of the state of security in Iraq indicates that in the period since the establishment of Iraq's new government, the number of Iraqi casualties has increased by more than 50%.

2 Sep A nine-hour sea battle between forces of the Sri Lankan government and the Liberation Tigers of Tamil Eelam (LTTE) takes place off the country's north coast; the government reports that it sank 12 LTTE boats and killed at least 80 rebels.

3 Sep A major battle takes place between NATO forces and Taliban insurgents in Kandahar province in southern Afghanistan; four Canadian soldiers and, according to a NATO spokesman, some 200 Taliban fighters are killed.

4 Sep After two days of talks in The Sudan, the government of Somalia and the fundamentalist Muslim group that controls most of the country's southern regions agree to form a unified army and a peace committee to work out details of the plan.

5 Sep Nine boats carrying 898 African migrants arrive at the Canary Islands, setting a record for arrivals on a single day; some 20,000 migrants have

traveled to the Canary Islands so far in 2006, and hundreds have died in the attempt.

6 Sep US Pres. George W. Bush announces that 14 prominent terrorism suspects who have been held in heretofore secret CIA prisons in undisclosed locations have been transferred to the military prison at Guantánamo Bay, Cuba.

7 Sep Tony Blair declares his intention to step down as British prime minister within the next year.

8 Sep The Naismith Memorial Basketball Hall of Fame in Springfield MA inducts as members players Charles Barkley, Dominique Wilkins, and Joe Dumars, men's coach Sandro Gamba of Italy and women's coach Geno Auriemma of the US, and college coach and executive Dave Gavitt.

9 Sep Mariya Sharapova of Russia wins the women's US Open tennis championship; the following day Roger Federer of Switzerland takes the men's title.

▶ The Detroit Shock wins the women's national basketball championship.

10 Sep Montenegro holds its first legislative elections.

▶ Sam Hornish, Jr., wins the overall IndyCar championship, his third.

11 Sep Palestinian Authority Pres. Mahmoud Abbas announces that he and Prime Minister Ismail Haniya have tentatively agreed to form a government of national unity.

12 Sep Remarks by Pope Benedict XVI in a speech in Regensburg, Germany, ignite a storm of criticism and protest in Muslim countries.

13 Sep Iraqi authorities report that 60 bodies have been found in Baghdad in the past 24 hours, and dozens more people are killed by several car bombs.

14 Sep US health officials tell consumers not to eat any bagged fresh spinach after an outbreak of a virulent strain of *E. coli* bacteria has sickened at least 50 people.

15 Sep An Iraqi government spokesman announces a plan to ring Baghdad with trenches so that all traffic into and out of the city must pass through one of 28 planned checkpoints; the scheme is intended to reduce violence in the city.

16 Sep In Côte d'Ivoire—in connection with the illegal dumping of toxic black sludge in several areas of Abidjan on 19 August that killed 7 people and sickened some 15,000 others—the ministers of transportation and environment are replaced.

17 Sep In a referendum in the secessionist province of Transnistria in Moldova, voters choose overwhelmingly to secede from Moldova and attach the province to Russia; the referendum is not internationally recognized.

18 Sep A suicide bomber on a bicycle kills 4 Canadian soldiers in Char Kota, Afghanistan; another kills 11 people in Herat; and a suicide car bomber in Kabul kills 4 policemen.

▶ A suicide car bomber fails in his attempt to kill Somalia's transitional president, Abdullahi Yusuf Ahmed, in Baidoa, Somalia, but does kill at least eight other people in the presidential convoy.

19 Sep Military leaders led by Gen. Sonthi Boonyaratkalin seize power in Thailand, suspending the constitution and all government bodies.

20 Sep ʻAli ʻAbdallah Salih resoundingly wins reelection as president of Yemen.

▶ At the UN General Assembly, Pres. Hugo Chávez of Venezuela makes an incendiary anti-American speech.

21 Sep The British entrepreneur Sir Richard Branson pledges to invest $3 billion in expected profit from his businesses in developing energy sources that do not increase global warming.

22 Sep Hundreds of thousands of people gather in the southern suburbs of Beirut to hear Hassan Nasrallah speak at what he calls a victory rally for Hezbollah over Israel.

> QUOTE OF THE MONTH
>
> " *And the devil came here yesterday. Yesterday the devil came here. Right here. And it smells of sulfur still today.* "
>
> —Hugo Chávez on 20 September in a speech to the UN General Assembly, referring to US Pres. George W. Bush, who addressed the assembly the previous day

23 Sep It is reported that the most recent National Intelligence Estimate in the US has concluded that the war in Iraq is stoking Islamic radicalism and increasing the threat of terrorism.

▶ A bomb in Baghdad kills at least 35 people, mostly women and children, in a line to receive cooking fuel; also, in Baiji, 9 people, including some policemen, are beheaded at a checkpoint.

24 Sep A sea battle between Sri Lankan naval forces and those of the Liberation Tigers of Tamil Eelam (LTTE) takes place off Sri Lanka's east coast; government spokesmen say 70 of the LTTE forces have been killed and 11 LTTE ships sunk.

25 Sep Security forces in Fraijanes, Guatemala, storm and take over Pavón prison, which had been under the control of the inmates for a decade.

26 Sep Shinzo Abe is installed as prime minister of Japan.

▶ The leader of the military junta that has seized power in Thailand, Gen. Sonthi Boonyaratkalin, announces that a civilian prime minister will be appointed soon but that the junta will remain in an advisory capacity.

27 Sep After many postponements, Iran's negotiator for nuclear issues, Ali Larijani, meets for talks with the head of foreign policy for the European Union, Javier Solana, in Berlin.

28 Sep Levy Mwanawasa is elected to a second term as president of Zambia.

▶ A Thai official discloses that Surayud Chulanont, an adviser to the king, has been chosen to serve as the country's interim prime minister.

29 Sep US Rep. Mark Foley of Florida resigns from the House of Representatives after the revelation of a number of sexually explicit e-mails that he sent to teenage pages; Foley was head of a caucus on missing and exploited children.

30 Sep A suicide bomber approaches the headquarters of the Ministry of the Interior in Kabul and detonates a device, killing at least 12 people.

October 2006

1 Oct Gun battles break out in Gaza between Fatahal-Islam-led protesters demonstrating their anger over unpaid government salaries and Hamas forces; six Palestinians are killed.

▶ Tiger Woods wins the world golf championship in London.

2 Oct In violence in Baghdad, eight US soldiers are killed; the following day violence throughout the country kills 51 civilians.

▶ A gunman invades an Amish schoolhouse in Nickel Mines PA and, after sending all the boys and adults out of the building, begins shooting the girls, killing four and wounding seven; he kills himself afterward.

▶ The Nobel Prize for Physiology or Medicine is awarded to Americans Andrew Z. Fire and Craig C. Mello.

3 Oct The Nobel Prize for Physics is awarded to American astronomers George F. Smoot and John C. Mather.

4 Oct The Nobel Prize for Chemistry is awarded to Roger D. Kornberg of the US.

5 Oct With its expansion into the east of the country, NATO officially takes charge of all peacekeeping and security in Afghanistan from the US military.

6 Oct The UN Security Council issues a statement to North Korea warning it not to engage in a nuclear test and pressing it to return to the six-party talks it abandoned in 2005.

7 Oct A suicide bomber kills 14 people at an Iraqi army checkpoint in Tal Afar, Iraq; in addition, 51 bodies are found in Baghdad.

▶ Anna Politkovskaya, a prominent, outspoken, and independent journalist, is shot dead at her home in Moscow.

8 Oct French Prime Minister Dominique de Villepin announces that smoking will be banned in most public places in France beginning on 1 Feb 2007.

9 Oct North Korea successfully tests a small nuclear weapon in the mountains above Kilju.

▶ The Nobel Memorial Prize for Economic Science goes to American Edmund S. Phelps.

▶ The search engine company Google agrees to buy the popular video-sharing Web site YouTube for $1.65 billion in stock.

10 Oct Three bombs in a single neighborhood in Baghdad kill a total of 17 people, and at least 50 bodies are found in various places in the city.

▶ The Man Booker Prize for Fiction goes to Anglo-Indian writer Kiran Desai for her novel *The Inheritance of Loss.*

11 Oct In a battle between the Sri Lankan army and forces of the Liberation Tigers of Tamil Eelam near Jaffna, at least 129 Sri Lankan soldiers are killed; it is the army's highest death toll since the start of the 2002 cease-fire.

12 Oct The Nobel Prize for Literature is awarded to Turkish novelist Orhan Pamuk.

▶ France's National Assembly passes a bill that makes it a crime punishable by jail and a heavy fine to deny that Armenians were subject to genocide by Turkey in 1915.

13 Oct The UN General Assembly appoints South Korea's foreign minister, Ban Ki-moon, the next secretary-general of the UN.

QUOTE OF THE MONTH

❝ *In too many places could I feel the dismay over inaction of the UN, or action that was too little or came too late.... I am determined to dispel the disillusionment.* ❞

—Ban Ki-moon, accepting his appointment as UN secretary-general, 13 October

---

▶ The Nobel Peace Prize is awarded to Bangladeshi economist Muhammad Yunus and the institution he founded, Grameen Bank.

14 Oct The UN Security Council, in response to North Korea's nuclear test, votes to impose strict sanctions on North Korea, including giving all countries the right to inspect all cargo going into or out of the country.

15 Oct A suicide truck bomber attacks a convoy of unarmed navy personnel in central Sri Lanka; at least 94 people are killed.

▶ After an investigation, police in Israel recommend that the attorney general file charges of rape and sexual assault against Israeli Pres. Moshe Katsav.

▶ Lorena Ochoa of Mexico wins the Ladies Professional Golf Association world championship.

16 Oct Scientists in California and Russia report that they have produced a new superheavy atom, element 118.

17 Oct The population of the United States reaches 300 million.

▶ US Pres. George W. Bush signs into law legislation that sets up new rules for interrogating and prosecuting terrorism suspects that differ from the rules for criminal suspects.

18 Oct The Liberation Tigers of Tamil Eelam detonate suicide boats near a navy base at Galle in southern Sri Lanka.

19 Oct A spokesman for the US military command in Iraq reports that the 12-week campaign to regain control of Baghdad has resulted in an increase in violence and a sharp rise in US combat deaths.

20 Oct Fighting breaks out in Al-'Amarah, Iraq, between members of the Mahdi Army and members of the Badr Organization, both Shi'ite militias; at least 25 people are left dead.

21 Oct Somali government troops retake the town of Buurhakaba from the Islamist forces that have occupied much of the country.

22 Oct Voters in Panama resoundingly approve a plan to enlarge the Panama Canal so that it will be able to handle modern ships; its capacity will be doubled.

23 Oct The Ford Motor Co. reports its biggest quarterly loss in 14 years.

24 Oct Government officials in Chad report that rebels seeking the overthrow of Pres. Idriss Déby have overrun the town of Goz Beida.

25 Oct For the first time in a month, battles take place between Taliban fighters and NATO troops; some 48 Taliban are killed near Kandahar, Afghanistan, and NATO bombing reportedly kills some 30 civilians in the village of Zangabad.

26 Oct A law that for the first time provides women with protection against domestic abuse from their husbands or partners goes into effect in India.

27 Oct Iran announces that it has begun enriching uranium in a second cascade of centrifuges, effectively doubling its capacity for nuclear enrichment.

▶ The St. Louis Cardinals defeat the Detroit Tigers 4–2 in St. Louis in the fifth game of the World Series to win their 10th Major League Baseball championship.

28 Oct Mexican Pres. Vicente Fox orders federal troops to end the crisis in Oaxaca, which has been riven by protests for five months; thousands of troops move into the area the following day.

29 Oct In runoff presidential elections, incumbent presidents Luiz Inácio Lula da Silva of Brazil, Joseph Kabila of the Democratic Republic of the Congo, and Georgi Purvanov of Bulgaria are victorious.

▶ In a nationwide vote in Serbia, the new constitution, which among other things asserts Serbia's claim to UN-administered Kosovo, is approved.

30 Oct A British report predicts cataclysmic effects from global warming and indicates the need for urgent action to forestall disaster.

▶ A bomb goes off in the morning near food stalls in Baghdad, killing 33 Shi'ite day laborers; five other bombs in the city bring the death toll to 46.

31 Oct North Korea agrees to return to nuclear disarmament talks.

November 2006

1 Nov The UN Security Council extends the mandate of the transitional government in Côte d'Ivoire for a further year, until 31 October 2007.

2 Nov The UN reports that militia attacks in the Darfur region of The Sudan in the past week have killed scores of civilians, including 27 young children.

▸ Ted Haggard, president of the National Association of Evangelicals, resigns as head pastor of the New Life megachurch in Colorado Springs CO after a former male prostitute says that he had a three-year affair with Haggard, who has publicly opposed gay sex and same-sex marriage.

▸ At the Latin Grammy Awards in New York City, Colombian singer Shakira wins four awards, including song of the year and record of the year.

3 Nov A study is published in the journal *Science* showing that if no adjustments are made in current fisheries practices, the entire marine ecosystem is likely to collapse by 2048.

4 Nov In ceremonies at the National Cathedral in Washington DC, Katharine Jefferts Schori is formally installed as the presiding bishop of the Episcopal Church, USA.

5 Nov Deposed Iraqi president Saddam Hussein is found guilty by an Iraqi court for the death of 148 people in Dujail in 1982; he is sentenced to be hanged.

▸ Voters go to the polls in Nicaragua to choose among five candidates for president; the winner is Daniel Ortega of the Sandinista National Liberation Front.

6 Nov Imomali Rakhmonov is reelected president of Tajikistan in elections that are boycotted by the main opposition and that fail to meet international standards.

7 Nov In legislative elections in the US, the Democratic Party gains control over the House of Representatives, with 233 of the 435 seats; with the aid of two independents, Democrats will also have a narrow majority in the Senate.

▸ The delivery company FedEx cancels its order for 10 Airbus A380s because of production delays for the giant plane, instead ordering 15 Boeing 777 freighters.

▸ Australian Prime Minister John Howard calls a meeting to address the country's worsening drought, the worst in 1,000 years.

8 Nov US Pres. George W. Bush announces the resignation of Donald Rumsfeld as secretary of defense and names Robert Gates, a former CIA director, as his successor.

9 Nov Israeli Prime Minister Ehud Olmert apologizes for the killing of 18 Palestinian civilians in Beit Hanun, Gaza, the previous day and offers to meet the Palestinian Authority president.

10 Nov In the Pakistani town of Shakai in South Waziristan, a roadside bomb kills pro-government tribal chief Malik Khajan and eight other people.

11 Nov The US vetoes a UN Security Council resolution taking Israel to task for disproportionate violence in Gaza and calling on Palestinians to take action to end rocket fire into Israel.

12 Nov The Houston Dynamo wins the Major League Soccer title.

13 Nov The US House of Representatives votes down a measure to grant permanent normal trade relations with Vietnam that is favored by US Pres. George W. Bush.

14 Nov In Baghdad, armed men in Iraqi police uniforms and driving trucks with Interior Ministry markings invade the Ministry of Higher Education, kidnapping at least 55 and possibly as many as 150 people.

▸ South Africa's legislature passes a bill that legalizes same-sex marriage, though it does not require officials to perform such marriages.

15 Nov As the UN climate conference opens in Nairobi, UN Secretary-General Kofi Annan, in his opening speech, decries the lack of leadership on the issue of climate change.

QUOTE OF THE MONTH

❝ *The impact of climate change will fall disproportionately on the world's poorest countries, many of them here in Africa. Poor people already live on the front lines of pollution, disaster, and the degradation of resources and land.* ❞

—UN Secretary-General Kofi Annan,
addressing the UN conference on climate
change in Nairobi, 15 November

---

16 Nov The much-anticipated Sony PlayStation 3 gaming system goes on sale at midnight throughout the US.

17 Nov Russia's State Duma (lower legislative house) approves new election laws that eliminate minimum turnout rules, allow the government to ban candidates, and forbid criticism of electoral opponents.

▸ The US Food and Drug Administration rescinds a 14-year-old ban on the use of silicone-gel breast implants, allowing them to be used for breast reconstruction and, for women over the age of 21, for cosmetic augmentation.

18 Nov In Madagascar, one day after Gen. Andrianafidisoa issued leaflets announcing a military coup, he is greeted by gunfire at a military base where he was seeking support; in an exchange of gunfire between his supporters and government forces, one government soldier is killed.

19 Nov The sudden illness of Alexander V. Litvinenko, a former KGB operative and outspoken opponent of the Russian government living in exile in Great Britain, attracts the attention of the British police because it appears to be a case of poisoning.

▸ The BC Lions capture the 94th Canadian Football League Grey Cup.

20 Nov Iraq and Syria reestablish diplomatic relations, which Syria had severed in 1982.

▸ The US Mint unveils four new one-dollar coins, each bearing the likeness of one of the first four US presidents.

21 Nov In Kathmandu, Nepali Prime Minister Girija Prasad Koirala and Maoist rebel leader Prachanda sign a peace agreement that will bring the Maoists into the transitional government, taking 73 seats in the country's legislature.

22 Nov In legislative elections in The Netherlands, the center-right Christian Democratic Party of Prime Minister Jan Peter Balkenende retains its majority.

▸ Pres. Vicente Fox of Mexico inaugurates the Large Millimeter Telescope (LMT), situated atop Sierra Negra in Puebla state.

23 Nov A judge in France calls for Pres. Paul Kagame of Rwanda to be tried in a UN court for complicity in the plane crash that killed Pres. Juvénal Habyarimana in 1994, igniting 100 days of genocide; some 25,000 Rwandans rally in protest.

24 Nov Authorities in London say they have determined that Russian opposition figure Alexander V. Litvinenko was killed by poisoning with the very rare radioactive substance polonium 210.

25 Nov Palestinian Authority Pres. Mahmoud Abbas and Israeli Prime Minister Ehud Olmert agree to a full cease-fire in the Gaza Strip.

▶ At least 47 Sunni insurgents are killed in gun battles with Iraqi security forces in Ba'qubah; 21 corpses are found in Balad Ruz and 17 in Baghdad, and the US military reports that it killed 22 insurgents and a civilian in battles north of Baghdad.

26 Nov A runoff presidential election in Ecuador is won by leftist candidate Rafael Correa.

27 Nov In a speech, Israeli Prime Minister Ehud Olmert offers a prisoner release, the release of embargoed moneys, and further negotiations if Palestine achieves a national unity government and releases the Israeli soldier captured earlier in the year.

28 Nov Pope Benedict XVI arrives in Turkey for a four-day visit.

29 Nov At the last minute, Iraqi Prime Minister Nuri Kamal al-Maliki cancels a planned dinner meeting with US Pres. George W. Bush and King Abdullah II of Jordan in Amman, Jordan; a breakfast meeting does take place the following day, however.

30 Nov Palestinian Authority Pres. Mahmoud Abbas announces that negotiations for a national unity government in Palestine have failed.

December 2006

1 Dec In a very brief ceremony accompanied by fisticuffs and catcalls in the Chamber of Deputies, Felipe Calderón is sworn in as president of Mexico.

▶ Hundreds of thousands of people turn out in the streets of Beirut to demand the resignation of Lebanese Prime Minister Fouad Siniora; demonstrations continue through the end of the year.

2 Dec Three car bombs explode in rapid succession in Baghdad, killing at least 51 people, while some 20 other people are killed throughout the city.

3 Dec Hugo Chávez wins reelection as president of Venezuela in a landslide.

▶ In an interview with the BBC, UN Secretary-General Kofi Annan says that Iraq is in a state of civil war.

▶ The annual Kennedy Center Honors are presented in Washington DC to film director Steven Spielberg, theater composer Andrew Lloyd Webber, orchestra conductor Zubin Mehta, and singers Dolly Parton and Smokey Robinson.

4 Dec A merger between the Bank of New York and Pittsburgh's Mellon Financial is announced; the new financial services giant is to be called Bank of New York Mellon Corp.

▶ John R. Bolton resigns as US ambassador to the UN.

5 Dec Military chief Frank Bainimarama announces that the military has taken over the government in Fiji in the country's fourth coup in 19 years.

6 Dec The bipartisan Iraq Study Group delivers its report to US Pres. George W. Bush; the blue-ribbon panel recommends moving toward a policy of disengagement.

▶ Joseph Kabila is sworn in as the first democratically elected president in the Democratic Republic of the Congo in over 40 years.

7 Dec At least 23 people are killed in various bombings and shootings in Iraq, and 35 bullet-riddled bodies are found in Baghdad.

▶ Gen. Bantz John Craddock of the US Army is sworn in as NATO's Supreme Allied Commander, Europe, replacing Gen. James L. Jones of the US Marines.

8 Dec The US House of Representatives passes a bill favored by Pres. George W. Bush permitting the sale of civilian nuclear reactors and fuel to India.

▶ The Commonwealth suspends Fiji's membership.

9 Dec In Darfur unidentified gunmen on horseback attack a truck carrying medical and aid supplies and kill about 30 civilians, some shot and some burned alive.

10 Dec Former Chilean dictator Augusto Pinochet dies in Santiago.

11 Dec The Organization for the Prohibition of Chemical Weapons grants the US and Russia a five-year extension, to 2012, of the deadline for destroying their stockpiles of chemical weapons under the Chemical Weapons Convention.

12 Dec At the end of a 12-year case in Addis Ababa, the Ethiopian High Court finds former dictator Mengistu Haile Mariam and 70 others guilty of genocide.

13 Dec The UN General Assembly unanimously adopts an international convention for civil and political rights of the disabled, including accessibility rights.

14 Dec South Korean Ban Ki-moon is sworn in as secretary-general of the United Nations.

▶ Israel stops Palestinian Prime Minister Ismail Haniya from returning to the Gaza Strip from Egypt for seven hours until he agrees to leave behind the large amounts of cash he is carrying; cash brought in from other countries is the only means now open to the Palestinian Authority to pay government expenses.

15 Dec US Pres. George W. Bush awards the Presidential Medal of Freedom to Ruth Johnson Colvin, Norman C. Francis, Paul Johnson, B.B. King, Joshua Lederberg, David McCullough, Norman Y. Mineta, Buck O'Neil, William Safire, and Natan Sharansky.

16 Dec King Jigme Singye Wangchuk of Bhutan abdicates, two years earlier than previously announced, in favor of his son, Jigme Khesar Namgyal Wangchuk, in order that his son may gain experience ahead of the country's first-ever legislative elections.

17 Dec Seven parishes in Virginia vote to secede from the Episcopal Church, USA, and affiliate themselves with the Convocation of Anglicans in North America, which is presided over by the conservative archbishop of Nigeria.

18 Dec Representatives of China, Japan, North Korea, South Korea, Russia, and the US meet in Beijing in renewed negotiations over North Korea's nuclear program.

▶ An arrest is made in the death of five prostitutes near Trimley St. Martin, Suffolk, England, in a case that has riveted the country; later a different man is charged with the murders.

19 Dec For the second time, five Bulgarian nurses and a Palestinian doctor are sentenced to death in Libya for having deliberately infected children in a hospital in Benghazi with HIV; experts have suggested that the 1998 outbreak of HIV in the hospital predated the arrival of the defendants.

▶ Battles between masked gunmen from Fatah and Hamas leave five people dead in Gaza City, in spite of public pleas from both Pres. Mahmoud Abbas and Prime Minister Ismail Haniya of Palestine.

20 Dec In a ceremony Al-Najaf becomes the third Iraqi province transferred to Iraqi control from US control; in Baghdad at least 114 people are killed or found dead.

21 Dec Saparmurad Niyazov, Turkmenistan's capricious and autocratic president, dies unexpectedly.

▶ The US Marine Corps charges four Marines with murder in the killing of 24 civilians in the Iraqi village of Haditha in November 2005; also, four officers are charged with dereliction of duty.

22 Dec Six-party talks on North Korea's nuclear program end with no discernible progress, owing largely to intransigence on the part of both North Korea and the US.

23 Dec The UN Security Council approves a limited program of sanctions against Iran intended to stop its program of uranium enrichment.

24 Dec Although it has been involved for some time, Ethiopia now massively enters the war against the forces of the Islamic Courts Union in Somalia.

25 Dec British and Iraqi forces storm a police station in Basra, Iraq, killing seven people and rescuing 127 prisoners who had been tortured and faced likely execution; the police unit had been infiltrated by death squads.

26 Dec An appeals court in Iraq upholds the death sentence against deposed president Saddam Hussein and rules that it must be carried out within 30 days.

▶ Former US president Gerald R. Ford (1974–77) dies in Rancho Mirage CA at the age of 93.

27 Dec The US Department of the Interior proposes listing polar bears as a threatened species; the proposal is the first step in a formal designation for which the final determination must be made within a year.

28 Dec Forces of Somalia's transitional national government, backed by the Ethiopian military, re-

take Mogadishu from the forces of the Union of Islamic Courts.

QUOTE OF THE MONTH

❝ *We always knew these Islamists weren't all they were cracked up to be. And now we are where they used to be, in control of Mogadishu—well, as much as anyone can be in control of Mogadishu.* ❞

—Abdirizad Adam Hassam, chief of staff for Somalia's transition president, after national forces retake the capital, 28 December

---

▶ A wave of violent attacks by drug gangs in Rio de Janeiro leaves at least 19 people dead.

29 Dec The Medicaid Commission established in 2005 by Secretary of Health and Human Services Michael O. Leavitt to find ways to modernize the US health care system delivers its final report.

30 Dec Former Iraqi president Saddam Hussein is hanged before dawn.

▶ Three car bombs in Baghdad kill 36 people, while another car bomb, in Kufah, kills 31.

31 Dec A video taken on a cell phone of the hanging of former Iraqi president Saddam Hussein is widely circulated; the execution has the look of a Shiʻite lynching, which causes international controversy.

▶ The death toll of American troops in Iraq since March 2003 reaches 3,000 with the death of Dustin Donica of Texas; estimates of total Iraqi deaths range from 30,000 (Pres. George W. Bush in December 2005) to 655,000 (Johns Hopkins University Bloomberg School of Public Health, October 2006).

January 2007

1 Jan With the beginning of the new year, Chancellor Angela Merkel of Germany assumes the presidency of the European Union.

▶ Bulgaria and Romania officially accede to the European Union, bringing the number of member states to 27; celebrations are held in Sofia and Bucharest, the respective capitals of the new members; Slovenia, meanwhile, becomes the 13th member of the European Union to adopt the euro as its official currency.

2 Jan The annual Hajj to Mecca, Saudi Arabia, ends without incident.

▶ In Australia, the Aborgine Githabul tribe reaches an agreement with the state government of New South Wales that gives the Githabul joint ownership with the government over an area of 6,000 sq km (2,300 sq mi), including national parks and forests.

▶ Oprah Winfrey officially opens the Oprah Winfrey Leadership Academy for Girls in Henley-on-Klip, South Africa; with an initial class of 152 girls, the eventual enrollment is planned to be 450.

3 Jan The US government announces that John D. Negroponte will resign as director of national intelligence in order to become deputy secretary of state, filling a post that has been vacant since the resignation of Robert B. Zoellick.

▶ Kenya closes its border with Somalia in an attempt to prevent fundamentalist Muslim militia members from entering the country.

4 Jan In Fiji, coup leader Frank Bainimarama restores Pres. Ratu Josefa Iloilo to power and dismisses Jona Senilagakali, whom Bainimarama had appointed interim prime minister; the following day Bainimarama is sworn in as interim prime minister.

▶ Democratic Rep. Nancy Pelosi of California becomes speaker of the US House of Representatives; she is the first woman to hold the post.

▶ Two bombs go off at a gas station in Baghdad, killing 13 people; in various other places in the city, the mutilated bodies of 47 people are found.

5 Jan US Pres. George W. Bush names Zalmay Khalilzad, currently US ambassador to Iraq, as his choice to become UN ambassador.

6 Jan A bomb on a passenger bus near Hikkaduwa, Sri Lanka, kills 11 people.

▶ Government officials in India say that a series of attacks by the United Liberation Front of Assam over the past two days has left at least 55 people dead.

7 Jan The US Air Force conducts a raid in Somalia, using a gunship against suspected al-Qaeda operatives.

▶ On the occasion that he was to be enthroned as Roman Catholic archbishop of Warsaw, Bishop Stanislaw Wielgus instead resigns after having admitted collaboration with the Polish secret police during the communist era; Jozef Cardinal Glemp is reappointed archbishop.

8 Jan Russia shuts down its oil pipeline that runs through Belarus, accusing Belarus of siphoning off fuel intended for other European countries; the cut-off affects supplies in Ukraine, Germany, Poland, Hungary, the Czech Republic, and Slovakia.

▸ The University of Florida defeats Ohio State University 41–14 to win college football's Bowl Championship Series title game in Glendale AZ as well as the national Division I-A championship.

9 Jan Hundreds of American and Iraqi troops fight insurgents in a daylong battle in downtown Baghdad.

▸ At the Macworld Expo trade show in San Francisco, Steven P. Jobs introduces the novel touch-screen-based iPhone, combining music player, camera, Web functions, and phone with other innovations.

▸ Cal Ripken, Jr., who played in 2,632 consecutive games, and Tony Gwynn are elected to the National Baseball Hall of Fame; slugger Mark McGwire is rejected.

10 Jan In a televised speech to the country, US Pres. George W. Bush acknowledges difficulties in Iraq and announces that he is sending 20,000 more US troops to Iraq in what he calls a "surge" to end the violence in Baghdad.

▸ China reports a record trade surplus for 2006 of $177.47 billion.

▸ Pres. Omar Hassan al-Bashir of The Sudan and leaders of several rebel groups in Darfur agree to a 60-day cease-fire in a truce brokered by New Mexico Gov. Bill Richardson.

11 Jan Alfred Gusenbauer is sworn in as chancellor of Austria at the head of a coalition government.

▸ Bangladeshi Pres. Iajuddin Ahmed declares a state of emergency, postpones elections, and resigns as caretaker prime minister.

▸ The Los Angeles Galaxy announces that it has signed Real Madrid star David Beckham to play Major League Soccer in the US starting in the summer.

12 Jan Pres. Iajuddin Ahmed of Bangladesh names Fakhruddin Ahmed head of the interim government ahead of elections and relaxes some controls imposed under the state of emergency.

13 Jan Meeting at Cebu, Philippines, the members of the Association of Southeast Asian Nations (ASEAN) agree to create a free-trade zone in the region by 2015 and approve the outline of a governing charter.

14 Jan Nicolas Sarkozy, French minister of the interior, is chosen as its presidential candidate by the ruling centre-right Union for a Popular Movement Party in Paris.

15 Jan A temporary constitution that makes the prime minister, rather than the king, head of state is approved in Nepal, and 83 Maoist rebels take seats in the interim legislature that the document grants them.

▸ Rafael Correa is sworn in as president of Ecuador and orders that a referendum be held on 18 March on amending the constitution to decrease the power of traditional parties.

16 Jan Two car bombs and a suicide bomber kill at least 70 people at Mustansiriyah University in Baghdad, and other assorted acts of violence kill 15 others throughout the city.

17 Jan In a speech to the European Parliament as president of the European Union, German Chancellor Angela Merkel states her goals of reviving the drive to pass the union's constitution and completing the Doha round of trade talks.

18 Jan US government officials reveal that China carried out a successful test of an antisatellite weapon some days ago, destroying an old weather satellite;

it was the first antisatellite test since the mid-1980s, when the US conducted such tests.

19 Jan After reports that United Nations Development Programme moneys may be being misused in North Korea, UN Secretary-General Ban Ki-moon calls for systemwide outside auditing of all UN activities.

▸ Prominent ethnic Armenian newspaper editor Hrant Dink is shot to death outside his office in Istanbul.

20 Jan A US helicopter crashes north of Baghdad, possibly shot down, killing all 13 aboard, and five American soldiers are killed in battle in Karbala.

21 Jan Sébastien Loeb, three-time world champion of automobile rally racing, wins the Monte Carlo Rally.

22 Jan Two car bombs in a market in Baghdad explode at noon, a very busy time, and kill at least 88 people.

▸ In fighting between antigovernment protesters and security forces in Conakry, Guinea, 17 people are killed.

▸ In the field of children's literature, the Newbery Medal is awarded to Susan Patron for *The Higher Power of Lucky,* a somewhat controversial book, and David Wiesner wins the Caldecott Medal for illustration for his book *Flotsam.*

▸ In Thoroughbred horse racing's 2006 Eclipse Awards, Invasor is named Horse of the Year.

23 Jan US Pres. George W. Bush delivers his sixth State of the Union address; he asks for support for his strategy in Iraq and makes modest health care proposals and plans to reduce gasoline consumption.

QUOTE OF THE MONTH

" *Ladies and gentlemen, on this day, at this hour, it is still within our power to shape the outcome of this battle. Let us find our resolve and turn events toward victory.* "

—US Pres. George W. Bush, asking for support for his planned troop "surge" in the Iraq war in his State of the Union Address, 23 January

---

▸ Government figures show that in 2006 Macau became the world's biggest gambling center, with gaming revenue exceeding that in Las Vegas.

24 Jan For the second time this month, US military forces conduct an air strike in Somalia.

25 Jan Charles Rabemananjara is sworn in as prime minister of Madagascar.

▸ A committee of the Knesset approves the request of Pres. Moshe Katsav to be suspended; Dalia Itzik is named acting president.

▸ The Ford Motor Co. announces a loss of $12.7 billion for 2006, its largest single-year loss ever.

26 Jan UN mediator Martti Ahtisaari presents his proposals for the future of the enclave of Kosovo in Serbia; the plan would allow Kosovo to declare independence but ensure international supervision to protect the rights of the Serbian minority in the region.

27 Jan Two car bombs go off at a busy market in Baghdad where crowds had gathered for a preparatory ritual for the Shiʿite holy day of ʿAshura; at least 15 people are killed.

▸ A suicide bomber kills 14 people, mostly police officers, just before a planned religious procession in Peshawar, Pakistan.

▸ American Serena Williams defeats Mariya Sharapova of Russia to win the Australian Open tennis tournament for the second successive year; the following day Roger Federer of Switzerland defeats Chilean Fernando González to win the men's title.

28 Jan A battle takes place outside Al-Najaf, Iraq, between Iraqi and American forces and a group of militants apparently intent on disrupting observations of the holy day 'Ashura; at least 250 people are killed.

▸ As violence between Hamas and Fatah that has claimed more than 20 lives in the past four days continues in Gaza, King Abdullah of Saudi Arabia invites both factions to hold reconciliation talks in Mecca in February; both sides say they will accept the invitation.

29 Jan China announces a plan to lend $3 billion in preferential credit to countries in Africa without placing political or other conditions on the loans.

▸ Meeting in Addis Ababa, Ethiopia, the African Union chooses Pres. John Kufuor of Ghana to assume the organization's rotating presidency, rebuffing The Sudan's bid for the second consecutive year because of worsening violence in Darfur.

30 Jan In violence connected with the observance of 'Ashura in Iraq, some 50 people are killed, at least 23 of them by a bomb in Karbala.

▸ Vice Pres. Cassim Chilumpha of Malawi goes on trial for treason; he is accused of having hired hit men to attempt to assassinate Pres. Bingu wa Mutharika.

▸ Vista, Microsoft's new Windows operating system, and its software suite Office 2007 go on sale.

31 Jan Venezuela's National Assembly grants Pres. Hugo Chávez the power to govern by decree for the next year and a half.

February 2007

1 Feb Two suicide bombers kill at least 60 people in a crowded market in Al-Hillah, Iraq, while at least 46 people die in assorted violent incidents in Baghdad.

▸ Taliban forces sack the town of Musa Qala, Afghanistan, which had been turned over to local control by British forces in October 2006 in an effort to end fighting.

2 Feb The Intergovernmental Panel on Climate Change releases the first section of its four-part report; it says that global warming is "unequivocal" and that human activity is almost certainly the cause and cites scientific evidence for these conclusions.

▸ In the Gaza Strip, 17 people are killed in fighting between adherents of Fatah and Hamas, and Fatah members attack the Islamic University in Gaza City.

3 Feb A suicide truck bomber detonates an estimated one ton of explosives in a crowded Shi'ite market in Baghdad, killing at least 130 people.

▸ British officials confirm that the H5N1 strain of avian flu has been found on a poultry farm in eastern England.

4 Feb Two days after a police officer was killed in rioting following an association football (soccer) match between Catania and Palermo in Sicily, the Italian Olympic Committee suspends all further matches.

▸ In Miami the Indianapolis Colts defeat the Chicago Bears 29–17 to win the National Football League's Super Bowl XLI.

5 Feb The computer company Apple Inc. and Apple Corps Ltd., which licenses Beatles music and related products, announce a new agreement whereby Apple Inc. will own all trademarks but license some of them back to Apple Corps; a dispute arose when Apple Computer began selling music through iTunes in 2003.

▸ Astronaut Lisa Nowak is arrested in Orlando FL after a bizarre attack on a perceived rival in a romantic triangle.

6 Feb US Pres. George W. Bush and Secretary of Defense Robert M. Gates announce that the United States Africa Command will be established by 30 Sep 2008; responsibility for Africa is now divided between three commands.

▸ For the second time in two days in England, a letter bomb explodes in a motoring-related company, this one in the offices of an accounting firm in Wokingham; the first was in a building near Scotland Yard headquarters in London.

7 Feb A Marine transport helicopter is shot down near Baghdad; it is the sixth helicopter to crash in combat in three weeks.

▸ A letter bomb explodes at the main British motor vehicle agency in Swansea, Wales; it seems to be of an incendiary nature, as were the ones that preceded it.

▸ British author Stef Penney wins the Costa (formerly Whitbread) Book of the Year Award for her first novel, *The Tenderness of Wolves*.

▸ Despite a loss in the final game to the host team (the Carolina Giants [Gigantes] of Puerto Rico), the Cibao Eagles (Águilas) from the Dominican Republic win baseball's Caribbean Series with a tournament record of 5–1.

▸ Sweden's Ministry of Agriculture gives the country's reindeer herders some $5.3 million in emergency aid to keep their animals from starving; thick ice has made it impossible for the reindeer to eat the lichen that is their usual diet.

8 Feb A paper published in *Nature* magazine describes an experiment by a team of researchers led by Lene Vestergaard Hau that used Bose-Einstein clouds to stop a pulse of light and reconstitute it in another location, where it continued on its way.

9 Feb Jim Samples resigns as general manager of the cable television Cartoon Network after a guerrilla marketing campaign involving electronic advertisements placed in unexpected places in several major cities caused a bomb scare in Boston.

10 Feb Gen. David H. Petraeus assumes responsibility for US troops in Iraq, replacing Gen. George W. Casey, Jr.

11 Feb Acting president Gurbanguly Berdymukhammedov wins the presidential election in Turkmenistan.

▸ Harvard University names Drew Gilpin Faust, dean of the Radcliffe Institute for Advanced Study, university president; she will be the first woman to serve in the post.

▸ At the Grammy Awards in Los Angeles, the top winner is the country music trio Dixie Chicks, who win five awards, including album of the year, for *Taking the Long Way,* and both record of the year and song of the year, for "Not Ready To Make Nice"; the best new artist is country singer Carrie Underwood.

12 Feb Four bombs at two markets in Baghdad leave at least 67 people dead and scores more injured.

▸ The World Health Organization for the first time approves a vaccine against rotavirus, which causes diarrhea and kills some 600,000 children a year; the approval means UN agencies can use it in mass-vaccination campaigns.

13 Feb In the six-country talks about North Korea's nuclear program, an agreement is reached that will give North Korea fuel oil and financial aid in exchange for starting to dismantle its nuclear facilities and for allowing UN inspectors back into the country.

▸ The US Department of Commerce reports that the country's trade deficit in 2006 reached $763.3 billion, a 6.5% increase over the previous year and a new record for the sixth consecutive year.

▸ Felicity's Diamond Jim, an English springer spaniel, wins Best in Show at the Westminster Kennel Club's 131st dog show.

14 Feb In the first major sweep by US and Iraqi forces through several Baghdad neighborhoods, very little resistance is encountered as the forces implement a new security plan for the city.

▸ In Zahedan, Iran, a car bomb explodes in front of a bus carrying Revolutionary Guard members; at least 11 people are killed.

▸ At the Brit Awards for popular music, the Arctic Monkeys win for best British group and best British album, and the Killers win best international group and best international album.

15 Feb The Hamas-led government of the Palestinian Authority resigns, and Pres. Mahmoud Abbas immediately asks the prime minister, Ismail Haniya, to form a new government.

▸ The US National Endowment for the Arts grants its inaugural International Literature Awards to Archipelago Books of Brooklyn, which is to publish Amaia Gabantxo's translation of *Vredaman* by Basque writer Unai Elorriaga; to Dalkey Archive Press of Champaign IL, which is to publish Karen Emmerich's translation of the short-story collection *I'd Like* by Amanda Michalopoulou of Greece; and to Etruscan Press of Wilkes-Barre PA, which is to publish Diane Thiel's translation of *Amerikaniki Fouga* by Greek writer Alexis Stamatis.

16 Feb A court in Italy brings indictments against 26 Americans, most of them alleged CIA officers, as well as the former head of Italy's spy agency, in connection with the disappearance of Egyptian cleric Hassan Mustafa Osama Nasr, who says he was kidnapped and sent to Egypt, where he was tortured; this is the first case ordered to trial involving the US program of "extraordinary renditions."

17 Feb In Quetta, Pakistan, a suicide bomber detonates his weapon in a small district courtroom, killing 15 people, including a senior judge.

▸ The Chinese film *Tuya de hun shi* (*Tuya's Marriage*), directed by Wang Quanan, wins the Golden Bear at the Berlin International Film Festival.

18 Feb Two bombs explode shortly before midnight just outside Diwana, India, on the Attari Express train traveling from Delhi to the border between India and Pakistan; at least 66 people are killed.

▸ Shortly after a US and Iraqi military patrol has passed through, two car bombs go off in rapid succession in a market in Baghdad; at least 60 people are killed.

▸ In Daytona Beach FL, Kevin Harvick wins the 49th Daytona 500, the premier NASCAR race, by an exceptionally close 0.02 second.

▸ In London, *Sunday in the Park with George* wins five Laurence Olivier Awards—outstanding musical production, best actor in a musical (Daniel Evans), best actress in a musical (Jenna Russell), best lighting design, and best set design.

19 Feb At the Anglican church gathering in Dar es Salaam, Tanzania, the Anglican Communion directs the Episcopal Church, USA, to ban the blessing of same-sex unions within eight months and establishes a council and vicar to address the concerns of conservative American congregations.

▸ The rival satellite radio companies XM and Sirius announce a merger; the combined company, with 14 million subscribers, will have Mel Karmazin of Sirius as CEO and will be called Project Big Sky by XM.

20 Feb Nigeria's Court of Appeal rules that the fact that Vice Pres. Atiku Abubakar is a presidential candidate for a political party not in power is not a valid reason for Pres. Olusegun Obasanjo to dismiss him.

21 Feb The $100,000 A.M. Turing Award for excellence in computer science is granted to Frances E. Allen for her work on optimizing compiler performance at IBM; she is the first woman to win the prize, which has been awarded since 1966.

22 Feb The International Atomic Energy Agency reports that Iran is steadily and quickly increasing its ability to enrich uranium, defying the United Nations.

▸ A federal jury orders Microsoft to pay $1.52 billion in royalties to Alcatel-Lucent for patents involved in the development of the MP3 audio file format.

▸ Executives of the All England Club announce that henceforth the prize money for men and women competing at the Wimbledon tennis tournament will be equal.

23 Feb The Supreme Court of Canada strikes down a law permitting the indefinite detention of foreign-born terrorism suspects; the ruling is suspended for a year so that the parliament may draft a law consistent with the ruling.

▸ Margaret M. Chiara is dismissed as US attorney in Grand Rapids MI; she is the eighth US attorney to be removed by the Department of Justice in the past few months in what is becoming a political scandal.

24 Feb A truck bomb goes off near a Sunni mosque, a school, an Iraqi police station, and a public market in Habbaniyah, Iraq, killing at least 36 people; in addition, US forces briefly detain Amar al-Hakim, son of a Shi'ite leader, provoking an international furor.

25 Feb Presidential elections are held in Senegal; voters reelect Pres. Abdoulaye Wade, who bests 14 challengers.

▸ At the 79th Academy Awards presentation, hosted by Ellen DeGeneres, Oscars are won by, among others, *The Departed* (best picture) and its director, Martin Scorsese, and actors Forest Whitaker, Helen Mirren, Alan Arkin, and Jennifer Hudson.

▸ Louis Farrakhan, leader of the Nation of Islam, gives what he intends to be his final major address, in Detroit.

QUOTE OF THE MONTH

❝ *Our lips are full of praise but our hearts are far removed from the prophets we all claim. That's why the world is in the shape that it's in.* ❞

—Louis Farrakhan, in his last public address as head of the Nation of Islam, in Detroit, 25 February

---

26 Feb Opening ceremonies are held in Washington DC, London, and Strasbourg, France, for the International Polar Year, a two-year project undertaken by scientists from more than 60 countries to learn as much as possible by studying the North and South poles.

▶ *Hold Me Close,* a memorial to the victims of the Indian Ocean tsunami of December 2004 by artist Louise Bourgeois, is unveiled in Hat Nopparat National Park in Thailand.

▶ Iraq's cabinet approves a draft law that will allow oil revenues to be distributed to regions on the basis of population and that will permit foreign companies to develop oil fields.

▶ Pres. Lansana Conté of Guinea appoints Lansana Kouyate prime minister; Kouyate was on a list of candidates deemed acceptable by union leaders.

▶ The PEN/Faulkner Award for fiction is granted to Philip Roth for his novel *Everyman;* Roth has won the award for a record third time.

27 Feb A sudden sell-off of stocks in the Shanghai market triggers a worldwide landslide in stock markets; in the US the Dow Jones industrial average suffers its biggest one-day point loss since 2001, the S&P 500 its largest drop in nearly four years, and the Nasdaq its biggest slide since 2002.

▶ A suicide bomber explodes outside the Bagram Air Base in Afghanistan, killing some 23 people; US Vice Pres. Dick Cheney is inside the base at the time.

28 Feb The NASA spacecraft *New Horizons,* launched in January 2006, reaches Jupiter; the craft will gather data on the planet and four of its moons until June, when it will continue on to Pluto.

March 2007

1 Mar Russian Pres. Vladimir Putin appoints Ramzan A. Kadyrov president of the republic of Chechnya; Kadyrov heads a security force that is believed to have been responsible for a number of atrocities.

▶ Japanese Prime Minister Shinzo Abe declares that there is no evidence to show that the country's military forced foreign women into sexual servitude during World War II; this contradicts the position held by the Japanese government since 1993.

2 Mar US Secretary of Defense Robert M. Gates dismisses Francis J. Harvey as army secretary over Harvey's response to revelations of poor care of soldiers at Walter Reed Army Medical Center, and Lieut. Gen. Kevin Kiley is replaced as temporary head of the hospital by Maj. Gen. Eric B. Schoomaker; Kiley is removed as army surgeon general on 12 March.

▶ Negotiators for the US and the European Union reach a preliminary agreement on a so-called "open skies" treaty that would eliminate almost all restrictions on cross-Atlantic air travel routes; full agreement is reached on 22 March.

3 Mar At the 20th Panafrican Film and Television Festival of Ouagadougou (Fespaco) in Burkina Faso, Africa's biggest film festival, the Golden Stallion goes to Nigerian director Newton I. Aduaka for his film *Ezra.*

4 Mar After a suicide car bombing near Jalalabad, Afghanistan, US troops open fire on a highway, killing at least 16 civilians; also, in response to a rocket attack, US forces in Afghanistan carry out an air strike on a compound near Kabul, reportedly killing 9 civilians, all members of a single family.

▶ Members of the Cherokee Nation in the US vote to deny membership in the tribe to African American descendants of slaves once owned by Cherokee.

5 Mar A car bomb goes off in Baghdad's historic literary quarter, leaving at least 20 people dead.

▶ The day after Australian forces struck at the stronghold of rebel leader Alfredo Reinado in East Timor, triggering massive demonstrations in support of Reinado, Timorese Pres. Xanana Gusmão declares a state of emergency.

6 Mar In various incidents in Iraq, at least 113 Shi'ite pilgrims preparing for the celebration of Arbaeen are killed, including at least 77 killed by back-to-back suicide bombers in Al-Hillah.

▶ Abu Dhabi signs an agreement with France to pay $520 million for use of the name of the Louvre Museum and $747 million more for art loans and management advice; the Louvre Abu Dhabi, de-

signed by architect Jean Nouvel, is scheduled to open after 2012.

▶ Fireworks and dancing in the streets as well as a recitation of the speech made in 1957 by Kwame Nkrumah, the country's first leader, mark the celebration of the 50th anniversary of Ghana's independence.

7 Mar At least 70 people are killed in assorted incidents in Iraq, 30 of them by a suicide bombing at a café in Ba'qubah.

▶ A scandal involving the murders of four Guatemalan police officers results in the resignation of the interior minister and police chief; the police officers, themselves in custody for the killing on 19 February of three Salvadoran lawmakers and their driver, were suspected of having ties to drug gangs.

▶ In comic books that arrive in stores today, the Marvel Entertainment superhero Captain America, who first appeared in 1941, is killed.

8 Mar The winners of the annual $100,000 TED Prize announce the projects that they intend to use the money for: former US president Bill Clinton has a foundation that is building a rural health-care system in Rwanda, biologist Edward O. Wilson is creating an Internet database to catalog all species of living things, and photographer James Nachtwey is creating a display of photographs about an unknown "big story."

▶ In New York City the winners of the National Book Critics Circle Awards are announced as Kiran Desai for *The Inheritance of Loss* (fiction), Simon Schama for *Rough Crossings* (nonfiction), Julie Phillips for *James Tiptree, Jr.* (biography), Daniel Mendelsohn for *The Lost* (autobiography), Troy Jollimore for *Tom Thomson in Purgatory* (poetry), and Lawrence Weschler for *Everything That Rises* (criticism); John Leonard is granted the Ivan Sandrof Lifetime Achievement Award.

9 Mar The European Union approves an agreement to reduce greenhouse gases by 20% from 1990 levels, obtain one-fifth of its energy from renewable resources, and run 10% of its vehicles on biofuels by 2020.

10 Mar Hundreds of thousands of people gather in Madrid to protest the granting of house arrest to José Ignacio de Juana Chaos, a leader of the Basque militant organization ETA who had been in prison.

11 Mar The energy services company Halliburton announces that it is moving its corporate headquarters to Dubai, though it will maintain its incorporation in the US.

12 Mar The Rock and Roll Hall of Fame in Cleveland inducts singer Patti Smith and the groups Van Halen, the Ronettes, R.E.M., and Grandmaster Flash and the Furious Five (the first hip-hop act to be inducted).

13 Mar Pres. Abdullahi Yusuf Ahmed of Somalia moves for the first time to Mogadishu, the capital, from the government stronghold of Baidoa; within hours a mortar attack is made on the presidential palace.

▶ Lance Mackey wins the 1,820-km (1,131-mi) Iditarod Trail Sled Dog Race, crossing the Burled Arch in Nome AK after a journey of 9 days 5 hours 8 minutes 41 seconds; Mackey's father and brother are previous winners of the race.

14 Mar The fruit company Chiquita Brands International agrees to pay a $25 million settlement in a case in which it was accused of having hired a rightwing militia to protect banana plantations in Colombia.

▶ Charles Taylor, a Canadian professor of law and philosophy, is named the winner of the Templeton Prize for Progress Toward Research or Discoveries About Spiritual Realities.

15 Mar A new Palestinian government composed of a unity coalition of Hamas and Fatah ministers is announced; led by Prime Minister Ismail Haniya, it fails to recognize Israel's right to exist or to promise not to use or support violence against Israel.

▶ In Athens the heads of state of Russia, Greece, and Bulgaria sign an agreement to build an oil pipeline that will run from Burgas, Bulgaria, to Alexandroupolis, Greece, bypassing the Bosporus strait in Turkey.

▶ In Bijapur in India's Chhattisgarh state, Maoist rebels attack a remote police post staffed largely by anti-Maoist counterinsurgents, slaughtering 49 police officers.

▶ NASA scientists announce that a radar instrument on the European Space Agency's Mars Express spacecraft has indicated huge ice deposits some 3.7 km (2.3 mi) thick at Mars's south pole.

16 Mar A five-year rebuilding plan for Iraq, called the International Compact with Iraq, is launched by Iraqi Vice Pres. Adil 'Abd al-Mahdi at the United Nations.

▶ A new law permitting same-sex civil unions goes into effect in Mexico City.

17 Mar Several brands of gravy-style pet food are recalled by manufacturer Menu Foods after the foods are linked to deaths from kidney failure of a number of dogs and cats.

▶ With its 46–19 defeat of Scotland, France wins the Six Nations Rugby Union championship, having achieved a won-lost record of 4–1.

18 Mar The coach of Pakistan's cricket team, Bob Woolmer, is found dead in his hotel room in Kingston, Jamaica, the day after Pakistan's ignominious defeat by Ireland in World Cup play; on 22 March the police report that he was murdered, but it is later reported that he died of natural causes.

▶ In his first race driving for Ferrari, Kimi Räikkönen of Finland wins the Australian Grand Prix, the inaugural event of the Formula One auto-racing season.

19 Mar US and Iranian officials report that Russia has told Iran that it must suspend uranium enrichment as demanded by the UN before Russia will deliver nuclear fuel for the nuclear power plant being built at Bushehr.

▶ Pres. Mahmoud Ahmadinejad of Iran and Pres. Robert Kocharyan of Armenia ceremonially open the first section of a natural-gas pipeline that will deliver gas from Iran as far as Yerevan, Armenia.

20 Mar Pakistani officials report that fighting in the South Waziristan region between foreign al-Qaeda adherents and local tribesmen has killed some 58 people in the past few days; by the following day the death toll has risen to 110.

21 Mar Bishops of the Episcopal Church USA, meeting outside Houston TX, reject an order from the Anglican Communion to accept a parallel leadership to serve conservative congregations who object to the Episcopal Church's stand on homosexuality.

▶ The US Food and Drug Administration announces new rules that will prevent advisers who receive substantial money from drug manufacturers from voting on whether to approve products made by those manufacturers.

▶ Musician Paul McCartney announces that he will be the first artist to sign with Hear Music, the record label of the coffee chain Starbucks.

22 Mar China ends six-nation talks on North Korea's nuclear program because funds that all agree are due to North Korea have not been transferred into the appropriate bank account.

▶ News Corp. and NBC Universal announce a new venture in which they will distribute videos, such as episodes of TV shows, on AOL, Yahoo!, MSN, and MySpace as well as on a new video site that the companies plan to launch.

▶ The Norwegian Academy of Science and Letters awards its annual Abel Prize for outstanding work in mathematics to American mathematician Srinivasa Varadhan for his work on calculating the probability of rare events.

23 Mar Fifteen British sailors and Marines on patrol in the Persian Gulf are seized by Iranian sailors, who say that the British personnel were in Iranian national waters; British authorities maintain that their naval forces were in Iraqi territory.

24 Mar In Iraq a truck bomb kills at least 20 people at a police compound in Baghdad; another suicide truck bomber in Haswah destroys a Shi'ite mosque and kills at least 11 people; three suicide car bombers kill 8 people in Al-Shuhadah; and a further 8 people are killed by a suicide bomber in Tal Afar.

25 Mar In a runoff presidential election, Sidi Ould Cheikh Abdallahi wins 53% of the vote to become Mauritania's first elected president.

▶ The European Union celebrates the 50th anniversary of the signing of the Treaty of Rome, which created the European Economic Community, the forerunner of the EU.

QUOTE OF THE MONTH

❝ *In short, European unification must be striven for and secured time and time again. That is our guiding mission for the future.* ❞

—German Chancellor and EU Pres. Angela Merkel, observing the 50th anniversary of the union, 25 March

---

26 Mar In their first direct talks ever, Ian Paisley of the Democratic Unionist Party and Gerry Adams of Sinn Féin agree to form a power-sharing government for Northern Ireland in a move that will return self-rule to the province for the first time since 2002.

▶ David Hicks, an Australian citizen who has been incarcerated in the US military base at Guantánamo Bay, Cuba, since he was captured in Afghanistan in

2001, is the first detainee to appear before a military tribunal under a law passed by the US Congress in fall 2006; after the military judge disallows two of his lawyers, he pleads guilty to having provided material support to a terrorist organization.

27 Mar A suicide truck bomb at a Shi'ite market in Tal Afar, Iraq, kills some 152 people.

▶ Pres. Laurent Gbagbo of Côte d'Ivoire agrees to appoint rebel leader Guillaume Soro prime minister as part of a new reunification plan.

28 Mar Portugal inaugurates a solar power plant in Serpa believed to be the world's most powerful one at 11 megawatts with 52,000 photovoltaic modules expected to produce 20 gigawatt hours annually; it eclipses the previous most powerful solar plant opened in Benejama, Spain, on 22 March.

29 Mar Ethiopian troops enter central Mogadishu, Somalia, provoking a violent reaction; more than 30 people, many of them civilians, are killed.

▶ Kurmanbek Bakiyev, the embattled president of Kyrgyzstan, names opposition figure Almaz Atambayev prime minister.

▶ British architect Richard Rogers is named winner of the 2007 Pritzker Architecture Prize; he is best known for his work on the Pompidou Centre in Paris, completed in 1977.

30 Mar US Secretary of Commerce Carlos M. Gutierrez announces that the US will begin imposing tariffs on imports from China; the US maintains that China illegally subsidizes some exports.

▶ Fighting between local tribesmen and Uzbek militants living in Pakistan's South Waziristan region begins anew; some 52 people are killed.

31 Mar US Pres. George W. Bush meets with Pres. Luiz Inácio Lula da Silva of Brazil at Camp David to discuss world trade negotiations and cooperation in ethanol development.

▶ At the swimming world championships in Melbourne, American swimmer Michael Phelps breaks his own world record in the 400-m individual medley to win a record seventh gold medal.

▶ Invasor, 2006 Horse of the Year, wins the Dubai World Cup, the world's richest horse race.

April 2007

1 Apr In an unusually brazen and deadly ambush, Sudanese rebels attack an African Union peacekeeping contingent that was traveling to provide a guard for a water source in Darfur; five peacekeepers are killed.

2 Apr The US Supreme Court rules that the Environmental Protection Agency is required by the Clean Air Act to regulate greenhouse gases in automobile emissions unless the agency can prove that such gases do not contribute to global warming.

▶ Negotiators for the US and South Korea announce that they have concluded a bilateral free-trade agreement that will eliminate tariffs on more than 90% of the categories of goods traded between the countries.

▶ In a complex financial transaction, real-estate tycoon Sam Zell becomes the owner of the Tribune Co., a media firm that includes several major newspapers, more than 20 television stations, and the Chicago Cubs baseball team.

▶ The music company EMI announces that it will begin offering songs that are free of copyright-protection software on Apple Inc.'s iTunes online music store.

▶ The National Collegiate Athletic Association (NCAA) championship in men's basketball is won for the second consecutive year by the University of Florida, which defeats Ohio State University 84–75; the following day the University of Tennessee defeats Rutgers University 59–46 to win the women's NCAA title.

3 Apr The French TGV bullet train, running three double-decker cars, reaches 574.8 km/h (357.2 mph) in a demonstration of its capabilities, setting a new world speed record for conventional trains.

4 Apr Reanne Evans of England wins her third consecutive women's world snooker championship in Cambridge, England.

5 Apr The 15 members of the British Royal Navy who had been held captive in Iran since they were seized in the Persian Gulf on 23 March are released; Iranian Pres. Mahmoud Ahmadinejad characterizes the move as a "gift" to the UK.

6 Apr The UN Intergovernmental Panel on Climate Change releases the second of its three reports; this one details the effects of global warming, describing changes already occurring and warning that action to cope with future changes, which will have a disproportionate impact on the world's poorest regions, is imperative.

▶ A suicide bomber driving a fuel tanker loaded with chlorine gas detonates a bomb on his truck in a residential area of Al-Ramadi, Iraq, killing some 30 people.

7 Apr Martin Strel of Slovenia becomes the first known person to swim the length of the Amazon River when he reaches Belem, Brazil, after having taken 66 days to complete an exceptionally challenging swim of 5,265 km (3,272 mi).

8 Apr The Roman Catholic bishops of Zimbabwe issue an Easter message that calls on Pres. Robert Mugabe to step down and demands a new constitution.

▶ Six NATO soldiers, all of them Canadian, are killed by a roadside bomb near Kandahar, Afghanistan.

▶ Zach Johnson wins the Masters golf tournament in Augusta GA by two strokes for his second PGA Tour victory.

9 Apr Donald Tsang is officially appointed to a second term as Hong Kong's chief executive by China after winning the first election for the post held since Hong Kong came under Chinese rule.

▶ In Al-Najaf, Iraq, tens of thousands of supporters of Shi'ite cleric Muqtada al-Sadr rally to demand that the US military leave Iraq.

10 Apr The US files two official complaints against China with the World Trade Organization, saying China tolerates trademark and copyright violation and unfairly limits the importation of books, films, and music.

▶ The winners of the annual Avery Fisher Career Grants for classical musicians are announced; they are violinist Yura Lee, double bassist DaXun Zhang, and the Borromeo String Quartet.

11 Apr Pak Pong Ju is removed from office as prime minister of North Korea; he is replaced by Kim Yong Il, who had been minister of transport.

▶ A suicide car bomb severely damages the Governmental Palace in Algiers, and a second car bomb destroys a police station in the suburb of Bab Ezzouar; at least 23 people are killed and 160 injured; an al-Qaeda-affiliated organization is thought responsible.

▶ US Secretary of Defense Robert Gates announces that tours of duty for most active-duty members of the US Army serving in Afghanistan and Iraq will be extended by 3 months, to 15 months.

▶ NBC News cancels its simulcasts of shock jock Don Imus's radio talk show in response to public outrage over Imus's gratuitous racist and sexist insults of the women's basketball team of Rutgers University; the following day CBS cancels the show altogether.

12 Apr The US Postal Service begins selling the "forever" stamp at the new rate of 41 cents per stamp; unlike any previous stamp, this one will remain valid in the event of future postal rate increases.

13 Apr The computer search company Google reaches an agreement to acquire the online advertising company DoubleClick.

▶ The opening ceremonies for the Museo Alameda, a new museum to showcase Latino culture, take place in San Antonio TX.

14 Apr In a market near a bus station in Karbala, Iraq, a suicide car bomber kills at least 37 people in the worst event of the day's carnage in Iraq.

▶ Up to 300,000 people turn out in Ankara, Turkey, to protest growing official Islamization in the country.

15 Apr The 60th anniversary of Jackie Robinson's major league baseball debut, which introduced racial integration to the sport, is observed by players throughout the league wearing Robinson's number, 42, on their uniforms, including the entire roster of the Los Angeles Dodgers; Robinson played for the Brooklyn Dodgers.

16 Apr A deranged and well-armed student methodically guns down 32 people, most of them in classrooms, at Virginia Polytech Institute (Virginia Tech) in Blacksburg before killing himself.

QUOTE OF THE MONTH

❝ *He didn't say, 'Get down.' He didn't say anything. He just came in and started shooting.* **❞**

—Virginia Tech sophomore Trey Perkins, describing the campus attack on a classroom Perkins was in, 16 April

---

▶ Shiʻite cleric Muqtada al-Sadr orders the six ministers in the Iraqi government who are members of his political bloc to withdraw from the government.

▶ In New York City the winners of the 2007 Pulitzer Prizes are announced: the top journalistic award goes to *The Wall Street Journal*, which is the only newspaper to win more than one award; winners in letters include Cormac McCarthy in fiction and Lawrence Wright in nonfiction, while Ornette Coleman wins in music.

▶ The 111th Boston Marathon is won for the second consecutive year by Robert K. Cheruiyot of Kenya, with a time of 2 hr 14 min 13 sec; the top woman finisher is Lidiya Grigoryeva of Russia, with a time of 2 hr 29 min 18 sec.

17 Apr For the first time the UN Security Council takes up the issue of global warming.

▶ A technical glitch disconnects more than 5,000 users of Blackberry personal digital assistants from e-mail; service is restored after 10 somewhat frantic hours.

▶ The pound sterling reaches an exchange rate of $2, its highest rate against the US dollar since 1992.

18 Apr A powerful car bomb in Baghdad near the Sadr City neighborhood kills at least 140 people; four other explosions in the city bring the death toll for the day to 171.

▶ In an ongoing pet-food crisis, melamine is found in rice protein concentrate imported from China, expanding the list of pet foods that must be recalled to some 100 brands in all; previously the toxic ingredient had been found only in wheat gluten from China.

▶ Officials in the US state of Georgia report that two wildfires are threatening the Okefenokee National Wildlife Refuge and have necessitated the evacuation of more than 1,000 people.

19 Apr Sidi Ould Cheikh Abdallahi is sworn into office as Mauritania's first democratically elected president; the following day he names Zeine Ould Zeidane prime minister.

▶ Joseph Nacchio, former CEO of Qwest Communications International, is convicted in Denver on 19 out of 42 counts of insider trading.

20 Apr Bollywood superstars Aishwarya Rai and Abhishek Bachchan marry in a Hindu ceremony in Mumbai (Bombay); thousands of fans outside the service strain for a glimpse of the couple.

21 Apr Chaotic and possibly flawed presidential elections take place in Nigeria; the ruling party's candidate, Umaru Musa Yar'Adua, is later declared the winner.

22 Apr Sunni Arabs in Mosul, Iraq, execute 23 members of the Yazidi religious sect; a car bomb kills 18 people in Baghdad; and Iraqi Prime Minister Nuri Kamal al-Maliki orders a halt to construction on a wall being built by the US military around a predominantly Sunni neighborhood in Baghdad.

▶ Martin Lel of Kenya wins the London Marathon, with a time of 2 hr 7 min 41 sec, and Zhou Chunxiu of China is the fastest woman in the race, with a time of 2 hr 20 min 38 sec.

23 Apr The Dutch banking giant ABN AMRO reaches an agreement to be acquired by Barclays of Great Britain and to sell LaSalle Bank to Bank of America.

▶ A suicide car bomb in Iraq's Diyala province kills nine US soldiers, and a suicide bomber kills several people in a popular restaurant in the International Zone (Green Zone) in Baghdad.

▶ The US Department of Veterans Affairs, faced with a lawsuit, agrees to add the pentacle, which is used in the Wiccan religion, to the list of symbols that may be engraved on the headstones of veterans.

24 Apr Rebel gunmen attack a Chinese-run oil field in the Ogaden region of Ethiopia, killing more than 70 people, 9 of whom are Chinese, and kidnapping 7 Chinese and 2 African workers.

▶ Japanese carmaker Toyota overtakes the American company General Motors to become the largest carmaker in the world, with sales of 2,348,000 vehicles in the first quarter of 2007.

▶ Astronomers led by Stéphane Udry of the Geneva Observatory say that a planet has been found orbiting the dim red star Gliese 581 about 20 light-years away in the constellation Libra; the new planet is within a distance from its sun called the habitable zone, which means that conditions on the planet could be such that life is possible.

25 Apr The Dow Jones Industrial Average closes above 13,000 for the first time.

26 Apr Pres. Vladimir Putin of Russia in his annual address to the legislature announces that Russia is suspending its compliance with the 1990 Treaty on Conventional Armed Forces in Europe (CFE), signed by members of NATO and the Warsaw Pact.

27 Apr In the first round of presidential voting in Turkey's legislature, the sole candidate, Abdullah Gul, who is associated with political Islam, fails to win enough votes to be confirmed because of a boycott of the vote by members of secular parties.

▸ The euro reaches a record high against the US dollar, with an exchange rate of $1.3682 to the euro.

28 Apr In the controversial final of the cricket World Cup in Barbados, Australia dominates Sri Lanka to win its third successive title; bowler Glenn McGrath,

with a record 26 wickets in the final match of his career, is named Player of the Tournament.

29 Apr In the Nascar Nextel Cup race series, Jeff Gordon wins the Aaron's 499 in Talladega AL, passing the late Dale Earnhardt's career victory total on the anniversary of Earnhardt's birth, to the displeasure of Earnhardt loyalists among the fans.

30 Apr Morocco and the Polisario Front agree to hold direct talks on the future of Western Sahara.

▸ Deutsche Börse, operator of the stock exchange in Frankfurt, Germany, acquires the US-based International Securities Exchange, the world's second largest options exchange.

May 2007

1 May It is reported that Rupert Murdoch, head of the international media empire the News Corp., has made an unsolicited offer to buy Dow Jones & Co., publisher of *The Wall Street Journal.*

▸ The Caribbean country of Saint Lucia restores diplomatic relations with Taiwan, which it broke in 1997, and ends relations with China.

▸ At the National Magazine Awards in New York City, the big winner is *New York* magazine, which wins five awards, including one for general excellence; other winners include *National Geographic, Rolling Stone, Bulletin of the Atomic Scientists, Wired,* and, in the online category, Belief.net.

2 May The day after Turkey's highest court annulled the Grand National Assembly's vote for president, the assembly votes to hold national elections on 22 July.

▸ An Afghan government investigation into the recent aerial bombardment of a valley in western Afghanistan by US military forces finds that the action left at least 42 civilians dead.

3 May The China National Petroleum Corp. announces that the oil field recently discovered in Bohai Bay has a reserve of some 7.35 billion bbl; it is the largest oil deposit found in the country in more than 40 years.

▸ Results of the 29 April presidential election in Mali are released; Amadou Toumani Touré was re-elected.

4 May Hubert Ingraham is sworn in as prime minister of The Bahamas, replacing Perry Christie, two days after the opposition Free National Movement won legislative elections.

▸ A large tornado nearly destroys the small town of Greensburg KS, killing at least 10 people and injuring 63.

▸ In Las Vegas challenger Floyd Mayweather defeats fellow American Oscar De La Hoya to become the World Boxing Council super welterweight (junior middleweight) champion.

5 May Over the objections of Rowan Williams, the archbishop of Canterbury, Archbishop Peter J. Akinola of Nigeria installs Martyn Minns as bishop of the Convocation of Anglicans in North America, a branch of the conservative Nigerian church, in Virginia.

▸ Street Sense wins the Kentucky Derby, the first race of Thoroughbred horse racing's US Triple Crown, before a crowd that includes Queen Elizabeth II of the United Kingdom.

6 May Nicolas Sarkozy is elected president of France in a runoff election against Ségolène Royale.

7 May Two car bombs kill some 25 people near Al-Ramadi, Iraq.

8 May Ian Paisley of the Democratic Unionists and Martin McGuinness of Sinn Féin are sworn in as leader and deputy leader of Northern Ireland's new executive government.

QUOTE OF THE MONTH

We cannot undo our sad and turbulent past. And none of us can forget the many victims of the Troubles. But we can, and are, shaping our future in a new and better way.

—Irish Prime Minister Bertie Ahern, on the inauguration of a new power-sharing government in Northern Ireland, 8 May

---

▸ Findings by geneticists that suggest that there was a single human migration to Australia and Papua New Guinea some 50,000 years ago and that that population remained in isolation until recent times are published in *The Proceedings of the National Academy of Sciences.*

9 May Former Nobel Peace Prize winner José Ramos-Horta easily wins the runoff elections for president of East Timor; he takes office on 20 May.

▸ The first pages of the Encyclopedia of Life, a Web-based compilation of all that is known about all the world's species of living things, are shown in Washington DC; it will take 10 years to finish the database.

▸ Officials in Afghanistan say that US air strikes during a battle against Taliban fighters in the village of Sarban Qala the previous day killed 21 civilians.

10 May Turkey's Grand National Assembly approves a constitutional amendment to allow the direct popular election of the president, presently chosen by the assembly; Pres. Ahmet Necdet Sezer vetoes the legislation on 25 May.

▸ The European Commission announces that its deal to produce a large satellite navigation system called Galileo in partnership with a consortium of private companies is off after the consortium missed the last of a number of important deadlines for management of the project.

▸ NASCAR driver Dale Earnhardt, Jr., announces that he will leave his late father's team, Dale Earnhardt Inc., at the end of the season, essentially making himself stock-car racing's first superstar free agent.

11 May In state elections in India's Uttar Pradesh state, the opposition Dalit-led Bahujan Samaj Party wins a majority of seats; the party leader, Mayawati, becomes chief minister.

12 May Competing rallies in Karachi held by supporters of the Pakistani government and supporters of the suspended chief justice, Iftikhar Muhammad Chaudhry, on the occasion of a planned speech by Chaudhry, result in violence in which at least 39 people die.

▶ Afghanistan's foreign minister is ousted by a no-confidence vote in the legislature, as was the minister of refugees earlier in the week; this is in response to the forcible repatriation of some 50,000 Afghans by Iran in the past three weeks.

▶ In Helsinki the Serbian singer Marija Serifovic wins the Eurovision Song Contest with her rendition of "Molitva."

13 May Government officials in Afghanistan report that the leading Taliban military commander, Mullah Dadullah, was killed in a joint operation by Afghan, US, and NATO forces in Helmand province.

▶ Nigeria launches Africa's first communications satellite; both satellite and launch service are provided by China.

▶ Canada defeats Finland 4–2 to win the gold medal in the ice hockey men's world championship tournament in Moscow.

14 May The automobile company DaimlerChrysler AG announces that the private equity company Cerberus Capital Management will buy Chrysler (including its health and pension obligations) from what will become Daimler AG.

15 May Serbia's legislature approves a new power-sharing government headed by Vojislav Kostunica as prime minister four months after inconclusive elections.

▶ A suicide bomber kills at least 22 people in a crowded restaurant in Peshawar, Pakistan.

▶ Officials in Nigeria say that protesters have taken over an oil hub in the Niger Delta, contributing to a 30% reduction in Nigeria's output in the wake of its recent election.

16 May At least 19 Palestinians are killed in Gaza on the fourth day of renewed violence between gunmen loyal to Fatah and those attached to Hamas.

▶ The Spanish association football (soccer) club Sevilla FC defeats RCD Espanyol of Barcelona to win the Union des Associations Européennes de Football (UEFA) Cup in Glasgow, Scotland; Sevilla is only the second side in the cup's history to have won the trophy in two consecutive years.

17 May Paul D. Wolfowitz resigns as president of the World Bank; his controversial tenure had been capped by a furor over a promotion package he arranged for his partner, Shaha Ali Riza, who also worked for the World Bank.

▶ Alex Salmond of the separatist and opposition Scottish National Party is sworn in as first minister of Scotland after his party's victory in elections for the Scottish Parliament on 3 May.

▶ Estonian Minister of Defense Jaak Aaviksoo declares that the devastating cyberattacks on the country's government and corporate Web sites over the past two weeks seem to have originated with the government of Russia.

▶ For the first time since the Korean War, two passenger trains traveling in opposite directions cross the border between North and South Korea.

18 May Officials in Panama say that some 6,000 tubes of toothpaste recently found to contain the poison diethylene glycol appear to have originated in China; in 2006 diethylene glycol from China that was mixed into mislabeled cough medicine killed at least 100 people in Panama.

▶ A bomb kills 11 people when it explodes in the historic Mecca Masjid mosque in Hyderabad, India; in resulting fighting between Muslims and government security forces, 5 more people die.

19 May In the Iraqi village of Hamid Shifi, men in Iraqi army uniforms, after having been waved through a checkpoint, pull 15 Shi'ite Kurds onto the street and kill them.

▶ Curlin noses out Kentucky Derby winner Street Sense to win the Preakness Stakes, the second event in US Thoroughbred horse racing's Triple Crown.

▶ In Durban, South Africa, the Bulls (Pretoria) defeat the Sharks (Durban) 20–19 to win the Super 14 rugby union tournament.

20 May Violence between Lebanese security forces and members of the group Fatah breaks out in the vicinity of a Palestinian refugee camp in Tripoli, Lebanon; 22 Lebanese soldiers and 17 militants die on the first day, and the death toll increases over the following days.

21 May The conglomerate General Electric agrees to sell its large plastics division to the Saudi Basic Industries Corp. (Sabic).

22 May Researchers report that a hammerhead shark born at the Henry Doorly Zoo in Omaha NE in 2001 to an isolated female has been found to be the result of a form of asexual reproduction called parthenogenesis, which had not previously been seen in sharks.

▶ Invitations to the Anglican Communion's Lambeth Conference scheduled for 2008 are sent out; neither openly gay bishop V. Gene Robinson nor conservative Martyn Minns, who was installed as bishop by Archbishop Peter J. Akinola of Nigeria, is invited.

▶ The Woodrow Wilson International Center for Scholars reports that diplomats attempting to visit one of its directors, Haleh Esfandiari, who was arrested in Iran while on a visit to her mother, have been denied access, as have her lawyers and her family members.

23 May A law is passed in Japan to fund the reorganization of US forces in the country and to pay $6 billion toward the movement of 8,000 US Marines from Okinawa to the US territory of Guam; the US will contribute $4 billion for the transfer.

▶ In association football (soccer), AC Milan defeats Liverpool to win the UEFA Champions League championship in Athens.

▶ The Ruth Lilly Poetry Prize is presented in Chicago to Lucille Clifton; Clifton is the first African American winner of the prize.

24 May In Fallujah, Iraq, a Sunni tribal leader who was working in opposition to al-Qaeda is assassinated, and hours later a car bomb kills at least 27 people when it explodes in a crowd of mourners for the slain leader.

▶ The US Congress passes a law raising the minimum hourly wage from $5.15 to $7.25 in three stages over two years; the wage was last increased in 1997.

25 May Shi'ite cleric Muqtada al-Sadr makes his first public appearance in months, making a speech in Kufah, Iraq, in which he exhorts Iraqis to stop fighting each other and concentrate on driving out US forces.

26 May Israel bombs several Hamas buildings and camps in Gaza; at least five Palestinians are killed.

27 May After days of jockeying for control of security forces, Ukrainian Pres. Viktor Yushchenko and

Prime Minister Viktor Yanukovich agree to hold early elections on 30 September.

▶ Pres. Bashar al-Assad of Syria is elected to a second seven-year term with 97.6% of the vote; he is the only candidate on the ballot.

▶ The 91st Indianapolis 500 auto race, delayed and shortened by 34 laps because of rain, is won by Dario Franchitti of Scotland.

▶ At the Cannes Festival, Romanian director Cristian Mungiu's film *4 luni, 3 saptamini, si 2 zite (4 Months, 3 Weeks, and 2 Days)* wins the Palme d'Or; the Grand Prix goes to Japanese director Naomi Kawase's *Mogari no mori (The Mourning Forest)*.

28 May Japanese Minister of Agriculture Toshikatsu Matsuoka commits suicide; he has been under investigation in scandals involving expense padding and bid rigging.

▶ Wildlife experts report that they have found a population of hundreds of wild elephants on an island south of The Sudan, an area that they had been unable to access until the end of the civil war in the region.

29 May Umaru Yar'Adua is sworn in as president of Nigeria.

▶ Zheng Xiaoyu, who was head of China's food and drug safety agency from its inception in 1998 to 2005, is sentenced to death after pleading guilty to corruption.

30 May The Standard & Poor's 500 index closes at a record high of 1,530.23, eclipsing its former record of 1,527.36, set on 24 Mar 2000; in addition, the Dow Jones Industrial Average sets a new record close of 13,633.08.

31 May The government of Niger falls after losing a no-confidence vote occasioned by an embezzlement scandal.

▶ Latvia's parliament chooses Valdis Zatlers to be the country's next president.

June 2007

1 Jun The Lebanese army attacks Fatah positions outside the Nahr al-Bared Palestinian refugee camp; at least 18 people are killed.

▶ The US Food and Drug Administration (FDA) reports that it has found the poison diethylene glycol in several brands of toothpaste made in China and warns consumers not to use Chinese-made toothpaste.

▶ British artist Damien Hirst unveils *For the Love of God*, an 18th-century human skull cast in platinum and encased in diamonds and valued at US$100 million, as part of a solo exhibition at London's White Cube gallery.

2 Jun The Derby, in its 228th year at Epsom Downs in Surrey, England, is won by favorite Authorized, ridden by Frankie Detorri; the following day Detorri wins the French Derby (Prix du Jockey Club) in Chantilly, France, aboard Lawman.

3 Jun A suicide truck-bomb attack on the Mogadishu residence of Somalia's transitional prime minister, Ali Muhammad Ghedi, kills six of his bodyguards and a civilian.

4 Jun China issues a national plan for addressing global warming; it sets a target of a 20% increase in efficiency by 2010, which would slow but not reverse the increase of greenhouse-gas emissions.

5 Jun Police in Nairobi crack down on the Mungiki, a murderous Kikuyu sect inspired by the Mau Mau movement of the 1950s, killing 22 and arresting 100.

▶ I. Lewis ("Scooter") Libby, former chief of staff to US Vice Pres. Dick Cheney, is sentenced to 30 months in prison for having lied to investigators looking into the exposure of the name of a covert CIA operative.

6 Jun The US FDA calls for the makers of the diabetes drugs Avandia and Actos to place black-box warnings onto packaging about the heart risks associated with the drugs.

▶ The Group of Eight industrialized countries' summit meeting begins in Heiligendamm, Germany, as thousands of people stage protests against US policy and against globalization.

▶ The Anaheim Ducks defeat the Ottawa Senators 6–2 to win the franchise's first Stanley Cup, the National Hockey League championship.

▶ Chimamanda Ngozi Adichie wins the Orange Broadband Prize, an award for fiction written by women and published in the UK, for her novel *Half of a Yellow Sun*.

7 Jun At the Group of Eight summit meeting, Pres. Vladimir Putin of Russia proposes a joint US-Russian missile defense system based in Azerbaijan in place of the systems that the US planned to place in the Czech Republic and Poland to the great displeasure of Russia.

▶ The organizers of the Tour de France bicycle race announce that Bjarne Riis of Denmark is no longer the winner of the 1996 race, which is now considered to have had no winner; Riis has admitted that he used performance-enhancing drugs during that race.

8 Jun In Iraq suicide bomb attacks kill at least 19 people in Daquq and at least 15 people in Al-Qurnah, while 14 people are killed in an attack on the home of a police chief in Kanaan.

▶ A report from an investigation for the Council of Europe is released; it gives detailed descriptions of secret prisons run by the US Central Intelligence Agency in Poland and Romania.

▶ The 2007 winners of the Kyoto Prize are announced: Hiroo Inokuchi (advanced technology), Hiroo Kanamori (basic sciences), and the choreographer Pina Bausch (arts and philosophy).

9 Jun In a daylong battle between Lebanese military forces and those of the militant group Fatah al-Islam at the Nahr al-Bared Palestinian refugee camp in Lebanon, 11 Lebanese soldiers are killed.

▶ Boeing Co. announces that it has signed a cooperation agreement with Russia's state-owned Unified Aircraft Corp. and that Aeroflot has purchased 22 Boeing 787 Dreamliners, with delivery scheduled to begin in 2014.

▶ Justine Henin of Belgium defeats Ana Ivanovic of Serbia to win her third consecutive women's French Open tennis title; the following day Rafael Nadal of Spain defeats Roger Federer of Switzerland to capture the men's championship for the third year in a row.

▶ After stumbling out of the gate, Rags to Riches wins the Belmont Stakes, the last event in Thoroughbred horse racing's US Triple Crown, by a head; she is the first filly to win the race in 102 years.

10 Jun The 61st annual Tony Awards are presented in New York City; winners include the productions *The Coast of Utopia* (which wins seven Tonys), *Spring Awakening* (with eight), *Journey's End*, and *Company* and the actors Frank Langella, Julie White, David Hyde Pierce, and Christine Ebersole.

▸ The 52nd Venice Biennale opens and for the first time features a pavilion for African art and another for Roma (Gypsy) art; the Malian photographer Malick Sidibé is awarded the festival's Golden Lion for lifetime achievement.

▸ Suzann Pettersen of Norway wins the Ladies Professional Golf Association championship.

11 Jun Guy Verhofstadt resigns as prime minister of Belgium the day after his party lost in legislative elections.

12 Jun Pres. Omar Hassan al-Bashir of The Sudan agrees to allow a combined United Nations and African Union force of some 20,000 troops to be deployed in the Darfur region.

▸ Chinua Achebe of Nigeria is named winner of the Man Booker International Prize, which is awarded every two years for a body of fictional work.

13 Jun Bombs destroy the golden minarets of the Askariya shrine in Samarra, Iraq, known as the Golden Mosque and revered by Shi'ites; an attack that destroyed the shrine's dome in February 2006 had set off greatly increased levels of violence.

▸ Walid Eido, a prominent anti-Syrian member of Lebanon's legislature, is assassinated in Beirut by a bomb that kills nine other people as well.

14 Jun As Hamas consolidates its control over Gaza, Palestinian Authority Pres. Mahmoud Abbas dissolves the government, dismisses Prime Minister Ismail Haniya, and declares a state of emergency.

QUOTE OF THE MONTH

❝ *This is the beginning of the separation of the Gaza Strip and the West Bank. This is the lowest point in our struggle. We Palestinians are writing the final chapters of our national enterprise.* ❞

—Mkhaimar Abusada, Palestinian political scientist, on the Hamas takeover of Gaza, 14 June

---

▸ The San Antonio Spurs defeat the Cleveland Cavaliers 83–82 in game four of the best-of-seven tournament to secure the team's fourth National Basketball Association championship.

15 Jun Samoa's legislature elects former prime minister Tuiatua Tupua Tamasese Efi head of state to replace Malietoa Tanumafili II, who died on 11 May.

▸ Bob Barker makes his final appearance as host of the CBS television game show *The Price Is Right;* he hosted the show for 35 years.

16 Jun A Sunni mosque in downtown Basra, Iraq, is blown up; it is the second Sunni mosque in the area destroyed in as many days.

17 Jun In Ram Allah in the West Bank, Palestinian Authority Pres. Mahmoud Abbas swears in an emergency government headed by Salam Fayyad as prime minister; Hamas declares the new government illegal.

▸ A bomb destroys a police bus in Kabul, killing at least 24 people, 22 of them police instructors.

▸ Angel Cabrera of Argentina bests Americans Tiger Woods and Jim Furyk to win the US Open golf tournament in Oakmont PA.

▸ Swimmer Kate Ziegler sets a new world record of 15 min 42.54 sec for the 1,500-m race, eclipsing the record 15 min 52.10 sec set in 1988 by fellow American Janet Evans.

18 Jun The US drops its embargo of the Palestinian Authority, freeing up financial aid for the new Fatah government in the West Bank, and the European Union (EU) announces that it will resume direct aid to the Palestinian Authority.

▸ The Japanese Geographical Survey Institute changes the official name of the island of Iwo Jima to Iwo To, its name before World War II.

19 Jun A suicide truck bomb is detonated in a large Shi'ite mosque in Baghdad; at least 87 people are killed.

▸ The government of Nicaragua files criminal charges against Enrique Bolaños, accusing him of having covered up human trafficking during his presidency of the country (2002–07).

▸ At a fire at a furniture warehouse in Charleston SC, the roof collapses; nine firefighters are killed in the deadliest event for firefighters in more than 30 years, aside from the events of 11 Sep 2001.

▸ The Samuel Johnson Prize, the most important award for nonfiction in the UK, goes to *Imperial Life in the Emerald City* by Rajiv Chandrasekaran; the book describes life in Baghdad's Green Zone during the time of the Coalition Provisional Authority (2003–04).

20 Jun The Netherlands Environmental Assessment Agency finds that China has surpassed the US in carbon dioxide emissions; carbon dioxide is the most significant greenhouse gas.

21 Jun A US federal judge finds that three major pharmaceutical companies had illegally inflated wholesale prices of their drugs paid for by Medicare, insurers, and patients and must pay damages.

▸ The World Health Organization releases a plan for a global campaign against drug-resistant tuberculosis.

▸ A rebel attack on a remote army base in Niger kills 13 soldiers; the rebels take at least 47 soldiers prisoner.

▸ Sammy Sosa of the Texas Rangers hits his 600th career home run against his former team, the Chicago Cubs; he is the fifth player in Major League Baseball history to reach that milestone.

22 Jun In a battle between Taliban militants and NATO forces in Kunjak, Afghanistan, some 30 Taliban and at least 25 civilians are killed.

23 Jun Drew Weaver becomes the first American since 1979 to win the British amateur golf championship, finishing ahead of Tim Stewart of Australia at Royal Lytham & St. Annes Golf Club in Lancashire, England.

24 Jun In southern Lebanon near the border with Israel, an apparent car bombing kills six UN peacekeepers.

▸ Ali Hassan al-Majid, known as "Chemical Ali" because of his guidance of poison gas attacks against Kurds in northern Iraq during the late 1980s, is found guilty of genocide in an Iraqi courtroom and is sentenced to be hanged.

▸ In Chicago the US defeats Mexico 2–1 to win the 2007 CONCACAF Gold Cup in association football (soccer).

▸ In the 148th running of the Queen's Plate Thoroughbred horse race in Toronto, Emma-Jayne Wilson becomes the first female jockey to win the race when her mount, long shot Mike Fox, wins by half a length.

25 Jun North Korea promises to shut down its main nuclear plant now that it has received the money pledged in the agreement made with the US, South Korea, Russia, China, and Japan on 13 February.

‣ In a hotel in Baghdad, a suicide bomber detonates his weapon in the lobby, killing 12 people, among them 4 Sunni sheikhs from Anbar province who were fighting against al-Qaeda in Mesopotamia and 2 Shi'ite sheikhs who were meeting with them; also, the leader of the US offensive to establish security in the Iraqi town of Ba'qubah says that more than half of the insurgents there have eluded US forces.

‣ Robert Zoellick is confirmed as president of the World Bank by that organization's executive board.

26 Jun The US Central Intelligence Agency releases to the public 702 pages of documents detailing illegal activities engaged in by the agency during the 1960s and '70s; these documents have long been known as the "family jewels."

27 Jun Tony Blair steps down as British prime minister; he is replaced by former chancellor of the Exchequer Gordon Brown.

28 Jun Pres. Álvaro Uribe of Colombia says that the Revolutionary Armed Forces of Colombia (FARC) killed 11 legislators the guerrilla group kidnapped in 2002; FARC had claimed that the hostages died in the cross fire during a rescue attempt, but Uribe says no attempt was made, as the location of the hostages was unknown.

‣ The US Supreme Court rules that a manufacturer may dictate minimum prices that dealers must charge for its products, overturning a 1911 ruling forbidding such a practice; in addition, it rules that public school systems may not consider race in admission policies, which have attempted to ensure diversity.

‣ The US Department of the Interior announces that the bald eagle is being removed from the list of animals requiring protection under the Endangered Species Act; there are now nearly 10,000 mating pairs in the US.

29 Jun Two Mercedes sedans that had been packed with explosives to make them into car bombs are discovered in London and defused by police.

‣ As a plane carrying Prime Minister Guillaume Soro of Côte d'Ivoire lands in Bouaké, it is attacked by heavy gunfire; three people are killed, but Soro escapes unharmed.

‣ The new Apple iPhone goes on sale throughout the US, to the elation of customers who stood in line for hours or, in some cases, days to make sure they were able to acquire the new gadget.

30 Jun Two men drive a burning SUV through the doors of the Glasgow, Scotland, airport; the men are arrested and no one at the airport is injured (though one of the men in the SUV later dies from his burns), but it is assumed that this incident is connected with the discovery the day before of car bombs in London.

Disasters

Listed here are major disasters between July 2006 and June 2007. The list includes natural and nonmilitary mechanical disasters that claimed 25 or more lives and/or resulted in significant damage to property.

July 2006

3 Jul Off the coast of Western Sahara. A boat carrying African migrants trying to reach the Canary Islands sinks, and bodies begin washing onshore; 30 corpses are found, but 40 additional people are thought to have drowned.

3 Jul South Asia. Mumbai (Bombay) is shut down by flooding caused by monsoon rains, and authorities report that landslides and collapsed houses in Orissa and Jharkand states have killed at least 30 people, while a further 17 deaths are reported from Pakistan.

3 Jul Valencia, Spain. A subway train derails while speeding on a curve; at least 41 passengers are killed.

5 Jul China. Storms and rain in China's Jiangsu and Anhui provinces have left at least 30 people dead; some 40,000 people have had to be evacuated.

6 Jul Shanxi province, China. An explosion at the home of a resident of the village of Dongzhai results in the death of at least 49 people; unlicensed explosives are a likely cause.

7 Jul Uttaranchal state, India. A bus skids off the road near Uttarkashi, causing the death of at least 26 people.

9 Jul Irkutsk, Siberia. After landing at the airport, an S7 Airlines Airbus A310 airplane arriving from Moscow crashes into a concrete wall and a row of buildings, breaking apart and catching fire; at least 122 of those aboard are killed.

10 Jul Multan, Pakistan. A Pakistan International Airlines plane bound for Lahore crashes shortly after takeoff, killing all 45 aboard; the dead include two judges, two army brigadiers, and a university vice-chancellor.

11 Jul Northern Bangladesh. At an unmanned railroad crossing, a train hits a passenger bus, knocking it into a ditch; at least 33 of the bus passengers perish.

14 Jul North Korea. The International Federation of Red Cross and Red Crescent Societies reports that flooding and landslides have left more than 100 people dead; later estimates of the death toll range from 549 to 55,000.

15 Jul Kaski district, Nepal. A landslide sweeps away houses; 17 bodies are recovered, but some 15 people are still missing.

17 Jul Java. Under the seabed of the Indian Ocean, a magnitude-7.7 earthquake sets off a 1.8-m (6-ft) tsunami that inundates the southern coast, with most of the damage centered on Pangandaran; though agencies in the US and Japan issued warnings, nearly 600 people are killed.

18 Jul Lagos, Nigeria. A four-story apartment building collapses, killing at least 43 people; the building consisted of 36 apartments, a penthouse, and shops.

21 Jul Hunan province, China. It is reported that 346 people have died in flooding resulting from Tropical Storm Bilis over several days, raising the death toll from that storm to 482; by the following day the death toll has reached 523, and it is reported that six provinces suffered major damage; the final toll passes 600.

25 Jul Southern China. Typhoon Kaemi hits the southern coast of China, leaving at least 25 people dead and more than 50 missing, mostly in Jiangxi province.

26 Jul France. Health officials say that the heat wave that has affected most of Europe for the past two weeks has claimed 64 lives in France, and the number is likely to rise.

27 Jul California. State authorities say that a heat wave that has seen temperatures of well over 38 °C (100 °F) over the past several days has left at least 100 people as well as some 16,500 dairy cows dead; the following day the human death toll climbs to 126.

27 Jul France and Italy. Authorities declare that the two-week heat wave has resulted in 80 deaths, and the French weather office says that this July has been the hottest month on record in the country.

28 Jul Jiangsu province, China. An explosion at a chemical plant producing the highly volatile liquid fluorobenzene kills at least 22 people, with 28 missing, and causes the evacuation of some 7,000 people.

August 2006

5 Aug Mardan, Pakistan. A bridge crowded with pedestrians and vehicles collapses; 39 bodies are pulled from the river below.

6 Aug Kenya. Heavy rains cause the Dechatu River to burst its banks, sweeping away homes and factories in Dire Dawa and leaving at least 250 people dead and 300 missing.

8 Aug South Asia. Indian officials report that flooding in Gujarat, Maharashtra, and Andhra Pradesh states has left some 300 people dead and hundreds of thousands stranded; some 140 people have died in flooding in Pakistan.

10 Aug China. Typhoon Saomai strikes the coastal provinces of Fujian and Zhejiang, leaving nearly 500 people dead; with winds of 216 km (134 mi) per hour, Saomai is the strongest storm to hit China in 50 years.

12 Aug India. It is reported that monsoon rains in the south and west have left more than 350 people dead and more than four million homeless; parts of Mumbai have been submerged.

13 Aug Southern Ethiopia. The Omo River floods, drowning at least 364 people and leaving tens of thousands stranded or homeless.

16 Aug Poura, Burkina Faso. In a long-closed gold mine, walls softened by rain collapse, killing some 50 of the people who continued to search for gold in the mine.

16 Aug Ethiopia. Officials say that after 11 days of heavy rains, the death toll from flooding has reached 626 and is likely to rise as the rains continue.

21 Aug Qalyub, Egypt. A train rams into another train stopped at the station; at least 58 people lose their lives, most of them commuters on their way to work in Cairo.

22 Aug Donetsk, Ukraine. A Pulkovo Airlines TU-154 flying from the Russian Black Sea resort of Anapa to St. Petersburg crashes north of Donetsk in bad weather; all 170 aboard are killed.

27 Aug Lexington KY. A small Comair jet takes off from the wrong runway at Blue Grass Airport, one that was also too short for the aircraft, and crashes into a field; 49 of the 50 people aboard the craft are killed.

27 Aug Rajasthan state, India. At a wrestling match in Bharatpur, a water tank onto which some 200 people had climbed for a better view collapses; at least 48 spectators are killed.

28 Aug Iraq. In Al-Diwaniyah residents begin siphoning gasoline from a government pipeline left unguarded because of a battle in the town; one of the residents lights a cigarette, igniting an explosion that incinerates at least 67 people.

28 Aug Rajasthan state, India. It is reported that unusually heavy rains have swept away almost all of the village of Malwa and killed at least 135 people.

29 Aug Karnataka state, India. A bus carrying passengers home from a pilgrimage site swerves to avoid a collision on a bridge near the Almatti reservoir and plunges into the Krishna River; at least 27 passengers drown.

September 2006

1 Sep Meshed, Iran. An Iran Air TU-154 flying from Bandar-e 'Abbas, Iran, slides off the runway as it is landing and catches fire; 29 of the 148 passengers die.

7 Sep Jharkand state, India. After an explosion and gas leak in a coal mine, 30 miners are found dead, with 23 still trapped inside and feared dead.

12 Sep Ibb, Yemen. At an election rally for Pres. 'Ali 'Abdallah Salih in a stadium, the crowd rushes the stage for a better view, which leads to a stampede in which at least 51 people are killed, most crushed under an iron fence that collapses under the force of the crowd.

20 Sep Kazakhstan. A methane explosion and fire kill at least 41 coal miners in the Karaganda region.

20 Sep South Asia. Officials report that a tropical depression in the Bay of Bengal has left more than 31 people dead, mostly from drowning and house collapses, in Andhra Pradesh state, at least 12 dead

in West Bengal state, and 18 fishermen drowned and more than 80 missing in Bangladesh.

22 Sep Germany. A high-speed maglev Transrapid train on a test run on an elevated track in northwestern Germany collides with a service train that had not left the track; though the maglev train does not derail, 25 people are killed.

24 Sep Near Quito, Ecuador. A bus overturns on a steep mountain road; at least 47 passengers, including 17 children, are killed.

28 Sep Philippines. Typhoon Xangsane roars through the central and northern provinces, leaving at least 63 people dead.

29 Sep Mato Grosso state, Brazil. A Boeing 737 airplane run by the low-cost Brazilian Gol Airlines nicks a smaller plane and crashes into the jungle; all 155 aboard perish.

29 Sep Near Greenville, Ghana. An overloaded canoe sinks in the Sinoe River; it is feared that some 45 passengers drowned.

October 2006

6 Oct Panama. After 19 people have mysteriously died of kidney failure, the government begins pulling a generic drug used to treat high blood pressure and heart failure that is believed to be connected with the deaths; it is learned that the deaths were caused by contamination of cough syrup and other medications with diethylene glycol, an ingredient of antifreeze, and the death toll later rises to 34.

9 Oct Guatemala. A passenger bus leaving Huehuetenango in foggy weather falls into a 90-m (300-ft) ravine; 42 passengers are killed.

12 Oct Southeast Asia. Severe flooding in Thailand and Myanmar (Burma) leaves at least 57 people dead despite widespread evacuation.

18 Oct The Nile River. Two steamboats carrying soldiers from the former Sudan People's Liberation Army from Malakal, Sudan, to their new post in the national army, in accordance with a 2005 peace treaty, collide in the Nile and sink; as many as 75 soldiers die.

23 Oct Meghna River, Bangladesh. A ferry carrying passengers home to celebrate 'Id al-Fitr collides with a cargo vessel and sinks; at least 15 people are killed, and a further 35 are missing.

25 Oct Sikkim state, India. A passenger bus carrying more than 60 people from Jorethang to Gangtok falls into the Teesta River; at least 21 people are killed.

28 Oct Russia. Authorities say that alcohol poisoning has broken out across the country, killing dozens and hospitalizing hundreds; the worst outbreak is reported to be in the Irkutsk region of Siberia, where 27 people have died.

29 Oct Abuja, Nigeria. A Boeing 737 crashes immediately after takeoff in bad weather, killing 96 of the 105 aboard; one of the dead is the sultan of Sokoto, the spiritual leader of Muslims in Nigeria.

31 Oct Ethiopia. Officials report that days of rain and the flooding of the Shebeli River in the past four days have left at least 67 people dead near the eastern border.

November 2006

5 Nov Shanxi province, China. A gas explosion in the Jiaojiazhai coal mine kills at least 17 miners, with a further 30 still missing; a day later the Chinese government reports that an astonishing 345 people died in mining accidents in October.

7 Nov Madhya Pradesh state, India. Near Hoshangabad a truck carrying farm workers falls into a ditch; 29 of the farm workers lose their lives.

13 Nov Near Cape Town. A trailer full of farm workers being pulled by a truck across an unmarked rail crossing is hit by a commuter train; 27 workers are killed.

25 Nov China. A gas explosion in a coal mine at Jixi, Heilongjiang province, kills at least 21 miners; a few hours later another explosion at a mine in Fuyuan, Yunnan province, kills 32.

27 Nov Tehran, Iran. A military plane crashes immediately after takeoff from Mehrabad Airport; all 39 aboard, 30 of them members of the Revolutionary Guards, die.

30 Nov Philippines. Typhoon Durian roars across the islands, triggering landslides, mostly on the slopes of Mt. Mayon, that sweep away entire villages and leave more than 1,000 people dead or missing.

December 2006

9 Dec Moscow. A nighttime fire breaks out at a drug-treatment facility; though some 160 people escape, 45 women die, mostly from smoke inhalation, when they are unable to escape because of locked doors and window grilles.

16 Dec Jhok Utra, Pakistan. In a wedding tent, heat from high-intensity lights ignites a fire, which triggers a stampede that results in the destruction of a newly built brick wall; 27 women and children, including the bride, are killed by the fire, the stampede, or the falling wall.

16 Dec Senegal. A wrecked boat carrying people who had been trying to get to the Canary Islands washes up on the coast of Senegal; it is believed that dozens of people died in the wreck. A similar disaster had occurred three days earlier.

24 Dec Southeast Asia. Indonesian officials report that flooding on the island of Sumatra has caused at least 87 people to perish, with dozens still missing; in neighboring Malaysia, 7 fatalities have been reported.

26 Dec Lagos, Nigeria. An oil pipeline breached by thieves explodes as people gather to siphon the leaking oil; the resultant fire incinerates at least 260 people.

27 Dec Off the coast of Yemen. Two boats filled with would-be refugees and being chased by Yemeni patrol boats capsize; at least 140 people are missing.

29 Dec Indonesia. A ferry nearing the completion of a 48-hour journey from Borneo to Java encounters bad weather that causes the boat to break apart; some 400 people are lost.

January 2007

1 Jan Indonesia. An Adam SkyConnection Airlines Boeing 737 flying from Java island to Sulawesi carrying 102 people disappears from radar screens and crashes; there are no survivors.

4 Jan Bangladesh. Government officials report that 40 deaths in poor areas during a cold snap bring the death toll for the week to at least 56.

6 Jan Comilla, Bangladesh. A speeding bus attempt-ing to pass another vehicle goes off the road and catches fire; at least 40 passengers are burned to death.

9 Jan Near Balad, Iraq. A chartered Moldovan Antonov-26 airplane carrying 35 people from Adana, Turkey, crashes while attempting to land in the fog; at least 30 people aboard are killed.

15 Jan US. An ice storm shuts down large parts of Oklahoma, Missouri, Texas, Iowa, and New York and is responsible for the deaths of at least 39 people.

15 Jan Sri Lanka. Landslides resulting from heavy rains kill at least 16 people.

17 Jan Australia. Steve Bracks, the premier of the state of Victoria, warns that the state is experiencing its worst fire conditions ever; close to 2.5 million acres have been burned.

18 Jan Andhra Pradesh, India. An overcrowded ferry carrying people to a religious festival capsizes on the Krishna River; at least 60 people drown.

18 Jan Europe. A ferocious storm, with winds in excess of 61 km/h (100 mph), sweeps through the British Isles and northern Europe; there are at least 47 storm-related deaths.

22 Jan Central Peru. Flooding and mud slides after days of heavy rainfall leave at least 16 people dead and thousands homeless.

25 Jan Angola. The minister of the interior reports that a weeklong storm in the country has resulted in at least 71 deaths, 65 of them in Luanda, and that thousands of people have been rendered homeless.

February 2007

2 Feb Central Florida. Thunderstorms and tornadoes leave at least 19 people dead and hundreds of homes destroyed.

2 Feb Indian-administered Kashmir. A minibus falls into a gorge near Dabhar, killing at least 18 people.

3 Feb Near Sardinata, Colombia. Explosions in a coal mine kill 32 miners; poisonous gases make rescue attempts difficult.

4 Feb Indonesia. Flooding from heavy rain traps hundreds of people in Jakarta, leaving at least 44 people dead as some 340,000 are forced to flee the floodwaters that inundate 40–70% of the city.

7 Feb Central and southern Somalia. Health officials report that a cholera outbreak that resulted from flooding has left at least 115 people dead in the past month.

12 Feb Off the coast of Yemen. A boat carrying refugees from Somalia and Ethiopia capsizes, and at least 112 migrants drown.

13 Feb Mozambique. Relief officials report that unusually catastrophic flooding of the Zambezi River has forced more than 68,000 people to evacuate and left at least 20 people dead.

14 Feb Mokambo, Democratic Republic of the Congo. A train accident in Katanga province leaves 22 people dead, 7 of them Zambian.

22 Feb Jakarta, Indonesia. A passenger ferry catches fire, killing at least 42 of those aboard; days later the wreckage sinks, killing 4 investigators and journalists.

23 Feb Alsunga, Latvia. A large fire, possibly caused by faulty wiring, destroys a home for the disabled, leaving 25 people dead or missing.

23 Feb Mediterranean Sea. African migrants rescued from a rubber dinghy traveling from Tunisia to Sicily say that 19 people died on the trip.

23 Feb Guatemala City, Guatemala. A sinkhole 100 m (330 ft) deep opens, swallowing several houses and killing at least two people.

25 Feb Bolivia. It is reported that the worst flooding in 25 years has left at least 35 people dead and thousands of homes as well as crops and roads destroyed.

25 Feb Northwestern Nigeria. A truck carrying traders and domestic animals from a local market suffers a burst tire and goes into a ditch; at least 40 of the passengers die.

26 Feb Punjab province, Pakistan. At the end of the annual two-day kite festival, 11 people have been killed, 2 of them cut by sharpened kite strings, 5 hit by celebratory gunfire, 2 electrocuted by kites tangled in power lines, and 2 fallen off roofs.

28 Feb Off the coast of Haiti. A sail-powered freighter catches fire and sinks; 52 people die.

March 2007

1 Mar US. A large storm system spawns tornadoes that leave at least 20 people in three states dead, among them 8 students at a high school in Enterprise AL who are killed when the roof collapses.

2 Mar Atlanta GA. A bus carrying members of the baseball team of Bluffton University in Bluffton OH to a series of games in Florida misses a turn on an elevated exit ramp and drives off an overpass onto the highway below; the bus driver, his wife, and five baseball players are killed.

5 Mar Chittagong, Bangladesh. A fire guts dozens of huts in a slum and leaves at least 21 people, mostly women and children, dead.

6 Mar Indonesia. Two earthquakes, with magnitudes of 6.3 and 6.1, occur near Solok, on Sumatra; at least 52 people perish.

6 Mar Zimbabwe. A bus is struck by a freight train at a crossing; 27 people on the bus perish.

7 Mar Yogyakarta, Indonesia. A Garuda Air Boeing 737 crashes upon landing and breaks apart; at least 22 of the passengers are killed.

7 Mar New York City. A fire started by a frayed cord on a space heater in a house in the Bronx leaves 10 members of an extended family from Mali, 9 of them young children, dead.

12 Mar Uttarakhand state, India. A road caves in after heavy rains, plunging a bus carrying wedding guests some 180 m (60 ft) into a ravine; at least 18 people aboard are killed.

19 Mar Siberia, Russia. A methane explosion at the Ulyanovskaya coal mine in Novokuznetsk kills at least 108 workers, including the mine's chief engineer, who was checking a hazard-monitoring system at the time; it later emerges that a device to detect methane had been deliberately disabled.

20 Mar Kamyshevatskaya, Russia. A fire at a home for the elderly and the disabled kills at least 62 people; numerous safety violations contribute to the high death toll.

20 Mar Koudou, Guinea. A truck traveling to a market goes off a bridge into a lake; 65 passengers die.

20 Mar Pakistani-administered Kashmir. Massive landslides caused by torrential rains kill at least 40 people in an area where many survivors of the destructive earthquake of October 2005 live in temporary tent shelters.

22 Mar Maputo, Mozambique. Intense heat causes an old Soviet-built arms depot to catch fire, igniting rockets and ammunition in a massive explosion that kills at least 117 people.

26 Mar Katugal, Nigeria. After an oil tanker rolls over while attempting to park, people rush to loot the truck's cargo; it explodes, killing at least 89 people.

26 Mar Gulf of Aden. After smugglers taking illegal migrants from Somalia to Yemen force them over-board in order to evade security forces, 31 bodies are found with a further 90 migrants reported missing.

29 Mar Guinea. An open boat traveling from Fore-cariah capsizes off the coast near Conakry; at least 60 people are drowned.

April 2007

2 Apr Solomon Islands. An earthquake of magnitude 8.1 occurs well below the sea floor, triggering a tsunami that damages property in the towns of Gizo and Munda and inundates several villages; at least 52 people lose their lives.

14 Apr Yemen. Officials report that at least 62 migrants from Somalia are believed to have drowned when the boat they were being smuggled in overturned; survivors say they were forced to jump into the sea when the smugglers saw the Yemeni coast guard.

16 Apr China. An explosion at the Wangzhuang coal mine in Henan province traps 33 miners under-ground, and in Zhouzhou in Hunan province 12 miners are trapped in a flooded pit.

18 Apr Liaoning province, China. In a metal factory, a huge ladle breaks, spilling molten steel across the floor; at least 32 workers die.

18 Apr Egypt. On the highway between Cairo and Assuit, a truck trying to pass another vehicle col-lides head-on with a school bus; at least 18 stu-dents are killed.

24 Apr Indian-administered Kashmir. An over-loaded minibus goes off the road near Kalai and falls down a hillside; at least 30 passengers die.

May 2007

2 May Himachal Pradesh state, India. A bus leaves the road and tumbles into a deep gorge near Kothkhai; at least 22 passengers perish.

4 May Greensburg KS. The town of Greensburg is de-molished by an exceptionally large tornado; 10 peo-ple die and at least 63 are injured.

4 May Off the Turks and Caicos Islands. A boat full of Haitian migrants capsizes under disputed circum-stances; some 90 people are drowned.

5 May Cameroon. A Kenya Airways Boeing 737 en route to Nairobi crashes near the village of Mbanga Pongo shortly after takeoff from Douala; 114 peo-ple were on board and no survivors are found.

7 May Lesotho. Near the village of Haramarupi, a speeding bus carrying workers from a textile fac-tory collides with a truck; at least 45 of the occu-pants are killed.

11 May Uttar Pradesh state, India. A storm causes the collapse of buildings in the town of Sultanpur, crushing 24 people, while 3 are killed by lightning in Pratapgarh.

13 May Port Harcourt, Nigeria. Three passenger buses are involved in a traffic accident and one of them catches fire; at least 25 people are killed.

21 May Liaoning province, China. A three-wheeled ve-hicle towing a trailer carrying women returning home after a day spent picking herbs overturns on a mountain road; 20 women are killed.

23 May Tiruppur, India. A dividing wall for a factory under construction collapses into an adjacent bar, crushing 27 bar patrons.

24 May Siberia. In the Yubileinaya coal mine in the town of Novokuznetsk, Russia, a methane explo-sion kills at least 38 miners.

June 2007

3 Jun Sierra Leone. A helicopter carrying Togolese sports officials and journalists crashes on the way to Lungi International Airport outside Freetown after an association football (soccer) game; 22 peo-ple, among them Togo's minister of sports, are killed.

5 Jun Victoria, Australia. A truck crashes into a Mel-bourne-bound passenger train at a crossing near Kerang; at least 11 of the train passengers are killed.

6 Jun Oman. Cyclone Gonu passes down the coast, forcing evacuations and shutting down oil installa-tions; at least 32 people are killed and some 30 are missing.

10 Jun Southern China. Officials in China report that days of torrential rain produced flooding in which at least 66 people died.

11 Jun Bangladesh. Mud slides caused by heavy rains leave some 119 people dead in Chittagong; elsewhere in the area rain and lightning kill roughly 16 more.

22 Jun Off Malta. The captain of an Italian fishing trawler reports that a dinghy carrying African mi-grants capsized and 24 of its occupants drowned; on 1 June at least 18 decomposing bodies were found in the same area.

24 Jun Karachi. A provincial health minister reports that unusually strong monsoon storms have caused the deaths of 228 people as well as flood-ing and extensive power failures.

24 Jun Bougainville, Papua New Guinea. A Bougain-ville Health Department boat carrying 15 people on a return trip to Buka from Nissan Island disap-pears.

25 Jun Southern Cambodia. A PMT Air An-24 airplane flying from Siem Reap to Sihanoukville crashes in the mountains; all 22 aboard lose their lives.

25 Jun India. In three days of monsoon rains, at least 144 people lose their lives: some 41 in Andhra Pradesh, 52 in Kerala, 39 in Karnataka, and 15 in Maharashtra.

26 Jun Europe. It is reported that a heat wave with temperatures as high as 46 °C (115 °F) has caused the deaths of 23 people in Romania, 7 peo-ple in Serbia, and 5 people in Greece; numerous wildfires in Greece and Italy are also blamed on the heat; later a death toll of 42 in Italy and the Balkans is reported.

People

The TIME 100, 2007

At the turn of the millennium in 2000, TIME selected 100 individuals as the most influential people of the 20th century. The resulting list provided such a revealing perspective on history that the magazine has now begun naming a TIME 100 each year, designating influential individuals in five categories. As with TIME's annual Person of the Year designation, the list includes both heroes and villains; inclusion reflects the power of an individual's impact on history, whether for good or for ill. The entries with bylines below are excerpts from articles commissioned for the TIME 100 issue.

LEADERS & REVOLUTIONARIES

Abdullah bin Abdul Aziz al-Saud The Saudi king's 2007 Arab peace initiative made him a dominant player in the troubled region.

Archbishop Peter Akinola Nigeria's top Episcopal prelate, a harsh critic of the American church, may lead a schism over gays in the pulpit.

Omar Hassan al-Bashir Clinging to power, The Sudan's dictator has devastated Darfur—and his nation.

Queen Elizabeth II At 81, Britain's monarch is willing to effect reforms without compromising her identity.

Osama bin Laden As long as al-Qaeda's leader remains at large, he remains a serious threat.

Michael Bloomberg New York City's billionaire mayor has presided brilliantly over the city's renaissance.

Raúl Castro Fidel's younger brother is in position to lead Cuba into the future.

Hillary Clinton New York's senator is the Democrats' frontrunner for '08. But Obama is gaining.

Sonia Gandhi The leader of India's Congress Party is an Italian—and her adopted nation's kingmaker.

Hu Jintao China's president, a tough technocrat, is riding an economic tiger. Can he control it?

Ayatollah Ali Khamenei Iran's Supreme Leader obstructs reform but also holds radicals in check.

Liu Qi The boss of the '08 Beijing Olympics is whipping his city into shape so the Games can begin.

Tzipi Livni "Tzipi [Israel's foreign affairs minister] has not been just a colleague; she has become my friend."   —Condoleezza Rice

Angela Merkel Germany's chancellor is helping revive stagnant European integration.

Pope Benedict XVI After John Paul II's Slavic sentiment, he brings German rigor to the papacy.

Barack Obama The Illinois senator's fresh face and ideas have roused Democrats' hopes for '08.

Nancy Pelosi "...the first woman ever to become Speaker of the House—and she earned it."
   —Newt Gingrich

General David Petraeus The warrior-scholar took on the toughest job on the planet: heading up the last-ditch US "surge" in Iraq.

Condoleezza Rice The US secretary of state handles a demanding job with grit and grace.

John Roberts Now 52, the conservative chief justice may head the Supreme Court for decades.

Arnold Schwarzenegger California's green governor is battling his own party over conserving resources and establishing new hydrocarbon emissions caps.

HEROES & PIONEERS

Maher Arar The Syrian-born Canadian, accused by US agents of being a terrorist, was sent to Syria and tortured. After his release, Canada found him was innocent.

Wesley Autrey New York City's "subway hero" claimed to be only an average citizen, yet he risked his life in saving the life of a stranger.

Tyra Banks The supermodel has become an advocate for women of all shapes, sizes, and races.

Warren Buffett America's oracle of investment has become a leader in a new approach to philanthropy that stresses strong oversight and clear results.

Youk Chhang The director of the Documentation Center of Cambodia is chronicling the genocide of the Khmer Rouge regime of the 1970s.

George Clooney The actor deploys his Hollywood wattage to shed light on the misery in Darfur.

Tony Dungy The coach of the Super Bowl champion Indianapolis Colts has a teacher's mentality and a strong faith in his mission.

Elizabeth Edwards The wife of presidential aspirant John Edwards became a courageous role model for millions of people diagnosed with cancer.

Drew Gilpin Faust Harvard University's first female president is setting an example for all women.

Roger Federer "...he's the best [tennis] player of his time and one of the most admirable champions on the planet."   —Rod Laver

Michael J. Fox The great comic actor, afflicted at 30 with Parkinson disease, has become a strong voice for stem-cell research.

Timothy Gittins TIME selected the decorated US Army captain to represent the one million Americans who have served in Iraq and Afghanistan.

Thierry Henry The French soccer star is heading up efforts to combat strains of ugly, persistent racism in Europe's favorite game.

Garry Kasparov The chess great is leading calls for reform in Vladimir Putin's corrupt modern Russia.

Amr Khaled At 39, the Egyptian commentator is a welcome voice for moderation in an Islamic world too often filled with the voices of extremists.

Judith Mackay The British-born Hong Kong doctor has taken a lead role in informing the world of the dangers of tobacco.

Chien-Ming Wang The New York Yankees pitcher is helping erode cultural barriers around the world.

Oprah Winfrey The girls' school she founded in South Africa "will change the trajectory of ... lives."
   —Nelson Mandela

Zeng Jinyan The Chinese blogger has built a global following by detailing the regime's injustices.

SCIENTISTS & THINKERS

Paul Allen Microsoft's cofounder has stimulated research science with his thoughtful philanthropy.

Chris Anderson The editor and physicist's 2006 book *The Long Tail* charted a new paradigm in accessing ideas.

Elizabeth Blackburn The California biologist is developing promising new ways to treat cancer.

Richard Dawkins Britain's evolutionary biologist explored religion and culture in *The God Delusion*.

Frans de Waal The Dutch-born primatologist studies apes to illuminate human behavior.

Al Gore The former vice president has led the way in putting global warming on the global agenda.

Monty Jones The native of Sierra Leone is creating a green revolution in Africa with new strains of rice.

John Mather The NASA scientist is building history's most powerful telescope, now scheduled to launch into Earth orbit in 2013.

Douglas Melton The codirector of Harvard's Stem Cell Institute has become a powerful, outspoken advocate for his field.

Steven Nissen The heart specialist is a respected, candid advocate for safer drugs and therapies.

Tullis Onstott The Princeton geosciences professor has found life forms two miles inside the Earth.

Svante Pääblo The Swedish genetics guru has decoded segments of the Neanderthal genome.

Lisa Randall The first female theoretical physicist to earn tenure at Harvard is now exploring gravity.

Klaus Schwab The German-born founder of the annual World Economic Forum at Davos, Switzerland, nurtures global understanding and action.

Kari Stefansson The biologist is fighting disease and illuminating heredity by charting the genetic code of his fellow Icelanders.

Alan Stern The new head of NASA's unmanned missions program has ambitious plans for the future.

Neil deGrasse Tyson The astronomer, director of New York City's Hayden Plantarium, is a Carl Sagan for the 21st century, guiding us through the stars.

J. Craig Venter After helping map the human genome, he is charting biodiversity in the planet's oceans.

Nora Volkow The director of the National Institute of Drug Abuse showed how drugs and addiction change the workings of the brain.

ARTISTS & ENTERTAINERS

Cate Blanchett A grown-up actress, she radiates natural aristocracy and a warm, alert intelligence.

Sacha Baron Cohen The British comic has created uniquely outrageous characters for our uniquely outrageous times.

Leonardo DiCaprio "He [is] *the* actor among a generation of gifted young actors."   —Martin Scorsese

Alber Elbaz The onetime Israeli soldier is now one of fashion's most admired and influential designers.

America Ferrera The Honduran-American star of TV hit *Ugly Betty* is spunky, driven, and real.

Tina Fey The force behind TV's witty *30 Rock* is a rising player in what has always been a man's game, the world of network comedy.

Simon Fuller The Briton behind the Spice Girls and *American Idol* is the P.T. Barnum of our times.

Brian Grazer The highly successful veteran film and TV producer is one of Hollywood's quickest-witted denizens.

John Mayer The white singer-songwriter explores the blues with sincerity, technique, and truth.

David Mitchell With *Cloud Atlas* and *Black Swan Green,* the British novelist is reinventing fiction.

Kate Moss Beauty may not be truth, but this longtime supermodel makes it very, very persuasive.

Youssou N'Dour Senegal's gifted pop singer uses his voice of gold to promote African progress.

Anna Netrebko The stunning Russian soprano blends vocal splendor with dramatic intensity. Bravo!

Rosie O'Donnell "... a fine actress, a great storyteller, and a woman of conviction."   —Barbara Walters

Brad Pitt The pretty-boy actor has developed into a thoughtful, provocative producer and activist.

Shonda Rhimes Overnight, the force behind TV hit *Grey's Anatomy* went from screenwriter and single mom to Hollywood eminence—with style and grace.

Nora Roberts The world's leading romance writer has the key to millions of gals'—and guys'—hearts.

Rick Rubin The top record producer "has the ability and patience to let music be discovered, not manufactured."   —Natalie Maines, Dixie Chicks

Martin Scorsese The director finally won an Oscar for *The Departed*—but that won't slow him down.

Justin Timberlake The onetime teen idol is now an accomplished entertainer, writer, and producer.

Kara Walker The artist's installations and films trace the twisted trajectories of race in America.

Brian Williams The NBC news anchor is a traditional journalist with an appreciation for hard news.

BUILDERS & TITANS

Bernard Arnault The French tycoon unites the competing interests of art and commerce with a businessman's skill and an artist's eye.

Richard Branson Britain's highest-flying entrepreneur is going even higher with his latest venture, Virgin Galactic, a foray into commercial spaceflight.

Rhonda Byrne She sold 2 million DVDs of her uplifting *The Secret* in a year—and 4 million books in six months.

Steven Cohen The billionaire head of hedge-fund phenomenon SAC Capital merges a deliberately low profile with earnings averaging 40% a year.

Clara Furse The CEO of the London Stock Exchange is bringing the world's business to Britain.

Ho Ching In four years, she doubled the equity of Temasek Holdings, the investment arm of Singapore's government, while raising accountability.

Chad Hurley & Steve Chen The YouTube founders fostered a community around sharing video, building a revolutionary platform for creative expression.

Steve Jobs The innovator did it again, turning the cell-phone industry upside down with the iPhone.

Ken Lewis While other big banks were letting workers go and fighting decline, the CEO of Bank of America saw '06 earnings surge by 28%.

Erik Lie The University of Iowa business professor led the investigations that revealed illegal stock-option transactions in US boardrooms.

Pony Ma The young visionary behind the monster online kids' community QQ and its 100 million users is shaping China's future.

Lakshmi Mittal The Indian steel magnate is the world's fifth-richest man and a noted philanthropist.

Shigeru Miyamoto With the Wii system, Nintendo's grand-master designer reinvented video games.

Michael Moritz The Welsh-born venture capitalist and his Sequoia Capital helped Apple, Oracle, Yahoo!, and Google start up; now he's going global.

Indra Nooyi PepsiCo's new boss knows the world is her market; she promotes sustainability in multiple arenas: human, talent, and environment.

Cyril Ramaphosa South Africa's noted union leader has left politics—but may be his nation's future.

Philip Rosedale The inventor of the online game *Second Life* helped millions connect in his cyberspace alternate world.

Stephen Schwarzman The cofounder of Wall Street's Blackstone Group uses his private equity firm to turn losing corporations into winners.

Katsuaki Watanabe Toyota's boss has invested in local communities in the US, creating jobs, being a good neighbor, and caring for the environment.

Celebrities and Newsmakers

These mini-biographies are intended to provide background information about people in the news. See also the Obituaries (below) for recently deceased persons.

Mahmoud (Ridha) Abbas (nom de guerre Abu Mazen; 1935, Zefat, Palestine), Palestinian politician; secretary general of the PLO executive committee and cofounder (with Yasir Arafat) of the Fatah movement; he served as the first prime minister of the Palestine Authority and was its president from 2005.

Sidi Muhammad Ould Cheikh Abdallahi (1938), Mauritanian politician; president from 2007.

A.P.J. Abdul Kalam (Avul Pakir Jainulabdeen Abdul Kalam; 15 Oct 1931, Rameswaram, Tamil Nadu state, British India), Indian aeronautical engineer; president of India, 2002–07.

Abdullah ('Abdallah ibn 'Abd al-'Aziz Al Saud; 1923, Riyadh, Saudi Arabia), Saudi royal and king of Saudi Arabia from 2005.

Abdullah II (Abdallah ibn al-Hussein al-Hashimi; 30 Jan 1962, Amman, Jordan), Jordanian royal and king from 1999.

Shinzo Abe (21 Sep 1954, Tokyo, Japan), Japanese politician (Liberal Democratic); prime minister of Japan from 2006.

Tuanku Mizan Zainal Abidin ibni al-Marhum Sultan Mahmud (22 Jan 1962, Kuala Terengganu, Malaysia), Malaysian politician; *yang di-pertuan agong* (head of state) in 2001 and again from 2006.

John (Philip) Abizaid (1 Apr 1951, Coleville CA), American military officer (lt. general, US Army) who was commander of the US Central Command and supreme commander of occupation forces in Iraq, 2003–07.

Jack A. Abramoff (28 Feb 1958, Atlantic City NJ), disgraced American lobbyist.

Aníbal Acevedo Vilá (13 Feb 1962, Hato Rey, Puerto Rico), American politician; governor of Puerto Rico from 2005.

Chinua Achebe (1930, Nigeria), Nigerian novelist and poet who won the second Man Booker International Prize for fiction in 2007.

Joe Ackermann (Josef Ackermann; 7 Feb 1948, Mels, Sankt Gallen, Switzerland), Swiss corporate executive and CEO of Deutsche Bank AG from 1997.

Valdas V. Adamkus (Valdas V. Adamkevicius; 3 Nov 1926, Kaunas, Lithuania), Lithuanian politician and president, 1998–2003 and again from 2004.

Gerry Adams (Gerard Adams; 6 Oct 1948, Belfast, Northern Ireland), Northern Irish resistance leader; president of Sinn Féin, the political wing of the Irish Republican Army.

John (Coolidge) Adams (15 Feb 1947, Worcester MA), American composer.

Scott Adams (8 Jun 1957, Windham NY), American cartoonist, creator of *Dilbert*.

Thomas Adès (27 Jun 1971, London, England), English composer, pianist, and conductor.

Ben Affleck (Benjamin Geza Affleck; 15 Aug 1972, Berkeley CA), American actor, director, and writer.

Isaias Afwerki (2 Feb 1946, Asmara, Ethiopia [now in Eritrea]), Eritrean independence leader, secretary-general of the Provisional Government, and first president of Eritrea from 1993.

Andre (Kirk) Agassi (29 Apr 1970, Las Vegas NV), American tennis player.

Christina (Maria) Aguilera (18 Dec 1980, Staten Island NY), American pop singer.

Bertie Ahern (Bartholomew Patrick Ahern; 12 Sep 1951, Dublin, Ireland), Irish politician; prime minister (*taoiseach*) of Ireland from 1997.

Iajuddin Ahmed (1 Feb 1931, Nayagaon, Bengal state, British India [now in Bangladesh]), Bangladeshi scientist and educator; president of Bangladesh from 2002.

Clay Aiken (Clayton Grissom Aiken; 30 Nov 1978, Raleigh NC), American entertainer.

Akihito (original name Tsugu Akihito; era name Heisei; 23 Dec 1933, Tokyo, Japan), Japanese royal; emperor of Japan from 1989.

Akil Akilov (1944, Tajikistan?), Tajik politician and prime minister from 1999.

Albert II (Albert Félix Humbert Théodore Christian Eugène Marie of Saxe-Coburg-Gotha; 6 Jun 1934, Brussels, Belgium), king of Belgium from 1993.

Albert II (Albert Alexandre Louis Pierre; 14 Mar 1958, Monaco), Monegasque prince who became ruler of Monaco upon the death of his father, Rainier III, in 2005.

Karl (1920, Germany) and **Theo Albrecht** (28 Mar 1922, Germany), German business executives who founded the Aldi supermarket chain.

Alan Alda (Alphonso Joseph D'Abruzzo; 28 Jan 1936, New York NY), American film and TV actor.

Sherman J. Alexie, Jr. (7 Oct 1966, Wellpinit, Spokane Indian Reservation, Washington), American poet and novelist who writes of his Native American upbringing.

Alexis II (Aleksey Mikhaylovich Ridiger; 23 Feb 1929, Tallinn, Estonia), Russian religious leader; Orthodox Patriarch of Moscow and All Russia, the 15th primate of Russia, from 1990.

Monica Ali (20 Oct 1967, Dacca, Pakistan [now Dhaka, Bangladesh]), Bangladesh-born British writer.

Muhammad Ali (Cassius Marcellus Clay, Jr., until 1964; 17 Jan 1942, Louisville KY), American boxer, the first to win the heavyweight championship three separate times.

Samuel A. Alito, Jr. (1 Apr 1950, Trenton NJ), American jurist; associate justice of the US Supreme Court from 2006.

Ilham Aliyev (Ilham Geidar ogly Aliev; 24 Dec 1961, Baku, USSR [now in Azerbaijan]), Azerbaijani politician; prime minister from 2003.

Ayad Allawi (31 May 1944, Baghdad, Iraq), Iraqi neurologist and prime minister, 2004–05.

Paul G. Allen (21 Jan 1953, Mercer Island WA), American corporate executive who cofounded Microsoft Corp. (1975) and owned several professional sports teams.

Woody Allen (Allen Stewart Konigsberg; 1 Dec 1935, Brooklyn NY), American filmmaker, actor, and comedian.

Isabel Allende (2 Aug 1942, Lima, Peru), Chilean writer in the magic realist tradition, considered one of the first successful women novelists in Latin America.

Kirstie Alley (12 Jan 1951, Wichita KS), American film and TV actress.

Pedro Almodóvar (24 Sep 1949, Calzada de Calatrava, Spain), Spanish film director specializing in melodrama.

Marin Alsop (1957?, New York NY), American conductor.

Amadou (Amadou Bagayoko; 24 Oct 1954, Bamako, French West Africa [now in Mali]), Malian guitarist (of Amadou and Mariam).

Anastacia (Newkirk) (7 Sep 1973, Chicago IL), American pop singer, songwriter, dancer, producer, and breast cancer activist.

Pamela (Denise) Anderson (1 Jul 1967, Ladysmith, BC, Canada), Canadian-born model and actress.

Tadao Ando (13 Sep 1941, Osaka, Japan), Japanese architect; recipient of the 1995 Pritzker Prize.

Marc Andreessen (July 1971, New Lisbon WI), American computer innovator, cofounder (1994) of Mosaic Communications Corp., and developer of Netscape, a software system for browsing the Internet.

Andrew (19 Feb 1960, Buckingham Palace, London, England), British prince; duke of York, the second son of Queen Elizabeth II and Prince Philip, duke of Edinburgh.

Maya Angelou (Marguerite Annie Johnson; 4 Apr 1928, St. Louis MO), American poet.

Jennifer Aniston (Jennifer Linn Anistassakis; 11 Feb 1969, Sherman Oaks CA), American TV and film actress.

Kofi (Atta) Annan (18 Apr 1938, Kumasi, Gold Coast [now Ghana]), Ghanaian diplomat; UN secretary-general, 1997–2006; corecipient, with the UN, of the 2001 Nobel Prize for Peace.

Anne (Elizabeth Alice Louise; 15 Aug 1950, Clarence House, London, England), British princess, the daughter of Queen Elizabeth II and Prince Philip, duke of Edinburgh.

Andrus Ansip (1 Oct 1956, Tartu, USSR [now in Estonia]), Estonian politician; prime minister from 2005.

Marc Anthony (Marco Antonio Muñiz; 16 Sep 1968, Spanish Harlem, New York NY), American salsa singer.

Louise Arbour (10 Feb 1947, Montreal, QC, Canada), Canadian judge; UN High Commissioner for Human Rights from 2004.

Denys Arcand (25 Jun 1941, Deschambault, QC, Canada), Canadian film director and screenwriter known first for his documentary films and later for gritty intellectual fare.

Martha Argerich (5 Jun 1941, Buenos Aires, Argentina), Argentine concert pianist.

Oscar Arias Sánchez (13 Sep 1941, Heredia, Costa Rica), Costa Rican statesman; president of Costa Rica, 1986–90 and from 2006; recipient of the 1987 Nobel Peace Prize.

Alan Arkin (Alan Wolf Arkin; 26 Mar 1934, Brooklyn NY), American film and TV actor.

Billie Joe Armstrong (17 Feb 1972, Rodeo CA), American punk-rock vocalist and guitarist (of Green Day).

Lance Armstrong (18 Sep 1971, Plano TX), American cyclist who won the Tour de France seven years in succession, 1999–2005.

Gerald Arpino (14 Jan 1928, Staten Island NY), American ballet choreographer, a cofounder and leader of the Joffrey Ballet from its founding in 1956 and its artistic director from 1988.

Courteney Cox Arquette (15 Jun 1964, Birmingham AL), American TV and film actress.

Owen Seymour Arthur (17 Oct 1949, Barbados), Barbadian politician and prime minister from 1994.

Ashanti (Ashanti S. Douglas; 13 Oct 1980, Glen Cove NY), American hip-hop singer.

Hanan Ashrawi (8 Oct 1946, Ram Allah, Palestine), Palestinian academic and spokeswoman for Palestine.

Bashar al-Assad (11 Sep 1965, Damascus, Syria), Syrian statesman and president from 2000.

Azali Assoumani (1959, Grand Comoro Island, Comoros), Comoran politician who was president, 1999–2002, and a second time, 2002–06.

Alaa Al Aswany (1957, Egypt), Egyptian dentist and popular writer.

Abdul Rahman ibn Hamad al-Attiyah (1950, Qatar), Qatari international official; secretary-general of the Gulf Cooperation Council from 2002.

Margaret (Eleanor) Atwood (18 Nov 1939, Ottawa, ON, Canada), Canadian poet, novelist, and critic.

Robert John Aumann (8 Jun 1930, Frankfurt am Main, Germany), American Israeli mathematician; corecipient of the 2005 Nobel Prize for Economic Sciences.

Daw Aung San Suu Kyi (19 Jun 1945, Rangoon, Burma [now Yangôn, Myanmar]), Burmese human rights activist and opposition leader; recipient in 1991 of the Nobel Prize for Peace.

Geno Auriemma (Luigi Auriemma; 1946, Montella, Italy), Italian-born American women's basketball coach.

Dan Aykroyd (1 Jul 1952, Ottawa, ON, Canada), Canadian-born comic actor.

Hank Azaria (25 Apr 1964, Forest Hills NY), American actor best known for comic film roles and for providing voices for TV's *The Simpsons*.

B-Real (Louis Freese; 2 Jun 1970, Los Angeles CA), American Latino rap artist.

'Abd al-Qadir al-Ba Jamal (1946, Yemen?), Yemeni politician; prime minister, 2001–07.

Michelle Bachelet (Verónica Michelle Bachelet Jeria; 29 Sep 1951, Santiago, Chile), Chilean politician (Socialist); president from 2006.

Kevin Bacon (8 Jul 1958, Philadelphia PA), American film and theater actor.

Datuk Seri Abdullah Ahmad Badawi (26 Nov 1939, Penang state, Malaysia), Malaysian politician; prime minister from 2003.

Erykah Badu (Erica Wright; 26 Feb 1972, Dallas TX), American singer-songwriter appreciated for the phrasing and emotive qualities of her smooth, jazz-inflected vocals.

Bob Baffert (13 Jan 1953, Nogales AZ), American trainer of Thoroughbred racehorses.

Jerry D. Bailey (29 Aug 1957, Dallas TX), American jockey.

Anita Baker (26 Jan 1958, Toledo OH), American singer.

Kurmanbek Bakiyev (1 Aug 1949, Masadan, Kirghiz SSR, USSR [now Teyyit, Kyrgyzstan]), Kyrgyz politician; president of Kyrgyzstan from 2005.

John Elias Baldacci (30 Jan 1955, Bangor ME), American Democratic politician and governor of Maine from 2003.

Alec Baldwin (Alexander Rae Baldwin III; 3 Apr 1958, Massapequa NY), American film and TV actor.

Jan Peter Balkenende (7 May 1956, Kapelle, Netherlands), Dutch Christian-Democratic politician and prime minister from 2002.

Steven A. Ballmer (24 Mar 1956, Detroit? MI), American corporate executive; CEO of Microsoft Corp. from 2000.

Ed(ward) Balls (25 Feb 1967, Norwich, England), British public official; chief economic adviser to the treasury.

David Baltimore (7 Mar 1938, New York NY), American microbiologist, corecipient of the 1975 Nobel Prize for Physiology or Medicine, and president of the California Institute of Technology, 1997–2006.

Ban Ki-moon (13 Jun 1944, Umsong, Japanese-occupied Korea [now in South Korea]), Korean government and international official; secretary-general of the United Nations from 2007.

Antonio Banderas (José António Domínguez Banderas; 10 Oct 1960, Málaga, Spain), Spanish actor and director.

Tyra Banks (4 Dec 1973, Los Angeles CA), American model, actress, and TV show host.

Patricia Barber (8 Nov 1955, Lisle IL), American jazz singer and pianist.

Haley Barbour (22 Oct 1947, Yazoo City MS), American Republican politician and governor of Mississippi from 2004.

Daniel Barenboim (15 Nov 1942, Buenos Aires, Argentina), Israeli pianist and conductor.

José Manuel Durão Barroso (23 Mar 1956, Lisbon, Portugal), Portuguese politician; prime minister, 2002–04; and president of the European Commission from 2004.

John D. Barrow (John David Barrow; 29 Nov 1952, London, England), British cosmologist, a specialist in the anthropic principle; recipient of the 2006 Templeton Prize.

Dave Barry (3 Jul 1947, Armonk NY), American humorist, syndicated newspaper columnist, and author of multiple best sellers.

Drew Barrymore (Andrew Blythe Barrymore; 22 Feb 1975, Culver City CA), American film actress.

Frederick Barthelme (10 Oct 1943, Houston TX), American writer of short stories and novels.

Richard Barton (2 Jun 1967, New Canaan CT), American Internet entrepreneur (Expedia.com, Zillow.com).

Mikhail Baryshnikov (28 Jan 1948, Riga, USSR [now Latvia]), Soviet-born American ballet dancer and director.

Traian Basescu (4 Nov 1951, Basarabi, Romania), Romanian politician; president from 2004.

Omar Hassan Ahmad al-Bashir (1944, Hosh Bannaga, Anglo-Egyptian Sudan [now The Sudan]), Sudanese military leader and president from 1989.

Angela Bassett (16 Aug 1958, New York NY), American film actress.

Beatrix (31 Jan 1938, Soestdijk, Netherlands), Dutch royal and queen of The Netherlands from 1980.

(Henry) Warren Beatty (30 Mar 1937, Richmond VA), American film actor, producer, director, and screenwriter.

Beck (Beck Hansen; 8 Jul 1970, Los Angeles CA), American singer and songwriter.

Margaret Beckett (Margaret Mary Jackson; 15 Jan 1943, Ashton-under-Lyne, Lancashire, England), British politician (Labour); foreign secretary of the UK from 2006.

David Beckham (2 May 1975, Leytonstone, England), British association football (soccer) player.

Victoria Beckham (Victoria Caroline Adams; 7 Apr 1975, Goff's Oak, England), British pop singer ("Posh Spice" of the Spice Girls) and wife of David Beckham.

Kate Beckinsale (26 Jul 1973, London, England), British actress.

Mike Beebe (Michael Dale Beebe; 28 Dec 1946, Amagon AR), American politician (Democrat); governor of Arkansas from 2007.

Kenenisa Bekele (13 Jun 1982, near Bekoji, Ethiopia), Ethiopian cross-country runner.

Carlos Filipe Ximenes Belo (3 Feb 1948, Wailacama, Portuguese Timor [now East Timor]), Timorese Roman Catholic bishop and advocate of independence for East Timor; corecipient of the 1996 Nobel Prize for Peace.

Arden L. Bement, Jr. (22 May 1932, Pittsburgh PA), American materials scientist; director of the National Science Foundation from 2004.

Zine al-Abidine Ben Ali (3 Sep 1936, Hammam-Sousse, Tunisia), Tunisian politician and president from 1987.

Benedict XVI (Joseph Alois Ratzinger; 16 Apr 1927, Marktl am Inn, Bavaria, Germany), German Roman Catholic churchman; pope from 2005.

Luciano Benetton (13 May 1935, Treviso, Italy), Italian retailer and cofounder (1965) of the Benetton company.

Annette Bening (29 May 1958, Topeka KS), American film actress.

Alan Bennett (9 May 1934, Leeds, England), British dramatist and writer.

Óscar Berger Perdomo (11 Aug 1946, Guatemala City, Guatemala), Guatemalan politician and president from 2004.

Sali Berisha (Sali Ram Berisha; 15 Oct 1944, Tropojë, Albania), Albanian cardiologist and politician (Democratic Party); president, 1992–97, and prime minister from 2005.

Silvio Berlusconi (29 Sep 1936, Milan, Italy), Italian businessman and politician; prime minister of Italy, 1994–95 and again, 2001–06.

Ben S. Bernanke (Benjamin Shalom Bernanke; 13 Dec 1953, Augusta GA), American economist and professor; chairman of the Board of Governors of the Federal Reserve System from 2006.

Tim Berners-Lee (Timothy J. Berners-Lee; 8 Jun 1955, London, England), British inventor of the World Wide Web and director of the World Wide Web Consortium (W3C) from 1994.

Halle (Maria) Berry (14 Aug 1968, Cleveland OH), American actress and model.

Guy Berryman (12 Apr 1978, Kirkcaldy, Fife, Scotland), British rock bassist (of Coldplay).

Liliane Bettencourt (October 1922, France), French daughter of the founder of the L'Oreal cosmetics company.

Beyoncé (Knowles) (4 Sep 1981, Houston TX), American R&B singer.

Jeffrey P. Bezos (12 Jan 1964, Albuquerque NM), American corporate executive; founder and CEO of Amazon.com from 1995.

Bhumibol Adulyadej (Rama IX; 5 Dec 1927, Cambridge MA), Thai royal; king of Thailand from 1946.

Joseph R(obinette) Biden, Jr. (20 Nov 1942, Scranton PA), American Democratic politician and senator from Delaware from 1973.

Big Boi (Antwan Andre Patton; 1 Feb 1975, Savannah GA), American hip-hop artist and a member of the duo OutKast.

James H(adley) Billington (1 Jun 1929, Bryn Mawr PA), American cultural historian; librarian of Congress from 1987.

Osama bin Laden (10 Mar 1957, Riyadh, Saudi Arabia), Saudi Arabian–born terrorist and leader of the al-Qaeda organization.

Pat Binns (8 Oct 1948, Weyburn, SK, Canada), Canadian politician; premier of Prince Edward Island from 1996.

Juliette Binoche (9 Mar 1964, Paris, France), French film actress.

Harrison Birtwistle (15 Jul 1934, Accrington, Lancashire, England), British composer of operas, chamber music, and orchestral music.

Paul Biya (13 Feb 1933, Mvomeka'a, Cameroon), Cameroonian politician; president from 1982.

Jonas Bjorkman (23 Mar 1972, Vaxjo, Sweden), Swedish tennis player best known for doubles play, especially with Todd Woodbridge.

Ole Einar Bjørndalen (27 Jan 1974, Drammen, Norway), Norwegian biathlete and cross-country skier.

Conrad (Moffat) Black (25 Aug 1944, Montreal, QC, Canada), Canadian financier and press baron.

Jack Black (28 Aug 1969, Hermosa Beach CA), American TV and film actor and comic rock bandleader.

Rubén Blades (16 Jul 1948, Panama City, Panama), Panamanian salsa singer and songwriter, actor, and politician.

Rod R. Blagojevich (10 Dec 1956, Chicago IL), American Democratic politician and governor of Illinois from 2003.

David Blaine (David Blaine White; 4 Apr 1973, Brooklyn NY), American magician known for his endurance stunts.

Tony Blair (Anthony Charles Lynton Blair; 6 May 1953, Edinburgh, Scotland), British politician, Labour Party leader, and prime minister of the UK, 1997–2007.

Robert Blake (Michael James Vijencio Gubitosi; 18 Sep 1933, Nutley NJ), American film and TV actor.

Cate Blanchett (Catherine Elise Blanchett; 14 May 1969, Melbourne, VIC, Australia), Australian film actress.

Kathleen Babineaux Blanco (15 Dec 1942, Coteau LA), American Democratic politician and governor of Louisiana from 2004.

Mary J. Blige (11 Jan 1971, New York NY), American hip-hop soul singer.

Harold (Irving) Bloom (11 Jul 1930, New York NY), American literary critic.

Orlando Bloom (13 Jan 1977, Canterbury, Kent, England), British film actor.

Michael R. Bloomberg (14 Feb 1942, Medford MA), American businessman, philanthropist, and Republican politician; mayor of New York City from 2002.

Matt Blunt (20 Nov 1970, Springfield MO), American Republican politician and governor of Missouri from 2005.

Andrea Bocelli (22 Sep 1958, Lajatico, Italy), Italian operatic tenor, blind from childhood.

Steven Bochco (16 Dec 1943, New York NY), American writer, producer, and creator of TV series.

Samuel Wright Bodman (26 Nov 1938, Chicago IL), American chemical engineer, corporate leader, and official; US secretary of energy from 2005.

Enrique Bolaños Geyer (13 May 1928, Masaya, Nicaragua), Nicaraguan politician and president from 2002.

Sir Haji Hassanal Bolkiah Mu'izzadin Waddaulah (15 Jul 1946, Brunei Town [now Bandar Seri Begawan], Brunei), sultan of Brunei from 1967.

Barry (Lamar) Bonds (24 Jul 1964, Riverside CA), American baseball player who tallied a record 73 home runs in 2001 and broke the all-time home run record in 2007.

Omar Bongo Ondimba (Albert-Bernard Bongo; 30 Dec 1935, Lewai, Gabon), Gabonese politician and president from 1967.

Yayi Boni (Thomas Yayi Boni; 1952, Tchaourou, French Dahomey [now Benin]), Beninois politician (independent); president from 2006.

Bono (Paul David Hewson; also known as Bono Vox; 10 May 1960, Dublin, Ireland), Irish lead singer and songwriter of the rock band U2; also a human rights activist and mediator.

Cherie Booth (23 Sep 1954, Bury, Lancashire, England), British barrister, the wife of former prime minister Tony Blair.

Umberto Bossi (19 Sep 1941, Cassano Magnano, Italy), Italian politician and leader of the separatist Northern League from 1991.

Bouasone Bouphavanh (3 Jun 1954, Ban Tao Poun, Salavan province, French Indochina [now in Laos]), Laotian politician and prime minister from 2006.

Lucien Bouchard (22 Dec 1938, Saint-Coeur-de-Marie, QC, Canada), French Canadian politician, an advocate of the separation of Quebec from the rest of Canada.

Ray Bourque (28 Dec 1960, Montreal, QC, Canada), American ice hockey defenseman and five-time James Norris Trophy winner.

Abdelaziz Bouteflika (2 Mar 1937, Tlemcen, Algeria), Algerian politician, diplomat, and president from 1999.

T. Coraghessan Boyle (Thomas John Boyle; 2 Dec 1948, Peekskill NY), American short-story writer and novelist.

François Bozizé (14 Oct 1946, Mouila, French Equatorial Africa [now in Gabon]), Central African Republic politician; president from 2003.

Ray (Douglas) Bradbury (22 Aug 1920, Waukegan IL), American author of science-fiction short stories and novels, nostalgic tales, poetry, radio drama, and TV and film screenplays.

Tom Brady (Thomas Brady; 3 Aug 1977, San Mateo CA), American professional football quarterback.

Lakhdar Brahimi (1 Jan 1934, Algeria), Algerian statesman, diplomat, and international official.

Kenneth (Charles) Branagh (10 Dec 1960, Belfast, Northern Ireland), British theater and film actor, director, and writer.

Brandy (Brandy Norwood; 11 Feb 1979, McComb MS), American R&B singer and TV actress.

Richard (Charles Nicholas) Branson (18 Jul 1950, Shamley Green, Surrey, England), British entrepreneur who founded the Virgin empire in 1973.

Benjamin Bratt (16 Dec 1963, San Francisco CA), American TV and film actor.

Anthony Braxton (4 Jun 1945, Chicago IL), American avant-garde reed player and composer.

Toni Braxton (7 Oct 1968, Severn MD), American R&B singer.

Phil Bredesen (Philip Norman Bredesen; 21 Nov 1943, Oceanport NJ), American Democratic politician; governor of Tennessee from 2003.

Thierry Breton (15 Jan 1955, Paris, France), French businessman and politician; executive chairman of France Télécom, 2002–05, and French economic minister from 2005.

Stephen (Gerald) Breyer (15 Aug 1938, San Francisco CA), American jurist; associate justice of the US Supreme Court from 1994.

Jeff Bridges (4 Dec 1949, Los Angeles CA), American actor.

Sergey Brin (21 Aug 1973, Moscow, USSR [now in Russia]), Russian-born computer scientist and Internet entrepreneur who cofounded (with Lawrence Page) in 1998 the Google Internet search engine.

Matthew Broderick (21 Mar 1962, New York NY), American comic actor of stage and screen.

Adrien Brody (14 Apr 1973, New York NY), American film actor.

Edgar M. Bronfman (20 Jun 1929, Montreal, QC, Canada), Canadian-born American businessman; chairman of the Seagram Co. Ltd. and, from 1981, president of the World Jewish Congress.

Garth Brooks (Troyal Garth Brooks; 7 Feb 1962, Tulsa OK), American country-and-western singer.

Kix Brooks (Leon Eric Brooks; 12 May 1955, Shreveport LA), American country-and-western singer in the duo Brooks & Dunn.

Pierce (Brendan) Brosnan (16 May 1953, Navan, County Meath, Ireland), Irish actor.

Dan Brown (22 Jun 1964, Exeter NH), American novelist (*The Da Vinci Code*).

Gordon Brown (20 Feb 1951, Glasgow, Scotland), British politician, chancellor of the Exchequer, 1997–2007, and prime minister from 2007.

Jerry Bruckheimer (21 Sep 1945, Detroit MI), American film and TV producer.

Kobe Bryant (23 Aug 1978, Philadelphia PA), American basketball player.

Bill Bryson (1951, Des Moines IA), American-born British journalist and travel writer.

Michael Bublé (9 Sep 1975, Burnaby, BC, Canada), Canadian pop singer.

Patrick J(oseph) Buchanan (2 Nov 1938, Washington DC), American conservative journalist.

Jon Buckland (11 Sep 1977, London, England), British rock guitarist (of Coldplay).

Christopher (Taylor) Buckley (1952, New York NY), American satiric novelist and magazine editor.

Warren (Edward) Buffett (30 Aug 1930, Omaha NE), American investor; CEO of Berkshire Hathaway Inc. from 1965.

Sandra (Annette) Bullock (26 Jul 1964, Arlington VA), American film actress.

Gisele Bündchen (Gisele Caroline Nonnenmacher Bündchen; 20 Jul 1980, Horizontina, Rio Grande do Sul state, Brazil), Brazilian fashion model.

Mark Burnett (17 Jul 1960, Myland, East London, England), English-born American reality-TV-show producer.

Ken Burns (Kenneth Lauren Burns; 29 Jul 1953, Brooklyn NY), American documentary filmmaker.

Gary Burton (23 Jan 1943, Anderson IN), American jazz vibraphonist and composer.

Tim Burton (Timothy William Burton; 25 Aug 1958, Burbank CA), American director and writer known for offbeat, imaginative films.

Steve Buscemi (13 Dec 1957, Brooklyn NY), American film actor.

Barbara Bush (Barbara Pierce; 8 Jun 1925, Rye NY), American first lady; wife of Pres. George H.W. Bush (married 6 Jan 1945).

Barbara Bush (25 Nov 1981, Dallas TX), American personality; daughter of Pres. George W. Bush.

George Herbert Walker Bush (12 Jun 1924, Milton MA), American statesman, vice president, 1981–89, and 41st president, 1989–93; he is the father of Pres. George W. Bush.

George Walker Bush (6 Jul 1946, New Haven CT), American statesman and 43rd president, from 2001; he is the son of Pres. George H.W. Bush.

Jeb Bush (John Ellis Bush; 11 Feb 1953, Midland TX), American Republican politician, governor of Florida, 1999–2007, and brother of Pres. George W. Bush.

Jenna Bush (25 Nov 1981, Dallas TX), American personality; daughter of Pres. George W. Bush.

Laura Bush (Laura Lane Welch; 4 Nov 1946, Midland TX), American first lady; wife of Pres. George W. Bush (married 5 Nov 1977).

Mangosuthu Gatsha Buthelezi (27 Aug 1928, Mahlabatini, Natal [now KwaZulu Natal] province, South Africa), South African Zulu chief, the founder (1975) and leader of the Inkatha Freedom Party.

Norbert Leo Butz (St. Louis MO), American actor.

A.S. Byatt (Antonia Susan Drabble; 24 Aug 1936, Sheffield, England), English scholar, literary critic, and novelist.

James Caan (26 Mar 1939, New York NY), American actor.

Nicolas Cage (Nicholas Kim Coppola; 7 Jan 1964, Long Beach CA), American film actor.

Santiago Calatrava (28 Jul 1951, Valencia, Spain), Spanish architect noted for his soaring designs for bridges and public buildings.

Felipe Calderón (Felipe de Jesús Calderón Hinojosa; 18 Aug 1962, Morelia, Michoacán, Mexico), Mexican politician (National Action Party); president from 2006.

Félix Pérez Camacho (30 Oct 1957, Camp Zama, Japan), American Republican politician and governor of Guam from 2003.

David Cameron (David William Donald Cameron; 9 Oct 1966, London, England), British politician and leader of the Conservative Party from 2005.

Camilla, duchess of Cornwall (Camilla Parker Bowles; Camilla Shand; 17 Jul 1947, London, England), English celebrity, the wife, from 9 Apr 2005, of Charles, prince of Wales.

Louis C. Camilleri (1955, Alexandria, Egypt), American corporate executive; president and CEO of Altria Group from 2002.

Sir Menzies Campbell (22 May 1941, Glasgow, Scotland), British politician, leader of the Liberal Democratic Party from 2006.

Naomi Campbell (22 May 1970, London, England), British runway and photographic model.

Fabio Cannavaro (13 Sep 1973, Naples, Italy), Italian association football (soccer) player who led his country's team to victory in the 2006 World Cup.

Jennifer Capriati (29 Mar 1976, New York NY), American tennis player, the youngest US player to turn professional (1989, at age 13).

Don Carcieri (16 Dec 1942, East Greenwich RI), American banker and Republican politician; governor of Rhode Island from 2003.

Drew (Allison) Carey (23 May 1958, Cleveland OH), American comic TV actor.

Mariah Carey (27 Mar 1970, Huntington, Long Island, NY), American pop singer.

Peter (Philip) Carey (7 May 1943, Bacchus Marsh, VIC, Australia), Australian author.

Carl XVI Gustaf (Carl Gustaf Folke Hubertus; 30 Apr 1946, Stockholm, Sweden), king of Sweden from 1973.

Lennart Carleson (Lennart Axel Edvard Carleson; 18 Mar 1928, Stockholm, Sweden), Swedish mathematician, a specialist in harmonic analysis; recipient of the 2006 Abel Prize.

Richard H. Carmona (22 Nov 1949, Harlem NY), American physician; surgeon general of the US, 2002–06.

Robert A. Caro (30 Oct 1935, New York NY), American biographer.

Caroline (Caroline Louise Margaret Grimaldi; 23 Jan 1957, Monte Carlo, Monaco), Monegasque princess, the elder daughter of Prince Rainier III and Princess Grace.

Jim Carrey (James Eugene Carrey; 17 Jan 1962, Newmarket, ON, Canada), Canadian-born American comic actor.

Edwin W. Carrington (1938, Tobago), Trinidadian international official; secretary-general of the Caribbean Community (CARICOM) from 1992.

Jimmy Carter (James Earl Carter, Jr.; 1 Oct 1924, Plains GA), American statesman and 39th president of the US, 1977–81; recipient of the 2002 Nobel Prize for Peace.

Marsh Carter (Marshall N. Carter; 1940, Washington DC?), American corporate executive; chairman of the New York Stock Exchange from 2005.

Rosalynn Carter (Eleanor Rosalynn Smith; 18 Aug 1927, Plains GA), American first lady (1977–81), the wife of Pres. Jimmy Carter, and mental health advocate.

David Caruso (7 Jan 1956, Forest Hills NY), American actor, mostly in TV.

James Carville, Jr. (25 Oct 1944, Carville LA), American political strategist and commentator.

Steve Case (Stephen McDonnell Case; 21 Aug 1958, Honolulu HI), American corporate executive; founder (1991) and former CEO of America Online and chairman of AOL Time Warner (2001–03).

Rosanne Cash (24 May 1955, Memphis TN), American country-and-western singer.

Fidel Castro Ruz (13 Aug 1926, near Birán, Cuba), Cuban revolutionary and leader of Cuba from 1959; he became a symbol of communist revolution in Latin America.

Raúl Castro (Raúl Modesto Castro Ruz; 3 Jun 1931, near Birán, Cuba), Cuban revolutionary leader and politician; acting president of Cuba from 2006.

Helio Castroneves (10 May 1975, São Paulo, Brazil), Brazilian race-car driver.

Kim Cattrall (21 Aug 1956, Liverpool, England), British-born film and TV actress.

Aníbal Cavaco Silva (Aníbal António Cavaco Silva; 15 Jul 1939, Boliqueime, Algarve, Portugal), Portuguese politician; prime minister, 1985–95, and president from 2006.

Jim Caviezel (James Patrick Caviezel; 26 Sep 1968, Mount Vernon WA), American film actor.

Riccardo Chailly (20 Feb 1953, Milan, Italy), Italian orchestra conductor; music director of the Leipzig Opera from 2005.

John T. Chambers (23 Aug 1949, Cleveland OH), American corporate executive; president and CEO of Cisco Systems, Inc., from 1997.

Will Champion (31 Jul 1978, Southampton, England), British rock drummer (of Coldplay).

Jackie Chan (Chan Kwong-Sang; 7 Apr 1954, Hong Kong), Chinese actor and director of martial arts films.

Margaret Chan (1947, Hong Kong), Hong Kong–born public health officer; director general of the World Health Organization from 2006.

Elaine Chao (26 Mar 1953, Taipei, Taiwan), American government official; US secretary of labor from 2001.

Manu Chao (Oscar Tramor; 26 Jun 1961, Paris, France), French-born Spanish international rock musician noted for his politics and his unstructured approach to the business side of music.

David Chappelle (24 Aug 1973, Washington DC), American film and TV comedian and actor who starred in TV's *Chappelle's Show*.

Jean Charest (John James Charest; 24 Jun 1958, Sherbrooke, QC, Canada), French Canadian politician; leader of the Quebec Liberal Party from 1998 and premier of Quebec from 2003.

Charles (Prince of Wales; 14 Nov 1948, Buckingham Palace, London, England), British royal, the eldest son of Queen Elizabeth II and Prince Philip, duke of Edinburgh, and heir apparent to the throne.

Yves Chauvin (10 Oct 1930, Menin, Belgium), French chemist; corecipient of the 2005 Nobel Prize for Chemistry for the development of the metathesis method in organic synthesis.

Hugo Chávez Frías (28 Jul 1954, Sabaneta, Venezuela), Venezuelan military leader, politician, and president of Venezuela from 1999.

Don Cheadle (29 Nov 1964, Kansas City MO), American film and TV actor.

Chen Shui-bian (Ch'en Shui-pian; 18 Feb 1951, Hsichuang village, Tainan county, Taiwan), Taiwanese politician and president from 2000.

Dick Cheney (Richard Bruce Cheney; 30 Jan 1941, Lincoln NE), American politician, secretary of defense, 1989–93, and vice president from 2001.

Lynne V. Cheney (Lynne Ann Vincent; 14 Aug 1941, Casper WY), American political commentator; she is the wife of Vice Pres. Dick Cheney (married 1964).

Cher (Cherilyn Sarkasian LaPier; 20 May 1946, El Centro CA), American pop singer and film actress.

Taïeb Chérif (29 Dec 1941, Kasr El Boukhari, Algeria), Algerian international official; secretary-general of the International Civil Aviation Organization from 2003.

Michael Chertoff (28 Nov 1953, Elizabeth NJ), American attorney, judge on the US Court of Appeals, and secretary of homeland security from 2005.

Robert Cheruiyot (Robert Kipkoech Cheruiyot; 26 Sep 1978, Eldoret, Kenya), Kenyan long-distance runner who won the Boston and Chicago marathons in 2006.

Kenny Chesney (26 Mar 1968, Luttrell TN), American country-and-western singer.

Judy Chicago (Judy Cohen; 20 Jul 1939, Chicago IL), American artist.

Dale Chihuly (20 Sep 1941, Tacoma WA), American glassblower and glass artist known for his vibrantly colored organic sculptures designed for large spaces.

Michael Chiklis (30 Aug 1963, Lowell MA), American TV actor; star of the TV series *The Shield* from 2002 and the Fantastic Four movies.

Jacques (René) Chirac (29 Nov 1932, Paris, France), French politician; prime minister of France, 1974–76 and 1986–88, and president, 1995–2007.

Fujio Cho (1937, Tokyo, Japan), Japanese corporate executive; chairman of Toyota Motor Corp. from 2005.

(Avram) Noam Chomsky (7 Dec 1928, Philadelphia PA), American linguist, writer, educator, and political activist; one of the founders of transformational, or generative, grammar.

Deepak Chopra (22 Oct 1946, New Delhi, British India), Indian-born American endocrinologist, alternative-medicine advocate, and best-selling author.

Choummaly Sayasone (6 Mar 1936, Attapu province, French Indochina [now in Laos]), Laotian political official; general secretary of the Lao People's Revolutionary Party from 2006 and president from 2006.

Chow Yun-Fat (Zhou Runfa; 18 May 1955, Lamma Island, Hong Kong), Hong Kong actor.

Perry (Gladstone) Christie (21 Aug 1943, Nassau, Bahamas), Bahamian politician and prime minister, 2002–07.

Steven Chu (28 Feb 1948, St. Louis MO), American physicist; recipient of the 1997 Nobel Prize for Physics.

Chang Chun-Hsiung (1938, Chia-i, China [now in Taiwan]), Taiwanese politician; president of the Executive Yuan (premier), 2000–02 and again from 2007.

Ralph J(ohn) Cicerone (2 May 1943, New Castle PA), American electrical engineer and atmospheric scientist; president of the National Academy of Sciences from 2005.

Aaron Ciechanover (1 Oct 1947, Haifa, Israel), Israeli biochemist; corecipient of the 2004 Nobel Prize for Chemistry.

Sandra Cisneros (20 Dec 1954, Chicago IL), American short-story writer and poet.

Tom Clancy (Thomas L. Clancy, Jr.; 12 Apr 1947, Baltimore MD), American best-selling writer on military-tinged current affairs topics.

Eric Clapton (Eric Patrick Clapp; 30 Mar 1945, Ripley, Surrey, England), British guitarist, singer, and songwriter.

Helen Clark (26 Feb 1950, Hamilton, New Zealand), New Zealand Labour politician and prime minister from 1999.

Mary Higgins Clark (24 Dec 1931, New York NY), American writer of best-selling books.

Victoria Clark (10 Oct 19??, Dallas TX), American stage actress.

Kelly Clarkson (24 Apr 1982, Burleson TX), American celebrity; winner of Fox TV's American Idol competition in 2002.

John (Marwood) Cleese (27 Oct 1939, Weston-super-Mare, England), British comic actor.

Van Cliburn (Harvey Lavan Cliburn, Jr.; 12 Jul 1934, Shreveport LA), American pianist.

Kim Clijsters (8 Jun 1983, Bilzen, Belgium), Belgian tennis player.

Bill Clinton (William Jefferson Blythe IV; 19 Aug 1946, Hope AR), American statesman and 42nd president of the US, 1993–2001.

Hillary Rodham Clinton (Hillary Diane Rodham; 26 Oct 1947, Chicago IL), American politician; wife of Pres. Bill Clinton; Democratic senator from New York from 2001.

George Clooney (6 May 1961, Lexington KY), American film and TV actor.

Chuck Close (Charles Thomas Close; 5 Jul 1940, Monroe WA), American painter best known for his large-scale, Photo-realist portraits.

Glenn Close (19 Mar 1947, Greenwich CT), American actress.

Paulo Coelho (August 1947, Rio de Janeiro, Brazil), Brazilian novelist.

Ethan (21 Sep 1958, St. Louis Park MN) and Joel Coen (29 Nov 1955, St. Louis Park MN), American filmmakers.

J(ohn) M(axwell) Coetzee (9 Feb 1940, Cape Town, South Africa), South African novelist and critic noted for his novels about the effects of apartheid; recipient of the 2003 Nobel Prize for Literature.

Leonard Cohen (21 Sep 1934, Montreal, QC, Canada), Canadian singer and songwriter.

Sacha Baron Cohen (Sacha Noam Baron Cohen; 13 Oct 1971, Hammersmith, London, England), British comedian and actor.

Stephen Colbert (13 May 1964, Charleston SC), American TV commentator and satirist, host of The Colbert Report from 2005.

Natalie (Maria) Cole (Stephanie Natalie Maria Cole; 6 Feb 1950, Los Angeles CA), American pop singer.

Pierluigi Collina (13 Feb 1960, Bologna, Italy), Italian association football (soccer) referee.

Billy Collins (1941, New York NY), American poet; poet laureate of the US, 2001–03.

Marva Collins (Marva Delores Knight; 31 Aug 1936, Monroeville AL), American educator.

Alan Colmes (24 Sep 1950, Long Island NY), American liberal radio and TV journalist and commentator.

Sean Combs (Puffy; Puff Daddy; P. Diddy; 4 Nov 1970, Harlem, New York, NY), American rap artist, impresario, fashion plate, and TV actor.

Blaise Compaoré (1951, Ziniane, Upper Volta [now Burkina Faso]), Burkinabe politician and president of Burkina Faso from 1987.

Philip M. Condit (2 Aug 1941, Berkeley CA), American aerospace engineer and corporate executive; chairman and CEO of the Boeing Co., 1997–2003.

Bill Condon (22 Oct 1955, New York NY), American screenwriter and film director.

Jennifer Connelly (12 Dec 1970, Catskill Mountains NY), American fashion model and film actress.

Sir Sean Connery (Thomas Connery; 25 Aug 1930, Edinburgh, Scotland), Scottish film actor known for portrayals of rugged leading men, including James Bond; he is also active in Scottish nationalist politics.

Lansana Conté (1934, Moussayah Loumbaya, French West Africa [now in Guinea]), Guinean military leader and president from 1984.

Cynthia Cooper (14 Apr 1963, Chicago IL), American collegiate, Olympic, and professional basketball player and coach.

Francis Ford Coppola (7 Apr 1939, Detroit MI), American film director, writer, and producer.

Sofia Coppola (14 May 1971, New York NY), American film actress, designer, writer, and director.

Chick Corea (Armando Anthony Corea; 12 Jun 1941, Chelsea MA), American jazz pianist, composer, and bandleader.

John Corigliano (16 Feb 1938, New York NY), American composer of lyrical, tonal, expressive works in orchestral music, opera, chamber music, and film scores.

Patricia Cornwell (Patricia Daniels; 9 Jun 1956, Miami FL), American author of mystery novels.

Rafael Correa (Rafael Vicente Correa Delgado; 6 Apr 1963, Guayaquil, Ecuador), Ecuadorian politician; president from 2007.

Jon Corzine (Jon Stevens Corzine; 1 Jan 1947, Willey's Station IL), American politician (Democrat); senator from New Jersey, 2001–06, and governor from 2006.

Bill Cosby (William Henry Cosby, Jr.; 12 Jul 1937, Philadelphia PA), American comedian and actor beloved for the groundbreaking TV series The Cosby Show (1984–92).

Bob Costas (Robert Quinlan Costas; 22 Mar 1952, New York NY), American TV sportscaster and host.

Kevin (Michael) Costner (18 Jan 1955, Lynwood CA), American film actor and director.

Ann (Hart) Coulter (8 Dec 1961, New Canaan CT), American attorney, political columnist, and author.

David Coulthard (27 Mar 1971, Twynholm, Scotland), Scottish Formula 1 race-car driver.

Katie Couric (7 Jan 1957, Arlington VA), American TV talk-show host and news anchor.

Simon Cowell (Simon Phillip Cowell; 7 Oct 1959, Brighton, East Sussex, England), British record producer and TV personality; a judge on the American Idol "reality TV" show.

Christopher Cox (16 Oct 1952, Saint Paul MN), American politician (Republican); chairman of the US Securities and Exchange Commission from 2005.

John Craddock (Bantz John Craddock; 1949, Doddridge county WV), American military official; Supreme Allied Commander, Europe (SACEUR) from 2006.

(John) Michael Crichton (23 Oct 1942, Chicago IL), American best-selling writer and director who specializes in novels on scientific themes.

Charlie Crist (Charles Joseph Crist, Jr.; 24 Jul 1956, Altoona PA), American politician (Republican); governor of Florida from 2007.

Walter (Leland) Cronkite, Jr. (4 Nov 1916, St. Joseph MO), American TV journalist, commentator, and TV news anchor.

Stanley Crouch (14 Dec 1945, Los Angeles CA), American journalist and critic.

Sheryl Crow (11 Feb 1962, Kennett MO), American singer-songwriter.

Russell (Ira) Crowe (7 Apr 1964, Wellington, New Zealand), New Zealand-born Australian film actor.

Tom Cruise (Thomas Cruise Mapother IV; 3 Jul 1962, Syracuse NY), American actor, one of the highest-paid film stars in the world.

Gastão Cruz (20 Jul 1941, Faro, Portugal), Portuguese poet and literary critic.

Nilo Cruz (1962?, Matanzas, Cuba), Cuban-born American playwright.

Penélope Cruz (Sánchez) (28 Apr 1974, Madrid, Spain), Spanish film actress.

Branko Crvenkovski (12 Oct 1962, Sarajevo, Yugoslavia [now in Bosnia and Herzegovina]), Macedonian politician and prime minister, 1992–98, and again, 2002–04, after which he took over as president.

Billy Crystal (14 Mar 1947, Long Beach NY), American comedic actor popular for light dramatic comedies.

Mihaly Csikszentmihalyi (1934, Fiume, Italy), American psychologist and sociologist who specializes in studies of creativity, especially in art, and social behavior and socialization.

Jamie Cullum (20 Aug 1979, Essex, England), British pop, jazz, and rock pianist and vocalist.

Chet Culver (Chester John Culver; 25 Jan 1966, Washington DC), American politician (Democrat); governor of Iowa from 2007.

Joan Cusack (11 Oct 1962, New York NY), American film and TV actress.

John Cusack (28 Jun 1966, Evanston IL), American film actor known for his intelligent, humorous characters.

Willem Dafoe (William Dafoe, Jr.; 22 Jul 1955, Appleton WI), American actor known for his complex, passionate portrayals.

Dalai Lama (the 14th Dalai Lama; Tenzin Gyatso, birth name Lhamo Dhondrub; 6 Jul 1935, Takster, Amdo province, Tibet [now Tsinghai province, China]), Tibetan spiritual leader (enthroned in 1940) and ruler-in-exile; head of the Tibetan Buddhists; recipient of the 1989 Nobel Prize for Peace.

Richard M. Daley (24 Apr 1942, Chicago IL), American Democratic politician; mayor of Chicago from 1989.

Matt Damon (Matthew Paige Damon; 8 Oct 1970, Cambridge MA), American film actor.

Mitchell E. Daniels, Jr. (7 Apr 1949, Monongahela PA), American businessman and politician; director of the US Office of Management and Budget, 2001–03; Republican governor of Indiana from 2005.

Edwidge Danticat (19 Jan 1969, Port-au-Prince, Haiti), Haitian-born American author.

Mahmoud Darwish (13 Mar 1942, Birwa, Palestine), Palestinian nationalist poet.

Larry David (2 Jul 1947, Brooklyn NY), American actor and writer.

Mario Davidovsky (4 Mar 1934, Médanos, Buenos Aires, Argentina), Argentine-born American composer best known for his electronic and electroacoustic works.

Shani Davis (13 Aug 1982, Chicago IL), American speed skater.

Patrick Day (13 Oct 1953, Brush CO), American jockey, the all-time top North American money winner with more than 8,000 career victories.

Carl R. de Boor (3 Dec 1937, Stolp, Germany), German-born American mathematician and computer scientist who specializes in numerical analysis, especially spline functions.

Inge De Bruijn (24 Aug 1973, Barendrecht, Netherlands), Dutch swimmer.

Jaap de Hoop Scheffer (Jakob Gijsbert de Hoop Scheffer; 3 Apr 1948, Amsterdam, Netherlands), Dutch international official; secretary-general of NATO from 2004.

John P. deJongh Jr. (13 Nov 1957, St. Thomas, US Virgin Islands), American politician (Democrat); governor of the Virgin Islands from 2007.

Robert De Niro (17 Aug 1943, New York NY), American film actor famous for his uncompromising portrayals of violent and abrasive characters.

Dominique (Galouzeau) de Villepin (14 Nov 1953, Rabat, Morocco), French diplomat; foreign minister, 2002–05, and prime minister from 2005.

Idriss Déby Itno (1952, Fada, Chad, French Equatorial Africa [now in Chad]), Chadian politician and president from 1990.

Ruby Dee (Ruby Ann Wallace; 27 Oct 1924, Cleveland OH), American film and TV actress.

Ellen DeGeneres (26 Jan 1958, Metairie LA), American comedian and TV personality.

Carla Del Ponte (9 Feb 1947, Lugano, Switzerland), Swiss jurist who has served as prosecutor for the International Criminal Tribunal for the former Yugoslavia (ICTY) from 1999.

Benicio Del Toro (19 Feb 1967, San Turce, Puerto Rico), American film actor.

Bertrand Delanoë (30 May 1950, Tunis, Tunisia), French politician and mayor of Paris from 2001.

Michael S. Dell (23 Feb 1965, Houston TX), American businessman, founder and CEO of Dell Computer Corp., 1984–2004, and again from 2007, and noted philanthropist.

Yelena Dementyeva (also spelled Elena Dementieva; 15 Oct 1981, Moscow, USSR [now in Russia]), Russian tennis player.

Patrick Dempsey (13 Jan 1966, Lewiston ME), American film and TV actor.

Dame Judi Dench (Judith Olivia Dench; 9 Dec 1934, York, England), British actress known for her powerful stage, TV, and screen roles.

Brian Dennehy (9 Jul 1938, Bridgeport CT), American TV, film, and stage actor known for serious dramatic roles.

Carl Dennis (17 Sep 1939, St. Louis MO), American poet.

Gérard Depardieu (27 Dec 1948, Châteauroux, France), French film actor.

Johnny Depp (John Christopher Depp II; 9 Jun 1963, Owensboro KY), American film and TV actor known for eccentric, brooding roles.

Kiran Desai (3 Sep 1971, New Delhi, India), Indian-born American novelist; recipient of the 2006 Booker Prize.

Frankie Dettori (Lanfranco Dettori; 15 Dec 1970, Milan, Italy), Italian-born English jockey.

Danny DeVito (Daniel Michaeli; 17 Nov 1944, Neptune NJ), American actor, director, and producer specializing in supporting comic roles.

Cameron M. Diaz (30 Aug 1972, San Diego CA), American model and actress.

Kate DiCamillo (25 Mar 1965, Philadelphia PA), American author of children's books.

Leonardo (Wilhelm) DiCaprio (11 Nov 1974, Los Angeles CA), American film actor.

Dido (Florian Cloude de Bourneville Armstrong; 25 Dec 1971, Islington, London, England), British pop singer.

Vin Diesel (Mark Vincent; 18 Jul 1967, New York NY), American film actor.

Matt Dillon (18 Feb 1964, New Rochelle NY), American film actor.

Fatou Diome (1968, Niodior island, Senegal), Senegalese French-language novelist.

Céline Dion (30 Mar 1968, Charlemagne, QC, Canada), French Canadian pop singer.

El Hadj Diouf (15 Jan 1981, Dakar, Senegal), Senegalese association football (soccer) star for French clubs and the Senegalese national team.

Waris Dirie (1967?, Somalia), Somali supermodel and women's rights activist.

Domenico Dolce (13 Aug 1958, Polizzi Generosa, near Palermo, Italy), Italian fashion designer who famously collaborates with partner Stefano Gabbana.

Plácido Domingo (21 Jan 1941, Madrid, Spain), Spanish-born Mexican operatic tenor.

Mary Donaldson (5 Feb 1972, Hobart, TAS, Australia), Australian-born marketing executive who wed Crown Prince Frederik of Denmark in 2004.

Sam Donaldson (Samuel Andrew Donaldson; 11 Mar 1934, El Paso TX), American TV newsman.

William Henry Donaldson (1931, Buffalo NY), American banker and corporate executive; chairman of the Security and Exchanges Commission from 2003.

Vincent D'Onofrio (30 Jul 1959, Brooklyn NY), American TV actor.

José Eduardo dos Santos (28 Aug 1942, Luanda, Angola), Angolan statesman and president from 1979.

James H. Douglas (21 Jun 1951, Springfield MA), American Republican politician; governor of Vermont from 2003.

Michael Douglas (25 Sep 1944, New Brunswick NJ), American film actor and producer.

Philippe Douste-Blazy (1 Jan 1953, Lourdes, France), French medical doctor and minister of foreign affairs from 2005.

Rita (Frances) Dove (28 Aug 1952, Akron OH), American writer and teacher; poet laureate of the US, 1993–95.

Jim Doyle (23 Nov 1945, Washington DC), American attorney and Democratic politician; governor of Wisconsin from 2003.

Kimberly Dozier (6 Jul 1966, Honolulu HI), American TV journalist and foreign correspondent.

Dr. Dre (Andre Young; 18 Feb 1965, Los Angeles CA), American rap musician and impresario, considered the pioneer of gangsta rap.

Stacy Dragila (25 Mar 1971, Auburn CA), American pole vaulter.

E. Linn Draper, Jr., American energy engineer and corporate executive; chairman, president, and CEO of American Electric Power, Inc., 1992–2003.

Deborah Drattell (1956, Brooklyn NY), American composer of operas.

Dré (Andre Benjamin; Andre 3000; 27 May 1975, Atlanta GA), American hip-hop artist and a member of the duo OutKast.

Paquito D'Rivera (Francisco Dejesus Rivera; 4 Jun 1948, Havana, Cuba), Cuban-born American jazz reed player and Afro-Cuban bandleader.

Janez Drnovsek (17 May 1950, Celje, Yugoslavia [now Slovenia]), Slovene politician, prime minister, 1992–2000 and 2000–02, and president from 2002.

Matt Drudge (27 Oct 1967, Maryland), American Internet journalist, editor of the *Drudge Report.*

Andres Duany (7 Sep 1949, New York NY), American urban planner and a leading exponent of New Urbanism who collaborates with his wife, Elizabeth Plater-Zyberk.

Nicanor Duarte Frutos (11 Oct 1956, Coronel Oviedo, Paraguay), Paraguayan politician and president from 2003.

David Duchovny (David William Ducovny; 7 Aug 1960, New York NY), American TV and film actor.

Hilary Duff (28 Sep 1987, Houston TX), American TV and film actress.

Avery Robert Cardinal Dulles (24 Aug 1918, Auburn NY), American Roman Catholic Jesuit theologian; cardinal from 2001.

(Dorothy) Faye Dunaway (14 Jan 1941, Bascom FL), American actress known for her tense, absorbing performances.

Tim Duncan (Timothy Theodore Duncan; 25 Apr 1976, St. Croix, US Virgin Islands), American basketball player (San Antonio Spurs).

Ronnie Gene Dunn (1 Jun 1953, Coleman TX), American country-and-western singer, a member of the duo Brooks & Dunn.

Kirsten Dunst (30 Apr 1982, Point Pleasant NJ), American film actress.

Robert Duvall (5 Jan 1931, San Diego CA), American actor, producer, and screenwriter.

Bob Dylan (Robert Allen Zimmerman; 24 May 1941, Duluth MN), American singer and songwriter.

Esther Dyson (14 Jul 1951, Zürich, Switzerland), American economist and journalist specializing in computer and cyberspace issues.

Freeman (John) Dyson (15 Dec 1923, Crowthorne, Berkshire, England), British-born American physicist and educator best known for his speculative work on extraterrestrial civilizations.

(Ralph) Dale Earnhardt, Jr. (10 Oct 1974, Concord NC), American NASCAR race-car driver.

Michael F. Easley (23 Mar 1950, Nash county NC), American Democratic politician; governor of North Carolina from 2001.

Clint Eastwood (Clinton Eastwood, Jr.; 31 May 1930, San Francisco CA), American film actor and moviemaker, originally famous for tough-guy roles.

Shirin Ebadi (1947, Hamadan, Iran), Iranian lawyer, writer, and advocate for democracy and human rights; recipient of the 2003 Nobel Prize for Peace.

Roger Ebert (18 Jun 1942, Urbana IL), American film critic.

Umberto Eco (5 Jan 1932, Alessandria, Italy), Italian literary critic, novelist, and semiotician.

Marian Wright Edelman (6 Jun 1939, Bennettsville SC), American attorney and civil rights advocate who founded the Children's Defense Fund.

Edward (Edward Anthony Richard Louis; 10 Mar 1964, Buckingham Palace, London, England), British prince; third son of Queen Elizabeth II and Prince Philip, duke of Edinburgh; and earl of Wessex.

John Edwards (10 Jun 1953, Seneca SC), American Democratic politician; senator from North Carolina, 1999–2005.

Tuiatua Tupua Tamasese Efi (1 Mar 1938, Samoan royal, *O le Ao o le Malo* (elective monarch) from 2007.

Edward Michael Cardinal Egan (2 Apr 1932, Oak Park IL), American Roman Catholic church leader; archbishop of New York from 2000 and cardinal from 2001.

Robert L. Ehrlich, Jr. (25 Nov 1957, Arbutus MD), American Republican politician and governor of Maryland from 2003.

Michael D(ammann) Eisner (7 Mar 1942, Mount Kisco NY), American corporate executive; CEO and chairman of the Walt Disney Co., 1984–2004.

Hicham El Guerrouj (14 Sep 1974, Berkane, Morocco), Moroccan distance runner.

Mohamed ElBaradei (Muhammad al-Baradei; 17 Jun 1942, Cairo, Egypt), Egyptian international official; director-general of the International Atomic Energy Agency from 1997.

Carmen Electra (Tara Leigh Patrick; 20 Apr 1972, Sharonville OH), American model, TV and film actress, and celebrity.

Danny Elfman (29 May 1943, Los Angeles CA), American pop musician (of Oingo Boingo) and composer of scores for films and TV, known especially for his collaborations with director Tim Burton.

Elizabeth II (21 Apr 1926, London, England), British royal; queen of the United Kingdom of Great Britain and Northern Ireland from 1952.

Missy Elliott (Melissa Elliott; 1 Jul 1971, Portsmouth VA), American rapper, singer, and songwriter.

George F.R. Ellis (George Francis Rayner Ellis; 11 Aug 1939, Johannesburg, South Africa), South African applied mathematician and professor; recipient of the 2004 Templeton Prize.

Lawrence J. Ellison (17 Aug 1944, Chicago IL), American corporate executive; founder and CEO of Oracle Corp. from 1977.

James Ellroy (Lee Earle Ellroy; 4 Mar 1948, Los Angeles CA), American mystery writer.

Ernie Els (Theodore Ernest Els; 17 Oct 1969, Johannesburg, South Africa), South African golfer.

Eminem (Marshall Bruce Mathers III; 17 Oct 1973, St. Joseph MO), American hip-hop artist.

Emmanuel III Delly (Emmanuel-Karim Delly; 6 Oct 1927, Telkaif, Iraq), Iraqi churchman, patriarch of Babylonia and the Chaldeans (leader of the Chaldean Catholic Church) from 2003.

Robert F(ry) Engle (November 1942, Syracuse NY), American mathematical economist; corecipient of the 2003 Nobel Memorial Prize for Economic Science.

Nambaryn Enhbayar (1 Jun 1958, Ulaanbaatar, Mongolia), Mongolian politician; prime minister of Mongolia, 2000–04, and president from 2005.

Miyeegombo Enkhbold (1964, Ulaanbaatar, Mongolia), Mongolian politician; prime minister from 2006.

Enya (Eithne Ní Bhraonáin; 17 May 1961, Gweedore, Ireland), Irish New Age singer.

Recep Tayyip Erdogan (26 Feb 1954, Istanbul, Turkey), Turkish politician, the leader of the Justice and Development Party, and prime minister from 2003.

Patricia Espinosa Cantellano (21 Oct 1958, Mexico City, Mexico), Mexican diplomat; secretary of foreign affairs of Mexico from 2006.

Gloria Estefan (Gloria Maria Milagrosa Fajardo; 1 Sep 1957, Havana, Cuba), Cuban-born American singer and lyricist.

Melissa Etheridge (29 May 1961, Leavenworth KS), American rock singer and songwriter.

Robin Eubanks (25 Oct 1955, Philadelphia PA), American jazz trombone player.

Jeffrey Eugenides (8 Mar 1960, Detroit MI), American novelist.

Sara Evans (5 Feb 1971, Boonville MO), American country-and-western musician.

Eve (Eve Jihan Jeffers; "Eve of Destruction"; 10 Nov 1979, Philadelphia PA), American rapper.

Richard D. Fairbank (18 Sep 1950, Menlo Park CA), American corporate executive; the founder, chairman, and CEO of Capital One Financial Corp. from 1988.

Edie Falco (Edith Falco; 5 Jul 1963, Brooklyn NY), American film and TV actress.

Lord Falconer of Thoroton (Charles Leslie Falconer; 19 Nov 1951, Edinburgh, Scotland), Scottish lord high chancellor and keeper of the great seal, the last to hold the office.

William J. Fallon (William Joseph Fallon; 30 Dec 1944, East Orange NJ), American military leader; commander of the US Central Command from 2007.

Sean Faris (25 Mar 1982, Parma OH), American film and TV actor.

Paul (Edward) Farmer (1959, North Adams MA), American medical anthropologist and physician.

Louis (Abdul) Farrakhan (Louis Eugene Walcott; 11 May 1933, Bronx NY), American leader of the Nation of Islam (Black Muslims) from 1978.

Colin (James) Farrell (31 May 1976, Dublin, Ireland), Irish actor.

Suzanne Farrell (Roberta Sue Ficker; 16 Aug 1945, Cincinnati OH), American ballet dancer.

Roger Federer (8 Aug 1981, Basel, Switzerland), Swiss tennis player.

Marc Feldmann (1944, Poland), Polish-born Australian immunologist; recipient of a 2000 Crafoord Prize and the 2003 Albert Lasker Clinical Medical Research Award.

Felipe (Felipe de Borbón y Grecia; 30 Jan 1968, Madrid, Spain), royal, prince of Asturias, and heir to the Spanish throne.

Eddie Fenech Adami (7 Feb 1934, Birkirkara, Malta), Maltese politician; prime minister, 1987–96 and 1998–2004, and president from 2004.

Craig Ferguson (17 May 1962, Glasgow, Scotland), Scottish film and TV actor; host of TV's *The Late Late Show* from 2005.

Sarah (Margaret) Ferguson (15 Oct 1959, London, England), British royal, duchess of York after her marriage (23 Jul 1986) to Prince Andrew; they divorced in 1996.

Lawrence Ferlinghetti (Lawrence Ferling; 24 Mar 1919, Yonkers NY), American poet, one of the founders of the Beat movement.

Leonel Fernández (26 Dec 1953, Santo Domingo, Dominican Republic), Dominican politician; president, 1996–2000 and again from 2004.

Gil de Ferran (11 Nov 1967, Paris, France), French-born Brazilian race-car driver.

Will Ferrell (16 Jul 1967, Irvine CA), American comedian and actor.

Robert Fico (15 Sep 1964, Topolcany, Czechoslovakia [now in Slovakia]), Slovak politician (Social Democrat) and prime minister from 2006.

Ralph (Nathaniel) Fiennes (22 Dec 1962, Suffolk, England), British dramatic actor known for intense roles.

Harvey (Forbes) Fierstein (6 Jun 1954, Brooklyn NY), American playwright and actor.

50 Cent (Curtis Jackson; 6 Jul 1976, Jamaica, Queens, NY), American hardcore rapper.

Luís (Filipe Madeira Caeiro) Figo (4 Nov 1972, Almada, Portugal), Portuguese association football (soccer) player; FIFA player of the year, 2001.

François Fillon (4 Mar 1954, Le Mans, France), French politician; prime minister from 2007.

Harvey V. Fineberg (15 Sep 1945, Pittsburgh PA), American public-health physician and medical administrator; president of the Institute of Medicine from 2002.

Andrew Z. Fire (Andrew Zachary Fire; 27 Apr 1959, Palo Alto CA), American geneticist; corecipient of the 2006 Nobel Prize for Physiology or Medicine.

Heinz Fischer (9 Oct 1938, Graz, Austria), Austrian Social Democratic politician and president of Austria from 2004.

Allison Fisher (24 Feb 1968, Cheshunt, Hertfordshire, England), British pocket-billiards champion.

Benigno Fitial (Benigno Repeki Fitial; 27 Nov 1945,

Saipan, Northern Mariana Islands), American politician (Covenant Party); governor of the Northern Marianas Islands from 2006.

Patrick Fitzgerald (22 Dec 1960, New York NY), American special prosecutor in a number of high-profile cases.

Renée Fleming (14 Feb 1959, Indiana PA), American operatic soprano.

Ernie Fletcher (12 Nov 1952, Mt. Sterling KY), American physician; Republican governor of Kentucky from 2003.

Carlisle Floyd (11 Jun 1926, Latta SC), American opera composer and librettist.

Larry (Claxton) Flynt (1 Nov 1942, Magoffin county KY), American publisher of *Hustler* magazine and freedom of the press advocate.

William H(erbert) Foege (12 Mar 1936, Decorah IA), American epidemiologist and director of various disease eradication initiatives.

Ken Follett (also published as Zachary Stone and Simon Myles; 5 Jun 1949, Cardiff, Wales), Welsh author of political thrillers.

Phil Fontaine (Larry Phillip Fontaine; "Buddy"; 20 Sep 1944, Fort Alexander Reserve, MB, Canada), Canadian Ojibway first-nations activist, grand chief of the Assembly of Manitoba Chiefs, 1989–97, and national chief of the Assembly of First Nations from 1997.

Harrison Ford (13 Jul 1942, Chicago IL), American film actor, a strong leading man, known especially for his work in action films.

Tom Ford (27 Aug 1961, Austin TX), American fashion designer.

William Clay Ford, Jr. (3 May 1957, Detroit MI), American corporate executive; chairman and CEO of Ford Motor Co. from 2001.

William Forsythe (1949, New York NY), American ballet dancer, choreographer, and director; artistic director of The Forsythe Company from 1984.

Steve Fossett (22 Apr 1944, Jackson TN), American commodities trader and adventurer who was the first to circle the globe solo in a hot-air balloon (2002), made the fastest transatlantic sailboat crossing (2001), and was the first to circle the globe solo in an airplane without refueling (2005).

Jodie Foster (Alicia Christian Foster; 19 Nov 1962, Los Angeles CA), American actress widely respected for her intense performances.

Sir Norman (Robert) Foster (1 Jun 1935, near Manchester, England), British architect; recipient of the 1999 Pritzker Prize and a 2002 Japanese Praemium Imperiale award.

Vicente Fox Quesada (2 Jul 1942, Mexico City, Mexico), Mexican businessman and politician; president, 2000–06.

Jamie Foxx (Eric Bishop; 13 Dec 1967, Terrell TX), American actor and comedian.

Mikhail Fradkov (1 Sep 1950, near Kuybyshev, USSR [now Samara, Russia]), Russian politician and prime minister, 2004–07.

Don Francisco (Mario Kreutzberger; 28 Dec 1940, Talca, Chile), Chilean-born American TV personality; host of the popular show *Sábado Gigante*.

Al Franken (21 May 1951, New York NY), American comedian and writer.

Dennis Franz (Dennis Schlachta; 28 Oct 1944, Maywood IL), American TV actor.

Jonathan Franzen (17 Aug 1959, Western Springs IL), American author.

Charles Frazier (1950, Asheville NC), American novelist.

Frederik (Frederik André Henrik Christian; 26 May 1968, Copenhagen, Denmark), Danish crown prince.

Morgan Freeman (1 Jun 1937, Memphis TN), American theater and film actor.

Dawn French (11 Oct 1957, Holyhead, Wales), British actress, comedian, and writer.

Lucian Freud (8 Dec 1922, Berlin, Germany), German-born British painter renowned for his portraits and nudes.

Dave Freudenthal (12 Oct 1950, Thermopolis WY), American attorney and Democratic politician; governor of Wyoming from 2003.

Benjamin M. Friedman, American political economist and expert on economic policy.

Thomas L. Friedman (20 Jul 1953, Minneapolis MN), American journalist and author, prominent foreign affairs columnist for the *New York Times.*

Akira Fujishima (3 Aug 1941, Tokyo, Japan), Japanese biologist, educator, and codeveloper of a photosynthetic method to split water into hydrogen and oxygen.

Takeo Fukui (28 Nov 1944, Tokyo, Japan), Japanese corporate executive; president and CEO of Honda Motor Co. from 2003.

Toshihiko Fukui (7 Sep 1935, Japan), Japanese banker; governor of the Bank of Japan from 2003.

Richard S. Fuld, Jr. (26 Apr 1946), American corporate executive; CEO of Lehman Brothers Holdings from 1993.

Nelly (Kim) Furtado (2 Dec 1978, Victoria, BC, Canada), Canadian singer and songwriter.

Stefano Gabbana (14 Nov 1962, Milan, Italy), Italian fashion designer who famously collaborates with partner Domenico Dolce.

Neil (Richard) Gaiman (10 Nov 1960, Portchester, England), British author of the multiple-award-winning *Sandman* series and of other graphic novels.

John (Charles) Galliano (28 Nov 1960, Gibraltar), British fashion designer and designer in chief at Christian Dior.

Christopher B. Galvin (21 Mar 1950, Chicago IL), American corporate executive; CEO of the Motorola Corp. from 1997.

Sonia Gandhi (Sonia Maino; 9 Dec 1947, Turin, Italy), Italian-born widow of Rajiv Gandhi and political force in India.

James Gandolfini (18 Sep 1961, Westwood NJ), American TV and film actor, star of the TV series *The Sopranos* from 1999.

Gao Xingjian (Kao Hsing-chien; 4 Jan 1940, Ganzhou, Jiangxi province, China), Chinese-born French novelist, playwright, critic, stage director, and artist; recipient of the 2000 Nobel Prize for Literature.

Mario Garcia (1947?, Cuba), Cuban-born American newspaper designer.

Gael García Bernal (30 Oct 1978, Guadalajara, Mexico), Mexican actor.

Gabriel García Márquez (6 Mar 1928, Aracataca, Colombia), Colombian novelist and short-story writer, a central figure in the magic realism movement in Latin American literature; recipient of the 1972 Neustadt Prize and the 1982 Nobel Prize for Literature.

Alan García Pérez (23 May 1949, Lima, Peru), Peruvian politician; president of Peru, 1985–90 and again from 2006.

Rulon Gardner (16 Aug 1971, Afton WY), American Greco-Roman wrestler.

Jennifer (Anne) Garner (17 Apr 1972, Houston TX), American TV actress.

Kenny Garrett (9 Oct 1960, Detroit MI), American jazz alto saxophone player.

Ivan Gasparovic (27 Mar 1941, Poltar, Czechoslovakia [now in Slovakia]), Slovak politician; president from 2004.

Bill Gates (William Henry Gates III; 28 Oct 1955, Seattle WA), American computer programmer, businessman and cofounder of the Microsoft Corp., and philanthropist; he is usually considered the richest person in the world.

Henry Louis Gates, Jr. ("Skip"; 16 Sep 1950, Keyser WV), American scholar of African American studies.

Melinda Gates (Melinda French; 15 Aug 1964, Dallas TX), American philanthropist, cofounder of the Bill & Melinda Gates Foundation.

Robert M. Gates (Robert Michael Gates; 25 Sep 1943, Wichita KS), American government official; CIA director, 1991–93, and secretary of defense from 2006.

Jean-Paul Gaultier (24 Apr 1952, Arcueil, France), French fashion designer known for his unusual and extravagant creations.

Maumoon Abdul Gayoom (29 Dec 1937, Malé, Maldives), Maldive politician and president from 1978.

Laurent Gbagbo (31 May 1945, Gagnoa, French West Africa [now in Côte d'Ivoire]), Ivorian politician and president of Côte d'Ivoire from 2000.

Haile Gebrselassie (18 Apr 1973, Assela, Ethiopia), Ethiopian runner and world-record holder in the 5,000-m and 10,000-m distances.

Frank O. Gehry (Frank Owen Goldberg; 28 Feb 1929, Toronto, ON, Canada), Canadian-born American architect and designer whose original, sculptural, often audacious work won him worldwide renown; recipient of the 1989 Pritzker Prize.

Sir Bob Geldof (5 Oct 1954, Dublin, Ireland), Irish musician (of the Boomtown Rats) who was knighted for his humanitarian work, notably arranging large-scale rock events for the benefit of the world's poor.

Murray Gell-Mann (15 Sep 1929, New York NY), American physicist who discovered that particles, including neutrons and protons, are composed of smaller, more fundamental building blocks that he named "quarks"; recipient of the 1969 Nobel Prize for Physics.

Sarah Michelle Gellar (14 Apr 1977, New York NY), American TV actress.

Francis (Eugene) Cardinal George (16 Jan 1937, Chicago IL), American Roman Catholic churchman; archbishop of Chicago from 1997 and cardinal from 1998.

(Susan) Elizabeth George (26 Feb 1949, Warren OH), American mystery writer.

Richard Gephardt (31 Jan 1941, St. Louis MO), American Democratic politician, congressman from Missouri (1977–2005), and House Democratic leader (1989–2003).

Richard (Tiffany) Gere (31 Aug 1949, Philadelphia PA), American film actor.

Valery Gergiev (2 May 1953, Moscow, USSR [now in Russia]), Russian conductor, the director of the Kirov Opera from 1998.

Mordicai Gerstein (1935, Los Angeles CA), American painter, designer, and writer and illustrator of children's books.

Ricky Gervais (25 Jun 1961, Reading, Berkshire, England), British comedian and actor who was the star of the British TV hit *The Office* (2001–03).

Mohamed Ghannouchi (18 Aug 1941, Al-Hamma, Tunisia), Tunisian politician and prime minister from 1999.

Jamal al-Ghitani (1945, Suhag, Egypt), Egyptian writer.

Riccardo Giacconi (6 Oct 1931, Genoa, Italy), Italian-born American X-ray astronomer; corecipient of the 2002 Nobel Prize for Physics.

Mossimo Giannulli (4 Jun 1963 California), American fashion designer known for his Mossimo line of sportswear and casual clothing for Target stores.

Jim Gibbons (James Arthur Gibbons; 16 Dec 1944, Sparks NV), American politician (Republican); governor of Nevada from 2007.

Mel Gibson (Mel Columcille Gerard Gibson; 3 Jan 1956, Peekskill NY), Australian American actor, producer, and director.

H.R. Giger (Hans Rudi Giger; 5 Feb 1940, Chur, Switzerland), Swiss illustrator, painter, sculptor, and film designer.

Gilberto Gil (Gilberto Passos Gil Moreira; 26 Jun 1942, Salvador, Bahia state, Brazil), Brazilian pop singer and songwriter; minister of culture from 2003.

Melissa Gilbert (8 May 1964, Los Angeles CA), American film and TV actress and president of the Screen Actors Guild from 2002.

João Gilberto (do Prado Pereira de Oliveira) (10 Jun 1931, Juazeiro, Bahia state, Brazil), Brazilian bossa-nova singer, songwriter, and guitarist.

Vince Gill (Vincent Grant Gill; 12 Apr 1957, Norman OK), American country and progressive-bluegrass instrumentalist and singer.

Ruth Bader Ginsburg (15 Mar 1933, Brooklyn NY), American jurist and associate justice of the US Supreme Court from 1993.

Vitaly L(azarevich) Ginzburg (21 Sep [4 Oct, New Style] 1916, Moscow, Russia), Russian theoretical physicist; corecipient of the 2003 Nobel Prize for Physics.

Dana Gioia (24 Dec 1950, Los Angeles CA), American poet and critic; chairman of the US National Endowment for the Arts from 2003.

Nikki Giovanni (Yolande Cornelia Giovanni, Jr.; 7 Jun 1943, Knoxville TN), American poet whose writings range from calls for violent revolution to poems for children and intimate personal statements.

Ira Glass (3 Mar 1959, Baltimore MD), American radio broadcaster, creator and host of *This American Life* on public radio and cable TV.

Philip Glass (31 Jan 1937, Baltimore MD), American composer of minimalist instrumental, vocal, and operatic music.

Roy J. Glauber (1 Sep 1925, New York NY), American quantum physicist; corecipient of the 2005 Nobel Prize for Physics.

Danny (Lebern) Glover (22 Jul 1947, San Francisco CA), American film and TV actor mostly cast in supporting roles.

Savion Glover (19 Nov 1973, Newark NJ), American dancer and choreographer known for a style of dance called "hitting," a combination of hip-hop music and tap dancing.

Louise (Elisabeth) Glück (22 Apr 1943, New York NY), American poet and poet laureate of the US, 2003–04.

Faure (Essozimna) Gnassingbé (Eyadéma) (6 Jun 1966, Afagnan, Togo), Togolese politician; president in February 2005 and again from May 2005.

Jean-Luc Godard (3 Dec 1930, Paris, France), French film director.

Whoopi Goldberg (Caryn Elaine Johnson; 13 Nov 1955, New York NY), American comedian and film actress.

Ralph E. Gonsalves (8 Aug 1946, Colonarie, Saint Vincent), St. Vincent politician and prime minister of Saint Vincent and the Grenadines from 2001.

Alberto R. Gonzales (4 Aug 1955, San Antonio TX), American attorney and judge who was White House counsel, 2001–05, and attorney general, 2005–07.

Alejandro González Iñárritu (15 Aug 1963, Mexico City, Mexico), Mexican film director.

Lawrence Gonzi (1 Jul 1953, Valletta, Malta), Maltese politician, leader of the Nationalist Party, and prime minister from 2004.

Roger Goodell (19 Feb 1959, Jamestown NY), American sports executive; commissioner of the National Football League from 2006.

Cuba Gooding, Jr. (2 Jan 1968, Bronx NY), American film actor.

John Goodman (20 Jun 1952, Affton MO), American film and TV actor.

Doris Kearns Goodwin (4 Jan 1943, Brooklyn NY), American historian, biographer, and TV commentator.

Al Gore (Albert A. Gore, Jr.; 31 Mar 1948, Washington DC), American Democratic politician, vice president of the US, 1993–2001, and environmental advocate.

Louis Gossett, Jr. (27 May 1936, Brooklyn NY), American film, stage, and TV actor.

Jorie Graham (9 May 1951, New York NY), American poet whose abstract, intellectual verse is known for its visual imagery, complex metaphors, and philosophical content.

(Allen) Kelsey Grammer (21 Feb 1955, St. Thomas, Virgin Islands), American TV actor, writer, and producer especially known for the TV series *Frasier* (1993–2004).

Clive W(illiam) J(ohn) Granger (4 Sep 1934, Swansea, Wales), Welsh economist; corecipient of the 2003 Nobel Memorial Prize for Economic Science.

Jennifer Granholm (5 Feb 1959, Vancouver, BC, Canada), Canadian-born American attorney and Democratic politician; governor of Michigan from 2003.

Hugh Grant (9 Sep 1960, London, England), British film actor.

Günter (Wilhelm) Grass (16 Oct 1927, Danzig, Germany [now Gdansk, Poland]), German poet, novelist, playwright, sculptor, and printmaker; recipient of the 1999 Nobel Prize for Literature.

Michael Graves (9 July 1934, Indianapolis IN), American architect and housewares designer in the Postmodernist style, known for his signature creations for Target stores.

Tom Green (30 Jul 1971, Pembroke, ON, Canada), Canadian comedian.

Richard Greenberg (1958, Long Island NY), American playwright.

Brian Greene (9 Feb 1963, New York NY), American physicist and expert on string theory.

Alan Greenspan (6 Mar 1926, New York NY), American monetary policymaker and chairman of the Board of Governors of the US Federal Reserve Bank, 1987–2006.

Colin (26 Jun 1969, Oxford, England) and **Jonny Greenwood** (Jonathan Richard Guy Greenwood; 5 Nov 1971, Oxford, England), British rock bassist and guitarist, respectively, of Radiohead.

Christine Gregoire (24 Mar 1947, Auburn WA), American politician and Democratic governor of Washington from 2005.

Grégoire III Laham (Lutfi Laham; 15 Dec 1933, Daraya, Syria), Syrian church leader; patriarch of Antioch in the Greek Melkite Catholic Church from 2000.

Kate Grenville (14 Oct 1950, Sydney, NSW, Australia), Australian writer.

Brad Grey (1958?, Bronx NY), American talent agent, producer, and film executive; chairman and CEO of Paramount Motion Picture Group from 2005.

Michael Griffin (Michael Douglas Griffin; 1 Nov 1949, Aberdeen MD), American aerospace engineer and businessman; administrator of NASA from 2005.

Ólafur Ragnar Grímsson (14 May 1943, Ísafjördhur, Iceland), Icelandic politician and president from 1996.

John Grisham (8 Feb 1955, Jonesboro AR), American lawyer and best-selling novelist.

Matt Groening (Matthew Abram Groening; 15 Feb 1954, Portland OR), American cartoonist and creator (1989) of TV's *The Simpsons*.

David J. Gross (19 Feb 1941, Washington DC), American quantum physicist; corecipient of the 2004 Nobel Prize for Physics for studies of quantum chromodynamics.

Gilbert M. Grosvenor (1933?), American executive; chairman of the board of the National Geographic Society.

Andrew S. Grove (Andras Grof; 2 Sep 1936, Budapest, Hungary), Hungarian-born American corporate executive; CEO of Intel Corp. from 1997.

Robert H. Grubbs (27 Feb 1942, Calvert City KY), American chemical engineer; corecipient of the 2005 Nobel Prize for Chemistry.

Jon Gruden (17 Aug 1963, Sandusky OH), American professional football coach.

Nikola Gruevski (31 Aug 1970, Skopje, Yugoslavia [now in Macedonia]), Macedonian politician (VMRO-DPMNE) and prime minister from 2006.

Armando (Emílio) Guebuza (20 Jan 1943, Marrupula, Portuguese Mozambique), Mozambican politician, secretary-general of the Frelimo political party from 2002, and president of Mozambique from 2005.

Ismail Omar Guelleh (27 Nov 1947, Diré-Dawa, Ethiopia), Djibouti politician and president from 1999.

Guillaume (Guillaume Jean Joseph Marie, Prince of Nassau and Bourbon-Parma; 11 Nov 1981, Château de Betzdorf, Luxembourg), Luxembourgian grand duke and heir to the throne.

Gilbert Guillaume (4 Dec 1930, Bois-Colombes, France), French jurist; president of the International Court of Justice from 2000.

Ozzie Guillen (Oswaldo José Guillen Barrios; 20 Jan 1964, Ocumare del Tuy, Venezuela), Venezuelan professional baseball manager (Chicago White Sox).

Kenny C. Guinn (24 Aug 1936, Garland AR), American Republican politician; governor of Nevada from 1999.

Abdullah Gul (29 Oct 1950, Kayseri, Turkey), Turkish economist and politician who was prime minister, 2002–03, and president from 2007.

James Edward Gunn (21 Oct 1938, Livingstone TX), American cosmologist; corecipient of the 2005 Crafoord Prize for research into the evolution of the universe.

Alfred Gusenbauer (8 Feb 1960, Sankt-Pölten, Austria), Austrian politician (Social Democrat); chancellor from 2007.

Xanana Gusmão (José Alexandre Gusmão; 20 Jun 1946, Laleia, Portuguese Timor [now East Timor]), Timorese independence leader who was first president of independent East Timor, 2002–07, and prime minister from 2007.

António (Manuel de Oliveira) Guterres (30 Apr 1949, Lisbon, Portugal), Portuguese Socialist politician; prime minister of Portugal, 1995–2002, and UN High Commissioner for Refugees from 2005.

David Guterson (4 May 1956, Seattle WA), American novelist.

Carlos M. Gutierrez (1953, Havana, Cuba), Cuban-born American corporate executive, former chairman and CEO of Kellogg Company, and US secretary of commerce from 2005.

Buddy Guy (George Guy; 30 Jul 1936, Lettsworth LA), American traditional guitarist and singer in the Delta blues tradition.

Gyanendra Bir Bikram Shah Dev (7 Jul 1947, Kathmandu, Nepal), Nepalese king, 1950–51 and again from 2001.

Jake Gyllenhaal (Jacob Benjamin Gyllenhaal; 19 Dec 1980, Los Angeles CA), American film actor.

Ferenc Gyurcsány (4 Jun 1961, Pápa, Hungary), Hungarian multimillionaire, politician, and prime minister from 2004.

Haakon (Haakon Magnus; 20 Jul 1973, Oslo, Norway), Norwegian crown prince (heir to the throne).

Geir Haarde (Geir Hilmar Haarde; 8 Apr 1951, Reykjavík, Iceland), Icelandic politician and prime minister from 2006.

Jürgen Habermas (18 Jun 1929, Düsseldorf, Germany), German philosopher, sociologist, and originator of the theory of communication ethics; he won a 2004 Kyoto Prize.

Charlie Haden (6 Aug 1937, Shenandoah IA), American jazz bass player.

Zaha Hadid (31 Oct 1950, Baghdad, Iraq), Iraqi-born architect; recipient of the 2004 Pritzker Prize.

Michael W. Hagee (1945, Hampton VA), American US Marine Corps general; commandant of the USMC from 2003.

Ted Haggard (Ted Arthur Haggard; Pastor Ted; 27 Jun 1956, Delphi IN), American evangelical church leader who resigned from his church position amidst a sexual scandal in 2006.

Hilary Hahn (27 Nov 1979, Lexington VA), American violinist.

Jörg Haider (26 Jan 1950, Bad Giosern, Austria), Austrian ultra-right-wing politician.

Zoltán Haiman (8 May 1971, Budapest, Hungary), Hungarian-born American cosmologist working on the early history of the universe.

Stelios Haji-Ioannou (14 Feb 1967, Athens, Greece), Greek entrepreneur and corporate executive (easyJet and easyGroup).

Donald Hall (Donald Andrew Hall, Jr.; 20 Sep 1928, New Haven CT), American poet, essayist, and critic; US poet laureate from 2006.

John L. Hall (John Lewis Hall; 21 Aug 1934, Denver CO), American physicist; corecipient of the 2005 Nobel Prize for Physics.

Tarja (Kaarina) Halonen (24 Dec 1943, Helsinki, Finland), Finnish politician and president from 2000.

Sam Hamill (1943, northern California?), American poet, editor, translator, and essayist; founder of Copper Canyon Press and catalyst of the Poets Against the War movement in 2003.

Mia Hamm (Mariel Margaret Hamm; 17 Mar 1972, Selma AL), American association football (soccer) player.

Herbie Hancock (Herbert Jeffrey Hancock; 12 Apr 1940, Chicago IL), American jazz keyboardist and composer.

Daniel Handler (pen name Lemony Snicket; 28 Feb 1970, San Francisco CA), American children's book author.

Ismail Haniya (1962, Shati refugee camp, Gaza, Palestine), Palestinian politician (Hamas); prime minister of the Palestine Authority from 2006.

Tom Hanks (9 Jul 1956, Concord CA), American film actor and director.

Daryl (Christine) Hannah (3 Dec 1960, Chicago IL), American film actress, director, and producer.

Hans Adam II (14 Feb 1945, Vaduz, Liechtenstein), prince of Liechtenstein from 1989.

Theodor W. Hänsch (Theodor Wolfgang Hänsch; 30 Oct 1941, Heidelberg, Germany), German physicist; corecipient of the 2005 Nobel Prize for Physics for work in laser spectroscopy.

Harald V (21 Feb 1937, Skaugum, Norway), king of Norway from 1991.

Marcia Gay Harden (14 Aug 1959, La Jolla CA), American film actress.

Roy Hargrove (16 Oct 1969, Waco TX), American jazz trumpeter.

Joy Harjo (9 May 1951, Tulsa OK), American poet, musician, and Native American (Muskogee) activist.

Nikolaus Harnoncourt (6 Dec 1929, Berlin, Germany), Austrian conductor, cellist, and viol player; cofounder in the 1950s of the Concentus Musicus Wien, an early-music group.

Stephen (Joseph) Harper (30 Apr 1959, Toronto, ON, Canada), Canadian Conservative politician and prime minister from 2006.

Ed Harris (Edward Allen Harris; 28 Nov 1950, Englewood NJ), American film and stage actor and director.

Emmylou Harris (2 Apr 1947, Birmingham AL), American folk and country singer.

William B. Harrison, Jr. (1943, Rocky Mount NC), American corporate executive; CEO of J.P. Morgan Chase & Co. from 2001.

Harry (Henry Charles Albert David; 15 Sep 1984, London, England), British prince; son of Charles and Diana, prince and princess of Wales; and third in line to the British throne.

Mary Hart (Mary Johanna Harum; 8 Nov 1950, Madison SD), American actress and TV personality, the co-host of *Entertainment Tonight* from 1982.

Dominik Hasek (29 Jan 1965, Pardubice, Czechoslovakia [now in the Czech Republic]), Czech ice-hockey goalie.

Robert Hass (1 Mar 1941, San Francisco CA), American poet and translator; US poet laureate, 1995–97.

Abdiqasim Salad Hassan (1942, Somaliland?), Somali politician and head of the Transitional National Government of Somalia from 2000.

J(ohn) Dennis Hastert (2 Jan 1942, Aurora IL), American politician, Republican congressman from Illinois, and speaker of the House, 1999–2007.

Tony Hawk (Anthony Frank Hawk; 12 May 1968, San Diego CA), American professional skateboarder.

Stephen W. Hawking (8 Jan 1942, Oxford, Oxfordshire, England), British theoretical physicist, a specialist in cosmology and quantum gravity.

Issa Hayatou (9 Aug 1945, Garoua, French Cameroun [now Cameroon]), Cameroonian sports executive, president of the African Football Confederation, vice president of FIFA from 1988, and member of the IOC from 2001.

Michael Hayden (Michael Vincent Hayden; 17 Mar 1945, Pittsburgh PA), American USAF general; director of the National Security Agency, 1999–2005, and director of the CIA from 2006.

Salma Hayek (Salma Hayek-Jiménez; 2 Sep 1966, Coatzacoalcos, Veracruz, Mexico), Mexican-born actress.

Roy Haynes (13 Mar 1926, Roxbury, Boston MA), American jazz drummer and bandleader.

Seamus (Justin) Heaney (13 Apr 1939, near Castledáwson, County Londonderry, Northern Ireland), Irish poet whose works evoke events in Irish history and allude to Irish myths; recipient of the 1995 Nobel Prize for Literature.

Chad Hedrick (17 Apr 1977, Spring TX), American speed skater, a champion inline (wheels) skater before switching to ice skating.

George H(arry) Heilmeier (22 May 1936, Philadelphia PA), American electronics engineer who led the team that developed the liquid-crystal display (LCD) screen.

Dave Heineman (12 May 1948, Falls City NE), American politician and Republican governor of Nebraska from 2005.

Heloise (Ponce Kiah Marchelle Heloise Cruse Evans; 15 Apr 1951, Waco TX), American newspaper columnist who writes the "Hints from Heloise" syndicated column.

Justine Henin (1 Jun 1982, Liège, Belgium), Belgian tennis player.

Jill Hennessy (Jillian Hennessy; 25 Nov 1969, Edmondton, AB, Canada), Canadian-born American TV actress.

Henri (16 Apr 1955, Château de Betzdorf, Luxembourg), grand duke of Luxembourg from 2000.

Brad Henry (10 Jun 1963, Shawnee OK), American attorney and Democratic politician; governor of Oklahoma from 2003.

Thierry (Daniel) Henry (17 Aug 1977, Châtillon, near Paris, France), French association football (soccer) player.

Seymour M(yron) Hersh (8 Apr 1937, Chicago IL), American investigative reporter and writer.

Avram Hershko (31 Dec 1937, Karcag, Hungary), Hungarian-born Israeli biochemist; corecipient of the 2004 Nobel Prize for Chemistry.

Mohamud Muse Hersi ("Adde"), Somali president of the secessionist republic of Puntland from 2005.

Jacques Herzog (19 Apr 1950, Basel, Switzerland), Swiss architect; corecipient of the 2001 Pritzker Prize.

Lleyton Hewitt (24 Feb 1981, Adelaide, SA, Australia), Australian tennis player.

Tommy Hilfiger (Thomas Jacob Hilfiger; 24 Mar 1951, Elmira NY), American fashion designer.

Faith Hill (Audrey Faith Perry; 21 Sep 1967, Jackson MS), American country singer.

Julia "Butterfly" Hill (18 Feb 1974, Mount Vernon MO), American environmental activist.

Lauryn Hill (25 May 1975, South Orange NJ), American hip-hop singer and actress.

Tony Hillerman (27 May 1925, Sacred Heart OK), American mystery writer.

Paris Hilton (17 Feb 1981, New York NY), American heiress and socialite.

Gertrude Himmelfarb (8 Aug 1922, Brooklyn NY), American historian and biographer who most often focuses on Victorian England and contemporary moral and cultural history.

Gordon B(itner) Hinckley (23 Jun 1910, Salt Lake City UT), American church official; president of the Church of Jesus Christ of Latter-day Saints from 1995.

Sam Hinds (1943), Guyanese politician; president in 1997 and prime minister, 1992–97, 1997–99, and again from 1999.

Damien Hirst (1965, Bristol, England), British artist.

Stanley Ho (Ho Hung-sun; 25 Nov 1921, Hong Kong), Macanese gaming magnate and multibillionaire.

Susan Hockfield (1951, Chicago IL), American neuroscientist; the first woman president of the Massachusetts Institute of Technology, from 2004.

John Hoeven (13 Mar 1957, Bismarck ND), American Republican politician who was governor of North Dakota from 2001.

James P. Hoffa (19 May 1941, Detroit MI), American labor leader; head of the International Brotherhood of Teamsters from 1999.

Dustin Hoffman (8 Aug 1937, Los Angeles CA), American film and stage actor.

Philip Seymour Hoffman (23 Jul 1967, Fairport NY), American film actor.

Hulk Hogan (Terry Gene Bollea; 11 Aug 1953, Augusta GA), American professional wrestler and actor.

Katie (Noelle) Holmes (18 Dec 1978, Toledo OH), American TV and film actress.

Evander Holyfield (19 Oct 1962, Atmore AL), American boxer and four-time heavyweight champion.

Kenichi Honda (23 Aug 1925, Tokyo, Japan), Japanese biologist, educator, and codeveloper of a method of artificial photosynthesis.

Gerardus 't Hooft (5 Jul 1946, Den Helder, Netherlands), Dutch physicist; corecipient of the 1999 Nobel Prize for Physics.

Sir (Philip) Anthony Hopkins (31 Dec 1937, Margam, West Glamorgan, Wales), British film and stage actor often in intense roles.

H. Robert Horvitz (8 May 1947, Chicago IL), American cell biologist, corecipient of the 2002 Nobel Prize for Physiology or Medicine.

Whitney (Elizabeth) Houston (9 Aug 1963, Newark NJ), American pop singer and film actress.

John Winston Howard (26 Jul 1939, Sydney, NSW, Australia), Australian politician, Liberal Party chairman, and prime minister from 1996.

Michael Howard (7 Jul 1941, Llanelli, Wales), British Conservative leader who served as home secretary, 1993–97, and shadow chancellor, 2001–05.

Ron Howard (1 Mar 1954, Duncan OK), American TV and film actor and director.

Hu Jintao (25 Dec 1942, Jixi, Anhui province, China), Chinese statesman; general secretary of the Communist Party of China, president of China from 2003, and vice chairman of the Military Commission.

Allan B. Hubbard (8 Sep 1947, Jackson TN), American economist; assistant to the president for economic policy and director of the National Economic Council from 2005.

Jan Huber (Johannes Huber; 1947?, The Netherlands), Dutch foreign ministry official; first executive secretary of the Antarctic Treaty system, from 2004.

Mike Huckabee (24 Aug 1955, Hope AR), American Republican politician; governor of Arkansas, 1996–2007.

Jennifer Hudson (Jennifer Kate Hudson; 12 Sep 1981, Chicago IL), American soul and gospel singer and film actress.

Dolores Huerta (Dolores Fernández; 10 Apr 1930, Dawson NM), American labor leader and activist whose work on behalf of migrant farmworkers led to the establishment of the United Farm Workers of America.

Arianna Huffington (Ariana Stassinopoulos; 1953?, Athens, Greece), Greek-born American political commentator, syndicated newspaper columnist, and author.

Robert (Studley Forrest) Hughes (28 Jul 1938, Sydney, NSW, Australia), Australian art critic and author.

Sarah Hughes (2 May 1985, Great Neck NY), American figure skater.

H. Wayne Huizenga (29 Dec 1939, Evergreen Park IL), American corporate executive and owner of the NFL's Miami Dolphins

John Hume (18 Jan 1937, Londonderry, Northern Ireland), Northern Ireland politician, corecipient of the Nobel Prize for Peace in 1998, and winner of the Gandhi Peace Prize in 2002.

Hun Sen (4 Apr 1951, Kompong Chom province, Cambodia), Cambodian politician and leader of the government from 1985.

Helen (Elizabeth) Hunt (15 Jun 1963, Culver City CA), American film and TV actress.

Holly Hunter (20 Mar 1958, Conyers GA), American film actress.

Jon M. Huntsman, Jr. (Jon Meade Huntsman, Jr.; 26 Mar 1960, Palo Alto CA), American businessman

(Huntsman Family Holdings), Republican politician, and philanthropist; governor of Utah from 2005.

Lubomyr Cardinal Husar (26 Feb 1933, Lwow, Poland [now Lviv, Ukraine]), Ukrainian Greek Catholic Church leader, patriarch of Lviv from 2000, and cardinal from 2001.

Nicholas Hytner (7 May 1956, Didsbury, near Manchester, England), British theater director who took over as artistic director of the Royal National Theatre in 2003.

Ice Cube (O'Shea Jackson; 15 Jun 1969), American rapper, songwriter, and actor.

Ice-T (Tracy Morrow; 16 Feb 1958, Newark NJ), American hip-hop artist, a founder of gangsta rap, and TV and film actor.

Nobuyuki Idei (22 Nov 1937, Tokyo, Japan), Japanese corporate executive; CEO of Sony Corp. from 1998 and chairman from 2000.

Eric Idle (29 Mar 1943, South Shields, Durham, England), British TV actor and author, a founding member of the Monty Python Flying Circus troupe.

Toomas Hendrik Ilves (26 Dec 1953, Stockholm, Sweden), Estonian diplomat; president from 2006.

Iman (Iman Mohamed Abdulmajid; 25 Jul 1955, Mogadishu, Somalia), Somali fashion model, actress, and cosmetics executive.

Natalie (Jane) Imbruglia (4 Feb 1975, Sydney, NSW, Australia), Australian pop singer.

Jeffrey R. Immelt (19 Feb 1956, Cincinnati OH), American corporate executive and CEO of the General Electric Co. from 2001.

India.Arie (India Arie Simpson; 3 Oct 1976, Denver CO), American singer and songwriter.

Hubert Alexander Ingraham (4 Aug 1947, Pine Ridge, Grand Bahama), Bahamian politician; prime minister, 1992–2002 and again from 2007.

Daisuke Inoue (10 May 1940, Osaka, Japan), Japanese pop drummer and inventor (1971) of the karaoke machine.

Shinya Inoué (5 Jan 1921, London, England), Japanese American cell biologist who developed techniques of microscopy to study intracellular structures.

José Miguel Insulza (2 Jun 1943, Santiago, Chile), Chilean Socialist government official; secretary-general of the Organization of American States from 2005.

Kathy Ireland (8 Mar 1963, Glendale CA), American fashion model, designer, and actress.

Bill Irwin (11 Apr 1950, Santa Monica CA), Tony Award-winning American actor and choreographer.

Walter Isaacson (20 May 1952, New Orleans LA), American corporate executive; chairman and CEO of the Cable News Network (CNN) from 2001.

Riduan Isamuddin (Encep Nurjaman; "Hambali"; 4 Apr 1966, Pamokolan, Indonesia), Indonesian militant and leader of the Jemaah Islamiya group.

Shintaro Ishihara (30 Sep 1932, Kobe, Japan), Japanese author and nationalist politician; governor of Tokyo from 1999.

Allen (Ezail) Iverson (7 Jun 1975, Hampton VA), American basketball player.

James (Francis) Ivory (7 Jun 1928, Berkeley CA), American film director famous for his collaboration with producer Ismail Merchant.

Ja Rule (Jeffrey Atkins; 29 Feb 1976, Queens NY), American rap performer.

Ibrahim (al-Eshaiker) al-Jaafari (1947, Karbala, Iraq), Iraqi Shi'ite politician and prime minister, 2005–06.

Alan (Eugene) Jackson (17 Oct 1958, Newnan GA), American country-music singer and guitarist.

Alphonso Jackson (Texas), American politician; secretary of housing and urban development from 2004.

Janet (Damita Jo) Jackson (16 May 1966, Gary IN), American singer and film and TV actress.

Jesse (Louis) Jackson (8 Oct 1941, Greenville SC), American civil rights leader, Baptist minister, and politician.

Michael (Joseph) Jackson (29 Aug 1958, Gary IN), American singer, songwriter, and dancer.

Peter Jackson (31 Oct 1961, Pukerua Bay, New Zealand), New Zealand film director and producer who directed the Lord of the Rings trilogy (2001–03).

Phil Jackson (Philip Douglas Jackson; 17 Sep 1945, Deer Lodge MT), American basketball player and coach.

Samuel L(eroy) Jackson (21 Dec 1948, Washington DC), American film actor.

Marc Jacobs (9 Apr 1963, New York NY), American fashion designer known for his sartorial interpretations of trends in contemporary art and modeling.

Jadakiss (Jason Phillips; 25 May 1975, Yonkers NY), American rapper.

Bharrat Jagdeo (23 Jan 1964, Unity village, Demarara, Guyana), Guyanese politician and president from 1999.

Sir Mick Jagger (Michael Philip Jagger; 26 Jul 1943, Dartford, Kent, England), British rock musician and lead singer of the Rolling Stones.

Helmut Jahn (4 Jan 1940, Nürnberg, Germany), German-born architect known especially for his use of light and color.

Zsuzsanna Jakab (17 May 1951, Hungary), Hungarian epidemiologist; the first director of the European Centre for Disease Prevention and Control (ECDC) in Stockholm, from 2005.

LeBron James (30 Dec 1984, Akron OH), American professional basketball player.

Judith Jamison (10 May 1944, Philadelphia PA), American dancer and choreographer who became artistic director of the Alvin Ailey American Dance Theater in 1989.

Yahya Jammeh (Alphonse Jamus Jebulai Jammeh; 25 May 1965, Kanilai village, Gambia), Gambian politician and president from 1994.

Janez Jansa (Ivan Jansa; 17 Sep 1958, Ljubljana, Yugoslavia [now in Slovenia]), Slovene dissident, defense official, politician (Social Democrat), and prime minister from 2004.

Mariss Jansons (14 Jan 1943, Riga, Latvia), Latvian-born American director; conductor of the Royal Concertgebouw Orchestra of Amsterdam from 2004.

Jim Jarmusch (22 Jan 1953, Akron OH), American avant-garde filmmaker.

Keith Jarrett (8 May 1945, Allentown PA), American jazz pianist, composer, and saxophonist.

Neeme Järvi (7 Jun 1937, Tallinn, Estonia), Estonian conductor and music director of the Detroit Symphony Orchestra from 1990.

Jay-Z (Shawn Corey Carter; 4 Dec 1970, Brooklyn NY), American rap performer.

Michaëlle Jean (6 Sep 1957, Port-au-Prince, Haiti), Haitian-born Canadian journalist; governor-general of Canada from 2005.

Katharine Jefferts Schori (26 Mar 1954, Pensacola FL), American church leader; presiding bishop of the US Episcopal Church from 2006.

Elfriede Jelinek (20 Oct 1946, Mürzzuschlag, Austria), Austrian playwright, novelist, and poet; recipient of the 2004 Nobel Prize for Literature.

Elwood V(ernon) Jensen (13 Jan 1920, Fargo ND),

American endocrinologist; corecipient of the 2004 Lasker Award for Basic Medical Research.

Jewel (Kilcher) (23 May 1974, Payson UT), American pop singer and songwriter.

Steven (Paul) Jobs (24 Feb 1955, San Francisco CA), American corporate executive, cofounder of Apple Computer, and CEO of Apple Computer, Inc., from 1997.

Billy Joel (William Joseph Martin Joel; 9 May 1949, Hicksville NY), American pop singer, pianist, and songwriter.

Mike Johanns (18 Jun 1950, Osage IA), American Republican politician who was governor of Nebraska, 1999–2005, and US secretary of agriculture from 2005.

Scarlett Johansson (22 Nov 1984, New York NY), American film actress.

Sir Elton John (Reginald Kenneth Dwight; 25 Mar 1947, Pinner, Middlesex, England), British singer, composer, and pianist.

Jasper Johns (15 May 1930, Augusta GA), American painter and graphic artist, a pioneer of Pop art.

Robert L. Johnson (8 Apr 1946, Hickory MS), American entrepreneur; creator (1980), chairman, and CEO of BET (Black Entertainment Television).

Stephen L. Johnson (21 Mar 1951, Washington DC), American government official; director of the US Environmental Protection Agency from 2005.

Ellen Johnson-Sirleaf (29 Oct 1938, Monrovia, Liberia), Liberian government and international official; president of Liberia from 2006.

Angelina Jolie (Angelina Jolie Voight; 4 Jun 1975, Los Angeles CA), American film actress.

Cherry Jones (21 Nov 1956, Paris TN), Tony Award-winning American stage actress.

James Earl Jones (17 Jan 1931, Arkabutla MS), American actor.

Norah Jones (30 Mar 1979, New York NY), American jazz-pop vocalist and pianist.

Quincy Jones (Quincy Delight Jones, Jr.; 14 Mar 1933, Chicago IL), American jazz and pop arranger, composer, and producer.

Tommy Lee Jones (15 Sep 1946, San Saba TX), American actor.

Michael (Jeffrey) Jordan (17 Feb 1963, Brooklyn NY), American basketball player; he was voted ESPN's Athlete of the Century and is believed by many to be the best basketball player in history.

Juan Carlos I (Juan Carlos Alfonso Víctor María de Borbón y Borbón; 5 Jan 1938, Rome, Italy), king of Spain from 1975.

Juanes (Juan Estebán Aristizábal Vásquez; 9 Aug 1972, Medellín, Colombia), Colombian singer, songwriter, and guitarist.

Ashley Judd (Ashley Tyler Ciminella; 19 Apr 1968, Granada Hills CA), American film actress.

Wynonna Judd (Christina Claire Ciminella; 30 May 1964, Ashland KY), American country-and-western singer.

Sir Aneerood Jugnauth (29 Mar 1930, Mauritius), Mauritian politician; prime minister, 1982–95 and again 2000–03, and president from 2003.

Jean-Claude Juncker (9 Dec 1954, Rédange-sur-Attert, Luxembourg), Luxembourgian politician and prime minister from 1995.

Ahmad Tejan Kabbah (16 Feb 1932, Pendembu, Sierra Leone), Sierra Leonean politician and president, 1996–97 and again from 1998.

Martinho Ndafa Kabi (1958?), Guinea-Bissau politician; prime minister from 2007.

Joseph Kabila (4 Jun 1971, Sud-Kivu province, Dem. Rep. of the Congo), Congolese politician and president of the Democratic Republic of the Congo from 2001.

Jaroslaw Kaczynski (18 Jun 1949, Warsaw, Poland), Polish politician (Law and Justice); prime minister from 2006.

Lech Kaczynski (18 Jun 1949, Warsaw, Poland), Polish politician (Law and Justice); president from 2005.

Ismail Kadare (28 Jan 1938, Gjirokastër, Albania), Albanian novelist and poet; recipient of the first Man Booker International Prize, in 2005.

Paul Kagame (October 1957, Gitarama, Ruanda-Urundi [now Rwanda]), Rwandan politician and president from 2000.

Dahir Riyale Kahin (1952), Somali politician; president of the secessionist Republic of Somaliland from 2002.

Daniel Kahneman (5 Mar 1934, Tel Aviv, British Palestine [now in Israel]), Israeli-born American economist; corecipient of the 2002 Nobel Memorial Prize for Economic Science.

Tim Kaine (Timothy Michael Kaine; 26 Feb 1958, St. Paul MN), American politician (Democrat); governor of Virginia from 2006.

Michiko Kakutani (9 Jan 1955, New Haven CT), American journalist; book critic at the *New York Times* from 1983.

Aivars Kalvitis (27 Jun 1966, Riga, USSR [now in Latvia]), Latvian politician and prime minister from 2004.

Dean Kamen (1951, Rockville Centre NY), American engineer and inventor of the Segway Human Transporter.

Ingvar Kamprad (1926, Småland province, Sweden), Swedish businessman and founder of the home-furnishing company IKEA.

Radovan Karadzic (19 Jun 1945, Petnjica, Yugoslavia [now in Montenegro]), Bosnian Serb politician and president of Republika Srpska (Bosnia and Herzegovina), 1992–96; he was wanted as a war criminal and was still at large in 2007.

Konstantinos Karamanlis (Kostas; 14 Sep 1956, Athens, Greece), Greek conservative politician; prime minister from 2004.

Donna Karan (Donna Faske; 2 Oct 1948, Forest Hills NY), American fashion designer known for the simplicity of her mostly black- and neutral-colored designs.

Islam Karimov (30 Jan 1938, Samarkand, Uzbek SSR, USSR [now Uzbekistan]), Uzbek politician and president from 1990.

Mel Karmazin (Melvin Alan Karmazin; 24 Aug 1943, New York NY), American media executive; president and CEO of CBS and president and COO of Viacom from 2000.

Hamid Karzai (24 Dec 1957, Karz, Afghanistan), Afghan statesman; head of the interim administration following the ousting of the Taliban; president of Afghanistan from 2001.

Garry Kasparov (Garri Kimovich Kasparov; original name Garri Weinstein or Harry Weinstein; 13 Apr 1963, Baku, USSR [now in Azerbaijan]), Azerbaijani-born Russian chess champion of the world, 1985–2000.

Moshe Katsav (1945, Iran), Iranian-born Israeli politician and president of Israel, 2000–07.

Jeffrey Katzenberg (21 Dec 1950, New York NY), American film producer and a cofounder (1994) of DreamWorks SKG.

Yoriko Kawaguchi (14 Jan 1941, Tokyo, Japan), Japanese politician and foreign minister from 2002.

Nobuhiko Kawamoto (3 Mar 1936, Tokyo, Japan), Japanese corporate executive; president of Honda Motor Co., Ltd., from 1990.

Alan (Curtis) Kay (1940, Springfield MA), American computer scientist who was instrumental in developing the personal computer, the local area network (LAN), and the graphical user interface (GUI), among other innovations.

Keb' Mo' (Kevin Moore; 3 Oct 1951, Los Angeles CA), American blues musician.

Garrison Keillor (Gary Edward Keillor; 7 Aug 1942, Anoka MN), American humorist and writer best known for his long-running radio variety show, *A Prairie Home Companion.*

Toby Keith (Toby Keith Covel; 8 Jul 1961, Clinton OK), American country-and-western singer.

Bill Keller (18 Jan 1949), American journalist; managing editor of the *New York Times,* 1997–2001, and executive editor from 2003.

David E. Kelley (4 Apr 1956, Waterville ME), American TV producer and screenwriter.

Ellsworth Kelly (31 May 1923, Newburgh NY), American painter and sculptor.

R. Kelly (Robert S. Kelly; 8 Jan 1969, Chicago IL), American R&B performer.

Yashar Kemal (Kemal Sadik Gogceli; 1922, Hemite, Turkey), Turkish novelist of Kurdish descent.

Dirk Kempthorne (29 Oct 1951, San Diego CA), American Republican politician; governor of Idaho, 1999–2006; and US secretary of the interior from 2006.

Thomas (Michael) Keneally (also published as William Coyle; 7 Oct 1935, Sydney, NSW, Australia), Australian novelist.

Anthony (McCleod) Kennedy (23 Jul 1936, Sacramento CA), American jurist; associate justice of the US Supreme Court from 1988.

Charles Kennedy (25 Nov 1959, Inverness, Scotland), British politician and leader of the Liberal Democratic Party from 1999.

Edward M(oore) Kennedy (22 Feb 1932, Brookline MA), American Democratic politician and senator from Massachusetts from 1962.

John F. Kerry (11 Dec 1943, Fitzsimons Army Hospital [now in Aurora CO]), American Democratic politician and senator from Massachusetts from 1985; the Democratic candidate for president in 2004.

Alicia Keys (Alicia Augello Cook; 25 Jan 1981, New York NY), American R&B singer.

Cheb Khaled (Khaled Hadj Brahim; 29 Feb 1960, Sidi-El-Houri, near Oran, French Algeria), Algerian *rai* performer.

Hamad ibn 'Isa al-Khalifah (28 Jan 1950, Bahrain), Bahraini sheikh; emir and chief of state from 1999; he proclaimed himself king in 2002.

Zalmay Khalilzad (1951, Mazar-i-Sharif, Afghanistan), Afghan-born American diplomat; US ambassador to Afghanistan, 2003–05, and to Iraq from 2005.

Hojatolislam Sayyed Ali Khamenei (15 Jul 1939, Meshed, Iran), Iranian Shi'ite clergyman and politician who served as president, 1981–89, and as that country's *rahbar,* or leader, from 1989.

Abdul Qadeer Khan (1935, Bhopal, Madhya Pradesh, British India), Pakistani nuclear engineer, "the father of the Islamic bomb."

Mikhail (Borisovich) Khodorkovsky (26 Jun 1963, Moscow, USSR [now in Russia]), Russian businessman, imprisoned former billionaire head of Yukos Oil Co.

Abbas Kiarostami (22 Jun 1940, Tehran, Iran), Iranian director and writer known for experimenting with the boundaries between reality and fiction.

Mwai Kibaki (15 Nov 1931, Gatuyaini village, Central province, Kenya), Kenyan politician and president from 2002.

Sue Monk Kidd (1949?, South Carolina), American author of best-selling novels about what she calls the "sacred feminine."

Angelique Kidjo (14 Jul 1960, Ouidah, Dahomey [now Benin]), Beninese pop singer.

Nicole (Mary) Kidman (20 Jun 1967, Honolulu HI), American-born Australian leading actress.

Anselm Kiefer (8 Mar 1945, Donaueschingen, Germany), German painter in the Neo-Expressionist movement known for works that deal ironically with 20th-century German history.

Jakaya Mrisho Kikwete (7 Oct 1950, Msoga, British Tanganyika [now in Tanzania]), Tanzanian military officer and government official; president from 2005.

Val (Edward) Kilmer (31 Dec 1959, Los Angeles CA), American film actor.

Jeong H. Kim (1961?, Seoul, South Korea), Korean-born American electronics industry executive who was founder (1992) of Yurie Systems, Inc., and president of Lucent Technologies' Bell Labs from 2005.

Kim Jong Il (16 Feb 1941, near Khabarovsk, USSR [now in Russia]), North Korean leader and successor to his father, Kim Il-Sung, as general secretary of the Central Committee of the Worker's Party of Korea (North Korea) from 1997.

Kim Soon Kwon (1 May 1945, Ulsan, Korea [now in South Korea]), Korean agricultural scientist specializing in developing high-yield, disease-resistant strains of corn; prominent for his work in aiding Korean reunification.

Kim Woo Choong (19 Dec 1936, Taegu, Korea [now in South Korea]), Korean businessman; founder and chairman of the Daewoo Group; chairman of the Federation of Korean Industries from 1998.

Jimmy Kimmel (13 Nov 1967, Brooklyn NY), American comedian and TV talk-show host.

Mick Kinane (22 Jun 1959, County Tipperary, Ireland), Irish jockey with a highly successful career in European Thoroughbred racing.

Jamaica Kincaid (Elaine Potter Richardson; 25 May 1949, St. Johns, Antigua), Antiguan American writer whose essays, stories, and novels are evocative portrayals of family relationships and her native country.

B.B. King (Riley B. King; 16 Sep 1925, Itta Bena, near Indianola MS), American guitarist and singer, a principal figure in the development of blues.

Carole King (Carole Klein; 9 Feb 1942, Brooklyn NY), American pop singer and songwriter.

Larry King (Lawrence Harvey Zeigler; 19 Nov 1933, Brooklyn NY), American TV journalist, longtime host of CNN's *Larry King Live* interview program.

Stephen (Edward) King (pseudonym Richard Bachman; 21 Sep 1947, Portland ME), American writer; author of novels combining horror, fantasy, and science fiction.

Galway Kinnell (1 Feb 1927, Providence RI), American poet whose poems examine the effects of personal confrontation with violence and inevitable death, attempts to hold death at bay, the plight of the urban dispossessed, and the regenerative powers of love and nature.

Michael Kinsley (9 Mar 1951, Detroit MI), American political commentator and editor; originator (1996) of the online magazine *Slate* and its editor 1996–2002.

Néstor Kirchner (25 Feb 1950, Río Gallegos, Argentina), Argentine politician and president from 2003.

Gediminas Kirkilas (30 Aug 1951, Vilnius, USSR [now in Lithuania]), Lithuanian politician and prime minister from 2006.

Vaclav Klaus (19 Jun 1941, Prague, Czechoslovakia [now in the Czech Republic]), Czech politician who served as prime minister, 1992–97, and president for one month in 1993 and again from 2003.

Calvin (Richard) Klein (19 Nov 1942, Bronx NY), American fashion designer.

Ralph Klein (1 Nov 1942, Calgary, AB, Canada), Canadian politician and leader of the Progressive Conservative Party from 1992.

August Kleinzahler (1949, Jersey City NJ), American poet.

Heidi Klum (1 Jun 1973, Bergisch Gladbach, Germany), German supermodel.

Evel Knievel (17 Oct 1938, Butte MT), American motorcycle stunt performer.

Bobby Knight (Robert Montgomery Knight; 25 Oct 1940, Massillon OH), American collegiate basketball coach.

Gladys Knight (28 May 1944, Atlanta GA), American R&B singer.

Keira Knightley (26 Mar 1985, Teddington, London, England), British film actress.

Alfred G(eorge) Knudson, Jr. (9 Aug 1922, Los Angeles CA), American geneticist and cancer researcher who developed the theory of tumor-suppressor genes; he received a 2004 Kyoto Prize.

Samuel Kobia (20 Mar 1947, Miathene, Kenya), Kenyan minister of the Methodist Church; general secretary of the World Council of Churches from 2004.

Robert (Sedraki) Kocharyan (31 Aug 1954, Stepanakert, Nagorno-Karabakh, USSR [now in Azerbaijan]), Armenian politician and president from 1998.

Horst Köhler (22 Feb 1943, Skierbieszow, Poland), German international economic official; president of Germany from 2004.

Jun'ichiro Koizumi (8 Jan 1942, Yokosuka, Kanagawa prefecture, Japan), Japanese politician and prime minister, 2001–06.

Willem J. Kolff (14 Feb 1911, Leyden, Netherlands), Dutch-born American biomechanical engineer and physician, a pioneer in artificial organ technology who invented the artificial kidney, devised the clinical membrane oxygenator, and helped develop the artificial heart.

Yusef Komunyakaa (29 Apr 1947, Bogalusa LA), American poet.

Alpha Oumar Konaré (2 Feb 1946, Kayes, French West Africa [now in Mali]), Malian statesman; president of Mali, 1992–2002; and chairman of the Commission of the African Union from 2003.

Tim Koogle (1951?, Alexandria VA), American corporate executive and CEO of Yahoo! Inc. from 1995.

Rem Koolhaas (17 Nov 1944, Rotterdam, Netherlands), Dutch architect known especially for his concepts of large-scale structures; recipient of the 2000 Pritzker Prize.

Jeff Koons (21 Jan 1955, York PA), American Pop-art painter and sculptor.

Dean (Ray) Koontz (9 Jul 1945, Everett PA), American writer of novels often with a grotesque or science-fiction atmosphere.

Ted Kooser (Theodore Kooser; 25 Apr 1939, Ames IA), American poet known for his deft use of images in describing rural Nebraska; US poet laureate, 2004–06.

Roger David Kornberg (24 Apr 1947, St. Louis MO), American chemist; recipient of the 2006 Nobel Prize for Chemistry for his studies of the molecular basis of eukaryotic transcription.

Michael Kors (Karl Anderson, Jr.; 1959, Merrick, Long Island NY), American fashion designer, creator of his own signature lines and artistic director for Celine.

Janica Kostelic ("The Croatian Sensation"; 5 Jan 1982, Zagreb, Yugoslavia [now in Croatia]), Croatian Alpine skier.

Vojislav Kostunica (24 Mar 1944, Belgrade, Yugoslavia [now in Serbia]), Serbian politician; president of Yugoslavia, 2000–03, and prime minister of Serbia from 2004.

Lansana Kouyaté (1950, Koba, Guinea), Guinean diplomat and statesman; prime minister from 2007.

Vladimir Kramnik (25 Jun 1975, Tuapse, USSR [now in Russia]), Russian chess grand master.

Alison Krauss (23 Jul 1971, Decatur IL), American bluegrass fiddle player and singer.

Lenny Kravitz (26 May 1964, Brooklyn NY), American rock performer.

Gidon Kremer (27 Feb 1947, Riga, USSR [now in Latvia]), Latvian-born violinist and conductor.

Léon Krier (1946, Luxembourg), Luxembourgian architect and urban planner in the New Urbanism style.

William Kristol (23 Dec 1952, New York NY), American editor and columnist.

Dennis J. Kucinich (8 Oct 1946, Cleveland OH), American Democratic politician; mayor of Cleveland, 1977–79; congressman from Ohio from 1996.

John (Kofi Agyekum) Kufuor (8 Dec 1938, Kumisi, Gold Coast [now Ghana]), Ghanaian politician and president from 2001.

Ted Kulongoski (5 Nov 1940 Missouri), American Democratic politician and governor of Oregon from 2003.

Harumi Kurihara (7 Mar 1947, Shimoda, Japan), Japanese chef, lifestyle celebrity, and cookbook author.

Raymond Kurzweil (12 Feb 1948, Queens NY), American computer scientist and visionary, a specialist in pattern recognition, whose work resulted in inventions of flatbed scanners, speech-recognition devices, and reading machines for the blind.

Tony Kushner (16 Jul 1956, New York NY), American playwright.

Michelle Kwan (Kwan Shan Wing; 7 Jul 1980, Torrance CA), American figure skater.

Finn E. Kydland (December 1943, Ålgård, near Stavanger, Norway), Norwegian economist; corecipient of the 2004 Nobel Memorial Prize for Economic Science.

Patti LaBelle (Patricia Louise Holt; 4 Oct 1944, Philadelphia PA), American soul and rock singer.

Andrew Lack (16 May 1947, New York NY), American communications executive; chairman and CEO of Sony Music Entertainment Corp. from 2003.

Emeril (John) Lagasse (15 Oct 1959, Fall River MA), American chef, restaurateur, and media personality known for his energetic TV cooking shows.

Karl Lagerfeld (10 Sep 1938, Hamburg, Germany), German-born French fashion designer known for his highly feminine creations for the houses of Chloé and Chanel.

Émile Jamil Lahoud (12 Jan 1936, Baabdat, Lebanon), Lebanese politician and president from 1998.

Guy Laliberté (1959, Quebec City, QC, Canada),

Canadian circus performer and founder of Cirque de Soleil.

Edward S. Lampert (1963?), American business executive and chairman of ESL Investments and Kmart Holding Corp. who engineered the takeover of Sears in 2005.

Pascal Lamy (8 Apr 1947, Levallois-Perret, Paris, France), French financial and government official; EU trade commissioner, 1999–2004; and director-general of the World Trade Organization from 2005.

Nathan Lane (Joseph Lane; 3 Feb 1956, Jersey City NJ), American comedic actor of stage and screen.

Helmut Lang (10 Mar 1956, Vienna, Austria), Austrian fashion designer.

k.d. lang (Kathryn Dawn Lang; 2 Nov 1961, Consort, AB, Canada), Canadian singer and songwriter.

Jessica Lange (Jesse Lange; 20 Apr 1949, Cloquet MN), American actress.

Sherry Lansing (Sherry Lee Heimann; 31 Jul 1944, Chicago IL), American actress and film executive.

Anthony M. LaPaglia (31 Jan 1959, Adelaide, SA, Australia), Australian film and TV actor.

Lewis H. Lapham (8 Jan 1935, San Francisco CA), American liberal political commentator, author, and editor of *Harper's Magazine* from 1983.

Lyndon (Hermyle) LaRouche, Jr. (8 Sep 1922, Rochester NH), American economist, populist politician, and presidential candidate.

John Larroquette (25 Nov 1947, New Orleans LA), American film and TV actor.

Mark Latham (28 Feb 1961, Sydney, NSW, Australia), Australian Labor politician and party leader.

Matt(hew Todd) Lauer (30 Dec 1957, New York NY), American TV journalist and news anchor; host of the *Today* show from 1997.

Ralph Lauren (Ralph Lipschitz; 14 Oct 1939, New York NY), American fashion designer known for his ready-to-wear collections and his use of unconventional materials.

Paul C. Lauterbur (6 May 1929, Sidney OH), American chemist and a pioneer of magnetic resonance imagery (MRI); corecipient of the 2003 Nobel Prize for Physiology or Medicine.

Avril (Ramona) Lavigne (27 Sep 1984, Napanee, ON, Canada), Canadian pop singer.

Sergey (Viktorovich) Lavrov (21 Mar 1950), Russian politician and foreign minister from 2004.

Jude Law (29 Dec 1972, Blackheath, London, England), British stage and screen actor.

Martin Lawrence (16 Apr 1965, Frankfurt am Main, West Germany [now in Germany]), American TV and film actor and comedian.

Nigella (Lucy) Lawson (6 Jan 1960, London, England), British cook and author of food-related books.

John H. Lawton (24 Sep 1943), British ecologist, head of the Natural Environment Research Council, and recipient of a 2004 Japan Prize for his studies and preservation of biodiversity.

John Le Carré (David John Moore Cornwell; 19 Oct 1931, Poole, Dorset, England), English novelist; author of suspenseful, realistic spy novels based on a wide knowledge of international espionage.

Ursula K. Le Guin (Ursula Kroeber; 21 Oct 1929, Berkeley CA), American author best known for tales of science fiction and fantasy distinctive for their character development and use of language.

Richard (Erskine Frere) Leakey (19 Dec 1944, Nairobi, Kenya), Kenyan physical anthropologist, paleontologist, conservationist, and politician.

Matt LeBlanc (25 Jul 1967, Newton MA), American TV actor.

Ang Lee (23 Oct 1954, P'ing-Tung county, Taiwan), Taiwanese-born film director.

Spike Lee (Shelton Lee; 20 Mar 1957, Atlanta GA), American filmmaker known for his uncompromising, provocative approach to controversial subject matter.

Stan Lee (Stanley Lieber; 1922, New York NY), American comic-book artist and creator of Spider-Man and other superheroes.

Lee Hsien Loong (10 Feb 1952, Singapore), Singaporean politician and economic expert; prime minister from 2004.

Lee Kun Hee (9 Jan 1942, Uiryung, Korea [now in South Korea]), Korean corporate executive and chairman of the Samsung Group from 1987.

Anthony J(ames) Leggett (26 Mar 1938, London, England), British physicist; corecipient of the 2003 Nobel Prize for Physics.

John Leguizamo (22 Jul 1964, Bogotá, Colombia), Colombian-born American comedian and actor.

Jim Lehrer (James C. Lehrer; 19 May 1934, Wichita KS), American TV journalist and author.

Annie Leibovitz (Anna-Lou Leibovitz; 2 Oct 1949, Westbury CT), American photographer and photojournalist known for her intense, often intimate portraits of celebrities.

Jean Lemierre (6 Jun 1950, Sainte Adresse, France), French international banking executive and president of the European Bank for Reconstruction and Development from 2000.

Jay Leno (James Douglas Muir Leno; 28 Apr 1950, Short Hills NJ), American comedian; host of *The Tonight Show with Jay Leno* from 1992.

Robert Lepage (12 Dec 1957, Quebec, QC, Canada), Canadian actor, director, and playwright.

Letsie III (David Mohato; 17 Jul 1963, Morija, Lesotho), king of Lesotho, 1990–95 and again from 1996.

David (Michael) Letterman (12 Apr 1947, Indianapolis IN), American TV personality; host of the *Late Show with David Letterman* from 1993.

Simon Asher Levin (22 Apr 1941, Baltimore MD), American biologist who specializes in the application of mathematics to problems in ecology; recipient of a 2005 Kyoto Prize for his role in establishing the field of spacial ecology.

James Levine (23 Jun 1943, Cincinnati OH), American conductor and pianist; principal conductor of the Boston Symphony Orchestra from 2004.

Bernard-Henri Lévy (5 Nov 1948, Béni-Saf, French Algeria), Algerian-born French media darling and author of best-selling "enhanced nonfiction" books.

Eugene Levy (17 Dec 1946, Hamilton, ON, Canada), Canadian comedian and writer.

Kenneth D. Lewis (9 Apr 1947, Meridian MS), American corporate executive, CEO of the Bank of America Corp. from 1999.

Lennox (Claudius) Lewis (2 Sep 1965, West Ham, London, England), British heavyweight boxer.

(Diane) Monique Lhuillier (1971, Cebu, Philippines), American couturier known for her bridal gowns for the stars.

Jet Li (Li Lian Jie; 26 Apr 1963, Beijing, China), Chinese-born wushu (acrobatic martial arts) champion who has starred in numerous martial arts films in China and the West.

Li Hongzhi (7 Jul 1952, Jilin province, China), Chinese religious leader who developed the Falun Dafa system.

Li Ka-shing (13 Jun 1928, Chaozhou, Guangdong province, China), Chinese (Hong Kong) corporate executive, chairman of Hutchison Whampoa Ltd. and Cheung Kong Holdings.

Li Ruigang (June 1969, Shanghai, China), Chinese business executive; president of Shanghai Media Group.

Li Zhaoxing (October 1940, Shandong province, China), Chinese politician and foreign minister from 2003.

Daniel Libeskind (12 May 1946, Lodz, Poland), Polish-born Israeli-American architect.

Joseph I. Lieberman (24 Feb 1942, Stamford CT), American Democratic/Independent politician, US senator from Connecticut, vice-presidential contender in 2000, and presidential candidate in 2004.

Lil Jon (Jonathan Smith; 1970, Atlanta GA), American "crunk" rapper and producer.

Lil' Kim (Kimberly Denise Jones; 11 Jul 1975, Bedford-Stuyvesant, Brooklyn NY), American hip-hop performer.

Rush Limbaugh (12 Jan 1951, Cape Girardeau MO), American radio talk-show host and conservative commentator.

Linda Lingle (4 Jun 1953, St. Louis MO), American Republican politician; governor of Hawaii from 2002.

John Lithgow (19 Oct 1945, Rochester NY), American comic and dramatic film and TV actor.

Lucy (Alexis) Liu (2 Dec 1968, Jackson Heights, Queens NY), American TV and film actress.

Nicholas (Joseph Orville) Liverpool (1934, Dominica?), West Indian politician and president of Dominica from 2003.

Kenneth Livingstone (17 Jun 1945, Lambeth, London, England), British Labour politician and mayor of London from 2000.

Tzipi Livni (5 Jul 1958, Tel Aviv, Israel), Israeli politician (Kadima); foreign minister from 2006.

LL Cool J (James Todd Smith; 14 Jan 1968, Queens NY), American hip-hop artist and actor.

Sir Andrew Lloyd Webber (22 Mar 1948, London, England), British composer whose eclectic stage musicals such as *Jesus Christ Superstar, Evita, Cats,* and *The Phantom of the Opera* blended pop, rock, and classical forms.

Keith Alan Lockhart (7 Nov 1959, Poughkeepsie NY), American conductor of the Boston Pops from 1993.

Lindsay (Morgan) Lohan (2 Jul 1986, New York NY), American actress and film starlet.

Bjørn Lomborg (6 Jan 1965, Copenhagen, Denmark), Danish statistician and controversial environmentalist.

Jonah Tali Lomu (12 May 1975, Auckland, New Zealand), New Zealand rugby winger of Tongan heritage.

Jennifer Lopez (24 Jul 1970, Bronx NY), American pop singer, actress, and fashion designer.

Andrés Manuel López Obrador (13 Nov 1953, Tepetitán, Mexico), Mexican politician and mayor of Mexico City; unsuccessful candidate for president in 2006.

Bernard Lord (27 Sep 1965, Moncton?, NB, Canada), Canadian politician and premier of New Brunswick from 1999.

Trent Lott (9 Oct 1941, Grenada MS), American Republican politician, senator from Mississippi from 1989, and Senate minority whip from 2006.

Joe Lovano (29 Dec 1952, Cleveland OH), American jazz tenor saxophone player, bandleader, and composer.

Courtney Love (Love Michelle Harrison; 9 Jul 1964, San Francisco CA), American pop-rock singer and actress.

Patty Loveless (Patricia Lee Ramey; 4 Jan 1957, Pikeville KY), American country-and-western singer.

Lyle (Pierce) Lovett (1 Nov 1957, Klein TX), American country-and-western singer.

Rob Lowe (17 Mar 1964, Charlottesville VA), American actor.

Henri Loyrette (31 May 1952, Neuilly-sur-Seine, France), French director of the Louvre museum in Paris from 2001.

George Lucas (George Walton Lucas, Jr.; 14 May 1944, Modesto CA), American film producer.

Susan Lucci (23 Dec 1947, Scarsdale NY), American TV soap opera star; she has played Erica Kane on *All My Children* since its premiere in 1970.

R. Duncan Luce (16 May 1925, Scranton PA), American cognitive scientist specializing in mathematical psychology and psychometrics.

Baz Luhrmann (Bazmark Anthony Luhrmann; 17 Sep 1962, near Sydney, NSW, Australia), Australian film and stage director and producer.

Alyaksandr (Hrygorevich) Lukashenka (30 Aug 1954, Kopys, Vitebsk oblast, Belorussian SSR, USSR [now Belarus]), Belarusian politician and president from 1994.

Luiz Inácio Lula da Silva ("Lula"; 27 Oct 1945, Garanhuns, Pernambuco state, Brazil), Brazilian labor leader and socialist politician; president from 2003.

Sidney Lumet (25 Jun 1924, Philadelphia PA), American film, TV, and stage director.

Hilary Lunke (7 Jun 1979, Edina MN), American golfer.

Uri Lupolianski (1951, Haifa, Israel), Israeli politician; mayor of Jerusalem from 2003.

Yury (Mikhaylovich) Luzhkov (21 Sep 1936, Moscow, USSR [now in Russia]), Russian politician and mayor of Moscow from 1992.

John Lynch (25 Nov 1952, Waltham MA), American businessman and Democratic politician; governor of New Hampshire from 2005.

Yo-Yo Ma (7 Oct 1955, Paris, France), American cellist noted for impeccable technique, the large number of commissions of new works he has attracted, and the breadth of his musical interests.

Wangari (Muta) Maathai (1 Apr 1940, Nyeri, British Kenya), Kenyan environmental activist who campaigned against the deforestation of Africa.

Lorin Maazel (6 Mar 1930, Neuilly, France), French-born American conductor and violinist; music director of the New York Philharmonic from 2002.

Bernie Mac (Bernard Jeffrey McCollough; 5 Oct 1958, Chicago IL), American TV and film entertainer.

Gloria (Macaraeg) Macapagal Arroyo (5 Apr 1947, San Juan, Philippines), Philippine politician and president from 2001.

Peter MacKay (27 Sep 1965, New Glasgow, NS, Canada), Canadian politician (Conservative Party); foreign minister from 2006.

Roderick MacKinnon (19 Feb 1956, Burlington MA), American chemist; corecipient of the 2003 Nobel Prize for Chemistry.

Alistair MacLeod (1936, North Batteford, SK, Canada), Canadian writer.

Elle Macpherson (Eleanor Gow; 29 Mar 1964, Cronulla, Sydney, NSW, Australia), Australian fashion model, actress, and lingerie designer.

Madonna (Madonna Louise Veronica Ciccone; 16 Aug 1958, Bay City MI), American singer, songwriter, actress, and entrepreneur.

Martie Maguire (Martha Elenor Erwin; Martie Seidel; 12 Oct 1969, York PA), American country musician and a member of the Dixie Chicks.

Tobey Maguire (Tobias Vincent Maguire; 27 Jun 1975, Santa Monica CA), American film actor known for playing unconventional leads.

Bill Maher (20 Jan 1956, New York NY), American satirist and host of controversial TV talk shows.

Roger Michael Cardinal Mahony (27 Feb 1936, Hollywood CA), American Roman Catholic churchman; archbishop of Los Angeles from 1985 and cardinal from 1991.

Natalie Maines (14 Oct 1974, Lubbock TX), American country musician; member of the Dixie Chicks.

Sir Ravinder N. Maini (1937, Ludhiana, Punjab, British India), Indian-born British immunologist and rheumatologist; corecipient of the 2000 Crafoord Prize and the 2003 Lasker Clinical Medical Research Award.

Mohammed ibn Rashid al-Maktum (1949, Dubai? [now in United Arab Emirates]), UAE sheikh; crown prince of Dubai from 1995 and prime minister from 2006; he is also a noted horse breeder and runs Godolphin Stables with his brothers.

Tuilaepa Sailele Malielegaoi (14 Apr 1945, Lepa, Samoa), Samoan politician and prime minister from 1998.

Nuri al-Maliki (Nuri Kamal al-Maliki; Jawad al-Maliki; Abu Isra; 1 Jul 1950, near Karbala, Iraq), Iraqi politician (Shi'ite); prime minister of Iraq from 2006.

John (Gavin) Malkovich (9 Dec 1953, Christopher IL), American film actor and filmmaker.

David (George Joseph) Malouf (20 Mar 1934, Brisbane, QLD, Australia), Australian poet and novelist; recipient of the 2000 Neustadt Prize.

David (Alan) Mamet (30 Nov 1947, Chicago IL), American playwright, director, and screenwriter noted for his often desperate working-class characters and for his distinctive, frequently profane dialogue.

Joe Manchin III (24 Aug 1947, Farmington WV), American businessman and Democratic politician; governor of West Virginia from 2005.

Nelson (Rolihlahla) Mandela (18 Jul 1918, Umtata, Cape of Good Hope, Union of South Africa), South African black nationalist leader and statesman; he was a political prisoner, 1962–90, president of South Africa, 1994–99, and corecipient of the 1993 Nobel Prize for Peace.

Winnie Madikizela Mandela (original name Nomzamo Winifred, original Xhosa name Nkosikazi Nobandle Nomzamo Madikizela; 26 Sep 1934/36?, Pondoland district, Transkei, British South Africa), South African social worker and black nationalist leader; second wife of Nelson Mandela.

Peter (Benjamin) Mandelson (21 Oct 1953, London, England), British Labour politician, cabinet minister, and international official; EU commissioner for trade from 2004.

Barry Manilow (Barry Alan Pincus; 17 Jun 1946, Brooklyn NY), American pop singer and songwriter.

Patrick (Augustus Merving) Manning (17 Aug 1946, San Fernando, Trinidad), Trinidadian politician and prime minister of Trinidad and Tobago, 1991–95 and again from 2001.

Preston Manning (10 Jun 1942, Edmonton, AB, Canada), Canadian politician and leader of the Reform Party.

Sir Peter Mansfield (9 Oct 1933, London, England), British physicist and a pioneer of magnetic resonance imaging (MRI); corecipient of the 2003 Nobel Prize for Physiology or Medicine.

Marilyn Manson (Brian Hugh Warner; 5 Jan 1969, Canton OH), American shock-rock performer who styles himself the "Antichrist Superstar."

John H. Marburger III (1941?, Staten Island NY), American physicist; presidential science adviser and head of the Office of Science and Technology Policy from 2001.

Geoffrey W. Marcy (29 Sep 1954, St. Clair Shores MI), American astronomer; discoverer of planetary systems outside the solar system.

Brice Marden (15 Oct 1938, Bronxville NY), American painter and printmaker who combines the techniques of Abstract Expressionism with the philosophies of Minimalism.

Margrethe II (Margrethe Alexandrine Thorhildur Ingrid; 16 Apr 1940, Copenhagen, Denmark), Danish royal, queen from 1972.

Mariza (Mariza Nunes; 1974?, Mozambique), Portuguese fado singer.

Mary Ellen Mark (20 Mar 1940, Philadelphia PA), American photojournalist whose compelling, empathetic images document the lives of marginalized people in the US and other countries.

Andranik Markaryan (12 Jun 1951, Yerevan, USSR [now in Armenia]), Armenian politician and prime minister, 2000–07.

Svetozar Marovic (31 Mar 1955, Kotor, Yugoslavia [now in Montenegro]), Montenegrin politician and president of Serbia and Montenegro, 2003–06.

Branford Marsalis (26 Aug 1960, Breaux Bridge LA), American jazz saxophonist and bandleader.

Wynton Marsalis (18 Oct 1961, New Orleans LA), American jazz trumpeter.

Barry J. Marshall (30 Sep 1951, Kalgoorlie, WA, Australia), Australian clinician; corecipient of the 2005 Nobel Prize for Physiology or Medicine.

Yann Martel (1963, Spain), Spanish-born Canadian novelist; recipient of the 2002 Man Booker Prize.

Chris Martin (2 Mar 1977, Exeter, Devon, England), British vocalist, guitarist, and pianist (of Coldplay).

Kevin Martin (14 Dec 1966, Charlotte NC), American politician and chairman of the Federal Communications Commission from 2005.

Paul Martin (28 Aug 1938, Windsor, ON, Canada), Canadian lawyer and businessman; prime minister of Canada, 2003–06.

Steve Martin (14 Aug 1945, Waco TX), American comedic actor, screenwriter, playwright, and author.

Masako (Masako Owada; 9 Dec 1963, Tokyo, Japan), Japanese royal, princess consort of Crown Prince Naruhito.

Master P (Percy Miller; 29 Apr 1970, New Orleans LA), American gangsta rap performer and producer.

Mary Matalin (19 Aug 1953, Chicago IL), American conservative political commentator and activist.

John C. Mather (John Cromwell Mather; 27 Aug 1946, Roanoke VA), American astrophysicist; corecipient of the 2006 Nobel Prize for Physics.

Mathilde (Mathilde d'Udekem d'Acoz; 21 Jan 1973, Uccle, Belgium), Belgian royal, princess consort of Prince Philippe (married 4 Dec 1999), and heir to the throne.

Hideki Matsui (12 Jun 1974, Ishikawa prefecture, Japan), Japanese baseball outfielder known for his hitting.

Koichiro Matsuura (1937, Tokyo, Japan), Japanese international official; director-general of UNESCO from 1999.

Dave Matthews (David John Matthews; 9 Jan 1967, Johannesburg, South Africa), South African–born American rock musician and songwriter, the leader of the Dave Matthews Band.

Amélie Mauresmo (5 Jul 1979, Saint-Germain-en-Laye, France), French tennis player.

Máxima (Máxima Zorreguieta Cerruti; 17 May 1971, Buenos Aires, Argentina), Argentine-born Dutch investment banker and princess consort of Crown Prince Willem-Alexander (married 2 Feb 2002).

Maxwell (23 May 1973, Brooklyn NY), American R&B and soul singer.

John (Dayton) Mayer (1979, Fairfield CT), American singer and songwriter.

Thom Mayne (19 Jan 1944, Waterbury CT), American architect, a cofounder (1972) of the architectural studio Morphosis, which specializes in schools and commercial buildings; recipient of the 2005 Pritzker Prize.

Kiran Mazumdar-Shaw (1954?, Bangalore, India), Indian business executive and founder (1978) of Biocon India, India's first biotechnology company.

Thabo (Mvuyelwa) Mbeki (18 Jun 1942, Idutywa, Transkei, South Africa), South African politician and president from 1999.

Mary Patricia McAleese (27 Jun 1951, Belfast, Northern Ireland), Irish politician, president from 1997.

Martina McBride (Martina Maria Schiff; 29 Jul 1966, Sharon KS), American country singer.

John McCain (John Sidney McCain III; 29 Aug 1936, Panama Canal Zone), American Republican politician and senator from Arizona.

Theodore Edgar Cardinal McCarrick (7 Jul 1930, New York NY), American Roman Catholic churchman; archbishop of Washington DC, 2001–06, and cardinal from 2001.

Cormac McCarthy (Charles McCarthy, Jr.; 20 Jul 1933, Providence RI), American writer in the Southern Gothic tradition whose novels about the rural American South are noted for their dark violence.

Sir Paul McCartney (James Paul McCartney; 18 Jun 1942, Liverpool, England), British singer, songwriter, and member of the Beatles.

Stella (Nina) McCartney (13 Sep 1971, London, England), British fashion designer for Chloé and for her own signature line.

Delbert McClinton (4 Nov 1940, Lubbock TX), American country-and-western singer and harmonica player, a pioneer of the Texas roots music revival.

Mike McConnell (John Michael McConnell; 26 Jul 1943, Greenville SC), American military intelligence officer; director of the National Security Agency, 1992–96, and director of national intelligence from 2007.

Eric McCormack (18 Apr 1963, Toronto, ON, Canada), American TV actor.

David McCullough (7 Jul 1933, Pittsburgh PA), American best-selling biographer and historian.

Audra (Ann) McDonald (3 Jul 1970, Berlin, Germany), Tony Award-winning American actress and singer on Broadway, on TV, and in classical music.

Frances McDormand (23 Jun 1957, Chicago IL), American film actress.

Malcolm McDowell (Malcolm Taylor; 13 Jun 1943, Leeds, England), British film actor.

John McEnroe (John Patrick McEnroe, Jr.; 16 Feb 1959, Wiesbaden, West Germany [now in Germany]), American tennis player and TV sportscaster.

Reba McEntire (28 Mar 1954, McAlester OK), American country singer and TV and film actress.

Ian (Russell) McEwan (21 Jun 1948, Aldershot, England), British novelist.

Daniel L. McFadden (29 Jul 1937, Raleigh NC), American economist; corecipient of the 2000 Nobel Memorial Prize for Economic Science.

Phil McGraw (Phillip C. McGraw; "Dr. Phil"; 1 Sep 1950, Vinita OK), American talk-show host, author, and psychologist-educator.

Tim McGraw (Samuel Timothy McGraw; 1 May 1967, Delhi LA), American country-and-western singer.

Dalton McGuinty (19 Jul 1955, Ottawa, ON, Canada), Canadian Liberal politician, premier of Ontario from 2003.

Mark (David) McGwire (1 Oct 1963, Pomona CA), American baseball player considered one of the most powerful hitters in the history of the game.

Dan Peter McKenzie (21 Feb 1942, Cheltenham, England), British geophysicist; recipient of the 2002 Crafoord Prize.

Kevin McKenzie (29 Apr 1954, Burlington VT), American ballet dancer, choreographer, and director who danced with the American Ballet Theatre, 1979–91, and became its artistic director in 1992.

Don McKinnon (Donald Charles McKinnon; 27 Feb 1939, Greenwich, England), New Zealand international official and secretary-general of the Commonwealth from 2000.

Sarah McLachlan (28 Jan 1968, Halifax, NS, Canada), Canadian singer and songwriter; she was the organizer and headliner of Lilith Fair, a traveling summer concert tour featuring female performers.

Beverley McLachlin (7 Sep 1943, Pincher Creek, AB, Canada), Canadian Supreme Court justice from 1989 and chief justice from 2000.

Vince McMahon (Vincent Kennedy McMahon, Jr.; 24 Aug 1945, Pinehurst NC), American wrestling promoter; owner of World Wrestling Entertainment, Inc., from 1982.

Larry McMurtry (3 Jun 1936, Wichita Falls TX), American writer noted for his novels set on the frontier, in contemporary small towns, and in increasingly urbanized and industrial areas of Texas.

Marian McPartland (Margaret Marian Turner; 20 Mar 1918, Slough, England), English-born American jazz pianist and composer; host of Piano Jazz, a weekly show on National Public Radio, from 1978.

James M. McPherson (11 Oct 1936, Valley City ND), American historian of slavery and the antislavery movement.

Ian McShane (29 Sep 1942, Blackburn, Lancashire, England), British film and TV actor.

Russell (Charles) Means (10 Nov 1939, Pine Ridge SD), American Lakota Sioux activist who was a leader of the American Indian Movement (AIM); he is best known for leading a 71-day siege at Wounded Knee SD to focus attention on rights for Native Americans.

Brad Mehldau (23 Aug 1970, Jacksonville FL), American jazz pianist and composer.

Zubin Mehta (29 Apr 1936, Bombay [now Mumbai], British India), Indian-born orchestral conductor; music director of the Israel Philharmonic from 1968.

John Mellencamp (Johnny Cougar; John Cougar Mellencamp; 7 Oct 1951, Seymour IN), American singer-songwriter who became popular in the 1980s by creating folk-inflected rock and presenting himself as a champion of small-town values.

Craig C. Mello (19 Oct 1960, New Haven CT), American geneticist; corecipient of the 2006 Nobel Prize for Physiology or Medicine.

Sam Mendes (Samuel Alexander Mendes; 1 Aug 1965, Reading, England), British film director.

Paulo Mendes da Rocha (25 Oct 1928, Vitória, Espírito Santo state, Brazil), Brazilian architect and professor; recipient of the 2006 Pritzker Prize.

Fradique de Menezes (1942), São Tomé and Príncipe politician; president of São Tomé and Príncipe from 2001 to 2003 and again from 2003.

Angela Merkel (Angela Dorothea Kasner; 17 Jul 1954, Hamburg, West Germany [now in Germany]),

German politician; leader of the Christian Democratic Union and chancellor of Germany from 2005.

W.S. Merwin (William Stanley Merwin; 30 Sep 1927, New York NY), American poet and translator.

Matthew Stanley Meselson (24 May 1930, Denver CO), American molecular biologist; the recipient of the 2004 Albert Lasker Special Achievement Award.

Stipe Mesic (Stjepan Mesic; 24 Dec 1934, Orahovica, Yugoslavia [now in Croatia]), Croatian politician and president from 2000.

Debra Messing (15 Aug 1968, Brooklyn NY), American TV and film actress.

Pat Metheny (12 Aug 1954, Lee's Summit MO), American jazz guitarist and bandleader.

Mette-Marit (Mette-Marit Tjessem Høiby; 19 Aug 1973, Kristiansand, Norway), Norwegian royal, princess consort of Crown Prince Haakon of Norway.

Pierre de Meuron (8 May 1950, Basel, Switzerland), Swiss architect; corecipient of the 2001 Pritzker Prize.

Michael (Michael Hohenzollern-Sigmaringen; ruled as Mihai I; 25 Oct 1921, Sinaia, Romania), Romanian king, 1927–30 (under regency) and 1940–47.

Lorne Michaels (Lorne Michael Lipowitz; 17 Nov 1944, Toronto, ON, Canada), Canadian-born TV and film producer who was the originator and executive producer of TV's *Saturday Night Live*.

James (Alix) Michel (16 Aug 1944, Mahe Island, Seychelles), Seychelles politician and president from 2004.

Michiko (Michiko Shoda; 20 Oct 1934, Tokyo, Japan), Japanese empress, consort of Emperor Akihito.

Midori (Midori Goto; 25 Oct 1971, Osaka, Japan), Japanese-born American violinist.

Dennis Miller (3 Nov 1953, Pittsburgh PA), American TV comedian and writer.

(Samuel) Bode Miller (12 Oct .1977, Easton NH), American Alpine skier.

Shannon (Lee) Miller (10 Mar 1977, Rolla MO), American gymnast.

Ming-Na (Wen) (20 Nov 1963, Macau), Macanese-born American TV actress.

Anthony Minghella (6 Jan 1954, Ryde, Isle of Wight, England), Academy Award-winning British film director and screenwriter.

Ruth Ann Minner (17 Jan 1935, Milford DE), American Democratic politician and governor of Delaware from 2001.

Kylie (Ann) Minogue (28 May 1968, Melbourne, VIC, Australia), Australian actress and pop singer.

Dame Helen Mirren (Ilyena Lydia Mironoff; 26 Jul 1945, Chiswick, London, England), British stage and film actress.

Joni Mitchell (Roberta Joan Anderson; 7 Nov 1943, Fort MacLeod, AB, Canada), Canadian singer, songwriter, and painter.

Keith (Claudius) Mitchell (12 Nov 1946, Grenada), Grenadan politician and prime minister from 1995.

Lakshmi Mittal (15 Jun 1950, Sadulpur, Rajastan state, India), Indian-born British steel magnate; owner of the LMN Group, the world's largest steel producer, and major shareholder in Ispat International.

Jun'ichiro Miyazu, Japanese corporate executive and CEO of Nippon Telephone & Telegraph from 2002.

Ratko Mladic (12 Mar 1943, Kalinovik village, Yugoslavia [now in Bosnia and Herzegovina]), Bosnian Serb military officer who led the Bosnian Serb army during the breakup of Yugoslavia and who was sought as a war criminal in the 1990s and 2000s.

Phumzile Mlambo-Ngcuka (3 Nov 1955, Claremont, Natal [now KwaZulu Natal] province, South Africa), South African politician, deputy president from 2005—the first woman to hold the position.

Festus (Gontebanye) Mogae (23 Jul 1939, Kanye, Botswana), Botswanan politician, president from 1998.

Alfred (Spiro) Moisiu (1 Dec 1929, Shkodër, Albania), Albanian military engineer, government official, and president, 2002–07.

N(avarre) Scott Momaday (27 Feb 1934, Lawton OK), American author of many works centered on his Kiowa heritage.

Sir Mark Moody-Stuart (1941, Antigua, West Indies), British corporate executive and CEO of the Royal Dutch/Shell Group (UK).

Alan Moore (18 Nov 1953), British author and creator of graphic novels such as the *Watchmen* series (1987), with intellectual, adult-oriented content.

Julianne Moore (Julie Anne Smith; 3 Dec 1960, Fayetteville NC), American film actress.

Lorrie Moore (Marie Lorena Moore; 13 Jan 1957, Glens Falls NY), American short-story writer and novelist.

Mandy Moore (Amanda Leigh Moore; 10 Apr 1984, Nashua NH), American pop singer and actress.

Michael Moore (23 Apr 1954, Davison MI), American film director and author.

Evo Morales (Juan Evo Morales Ayma; 26 Oct 1959, Orinoca, Bolivia), Bolivian farm-union leader; president of Bolivia from 2006.

Jason Moran (21 Jan 1975, Houston TX), American jazz pianist and bandleader.

Airto Moreira (5 Aug 1941, Itaiopolis, Santa Catarina state, Brazil), Brazilian jazz percussionist.

Luis Moreno Ocampo (4 Jun 1952, Buenos Aires, Argentina), Argentine lawyer; the first chief prosecutor of the International Criminal Court, from 2003.

Rhodri Morgan (29 Sep 1939, Cardiff, Wales), Welsh Labour politician, first minister of Wales from 2000.

Manny Mori (1948), Micronesian politician; president from 2007.

Alanis Morissette (1 Jun 1974, Ottawa, ON, Canada), Canadian-born American pop singer and songwriter.

Mark Morris (29 Aug 1956, Seattle WA), American dancer and leading choreographer for several international dance companies; founder of the Mark Morris Dance Group in 1980.

Toni Morrison (Chloe Anthony Wofford; 18 Feb 1931, Lorain OH), American novelist noted for her examination of the black experience (particularly the black female experience) within the African American community; recipient of the 1993 Nobel Prize for Literature.

Viggo (Peter) Mortensen (20 Oct 1958, New York NY), American film actor.

Walter Mosley (12 Jan 1952, Los Angeles CA), American writer of science-fiction and mystery novels interwoven with a progressive voice on social matters.

Kate Moss (16 Jan 1974, Croydon, Surrey, England), British fashion model known for her work for Calvin Klein and for introducing the "waif" look to fashion.

Andrew Motion (26 Oct 1952, London, England), English poet, teacher, editor, and biographer; poet laureate of England from 1999.

Alonzo Mourning (8 Feb 1970, Chesapeake VA), American basketball player.

Bill Moyers (Billy Don Moyers; 5 Jun 1934, Hugo OK), American TV journalist, government official, and author.

Ms. Dynamite (Niomi McLean-Daley; 1982, London, England), British R&B singer.

Mswati III (19 Apr 1968, Swaziland), Swazi royal; king of Swaziland from 1986.

(Muhammed) Hosni Mubarak (4 May 1928, Al-Minu-fiyah governorate, Egypt); Egyptian politician and president from 1981.

Lisel Mueller (Lisel Neumann; 8 Feb 1924, Hamburg, Germany), German-born American poet.

Robert S(wan) Mueller III (7 Aug 1944, New York NY), American government official; FBI director from 2001.

Robert (Gabriel) Mugabe (21 Feb 1924, Kutama, Southern Rhodesia [now Zimbabwe]), Zimbabwean politician; the first prime minister (1980–87) of the reconstituted state of Zimbabwe and president from 1987.

Muhammad VI (Muhammad ibn al-Hassan; 21 Aug 1963, Rabat, Morocco), king of Morocco from 1999.

Ali Muhammad Mujawar (1953), Yemeni politician; prime minister from 2007.

Paul Muldoon (20 Jun 1951, Portadown, Northern Ireland), Irish-born American poet known for his in-genious verses and flashy wordplay.

Marcia Muller (28 Sep 1944, Detroit MI), American mystery writer; author of a series of novels (from 1977) featuring a female detective, Sharon McCone.

Alice Munro (10 Jul 1931, Wingham, ON, Canada), Canadian short-story writer who gained interna-tional recognition with her exquisitely drawn sto-ries, usually set in southwestern Ontario.

(Keith) Rupert Murdoch (11 Mar 1931, Melbourne, VIC, Australia), Australian-born British newspaper publisher and media entrepreneur, founder of the global media holding company News Corporation Ltd.

Eddie Murphy (3 Apr 1961, Brooklyn NY), American comedian and film actor.

Cormac Cardinal Murphy-O'Connor (24 Aug 1932, Reading, Berkshire, England), British church leader; archbishop of Westminster (leader of the Roman Catholic church in the UK) from 2000 and cardinal from 2001.

Bill Murray (21 Sep 1950, Wilmette IL), American co-median and film actor known for eccentric charac-terizations.

Said Musa (19 Mar 1944, San Ignacio, British Hon-duras [now Belize]), Belizean politician and prime minister from 1998.

Yoweri Museveni (15 Aug 1944, Mbarra district, Uganda), Ugandan politician and president from 1986.

Pervez Musharraf (11 Aug 1943, New Delhi, British India), Pakistani military leader and politician; head of Pakistan's government, 1999–2001, and presi-dent from 2001.

Bingu wa Mutharika (24 Feb 1934, Thyolo district, British Nyasaland [now Malawi]), Malawian politi-cian; president from 2004.

Riccardo Muti (28 Jul 1941, Naples, Italy), Italian conductor of both opera and the symphonic reper-tory; principal conductor of La Scala Orchestra in Milan from 1987.

Halil Mutlu (Huben Hubenov; "Little Dynamo"; 14 Jul 1973, Postnik, Bulgaria), Bulgarian-born Turkish weightlifter in the 54/56-kg class who has set more than 20 world records during his career.

Anne-Sophie Mutter (29 Jun 1963, Rheinfelden, West Germany [now in Germany]), German violinist known for her striking onstage appearance, impec-cable technique, and idiosyncratic interpretations of the standard repertoire.

Levy Mwanawasa (3 Sep 1948, Mufulira, Southern Rhodesia [now Zambia]), Zambian politician and president from 2002.

Mike Myers (25 May 1963, Scarborough, ON, Canada), Canadian comedian and actor famous for offbeat comedy.

Youssou N'Dour (1 Oct 1959, Dakar, French West Africa [now in Senegal]), Senegalese singer and songwriter.

James Nachtwey (14 Mar 1948, Syracuse NY), Amer-ican photojournalist known for his award-winning work typically in zones of war and other turmoil.

Ralph Nader (27 Feb 1934, Winsted CT), American social activist and politician; he was a presidential candidate in 2000 and 2004.

Ray Nagin (Clarence Ray Nagin, Jr.; 11 Jun 1956, New Orleans LA), American politician (Democrat); mayor of New Orleans from 2002.

Parminder K. Nagra (5 Oct 1975, Leicester, Leices-tershire, England), British film and TV actress.

V.S. Naipaul (Vidiadhar Surajprasad Naipaul; 17 Aug 1932, Chaguanas, Trinidad), Trinidadian-born British writer known for his pessimistic novels about exile and alienation among postcolonial peoples; re-cipient of the 2001 Nobel Prize for Literature.

Mira Nair (15 Oct 1957, Bhubaneshwar, Orissa state, India), Indian film director and screenwriter.

Giorgio Napolitano (29 Jun 1925, Naples, Italy), Ital-ian politician (Communist) and president from 2006.

Janet Napolitano (29 Nov 1957, New York NY), Amer-ican Democratic politician and governor of Arizona from 2003.

Murthy Narayana (20 Aug 1946, Karnataka state, British India), Indian international business execu-tive and pioneer in India's high-tech industry; co-founder and CEO of Infosys Technologies Ltd., a technology and consulting firm.

Robert Louis Nardelli (17 May 1948, Old Forge PA), American corporate executive and CEO of the Home Depot, Inc., from 2000.

Naruhito (23 Feb 1960, Tokyo, Japan), Japanese crown prince.

Milton Nascimento (1942, Rio de Janeiro, Brazil), Brazilian pop singer and songwriter.

Sayyed Hassan Nasrallah (31 Aug 1960, Borj Ham-moud, Beirut, Lebanon), Lebanese Islamist military leader and secretary-general of Hezbollah from 1992.

Taslima Nasrin (25 Aug 1962, Mymensingh, Bangladesh), Bangladeshi Islamic feminist writer.

S.R. Nathan (Sellapan Ramanathan Nathan; 3 Jul 1924, Singapore?), Singaporean diplomat and president from 1999.

Nursultan Nazarbayev (6 Jul 1940, Chemolgan, USSR [now in Kazakhstan]), Kazakh statesman and president of Kazakhstan from 1990.

Liam Neeson (William Neeson; 7 Jun 1952, Bally-mena, Northern Ireland), British film actor.

John D(imitri) Negroponte (21 Jul 1939, London, England), British-born American diplomat; US rep-resentative to the United Nations, 2001–04, and US ambassador to Iraq, 2004–05; the first director of national intelligence, 2005–07.

Nelly (Cornell Haynes, Jr.; 2 Nov 1978, Austin TX), American rap artist.

Willie (Hugh) Nelson (30 Apr 1933, Fort Worth TX), American songwriter and guitarist.

Nerses Bedros XIX (Boutros Tarmouni; 17 Jan 1940, Cairo, Egypt), Armenian churchman and patriarch of the Catholic Armenians from 1999.

Randy Newman (Randall Stuart Newman; 28 Nov 1943, Los Angeles CA), American composer, song-writer, singer, and pianist known for character-dri-ven, ironic, and often humorous compositions.

(Carson) Wayne Newton (3 Apr 1942, Roanoke VA), American pop singer.

Teodoro Obiang Nguema Mbasogo (1942, Acoacan, Río Muni [now Equatorial Guinea]), Equatorial Guinean politician and president of Equatorial Guinea from 1979.

Ngugi wa Thiong'o (James Thiong'o Ngugi; 5 Jan 1938, Limuru, Kenya), Kenyan novelist.

Nguyen Minh Triet (8 Oct 1942, Ben Cat district, French Indochina [now in Vietnam]), Vietnamese politician and president from 2006.

Nguyen Tan Dung (17 Nov 1949, Ca Mau, French Indochina [now in Vietnam]), Vietnamese politician and prime minister from 2006.

Mike Nichols (Michael Igor Peschkowsky; 6 Nov 1931, Berlin, Germany), American film and stage director whose productions focus on the absurdities and horrors of modern life as revealed in personal relationships.

Jim Nicholson (R. James Nicholson; 4 Feb 1938, near Struble IA), American army officer and lawyer; chairman of the Republican National Committee, 1997–2000; ambassador to the Vatican, 2001–04; and secretary of veterans affairs from 2005.

Uichiro Niwa (c. 1941, Aichi prefecture, Japan), Japanese corporate executive who was CEO and president of Itochu Corp. from 1998.

Pierre Nkurunziza (18 Dec 1963, Ngozi province, Burundi), Burundian Hutu rebel leader; president of Burundi from 2005.

Christopher (Jonathan James) Nolan (30 Jul 1970, London, England), British film director known for his psychologically challenging pictures.

Donald A. Norman (25 Dec 1935, New York NY), American cognitive scientist specializing in problems of systems and design.

Norodom Sihamoni (14 May 1953, Phnom Penh, Cambodia), Cambodian prince trained in classical dance and filmmaking; king from 2004, following the abdication of his father, King Norodom Sihanouk.

Norodom Sihanouk (Preah Baht Samdach Preah Norodom Sihanuk Varman; 31 Oct 1922, Phnom Penh, Cambodia), Cambodian king, 1941–55 and again 1993–2004; head of state, 1960–70 and again in 1991–93.

Elwood "Woody" Norris (1942?), American inventor of HyperSonic Sound (a device to focus sound waves), the AirScooter, and other devices.

Deborah Norville (8 Aug 1958, Dalton GA), American TV anchor.

Kessai Note (1950, Ailinglaplap atoll, Marshall Islands), Marshallese politician and president from 2000.

Richard C. Notebaert (1948?, Montreal, QC, Canada), Canadian-born corporate executive; chairman and CEO of Ameritech Corp., 1993–99, and of Qwest Communications International Inc. from 2002.

Chris Noth (13 Nov 1954, Madison WI), American film and TV actor.

Lynn Nottage (1971?, Brooklyn NY), American playwright.

Robert Novak (26 Feb 1931, Joliet IL), American newspaper and TV journalist.

Conan O'Brien (18 Apr 1963, Brookline MA), American TV personality; host of *Late Night with Conan O'Brien* from 1993.

Ed O'Brien (Edward John O'Brien; 15 Apr 1968, Oxford, England), British rock guitarist and member of Radiohead.

Mark O'Connor (5 Aug 1961, Seattle WA), American country fiddle player.

Sandra Day O'Connor (26 Mar 1930, El Paso TX), American jurist and associate justice of the US Supreme Court, 1981–2005, the first woman appointed to the court.

Rosie O'Donnell (Rosanne O'Donnell; 21 Mar 1962, Commack NY), American TV personality.

Martin O'Malley (Martin Joseph O'Malley; 18 Jan 1963, Washington DC), American politician (Democrat); mayor of Baltimore, 1999–2007; governor of Maryland from 2007.

Sean Patrick O'Malley (29 Jun 1944, Lakewood OH), American Roman Catholic churchman; archbishop of Boston from 2003.

Shaquille (Rashaun) O'Neal (6 Mar 1972, Newark NJ), American professional basketball center who won NBA titles with the Los Angeles Lakers in 2000–02 and with the Miami Heat in 2006.

Bill O'Reilly (William James O'Reilly, Jr.; 10 Sep 1949, New York NY), American TV journalist and talk-show host; anchorman of *The O'Reilly Factor* on cable TV's Fox News Channel from 1996.

David J. O'Reilly (January 1947, Dublin, Ireland), Irish-born American corporate executive; chairman and CEO of ChevronTexaco Corp. from 2001.

P.J. O'Rourke (Patrick Jake O'Rourke; 14 Nov 1947, Toledo OH), American political satirist.

Peter (Seamus) O'Toole (2 Aug 1932, Connemara, County Galway, Ireland), British stage and film actor.

Joyce Carol Oates (16 Jun 1938, Lockport NY), American novelist, short-story writer, and essayist noted for her depictions of violence and evil in modern society.

Thoraya Obaid (2 Mar 1945, Baghdad, Iraq), Iraqi-born Saudi Arabian civil servant; executive director of the UN Population Fund from 2001.

Barack Obama (4 Aug 1961, Honolulu HI), American Democratic politician; senator from Illinois from 2005.

Olusegun Obasanjo (5 Mar 1937, Abeokuta, Nigeria), Nigerian military leader, politician, and president, 1999–2007.

Piermaria J. Oddone (26 Mar 1944, Arequipa, Peru), Peruvian-born American experimental particle physicist and administrator; director of the Fermi National Accelerator Laboratory from 2005.

Kenzaburo Oe (31 Jan 1935, Ose, Ehime prefecture, Japan), Japanese novelist whose works express the disillusionment of his post–World War II generation; recipient of the 1994 Nobel Prize for Literature.

Sadaharu Oh (20 May 1940, Tokyo, Japan), Japanese baseball player who holds the world record for most professional career home runs (868) and holds the Japanese single-season home-run record (55).

Paul Okalik (26 May 1964, Pangnirtung, NWT [now in Nunavut], Canada), Canadian politician and premier of Nunavut from 1999.

Claes (Thure) Oldenburg (28 Jan 1929, Stockholm, Sweden), Swedish-born Pop-art sculptor, best known for his giant soft sculptures of everyday objects.

Sharon Olds (19 Nov 1942, San Francisco CA), American poet best known for her powerful, often erotic, imagery of the body and her examination of the family.

Jamie Oliver (27 May 1975, Essex, England), British chef and TV personality who is known by the title of his TV program, *The Naked Chef,* and for his hip, down-to-earth, and fun style of food preparation.

Ehud Olmert (30 Sep 1945, near Binyamina, Palestine [now in Israel]), Israeli politician; prime minister of Israel from 2006.

Ashley (Fuller) and **Mary-Kate Olsen** (13 Jun 1986, Sherman Oaks CA), American twin child stars and a marketing phenomenon in modeling, films, TV, and music videos.

Omarion (Omari Ishmael Grandberry; 12 Nov 1984, Los Angeles CA), American soul-pop singer, originally of the group B2K but beginning in 2005 also a successful solo act.

(Philip) Michael Ondaatje (12 Sep 1943, Colombo, Ceylon [now Sri Lanka]), Canadian novelist and poet whose musical prose and poetry are created from a blend of myth, history, jazz, memoir, and other forms.

Ong Keng Yong (1954), Singaporean diplomat and international official; secretary general of the Association of Southeast Asian Nations from 2003.

Ami Onuki (18 Sep 1973, Tokyo, Japan), Japanese pop singer, of the pop group Puffy AmiYumi.

Makoto Ooka (16 Feb 1931, Mishima, Shizuoka prefecture, Japan), Japanese poet and literary critic, a prolific writer largely responsible for bringing contemporary Japanese poetry to the attention of the Western world.

Suze Orman (5 Jun 1951, Chicago IL), American financial adviser and best-selling author.

Daniel Ortega Saavedra (José Daniel Ortega Saavedra; 11 Nov 1945, La Libertad, Nicaragua), Nicaraguan guerrilla leader and politician; president, 1984–90 and again from 2007.

Yury (Sergeyevich) Osipov (7 Jul 1936, Tobolsk, USSR [now in Russia]), Russian mathematician and computer scientist; president of the Russian Academy of Sciences from 1991.

Joel Osteen (5 Mar 1963, Houston TX), American evangelist; head of the Lakewood Church in Houston.

Albert Osterhaus (1949?, The Netherlands), Dutch virologist famed for his knack for isolating and identifying pathogenic human and animal viruses, including, in 2003, the SARS (severe acute respiratory syndrome) virus.

Butch Otter (Clement Leroy Otter; 3 May 1942, Caldwell ID), American politician (Republican); governor of Idaho from 2007.

Michael Ovitz (14 Dec 1946, Encino CA), American entertainment executive; cofounder (1975) of the Creative Artists Agency.

Amos Oz (4 May 1939, Jerusalem, British-mandated Palestine), Israeli novelist, short-story writer, and essayist.

Cynthia Ozick (17 Apr 1928, New York NY), American novelist, short-story writer, and playwright.

Makoto Ozone (25 Mar 1961, Kobe, Japan), Japanese jazz pianist known for his performances with vibraphonist Gary Burton as well as for his solo work.

Peter Pace (1945, Brooklyn NY), American Marine Corps general; chairman of the Joint Chiefs of Staff, 2005–07.

Rajendra K. Pachauri (20 Aug 1940, Nainital, Uttar Pradesh [now in Uttaranchal] state, British India), Indian businessman and head of the Intergovernmental Panel on Climate Change from 2002.

Al Pacino (Alfredo James Pacino; 25 Apr 1940, New York NY), American film actor known for intense, explosive roles.

Lawrence Page (1972, East Lansing MI), American computer scientist and Internet entrepreneur who cofounded (1998) the Google Internet search engine.

Ian Paisley (6 Apr 1926, Armagh, Northern Ireland), Northern Irish politician; first minister for Northern Ireland from 2007.

Michael Palin (5 May 1943, Sheffield, Yorkshire, England), British comedian and actor; a founding member of the Monty Python comedy troupe.

Sarah Palin (Sarah Heath; 11 Feb 1964, Sandpoint ID), American politician; governor of Alaska from 2006.

Eddie Palmieri (15 Dec 1936, New York NY), American jazz-salsa pianist.

Samuel J. Palmisano (29 Jul 1951), American corporate executive; president and CEO of the International Business Machines (IBM) Corp. from 2002.

Gwyneth Paltrow (28 Sep 1972, Los Angeles CA), American film and stage actress.

Orhan Pamuk (7 Jun 1952, Istanbul, Turkey), Turkish novelist; recipient of the 2006 Nobel Prize for Literature.

Paola (Paola dei Principi Ruffo di Calabria; 11 Sep 1937, Forte dei Marmi, Italy), Italian-born Belgian queen consort of King Albert II (married 2 Jul 1959).

Tassos Papadopoulos (7 Jan 1934, Nicosia, Cyprus), Greek Cypriot lawyer, politician, and government official; president of the Republic of Cyprus from 2003.

Karolos Papoulias (4 Jun 1929, Ioannina, Greece), Greek PASOK politician and president from 2005.

Anna (Helene) Paquin (24 Jul 1982, Winnipeg, MB, Canada), New Zealand film actress.

Sara Paretsky (8 Jun 1947, Ames IA), American mystery writer who created the detective VI Warshawski.

Nick Park (Nicholas Wulstan Park; 6 Dec 1958, Preston, Lancashire, England), Academy Award-winning British film animator.

Sir Alan (William) Parker (14 Feb 1944, Islington, London, England), British advertising copywriter and film director.

Eugene N(ewman) Parker (10 Jun 1927, Houghton MI), American physicist and astronomer; recipient of the 2003 Kyoto Prize in the basic science section for his prediction of the existence of the solar wind.

Mary-Louise Parker (2 Aug 1964, Fort Jackson SC), American actress successful in equal measure on stage, in film, and on TV.

Sarah Jessica Parker (25 Mar 1965, Nelsonville OH), American TV and film actress and model who starred in TV's *Sex and the City* (1998–2004).

Trey Parker (Randolph Severn Parker III; 19 Oct 1969, Conifer CO), American animator and cocreator (with Matt Stone) of *South Park,* an animated TV show.

Bradford W. Parkinson (1935, Wisconsin), American aerospace engineer and developer of the NAVSTAR global positioning system; corecipient of the 2003 Charles Stark Draper Prize of the National Academy of Engineering.

Suzan-Lori Parks (10 May 1963, Fort Knox KY), American playwright.

Richard D(ean) Parsons (4 Apr 1949, Bedford-Stuyvesant, Brooklyn NY), American corporate executive; CEO of AOL Time Warner from 2002 and chairman from 2003.

Timothy (Richard) Parsons (1 Nov 1932, Colombo, Ceylon [now Sri Lanka]), Canadian oceanographer; recipient of the 2001 Japan Prize for his work in fisheries management.

Arvo Pärt (11 Sep 1935, Paide, Estonia), Estonian composer whose works display a simplicity and a medieval liturgical sound.

Dolly (Rebecca) Parton (19 Jan 1946, Locust Ridge TN), American country-and-western singer, songwriter, and actress.

Amy Pascal (1959, Los Angeles CA), American film executive; president of Turner Pictures from 1994 and, from Turner's merger in 1996 with Time Warner, president of Sony Corp.'s Columbia Pictures.

George E. Pataki (24 Jun 1945, Peekskill NY), American Republican politician and governor of New York, 1995–2007.

Ann Patchett (2 Dec 1963, Los Angeles CA), American novelist.

Pratibha Patil (19 Dec 1934, Jalgaon, British India), Indian politician; first female president, from 2007.

Deval Patrick (Deval Laurdine Patrick; 31 Jul 1956, Chicago IL), American politician (Democrat); governor of Massachusetts from 2007.

Arnall Patz (14 Jun 1920), American ophthalmologist and researcher on the causes and treatment of eye disease, especially among children.

Sean Paul (Sean Paul Henriques; 8 Jan 1973, St. Andrew, Jamaica), Jamaican reggae musician.

(Margaret) Jane Pauley (31 Oct 1950, Indianapolis IN), American TV personality.

Henry M. Paulson (Henry Merritt Paulson, Jr.; 28 Mar 1946, Palm Beach FL), American corporate executive; CEO of Goldman Sachs Group; secretary of the treasury from 2006.

Tim Pawlenty (Timothy James Pawlenty; 21 Nov 1960, St. Paul MN), American Republican politician and governor of Minnesota from 2003.

Peaches (Merrill Nisker; 1968, Toronto, ON, Canada), Canadian electro-techno rapper known for her brash, sexually explicit material.

Claudia Pechstein (22 Feb 1972, East Berlin, East Germany [now Berlin, Germany]), German speed skater.

Amanda Peet (11 Jan 1972, New York NY), American film and TV actress.

Harvey Pekar (1939, Cleveland OH), American file clerk and alternative comic-book artist.

Pelé (Edson Arantes do Nascimento; 23 Oct 1940, Três Corações, Minas Gerais state, Brazil), Brazilian soccer (association football) inside-forward who was revered as much for his sportsmanship as for his extraordinary skill and innovative style; in his time he was probably the most famous and possibly the best-paid athlete in the world.

David Pelletier (22 Nov 1974, Sayabec, QC, Canada), Canadian pairs figure skater (with Jamie Salé).

Cesar Pelli (12 Oct 1926, Tucumán, Argentina), Argentine architect known for the lightweight, almost tentlike, appearance of his buildings, which are often surfaced in glass or with a thin stone veneer.

Nancy Pelosi (Nancy D'Alesandro; 26 Mar 1940, Baltimore MD), American Democratic politician; congresswoman from California from 1987, House Democratic leader from 2003, and speaker of the House from 2007 (the first woman to hold the post).

Leonard Peltier (12 Sep 1944, Grand Forks ND), American Ojibwa and Lakota activist and a leader in the American Indian Movement; his conviction in 1977 and imprisonment for the murder of two FBI agents at South Dakota's Pine Ridge Reservation in 1975 became a cause célèbre.

Sean (Justin) Penn (17 Aug 1960, Santa Monica CA), American film actor and director known for his intense, brooding roles.

Murray Perahia (19 Apr 1947, New York NY), American concert pianist.

Sonny Perdue (20 Dec 1946, Perry GA), American agribusinessman, Republican politician, and governor of Georgia from 2003.

Grigory Perelman (Grigory Yakovlevich Perelman; 13 Jun 1966, Leningrad, USSR [now St. Petersburg, Russia]), Russian-born mathematician who offered a solution to the famous Poincaré conjecture.

Shimon Peres (2 Aug 1923, Wieniawa, Poland [now Vishniev, Belarus]), Israeli statesman, prime minister, 1984–86 and 1995–96, and president from 2007; he won the Nobel Peace Prize in 1994 for his efforts to work with the PLO.

Kieran Perkins (14 Aug 1973, Brisbane, QLD, Australia), Australian swimmer who held 12 world records in distance freestyle events.

Grayson Perry (24 Mar 1960, Chelmsford, Essex, England), British artist; recipient of the 2003 Turner Prize for ceramic pots decorated with his drawings.

Matthew Perry (19 Aug 1969, Williamstown MA), American TV and film actor.

Rick Perry (4 Mar 1950, West Texas), American Republican politician and governor of Texas from 2000.

Joe Pesci (9 Feb 1943, Newark NJ), American film actor best known for roles in gangster movies and comedies.

Bernadette Peters (Bernadette Lazzaro; 28 Feb 1948, Queens NY), American singer and actress on Broadway, on TV, and in films.

Jürgen Peters (17 Mar 1944, Bolko, Germany [now Oppeln, Poland]), German trade union leader and chairman of IG Metall, the most powerful German trade union, from 2003.

Mary E. Peters (Arizona), American transportation official; secretary of transportation from 2006.

David Petraeus (David Howell Petraeus; 7 Nov 1952), American military leader; commander of Multinational Force Iraq (MNF-I) from 2007.

Tom Petty (20 Oct 1953, Gainesville FL), American singer and songwriter whose roots-oriented guitar rock arose in the late 1970s and resulted in a string of hit singles and albums.

Madeleine Peyroux (1973, Athens GA), American jazz singer.

Michelle Pfeiffer (29 Apr 1958, Santa Ana CA), American film actress.

Liz Phair (Elizabeth Clark Phair; 17 Apr 1967, New Haven CT), American rock singer and songwriter.

Michael Phelps (30 Jun 1985, Baltimore MD), American swimmer, holder of numerous records.

Regis (Francis Xavier) Philbin (25 Aug 1934, New York NY), American TV personality.

Philip (Prince Philip of Greece; 3rd Duke of Edinburgh; 10 Jun 1921, Corfu, Greece), British royal; consort of Queen Elizabeth II (married 20 Nov 1947).

Philippe (Philippe Leopold Louis Marie; 15 Apr 1960, Brussels, Belgium), duke of Brabant and crown prince of Belgium.

Stone Phillips (2 Dec 1954, Texas City TX), American TV host and anchorman for Dateline NBC from 1992.

Renzo Piano (14 Sep 1937, Genoa, Italy), Italian architect; recipient of the 1998 Pritzker Prize and the 2002 UIA Gold Medal for Architecture.

Heinrich von Pierer (26 Jan 1941, Erlangen, Germany), German corporate executive and CEO of Siemens AG from 1992.

DBC Pierre (Peter Finlay; June 1961, Australia), Australian-born British novelist; winner of the Man Booker Prize.

Laffit Pincay, Jr. (29 Dec 1946, Panama City, Panama), Panamanian-born American jockey.

Pink (Alecia Moore; 8 Sep 1979, Doylestown PA), American pop vocalist.

Robert Pinsky (20 Oct 1940, Long Branch NJ), American poet and critic; poet laureate of the US, 1997–2000.

Harold Pinter (10 Oct 1930, London, England), English playwright regarded as one of the most complex and challenging post-World War II dramatists; recipient of the 2005 Nobel Prize for Literature.

Pedro Pires (April 1934, Ilha do Fogo, Cape Verde), Cape Verdean politician and president from 2001.

Bernd Pischetsrieder (15 Feb 1948, Munich, West Germany [now in Germany]), German corporate executive and CEO of Volkswagen AG from 2001.

Brad Pitt (William Bradley Pitt; 18 Dec 1963, Shawnee OK), American actor and one of the biggest box-office draws in America.

Elizabeth Plater-Zyberk (20 Dec 1950, Bryn Mawr PA), American urban planner who collaborates with her husband, Andres Duany.

Yevgeny (Viktorovich) Plushchenko (also written Evgeni Plushenko; 3 Nov 1982, Solnechny, USSR [now in Russia]), Russian figure skater.

Norman Podhoretz (16 Jan 1930, Brooklyn NY), American political commentator and editor of the journal *Commentary*, 1960–95.

Sylvia Poggioli (194?, Providence RI), American foreign correspondent for National Public Radio.

Hifikepunye (Lucas) Pohamba (18 Aug 1935, Okanghudi, South West Africa [now Namibia]), Namibian independence leader and politician; president from 2005.

Sidney Poitier (20 Feb 1927?, Miami FL), Bahamian American stage and film actor and director.

Roman Polanski (Raimund Liebling; 18 Aug 1933, Paris, France), Polish film director, scriptwriter, and actor.

Judit Polgar (23 Jul 1976, Budapest, Hungary), Hungarian chess player.

H. David Politzer (31 Aug 1949, New York NY), American quantum physicist; corecipient of the 2004 Nobel Prize for Physics.

Sigmar Polke (13 Feb 1941, Oels, Germany [now Olesnica, Poland]), German painter, one of the founders of Capitalist Realism, a movement that depicts popular and mundane cultural artifacts with ironic seriousness.

John (Charlton) Polkinghorne (16 Oct 1930, Weston-super-Mare, Somerset, England), British Anglican priest and particle physicist; recipient of the 2002 Templeton Prize.

Natalie Portman (Natalie Hershlag; 9 Jun 1981, Jerusalem, Israel), Israeli-born American film actress.

Rob Portman (Robert Jones Portman; 19 Dec 1955, Cincinnati OH), American politician (Republican); director of the Office of Management and Budget from 2006.

John E. Potter (195?), American corporate executive; CEO and postmaster general of the US Postal Service from 2001.

Earl A. ("Rusty") Powell III (24 Oct 1943, Spartanburg SC), American museum official; director of the National Gallery of Art in Washington DC from 1992.

Samantha Power (1970, Ireland), Irish-born American writer.

Velupillai Prabhakaran (26 Nov 1954, Jaffna, Sri Lanka), Sri Lankan secessionist, the founder and leader of the Liberation Tigers of Tamil Eelam (Tamil Tigers) from the early 1970s.

Miuccia Prada (1949, Milan, Italy), Italian fashion designer whose clothing, footwear, and accessories designs are characterized by casual luxury.

John M(ichael) Prausnitz (1928, Berlin, Germany), German-born American applied physical chemist who specialized in the design of industrial-scale chemical separation processes to make them more efficient and environmentally sound.

Azim Hasham Premji (24 Jul 1945, Bombay [now Mumbai], British India), Indian corporate executive; chairman of the Wipro Corp. of Bangalore from 1977.

Edward C. Prescott (26 Dec 1940, Glens Falls NY), American economist; corecipient of the 2004 Nobel Memorial Prize for Economic Science.

René Préval (René García Préval; 17 Jan 1943, Port-au-Prince, Haiti), Haitian politician; president from 2006.

André (George) Previn (6 Apr 1929, Berlin, Germany), German-born American pianist, composer, and conductor; music director of the Oslo Symphony Orchestra from 2002.

Prince (Prince Rogers Nelson; 7 Jun 1958, Minneapolis MN), American singer and songwriter.

Richard B. Priory (15 May 1946, Lakehurst NJ), American energy engineer, corporate executive, and CEO of Duke Energy from 1997.

Romano Prodi (9 Aug 1939, Scandiano, Italy), Italian politician and prime minister, 1996–98 and again from 2006.

E(dna) Annie Proulx (22 Aug 1935, Norwich CT), American writer whose darkly comic yet sad fiction is peopled with quirky, memorable individuals and unconventional families.

Stanley Ben Prusiner (28 May 1942, Des Moines IA), American biochemist who discovered the prion; recipient of the 1997 Nobel Prize for Physiology or Medicine.

Georgi Purvanov (28 Jun 1957, Kovachevtsi, Bulgaria), Bulgarian politician and president from 2002.

Vladimir (Vladimirovich) Putin (7 Oct 1952, Leningrad, USSR [now St. Petersburg, Russia]), Russian intelligence officer, politician, and president from 1999.

(Sayyid) Qabus ibn Sa'id (18 Nov 1940, Salalah, Oman), sultan of Oman from 1970.

Muammar al-Qaddafi (also spelled Muammar Khadafy, Moammar Gadhafi, or Mu'ammar al-Qadh-dhafi; spring 1942, near Surt, Libya), Libyan military leader and Arab statesman; de facto chief of state from 1969.

Dennis Quaid (9 Apr 1954, Houston TX), American film actor.

Thomas Quasthoff (9 Nov 1959, Hildesheim, Germany), German bass-baritone who overcame being severely disabled to become one of the world's preeminent classical music artists.

Queen Latifah (Dana Elaine Owens; 18 Mar 1970, Newark NJ), American rap musician, film actress, and TV personality.

Anna Quindlen (8 Jul 1953, Philadelphia PA), American political commentator and author.

Daniel Radcliffe (23 July 1989, London, England), British actor who played the title character in the *Harry Potter* series of films from 2001.

Paula Radcliffe (17 Dec 1973, Northwich, Cheshire, England), British long-distance runner.

Aishwarya Rai (1 Nov 1973, Mangalore, Karnataka state, India), Indian beauty queen and film actress.

Sam Raimi (Samuel M. Raimi; 23 Oct 1959, Franklin MI), American cult filmmaker who struck it big with the Spider-Man movies.

Franklin D. Raines (14 Jan 1949, Seattle WA), American corporate executive and CEO of Fannie Mae from 1999.

Konrad Raiser (25 Jan 1938, Magdeburg, Germany), German church official and general secretary of the World Council of Churches from 1993.

Bonnie Raitt (8 Nov 1949, Burbank CA), American blues and R&B singer and bottleneck guitarist.

Mahinda Rajapakse (18 Nov 1945, British Ceylon [now Sri Lanka]), Sri Lankan politician who was prime minister, 2004–05, and president from 2005.

Imomali Rakhmonov (5 Oct 1952, Dangara, Tadzhik

SSR, USSR [now Tajikistan]), Tajik politician and president from 1992.

Samuel Ramey (28 Mar 1942, Colby KS), American operatic bass.

José Ramos-Horta (26 Dec 1949, Dili, Portuguese Timor [now East Timor]), Timorese nationalist leader and prime minister from 2006; corecipient of the 1996 Nobel Peace Prize.

Rania, al-Abdullah (Rania al-Yaseen; 31 Aug 1970, Kuwait), Kuwaiti-born Jordanian royal, queen consort of King Abdullah II.

Ian Rankin (28 Apr 1960, Cardenden, Fife, Scotland), Scottish author, one of the top-selling crime writers in the UK and creator of Inspector John Rebus.

Anders Fogh Rasmussen (26 Jan 1953, Ginnerup, Denmark), Danish politician and prime minister from 2001.

Aleksei Ratmansky (1968, Leningrad, USSR [now St. Petersburg, Russia]), Russian dancer, choreographer, and director; artistic director of the Bolshoi Ballet from 2003.

Rodrigo de Rato y Figaredo (18 Mar 1949, Madrid, Spain), Spanish government and international official; managing director and chairman of the International Monetary Fund from 2004.

Sir Simon (Denis) Rattle (19 Jan 1955, Liverpool, England), British orchestra conductor; principal conductor and artistic director of the Berlin Philharmonic from the 2002–03 season.

Marc Ravalomanana (1949, near Atananarivo, French Madagascar), Malagasy politician and president of Madagascar from 2002.

Rachael (Domenica) Ray (25 Aug 1968, Cape Cod MA), American TV cook and cookbook author.

Lee R. Raymond (1938, Waterstown SD), American corporate executive; chairman and CEO of Exxon Mobil Corp. from 1994.

Giovanni Battista Cardinal Re (30 Jan 1934, Borno, Italy), Italian Roman Catholic churchman and official of the Roman Curia; cardinal from 2001.

Nancy Davis Reagan (Anne Frances Robbins; 6 Jul 1921, New York NY), American first lady; second wife and widow of Pres. Ronald Reagan.

Robert Redford (18 Aug 1937, Santa Monica CA), American film actor and director and founder of the Sundance Institute and Film Festival.

Lynn Redgrave (8 Mar 1943, London, England), British stage, screen, and TV actress.

Vanessa Redgrave (30 Jan 1937, London, England), British stage and screen actress and political activist.

Joshua Redman (1 Feb 1969, Berkeley CA), American jazz-saxophone player.

Sumner Redstone (Sumner Rothstein; 27 May 1923, Boston MA), American corporate executive; chairman of the board (from 1987) and CEO (from 1996) of Viacom Inc.

David Rees (1973?), American comic artist, creator (2001) of the topical, profane *Get Your War On* comic strip on the Internet.

Sir Martin J(ohn) Rees (23 Jun 1942, Shropshire, England), British astronomer royal whose controversial book *Our Final Century* (2003; published in the US as *Our Final Hour*) argued that the pace of technological change threatened to outstrip the ability of humans to control it.

Keanu (Charles) Reeves (2 Sep 1964, Beirut, Lebanon), American actor.

Harry Reid (2 Dec 1939, Searchlight NV), American Democratic politician, senator from Nevada (from 1987), Senate minority whip (1998–2005), and Democratic leader from 2005.

Tara Reid (8 Nov 1975, Wyckoff NJ), American film actress.

Rob Reiner (6 Mar 1947, Bronx NY), American actor, director, writer, and producer.

Fredrik Reinfeldt (John Fredrik Reinfeldt; 4 Aug 1965, Österhaninge, Sweden), Swedish politician (Moderate Party); prime minister of Sweden from 2006.

M(argaret) Jodi Rell (16 Jun 1946, Norfolk VA), American Republican politician and governor of Connecticut from 2004.

Tommy Remengesau, Jr. (1956), Palauan politician and president from 2001.

Edward Gene Rendell (5 Jan 1944, New York NY), American Democratic politician, mayor of Philadelphia, 1992–2000, and governor of Pennsylvania from 2003.

Ruth Rendell (Baroness Rendell of Babergh; pseudonym Barbara Vine; 17 Feb 1930, London, England), British mystery novelist and creator of Chief Inspector Wexford.

Yasmina Reza (1 May 1959, Paris, France), French playwright best known for her play *Art*.

Busta Rhymes (Trevor Smith, Jr.; 20 May 1972, Brooklyn NY), American rap performer.

Anne Rice (Howard Allen O'Brien; pseudonyms A.N. Roquelaure and Anne Rampling; 4 Oct 1941, New Orleans LA), American Gothic novelist known especially for her six-volume *Vampire Chronicles*.

Condoleezza Rice (14 Nov 1954, Birmingham AL), American academic and government official; national security adviser, 2001–05, and US secretary of state from 2005.

Adrienne (Cecile) Rich (16 May 1929, Baltimore MD), American poet, scholar, teacher, and critic.

Denise (Lee) Richards (17 Feb 1971, Downers Grove IL), American model and TV and film actress.

Keith Richards (18 Dec 1943, Dartford, Kent, England), British guitarist and singer with the Rolling Stones.

Maxwell Richards (1931, San Fernando, Trinidad), Trinidadian chemical engineer and university professor; president of Trinidad and Tobago from 2003.

Bill Richardson (15 Nov 1947, Pasadena CA), American government official; governor of New Mexico from 2003.

Lionel B. Richie, Jr. (20 Jun 1949, Tuskegee AL), American R&B songwriter and singer.

Nicole Richie (15 Sep 1981, Berkeley CA), American celebrity entertainer.

Gerhard Richter (9 Feb 1932, Dresden, Germany), German artist and cofounder of the movement known as Capitalist Realism, in which ordinary objects such as furniture and food, and sometimes the artists themselves, are depicted as art.

Kai-Uwe Ricke (Oct 1961, Krefeld, West Germany [now in Germany]), German corporate executive and CEO of Deutsche Telekom from 2002.

Sally K(risten) Ride (26 May 1951, Encino CA), American astronaut and astrophysicist who was the first American woman to fly in space (1983).

Robert R. Riley (3 Oct 1944, Ashland AL), American Republican politician and governor of Alabama from 2003.

LeAnn Rimes (28 Aug 1982, Jackson MS), American country-and-western singer.

Bill Ritter (August William Ritter, Jr.; 6 Sep 1956, Denver CO), American politician (Democrat); governor of Colorado from 2007.

Rivaldo (Vítor Borba Ferreira; 19 Apr 1972, Recife, Brazil), Brazilian association football (soccer) player.

Geraldo (Miguel) Rivera (4 Jul 1943, Brooklyn NY), American TV journalist and talk-show host.

Tim Robbins (16 Oct 1958, West Covina CA), American actor.

Cecil E(dward) Roberts, Jr. (31 Oct 1946, Kayford WV), American labor leader; president of the United Mine Workers of America from 1995.

John G(lover) Roberts (27 Jan 1955, Buffalo NY), American trial lawyer and federal appeals court judge; chief justice of the US from 2005.

Julia Roberts (Julie Fiona Roberts; 28 Oct 1967, Smyrna GA), American film actress.

Nora Roberts (Eleanor Marie Robertson; 10 Oct 1950, Silver Spring MD), American author of best-selling novels that blur the distinction between the romance, fantasy, and suspense genres.

Smokey Robinson (William Robinson, Jr.; 19 Feb 1940, Detroit MI), American R&B singer and song-writer.

Emily Robison (Emily Burns Erwin; 16 Aug 1972, Pittsfield MA), American country musician, a member of the Dixie Chicks.

Chris Rock (7 Feb 1966, Georgetown SC), American stand-up comedian and actor known for his brash style.

Kid Rock (Robert James Ritchie; 17 Jan 1971, Romeo MI), American rap-rock artist.

The Rock (Dwayne Douglas Johnson; 2 May 1972, Hayward CA), American professional wrestler turned actor.

Andy Roddick (30 Aug 1982, Omaha NE), American tennis player.

Alex Rodriguez (27 Jul 1975, New York NY), American baseball shortstop and third baseman.

Narciso Rodríguez (1961, New Jersey), American fashion designer.

Oscar Andrés Cardinal Rodríguez Maradiaga (29 Dec 1942, Tegucigalpa, Honduras), Honduran Roman Catholic churchman; archbishop of Tegucigalpa from 1993 and cardinal from 2001.

Robert G. Roeder (1942, Boonville IN), American bio-chemist; recipient of the 2003 Lasker Award for Basic Medical Research for his investigations into DNA/RNA transcription.

Jacques Rogge (2 May 1942, Ghent, Belgium), Belgian Olympic yachtsman, surgeon, and sports executive; president of the International Olympic Committee from 2001.

Roh Moo Hyun (6 Aug 1946, near Pusan, Korea [now in South Korea]), Korean politician; president of the Republic of Korea from 2003.

Sonny Rollins (Theodore Walter Rollins; 7 Sep 1930, Harlem, New York NY), American jazz tenor and soprano saxophonist.

Holmes Rolston III (19 Nov 1932, Staunton VA), American Presbyterian minister and environmental ethicist; founder of the journal *Environmental Ethics* (1979); recipient of the 2003 Templeton Prize.

Ray Romano (21 Dec 1957, Queens NY), American comic actor best known for the award-winning TV series *Everybody Loves Raymond* (1996–2005).

Mitt Romney (12 Mar 1947, Bloomfield MI), American businessman, sports executive, and Republican governor of Massachusetts, 2003–07.

Ronaldo (Ronaldo Luiz Nazario de Lima; 22 Sep 1976, Itaguai, Rio de Janeiro state, Brazil), Brazilian association football (soccer) player.

Andy Rooney (14 Jan 1919, Albany NY), American TV journalist.

Charlie Rose (5 Jan 1942, Henderson NC), American TV journalist and interviewer; host of *The Charlie Rose Show* since 1991.

Irwin A. Rose (16 Jul 1926, Brooklyn NY), American biochemist; corecipient of the 2004 Nobel Prize for Chemistry.

Roseanne (Roseanne Cherrie Barr; Roseanne Arnold; 3 Nov 1952, Salt Lake City UT), American TV, film, stage, and nightclub comedian and actress.

Wilbur Ross (28 Nov 1937, North Bergen NJ), American financier and turnaround specialist; chairman of International Steel Group, Inc.

Philip (Milton) Roth (19 Mar 1933, Newark NJ), American novelist and short-story writer whose works are characterized by an acute ear for dialogue, a concern with Jewish middle-class life, and the painful entanglements of sexual and familial love.

Mike Rounds (24 Oct 1954, Huron SD), American Republican politician and governor of South Dakota from 2003.

Karl Rove (25 Dec 1950, Denver CO), American right-wing political operative; chief strategist for Pres. George W. Bush and deputy chief of staff, 2005–07.

J.K. Rowling (Joanne Rowling; 31 Jul 1965, Chipping Sodbury, near Bristol, Gloucestershire, England), British author, creator of the *Harry Potter* series of novels about a young sorcerer in training.

Patrick Roy (5 Oct 1965, Quebec City, QC, Canada), Canadian ice-hockey goalie.

Donald (Henry) Rumsfeld (9 Jul 1932, Chicago IL), American government official who was US secretary of defense, 1975–77, and again 2001–06.

Erkki Ruoslahti (16 Feb 1940, Helsinki, Finland), Finnish-born American cell biologist and distinguished professor at the Burnham Institute, La Jolla CA; corecipient of the 2005 Japan Prize in Cell Biology.

Ed Ruscha (Edward Joseph Ruscha; 16 Dec 1937, Omaha NE), American artist known for his deadpan take on American pop culture.

Geoffrey Rush (6 Jul 1951, Toowoomba, QLD, Australia), Australian film actor.

(Ahmed) Salman Rushdie (19 Jun 1947, Bombay [now Mumbai], British India), Anglo-Indian novelist who was condemned to death by leading Iranian Muslim clerics in 1989 for allegedly having blasphemed Islam in his novel *The Satanic Verses* (1988).

Tim Russert (7 May 1950, Buffalo NY), American TV talk-show host and moderator of *Meet the Press* from 1991.

Patricia F(iorello) Russo (12 Jun 1952, Trenton NJ), American business executive and CEO of Lucent Technologies from 2002.

Burt Rutan (Elbert L. Rutan; 17 Jun 1943, Portland OR), American test pilot, aerospace engineer, and designer of specialized aircraft.

John A. Ruthven (1927, Cincinnati OH), American wildlife artist.

John Rutter (24 Sep 1945, London, England), British composer and conductor; founder (1981) and leader of the Cambridge Singers.

Kay Ryan (11 Sep 1945, San Jose CA), American poet.

Meg Ryan (Margaret Mary Emily Anne Hyra; 19 Nov 1961, Fairfield CT), American film star.

Winona Ryder (Winona Laura Horowitz; 29 Oct 1971, Winona MN), American film actress.

Mikheil Saakashvili (21 Dec 1967, Tbilisi, USSR [now in Georgia]), Georgian politician; president from 2004.

Charles Saatchi (9 Jun 1943, Baghdad, Iraq), Iraqi-born British advertising executive; cofounder of the Saatchi & Saatchi firm in London; art collector and patron and owner of the Saatchi Gallery.

Sabah al-Ahmad al-Jabir Al Sabah (1929?, Kuwait), Kuwaiti sheikh; emir from 2006.

Antonio Saca (Antonio Elías Saca González; 9 Mar 1965, Usulután, El Salvador), Salvadoran communications executive and politician; president of El Salvador from 2004.

Jeffrey D. Sachs (Jeffrey David Sachs; 5 Nov 1954, Detroit MI), American economist.

Oliver (Wolf) Sacks (9 Jul 1933, London, England), British-born American neurologist and best-selling author.

Sade (Helen Folasade Adu; 16 Jan 1959, Ibadan, Nigeria), Nigerian-born British singer and songwriter.

Muqtada al-Sadr (1974?, Baghdad, Iraq), Iraqi Muslim cleric, a charismatic figure in the anti-American and anti-Western insurrection in Iraq following the US-led occupation of March 2003.

Keith J. Sainsbury (22 Feb 1951, Christchurch, NZ), New Zealand–born ecologist who researched marine-shelf ecosystems and their sustainable use; recipient of a Japan Prize in 2004.

Yves Saint Laurent (Yves-Henri-Donat-Mathieu Saint Laurent; 1 Aug 1936, Oran, Algeria), French fashion designer noted for his popularization of women's trousers for all occasions.

Jamie Salé (21 Apr 1977, Calgary, AB, Canada), Canadian pairs figure skater (with David Pelletier).

Sebastião (Ribeiro) Salgado (8 Feb 1944, Aimorés, Minas Gerais state, Brazil), Brazilian photographer whose work powerfully expresses the suffering of the homeless and downtrodden.

'Ali 'Abdallah Salih (21 Mar 1942, Beit al-Ahmar, Yemen), Yemeni politician; president of Yemen (San'a), 1978–90, and of the unified Yemen thereafter.

Esa-Pekka Salonen (30 Jun 1958, Helsinki, Finland), Finnish conductor and musical director of the Los Angeles Philharmonic from 1992.

Ahmed Abdallah Sambi (5 Jun 1958, Mutsamudu, Anjouan, French Comoro Islands), Comoran Muslim religious leader and president from 2006.

Ivo Sanader (8 Jun 1953, Split, Croatia, Yugoslavia), Croatian scholar, politician, and prime minister from 2003.

Pedro A. Sánchez (1940, Havana, Cuba), Cuban-born American soil scientist; recipient of the 2002 World Food Prize.

Adam Sandler (9 Sep 1966, Brooklyn NY), American comic actor.

Mark Sanford (15 Jan 1960, Fort Lauderdale FL), American Republican politician and governor of South Carolina from 2003.

Carlos Santana (20 Jul 1947, Autlán de Navarro, Mexico), Mexican-born guitarist and bandleader.

Alejandro Sanz (Alejandro Sánchez Pizarro; 18 Dec 1968, Madrid, Spain), Spanish pop singer-songwriter and flamenco-pop artist.

Cristina Saralegui (29 Jan 1948, Havana, Cuba), Cuban-born American Spanish-language TV talk-show host.

José Saramago (16 Nov 1922, Azinhaga, Portugal), Portuguese novelist and man of letters; recipient of the 1998 Nobel Prize for Literature.

Susan Sarandon (Susan Abigail Tomalin; 4 Oct 1946, New York NY), American film actress.

Serzh Sarkisyan (30 Jun 1954, Stepanakert, Armenia [now Xankändi, Azerbaijan]), Armenian politician; prime minister from 2007.

Nicolas Sarkozy (Nicolas Paul-Stéphane Sarközy de Nagy-Bocsa; 28 Jan 1955, Paris, France), French conservative politician; interior minister from 2005 and president from 2007.

Mikio Sasaki (1937?), Japanese corporate executive; president and CEO of Mitsubishi Motors Corp. from 1998.

Denis Sassou-Nguesso (1943, Edou, French Equatorial Africa [now in the Republic of the Congo]), Congolese politician and president of the Republic of the Congo, 1979–92 and again from 1997.

Jennifer Saunders (6 Jul 1958, Sleaford, Lincolnshire, England), British TV actress and comedienne.

Michael Savage (Michael Alan Weiner; 31 Mar 1942, Bronx NY), American nutrition expert.

Diane K. Sawyer (Lila Sawyer; 22 Dec 1945, Glasgow KY), American TV journalist.

Antonin Scalia (11 Mar 1936, Trenton NJ), American jurist and associate justice of the US Supreme Court from 1986.

Dame Marjorie Scardino (Marjorie Morris; 25 Jan 1947, Flagstaff AZ), American-born British CEO (from 1997) of the media firm Pearson PLC, which owns the *Financial Times* newspaper among others.

Thomas C. Schelling (Thomas Crombie Schelling; 14 Apr 1921, Oakland CA), American economist; corecipient of the 2005 Nobel Prize for Economic Sciences.

Claudia Schiffer (25 Aug 1970, Düsseldorf, West Germany [now in Germany]), German fashion model.

Eric E. Schmidt (1955?), American computer scientist and corporate executive; CTO of Sun Microsystems, Inc., chairman and CEO of Novell, Inc., and chairman and CEO of Google, Inc., from 2001.

Christoph Cardinal Schönborn (22 Jan 1945, Skalsko, Czechoslovakia [now in the Czech Republic]), Austrian Roman Catholic churchman, archbishop of Vienna from 1995, bishop of Austria for the Faithful of Eastern Rite (Byzantine) from 1995, and cardinal from 1998.

Peter J. Schoomaker (12 Feb 1946, Detroit MI), American military officer; chief of staff of the US Army from 2003.

Daniel Schorr (31 Aug 1916, New York NY), American TV and radio journalist and political commentator.

Richard Royce Schrock (4 Jan 1945, Berne IN), American chemist; corecipient of the 2005 Nobel Prize for Chemistry for the development of the metathesis method in organic synthesis.

Dieter Schulte (13 Jan 1940, Duisberg, Germany), German labor leader and head of the German Trade Union Federation from 1994.

Henning Schulte-Noelle (26 Aug 1942, Essen, Germany), German corporate executive and CEO of Allianz AG from 1991.

Howard Schultz (19 Jul 1953, Brooklyn NY), American businessman, CEO of Starbucks Corp. from 1987, and principal owner of the Seattle SuperSonics professional basketball team from 2001.

Michael Schumacher (3 Jan 1969, Hürth-Hermülheim, West Germany [now in Germany]), German Formula 1 race-car driver who dominated Grand Prix racing in the early 2000s.

Wolfgang Schüssel (7 Jun 1945, Vienna, Austria), Austrian politician and chancellor from 2000.

Susan Schwab (Susan Carol Schwab; 23 Mar 1955, Washington DC), American trade official; US trade representative from 2006.

Arnold (Alois) Schwarzenegger (30 Jul 1947, Thal bei Graz, Austria), Austrian-born American bodybuilder, Hollywood film star, and governor of California from 2003.

Christian Schwarz-Schilling (19 Nov 1930, Innsbruck, Austria), German politician and diplomat; International High Representative in Bosnia and Herzegovina from 2006.

Brian Schweitzer (4 Sep 1955, Havre MT), American politician and Democratic governor of Montana from 2005.

David Schwimmer (2 Nov 1966, Astoria, Queens NY), American TV and film actor.

John Scofield (26 Dec 1951, Dayton OH), American jazz electric guitarist, composer, and bandleader.

Martin Scorsese (17 Nov 1942, Flushing, Long Island NY), American film director, writer, and producer known for harsh, violent depictions.

H. Lee Scott, Jr. (1949?, Joplin MO), American executive; president and CEO of Wal-Mart Stores from 2000.

Sir Ridley Scott (30 Nov 1937, South Shields, Durham, England), British film director and producer known for visual style and rich details.

Kristin Scott Thomas (24 May 1960, Redruth, Cornwall, England), British actress.

Ludwig Scotty, Nauruan politician and president, 2003 and again from 2004.

Vincent J. Scully, Jr. (New Haven CT), American architectural historian and critic.

Seal (Sealhenry Olusegun Olumide Samuel; 19 Feb 1963, Kilburn, London, England), British soul singer.

Son Seals (13 Aug 1942, Osceola AR), American blues singer.

John (Rogers) Searle (31 Jul 1932, Denver CO), American philosopher of language.

Kathleen Sebelius (15 May 1948, Cincinnati OH), American Democratic politician and governor of Kansas from 2003.

Alice Sebold (1963, Madison WI), American author.

David Sedaris (26 Dec 1956, Johnson City NY), American writer and humorist.

Ivan G. Seidenberg (1947?, Bronx NY), American corporate executive and CEO of Verizon Communications from 2002.

Jerry Seinfeld (29 Apr 1954, Brooklyn NY), American comic and TV personality made famous by his series *Seinfeld* (1990–98).

Bud Selig (Allan H. Selig; 30 Jul 1934, Milwaukee WI), American sports executive; Major League Baseball commissioner from 1998 (and de facto commissioner for six years before that).

Tom Selleck (29 Jan 1945, Detroit MI), American film and TV actor.

Phil Selway (23 May 1967, Hemingford Grey, Cambridgeshire, England), British rock drummer (of Radiohead).

Amartya (Kumar) Sen (3 Nov 1933, Santiniketan, Bengal state, British India), Indian economist; recipient of the 1998 Nobel Memorial Prize for Economic Science for his contributions to welfare economics.

Senait (Senait G. Mehari; 3 Dec 1976, Asmara, Ethiopia [now Eritrea]), Eritrean-born German singer who was a child soldier during the Eritrean war of independence before becoming a pop star in Germany.

Paul Sereno (11 Oct 1957, Aurora IL), American paleontologist credited with a number of significant dinosaur finds.

Jean-Pierre Serre (15 Sep 1926, Bages, France), French mathematician, a specialist in algebraic topology; recipient of the 1954 Fields Medal and the first winner (2003) of the Abel Prize.

Vikram Seth (20 Jun 1952, Calcutta [now Kolkata], India), Indian poet, novelist, and travel writer.

Ahmed Necdet Sezer (13 Sep 1941, Ayfon, Turkey), Turkish politician and president from 2000.

Nasrallah Pierre Cardinal Sfeir (Nasrallah Boutros Pierre Sfeir; 15 May 1920, Reyfoun, Lebanon), Lebanese (Maronite Catholic) Patriarch of Antioch and All the East and Roman Catholic cardinal from 1994.

Shaggy (Orville Richard Burrell; 22 Oct 1968, Rae Town, Kingston, Jamaica), Jamaican reggae artist.

Gil Shaham (19 Feb 1971, Champaign-Urbana IL), American violinist.

Shakira (Shakira Isabel Mebarak Ripoll; 2 Feb 1977, Barranquilla, Colombia), Colombian-born pop singer.

Tony Shalhoub (9 Oct 1953, Green Bay WI), American TV and film actor best known for his work in the detective show *Monk*, from 2002.

Gene Shalit (25 Mar 1932, New York NY), American film critic.

John Patrick Shanley (1950, Bronx NY), American screenwriter and playwright.

Mariya Sharapova (19 Apr 1987, Nyagan, USSR [now in Russia]), Russian tennis player.

Ariel Sharon (Ariel Sheinerman; 26 Feb 1928, Kefar Malal, Palestine [now in Israel]), Israeli politician and prime minister, 2001–06.

Al Sharpton (3 Oct 1954, New York NY), American Democratic political activist, civil rights leader, and presidential candidate.

William Shatner (22 Mar 1931, Montreal, QC, Canada), Canadian TV actor, author, and personality.

Charlie Sheen (Carlos Irwin Estevez; 3 Sep 1965, New York NY), American film and TV actor.

Martin Sheen (Ramon Estevez; 3 Aug 1940, Dayton OH), American stage, film, and TV actor.

Judith Sheindlin (21 Oct 1942, Brooklyn NY), American TV judge (*Judge Judy*).

Sam Shepard (Samuel Shepard Rogers; 5 Nov 1943, Fort Sheridan IL), American playwright and actor whose plays adroitly blend images of the American West, Pop motifs, science fiction, and other elements of popular and youth culture.

Cindy Sherman (Cynthia Morris Sherman; 19 Jan 1954, Glen Ridge NJ), American photographer known for her elaborately disguised self-portraits that comment on social role-playing and sexual stereotypes.

Vandana Shiva (1952, Dehra Dun, Uttar Pradesh [now in Uttaranchal] state, India), Indian biologist and social activist against the "biological theft" of the resources of poor countries by the richer ones; director of the Research Foundation on Science, Technology, and Ecology in India.

Martin Short (26 Mar 1950, Hamilton, ON, Canada), Canadian actor and comedian.

Will Shortz (1952), American "enigmatologist" and "puzzlemaster"; crossword-puzzle editor at the *New York Times*.

Etsuhiko Shoyama (c. 1937), Japanese corporate executive and CEO of Hitachi, Ltd., from 1999.

Maria (Owings) Shriver (6 Nov 1955, Chicago IL), American TV journalist and wife of actor and California governor Arnold Schwarzenegger.

M. Night Shyamalan (6 Aug 1970, Pondicherry, India), Indian-born American film director and screenwriter.

John W. Sidgmore (1950?), American corporate executive; CEO of WorldCom, Inc., from 2002.

Thomas M. Siebel (February 1953, Chicago IL), American corporate executive, the founder and CEO of Siebel Systems from 1993.

Alicia Silverstone (4 Oct 1976, San Francisco CA), American film and TV actress.

Silvia (Silvia Renate Sommerlath; 23 Dec 1943, Heidelberg, Germany), Swedish royal and social activist, queen consort of King Carl XVI Gustaf (married 19 Jun 1976).

Charles Simic (9 May 1938, Belgrade, Yugoslavia [now in Serbia]), Yugoslav-born American poet who evoked his Eastern European heritage and his childhood experiences during World War II to comment on the dearth of spirituality in contemporary life.

Russell Simmons ("Rush"; 4 Oct 1957, Queens NY), American hip-hop impresario and cofounder of Def Jam Records.

Paul Simon (13 Oct 1941, Newark NJ), American singer and songwriter known first for his folk-rock albums with partner Art Garfunkel and later for his innovative solo work.

Ashlee Simpson (3 Oct 1984, Dallas TX), American singer and TV and film actress, the younger sister of Jessica Simpson.

Jessica Simpson (10 Jul 1980, Dallas TX), American dance-pop singer.

Portia (Lucretia) Simpson Miller (12 Dec 1945, Wood Hall, St. Catherine parish, Jamaica), Jamaican politician; prime minister, 2006–07 (the country's first female prime minister).

Manmohan Singh (26 Sep 1932, Gah, Punjab, British India [now in Pakistan]), Indian Sikh economist, professor, and government official; prime minister from 2004.

Fouad Siniora (1943, Sidon, Lebanon), Lebanese banker and Sunni politician; prime minister from 2005.

Gary Sinise (17 Mar 1955, Blue Island IL), American TV and film actor and director.

(Sayyid) Ali (Hussaini) al-Sistani (4 Aug 1930?, near Meshed, Iran), Iranian Shi'ite Muslim cleric, a grand ayatollah, and one of the top two religious and legal authorities in Shi'i Islam.

Ricky Skaggs (18 Jul 1954, Cordell KY), American bluegrass and country musician.

Antonio Skármeta (7 Nov 1940, Antofagasta, Chile), Chilean novelist and screenwriter.

Jeffrey S. Skoll (16 Jan 1965, Montreal, QC, Canada), Canadian entrepreneur, a cofounder of eBay and, from 1999, the president of the philanthropic Skoll Foundation.

Leonard (Edward) Slatkin (1 Sep 1944, Los Angeles CA), American conductor; music director of the National Symphony Orchestra from 1996.

Carlos Slim Helú (1940, Mexico?), Mexican investor; head of Grupo Carso, SA de CV, and longtime owner of the national telephone monopoly, Teléfonos de México (Telmex).

Irina Slutskaya (9 Feb 1979, Moscow, USSR [now in Russia]), Russian figure skater.

Lawrence M. Small (14 Sep 1941, New York NY), American businessman, president and COO of Fannie Mae, and secretary of the Smithsonian Institution from 2000.

Tavis Smiley (13 Sep 1964, Gulfport MS), American advocacy journalist on radio and TV.

Marc (Kelly) Smith ("Slampapi"; 195?, Chicago IL), American poet and originator of the "poetry slam"—performance-poetry competition—in the mid-1980s.

Michael W. Smith (7 Oct 1957, Kenova WV), American Christian singer.

Patti Smith (30 Dec 1946, Chicago IL), American musician, poet, and visual artist.

Vernon L. Smith (1 Jan 1927, Wichita KS), American economist; corecipient of the 2002 Nobel Memorial Prize for Economic Science.

Will Smith (Willard Christopher Smith, Jr.; 25 Sep 1968, Philadelphia PA), American rapper and actor on TV and in films.

Zadie Smith (Sadie Smith; 1975, Willesden Green, London, England), British novelist whose work is acclaimed for its eccentric characters, savvy humor, and snappy dialogue.

Jimmy Smits (9 Jul 1955, Brooklyn NY), American TV and film actor.

George F. Smoot (George Fitzgerald Smoot III; 20 Feb 1945, Yukon FL), American astrophysicist; corecipient of the 2006 Nobel Prize for Physics for work concerning cosmic background radiation.

Wesley Snipes (31 Jul 1962, Orlando FL), American film actor, principally in action movies.

Snoop Dogg (Calvin Broadus; 20 Oct 1972, Long Beach CA), American gangsta rap musician.

Gary (Sherman) Snyder (8 May 1930, San Francisco CA), American poet early identified with the Beat movement and a spokesman for the concerns of communal living and ecological activism.

Solomon Halbert Snyder (26 Dec 1938, Washington DC), American neuroscientist who discovered opiate receptors in the brain and determined that gases can serve as neural messengers.

José Sócrates (Carvalho Pinto de Sousa) (6 Sep 1957, Vilar de Maçada, Portugal), Portuguese civil engineer and Socialist politician; prime minister from 2005.

Angelo Cardinal Sodano (23 Nov 1927, Isola d'Asto, Italy), Italian Roman Catholic churchman who became secretary of state of the Vatican in 1991 and was elevated to cardinal in the same year.

Steven Soderbergh (14 Jan 1963, Atlanta GA), American film director.

Sofia (Princess Sophie of Greece; Sofia de Grecia y Hannover; 2 Nov 1938, Athens, Greece), Spanish royal, queen consort of King Juan Carlos I of Spain (married 12 May 1962).

Javier Solana Madariaga (14 Jul 1942, Madrid, Spain), Spanish statesman, NATO secretary-general, 1995–99, and secretary-general of the Council of the European Union from 1999.

Susan Solomon (19 Jan 1956, Chicago IL), American photochemist specializing in the chemistry of the stratosphere, especially the science of the Antarctic ozone hole.

László Sólyom (3 Jan 1942, Pécs, Hungary), Hungarian jurist; president from 2005.

Sir Michael Somare (9 Apr 1936, Rabaul, Australian-mandated New Guinea [now Papua New Guinea]), politician who was the first prime minister of independent Papua New Guinea, 1975–80, served a second time, 1982–85, and again from 2002.

Stephen (Joshua) Sondheim (22 Mar 1930, New York NY), American composer and lyricist for musical theater.

Sonja (Sonja Haraldsen; 4 Jul 1937, Oslo, Norway), Norwegian royal, queen consort of King Harald V (married 29 Aug 1968).

Sophie, countess of Wessex (Sophie Helen Rhys-Jones; 20 Jan 1965, Oxford, England), British royal, the wife of Prince Edward, earl of Wessex.

Annika Sörenstam (9 Oct 1970, Stockholm, Sweden), Swedish golfer.

Aaron Sorkin (9 Jun 1961, Scarsdale NY), American screenwriter, playwright, and TV producer.

Guillaume Soro (8 May 1972, Kofiplé, Côte d'Ivoire), Ivorian politician; prime minister from 2007.

Mira Sorvino (28 Sep 1967, Tenafly NJ), American film actress.

Sammy Sosa (Samuel Sosa Peralta; 12 Nov 1968, San Pedro de Macorís, Dominican Republic), Dominican baseball outfielder for the Texas Rangers.

David H(ackett) Souter (17 Sep 1939, Melrose MA),

American jurist and associate justice of the US Supreme Court from 1990.

Wole Soyinka (Akinwande Oluwole Soyinka; 13 Jul 1934, Abeokuta, Nigeria), Nigerian playwright, poet, novelist, and critic; recipient of the 1986 Nobel Prize for Literature.

Kevin Spacey (Kevin Matthew Fowler; 26 Jul 1959, South Orange NJ), American stage and film actor.

James (Todd) Spader (7 Feb 1960, Boston MA), American film and TV actor.

Nicholas Sparks (31 Dec 1965, Omaha NE), American author of best-selling novels.

Britney (Jean) Spears (2 Dec 1981, Kentwood LA), American pop singer and celebrity.

Margaret Spellings (30 Nov 1957, Michigan), American political adviser, education expert, and US secretary of education from 2005.

Sir Baldwin Spencer (8 Oct 1948), West Indian politician and prime minister of Antigua and Barbuda from 2004.

Steven Spielberg (18 Dec 1947, Cincinnati OH), American film director and producer, one of the foremost of all time.

Nikola Spiric (4 Sep 1956, Drvar, Yugoslavia [now in Bosnia and Herzegovina]), Bosnia and Herzegovinian politician; chairman of the Council of Ministers (prime minister) from 2007.

Eliot Spitzer (10 Jun 1959, Riverdale, Bronx NY), American attorney and Democratic politician; governor of New York from 2007.

Jerry Springer (Gerald N. Springer; 13 Feb 1944, London, England), American TV personality and politician.

Timothy A. Springer (23 Feb 1948, Fort Benning GA), American pathologist.

Bruce Springsteen ("The Boss"; 23 Sep 1949, Freehold NJ), American rock singer and songwriter who became the archetypal rock performer of the 1970s and '80s.

Sylvester Stallone (Michael Sylvester Enzio Stallone; "Sly"; 6 Jul 1946, New York NY), American film actor and director best known for macho acting roles.

Sergey Stanishev (Sergey Dmitriyevich Stanishev; 5 May 1966, Kherson, USSR [now in Ukraine]), Bulgarian politician (Socialist); prime minister from 2005.

Mavis Staples (1940, Chicago IL), American gospel vocalist, the lead singer of the Staples Singers.

Danielle Steel (Danielle Fernande Schuelein-Steel; 14 Aug 1947, New York NY), American romance novelist.

Shelby Steele (1 Jan 1946, Chicago IL), American critic and scholar of race issues who has opposed quota-based affirmative action.

Gwen Stefani (3 Oct 1969, Fullerton CA), American rock vocalist who led the group No Doubt from 1987 and established herself as a successful solo artist.

Frank-Walter Steinmeier (5 Jan 1956, Detmold, Germany), German government official; foreign minister of Germany from 2005.

Frank P(hilip) Stella (12 May 1936, Malden MA), American painter, a leading figure in the Minimal art movement, known for paintings that are austere yet monumental in the simplicity of their design.

Stephanie (Stéphanie Marie Elizabeth Grimaldi; 1 Feb 1965, Monaco), Monegasque princess, the youngest child of Prince Rainier III and Grace Kelly.

George Stephanopoulos (10 Feb 1961, Fall River MA), American journalist, political commentator, and presidential adviser.

Stéphanos II (Amba Andraos Ghattas; Stéphanos Cardinal Ghattas; 16 Jan 1920, Cheikh Zein-el-Dine, Egypt), Egyptian churchman, patriarch of Alexandria of the Coptics from 1986; Roman Catholic cardinal from 2001.

Howard Stern (12 Jan 1954, Roosevelt NY), American radio and TV "shock jock," actor, and author.

John Paul Stevens (20 Apr 1920, Chicago IL), American jurist; associate justice of the US Supreme Court from 1975.

Ted Stevens (18 Nov 1923, Indianapolis IN), American Republican politician, senator from Alaska, and president pro tempore of the Senate, 2003–2007.

Jon Stewart (Jonathan Stewart Leibowitz; 28 Nov 1962, New York NY), American actor, writer, and comedian; anchor of TV's *The Daily Show with Jon Stewart* from 1999.

Martha Stewart (Martha Helen Kostyra; 3 Aug 1941, Nutley NJ), American homemaking adviser, TV personality, and entrepreneur.

Rod(erick) (David) Stewart (10 Jan 1945, London, England), British singer whose soulful, raspy voice has graced rock and pop hits since the late 1960s.

Joseph E. Stiglitz (9 Feb 1943, Gary IN), American economist; corecipient of the 2001 Nobel Memorial Prize for Economic Science.

Ben Stiller (30 Nov 1965, New York NY), American comedian, actor, and film director.

Sting (Gordon Matthew Sumner; 2 Oct 1951, Wallsend, Newcastle upon Tyne, England), British musician, singer, songwriter, and actor.

Jens Stoltenberg (16 Mar 1959, Oslo, Norway), Norwegian economist, politician (Norwegian Labor Party), and prime minister, 2000–01 and again from 2005.

Joss Stone (Joscelyn Eve Stoker; 11 Apr 1987, Dover, Kent, England), English soul singer.

Matt Stone (26 May 1971, Houston TX), American cocreator (with Trey Parker) of *South Park*, an animated TV show.

Oliver (William) Stone (15 Sep 1946, New York NY), American director, writer, and producer of films with often politically controversial content.

Sharon (Vonne) Stone (10 Mar 1958, Meadville PA), American fashion model and film actress.

Sir Tom Stoppard (Tomas Straussler; 3 Jul 1937, Zlin, Czechoslovakia [now in the Czech Republic]), British playwright and screenwriter whose work is marked by verbal brilliance, ingenious action, and structural dexterity.

Mark Strand (11 Apr 1934, Summerside, PE, Canada), Canadian writer whose poetry, noted for its surreal quality, explores the boundaries of the self and the external world.

Meryl Streep (Mary Louise Streep; 22 Jun 1949, Summit NJ), American film actress.

John F. Street (1943, Norristown PA), American Democratic politician; mayor of Philadelphia from 2000.

Barbra Streisand (Barbara Joan Streisand; 24 Apr 1942, Brooklyn NY), American singer, actress, and film director.

Ted Strickland (4 Aug 1941, Lucasville OH), American politician (Democrat); governor of Ohio from 2007.

Sir Howard Stringer (19 Feb 1942, Cardiff, Wales), Welsh-born business executive; chairman and CEO of Sony Corp. from 2005.

Susan Stroman (17 Oct 1954, Wilmington DE), American theater director.

(Christopher) Ruben Studdard (12 Sep 1978, Frankfurt am Main, West Germany [now in Germany]), American singer.

Zeljko Sturanovic (31 Jan 1960, Niksic, Yugoslavia [now in Montenegro]), Montenegrin politician; prime minister from 2006.

Su Tseng-chang (28 Jul 1947, Ping-Tung, China [now

in Taiwan]), Taiwanese politician; prime minister, 2006–07.

Raman Sukumar (3 Apr 1955, Madras [now Chennai], India), Indian animal ecologist who studies Asian elephants in the wild in an effort to preserve the species.

John E. Sulston (27 Mar 1942, Cambridge, England), British cell biologist; corecipient of the 2002 Nobel Prize for Physiology or Medicine.

Arthur Ochs Sulzberger, Jr. (22 Sep 1951, Mt. Kisco NY), American newspaper executive, publisher of the *New York Times* from 1992 and CEO from 1997.

Pat Summitt (Patricia Head; 14 Jun 1952, Henrietta TN), American basketball coach; longtime coach of the University of Tennessee Lady Volunteers teams and the winningest coach in Division I basketball.

Surayud Chulanont (28 Aug 1943, Phetchaburi province, Thailand), Thai politician and prime minister from 2006.

Kiefer Sutherland (William Frederick Dempsey George Sutherland; 21 Dec 1966, London, England), Canadian film and TV actor.

Ichiro Suzuki (22 Oct 1973, Kasugai, Aichi prefecture, Japan), Japanese baseball player, right fielder for the American League Seattle Mariners.

Hilary Swank (30 Jul 1974, Lincoln NE), American film actress.

John J. Sweeney (5 May 1934, New York NY), American labor leader and president of the AFL-CIO from 1995.

Azadeh Tabazadeh (1965?, Iran), Iranian-born American atmospheric scientist whose work was instrumental in proving that naturally produced materials cannot be responsible for the degradation of the Earth's ozone layer.

Keiji Tachikawa (27 May 1939, Ogaki, Gifu prefecture, Japan), Japanese communications executive; president of DoCoMo, a wireless provider.

Paul Tagliabue (24 Nov 1940, Jersey City NJ), American sports executive and commissioner of the National Football League, 1989–2006.

Masatoshi Takeichi (27 Nov 1943, Nagoya, Japan), Japanese developmental biologist, professor, and director of the RIKEN Center for Developmental Biology; corecipient of the 2005 Japan Prize in Cell Biology.

Jalal Talabani (1933, Kalkan, Iraq), Iraqi Kurdish politician who created (1976) and led the Patriotic Union of Kurdistan and was the first democratically elected president of Iraq, from 2005.

Mehmet Ali Talat (6 Jul 1952, Girne, Cyprus), Turkish Cypriot politician, prime minister of the Turkish Republic of Northern Cyprus, 2004–05, and president from 2005.

Koichi Tanaka (3 Aug 1959, Toyama, Toyama prefecture, Japan), Japanese chemist; corecipient of the 2002 Nobel Prize for Chemistry.

Mamadou Tandja (1938), Nigerois politician and president of Niger from 1999.

Quentin (Jerome) Tarantino (27 Mar 1963, Knoxville TN), American film director.

Calin Popescu Tariceanu (14 Jan 1952), Romanian industrial engineer, politician, and prime minister from 2004.

Vasile Tarlev (9 Oct 1963, Bascalia, Moldavian SSR, USSR [now Moldova]), Moldovan politician and prime minister from 2001.

Audrey Tautou (9 Aug 1978, Beaumont, France), French film actress.

Sir John Tavener (28 Jan 1944, London, England), British composer whose works were inspired by sacred and spiritual texts and drew from Russian, Byzantine, and Greek influences.

Charles (McArthur Ghankay) Taylor (27 Jan 1948, Athington, Liberia), Liberian coup leader and president of Liberia from 1997 until 2003, when he stepped down and went into exile.

Elizabeth Taylor (27 Feb 1932, London, England), American film actress of great distinction noted for emotionally volatile characters.

Studs Terkel (Louis Terkel; 16 May 1912, New York NY), American author, radio host, and oral historian.

Adnan Terzic (1960, Zagreb, Croatia, Yugoslavia [now in Croatia]), Bosnian and Herzegovinian politician and chairman of the Council of Ministers (prime minister), 2002–07.

Dionigi Cardinal Tettamanzi (14 Mar 1934, Renate, Italy), Italian Roman Catholic churchman; archbishop of Milan from 2002 and cardinal from 1998.

Bal (Keshav) Thackeray (23 Jan 1927), Indian political cartoonist, newspaper publisher, and politician; founder (1966) and president of the ultra-Hindu-nationalist Shivsena party.

John A. Thain (1955?), American financial official; CEO of the New York Stock Exchange from 2004.

Hamad ibn Khalifah al-Thani (1950, Doha, Qatar), Qatari sheikh; emir from 1995.

Twyla Tharp (1 Jul 1941, Portland IN), American dancer, director, and choreographer noted for her innovation and her humor.

Charlize Theron (7 Aug 1975, Benoni, South Africa), South African actress.

Thich Nhat Hanh (1926, central Vietnam), Vietnamese Buddhist monk, pacifist, and teacher.

Clarence Thomas (23 Jun 1948, Pinpoint community, near Savannah GA), American jurist; associate justice of the US Supreme Court from 1991.

Michael Tilson Thomas (21 Dec 1944, Hollywood CA), American conductor and composer; music director of the San Francisco Symphony from 1995.

Emma Thompson (15 Apr 1959, London, England), British film actress known especially for serious dramatic roles and period pieces.

Jenny Thompson (26 Feb 1973, Danvers MA), American swimmer.

James Thomson (20 Dec 1958, Chicago IL), American cell biologist and stem-cell researcher, the first person to isolate stem cells from human embryos.

Robert Thomson (11 Mar 1961, Echuca, VIC, Australia), Australian journalist; editor of *The Times* of London from 2002.

Billy Bob Thornton (4 Aug 1955, Hot Springs AR), American director and actor.

Ian Thorpe ("The Thorpedo"; 13 Oct 1982, Sydney, NSW, Australia), Australian swimmer.

Uma (Karuna) Thurman (29 Apr 1970, Boston MA), American film actress often cast in sultry roles.

Justin (Randall) Timberlake (31 Jan 1981, Memphis TN), American singer, a member of the group *NSYNC and, after 2001, a solo artist.

Claire Tomalin (Claire Delavenay; 20 Jun 1933, London, England), English biographer and journalist.

Anote Tong (1952), Kiribati politician and president from 2003.

Bamir Topi (24 Apr 1957, Tiranë, Albania), Albanian biologist and politician; president from 2007.

Mirek Topolánek (15 May 1956, Vsetin, Moravia, Czechoslovakia [now in Czech Republic]), Czech industrial engineer and businessman, politician, and prime minister of the Czech Republic from 2006.

Martín Torrijos Espino (18 Jul 1963, Panama City, Panama), Panamanian politician and president from 2004.

Linus (Benedict) Torvalds (28 Dec 1969, Helsinki,

Finland), Finnish-born computer scientist who developed the Linux operating system.

Amadou Toumani Touré (4 Nov 1948, Mpoti, French Sudan [now in Mali]), Malian politician and president, 1991–92 and again from 2002.

Randy Travis (Randy Traywick; 4 May 1959, Marshville NC), American country-and-western singer, songwriter, and actor.

John (Joseph) Travolta (18 Feb 1955, Englewood NJ), American actor known for TV roles and trendsetting films.

Jean-Claude Trichet (20 Dec 1942, Lyons, France), French banker, two-term governor of the Banque de France, and president of the European Central Bank from 2003.

Calvin Trillin (5 Dec 1935, Kansas City MO), American author, commentator, and occasional poet.

(William) David Trimble (15 Oct 1944, Belfast, Northern Ireland), Northern Irish politician and first minister of Northern Ireland, 1998–2002; corecipient of the 1998 Nobel Prize for Peace.

Travis Tritt (9 Feb 1963, Marietta GA), American country-and-western singer who found great success from 1990 onward with a blues- and rock-tinged style.

Garry Trudeau (21 Jul 1948, New York NY), American cartoonist, creator of the durable *Doonesbury* syndicated comic strip.

Donald (John) Trump (14 Jun 1946, New York NY), American real-estate developer known for his high-profile real-estate developments; he also starred in a reality-TV series, *The Apprentice*, from 2004.

Kostya Tszyu (Konstantin Tszyu; "The Thunder from Down Under"; 19 Sep 1969, Serov, USSR [now in Russia]), Russian-born Australian boxer, the undisputed junior welterweight (super-lightweight) champion from 2001.

Togiola Tulafono (28 Feb 1947, American Samoa), American Democratic politician and governor of American Samoa from 2003.

Tommy Tune (28 Feb 1939, Wichita Falls TX), American musical comedy dancer and actor noted especially for his work on Broadway.

Christy Turlington (2 Jan 1969, Oakland CA), American fashion model.

Ted Turner (Robert Edward Turner III; 19 Nov 1938, Cincinnati OH), American TV executive, the founder of Turner Broadcasting System and owner of Cable News Network (CNN), a pioneer in the use of satellite and cable technology; he is also a sports club owner (Atlanta Braves and others), a noted yachtsman, and a philanthropist.

Scott Turow (12 Apr 1949, Chicago IL), American best-selling novelist, the author of crime and suspense novels dealing with law and the legal profession.

John Turturro (27 Feb 1957, Brooklyn NY), American stage, film, and TV actor, often cast as disturbed or eccentric characters.

Desmond (Mpilo) Tutu (7 Oct 1931, Klerksdorp, South Africa), South African Anglican cleric who in 1984 received the Nobel Prize for Peace for his role in the opposition to apartheid in South Africa.

Shania Twain (Eileen Regina Edwards; 28 Aug 1965, Windsor, ON, Canada), Canadian country singer.

Cy Twombly (Edwin Parker Twombly, Jr.; 25 Apr 1928, Lexington VA), American abstract artist and sculptor.

Anne Tyler (25 Oct 1941, Minneapolis MN), American novelist and short-story writer whose comedies of manners are marked by compassionate wit and precise details of domestic life.

Liv Tyler (Liv Rundgren; 1 Jul 1977, Portland ME), American actress and model.

Steven Tyler (Steven Tallarico; 26 Mar 1948, New York NY), American rock vocalist (of Aerosmith).

(Alfred) McCoy Tyner (later Sulaimon Saud; 11 Dec 1938, Philadelphia PA), American jazz pianist and composer.

João Ubaldo Ribeiro (João Ubaldo Osório Pimentel Ribeiro; 23 Jan 1941, Itaparica, Bahia state, Brazil), Brazilian novelist.

Robert J. Ulrich (Minneapolis MN), American corporate executive and CEO of Target Corp. from 1994.

Carrie Underwood (10 Mar 1983, Muskogee OK), American country singer.

John (Hoyer) Updike (18 Mar 1932, Shillington PA), American writer of novels, short stories, and poetry, known for his careful craftsmanship and realistic, subtle depiction of American, Protestant, small-town, middle-class life.

Álvaro Uribe Vélez (4 Jul 1952, Medellín, Colombia), Colombian politician and president from 2002.

Joseph J. Urusemal (19 Mar 1952, Woleai, Yap, Trust Territory of the Pacific Islands [now in the Federated States of Micronesia]), Micronesian politician and president of the Federated States of Micronesia, 2003–07.

Greg Urwin (1947?, Lithgow, NSW, Australia), Australian diplomat and international official; secretary-general of the Pacific Islands Forum from 2004.

Usher (Usher Raymond IV; 14 Oct 1978, Chattanooga TN), American R&B singer.

Jørn Utzon (9 Apr 1918, Copenhagen, Denmark), Danish architect best known for his dynamic, imaginative, but problematic design for the Sydney Opera House, Australia; recipient of the 2003 Pritzker Prize.

Jochem Uytdehaage (9 Jul 1976, Utrecht, Netherlands), Dutch speed skater.

Ely Ould Mohamed Vall (1953, Nouakchott, French West Africa [now in Mauritania]), Mauritanian military officer and coup leader; chairman of the Military Council for Justice and Democracy (head of state), 2005–07.

Dick Van Dyke (13 Dec 1925, West Plains MO), American actor and comedian.

Martine Van Hamel (16 Nov 1945, Brussels, Belgium), Belgian dancer and leading choreographer for the American Ballet Theatre.

Gus van Sant (24 Jul 1952, Louisville KY), American film director.

Matti Vanhanen (4 Nov 1955, Jyväskylä, Finland), Finnish politician and prime minister from 2003.

(Jorge) Mario (Pedro) Vargas Llosa (28 Mar 1936, Arequipa, Peru), Peruvian-born Spanish novelist and presidential candidate; recipient of the Cervantes Prize in 1994.

Harold (Eliot) Varmus (18 Dec 1939, Oceanside NY), American virologist; corecipient of 1989 Nobel Prize for Physiology or Medicine; director of the National Institutes of Health, 1993–99; and president of Memorial Sloan-Kettering Cancer Center in New York City from 2000.

Tabaré (Ramón) Vázquez Rosas (17 Jan 1940, Barrio La Teja, Montevideo, Uruguay), Uruguayan physician and Socialist politician; president from 2005.

Jeroen van der Veer (1947, Utrecht, Netherlands), Dutch corporate executive; CEO of Royal Dutch/Shell Group (Netherlands).

Jaci Velasquez (Jacquelyn Davette Velasquez; 15 Oct 1979, Houston TX), American Latin and gospel singer.

Ann M. Veneman (29 Jun 1949, Modesto CA), American government official; US secretary of agriculture, 2001–05; and executive secretary of UNICEF from 2005.

(Runaldo) Ronald Venetiaan (18 Jun 1936, Paramaribo, Dutch Gujana [now Suriname]), Surinamese politician; president, 1991–96 and again from 2000.

Maxim Vengerov (20 Aug 1974, Novosibirsk, USSR [now in Russia]), Russian-born concert violinist known for his mastery of technique and his ardent, lyrical playing.

J. Craig Venter (14 Oct 1946, Salt Lake City UT), American geneticist and researcher into the human genome; he was the founder of Celera Genomics.

Guy Verhofstadt (11 Apr 1953, Dendermonde, Belgium), Belgian politician and prime minister from 1999.

Donatella Versace (2 May 1955, Reggio di Calabria, Italy), Italian fashion designer; creative director at the Versace design house from 1997.

Ben Verwaayen (Feb 1952), Dutch corporate executive and CEO of British Telecommunications PLC from 2002.

Jack Vettriano (Jack Hoggan; 17 Nov 1951, St. Andrews, Fife, Scotland), British painter of realistic natural scenes, sometimes with erotic overtones.

Victoria (Victoria Ingrid Alice Desirée; Duchess of Västergötland; 14 Jul 1977, Stockholm, Sweden), Swedish crown princess.

João Bernardo Vieira (27 Apr 1939, Bissau, Portuguese Guinea [now Guinea-Bissau]), Guinea-Bissau politician; president, 1973–84, 1984–99, and again from 2005.

Vaira Vike-Freiberga (1 Dec 1937, Riga, Latvia), Canadian Latvian folklorist and politician; president of Latvia, 1999–2007.

Antonio Villaraigosa (Antonio Villar; 23 Jan 1953, East Los Angeles CA), American Democratic politician and mayor of Los Angeles from 2005.

Lars von Trier (30 Apr 1956, Copenhagen, Denmark), Danish film director and cinematographer known for his avant-garde approach to filmmaking.

Vladimir Voronin (25 May 1941, Corjova, Moldavian SSR, USSR [now Moldova]), Moldovan politician and president from 2001.

Filip Vujanovic (1 Sep 1954, Belgrade, Yugoslavia [now in Serbia]), Montenegrin politician and president of the republic of Montenegro, before and after its independence, 2002–03 (acting) and again from 2003.

Rem (Ivanovich) Vyakhirev (23 Aug 1934, Bolshaya Chernigovka, USSR [now in Russia]), Russian billionaire head (1992–2001) of Gazprom, the largest company in Russia, and chairman of Siberia Oil Co. from 1996.

Norio Wada (17 Nov 1949, Osaka, Japan), Japanese corporate executive; president and CEO of Nippon Telegraph & Telephone from 2002.

Abdoulaye Wade (29 May 1926, Kébémer, French West Africa [now in Senegal]), Senegalese politician and president from 2000.

G. Richard Wagoner, Jr. (9 Feb 1953, Wilmington DE), American corporate executive and CEO of General Motors Corp. from 2000.

Rufus Wainwright (22 Jul 1973, Rhinebeck NY), American-born Canadian singer and songwriter.

Ted Waitt (18 Jan 1963, Sioux City IA), American computer executive and philanthropist; cofounder of Gateway Inc. in 1985 and chairman and CEO of the charitable Waitt Family Foundation from 1993.

Derek (Alton) Walcott (23 Jan 1930, Castries, Saint Lucia), Saint Lucian poet and playwright noted for works that explored the Caribbean cultural experience; recipient of the 1992 Nobel Prize for Literature.

Jimmy (Donal) Wales (7 Aug 1966, Huntsville AL), American Internet publisher and founder of Wikipedia.

Lech Walesa (29 Sep 1943, Popowo, near Wloclawek, Poland), Polish labor activist; president of Poland, 1990–95; recipient of the 1983 Nobel Prize for Peace.

Al-Walid ibn Talal ibn Abdulaziz al-Saud (1954, Riyadh, Saudi Arabia), Saudi Arabian prince and billionaire businessman.

Alice (Malsenior) Walker (9 Feb 1944, Eatonton GA), American writer whose novels, short stories, and poems are noted for their insightful treatment of women and African American culture.

Mike Wallace (Myron Leon Wallace; 9 May 1918, Brookline MA), American TV journalist, interviewer, and coeditor of CBS's 60 Minutes.

Immanuel Wallerstein (28 Sep 1930, New York NY), American sociologist of systems theory.

Mark J. Walport (1953, England), British immunologist and specialist in lupus and other autoimmune diseases; director of the Wellcome Trust from 2003.

Barbara Walters (25 Sep 1931, Boston MA), American broadcast journalist known especially as an interviewer.

Alice L. (c. 1949), Helen R. (c. 1920), and Jim C. (c. 1948) Walton, American heirs to the Wal-Mart fortune left by Sam Walton, who died in 1992.

Michael Waltrip (30 Apr 1963, Owensboro KY), American NASCAR race car driver.

Vera Wang (27 June 1949, New York NY), American fashion designer known for her elegant and luxurious wedding gowns.

Jigme Khesar Namgyal Wangchuk (21 Feb 1980, Thimphu, Bhutan), king of Bhutan from 2006.

Shane Keith Warne (13 Sep 1969, Ferntree Gully, VIC, Australia), Australian cricketer, a spin bowler named one of Wisden's Five Cricketers of the Century.

J. Robin Warren (11 Jun 1937, Adelaide, SA, Australia), Australian pathologist; corecipient of the 2005 Nobel Prize for Physiology or Medicine.

Rick Warren (1954, San Jose CA), American evangelist minister.

Denzel Washington (28 Dec 1954, Mount Vernon NY), American film and TV actor.

(Chaudhry) Wasim Akram (3 Jun 1966, Lahore, Pakistan), Pakistani cricketer, called the greatest left-handed fast bowler, pioneer of "reverse swing" bowling.

John Waters (22 Apr 1946, Baltimore MD), American filmmaker.

Charlie Watts (2 Jun 1941, Islington, England), British rock drummer (of the Rolling Stones).

Naomi Watts (28 Sep 1968, Shoreham, Kent, England), Australian film actress.

Keenen Ivory Wayans (8 Jun 1958, New York NY), American TV and film actor, writer, director, and producer.

George Weah (George Manneh Oppong Ousman Weah; 1 Oct 1966, Monrovia, Liberia), Liberian-born association football (soccer) star who in 1995–96 was elected European, African, and FIFA World Footballer of the Year.

Sigourney Weaver (Susan Alexandra Weaver; 8 Oct 1949, New York NY), American film actress.

Hugo Weaving (4 Apr 1960, Austin, Nigeria), Nigerian-born Australian film actor.

Karrie Webb (21 Dec 1974, Ayr, QLD, Australia), Australian golfer.

Andrew Thomas Weil (8 Jun 1942, Philadelphia PA), American physician and champion of alternative medicine.

Sandy Weill (Sanford I. Weill; 16 Mar 1933, Brooklyn NY), American corporate executive; CEO of Travelers Group and, after its merger in 1998 with Citicorp, CEO of Citigroup.

Harvey (19 Mar 1952, Queens NY) and **Bob** (1954, Queens NY) **Weinstein**, American film executives; cofounders of Miramax Films.

Alek Wek (16 Apr 1977, Wau, Sudan), Sudanese fashion model.

Gillian Welch (1967, New York NY), American folk and country-and-western singer.

Rachel Weisz (7 Mar 1971, London, England), British film actress.

Wen Jiabao (September 1942, Tianjin, China), Chinese geologist and party and state official; premier of China from 2003.

Jann S. Wenner (7 Jan 1946, New York NY), American journalist, originator (1967), and publisher of *Rolling Stone* magazine.

Kanye West (8 Jun 1977, Atlanta GA), American rapper and music producer.

Randy Weston (Randolph Edward Weston; 6 Apr 1926, Brooklyn NY), American jazz pianist and composer.

Vivienne Westwood (Vivienne Swire; 8 Apr 1941, Tintwistle, Derbyshire, England), British fashion designer whose radical, antiestablishment creations started the 1970s punk fashion trend.

Christopher Wheeldon (22 Mar 1973, Yeovil, Somerset, England), British dancer and choreographer with the New York City Ballet.

Forest Whitaker (Forest Steven Whitaker; 15 Jul 1961, Longview TX), American film actor and director.

Shaun White (3 Sep 1986, San Diego CA), American snowboarder who won a 2006 Olympic gold medal in halfpipe.

Meg Whitman (Margaret C. Whitman; 4 Aug 1956, Cold Spring Harbor NY), American corporate executive and president and CEO of eBay from 1998.

John Edgar Wideman (14 Jun 1941, Washington DC), American writer regarded for his intricate literary style in novels about the experiences of black men in contemporary urban America.

Carl E. Wieman (26 Mar 1951, Corvallis OR), American physicist; corecipient of the 2001 Nobel Prize for Physics for work in the creation of the Bose-Einstein condensate.

Richard (Purdy) Wilbur (1 Mar 1921, New York NY), American poet associated with the New Formalist movement; poet laureate of the US, 1987–88.

Frank A. Wilczek (15 May 1951, New York NY), American quantum physicist; corecipient of the 2004 Nobel Prize for Physics.

George F(rederick) Will (4 May 1941, Champaign IL), American conservative political commentator.

Willem-Alexander (27 Apr 1967, Utrecht, Netherlands), Dutch crown prince.

William (William Arthur Philip Louis; 21 Jun 1982, London, England), British prince; son of Charles and Diana, prince and princess of Wales; and second in line to the British throne.

C(harles) K(enneth) Williams (4 Nov 1936, Newark NJ), American poet.

John Williams (24 Apr 1941, Melbourne, VIC, Australia), Australian-born classical guitarist.

John (Towner) Williams (8 Feb 1932, Queens NY), American conductor and composer; conductor of the Boston Pops Orchestra, 1980–93, known especially for composing scores for blockbuster films.

Lucinda Williams (26 Jan 1953, Lake Charles LA), American contemporary folk and country singer and songwriter.

Montel (Brian Anthony) Williams (3 Jul 1956), American TV personality.

Robbie Williams (Robert Peter Maximillian Williams; 13 Feb 1974, Tunstall, Stoke-on-Trent, Staffordshire, England), British singer.

Robin Williams (21 Jul 1952, Chicago IL), American comedian and actor known for his eccentricity, rapid-fire wit, and energy.

Rowan Williams (14 Jun 1950, Swansea, Wales), Welsh-born Anglican clergyman; archbishop of Canterbury from 2003.

Serena Williams (26 Sep 1981, Saginaw MI), American tennis player.

Treat Williams (Richard Williams; 1 Dec 1951, Rowayton CT), American TV and film actor who starred in the TV series *Everwood*, 2002–06.

Venus Williams (17 Jun 1980, Lynwood CA), American tennis player, the sister of Serena Williams, with whom she has also won doubles titles.

Bruce Willis (Walter Willison; 19 Mar 1955, Idar-Oberstein, West Germany [now in Germany]), American actor.

August Wilson (27 Apr 1945, Pittsburgh PA), American playwright.

Cassandra Wilson (4 Dec 1955, Jackson MS), American jazz singer who applies her wide-ranging "smoky contralto" voice to jazz standards, folk songs, Delta blues, and pop classics.

Lanford Wilson (13 Apr 1937, Lebanon MO), American playwright, a pioneer of the Off-Off-Broadway and regional theater movements.

Robert Wilson (4 Oct 1941, Waco TX), American avant-garde theater director.

William Julius Wilson (20 Dec 1935, Derry township, Westmoreland county PA), American sociologist of race and urban society; government adviser.

Oprah Winfrey (29 Jan 1954, Kosciusko MS), American TV personality; host and producer of *The Oprah Winfrey Show* from 1985.

Kate Winslet (5 Oct 1975, Reading, England), British film actress.

Anna Wintour (3 Nov 1949, London, England), British-born fashion magazine editor, editor in chief of American *Vogue* from 1988.

Reese Witherspoon (Laura Jean Reese Witherspoon; 22 Mar 1976, Baton Rouge LA), American film actress.

Patricia A. Woertz (Patricia Ann Woertz; 17 Mar 1953, Pittsburgh PA), American corporate executive; CEO of Archer Daniels Midland from 2006.

Carl R. Woese (15 Jul 1928, Syracuse NY), American microbiologist; recipient of the 2003 Crafoord Prize for his discovery of archaea, a third domain of life (besides eukaryotes and prokaryotes).

Girma Wolde-Giorgis (December 1924, Addis Ababa, Ethiopia), Ethiopian military officer and president from 2001.

Tom Wolfe (Thomas Kennerly Wolfe, Jr.; 2 Mar 1930, Richmond VA), American novelist, journalist, and social commentator, a leading critic of contemporary life, and a proponent of New Journalism (the application of fiction-writing techniques to journalism).

Tobias (Jonathan Ansell) Wolff (19 Jun 1945, Birmingham AL), American writer primarily known for his short stories.

Paul Wolfowitz (22 Dec 1943, New York NY), American deputy secretary of defense, 2001–05; president of the World Bank, 2005–07.

Stephen Wolfram (29 Aug 1959, London, England), British-born American physicist who has attacked the inadequacy of math-based science and proposed "cellular automata" as a better key to understanding the patterns of nature.

Lee Ann Womack (19 Aug 1966, Jacksonville TX), American country singer.

Stevie Wonder (Steveland Judkins; Steveland Morris; 13 May 1950, Saginaw MI), American pop composer, singer, and pianist.

Elijah (Jordan) Wood (28 Jan 1981, Cedar Rapids IA), American film actor.

Fiona Wood (1958, Yorkshire, England), Australian plastic surgeon who invented "spray-on skin."

Todd Woodbridge (2 Apr 1971, Sydney, NSW, Australia), Australian tennis player best known for doubles play, especially with Jonas Bjorkman.

Tiger Woods (Eldrick Woods; 30 Dec 1975, Cypress CA), American golfer, perhaps the greatest of all time.

Bob Woodward (Robert Upshur Woodward; 26 Mar 1943, Geneva IL), American journalist and author of nonfiction political best sellers.

Stephen Wozniak (11 Aug 1950, San Jose CA), American electrical engineer, cofounder of Apple Computer Corp., and youth leader.

William A. Wulf (8 Dec 1939, Chicago IL), American computer scientist who was president of the National Academy of Engineering from 1997.

Kurt Wüthrich (4 Oct 1938, Aarberg, Bern canton, Switzerland), Swiss chemist; corecipient of the 2002 Nobel Prize for Chemistry for his work in the study of macromolecules.

Aleksey (Konstantinovich) Yagudin (18 Mar 1980, Leningrad, USSR [now St. Petersburg, Russia]), Russian figure skater.

Viktor (Fedorovych) Yanukovych (9 Jul 1950, Yenakiyevo, USSR [now in Ukraine]), Ukrainian politician; prime minister, 2002–05 and again from 2006.

Yao Ming (12 Sep 1980, Shanghai, China), Chinese basketball player.

Umaru Musa Yar'Adua (1951, Katsina, Nigeria), Nigerian politician; president from 2007.

Yury (Fyodorvich) Yarov (2 Apr 1942, Leningrad, USSR [now St. Petersburg, Russia]), Russian international official and executive secretary of the Commonwealth of Independent States from 1999.

Catherine Yass (1963, London, England), British photographic artist whose work often combines positive and negative photographic images to eerie effect.

Trisha Yearwood (Patricia Lynn Yearwood; 19 Sep 1964, Monticello GA), American country singer.

Michelle Yeoh (Yang Zi Chong or Yeoh Chu-keng; 6 Aug 1962, Ipoh, Malaysia), Malaysian-born film actress.

Gloria Yerkovich (1942), American founder of CHILDFIND, an organization that helps locate missing children.

Frances Yip (Frances Yip Lai Yee; 1948, Hong Kong), Hong Kong popular singer.

Dwight (David) Yoakam (23 Oct 1956, Pikesville KY), American country-and-western singer, songwriter, and actor.

Thom Yorke (7 Oct 1968, Wellingborough, Northamptonshire, England), British vocalist (of Radiohead).

Banana Yoshimoto (Yoshimoto Mahoko; 24 Jul 1964, Tokyo, Japan), Japanese writer of best-selling fiction.

Yumi Yoshimura (30 Jan 1975, Osaka, Japan), Japanese pop singer (of Puffy AmiYumi).

Will Young (William Robert Young; 20 Jan 1979, Hungerford, Berkshire, England), British rock singer.

Yu Miri (22 Jun 1968, Yokohama, Japan), Japanese writer of Korean ancestry.

Susilo Bambang Yudhoyono (9 Sep 1949, Pacitan, East Java, Indonesia), Indonesian military officer and politician; president from 2004.

Muhammad Yunus (28 Jun 1940, Chittagong, East Bengal, British India [now Bangladesh]), Bangladeshi economist (microcredit) and founder of the Grameen Bank; winner of the 1994 World Food Prize and corecipient of the 2006 Nobel Peace Prize.

Viktor (Andriyovych) Yushchenko (23 Feb 1954, Khoruzhivka, USSR [now in Ukraine]), Ukrainian banker and politician; prime minister, 1999–2001, and president from 2005.

Sadi Yusuf (1934, near Basra, Iraq), Iraqi-born poet.

Raúl Yzaguirre (22 Jul 1939, south Texas), American Hispanic rights activist; president and CEO of the National Council of La Raza from 1974.

Adam Zagajewski (21 Jun 1945, Lwow, Poland [now Lviv, Ukraine]), Polish poet, novelist, and essayist; recipient of the 2004 Neustadt Prize.

Paula Zahn (24 Feb 1956, Omaha NE), American TV anchorwoman and journalist.

José Luis Rodríguez Zapatero (4 Aug 1960, Valladolid, Spain), Spanish politician and prime minister from 2004.

Valdis Zatlers (22 Mar 1955), Latvian politician; president from 2007.

Ayman al-Zawahiri (19 Jun 1951, Maadi, Egypt), Egyptian-born physician and militant Islamist leader.

Manuel Zelaya (José Manuel Zelaya Rosales; 20 Sep 1952, Catacamas, Honduras), Honduran politician (Liberal Party) and president from 2006.

Renée (Kathleen) Zellweger (25 Apr 1969, Katy TX), American actress.

Robert Zemeckis (14 May 1952, Chicago IL), American director and producer of popular mainstream films.

Meles Zenawi (8 May 1955, Adoua, Ethiopia), Ethiopian politician and prime minister from 1995.

Elias (Adam) Zerhouni (1 Apr 1951, Nedroma, Algeria), Algerian-born American radiologist and medical administrator; director of the National Institutes of Health from 2002.

Catherine Zeta-Jones (Catherine Jones; 25 Sep 1969, Swansea, West Glamorgan, Wales), Welsh-born American actress.

Zhang Yimou (14 Nov 1951, Xi'an, Shaanxi province, China), Chinese film director.

Zhang Ziyi (9 Feb 1979, Beijing, China), Chinese actress.

Zhou Guangzhao (May 1929, Changsha, Hunan province, China), Chinese mechanical engineer; president of the Chinese Academy of Sciences, 1987–97; and chairman of the China Association of Science and Technology from 1996.

Zinedine Zidane (23 Jun 1972, Marseille, France), French association football (soccer) player.

Mary (Alice) Zimmerman (23 Aug 1960, Lincoln NE), American stage director.

Robert B. Zoellick (25 Jul 1953, Evergreen Park IL), American businessman and government official; US Trade Representative, 2001–05, deputy secretary of state, 2005–06, and president of the World Bank from 2007.

Mortimer B. Zuckerman (4 Jun 1937, Montreal, QC, Canada), Canadian-born American publisher, columnist, and editor in chief of *U.S. News & World Report*.

Jacob (Gedleyihlekisa) Zuma (12 Apr 1942, Inkandla, British South Africa), South African politician.

Obituaries

Death of notable people since 1 Jul 2006

Abbé Pierre (Henri-Antoine Grouès; the "ragpickers' saint"; 5 Aug 1912, Lyons, France—22 Jan 2007, Paris, France), French Roman Catholic priest and social activist, founder of the Emmaus movement, who championed the cause of the homeless in France and throughout the world.

Ladislav Adamec (10 Sep 1926, Frenstat pod Radhostem, Moravia, Czechoslovakia [now in Czech Republic]—14 Apr 2007, Prague, Czech Republic), Czech politician who witnessed the end of communist rule in his country as federal prime minister (1988–89); during the 1989 Velvet Revolution, Adamec opened the country's borders and refused to authorize military intervention; he stepped down as Communist Party leader in 1990 but remained a member of the new Czech parliament until 1992.

Lloyd Alexander (30 Jan 1924, Philadelphia PA—17 May 2007, Drexel Hill PA), American author who transported readers to a world of fantasy with a five-book series that was known as the Prydain Chronicles, the second novel of which, *The Black Cauldron* (1965), was chosen as a Newbery Honor Book in 1966, and the last installment of which, *The High King* (1968), received the Newbery Medal; Alexander also received the National Book Award in 1971 and in 1982.

Robert Altman (20 Feb 1925, Kansas City MO—20 Nov 2006, Los Angeles CA), American filmmaker, an unconventional and independent director whose works emphasized character and atmosphere over plot in exploring themes of innocence, corruption, and survival.

William Robert Anderson (17 Jun 1921, Bakerville TN—25 Feb 2007, Leesburg VA), commander, US Navy, and American politician who piloted the world's first nuclear-powered submarine, the *Nautilus*, beneath the North Pole in August 1958; in 1964 he was elected to the US House of Representatives, and he became a staunch critic of the Vietnam War.

Michelangelo Antonioni (29 Sep 1912, Ferrara, Italy—30 Jul 2007, Rome, Italy), Italian film director, cinematographer, and producer who eschewed "realistic" narrative and traditional plots in favor of character study and poetic visual imagery that used film as a metaphor for human experience; his most successful motion picture was the English-language *Blowup* (1966), which won the Golden Palm at the Cannes Festival and came to epitomize "swinging '60s" London.

Hassan Gouled Aptidon (15 Oct 1916, Garissa, Lughaya district, French Somaliland [now Djibouti]—21 Nov 2006, Djibouti, Djibouti), Djibouti politician who was founding president for 22 years, from 1977, when Djibouti gained independence from France, until ill health compelled him to step down in 1999.

Paul Arizin ("Pitchin' Paul"; 9 Apr 1928, Philadelphia PA—12 Dec 2006, Philadelphia PA), American basketball player, a jump-shot specialist who was hailed in 1996 as one of the 50 greatest players in the National Basketball Association.

Duygu Asena (19 Apr 1946, Istanbul, Turkey—30 Jul 2006, Istanbul, Turkey), Turkish feminist writer who fought for women's rights in her native Turkey, both as a journalist and through her novels, notably *Kadinin adi yok* (1987; "Woman Has No Name").

Lucie Aubrac (Lucie Bernard) (29 Jun 1912, Mâcon, France—14 Mar 2007, Issy-les-Moulineaux, France), French Resistance heroine who was hailed for her courageous actions in the underground network Libération Sud in southern France during World War II; she was awarded the Legion of Honour for her wartime activities, and her somewhat fictionalized memoir, *Ils partiront dans l'ivresse* (1984; *Outwitting the Gestapo*, 1993), served as the inspiration for *Lucie Aubrac* (1997).

Red Auerbach (Arnold Jacob Auerbach; 20 Sep 1917, Brooklyn NY—28 Oct 2006, Washington DC), American basketball coach who led the Boston Celtics to nine NBA championships and 1,037 wins against 548 losses.

Robert Austrian (12 Apr 1916, Baltimore MD—25 Mar 2007, Philadelphia PA), American physician and educator who devoted his life to identifying the various strains associated with pneumococcal infections; his 10-year (1952–62) groundbreaking study led to his development of a vaccine in 1977 that treated antibiotic-resistant strains of pneumonia.

Warren Edward Avis (4 Aug 1915, Bay City MI—24 Apr 2007, Ann Arbor MI), American businessman who was the pioneering founder in 1946 of Avis Rent-a-Car, which became the first car-rental agency to be based at an airport and within a few years established itself as the second largest car-rental company worldwide.

John Warner Backus (3 Dec 1924, Philadelphia PA—17 Mar 2007, Ashland OR), American computer scientist who led the team at IBM that during the 1950s designed FORTRAN (formula translation), the first important algorithmic language for computers, the development of which was instrumental in paving the way for modern software; Backus received the 1977 Turing Award and the 1975 National Medal of Science.

Alan James Ball (12 May 1945, Farnworth, Lancashire, England—25 Apr 2007, Warsash, Hampshire, England), British association football (soccer) player and manager who represented his country in 72 matches from 1965 to 1975 and was, at age 21, the youngest player on the team that won the Fédération Internationale de Football Association (FIFA) World Cup for England in 1966; he was appointed MBE in 2000.

Joseph Barbera (Joseph Roland Barbera; 24 Mar 1911, New York NY—18 Dec 2006, Los Angeles CA), American film animator who collaborated for more than half a century with William Hanna; the two created some of the most beloved characters on the big and small screen, including Tom (the cat) and Jerry (the mouse), Huckleberry Hound, Yogi Bear, the Flintstones, and the Jetsons.

Syd Barrett (Roger Keith Barrett; 6 Jan 1946, Cambridge, England—7 Jul 2006, Cambridge, England), British singer-songwriter and guitarist who was an original creative force behind the rock group Pink Floyd.

Jean Baudrillard (29 Jul 1929, Reims, France—6 Mar 2007, Paris, France), French sociologist and cultural theorist who imparted theoretical ideas of "hyperreality" and "simulacrum" that influenced academia and spread into popular culture through the 1999 film *The Matrix*; Baudrillard espoused an account of postmodern society in which consumer and electronic images have become more real (hyperreal) than physical reality and in which simulations of reality (simulacra) have displaced their originals, leaving only "the desert of the real."

Hank Bauer (Henry Albert Bauer; 31 Jul 1922, East St. Louis IL—9 Feb 2007, Shawnee Mission KS), American baseball player and manager who, as an outfielder and slugger for the New York Yankees in 1948–59, helped the team win nine American League pennants and seven World Series championships; he also managed the Baltimore Orioles when they won their first World Series in 1966.

Edward Samuel Behr (7 May 1926, Paris, France—26 May 2007, Paris, France), British journalist and author who covered wars in Africa, Asia, and the Middle East, as well as such international emergencies as the 1962 Cuban missile crisis, in his role as a foreign correspondent for Reuters news agency (1950–54) and *Time* (1957–63), *The Saturday Evening Post* (1963–65), and *Newsweek* (1965–87); Behr's *The Last Emperor* (1987) was released in conjunction with a film of the same name.

Carey Bell (Harrington) (14 Nov 1936, Macon MS—7 May 2007, Chicago IL), American blues harmonica player who was a fixture on the Chicago blues scene; after perfecting his playing under the tutelage of such masters as "Little Walter" Jacobs and "Big Walter" Horton, he toured and recorded with stars including Muddy Waters and Willie Dixon.

Louise Bennett-Coverly ("Miss Lou"; 7 Sep 1919, Kingston, Jamaica—26 Jul 2006, Toronto, ON, Canada), Jamaican folklorist, poet, and radio and TV personality who was regarded by many as the "mother of Jamaican culture" for her efforts to popularize Jamaican patois and to celebrate the lives of ordinary Jamaicans.

Trevor Berbick (1 Aug 1954, Port Antonio, Jamaica—28 Oct 2006, Norwich, Jamaica), Jamaican-born Canadian boxer who defeated Muhammad Ali on 12 Dec 1981 in a unanimous decision in a fight that would end Ali's career.

Patty Berg (Patricia Jane Berg; 13 Feb 1918, Minneapolis MN—10 Sep 2006, Fort Myers FL), American professional golfer who won more than 80 tournaments, including a record 15 major women's championships, and was the first president of the Ladies Professional Golf Association.

Heinz Berggruen (5 Jan 1914, Berlin, Germany—23 Feb 2007, Neuilly-sur-Seine, France), German-born art collector who amassed a collection of 20th-century art, the core of which consisted of some 130 works by Pablo Picasso, with whom Berggruen had become friends in 1949; in 2000 he sold 165 works to the Berggruen Museum for a fraction of their true value.

(Ernst) Ingmar Bergman (14 Jul 1918, Uppsala, Sweden—30 Jul 2007, Fårö, Sweden), Swedish writer-director who achieved worldwide fame for creating films that examine issues of morality by exploring man's relationship to himself, to others, and to God and were noted for their versatile camera work and fragmented narrative style; though Bergman never won an individual Academy Award (despite nine nominations), three of his movies won Oscars for best foreign language film—*Jungfrukällan* (1960; *The Virgin Spring*), *Såsom i en spegel* (1961; *Through a Glass Darkly*), and *Fanny och Alexander* (1983; *Fanny and Alexander*), and in 1971 the Academy presented him with a lifetime achievement award; the trilogy he made in the 1960s—*Through a Glass Darkly*, *Nattsvardsgästerna* (1962; *Winter Light*), and *Tystnaden* (1963; *The Silence*)—was regarded by many

as his crowning achievement. In 1977 he received the Swedish Academy of Letters Great Gold Medal, and in the following year the Swedish Film Institute established a prize in his name.

Lesley Blanch (6 Jun 1904, London, England—7 May 2007, Menton, France), British writer and traveler who delighted readers with many books that, like her life, were full of romance and adventure; her best-known book was *The Wilder Shores of Love* (1954), in which she recounted the real-life exotic adventures of four 19th-century women; she was appointed MBE in 2001.

Isabella Blow (Isabella Delves Broughton; 19 Nov 1958, London, England—7 May 2007, Gloucester, Gloucestershire, England), British fashion editor who discovered and promoted fashion designers (Alexander McQueen, John Galliano, Jun Takahashi, and Hussein Chalayan) and models (Stella Tennant, Honor Fraser, and Sophie Dahl) while becoming memorable for her own flamboyant style of dress.

Bo Yibo (Bo Shucun; 17 Feb 1908, Jiang village, Dingxiang county, China—15 Jan 2007, Beijing, China), Chinese political leader, the last surviving member of the Eight Immortals, the highly influential group of Chinese Communist Party leaders who had been purged during Mao Zedong's Cultural Revolution (1966–76) but brought back to assert power under the country's de facto leader, Deng Xiaoping, in the 1980s and '90s.

Egon Bondy (Zbynek Fiser) (20 Jan 1930, Prague, Czechoslovakia [now in Czech Republic]—9 Apr 2007, Bratislava, Slovakia), Czech writer who produced dozens of surrealist novels, poems, and philosophical treatises, most of which were disseminated through underground samizdat publications, but whose veiled criticisms of Czechoslovakia's communist government reached a wider audience.

P.W. Botha (Pieter Willem Botha; "Die Groot Krokodil"; "The Great Crocodile"; 12 Jan 1916, Paul Roux, Orange Free State, Union of South Africa—31 Oct 2006, Wilderness, near George, Western Cape, South Africa), South African politician who, as prime minister (1978–84) and president (1984–89), was fully committed to white supremacy, but who sought to find middle ground between those who supported apartheid and the increasingly frustrated and militant nonwhite population.

Edward Francis Boyd (27 Jun 1914, Riverside CA—30 Apr 2007, Los Angeles CA), American business executive who was the trailblazing creator of advertisements for Pepsi-Cola that, rather than containing caricatures of blacks, featured middle-class African American consumers in fun-loving scenarios, introducing niche marketing and helping Pepsi to overtake Coke in the cola wars for the first time.

Gerald Boyd (Gerald Michael Boyd; 3 Oct 1950, St. Louis MO—23 Nov 2006, New York NY), American journalist who rose from serving as a political reporter for the *New York Times* to become in 2001 the newspaper's first black managing editor.

Clete Boyer (Cletis Leroy Boyer; 9 Feb 1937, Cassville MO—4 Jun 2007, Atlanta GA), American baseball player who helped the New York Yankees professional baseball team capture five consecutive pennants (1960–64) and two World Series (1961 and 1962) as the team's acrobatic third baseman.

Peter Boyle (Peter Lawrence Boyle; 18 Oct 1935, Norristown PA—12 Dec 2006, New York NY), American actor who showcased his comedic talents in a series of films, notably as the creature in Mel Brooks's *Young Frankenstein* (1974) and as the curmudgeonly Frank Barone (1996–2005) in the TV sitcom *Everybody Loves Raymond.*

Ed Bradley (Edward Rudolph Bradley, Jr.; 22 Jun 1941, Philadelphia PA–9 Nov 2006, New York NY), American broadcast journalist who was affiliated with CBS news for more than three decades and was rewarded with 19 Emmy Awards, most of them for his insightful reporting as a roving correspondent for the CBS news magazine program *60 Minutes.*

Jean-Claude Brialy (30 Mar 1933, Aumale, French Algeria [now Sour el-Ghozlane, Algeria]–30 May 2007, Paris, France), French actor who epitomized New Wave (Nouvelle Vague) cinema in such classics of the genre as Claude Chabrol's *Le Beau Serge* (1958; *Handsome Serge*) and *Les Cousins* (1959; *The Cousins*); he was inducted into the Legion of Honor in 1986.

Herman Brix (Bruce Bennett; 19 May 1906, Tacoma WA–24 Feb 2007, Los Angeles CA), American athlete and actor who, after winning the silver medal in shot put at the 1928 Olympic Games went on to appear in more than 100 movies and dozens of TV shows.

Peter Brock ("Brocky"; 26 Feb 1945, Australia–8 Sep 2006, near Perth, WA, Australia), Australian racecar driver who dominated the Australian Touring Car circuit over a career of almost 40 years.

James Brown (James Joseph Brown, Jr.; 3 May 1933, Barnwell SC–25 Dec 2006, Atlanta GA), American singer, songwriter, arranger, and dancer, one of the most important and influential entertainers in 20th-century popular music; his remarkable achievements earned him description as "the hardest-working man in show business."

Roscoe Lee Browne (2 May 1925, Woodbury NJ–11 Apr 2007, Los Angeles CA), American character actor who had a regal bearing and a sonorous voice that he used to memorable effect in a string of films, in Broadway plays, and as the narrator of films; he won an Obie Award in 1965 for his role in *Benito Cereno* and an Emmy Award in 1986 for his guest role on an episode of *The Cosby Show.*

Lothar-Günther Buchheim (6 Feb 1918, Weimar, Germany–22 Feb 2007, Starnberg, Germany), German art collector and author who wrote the autobiographical novel *Das Boot* (1973; *The Boat,* 1974); he served on the German submarine *U-96* in 1941 and photographed and wrote about the experience in several fiction and nonfiction works.

Art Buchwald (Arthur Buchwald; 20 Oct 1925, Mount Vernon NY–17 Jan 2007, Washington DC), American humorist who wrote a newspaper column of observational satire that was an institution for some 40 years.

Susan Butcher (Susan Howlet Butcher; 26 Dec 1954, Boston MA–5 Aug 2006, Seattle WA), American sled-dog racer and trainer who dominated her sport for more than a decade and won the challenging 1,770-km (1,100-mi) Iditarod Trail Sled Dog Race in Alaska four times.

Red Buttons (Aaron Chwatt; 5 Feb 1919, New York NY–13 Jul 2006, Los Angeles CA), American actor and comedian who performed in burlesque before fronting his own TV show (1952–55) and creating a cast of unforgettable characters—notably Rocky, a punch-drunk boxer; he won an Academy Award for best supporting actor for a dramatic role in the film *Sayonara* (1957).

Bebe Moore Campbell (Elizabeth Moore; 18 Feb 1950, Philadelphia PA–27 Nov 2006, Los Angeles CA), American novelist who examined race relations in the US in a series of fact-based novels; her debut novel, *Your Blues Ain't Like Mine* (1992), fol-

lowed the killing of a black Chicago boy by a white man in Mississippi and the killing's aftermath.

Kitty Carlisle (Catherine Conn; Kitty Carlisle Hart) (3 Sep 1910, New Orleans LA–17 Apr 2007, New York NY), American actress who was an effervescent entertainer onstage and in films but was best remembered as a guest panelist on the TV game shows *What's My Line?* and *To Tell the Truth;* in 1991 she was awarded the National Medal of Arts.

Alfred DuPont Chandler (15 Sep 1918, Guyencourt DE–9 May 2007, Cambridge MA), American business historian who won the Pulitzer Prize for history in 1978 for his groundbreaking study *The Visible Hand: The Managerial Revolution in American Business,* in which he stressed the importance of professional managers in the rise of modern-day corporations.

Jagjit Singh Chauhan (1927, Tanda, Punjab, British India–4 Apr 2007, Tanda, Punjab state, India), Indian Sikh separatist leader who, as a prominent figure in the movement for an independent Sikh state (called Khalistan) in Punjab, organized a government-in-exile in London, appointing a cabinet, issuing passports and currency, and opening embassies in several countries.

Don Chipp (Donald Leslie Chipp; 21 Aug 1925, Melbourne, VIC, Australia–28 Aug 2006, Melbourne, VIC, Australia), Australian politician who founded (1977) the left-wing Australian Democrats as a reaction to policies of the ruling Liberal Party that he considered too conservative.

Choi Kyu Hah (16 Jul 1919, Wonju, Kangwon province, Japanese-occupied Korea [now in South Korea]–22 Oct 2006, Seoul, South Korea), South Korean politician who briefly served as president (October 1979–September 1980) of South Korea during the tumultuous period after Pres. Park Chung Hee was assassinated.

Dorothea Towles Church (26 Jul 1922, Texarkana TX–7 Jul 2006, New York NY), American model who found stardom in the 1950s as the first black model on the runways of Paris, where she was hired by Christian Dior.

Liz Claiborne (Anne Elisabeth Jane Claiborne; Elisabeth Claiborne Ortenberg; 31 Mar 1929, Brussels, Belgium–26 Jun 2007, New York NY), American fashion designer who revolutionized the women's apparel industry as the head designer and cofounder in 1976 of the company that bears her name (the first Fortune 500 company to be headed by a woman); at a time when career women were looking for an alternative to suits, her line of casual and colorful sportswear separates allowed customers to mix and match elements of their wardrobe at realistic prices.

Paul Joseph Cohen (2 Apr 1934, Long Branch NJ–23 Mar 2007, Stanford CA), American mathematician who was awarded the Fields Medal in 1966 for his proof of the independence of the continuum hypothesis from the other axioms of set theory (the first problem on David Hilbert's influential 1900 list of important unsolved problems); his publications included *Set Theory and the Continuum Hypothesis* (1966).

Alice Coltrane (Alice McLeod; Turiya Sagittinanda; 27 Aug 1937, Detroit MI–12 Jan 2007, Los Angeles CA), American jazz keyboard artist who played bop piano with Detroit musicians and with Terry Gibbs (1962–63) and impressionist piano with her husband John Coltrane's combos (1965–67).

Betty Comden (Basya Cohen; Betty Comden Kyle; 3 May 1919, Brooklyn NY–23 Nov 2006, New York NY), American lyricist who collaborated with Adolph

Green, and the two made up a musical-comedy team that wrote scripts—and often the lyrics—for many Broadway shows and Hollywood film musicals; they were paired longer than any other writing team in the history of Broadway.

Diego Corrales (25 Aug 1977, Sacramento CA—7 May 2007, Las Vegas, NV), American boxer fighting mainly at the junior lightweight (130-lb) weight class who accrued a record of 40 wins (33 knockouts) and 5 losses; he variously held the International Boxing Federation and the World Boxing Organization junior lightweight title (1999–2000) and the World Boxing Council lightweight title (2005–06).

Mullah Dadullah (Dadullah Akhund; 1966?, Uruzgan province, Afghanistan—12 May 2007, Helmand province, Afghanistan), ethnic Pashtun Afghan guerrilla commander who was a notoriously ruthless senior leader of the Taliban insurgency; he fought against the Soviet occupation of Afghanistan in the 1980s and rose to prominence in the 1990s with the Taliban army that conquered most of the country; he was killed by US-led coalition forces.

Iva Toguri D'Aquino (Ikuko Toguri; "Tokyo Rose"; 4 Jul 1916, Los Angeles CA—26 Sep 2006, Chicago IL), American broadcaster who was stranded in Japan when the US entered World War II and was forced to make propagandist broadcasts to US troops; she was one of 13 women announcers, all native speakers of American English, who came to be collectively known as Tokyo Rose.

James Bodie Davis (6 Jun 1916, Greenville SC—17 Apr 2007, Philadelphia PA), American gospel singer who was a founding member of the Dixie Hummingbirds, an a cappella group that influenced Little Richard, James Brown, and others and who pioneered a style called "trickeration," in which one vocalist would pick up a note where another left off; the Hummingbirds scored a hit in 1973 with their interpretation of Paul Simon's "Loves Me Like a Rock," for which they won a Grammy Award.

Mary Day (25 Jan 1910, Washington DC—11 Jul 2006, Washington DC), American dance teacher and artistic director who cofounded (with Lisa Gardiner) in 1944 the Washington School of Ballet, which attracted students from throughout the country and turned out such illustrious talents as Kevin McKenzie, Amanda McKerrow, and Virginia Johnson.

Yvonne DeCarlo (Margaret Yvonne Middleton; "Peggy"; 1 Sep 1922, Vancouver, BC, Canada—8 Jan 2007, Woodland Hills CA), Canadian-born American actress who appeared in a string of B-Westerns; she was best remembered on the big screen for her role as the wife of Moses in The Ten Commandments (1956) and on TV as Lily Munster, the vampirelike matriarch of The Munsters (1964–66).

Brad Delp (Bradley E. Delp) (12 Jun 1951, Danvers MA—9 Mar 2006, Atkinson NH), American guitarist and singer who was the lead singer for the rock group Boston, whose unique hard-rock–pop sound was created by Delp's distinctive high-register vocals and Tom Scholz's soaring guitar and whose eponymous first album was for years the biggest-selling debut in rock history.

Jupp Derwall (Josef Derwall; 10 Mar 1927, Würselen, Germany—26 Jun 2007, Sankt Ingbert, Germany), German association football (soccer) manager who during his tenure as national coach (1978–84) guided West Germany to 45 wins (including a record 23 straight), the 1980 European championship title, and the final of the 1982 World Cup.

Michael John Dibdin (21 Mar 1947, Wolverhampton, Staffordshire [now in West Midlands], England—30 Mar 2007, Seattle WA), British crime novelist who delighted fans of detective fiction with a series of novels featuring idiosyncratic Italian police inspector Aurelio Zen; his third novel, Ratking (1988), introduced the cerebral, world-weary Zen and won the Crime Writers' Association Gold Dagger for Fiction.

Hrant Dink (15 Sep 1954, Matalya, Turkey—19 Jan 2007, Istanbul, Turkey), Turkish journalist who campaigned for the rights of ethnic Armenians; he was shot dead outside the offices of the bilingual Turkish-Armenian newspaper Agos, which he edited.

Floyd Dixon (Jay Riggins, Jr.; 8 Feb 1929, Marshall TX—26 Jul 2006, Orange CA), American R&B musician who was one of the principal exponents of the West Coast jump blues style.

Denny Doherty (Dennis Doherty; 29 Nov 1940, Halifax, NS, Canada—19 Jan 2007, Mississauga, ON, Canada), Canadian singer, a member with John Phillips, Michelle Phillips, and "Mama" Cass Elliot of the original Mamas and the Papas vocal quartet, whose intricate harmonies brought them to the forefront of the folk rock movement of the 1960s.

Mike Douglas (Michael Delaney Dowd, Jr; 11 Aug 1925, Chicago IL—11 Aug 2006, Palm Beach Gardens FL), American TV personality and singer, the laid-back host of the daytime The Mike Douglas Show (1961–82), which featured musical acts, top celebrities of the day, and politicians, including seven US presidents.

Charlie Drake (Charles Edward Springall; 19 Jun 1925, Elephant and Castle, London, England—23 Dec 2006, Twickenham, Middlesex, England), British comedian and actor who delighted audiences with his slapstick comic antics in stage variety shows and on TV for more than 50 years, often playing a downtrodden "everyman" who failed at everything he tried.

Thomas F. Eagleton (Thomas Francis Eagleton; 4 Sep 1929, St. Louis MO—4 Mar 2007, Richmond Heights MO), American politician who was Democratic presidential candidate George McGovern's running mate in the 1972 election but was asked to step down after it became known that he had been voluntarily hospitalized for a nervous condition in the early 1960s and treated with electroshock therapy.

Bulent Ecevit (28 May 1925, Constantinople [now Istanbul], Turkey—5 Nov 2006, Ankara, Turkey), Turkish poet, journalist, and politician who intermittently served as prime minister of Turkey (1974, 1977, 1978–79, and 1999–2002).

Ahmet Ertegun (31 Jul 1923, Constantinople [now Istanbul], Turkey—14 Dec 2006, New York NY), Turkish-born American music magnate, a jazz enthusiast who together with Herb Abramson founded (1947) Atlantic Records in New York City.

David Walter Ervine (21 Jul 1953, East Belfast, Northern Ireland—8 Jan 2007, Belfast, Northern Ireland), Northern Irish Protestant militant and politician who abandoned the illegal loyalist paramilitary Ulster Volunteer Force to join its political wing, the Progressive Unionist Party, which he headed from 2002.

Vilma Espín Guillois (7 Apr 1930, Santiago, Cuba—18 Jun 2007, Havana, Cuba), Cuban revolutionary and women's rights activist who, as the wife of Raúl Castro, longtime Cuban leader Fidel Castro's younger brother, was regarded as the unofficial first lady of Cuba and the most politically powerful woman in the country; she held key positions in the

Cuban Communist Party and the country's influential Council of State, founded the Cuban Federation of Women, and frequently represented Cuba at the UN General Assembly.

Bob Evans (30 May 1918, Sugar Ridge OH—21 Jun 2007, Cleveland OH), American farmer and restaurateur who parlayed a 12-stool restaurant into a popular nationwide chain of more than 500 restaurants that bore his name and featured home-style meals and by 2007 had revenue of $1.6 billion annually.

Ray Evans (Raymond B. Evans; 4 Feb 1915, Salamanca NY—15 Feb 2007, Los Angeles CA), American lyricist who, in collaboration with Jay Livingston, created songs for some 80 motion pictures, including three songs that won Academy Awards—"Buttons and Bows," "Mona Lisa," and "Que Sera, Sera."

Jerry (Laymon) Falwell, Sr. (11 Aug 1933, Lynchburg VA—15 May 2007, Lynchburg VA), American religious leader who was a charismatic televangelist who, as the founder in 1979 of the Moral Majority, a political organization for the promotion of conservative social values, was largely responsible for making American Christian conservatives politically active; the pro-family, pro-American organization, which quickly grew to several million members, was credited with playing an important role in the election of Republican Ronald Reagan as president in 1980, and it remained a force in American politics until it was disbanded in 1989; in 1956 Falwell started broadcasting sermons on a radio program, the *Old-Time Gospel Hour,* which later began appearing on a local television network, eventually going into international syndication and claiming more than 50 million regular viewers; he opposed abortion, feminism, and gay rights.

Freddy Fender (Baldemar G. Huerta; 4 Jun 1937, San Benito TX—14 Oct 2006, Corpus Christi TX), American country and Tex-Mex rock singer and guitarist who scored number one hits on the country charts in 1975 with "Wasted Days and Wasted Nights" and "Before the Next Teardrop Falls," which also reached number one on the pop charts.

Gianfranco Ferré (15 Aug 1944, Legnano, Italy—17 Jun 2007, Milan, Italy), Italian fashion designer who earned the nickname "L'Architteto" ("Architect of Fashion") after he applied his architecture degree to the design of sculptural, carefully constructed couture, ready-to-wear, and fashion accessories.

Len Fitzgerald (17 May 1929—17 Apr 2007), Australian rules football player who was one of Australia's finest "footy" players in the era before the separate state leagues evolved into the national Australian Football League (AFL); he was an inaugural inductee into the AFL Hall of Fame (1996).

Eugene Bennett Fluckey (5 Oct 1913, Washington DC—29 Jun 2007, Annapolis MD), rear admiral (ret.), US Navy, who was the commander during World War II of the submarine USS *Barb* and earned the nickname the "Galloping Ghost" because of his ability to move undetected through enemy-laden waters; he was awarded four Navy Crosses and a Medal of Honor for his exploits during the war, and he later became an aide to Navy Secretary James Forrestal and to Adm. Chester W. Nimitz, the chief of naval operations.

Gerald R. Ford (Leslie Lynch King, Jr.; Gerald Rudolph Ford; 14 Jul 1913, Omaha NE—26 Dec 2006, Rancho Mirage CA), American statesman; 38th president of the US, 1974–77 (*see full biography at Presidents*).

Glenn Ford (Gwyllyn Samuel Newton Ford; 1 May 1916, Sainte-Christine, QC, Canada—30 Aug 2006, Beverly Hills CA), Canadian-born American actor who portrayed strong-willed yet soft-spoken characters in more than 80 films during a career that spanned some 50 years.

Charles Forte, Baron Forte of Ripley (Carmine Monforte; 26 Nov 1908, Mortale [later renamed Monforte], Italy—28 Feb 2007, London, England), British entrepreneur who expanded a tiny London snack bar, which he opened in 1934, into Trusthouse Forte PLC, a vast international enterprise that included highway service centers, restaurants, airport caterers, breweries, wine merchants, a motel chain, and luxury hotels.

Bill France, Jr. (4 Apr 1933, Washington DC—4 Jun 2007, Daytona Beach FL), American sports executive who served as chairman (1972–2003) of NASCAR (the National Association for Stock Car Auto Racing) and oversaw its growth from a relatively small regional attraction into a multibillion-dollar racing circuit with a nationwide following; in 1979 he persuaded CBS to air live coverage of the Daytona 500; by 2001 NASCAR commanded a $2.4-billion multinetwork television contract and generated another $2 billion annually in merchandise sales.

Freddie Francis (Frederick William Francis) (22 Dec 1917, London, England—17 Mar 2007, Isleworth, Middlesex, England), British cinematographer and director who won two Academy Awards during a 60-year career (1937–96) in the film industry, for the black-and-white classic *Sons and Lovers* (1960) and the American Civil War drama *Glory* (1989); in 1997 he earned a lifetime achievement award from the British Society of Cinematographers.

Leonard Freed (23 Oct 1929, Brooklyn NY—29 Nov 2006, Garrison NY), American photojournalist who joined the Magnum Photos cooperative agency in 1972 and was renowned for the gripping magazine photo-essays he produced, especially those that documented the lives of African Americans and the injustices they suffered.

Alan Freeman (Alan Leslie Freeman; "Fluff"; 6 Jul 1927, Melbourne, VIC, Australia—27 Nov 2006, Twickenham, Middlesex, England), Australian-born British radio personality who, as the host (1961–72, 1989–93, 1997–2000), of BBC radio's *Pick of the Pops,* made that musical chart program required listening across Britain.

Milton Friedman (31 Jul 1912, Brooklyn NY—16 Nov 2006, San Francisco CA), American laissez-faire economist, professor at the University of Chicago, and one of the leading conservative economists in the 20th century; he was awarded the 1976 Nobel Memorial Prize for Economic Science for work in the fields of economic consumption, monetary history and theory, and stabilization policy.

Harold Edward Froehlich ("Bud"; 13 Jul 1922, Minneapolis MN—19 May 2007, Maplewood MN), American engineer who led the team at General Mills that designed *Alvin,* a three-person submersible built to withstand pressures in the deep sea; launched in 1964, *Alvin* was used to map the Mid-Atlantic Ridge (the underwater mountain chain in the center of the Atlantic Ocean), to recover an errant hydrogen bomb, and to find the wreckage of the *Titanic.*

Ernest Gallo (18 Mar 1909, Jackson CA—6 Mar 2007, Modesto CA), American winemaker and marketer who, together with his older brother, Julio, founded (1933) E.&J. Gallo Winery in Modesto CA and built an empire by shaping American drinking tastes with inexpensive nonvintage wines.

David Gemmell (1 Aug 1948, London, England—28 Jul 2006, Udimore, East Sussex, England), British novelist who wrote more than 30 historic fantasy stories, notably his first novel, *Legend* (1984), and its sequels *Waylander* (1986) and the Drenai saga.

Pierre-Gilles de Gennes (24 Oct 1932, Paris, France—18 May 2007, Orsay, France), French physicist, described as "the Isaac Newton of our time," who was awarded the 1991 Nobel Prize for Physics for his discoveries about the behavior of molecules in liquid crystals and polymers during the transition from order to disorder; his findings are used in liquid-crystal displays.

Ralph Ginzburg (28 Oct 1929, New York NY—6 Jul 2006, New York NY), American publisher, author, and photojournalist who was at the center of two highly publicized 1960s court cases involving freedom of speech rights.

Merv Griffin (Mervyn Edward Griffin; 6 Jul 1925, San Mateo CA—12 Aug 2007, Los Angeles CA), American television personality and producer who was the congenial host of *The Merv Griffin Show* (1962–63, 1965–86) and the creator of two of television's most successful game shows, *Jeopardy!* (1964–75, 1984–) and *Wheel of Fortune* (1975–); he sold Merv Griffin Enterprises for $250 million in 1986, becoming one of the richest entertainers in Hollywood history; in 2005 he was honored with a Daytime Emmy Lifetime Achievement Award.

David Halberstam (10 Apr 1934, New York NY—23 Apr 2007, Menlo Park CA), American journalist and author who received a Pulitzer Prize in 1964 for his penetrating coverage of the Vietnam War as a staff reporter (1960–67) for the *New York Times* and went on to become the best-selling author of 21 meticulously researched books, including *The Best and the Brightest* (1972), *War in a Time of Peace: Bush, Clinton, and the Generals* (2001), and *Playing for Keeps: Michael Jordan and the World He Made* (1999).

Mark Harris (Mark Harris Finkelstein; 19 Nov 1922, Mount Vernon NY—30 May 2007, Santa Barbara CA), American novelist who was the author of a baseball tetralogy; the second novel in the series, *Bang the Drum Slowly* (1956), was hailed as one of the 100 greatest sports novels of all time and was adapted in 1956 as a television play with Paul Newman and in 1973 as a film starring Robert De Niro.

Johnny Hart (John Lewis Hart) (18 Feb 1931, Endicott NY—7 Apr 2007, Nineveh NY), American cartoonist who created a formidable following of more than 100 million readers as the creator in 1958 of the comic strip *B.C.*, which focused on prehistoric cave dwellers and anthropomorphic animals and plants while being laced with puns and clever satire about modern society.

Ryutaro Hashimoto (29 Jul 1937, Soja, Okayama prefecture, Japan—1 Jul 2006, Tokyo, Japan), Japanese politician who served (1996–98) as prime minister but left office after having failed in his attempts to end a long-lasting economic recession in Japan.

Sir Wally Herbert (Walter William Herbert; 24 Oct 1934, York, England—12 June 2007, Inverness, Scotland), British polar explorer who led the British Transarctic Expedition that crossed the Arctic Ocean via the North Pole on an epic 15-month trek covering more than 5,800 km (3,600 mi); his books included *The Noose of Laurels* (1989), in which he determined that American explorer Robert Peary,

famed for being the first man to reach the North Pole, had actually fallen short in his attempt.

María Julia Hernández (30 Jan 1939, Honduras—30 Mar 2007, San Salvador, El Salvador), El Salvadoran human rights activist who devoted her life to chronicling and investigating the abuses and massacres committed by right-wing paramilitary death squads during El Salvador's civil war (1980s and early '90s) as the founder (1983) of Tutela Legal, a Roman Catholic-based human rights group.

Arthur Edward Spence Hill (1 Aug 1922, Melfort, SK, Canada—22 Oct 2006, Pacific Palisades CA), Canadian-born American actor who appeared in some 50 TV series but was best remembered for his starring role in *Owen Marshall: Counselor at Law* (1971–74) and as George in the play *Who's Afraid of Virginia Woolf?* (1962).

Don Ho (Donald Tai Loy Ho) (13 Aug 1930, Honolulu, HI—14 Apr 2007, Honolulu), American singer who became an icon of the relaxed Hawaiian lifestyle with his rich baritone in songs such as "Tiny Bubbles," a hit single in 1967 that became his signature tune; his success on the mainland sparked the TV variety program *The Don Ho Show* (1976–77).

Martha Louise Holmes (7 Feb 1923, Louisville KY—19 Sep 2006, New York NY), American photographer who specialized in taking intimate portraits of celebrities, politicians, and sports figures while working for 35 years as a freelancer for *Life* magazine.

F(rancis) Clark Howell (27 Nov 1925, Kansas City MO—10 Mar 2007, Berkeley CA), American anthropologist who established paleoanthropology as a multidisciplinary science in the study of early human origins and founded the Human Evolution Research Center at the University of California, Berkeley; Howell was also a recipient of the Charles Darwin Award for Lifetime Achievement in Physical Anthropology and an adviser for *Encyclopædia Britannica*.

Elias Hrawi (4 Sep 1925, Hawch Al-Umara, Lebanon—7 Jul 2006, Beirut, Lebanon), Lebanese politician who, as president of Lebanon (1989–98), helped bring stability to the country after its prolonged civil war and the 1982–85 occupation by Israel.

Huang Ju (September 1938, Jiashin, China—2 Jun 2007, Beijing, China), Chinese politician who served as vice-premier of China from 2003 until his death and was responsible for reforms to China's banking and financial systems; he was a protégé of Jiang Zemin, a Shanghai party boss who became president of China.

Barnard Hughes (Bernard Hughes; 16 Jul 1915, Bedford Hills NY—11 Jul 2006, New York NY), American character actor, a veteran who appeared in more than 400 plays and in dozens of films and TV shows.

E. Howard Hunt (Everette Howard Hunt, Jr.; 9 Oct 1918, Hamburg NY—23 Jan 2007, Miami FL), American spy who spent 33 months in prison after he pleaded guilty to wiretapping and conspiracy in the 1972 break-in at the Democratic National Committee headquarters in the Watergate complex, Washington DC.

Lamar Hunt (2 Aug 1932, El Dorado AR—13 Dec 2006, Dallas TX), American sports executive who was the founder in 1959 of the upstart American Football League, which rivaled the National Football League in influence before the two agreed to merge in 1966.

Saddam Hussein (Saddam Hussein al-Majid al-Tikriti; 28 Apr 1937, near Tikrit, Iraq—30 Dec 2006, Baghdad, Iraq), Iraqi military leader and politician, the despotic president of Iraq from 1979 until 2003, when he was deposed by the invasion of Iraq by US-led coalition forces; he was tried by the Iraqi High Tribunal, convicted of crimes against humanity, and condemned to death by hanging.

Marmaduke James Hussey, Baron Hussey of North Bradley (29 Aug 1923, London, England–27 Dec 2006, London, England), British newspaper and TV executive who was appointed (1986) BBC chairman by Prime Minister Margaret Thatcher, reportedly in order to "sort out" the corporation, which the Thatcher administration accused of leftist antigovernment programming.

William Ian deWitt Hutt (2 May 1920, Toronto, ON, Canada–27 Jun 2007, Stratford, ON, Canada), Canadian theatrical actor and director who became a member of the Stratford Festival of Canada during its inaugural season (1953) and earned international acclaim in the title roles of such Shakespearean tragedies as King Lear, Titus Andronicus, Macbeth, and Richard II; among his many accolades were a Companion of the Order of Canada (1969).

Vernon Martin Ingram (Werner Adolf Martin Immerwahr; 19 May 1924, Breslau, Germany [now Wroclaw, Poland]–17 Aug 2006, Boston MA), American biochemist who was hailed as the father of molecular medicine for having discovered in the mid-1950s the amino acid in the oxygen-carrying molecule called hemoglobin responsible for sickle-cell anemia.

Steve Irwin (Stephen Robert Irwin; "The Crocodile Hunter"; 22 Feb 1962, Essendon, VIC, Australia–4 Sep 2006, off the coast of Port Douglas, QLD, Australia), Australian wildlife conservationist and TV personality who achieved worldwide fame as the exuberant host of The Crocodile Hunter (1992–2006) TV series; Irwin shared with his audiences a passion for preserving wildlife and emphasized the beauty in some not-so-popular animals, such as venomous snakes and spiders.

Molly Ivins (Mary Tyler Ivins; 30 Aug 1944, Monterey CA–31 Jan 2007, Austin TX), American political satirist who wrote a newspaper column from a staunchly liberal point of view that mercilessly and humorously skewered politicians in both her home state of Texas and the federal government.

Dennis Wayne Johnson ("D.J."; 18 Sep 1954, Compton CA–22 Feb 2007, Austin TX), American basketball player who, in a 13-year career as an exceptional defensive guard, on three occasions helped two different teams capture the National Basketball Association championships.

Lady Bird Johnson (Claudia Alta Taylor; 22 Dec 1912, Karnack TX–11 Jul 2007, Austin TX), American first lady who was the wife of Lyndon B. Johnson, 36th president of the United States (1963–69), and was a noted environmentalist; she married Johnson on 17 Nov 1934, just a few months after their first meeting, and she gave birth to two daughters, Lynda Bird in 1944 and Luci Baines in 1947; following her husband's 1964 election she concentrated on Head Start, a program aimed at helping preschool children from disadvantaged backgrounds, but she was most closely identified with an environmental program, called "beautification," that sought to encourage people to make their surroundings more attractive, and she urged Congress to pass the Highway Beautification Bill, which was strenuously opposed by billboard advertisers. After the Johnsons retired to their ranch in Texas, she established the National Wildflower Research Center (now the Lady Bird Johnson Wildlife Center); in 1977 she was awarded the Medal of Freedom for her conservation efforts.

Duke Jordan (Irving Sidney Jordan; 1 Apr 1922, New York NY–8 Aug 2006, Valby, Denmark), American jazz pianist who first became noted during the heyday of bebop as a member of Charlie Parker's classic late 1940s quintet and then enjoyed a long career as a lyrical soloist.

Winthrop Donaldson Jordan (11 Nov 1931, Worcester MA–23 Feb 2007, Oxford MS), American historian, educator, and author who explored the nature of race in meticulously researched works that included White over Black: American Attitudes Toward the Negro, 1550–1812 (1968), which won a National Book Award, and The White Man's Burden: Historical Origins of Racism in the United States (1974).

Ghulam Ishaq Khan (20 Jan 1915, Ismail Khel, North-West Frontier Province, British India [now in Pakistan]–27 Oct 2006, Peshawar, Pakistan), Pakistani politician who served as president (1988–93).

Benedict Kiely (15 Aug 1919, near Dromore, County Tyrone, Ireland [now in Northern Ireland]–9 Feb 2007, Dublin, Ireland), Irish novelist and short-story writer who explored everyday life in Ireland, especially after partition in the 1920s, in a rich narrative voice that drew on Irish oral tradition; he was elected Saoi of Aosdána, Ireland's highest artistic honor, in 1996.

Pete Kleinow ("Sneaky"; 1934, South Bend IN–6 Jan 2007, Petaluma CA), American pedal-steel guitarist, an original member of the Flying Burrito Brothers, a popular musical group of the late 1960s and '70s that was one of the chief influences on the development of country rock.

Lars Korvald (29 Apr 1916, near Nedre Eiker, Norway–4 Jul 2006, Oslo, Norway), Norwegian politician who was the first Christian Democratic prime minister of the country, at the head of a three-party minority coalition (1972–73).

Bowie Kent Kuhn (28 Oct 1926, Takoma Park MD–15 Mar 2007, Jacksonville FL), American sports executive who strove to uphold the integrity of Major League Baseball (MLB) while serving as its commissioner (1969–84); during his tenure five MLB work stoppages occurred, but he was at the forefront of the movement to bring night games to the World Series, an action that resulted in millions of dollars in TV advertising revenue, and he was also noted for the many fines and suspensions he imposed.

Mazisi Kunene (Mazisi Raymond Fakazi Mngoni Kunene; 12 May 1930, Durban, Union of South Africa–11 Aug 2006, Durban, South Africa), South African–born poet and educator whose verse explored the culture and history of the Zulu people; he was named poet laureate of Africa by UNESCO in 1993 and in 2005 was appointed the first poet laureate of South Africa.

Frankie Laine (Francesco Paolo LoVecchio; 30 Mar 1913, Chicago IL–6 Feb 2007, San Diego CA), American singer who had a string of hit songs in the 1950s but was perhaps best remembered for recording the theme song to the long-running TV show Rawhide (1959–66).

Paul Christian Lauterbur (6 May 1929, Sidney OH–27 Mar 2007, Urbana IL), American chemist who won the Nobel Prize for Physiology or Medicine in 2003, together with British physicist Sir Peter Mansfield, for the development of magnetic resonance imaging (MRI); Mansfield transformed Lauterbur's research on nuclear magnetic resonance, the selective absorption of radio waves by certain atomic nuclei subjected to a strong, nonuniform magnetic field, into a practical medical tool that was noninvasive and lacking the harmful side effects of X-ray and computed tomography (CT) examinations.

Kenneth Lay (Kenneth Lee Lay; 15 Apr 1942, Tyrone MO—5 Jul 2006, Aspen CO), American business executive and CEO of Enron Corp. until his resignation in 2002; he was indicted by a federal jury in Houston in 2004 for his role in the catastrophic crash of the company in 2001.

Gerald Levert (13 Jul 1966, Philadelphia PA—10 Nov 2006, Cleveland OH), American singer, a powerful and soulful vocalist whose string of R&B hits included "I Swear," "I'd Give Anything," and "Baby Hold on to Me," a duet with his father, Eddie Levert, Sr.

Sol LeWitt (Solomon LeWitt) (9 Sep 1928, Hartford CT—8 Apr 2007, New York NY), American sculptor, printmaker, and draftsman who was credited with helping to usher in conceptual art and minimalism as major movements of the post-World War II era with wall drawings that featured basic geometric forms and four basic colors (red, yellow, blue, and black).

Alexander Litvinenko (Aleksandr Valterovich Litvinenko; 4 Dec 1962, Voronezh, near Moscow, USSR [now in Russia]—23 Nov 2006, London, England), Russian security agent who investigated domestic organized crime in his role as a member (1988–99) of the KGB (from 1994 the FSB); his death by plutonium-210 poisoning under suspicious circumstances was a cause célèbre in 2006.

Robert Lockwood, Jr. (Robert Jr. Lockwood; 27 Mar 1915, Turkey Scratch AR—21 Nov 2006, Cleveland OH), American blues musician who was perhaps best known for his relationship with blues legend Robert Johnson.

Lobby Loyde (John Baslington Lyde; 18 May 1951, Longreach, QLD, Australia—21 Apr 2007, Melbourne, VIC, Australia), Australian rock musician who championed the loud, aggressive musical style that dominated Australian pub rock and influenced such heavy metal bands as AC/DC; a member of the Aztecs, Loyde was inducted into the Australian Recording Industry Association Hall of Fame in 2006.

Muhammadu Maccido (Alhaji Muhammadu Maccido Abubakar; 20 Apr 1926, Sokoto, Nigeria—29 Oct 2006, near Abuja, Nigeria), Nigerian religious figure, the 19th sultan of Sokoto, head of the Sokoto caliphate, and the spiritual leader of about 70 million Muslims in Nigeria.

Alan Graham MacDiarmid (14 Apr 1927, Masterton, New Zealand—7 Feb 2007, Drexel Hill PA), New Zealand-born American chemist who was awarded the Nobel Prize for Chemistry in 2000 (together with Alan J. Heeger and Hideki Shirakawa) for the discovery that certain plastics can be chemically modified to conduct electricity almost as readily as metals.

Naguib Mahfouz (11 Dec 1911, Cairo, Egypt—30 Aug 2006, Cairo, Egypt), Egyptian novelist and screenwriter noted for works dealing with social issues involving women and political prisoners; he was awarded the 1988 Nobel Prize for Literature, the first Arabic writer to be so honored.

Theodore Harold Maiman (11 Jul 1927, Los Angeles CA—5 May 2007, Vancouver, BC, Canada), American physicist who constructed the first laser, which found numerous practical uses, ranging from delicate surgery to measurement of the distance between the Earth and the Moon; his autobiography, *The Laser Odyssey*, was published in 2000.

Malietoa Tanumafili II (4 Jan 1912—11 May 2007, Apia, Samoa), Samoan head of state who was the world's oldest reigning monarch and the third longest serving, having succeeded to the chiefly title Malietoa in 1939; he was appointed (1940) an adviser to the New Zealand colonial administration and played a large role in the independence negotiations with New Zealand.

Bernard John Manning (13 Aug 1930, Manchester, England—18 Jun 2007, Manchester, England), British comedian who was as well known for the inflammatory invective with which he pilloried other races and nationalities as he was for his pointed satire and bawdy jokes; he was named National Club Comedian of the Year in 1982 and 1985.

Bob Mathias (Robert Bruce Mathias; 17 Nov 1930, Tulare CA—2 Sep 2006, Fresno CA), American athlete, the youngest to win a gold medal in the decathlon in Olympic competition; after his victory in 1948, at the age of 17, he returned to win a second Olympic gold medal in 1952.

Robert McFerrin, Sr. (19 Mar 1921, Marianna AR—24 Nov 2006, St Louis MO), American opera singer who became the first black male to solo at the Metropolitan Opera when he made his 1955 debut as Amonasro in *Aïda*.

Enolia Pettigen McMillan (20 Oct 1904, Willow Grove PA—24 Oct 2006, Stevenson MD), American civil rights leader who served (1984–89) as the first woman president of the National Association for the Advancement of Colored People.

Barbara McNair (Barbara Joan McNair; 4 Mar 1934, Racine WI—4 Feb 2007, Los Angeles CA), American singer and actress who starred (1969–71) in the TV variety program *The Barbara McNair Show* as well as movies and stage shows and was a recording artist during the 1960s and early 1970s.

Josefina Méndez (8 Mar 1941, Havana, Cuba—26 Jan 2007, Havana, Cuba), Cuban ballerina regarded as one of the "four jewels" of the National Ballet of Cuba (together with Loipa Araújo, Aurora Bosch, and Mirta Plá) and who enjoyed a 35-year career as a dancer and as the company's ballet mistress.

William Morris Meredith, Jr. (9 Jan 1919, New York NY—30 May 2007, New London CT), American poet who was awarded (1988) a Pulitzer Prize for *Partial Accounts: New and Selected Poems* (1987), a collection that showcased his formal and unadorned verse, which was compared to that of Robert Frost; from 1978 to 1980 he was the poetry consultant to the Library of Congress (now the poet laureate consultant in poetry).

Tammy Faye Messner (Tammy Faye LaValley; Tammy Faye Bakker; 7 Mar 1942, International Falls MN—20 Jul 2007, near Kansas City MO), American televangelist who was best remembered as the diminutive wife of Jim Bakker and as his cohost on the televised Jim and Tammy Show, which was syndicated on the Praise the Lord Network, founded by the couple in 1974; the couple built a $125 million empire that included Heritage USA, a religious theme park, and were often criticized for their lavish spending; in 1987 they lost their TV ministry following a series of sex and money scandals, and she and Bakker divorced after he was convicted in 1989 of having bilked followers of $158 million.

Joseph Metcalf III (20 Dec 1927, Holyoke MA—2 Mar 2007, Washington DC), vice admiral in the US Navy who commanded the US military invasion of Grenada in October 1983, after a bloody Marxist coup resulted in the execution of the country's prime minister and 15 of his supporters.

Stanley Miller (7 Mar 1930, Oakland CA—20 May 2007, National City CA), American chemist who designed the first experiment to produce organic molecules from some of the inorganic components of the Earth's prebiotic atmosphere; Miller's procedure (which was known as the Miller-Urey experiment) was a groundbreaking moment for research into the origin of life on Earth and gave rise to the term *prebiotic soup.*

Parren James Mitchell (29 Apr 1922, Baltimore MD—28 May 2007, Baltimore MD), American politician who as a liberal Democrat from Maryland spent eight terms (1971–87) in the US House of Representatives and was the first African American since 1898 to be elected to Congress from a state below the Mason-Dixon Line.

Kiichi Miyazawa (8 Oct 1919, Tokyo, Japan—28 Jun 2007, Tokyo, Japan), Japanese politician who served (1991–93) as prime minister of Japan but was unable to implement promised anticorruption measures; in 1953 he was elected to the Diet (parliament), and along with other senior politicians, he was tainted by bribery scandals—he was forced to resign as finance minister in December 1988; he soon returned to power, however, and became prime minister on 5 November.

Sheridan Robert Morley (5 Dec 1941, Ascot, Berkshire, England—16 Feb 2007, London, England), British theater critic and biographer who was nearly ubiquitous in the theater scene in London, writing reviews for an assortment of newspapers and magazines and appearing on several TV and radio shows.

Byron Nelson (John Byron Nelson, Jr.; 4 Feb 1912, near Waxahachie TX—26 Sep 2006, Roanoke TX), American golfer who dominated the sport in the late 1930s and '40s; known for his fluid swing, he won a record 11 consecutive professional tournaments in 1945.

David Nicholson ("The Duke"; 19 Mar 1939, Epsom, Surrey, England—27 Aug 2006), British steeplechase jockey and trainer who, as one of England's finest jump trainers (1968–99), saddled 1,499 winning horses and was named champion National Hunt trainer in 1993–94 and 1994–95.

Joe Niekro (Joseph Franklin Niekro; 7 Nov 1944, Martins Ferry OH—27 Oct 2006, Tampa FL), American baseball player who won 221 games in 22 seasons as a major league pitcher after making his big-league debut in 1967 with the Chicago Cubs.

Saparmurad (Atayevich) Niyazov ("Turkmenbashi"; 19 Feb 1940, Kipchak, near Ashkhabad [now Ashgabat], USSR [now in Turkmenistan]—21 Dec 2006, Ashgabat, Turkmenistan), Turkmen politician, the despotic and idiosyncratic ruler of Turkmenistan for more than 15 years, from 1991 when the former Soviet republic declared independence from the USSR.

(William) Parry O'Brien (28 Jan 1932, Santa Monica CA—21 Apr 2007, Santa Clarita CA), American shotputter who won two gold and one silver Olympic medal and developed a style that revolutionized the event (the maneuver called for the athlete to turn 180° before the release of the shot); he was inducted into the US Track and Field Hall of Fame in 1974 and the US Olympic Hall of Fame in 1984.

Robin Olds (14 Jul 1922, Honolulu, Hawaiian Islands—14 Jun 2007, Steamboat Springs CO), brigadier general (ret.), US Air Force, who was an ace fighter pilot who flew 107 combat missions during World War II and 152 combat missions during the Vietnam War; he was perhaps best known for commanding the air force wing over North Vietnam in the war's biggest air battle; he later served as commandant of cadets at the US Air Force Academy (1967–71).

Buck O'Neil (John Jordan O'Neil, Jr.; 13 Nov 1911,

Carrabelle FL—6 Oct 2006, Kansas City MO), American baseball player who starred as a first baseman and manager in the Negro leagues.

Antonio Ortíz Mena (16 Apr 1907, Parral, Mexico—12 Mar 2007, Mexico City, Mexico), Mexican politician who was credited with fueling Mexico's phenomenal growth (the "Mexican miracle" that elevated millions of Mexicans into the middle class) while serving as the country's finance minister (1958–70); from 1971 to 1988 he led the Inter-American Development Bank (IDB) and was responsible for increasing its lending from $4 billion to $40 billion and its membership from 23 countries to 44.

Aden Abdullah Osman (1908, Belet Weyne, Italian Somaliland [now in Somalia]—8 Jun 2007, Nairobi, Kenya), Somali politician who served as independent Somalia's first president (1961–67) and was the first post-colonial African head of state to voluntarily step down after losing an election.

Jack Palance (Volodymyr Palanyuk; Walter Jack Palance; 18 Feb 1919, Lattimer Mines PA—10 Nov 2006, Montecito CA), American actor who was often typecast in menacing roles but won the Oscar for best supporting actor for a comedic self-parody as Curly in *City Slickers* (1991).

Valentín Paniagua (23 Sep 1936, Cuzco, Peru—16 Oct 2006, Lima, Peru), Peruvian politician who, as caretaker president of Peru (2000–01), was instrumental in guiding the country back to democracy following the collapse of the autocratic government of Pres. Alberto Fujimori.

Maurice-Arthur-Jean Papon (3 Sep 1910, Gretz-Armainvilliers, France—17 Feb 2007, Paris, France), French official (1942–44) under the collaborationist Vichy government, who authorized the arrest and deportation of more than 1,600 Jews, most of whom died in concentration camps.

Luciano Pavarotti (12 Oct 1935, Modena, Italy—6 Sep 2007, Modena, Italy), Italian operatic lyric tenor who, as one of the "Three Tenors" (with Plácido Domingo and José Carreras), was one of the most popular singers of his time.

Willie Pep (Guglielmo Papaleo; 19 Sep 1922, Middletown CT—23 Nov 2006, Rocky Hill CT), American boxer who reigned (1942–48 and 1949–50) as featherweight champion of the world and compiled a remarkable 230–11–1 record (65 wins by knockout).

Robert Einar Petersen (10 Sep 1926, Los Angeles CA—23 Mar 2007, Santa Monica CA), American publisher who established a multimillion-dollar publishing empire, starting with his founding of *Hot Rod* (1948) and *Motor Trend* (1949) magazines and later, titles such as *Car Craft, Guns & Ammo,* and *Photographic;* Petersen helped establish the Petersen Automotive Museum in Los Angeles.

Augusto Pinochet (Augusto José Ramón Pinochet Ugarte; 25 Nov 1915, Valparaíso, Chile—10 Dec 2006, Santiago, Chile), Chilean dictator, leader of the military junta that overthrew the socialist government of Pres. Salvador Allende on 11 Sep 1973, and head of Chile's military government (1974–90).

Anna Politkovskaya (Anna Stepanovna Mazepa; 30 Aug 1958, New York NY—7 Oct 2006, Moscow, Russia), Russian investigative journalist who denounced the government of Russian Pres. Vladimir Putin for corruption and human rights abuses, particularly during the Chechen war of secession; she was found shot in the elevator of her apartment building.

Carlo Ponti (Carlo Fortunaro Pietro Ponti; 11 Dec 1912, Magenta, near Milan, Italy—10 Jan 2007, Geneva, Switzerland), Italian film producer who was responsible for producing (or co-producing) more than 150 films, including the Oscar-winning *La strada* (1954), *War and Peace* (1955), *Doctor Zhivago* (1965), and *Blowup* (1966).

Tom Poston (Thomas Gordon Poston; 17 Oct 1921, Columbus OH—30 Apr 2007, Los Angeles CA), American actor who was best remembered for TV roles in which he portrayed a bumbling funnyman, including his Emmy Award-winning role as one of the interviewees on *The Steve Allen Show* (1956–60), befuddled drunkard Franklin Delano Bickley on *Mork and Mindy* (1978–82), and inept handyman George Utley on *Newhart* (1982–90).

Warren Eversleigh Preece (17 Apr 1921, Norwalk CT—11 Apr 2007, Philadelphia PA), American encyclopedist who was general editor of *Encyclopædia Britannica* in the creation of the 15th edition (1974), which consists of 30 volumes in three parts (the *Propædia*, the *Micropædia*, and the *Macropædia*); after publication of the 15th edition he resigned as editor, but he continued to serve as a member of the board of editors (vice-chairman, 1975–79).

Ivica Racan (24 Feb 1944, Ebersbach, Germany—29 Apr 2007, Zagreb, Croatia), Croatian politician who, as prime minister (2000–03), moved the country away from the nationalistic authoritarianism of Pres. Franjo Tudjman, the country's first leader (1991–99) after independence, and toward a more liberal Western-oriented future, introducing economic reforms such as the privatization of state monopolies and political reforms that increased the power of the legislature and cut down on the pervasive corruption of the previous regime.

Fons Rademakers (Alphonse Marie Rademakers; 5 Sep 1920, Roosendaal, Netherlands—22 Feb 2007, Geneva, Switzerland), Dutch filmmaker, the first from The Netherlands to win an Academy Award for best foreign-language film, for his poignant drama *De Aanslag* (1986; *The Assault*).

Charles Nelson Reilly (13 Jan 1931, New York NY—25 May 2007, Los Angeles CA), American actor who won a Tony Award in 1962 for his portrayal of Bud Frump in *How To Succeed in Business Without Really Trying* (1961) and was nominated for a Tony in 1997 for directing *The Gin Game;* he was best remembered for his comic double entendres while appearing as a fixture on the television game show *The Hollywood Squares* (1965–82).

Ann W. Richards (Dorothy Ann Willis; 1 Sep 1933, Lakeview TX—13 Sep 2006, Austin TX), American politician who served (1991–95) as the governor of Texas and was the first woman to gain the office in her own right (rather than as a surrogate for a husband).

Ian Richardson (Ian William Richardson; 7 Apr 1934, Edinburgh, Scotland—9 Feb 2007, London, England), British actor who was an accomplished actor and a founding member (1960–75) of the Royal Shakespeare Company; he gained international recognition for his performance in the BBC TV trilogy *House of Cards* (1990), *To Play the King* (1993), and *The Final Cut* (1995).

Eddie Robinson (Edward Gay Robinson) (13 Feb 1919, Jackson LA—3 Apr 2007, Ruston LA), American collegiate football coach who set the record for most career wins (the mark was surpassed in 2003 by John Gagliardi of St. John's University); Robinson spent his entire head-coaching career (1941–97) at Grambling (LA) State University, where his Tigers recorded 3 perfect seasons and captured 17 conference titles; he retired with a record of

408-165-15 and was inducted into the College Football Hall of Fame in 1997.

Joe Rosenthal (Joseph John Rosenthal; 9 Oct 1911, Washington DC—20 Aug 2006, Novato CA), American photographer who captured the Pulitzer Prize-winning image of five Marines and a navy corpsman hoisting an American flag on Mt. Suribachi on the island of Iwo Jima near the end of World War II.

Baron Guy de Rothschild (Guy Édouard Alphonse Paul de Rothschild; 21 May 1908, Paris, France—12 Jun 2007, Paris, France), French banker who, as the scion of the French branch of the Rothschild international banking dynasty, restored his family's fortunes after their holdings were confiscated during the Nazi occupation of France; he was also a successful breeder of Thoroughbred racehorses and was involved in the family's wine interests in Bordeaux.

Bo Schembechler (Glenn Edward Schembechler; 1 Apr 1929, Barberton OH—17 Nov 2006, Southfield MI), American football coach who was head coach (1969–89) at the University of Michigan and had an impressive lifetime record of 234-65-8.

Wally Schirra (Walter Marty Schirra, Jr.; 12 Mar 1923, Hackensack NJ—3 May 2007, La Jolla CA), US astronaut, the only one to fly in the Mercury, Gemini, and Apollo space programs, who manned the Mercury *Sigma 7* (1962) and was command pilot of Gemini 6 (1965), which made the first rendezvous in space; Schirra was one of the original seven astronauts named in 1959 and the fifth to go into space.

Arthur Meier Schlesinger, Jr. (Arthur Bancroft Schlesinger) (15 Oct 1917, Columbus OH—28 Feb 2007, New York NY), American historian, educator, and public official who reinterpreted the American era of Jacksonian democracy in the Pulitzer Prize-winning *The Age of Jackson* (1946); he was an adviser to Adlai Stevenson and John F. Kennedy during their presidential campaigns, and Kennedy appointed him a special assistant for Latin American affairs—Schlesinger's study of the Kennedy administration, *A Thousand Days: John F. Kennedy in the White House* (1965), also won a Pulitzer Prize.

Melvin Schwartz (2 Nov 1932, New York NY—28 Aug 2006, Twin Falls ID), American physicist and entrepreneur who was the corecipient of the Nobel Prize for Physics in 1988 for research concerning neutrinos (subatomic particles that have no electric charge and virtually no mass).

Ousmane Sembène (1 Jan 1923, Ziguinchor-Casamance, French West Africa [now in Senegal]—9 Jun 2007, Dakar, Senegal), Senegalese writer and film director who was the first internationally known African filmmaker and whose *La Noire de …* (1966; *Black Girl*) is considered the first major motion picture produced by a sub-Saharan African filmmaker; his *Moolaadé* (2004; "Protection") received the Prix Un Certain Regard at the Cannes Festival.

Sidney Sheldon (Sidney Schechtel; 11 Feb 1917, Chicago IL—30 Jan 2007, Rancho Mirage CA), American writer of award-winning film and TV screenplays and, later, best-selling novels.

Beverly Sills (Belle Miriam Silverman; 25 May 1929, Brooklyn NY—2 Jul 2007, New York NY), American operatic soprano and administrator; she made her operatic debut in 1947 with the Philadelphia Civic Opera, and in 1955 she became a member of the company of the New York City Opera; besides serving (1979–89) as director of that company, Sills was chairman of the board of New York's Lincoln Center (1994–2002) and of the Metropolitan Opera (2002–05).

Anna Nicole Smith (Vickie Lynn Hogan; married name Marshall; 28 Nov 1967, Mexia TX—8 Feb 2007, Hollywood FL), American model and *Playboy* magazine's Playmate of the Year 1993; known for her brief marriage (1994–95) to aged billionaire J. Howard Marshall, her reality-based TV series in 2002–04, and other aspects of her flamboyant lifestyle that kept her prominent in the tabloids.

Tom Snyder (12 May 1936, Milwaukee WI—29 Jul 2007, San Francisco CA), American TV newsman who served as host of *The Tomorrow Show* (1973–82) and *The Late Late Show with Tom Snyder* (1995–99) and helped to establish the popularity of the late-night talk-show format; he was best known for his ability to connect with audiences and for his unusual questions and no-nonsense style of interviewing an array of guests.

Mickey Spillane (Frank Morrison Spillane; 9 Mar 1918, Brooklyn NY—17 Jul 2006, Murrells Inlet SC), American writer who flouted literary taste in detective fiction that was characterized by violence and sexual licentiousness, vigorous narrative, and captivating central characters.

Darryl Floyd Stingley (18 Sep 1951, Chicago IL—5 Apr 2007, Chicago), American football player whose career was ended during a preseason game in 1978, after what many believed to have been an intentionally brutal tackle by Oakland Raiders safety Jack ("The Assassin") Tatum; Stingley was left a quadriplegic, and his injuries prompted the NFL to institute rules to protect receivers and to penalize overly aggressive tacklers.

Alfredo Stroessner (Alfredo Stroessner Matiauda; 3 Nov 1912, Encarnación, Paraguay—16 Aug 2006, Brasília, Brazil), Paraguayan military leader who became president of Paraguay after leading an army coup in 1954 and was one of Latin America's longest-serving rulers before he was overthrown in 1989.

William Styron (William Clark Styron, Jr.; 11 Jun 1925, Newport News VA—1 Nov 2006, Martha's Vineyard MA), American novelist noted for his treatment of tragic themes and his use of a rich, classical style.

Ta Mok (c. 1926, Takeo province, French Indochina [now in Cambodia]—21 Jul 2006, Phnom Penh, Cambodia), Cambodian guerrilla leader who, as a senior leader of the Khmer Rouge, was believed to have been responsible for many of the worst atrocities of that bloody regime.

Adelaide Tambo (Adelaide Frances Tshukudu; 18 Jul 1929, near Vereeniging, Union of South Africa—31 Jan 2007, Johannesburg, South Africa), South African political activist who was a prominent figure in the struggle against apartheid in South Africa; she was married to nationalist leader Oliver Tambo.

Dame Te Atairangikaahu (Princess Piki Mahuta; Princess Piki Paki; Te Arikinui Dame Te Atairangikaahu; Dame Te Ata; 23 Jul 1931, Waahi Marae Huntly, New Zealand—15 Aug 2006, Ngaruawahia, New Zealand), Maori queen, the sixth and longest-serving monarch of the Kingitanga movement and the Maori people's first reigning queen.

Marie Tharp (30 Jul 1920, Ypsilanti MI—23 Aug 2006, Nyack NY), American oceanographic cartographer who pioneered ocean-floor mapping, which provided crucial support for acceptance of the theories of seafloor spreading and continental drift.

Bob Thaves (Robert Lee Thaves; 5 Oct 1924, Burt IA—1 Aug 2006, Torrance CA), American comic-strip artist who sketched the award-winning nationally syndicated *Frank and Ernest*, a one-panel comic feature that followed the adventures of the pun-cracking tramps as they delivered their wry commentary, usually from a park bench.

Billy Thorpe (William Richard Thorpe; 29 Mar 1946, Manchester, England—28 Feb 2007, Sydney, NSW, Australia), British-born Australian rock icon who, as front man for the Aztecs, was regarded as the father of Australian pub rock; he was inducted into the Australian Recording Industry Association Hall of Fame in 1991.

Tomasi Kulimoetoke II (26 Jul 1918, Mata-Utu, Wallis [Uvea] Island—7 May 2007, Mata-Utu, Wallis and Futuna), Wallisian monarch who, as the 50th lavelua (paramount chief, or king, of Wallis), was the longest-serving traditional leader in the French South Pacific island dependency Wallis and Futuna (1959 until his death).

Henry Townsend (27 Oct 1909, Shelby MS—24 Sep 2006, Grafton WI), American blues musician who was one of the principal figures of the St. Louis blues scene and the last blues musician known to have recorded in the 1920s.

Tupou IV (King Taufa'ahau Tupou IV; 4 Jul 1918, Nuku'alofa, Tongatapu island, British-protected Tonga—10 Sep 2006, Auckland, New Zealand), Tongan monarch, the absolute ruler of Tonga for 41 years; he expanded Tonga's contact with the outside world and guided the 170-island territory's emergence as a fully independent country in 1970.

Jack Joseph Valenti (5 Sep 1921, Houston TX—26 Apr 2007, Washington DC), American public figure who was a longtime lobbyist and publicist for the Motion Picture Association of America, of which he was president (1966–2004), and the brainchild behind the creation of the film-rating system that assigned labels for audience suitability (currently G, PG, PG-13, R, or NC-17).

Marais Viljoen (2 Dec 1915, Robertson, Cape province, Union of South Africa—4 Jan 2007, Pretoria, South Africa), South African politician; the fifth president (1979–84) of independent South Africa and the last to serve as a purely ceremonial head of state before the revised constitution of 1984 gave presidents greater power.

Kurt Vonnegut, Jr. (11 Nov 1922, Indianapolis IN—11 Apr 2007, New York NY), American novelist who was noted for his pessimistic and satiric novels that used fantasy and science fiction to highlight the horrors and ironies of 20th-century civilization; Vonnegut was captured by the Germans while serving in the US Air Force in World War II, and he was a survivor of the fire bombing of Dresden, Germany, in February 1945—his *Slaughterhouse-Five; or, The Children's Crusade, a Duty-Dance with Death* (1969), used that bombing raid as a symbol of the cruelty and destructiveness of war; *The Sirens of Titan* (1959) was a quasi-science-fiction novel in which the entire history of the human race is considered an accident attendant on an alien planet's search for a spare part for a spaceship; his other novels included *Cat's Cradle* (1963), *Mother Night* (1961), and *Breakfast of Champions* (1973); he also wrote plays, nonfiction, and collections of short stories, and in 2005 he published *A Man Without a Country*, a collection of essays and speeches.

Kurt Josef Waldheim (21 Dec 1918, Sankt Andrä-Wördern, Austria—14 Jun 2007, Vienna, Austria), Austrian diplomat and statesman who served two terms as the fourth UN secretary-general (1972–81) and one as president of Austria (1986–92) before an international scandal concerning his alleged complicity in Nazi atrocities during World War II ended his career; at the UN he oversaw effective relief efforts in Bangladesh, Nicaragua, the Sudan-Sahel area of Africa, and Guatemala.

Bill Walsh (30 Nov 1931, Los Angeles CA–30 Jul 2007, Woodside CA), American football coach who was the architect of the "West Coast offense," which featured short passes and quick slanting pass routes by receivers, and helped build the San Francisco 49ers into a powerhouse NFL team—under Walsh the 49ers won Super Bowls XVI (1981), XIX (1985) and XXIII (1989) and registered a record of 102-63-1; he was inducted into the Pro Football Hall of Fame in 1993.

Wang Guangmei (26 Sep 1921, China–13 Oct 2006, Beijing, China), Chinese first lady who was renowned for her beauty and her bourgeois lifestyle as the fifth wife of Liu Shaoqi, chairman (1959–68) of the People's Republic of China.

Nina Wang ("Little Sweetie"; 29 Sep 1937, Shanghai, China–3 Apr 2007, Hong Kong, China), Chinese businesswoman who became Asia's richest woman after she inherited the estate of her husband, Teddy Wang, the founder of Chinachem Group, a private property firm, and built it into a multinational empire; at the time of her death, the eccentric Wang reportedly had a fortune of $4.2 billion.

Jack Warden (John H. Lebzelter; 18 Sep 1920, Newark NJ–19 Jul 2006, New York NY), American actor who specialized in gruff character roles on the large and small screen.

Bradford Washburn (Henry Bradford Washburn, Jr.; 7 Jun 1910, Cambridge MA–10 Jan 2007, Lexington MA), American mountaineer, pioneer of aerial photography, cartographer, and museum director who mapped the Grand Canyon during the 1970s and made Boston's Museum of Science a leading institution of its kind.

Kate Webb (Catherine Merrial Webb; 24 Mar 1943, Christchurch, New Zealand–13 May 2007, Sydney, NSW, Australia), New Zealand-born journalist who, in her role as a reporter (1967–71) and Phnom Penh bureau chief (1971–77) for United Press International news agency, was one of the few women war correspondents to cover the Vietnam War; she later reported on wars, coups, and other civil strife in such places as Sri Lanka, Afghanistan, Nepal, Iraq, Indonesia, and East Timor.

Sandy West (Sandy Pesavento; 1959, Los Angeles CA–21 Oct 2006, San Dimas CA), American musician who used her powerful drumming to ignite the influential all-female rock band the Runaways, which she founded in 1975 with Joan Jett.

Milan B. Williams (28 Mar 1948, Okolona MS–9 Jul 2006, Houston TX), American keyboard player who was a founding member in 1968 of the soul-funk band the Commodores and scored the group's first hit after writing the instrumental "Machine Gun" (1974).

Ellen Jane Willis (14 Dec 1941, New York NY–9 Nov 2006, Queens NY), American feminist and journalist who agitated for women's rights, especially abortion rights, as the author of numerous articles; as a founder in 1969 of the short-lived Redstockings, an influential radical feminist group; and as a founder of No More Nice Girls, a street-theater group.

Bertha Wilson (Bertha Wernham; 18 Sep 1923, Kirkcaldy, Scotland–28 Apr 2007, Ottawa, ON, Canada), Canadian jurist who was appointed the first woman to serve on the Supreme Court of Canada (1982–91), after having been appointed the first woman on the Ontario Court of Appeal in

1975; she was the author of the 1988 Supreme Court decision that overturned Canada's restrictions on abortion, and she wrote the judgment in 1990 that recognized the battered-wife syndrome as a valid self-defense.

Ian Edmund Wooldridge ("Woolers") (14 Jan 1932–4 Mar 2007, London, England), British writer who was considered one of England's best sports journalists, writing with wit and a passionate enthusiasm for sports in a career that lasted almost 60 years (1948–2007); he was employed in 1961 by the *Daily Mail*, where he covered the cricket beat before being named sports editor in 1972; he was named Sportswriter of the Year four times and was appointed OBE in 1991.

Bob Woolmer (14 May 1948, Kanpur, Uttar Pradesh, India–18 Mar 2007, Kingston, Jamaica), English cricketer and coach whose sudden death, the night after the Pakistani cricket team that he coached was eliminated from the World Cup, made international news after a local medical examiner initially indicated that death had occurred by strangulation (it was later ruled that Woolmer died of natural causes); at the Test level he coached South Africa (1994–99) before taking over the Pakistani team in 2004.

Boris Nikolayevich Yeltsin (1 Feb 1931, Sverdlovsk [now Yekaterinburg], Russia, USSR–23 Apr 2007, Moscow, Russia), Russian politician who, as independent Russia's first popularly elected president (1991–99), guided the country through a stormy decade of political and economic retrenching but was plagued by an ongoing war with the breakaway republic of Chechnya and the failure of his free-market reforms to spur economic growth; Yeltsin joined the Communist Party in 1961, and after Mikhail Gorbachev came to national power, he chose Yeltsin to clean out the corruption in the Moscow party organization, and the next year he elevated Yeltsin to the Politburo. As the mayor of Moscow, Yeltsin began condemning the slow pace of reform, challenging party conservatives, and criticizing Gorbachev, and he was forced to resign from the Moscow party leadership (1987) and from the Politburo (1988); in May 1990 the parliament of the Russian SFSR elected him president of the republic against Gorbachev's wishes, and Yeltsin took steps to give the Russian republic more autonomy, declared himself in favor of a market-oriented economy and a multiparty political system, and quit the Communist Party. His victory in the first direct popular elections for the presidency of the Russian republic (June 1991) was seen as a mandate for economic reform; when the Soviet Union collapsed on Christmas, the Russian government under his leadership assumed many of the former superpower's responsibilities.

Mohammad Zahir Shah (15 Oct 1914, Kabul, Afghanistan–23 Jul 2007, Kabul, Afghanistan), Afghan monarch who, as Afghanistan's last reigning king (1933–73), provided an era of stable government while maintaining a neutral position for his country in international politics; he established a constitutional monarchy, prohibited royal relatives from holding public office, and undertook a number of economic-development projects, including irrigation and highway construction, but in a bloodless coup on 17 Jul 1973, he was deposed, and he went into exile in Italy soon after; following the US overthrow of the Taliban, he returned to Afghanistan in 2002, and he was later given the honorary title Father of the Nation.

Awards

TIME's Top 100 Films

There's nothing like a list to stimulate a strong discussion, so in the hopes of striking a few sparks among movie lovers, TIME asked its long-time film critics Richard Corliss and Richard Schickel to compile a list of the 100 greatest films ever made. Of course, the discussions that followed between the two critics were entirely civil at all times. Below, the films and the year they were released.

A–C
Aguirre: The Wrath of God (1972)
The Apu Trilogy (1955, 1956, 1959)
The Awful Truth (1937)
Baby Face (1933)
Bande à part (1964)
Barry Lyndon (1975)
Berlin Alexanderplatz (1980)
Blade Runner (1982)
Bonnie and Clyde (1967)
Brazil (1985)
Bride of Frankenstein (1935)
Camille (1936)
Casablanca (1942)
Charade (1963)
Children of Paradise (1945)
Chinatown (1974)
Chungking Express (1994)
Citizen Kane (1941)
City Lights (1931)
City of God (2002)
Closely Watched Trains (1966)
The Crime of Monsieur Lange (1936)
The Crowd (1928)

D–F
Day for Night (1973)
The Decalogue (1989)
Detour (1945)
The Discreet Charm of the Bourgeoisie (1972)
Dodsworth (1936)
Double Indemnity (1944)
Dr. Strangelove or: How I Learned To Stop Worrying and Love the Bomb (1964)
Drunken Master II (1994)
E.T.: The Extra-Terrestrial (1982)
8 1/2 (1963)
The 400 Blows (1959)
Farewell My Concubine (1993)
Finding Nemo (2003)
The Fly (1986)

G–J
The Godfather, Parts I and II (1972, 1974)
The Good, the Bad, and the Ugly (1966)
Goodfellas (1990)
A Hard Day's Night (1964)
His Girl Friday (1940)
Ikiru (1952)
In a Lonely Place (1950)
Invasion of the Body Snatchers (1956)
It's a Gift (1934)
It's a Wonderful Life (1946)

K–M
Kandahar (2001)
Kind Hearts and Coronets (1949)
King Kong (1933)
The Lady Eve (1941)
The Last Command (1928)
Lawrence of Arabia (1962)
Léolo (1992)
The Lord of the Rings (2001, 2002, 2003)
The Man with a Camera (1929)
The Manchurian Candidate (1962)
Meet Me in St. Louis (1944)
Metropolis (1927)
Miller's Crossing (1990)
Mon oncle d'Amérique (1980)
Mouchette (1967)

N–P
Nayakan (1987)
Ninotchka (1939)
Notorious (1946)
Olympia, Parts 1 and 2 (1938)
On the Waterfront (1954)
Once upon a Time in the West (1968)
Out of the Past (1947)
Persona (1966)
Pinocchio (1940)
Psycho (1960)
Pulp Fiction (1994)
The Purple Rose of Cairo (1985)
Pyaasa (1957)

Q–S
Raging Bull (1980)
Schindler's List (1993)
The Searchers (1956)
Sherlock, Jr. (1924)
The Shop Around the Corner (1940)
Singin' in the Rain (1952)
The Singing Detective (1986)
Smiles of a Summer Night (1955)
Some Like It Hot (1959)
Star Wars (1977)
A Streetcar Named Desire (1951)
Sunrise (1927)
Sweet Smell of Success (1957)
Swing Time (1936)

T–Z
Talk to Her (2002)
Taxi Driver (1976)
Tokyo Story (1953)
A Touch of Zen (1971)
Ugetsu (1953)
Ulysses' Gaze (1995)
Umberto D (1952)
Unforgiven (1992)
White Heat (1949)
Wings of Desire (1987)
Yojimbo (1961)

TIME's Person of the Year, 1927—2006

Every year since 1927, TIME has named a Person of the Year, identifying the individual who has done the most to affect the news in the past twelve months. The designation is often mistaken for an honor, but the magazine has always pointed out that inclusion on the list is not a recognition of good works (like the Nobel Peace prize, for example), but rather a reflection of the sheer power of one's actions, whether for good or for ill. Hence, both Adolf Hitler and Ayatollah Ruhollah Khomeini were chosen Person of the Year at the time when their actions commanded the attention of the world. Below, the complete list of Persons of the Year.

1927	Charles Lindbergh
1928	Walter Chrysler
1929	Owen Young
1930	Mahatma Gandhi
1931	Pierre Laval
1932	Franklin Delano Roosevelt
1933	Hugh Johnson
1934	Franklin Delano Roosevelt
1935	Haile Selassie
1936	Wallis Simpson
1937	Chiang Kai-Shek and Soong Mei-ling
1938	Adolf Hitler
1939	Joseph Stalin
1940	Winston Churchill
1941	Franklin Delano Roosevelt
1942	Joseph Stalin
1943	George Marshall
1944	Dwight Eisenhower
1945	Harry Truman
1946	James F. Byrnes
1947	George Marshall
1948	Harry Truman
1949	Winston Churchill ("Man of the Half-Century")
1950	The American Fighting-Man (representing US troops fighting in the Korean War; first abstract chosen)
1951	Mohammed Mossadegh
1952	Queen Elizabeth II
1953	Konrad Adenauer
1954	John Foster Dulles
1955	Harlow Curtice
1956	Hungarian Freedom Fighter (representing the citizens' uprising against Soviet domination)
1957	Nikita Khrushchev
1958	Charles De Gaulle
1959	Dwight Eisenhower
1960	US Scientists (represented by Linus Pauling, Isidor Rabi, Edward Teller, Joshua Lederberg, Donald A. Glaser, Robert Woodward, Charles Draper, William Shockley, Emilio Segrè, John Enders, Charles Townes, George Beadle, James Van Allen, and Edward Purcell)
1961	John F. Kennedy
1962	Pope John XXIII
1963	Martin Luther King, Jr.
1964	Lyndon Johnson
1965	William Westmoreland
1966	The Generation Twenty-Five and Under (representing American youth)
1967	Lyndon Johnson
1968	Apollo 8 astronauts Frank Borman, Jim Lovell, and William Anders
1969	The Middle Americans (representing the American electorate's turn to the right)
1970	Willy Brandt
1971	Richard Nixon
1972	Richard Nixon and Henry Kissinger
1973	John Sirica
1974	King Faisal
1975	American Women (represented by Betty Ford, Carla Hills, Ella Grasso, Barbara Jordan, Susie Sharp, Jill Conway, Billie Jean King, Susan Brownmiller, Addie Wyatt, Kathleen Byerly, Carol Sutton, and Alison Cheek)
1976	Jimmy Carter
1977	Anwar el-Sadat
1978	Deng Xiaoping
1979	Ayatollah Ruhollah Khomeini
1980	Ronald Reagan
1981	Lech Walesa
1982	The Computer (first non-human abstract chosen; termed "Machine of the Year")
1983	Ronald Reagan and Yuri Andropov
1984	Peter Ueberroth
1985	Deng Xiaoping
1986	Corazon Aquino
1987	Mikhail Gorbachev
1988	Endangered Earth ("Planet of the Year")
1989	Mikhail Gorbachev ("Man of the Decade")
1990	George H.W. Bush (termed "The Two George Bushes"; commended for his role in international affairs and criticized for his management of domestic affairs)
1991	Ted Turner
1992	Bill Clinton
1993	The Peacemakers (represented by Nelson Mandela and F.W. de Klerk of South Africa and Yasir Arafat and Yitzhak Rabin of the Middle East)
1994	Pope John Paul II
1995	Newt Gingrich
1996	David Ho
1997	Andy Grove
1998	Bill Clinton and Kenneth Starr
1999	Jeffrey P. Bezos
2000	George W. Bush
2001	Rudolph Giuliani
2002	The Whistleblowers (represented by Cynthia Cooper of Worldcom, Sherron Watkins of Enron, and Coleen Rowley of the FBI)
2003	The American Soldier (representing US troops fighting in Iraq and Afghanistan)
2004	George W. Bush
2005	The Good Samaritans (represented by Bono [Paul Hewson], Bill Gates, and Melinda Gates)
2006	You (representing the new age of user-generated Internet content)

The Nobel Prizes

The Alfred B. Nobel Prizes are widely regarded as the world's most prestigious awards given for intellectual achievement. They are awarded annually from a fund bequeathed for that purpose by the Swedish inventor and industrialist Alfred Bernhard Nobel and administered by the Nobel Foundation. Nobel's 1895 will established five of the six prizes: those for physics, chemistry, literature, physiology or medicine, and peace. The prize for economic sciences was added in 1969. Each year thousands of invitations are sent out to members of scholarly academies, scientists, university professors, previous Nobel laureates, members of parliaments and other assemblies, and others, requesting nominations for the various prizes. The country given is the citizenship of the recipient at the time that the award was made. Prizes may be withheld or not awarded in years when no worthy recipient can be found or when the world situation (e.g., World Wars I and II) prevents the gathering of information needed to reach a decision. Prizes are announced in mid-October and awarded in December in Stockholm and Oslo. A cash award of SEK 10 million (about $1,450,000), a personal diploma, and a commemorative medal are given for each prize category.
Web site: <nobelprize.org>

Physics

YEAR	WINNER(S)	COUNTRY	ACHIEVEMENT
1901	Wilhelm Conrad Röntgen	Germany	discovery of X rays
1902	Hendrik Antoon Lorentz	Neth.	investigation of the influence
	Pieter Zeeman	Neth.	of magnetism on radiation
1903	Henri Becquerel	France	discovery of spontaneous radioactivity
	Marie Curie	France	investigations of radiation phenomena
	Pierre Curie	France	discovered by Becquerel
1904	John William Strutt, 3rd Baron Rayleigh (of Terling Place)	UK	discovery of argon
1905	Philipp Lenard	Germany	research on cathode rays
1906	Sir J.J. Thomson	UK	researches into electrical conductivity of gases
1907	A.A. Michelson	US	spectroscopic and metrological investigations
1908	Gabriel Lippmann	France	photographic reproduction of colors
1909	Ferdinand Braun	Germany	development of
	Guglielmo Marconi	Italy	wireless telegraphy
1910	Johannes Diederik van der Waals	Neth.	research concerning the equation of state of gases and liquids
1911	Wilhelm Wien	Germany	discoveries regarding laws governing heat radiation
1912	Nils Dalén	Sweden	invention of automatic regulators for lighting coastal beacons and light buoys
1913	Heike Kamerlingh Onnes	Neth.	investigation into the properties of matter at low temperatures; production of liquid helium
1914	Max von Laue	Germany	discovery of diffraction of X rays by crystals
1915	Sir Lawrence Bragg	UK	analysis of crystal structure
	Sir William Bragg	UK	by means of X rays
1917	Charles Glover Barkla	UK	discovery of characteristic X-radiation of elements
1918	Max Planck	Germany	discovery of the elemental quanta
1919	Johannes Stark	Germany	discovery of Doppler effect in positive ion rays and division of spectral lines in electric field
1920	Charles Édouard Guillaume	Switz.	discovery of anomalies in alloys
1921	Albert Einstein	Switz.	work in theoretical physics
1922	Niels Bohr	Denmark	investigation of atomic structure and radiation
1923	Robert Andrews Millikan	US	work on elementary electric charge and the photoelectric effect
1924	Karl Manne Georg Siegbahn	Sweden	work in X-ray spectroscopy
1925	James Franck	Germany	discovery of the laws governing the
	Gustav Hertz	Germany	impact of an electron upon an atom
1926	Jean Perrin	France	work on discontinuous structure of matter
1927	Arthur Holly Compton	US	discovery of wavelength change in diffused X rays
	C.T.R. Wilson	UK	method of making visible the paths of electrically charged particles
1928	Sir Owen Willans Richardson	UK	work on electron emission by hot metals
1929	Louis-Victor, 7e duc (duke) de Broglie	France	discovery of the wave nature of electrons

Physics (continued)

YEAR	WINNER(S)	COUNTRY	ACHIEVEMENT
1930	Sir Chandrasekhara Venkata Raman	India	work on light diffusion; discovery of Raman effect, light wavelength variation that occurs when a light beam is deflected by molecules
1932	Werner Heisenberg	Germany	creation of quantum mechanics
1933	P.A.M. Dirac	UK	introduction of wave equations
	Erwin Schrödinger	Austria	in quantum mechanics
1935	Sir James Chadwick	UK	discovery of the neutron
1936	Carl David Anderson	US	discovery of the positron
	Victor Francis Hess	Austria	discovery of cosmic radiation
1937	Clinton Joseph Davisson	US	experimental demonstration of the interference
	Sir George Paget Thomson	UK	phenomenon in crystals irradiated by electrons
1938	Enrico Fermi	Italy	disclosure of artificial radioactive elements produced by neutron irradiation
1939	Ernest Orlando Lawrence	US	invention of the cyclotron
1943	Otto Stern	US	discovery of the magnetic moment of the proton
1944	Isidor Isaac Rabi	US	resonance method for registration of various properties of atomic nuclei
1945	Wolfgang Pauli	Austria	discovery of the exclusion principle of electrons
1946	Percy Williams Bridgman	US	discoveries in the domain of high-pressure physics
1947	Sir Edward V. Appleton	UK	discovery of Appleton layer in upper atmosphere
1948	Patrick M.S. Blackett	UK	discoveries in the domain of nuclear physics and cosmic radiation
1949	Hideki Yukawa	Japan	prediction of the existence of mesons
1950	Cecil Frank Powell	UK	photographic method of studying nuclear processes; discoveries concerning mesons
1951	Sir John D. Cockcroft	UK	work on transmutation of atomic nuclei
	Ernest T.S. Walton	Ireland	by accelerated particles
1952	Felix Bloch	US	discovery of nuclear magnetic
	E.M. Purcell	US	resonance in solids
1953	Frits Zernike	Neth.	method of phase-contrast microscopy
1954	Max Born	UK	statistical studies of atomic wave functions
	Walther Bothe	W.Ger.	invention of coincidence method
1955	Polykarp Kusch	US	measurement of magnetic moment of electron
	Willis Eugene Lamb, Jr.	US	discoveries in the hydrogen spectrum
1956	John Bardeen	US	investigations on
	Walter H. Brattain	US	semiconductors and
	William B. Shockley	US	invention of the transistor
1957	Tsung-Dao Lee	China	discovery of violations of the principle of parity, the
	Chen Ning Yang	China	symmetry between phenomena in coordinate systems
1958	Pavel Alexeyevich Cherenkov	USSR	discovery and interpretation of the Cherenkov effect, which indicates that electrons emit light as they
	Ilya Mikhaylovich Frank	USSR	pass through a transparent medium at a speed
	Igor Yevgenyevich Tamm	USSR	higher than the speed of light in that medium
1959	Owen Chamberlain	US	confirmation of the existence
	Emilio Segrè	US	of the antiproton
1960	Donald A. Glaser	US	development of the bubble chamber
1961	Robert Hofstadter	US	determination of shape and size of atomic nucleons
	Rudolf Ludwig Mössbauer	W.Ger.	discovery of the Mössbauer effect, a nuclear process permitting the resonance absorption of gamma rays
1962	Lev Davidovich Landau	USSR	contributions to the understanding of condensed states of matter
1963	J. Hans D. Jensen	W.Ger.	development of shell model theory of
	Maria Goeppert Mayer	US	the structure of the atomic nuclei
	Eugene Paul Wigner	US	principles governing interaction of protons and neutrons in the nucleus
1964	Nikolay G. Basov	USSR	work in quantum electronics leading to
	Aleksandr M. Prokhorov	USSR	construction of instruments based on
	Charles Hard Townes	US	maser-laser principles
1965	Richard P. Feynman	US	work in quantum electrodynamics, which
	Julian Seymour Schwinger	US	describes mathematically all interactions of light with
	Shin'ichiro Tomonaga	Japan	matter and of charged particles with one another
1966	Alfred Kastler	France	discovery of optical methods for studying Hertzian resonances in atoms
1967	Hans Albrecht Bethe	US	discoveries concerning the energy production of stars
1968	Luis W. Alvarez	US	work with elementary particles, discovery of resonance states
1969	Murray Gell-Mann	US	classification of elementary particles and their interactions

Physics (continued)

YEAR	WINNER(S)	COUNTRY	ACHIEVEMENT
1970	Hannes Alfvén	Sweden	work in magnetohydrodynamics and
	Louis-Eugène-Félix Néel	France	in antiferromagnetism and ferrimagnetism
1971	Dennis Gabor	UK	invention of holography
1972	John Bardeen	US	development of the theory of superconductivity, the
	Leon N. Cooper	US	disappearance of electrical resistance in various solids
	John Robert Schrieffer	US	when they are cooled below certain temperatures
1973	Leo Esaki	Japan	experimental disoveries in tunneling in
	Ivar Giaever	US	semiconductors and superconductors
	Brian D. Josephson	UK	predictions of supercurrent properties through a tunnel barrier
1974	Antony Hewish	UK	work in radio
	Sir Martin Ryle	UK	astronomy
1975	Aage N. Bohr	Denmark	work on the atomic nucleus
	Ben R. Mottelson	Denmark	that paved the way for nuclear
	James Rainwater	US	fusion
1976	Burton Richter	US	discovery of new class of
	Samuel C.C. Ting	US	elementary particles (psi, or J)
1977	Philip W. Anderson	US	contributions to understanding the
	Sir Nevill F. Mott	UK	behavior of electrons in
	John H. Van Vleck	US	magnetic, noncrystalline solids
1978	Pyotr L. Kapitsa	USSR	research in magnetism and low-temperature physics
	Arno Penzias	US	discovery of cosmic microwave background
	Robert Woodrow Wilson	US	radiation, providing support for the big-bang theory
1979	Sheldon Lee Glashow	US	contributions to the theory of the
	Abdus Salam	Pakistan	unified weak and electromagnetic
	Steven Weinberg	US	interactions of subatomic particles
1980	James Watson Cronin	US	demonstration of simultaneous violation of both
	Val Logsdon Fitch	US	charge-conjugation and parity-inversion symmetries
1981	Nicolaas Bloembergen	US	applications of lasers
	Arthur L. Schawlow	US	in spectroscopy
	Kai M.B. Siegbahn	Sweden	development of electron spectroscopy
1982	Kenneth G. Wilson	US	analysis of continuous phase transitions
1983	Subrahmanyan Chandrasekhar	US	contributions to understanding the evolution and devolution of stars
	William A. Fowler	US	studies of nuclear reactions key to the formation of chemical elements
1984	Simon van der Meer	Neth.	discovery of subatomic particles W and Z,
	Carlo Rubbia	Italy	which supports the electroweak theory
1985	Klaus von Klitzing	W.Ger.	discovery of the quantized Hall effect, permitting exact measurements of electrical resistance
1986	Gerd Binnig	W.Ger.	development of the scanning tunneling
	Heinrich Rohrer	Switz.	electron microscope
	Ernst Ruska	W.Ger.	development of the electron microscope
1987	J. Georg Bednorz	W.Ger.	discoveries of superconductivity in
	Karl Alex Müller	Switz.	ceramic materials
1988	Leon Max Lederman	US	research in
	Melvin Schwartz	US	subatomic
	Jack Steinberger	US	particles
1989	Hans Georg Dehmelt	US	development of methods to isolate atoms
	Wolfgang Paul	W.Ger.	and subatomic particles for study
	Norman Foster Ramsey	US	development of the atomic clock
1990	Jerome Isaac Friedman	US	discovery of
	Henry Way Kendall	US	atomic
	Richard E. Taylor	Canada	quarks
1991	Pierre-Gilles de Gennes	France	discovery of general rules for behavior of molecules
1992	Georges Charpak	France	invention of detector that traces subatomic particles
1993	Russell Alan Hulse	US	identification of
	Joseph H. Taylor, Jr.	US	binary pulsars
1994	Bertram N. Brockhouse	Canada	development of
	Clifford G. Shull	US	neutron-scattering techniques
1995	Martin Lewis Perl	US	discovery of tau subatomic particle
	Frederick Reines	US	discovery of neutrino subatomic particle
1996	David M. Lee	US	discovery of
	Douglas D. Osheroff	US	superfluidity in
	Robert C. Richardson	US	isotope helium-3
1997	Steven Chu	US	process of
	Claude Cohen-Tannoudji	France	cooling and trapping atoms with
	William D. Phillips	US	laser light

Physics (continued)

YEAR	WINNER(S)	COUNTRY	ACHIEVEMENT
1998	Robert B. Laughlin	US	discovery of fractional quantum Hall effect, demonstrating that electrons in a powerful low-temperature magnetic field can form a quantum fluid whose particles have fractional electric charges
	Horst L. Störmer	US	
	Daniel C. Tsui	US	
1999	Gerardus 't Hooft	Neth.	study of quantum structure of electroweak interactions
	Martinus J.G. Veltman	Neth.	
2000	Zhores I. Alferov	Russia	development of fast semiconductors for use in microelectronics
	Herbert Kroemer	Germany	
	Jack S. Kilby	US	development of the integrated circuit (microchip)
2001	Eric A. Cornell	US	achievement of Bose-Einstein condensation in dilute gases of alkali atoms, and for early fundamental studies of the properties of the condensates
	Wolfgang Ketterle	Germany	
	Carl E. Wieman	US	
2002	Raymond Davis, Jr.	US	pioneering contributions to astrophysics, in particular for the detection of cosmic neutrinos
	Masatoshi Koshiba	Japan	
	Riccardo Giacconi	US	pioneering contributions to astrophysics, which have led to the discovery of cosmic X-ray sources
2003	Alexei A. Abrikosov	US/Russia	pioneering contributions to the theory of superconductors and superfluids
	Vitaly L. Ginzburg	Russia	
	Anthony J. Leggett	UK/US	
2004	David J. Gross	US	discovery of asymptotic freedom in the theory of the strong interaction
	H. David Politzer	US	
	Frank Wilczek	US	
2005	Roy J. Glauber	US	contributions to quantum theory of optical coherence
	John L. Hall	US	contributions to the development of laser-based precision spectroscopy, including the optical frequency comb technique
	Theodor W. Hänsch	Germany	
2006	John C. Mather	US	discovery of the blackbody form and variability of cosmic microwave background radiation
	George F. Smoot	US	

Chemistry

YEAR	WINNER(S)	COUNTRY	ACHIEVEMENT
1901	Jacobus H. van 't Hoff	Neth.	discovery of the laws of chemical dynamics and osmotic pressure
1902	Emil Fischer	Germany	work on sugar and purine syntheses
1903	Svante Arrhenius	Sweden	theory of electrolytic dissociation
1904	Sir William Ramsay	UK	discovery of inert gas elements and their places in the periodic system
1905	Adolf von Baeyer	Germany	work on organic dyes, hydroaromatic compounds
1906	Henri Moissan	France	isolation of fluorine; introduction of Moissan furnace
1907	Eduard Buchner	Germany	discovery of noncellular fermentation
1908	Ernest Rutherford	UK	investigations into the disintegration of elements and the chemistry of radioactive substances
1909	Wilhelm Ostwald	Germany	pioneer work on catalysis, chemical equilibrium, and reaction velocities
1910	Otto Wallach	Germany	pioneer work in alicyclic combinations
1911	Marie Curie	France	discovery of radium and polonium; isolation of radium
1912	Victor Grignard	France	discovery of the Grignard reagents
	Paul Sabatier	France	method of hydrogenating organic compounds
1913	Alfred Werner	Switz.	work on the linkage of atoms in molecules
1914	Theodore W. Richards	US	accurate determination of the atomic weights of numerous elements
1915	Richard Willstätter	Germany	research in plant pigments, especially chlorophyll
1918	Fritz Haber	Germany	synthesis of ammonia
1920	Walther Hermann Nernst	Germany	work in thermochemistry
1921	Frederick Soddy	UK	investigation into the chemistry of radioactive substances and the occurrence and nature of isotopes
1922	Francis William Aston	UK	work with mass spectrograph; whole-number rule
1923	Fritz Pregl	Austria	method of microanalysis of organic substances
1925	Richard Zsigmondy	Austria	elucidation of the heterogenous nature of colloidal solutions
1926	Theodor H.E. Svedberg	Sweden	work on disperse systems
1927	Heinrich Otto Wieland	Germany	research into the constitution of bile acids
1928	Adolf Windaus	Germany	research into the constitution of sterols and their connection with vitamins
1929	Hans von Euler-Chelpin	Sweden	investigations in the fermentation of sugars and the enzyme action involved
	Sir Arthur Harden	UK	

Chemistry (continued)

YEAR	WINNER(S)	COUNTRY	ACHIEVEMENT
1930	Hans Fischer	Germany	hemin, chlorophyll research; synthesis of hemin
1931	Friedrich Bergius	Germany	} invention and development of
	Carl Bosch	Germany	} chemical high-pressure methods
1932	Irving Langmuir	US	discoveries and investigations in surface chemistry
1934	Harold C. Urey	US	discovery of heavy hydrogen
1935	Frédéric and Irène Joliot-Curie	France	synthesis of new radioactive elements
1936	Peter Debye	Neth.	work on dipole moments and diffraction of X rays and electrons in gases
1937	Sir Norman Haworth	UK	research on carbohydrates and vitamin C
	Paul Karrer	Switz.	research on carotenoids, flavins, and vitamins
1938	Richard Kuhn (declined)	Germany	carotenoid and vitamin research
1939	Adolf Butenandt (declined)	Germany	work on sexual hormones
	Leopold Ruzicka	Switz.	work on polymethylenes and higher terpenes
1943	Georg Charles von Hevesy	Hungary	use of isotopes as tracers in chemical research
1944	Otto Hahn	Germany	discovery of the fission of heavy nuclei
1945	Artturi Ilmari Virtanen	Finland	invention of fodder preservation method
1946	John Howard Northrop	US	} preparation of enzymes and
	Wendell M. Stanley	US	} virus proteins in pure form
	James B. Sumner	US	discovery of enzyme crystallization
1947	Sir Robert Robinson	UK	investigation of alkaloids and other plant products
1948	Arne Tiselius	Sweden	research on electrophoresis and adsorption analysis; discoveries concerning serum proteins
1949	William Francis Giauque	US	behavior of substances at extremely low temperatures
1950	Kurt Alder	W.Ger.	} discovery and development of
	Otto Paul Hermann Diels	W.Ger.	} diene synthesis
1951	Edwin M. McMillan	US	} discovery of and research on
	Glenn T. Seaborg	US	} transuranium elements
1952	A.J.P. Martin	UK	} development of partition
	R.L.M. Synge	UK	} chromatography
1953	Hermann Staudinger	W.Ger.	work on macromolecules
1954	Linus Pauling	US	study of the nature of the chemical bond
1955	Vincent du Vigneaud	US	first synthesis of a polypeptide hormone
1956	Sir Cyril N. Hinshelwood	UK	} work on the kinetics of
	Nikolay N. Semyonov	USSR	} chemical reactions
1957	Alexander Robertus Todd, Baron Todd (of Trumpington)	UK	work on nucleotides and nucleotide coenzymes
1958	Frederick Sanger	UK	determination of the structure of the insulin molecule
1959	Jaroslav Heyrovsky	Czecho-slovakia	discovery and development of polarography
1960	Willard Frank Libby	US	development of radiocarbon dating
1961	Melvin Calvin	US	study of chemical steps that take place during photosynthesis
1962	Sir John C. Kendrew	UK	} determination of the structure of
	Max Ferdinand Perutz	UK	} hemoproteins
1963	Giulio Natta	Italy	} structure and synthesis of polymers
	Karl Ziegler	W.Ger.	} in the field of plastics
1964	Dorothy M.C. Hodgkin	UK	determination of the structure of biochemical compounds essential in combating pernicious anemia
1965	R.B. Woodward	US	synthesis of sterols, chlorophyll, and other substances
1966	Robert S. Mulliken	US	work concerning chemical bonds and the electronic structure of molecules
1967	Manfred Eigen	W.Ger.	studies of extremely fast chemical reactions
	Ronald G.W. Norrish	UK	} studies of extremely fast
	Sir George Porter	UK	} chemical reactions
1968	Lars Onsager	US	work on theory of thermodynamics of irreversible processes
1969	Sir Derek H.R. Barton	UK	} work in determining actual
	Odd Hassel	Norway	} three-dimensional shape of molecules
1970	Luis Federico Leloir	Argentina	discovery of sugar nucleotides and their role in the biosynthesis of carbohydrates
1971	Gerhard Herzberg	Canada	research in the structure of molecules
1972	Christian B. Anfinsen	US	fundamental contributions to enzyme chemistry
	Stanford Moore	US	} fundamental contributions
	William H. Stein	US	} to enzyme chemistry

Chemistry (continued)

YEAR	WINNER(S)	COUNTRY	ACHIEVEMENT
1973	Ernst Otto Fischer	W.Ger.	} organometallic
	Sir Geoffrey Wilkinson	UK	} chemistry
1974	Paul J. Flory	US	studies of long-chain molecules
1975	Sir John W. Cornforth	UK	} work in
	Vladimir Prelog	Switz.	} stereochemistry
1976	William N. Lipscomb, Jr.	US	studies on the structure of boranes
1977	Ilya Prigogine	Belgium	widening the scope of thermodynamics
1978	Peter Dennis Mitchell	UK	formulation of a theory of energy transfer processes in biological systems
1979	Herbert Charles Brown	US	introduction of compounds of boron and phosphorus in the synthesis of organic substances
	Georg Wittig	W.Ger.	introduction of compounds of boron and phosphorus in the synthesis of organic substances
1980	Paul Berg	US	first preparation of a hybrid DNA
	Walter Gilbert	US	} development of chemical and
	Frederick Sanger	UK	} biological analyses of DNA structure
1981	Kenichi Fukui	Japan	} orbital symmetry interpretation
	Roald Hoffmann	US	} of chemical reactions
1982	Aaron Klug	UK	determination of structure of biological substances
1983	Henry Taube	US	study of electron transfer reactions
1984	Bruce Merrifield	US	development of a method of polypeptide synthesis
1985	Herbert A. Hauptman	US	} development of a way to map the
	Jerome Karle	US	} chemical structure of small molecules
1986	Dudley R. Herschbach	US	} development of methods
	Yuan T. Lee	US	} for analyzing basic
	John C. Polanyi	Canada	} chemical reactions
1987	Donald J. Cram	US	} development of molecules
	Jean-Marie Lehn	France	} that can link with
	Charles J. Pedersen	US	} other molecules
1988	Johann Deisenhofer	W.Ger.	discovery of structure
	Robert Huber	W.Ger.	} proteins needed
	Hartmut Michel	W.Ger.	} in photosynthesis
1989	Sidney Altman	US	} discovery of certain
	Thomas Robert Cech	US	} basic properties of RNA
1990	Elias James Corey	US	development of retrosynthetic analysis for synthesis of complex molecules
1991	Richard R. Ernst	Switz.	improvements in nuclear magnetic resonance spectroscopy
1992	Rudolph A. Marcus	US	explanation of how electrons transfer between molecules
1993	Kary B. Mullis	US	} invention of techniques for
	Michael Smith	Canada	} gene study and manipulation
1994	George A. Olah	US	development of techniques to study hydrocarbon molecules
1995	Paul Crutzen	Neth.	explanation of processes
	Mario Molina	US	} that deplete Earth's
	F. Sherwood Rowland	US	} ozone layer
1996	Robert F. Curl, Jr.	US	} discovery of new
	Sir Harold W. Kroto	UK	} carbon compounds
	Richard E. Smalley	US	} called fullerenes
1997	Paul D. Boyer	US	} explanation of the enzymatic
	John E. Walker	UK	} conversion of adenosine triphosphate
	Jens C. Skou	Denmark	discovery of sodium-potassium-activated adenosine triphosphatase
1998	Walter Kohn	US	development of the density-functional theory
	John A. Pople	UK	development of computational methods in quantum chemistry
1999	Ahmed H. Zewail	Egypt/US	study of the transition states of chemical reactions using femtosecond spectroscopy
2000	Alan J. Heeger	US	discovery of plastics
	Alan G. MacDiarmid	US	} that conduct
	Hideki Shirakawa	Japan	} electricity
2001	William S. Knowles	US	} work on chirally catalyzed
	Ryoji Noyori	Japan	} hydrogenation reactions
	K. Barry Sharpless	US	work on chirally catalyzed oxidation reactions
2002	John B. Fenn	US	} development of soft desorption ionization methods
	Koichi Tanaka	Japan	} for mass spectrometric analyses of biological macromolecules

Chemistry (continued)

YEAR	WINNER(S)	COUNTRY	ACHIEVEMENT
2002 (cont.)	Kurt Wüthrich	Switz.	development of nuclear magnetic resonance spectroscopy for determining the three-dimensional structure of biological macromolecules in solution
2003	Peter Agre	US	} cell membrane channel
	Roderick MacKinnon	US	discoveries
2004	Aaron Ciechanover	Israel	discovery of
	Avram Hershko	Israel	} ubiquitin-mediated
	Irwin Rose	US	protein degradation
2005	Yves Chauvin	France	development of the
	Robert H. Grubbs	US	} metathesis method in
	Richard R. Schrock	US	organic synthesis
2006	Roger D. Kornberg	US	studies of the molecular basis of eukaryotic transcription

Physiology or Medicine

YEAR	WINNER(S)	COUNTRY	ACHIEVEMENT
1901	Emil von Behring	Germany	work on serum therapy
1902	Sir Ronald Ross	UK	discovery of how malaria enters an organism
1903	Niels Ryberg Finsen	Denmark	treatment of skin diseases with light
1904	Ivan Petrovich Pavlov	Russia	work on the physiology of digestion
1905	Robert Koch	Germany	tuberculosis research
1906	Camillo Golgi	Italy	} work on the structure
	Santiago Ramón y Cajal	Spain	of the nervous system
1907	Alphonse Laveran	France	discovery of the role of protozoa in diseases
1908	Paul Ehrlich	Germany	} work on
	Élie Metchnikoff	Russia	immunity
1909	Emil Theodor Kocher	Switz.	work on aspects of the thyroid gland
1910	Albrecht Kossel	Germany	researches in cellular chemistry
1911	Allvar Gullstrand	Sweden	work on dioptrics of the eye
1912	Alexis Carrel	France	work on vascular suture; transplantation of organs
1913	Charles Richet	France	work on anaphylaxis
1914	Robert Bárány	Austria-Hungary	work on vestibular apparatus
1919	Jules Bordet	Belgium	work on immunity factors in blood serum
1920	August Krogh	Denmark	discovery of capillary motor-regulating mechanism
1922	A.V. Hill	UK	discoveries concerning heat production in muscles
	Otto Meyerhof	Germany	work on metabolism of lactic acid in muscles
1923	Sir Frederick G. Banting	Canada	} discovery of
	J.J.R. Macleod	UK	insulin
1924	Willem Einthoven	Neth.	discovery of electrocardiogram mechanism
1926	Johannes Fibiger	Denmark	contributions to cancer research
1927	Julius Wagner-Jauregg	Austria	work on malaria inoculation in dementia paralytica
1928	Charles-Jules-Henri Nicolle	France	work on typhus
1929	Christiaan Eijkman	Neth.	discovery of the antineuritic vitamin
	Sir Frederick Gowland Hopkins	UK	discovery of growth-stimulating vitamins
1930	Karl Landsteiner	US	discovery of human blood groups
1931	Otto Warburg	Germany	discovery of nature and action of respiratory enzyme
1932	Edgar Douglas Adrian, 1st Baron Adrian (of Cambridge)	UK	discoveries regarding function of neurons
	Sir Charles Scott Sherrington	UK	discoveries regarding function of neurons
1933	Thomas Hunt Morgan	US	discoveries concerning chromosomal heredity functions
1934	George Richards Minot	US	discoveries concerning
	William P. Murphy	US	} liver treatment
	George H. Whipple	US	for anemia
1935	Hans Spemann	Germany	discovery of the organizer effect in embryos
1936	Sir Henry Dale	UK	} work on chemical
	Otto Loewi	Germany	transmission of nerve impulses
1937	Albert Szent-Gyorgyi	Hungary	work on biological combustion
1938	Corneille Heymans	Belgium	discovery of role of sinus and aortic mechanisms in respiration regulation
1939	Gerhard Domagk (declined)	Germany	discovery of the antibacterial effect of Prontosil

Physiology or Medicine (continued)

YEAR	WINNER(S)	COUNTRY	ACHIEVEMENT
1943	Henrik Dam	Denmark	discovery of vitamin K
	Edward Adelbert Doisy	US	discovery of chemical nature of vitamin K
1944	Joseph Erlanger	US	researches on differentiated
	Herbert S. Gasser	US	functions of nerve fibers
1945	Sir Ernst Boris Chain	UK	discovery of penicillin
	Sir Alexander Fleming	UK	and its curative value
	Howard Walter Florey, Baron Florey	Australia	discovery of penicillin and its curative value
1946	Hermann J. Muller	US	production of mutations by X-ray irradiation
1947	Carl and Gerty Cori	US	discovery of how glycogen is catalytically converted
	Bernardo A. Houssay	Argentina	discovery of the pituitary hormone function in sugar metabolism
1948	Paul Hermann Müller	Switz.	discovery of properties of DDT
1949	António Egas Moniz	Portugal	discovery of therapeutic value in leucotomy for psychoses
	Walter Rudolf Hess	Switz.	discovery of function of interbrain
1950	Philip Showalter Hench	US	research on adrenal cortex
	Edward Calvin Kendall	US	hormones, their structure and
	Tadeus Reichstein	Switz.	biological effects
1951	Max Theiler	South Africa	yellow fever discoveries
1952	Selman A. Waksman	US	discovery of streptomycin
1953	Sir Hans Adolf Krebs	UK	discovery of coenzyme A citric acid cycle in
	Fritz Albert Lipmann	US	metabolism of carbohydrates
1954	John Franklin Enders	US	cultivation of the
	Frederick C. Robbins	US	poliomyelitis virus in
	Thomas H. Weller	US	tissue cultures
1955	Axel H.T. Theorell	Sweden	discoveries concerning oxidation enzymes
1956	André F. Cournand	US	discoveries concerning
	Werner Forssmann	W.Ger.	heart catheterization and
	Dickinson W. Richards	US	circulatory changes
1957	Daniel Bovet	Italy	production of synthetic curare
1958	George Wells Beadle	US	discovery of the genetic regulation
	Edward L. Tatum	US	of chemical processes
	Joshua Lederberg	US	discoveries concerning genetic recombination
1959	Arthur Kornberg	US	work on producing nucleic
	Severo Ochoa	US	acids artificially
1960	Sir Macfarlane Burnet	Australia	discovery of acquired immunity to
	Sir Peter B. Medawar	UK	tissue transplants
1961	Georg von Békésy	US	discovery of functions of the inner ear
1962	Francis H.C. Crick	UK	discoveries concerning
	James Dewey Watson	US	the molecular structure
	Maurice Wilkins	UK	of DNA
1963	Sir John Carew Eccles	Australia	study of the transmission
	Sir Alan Hodgkin	UK	of impulses along
	Sir Andrew F. Huxley	UK	a nerve fiber
1964	Konrad Bloch	US	discoveries concerning
	Feodor Lynen	W.Ger.	cholesterol and fatty-acid metabolism
1965	François Jacob	France	discoveries concerning
	André Lwoff	France	regulatory activities
	Jacques Monod	France	of the body cells
1966	Charles B. Huggins	US	research on causes and
	Peyton Rous	US	treatment of cancer
1967	Ragnar Arthur Granit	Sweden	discoveries about chemical
	Haldan Keffer Hartline	US	and physiological visual
	George Wald	US	processes in the eye
1968	Robert William Holley	US	deciphering
	Har Gobind Khorana	US	of the
	Marshall W. Nirenberg	US	genetic code
1969	Max Delbrück	US	research and discoveries
	A.D. Hershey	US	concerning viruses and
	Salvador Luria	US	viral diseases
1970	Julius Axelrod	US	discoveries concerning
	Ulf von Euler	Sweden	the chemistry of
	Sir Bernard Katz	UK	nerve transmission
1971	Earl W. Sutherland, Jr.	US	discoveries concerning the action of hormones
1972	Gerald M. Edelman	US	research on the chemical
	Rodney Robert Porter	UK	structure of antibodies

Physiology or Medicine (continued)

YEAR	WINNER(S)	COUNTRY	ACHIEVEMENT
1973	Karl von Frisch	Austria	discoveries in
	Konrad Lorenz	Austria	animal behavior
	Nikolaas Tinbergen	UK	patterns
1974	Albert Claude	US	research on structural
	Christian René de Duve	Belgium	and functional organization
	George E. Palade	US	of cells
1975	David Baltimore	US	discoveries concerning the interaction between
	Renato Dulbecco	US	tumor viruses and the genetic
	Howard Martin Temin	US	material of the cell
1976	Baruch S. Blumberg	US	studies of origin and
	D. Carleton Gajdusek	US	spread of infectious diseases
1977	Roger C.L. Guillemin	US	research on pituitary
	Andrew Victor Schally	US	hormones
	Rosalyn S. Yalow	US	development of radioimmunoassay
1978	Werner Arber	Switz.	discovery and application
	Daniel Nathans	US	of enzymes that
	Hamilton O. Smith	US	fragment DNA
1979	Allan M. Cormack	US	development of
	Sir Godfrey N. Hounsfield	UK	the CAT scan
1980	Baruj Benacerraf	US	investigations of genetic
	Jean Dausset	France	control of the response of the
	George Davis Snell	US	immune system to foreign substances
1981	David Hunter Hubel	US	discoveries concerning the processing of visual
	Torsten Nils Wiesel	Sweden	information by the brain
	Roger Wolcott Sperry	US	discoveries concerning cerebral hemisphere functions
1982	Sune K. Bergström	Sweden	discoveries concerning the biochemistry
	Bengt I. Samuelsson	Sweden	and physiology of
	John Robert Vane	UK	of prostaglandins
1983	Barbara McClintock	US	discovery of mobile plant genes that affect heredity
1984	Niels K. Jerne	Denmark	theory and development
	Georges J.F. Köhler	W.Ger.	of a technique
	César Milstein	UK/	for producing
		Argentina	monoclonal antibodies
1985	Michael S. Brown	US	discovery of cell receptors relating to
	Joseph L. Goldstein	US	cholesterol metabolism
1986	Stanley Cohen	US	discovery of chemical agents
	Rita Levi-Montalcini	Italy	that help regulate the growth of cells
1987	Susumu Tonegawa	Japan	study of genetic aspects of antibodies
1988	Sir James Black	UK	development of new
	Gertrude Belle Elion	US	classes of drugs for
	George H. Hitchings	US	combating disease
1989	J. Michael Bishop	US	study of cancer-causing
	Harold Varmus	US	genes called oncogenes
1990	Joseph E. Murray	US	development of kidney and
	E. Donnall Thomas	US	bone-marrow transplants
1991	Erwin Neher	Germany	discovery of how cells
	Bert Sakmann	Germany	communicate, as related to diseases
1992	Edmond H. Fischer	US	discovery of class of enzymes
	Edwin Gerhard Krebs	US	called protein kinases
1993	Richard J. Roberts	UK	discovery of "split," or
	Phillip A. Sharp	US	interrupted, genetic structure
1994	Alfred G. Gilman	US	discovery of cell signalers
	Martin Rodbell	US	called G-proteins
1995	Edward B. Lewis	US	identification of genes
	Christiane	Germany	that control the body's
	Nüsslein-Volhard		early structural
	Eric F. Wieschaus	US	development
1996	Peter C. Doherty	Australia	discovery of how the immune
	Rolf M. Zinkernagel	Switz.	system recognizes virus-infected cells
1997	Stanley B. Prusiner	US	discovery of the prion, a type of disease-causing protein
1998	Robert F. Furchgott	US	discovery that nitric oxide (NO)
	Louis J. Ignarro	US	acts as a signaling molecule in
	Ferid Murad	US	the cardiovascular system
1999	Günter Blobel	US	discovery that proteins have signals
			governing cellular organization
2000	Arvid Carlsson	Sweden	discovery of how signals
	Paul Greengard	US	are transmitted between nerve
	Eric Kandel	US	cells in the brain

Physiology or Medicine (continued)

YEAR	WINNER(S)	COUNTRY	ACHIEVEMENT
2001	Leland H. Hartwell	US	discovery of key
	R. Timothy Hunt	UK	regulators of
	Sir Paul M. Nurse	UK	the cell cycle
2002	Sydney Brenner	UK	discoveries concerning how genes
	H. Robert Horvitz	US	regulate and program organ
	John E. Sulston	UK	development and cell death
2003	Paul C. Lauterbur	US	discoveries concerning magnetic
	Sir Peter Mansfield	UK	resonance imaging
2004	Richard Axel	US	discoveries of odorant receptors and the
	Linda B. Buck	US	organization of the olfactory system
2005	Barry J. Marshall	Australia	discovery of the bacterium *Helicobacter pylori* and its
	J. Robin Warren	Australia	role in peptic ulcer disease and gastritis
2006	Andrew Z. Fire	US	discovery of RNA interference: gene silencing
	Craig C. Mello	US	by double-stranded RNA

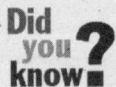

Did you know? Although he is remembered as the "Rebel General," Robert E. Lee was a disbeliever in slavery and was devoutly attached to the republic that his father and kinsmen had helped bring into being. Moreover, he rejected war as a means of resolving political conflict. In late 1860 he wrote, "[If] strife and civil war are to take the place of brotherly love and kindness, I shall mourn for my country and for the welfare and progress of mankind."

Literature

YEAR	WINNER(S)	COUNTRY	FIELD
1901	Sully Prudhomme	France	poetry
1902	Theodor Mommsen	Germany	history
1903	Bjørnstjerne Martinus Bjørnson	Norway	prose fiction, poetry, drama
1904	José Echegaray y Eizaguirre	Spain	drama
	Frédéric Mistral	France	poetry
1905	Henryk Sienkiewicz	Poland	prose fiction
1906	Giosuè Carducci	Italy	poetry
1907	Rudyard Kipling	UK	poetry, prose fiction
1908	Rudolf Christoph Eucken	Germany	philosophy
1909	Selma Lagerlöf	Sweden	prose fiction
1910	Paul Johann Ludwig von Heyse	Germany	poetry, prose fiction, drama
1911	Maurice Maeterlinck	Belgium	drama
1912	Gerhart Hauptmann	Germany	drama
1913	Rabindranath Tagore	India	poetry
1915	Romain Rolland	France	prose fiction
1916	Verner von Heidenstam	Sweden	poetry
1917	Karl Gjellerup	Denmark	prose fiction
	Henrik Pontoppidan	Denmark	prose fiction
1918	Erik Axel Karlfeldt (declined)	Sweden	poetry
1919	Carl Spitteler	Switz.	poetry, prose fiction
1920	Knut Hamsun	Norway	prose fiction
1921	Anatole France	France	prose fiction
1922	Jacinto Benavente y Martínez	Spain	drama
1923	William Butler Yeats	Ireland	poetry
1924	Wladyslaw Stanislaw Reymont	Poland	prose fiction
1925	George Bernard Shaw	Ireland	drama
1926	Grazia Deledda	Italy	prose fiction
1927	Henri Bergson	France	philosophy
1928	Sigrid Undset	Norway	prose fiction
1929	Thomas Mann	Germany	prose fiction
1930	Sinclair Lewis	US	prose fiction
1931	Erik Axel Karlfeldt (posthumous award)	Sweden	poetry
1932	John Galsworthy	UK	prose fiction
1933	Ivan Alekseyevich Bunin	USSR	poetry, prose fiction
1934	Luigi Pirandello	Italy	drama
1936	Eugene O'Neill	US	drama
1937	Roger Martin du Gard	France	prose fiction
1938	Pearl Buck	US	prose fiction
1939	Frans Eemil Sillanpää	Finland	prose fiction

Literature (continued)

YEAR	WINNER(S)	COUNTRY	FIELD
1944	Johannes V. Jensen	Denmark	prose fiction
1945	Gabriela Mistral	Chile	poetry
1946	Hermann Hesse	Switz.	prose fiction
1947	André Gide	France	prose
1948	T.S. Eliot	UK	poetry, criticism
1949	William Faulkner	US	prose fiction
1950	Bertrand Russell	UK	philosophy
1951	Pär Lagerkvist	Sweden	prose fiction
1952	François Mauriac	France	poetry, prose fiction, drama
1953	Sir Winston Churchill	UK	history, oration
1954	Ernest Hemingway	US	prose fiction
1955	Halldór Laxness	Iceland	prose fiction
1956	Juan Ramón Jiménez	Spain	poetry
1957	Albert Camus	France	prose fiction, drama
1958	Boris L. Pasternak (declined)	USSR	prose fiction, poetry
1959	Salvatore Quasimodo	Italy	poetry
1960	Saint-John Perse	France	poetry
1961	Ivo Andric	Yugoslavia	prose fiction
1962	John Steinbeck	US	prose fiction
1963	George Seferis	Greece	poetry
1964	Jean-Paul Sartre (declined)	France	philosophy, drama
1965	Mikhail A. Sholokhov	USSR	prose fiction
1966	S.Y. Agnon	Israel	prose fiction
	Nelly Sachs	Sweden	poetry
1967	Miguel Ángel Asturias	Guatemala	prose fiction
1968	Yasunari Kawabata	Japan	prose fiction
1969	Samuel Beckett	Ireland	prose fiction, drama
1970	Aleksandr I. Solzhenitsyn	USSR	prose fiction
1971	Pablo Neruda	Chile	poetry
1972	Heinrich Böll	W.Ger.	prose fiction
1973	Patrick White	Australia	prose fiction
1974	Eyvind Johnson	Sweden	prose fiction
	Harry Martinson	Sweden	prose fiction, poetry
1975	Eugenio Montale	Italy	poetry
1976	Saul Bellow	US	prose fiction
1977	Vicente Aleixandre	Spain	poetry
1978	Isaac Bashevis Singer	US	prose fiction
1979	Odysseus Elytis	Greece	poetry
1980	Czeslaw Milosz	US	poetry
1981	Elias Canetti	Bulgaria	prose
1982	Gabriel García Márquez	Colombia	prose fiction, journalism, social criticism
1983	Sir William Golding	UK	prose fiction
1984	Jaroslav Seifert	Czechoslovakia	poetry
1985	Claude Simon	France	prose fiction
1986	Wole Soyinka	Nigeria	drama, poetry
1987	Joseph Brodsky	US	poetry, prose
1988	Naguib Mahfouz	Egypt	prose fiction
1989	Camilo José Cela	Spain	prose fiction
1990	Octavio Paz	Mexico	poetry, prose
1991	Nadine Gordimer	South Africa	prose fiction
1992	Derek Walcott	St. Lucia	poetry
1993	Toni Morrison	US	prose fiction
1994	Kenzaburo Oe	Japan	prose fiction
1995	Seamus Heaney	Ireland	poetry
1996	Wislawa Szymborska	Poland	poetry
1997	Dario Fo	Italy	drama
1998	José Saramago	Portugal	prose fiction
1999	Günter Grass	Germany	prose fiction
2000	Gao Xingjian	France	prose fiction, drama
2001	Sir V.S. Naipaul	UK	prose fiction
2002	Imre Kertész	Hungary	prose fiction
2003	J.M. Coetzee	South Africa	prose fiction
2004	Elfriede Jelinek	Austria	prose fiction, drama
2005	Harold Pinter	UK	drama
2006	Orhan Pamuk	Turkey	prose fiction

Peace

YEAR	WINNER(S)	COUNTRY
1901	Henri Dunant	Switzerland
	Frédéric Passy	France
1902	Élie Ducommun	Switzerland
	Charles-Albert Gobat	Switzerland
1903	Sir Randal Cremer	UK
1904	Institute of International Law	(founded 1873)
1905	Bertha, Freifrau von Suttner	Austria-Hungary
1906	Theodore Roosevelt	US
1907	Ernesto Teodoro Moneta	Italy
	Louis Renault	France
1908	Klas Pontus Arnoldson	Sweden
	Fredrik Bajer	Denmark
1909	Auguste-Marie-François Beernaert	Belgium
	Paul-H.-B. d'Estournelles de Constant	France
1910	International Peace Bureau	(founded 1891)
1911	Tobias Michael Carel Asser	Netherlands
	Alfred Hermann Fried	Austria-Hungary
1912	Elihu Root	US
1913	Henri-Marie Lafontaine	Belgium
1917	International Committee of the Red Cross	(founded 1863)
1919	Woodrow Wilson	US
1920	Léon Bourgeois	France
1921	Karl Hjalmar Branting	Sweden
	Christian Lous Lange	Norway
1922	Fridtjof Nansen	Norway
1925	Sir Austen Chamberlain	UK
	Charles G. Dawes	US
1926	Aristide Briand	France
	Gustav Stresemann	Germany
1927	Ferdinand-Édouard Buisson	France
	Ludwig Quidde	Germany
1929	Frank B. Kellogg	US
1930	Nathan Söderblom	Sweden
1931	Jane Addams	US
	Nicholas Murray Butler	US
1933	Sir Norman Angell	UK
1934	Arthur Henderson	UK
1935	Carl von Ossietzky	Germany
1936	Carlos Saavedra Lamas	Argentina
1937	Robert Gascoyne-Cecil, 1st Viscount Cecil (of Chelwood)	UK
1938	Nansen International Office for Refugees	(founded 1931)
1944	International Committee of the Red Cross	(founded 1863)
1945	Cordell Hull	US
1946	Emily Greene Balch	US
	John R. Mott	US
1947	American Friends Service Committee	US
	Friends Service Council (FSC)	UK
1949	John Boyd Orr, Baron Boyd-Orr of Brechin Mearns	UK
1950	Ralph Bunche	US
1951	Léon Jouhaux	France
1952	Albert Schweitzer	France
1953	George C. Marshall	US
1954	Office of the United Nations High Commissioner for Refugees	(founded 1951)
1957	Lester B. Pearson	Canada

YEAR	WINNER(S)	COUNTRY
1958	Dominique Pire	Belgium
1959	Philip John Noel-Baker, Baron Noel-Baker (of the City of Derby)	UK
1960	Albert John Luthuli	South Africa
1961	Dag Hammarskjöld	Sweden
1962	Linus Pauling	US
1963	International Committee of the Red Cross	(founded 1863)
	League of Red Cross Societies	
1964	Martin Luther King, Jr.	US
1965	United Nations Children's Fund	(founded 1946)
1968	René Cassin	France
1969	International Labour Organisation	(founded 1919)
1970	Norman Ernest Borlaug	US
1971	Willy Brandt	West Germany
1973	Henry Kissinger	US
	Le Duc Tho (declined)	North Vietnam
1974	Seán MacBride	Ireland
	Eisaku Sato	Japan
1975	Andrey Dmitriyevich Sakharov	USSR
1976	Mairéad Corrigan	Northern Ireland
	Betty Williams	Northern Ireland
1977	Amnesty International	(founded 1961)
1978	Menachem Begin	Israel
	Anwar el-Sadat	Egypt
1979	Mother Teresa	India
1980	Adolfo Pérez Esquivel	Argentina
1981	Office of the United Nations High Commissioner for Refugees	(founded 1951)
1982	Alfonso García Robles	Mexico
	Alva Myrdal	Sweden
1983	Lech Walesa	Poland
1984	Desmond Tutu	South Africa
1985	International Physicians for the Prevention of Nuclear War	(founded 1980)
1986	Elie Wiesel	US
1987	Oscar Arias Sánchez	Costa Rica
1988	United Nations Peace-keeping Forces	
1989	Dalai Lama	Tibet
1990	Mikhail Gorbachev	USSR
1991	Aung San Suu Kyi	Myanmar
1992	Rigoberta Menchú	Guatemala
1993	F.W. de Klerk	South Africa
	Nelson Mandela	South Africa
1994	Yasir Arafat	Palestinian
	Shimon Peres	Israel
	Yitzhak Rabin	Israel
1995	Pugwash Conferences	(founded 1957)
	Joseph Rotblat	UK
1996	Carlos Filipe Ximenes Belo	East Timor
	José Ramos-Horta	East Timor
1997	International Campaign to Ban Landmines	(founded 1992)
	Jody Williams	US
1998	John Hume	Northern Ireland

Peace (continued)

YEAR	WINNER(S)	COUNTRY	YEAR	WINNER(S)	COUNTRY
	David Trimble	Northern Ireland	2003	Shirin Ebadi	Iran
1999	Doctors Without Borders	(founded 1971)	2004	Wangari Maathai	Kenya
2000	Kim Dae Jung	South Korea	2005	Mohamed ElBaradei	Egypt
2001	Kofi Annan	Ghana		International Atomic	(founded 1957)
	United Nations	(founded 1945)		Energy Agency	
2002	Jimmy Carter	US	2006	Muhammad Yunus	Bangladesh
				Grameen Bank	Bangladesh

Economics

YEAR	WINNER(S)	COUNTRY	ACHIEVEMENT
1969	Ragnar Frisch	Norway	work in
	Jan Tinbergen	Neth.	econometrics
1970	Paul Samuelson	US	work in scientific analysis of economic theory
1971	Simon Kuznets	US	extensive research on the economic growth of nations
1972	Kenneth J. Arrow	US	contributions to general economic
	Sir John R. Hicks	UK	equilibrium theory and welfare theory
1973	Wassily Leontief	US	development of input-output analysis
1974	Friedrich von Hayek	UK	pioneering analysis of the interdependence of
	Gunnar Myrdal	Sweden	economic, social, and institutional phenomena
1975	Leonid V. Kantorovich	USSR	contributions to the theory of
	Tjalling C. Koopmans	US	optimum allocation of resources
1976	Milton Friedman	US	work in consumption analysis, monetary theory, and economic stabilization
1977	James Edward Meade	UK	contributions to theory
	Bertil Ohlin	Sweden	of international trade
1978	Herbert A. Simon	US	decision-making processes in economic organizations
1979	Sir Arthur Lewis	UK	analyses of economic processes
	Theodore W. Schultz	US	in developing nations
1980	Lawrence Robert Klein	US	development and analysis of empirical models of business fluctuations
1981	James Tobin	US	portfolio-selection theory of investment
1982	George J. Stigler	US	studies of economic effects of governmental regulation
1983	Gerard Debreu	US	mathematical proof of supply and demand theory
1984	Sir Richard Stone	UK	development of national income accounting system
1985	Franco Modigliani	US	analyses of household savings and financial markets
1986	James M. Buchanan	US	public-choice theory bridging economics and political science
1987	Robert Merton Solow	US	contributions to the theory of economic growth
1988	Maurice Allais	France	contributions to the theory of markets and efficient use of resources
1989	Trygve Haavelmo	Norway	development of statistical techniques for economic forecasting
1990	Harry M. Markowitz	US	study of financial
	Merton H. Miller	US	markets and investment
	William F. Sharpe	US	decision making
1991	Ronald Coase	US	application of economic principles to the study of law
1992	Gary S. Becker	US	application of economic theory to social sciences
1993	Robert William Fogel	US	contributions to
	Douglass C. North	US	economic history
1994	John C. Harsanyi	US	development
	John F. Nash	US	of game
	Reinhard Selten	Germany	theory
1995	Robert E. Lucas, Jr.	US	incorporation of rational expectations in macroeconomic theory
1996	James A. Mirrlees	UK	contributions to theory of incentives under
	William Vickrey	US	conditions of asymmetric information
1997	Robert C. Merton	US	method for determining the value of
	Myron S. Scholes	US	stock options and other derivatives
1998	Amartya Sen	India	contribution to welfare economics
1999	Robert A. Mundell	Canada	analysis of optimum currency areas and of policy under different exchange-rate regimes
2000	James J. Heckman	US	development of methods of statistical
	Daniel L. McFadden	US	analysis of individual and household behavior
2001	George A. Akerlof	US	analyses of
	A. Michael Spence	US	markets with asymmetric
	Joseph E. Stiglitz	US	information

Economics (continued)

YEAR	WINNER(S)	COUNTRY	ACHIEVEMENT
2002	Daniel Kahneman	US/Israel	integration of psychological research into economics, particularly concerning decision-making under circumstances of uncertainty
	Vernon L. Smith	US	establishment of laboratory experiments for empirical economic analysis, particularly in the area of alternative market mechanisms
2003	Robert F. Engle	US	methods of analysis of economic time series with time-varying volatility
	Clive W.J. Granger	UK	methods of analysis of economic time series with common trends
2004	Finn E. Kydland	Norway	} macroeconomic analysis of time consistency of
	Edward C. Prescott	US	economic policy and the driving forces behind business cycles
2005	Robert J. Aumann	Israel/US	} enhancement of the understanding of conflict and
	Thomas C. Schelling	US	cooperation through game-theory analysis
2006	Edmund S. Phelps	US	analysis of intertemporal tradeoffs in macroeconomic policy

Special Achievement Awards

Templeton Prize Winners

Formerly the Templeton Prize for Progress in Religion, the Templeton Prize for Progress Toward Research or Discoveries About Spiritual Realities was established in 1972 by American-born British businessman and philanthropist Sir John Templeton. It recognizes the diversity of and rewards advancement in the ideas and perceptions of divinity. Each year an international interfaith group of judges chooses a winner from any of the world's religions. Award amount: £800,000 (about $1.6 million). Templeton Prize Web site: <www.templetonprize.org>

YEAR	NAME	FIELD
1973	Mother Teresa	founder, Missionaries of Charity
1974	Brother Roger	founder, Taizé Community
1975	Sir Sarvepalli Radhakrishnan	president of India, 1962–67
1976	Leon Joseph Cardinal Suenens	pioneer, Charismatic Renewal Movement
1977	Chiara Lubich	founder, Focolare Movement
1978	Thomas F. Torrance	educator, writer on religion and science
1979	Nikkyo Niwano	founder, Rissho Kosei-Kai
1980	Ralph Wendell Burhoe	founder and editor, *Zygon, Journal of Religion and Science*
1981	Dame Cicely Saunders	founder, Hospice and Palliative Care Movement
1982	Billy Graham	Christian evangelist
1983	Aleksandr Solzhenitsyn	writer, dissident
1984	Michael Bourdeaux	scholar, religious freedom activist
1985	Sir Alister Hardy	scientist, educator
1986	James McCord	chancellor, Center of Theological Inquiry; president, Princeton Theological Seminary
1987	Stanley L. Jaki	Benedictine monk, professor of astrophysics
1988	Inamullah Khan	interfaith peace activist; founder, Modern World Muslim Congress
1989	Lord George MacLeod	founder, Iona Community
	Carl Friedrich von Weizsäcker	physics and theology scholar
1990	Baba Amte	social activist, philanthropist
	L. Charles Birch	natural scientist
1991	Lord Immanuel Jakobovits	Chief Rabbi of Great Britain and the Commonwealth, 1967–91
1992	Kyung-Chik Han	founder, Young Nak Presbyterian Church
1993	Charles W. Colson	prison ministry founder
1994	Michael Novak	theologian, writer on theology and economics
1995	Paul Charles William Davies	mathematical physicist
1996	William R. Bright	founder, Campus Crusade for Christ
1997	Pandurang Shastri Athavale	founder, *swadhyaya* self-study
1998	Sir Sigmund Sternberg	philanthropist, businessman
1999	Ian Graeme Barbour	technology ethicist
2000	Freeman J. Dyson	physicist, social activist
2001	Arthur Peacocke	founder, Society of Ordained Scientists
2002	John C. Polkinghorne	Anglican priest, mathematical physicist
2003	Holmes Rolston III	Presbyterian minister, environmental ethicist
2004	George Ellis	cosmologist, scholar of the relationship between science and faith

Templeton Prize Winners (continued)

YEAR	NAME	FIELD
2005	Charles Townes	physicist, proponent of exploring commonalities between science and religion
2006	John D. Barrow	cosmologist, scholar of multidisciplinary perspectives integrating astronomy, physics, mathematics, and philosophy
2007	Charles Taylor	philosopher, advocate for inclusion of spiritual considerations in public policy discussions and in the humanities and social sciences

Congressional Gold Medal

Individuals, institutions, or events of distinguished achievement are honored by the Congressional Gold Medal. The medal was first awarded in 1776, and 132 others have since been given out. Early medals went primarily to military figures; beginning in the mid-19th century, they were given to a wide variety of people. Past recipients include George Washington, Zachary Taylor, the Wright Brothers, inventor Thomas Edison, entertainer Bob Hope, singers Marion Anderson and Frank Sinatra, Queen Beatrix I of The Netherlands, human rights activist Elie Wiesel, South African President Nelson Mandela, cartoonist Charles M. Schulz, and the Navajo code talkers of World War II. In 2007 Congress awarded the medal to the Tuskegee Airmen, the first African American flying unit in the US military.

The Kennedy Center Honors

The Kennedy Center Honors are bestowed annually by the John F. Kennedy Center for the Performing Arts in Washington DC. First conferred in 1978, the honors salute five artists each year for lifetime achievement in the performing arts and are celebrated by a televised gala in December. Web site: <www.kennedy-center.org/programs/specialevents/honors/>.

YEAR	NAME	FIELD
1978	Marian Anderson	opera singer
	Fred Astaire	dancer, actor
	George Balanchine	choreographer
	Richard Rodgers	composer
	Arthur Rubenstein	pianist
1979	Aaron Copland	composer
	Ella Fitzgerald	singer
	Henry Fonda	actor
	Martha Graham	dancer, choreographer
	Tennessee Williams	playwright
1980	Leonard Bernstein	conductor
	James Cagney	actor
	Agnes de Mille	dancer, choreographer
	Lynn Fontanne	actress
	Leontyne Price	opera singer
1981	Count Basie	jazz pianist
	Cary Grant	actor
	Helen Hayes	actress
	Jerome Robbins	dancer, choreographer
	Rudolf Serkin	pianist
1982	George Abbott	theater producer, director, writer
	Lillian Gish	actress
	Benny Goodman	swing musician
	Gene Kelly	dancer, actor
	Eugene Ormandy	conductor
1983	Katherine Dunham	dancer, choreographer
	Elia Kazan	theater and film director
	Frank Sinatra	singer, actor
	James Stewart	actor
	Virgil Thomson	composer, music critic
1984	Lena Horne	singer, actress
	Danny Kaye	actor, comedian
	Gian Carlo Menotti	composer
	Arthur Miller	playwright
	Isaac Stern	violinist
1985	Merce Cunningham	dancer, choreographer
	Irene Dunne	actress
1985 (cont.)	Bob Hope	entertainer, actor
	Alan Jay Lerner	playwright, lyricist
	Frederick Loewe	composer
	Beverly Sills	opera singer
1986	Lucille Ball	actress
	Ray Charles	soul musician
	Hume Cronyn	actor
	Jessica Tandy	actress
	Yehudi Menuhin	violinist
	Antony Tudor	choreographer
1987	Perry Como	singer
	Bette Davis	actress
	Sammy Davis, Jr.	singer, dancer, entertainer
	Nathan Milstein	violinist
	Alwin Nikolais	choreographer
1988	Alvin Ailey	dancer, choreographer
	George Burns	actor, comedian
	Myrna Loy	actress
	Alexander Schneider	violinist, conductor
	Roger L. Stevens	arts administrator
1989	Harry Belafonte	folk singer, actor
	Claudette Colbert	actress
	Alexandra Danilova	ballet dancer
	Mary Martin	actress, singer
	William Schuman	composer
1990	Dizzy Gillespie	jazz musician
	Katharine Hepburn	actress
	Risë Stevens	opera singer
	Jule Styne	composer
	Billy Wilder	film director
1991	Roy Acuff	country musician
	Betty Comden	theater and film writer
	Adolph Green	theater and film writer
	Fayard Nicholas	dancer
	Harold Nicholas	dancer
	Gregory Peck	actor
	Robert Shaw	choral and orchestral conductor

The Kennedy Center Honors (continued)

YEAR	NAME	FIELD
1992	Lionel Hampton	swing musician
	Paul Newman	actor
	Joanne Woodward	actress
	Ginger Rogers	dancer, actress
	Mstislav Rostro-povich	musician, conductor
	Paul Taylor	dancer, choreographer
1993	Johnny Carson	television entertainer
	Arthur Mitchell	dancer, choreographer
	George Solti	conductor
	Stephen Sondheim	composer, lyricist
	Marion Williams	gospel singer
1994	Kirk Douglas	actor
	Aretha Franklin	soul singer
	Morton Gould	composer
	Harold Prince	theater director, producer
	Pete Seeger	folk musician
1995	Jacques d'Amboise	dancer, choreographer
	Marilyn Horne	opera singer
	B.B. King	blues musician
	Sidney Poitier	actor
	Neil Simon	playwright
1996	Edward Albee	playwright
	Benny Carter	jazz musician
	Johnny Cash	country musician
	Jack Lemmon	actor
	Maria Tallchief	ballet dancer
1997	Lauren Bacall	actress
	Bob Dylan	singer, songwriter
	Charlton Heston	actor
	Jessye Norman	opera singer
	Edward Villella	dancer, choreographer
1998	Bill Cosby	actor, comedian
	Fred Ebb and John Kander	lyricist and composer
	Willie Nelson	country musician
	André Previn	pianist, composer, conductor
	Shirley Temple Black	actress
1999	Victor Borge	pianist, comedian
	Sean Connery	actor
	Judith Jamison	dancer, choreographer

YEAR	NAME	FIELD
1999 (cont.)	Jason Robards	actor
	Stevie Wonder	musician
2000	Mikhail Baryshnikov	dancer
	Chuck Berry	musician
	Plácido Domingo	opera singer
	Clint Eastwood	actor, director
	Angela Lansbury	actress
2001	Julie Andrews	actress
	Van Cliburn	pianist
	Quincy Jones	music producer, composer
	Jack Nicholson	actor
	Luciano Pavarotti	opera singer
2002	James Earl Jones	actor
	James Levine	conductor
	Chita Rivera	musical theater performer
	Paul Simon	singer
	Elizabeth Taylor	actress
2003	James Brown	musician
	Carol Burnett	actress
	Loretta Lynn	musician
	Mike Nichols	director
	Itzhak Perlman	musician
2004	Warren Beatty	film actor, director
	Ossie Davis and Ruby Dee	actors, writers, producers
	Elton John	musician
	Joan Sutherland	opera singer
	John Williams	composer
2005	Tony Bennett	singer
	Suzanne Farrell	dancer, teacher
	Julie Harris	actress
	Robert Redford	film actor, director, producer
	Tina Turner	singer, actress
2006	Zubin Mehta	conductor
	Dolly Parton	singer, actress
	Andrew Lloyd Webber	composer
	Steven Spielberg	film director, producer
	William "Smokey" Robinson	singer

The National Medal of Arts

The National Medal of Arts, awarded annually since 1985 by the National Endowment for the Arts (NEA) and the president of the United States, honors artists and art patrons for remarkable contributions to American arts. As many as 12 medals may be given out each year. Both the NEA and the president choose candidates for the award, and the winners are selected by the president. Web site: <www.nea.gov/honors/medals/medalists_year.html>.

YEAR	NAME	FIELD
1985	Elliott Carter, Jr.	composer
	Ralph Ellison	writer
	José Ferrer	actor
	Martha Graham	dancer, choreographer
	Louise Nevelson	sculptor
	Georgia O'Keeffe	painter
	Leontyne Price	opera singer
	Dorothy Buffum Chandler	patron
	Lincoln Kirstein	patron
	Paul Mellon	patron
	Alice Tully	patron
	Hallmark Cards, Inc.	patron

YEAR	NAME	FIELD
1986	Marian Anderson	opera singer
	Frank Capra	film director
	Aaron Copland	composer
	Willem de Kooning	painter
	Agnes de Mille	dancer, choreographer
	Eva Le Gallienne	actress, theater producer
	Alan Lomax	ethnomusicologist
	Lewis Mumford	architectural critic, historian
	Eudora Welty	writer
	Dominique de Menil	patron
	Exxon Corporation	patron
	Seymour H. Knox	patron

The National Medal of Arts (continued)

YEAR	NAME	FIELD
1987	Romare Bearden	painter
	Ella Fitzgerald	singer
	Howard Nemerov	writer, scholar
	Alwin Nikolais	choreographer
	Isamu Noguchi	sculptor
	William Schuman	composer
	Robert Penn Warren	writer
	J.W. Fisher	patron
	Armand Hammer	patron
	Sydney and Frances Lewis	patrons
1988	Saul Bellow	writer
	Helen Hayes	actress
	Gordon Parks	photographer, writer
	I.M. Pei	architect
	Jerome Robbins	dancer, choreographer
	Rudolf Serkin	pianist
	Virgil Thomson	composer, music critic
	Sydney J. Freedberg	art historian, museum curator
	Roger L. Stevens	arts administrator
	Brooke Astor	patron
	Francis Goelet	patron
	Obert C. Tanner	patron
1989	Leopold Adler	historic preservationist, civic leader
	Katherine Dunham	dancer, choreographer
	Alfred Eisenstaedt	photojournalist
	Martin Friedman	museum director
	Leigh Gerdine	civic leader, patron
	Dizzy Gillespie	jazz musician
	Walker K. Hancock	sculptor
	Vladimir Horowitz[1]	pianist
	Czeslaw Milosz	writer
	Robert Motherwell	painter
	John Updike	writer
	Dayton Hudson Corp.	patron
1990	George Abbott	theater producer, director, writer
	Hume Cronyn	actor, director
	Jessica Tandy	actress
	Merce Cunningham	dancer, choreographer
	Jasper Johns	painter, sculptor
	Jacob Lawrence	painter
	B.B. King	blues musician
	Beverly Sills	opera singer
	Ian McHarg	landscape architect
	Harris & Carroll Sterling Masterson	patrons
	David Lloyd Kreeger	patron
	Southeastern Bell Corporation	patron
1991	Maurice Abravanel	conductor, music director
	Roy Acuff	country musician
	Pietro Belluschi	architect
	J. Carter Brown	museum director
	Charles "Honi" Coles	tap dancer
	John O. Crosby	opera director, conductor
	Richard Diebenkorn	painter
	Isaac Stern	violinist
	Kitty Carlisle Hart	actress, singer
	R. Philip Hanes, Jr.	patron
	Pearl Primus	choreographer, anthropologist
	Texaco Inc.	patron
1992	Marilyn Horne	opera singer
	James Earl Jones	actor
	Allan Houser	sculptor
	Minnie Pearl	Grand Ole Opry performer
	Robert Saudek	television producer, museum director
	Earl Scruggs	banjo player
	Robert Shaw	choral and orchestral conductor
	Billy Taylor	jazz pianist
	Robert Venturi and Denise Scott Brown	architects
	Robert Wise	film director
	AT&T	patron
	Lila Wallace–Reader's Digest Fund	patron
1993	Cabell "Cab" Calloway	jazz musician
	Ray Charles	soul musician
	Bess Lomax Hawes	folklorist, musician
	Stanley Kunitz	poet
	Robert Merrill	opera singer
	Arthur Miller	playwright
	Robert Rauschenberg	painter
	Lloyd Richards	theater director
	William Styron	writer
	Paul Taylor	dancer, choreographer
	Billy Wilder	film director, producer, writer
	Walter and Leonore Annenberg	patrons
1994	Harry Belafonte	folk singer, actor
	Dave Brubeck	jazz musician
	Celia Cruz	salsa singer
	Dorothy DeLay	violin instructor
	Julie Harris	actress
	Erick Hawkins	dancer, choreographer
	Gene Kelly	dancer, actor
	Pete Seeger	folk musician
	Wayne Thiebaud	painter
	Richard Wilbur	poet
	Young Audiences	arts organization
	Catherine Filene Shouse	patron
1995	Licia Albanese	opera singer
	Gwendolyn Brooks	poet
	Ossie Davis and Ruby Dee	actors
	David Diamond	composer
	James Ingo Freed	architect
	Bob Hope	entertainer
	Roy Lichtenstein	painter
	Arthur Mitchell	dancer, choreographer
	William S. Monroe	bluegrass musician
	Urban Gateways	arts education organization
	B. Gerald and Iris Cantor	patrons
1996	Edward Albee	playwright
	Sarah Caldwell	opera conductor, producer
	Harry Callahan	photographer
	Zelda Fichandler	theater founder, director
	Eduardo "Lalo" Guerrero	Chicano musician
	Lionel Hampton	swing musician

The National Medal of Arts (continued)

YEAR	NAME	FIELD
1996 (cont.)	Bella Lewitzky	dancer, choreographer
	Robert Redford	actor, film director
	Maurice Sendak	illustrator, writer
	Stephen Sondheim	composer, lyricist
	Boys Choir of Harlem	youth performance group
	Vera List	patron
1997	Louise Bourgeois	sculptor
	Betty Carter	jazz singer
	Daniel Urban Kiley	landscape architect
	Angela Lansbury	actress
	James Levine	opera conductor, pianist
	Tito Puente	jazz and mambo musician
	Jason Robards	actor
	Edward Villella	dancer, choreographer
	Doc Watson	folk and country musician
	MacDowell Colony	artists' colony
	Agnes Gund	patron
1998	Jacques d'Amboise	dancer, choreographer
	Antoine "Fats" Domino	rock-and-roll musician
	Ramblin' Jack Elliott	folk musician
	Frank O. Gehry	architect
	Agnes Martin	painter
	Gregory Peck	actor
	Roberta Peters	opera singer
	Philip Roth	writer
	Gwen Verdon	actress, dancer
	Steppenwolf Theatre Company	arts organization
	Sara Lee Corporation	patron
	Barbara Handman	patron
1999	Aretha Franklin	soul singer
	Michael Graves	architect, designer
	Odetta	folk singer
	Norman Lear	television producer, writer
	Rosetta LeNoire	actress, theater founder
	Harvey Lichtenstein	arts administrator
	Lydia Mendoza	Tejano musician
	George Segal	sculptor
	Maria Tallchief	ballet dancer
	The Juilliard School	performing arts school
	Irene Diamond	patron
2000	Maya Angelou	poet, writer
	Eddy Arnold	country musician
	Mikhail Baryshnikov	dancer, dance company director
	Benny Carter	jazz musician
	Chuck Close	painter
	Horton Foote	dramatist
	Claes Oldenburg	sculptor
	Itzhak Perlman	violinist
	Harold Prince	theater director, producer
	Barbra Streisand	singer, actress, film director
	Lewis Manilow	patron
	NPR Cultural Programming Division	broadcaster

YEAR	NAME	FIELD
2001	Alvin Ailey Dance Foundation	modern dance company and school
	Rudolfo Anaya	writer
	Johnny Cash	country musician
	Kirk Douglas	actor
	Helen Frankenthaler	painter
	Judith Jamison	dancer, choreographer
	Yo-Yo Ma	cellist
	Mike Nichols	theater and film director
2002	Florence Knoll Bassett	designer, architect
	Trisha Brown	dancer, choreographer
	Philippe de Montebello	museum director
	Uta Hagen	actress, educator
	Lawrence Halprin	landscape architect
	Al Hirschfeld[1]	artist, caricaturist
	George Jones	singer, songwriter
	Ming Cho Lee	painter, stage designer
	William "Smokey" Robinson, Jr.	singer, songwriter
2003	Austin City Limits	television show
	Beverly Cleary	children's book author
	Rafe Esquith	arts educator
	Suzanne Farrell	dancer, artistic director, arts educator
	Buddy Guy	blues musician
	Ron Howard	actor, director, writer, producer
	The Mormon Tabernacle Choir	choir
	Leonard Slatkin	conductor
	George Strait	singer, songwriter
	Tommy Tune	director, actor
2004	Andrew W. Mellon Foundation	arts patron
	Ray Bradbury	writer
	Carlisle Floyd	opera composer
	Frederick "Rick" Hart[1]	sculptor
	Anthony Hecht[1]	poet
	John Ruthven	painter
	Vincent Scully	architectural historian
	Twyla Tharp	dancer, choreographer
2005	Louis Auchincloss	writer
	James DePreist	conductor
	Paquito D'Rivera	musician
	Robert Duvall	actor
	Leonard Garment	arts advocate
	Ollie Johnston	animator, artist
	Wynton Marsalis	musician, educator
	Pennsylvania Academy of the Fine Arts	arts academy
	Tina Ramirez	dancer, choreographer
	Dolly Parton	singer, songwriter
2006	William Bolcom	composer
	Cyd Charisse	dancer
	Roy R. DeCarava	photographer
	Wilhelmina C. Holladay	patron
	Interlochen Center for the Arts	music school
	Erich Kunzel	conductor
	Preservation Hall Jazz Band	
	Gregory Rabassa	translator
	Viktor Schreckengost	industrial designer
	Dr. Ralph Stanley	bluegrass musician

[1]Awarded posthumously.

American Academy of Arts and Letters

The American Academy of Arts and Letters is a 250-member organization founded in 1898. Members elected in 2007 were: ▶ **Art:** Robert Irwin, Billie Tsien; ▶ **Literature:** Deborah Eisenberg, Mary Gordon, Allan Gurganus, Jim Harrison, Harper Lee, Annie Proulx; ▶ **Music:** Steven Stucky. The academy also confers 26 awards for excellence. The Academy Awards in each field are the most prestigious. Winners receive $7,500; music winners receive an additional $7,500 to be used for the recording of a musi-

cal piece. Recipients for 2007 were: ▶ **Architecture:** Wes Jones, Tom Kundig, Lebbeus Woods; ▶ **Art:** Jackie Gendel, Julian Hatton, Bryan Hunt, Sarah Oppenheimer, Dana Schutz; ▶ **Literature:** Joan Acocella, Charles D'Ambrosio, Barbara Ehrenreich, David Markson, Robert Morgan, Joan Silber, William T. Vollmann, Dean Young; ▶ **Music:** Leonardo Balada, Mason Bates, Chester Biscardi, Ben Johnston.

Web site: <www.artsandletters.org>

National Humanities Medal

The National Humanities Medal (originally known as the Charles Frankel Prize, 1988–96) is awarded by the National Endowment for the Humanities for notable contributions to Americans' understanding of and involvement with the humanities. As many as 12 medals may be conferred each year. The recipients for 2006 were Fouad Ajami, scholar; James Buchanan, economist; Nickolas

Davatzes, historian; Robert Fagles, translator and classicist; Mary Lefkowitz, classicist; Bernard Lewis, scholar; Mark Noll, historian; Meryle Secrest, biographer; Kevin Starr, historian; and the Hoover Institution.

Web site: <www.neh.gov/whoweare/awards.html>

The Spingarn Medal

The National Association for the Advancement of Colored People (NAACP) presents the medal for distinguished achievement among African Americans. The medal is named for early NAACP activist Joel E. Spingarn.

YEAR	NAME	FIELD	YEAR	NAME	FIELD
1915	Ernest Everett Just	zoologist, marine biologist	1942	A. Philip Randolph	labor and civil rights leader
1916	Charles Young	army officer	1943	William H. Hastie	lawyer, judge
1917	Harry Thacker Burleigh	singer, composer	1944	Charles Richard Drew	surgeon, research scientist
1918	William Stanley Braithwaite	poet, literary critic	1945	Paul Robeson	actor, singer, social activist
1919	Archibald Henry Grimké	lawyer, diplomat, social activist	1946	Thurgood Marshall	lawyer, US Supreme Court justice
1920	W.E.B. Du Bois (William Edward Burghardt Du Bois)	sociologist, social activist	1947	Percy L. Julian	chemist
1921	Charles S. Gilpin	actor	1948	Channing H. Tobias	civil rights leader
1922	Mary Burnett Talbert	civil rights activist	1949	Ralph Bunche	diplomat, scholar
1923	George Washington Carver	agricultural chemist	1950	Charles Hamilton Houston	lawyer
1924	Roland Hayes	singer, composer	1951	Mabel Keaton Staupers	nurse, social activist
1925	James Weldon Johnson	writer, diplomat, anthologist	1952	Harry T. Moore	civil rights activist, educator
1926	Carter G. Woodson	historian	1953	Paul R. Williams	architect
1927	Anthony Overton	businessman	1954	Theodore K. Lawless	dermatologist, philanthropist
1928	Charles W. Chesnutt	writer	1955	Carl Murphy	journalist, civil rights activist
1929	Mordecai W. Johnson	minister, university president	1956	Jackie Robinson (Jack Roosevelt Robinson)	baseball player
1930	Henry Alexander Hunt	educator, government official	1957	Martin Luther King, Jr.	civil rights leader
1931	Richard B. Harrison	actor	1958	Daisy Bates and the Little Rock Nine	school integration activists
1932	Robert Russa Moton	educator, civil rights leader	1959	Duke Ellington (Edward Kennedy Ellington)	jazz musician
1933	Max Yergan	civil rights leader	1960	Langston Hughes	writer
1934	William T.B. Williams	educator	1961	Kenneth Bancroft Clark	educator
1935	Mary McLeod Bethune	educator, social activist	1962	Robert C. Weaver	economist, government official
1936	John Hope	educator	1963	Medgar Evers	civil rights activist
1937	Walter White	civil rights leader	1964	Roy Wilkins	civil rights leader
1938	*no medal awarded*		1965	Leontyne Price	opera singer
1939	Marian Anderson	opera singer	1966	John H. Johnson	publisher
1940	Louis T. Wright	surgeon, civil rights leader	1967	Edward W. Brooke III	lawyer, US senator
1941	Richard Wright	writer			

The Spingarn Medal (continued)

YEAR	NAME	FIELD	YEAR	NAME	FIELD
1968	Sammy Davis, Jr.	singer, dancer, entertainer	1989	Jesse Jackson	minister, politician, civil rights leader
1969	Clarence M. Mitchell, Jr.	civil rights lobbyist	1990	L. Douglas Wilder	politician
1970	Jacob Lawrence	painter	1991	Colin Powell	army general, government official
1971	Leon H. Sullivan	minister, civil rights activist	1992	Barbara Jordan	lawyer, politician
1972	Gordon Parks	photographer, writer	1993	Dorothy I. Height	social activist
1973	Wilson C. Riles	educator	1994	Maya Angelou	poet
1974	Damon Keith	lawyer, judge	1995	John Hope Franklin	historian, educator
1975	Hank Aaron	baseball player	1996	A. Leon Higginbotham	lawyer, judge, scholar
1976	Alvin Ailey	dancer, choreographer	1997	Carl T. Rowan	journalist, commentator
1977	Alex Haley	writer			
1978	Andrew Young	politician, civil rights leader	1998	Myrlie Evers-Williams	civil rights activist
1979	Rosa Parks	civil rights activist	1999	Earl G. Graves	publisher
1980	Rayford W. Logan	educator, writer	2000	Oprah Winfrey	television host, media personality
1981	Coleman A. Young	labor activist, politician	2001	Vernon E. Jordan, Jr.	lawyer, civil rights activist
1982	Benjamin E. Mays	educator, minister	2002	John Lewis	politician, civil rights activist
1983	Lena Horne	singer, actress			
1984	Thomas Bradley	politician	2003	Constance Baker Motley	judge, lawyer, civil rights activist
1985	Bill Cosby	actor, comedian			
1986	Benjamin L. Hooks	civil rights leader, government official	2004	Robert L. Carter	judge, lawyer, civil rights activist
1987	Percy Ellis Sutton	civil rights activist, politician	2005	Oliver W. Hill	lawyer, civil rights activist
1988	Frederick Douglass Patterson	educator	2006	Benjamin S. Carson	physician
			2007	John Conyers, Jr.	politician

Science Honors

Fields Medal

The Fields Medal, officially known as the International Medal for Outstanding Discoveries in Mathematics, is granted every four years to between two and four mathematicians for outstanding or groundbreaking research. It is traditionally given to mathematicians under the age of 40. Prize: Can$15,000 (about US$13,000).

YEAR	NAME	BIRTHPLACE	PRIMARY RESEARCH
1936	Lars Ahlfors	Helsinki, Finland	Riemann surfaces
	Jesse Douglas	New York NY	Plateau problem
1950	Laurent Schwartz	Paris, France	functional analysis
	Atle Selberg	Langesund, Norway	number theory
1954	Kunihiko Kodaira	Tokyo, Japan	algebraic geometry
	Jean-Pierre Serre	Bages, France	algebraic topology
1958	Klaus Roth	Breslau, Germany	number theory
	René Thom	Montbéliard, France	topology
1962	Lars Hörmander	Mjällby, Sweden	partial differential equations
	John Milnor	Orange NJ	differential topology
1966	Michael Atiyah	London, England	topology
	Paul Cohen	Long Branch NJ	set theory
	Alexandre Grothendieck	Berlin, Germany	algebraic geometry
	Stephen Smale	Flint MI	topology
1970	Alan Baker	London, England	number theory
	Heisuke Hironaka	Yamaguchi prefecture, Japan	algebraic geometry
	Sergey Novikov	Gorky, Russia	topology
	John Thompson	Ottawa KS	group theory
1974	Enrico Bombieri	Milan, Italy	number theory
	David Mumford	Worth, Sussex, UK	algebraic geometry
1978	Pierre Deligne	Brussels, Belgium	algebraic geometry
	Charles Fefferman	Washington DC	classical analysis
	Gregory Margulis	Moscow, Russia	Lie groups
	Daniel Quillen	Orange NJ	algebraic K-theory
1983	Alain Connes	Darguignan, France	operator theory
	William Thurston	Washington DC	topology
	Shing-Tung Yau	Swatow, China	differential geometry

Fields Medal (continued)

YEAR	NAME	BIRTHPLACE	PRIMARY RESEARCH
1986	Simon Donaldson	Cambridge, UK	topology
	Gerd Faltings	Gelsenkirchen, West Germany	Mordell conjecture
	Michael Freedman	Los Angeles CA	Poincaré conjecture
1990	Vladimir Drinfeld	Kharkov, Ukraine, USSR	algebraic geometry
	Vaughan Jones	Gisborne, New Zealand	knot theory
	Shigefumi Mori	Nagoya, Japan	algebraic geometry
	Edward Witten	Baltimore MD	superstring theory
1994	Jean Bourgain	Ostend, Belgium	analysis
	Pierre-Louis Lions	Grasse, France	partial differential equations
	Jean-Christophe Yoccoz	France	dynamical systems
	Yefim Zelmanov	Khabarovsk, USSR	group theory
1998	Richard Borcherds	Cape Town, South Africa	mathematical physics
	William Gowers	Marlborough, Wiltshire, UK	functional analysis
	Maksim Kontsevich	Khimki, Russia	mathematical physics
	Curt McMullen	Berkeley CA	chaos theory
2002	Laurent Lafforgue	Antony, France	number theory and analysis
	Vladimir Voevodsky	USSR	algebraic geometry
2006	Andrei Okounkov	Moscow, USSR	algebraic geometry
	Grigory Perelman (declined)	USSR	Ricci flow
	Terence Tao	Adelaide, Australia	prime numbers, nonlinear equations
	Wendelin Werner	Germany	mathematics of critical phenomena

Japan Prize

The Science and Technology Foundation of Japan awards the Japan Prize annually to living individuals or small groups whose achievements in science and technology have advanced knowledge and promoted human peace and prosperity. A cash award of ¥50 million (about $420,000), a certificate of merit, and a commemorative medal are also given for each prize category. Web site: <www.japanprize.jp>.

YEAR	LAUREATE	COUNTRY	AREA OF ACHIEVEMENT
1985	John R. Pierce	US	electronics and communications technologies
	Ephraim Katchalski-Katzir	Israel	basic theory of immobilized enzymes
1986	David Turnbull	US	new materials technology such as amorphous solids
	Willem J. Kolff	US	artificial organs
1987	Henry M. Beachell	US	high-yield rice
	Gurdev S. Khush	India	hardy rice
	Theodore H. Maiman	US	lasers
1988	Georges Vendryes	France	fast-breeder reactor technology
	Donald A. Henderson	US	} eradication of smallpox
	Isao Arita	Japan	
	Frank Fenner	Australia	
	Luc Montagnier	France	discovery of HIV
	Robert C. Gallo	US	isolation of HIV and development of AZT
1989	Frank Sherwood Rowland	US	stratospheric ozone depletion by chlorofluorocarbons
	Elias James Corey	US	syntheses of prostaglandins and related compounds
1990	Marvin Minsky	US	artificial intelligence
	William Jason Morgan	US	} plate tectonics
	Dan Peter Mckenzie	UK	
	Xavier Le Pichon	France	
1991	Jacques-Louis Lions	France	analysis and control of distributed systems, applied analysis
	John Julian Wild	US	ultrasound imaging
1992	Gerhard Ertl	Germany	chemistry and physics of solid surfaces
	Ernest John Christopher Polge	UK	cryopreservation of semen and embryos in farm animals
1993	Frank Press	US	seismology and disaster science
	Kary B. Mullis	US	polymerase chain reaction
1994	William Hayward Pickering	US	space travel and unmanned space exploration
	Arvid Carlsson	Sweden	dopamine's role in mental and motor functions
1995	Nick Holonyak, Jr.	US	light-emitting diodes and lasers
	Edward F. Knipling	US	pest management
1996	Charles K. Kao	Hong Kong	wide-band, low-loss optical fiber communications
	Masao Ito	Japan	cerebellum function
1997	Takashi Sugimura	Japan	} cancer
	Bruce N. Ames	US	
	Joseph F. Engelberger	US	} robotics
	Hiroyuki Yoshikawa	Japan	

Japan Prize (continued)

YEAR	LAUREATE	COUNTRY	AREA OF ACHIEVEMENT
1998	Leo Esaki	Japan	man-made superlattice crystals
	Jozef S. Schell	Belgium	} transgenic plants
	Marc C.E. Van Montagu	Belgium	
1999	W. Wesley Peterson	US	algebraic coding theory
	Jack L. Strominger	US	} human histocompatibility
	Don C. Wiley	US	antigens and their bound peptides
2000	Ian L. McHarg	US	ecological city planning and land-use evaluation
	Kimishige Ishizaka	Japan	immunoglobulin E and IgE-mediated allergic reactions
2001	John B. Goodenough	US	environmentally benign electrode materials for rechargeable lithium batteries
	Timothy R. Parsons	Canada	fishery resources and marine environment conservation
2002	Timothy John Berners-Lee	UK	World Wide Web
	Anne McLaren	UK	} study and manipulation of early-
	Andrzej K. Tarkowski	Poland	stage mammalian embryos
2003	Benoit B. Mandelbrot	France	fractals
	James A. Yorke	US	concept of chaos in complex systems
	Seiji Ogawa	Japan	magnetic resonance imaging
2004	Kenichi Honda	Japan	} photochemical
	Akira Fujishima	Japan	catalysis
	Keith Sainsbury	New Zealand	sustainable usage of seabed-shelf ecosystems
	John H. Lawton	UK	conservation of biodiversity
2005	Makoto Nagao	Japan	contributions to natural language processing and intelligent image processing
	Masatoshi Takeichi	Japan	} contributions to clarifying the molecular mechanisms
	Erkki Ruoslahti	US	of cell adhesion
2006	Sir John Houghton	UK	research of atmospheric structure based on satellite observation technology and promotion of transglobal assessments of climate change
2007	Albert Fert	France	} discovery of Giant Magneto-
	Peter Grünberg	Germany	Resistance (GMR)
	Peter Shaw Ashton	UK	conservation of tropical forests

National Medal of Science

The National Medal of Science was established by Congress in 1959. Awarded annually since 1962 by the National Science Foundation and the president of the United States, it recognizes notable achievements in mathematics, engineering, and the physical, natural, and social sciences. A presidentially appointed committee selects the winners from a pool of nominees. Medals have been given out in the second year after the date of the award: e.g., 2005 medals were awarded in May 2007. For more information, see the National Science Foundation Web site at <www.nsf.gov/nsb/od/nms/medal.htm>.

YEAR	NAME	FIELD
1962	Theodore von Karman	aerospace engineering
1963	Luis W. Alvarez	physics
	Vannevar Bush	electrical engineering
	John Robinson Pierce	communications engineering
	Cornelius Barnardus van Niel	biology
	Norbert Wiener	mathematics
1964	Roger Adams	chemistry
	Othmar Herman Ammann	civil engineering
	Theodosius Dobzhansky	genetics
	Charles Stark Draper	aerospace engineering
	Solomon Lefschetz	mathematics
	Neal Elgar Miller	psychology
	H. Marston Morse	mathematics
	Marshall Warren Nirenberg	biochemistry

YEAR	NAME	FIELD
1964 (cont.)	Julian Seymour Schwinger	physics
	Harold C. Urey	chemistry
	Robert Burns Woodward	chemistry
1965	John Bardeen	physics
	Peter J.W. Debye	physical chemistry
	Hugh L. Dryden	physics
	Clarence L. Johnson	aerospace engineering
	Leon M. Lederman	physics
	Warren K. Lewis	chemical engineering
	Francis Peyton Rous	pathology
	William W. Rubey	geology
	George Gaylord Simpson	paleontology
	Donald D. Van Slyke	chemistry
	Oscar Zariski	mathematics
1966	Jacob A.B. Bjerknes	meteorology
	Subrahmanyan Chandrasekhar	astrophysics
	Henry Eyring	chemistry

National Medal of Science (continued)

YEAR	NAME	FIELD	YEAR	NAME	FIELD
1966 (cont.)	Edward F. Knipling	entomology	1973 (cont.)	John Wilder Tukey	statistics
	Fritz Albert Lipmann	biochemistry		Richard T. Whitcomb	aerospace engineering
	John Willard Milnor	mathematics			
	William C. Rose	biochemistry		Robert Rathbun Wilson	particle physics
	Claude E. Shannon	mathematics, electrical engineering	1974	Nicolaas Bloembergen	physics
	John H. Van Vleck	physics		Britton Chance	biophysics
	Sewall Wright	genetics		Erwin Chargaff	biochemistry
	Vladimir Kosma Zworykin	electrical engineering		Paul J. Flory	physical chemistry
				William A. Fowler	nuclear astrophysics
1967	Jesse W. Beams	physics		Kurt Gödel	mathematics
	Francis Birch	geophysics		Rudolf Kompfner	physics
	Gregory Breit	physics		James Van Gundia Neel	genetics
	Paul Joseph Cohen	mathematics			
	Kenneth S. Cole	biophysics		Linus Pauling	chemistry
	Louis P. Hammett	chemistry		Ralph Brazelton Peck	geotechnical engineering
	Harry F. Harlow	psychology			
	Michael Heidelberger	immunology		Kenneth Sanborn Pitzer	physical chemistry
	George B. Kistiakowsky	chemistry			
				James Augustine Shannon	physiology
	Edwin Herbert Land	physics			
	Igor I. Sikorsky	aircraft design		Abel Wolman	sanitary engineering
	Alfred H. Sturtevant	genetics	1975	John W. Backus	computer science
1968	Horace A. Barker	biochemistry		Manson Benedict	nuclear engineering
	Paul D. Bartlett	chemistry		Hans Albrecht Bethe	theoretical physics
	Bernard B. Brodie	pharmacology		Shiing-shen Chern	mathematics
	Detlev W. Bronk	biophysics		George B. Dantzig	mathematics
	J. Presper Eckert, Jr.	engineering, computer science		Hallowell Davis	physiology
				Paul Gyorgy	medicine, vitamin research
	Herbert Friedman	astrophysics			
	Jay L. Lush	livestock genetics		Sterling Brown Hendricks	chemistry
	Nathan M. Newmark	civil engineering			
	Jerzy Neyman	mathematics, statistics		Joseph O. Hirschfelder	chemistry
				William Hayward Pickering	physics
	Lars Onsager	chemistry			
	B.F. Skinner	psychology		Lewis H. Sarett	chemistry
	Eugene Paul Wigner	mathematical physics		Frederick Emmons Terman	electrical engineering
1969	Herbert C. Brown	chemistry		Orville Alvin Vogel	research agronomy
	William Feller	mathematics		Wernher von Braun	aerospace engineering
	Robert J. Huebner	virology			
	Jack Kilby	electrical engineering		E. Bright Wilson, Jr.	chemistry
	Ernst Mayr	biology		Chien-Shiung Wu	physics
	Wolfgang K.H. Panofsky	physics	1976	Morris Cohen	materials science
1970	Richard Dagobert Brauer	mathematics		Kurt Otto Friedrichs	mathematics
				Peter C. Goldmark	communications engineering
	Robert H. Dicke	physics			
	Barbara McClintock	genetics		Samuel Abraham Goudsmit	physics
	George E. Mueller	physics			
	Albert Bruce Sabin	medicine, vaccine development		Roger Charles Louis Guillemin	physiology
	Allan R. Sandage	astronomy		Herbert S. Gutowsky	chemistry
	John C. Slater	physics		Erwin W. Mueller	physics
	John Archibald Wheeler	physics		Keith Roberts Porter	cell biology
				Efraim Racker	biochemistry
	Saul Winstein	chemistry		Frederick D. Rossini	chemistry
1971	no awards given			Verner E. Suomi	meteorology
1972	no awards given			Henry Taube	chemistry
1973	Daniel I. Arnon	biochemistry		George Eugene Uhlenbeck	physics
	Carl Djerassi	chemistry			
	Harold E. Edgerton	electrical engineering, photography		Hassler Whitney	mathematics
				Edward O. Wilson	biology
	Maurice Ewing	geophysics	1977	no awards given	
	Arie Jan Haagen-Smit	biochemistry	1978	no awards given	
	Vladimir Haensel	chemical engineering	1979	Robert H. Burris	biochemistry
	Frederick Seitz	physics		Elizabeth C. Crosby	neuroanatomy
	Earl W. Sutherland, Jr.	biochemistry		Joseph L. Doob	mathematics

National Medal of Science (continued)

YEAR	NAME	FIELD
1979 (cont.)	Richard P. Feynman	theoretical physics
	Donald E. Knuth	computer science
	Arthur Kornberg	biochemistry
	Emmett N. Leith	electrical engineering
	Herman F. Mark	chemistry
	Raymond D. Mindlin	mechanical engineering
	Robert N. Noyce	computer science
	Severo Ochoa	biochemistry
	Earl R. Parker	materials science
	Edward M. Purcell	physics
	Simon Ramo	electrical engineering
	John H. Sinfelt	chemical engineering
	Lyman Spitzer, Jr.	astrophysics
	Earl Reece Stadtman	biochemistry
	George Ledyard Stebbins	botany, genetics
	Victor F. Weisskopf	physics
	Paul Alfred Weiss	biology
1980	*no awards given*	
1981	Philip Handler	biochemistry
1982	Philip W. Anderson	physics
	Seymour Benzer	molecular biology
	Glenn W. Burton	genetics
	Mildred Cohn	biochemistry
	F. Albert Cotton	chemistry
	Edward H. Heinemann	aerospace engineering
	Donald L. Katz	chemical engineering
	Yoichiro Nambu	theoretical physics
	Marshall H. Stone	mathematics
	Gilbert Stork	organic chemistry
	Edward Teller	nuclear physics
	Charles Hard Townes	physics
1983	Howard L. Bachrach	biochemistry
	Paul Berg	biochemistry
	E. Margaret Burbidge	astronomy
	Maurice Goldhaber	physics
	Herman H. Goldstine	computer science
	William R. Hewlett	electrical engineering
	Roald Hoffmann	chemistry
	Helmut E. Landsberg	climatology
	George M. Low	aerospace engineering
	Walter H. Munk	oceanography
	George C. Pimentel	chemistry
	Frederick Reines	physics
	Wendell L. Roelofs	chemistry, entomology
	Bruno B. Rossi	astrophysics
	Berta V. Scharrer	neuroscience
	John Robert Schrieffer	physics
	Isadore M. Singer	mathematics
	John G. Trump	electrical engineering
	Richard N. Zare	chemistry
1984	*no awards given*	
1985	*no awards given*	
1986	Solomon J. Buchsbaum	physics
	Stanley Cohen	biochemistry
	Horace R. Crane	physics
	Herman Feshbach	physics
	Harry Gray	chemistry
	Donald A. Henderson	medicine, public health
	Robert Hofstadter	physics
	Peter D. Lax	mathematics
	Yuan Tseh Lee	chemistry

YEAR	NAME	FIELD
1986 (cont.)	Hans Wolfgang Liepmann	aerospace engineering
	T.Y. Lin	civil engineering
	Carl S. Marvel	chemistry
	Vernon B. Mountcastle	neurophysiology
	Bernard M. Oliver	electrical engineering
	George Emil Palade	cell biology
	Herbert A. Simon	social science
	Joan A. Steitz	molecular biology
	Frank H. Westheimer	chemistry
	Chen Ning Yang	theoretical physics
	Antoni Zygmund	mathematics
1987	Philip Hauge Abelson	physical chemistry
	Anne Anastasi	psychology
	Robert Byron Bird	chemical engineering
	Raoul Bott	mathematics
	Michael E. DeBakey	heart surgery
	Theodor O. Diener	plant pathology
	Harry Eagle	cell biology
	Walter M. Elsasser	physics
	Michael H. Freedman	mathematics
	William S. Johnson	chemistry
	Har Gobind Khorana	biochemistry
	Paul C. Lauterbur	chemistry
	Rita Levi-Montalcini	neurology
	George E. Pake	research, physics
	H. Bolton Seed	civil engineering
	George J. Stigler	economics
	Walter H. Stockmayer	chemistry
	Max Tishler	chemistry
	James Alfred Van Allen	physics
	Ernst Weber	electrical engineering
1988	William O. Baker	chemistry
	Konrad E. Bloch	biochemistry
	David Allan Bromley	physics
	Michael S. Brown	molecular genetics
	Paul C.W. Chu	physics
	Stanley N. Cohen	genetics
	Elias James Corey	chemistry
	Daniel C. Drucker	engineering education
	Milton Friedman	economics
	Joseph L. Goldstein	molecular genetics
	Ralph E. Gomory	mathematics, research
	Willis M. Hawkins	aerospace engineering
	Maurice R. Hilleman	vaccine research
	George W. Housner	earthquake engineering
	Eric Kandel	neurobiology
	Joseph B. Keller	mathematics
	Walter Kohn	physics
	Norman Foster Ramsey	physics
	Jack Steinberger	physics
	Rosalyn S. Yalow	medical physics
1989	Arnold O. Beckman	chemistry
	Richard B. Bernstein	chemistry
	Melvin Calvin	biochemistry
	Harry G. Drickamer	chemistry, physics
	Katherine Esau	botany
	Herbert E. Grier	aerospace engineering
	Viktor Hamburger	biology
	Samuel Karlin	mathematics

National Medal of Science (continued)

YEAR	NAME	FIELD
1989 (cont.)	Philip Leder	genetics
	Joshua Lederberg	genetics
	Saunders Mac Lane	mathematics
	Rudolph A. Marcus	chemistry
	Harden M. McConnell	chemistry
	Eugene N. Parker	theoretical astrophysics
	Robert P. Sharp	geology
	Donald C. Spencer	mathematics
	Roger Wolcott Sperry	neurobiology
	Henry M. Stommel	oceanography
	Harland G. Wood	biochemistry
1990	Baruj Benacerraf	pathology, immunology
	Elkan R. Blout	chemistry
	Herbert W. Boyer	biochemistry, genetics
	George F. Carrier	mathematics
	Allan MacLeod Cormack	physics
	Mildred S. Dresselhaus	physics
	Karl August Folkers	chemistry
	Nick Holonyak, Jr.	electrical engineering
	Leonid Hurwicz	economics
	Stephen Cole Kleene	mathematics
	Daniel E. Koshland, Jr.	biochemistry
	Edward B. Lewis	developmental genetics
	John McCarthy	computer science
	Edwin Mattison McMillan	nuclear physics
	David G. Nathan	pediatrics
	Robert V. Pound	physics
	Roger R.D. Revelle	oceanography
	John D. Roberts	chemistry
	Patrick Suppes	philosophy, statistics education
	E. Donnall Thomas	medicine
1991	Mary Ellen Avery	pediatrics
	Ronald Breslow	chemistry
	Alberto P. Calderon	mathematics
	Gertrude B. Elion	pharmacology
	George H. Heilmeier	electrical engineering
	Dudley R. Herschbach	chemistry
	G. Evelyn Hutchinson	zoology
	Elvin A. Kabat	immunology
	Robert W. Kates	geography
	Luna B. Leopold	hydrology, geology
	Salvador Luria	biology
	Paul A. Marks	hematology, cancer research
	George A. Miller	psychology
	Arthur L. Schawlow	physics
	Glenn T. Seaborg	nuclear chemistry
	Folke K. Skoog	botany
	H. Guyford Stever	aerospace engineering
	Edward C. Stone	physics
	Steven Weinberg	nuclear physics
	Paul C. Zamecnik	molecular biology
1992	Eleanor J. Gibson	psychology
	Allen Newell	computer science
	Calvin F. Quate	electrical engineering
	Eugene M. Shoemaker	planetary geology
1992 (cont.)	Howard E. Simmons, Jr.	chemistry
	Maxine F. Singer	biochemistry, administration
	Howard Martin Temin	virology
	John Roy Whinnery	electrical engineering
1993	Alfred Y. Cho	electrical engineering
	Donald J. Cram	chemistry
	Val Logsdon Fitch	particle physics
	Norman Hackerman	chemistry
	Martin D. Kruskal	mathematics
	Daniel Nathans	microbiology
	Vera C. Rubin	astronomy
	Salome G. Waelsch	molecular genetics
1994	Ray W. Clough	civil engineering
	John Cocke	computer science
	Thomas Eisner	chemical ecology
	George S. Hammond	chemistry
	Robert K. Merton	sociology
	Elizabeth F. Neufeld	biochemistry
	Albert W. Overhauser	physics
	Frank Press	geophysics, administration
1995	Thomas Robert Cech	biochemistry
	Hans Georg Dehmelt	physics
	Peter M. Goldreich	astrophysics
	Hermann A. Haus	electrical engineering
	Isabella L. Karle	chemistry
	Louis Nirenberg	mathematics
	Alexander Rich	molecular biology
	Roger N. Shepard	psychology
1996	Wallace S. Broecker	geochemistry
	Norman Davidson	chemistry, molecular biology
	James L. Flanagan	electrical engineering
	Richard M. Karp	computer science
	C. Kumar N. Patel	electrical engineering
	Ruth Patrick	limnology
	Paul Samuelson	economics
	Stephen Smale	mathematics
1997	William K. Estes	psychology
	Darleane C. Hoffman	chemistry
	Harold S. Johnston	chemistry
	Marshall N. Rosenbluth	theoretical plasma physics
	Martin Schwarzschild	astrophysics
	James Dewey Watson	genetics, biophysics
	Robert A. Weinberg	biology, cancer research
	George W. Wetherill	planetary science
	Shing-Tung Yau	mathematics
1998	Bruce N. Ames	biochemistry, cancer research
	Don L. Anderson	geophysics
	John N. Bahcall	astrophysics
	John W. Cahn	materials science
	Cathleen Synge Morawetz	mathematics
	Janet D. Rowley	medicine, cancer research
	Eli Ruckenstein	chemical engineering
	George M. Whitesides	chemistry
	William Julius Wilson	sociology
1999	David Baltimore	virology, administration
	Felix E. Browder	mathematics
	Ronald R. Coifman	mathematics

National Medal of Science (continued)

YEAR	NAME	FIELD
1999 (cont.)	James Watson Cronin	particle physics
	Jared Diamond	physiology
	Leo P. Kadanoff	theoretical physics
	Lynn Margulis	microbiology
	Stuart A. Rice	chemistry
	John Ross	chemistry
	Susan Solomon	atmospheric science
	Robert M. Solow	economics
	Kenneth N. Stevens	electrical engineering, speech
2000	Nancy C. Andreasen	psychiatry
	John D. Baldeschwieler	chemistry
	Gary S. Becker	economics
	Yuan-Cheng B. Fung	bioengineering
	Ralph F. Hirschmann	chemistry
	Willis Eugene Lamb, Jr.	physics
	Jeremiah P. Ostriker	astrophysics
	Peter H. Raven	botany
	John Griggs Thompson	mathematics
	Karen K. Uhlenbeck	mathematics
	Gilbert F. White	geography
	Carl R. Woese	microbiology
2001	Andreas Acrivos	chemical engineering
	Francisco J. Ayala	molecular biology
	George F. Bass	nautical archaeology
	Mario R. Capecchi	genetics
	Marvin L. Cohen	materials science
	Ernest R. Davidson	chemistry
	Raymond Davis, Jr.	chemistry, astrophysics
	Ann M. Graybiel	neuroscience
	Charles D. Keeling	oceanography
	Gene E. Likens	ecology
	Victor A. McKusick	medical genetics
	Calyampudi R. Rao	mathematics, statistics
	Gabor A. Somorjai	chemistry

YEAR	NAME	FIELD
2001 (cont.)	Elias M. Stein	mathematics
	Harold Varmus	virology, administration
2002	Leo L. Beranek	engineering
	John I. Brauman	chemistry
	James E. Darnell	cell biology
	Richard L. Garwin	physics
	James G. Glimm	mathematics, statistics
	W. Jason Morgan	geophysics
	Evelyn M. Witkin	genetics
	Edward Witten	mathematical physics
2003	J. Michael Bishop	microbiology
	G. Brent Dalrymple	geology
	Carl R. de Boor	mathematics
	Riccardo Giacconi	astrophysics
	R. Duncan Luce	cognitive science
	John M. Prausnitz	chemical engineering
	Solomon H. Snyder	neuroscience
	Charles Yanofsky	molecular biology
2004	Kenneth J. Arrow	economics
	Norman E. Borlaug	agriculture
	Robert N. Clayton	geochemistry
	Edwin N. Lightfoot	engineering
	Stephen J. Lippard	chemistry
	Phillip A. Sharp	molecular biology, biochemistry
	Thomas E. Starzl	medicine
	Dennis P. Sullivan	mathematics
2005	Jan D. Achenbach	mechanical engineering
	Ralph A. Alpher	astronomy
	Gordon H. Bower	psychology
	Bradley Efron	statistics
	Anthony S. Fauci	immunology
	Tobin J. Marks	chemistry
	Lonnie G. Thompson	glaciology
	Torsten N. Wiesel	neurobiology

The National Inventor of the Year Award

The National Inventor of the Year Award is given by the Intellectual Property Owners Association, a trade organization established in 1972. Patented American inventions from the preceding four years are eligible for nomination annually; runners-up receive recognition as Distinguished Inventors. The winner for 2007 was physician Raymond Damadian, honored for his development of the Upright MRI scanner, which allows magnetic reso- nance imaging of patients in standing, sitting, or other positions other than the standard prone position, greatly increasing the patients' comfort level as well as making possible images of tissue and bone while the patients are approximating the weight-bearing effects of normal circumstances. Award amount: $25,000.

Web site: <www.ipo.org>.

Intel Science Talent Search

The Intel Science Talent Search encourages American high school seniors to pursue careers in the sciences by awarding scholarships for outstanding science projects. Created in 1942 by Science Service, a nonprofit organization devoted to public appreciation of science, and Westinghouse Electric Corporation, the contest brings 40 finalists each year to exhibit their projects at the Science Talent Institute in Washington DC and compete for the top prizes. Since 1998 the talent search has been sponsored by Intel Corp. The highest-place winners for 2007 were **Mary Masterman** of Oklahoma City OK (first prize, $100,000), **John Pardon** of Chapel Hill NC (second prize, $75,000), and **Dmitry Vaintrob** of Eugene OR (third prize, $50,000).

Masterman designed and built an accurate spectrograph, a machine that identifies specific characteristics of different kinds of molecules. Pardon solved a classical open problem from differential geometry related to making a closed curve convex in a continuous manner. Vaintrob investigated ways to associate algebraic structures to topological spaces.

Web site: <www.sciserv.org/sts>.

Nature, Science, Medicine, & Technology

Environment: Global Warming

by Jeffrey Kluger, TIME

It was probably always too much to believe that human beings would be responsible stewards of the planet. We may be the smartest of all the animals, endowed with exponentially greater powers of insight and abstraction than the rest, but we're animals all the same. That means that we can also be shortsighted and brutish, hungry for food, resources, land—and heedless of the mess we leave behind trying to get them.

And make a mess we have. If droughts and wildfires, floods and crop failures, collapsing climate-sensitive species, and the images of drowning polar bears didn't quiet most of the remaining global-warming doubters, the hurricane-driven destruction of New Orleans did. Dismissing a scientist's temperature chart is one thing. Dismissing the death of a major American city is something else entirely. What's more, the heat is only continuing to rise. The year 2006 was the hottest on record in the US. The deceptively normal average temperature in the winter of 2006-07 masked record-breaking highs in December and record-breaking lows in February. That's the sign not of a planet keeping an even strain but of one thrashing through the alternating chills and night sweats of a serious illness.

The UN's Intergovernmental Panel on Climate Change issued a report on the state of planetary warming in February 2007 that was surprising only in its utter lack of hedging. "Warming of the climate system is unequivocal," the report stated. What's more, there is "very high confidence" that human activities since 1750 have played a significant role by overloading the atmosphere with carbon dioxide (CO_2), hence retaining solar heat that would otherwise radiate away. The report concludes that while the long-term solution is to reduce the levels of carbon dioxide in the atmosphere, for now we're going to have to dig in and prepare, building better levees, moving to higher ground, abandoning vulnerable floodplains altogether.

Some lingering critics still found wiggle room in the UN panel's findings. "I think there is a healthy debate ongoing, even though the scientists who are in favor of doing something on greenhouse gases are in the majority," says Republican Rep. James Sensenbrenner of Wisconsin. But when your last good position is to debate the difference between certain and extra certain, you're playing a losing hand. "The science," says Christine Todd Whitman, former administrator of the Environmental Protection Agency (EPA), "now is getting to the point where it's pretty hard to deny." Indeed it is. Atmospheric levels of CO_2 were 379 parts per million (ppm) in 2005, higher than at any time in the past 650,000 years. Of the 12 warmest years on record, 11 occurred between 1995 and 2006.

So if the diagnosis is in, what's the cure? A crisis of this magnitude clearly calls for action that is both bottom-up and top-down. Though there is some debate about how much difference individuals can make, there is little question that the most powerful players—government and industry—have to take the lead.

Still, individuals too can move the carbon needle, but how much and how fast? Different green strategies, after all, yield different results. You can choose a hybrid vehicle, but simply tuning up your car and properly inflating the tires will help too. Buying carbon offsets can reduce the impact of your cross-continental travel, provided you can ensure where your money's really going. Planting trees is great, but in some parts of the world, the light-absorbing color of the leaves causes them to retain heat and paradoxically increases warming.

Even the most effective individual action, however, is not enough. Cleaning up the wreckage left by our 250-year industrial bacchanal will require fundamental changes in a society hooked on its fossil fuels. Beneath the grassroots action, larger tectonic plates are shifting. Science is attacking the problem more aggressively than ever. So is industry. So are architects and lawmakers and urban planners. The world is awakened to the problem in a way it never has been before. Says Carol Browner, onetime administrator of the EPA: "It's a sea change from where we were on this issue."

The Scientists' Solutions. If the Earth is choking on greenhouse gases, it's not hard to see why. Global carbon dioxide output in 2006 approached a staggering 32 billion tons, with about 25% of that coming from the US. Turning off the carbon spigot is the first step, and many of the solutions are familiar: windmills, solar panels, nuclear plants. All three technologies are part of the energy mix, although each has its issues, including noise from windmills and radioactive waste from nukes.

Biofuels, however, are the real growth science, particularly after Pres. George W. Bush, in his 2007 state of the union address, called for the US to quintuple its production of biofuels, primarily ethanol. That was good news to American corn farmers, who produce the crop from which the overwhelming share of domestic ethanol is made. But the manufacture of corn ethanol is still inefficient: the process burns up almost as much energy as it produces.

A better answer is sugarcane ethanol, which yields eight times the energy it takes to make and provides 40% of all the fuel sold in Brazil. But such ethanol causes environmental problems of its own, as forests are cleared for cane fields. Better still would be to process ethanol from agricultural waste like wood chips or the humble summer grass called switchgrass. The cellulosic ethanol they produce packs more energy than corn ethanol, but it also takes more energy to manufacture. "If you make ethanol by burning coal, you defeat the purpose," says Sarah Hessenflow Harper, an analyst for the advocacy group Environmental Defense.

Until we can dial down our carbon emissions, a more immediate strategy might be to find somewhere to put it all—to sequester it underground. In the same way we store radioactive waste from nuclear reactors, so too could we collect the gaseous CO_2 from power plants.

The earth is full of safe, stable places to store gases we don't want, and scientists know precisely where they are. The natural gas that heats homes, fires stoves, and runs factories is found in deep, saline-rich limestone and sandstone cavities, where spongelike pores store gas and help keep it from leaking away. When the energy industry pumps a deposit clean, the chambers stand empty. Not only are the shape and capacity of the cavities mapped, but also in many cases drilling equipment is still on hand that could easily be repurposed from extraction to injection.

The US Department of Energy is funding seven research partnerships to test sequestration technologies. In the summer of 2007, one of those projects is prepared to inject a modest 2,000 metric tons of CO_2 into the sandstone subsurface beneath a spread of tomato fields near Thornton CA, where it would stay, in effect, forever.

Would that be safe? Carbon dioxide can be lethal, a fact grimly illustrated in 1986 when a giant surge of the stuff bubbled up from Lake Nyos in Cameroon, asphyxiating 1,700 people as they slept. Nonetheless, investigators involved in the Thornton project insist there is little cause for worry. "The fields held oil and gas for millennia," says Larry Myer, an earth scientist with Lawrence Berkeley National Laboratory in Berkeley CA and the project's director, "so geologically we know they're going to hold CO_2."

Even if researchers master the mechanics of sequestration, they must still develop a way to separate CO_2 from power-plant exhaust so that there will be something to stash in the cavities in the first place. There are two promising methods. One is to gasify coal before it's burned, reducing it to a high-pressure synthetic gas that can be stripped of its carbon, leaving mostly hydrogen behind. The alternative is to pulverize coal as power-plant operators do now but then rely on new hardware to separate the CO_2 after burning. Both methods are at least 20 years away from being fully developed, predicts Ernest Moniz, codirector of the Massachusetts Institute of Technology Laboratory for Energy and the Environment and a former under secretary of the Department of Energy. "We're very early in the process," he says.

The Twin Elephants. While legislators in Washington debate the urgency of global warming, states and cities aren't waiting for Congress to act. California Gov. Arnold Schwarzenegger committed the state to a 25% reduction in greenhouse gases by 2020; he was promptly sued by carmakers that would have to increase fuel efficiency to sell there. If California prevails, the size of its market could turn its regulations into a de facto national standard.

States are also joining hands to curb emissions from power plants—the coal burned in Pennsylvania,

after all, doesn't pause at the New Jersey state line. In 2003 then governor George Pataki of New York launched the Regional Greenhouse Gas Initiative, a confederation of northeastern and mid-Atlantic states that has created its own cap-and-trade program, with the goal of reducing emissions 10% below the current level by 2019. Ten states are now part of the group; in 2007 five Western states embraced a similarly ambitious goal. And New York City Mayor Michael Bloomberg has proposed strong measures to make his metropolis greener.

Yet no matter how aggressively the US tackles its carbon problem, the global outlook hinges on the coal-fired economies of the world's two looming giants: China and India. Between 1990 and 2004, energy consumption rose 37% in India and 53% in China. Beijing is building new coal-fired power plants at the rate of one every week. While the most technologically sophisticated coal plants operate at almost 45% efficiency, China's top out at just 33%.

But China and India are hardly energy hogs—not if you consider the amount of emissions that any single person living there generates. Americans' per capita emission of carbon dioxide is about 21.75 tons. In China it's just 4.03; in India it's an even smaller 1.12. Yet that is going to change. Up to 50% of the Indian population lives almost entirely off the grid, and the government is determined to bring them aboard. The Chinese economy has been growing at the rate of 10% a year, and Beijing is not inclined to slow down. China is expected to pass the US in total greenhouse emissions before 2010.

Not all is bleak. The American-based Natural Resources Defense Council is trying to help the Chinese clean up, working with their businesses to audit energy consumption and developing a fund to bankroll the installation of more efficient equipment in factories. Barbara Finamore of the China Clean Energy Program estimates that this could eliminate the need for 3,000 new power plants over the next few decades. China also imposes higher taxes on large cars than on small ones; subsidizes wind, solar and other renewables; and has passed a law that aims to make 15% of the country's power come from renewables by 2020.

India is further behind China in developing renewable-energy sources, but the need for power is spurring innovation. India has an aggressive solar and wind industry, with one company, Suzlon, generating US$1.5 billion in wind-turbine revenue in 2006. But India, with its less-developed economy, cannot as easily afford the cost of going green—or at least greener. "The Indian government has not taken the problem seriously," says Steve Sawyer, a policy adviser for Greenpeace International.

It sometimes seems that the same can be said for the entire world. It's not surprising that faced with a problem of this magnitude, people will yield to the impulse to lay blame. Voters blame politicians. Politicians blame industry. Industry blames an overweening government. Prius owners blame Hummer drivers. But never mind who caused the problem, its very enormity means that all of the finger pointers will have to assume a role in cleaning it up.

It took generations to foul the planet as badly as we have, and it will surely take generations to reverse things. The difference is we had the leisure of beginning our long industrial climb whenever we wanted to. We don't have the leisure of waiting to clean up after it.

Time

Measuring Time

The measurement of time is an ancient science. The **Cro-Magnons** recorded the phases of the Moon some 30,000 years ago—but the first minutes were counted accurately only 400 years ago, and the atomic clocks that allow us to track time to the billionth of a second are less than 50 years old. Timekeeping has been both a lens through which humanity has observed the heavens and a mirror reflecting the progress of science and civilization. Our millennia-long struggle to **define and calibrate** time through calendars and clocks has meant trying to bring the register of human affairs in line with natural cycles—of the Earth, Sun, Moon, and stars, of the physics of matter—but always cycles. What vary are the cultural values and goals that dictate which cycles are significant.

With a religious culture dominated by gods of the Sun and sky and a civilization dependent on the annual cycle of a river, the **ancient Egyptians** were expert astronomers who studied the Sun's recurrent movements and their effects on the Earth very closely. By plotting the beginning of the Nile's flood each year, a reliable harbinger of seasonal change, they measured a cycle 365 days long—a reasonable approximation of the duration of the solar year. Observations of the star Sirius eventually allowed Egyptian astronomers to adjust the solar year to 365.25 days. Astronomic studies by the Mayan civilization of the first millennium AD underlay a complex calendrical system involving an accurately determined solar year (18 months of days, plus an unlucky 5-day period) and a sacred year of 260 days (13 cycles of 20 named days).

About 127 BC the **Greek astronomer Hipparchus** further refined the year. His adjustments centered on the equinoxes—which he discovered to be shifting to the west at the barely perceptible rate of two degrees in 150 years. Because of this discovery Hipparchus realized that the solar year was slightly shorter than the accepted 365.25 days. His calculation of 365.242 days was remarkably close to the present calculation of 365.242199 days.

Unfortunately for people of the next 1,600 years, Hipparchus's discoveries were virtually ignored by calendar makers. **Julius Caesar's** calendrical reforms in 46 BC left the calendar year at 365.25 days—more than 11 minutes too long. By the 1500s the Julian calendar was 10 days behind the solar year. The shortfall alarmed Christian religious leaders because it meant that holy days, including Easter, were being observed at the wrong times. In 1582, **Pope Gregory XIII** officially revised the accepted length of the year to 365.2422 days, adjusted the leap-year rule, and lopped off the 10 extra days, creating in the process the calendar in most widespread use today.

Meanwhile, the quest to measure time accurately on a much smaller scale was still in its early phases. The invention of the **weight-driven mechanical clock** some 200 years earlier had revolutionized timekeeping, making it possible to count equal units of time and radically changing the way people thought about time and the best ways to measure it.

Calendars are deemed accurate according to how well they accommodate the variations in larger celestial cycles. Clocks, on the other hand, have historically been judged accurate in relation to the average duration of the Earth's rotation around the Sun—that is, by how well they keep "**mean time.**" While calendrical standards have remained fairly stable, the clock's units of measure have gradually shifted away from using the Earth-Sun relationship as a norm. With the introduction of mechanical clocks, clock time became increasingly removed from cyclical events in the sky, for the cycles on which mechanical clocks base their measures are independent of Earth and Sun. A **pendulum clock**, for example, measures only the beat of its pendulum, not any part of a "real" day.

The pendulum clock kicked off the modern search for the perfect clock, a timepiece governed by a naturally cycling period that operated free from mechanical friction and fatigue. In 1927 W.A. Marrison invented a clock that operated via a tiny **quartz crystal**. The crystal vibrated at an ultrasonic frequency when exposed to an electric field. These vibrations were constant and delivered a virtually frictionless beat to the counting mechanism of the clock. Accurate to thousandths of a second, quartz clocks led scientists to make the belated discovery that the Earth was not a reliable clock to begin with. Disparities between the measurements of quartz clocks and the rotation of the Earth revealed unpredictable irregularities in the rotation, which had to that point defined the duration of a second (1/86,400 of the mean solar day).

In 1967 the **definition of a second** was officially divorced from the Earth's rotation when the 13th General Conference of Weights and Measures redefined the second as "9,192,631,770 periods of the radiation corresponding to the transition between the two hyperfine levels of the ground state of the cesium-133 atom." **Cesium atoms** are superior to quartz crystals because they do not wear out and have cycles that comprise oscillations between precisely defined energy states that can oscillate forever without any distortion. Furthermore, each atom of cesium oscillates at exactly the same frequency as all others, making each one a perfect timekeeper. To keep solar time and atomic time from drifting too far apart, the two were combined in 1964 to form **Coordinated Universal Time**, which is based on the atomic second and kept within 0.9 second of solar time by adding a leap second as needed.

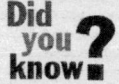
Did you know? The liger is the offspring of a lion and a tigress, whereas the tigon is the result of mating a tiger with a lioness. Both are zoo-bred hybrids, and it is probable that neither occurs in the wild, as differences in the behavior and habitat of the lion and tiger make interbreeding unlikely. The liger and the tigon possess features of both parents, in variable proportions, but are generally larger and darker than either.

Time Zone Map

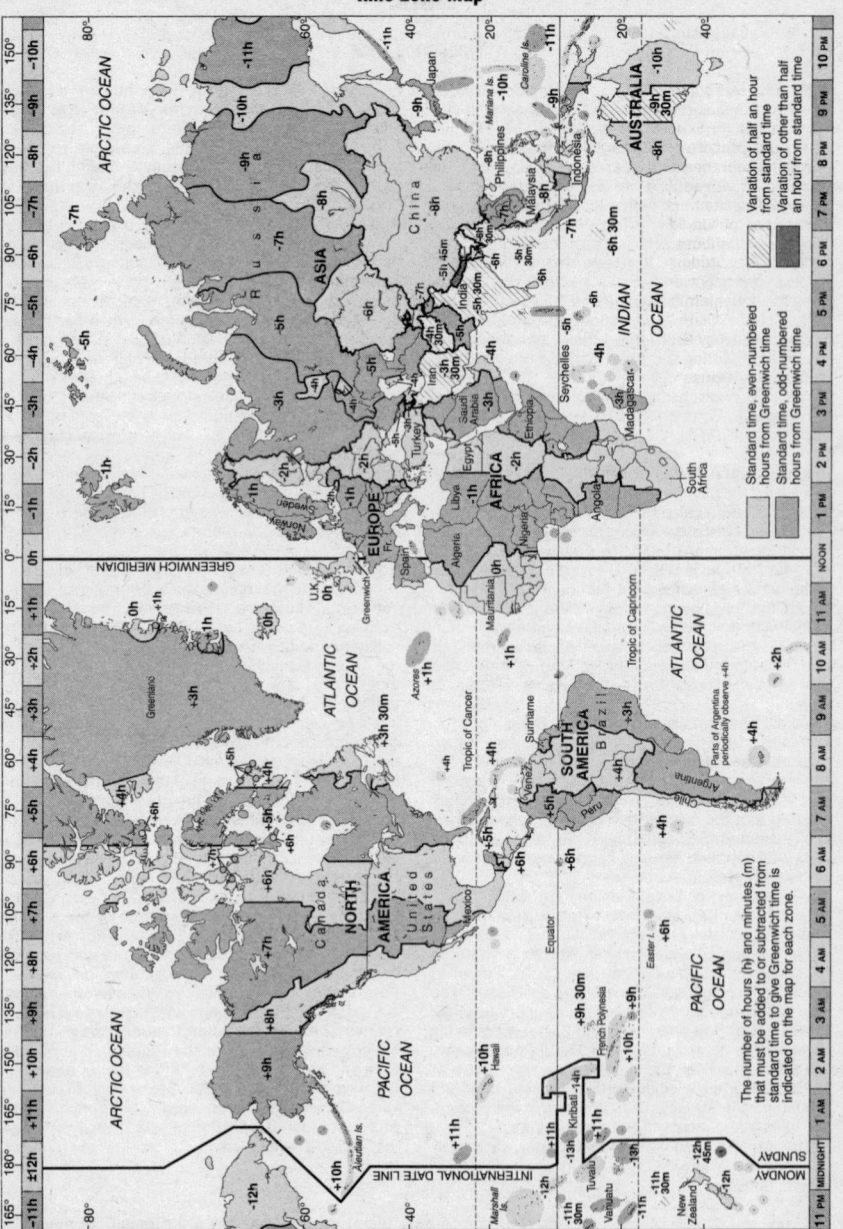

Based on data from the US Defense Mapping Agency Hydrographic/Topographic Center

Daylight Saving Time

Also called **summer time, daylight saving time** is a system for uniformly advancing clocks, especially in summer, so as to extend daylight hours during conventional waking time. In the Northern Hemisphere, clocks are usually set ahead one hour in late March or in April and are set back one hour in late September or in October; most Southern Hemisphere countries that observe daylight saving time set clocks ahead in October or November and reset them in March or April. Equatorial countries do not observe daylight saving time because daylight hours stay about the same from season to season in the lower latitudes.

The practice was first suggested in a whimsical essay by **Benjamin Franklin** in 1784. In 1907 an Englishman, William Willett, campaigned for setting the clock ahead by 80 minutes in four moves of 20 minutes each during the spring and summer months. In 1908 the House of Commons rejected a bill to advance the clock by one hour in the spring and return to Greenwich Mean (standard) Time in the autumn.

Several countries, including Australia, Great Britain, Germany, and the United States, adopted **summer daylight saving time** during World War I to conserve fuel by reducing the need for artificial light. During World War II, clocks were kept continuously advanced by an hour in some nations—e.g., in the US from 9 Feb 1942 to 30 Sep 1945; and England used "double summer time" during part of the year, advancing clocks two hours from the standard time during the summer and one hour during the winter months.

In 2005 the US Congress changed the law governing daylight saving time, moving the start of daylight saving time from the first Sunday in April to the second Sunday in March, while moving the end date from the last Sunday in October to the first Sunday in November starting in 2007. In most of the countries of Western Europe, daylight saving time starts on the last Sunday in March and ends on the last Sunday in October.

Julian and Gregorian Calendars

The **Julian calendar**, also called the Old Style calendar, is a dating system established by Julius Caesar as a reform of the Roman republican calendar. Caesar, advised by the Alexandrian astronomer Sosigenes, made the new calendar solar, not lunar, and he took the length of the solar year as 365¼ days. The year was divided into 12 months, all of which had either 30 or 31 days except February, which contained 28 days in common (365-day) years and 29 in every fourth year (a leap year, of 366 days). Because of misunderstandings, the calendar was not established in smooth operation until AD 8. Further, Sosigenes had overestimated the length of the year by 11 minutes 14 seconds, and by the mid-1500s, the cumulative effect of this error had shifted the dates of the seasons by about 10 days from Caesar's time.

This inaccuracy led **Pope Gregory XIII** to reform the Julian calendar. His **Gregorian calendar**, also called the **New Style calendar**, is still in general use. Gregory's proclamation in 1582 restored the calendar to the seasonal dates of AD 325, an adjustment of 10 days. Although the amount of regression was some 14 days by Pope Gregory's time, Gregory based his reform on restoration of the vernal equinox, then falling on 11 March, to the date (21 March) it had in AD 325, the time of the Council of Nicaea. Advancing the calendar 10 days after 4 Oct 1582, the day following being reckoned as 15 October, effected the change.

The Gregorian calendar differs from the Julian only in that no century year is a leap year unless it is exactly divisible by 400 (e.g., 1600, 2000). A further refinement, the designation of years evenly divisible by 4,000 as common (not leap) years, will keep the Gregorian calendar accurate to within one day in 20,000 years.

Jewish Calendar

The **Jewish calendar** is **lunisolar**—i.e., regulated by the positions of both the Moon and the Sun. It consists usually of 12 alternating lunar months of 29 and 30 days each (except for Heshvan and Kislev, which sometimes have either 29 or 30 days), and totals 353, 354, or 355 days per year. The average lunar year (354 days) is adjusted to the solar year (365¼ days) by the periodic introduction of leap years in order to assure that the major festivals fall in their proper season. The leap year consists of an additional 30-day month called **First Adar**, which always precedes the month of (Second) Adar. (During leap year, the Adar holidays are postponed to Second Adar.) A leap year consists of either 383, 384, or 385 days and occurs seven times during every 19-year period (the so-called Metonic cycle). Among the consequences of the lunisolar structure are these: (1) The number of days in a year may vary considerably, from 353 to 385 days. (2) The first day of a month can fall on any day of the week, that day varying from year to year. Consequently, the days of the week upon which an annual Jewish festival falls vary from year to year despite the festival's fixed position in the Jewish month. The months of the Jewish calendar and their Gregorian equivalents are as follows:

JEWISH MONTH	GREGORIAN MONTH(S)	JEWISH MONTH	GREGORIAN MONTH(S)
Tishri	September–October	Nisan	March–April
Heshvan, or Marheshvan	October–November	Iyyar	April–May
Kislev	November–December	Sivan	May–June
Tevet	December–January	Tammuz	June–July
Shevat	January–February	Av	July–August
Adar	February–March	Elul	August–September

Muslim Calendar

The **Muslim calendar** (also called the **Islamic calendar**, or **Hijrah**) is a dating system used in the Muslim world that is based on a year of 12 months. Each month begins approximately at the time of the New Moon. The **months** of the Muslim calendar are: Muharram, Safar, Rabi I, Rabi II, Jumada I, Jumada II, Rajab, Sha'ban, Ramadan, Shawwal, Dhu al-Qa'dah, and Dhu al-Hijjah.

In the standard Muslim calendar the months are alternately 30 and 29 days long except for the 12th month, Dhu al-Hijjah, the length of which is varied in a 30-year cycle intended to keep the calendar in step with the true phases of the Moon. In 11 years of this cycle, Dhu al-Hijjah has 30 days, and in the other 19 years it has 29. Thus the year has either 354 or 355 days. No months are intercalated, so that the named months do not remain in the same seasons but retrogress through the entire solar, or seasonal, year (of about 365.25 days) every 32.5 solar years.

There are some exceptions to this calendar in the Muslim world. **Turkey** uses the Gregorian calendar, while the **Iranian Muslim calendar** is based on a solar year. The Iranian calendar still begins from the same dating point as other Muslim calendars (that is, some 10 years prior to the death of Muhammad in AD 632). Thus, the Gregorian year AD 2008 corresponds to the Hijrah years of AH 1428–30.

Chinese Calendar

The **Chinese calendar** is a dating system used concurrently with the Gregorian (Western) calendar in China and Taiwan and in neighboring countries (e.g., Japan). The calendar consists of 12 months of alternately 29 and 30 days, equal to 354 or 355 days, or approximately 12 full lunar cycles. Intercalary months have been inserted to keep the calendar year in step with the solar year of about 365 days. **Months** have no names but are instead referred to by numbers within a year and sometimes also by a series of 12 animal names that from ancient times have been attached to years and to hours of the day.

The calendar also incorporates a **meteorologic cycle** that contains 24 points, each beginning one of the periods named. The establishment of this cycle required a fair amount of astronomical understanding of the Earth as a celestial body. Modern scholars acknowledge the superiority of pre-Sung **Chinese astronomy** (at least until about the 13th century AD) over that of other, contemporary nations.

The **24 points** within the meteorologic cycle coincide with points 15° apart on the ecliptic (the plane of the Earth's yearly journey around the Sun or, if it is thought that the Sun turns around the Earth, the apparent journey of the Sun against the stars). It takes about 15.2 days for the Sun to travel from one of these points to another (because the ecliptic is a complete circle of 360°), and the Sun needs 365¼ days to finish its journey in this cycle. Supposedly, each of the 12 months of the year contains two points, but, because a lunar month has only 29½ days and the two points share about 30.4 days, there is always the chance that a lunar month will fail to contain both points, though the distance between any two given points is only 15°. If such an occasion occurs, the intercalation of an extra month takes place. For instance, one may find a year with two "Julys" or with two "Augusts" in the Chinese calendar. In fact, the exact length of the month in the Chinese calendar is either 30 days or 29 days—a phenomenon that reflects its lunar origin.

SOLAR TERMS—CHINESE (ENGLISH EQUIVALENTS)	GREGORIAN DATE (APPROXIMATE)	LUNAR MONTH (CORRESPONDENCE OF LUNAR AND SOLAR MONTHS APPROXIMATE)
Lichun (spring begins)	5 February	1—tiger
Yushui (rain water)	19 February	
Jingzhe (excited insects)	5 March	2—rabbit/hare
Chunfen (vernal equinox)	20 March	
Qingming (clear and bright)	5 April	3—dragon
Guyu (grain rains)	20 April	
Lixia (summer begins)	5 May	4—snake
Xiaoman (grain fills)	21 May	
Mangzhong (grain in ear)	6 June	5—horse
Xiazhi (summer solstice)	21 June	
Xiaoshu (slight heat)	7 July	6—sheep/ram
Dashu (great heat)	23 July	
Liqiu (autumn begins)	7 August	7—monkey
Chushu (limit of heat)	23 August	
Bailu (white dew)	8 September	8—chicken/rooster
Qiufen (autumn equinox)	23 September	
Hanlu (cold dew)	8 October	9—dog
Shuangjiang (hoar frost descends)	24 October	
Lidong (winter begins)	8 November	10—pig/boar
Xiaoxue (little snow)	22 November	
Daxue (heavy snow)	7 December	11—rat
Dongzhi (winter solstice)	22 December	
Xiaohan (little cold)	6 January	12—cow/ox
Dahan (severe cold)	20 January	

Chinese Calendar (continued)

CHINESE NEW YEAR	GREGORIAN DATE	ANIMAL	CHINESE NEW YEAR	GREGORIAN DATE	ANIMAL
4698	5 Feb 2000	dragon	4705	18 Feb 2007	pig/boar
4699	24 Jan 2001	snake	4706	7 Feb 2008	rat
4700	12 Feb 2002	horse	4707	26 Jan 2009	cow/ox
4701	1 Feb 2003	sheep/ram	4708	14 Feb 2010	tiger
4702	22 Jan 2004	monkey	4709	3 Feb 2011	rabbit/hare
4703	9 Feb 2005	chicken/rooster	4710	23 Jan 2012	dragon
4704	29 Jan 2006	dog	4711	10 Feb 2013	snake

Did you know? Popcorn king Orville Redenbacher developed a hybrid popcorn with his partner, Charles Bowman. The hybrid produced plumper and more tender kernels, but no company would buy the product because it was so expensive to produce. Redenbacher went into business for himself, promoting his "gourmet" popcorn as "The World's Most Expensive," a marketing ploy that made Redenbacher's product an enormous success starting in the 1970s.

Religious and Traditional Holidays

The word holiday comes from "holy day," and it was originally a day of dedication to religious observance; in modern times a holiday may be of either religious or secular commemoration. All dates in this article are Gregorian.

Jewish holidays—The major holidays are the Pilgrim Festivals: **Pesach** (Passover), **Shavuot** (Feast of Weeks, or Pentecost), and **Sukkot** (Tabernacles); and the High Holidays: **Rosh Hashana** (New Year) and **Yom Kippur** (Day of Atonement).

Pesach commemorates the Exodus from Egypt and the servitude that preceded it. As such, it is the most significant of the commemorative holidays, for it celebrates the very inception of the Jewish people–i.e., the event that provided the basis for the covenant between God and Israel. The term Pesach refers originally to the paschal (Passover) lamb sacrificed on the eve of the Exodus, the blood of which marked the Jewish homes to be spared from God's plague. Leaven (se'or) and foods containing leaven (hametz) are neither to be owned nor consumed during Pesach. Aside from meats, fresh fruits, and vegetables, it is customary to consume only those foods prepared under rabbinic supervision and labeled "kosher for Passover." The unleavened bread (matzo) consists entirely of flour and water. On the eve of Pesach families partake of the Seder, an elaborate festival meal. The table is bedecked with an assortment of foods symbolizing the passage from slavery (e.g., bitter herbs) into freedom (e.g., wine). Pesach will begin at sundown on 19 April and end on 27 April in 2008. (All Jewish holidays begin at sundown.)

A distinctive Rosh Hashana observance is the sounding of the ram's horn (shofar) at the synagogue service. Symbolic ceremonies, such as eating bread and apples dipped in honey, accompanied by prayers for a "sweet" and propitious year, are performed at the festive meals. In 2008 Rosh Hashana will begin at sundown on 29 September and will end on 1 October. Yom Kippur is a day when sins are confessed and expiated and man and God are reconciled. It is the holiest and most solemn day of the Jewish year. It is marked by fasting, penitence, and prayer. Working, eating, drinking, washing, anointing one's body, engaging in sexual intercourse, and don-

ning leather shoes are all forbidden. Yom Kippur begins at sundown on 8 October in 2008.

Though not as important theologically, the feast of **Hanukka** has become socially significant, especially in Western cultures. Hanukka commemorates the rededication (164 BCE) of the Second Temple of Jerusalem after its desecration three years earlier. Though modern Israel tends to emphasize the military victory of the general Judas Maccabeus, the distinctive rite of lighting the menorah also recalls the Talmud story of how the small supply of nondesecrated oil—enough for one day—miraculously burned in the Temple for eight full days until new oil could be obtained. During Hanukka, in addition to the lighting of the ceremonial candles, gifts are exchanged and children play holiday games. The festival occurs 4 through 12 Dec 2007, subsequently spanning 21 through 29 Dec 2008.

Christian holidays—The major holidays celebrated by nearly all Christians are **Easter** and **Christmas**.

Easter celebrates the Resurrection of Jesus on the third day after his Crucifixion. In the Christian liturgical year, Easter is preceded by the period of **Lent**, the 40 days (not counting Sundays) before Easter, which traditionally were observed as a period of penance and fasting. Lent begins on **Ash Wednesday**, a day devoted to penitence. Holy Week precedes **Easter Sunday** and includes **Maundy Thursday**, the commemoration of Jesus' last supper with his disciples; **Good Friday**, the day of his Crucifixion; and **Holy Saturday**, the transition between Crucifixion and Resurrection. Easter shares with Christmas the presence of numerous customs, some of which have little to do with the Christian celebration of the resurrection but clearly derive from folk customs. In 2008 the Western churches (nearly all Christian denominations) will observe Ash Wednesday on 6 February and Easter on 23 March. For Eastern Orthodox Christians, Lent begins on 10 March and Easter will be observed on 27 Apr 2008.

Christmas commemorates the birth of Jesus Christ. Since the early part of the 20th century, Christmas has also become a secular family holiday, observed by non-Christians, devoid of Christian elements, and marked by an increasingly elaborate exchange of gifts. In this secular Christmas celebration, a mythical figure named Santa Claus plays the pivotal role. Christmas is held on 25 December in most Christian cultures but occurs on the following 7 January in some Eastern Orthodox churches.

Islamic holidays—**Ramadan** is the holy month of fasting for Muslims. The Islamic ordinance prescribes abstention from evil thoughts and deeds as well as from food, drink, and sexual intercourse from dawn until dusk throughout the month. The beginning and end of Ramadan are announced when one trustworthy witness testifies before the authorities that the new moon has been sighted; a cloudy sky may therefore delay or prolong the fast. The end of the fast is celebrated as the feast of 'Id al-Fitr. Ramadan begins on 1 September in 2008 and 'Id al-Fitr falls on 1 October of that year (all Islamic holidays begin at sundown). The Muslim New Year, **Hijra**, is on 9 January in 2008.

After 'Id al-Fitr, the second major Islamic festival is **'Id al-Adha**. Throughout the Muslim world, all who are able sacrifice sheep, goats, camels, or cattle and then divide the flesh equally among themselves, the poor, and friends and neighbors to commemorate the ransom of Ishmael with a ram. This festival falls at the end of the hajj, the pilgrimage to the holy city of Mecca in Saudi Arabia, which every adult Muslim of either sex must make at least once in his or her lifetime. 'Id al-Adha will be observed on 7 December in 2008.

Ashura was originally designated in AD 622 by Muhammad as a day of fasting from sunset to sunset, probably patterned on the Jewish Day of Atonement, Yom Kippur. Among the Shi'ites, Ashura is a major festival that commemorates the death of Husayn (Hussein), son of Ali and grandson of Muhammad. It is a period of expressions of grief and of pilgrimage to Karbala (the site of Husayn's death, now in present-day Iraq). Ashura is on 18 January in 2008.

Buddhist holidays—Holidays practiced by a large number of Buddhists are *uposatha* days and days that commemorate events in the life of the Buddha.

The four monthly holy days of ancient Buddhism continue to be observed in the Theravada countries of Southeast Asia. These *uposatha* days—the new moon and full moon days of each lunar month and the eighth day following the new and full moons—have their origin, according to some scholars, in the fast days that preceded the Vedic soma sacrifices.

The three major events of the Buddha's life—his birth, Enlightenment, and entrance into final nirvana—are commemorated in all Buddhist countries but not everywhere on the same day. In the Theravada countries the three events are all observed together on **Vesak**, the full moon day of the sixth lunar month, which usually occurs in May. In Japan and other Mahayana countries, the three anniversaries of the Buddha are observed on separate days (in some countries the birth date is 8 April, the Enlightenment date is 8 December, and the death date is 15 February).

Chinese holidays—The **Chinese New Year** is celebrated with a big family meal, and presents of cash are given to children in red envelopes. In 2008 the Chinese New Year will be on 7 February.

During the **Chinese Moon Festival**, on the 15th day of the 8th month of the lunar calendar, people return to their homes to visit with their family. The traditional food is moon cakes, round pastries stuffed with food such as red bean paste. The Moon Festival will occur on 14 September in 2008.

Japanese holidays—The Japanese celebrate **3-5-7 day** (Shichigosan no hi), in which parents bring children of those ages to the Shinto shrine to pray for their continued health. This day is held on 15 November.

In mid-July (or mid-August, in some areas) the Japanese celebrate **Obon** (also known as Bon Matsuri, or Urabon). The festival honors the spirits of deceased householders and of the dead generally. Memorial stones are cleaned, community dances are performed, and paper lanterns and fires are lit to welcome the dead and to bid them farewell at the end of their visit. The Shinto New Year, **Gantan-sai**, is celebrated on 1–3 January.

Hindu holidays—**Dussehra** celebrates the victory of Rama over Ravana, the symbol of evil on earth. In 2008 Dussehra falls on 9 October. **Diwali** is a festival of lights devoted to Laksmi, the goddess of wealth. During the festival, small earthenware lamps filled with oil are lighted and placed in rows along the parapets of temples and houses and set adrift on rivers and streams. Diwali is on 28 October in 2008. **Sivaratri**, the most important sectarian festival of the year for devotees of the Hindu god Shiva, occurs on 6 March in 2008. **Holi** is a spring festival, probably of ancient origin. Participants throw colored waters and powders on one another, and, on this day, the usual restrictions of caste, sex, status, and age are disregarded. It will be on 22 March in 2008.

Sikh holidays—Sikhs observe all festivals celebrated by the Hindus of northern India. In addition, they celebrate the birthdays of the first and the last Gurus and the martyrdom of the fifth (Arjun) and the ninth (Tegh Bahadur). In 2008 **Guru Nanak Dev Sahib's birthday** is celebrated on 13 November, and that of **Guru Gobind Singh Sahib** is celebrated on 5 January. On 16 June **Arjun's martyrdom** is observed. *Kachi lassi* (sweetened milk) is offered to passersby to commemorate his death. On 24 November the **martyrdom of Tegh Bahadur** is observed.

Baha'i holidays—The Baha'i New Year (**Naw Ruz**) in 2008 will fall on 20 March (all Baha'i holidays begin at sundown). Other important observances include the **declaration of the Bab** on 22 May, the **Baha 'Ullah's birth** (11 November), and **Ascension** (28 May).

Zoroastrian holidays—**Noruz** (New Day) is on 21 March for 2008, and the 26th of that month is **Khordad Sal**, the birth of the prophet Zarathustra.

The **African American holiday** of **Kwanzaa** (Swahili for "First Fruits") is celebrated each year from 26 December to 1 January and is patterned after various African harvest festivals. Maulana Karenga, a blackstudies professor, created Kwanzaa in 1966 as a nonreligious celebration of family and social values. Each day of Kwanzaa is dedicated to one of seven principles: unity (*umoja*), self-determination (*kujichagulia*), collective responsibility (*ujima*), cooperative economics (*ujamaa*), purpose (*nia*), creativity (*kuumba*), and faith (*imani*).

Perpetual Calendar

The perpetual calendar is a type of dating system that makes it possible to find the correct day of the week for any date over a wide range of years. Aspects of the perpetual calendar can be found in the Jewish religious and the Julian calendars, and some form of it has appeared in many proposed calendar reforms.

To find the day of the week for any Gregorian or Julian date in the perpetual calendar provided in this table, first find the proper dominical letter (one of the letters A through G) for the year in the upper table. Leap years have two dominical letters, the first applicable to dates in January and February, the second to dates in the remaining months. Then find the same dominical letter in the lower table, in whichever column it appears opposite the month in question. The days then fall as given in the lowest section of the column.

YEAR				JULIAN CALENDAR							CENTURY 1500**	GREGORIAN CALENDAR			
				0 / 700 / 1400	100 / 800 / 1500*	200 / 900	300 / 1000	400 / 1100	500 / 1200	600 / 1300	1500**	1600 / 2000	1700 / 2100	1800 / 2200	1900 / 2300
0				DC	ED	FE	GF	AG	BA	CB	...	BA	C	E	G
1	29	57	85	B	C	D	E	F	G	A	F	G	B	D	F
2	30	58	86	A	B	C	D	E	F	G	E	F	A	C	E
3	31	59	87	G	A	B	C	D	E	F	D	E	G	B	D
4	32	60	88	FE	GF	AG	BA	CB	DC	ED	CB	DC	FE	AG	CB
5	33	61	89	D	E	F	G	A	B	C	A	B	D	F	A
6	34	62	90	C	D	E	F	G	A	B	G	A	C	E	G
7	35	63	91	B	C	D	E	F	G	A	F	G	B	D	F
8	36	64	92	AG	BA	CB	DC	ED	FE	GF	ED	FE	AG	CB	ED
9	37	65	93	F	G	A	B	C	D	E	C	D	F	A	C
10	38	66	94	E	F	G	A	B	C	D	B	C	E	G	B
11	39	67	95	D	E	F	G	A	B	C	A	B	D	F	A
12	40	68	96	CB	DC	ED	FE	GF	AG	BA	GF	AG	CB	ED	GF
13	41	69	97	A	B	C	D	E	F	G	E	F	A	C	E
14	42	70	98	G	A	B	C	D	E	F	D	E	G	B	D
15	43	71	99	F	G	A	B	C	D	E	C	D	F	A	C
16	44	72		ED	FE	GF	AG	BA	CB	DC	...	CB	ED	GF	BA
17	45	73		C	D	E	F	G	A	B	...	A	C	E	G
18	46	74		B	C	D	E	F	G	A	...	G	B	D	F
19	47	75		A	B	C	D	E	F	G	...	F	A	C	E
20	48	76		GF	AG	BA	CB	DC	ED	FE	...	ED	GF	BA	DC
21	49	77		E	F	G	A	B	C	D	...	C	E	G	B
22	50	78		D	E	F	G	A	B	C	...	B	D	F	A
23	51	79		C	D	E	F	G	A	B	...	A	C	E	G
24	52	80		BA	CB	DC	ED	FE	GF	AG	...	GF	BA	DC	FE
25	53	81		G	A	B	C	D	E	F	...	E	G	B	D
26	54	82		F	G	A	B	C	D	E	C	D	F	A	C
27	55	83		E	F	G	A	B	C	D	B	C	E	G	B
28	56	84		DC	ED	FE	GF	AG	BA	CB	AG	BA	DC	FE	AG

MONTH	DOMINICAL LETTER						
January, October	A	B	C	D	E	F	G
February, March, November	D	E	F	G	A	B	C
April, July	G	A	B	C	D	E	F
May	B	C	D	E	F	G	A
June	E	F	G	A	B	C	D
August	C	D	E	F	G	A	B
September, December	F	G	A	B	C	D	E
1 8 15 22 29	Sunday	Saturday	Friday	Thursday	Wednesday	Tuesday	Monday
2 9 16 23 30	Monday	Sunday	Saturday	Friday	Thursday	Wednesday	Tuesday
3 10 17 24 31	Tuesday	Monday	Sunday	Saturday	Friday	Thursday	Wednesday
4 11 18 25	Wednesday	Tuesday	Monday	Sunday	Saturday	Friday	Thursday
5 12 19 26	Thursday	Wednesday	Tuesday	Monday	Sunday	Saturday	Friday
6 13 20 27	Friday	Thursday	Wednesday	Tuesday	Monday	Sunday	Saturday
7 14 21 28	Saturday	Friday	Thursday	Wednesday	Tuesday	Monday	Sunday

*On and before 1582, 4 October only.   **On and after 1582, 15 October only.
Source: Smithsonian Physical Tables, 9th edition, rev. 1956.

Civil Holidays

DAY	EVENT
1 January	New Year's Day, the first day of the modern calendar (various countries)
20 January	Inauguration Day, for quadrennial inauguration of US president
26 January	Australia Day, commemorates the establishment of the first British settlement in Australia
3rd Monday in January	Martin Luther King Day, for birth of US civil rights leader
2nd new moon after winter solstice (at the earliest 21 January and at the latest 19 February)	New Year, for Chinese lunar year, inaugurating a 15-day celebration
6 February	Waitangi Day, for Treaty of Waitangi, granting British sovereignty (New Zealand)
11 February	National Foundation Day, for founding by first emperor (Japan)
14 February	St. Valentine's Day, celebrating the exchange of love messages and named for either of two 3rd-century Christian martyrs (various)
3rd Monday in February	Presidents' Day, Washington-Lincoln Day, or Washington's Birthday, for birthdays of US Presidents George Washington and Abraham Lincoln
8 March	International Women's Day, celebration of the women's liberation movement
17 March	St. Patrick's Day, for patron saint of Ireland (Ireland and various)
21 or 22 March	Vernal Equinox Day, for beginning of spring (Japan)
25 March	Independence Day, for proclamation of independence from the Ottoman Empire (Greece)
4th Sunday in Lent	Mothering Day (UK)
1 April	April Fools' Day, or All Fools' Day, day for playing jokes, falling one week after the old New Year's Day of 25 March (various)
5 April	Qingming, for sweeping tombs and honoring the dead (China)
7 April	World Health Day, for founding of World Health Organization
22 April	Earth Day, for conservation and reclaiming of the natural environment (various)
25 April	ANZAC Day, for landing at Gallipoli (Australia/New Zealand/Samoa/Tonga)
29 April	Green Day, national holiday for environment and nature (Japan)
30 April	Queen's Birthday, for Queen Beatrix's investiture and former queen Juliana's birthday (The Netherlands)
1 May	May Day, celebrated as labor day or as festival of flowers (various)
3 May	Constitution Memorial Day, for establishment of democratic government (Japan)
5 May	Children's Day, honoring children (Japan/South Korea)
5 May	Cinco de Mayo, anniversary of Mexico's victory over France in the Battle of Puebla (Mexico)
8/9 May	V-E Day, or Liberation Day, for end of World War II in Europe (various)
2nd Sunday in May	Mother's Day, honoring mothers (US)
Monday on or preceding 25 May	Victoria Day, for Queen Victoria's birthday (Canada)
30 or last Monday in May	Memorial Day, or Decoration Day, in honor of the deceased, especially the war dead (US)
2 June	Anniversary of the Republic, for referendum establishing republic (Italy)
5 June	Constitution Day (Denmark)
6 June	National Day, for Gustav I Vasa's ascension to the throne and adoption of Constitution (Sweden)
10 June	Portugal's Day, or Camões Memorial Day, anniversary of Luis de Camões's death
14 June	Flag Day, honoring flag (US)
3rd Saturday in June	Queen's Official Birthday, for Queen Elizabeth II (UK/New Zealand)
3rd Sunday in June	Father's Day, honoring fathers (US)
23 June	National Day, for Grand Duke Jean's official birthday (Luxembourg)
23–24 June	Midsummer Eve and Midsummer Day, celebrating the return of summer (various European)
last Sunday in June	Gay and Lesbian Pride Day, final day of weeklong advocacy of rights of gay men and lesbians (international)
1 July	Canada Day (formerly Dominion Day), for establishment of dominion
4 July	Independence Day, for Declaration of Independence from Britain (US)
12 July	Orangemen's Day, or Orange Day, anniversary of the Battle of the Boyne (Northern Ireland)
14 July	Bastille Day, for fall of the Bastille and onset of French Revolution (France)
21 July	National Day, for separation from The Netherlands (Belgium)
1 August	National Day, anniversary of the founding of the Swiss Confederation (Switzerland)
6 August	Hiroshima Day, for dropping of atomic bomb (Japan)
full-moon day of 8th lunar month	Chusok, harvest festival (Korea)
1st Monday in September	Labor Day, tribute to workers (US/Canada)
15 September	Respect-for-the-Aged Day, for the elderly (Japan)
16 September	Independence Day, for independence from Spain (Mexico)
23 or 24 September	Autumnal Equinox Day, for beginning of autumn; in honor of ancestors (Japan)

Civil Holidays (continued)

DAY	EVENT
two weeks ending on 1st Sunday in October	Oktoberfest, festival of food and drink, formerly commemorating marriage of King Louis (Ludwig) I (Germany)
3 October	Day of German Unity, for reunification of Germany
5 October	Republic Day, for founding of the republic (Portugal)
12 or 2nd Monday in October	Hispanic Day, Columbus Day, Discovery Day, or Day of the Race, for Christopher Columbus's discovery of the New World on behalf of Spain (Spain and various)
2nd Monday in October	Thanksgiving Day, harvest festival (Canada)
24 October	United Nations Day, for effective date of UN Charter (international)
26 October	National Day, for end of postwar occupation and return of sovereignty (Austria)
31 October	Halloween, or All Hallows' Eve, festive celebration of ghosts and spirits, on eve of All Saints' Day (various)
5 November	Guy Fawkes Day, anniversary of the Gunpowder Plot to blow up the king and Parliament (UK)
11 November	Armistice Day, Remembrance Day, or Veterans Day, honoring participants in past wars and recalling the Armistice of World War I (various)
23 November	Labor Thanksgiving Day, honoring workers (Japan)
4th Thursday in November	Thanksgiving Day, harvest festival (US)
16 December	Day of Reconciliation, for promoting national unity (South Africa)
23 December	Emperor's Birthday, for birthday of Emperor Akihito (Japan)
26 December	Boxing Day, second day of Christmas, for giving presents to service people (various)
31 December	New Year's Eve, celebration ushering out the old year and in the new year (various)

The Universe

Cosmogony (Theories of the Origin of the Universe)

Three great ages of scientific thinking about the universe can be distinguished. The first began in Greece in the 6th century BC when the **Pythagoreans** introduced the concept of a **spherical Earth** and postulated a universe in which the motions of heavenly bodies were governed by natural laws. The **infinite atomist universe** of Leucippus and Democritus followed, wherein countless worlds, teeming with life, were the result of chance aggregations of atoms. The **geocentric Aristotelian universe** arose in the 4th century BC. It consisted of a central Earth surrounded by revolving, translucent spheres to which were attached the Sun and the planets; the outermost sphere supported the fixed stars.

The **Copernican revolution** ushered in the second great age. In the 16th century, Nicolaus Copernicus revived ancient ideas and proposed a heliocentric universe, which during the following century was transformed into the mechanistic, infinite **Newtonian universe** that flourished until the early 1900s. In the mid-18th century, Thomas Wright proposed the influential notion of a universe composed of numerous **galaxies**, and William Herschel, followed by many other astronomers, made rapid strides in the study of stars and of the Milky Way Galaxy, of which the Earth is a component.

The third great age began in the early years of the 20th century, with the discovery of **special relativity** and its development into **general relativity** by **Albert Einstein**. These years also saw momentous developments in astronomy: extragalactic redshifts were detected by Vesto Slipher; extragalactic nebulae were shown to be galaxies comparable with the Milky Way; and **Edwin Hubble** began to estimate the distances of these galactic systems. Such discoveries and the application of general relativity to cosmology eventually gave rise to the view that the **universe is expanding**. The basic premise of modern thinking on the universe is the principle that asserts that the universe is

homogeneous in space (on the average all places are alike at any time) and that the laws of physics are everywhere the same.

Two theories of the origin of the universe have been the most influential during the last century—the steady state theory and the big bang theory. The **steady state theory** posits that the universe is always expanding but maintains a constant average density, matter being continuously created to form new stars and galaxies at the same rate that old ones become unobservable as a consequence of their increasing distance and velocity of recession. A steady-state universe has no beginning or end in time; and from any point within it the view on the grand scale—i.e., the average density and arrangement of galaxies—is the same. Galaxies of all possible ages are intermingled. Observations since the 1950s have produced much evidence contradictory to the steady-state picture and supportive of the big-bang model.

The essential feature of the widely-held **big bang theory** is the emergence of the universe from a state of extremely high temperature and density—the so-called big bang that occurred at least 10,000,000,000 years ago. Although this type of universe was proposed by Alexander Friedmann and Abbé Georges Lemaître in the 1920s, the modern version was developed by George Gamow and colleagues in the 1940s.

One current problem that scientists are studying is the **amount of matter in the universe**. Based upon such things as the rate of the motion of galaxies, scientists realized that there is some 90% more matter in the universe than can be seen. Scientists refer to the matter that can be observed as **"bright matter"** and this other 90% is called **"dark matter."** Whether dark matter is of a different and exotic nature from the matter with which we are familiar, or whether dark matter is just like luminous matter (and for some reason we cannot detect it), is something a large number of scientists are studying.

Astronomical Constants

QUANTITY	SYMBOL	VALUE
astronomical unit	AU	length of the semimajor axis of the Earth's orbit around the Sun—149,597,870 km (92,955,808 mi)

measures large distances in space; equals the average distance from the Earth to the Sun

| parsec | pc | one parsec equals 3.26 light-years |

measures the distance at which the radius of the Earth's orbit subtends an angle of one second of arc

| light-year | ly | 9.46089×10^{12} km (5.8787×10^{12} mi) |

measures the distance traveled by light moving in a vacuum in the course of one year

| solar parallax | | 8.79414 seconds of arc |

quantifies the angular difference in direction of the Sun as seen from the Earth's center and a point one Earth radius away

| lunar parallax | | 57 minutes 02.608 seconds of arc |

quantifies the angular difference in direction of the Moon as seen from the Earth's center and a point one Earth radius away

| general precession | | 50.29 seconds of arc per year |

measures the cyclic wobbling in the orientation of the Earth's axis of rotation with a period of almost 26,000 years

| constant of aberration | | about 20.49 seconds of arc |

the maximum amount of the apparent yearly aberrational displacement of a star or other celestial body, resulting from the Earth's orbital motion around the Sun

| constant of nutation | | 9.202 seconds of arc |

a small irregularity in the Earth's axial precession of that occurs over a period of 18.6 years

| speed of light (in a vacuum) | c | $2.99792458 \times 10^{10}$ cm per sec (186,282 mi per sec) |

| radius of the Sun | Sun $R_\odot$ | 6.96×10^{8} m (109 times the radius of Earth) |

| mass of the Sun | Sun $M_\odot$ | 1.989×10^{30} kg (330,000 times the mass of the Earth) |

| Earth's mean radius | | 6,378 km (3,963 mi) |

| sidereal day (on Earth) | | 23 h 56 min 4.10 sec of mean solar time |

defined by the period between two successive passages of a star across the same meridian; it is the time required for the Earth to rotate once relative to the distant stars

| mean solar day (on Earth) | | 24 h 3 min 56.55 sec of mean sideral time |

the interval between two successive passages of the Sun across the same meridian is a solar day; in practice, since the rate of the Sun's motion varies with the seasons, use is made of a fictitious Sun that always moves across the sky at an even rate

| tropical (or solar) year (on Earth) | | 365.242 days |

the time required for the Earth's orbital motion to return the Sun's position to the spring equinoctial point

| sidereal year (on Earth) | | 365.256 days |

the time required for the Earth in its orbit to return to the longitude of a distant star

| synodic month (on Earth) | | 29.53 days |

the time required for the Moon to pass through one complete cycle of phases

| sidereal month (on Earth) | | 27.32 days |

the time required for the Moon to return to the same place in relation to distant stars

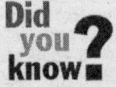

Did you know?

The speed of steamboats increased dramatically over the years; the run from New Orleans to Louisville KY, which took 25 days in 1816, required only 4 days by 1853. The average life span of a steamboat was only four to five years because of poor construction and maintenance, exploding boilers, and sinkings due to river construction. Spontaneous races were common and contributed greatly to the approximately 4,000 deaths in steamboat disasters between 1810 and 1850.

Definitions of Astronomical Positions

A conjunction is an apparent meeting or passing of two or more celestial bodies. For example, the Moon is in conjunction with the Sun at the phase of new Moon, when it moves between the Earth and Sun and the side turned toward the Earth is dark. Inferior planets—those with orbits smaller than the Earth's (namely, Venus and Mercury)—have two kinds of conjunctions with the Sun. An **inferior conjunction** occurs when the planet passes approximately between Earth and Sun; if it passes exactly between them, moving across the Sun's face as seen from Earth, it is said to be in transit (*see below*). A **superior conjunction** occurs when Earth and the other planet are on opposite sides of the Sun, but all three bodies are again nearly in a straight line. Superior planets, those having orbits larger than the Earth's can have only superior conjunctions with the Sun.

When celestial bodies appear in opposite directions in the sky they are said to be in **opposition**. The Moon, when full, is said to be in opposition to the Sun (the Earth is then approximately between them). A superior planet (one with an orbit farther from the Sun than Earth's) is in opposition when Earth passes between it and the Sun. The opposition of a planet is a good time to observe it, because the planet is then at its nearest point to the Earth and in its full phase. The inferior planets, Venus and Mercury, can never be in opposition to the Sun.

When a celestial body as seen from the Earth makes a right angle with the direction of the Sun it is said to be in **quadrature**. The Moon at first or last quarter is said to be at east or west quadrature, respectively. A superior planet is at west quadrature when its position is 90° west of the Sun.

The east–west coordinate by which the position of a celestial body is ordinarily measured is known as the **right ascension**. Right ascension in combination with **declination** defines the position of a celestial object. Declination is the angular distance of a body north or south of the celestial equator. North declination is considered positive and south, negative. Thus, +90° declination marks the north celestial pole, 0° the celestial equator, and −90° the south celestial pole. The symbol for right ascension is the Greek letter α (alpha) and for declination the lowercase Greek letter Δ (delta).

The angular distance in celestial longitude separating the Moon or a planet from the Sun is known as **elongation**. The greatest elongation possible for the two inferior planets is about 48° in the case of Venus and about 28° in that of Mercury. Elongation may also refer to the angular distance of any celestial body from another around which it revolves or from a particular point in the sky; e.g., the extreme east or west position of a star with reference to the north celestial pole.

The point at which a planet is closest to the Sun is called the **perihelion**, and the most distant point in that planet's orbit is the **aphelion**. The term helion refers specifically to the Sun as the primary body about which the planet is orbiting.

Occultation refers to the obscuring of the light of an astronomical body, most commonly a star, by another astronomical body, such as a planet or a satellite. Hence, a solar eclipse is the occultation of the Sun by the Moon. From occultations of stars by planets, asteroids, and satellites, astronomers are able to determine the precise sizes and shapes of the latter bodies in addition to the temperatures of planetary atmospheres. For example, astronomers unexpectedly discovered the rings of Uranus during a stellar occultation on 10 Mar 1977.

A complete or partial obscuring of a celestial body by another is an **eclipse**; these occur when three celestial objects become aligned. The Sun is eclipsed when the Moon comes between it and the Earth; the Moon is eclipsed when it moves into the shadow of the Earth cast by the Sun. Eclipses of natural or artificial satellites of a planet occur as the satellites move into the planet's shadow. When the apparent size of the eclipsed body is much smaller than that of the eclipsing body, the phenomenon is known as an **occultation** (*see above*). Examples are the disappearance of a star, nebula, or planet behind the Moon, or the vanishing of a natural satellite or space probe behind some body of the solar system. A **transit** (*see above*) occurs when, as viewed from the Earth, a relatively small body passes across the disk of a larger body, usually the Sun or a planet, eclipsing only a very small area: Mercury and Venus periodically transit the Sun, and a satellite may transit its planet.

When an object orbiting the Earth is at the point in its orbit that is the greatest distance from the center of the Earth, this point is known as **apogee**; the term is also used to describe the point farthest from a planet or a satellite (as the Moon) reached by an object orbiting it. **Perigee** is the opposite of apogee.

The difference in direction of a celestial object as seen by an observer from two widely separated points is termed **parallax**. The measurement of parallax is used directly to find the distance of the body from the Earth (geocentric parallax) and from the Sun (heliocentric parallax). The two positions of the observer and the position of the object form a triangle; if the base line between the two observing points is known and the direction of the object as seen from each has been measured, the apex angle (the parallax) and the distance of the object from the observer can be determined.

An **hour angle** is the angle between an observer's meridian (a great circle passing over his head and through the celestial poles) and the hour circle (any other great circle passing through the poles) on which some celestial body lies. This angle, when expressed in hours and minutes, is the time elapsed since the celestial body's last transit of the observer's meridian. The hour angle can also be expressed in degrees, 15° of arc being equal to one hour.

Constellations

C onstellations are certain groupings of stars that were imagined—at least by those who named them—to form conspicuous configurations of objects or creatures in the sky. Constellations are useful in tracking artificial satellites and in assisting astronomers and navigators to locate certain stars.

From the earliest times the star groups known as constellations, the smaller groups (parts of constellations) known as **asterisms**, and, also, **individual stars** have received names connoting some meteorological phenomena or symbolizing religious or mythological beliefs. At one time it was held that the constellation

Constellations (continued)

names and myths were of Greek origin; this view has now been disproved. It is now thought that the Greek constellation system and the cognate legends are primarily of Semitic or even pre-Semitic origin and that they came to the Greeks through the Phoenicians.

The Alexandrian astronomer **Ptolemy** lists the names and orientation of the 48 constellations in his *Almagest*, and, with but few exceptions, they are iden-

tical with those used at the present time. The majority of the remaining 40 constellations that are now accepted were added by European astronomers in the 17th and 18th centuries. In the 20th century the delineation of precise boundaries for all the 88 constellations was undertaken by a committee of the International Astronomical Union. By 1930 it was possible to assign any star to a constellation.

NAME	GENITIVE	MEANING	NOTES
Constellations described by Ptolemy: the zodiac			(First-magnitude stars are given in italics in this column)
Aries	Arietis	Ram	
Taurus	Tauri	Bull	*Aldebaran* is the constellation's brightest star. Taurus also contains the Pleiades star cluster and the Crab Nebula.
Gemini	Geminorum	Twins	The brightest stars in Gemini are Castor and *Pollux.*
Cancer	Cancri	Crab	Cancer contains the well-known star cluster Praesepe.
Leo	Leonis	Lion	*Regulus* is the brightest star in Leo.
Virgo	Virginis	Virgin	*Spica* is the brightest star in Virgo.
Libra	Librae	Balance	
Scorpius	Scorpii	Scorpion	*Antares* is the brightest star of Scorpius, which also contains many star clusters.
Sagittarius	Sagittarii	Archer	The center of the Milky Way Galaxy lies in Sagittarius, with the densest star clouds of the galaxy.
Capricornus	Capricorni	Sea-goat	
Aquarius	Aquarii	Water-bearer	
Pisces	Piscium	Fishes	
Other Ptolemaic constellations			
Andromeda	Andromedae	Andromeda (an Ethiopian princess of Greek legend, daughter of Cepheus and Cassiopeia)	The constellation's most notable feature is the great spiral galaxy Andromeda (also called M31).
Aquila	Aquilae	Eagle	The brightest star in Aquila is *Altair.*
Ara	Arae	Altar	
Argo Navis	Argus Navis	the ship *Argo*	Argo Navis is now divided into smaller constellations that include Carina, Puppis, Pyxis, and Vela.
Auriga	Aurigae	Charioteer	The brightest star in Auriga is *Capella.* The constellation also contains open star clusters M36, M37, and M38.
Boötes	Boötis	Herdsman	*Arcturus* is the brightest star in Boötes.
Canis Major	Canis Majoris	Greater Dog	*Sirius* is the brightest star in Canis Major.
Canis Minor	Canis Minoris	Smaller Dog	*Procyon* is the brightest star in Canis Minor.
Cassiopeia	Cassiopeiae	Cassiopeia was a legendary queen of Ethiopia	Tycho's nova, one of the few recorded supernovae in the Galaxy, appeared in Cassiopeia in 1572.
Centaurus	Centauri	Centaur (possibly represents Chiron)	*Alpha Centauri* in Centaurus contains Proxima, the nearest star to the Sun.
Cepheus	Cephei	Cepheus (legendary king of Ethiopia)	Delta Cephei was the prototype for cepheid variables (a class of variable stars).
Cetus	Ceti	Whale	Mira Ceti was the first recognized variable star.
Corona Austrina	Coronae Austrinae	Southern Crown	
Corona Borealis	Coronae Borealis	Northern Crown	
Corvus	Corvi	Raven	
Crater	Crateris	Cup	
Cygnus	Cygni	Swan	Cygnus contains the asterism (grouping of stars) known as the Northern Cross; the constellation's brightest star is *Deneb.*
Delphinus	Delphini	Dolphin	Delphinus contains the asterism known as Job's Coffin.
Draco	Draconis	Dragon	Draco contains the star Thuban, which was the polestar in 3000 BC.

Constellations (continued)

NAME	GENITIVE	MEANING	NOTES
Other Ptolemaic constellations (continued)			
Equuleus	Equulei	Little Horse	
Eridanus	Eridani	River Eridanus or river god	*Achernar* is the brightest star in Eridanus.
Hercules	Herculis	Hercules (Greek hero)	Hercules contains the great globular star cluster M13.
Hydra	Hydrae	Water Snake	
Lepus	Leporis	Hare	
Lupus	Lupi	Wolf	
Lyra	Lyrae	Lyre	The brightest star in Lyra is *Vega*. In some 10,000 years, *Vega* will become the polestar. Lyra also contains the Ring Nebula (M57).
Ophiuchus	Ophiuchi	Serpent-bearer	When the Zodiac was conceived of, Ophiuchus was not in the Sun's path, but the Sun does now pass through Ophiuchus each December.
Orion	Orionis	Hunter	*Rigel* is the brightest star in Orion, followed closely by *Betelgeuse;* M42 (the Great Nebula) resides in Orion.
Pegasus	Pegasi	Pegasus (winged horse)	The constellation contains stars of the Great Square of Pegasus.
Perseus	Persei	Perseus (legendary Greek hero)	
Piscis Austrinus	Piscis Austrini	Southern Fish	The brightest star in Piscis Austrinus is *Fomalhaut*.
Sagitta	Sagittae	Arrow	
Serpens	Serpentis	Serpent	
Triangulum	Trianguli	Triangle	The constellation contains M33, a nearby spiral galaxy.
Ursa Major	Ursae Majoris	Great Bear	The seven brightest stars of this constellation are the Big Dipper (also called the Plough).
Ursa Minor	Ursae Minoris	Lesser Bear	Ursa Minor contains Polaris (the north polestar).
Southern constellations, added c. 1600			
Apus	Apodis	Bird of Paradise	
Chamaeleon	Chamaeleontis	Chameleon	
Dorado	Doradus	Swordfish	The most notable object in Dorado is the Large Magellanic Cloud.
Grus	Gruis	Crane	
Hydrus	Hydri	Water Snake	
Indus	Indi	Indian	
Musca	Muscae	Fly	
Pavo	Pavonis	Peacock	
Phoenix	Phoenicis	Phoenix (mythical bird)	
Triangulum Australe	Trianguli Australis	Southern Triangle	
Tucana	Tucanae	Toucan	The most notable object in Tucana is the Small Magellanic Cloud.
Volans	Volantis	Flying Fish	
Constellations of Bartsch, 1624			
Camelopardalis	Camelopardalis	Giraffe	
Columba	Columbae	Dove	The constellation was formed by Petrus Plancius in the early 1600s.
Monoceros	Monocerotis	Unicorn	
Constellations of Hevelius, 1687			
Canes Venatici	Canum Venaticorum	Hunting Dogs	The constellation contains M51 (the Whirlpool Galaxy).
Lacerta	Lacertae	Lizard	
Leo Minor	Leonis Minoris	Lesser Lion	
Lynx	Lyncis	Lynx	
Scutum	Scuti	Shield	Scutum contains the Scutim star cloud in the Milky Way.
Sextans	Sextantis	Sextant	
Vulpecula	Vulpeculae	Fox	Vulpecula contains M27 (the Dumbbell Nebula).

Constellations (continued)

NAME	GENITIVE	MEANING	NOTES
Ancient asterisms that are now separate constellations			
Carina	Carinae	Keel [of the leg-endary ship the *Argo*]	The brightest star in Carina is *Canopus*.
Coma Berenices	Comae Berenices	Berenice's Hair	The constellation contains both a coma (star cluster) and the north galactic pole (a point that lies perpendicular to the Milky Way).
Crux	Crucis	[Southern] Cross	
Puppis	Puppis	Stern [of the *Argo*]	
Pyxis	Pyxidis	Compass [of the *Argo*]	
Vela	Velorum	Sails [of the *Argo*]	
Southern constellations of Lacaille, c. 1750			
Antlia	Antliae	Pump	
Caelum	Caeli	[Sculptor's] Chisel	
Circinus	Circini	Drawing Compasses	
Fornax	Fornacis	[Chemical] Furnace	
Horologium	Horologii	Clock	
Mensa	Mensae	Table [Mountain]	
Microscopium	Microscopii	Microscope	
Norma	Normae	Square	
Octans	Octantis	Octant	Octans contains the south celestial pole.
Pictor	Pictoris	Painter's [Easel]	
Reticulum	Reticuli	Reticle	
Sculptor	Sculptoris	Sculptor's [Work-shop]	Sculptor contains the south galactic pole.
Telescopium	Telescopii	Telescope	

Astrology: The Zodiac

Signs of the zodiac are popularly used for divination as well as for designation of constellations.

NAME	SYMBOL	DATES	SEX/NATURE	TRIPLICITY	HOUSE	EXALTATION
Aries the Ram	♈	21 Mar–19 Apr	masculine/moving	fire	Mars	Sun (19°)
Taurus the Bull	♉	20 Apr–20 May	feminine/fixed	earth	Venus	Moon (3°)
Gemini the Twins	♊	21 May–21 Jun	masculine/common	air	Mercury	
Cancer the Crab	♋	22 Jun–22 Jul	feminine/moving	water	Moon	Jupiter (15°)
Leo the Lion	♌	23 Jul–22 Aug	masculine/fixed	fire	Sun	
Virgo the Virgin	♍	23 Aug–22 Sep	feminine/common	earth	Mercury	Mercury (15°)
Libra the Balance	♎	23 Sep–23 Oct	masculine/moving	air	Venus	Saturn (21°)
Scorpius the Scorpion	♏	24 Oct–21 Nov	feminine/fixed	water	Mars	
Sagittarius the Archer	♐	22 Nov–21 Dec	masculine/common	fire	Jupiter	
Capricorn the Goat	♑	22 Dec–19 Jan	feminine/moving	earth	Saturn	Mars (28°)
Aquarius the Water Bearer	♒	20 Jan–18 Feb	masculine/fixed	air	Saturn	
Pisces the Fish	♓	19 Feb–20 Mar	feminine/common	water	Jupiter	Venus (27°)

Classification of Stars

The spectral sequence O–M represents stars of essentially the same chemical composition but of different temperatures and atmospheric pressures. Stars belonging to other, more rare types of spectral classifications differ in chemical composition from O–M stars.

Each spectral class is additionally subdivided into 10 spectral types. For example, spectral class A is subdivided into spectral types A0–A9 with 0 being the hottest and 9 the coolest. (Spectral class O is unusual in that it is subdivided into O4–O9.) Between two stars of the same spectral type, the more luminous star will also be larger in diameter. Thus the Yerkes system of luminosity also tells something of a star's radius, with Ia being the largest and V the smallest. Approximately 90% of all stars are main sequence, or type V, stars.

Based upon these systems, the Sun would be a G2 V star (a yellow, relatively hot dwarf star).

SPECTRAL CLASS	COLOR	APPROXIMATE SURFACE TEMP (°C)	EXAMPLES
O	blue	30,000 or greater	These stars are relatively rare
B	blue-white	20,000 to 30,000	Rigel, Alpha Crucis, Beta Crucis
A	white	10,000 to 20,000	Sirius, Vega, Fomalhaut
F	yellow-white	7,000 to 10,000	Canopus, Procyon

Classification of Stars (continued)

SPECTRAL CLASS	COLOR	APPROXIMATE SURFACE TEMP (°C)	EXAMPLES
G	yellow	6,000 to 7,000	Sun
K	orange	4,500 to 6,000	Arcturus, Aldebaran
M	red	3,000 to 4,500	Betelgeuse, Antares

LUMINOSITY CLASSES (BASED UPON THE YERKES SYSTEM)

Ia	most luminous supergiants
Ib	luminous supergiants
II	bright giants
III	normal giants
IV	subgiants
V	main sequence stars (dwarfs)

The 20 Brightest Stars in the Night Sky

This table lists the stars in descending order from brightest to least bright, based on apparent visual magnitude. Formal names of stars, such as Alpha Carinae, refer to the constellation in which the star appears (Carina) and to which star appears the brightest in that constellation; the second highest would be designated Beta, etc. Some anomalies exist within the naming convention: Betelgeuse, for example, is the Alpha star of Orion, though Rigel appears brighter.

On the scale of brightness, negative magnitudes are brightest, and one magnitude difference corresponds to a difference in brightness of 2.5 times; e.g., a star of magnitude −1 is 10 times brighter than one of magnitude +1.5.

Apparent magnitude is a measure of how bright a star appears to a viewer on Earth. Absolute magnitude, another designation used by astronomers, represents the brightness one would perceive if all stars were located 10 parsecs (about 32.6 light-years; one light-year equals about 9.46×10^{12} km) from Earth. The Sun, for purposes of comparison with the stars in the table, has an apparent magnitude of −26.8; it is a yellow dwarf star that is 8.3 light-minutes (one light-minute equals about 18 million km) from Earth.

STAR	APPARENT VISUAL MAGNITUDE	DISTANCE FROM THE SOLAR SYSTEM (LIGHT-YEARS)	CONSTELLATION
Sirius (Alpha Canis Majoris, or Dog Star)	−1.44	8.6	Canis Major

Sirius is a blue-white dwarf with a white-dwarf companion; among the ancient Romans, the hottest part of the year was associated with the time in which the Dog Star rose just before dawn; this connection survives in the expression "dog days."

| Canopus (Alpha Carinae) | −0.73 (reported values vary) | 312.0 (reported values vary) | Carina |

A yellow-white supergiant, Canopus is sometimes used as a guide in the attitude control of spacecraft because of its angular distance from the Sun and the contrast of its brightness among nearby celestial objects.

| Arcturus (Alpha Boötis) | −0.05 | 36.7 | Boötes |

An orange-colored giant, Arcturus lies in an almost direct line with the tail of Ursa Major (the Great Bear), hence its name, derived from the Greek words for "bear guard."

| Alpha Centauri (Rigel Kentaurus) | 0.00 | 4.4 | Centaurus |

Alpha Centauri is a triple star—a binary yellow dwarf circled by a red dwarf with a much smaller red dwarf; the faintest of Alpha Centauri's three stars, Proxima, is the star closest to the Sun.

| Vega (Alpha Lyrae) | +0.03 | 25.3 | Lyra |

A blue dwarf, Vega will become the northern polestar by about AD 14,000 because of the precession of the equinoxes.

| Capella (Alpha Aurigae) | +0.08 | 42.2 | Auriga |

Capella is actually four stars, two yellow giants and two red-dwarf companion stars. Scientists are studying Capella to determine why it emits more X-rays than other stars of its type.

| Rigel (Beta Orionis) | +0.18 (reported values vary) | 773.0 | Orion |

Rigel is a blue-white supergiant with two smaller companion stars. The name Rigel derives from an Arabic term meaning "the left leg of the giant," referring to the figure of Orion.

The 20 Brightest Stars in the Night Sky (continued)

STAR	APPARENT VISUAL MAGNITUDE	DISTANCE FROM THE SOLAR SYSTEM (LIGHT-YEARS)	CONSTELLATION
Procyon (Alpha Canis Minoris)	+0.40	11.4	Canis Minor

Procyon is a yellow-white subgiant with a faint white-dwarf companion. The name Procyon apparently derives from Greek words for "before the dog," as in northern latitudes the star rises just before Sirius, the Dog Star.

| Achernar (Alpha Eridani) | +0.45 | 144.0 | Eridanus |

Achernar is a blue dwarf. The name Achernar probably derives from an Arabic phrase meaning "the end of the river," in which the river referred to is the constellation.

| Betelgeuse (Alpha Orionis) | +0.45 (reported values vary) | 427.0 | Orion |

A red supergiant, Betelgeuse has a diameter that varies between 430 and 625 times the diameter of the Sun over a period of 5.8 years.

| Beta Centauri (Hadar) | +0.58 | 526.0 | Centaurus |

Beta Centauri is a blue-white supergiant with two smaller companion stars; the constellation Centaurus most likely is meant to represent the centaur Chiron. In Greek mythology Chiron was renowned for his wisdom and knowledge of medicine. He renounced his immortality to escape a painful wound, and Zeus placed him in the Southern sky.

| Altair (Alpha Aquilae) | +0.76 | 16.8 | Aquila |

A blue dwarf, Altair spins nearly 760,000 km/h (470,000 mph), as compared with Earth, which spins some 1,600 km/h (1,000 mph). This rapid spinning flattens Altair from a spherical into an oblate shape.

| Aldebaran (Alpha Tauri) | +0.87 | 65.1 | Taurus |

A red giant, Aldebaran has a name derived from the Arabic for "the follower," perhaps because it rises after the Pleiades cluster of stars.

| Spica (Alpha Virginis) | +0.98 | 262.0 | Virgo |

A binary blue-white dwarf with a nonvisible companion, Spica has a name derived from the Latin for "ear of wheat"; the star is said to represent the wheat being held by the Virgin/fertility goddess (for whom Virgo is named).

| Antares (Alpha Scorpii) | +1.06 (reported values vary) | 604.0 | Scorpio |

Antares is a red supergiant. The name Antares seems to come from a Greek phrase meaning "rival of Ares" (i.e., rival of the planet Mars) and was probably given because of the star's color and brightness.

| Pollux (Beta Geminorum) | +1.16 | 96.7 | Gemini |

A red giant, Pollux is named for one of the twins of ancient Greek mythology (the other is Castor).

| Fomalhaut (Alpha Piscis Austrini) | +1.17 | 25.1 | Piscis Austrinus |

The blue-white dwarf Fomalhaut's name is derived from the Arabic for "mouth of the fish."

| Becrux (Beta Crucis, or Mimosa) | +1.25 | 352.0 | Crux (The Southern Cross) |

A blue-white giant, Becrux forms the eastern tip of the Southern Cross.

| Deneb (Alpha Cygni) | +1.25 | 3,230.0 | Cygnus |

A blue-white supergiant, Deneb gained its name from an Arabic word meaning "tail," as it is considered the tail of the swan Cygnus.

| Acrux (Alpha Crucis) | +1.40 | 321.0 | Crux (The Southern Cross) |

Acrux is a double star that stands at the foot of the Southern Cross.

*Data for apparent visual magnitudes taken from Encyclopædia Britannica Online.

Astronomical Phenomena for 2008

Source: The Astronomical Almanac 2008.

MONTH	DAY	HOUR (GMT)	EVENT	MONTH	DAY	HOUR (GMT)	EVENT
January	1	18	Ceres statonary	March	20	06	equinox
	3	00	Earth at perihelion		21	19	full moon
	5	06	Venus 7° N of Moon		23	10	Mercury 1°0 S of Venus
	5	10	Antares 0°05 N of Moon[1]		26	20	Moon at apogee
					27	10	Antares 0°5 N of Moon[1]
	7	02	Venus 7° N of Antares		29	22	last quarter
	8	12	new moon		30	00	Pallas in conjunction with Sun
	11	01	Neptune 0°04 N of Moon[1]		30	17	Jupiter 3° N of Moon
	13	01	Uranus 3° S of Moon	April	2	09	Neptune 0°002 S of Moon[1]
	15	20	first quarter				
	19	09	Moon at perigee		2	09	Pluto stationary
	20	00	Mars 1°1 S of Moon[1]		4	10	Uranus 3° S of Moon
	22	05	Mercury greatest elongation E (19°)		5	01	Venus 5° S of Moon
					6	04	new moon
	22	14	full moon		7	19	Moon at perigee
	24	15	Regulus 0°7 N of Moon[1]		12	06	Mars 1°2 S of Moon[1]
	25	06	Saturn 3° N of Moon		12	19	first quarter
	28	07	Mercury stationary		15	14	Regulus 0°9 N of Moon
	30	05	last quarter		15	18	Saturn 3° N of Moon
	30	21	Mars stationary		16	07	Mercury in superior conjunction
	31	04	Moon at apogee		18	14	Juno stationary
February	1	13	Venus 0°6 N of Jupiter		20	10	full moon
	1	18	Antares 0°6 N of Moon[1]		23	10	Moon at apogee
	4	06	Jupiter 4° N of Moon		23	17	Antares 0°3 N of Moon[1]
	4	12	Venus 4° N of Moon		27	05	Jupiter 3° N of Moon
	6	18	Mercury in inferior conjunction		28	14	last quarter
					28	20	Mars 5° S of Pollux
	7	04	new moon[3]		29	19	Neptune 0°3 S of Moon[1]
	9	10	Uranus 3° S of Moon				
	11	02	Neptune in conjunction with Sun	May	1	23	Uranus 3° S of Moon
					3	13	Saturn stationary
	14	01	Moon at perigee		5	12	new moon
	14	04	first quarter		6	03	Moon at perigee
	16	08	Mars 1°6 S of Moon		6	22	Mercury 3° S of Moon
	18	16	Mercury stationary		9	15	Jupiter stationary
	20	15	Vesta in conjunction with Sun		10	06	Mercury 8° N of Aldebaran
	21	00	Regulus 0°7 N of Moon[1]		10	14	Mercury 0°2 S of Moon[1]
	21	04	full moon[2]		12	04	first quarter
	21	12	Saturn 3° N of Moon		12	19	Regulus 1°2 N of Moon[1]
	24	10	Saturn at opposition		13	00	Saturn 3° N of Moon
	26	03	Mercury 1°3 N of Venus		14	04	Mercury greatest elongation E (22°)
	28	01	Moon at apogee				
	29	02	last quarter		20	02	full moon
	29	03	Antares 0°6 N of Moon[1]		20	14	Moon at apogee
March	3	01	Jupiter 4° N of Moon		20	23	Antares 0°2 N of Moon[1]
	3	11	Mercury greatest elongation W (27°)		24	11	Jupiter 2° N of Moon
					26	21	Mercury stationary
	5	14	Mercury 0°2 N of Moon[1]		26	22	Neptune stationary
	5	19	Venus 0°2 N of Moon[1]		27	03	Neptune 0°6 S of Moon[1]
	5	22	Neptune 0°2 N of Moon[1]				
					28	03	last quarter
	6	20	Venus 0°6 S of Neptune		29	09	Uranus 4° S of Moon
	7	17	new moon	June	3	13	Moon at perigee
	8	20	Uranus in conjunction with Sun		3	19	new moon
					7	15	Mercury in inferior conjunction
	9	03	Mercury 0°9 S of Neptune				
	10	22	Moon at perigee		8	02	Mars 1°1 N of Moon[1]
	14	11	first quarter		9	04	Venus in superior conjunction
	15	03	Mars 1°7 S of Moon				
	19	08	Regulus 0°8 N of Moon[1]		9	09	Saturn 3° N of Moon
	19	15	Saturn 3° N of Moon				

Astronomical Phenomena for 2008 (continued)

MONTH	DAY	HOUR (GMT)	EVENT	MONTH	DAY	HOUR (GMT)	EVENT
June	10	15	first quarter	September	4	02	Saturn in conjunction with Sun
	12	16	Juno at opposition		7	03	Antares 0°3 N of Moon[1]
	16	18	Moon at apogee		7	14	first quarter
	17	05	Antares 0°2 N of Moon[1]		7	15	Moon at apogee
	18	18	full moon		8	03	Jupiter stationary
	19	15	Mercury stationary		9	20	Jupiter 3° N of Moon
	20	13	Jupiter 2° N of Moon		11	04	Mercury greatest elongation E (27°)
	20	20	Pluto at opposition		11	05	Mercury 4° S of Moon
	21	00	Solstice		11	21	Venus 0°3 N of Mars
	23	09	Neptune 0°8 S of Moon[1]		12	21	Mercury 3° S of Mars
	25	16	Uranus 4° S of Moon		12	22	Vesta stationary
	26	12	last quarter		13	02	Neptune 0°8 S of Moon[1]
	27	08	Uranus stationary		13	02	Uranus at opposition
	28	17	Ceres in conjunction with Sun		15	08	Uranus 4° S of Moon
July	1	04	Mars 0°7 N of Regulus		15	09	full moon
	1	15	Mercury 8° S of Moon		18	09	Venus 3° N of Spica
	1	18	Mercury greatest elongation W (22°)		19	05	Mercury 4° S of Mars
	1	21	Moon at perigee		20	03	Moon at perigee
	3	02	new moon		22	05	last quarter
	4	08	Earth at aphelion		22	16	Equinox
	6	18	Mars 3° N of Moon		23	19	Mars 2° N of Spica
	6	22	Saturn 3° N of Moon		24	05	Mercury stationary
	9	08	Jupiter at opposition		27	20	Saturn 5° N of Moon
	10	05	first quarter		29	08	new moon
	11	06	Mars 0°7 S of Saturn	October	1	04	Mars 5° N of Moon
	14	04	Moon at apogee		2	02	Venus 5° N of Moon
	14	12	Antares 0°3 N of Moon[1]		4	11	Antares 0°1 N of Moon[1]
	17	12	Jupiter 3° N of Moon		5	11	Moon at apogee
	18	08	full moon		6	21	Mercury in inferior conjunction
	20	13	Neptune 0°9 S of Moon[1]		7	07	Jupiter 2° N of Moon
	22	22	Uranus 4° S of Moon		7	09	first quarter
	25	19	last quarter		10	10	Neptune 0°9 S of Moon[1]
	29	20	Mercury in superior conjunction		12	16	Uranus 4° S of Moon
	29	23	Moon at perigee		14	20	full moon
	31	05	Ceres 0°9 N of Moon[1]		15	05	Mercury stationary
August	1	10	new moon[3]		17	06	Moon at perigee
	3	14	Saturn 4° N of Moon		21	12	last quarter
	4	12	Mars 4° N of Moon		22	10	Mercury greatest elongation W (18°)
	5	20	Venus 1°1 N of Regulus		25	08	Saturn 5° N of Moon
	8	20	first quarter		26	13	Venus 3° N of Antares
	10	02	Juno stationary		27	18	Mercury 7° N of Moon
	10	05	Mercury 1°1 N of Regulus		28	23	new moon
	10	19	Antares 0°4 N of Moon[1]		29	09	Pallas stationary
	10	20	Moon at apogee		30	02	Vesta at opposition
	13	14	Jupiter 3° N of Moon		30	20	Mercury 4° N of Spica
	13	19	Venus 0°2 S of Saturn		31	18	Antares 0°06 S of Moon[1]
	15	08	Neptune at opposition	November	1	08	Venus 3° N of Moon
	16	00	Mercury 0°7 S of Venus		2	05	Moon at apogee
	16	19	Neptune 0°8 S of Moon[1]		2	07	Neptune stationary
	16	21	full moon[2]		3	22	Jupiter 1°9 N of Moon
	19	02	Uranus 4° S of Moon		6	04	first quarter
	23	05	Mercury 1°2 S of Venus		6	19	Neptune 1°1 S of Moon[1]
	24	00	last quarter		9	01	Uranus 4° S of Moon
	26	04	Moon at perigee		13	06	full moon
	30	20	new moon		14	10	Moon at perigee
September	1	21	Venus 5° N of Moon				
	1	23	Mercury 3° N of Moon				
	2	08	Mars 5° N of Moon				

Astronomical Phenomena for 2008 (continued)

MONTH	DAY	HOUR (GMT)	EVENT	MONTH	DAY	HOUR (GMT)	EVENT
November	19	22	last quarter	December	19	03	Saturn 6.° N of Moon
	21	18	Saturn 6° N of Moon		19	10	last quarter
	25	17	Mercury in superior conjunction		19	20	Vesta stationary
					21	12	solstice
	27	17	new moon		22	09	Pluto in conjunction with Sun
	28	00	Uranus stationary				
	29	17	Moon at apogee		25	07	Antares 0.°09 S of Moon[1]
December	1	01	Venus 2° S of Jupiter		26	18	Moon at apogee
	1	15	Jupiter 1.°3 N of Moon		27	02	Venus 1.°5 S of Neptune
	1	16	Venus 0.°8 S of Moon[1]				
	4	03	Neptune 1.°4 S of Moon		27	12	new moon
					29	04	Mercury 0.°7 S of Moon[1]
	4	17	Pallas at opposition				
	5	21	first quarter		29	09	Jupiter 0.°06 N of Moon[1]
	5	22	Mars in conjunction with Sun		31	06	Mercury 1.°3 S of Jupiter
	6	09	Uranus 4° S of Moon				
	12	17	full moon		31	11	Neptune 1.°7 S of Moon
	12	22	Moon at perigee		31	21	Venus 3° S of Moon

[1]Occultation. [2]Eclipse. [3]Penumbral eclipse.

Morning and Evening Stars

This table gives the morning and evening stars for autumn 2007 through 2008. The morning and evening stars are actually planets visible to the naked eye during the early morning and at evening twilight.

PLANET	MORNING STAR	EVENING STAR
Mercury	November 2007; 13 Feb–8 Apr, 17 Jun–22 Jul, 14 Oct–10 Nov 2008	2–31 Jan, 24 Apr–29 May, 8 Aug–30 Sep, 13–31 Dec 2008
Venus	October 2007–3 May 2008	16 Jul–31 Dec 2008
Mars	October–December 2007	1 Jan–16 Oct 2008
Jupiter	5 Jan–9 Jul 2008	October–4 Dec 2007; 9 Jul–31 Dec 2008
Saturn	October 2007–24 Feb 2008 22 Sep–31 Dec 2008	24 Feb–17 Aug 2008
Uranus	late March–September 2008	January–mid-February 2008 late December 2008
Neptune	early March–August 2008	early January 2008 mid-November–31 Dec 2008

Meteors, Meteorites, and Meteor Showers

A meteor (also called a **shooting star** or **falling star**) is a streak of light in the sky that results when a particle or small chunk of stony or metallic matter enters the Earth's atmosphere and vaporizes. The term is sometimes applied to the falling object itself, but the latter is properly called a **meteoroid**. The vast majority of meteoroids burn up in the upper atmosphere, but occasionally one of relatively large mass survives its fiery plunge and reaches the surface as a solid body. Such an object is known as a **meteorite**.

On any clear night in the countryside beyond the bright lights of cities, one can observe with the naked eye several meteors per hour as they streak through the sky. Quite often they vary in brightness along the path of their flight, appear to emit "sparks" or flares, and sometimes leave a luminous train that lingers after their flight has ended. These meteors are the result of the high-velocity collision of meteoroids with the Earth's atmosphere. Nearly all such interplanetary bodies are small fragments derived from comets or asteroids.

The brightest meteor (possibly of cometary origin) for which historical documentation exists—called the **Tunguska event**—struck on 30 Jun 1908 in central Siberia and rivaled the Sun in brightness. The energy delivered to the atmosphere by this impact was roughly equivalent to that of a 10-megaton thermonuclear explosion and caused the destruction of forest over an area of about 2,000 sq km (772.2 sq mi). The geologic record of cratering attests to the impact of much more massive meteorites. Fortunately, impacts of this magnitude occur only once or twice every 100 million years. It is hypothesized that large impacts of this kind may have played a major role in determining the course of biological evolution by causing simultaneous **mass extinctions** of many species of organisms, possibly including the dinosaurs some 65 million years ago. If so, the replacement of reptiles by mammals as the dominant land animals, the eventual consequence of which was the rise of the human species, would be the result of a grand example of a phenomenon observable every clear night.

The **visibility of meteors** is a consequence of the high velocity of meteoroids in interplanetary space. Before entering the region of the Earth's gravitational influence, their **velocities** range from a few kilometers per second up to as high as 72 km (44.7 mi) per second. As they approach the Earth, the Earth's gravitational field accelerates them to even higher velocities. This great release of energy destroys meteoroids of small mass—particularly those with relatively high ve-

locities—very quickly. Numerous meteors end their observed flight at altitudes above 80 km (49.7 mi), and penetration to as low as 50 km (31 mi) is unusual.

"**Showers**" of meteors have been known since ancient times. On rare occasions, these showers are very dramatic, with thousands of meteors falling per hour. More often, the background hourly rate of roughly 5 observed meteors increases up to about 10–50. Some of the best-known meteor showers are listed below, with their average date of maximum strength and associated comet, if known: **Quadrantid** (3 January); **Lyrid** (22 April; 1861 I [Thatcher]); **Eta Aquarid** (3 May; Halley); **S. Delta Aquarid** (29 July); **Capricornid** (30 July); **Perseid** (12 August; Swift-Tuttle); **Andromedid** (3 October; Biela); **Draconid** (9 October; Giacobini-Zinner); **Orionid** (21 October; Halley); **Taurid** (8 November; Encke); **Leonid** (17 November; Temple-Tuttle); **Germinid** (14 December; 3200 Phaeton [this body exhibits no cometary activity and may be of asteroidal rather than cometary origin]).

Auroras

Auroras are **luminous phenomena** of the upper atmosphere that occur primarily in high latitudes of both hemispheres; auroras in the Northern Hemisphere are called **aurora borealis,** or **northern lights**; in the Southern Hemisphere, **aurora australis,** or **southern lights**.

Auroras are caused by the interaction of energetic particles (electrons and protons) from outside the atmosphere with atoms of the upper atmosphere. Such interaction occurs in zones surrounding the Earth's magnetic poles. During periods of intense solar activity, auroras occasionally extend to the middle latitudes; for example, the aurora borealis has been seen at latitudes as far south as 40° in the US.

Auroras take many **forms,** including luminous curtains, arcs, bands, and patches. The uniform arc is the most stable form of aurora, sometimes persisting for hours without noticeable variation. In a great display, however, other forms appear, commonly under-

going dramatic variation. The lower edges of the arcs and folds are usually much more sharply defined than the upper parts. Greenish rays may cover most of the sky poleward of the magnetic zenith, ending in an arc that is usually folded and sometimes edged with a lower red border that may ripple like drapery. The display ends with a poleward retreat of the auroral forms, the rays gradually degenerating into diffuse areas of white light.

The **mechanisms** that produce auroral displays are not completely understood. It is known, however, that charged particles arriving in the vicinity of Earth as part of the solar wind are captured by the Earth's magnetic field and conducted downward toward the magnetic poles. They collide with oxygen and nitrogen atoms, knocking away electrons to leave ions in excited states. These ions emit radiation at various wavelengths, creating the characteristic colors (red or greenish blue) of the aurora.

Eclipses

An **eclipse** is a complete or partial obscuring of one celestial body by another; this event occurs when three celestial objects become aligned.

The Sun is eclipsed when the Moon comes between it and the Earth. (Hence, a **solar eclipse** can only occur during a new moon.) The Moon's shadow sweeps across the Earth, darkening the sky, while the Moon blocks out some portion of the view of the Sun. During a total eclipse of the Sun, the Moon's elliptical orbit brings the satellite closer to Earth and causes it to appear larger than the Sun. When the Moon's orbit places it at its farthest distance from Earth, the Moon appears smaller than the Sun and the eclipse will appear as a ring or "annulus" of bright sunlight around the Moon.

A **lunar eclipse** occurs when the Moon moves into the shadow of the Earth cast by the Sun. A lunar eclipse can only occur during a full moon. Lunar eclipses can be penumbral, partial, or total. The first type is of interest to astronomers but is difficult to detect because the Moon's dimming is so slight. With the next two types either a portion of the Moon or the entire Moon passes through Earth's umbral shadow.

It is safe to watch a lunar eclipse, but solar eclipses must be viewed via a projection onto another surface or through protective filters designed specially for eclipses.

The eclipses for 2008 are given in the table below.

	DATE	TYPE	VISIBLE IN
Solar eclipses	7 February	annular eclipse	Antarctica, eastern Australia, and the southwestern Pacific
	1 August	total eclipse	the Arctic, northern Europe, and northern Asia
Lunar eclipses	21 February	total eclipse	eastern Asia, Africa, Europe, the Arctic, and the Americas
	16 August	partial eclipse	western Asia, eastern Europe, Africa, and Antarctica

Characteristics of Celestial Bodies

Mean orbital velocity indicates the average speed with which a planet orbits the Sun unless otherwise specified. *Inclination of orbit to ecliptic* indicates the angle of tilt between a planet's orbit and the plane of the Earth's orbit (essentially the plane of the solar system). *Orbital period* indicates the planet's sidereal year (in Earth days except where noted). *Rotation period* indicates the planet's sidereal day (in Earth days except where noted). *Inclination of equator to orbit* indicates the angle of tilt between a planet's orbit and its equator. *Gravitational acceleration* is a measure of the body's gravitational pull on other objects. *Escape velocity* is the speed needed at the surface to escape the planet's gravitational pull.

Sun

diameter (at equator): 1,390,000 km (863,705 mi)
mass (in 10^{20} kg): 19.8 billion
density (mass/volume, in kg/m^3): 1,408
mean orbital velocity: the Sun orbits the Milky Way's center at around 220 km/sec (136.7 mi/sec)
orbital period: the Sun takes approximately 250 million Earth years to complete its orbit around the Milky Way's center
rotation period: 25–36 Earth days
gravitational acceleration: 275 m/sec^2 (902.2 ft/sec^2)
escape velocity: 618.02 km/sec (384.01 mi/sec)
mean temperature at visible surface: 5,527 °C (9,980 °F)
probes and space missions: US—Pioneer 5-9, launched 1959–87; Skylab, launched 1973; Ulysses, 1990; Genesis, 2001; Japan—Yohkoh, 1991; US/European Space Agency (ESA)—SOHO, 1995.

Mercury

average distance from Sun: 58 million km (36 million mi)
diameter (at equator): 4,879 km (3,032 mi)
mass (in 10^{20} kg): 3,300
density (mass/volume, in kg/m^3): 5,427
eccentricity of orbit*: 0.205
mean orbital velocity: 47.9 km/sec (29.7 mi/sec)
inclination of orbit to ecliptic: 7.0°
orbital period: 88 Earth days
rotation period: 58.6 Earth days
inclination of equator to orbit: probably 0°
gravitational acceleration: 3.7 m/sec^2 (12.1 ft/sec^2)
escape velocity: 4.3 km/sec (2.7 mi/sec)
mean temperature at surface†: 167 °C (333 °F)
satellites: none known
probes and space missions: US—Mariner 10, 1973; Messenger, 2004.

Venus

average distance from Sun: 108.2 million km (67.2 million mi)
diameter (at equator): 12,104 km (7,521 mi)
mass (in 10^{20} kg): 48,700
density (mass/volume, in kg/m^3): 5,243
eccentricity of orbit*: 0.007
mean orbital velocity: 35.0 km/sec (21.8 mi/sec)
inclination of orbit to ecliptic: 3.4°
orbital period: 224.7 Earth days
rotation period: 243.0 Earth days (retrograde)
inclination of equator to orbit: 177.4°
gravitational acceleration: 8.9 m/sec^2 (29.1 ft/sec^2)
escape velocity: 10.4 km/sec (6.4 mi/sec)
mean temperature at surface†: 464 °C (867 °F)
satellites: none known
probes and space missions: USSR—Venera 1-16, 1961–83; Vega 1 and 2, 1984; US—Mariner 2, 5, and 10, 1962, 1967, and 1973; Pioneer Venus 1 and 2, 1978; Galileo, 1989; Magellan, 1989.

Earth

average distance from Sun: 149.6 million km (93 million mi)
diameter (at equator): 12,756 km (7,926 mi)
mass (in 10^{20} kg): 59,700
density (mass/volume, in kg/m^3): 5,515
eccentricity of orbit*: 0.017
mean orbital velocity: 29.8 km/sec (18.5 mi/sec)
inclination of orbit to ecliptic: 0.00°
orbital period: 365.25 days
rotation period: 23 hours, 56 minutes, and 4 seconds of mean solar time
inclination of equator to orbit: 23.5°
gravitational acceleration: 9.8 m/sec^2 (32.1 ft/sec^2)
escape velocity: 11.2 km/sec (7.0 mi/sec)
mean temperature at surface†: 15 °C (59 °F)
satellites: 1 known—the Moon.

Moon (of Earth)

average distance from Earth: 384,401 km (238,855.7 mi)
diameter (at equator): 3,475 km (2,159 mi)
mass (in 10^{20} kg): 730
density (mass/volume, in kg/m^3): 3,340
eccentricity of orbit*: orbital eccentricity of Moon around Earth is 0.055
mean orbital velocity: the Moon orbits Earth at 1.0 km/sec (0.64 mi/sec)
inclination of orbit to ecliptic: 5.1°
orbital period: the Moon revolves around the Earth in 27.32 Earth days
rotation period: the Moon rotates on its axis every 27.32 Earth days (synchronous with orbital period)
inclination of equator to orbit: 6.7°
gravitational acceleration: 1.6 m/sec^2 (5.3 ft/sec^2)
escape velocity: 2.4 km/sec (1.5 mi/sec)
mean temperature at surface†: daytime: 107 °C (224.6 °F); nighttime: −153 °C (−243.4 °F)
probes and space missions: USSR, US, ESA, Japan—collectively about 70 missions since 1959, including 9 manned missions by the US. On 20 Jul 1969 humans first set foot on the Moon, from NASA's Apollo 11.

Mars

average distance from Sun: 227.9 million km (141.6 million mi)
diameter (at equator): 6,794 km (4,222 mi)
mass (in 10^{20} kg): 6,420
density (mass/volume, in kg/m^3): 3,933
eccentricity of orbit*: 0.094
mean orbital velocity: 24.1 km/sec (15 mi/sec)
inclination of orbit to ecliptic: 1.9°
orbital period: 687 Earth days (1.88 Earth years)
rotation period: 24.6 Earth hours
inclination of equator to orbit: 24.9°
gravitational acceleration: 3.7 m/sec^2 (12.1 ft/sec^2)
escape velocity: 5.0 km/sec (3.1 mi/sec)
mean temperature at surface†: −65 °C (−85 °F)
satellites: 2 known—Phobos and Deimos

probes and space missions: US—Mariner 4, 6, 7, and 9, 1964–71; Viking 1 and 2, 1975; Mars Global Surveyor, 1996; Mars Pathfinder, 1996; 2001 Mars Odyssey, 2001; Mars Exploration Rovers, 2003; USSR—Mars 2–7, 1971–73; Phobos 1 and 2, 1988; ESA—Mars Express, 2003.

asteroids
(several hundred thousand small rocky bodies, about 1,000 km [610 mi] or less in diameter, that orbit the Sun primarily between the orbits of Mars and Jupiter)
distance from Sun: between approximately 300 million km (190 million mi) and 600 million km (380 million mi), with notable outlyers
estimated mass: 2.3×10^{21} kg
probes and space missions: US—Galileo, 1989; Ulysses, 1990; NEAR Shoemaker, 1996; Deep Space 1, 1998; Stardust, 1999; US/ESA/Italy—Cassini-Huygens, 1997; ESA—Rosetta, 2004; Japan—Hayabusa, 2003.

Jupiter
average distance from Sun: 778.6 million km (483.8 million mi)
diameter (at equator): 142,984 km (88,846 mi)
mass (in 10^{20} kg): 18,990,000
density (mass/volume, in kg/m³): 1,326
eccentricity of orbit*: 0.049
mean orbital velocity: 13.1 km/sec (8.1 mi/sec)
inclination of orbit to ecliptic: 1.3°
orbital period: 11.86 Earth years
rotation period: 9.9 Earth hours
inclination of equator to orbit: 3.1°
gravitational acceleration: 23.1 m/sec² (75.9 ft/sec²)
escape velocity: 59.5 km/sec (37.0 mi/sec)
mean temperature at surface†: −110 °C (−166 °F)
satellites: more than 60 moons—including Callisto, Ganymede, Europa, and Io—plus rings
probes and space missions: US—Pioneer 10 and 11, 1972–73; Voyager 1 and 2, 1977; Galileo, 1989; Ulysses, 1990; US/ESA/Italy—Cassini-Huygens, 1997.

Saturn
average distance from Sun: 1.433 billion km (890.8 million mi)
diameter (at equator): 120,536 km (74,897 mi)
mass (in 10^{20} kg): 5,680,000
density (mass/volume, in kg/m³): 687
eccentricity of orbit*: 0.057
mean orbital velocity: 9.7 km/sec (6 mi/sec)
inclination of orbit to ecliptic: 2.5°
orbital period: 29.43 Earth years
rotation period: 10.7 Earth hours
inclination of equator to orbit: 26.7°
gravitational acceleration: 9.0 m/sec² (29.4 ft/sec²)
escape velocity: 35.5 km/sec (22.1 mi/sec)
mean temperature at surface†: −140 °C (−220 °F)
satellites: more than 45 moons—including Titan—plus rings
probes and space missions: US—Pioneer 11, 1973; Voyager 1 and 2, 1977; US/ESA/Italy—Cassini/Huygens, 1997.

Uranus
average distance from Sun: 2.872 billion km (1.784 billion miles)

diameter (at equator): 51,118 km (31,763 mi)
mass (in 10^{20} kg): 868,000
density (mass/volume, in kg/m³): 1,270
eccentricity of orbit*: 0.046
mean orbital velocity: 6.8 km/sec (4.2 mi/sec)
inclination of orbit to ecliptic: 0.8°
orbital period: 84.01 Earth years
rotation period: 17.2 Earth hours (retrograde)
inclination of equator to orbit: 97.8°
gravitational acceleration: 8.7 m/sec² (28.5 ft/sec²)
escape velocity: 21.3 km/sec (13.2 mi/sec)
mean temperature at surface†: −195 °C (−320 °F)
satellites: at least 27 moons, plus rings
probes and space missions: US—Voyager 2, 1977.

Neptune
average distance from Sun: 4.495 billion km (2.793 billion mi)
diameter (at equator): 49,528 km (30,775 mi)
mass (in 10^{20} kg): 1,020,000
density (mass/volume, in kg/m³): 1,638
eccentricity of orbit*: 0.009
mean orbital velocity: 5.4 km/sec (3.4 mi/sec)
inclination of orbit to ecliptic: 1.8°
orbital period: 164.79 Earth years
rotation period: 16.1 Earth hours
inclination of equator to orbit: 28.3°
gravitational acceleration: 11.0 m/sec² (36.0 ft/sec²)
escape velocity: 23.5 km/sec (14.6 mi/sec)
mean temperature at surface†: −200 °C (−330 °F)
satellites: at least 13 moons, plus rings
probes and space missions: US—Voyager 2, 1977.

Pluto
average distance from Sun: 5.910 billion km (3.67 billion mi); Pluto lies within the Kuiper belt and can be considered its largest known member.
diameter (at equator): 2,344 km (1,485 mi)
mass (in 10^{20} kg): 125
density (mass/volume, in kg/m³): about 2,000
eccentricity of orbit*: 0.249
mean orbital velocity: 4.72 km/sec (2.93 mi/sec)
inclination of orbit to ecliptic: 17.2°
orbital period: 248 Earth years
rotation period: 6.4 Earth days (retrograde)
inclination of equator to orbit: 122.5°
gravitational acceleration: 0.6 m/sec² (1.9 ft/sec²)
escape velocity: 1.1 km/sec (0.7 mi/sec)
mean temperature at surface†: −225 °C (−375 °F)
satellites: 1 known—Charon.

Charon (moon of Pluto)
average distance from Pluto: 19,600 km (12,178.8 mi)
diameter (at equator): 1,250 km (777 mi)
mass (in 10^{20} kg): 19
density (mass/volume, in kg/m³): about 1,700
eccentricity of orbit*: 0
mean orbital velocity: Charon orbits Pluto at 0.23 km/sec (0.142 mi/sec)
inclination of orbit to Pluto's equator: close to 0°
orbital period: 6.3873 Earth days
rotation period: 6.3873 Earth days
gravitational acceleration: 0.21 m/sec² (0.69 ft/sec²)
escape velocity: 0.58 km/sec (0.36 mi/sec)
mean temperature at surface†: as low as −240 °C (−400 °F).

Comet 1P Halley
distance from Sun at closest point of orbit is 87.8 million km (54 million mi). Farthest distance from Sun is 5.2 billion km (3.2 billion mi).
diameter (at equator): 16 x 8 x 8 km (9.9 x 4.9 x 4.9 mi)
density (mass/volume, in kg/m³): possibly as low as 200
eccentricity of orbit*: 0.967
inclination of orbit to ecliptic: 18°
orbital period: 76.1 to 79.3 Earth years. The next appearance will be 2061. The comet's orbit is retrograde.
rotation period: 52 Earth hours
probes and space missions: ESA—Giotto, 1985; USSR—Vega 1 and 2, 1985; Japan—Sakigake and Suisei, 1985.

Comet 2P Encke
distance from Sun at closest point of orbit is 50 million km (31 million mi). Farthest distance from Sun is 658 million km (408 million mi).
eccentricity of orbit*: 0.847
orbital period: 3.3 Earth years (shortest known for a comet); next closest pass of Sun is on 19 Apr 2007.

Comet 9P Tempel 1
distance from Sun at closest point of orbit is 225 million km (140 million mi). Farthest distance from Sun is 708 million km (440 million mi).
eccentricity of orbit*: 0.52
orbital period: 5.52 Earth years; next closest pass of Sun is in January 2011.
rotation period: 41 Earth hours
probes and space missions: US—Deep Impact, 2005

Comet 81P Wild 2
distance from Sun at closest point of orbit is 236.8 million km (147.1 million mi). Farthest distance from Sun is 10 billion km (6.2 billion mi).
eccentricity of orbit*: 0.54
orbital period: 6.39 Earth years; next closest pass of Sun is in February 2010.
probes and space missions: US—Stardust, 1999.

Comet Hale-Bopp
distance from Sun at closest point of orbit is 136 million km (84.5 million mi). Farthest distance from Sun is 74.7 billion km (46.4 billion mi).
eccentricity of orbit*: 0.995
orbital period: 4,000 Earth years; last closest pass of Sun was on 31 Mar 1997.

Comet Hyakutake
distance from Sun at closest point of orbit is 34 million km (21 million mi). Farthest distance from Sun is 344 billion km (213 billion mi).
eccentricity of orbit*: 0.9998
orbital period: about 40,000 Earth years; last closest pass of Sun was on 1 May 1996.

Kuiper belt
(a huge flat ring located beyond Neptune containing residual icy material from the formation of the outer planets)
average distance from Sun (main concentration): 4.5–7.5 billion km (2.8–4.7 billion mi)
mass: Scientists estimate there may be as many as 100,000 icy, cometlike bodies of a size greater than 100 km in the Kuiper belt; the belt is estimated to have a mass of 6,000 x 10²⁰ kg.

Oort cloud
(an immense, roughly spherical cloud of icy, cometlike bodies inferred to orbit Sun at distances roughly 1,000 times that of the orbit of Pluto)
average distance from Sun: 3–7 trillion km (1.9–4.3 trillion mi)
mass: some trillions of the cloud's icy objects have an estimated total mass of at least 600,000 x 10²⁰ kg (10 times the mass of Earth).

*Eccentricity of orbit measures circularity or elongation of an orbit; 0 indicates circular orbits, and closer to 1 more elliptical ones.   †For planets with no surface, temperature given is at a level in the atmosphere equal to 1 bar of pressure.

Solar System Superlatives

Largest planet in solar system: Jupiter (142,984 km [88,846 mi] diameter); all of the other planets in the solar system could fit inside Jupiter.
Largest moon in the solar system: Jupiter's moon Ganymede (5,270 km [3,275 mi]).
Smallest planet in solar system: Mercury (4,879 km [3,032 mi] diameter).
Smallest moons in the solar system: Saturn and Jupiter both have numerous satellites that are smaller than 10 km (6 mi) in diameter.
Planet closest to the Sun: Mercury (average distance from the Sun 58 million km [36 million mi]).
Planet farthest from the Sun: Neptune (average distance from the Sun 4.50 billion km [2.80 billion mi]); Pluto, demoted to the status of dwarf planet in 2006, was the farthest planet from the Sun for all but 20 years of its 248-year orbital period.

Planet with the most eccentric (least circular) orbit: Mercury (eccentricity of 0.206).
Moon with the most eccentric orbit: Neptune's moon Nereid (eccentricity of 0.75).
Planet with the least eccentric orbit: Venus (eccentricity of 0.007).
Moon with the least eccentric orbit: Saturn's moon Tethys (eccentricity of 0.00000).
Planet most tilted on its axis: Uranus (axial tilt of 98° from its orbital plane).
Planet with the most moons: Jupiter (more than 60).
Planets with the fewest moons: Mercury and Venus (no moons).
Planet with the longest day: Venus (1 day on Venus equals 243 Earth days).
Planet with the shortest day: Jupiter (1 day on Jupiter equals 9.9 hours).

Planet with the longest year: Neptune (1 year on Neptune equals 165 Earth years).

Planet with the shortest year: Mercury (1 year on Mercury equals 88 Earth days).

Fastest orbiting planet in the solar system: Mercury (47.9 km per second [29.7 mi per second] average orbital speed).

Slowest orbiting planet in the solar system: Neptune (5.48 km per second [3.40 mi per second] average orbital speed).

Hottest planet in solar system: Venus (464 °C [867 °F] average temperature); although Mercury is closer to the Sun, Venus is hotter because Mercury has no atmosphere, whereas the atmosphere of Venus traps heat via a strong greenhouse effect.

Coldest planet in the solar system: Neptune (–220 °C [–364 °F] average temperature).

Brightest visible star in the night sky: Sirius (–1.46 apparent visual magnitude).

Brightest planet in the night sky: Venus (apparent visual magnitude –4.5 to –3.77).

Densest planet: Earth (density of 5,515 kg/m³).

Least dense planet: Saturn (density of 687 kg/m³); Saturn in theory would float in water.

Planet with strongest gravity: Jupiter (more than twice the gravitational force of Earth at an altitude at which 1 bar of atmospheric pressure is exerted).

Planet with weakest gravity: Mars (slightly more than ⅓ the gravitational force of Earth).

Planet with the largest mountain: Mars (Olympus Mons, an extinct volcano, stands some 21 km [13 mi] above the planet's mean radius and 540 km [335 mi] across).

Planet with deepest valley: Mars (Valles Marineris, a system of canyons, is some 4,000 km [2,500 mi] long and from about 2 to 9 km [1 to 5.6 mi] deep).

Largest known impact crater: Valhalla, a crater on Jupiter's moon Callisto, has a bright central area that is about 600 km (370 mi) across with sets of concentric ridges extending about 1,500 km (900 mi) from the center. For contrast, the largest crater on Earth believed to be of impact origin is the Vredefort ring structure in South Africa, which is about 300 km (190 mi) across.

The Sun

The Sun is the star around which the Earth and the other components of the solar system revolve. It is the dominant body of the system, constituting more than 99% of the system's entire mass. The Sun is the source of an enormous amount of energy, a portion of which provides the Earth with the light and heat necessary to support life. The geologic record of the Earth and Moon reveals that the Sun was formed about 4.5 billion years ago. The energy radiated by the Sun is produced during the conversion of hydrogen atoms to helium. The Sun is at least 90% hydrogen by number of atoms, so the fuel is readily available.

The Sun is classified as a G2 V star, where G2 stands for the second hottest stars of the yellow G class—of surface temperature about 5,500 °C (10,000 °F)—and V represents a main sequence, or dwarf, star, the typical star for this temperature class (see also "Classification of Stars"). The Sun exists in the outer part of the Milky Way Galaxy and was formed from material that had been processed inside other stars and supernovas.

The mass of the Sun is 743 times the total mass of all the planets in the solar system and 330,000 times that of the Earth. All the interesting planetary and interplanetary gravitational phenomena are negligible effects in comparison to the gravitational force exerted by the Sun. Under the force of gravity, the great mass of the Sun presses inward, and to keep the star from collapsing, the central pressure outward must be great enough to support its weight. The Sun's core, which occupies approximately 25% of the star's radius, has a density about 100 times that of water (roughly 6 times that at the center of the Earth), but the temperature at the core is at least 15 million °C (27 million °F), so the central pressure is at least 10,000 times greater than that at the center of the

Earth. In this environment atoms are completely stripped of their electrons, and at this high temperature the bare nuclei collide to produce the nuclear reactions that are responsible for generating the energy vital to life on Earth.

The temperature of the Sun's surface is so high that no solid or liquid can exist; the constituent materials are predominantly gaseous atoms, with a very small number of molecules. As a result, there is no fixed surface. The surface viewed from Earth, the photosphere, is approximately 400 km (250 mi) thick and is the layer from which most of the radiation reaches us; the radiation from below the photosphere is absorbed and reradiated, while the emission from overlying layers drops sharply, by about a factor of six every 200 km (124 mi).

While the temperature of the Sun drops from 15 million °C (27 million °F) at the core to around 5,500 °C (10,000 °F) at the photosphere, a surprising reversal occurs above that point; the temperature begins to rise in the chromosphere, a layer several thousand kilometers thick. Temperatures there range from 4,200 °C (7,600 °F) to 100,000 °C (180,000 °F). Above the chromosphere is a comparatively dim, extended halo called the corona, which has a temperature of 1 million °C (1.8 million °F) and reaches far past the planets. Beyond a distance of around 3.5 million km (2.2 million mi) from the Sun, the corona flows outward at a speed (near the Earth) of 400 km/sec (250 mi/sec); this flow of charged particles is called the solar wind.

The Sun is a very stable source of energy. Superposed on this stability, however, is an interesting 11-year cycle of magnetic activity manifested by regions of transient strong magnetic fields called sunspots. The largest sunspots can be seen on the solar surface even without a telescope.

Mercury

Mercury is the planet closest to the Sun, revolving around it at an average distance of 58 million km (36 million mi). In Sumerian times, some 5,000 years ago, it was already known

in the night sky. In classical Greece the planet was called Apollo when it appeared as a morning star and Hermes, for the Greek equivalent of the Roman god Mercury, when it appeared as an evening star.

Mercury's orbit lies inside the orbit of the Earth and is more elliptical than those of most of the other planets. At its closest approach (perihelion), Mercury is only 46 million km (28.5 million mi) from the Sun, while its greatest distance (aphelion) approaches 70 million km (43.5 million mi). Mercury orbits the Sun in 88 Earth days at an average speed of 48 km per second (29.8 mi per sec), allowing it to overtake and pass Earth every 116 Earth days (synodic period).

Because of its proximity to the Sun, the surface of Mercury can become extremely hot. High temperatures at "noon" may reach 400 °C (755 °F) while the "predawn" lowest temperature is −173 °C (−280 °F). Mercury's equator is almost exactly in its orbital plane (its spin-axis inclination is nearly zero), and thus Mercury does not have seasons as does the Earth. Because of its elliptical orbit and a peculiarity of its rotational period (see below), however, certain longitudes experience cyclical variations in temperatures on a "yearly" as well as on a "diurnal" basis.

Mercury is about 4,879 km (3,032 mi) in diameter, the smallest of the planets. Mercury is only a bit larger than the Moon. Its mass, as measured by the gravitational perturbation of the path of the Mariner 10 spacecraft during close flybys in 1974 and 1975, is about one-eighteenth of the mass of the Earth. Escape velocity, the speed needed to escape from a planet's gravitational field, is about 4.3 km per second (2.7 mi per second)—compared with 11.2 km per sec (7 mi per sec) for the Earth.

The mean density of Mercury, calculated from its mass and radius, is about 5.43 grams per cubic cm, nearly the same as that of the Earth (5.52 grams per cubic cm).

Photographs relayed by the Mariner 10 spacecraft showed that Mercury spins on its axis (rotates) once every 58.646 Earth days, exactly two-thirds of the orbital period of 87.9694 Earth days. This observation confirmed that Mercury is in a 3:2 spin-orbit tidal resonance—i.e., that tides raised on Mercury by the Sun have forced it into a condition that causes it to rotate three times on its axis in the same time it takes to revolve around the Sun twice. The 3:2 spin-orbit coupling combines with Mercury's eccentric orbit to create very unusual temperature effects.

Although Mercury rotates on its axis once every 58.646 Earth days, one rotation does not bring the Sun back to the same part of the sky, because during that time Mercury has moved partway around the Sun. A solar day on Mercury (for example, from one sunrise to another, or one noon to another) is 176 Earth days (exactly two Mercurian years).

Mercury's low escape velocity and high surface temperatures do not permit it to retain a significant atmosphere.

Venus

Venus is the second planet from the Sun and the planet whose orbit is closest to that of the Earth. When visible, Venus is the brightest planet in the sky. Viewed through a telescope, it presents a brilliant, yellow-white, essentially featureless face to the observer. The obscured appearance results because the surface of the planet is hidden from sight by a continuous and permanent cover of clouds.

Venus's orbit is the most nearly circular of that of any planet, with a deviation from perfect circularity of only about 1 part in 150. The period of the orbit—that is, the length of the Venusian year—is 224.7 Earth days. The rotation of Venus is unusual in both its direction and speed. Most of the planets in the solar system rotate in a counterclockwise direction when viewed from above their north poles; Venus, however, rotates in the opposite, or retrograde, direction. Were it not for the planet's clouds, an observer on Venus's surface would see the Sun rise in the west and set in the east.

Venus spins on its axis very slowly, taking 243 Earth days to complete one rotation. Venus's spin and orbital periods are nearly synchronized with the Earth's orbit such that Venus presents almost the same face toward the Earth when the two planets are at their closest approach.

Venus is nearly the Earth's twin in terms of size and mass. Venus's equatorial diameter is about 95% of the Earth's diameter, while its mass is 81.5% that of the Earth. The similarities to the Earth in size and mass also produce a similarity in density; Venus's density is 5.24 grams per cubic cm, as compared with 5.52 for the Earth.

In terms of its shape, Venus is more nearly a perfect sphere than are most planets. A planet's rotation generally causes a slight flattening at the poles and bulging at the equator, but Venus's very slow rotation rate allows it to maintain its highly spherical shape.

Venus has the most massive atmosphere of all the terrestrial planets (Mercury, Venus, Earth, and Mars). Its atmosphere is composed of 96.5% carbon dioxide and 3.5% nitrogen. The atmospheric pressure at the planet's surface varies with the surface elevation but averages about 90 bars, or 90 times the atmospheric pressure at the Earth's surface. This is the same pressure found at a depth of about one kilometer in the Earth's oceans. Temperatures range between a minimum temperature of −45 °C (−49 °F) and a maximum temperature of 500 °C (932 °F); the average temperature is 464 °C (867 °F).

Earth

The Earth is the third planet in distance outward from the Sun. It is the only planetary body in the solar system that has conditions suitable for life, at least as known to modern science.

The average distance of the Earth from the Sun—149.6 million km (93 million mi)—is designated as the distance of the unit of measurement known as the AU (astronomical unit). The Earth orbits the Sun at a speed of 29.8 km (18.5 mi) per second, making one complete revolution in 365.25 days. As it

revolves around the Sun, the Earth spins on its axis and rotates completely once every 23 hr 56 min 4 sec. The Earth has a single natural satellite, the Moon.

The fifth largest planet of the solar system, the Earth has a total surface area of roughly 509.6 million sq km (197 million sq mi), of which about 29%, or 148 million square km (57 million square mi), is land. Oceans and smaller seas cover the balance of the surface. The Earth is the only planet known to have liquid water. Together with ice, the liquid water constitutes the hydrosphere. Seawater makes up more than 98% of the total mass of the hydrosphere and covers about 71% of the Earth's surface. Significantly, seawater constituted the environment of the earliest terrestrial life forms.

The Earth's atmosphere consists of a mixture of gases, chiefly nitrogen (78%) and oxygen (21%). Argon makes up much of the remainder of the gaseous envelope, with trace amounts of water vapor, carbon dioxide, and various other gases also present.

The Earth's structure consists of an inner core of nearly solid iron, surrounded by successive layers of molten metals and solid rock, and a thin layer at the surface comprising the continental crust.

The Earth is surrounded by a magnetosphere, a region dominated by the Earth's magnetic field and extending upward from about 140 km (90 mi) in the upper atmosphere. In the magnetosphere, the magnetic field of the Earth traps rapidly moving charged particles (mainly electrons and protons), the majority of which flow from the Sun (as solar wind). If it were not for this shielding effect, such particles would bombard the terrestrial surface and destroy life. High concentrations of the trapped particles make up two doughnut-shaped zones called the Van Allen radiation belts. These belts play a key role in certain geophysical phenomena, such as auroras.

The Moon

The Moon is the sole natural satellite of the Earth. It revolves around the planet from west to east at a mean distance of about 384,400 km (238,900 mi). The Moon is less than one-third the size of the Earth, having a diameter of only about 3,475 km (2,159 mi) at its equator. The Moon shines by reflecting sunlight, but its albedo—i.e., the fraction of light received that is reflected—is only 0.073.

The Moon rotates about its own axis in about 27.32 days, which is virtually identical to the time it takes to complete its orbit around the Earth. As a result, the Moon always presents nearly the same face to the Earth. The rate of actual rotation is uniform, but the arc through which the Moon moves from day to day varies somewhat, causing the lunar globe (as seen by a terrestrial observer) to oscillate slightly over a period nearly equal to that of revolution.

The surface of the Moon has been a subject of continuous telescopic study from the time of Galileo's first observation in 1609. The Italian-Jesuit astronomer Giovanni B. Riccioli designated the dark areas on the Moon as seas (maria), with such fanciful names as Mare Imbrium ("Sea of Showers") and Mare Nectaris ("Sea of Nectar"). This nomenclature continues to be used even though it is now known that the Moon is completely devoid of surface water. During the centuries that followed the publication of these early studies, more detailed maps and, eventually, photographs were produced. A Soviet space probe photographed the side of the Moon facing away from the Earth in 1959. By the late 1960s the US Lunar Orbiter missions had yielded close-up photographs of the entire lunar surface. On 20 Jul 1969, Apollo 11 astronauts Neil Armstrong and Edwin ("Buzz") Aldrin set foot on the Moon.

The most striking formations on the Moon are its craters. These features, which measure up to about 200 km (320 mi) or more in diameter, are scattered over the surface in great profusion and often overlap one another. Meteorites hitting the lunar surface at high velocity produced most of the large craters. Many of the smaller ones—those measuring less than 1 km (0.6 mi) across—appear to have been formed by explosive volcanic activity, however. The Moon's maria have relatively few craters. These lava outpourings spread over vast areas after most of the craters had already been formed.

Various theories for the Moon's origin have been proposed. At the end of the 19th century, the English astronomer Sir George H. Darwin advanced a hypothesis stating that the Moon had been originally part of the Earth but had broken away as a result of tidal gravitational action and receded from the planet. This was proved unlikely in the 1930s. A theory that arose during the 1950s postulated that the Moon had formed elsewhere in the solar system and was then later captured by the Earth. This idea was also proved to be physically implausible and was dismissed. Today, most investigators favor an explanation known as the giant-impact hypothesis, which postulates that a Mars-sized body struck the proto-Earth early in the history of the solar system. As a result, a cloud of fragments from both bodies was ejected into orbit around the Earth, and this later accreted into the Moon.

Moon Phases, 2007–2008

As the Moon orbits the Earth, more or less of the half of the Moon illuminated by the Sun is visible on Earth. During the lunar month the Moon's appearance changes from dark (the new moon) to being illuminated more and more on the right side (waxing crescent, first quarter, and waxing gibbous) to the full disc being illuminated (the full moon). The phases of the Moon are completed by the Moon being illuminated less and less on the left side (waning gibbous, last quarter, and waning crescent) and end with another new moon. The cycle of the Moon takes place over a period of around 29 days; the time from new moon to new moon is referred to as a lunation.

The phases of the Moon are caused by the positions of the Sun in relationship to the Moon. Thus, when the Sun and Moon are close in the sky a dark new moon is the result (the Sun is lighting the half of the Moon not visible to Earth). When the Sun and Moon are at opposition (in opposite parts of the sky) the full moon occurs (the Sun illuminates fully the half of the Moon seen on Earth). When the Sun and Moon are at about a 90-degree angle, one sees either a first quarter or last quarter moon.

The dates for the new moon, first quarter, full moon, and last quarter for June 2007–December 2008 are given in the table below.

Moon Phases, 2007–2008 (continued)

	NEW MOON	FIRST QUARTER	FULL MOON	LAST QUARTER
June 2007	15	22	1/30	8
July 2007	14	22	30	7
August 2007	12	20	28	5
September 2007	11	19	26	4
October 2007	11	19	26	3
November 2007	9	17	24	1
December 2007	9	17	24	1/31
January 2008	8	15	22	30
February 2008	7	14	21	29
March 2008	7	14	21	29
April 2008	6	12	20	28
May 2008	5	12	20	28
June 2008	3	10	18	26
July 2008	3	10	18	25
August 2008	1	8	16	23
September 2008	(30 August)	7	15	22
October 2008	(29 September	7	14	21
November 2008	(28 October)	6	13	19
December 2008	(27 November)	5	12	19
	27			

Moon's Apogee and Perigee, 2008

The distance between the centers of mass of the Earth and the Moon varies rather widely due to the combined gravity of the Earth, the Sun, and the planets. For example, during the period 1969–2000, apogee (when the Moon is at the greatest distance from Earth) varied from 404,063 to 406,711 km (251,073 to 252,719 mi), while perigee (when the Moon is closest to Earth) varied from 356,517 to 370,354 km (221,529 to 230,127 mi). Tidal interactions have braked the Moon's spin so that presently the same side always faces the Earth. Dates are Universal Time/GMT.

Moon at apogee

DATE	OCCURS
3 January	between last quarter and new moon
31 January	between last quarter and new moon
28 February	between full moon and last quarter
26 March	between full moon and last quarter
23 April	between full moon and last quarter
20 May	at full moon
16 June	between first quarter and full moon
14 July	between first quarter and full moon
10 August	between first quarter and full moon
7 September	at first quarter
5 October	between new moon and first quarter
2 November	between new moon and first quarter
29 November	between new moon and first quarter
26 December	between last quarter and new moon

Moon at perigee

DATE	OCCURS
19 January	between first quarter and full moon
14 February	at first quarter
10 March	between new moon and first quarter
7 April	between new moon and first quarter
6 May	between new moon and first quarter
3 June	at new moon
1 July	between last quarter and new moon
29 July	between last quarter and new moon
26 August	between last quarter and new moon
20 September	between full moon and last quarter
17 October	between full moon and last quarter
14 November	between full moon and last quarter
12 December	at full moon

Mars

Mars is the fourth planet in order of distance from the Sun and the seventh in order of diminishing size and mass. It orbits the Sun once in 687 Earth days and spins on its axis once every 24 hr 37 min.

Owing to its blood-red color, Mars has often been associated with warfare and slaughter. It is named for the Roman god of war; as far back as 3,000 years ago, Babylonian astronomer-astrologers called the planet Nergal for their god of death and pestilence. The Greeks called it Ares for their god of battle; the planet's two satellites, Phobos (Fear) and Deimos (Terror), were later named for the two sons of Ares and Aphrodite.

Mars moves around the Sun at a mean distance of approximately 1.52 times that of the Earth from the Sun. Because the orbit of Mars is relatively elongated, the distance between Mars and the Sun varies from 206.6 to 249.2 million km (128.4 to 154.8 million mi). Mars completes a single orbit in roughly the time in which the Earth completes two. At its closest approach, Mars is less than 56 million km (34.8 million mi) from the Earth, but it recedes to almost 400 million km (248.5 million mi). Mars is a small planet. Its equatorial radius is about half that of Earth, and its mass is only one-tenth the terrestrial value.

The axis of rotation is inclined to the orbital plane at an angle of 24.9°, and, as for the Earth, the tilt gives rise to the seasons on Mars. The Martian year consists of 668.6 Martian solar days (called sols). The orientation and eccentricity of the orbit (eccentricity denotes how much the orbit deviates from a perfect circle, the more elongated the more eccentric) leads to seasons that are quite uneven in length.

The Martian atmosphere is composed mainly of carbon dioxide. It is very thin (less than 1% of the Earth's atmospheric pressure). Evidence suggests that the atmosphere was much denser in the remote past and that water was once much more abundant at the surface. Only small amounts of water are found in the lower atmosphere today, occasionally forming thin ice clouds at high altitudes and, in several localities, morning ice fogs. Mars's polar caps consist of frozen carbon dioxide and water ice. Intriguing spacecraft observations confirm that water ice also is present under large areas of the Martian surface and hint that liquid water may have flowed in geologically recent times.

The characteristic temperature in the lower atmosphere is about −70 °C (−100 °F). Unlike that of Earth, the total mass (and pressure) of the atmosphere experiences large seasonal variations, as carbon dioxide "snows out" at the winter pole.

The surface of Mars shows some of the most dramatic variation in the solar system: the massive extinct volcano Olympus Mons stands some 21 km (13 mi) above the planet's mean radius and is 540 km (335 mi) across, and Valles Marineris, a system of canyons, is some 4,000 km (2,500 mi) long and from about 2 to 9 km (1 to 5.6 mi) deep.

The two satellites of Mars—Phobos and Deimos—were discovered in 1877 by Asaph Hall of the United States Naval Observatory. Little was known about these bodies until observations were made by NASA's orbiting Mariner 9 spacecraft nearly a century later. The moons of Mars cannot be seen from all locations on the planet because of their small size, proximity to the planet, and near-equatorial orbits.

Small Celestial Bodies

Small bodies are defined as all the natural objects in the solar system other than the Sun and the major planets and their satellites. The solar system is populated by vast numbers of these small bodies, which can be grouped as asteroids, comets, and meteoroids (at times, however, the distinctions between these groupings can be somewhat blurred).

Small bodies in stable orbits are found in several regions of the solar system. Most asteroids reside in a belt between Mars and Jupiter at approximately 300–600 million km (190–380 million mi). Others, called Trojan asteroids, are found at gravitationally stable points near the orbits of Mars and Jupiter.

The trans-Neptunian objects (considered comets) are located outside the orbit of Neptune, from around 4.5–7.5 billion km (2.8–4.7 billion mi) in the area known as the Kuiper belt. A spherical cloud known as the Oort cloud also contains comets at a distance of some 3–15 trillion km (1.8–9 trillion mi).

Other small bodies travel in unstable paths which cross planetary orbits. These include: all observed comets; near-Earth asteroids, whose orbits either cross or closely approach Earth's orbit; and other planet-crossing objects (a mixture of both asteroids and icy cometlike bodies). All objects on planet-crossing orbits will eventually collide with the Sun or a planet or be permanently ejected from the solar system, although some of these objects do survive for long periods of time due to stabilizing orbital resonances.

Comets originate, and most are still located, in the Kuiper belt and Oort cloud. Even though comets are brief visitors to the inner solar system, their population is constantly replenished through perturbations of the comets in these areas.

There are several characteristics that traditionally have distinguished asteroids, comets, and meteoroids. These are based upon origin, orbital, and physical differences. An object is classified as a comet when it displays a coma or tail (or any evidence of gas or dust coming from it). In addition, the icy objects found in the Kuiper belt (and the Oort cloud, though none of these are observable) are also considered to be comets. They do not display cometary activity because of their great distance from the Sun. Nevertheless, they are believed to be made up of the same volatile material—primarily water and carbon dioxide—as the nuclei of observed comets, and it is the presence of these volatiles on the surface that is responsible for cometary activity. Finally, objects on parabolic or hyperbolic (nonreturning) orbits are generally considered to be comets.

Meteoroids are defined as any small object in space, especially one less than a few tens of meters in size. When a meteoroid enters the Earth's atmosphere, the heat of friction creates a glowing trail of hot gases called a meteor. Should any part of a meteoroid reach the ground without being completely vaporized, that object is termed a meteorite. The term asteroid is traditionally reserved for the larger rocky bodies in solar orbit, which range up to nearly 1,000 km (600 mi) in size.

Asteroids and the Asteroid Belt

Asteroids are any of a host of small rocky bodies, about 1,000 km (600 mi) or less in diameter, that orbit the Sun. About 95% of the known asteroids move in orbits between those of Mars and Jupiter in an area known as the asteroid belt. The orbits of the asteroids, however, are not uniformly distributed within the asteroid belt, but exhibit "gaps." Known as Kirkwood gaps, these asteroid-less areas are maintained by the gravitational force exerted by Jupiter upon asteroids in certain orbits.

The vast majority of asteroids have orbital periods between three years and six years—i.e., between one-fourth and one-half of Jupiter's orbital period. These asteroids are said to be main-belt asteroids. Within the main belt are asteroids that share certain traits. Known as families, about 40% of all known asteroids belong to such groupings. Families are usually assigned the name of the lowest numbered (first discovered) asteroid in the family. The three largest families (Eos, Koronis, and Themis) have been determined to be compositionally homogeneous; each is thought to comprise fragments from a larger parent body that broke apart in a collision.

Besides the few asteroids in highly unusual orbits, there are a number of groups that fall outside the main belt. Those that have orbital periods greater than one-half that of Jupiter are called outer-belt asteroids. There are four such groups: the Cybeles, Hildas, Thule, and Trojan groups.

There is only one known group of inner-belt asteroids—namely, the Hungarias. The Hungaria asteroids have orbital periods that are less than one-fourth that of Jupiter. Finally, asteroids that pass inside the orbit of Mars are said to be near-Earth asteroids. There are two groups of near-Earth asteroids that deeply cross the Earth's orbit on an almost continuous basis. The first of these to be discovered were the Apollo asteroids. The other group of Earth-crossing asteroids is named Atens. A third group, the Amors, comprises part-time Earth crossers.

Asteroids are thought to be made of the same rocky (stony, metallic, and carbon-rich) material that formed the planets. Scientists believe that at the time the planets were forming the gravitational influence of what became Jupiter kept the asteroids from aggregating into a single planet. Since that time they have been evolving through ongoing collisions so that most of the present-day asteroids are remnants or fragments of larger bodies. As of 2007 astronomers had detected and numbered more than 90,000 asteroids.

Jupiter

Jupiter is the most massive of the planets and is fifth in distance from the Sun. When ancient astronomers named the planet Jupiter for the ruler of the gods in the Greco-Roman pantheon, they had no idea of the planet's true dimensions, but the name is appropriate, for Jupiter is larger than all the other planets combined. It has a narrow ring system and at least 63 known satellites, 3 larger than the Earth's Moon. Jupiter also has an internal heat source—i.e., it emits more energy than it receives from the Sun. This giant has the strongest magnetic field of any planet, with a magnetosphere so large that, if it could be seen from Earth, its apparent diameter would exceed that of the Moon. Jupiter's system is the source of intense bursts of radio noise, at some frequencies occasionally radiating more energy than the Sun.

Of special interest concerning Jupiter's physical properties is the low mean density of 1.33 grams per cubic cm—in contrast with Earth's 5.52 grams/cm³—coupled with the large dimensions and mass and the short rotational period. The low density and large mass indicate that Jupiter's composition and structure are quite unlike those of the Earth and the other inner planets, a deduction that is supported by detailed investigations of the giant planet's atmosphere and interior.

Jupiter has no solid surface; the transition from the atmosphere to its highly compressed core occurs gradually at great depths. The close-up views of Jupiter from the Voyager spacecraft revealed a variety of cloud forms, with a predominance of elliptical features reminiscent of cyclonic and anticyclonic storm systems on the Earth. All these systems are in motion, appearing and disappearing on time scales dependent on their sizes and locations. Also observed to vary are the pastel shades of various colors present in the cloud layers—from the tawny yellow that seems to characterize the main layer, through browns and blue-grays, to the well-known salmon-colored Great Red Spot, Jupiter's largest, most prominent, and longest-lived feature.

Because Jupiter has no solid surface, it has no topographic features, and latitudinal currents dominate the planet's large-scale circulation. The lack of a solid surface with physical boundaries and regions with different heat capacities makes the persistence of these currents and their associated cloud patterns all the more remarkable. The Great Red Spot, for example, moves in longitude with respect to Jupiter's rotation, but it does not move in latitude.

The Voyager 1 spacecraft verified the existence of a ring system surrounding Jupiter when it crossed the planet's equatorial plane. Subsequently, images from the Galileo spacecraft revealed that the ring system consists principally of four concentric components whose boundaries are associated with the orbits of Jupiter's four innermost moons. The ring system is comprised of large numbers of micrometer-sized particles that produce strong forward scattering of incident sunlight. The presence of such small particles requires a source, and the association of the ring boundaries with the four moons makes the source clear. The particles are generated by impacts on these moons (and on still smaller bodies within the main part of the ring) by micrometeoroids, cometary debris, and possibly volcanically produced material from Jupiter's moon Io.

Did you know? With the exception of snakes and bees, scorpions cause more deaths than any other non-parasitic group of animals. It is thought that more than 5,000 people die each year from scorpion stings. A long curved tail with a venomous stinger and grasping, fingerlike first appendages are typical scorpion features.

Jovian Moons

The satellites orbiting Jupiter are numerous; there are at least 63 Jovian moons and likely additional ones to be discovered.

The first objects in the solar system discovered by means of a telescope (by Galileo in 1610) were the four brightest moons of Jupiter. Now known as the Galilean satellites, they are (in order of increasing distance from Jupiter) Io, Europa, Ganymede, and Callisto. Each is a unique world in its own right. Callisto and Ganymede, for example, are as large or larger than the planet Mercury, but, while Callisto's icy surface is ancient and heavily cratered from impacts, Ganymede's appears to have been extensively modified by internal activity. Europa may still be geologically active and may harbor an ocean of liquid water, and possibly even life, beneath its frozen surface. Io is the most volcanically active body in the solar system; its surface is a vividly colored landcape of erupting vents, pools and solidified flows of lava, and sulfurous deposits.

Data for the first 16 known Jovian moons (discovered 1610–1979) are summarized below. The orbits of the inner eight satellites have low inclinations (they are not tilted relative to the planet's equator) and low eccentricities (their orbits are relatively circular). The orbits of the outer eight have much higher inclinations and eccentricities, and four of them are retrograde (they are opposite to Jupiter's spin and orbital motion around the Sun). The innermost four satellites are thought to be intimately associated with Jupiter's ring and are the sources of the fine particles within the ring itself.

Beginning in 1999 some 47 tiny moons (including one seen in 1975 and then lost) were discovered photographically in observations from Earth. All have high orbital eccentricities and inclinations and large orbital radii; nearly all of the orbits are retrograde. Rough size estimates based on their brightness place them between 2 and 8 km (1.2 and 5 mi) in diameter. They were assigned provisional numerical designations on discovery; many also have received official names.

In the table, "sync" denotes that the orbital period and rotational period are the same, or synchronous; hence, the moon always keeps the same face toward Jupiter. "R" following the orbital period indicates a retrograde orbit. Unspecified quantities are unknown.

NAME (DESIGNATION)	MEAN DISTANCE FROM JUPITER	DIAMETER	MASS (10^{20} KG)	ORBITAL PERIOD (EARTH DAYS)	ROTATIONAL PERIOD (EARTH DAYS)
Metis (JXVI)	128,000 km (79,500 mi)	40 km (25 mi)	0.001	0.295	sync
Adrastea (JXV)	129,000 km (80,000 mi)	20 km (12 mi)	0.0002	0.298	sync
Amalthea (JV)[1]	181,000 km (112,500 mi)	189 km (117 mi)	0.075	0.498	sync
Thebe (JXIV)	222,000 km (138,000 mi)	100 km (62 mi)	0.008	0.675	sync
Io (JI)[1]	422,000 km (262,000 mi)	3,630 km (2,256 mi)	893.2	1.769	sync
Europa (JIII)[1]	671,000 km (417,000 mi)	3,130 km (1,945 mi)	480.0	3.551	sync
Ganymede (JIII)[1]	1,070,000 km (665,000 mi)	5,268 km (3,273 mi)	1,482.0	7.155	sync
Callisto (JIV)[1]	1,883,000 km (1,170,000 mi)	4,806 km (2,986 mi)	1,076.0	16.689	sync
Leda (JXIII)	11,127,000 km (6,914,000 mi)	10 km (6 mi)	0.00006	234	
Himalia (JVI)	11,480,000 km (7,133,000 mi)	170 km (106 mi)	0.095	251	0.4
Lysithea (JX)	11,686,000 km (7,261,300 mi)	24 km (15 mi)	0.0008	258	0.5
Elara (JVII)	11,737,000 km (7,293,000 mi)	80 km (50 mi)	0.008	256	0.5
Ananke (JXII)	21,269,000 km (13,216,000 mi)	20 km (12.5 mi)	0.0004	634 R	0.4
Carme (JXI)	23,350,000 km (14,509,000 mi)	30 km (18.6 mi)	0.001	729 R	0.4
Pasiphae (JVIII)	23,500,000 km (14,602,000 mi)	36 km (22.3 mi)	0.003	735 R	
Sinope (JIX)	23,700,000 km (14,726,500 mi)	28 km (17.3 mi)	0.0008	758 R	0.5

[1]Densities are known for these moons. They are: Amalthea (0.86 grams/cm³), Io (3.53 grams/cm³), Europa (3.01 grams/cm³), Ganymede (1.94 grams/cm³), Callisto (1.83 grams/cm³).

Jovian Ring

Jupiter's complex ring was discovered and first studied by the twin Voyager spacecraft during their flybys of the giant planet in 1979. It is now known to consist of four main components: an outer gossamer ring, whose outer radius coincides with the orbital radius of the Jovian moon Thebe (222,000 km; 138,000 mi); an inner gossamer ring bounded on its outer edge by the orbit of Amalthea (181,000 km; 112,500 mi); the main ring, extending inward some 6,000 km (3,700 mi) from the orbits of Adrastea (129,000 km; 80,000 mi) and Metis (128,000 km; 79,500 mi); and a halo of particles with a thickness of 25,000 km (15,500 mi) that extends from the main ring inward to a radius of about 95,000 km (59,000 mi). For comparison, Jupiter's visible surface lies at a radius of about 71,500 km (44,400 mi) from its center. The four moons involved with the ring are believed to supply the fine particles that compose it.

Saturn

Saturn is the sixth planet in order of distance from the Sun and the second largest of the planets in mass and size. Its dimensions are almost equal to those of Jupiter, while its mass is about a third as large; it has the lowest mean density of any object in the solar system.

Both Saturn and Jupiter resemble stellar bodies in that the light gas hydrogen dominates their bulk **chemical composition.** Saturn's atmosphere is 91% hydrogen by mass and is thus the most hydrogen-rich atmosphere in the solar system. Saturn's structure and **evolutionary history,** however, differ significantly from those of its larger counterpart. Like the other giant planets—Jupiter, Uranus, and Neptune—Saturn has extensive satellite and ring systems, which may provide clues to its origin and evolution. The planet has at least 56 moons, including the second largest in the solar system. Saturn's dense and extended rings, which lie in its equatorial plane, are the most impressive in the solar system.

Saturn has no single **rotation period.** Cloud motions in its massive upper atmosphere can be used to trace out a variety of rotation periods, with periods as short as about 10 hours 10 minutes near the equator and increasing with some oscillation to about 30 minutes longer at latitudes higher than 40°. The rotation period of Saturn's deep interior can be determined from the rotation period of the magnetic field, which is presumed to be rooted in an outer core of hydrogen compressed to a metallic state. The "surface" of Saturn that is seen through telescopes and in spacecraft images is actually a complex layer of clouds.

The **atmosphere** of Saturn shows many smaller-scale time-variable features similar to those found in Jupiter, such as red, brown, and white spots, bands, eddies, and vortices. The atmosphere generally has a much blander appearance than Jupiter's, however, and is less active on a small scale. A spectacular exception occurred during September–November 1990, when a large white spot appeared near the equator, expanded to a size exceeding 20,000 km (12,400 mi), and eventually spread around the equator before fading.

Saturnian Moons

At least 56 natural satellites are known to circle the planet Saturn. Data for the first 18 Saturnian moons (discovered 1655–1990) are summarized below. As with the other giant planets, those satellites closest to Saturn are mostly regular, meaning that their orbits are fairly circular and not greatly inclined (tilted) with respect to the planet's equator. All of the satellites in the table except distant Phoebe are regular.

Titan is Saturn's largest moon and the only satellite in the solar system known to have clouds and a dense atmosphere (composed mostly of nitrogen and methane). The moon is also enveloped in a reddish haze, which is thought to be composed of complex organic compounds that are produced by the action of sunlight on its clouds and atmosphere. That organic molecules may have been settling out of the haze onto Titan's surface for much of its history has encouraged some scientists to speculate on the possibility that life may have evolved there. Observations by the Cassini-Huygens spacecraft showed Titan to have a varied surface sculpted by rains of hydro-carbon compounds, flowing liquids, wind, impacts, and possibly volcanic and tectonic activity. Saturn's second largest moon is **Rhea,** followed by **Iapetus** and **Dione.**

An unusual Saturnian satellite is **Hyperion.** Owing to its highly irregular shape and eccentric orbit, it does not rotate stably about a fixed axis. Unlike any other known object in the solar system, Hyperion rotates chaotically, alternating unpredictably between periods of tumbling and seemingly regular rotation.

Between 2000 and 2005 about 30 additional tiny moons occupying various (mostly distant) orbits were discovered. Like the numerous outer moons of Jupiter, nearly all of the recent finds around Saturn belong to the irregular class, meaning that their orbits are highly inclined and elliptical. More than half of them, plus Phoebe, are in retrograde orbits (they move opposite to Saturn's spin and orbital motion around the Sun).

In the table, "sync" denotes that the orbital period and rotational period are the same, or synchronous. Unspecified quantities are unknown.

NAME (DESIGNATION)	MEAN DISTANCE FROM SATURN	DIAMETER	MASS (10^{20} KG)	DENSITY (GRAMS/CM³)	ORBITAL PERIOD (EARTH DAYS)	ROTATIONAL PERIOD (EARTH DAYS)
Pan (SXVIII)	133,580 km (83,000 mi)	20 km (12 mi)	0.00003	0.63	0.5750	
Atlas (SXV)	137,670 km (85,540 mi)	28 km (17 mi)	0.0001	0.63	0.6019	

Saturnian Moons (continued)

NAME (DESIGNATION)	MEAN DISTANCE FROM SATURN	DIAMETER	MASS (10^{20} KG)	DENSITY (GRAMS/CM³)	ORBITAL PERIOD (EARTH DAYS)	ROTATIONAL PERIOD (EARTH DAYS)
Prometheus (SXVI)	139,350 km (86,590 mi)	92 km (57 mi)	0.0033	0.63	0.6130	
Pandora (SXVII)	141,700 km (88,050 mi)	92 km (57 mi)	0.002	0.63	0.6285	
Epimetheus (SXI)	151,420 km (94,090 mi)	114 km (71 mi)	0.0054	0.60	0.6942	sync
Janus (SX)	151,470 km (94,120 mi)	178 km (111 mi)	0.0192	0.65	0.6945	sync
Mimas (SI)	185,520 km (115,280 mi)	392 km (244 mi)	0.375	1.14	0.94	sync
Enceladus (SII)	238,020 km (147,900 mi)	520 km (323 mi)	0.7	1.0	1.37	sync
Tethys (SIII)	294,660 km (183,090 mi)	1,060 km (659 mi)	6.27	1.0	1.88	sync
Telesto (SXIII)*	294,660 km (183,090 mi)	30 km (19 mi)	0.00007	1.0	1.88	
Calypso (SXIV)*	294,660 km (183,090 mi)	26 km (16 mi)	0.00004	1.0	1.88	
Dione (SIV)	377,400 km (234,510 mi)	1,120 km (696 mi)	11	1.5	2.73	sync
Helene (SXII)†	377,400 km (234,510 mi)	32 km (20 mi)	0.0003	1.5	2.73	
Rhea (SV)	527,040 km (327,490 mi)	1,530 km (951 mi)	23.1	1.24	4.51	sync
Titan (SVI)	1,221,830 km (759,210 mi)	5,150 km (3,200 mi)	1,350	1.881	15.94	sync
Hyperion (SVII)	1,481,100 km (920,310 mi)	286 km (178 mi)	0.2	1.50	21.27	chaotic
Iapetus (SVIII)	3,561,300 km (2,212,890 mi)	1,460 km (907 mi)	16	1.02	79.33	sync
Phoebe (SIX)	12,952,000 km (8,048,000 mi)	220 km (137 mi)	0.004	1.3	550.5 (retrograde)	0.4

*Telesto and Calypso occupy the same orbit as Tethys but about 60° ahead and behind, respectively.
†Helene occupies the same orbit as Dione but about 60° behind.

Saturnian Rings

Saturn's rings rank among the most spectacular phenomena in the solar system. They have intrigued astronomers ever since they were discovered telescopically by Galileo in 1610, and their mysteries have only deepened since they were photographed and studied by Voyagers 1 and 2 in the early 1980s. The **particles** that make up the rings are composed primarily of water ice and range from dust specks to car- and house-sized chunks. The rings exhibit a great amount of structure on many scales, from the broad **A, B, and C rings** visible from Earth down to myriad narrow component ringlets. Odd structures resembling spokes, braids, and spiral waves are also present. Some of this detail is explained by gravitational interaction with a number of Saturn's 56 moons (the orbits of well more than a dozen known moons, from Pan to Dione and Helene, lie within the rings), but much of it remains unaccounted for.

Numerous divisions or **gaps** are seen in the major ring regions. A few of the more prominent ones are named for famous astronomers who were associated with studies of Saturn.

The major rings and gaps, listed outward from Saturn, are given below. For comparison, Saturn's visible surface lies at a radius of about 60,300 km (37,500 mi).

RING (OR DIVISION)	RADIUS OF RING'S INNER EDGE	WIDTH	COMMENTS
D ring	66,900 km (41,600 mi)	7,500 km (4,700 mi)	faint, visible only in reflected light
(Guerin division)			
C ring	74,500 km (46,300 mi)	17,500 km (10,900 mi)	also called Crepe ring
(Maxwell division)			
B ring	92,000 km (57,200 mi)	25,500 km (15,800 mi)	brightest ring
(Cassini division, Huygens gap)			Cassini division is the largest ring gap
A ring	122,200 km (75,900 mi)	14,600 km (9,100 mi)	the outermost ring visible from Earth

Saturnian Rings (continued)

RING (OR DIVISION)	RADIUS OF RING'S INNER EDGE	WIDTH	COMMENTS
(Encke division)			located within the A ring, near its outer edge
F ring	140,200 km (87,100 mi)	30–500 km (20–300 mi)	faint, narrowest major ring
G ring	165,800 km (103,000 mi)	8,000 km (5,000 mi)	faint
E ring	180,000 km (111,800 mi)	300,000 km (186,400 mi)	faint

Uranus

Uranus is the seventhth planet in order of distance from the Sun and the first found with the aid of a telescope. Its low density and large size place it among the four giant planets, all of which are composed primarily of hydrogen, helium, water, and other volatile compounds and which thus are without solid surfaces. Absorption of red light by methane gas gives the planet a blue-green color. The planet has at least 27 satellites, ranging up to 789 km (490 mi) in radius, and 10 narrow rings.

Uranus spins on its side; its **rotation axis** is tipped at an angle of 98° relative to its orbit axis. The 98° tilt is thought to have arisen during the final stages of planetary accretion when bodies comparable in size to the present planets collided in a series of violent events that knocked Uranus onto its side.

Although Uranus is nearly featureless, extreme contrast enhancement of images taken by the Voyager spacecraft reveals faint bands oriented parallel to circles of constant latitude. Apparently the rotation of the planet and not the distribution of absorbed sunlight controls the cloud patterns.

Wind is the motion of the atmosphere relative to the rotating planet. At high latitudes on Uranus, as on the Earth, this relative motion is in the direction of the planet's rotation. At low (that is, equatorial) latitudes, the relative motion is in the opposite direction. On the Earth these directions are called east and west, respectively, but the more general terms are prograde and retrograde. The winds that exist on Uranus are several times stronger than are those of the Earth. The wind is 200 m (656 ft) per second (prograde) at a latitude of 55° S and 110 m (360.8 ft) per second (retrograde) at the equator. Neptune's equatorial winds are also retrograde, although those of Jupiter

and Saturn are prograde. No satisfactory theory exists to explain these differences.

Uranus has no large **spots** like the Great Red Spot of Jupiter or the Great Dark Spot of Neptune. Since the giant planets have no solid surfaces, the spots represent atmospheric storms. For reasons that are not clear, Uranus seems to have the smallest number of storms of any of the giant planets. Most of the mass of Uranus (roughly 80%) is in the form of a liquid core made primarily of icy materials (water, methane, and ammonia).

Uranus was discovered in 1781 by the English astronomer **William Herschel,** who had undertaken a survey of all stars down to eighth magnitude—i.e., those about five times fainter than stars visible to the naked eye. Herschel suggested naming the new planet the Georgian Planet after his patron, King George III of England, but the planet was eventually named according to the tradition of naming planets for the gods of Greek and Roman mythology; Uranus is the father of Saturn, who is in turn the father of Jupiter.

After the discovery, Herschel continued to observe the planet with larger and better telescopes and eventually discovered its two largest satellites, Titania and Oberon, in 1787. Two more satellites, Ariel and Umbriel, were discovered by the British astronomer William Lassell in 1851. The names of the four satellites come from English literature—they are characters in works by Shakespeare and Pope—and were proposed by Herschel's son, John Herschel. A fifth satellite, Miranda, was discovered by Gerard P. Kuiper in 1948. The tradition of naming the satellites after characters in Shakespeare's and Pope's works continues to the present.

Uranian Moons and Rings

Uranus has 27 known **satellites** forming three distinct groups: 13 small moons orbiting quite close to the planet, 5 large moons located somewhat farther out, and finally another 9 small and much more distant moons. The members of the first two groups are in nearly circular orbits with low inclinations with respect to the planet.

The densities of the four largest satellites, **Ariel, Umbriel, Titania,** and **Oberon,** suggest that they are about half (or more) water ice and the rest rock. Oberon and Umbriel are heavily scarred with large impact craters dating back to the very early history of the solar system, evidence that their surfaces probably have been stable since their formation. In contrast, Titania and Ariel have far fewer large craters, indicating relatively young surfaces shaped over time by internal geological activity. Miranda, though small compared with the other major moons, has a unique jumbled patchwork of varied surface terrain revealing surprisingly extensive past activity. Data for the major satellites are summarized below.

The 5 major moons were **discovered** telescopically from Earth between 1787 and 1948. Eleven of the 13 innermost moons, with diameters of about 40–160 km (25–100 mi), were found in Voyager 2 images. The rest of the moons, with diameters of 10–200 km (6–120 mi), were detected in Earth-based observations between 1997 and 2003; the orbital motion of nearly all of the outermost moons is retrograde (opposite to the direction of Uranus's spin and revolution around the Sun).

Ten very narrow rings are known to encircle Uranus, with radii from 41,800 to 51,100 km (26,000 to 31,800 mi), for the most part within the orbits of the innermost moons. For comparison, Uranus's visible surface lies at a radius of about 25,600 km (15,900 mi). The ring system was first detected in 1977 during Earth-based observations of Uranus when the planet was passing in front of a star. Subsequent observations from Earth and images from Voyager 2 clarified the number and other features of the rings.

Uranian Moons and Rings (continued)

NAME (DESIGNATION)	MEAN DISTANCE FROM URANUS	DIAMETER	MASS (10^{20} KG)	DENSITY (GRAMS/CM³)	ORBITAL PERIOD/ ROTATIONAL PERIOD (EARTH DAYS)*
Miranda (V)	129,390 km (80,400 mi)	472 km (293 mi)	0.66	1.2	1.41
Ariel (I)	191,020 km (118,690 mi)	1,158 km (720 mi)	13.5	1.67	2.52
Umbriel (II)	266,300 km (165,470 mi)	1,169 km (726 mi)	11.7	1.4	4.14
Titania (III)	435,910 km (270,860 mi)	1,578 km (981 mi)	35.3	1.71	8.71
Oberon (IV)	583,520 km (362,580 mi)	1,523 km (946 mi)	30.1	1.63	13.46

*The orbital period and rotational period are the same, or synchronous, for the listed moons.

Neptune

Neptune is the eighth planet in average distance from the Sun. It was named for the Roman god of the sea. The sea god's trident serves as the planet's astronomical symbol.

Neptune's **distance** from the Sun varies between 29.8 and 30.4 astronomical units (AUs). Its **diameter** is about four times that of the Earth, but because of its great distance Neptune cannot be seen from the Earth without the aid of a telescope. Neptune's deep blue **color** is due to the absorption of red light by methane gas in its atmosphere. It receives less than half as much sunlight as Uranus, but heat escaping from its interior makes Neptune slightly warmer than the latter. The heat released may also be responsible for Neptune's stormier **atmosphere**, which exhibits the fastest winds seen on any planet in the solar system.

Neptune's **orbital period** is 164.8 Earth years. It has not completely circled the Sun since its discovery in 1846, so some refinements in calculations of its orbital size and shape are still expected. The planet's orbital eccentricity of 0.009 means that its orbit is very nearly circular; among the planets in the solar system, only Venus has a smaller eccentricity. Neptune's seasons (and the seasons of its moons) are therefore of nearly equal length, each about 41 Earth years in duration. The length of Neptune's day, as determined by Voyager 2, is 16.11 hours.

As with the other giant planets of the outer solar system, Neptune's atmosphere is composed predominantly of hydrogen and helium. The **temperature** of Neptune's atmosphere varies with altitude. A minimum temperature of about −223 °C (−369 °F) occurs at pressure near 0.1 bar. The temperature increases with altitude to about 477 °C (891 °F) at 2,000 km (1,240 mi, which corresponds to a pressure of 10^{-11} bar) and remains uniform above that altitude. It also increases with depth to about 6,730 °C (12,140 °F) near the center of the planet.

As with the other giant planets of the outer solar system, the **winds** on Neptune are constrained to blow generally along lines of constant latitude and are relatively invariable with time. Winds on Neptune vary from about 100 m/sec (328 ft/sec) in an easterly (prograde) direction near latitude 70° S to as high as 700 m/sec (2,300 ft/sec) in a westerly (retrograde) direction near latitude 20° S.

The high winds and relatively large contribution of escaping internal heat may be responsible for the observed turbulence in Neptune's visible atmosphere. Two large dark ovals are clearly visible in images of Neptune's southern hemisphere taken by Voyager 2 in 1989, although they are not present in Hubble Space Telescope images made 2 years later. The largest, called the **Great Dark Spot** because of its similarity in latitude and shape to Jupiter's Great Red Spot, is comparable to the entire Earth in size. It was near this feature that the highest wind speeds were measured. Atmospheric storms such as the Great Dark Spot may be centers where strong upwelling of gases from the interior takes place.

Neptune's mean **density** is about 30% of the Earth's; nevertheless, it is the densest of the giant planets. Neptune's greater density implies that a larger percentage of its interior is composed of melted ices and molten rocky materials than is the case for the other gas giants.

Neptunian Moons and Rings

Neptune has at least 13 natural satellites, but Earth-based observations had found only 2 of them, Triton in 1846 and Nereid in 1949, before Voyager 2 flew by the planet. The spacecraft observed 5 small moons orbiting close to Neptune and verified the existence of a 6th that had been detected from Earth in 1981. Data for these 8 moons are summarized in the table below. In 2002–03, 5 additional small moons (diameters roughly 30–60 km [20–40 mi]) were discovered telescopically from Earth; they all occupy highly inclined and elliptical orbits that are comparatively far from Neptune.

Triton is Neptune's only large moon and the only large satellite in the solar system to orbit its planet in the retrograde direction (opposite the planet's rotation and orbital motion around the Sun). Thus, as is also suspected of the solar system's other retrograde moons, Triton likely was captured by its planet rather than formed in orbit with its planet from the solar nebula. Its density (2 grams/cm³) suggests that it is about 25% water ice and the rest rock. Triton has a tenuous atmosphere, mostly of nitrogen. Its varied icy surface, imaged by Voyager 2, contains giant faults and dark markings that have been interpreted as the product of geyserlike

Neptunian Moons and Rings (continued)

"ice volcanoes" in which the eruptive material may be gaseous nitrogen and methane. Nereid has the most elliptical orbit of any planet or moon in the solar system; it also is probably a captured object.

Neptune's system of six faint rings, with radii from about 42,000 to 63,000 km (26,000–39,000 mi), straddles the orbits of its 4 innermost moons. (Neptune's visible surface lies at a radius of 24,800 km, or 15,400 mi.) The outermost ring, named Adams, is unusual in that it contains several clumps, or concentrations of material, that before Voyager 2's visit had been interpreted incorrectly as independent ring arcs. What created and has maintained this structure has not yet been fully explained; it has been suggested that the clumps resulted from the relatively recent breakup of a small moon and are being temporarily held together by the gravitational effects of the nearby moon Galatea.

NAME (DESIGNATION)	MEAN DISTANCE FROM NEPTUNE	DIAMETER	MASS (10^{20} KG)	ORBITAL PERIOD (EARTH DAYS)
Naiad (III)	48,230 km (29,970 mi)	58 km (36 mi)	0.002	0.294
Thalassa (IV)	50,070 km (31,110 mi)	80 km (50 mi)	0.004	0.311
Despina (V)	52,530 km (32,640 mi)	148 km (92 mi)	0.02	0.335
Galatea (VI)	61,950 km (38,490 mi)	158 km (98 mi)	0.04	0.429
Larissa (VII)	73,550 km (45,700 mi)	192 km (119 mi)	0.05	0.555
Proteus (VIII)	117,640 km (73,100 mi)	416 km (258 mi)	0.5	1.122
Triton (I)*	354,800 km (220,460 mi)	2,700 km (1,678 mi)	214	5.877 (retrograde)
Nereid (II)	5,509,100 km (3,423,200 mi)	340 km (211 mi)	0.2	359.632

*Among the rotational periods of Neptune's moons, only Triton's has been established; it is the same as (synchronous with) the orbital period.

Pluto

Pluto is named for the god of the underworld in Roman mythology. It was long considered the planet normally farthest from the Sun, but on 24 Aug 2006, the International Astronomical Union announced that it was downgrading the status of Pluto to a dwarf planet. The key criterion in this classification was that Pluto, which orbits in the cluttered, icy Kuiper belt, had not cleared the neighborhood around its orbit. This was a controversial decision sure to be revisited.

Pluto has three natural satellites, Charon, Hydra, and Nix. Because Charon's diameter is more than half the size of Pluto's and they orbit around a common center of gravity, it was common to speak of the Pluto-Charon system as a double planet. Charon, named for the boatman in Greek mythology who carried the souls of the dead across the river Styx, was discovered in 1978, while Hydra and Nix were both first seen in 2005. The New Horizons spacecraft, launched in January 2006 and scheduled to arrive at Pluto in 2015, will search for yet more new satellites.

Pluto is so distant (its average distance from the Sun is 39.6 astronomical units, or AU) that sunlight traveling at 299,792 km/sec (186,282.1 mi/sec) takes more than five hours to reach it. An observer standing on the dwarf planet's surface would see the Sun as an extremely bright star in the dark sky, providing Pluto with only 1/1600 the amount of sunlight reaching the Earth.

Pluto has a diameter less than half that of Mercury; it is about two-thirds the size of the Moon. Pluto's physical characteristics are unlike those of any of the planets. Pluto resembles most closely Neptune's icy satellite Triton, which implies a similar origin for these two bodies. Most scientists now believe that Pluto and Charon are large icy planetesimals left over from the formation of the giant outer planets of the solar system. Accordingly, Pluto can be interpreted to be the largest known member of the Kuiper belt (which, as discussed, includes the outer part of Pluto's orbit). Observations of Pluto show that it appears slightly red, though not as red as Mars or Io. Thus, the surface of Pluto cannot be composed simply of pure ices. Its overall reflectivity, or albedo, ranges from 0.3 to 0.5, as compared with 0.1 for the Moon and 0.8 for Triton.

The surface temperature of Pluto has proved very difficult to measure. Observations made from the Infrared Astronomical Satellite suggest values in the range of −228 to −215 °C (−379 to −355 °F), whereas measurements at radio wavelengths imply a range of −238 to −223 °C (−397 to −370 °F). The temperature certainly must vary over the surface, depending on the local reflectivity and solar zenith angle. There is also expected to be a seasonal decrease in incident solar energy by a factor of roughly three as Pluto moves from perihelion to aphelion.

The detection of methane ice on Pluto's surface made scientists confident that it had an atmosphere before one was actually discovered. The atmosphere was finally detected in 1988 when Pluto passed in front of a star as observed from the Earth. The light of the star was dimmed before disappearing entirely behind Pluto during the occultation. This proved that a thin, greatly distended atmosphere was present. Because that atmosphere must consist of vapors in equilibrium with their ices, small changes in temperature will have a large effect on the amount of gas in the atmosphere.

Comets

Comets are a class of small bodies orbiting the Sun and developing diffuse gaseous envelopes. They also often form long luminous tails when near the Sun. The comet makes a transient appearance in the sky and is often said to have a "hairy" tail. In fact, the word comes from the Greek *kometes*, meaning "hairy one," a description that fits the bright comets noticed by the ancients.

Despite their name, many comets do not develop tails. Moreover, a comet is not surrounded by nebulosity during most of its lifetime. The only permanent feature of a comet is its **nucleus**, which is a small body that may be seen as a starlike object in large telescopes when tail and nebulosity do not exist, particularly when the comet is still far away from the Sun. Two characteristics differentiate the cometary nucleus from a rocky body such as an asteroid or meteoroid—its orbit and its chemical nature. A comet's **orbit** is more eccentric (less circular); therefore, its distance to the Sun varies considerably. Its material contains more volatile components, with water ice the predominant compound. They have been described as "dirty snowballs" or "icy mudballs." When far from the Sun, however, a comet remains in its pristine state for eons without losing any volatile components because of the deep cold of space. For this reason, astronomers believe that pristine cometary nuclei may represent the oldest and best-preserved material in the solar system.

During a close passage near the Sun, the nucleus of a comet loses water vapor and other more volatile compounds, as well as dust dragged away by the sublimating gases. It is then surrounded by a transient dusty "atmosphere" that is steadily lost to space. This feature is the **coma**, which gives a comet its nebulous appearance.

The astronomer **Edmond Halley**, a friend of Isaac Newton, endeavored to compute the orbits of 24 comets for which he had found fairly accurate historical documents. Applying a method Newton had developed, Halley predicted that the comet that now bears his name would return to Earth in 1758, and that proved correct. Since its prediction by astronomers and its appearance in 1758/59, Comet Halley has reappeared three times—in 1835, 1910, and 1986.

Each century, a score of comets brighter than Comet Halley have been discovered. Many are **periodic** (returning) **comets** like Comet Halley, but their periods are extremely long (millennia or even scores or hundreds of millennia), and they have not left any identifiable trace in prehistory. Bright Comet Bennett (1970) will return in 17 centuries, whereas the spectacular Comet West (1976) will reappear in about 500,000 years. Among the comets that can easily be seen with the unaided eye, Comet Halley is the only one that returns in a single lifetime. About 200 comets whose periods are between 3 and 200 years are known, however. Unfortunately, they are or have become too faint to be readily seen without the aid of telescopes.

For faraway objects that contain volatile ices, the distinction between **asteroids and comets** becomes a matter of semantics because many orbits are unstable; an asteroid that comes closer to the Sun than usual may become a comet by producing a transient atmosphere that gives it a fuzzy appearance and that may develop into a tail. Some objects have been reclassified as a result of such occurrences. For example, asteroid 1990 UL3, which crosses the orbit of Jupiter, was reclassified as Comet P/Shoemaker-Levy 2 late in 1990. Conversely, it is suspected that some of the Earth-approaching asteroids (Amors, Apollos, and Atens) could be the extinct nuclei of comets that have now lost most of their volatile ices.

Measurements and Numbers

The International System of Units (SI)

Rapid advances in science and technology in the 19th and 20th centuries fostered the development of several overlapping systems of units of measurements as scientists improvised to meet the practical needs of their disciplines. The **General Conference on Weights and Measures** was chartered by international convention in 1875 to produce standards of physical measurement based upon an earlier international standard, the meter-kilogram-second (MKS) system. The convention calls for regular General Conference meetings to consider improvements or modifications in standards, an International Committee of Weights and Measures elected by the Conference (meets annually), and several consultative committees. **The International Bureau of Weights and Measures** (Bureau International des Poids et Mesures) at Sèvres, France, serves as a depository for the primary international standards and as a laboratory for certification and intercomparison of national standard copies.

The 1960 **International System** (universally abbreviated as **SI**, from *système international*) builds upon the MKS system. Its **seven basic units**, from which other units are derived, are currently defined as follows: the **meter**, defined as the distance traveled by light in a vacuum in 1/299,792,458 second; the **kilogram** (about 2.2 pounds avoirdupois), which equals 1,000 grams as defined by the international prototype kilogram of platinum-iridium in the keeping of the International Bureau of Weights and Measures; the **second**, the duration of 9,192,631,770 periods of radiation associated with a specified transition of the cesium-133 atom; the **ampere**, which is the current that, if maintained in two wires placed one meter apart in a vacuum, would produce a force of 2×10^{-7} newton per meter of length; the **candela**, defined as the intensity in a given direction of a source emitting radiation of frequency 540×10^{12} hertz and that has a radiant intensity in that direction of 1/683 watt per steradian; the **mole**, defined as containing as many elementary entities of a substance as there are atoms in 0.012 kilogram of carbon-12; and the **kelvin**, which is 1/273.16 of the thermodynamic temperature of the triple point (equilibrium among the solid, liquid, and gaseous phases) of pure water.

International Bureau of Weights and Measures Web site: <www.bipm.fr>.

Elemental and Derived SI Units and Symbols

Quantity	SI Units		
	UNIT	FORMULA/EXPRESSION IN BASE UNITS	SYMBOL
elemental units			
length	meter	—	m
mass	kilogram	—	kg
time	second	—	s
electric current	ampere	—	A
luminous intensity	candela	—	cd
amount of substance	mole	—	mol
thermodynamic temperature	kelvin	—	K
derived units			
acceleration	meter/second squared	m/s^2	
area	square meter	m^2	
capacitance	farad	$A \times s/V$	F
charge	coulomb	$A \times s$	C
Celsius temperature	degree Celsius	K	°C
density	kilogram/cubic meter	kg/m^3	
electric field strength	volt/meter	V/m	
electrical potential	volt	W/A	V
energy	joule	$N \times m$	J
force	newton	$kg \times m/s^2$	N
frequency	hertz	s^{-1}	Hz
illumination	lux	lm/m^2	lx
inductance	henry	$V \times s/A$	H
kinematic viscosity	square meter/second	m^2/s	
luminance	candela/square meter	cd/m^2	
luminous flux	lumen	$cd \times sr$	lm
magnetic field strength	ampere/meter	A/m	
magnetic flux	weber	$V \times s$	Wb
magnetic flux density	tesla	Wb/m^2	T
plane angle	radian	$m \times m^{-1}=1$	rad
power	watt	J/s	W
pressure	pascal (newton/square meter)	N/m^2	Pa
resistance	ohm	V/A	Ω
solid angle	steradian	$m^2 \times m^{-2}=1$	sr
stress	pascal (newton/square meter)	N/m^2	Pa
velocity	meter/second	m/s	
viscosity	newton-second/square meter	$N \times s/m^2$	
volume	cubic meter	m^3	

Conversion of Metric Weights and Measures

The International System of Units is a decimal system of weights and measures derived from and extending the metric system of units. Adopted by the 11th General Conference on Weights and Measures in 1960, it is abbreviated "SI" in all languages. Below are common equivalents and conversion factors for US customary and SI systems.

approximate common equivalents		conversions accurate within 10 parts per million	
1 inch	= 25 millimeters	inches × 25.4[1]	= millimeters
1 foot	= 0.3 meter	feet × 0.3048[1]	= meters
1 yard	= 0.9 meter	yards × 0.9144[1]	= meters
1 mile	= 1.6 kilometers	miles × 1.60934	= kilometers
1 square inch	= 6.5 sq. centimeters	square inches × 6.4516[1]	= square centimeters
1 square foot	= 0.09 square meter	square feet × 0.0929030	= square meters
1 square yard	= 0.8 square meter	square yards × 0.836127	= square meters
1 acre	= 0.4 hectare[2]	acres × 0.404686	= hectares
1 cubic inch	= 16 cubic centimeters	cubic inches × 16.3871	= cubic centimeters
1 cubic foot	= 0.03 cubic meter	cubic feet × 0.0283168	= cubic meters
1 cubic yard	= 0.8 cubic meter	cubic yards × 0.764555	= cubic meters
1 quart (liq)	= 1 liter[2]	quarts (liquid) × 0.946353	= liters
1 gallon	= 0.004 cubic meter	gallons × 0.00378541	= cubic meters
1 ounce (avdp)[3]	= 28 grams	ounces (avdp)[3] × 28.3495	= grams
1 pound (avdp)[3]	= 0.45 kilogram	pounds (avdp)[3] × 0.453592	= kilograms
1 horsepower	= 0.75 kilowatt	horsepower × 0.745700	= kilowatts
1 millimeter	= 0.04 inch	millimeters × 0.0393701	= inches
1 meter	= 3.3 feet	meters × 3.28084	= feet

Conversion of Metric Weights and Measures (continued)

1 meter	= 1.1 yards	meters × 1.09361	= yards
1 kilometer	= 0.6 mile (statute)	kilometers × 0.621371	= miles (statute)
1 square centimeter	= 0.16 square inch	square centimeters × 0.155000	= square inches
1 square meter	= 11 square feet	square meters × 10.7639	= square feet
1 square meter	= 1.2 square yards	square meters × 1.19599	= square yards
1 hectare[2]	= 2.5 acres	hectares × 2.47105	= acres
1 cubic centimeter	= 0.06 cubic inch	cubic centimeters × 0.0610237	= cubic inches
1 cubic meter	= 35 cubic feet	cubic meters × 35.3147	= cubic feet
1 cubic meter	= 1.3 cubic yards	cubic meters × 1.30795	= cubic yards
1 liter[2]	= 1 quart (liq)	liters × 1.05669	= quarts (liq)
1 cubic meter	= 264 gallons	cubic meters × 264.172	= gallons
1 gram	= 0.035 ounce (avdp)[3]	grams × 0.0352740	= ounces (avdp)[3]
1 kilogram	= 2.2 pounds (avdp)[3]	kilograms × 2.20462	= pounds (avdp)[3]
1 kilowatt	= 1.3 horsepower	kilowatts × 1.34102	= horsepower

[1]Exact.   [2]Common term not used in SI.   [3]avdp = avoirdupois.
Source: National Institute of Standards and Technology.

Tables of Equivalents: Metric System Units and Prefixes

base unit*

QUANTITY	NAME OF UNIT	SYMBOL
length	meter	m
area	square meter	square m, or m²
	are (100 square meters)	a
volume	cubic meter	cubic m, or m³
	stere (1 cubic meter)	s
mass	gram	g
	metric ton (1,000,000 grams)	t
capacity	liter	l
temperature	degree Celsius	°C

prefixes designating multiples and submultiples

PREFIX	SYMBOL	FACTOR BY WHICH UNIT IS MULTIPLIED		EXAMPLES
exa-	E	10^{18} =	1,000,000,000,000,000,000	
peta-	P	10^{15} =	1,000,000,000,000,000	
tera-	T	10^{12} =	1,000,000,000,000	
giga-	G	10^{9} =	1,000,000,000	
mega-	M	10^{6} =	1,000,000	megaton (Mt)
kilo-	k	10^{3} =	1,000	kilometer (km)
hecto-, hect-	h	10^{2} =	100	hectare (ha)
deca- dec-	da	10 =	10	decastere (das)
			1	
deci-	d	10^{-1} =	0.1	decigram (dg)
centi-, cent-	c	10^{-2} =	0.01	centimeter (cm)
milli-	m	10^{-3} =	0.001	milliliter (ml)
micro-, micr-	μ	10^{-6} =	0.000001	microgram (μg)
nano-	n	10^{-9} =	0.000000001	
pico-	p	10^{-12} =	0.000000000001	
femto-	f	10^{-15} =	0.000000000000001	
atto-	a	10^{-18} =	0.000000000000000001	

*The metric system of bases and prefixes has been applied to many other units, such as decibel (0.1 bel), kilowatt (1,000 watts), and microhm (one-millionth of an ohm).

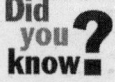
Did you know?

The US was an independent nation for 13 years before the Constitution was signed in 1789, the same year George Washington was elected the country's first president. In 1781, American Revolutionary leader John Hanson was elected by the Continental Congress "President of the United States in Congress Assembled." Hanson is thus referred to by some as the first US president, but he was a congressional presiding officer and had none of the presidential powers that would be granted under the Constitution.

British/US system (ft-lb-second, fps)

length

1 statute mi	= 5,280 ft	= 1,760 yd	= 320 rods	= 8 furlongs
1 nautical mi	= 6,076 ft	= 1.151 mi		
1 furlong	= 660 ft	= 220 yd	= 40 rods	= 1/8 mi
1 chain (Gunter's)	= 66 ft	= 22 yd	= 100 links	= 4 rods
1 rod	= 16.5 ft	= 5.5 yd	= 25 links	
1 fathom	= 6 ft	= 72 in		
1 yd	= 3 ft	= 36 in		
1 ft	= 12 in			
1 link (Gunter's)	= 0.66 ft	= 7.92 in		
1 hand	= 4 in			
1 mil	= 0.001 in			

area

1 sq mi	= 640 acres	= 102,400 sq rods	= 3,097,600 sq yd	= 27,878,400 sq ft
1 acre	= 10 sq chains	= 160 sq rods	= 4,840 sq yd	= 43,560 sq ft
1 sq ft	= 144 sq in			

volume

1 cu ft	= 1/27 cu yd	= 12 board ft	= 1,728 cu in
1 cu in	= 1/46,656 cu yd	= 1/1,728 cu ft	
1 acre-ft	= 43,560 cu ft	= 1,613 cu yd	
1 board ft	= 144 cu in	= 1/12 cu ft	= 1 super ft (lumber)
1 cord (US)	= 128 cu ft		

capacity

1 cu ft	= 7.481 gal (US)	= 6.229 gal (British)

liquid measure (US)

1 barrel, oil	= 42 gal (US)	= 34.97 gal (British)		
1 gal	= 0.833 gal (British)	= 4 quarts	= 231.00 cu in	= 128 fl oz
1 quart	= 1/4 gal	= 2 pints	= 57.75 cu in	= 32 fl oz
1 pint	= 1/8 gal	= 1/2 quart	= 28.88 cu in	= 16 fl oz
1 gill	= 1/32 gal	= 1/4 pint	= 7.22 cu in	= 4 fl oz
1 fl oz	= 1/128 gal	= 1/16 pint	= 1.80 cu in	

dry measure (US)

1 bushel	= 0.97 bushel (British)	= 4 pecks	= 2,150.4 cu in	= 1.24 cu ft
1 peck	= 1/4 bushel	= 8 quarts	= 537.6 cu in	= 0.31 cu ft
1 quart	= 1/32 bushel	= 2 pints	= 67.2 cu in	= 1/8 peck
1 pint	= 1/64 bushel	= 1/2 quart	= 33.6 cu in	

liquid and dry measure (British)

1 bushel	= 1.03 bushels (US)	= 8 gal	= 4 pecks	= 2,219.36 cu in	= 1.284 cu ft
1 peck	= 0.25 bushel	= 2 gal	= 8 quarts	= 554.84 cu in	
1 gal	= 1.20 gal (US)	= 4 quarts		= 277.42 cu in	
1 quart	= 0.30 gal	= 2 pints	= 1/8 peck	= 69.36 cu in	
1 pint	= 4.80 gills (US)	= 4 gills		= 34.68 cu in	= 20 fl oz
1 gill	= 1.20 gills (US)			= 8.67 cu in	= 5 fl oz
1 fl oz	= 0.96 fl oz (US)			= 1.73 cu in	

weight

1 short ton (US)	= 0.89 long ton	= 2,000 lbs	= 20 short cwt*
1 long ton (British)	= 1.12 short tons	= 2,240 lbs	= 22.4 short cwt*
1 short cwt* (US)	= 0.05 short ton	= 100 lbs	
1 long cwt* (British)	= 0.05 long ton	= 112 lbs	
1 stone (person)	= 0.14 short cwt*	= 14 lbs	
1 lb	= 0.07 stone (British)		
1 oz avdp†	= 437.50 grains	= 1/16 lb	= 0.911 oz troy
1 oz troy	= 480.00 grains	= 1/12 lb	= 1.097 oz
1 grain		= 0.0023 oz	= 0.0021 oz troy

*cwt = hundredweight.   †avdp = avoirdupois..

Electrical Units

UNIT	SYMBOL	ATTRIBUTE MEASURED	EXPRESSION IN OTHER UNITS (S = SECOND)
ampere	A	current	C/s or V/Ω

the basic electrical unit of the International System of Units (SI), since 1948 defined by the International Bureau of Weights and Measures as the constant current which, if maintained in two straight parallel conductors of infinite length, of negligible circular cross section, and placed one meter apart in a vacuum, would produce between these conductors a force equal to 2×10^{-7} newton per meter of length. One ampere is equal to a flow of one coulomb of electricity per second; or, the flow produced in a conductor with a resistance of one ohm by a potential difference of one volt.

farad	F	capacitance (ability to hold a charge)	A × s/V or C/V

the ability of two parallel, oppositely charged plates (a capacitor) to hold an electric charge equals one farad when one coulomb of electricity changes the potential between the plates by one volt.

coulomb	C	charge	A × s

the quantity of electricity transported in one second by a current of one ampere. Approximately equal to 6.24×10^{18} electrons.

watt	W	power	J/s or V × A

one joule of work performed per second; or, the power dissipated in an electrical conductor carrying one ampere current between points at one volt potential difference.

ohm	Ω	resistance	V/A or W/A^2

resistance of a circuit in which a potential difference of one volt produces a current of one ampere; or, the resistance in which one watt of power is dissipated when one ampere flows through it.

volt	V	potential	W/A or A × Ω

the difference in potential between two points in a conductor carrying one ampere current when the power dissipated between the points is one watt; or, the difference in potential between two points in a conductor across a resistance of one ohm when one ampere is flowing through it.

Temperature Equivalents

Instructions for converting °F into °C or K*, and °C into °F: Find the figure you wish to convert in the second column. If this figure is in °F, the corresponding temperature in °C and K will be found in the third and fourth columns; if the figure is in °C, the corresponding temperature in °F will be found in the first column. To convert a temperature range between two scales, rather than finding equivalent temperatures, see the temperature conversion instructions, below.

°FAHRENHEIT (°F)	FIGURE TO BE CONVERTED	°CELSIUS (°CENTIGRADE) (°C)	KELVIN (K)	°FAHRENHEIT (°F)	FIGURE TO BE CONVERTED	°CELSIUS (°CENTIGRADE) (°C)	KELVIN (K)
...	−459.67	−273.15	0	+46.4	+8	−13.33	+259.82
				+48.2	+9	−12.78	+260.37
...	−400	−240.00	+33.15				
...	−300	−184.44	+88.71	+50.0	+10	−12.22	+260.93
−459.67	−273.15	−169.53	+103.62	+68.0	+20	−6.67	+266.48
				+86.0	+30	−1.11	+272.04
−328.0	−200	−128.89	+144.26	+89.6	+32	0.00	+273.15
−148.0	−100	−73.33	+199.82	+104.0	+40	+4.44	+277.59
				+122.0	+50	+10.00	+283.15
−130.0	−90	−67.78	+205.37	+140.0	+60	+15.56	+288.71
−112.0	−80	−62.22	+210.93	+158.0	+70	+21.11	+294.26
−94.0	−70	−56.67	+216.48	+176.0	+80	+26.67	+299.82
−76.9	−60	−51.11	+222.04	+194.0	+90	+32.22	+305.37
−58.0	−50	−45.56	+227.59				
−40.0	−40	−40.00	+233.15	+212.0	+100	+37.78	+310.93
−22.0	−30	−34.44	+238.71	+392.0	+200	+93.33	+366.48
−4.0	−20	−28.89	+244.26	+572.0	+300	+148.89	+422.04
+14.0	−10	−23.33	+249.82	+752.0	+400	+204.44	+477.59
				+932.0	+500	+260.00	+533.15
+32.0	0	−17.78	+255.37	+1112.0	+600	+315.56	+588.71
+33.8	+1	−17.22	+255.93	+1292.0	+700	+371.11	+644.26
+35.6	+2	−16.67	+256.48	+1472.0	+800	+426.67	+699.82
+37.4	+3	−16.11	+257.04	+1652.0	+900	+482.22	+755.37
+39.2	+4	−15.56	+257.59				
+41.0	+5	−15.00	+258.15	+1832.0	+1000	+537.78	+810.93
+42.8	+6	−14.44	+258.71	+3632.0	+2000	+1093.33	+1366.45
+44.6	+7	−13.89	+259.26	+5432.0	+3000	+1648.89	+1922.05

Temperature Equivalents (continued)

All systems of measuring temperature in degrees or units (kelvins) on a scale are based on the interval between the freezing and boiling points of water and differ only in the number of degrees or units into which this interval is divided.

Fahrenheit: interval is divided into 180 degrees (32° to 212°); 0° is at 32° below the freezing point of water.

Rankine: degree is the same as the Fahrenheit degree; 0° is at absolute zero (the theoretical point at which a thermodynamic system has the lowest energy, –459.67 °F). Once common in engineering applications in the US, the Rankine scale is now rarely used.

Celsius: interval is divided into 100 degrees; 0° is at the freezing point of water.

Kelvin: interval is the same as the Celsius degree; 0 K is at absolute zero (the theoretical point at which a thermodynamic system has the lowest energy, –273.15 °C).

Réaumur: interval is divided into 80 degrees; 0° is at the freezing point of water. One of the earliest (1730) temperature scales in widespread use, the Réaumur scale had been supplanted by other scales by the late 19th century.

*temperature conversion instructions:***

°Fahrenheit	into	°Celsius	subtract 32, divide by 1.8**
°Celsius	into	°Fahrenheit	multiply by 1.8, add 32**
°Celsius	into	kelvin	add 273.15

**Because a kelvin is itself a unit of measurement, it is incorrect to use "degree" or the ° symbol with it, as is necessary with the units of the Rankine, Fahrenheit, Celsius, and Réaumur scales. One kelvin is equal to one degree Celsius. **Instructions are for finding equivalent temperatures; to find the equivalent number of degrees in a temperature range (e.g., tomorrow's temperature will be 11.0 °F, or 6.1 °C, warmer than today's temperature), omit the step of adding or subtracting 32.*

Cooking Measurements

MEASURE	CONVENTIONAL EQUIVALENTS*	METRIC EQUIVALENT
drop	1⁄60 teaspoon	0.08 ml
dash	⅛ teaspoon	0.62 ml
teaspoon	8 dashes; ⅓ tablespoon; ⅙ fluid ounce	4.93 ml
tablespoon	3 teaspoons; ½ fluid ounce	14.79 ml
ounce (weight)	1⁄16 pound	28.35 g
fluid ounce (volume)	2 tablespoons	29.57 ml
cup	8 fluid ounces; 16 tablespoons; ½ pint	236.59 ml
pound	16 ounces	453.6 g
pint	16 fluid ounces; 2 cups; ½ quart	473.18 ml
quart	32 fluid ounces; 4 cups; 2 pints; ¼ gallon	946.36 ml
gallon	128 fluid ounces; 16 cups; 8 pints; 4 quarts	3.785 l
peck	2 gallons	7.57 l
bushel	8 gallons; 4 pecks	30.28 l

**All ounce measurements are in US ounces or fluid ounces.*

OVEN TEMPERATURE EQUIVALENTS

°F	°C	AMERICAN OVEN TEMPERATURE TERMS	FRENCH OVEN TEMPERATURE TERMS AND THERMOSTAT SETTINGS	BRITISH "GAS MARK" OVEN THERMOSTAT SETTINGS
160	71		#1	
170	77			
200	93		très doux; étuve	
212	100			
221	105		#2	
225	107	very slow	doux	
230	110		#3	#¼ (241 °F)
250	121			
275	135			#½ (266 °F)
284	140	slow	moyen; modéré	#1 (291 °F)
300	149			
302	150		#4	
320	160			#2 (313 °F)
325	163			
350	177	moderate	assez chaud; bon four	#3 (336 °F)

Cooking Measurements (continued)

OVEN TEMPERATURE EQUIVALENTS (CONTINUED)

°F	°C	AMERICAN OVEN TEMPERATURE TERMS	FRENCH OVEN TEMPERATURE TERMS AND THERMOSTAT SETTINGS	BRITISH "GAS MARK" OVEN THERMOSTAT SETTINGS
356	180			#4 (358 °F)
375	190		#5	
390	200			#5 (379 °F)
400	·205			#6 (403 °F)
410	210	hot	chaud	
425	218		#6	#7 (424 °F)
428	220			
437	225			
450	232			#8 (446 °F)
475	246	very hot	très chaud; vif	#9 (469 °F)
500	260		#7	
525	274		#8	
550	288		#9	

Spirits Measure

Many specific volumes have varied over time and from place to place, but the proportional relationships within families of measures have generally remained the same. All ounce measures are in US fluid ounces.

MEASURE	CONVENTIONAL EQUIVALENTS	METRIC EQUIVALENT
pony	0.75 oz = ¾ shot= ½ jigger	22.17 ml
shot/ounce/finger	1 oz = 1⅓ ponies = ⅔ jigger	29.57 ml
jigger	1.5 oz = 2 ponies = 1½ shots	44.36 ml
double	2 oz = 2 shots	59.15 ml
triple	3 oz = 3 shots	88.72 ml
noggin/imperial gill/drink (whiskey)	4.8 oz	142.1 ml
pint	16 oz = ⅝ fifth = ½ quart	473.2 ml
quarter yard	20 oz = 1¼ pints	591.5 ml
bottle (champagne or other wine)	about 25.5 oz or ⅙ imperial gallon	750 ml (industry standard)
fifth	25.6 oz = ⅘ quart = ⅕ gallon	757.1 ml
quart	32 oz = ½ magnum = ¼ gallon	946.3 ml
half yard	40 oz = 2½ pints	1.182 l
magnum	2 bottles (champagne or other wine)	1.5 l
magnum	64 oz = 2 quarts = ½ gallon	1.893 l
yard	80 oz = 5 pints	2.365 l
jeroboam	4 bottles (champagne or other wine)	3 l
gallon/double magnum	128 oz = 4 quarts = 5 fifths = 2 magnums	3.785 l
rehoboam	6 bottles (champagne or other wine)	4 l
imperial gallon	1.20 gallons = ⅖ barn gallon = ¹⁄₁₀ anker	4.546 l
ale/beer gallon	1.22 gallons	4.620 l
methuselah	8 bottles (champagne or other wine)	6 l
salmanazar	12 bottles (champagne or other wine) .	9 l
barn gallon	2½ imperial gallons = ¼ anker	11.37 l
balthazar	16 bottles (champagne or other wine)	12 l
half keg	5 gallons (type varies)	varies
nebuchadnezzar	20 bottles (champagne or other wine)	15 l
firkin	9 gallons	34.07 l
keg	10 gallons (type varies)	varies
anker	60 bottles = 10 imperial gallons = 4 barn gallons	45.46 l
runlet/rundlet/rudlet	144 pints = 72 quarts = 18 gallons = 2 firkins	68.14 l
octave	15.75 imperial gallons = ⅛ butt (wine)	71.60 l
British bottle	126 bottles = 21 imperial gallons	95.47 l
aum	120 quarts = 30 gallons	113.6 l
barrel (wine)	126 quarts = 31½ gallons = ¾ tierce	119.2 l
barrel (ale/beer)	144 quarts = 36 gallons = ½ puncheon (ale/beer)	136.3 l
tierce	168 quarts = 42 gallons = ½ puncheon (wine)	159.0 l
British hogshead (ale/beer)	54 imperial gallons = ½ butt (ale/beer) = ¼ tun (ale/beer)	245.5 l
puncheon (ale/beer)	72 gallons = 2 barrels (ale/beer)	272.5 l
British hogshead (wine)	63 imperial gallons = ½ butt (wine) = ¼ tun (wine)	286.4 l
puncheon (wine)	84 gallons = 2 tierces	318.0 l
butt/pipe (ale/beer)	108 imperial gallons = ½ tun (ale/beer)	491.0 l
butt/pipe (wine)	126 imperial gallons = ½ tun (wine)	572.8 l
tun (ale/beer)	216 imperial gallons = 4 British hogsheads (ale/beer) = 2 butts (ale/beer)	982.0 l
tun (wine)	252 imperial gallons = 12 British bottles = 2 butts (wine)	1,146 l

Playing Cards and Dice Chances

Blackjack

Number of two-card combinations in a 52-card deck (where aces equal 11 and face cards equal 10) for each number between 13 and 21

Approximate chances of various hands reaching or exceeding 21

TOTAL WITH TWO CARDS	POSSIBLE COMBINATIONS FROM 52 CARDS
21	64
20	136
19	80
18	86
17	96
16	86
15	96
14	102
13	118

TOTAL IN HAND BEFORE DEAL (TWO OR MORE CARDS)	CHANCE OF REACHING A COUNT OF 17 TO 21 (%)	CHANCE OF EXCEEDING 21	
		ONE CARD (%)	ANY NUMBER OF CARDS (%)
16	38	62	62
15	42	54	58
14	44	46	56
13	48	38	52

Poker

Number of ways to reach and odds of reaching various five-card combinations on a single deal (52-card deck, no wild cards)

HAND	NUMBER OF COMBINATIONS	ODDS OF RECEIVING ON A SINGLE DEAL
royal flush	4	1 in 649,740
straight flush	36	1 in 72,193
four of a kind	624	1 in 4,165
full house	3,744	1 in 694
flush	5,108	1 in 509
straight	10,200	1 in 255
three of a kind	54,912	1 in 47
two pairs	123,552	1 in 21
one pair	1,098,240	1 in 2

Dice

Probabilities of two-die totals

TWO-DIE TOTAL	NUMBER OF COMBINATIONS	PROBABILITY (%)	TWO-DIE TOTAL	NUMBER OF COMBINATIONS	PROBABILITY (%)
2	1	2.78	8	5	13.89
3	2	5.56	9	4	11.11
4	3	8.33	10	3	8.33
5	4	11.11	11	2	5.56
6	5	13.89	12	1	2.78
7	6	16.67	total	36	100[1]

[1] Detail does not add to total because of rounding.

Ancient Measures

The standard unit of measure is listed first, with a rough modern equivalent in parentheses. Often, standard units varied over time, so a range is sometimes given. The subdivisions below relate to the standard unit of measure given first.

CULTURE	LENGTH	WEIGHT	LIQUID
Egyptian	cubit (524 mm; 20.62 in)	kite (4.5–29.9 g; 0.16–1.05 oz)	cubic cubit (0.14 cubic m; 37 gal)[1]
	digit (1/28 of a cubit)	deben (10 kites)	khar
	palm (4 digits)	sep (10 debens)	hekat
	hand (5 digits)		hin
	small span (12 digits, or 3 palms)		ro
	large span (14 digits, or 1/2 cubit)		
	t'ser (16 digits, or 4 palms)		
	small cubit (24 digits, or 6 palms)		
Babylonian	kus[2] (530 mm; 20.9 in)	mina (640–978 g; 23–34 oz)	ka (99–102 cubic mm; 3.9–4.0 cubic in)
	foot (2/3 kus)	shekel	gur (300 ka)
	shusi (1/30 kus)		

CULTURE	LENGTH	WEIGHT	LIQUID
Hebrew[3]		sacred mina (60 shekels)	bat[4]
		sacred talent (3,000 shekels, or 50 sacred minas)	hin
			log
		Talmudic mina (25 shekels)	
		Talmudic talent (1,500 shekels, or 60 Talmudic minas)	
Greek	finger (19.3 mm; 0.76 in)	talent (25.8 kg; 56.9 lb)	metretes (39.4 l; 10.4 gal)
	foot (16 fingers)		
	Olympic cubit (24 fingers)		
Roman	foot (subdivided into the uncia [plural unciae; $\frac{1}{12}$ ft])	libra (327.45 g; 11.55 oz)	sextarius (0.53 l; 0.14 gal)
	pace, or double step (5 ft)	uncia ($\frac{1}{12}$ lb)	amphora (48 sextarii)
	mille passus (1,000 paces)		
Chinese[5]	chih (25 cm; 9.8 in)	shih, or tan (60 kg; 132 lb)	
	chang (3 m; 9.8 ft)		

[1]Measures given below the cubic cubit run from small to large. [2]Also called the Babylonian cubit. [3]The Hittites, Assyrians, Phoenicians, and Hebrews derived their systems from the Babylonians and Egyptians. Hebrew standards were based on the relationship between the mina, the talent (the basic unit), and the shekel. [4]Volumes are not definitely known but are listed from largest to smallest. [5]The Chinese system of measurement exhibited all the principal characteristics of the Western. It was, however, fundamentally chaotic in that there was no relationship between different types of units, such as those of length and those of volume. It also fluctuated from region to region. The first emperor of China, Shi Huangdi (221–210/09 BC), fixed the basic units given here.

Roman Numerals

Seven numeral-characters compose the Roman numeral system. When a numeral appears with a line above it, it represents the base value multiplied by 1,000. However, because Roman numerals are now seldom utilized for values beyond 4,999, this convention is no longer in use.

ARABIC	ROMAN	ARABIC	ROMAN	ARABIC	ROMAN	ARABIC	ROMAN
1	I	15	XV	70	LXX	1,000	M
2	II	16	XVI	80	LXXX	1,001	MI
3	III	17	XVII	90	XC	1,002	MII
4	IV	18	XVIII	100	C	1,003	MIII
5	V	19	XIX	101	CI	1,900	MCM
6	VI	20	XX	102	CII	2,000	MM
7	VII	21	XXI	200	CC	2,001	MMI
8	VIII	22	XXII	300	CCC	2,002	MMII
9	IX	23	XXIII	400	CD	2,100	MMC
10	X	24	XXIV	500	D	3,000	MMM
11	XI	30	XXX	600	DC	4,000	MMMM or MV̄
12	XII	40	XL	700	DCC	5,000	V̄
13	XIII	50	L	800	DCCC		
14	XIV	60	LX	900	CM		

Mathematical Formulas

The ratio of the circumference of a circle to its diameter is π (3.14159265358979323846264338327 9..., generally rounded to $\frac{22}{7}$ or 3.1416). It occurs in various mathematical problems involving the lengths of arcs or other curves, the areas of surfaces, and the volumes of many solids.

	SHAPE	ACTION	FORMULA
circumference	circle	multiply diameter by π	πd
area	circle	multiply radius squared by π	πr^2
	rectangle	multiply height by length	hl
	sphere surface	multiply radius squared by π by 4	$4\pi r^2$
	square	length of one side squared	s^2
	trapezoid	parallel side length A + parallel side length B multiplied by height and divided by 2	$(A+B)h/2$
	triangle	multiply base by height and divide by 2	$hb/2$
volume	cone	multiply base radius squared by π by height and divide by 3	$br^2\pi h/3$
	cube	length of one edge cubed	$a3$
	cylinder	multiply base radius squared by π by height	$br^2\pi h$
	pyramid	multiply base area by height and divide by 3	$hb/3$
	sphere	multiply radius cubed by π by 4 and divide by 3	$4\pi r^3/3$

Large Numbers

The American system of numeration for denominations above one million was modeled on a French system, but subsequently the French system changed to correspond to the German and British systems. In recent years, British usage reflects widespread and increasing use of the values of the American system. In the American system each of the denominations above 1,000 millions (the American billion) is 1,000 times the preceding one (one trillion = 1,000 billions; one quadrillion = 1,000 trillions). In the British system the first denomination above 1,000 millions (the British milliard) is 1,000 times the preceding one, but each of the denominations above 1,000 milliards (the British billion) is 1,000,000 times the preceding one (one trillion = 1,000,000 billions; one quadrillion = 1,000,000 trillions).

Source: Merriam-Webster's Collegiate Dictionary, Eleventh Edition, Merriam-Webster, Inc., 2003.

AMERICAN NAME	VALUE IN POWERS OF TEN	NUMBER OF ZEROS	BRITISH NAME	VALUE IN POWERS OF TEN	NUMBER OF ZEROS
billion	10^9	9	milliard	10^9	9
trillion	10^{12}	12	billion	10^{12}	12
quadrillion	10^{15}	15	trillion	10^{18}	18
quintillion	10^{18}	18	quadrillion	10^{24}	24
sextillion	10^{21}	21	quintillion	10^{30}	30
septillion	10^{24}	24	sextillion	10^{36}	36
octillion	10^{27}	27	septillion	10^{42}	42
nonillion	10^{30}	30	octillion	10^{48}	48
decillion	10^{33}	33	nonillion	10^{54}	54
undecillion	10^{36}	36	decillion	10^{60}	60
duodecillion	10^{39}	39	undecillion	10^{66}	66
tredecillion	10^{42}	42	duodecillion	10^{72}	72
quattuordecillion	10^{45}	45	tredecillion	10^{78}	78
quindecillion	10^{48}	48	quattuordecillion	10^{84}	84
sexdecillion	10^{51}	51	quindecillion	10^{90}	90
septendecillion	10^{54}	54	sexdecillion	10^{96}	96
octodecillion	10^{57}	57	septendecillion	10^{102}	102
novemdecillion	10^{60}	60	octodecillion	10^{108}	108
vigintillion	10^{63}	63	novemdecillion	10^{114}	114
centillion	10^{303}	303	vigintillion	10^{120}	120
			centillion	10^{600}	600

Decimal Equivalents of Common Fractions

4THS	8THS	16THS	32NDS	DECIMAL	4THS	8THS	16THS	32NDS	DECIMAL
				0.015625			15	30	0.9375
			1	0.03125				31	0.96875
		1	2	0.0625	4	8	16	32	1
			3	0.09375					
	1	2	4	0.125					
			5	0.15625					
		3	6	0.1875					
			7	0.21875		**3RDS**	**6THS**	**12THS**	**DECIMAL**
1	2	4	8	0.25				1	0.833334
			9	0.28125			1	2	0.166667
		5	10	0.3125				3	0.25
			11	0.34375		1	2	4	0.333334
	3	6	12	0.375				5	0.416667
			13	0.40625			3	6	0.5
		7	14	0.4375				7	0.583333
			15	0.46875		2	4	8	0.666667
2	4	8	16	0.5				9	0.75
			17	0.53125			5	10	0.833333
		9	18	0.5625				11	0.916667
			19	0.59375			6	12	1
	5	10	20	0.625					
			21	0.65625					
		11	22	0.6875		**5THS**	**DECIMAL**	**7THS**	**DECIMAL**
			23	0.71875		1	0.2	1	0.142857
3	6	12	24	0.75		2	0.4	2	0.285714
			25	0.78125		3	0.6	3	0.428571
		13	26	0.8125		4	0.8	4	0.571428
			27	0.84375		5	1	5	0.714285
	7	14	28	0.875				6	0.857142
			29	0.90625				7	1

Periodic Table of the Elements

The periodic table arranges the elements into groups (vertically) of elements sharing common physical and chemical characteristics and into periods (horizontally) of sequentially increasing atomic number and electron-shell configuration. Elements 112–116 and 118 have been created experimentally and have temporary names. Atomic weights in parentheses indicate the number of the most stable isotope of a radioactive element.

1																	18
1 H	2											13	14	15	16	17	2 He
3 Li	4 Be											5 B	6 C	7 N	8 O	9 F	10 Ne
11 Na	12 Mg	3	4	5	6	7	8	9	10	11	12	13 Al	14 Si	15 P	16 S	17 Cl	18 Ar
19 K	20 Ca	21 Sc	22 Ti	23 V	24 Cr	25 Mn	26 Fe	27 Co	28 Ni	29 Cu	30 Zn	31 Ga	32 Ge	33 As	34 Se	35 Br	36 Kr
37 Rb	38 Sr	39 Y	40 Zr	41 Nb	42 Mo	43 Tc	44 Ru	45 Rh	46 Pd	47 Ag	48 Cd	49 In	50 Sn	51 Sb	52 Te	53 I	54 Xe
55 Cs	56 Ba	57 La	72 Hf	73 Ta	74 W	75 Re	76 Os	77 Ir	78 Pt	79 Au	80 Hg	81 Tl	82 Pb	83 Bi	84 Po	85 At	86 Rn
87 Fr	88 Ra	89 Ac	104 Rf	105 Db	106 Sg	107 Bh	108 Hs	109 Mt	110 Ds	111 Rg	112 Uub	113 Uut	114 Uuq	115 Uup	116 Uuh		118 Uuo

Lanthanide Series

58 Ce	59 Pr	60 Nd	61 Pm	62 Sm	63 Eu	64 Gd	65 Tb	66 Dy	67 Ho	68 Er	69 Tm	70 Yb	71 Lu

Actinide Series

90 Th	91 Pa	92 U	93 Np	94 Pu	95 Am	96 Cm	97 Bk	98 Cf	99 Es	100 Fm	101 Md	102 No	103 Lr

Element	Symbol	Atomic no.	Atomic weight	Element	Symbol	Atomic no.	Atomic weight
Actinium	Ac	89	(227)	Molybdenum	Mo	42	95.94
Aluminum	Al	13	26.98154	Neodymium	Nd	60	144.242
Americium	Am	95	(243)	Neon	Ne	10	20.1797
Antimony	Sb	51	121.760	Neptunium	Np	93	(237)
Argon	Ar	18	39.948	Nickel	Ni	28	58.6934
Arsenic	As	33	74.92160	Niobium	Nb	41	92.90638
Astatine	At	85	(210)	Nitrogen	N	7	14.0067
Barium	Ba	56	137.327	Nobelium	No	102	(259)
Berkelium	Bk	97	(247)	Osmium	Os	76	190.23
Beryllium	Be	4	9.01218	Oxygen	O	8	15.9994
Bismuth	Bi	83	208.98040	Palladium	Pd	46	106.42
Bohrium	Bh	107	(272)	Phosphorus	P	15	30.97376
Boron	B	5	10.811	Platinum	Pt	78	195.084
Bromine	Br	35	79.904	Plutonium	Pu	94	(244)
Cadmium	Cd	48	112.411	Polonium	Po	84	(209)
Calcium	Ca	20	40.078	Potassium	K	19	39.0983
Californium	Cf	98	(251)	Praseodymium	Pr	59	140.90765
Carbon	C	6	12.0107	Promethium	Pm	61	(145)
Cerium	Ce	58	140.116	Protactinium	Pa	91	231.03588
Cesium	Cs	55	132.90545	Radium	Ra	88	(226)
Chlorine	Cl	17	35.453	Radon	Rn	86	(222)
Chromium	Cr	24	51.9961	Rhenium	Re	75	186.207
Cobalt	Co	27	58.93320	Rhodium	Rh	45	102.90550
Copper	Cu	29	63.546	Roentgenium	Rg	111	(280)
Curium	Cm	96	(247)	Rubidium	Rb	37	85.4678
Darmstadtium	Ds	110	(281)	Ruthenium	Ru	44	101.07
Dubnium	Db	105	(268)	Rutherfordium	Rf	104	(267)
Dysprosium	Dy	66	162.500	Samarium	Sm	62	150.36
Einsteinium	Es	99	(252)	Scandium	Sc	21	44.9559
Erbium	Er	68	167.259	Seaborgium	Sg	106	(271)
Europium	Eu	63	151.964	Selenium	Se	34	78.96
Fermium	Fm	100	(257)	Silicon	Si	14	28.0855
Fluorine	F	9	18.99840	Silver	Ag	47	107.8682
Francium	Fr	87	(223)	Sodium	Na	11	22.98977
Gadolinium	Gd	64	157.25	Strontium	Sr	38	87.62
Gallium	Ga	31	69.723	Sulfur	S	16	32.065
Germanium	Ge	32	72.64	Tantalum	Ta	73	180.94788
Gold	Au	79	196.96657	Technetium	Tc	43	(98)
Hafnium	Hf	72	178.49	Tellurium	Te	52	127.60
Hassium	Hs	108	(270)	Terbium	Tb	65	158.92535
Helium	He	2	4.00260	Thallium	Tl	81	204.3833
Holmium	Ho	67	164.93032	Thorium	Th	90	232.03806
Hydrogen	H	1	1.00794	Thulium	Tm	69	168.93421
Indium	In	49	114.818	Tin	Sn	50	118.710
Iodine	I	53	126.90447	Titanium	Ti	22	47.867
Iridium	Ir	77	192.217	Tungsten (wolfram)	W	74	183.85
Iron	Fe	26	55.845	Ununbium	Uub	112	(285)
Krypton	Kr	36	83.798	Ununhexium	Uuh	116	(293)
Lanthanum	La	57	138.90547	Ununoctium	Uuo	118	(294)
Lawrencium	Lr	103	(262)	Ununpentium	Uup	115	(288)
Lead	Pb	82	207.2	Ununquadium	Uuq	114	(289)
Lithium	Li	3	6.941	Ununtrium	Uut	113	(284)
Lutetium	Lu	71	174.967	Uranium	U	92	238.02891
Magnesium	Mg	12	24.3050	Vanadium	V	23	50.9415
Manganese	Mn	25	54.93805	Xenon	Xe	54	131.293
Meitnerium	Mt	109	(276)	Ytterbium	Yb	70	173.04
Mendelevium	Md	101	(258)	Yttrium	Y	39	88.90585
Mercury	Hg	80	200.59	Zinc	Zn	30	65.409
				Zirconium	Zr	40	91.224

Applied Science

Chemistry

Chemistry is the science that deals with the properties, composition, and structure of substances (defined as elements and compounds), the transformations that they undergo, and the energy that is released or absorbed during these processes. Every substance, whether naturally occurring or artificially produced, consists of one or more of the hundred-odd species of atoms that have been identified as elements. Although these atoms, in turn, are composed of more elementary particles, they are the basic building blocks of chemical substances; there is no quantity of oxygen, mercury, or gold, for example, smaller than an atom of that substance. Chemistry, therefore, is concerned not with the subatomic domain but with the properties of atoms and the laws governing their combinations and with how the knowledge of these properties can be used to achieve specific purposes.

Common Alloys

ALLOY	COMPOSITION	ALLOY	COMPOSITION
brass	55% copper, 45% zinc	pewter	tin, antimony, copper
bronze	copper, tin	solder	tin, lead
cast iron	iron, carbon, silicon, manganese, trace impurities	stainless steel	iron, carbon, chromium, nickel
		steel	iron, carbon
cupronickel	copper, nickel	sterling silver	silver, copper

Physics

Physics is the science that deals with the structure of matter and the interactions between the fundamental constituents of the observable universe. The basic physical science, its aim is the discovery and formulation of the fundamental laws of nature. In the broadest sense, physics (from the Greek physikos) is concerned with all aspects of nature on both the macroscopic and submicroscopic levels. Its scope of study encompasses not only the behavior of objects under the action of given forces but also the nature and origin of gravitational, electromagnetic, and nuclear force fields. Its ultimate objective is the formulation of a few comprehensive principles that bring together and explain all such disparate phenomena. Physics can, at base, be defined as the science of matter, motion, and energy. Its laws are typically expressed with economy and precision in the language of mathematics.

Weight, Mass, and Density

Mass, strictly defined, is the quantitative measure of inertia, the resistance a body offers to a change in its speed or position when force is applied to it. The greater the mass of a body, the smaller the change produced by an applied force. In more practical terms, it is the measure of the amount of material in an object, and in common usage is often expressed as weight. However, the mass of an object is constant regardless of its position, while weight varies according to gravitational pull.

In the International System of Units (SI, the metric system), the kilogram is the standard unit of mass, defined as equaling the mass of the international prototype of the kilogram, currently a platinum-iridium cylinder kept at Sèvres, near Paris, France; it is roughly equal to the mass of 1,000 cubic centimeters of pure water at the temperature of its maximum density. In the US customary system, the unit is the slug, defined as the mass which a one pound force can accelerate at a rate of one foot per second per second, which is the same as the mass of an object weighing 32.17 pounds on the earth's surface.

Weight is the gravitational force of attraction on an object, caused by the presence of a massive second object, such as the Earth or Moon. Weight is the product of an object's mass and the acceleration of gravity at the point where the object is located. A given object will have the same mass on the Earth's surface, on the Moon, or in the absence of gravity, while weight on the Moon would be about one sixth of its weight on the Earth's surface, because of the Moon's smaller gravitational pull (due in turn to the Moon's smaller mass and radius), and in the absence of gravity the object would have no weight at all.

Weight is measured in units of force, not mass, though in practice units of mass (such as the kilogram) are often substituted because of mass's relatively constant relation to weight on the Earth's surface. The weight of a body can be obtained by multiplying the mass by the acceleration of gravity. In SI, weight is expressed in newtons, or the force required to impart an acceleration of one meter per second per second to a mass of one kilogram. In the US customary system, it is expressed in pounds.

Density is the mass per unit volume of a material substance. It offers a convenient means of obtaining the mass of a body from its volume, or vice versa; the mass is equal to the volume multiplied by the density, while the volume is equal to the mass divided by the density. In SI, density is expressed in kilograms per cubic meter.

Communications

Introduction to the Internet

The **Internet** is a dynamic collection of computer networks that has revolutionized communications and methods of commerce by enabling those networks around the world to interact with each other. Sometimes referred to as a "**network of networks**," the Internet was developed in the United States in the 1970s but was not widely used by the general public until the early 1990s. By early 2007 approximately 1.1 billion people, or roughly 17% of the world's population, were estimated to have access to the Internet. It is widely assumed that at least half of the world's population will have some form of Internet access by 2010 and that wireless access will play a growing role.

The Internet is so powerful and general that it can be used for almost any purpose that depends on the processing of information, and it is accessible by every individual who connects to one of its constituent networks. It supports human communication via **electronic mail** (e-mail), real-time "chat rooms," instant messaging (IM), newsgroups, and audio and video transmission and allows people to work collaboratively at many different locations. It supports access to information by many applications, including the **World Wide Web**, which uses text and graphical presentations. Publishing has been revolutionized, as whole novels and reference works are available on the Web, and periodicals, including data prepared daily for an individual subscriber (such as stock market reports or news summaries), are also common. The Internet has attracted a large and growing number of "e-businesses" (including subsidiaries of traditional "brick-and-mortar" companies) that carry out most of their sales and services over the Internet.

While the precise structure of the future Internet is not yet clear, many directions of growth seem apparent. One is the increased availability of wireless access, enabling better real-time use of web-managed information. Another future development is toward higher backbone and network access speeds. Backbone data rates of 10 billion bits (10 gigabits) per second are readily available today, but data rates of 1 trillion bits (1 terabit) per second or higher will eventually become commercially feasible. At very high data rates, high-resolution video, for example, would occupy only a small fraction of available bandwidth, and remaining bandwidth could be used to transmit auxiliary information about the data being sent, which in turn would enable rapid customization of displays and prompt resolution of certain local queries.

Communications connectivity will be a key function of a future Internet as more machines and devices are interconnected. Since the Internet Engineering Task Force published its 128-bit IP address standard in 1998, the increased number of available addresses (2^{128}, as opposed to 2^{32} under the previous standard) allowed almost every electronic device imaginable to be assigned a unique address. Thus the expressions "wired" office, home, and car may all take on new meanings, even if the access is really wireless.

Growth of Internet Use

Sources: International Telecommunications Union, Yearbook of Statistics; ICT Statistics Database.

YEAR	US USERS	WORLD USERS	YEAR	US USERS	WORLD USERS
1994	13,000,000	22,000,000	2000	124,000,000	390,251,600
1995	25,000,000	28,700,000	2001	142,823,000	489,924,200
1996	45,000,000	70,000,000	2002	159,000,000	618,434,100
1997	60,000,000	116,000,000	2003	161,632,400	718,772,300
1998	84,587,000	171,587,000	2004	185,000,000	851,804,400
1999	102,000,000	275,518,600	2005	197,800,000	980,386,700

Worldwide Cellular Mobile Telephone Subscribers, 2005

Source: International Telecommunication Union, ICT Statistics Database.

COUNTRY	SUBSCRIBERS	SUBSCRIBERS PER 1,000 RESIDENTS	COUNTRY	SUBSCRIBERS	SUBSCRIBERS PER 1,000 RESIDENTS
China	393,406,000	299	Indonesia	46,910,000	211
United States	213,000,000	714	Turkey	43,609,000	596
Russia	120,000,000	836	Spain	41,327,900	968
Japan	96,484,000	753	South Korea	38,342,300	794
India	90,000,000	82	Philippines	34,779,000	413
Brazil	86,210,000	463	South Africa	33,960,000	716
Germany	79,200,000	958	Poland	29,166,400	757
Italy	72,200,000	1,243	Thailand	27,378,700	430
United Kingdom	65,500,000	1,098	Taiwan	22,171,000	974
			Argentina	22,156,400	574
France	48,099,000	795	Colombia	21,850,000	479
Mexico	47,141,000	440	Malaysia	19,545,000	752

Growth of Cell Phone Use in the US

Estimated number of cellular mobile telephone subscribers in the US, 1995–2006. Source: CTIA-The Wireless Association's Annualized Wireless Industry Survey Results December 1985–December 2006.

YEAR	SUBSCRIBERS	YEAR	SUBSCRIBERS	YEAR	SUBSCRIBERS	YEAR	SUBSCRIBERS
1995	33,786,000	1998	69,209,000	2001	128,375,000	2004	182,140,000
1996	44,043,000	1999	86,047,000	2002	140,767,000	2005	207,896,000
1997	55,312,000	2000	109,478,000	2003	158,722,000	2006	233,041,000

Aerospace Technology

Space Exploration

Three men were the first scientists to conceive pragmatically of spaceflight: the Russian **Konstantin Tsiolkovsky**, the American **Robert Goddard**, and the German **Hermann Oberth**. Technology in the early 20th century, however, was a long way from the level required for rocket-powered flight. Nonetheless, the theory and dynamics of such flights were rigorously studied. By the end of World War II, the German development of rocket propulsion for aircraft and guided missiles (notably the V-2) had reached a high level. With the German surrender in 1945, the US and its Allies fell heir to the technical knowledge of rocket power developed by the Germans. The technical director of the German missile effort, **Wernher von Braun**, and some 150 of his top aides surrendered to US troops. Most emigrated to the US, where they assembled and launched V-2 missiles that had been captured and shipped there. The USSR carried out an unpublicized but extensive and likely similar program; Britain and France conducted smaller programs.

In both the US and the USSR the development of **military missile technology** was essential to the achievement of satellite flight. Preparations for the International Geophysical Year (IGY, 1957–58) stimulated discussion of the possibility of launching **artificial Earth satellites** for scientific investigations. Both the US and the USSR became determined to prepare scientific satellites for launching during the IGY. While the US was still developing a space launch vehicle, the USSR startled the world by placing **Sputnik 1** in orbit on 4 Oct 1957. This was followed a month later by **Sputnik 2** carrying a live dog. The failure by the US to launch its small payload on 6 Dec 1957 heightened that nation's political discomfiture in view of its supposed advanced status in science. Following debates on the necessity of achieving parity, the US government established the **National Aeronautics and Space Administration (NASA)** in 1958. Since that time, NASA has conducted virtually all major aspects of the US space program.

The first successful US satellite, **Explorer 1**, was launched about 4 months after Sputnik 1. During the next decades the two nations participated in a space race, conducting thousands of successful launches of spacecraft of all varieties including scientific-research,

Significant space programs and missions:

Sputnik (Russian for "fellow traveler")
Years launched: 1957–58. **Country or space agency:** USSR. **Designation:** 1 through 3 (first series). **Not manned. Events of note:** Sputnik 1 was the first satellite to be successfully launched into space; Sputnik 2 carried a small dog named Laika ("Barker"); Sputnik 3 became the first multipurpose space-science satellite.

communications, meteorological, remote-sensing, military-reconnaissance, early-warning, and navigation satellites, lunar and planetary probes, and manned craft. The USSR launched the first human, **Yury Gagarin**, into orbit around Earth on 12 Apr 1961. On 20 July 1969, the US landed two men, **Neil Armstrong** and **Edwin ("Buzz") Aldrin**, on the surface of the Moon as part of the **Apollo 11** mission. On 12 Apr 1981, the 20th anniversary of manned space flight, the US launched the first reusable manned space transportation system, the space shuttle. From the 1960s the European nations, Japan, India, and other countries have formed their own agencies for space exploration and development. The **European Space Agency (ESA)** consists of 15 member nations. Private corporations, too, offer space launches for communications and remote-sensing satellites.

In the post-Apollo decades, while the US focused much of its manned space program on the **shuttle**, the USSR concentrated on launching a series of increasingly sophisticated Earth-orbiting **space stations**, beginning with the world's first in 1971. Station crews, who were carried up in two- and three-person spacecraft, carried out mostly scientific missions while gaining experience in living and working for long periods in the space environment. After the USSR was dissolved in 1991, its space program was continued by Russia on a much smaller scale owing to economic constraints. The US launched a space station in 1973 using surplus Apollo hardware and conducted shuttle missions to a Russian station, Mir, in the 1990s. In 1998, at the head of a 16-nation consortium and with Russia as a major partner, it began in-orbit assembly of the **International Space Station (ISS)**, using the shuttle and Russian expendable launch vehicles to ferry the facility's modular components and crews into space. In addition to manned and unmanned lunar exploration, space exploration programs have included deep-space robotic missions to the planets, their moons, and smaller bodies such as comets and asteroids. Also important has been the development of unmanned space-based astronomical observatories, which allow observation of near and distant cosmic objects above the filtering and distorting effects of Earth's atmosphere.

Vanguard
Years launched: 1958–59. **Country or space agency:** US. **Designation:** 1 through 3. **Events of note:** The first attempted Vanguard launch, hastily mounted in December 1957 after the USSR's Sputnik successes, failed with the launch vehicle's explosion.

Explorer
Years launched: 1958–75. **Country or space agency:** US. **Designation:** 1 through 55. **Not manned. Events of note:** Explorer 1, the first successful US satellite,

discovered Earth's inner radiation belt. Other Explorers in this long series conducted pioneering studies over a broad spectrum of Earth and space sciences.

Pioneer

Years launched: 1958–78. **Country or space agency:** US. **Designation:** 1 through 13. **Not manned. Events of note:** Pioneer 10 was the first spacecraft to travel through the asteroid belt, to fly by Jupiter, and to escape the solar system; Pioneer 11 was the first to visit Saturn. Complementary Pioneer 12 and 13 spacecraft (also called Pioneer Venus) explored Venus, one conducting radar mapping of the planet's cloud-shrouded surface from orbit while the other dropped atmospheric probes.

Luna (Russian for "Moon")

Years launched: 1959–76. **Country or space agency:** USSR. **Designation:** 1 through 24. **Not manned. Events of note:** Luna 2 was the first spacecaft to crash-land on the lunar surface; Luna 3 took the first photographs of the Moon's far side; three Lunas (16, 20, and 24) returned with samples of lunar soil.

Mercury

Years launched: 1961–63 (manned missions). **Country or space agency:** US. **Designation:** Mercury spacecraft had program designations, but they became better known by the individual names bestowed on them, such as "Freedom," followed by a "7" to honor the seven NASA astronauts chosen for the program. **Events of note:** Some 20 preliminary unmanned Mercury missions took place between 1959 and 1961. Of the six manned missions, *Freedom 7* was launched in 1961 with Alan Shepard (the first American in space) aboard; *Liberty Bell 7* in 1961 with Virgil "Gus" Grissom; *Friendship 7* in 1962 with John Glenn (the first American to orbit Earth); *Aurora 7* in 1962 with Scott Carpenter; *Sigma 7* in 1962 with Walter Schirra; and *Faith 7* in 1963 with Gordon Cooper.

Vostok (Russian for "east")

Years launched: 1961–63. **Country or space agency:** USSR. **Designation:** 1 through 6. **Manned. Events of note:** The first man in space and to orbit Earth was Soviet cosmonaut Yury Gagarin in Vostok 1, launched on 12 April 1961. Vostok 2 was launched with Gherman Titov in 1961, Vostok 3 with Andriyan Nikolayev in 1962, Vostok 4 with Pavel Popovich in 1962, Vostok 5 with Valery Bykovsky in 1963, and Vostok 6 with Valentina Tereshkova, the first woman in space, in 1963.

Venera (Russian for "Venus")

Years launched: 1961–83. **Country or space agency:** USSR. **Designation:** 1 through 16. **Not manned. Events of note:** Venera 1 carried out the first Venus flyby. Venera 3 was the first spacecraft to impact on another planet, and Venera 7 was the first to soft-land on another planet. Venera 9 and 10 sent back the first close-up pictures of Venus's surface.

Ranger

Years launched: 1961–65. **Country or space agency:** US. **Designation:** 1 through 9. **Not manned. Events of note:** Ranger 4 was the first US spacecraft to crash-land on the Moon; the last three Rangers returned thousands of images of the lunar surface before impacting the lunar surface as planned.

Mariner

Years launched: 1962–73. **Country or space agency:** US. **Designation:** 1 through 10. **Not manned. Events of note:** Various Mariners in the program flew by Venus, Mercury, and Mars. Mariner 9 mapped Mars in detail from orbit, becoming the first spacecraft to orbit another planet. Mariner 10 is the only spacecraft to have visited the vicinity of Mercury.

Voskhod (Russian for "sunrise" or "ascent")

Years launched: 1964–65. **Country or space agency:** USSR. **Designation:** 1 and 2. **Manned. Events of note:** Voskhod 1 was the first spacecraft to carry more than one person; Aleksey Leonov performed the first space walk, from the Voskhod 2 spacecraft, on 18 Mar 1965.

Gemini

Years launched: 1965–66. **Country or space agency:** US. **Designation:** 1 through 12. **Manned. Events of note:** Ten two-person manned missions followed two unmanned test flights. Gemini 8 was the first spacecraft to dock with another craft, an unmanned launcher stage. The Gemini program showed that astronauts could carry out rendezvous and docking maneuvers and could live and work in space for the time needed for a round-trip to the Moon.

Lunar Orbiter

Years launched: 1966–67. **Country or space agency:** US. **Designation:** 1 through 5. **Not manned. Events of note:** Five consecutive spacecraft made detailed photographic surveys of most of the Moon's surface, providing the mapping essential for choosing landing sites for the manned Apollo missions.

Soyuz (Russian for "union")

Years launched: 1967–present. **Country or space agency:** USSR. **Designation:** 1 through 40 (first series). Three subsequent series of upgraded spacecraft received the additional suffix letters T, TM, or TMA and were renumbered from 1. **Manned. Events of note:** On 24 Apr 1967 cosmonaut Vladimir Komarov conducted the inaugural test flight (Soyuz 1) of this multiperson transport craft but died returning to Earth after the parachute system failed, becoming the first fatality during a spaceflight. Soyuz 11 ferried the crew of the first space station, Salyut 1. Soyuz TM-2 made the inaugural manned flight of this TM upgrade while transporting the second crew of the Mir space station. Soyuz TM-31 carried up the International Space Station's first three-man crew. An automated unmanned cargo ferry, called Progress, was derived from the Soyuz design. High-resolution remote observations of Earth were made possible in 2006 with the launch of the Resurs–DK1 satellite.

Apollo

Years launched: 1968–72. **Country or space agency:** US. **Designation:** 7 through 17. **Manned. Events of note:** Several unmanned test flights preceded 11 manned Apollo missions, including two in Earth orbit (7 and 9), two in lunar orbit (8 and 10), one lunar swingby (13), and six lunar landings (11, 12, and 14–17) in which a total of 12 astronauts walked on the Moon. Apollo 11, crewed by Neil Armstrong, Michael Collins, and Buzz Aldrin, was the first mission to land humans on the Moon, on 20 Jul 1969. Apollo 13, planned as a lunar landing mission, experienced an onboard explosion en route to the Moon; after a swing around the Moon, the crippled spacecraft made a harrowing but safe return journey to Earth with its crew, James Lovell, John Swigert, and Fred Haise. The six landing missions collectively returned almost 382 kg (842 pounds) of lunar rocks and soil for study on Earth.

Salyut (Russian for "salute")

Years launched: 1971–82. **Country or space agency:** USSR. **Designation:** 1 through 7 (two designs). **Manned. Events of note:** Salyut 1, launched 19 Apr 1971, was the world's first space station; its crew, cosmonauts Georgy Dobrovolsky, Vladislav Volkov, and Viktor Patsayev, died returning to Earth when their Soyuz spacecraft depressurized. Salyut 6, the first of an improved design, operated as a highly successful scientific space platform, supporting a series of crews and international visitors over a four-year period.

Skylab

Year launched: 1973. **Country or space agency:** US. **Manned. Events of note:** Skylab, based on the outfitted and pressurized upper stage of a Saturn V Moon rocket, was the first US space station. Three successive astronaut crews carried out solar astronomy studies, materials-sciences research, and biomedical experiments on the effects of weightlessness.

Apollo-Soyuz

Year launched: 1975. **Countries or space agencies:** US and USSR. **Manned. Events of note:** As a sign of improved US-Soviet relations, an Apollo spacecraft carrying three astronauts docked in Earth orbit with a Soyuz vehicle carrying two cosmonauts. It was the first cooperative multinational space mission and the last use of an Apollo craft.

Viking

Year launched: 1975. **Country or space agency:** US. **Designation:** 1 and 2. **Not manned. Events of note:** Both space probes traveled to Mars, released landers, and took photographs of large expanses of Mars from orbit. The Viking 1 lander transmitted the first pictures from the Martian surface; both landers carried experiments designed to detect living organisms or life processes but found no convincing signs of life.

Voyager

Years launched: 1977. **Country or space agency:** US. **Designation:** 1 and 2. **Not manned. Events of note:** Both Voyager spacecraft flew past Jupiter and Saturn, transmitting measurements and photographs; Voyager 2 went on to Uranus in 1986 and then to Neptune. Both craft continued out of the solar system, with Voyager 1 overtaking Pioneer 10 in 1998 to become the most distant human-made object in space.

space shuttle (Space Transportation System, or STS)

Years launched: 1981–present. **Country or space agency:** US. **Designation:** Individual missions were designated STS with a number (and sometimes letter) suffix, although the orbiter spacecraft themselves were reused. **Manned. Events of note:** The first flight of a manned space shuttle, STS-1, was on 12 Apr 1981 with the orbiter *Columbia*. Other original operational orbiters included *Challenger*, *Discovery*, and *Atlantis*. During shuttle mission STS-51-L, *Challenger* exploded after liftoff on 28 Jan 1986, killing all seven astronauts aboard, including a private citizen, Christa McAuliffe; the orbiter *Endeavour* was built as a replacement vehicle. Space shuttle missions were used to deploy satellites, space observatories, and planetary probes; to carry out in-space repairs of orbiting spacecraft; and to take US astronauts to the Russian space station Mir. Beginning in 1998 a series of shuttle missions ferried components, supplies, and crews to the International Space Station during its assembly and operation. In 2003 the orbiter *Columbia* disintegrated while returning from a space mission, claiming the lives of its seven-person crew, including Ilan Ramon, the first Israeli astronaut to go into space.

Giotto (named for the Italian artist)

Year launched: 1985. **Countries or space agency:** ESA. **Not manned. Events of note:** This first deep-space probe launched by ESA made a close flyby of Halley's Comet, collecting data and transmitting images of the icy nucleus. It was then redirected to a second comet, using a gravity-assist flyby of Earth, the first time that a spacecraft coming back from deep space had made such a maneuver.

Mir (Russian for "peace" and "world")

Years launched: 1986–96. **Country or space agency:** USSR/Russia. **Manned. Events of note:** The core of this modular space station was launched on 20 Feb 1986; five additional modules were added over the next decade to create a large, versatile space laboratory. Although intended for a five-year life, it supported human habitation between 1986 and 2000, including an uninterrupted stretch of occupancy of almost 10 years, and it hosted a series of US astronauts as part of a Mir–space shuttle cooperative endeavor. In 1995, Mir cosmonaut Valery Polyakov set a space endurance record of nearly 438 days.

Magellan

Year launched: 1989. **Country or space agency:** US. **Not manned. Events of note:** Magellan was the first deep-space probe deployed by the space shuttle. During four years in orbit above Venus, it mapped some 98% of the surface of the cloud-covered planet with radar at high resolution. At the end of its mission, it was sent on a gradual dive into the Venusian atmosphere, where it measured various properties before burning up.

Galileo

Year launched: 1989. **Country or space agency:** US. **Not manned. Events of note:** En route to Jupiter, Galileo took the first detailed pictures of two asteroids and returned unique images of a comet as it impacted Jupiter's atmosphere. Near the Jovian planet, it released an atmospheric probe and then went into orbit around Jupiter for an extended study of the giant planet and its Galilean moons. Among many discoveries, Galileo found evidence of a liquid-water ocean below the moon Europa's icy surface.

Ulysses

Year launched: 1990. **Countries or space agency:** US and ESA. **Not manned. Events of note:** Ulysses traveled first to Jupiter in order to use the giant planet's gravity to sling the probe out of the plane of the planets. Ulysses successively passed over the Sun's south and north poles, studying properties of the corona, solar wind, and interplanetary space at high solar latitudes.

Clementine

Year launched: 1994. **Country or space agency:** US. **Not manned. Events of note:** This probe was designed to test new imaging sensors in space for defense applications. It mapped the Moon in various wavelengths from lunar orbit, determining mineral content of the surface and producing tantalizing hints of the existence of frozen water in permanently shadowed craters near the Moon's south pole.

NEAR Shoemaker (Near Earth Asteroid Rendezvous Shoemaker)

Year launched: 1996. Country or space agency: US. **Not manned. Events of note:** This spacecraft was the first to orbit a small body (the Earth-approaching asteroid Eros) to touch down on its surface. It studied Eros for a year with cameras and instruments, then made a slow descent and a soft landing and transmitted gamma-ray data from the surface for more than two weeks.

Mars Global Surveyor (MGS)

Year launched: 1996. Country or space agency: US. **Not manned. Events of note:** MGS conducted long-term mapping from Martian orbit of the planet's entire surface and studies of its magnetic, atmospheric, and internal properties. Close-up images suggested, controversially, that liquid water may have flowed on or near the planet's surface in geologically recent times and still may exist in protected areas. They also showed that the "face on Mars" formation first photographed by Viking 1 was of natural origin and not a product of alien intelligence, as some had purported.

Mars Pathfinder

Year launched: 1996. Country or space agency: US. **Not manned. Events of note:** The first spacecraft to land on Mars since the 1976 Viking missions, Pathfinder descended to the Martian surface using a novel combination of parachutes, rockets, and air bags. The lander and its robotic surface rover, Sojourner, which together successfully collected 17,000 images and other data, added to evidence that ancient Mars was much more Earth-like than it is today.

Cassini-Huygens

Year launched: 1997. Country or space agency: US, ESA, and Italy. **Not manned. Events of note:** Consisting of an orbiter (Cassini) and a descent probe (Huygens), the spacecraft traveled seven years to the Saturnian system. En route it flew by Jupiter and returned detailed images. At Saturn, Cassini established an orbit around the planet for several years of studies, while the Huygens probe parachuted through the atmosphere of the moon Titan, transmitting pictures and other data for about three hours during its descent and once on the moon's surface.

Lunar Prospector

Year launched: 1998. Country or space agency: US. **Not manned. Events of note:** Equipped with radiation- and particle-measuring equipment to assay the geochemistry of the Moon's surface from orbit, the probe strengthened the evidence for water (first found by Clementine) in the south polar region. It later was deliberately crashed into a permanently shadowed crater at the south pole in an unsuccessful attempt to liberate water vapor, which could be detected from Earth.

International Space Station (ISS)

Years launched: 1998–present. Countries or space agencies: US, Russia, ESA, Canada, Japan, and Brazil. **Manned. Events of note:** A large modular complex of habitat modules and laboratories powered by solar arrays, the ISS continued to be assembled in Earth orbit by means of space-shuttle and Proton and Soyuz rocket flights that ferried components, crews, and supplies between Earth and the station. The first component, a US-funded, Russian-built module called Zarya, was launched on 20 Nov 1998. The ISS received its first resident crew on 2 Nov 2000.

Chandra X-Ray Observatory

Year launched: 1999. Country or space agency: US. **Not manned. Events of note:** The world's most powerful X-ray telescope, it revolves in an elliptical orbit around Earth, delivering roughly 1,000 observations annually of the universe. To scientists, the stunning images of the universe's outer limits (including images of black holes and distant galaxies) help clarify its origin and evolution.

2001 Mars Odyssey

Year launched: 2001. Country or space agency: US. **Not manned. Events of note:** This spacecraft was launched to study Mars from orbit and serve as a communications relay for future US and multinational landers. Its instruments mapped the distribution of various elements on or near the surface; some of its data suggested the presence of huge subsurface reservoirs of frozen water in both polar regions.

Mars Express

Year launched: 2003. Country or space agency: ESA. **Not manned. Events of note:** Carrying instruments to study the atmosphere, surface, and subsurface from Mars orbit, the spacecraft detected vast fields of water ice as well as carbon-dioxide ice at the planet's south pole. Its lander, Beagle 2, which was designed to examine the rocks and soil for signs of past or present life, failed to establish radio contact after presumably reaching the Martian surface.

Mars Exploration Rover Mission

Year launched: 2003. Country or space agency: US. **Designation:** Spirit and Opportunity. **Not manned. Events of note:** Twin six-wheeled robotic rovers, each equipped with cameras, a microscopic imager, a rock-grinding tool, and other instruments, landed on opposite sides of Mars. Both rovers found evidence of past water; particularly dramatic was the discovery by Opportunity of rocks that appeared to have been laid down at the shoreline of an ancient body of salty water.

Deep Impact

Year launched: 2005. Country or space agency: US. **Not manned. Events of note:** Deep Impact was the first spacecraft designed to study the interior composition of a comet. As it traveled past Comet Tempel 1, it released a 370-kg (820-lb) instrumented impactor into the path of the comet's icy nucleus. A high-resolution camera and other apparatuses on the flyby portion of the probe studied the impact and the resulting crater and excavated debris. The collision occurred at a relative speed of about 37,000 km/hr (23,000 mi/hr).

Mars Reconnaissance Orbiter

Year launched: 2005. Country or space agency: US. **Not manned. Events of note:** It carries the most powerful camera ever flown on a space mission. The Orbiter is expected to be an important communications link between other spacecraft, Mars, and Earth.

Space Exploration Firsts

EVENT	DETAILS	COUNTRY OR AGENCY	DATE ACCOMPLISHED
earliest known person to write about spaceflight	Lucian, in *True History,* which includes a visit to the Moon	ancient Greece	2nd century
earliest appearance of rocket propulsion technology	recorded use of gunpowder-propelled arrows in battle	China	by 13th century
first person to study in detail the use of rockets for spaceflight	Konstantin Tsiolkovsky	Russia	late 19th–early 20th centuries
first launch of a liquid-fueled rocket	Robert Goddard	US	16 Mar 1926
first launch of the V-2 ballistic missile, the forerunner of modern space rockets	Wernher von Braun	Germany	3 Oct 1942
first artificial Earth satellite	Sputnik 1	USSR	4 Oct 1957
first animal launched into space	dog Laika aboard Sputnik 2	USSR	3 Nov 1957
first spacecraft to hard-land on another celestial object (the Moon)	Luna 2	USSR	14 Sep 1959
first pictures of the far side of the Moon	Luna 3	USSR	7 Oct 1959
first applications satellite launched	TIROS 1 (weather observation)	US	1 Apr 1960
first recovery of a payload from Earth orbit	*Discoverer 13* (part of Corona reconnaissance satellite program)	US	11 Aug 1960
first piloted spacecraft to orbit Earth	Yury Gagarin on Vostok 1	USSR	12 Apr 1961
first US citizen in space	Alan Shepard on *Freedom 7*	US	5 May 1961
first piloted US spacecraft to orbit Earth	John Glenn on *Friendship 7*	US	20 Feb 1962
first active communications satellite	Telstar 1	US	10 July 1962
first data transmitted to Earth from vicinity of another planet (Venus)	Mariner 2	US	14 Dec 1962
first woman in space	Valentina Tereshkova on Vostok 6	USSR	16 Jun 1963
first satellite to operate in geostationary orbit	Syncom 2 (telecommunications satellite)	US	26 Jul 1963
first space walk	Aleksey Leonov on Voskhod 2	USSR	18 Mar 1965
first spacecraft pictures of Mars	Mariner 4	US	14 Jul 1965
first spacecraft to soft-land on the Moon	Luna 9	USSR	3 Feb 1966
first death during a space mission	Vladimir Komarov on Soyuz 1	USSR	24 Apr 1967
first humans to orbit the Moon	Frank Borman, James Lovell, and William Anders on Apollo 8	US	24 Dec 1968
first human to walk on the Moon	Neil Armstrong on Apollo 11	US	20 Jul 1969
first unmanned spacecraft to carry lunar samples back to Earth	Luna 16	USSR	24 Sep 1970
first soft landing on another planet (Venus)	Venera 7	USSR	15 Dec 1970
first space station launched	Salyut 1	USSR	19 Apr 1971
first spacecraft to orbit another planet (Mars)	Mariner 9	US	13 Nov 1971
first spacecraft to soft-land on Mars	Mars 3	USSR	2 Dec 1971
first spacecraft to fly by Jupiter	Pioneer 10	US	3 Dec 1973
first international docking in space	Apollo and Soyuz spacecraft during Apollo-Soyuz Test Project	US/USSR	17 Jul 1975
first pictures transmitted from the surface of Mars	Viking 1	US	20 Jul 1976
first spacecraft to fly by Saturn	Pioneer 11	US	1 Sep 1979
first reusable spacecraft launched and returned from space	space shuttle *Columbia*	US	12–14 Apr 1981
first spacecraft to fly by Uranus	Voyager 2	US	24 Jan 1986
first spacecraft to make a close flyby of a comet's nucleus	Giotto at Halley's Comet	European Space Agency	13 Mar 1986
first spacecraft to fly by Neptune	Voyager 2	US	24 Aug 1989
first large optical space telescope launched	Hubble Space Telescope	US/European Space Agency	25 Apr 1990
first spacecraft to orbit Jupiter	Galileo	US	7 Dec 1995
first confirmed case of a large black hole outside of the nucleus of a galaxy	Chandra X-Ray Observatory	US	28 Oct 1999/ 20 Jan 2000
first resident crew to occupy the International Space Station	William Shepherd, Yury Gidzenko, Sergey Krikalev	US/Russia	2 Nov 2000
first spacecraft to orbit and land on an asteroid	NEAR Shoemaker at the asteroid Eros	US	14 Feb 2000/ 12 Feb 2001
first piloted Chinese spacecraft to orbit Earth	Shenzhou 5, piloted by Yang Liwei	China	15 Oct 2003
first privately funded human spaceflight (to 100 km [62 mi])	*SpaceShipOne,* piloted by Michael W. Melvill (private venture)	US	21 Jun 2004
first spacecraft to strike a comet's nucleus and study its interior composition	Deep Impact at Comet Tempel 1	US	4 Jul 2005

Air Travel

Flight History

Humanity has been fascinated with the possibility of flight for millennia. The history of flight began at least as early as about AD 400 with historical references to a Chinese kite that used a rotary wing as a source of lift. Other toys using the principle of the helicopter—in this case a rotary blade turned by the pull of a string—were known during the Middle Ages. During the latter part of the 15th century, Leonardo da Vinci made drawings pertaining to flight. In the 1700s experiments were made with the ornithopter, a machine with flapping wings.

The history of successful flight begins with the hot-air balloon. In southwestern France, two brothers, Joseph and Étienne Montgolfier, papermakers, experimented with a large cell contrived of paper in which they could collect heated air. On 19 Sep 1783 the Montgolfiers sent aloft a balloon with a rooster, a duck, and a sheep, and on 21 November the first manned flight was made. Balloons gained importance as their flights increased into hundreds of miles, but they were essentially unsteerable.

A former military man, Count Ferdinand von Zeppelin, spent much of his life after retiring in 1890 working with balloons, particularly on the steering problem. As his experimentation continued, hydrogen and illuminating gas were substituted for hot air, and a motor was mounted on a bag filled with gas that had been fitted with propellers and rudders. It was Zeppelin who first saw clearly that maintaining a steerable shape was essential, so he created a rigid but light frame. On 2 Jul 1900 Zeppelin undertook the first experimental flight of what he called an airship. The development of the dirigible went well until the docking procedure at Lakehurst NJ on 6 May 1937, when the Hindenburg burst into flames and exploded, with a loss of 36 lives. Public feeling about the craft made further development futile.

It should be remembered, however, that neither balloons nor dirigibles had produced true flight: what they had done was harness the dynamics of the atmosphere to lift a craft off the ground, using what power (if any) they supplied primarily to steer. The first scientific exposition of the principles that ultimately led to the successful flight with a heavier-than-air device came in 1843 from Sir George Cayley, who is also regarded by many as the father of fixed-wing flight. It was Cayley who built the successful man-carrying glider that came closest to permitting real flight. Cayley's work was built upon in the experiments and writings on gliders from the late 1800s by aviation pioneers Otto Lilienthal of Germany and Octave Chanute of the United States. The works of Cayley, Lilienthal, and Chanute would eventually inspire and form the basis of the Wright brothers' work.

The Americans Wilbur and Orville Wright by 1902 had developed a fully practical biplane glider that could be controlled in every direction. Fitting a small engine and two propellers to another biplane, the Wrights on 17 Dec 1903 made the world's first successful flight of a man-carrying, engine-powered, heavier-than-air craft at a site near Kitty Hawk NC.

The Wright brothers' success soon inspired successful aircraft designs and flights by others, and World War I (1914–18) further accelerated the expansion of aviation. Though initially used for aerial reconnaissance, aircraft were soon fitted with machine guns to shoot at other aircraft and with bombs to drop on ground targets; military aircraft with these types of missions and armaments became known, respectively, as fighters and bombers.

By the 1920s the first small commercial airlines had begun to carry mail, and the increased speed and range of aircraft made nonstop flights over the world's oceans, poles, and continents possible. In the 1930s more efficient monoplane aircraft with an all-metal fuselage and a retractable undercarriage became standard. Aircraft played a key role in World War II (1939–45), developing in size, weight, speed, power, range, and armament. The war marked the high point of piston-engined propeller craft while also introducing the first aircraft with jet engines, which could fly at higher speeds. Jet-engined craft became the norm for fighters in the late 1940s and proved their superiority as commercial transports beginning in the '50s. The high speeds and low operating costs of jet airliners led to a massive expansion of commercial air travel in the second half of the 20th century.

The next great aviation innovation after the jet engine was aircraft able to fly at supersonic speeds. The first was a Bell XS-1 rocket-powered research plane piloted by Maj. Charles E. Yeager of the US Air Force on 14 Oct 1947. The XS-1 broke the sound barrier at 1,066 km/hr (662 mph) and attained a top speed of 1,126 km/hr (700 mph). Thereafter many military aircraft capable of supersonic flight were built. The first supersonic, passenger-carrying, commercial airplane, the Concorde, was built jointly by aircraft manufacturers in Great Britain and France and was in regular commercial service between 1976 and 2003. In the 21st century aircraft manufacturers strove to produce larger planes. A huge new passenger airliner, the double-decker Airbus A380, with a passenger capacity of 555 (40% greater than the next largest airplane), was scheduled to begin commercial flights in late 2007.

Airlines in the US: Best On-Time Arrival Performance

Source: US Department of Transportation, July 2007.

	AIRLINE	% OF ALL FLIGHTS		AIRLINE	% OF ALL FLIGHTS		AIRLINE	% OF ALL FLIGHTS
1	Hawaiian Airlines	92.8	9	Atlantic Southeast Airlines	78.8	16	Continental Airlines	75.1
2	Aloha Airlines	88.4	10	JetBlue Airways	78.2	17	Northwest Airlines	74.6
3	AirTran Airways	85.5	11	Frontier Airlines	77.1	18	American Eagle Airlines	73.4
4	Delta Air Lines	84.0	12	ExpressJet Airlines	76.8	19	American Airlines	71.0
5	Pinnacle Airlines	83.6	13	Comair	76.5	20	US Airways	67.9
6	Southwest Airlines	83.2	14	Alaska Airlines	76.2			
7	SkyWest Airlines	80.9	15	United Airlines	75.7			
8	Mesa Airlines	80.1						

US Aviation Safety, 1987–2006

2006 data are preliminary.
Source: US National Transportation Safety Board.

| | US AIRLINES[1] | | | | US GENERAL AVIATION | | | |
YEAR	NO. OF ACCIDENTS	NO. OF ACCIDENTS WITH FATALITIES	TOTAL NO. OF DEATHS	HOURS FLOWN	ALL ACCIDENTS	FATAL ACCIDENTS	TOTAL FATALITIES	HOURS FLOWN
1987	34	5	232	10,645,192	2,494	446	837	26,972,000
1988	30	3	285	11,140,548	2,388	460	797	27,446,000
1989	28	11	278	11,274,543	2,242	432	769	27,920,000
1990	24	6	39	12,150,116	2,242	444	770	28,510,000
1991	26	4	62	11,780,610	2,197	439	800	27,678,000
1992	18	4	33	12,359,715	2,111	451	867	24,780,000
1993	23	1	1	12,706,206	2,064	401	744	22,796,000
1994	23	4	239	13,124,315	2,021	404	730	22,235,000
1995	36	3	168	13,505,257	2,056	413	735	24,906,000
1996	37	5	380	13,746,112	1,908	361	636	24,881,000
1997	49	4	8	15,838,109	1,845	350	631	25,591,000
1998	50	1	1	16,816,555	1,905	365	625	25,518,000
1999	51	2	12	17,555,208	1,905	340	619	29,246,000
2000	56	3	92	18,299,257	1,837	345	596	27,838,000
2001	46	6	531	17,814,191	1,727	325	562	25,431,000
2002	41	0	0	17,290,198	1,715	345	581	25,545,000
2003	54	2	22	17,467,700	1,740	352	633	25,998,000
2004	30	2	14	18,882,503	1,619	314	559	24,888,000
2005	40	3	22	19,390,029	1,669	321	563	23,168,000
2006	31	2	50	19,560,000	1,515	303	698	22,800,000

[1]Scheduled and nonscheduled service.

World's Busiest Airports

Ranked by total aircraft movement (takeoffs and landings), 2006.
Source: Airports Council International (preliminary statistics). Web site: <www.airports.org>.

RANK	AIRPORT	LOCATION	AIRPORT CODE	TOTAL MOVEMENTS
1	Hartsfield-Jackson Atlanta International Airport	Atlanta GA	ATL	976,447
2	O'Hare International Airport	Chicago IL	ORD	958,643
3	Dallas/Fort Worth International Airport	Dallas/Fort Worth TX	DFW	700,409
4	Los Angeles International Airport	Los Angeles CA	LAX	656,842
5	McCarran International Airport	Las Vegas NV	LAS	619,486
6	George Bush Intercontinental Airport	Houston TX	IAH	602,672
7	Denver International Airport	Denver CO	DEN	597,290
8	Paris Charles de Gaulle International Airport	Paris, France	CDG	541,566
9	Phoenix Sky Harbor International Airport	Phoenix AZ	PHX	541,273
10	Philadelphia International Airport	Philadelphia PA	PHL	515,809
11	Charlotte Douglas International Airport	Charlotte NC	CLT	509,559
12	Frankfurt Airport	Frankfurt, Germany	FRA	489,406
13	Detroit Metropolitan Wayne County Airport	Detroit MI	DTW	481,740
14	Heathrow Airport	London, UK	LHR	477,029
15	Minneapolis–St. Paul International Airport	Minneapolis/St. Paul MN	MSP	475,600
16	Newark Liberty International Airport	Newark NJ	EWR	444,075
17	Amsterdam Airport Schiphol	Amsterdam, Netherlands	AMS	440,163
18	Madrid Barajas International Airport	Madrid, Spain	MAD	435,018
19	Salt Lake City International Airport	Salt Lake City UT	SLC	420,643
20	Toronto Pearson International Airport	Toronto, ON, Canada	YYZ	418,244
21	Munich International Airport	Munich, Germany	MUC	411,335
22	Boston Logan International Airport	Boston MA	BOS	406,119
23	LaGuardia Airport	New York NY	LGA	399,036
24	Van Nuys Airport	Los Angeles CA	VNY	394,915
25	Miami International Airport	Miami FL	MIA	385,538
26	Memphis International Airport	Memphis TN	MEM	384,823
27	Washington Dulles International Airport	Washington DC	IAD	379,280
28	Beijing Capital International Airport	Beijing, China	PEK	376,340
29	John F. Kennedy International Airport	New York NY	JFK	375,377
30	Long Beach Airport	Long Beach CA	LGB	369,708

Meteorology

Global Temperatures and Precipitation

Listed in alphabetical order by city. For more information see <www.weatherbase.com>.

CITY	JAN	APR	JUL	OCT	AVERAGE ANNUAL PRECIPITATION LEVELS IN INCHES (MM)
Ankara, Turkey	27 (−2)	49 (9)	69 (20)	52 (11)	13.6 (346)
Beijing, China	26 (−3)	57 (13)	79 (26)	57 (13)	25.1 (630)
Buenos Aires, Argentina	75 (23)	62 (16)	50 (10)	61 (16)	38.5 (970)
Cairo, Egypt	57 (13)	71 (21)	83 (28)	75 (23)	1 (25)
Casablanca, Morocco	55 (12)	60 (15)	73 (22)	66 (18)	16.1 (400)
Christchurch, New Zealand	63 (17)	54 (12)	44 (6)	53 (11)	25.5 (640)
Colombo, Sri Lanka	81 (27)	84 (28)	83 (28)	82 (27)	87.8 (2,230)
Doha, Qatar	63 (17)	80 (26)	96 (35)	85 (29)	3.2 (80)
Hanoi, Vietnam	62 (16)	76 (24)	86 (30)	78 (25)	66.2 (1,682)
Havana, Cuba	71 (21)	76 (24)	82 (27)	78 (25)	48.2 (1,225)
Jerusalem, Israel	46 (7)	59 (15)	73 (22)	66 (18)	23 (580)
Johannesburg, South Africa	69 (20)	61 (16)	52 (11)	64 (17)	28.7 (720)
Kandahar, Afghanistan	44 (6)	68 (19)	89 (31)	64 (17)	7.4 (180)
Lima, Peru	74 (23)	71 (21)	64 (17)	65 (18)	0.3 (7.6)
Lisbon, Portugal	51 (10)	58 (14)	73 (22)	64 (17)	27.9 (708)
London, UK	39 (3)	46 (7)	62 (16)	51 (10)	29.7 (750)
Mbarara, Uganda	69 (20)	69 (20)	68 (20)	69 (20)	35.3 (890)
Moscow, Russia	16 (−8)	42 (5)	63 (17)	39 (3)	23.6 (590)
Nice, France	48 (8)	55 (12)	74 (23)	62 (16)	32.4 (820)
Nuuk, Greenland	17 (−8)	25 (−3)	45 (7)	31 (0)	23.9 (600)
Pala, Chad	77 (25)	87 (31)	77 (25)	78 (26)	40.4 (1,027)
Reykjavík, Iceland	31 (0)	37 (2)	52 (11)	40 (4)	32.2 (810)
Rotterdam, The Netherlands	38 (3)	47 (8)	63 (17)	52 (11)	N/A
Santiago, Chile	70 (21)	59 (15)	47 (8)	58 (14)	13.4 (340)
São Paulo, Brazil	74 (23)	70 (21)	63 (17)	69 (20)	53.2 (1,350)
South Pole, Antarctica	−16 (−26)	−69 (−56)	−74 (−58)	−58 (−50)	0.1 (2.5)
Sydney, Australia	72 (22)	65 (18)	53 (11)	64 (17)	44.5 (1,130)
Tokyo, Japan	42 (5)	57 (13)	77 (25)	64 (17)	60.2 (1,520)
Toronto, ON, Canada	21 (−6)	44 (6)	70 (21)	48 (8)	30.1 (760)
Vilnius, Lithuania	23 (−5)	41 (5)	62 (17)	42 (6)	26.3 (669)

N/A: not available.

World Temperature Extremes

REGION	highest recorded air temperature PLACE (ELEVATION)	°F	°C	lowest recorded air temperature PLACE (ELEVATION)	°F	°C
Africa	Al-'Aziziyah, Libya (112 m [367 ft]; 13 Sep 1922)	136.0	57.8	Ifrane, Morocco (1,635 m [5,364 ft]; 11 Feb 1935)	−11.0	−23.9
Antarctica	Vanda Station, Scott Coast (15 m [49 ft]; 5 Jan 1974)	59.0	15.0	Vostok, 78° 27″ S, 106° 52′ E (3,420 m [11,220 ft]; 21 Jul 1983)	−129.0	−89.4
Asia	Tirat Zevi, Israel (−220 m [−722 ft]; 21 Jun 1942)	129.0	53.9	Oymyakon, Russia (806 m [2,625 ft]; 6 Feb 1933)	−90.0	−67.8
Australia	Cloncurry, Queensland (190 m [622 ft]; 16 Jan 1889)	128.0	53.3	Charlotte Pass, New South Wales (1,755 m [5,758 ft]; 29 Jun 1994)	−9.4	−23.0
Europe	Seville, Spain (8 m [26 ft]; 4 Aug 1881)	122.0	50.0	Ust-Shchuger, Russia (85 m [279 ft]; exact date unknown)	−67.0	−55.0
North America	Greenland Ranch, Death Valley, California (−54 m [−178 ft]; 10 Jul 1913)	134.0	56.7	Snag, Yukon (646 m [2,120 ft]; 3 Feb 1947)	−81.4	−63.0
South America	Rivadavia, Argentina (206 m [676 ft]; 11 Dec 1905)	120.0	48.9	Colonia, Sarmiento, Argentina (268 m [879 ft]; 1 Jun 1907)	−27.0	−32.8
Tropical Pacific	Tuguegarao, Philippines (22 m [72 ft]; 29 Apr 1912)	108.0	42.2	Haleakala, Hawaii (2,972 m [9,750 ft]; 17 May 1979)	12.0	−11.1

Normal Temperatures and Precipitation for Selected US Cities

Statistics from city airports, 1971–2000. Alphabetical by state.
Source: National Oceanic and Atmospheric Administration, National Climatic Data Center, Asheville NC.

CITY	JAN	APR	JUL	OCT	ANNUAL PRECIPITATION (IN)
Montgomery AL	46.6	64.3	81.8	65.4	54.77
Anchorage AK	15.8	36.3	58.4	34.1	16.08
Phoenix AZ	54.2	70.2	92.8	74.6	8.29
Little Rock AR	40.1	61.4	82.4	63.3	50.93
Los Angeles CA	57.1	60.8	69.3	66.9	13.15
San Francisco CA	49.4	56.2	62.8	61.0	20.11
Denver CO	29.2	47.6	73.4	51.0	15.81
Hartford CT	25.7	48.9	73.7	51.9	46.16
Wilmington DE	31.5	52.4	76.6	55.8	42.81
Miami FL	68.1	75.7	83.7	78.8	58.53
Atlanta GA	42.7	61.6	80.0	62.8	50.20
Honolulu HI	73.0	75.6	80.8	80.2	18.29
Boise ID	30.2	50.6	74.7	52.8	12.19
Chicago IL[1]	22.0	47.8	73.3	52.1	36.27
Indianapolis IN	26.5	52.0	75.4	54.6	40.95
Des Moines IA	20.4	50.6	76.1	52.8	34.72
Topeka KS	27.2	54.5	78.4	56.6	35.64
Louisville KY	33.0	56.4	78.4	58.5	44.54
New Orleans LA	52.6	68.2	82.7	70.0	64.16
Portland ME	21.7	43.7	68.7	47.7	45.83
Baltimore MD	32.3	53.2	76.5	55.4	41.94
Boston MA	29.3	48.3	73.9	54.1	42.53
Detroit MI	24.5	48.1	73.5	51.9	32.89
Minneapolis MN	13.1	46.6	73.2	48.7	29.41
Jackson MS	45.0	63.4	81.4	64.4	55.95
St. Louis MO	29.6	56.6	80.2	58.3	38.75
Missoula MT	23.5	45.2	66.9	44.4	13.82
Lincoln NE	22.4	51.2	77.8	53.5	28.37
Las Vegas NV	47.0	66.0	91.2	68.7	4.49
Concord NH	20.1	44.6	70.0	47.8	37.60
Newark NJ	31.3	52.3	77.2	56.4	46.25
Albuquerque NM	35.7	55.6	78.5	57.3	9.47
New York NY[2]	31.8	50.1	74.8	56.5	42.46
Charlotte NC	41.7	60.9	80.3	61.7	43.51
Fargo ND	6.8	43.5	70.6	45.3	21.19
Cleveland OH	25.7	47.6	71.9	52.2	38.71
Tulsa OK	36.4	60.8	83.5	62.6	42.42
Portland OR	39.9	51.2	68.1	54.3	37.07
Philadelphia PA	32.3	53.1	77.6	57.2	42.05
Providence RI	28.7	48.6	73.3	53.0	46.45
Charleston SC	47.9	64.2	81.7	66.2	51.53
Rapid City SD	22.4	44.7	71.7	48.2	16.64
Memphis TN	39.9	62.1	82.5	63.8	54.65
Dallas TX[3]	44.1	65.0	85.0	67.2	34.73
Salt Lake City UT	29.2	50.0	77.0	52.5	16.50
Burlington VT	18.0	43.5	70.6	47.7	36.05
Richmond VA	36.4	57.1	77.9	58.3	43.91
Seattle WA	40.9	50.2	65.3	52.7	37.07
Charleston WV	33.4	54.3	73.9	55.1	44.05
Milwaukee WI	20.7	45.2	72.0	51.4	34.81
Casper WY	22.3	42.7	70.0	45.7	13.03

[1]Data from O'Hare International Airport.   [2]Data from John F. Kennedy International Airport.   [3]Data from Dallas/Fort Worth International Airport.

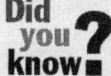
Did you know?

The oldest detected meteorite impact on Earth occurred 3.47 billion years ago. The meteor left geochemical evidence of its impact in southern Africa and Australia and is thought to have been about 20 km (12 mi) wide. It would have taken less than two seconds to pass through the atmosphere and slam into the surface of the planet, causing immense tsunamis and devastating erosion to the ocean floor and small continents.

Indexes

Wind Chill Table

The wind chill index is based upon a formula that determines how cold the atmosphere feels by combining the temperature and wind speed and applying other factors. For more information, see <www.nws.noaa.gov/om/windchill/index.shtml>.

WIND SPEED (MPH) CALM	40	35	30	25	20	15	10	5	0	-5	-10	-15	-20	-25	-30
5	36	31	25	19	13	7	1	-5	-11	-16	-22	-28	-34	-40	-46
10	34	27	21	15	9	3	-4	-10	-16	-22	-28	-35	-41	-47	-53
15	32	25	19	13	6	0	-7	-13	-19	-26	-32	-39	-45	-51	-58
20	30	24	17	11	4	-2	-9	-15	-22	-29	-35	-42	-48	-55	-61
25	29	23	16	9	3	-4	-11	-17	-24	-31	-37	-44	-51	-58	-64
30	28	22	15	8	1	-5	-12	-19	-26	-33	-39	-46	-53	-60	-67
35	28	21	14	7	0	-7	-14	-21	-27	-34	-41	-48	-55	-62	-69
40	27	20	13	6	-1	-8	-15	-22	-29	-36	-43	-50	-57	-64	-71
45	26	19	12	5	-2	-9	-16	-23	-30	-37	-44	-51	-58	-65	-72
50	26	19	12	4	-3	-10	-17	-24	-31	-38	-45	-52	-60	-67	-74
55	25	18	11	4	-3	-11	-18	-25	-32	-39	-46	-54	-61	-69	-75
60	25	17	10	3	-4	-11	-19	-26	-33	-40	-48	-55	-62	-69	-76

Column header: TEMPERATURE (°F)

Heat Index

The Heat Index shows the effects of the combination of heat and humidity. Apparent temperature is the temperature as it feels to your body. For more information see <www.jeonet.com/heat.htm>.

relative humidity	70	75	80	85	90	95	100	105	110	115	120
0%	64	69	73	78	83	87	91	95	99	103	107
10%	65	70	75	80	85	90	95	100	105	111	116
20%	66	72	77	82	87	93	99	105	112	120	130
30%	67	73	78	84	90	96	104	113	123	135	148
40%	68	74	79	86	93	101	110	123	137	151	
50%	69	75	81	88	96	107	120	135	150		
60%	70	76	82	90	100	114	132	149			
70%	70	77	85	93	106	124	144				
80%	71	78	86	97	113	136	157				
90%	71	79	88	102	122	150	170				
100%	72	80	91	108	133	166					

Column header: AIR TEMPERATURE (°F); sub-header: apparent temperature

HEAT INDEX/HEAT DISORDERS

Heat Index	Possible heat disorders for people in higher risk groups*
130°F or higher	Heatstroke/sunstroke highly likely with continued exposure.
105°–130°F	Sunstroke, heat cramps, or heat exhaustion likely, and heatstroke possible with prolonged exposure and/or physical activity.
90°–105°F	Sunstroke, heat cramps, and heat exhaustion possible with prolonged exposure and/or physical activity.
80°–90°F	Fatigue possible with prolonged exposure and/or physical activity.

Small children, the elderly, the chronically ill, those on certain medications or drugs (especially tranquilizers and anticholinergics), and persons with weight and alcohol problems are particularly susceptible to heat reactions, especially during heat waves in areas where moderate climate usually prevails.

Ultraviolet (UV) Index

The Ultraviolet (UV) Index predicts the intensity of the sun's ultraviolet rays. It was developed by the National Weather Service and the US Environmental Protection Agency to provide a daily forecast of the expected risk of overexposure to the sun. The Index is calculated on a next-day basis for dozens of cities across the US. Other local conditions, such as cloud cover, are taken into account in determining the UV Index number. UV Index numbers are: 0–2 (minimal exposure); 3–4 (low exposure); 5–6 (moderate exposure); 7–9 (high exposure); and 10 and over (very high exposure).

Some simple precautions can be taken to reduce the risk of sun-related illness: limit time in the sun between 10 AM and 4 PM, when rays are generally the strongest; seek shade whenever possible; use a broad spectrum sunscreen with an SPF of at least 15; wear a wide-brimmed hat and, if possible, tightly woven, full-length clothing; wear UV-protective sunglasses; avoid sunlamps and tanning salons; and watch for the UV Index daily. The UV Index should not be used by seriously sun-sensitive individuals, who should consult their doctors and take additional precautions regardless of the exposure level.

Hurricanes

Hurricane and Tornado Classifications

The Saffir/Simpson Hurricane Scale[1] is used to rank tropical cyclones in the North Atlantic Ocean and the eastern North Pacific.

Category 1. *Barometric pressure:* 28.91 in or more; *wind speed:* 74–95 mph; *storm surge:* 4–5 ft; *damage:* minimal.

Category 2. *Barometric pressure:* 28.50–28.91 in; *wind speed:* 96–110 mph; *storm surge:* 6–8 ft; *damage:* moderate.

Category 3. *Barometric pressure:* 27.91–28.47 in; *wind speed:* 111–130 mph; *storm surge:* 9–12 ft; *damage:* extensive.

Category 4. *Barometric pressure:* 27.17–27.88 in; *wind speed:* 131–155 mph; *storm surge:* 13–18 ft; *damage:* extreme.

Category 5. *Barometric pressure:* less than 27.17 in; *wind speed:* 155 mph or more; *storm surge:* 18 ft or more; *damage:* catastrophic.

Tornado classifications.
Tornado intensity is commonly estimated after the fact by analyzing damaged structures and then correlating the damage with the wind speeds known to produce various degrees of damage. Tornadoes are assigned specific values on the Fujita Scale, or F-Scale, of tornado intensity established by meteorologist T. Theodore Fujita.
Categories:

F0. *Wind speed:* 40–72 mph; *damage:* light.

F1. *Wind speed:* 73–112 mph; *damage:* moderate.

F2. *Wind speed:* 113–157 mph; *damage:* considerable.

F3. *Wind speed:* 158–206 mph; *damage:* severe.

F4. *Wind speed:* 207–260 mph; *damage:* devastating.

F5. *Wind speed:* 261–318 mph; *damage:* incredible.

[1]*Published by permission of Herbert Saffir, consulting engineer, and Robert Simpson, meteorologist.*

Hurricane Names
Source: National Hurricane Center.

In 1953, the National Hurricane Center developed a list of given names for Atlantic tropical storms. This list is now maintained by the World Meteorological Organization (WMO). Until 1979 only women's names were used, but since then men's and women's names have alternated. There are six lists currently in rotation, so names can be reused every six years. Any country affected by a hurricane, however, can request its name be retired for ten years. Also, if a storm has been particularly destructive, the WMO can remove it from the list and replace it with a different name.

Deadliest Hurricanes in the US

Listed below, in order of number of deaths, are the 30 deadliest hurricanes to hit the US mainland 1900–2006. Hurricane names are given in parentheses after the location, when applicable. The list includes Atlantic/Gulf Coast hurricanes only. Source: National Hurricane Center. Web site: <www.nhc.noaa.gov/Deadliest_Costliest.shtml>.

	HURRICANE LOCATION	YEAR	CATEGORY	DEATHS
1	Galveston TX	1900	4	8,000[1]
2	Lake Okeechobee FL	1928	4	2,500[2]
3	southeast LA; MS; FL (Katrina)	2005	3	1,500
4	New Orleans LA	1915	4	600[3]
5	southwest LA; north TX (Audrey)	1957	4	416
6	Florida Keys	1935	5	408
7	northeast US	1944	3	390[4]
8	FL; MS; AL	1926	4	372
9	Grand Isle LA	1909	3	350
10	south TX; Florida Keys	1919	4	287
11	Galveston TX	1915	4	275
12	MS; LA; VA (Camille)	1969	5	256
12	New England	1938	3	256
14	northeast US (Diane)	1955	1	184
15	southeast FL	1906	3	164
16	FL; MS; AL	1906	2	134
17	FL; northeast US (Agnes)	1972	1	122
18	SC; NC (Hazel)	1954	4	95
19	southeast FL; southeast LA (Betsy)	1965	3	75
20	northeast US (Carol)	1954	3	60
21	eastern US (Floyd)	1999	2	56
22	southeast FL; LA; MS	1947	4	51
23	FL; eastern US (Donna)	1960	4	50
23	GA; SC; NC	1940	2	50
25	TX (Carla)	1961	4	46
26	Velasco TX	1909	3	41
26	east Texas; southeast US (Allison)	2001	TS[5]	41
28	Freeport TX	1932	4	40
29	south TX	1933	3	40
30	LA (Hilda)	1964	3	38

[1]*Death toll may actually have been as high as 12,000.* [2]*Death toll may have been as high as 3,000.* [3]*325 of these lost on ships at sea.* [4]*326 of these lost on ships at sea.* [5]*Tropical storm.*

Costliest Hurricanes in the US

This table shows cyclones that caused the most damage on the US mainland. For more information see <www.nhc.noaa.gov/Deadliest_Costliest.shtml>. Note: ranking numbers 19 and 30 on the list are repeated due to the equal damage amount in dollars of multiple separate hurricanes.

RANK	HURRICANE (LOCATION)	YEAR	CATEGORY	ESTIMATED DAMAGE ($), NOT ADJUSTED	DAMAGE IN CONSTANT 2006 DOLLARS
1	Katrina (southeastern LA; MS; FL)	2005	3	81,000,000,000	84,645,000,000
2	Andrew (southeastern FL; southeastern LA)	1992	5	26,500,000,000	48,058,000,000
3	Wilma (southern FL)	2005	3	20,600,000,000	21,527,000,000
4	Charley (southwestern FL)	2004	4	15,000,000,000	16,322,000,000
5	Ivan (northwestern FL; AL)	2004	3	14,200,000,000	15,541,000,000
6	Rita (southwestern LA; TX; FL)	2005	3	11,300,000,000	11,808,000,000
7	Frances (FL)	2004	2	8,900,000,000	9,684,000,000
8	Hugo (SC)	1989	4	7,000,000,000	13,480,000,000
9	Jeanne (FL)	2004	3	6,900,000,000	7,508,000,000
10	Allison (northern TX)	2001	TS[1]	5,000,000,000	6,414,000,000
11	Floyd (mid-Atlantic US; northeastern US)	1999	2	4,500,000,000	6,342,000,000
12	Isabel (NC; eastern US)	2003	2	3,370,000,000	3,985,000,000
13	Fran (NC)	1996	3	3,200,000,000	4,979,000,000
14	Opal (northwestern FL; AL)	1995	3	3,000,000,000	4,758,000,000
15	Frederic (AL; MS)	1979	3	2,300,000,000	6,922,000,000
16	Dennis (northwestern FL)	2005	3	2,230,000,000	2,330,000,000
17	Agnes (FL; northeastern US)	1972	1	2,100,000,000	12,424,000,000
18	Alicia (northern TX)	1983	3	2,000,000,000	4,825,000,000
19	Bob (NC; northeastern US)	1991	2	1,500,000,000	2,853,000,000
	Juan (LA)	1985	1	1,500,000,000	3,417,000,000
21	Camille (MS; southeastern LA; VA)	1969	5	1,420,700,000	9,781,000,000
22	Betsy (southeastern FL; southeastern LA)	1965	3	1,420,500,000	11,883,000,000
23	Elena (MS; AL; northwestern FL)	1985	3	1,250,000,000	2,848,000,000
24	Georges (Florida Keys; MS; AL)	1998	2	1,155,000,000	1,645,000,000
25	Gloria (eastern US)	1985	3[2]	900,000,000	2,050,000,000
26	Lili (LA; MS)	2002	1	860,000,000	1,249,000,000
27	Diane (northeastern US)	1955	1	831,700,000	7,700,000,000
28	Bonnie (NC; VA)	1998	2	720,000,000	1,025,000,000
29	Erin (northwestern FL)	1998	2	700,000,000	997,000,000
30	Allison (northern TX)	1989	TS[1]	500,000,000	962,857,000
	Frances (TX)	1998	TS[1]	500,000,000	712,143,000
non-Atlantic or non–Gulf Coast systems					
19	Georges (USVI; Puerto Rico)	1998	3	1,800,000,000	2,276,000,000
19	Iniki (Kauai, Hawaii)	1992	3–4	1,800,000,000	2,576,000,000
19	Marilyn (USVI; Puerto Rico)	1995	2	1,500,000,000	1,900,000,000
25	Hugo (USVI; Puerto Rico)	1989	4	1,000,000,000	1,502,000,000

[1]*Of tropical storm intensity but included because of high damage.*   [2]*Moving more than 30 mph.*

Geologic Disasters

Measuring Earthquakes

The seismologists Beno Gutenberg and Charles Francis Richter introduced measurement of the seismic energy released by earthquakes on a magnitude scale in 1935. Each increase of one unit on the scale represents a 10-fold increase in the magnitude of an earthquake. Seismographs are designed to measure different components of seismic waves, such as wave type, intensity, and duration. This table shows the typical effects of earthquakes in various magnitude ranges. For further information, see <www.seismo.unr.edu/ftp/pub/louie/class/100/magnitude.html>.

MAGNITUDE	EARTHQUAKE EFFECTS
Less than 3.5	Generally not felt, but recorded.
3.5–5.4	Often felt, but rarely causes damage.
Less than 6.0	At most, slight damage to well-designed buildings. Can cause major damage to poorly constructed buildings over small regions.
6.1–6.9	Can be destructive in areas up to about 100 km (61 mi) across where people live.
7.0–7.9	Major earthquake. Can cause serious damage over larger areas.
8 or greater	Great earthquake. Can cause serious damage in areas several hundred km across.

Major Historical Earthquakes

Magnitudes given for pre-20th-century events are generally estimations from intensity data. When no magnitude was available, the earthquake's maximum intensity, written as a Roman numeral from I to XII, is given.

YEAR (AD)	AFFECTED AREA	MAGNITUDE OR INTENSITY	DEATHS	YEAR (AD)	AFFECTED AREA	MAGNITUDE OR INTENSITY	DEATHS
365	Knossos, Crete, Greece	XI	50,000	1939	Chillán, Chile	7.8	28,000
526	Antioch, Syria	unknown	250,000	1944	Nankaido, Japan	8.1	1,223
844	Damascus, Syria	VIII	50,000	1944	San Juan, Argentina	7.8	c. 8,000
847	Damascus, Syria	X	70,000	1945	off the coast of Pakistan	8.0	4,000
847	Mosul, Iraq	unknown	50,000	1946	Tonankai, Japan	8.1	1,330
856	Qumis, Damghan, Iran	unknown	200,000	1948	Ashgabat, Turkmenistan	7.3	110,000
893	Daipur, India	unknown	180,000	1950	China-India border, near Myanmar (Burma)	8.6	1,526
893	Ardabil, Iran	unknown	150,000	1960	Puerto Montt, Chile	9.5	5,700
893	Caucasus	unknown	82,000	1960	Agadir, Morocco	5.7	10,000–15,000
1042	Palmyra, Baalbek, Syria	X	50,000	1964	Prince William Sound AK	8.3	131
1138	Ganzah, Aleppo, Syria	unknown	230,000	1968	Khorasan, Iran	7.3	12,000–20,000
1201	Upper Egypt or Syria	IX	1,100,000	1970	northern Peru	7.9	66,000
1268	Cilicia, Anatolia, Turkey	unknown	60,000	1970	southern Yunnan province, China	7.7	10,000
1290	Chihli, China	unknown	100,000	1972	Fars, Iran	7.1	5,054
1556	Shaanxi province, China	8.0	830,000	1972	Managua, Nicaragua	6.2	5,000
1667	Shemakha, Azerbaijan	unknown	80,000	1974	Yunnan province, China	6.8	20,000
1668	Shandong province, China	XII	50,000	1974	North-West Frontier, Pakistan	6.2	5,300
1693	Sicily, Italy	7.5	60,000	1975	Liaoning province, China	7.0	10,000
1703	Jeddo, Japan	unknown	200,000	1976	Mindanao, Philippines	7.9	8,000
1727	Tabriz, Iran	unknown	77,000	1976	Tangshan, China	7.5	255,000
1730	Hokkaido, Japan	unknown	137,000	1976	Guatemala City, Guatemala	7.5	23,000
1731	Beijing, China	unknown	100,000	1976	Turkey-Iran border	7.3	5,000
1739	China	X	50,000	1977	Bucharest, Romania	7.2	1,581
1755	Lisbon, Portugal; Spain; Morocco	8.7	70,000	1978	Khorasan, Iran	7.8	15,000
1780	Tabriz, Iran	unknown	100,000	1979	Colombia; Ecuador	7.9	579
1783	Calabria, Italy	unknown	50,000	1980	El-Asnam, Algeria	7.7	5,000
1811	New Madrid MO	8.6	unknown	1980	southern Italy	6.9	3,114
1835	northern Japan	7.6	28,300	1985	Michoacán, Mexico	8.0	9,500–30,000
1857	Tejon Pass (Palmdale) CA	8.3	unknown	1988	Leninakan (Kumayri), Armenia	6.8	25,000
1868	Ecuador; Colombia	7.7	70,000	1990	Luzon, Philippines	7.8	1,621
1883	Java, Indonesia	unknown	100,000	1990	Rasht, Iran	7.7	40,000–50,000
1905	Calabria, Italy	7.9	2,500	1991	northern India	7.1	2,000
1905	Kangra, India	7.5	19,000	1992	Flores Island, Indonesia	7.5	2,500
1906	off the coast of Ecuador	8.8	1,000	1993	Latur, India	6.2	9,748
1906	Valparaíso, Chile	8.2	20,000	1995	Sakhalin Island, Russia	7.5	2,000
1906	San Francisco CA	7.8	c. 3,000	1995	Kobe, Japan	6.9	5,502
1907	southwestern Tajikistan	8.0	12,000	1997	eastern Iran	7.1	1,560
1908	Calabria, Italy	7.2	70,000–100,000	1998	Feyzabad, Afghanistan	6.6	4,000
1912	Sea of Marmara, Turkey	7.8	1,950	1999	Taiwan	7.7	2,400
1915	Abruzzi, Italy	7.0	29,980	1999	Golcuk, Turkey	7.6	17,118
1920	Gansu province, China	7.8	200,000	2001	El Salvador	7.7	844
1923	Tokyo; Yokohama, Japan	7.9	143,000	2001	Gujarat, India	7.6	20,085
1927	Qinghai province, China	7.9	200,000	2003	northern Algeria	6.8	2,266
1932	Gansu province, China	7.6	70,000	2003	Bam, Iran	6.6	26,200
1933	Sanriku, Japan	8.4	2,990	2004	off the west coast of northern Sumatra, Indonesia	9.1	283,106
1935	Quetta, Pakistan	7.5	30,000	2005	northern Sumatra, Indonesia	8.6	1,313
1939	Erzincan, Turkey	7.8	32,700	2005	Kashmir, Pakistan	7.6	80,361
				2006	Bantul, Indonesia	6.3	5,749

Tsunami

A tsunami is a catastrophic ocean wave, usually caused by a submarine earthquake occurring less than 30 mi (50 km) beneath the seafloor, with a magnitude greater than 6.5. Underwater or coastal landslides or volcanic eruptions also may cause a tsunami. The often-used term tidal wave is a misnomer: the wave has no connection with the tides. After the earthquake or other generating impulse, a train of simple, progressive oscillatory waves is propagated great distances at the ocean surface in ever-widening circles, much like the waves produced by a pebble falling into a shallow pool. In deep water, the wavelengths are enormous, about 60 to 125 mi (100 to 200 km), and the wave heights are very small, only 1 to 2 ft (0.3 to 0.6 m). The resulting wave steepness is extremely low; coupled with the waves' long periods that vary from five minutes to an hour, this enables

normal wind waves and swell to completely obscure the waves in deep water. Thus, a ship in the open ocean experiences the passage of a tsunami as an insignificant rise and fall. As the waves approach the continental coasts, friction with the increasingly shallow bottom reduces the velocity of the waves. The period must remain constant; consequently, as the velocity lessens, the wavelengths become shortened and the wave amplitudes increase, coastal waters rising as high as 100 feet (30 m) in 10 to 15 minutes. By a poorly understood process, the continental shelf waters begin to oscillate after the rise in sea level. Between three and five major oscillations generate most of the damage; the oscillations cease, however, only several days after they begin. Occasionally, the first arrival of a tsunami at a coast may be a trough, the water receding and exposing the shallow seafloor.

Deadly Volcano Eruptions

Casualty figures are approximate.

VOLCANO (LOCATION)	YEAR	CASUALTIES	VOLCANO (LOCATION)	YEAR	CASUALTIES
Tambora (Indonesia)	1815	92,000[1]	Raung (Indonesia)	1730	3,000
Krakatoa (Indonesia)	1883	36,000[1]	Lamington (Papua New Guinea)	1951	3,000
Pelée (Martinique)	1902	30,000	Awu (Indonesia)	1856	2,800
Ruiz (Colombia)	1985	25,000[2]	Taal, Luzon (Philippines)	1906	1,500
Etna (Italy)	1669	20,000	Taal, Luzon (Philippines)	1911	1,300
Unzen (Japan)	1792	15,000	Etna (Italy)	1536	1,000
Kelud (Indonesia)	1586	10,000	Paricutín (Mexico)	1949	1,000
Laki (Iceland)	1783	9,000	Purace (Colombia)	1949	1,000
Kelud (Indonesia)	1919	5,000	Pinatubo (Philippines)	1991	350
Vesuvius (Italy)	79	3,360	El Chichón (Mexico)	1982	100
Awu (Indonesia)	1711	3,200	St. Helens (Washington, US)	1980	66[3]
Raung (Indonesia)	1638	3,000			

[1]Includes tidal wave triggered by eruption.   [2]Includes mudflow triggered by eruption.   [3]Includes persons missing.

Civil Engineering

The Seven Wonders of the Ancient World

The seven wonders of the ancient world were considered to be the preeminent architectural and sculptural achievements of the Mediterranean and Middle East. The best known are those of the 2nd-century-BC writer Antipater of Sidon. Some early lists included the Walls of Babylon or the Palace of King Cyrus of Persia, but the established list usually contained the following:

Pyramids of Giza. The oldest of the wonders and the only one substantially in existence today, the pyramids of Giza were erected c. 2575–c. 2465 BC on the west bank of the Nile River near Al-Jizah in northern Egypt. The designations of the pyramids—Khufu, Khafre, and Menkaure—correspond to the kings for whom they were built. Khufu (also called the Great Pyramid) is the largest of the three, the length of each side at the base averaging 230 m (755 ¾ ft). Its original height was 147 m (481.4 ft); none of the pyramids reach their original heights because they have been almost entirely stripped of their outer casings of smooth white limestone. According to Herodotus, the Great Pyramid took 20 years to construct and demanded the labor of 100,000 men.

Hanging Gardens of Babylon. A series of landscaped terraces ascribed to either Queen Sammu-ramat (810–783 BC) or King Nebuchadrezzar II (c. 605–c. 561 BC), the gardens were built within the walls of the royal palace at Babylon (in present-day southern Iraq). They did not actually "hang" but were instead "up in the air"—that is, they were roof gardens laid out on a series of ziggurat terraces that were irrigated by pumps from the Euphrates River. Although no traces of the Hanging Gardens have been found, classical authors related that the terraces were roofed with stone balconies on which were layered various materials, such as reeds, bitumen, and lead, so that the irrigation water would not seep through them.

Statue of Zeus. A large, ornate figure of Zeus on his throne, this wonder was made around 430 BC by Phidias of Athens. It was placed in the huge Temple of Zeus at Olympia in western Greece. The statue, almost 12 m (40 ft) high and plated with gold and ivory, represented the god sitting on an elaborate cedarwood throne ornamented with ebony, ivory, gold, and precious stones. On his outstretched right hand was a statue of Nike (Victory), and in the god's left hand was a scepter on which an eagle was perched. The statue, which took eight years to construct, may have been destroyed along with the temple in AD 426, or in a fire at Constantinople (Istanbul) about 50 years later.

Temple of Artemis. The great temple was built by Croesus, king of Lydia, in about 550 BC and was re-built after being burned by a madman named Hero-stratus in 356 BC. The artemesium was famous not only for its great size (over 110 by 55 m [350 by 80 ft]) but also for the magnificent works of art that adorned it. It was destroyed by invading Goths in AD 262 and was never rebuilt. Little remains of the temple, but excavation has revealed traces of it, and copies survive of the famous statue of Artemis. A mummylike figure, this early representation of the goddess stands stiffly straight, with her hands extended outward. The original statue was made of gold, ebony, silver, and black stone, the legs and hips covered by a garment decorated with reliefs of animals and bees and the head adorned with a high-pillared headdress.

Mausoleum of Halicarnassus. Monumental tomb of Mausolus, the tyrant of Caria in southwestern Asia Minor, the mausoleum was built between about 353 and 351 BC by Mausolus' sister and widow, Artemisia. The architect was Pythius (Pytheos), and the sculptures that adorned the building were the work of four leading Greek artists. According to the description of Pliny the Elder, the monument was almost square, with a total periphery of 125 m (411 ft). It was bounded by 36 columns, and the top formed a 24-step pyramid surmounted by a four-horse marble chariot. Fragments of the mausoleum's sculpture are preserved in the British Museum. The mausoleum was probably destroyed by an earthquake between the 11th and 15th century AD, and the stones were reused in local buildings.

Colossus of Rhodes. This huge bronze statue was built at the harbor of Rhodes in ancient Greece in commemoration of the raising of the siege of Rhodes (305–304 BC). The sculptor was Chares of Lyndus, and the statue was made of bronze, reinforced with iron, and weighted with stones. The Colossus was said to be 70 cubits (32 m [105 ft]) high and stood beside Mandrákion harbor. It is technically impossible that the statue could have straddled the harbor entrance, and the popular belief that it did so dates only from the Middle Ages. The Colossus took 12 years to build (c. 294–282 BC) and was toppled by an earthquake about 225 BC. The fallen Colossus was left in place until AD 654, when Arabian forces raided Rhodes and had the statue broken up and the bronze sold for scrap.

Pharos of Alexandria. The most famous lighthouse of the ancient world, it was built by Sostratus of Cnidus, perhaps for Ptolemy I Soter, but was finished during the reign of his son, Ptolemy II of Egypt, about 280 BC. The lighthouse stood on the island of Pharos off Alexandria and is said to have been more than 100 m (350 ft) high; the only taller man-made structures at the time would have been the pyramids of Giza. It was a technological triumph and is the archetype of all lighthouses since. According to ancient sources, a broad spiral ramp led to the top, where a fire burned at night. The lighthouse was destroyed by an earthquake in the 1300s. In 1994 a large amount of masonry blocks and statuary was found in the waters off Pharos.

25 Tallest Buildings in the World

Building height equals the distance from the sidewalk level of the main entrance to the structural top of the building, including spires. Source: Council on Tall Buildings and Urban Habitat.

RANK	BUILDING	CITY	YEAR COMPLETED	HEIGHT IN FT/M	STORIES
1	Taipei 101	Taipei, Taiwan	2004	1,667/508	101
2	Petronas Tower 1	Kuala Lumpur, Malaysia	1998	1,483/452	88
3	Petronas Tower 2	Kuala Lumpur, Malaysia	1998	1,483/452	88
4	Sears Tower	Chicago IL	1974	1,451/442	110
5	Jin Mao Building	Shanghai, China	1999	1,381/421	88
6	Two International Finance Centre	Hong Kong, China	2003	1,362/415	88
7	CITIC Plaza	Guangzhou, China	1996	1,283/391	80
8	Shun Hing Square	Shenzhen, China	1996	1,260/384	69
9	Empire State Building	New York NY	1931	1,250/381	102
10	Central Plaza	Hong Kong, China	1992	1,227/374	78
11	Bank of China	Hong Kong, China	1989	1,205/367	70
12	Emirates Tower One	Dubai, UAE	1999	1,165/355	54
13	Tuntex Sky Tower	Kaohsiung, Taiwan	1997	1,140/348	85
14	Aon Centre	Chicago IL	1973	1,136/346	83
15	The Center	Hong Kong, China	1998	1,135/346	73
16	John Hancock Center	Chicago IL	1969	1,127/344	100
17	Shimao International Plaza	Shanghai, China	2006	1,093/333	60
18	Q1	Gold Coast, QLD, Australia	2005	1,058/323	78
19	Burj Al Arab	Dubai, UAE	1999	1,053/321	60
20	Chrysler Building	New York NY	1930	1,046/319	77
21	Nina Tower I	Hong Kong, China	2006	1,046/319	80
22	Bank of America Plaza	Atlanta GA	1993	1,039/317	55
23	US Bank Tower	Los Angeles CA	1990	1,018/310	73
24	Menara Telekom Headquarters	Kuala Lumpur, Malaysia	1999	1,017/310	55
25	Emirates Tower Two	Dubai, UAE	2000	1,014/309	56

World's Longest-Span Structures by Type

Bridges

SUSPENSION	LOCATION	YEAR OF COMPLETION	MAIN SPAN (M)
Akashi Kaikyo	Kobe–Awaji Island, Japan	1998	1,991
part of eastern link between islands of Honshu and Shikoku			
Store Baelt (Great Belt)	Zealand–Funen, Denmark	1998	1,624
part of link between Copenhagen and mainland Europe			
Nancha	Zhenjiang, China	2005	1,490
world's third longest suspension bridge			
Humber	near Hull, England	1981	1,410
crosses Humber estuary between Yorkshire and Lincolnshire			
Jiangyin	Jiangsu province, China	1999	1,385
crosses Chang Jiang (Yangtze River) near Shanghai			
Tsing Ma	Hong Kong, China	1997	1,377
connects Hong Kong city with airport on Landao Island			
Verrazano-Narrows	New York NY	1964	1,298
spans New York Harbor between Brooklyn and Staten Island			
Golden Gate	San Francisco CA	1937	1,280
spans entrance to San Francisco Bay			
Höga Kusten (High Coast)	Kramfors, Sweden	1997	1,210
crosses Angerman River on scenic coastal route in northern Sweden			
Mackinac	Mackinaw City–St. Ignace MI	1957	1,158
spans Mackinac Straits between upper and lower peninsulas of Michigan			
CABLE-STAYED (STEEL)			
Tatara	Onomichi–Imabari, Japan	1999	890
part of western link between islands of Honshu and Shikoku			
Normandie	near Le Havre, France	1995	856
crosses Seine estuary between upper and lower Normandy			
Nanjing Yangtze Sanqiao	Nanjing, China	2005	648
world's third longest cable-stayed bridge			
Nancha	Nanjing, China	2001	628
southern span of Second Nanjing Yangtze Bridge			
Wuhan Baishazhou	Hubei province, China	2000	618
provides third crossing of Chang Jiang (Yangtze River) in city of Wuhan			
Rion–Antirion	near Patrai, Greece (Gulf of Corinth)	2004	560
world's second largest cable-stayed bridge			
Millau Viaduct	Tarn Gorge, France	2004	342
world's highest bridge (270 m) and longest cable-stayed bridge (2,460 m)			
ARCH			
steel			
Lupu	Shanghai, China	2003	550
crosses Huangpujiang (Huang-p'u River) between central Shanghai and Pudong New District			
New River Gorge	Fayetteville WV	1977	518
provides road link through scenic New River Gorge National River area			
Bayonne	Bayonne NJ–New York NY	1931	504
spans the Kill Van Kull between New Jersey and Staten Island			
Sydney Harbour	Sydney, NSW, Australia	1932	503
links the City of Sydney with North Sydney			
concrete			
Wanxian	Sichuan province, China	1997	420
crosses Chang Jiang (Yangtze River) in Three Gorges area			
Krk I	Krk Island, Croatia	1980	390
links scenic Krk Island with mainland Croatia			
Jiangjiehe	Guizhou province, China	1995	330
spans gorge of Wujiang (Wu River)			
CANTILEVER			
steel truss			
Pont de Québec	Quebec City, QC, Canada	1917	549
provides rail crossing over St. Lawrence River			
Forth	Queensferry, Scotland	1890	2 spans, each 521
provides rail crossing over Firth of Forth			
Minato	Osaka–Amagasaki, Japan	1974	510
carries road traffic across Osaka's harbor			
Commodore John J. Barry	Bridgeport NJ–Chester PA	1974	501
provides road crossing over Delaware River			

World's Longest-Span Structures by Type (continued)

	LOCATION	YEAR OF COMPLETION	MAIN SPAN (M)
CANTILEVER (CONTINUED)			
prestressed concrete			
Shibanpo-2	Chongqing, China	2006	336
world's longest prestressed-concrete box girder bridge			
Stolmasundet	Austevoll, Norway	1998	301
links islands of Stolmen and Sjelbörn south of Bergen			
Raftsundet	Lofoten, Norway	1998	298
crosses Raft Sound in arctic Lofoten Islands			
Sundøy	Leirfjord, Norway	2003	298
links Alsten Island to mainland Norway			
BEAM			
steel truss			
Ikitsuki Ohashi	Nagasaki prefecture, Japan	1991	400
connects islands of Iki and Hirado off northwest Kyushu			
Astoria	Astoria OR	1966	376
carries Pacific Coast Highway across Columbia River between Oregon and Washington			
Francis Scott Key	Baltimore MD	1977	366
spans Patapsco River at Baltimore Harbor			
Oshima	Yamaguchi prefecture, Japan	1976	325
links Yanai City and Oshima Island			
steel plate and box girder			
Presidente Costa e Silva	Rio de Janeiro state, Brazil	1974	300
crosses Guanabara Bay between Rio de Janeiro and suburb of Niterói			
Neckartalbrücke-1	Weitingen, Germany	1978	263
carries highway across Neckar River Valley			
Brankova	Belgrade, Serbia	1956	261
provides road crossing of Sava River between Old and New Belgrade			
Ponte de Vitória-3	Espírito Santo state, Brazil	1989	260
provides road link to state capital on Vitória Island			
MOVABLE			
vertical lift			
Arthur Kill	Elizabeth NJ–New York NY	1959	170
provides rail link between port of Elizabeth and Staten Island			
Cape Cod Canal	Cape Cod MA	1935	166
provides rail crossing over waterway near Buzzard's Bay			
Delair	Delair NJ–Philadelphia PA	1960	165
provides rail link across Delaware River between Philadelphia and South Jersey shore			
Marine Parkway–Gil Hodges Memorial	New York NY	1937	165
carries road traffic over mouth of Jamaica Bay between Brooklyn and the Rockaways, Queens			
swing span			
Al-Firdan (El-Ferdan)	Suez Canal, Egypt	2001	340
provides road and rail link between Sinai Peninsula and eastern Nile Delta region			
Santa Fe	Fort Madison IA–Niota IL	1927	160
provides road and rail crossing of Mississippi River			
BASCULE			
South Capitol Street/Frederick Douglass Memorial	Washington DC	1949	118
carries road traffic over Anacostia River			
Sault Sainte Marie	Sault Sainte Marie MI–Ontario, Canada	1941	102
connects rail systems of United States and Canada			
Charles Berry	Lorain OH	1940	101
carries road traffic over Black River			
Market Street/Chief John Ross	Chattanooga TN	1917	94
carries road traffic over Tennessee River			
Causeways (fixed link over water only)			
Lake Pontchartrain-2	Metairie–Mandeville LA	1969	38,422
carries northbound road traffic from suburbs of New Orleans to north lakeshore			
Lake Pontchartrain-1	Mandeville–Metairie LA	1956	38,352
carries southbound road traffic from north lakeshore to suburbs of New Orleans			
King Fahd Causeway	Bahrain–Saudi Arabia	1986	24,950
carries road traffic across Gulf of Bahrain in Persian Gulf			
Confederation Bridge	Borden-Carleton, PE–Cape Jourimain, NB, Canada	1997	12,900
carries road traffic over Northumberland Strait			

Basic Types of Bridges

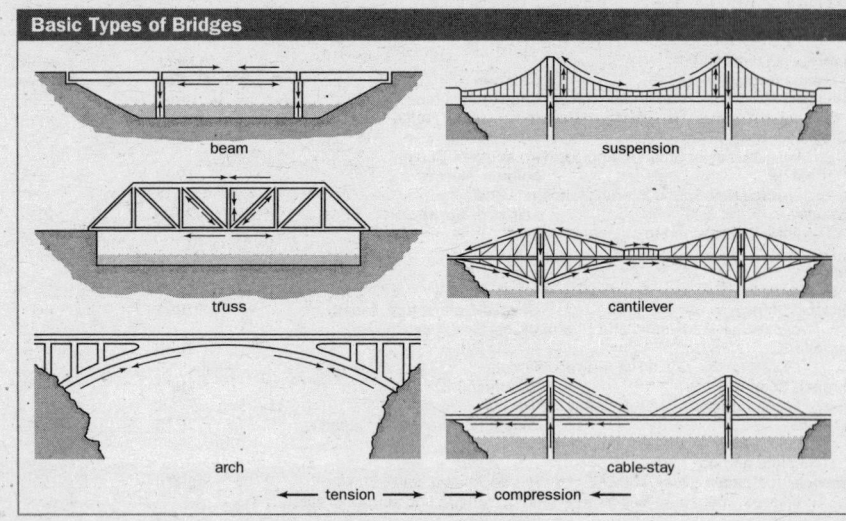

beam

suspension

truss

cantilever

arch

cable-stay

← tension →   → compression ←

The World's 25 Longest Tunnels

TUNNEL	LOCATION	LENGTH IN KM (MI)	COMPLETED	USE
Seikan	Japan	53.9 (33.5)	1988	railway
passes under the Tsugaru Strait between islands of Honshu and Hokkaido				
Channel Tunnel (Eurotunnel)	UK–France	50.5 (31.4)	1994	railway
passes under English Channel between Folkestone (UK) and Sangatte (France)				
Lötschberg Base	Switzerland	34.6 (21.5)	2007	railway
world's longest land tunnel (under Alps between Frutigen and Raron)				
Guadarrama	Spain	28.4 (17.6)	2007	railway
on high-speed rail line between Madrid and Valladolid				
Iwate-Ichinohe	Japan	25.8 (15.7)	2002	railway
carries Tohoku high-speed line through mountains between Tokyo and northern Honshu				
Lærdal	Norway	24.5 (15.3)	2000	highway
carries main cross-country highway through mountains in central Norway				
Dai-Shimizu	Japan	22.2 (13.8)	1982	railway
on Joetsu "Bullet" Line across Honshu between Tokyo and Niigata				
Wushaoling I and II (dual-bore)	China	21.0 (13.1)	2006	railway
between Lanzhou and Wuwei				
Simplon I	Italy–Switzerland	19.8 (12.3)	1906	railway
Simplon II	Italy–Switzerland	19.8 (12.3)	1922	railway
rail links under Simplon Pass, traditional divide between northern and southern Europe				
Vereina	Switzerland	19.1 (11.9)	1999	railway
rail link under Flüela Pass between upper Rhine and lower Engadin valleys				
Shin-Kanmon	Japan	18.7 (11.6)	1975	railway
carries Sanyo high-speed line under Kanmon Strait between islands of Honshu and Kyushu				
Great Apennine	Italy	18.5 (11.5)	1934	railway
rail link through mountains between Bologna and Florence				
Qinling	China	18.5 (11.5)	2001	railway
traverses Qinling (Tsinling) Mountains, historic barrier between northern and southern China				
Zhongnanshan	China	18.0 (11.2)	2007	highway
world's longest double-tube four-lane highway tunnel				
St. Gotthard	Switzerland	16.9 (10.5)	1980	highway
links Uri and Ticino cantons under St. Gotthard Pass				
Rokko	Japan	16.3 (10.1)	1972	railway
carries Sanyo high-speed line through Rokko Mountains near Kobe				
Furka	Switzerland	15.4 (9.6)	1982	railway
carries scenic Glacier Express Line under Furka Pass				
Haruna	Japan	15.4 (9.6)	1982	railway
on Joetsu "Bullet" Line across Honshu between Tokyo and Niigata				
Severomuyskiy	Russia	15.3 (9.5)	2001	railway
on the Baikal–Amur Line to the northeast of Lake Baikal				

The World's 25 Longest Tunnels (continued)

TUNNEL	LOCATION	LENGTH IN KM (MI)	COMPLETED	USE
Gorigamine	Japan	15.2 (9.4)	1997	railway
on the Hokuriku high-speed line between Takasaki and Nagano				
Monte Santomarco	Italy	15.0 (9.3)	1987	railway
tunnel in Calabria between Paola and Cosenza				
St. Gotthard	Switzerland	15.0 (9.3)	1882	railway
carries Luzern–Milan line under St. Gotthard Pass between Uri and Ticino cantons				
Nakayama	Japan	14.9 (9.2)	1982	railway
on Joetsu "Bullet" Line across Honshu between Tokyo and Niigata				
Mount MacDonald	BC, Canada	14.7 (9.2)	1988	railway
longest tunnel in Western Hemisphere; in Canada's Glacier National Park				

World's Largest Dams

Source: International Water Power and Dam Construction Yearbook (1996).

NAME	TYPE*	DATE OF COMPLETION	RIVER	COUNTRY	
by height					**height (m)**
Nurek	E	1980	Vakhsh	Tajikistan	300
Grand Dixence	G	1961	Dixence	Switzerland	285
Inguri	A	1980	Inguri	Georgia	272
Vaiont[1]	A	1961	Vaiont	Italy	262
Chicoasen	ER	1980	Grijalva	Mexico	261
Tehri	ER	2002[2]	Bhagirathi	India	261
Mauvoisin	A	1957	Drance de Bagnes	Switzerland	250
by volume					**volume ('000 cubic m)**
Syncrude Tailings	E	N/A	...[3]	Canada	540,000
New Cornelia Tailings	E	1973	Ten Mile Wash	US	209,500
Tarbela	ER	1976	Indus	Pakistan	106,000
Fort Peck	E	1937	Missouri	US	96,050
Lower Usuma	E	1990	Usuma	Nigeria	93,000
Tucurui	EGR	1984	Tocantins	Brazil	85,200
Ataturk	ER	1990	Euphrates	Turkey	84,500
by size of reservoir					**reservoir capacity ('000 cubic m)**
Owen Falls	G	1954	Victoria Nile	Uganda	2,700,000,000[4]
Kakhovsk	EG	1955	Dnieper	Ukraine	182,000,000
Kariba	A	1959	Zambezi	Zimbabwe–Zambia	180,600,000
Bratsk	EG	1964	Angara	Russia	169,270,000
Aswan High	ER	1970	Nile	Egypt	168,900,000
Akosombo	ER	1965	Volta	Ghana	153,000,000
Daniel Johnson	M	1968	Manicouagan	Canada	141,852,000
Guri (Raúl Leoni)	EGR	1986	Caroní	Venezuela	138,000,000
by power capacity					**power capacity (megawatts)**
Itaipú	EGR	1983	Paraná	Brazil–Paraguay	13,320
Guri (Raúl Leoni)	EGR	1986	Caroní	Venezuela	10,055
Grand Coulee	G	1942	Columbia	US	6,809
Sayano-Shushenskoye	GA	1989	Yenisey	Russia	6,400
Krasnoyarsk	G	1968	Yenisey	Russia	6,000
Churchill Falls	E	1971	Churchill	Canada	5,428
La Grande 2	R	1979	LaGrande	Canada	5,328
Three Gorges	G	2003	Yangtze	China	4,970

*Key: A, arch; B, buttress; E, earth fill; G, gravity; M, multi-arch; R, rock fill. N/A indicates "not available." [1]Vaiont Dam was the scene of a massive landslide and flood in 1963 and no longer operates. [2]Diversion tunnels closed and reservoir filling begun December 2002. [3]Near Fort McMurray AB. [4]Most of this reservoir is a natural lake.

Notable Civil Engineering Projects (in progress or completed as of December 2006)

NAME	LOCATION		YEAR OF COMPLETION	NOTES
airports		**terminal area (sq m)**		
Beijing Capital (Terminal 3)	northeast of Beijing	904,000	2007	to be world's largest terminal
New Doha International	near Doha, Qatar	140,000	2009	first airport built for Airbus A380-800 (world's largest passenger plane)
Heathrow (new Terminal 5)	southwest of London	70,000	2008	biggest construction project in the UK from 2002
bridges		**length (main span; m)**		
Hangzhou Bay	near Jiaxing, China– near Cixi, China	2,600	2008	to be world's longest transoceanic bridge/ causeway; begun 2003
I-95 (Woodrow Wilson #2)	Alexandria VA– Maryland suburbs of Washington DC	1,829 each	2006–08	2 bascule spans forming higher inverted V shape for ships; begun 2000
Sutong	Nantong, China (100 km from Yangtze mouth)	1,088	2008	to have world's longest cable-stayed main span
Stonecutters	Hong Kong	1,018	2008	to be world's longest cable-stayed bridge
buildings		**height (m)**		
Burj ("Tower") Dubai	Dubai, United Arab Emirates	805	2008	to be the world's tallest building
Freedom Tower	New York City	541 (1,776 ft)	2011	to be tallest building in North America
Shanghai World Financial Center	Shanghai	492	2007	begun 1997, resumed 2003; to be world's 2nd tallest building
Union Square Phase 7	Hong Kong	474	2007	begun 2002; 16-building complex
dams and hydrologic projects		**crest length (m)**		
Three Gorges (3rd phase)	west of Yichang, China	1,983	2008	to create world's largest reservoir (620 km long) beginning 2003 and ⅕ of national total generated power
Sardar Sarovar (Narmada) Project	Narmada River, Madhya Pradesh, India	1,210	2007	largest dam of controversial 30-dam project; drinking water for Gujarat
Bakun Hydroelectric Project	Balui River, Sarawak, Borneo, Malaysia	740	2008	to be world's largest concrete-faced rockfill dam
Caruachi (3rd of 5-dam Lower Caroní Development scheme)	Caroní River, northern Bolívar, Venezuela	360	2003–06	hydroelectric generation began 28 Feb 2003
Belo Monte	Xingù River, Pará state, Brazil	?	2008	to be 3rd largest dam in the world in terms of electricity output
Project Moses (flood-protection plan)	lagoon openings near Venice	—	2011	rows of 79 20-m-wide submerged gates in three lagoon openings will rise in flood conditions
highways		**length (km)**		
Golden Quadrilateral superhighway	Mumbai– Chennai–Kolkata– Delhi, India	5,846	2007	upgrade to 4 lanes; Mumbai–Delhi (2005), Delhi–Kolkata (2007)
East–West Highway	Annaba–Tlemcen, Algeria	1,216	2009	to facilitate trade across North Africa
Highway 1	Kabul–Kandahar– Herat, Afghanistan	1,048	2007	final, 556-km Kandahar–Herat section 80% complete in November 2006
land reclamation		**area (sq km)**		
The Palms ("Jumeirah, Jebel Ali, and Deira islands")	in the Persian Gulf, near Dubai, UAE	20, 44, and 94	2007–09	3 date-palm-tree-shaped arrays of ultraexclusive islands

Notable Civil Engineering Projects (in progress or completed as of December 2006) (continued)

NAME	LOCATION		YEAR OF COMPLETION	NOTES
land reclamation (continued)		area (sq km)		
The World	in the Persian Gulf, near Dubai, UAE	c. 56	2008	300 private artificial islands arrayed as a map of the world
railways (heavy)		length (km)		
Trans-Kazakhstan	Dostyq (Druzhba), Kazakhstan– Gorgan, Iran	3,943	2008	China to Europe link, bypassing Russia and Uzbekistan; 3,083 km in Kazakhstan
Qinghai–Tibet	China: Golmud, Qinghai–Lhasa, Tibet	1,142	2007	world's highest railway (5,072 m at summit); 86% above 4,000 m
Xi'an–Nanjing	China: Xi'an, Shaanxi– Nanjing, Jiangsu	1,129	2007	for economic growth in interior; 954-km Xi'an-Hefei section finished 2003
Ferronorte (extension to Rondonópolis)	Alto Araguaia– Rondonópolis, Brazil	270	2007	for agricultural exports from Mato Grosso (Brazil interior)
railways (high speed)		length (km)		
Spanish high speed (second line)	Madrid, Spain–France (via Barcelona)	719	2009	to reach Barcelona in 2007; Madrid–Lleida corridor opened 11 Oct 2003
Italian high speed	Turin–Naples, Italy	844	2009	high-speed route to link the major cities of Italy from north to south
Korea Train Express (KTX)	Seoul–Pusan, South Korea	412	2008	will connect largest and 2nd largest cities; to Taegu as of 1 Apr 2004
Taiwan high speed	Hsi-chih–Tso-ying, Taiwan	345	2007	links Taiwan's two largest cities; opened January 2007
Eastern France high speed	eastern outskirts of Paris–near Metz, France	300	2007	106-km extension to Strasbourg in planning stage
Channel Tunnel Rail Link	near Folkestone, England–central London	109	2007	74-km section (Folkestone-north Kent) opened 16 Sep 2003
subways/metros/light rails		length (km)		
Guangzhou Metro (including suburbs)	Guangzhou (Canton), China	313.9	2010	9-line system planned
Shanghai Metro	Shanghai	147.4	. . .	18-line system planned; 9 lines under construction in 2007
Shenzhen Metro	Shenzhen, China (adjacent to Hong Kong)	78.1	2010	construction of Lines 2 and 3; extension of Lines 1 and 4
Dubai Metro (Red and Green Lines)	Dubai, UAE	69.7	2010	to be world's longest fully automated driverless transport system
Barcelona Metro (Line 9)	airport–northeast Barcelona	47.0	2011	connects to other metro lines and future high-speed rail
tunnels		length (m)		
Apennine Range tunnels (9)	Bologna–Florence, Italy (high-speed railway)	73,400	2008	longest tunnel (Vaglia, 18.6 km); tunnels to cover 93% of railway
Lötschberg #2	Frutigen–Raron, Switzerland	34,577	2007	to be world's 3rd longest rail tunnel; France–Italy link
Guadarrama	50 km north-northwest of Madrid	28,377	2007	to be world's 4th longest rail tunnel; Valladolid high-speed link

1 m=3.28 ft; 1 km=0.62 mi

Life on Earth

Taxonomy

Taxonomy is the classification of living and extinct organisms. The term is derived from the Greek *taxis* ("arrangement") and *nomos* ("law") and refers to the methodology and principles of systematic botany and zoology by which the various kinds of plants and animals are arranged in hierarchies of superior and subordinate groups.

Popularly, classifications of living organisms arise according to need and are often superficial; for example, although the term fish is common to the names shellfish, crayfish, and starfish, there are more anatomical differences between a shellfish and a starfish than there are between a bony fish and a human. Also, vernacular names vary widely. Biologists have attempted to view all living organisms with equal thoroughness and thus have devised a formal classification. A formal classification supports a relatively uniform and internationally understood nomenclature, thereby simplifying cross-referencing and retrieval of information.

Carolus Linnaeus, who is usually regarded as the founder of modern taxonomy and whose books are considered the beginning of modern botanical and zoological nomenclature, drew up rules for assigning names to plants and animals and was the first to use binomial nomenclature consistently, beginning in 1758. Classification since Linnaeus has incorporated newly discovered information and more closely approaches a natural system, and the process of clarifying relationships continues to this day. The table below shows the seven ranks that are accepted as obligatory by zoologists and botanists and sample listings for animals and plants.

	ANIMALS	PLANTS
Kingdom	Animalia	Plantae
Phylum/Division	Chordata	Tracheophyta
Class	Mammalia	Pteropsida
Order	Primates	Coniferales
Family	Hominidae	Pinaceae
Genus	*Homo*	*Pinus*
Species	*Homo sapiens* (human)	*Pinus strobus* (white pine)

Animals

Period of Gestation and Longevity of Selected Mammals

ANIMAL	AVERAGE GESTATION (DAYS)	AVERAGE LONGEVITY (YEARS)	ANIMAL	AVERAGE GESTATION (DAYS)	AVERAGE LONGEVITY (YEARS)
bear (black)	219	18	horse	330	20
bear (grizzly)	225	25	human (worldwide)	266–70	Men: 64.7; Women: 68.9
bear (polar)	240	20			
cat (domestic)	63	12	monkey (rhesus)	164	15
dog (domestic)	61	12	mouse (domestic white)	19	3
elephant (Asian)	645	40	pig (domestic)	112	10
fox (red)	52	7	rabbit (domestic)	31	5
guinea pig	68	4	sheep (domestic)	154	12
hippopotamus	238	25–30	squirrel (gray)	44	9–10

Names of the Male, Female, Young, and Group of Animals

ANIMAL	MALE	FEMALE	YOUNG	GROUP
ape	male	female	baby	shrewdness
bear	boar	sow	cub	sleuth, sloth
camel	bull	cow	calf	flock
cattle	bull	cow	calf	drift, drove, herd, mob
chicken	rooster	hen	chick, pullet (hen), cockrell (rooster)	flock, brood (hens), clutch & peep (chicks)
deer	buck, stag	doe	fawn	herd
donkey	jack, jackass	jennet, jenny	colt, foal	drove, herd
elephant	bull	cow	calf	herd, parade
ferret	hob	jill	kit	business, fesynes
fox	reynard	vixen	kit, cub, pup	skulk, leash
giraffe	bull	doe	calf	herd, corps, tower, group
goat	buck, billy	doe, nanny	kid, billy	herd, tribe, trip
gorilla	male	female	infant	band

Names of the Male, Female, Young, and Group of Animals (continued)

ANIMAL	MALE	FEMALE	YOUNG	GROUP
hamster	buck	doe	pup	horde
hippopotamus	bull	cow	calf	herd, bloat
horse	stallion, stud	mare, dam	foal, colt (male), filly (female)	stable, harras, herd, team (working) string or field (racing)
human	man	woman	baby, infant, toddler	clan (related), crowd, family (closely related), community, gang, mob, tribe, etc.
lion	lion	lioness	cub	pride
louse	male	female	nymph	lice, colony, infestation
mouse	buck	doe	pup, pinkie, kitten	horde, mischief
ostrich	cock	hen	chick	flock
pig	boar	sow	piglet, shoat, farrow	drove, herd, litter (of pups), sounder
quail	cock	hen	chick	bevy, covey, drift
rhinoceros	bull	cow	calf	crash
seal	bull	cow	pup	herd, pod, rookery, harem
sheep	buck, ram	ewe, dam	lamb, lambkin, cosset	drift, drove, flock, herd, mob, trip
turkey	tom	hen	poult	rafter
turtle	male	female	hatchling	bale
whale	bull	cow	calf	gam, grind, herd, pod, school
wolf	dog	bitch	pup, whelp	pack, rout
zebra	stallion	mare	colt, foal	herd, crossing

Plants

World's Oldest Trees and Flowering Plants

	MAXIMUM AGE IN YEARS		
	ESTIMATED	VERIFIED	LOCATION
trees			
Bristlecone pine		4,900	Wheeler Peak, Humboldt National Forest, Nevada
Sierra redwood	4,000	2,200–2,300	northern California
Swiss stone pine	1,200	750	Riffel Alp, Switzerland
common juniper	2,000	544	Kola Peninsula, northeastern Russia
European larch	700	417	Riffel Alp, Switzerland
Norway spruce	1,200	350–400	Eichstätt, Bavaria, Germany
flowering plants			
bo tree	2,000–3,000		Bodh Gaya, India; Anuradhapura, Sri Lanka
English oak	2,000	1,500	Hasbruch Forest, Lower Saxony, Germany
linden		815	Lithuania
European beech	900	250	Montigny, Normandy, France
English ivy	440		Ginac, near Montpellier, France
dragon tree	200		Tenerife, Canary Islands
dwarf birch		80	eastern Greenland

The World's Forests

This table shows the 50 countries that either lost or gained the most forest area between 1990 and 2000 as well as forest losses or gains by continent. Source: State of the World's Forests 2001. 1 hectare (ha) = x .01 sq km, .004 sq mi. Web site: <www.fao.org/forestry>.

COUNTRY/AREA	LAND AREA ('000 HA)	TOTAL FOREST IN 1990 ('000 HA)	TOTAL FOREST IN 2000 ('000 HA)	PERCENTAGE OF LAND AREA IN 2000 (%)	% CHANGE 1990–2000
Burundi	2,568	241	94	3.7	−61.00
Haiti	2,756	158	88	3.2	−44.30
Micronesia	69	24	15	21.7	−37.50
El Salvador	2,072	193	121	5.8	−37.31
Saint Lucia	61	14	9	14.8	−35.71
Comoros	186	12	8	4.3	−33.33
Rwanda	2,466	457	307	12.4	−32.82
Niger	126,670	1,945	1,328	1	−31.72
Togo	5,439	719	510	9.4	−29.07
Côte d'Ivoire	31,800	9,766	7,117	22.4	−27.12
Nicaragua	12,140	4,450	3,278	27	−26.34

The World's Forests (continued)

COUNTRY/AREA	LAND AREA ('000 HA)	TOTAL FOREST IN 1990 ('000 HA)	TOTAL FOREST IN 2000 ('000 HA)	PERCENTAGE OF LAND AREA IN 2000 (%)	% CHANGE 1990–2000
Sierra Leone	7,162	1,416	1,055	14.7	−25.49
Mauritania	102,522	415	317	0.3	−23.61
Nigeria	91,077	17,501	13,517	14.8	−22.76
Malawi	9,409	3,269	2,562	27.2	−21.63
Zambia	74,339	39,755	31,246	42	−21.40
Belize	2,280	1,704	1,348	59.1	−20.89
Benin	11,063	3,349	2,650	24	−20.87
Samoa	282	130	105	37.2	−19.23
Liberia	11,137	4,241	3,481	31.3	−17.92
Uganda	19,964	5,103	4,190	21	−17.89
Yemen	52,797	541	449	0.9	−17.01
Nepal	14,300	4,683	3,900	27.3	−16.72
Ghana	22,754	7,535	6,335	27.8	−15.93
Guatemala	10,843	3,387	2,850	26.3	−15.85
Greece	12,890	3,299	3,599	27.9	9.09
The Gambia	1,000	436	481	48.1	10.32
China	932,743	145,417	163,480	17.5	12.42
Swaziland	1,721	464	522	30.3	12.50
Cuba	10,982	2,071	2,348	21.4	13.38
Azerbaijan	8,359	964	1,094	13.1	13.49
Armenia	2,820	309	351	12.4	13.59
Bangladesh	13,017	1,169	1,334	10.2	14.11
Algeria	238,174	1,879	2,145	0.9	14.16
Libya	175,954	311	358	0.2	15.11
Liechtenstein	15	6	7	46.7	16.67
Portugal	9,150	3,096	3,666	40.1	18.41
Guadeloupe	169	67	82	48.5	22.39
Iceland	10,025	25	31	0.3	24.00
Kazakhstan	267,074	9,758	12,148	4.5	24.49
Kyrgyzstan	19,180	775	1,003	5.2	29.42
United Arab Emirates	8,360	243	321	3.8	32.10
Ireland	6,889	489	659	9.6	34.76
Belarus	20,748	6,840	9,402	45.3	37.46
Egypt	99,545	52	72	0.1	38.46
Cyprus	925	119	172	18.6	44.54
Israel	2,062	82	132	6.4	60.98
Uruguay	17,481	791	1,292	7.4	63.34
Kuwait	1,782	3	5	0.3	66.67
Cape Verde	403	35	85	21.1	142.86
Africa	2,978,394	702,502	649,866	21.8	−7.5
Asia	3,084,746	551,448	547,793	17.8	−0.7
Europe	2,259,957	1,030,475	1,039,251	46	0.9
North and Central America	2,136,966	555,002	549,304	25.7	−1.0
Oceania	849,096	201,271	197,623	23.3	−1.8
South America	1,754,741	922,731	885,618	50.5	−4.0
World	13,063,900	3,963,429	3,869,455	29.6	−2.4

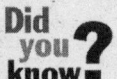

Did you know? In 17th-century Holland a speculative frenzy erupted over the sale of tulip bulbs. Tulips had been introduced into Europe from Turkey shortly after 1550. Demand for new varieties soon exceeded the supply, and prices rose to astonishing heights. The craze, known as the tulip mania, reached its peak in Holland in 1633–37. Homes, estates, and industries were mortgaged so that bulbs could be purchased; bulbs of rare varieties sold for the equivalent of hundreds of dollars each. The crash came in 1637, when almost overnight the price structure collapsed, sweeping away fortunes and leaving behind financial ruin for many Dutch families.

Geology

The Continents

Figures given are approximate. Area and population as of 2004. Lowest points listed are all below sea level.

CONTINENT	POPULATION	AREA	% OF TOTAL LAND AREA[1]	HIGHEST/LOWEST POINT
Africa	852,637,200	30,263,037 sq km 11,684,711 sq mi	20.2	Mt. Kilimanjaro (Tanzania): 5,895 m (19,340 ft) Lake Assal (Djibouti): −157 m (−515 ft)
Antarctica	N/A	14,000,000 sq km 5,400,000 sq mi	9.4	Vinson Massif: 4,897 m (16,066 ft) Bentley Subglacial Trench: −5,538 m (−8,327 ft)
Asia	3,879,428,240	44,887,537 sq km 17,331,069 sq mi	30.0	Mount Everest (China, Nepal): 8,848 m (29,028 ft) Dead Sea (Israel, Jordan): −400 m (−1,312 ft)
Europe	691,509,155	9,859,691 sq km 3,806,906 sq mi	6.6	Mt. Elbrus (Russia): 5,642 m (18,510 ft) Caspian Sea (Russia): −27 m (−90 ft)
North America	509,198,900	24,238,486 sq km 9,358,532 sq mi	16.2	Mt. McKinley (Alaska): 6,194 m (20,320 ft) Death Valley (California): −86 m (−282 ft)
Oceania	32,813,267	8,514,986 sq km 3,287,656 sq mi	5.7	Mt. Wilhelm (Papua New Guinea): 4,509 m (14,793 ft) Lake Eyre: −15 m (−50 ft)
South America	364,018,500	17,822,497 sq km 6,881,304 sq mi	11.9	Mt. Aconcagua (Argentina): 6,959 m (22,831 ft) Valdés Peninsula (Argentina): −40 m (−131 ft)

[1]*Together, the continents make up about 29.2% of the Earth's surface.*

Earth's interior layers (depths below surface)

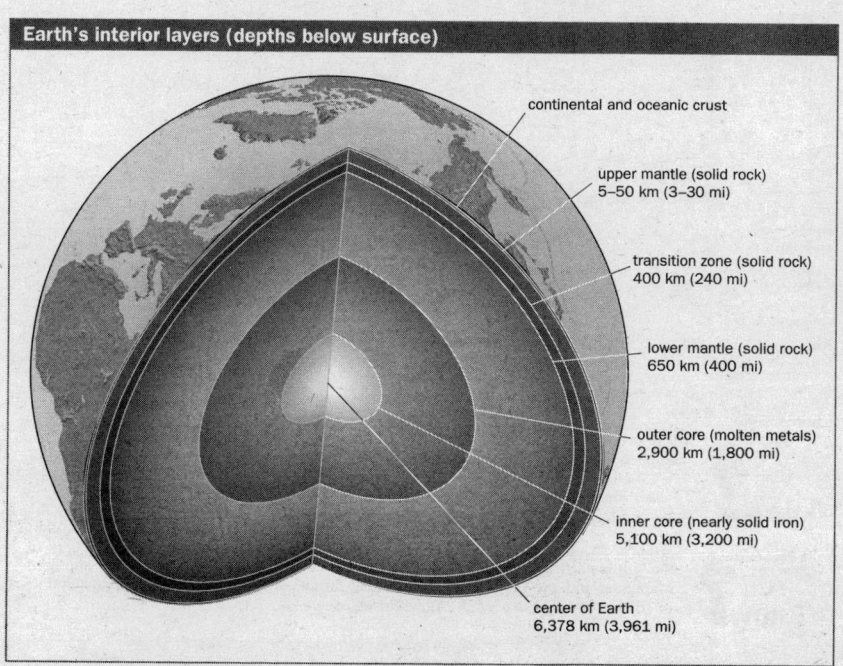

continental and oceanic crust

upper mantle (solid rock)
5–50 km (3–30 mi)

transition zone (solid rock)
400 km (240 mi)

lower mantle (solid rock)
650 km (400 mi)

outer core (molten metals)
2,900 km (1,800 mi)

inner core (nearly solid iron)
5,100 km (3,200 mi)

center of Earth
6,378 km (3,961 mi)

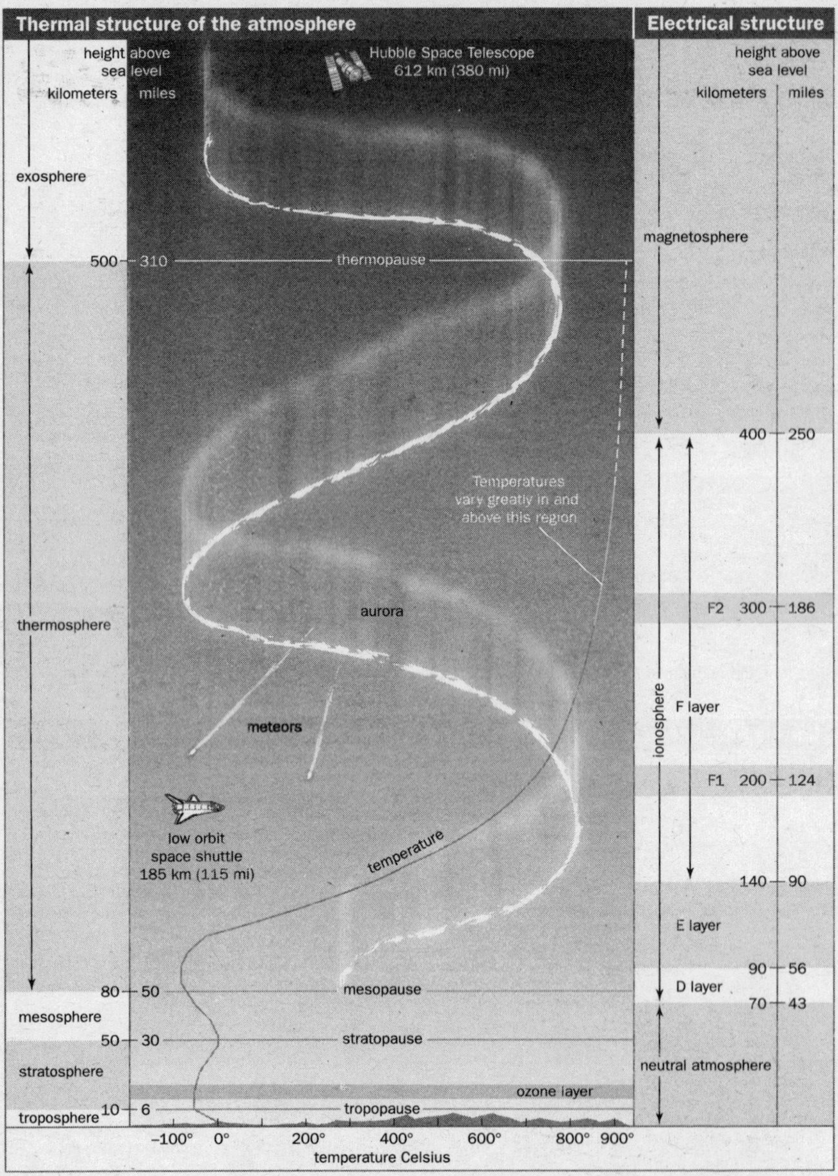

Thermal structure of the atmosphere

Electrical structure

height above sea level

kilometers | miles

Hubble Space Telescope
612 km (380 mi)

height above sea level

kilometers | miles

exosphere

500 — 310 ———————— thermopause ————————

magnetosphere

thermosphere

Temperatures vary greatly in and above this region

400 — 250

aurora

F2 300 — 186

F layer

meteors

F1 200 — 124

low orbit space shuttle
185 km (115 mi)

temperature

140 — 90

E layer

ionosphere

80 — 50 ———————— mesopause ————————

90 — 56

D layer

70 — 43

mesosphere

50 — 30 ———————— stratopause ————————

neutral atmosphere

stratosphere

ozone layer

troposphere 10 — 6 ———————— tropopause ————————

−100°   0°   200°   400°   600°   800° 900°

temperature Celsius

Did you know?

Wall Street, which was recognized even before the Civil War as the financial capital of the US, is narrow and short, extending only about seven blocks across part of southern Manhattan in New York City. It was named for an earthen wall built by Dutch settlers in 1653 to repel an expected English invasion.

Geologic Time Scale

Cenozoic Era

period	epoch	age	boundaries*
Quaternary	Holocene		0.01
	Pleistocene	Calabrian	1.8
Tertiary — Neogene	Pliocene L	Piacenzian	3.6
	Pliocene E	Zanclean	5.3
	Miocene L	Messinian	7.1
		Tortonian	11.2
	Miocene M	Serravallian	14.8
		Langhian	16.4
	Miocene E	Burdigalian	20.5
		Aquitanian	23.8
Tertiary — Paleogene	Oligocene L	Chattian	28.5
	Oligocene E	Rupelian	33.7
	Eocene L	Priabonian	37.0
	Eocene M	Bartonian	41.3
		Lutetian	49.0
	Eocene E	Ypresian	54.8
	Paleocene L	Thanetian	57.9
		Selandian	61.0
	Paleocene E	Danian	65.0

Mesozoic Era

period	epoch	age	boundaries*
Cretaceous	L	Maastrichtian	65.0
		Campanian	71.3
		Santonian	83.5
		Coniacian	85.8
		Turonian	89.0
		Cenomanian	93.5
	E	Albian	99.0
		Aptian	112
		Barremian	121
	Neocomian	Hauterivian	127
		Valanginian	132
		Berriasian	137
Jurassic	L	Tithonian	144
		Kimmeridgian	151
		Oxfordian	154
	M	Callovian	159
		Bathonian	164
		Bajocian	169
		Aalenian	176
	E	Toarcian	180
		Pliensbachian	190
		Sinemurian	195
		Hettangian	202
Triassic	L	Rhaetian	206
		Norian	210
		Carnian	221
	M	Ladinian	227
		Anisian	234
	E	Olenekian	242
		Induan	245 / 248

Paleozoic Era

period	epoch	age	boundaries*
Permian	L	Tatarian	248
		Ufimian-Kazanian	256
		Kungurian	260
	E	Artinskian	269
		Sakmarian	282
		Asselian	290
Carboniferous — Pennsylvanian	L	Gzelian	296
		Kasimovian	303
		Moscovian	311
		Bashkirian	323
Carboniferous — Mississippian		Serpukhovian	327
	E	Visean	342
		Tournaisian	354
Devonian	L	Famennian	364
		Frasnian	370
	M	Givetian	380
		Eifelian	391
	E	Emsian	400
		Praghian	412
		Lochkovian	417
Silurian	L	Pridoli	419
		Ludlovian	423
	E	Wenlockian	428
		Llandoverian	443
Ordovician	L	Ashgillian	449
		Caradocian	458
	M	Llandeilian	464
		Llanvirnian	470
	E	Arenigian	485
		Tremadocian	490
Cambrian**	D	Sunwaptan**	495
		Steptoean**	500
	C	Marjuman**	506
		Delamaran**	512
	B	Dyeran**	516
	A	Montezuman**	520 / 543

Precambrian time

eon	era	boundaries*
Proterozoic	L	543
	M	900
	E	1,600
Archean	L	2,500
	M	3,000
	E	3,400
		3,800?

Published with permission of the Geological Society of America.

* Millions of years before the present.
** International ages have not been established. These are regional (Laurentian) only.

Largest Islands of the World

NAME AND LOCATION	CONTINENT	AREA* SQ MI	AREA* SQ KM
Greenland	North America	822,700	2,130,800
New Guinea, Papua New Guinea–Indonesia	Oceania	309,000	800,000
Borneo, Indonesia–Malaysia–Brunei	Asia	283,400	734,000
Madagascar	Africa	226,658	587,041
Baffin, Nunavut, Canada	North America	195,928	507,451
Sumatra, Indonesia	Asia	167,600	434,000
Honshu, Japan	Asia	87,805	227,414
Victoria, Northwest Territories–Nunavut, Canada	North America	83,897	217,291
Great Britain	Europe	83,698	216,777
Ellesmere, Nunavut, Canada	North America	75,767	196,236
Celebes, Indonesia	Asia	69,100	179,000
South Island, New Zealand	Oceania	58,676	151,971
Java, Indonesia	Asia	49,000	126,900
North Island, New Zealand	Oceania	44,204	114,489
Newfoundland, Canada	North America	42,031	108,860
Cuba	North America	40,519	104,945
Luzon, Philippines	Asia	40,420	104,688
Iceland	Europe	39,699	102,819
Mindanao, Philippines	Asia	36,537	94,630
Ireland, Ireland–UK	Europe	32,589	84,406
Hokkaido, Japan	Asia	30,144	78,073
Sakhalin, Russia	Asia	29,500	76,400
Hispaniola, Haiti–Dominican Republic	North America	29,418	76,192
Banks, Northwest Territories, Canada	North America	27,038	70,028
Sri Lanka, Ceylon	Asia	25,332	65,610
Tasmania, Australia	Oceania	24,868	64,409
Devon, Nunavut, Canada	North America	21,331	55,247

*Area given may include small adjoining islands. Conversions for rounded figures are rounded to nearest hundred.

Highest Mountains of the World

"I" in the name of a peak refers to the highest in a group of numbered peaks of the same name.

NAME AND LOCATION	HEIGHT IN M	HEIGHT IN FT	YEAR FIRST CLIMBED
Africa			
Kilimanjaro (Kibo peak), Tanzania	5,895	19,340	1889
Mt. Kenya (Batian peak), Kenya	5,199	17,058	1899
Margherita, Ruwenzori Range, Zaire–Uganda	5,119	16,795	1906
Ras Dashen, Simen Mtns., Ethiopia	4,620	15,157	1841
Antarctica			
Vinson Massif, Sentinel Range, Ellsworth Mtns.	4,897	16,066	1966
Tyree, Sentinel Range, Ellsworth Mtns.	4,852	15,919	1967
Shinn, Sentinel Range, Ellsworth Mtns.	4,801	15,751	1966
Asia			
Everest, Chomolungma), Himalayas, Nepal–Tibet, China	8,848	29,028	1953
K2 (Godwin Austen) (Chogori), Karakoram Range, Pakistan–Sinkiang, China	8,611	28,251	1954
Kanchenjunga I (Gangchhendzonga), Himalayas, Nepal–India	8,586	28,169	1955
Lhotse I, Himalayas, Nepal–Tibet, China	8,516	27,940	1956
Makalu I, Himalayas, Nepal–Tibet, China	8,463	27,766	1955
Caucasus			
Elbrus, Russia	5,642	18,510	1874
Dykh–Tau, Russia	5,204	17,073	1888
Koshtan–Tau, Russia	5,151	16,900	1889
Shkhara, Russia–Georgia	5,068	16,627	1888
Europe			
Mont Blanc, Alps, France–Italy	4,807	15,771	1786
Dufourspitze (Monte Rosa), Alps, Switzerland–Italy	4,634	15,203	1855

Highest Mountains of the World (continued)

NAME AND LOCATION	HEIGHT IN M	HEIGHT IN FT	YEAR FIRST CLIMBED
Europe (continued)			
Dom (Mischabel), Alps, Switzerland	4,545	14,911	1858
Weisshorn, Alps, Switzerland	4,505	14,780	1861
North America			
McKinley, Alaska Range, Alaska	6,194	20,320	1913
Logan, St. Elias Mtns., Yukon, Canada	5,951	19,524	1925
Citlaltépetl (Orizaba), Cordillera Neo-Volcánica, Mexico	5,610	18,406	1848
St. Elias, St. Elias Mtns., Alaska–Canada	5,489	18,009	1897
Oceania			
Jaya (Sukarno, Carstensz), Sudirman Range, Indonesia	5,030	16,500[1]	1962
Pilimsit (Idenburg), Sudirman Range, Indonesia	4,800	15,750[1]	1962
Trikora (Wilhelmina), Jayawijaya Mtns., Indonesia	4,750	15,580[1]	1912
Mandala (Juliana), Jayawijaya Mtns., Indonesia	4,700	15,420[1]	1959
South America			
Aconcagua, Andes, Argentina–Chile	6,959	22,831	1897
Ojos del Salado, Andes, Argentina–Chile	6,893	22,615	1937
Bonete, Andes, Argentina	6,872	22,546	1913
Tupungato, Andes, Argentina–Chile	6,800	22,310	1897

[1]Conversions rounded to the nearest 10 ft.

Major Caves and Cave Systems of the World by Continent

NAME AND LOCATION	DEPTH[1] FEET	DEPTH[1] M	LENGTH[2] MILES	LENGTH[2] KM
Africa				
Ambatoharanana, Madagascar	N/A	N/A	11.2	18.1
Apocalypse Pothole, South Africa	279	85	7.5	12.1
Ifflis, Algeria	3,802	1,159	1	1.6
Sof 'Umar, Ethiopia	N/A	N/A	9.4	15.1
Tafna (Bou Ma'za), Algeria	N/A	N/A	11.4	18.4
Antarctica: no significant caves				
Asia				
Air Jernih, Malaysia	1,165	355	32.1	51.6
Faouar Dara, Lebanon	2,041	622	1.5	2.5
Kap-Kutan/Promezhutochnaya, Uzbekistan	N/A	N/A	31.3	50.3
Kiev, Uzbekistan	3,248	990	1.1	1.8
Oreshnaya, Russia	623	190	25.5	41
Europe				
Hölloch, Switzerland	2,844	867	82.7	133.1
Jean Bernard, France	5,036	1,535	11.1	17.9
Optimisticheskaya, Ukraine	N/A	N/A	102.5	165
Trave, Spain	4,528	1,380	1.8	2.9
Vyacheslav Pantyukhin, Georgia	4,948	1,508	N/A	N/A
Oceania				
Atea, Papua New Guinea	1,148	350	21.4	34.5
Bulmer, New Zealand	2,388	728	6.8	11
H.H. Hole, New Zealand	2,044	623	N/A	N/A
Muruk, Papua New Guinea	2,090	637	2.9	4.6
Nettlebed, New Zealand	2,917	889	15.2	24.4
North America				
Cuicateca, Mexico	4,035	1,230	5.8	9.3
Friars Hole, West Virginia	617	188	42.8	68.8
Guixani Ndia Guinjao, Mexico	3,084	940	1.2	2
Jewel, South Dakota	443	135	76.9	123.8
Mammoth–Flint Ridge, Kentucky	360	110	329.3	530

Major Caves and Cave Systems of the World (continued)

NAME AND LOCATION	DEPTH[1]		LENGTH[2]	
	FEET	M	MILES	KM
South America				
Aonda, Venezuela	1,188	362	N/A	N/A
Auyantepuy Norte, Venezuela	1,050	320	N/A	N/A
Kaukiran, Peru	1,335	407	1.3	2.1
San Andrés, Peru	1,096	334	N/A	N/A
São Mateus–Imbira, Brazil	N/A	N/A	12.7	20.5

[1]Below highest entrance.   [2]Explored portion of cave.
Source: Paul Courbon et al., Atlas of the Great Caves of the World (1989).

Major Deserts of the World by Continent

DESERT (LOCATION)	AREA		DESERT (LOCATION)	AREA	
	SQ KM	SQ MI		SQ KM	SQ MI
Africa			**Australia**		
Sahara, northern Africa	8,600,000	3,320,000	Great Victoria, Western and South Australia	647,000	250,000
Libyan, Libya, Egypt, and Sudan	N/A	N/A	Great Sandy, northern Western Australia	400,000	150,000
Kalahari, southwestern Africa	930,000	360,000	Gibson, Western Australia	N/A	N/A
Namib, southwestern Africa	135,000	52,000	Simpson, Northern Territory	145,000	56,000
			North America		
Asia			Great Basin, southwestern US	492,000	190,000
Arabia, southwestern Asia	2,330,000	900,000			
Rub'al-Khali, southern Arabian Peninsula	650,000	250,000	Chihuahuan, northern Mexico	450,000	175,000
Gobi, Mongolia and northeastern China	1,300,000	500,000	Sonoran, southwestern US and Baja California	310,000	120,000
Kyzylkum, Kazakhstan-Uzbekistan	300,000	115,000	Colorado, California and northern Mexico	N/A	N/A
Takla Makan, northern China	270,000	105,000	Yuma, Arizona and Sonora, Mexico	N/A	N/A
Karakum, Turkmenistan	350,000	135,000	Mojave, southwestern US	65,000	25,000
Kavir, central Iran	260,000	100,000			
Syrian, Saudi Arabia, Jordan, Syria, and Iraq	260,000	100,000	**South America**		
Thar, India and Pakistan	200,000	77,000	Patagonian, southern Argentina	673,000	260,000
Lut, eastern Iran	52,000	20,000	Atacama, northern Chile	140,000	54,000

Major Volcanoes of the World by Continent

VOLCANO, LOCATION	ELEVATION		FIRST RECORDED ERUPTION	MOST RECENT ERUPTION
	M	FT		
Africa				
Kilimanjaro, Tanzania[1]	5,895	19,340	N/A	N/A
Cameroon, Cameroon	4,095	13,435	1650	2000
Teide (Tenerife), Canary Islands	3,715	12,188	N/A	1909
Nyiragongo, Dem. Rep. of the Congo	3,470	11,384	1884	2007
Nyamuragira, Dem. Rep. of the Congo	3,058	10,033	1882	2006
Antarctica				
Erebus, Ross Island	3,794	12,447	1841	2007
Darnley, Sandwich Islands	1,100	3,609	1823	N/A
Asia, Oceania, and the Pacific				
Klyuchevskaya, Kamchatka, Russia[2]	4,835	15,863	1697	2007
Mauna Kea, Hawaii	4,205	13,796	N/A	c. 2460 BC
Mauna Loa, Hawaii	4,170	13,681	1750	1984
Kerinci, Sumatra, Indonesia	3,800	12,467	1838	2004
Fuji, Honshu, Japan	3,776	12,388	1050 BC	1708
Rinjani, Lombok, Indonesia	3,726	12,224	1847	2004
Tolbachik, Kamchatka, Russia	3,682	12,080	1740	1976
Semeru, Java, Indonesia	3,676	12,060	1818	2007

Major Volcanoes of the World (continued)

VOLCANO, LOCATION	ELEVATION M	ELEVATION FT	FIRST RECORDED ERUPTION	MOST RECENT ERUPTION
Europe and the Atlantic				
Etna, Italy	3,350	10,991	N/A	2007
Askja, Iceland	1,516	4,974	1875	1961
Hekla, Iceland	1,491	4,892	1104	2000
Vesuvius, Italy	1,281	4,203	N/A	1944
Stromboli, Italy	924	3,031	N/A	2007
North America				
Citlaltépetl, Mexico	5,675	18,619	N/A	1846
Popocatépetl, Mexico	5,426	17,802	1347	2007
Rainier, Washington	4,392	14,409	N/A	1894
Shasta, California	4,317	14,163	1786	1786
Colima, Mexico	3,850	12,631	1576	2007
St. Helens, Washington	2,549	8,363	N/A	2007
South America				
Guallatiri, Chile	6,071	19,918	1825	1960
Tupungatito, Chile	6,000	19,685	1829	1987
Cotopaxi, Ecuador	5,911	19,393	1532	1940
Láscar, Chile	5,592	18,346	1848	2007
Nevado del Ruiz, Colombia	5,321	17,457	1595	1991

[1]Includes three dormant volcanoes (Kibo, Mawensi, and Shira) that have not erupted in historic times.   [2]Highest active volcano on the Kamchatka Peninsula.

Oceans & Seas

	AREA SQ KM	AREA SQ MI	VOLUME CU KM	VOLUME CU MI
Pacific Ocean				
without marginal seas	165,250,000	63,800,000	707,600,000	169,900,000
with marginal seas	179,680,000	69,370,000	723,700,000	173,700,000
Atlantic Ocean				
without marginal seas	82,440,000	31,830,000	324,600,000	77,900,000
with marginal seas	106,460,000	41,100,000	354,700,000	85,200,000
Indian Ocean				
without marginal seas	73,440,000	28,360,000	291,000,000	69,900,000
with marginal seas	74,920,000	28,930,000	291,900,000	70,100,000
Arctic Ocean	14,090,000	5,440,000	17,000,000	4,100,000
Australasian Central Sea	8,140,000	3,140,000	9,900,000	2,400,000
Gulf of Mexico and Caribbean Sea	4,320,000	1,670,000	9,600,000	2,300,000
Mediterranean and Black Seas	2,970,000	1,150,000	4,200,000	100,000
Bering Sea	2,304,000	890,000	3,330,000	80,000
Sea of Okhotsk	1,583,000	611,000	1,300,000	30,000
Hudson Bay	1,230,000	470,000	160,000	40,000
North Sea	570,000	220,000	50,000	10,000
Baltic Sea	420,000	160,000	20,000	5,000
Irish Sea	100,000	40,000	6,000	1,000
English Channel	75,000	29,000	4,000	1,000

	AVERAGE DEPTH M	AVERAGE DEPTH FT	DEEPEST POINT
Pacific Ocean			
without marginal seas	4,280	14,040	Mariana Trench
with marginal seas	4,030	13,220	(11,034 m; 36,201 ft)
Atlantic Ocean			
without marginal seas	3,930	12,890	Puerto Rico Trench
with marginal seas	3,330	10,920	(8,380 m; 27,493 ft)
Indian Ocean			
without marginal seas	3,960	10,040	Sunda Deep of the Java
with marginal seas	3,900	12,790	Trench (7,450 m; 24,442 ft)
Arctic Ocean	1,205	3,950	(5,502 m; 18,050 ft)

Oceans & Seas (continued)

	AVERAGE DEPTH		
	M	FT	DEEPEST POINT
Australasian Central Sea	1,210	3,970	N/A
Gulf of Mexico and Caribbean Sea	2,220	7,280	Cayman Trench (7,686 m; 25,216 ft)
Mediterranean and Black Seas	1,430	4,690	Ionian Basin (4,900 m; 16,000 ft)
Bering Sea	1,440	4,720	Bowers Basin (4,097 m; 13,442 ft)
Sea of Okhotsk	838	2,750	Kuril Basin (2,499 m; 8,200 ft)
Hudson Bay	128	420	(867 m; 2,846 ft)
North Sea	94	310	Skagerrak (700 m; 2,300 ft)
Baltic Sea	55	180	Landsort Deep (459 m; 1,506 ft)
Irish Sea	60	200	Mull of Galloway (175 m; 576 ft)
English Channel	54	180	Hurd Deep (172 m; 565 ft)

Major Natural Lakes of the World

Conversions for figures have been rounded, thousands to the nearest hundred and hundreds to the nearest ten.

NAME	LOCATION	AREA SQ MI	AREA SQ KM	NAME	LOCATION	AREA SQ MI	AREA SQ KM
Caspian Sea	Central Asia	149,200	386,400	Nyasa (Malawi)	eastern Africa	11,430	29,604
Superior	Canada-US	31,700	82,100	Great Slave	Northwest Territories, Canada	11,031	28,570
Victoria	eastern Africa	26,828	69,485				
Huron	Canada-US	23,000	59,600				
Michigan	US	22,300	57,800	Erie	Canada-US	9,910	25,667
Aral Sea[1]	Central Asia	13,000	33,800	Winnipeg	Manitoba, Canada	9,417	24,390
Tanganyika	eastern Africa	12,700	32,900				
Great Bear	Northwest Territories, Canada	12,028	31,153	Ontario	Canada-US	7,340	19,010

[1]Salt lake.

Longest Rivers of the World

This list includes both rivers and river systems. Conversions of rounded figures are rounded to nearest 10 or 100 miles or kilometers.

NAME	OUTFLOW	LENGTH MI	LENGTH KM
Africa			
Nile	Mediterranean Sea	4,132	6,650
Congo	South Atlantic Ocean	2,900	4,700
Niger	Bight of Biafra	2,600	4,200
Zambezi	Mozambique Channel	2,200	3,500
Kasai	Congo River	1,338	2,153
Asia			
Yangtze	East China Sea	3,915	6,300
Yenisey-Baikal-Selenga	Kara Sea	3,442	5,540
Huang Ho (Yellow)	Gulf of Chihli	3,395	5,464
Ob–Irtysh	Gulf of Ob	3,362	5,410
Amur–Argun	Sea of Okhotsk	2,761	4,444
Europe			
Volga	Caspian Sea	2,193	3,530
Danube	Black Sea	1,770	2,850
Ural	Caspian Sea	1,509	2,428
Dnieper	Black Sea	1,367	2,200
Don	Sea of Azov	1,162	1,870
North America			
Mississippi–Missouri–Red Rock	Gulf of Mexico	3,710	5,971
Mackenzie–Slave–Peace	Beaufort Sea	2,635	4,241
Missouri–Red Rock	Mississippi River	2,540	4,090
St. Lawrence–Great Lakes	Gulf of St. Lawrence	2,500	4,000
Mississippi	Gulf of Mexico	2,340	3,770

Longest Rivers of the World (continued)

NAME	OUTFLOW	LENGTH	
		MI	KM
Oceania			
Darling	Murray River	1,702	2,739
Murray	Great Australian Bight	1,609	2,589
Murrumbidgee	Murray River	981	1,579
Lachlan	Murrumbidgee River	922	1,484
Cooper Creek	Lake Eyre	882	1,420
South America			
Amazon–Ucayali–Apurimac	South Atlantic Ocean	4,000	6,400
Paraná	Río de la Plata	3,032	4,880
Madeira–Mamoré–Guaporé	Amazon River	2,082	3,350
Jurua	Amazon River	2,040	3,283
Purus	Amazon River	1,995	3,211

Preserving Nature

US National Parks

Dates in parentheses indicate when the area was first designated a park, in most cases under a different name. Web site: <www.nps.gov/parks.html>.

PARK	LOCATION	DESIGNATION DATE	SQ MI	SQ KM
Acadia	Bar Harbor ME	1929 (1916)	74	192
American Samoa	American Samoa	1993 (1988)	14	36
Arches	Moab UT	1971 (1929)	120	311
Badlands	southwestern South Dakota	1978 (1939)	379	982
Big Bend	curve of the Rio Grande river, Texas	1944	1,252	3,243
Biscayne	near Miami FL	1980 (1968)	270	699
Black Canyon of the Gunnison	near Montrose CO	1999 (1933)	43	112
Bryce Canyon	Bryce Canyon, Utah	1928 (1923)	56	145
Canyonlands	near Moab UT	1964	527	1,366
Capitol Reef	near Torrey UT	1971 (1937)	379	982
Carlsbad Caverns	near Carlsbad NM	1930 (1923)	73	189
Channel Islands	Ventura CA	1980 (1938)	75	194
Congaree	Hopkins SC	2003	34	88
Crater Lake	Crater Lake OR	1902	286	741
Cuyahoga Valley	near Cleveland and Akron OH	2000 (1974)	51	133
Death Valley	Death Valley, California	1994 (1933)	5,219	13,518
Denali	central Alaska	1980 (1917)	9,492	24,584
Dry Tortugas	Key West FL	1992 (1935)	101	262
Everglades	southern Florida	1947	2,358	6,107
Gates of the Arctic	Bettles AK	1980 (1978)	13,238	34,287
Glacier	northwest Montana	1910	1,584	4,102
Glacier Bay	Gustavus AK	1980 (1925)	5,130	13,287
Grand Canyon	Grand Canyon, Arizona	1919 (1908)	1,902	4,927
Grand Teton	Moose WY	1950 (1929)	484	1,255
Great Basin	near Baker NV	1986 (1922)	121	313
Great Sand Dunes	Mosca CO	2000 (1932)	132	343
Great Smoky Mountains	Tennessee and North Carolina	1934	815	2,110
Guadalupe Mountains	Salt Flat TX	1972	135	350
Haleakala	Kula, Maui HI	1960 (1916)	47	121
Hawaii Volcanoes	near Hilo HI	1961 (1916)	328	849
Hot Springs	Hot Springs AR	1921 (1832)	9	22
Isle Royale	Houghton MI	1940 (1931)	893	2,314
Joshua Tree	near Palm Springs CA	1994 (1936)	1,591	4,120
Katmai	near King Salmon AK	1980 (1918)	7,385	19,128
Kenai Fjords	Seward AK	1980 (1978)	1,047	2,711
Kobuk Valley	Kotzebue AK	1980 (1978)	2,672	6,920
Lake Clark	Port Alsworth AK	1980 (1978)	6,297	16,309
Lassen Volcanic	Mineral CA	1916 (1907)	166	430
Mammoth Cave	Mammoth Cave, Kentucky	1941	83	214
Mesa Verde	near Cortez and Mancos CO	1906	81	211
Mount Rainier	near Ashford WA	1899	368	954
North Cascades	near Marblemount WA	1968	1,069	2,769
Olympic	near Port Angeles WA	1938	1,442	3,734

US National Parks (continued)

PARK	LOCATION	DESIGNATION DATE	SQ MI	SQ KM
Petrified Forest	Arizona	1962 (1906)	146	379
Redwood	Crescent City CA	1994	172	445
Rocky Mountain	near Estes Park and Grand Lake CO	1915	415	1,076
Saguaro	Tucson AZ	1994 (1933)	143	370
Sequoia & Kings Canyon	near Three Rivers CA	1940 (1890)	1,351	3,498
Shenandoah	near Luray VA	1935	311	805
Theodore Roosevelt	Medora ND (south unit); near Watford City ND (north unit)	1978 (1947)	110	285
Virgin Islands	St. John, US Virgin Islands	1956	23	59
Voyageurs	International Falls MN	1975	341	883
Wind Cave	near Hot Springs SD	1903	44	115
Wolf Trap	Vienna VA	2002 (1966)	130 acres	
Wrangell–St. Elias	near Copper Center AK	1980	20,587	53,320
Yellowstone	Idaho, Montana, and Wyoming	1872	3,468	8,983
Yosemite	in the Sierra Nevada, California	1890 (1864)	1,189	3,081
Zion	Springdale UT	1919 (1909)	229	593

Did you know? On 13 May 1864, a Confederate prisoner who died in a local hospital became the first soldier laid to rest at Arlington National Cemetery. Dead from every war in which the US has participated have since been buried there. More than 300,000 people are interred at Arlington, and the Fields of the Dead, with their seemingly endless lines of plain stones, follow a pattern adopted in 1872 for use in all national cemeteries.

Health

Worldwide Health Indicators

*Column data as follows: **Life expectancy** in 2003; **Doctors** = persons per doctor[1]; **Infant mortality** per 1,000 births in 2003; **Water** = percentage (%) of population with access to safe drinking water (2000); **Food** = percentage (%) of the FAO recommended minimum (2004)[2].*

REGION/BLOC	LIFE EXPECTANCY		DOCTORS	INFANT MORTALITY	WATER	FOOD
	MALE	FEMALE				
World	65.5	69.5	730	39.6	82	118
Africa	**51.0**	**53.2**	**2,560**	**78.1**	**64**	**103**
Central Africa	45.7	49.1	12,890	102.1	46	80
East Africa	45.1	46.5	13,620	93.6	50	86
North Africa	66.4	70.4	890	42.6	87	125
Southern Africa	44.1	45.3	1,610	64.1	85	119
West Africa	49.2	50.6	6,260	81.7	65	109
Americas	**71.0**	**77.3**	**520**	**18.8**	**91**	**129**
Anglo-America[3]	74.6	80.4	370	6.6	100	140
Canada	76.4	83.4	540	5.0	100	136
United States	74.4	80.1	360	6.8	100	141
Latin America	68.9	75.4	690	26.1	86	123
Caribbean	67.1	71.4	380	29.3	79	118
Central America	66.9	70.9	950	29.5	88	106
Mexico	71.9	77.6	810	17.4	88	134
South America	68.4	75.7	710	27.9	86	122
Andean Group	68.9	75.0	830	26.5	86	108
Brazil	67.2	75.3	770	31.8	87	132
Other South America	71.5	78.9	410	17.7	82	120
Asia	**66.6**	**69.7**	**970**	**41.8**	**81**	**116**
Eastern Asia	70.9	74.6	610	23.4	78	121
China	70.1	73.3	620	26.4	75	123
Japan	78.4	85.3	530	3.0	97	110
South Korea	71.7	79.3	740	7.3	92	123
Other Eastern Asia	71.3	76.9	500	14.1	94	93

Worldwide Health Indicators (continued)

REGION/BLOC	LIFE EXPECTANCY MALE	LIFE EXPECTANCY FEMALE	DOCTORS	INFANT MORTALITY	WATER	FOOD
Asia (continued)						
South Asia	62.3	63.7	2,100	63.4	85	108
India	62.9	64.4	1,920	59.6	84	112
Pakistan	61.3	63.2	1,840	76.6	90	100
Other South Asia	60.0	60.3	5,080	73.7	85	97
Southeast Asia	66.1	71.0	3,120	36.2	78	123
Southwest Asia	66.4	70.5	610	43.1	85	118
Central Asia	62.0	68.7	330	55.9	82	99
Gulf Cooperation Council	68.5	72.2	620	39.3	95	117
Iran	68.0	70.7	1,200	44.2	92	131
Other Southwest Asia	66.9	70.8	690	39.1	82	119
Europe	**70.0**	**78.3**	**300**	**9.2**	**98**	**130**
European Union (EU)	74.8	81.3	290	5.2	100	137
France	75.6	83.1	330	4.4	100	142
Germany	75.5	81.6	290	4.2	100	131
Italy	76.5	82.5	180	6.2	100	151
Spain	75.7	83.1	240	3.6	99	138
United Kingdom	75.7	80.7	720	5.3	100	137
Other EU	72.8	79.7	320	6.2	100	133
Non-EU[4]	77.2	82.6	480	4.2	100	131
Eastern Europe	61.3	72.7	290	16.4	95	119
Russia	58.5	71.9	240	13.3	99	117
Ukraine	61.1	72.2	330	20.8	98	120
Other Eastern Europe	67.2	74.8	370	20.1	84	121
Oceania	**73.4**	**79.1**	**480**	**15.0**	**87**	**117**
Australia	77.0	83.1	400	4.8	100	116
Pacific Ocean Islands	67.7	72.7	770	31.3	67	118

[1]Latest data available for individual countries. [2]The Food and Agriculture Organization of the United Nations (FAO) calculates this percentage by dividing the caloric equivalent to the known average daily supply of foodstuffs for human consumption in a given country by its population, thus arriving at a minimum daily per capita caloric intake. The higher the percentage, the more calories consumed. [3]Includes Canada, the US, Greenland, Bermuda, and St. Pierre and Miquelon. [4]Western Europe only; includes Andorra, Faroe Islands, Gibraltar, Guernsey, Iceland, Isle of Man, Jersey, Liechtenstein, Monaco, Norway, San Marino, and Switzerland.

Causes of Death, Worldwide, by Sex

Global estimates for 2002 as published in the World Health Organization World Health Report 2003. Data are percentages of total deaths in each category. Ranking is based on categories defined by the International Classification of Diseases, Tenth Revision. All other causes of death (mostly residual) make up approximately 3.7 percent of all deaths.

	LEADING CAUSES OF DEATH	ALL CATEGORIES (%)	MALES (%)	FEMALES (%)
1	Major cardiovascular diseases	29.2	27.0	31.7
	Ischemic heart diseases	12.6	12.6	12.5
	Cerebrovascular diseases	9.6	8.5	10.9
	Hypertensive heart disease	1.6	1.4	1.8
2	Infectious and parasitic diseases	19.5	19.9	19.0
	HIV/AIDS	4.9	5.1	4.8
	Diarrheal diseases	3.1	3.1	3.1
	Tuberculosis	2.8	3.5	2.0
	Childhood diseases	2.4	2.3	2.5
	Malaria	2.1	2.0	2.4
3	Malignant neoplasms	12.5	13.2	11.6
	Trachea, bronchus, and lung	2.2	3.0	1.3
	Stomach	1.5	1.7	1.2
	Colon, rectum, and anus	1.1	1.1	1.1
	Liver	1.1	1.4	0.7
4	Respiratory infections	6.7	6.4	7.1
5	Respiratory diseases	6.5	6.4	6.6
	Chronic obstructive pulmonary disease	4.8	4.7	4.9

Causes of Death, Worldwide, by Sex (continued)

	LEADING CAUSES OF DEATH	ALL CATE-GORIES (%)	MALES (%)	FEMALES (%)
6	Accidents (unintentional injuries)	6.2	7.7	4.6
	Road traffic injuries	*2.1*	*2.9*	*1.2*
	Falls	*0.7*	*0.8*	*0.6*
7	Perinatal conditions	4.3	4.6	4.0
8	Digestive diseases	3.4	3.6	3.2
	Chronic liver disease and cirrhosis of the liver	*1.4*	*1.7*	*1.0*
9	Neuropsychiatric disorders	1.9	1.9	2.0
	Alzheimer and other dementias	*0.7*	*0.5*	*0.9*
10	Diabetes mellitus	1.7	1.5	2.0
11	Nephritis, nephrotic syndrome, and nephrosis	1.2	1.2	1.2
12	Intentional injuries	2.9	3.9	1.7
	Intentional self-harm (suicide)	*1.5*	*1.8*	*1.2*
	Violence (assault)	*1.0*	*1.5*	*0.4*

Causes of Death, Worldwide, by Region

Global estimates for 2001 as published in the World Health Organization (WHO) World Health Report 2002. Regions are as defined by the WHO. Numbers are in thousands ('000).

	LEADING CAUSES OF DEATH	ALL CATE-GORIES (%)	ALL CATE-GORIES	AFRI-CAN	AMER-ICAN	EASTERN MEDITER-RANEAN	EURO-PEAN	SOUTHEAST ASIAN	WESTERN PACIFIC
1	Ischemic heart disease	12.7	7,181	333	967	523	2,423	1,972	963
2	Cerebrovascular disease	9.6	5,454	307	454	218	1,480	1,070	1,926
3	Lower respiratory infections	6.8	3,871	1,026	225	383	298	1,355	586
4	HIV disease	5.1	2,866	2,197	88	58	26	445	53
5	Chronic obstructive pulmonary disease	4.7	2,672	116	222	88	285	614	1,347
6	Perinatal conditions	4.4	2,504	577	167	313	70	1,023	353
7	Diarrheal diseases	3.5	2,001	703	76	326	21	802	74
8	Tuberculosis	2.9	1,644	336	46	133	77	701	351
9	Road traffic accidents	2.1	1,194	179	141	103	125	353	292
10	Trachea, bronchus, lung cancers	2.1	1,213	23	227	30	371	162	399
11	Malaria	2.0	1,124	963	1	55	0	95	10
12	Diabetes mellitus	1.6	895	55	230	52	141	238	179
13	Hypertensive heart disease	1.5	874	54	131	91	175	138	285
14	Stomach cancer	1.5	850	37	76	21	172	65	480
15	Self-inflicted injuries	1.5	849	28	65	35	168	234	318
16	Cirrhosis of the liver	1.4	796	70	104	60	166	214	183
17	Measles	1.3	745	426	0	85	6	193	32
18	Nephritis and nephrosis	1.1	625	80	95	61	77	155	157
19	Liver cancer	1.1	616	64	39	14	64	65	371
20	Colon and rectum cancers	1.1	615	27	108	15	235	58	174
21	Congenital anomalies	0.9	507	67	62	75	38	149	116
22	Violence	0.9	500	116	150	22	70	77	65
23	Breast cancer	0.8	479	38	90	28	154	90	79
24	Esophagus cancer	0.8	438	27	31	13	50	80	236
25	Drowning	0.7	403	92	24	27	37	91	132
26	Alzheimer's and other dementias	0.7	368	5	94	10	97	100	62
27	Poisoning	0.6	343	37	17	18	104	95	73
28	Mouth and oropharynx cancers	0.6	326	34	22	21	52	144	54
29	Whooping cough	0.5	285	157	7	59	0	60	2
30	Tetanus	0.5	282	110	0	53	0	101	18
31	Prostate cancer	0.5	269	45	77	8	95	26	19
32	Cervix uteri cancer	0.5	258	59	30	12	27	99	33
33	War	0.4	230	122	11	59	16	20	3

Ten Leading Causes of Death in the US, by Age

Preliminary data for 2003. Numbers in thousands. Rates per 100,000 population. Numbers are based on weighted data rounded to the nearest individual, so category percentages and rates may not add to totals.
Source: National Vital Statistics Report, <www.cdc.gov/nchs>.

CAUSE	NUMBER	RATE	%
1–4 YEARS			
1 Accidents	1,679	10.6	34.2%
Motor vehicle accidents	591	3.7	12.0%
All other accidents	1,088	6.9	22.2%
2 Congenital malformations, deformations, and chromosomal abnormalities	514	3.3	10.5%
3 Malignant neoplasms	383	2.4	7.8%
4 Assault (homicide)	342	2.2	7.0%
5 Diseases of heart	186	1.2	3.8%
6 Influenza and pneumonia	151	1.0	3.1%
7 Septicemia	82	0.5	1.7%
8 Conditions of perinatal origin	76	0.5	1.5%
9 Nonmalignant/unknown neoplasms	53	0.3	1.1%
10 Chronic lower respiratory diseases	47	0.3	1.0%
All other causes	1,398	8.9	28.5%
All causes, 1–4 years	**4,911**	**31.1**	**100.0%**

CAUSE	NUMBER	RATE	%
5–14 YEARS			
1 Accidents	2,561	6.3	37.0%
Motor vehicle accidents	1,592	3.9	23.0%
All other accidents	970	2.4	14.0%
2 Malignant neoplasms	1,060	2.6	15.3%
3 Congenital malformations, deformations, and chromosomal abnormalities	370	0.9	5.3%
4 Assault (homicide)	310	0.8	4.5%
5 Intentional self-harm (suicide)	255	0.6	3.7%
6 Diseases of heart	252	0.6	3.6%
7 Influenza and pneumonia	77	0.2	1.1%
8 Chronic lower respiratory diseases	134	0.3	1.9%
9 Septicemia	107	0.3	1.5%
10 Nonmalignant/unknown neoplasms	76	0.2	1.1%
All other causes	1,728	4.2	24.9%
All causes, 5–14 years	**6,930**	**16.9**	**100.0%**

CAUSE	NUMBER	RATE	%
15–24 YEARS			
1 Accidents	14,966	36.3	45.3%
Motor vehicle accidents	10,857	26.3	32.9%
All other accidents	4,109	10.0	12.4%
2 Assault (homicide)	5,148	12.5	15.6%
3 Intentional self-harm (suicide)	3,921	9.5	11.9%
4 Malignant neoplasms	1,628	4.0	4.9%
5 Diseases of heart	1,083	2.6	3.3%
6 Congenital malformations, deformations, and chromosomal abnormalities	425	1.0	1.3%
7 Influenza and pneumonia	216	0.5	0.7%
8 Cerebrovascular diseases	204	0.5	0.6%
9 Chronic lower respiratory diseases	172	0.4	0.5%
10 HIV disease	171	0.4	0.5%
All other causes	5,088	12.3	15.4%
All causes, 15–24 years	**33,022**	**80.1**	**100.0%**

CAUSE	NUMBER	RATE	%
25–44 YEARS			
1 Accidents	27,844	33.1	22.0%
Motor vehicle accidents	13,582	16.1	10.5%
All other accidents	14,261	16.9	11.1%
2 Malignant neoplasms	19,041	22.6	14.8%
3 Diseases of heart	16,283	19.3	12.6%
4 Intentional self-harm (suicide)	11,251	13.4	8.7%
5 Assault (homicide)	7,367	8.7	5.7%
6 HIV disease	6,879	8.2	5.3%
7 Chronic liver disease and cirrhosis	3,288	3.9	2.6%
8 Cerebrovascular diseases	3,004	3.6	2.3%
9 Diabetes mellitus	2,662	3.2	2.1%
10 Influenza and pneumonia	1,337	1.6	1.0%
All other causes	29,968	35.6	23.2%
All causes, 25–44 years	**128,924**	**153.0**	**100.0%**

CAUSE	NUMBER	RATE	%
45–64 YEARS			
1 Malignant neoplasms	144,936	211.0	33.2%
2 Diseases of heart	101,713	148.0	23.3%
3 Accidents	23,669	34.5	5.4%
Motor vehicle accidents	9,891	14.4	2.3%
All other accidents	13,778	20.1	3.2%
4 Diabetes mellitus	16,326	23.8	3.7%
5 Cerebrovascular diseases	15,971	23.2	3.7%
6 Chronic lower respiratory diseases	15,409	22.4	3.5%
7 Chronic liver disease and cirrhosis	13,649	19.9	3.1%
8 Intentional self-harm (suicide)	10,057	14.6	2.3%
9 HIV disease	5,917	8.6	1.4%
10 Septicemia	5,827	8.5	1.3%
All other causes	83,584	121.7	19.1%
All causes, 45–64 years	**437,058**	**636.1**	**100.0%**

CAUSE	NUMBER	RATE	%
65 YEARS AND OVER			
1 Diseases of heart	564,204	1570.8	31.3%
2 Malignant neoplasms	387,475	1078.7	21.5%
3 Cerebrovascular diseases	138,397	385.3	7.7%
4 Chronic lower respiratory diseases	109,199	304.0	6.1%
5 Alzheimer disease	62,707	174.6	3.5%
6 Influenza and pneumonia	57,507	160.1	3.2%
7 Diabetes mellitus	54,770	152.5	3.0%
8 Nephritis, nephrotic syndrome, and nephrosis	35,392	98.5	2.0%
9 Accidents	26,597	94.6	1.5%
Motor vehicle accidents	7,379	20.5	0.4%
All other accidents	26,597	74.0	1.5%
10 Septicemia	26,609	74.1	1.5%
All other causes	333,895	929.6	18.5%
All causes, 65 years and over	**1,804,131**	**5022.8**	**100.0%**

Twenty Leading Causes of Death in the US for All Ages

Data for 2003. Rates per 100,000 population. Source: National Vital Statistics Report, <www.cdc.gov/nchs>.

	CAUSE	NUMBER	RATE	TOTAL %	% MALE (RANK)	% FEMALE (RANK)
1	Diseases of heart	685,089	235.3	28.0	28.0 (1)	28.0 (1)
	Ischemic heart diseases	480,028	165.0	19.6	20.5	18.8
	Heart failure	57,448	19.7	2.3	1.9	2.8
2	Malignant neoplasms	556,902	191.3	22.7	24.0 (2)	21.6 (2)
	Neoplasms of the trachea, bronchus, and lung	158,086	54.3	6.5	7.5	5.5
	Neoplasms of the colon, rectum, and anus	55,958	19.2	2.3	2.3	2.2
	Neoplasms of the breast	42,000	14.4	1.7	0.03	3.3
3	Cerebrovascular diseases	157,689	54.2	6.4	5.1 (4)	7.7 (3)
4	Chronic lower respiratory diseases	126,382	43.4	5.2	5.1 (5)	5.3 (4)
	Emphysema	14,861	5.1	0.6	0.6	0.6
5	Accidents	109,277	37.5	4.5	5.9 (3)	3.1 (7)
	Motor-vehicle accidents	44,757	15.4	1.8	2.6	1.1
	Accidental poisoning and exposure to noxious substances	19,457	6.7	0.8	1.1	0.5
	Falls	17,299	5.9	0.7	0.7	0.7
6	Diabetes mellitus	74,219	25.5	3.0	2.9 (6)	3.1 (6)
7	Influenza and pneumonia	65,163	22.4	2.7	2.4 (7)	2.9 (8)
	Pneumonia	63,371	21.8	2.6	2.3	2.8
8	Alzheimer disease	63,457	21.8	2.6	1.5 (10)	3.6 (5)
9	Nephritis, nephrotic syndrome, and nephrosis	42,453	14.6	1.7	1.7 (9)	1.8 (9)
10	Septicemia	34,069	11.7	1.4	1.2 (12)	1.5 (10)
11	Intentional self-harm (suicide)	31,484	10.8	1.3	2.1 (8)	0.5 (17)
12	Chronic liver disease and cirrhosis	27,503	9.4	1.1	1.5 (11)	0.8 (12)
13	Essential (primary) hypertension and hypertensive renal disease	21,940	7.5	0.9	0.7 (18)	1.1 (11)
14	Parkinson disease	17,997	6.2	0.7	0.8 (14)	0.6 (15)
15	Assault (homicide)	17,732	6.1	0.7	1.2 (13)	0.3 (21)
16	Pneumonitis due to solids and liquids	17,335	6.0	0.7	0.7 (17)	0.7 (13)
17	Aortic aneurysm and dissection	14,810	5.1	0.6	0.7 (16)	0.5 (19)
18	Conditions of perinatal origin	14,378	4.9	0.6	0.7 (19)	0.5 (18)
19	HIV disease	13,658	4.7	0.6	0.8 (15)	0.3 (22)
20	Benign and in situ neoplasms	13,563	4.7	0.6	0.6 (20)	0.6 (16)

HIV/AIDS

Acquired Immunodeficiency Syndrome, or AIDS, is a fatal transmissable disorder of the immune system that is caused by the human immunodeficiency virus (HIV). HIV was first isolated in 1983. In most cases, HIV slowly attacks and destroys the **immune system**, leaving the infected individual vulnerable to malignancies and infections that eventually cause death. AIDS is the last stage of HIV infection, during which time these diseases arise. An average interval of 10 years exists between infection with HIV and development of the conditions typical of AIDS. **Pneumonia** and **Kaposi's sarcoma** are two of the most common diseases seen in AIDS patients.

HIV is contracted through semen, vaginal fluid, breast milk, blood, or other body fluids containing blood. Health care workers may come into contact with other body fluids that may transmit the HIV virus, including amniotic and synovial fluids. Although it is a transmissable virus, it is not contagious and it cannot be spread through coughing, sneezing, or casual physical contact. Other **STDs**, such as genital herpes, may increase the risk of contracting AIDS through sexual contact.

The main **cellular target** of HIV is a special class of white blood cells critical to the immune system known as T4 helper cells. Once HIV has entered a helper T cell, it can cause the cell to function poorly or it can destroy the cell. A hallmark of the onset of AIDS is a drastic reduction in the number of helper T cells in the body. Two predominant strains of the virus, designated HIV-1 and HIV-2, are known. Worldwide the most common strain is HIV-1, with HIV-2 more common primarily in western Africa; the two strains act in a similar manner, but the latter causes a form of AIDS that progresses much more slowly.

Diagnosis is made on the basis of blood tests approved by the Centers for Disease Control and Prevention that may be administered by a doctor or at a local health department. Alternately, a home collection kit may be purchased at many pharmacies. No vaccine or cure has yet been developed that can prevent HIV infection. Several **drugs** are now used to slow the development of AIDS, including azidothymidine (AZT). **Protease inhibitors**, such as ritonavir and indinavir, have been shown to block the development of AIDS, at least temporarily. Protease inhibitors are most effective when used in conjunction with two different reverse transcriptase inhibitors—the so-called "triple-drug therapy."

HIV/AIDS is a major problem in developing countries, particularly sub-Saharan Africa. At the end of 2006, as many as 47 million people were estimated to have contracted HIV (as many as 6.6 million in 2006 alone),

with 95% of those living in the developing world.

For information on **prevention**, see "Safer Sex Defined," below.

For confidential information on HIV/AIDS, call 1-800-342-AIDS.

Internet resources: <www.cdc.gov/hiv>

Sexually Transmitted Diseases (STDs)

A sexually transmitted disease (STD) is usually passed from person to person by direct sexual contact. It may also be transmitted from a mother to her child before or at birth or, less frequently, may be passed from person to person in nonsexual contact. STDs usually initially affect the genitals, the reproductive tract, the urinary tract, the oral cavity, the anus, or the rectum but may mature in the body to attack various organs and systems. Following are some of the major STDs:

Syphilis was first widely reported by European writers in the 16th century, and a virtual epidemic swept Europe around the year 1500. Syphilis is spread through direct contact with a syphilis sore (chancre); development of this sore is the first stage of the disease. The second stage manifests itself as a rash on the palms and the bottoms of the feet. In the last stage, symptoms disappear, but the disease remains in the body and may damage internal organs and lead to paralysis, blindness, dementia, and even death. For individuals infected less than a year, a single dose of penicillin will cure the disease. Larger doses are needed for those who have had it for a longer period of time.

Gonorrhea, a form of urethritis (an infection and inflammation of the urethra), is one of the most common STDs. Although spread through sexual contact, the gonorrhea infection can also be spread to other parts of the body after touching the infected area. Men manifest symptoms, which include discharge and a burning sensation when urinating, more often than women. If gonorrhea is left untreated, women may develop pelvic inflammatory disease (PID) and men may become infertile. The disease can also spread to the blood or joints and is potentially life threatening.

Chlamydia, another form of urethritis, can be transmitted during vaginal, anal, or oral sex. Since there are frequently no symptoms, most infected individuals do not know they have the disease until complications develop. Untreated chlamydia can cause pain during urination or sex in men and PID in women. Antibiotics can successfully cure the disease.

Genital herpes, a disease that became especially widespread in the 1960s and 1970s, often presents minimal symptoms upon infection. The most common sign, however, is blistering in the genital area; outbreaks can occur over many years but generally decrease in severity and number. Genital herpes is caused by the herpes simplex viruses type 1 (HSV-1) and type 2 (HSV-2). The former causes infections on and around the mouth but may be spread through the saliva to the genitals; the latter is transmitted during sexual contact with someone who has a genital infection. The HSV-2 infection can cause problems for people with suppressed immune systems and for infants who contract the disease upon delivery. Herpes can also leave individuals more susceptible to HIV infection and make those carrying the disease more infectious. A variety of treatments, including antiviral medications, have been used to help manage genital herpes, but currently there is no cure for the disease.

Almost all STDs have reasonably effective drug cures. For information on STD **prevention**, see below, "Safer Sex Defined." For information on **HIV disease**, see individual entry.

Internet resources:
<www.cdc.gov/nchstp/od/nchstp.html>

Safer Sex Defined

Defining risky sexual behavior. Any activity involving the exchange of body fluids—vaginal secretions, semen, or blood—could result in the transmission of AIDS and other STDs. Unprotected vaginal and anal intercourse present the highest risks for contraction of STDs. Women are at greater risk than men of developing an infection as a result of heterosexual intercourse, though many STDs present fewer symptoms in women than in men. Men and women of all sexual orientations should practice safer sex to reduce their risk of contracting an STD.

HIV testing. It can take years to develop symptoms of HIV disease, so it is important to be tested for HIV after any behavior that might have resulted in infection. The CDC recommends undergoing two separate HIV-antibody tests, six months apart. If the second test is negative, there is a reasonable certainty that HIV is not present.

STD testing. It is important to get checked for other STDs at least once a year. Do not assume that STD testing is part of a routine checkup.

Abstinence. Refraining from any sexual activity that would allow the exchange of body fluids is by far the most effective method of birth control and disease prevention.

Monogamous intercourse. Sexual intercourse with only one partner can be as effective as abstinence in preventing disease transmission, if both partners have been properly tested for AIDS and other STDs. Most health professionals, however, recommend continuing to practice safer sex, even in monogamous relationships, as there is no way to be sure a partner is being faithful.

Condoms. Using a latex or female condom correctly and consistently significantly reduces the chance of unplanned pregnancy. Condoms also reduce the risk of transmission of HIV, vaginitis, chlamydia, honeymoon cystitis, syphilis, pelvic inflammatory disease, chancroid, and gonorrhea. Condoms may be less effective in preventing genital warts, herpes, and hepatitis B. Male and female condoms should not be worn simultaneously.

Birth control. There are many methods of birth control that can help prevent unwanted pregnancy, including birth-control pills, Norplant, Depo-Provera, condoms, diaphragms, and cervical caps. However, of these, only condoms protect against STDs. Emergency contraception, including the "morning-after" pill, should be used only when necessary and not relied upon as a regular method of birth control. Withdrawal and family planning are not recommended forms of birth control.

Internet resources: <www.sexualhealth.com>

Contraceptive Use by US Women

Percent distribution by age. Source: Fertility, Family Planning, and Reproductive Health of U.S. Women: Data from the 2002 National Survey of Family Growth *(CDC/National Center for Health Statistics).*

	AGE 15–44	AGE 15–19	20–24	25–29	30–34	35–39	40–44
Using contraception							
Pill	19.0	16.7	31.8	25.6	21.8	13.2	7.6
Condom	11.1	8.5	14.0	14.0	11.8	11.1	8.0
Female sterilization	16.7	—	2.2	10.3	19.0	29.2	34.7
Male sterilization	5.7	—	0.5	2.8	6.4	10.0	12.7
Implant or patch[1]	0.8	0.4	0.9	1.7	0.9	0.5	0.2
Injectable[2]	3.3	4.4	6.1	4.4	2.9	1.5	1.1
Intrauterine device (IUD)	1.3	0.1	1.1	2.5	2.2	1.0	0.8
Diaphragm	0.2	—	0.1	0.3	0.1	—	0.4
Periodic abstinence (rhythm)	0.7	—	0.8	0.3	0.9	1.1	1.2
Natural family planning	0.2	—	—.	0.4	0.2	0.3	0.4
Withdrawal	2.5	0.8	3.1	5.3	2.6	2.4	1.0
Other[3]	0.6	0.6	0.2	0.4	0.4	0.5	1.1
Total using contraception[4]	**61.9**	**31.5**	**60.7**	**68.0**	**69.2**	**70.8**	**69.1**
Not using contraception							
Surgically sterile female or male	1.5	—	...	0.4	0.9	2.1	4.9
Nonsurgically sterile female or male	1.6	0.7	0.7	0.9	1.4	1.2	4.4
Pregnant or postpartum	5.3	3.5	9.5	8.4	6.9	3.8	0.8
Seeking pregnancy	4.2	1.2	2.8	5.5	7.0	5.1	3.3
Other							
Never had intercourse	10.9	49.5	11.4	2.7	1.5	1.6	1.1
No intercourse in last 3 months	7.2	6.7	6.6	6.2	6.1	7.5	9.7
Had intercourse in last 3 months	7.4	6.9	8.4	8.0	7.0	7.7	6.7
Total not using contraception[4]	**38.1**	**68.5**	**39.3**	**32.0**	**30.8**	**29.2**	**30.9**

— None.   ... Less than 0.05.

[1]*Includes Lunelle™.*   [2]*Depo-Provera™.*   [3]*Includes female condom, cervical cap, Today™ sponge, and other methods.*   [4]*Includes other categories not listed. Totals may not add to 100% because of rounding.*

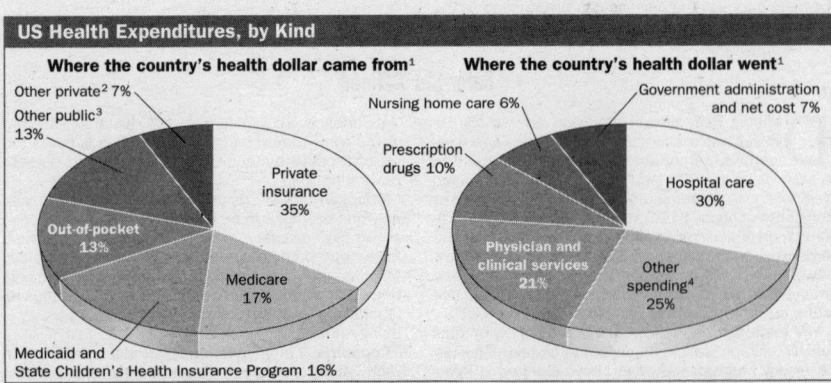

US Health Expenditures, by Kind

Where the country's health dollar came from[1]

- Other private[2] 7%
- Other public[3] 13%
- Private insurance 35%
- Out-of-pocket 13%
- Medicare 17%
- Medicaid and State Children's Health Insurance Program 16%

Where the country's health dollar went[1]

- Nursing home care 6%
- Government administration and net cost 7%
- Prescription drugs 10%
- Hospital care 30%
- Physician and clinical services 21%
- Other spending[4] 25%

[1] Calendar year 2005. Details may not add to 100% because of rounding.
[2] Other private includes industrial in-plant, privately funded construction, and non-patient revenues, including philanthropy.
[3] Other public includes programs such as workers' compensation, public health activity, US Department of Defense, US Department of Veterans Affairs, Indian Health Service, state and local hospital subsidies, and school health.
[4] Other spending includes dentist and other professional services, home health care, durable medical equipment, other nondurable medical products, government public health activities, and research and construction.
Source: Centers for Medicare and Medicaid Services, Office of the Actuary, National Health Statistics Group.

Diet and Exercise

The Food and Drug Administration (FDA)

The FDA is a division of the US Department of Health and Human Services. FDA Web site: <www.fda.gov>.

Mission: To promote and protect the public health by helping safe and effective products reach the market in a timely way and monitoring products for continued safety after they are in use. **History:** The FDA celebrated its 100th anniversary in 2006, having been created by the passing of the Food and Drugs Act, or Wiley Act, in 1906. The Food, Drug, and Cosmetic Act of 1938 then brought cosmetics and medical devices under the authority of the FDA. The Food and Drug Administration Act of 1988 officially established the body as an agency of the Department of Health and Human Services, with a commissioner of food and drugs appointed by the president with the consent of the Senate. **Location:** Rockville MD (with a transfer to Silver Spring MD in progress and scheduled to be completed in 2012). **Commissioner of Food and Drugs:** Andrew C. von Eschenbach. **Budget:** FY 2008 (requested) $2.1 billion. **Functions:** The FDA is the agency of the US federal government authorized by Congress to inspect, test, approve, and set safety standards for foods and food additives, drugs, chemicals, cosmetics, and household and medical devices. Generally, the FDA is empowered to prevent untested products from being sold and to take legal action to halt sale of undoubtedly harmful products or of products which involve a health or safety risk. Through court procedure, the FDA can seize products and prosecute the persons or firms responsible for legal violation. FDA authority is limited to interstate commerce. The agency cannot control prices nor directly regulate advertising except of prescription drugs and medical devices.

Vitamins, with Daily Recommendations

Vitamins are organic substances that are usually divided into two types: water-soluble and fat-soluble. Small quantities are necessary for normal health and growth in higher forms of animal life, as they work to regulate reactions that occur in metabolism (in contrast to macronutrients such as fats, carbohydrates, and proteins, which are the compounds utilized in the reactions regulated by vitamins). Absence of a vitamin blocks one or more specific metabolic reactions in a cell; thus, vitamin deficiency may result in specific diseases. As they generally cannot be synthesized by humans, vitamins must be obtained from the diet or from a synthetic source.

The name of each vitamin is followed by its alternative name and usual pharmaceutical preparation, respectively. Amounts shown indicate recommended daily consumption.

Abbreviations—mg: milligram; mcg: microgram; RAE: retinol activity equivalent; IU: international unit; N/A: not applicable.

Water-soluble vitamins

Thiamin (vitamin B_1; thiamine hydrochloride)
  Purpose: energy metabolism and initiation of nerve impulses. **Dietary sources:** pork, nuts, peas. **Men over 13:** 1.2 mg; **women over 18:** 1.1 mg; **pregnant women:** 1.4 mg; **lactating women:** 1.4 mg.

Riboflavin (vitamin B_2; riboflavin)
  Purpose: release of energy from carbohydrates, fats, and proteins; maintaining integrity of red blood cells. **Dietary sources:** milk, eggs, kidney, liver, peas, soybeans, leafy vegetables. **Men over 13:** 1.3 mg; **women over 18:** 1.1 mg; **pregnant women:** 1.4 mg; **lactating women:** 1.6 mg.

Niacin (nicotinic acid; nicotinamide or niacinamide)
  Purpose: release of energy from carbohydrates and fats; red-blood-cell formation; metabolism of proteins. **Dietary sources:** cereal grains, nuts, green vegetables, liver, kidney. **Men over 13:** 16.0 mg; **women over 18:** 14.0 mg; **pregnant women:** 18.0 mg; **lactating women:** 17.0 mg.

Pantothenic acid (vitamin B_5; calcium pantothenate)
  Purpose: metabolism of carbohydrates; synthesis and degradation of fats; synthesis of sterols and other compounds. **Dietary sources:** liver, kidney, eggs, avocados, bananas. **All adults:** 4.0–7.0 mg.

Did you know? The celebrated "four-color map problem," framed in 1850 and publicized in 1878, bears little relation to cartography. The question is mathematical: how many colors are needed to color any map so that no two regions sharing a common border will have the same color? The proof, in 1977, that four colors are always sufficient occupied 170 pages of text and diagrams derived from more than 1,000 hours of calculations on a large computer.

Vitamins, with Daily Recommendations (continued)

Water-soluble vitamins (continued)

Vitamin B6 (pyroxidine; pyroxidine hydrochloride)
Purpose: amino acid, carbohydrate, and fat metabolism. **Dietary sources:** bananas, cereal grains, fish, nuts, spinach. **Men 14–50:** 1.3 mg; **men over 50:** 1.7 mg; **women 19–50:** 1.3 mg; **women over 50:** 1.5 mg; **pregnant women:** 1.9 mg; **lactating women:** 2.0 mg.

Biotin (N/A; biotin)
Purpose: carbohydrate and fat metabolism. **Dietary sources:** beef liver, yeast, oatmeal. **Adults:** 30 mcg; **pregnant women:** 30 mcg; **lactating women:** 35 mcg.

Folate (folacin or vitamin B9; folacin or folic acid)
Purpose: cellular metabolism, including synthesis of DNA components; normal red-blood-cell formation. **Dietary sources:** chicken, liver, green leafy vegetables, wheat bran and germ, citrus fruits, cereals, beans, asparagus. **Adults:** 400 mcg; **pregnant women:** 600 mcg; **lactating women:** 500 mcg.

Vitamin B12 (cobalamin; cyanocobalamin or hydroxocobalamin)
Purpose: proper functioning of many enzymes involved in carbohydrate, fat, and protein metabolism; synthesis of the insulating sheath around nerve cells; cell reproduction and normal growth; red-blood-cell formation. **Dietary sources:** eggs, meat, milk, nutritional yeast, fortified cereals. **Adults:** 2.4 mcg; **pregnant women:** 2.6 mcg; **lactating women:** 2.8 mcg.

Vitamin C (ascorbic acid; ascorbic acid)
Purpose: prevention of oxidative damage to DNA, membrane lipids, and proteins; synthesis of collagen, hormones, transmitters of the nervous sytem, lipids, and proteins; proper immune function. **Dietary sources:** citrus fruits, green peppers, broccoli, cantaloupe, green leafy vegetables. **Men over 18:** 90 mg;   **women over 18:** 75 mg; **pregnant women:** 80–85 mg; **lactating women:** 115–120 mg.

Fat-soluble vitamins

Vitamin A (retinol; retinol)
Purpose: functioning of the retina; growth and maturation of epithelial cells; growth of bone; reproduction and embryonic development. **Dietary sources:** fish and fish-liver oils, liver, butter, orange vegetables and fruits, dark green leafy vegetables; tomatoes. **Men over 13:** 900 RAE; **women over 13:** 700 RAE; **pregnant women:** 750–770 RAE; **lactating women:** 1,200–1,300 RAE.

Vitamin D (vitamins D2 and D3; [ergo] calciferol)
Purpose: promotes formation of bone by increasing the blood levels of calcium and phosphorus. **Dietary sources:** fish-liver oils, eggs, milk enriched with Vitamin D. **All adults:** 200–600 IU.

Vitamin E (N/A; tocopherol)
Purpose: protection of cell membranes and prevention of damage to membrane-associated enzymes. **Dietary sources:** nuts, vegetable oils, margarine, cereal grains. **Adults:** 15 mg; **pregnant women:** 15 mg; **lactating women:** 19 mg.

Vitamin K (N/A; vitamin K1)
Purpose: formation of several blood clotting factors. **Dietary sources:** green leafy vegetables, vegetable oils. **Men over 18:** 120 mcg; **women over 18:** 90 mcg; **pregnant women:** 75–90 mcg; **lactating women:** 75–90 mcg.

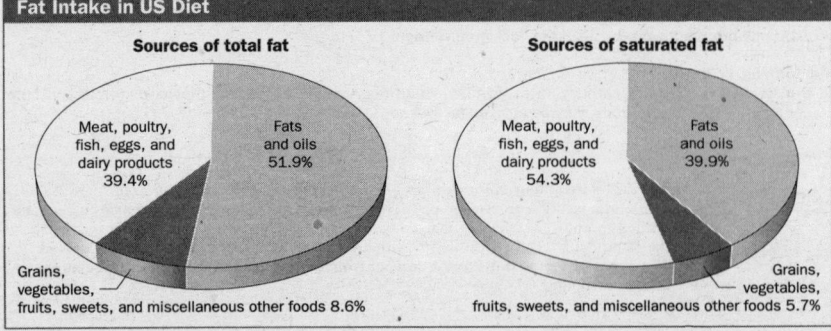

Fat Intake in US Diet

Sources of total fat

Meat, poultry, fish, eggs, and dairy products 39.4%

Fats and oils 51.9%

Grains, vegetables, fruits, sweets, and miscellaneous other foods 8.6%

Sources of saturated fat

Meat, poultry, fish, eggs, and dairy products 54.3%

Fats and oils 39.9%

Grains, vegetables, fruits, sweets, and miscellaneous other foods 5.7%

Food Guide Pyramid

In 2005 the USDA released an update of its food-pyramid guide to a healthy diet. It is designed to help individuals get proper nutrients while at the same time consuming the appropriate amount of calories necessary to maintain healthy weight. The 2005 pyramid also provides information about exercise and weight loss. Diets should be low in added sugars, salt, saturated fat and cholesterol and moderate in overall fat.

Find your balance between food and physical activity:

- Be sure to stay within your daily calorie needs.
- Be physically active for at least 30 minutes most days of the week.
- About 60 minutes a day of physical activity may be needed to prevent weight gain.
- For sustaining weight loss, at least 60 to 90 minutes a day of physical activity may be required.
- Children and teenagers should be physically active for 60 minutes every day or most days.

MyPyramid.gov

Recommended daily intake
These amounts are appropriate for individuals who get less than 30 minutes per day of moderate physical activity, beyond normal daily activities. Those who are more physically active may be able to consume more because they may have greater calorie needs.

	Grains	Vegetables	Fruits	Fats and Oils—limit your intake	Milk	Meat and Beans
Children 2–3 years old	3 ounce equivalents[1]	1 cup[2]	1 cup[3]		2 cups[4]	2 ounce equivalents[5]
Children 4–8 years old	4–5 ounce equivalents[1]	1.5 cups[2]	1–1.5 cups[3]		2 cups[4]	3–4 ounce equivalents[5]
Girls 9–13 years old	5 ounce equivalents[1]	2 cups[2]	1.5 cups[3]		3 cups[4]	5 ounce equivalents[5]
Boys 9–13 years old	6 ounce equivalents[1]	2.5 cups[2]	1.5 cups[3]		3 cups[4]	5 ounce equivalents[5]
Girls 14–18 years old	6 ounce equivalents[1]	2.5 cups[2]	1.5 cups[3]		3 cups[4]	5 ounce equivalents[5]
Boys 14–18 years old	7 ounce equivalents[1]	3 cups[2]	2 cups[3]		3 cups[4]	6 ounce equivalents[5]
Women 19–30 years old	6 ounce equivalents[1]	2.5 cups[2]	2 cups[3]		3 cups[4]	5.5 ounce equivalents[5]
Men 19–30 years old	8 ounce equivalents[1]	3 cups[2]	2 cups[3]		3 cups[4]	6.5 ounce equivalents[5]
Women 31–50 years old	6 ounce equivalents[1]	2.5 cups[2]	1.5 cups[3]		3 cups[4]	5 ounce equivalents[5]
Men 31–50 years old	7 ounce equivalents[1]	3 cups[2]	2 cups[3]		3 cups[4]	6 ounce equivalents[5]
Women 51+ years old	5 ounce equivalents[1]	2 cups[2]	1.5 cups[3]		3 cups[4]	5 ounce equivalents[5]
Men 51+ years old	6 ounce equivalents[1]	2.5 cups[2]	2 cups[3]		3 cups[4]	5.5 ounce equivalents[5]

[1] 1 slice of bread, 1 cup of ready-to-eat cereal, or ½ cup of cooked rice, cooked pasta, or cooked cereal can be considered as 1 ounce equivalent from the grains group.
[2] 1 cup of raw or cooked vegetables or vegetable juice or 2 cups of raw leafy greens can be considered as 1 cup from the vegetable group.
[3] 1 cup of fruit or 100% fruit juice or ½ cup of dried fruit can be considered as 1 cup from the fruit group.
[4] 1 cup of milk or yogurt, 1½ ounces of natural cheese, or 2 ounces of processed cheese can be considered as 1 cup from the milk group.
[5] 1 ounce of meat, poultry, or fish, ¼ cup cooked dry beans, 1 egg, 1 tablespoon of peanut butter, or ½ ounce of nuts or seeds can be considered as 1 ounce equivalent from the meat and beans group.

Source: USDA.

Individuals Meeting Dietary Guidelines
1977–78 and 1994–96.

Percentages of US population that meet or exceed the minimum dietary guidelines given in *Nutrition and Your Health: Dietary Guidelines for Americans, 5th edition (2000)*, a joint publication of the depart- ments of Health and Human Services and Agricul- ture. To view the complete publication or to order a print copy, visit <www.health.gov/dietaryguidelines>. Next update: 2005.

AGE AND GENDER	CALORIES	TOTAL FAT	SATURA- TED FAT	CHOL- ESTEROL	SODIUM	FIBER	CALCIUM	IRON
1977–78								
Children (2–17)	33	14	N/A	N/A	N/A	N/A	37	39
Adults (18 and over)	23	13	N/A	N/A	N/A	N/A	15	43
Males 60 and over	29	12	N/A	N/A	N/A	N/A	11	66
Females 60 and over	18	17	N/A	N/A	N/A	N/A	4	40
All individuals 2 and over	26	13	N/A	N/A	N/A	N/A	22	42
1994–96								
Children (2–17)	38	37	31	77	39	39	37	59
Adults (18 and over)	27	37	43	69	34	20	21	60
Males 60 and over	28	36	43	65	30	26	16	77
Females 60 and over	18	41	49	79	54	35	6	56
All individuals 2 and over	30	37	40	71	35	25	25	59

N/A indicates data not available.

Nutrient Composition of Selected Fruits and Vegetables
Values shown are approximations for 100 grams (3.57 oz.). Foods are raw unless otherwise noted. Source: USDA Nutrient Data Laboratory. kcal: kilocalorie; g: gram; mg: milligram; IU: international unit.

	ENERGY (KCAL)	WATER (G)	CARBO- HYDRATE (G)	PROTEIN (G)	FAT (G)	VITAMIN A (IU)	VITAMIN C (MG)	THIAMINE (MG)	RIBO- FLAVIN (MG)	NIACIN (MG)
Fruits										
Apple	59	83.93	15.25	0.19	0.36	53	5.7	0.017	0.014	0.077
Apricot	48	86.35	11.12	1.40	0.39	2,612	10.0	0.030	0.040	0.600
Avocado	161	74.27	7.39	1.98	15.32	61	7.9	0.108	0.122	1.921
Banana	92	74.26	23.43	1.03	0.48	81	9.1	0.045	0.100	0.540
Blackberries	52	85.64	12.76	0.72	0.39	165	21.0	0.030	0.040	0.400
Blueberries	56	84.61	14.13	0.67	0.38	100	13.0	0.048	0.050	0.359
Cantaloupe	35	89.78	8.36	0.88	0.28	3,224	42.2	0.036	0.021	0.574
Cherries (sweet)	72	80.76	16.55	1.20	0.96	214	7.0	0.050	0.060	0.400
Grapes	67	81.30	17.15	0.63	0.35	100	4.0	0.092	0.057	0.300
Grapefruit	32	90.89	8.08	0.63	0.10	124	34.4	0.036	0.020	0.250
Kiwi	61	83.05	14.88	0.99	0.44	175	98.0	0.020	0.050	0.500
Lemon	29	88.98	9.32	1.10	0.30	29	53.0	0.040	0.020	0.100
Lime	30	88.26	10.54	0.70	0.20	10	29.1	0.030	0.020	0.200
Mango	65	81.71	17.00	0.51	0.27	3,894	27.7	0.058	0.057	0.584
Nectarine	49	86.28	11.78	0.94	0.46	736	5.4	0.017	0.041	0.990
Orange	47	86.75	11.75	0.94	0.12	205	53.2	0.087	0.040	0.282
Peach	43	87.66	11.10	0.70	0.09	535	6.6	0.017	0.041	0.990
Pear	59	83.81	15.11	0.39	0.40	20	4.0	0.020	0.040	0.100
Pineapple	49	86.50	12.39	0.39	0.43	23	15.4	0.092	0.036	0.420
Plum	55	85.20	13.01	0.79	0.62	323	9.5	0.043	0.096	0.500
Raspberries	49	86.57	11.57	0.91	0.55	130	25.0	0.030	0.090	0.900
Strawberries	30	91.57	7.02	0.61	0.37	27	56.7	0.020	0.066	0.230
Tangerine	44	87.60	11.19	0.63	0.19	920	30.8	0.105	0.022	0.160
Watermelon	32	91.51	7.18	0.62	0.43	366	9.6	0.080	0.020	0.200
Vegetables										
Artichoke[1]	50	83.97	11.18	3.48	0.16	177	10.0	0.065	0.066	1.001
Asparagus[1]	24	92.20	4.23	2.59	0.31	539	10.8	0.123	0.126	1.082
Beans (snap, green)	31	90.27	7.14	1.82	0.12	668	16.3	0.084	0.105	0.752
Beet	43	87.58	9.56	1.61	0.17	38	4.9	0.031	0.040	0.334
Broccoli	28	90.69	5.24	2.98	0.35	1,542	93.2	0.065	0.119	0.638
Brussels sprout	43	86.00	8.96	3.38	0.30	883	85.0	0.139	0.090	0.745
Cabbage	25	92.15	5.43	1.44	0.27	133	32.2	0.050	0.040	0.300
Carrot	43	87.79	10.14	1.03	0.19	28,129	9.3	0.097	0.059	0.928
Cauliflower	25	91.91	5.20	1.98	0.21	19	46.4	0.057	0.063	0.526

Nutrient Composition of Selected Fruits and Vegetables (continued)

	ENERGY (KCAL)	WATER (G)	CARBO-HYDRATE (G)	PROTEIN (G)	FAT (G)	VITAMIN A (IU)	VITAMIN C (MG)	THIAMINE (MG)	RIBO-FLAVIN (MG)	NIACIN (MG)
Vegetables (continued)										
Celery	16	94.64	3.65	0.75	0.14	134	7.0	0.046	0.045	0.323
Collards[1]	26	91.86	4.90	2.11	0.36	3,129	18.2	0.040	0.106	0.575
Corn (sweet, yellow)[1]	108	69.57	25.11	3.32	1.28	217	6.2	0.215	0.072	1.614
Cucumber	13	96.01	2.76	0.69	0.13	215	5.3	0.024	0.022	0.221
Eggplant[1]	28	91.77	6.64	0.83	0.23	64	1.3	0.076	0.020	0.600
Lettuce (iceberg)	12	95.89	2.09	1.01	0.19	330	3.9	0.046	0.030	0.187
Mushroom[1]	27	91.08	5.14	2.17	0.47	0	4.0	0.073	0.300	4.460
Okra[1]	32	89.91	7.21	1.87	0.17	575	16.3	0.132	0.055	0.871
Onion[1]	44	87.86	10.15	1.36	0.19	0	5.2	0.042	0.023	0.165
Pepper (sweet, green)	27	92.19	6.43	0.89	0.19	632	89.3	0.066	0.030	0.509
Pepper (sweet, red)	27	92.19	6.43	0.89	0.19	5,700	190.0	0.066	0.030	0.509
Potato[2]	93	75.42	21.56	1.96	0.10	0	12.8	0.105	0.021	1.395
Spinach	22	91.58	3.50	2.86	0.35	6,715	28.1	0.078	0.189	0.724
Sweet potato[2]	103	72.85	24.27	1.72	0.11	21,822	24.6	0.073	0.127	0.604
Tomato (red)	21	93.76	4.64	0.85	0.33	623	19.1	0.059	0.048	0.628

[1]Boiled. [2]Baked.

Nutritional Value of Selected Foods

Values shown are approximations. Source: *Home and Garden Bulletin No. 72, USDA. kcal: kilocalorie; g: gram; mg: milligram; oz: ounce; fl oz: fluid ounce.*

FOOD	AMOUNT	GRAMS	ENERGY (KCAL)	CARBO-HYDRATE (G)	PROTEIN (G)	TOTAL FAT (G)	SATU-RATED FAT (G)	CALCIUM (MG)	IRON (MG)	SODIUM (MG)
Beverages										
Beer	12 fl oz	360	150	13	1	0	0	14	0.1	18
Cola, regular	12 fl oz	369	160	41	0	0	0	11	0.2	18
Cola, diet (w/aspartame and saccharine)	12 fl oz	355	0	0	0	0	0	14	0.2	32
Coffee, brewed	6 fl oz	180	0	0	0	0	0	4	0	2
Orange juice, canned	8 fl oz	249	105	25	1	0	0	20	1.1	5
Tea, instant, prepared, unsweetened	8 fl oz	241	0	1	0	0	0	1	0	1
Wine, table, red	3.5 fl oz	102	75	3	0	0	0	8	0.4	5
Dairy										
Butter, salted	4 oz	113	810	0	1	92	57.1	27	0.2	933
Cheese, American (pasteurized, processed)	1 oz	28.35	105	0	6	9	5.6	174	0.1	406
Cheese, cheddar	1 oz	28.35	115	0	7	9	6	204	0.2	176
Cheese, mozzarella (whole milk)	1 oz	28.35	80	1	6	6	3.7	147	0.1	106
Cheese, swiss	1 oz	28.35	105	1	8	8	5	272	0	74
Cottage cheese, small curd	8 oz	210	215	6	26	9	6	126	0.3	850
Cream cheese	1 oz	28.35	100	1	2	10	6.2	23	0.3	84
Cream, half and half	0.5 oz	15	20	1	0	2	1.1	16	0	6
Cream, sour	8 oz	230	495	10	7	48	30	268	0.1	123
Eggs, cooked, fried	1 egg	46	90	1	6	7	1.9	25	0.7	162
Eggs, cooked, hard-cooked	1 egg	50	75	1	6	5	1.6	25	0.6	62
Eggs, cooked, scrambled	1 egg	61	100	1	7	7	2.2	44	0.7	171
Ice cream, vanilla, 11% fat	8 oz	133	270	32	5	14	8.9	176	0.1	116
Milk, whole, 3.3% fat	8 oz	244	150	11	8	8	5.1	291	0.1	120
Milk, low fat, 2% fat	8 oz	244	120	12	8	5	2.9	297	0.1	122
Milk, skim	8 oz	245	85	12	8	0	0.3	302	0.1	126
Milk, chocolate	8 oz	250	210	26	8	8	5.3	280	0.6	149
Yogurt, plain, low fat	8 oz	227	145	16	12	4	2.3	415	0.2	159
Fats, oils										
Lard	0.5 oz	13	115	0	0	13	5.1	0	0	0
Margarine, hard, 80% fat	0.5 oz	14	100	0	0	11	2.2	4	0	132

Nutritional Value of Selected Foods (continued)

FOOD	AMOUNT	GRAMS	ENERGY (KCAL)	CARBO-HYDRATE (G)	PROTEIN (G)	TOTAL FAT (G)	SATU-RATED FAT (G)	CALCIUM (MG)	IRON (MG)	SODIUM (MG)
Fats, oils (continued)										
Olive oil	0.5 oz	14	125	0	0	14	1.9	0	0	0
Vegetable shortening	0.5 oz	13	115	0	0	13	3.3	0	0	0
Fish										
Crabmeat, canned	8 oz	135	135	1	23	3	0.5	61	1.1	1350
Fish sticks, frozen	1 piece	28	70	4	6	3	0.8	11	0.3	53
Ocean perch, breaded, fried	1 piece	85	185	7	16	11	2.6	31	1.2	138
Oysters, raw	8 oz	240	160	8	20	4	1.4	226	15.6	175
Salmon, baked, red	3 oz	85	140	0	21	5	1.2	26	0.5	55
Shrimp, fried	3 oz	85	200	11	16	10	2.5	61	2	384
Trout, broiled, w/butter and lemon juice	3 oz	85	175	0	21	9	4.1	26	1	122
Tuna, canned, white, in water	3 oz	85	135	0	30	1	0.3	17	0.6	468
Fruits, fruit products										
Apples, peeled, sliced	8 oz	110	65	16	0	0	0.1	4	0.1	0
Applesauce, canned, sweetened	8 oz	255	195	51	0	0	0.1	10	0.9	8
Apricots	3 apricots	106	50	12	1	0	0	15	0.6	1
Bananas	1 banana	114	105	27	1	1	0.2	7	0.4	1
Blackberries	8 oz	144	75	18	1	1	0.2	46	0.8	0
Blueberries	8 oz	145	80	20	1	1	0	9	0.2	9
Grapefruit, pink	½ grapefruit	120	40	10	1	0	0	14	0.1	0
Grapes, European, Thompson	10 grapes	50	35	9	0	0	0.1	6	0.1	1
Oranges	1 orange	131	60	15	1	0	0	52	0.1	0
Peaches	1 peach	87	35	10	1	0	0	4	0.1	0
Pears, Bartlett	1 pear	166	100	25	1	1	0	18	0.4	0
Pineapple, canned, heavy syrup	8 oz	255	200	52	1	0	0	36	1	3
Plums, 2⅛-in. diam.	1 plum	66	35	9	1	0	0	3	0.1	0
Prunes, dried, large	5 prunes	49	115	31	1	0	0	25	1.2	2
Raisins	8 oz	145	435	115	5	1	0.2	71	3	17
Strawberries	8 oz	149	45	10	1	1	0	21	0.6	1
Watermelon	1 piece	482	155	35	3	2	0.3	39	0.8	10
Grains										
Bagels, plain	1 bagel	68	200	38	7	2	0.3	29	1.8	245
Bread, rye, light	1 slice	25	65	12	2	1	0.2	20	0.7	175
Bread, wheat	1 slice	25	65	12	2	1	0.2	32	0.9	138
Bread, white	1 slice	25	65	12	2	1	0.3	32	0.7	129
Bread, whole wheat	1 slice	28	70	13	3	1	0.4	20	1	180
Cereal, Cheerios	1 oz	28.35	110	20	4	2	0.3	48	4.5	307
Cereal, Kellogg's Corn Flakes	1 oz	28.35	110	24	2	0	0	1	1.8	351
Cereal, Lucky Charms	1 oz	28.35	110	23	3	1	0.2	32	4.5	201
Cereal, Post Raisin Bran	1 oz	28.35	85	21	3	1	0.1	13	4.5	185
Cake, white, w/white frosting, commercial	1 piece	71	260	42	3	9	2.1	33	1	176
Cheesecake	1 piece	92	280	26	5	18	9.9	52	0.4	204
Chocolate chip cookies, commercial	4 cookies	42	180	28	2	9	2.9	13	0.8	140
Cornmeal, whole-ground, dry	8 oz	122	435	90	11	5	0.5	24	2.2	1
Doughnuts, cake, plain	1 doughnut	50	210	24	3	12	2.8	22	1	192
English muffins, plain	1 muffin	57	140	27	5	1	0.3	96	1.7	378
Oatmeal, instant, cooked, w/salt	8 oz	234	145	25	6	2	0.4	19	1.6	374
Macaroni, cooked, firm	8 oz	130	190	39	7	1	0.1	14	2.1	1
Muffins, blueberry, commercial mix	1 muffin	45	140	22	3	5	1.4	15	0.9	225
Pancakes, plain, commercial mix	1 pancake	27	60	8	2	2	0.5	36	0.7	160
Pie, apple	1 piece	158	405	60	3	18	4.6	13	1.6	476

Nutritional Value of Selected Foods (continued)

FOOD	AMOUNT	GRAMS	ENERGY (KCAL)	CARBO-HYDRATE (G)	PROTEIN (G)	TOTAL FAT (G)	SATU-RATED FAT (G)	CALCIUM (MG)	IRON (MG)	SODIUM (MG)
Grains (continued)										
Popcorn, air-popped, unsalted	8 oz	8	30	6	1	0	0	1	0.2	0
Pretzels, stick	10 pieces	3	10	2	0	0	0	1	0.1	48
Rice, brown, cooked	8 oz	195	230	50	5	1	0.3	23	1	0
Rice, white, instant, cooked	8 oz	165	180	40	4	0	0.1	5	1.3	0
Saltines	4 pieces	12	50	9	1	1	0.5	3	0.5	165
Spaghetti, cooked, tender	8 oz	140	155	32	5	1	0.1	11	1.7	1
Waffles, from commercial mix	1 waffle	75	205	27	7	8	2.7	179	1.2	515
Meat, poultry										
Bacon, regular, cooked	3 slices	19	110	0	6	9	3.3	2	0.3	303
Beef, chuck, lean, cooked	2.2 oz	62	170	0	19	9	3.9	8	2.3	44
Chicken, breast, roasted	3 oz	86	140	0	27	3	0.9	13	0.9	64
Chicken, drumstick, floured, fried	1.7 oz	49	120	1	13	7	1.8	6	0.7	44
Ground beef, broiled	3 oz	85	245	0	20	18	6.9	9	2.1	70
Ham, roasted, lean and fat	3 oz	85	205	0	18	14	5.1	6	0.7	1009
Hamburger	4-oz patty	174	445	38	25	21	7.1	75	4.8	763
Lamb chops, braised, lean	1.7 oz	48	135	0	17	7	2.9	12	1.3	36
Turkey, roasted, light and dark	8 oz	140	240	0	41	7	2.3	35	2.5	98
Veal cutlet, med. fat, braised or broiled	3 oz	85	185	0	23	9	4.1	9	0.8	56
Nuts, legumes, seeds										
Mixed nuts w/peanuts, dry, salted	1 oz	28.35	170	7	5	15	2	20	1	190
Peanuts, oil-roasted, unsalted	8 oz	145	840	27	39	71	9.9	125	2.8	22
Peanut butter	0.5 oz	16	95	3	5	8	1.4	5	0.3	75
Pinto beans, dry, cooked	8 oz	180	265	49	15	1	0.1	86	5.4	3
Sunflower seeds	1 oz	28.35	160	5	6	14	1.5	33	1.9	1
Tofu	1 piece	120	85	3	9	5	0.7	108	2.3	8
Sauces, dressings, condiments										
Catsup	0.5 oz	15	15	4	0	0	0	3	0.1	156
Cheese sauce w/milk, from mix	8 fl oz	279	305	23	16	17	9.3	569	0.3	1565
Honey	0.5 oz	21	65	17	0	0	0	1	0.1	1
Jams/preserves	0.5 oz	20	55	14	0	0	0	4	0.2	2
Mayonnaise	0.5 oz	14	100	0	0	11	1.7	3	0.1	80
Mustard, yellow	0.17 oz	5	5	0	0	0	0	4	0.1	63
Salad dressing, French	0.5 oz	16	85	1	0	9	1.4	2	0	188
Salad dressing, Italian, low calorie	0.5 oz	15	5	2	0	0	0	1	0	136
Syrup, table	1 oz	42	122	32	0	0	0	1	0	19
Sugars, sweets, miscellaneous snacks										
Caramels, plain or chocolate	1 oz	28.35	115	22	1	3	2.2	42	0.4	64
Chocolate, milk, candy, w/almonds	1 oz	28.35	150	15	3	10	4.8	65	0.5	23
Chocolate, dark, sweet	1 oz	28.35	150	16	1	10	5.9	7	0.6	5
Gelatin dessert, prepared	4 oz	120	70	17	2	0	0	2	0	55
Hard candy	1 oz	28.35	110	28	0	0	0	0	0.1	7
Popsicle	1 popsicle	95	70	18	0	0	0	0	0	11
Potato chips	10 chips	20	105	10	1	7	1.8	5	0.2	94
Pudding, chocolate, instant	4 oz	130	155	27	4	4	2.3	130	0.3	440
Sugar, brown	8 oz	220	820	212	0	0	0	187	4.8	97
Sugar, white, granulated	8 oz	200	770	199	0	0	0	3	0.1	5
Vegetables										
Beans, snap, yellow, canned, no salt	8 oz	135	25	6	2	0	0	35	1.2	3
Broccoli	1 spear	151	40	8	4	1	0.1	72	1.3	41

Nutritional Value of Selected Foods (continued)

FOOD	AMOUNT	GRAMS	ENERGY (KCAL)	CARBO-HYDRATE (G)	PROTEIN (G)	TOTAL FAT (G)	SATU-RATED FAT (G)	CALCIUM (MG)	IRON (MG)	SODIUM (MG)
Vegetables (continued)										
Carrots, cooked from frozen	8 oz	146	55	12	2	0	0	41	0.7	86
Cauliflower, cooked from raw	8 oz	125	30	6	2	0	0	34	0.5	8
Celery, Pascal, raw	1 stalk	40	5	1	0	0	0	14	0.2	35
Corn, yellow, cooked from frozen	8 oz	165	135	34	5	0	0	3	0.5	8
Cucumber, w/peel	6 slices	28	5	1	0	0	0	4	0.1	1
Lettuce, crisphead	1 wedge	135	20	3	1	0	0	26	0.7	12
Mushrooms	8 oz	70	20	3	1	0	0	4	0.9	3
Onions, sliced	8 oz	115	40	8	1	0	0.1	29	0.4	2
Peas, green, cooked from frozen	8 oz	160	125	23	8	0	0.1	38	2.5	139
Potatos, boiled, peeled after	1 potato	136	120	27	3	0	0	7	0.4	5
Tomatoes, raw	1 tomato	123	25	5	1	0	0	9	0.6	10

Reading Food Labels

The FDA requires most food manufacturers to provide standardized information about certain nutrients. Within strict guidelines the nutritional labels are designed to aid the consumer in making informed dietary decisions as well as to regulate claims made by manufacturers about their products.

The percent daily value is based on a 2,000-calorie-per-day diet. Some larger packages will have listings for both 2,000-calorie and 2,500-calorie diets. For products that require additional preparation before eating, such as dry cake mixes, manufacturers often provide two columns of nutritional information, one with the values of the food as purchased, the other with the values of the food as prepared.

The FDA selects mandatory label components (see sample label at right) based on current understanding of nutrition concerns, and component order on the label is consistent with the priority of dietary recommendations. Components that may appear in addition to the mandatory components are limited to the following: calories from saturated fat, polyunsaturated fat, monounsaturated fat, potassium, soluble fiber, insoluble fiber, sugar alcohol (for example, the sugar substitutes xylitol, mannitol, and sorbitol), other carbohydrate (the difference between total carbohydrate and the sum of dietary fiber, sugars, and sugar alcohol if declared), percent of vitamin A present as beta-carotene, and other essential vitamins and minerals. Any of these optional components that form the basis of product claims, fortification, or enrichment must appear in the nutrition facts. In 2006 labels were required to specify amounts of trans fatty acids.

Certain key descriptions are also regulated by the FDA. They include the following, in amounts per serving:

Low fat: 3 g or less
Low saturated fat: 1 g or less
Low sodium: 140 mg or less
Low cholesterol: 20 mg or less and 2 g or less of saturated fat
Low calorie: 40 calories or less

Dietary Guidelines for Americans, 2005
Web site: <www.health.gov/dietaryguidelines>.

Nutrition Facts

Serving Size 1 cup (228g)
Servings Per Container 2

Amount Per Serving

Calories 250 — Calories from Fat 110

%Daily Value*

Total Fat 12g — **18%**
Saturated Fat 3g — **15%**
Trans Fat 3g
Cholesterol 30mg — **10%**
Sodium 470mg — **20%**
Potassium 700mg — **20%**
Total Carbohydrate 31g — **10%**
Dietary Fiber 0g — **0%**
Sugars 5g
Protein 5g

Vitamin A — **4%**
Vitamin C — **2%**
Calcium — **20%**
Iron — **4%**

* Percent Daily Values are based on a 2,000 calorie diet. Your Daily Values may be higher or lower depending on your calorie needs:

	Calories	2,000	2,500
Total Fat	Less than	65g	80g
Sat Fat	Less than	20g	25g
Cholesterol	Less than	300mg	300mg
Sodium	Less than	2,400mg	2,400mg
Total Carbohydrate		300g	375g
Dietary Fiber		25g	30g

Americans and Physical Activity

This table shows selected data illustrating the number of leisure-time periods of vigorous physical activity per week (lasting 10 minutes or longer) among persons 18 years of age and over. Numbers are in thousands ('000). Details may not add to totals due to rounding. Data from the Centers for Disease Control and Prevention National Center for Health Statistics National Health Interview Survey, 2002.

SELECTED CHARACTERISTIC	ALL PERSONS 18 YEARS OF AGE AND OVER	NEVER	LESS THAN 1	1–2	3–4	5 OR MORE
Total	205,825	119,634	6,022	24,914	26,655	24,911
Age						
18–44 years	108,114	52,714	3,901	16,583	17,183	15,671
45–64 years	64,650	40,137	1,746	6,957	7,718	6,931
65–74 years	17,809	13,513	238	1,038	1,174	1,566
75 years and over	15,252	13,270	138	336	580	743
Sex and ethnicity						
Hispanic male or Latino	11,145	6,738	239	1,500	1,112	1,341
Hispanic female or Latina	11,546	8,632	180	852	928	790
Not Hispanic or Latino						
White male	71,855	35,539	2,689	10,554	10,495	11,216
White female	77,729	47,741	1,980	8,351	10,227	8,139
Black male	10,292	5,617	249	1,281	1,543	1,389
Black female	12,773	9,225	320	1,139	1,009	829
Education (respondents 25 and older)						
Less than a high school diploma	28,248	23,044	372	1,451	1,154	1,821
High school diploma or GED	52,556	35,412	1,263	5,008	4,479	5,384
Some college	48,091	26,867	1,595	6,230	6,894	5,694
Bachelor's degree or higher	47,197	20,254	1,892	8,013	9,455	7,083
Family income						
Less than $20,000	37,369	27,175	618	2,856	2,788	3,465
$20,000 or more	155,166	83,864	5,174	20,835	22,758	20,288
$20,000–$34,999	29,671	19,443	731	2,978	2,974	3,278
$35,000–$54,999	31,814	17,666	987	4,425	4,279	4,139
$55,000–$74,999	23,984	12,212	985	3,661	3,666	3,254
$75,000 or more	41,572	17,538	1,789	7,021	8,429	6,341
Marital status						
Married	118,960	69,003	3,693	15,198	15,219	13,618
Widowed	13,093	11,004	148	444	626	735
Divorced or separated	21,203	13,386	529	2,083	2,580	2,230
Never married	39,981	19,103	1,327	5,492	6,695	6,791
Living with a partner	11,978	6,842	312	1,648	1,473	1,497

Ways To Burn 150 Calories

Values shown are approximations. Activities are listed from more to less vigorous—the more vigorous an activity, the less time it takes to burn a calorie. When specific distances are given, the activity must be performed in the time shown (for example, one must run 1.5 miles in 15 minutes to burn 150 calories).

ACTIVITY	DURATION (MINUTES)
Climbing stairs	15
Shoveling snow	15
Running 1.5 miles (10 minutes/mile)	15
Jumping rope	15
Bicycling 4 miles	15
Playing basketball	15–20
Playing wheelchair basketball	20
Swimming laps	20
Performing water aerobics	30
Walking 2 miles (15 minutes/mile)	30
Raking leaves	30

ACTIVITY	DURATION (MINUTES)
Pushing a stroller 1.5 miles	30
Dancing fast	30
Bicycling 5 miles	30
Shooting baskets	30
Walking 1.75 miles (20 minutes/mile)	35
Wheeling oneself in a wheelchair	30–40
Gardening (standing)	30–45
Playing touch football	30–45
Playing volleyball	45
Washing windows or floors	45–60
Washing and waxing a car or boat	45–60

Target Heart Rate Training Zones

Measuring **target heart rate** involves monitoring your pulse periodically as you exercise. To use the Target Heart Rate chart:

1. Calculate your maximum heart rate by subtracting your age from 220.
2. Determine your target heart rate zone (50–70% of your maximum heart rate).
3. While exercising, monitor your pulse regularly. Count the number of beats for 10 seconds, then multiply by 6 to determine in what zone you are working.

The American Heart Association recommends using the target heart rate scale when participating in more vigorous athletic activity, such as jogging or aerobics. If your activity is moderate or taking your pulse is too bothersome, a "talk test" can be used as a substitute. If you can converse with someone with minimal effort, you are not working too hard. Alternately, if you can sing without difficulty, you are not working hard enough.

Note: For optimal cardiovascular fitness, you should work toward the middle of your 50 and 70% zones. Always check with your physician before starting any fitness routine, especially if you have heart or respiratory concerns.

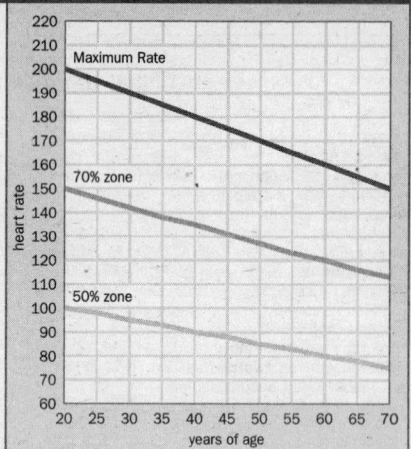

Body Mass Index (BMI)

The BMI is a measure expressing the relationship of weight to height determined by dividing body weight in kilograms by the square of height in meters (for convenience, the information has been converted to standard US measurements in the table below). It is more highly correlated with body fat than any other indicator of height and weight. The National Institutes of Health recommend using the BMI scale to help assess the risk of diseases and disabilities associated with an unhealthy weight. Individuals with a BMI below 18.5 are considered underweight; those with a BMI from 18.5 to 24.9 are considered normal; those with a BMI between 25.0 and 29.9 are considered overweight; and those with a BMI of 30.0 or more are considered obese. The BMI may overestimate body fat in athletes and others who have a muscular build, and it may underestimate body fat in older persons and others who have lost muscle mass.
Source: <www.nhlbi.nih.gov>.

HEIGHT (INCHES)							BODY WEIGHT (POUNDS)														
58	91	96	100	105	110	115	119	124	129	134	138	143	148	153	158	162	167	172	177	181	186
59	94	99	104	109	114	119	124	128	133	138	143	148	153	158	163	168	173	178	183	188	193
60	97	102	107	112	118	123	128	133	138	143	148	153	158	163	168	174	179	184	189	194	199
61	100	106	111	116	122	127	132	137	143	148	153	158	164	169	174	180	185	190	195	201	206
62	104	109	115	120	126	131	136	142	147	153	158	164	169	175	180	186	191	196	202	207	213
63	107	113	118	124	130	135	141	146	152	158	163	169	175	180	186	191	197	203	208	214	220
64	110	116	122	128	134	140	145	151	157	163	169	174	180	186	192	197	204	209	215	221	227
65	114	120	126	132	138	144	150	156	162	168	174	180	186	192	198	204	210	216	222	228	234
66	118	124	130	136	142	148	155	161	167	173	179	186	192	198	204	210	216	223	229	235	241
67	121	127	134	140	146	153	159	166	172	178	185	191	198	204	211	217	223	230	236	242	249
68	125	131	138	144	151	158	164	171	177	184	190	197	203	210	216	223	230	236	243	249	256
69	128	135	142	149	155	162	169	176	182	189	196	203	209	216	223	230	236	243	250	257	263
70	132	139	146	153	160	167	174	181	188	195	202	209	216	222	229	236	243	250	257	264	271
71	136	143	150	157	165	172	179	186	193	200	208	215	222	229	236	243	250	257	265	272	279
72	140	147	154	162	169	177	184	191	199	206	213	221	228	235	242	250	258	265	272	279	287
73	144	151	159	166	174	182	189	197	204	212	219	227	235	242	250	257	265	272	280	288	295
74	148	155	163	171	179	186	194	202	210	218	225	233	241	249	256	264	272	280	287	295	303
75	152	160	168	176	184	192	200	208	216	224	232	240	248	256	264	272	279	287	295	303	311
76	156	164	172	180	189	197	205	213	221	230	238	246	254	263	271	279	287	295	304	312	320
BMI	19	20	21	22	23	24	25	26	27	28	29	30	31	32	33	34	35	36	37	38	39
			NORMAL					OVERWEIGHT						OBESE							

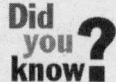

The colorful onion domes of Saint Basil the Blessed above Red Square are perhaps the most common vision Westerners conjure up in Moscow. The church was commissioned by Ivan the Terrible in honor of the Russian victory over the Tatars in Kazan and Astrakhan.

World

China: Dawn of a New Dynasty

by Michael Elliott, TIME

The railroad station in the Angolan town of Dondo hasn't seen a train in years. Its windows are boarded up, its pale pink facade crumbling away; the local coffee trade that Portuguese colonialists founded long ago is a distant memory, victim of a civil war that lasted for 27 years. Dondo's fortunes, however, may be looking up. In January 2007, laborers began restoring the local section of the line that links the town to the deep harbor at Luanda, Angola's capital. The work will be done by Chinese construction firms, and as two of their workers survey the track, an Angolan security guard sums up his feelings. "Thank you, God," he says, "for the Chinese."

That sentiment, or something like it, can be heard a lot these days in Africa, where Chinese investment is building roads and railways, opening textile factories, and digging oil wells. You hear it on the farms of Brazil, where Chinese appetite for soy and beef has led to a booming export trade. And you hear it in Chiang Saen, a town on the Mekong River in northern Thailand, where locals used to subsist on whatever they could make from farming and smuggling—until Chinese engineers began blasting the rapids and reefs on the upper Mekong so that large boats could take Chinese-manufactured goods to markets in Southeast Asia.

You may know all about the world coming to China—about the hordes of foreign businesspeople setting up factories and boutiques and showrooms in places like Shanghai and Shenzhen. But you probably know less about how China is going out into the world. Through its foreign investments and appetite for raw materials, the world's most populous country has already transformed economies from Angola to Australia. Now China is turning that commercial might into real political muscle, striding onto the global stage and acting like a nation that very much intends to become the world's next great power.

Reaching Out to the World. In recent years China established itself as the key dealmaker in nuclear negotiations with North Korea, allied itself with Russia in an attempt to shape the future of Central Asia, launched a diplomatic offensive in Europe and Latin America, and contributed troops to the UN peacekeeping mission in Lebanon. With the US preoccupied with the threat of Islamic terrorism and struggling to extricate itself from a failing war in Iraq, China seems ready to challenge—possibly even undermine—some of Washington's other foreign policy goals, from halting the genocide in Darfur to toughening sanctions against Iran.

Blink for a moment and you can imagine that—as many Chinese would tell the tale—after nearly 200 years of foreign humiliation, invasion, civil war, revolution, and unspeakable horrors, China is at last preparing for a date with destiny.

"China is thinking in much more active terms about its strategy, not only regionally, but globally, than it has done in the past," says Kenneth Lieberthal of the University of Michigan, who served as senior director at the National Security Council's Asia desk under Pres. Bill Clinton. "We have seen a sea change in China's fundamental level of confidence. The Chinese wouldn't put it this way themselves, but in their hearts I think they believe that the 21st century is China's century," says Lieberthal.

That's quite something to believe. Is it true? Or rather—since the century is yet young—will it be true? If so, when, and how will it happen? How comfortable would such a development be for the West? Can China's rise be managed peaceably by the international system? Or will China so threaten the interests of established powers that, as with Germany at the end of the 19th century and Japan in the 1930s, war one day comes? Those questions are going to be nagging at us for some time—but a peaceful, prosperous future for both China and the West depends on trying to answer them now.

What China Wants—and Fears. If you ever feel mesmerized by the usual stuff you hear about China—20% of the world's population, gazillions of brainy engineers, serried ranks of soldiers, 10% economic growth from now until the crack of doom—remember this: China is still a poor country (GDP per head in 2005 was US$1,700, compared with US$42,000 in the US) whose leaders face so many problems that it is reasonable to wonder how they ever sleep. The country's urban labor market recently exceeded by 20% the number of new jobs created. Its pension system is nonexistent. China is an environmental dystopia, its cities' air foul beyond imagination, and its clean water scarce. Corruption is endemic and growing. Protests and riots by rural workers are measured in the thousands each year. The most immediate priority for China's leadership is less how to project itself internationally than how to maintain stability in a society that is going through the sort of social and economic change that, in the past, has led to chaos and violence.

And yet for all their internal challenges, the Chinese seem to want their nation to be a bigger player in the world. The most striking aspect of Pres. Hu Jintao's leadership has been China's remarkable success in advancing its interests abroad despite turmoil at home.

Surprisingly for those who thought they knew his type, Hu has placed himself at the forefront of China's new assertiveness. Hu, 64, has never studied outside China and is steeped in the ways of the Communist Party. Despite a public stiffness in front of foreigners, Hu has been a vigorous ambassador for China: the pattern was set in 2004, when Hu spent two weeks in South America and pledged billions of dollars in investments in Argentina, Brazil, Chile, and Cuba. While Wen Jiabao, China's premier, was visiting 15 countries in 2006, Hu spent time in the US, Russia, Saudi Arabia, Morocco, Nigeria, and Kenya. In a three-week period toward the end of 2006, he played host to leaders from 48 African countries in Beijing, went to Vietnam for the annual

Asia-Pacific Economic Cooperation summit, slipped over to Laos for a day, and then popped off for a six-day tour of India and Pakistan. For a man whose comfort zone is thought to be domestic affairs, that's quite a schedule.

Great Wall Stonewall. As it follows Hu's lead and steps out in the world, what will be China's priorities? The first item on the agenda is straightforward: it is to be left alone. China brooks no interference in its internal affairs, and its definition of what is internal is not in doubt. The status of Tibet, for example, is an internal matter; the Dalai Lama is not a spiritual leader but a "splittist" whose real aim is to break up China. As for Taiwan, China is prepared to tolerate all sorts of temporary uncertainties as to how its status might one day be resolved—but not the central point that there is only one China. Cross that line, and you will hear about it.

China's commitment to nonintervention means that it doesn't inquire closely into the internal arrangements of others. As a 2005 report by the Council on Foreign Relations notes, "China's aid and investments are attractive to Africans precisely because they come with no conditionality related to governance, fiscal probity, or other concerns of Western donors." In 2004, when an International Monetary Fund loan to Angola was held up due to suspected corruption, China ponied up US$2 billion in credit. Beijing has sent weapons and money to Zimbabwe's President Robert Mugabe, whose government is widely accused of massive human-rights violations.

China doesn't support unsavory regimes for the sake of it. Instead China's key objective is to ensure a steady supply of natural resources, so that its economy can sustain the growth that officials hope will keep a lid on unrest at home. That is why China has reached out to resource-rich democracies like Australia and Brazil as much as it has to such international pariahs as The Sudan and Myanmar (Burma), both of which have underdeveloped hydrocarbon reserves.

There's nothing particularly surprising about any of this; it is how all nations behave when domestic supplies of primary goods are no longer sufficient to sustain their economies. But China has never needed such resources in such quantities before, so its politicians have never had to learn the skills of getting them without looking like a dictator's friend. Now they have to.

Working with China. Assuming a bigger global presence has forced Beijing to learn the art of international diplomacy. Until recently, China's foreign policy consisted of little more than bloodcurdling condemnations of hegemonic imperialism. But today, when the stars align—when China's perception of its own national interest matches what the US and other international powers seek—change is in the air.

Exhibit A is North Korea, long a Chinese ally, with whom China once fought a war against the US. As North Korea's leader Kim Jong Il developed a nuclear-weapons program in the 1990s, China was forced to choose between irking the US—which would have implied doing little to rein in Pyongyang—or stiffing its former protégé.

Hu's personal preferences seem to have helped shape the choice. He is known to have been stingingly critical of Kim in meetings with US officials. When the North finally tested a nuke in 2006, China joined the US and other regional powers in condemning Kim and supported a UN Security Council resolution that sanctioned Pyongyang.

But nobody in Washington is getting carried away. Beijing has been helpful on North Korea because it's more important to China that Pyongyang not provoke a regional nuclear arms race than it is to deny the US diplomatic support. Contrast such helpfulness with China's behavior on the dispute over Iran's nuclear ambitions. In December 2006, China signed a US$16 billion contract with Iran to buy natural gas and help develop some oil fields, and it has consistently joined Russia in refusing to back the tough sanctions against Tehran sought by the US and Europe.

Within its own neighborhood, there are signs that China's behavior is changing in more constructive ways. China fought a war with India in 1962 and another with Vietnam in 1979. For years, it supported communist movements dedicated to undermining governments in nations such as Indonesia, Singapore, and Malaysia. Yet today China's relations with its neighbors are nothing but sweetness and light, often at the expense of the US. Absorbed by the arc of crisis spreading from the Middle East, the US is simply less visible in Southeast Asia than it once was, and China is stepping into the vacuum.

While American exports to Southeast Asia have been virtually stagnant for the past five years, Chinese trade with the region is soaring. It is not aid from the US but trade with China that is transforming much of Southeast Asia. Nor is China's smiling face visible only to its south. In a cordial state visit in 2006, Hu reached out to India—an old rival with which it still has some disputed borders. Hu has also sought to mend ties with Japan, another longtime rival, with whom China's relations have deteriorated in recent years.

Good News, Bad News. So, a China whose influence is growing but that is trying to ease old antagonisms—what's not to like? But other aspects of China's rise are real and troubling. China is a one-party state, not a democracy. Some US policymakers and business leaders like to say there is something inevitable about political change in China—that as China gets richer, its population will press for more democratic freedoms and its ruling elite, mindful of the need for change, will grant them. Could be. But China is becoming richer now, and if there is any sign of substantial political reform—or any sign that the absence of such reform is hurting China's economic growth—it is, to put it mildly, hard to find.

For Americans, working with China involves cozying up to a nation that is not a democracy—and does not look as if it will become one soon. But China is now so significant a player in the global economy that the alternative—waiting until China changes its ways—won't fly. There is still time to hope that China's way into the world will be a smooth one. Perhaps above anything else, the sheer scale of China's domestic agenda is likely to act as a brake on its doing anything dramatically destabilizing abroad.

On the optimistic view, then, China's rise to global prominence can be managed. It doesn't have to lead to the sort of horror that accompanied the emerging power of Germany or Japan. Raise a glass to that, but don't get too comfortable. There need be no wars between China and the US, no catastrophes, no economic competition that gets out of hand. But in this century the relative power of the US is going to decline, and that of China is going to rise. That cake was baked long ago.

Countries of the World

The information about the countries of the world that follows has been assembled and analyzed by Encyclopædia Britannica editors from hundreds of private, national, and international sources. Included are all the sovereign states of the world as well as the major dependent, or nonsovereign, areas. The historical background sketches have been adapted, augmented, and updated from *Britannica Concise Encyclopedia* and the statistical sections from *Britannica World Data*, which is published annually in conjunction with *Britannica Book of the Year*. The section called "Recent Developments" also has been adapted from material appearing in recent issues of the yearbook, as well as from other sources inside and outside Britannica. The locator maps have been prepared by Britannica's Cartography Department, and the recommended Web sites are from Britannica Online.

All information is the latest available to Britannica. It must be understood that in many cases it takes several years for the various countries or agencies to gather and process statistics—the most current data available will normally be dated several years earlier.

A few definitions of terms used in the articles may be useful. **Gross domestic product** (GDP) is the total value of goods and services produced in a country during a given accounting period, usually a year. Unless otherwise noted, the value is given in current prices of the year indicated. **Gross national product** (GNP) is essentially GDP plus income from foreign transactions minus payments made outside the country (the World Bank refers to GNP as Gross National Income [GNI]). **Imports** are material goods legally entering a country (or customs area) and subject to customs regulations and exclude financial movements. The value of goods imported is given free on board (**f.o.b.**) unless otherwise specified; the value of goods exported and imported f.o.b. is calculated from the cost of production and excludes the cost of transport. The principal alternate basis for valuation of goods in international trade is that of cost, insurance, and freight (**c.i.f.**); its use is restricted to imports, as it comprises the principal charges needed to bring the goods to the customs house in the country of destination. **Exports** are material goods legally leaving a country and subject to customs regulations. Valuation of goods exported is free on board (f.o.b.) unless otherwise specified. The **FAO recommended minimum daily per capita caloric intake** varies by region and is calculated from age and sex distributions, average body weights, and environmental temperatures.

The symbol **$** indicates US dollars unless otherwise indicated. "**CFA franc**" stands for Communauté Financière Africaine franc. A few helpful **conversions** for the statistical section are given at the foot of the left-hand pages.

Afghanistan

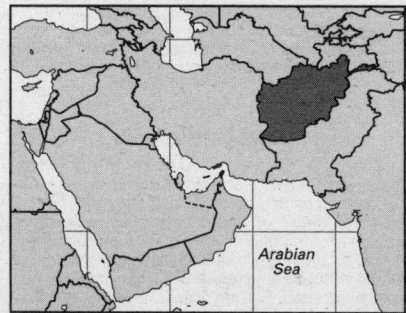

Arabian Sea

Official name: Islamic Republic of Afghanistan (Jomhuri-ye Eslami-ye Afghanestan [Dari (Persian)] Da Afghanestan Eslami Jamhuriyat [Pashto]). **Form of government:** Islamic republic. **Chief of state and head of government:** President Hamid Karzai (from 2002). **Capital:** Kabul. **Official languages:** Dari (Persian); Pashto; six additional local languages have official status per the 2004 constitution. **Official religion:** Islam. **Monetary unit:** 1 (new) afghani (Af) = 100 puls (puli); valuation (1 Jul 2007) US$1 = Af 49.53.

Demography

Area: 249,347 sq mi, 645,807 sq km. **Population** (2006): 24,592,000 (excludes Afghan refugees in Pakistan and Iran and other Afghans abroad; includes nomadic population). **Density** (2006): persons per sq mi 98.6, persons per sq km 38.1. **Urban** (2003): 22.4%. **Sex distribution** (2003): male 51.17%; female 48.83%. **Age breakdown** (2003): under 15, 44.8%; 15–29, 26.8%; 30–44, 15.9%; 45–59, 8.5%; 60–74, 3.4%; 75 and over, 0.6%. **Ethnolinguistic composition** (early 1990s): Pashtun 52.4%; Tajik 20.4%; Hazara 8.8%; Uzbek 8.8%; Chahar Aimak 2.8%; Turkmen 1.9%; other 4.9%. **Religious affiliation** (2000): Sunni Muslim 89.2%; Shi'i Muslim 8.9%; Zoroastrian 1.4%; Hindu 0.4%; other 0.1%. **Major cities** (2003–04): Kabul 2,799,300 (urban agglomeration); Kandahar (Qandahar) 323,900; Herat 254,800; Mazar-e Sharif 187,700; Jalalabad 97,900. **Location:** southern Asia, bordering Uzbekistan, Tajikistan, China, Pakistan, Iran, and Turkmenistan.

Vital statistics

Birth rate per 1,000 population (2003): 47.5 (world avg. 21.3). **Death rate** per 1,000 population (2003): 21.5 (world avg. 9.1). **Total fertility rate** (avg. births per childbearing woman; 2003): 6.8. **Life expectancy** at birth (2003): male 41.8 years; female 42.2 years.

National economy

Budget (2003–04). *Revenue:* $208,000,000 (domestic revenue only; excludes heavy reliance on foreign assistance; tax revenue 63.0%, of which import duties 53.4%; nontax revenue 37.0%). *Expenditures:* $2,826,000,000 (development expenditure 84.0%; current expenditure 16.0%). **Gross domestic product** (2003): $7,000,000,000 (one-third of which is illegal opiate receipts; $340 per capita). **Public debt** (external, outstanding; 2000): $5,319,000,000. **Production** (metric tons except as noted). *Agriculture, forestry, fish-*

ing (2002): wheat 2,686,000, rice 388,000, grapes 365,000, opium poppy 3,400 (represents 74% of world production); livestock (number of live animals; 2003) 8,700,000 sheep, 7,200,000 goats, 3,600,000 cattle; roundwood (2002) 1,404,208 cu m; fish catch (2001) 2,000. *Mining and quarrying* (2000): salt 13,000; copper (metal content) 5,000. *Manufacturing* (by production value in Af '000,000; 1988–89): food products 4,019; leather and fur products 2,678; textiles 1,760. *Energy production (consumption):* electricity (kW-hr; 2002) 557,000,000 ([2000] 480,000,000); coal (metric tons; 2000) 2,000 (2,000); petroleum products (metric tons; 2000) none (206,000); natural gas (cu m; 2000) 116,603,000 (116,603,000). **Household income and expenditure** (2003). Average household size 8.0; sources of income: wages and salaries 49%, self-employed 47%, other 4%. **Population economically active** (1994; based on settled population only): total 5,557,000; activity rate of total population 29.4% (participation rates: female 9.0%; unemployed [1995] c. 8%). **Tourism** (1997): receipts $1,000,000; expenditures $1,000,000. **Land use** as % of total land area (2000): in temporary crops 12.1%, in permanent crops 0.2%, in pasture 46.0%; overall forest area 2.1%.

Foreign trade

Imports (2002–03-c.i.f.): $880,000,000 (machinery 36.8%, consumer goods and medicine 26.8%, clothing 14.9%, food 8.9%). *Major import sources:* Pakistan 23.5%; South Korea 12.8%; Japan 9.7%; Kenya 6.5%; Turkmenistan 5.6%; Germany 5.6%. **Exports** (2002–03-f.o.b.): $97,000,000 (carpets and rugs 47.4%, dried fruits and nuts 40.5%). *Major export destinations:* India 27.8%; Pakistan 23.7%; Germany 6.2%; Finland 6.2%; UAE 5.2%.

Transport and communications

Transport. *Roads* (2001): total length 20,720 km (paved 12%). *Vehicles* (2000): passenger cars 39,707; trucks and buses 7,000. *Air transport* (Ariana Afghan Airlines only): passenger-km (1999) 129,000,000; metric ton-km cargo 19,000,000; airports (2002) 2. **Communications**, in total units (units per 1,000 persons). Daily newspaper circulation (2000): 129,000 (5); radios (2000): 2,950,000 (114); televisions (2000): 362,000 (14); telephone main lines (2002): 33,100 (1.6); cellular telephone subscribers (2002): 12,000 (0.6); Internet users (2002): 1,000 (0.04).

Education and health

Literacy (2003; based on settled population only): total population age 15 and over literate 29%; males 43%; females 14%. **Health:** physicians (2002) 2,880 (1 per 7,128 persons); infant mortality rate per 1,000 live births (2003) 115.0. **Food** (1999): daily per capita caloric intake 1,755 (vegetable products 79%, animal products 21%); 72% of FAO recommended minimum.

Military

Total active duty personnel (2004): 13,000 (army 100%); size of planned army is 65,000, size of

planned air force 8,000· Foreign troops (2004): 8,000-member, NATO-controlled, 31-nation International Security Assistance Force (ISAF) and more than 18,000-member, non-ISAF US troops searching for al-Qaeda and Taliban fighters.

Did you know? The town of Bamian is northwest of Kabul, the nation's capital, in the Bamian Valley. Two great figures of Buddha were erected there in the 4th and 5th centuries. Despite international pleas to preserve them, the statues were destroyed in early 2001 after the Taliban condemned them as idolatrous.

Background

The area was part of the Persian empire in the 6th century BC and was conquered by Alexander the Great in the 4th century BC. Hindu influence entered with the Hephthalites and Sasanians; Islam became entrenched during the rule of the Saffarids, c. AD 870. Afghanistan was divided between the Mughal empire of India and the Safavid empire of Persia until the 18th century, when other Persians under Nadir Shah took control. Great Britain and Russia fought several wars in the area in the 19th century. From the 1930s Afghanistan had a stable monarchy; it was overthrown in the 1970s. The rebels' intention was to institute Marxist reforms, but the reforms sparked rebellion, and troops from the USSR invaded to establish order. Afghan guerrillas prevailed, and the Soviet Union withdrew in 1988–89. In 1992 rebel factions overthrew the government and established an Islamic republic, but fighting among factions continued. In 1996 the government was taken over by the Taliban faction. A US-led coalition invaded Afghanistan and overthrew the Taliban government in late 2001.

Recent Developments

In 2006, five years after the defeat of the Taliban, the government of Pres. Hamid Karzai remained dependent upon international military assistance to face the threat of armed resistance. A coalition-trained Afghan National Army undertook its first serious engagement in Operation Mountain Thrust, an offensive in which hundreds of Taliban militants were reportedly killed, but the army's reliability remained uncertain. The inability of Kabul to control or develop many rural areas left thousands of farmers with little choice but to cultivate highly profitable opium crops—already growing most of the world's opium, Afghans planted half again as much land as the previous year. Despite having stationed 80,000 of its soldiers along the border with Afghanistan, Pakistan appeared unable to prevent penetration by those wishing to join the revitalized Taliban. It became obvious that Helmand province in the south had become an effective base of Taliban operations. Other groups, such as followers of former mujahideen leader Gulbuddin Hekmatyar, were also blamed for violence.

Internet resources: <www.afghan-web.com/politics>.

1 metric ton = about 1.1 short tons;   1 kilometer = 0.6 mi (statute);   1 metric ton-km cargo = about 0.68 short ton-mi cargo;   c.i.f.: cost, insurance, and freight;   f.o.b.: free on board

Albania

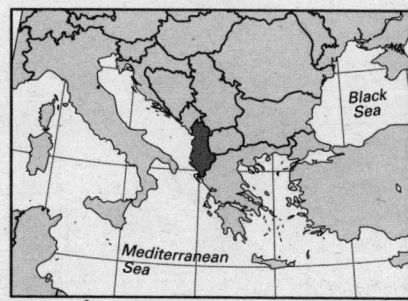

Black Sea

Mediterranean Sea

Official name: Republika e Shqipërisë (Republic of Albania). **Form of government:** unitary multiparty republic with one legislative house (Assembly [140]). **Chief of state:** President Bamir Topi (from 2007). **Head of government:** Prime Minister Sali Berisha (from 2005). **Capital:** Tirana (Tiranë). **Official language:** Albanian. **Official religion:** none. **Monetary unit:** 1 lek = 100 qindars; valuation (1 Jul 2007) US$1 = 90.15 leks.

Demography

Area: 11,082 sq mi, 28,703 sq km. **Population** (2006): 3,161,000. **Density** (2006): persons per sq mi 285.2, persons per sq km 110.1. **Urban** (2001): 42.1%. **Sex distribution** (2001): male 49.88%; female 50.12%. **Age breakdown** (2003): under 15, 27.1%; 15–29, 26.0%; 30–44, 20.6%; 45–59, 14.6%; 60–74, 8.8%; 75 and over, 2.9%. **Ethnic composition** (2000): Albanian 91.7%; Vlach (Aromanian) 3.6%; Greek 2.3%; other 2.4%. **Religious affiliation** (2000): Muslim 38.8%; Roman Catholic 16.7%; nonreligious 16.6%; Albanian Orthodox 10.4%; other Orthodox 5.7%; other 11.8%. **Major cities** (2001): Tirana (Tiranë) 343,078; Durrës 99,546; Elbasan 87,797; Shkodër 82,455. **Location:** southeastern Europe, bordering Serbia and Montenegro, Macedonia, Greece, and the Mediterranean Sea.

Vital statistics

Birth rate per 1,000 population (2002): 18.6 (world avg. 21.3). **Death rate** per 1,000 population (2002): 6.5 (world avg. 9.1). **Natural increase rate** per 1,000 population (2002): 12.1 (world avg. 12.2). **Total fertility rate** (avg. births per childbearing woman; 2002): 2.3. **Marriage rate** per 1,000 population (1998): 7.4. **Life expectancy** at birth (2002): male 69.3 years; female 75.1 years.

National economy

Budget (2002). *Revenue:* 149,487,000,000 leks (taxes 86.3%, of which value-added tax 30.8%, social security contributions 17.1%, income tax 14.0%, import duties and export taxes 9.0%, other taxes 15.4%; nontax revenue 13.7%). *Expenditures:* 196,-549,000,000 leks (current expenditure 78.7%, of which wages 21.4%, social security 20.4%, interest on debt 12.6%, government operations 10.4%, other 13.9%; capital expenditure 21.3%). **Public debt** (2002): $1,187,000,000. **Production** (metric tons except as noted). *Agriculture, forestry, fishing* (2002): vegetables and melons 650,000 (mainly beans, peas, onions, tomatoes, cabbage, eggplants, and carrots), cereals 472,500, watermelons 293,000; livestock (number of live animals) 1,844,000 sheep, 929,000 goats, 690,000 cattle; roundwood (2002) 304,800 cu m; fish catch (2001) 3,596. *Mining and quarrying* (2001): chromium ore 165,000; copper ore 45,000. *Manufacturing* (value added in $'000,000; 2001): textiles 17; glass products 14; leather (all forms) 11. *Energy production (consumption):* electricity (kW-hr; 2002) 3,880,-000,000 (3,880,000,000); lignite (metric tons; 2001) 17,300 (17,300); crude petroleum (barrels; 2001) 2,136,000 ([2000] 2,090,000); petroleum products (metric tons; 2000) 228,000 (390,000); natural gas (cu m; 2001) 10,000,000 (10,000,000). **Gross national product** (2003): $5,517,000,000 ($1,740 per capita). **Population economically active** (2001): total 1,244,000; activity rate of total population 40.3% (participation rates: ages 15–64, 55.4%; female 49.8%; unemployed [2002] 15.8%). **Households.** Average household size (2002): 4.2. **Tourism** (2002): receipts $487,000,000; expenditures $366,000,000. **Land use** as % of total land area (2000): in temporary crops 21.1%, in permanent crops 4.4%, in pasture 16.2%; overall forest area 36.2%.

Foreign trade

Imports (2002): $1,487,000,000 (food and beverages 20.0%; nonelectrical and electrical machinery 16.2%; mineral fuels 12.9%; textiles and clothing 11.0%; base and fabricated metals 8.9%). *Major import sources:* Italy 47.9%; Greece 34.3%; Germany 6.3%; UK 3.6%. **Exports** (2002): $330,000,000 (textiles and clothing 37.7%; footwear and related products 28.9%; base and fabricated metals 9.3%). *Major export destinations:* Italy 71.7%; Greece 12.8%; Germany 5.5%; Yugoslavia 1.5%.

Transport and communications

Transport. *Railroads* (2001): length 670 km; passenger-km 138,000,000; metric ton-km cargo 19,000. *Roads* (2000): total length 18,000 km (paved 30%). *Vehicles* (2001): passenger cars 133,533; trucks and buses 70,413. *Air transport* (2001; Albanian Air only): passenger-km 82,298,-000; airports (2002) 1. **Communications,** in total units (units per 1,000). Daily newspaper circulation (2000): 109,000 (35); radios (2000): 756,000 (243); televisions (2001): 480,000 (157); telephone main lines (2003): 255,000 (83); cellular telephone subscribers (2003): 1,100,000 (358); Internet users (2003): 30,000 (9.8).

Education and health

Educational attainment (1989). Population age 10 and over having: primary education 65.3%; secondary 29.1%; higher 5.6%. **Literacy** (2001): total population age 10 and over literate 85.3%; males 92.5%; females 77.8%. **Health** (1999): physicians 4,325 (1 per 724 persons); hospital beds 10,237 (1 per 306 persons); infant mortality rate per 1,000 live births (2002) 38.6. **Food** (2001): daily per capita caloric intake 2,900 (vegetable products 72%, animal products 28%); 110% of FAO recommended minimum.

Military

Total active duty personnel (2003): 22,000 (army 72.7%, navy 11.4%, air force 15.9%). **Military expenditure as percentage of GNP** (1999): 1.3% (world 2.4%); per capita expenditure $21.

Background

The Albanians are descended from the Illyrians, an ancient Indo-European people who lived in central Europe and migrated south by the beginning of the Iron Age. Of the two major Illyrian migrating groups, the Ghegs settled in the north and the Tosks in the south, along with Greek colonizers. The area was under Roman rule by the 1st century BC; after AD 395 it was connected administratively to Constantinople. Turkish invasion began in the 14th century and continued into the 15th century; though the national hero, Skanderbeg, was able to resist them for a time, after his death (1468) the Turks consolidated their rule. The country achieved independence in 1912 and was admitted into the League of Nations in 1920. It was briefly a republic in 1925–28, then became a monarchy under Zog I, whose initial alliance with Benito Mussolini led to Italy's invasion of Albania in 1939. After the war a socialist government under Enver Hoxha was installed. Gradually Albania cut itself off from the nonsocialist international community and eventually from all nations, including China, its last political ally. By 1990 economic hardship had produced antigovernment demonstrations, and in 1992 a non-Communist government was elected and Albania's international isolation ended. In 1997 it plunged into chaos, brought on by the collapse of pyramid investment schemes. In 1999 it was overwhelmed by ethnic Albanians seeking refuge from Yugoslavia.

Recent Developments

The Democratic Party, under former president Sali Berisha, gained control in elections held in July 2005. Local elections of February 2007, however, saw the rival Socialist Party regain control of many mayoralties and city council seats. In an accord signed in January 2007, Albania, Macedonia, and Bulgaria agreed to construct a 917-km (570-mi) petroleum pipeline terminating in the Adriatic port of Vlorë in Albania.

Internet resources: <www.albanian.com>.

Algeria

Official name: Al-Jumhuriyah al-Jazairiyah al-Dimuqratiyah al-Sha'biyah (Arabic) (People's Democratic Republic of Algeria). **Form of government:** multiparty republic with two legislative bodies (Council of the Nation [144; includes 48 nonelected seats appointed by the president]; National People's Assembly [389]). **Chief of state:** President Abdelaziz Bouteflika (from 1999). **Head of government:** Prime Minister Abdelaziz Belkhadem (from 2006). **Capital:** Algiers. **Official languages:** Arabic; Tamazight is designated as a national language. **Official religion:** Islam. **Monetary unit:** 1 Algerian dinar (DA) = 100 centimes; valuation (1 Jul 2007) US$1 = DA 69.73.

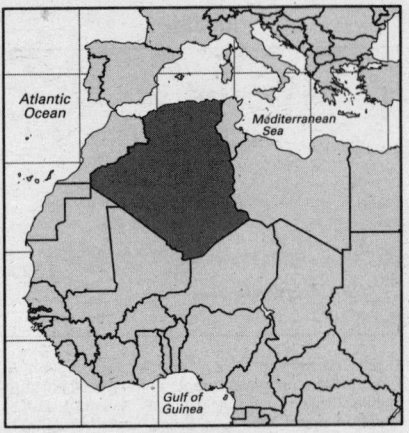

Demography

Area: 919,595 sq mi, 2,381,741 sq km. **Population** (2004): 32,322,000. **Density** (2004): persons per sq mi 35.1, persons per sq km 13.6. **Urban** (1998): 80.8%. **Sex distribution** (2003): male 50.40%; female 49.60%. **Age breakdown** (1998): under 15, 29.9%; 15–29, 30.6%; 30–44, 17.7%; 45–59, 8.9%; 60–74, 5.1%; 75 and over, 1.5%. **Ethnic composition** (2000): Algerian Arab 59.1%; Berber 26.2%, of which Arabized Berber 3.0%; Bedouin Arab 14.5%; other 0.2%. **Religious affiliation** (2000): Muslim 99.7%, of which Sunni 99.1%, Ibadiyah 0.6%; Christian 0.3%. **Major cities** (1998): Algiers 1,519,570; Oran 692,516; Constantine 462,187; Annaba 348,554; Batna 242,514. **Location:** northern Africa, bordering the Mediterranean Sea, Tunisia, Libya, Niger, Mali, Mauritania, Western Sahara, and Morocco.

Vital statistics

Birth rate per 1,000 population (2003): 18.3 (world avg. 21.3). **Death rate** per 1,000 population (2003): 4.6 (world avg. 9.1). **Natural increase rate** per 1,000 population (2003): 13.7 (world avg. 12.2). **Total fertility rate** (avg. births per childbearing woman; 2003): 2.2. **Marriage rate** per 1,000 population (2000): 5.8. **Life expectancy** at birth (2003): male 71.0 years; female 74.0 years.

National economy

Budget (2002). *Revenue:* DA 1,603,200,000,000 (taxes on hydrocarbons 62.9%, value-added taxes 7.0%, other 30.1%). *Expenditures:* DA 1,550,-600,000,000 (current expenditure 70.8%, development expenditure 29.2%). **Land use** as % of total land area (2000): in temporary crops 3.2%, in permanent crops 0.2%, in pasture 13.4%; overall forest area 0.9%. **Production** (metric tons except as noted). *Agriculture, forestry, fishing* (2002): wheat 1,502,000, potatoes 1,000,000, tomatoes 830,000; livestock (number of live animals) 17,300,000 sheep, 3,200,000 goats; roundwood (2002) 7,526,000 cu m; fish catch (2001) 100,300. *Mining and quarrying* (2002): iron ore 1,202,000; phosphate rock 740,000;

1 metric ton = about 1.1 short tons;   1 kilometer = 0.6 mi (statute);   1 metric ton-km cargo = about 0.68 short ton-mi cargo;   c.i.f.: cost, insurance, and freight;   f.o.b.: free on board

zinc (metal content) 8,576. *Manufacturing* (value added in $'000,000; 1997): food products 463; cement, bricks, and tiles 393. *Energy production (consumption):* electricity (kW-hr; 2001) 24,690,000,000 (22,900,000,000); coal (metric tons; 2000) 25,000 (583,000); crude petroleum (barrels; 2001) 305,-599,000 ([2000] 168,338,000); petroleum products (metric tons; 2000) 44,689,000 (10,584,000); natural gas (cu m; 2001) 80,300,000,000 (22,320,000,000). **Household income and expenditure**. Average household size (2000) 6.3; income per household (2001) c. $6,700; sources of income (2001): wages and salaries 39.9%, self-employment 39.2%, transfers 20.9%; expenditure (2001): food and beverages 44.1%, clothing and footwear 11.6%, transportation and communications 11.5%, furniture 6.8%, education 6.5%. **Gross national product** (2003): $60,221,000,000 ($1,890 per capita). **Population economically active** (2002): total 9,303,000; activity rate of population 29.2% (participation rates: ages 15–64 [1998] 52.6%; unemployed [2002] 25.9%). **Public debt** (external, outstanding; 2002): $21,255,000,000. **Tourism:** receipts from visitors (2002) $133,000,000; expenditures by nationals abroad (2000) $193,000,000.

Foreign trade

Imports (2001-c.i.f.): $9,482,000,000 (industrial equipment 34.7%, food 24.7%, semifinished products 18.4%, consumer goods 14.8%). *Major import sources* (2002): France 22.7%; US 9.8%; Italy 9.6%; Germany 7.2%; Spain 5.3%. **Exports** (2001-f.o.b.): $19,091,000,000 (crude petroleum 38.9%, natural and manufactured gas 36.6%, refined petroleum 17.1%). *Major export destinations* (2002): Italy 20.1%; US 14.2%; France 13.6%; Spain 12.1%; The Netherlands 9.0%; Turkey 5.1%; Canada 5.0%.

Transport and communications

Transport. *Railroads* (2003): route length 3,973 km; (2000) passenger-km 1,142,000,000; metric ton-km cargo 2,029,000,000. *Roads* (1999): total length 104,000 km (paved 69%). *Vehicles* (2001): passenger cars 1,692,148; trucks and buses 948,553. *Air transport* (2003; Air Algérie only): passenger-km 3,343,000,000; metric ton-km cargo 19,091,000; airports (1996) 28. **Communications**, in total units (units per 1,000 persons). Daily newspaper circulation (2000): 817,000 (27); radios (2000): 7,380,000 (244); televisions (2000): 3,300,000 (110); telephone main lines (2003): 2,199,600 (69); cellular telephone subscribers (2003): 1,447,310 (45); personal computers (2003): 242,000 (7.6); Internet users (2002): 500,000 (16).

Education and health

Educational attainment (1998). Percentage of economically active population age 6 and over having: no formal schooling 30.1%; primary education 29.9%; lower secondary 20.7%; upper secondary 13.4%; higher 4.3%; other 1.6%. **Literacy** (1998): total population age 10 and over literate 15,314,109 (68.1%); males literate 8,650,719 (76.3%); females literate 6,663,392 (59.7%). **Health** (1996): physicians 27,650 (1 per 1,015 persons); hospital beds 34,544 (1 per 812 persons); infant mortality rate per 1,000 live births (2003) 33.4. **Food** (2000): daily per capita caloric intake 2,987 (vegetable products 90%, animal products 10%); 124% of FAO recommended minimum.

Military

Total active duty personnel (2003): 127,500 (army 86.3%, navy 5.9%, air force 7.8%). **Military expenditure as percentage of GNP** (1999): 4.0% (world 2.4%); per capita expenditure $60.

 **Did you know?** Algeria is Africa's only producer of mercury and produces about one-tenth of the world's supply.

Background

Phoenician traders settled the area early in the 1st millennium BC; several centuries later the Romans invaded, and by AD 40 they had control of the Mediterranean coast. The fall of Rome in the 5th century led to invasion by the Vandals and later by Byzantium. The Islamic invasion began in the 7th century; by 711 all of northern Africa was under the control of the Umayyad caliphate. Several Islamic Berber empires followed, most prominently the Almoravid (c. 1054–1130), which extended its domain to Spain, and the Almohad (c. 1130–1269). The Barbary Coast pirates, operating in the area, had menaced Mediterranean trade for centuries, and France seized this pretext to enter Algeria in 1830. By 1847 France had established control in the region, and by the late 19th century it had instituted civil rule. Popular movements resulted in the bloody Algerian War (1954–62); independence was achieved following a referendum in 1962. In the 1990s Islamic fundamentalists opposing the military brought Algeria to a state of civil war.

Recent Developments

A charter for national reconciliation went into effect in February 2006 and proved controversial, as it granted immunity to security forces believed to be responsible for abuses during Algeria's civil war and offered a limited amnesty for members of rebel groups such as the Salafist Group for Preaching and Combat (GSPC). The GSPC renamed itself the al-Qaeda Organization in the Islamic Maghreb in January 2007. It was responsible for two bombings in April that killed at least 23.

Internet resources: <www.algeria.com>.

American Samoa

Official name: American Samoa (English); Amerika Samoa (Samoan). **Political status:** unincorporated and unorganized territory of the US with two legislative houses (Senate [18]; House of Representatives [20; excludes nonvoting delegate representing Swains Island]). **Chief of state:** President George W. Bush (from 2001). **Head of government:** Governor Togiola Tulafono (from 2003). **Capital:** Fagatogo (legislative and judicial) and Utulei (executive). **Official languages:** English; Samoan. **Official religion:** none. **Monetary unit:** 1 US dollar ($) = 100 cents.

Demography

Area: 77 sq mi, 200 sq km. **Population** (2006): 67,000. **Density** (2006): persons per sq mi 870.1,

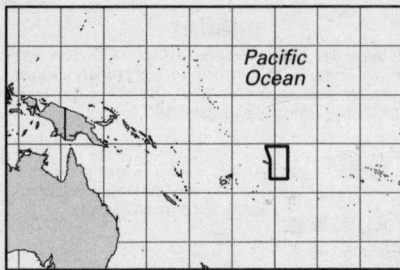

persons per sq km 335.0. **Urban** (2000): 53.4%. **Sex distribution** (2000): male 51.08%; female 48.92%. **Age breakdown** (2000): under 15, 38.8%; 15–29, 25.5%; 30–44, 19.4%; 45–59, 10.8%; 60–74, 4.5%; 75 and over, 1.0%. **Ethnic composition** (2000): Samoan 88.2%; Tongan 2.8%; Asian 2.8%; Caucasian 1.1%; other 5.1%. **Religious affiliation** (1995): 4 major Protestant groups 60.1%; Roman Catholic 19.4%; Mormon 12.5%; other 8.0%. **Major villages** (2000): Tafuna 8,406; Nu'uuli 5,154; Pago Pago 4,278 (urban agglomeration [2001] 15,000); Leone 3,568; Fagatogo 2,096 (within Pago Pago). **Location:** group of islands in the south Pacific Ocean.

Vital statistics

Birth rate per 1,000 population (2003): 25.9 (world avg. 21.3); legitimate (2001) 71.7%; illegitimate 28.3%. **Death rate** per 1,000 population (2003): 3.4 (world avg. 9.1). **Natural increase rate** per 1,000 population (2003): 22.5 (world avg. 12.2). **Total fertility rate** (avg. births per childbearing woman; 2003): 3.6. **Marriage rate** per 1,000 population (2000): 4.7. **Divorce rate** per 1,000 population (1993): 0.5. **Life expectancy** at birth (2003): male 71.8 years; female 79.2 years.

National economy

Budget (1997). *Revenue:* $144,438,095 (US government grants 67.4%; taxes 23.6%; insurance claims 4.9%; other 4.1%). *Expenditures:* $152,912,308 (education and culture 28.5%; health and welfare 27.3%; general government 14.1%; public works and parks 12.8%; public safety 6.9%; economic development 6.1%; capital projects 3.4%; debt 0.9%). **Gross national product** (1997): $253,000,000 ($4,300 per capita). **Production** (metric tons except as noted). *Agriculture, forestry, fishing* (2002): coconuts 4,700, taros 1,500, fruits (excluding melons) 1,200; livestock (number of live animals; 2002) 10,700 pigs, 37,000 chickens; fish catch (2000) 866, of which tunas, bonitos, and billfish 820. *Manufacturing* (value of export in $; 2003): canned tuna 467,700,000; pet food 9,800,000; other manufactures include garments, handicrafts, soap, and alcoholic beverages. *Energy production* (consumption): electricity (kW-hr; 2001) 171,101,000 (148,109,000); petroleum products (1999) none (93,000). **Population economically active** (2000): total 17,664, activity rate of total population 30.8% (participation rates: ages 16 and over 52.0%; female 41.5%; unemployed 5.1%). **Household income and expenditure.** Average

household size (2000) 6.0; income per household (2000): $24,000; expenditure (1995): food and beverages 30.9%, housing and furnishings 25.8%, church donations 20.7%, transportation and communications 9.4%, clothing 2.9%, other 10.3%. **Tourism:** receipts from visitors (1997) $10,000,000; expenditures by nationals abroad (1996) $2,000,000. **Land use** as % of total land area (2000): in temporary crops 10%, in permanent crops 15%; overall forest area 60%.

Foreign trade

Imports (2001): $520,000,000 (fish for cannery 50.9%, consumer goods 16.4%, other food 12.8%, mineral fuels 5.0%). *Major import sources* (2000): US 56.7%; Australia 14.9%; New Zealand 11.1%; Fiji 5.7%; Samoa 3.1%. **Exports** (2001; to the US only): $317,000,000 (tuna in airtight containers 86.3%, fish meal 8.9%, pet food 4.8%). *Major export destinations* (2000): US 99.6%.

Transport and communications

Transport. *Roads* (1991): total length 350 km (paved 43%). *Vehicles* (2001): passenger cars 6,579; trucks and buses 625. *Air transport* (2001): incoming flights 7,805; incoming passengers 74,543; incoming cargo 890 metric tons; airports (2000) with scheduled flights 3. **Communications**, in total units (units per 1,000 persons). Daily newspaper circulation (1996): 5,000 (85); radios (1997): 57,000 (929); televisions (2000): 13,200 (211); telephone main lines (2002): 14,700 (252); cellular telephone subscribers (2001): 2,156 (38).

Education and health

Educational attainment (2000). Percentage of population age 25 and over having: no formal schooling to some secondary education 33.9%; completed secondary 39.3%; some college 19.4%; undergraduate degree 4.8%; graduate degree 2.6%. **Literacy** (2000): total population age 10 and over literate 33,993 (99.4%); males literate 17,704 (99.4%); females literate 16,589 (99.5%). **Health** (1991): physicians 26 (1 per 1,888 persons); hospital beds (1995) 140 (1 per 4.7 persons); infant mortality rate per 1,000 live births (2003) 9.7.

Military

Military defense is the responsibility of the United States.

Background

The Samoan islands were probably inhabited by Polynesians 2,500 years ago. Dutch explorers first arrived in 1722. A haven for runaway sailors and escaped convicts, the islands were ruled by native chiefs until c. 1860. The US gained the right to establish a naval station at Pago Pago in 1878, and the US, Britain, and Germany administered a tripartite protectorate in 1889–99. The eastern islands were ceded to the US in 1904, and Swains Island was added in 1925. The first constitution was approved in 1960, and in 1977 the territory's first elected governor took office.

1 metric ton = about 1.1 short tons;   1 kilometer = 0.6 mi (statute);   1 metric ton-km cargo = about 0.68 short ton-mi cargo;   c.i.f.: cost, insurance, and freight;   f.o.b.: free on board

Recent Developments

Military activity on American Samoa was a focus with the US involvement in Iraq and Afghanistan. In November 2006 Eni Faleomavaega was elected to a 10th consecutive term as American Samoa's nonvoting delegate to the US Congress.

Internet resources: <www.amsamoa.com/tourism>.

Andorra

Official name: Principat d'Andorra (Principality of Andorra). **Form of government:** parliamentary coprincipality with one legislative house (General Council [28]). **Chiefs of state:** President of France Nicolas Sarkozy (from 2007); Bishop of Urgell, Spain, Joan Enric Vives Sicilia (from 2003). **Head of government:** Chief Executive Albert Pintat Santolaria (from 2005). **Capital:** Andorra la Vella. **Official language:** Catalan. **Official religion:** none (Roman Catholicism enjoys special recognition in accordance with Andorran tradition). **Monetary unit:** 1 euro (€) = 100 cents; valuation (1 Jul 2007) US$1 = €0.74.

Demography

Area: 179 sq mi, 464 sq km. **Population** (2006): 77,800. **Density** (2006): persons per sq mi 434.6, persons per sq km 167.7. **Urban** (2003): 93%. **Sex distribution** (2002): male 51.82%; female 48.18%. **Age breakdown** (2002): under 15, 15.1%; 15–29, 18.0%; 30–44, 29.1%; 45–59, 20.5%; 60–74, 11.1%; 75 and over, 6.2%. **Ethnic composition** (by nationality; 2000): Spanish 40.6%; Andorran 36.0%; Portuguese 10.2%; French 6.5%; British 1.4%; Moroccan 0.7%; German 0.5%; other 4.1%. **Religious affiliation** (2000): Roman Catholic 89.1%; other Christian 4.3%; Muslim 0.6%; Hindu 0.5%; nonreligious 5.0%; other 0.5%. **Major urban areas** (2002): Andorra la Vella 20,787; Les Escaldes–Engordany 15,519; Encamp 10,627. **Location:** southwestern Europe, between France and Spain.

Vital statistics

Birth rate per 1,000 population (2002): 11.1 (world avg. 21.3). **Death rate** per 1,000 population (2002): 3.3 (world avg. 9.1). **Natural increase rate** per 1,000 population (2002): 7.8 (world avg. 12.2). **Total fertility rate** (avg. births per childbearing woman; 2003):

1.3. **Marriage rate** per 1,000 population (2002): 2.8. **Life expectancy** at birth (2003): male 80.6 years; female 86.6 years.

National economy

Budget (2003). *Revenue:* €246,610,000 (indirect taxes 75.0%, taxes from government enterprises 15.6%, revenue from capital 9.4%). *Expenditures:* €253,835,000 (current expenditures 51.3%, of which education 13.9%, tourism 7.7%, public order 6.5%, health 4.3%, environment 3.5%; development expenditures 48.7%). **Production.** *Agriculture* (2002): tobacco 321 metric tons; other traditional crops include hay, potatoes, and grapes; livestock (number of live animals; 2002) 2,683 sheep, 1,194 cattle, 741 horses. *Quarrying:* small amounts of marble are quarried. *Manufacturing* (value of recorded exports in €'000; 2000): electrical machinery and apparatus 11,090; motor vehicles and parts 8,500; newspapers and periodicals 4,690. *Energy production (consumption):* electricity (kW-hr; 1997) 116,000,000 ([2002] 463,000,000); petroleum products, none ([2000] 201,677,000 liters). **Household expenditure** (1997): food, beverages, and tobacco 25.5%, housing and energy 19.4%, transportation 17.7%, clothing and footwear 9.2%. **Land use** as % of total land area (2000): in temporary and permanent crops 4%, in pasture 45%; overall forest area 35%. **Population economically active** (2002): total 44,058; activity rate of total population 66.4% (participation rate: ages 15–64 [2000] 72.6%). **Gross domestic product** (at current market prices; 2001): $1,462,000,000 ($22,120 per capita). **Public debt** (1995): c. $500,000,000. **Tourism** (2002): 11,500,698 visitors; number of hotels 271.

Foreign trade

Imports (2002): €1,269,200,000 (food, beverages, and tobacco 19.2%; machinery and apparatus 19.1%; chemicals and chemical products 10.0%; transport equipment 9.9%; textiles and wearing apparel 8.4%; photographic and optical goods and watches and clocks 5.7%). *Major import sources:* Spain 50.0%; France 24.5%; Germany 5.1%; Italy 3.2%; UK 2.0%. **Exports** (2002): €64,900,000 (motor vehicles and parts 29.7%; optical and photo equipment 17.7%; electrical machinery and apparatus 16.3%; chemicals and chemical products 7.0%; clothing 4.8%). *Major export destinations:* Spain 54.8%; France 30.3%; Germany 9.8%; Hong Kong 3.2%.

Transport and communications

Transport. *Railroads:* none; however, both French and Spanish railways stop near the border. *Roads* (1999): total length 269 km (paved 74%). *Vehicles* (2002): passenger cars 63,616; trucks and buses 4,809. **Communications,** in total units (units per 1,000 persons). Daily newspaper circulation (1996): 4,000 (62); radios (1997): 16,000 (247); televisions (2000): 30,400 (458); telephones (2002): 43,561 (653); cellular telephone subscribers (2002): 31,323 (469); Internet users (2001): 7,000 (88).

Education and health

Educational attainment (mid-1980s). Percentage of population age 15 and over having: no formal

schooling 5.5%; primary education 47.3%; secondary education 21.6%; postsecondary education
24.9%; unknown 0.7%. **Literacy:** resident population
is virtually 100% literate. **Health** (1999): physicians
218 (1 per 303 persons); hospital beds 203 (1 per
323 persons); infant mortality rate per 1,000 live
births (1999–2001 avg.) 4.1.

Military

France and Spain are responsible for Andorra's external security; the police force is assisted in alternate years by either French gendarmerie or
Barcelona police.

 Andorra has the world's highest
life expectancy rate: 83.5 years
overall, with 80.6 for males and
86.6 for females.

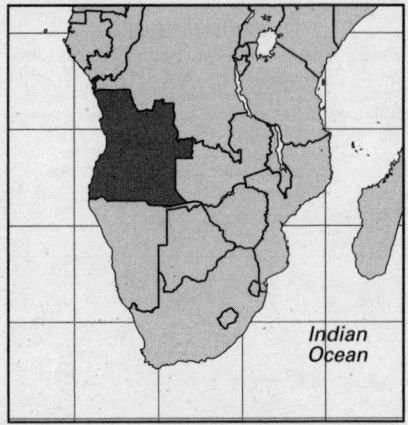

*Indian
Ocean*

Background

Andorra's independence is traditionally ascribed to
Charlemagne, who recovered the region from the
Muslims in 803. It was placed under the joint
suzerainty of the French counts of Foix and the Spanish bishops of the See of Urgell in 1278, and it was
subsequently governed jointly by the Spanish bishop
of Urgell and the French head of state. This feudal
system of government, the last in Europe, lasted until
1993, when a constitution was adopted that transferred most of the coprinces' powers to the Andorran
General Council, a body elected by universal suffrage. Andorra has long had a strong affinity with Catalonia; its institutions are based in Catalonian law,
and it is part of the diocese of the See of Urgell
(Spain). The traditional economy was based on sheep
raising, but tourism has been very important since
the 1950s.

Recent Developments

Andorra continued working to develop more modern
institutions in order to achieve fuller alignment with
those of the EU, members of which completely surrounded Andorra. Only one-third of Andorran residents were actual citizens of the country, and residency of 25 years was required for citizenship
eligibility.

Internet resources: <www.turisme.ad>.

Angola

Official name: República de Angola (Republic of Angola). **Form of government:** unitary multiparty republic with one legislative house (National Assembly
[220]). **Head of state and government:** President
José Eduardo dos Santos (from 1979), assisted by
Prime Minister Fernando da Piedade Dias dos Santos
(from 2002). **Capital:** Luanda. **Official language:** Portuguese. **Official religion:** none. **Monetary unit:** 1 re-
floated kwanza = 100 lwei; valuation (1 Jul 2007)
US$1 = refloated kwanza 79.01.

Demography

Area: 481,354 sq mi, 1,246,700 sq km. **Population**
(2006): 12,127,000. **Density** (2006): persons per sq
mi 25.2, persons per sq km 9.7. **Urban** (2001): 34.9%.
Sex distribution (2003): male 50.53%; female 49.47%.
Age breakdown (2003): under 15, 43.5%; 15–29,
26.5%; 30–44, 16.8%; 45–59, 8.5%; 60–74, 4.1%; 75
and over, 0.6%. **Ethnic composition** (2000): Ovim-
bundu 25.2%; Kimbundu 23.1%; Kongo 12.6%; Lwena
(Luvale) 8.2%; Chokwe 5.0%; Kwanyama 4.1%;
Nyaneka 3.9%; Luchazi 2.3%; Ambo (Ovambo) 2.0%;
Mbwela 1.7%; Nyemba 1.7%; other 10.2%. **Religious
affiliation** (2001): Christian 94.1%, of which Roman
Catholic 62.1%, Protestant 15.0%; traditional beliefs
5.0%; other 0.9%. **Major cities** (2004): Luanda
2,783,000; Huambo 173,600; Lobito 137,400;
Benguela 134,500; Namibe 132,900. **Location:**
southern Africa, bordering Democratic Republic of the
Congo, Zambia, Namibia, and the Atlantic Ocean.

Vital statistics

Birth rate per 1,000 population (2003): 45.6 (world
avg. 21.3). **Death rate** per 1,000 population (2003):
25.8 (world avg. 9.1). **Natural increase rate** per
1,000 population (2003): 19.8 (world avg. 12.2).
Total fertility rate (avg. births per childbearing
woman; 2003): 6.4. **Life expectancy** at birth (2003):
male 36.1 years; female 37.8 years.

National economy

Budget (2002). *Revenue:* $4,367,000,000 (oil rev-
enue 76.7%; non-oil revenue 23.3%, of which tax on
goods 7.7%, income tax 6.6%, import duties 5.6%,
other 3.4%). *Expenditure:* $5,370,000,000 (defense
and internal security 15.0%, social security 7.0%, education 6.0%, economic services 5.2%, health 4.0%,
interest payment 2.1%, other 60.7%). **Public debt** (external, outstanding; 2002): $8,883,000,000. **House-
hold.** Average household size (2000) 4.7. **Production**
(metric tons except as noted). *Agriculture, forestry,
fishing* (2002): cassava 5,400,000, corn (maize)
430,000, sugarcane 360,000; livestock (number of

---

*1 metric ton = about 1.1 short tons;   1 kilometer = 0.6 mi (statute);   1 metric ton-km cargo = about 0.68 short
ton-mi cargo;   c.i.f.: cost, insurance, and freight;   f.o.b.: free on board*

live animals) 4,150,000 cattle, 2,050,000 goats, 780,000 pigs; roundwood (2002) 4,436,271 cu m; fish catch (2001) 252,518. *Mining and quarrying* (2002): diamonds 5,022,000 carats. *Manufacturing* (1999): bread 87,500; frozen fish 57,700; wheat flour 57,500. *Energy production (consumption):* electricity (kW-hr; 2002) 1,710,000,000 ([2000] 1,235,000,-000); crude petroleum (barrels; 2001) 270,800,000 ([2000] 14,114,000); petroleum products (2000) 1,658,000 (976,000); natural gas (cu m; 2001) 710,000,000 (710,000,000). **Tourism:** receipts from visitors (2002) $60,000,000; expenditures by nationals abroad (2001) $66,000,000. **Gross national product** (at current market prices; 2003): $10,004,000,-000 ($740 per capita). **Population economically active** (1999): total 5,729,000; activity rate of total population 57.7% (participation rates over age 10 [1991] 60.1%; female 38.4%; unemployed [2002] 70%). **Land use** as % of total land area (2000): in temporary crops 2.4%, in permanent crops 0.2%, in pasture 43.3%; overall forest area 56.0%.

Foreign trade

Imports (2001): $3,179,000,000 (consumer goods 68.4%, capital goods 22.1%, intermediate goods 9.5%). *Major import sources* (2001): South Korea 22.4%; Portugal 14.5%; South Africa 12.3%; US 8.9%; France 4.8%. **Exports** (2001): $6,534,000,000 (crude petroleum 90.5%, diamonds 7.6%, refined petroleum 1.4%, coffee 0.1%). *Major export destinations* (2001): US 44.3%; China 18.7%; France 9.0%; Belgium 8.8%; Taiwan 6.8%.

Transport and communications

Transport. *Railroads* (2001): route length 2,771 km; (1991) passenger-km 246,200,000; metric ton-km cargo 45,300,000. *Roads* (1998): total length 72,626 km (paved 25%). *Vehicles* (1997): passenger cars 207,000; trucks and buses 25,000. Air transpórt (2001; TAAG airline): passenger-km 732,-968,000; metric ton-km cargo 57,662,000; airports (1999) with scheduled flights 17. **Communications,** in total units (units per 1,000 persons). Daily newspaper circulation (2000): 111,000 (11); televisions (2000): 193,000 (19); telephones (2003): 96,300 (6.7); cellular telephone subscribers (2002): 130,-000 (9.3); personal computers (2002): 27,000 (1.9); Internet users (2002): 41,000 (2.9).

Education and health

Literacy (1998): percentage of population age 15 and over literate 41.7%; males literate 55.6%; females literate 28.5%. **Health** (1997): physicians 736 (1 per 12,985 persons); hospital beds (1990) 11,857 (1 per 845 persons); infant mortality rate per 1,000 live births (2003) 193.8. **Food** (2000): daily per capita caloric intake 1,953 (vegetable products 92%, animal products 8%); 81% of FAO recommended minimum.

Military

Total active duty personnel (2003): 131,000 (army 91.6%, navy 2.3%, air force 6.1%). **Military expenditure as percentage of GNP** (1999): 21.2% (world 2.4%); per capita expenditure $248.

Background

An influx of Bantu-speaking peoples in the 1st millennium AD led to their dominance in the area by c. 1500. The most important Bantu kingdom was the Kongo; south of the Kongo was the Ndongo kingdom of the Mbundu people. Portuguese explorers arrived in 1483 and over time gradually extended their rule. Angola's frontiers were largely determined with other European nations in the 19th century, but not without severe resistance by the indigenous peoples. Its status as a Portuguese colony was changed to that of an overseas province in 1951. Resistance to colonial rule led to the outbreak of fighting in 1961, which led ultimately to independence in 1975. Rival factions continued fighting after independence; although a peace accord was reached in 1994, forces led by Jonas M. Savimbi continued to resist government control. The killing of Savimbi in February 2002 changed the political balance and led to the signing of a cease-fire agreement in Luanda in April that effectively ended the civil war.

Recent Developments

Instability continued in the exclave of Cabinda, where local leaders were demanding independence. A major issue here and in the rest of Angola was the increased production of crude petroleum and the profits derived from it. Already China's largest supplier of crude petroleum, Angola in 2006 became the second largest petroleum producer in Africa as well as the 12th full member of OPEC. Although questions remained over the transparency of the process to distribute this oil wealth, China offered $5 billion in loans in 2006.

Internet resources: <www.angola.org>.

Antigua and Barbuda

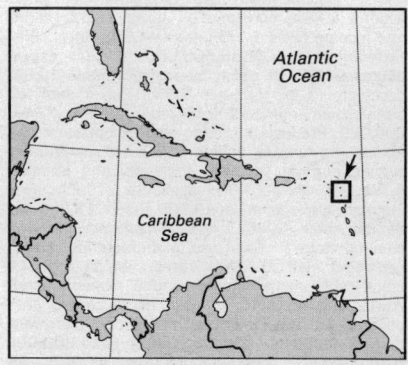

Official name: Antigua and Barbuda. **Form of government:** constitutional monarchy with two legislative houses (Senate [17]; House of Representatives [17 directly elected seats; attorney general and speaker may serve ex officio if they are not elected to House of Representatives]). **Chief of state:** British Monarch

Queen Elizabeth II (from 1952), represented by Governor-General Sir James B. Carlisle (from 1993). **Head of government:** Prime Minister Baldwin Spencer (from 2004). **Capital:** Saint John's. **Official language:** English. **Official religion:** none. **Monetary unit:** 1 Eastern Caribbean dollar (EC$) = 100 cents; valuation (1 Jul 2007) US$1 = EC$2.67.

Demography

Area: 171 sq mi, 442 sq km. **Population** (2006): 78,200. **Density** (2006): persons per sq mi 457.3, persons per sq km 176.9. **Urban** (2001): 36.9%. **Sex distribution** (2001): male 48.25%; female 51.75%. **Age breakdown** (2001): under 15, 26.4%; 15–29, 25.4%; 30–44, 23.9%; 45–59, 13.9%; 60 and over, 10.4%. **Ethnic composition** (2000): black 82.4%; US white 12.0%; mulatto 3.5%; British 1.3%; other 0.8%. **Religious affiliation** (1991): Protestant 73.7%, of which Anglican 32.1%, Moravian 12.0%, Methodist 9.1%, Seventh-day Adventist 8.8%; Roman Catholic 10.8%; Jehovah's Witness 1.2%; Rastafarian 0.8% (increased to more than 3% of population by 2000); other religion/no religion/not stated 13.5%. **Major city** (2004): Saint John's 23,600. **Location:** eastern Caribbean Sea.

Vital statistics

Birth rate per 1,000 population (2003): 18.2 (world avg. 21.3). **Death rate** per 1,000 population (2003): 5.6 (world avg. 9.1). **Natural increase rate** per 1,000 population (2003): 12.6 (world avg. 12.2). **Total fertility rate** (avg. births per childbearing woman; 2003): 2.3. **Marriage rate** per 1,000 population (1995): 22.1. **Divorce rate** per 1,000 population (1988): 0.2. **Life expectancy** at birth (2003): male 69.0 years; female 73.8 years.

National economy

Budget (2002). *Revenue:* EC$418,000,000 (tax revenue 92.9%, of which taxes on international transactions 49.8%, consumption taxes 18.9%, corporate income taxes 14.7%; grants 4.3%; other 2.8%). *Expenditures:* EC$535,500,000 (current expenditures 94.5%, of which interest payments 10.8%; development expenditures 5.5%). **Public debt** (external, outstanding; 2004): more than US$740,-000,000. **Production** (metric tons except as noted). *Agriculture, forestry, fishing* (2002): tropical fruit (including papayas, guavas, soursops, and oranges) 6,750, mangoes 1,400, eggplants 270; livestock (number of live animals) 18,500 sheep, 13,800 cattle; fish catch (2000) 1,481. *Mining and quarrying:* crushed stone for local use. *Manufacturing* (1994): beer and malt 166,000 cases; T-shirts 179,000 units; other manufactures include cement, handicrafts, and furniture, as well as electronic components for export. *Energy production (consumption):* electricity (kW-hr; 2002) 110,000,000 (110,000,000); petroleum products (2000) negligible (115,000). **Population economically active** (1991): total 26,753; activity rate of total population 45.1% (participation rates: ages 15–64, 69.7%; female 45.6%; unemployed [2000] 11.0%). **Households.** Average household size (2001) 3.1. **Gross national product** (2003): US$719,000,000

(US$9,160 per capita). **Land use** as % of total land area (2000): in temporary crops c. 18%, in permanent crops c. 5%, in pasture c. 9%; overall forest area c. 20%. **Tourism:** receipts from visitors (2001) US$272,000,000; expenditures by nationals abroad US$32,000,000.

Foreign trade

Imports (1999): US$356,000,000 (machinery and equipment 32.2%, agricultural products 24.7%, basic manufactures 15.4%, petroleum products 10.5%). *Major import sources:* US 49.5%; Japan 10.2%; UK 6.3%; Trinidad and Tobago 6.0%; Netherlands Antilles 5.5%. **Exports** (1999): US$37,800,000 (reexports [significantly, petroleum products reexported to neighboring islands] 60.3%, domestic exports 39.7%). *Major export destinations* (1998): Barbados 9.5%; Trinidad and Tobago 7.3%; St. Lucia 7.3%; UK 6.1%; unspecified 52.5%.

Transport and communications

Transport. *Roads* (1998): total length 250 km. *Vehicles* (1995): passenger cars 13,588; trucks and buses 1,342. *Air transport* (1999): passenger-km 276,300,000; metric ton-km cargo 300,000; airports (2001) with scheduled flights 2. **Communications,** in total units (units per 1,000 persons). Daily newspaper circulation (1996): 6,000 (87); radios (1997): 36,000 (523); televisions (1999): 33,000 (501); telephones (2002): 38,000 (488); cellular telephone subscribers (2002): 38,200 (490); Internet users (2002): 10,000 (128).

Education and health

Educational attainment (1991). Percentage of population age 25 and over having: no formal schooling 1.1%; primary education 50.5%; secondary 33.4%; higher (not university) 5.4%; university 6.2%; other/unknown 3.4%. **Literacy** (2000): percentage of total population age 15 and over literate 86.6%. **Health** (1996): physicians 75 (1 per 915 persons); hospital beds 255 (1 per 269 persons); infant mortality rate per 1,000 live births (2003) 20.9. **Food** (2000): daily per capita caloric intake 2,381 (vegetable products 67%, animal products 33%); 102% of FAO recommended minimum.

Military

Total active duty personnel (2003): a 170-member defense force (army 73.5%, navy 26.5%) is part of the Eastern Caribbean regional security system. **Military expenditure as percentage of GNP** (1998): 0.7% (world 2.5%); per capita expenditure US$57.

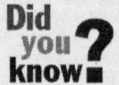

Did you know? Antigua, the "gateway to the Caribbean," is home to Nelson's Dockyard, named for British Adm. Horatio Nelson. The collection of buildings, most built between 1785 and 1792, is considered an architectural treasure and is a major tourist attraction.

---

1 metric ton = about 1.1 short tons;   1 kilometer = 0.6 mi (statute);   1 metric ton-km cargo = about 0.68 short ton-mi cargo;   c.i.f.: cost, insurance, and freight;   f.o.b.: free on board

Background

Christopher Columbus visited Antigua in 1493 and named it after a church in Seville, Spain. It was colonized in 1632 by English settlers, who imported African slaves to grow tobacco and sugarcane. Barbuda was colonized by the English in 1678. In 1834 its slaves were emancipated. Antigua (with Barbuda) was part of the British colony of the Leeward Islands from 1871 until that colony was defederated in 1956. The islands achieved full independence in 1981.

Recent Developments

In March 2004 Antigua and Barbuda won a ruling against the United States from the World Trade Organization; the US had sought a prohibition on Internet gambling, while Antigua and Barbuda held that such a ban would be against normal international trade. As of early 2007 the US had not complied with the ruling, and the EU, with significant interests in online gambling, was considering joining the fight with legal action of its own.

Internet resources: <www.antigua-barbuda.org>.

Argentina

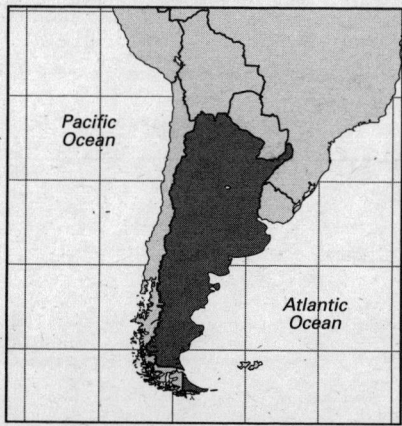

Pacific Ocean

Atlantic Ocean

Official name: República Argentina (Argentine Republic). **Form of government:** federal republic with two legislative houses (Senate [72]; Chamber of Deputies [257]). **Head of state and government:** President Néstor Kirchner (from 2003), assisted by Cabinet Chief Alberto Fernández (from 2003). **Capital:** Buenos Aires. **Official language:** Spanish. **Official religion:** Roman Catholicism. **Monetary unit:** 1 peso (pl. pesos) (Arg$) = 100 centavos; valuation (1 Jul 2007) US$1 = Arg$3.09.

Demography

Area: 1,073,400 sq mi, 2,780,092 sq km. **Population** (2006): 38,971,000. **Density** (2006): persons per sq mi 36.3, persons per sq km 14.0. **Urban** (2000): 89.6%. **Sex distribution** (2001): male 48.70%; female 51.30%. **Age breakdown** (2001):

under 15, 28.3%; 15–29, 25.0%; 30–44, 18.6%; 45–59, 14.7%; 60–74, 9.3%; 75 and over, 4.1%. **Ethnic composition** (2000): European extraction 86.4%; mestizo 6.5%; Amerindian 3.4%; Arab 3.3%; other 0.4%. **Religious affiliation** (2000): Roman Catholic 79.8%; Protestant 5.4%; Muslim 1.9%; Jewish 1.3%; other 11.6%. **Major cities** (2001): Buenos Aires 2,768,772 (16,603,341 combined population of Gran Buenos Aires and Buenos Aires city); Córdoba 1,267,774; San Justo 1,256,724; Rosario 906,004; La Plata 553,002. **Location:** southern South America, bordering Bolivia, Paraguay, Brazil, Uruguay, the South Atlantic Ocean, and Chile.

Vital statistics

Birth rate per 1,000 population (2003): 17.5 (world avg. 21.3). **Death rate** per 1,000 population (2003): 7.6 (world avg. 9.1). **Natural increase rate** per 1,000 population (2003): 9.9 (world avg. 12.2). **Total fertility rate** (avg. births per childbearing woman; 2003): 2.3. **Life expectancy** at birth (2003): male 71.7 years; female 79.4 years.

National economy

Budget (2001). *Revenue:* Arg$37,093,900,000 (tax revenue 90.3%, of which sales tax 36.0%, social security tax 22.8%, income tax 17.9%, property tax 9.3%; nontax revenue 9.7%). *Expenditure:* Arg$46,013,400,000 (social security 47.8%; debt service 22.1%; education 5.7%; defense 3.8%; health 1.8%). **Public debt** (external, outstanding; 2002): US$74,661,000,000. **Gross national product** (at current market prices; 2003): US$140,113,000,000 (US$3,650 per capita). **Production** (metric tons except as noted). *Agriculture, forestry, fishing* (2002): soybeans 30,000,000, sugarcane 16,500,000, corn (maize) 14,710,000; livestock (number of live animals) 50,669,000 cattle, 14,000,000 sheep; roundwood (2002) 9,307,000 cu m; fish catch (2001) 924,700. *Mining and quarrying* (2001): silver 152,802 kg; gold 30,630 kg. *Manufacturing* (value added in US$'000,000; 1999): food products 5,601; beverages 2,146; refined petroleum products 1,361. *Energy production (consumption):* electricity (kW-hr; 2002) 81,390,000,000 ([2000] 89,014,000,000); coal (2001) 259,000 (1,058,000); crude petroleum (barrels; 2001) 277,000,000 ([2000] 191,379,000); petroleum products (2000) 23,197,000 (20,460,000); natural gas (cu m; 2001) 53,298,000,000 ([2000] 40,817,400,000). **Land use** as % of total land area (2000): in temporary crops 12.2%, in permanent crops 0.5%, in pasture 51.9%; overall forest area 12.7%. **Tourism** (2002): receipts US$1,476,000,000; expenditures US$2,256,000,000. **Population economically active** (2001): total 15,264,783; activity rate of total population 42.1% (participation rates: ages 14 and over 57.2%; female 40.9%; unemployed [2004] c. 12%). **Households.** Average household size (2001) 3.6.

Foreign trade

Imports (2001-f.o.b. in balance of trade and c.i.f. in commodities and trading partners): US$20,311,600,000 (chemicals and chemical products 17.8%, nonelectrical machinery 17.4%, electrical machinery 12.6%, transport equipment 10.5%). *Major import sources:* Brazil 26.0%; US 18.6%; Germany 5.2%; China 5.2%; Italy 4.1%; Japan 3.8%. **Exports** (2001):

US$26,655,200,000 (food products and live animals 44.2%, crude petroleum and petroleum products 16.9%, road vehicles 8.3%, nonelectrical machinery 4.3%). *Major export destinations:* Brazil 23.3%; US 10.9%; Chile 10.7%; China 4.2%; Spain 4.1%.

Transport and communications

Transport. *Railroads:* (2000) route length 35,753 km; (2001) passenger-km 7,934,000,000; (2001) metric ton-km cargo 8,989,000,000. *Roads* (1999): total length 215,471 km (paved 29%). *Vehicles:* passenger cars (2000) 5,386,700; commercial vehicles and buses (1998) 1,496,567. *Air transport* (2003; Aerolineas Argentinas): passenger-km 9,514,000,000; metric ton-km cargo 103,435,000. **Communications**, in total units (units per 1,000 persons). Daily newspaper circulation (2000): 1,320,000 (37); radios (2000): 24,300,000 (681); televisions (2000): 10,500,000 (293); telephones (2002): 8,009,400 (219); cellular telephone subscribers (2002): 6,500,000 (178); personal computers (2002): 3,000,000 (82); Internet users (2002): 4,100,000 (112).

Education and health

Educational attainment (2001). Percentage of population age 15 and over having: no formal schooling 3.7%; incomplete primary education 14.2%; complete primary 28.0%; secondary 37.1%; some higher 8.3%; complete higher 8.7%. **Literacy** (2001): percentage of total population age 10 and over literate 97.4%; males literate 97.4%; females literate 97.4%. **Health:** physicians (1992) 88,800 (1 per 376 persons); hospital beds (1996) 115,803 (1 per 304 persons); infant mortality rate (2003) 16.2. **Food** (2001): daily per capita caloric intake 3,171 (vegetable products 70%, animal products 30%); 135% of FAO recommended minimum.

Military

Total active duty personnel (2003): 71,400 (army 58.0%, navy 24.5%, air force 17.5%). **Military expenditure as percentage of GNP** (1999): 1.6% (world 2.4%); per capita expenditure US$118.

Background

Little is known of Argentina's indigenous population before the Europeans' arrival. The area was explored for Spain by Sebastian Cabot in 1526–30; by 1580, Asunción, Santa Fe, and Buenos Aires had been settled. At first attached to the viceroyalty of Perú (1620), it was later included with regions of modern Uruguay, Paraguay, and Bolivia in the viceroyalty of La Plata, or Buenos Aires (1776). With the establishment of the United Provinces of the Plate River in 1816, Argentina achieved its independence from Spain, but its boundaries were not set until the early 20th century. In 1943 the government was overthrown by the military; Col. Juan Perón took control in 1946. He in turn was overthrown in 1955. He returned to power in 1973 after two decades of turmoil. His second wife, Isabel, became president on his death in 1974 but lost power after a military coup in 1976. The military government tried to take the Falkland Islands (Islas Malvinas) in 1982 but was de-feated by the British, with the result that the government returned to civilian rule in 1983. The government of Raúl Alfonsín worked to end the human rights abuses that characterized the former regimes. Hyperinflation led to public riots and Alfonsín's electoral defeat in 1989; his Peronist successor, Carlos Menem, instituted laissez-faire economic policies. In 1999 Fernando de la Rúa of the Alliance coalition was elected president, and his administration struggled with rising unemployment, foreign debt, and government corruption until the collapse of the government late in 2001.

Recent Developments

The Argentine economy experienced robust growth, fueled by the success of the agricultural sector (particularly soybean exports), an increase in local industrial production as consumers substituted locally manufactured products for imports (which were now prohibitively expensive because of the three-to-one exchange rate with the US dollar), and the boom experienced by the construction sector. The country's GDP increased by 9% in 2005 and 8.5% in 2006, while unemployment dropped to 10%. Inflation reached double digits in both years, however, causing fear in the international community about investing in the country. Lack of investment in the electricity and mineral-fuels industries led some to predict severe energy shortages for Argentina in the near future. The government imposed price controls and export restrictions to try to tame the inflation.

Internet resources: <www.sectur.gov.ar>.

Armenia

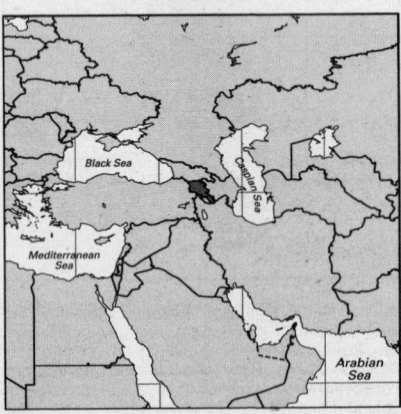

Official name: Hayastani Hanrapetut'yun (Republic of Armenia). **Form of government:** unitary multiparty republic with a single legislative body (National Assembly [131]). **Head of state:** President Robert Kocharyan (from 1998). **Head of government:** Prime Minister Serzh Sarkisyan (from 2007). **Capital:** Yerevan. **Official language:** Armenian. **Official religion:** none, but the Armenian Apostolic Church (Armenian Orthodox

Church) has special status per 1991 religious law. **Monetary unit:** 1 dram = 100 lumas; valuation (1 Jul 2007) US$1 = 345.41 drams.

Demography

Area: 11,484 sq mi, 29,743 sq km; in addition, about 16% of neighboring Azerbaijan (including the 1,700-sq mi [4,400-sq km] geographic region of Nagorno-Karabakh [Armenian: Artsakh]) has been occupied by Armenian forces since 1993. **Population** (2006): 2,976,000. **Density** (2006): persons per sq mi 259.1, persons per sq km 100.1. **Urban** (2001): 64.8%. **Sex distribution** (2001): male 46.87%; female 53.13%. **Age breakdown** (2001): under 15, 24.8%; 15–29, 24.9%; 30–44, 21.8%; 45–59, 13.6%; 60–74, 12.1%; 75 and over, 2.8%. **Ethnic composition** (2001): Armenian 97.9%; Kurdish 1.3%; Russian 0.5%; other 0.3%. **Religious affiliation** (1995): Armenian Apostolic 64.5%; other Christian 1.3%; other (mostly nonreligious) 34.2%. **Major cities** (2001): Yerevan 1,091,235; Gyumri 150,917; Vanadzor (Kirovakan) 107,394; Vagharshapat 56,388; Hrazdan 52,808. **Location:** southwestern Asia, bordering Georgia, Azerbaijan, Iran, and Turkey.

Vital statistics

Birth rate per 1,000 population (2002): 10.1 (world avg. 21.3); legitimate 86.8%; illegitimate 13.2%. **Death rate** per 1,000 population (2002): 8.0 (world avg. 9.1). **Natural increase rate** per 1,000 population (2002): 2.1 (world avg. 12.2). **Total fertility rate** (avg. births per childbearing woman; 2001): 1.1. **Marriage rate** per 1,000 population (2002): 4.3. **Divorce rate** per 1,000 population (2002): 0.5. **Life expectancy** at birth (2002): male 70.0 years; female 76.1 years.

National economy

Budget (2002). *Revenue:* 228,317,000,000 drams (tax revenue 87.0%, of which value-added tax 41.6%, excise tax 15.5%, enterprise profit tax 7.6%, stamp duties 5.8%; nontax revenue 13.0%). *Expenditures:* 263,912,000,000 drams (public services and social welfare 18.2%, defense 13.9%, education 11.0%, housing and energy 6.4%, public health 6.0%, unspecified 27.2%). **Public debt** (external, outstanding; 2002): $920,000,000. **Tourism** (2002): receipts from visitors $162,000,000; expenditures by nationals abroad $54,000,000. **Land use** as % of total land area (2000): in temporary crops 17.6%, in permanent crops 2.3%, in pasture 28.4%; overall forest area 12.4%. **Gross national product** (2003): $2,910,-000,000 ($950 per capita). **Production** (metric tons except as noted). *Agriculture, forestry, fishing* (2002): potatoes 374,263, wheat 280,477, tomatoes 171,000; livestock (number of live animals) 546,136 sheep, 514,244 cattle, 97,884 pigs; roundwood (2002) 54,000 cu m; fish catch (2001) 2,100. *Mining and quarrying* (2000): copper (metal content) 14,000; molybdenum (metal content) 6,044; gold (metal content) 400 kg. *Manufacturing* (value of production in '000,000 drams; 2001): food products 109,300; metals 24,600; jewelry 16,600. *Energy production (consumption):* electricity (kW-hr; 2002) 5,519,000,000 (5,519,000,000); coal (2001) none (5,000); crude petroleum (barrels; 1998) none (1,035,000); petroleum products (2000) none (273,000); natural gas (cu m; 2000) none (1,336,000,000). **Population economically active:** total (2003) 1,232,400; activity rate of total population (2001) 49.5% (participation rates [2001]: ages 15–64, 72.1%; female [2003] 49.5%; unemployed [2003] 10.1%). **Household income and expenditure.** Average household size (2001) 4.1; income per household (2002) 750,400 drams; sources of income (1999): agricultural income 32.1%, wages and salaries 24.6%, transfers 19.3%, help from abroad 12.8%, self-employment 10.6%, other 0.6%; expenditure (1999): food 67.0%, beverages and tobacco 19.2%, services 12.4%, other 1.4%.

Foreign trade

Imports (2001-f.o.b. in balance of trade and c.i.f. in commodities and trading partners): $877,434,000 (2000: mineral fuels 20.8%; food 20.6%, of which cereals 9.8%; rough diamonds 11.0%; nonelectrical machinery 10.9%). *Major import sources* (2001): Russia 19.5%; UK 10.4%; US 9.6%; Iran 8.9%; UAE 5.4%; Belgium 4.8%. **Exports** (2001): $341,836,000 (2000: cut diamonds 33.5%; alcoholic beverages 7.5%; electric current 7.0%; metal scrap 6.8%; nonelectrical machinery 6.4%). *Major export destinations* (2001): Russia 17.7%; US 15.3%; Belgium 13.6%; Iran 9.5%; UK 5.9%.

Transport and communications

Transport. *Railroads* (2003): length 711 km; (2002) passenger-km 48,400,000; metric ton-km cargo 451,800,000. *Roads* (2003): length 7,527 km (paved 100%). *Vehicles* (1996): passenger cars 1,300; trucks and buses 4,460. *Air transport* (2002): passenger-km 755,300,000; metric ton-km cargo 5,800,000; airports (2003) 1. **Communications,** in total units (units per 1,000 persons). Daily newspaper circulation (2000): 18,700 (6.2); radios (2000): 700,000 (225); televisions (2000): 759,000 (244); telephone main lines (2003): 562,600 (148); cellular telephone subscribers (2003): 114,400 (30); personal computers (2002): 60,000 (16); Internet users (2003): 150,000 (39).

Education and health

Educational attainment (2001). Percentage of population age 26 and over having: no formal schooling 0.7%; primary education 13.0%; completed secondary and some postsecondary 66.0%; higher 20.3%. **Literacy** (2001): total population age 15 and over literate 99.4%; male 99.7%; female 99.2%. **Health** (2002): physicians 11,508 (1 per 279 persons); hospital beds 13,968 (1 per 230 persons); infant mortality rate per 1,000 live births (2002) 14.0. **Food** (2001): daily per capita caloric intake 1,991 (vegetable products 84%, animal products 16%); 80% of FAO recommended minimum.

Military

Total active duty personnel (2003): 44,660 (army 92.9%, air force 7.1%); Russian troops (August 2004) 3,500. **Military expenditure as percentage of GNP** (1999): 5.8% (world 2.4%); per capita expenditure $170.

Did you know? Though first historically recorded in AD 607, Armenia's capital, Yerevan, dates by archaeological evidence to a settlement on the site in the 6th-3rd millennia BC.

Background

Armenia is a successor state to a historical region in southwestern Asia. Historical Armenia's boundaries have varied considerably, but the region extended over what is now northeastern Turkey and the Republic of Armenia. The area was later conquered by the Medes and Macedonia and still later allied with the Roman Empire. Armenia adopted Christianity as its national religion in AD 303. It came under the rule of the Ottoman Turks in 1514. Over the next centuries, as parts were ceded to other rulers, nationalism arose among the scattered Armenians; by the late 19th century it was causing widespread disruption. Fighting between Turks and Russians escalated when part of Armenia was ceded to Russia in 1878, and it continued through World War I, leading to Armenian deaths on a genocidal scale. With the Turkish defeat, the Russian-controlled part of Armenia was set up as a Soviet republic in 1921. Armenia became a constituent republic of the USSR in 1936. With the latter's dissolution in the late 1980s, Armenia declared its independence in 1990. It fought Azerbaijan for control over Nagorno-Karabakh until a cease-fire in 1994. About one-fifth of the population left the country beginning in 1993 because of an energy crisis. Political tension escalated, and in 1999 the prime minister and some legislators were killed in a terrorist attack on the legislature.

Recent Developments

Antagonism between the Armenian three-party coalition government and the opposition generated by the flawed elections in 2003 continued to pervade domestic politics. One provision of contentious proposed constitutional amendments—legalizing dual citizenship for Armenians—passed in February 2007. This allowed millions from the Armenian diaspora worldwide to vote. Energy cooperation with Iran continued. In January 2007 it was announced that a $1.7 billion refinery for Iranian crude petroleum was to be built in Armenia.

Internet resources: <www.armeniaemb.org>.

Aruba

Official name: Aruba. Political status: nonmetropolitan territory of The Netherlands with one legislative house (States of Aruba [21]). Chief of state: Dutch Monarch Queen Beatrix (from 1980), represented by Governor Fredis Refunjol (from 2004). Head of government: Prime Minister Nelson O. Oduber (from 2001). Capital: Oranjestad. Official language: Dutch. Official religion: none. Monetary unit: 1 Aruban florin (Af.) = 100 cents; pegged to the US dollar at a fixed rate of Af. 1.79 = $1.

Demography

Area: 75 sq mi, 193 sq km. Population (2006): 101,000. Density (2006): persons per sq mi 1,346.7, persons per sq km 523.3. Urban (2001): 67.0%. Sex distribution (2002): male 47.81%; female 52.19%. Age breakdown (2002): under 15, 22.9%; 15–29, 19.4%; 30–44, 27.5%; 45–59, 18.7%; 60–74, 8.7%; 75 and

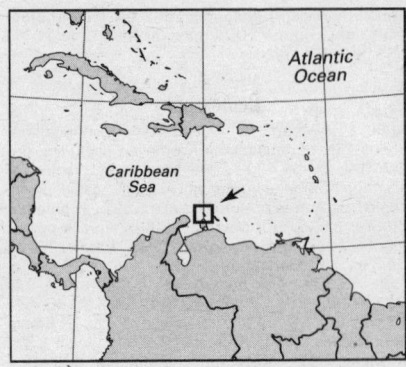

over, 2.7%; unknown 0.1%. Linguistic composition (2000): Papiamento 69.4%; Spanish 13.2%; English 8.1%; Dutch 6.1%; Portuguese 0.3%; other 2.0%; unknown 0.9%. Most Arubans are racially and ethnically mixed; ethnic composition (1998): Amerindian/other 80%; other (primarily Dutch, Spanish and/or black) 20%. Religious affiliation (2000): Christian 96.2%, of which Roman Catholic 81.9%, Protestant 7.3%, other Christian (Jehovah's Witness) 1.3%; Spiritist 1.0%; nonreligious 1.4%; other 1.4%. Major urban areas (2000): Oranjestad 26,355; San Nicolas 15,848. Location: southern Caribbean, north of Venezuela.

Vital statistics

Birth rate per 1,000 population (2002): 14.6 (world avg. 21.3); legitimate 52.5%; illegitimate 47.5%. Death rate per 1,000 population (2002): 5.2 (world avg. 9.1). Natural increase rate per 1,000 population (2002): 9.4 (world avg. 12.2). Total fertility rate (avg. births per childbearing woman; 2002): 1.8. Marriage rate per 1,000 population (2002): 6.9. Divorce rate per 1,000 population (2002): 5.2. Life expectancy at birth (2002): male 70.0 years; female 76.0 years.

National economy

Budget (2002). Revenue: Af. 751,200,000 (tax revenue 81.2%, of which taxes on income and profits 40.1%, sales tax 28.4%; nontax revenue 13.8%; grants 5.0%). Expenditures: Af. 816,400,000 (wages 32.1%, goods and services 18.3%, subsidies 13.2%, social security contributions 8.1%). Production (metric tons except as noted). Agriculture, forestry, fishing: aloes are cultivated for export; small amounts of tomatoes, beans, cucumbers, gherkins, watermelons, and lettuce are grown on hydroponic farms; divi-divi pods, sour orange fruit, sorghum, and peanuts (groundnuts) are nonhydroponic crops of limited value; fish catch (2001) 163. Mining and quarrying: excavation of sand for local use. Manufacturing: rum, cigarettes, aloe products, and soaps. Service facilities include a free zone, offshore corporate banking facilities, casino/resort complexes, a petroleum transshipment terminal, a cruise ship terminal, and ship repair and bunkering facilities. Energy production (consumption): electricity (kW-hr; 2002) 824,649,000 (690,129,000); crude petroleum (barrels; 2000) none (2,382,000); petroleum products (2000) none (302,000). **Gross domestic product** (2003): $2,011,000,000 ($21,160 per capita). **Population economically active** (2000): total 45,036; activity rate of total population 49.5% (participation rates: ages 15–64, 71.9%; female 46.6%; unemployed [2003] 8.0%). **Public debt** (external, outstanding; 2003): $407,800,000. **Household income and expenditure** (1999): average household size 3.6; average annual income per household: Af. 39,000; expenditure (1994): transportation and communications 20.7%, food and beverages 18.4%, clothing and footwear 11.3%, household furnishings 10.4%, housing 9.8%. **Tourism:** receipts from visitors (2003) $844,000,000; expenditures by nationals abroad (2002) $154,000,000. **Land use** as % of total land area (2000): in temporary crops c. 11%, in pasture, negligible; overall forest area, negligible.

Foreign trade

Imports (2001): $2,362,000,000 (petroleum [all forms] and free-zone imports 68.8%, food and beverages 7.1%, electrical and nonelectrical machinery 5.5%). *Major import sources* (excludes petroleum [all forms] and free-zone trade): US 61.9%; The Netherlands 11.6%; Netherlands Antilles 3.6%; Venezuela 3.1%. **Exports** (2001): $2,439,000,000 (petroleum [all forms] and free-zone exports 98.8%, food and beverages 0.5%). *Major export destinations:* US 25.9%; Venezuela 21.3%; Netherlands Antilles 19.8%; The Netherlands 14.5%.

Transport and communications

Transport. *Roads* (1995): total length 800 km (paved 64%). *Vehicles* (2002): passenger cars 42,802; trucks and buses 1,072. *Air transport* (2001; Air Aruba only): passenger-km 800,000,000; airports (2001) with scheduled flights 1. **Communications,** in total units (units per 1,000 persons). Daily newspaper circulation (1996): 73,000 (851); radios (2000): 51,000 (562); televisions (2000): 20,000 (224); telephone main lines (2001): 37,100 (350); cellular telephone subscribers (2001): 53,000 (500); Internet users (2001): 24,000 (226).

Education and health

Educational attainment (2000). Percentage of population age 25 and over having: no formal schooling or incomplete primary education 9.7%; primary education 33.9%; secondary/vocational 39.2%; advanced vocational/higher 16.2%; unknown status 1.0%. **Literacy** (2000): percentage of total population age 13 and over literate 97.3%. **Health** (2002): physicians 99 (1 per 944 persons); hospital beds 305 (1 per 306 persons); infant mortality rate per 1,000 live births (2000) 6.5.

Military

Total active duty personnel (2003): a small Dutch naval/coast guard contingent is stationed in Aruba and the Netherlands Antilles to combat organized crime and drug smuggling.

Background

Aruba's earliest inhabitants were Arawak Indians, whose cave drawings can still be seen. Though the Dutch took possession of Aruba in 1636, they did not begin to develop it aggressively until 1816. In 1986 Aruba seceded from the Federation of the Netherlands Antilles in an initial step toward independence.

Recent Developments

Tourism, the economic mainstay of Aruba, grew in 2006, as almost 600,000 cruise-ship passengers visited the island that year (a 7% increase over the numbers for 2005). Some $350 million had been invested in the tourism sector, and in 2007 improvements to Queen Beatrix International Airport, the cruise terminal facility and marina, and numerous hotels and resorts were under way.

Internet resources: <www.aruba.com>.

Australia

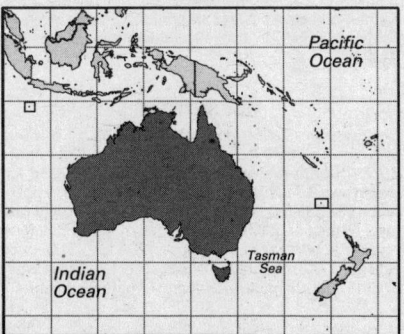

Official name: Commonwealth of Australia. **Form of government:** federal parliamentary state (formally a constitutional monarchy) with two legislative houses (Senate [76]; House of Representatives [150]). **Chief of state:** British Monarch Queen Elizabeth II (from 1952), represented by Governor-General Michael Jeffery (from 2003). **Head of government:** Prime Minister John Howard (from 1996). **Capital:** Canberra. **Official language:** English. **Official religion:** none. **Monetary unit:** 1 Australian dollar ($A) = 100 cents; valuation (1 Jul 2007) US$1 = $A 1.18.

Demography

Area: 2,969,978 sq mi, 7,692,208 sq km. **Population** (2006): 20,680,000. **Density** (2006): persons per sq mi 7.0, persons per sq km 2.7. **Urban** (2002): 85.0%. **Sex distribution** (2003): male 49.80%; female 50.20%. **Age breakdown** (2003): under 15, 20.3%; 15–29, 20.7%; 30–44, 22.7%; 45–59, 19.3%; 60–74, 11.0%; 75 and over, 6.0%. **Ethnic composition** (2001): white c. 92%; Asian c. 6%; aboriginal c. 2%. **Religious affiliation** (2001): Christian 68.0%, of which Roman Catholic 26.6%, Anglican Church of Australia 20.7%, other Protestant 15.8% (Uniting Church 6.7%, Presbyterian 3.4%), Orthodox 2.8%, other Christian 2.1%; Buddhist 1.9%; Muslim 1.5%; Hindu 0.5%; Jewish 0.4%; no religion 15.5%; other 12.2%. **Metropolitan areas** (2001): Sydney 3,997,321; Melbourne 3,366,542; Brisbane 1,627,535; Perth 1,339,993; Adelaide 1,072,585; Newcastle 470,610; Gold Coast 444,077; Canberra 353,149; Wollongong 257,510;

Caloundra 192,397; Hobart 191,169. **Location:** Oceania; a continent between the Indian Ocean and the South Pacific Ocean. **Place of birth** (2001): 76.9% native-born; 23.1% foreign-born, of which Europe 9.7% (UK and Republic of Ireland 5.5%, Italy 1.2%, Greece 0.7%, Germany 0.7%, The Netherlands 0.5%, other Europe 1.1%), Asia and Middle East 3.9%, New Zealand 1.9%, Africa, the Americas, and other 7.6%. **Mobility** (1995–96). Population age 15 and over living in the same residence as in 1994: 81.6%; different residence between states, regions, and neighborhoods 18.4%. **Households** (2000). Total number of households 7,510,000. Average household size 3.0; 1 person 25.1%, 2 persons 33.4%, 3 or more persons 41.5%. Family households 5,367,000 (71.5%), nonfamily 2,143,000 (28.5%), of which 1-person 25.1%. **Immigration** (2001–02): permanent immigrants admitted 88,900, from New Zealand 17.6%, UK and Ireland 10.4%, China 7.5%, India 5.7%, Indonesia 4.7%, South Africa 4.0%, Vietnam 2.3%, Philippines 2.3%, former Yugoslavia 2.3%, Sri Lanka 2.3%. Refugee arrivals (2001–02): 12,349. Emigration (2001–02): 48,241.

Vital statistics

Birth rate per 1,000 population (2003): 12.6 (world avg. 21.3); (2000) legitimate 69.3%; illegitimate 30.7%. **Death rate** per 1,000 population (2003): 7.3 (world avg. 9.1). **Natural increase rate** per 1,000 population (2003): 5.3 (world avg. 12.2). **Total fertility rate** (avg. births per childbearing woman; 2003): 1.8. **Marriage rate** per 1,000 population (2001): 5.3. **Divorce rate** per 1,000 population (2001): 2.8. **Life expectancy** at birth (2003): male 77.3 years; female 83.1 years.

Social indicators

Educational attainment (1999). Percentage of population age 15 to 64 having: no formal schooling and incomplete secondary education 38.0%; completed secondary 18.3%; postsecondary, technical, or other certificate/diploma 28.3%; university 15.4%. **Quality of working life** (2003). Average workweek: 34.7 hours. Working 50 hours a week or more 28.8%. Annual rate per 100,000 workers for: accidental injury and industrial disease, 3,200 (1992–93). Proportion of employed persons insured for damages or income loss resulting from: injury 100%; permanent disability 100%; death 100%. Working days lost to industrial disputes per 1,000 employees (2000): 52. Means of transportation to work (2000): private automobile 76.0%; public transportation 12.0%; motorcycle, bicycle, and foot 12.0%. Discouraged job seekers (2002): 78,000 (0.8% of labor force). **Social participation.** Eligible voters participating in last national election (2001): 95.0%; voting is compulsory. Trade union membership in total workforce (2002): 23.1%. **Social deviance** (2003). Offense rate per 100,000 population for: murder 1.5; sexual assault 92; assault 798; auto theft 497; burglary and housebreaking 1,776; armed robbery 99. Incidence per 100,000 in general population of: prisoners 139 (2001); suicide 13.0 (2001).

National economy

Gross national product (2003): US$430,533,000,000 (US$21,650 per capita). **Budget** (2002–03). *Revenue:*

$A 175,014,000,000 (tax revenue 93.2%, of which individual 52.5%, corporate 19.1%, excise duties and sales tax 15.6%; nontax revenue 6.8%). *Expenditures:* $A 169,247,000,000 (social security and welfare 42.1%; health 17.4%; defense 7.9%; public services 7.7%; economic services 7.5%; education 7.2%; interest on public debt 2.7%; other 7.5%). **Public debt** (2002–03): $A 69,926,000,000. **Tourism** (2002): receipts from visitors US$8,087,000,000; expenditures by nationals abroad US$6,116,000,000. **Production** (gross value in $A '000 except as noted). *Agriculture, forestry, fishing* (1999–2000): livestock (slaughtered value) 7,946,900 (cattle 5,050,900, sheep and lambs 1,053,900, poultry 1,031,000, pigs 791,700); wheat 4,831,200, wool 2,149,000, vegetables 1,861,900, fruits and nuts 1,761,100, seed cotton 1,400,000, grapes 1,118,200, sugarcane 881,900, barley 864,-800, canola 638,000, oats 118,400, sunflower seeds 74,000, corn (maize) 60,000, tobacco 40,000, other cereal crops 4,735,100; livestock (number of live animals; 2002) 113,000,000 sheep, 30,500,000 cattle, 2,912,000 pigs, 93,000,000 poultry; roundwood (2002) 31,212,000 cu m; fish catch (2001) 236,300 metric tons. *Mining and quarrying* (metric tons except as noted; 2001): iron ore 112,592,000 (world rank: 2), bauxite 53,285,000 (world rank: 1), ilmenite 2,017,-000, zinc (metal content) 1,519,000, copper (metal content) 873,000 (world rank: 4), lead (metal content) 432,000, rutile 206,000, nickel (metal content) 205,000, cobalt (metal content) 6,100, opal (value of production) US$140,000,000, sapphire (value of production) US$40,000,000; gem diamonds 14,397,000 carats, gold 285,030 kilograms (world rank: 3). *Manufacturing* (value added in $A '000,000; 2000–01): food products 11,026; printing and publishing 6,599; chemicals and chemical products 5,756; nonferrous base metals 5,678; fabricated metal products 5,402; motor vehicles and parts 4,657; electrical machinery and apparatus 3,366; beverages 3,185. **Population economically active** (2003): total 10,066,000; activity rate of total population 50.6% (participation rates: ages 15–64, 74.2%; female 44.8%; unemployed [September 2003–August 2004] 5.7%). **Household income and expenditure** (1999–2000). Average household size (2002) 3.0; average annual income per household $A 37,752; sources of income: wages and salaries 56.7%, transfer payments 28.0%, self-employment 6.0%, other 9.3%; expenditure (1998–99): food and nonalcoholic beverages 18.2%, transportation and communications 16.9%, housing 13.9%, recreation 12.7%, household durable goods 6.0%. *Energy production (consumption):* electricity (kW-hr; 2002) 210,320,000,000 (210,320,000,000); hard coal (metric tons; 2001) 264,680,000 ([1999] 60,643,-000); lignite (metric tons; 2001) 70,000,000 (70,000,-000); crude petroleum (barrels; 2000) 187,500,000 (224,810,000); petroleum products (metric tons; 1999) 34,381,000 (32,001,000); natural gas (cu m; 2002) 31,188,000,000 ([2000] 24,095,000,000). **Land use** as % of total land area (2000): in temporary crops 6.5%, in permanent crops 0.04%, in pasture 52.7%; overall forest area 20.1%.

Foreign trade

Imports (2000–01-f.o.b.): $A 118,264,000,000 (machinery and transport equipment 45.2%, of which road motor vehicles 12.1%, office machines and au-

1 metric ton = about 1.1 short tons;   1 kilometer = 0.6 mi (statute);   1 metric ton-km cargo = about 0.68 short ton-mi cargo; c.i.f.: cost, insurance, and freight;   f.o.b.: free on board

tomatic data-processing equipment 7.0%, telecommunications equipment 6.7%; chemicals and related products 12.0%, of which medicines and pharmaceuticals 3.7%; mineral fuels and lubricants 8.9%; food and live animals 3.6%). *Major import sources:* US 18.9%; Japan 13.0%; China 8.4%; UK 5.3%; Germany 5.2%; South Korea 4.0%; New Zealand 3.9%; Malaysia 3.5%; Singapore 3.3%; Taiwan 2.8%. **Exports** (2000–01): $A 119,602,000,000 (mineral fuels 21.1%, of which coal [all forms] 9.1%, petroleum products and natural gas 9.1%; crude materials excluding fuels 19.7%, of which metalliferous ores and metal scrap [mostly iron ore and alumina] 12.3%, textile fibers 4.7%; food 16.8%, of which meat and meat preparations 4.8%, cereals and cereal preparations 4.5%; nonferrous metals 7.9%). *Major export destinations:* Japan 19.6%; US 9.7%; South Korea 7.7%; China 5.7%; New Zealand 5.7%; Singapore 5.0%; Taiwan 4.9%; UK 3.9%; Hong Kong 3.3%; Indonesia 2.6%.

Transport and communications

Transport. *Railroads* (1999–2000; government railways only): route length 35,780 km; passengers carried 629,200,000; metric ton-km cargo 134,200,000,000. *Roads* (2000): total length 808,465 km (paved 40%). *Vehicles* (2002): passenger cars 10,100,000; trucks and buses 2,355,400. *Air transport* (2002; Qantas only): passenger-km 72,890,571,000; metric ton-km cargo 1,466,937,000; airports (1996) with scheduled flights 400. **Communications**, in total units (units per 1,000 persons). Daily newspaper circulation (2000): 5,630,000 (293); radios (2000): 36,700,000 (1,908); televisions (2000): 14,200,000 (738); telephone main lines (2003): 10,815,000 (542); cellular telephone subscribers (2003): 14,347,000 (720); personal computers (2002): 11,100,000 (564); Internet users (2002): 9,472,000 (482).

Education and health

Literacy (1996): total population literate, virtually 100% (a national survey conducted in 1996 put the number of persons who had very poor literacy and numeracy skills at about 17% of the total population [age 15 to 64]). **Health:** physicians (2001) 48,211 (1 per 404 persons); hospital beds (2001) 79,900 (1 per 244 persons); infant mortality rate per 1,000 live births (2003) 4.8. **Food** (2001): daily per capita caloric intake 3,126 (vegetable products 66%, animal products 34%); 117% of FAO recommended minimum.

Military

Total active duty personnel (2003): 53,650 (army 49.5%, navy 24.0%, air force 26.5%). **Military expenditure as percentage of GNP** (1999): 1.8% (world 2.4%); per capita expenditure US$372.

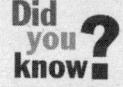
Background

Australia has long been inhabited by Aboriginals, who arrived on the continent 40,000–60,000 years ago. Estimates of the population at the time of European settlement in 1788 range from 300,000 to more than 1,000,000. Widespread European knowledge of Australia began with 17th-century explorations. The Dutch landed in 1616 and the British in 1688, but the first large-scale expedition was that of James Cook in 1770, which established Britain's claim to Australia. The first English settlement, at Port Jackson (1788), consisted mainly of convicts and seamen; convicts were to make up a large proportion of the incoming settlers. By 1859 the colonial nuclei of all Australia's states had been formed, but with devastating effects on the Aboriginals, whose population declined sharply with the introduction of European diseases and weaponry. Britain granted its colonies limited self-government in the mid-19th century, and Australia achieved federation in 1901. Australia fought alongside the British in World War I, notably at Gallipoli, and again in World War II, preventing the occupation of Australia by the Japanese. It joined the US in the Korean and Vietnam wars. Since the 1960s the government has sought to deal more fairly with the Aboriginals, and a loosening of immigration restrictions has led to a more heterogeneous population. Constitutional links allowing British interference in government were formally abolished in 1968, and Australia has assumed a leading role in Asian and Pacific affairs. During the 1990s it experienced several debates about giving up its British ties and becoming a republic.

Recent Developments

The relationship between Australia and Indonesia was harmed when Australia granted 43 Papuans fleeing Indonesian West Papua temporary protection visas, which entitled them to stay in Australia for three years, in early 2006. When the Australian government later failed to pass new asylum-seeker laws, Indonesia warned that Canberra's action could be interpreted as opening the door to asylum seekers, including illegal immigrants who had been resident in Indonesia for many years. Australian Prime Minister John Howard, in turn, wrote to the Indonesian government protesting the early release from prison of the hard-line Islamic cleric Abu Bakar Bashir, who had been jailed in Jakarta for his part in the 2002 Bali bombings in which nearly 100 Australian tourists died. Howard faced his biggest party revolt and public defeat in August when he was forced to withdraw proposed laws that would have extended the offshore processing of asylum seekers, with public opinion critical of the practice. The prospects for future trade with Iraq were damaged when Australia's monopoly wheat exporter, the Australian Wheat Board, was accused of having paid bribes to former Iraqi president Saddam Hussein's regime while participating in the UN's oil-for-food program in Iraq. Australia's international and regional security difficulties increased in 2006. The government continued to support the US-led "war against terrorism" and decided to redeploy its 460 troops from their position in southern Iraq to Tallil, where there was a US air base. Howard explained that even though the Japanese soldiers that the troops had been protecting were leaving Iraq, the Australian forces would remain to support the US with intelligence and surveillance and in extreme cases "through direct military action." Tension between renegade soldiers and East Timorese Prime Minister Mari Alkatiri led to a breakdown of law and order. Some 2,000 Australians were deployed to restore stability during the political crisis. A severe drought, considered by some to be the worst in 1,000 years, continued to afflict Australia into 2007.

Internet resources: <www.australia.com>.

Austria

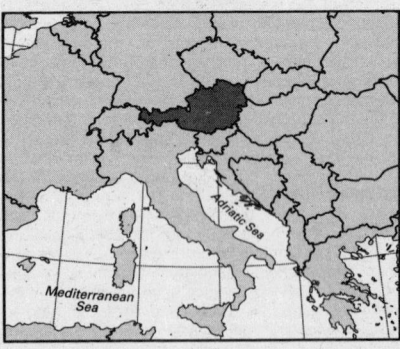

Official name: Republik Österreich (Republic of Austria). **Form of government:** federal state with two legislative houses (Federal Council [64]; National Council [183]). **Chief of state:** President Heinz Fischer (from 2004). **Head of government:** Chancellor Alfred Gusenbauer (from 2007). **Capital:** Vienna. **Official language:** German. **Official religion:** none. **Monetary unit:** 1 euro (€) = 100 cents; valuation (1 Jul 2007) US$1 = €0.74; the Austrian Schilling (S) was the former monetary unit; on 1 Jan 2002, S13.76 = €1.

Demography

Area: 32,383 sq mi, 83,871 sq km. **Population** (2006): 8,263,000. **Density** (2006): persons per sq mi 255.2, persons per sq km 98.5. **Urban** (2001): 66.8%. **Sex distribution** (2001): male 48.41%; female 51.59%. **Age breakdown** (2001): under 15, 16.9%; 15–29, 18.6%; 30–44, 24.9%; 45–59, 18.6%; 60–74, 13.8%; 75 and over, 7.2%. **Ethnic composition** (national origin; 1998): Austrian 91.2%; citizens of former Yugoslavia 4.0%; Turkish 1.6%; other 3.2%. **Religious affiliation** (1995): Roman Catholic 75.1%; nonreligious and atheist 8.6%; Protestant (mostly Lutheran) 5.4%; Muslim 2.1%; Eastern Orthodox 0.7%; Jewish 0.1%; other 1.9%; unknown 6.1%. **Major cities** (2001): Vienna 1,550,123 (2003; urban agglomeration 2,179,000); Graz 226,244; Linz 183,504; Salzburg 142,662; Innsbruck 113,392. **Location:** central Europe, bordering the Czech Republic, Slovakia, Hungary, Slovenia, Italy, Switzerland, Liechtenstein, and Germany.

Vital statistics

Birth rate per 1,000 population (2002): 9.7 (world avg. 21.3); (2002) legitimate 73.6%; illegitimate 26.4%. **Death rate** per 1,000 population (2002): 9.5 (world avg. 9.1). **Natural increase rate** per 1,000 population (2002): 0.2 (world avg. 12.2). **Total fertility rate** (avg. births per childbearing woman; 2002): 1.3. **Marriage rate** per 1,000 population (2002): 4.5. **Divorce rate** per 1,000 population (2002): 2.5. **Life expectancy** at birth (2002): male 75.8 years; female 81.7 years.

National economy

Budget (2003). *Revenue:* €57,414,000,000 (tax revenue 93.6%, of which individual income taxes 29.3%, turnover tax 28.4%, corporate income tax 7.1%, other taxes 28.8%; nontax revenue 6.4%). *Expenditures:* €61,355,000,000 (social security, health, and welfare 34.3%; education 14.3%; interest 14.2%; transportation 9.9%; public safety 6.6%; defense 2.6%). **Public debt** (2001): $117,420,000,000. **Production** (metric tons except as noted). *Agriculture, forestry, fishing* (2002): sugar beets 3,005,000, corn (maize) 2,000,000, wheat 1,460,000; livestock (number of live animals) 3,440,405 pigs, 2,118,454 cattle, 11,000,000 chickens; roundwood (2002) 14,845,000 cu m; fish catch (2001) 2,755. *Mining and quarrying* (2002): iron ore 1,941,800; magnesite 728,200; talc 140,000. *Manufacturing* (value added in $'000,000; 2000): nonelectrical machinery and apparatus 3,907; electrical machinery and apparatus 3,786; food products and beverages 3,112. *Energy production (consumption):* electricity (kW-hr; 2002) 58,490,000,000 ([2001] 62,250,000,000); hard coal (2002) negligible ([2000] 3,710,000); lignite (2002) 1,411,800 ([2000] 1,290,000); crude petroleum (barrels; 2001) 7,139,000 ([2000] 58,639,000); petroleum products (2000) 7,461,000 (10,297,000); natural gas (cu m; 2002) 2,014,600,000 ([2001] 7,333,000,000). *Tourism* ($'000,000; 2002): receipts $11,237; expenditures $9,391. **Population economically active** (2002): total 3,996,700; activity rate of total population 49.6% (participation rates: ages 15–64 [2001] 72.0%; female 44.4%; unemployed [April 2003–March 2004] 7.1%). **Gross national product** (2003): $215,372,000,000 ($26,720 per capita). **Household income and expenditure.** Average household size (2001) 2.4; sources of income (1995): wages and salaries 54.8%, transfer payments 25.9%; expenditure (2001): housing and energy 19.3%, transportation 12.6%, food and nonalcoholic beverages 12.6%, cafe and hotel expenditures 12.2%, recreation 11.5%, household furnishings 8.3%. **Land use** as % of total land area (2000): in temporary crops 16.9%, in permanent crops 0.9%, in pasture 23.2%; overall forest area 47.0%.

Foreign trade

Imports (2002-c.i.f.): €77,104,000,000 (machinery and transport equipment 38.9%, of which road vehicles 11.2%, electrical machinery and apparatus 7.6%; chemicals and related products 11.3%; mineral fuels 7.4%; food products 5.2%). *Major import sources:* Germany 40.3%; Italy 7.2%; US 4.8%;

---

1 metric ton = about 1.1 short tons;   1 kilometer = 0.6 mi (statute);   1 metric ton-km cargo = about 0.68 short ton-mi cargo;   c.i.f.: cost, insurance, and freight;   f.o.b.: free on board

France 3.9%; Hungary 3.3%; Switzerland 3.3%. **Exports** (2002-f.o.b.): €77,400,000,000 (machinery and apparatus 32.9%; chemical products 10.2%; transportation equipment 9.8%; paper and paper products 4.6%; fabricated metals 4.3%; iron and steel 4.1%). *Major export destinations:* Germany 32.0%; Italy 8.5%; Switzerland 5.3%; US 5.2%; UK 4.7%; France 4.4%; Hungary 4.3%.

Transport and communications

Transport. *Railroads:* (2002) length 5,616 km; (2000) passenger-km 8,206,000,000; (2001) metric ton-km cargo 17,387,000,000. *Roads* (2001): total length 210,483 km (paved 100%). *Vehicles* (2002): passenger cars 3,987,093; trucks and buses 313,434. *Air transport* (2003; Austrian Airlines Group): passenger-km 17,965,000,000; metric ton-km cargo 442,549,000; airports (2002) with scheduled flights 6. **Communications,** in total units (units per 1,000 persons). Daily newspaper circulation (2000): 2,380,000 (296); radios (2000): 6,050,000 (753); televisions (2000): 4,310,000 (536); telephone main lines (2003): 3,881,000 (481); cellular telephone subscribers (2003): 7,094,500 (879); personal computers (2002): 3,013,000 (374); Internet users (2003): 3,730,000 (462).

Education and health

Educational attainment (1993). Percentage of population age 25 and over having: lower-secondary education 37.5%; vocational education ending at secondary level 44.6%; completed upper secondary 6.1%; higher vocational 5.5%; higher 6.3%. **Literacy:** virtually 100%. **Health:** physicians (2003) 36,531 (1 per 213 persons); hospital beds (2002) 66,299 (1 per 118 persons); infant mortality rate per 1,000 live births (2002) 4.1. **Food** (2001): daily per capita caloric intake 3,799 (vegetable products 67%; animal products 33%); 144% of FAO recommended minimum.

Military

Total active duty personnel (2003): 34,600 (army 80.2%; air force 19.8%). **Military expenditure as percentage of GNP** (1999): 0.8% (world 2.4%); per capita expenditure $208.

Background

Settlement in Austria goes back some 3,000 years, when Illyrians were probably the main inhabitants. The Celts invaded c. 400 BC and established Noricum. The Romans arrived after 200 BC and established the provinces of Raetia, Noricum, and Pannonia; prosperity followed and the population became romanized. With the fall of Rome in the 5th century AD, many tribes invaded, including the Slavs; they were eventually subdued by Charlemagne, and the area became ethnically Germanic. The distinct political entity that would become Austria emerged in 976 with Leopold I of Babenberg as margrave. In 1278 Rudolf I of the Holy Roman Empire (formerly Rudolf IV of Habsburg) conquered the area; Habsburg rule lasted until 1918. While in power the Habsburgs created a kingdom centered on Austria, Bohemia, and Hungary. The Napoleonic Wars brought about the creation of the Austrian empire (1804) and the end of the Holy Roman Empire (1806). Count von Metternich

tried to assure Austrian supremacy among Germanic states, but war with Prussia led Austria to divide the empire into the Dual Monarchy of Austria-Hungary. Nationalist sentiment plagued the kingdom, and the assassination of Francis Ferdinand by a Serbian nationalist in 1914 triggered World War I, which destroyed the Austrian empire. In the postwar carving up of Austria-Hungary, Austria became an independent republic. It was annexed by Nazi Germany in 1938 and joined the Axis powers in World War II. The republic was restored in 1955 after 10 years of Allied occupation. Austria became a member of the European Union in 1995.

Recent Developments

In 2005 Austria celebrated the 60th anniversary of the founding of the Second Republic following the end of World War II, the 50th anniversary of regaining total independence from occupying Allied forces, and the 10th anniversary of its membership in the European Union. The Regional Employment and Growth Campaign, a $1.5 billion unemployment program, was presented in August of that year. The Austrian economy in 2006 grew at its fastest pace in six years, helped by a healthy foreign trade (especially with neighboring Germany) and strong investment. In February 2006 British historian David Irving was sentenced to three years in prison for allegedly having violated Austria's stringent Holocaust-denial laws in a speech he gave in 1989. He was released in December and expelled from the country.

Internet resources: <www.austria.org>.

Azerbaijan

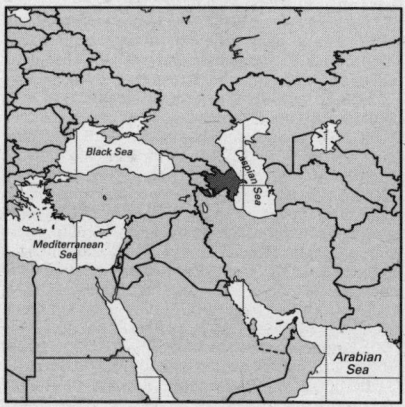

Official name: Azerbaycan Respublikasi (Republic of Azerbaijan). **Form of government:** unitary multiparty republic with a single legislative body (National Assembly [124, excluding one vacant seat reserved for Nagorno-Karabakh representative]). **Head of state and government:** President Ilham Aliyev (from 2003), assisted by Prime Minister Artur Rasizade (from 2003). **Capital:** Baku. **Official language:** Azerbaijani. **Official religion:** none. **Monetary unit:** 1 new manat (A.M.) = 100 gopik; valuation (1 Jul 2007) free rate, US$1 = A.M. 0.91.

Demography

Area: 33,400 sq mi, 86,600 sq km. **Population** (2006): 8,474,000. **Density** (2006): persons per sq mi 253.7, persons per sq km 97.9. **Urban** (2004): 50.6%. **Sex distribution** (2001): male 48.94%; female 51.06%. **Age breakdown** (2004): under 15, 27.4%; 15–29, 27.1%; 30–44, 24.5%; 45–59, 11.5%; 60 and over, 9.5%. **Ethnic composition** (1995): Azerbaijani 89.0%; Russian 3.0%; Lezgian 2.2%; Armenian 2.0%; other 3.8%. **Religious affiliation** (1995): Muslim 93.4%, of which Shi'i 65.4%, Sunni 28.0%; Russian Orthodox 1.1%; Armenian Apostolic (Orthodox) 1.1%; other 4.4%. **Major cities** (2003): Baku 1,828,800; Ganca 302,200; Sumqayit (Sumgait) 289,700; Mingacevir (Mingechaur) 94,900. **Location:** eastern Transcaucasia, bordering Russia, the Caspian Sea, Iran, Turkey, Armenia, and Georgia.

Vital statistics

Birth rate per 1,000 population (2004): 14.0 (world avg. 21.3); (2003) legitimate 92.4%; illegitimate 7.6%. **Death rate** per 1,000 population (2004): 6.0 (world avg. 9.1). **Natural increase rate** per 1,000 population (2004): 8.0 (world avg. 12.2). **Total fertility rate** (avg. births per childbearing woman; 2001): 1.6. **Life expectancy** at birth (2003): male 69.5 years; female 75.1 years.

National economy

Budget (2003). *Revenue:* A.M. 6,131,900,000,000 (tax revenue 82.5%, of which value-added tax 33.4%, enterprise profits tax 14.5%, personal income tax 12.3%, import duties 7.6%, excise taxes 5.5%; nontax revenue 17.5%). *Expenditures:* A.M. 6,173,000,-000,000 (national economy 19.7%; education 19.0%; social security 17.3%; defense 9.8%; health 5.0%). **Public debt** (external, outstanding; 2002): $964,000,000. **Production** (metric tons except as noted). *Agriculture, forestry, fishing* (2003): cereals 2,057,800, vegetables (except potatoes) 1,046,300, potatoes 769,000; livestock (number of live animals) 7,280,100 sheep and goats, 2,241,800 cattle; roundwood (2002) 13,500 cu m; fish catch (2001) 11,063. *Mining and quarrying* (2000): alumina 200,000; gypsum 60,000. *Manufacturing* (gross value of production in A.M. '000,000; 2003): food, beverages, and tobacco products 4,216,600; petroleum products 3,162,800; chemicals and chemical products 697,000. *Energy production (consumption):* electricity (kW-hr; 2002) 18,708,000,000 ([2001] 19,193,000,000); coal (2002) none (1,000); crude petroleum (barrels; 2002) 113,418,000 (63,384,-000); petroleum products (2003) 5,476,000 ([1999] 5,030,000); natural gas (cu m; 2003) 5,100,000,000 (5,100,000,000). **Households.** Average household size (2000) 5.3; income per household (2000) $460; sources of money income (2003): self-employment 55.2%, wages and salaries 7.5%, transfers 7.5%, other 29.8%. **Tourism** (2002): receipts $51,000,000; expenditures $106,000,000. **Gross national product** (at current market prices; 2003): $6,709,000,000 ($810 per capita). **Population economically active** (2003): total 3,801,400; activity rate of total population 46.3% (participation rates: ages 15–64, 75.6%; female 47.7%; unemployed 1.4%). **Land use** as % of

total land area (2000): in temporary crops 19.2%, in permanent crops 2.8%, in pasture 29.6%; overall forest area 13.1%.

Foreign trade

Imports (2002): $1,665,000,000 (machinery and equipment 23.8%, natural gas 12.9%, iron and steel 11.6%, food 10.3%, transport equipment 7.4%). *Major import sources* (2002): Russia 16.9%; Turkey 9.4%; Kazakhstan 9.0%; Turkmenistan 7.2%; France 7.1%; US 5.9%. **Exports** (2002): $2,167,000,000 (crude petroleum 68.1%, refined petroleum 19.6%, food products 1.8%). *Major export destinations* (2002): Italy 50.0%; France 7.7%; Israel 7.1%; Spain 4.8%; Russia 4.4%.

Transport and communications

Transport. *Railroads* (2003): length 2,116 km; passenger-km 636,000,000; metric ton-km cargo 7,696,000,000. *Roads* (2002): total length 45,870 km (paved 94%). *Vehicles* (2003): passenger cars 370,439; trucks and buses 95,800. *Air transport* (2003; Azerbaijan Airlines): passenger-km 755,-000,000; metric ton-km cargo 67,109,000; airports (2002) 3. **Communications,** in total units (units per 1,000 persons). Daily newspaper circulation (2000): 217,000 (27); radios (2000): 177,000 (22); televisions (2000): 2,080,000 (259); telephone main lines (2003): 976,500 (119); cellular telephone subscribers (2003): 1,055,000 (128); Internet users (2002): 300,000 (37).

Education and health

Educational attainment (1995). Percentage of population age 15 and over having: primary education or no formal schooling 12.1%; some secondary 9.1%; completed secondary and some postsecondary 27.5%; higher 7.6%. **Literacy** (1995): percentage of total population 15 and over literate 99.6%. **Health** (2003): physicians 29,500 (1 per 280 persons); hospital beds 68,600 (1 per 120 persons); infant mortality rate per 1,000 live births (2003) 12.8. **Food** (2001): daily per capita caloric intake 2,474 (vegetable products 86%, animal products 14%); 96% of FAO recommended minimum.

Military

Total active duty personnel (2003): 66,490 (army 85.5%, navy 2.6%, air force 11.9%). **Military expenditure as percentage of GNP** (1999): 6.6% (world 2.4%); per capita expenditure $120.

Background

Azerbaijan adjoins the Iranian region of the same name, and the origin of their respective inhabitants is the same. By the 9th century AD the area had come under Turkish influence, and in ensuing centuries it was fought over by Arabs, Mongols, Turks, and Iranians. Russia acquired the territory of what is now independent Azerbaijan in the early 19th century. After the Russian Revolution of 1917, Azerbaijan declared its independence; it was subdued by the Red Army in 1920 and became a Soviet Socialist Republic. It de-

1 metric ton = about 1.1 short tons; 1 kilometer = 0.6 mi (statute); 1 metric ton-km cargo = about 0.68 short ton-mi cargo; c.i.f.: cost, insurance, and freight; f.o.b.: free on board

clared independence from the collapsing Soviet Union in 1991. Azerbaijan has two geographic peculiarities. The exclave Nakhichevan is separated from the rest of Azerbaijan by Armenian territory. Nagorno-Karabakh, which lies within Azerbaijan and is administered by it, has a Christian Armenian majority. Azerbaijan and Armenia went to war over both territories in the 1990s, causing great economic disruption. Though a cease-fire was declared in 1994, the political situation remained unresolved.

Recent Developments

The vast mineral wealth of Azerbaijan drove its economy. The country's GDP grew by 34.5% in 2006. In July 2006 a pipeline with a capacity for pumping 1,000,000 barrels of crude oil a day from Azerbaijan's Caspian Sea fields to the Turkish port of Ceyhan opened. Azerbaijan developed its natural-gas fields as well, and in December 2006 the Baku–Tbilisi–Erzerum gas pipeline opened to supply Turkey. There remained significant concerns, however, that the mineral wealth would not be handled transparently. Inflation stood at 11.4% and the foreign debt grew by 19.5% in 2006.

Internet resources: <www.president.az>.

The Bahamas

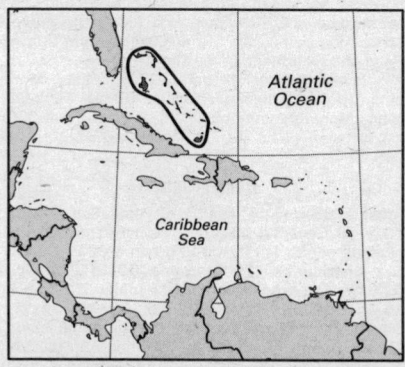

Official name: The Commonwealth of The Bahamas. Form of government: constitutional monarchy with two legislative houses (Senate [16]; House of Assembly [41]). Chief of state: Queen Elizabeth II (from 1952), represented by Governor-General Arthur Dion Hanna (from 2006). Head of government: Prime Minister Hubert Ingraham (from 2007). Capital: Nassau. Official language: English. Official religion: none. Monetary unit: 1 Bahamian dollar (B$) = 100 cents; valuation (1 Jul 2007) US$1 = B$1.00.

Demography

Area: 5,382 sq mi, 13,939 sq km. Population (2006): 327,000. Density (2006): persons per sq mi 84.1, persons per sq km 32.5. Urban (2000): 88.4%. Sex distribution (2000): male 48.65%; female 51.35%. Age breakdown (2000): under 15, 29.6%; 15–29, 25.8%; 30–44, 24.2%; 45–59, 12.6%; 60–74, 5.9%; 75 and over, 1.9%. Ethnic composition (2000): local

black 67.5%; mulatto 14.2%; British 12.0%; Haitian black 3.0%; US white 2.4%; other 0.9%. Religious affiliation (1995): non-Anglican Protestant 45.4%, of which Baptist 17.5%; Roman Catholic 16.8%; Anglican 10.8%; nonreligious 5.3%; Spiritist 1.5%; other (mostly independent and unaffiliated Christian) 20.2%. Major cities (2002): Nassau 179,300; Freeport 42,600; West End 7,800; Cooper's Town 5,700; Marsh Harbour 3,600. Location: chain of islands in the Caribbean Sea, southeast of Florida.

Vital statistics

Birth rate per 1,000 population (2003): 18.6 (world avg. 21.3); (2000) legitimate 43.2%; illegitimate 56.8%. Death rate per 1,000 population (2003): 8.7 (world avg. 9.1). Natural increase rate per 1,000 population (2003): 9.9 (world avg. 12.2). Total fertility rate (avg. births per childbearing woman; 2003): 2.3. Marriage rate per 1,000 population (2000): 7.8. Life expectancy at birth (2003): male 62.3 years; female 69.2 years.

National economy

Budget (2003). Revenue: B$991,503,000 (import taxes 45.0%, stamp taxes from imports 11.3%, departure taxes 6.6%, business and professional licenses 5.5%). Expenditures: B$1,088,643,000 (education 19.2%, health 15.9%, public order 11.6%, interest on public debt 10.3%, defense 3.1%). National debt (2003): US$1,647,600,000. Production (value of production in B$'000 except as noted). Agriculture, forestry, fishing (2001): crayfish 56,500, poultry products 28,300 (1998), citrus and other fruit 21,300 (1998), roundwood (2002) 17,000 cu m. Mining and quarrying (value of export production; 2000): aragonite 26,086; salt 12,447. Manufacturing (value of export production; 2000): chemical products 42,787; rum 18,856. Energy production (consumption): electricity (kW-hr; 2003) 1,797,-029,000 (1,656,600,000); petroleum products (metric tons; 2000) none (584,000). Tourism (US$'000,-000): receipts (2003) 1,763; expenditures (2001) 297. Household income and expenditure. Average household size (2000) 3.5; income per household (1996) B$27,252; expenditure (1995): housing 32.8%, transportation and communications 14.8%, food and beverages 13.8%, household furnishings 8.9%. Gross national product (at current market prices; 2002): US$4,684,000,000 (US$14,920 per capita). Population economically active (2000): total 154,396; activity rate of total population 50.9% (participation rates: ages 15–64, 76.6%; female 47.5%; unemployed [2001] 6.9%). Land use as % of total land area (2000): in temporary crops 0.7%, in permanent crops 0.4%, in pasture 0.2%; overall forest area 84.1%.

Foreign trade

Imports (2001-c.i.f.): B$1,927,000,000 (machinery and apparatus 16.0%; food products 14.2%; refined petroleum 14.1%; transport equipment 10.3%). Major import sources: US 83.3%; Venezuela 5.5%; Netherlands Antilles 2.6%; Japan 1.2%. Exports (2001-f.o.b.): B$376,000,000 (crustaceans and mollusks [primarily crayfish] 19.1%; polystyrene 19.1%; refined petroleum 18.3%; alcoholic beverages 10.5%). Major export destinations: US 77.5%; France 5.7%; Germany 3.9%; Spain 3.3%.

Transport and communications

Transport. *Roads* (2000): total length 2,693 km (paved 57%). *Vehicles* (1998): passenger cars 67,400; trucks and buses 16,800. *Air· transport* (2001; Bahamasair only): passenger-km 374,-000,000; metric ton-km cargo 1,764,000; airports (1997) with scheduled flights 22. **Communications,** in total units (units per 1,000 persons). Daily news-paper circulation (1996): 28,000 (99); radios (1997): 215,000 (744); televisions (2000): 75,200 (247); telephone main lines (2003): 131,700 (419); cellular telephone subscribers (2002): 121,800 (390); Inter-net users (2003): 84,000 (264).

Education and health

Educational attainment (2000). Percentage of pop-ulation age 15 and over having: no formal school-ing 1.5%; primary education 8.7%; incomplete sec-ondary 19.9%; complete secondary 53.7%; incomplete higher 8.1%; complete higher 7.1%; not stated 1.0%. **Literacy** (2001): total percentage age 15 and over literate 95.5%; males literate 94.6%; females literate 96.3%. **Health** (2001): physicians 458 (1 per 672 persons); hospital beds 1,540 (1 per 200 persons); infant mortality rate per 1,000 live births (2000) 17.0. **Food** (2001): daily per capita caloric intake 2,777 (vegetable products 67%, animal products 33%); 104% of FAO recom-mended minimum.

Military

Total active duty personnel (2003): 860 (paramilitary coast guard 100%). **Military expenditure as percent-age of GNP** (2000): 0.6% (world, n.a.); per capita ex-penditure US$85.

Background

The islands were inhabited by Lucayan Indians when Christopher Columbus sighted them on 12 Oct 1492. He is thought to have landed on San Salvador (Watling) Island. The Spaniards made no attempt to settle but carried out slave raids that depopulated the islands; when English settlers ar-rived in 1648 from Bermuda, the islands were un-inhabited. They became a haunt of pirates, and few of the ensuing settlements prospered. The is-lands enjoyed some prosperity following the Ameri-can Revolution, when Loyalists fled the US and es-tablished cotton plantations. The islands were a center for blockade runners during the American Civil War. Not until the development of tourism after World War II did permanent economic pros-perity arrive. The Bahamas was granted internal self-government in 1964 and became independent in 1973.

Recent Developments

In January 2007 The Bahamas officially unveiled nu-clear-weapon-detection equipment in its port at Freeport, Grand Bahama, installed under the US Container Security Initiative. In a related matter, how-ever, The Bahamas continued to resist signing the Proliferation Security Initiative, which would allow US forces to board and search any Bahamanian-flagged vessel.

Internet resources: <www.bahamas.com>.

Bahrain

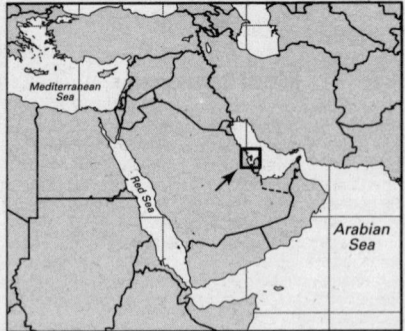

Official name: Mamlakat al-Bahrayn (Kingdom of Bahrain). **Form of government:** constitutional monar-chy (declared 14 Feb 2002) with two legislative houses (Chamber of Deputies [40; elected] and Con-sultative Council [40; appointed by the king]). **Chief of state:** King Hamad ibn 'Isa al-Khalifah (from 2002). **Head of Government:** Prime Minister Sheikh Khalifah ibn Sulman al-Khalifah (from 1970). **Capital:** Man-ama. **Official language:** Arabic. **Official religion:** Islam. **Monetary unit:** 1 Bahrain dinar (BD) = 1,000 fils; valuation (1 Jul 2007) US$1 = BD 0.38.

Demography

Area: 278 sq mi, 720 sq km. **Population** (2006): 727,000. **Density** (2004): persons per sq mi 2,615.1, persons per sq km 1,009.7. **Urban** (2001): 88.4%. **Sex distribution** (2002): male 57.46%; female 42.54%. **Age breakdown** (2001): under 15, 27.9%; 15–29, 27.5%; 30–44, 29.6%; 45–59, 11.0%; 60–74, 3.2%; 75 and over, 0.8%. **Ethnic composition** (2000): Bahraini Arab 63.9%; Indo-Pakistani 14.8%, of which Urdu 4.5%, Malayali 3.5%; Persian 13.0%; Filipino 4.5%; British 2.1%; other 1.7%. **Religious af-filiation** (2000): Muslim 82.4%, of which Shi'i c. 41%, Sunni c. 41%; Christian 10.5%; Hindu 6.3%; other 0.8%. **Major urban areas** (2001): Manama 143,035; Muharraq 91,307; Ar-Rifa' 79,550; Madinat Hamad 52,718; Madinat 'Isa 36,833. **Location:** Middle East, archipelago in the Persian Gulf, east of Saudi Arabia.

Vital statistics

Birth rate per 1,000 population (2002): 20.2 (world avg. 21.3). **Death rate** per 1,000 population (2002): 3.0 (world avg. 9.1). **Natural increase rate** per 1,000 popu-lation (2002): 17.2 (world avg. 12.2). **Total fertility rate** (avg. births per childbearing woman; 2002): 3.0. **Mar-riage rate** per 1,000 population (2002): 7.3. **Divorce rate** per 1,000 population (2002): 1.2. **Life expectancy** at birth (2002): male 73.2 years; female 76.2 years.

---

1 metric ton = about 1.1 short tons;   1 kilometer = 0.6 mi (statute);   1 metric ton-km cargo = about 0.68 short ton-mi cargo;   c.i.f.: cost, insurance, and freight;   f.o.b.: free on board

National economy

Budget (2002). *Revenue:* BD 1,026,800,000 (petroleum revenue 67.3%, non-petroleum revenue 32.7%). *Expenditures:* BD 1,031,000,000 (infrastructure 35.4%, general administration and public order 26.3%, social services 18.3%, transfers 12.9%, economic services 5.8%, other 1.3%). **Production** (metric tons except as noted). *Agriculture, forestry, fishing* (2002): dates 16,508, fruit (excluding dates) 8,336, vegetables 7,922 (of which tomatoes 2,048, onions 1,213); livestock (number of live animals; 2003) 17,500 sheep, 16,000 goats, 13,000 cattle; fish catch (2002) 11,204. *Manufacturing* (barrels; 2002): gas oil 31,575,000; fuel oil 18,878,000; kerosene and jet fuel 18,804,000. *Energy production (consumption):* electricity (kW-hr; 2002) 7,278,000,000 (6,454,658,000); crude petroleum (barrels; 2003) 68,900,000 ([2000] 93,886,000); petroleum products (2000) 11,105,000 (913,000); natural gas (cu m; 2002) 9,429,000,000 (9,429,000,000). **Public debt** (2001): BD 773,600,000 ($2,057,800,000). **Gross national product** (2002): $7,977,000,000 ($11,900 per capita). **Population economically active** (2002): total 319,000; activity rate of total population 46.3% (participation rates: ages 15 and over 64.1%; female 21.7%; unemployed [2001] 5.5%). **Tourism** (2002): receipts from visitors $741,-000,000; expenditures by nationals abroad $378,-000,000. **Household income and expenditure.** Average household size (2001) 6.2; expenditure (1984): food and tobacco 33.3%, housing 21.2%, household durable goods 9.8%, transportation and communications 8.5%, recreation 6.4%, clothing and footwear 5.9%. **Land use** as % of total land area (2000): in temporary crops 3%, in permanent crops 6%, in pasture 6%; overall forest area, negligible.

Foreign trade

Imports (2002-c.i.f.): BD 1,881,300,000 (petroleum products 33.4%, machinery and transport equipment 23.6%, food, beverages, and tobacco products 11.1%). *Major import sources* (2001; excludes trade in petroleum): Australia 10.0%; Saudi Arabia 9.0%; Japan 8.3%; US 7.8%; UK 6.4%; Germany 6.0%. **Exports** (2002): BD 2,178,800,000 (petroleum products 68.3%, aluminum [all forms] 15.0%, textiles and clothing 7.8%). *Major export destinations* (2001; excludes trade in petroleum): US 23.8%; Saudi Arabia 14.2%; Taiwan 9.8%; Malaysia 4.3%; India 4.2%.

Transport and communications

Transport. *Roads* (2002): total length 3,459 km (paved 79%). *Vehicles* (2002): passenger cars 176,261; trucks and buses 36,231. *Air transport* (2003; one-fourth apportionment of international flights of Gulf Air [jointly administered by the governments of Bahrain, Oman, Qatar, and the UAE]): passenger-km 3,369,800,000; metric ton-km cargo 140,000,000; airports (2002) with scheduled flights 1. **Communications,** in total units (units per 1,000 persons). Daily newspaper circulation (1996): 67,000 (117); radios (2000): 48,500 (76); televisions (2000): 256,000 (402); telephone main lines (2003): 185,800 (268); cellular telephone subscribers (2003): 443,100 (638); personal computers (2002): 108,000 (159); Internet users (2003): 195,700 (282).

Education and health

Educational attainment (2001). Percentage of population age 15 and over having: no formal education 24.0%; primary education 37.1%; secondary 26.4%; higher 12.5%. **Literacy** (2001): percentage of population age 15 and over literate 87.7%; males literate 92.5%; females literate 83.0%. **Health** (2002): physicians 1,189 (1 per 565 persons); hospital beds 1,814 (1 per 371 persons); infant mortality rate per 1,000 live births (2001) 8.7.

Military

Total active duty personnel (2003): 11,200 (army 75.9%, navy 10.7%, air force 13.4%); US troops in Bahrain (2004): 4,500. **Military expenditure as percentage of GNP** (1999): 8.1% (world 2.4%); per capita expenditure $666.

Background

The area has long been an important trading center and is mentioned in Persian, Greek, and Roman references. It was ruled by Arabs from the 7th century AD but was then occupied by the Portuguese in 1521–1602. Since 1783 it has been ruled by the Khalifah family, though through a series of treaties its defense remained a British responsibility from 1820 to 1971. After Britain withdrew its forces from the Persian Gulf (1968), Bahrain declared its independence in 1971. It served as a center for the allies in the Persian Gulf War (1990–91). Since 1994 it has experienced bouts of political unrest, mainly by Shi-'ites, who attempted to get the government to restore the parliament (abolished in 1975).

Recent Developments

Lacking important oil resources, Bahrain continued to position itself as a center of trade and finance. In July 2005 the king ratified the US-Bahrain Free Trade Agreement. This agreement, the first between a Gulf state and the US, went into effect in August 2006 and eliminated most of the tariffs between the two countries.

Internet resources: <www.bahraintourism.com>.

Bangladesh

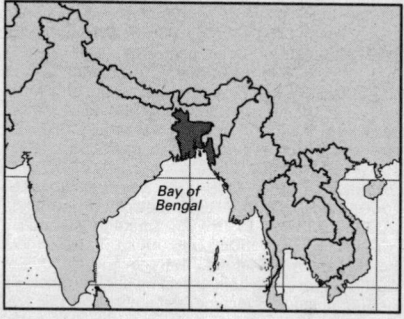

Official name: Gana Prajatantri Bangladesh (People's Republic of Bangladesh). **Form of government:**

unitary multiparty republic with one legislative house (Parliament [300 seats, excluding 45 reserved for women to be reinstated as of 2006 elections]). **Chief of state:** President Iajuddin Ahmed (from 2002). **Head of government:** Chief Adviser Fakhruddin Ahmed (from 2007). **Capital:** Dhaka. **Official language:** Bengali. **Official religion:** Islam. **Monetary unit:** 1 Bangladesh taka (Tk) = 100 paisa; valuation (1 Jul 2007) US$1 = Tk 68.59.

Demography

Area (including river area): 56,977 sq mi, 147,570 sq km. **Population** (2006): 138,835,000. **Density** (2006): persons per sq mi 2,436.7, persons per sq km 940.8. **Urban** (2001): 23.4%. **Sex distribution** (2003): male 51.30%; female 48.70%. **Age breakdown** (2003): under 15, 34.1%; 15–29, 32.4%; 30–44, 18.0%; 45–59, 10.2%; 60–74, 4.3%; 75 and over, 1.0%. **Ethnic composition** (1997): Bengali 97.7%; tribal 1.9%, of which Chakma 0.4%, Saontal 0.2%, Marma 0.1%; other 0.4%. **Religious affiliation** (2000): Muslim 85.8%; Hindu 12.4%; Christian 0.7%; Buddhist 0.6%; other 0.5%. **Major cities/urban agglomerations** (2001): Dhaka 5,644,235/10,403,-597; Chittagong 2,199,590/3,361,244; Khulna 811,490/1,287,987; Rajshahi 402,646/ 678,728. **Location:** South Asia, bordering India, Myanmar (Burma), and the Bay of Bengal.

Vital statistics

Birth rate per 1,000 population (2003): 29.9 (world avg. 21.3). **Death rate** per 1,000 population (2003): 8.6 (world avg. 9.1). **Natural increase rate** per 1,000 population (2003): 21.3 (world avg. 12.2). **Total fertility rate** (avg. births per childbearing woman; 2003): 3.2. **Marriage rate** per 1,000 population (1998): 9.2. **Life expectancy** at birth (2003): male 61.5 years; female 61.2 years.

National economy

Budget (2002–03). *Revenue:* Tk 326,000,000,000 (value-added tax 39.3%, international trade 36.2%, income taxes 14.7%, other 9.8%). *Expenditures:* Tk 448,000,000,000 (development program 42.4%, wages 16.5%, subsidies 14.7%, interest payments 10.3%, goods and services 8.3%, other 7.8%). **Production** (metric tons except as noted). *Agriculture, forestry, fishing* (2002): paddy rice 38,134,000, sugarcane 6,502,000, potatoes 3,216,000; livestock (number of live animals) 34,400,000 goats, 24,000,-000 cattle, 140,000,000 chickens; roundwood (2002) 28,386,000 cu m; fish catch (2001) 1,687,-000. *Mining and quarrying* (2002): marine salt 350,000; industrial limestone 32,000. *Manufacturing* (value added in $'000,000; 1998): wearing apparel 839; tobacco products 634; textiles 567. *Energy production (consumption):* electricity (kW-hr; 2002) 17,021,000,000 (17,021,000,000); coal (2000) none (660,000); crude petroleum (barrels; 2000) none (10,054,000); petroleum products (2002) 1,323,000 (3,769,000); natural gas (cu m; 2002) 6,568,000,000 (3,096,000,000). **Household income and expenditure.** Average household size (2000) 5.7; average annual income per household Tk 52,389; sources of income: self-employment 56.9%,

wages and salaries 28.1%, transfer payments 9.1%, other 5.9%; expenditure (2002–03): food and drink 64.5%, housing and energy 15.0%, clothing and footwear 5.9%, transport 3.3%, other 11.3%. **Population economically active** (2000): total 52,847,000; activity rate of total population 47.3% (participation rates: over age 15, 58.8%; female 37.5%; unemployed 2.0%). **Public debt** (external, outstanding; 2002): $16,445,000,000. **Gross national product** (2003): $54,587,000,000 ($400 per capita). **Land use** as % of total land area (2000): in temporary crops 62.5%, in permanent crops 2.7%, in pasture 4.6%; overall forest area 10.2%. **Tourism** (2002): receipts $57,000,000; expenditures $202,000,000.

Foreign trade

Imports (2002–03-f.o.b. in balance of trade and c.i.f. in commodities and trading partners): $9,648,-000,000 (capital goods 28.3%; textile yarn, fabrics, and made-up articles 14.3%; imports for export processing zone 7.5%; rice and wheat 4.3%; cotton 4.1%). *Major import sources* (2001): China 11.0%; India 10.9%; Singapore 8.1%; Japan 7.3%; South Korea 6.5%; Hong Kong 6.2%. **Exports** (2002–03): $6,548,000,000 (ready-made garments 49.8%; hosiery and knitwear 25.3%; frozen fish and shrimp 4.9%; jute manufactures 3.9%). *Major export destinations* (2001): US 39.0%; Germany 11.1%; UK 8.8%; France 5.7%; The Netherlands 5.3%.

Transport and communications

Transport. *Railroads* (1998–99): route length 2,734 km; passenger-km 4,980,000,000; metric ton-km cargo 828,000,000. *Roads* (1999): total length 207,486 km (paved 10%). *Vehicles* (1999): passenger cars 66,723; trucks and buses 82,025. *Air transport* (2002; Bangladesh Biman only): passenger-km 4,584,000,000; metric ton-km cargo 205,896,000; airports with scheduled flights (2001) 8. **Communications**, in total units (units per 1,000 persons). Daily newspaper circulation (2000): 6,880,000 (53); radios (2000): 6,360,000 (49); televisions (2000): 909,000 (7); telephone main lines (2003): 740,000 (5.5); cellular telephone subscribers (2003): 1,365,-000 (10.1); personal computers (2002): 450,000 (3); Internet users (2003): 243,000 (1.8).

Education and health

Educational attainment (1991). Percentage of population age 25 and over having: no formal schooling 65.4%; primary education 17.1%; secondary 13.8%; postsecondary 3.7%. **Literacy** (2000): total population age 15 and over literate 41.3%; males literate 52.3%; females literate 29.9%. **Health** (1999): physicians 30,864 (1 per 4,150 persons); hospital beds 44,374 (1 per 2,886 persons); infant mortality rate per 1,000 live births (2002) 68.0. **Food** (2001): daily per capita caloric intake 2,187 (vegetable products 97%, animal products 3%); 95% of FAO recommended minimum.

Military

Total active duty personnel (2003): 125,500 (army 87.6%, navy 7.2%, air force 5.2%). **Military expendi-**

1 metric ton = about 1.1 short tons;   1 kilometer = 0.6 mi (statute);   1 metric ton-km cargo = about 0.68 short ton-mi cargo;   c.i.f.: cost, insurance, and freight;   f.o.b.: free on board

ture as percentage of GNP (1999): 1.4% (world 2.4%); per capita expenditure $5.

Did you know? The Sundarbans is a vast tract of forests and saltwater swamps in Bangladesh that forms the lower part of the Ganges delta, extending about 160 mi (260 km) along the Bay of Bengal. The Sundarbans is one of the last preserves of the Bengal tiger.

Background

In its early years Bangladesh was known as Bengal. When the British left the subcontinent in 1947, the area that was East Bengal became the part of Pakistan called East Pakistan. Bengali nationalist sentiment increased after the creation of an independent Pakistan. In 1971 violence erupted; some one million Bengalis were killed, and millions more fled to India, which finally entered the war on the side of the Bengalis, ensuring West Pakistan's defeat. East Pakistan became the independent nation of Bangladesh. Little of the devastation caused by the war has been repaired, and political instability, including the assassination of two presidents, has continued. In addition, the low-lying country has been repeatedly battered by natural disasters, notably tropical storms and flooding.

Recent Developments

In 2006 Bangladesh experienced severe unrest—at least 25 people protesting against poor living and working conditions were killed by security forces, and thousands of laborers in the ready-made-garment industry damaged hundreds of factories, including some foreign-owned ones. The monthlong agitation and chaos seriously hurt the country's main source of foreign-exchange earnings. A positive development in the country was the arrest in March of the alleged masterminds of the August 2005 terrorist attacks in which some 500 bombs exploded nearly simultaneously throughout the country.

Internet resources: <www.bangladesh.gov.bd/>.

Barbados

Official name: Barbados. **Form of government:** constitutional monarchy with two legislative houses (Senate [21]; House of Assembly [30]). **Chief of state:** Queen Elizabeth II, represented by Governor-General Sir Clifford Husbands (from 1996). **Head of government:** Prime Minister Owen Arthur (from 1994). **Capital:** Bridgetown. **Official language:** English. **Official religion:** none. **Monetary unit:** 1 Barbados dollar (BDS$) = 100 cents; valuation (1 Jul 2007) US$1 = BDS$1.99.

Demography

Area: 166 sq mi, 430 sq km. **Population** (2006): 270,000. **Density** (2006): persons per sq mi 1,626.5, persons per sq km 627.9. **Urban** (2001): 50.5%. **Sex distribution** (2003): male 48.26%; female 51.74%. **Age breakdown** (2003): under 15, 21.2%; 15–29, 23.1%; 30–44, 25.8%; 45–59, 17.8%; 60–74, 8.1%; 75 and over, 4.0%. **Ethnic composition** (2000): local black 87.1%; mulatto 6.0%; British expatriates 4.3%;

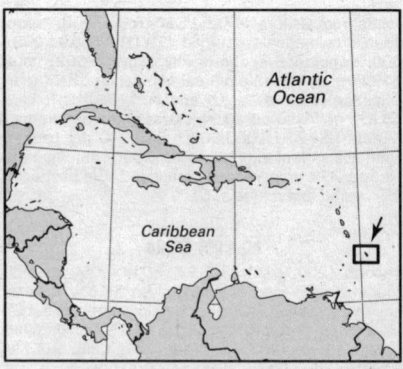

US white 1.2%; Indo-Pakistani 1.1%; other 0.3%. **Religious affiliation** (1995): Protestant 63.0%, of which Anglican 26.3%, Pentecostal 10.6%, Methodist 5.7%; Roman Catholic 4.8%; other Christian 2.0%; nonreligious/other 30.2%. **Major cities** (1990): Bridgetown 6,070 (urban agglomeration [2003] 140,000); Speightstown c. 3,500. **Location:** northeast of Venezuela at the eastern edge of the Caribbean Sea where it adjoins the North Atlantic Ocean.

Vital statistics

Birth rate per 1,000 population (2001): 15.0 (world avg. 21.3). **Death rate** per 1,000 population (2001): 8.9 (world avg. 9.1). **Natural increase rate** per 1,000 population (2001): 6.1 (world avg. 12.2). **Total fertility rate** (avg. births per childbearing woman; 2000): 1.6. **Marriage rate** per 1,000 population (1995): 13.5. **Divorce rate** per 1,000 population (1995): 1.5. **Life expectancy** at birth (2000): male 70.4 years; female 75.6 years.

National economy

Budget (2003). *Revenue:* BDS$1,843,800,000 (tax revenue c. 94%, of which personal income and company taxes 31.4%, value-added tax 29.8%, import duties 9.3%; nontax revenue c. 6%). *Expenditures:* BDS$2,009,200,000 (current expenditure 86.4%, of which wages and salaries 31.5%, debt payment 13.5%; capital expenditure 13.6%). **Public debt** (external, outstanding; 2002): US$958,000,000. **Production** (metric tons except as noted). *Agriculture, forestry, fishing* (2002): raw sugar 50,000, sweet potatoes 5,300, yams 1,450; livestock (number of live animals) 41,300 sheep, 35,000 pigs, 21,000 cattle; roundwood (2002) 5,000; fish catch (2001) 2,676. *Manufacturing* (value added in US$'000,000; 1997): industrial chemicals 87; food products 63; beverages (significantly rum and beer) 58. *Energy production (consumption):* electricity (kW-hr; 2002) 741,300,000 (741,300,000); crude petroleum (barrels; 2002) 390,600 ([2000] 1,778,000); petroleum products (2000) 1,000 (332,000); natural gas (cu m; 2001) 34,900,000 (34,900,000). **Household income and expenditure.** Average household size (2000) 2.8; income per household (1988) BDS$13,455; expenditure (1994): food 39.4%, housing 16.8%, transportation 10.5%, household operations 8.1%, alcohol and tobacco 6.4%, fuel and light 5.2%, clothing and footwear 5.0%, other 8.6%. **Tourism:** receipts from visitors (2002) US$648,000,000; expenditures by nationals abroad (2001) US$101,000,000. **Population economically active** (2002): total 143,200; activity rate of total population 52.8% (participation rates: ages 15 and over, 68.5%; female 48.4%; unemployed 10.3%). **Gross national product** (2003): US$2,512,000,000 (US$9,270 per capita). **Land use** as % of total land area (2000): in temporary crops c. 37%, in permanent crops c. 2%, in pasture c. 5%; overall forest area c. 5%.

Foreign trade

Imports (2003-c.i.f.): BDS$2,050,000,000 (capital goods 20.9%; food and beverages 15.5%; mineral fuels 11.1%; chemicals and chemical products 5.1%). *Major import sources* (2002): US 44.1%; Trinidad and Tobago 11.7%; UK 7.9%; Japan 4.5%; Canada 3.7%. **Exports** (2003-f.o.b.): BDS$542,000,000 (food and beverages 25.3%, of which sugar and molasses 9.2%; rum 7.0%; chemicals and chemical products 8.3%; electrical components 5.2%; other manufactures 17.5%). *Major export destinations* (2002): US 16.5%; UK 11.9%; Trinidad and Tobago 11.0%; Jamaica 7.0%; bunkers and ships' stores 9.3%.

Transport and communications

Transport. *Roads* (2000): total length 1,600 km (paved 99%). *Vehicles* (2001): passenger cars 64,900; trucks and buses 11,400. *Air transport:* (2001) passenger arrivals and departures 1,760,000; (2000) cargo unloaded and loaded 14,000 metric tons; airports (2002) with scheduled flights 1. **Communications,** in total units (units per 1,000 persons). Daily newspaper circulation (1996): 53,000 (199); radios (2001): 202,000 (749); televisions (2001): 83,700 (310); telephone main lines (2003): 134,000 (497); cellular telephone subscribers (2003): 140,000 (519); personal computers (2002): 28,000 (104); Internet users (2003): 100,000 (371).

Education and health

Educational attainment (1990). Percentage of population age 25 and over having: no formal schooling 0.4%; primary education 23.7%; secondary 60.3%; higher 11.2%; other 4.4%. **Literacy** (1995): total population age 15 and over literate 97.4%; males literate 98.0%; females literate 96.8%. **Health:** physicians (2002) 376 (1 per 721 persons); hospital beds (1992) 1,966 (1 per 134 persons); infant mortality rate per 1,000 live births (2002) 12.6. **Food** (2001): daily per capita caloric intake 2,992 (vegetable products 75%, animal products 25%); 124% of FAO recommended minimum.

Military

Total active duty personnel (2003): 500 (army 82.0%, navy 18.0%). **Military expenditure as percentage of GNP** (1999): 0.5% (world 2.4%); per capita expenditure US$44.

Background

The island of Barbados was probably inhabited by Arawak Indians who originally came from South America. Spaniards may have landed by 1518, and by 1536 they had apparently wiped out the Indian population. Barbados was settled by the English in the 1620s. Slaves were brought in to work the sugar plantations, which were especially prosperous in the 17th–18th centuries. The British Empire abolished slavery in 1834, and all the Barbados slaves were freed by 1838. In 1958 Barbados joined the West Indies Federation. When the latter dissolved in 1962, Barbados sought independence from Britain; it achieved it and joined the Commonwealth in 1966.

Recent Developments

In August 2006 it was announced that the country's two remaining sugar refineries could be converted for use in ethanol production.

Internet resources: <www.barbados.org>.

Belarus

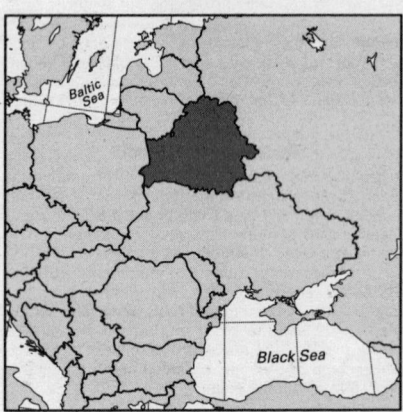

Official name: Respublika Belarus (Republic of Belarus). **Form of government:** republic with two legislative bodies (Council of the Republic [64]; House of Representatives [110]). **Head of state and government:** President Alyaksandr H. Lukashenka (from 1994), assisted by Prime Minister Syarhey Sidorski (from 2003). **Capital:** Minsk. **Official languages:** Belarusian; Russian. **Official religion:** none. **Monetary unit:** rubel (Rbl; plural rubli); valuation (1 Jul 2007) US$1 = (new) Rbl 2,152; rubel re-denominated 1 Jan 2000; as of that date 1,000 (old) rubli = 1 (new) rubel.

Demography

Area: 80,153 sq mi, 207,595 sq km. **Population** (2006): 10,517,000. **Density** (2006): persons per sq mi 121.3, persons per sq km 46.8. **Urban** (2004): 71.5%. **Sex distribution** (2004): male 46.61%; female 53.39%. **Age breakdown** (2003): under 15, 16.8%; 15–29, 23.5%; 30–44, 22.7%; 45–59,

18.1%; 60–74, 13.4%; 75 and over, 5.5%. **Ethnic composition** (1999): Belarusian 81.2%; Russian 11.4%; Polish 3.9%; Ukrainian 2.4%; Jewish 0.3%; other 0.8%. **Religious affiliation** (1995): Belarusian Orthodox 31.6%; Roman Catholic 17.7%; other (mostly nonreligious) 50.7%. **Major cities** (2004): Minsk 1,682,900; Homyel 497,200; Mahilyow 365,400; Vitsyebsk 355,200; Hrodna 315,500. **Location:** Eastern Europe, bordering Latvia, Russia, Ukraine, Poland, and Lithuania.

Vital statistics

Birth rate per 1,000 population (2003): 10.1 (world avg. 21.3); (2000) legitimate 81.4%; illegitimate 18.6%. **Death rate** per 1,000 population (2003): 14.1 (world avg. 9.1). **Natural increase rate** per 1,000 population (2003): –4.0 (world avg. 12.2). **Total fertility rate** (avg. births per childbearing woman; 2003): 1.3. **Marriage rate** per 1,000 population (2000): 6.2. **Divorce rate** per 1,000 population (2000): 4.3. **Life expectancy** at birth (2003): male 62.5 years; female 74.6 years.

National economy

Budget (2003). *Revenue:* Rbl 12,154,223,000,000 (tax revenue 76.8%, of which value-added tax 23.8%, income tax 8.4%, profit tax 7.7%, excise tax 6.9%, property tax 6.0%, other 24.0%; nontax revenue 23.2%). *Expenditures:* Rbl 12,646,135,-000,000 (education 18.5%, target budgetary fund 15.3%, health 14.3%, subsidies 7.4%, public order 5.2%, capital expenditure 4.2%, defense 3.0%). **Public debt** (external, outstanding; 2002): $709,-500,000. **Household income and expenditure.** Average household size (2000) 3.4; sources of money income (2003): wages and salaries 49.2%, business activities 31.6%, transfers 18.1%; expenditure (2001): food and nonalcoholic beverages 53.6%, clothing and footwear 9.4%, housing and energy 7.2%, transport 6.3%, alcoholic beverages and tobacco products 5.9%. **Population economically active** (2003): 4,446,000; activity rate of total population 45.1% (participation rate: ages 16–59 [male], 16–54 [female] 74.0%; female 53.5%; unemployed 3.1%). **Production** (metric tons except as noted). *Agriculture, forestry, fishing* (2003): potatoes 8,649,000, maize for forage 6,500,000, sugar beets 1,920,000; livestock (number of live animals) 3,921,000 cattle, 3,277,000 pigs, 30,600,000 poultry; roundwood (2002) 6,947,000 cu m; fish catch (2001) 5,609. *Mining and quarrying* (2000): potash 3,400,000; peat 2,211,000. *Manufacturing* (value of production in [old] Rbl '000,000; 1994): machine-building equipment 1,086,650; chemical products 659,438; food products 562,438. *Energy production (consumption):* electricity (kW-hr; 2003) 26,615,000,000 (33,228,000,000); coal (2000) none (504,000); crude petroleum (barrels; 2000) 13,600,000 (98,640,000); petroleum products (2003) 15,774,000 (6,240,000); natural gas (cu m; 2003) 254,000,000 (18,448,000,000). **Gross national product** (2003): $15,700,000,000 ($1,590 per capita). **Tourism** (2002): receipts $193,000,000; expenditures $559,000,000. **Land use** as % of total land area (2000): in temporary crops 29.6%, in permanent crops 0.6%, in pasture 14.4%; overall forest area 45.3%; 25% of Belarusian territory severely affected by radioactive fallout from Chernobyl.

Foreign trade

Imports (2002-c.i.f.): $8,980,000,000 (crude petroleum 16.8%, machinery and apparatus 15.5%, chemicals and chemical products 10.2%, food and beverages 8.8%, natural and manufactured gas 6.3%, iron and steel 6.2%). *Major import sources:* Russia 65.1%; Germany 7.7%; Ukraine 3.2%; Poland 2.4%; Italy 2.4%. **Exports** (2002-f.o.b.): $8,098,000,000 (refined petroleum 18.3%, road vehicles 8.9%, nonelectrical machinery 8.3%, food 6.7%, potassium chloride 5.7%, electrical machinery 5.7%). *Major export destinations:* Russia 50.1%; Latvia 6.4%; UK 6.1%; Germany 4.3%; The Netherlands 3.4%.

Transport and communications

Transport. *Railroads* (2002): length 5,533 km; passenger-km 14,349,000,000; metric ton-km cargo 34,169,000,000. *Roads* (2000): total length 74,400 km (paved 89%). *Vehicles* (2001): passenger cars 1,448,461; trucks and buses 85,791. *Air transport* (2002): passenger-km 553,000,000; metric ton-km cargo 37,000,000; airports 1. **Communications,** in total units (units per 1,000 persons). Daily newspaper circulation (2000): 1,550,000 (155); radios (2000): 2,990,000 (299); televisions (2000): 3,420,000 (342); telephone main lines (2003): 3,071,300 (311); cellular telephone subscribers (2003): 1,118,000 (113); Internet users (2003): 1,391,900 (141).

Education and health

Literacy (2001): total population age 15 and over literate 99.7%; males literate 99.8%; females literate 99.6%. **Health:** physicians (2003) 44,800 (1 per 220 persons); hospital beds (2000) 126,209 (1 per 79 persons); infant mortality rate per 1,000 live births (2003) 7.7. **Food** (2001): daily per capita caloric intake 2,925 (vegetable products 72%, animal products 28%); 113% of FAO recommended minimum.

Military

Total active duty personnel (2003): 72,940 (army 40.6%, air force and air defense 24.9%, other 34.5%). **Military expenditure as percentage of GNP** (1999): 1.3% (world 2.4%); per capita expenditure $89.

Background

While Belarusians share a distinct identity and language, they did not enjoy political sovereignty until the late 20th century. The territory that is now Belarus underwent partition and changed hands often; as a result its history is entwined with those of its neighbors. In medieval times the region was ruled by Lithuanians and Poles. Following the Third Partition of Poland, it was ruled by Russia. After World War I, the western part was assigned to Poland, and the eastern part became Soviet Russian territory. After World War II, the Soviets expanded what had been the Belorussian SSR by annexing more of Poland. Much of the area suffered contamination from the Chernobyl accident in 1986, forcing many to evacuate. Belarus declared its independence in 1991 and later joined the Commonwealth of Independent States. Amid increasing political turmoil in the 1990s, it proposed a union with Russia in 1997 that was still being debated at the start of the 21st century.

Recent Developments

Poland recalled its ambassador to Belarus in July 2005 after the government in Minsk replaced the newly elected head of the Belarusian Union of Poles, which represented Belarus's 400,000-strong Polish minority. Russia announced that the price of its natural gas for Belarus would double in 2007 (though this price was still below the world average). In response, in February 2007 Belarus increased the transit fees for Russian oil flowing to Europe through Belarus. Relations with The Sudan, which had a large and developing oil sector, improved as Belarus called for the opening of a Sudanese embassy. Venezuela, another country with huge oil reserves, cultivated ties in March 2007 by offering Belarus the rights to develop Venezuelan oil fields with an estimated annual yield of 2,000,000 tons.

Internet resources: <www.belarusembassy.org>.

Belgium

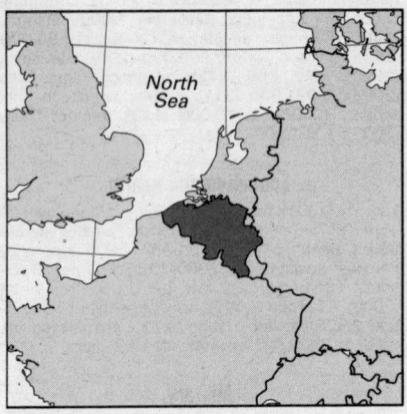

Official name: Koninkrijk België (Dutch); Royaume de Belgique (French) (Kingdom of Belgium). **Form of government:** federal constitutional monarchy with a Parliament composed of two legislative chambers (Senate [71, excluding children of the monarch serving ex officio from age 18]; House of Representatives [150]). **Chief of state:** King Albert II (from 1993). **Head of government:** Prime Minister Guy Verhofstadt (from 1999). **Capital:** Brussels. **Official languages:** Dutch; French; German. **Official religion:** none. **Monetary unit:** 1 euro (€) = 100 cents; US$1 = €0.74 (1 Jul 2007). The Belgian franc (BF) was the former monetary unit; at conversion on 1 Jan 2002, €1 = BF40.34.

Demography

Area: 11,787 sq mi, 30,528 sq km. **Population** (2006): 10,517,000. **Density** (2006): persons per sq mi 892.3, persons per sq km 344.5. **Urban** (2002): 97.0%. **Sex distribution** (2003): male 48.95%; female 51.05%. **Age breakdown** (2003): under 15, 17.2%; 15–29, 18.2%; 30–44, 22.5%; 45–59,

20.1%; 60–74, 14.1%; 75 and over, 7.9%. **Ethnic composition** (2000): Flemish 53.7%; Walloon (French) 31.6%; Italian 2.6%; French 2.0%; Arab 1.8%; German 1.5%; Berber 0.9%; other 5.9%. **Religious affiliation** (1995): Roman Catholic 87.9%; Muslim 2.5%; other Christian 2.4%, of which Protestant 1.0%; Jewish 0.3%; other 6.9%. **Major cities** (2004): Brussels 999,899; Antwerp 455,148; Ghent 229,344; Charleroi 200,608; Liège 185,488. **Location:** western Europe, bordering The Netherlands, Germany, Luxembourg, France, and the North Sea.

Vital statistics

Birth rate per 1,000 population (2003): 10.7 (world avg. 21.3). **Death rate** per 1,000 population (2003): 10.2 (world avg. 9.1). **Natural increase rate** per 1,000 population (2003): 0.5 (world avg. 12.2). **Total fertility rate** (avg. births per childbearing woman; 2003): 1.6. **Marriage rate** per 1,000 population (2001): 4.1. **Divorce rate** per 1,000 population (2000): 2.6. **Life expectancy** at birth (2002): male 75.1 years; female 81.6 years.

National economy

Budget (2003). *Revenue:* €137,781,000,000 (social security contributions 28.4%, income tax 24.5%, taxes on goods and services 21.9%, property tax 6.7%). *Expenditures:* €137,348,000,000 (social security payments 25.7%, wages 23.5%, health 12.1%, interest on debt 11.0%, capital expenditure 6.1%). **Public debt** (2001): $244,540,000,000. **Production** (metric tons except as noted). *Agriculture, forestry, fishing* (2003): sugar beets 6,450,000, potatoes 2,522,000, wheat 1,640,000; livestock (number of live animals) 6,539,000 pigs, 2,778,000 cattle; roundwood (2002) 4,500,000 cu m; fish catch (2001; includes Luxembourg) 31,839. *Mining and quarrying* (2002): limestone 30,000,000; granite (Belgium bluestone) 1,200,000 cu m. *Manufacturing* (value added in $'000,000; 1997): chemicals and chemical products 7,702; food products 4,513; motor vehicles and parts 3,287; electrical machinery 3,278; base metals 3,126; value of traded diamonds handled in Antwerp (2002) $26,000,-000,000. *Energy production (consumption):* electricity (kW-hr; 2002) 76,580,000,000 ([2000] 88,225,000,000); coal (2000) 375,000 (11,266,-000); crude petroleum (barrels; 2000) none (248,700,000); petroleum products (2000) 29,525,-000 (15,991,000); natural gas (cu m; 2000) 3,017,000 (19,544,000,000). **Household income and expenditure.** Average household size (2000) 2.5; sources of income (2003): wages and transfer payments 69.3%, property income 11.1%, mixed income 19.6%; expenditure (1992): food 18.0%, housing 17.0%, transportation 13.3%, health 11.8%, durable goods 10.7%, clothing 7.7%. **Tourism** (2002): receipts $6,892,000,000; expenditures $10,435,000,000. **Population economically active** (2003): total 4,708,000; activity rate 45.5% (participation rates: ages 15–64, 69.3%; female [2000] 43.1%; unemployed 11.4%). **Gross national product** (2003): $267,227,000,000 ($25,820 per capita). **Land use** as % of total land area (2000): in temporary crops 25.6%, in permanent crops 0.7%, in pasture 20.5%; overall forest area 21.1%.

---

1 metric ton = about 1.1 short tons;   1 kilometer = 0.6 mi (statute);   1 metric ton-km cargo = about 0.68 short ton-mi cargo;   c.i.f.: cost, insurance, and freight;   f.o.b.: free on board

Foreign trade

Imports (2002-c.i.f.): €209,720,700,000 (machinery and apparatus 16.3%, road vehicles 12.0%, medicine and pharmaceuticals 10.6%, food 6.8%). *Major import sources:* Germany 17.3%; The Netherlands 15.8%; France 12.6%; UK 7.5%; Ireland 7.0%. **Exports** (2002-f.o.b.): €228,561,700,000 (machinery and apparatus 14.0%, road vehicles 13.8%, pharmaceuticals 10.1%, food 7.6%, organic chemicals 5.9%). *Major export destinations:* Germany 18.6%; France 16.3%; The Netherlands 11.7%; UK 9.6%; US 7.8%.

Transport and communications

Transport. *Railroads* (2001): route length 3,380 km; passenger-km 8,038,000,000; metric ton-km cargo 7,080,000,000. *Roads* (1997): total length 143,800 km (paved 97%). *Vehicles* (2001): passenger cars 4,739,850; trucks and buses 541,056. *Air transport* (2000; Sabena airlines only; shut down November 2001. SN Brussels Airlines was founded in February 2002): passenger-km 19,378,689,000; metric ton-km cargo 568,244,000; airports 2. **Communications,** in total units (units per 1,000 persons). Daily newspaper circulation (2000): 1,640,000 (160); radios (2000): 8,130,000 (793); televisions (2000): 5,550,000 (541); telephone main lines (2002): 5,120,400 (494); cellular telephone subscribers (2002): 8,135,500 (786); personal computers (2002): 2,500,000 (242); Internet users (2002): 3,400,000 (329).

Education and health

Educational attainment (1991). Percentage of population age 18 and over having: less than secondary education 46.8%; lower secondary 16.6%; upper secondary 21.6%; teacher's college 3.7%; university 11.3%. **Health:** physicians (2002) 46,268 (1 per 223 persons); hospital beds (2001) 71,907 (1 per 143 persons); infant mortality rate (2001) 5.1. **Food** (2001; includes Luxembourg): daily per capita caloric intake 3,682 (vegetable products 69%, animal products 31%); 140% of FAO recommended minimum.

Military

Total active duty personnel (2003): 40,800 (army 60.8%, navy 6.0%, air force 25.1%, medical service 4.4%, other 3.7%). **Military expenditure as percentage of GNP** (1999): 1.4% (world 2.4%); per capita expenditure $352.

Background

Inhabited in ancient times by the Belgae, a Celtic people, the area was conquered by Caesar in 57 BC; under Augustus it became the Roman province of Gallia Belgica. Conquered by the Franks, it later broke up into semi-independent territories, including Brabant and Luxembourg. By the late 15th century, the territories of the Netherlands, of which the future Belgium was a part, had gradually united and passed to the Habsburgs. In the 16th century, it was a center for European commerce. The basis of modern Belgium was laid in the southern Catholic provinces that split from the northern provinces after the Union of Utrecht in 1579. Overrun by the French and incorporated into France in 1801, it was reunited to Holland and with it became the independent Kingdom of The Netherlands in 1815. After the revolt of its citizens in 1830, it became the independent Kingdom of Belgium. Under Léopold II it acquired vast lands in Africa. Overrun by the Germans in World Wars I and II, Belgium was the scene of the Battle of the Bulge. Internal discord led to legislation in the 1970s and 1980s that created three nearly autonomous regions in accordance with language distribution: Flemish Flanders, French Wallonia, and bilingual Brussels. In 1993 it became a federation comprising the three regions. It is a member of the European Union.

Recent Developments

In 2005 Belgium celebrated two anniversaries—the 175th anniversary of independence from The Netherlands and the 25th anniversary of the forming of its federal system of government. That year controversy arose over a plan to split up the Brussels-Hal-Vilvoorde parliamentary constituency, the largest in Belgium. Under the plan Hal and Vilvoorde would be added to the existing Dutch-speaking constituency of Leuven, creating a purely Flemish bloc. A solution was reached whereby the issue would be addressed after the planned May 2007 general election. In 2006 the country had a balanced budget for the seventh straight year, the GDP grew by 2.9%, and the national debt fell below 90% of the GDP (still one of the highest in the European Union but down from 137% in 1993), though unemployment stood at 8.2%. In April 2006 legislation was passed that allowed same-sex couples to adopt children.

Internet resources: <www.visitbelgium.com>.

Belize

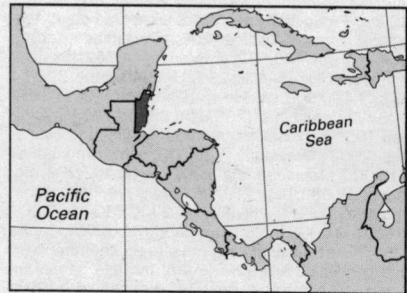

Official name: Belize. **Form of government:** constitutional monarchy with two legislative houses (Senate [8, excluding president of the Senate]; House of Representatives [29, excluding speaker of the House of Representatives]). **Chief of state:** Queen Elizabeth II, represented by Governor-General Sir Colville Young (from 1993). **Head of government:** Prime Minister Said Musa (from 1998). **Capital:** Belmopan. **Official language:** English. **Official religion:** none. **Monetary unit:** 1 Belize dollar (BZ$) = 100 cents; valuation (1 Jul 2007) US$1 = BZ$1.99 (pegged to the US dollar).

Demography

Area: 8,867 sq mi, 22,965 sq km (includes offshore cays totaling 266 sq mi (689 sq km). **Population** (2006): 301,000. **Density** (2006): persons per sq mi 33.9, persons per sq km 13.1. **Urban** (2004): 49.9%. **Sex distribution** (2004): male 50.50%; female 49.50%. **Age breakdown** (2004): under 15, 40.8%; 15–29, 27.7%; 30–44, 17.4%; 45–59, 8.1%; 60–74, 4.3%; 75 and over, 1.7%. **Ethnic composition** (2000): mestizo (Spanish-Indian) 48.7%; Creole (predominantly black) 24.9%; Mayan Indian 10.6%; Garifuna (black-Carib Indian) 6.1%; white 4.3%; East Indian 3.0%; other or not stated 2.4%. **Religious affiliation** (2000): Roman Catholic 49.6%; Protestant 31.8%, of which Pentecostal 7.4%, Anglican 5.3%, Seventh-day Adventist 5.2%, Mennonite 4.1%; other Christian 1.9%; nonreligious 9.4%; other 7.3%. **Major cities** (2004): Belize City 59,400; San Ignacio/Santa Elena 16,100; Orange Walk 15,000; Belmopan 12,300; Dangriga 10,400. **Location:** Central America, bordering Mexico, the Caribbean Sea, and Guatemala.

Vital statistics

Birth rate per 1,000 population (2002): 27.7 (world avg. 21.3); (1997) legitimate 40.3%; illegitimate 59.7%. **Death rate** per 1,000 population (2002): 4.8 (world avg. 9.1). **Natural increase rate** per 1,000 population (2002): 22.9 (world avg. 12.2). **Total fertility rate** (avg. births per childbearing woman; 2003): 3.9. **Marriage rate** per 1,000 population (2002): 6.1. **Divorce rate** per 1,000 population (2002): 0.2. **Life expectancy** at birth (2003): male 65.2 years; female 69.6 years.

National economy

Budget (2002–03). *Revenue:* BZ$431,300,000 (tax revenue 83.4%, of which import duties 38.3%, general sales tax 26.3%, income tax 18.3%; nontax revenue 12.2%; grants 4.4%). *Expenditures:* BZ$600,900,000 (current expenditure 60.2%; capital expenditure 39.8%). **Production** (metric tons except as noted). *Agriculture, forestry, fishing* (2002): sugarcane 1,150,-656, oranges 168,652, grapefruits 44,762; livestock (number of live animals; 2002) 56,949 cattle, 22,874 pigs, 1,400,000 chickens; roundwood (2002) 187,-600 cu m; fish catch (2001) 18,830, of which marine fish 10,155, crustaceans 4,983. *Mining and quarrying* (2002): limestone 700,000; sand and gravel 415,000. *Manufacturing* (2002): sugar 107,209; molasses 35,633; flour 26,078. *Energy production (consumption):* electricity (kW-hr; 2000) 137,000,000 (162,000,000); petroleum products (2000) none (258,000). **Household income and expenditure.** Average household size (2000) 4.5; average annual income of employed head of household (1993) BZ$6,450 (estimated); expenditure (1990): food, beverages, and tobacco 34.0%, transportation 13.7%, energy and water 9.1%, housing 9.0%, clothing and footwear 8.8%, household furnishings 8.0%. **Tourism** (2002): receipts from visitors US$132,800,000; expenditures by nationals abroad US$43,000,000. **Land use** as % of total land area (2000): in temporary crops 2.8%, in permanent crops 1.7%, in pasture 2.2%; overall forest area 59.1%. **Population economically active** (2002): total 94,172; activity rate of total population 35.5% (participation rates: ages 14 and over 58.4%; female [2001] 29.6%; unemployed 10.0%). **Gross national product** (2002): US$807,-000,000 (US$3,190 per capita). **Public debt** (external, outstanding; 2002): US$789,600,000.

Foreign trade

Imports (2002): BZ$995,900,000 (machinery and transport equipment 19.4%; mineral fuels and lubricants 13.0%; manufactured goods 11.9%; food 10.0%; chemicals and chemical products 7.9%). *Major import sources:* US 43.3%; EU 7.9%; Mexico 7.8%; Canada 3.1%; Caricom 3.0%. **Exports** (2002): BZ$619,400,000 (domestic exports 51.6%, of which seafood products [significantly shrimp] 11.8%, raw sugar 11.3%, citrus concentrate 9.3%, bananas 7.0%, garments 5.1%; reexports [principally to Mexico] 48.4%). *Major export destinations* (domestic exports only): US 49.0%; UK 22.7%; other EU 8.6%; Caricom 6.5%.

Transport and communications

Transport. *Roads* (1999): total length 2,872 km (paved 18%). *Vehicles* (1998): passenger cars 9,929; trucks and buses 11,755. *Air transport* (2001; Belize international airport only): passenger arrivals 256,564, passenger departures 240,900; cargo loaded 186 metric tons, cargo unloaded 1,272 metric tons. Airports (1997) with scheduled flights 9. **Communications,** in total units (units per 1,000 persons). Radios (1997): 133,000 (571); televisions (1998): 42,000 (183); telephone main lines (2003): 33,300 (113); cellular telephone subscribers (2003): 60,400 (205); personal computers (2002): 35,000 (138); Internet users (2002): 30,000 (109).

Education and health

Educational attainment (2000). Percentage of population age 25 and over having: no formal schooling 36.6%; primary education 40.9%; secondary 11.7%; postsecondary/advanced vocational 6.4%; university 3.8%; other/unknown 0.6%. **Literacy** (2001): total population age 14 and over literate 93.4%; males 93.6%; females 93.3%. **Health** (1998): physicians 155 (1 per 1,558 persons); hospital beds 554 (1 per 435 persons); infant mortality rate per 1,000 live births (2003) 27.1. **Food** (2001): daily per capita caloric intake 2,885 (vegetable products 79%, animal products 21%); 128% of FAO recommended minimum.

Military

Total active duty personnel (2003): 1,050 (army 100%; British army 30. **Military expenditure as percentage of GNP** (1999): 1.6% (world 2.4%); per capita expenditure US$47.

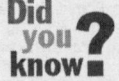

Did you know? The Maya Mountains form a plateau in southern Belize. The range's highest point is Victoria Peak, which rises to 3,681 ft. (1,122 m) in a spur of the Maya range.

1 metric ton = about 1.1 short tons;   1 kilometer = 0.6 mi (statute);   1 metric ton-km cargo = about 0.68 short ton-mi cargo;   c.i.f.: cost, insurance, and freight;   f.o.b.: free on board

Background

The area was inhabited by the Maya c. 300 BC–AD 900; the ruins of their ceremonial centers, including Caracol and Xunantunich, can still be seen. The Spanish claimed sovereignty from the 16th century but never tried to settle Belize, though they regarded as interlopers the British who did. British logwood cutters arrived in the mid-17th century; Spanish opposition was finally overcome in 1798. When settlers began to penetrate the interior they met with Indian resistance. In 1871 British Honduras became a crown colony, but an unfulfilled provision of an 1859 British-Guatemalan treaty led Guatemala to claim the territory. The situation had not been resolved when Belize was granted its independence in 1981. A British force, stationed there to ensure the new nation's security, was withdrawn after Guatemala officially recognized the territory's independence in 1991.

Recent Developments

Public debt, the rising price of fuel, and dropping world prices for sugar and bananas, two major exports for Belize, were major concerns. In April 2005 labor unions mounted unprecedented strikes against failures of the government to maintain transparency in financial matters. A Belizean company discovered petroleum in 2006 and began exporting it to the US.

Internet resources: <www.belize.gov.bz>.

Benin

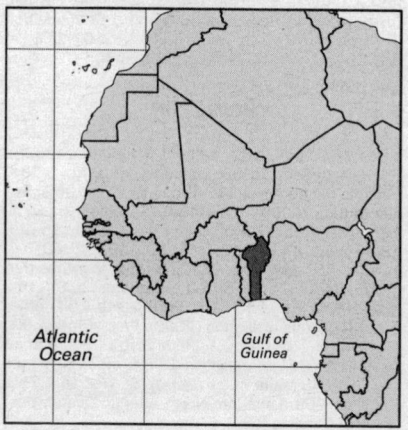

Atlantic Ocean

Gulf of Guinea

Official name: République du Bénin (Republic of Benin). **Form of government:** multiparty republic with one legislative house (National Assembly [83]). **Head of state and government:** President Yayi Boni (from 2006). **Capital:** Porto-Novo (official capital and seat of legislature; administrative seat in Cotonou). **Official language:** French. **Official religion:** none. **Monetary unit:** 1 CFA franc (CFAF) = 100 centimes; valuation (1 Jul 2007) US$1 = CFAF 485.18 (formerly pegged to the French franc and since 1 Jan 2002 to the euro at €1 = CFAF 655.96).

Demography

Area: 43,483 sq mi, 112,622 sq km. **Population** (2006): 7,687,000. **Density** (2006): persons per sq mi 176.8, persons per sq km 68.3. **Urban** (2002): 43.0%. **Sex distribution** (2003): male 49.36%; female 50.64%. **Age breakdown** (2003): under 15, 47.1%; 15–29, 27.7%; 30–44, 14.5%; 45–59, 7.0%; 60–74, 3.1%; 75 and over, 0.6%. **Ethnic composition** (1992): Fon 39.7%; Yoruba (Nago) 12.1%; Adjara 11.1%; Bariba 8.6%; Aizo 8.6%; Somba (Otomary) 6.6%; Fulani 5.6%; other 7.7%. **Religious affiliation** (1992): Christian 35.4%, of which Roman Catholic 25.9%, Protestant 9.5%; traditional beliefs, including voodoo 35.0%; Muslim 20.6%; other 9.0%. **Major cities** (2004): Cotonou 818,100; Porto-Novo 234,300; Parakou 227,900; Djoúgou 206,500; Abomey 126,800. **Location:** western Africa, bordering Burkina Faso, Niger, Nigeria, the Atlantic Ocean, and Togo.

Vital statistics

Birth rate per 1,000 population (2003): 43.2 (world avg. 21.3). **Death rate** per 1,000 population (2003): 13.7 (world avg. 9.1). **Natural increase rate** per 1,000 population (2003): 29.5 (world avg. 12.2). **Total fertility rate** (avg. births per childbearing woman; 2003): 6.0. **Life expectancy** at birth (2003): male 50.4 years; female 51.8 years.

National economy

Budget (2002). *Revenue:* CFAF 300,200,000,000 (tax revenue 80.5%, of which tax on international trade 44.3%, income tax 19.8%, sales tax 16.3%; nontax revenue 12.8%; grants 6.7%). *Expenditures:* CFAF 352,800,000,000 (current expenditures 61.6%, of which salaries 22.9%, pensions and other transfers 17.6%, interest on debt 4.3%; development expenditure 38.4%). **Production** (metric tons except as noted). *Agriculture, forestry, fishing* (2002): cassava 2,452,050, yams 1,785,000, corn (maize) 622,136; livestock (number of live animals; 2002) 1,550,000 cattle, 1,270,000 goats, 10,000,000 chickens; roundwood (2002) 6,297,969 cu m; fish catch (2001) 38,415. *Mining* (2002): gold 20 kg. *Manufacturing* (value added in $'000,000; 1999): food products 74; textiles 42; beverages 36. *Energy production (consumption):* electricity (kW-hr; 2001) 55,888,000 (413,587,000); crude petroleum (barrels; 2001) 365,000 (negligible); petroleum products (2001) none (150,000). **Gross national product** (2003): $2,990,000,000 ($440 per capita). **Public debt** (external, outstanding; 2002): $1,690,000,000. **Population economically active** (1997): total 2,608,000; activity rate of total population 44.2% (participation rates: ages 15–64, 84.3%; female 48.3%). **Households.** Average household size (2000) 6.1. **Land use** as % of total land area (2000): in temporary crops 17.6%, in permanent crops 2.4%, in pasture 5.0%; overall forest area 24.0%. **Tourism** (2002): receipts from visitors $60,000,000; expenditures by nationals abroad $7,000,000.

Foreign trade

Imports (2002-f.o.b. in balance of trade and commodities and c.i.f. in trading partners): CFAF 389,800,000,000 (food products 22.8%; petroleum products 22.4%; machinery and transport equipment 18.0%). *Major import sources* (2001): France c. 23%;

China c. 8%; free-trade zones c. 6%; Côte d'Ivoire c. 5%; Ghana c. 5%; Nigeria c. 5%. **Exports** (2002): CFAF 261,400,000,000 (domestic exports 60.2%, of which cotton yarn 33.3%; reexports 39.8%). *Major export destinations* (2001): India c. 31%; Brazil c. 6%; Indonesia c. 6%; Ghana c. 6%; Nigeria c. 5%.

Transport and communications

Transport. *Railroads* (2000): length 578 km; passenger-km 156,600,000; metric ton-km cargo 153,200,-000. *Roads* (1999): total length 6,787 km (paved 20.0%). *Vehicles* (1996): passenger cars 37,772; trucks and buses 8,058. *Air transport:* Air Afrique, an airline jointly owned by 11 African countries (including Benin) was declared bankrupt in February 2002; airports (2002) with scheduled flights 1. **Communications,** in total units (units per 1,000 persons). Daily newspaper circulation (2000): 12,900 (2); radios (2000): 2,820,000 (439); televisions (2000): 289,-000 (45); telephone main lines (2003): 66,500 (9.5); cellular telephone subscribers (2003): 236,200 (34); personal computers (2003): 26,000 (3.7); Internet users (2003): 70,000 (10.0).

Education and health

Educational attainment (1992). Percentage of population age 25 and over having: no formal schooling 78.5%; primary education 10.8%; some secondary 8.2%; secondary 1.2%; postsecondary 1.3%. *Literacy* (1998): total percentage of population age 15 and over literate 37.7%; males literate 53.8%; females literate 22.6%. **Health:** physicians (1995) 313 (1 per 17,520 persons); hospital beds (1994) 1,230 (1 per 4,342 persons); infant mortality rate per 1,000 live births (2003) 86.7. **Food** (2001): daily per capita caloric intake 2,455 (vegetable products 96%, animal products 4%); 107% of FAO recommended minimum.

Military

Total active duty personnel (2003): 4,550 (army 94.5%, navy 2.2%, air force 3.3%). **Military expenditure as percentage of GNP** (1999): 1.4% (world 2.4%); per capita expenditure $5.

Background

In southern Benin, the Dahomey, or Fon, established the Abomey kingdom in 1625. In the 18th century, the kingdom became known as Dahomey when it expanded to include Allada and Ouidah, where French forts had been established in the 17th century. In 1857 the French reestablished themselves in the area, and eventually fighting ensued. In 1894 Dahomey became a French protectorate; it was incorporated into the federation of French West Africa in 1904. It achieved independence in 1960. The area called Dahomey was renamed Benin in 1975. At the end of the 20th century, its chronically weak economy produced tension between laborers and the government.

Recent Developments

Despite predictions of healthy economic growth in Benin in 2005 and 2006, it remained one of the world's poorest countries. Assistance came in the form of the cancellation of $800 million of debt owed to the World Bank (equaling 63% of Benin's foreign debt) in June 2005. In February 2006 the US signed an agreement offering $307 million in antipoverty aid.

Internet resources:
<www.siftthru.com/benintrav.htm>.

Bermuda

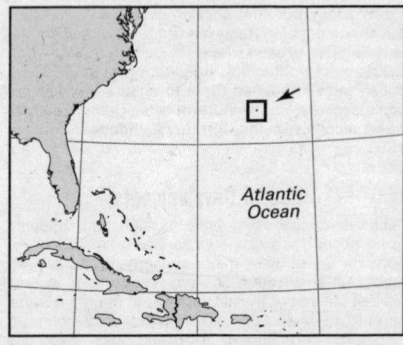

Official name: Bermuda. **Political status:** colony (UK) with two legislative houses (Senate [11]; House of Assembly [36]). **Chief of state:** Queen Elizabeth II, represented by Governor Sir John Vereker (from 2002). **Head of government:** Premier Ewart Brown (from 2006). **Capital:** Hamilton. **Official language:** English. **Official religion:** none. **Monetary unit:** 1 Bermuda dollar (Bd$) = 100 cents; valuation (1 Jul 2007) US$1 = Bd$1.00.

Demography

Area: 20.5 sq mi, 53.1 sq km (includes 0.4 sq mi [1.1 sq km] of uninhabited islands). **Population** (2006): 65,500. **Density** (2006): persons per sq mi 3,195, persons per sq km 1,234. **Urban** (2003): 100%. **Sex distribution** (2000): male 48.03%; female 51.97%. **Age breakdown** (2000): under 15, 19.1%; 15–29, 18.4%; 30–44, 27.9%; 45–59, 19.6%; 60–74, 10.9%; 75 and over, 4.1%. **Ethnic composition** (2000): black 50.4%; British expatriates 29.0%; mulatto 10.0%; US white 6.0%; Portuguese 4.5%; other 0.1%. **Religious affiliation** (2000): Protestant 64.3%, of which Anglican 22.6%, Methodist 14.9%; Roman Catholic 14.9%; nonreligious 13.8%; other 6.0%; unknown 1.0%. **Major cities** (2000): St. George 1,752; Hamilton 969. **Location:** North Atlantic Ocean, east of North Carolina (US).

Vital statistics

Birth rate per 1,000 population (2001): 13.2 (world avg. 21.3); legitimate 62.3%. **Death rate** per 1,000 population (2001): 7.0 (world avg. 9.1). **Natural increase rate** per 1,000 population (2001): 6.2 (world avg. 12.2). **Total fertility rate** (avg. births per childbearing woman; 2000): 1.8. **Marriage rate** per 1,000

---

1 metric ton = about 1.1 short tons;   1 kilometer = 0.6 mi (statute);   1 metric ton-km cargo = about 0.68 short ton-mi cargo;   c.i.f.: cost, insurance, and freight;   f.o.b.: free on board

population (2001): 14.6. **Divorce rate** per 1,000 population (2000): 3.5. **Life expectancy** at birth (2000): male 74.9 years; female 78.9 years.

National economy

Budget (2002). *Revenue:* Bd$631,100,000 (customs duty 30.1%; payroll tax 27.1%; tax on international companies 7.2%; land tax 6.3%; stamp duties 4.5%; other 24.8%). *Expenditures:* Bd$607,500,000 (current expenditure 89.4%, of which wages 41.9%, goods and services 25.6%, grants and contributions 21.9%; development expenditure 10.6%). **Production** (value in Bd$'000 except as noted). *Agriculture, forestry, fishing* (1999): vegetables 3,000, milk 1,657, fruits 900; livestock (number of live animals; 2002) 900 horses, 600 cattle, 45,000 chickens; fish catch (metric tons; 2001) 315, of which crustaceans and mollusks 25. *Mining and quarrying:* crushed stone for local use. *Manufacturing:* industries include pharmaceuticals, cosmetics, and electronics. *Energy production (consumption):* electricity (kW-hr; 2003) 664,000,000 (664,000,000); petroleum products (metric tons; 2000) none (151,000). **Tourism:** receipts from visitors (2003) US$342,-000,000; expenditures by nationals abroad (1997) US$148,000,000. **Population economically active** (2002): total 37,815; activity rate of total population 59.1% (participation rates [2000]: ages 15–64, 88.1%; female 49.0%; unemployed 2.9%). **Gross domestic product** (at current market prices; 2000–01): US$3,023,000,000 (US$48,580 per capita). **Household income and expenditure.** Average household size (2000) 2.4; average annual income per household (2001) Bd$72,500; sources of income (1993): wages and salaries 65.3%, imputed income from owner occupancy 10.6%, self-employment 9.0%, net rental income 4.8%, other 10.3%; expenditure (2002): housing 26.1%, food and nonalcoholic beverages 16.0%, household furnishings 15.0%, clothing and footwear 4.2%, other goods and services 38.7%.

Foreign trade

Imports (2002): Bd$746,000,000 (food, beverages, and tobacco 20.2%; machinery 16.5%; chemicals and chemical products 13.9%; mineral fuels 7.8%; transport equipment 6.0%). *Major import sources:* US 76%; Canada 5%; UK 5%; Caribbean countries (mostly Netherlands Antilles) 3%. **Exports** (2002): Bd$57,000,000 (nearly all reexports; diamond market was established in 1990s). *Major export destinations* (2002): mostly US, UK, Norway, and Spain.

Transport and communications

Transport. *Roads* (2000): total length 225 km (paved 100%). *Vehicles* (2002): passenger cars 21,594; trucks and buses 3,768. *Air transport* (2001): passenger arrivals 826,000, passenger departures 826,000; cargo loaded and unloaded 4,200 metric tons; airports (2002) with scheduled flights 1. **Communications,** in total units (units per 1,000 persons). Daily newspaper circulation (1996): 17,000 (277); radios (1997): 82,000 (1,328); televisions (1997): 66,000 (1,069); telephone main lines (2001): 56,300 (872); cellular telephone subscribers (2001): 13,300 (206); personal computers (2001): 32,000 (495); Internet users (2001): 30,000 (464).

Education and health

Educational attainment (2000). Percentage of total population age 16 and over having: no formal schooling 0.4%; primary education 7.0%; secondary 39.3%; postsecondary technical 25.7%; higher 26.8%; not stated 0.8%. **Literacy** (1997): total population age 15 and over literate 98%. **Health** (2002): physicians 122 (1 per 524 persons); hospital beds 226 (1 per 283 persons); infant mortality rate per 1,000 live births (2003) 9.1. **Food** (2001): daily per capita caloric intake 2,904 (vegetable products 74%, animal products 26%); 115% of FAO recommended minimum.

Military

Total active duty personnel (2003): 700; part-time defense force assists police and is drawn from Bermudian conscripts.

Background

The Bermuda archipelago was named for Juan de Bermúdez, who may have visited the islands in 1503. Colonized by the English in 1612, Bermuda became a crown colony in 1684 and a British overseas territory in 2002. Its economy is based on tourism and international finance; its per capita gross national product is among the world's highest.

Recent Developments

Although most marked the date of its sighting by Bermúdez as 1503, Bermuda celebrated its 500th anniversary in 2005. Polls over the years showed that about two-thirds of Bermudans did not favor changing the island's status from British overseas territory to independent republic, yet the question has continued to be raised periodically.

Internet resources: <www.bermudatourism.org>.

Bhutan

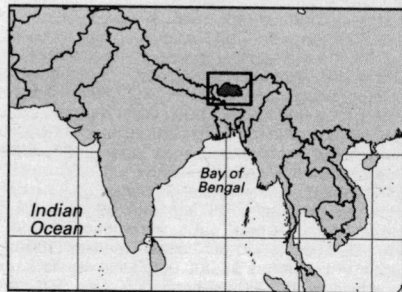

Official name: Druk-Yul (Kingdom of Bhutan). **Form of government:** de facto constitutional monarchy with one legislative house (National Assembly [152 seats, including 36 nonelective seats representing the king and religious groups]). **Chief of state:** King Jigme Khesar Namgyal Wangchuk (from 2006). A constitution commissioned by the monarch is to become effective in 2005; reforms in July 1998 curtailed the powers of the monarchy. **Head of government:** Prime Minister Lyonpo Khandu Wangchuk (from 2006). **Capital:**

Thimphu. **Official language:** Dzongkha (a Tibetan dialect). **Official religion:** Mahayana Buddhism. **Monetary unit:** 1 ngultrum (Nu) = 100 chetrum; valuation (1 Jul 2007) US$1 = Nu 44.42; the Indian rupee is also accepted legal tender.

Demography

Area: 14,824 sq mi, 38,394 sq km. **Population** (2006): 790,000. **Density** (2006): persons per sq mi 53.3, persons per sq km 20.6. **Urban** (2000): 21.0%. **Sex distribution** (2003): male 50.50%; female 49.50%. **Age breakdown** (2003): under 15, 42.1%; 15–29, 23.7%; 30–44, 16.4%; 45–59, 10.6%; 60–74, 5.9%; 75 and over, 1.3%. **Ethnic composition** (1993): Bhutia (Ngalops) 50.0%; Nepalese (Gurung) 35.0%; Sharchops 15.0%. **Religious affiliation** (2000): Buddhist 74.0%; Hindu 20.5%; other 5.5%. **Major cities** (2002): Thimphu 45,000; Phuntsholing (1997) 45,000. **Location:** southern Asia, bordering China and India.

Vital statistics

Birth rate per 1,000 population (2002): 34.9 (world avg. 21.3). **Death rate** per 1,000 population (2002): 8.7 (world avg. 9.1). **Natural increase rate** per 1,000 population (2002): 26.2 (world avg. 12.2). **Total fertility rate** (avg. births per childbearing woman; 2003): 4.9. **Life expectancy** at birth (2002): male 62.0 years; female 64.0 years.

National economy

Budget (2003–04). *Revenue:* Nu 11,154,500,000 (domestic revenue 46.8%, grants 44.6%, other 8.6%). *Expenditures:* Nu 11,537,700,000 (capital expenditures 54.4%, current expenditures 43.3%, repayments 2.3%). **Public debt** (external, outstanding; 2002): $376,900,000. **Production** (metric tons except as noted). *Agriculture, forestry, fishing* (2002): corn (maize) 48,500, rice 44,300, oranges 30,000; livestock (number of live animals) 355,400 cattle, 41,400 pigs, 31,300 goats; roundwood (2002) 4,482,000 cu m; fish catch (2001) 330. *Mining and quarrying* (2001): limestone 434,900; dolomite 283,700; gypsum 87,000. *Manufacturing* (value in Nu '000,000; 2000): cement 696.7; chemical products 474.6; alcoholic beverages 255.0. *Energy production (consumption):* electricity (kW-hr; 2002) 2,059,400,000 (489,260,000); coal (2000) 50,000 (66,000); petroleum products (2000) none (47,000). **Households.** Average household size (2000) 5.5. **Population economically active** (1999): total 358,950; activity rate of total population 52.9% (participation rates: ages 15 and over 69.6%; unemployed 1.4%). **Gross national product** (2003): $578,000,000 ($660 per capita). **Tourism** (2002): receipts from visitors $8,000,000. **Land use** as % of total land area (2000): in temporary crops 3.0%, in permanent crops 0.4%, in pasture 8.8%; overall forest area 64.2%.

Foreign trade

Imports (2001-c.i.f.): $188,300,000 (1999; machinery and transport equipment 41.7%, of which computers and related goods 11.0%, road vehicles 10.5%; food 13.9%, of which cereals 7.6%; refined petroleum 7.2%). *Major import sources* (2001): India 81.1%; Japan 7.2%; Thailand 3.4%; Singapore 2.5%. **Exports** (2001-f.o.b.): $97,700,000 (electricity 48.1%, calcium carbide 13.3%, ferro-silicon 12.6%, cement 9.6%). *Major export destinations* (2001): India 94.1%; Bangladesh 4.5%; Nepal 0.8%.

Transport and communications

Transport. *Roads* (2003): total length 4,007 km (paved 60%). *Vehicles* (2003): passenger cars 10,574; trucks and buses 3,852. *Air transport* (1999): passenger-km 49,000,000; metric ton-km cargo 4,000,000; airports (2002) with scheduled flights 1. **Communications,** in total units (units per 1,000 persons). Radios (1997): 37,000 (19); televisions (1999): 13,000 (20); telephone main lines (2002): 20,168 (33); personal computers (2002): 10,000 (15); Internet users (2002): 17,980 (27).

Education and health

Literacy (1995): total population age 15 and over literate 42.2%; males literate 56.2%; females literate 28.1%. **Health** (2002): physicians 122 (1 per 6,019 persons); hospital beds 1,023 (1 per 696 persons); infant mortality rate per 1,000 live births 55.0.

Military

Total active duty personnel (2002): about 6,000 (army 100%).

Background

Bhutan's mountains and forests long made it inaccessible to the outside world, and its feudal rulers banned foreigners until well into the 20th century. It nevertheless became the object of foreign invasions; in 1865 it came under British influence, and in 1910 it agreed to be guided by Britain in its foreign affairs. It later became oriented toward British-ruled India, though much of its trade was with Tibet. India took over Britain's role in 1949, and Communist China's 1950 occupation of neighboring Tibet further strengthened Bhutan's ties with India. The apparent Chinese threat made Bhutan's rulers aware of the need to modernize, and it embarked on a program to build roads and hospitals and to create a system of secular education.

Recent Developments

In December 2006 King Jigme Singye Wangchuk, ruler of Bhutan for 34 years, abdicated in favor of his son Crown Prince Jigme Khesar Namgyal Wangchuk. The new king was committed to transforming one of the world's few remaining absolute monarchies into a two-party democracy by 2008, although no referendum had been held to ratify a draft constitution that would legislate the change. More than 100,000 Bhutanese refugees continued to languish in camps in Nepal. In 2005 Bhutan banned smoking in public places and the broadcast of foreign television channels.

Internet resources: <www.kingdomofbhutan.com>.

---

1 metric ton = about 1.1 short tons;   1 kilometer = 0.6 mi (statute);   1 metric ton-km cargo = about 0.68 short ton-mi cargo;   c.i.f.: cost, insurance, and freight;   f.o.b.: free on board

Bolivia

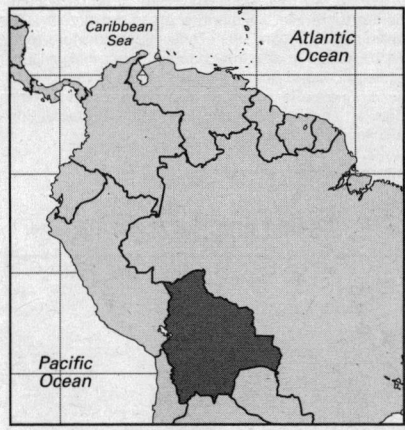

Official name: República de Bolivia (Republic of Bolivia). **Form of government:** unitary multiparty republic with two legislative houses (Chamber of Senators [27]; Chamber of Deputies [130]). **Head of state and government:** President Evo Morales (from 2006). **Capitals:** La Paz (administrative); Sucre (judicial). **Official languages:** Spanish, Aymara, Quechua. **Official religion:** Roman Catholicism. **Monetary unit:** 1 boliviano (Bs) = 100 centavos; valuation (1 Jul 2007) US$1 = Bs 8.01.

Demography

Area: 424,164 sq mi, 1,098,581 sq km. **Population** (2006): 9,354,000. **Density** (2006): persons per sq mi 22.1, persons per sq km 8.5. **Urban** (2001): 62.4%. **Sex distribution** (2003): male 49.81%; female 50.19%. **Age breakdown** (2001): under 15, 38.6%; 15–29, 27.4%; 30–44, 17.0%; 45–59, 10.0%; 60–74, 5.2%; 75 and over, 1.8%. **Ethnic composition** (2000): Amerindian 65%, of which Quechua 40%, Aymara 24%; mestizo 27%; white 8%, of which German 3%. **Religious affiliation** (1995): Roman Catholic 88.5%; Protestant 9.0%; other 2.5%. **Major cities** (2001): Santa Cruz 1,116,059; La Paz 789,585 (urban agglomeration [2003] 1,477,000); El Alto 647,350 (within La Paz agglomeration); Cochabamba 516,683; Oruro 201,230. **Location:** central South America, bordering Brazil, Paraguay, Argentina, Chile, and Peru.

Vital statistics

Birth rate per 1,000 population (2003): 25.5 (world avg. 21.3). **Death rate** per 1,000 population (2003): 7.9 (world avg. 9.1). **Natural increase rate** per 1,000 population (2003): 17.6 (world avg. 12.2). **Total fertility rate** (avg. births per childbearing woman; 2003): 3.2. **Life expectancy** at birth (2003): male 62.2 years; female 67.4 years.

National economy

Budget (2002). *Revenue:* Bs 13,558,000,000 (tax revenue 74.3%, of which value-added taxes 25.2%, taxes on hydrocarbons 19.3%, import duties 12.7%;

nontax revenue 11.3%; foreign grants 9.4%; other 5.0%). *Expenditures:* Bs 18,857,000,000 (current expenditure 75.1%; capital expenditure 24.9%). **Production** (metric tons except as noted). *Agriculture, forestry, fishing* (2002): sugarcane 4,320,784, soybeans 1,166,660, potatoes 944,216; livestock (number of live animals) 8,901,631 sheep, 6,576,277 cattle, 2,850,547 pigs; roundwood (2002) 10,237,753 cu m; fish catch (2001) 6,260. *Mining and quarrying* (pure metal; 2003): zinc 145,490; tin 16,386; lead 9,353. *Manufacturing* (value added in $'000,000; 1998): petroleum products 399; food products 222; beverages 141. *Energy production (consumption):* electricity (kW-hr; 2003) 4,318,000,000 (2,905,000,000); crude petroleum (barrels; 2000) 11,877,000 (11,877,000); petroleum products (2000) 1,345,000 (1,641,000); natural gas (cu m; 2000) 3,904,000,000 (1,815,000,000). **Population economically active** (2002): total 3,823,500; activity rate of total population 44.5% (participation rates: ages 10 and over 78.2%; female 45.9%; unemployed [2000] 7.4%). **Tourism:** receipts (2002) $104,000,000; expenditures (2001) $118,000,000. **Gross national product** (at current market prices; 2003): $7,985,000,000 ($890 per capita). **Public debt** (external, outstanding; 2002): $3,378,000,000. **Household income and expenditure.** Average household size (2000): 4.0; expenditure (1988): food 35.5%, transportation and communications 17.7%, housing 14.8%, household durable goods 7.3%, clothing and footwear 5.1%, beverages and tobacco 4.5%, recreation 2.7%, health 2.1%. **Land use** as % of total land area (2000): in temporary crops 2.7%, in permanent crops 0.2%, in pasture 31.2%; overall forest area 48.9%.

Foreign trade

Imports (2001-f.o.b. in balance of trade and c.i.f. for commodities and trading partners): $1,706,800,000 (machinery and transport equipment 27.6%; chemicals and chemical products 17.0%; food 11.4%; refined petroleum 6.2%; iron and steel 5.8%). *Major import sources:* Argentina 16.9%; US 16.6%; Brazil 16.2%; Chile 8.4%; Peru 6.3%. **Exports** (2001): $1,351,200,000 (food 20.7%, of which soybean oilcake 13.7%; natural gas 17.9%; zinc ores and concentrates 8.9%; soybean oil 5.5%; gold 3.7%). *Major export destinations:* Brazil 22.1%; Colombia 14.1%; US 13.9%; Switzerland 13.0%; Venezuela 7.3%.

Transport and communications

Transport. *Railroads* (2000): route length 3,608 km; (1997) passenger-km 224,900,000; metric ton-km cargo 838,900,000. *Roads* (2001): total length 53,259 km (paved 6%). *Vehicles* (2001): passenger cars 254,175; trucks and buses 194,510. *Air transport* (2003): passenger-km 1,704,000,000; metric ton-km cargo 24,348,000; airports (2000) with scheduled flights 14. **Communications,** in total units (units per 1,000 persons). Daily newspaper circulation (2000): 448,000 (65); radios (2000): 5,510,000 (676); televisions (2000): 970,000 (119); telephone main lines (2003): 600,100 (71); cellular telephone subscribers (2003): 1,401,500 (167); personal computers (2002): 190,000 (23); Internet users (2002): 270,000 (32).

Education and health

Educational attainment (1992). Percentage of population age 25 and over having: no formal schooling 23.3%; some primary 20.3%; primary education 21.7%; some secondary 9.0%; secondary 6.5%; some higher 5.0%; higher 4.8%; not specified 9.4%. **Literacy** (2001): total population age 15 and over literate 86.0%; males literate 92.3%; females literate 79.9%. **Health** (2002): physicians 2,987 (1 per 2,827 persons); hospital beds 11,921 (1 per 708 persons); infant mortality rate per 1,000 live births (2003) 56.1. **Food** (2001): daily per capita caloric intake 2,267 (vegetable products 84%, animal products 16%); 95% of FAO recommended minimum.

Military

Total active duty personnel (2003): 31,500 (army 79.4%, navy 11.1%, air force 9.5%). **Military expenditure as percentage of GNP** (1998): 1.8% (world 2.5%); per capita expenditure $18.

Did you know? Lake Titicaca, the world's highest lake navigable to large vessels, lies 12,500 ft (3,810 m) above sea level in the Andes Mountains of South America, astride the Peru-Bolivia border.

Background

The Bolivian highlands were the location of the advanced Tiwanaku culture in the 7th–11th centuries and, with its passing, became the home of the Aymara, an Indian group conquered by the Incas in the 15th century. The Incas were overrun by the invading Spanish under Francisco Pizarro in the 1530s. By 1600 Spain had established the cities of Charcas (now Sucre), La Paz, Santa Cruz, and what would become Cochabamba, and had begun to exploit the silver wealth of Potosí. Bolivia flourished in the 17th century, and for a time Potosí was the largest city in the Americas. By the end of the century, the mineral wealth had dried up. Talk of independence began as early as 1809, but not until 1825 were Spanish forces finally defeated. Bolivia shrank in size when it lost Atacama province to Chile in 1884 at the end of the War of the Pacific and again in 1939 when it lost most of Gran Chaco to Paraguay. One of South America's poorest countries, it was plagued by governmental instability for much of the 20th century. By the 1990s Bolivia had become one of the world's largest producers of coca, from which cocaine is derived. The government subsequently instituted a largely successful program to eradicate the crop, although such efforts were resisted by the many poor farmers who depended on coca.

Recent Developments

Protests against the government's stewardship over Bolivia's huge natural-gas reserves took place, and in May 2005 a law was passed increasing taxes on gas firms. In January 2006 Evo Morales, a former coca grower and protest leader, was inaugurated, becoming Bolivia's first Indian president. His administration passed a law that required foreign oil and gas companies to transfer a majority share to the state-owned petroleum company. Venezuela provided more than $165 million in antidrug, humanitarian, and military assistance, and Bolivia's coca growers were aided by Venezuela's offer to buy all legal products made from Bolivian coca at the same time that US eradication aid was being reduced.

Internet resources: <www.boliviabiz.com>.

Bosnia and Herzegovina

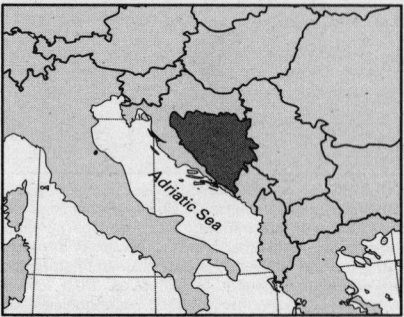

Official name: Bosna i Hercegovina (Bosnia and Herzegovina). **Form of government:** federal multiparty republic with bicameral legislature (House of Peoples [15; all seats are nonelective]; House of Representatives [42]). **Chiefs of state:** Tripartite presidency with 8-month-long rotating chairmanship (final authority rests with International High Representative Christian Schwarz-Schilling (from 2006). **Head of government:** Prime Minister Nikola Spiric (chairman of Council of Ministers; from 2007). **Capital:** Sarajevo. **Official language:** Bosnian (Serbo-Croatian). **Official religion:** none. **Monetary unit:** 1 marka (KM) = 100 fenning; valuation (1 Jul 2007) US$1 = KM 1.44 (pegged to the euro from 1 Jan 2002; the euro also circulates as semiofficial legal tender).

Demography

Area: 19,772 sq mi, 51,209 sq km. **Population** (2006; excludes refugees in adjacent countries and western Europe): 3,860,000. **Density** (2006): persons per sq mi 195.2, persons per sq km 75.4. **Urban** (2002): 43.4%. **Sex distribution** (2002): male 48.80%; female 51.20%. **Age breakdown** (2002): under 15, 18.4%; 15–29, 21.8%; 30–44, 23.0%; 45–59, 18.5%; 60–74, 15.2%; 75 and over, 3.1%. **Ethnic composition** (1999): Bosniac 44.0%; Serb 31.0%; Croat 17.0%; other 8.0%. **Religious affiliation** (1999): Sunni Muslim 43.0%; Serbian Orthodox 30.0%; Roman Catholic 18.0%; other (mostly nonreligious) 9.0%. **Major cities** (2004): Sarajevo 428,600 (urban agglomeration 602,500); Banja Luka 170,000; Zenica 139,800; Tuzla 123,500; Mostar 94,100. **Location:** southeastern Europe, bordered by Croatia, Serbia and Montenegro, and the Adriatic Sea.

---

1 metric ton = about 1.1 short tons;   1 kilometer = 0.6 mi (statute);   1 metric ton-km cargo = about 0.68 short ton-mi cargo;   c.i.f.: cost, insurance, and freight;   f.o.b.: free on board

Vital statistics

Birth rate per 1,000 population (2002): 9.5 (world avg. 21.3); (2001) legitimate 89.4%. **Death rate** per 1,000 population (2002): 8.0 (world avg. 9.1). **Natural increase rate** per 1,000 population (2002): 1.5 (world avg. 12.2). **Total fertility rate** (avg. births per childbearing woman; 2002): 1.4. **Marriage rate** per 1,000 population (2002): 5.4. **Life expectancy** at birth (2001): male 64.6 years; female 70.2 years.

National economy

Budget (2001). *Revenue:* KM 1,653,100,000 (tax revenue 90.8%, nontax revenue 6.4%, grants 2.8%). *Expenditures:* KM 1,887,600,000 (wages and contributions 24.1%, transfers to households 22.6%, defense 15.4%). **Gross national product** (2003): $6,386,000,000 ($1,540 per capita). **Production** (metric tons except as noted). *Agriculture, forestry, fishing* (2002): corn (maize) 530,000, potatoes 310,000, wheat 297,000; livestock (number of live animals) 670,000 sheep, 440,000 cattle, 300,000 pigs; roundwood (2002) 4,226,000 cu m; fish catch (2001) 2,500. *Mining* (2001): iron ore (gross weight) 100,000; bauxite 75,000; kaolin 3,000. *Manufacturing* (2001): cement 300,000; crude steel 80,000; pig iron 60,000. *Energy production (consumption):* electricity (kW-hr; 2000) 10,429,000,000 (9,365,-000,000); hard coal (2000) 3,553,000 (3,553,000); lignite (2000) 5,330,000 (5,330,000); petroleum products (2000) none (842,000,000); natural gas (cu m; 2000) none (276,800,000). **Public debt** (external, outstanding; 2002): $2,282,000,000. **Population economically active** (2001): total 1,015,169; activity rate of total population 27.4% (participation rates: ages 15–64 [1991] 35.6%; female [1990] 37.7%; unemployed [2002] 42.7%). **Households.** Average household size (1991) 3.4; sources of income (1990): wages 53.2%, transfers 18.2%, self-employment 12.0%, other 16.6%. **Tourism** (2002): receipts from visitors $112,000,000; expenditures by nationals abroad $49,000,000. **Land use** as % of total land area (2000): in temporary crops 13.0%, in permanent crops 3.0%, in pasture 23.7%; overall forest area 44.6%.

Foreign trade

Imports (2003): KM 7,920,191,000. *Major import sources:* Croatia 17.3%; Germany 13.2%; Italy 9.6%; Slovenia 9.6%; Serbia and Montenegro 7.6%. **Exports** (2003): KM 2,349,189,000. *Major export destinations:* Croatia 17.9%; Germany 15.4%; Serbia and Montenegro 15.3%; Italy 13.4%; Slovenia 9.7%.

Transport and communications

Transport. *Railroads* (2001): length 1,031 km; passenger-km 38,740,000; metric ton-km cargo 239,138,000. *Roads* (2001): total length 21,846 km (paved 64%). *Vehicles* (1996): passenger cars 96,182; trucks and buses 10,919. *Air transport* (2000): passenger-km 48,000,000; airports (2000) with scheduled flights 1. **Communications,** in total units (units per 1,000 persons). Daily newspaper circulation (2000): 563,000 (152); radios (2000): 900,000 (243); televisions (2000): 411,000 (111); telephone main lines (2003): 938,000 (244); cellular telephone subscribers (2003): 1,050,000 (274); Internet users (2002): 100,000 (24).

Health

Health: physicians (2000) 5,293 (1 per 714 persons); hospital beds (1999) 13,783 (1 per 270 persons); infant mortality rate per 1,000 live births (2002) 23.5. **Food** (2001): daily per capita caloric intake 2,845 (vegetable products 85%, animal products 15%); 112% of FAO recommended minimum.

Military

Total active duty personnel: EU peacekeeping troops (also includes Canadian and Turkish troops; 2004) 7,000. **Military expenditure as percentage of GNP** (1999): 4.5% (world 2.4%); per capita expenditure $75.

Did you know? Slivovitz, distilled from plums, particularly those from the Posavina region in the far north of Bosnia and Herzegovina, is the liquor of choice for men here and in many other Balkan countries.

Background

Habitation long predates the era of Roman rule, when much of the country was included in the province of Dalmatia. Slav settlement began in the 6th century AD. For the next several centuries, parts of the region fell under the rule of Serbs, Croats, Hungarians, Venetians, and Byzantines. The Ottoman Turks invaded Bosnia in the 14th century, and after many battles it became a Turkish province in 1463. Herzegovina, then known as Hum, was taken in 1482. In the 16th–17th century the area was an important Turkish outpost, constantly at war with the Habsburgs and Venice. During this period much of the native population converted to Islam. At the Congress of Berlin after the Russo-Turkish War of 1877–78, Bosnia and Herzegovina was assigned to Austria-Hungary and annexed in 1908. Growing Serb nationalism resulted in the 1914 assassination of the Austrian Archduke Francis Ferdinand at Sarajevo by a Bosnian Serb, an event that precipitated World War I. After the war the area was annexed to Serbia. Following World War II the twin territory became a republic of communist Yugoslavia. With the collapse of communist regimes in Eastern Europe, Bosnia and Herzegovina declared its independence in 1992; its Serb population objected, and conflict ensued among Serbs, Croats, and Muslims. The 1995 peace accord established a loosely federated government roughly divided between a Muslim-Croat federation and a Serb Republic (Republika Srpska). In 1996 a NATO peacekeeping force was installed there.

Recent Developments

In November 2006 Bosnia and Herzegovina was invited to join the NATO Partnership for Peace program, a first step toward NATO membership, and the European Union announced in early 2007 that it would reduce its peacekeeping force there from 6,800 to 2,500 by June as a result of improved conditions. In February 2007 the International Court of Justice declared that the 1995 slaughter of almost 8,000 Bosnian Muslims in Srebrenica by Bosnian Serbs had been genocide but stopped short of blaming the Serbian government for it.

Internet resources: <www.bhembassy.org>.

Botswana

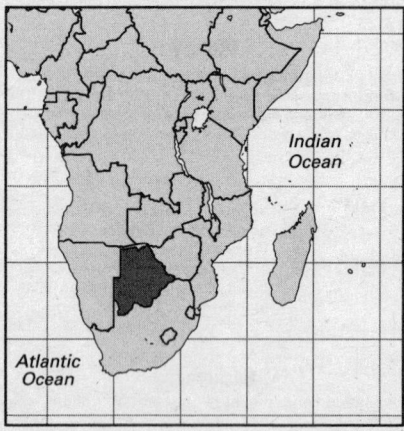

Official name: Republic of Botswana. **Form of government:** multiparty republic with one legislative body (National Assembly [63]) and a 15-member advisory board, the House of Chiefs. **Head of state and government:** President Festus Mogae (from 1998). **Capital:** Gaborone. **Official language:** English (Tswana is the national language). **Official religion:** none. **Monetary unit:** 1 pula (P) = 100 thebe; valuation (1 Jul 2007) US$1 = P 6.31.

Demography

Area: 224,848 sq mi, 582,356 sq km. **Population** (2006): 1,760,000. **Density** (2006): persons per sq mi 7.8, persons per sq km 3.0. **Urban** (2002): 49.4%. **Sex distribution** (2001): male 48.40%; female 51.60%. **Age breakdown** (2000): under 15, 40.6%; 15–29, 30.8%; 30–44, 15.0%; 45–59, 7.7%; 60–74, 4.3%; 75 and over, 1.6%. **Ethnic composition** (2000): Tswana 66.8%; Kalanga 14.8%; Ndebele 1.7%; Herero 1.4%; San (Bushman) 1.3%; Afrikaner 1.3%. **Religious affiliation** (2000): traditional beliefs 38.8%; African Christian 30.7%; Protestant 10.9%; Roman Catholic 3.7%. **Major cities** (2001): Gaborone 186,007; Francistown 83,023; Molepolole 54,561; Selebi-Pikwe 49,849; Maun 43,776. **Location:** southern Africa, bordered by Namibia, Zimbabwe, and South Africa.

Vital statistics

Birth rate per 1,000 population (2002): 28.0 (world avg. 21.3). **Death rate** per 1,000 population (2002): 26.3 (world avg. 9.1). **Natural increase rate** per 1,000 population (2002): 1.7 (world avg. 12.2). **Total fertility rate** (avg. births per childbearing woman; 2002): 3.6. **Life expectancy** at birth (2002): male 36.9 years;

female 37.6 years. **Adult population** (ages 15–49) **living with HIV** (2004): 37.3% (world avg. 1.1%).

National economy

Budget (2002–03). *Revenue:* P 14,311,000,000 (tax revenue 85.7%, of which mineral royalties 52.4%, income tax 12.9%, value-added tax 8.8%; nontax revenue 13.7%, of which property income 7.4%; grants 0.6%). *Expenditures:* P 15,710,100,000 (education 22.6%, health 8.8%, defense 8.3%, public order 4.0%). **Public debt** (external, outstanding; 2002): $463,900,000. **Population economically active** (2000): total 574,160; activity rate of total population 35.1% (participation rates: ages 15–64, 58.3%; female 44.3%; unemployed 15.8%). **Production** (metric tons except as noted). *Agriculture, forestry, fishing* (2002): sorghum 32,298, pulses 17,500, corn (maize) 10,000; livestock (number of live animals) 2,250,000 goats, 1,700,000 cattle, 370,000 sheep; roundwood 749,515 cu m; fish catch (2001) 118. *Mining and quarrying* (2003): soda ash 234,520; nickel ore (metal content) 27,400; copper ore (metal content) 24,289. *Manufacturing* (value added in $'000,000; 1997): motor vehicles 33; beverages 26; bricks, cement, and tiles 20. *Energy production (consumption):* electricity (kW-hr; 2003) 624,000,000 ([2000] 1,450,000,000); coal (2003) 822,780 ([2000] 971,000). **Tourism:** receipts (2002) $309,000,000; expenditures $184,000,000. **Gross national product** (at current market prices; 2003): $5,911,000,000 ($3,430 per capita). **Household expenditure.** Average household size (2001) 4.2; expenditure (2000): food and nonalcoholic beverages 30.6%, housing and energy 13.4%, alcoholic beverages and tobacco 12.3%, education 7.0%, transportation 5.7%. **Land use** as % of total land area (2000): in temporary crops 0.7%, in permanent crops 0.01%, in pasture 45.2%; overall forest area 21.9%.

Foreign trade

Imports (2002-c.i.f.): P 10,169,000,000 (machinery and apparatus 19.6%; food, beverages, and tobacco 13.9%; transport equipment 12.1%; chemical and rubber products 10.3%; wood and paper products 8.8%). *Major import sources* (2001): Customs Union of Southern Africa (CUSA) 77.6%; Europe 12.3%, of which UK 4.4%; Zimbabwe 3.2%; US 1.8%. **Exports** (2002-f.o.b.): P 14,983,000,000 (diamonds 83.3%; copper-nickel matte 3.2%; textiles 2.0%; meat products 1.9%). *Major export destinations* (2001): UK 85.9%; CUSA 6.5%; Zimbabwe 2.6%.

Transport and communications

Transport. *Railroads* (2000–01): length 1,135 km; passenger-km 106,000,000; metric ton-km cargo 747,000. *Roads* (2002): total length 10,528 km (paved 55%). *Vehicles* (2003): passenger cars 64,681; trucks and buses 70,923. *Air transport* (2002; Air Botswana only): passenger-km 96,000,000; metric ton-km cargo 300,000; airports (1998) 7. **Communications,** in total units (units per 1,000 persons). Daily newspaper circulation (2000): 44,200 (27); radios (2000): 254,000 (155); televisions (2000): 40,900 (25); telephone main lines

---

1 metric ton = about 1.1 short tons;   1 kilometer = 0.6 mi (statute);   1 metric ton-km cargo = about 0.68 short ton-mi cargo;   c.i.f.: cost, insurance, and freight;   f.o.b.: free on board

(2002): 142,400 (83); cellular telephone subscribers (2002): 435,000 (253); personal computers (2002): 70,000 (41); Internet users (2002): 60,000 (35).

Education and health

Educational attainment (1993). Percentage of population age 25 and over having: no formal schooling 34.7%; primary education 44.1%; some secondary 19.8%; postsecondary 1.4%. **Literacy** (2001): total population over age 15 literate 78.1%; males literate 75.3%; females literate 80.6%. **Health** (2003): physicians 510 (1 per 3,261 persons); hospital beds 3,088 (1 per 539 persons); infant mortality rate per 1,000 live births (2002) 64.7. **Food** (2001): daily per capita caloric intake 2,292 (vegetable products 83%, animal products 17%); 99% of FAO recommended minimum.

Military

Total active duty personnel (2003): 9,000 (army 94.4%, air force 5.6%). **Military expenditure as percentage of GNP** (1999): 4.7% (world 2.4%); per capita expenditure $142.

Did you know? Gaborone is the capital of Botswana. The seat of government was transferred there from Mafeking, South Africa, in 1965, one year before Botswana became independent of Great Britain. It is the seat of the University of Botswana (founded 1976), and it also has a national museum and art gallery (1968).

Background

The region's earliest inhabitants were the Khoekhoe and San (Bushmen). Sites were settled as early as AD 190 during the southerly migration of Bantu-speaking farmers. Tswana dynasties, which developed in the western Transvaal in the 13th–14th century, moved into Botswana in the 18th century and established several powerful states. European missionaries arrived in the early 19th century, but it was the discovery of gold in 1867 that excited European interest. In 1885 the area became the British Bechuanaland Protectorate. The next year the region south of the Molopo River became a crown colony, and it was annexed by the Cape Colony 10 years later. Bechuanaland itself continued as a British protectorate until the 1960s. In 1966 the Republic of Bechuanaland (later Botswana) was proclaimed an independent member of the British Commonwealth. Independent Botswana tried to maintain a delicate balance between its economic dependence on South Africa and its relations with the surrounding black countries; the independence of Namibia in 1990 and South Africa's rejection of apartheid eased tensions.

Recent Developments

Botswana, one of the most mineral-rich countries in the world, saw its per capita GDP rise to more than $5,000 in mid-2006. The country, the world's leading diamond producer, announced plans in early 2007 to expand its entire diamond industry, including cutting and polishing operations, grading, banking and insurance, security, and technology and engineering. De Beers, the international diamond giant, entered into an agreement with the government to build a diamond-sorting center in Botswana by 2008.

Internet resources: <www.botswana-tourism.gov.bw>.

Brazil

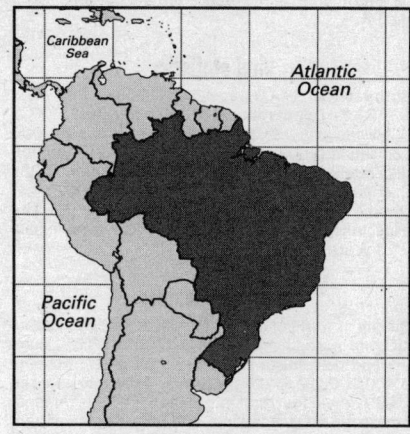

Official name: República Federativa do Brasil (Federative Republic of Brazil). **Form of government:** multiparty federal republic with two legislative houses (Federal Senate [81]; Chamber of Deputies [513]). **Chief of state and government:** President Luiz Inácio Lula da Silva (from 2003). **Capital:** Brasília. **Official language:** Portuguese. **Official religion:** none. **Monetary unit:** 1 real (R$) = 100 centavos; valuation (1 Jul 2007) US$1 = 1.93 reais.

Demography

Area (including inland water): 3,287,612 sq mi, 8,514,877 sq km. **Population** (2006): 186,771,000. **Density** (2006): persons per sq mi 56.8, persons per sq km 21.9. **Urban** (2000): 81.2%. **Sex distribution** (2000): male 49.21%; female 50.79%. **Age breakdown** (2000): under 15, 29.6%; 15–29, 28.2%; 30–44, 21.1%; 45–59, 12.5%; 60–74, 6.5%; 75 and over, 2.1%. **Racial composition** (1999; excludes rural population of Acre, Amapá, Amazonas, Pará, Rondônia, and Roraima): white 54.0%; mulatto and mestizo 39.9%; black and black/Amerindian 5.4%; Asian 0.5%; Amerindian 0.2%. **Religious affiliation** (1995): Catholic 74.3%, of which Roman Catholic 72.3%; Protestant 23.2%, of which Pentecostal 19.1%; other Christian 0.9%; New-Religionist 0.3%; Buddhist 0.3%; Jewish 0.2%; Muslim 0.1%; other 0.7%. **Major cities and metropolitan areas** (2003): São Paulo 10,041,500 (18,628,444); Rio de Janeiro 5,974,100 (11,226,729); Salvador 2,555,400 (3,183,327); Belo Horizonte 2,305,800 (5,100,359); Fortaleza 2,256,200 (3,164,225); Brasília 2,094,100 (3,199,451); Curitiba 1,671,200 (2,930,772); Manaus 1,517,500 (1,527,314); Recife 1,461,300 (3,466,214); Porto Alegre 1,353,300 (3,815,447); Belém 1,333,500 (1,916,982); Goiânia 1,138,600

(1,766,588); Guarulhos 1,135,500 (within São Paulo metropolitan area); Campinas 990,100 (2,483,594). **Location:** eastern South America, bordered by Venezuela, Guyana, Suriname, French Guiana, Uruguay, Argentina, Paraguay, Bolivia, Peru, and Colombia. **Families** (1999). Average family size 3.3; (1996) 1–2 persons 25.2%, 3 persons 20.3%, 4 persons 22.2%, 5–6 persons 23.3%, 7 or more persons 9.0%. **Number of emigrants/immigrants** (1986–96): 2,355,057/169,303. Emigrants' most popular destinations in order of preference are the US, Japan, and the UK.

Vital statistics

Birth rate per 1,000 population (2003): 19.5 (world avg. 21.3). **Death rate** per 1,000 population (2003): 6.7 (world avg. 9.1). **Natural increase rate** per 1,000 population (2003): 12.8 (world avg. 12.2). **Total fertility rate** (avg. births per childbearing woman; 2003): 2.2. **Marriage rate** per 1,000 population (2002): 4.1. **Divorce rate** per 1,000 population (2001): 0.7. **Life expectancy** at birth (2003): male 67.2 years; female 75.3 years.

Social indicators

Quality of working life. Proportion of employed population receiving minimum wage (2002): 53.5%. Number and percentage of children (age 5–17) working: 5,400,000 (12.6% of age group). **Access to services** (1999; excludes rural population of Acre, Amapá, Amazonas, Pará, Rondônia, and Roraima). Proportion of households having access to: electricity 94.8%, of which urban households having access 99.2%, rural households having access 75.4%; safe public (piped) water supply 79.8%, of which urban households having access 92.3%, rural households having access 24.9%; public (piped) sewage system 43.6%, of which urban households having access 52.5%, rural households having access 4.5%; no sewage disposal 8.5%, of which urban households having no disposal 2.9%, rural households having no disposal 32.9%. **Social participation.** Voting is mandatory for national elections; abstention is punishable by a fine. Trade union membership in total workforce (2001): 19,500,000. Practicing Roman Catholic population in total affiliated Roman Catholic population (2000): large cities 10–15%; towns and rural areas 60–70%. **Social deviance.** Annual murder rate per 100,000 population (1996): Brazil 23, Rio de Janeiro only 69, São Paulo only 55. **Leisure.** Favorite leisure activities include: playing soccer, dancing, rehearsing all year in neighborhood samba groups for celebrations of Carnival, and competing in water sports, volleyball, and basketball. **Material well-being** (1999; excludes rural population of Acre, Amapá, Amazonas, Pará, Rondônia, and Roraima). Households possessing: television receiver 87.7%, of which urban 93.2%, rural 63.8%; refrigerator 82.8%, of which urban 89.7%, rural 52.5%; washing machine 32.8%, of which urban 38.0%, rural 10.0%.

National economy

Gross national product (at current market prices; 2003): US$478,922,000,000 (US$2,710 per capita). **Budget** (1998). *Revenue:* R$237,187,-

000,000 (current revenue 95.8%, of which social contributions 32.6%, sales tax 20.3%, tax on income and profit 19.4%, nontax revenue 16.3%; capital revenue 4.2%). *Expenditures:* R$245,-032,100,000 (social security and welfare 47.3%; interest on debt 14.3%; defense and public order 6.6%; health 6.2%; education 6.1%; economic affairs 4.8%; other 14.7%). **Public debt** (external, outstanding; 2002): US$96,565,000,000. **Production** ('000 metric tons except as noted). *Agriculture, forestry, fishing* (2002): sugarcane 360,566, soybeans 41,903, corn (maize) 35,479, cassava 23,108, oranges 18,694, rice 10,489, bananas 6,369, tomatoes 3,518, dry beans 3,017, wheat 2,926, potatoes 2,865, coconuts 2,695, coffee 2,390, seed cotton 2,172, cashew apples 1,600, papayas 1,500, pineapples 1,469, onions 1,132, grapes 1,099, apples 858, sorghum 814, tobacco 654, lemons and limes 580, maté 535, oil palm fruit 450, peanuts (groundnuts) 192, cashews 184, sisal 177, cacao beans 172, garlic 113, natural rubber 96, Brazil nuts 26; livestock (number of live animals) 176,000,000 cattle, 30,000,000 pigs, 15,000,000 sheep, 5,900,000 horses; roundwood (2002) 237,467,063 cu m, of which fuelwood 134,473,063 cu m, sawlogs and veneer logs 49,290,000 cu m, pulpwood 45,860,000 cu m; fish catch (2001) 847, of which freshwater fishes 299. *Mining and quarrying* (value of export production in US$'000,000; 1998): iron ore 3,066; ferroniobium 242; silicon 135; bauxite 122; kaolin (clay) 106; ferrosilicon 101; granite (1996) 97; copper 89; manganese 52; nickel 52; gold production for both domestic use and export 1,594,000 troy oz; Brazil is also a world-leading producer of high-quality grade quartz and tantalum. *Manufacturing* (value added in US$'000,000; 2001): food products 15,387; petroleum products 11,046; transport equipment 10,632, of which cars 8,103; electrical machinery 7,248; iron, steel, and nonferrous metals 7,209; industrial chemicals 5,457; paper and paper products 4,740; printing and publishing 4,304; plastics and rubber products 4,201. *Energy production (consumption):* electricity (kW-hr; 2000) 349,000,000,000 (393,000,000,000); coal (metric tons; 2001) 6,600,000 ([2000] 20,270,000); crude petroleum (barrels; 2002) 536,000,000 ([2000] 583,000,000); petroleum products (metric tons; 2000) 67,910,000 (71,664,000); natural gas (cu m; 2002) 15,517,000,000 ([2000] 7,938,000,-000). **Land use** as % of total land area (2000): in temporary crops 6.8%, in permanent crops 0.9%, in pasture 23.2%; overall forest area 64.3%. **Population economically active** (2000; excludes rural population of Acre, Amapá, Amazonas, Pará, Rondônia, and Roraima): total 77,467,473; activity rate of total population 45.6% (participation rates: ages 15–59, 73.8%; female [1999] 40.2%; unemployed [2004] 11.2%). **Tourism** (2002): receipts from visitors US$3,120,000,000; expenditures by nationals abroad US$2,380,000,000. **Households.** Average household size (2002) 3.8. **Family income and expenditure.** Average family size (1999; excludes rural population of Acre, Amapá, Amazonas, Pará, Rondônia, and Roraima) 3.3; annual income per family (1999) R$10,500 (excludes rural population of Acre, Amapá, Amazonas, Pará, Rondônia, and Roraima); expenditure (1995–96; based on survey

---

1 metric ton = about 1.1 short tons; 1 kilometer = 0.6 mi (statute); 1 metric ton-km cargo = about 0.68 short ton-mi cargo; c.i.f.: cost, insurance, and freight; f.o.b.: free on board

of 11 metropolitan areas only): housing, energy, and household furnishings 28.8%, food and beverages 23.4%, transportation and communications 13.8%, health care 9.2%, education and recreation 8.4%.

Foreign trade

Imports (2001-f.o.b.): US$55,581,000,000 (machinery and apparatus 43.0%; chemicals and chemical products 18.1%; mineral fuels 14.4%; motor vehicles 9.5%; food products 5.0%). *Major import sources* (2002): US 21.8%; Argentina 10.1%; Germany 9.3%; Japan 5.0%; Italy 3.7%; France 3.7%; China 3.3%; UK 2.8%; Algeria 2.3%; South Korea 2.3%. **Exports** (2001): US$58,223,000,000 (food products 20.0%, of which meat 5.0%, sugar 4.1%, animal food 3.7%, coffee 3.0%; transportation equipment 13.6%, of which road vehicles 7.4%; machinery and apparatus 13.1%; iron and steel 5.5%; chemicals and chemical products 5.4%; iron ore and concentrates 5.0%; soybeans 4.7%). *Major export destinations* (2002): US 25.4%; The Netherlands 5.3%; Germany 4.2%; China 4.2%; Argentina 3.9%; Mexico 3.9%; Japan 3.5%; Belgium 3.1%; UK 2.9%; France 2.5%.

Transport and communications

Transport. *Railroads* (2000): route length 29,283 km; passenger-km 5,852,000,000; metric ton-km cargo 154,870,000,000. *Roads* (2000): total length 1,724,924 km (paved 10%). *Vehicles* (2001): passenger cars 23,241,966; trucks and buses 3,897,140. *Air transport* (2002; TAM, VARIG, and VASP airlines only): passenger-km 40,861,000,000; metric ton-km cargo 1,327,000,000; airports (1995) with scheduled flights 139. **Communications**, in total units (units per 1,000 persons). Daily newspaper circulation (2000): 7,390,000 (43); radios (2000): 74,400,000 (433); televisions (2000): 58,900,000 (343); telephone main lines (2002): 38,810,000 (223); cellular telephone subscribers (2003): 46,373,000 (264); personal computers (2002): 13,000,000 (75); Internet users (2002): 14,300,000 (82).

Education and health

Educational attainment (1996). Percentage of population age 25 and over having: no formal schooling or less than one year of primary education 17.7%; lower primary only 19.1%; upper primary 30.7%; complete primary to some secondary 11.6%; complete secondary to some higher 13.9%; complete higher 6.2%; unknown 0.8%. **Literacy** (2000): total population age 15 and over literate 86.4%. **Health:** physicians (1999) 429,808 (1 per 395 persons); hospital beds (1999) 484,945 (1 per 343 persons); infant mortality rate per 1,000 live births (2002) 31.8. **Food** (2001): daily per capita caloric intake 3,002 (vegetable products 80%, animal products 20%); 126% of FAO recommended minimum.

Military

Total active duty personnel (2003): 287,600 (army 65.7%, navy 16.9%, air force 17.4%). **Military expenditure as percentage of GNP** (1999): 1.9% (world 2.4%); per capita expenditure US$59.

Did you know? Iguaçu Falls is a series of cataracts on the Iguaçu River, 14 miles (23 km) above its confluence with the Alto Paraná River, at the Argentina-Brazil border. The falls resemble an elongated horseshoe that extends for 1.7 miles (2.7 km)—nearly three times wider than Niagara Falls in North America. In 1897 Edmundo de Barros, a Brazilian army officer, envisaged the establishment of a national park at Iguaçu Falls. Following boundary rectifications between Brazil and Argentina, two separate national parks were established, one by each country—Iguaçu National Park (1939) in Brazil and Iguazú National Park (1934) in Argentina.

Background

Little is known about Brazil's early indigenous inhabitants. Though the area was theoretically allotted to Portugal by the 1494 Treaty of Tordesillas, it was not formally claimed by discovery until Pedro Álvares Cabral accidentally touched land in 1500. It was first settled by the Portuguese in the early 1530s on the southeastern coast and at São Vicente (near modern São Paulo); the French and Dutch created small settlements over the next century. A viceroyalty was established in 1640, and Rio de Janeiro became the capital in 1763. In 1808 Brazil became the refuge and seat of the government of John VI of Portugal when Napoleon invaded Portugal; ultimately the Kingdom of Portugal, Brazil, and the Algarves was proclaimed, and John ruled from Brazil in 1815–21. On John's return to Portugal, his son Pedro I proclaimed Brazilian independence. In 1889 his successor, Pedro II, was deposed, and a constitution mandating a federal republic was adopted. The 20th century saw increased immigration and growth in manufacturing along with frequent military coups and suspensions of civil liberties. Construction of a new capital at Brasília, intended to spur development of the country's interior, worsened the inflation rate. After 1979 the military government began a gradual return to democratic practices, and in 1989 the first popular presidential election in 29 years was held.

Recent Developments

In April 2006 Pres. Luiz Inácio Lula da Silva proclaimed Brazil's self-sufficiency in petroleum. In May, however, Bolivian Pres. Evo Morales nationalized his country's petroleum and gas industries, threatening the industries in southern Brazil that relied on Bolivian natural gas. Meanwhile, state-owned Petrobrás announced that it would pursue expansion of domestic capacity in the Santos basin. Protesting prison conditions and the transfer of its leaders to maximum-security installations, a criminal gang launched widespread attacks and prison rebellions against civil and military police in the states of São Paulo and Mato Grosso starting in May. The attacks, coordinated inside prison walls via cell phones, paralyzed the nation and left more than 200 dead. In 2006 the Brazilian economy showed mixed signs. A 16.7% minimum-wage increase went into effect in April. GDP growth of 2.95% was forecast, and the government aimed to achieve 5% growth in 2007. In October Lula won reelection to a second term in office, claiming victory with five million more votes than he had achieved in winning his first term in 2002.

Internet resources: <www.embratur.gov.br>.

Brunei

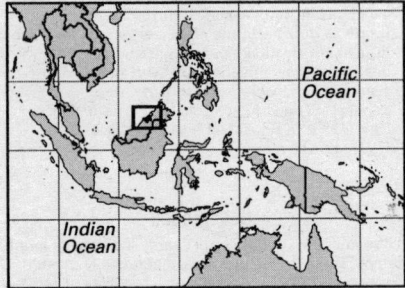

Official name: Negara Brunei Darussalam (State of Brunei, Abode of Peace). Form of government: monarchy (monarch is advised on legislative matters by a 21-member appointed body). Head of state and government: Sultan Haji Hassanal Bolkiah Mu'izzadin Waddaulah (from 1967). Capital: Bandar Seri Begawan. Official language: Malay. Official religion: Islam. Monetary unit: 1 Brunei dollar (B$) = 100 cents; valuation (1 Jul 2007) US$1 = B$1.54.

Demography

Area: 2,226 sq mi, 5,765 sq km. Population (2006): 375,000. Density (2006): persons per sq mi 168.5, persons per sq km 65.0. Urban (2002): 73.0%. Sex distribution (2002): male 52.35%; female 47.65%. Age breakdown (2002): under 15, 30.2%; 15–29, 27.0%; 30–44, 25.2%; 45–59, 13.2%; 60–74, 3.6%; 75 and over, 0.8%. Ethnic composition (2001): Malay 66.8%; Chinese 11.1%; other indigenous 3.5%; other 18.6%. Religious affiliation (2000): Muslim 64.4%; traditional beliefs 11.2%; Buddhist 9.1%; Christian 7.7%; other religions and nonreligious 7.6%. Major cities: Bandar Seri Begawan (2001) 27,285 (urban agglomeration [2002] 74,700); Kuala Belait (2002) 27,200; Seria (2002) 23,200. Location: southeastern Asia, bordering the South China Sea and Malaysia.

Vital statistics

Birth rate per 1,000 population (2002): 20.1 (world avg. 21.3). Death rate per 1,000 population (2002): 3.4 (world avg. 9.1). Natural increase rate per 1,000 population (2002): 16.7 (world avg. 12.2). Total fertility rate (avg. births per childbearing woman; 2002): 2.4. Marriage rate per 1,000 population (2000): 6.7. Divorce rate per 1,000 population (2000): 1.1. Life expectancy at birth (2002): male 71.7 years; female 76.6 years.

National economy

Budget (2000). Revenue: B$5,084,000,000 (nontax revenue 52.1%, of which government property in-

come 39.7%, commercial receipts 12.4%; tax revenue 47.6%). Expenditures: B$4,196,000,000 (current expenditure 83.5%; capital expenditure 9.1%; other 7.4%). Public debt (external, outstanding; 1999): US$902,000,000. Tourism (1998): receipts from visitors US$37,000,000; expenditures by nationals abroad US$1,000,000. Production (metric tons except as noted). Agriculture, forestry, fishing (2002): vegetables and melons 9,800, fruits (excluding melons) 4,150, cassava 1,800; livestock (number of live animals) 7,000 buffalo, 6,500 pigs, 12,500,-000 chickens; roundwood (2001) 228,550 cu m; fish catch (2001) 1,591. Mining and quarrying: sand and gravel for construction. Manufacturing (2003): gasoline 1,717,000 barrels; kerosene 634,000 barrels; distillate fuel oils 1,195 barrels. Energy production (consumption): electricity (kW-hr; 2000) 2,434,-000,000 (2,434,000,000); crude petroleum (barrels; 2003) 75,600,000 ([2000] 1,700,000); petroleum products (2000) 985,000 (987,000); natural gas (cu m; 2003) 12,000,000,000 ([2001] 1,371,000,000). Gross national product (at current market prices; 2001): US$8,169,000,000 (US$24,630 per capita). Population economically active (2001): total 145,600; activity rate of total population 43.9% (participation rates: ages 15–64, 65.9%; female 41.4%; unemployed [2002] 4.6%). Households. Average household size (2000) ; expenditure (1990): food 38.7%, transportation and communications 19.9%, housing 18.6%, clothing 6.4%, other 16.4%. Land use as % of total land area (2000): in temporary crops 0.6%, in permanent crops 0.8%, in pasture 1.1%; overall forest area 83.9%.

Foreign trade

Imports (2001-c.i.f.): B$2,076,000,000 (basic manufactures 30.7%, machinery and transport equipment 30.3%, food and live animals 16.4%, chemicals and chemical products 7.6%). Major import sources: Singapore 23.4%; Malaysia 22.0%; US 9.2%; Japan 6.4%; Hong Kong 5.0%. Exports (2001-f.o.b.): B$6,522,000,000 ([1999] crude petroleum and partly refined petroleum 43.4%, natural gas 37.7%, petroleum products 2.2%). Major export destinations (2001): Japan 46.0%; South Korea 11.9%; Thailand 11.8%; Singapore 8.4%; US 7.5%.

Transport and communications

Transport. Railroads: length 19 km. Roads (2000): total length 3,272 km (paved 73%). Vehicles (2001): passenger cars 188,720; trucks and buses 17,828. Air transport (2003; Royal Brunei Airlines): passenger-km 3,588,000,000; metric ton-km cargo 148,703,000; airports (2001) with scheduled flights 1. Communications, in total units (units per 1,000 persons). Daily newspaper circulation (2002): 72,-000 (213); radios (2000): 362,712 (1,120); televisions (2000): 216,223 (668); telephone main lines (2002): 90,000 (256); cellular telephone subscribers (2001): 137,000 (401); personal computers (2002): 27,000 (77); Internet users (2001): 35,000 (102).

Education and health

Educational attainment (1991). Percentage of population age 25 and over having: no formal schooling

---

1 metric ton = about 1.1 short tons;   1 kilometer = 0.6 mi (statute);   1 metric ton-km cargo = about 0.68 short ton-mi cargo;   c.i.f.: cost, insurance, and freight;   f.o.b.: free on board

17.0%; primary education 43.3%; secondary 26.3%; postsecondary and higher 12.9%; not stated 0.5%. **Literacy** (2000): percentage of total population age 15 and over literate 91.5%; males literate 95.0%; females literate 88.0%. **Health** (2001): physicians 371 (1 per 929 persons); hospital beds 908 (1 per 379 persons); infant mortality rate per 1,000 live births (2002) 14.0. **Food** (2001): daily per capita caloric intake 2,814 (vegetable products 80%, animal products 20%); 120% of FAO recommended minimum.

Military

Total active duty personnel (2003): 7,000 (army 70.0%, navy 14.3%, air force 15.7%). British troops (a Gurkha batallion): 1,100. **Military expenditure as percentage of GNP** (1999): 4.0% (world 2.4%); per capita expenditure US$897.

Background

Brunei traded with China in the 6th century AD. Through allegiance to the Javanese Majapahit kingdom (13th–15th century), it came under Hindu influence. In the early 15th century, with the decline of the Majapahit kingdom, many people converted to Islam, and Brunei became an independent sultanate. When Ferdinand Magellan's ships visited in 1521, the sultan of Brunei controlled almost all of Borneo and its neighboring islands. Beginning in the late 16th century, Brunei lost power because of the Portuguese, Dutch, and, later, British activities in the region. By the 19th century, the sultanate of Brunei included Sarawak (present-day Brunei) and part of North Borneo (now part of Sabah). In 1841 a revolt took place against the sultan, and a British soldier, James Brooke, helped put it down; he was later proclaimed governor. In 1847 the sultanate entered into a treaty with Great Britain and by 1906 had yielded all administration to a British resident. Brunei rejected membership in the Federation of Malaysia in 1963, negotiated a new treaty with Britain in 1979, and achieved independence in 1984, with membership in the Commonwealth.

Recent Developments

On 15 Jul 2004, Brunei's Sultan Haji Hassanal Bolkiah Mu'izzaddin Waddaulah announced that the Legislative Council, which was suspended in 1984, would be revitalized. He also stated that the 1959 constitution was being reviewed and draft amendments would soon be debated by the Legislative Council. The sultan appointed 21 Legislative Council members on 6 September; 11 were state officials, including the sultan himself. In March 2006 legal action was taken against the sultan's brother Prince Jefri to compel him to surrender assets worldwide as part of a court case involving billions of dollars missing from the country's treasury.

Internet resources: <www.brunei.gov.bn>.

Bulgaria

Official name: Republika Bulgariya (Republic of Bulgaria). **Form of government:** unitary multiparty republic with one legislative body (National Assembly

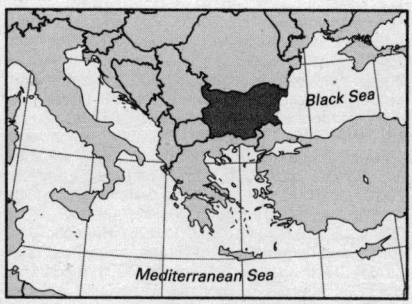

[240]). **Chief of state:** President Georgi Purvanov (from 2002). **Head of government:** Prime Minister Sergey Stanishev (from 2005). **Capital:** Sofia. **Official language:** Bulgarian. **Official religion:** none. **Monetary unit:** 1 lev (Lw; leva) = 100 stotinki; valuation (1 Jul 2007) US$1 = 1.45 (new) leva (re-denominated in 1999 to 1 new lev = 1,000 old leva).

Demography

Area: 42,858.1 sq mi, 111,002 sq km. **Population** (2006): 7,681,000. **Density** (2006): persons per sq mi 179.2, persons per sq km 69.2. **Urban** (2001): 69.0%. **Sex distribution** (2002): male 48.68%; female 51.32%. **Age breakdown** (2002): under 15, 15.0%; 15–29, 21.3%; 30–44, 20.4%; 45–59, 20.9%; 60–74, 16.1%; 75 and over, 6.3%. **Ethnic composition** (2001): Bulgarian 83.9%; Turkish 9.4%; Rom (Gypsy) 4.7%; other 2.0%. **Religious affiliation** (2001): Christian 83.7%, of which Bulgarian Orthodox c. 72%, independent Christian c. 7%; Sunni Muslim 12.2%; other/nonreligious 4.1%. **Major cities** (2001): Sofia 1,099,507; Plovdiv 340,122; Varna 313,408; Burgas 193,316; Ruse 162,128. **Location:** southeastern Europe, bordering Romania, the Black Sea, Turkey, Greece, Macedonia, and Serbia and Montenegro.

Vital statistics

Birth rate per 1,000 population (2001): 8.6 (world avg. 21.3). **Death rate** per 1,000 population (2001): 14.2 (world avg. 9.1). **Natural increase rate** per 1,000 population (2001): -5.6 (world avg. 12.2). **Total fertility rate** (avg. births per childbearing woman; 2001): 1.2. **Life expectancy** at birth (2001): male 68.5 years; female 75.2 years.

National economy

Budget (2003). *Revenue:* 13,222,000,000 leva (tax revenue 77.7%, of which value-added tax 23.5%, social insurance 21.2%, income and profit tax 16.8%; nontax revenue 20.0%; grants 2.3%). *Expenditures:* 13,221,000,000 leva (social insurance 35.0%; capital expenditure 10.3%; health 9.5%; administration and defense 8.4%; interest on debt 5.5%). **Public debt** (external, outstanding; 2002): $7,474,000,000. **Gross national product** (2003): $16,639,000,000 ($2,130 per capita). **Production** (metric tons except as noted). *Agriculture, forestry, fishing* (2002): wheat 4,888,648, corn (maize) 1,206,000, barley 1,187,-859; livestock (number of live animals) 2,418,490 sheep, 1,013,740 pigs, 898,559 goats; roundwood (2002) 4,833,000 cu m; fish catch (2001) 8,100.

Mining and quarrying (2000): iron (metal content) 178,000; copper (metal content) 107,000; gold 2,347 kg. *Manufacturing* (value added in $'000,000; 2001): nonelectrical machinery and apparatus 188; wearing apparel 168; food products 158. *Energy production (consumption):* electricity (kW-hr; 2001) 43,968,000,000 (43,968,000,000); hard coal (2000) 118,000 (3,379,000); lignite (2003) 27,156,-000 ([2000] 25,844,000); crude petroleum (barrels; 2000) 308,000 (39,100,000); petroleum products (2000) 4,459,000 (3,064,000); natural gas (cu m; 2000) 16,313,000 (3,883,000,000). **Household income and expenditure.** Average household size (2001) 3.0; income per household (2001) 4,532 leva ($2,280); sources of income: wages and salaries 37.8%, transfer payments 24.4%, self-employment in agriculture 14.2%; expenditure (2001): food 42.7%, housing and energy 11.5%, transportation 5.0%, health 3.7%, clothing 3.4%. **Population economically active** (2003): total 3,237,100; activity rate of total population 41.5% (participation rates [2001] age 16–59 [male], 16–54 [female] 54.2%; female [2001] 46.4%; unemployed 12.7%). **Tourism** (2002): receipts $1,344,000,000; expenditures $616,000,-000. **Land use** as % of total land area (2000): in temporary crops 40.0%, in permanent crops 1.9%, in pasture 14.6%; overall forest area 33.4%.

Foreign trade

Imports (2003-f.o.b. in balance of trade and c.i.f. for commodities and trading partners): $10,836,-000,000 (textiles 13.7%; crude petroleum and natural gas 13.6%; machinery and apparatus 13.1%; transport equipment 9.4%; plastics and rubber 4.6%). *Major import sources:* Germany 14.3%; Russia 12.6%; Italy 10.2%; Turkey 6.1%; France 5.6%. **Exports** (2003): $7,520,000,000 (clothing and footwear 21.9%; base and fabricated metals 16.1%, of which iron and steel 8.1%; machinery and transport equipment 10.3%; mineral fuels 8.4%, of which petroleum products 5.8%). *Major export destinations:* Italy 14.0%; Germany 10.8%; Greece 10.4%; Turkey 9.2%; Belgium 6.1%; France 5.1%.

Transport and communications

Transport. *Railroads* (2002): track length 6,384 km; passenger-km 2,598,000,000; metric ton-km cargo 4,628,000,000. *Roads* (2001): length 37,296 km (paved 92%). *Vehicles* (2001): cars 2,085,730; trucks and buses 288,832. *Air transport* (2001): passenger-km 1,795,400,000; metric ton-km cargo 2,335,000; airports (2000) with scheduled flights 3. **Communications,** in total units (units per 1,000 persons). Daily newspaper circulation (2000): 2,060,000 (257); radios (2001): 4,340,000 (543); televisions (2002): 3,620,000 (453); telephone main lines (2002): 2,868,200 (368); cellular telephone subscribers (2002): 2,597,500 (330); personal computers (2002): 405,000 (52); Internet users (2002): 630,000 (81).

Education and health

Educational attainment (1992). Percentage of population age 25 and over having: no formal schooling 4.7%; incomplete primary education 12.5%; primary 31.9%; secondary 35.7%; higher 15.0%. **Literacy** (2001): total population age 15 and over literate 98.5%; males 99.0%; females 98.0%. **Health** (2002): physicians 27,186 (1 per 290 persons); hospital beds 56,984 (1 per 138 persons); infant mortality rate per 1,000 live births (2001) 13.5. **Food** (2001): daily per capita caloric intake 2,626 (vegetable products 73%, animal products 27%); 105% of FAO recommended minimum.

Military

Total active duty personnel (2003): 51,000 (army 49.0%, navy 8.6%, air force 25.7%, other 16.7%). **Military expenditure as percentage of GNP** (1999): 3.0% (world 2.4%); per capita expenditure $158.

Background

Evidence of human habitation in Bulgaria dates from prehistoric times. Thracians were its first recorded inhabitants, dating from c. 3500 BC, and their first state dates from about the 5th century BC; the area was subdued by the Romans, who divided it into the provinces of Moesia and Thrace. In the 7th century AD the Bulgars took the region to the south of the Danube. The Byzantine Empire in 681 formally recognized Bulgar control over the area between the Balkans and the Danube. In the second half of the 14th century, Bulgaria fell to the Turks and ultimately lost its independence. At the end of the Russo-Turkish War (1877–78), Bulgaria rebelled. The ensuing Treaty of San Stefano was unacceptable to the Great Powers, and the Congress of Berlin (1878) resulted. In 1908 the Bulgarian ruler, Ferdinand, declared Bulgaria's independence. After its involvement in the Balkan Wars (1912–13), Bulgaria lost territory. It sided with the Central Powers in World War I and with Germany in World War II. A communist coalition seized power in 1944, and in 1946 a people's republic was declared. Like other eastern European countries in the late 1980s, Bulgaria experienced political unrest; its communist leader resigned in 1989. A new constitution proclaiming a republic was implemented in 1991. The rest of the decade brought economic turmoil.

Recent Developments

On 1 January 2007, Bulgaria was admitted into the European Union. Although Bulgaria had received roughly $1.9 billion in foreign direct investment in 2006 (a 15-year high), it came into the EU as one of its poorest members. It stood to receive $873 million in financial assistance during its first year of membership. In an accord signed in January 2007, Bulgaria, Macedonia, and Albania agreed to construct a 917-km (570-mi) petroleum pipeline from the Bulgarian port of Burgas on the Black Sea to Albania. Five Bulgarian nurses who, with a Palestinian doctor, had been convicted of having deliberately infected 426 Libyan children with HIV and sentenced to death appealed the verdict in February 2007.

Internet resources: <www.bulgaria-embassy.org>.

---

1 metric ton = about 1.1 short tons;   1 kilometer = 0.6 mi (statute);   1 metric ton-km cargo = about 0.68 short ton-mi cargo;   c.i.f.: cost, insurance, and freight;   f.o.b.: free on board

Burkina Faso

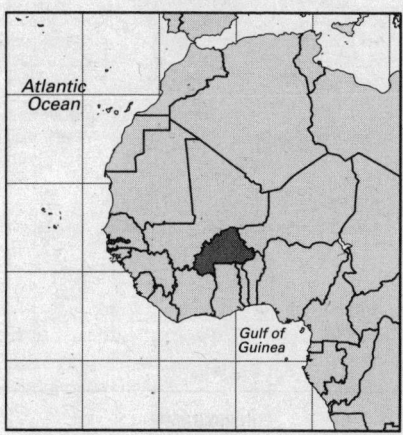

Official name: Burkina Faso. **Form of government:** multiparty republic with one legislative body (National Assembly [111]). **Chief of state:** President Blaise Compaoré (from 1987). **Head of government:** Prime Minister Tertius Zongo (from 2007). **Capital:** Ouagadougou. **Official language:** French. **Official religion:** none. **Monetary unit:** 1 CFA franc (CFAF) = 100 centimes; valuation (1 Jul 2007) US$1 = CFAF 485.18 (formerly pegged to the French franc and since 1 Jan 2002 to the euro (€) at €1 = CFAF 655.96).

Demography

Area: 103,456 sq mi, 267,950 sq km. **Population** (2006): 13,558,000. **Density** (2006): persons per sq mi 131.1, persons per sq km 50.6. **Urban** (2002): 16.9%. **Sex distribution** (2003): male 49.26%; female 50.74%. **Age breakdown** (2003): under 15, 46.1%; 15–29, 27.4%; 30–44, 14.8%; 45–59, 7.4%; 60–74, 3.7%; 75 and over, 0.8%. **Ethnic composition** (1995): Mossi 47.9%; Fulani 10.3%; Lobi 6.9%; Bobo 6.9%; Mande 6.7%; Senufo 5.3%; Grosi 5.0%; Gurma 4.8%; Tuareg 3.1%. **Religious affiliation** (2000): Muslim 48.6%; traditional beliefs 34.1%; Christian 16.7%, of which Roman Catholic 9.5%. **Major cities** (1996): Ouagadougou 709,736; Bobo-Dioulasso 309,771; Koudougou 72,490; Ouahigouya 52,193; Banfora 49,724. **Location:** western Africa, bordering Mali, Niger, Benin, Togo, Ghana, and Côte d'Ivoire.

Vital statistics

Birth rate per 1,000 population (2003): 44.8 (world avg. 21.3). **Death rate** per 1,000 population (2003): 18.8 (world avg. 9.1). **Natural increase rate** per 1,000 population (2003): 26.0 (world avg. 12.2). **Total fertility rate** (avg. births per childbearing woman; 2003): 6.3. **Life expectancy** at birth (2003): male 43.0 years; female 45.9 years. **Adult population** (ages 15–49) **living with HIV** (2004): 4.2% (world avg. 1.1%).

National economy

Budget (2002). *Revenue:* CFAF 377,000,000,000 (tax revenue 63.9%, of which sales tax 34.5%, income taxes 16.4%, import duties 11.2%; grants 31.5%; nontax revenue 4.6%). *Expenditures:* CFAF 489,100,000,000 (current expenditure 52.9%, of which wages and salaries 21.1%, transfers 14.3%, goods and services 12.8%, debt service 3.4%; investment expenditure 47.1%). **Public debt** (external, outstanding; 2002): $1,399,000,000. **Households.** Average household size (2000) 6.0; expenditure (1998; Ouagadougou only): food 33.9%, transportation 15.6%, electricity and fuel 10.5%, clothing 6.4%, health 4.2%, education 3.4%. **Production** (metric tons except as noted). *Agriculture, forestry, fishing* (2002): sorghum 1,373,300, millet 994,700, corn (maize) 653,100; livestock (number of live animals) 9,450,000 goats, 7,411,000 sheep, 23,000,000 chickens; roundwood (2002) 11,994,000 cu m; fish catch (2001) 8,505. *Mining and quarrying* (2002): gold 624 kg (does not include substantial illegal production). *Manufacturing* (2002): sugar 47,743; edible oils 19,636; flour 10,005. *Energy production (consumption):* electricity (kW-hr; 2002) 361,-000,000 (361,000,000); petroleum products (2001) none (294,000). **Tourism:** receipts (2002) $39,000,-000; expenditures (1994) $23,000,000. **Population economically active** (1996): total 5,075,615; activity rate 49.2% (participation rates: over age 10, 70.0%; female 48.2%; unemployed 1.4%). **Gross national product** (at current market prices; 2003): $3,587,-000,000 ($300 per capita). **Land use** as % of total land area (2000): in temporary crops 13.9%, in permanent crops 0.2%, in pasture 21.9%; overall forest area 25.9%.

Foreign trade

Imports (2002): CFAF 381,700,000,000 (capital equipment 32.6%, petroleum products 18.6%, food products 12.7%, raw materials 10.1%). *Major import sources:* France 19.6%; Côte d'Ivoire 18.8%; Japan 9.3%; Germany 6.0%; US 3.3%. **Exports** (2002): CFAF 164,200,000,000 (raw cotton 54.1%, hides and skins 11.0%, live animals 8.8%, shea nuts 2.6%, gold 2.0%). *Major export destinations:* France 45.3%; Côte d'Ivoire 9.2%; Singapore 5.1%; Mali 4.0%; Japan 3.0%.

Transport and communications

Transport. *Railroads:* (2002) route length 622 km; (1995) passenger-km 202,000,000; (1995) metric ton-km cargo 45,000,000. *Roads* (1999): total length 10,469 km (paved 19%). *Vehicles* (1999): passenger cars 26,300; trucks and buses 19,600. *Air transport* (2000; Air Afrique, an airline jointly owned by 11 African countries including Burkina Faso, was declared bankrupt in February 2002): passenger-km 247,000,000; airports 2. **Communications**, in total units (units per 1,000 persons). Daily newspaper circulation (2000): 12,200 (1); radios (2000): 428,000 (35); televisions (2000): 147,000 (12); telephone main lines (2003): 65,400 (5.3); cellular telephone subscribers (2003): 227,000 (19); personal computers (2003): 26,000 (2.1); Internet users (2003): 48,000 (3.9).

Education and health

Educational attainment (1985). Percentage of population age 10 and over having: no formal schooling 86.1%; some primary 7.3%; general secondary 2.2%; specialized secondary and postsecondary 3.8%; other 0.6%. **Literacy** (2000): percentage of total population age 15 and over literate 23.9%; males literate 33.9%; females literate 14.1%. **Health** (1995): physicians 361 (1 per 29,385 persons); hospital beds (1991) 5,041 (1 per 1,837 persons); infant mortality rate per 1,000 live births (2003) 99.8. **Food** (2001): daily per capita caloric intake 2,485 (vegetable products 95%, animal products 5%); 105% of FAO recommended minimum.

Military

Total active duty personnel (2003): 10,800 (army 98.1%, air force 1.9%). **Military expenditure as percentage of GNP** (1999): 1.6% (world 2.4%); per capita expenditure $4.

Background

Probably in the 14th century, the Mossi and Gurma peoples established themselves in eastern and central areas of what is now Burkina Faso. The Mossi kingdoms of Yatenga and Ouagadougou existed into the early 20th century. A French protectorate was established over the region (1895–97), and its southern boundary was demarcated through an Anglo-French agreement. It was part of the Upper Senegal–Niger colony, then became a separate colony in 1919. Named Upper Volta, it was constituted an overseas territory within the French Union in 1947, became an autonomous republic within the French Community in 1958, and achieved total independence in 1960. Since then, the country has been ruled primarily by the military and has experienced several coups; following one in 1983, the country received its present name. A new constitution, adopted in 1991, restored multiparty rule.

Recent Developments

Despite a 2000 amendment to Burkina Faso's constitution that held ambiguous provisions containing term limits, Blaise Compaoré was allowed to run in the November 2005 presidential election, which he won to set up his third term. The World Bank approved grants totaling $65 million in May 2005 for poverty-reduction and AIDS programs, and in June of that year the Group of Eight nations canceled Burkina Faso's $18 million in outstanding debt. A major locust infestation in 2004, coupled with severe flooding that destroyed homes and wiped out crops in August 2006, raised concerns about food shortages in 2007.

Internet resources: <www.burkinaembassy-usa.org>.

Burundi

Official name: Republika y'u Burundi (Rundi); République du Burundi (French) (Republic of Burundi). **Form of government:** transitional regime with one legislative body (Transitional Assembly [178]). **Head of state and government:** President Pierre Nkurunziza (from 2005), assisted by Vice President Martin Nduwimana (from 2005). **Capital:** Bujumbura. **Official languages:** Rundi; French. **Official religion:** none. **Monetary unit:** 1 Burundi franc (FBu) = 100 centimes; valuation (1 Jul 2007) US$1 = FBu 1,109.

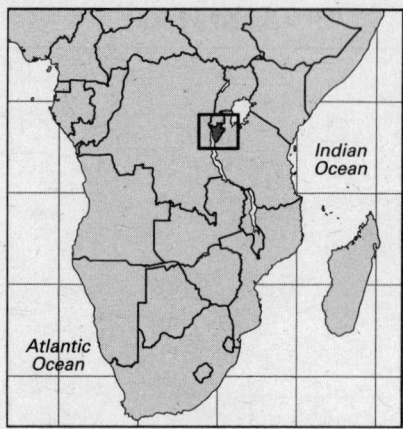

Demography

Area: 10,740 sq mi, 27,816 sq km. **Population** (2006): 8,090,000. **Density** (2006): persons per sq mi 753.3, persons per sq km 290.8. **Urban** (2002): 9.3%. **Sex distribution** (2003): male 49.57%; female 50.43%. **Age breakdown** (2003): under 15, 46.7%; 15–29, 28.8%; 30–44, 13.4%; 45–59, 7.1%; 60–74, 3.1%; 75 and over, 0.9%. **Ethnic composition** (2000): Hutu 80.9%; Tutsi 15.6%; Lingala 1.6%; Twa Pygmy 1.0%; other 0.9%. **Religious affiliation** (2000): Roman Catholic 57.2%; Protestant 19.5%; unaffiliated Christian 14.7%; traditional beliefs 6.7%; Muslim 1.4%; other 0.5%. **Major cities** (2004): Bujumbura 340,300; Gitega 46,900; Muyinga 45,300; Ngozi 40,200; Ruyigi 36,800. **Location:** central Africa, bordering Rwanda, Tanzania, Lake Tanganyika, and the Democratic Republic of the Congo.

Vital statistics

Birth rate per 1,000 population (2003): 39.7 (world avg. 21.3). **Death rate** per 1,000 population (2003): 17.8 (world avg. 9.1). **Natural increase rate** per 1,000 population (2003): 21.9 (world avg. 12.2). **Total fertility rate** (avg. births per childbearing woman; 2003): 6.0. **Life expectancy** at birth (2003): male 42.5 years; female 43.9 years. **Adult population** (ages 15–49) **living with HIV** (2004): 6.0% (world avg. 1.1%).

National economy

Budget (2002). *Revenue:* FBu 118,400,000,000 (tax revenue 88.5%, of which taxes on goods and services 43.8%, income tax 24.8%, taxes on international trade 19.6%; nontax revenue 11.5%). *Expenditures:* FBu 151,600,000,000 (current expenditure 79.0%; capital expenditure 21.0%). **Public debt** (external, outstanding; 2002): $1,095,000,000. **Production** (metric tons except as noted). *Agriculture, forestry, fishing* (2003): bananas 1,600,000, sweet potatoes 835,000, cassava 750,000; livestock (number of live animals) 750,000 goats, 325,000 cattle, 4,300,000 chickens; roundwood (2002) 8,428,000 cu m; fish catch (2001) 9,064. *Mining and quarrying* (2001): gemstones 16,500 kg; gold 415 kg. *Manufacturing*

1 metric ton = about 1.1 short tons;   1 kilometer = 0.6 mi (statute);   1 metric ton-km cargo = about 0.68 short ton-mi cargo;   c.i.f.: cost, insurance, and freight;   f.o.b.: free on board

(2003): beer 580,226 hectoliters; carbonated beverages 82,367 hectoliters; cottonseed oil 25,000 liters. *Energy production (consumption):* electricity (kW-hr; 2001) 107,774,000 (108,800,000); petroleum products (2001) none (48,093); peat (2000) 12,000 (12,000). **Households.** Average household size (2000) 5.1; expenditure: (1991) food 51.9%, energy and housing 27.0%, transportation 5.3%, clothing 5.3%. **Land use** as % of total land area (2000): in temporary crops 35.0%, in permanent crops 14.0%, in pasture 36.4%; overall forest area 3.7%. **Gross national product** (at current market prices; 2003): $702,000,000 ($100 per capita). **Population economically active** (1997): total 3,475,000; activity rate of total population 63.1% (participation rates [1991]: ages 15–64, 91.4%; female 48.9%). **Tourism** (2002): receipts from visitors $1,100,000; expenditures by nationals abroad $14,000,000.

Foreign trade

Imports (2002): $103,900,000 (consumption goods 45.0%, of which food and food products 12.4%; capital goods 30.8%; petroleum products 15.3%). *Major import sources:* Belgium 16.4%; Kenya 12.1%; Tanzania 10.3%; France 7.0%; Japan 5.7%. **Exports** (2002): $31,200,000 (coffee 53.9%, tea 28.5%, manufactured products 12.9%). *Major export destinations:* UK 18.9%; Kenya 18.7%; Rwanda 10.1%; Belgium 8,5%; The Netherlands 5.2%.

Transport and communications

Transport. *Roads* (1999): total length 14,480 km (paved 7%). *Vehicles* (1999): passenger cars 6,900; trucks and other vehicles 9,300. *Air transport* (2000; Bujumbura airport only): passenger arrivals and departures 58,402; cargo loaded and unloaded 3,905 metric tons; airports (2002) 1. **Communications,** in total units (units per 1,000 persons). Daily newspaper circulation (1996): 20,000 (3.2); radios (2000): 1,260,000 (220); televisions (2002): 220,000 (31); telephone main lines (2003): 23,900 (3.4); cellular telephone subscribers (2003): 64,000 (9); Internet users (2003): 14,000 (1.8).

Education and health

Literacy (2000): percentage of total population age 15 and over literate 48.0%; males literate 56.2%; females literate 40.4%. **Health** (1999): physicians 357 (1 per 15,695 persons); hospital beds 3,380 (1 per 1,657 persons); infant mortality rate per 1,000 live births (2003) 71.5. **Food** (2001): daily per capita caloric intake 1,612 (vegetable products 98%, animal products 2%); 72% of FAO recommended minimum.

Military

Total active duty personnel (2003): 50,500 (army 100%); UN peacekeeping troops (2004) 2,700. **Military expenditure as percentage of GNP** (1999): 7.0% (world 2.4%); per capita expenditure $8.

Background

Original settlement by the Twa people was followed by Hutu settlement, which occurred gradually and was completed by the 11th century. The Tutsi arrived 300–400 years later; though a minority, they established the kingdom of Burundi in the 16th century. In the 19th century the area came within the German sphere of influence, but the Tutsi remained in power. Following World War I the Belgians took control of the area, which became a UN trusteeship after World War II. Colonial-period conditions had intensified Hutu-Tutsi ethnic animosities, and as independence neared, hostilities flared. Independence was granted in 1962 in the form of a kingdom ruled by the Tutsi. In 1965 the Hutu rebelled but were brutally repressed. The rest of the 20th century saw violent clashes between the two groups, leading to charges of genocide in the 1990s. The very unstable government that existed in these surroundings was overthrown by the military in 1996.

Recent Developments

A new constitution under which power would be divided according to a formula between Hutu and Tutsi was overwhelmingly approved on schedule by voters in February 2005, and after elections in August of that year, Pierre Nkurunziza was sworn in as the first democratically elected president since the genocide of 1993 and ensuing 12-year civil war that killed 300,000 people. In September 2006 the government signed a cease-fire agreement with the one remaining rebel group.

Internet resources: <www.burundi.gov.bi>.

Cambodia

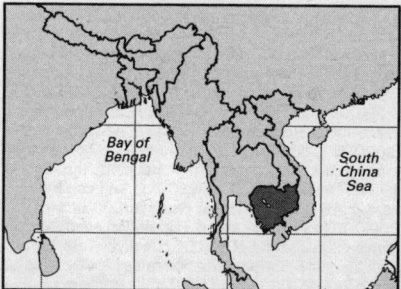

Official name: Preah Reach Ana Pak Kampuchea (Kingdom of Cambodia). **Form of government:** constitutional monarchy with two legislative houses (Senate [61; all seats appointed in 1999; all seats to be elected in future]; National Assembly [123]). **Chief of state:** King Norodom Sihamoni (from 2004). **Head of government:** Prime Minister Hun Sen (from 1998). **Capital:** Phnom Penh. **Official language:** Khmer. **Official religion:** Buddhism. **Monetary unit:** 1 riel = 100 sen; valuation (1 Jul 2007) US$1 = 4,075 riels.

Demography

Area: 69,898 sq mi, 181,035 sq km. **Population** (2006): 13,648,000. **Density** (2006): persons per sq mi 195.3, persons per sq km 75.4. **Urban** (2002): 17.0%. **Sex distribution** (2003): male 48.60%; female 51.40%. **Age breakdown** (2003): under 15, 39.3%; 15–29, 28.8%; 30–44, 18.5%; 45–59, 8.8%; 60–74, 3.7%; 75 and over, 0.9%. **Ethnic composition** (2000): Khmer 85.2%; Chinese 6.4%; Vietnamese 3.0%; Cham 2.5%; Lao 0.6%; other 2.3%. **Religious affilia-**

tion (2000): Buddhist 84.7%; Chinese folk religionist 4.7%; traditional beliefs 4.3%; Muslim 2.3%; Christian 1.1%; other 2.9%. **Major urban areas** (1998): Phnom Penh (2003) 1,157,000; Bat Dambang 124,290; Sisophon 85,382; Siem Reab 83,715; Preah Sihanouk 66,723. **Location:** southeastern Asia, bordering Thailand, Laos, Vietnam, and the Gulf of Thailand.

Vital statistics

Birth rate per 1,000 population (2003): 27.3 (world avg. 21.3). **Death rate** per 1,000 population (2003): 9.3 (world avg. 9.1). **Natural increase rate** per 1,000 population (2003): 18.0 (world avg. 12.2). **Total fertility rate** (avg. births per childbearing woman; 2003): 3.7. **Life expectancy** at birth (2003): male 55.5 years; female 60.5 years.

National economy

Budget (2001). *Revenue:* 1,520,000,000,000 riels (indirect taxes 37.6%, of which value-added taxes 26.5%; taxes on international trade 24.7%; nontax revenue 27.9%). *Expenditures:* 2,329,000,000,000 riels (current expenditure 58.1%, of which civil administration 30.2%, defense and security 16.7%; development expenditure 41.9%). **Public debt** (external, outstanding; 2002): $2,594,000,000. **Production** (metric tons except as noted). *Agriculture, forestry, fishing* (2002): rice 3,740,002, cassava 186,800, corn (maize) 168,700; livestock (number of live animals) 2,924,457 cattle, 2,105,435 pigs, 625,912 buffalo; roundwood (2002) 9,858,000 cu m; fish catch (2001) 412,700. *Mining and quarrying:* legal mining is confined to fertilizers, salt, and construction materials. *Manufacturing* (value added in $'000,000; 2000): wearing apparel 626; textiles 479; leather products 105. *Energy production (consumption):* electricity (kW-hr; 2000) 229,000,000 (229,000,000); petroleum products (2000) negligible (173,000). **Households.** Average household size (2000) 5.7; household expenditure (2002): food, beverages, and tobacco 62.6%, housing and energy 19.7%, health 6.0%, transportation and communications 3.4%. **Gross national product** (2003): $4,105,-000,000 ($310 per capita). **Population economically active** (2002): total 6,399,677; activity rate of total population 48.8% (participation rates [2000]: ages 15 and over, 69.9%; female 54.6%; unemployed 5.3%). **Tourism** (2002): receipts $379,000,000; expenditures $38,000,000. **Land use** as % of total land area (2000): in temporary crops 21.0%, in permanent crops 0.6%, in pasture 8.5%; overall forest area 52.9%.

Foreign trade

Imports (2001): $1,951,000,000 (retained imports 91.1%; imports for reexport 8.9%). *Major import sources* (2002): Thailand 30.2%; Singapore 21.5%; Hong Kong 10.2%; China 7.7%; Vietnam 6.6%. **Exports** (2001): $1,475,000,000 (domestic exports 87.8%, of which garments c. 75%, rubber 3.4%, sawn timber and logs 2.2%; reexports 12.2%). *Major export destinations* (2002): US 61.4%; Germany 8.9%; UK 7.2%.

Transport and communcations

Transport. *Railroads* (1999): length 649 km; passenger-km 49,894,000; metric ton-km 76,171,000.

Roads (1999): total length 35,769 km (paved 12%). *Vehicles* (2002): passenger cars 209,128; trucks and buses 33,164. *Air transport* (2002; combined total of Imtrec Aviation, Phnom Penh Airways, President Airlines, and Siem Reap Airways): passenger-km 60,900,000; metric ton-km cargo 4,100,000; airports (1997) with scheduled flights 8. **Communications,** in total units (units per 1,000 persons). Daily newspaper circulation (2000): 24,000 (2); radios (2000): 1,480,000 (119); televisions (2000): 99,500 (8); telephone main lines (2002): 35,400 (2.6); cellular telephone subscribers (2002): 380,000 (28); personal computers (2002): 27,000 (2); Internet users (2002): 30,000 (2.2).

Education and health

Educational attainment (1998). Percentage of population age 25 and over having: no formal schooling 2.1%; some primary education 56.6%; primary 24.7%; some secondary 11.8%; secondary and above 4.8%. **Literacy** (2000): percentage of total population age 15 and over literate 68.5%; males literate 79.8%; females literate 57.1%. **Health** (2001): physicians 2,047 (1 per 5,862 persons); hospital beds 10,900 (1 per 1,100 persons); infant mortality rate per 1,000 live births (2003) 75.9. **Food** (2001): daily per capita caloric intake 1,967 (vegetable products 91%, animal products 9%); 89% of FAO recommended minimum.

Military

Total active duty personnel (2003; excludes paramilitary forces): 125,000 (army 60.0%, navy 2.4%, air force 1.6%, provincial forces 36.0%). **Military expenditure as percentage of GNP** (1999): 4.0% (world 2.4%); per capita expenditure $28.

Did you know? Angkor was the capital of the Khmer (Cambodian) empire from the 9th to the 15th century AD. Its most imposing monuments are Angkor Wat, a temple complex built in the 12th century by King Suryavarman II (reigned 1113-c. 1150), and Angkor Thom, a temple complex built about 1200 by King Jayavarman VII.

Background

In the early Christian era, what is now Cambodia was under Hindu and, to a lesser extent, Buddhist influence. The Khmer state gradually spread in the early 7th century and reached its height under Jayavarman II and his successors in the 9th–12th centuries, when it ruled the Mekong Valley and the tributary Shan states and built Angkor. Widespread adoption of Buddhism occurred in the 13th century, resulting in a script change from Sanskrit to Pali. From the 13th century Cambodia was attacked by Annam and Siamese city-states and was alternately a province of one or the other. The area became a French protectorate in 1863. It was occupied by the Japanese in World War II and became independent in 1954. Cambodia's borders were the scene of fighting in the Vietnam War from 1961, and in 1970 its northeastern

---

1 metric ton = about 1.1 short tons; 1 kilometer = 0.6 mi (statute); 1 metric ton-km cargo = about 0.68 short ton-mi cargo; c.i.f.: cost, insurance, and freight; f.o.b.: free on board

and eastern areas were occupied by the North Vietnamese and penetrated by US and South Vietnamese forces. An indiscriminate US bombing campaign alienated much of the population, enabling the communist Khmer Rouge under Pol Pot to seize power in 1975. Their regime of terror resulted in the deaths of at least one million Cambodians. Vietnam invaded in 1979 and drove the Khmer Rouge into the western hinterlands, but it was unable to effect reconstruction of the country, and Cambodian infighting continued. A peace accord was reached by most Cambodian factions under UN auspices in 1991, and elections were held in 1993. In 2004 King Norodom Sihanouk abdicated, and his son Sihamoni was named his successor.

Recent Developments

At the beginning of 2005, US quotas for Cambodian textile products (which made up 90% of the country's exports) were removed, resulting in the immediate loss of 20,000 jobs. The US began setting limits on cheaper Chinese imports, however, and Cambodia's prospects brightened. In 2005 garment exports actually gained 10% over 2004 figures, though workers' earnings decreased by 8.5% in the same period. In 2005 oil was discovered in Cambodian waters, and the oil reserves were estimated to contain 2 billion barrels, while natural gas reserves were estimated to contain 10 trillion cu ft. A tribunal was set up to try former leaders of Pol Pot's Khmer Rouge regime for crimes against humanity, and in July 2006 judges and prosecutors were sworn in, but by March 2007 no defendants had been tried.

Internet resources: <www.cambodia.org>.

Cameroon

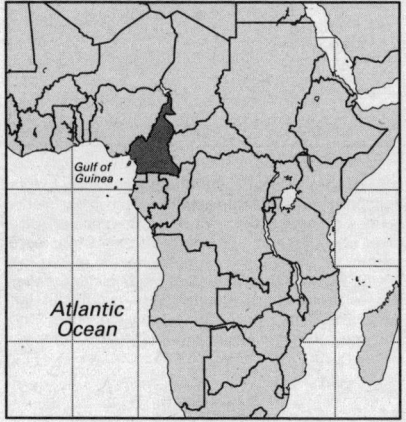

Official name: République du Cameroun (French); Republic of Cameroon (English). **Form of government:** unitary multiparty republic with one legislative house (National Assembly [180]). **Chief of state:** President Paul Biya (from 1982). **Head of government:** Prime Minister Ephraïm Inoni (from 2004). **Capital:** Yaoundé. **Official languages:** French; English. **Official

religion: none. **Monetary unit:** 1 CFA franc (CFAF) = 100 centimes; valuation (1 Jul 2007) US$1 = CFAF 485.18 (formerly pegged to the French franc and, since 1 Jan 2002, to the euro [€] at the rate of €1 = CFAF 655.96).

Demography

Area: 183,569 sq mi, 475,442 sq km. **Population** (2006): 17,341,000. **Density** (2006; based on land area): persons per sq mi 96.6, persons per sq km 37.3. **Urban** (2002): 49.7%. **Sex distribution** (2003): male 50.27%; female 49.73%. **Age breakdown** (2003): under 15, 42.3%; 15–29, 29.0%; 30–44, 15.3%; 45–59, 8.4%; 60–74, 4.0%; 75 and over, 0.9%. **Ethnic composition** (1983): Fang 19.6%; Bamileke and Bamum 18.5%; Duala, Luanda, and Basa 14.7%; Fuani 9.6%; Tikar 7.4%; Mandara 5.7%; Maka 4.9%; Chamba 2.4%; Mbum 1.3%; Hausa 1.2%; French 0.2%; other 14.5%. **Religious affiliation** (2000): Roman Catholic 26.4%; traditional beliefs 23.7%; Muslim 21.2%; Protestant 20.7%. **Major cities** (2003): Douala 1,239,100; Yaoundé 1,122,500; Garoua 185,800; Maroua 169,200; Bafoussam 151,800. **Location:** western Africa, bordering Chad, Central African Republic, Republic of the Congo, Gabon, Equatorial Guinea, the Bight of Biafra and Nigeria.

Vital statistics

Birth rate per 1,000 population (2003): 35.5 (world avg. 21.3). **Death rate** per 1,000 population (2003): 15.3 (world avg. 9.1). **Natural increase rate** per 1,000 population (2003): 20.2 (world avg. 12.2). **Total fertility rate** (avg. births per childbearing woman; 2003): 4.6. **Life expectancy** at birth (2003): male 47.2 years; female 49.0 years. **Adult population** (ages 15–49) living with HIV (2004): 6.9% (world avg. 1.1%).

National economy

Budget (2000–01). *Revenue:* CFAF 1,326,000,000,000 (oil revenue 33.0%; taxes on goods and services 32.9%; income tax 16.6%; customs duties 11.2%). *Expenditures:* CFAF 1,175,000,000,000 (current expenditure 80.9%, of which wages and salaries 28.8%, debt service 20.9%, goods and services 20.0%, transfers 11.3%; capital expenditure 19.1%). **Public debt** (external, outstanding; 2002): $7,240,000,000. **Gross national product** (2003): $10,287,000,000 ($640 per capita). **Households.** Average household size (2000) 5.5; expenditure (1993): food 49.1%, housing 18.0%, transportation and communications 13.0%, health 8.6%, clothing 7.6%, recreation 2.4%. **Tourism** (2000): receipts $39,000,000; expenditures (1995) $105,000,000. **Population economically active** (1991): total 4,740,000; activity rate of total population 40.0% (participation rates [1985]: ages 15–69, 66.3%; female 38.5%). **Production** (metric tons except as noted). *Agriculture, forestry, fishing* (2002): cassava 1,900,000, sugarcane 1,350,000, plantains 1,200,000; livestock (number of live animals) 5,900,000 cattle, 4,400,000 goats, 3,800,000 sheep; roundwood (2002) 10,526,000 cu m; fish catch (2001) 111,100. *Mining and quarrying* (2002): pozzolana 620,000; aluminum 80,000; gold 1,000 kg. *Manufacturing* (value added in $'000; 1999): beverages 182; food products 149; textiles 112. *Energy production (consumption):* electricity (kW-hr; 2000) 3,441,000,000 (3,441,000,000); coal (2000) 1,000 (1,000); crude petroleum (barrels; 2000) 52,000,000

(10,700,000); petroleum products (2000) 1,530,000 (898,000). **Land use** as % of total land area (2000): in temporary crops 12.8%, in permanent crops 2.6%, in pasture 4.3%; overall forest area 51.3%.

Foreign trade

Imports (2000–01): CFAF 1,157,800,000,000 (minerals and other raw materials c. 21%, semifinished goods c. 16%, industrial equipment c. 13%, food and beverages c. 11%, transport equipment c. 10%). *Major import sources:* France c. 24%; Nigeria c. 20%; Germany c. 5%; US c. 5%; Japan c. 5%; Belgium-Luxembourg c. 5%. **Exports** (2000–01): CFAF 1,540,200,-000,000 (crude petroleum c. 50.6%, lumber c. 13.4%, cocoa beans c. 6.3%, aluminum c. 4.6%, cotton c. 4.2%, coffee c. 3.7%). *Major export destinations:* Italy c. 24%; France c. 9%; Spain c. 9%; The Netherlands c. 7%; China c. 7%; Taiwan c. 7%.

Transport and communications

Transport. *Railroads* (2001): route length 1,016 km; passenger-km 237,800,000; metric ton-km cargo 854,600,000. *Roads* (1999): total length 49,300 km (paved 8%). *Vehicles* (1997): passenger cars 98,000; trucks and buses 64,350. *Air transport* (2001): passenger-km 796,567,000; metric ton-km cargo 23,255,000; airports (1998) with scheduled flights 5. **Communications,** in total units (units per 1,000 persons). Daily newspaper circulation (2000): 104,-000 (7); radios (2000): 2,410,000 (163); televisions (2000): 503,000 (34); telephone main lines (2002): 110,900 (7); cellular telephone subscribers (2003): 1,077,000 (66); personal computers (2002): 90,000 (5.7); Internet users (2002): 60,000 (3.8).

Education and health

Literacy (2001): percentage of total population age 15 and over literate 72.5%; males literate 79.9%; females literate 65.1%. **Health:** physicians (1996) 1,031 (1 per 13,510 persons); hospital beds (1988) 29,285 (1 per 371 persons); infant mortality rate per 1,000 live births (2003) 70.1. **Food** (2001): daily per capita caloric intake 2,242 (vegetable products 94%, animal products 6%); 97% of FAO recommended minimum.

Military

Total active duty personnel (2003): 14,100 (army 88.7%, navy 9.2%, air force 2.1%). **Military expenditure as percentage of GNP** (1999): 1.8% (world 2.4%); per capita expenditure $10.

Background

The Cameroon area had long been inhabited before European colonization. Bantu speakers from equatorial Africa settled in the south, followed by Muslim Fulani from the Niger River basin, who settled in the north. Portuguese explorers visited in the late 15th century and established a foothold, but they lost control to the Dutch in the 17th century. In 1884 the Germans took control and extended their protectorate over Cameroon. In World War I joint French-British action forced the Germans to retreat, and after the war the region was divided into French and British admin-

istrative zones. After World War II the two areas became UN trusteeships. In 1960 the French trust territory became an independent republic. In 1961 the southern part of the British trust territory voted for union with the new republic of Cameroon, and the northern part voted for union with Nigeria. In recent decades economic problems have produced unrest in the country.

Recent Developments

In August 2006 a ceremony was held marking the transfer of sovereignty of the petroleum-rich Bakassi peninsula from Nigeria to Cameroon. It had been the source of contention for years, and the resolution brought the possibility of significant oil revenue to Cameroon. In May 2006 the IMF announced the cancellation of 27% of Cameroon's public debt. Although various anticorruption measures were in effect, in July 2005 and April 2006 prominent editors were imprisoned for alleging that high-ranking civil servants had embezzled hundreds of thousands of dollars.

Internet resources:
<www.cameroon.net/cameroon-guide.php>.

Canada

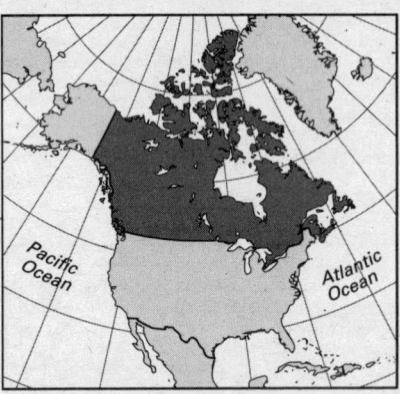

Official name: Canada. **Form of government:** federal multiparty parliamentary state with two legislative houses (Senate [105]; House of Commons [308]). **Chief of state:** Queen Elizabeth II (from 1952), represented by Governor-General Michaëlle Jean (from 2005). **Head of government:** Prime Minister Stephen Harper (from 2006). **Capital:** Ottawa. **Official languages:** English; French. **Official religion:** none. **Monetary unit:** 1 Canadian dollar (Can$) = 100 cents; valuation (1 Jul 2007) US$1 = Can$1.06.

Demography

Area: 3,855,103 sq mi, 9,984,670 sq km. **Population** (2006): 32,547,000. **Density** (2006; based on land area of 3,511,023 sq mi [9,093,507 sq km]): persons per sq mi 9.3, persons per sq km 3.6. **Urban** (2001): 78.9%. **Sex distribution** (2003): male 49.51%; female

---

1 metric ton = about 1.1 short tons;   1 kilometer = 0.6 mi (statute);   1 metric ton-km cargo = about 0.68 short ton-mi cargo;   c.i.f.: cost, insurance, and freight;   f.o.b.: free on board

50.49%. **Age breakdown** (2003): under 15, 18.3%; 15–29, 20.3%; 30–44, 23.4%; 45–59, 20.7%; 60–74, 11.3%; 75 and over, 6.0%. **Ethnic origin** (2000): Anglo-Canadian 45.5%; French-Canadian 23.5%; Chinese 3.4%; British expatriates 3.3%; Indo-Pakistani 2.6%, of which Punjabi 2.3%; German 2.4%; Italian 2.2%; US white 1.8%; Métis (part-Indian) 1.8%; Indian 1.5%, of which detribalized 0.5%; Jewish 1.4%; Arab 1.3%; Ukrainian 1.2%; Eskimo (Inuit) 0.1%; other 8.0%. **Religious affiliation** (2001): Christian 77.1%, of which Roman Catholic 43.2%, Protestant 28.3%, unspecified Christian 2.6%, Orthodox 1.7%, other Christian 1.3%; Muslim 2.0%; Jewish 1.1%; Hindu 1.0%; Buddhist 1.0%; Sikh 0.9%; nonreligious 16.5%; other 0.4%. **Major metropolitan areas** (2002): Toronto 5,029,900; Montreal 3,548,800; Vancouver 2,122,-700; Ottawa-Hull 1,128,900; Calgary 993,200; Edmonton 967,200; Quebec 697,800; Hamilton 686,900; Winnipeg 685,500; Kitchener 438,000. **Location:** northern North America, bordering the Arctic Ocean, the North Atlantic Ocean, the US, and the North Pacific Ocean. **Place of birth** (2001): 81.6% native-born; 18.4% foreign-born, of which UK 2.0%, other European 5.7%, Asian countries 5.8%, US 0.8%, other 4.1%. **Mobility** (2001). Population living in the same residence as in 1996: 58.1%; different residence, same municipality 22.4%; same province, different municipality 3.3%; different province 12.7%; different country 3.5%. **Households.** Total number of households (2002) 11,657,730. Average household size (2002) 2.7; 1 person (1997) 25.2%, 2 persons 33.0%, 3 persons 16.7%, 4 persons 16.3%, 5 or more persons 8.8%. Family households (2001): 8,371,020 (72.4%), nonfamily 3,191,955 (27.6%, of which 1 person 75.6%). **Immigration** (2002): permanent immigrants admitted 222,447; (2000) from Asia 62.1%, of which India 11.6%, Philippines 5.6%, Vietnam 0.7%, Hong Kong 0.3%; US 2.4%; UK 2.1%; refugee arrivals (2002) 27,899.

Vital statistics

Birth rate per 1,000 population (2003): 10.5 (world avg. 21.3); (1997) legitimate 72.3%. **Death rate** per 1,000 population (2003): 7.2 (world avg. 9.1). **Natural increase rate** per 1,000 population (2003): 3.3 (world avg. 12.2). **Total fertility rate** (avg. births per child-bearing woman; 2002): 1.6. **Marriage rate** per 1,000 population (2003): 4.8. **Divorce rate** per 1,000 population (2003): 2.2. **Life expectancy** at birth (2003): male 76.4 years; female 83.4 years.

Social indicators

Quality of working life. Average workweek (2000): 31.6 hours. Annual rate per 100,000 workers for (1997): injury, accident, or industrial illness 1,330; death 2.7. Average days lost to labor stoppages per 1,000 employee-workdays (2001): 0.7. Average commuting distance (2001): 4.5 mi, 7.2 km; mode of transportation: automobile 80.7%, public transportation 10.5%, walking 6.6%, other 2.2%. Labor force covered by a pension plan (2001): 33.6%. **Access to services.** Proportion of households having access to: electricity (2002) 100.0%; public water supply (1996) 99.8%; public sewage collection (1996) 99.3%. **Social participation.** Eligible voters participating in last national election (June 2004): 60.5%. Population over 18 years of age participating in voluntary work (2000): 26.7%. Union membership as percentage of civilian labor force (2003) 25.0%. Attendance at reli-

gious services on a weekly basis (2001): 20.0%. **Social deviance** (2003). Offense rate per 100,000 population for: violent crime 962.8, of which assault 746.5, sexual assault 74.1, homicide 1.7; property crime 4,121, of which auto theft 541, burglary 900. **Leisure** (1998). Favorite leisure activities (hours weekly): television (2002) 21.6; social time 13.3; reading 2.8; sports and entertainment 1.4. **Material well-being** (1999). Households possessing: automobile 64.4%; telephone 98.2%; cellular phone 31.9%; color television 99.9%; central air conditioner 34.0%; cable television 73.3%; home computers 49.8%; Internet access 33.1%.

National economy

Gross national product (2003): US$756,770,-000,000 (US$23,930 per capita). **Budget** (2003–04; federal revenues and expenditures). *Revenue:* Can$204,075,000,000 (income tax 60.8%, sales tax 21.6%, contributions to social security 10.8%, other 6.8%). *Expenditures:* Can$197,296,000,000 (social services and welfare 37.9%, defense and social protection 13.0%, public debt interest 12.1%, economy 3.9%, health 3.1%, education 2.4%). **Public debt** (2001): US$406,000,000,000. **Tourism** (2002): receipts US$9,700,000,000; expenditures US$9,929,-000,000. **Production** (metric tons except as noted). *Agriculture, forestry, fishing* (2002): wheat 15,689,-000, corn (maize) 9,069,000, barley 7,282,600, potatoes 4,645,000, rapeseed 3,577,100, oats 2,748,000, vegetables 2,435,000 (of which tomatoes 690,000, carrots 280,000, onions 190,000, cabbage 160,000), soybeans 2,334,000, dry peas 1,365,000, linseed 679,400, sugar beets 540,000, apples 460,000; livestock (number of live animals) 14,367,100 pigs, 13,699,500 cattle, 993,600 sheep; roundwood (2002) 193,168,000 cu m; fish catch (2001) 1,116,902. *Mining and quarrying* (value of production in Can$'000,000; 2002): gold 2,292; nickel 1,883; potash 1,598; copper 1,419; iron ore 1,392; zinc 1,090; sand and gravel 1,047; stone 972; diamonds 802. *Manufacturing* (value of shipments in Can$'000,000; 2002): transportation equipment 119,746; food 62,911; chemicals 37,679; paper products 32,726; petroleum and coal 32,250; primary metals 32,216; wood industries 29,498; fabricated metal products 27,510; machinery 24,113; rubber and plastic products 23,002; computers and electronic products 21,255. *Energy production (consumption):* electricity (kW-hr; 2000) 590,134,000,000 (554,411,000,000); hard coal (2000) 33,804,000 (21,620,000); lignite (2000) 35,359,000 (40,459,000); crude petroleum (barrels; 2000) 655,400,000 (554,300,000); petroleum products (2000) 103,972,000 (88,296,000); natural gas (cu m; 2000) 164,352,000,000 (76,277,000,000). **Population economically active** (2003): total 17,046,800; activity rate of total population 54.0% (participation rates: ages 15 and over 67.5%; female 46.4%; unemployed [August 2004] 7.2%). **Household income and expenditure** (2002). Average household size 2.6; average annual income per family (2002) Can$73,200; sources of income (1995): wages and salaries 57.0%, transfer payments 20.7%, property and entrepreneurial income 13.7%, profits 8.6%; expenditure (2002): housing 25.9%, food, alcohol, and tobacco 18.9%, transportation and communications 19.5%, recreation 8.2%, utilities 6.4%, clothing 5.7%, household durable goods 4.1%, health 3.7%, education 2.1%, other 5.5%. **Land use** as % of total land area (2000): in temporary crops 4.9%, in permanent crops 0.02%, in pasture 3.1%; overall forest area 26.5%.

Foreign trade

Imports (2002): Can$348,198,000,000 (machinery and apparatus 27.8%; transport equipment 21.5%, of which road vehicles 19.1%; chemicals and chemical products 9.4%; food products 5.1%; crude petroleum 3.4%). *Major import sources:* US 62.6%; China 4.6%; Japan 4.4%; Mexico 3.6%; UK 2.8%; Germany 2.4%; France 1.7%. **Exports** (2002): Can$396,020,-000,000 (transport equipment 24.8%, of which road vehicles 21.4%; machinery and apparatus 13.3%; food products 6.4%; chemicals and chemical products 5.9%; natural gas 5.2%; wood and wood pulp 4.7%; crude petroleum 4.5%; paper and paperboard 4.4%). *Major export destinations:* US 87.2%; Japan 2.1%; UK 1.1%; China 1.0%; Germany 0.7%.

Transport and communications

Transport. *Railroads* (2000): length 65,403 km; passenger-km 1,571,000,000; metric ton-km cargo 319,382,000,000. *Roads* (1999): total length 901,-903 km (paved 35%). *Vehicles* (1998): passenger cars 13,887,270; trucks and buses 3,694,125. *Air transport* (2003): passenger-km 59,016,000,000; metric ton-km cargo 1,284,800,000; airports (1997) 269. **Communications,** in total units (units per 1,000 persons). Daily newspaper circulation (2000): 4,890,000 (159); radios (2000): 32,200,000 (1,047); televisions (2000): 21,700,000 (691); telephone main lines (2003): 19,950,900 (658); cellular telephone subscribers (2003): 13,221,800 (417); personal computers (2002): 15,300,000 (487); Internet users (2002): 16,110,000 (513).

Education and health

Educational attainment (2001). Percentage of population age 15 and over having: incomplete primary education 2.2%; complete primary education 7.6%; some secondary and complete secondary 49.5%; postsecondary 25.3%; undergraduate degree 10.1%; graduate degree 5.3%. **Literacy** (2003): total population age 15 and over literate virtually 100%. **Health:** physicians (2000) 60,559 (1 per 508 persons); hospital beds (1997) 161,867 (1 per 185 persons); infant mortality rate per 1,000 live births (2001) 5.0. **Food** (2001): daily per capita caloric intake 3,176 (vegetable products 70%, animal products 30%); 121% of FAO recommended minimum.

Military

Total active duty personnel (2003): 52,300 (army 36.9%, navy 17.2%, air force 25.8%, not identified by service 20.1%). **Military expenditure as percentage of GNP** (1999): 1.4% (world 2.4%); per capita expenditure US$269.

Background

Originally inhabited by American Indians and Inuit, Canada was visited c. AD 1000 by Scandinavian explorers, whose discovery is confirmed by archaeological evidence from Newfoundland. Fishing expeditions off Newfoundland by the English, French, Spanish, and Portuguese began as early as 1500. The French claim to Canada was made in 1534 when Jacques Cartier entered the Gulf of St. Lawrence. A small settlement was made in Nova Scotia (Acadia) in 1605, and in 1608 Samuel de Champlain founded Quebec. Fur trading was the impetus behind the early colonizing efforts. In response to French activity, the English in 1670 formed the Hudson's Bay Company.

The British-French rivalry for the interior of upper North America lasted almost a century. The first French loss occurred in 1713 at the conclusion of Queen Anne's War (War of the Spanish Succession) when Nova Scotia and Newfoundland were ceded to the British. The Seven Years' War (French and Indian War) resulted in France's expulsion from continental North America in 1763. After the US War of Independence, the population was augmented by Loyalists fleeing the US, and the increasing number arriving in Quebec led the British to divide the colony into Upper and Lower Canada in 1791. The British reunited the two provinces in 1841. Canadian expansionism resulted in the confederation movement of the mid-19th century, and in 1867 the Dominion of Canada, comprising Nova Scotia, New Brunswick, Quebec, and Ontario, came into existence. After confederation, Canada entered a period of westward expansion.

The prosperity that accompanied Canada into the 20th century was marred by continuing conflict between the English and French communities. Through the Statute of Westminster (1931), Canada was recognized as an equal of Great Britain. With the Constitution Act of 1982, the British gave Canada total control over its constitution and severed the remaining legal connections between the two countries. French Canadian unrest continued to be a major concern, with a movement growing for Quebec separatism in the late 20th century. Referendums for more political autonomy for Quebec were rejected in 1992 and 1995, but the issue remained unresolved. In 1999 Canada formed the new territory of Nunavut, and in December 2001 Newfoundland was renamed Newfoundland and Labrador.

Recent Developments

In 2006 Canada gained a new Conservative government and a new prime minister, Stephen Harper. A plan to give the parents of children under age six a monthly child-care grant was quickly implemented. The government also moved swiftly on a promise to cut 1% from the federal goods and services tax. The government concluded that the Kyoto Treaty targets for reducing greenhouse-gas emissions were unattainable, and in October the Clean Air Act, which promised to limit smog levels beginning in 2010 and cut greenhouse-gas emissions in half by 2050, was introduced.

The year 2006 had opened on a confident note with the announcement that in 2005, for the first time, Canada had enjoyed a surplus in trade. The tar sands of northern Alberta constituted one of the largest energy reserves in the world, second only to Saudi Arabia. Canada was the world's fifth largest energy producer, which, the International Monetary Fund reported, would help Canada achieve economic

---

1 metric ton = about 1.1 short tons;   1 kilometer = 0.6 mi (statute);   1 metric ton-km cargo = about 0.68 short ton-mi cargo;   c.i.f.: cost, insurance, and freight;   f.o.b.: free on board

growth of 3% in 2006. This result greatly strengthened the Canadian dollar (in May it reached its highest standing against the US dollar in 28 years). The
overall unemployment rate fell to 6.1% in May, its lowest level since 1972. In the face of this impressive
economic performance, the Harper government was
able to deliver its first budget that month, with 28
separate tax reductions and concessions aimed at
middle-class voters and tax cuts amounting to
Can$26 billion planned over the next three years.
Extra funds would go to the military, and there would
be more funding for aboriginal housing and education. A budget surplus of Can$12 billion was recorded
for the fiscal year 2005–06, the ninth consecutive
federal surplus, and a higher surplus was predicted
for fiscal 2006–07.

Canada cut off aid to the Palestinian Authority after
Hamas won the general election, fearing that some of
the funds might be diverted to terrorist operations.
Canada strongly supported efforts to bring stability to
Afghanistan. It had stationed troops in Kandahar in
southern Afghanistan in 2005, and in early 2006 it
sent 2,300 soldiers to work with US and British troops
stationed in the area. In May the government asked
Parliament to extend the country's mandate in
Afghanistan until 2009. On that same day, however, a
woman officer had been killed by gunfire in
Afghanistan, the first woman in Canadian history to
die in combat. The mandate was extended by a vote
of only 149 to 145. Harper sought to restore close relations with the administration of US Pres. George W.
Bush, ties that he claimed had been weakened by the
previous government. At a meeting in March, the two
declared their intention to resolve a five-year dispute
over the US imposition of tariffs on softwood-lumber
imports from Canada, which had damaged a trade
valued at some Can$50 billion annually. In April a
deal was announced under which Canada was allowed to ship as much lumber as it wished to the US.
If the price of the Canadian lumber fell below a settled
point, then Canada would be required to impose an
export tax on lumber shipments or submit to a quota
system. It was hoped that the dispute between the
two countries, which shared the largest bilateral trade
flow in the world, would be brought to a conclusion.

Internet resources: <www.travelcanada.ca>.

Cape Verde

Official name: República de Cabo Verde (Republic of
Cape Verde). **Form of government:** multiparty republic with one legislative house (National Assembly
[72]). **Chief of state:** President Pedro Pires (from
2001). **Head of government:** Prime Minister José
Maria Neves (from 2001). **Capital:** Praia. **Official language:** Portuguese. **Official religion:** none. **Monetary
unit:** 1 escudo (C.V.Esc.) = 100 centavos; valuation (1
Jul 2007) US$1 = C.V.Esc. 81.46 (formerly pegged to
the Portuguese escudo and, since 1 Jan 2002, to the
euro [€] at the rate of €1 = C.V.Esc. 110.27).

Demography

Area: 1,557 sq mi, 4,033 sq km. **Population** (2006):
485,000. **Density** (2004): persons per sq mi 311.5,
persons per sq km 120.3. **Urban** (2002) 63.5%. **Sex
distribution** (2003): male 48.39%; female 51.61%.
Age breakdown (2003): under 15, 41.0%; 15–29,
26.7%; 30–44, 17.0%; 45–59, 6.8%; 60–74, 5.8%;

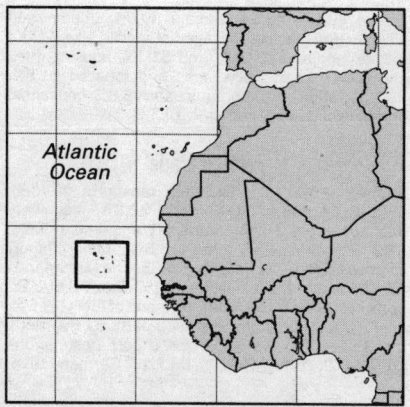

75 and over, 2.7%. **Ethnic composition** (2000): Cape
Verdean *mestico* (black-white admixture) 69.6%; Fulani 12.2%; Balanta 10.0%; Mandyako 4.6%; Portuguese white 2.0%; other 1.6%. **Religious affiliation**
(2000): Roman Catholic 91.4%; Muslim 2.8%; other
5.8%. **Major cities** (2000): Praia 94,757; Mindelo
62,970; São Filipe 7,894. **Location:** off the coast of
western Africa; consists of 10 islands in the North Atlantic Ocean.

Vital statistics

Birth rate per 1,000 population (2003): 27.0 (world
avg. 21.3); (1989) legitimate 28.9%. **Death rate** per
1,000 population (2002): 6.9 (world avg. 9.1). **Natural increase rate** per 1,000 population (2002): 20.1
(world avg. 12.2). **Total fertility rate** (avg. births per
childbearing woman; 2003): 3.8. **Marriage rate** per
1,000 population (1994): 3.1. **Life expectancy** at
birth (2003): male 66.5 years; female 73.2 years.

National economy

Budget (2001). *Revenue:* C.V.Esc. 14,900,000,000
(tax revenue 87.2%, of which taxes on international
trade 35.6%, income taxes 32.2%, sales taxes 14.1%;
nontax revenue 12.8%). *Expenditures:* C.V.Esc.
21,200,000,000 (current expenditure 69.8%, of
which wages and salaries 31.1%, transfers 26.9%,
public debt 6.6%, goods and services 2.9%; capital expenditure 30.2%). **Public debt** (external, outstanding;
2002): $385,000,000. **Production** (metric tons ex-
cept as noted). *Agriculture, forestry, fishing* (2002):
corn (maize) 20,000, sugarcane 14,000, bananas
6,000; livestock (number of live animals) 200,000
pigs, 112,000 goats, 22,000 cattle; fish catch (2000)
10,821. *Mining and quarrying* (2000): salt 2,000.
Manufacturing (1999): flour 15,901; bread 5,628
(1995); soap 833. *Energy production (consumption):*
electricity (kW-hr; 2001) 43,000,000 (43,000,000);
petroleum products (2001) none (101,619). **Tourism**
(2002): receipts from visitors $66,000,000; expendi-
tures by nationals abroad $56,000,000. **Land use** as
% of total land area (2000): in temporary crops 9.7%,
in permanent crops 0.5%, in pasture 6.2%; overall forest area 21.1%. **Gross national product** (2003):
$701,000,000 ($1,490 per capita). **Population economically active** (2000): total 174,644; activity rate
of total population 40.2% (participation rates: ages

15–64 [1990] 64.3%; female 39.0%; unemployed 17.4%). **Households.** Average household size (2000) 4.6; expenditure (1988): food 51.1%, housing, fuel, and power 13.5%, beverages and tobacco 11.8%, transportation and communications 8.8%, household durable goods 6.9%, other 7.9%.

Foreign trade

Imports (2000-c.i.f.; excludes reexports of fuel): C.V.Esc. 27,585,000,000 (food 32.8%, machinery and apparatus 16.1%, transport equipment 9.5%, base and fabricated metals 6.5%). *Major import sources* (2001–02): Portugal 54.8%; The Netherlands 13.4%; Spain 4.9%; Belgium 4.1%; Brazil 3.6%. **Exports** (2000-f.o.b.; excludes reexports of fuel): C.V.Esc. 1,272,000,000 (shoes and shoe parts 51.8%, clothing 35.1%, fish 4.8%). *Major export destinations* (2001–02): Portugal 91.7%; US 2.1%; Germany 1.6%.

Transport and communications

Transport. *Roads* (1999): total length 1,100 km (paved [1996] 78%). *Vehicles* (2000): passenger cars 13,473; trucks and buses 3,085. *Air transport* (2001; TACV airline only): passenger-km 276,000,-000; metric ton-km cargo 26,000,000; airports (1997) with scheduled flights 9. **Communications,** in total units (units per 1,000 persons). Radios (1997): 71,000 (179); televisions (2000): 2,000 (4.6); telephone main lines (2003): 71,700 (156); cellular telephone subscribers (2003): 53,300 (116); personal computers (2002): 35,000 (78); Internet users (2003): 20,400 (44).

Education and health

Educational attainment (1990). Percentage of population age 25 and over having: no formal schooling 47.9%; primary 40.9%; incomplete secondary 3.9%; complete secondary 1.4%; higher 1.5%; unknown 4.4%. **Literacy** (2000): total population age 15 and over literate 73.8%; males 84.5%; females 65.7%. **Health** (2000): physicians 102 (1 per 4,274 persons); hospital beds 689 (1 per 631 persons); infant mortality rate per 1,000 live births (2002) 50.5. **Food** (2001): daily per capita caloric intake 3,308 (vegetable products 85%, animal products 15%); 141% of FAO recommended minimum.

Military

Total active duty personnel (2003): 1,200 (army 83.3%, air force 8.3%, coast guard 8.4%). **Military expenditure as percentage of GNP** (1999): 0.9% (world 2.4%); per capita expenditure $13.

Background

When visited by the Portuguese in 1456–60, the islands were uninhabited. In 1460 Diogo Gomes sighted and named Maio and São Tiago, and in 1462 the first settlers landed on São Tiago, founding the city of Ribeira Grande. The city's importance grew with the development of the slave trade, but its wealth attracted pirates so often that it was abandoned after 1712. The prosperity of the Portuguese-controlled islands vanished with the decline of the

slave trade in the 19th century but later improved because of their position on the great trade routes between Europe, South America, and southern Africa. In 1951 the colony became an overseas province of Portugal. Many islanders preferred outright independence, and it was finally granted in 1975. At one time associated politically with Guinea-Bissau, Cape Verde split from it in 1981.

Recent Developments

The UN Economic and Social Council decided to remove Cape Verde from its list of "least developed countries." This would take effect in 2008 if there were no significant setbacks. Although this represented recognition of strong economic growth and sound policies, there was some concern as well, as graduation from the list would bring with it a drop in the availability of development funds, low-interest loans, and aid. Cape Verde's main sources of income remained aid, overseas remittances, and fish exports.

Internet resources: <www.ine.cv>.

Central African Republic

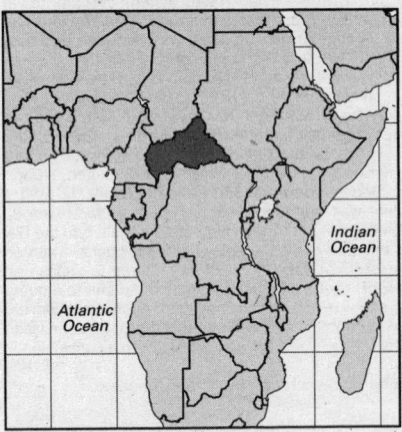

Official name: République Centrafricaine (Central African Republic). **Form of government:** military regime with one advisory body (National Transitional Council [63]). **Chief of state:** President François Bozizé (from 2003). **Head of government:** Prime Minister Élie Doté (from 2005). **Capital:** Bangui. **Official languages:** French; Sango. **Official religion:** none. **Monetary unit:** 1 CFA franc (CFAF) = 100 centimes; valuation (1 Jul 2007) US$1 = CFAF 485.18 (formerly pegged to the French franc and, since 1 Jan 2002, to the euro [€] at the rate of €1 = CFAF 655.96).

Demography

Area: 240,324 sq mi, 622,436 sq km. **Population** (2006): 4,039,000. **Density** (2006): persons per sq mi 16.8, persons per sq km 6.5. **Urban** (2002): 41.7%. **Sex distribution** (2003): male 49.47%; female

---

1 metric ton = about 1.1 short tons;   1 kilometer = 0.6 mi (statute);   1 metric ton-km cargo = about 0.68 short ton-mi cargo;   c.i.f.: cost, insurance, and freight;   f.o.b.: free on board

50.53%. **Age breakdown** (2003): under 15, 43.1%; 15–29, 28.9%; 30–44, 14.6%; 45–59, 8.2%; 60–74, 4.2%; 75 and over, 1.0%. **Ethnolinguistic composition** (1988): Gbaya (Baya) 23.7%; Banda 23.4%; Mandjia 14.7%; Ngbaka 7.6%; Sara 6.5%; Mbum 6.3%; Kare 2.4%; French 0.1%; other 15.3%. **Religious affiliation** (2000): Christian 67.8%, of which Roman Catholic 18.4%, Protestant 14.4%, African Christian 11.6%, other Christian 23.4%; Muslim 15.6%; traditional beliefs 15.4%; other 1.2%. **Major cities** (1994): Bangui 524,000; Berbérati 47,000; Bouar 43,000; Bambari 41,000; Carnot 41,000. **Location**: central Africa, bordering Chad, The Sudan, Democratic Republic of the Congo, Republic of the Congo, and Cameroon.

Vital statistics

Birth rate per 1,000 population (2003): 35.9 (world avg. 21.3). **Death rate** per 1,000 population (2003): 19.7 (world avg. 9.1). **Natural increase rate** per 1,000 population (2003): 16.2 (world avg. 12.2). **Total fertility rate** (avg. births per childbearing woman; 2003): 4.7. **Life expectancy** at birth (2003): male 40.2 years; female 43.3 years. **Adult population** (ages 15–49) living with HIV (2004): 13.5% (world avg. 1.1%).

National economy

Budget (2001). *Revenue:* CFAF 63,200,000,000 (1999; taxes 88.0%, of which international trade tax 38.0%, indirect domestic tax 30.1%, taxes on income and profits 19.9%; nontax receipts 12.0%). *Expenditures:* CFAF 97,200,000,000 (current expenditure 61.2%, of which wages 30.5%; public investment program 38.8%. **Public debt** (external, outstanding; 2002): $980,000,000. **Production** (metric tons except as noted). *Agriculture, forestry, fishing* (2002): cassava 563,000, yams 400,000, peanuts (groundnuts) 127,800; livestock (number of live animals; 2002) 3,273,000 cattle, 2,921,000 goats, 4,575,000 chickens; roundwood (2001) 3,058,000 cu m; fish catch (2001) 15,125. *Mining and quarrying* (2002): gold 20 kg, diamonds 415,000 carats (official figure; at least an equal amount was smuggled out of the country in 2002). *Manufacturing* (value added in $'000; 1994): food, beverages, and tobacco 19,000; chemical products 3,000; wood products 2,000. *Energy production (consumption):* electricity (kW-hr; 2000) 107,000,000 (107,000,000); petroleum products (2000) none (88,000). **Household income and expenditure.** Average household size (2000) 5.9; average annual income per household (1988) CFAF 91,985; expenditure (1991): food 70.5%, clothing 8.5%, other manufactured products 7.6%, energy 7.3%, services (including transportation and communications, recreation, and health) 6.1%. **Gross national product** (2003): $1,019,000,000 ($260 per capita). **Population economically active** (2000): total 1,752,000; activity rate of total population 50.0% (participation rates [1988]: ages 15–64, 78.3%; female 46.8%). **Land use** as % of total land area (2000): in temporary crops 3.1%, in permanent crops 0.1%, in pasture 5.0%; overall forest area 36.8%. **Tourism** (2002): receipts $3,000,000; expenditures $29,000,000.

Foreign trade

Imports (2001): CFAF 84,800,000,000 (1996; road vehicles 18.3%, machinery and apparatus 15.8%, raw cotton 9.7%, refined petroleum 8.0%, food 7.0%).

Major import sources (1999): France 34%; Cameroon 12%; Belgium 7%; UK 4%; Japan 3%. **Exports** (2001): CFAF 100,500,000,000 (wood 41.3%, diamonds 41.0%, cotton 7.4%, coffee 1.8%). *Major export destinations* (1999): Belgium 65%; Spain 6%; Indonesia 4%; France 3%; UK 3%.

Transport and communications

Transport. *Roads* (1999): total length 23,810 km (paved 3%). *Vehicles* (1996): passenger cars 8,900; trucks and buses 7,000. *Air transport* (1998: Air Afrique, an airline jointly owned by 11 African countries [including the Central African Republic], was declared bankrupt in February 2002): passenger-km 258,000,000; metric ton-km cargo 38,000,000; airports (2001) 1. **Communications,** in total units (units per 1,000 persons). Daily newspaper circulation (2000): 7,000 (2); radios (2000): 280,000 (80); televisions (2002): 22,800 (6); telephone main lines (2002): 9,000 (2.3); cellular telephone subscribers (2002): 13,000 (3.1); personal computers (2002): 8,000 (2); Internet users (2002): 5,000 (1.3).

Education and health

Educational attainment (1988). Percentage of population age 10 and over having: no formal schooling 59.3%; primary education 29.6%; lower secondary 7.5%; upper secondary 2.3%; higher 1.3%. **Literacy** (2000): total population age 15 and over literate 46.7%; males literate 59.7%; females literate 34.9%. **Health** (1995): physicians 112 (1 per 28,600 persons); hospital beds (1998) 3,044 (1 per 1,111 persons); infant mortality rate per 1,000 live births (2003) 93.3. **Food** (2002): daily per capita caloric intake 1,980 (vegetable products 90%, animal products 10%); 86% of FAO recommended minimum.

Military

Total active duty personnel (2003): 2,550 (army 54.9%; air force 5.9%; paramilitary [gendarmerie] 39.2%). **Military expenditure as percentage of GNP** (1999): 2.8% (world 2.4%); per capita expenditure $8.

Background

For several centuries before the arrival of Europeans, the territory was subjected to slave traders. The French explored and claimed central Africa and in 1889 established a post at Bangui. In 1898 they partitioned the colony among commercial concession-aires. United with Chad in 1906 to form the French colony of Ubangi-Shari, it later became part of French Equatorial Africa. It was separated from Chad in 1920 and became an overseas territory in 1946. Named an autonomous republic within the French Community in 1958, the country achieved independence in 1960. In 1966 the military overthrew a civilian government and installed Jean-Bédel Bokassa, who in 1976 declared himself Emperor Bokassa I and renamed the country the Central African Empire. He was overthrown in 1979, but the military again seized power in the 1980s. Elections in 1993 led to the installation of a civilian government.

Recent Developments

In light of the deteriorating security situation in the Darfur region of The Sudan and neighboring Central

African Republic (CAR) and Chad, the UN Security Council in January 2007 agreed to send a team to the CAR and Chad to assess the requirements for establishing a UN peacekeeping force in the two countries. The UN estimated that by the end of 2005 more than 43,000 CAR refugees resided in Chad, and in mid-2006 relief agencies announced that some 90,000 people had been displaced in the CAR by fighting between government troops and rebels in the north. Additionally, thousands of refugees from The Sudan continued to live in the CAR.

Internet resources:
<www.sas.upenn.edu/African_Studies/Country_Specific/CAR.html>.

Chad

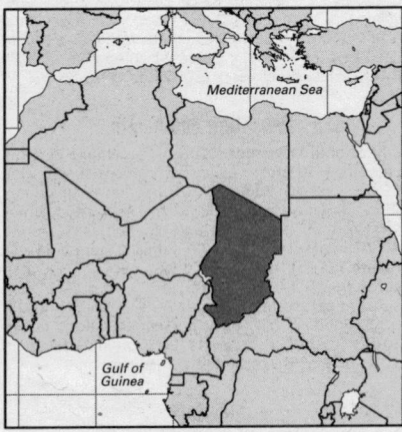

Official name: Jumhuriyah Tshad (Arabic); République du Tchad (French) (Republic of Chad). **Form of government:** unitary republic with one legislative body (National Assembly [155]). **Chief of state:** President Idriss Déby (from 1990). **Head of government:** Prime Minister Delwa Kassire Koumakoye (from 2007). **Capital:** N'Djamena. **Official languages:** Arabic; French. **Official religion:** none. **Monetary unit:** 1 CFA franc (CFAF) = 100 centimes; valuation (1 Jul 2007) US$1 = CFAF 485.18 (formerly pegged to the French franc and, since 1 Jan 2002, to the euro [€] at the rate of €1 = CFAF 655.96).

Demography

Area: 495,755 sq mi, 1,284,000 sq km. **Population** (2006): 9,944,000. **Density** (2006): persons per sq mi 20.1, persons per sq km 7.7. **Urban** (2002): 24.1%. **Sex distribution** (2002): male 48.62%; female 51.38%. **Age breakdown** (2002): under 15, 47.8%; 15–29, 26.2%; 30–44, 14.1%; 45–59, 7.5%; 60–74, 3.6%; 75 and over, 0.8%. **Ethnolinguistic composition** (1993): Sara 27.7%; Sudanic Arab 12.3%; Mayo-Kebbi peoples 11.5%; Kanem-Bornu peoples 9.0%; Ouaddaï peoples 8.7%; Hadjeray (Hadjaraï) 6.7%; Tangale (Tandjilé) peoples 6.5%; Gorane

peoples 6.3%; Fitri-Batha peoples 4.7%; Fulani (Peul) 2.4%; other 4.2%. **Religious affiliation** (1993): Muslim 53.9%; Christian 34.7%, of which Roman Catholic 20.3%, Protestant 14.4%; traditional beliefs 7.4%; other 4.0%. **Major cities** (1993): N'Djamena 530,-965; Moundou 282,103; Bongor 196,713; Sarh 193,753; Abéché 187,936. **Location:** central Africa, bordered by Libya, The Sudan, Central African Republic, Cameroon, Nigeria, and Niger.

Vital statistics

Birth rate per 1,000 population (2003): 47.1 (world avg. 21.3). **Death rate** per 1,000 population (2003): 16.4 (world avg. 9.1). **Natural increase rate** per 1,000 population (2003): 30.7 (world avg. 12.2). **Total fertility rate** (avg. births per childbearing woman; 2003): 6.4. **Life expectancy** at birth (2003): male 47.0 years; female 50.1 years. **Adult population** (ages 15–49) **living with HIV** (2004): 4.8% (world avg. 1.1%).

National economy

Budget (2000). *Revenue:* CFAF 128,200,000,000 (tax revenue 53.3%, of which income tax 19.0%, taxes on international trade 17.0%, taxes on goods and services 14.7%, other taxes 2.6%; grants 37.4%; nontax revenue 9.3%). *Expenditures:* CFAF 203,200,000,000 (current expenditure 49.2%, of which government salaries 19.7%, materials and supply 10.2%, defense 7.5%, transfer payments 5.9%, debt service 5.1%, other 0.8%; capital expenditure 50.8%). **Tourism** (2001): receipts from visitors $23,000,000; expenditures by nationals abroad $56,000,000. **Production** (metric tons except as noted). *Agriculture, forestry, fishing* (2002): peanuts (groundnuts) 448,089, sorghum 428,000, millet 369,000; livestock (number of live animals) 5,900,000 cattle, 5,500,000 goats, 5,000,000 chickens; roundwood (2001) 6,761,676 cu m; fish catch (2001) 84,000. *Mining and quarrying* (1997): aggregate (gravel) 170,000; limited commercial production of natron (10,000) and salt; artisanal gold production. *Manufacturing* (2000): cotton fiber (1998) 86,260; refined sugar 27,000; gum arabic 3,420. *Energy production (consumption):* electricity (kW-hr; 2000) 92,000,000 (92,000,000); crude petroleum (barrels; 2003) production began in 2003 at 50,000 barrels per day and was expected to increase to 225,000 barrels per day by the end of the first quarter 2004 (none); petroleum products (2000) none (41,000). **Household income and expenditure.** Average household size (2000) 4.2; average annual income per household (1993) CFAF 96,806; sources of income (1995–96; urban): informal-sector employment and entrepreneurship 36.7%, transfers 24.8%, wages 23.6%, ownership of real estate 8.6%; expenditure (1983; capital city only): food 45.3%, health 11.9%, energy 5.8%, clothing 3.3%. **Population economically active** (1997): total 3,433,000; activity rate of total population 47.9% (participation rates: over age 15, 72.3%; female 44.5%; unemployed [1993] 0.6%). **Public debt** (external, outstanding; 2002): $1,148,000,000. **Gross national product** (2003): $2,104,000,000 ($250 per capita). **Land use** as % of total land area (2000): in temporary crops 2.8%, in permanent crops 0.02%, in pasture 35.7%; overall forest area 10.1%.

1 metric ton = about 1.1 short tons;   1 kilometer = 0.6 mi (statute);   1 metric ton-km cargo = about 0.68 short ton-mi cargo;   c.i.f.: cost, insurance, and freight;   f.o.b.: free on board

Foreign trade

Imports (2001): CFAF 328,700,000,000 (petroleum sector 61.3%; non-petroleum sector 38.7%). *Major import sources* (1999): France 37%; Cameroon 22%; Nigeria 10%; India 4%. **Exports** (2001): CFAF 129,600,000,000 (cattle, sheep, and goats 39.5%; cotton fiber 37.2%; other 23.3%). *Major export destinations* (1999): Portugal 29%; Germany 15%; Taiwan 8%; US 7%; France 5%; Brazil 5%.

Transport and communications

Transport. *Roads* (1999): total length 33,400 km (paved 1%). *Vehicles* (1996): passenger cars 10,560; trucks and buses 14,550. *Air transport* (1996; data represent 1/11 of the total traffic of Air Afrique; Air Afrique, an airline jointly owned by 11 African countries [including Chad], was declared bankrupt in 2002): passenger-km 233,000,000; metric ton-km cargo 37,000,000; airports (2000) with scheduled flights 1. **Communications**, in total units (units per 1,000 persons). Daily newspaper circulation (1997): 2,000 (0.2); radios (2000): 1,990,000 (236); televisions (2002): 16,600 (2); telephone main lines (2002): 11,800 (1.5); cellular telephone subscribers (2003): 65,000 (8); personal computers (2002): 13,000 (1.7); Internet users (2002): 15,000 (1.9).

Education and health

Educational attainment (1993). Percentage of economically active population age 15 and over having: no formal schooling 81.1%; Koranic education 4.2%; primary education 11.2%; secondary education 2.7%; higher education 0.3%; professional education 0.5%. **Literacy** (2000): percentage of total population age 15 and over literate 42.6%; males literate 51.6%; females literate 34.0%. **Health** (2000): physicians 1,667 (1 per 4,471 persons); hospital beds (1993) 3,962 (1 per 1,521 persons); infant mortality rate per 1,000 live births (2002) 96.7. **Food** (2001): daily per capita caloric intake 2,245 (vegetable products 94%, animal products 6%); 94% of FAO recommended minimum.

Military

Total active duty personnel (2003): 30,350 (army 82.4%; air force 1.2%; paramilitary [gendarmerie] 16.4%); French peacekeeping troops (August 2004) 1,000. **Military expenditure as percentage of GNP** (1999): 2.4% (world 2.4%); per capita expenditure $5.

Background

Around AD 800 the kingdom of Kanem was founded in north-central Africa, and by the early 1200s its borders had expanded to form a new kingdom, Kanem-Bornu, in the northern regions of the area. Its power peaked in the 16th century with its command of the southern terminus of the trans-Sahara trade route to Tripoli. Around this time the rival kingdoms of Baguirmi and Wadai evolved in the south. In the years 1883–93 all three kingdoms fell to the Sudanese adventurer Rabih al-Zubayr, who was in turn pushed out by the French in 1900. Extending their power, the French in 1910 made Chad a part of French Equatorial Africa. Chad became a separate colony in 1920 and was made an overseas territory in 1946. The country achieved independence in 1960. This was followed by decades of civil war and frequent intervention by France and Libya.

Recent Developments

Chad earned tremendous royalties from its oil projects, but despite this wealth an estimated 80% of the population lived on less than $1 a day in 2005. After constitutional amendments were passed in 2005 that removed presidential term limits and replaced the Senate with a council whose members were all nominated by the president, Lieut. Gen. Idriss Déby was elected to a third term in May 2006. Fighting before the election caused many to flee into neighboring Cameroon, and 200,000 refugees from the Darfur region of The Sudan and thousands more from the Central African Republic (CAR) fled to Chad in 2006. In July the president pledged that 70% of the oil revenues in 2007 would be set aside for poverty-reduction programs. The UN called in February 2007 for up to 11,000 peacekeepers to deploy to Chad and the CAR.

Internet resources: <www.chadembassy.org>.

Chile

Pacific Ocean

Atlantic Ocean

Official name: República de Chile (Republic of Chile). **Form of government:** multiparty republic with two legislative houses (Senate [48, including 9 nonelective seats and excluding one senator-for-life]; Chamber of Deputies [120]). **Head of state and government:** President Michelle Bachelet (from 2006). **Capital:** Santiago (legislative bodies meet in Valparaíso). **Official language:** Spanish. **Official religion:** none. **Monetary unit:** 1 peso (Ch$) = 100 centavos; valuation (1 Jul 2007) US$1 = Ch$527.46.

Demography

Area: 291,930 sq mi, 756,096 sq km. **Population** (2006): 16,436,000. **Density** (2006): persons per sq mi 56.3, persons per sq km 21.7. **Urban** (2002): 86.6%. **Sex distribution** (2002): male 49.27%; female 50.73%. **Age breakdown** (2002): under 15, 25.7%; 15–29, 24.3%; 30–44, 23.6%; 45–59, 15.0%; 60–74, 8.3%; 75 and over, 3.1%. **Ethnic composition** (2000): mestizo 72.4%; local white 20.8%;

Araucanian (Mapuche) 4.7%; European 1.0%; other 1.1%. **Religious affiliation** (2002; for population age 15 and older): Roman Catholic 70.0%; Protestant 15.4%; other Christian 2.1%; atheist/nonreligious 4.6%; other 7.9%. **Major cities** (2002): Greater Santiago 4,647,444; Puente Alto 501,042; Concepción 376,043; Viña del Mar 298,828; Antofagasta 298,153. **Location:** southern South America, bordering Peru, Bolivia, Argentina, the South Atlantic Ocean, and the South Pacific Ocean.

Vital statistics

Birth rate per 1,000 population (2003): 16.1 (world avg. 21.3). **Death rate** per 1,000 population (2003): 5.7 (world avg. 9.1). **Natural increase rate** per 1,000 population (2003): 10.4 (world avg. 12.2). **Total fertility rate** (avg. births per childbearing woman; 2003): 2.1. **Life expectancy** at birth (2003): male 72.9 years; female 79.6 years.

National economy

Budget (2001). *Revenue:* Ch$9,537,200,000,000 (income from taxes 76.2%, nontax revenue 23.5%, capital 0.3%). *Expenditures:* Ch$9,932,200,000,000 (pensions 29.5%, wages 19.0%, capital expenditure 15.0%, interest 2.1%). **Population economically active** (1999): total 5,822,700; activity rate of total population 38.6% (participation rates [1995]: ages 15–64, 58.6%; female 32.4%; unemployed [2002] 9.0%). **Production** (metric tons except as noted). *Agriculture, forestry, fishing* (2003): sugar beets 2,100,000, wheat 1,797,084, grapes 1,750,000; livestock (number of live animals) 4,105,000 sheep, 3,927,000 cattle, 3,100,000 pigs; roundwood (2001) 37,790,000 cu m; fish catch (2001) 3,717,000. *Mining* (metal content; 2002): iron ore (2001) 5,520,000; copper 4,580,600; molybdenum 29,500. *Manufacturing* (value added in US$'000,000; 2000): food products 3,251; nonferrous base metals 1,947; paints, soaps, pharmaceuticals 1,206. *Energy production (consumption):* electricity (kW-hr; 2001) 41,292,000,000 (41,292,000,000); coal (2001) 480,000 ([2000] 4,590,000); crude petroleum (barrels; 2000) 2,027,000 (72,771,000); petroleum products (2000) 8,943,000 (10,270,000); natural gas (cu m; 2000) 2,188,300,000 (6,407,400,000). **Gross national product** (2003): US$69,193,000,000 (US$4,390 per capita). **Public debt** (external, outstanding; 2002): US$6,792,000,000. **Household income and expenditure.** Average household size (2002) 3.4; average annual income per household (1994) Ch$5,981,706 at November prices; sources of income (1990): wages and salaries 75.1%, transfer payments 12.0%, other 12.9%; expenditure (1989): food 27.9%, clothing 22.5%, housing 15.2%, transportation 6.4%. **Tourism** (2002): receipts US$845,000,000; expenditures US$793,000,000. **Land use** as % of total land area (2000): in temporary crops 2.6%, in permanent crops 0.4%; in pasture 17.3%; overall forest area 20.7%.

Foreign trade

Imports (2001-f.o.b. in balance of trade and c.i.f. in commodities and trading partners): US$17,181,000,000 (machinery and fabricated metals 29.4%; chemical products and mineral fuels 19.7%; copper 12.5%). *Major import sources:* Argentina 17.8%; US 16.8%; Brazil 8.7%; Germany 4.0%; Japan 3.3%. **Exports** (2001): US$17,620,000,000 (copper 37.9%; food products 24.8%, of which raw fruit 7.8%; paper and paper products 6.4%). *Major export destinations:* US 19.4%; Japan 12.1%; UK 7.0%; Brazil 4.8%; France 3.4%.

Transport and communications

Transport. *Railroads* (2001): route length 8,501 km; passenger-km 870,836,000; metric ton-km cargo 3,318,000,000. *Roads* (1996): total length 79,800 km (paved 14%). *Vehicles* (2001): passenger cars 1,351,900; trucks and buses 693,000. *Air transport* (1999): passenger-km 10,650,500,000; metric ton-km cargo 2,107,000,000; airports (1998) with scheduled flights 23. **Communications,** in total units (units per 1,000 persons). Daily newspaper circulation (2000): 1,450,000 (98); radios (2000): 5,230,000 (354); televisions (2000): 3,580,000 (242); telephone main lines (2002): 3,467,200 (230); cellular telephone subscribers (2002): 6,446,000 (428); personal computers (2002): 1,796,000 (119); Internet users (2002): 3,575,000 (236).

Education and health

Educational attainment (1992). Percentage of population age 25 and over having: no formal schooling 5.7%; primary education 44.2%; secondary 42.2%; higher 7.9%. **Literacy** (1995): total population age 15 and over literate 95.2%; males literate 95.4%; females literate 95.0%. **Health:** physicians (2000) 17,720 (1 per 834 persons); hospital beds (1999) 42,163 (1 per 346 persons); infant mortality rate per 1,000 live births (2003) 9.3. **Food** (2001): daily per capita caloric intake 2,868 (vegetable products 78%, animal products 22%); 118% of FAO recommended minimum.

Military

Total active duty personnel (2003): 77,300 (army 61.7%, navy 24.6%, air force 13.7%). **Military expenditure as percentage of GNP** (1999): 3.0% (world 2.4%); per capita expenditure US$133.

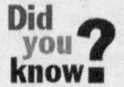 Some 2,200 miles west of Chile is the island known to its original inhabitants as Rapa Nui ("Great Rapa") or Te Pito te Henua ("Navel of the World"). Its first European visitors, the Dutch, named it Paaseiland ("Easter Island") in memory of their own day of arrival.

Background

Originally inhabited by native peoples, including the Mapuche, the Chilean coast was invaded by the Spanish in 1536. A settlement begun at Santiago in 1541 was governed under the viceroyalty of Peru but became a separate captaincy general in 1778. It revolted against Spanish rule in 1810; its independence was finally assured by the victory of José de

---

1 metric ton = about 1.1 short tons;   1 kilometer = 0.6 mi (statute);   1 metric ton-km cargo = about 0.68 short ton-mi cargo;   c.i.f.: cost, insurance, and freight;   f.o.b.: free on board

San Martín in 1818, and the area was then governed by Bernardo O'Higgins to 1823. In the War of the Pacific against Peru and Bolivia, it won the rich nitrate fields on the coast of Bolivia, effectively forcing that country into a landlocked position. Chile remained neutral in World War I and in World War II but severed diplomatic ties with the Axis in 1943. In 1970 Salvador Allende was elected president, becoming the first avowed Marxist to be elected chief of state in Latin America. Following economic upheaval, he was ousted in 1973 in a coup led by Gen. Augusto Pinochet, whose military junta for many years harshly suppressed all internal opposition. A national referendum in 1988 rejected Pinochet, and elections held in 1989 returned the country to civilian rule.

Recent Developments

In January 2006 Michelle Bachelet was elected the first woman president of Chile. Some of Bachelet's first actions as president were to extend free medical attention in public hospitals to the elderly poor and increase the pensions of the poorest Chileans by 10%. She also met with the families of Chileans who had been "disappeared" during the rule of former president Gen. Augusto Pinochet, and she declared 30 August a National Day of the Detained and Disappeared. News of Pinochet's death in December prompted thousands to celebrate in the streets of the capital city. The government refused a state funeral for Pinochet, who died without ever having stood trial for human rights abuses that occurred while he was in power. Record prices for copper, Chile's largest export earner, brought high revenues to Chile's coffers. The government concluded negotiations on a historic free-trade agreement (FTA) with China, progressed in its FTA negotiations with Japan, and signed a trade agreement with India.

Internet resources: <www.visit-chile.org>.

China

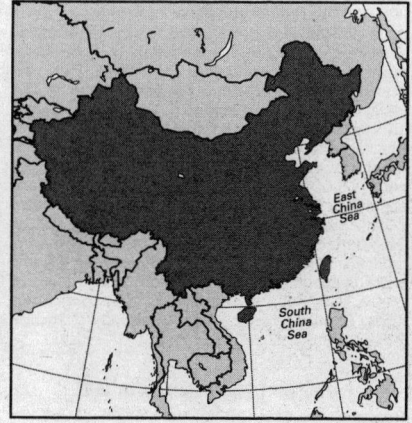

Official name: Zhonghua Renmin Gongheguo (People's republic of China). **Form of government:** single-party people's republic with one legislative house (National People's Congress [2,985; 36 seats are allotted to Hong Kong and 12 to Macau]). **Chief of** state: President Hu Jintao (from 2003). **Head of government:** Premier Wen Jiabao (from 2003). **Capital:** Beijing (Peking). **Official language:** Mandarin Chinese. **Official religion:** none. **Monetary unit:** 1 Renminbi (yuan) (Y) = 10 jiao = 100 fen; valuation (1 Jul 2007) US$1 = Y 7.61 (devalued on 21 Jul 2005 to 8.11).

Demography

Area: 3,696,100 sq mi, 9,572,900 sq km. **Population** (2006): 1,311,381,000. **Density** (2006): persons per sq mi 354.8, persons per sq km 137.0. **Urban** (2002): 37.7%. **Sex distribution** (2002): male 51.46%; female 48.54%. **Age breakdown** (2000): under 15, 22.9%; 15–29, 25.4%; 30–44, 25.6%; 45–59, 15.7%; 60–74, 8.2%; 75 and over, 2.2%. **Ethnic composition** (2000): Han (Chinese) 91.53%; Chuang 1.30%; Manchu 0.86%; Hui 0.79%; Miao 0.72%; Uighur 0.68%; Tuchia 0.65%; Yi 0.62%; Mongolian 0.47%; Tibetan 0.44%; Puyi 0.24%; Tung 0.24%; Yao 0.21%; Korean 0.15%; Pai 0.15%; Hani 0.12%; Kazakh 0.10%; Li 0.10%; Tai 0.09%; other 0.54%. **Religious affiliation** (2000): nonreligious 42.1%; Chinese folk-religionist 28.5%; Buddhist 8.4%; atheist 8.1%; Christian 7.1%; traditional beliefs 4.3%; Muslim 1.5%. **Major cities** (2003): Shanghai 10,030,800; Beijing 7,699,300; Tianjin 4,933,100; Guangzhou 4,653,100; Wuhan 4,593,400; Chongqing 4,239,700; Shenyang 3,995,500; Nanjing 2,966,000; Harbin 2,735,100; Chengdu 2,664,000; Xi'an 2,657,900; Jinan 2,346,000; Changchun 2,283,800; Dalian 2,181,600; Hangzhou 2,059,800; Shijiazhuang 1,971,000; Taiyuan 1,970,300; Qingdao 1,930,200; Zhengzhou 1,770,800; Kunming 1,597,800; Lanzhou 1,576,400; Changsha 1,562,200; Zibo 1,519,300. **Location:** eastern Asia, bordering Mongolia, Russia, North Korea, the Yellow Sea, the East China Sea, the South China Sea, Vietnam, Laos, Myanmar (Burma), India, Bhutan, Nepal, Pakistan, Afghanistan, Tajikistan, Kyrgyzstan, and Kazakhstan. **Households.** Average household size (2000) 3.4; total households 351,233,698, of which family households 340,491,197 (96.9%), collective 10,742,501 (3.1%).

Vital statistics

Birth rate per 1,000 population (2003): 13.0 (world avg. 21.3). **Death rate** per 1,000 population (2003): 6.9 (world avg. 9.1). **Natural increase rate** per 1,000 population (2003): 6.1 (world avg. 12.2). **Total fertility rate** (avg. births per childbearing woman; 2003): 1.7. **Marriage rate** per 1,000 population (2001): 6.3. **Divorce rate** per 1,000 population (2001): 1.0. **Life expectancy** at birth (2003): male 70.1 years; female 73.3 years.

Social indicators

Educational attainment (2000). Percentage of population age 15 and over having: no schooling and incomplete primary 15.6%; completed primary 35.7%; some secondary 34.0%; complete secondary 11.1%; some postsecondary through advanced degree 3.6%. **Quality of working life.** Average workweek (1998): 40 hours. Annual rate per 100,000 workers for (1997): injury or accident 0.7; death 1.4. Funds for pensions and social welfare relief (2001): Y 26,668,000,000. **Access to services.** Proportion of communes having access to electricity (1979) 87.1%. Percentage of urban population with: safe public water supply (1996) 95.0%. **Social participation.** Trade union membership in total labor force (1996): 14.7%. **Social deviance.** Annual reported arrest rate per 100,000 population (1986) for: property violation 20.7; infringing personal rights 7.2; disruption of social administration 3.3; endangering public security 1.0 (excludes arrests for anti-Communist activities). **Material well-being.** Urban households possessing (number per household; 2002): bicycles 1.6; color televisions 1.2; washing machines 0.9; refrigerators 0.8; cameras 0.4; rural families possessing (number per family; 2002): bicycles 1.2; color televisions 0.5; washing machines 0.3; refrigerators 0.1; cameras 0.03.

National economy

Gross national product (2003): $1,417,301,000,000 ($1,100 per capita). **Budget** (2001). *Revenue:* Y 1,638,604,000,000 (tax revenue 93.4%, of which VAT 32.7%, corporate income taxes 12.6%, consumption tax 5.6%; nontax revenue 6.6%). *Expenditures:* Y 1,890,258,000,000 (economic development 34.2%; education, health, and science 27.6%; administration 18.9%; debt payment 10.6%; defense 7.6%; other 1.1%). **Public debt** (external, outstanding; 2002): $88,531,000,000. **Tourism** (2002): receipts from visitors $20,385,000,000; expenditures by nationals abroad $15,398,000,000. **Production** (metric tons except as noted). *Agriculture, forestry, fishing* (2002): grains—rice 176,553,000, corn (maize) 123,175,000, wheat 91,290,000, sorghum 2,731,000, barley 2,470,000, millet 2,071,000; oilseeds—soybeans 16,900,000, peanuts (groundnuts) 15,006,000, rapeseed 10,530,000, sunflower seeds 1,900,000; fruits and nuts—watermelons 57,530,000, apples 20,435,000, pears 9,091,000, cantaloupes 8,631,000, oranges 3,676,000; other—sweet potatoes 114,289,000, sugarcane 82,278,000, potatoes 65,052,000, cabbage 26,812,000, tomatoes 25,466,000, cucumbers 22,924,000, onions 15,622,000, eggplants 15,430,000, seed cotton 14,760,000, sugar beets 11,562,000, garlic 8,694,000, tobacco leaves 2,394,000, tea 760,000; livestock (number of live animals) 464,695,000 pigs, 161,492,000 goats, 136,972,000 sheep, 106,175,000 cattle, 22,249,000 water buffalo, 8,815,000 asses, 8,262,000 horses, 3,923,600,000 chickens, 661,250,000 ducks; roundwood (2001) 284,910,000 cu m; fish catch (2002) 44,320,000, of which aquaculture 27,767,000. *Mining and quarrying* (2002): metal content of mine output—zinc 1,550,000, lead 641,000, copper 568,000, antimony 100,000, tin 62,000, tungsten 49,500; metal ores—iron ore 231,000,000, bauxite 11,000,000, manganese ore 4,500,000, vanadium 33,000, silver 2,950, gold 192; nonmetals—salt 36,024,000, soda ash 10,330,000, gypsum 6,850,000, magnesite 3,700,000, talc 3,600,000, barite 3,100,000, fluorspar 2,450,000, asbestos 270,000. *Manufacturing* (2001): cement 661,040,000; steel products 160,676,000; pig iron 155,554,000; rolled steel 151,634,000; paper and paperboard 37,771,000; chemical fertilizer 33,830,000; sulfuric acid 22,300,000; cotton fabrics 11,716,000; cotton yarn 7,606,000; sugar 6,531,000; color television sets 40,937,000 units; bicycles 29,023,000 units; household refrigerators 13,513,000 units; household washing machines 13,416,000 units; motor vehicles 2,342,000 units. Distribution of industrial production (percentage of total value of output by sector; 2001): state-operated enterprises 26.8%; urban collectives 16.6%; rural collectives 23.2%; privately operated enterprises 33.4%. Retail sales (percentage of total sales by sector; 2001): state-operated enterprises 25.3%; collectives 29.8%; privately operated enterprises 44.9%. *Energy production (consumption):* electricity (kW-hr; 2003) 1,838,748,000,000 ([2002] 1,602,156,000,000); coal (2003) 1,315,224,000 ([2000] 981,776,000); crude petroleum (barrels; 2003) 1,247,679,000 ([2000] 1,565,236,000); petroleum products (2000) 157,629,000 (174,016,000); natural gas (cu m; 2003) 34,243,412,000 ([2000] 33,542,000,000). **Household income and expenditure.** Average household size (2001) 3.5; rural households 4.4, urban households 3.1. Average annual per capita income of household (2001): rural households Y 2,366, urban households Y 6,907. Sources of income (2001): rural households—income from household businesses 77.9%, wages 16.6%, transfers 4.3%, other 1.2%; urban households—wages 73.9%, transfers 19.7%, business income 5.8%, other 0.6%. Expenditure: rural (urban) households—food 47.7% (37.9%), housing 16.0% (10.3%), education and recreation 11.1% (13.0%), transportation and communications 6.3% (8.6%), clothing 5.7% (10.1%), health and personal effects 5.6% (6.5%), household furnishings 4.4% (8.3%). **Population economically active** (2001): total 744,320,000; activity rate of total population 58.5% (participation rates: over age 15, 77.7%; female 37.8%; registered unemployed in urban areas 3.6%). Urban employed workforce (2001): 239,400,000; by sector: state enterprises 76,400,000, collectives 28,130,000, self-employment or privately run enterprises 134,870,000. Rural employed workforce 490,850,000. **Land use** as % of total land area (2000): in temporary crops 14.7%, in permanent crops 1.2%, in pasture 42.9%; overall forest area 17.5%.

Foreign trade

Imports (2000-f.o.b. in balance of trade and c.i.f. in commodities and trading partners): $225,094,000,000 (machinery and apparatus 38.0%, of which transistors/microcircuits 9.4%, telecommunications equipment 5.5%; crude petroleum 6.6%; artificial resins and plastic materials 5.8%; textile yarn, fabrics, and made-up articles 5.8%; iron and steel 4.4%). *Major import sources:* Japan 18.4%; unspecified Asia (mostly Taiwan) 11.3%; South Korea 10.3%; US 9.9%; Germany 4.6%; Hong Kong 4.2%; free zones 3.2%; Russia 2.6%; Malaysia 2.4%; Singapore 2.2%. **Exports** (2000): $249,203,000,000 (machinery and apparatus 29.5%, of which computers and related units 7.5%, telecommunications equipment and related parts 5.0%; wearing apparel 14.5%; textile yarn, fabrics, and made-up articles 6.5%; toys, games, and sporting goods 4.1%). *Major export destinations:* US 20.9%; Hong Kong 17.9%; Japan 16.7%; South Korea 4.5%; Germany 3.7%; The Netherlands 2.7%; UK 2.5%; Singapore 2.3%.

Transport and communications

Transport. *Railroads* (2001): route length 70,057 km; passenger-km 476,680,000,000; metric ton-km cargo 1,457,510,000,000. *Roads* (2001): total length 1,698,012 km. *Vehicles* (2001): passenger cars

---

1 metric ton = about 1.1 short tons;   1 kilometer = 0.6 mi (statute);   1 metric ton-km cargo = about 0.68 short ton-mi cargo;   c.i.f.: cost, insurance, and freight;   f.o.b.: free on board

9,939,600; trucks and buses 7,652,400. *Air transport* (2001): passenger-km 109,140,000,000; metric ton-km cargo 4,372,000,000; airports (1996) with scheduled flights 113. **Communications,** in total units (units per 1,000 persons). Daily newspaper circulation (1994): 27,790,000 (23); radios (2000): 428,000,000 (339); televisions (2000): 448,000,000 (350); telephone main lines (2003): 263,000,000 (209); cellular telephone subscribers (2003): 269,000,000 (214); personal computers (2002): 35,500,000 (28); Internet users (2003): 79,500,000 (63).

Education and health

Literacy (2000): total population age 15 and over literate 90.9%; males literate 95.1%; females literate 86.5%. **Health** (2004): physicians 1,830,000 (1 per 708 persons); hospital beds 2,900,000 (1 per 447 persons); infant mortality rate per 1,000 live births (2003) 26.4. **Food** (2002): daily per capita caloric intake 2,951 (vegetable products 79%, animal products 21%); 125% of FAO recommended minimum.

Military

Total active duty personnel (2003): 2,250,000 (army 75.6%, navy 11.1%, air force 13.3%). **Military expenditure as percentage of GNP** (1999): 2.3% (world 2.4%); per capita expenditure $71.

 **Did you know?** The Forbidden City is the imperial palace complex at the heart of Beijing, China. Commissioned in 1406 by the Yung-lo emperor of the Ming dynasty, it was first officially occupied by the court in 1420. It was so named because access to the area was barred to most of the subjects of the realm.

Background

The discovery of Peking man (*Homo erectus*) in 1927 dated the advent of early humans in what is now China to the Middle Pleistocene, about 900,000 to 130,000 years ago. Chinese civilization probably spread from the Huang He (Yellow River) valley, where it existed c. 3000 BC. The first dynasty for which there is definite historical material is the Shang (c. 16th century BC), which had a writing system and a calendar. The Zhou, a subject state of the Shang, overthrew its Shang rulers in the 11th century BC and ruled until the 3rd century BC. Taoism and Confucianism were founded in this era.

A time of conflict, called the Warring States Period, lasted from the 5th century BC until 221 BC, when the Qin (Ch'in) dynasty (from whose name China is derived) was established after its rulers had conquered rival states and created a unified empire. The Han dynasty was established in 206 BC and ruled until AD 220. A time of turbulence followed, and Chinese reunification was not achieved until the Sui dynasty was established in 581.

After the founding of the Song dynasty in 960, the capital was moved to the south because of northern invasions. In 1279 this dynasty was overthrown and Mongol (Yuan) domination began. During this time Marco Polo visited Kublai Khan. The Ming dynasty followed the period of Mongol rule and lasted from 1368 to 1644, cultivating antiforeign feelings to the point

that China closed itself off from the rest of the world.

Peoples from Manchuria overran China in 1644 and established the Qing (Manchu) dynasty. Ever-increasing incursions by Western and Japanese interests led in the 19th century to the Opium Wars, the Taiping Rebellion, and the Sino-Japanese War, all of which weakened the Manchus.

The dynasty fell in 1911, and a republic was proclaimed in 1912 by Sun Yat-sen. The power struggles of warlords weakened the republic. Under Sun's successor, Chiang Kai-shek, some national unification was achieved in the 1920s, but Chiang soon broke with the Communists, who then formed their own armies. Japan invaded northern China in 1937; its occupation lasted until 1945. The Communists gained support after the Long March (1934–35), in which Mao Zedong emerged as their leader.

Upon Japan's surrender at the end of World War II, a fierce civil war began; in 1949 the Nationalists fled to Taiwan and the Communists proclaimed the People's Republic of China. The Communists undertook extensive reforms, but pragmatic policies alternated with periods of revolutionary upheaval, most notably in the Great Leap Forward and the Cultural Revolution. The chaos of the latter led, after Mao's death in 1976, to a turn to moderation under Deng Xiaoping, who undertook economic reforms and renewed China's ties to the West. The government established diplomatic ties with the US in 1979. It suppressed the Tiananmen Square student demonstration in 1989. The economy has been in transition since the late 1970s, moving from central planning and state-run industries to a mixture of state-owned and private enterprises in manufacturing and services. The death of Deng in 1997 marked the end of a political era, but power passed peacefully to Jiang Zemin. In 1997 Hong Kong reverted to Chinese rule, as did Macao in 1999.

Recent Developments

In 2006 the Chinese economy set records at every turn. Tax revenue climbed to $385 billion; the trade surplus tripled and broke $100 billion; domestic tourism hit 1.2 billion visits; and businesses brought in $18.9 billion in Hong Kong alone—all by the new year of 2006. Individual savings exceeded $1.75 billion at the beginning of 2006, and real-estate investment rocketed to $660 billion over five years. There were at least 320,000 millionaires in China. Foreign-exchange reserves stood at $853 billion in February 2006 (China surpassed Japan to become the world's largest reserve holder) and reached $954 billion in July. GDP growth rate was 10.7% for 2006. The Chinese automobile industry was especially hot. For the first time, China exported more cars than it imported. After having bought MG Rover in 2005, Nanjing Automobile planned to build cars in Oklahoma; it would be the first Chinese assembler in the United States.

Although Beijing increased grain donations to the country, China openly criticized North Korea for having conducted a nuclear test, and it pressured Pyongyang to return to the six-party talks on its nuclear program. China offered loan packages of $600 million to Cambodia and $2 billion each year for the next three years to the Philippines. China and the US exchanged high-level military visits. During a visit by Vice-Premier Wu Yi in April, the signing of contracts with American companies valued at $16.2 billion was announced. China was a leading financier of the US current-account deficit. Because China was consuming 8% of the world's energy, the security of energy resources was a focal point of Beijing's diplomacy. After his visit to the US, President Hu made stops in Saudi Arabia, Morocco, Nigeria, and Kenya. Premier Wen Jiabao later traveled to seven other African countries, including Angola, the continent's second largest oil producer. Hu signed an agreement with visiting Russian Pres. Vladimir Putin to build gas pipelines from Russia to China, and the largest Chinese oil company bought a $500 million stake in the newly listed Russian petroleum giant Rosneft. Russian oil exports to China in 2006 nearly doubled from the previous year. China also had started building a 900-km (560-mi) oil pipeline through Myanmar (Burma).

Internet resources: <www.chinaonline.com>.

Colombia

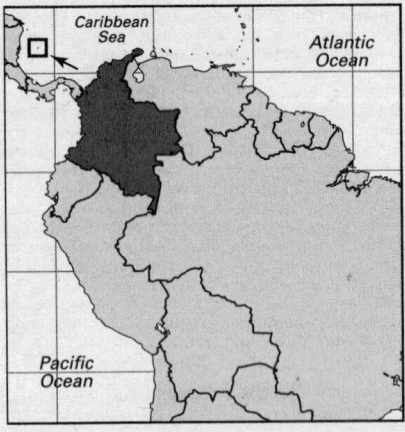

Official name: República de Colombia (Republic of Colombia). **Form of government:** unitary, multiparty republic with two legislative houses (Senate [102]; House of Representatives [166, including two representatives from indigenous communities]). **Head of state and government:** President Álvaro Uribe Vélez (from 2002). **Capital:** Bogotá. **Official language:** Spanish. **Official religion:** none. **Monetary unit:** 1 peso (Col$) = 100 centavos; valuation (1 Jul 2007) US$1 = Col$1,954.

Demography

Area: 440,762 sq mi, 1,141,568 sq km. **Population** (2006): 43,593,000. **Density** (2006): persons per sq mi 98.9, persons per sq km 38.2. **Urban** (2003) 76.5%. **Sex distribution** (2003): male 49.08%; female 50.92%. **Age breakdown** (2003): under 15, 31.3%; 15–29, 25.8%; 30–44, 22.8%; 45–59, 12.8%; 60–74, 5.8%; 75 and over, 1.5%. **Ethnic composition** (2000): mestizo 47.3%; mulatto 23.0%; white 20.0%; black 6.0%; black-Amerindian 1.0%; Amerindian/other 2.7%. **Religious affiliation** (1995): Roman Catholic 91.9%; other 8.1%. **Major cities** (1999): Bogotá, D.C., 6,276,428; Cali 2,110,571; Medellín 1,957,928; Barranquilla 1,226,292; Bucaramanga 520,874. **Location:** northern South Amer-

ica, bordering the Caribbean Sea, Venezuela, Brazil, Peru, Ecuador, the Pacific Ocean, and Panama.

Vital statistics

Birth rate per 1,000 population (2003): 21.6 (world avg. 21.3). **Death rate** per 1,000 population (2003): 5.6 (world avg. 9.1). **Natural increase rate** per 1,000 population (2003): 16.0 (world avg. 12.2). **Total fertility rate** (avg. births per childbearing woman; 2003): 2.6. **Life expectancy** at birth (2003): male 67.3 years; female 75.1 years.

National economy

Budget (1999). *Revenue:* Col$41,457,000,000,000 (tax revenue 61.7%, nontax revenue 38.3%). *Expenditures:* Col$50,441,000,000,000 (current expenditure 73.6%, capital expenditure 26.4%). **Public debt** (external, outstanding; 2002): US$21,177,000,000. **Population economically active** (2000): total 15,417,000; activity rate 38.8% (participation rates: ages 15–69, 64.3%; female 38.0%; unemployed 20.2%). *Production* (metric tons except as noted). *Agriculture, forestry, fishing* (2002): sugarcane 38,200,000, plantains 2,827,024, potatoes 2,697,980; livestock (number of live animals) 27,000,000 cattle, 2,260,000 sheep, 2,150,000 pigs; roundwood (2001) 12,501,000 cu m; fish catch (2001) 190,000. *Mining and quarrying* (2001): nickel (metal content) 52,962; gold 21,813 kg; emeralds 5,500,000 carats. *Manufacturing* (value added in Col$'000,000; 1997): processed food 11,133,000; beverages 3,165,400; petroleum products 2,483,600. *Energy production (consumption):* electricity (kW-hr; 2000) 43,943,000,000 (43,983,000,000); coal (2000) 38,365,000 (4,551,000); crude petroleum (barrels; 2001) 243,208,000 ([2000] 110,482,000); petroleum products (2000) 13,050,000 (8,656,000); natural gas (cu m; 2000) 7,337,400,000 (7,337,400,000). **Gross national product** (2003): US$80,488,000,000 (US$1,810 per capita). **Land use** as % of total land area (2000): in temporary crops 2.7%, in permanent crops 1.7%, in pasture 39.4%; overall forest area 47.8%. **Households.** Average household size (2000) 5.0; expenditure (1992): food 34.2%, transportation 18.5%, housing 7.8%, health care 6.4%. **Tourism** (2002): receipts US$962,000,000; expenditures US$1,072,000,000.

Foreign trade

Imports (2002-c.i.f.): US$12,690,000,000 (capital goods 32.5%, consumer goods 21.3%). *Major import sources:* US 31.7%; Venezuela 6.2%; Mexico 5.3%; Brazil 5.1%; Japan 4.9%. **Exports** (2002-f.o.b.): US$11,900,000,000 (crude and refined petroleum 27.5%, chemicals and chemical products 12.4%, coal 8.3%, food, beverages, and tobacco 7.9%, machinery and equipment 7.6%, coffee 6.5%). *Major export destinations:* US 43.0%; Venezuela 9.4%; Ecuador 6.8%; Peru 2.9%; Germany 2.8%.

Transport and communications

Transport. *Railroads* (2000): route length 3,154 km; passenger-km (1992) 15,524,000; metric ton-km cargo (1999) 473,000,000. *Roads* (1999): total

---

1 metric ton = about 1.1 short tons;   1 kilometer = 0.6 mi (statute);   1 metric ton-km cargo = about 0.68 short ton-mi cargo;   c.i.f.: cost, insurance, and freight;   f.o.b.: free on board

length 114,912 km (paved 14%). *Vehicles* (1999): cars 762,000; trucks 672,000. *Air transport* (2001): passenger-km 5,858,369,000; metric ton-km cargo 33,037,000; airports (1998) 43. **Communications,** in total units (units per 1,000 persons). Daily newspaper circulation (1996): 1,800,000 (46); radios (2001): 25,968,000 (549); televisions (2002): 13,241,000 (303); telephone main lines (2003): 8,768,000 (200); cellular telephone subscribers (2003): 6,186,000 (141); personal computers (2002): 2,133,000 (49); Internet users (2003): 2,732,000 (62).

Education and health

Educational attainment (1985). Percentage of population age 25 and over having: no schooling 15.3%; primary education 50.1%; secondary 25.4%; higher 6.8%; not stated 2.4%. **Literacy** (2002): population age 15 and over literate 92.1%; males literate 92.1%; females literate 92.2%. **Health** (2003): physicians 57,000 (1 per 729 persons); hospital beds 49,000 (1 per 850 persons); infant mortality rate per 1,000 live births 24.2. **Food** (2001): daily per capita caloric intake 2,580 (vegetable products 84%, animal products 16%); 111% of FAO recommended minimum.

Military

Total active duty personnel (2003): 200,000 (army 89.0%, navy 7.5%, air force 3.5%). **Military expenditure as percentage of GNP** (1999): 3.2% (world 2.4%); per capita expenditure US$68.

Background

The Spanish arrived in what is now Colombia c. 1500 and by 1538 had defeated the area's Chibchan-speaking Indians and made the area subject to the viceroyalty of Peru. After 1740 authority was transferred to the newly created viceroyalty of New Granada. Parts of Colombia threw off Spanish jurisdiction in 1810, and full independence came after Spain's defeat by Simón Bolívar in 1819. Civil war in 1840 checked development. Conflict between the Liberal and Conservative parties led to the War of a Thousand Days (1899–1903). Years of relative peace followed, but hostility erupted again in 1948; the two parties agreed in 1958 to a scheme for alternating governments. A new constitution was adopted in 1991, but democratic power remained threatened by civil unrest. Many leftist rebels and right-wing paramilitary groups funded their activities through kidnappings and narcotics trafficking.

Recent Developments

In elections in May 2006 Pres. Álvaro Uribe, the first Colombian president legally allowed to pursue reelection under an amended constitution, garnered 62% of the vote. A major challenge confronting Uribe was the paramilitary groups on the right and the guerrilla groups on the left. Implementation of a disarmament agreement signed with the paramilitaries in 2005 continued at a much slower pace than was officially called for, and there were revelations of close relations and cooperation between the paramilitaries and the government's secret police force. President Uribe offered to respond to any gesture related to peace talks by the leftist Revolutionary Armed Forces of Colombia (FARC), the largest guerrilla group. In June FARC agreed to enter into peace talks and to implement a prisoner exchange if the government ceased operations against it and again demilitarized portions of the countryside. The government agreed and demilitarized two municipalities in the Valle del Cauca department in response.

Internet resources: <www.dane.gov.co>.

Comoros

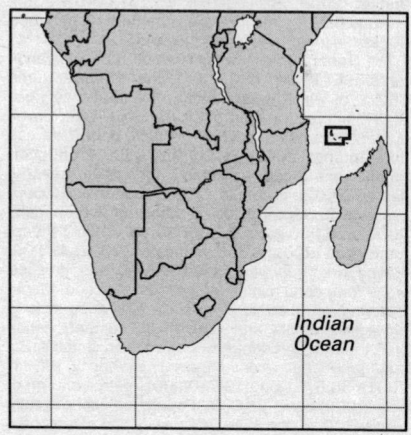

Indian Ocean

Official name: Udzima wa Komori (Comorian); L'Union des Comores (French) (Union of the Comoros). **Form of government:** federal republic with one legislative house (Federal Assembly [33, including 15 non-elected seats]). **Head of state and government:** President Ahmed Abdallah Mohamed Sambi (from 2006), assisted by vice presidents. **Capital:** Moroni. **Official languages:** Comorian (Shikomor); Arabic; French. **Official religion:** Islam. **Monetary unit:** 1 Comorian franc (formerly pegged to the French franc and, since 1 Jan 2002, to the euro [€] at the rate of €1 = CF 491.97) (CF) = 100 centimes; valuation (1 Jul 2007) US$1 = CF 364.50.

Demography

Area: 719 sq mi, 1,862 sq km. **Population** (2006): 632,000 (includes Comorians living abroad in France or Mayotte). **Density** (2006): persons per sq mi 879.0, persons per sq km 339.4. **Urban** (2002): 33.8%. **Sex distribution** (2002): male 49.62%; female 50.38%. **Age breakdown** (2002): under 15, 42.9%; 15–29, 27.8%; 30–44, 16.6%; 45–59, 8.1%; 60–74, 3.9%; 75 and over, 0.7%. **Ethnic composition** (2000): Comorian (a mixture of Bantu, Arab, Malay, and Malagasy peoples) 97.1%; Makua 1.6%; French 0.4%; Arab 0.1%; other 0.8%. **Religious affiliation** (2000): Sunni Muslim 98.0%; Christian 1.2%; other 0.8%. **Major cities** (1991): Moroni (2003) 41,557 (urban agglomeration [2001] 49,000); Mutsamudu 16,785; Domoni 10,400; Fomboni 5,633. **Location:** western Indian Ocean, lying between Madagascar and Mozambique.

Vital statistics

Birth rate per 1,000 population (2003): 38.5 (world avg. 21.3). **Death rate** per 1,000 population (2003):

8.9 (world avg. 9.1). **Natural increase rate** per 1,000 population (2003): 29.6 (world avg. 12.2). **Total fertility rate** (avg. births per childbearing woman; 2002): 5.2. **Marriage rate** per 1,000 population: n.a. (in the early 1990s, 20% of adult men had more than one wife). **Life expectancy** at birth (2003): male 58.9 years; female 63.5 years.

National economy

Budget (2000). *Revenue:* CF 15,557,000,000 (tax revenue 62.5%, of which taxes on international trade 40.9%, income and profit taxes 12.2%, sales tax 7.7%; grants 29.2%; nontax revenue 8.3%). *Expenditures:* CF 17,649,000,000 (current expenditures 68.4%, of which wages 34.5%, goods and services 23.3%, interest on debt 5.4%, transfers 4.8%; development expenditures 31.6%). **Public debt** (external, outstanding; 2002): $239,900,000. **Production** (metric tons except as noted). *Agriculture, forestry, fishing* (2002): coconuts 76,000, bananas 60,000, cassava 55,000; livestock (number of live animals; 2002) 115,000 goats, 52,000 cattle, 21,000 sheep; roundwood (2001) 8,650; fish catch (2002) 12,200. *Mining and quarrying:* sand, gravel, and crushed stone from coral mining for local construction. *Manufacturing:* products of small-scale industries include processed vanilla and ylang-ylang, cement, handicrafts, soaps, soft drinks, woodwork, and clothing. *Energy production (consumption):* electricity (kW-hr; 2001) 36,578,000 (19,780,000); petroleum products (2000) none (26,000). **Population economically active** (2000): total 156,000; activity rate of total population 28.4% (participation rates: [1991] ages 10 years and over, 57.8%; female 40.0%; unemployed [2000] 20%). **Tourism:** receipts from visitors (2002) $11,000,000; expenditures by nationals abroad (1998) $3,000,000. **Household income and expenditure.** Average household size (1995) 6.3; average annual income per household (1995) CF 188,985; expenditure (1993): food and beverages 67.3%, clothing and footwear 11.6%, tobacco and cigarettes 4.1%, energy 3.8%, health 3.2%, education 2.5%, transportation 2.2%, other 5.3%. **Gross national product** (at current market prices; 2003): $269,000,000 ($450 per capita). **Land use** as % of total land area (2000; includes Mayotte): in temporary crops 36%, in permanent crops 22%, in pasture 7%; overall forest area 4%.

Foreign trade

Imports (2001-c.i.f.): CF 27,776,000,000 (food products 28.1%, of which rice 11.3%, meat and fish 8.0%; vehicles 15.6%; petroleum products 15.3%; unspecified 30.1%). *Major import sources:* EU 49%; UAE 11%; South Africa 10%; Pakistan 9%. **Exports** (2001-f.o.b.): CF 9,144,000,000 (vanilla 59.1%, cloves 26.6%, ylang-ylang 10.9%). *Major export destinations:* France 47%; US 30%.

Transport and communications

Transport. *Roads* (1996): total length 900 km (paved 76%). *Vehicles* (1996): passenger cars 9,100; trucks and buses 4,950. *Air transport* (1996): passenger-km 3,000,000; airports (2002) with scheduled flights 4. **Communications,** in total units (units per 1,000 persons). Radios (1997): 90,000 (170); televisions

(1997): 1,000 (1.8); telephone main lines (2003): 13,200 (17); cellular telephone subscribers (2003): 2,000 (2.5); personal computers (2003): 5,000 (5.8); Internet users (2003): 5,000 (5.8).

Education and health

Educational attainment (1980). Percentage of population age 25 and over having: no formal schooling 56.7%; Koranic school education 8.3%; primary 3.6%; secondary 2.0%; higher 0.2%; not specified 29.2%. **Literacy** (2003): total population age 15 and over literate 55.9%; males literate 63.2%; females literate 48.7%. **Health** (1995): physicians 64 (1 per 7,800 persons); hospital beds 1,450 (1 per 342 persons); infant mortality rate per 1,000 live births (2003) 79.5. **Food** (2002): daily per capita caloric intake 1,754 (vegetable products 95%, animal products 5%); 75% of FAO recommended minimum.

Military

Total active duty personnel (1997): 1,500.

 **Did you know?** Elaborate public wedding celebrations, some lasting as long as 3 weeks, are common in the Comoros, and tourists are generally welcome to attend.

Background

The Comoros islands were known to European navigators from the 16th century. In 1843 France officially took possession of Mayotte and in 1886 placed the other three islands under protection. Subordinated to Madagascar in 1912, the Comoros became an overseas territory of France in 1947. In 1961 they were granted autonomy. In 1974 majorities on three of the islands voted for independence, which was granted in 1975. The following decade saw several coup attempts, which culminated in the assassination of the president in 1989. French intervention permitted multiparty elections in 1990, but the country remained in a state of chronic instability. Anjouan seceded from the Comoros federation in 1997. The army took control of the government in 1999. A referendum at the end of 2001 renamed the country the Union of the Comoros and granted the three main islands partially autonomous status.

Recent Developments

Pres. Col. Azali Assoumani made a historic state visit to France in January 2005, the first such visit by a head of state since independence. Relations between the two countries had been strained since the 1999 coup that brought Assoumani to power (the island country had suffered more than 20 coups since gaining independence from France). The government in 2006 focused on development plans in the face of the decline in prices of the country's three leading exports—vanilla, cloves, and ylang-ylang.

Internet resources:
<http://travel.state.gov/comoros>.

1 metric ton = about 1.1 short tons; 1 kilometer = 0.6 mi (statute); 1 metric ton-km cargo = about 0.68 short ton-mi cargo; c.i.f.: cost, insurance, and freight; f.o.b.: free on board

Democratic Republic of the Congo

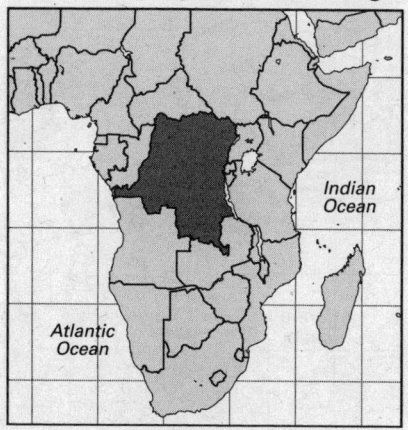

Indian
Ocean

Atlantic
Ocean

Official name: République Democratique du Congo (Democratic Republic of the Congo). **Form of government:** transitional regime (five-year civil war began in 1998; peace accord and transitional constitution effective from 5–6 Apr 2003 created a two-year interim administration) with two legislative bodies (Senate [120]; National Assembly [500]). **Head of state and government:** President Joseph Kabila (from 2001), assisted by vice presidents. **Head of government:** Prime Minister Antoine Gizenga (from 2006). **Capital:** Kinshasa. **Official languages:** French; English. **Official religion:** none. **Monetary unit:** Congo franc (FC); valuation (1 Jul 2007) US$1 = FC 437.00.

Demography

Area: 905,355 sq mi, 2,344,858 sq km. **Population** (2006): 59,320,000. **Density** (2006): persons per sq mi 65.5, persons per sq km 25.3. **Urban** (2002): 30.7%. **Sex distribution** (2002): male 49.38%; female 50.62%. **Age breakdown** (2002): under 15, 48.3%; 15–29, 27.2%; 30–44, 13.6%; 45–59, 6.9%; 60–74, 3.2%; 75 and over, 0.8%. **Ethnic composition** (1983): Luba 18.0%; Kongo 16.1%; Mongo 13.5%; Rwanda 10.3%; Azande 6.1%; Bangi and Ngale 5.8%; Rundi 3.8%; Teke 2.7%; Boa 2.3%; Chokwe 1.8%; Lugbara 1.6%; Banda 1.4%; other 16.6%. **Religious affiliation** (1995): Roman Catholic 41.0%; Protestant 32.0%; indigenous Christian 13.4%, of which Kimbanguist 13.0%; other Christian 0.8%; Muslim 1.4%; traditional beliefs and other 11.4%. **Major cities** (1994): Kinshasa 4,655,313; Lubumbashi 851,381; Mbuji-Mayi 806,475; Kolwezi 417,800; Kisangani 417,517. **Location:** central Africa, bordering the Central African Republic, The Sudan, Uganda, Rwanda, Burundi, Tanzania, Zambia, Angola, the South Atlantic Ocean, and the Republic of the Congo.

Vital statistics

Birth rate per 1,000 population (2003): 45.1 (world avg. 21.3). **Death rate** per 1,000 population (2003): 14.9 (world avg. 9.1). **Natural increase rate** per 1,000 population (2003): 30.2 (world avg. 12.2). **Total fertility rate** (avg. births per childbearing woman; 2003): 6.7. **Life expectancy** at birth (2003):

male 46.8 years; female 51.1 years. **Adult population** (ages 15–49) **living with HIV** (beginning of 2004): 4.2% (world avg. 1.1%).

National economy

Budget (2000). *Revenue:* FC 15,091,000,000 (tax revenue 83.3%, of which sales tax 24.4%, taxes on international trade 23.8%, corporate tax 23.8%; nontax revenue 16.7%). *Expenditures:* FC 32,988,000,000 (goods and services 45.4%; wages and salaries 22.2%; interest on debt 18.7%). **Public debt** (external, outstanding; 2002): $7,391,000,000. **Production** (metric tons except as noted). *Agriculture, forestry, fishing* (2002): cassava 14,929,410, sugarcane 1,550,000, plantains 1,200,000; livestock (number of live animals) 4,003,880 goats, 953,066 pigs; roundwood (2001) 69,733,688 cu m; fish catch (2001) 208,848. *Mining and quarrying* (2002): copper (metal content) 30,000; cobalt (metal content) 3,000; diamonds 18,556,000 carats. *Manufacturing* (2000): butter 2,052,000; steel 259,000; explosives 246,000. *Energy production (consumption):* electricity (kW-hr; 2000) 5,458,000,000 (4,414,000,000); coal (2000) 986,000 (136,000); crude petroleum (barrels; 2000) 9,553,000 (1,358,000); petroleum products (2000) 176,000 (612,000). **Households.** Average household size (1998) 2.3; expenditure (1985): food 61.7%, housing and energy 11.5%, clothing and footwear 9.7%, transportation 5.9%, furniture and utensils 4.9%. **Gross national product** (at current market prices; 2002): $5,369,000,000 ($100 per capita). **Population economically active** (2000): total 20,686,000; activity rate 42.6%. **Tourism** (1998): receipts $2,000,000; expenditures (1997) $7,000,000. **Land use** as % of total land area (2000): in temporary crops 3.0%, in permanent crops 0.5%, in pasture 6.6%; overall forest area 59.6%.

Foreign trade

Imports (2000): $680,000,000 (non-petroleum sector 92.9%, petroleum sector 7.1%). *Major import sources* (2001): Belgium 17.5%; South Africa 15.9%; Nigeria 10.3%; France 5.1%; Kenya 5.0%. **Exports** (2000): $892,000,000 (diamonds 52.5%, crude petroleum 22.8%, cobalt 8.0%, coffee 6.2%, copper 4.8%, gold 2.4%). *Major export destinations* (2001): Belgium 62.1%; US 14.7%; Finland 8.0%; India 4.8%; Italy 2.0%.

Transport and communications

Transport. *Railroads* (1996; Zaire National Railway only): length 5,138 km; passenger-km (1994) 29,000,000; metric ton-km cargo (1994) 176,000,-000. *Roads* (1996): total length 154,027 km (paved 2%). *Vehicles* (1996): passenger cars 787,000; trucks and buses 60,000. *Air transport* (1996): passenger-km 279,000,000; metric ton-km cargo 42,000,000; airports (1997) with scheduled flights 22. **Communications,** in total units (units per 1,000 persons). Daily newspaper circulation (1996): 124,000 (2.7); radios (2000): 18,700,000 (386); televisions (1997): 6,478,000 (135); telephone main lines (2002): 10,000 (0.2); cellular telephone subscribers (2003): 1,000,000 (19); Internet users (2002): 50,000 (0.9).

Education and health

Literacy (2000): percentage of total population age 15 and over literate 61.4%; males literate 73.1%;

females literate 50.2%. **Health:** physicians (1996) 3,129 (1 per 14,494 persons); infant mortality rate per 1,000 live births (2003) 96.6. **Food** (2001): daily per capita caloric intake 1,535 (vegetable products 98%, animal products 2%); 68% of FAO recommended minimum.

Military

Total active duty personnel: new national army being created from August 2003; UN peacekeepers (August 2004): 10,000. **Military expenditure as percentage of GNP** (1997): 14.4% (world 2.4%); per capita expenditure $102.

Background

Prior to European colonization, several native kingdoms had emerged in the Congo region, including the 16th-century Luba kingdom and the Kuba federation, which reached its peak in the 18th century. European development began late in the 19th century when King Léopold II of Belgium financed Henry Morton Stanley's exploration of the Congo River. The 1884–85 Berlin West Africa Conference recognized the Congo Free State with Léopold as its sovereign. The growing demand for rubber helped finance the exploitation of the Congo, but abuses against native peoples outraged Western nations and forced Léopold to grant the Free State a colonial charter as the Belgian Congo (1908). Independence was granted in 1960, and the country's name was changed to Zaire. The post-independence period was marked by unrest, culminating in a military coup that brought Gen. Mobutu Sese Seko to power in 1965. Mismanagement, corruption, and increasing violence devastated the infrastructure and economy. Mobutu was deposed in 1997 by Laurent Kabila, who restored the country's name to Congo. Regional instability and desire for Congo's mineral wealth led to military involvement by numerous African countries. Kabila was assassinated in 2001 and succeeded by his son Joseph.

Recent Developments

Efforts by the Congolese army and the 17,500-strong UN Organization Mission in the Democratic Republic of the Congo to control the activities of rival militias produced only mixed results in 2006. A constitution was promulgated by President Kabila in February, however, and shortly afterward the parliament adopted a bill authorizing the Independent Electoral Commission to organize multiparty elections. The resulting presidential and parliamentary elections held in July (the first since 1960) went ahead successfully. More than 70% of registered voters cast their ballots, and observers commented favorably on the conduct of the elections. President Kabila won almost 45% of the vote, while Vice Pres. Jean-Pierre Bemba gained only 20% of the vote. Since neither candidate won more than 50%, however, a runoff election was required. It was announced on 29 October that Kabila had received 58%. Violent clashes between Bemba's supporters and government forces took place into 2007, and in April of that year Bemba fled to Portugal.

Internet resources: <www.un.int/drcongo>.

Republic of the Congo

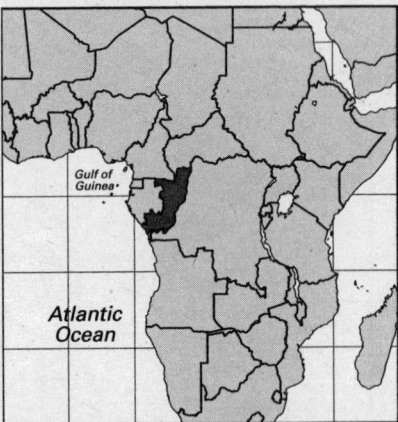

Gulf of Guinea

Atlantic Ocean

Official name: République du Congo (Republic of the Congo). **Form of government:** republic with two legislative houses (Senate [66]; National Assembly [137]). **Chief of state:** President Denis Sassou-Nguesso (from 1997). **Head of government:** Isidore Mvouba (from 2005). **Capital:** Brazzaville. **Official language:** French (Lingala and Monokutuba are "functional" national languages). **Official religion:** none. **Monetary unit:** 1 CFA franc (CFAF) = 100 centimes; valuation (1 Jul 2007) US$1 = CFAF 485.18 (formerly pegged to the French franc and, since 1 Jan 2002, to the euro at the rate of €1 = CFAF 655.96).

Demography

Area: 132,047 sq mi, 342,000 sq km. **Population** (2006): 3,702,000. **Density** (2006): persons per sq mi 28.0, persons per sq km 10.8. **Urban** (2002): 66.1%. **Sex distribution** (2002): male 49.36%; female 50.64%. **Age breakdown** (2002): under 15, 38.9%; 15–29, 29.6%; 30–44, 17.7%; 45–59, 8.4%; 60–74, 4.4%; 75 and over, 1.0%. **Ethnic composition** (1983): Kongo 51.5%; Teke 17.3%; Mboshi 11.5%; Mbete 4.9%; Punu 3.0%; Sango 2.7%; Maka 1.8%; Pygmy 1.5%; other 5.8%. **Religious affiliation** (2000): Roman Catholic 49.3%; Protestant 17.0%; African Christians 12.6%; unaffiliated Christians 11.9%; traditional beliefs 4.8%; other 4.4%. **Major cities** (1992): Brazzaville (urban agglomeration; 2001) 1,360,000; Pointe-Noire (1996) 455,131; Dolisie (known as Loubomo between 1980 and 2000) 83,605; Nkayi 42,465; Mossendjo 16,405. **Location:** west-central Africa, bordering Cameroon, the Central African Republic, the Democratic Republic of the Congo, Angola, the South Atlantic Ocean, and Gabon.

Vital statistics

Birth rate per 1,000 population (2003): 29.5 (world avg. 21.3). **Death rate** per 1,000 population (2003): 14.2 (world avg. 9.1). **Natural increase rate** per 1,000 population (2002): 15.3 (world avg. 12.2). **Total fertility rate** (avg. births per childbearing

---

1 metric ton = about 1.1 short tons;   1 kilometer = 0.6 mi (statute);   1 metric ton-km cargo = about 0.68 short ton-mi cargo;   c.i.f.: cost, insurance, and freight;   f.o.b.: free on board

woman; 2003): 3.7. **Life expectancy** at birth (2003): male 49.0 years; female 51.0 years. **Adult population** (ages 15–49) **living with HIV** (beginning of 2004): 4.9% (world avg. 1.1%).

National economy

Budget (2001). *Revenue:* CFAF 631,800,000,000 (petroleum revenue 68.2%; nonpetroleum receipts 31.2%; grants 0.6%). *Expenditures:* CFAF 645,900,-000,000 (current expenditure 68.2%, of which debt service 23.5%, salaries 18.3%, transfers and subsidies 11.3%; capital expenditure 31.8%). **Public debt** (external, outstanding; 2002): $3,974,000,000. **Households**. Average household size (1984) 5.2. **Gross national product** (at current market prices; 2002): $2,407,000,000 ($640 per capita). **Production** (metric tons except as noted). *Agriculture, forestry, fishing* (2002): cassava 862,000, sugarcane 459,000, oil palm fruit 90,000; livestock (number of live animals) 294,000 goats, 96,000 sheep, 93,000 cattle; roundwood (2001) 2,420,000 cu m; fish catch (2002) 43,000. *Mining and quarrying* (2002): gold 10 kg; diamonds, no reported production (annual volume of large-scale diamond smuggling as of July 2004 equaled 5,200,000 carats). *Manufacturing* (2000): residual fuel oil 262,000; distillate fuel oils 96,000; refined sugar 74,726. *Energy production (consumption):* electricity (kW-hr; 2000) 300,000,000 (490,000,000); crude petroleum (barrels; 2000) 99,200,000 (4,444,000); petroleum products (2001) 383,000 (165,400); natural gas (cu m; 2000) 124,983,000 (124,983,000). **Population economically active** (2000): total 1,232,000; activity rate of total population 35.7% (participation rates [1984]: ages 15–64, 54.0%; female [1997] 43.4%). **Land use** as % of total land area (2000): in temporary crops 0.5%, in permanent crops 0.1%, in pasture 29.3%; overall forest area 64.6%. **Tourism** (2002): receipts $25,000,000; expenditures $70,000,000.

Foreign trade

Imports (2001): CFAF 486,200,000,000 (nonpetroleum sector 84.0%; petroleum sector 16.0%). *Major import sources* (1999): France 23%; US 8%; Italy 8%; Hong Kong 5%; Belgium 4%. **Exports** (2001): CFAF 1,443,200,000,000 (crude petroleum 89.6%, wood and wood products 5.1%, petroleum products 1.3%, sugar 0.7%). *Major export destinations* (1999): Taiwan 32%; US 23%; South Korea 15%; Germany 7%; China 3%.

Transport and communications

Transport. *Railroads:* (1998) length 894 km; passenger-km 242,000,000; metric ton-km cargo 135,-000,000. *Roads* (2001): total length 17,244 km (paved 7%). *Vehicles* (1997): passenger cars 37,240; trucks and buses 15,500. *Air transport* (1998; represents 1/11 of the traffic of Air Afrique; Air Afrique, an airline jointly owned by 11 African countries [including Republic of the Congo], was declared bankrupt in February 2002): passenger-km 258,272,000; metric ton-km cargo 13,524,000; airports (1998) with scheduled flights 10. **Communications**, in total units (units per 1,000 persons). Daily newspaper circulation (2000): 10,300 (3); radios (2000): 403,300 (109); televisions (2000): 114,000 (13); telephone main lines (2003): 7,000 (2); cellular telephone subscribers (2003): 330,000

(94); personal computers (2003): 15,000 (4.3); Internet users (2003): 15,000 (4.3).

Education and health

Educational attainment (1984). Percentage of population age 25 and over having: no formal schooling 58.7%; primary education 21.4%; secondary education 16.9%; postsecondary 3.0%. **Literacy** (2000): total population age 15 and over literate 80.7%; males literate 87.5%; females literate 74.4%. **Health**: physicians (1995) 632 (1 per 4,083 persons); hospital beds (1989) 4,817 (1 per 446 persons); infant mortality rate per 1,000 live births (2003) 95.3. **Food** (2002): daily per capita caloric intake 2,162 (vegetable products 94%, animal products 6%); 97% of FAO recommended minimum.

Military

Total active duty personnel (2003): 10,000 (army 80.0%, navy 8.0%, air force 12.0%). **Military expenditure as percentage of GNP** (1999): 3.5% (world 2.4%); per capita expenditure $21.

Background

In precolonial days the Congo area was home to several thriving kingdoms, including the Kongo, which had its beginnings in the 1st millennium AD. The slave trade began in the 15th century with the arrival of the Portuguese; it supported the local kingdoms and dominated the area until its suppression in the 19th century. The French arrived in the mid-19th century and established treaties with two of the kingdoms, placing them under French protection prior to their becoming part of the colony of French Congo. In 1910 the French possessions were renamed French Equatorial Africa, and Congo became known as Middle (Moyen) Congo. In 1946 Middle Congo became a French overseas territory and in 1958 voted to become an autonomous republic within the French Community. Full independence came two years later. The area has suffered from political instability since independence. Congo's first president was ousted in 1963. A Marxist party, the Congolese Labor Party, gained strength, and in 1968 another coup, led by Maj. Marien Ngouabi, created the People's Republic of the Congo. Ngouabi was assassinated in 1977. A series of military rulers followed, at first militantly socialist but later oriented toward social democracy. Fighting between local militias that began in 1997 badly disrupted the economy.

Recent Developments

Although the World Bank granted $17 million in January 2006 for the disarmament and reintegration of 30,000 members of "Ninja" militias, in March Ninja leader Frédéric Bitsangou announced that he would not allow his men to be disarmed until a final political settlement had been agreed upon with the government. Despite an 8.5% increase in oil production, the country suffered fuel shortages throughout the year. In March the World Bank announced that the country would receive $2.9 billion in debt relief under the Heavily Indebted Poor Countries Initiative.

Internet resources:
<www.cia.gov/cia/publications/factbook/geos/cf.html>.

Costa Rica

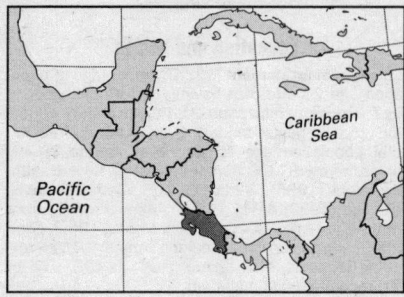

Official name: República de Costa Rica (Republic of Costa Rica). **Form of government:** unitary multiparty republic with one legislative house (Legislative Assembly [57]). **Head of state and government:** President Óscar Arias Sánchez (from 2006). **Capital:** San José. **Official language:** Spanish. **Official religion:** Roman Catholicism. **Monetary unit:** 1 Costa Rican colón (₡) = 100 céntimos; valuation (1 Jul 2007) US$1 = ₡517.84.

Demography

Area: 19,730 sq mi, 51,100 sq km. **Population** (2006): 4,274,000. **Density** (2006): persons per sq mi 216.6, persons per sq km 83.6. **Urban** (2003): 60.6%. **Sex distribution** (2003): male 50.86%; female 49.14%. **Age breakdown** (2002): under 15, 30.7%; 15–29, 27.3%; 30–44, 21.7%; 45–59, 12.5%; 60–74, 5.7%; 75 and over, 2.1%. **Ethnic composition** (2000): white 77.0%; mestizo 17.0%; black/mulatto 3.0%; East Asian (mostly Chinese) 2.0%; Amerindian 1.0%. **Religious affiliation** (1995): Roman Catholic 86.0%; Protestant 9.3%, of which Pentecostal 4.9%; other Christian 2.4%; other 2.3%. **Major cities** (2000): San José 309,672 (San José canton; urban agglomeration 983,000 [2001]); Limón 60,298 (district population); Alajuela 42,889 (district population); San Isidro de El General 41,221 (district population); Cartago 39,958 (three districts). **Location:** Central America, bordering Nicaragua, the Caribbean Sea, Panama, and the North Pacific Ocean.

Vital statistics

Birth rate per 1,000 population (2003): 19.4 (world avg. 21.3); (1999) legitimate 51.0%. **Death rate** per 1,000 population (2003): 4.3 (world avg. 9.1). **Natural increase rate** per 1,000 population (2003): 15.1 (world avg. 12.2). **Total fertility rate** (avg. births per childbearing woman; 2003): 2.4. **Marriage rate** per 1,000 population (1999): 7.1. **Divorce rate** per 1,000 population (1995): 1.4. **Life expectancy** at birth (2003): male 73.9 years; female 79.1 years.

National economy

Budget (2000). *Revenue:* ₡610,138,000,000 (taxes on goods and services 63.8%, income and profit taxes 21.8%, import duties 7.7%, other 6.7%). *Ex-*

penditures: ₡761,306,000,000 (current expenditures 90.1%, of which transfers 30.5%, wages 29.7%, interest on debt 23.0%; development expenditures 9.9%). **Public debt** (external, outstanding; 2002): $3,139,000,000. **Gross national product** (2003): $17,157,000,000 ($4,280 per capita). **Production** (metric tons except as noted). *Agriculture, forestry, fishing* (2003): sugarcane 3,923,870, bananas 1,862,978, green coffee 731,126; livestock (number of live animals) 1,150,000 cattle, 500,000 pigs, 18,500,000 chickens; roundwood (2001) 5,140,781 cu m; fish catch (2001) 35,000. *Mining and quarrying* (2002): limestone 900,000; gold 100 kg. *Manufacturing* (value added in $'000,000; 2001): food products 777; beverages 211; paints, soaps, and pharmaceuticals 148. *Energy production (consumption):* electricity (kW-hr; 2000) 7,227,000,000 (7,226,000,000); crude petroleum (barrels; 2000) none (80,630); petroleum products (2000) 6,000 (1,597,000). **Population economically active** (2000): total 1,390,560; activity rate of total population 39.9% (participation rates: ages 12–59, 53.4%; female 32.1%; unemployed 5.2%). **Tourism** (2002): receipts $1,078,000,000; expenditures $367,000,000. **Household income and expenditure.** Average household size (2000) 4.1; average annual household income (1997) ₡1,468,597; sources of income (1987–88): wages and salaries 61.0%, self-employment 22.6%, transfers 9.6%; expenditure (1987–88): food and beverages 39.1%, housing and energy 12.1%, transportation 11.6%, household furnishings 10.9%. **Land use** as % of total land area (2000): in temporary crops 4.4%, in permanent crops 5.9%, in pasture 45.8%; overall forest area 38.5%.

Foreign trade

Imports (2000-c.i.f.): $6,380,000,000 (estimated figures: general merchandise 68%; goods for reassembly 32%). *Major import sources:* US 53.1%; Mexico 6.2%; Venezuela 5.3%; Japan 3.4%; Spain 2.3%. **Exports** (2000-f.o.b.): $5,897,000,000 (components for microprocessors 28.0%, bananas 9.0%, processed food and tobacco products 6.5%, coffee 4.7%, tropical fruit 3.4%). *Major export destinations:* US 51.8%; The Netherlands 6.7%; UK 5.1%; Guatemala 3.3%; Nicaragua 3.0%.

Transport and communications

Transport. *Roads* (1999): total length 35,876 km (paved 17%). *Vehicles* (1999): passenger cars 326,524; trucks and buses 181,272. *Air transport* (2001; Lacsa [Costa Rican Airlines] only): passenger-km 2,143,000,000; metric ton-km cargo 84,697,000; airports (1996) 14. **Communications,** in total units (units per 1,000 persons). Daily newspaper circulation (1996): 320,000 (94); radios (2000): 3,200,000 (816); televisions (2000): 907,000 (231); telephone main lines (2002): 1,038,000 (251); cellular telephone subscribers (2003): 459,800 (141); personal computers (2002): 800,000 (193); Internet users (2002): 817,000 (197).

Education and health

Educational attainment (1996). Percentage of population age 5 and over having: no formal schooling

---

1 metric ton = about 1.1 short tons;   1 kilometer = 0.6 mi (statute);   1 metric ton-km cargo = about 0.68 short ton-mi cargo;   c.i.f.: cost, insurance, and freight;   f.o.b.: free on board

11.7%; incomplete primary education 28.5%; complete primary 25.8%; incomplete secondary 16.0%; complete secondary 9.0%; higher 8.5%; other/unknown 0.5%. **Literacy** (2002): total population age 15 and over literate 95.8%; males literate 95.7%; females literate 95.9%. **Health** (2003): physicians (2000) 6,800 (1 per 625 persons); hospital beds 6,000 (1 per 700 persons); infant mortality rate per 1,000 live births 10.6. **Food** (2001): daily per capita caloric intake 2,761 (vegetable products 80%, animal products 20%); 123% of FAO recommended minimum.

Military

Paramilitary expenditure as percentage of GNP (1999): 0.5% (world 2.4%); per capita expenditure $19. The army was officially abolished in 1948. Paramilitary (police) forces had 8,400 members in 2003.

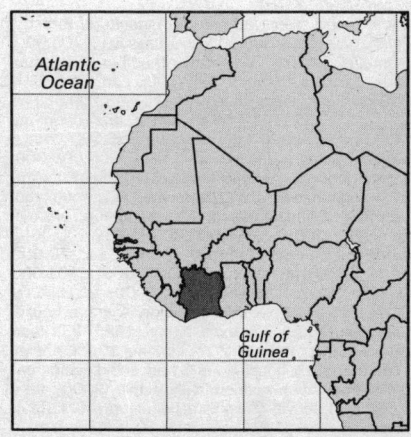

Background

Christopher Columbus landed in Costa Rica in 1502 in an area inhabited by a number of small, independent Indian tribes. These peoples were not easily dominated, and it took almost 60 years for the Spanish to establish a permanent settlement. Ignored by the Spanish crown because of its lack of mineral wealth, the colony grew slowly. Coffee exports and the construction of a rail line improved its economy in the 19th century. It joined the short-lived Mexican Empire in 1821, was a member of the United Provinces of Central America 1823–38, and adopted a constitution in 1871. In 1890 Costa Ricans held what is considered to be the first free and honest election in Central America, beginning a tradition of democracy for which Costa Rica is renowned. In 1987 then president Óscar Arias Sánchez was awarded the Nobel Peace Prize. During the 1990s Costa Rica struggled with its economic policies. It suffered severe damage from a hurricane in 1996.

Recent Developments

National attention in Costa Rica was riveted on the Central America–Dominican Republic Free Trade Agreement (CAFTA–DR) with the United States. Although protests continued in 2005 and 2006 against the agreement, which would create the 10th largest US export market and which Costa Rica had earlier signed, newly elected president Óscar Arias Sánchez acted in 2006 to fulfill campaign promises to pursue its ratification. As of February 2007, however, this ratification had not occurred. Costa Rica remained the only signatory that had not also ratified the agreement, leaving some supporters to worry that Costa Rica would eventually be excluded from it.

Internet resources: <www.casapres.go.cr>.

Côte d'Ivoire

Official name: République de Côte d'Ivoire (Republic of Côte d'Ivoire). **Form of government:** republic with one legislative house (National Assembly [225, including unoccupied seats]); constitutional referendum approved July 2000, but status of new constitution unclear in 2004. **Chief of state and government:** President Laurent Gbagbo (from 2000), assisted by

Prime Minister Guillaume Soro (from 2007). **Capital:** Abidjan. **Official language:** French. **Official religion:** none. **Monetary unit:** 1 CFA franc (CFAF) = 100 centimes; valuation (1 Jul 2007) US$1 = CFAF 485.18 (formerly pegged to the French franc and, since 1 Jan 2002, to the euro at the rate of €1 = CFAF 655.96).

Demography

Area: 123,863 sq mi, 320,803 sq km. **Population** (2006): 17,655,000. **Density** (2006): persons per sq mi 142.5, persons per sq km 55.0. **Urban** (2003): 44.9%. **Sex distribution** (2002): male 50.28%; female 49.72%. **Age breakdown** (2002): under 15, 45.6%; 15–29, 28.7%; 30–44, 14.4%; 45–59, 7.6%; 60–74, 3.0%; 75 and over, 0.7%. **Ethnolinguistic composition** (1998; local population only; foreigners constituted 26% of the population and two-thirds of all foreigners were from Burkina Faso): Akan 42.1%; Mande 26.5%; other 31.4%. **Religious affiliation** (1998): Muslim 38.6%; Christian 30.4%; nonreligious 16.7%; animist 11.9%; other 2.4%. **Major cities** (1998): Abidjan (1999) 3,199,000; Bouaké 462,000; Daloa 173,000; Yamoussoukro 110,000. **Location:** western Africa, bordering Mali, Burkina Faso, Ghana, the Atlantic Ocean, Liberia, and Guinea.

Vital statistics

Birth rate per 1,000 population (2002): 40.4 (world avg. 21.3). **Death rate** per 1,000 population (2001): 18.4 (world avg. 9.1). **Natural increase rate** per 1,000 population (2002): 22.0 (world avg. 12.2). **Total fertility rate** (avg. births per childbearing woman; 2002): 5.6. **Life expectancy** at birth (2002): male 40.4 years; female 45.3 years. **Adult population** (ages 15–49) **living with HIV** (2004): 7.0% (world avg. 1.1%).

National economy

Budget (2000). *Revenue:* CFAF 1,237,100,000,000 (tax revenue 87.1%, of which import taxes and duties 29.2%, export taxes 13.2%, taxes on profits 11.6%, income tax 10.2%; nontax revenue 12.9%). *Expenditures:* CFAF 1,358,200,000,000 (wages and salaries 33.0%; debt service 22.7%; capital expenditure 15.4%; transfers 13.1%; other 15.8%). **Production**

(metric tons except as noted). *Agriculture, forestry, fishing* (2002): yams 3,000,000, cassava 1,700,000, plantains 1,410,000; livestock (number of live animals) 1,522,000 sheep, 1,476,000 cattle, 32,625,-000 chickens; roundwood (2001) 12,083,092 cu m; fish catch (2001) 74,581. *Mining and quarrying* (2002): gold 2,000 kg; diamonds 306,500 carats. *Manufacturing* (value added in CFAF '000,000,000; 1997): food 156.6, of which cocoa and chocolate 72.4, vegetable oils 62.7; chemicals 60.2; wood products 55.9. *Energy production (consumption):* electricity (kW-hr; 2000) 3,619,000,000 (3,619,000,000); crude petroleum (barrels; 2000) 11,270,000 (30,087,000); petroleum products (2000) 2,801,000 (1,242,000); natural gas (cu m; 2000) 1,510,400,-000 (1,510,400,000). **Households.** Average household size (2000) 7.8; expenditure (1992–93): food 48.0%, transportation 12.2%, clothing 10.1%, energy and water 8.5%, housing 7.8%, household equipment 3.4%. **Population economically active** (2000): total 6,531,000; activity rate of total population 40.9% (participation rates [1994] over age 10, 64.3%; female 33.0%; unemployed [1996] 38.8%). **Gross national product** (2003): $11,159,000,000 ($660 per capita). **Public debt** (external, outstanding; 2002): $9,110,-000,000. **Tourism** (2001): receipts $48,000,000; expenditures $192,000,000. **Land use** as % of total land area (2000): in temporary crops 9.7%, in permanent crops 13.8%, in pasture 40.9%; overall forest area 22.4%.

Foreign trade

Imports (2001-f.o.b. in balance of trade and commodities and c.i.f. for trading partners): CFAF 1,768,000,000,000 (crude and refined petroleum 28.8%, food products 22.5%, machinery and transport equipment 20.4%). *Major import sources* (2000): Nigeria 26.6%; France 20.3%; Belgium 4.0%; Italy 3.6%; Germany 3.6%. **Exports** (2001): CFAF 2,891,000,000,000 (cocoa beans and products 33.2%, crude petroleum and petroleum products 13.7%, wood and wood products 7.1%, coffee beans 3.6%). *Major export destinations* (2000): France 14.9%; The Netherlands 9.7%; US 8.3%; Mali 5.7%; Italy 4.8%; Senegal 4.0%.

Transport and communications

Transport. *Railroads* (1999): route length 655 km; passenger-km 93,100,000; metric ton-km cargo 537,600,000. *Roads* (1999): total length 50,400 km (paved 9.7%). *Vehicles* (1999): passenger cars 109,600; trucks and buses 54,100. *Air transport* (1998): passenger-km 318,000,000; metric ton-km cargo 44,000,000; airports (1999) 5. **Communications,** in total units (units per 1,000 persons). Daily newspaper circulation (2000): 1,440,000 (91); radios (2001): 3,053,000 (185); televisions (2002): 1,007,000 (61); telephone main lines (2003): 328,000 (20); cellular telephone subscribers (2003): 1,236,000 (74); personal computers (2002): 154,000 (9.3); Internet users (2002): 90,000 (5.5).

Education and health

Educational attainment (1988). Percentage of population age 6 and over having: no formal schooling

60.0%; Koranic school 3.6%; primary education 24.8%; secondary 10.7%; higher 0.9%. **Literacy** (2000): percentage of population age 15 and over literate 46.8%; males 54.5%; females 38.6%. **Health:** physicians (1996) 1,318 (1 per 11,111 persons); hospital beds (1993) 7,928 (1 per 1,698 persons); infant mortality rate per 1,000 live births (2001) 99.6. **Food** (2001): daily per capita caloric intake 2,594 (vegetable products 97%, animal products 3%); 112% of FAO recommended minimum.

Military

Total active duty personnel: New national army to be created pending final resolution of 2002–03 civil war. Peacekeeping troops (August 2004): UN 5,800; French 4,000. **Military expenditure as percentage of GNP** (1999): 0.8% (world avg. 2.4%); per capita expenditure $5.

Background

Europeans came to the area to trade in ivory and slaves beginning in the 15th century, and local kingdoms gave way to French influence in the 19th century. The French colony of Côte d'Ivoire was founded in 1893, and full occupation took place 1908–18. In 1946 it became a territory in the French Union. Côte d'Ivoire achieved independence in 1960, when Félix Houphouët-Boigny was elected president. The country's first multiparty presidential elections were held in 1990. In 2002 the country began to fracture politically into north and south, and civil war ensued.

Recent Developments

In 2006 members of the rebellious New Forces alliance (FN) continued to hold the north, while the government controlled the south. Spasmodic outbreaks of ethnic and religious violence dominated the year. In March 2007, however, Pres. Laurent Gbagbo and rebel leader Guillaume Soro signed a peace agreement that called for the dissolution of the buffer zone patrolled by UN and French forces and for a transitional government ahead of planned elections at the end of the year. The forces of both sides would be integrated and an amnesty for those forces offered. France announced that month that it was reducing the size of its military contingent to 3,000.

Internet resources: <www.africaonline.co.ci>.

Croatia

Official name: Republika Hrvatska (Republic of Croatia). **Form of government:** multiparty republic with one legislative house (House of Representatives [152, including six seats representing Croatians living abroad and two seats for minorities]). **Head of state:** President Stipe Mesic (from 2000). **Head of government:** Prime Minister Ivo Sanader (from 2003). **Capital:** Zagreb. **Official language:** Croatian (Serbo-Croatian). **Official religion:** none. **Monetary unit:** 1 kuna (HrK; plural kune) = 100 lipa; valuation (1 Jul 2007) US$1 = HrK 5.39.

1 metric ton = about 1.1 short tons;   1 kilometer = 0.6 mi (statute);   1 metric ton-km cargo = about 0.68 short ton-mi cargo;   c.i.f.: cost, insurance, and freight;   f.o.b.: free on board

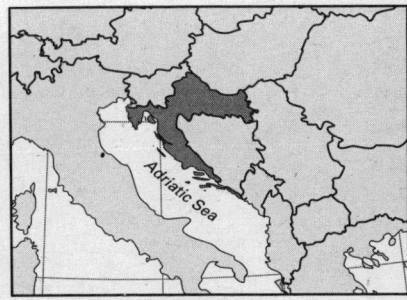

Adriatic Sea

Demography

Area: 21,851 sq mi, 56,594 sq km. **Population** (2006): 4,450,000. **Density** (2006): persons per sq mi 203.7, persons per sq km 78.6. **Urban** (2002): 59.0%. **Sex distribution** (2001): male 48.13%; female 51.87%. **Age breakdown** (2001): under 15, 17.1%; 15–29, 20.4%; 30–44, 21.4%; 45–59, 19.5%; 60–74, 16.3%; 75 and over, 5.3%. **Ethnic composition** (2001): Croat 89.6%; Serb 4.5%; Bosniac 0.5%; Italian 0.4%; Hungarian 0.4%; other 4.6%. **Religious affiliation** (2000): Christian 95.2%, of which Roman Catholic 88.5%, Eastern Orthodox 5.6%, Protestant 0.6%; Sunni Muslim 2.3%; nonreligious/atheist 2.5%. **Major cities** (2001): Zagreb 691,724; Split 175,140; Rijeka 143,800; Osijek 90,411; Zadar 69,556. **Location:** southeastern Europe, bordering Slovenia, Hungary, Serbia and Montenegro, Bosnia and Herzegovina, and the Adriatic Sea.

Vital statistics

Birth rate per 1,000 population (2003): 9.5 (world avg. 21.3); (1999) legitimate 91.8%. **Death rate** per 1,000 population (2003): 11.2 (world avg. 9.1). **Natural increase rate** per 1,000 population (2001): –1.7 (world avg. 12.2). **Total fertility rate** (avg. births per childbearing woman; 2003): 1.4. **Marriage rate** per 1,000 population (2001): 5.0. **Divorce rate** per 1,000 population (2001): 1.1. **Life expectancy** at birth (2003): male 69.6 years; female 78.3 years.

National economy

Budget (2001). *Revenue:* HrK 55,303,800,000 (tax revenue 84.9%, of which sales tax 40.7%, excise taxes 14.2%, income tax 6.8%; nontax revenue 15.1%). *Expenditures:* HrK 57,308,100,000 (social security and welfare 43.2%; education 10.7%; public order 8.3%; defense 7.4%). **Population economically active** (2001): total 1,728,503; activity rate 39.0% (participation rates: ages 15–64, 57.9%; female 43.0%; unemployed 22.0%). **Production** (metric tons except as noted). *Agriculture, forestry, fishing* (2002): corn (maize) 2,502,000, sugar beets 1,183,000, wheat 988,000; livestock (number of live animals) 1,286,000 pigs, 580,000 sheep, 11,665,000 poultry; roundwood (2001) 3,468,000 cu m; fish catch (2002) 30,000. *Mining and quarrying* (2002): gypsum 145,000; ornamental stone 1,128,000 sq m. *Manufacturing* (value added in $'000,000; 1996): food products 895; transport equipment 425; electrical machinery 362. *Energy production (consumption):* electricity (kW-hr; 2001) 11,674,000,000 ([2000] 14,702,000,000); hard coal (2000) none ([623,000]); lignite (2000) none

(80,000); crude petroleum (barrels; 2000) 8,158,000 (37,845,000); petroleum products (2000) 4,827,000 (3,534,000); natural gas (cu m; 2001) 2,009,000,000 ([2000] 2,633,994,000). **Gross national product** (2003): $23,839,000,000 ($5,350 per capita). **Public debt** (external, outstanding; 2002): $7,679,000,000. **Household income and expenditure.** Average household size (2001) 3.0; income per household HrK 64,288; sources: wages 42.8%, self-employment 22.5%, pension 20.6%, other 14.1%; expenditure (2001): food and nonalcoholic beverages 33.7%, housing and energy 13.4%, transportation 11.5%, clothing 9.1%, recreation and culture 5.9%, household furnishings 5.6%, alcoholic beverages and tobacco 4.1%, other 16.7%. **Tourism** (2002): receipts $3,811,000,000; expenditures $781,000,000. **Land use** as % of total land area (2000): in temporary crops 26.1%, in permanent crops 2.3%, in pasture 28.1%; overall forest area 31.9%.

Foreign trade

Imports (2001-f.o.b. in balance of trade and c.i.f. for commodities and trading partners): $9,044,000,000 (machinery and transport equipment 33.2%, chemical products 11.5%, base and fabricated metals 10.1%, crude and refined petroleum 9.2%). *Major import sources:* Germany 17.1%; Italy 16.9%; Slovenia 7.9%; Russia and other countries of former USSR 7.2%; Austria 7.0%. **Exports** (2001): $4,659,000,000 (machinery and transport equipment 29.4%, chemical and chemical products 10.6%, clothing 10.5%, crude petroleum and petroleum products 7.4%, food 6.9%). *Major export destinations:* Italy 23.7%; Germany 14.8%; Bosnia and Herzegovina 12.0%; Slovenia 9.1%; Austria 5.7%.

Transport and communications

Transport. *Railroads* (2001): length 2,726 km; passenger-km 1,234,000,000; metric ton-km cargo 2,148,000,000. *Roads* (2001): total length 28,275 km (paved 82%). *Vehicles* (2001): passenger cars 1,195,450; trucks and buses 124,669. *Air transport* (2001): passenger-km 921,053,000; metric ton-km cargo 3,597,000; airports (2001) 4. **Communications,** in total units (units per 1,000 persons). Daily newspaper circulation (1996): 515,000 (118); radios (2000): 1,120,000 (252); televisions (2000): 1,693,-000 (380); telephone main lines (2002): 1,825,000 (417); cellular telephone subscribers (2003): 2,553,000 (584); personal computers (2002): 760,000 (174); Internet users (2003): 1,014,000 (232).

Education and health

Educational attainment (1991). Percentage of population age 15 and over having: no schooling or unknown 10.1%; less than full primary education 21.2%; primary 23.4%; secondary 36.0%; postsecondary and higher 9.3%. **Literacy** (1999): population age 15 and over literate 98.2%; males 99.3%; females 97.1%. **Health** (1999): physicians 8,046 (1 per 529 persons); hospital beds 27,000 (1 per 158 persons); infant mortality rate per 1,000 live births (2003) 7.1. **Food** (2002): daily per capita caloric intake 2,799 (vegetable products 81%, animal products 19%); 110% of FAO recommended minimum.

Military

Total active duty personnel (2003): 20,800 (army 67.5%, navy 12.0%, air force and air defense 11.1%, headquarters staff 9.4%). **Military expenditure as percentage of GNP** (1999): 6.4% (world 2.4%); per capita expenditure $491.

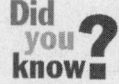 The seaport and resort of Split is the chief city of Dalmatia, Croatia. The city is best known for the ruins of the Palace of Diocletian (built AD 295–305).

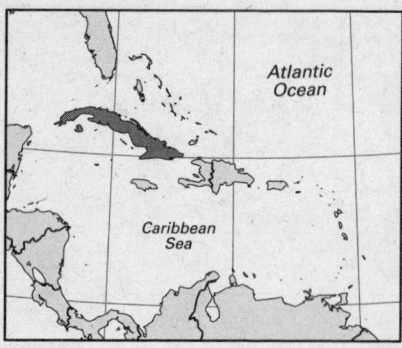

Background

The Croats, a southern Slavic people, arrived in the area in the 7th century AD and in the 8th century came under Charlemagne's rule. They converted to Christianity soon afterward and formed a kingdom in the 10th century. Most of Croatia was taken by the Turks in 1526; the rest voted to accept Austrian rule. In 1867 it became part of Austria-Hungary, with Dalmatia and Istria ruled by Vienna and Croatia-Slavonia a Hungarian crown land. In 1918, after the defeat of Austria-Hungary in World War I, it joined other south Slavic territories to form the Kingdom of Serbs, Croats, and Slovenes, renamed Yugoslavia in 1929. During World War II an independent state of Croatia was established by Germany and Italy, embracing Croatia-Slavonia, part of Dalmatia, and Bosnia and Herzegovina; after the war Croatia was rejoined to Yugoslavia as a people's republic. It declared its independence in 1991, sparking insurrections by Croatian Serbs, who carved out autonomous regions with Serbian-led Yugoslav army help; Croatia had taken back most of these regions by 1995. With some stability returning, Croatia's economy began to revive in the late 1990s.

Recent Developments

Croatia entered 2006 with great optimism that it would achieve its principal foreign-policy goal, full membership in the European Union, by 2009. While the government publicly attributed a delay in the accession screening of Croatia's judiciary to "technical difficulties," independent observers cited widespread corruption as the real culprit. In response, in April the government adopted an anticorruption strategy that consisted of new legislation, stronger enforcement mechanisms, and educational and awareness campaigns. Talks with the EU continued, though in early 2007 the EU still expressed reservations about the judiciary. Overall, the Croatian economy proved robust in 2006, with GDP growing an estimated 6%, inflation holding at a low 3.6%, and unemployment dipping to 15.7%. Tourism continued its upward trend, growing 3% with total revenues of $7.5 billion.

Internet resources: <www.croatia.hr>.

Cuba

Official name: República de Cuba (Republic of Cuba). **Form of government:** unitary socialist republic with one legislative house (National Assembly of the People's Power [609]). **Head of state and government:** President Fidel Castro (from 1976). **Capital:** Havana. **Official language:** Spanish. **Official religion:** none. **Monetary unit:** 1 Cuban peso (CUP) = 100 centavos; valuation (1 Jul 2007) US$1 = 0.93 CUP.

Demography

Area: 42,804 sq mi, 110,861 sq km. **Population** (2006): 11,294,000. **Density** (2006): persons per sq mi 263.9, persons per sq km 101.9. **Urban** (2003): 75.6%. **Sex distribution** (2003): male 50.02%; female 49.98%. **Age breakdown** (2003): under 15, 20.5%; 15–29, 21.2%; 30–44, 27.7%; 45–59, 16.5%; 60–74, 9.9%; 75 and over, 4.2%. **Ethnic composition** (1994): mixed 51.0%; white 37.0%; black 11.0%; other 1.0%. **Religious affiliation** (1995): Roman Catholic 39.5%; Protestant 2.4%; other Christian 0.2%; other (mostly Santería) 57.9%. **Major cities** (1999): Havana (2002) 2,175,900; Santiago de Cuba 441,524; Camagüey 306,049; Holguín 259,300; Santa Clara 210,100. **Location:** island southeast of Florida, US, between the North Atlantic Ocean and the Caribbean Sea.

Vital statistics

Birth rate per 1,000 population (2003): 12.4 (world avg. 21.3). **Death rate** per 1,000 population (2003): 7.2 (world avg. 9.1). **Natural increase rate** per 1,000 population (2003): 5.2 (world avg. 12.2). **Total fertility rate** (avg. births per childbearing woman; 2003): 1.7. **Marriage rate** per 1,000 population (2001): 4.8. **Divorce rate** per 1,000 population (2001): 2.3. **Life expectancy** at birth (2003): male 74.6 years; female 79.2 years.

National economy

Budget (2000). *Revenue:* CUP 14,505,000,000. *Expenditures:* CUP 15,243,000,000 (capital expenditure 18.0%, education 13.9%, health 11.3%, defense 6.1%, other 50.7%). **Public debt** (external, outstanding; 2002): $12,300,000,000. **Production** (metric tons except as noted). *Agriculture, forestry, fishing* (2003): sugarcane 22,901,600, fresh vegetables 1,930,870, plantains 797,200; livestock (number of live animals) 4,025,000 cattle, 3,121,000 sheep, 23,210,000 chickens; roundwood (2003) 3,597,000 cu m; fish catch (2001) 110,330. *Mining and quarrying* (2001):

---

1 metric ton = about 1.1 short tons; 1 kilometer = 0.6 mi (statute); 1 metric ton-km cargo = about 0.68 short ton-mi cargo; c.i.f.: cost, insurance, and freight; f.o.b.: free on board

nickel (metal content) 72,619; cobalt (metal content) 3,910. *Manufacturing* (value added in $'000,000; 1990): tobacco products 2,629; food products 1,033; beverages 358. *Energy production (consumption):* electricity (kW-hr; 2001) 15,301,000,000 (15,301,-000,000); coal (2000) none (15,000); crude petroleum (2003) 26,020,000 ([2000] 28,240,000); petroleum products (2000) 2,068,000 (5,888,000); natural gas (cu m; 2003) 653,000,000 ([2000] 574,000,-000). **Population economically active** (2002): total 4,300,000; activity rate 38.2% (participation rates: female [1998] 37.0%; unemployed [2002] 3.5%). **Gross domestic product** (2002): $25,900,000,000 ($2,300 per capita). **Households.** Average household size (2000) 3.6. **Tourism** (2002): $1,633,000,000. **Land use** as % of total land area (2000): in temporary crops 33.1%, in permanent crops 7.6%, in pasture 20.0%; overall forest area 21.4%.

Foreign trade

Imports (1996-f.o.b. in balance of trade and trading partners and c.i.f. for commodities): $3,481,000,000 (refined petroleum 20.2%; food and live animals 19.8%, of which cereals 11.4%; machinery and transport equipment 16.1%, of which power-generating machinery 7.4%; crude petroleum 7.2%). *Major import sources* (2001): Spain 12.7%; France 6.5%; Canada 5.7%; China 5.3%; Italy 5.0%. **Exports** (1996): $1,849,000,000 (raw sugar 51.5%; nickel [all forms] 22.6%; fresh and frozen fish 6.7%; raw tobacco and tobacco products 5.9%; medicinal and pharmaceutical products 2.8%). *Major export destinations* (2001): The Netherlands 22.4%; Russia 13.3%; Canada 13.3%; Spain 7.3%; China 6.2%.

Transport and communications

Transport. *Railroads* (2001): length 4,807 km; (1997) passenger-km 1,684,000; metric ton-km cargo 821,500,000. *Roads* (1997): total length 60,858 km (paved 49%). *Vehicles* (1998): passenger cars 172,574; trucks and buses 185,495. *Air transport* (2000): passenger-km 2,769,162,000; metric ton-km cargo 49,294,000; airports with scheduled flights (1999) 14. **Communications,** in total units (units per 1,000 persons). Daily newspaper circulation (2000): 1,280,000 (114); radios (2001): 2,091,000 (185); televisions (2000): 3,580,000 (242); telephone main lines (2001): 574,000 (51); cellular telephone subscribers (2002): 179,000 (1.6); personal computers (2002): 359,000 (32); Internet users (2001): 120,000 (11).

Education and health

Literacy (2004): total population age 15 and over literate 96.9%; males 97.0%; females 96.8%. **Health** (2002): physicians 67,000 (1 per 168 persons); hospital beds 70,424 (1 per 161 persons); infant mortality rate per 1,000 live births 6.5. **Food** (2001): daily per capita caloric intake 2,564 (vegetable products 86%, animal products 14%); 111% of FAO recommended minimum.

Military

Total active duty personnel (2003): 46,000 (army 76.1%, navy 6.5%, air force 17.4%). **Military expenditure as percentage of GDP** (1999): 1.9% (world 2.4%); per capita expenditure: $57.

 Located on Cuba's north coast, Havana is the country's capital and one of the great treasuries of colonial architecture in the Western Hemisphere.

Background

Several Indian groups, including the Ciboney, the Taino, and the Arawak, inhabited Cuba at the time of the first Spanish contact. Christopher Columbus claimed the island for Spain in 1492, and the Spanish conquest began in 1511, when the settlement of Baracoa was founded. The native Indians were eradicated over the succeeding centuries, and African slaves, from the 18th century until slavery was abolished in 1886, were imported to work the sugar plantations. Cuba revolted unsuccessfully against Spain in the Ten Years' War (1868–78); a second war of independence began in 1895. In 1898 the US entered the war; Spain relinquished its claim to Cuba, which was occupied by the US for three years before gaining its independence in 1902. The US invested heavily in the Cuban sugar industry in the first half of the 20th century, and this, combined with tourism and gambling, caused the economy to prosper. Inequalities in the distribution of wealth persisted, however, as did political corruption. In 1958–59 the communist revolutionary Fidel Castro overthrew Cuba's longtime dictator, Fulgencio Batista, and established a socialist state aligned with the Soviet Union, abolishing capitalism and nationalizing foreign-owned enterprises. Relations with the US deteriorated, reaching a low point with the 1961 Bay of Pigs invasion and the 1962 Cuban missile crisis. In 1980 about 125,000 Cubans, including many that their government officially labeled "undesirables," were shipped to the US in the so-called Mariel Boat Lift. When communism collapsed in the USSR, Cuba lost important financial backing and its economy suffered greatly. The latter gradually improved in the 1990s with the encouragement of tourism, though diplomatic relations with the US were not resumed.

Recent Developments

In July 2006 Cuban Pres. Fidel Castro passed power temporarily to his brother and head of the armed forces, Raúl Castro, when serious internal bleeding forced the Cuban leader to undergo emergency surgery, marking the first time that the elder Castro had relinquished control since the revolution. Cuba continued to strengthen its ties with Venezuelan Pres. Hugo Chávez. Annual trade between the two countries neared $3 billion, with Venezuela exporting nearly 100,000 barrels of oil a day on preferential financing terms, and the countries continued to administer several joint programs, including a regional oil pact known as PetroCaribe. In September Cuba hosted the 14th summit of the Non-Aligned Movement, a 118-member grouping of less-developed countries, and the leaders of Pakistan, India, Iran, and Malaysia attended, among others. China emerged as Cuba's second largest trading partner, with nearly $1.8 billion in trade in 2006. Foreign companies continued exploring Cuba's offshore energy reserves, which the US Geological Survey estimated could hold 4.6 billion barrels of oil and 278 billion cu m of natural gas.

Internet resources: <www.cubatravel.cu>.

Cyprus

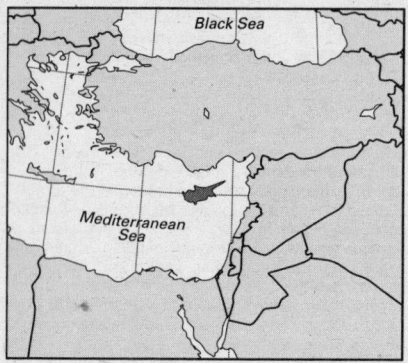

Two de facto states currently exist on the island of Cyprus: the Republic of Cyprus (ROC), predominantly Greek in character, occupying the southern two-thirds of the island, which is the original and still the internationally recognized de jure government of the whole island; and the Turkish Republic of Northern Cyprus (TRNC), proclaimed unilaterally 15 Nov 1983, on territory originally secured for the Turkish Cypriot population by the 20 Jul 1974 intervention of Turkey. Only Turkey recognizes the TRNC, and the two ethnic communities have failed to reestablish a single state. Provision of separate data below does not imply recognition of either state's claims but is necessitated by the lack of unified data.

Area: 3,572 sq mi, 9,251 sq km. **Population** (2004): 937,000; includes 80,000 "settlers" from Turkey and 38,000 Turkish military in the TRNC; excludes 3,300 British military in the Sovereign Base Areas (SBA) in the ROC and 1,200 UN peacekeeping forces. **Location:** Middle East, island in the Mediterranean Sea, south of Turkey.

Republic of Cyprus

Official name: Kipriakí Dhimokratía (Greek); Kibris Cumhuriyeti (Turkish) (Republic of Cyprus). **Form of government:** unitary multiparty republic with a unicameral legislature (House of Representatives [80; 24 seats reserved for Turkish Cypriots are not occupied]). **Head of state and government:** President Tassos Papadopoulos (from 2003). **Capital:** Lefkosia (Nicosia). **Official languages:** Greek; Turkish. **Monetary unit:** 1 Cyprus pound (£C) = 100 cents; valuation (1 Jul 2007) US$1 = £C 0.43.

Demography

Area (includes 99 sq mi [256 sq km] of British military SBA and c. 107 sq mi (c. 278 sq km) of the UN Buffer Zone): 2,276 sq mi, 5,896 sq km. **Population** (2006; excludes British and UN military forces): 781,000. **Urban** (2001): 68.8%. **Age breakdown** (2002): under 15, 21.5%; 15–29, 22.6%; 30–44, 22.0%; 45–59, 17.8%; 60–74, 11.2%; 75 and over,

4.9%. **Ethnic composition** (2000): Greek Cypriot 91.8%; Armenian 3.3%; Arab 2.9%, of which Lebanese 2.5%; British 1.4%; other 0.6%. **Religious affiliation** (2001): Greek Orthodox 94.8%; Roman Catholic 2.1%, of which Maronite 0.6%; Anglican 1.0%; Muslim 0.6%; other 1.5%. **Urban areas** (2001): Lefkosia 200,686 (ROC only); Limassol 156,939; Larnaca 70,502.

Vital statistics

Birth rate per 1,000 population (2003): 11.2 (world avg. 21.3). **Death rate** per 1,000 population (2003): 7.2 (world avg. 9.1). **Natural increase rate** per 1,000 population (2003): 4.0 (world avg. 12.2). **Life expectancy** at birth (2002–03): male 77.0 years; female 81.4 years.

National economy

Budget (2001). *Revenue:* £C 2,073,100,000 (indirect taxes 34.8%, direct taxes 31.8%, social security contributions 19.7%). *Expenditures:* £C 2,239,700,000 (current expenditures 90.0%, development expenditures 10.0%). **Tourism** (2002): receipts $1,863,-000,000; expenditures $424,000,000. **Household expenditure** (2000): housing and energy 21.3%, food and beverages 20.0%, transportation and communications 19.2%. **Gross national product** (2003): $9,373,000,000 ($12,320 per capita). *Production. Agriculture* (in '000 metric tons; 2002): potatoes 142.0, barley 125.7, grapes 88.0. *Manufacturing* (value added in £C '000,000; 1999): food 102.7; cement, bricks, and tiles 47.1; tobacco products 46.3. *Energy production:* electricity (kW-hr; 2001) 3,552,000,000.

Foreign trade

Imports (2001-c.i.f.): £C 2,528,700,000 (consumer goods 24.4%; for reexport 13.9%; mineral fuels 10.5%; capital goods 10.2%). *Major import sources:* US 9.4%; Greece 8.9%; UK 8.8%; Italy 8.8%; Germany 6.8%; Japan 6.1%. **Exports** (2001-f.o.b.): £C 628,000,000 (reexports 53.7%; domestic exports 37.2%, of which pharmaceuticals 6.3%, clothing 3.1%; ships' stores 9.1%). *Major export destinations:* UK 18.7%; Russia 8.6%; Greece 8.4%; UAE 7.8%; Syria 6.0%.

Transport and communications

Transport. *Roads* (2001): total length 11,408 km (paved 58%). *Vehicles* (2001): cars 268,200; trucks and buses 136,200. *Air transport* (2002; Cyprus Airways): passenger-km 3,276,000,000; metric ton-km cargo 40,392,000; airports (2000) 2. **Communications,** in total units (units per 1,000 persons). Televisions (1999): 120,000 (180); telephone main lines (2002): 492,000 (688); cellular telephone subscribers (2002): 417,900 (597); personal computers (2002): 193,000 (270); Internet users (2002): 210,000 (294).

Education and health

Educational attainment (2001). Percentage of population age 15 and over having: no formal schooling

---

1 metric ton = about 1.1 short tons;   1 kilometer = 0.6 mi (statute);   1 metric ton-km cargo = about 0.68 short ton-mi cargo;   c.i.f.: cost, insurance, and freight;   f.o.b.: free on board

2.1%; incomplete primary 6.4%; complete primary 20.6%; secondary 48.3%; higher education 22.3%; not stated 0.3%. **Health** (2002): physicians 1,864 (1 per 381 persons); hospital beds 3,092 (1 per 229 persons); infant mortality rate per 1,000 live births (2003) 4.1.

Turkish Republic of Northern Cyprus

Official name: Kuzey Kibris Türk Cumhuriyeti (Turkish Republic of Northern Cyprus). **Capital:** Lefkosa (Nicosia). **Official language:** Turkish. **Monetary unit:** 1 new Turkish lira (YTL) = 100 kurush; valuation (1 Jul 2007) US$1 = YTL 1.31. **Population** (2004; includes 80,000 "settlers" from Turkey and 38,000 Turkish military in the TRNC; excludes 3,300 British military in the Sovereign Base Areas (SBA) in the ROC and 1,200 UN peacekeeping forces): 211,000 (Lefkosa 39,176 [1996]; Gazimagusa [Famagusta] 27,637 [1996]; Girne [Kyrenia] 14,205 [1996]). **Ethnic composition** (1996): Turkish Cypriot/Turkish 96.4%; other 3.6%. **Budget** (2001). *Revenue:* US$418,200,000 (foreign aid 46.8%, direct taxes 24.2%, indirect taxes 18.8%, loans 6.4%). *Expenditures:* US$418,200,000 (wages 32.9%, social transfers 29.8%, defense 8.3%, investments 8.2%). **Imports** (2001): US$272,000,-000 (machinery and transport equipment 21.7%, food 21.7%). *Major import sources:* Turkey 63.7%; UK 10.5%. **Exports** (2001): US$34,600,000 (ready-made garments 32.1%, citrus fruits 28.6%). *Major export destinations:* Turkey 37.0%; UK 33.2%. **Health** (2002): physicians 523 (1 per 408 persons); hospital beds 1,121 (1 per 190 persons); infant mortality rate per 1,000 live births (1999) 3.7.

Internet resources:
<www.visitcyprus.org.cy>; <www.trncwashdc.org>.

Background

Cyprus was inhabited by the early Neolithic Age; by the late Bronze Age it had been visited and settled by Mycenaeans and Achaeans, who introduced Greek culture and language, and it became a trading center. By 800 BC Phoenicians had begun to settle there. Ruled over the centuries by the Assyrian, Persian, and Ptolemaic empires, it was annexed by Rome in 58 BC. It was part of the Byzantine empire in the 4th–12th centuries AD. Cyprus was conquered by the English king Richard I in 1191. A part of the Venetian empire from 1489, it was taken by Ottoman Turks in 1571. In 1878 the British assumed control, and Cyprus became a British crown colony in 1925. It gained independence in 1960. Conflict between Greek and Turkish Cypriots led to the establishment of a UN peacekeeping mission in 1964. In 1974, fearing a movement to unite Cyprus with Greece, Turkish soldiers occupied the northern third of the country, and Turkish Cypriots established a functioning government, which obtained recognition only from Turkey. Conflict has continued to the present, and the UN peacekeeping mission has remained in place. Reunification talks have remained deadlocked.

Recent Developments

The Greek part of Cyprus joined the European Union on 1 May 2004. The election of Mehmet Ali Talat as president of the Turkish Republic of Northern Cyprus in April 2005 was promising, as he was seen as both pro-unification and pro-European. Border crossing between the two sectors became commonplace. Greek Cyprus planned to convert its currency to the euro in 2008. The island became the center for the evacuation of refugees from Lebanon following the Israeli incursion in July 2006. Some 47,000 persons transited the island, and in addition, Cyprus made an airfield and a military camp available for the UN peacekeepers in Lebanon.

Czech Republic

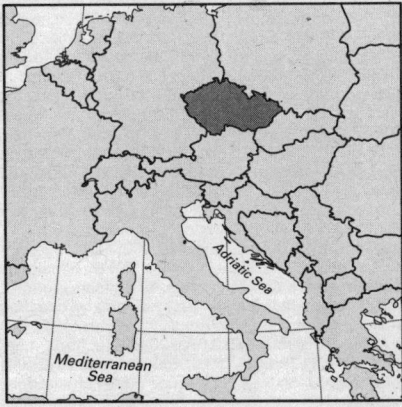

Official name: Ceska Republika (Czech Republic). **Form of government:** unitary multiparty republic with two legislative houses (Senate [81]; Chamber of Deputies [200]). **Chief of state:** President Vaclav Klaus (from 2003). **Head of government:** Prime Minister Mirek Topolanek (from 2006). **Capital:** Prague. **Official language:** Czech. **Official religion:** none. **Monetary unit:** 1 koruna (Kc) = 100 halura; valuation (1 Jul 2007) US$1 = 21.23 Kc.

Demography

Area: 30,450 sq mi, 78,866 sq km. **Population** (2006): 10,260,000. **Density** (2006): persons per sq mi 336.9, persons per sq km 130.1. **Urban** (2003): 74.3%. **Sex distribution** (2002): male 48.68%; female 51.32%. **Age breakdown** (2001): under 15, 16.3%; 15–29, 23.5%; 30–44, 20.1%; 45–59, 21.8%; 60–74, 12.8%; 75 and over, 5.5%. **Ethnic composition** (2001): Czech 90.4%; Moravian 3.7%; Slovak 1.9%; Polish 0.5%; German 0.4%; Silesian 0.1%; Rom (Gypsy) 0.1%; other 2.9%. **Religious affiliation** (2000): Catholic 43.8%, of which Roman Catholic 40.4%, Hussite Church of the Czech Republic 2.2%; nonreligious 31.9%; atheist 5.0%; Protestant 3.1%; Orthodox Christian 0.6%; Jewish 0.1%; other (mostly unaffiliated Christian) 15.5%. **Major cities** (2003): Prague 1,161,938; Brno 370,505; Ostrava 314,102; Plzen 163,791; Olomouc 101,624. **Location:** central Europe, bordering Germany, Poland, Slovakia, and Austria.

Vital statistics

Birth rate per 1,000 population (2003): 9.2 (world avg. 21.3); (2002) legitimate 74.5%. **Death rate** per

1,000 population (2003): 10.9 (world avg. 9.1). **Natural increase rate** per 1,000 population (2003): –1.7 (world avg. 12.2). **Total fertility rate** (avg. births per childbearing woman; 2001): 1.1. **Marriage rate** per 1,000 population (2003): 4.8. **Divorce rate** per 1,000 population (2003): 3.2. **Life expectancy** at birth (2002): male 72.1 years; female 78.5 years.

National economy

Budget (2001). *Revenue:* Kc 626,216,000,000 (tax revenue 95.6%, of which social security contributions 37.4%, value-added tax 18.6%, personal income tax 13.4%, corporate tax 9.4%, excise tax 9.3%; nontax revenue 4.4%). *Expenditures:* Kc 693,920,000,000 (social security and welfare 39.3%; education 11.6%; health 6.1%; defense 5.4%; police 3.9%). **Production** (metric tons except as noted). *Agriculture, forestry, fishing* (2002): cereals 6,771,000 (of which wheat 3,867,000, barley 1,793,000, corn [maize] 616,000), sugar beets 3,833,000, potatoes 901,000; livestock (number of live animals) 3,363,000 pigs, 1,474,000 cattle, 16,564,000 chickens; roundwood (2001) 14,374,000 cu m; fish catch (2002) 24,000. *Mining and quarrying* (2001): kaolin 6,300,000; feldspar 410,000. *Manufacturing* (value added in Kc '000,000,000; 1998): nonelectrical machinery and apparatus 47.0; food products 37.4; fabricated metals 35.2. *Energy production (consumption):* electricity (kW-hr; 2001) 74,647,000,000 (65,108,000,000); hard coal (2001) 15,138,000 (15,138,000); lignite (2001) 50,968,000 (50,968,000); crude petroleum (barrels; 2000) 1,186,500 (39,771,000); petroleum products (2000) 6,132,000 (7,998,000); natural gas (cu m; 2000) 238,462,000 (10,564,000,000). **Household income and expenditure.** Average household size (2001) 2.5; disposable income per household (2000) Kc 286,920; sources of income (2001): wages and salaries 67.4%, transfer payments 21.5%, self-employment 6.7%, other 4.4%; expenditure (2001): food and beverages 25.3%, housing and utilities 19.8%, transportation and communications 14.4%, recreation 10.5%, household furnishings 6.9%. **Population economically active** (2002): total 4,769,727; activity rate of total population 46.6% (participation rates: ages 15–64, 60.9%; female 44.3%; unemployed [2003] 9.9%). **Public debt** (external, outstanding; 2002): $6,904,000,000. **Gross national product** (2003): $68,711,000,000 ($6,740 per capita). **Tourism** (2002): receipts from visitors $2,941,000,000; expenditures by nationals abroad $1,575,000,000. **Land use** as % of total land area (2000): in temporary crops 39.9%, in permanent crops 3.1%, in pasture 12.4%; overall forest area 34.1%.

Foreign trade

Imports (2002): Kc 1,326,339,000,000 (machinery and apparatus 31.2%; base and fabricated metals 10.9%; chemicals and chemical products 10.4%; motor vehicles 9.7%). *Major import sources:* Germany 32.5%; Italy 5.4%; Slovakia 5.2%; France 4.8%; China 4.6%; Russia 4.5%. **Exports** (2002): Kc 1,251,884,000,000 (machinery and apparatus 31.9%, of which computers 6.2%; motor vehicles 16.7%; fabricated metals 6.5%; base metals 5.4%; chemicals and chemical products 5.4%). *Major export destinations:*

Germany 36.5%; Slovakia 7.7%; UK 5.8%; Austria 5.5%; Poland 4.7%; France 4.7%.

Transport and communications

Transport. *Railroads* (2001): length 9,444 km; passenger-km 7,299,000,000; metric ton-km cargo 16,882,000,000. *Roads* (2001): total length 125,905 km. *Vehicles* (2001): passenger cars 3,529,791; trucks and buses 381,876. *Air transport* (2001): passenger-km 6,398,920,000; metric ton-km 29,209,000; airports (2001) with scheduled flights 22. **Communications,** in total units (units per 1,000 persons). Daily newspaper circulation (2000): 1,210,000 (118); televisions (2000): 3,289,000 (341); telephone main lines (2003): 3,626,000 (360); cellular telephone subscribers (2003): 9,709,000 (965); personal computers (2002): 1,800,000 (177); Internet users (2003): 2,700,000 (268).

Education and health

Educational attainment (2001). Percentage of population age 15 and over having: no formal schooling 0.2%; primary education 21.6%; secondary 68.7%; higher 9.5%. **Literacy** (2001): 99.8%. **Health** (2002): physicians 43,824 (1 per 233 persons); hospital beds 66,668 (1 per 153 persons); infant mortality rate per 1,000 live births (2003) 3.9. **Food** (2002): daily per capita caloric intake 3,171 (vegetable products 73%, animal products 27%); 128% of FAO recommended minimum.

Military

Total active duty personnel (2003): 57,050 (army 69.9%, air force 23.0%, ministry of defense 7.1%). **Military expenditure as percentage of GNP** (1999): 2.3% (world 2.4%); per capita expenditure: $292.

Background

Until 1918 the history of what is now the Czech Republic was largely that of Bohemia. In that year the independent republic of Czechoslovakia was born through the union of Bohemia and Moravia with Slovakia. Czechoslovakia came under the domination of the Soviet Union after World War II, and from 1948 to 1989 it was ruled by a communist government. Its growing political liberalization was suppressed by a Soviet invasion in 1968. After communist rule collapsed in 1989–90, separatist sentiments emerged among the Slovaks, and in 1992 the Czechs and Slovaks agreed to break up their federated state. On 1 Jan 1993 the Czechoslovakian republic was peacefully dissolved and replaced by two new countries, the Czech Republic and Slovakia, with the region of Moravia remaining in the former. In 1999 the Czech Republic entered NATO and in 2004 the EU.

Recent Developments

The Czech Republic experienced considerable political turmoil in 2006 as the parliamentary elections of June and October saw the right-wing opposition Civic Democratic Party emerge as the largest party, with 122 seats in the 281-seat legislature. The most im-

---

1 metric ton = about 1.1 short tons; 1 kilometer = 0.6 mi (statute); 1 metric ton-km cargo = about 0.68 short ton-mi cargo; c.i.f.: cost, insurance, and freight; f.o.b.: free on board

portant bill requiring parliamentary approval following the elections was the state-budget draft for 2007. Local economists strongly criticized the budget because the public-finance deficit was scheduled to rise to 4% of GDP, far above the Maastricht limit for entry to the euro zone. By late 2006 politicians and economists from across the political spectrum had accepted that the Czech Republic would miss the target date of January 2010 to adopt the euro. Otherwise, the Czech economic situation was quite good in 2006, with an estimated 6% growth in GDP, declining unemployment (7.1%), and a foreign-trade surplus.

Internet resources: <www.czechtourism.com>.

Denmark

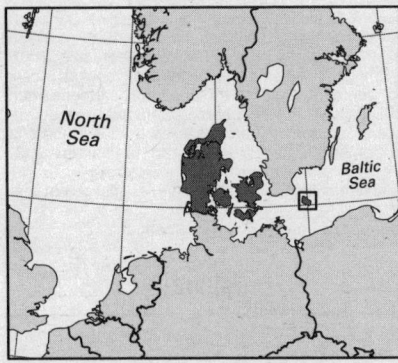

Official name: Kongeriget Danmark (Kingdom of Denmark). **Form of government:** parliamentary state and constitutional monarchy with one legislative house (Folketing [179]). **Chief of state:** Queen Margrethe II (from 1972). **Head of government:** Prime Minister Anders Fogh Rasmussen (from 2001). **Capital:** Copenhagen. **Official language:** Danish. **Official religion:** Evangelical Lutheran. **Monetary unit:** 1 Danish krone (Dkr; plural kroner) = 100 øre; valuation (1 Jul 2007) US$1 = Dkr 5.49.

Demography

Area: 16,640 sq mi, 43,098 sq km (excludes the Faroe Islands and Greenland). **Population** (2006): 5,435,000. **Density** (2006): persons per sq mi 326.6, persons per sq km 126.1. **Urban** (2003): 85.3%. **Sex distribution** (2003): male 49.46%; female 50.54%. **Age breakdown** (2003): under 15, 18.8%; 15–29, 17.9%; 30–44, 22.3%; 45–59, 20.9%; 60–74, 13.1%; 75 and over, 7.0%. **Ethnic composition** (2001; based on nationality): Danish 95.2%; Asian 1.7%, of which Turkish 0.7%; residents of pre-1992 Yugoslavia 0.7%; African 0.5%; German 0.2%; English 0.2%; other 1.5%. **Religious affiliation** (1998): Christian 87.5%, of which Evangelical Lutheran 85.8%; Muslim 2.2%; other/nonreligious 10.3%. **Major urban areas** (2003): Greater Copenhagen 1,085,813; Århus 222,559; Odense 145,374; Ålborg 121,100; Esbjerg 72,613. **Location:** northern Europe, bordering the North Sea, the Baltic Sea, and Germany.

Vital statistics

Birth rate per 1,000 population (2003): 12.0 (world avg. 21.3). **Death rate** per 1,000 population (2003): 10.7 (world avg. 9.1). **Natural increase rate** per 1,000 population (2003): 1.3 (world avg. 12.2). **Total fertility rate** (avg. births per childbearing woman; 2003): 1.8. **Marriage rate** per 1,000 population (2003): 6.5. **Divorce rate** per 1,000 population (2003): 2.9. **Life expectancy** at birth (2003): male 74.9 years; female 79.5 years.

National economy

Budget (2002). *Revenue:* Dkr 498,382,000,000 (tax revenue 82.8%, nontax revenue 11.9%, other 5.3%). *Expenditures:* Dkr 482,437,000,000 (health and social protection 39.6%, education 12.9%, economic affairs 7.1%, defense 4.8%, public order 2.7%). **National debt** (end of year; 2001): Dkr 679,957,000,000. **Tourism** (2002): receipts $5,785,000,000; expenditures $6,856,000,000. **Population economically active** (2002): total 2,892,800; activity rate of total population 53.9% (participation rates: ages 16–66, 77.8%; female 46.9%; unemployed 3.8%). **Household income and expenditure.** Average household size (2001) 2.2; annual disposable income per household (2000) Dkr 259,589; expenditure (2000): housing 22.3%, transportation and communications 16.1%, food 11.3%, recreation 11.1%, energy 6.8%, household furnishings 6.3%. **Production** (in Dkr '000,000 except as noted). *Agriculture, forestry, fishing* (value added; 2001): meat 24,884 (of which pork 21,069, beef 2,178), milk 11,327, cereals 8,095 (of which wheat 4,012, barley 3,469); livestock (number of live animals) 12,732,035 pigs, 1,796,118 cattle; roundwood (2002) 1,446,000 cu m; fish catch (2001) 1,552,000 metric tons. *Mining and quarrying* (2001): sand and gravel 23,000,000 cu m; chalk 410,000 metric tons. *Manufacturing* (value added in $'000,000; 1998): nonelectrical machinery and apparatus 3,874; food products 3,848; fabricated metals 2,228. *Energy production (consumption):* electricity (kW-hr; 2003) 43,752,000,000 ([2000] 44,284,000,000); coal (metric tons; 2001) none (6,984,000); crude petroleum (barrels; 2003) 140,800,000 ([2000] 61,812,000); petroleum products (metric tons; 2001) 8,860,000 (7,547,000); natural gas (cu m; 2003) 4,427,000,000 ([2001] 4,366,000,000). **Gross national product** (2003): $181,825,000,000 ($33,750 per capita). **Land use** as % of total land area (2000): in temporary crops 53.8%, in permanent crops 0.2%, in pasture 8.4%; overall forest area 10.7%.

Foreign trade

Imports (2001-c.i.f.): Dkr 369,582,000,000 (machinery and apparatus [including parts] 22.9%; transport equipment and parts 10.5%; food, beverages, and tobacco 8.5%; clothing and footwear 5.0%; fuels 4.7%). *Major import sources:* Germany 22.0%; Sweden 12.0%; UK 7.5%; The Netherlands 7.0%; France 5.7%. **Exports** (2001-f.o.b.): Dkr 422,877,000,000 (machinery and apparatus 27.5%; agricultural products 19.2%, of which swine 5.7%; mineral fuels and lubricants 6.8%; pharmaceuticals 6.7%; furniture 3.8%). *Major export destinations:* Germany 19.7%; Sweden 11.7%; UK 9.4%; US 7.0%; Norway 5.6%; France 5.1%.

Transport and communications

Transport. *Railroads* (2001): route length 2,743 km; passenger-km 5,318,000,000; metric ton-km cargo 2,025,000,000. *Roads* (2001): total length 71,663 km (paved 100%). *Vehicles* (2001): passenger cars 1,854,060; trucks and buses 335,690. *Air transport* (2001; Danish share of Scandinavian Airlines System [scheduled air service only] and Maersk Air): passenger-km 8,942,000,000; metric ton-km cargo 183,152,000; airports (1996) with scheduled flights 13. **Communications,** in total units (units per 1,000 persons). Daily newspaper circulation (2000): 1,510,000 (283); radios (2000): 7,200,000 (1,349); televisions (2000): 4,310,000 (807); telephone main lines (2003): 3,610,100 (669); cellular telephone subscribers (2003): 4,785,300 (887); personal computers (2002): 2,756,000 (513); Internet users (2002): 3,100,000 (577).

Education and health

Educational attainment (2000). Percentage of population age 25–69 having: completed lower secondary or not stated 34.6%; completed upper secondary or vocational 42.3%; undergraduate 17.6%; graduate 5.5%. **Literacy:** 100%. **Health:** physicians (2002) 19,600 (1 per 276 persons); hospital beds (2001) 22,604 (1 per 239 persons); infant mortality rate per 1,000 live births (2003) 4.0. **Food** (2001): daily per capita caloric intake 3,454 (vegetable products 60.5%, animal products 39.5%); 128% of FAO recommended minimum.

Military

Total active duty personnel (2003): 22,880 (army 64.2%, navy 17.5%, air force 18.3%). **Military expenditure as percentage of GNP** (1999): 1.6% (world 2.4%); per capita expenditure $524.

 **Did you know?** The city of Copenhagen, located on the islands of Zealand and Amager, has been the capital of Denmark since 1445. It is the residence of the Danish royal family and is a cultural center of northern Europe.

Background

The Danes, a Scandinavian branch of the Teutons, settled the area in c. 6th century AD. During the Viking period the Danes expanded their territory, and by the 11th century the united Danish kingdom included parts of what are now Germany, Sweden, England, and Norway. Scandinavia was united under Danish rule from 1397 until 1523, when Sweden became independent; a series of debilitating wars with Sweden in the 17th century resulted in the Treaty of Copenhagen (1660), which established the modern Scandinavian frontiers. Denmark gained and lost various other territories, including Norway, in the 19th and 20th centuries; it went through three constitutions between 1849 and 1915 and was occupied by Nazi Germany in 1940–45. A founding member of NATO (1949), Denmark adopted its current constitution in 1953. It became a member of the European Community in 1973 and modified its membership during the 1990s. The island of Zealand, on which Copenhagen stands, was connected to the central island of Funen by a rail tunnel and bridge in 1997. This ended more than 100 years of ferry service and cut the crossing time from an hour to under 10 minutes.

Recent Developments

Denmark's restrictive immigration policies continued to draw criticism from international bodies, including the European Commission Against Racism and Intolerance and the UN Committee on the Elimination of Racial Discrimination. Despite this, in 2005 the government passed new laws containing an "integration pact" with potential immigrants that called for them to learn Danish, secure employment, and refrain from illegal activity or risk losing state benefits. Controversy worldwide also followed the publication of satiric caricatures depicting the Prophet Muhammad in the leading Danish paper *Jyllands-Posten* in September 2005. A January 2006 Arab League meeting resulted in calls for Denmark to punish the paper for "cartoons offensive to Islam." After Denmark refused, protests ensued, and demonstrators sacked Danish embassies in Damascus, Beirut, and Tehran. In February 2007 Denmark announced plans to withdraw its roughly 460 remaining troops from Iraq by August of that year.

Internet resources: <www.denmark.dk>.

Djibouti

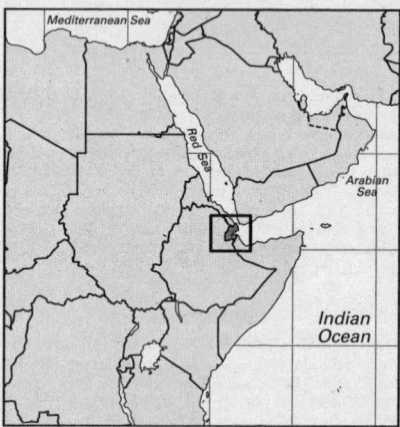

Official name: Jumhuriyah Jibuti (Arabic); République de Djibouti (French) (Republic of Djibouti). **Form of government:** multiparty republic with one legislative house (National Assembly [65]). **Chief of state and head of government:** President Ismail Omar Guelleh (from 1999), assisted by Prime Minister Dileita Muhammad Dileita (from 2001). **Capital:** Djibouti. **Official languages:** Arabic; French. **Official religion:** none. **Monetary unit:** 1 Djibouti franc (DF) = 100 centimes; valuation (1 Jul 2007) US$1 = DF 178.82.

---

1 metric ton = about 1.1 short tons;   1 kilometer = 0.6 mi (statute);   1 metric ton-km cargo = about 0.68 short ton-mi cargo;   c.i.f.: cost, insurance, and freight;   f.o.b.: free on board

Demography

Area: 8,950 sq mi, 23,200 sq km. **Population** (2006): 487,000. **Density** (2006): persons per sq mi 54.4, persons per sq km 21.0. **Urban** (2003): 83.7%. **Sex distribution** (2002): male 51.55%; female 48.45%. **Age breakdown** (2002): under 15, 43.0%; 15–29, 28.1%; 30–44, 13.2%; 45–59, 10.5%; 60–74, 4.6%; 75 and over, 0.6%. **Ethnic composition** (2000): Somali 46.0%; Afar 35.4%; Arab 11.0%; mixed African and European 3.0%; French 1.6%; other/unspecified 3.0%. **Religious affiliation** (1995): Sunni Muslim 97.2%; Christian 2.8%, of which Roman Catholic 2.2%, Orthodox 0.5%, Protestant 0.1%. **Major city and towns** (1991): Djibouti 465,300 (2004); 'Ali Sabih 8,000; Tadjoura 7,500; Dikhil 6,500. **Location:** eastern Africa, bordering Eritrea, the Red Sea, the Gulf of Aden, Somalia, and Ethiopia.

Vital statistics

Birth rate per 1,000 population (2003): 40.8 (world avg. 21.3). **Death rate** per 1,000 population (2003): 19.5 (world avg. 9.1). **Natural increase rate** per 1,000 population (2003): 21.3 (world avg. 12.2). **Total fertility rate** (avg. births per childbearing woman; 2003): 5.6. **Life expectancy** at birth (2003): male 41.8 years; female 44.5 years.

National economy

Budget (2000). *Revenue:* DF 23,739,000,000 (tax revenue 91.2%, of which indirect taxes 45.3%, direct taxes 38.9%, income and profit tax 6.7%; nontax revenue 8.8%). *Expenditures:* DF 32,813,000,000 (current expenditures 92.0%, of which general administration 22.7%, defense 13.7%, education 10.0%, health 4.6%; capital expenditures 8.0%). **Tourism** (1998): receipts from visitors $4,000,000; expenditures by nationals abroad $4,000,000. **Production** (metric tons except as noted). *Agriculture, forestry, fishing* (2002): vegetables and melons 24,000 (of which tomatoes 1,100, onions 110, eggplant 33), lemons and limes 1,800, tropical fruit 1,100; livestock (number of live animals) 512,000 goats, 475,000 sheep, 270,000 cattle; fish catch (2001) 350. *Mining and quarrying:* mineral production limited to locally used construction materials and evaporated salt (2001) 173,000. *Manufacturing* (2000): main products include furniture, nonalcoholic beverages, meat and hides, light electromechanical goods, and mineral water. *Energy production (consumption):* electricity (kW-hr; 2001) 235,262,000 (182,870,000); petroleum products (2000) none (126,000); geothermal, wind, and solar resources are substantial but largely undeveloped. **Population economically active** (1991): total 282,000; activity rate of total population 61.5% (participation rates: over age 10, 70.4%; female 40.8%; unemployed [2000] c. 50%). **Households**. Average household size (2000) 5.3; expenditure (expatriate households; 1984): food 50.3%, energy 13.1%, recreation 10.4%, housing 6.4%, clothing 1.7%, personal effects 1.4%, health care 1.0%, household goods 0.3%, other 15.4%. **Gross national product** (2003): $643,000,000 ($910 per capita). **Public debt** (external, outstanding; 2002): $305,200,000. **Land use** as % of total land area (2000): in temporary crops, negligible, in permanent crops, negligible, in pasture 56.1%; overall forest area 0.3%.

Foreign trade

Imports (1999; excludes Ethiopian trade via rail): $152,700,000 (food and beverages 25.0%; machinery and electric appliances 12.5%; khat 12.2%; petroleum products 10.9%; transport equipment 10.3%. *Major import sources* (2001): Saudi Arabia 18.5%; France 16.1%; Ethiopia 10.3%; China 8.1%; Italy 3.8%. **Exports** (2001; excludes Ethiopian trade via rail): $10,200,000 (aircraft parts 24.5%; hides and skins of cattle, sheep, goats, and camels 20.6%; unspecified special transactions 8.8%; leather 7.8%; live animals 6.9%). *Major export destinations* (2001): Somalia 44.8%; France 23.5%; Yemen 19.2%; Ethiopia 3.5%; UAE 3.3%.

Transport and communications

Transport. *Railroads* (2000): length 100 km; (1999) passenger-km 81,000,000; metric ton-km cargo 266,100,000. *Roads* (1999): total length 2,890 km (paved 13%). *Vehicles* (1996): passenger cars 9,200; trucks and buses 2,040. *Air transport* (2001): passengers handled 94,590; metric tons of freight handled 6,652; airports (2000) with scheduled flights 1. **Communications,** in total units (units per 1,000 persons). Daily newspaper circulation (1995): 500 (0.8); radios (1997): 52,000 (84); televisions (2000): 45,000 (104); telephone main lines (2003): 9,500 (14); cellular telephone subscribers (2003): 23,000 (34); personal computers (2003): 15,000 (22); Internet users (2003): 6,500 (9.7).

Education and health

Literacy (2000): percentage of population age 15 and over literate 64.6%; males literate 75.6%; females literate 54.4%. **Health:** physicians (1996) 60 (1 per 7,100 persons); hospital beds (1990; public health facilities only) 930 (1 per 394 persons); infant mortality rate per 1,000 live births (2003) 107.0. **Food** (2002): daily per capita caloric intake 2,220 (vegetable products 87%, animal products 13%); 96% of FAO recommended minimum.

Military

Total active duty personnel (2003; excludes foreign troops): 9,850 (army 81.3%, navy 2.0%, air force 2.5%, paramilitary 14.2%). Foreign troops (March 2004): French 2,700; US 1,800; German 800. **Military expenditure as percentage of GNP** (1999): 4.3% (world 2.4%); per capita expenditure $51.

Did you know? Djibouti, virtually a city-state, is a deepwater port city and railhead bordered on three sides by a sparsely-populated hot, arid landscape. In 1985 this small country won the first world cup men's team marathon.

Background

Settled around the 3rd century BC by the Arab ancestors of the Afars, Djibouti was later populated by Somali Issas. In AD 825 Islam was brought to the area by missionaries. Arabs controlled the trade in this region until the 16th century; it became the French protectorate of French Somaliland in 1888. In 1946 it became a French overseas territory, and in 1977 it gained its independence. In the late 20th century, the country received refugees from the Ethiopian-Somali war and from civil conflicts in Eritrea. In the 1990s it suffered from political unrest.

Recent Developments

Djibouti continued to host the roughly 1,500 American troops of the Combined Joint Task Force–Horn of Africa at the former French Foreign Legion base Camp Lemonier. Their mission was to monitor and disrupt terrorist networks in six countries of and around the Horn. The camp proved controversial in January 2007 when US aircraft based there bombed suspected al-Qaeda members in Somalia during clashes between Somali government forces and fighters of the Islamic Courts Union, who had controlled most of Somalia for much of the previous year.

Internet resources: <www.office-tourisme.dj>.

Dominica

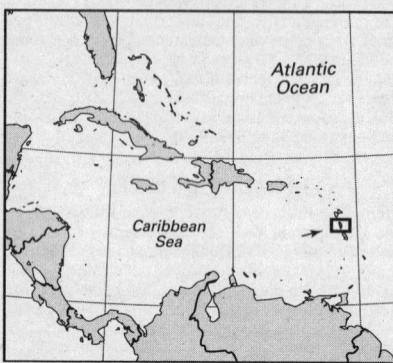

Official name: Commonwealth of Dominica. **Form of government:** multiparty republic with one legislative house (House of Assembly [32; includes 22 seats that are elective [including speaker if elected from outside of the House of Assembly] and 10 seats that are nonelective [including 9 appointees of the president and the attorney general serving ex officio]). **Chief of state:** President Nicholas Liverpool (from 2003). **Head of government:** Prime Minister Roosevelt Skerrit (from 2004). **Capital:** Roseau. **Official language:** English. **Official religion:** none. **Monetary unit:** 1 East Caribbean dollar (EC$) = 100 cents; valuation (1 Jul 2007) US$1 = EC$2.67.

Demography

Area: 290 sq mi, 750 sq km. **Population** (2006): 69,500. **Density** (2006): persons per sq mi 239.7, persons per sq km 92.7. **Urban** (2003): 72.0%. **Sex distribution** (2003): male 50.33%; female 49.67%. **Age breakdown** (2002): under 15, 27.8%; 15–29, 24.8%; 30–44, 26.3%; 45–59, 10.7%; 60–74, 7.0%; 75 and over, 3.4%. **Ethnic composition** (2000): black 88.3%; mulatto 7.3%; black-Amerindian 1.7%; British expatriates 1.0%; Indo-Pakistani 1.0%; other 0.7%. **Religious affiliation** (1991): Roman Catholic 70.1%; six largest Protestant groups 17.2%, of which Seventh-day Adventist 4.6%, Pentecostal 4.3%, Methodist 4.2%; other 8.9%; nonreligious 2.9%; unknown 0.9%. **Major towns** (1991): Roseau 15,853; Portsmouth 3,621; Marigot 2,919. **Location:** island in the southern Caribbean Sea, south of Guadeloupe and north of Martinique.

Vital statistics

Birth rate per 1,000 population (2003): 17.8 (world avg. 21.3); (1991) legitimate 24.1%. **Death rate** per 1,000 population (2003): 7.0 (world avg. 9.1). **Natural increase rate** per 1,000 population (2003): 10.8 (world avg. 12.2). **Total fertility rate** (avg. births per childbearing woman; 2003): 2.0. **Marriage rate** per 1,000 population (1996): 3.1. **Divorce rate** per 1,000 population (1996): 0.7. **Life expectancy** at birth (2002): male 71.0 years; female 75.8 years.

National economy

Budget (2000–01). *Revenue:* EC$194,900,000 (tax revenue 79.2%, of which consumption taxes on imports 39.1%, income taxes 19.9%; nontax revenue 13.8%; grants 7.0%). *Expenditures:* EC$270,800,-000 (current expenditures 84.2%, of which wages 42.8%, debt payment 13.6%; development expenditures 15.8%). **Tourism:** receipts from visitors (2002) US$45,000,000; expenditures by nationals abroad (2001) US$9,000,000. **Gross national product** (2003): US$239,000,000 (US $3,360 per capita). **Land use** as % of total land area (2000): in temporary crops 7%, in permanent crops 19%, in pasture 3%; overall forest area 61%. **Public debt** (external, outstanding; 2002): US$178,300,000. **Population economically active** (1997): total 33,420; activity rate of total population 45.8% (participation rates: ages 15–64 [1991] 62.4%; female 45.8%; unemployed 23.1%). **Households.** Average household size (1991) 3.6; expenditure (1984): food and nonalcoholic beverages 43.1%, housing and utilities 16.1%, transportation 11.6%, clothing and footwear 6.5%, household furnishings 6.0%. **Production** (metric tons except as noted). *Agriculture, forestry, fishing* (2003): bananas 29,000, root crops 23,750 (of which taro 11,200, yams 8,000, yautia 4,550), grapefruit and pomelos 17,000; livestock (number of live animals; 2003) 13,400 cattle, 9,700 goats, 7,600 sheep; fish catch (2001) 1,157. *Mining and quarrying:* pumice, limestone, and sand and gravel are quarried primarily for local consumption. *Manufacturing* (value of production in EC$'000; 2000): toilet and laundry soap 18,815; toothpaste 10,063; crude coconut oil 1,758. *Energy production (consumption):* electricity (kW-hr; 2000) 77,000,000 (77,000,000); petroleum products (2000) none (33,000).

Foreign trade

Imports (2000–c.i.f.): EC$397,700,000 (food and beverages 19.3%; machinery and apparatus 17.7%; refined petroleum 8.6%; road vehicles 8.3%). *Major import sources:* US 37.5%; Trinidad and Tobago 16.3%; UK 7.7%; Japan 6.3%; Canada 4.2%. **Exports**

---

1 metric ton = about 1.1 short tons;   1 kilometer = 0.6 mi (statute);   1 metric ton-km cargo = about 0.68 short ton-mi cargo;   c.i.f.: cost, insurance, and freight;   f.o.b.: free on board

(2000-f.o.b.): EC$147,300,000 (agricultural exports 37.5%, of which bananas 25.9%; coconut-based soaps 25.0%; perfumery and cosmetics 13.7%). *Major export destinations:* UK 24.8%; Jamaica 23.7%; France (significantly Guadeloupe) 8.5%; US 7.4%; Antigua and Barbuda 7.4%.

Transport and communications

Transport. *Roads* (1999): total length 780 km (paved 50%). *Vehicles* (1998): passenger cars 8,700; trucks and buses 3,400. *Air transport:* (1997) passenger arrivals and departures 74,100; (1997) cargo unloaded 575 metric tons, cargo loaded 363 metric tons; airports (1996) with scheduled flights 2. **Communications,** in total units (units per 1,000 persons). Radios (1997): 46,000 (608); televisions (2000): 15,700 (220); telephone main lines (2002): 23,700 (265); cellular telephone subscribers (2002): 9,400 (120); personal computers (2002): 7,000 (90); Internet users (2002): 12,500 (160).

Education and health

Educational attainment (1991). Percentage of population age 25 and over having: no formal schooling 4.2%; primary education 78.4%; secondary 11.0%; higher vocational 2.3%; university 2.8%; other/unknown 1.3%. **Literacy** (1996): total population age 15 and over literate, 94.0%. **Health** (2002): physicians 34 (1 per 2,041 persons); hospital beds 270 (1 per 257 persons); infant mortality rate per 1,000 live births 15.9. **Food** (2001): daily per capita caloric intake 2,995 (vegetable products 77%, animal products 23%); 124% of FAO recommended minimum.

Military

Total active duty personnel (2003): none; 300-member police force includes a coast guard unit.

Background

At the time of the arrival of Christopher Columbus in 1493, Dominica was inhabited by the Caribs. With its steep coastal cliffs and inaccessible mountains, it was one of the last islands to be explored by Europeans, and the Caribs remained in possession until the 18th century; it was then settled by the French and ultimately taken by Britain in 1783. Subsequent hostilities between the settlers and the native inhabitants resulted in the Caribs' near extinction. Incorporated with the Leeward Islands in 1883 and with the Windward Islands in 1940, it became a member of the West Indies Federation in 1958. Dominica became independent in 1978.

Recent Developments

The IMF came to Dominica's aid in January 2004 with a three-year, $11.4 million credit from its Poverty Reduction and Growth Facility, which was designed, among other purposes, to help restore economic growth and preserve the public-sector investment program. China, having established diplomatic relations with Dominica in 2004, pledged in 2005 to build roads, schools, a hospital, and a $12.3 million stadium.

Internet resources: <www.ndcdominica.dm>.

Dominican Republic

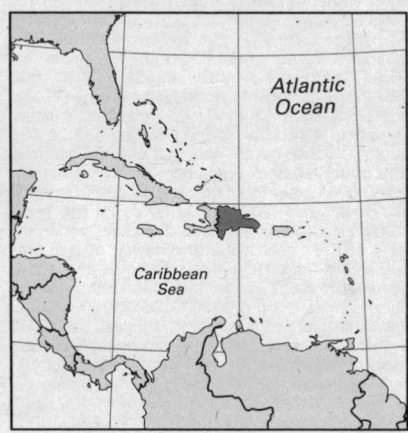

Official name: República Dominicana (Dominican Republic). **Form of government:** multiparty republic with two legislative houses (Senate [32]; Chamber of Deputies [150]). **Head of state and government:** President Leonel Fernández Reyna (from 2004). **Capital:** Santo Domingo. **Official language:** Spanish. **Official religion:** none (Roman Catholicism is the state religion per concordat with Vatican City). **Monetary unit:** 1 Dominican peso (RD$) = 100 centavos; valuation (1 Jul 2007) US$1 = RD$32.95.

Demography

Area: 18,792 sq mi, 48,671 sq km. **Population** (2006): 9,021,000. **Density** (2006): persons per sq mi 480.0, persons per sq km 185.3. **Urban** (2002): 63.6%. **Sex distribution** (2002): male 49.81%; female 50.19%. **Age breakdown** (2002): under 15, 34.0%; 15–29, 27.1%; 30–44, 20.2%; 45–59, 11.2%; 60–74, 5.9%; 75 and over, 1.6%. **Ethnic composition** (2000): mulatto 69.5%; white 17.0%; local black 9.4%; Haitian black 2.4%; other/unknown 1.7%. **Religious affiliation** (1995): Roman Catholic 81.8%; Protestant 6.4%; other Christian 0.6%; other 11.2%. **Major urban centers** (2004): Santo Domingo 1,817,754; Santiago 505,600; La Romana 171,500; San Francisco de Macorís 152,600; San Cristóbal 120,200. **Location:** eastern two-thirds of the island of Hispaniola, bordered by the North Atlantic Ocean, the Caribbean Sea, and Haiti.

Vital statistics

Birth rate per 1,000 population (2003): 23.0 (world avg. 21.3). **Death rate** per 1,000 population (2003): 7.2 (world avg. 9.1). **Natural increase rate** per 1,000 population (2003): 15.8 (world avg. 12.2). **Total fertility rate** (avg. births per childbearing woman; 2003): 2.7. **Marriage rate** per 1,000 population (2001): 2.9. **Divorce rate** per 1,000 population (2001): 1.0. **Life expectancy** at birth (2003): male 66.4 years; female 69.6 years.

National economy

Budget (2002). *Revenue:* RD$67,009,000,000 (tax revenue 94.5%, of which taxes on goods and services

45.5%, income taxes 25.0%, import duties 21.2%; nontax revenue 5.5%). *Expenditures:* RD$75,789,-000,000 (current expenditures 63.1%; development expenditures 36.9%). **Public debt** (external, outstanding; 2002): US$4,035,000,000. **Gross national product** (2003): US$18,078,000,000 (US$2,070 per capita). **Households.** Average household size (2002) 3.5. **Production** (metric tons except as noted). *Agriculture, forestry, fishing* (2002): sugarcane 4,846,000, rice 731,000, bananas 503,000; livestock (number of live animals) 2,160,000 cattle, 577,000 pigs, 46,000,000 chickens; roundwood (2001) 562,000 cu m; fish catch (2001) 15,864. *Mining* (2002): nickel (metal content) 38,859; gold, none (the mining of gold was suspended from 1999 through late 2003). *Manufacturing* (1998; excludes free-zone sector for reexport employing [2000] 195,000): cement 1,872,000; refined sugar 105,000; beer 2,990,000 hectoliters. *Energy production (consumption):* electricity (kW-hr; 2002) 10,449,000,000 (6,808,-000,000); coal (2000) none (193,000); crude petroleum (barrels; 2002) none (14,400,000); petroleum products (2000) 1,859,000 (7,325,000). **Tourism** (2002): receipts US$2,738,000,000; expenditures US$295,000,000. **Population economically active** (1997): total 3,155,500; activity rate of total population 39.5% (participation rates: ages 15–64 [1993] 54.3%; female [1993] 24.9%; unemployed [2002] 16.1%). **Land use** as % of total land area (2000): in temporary crops 22.7%, in permanent crops 10.3%, in pasture 43.4%; overall forest area 28.4%.

Foreign trade

Imports (2002): US$8,882,000,000 (imports for free zones 29.8%, refined petroleum 14.6%, machinery and apparatus 11.4%, transport equipment 10.5%, food 5.4%). *Major import sources* (1998): US 65%; Venezuela 6%; Mexico 4%; Japan 3%. **Exports** (2002): US$5,183,000,000 (reexports of free zones 83.6%, ferronickel 3.0%, ships' stores 2.2%, raw sugar 1.4%, cacao and cocoa 1.3%). *Major export destinations* (1998): US 87%; Belgium-Luxembourg 2%; UK 2%.

Transport and communications

Transport. *Railroads* (1997; most track is privately owned and serves the sugar industry only): route length 1,743 km. *Roads* (1999): total length 12,600 km (paved 49%). *Vehicles* (1998): passenger cars 353,177; trucks and buses 200,347. *Air transport* (1997; Aerochago and Dominair airlines): passenger-km, 15,808,000; metric ton-km cargo 11,624,000; airports (2002) 6. **Communications,** in total units (units per 1,000 persons). Daily newspaper circulation (1996): 416,000 (53); radios (2000): 1,510,000 (181); televisions (2000): 810,000 (97); telephone main lines (2003): 901,800 (115); cellular telephone subscribers (2003): 2,120,400 (271); Internet users (2003): 500,000 (64).

Education and health

Literacy (1995): total population age 15 and over literate, 4,164,000 (82.1%); males literate, 2,118,000

(82.0%); females literate, 2,046,000 (82.2%). **Health** (1999): physicians 15,422 (1 per 526 persons); hospital beds 16,234 (1 per 500 persons); infant mortality rate per 1,000 live births (2003) 34.2. **Food** (2002): daily per capita caloric intake 2,347 (vegetable products 85%, animal products 15%); 104% of FAO recommended minimum.

Military

Total active duty personnel (2003): 24,500 (army 61.2%, navy 16.3%, air force 22.4%). **Military expenditure as percentage of GNP** (1999): 0.7% (world 2.4%); per capita expenditure US$15.

Did you know? The island of Hispaniola was the first area in the New World to receive the full imprint of Spanish colonial policy. The oldest cathedral, monastery, and hospital in the Americas were established on the island, and the first university was chartered in Santo Domingo in 1538.

Background

The Dominican Republic was originally part of the Spanish colony of Hispaniola. In 1697 the western third of the island, which later became Haiti, was ceded to France; the remainder of the island passed to France in 1795. The eastern two-thirds of the island was returned to Spain in 1809, and the colony declared its independence in 1821. Within a matter of weeks it was overrun by Haitian troops and occupied until 1844. Since then the country has been under the rule of a succession of dictators, except for short interludes of democratic government, and the US has frequently been involved in its affairs. The termination of the dictatorship of Rafael Trujillo in 1961 led to civil war in 1965 and US military intervention. The country suffered from severe hurricanes in 1979 and 1998.

Recent Developments

The government of Pres. Leonel Fernández continued to implement the austerity programs that had been promised in the presidential campaign of 2004, to positive effect. GDP growth in 2005 was estimated at 9%, and inflation fell to only 4%, from 52% the previous year. In January 2005 the IMF awarded the Dominican Republic a standby agreement totaling more than $653 million, to be disbursed over 28 months. In February 2007 the IMF completed the fifth and sixth reviews of the country's economic performance and released more than $57 million, bringing the total disbursement to more than $423 million. It also extended the agreement by eight months. The Central America–Dominican Republic Free Trade Agreement (CAFTA–DR), which sought to create the 10th largest US export market, went into effect in March 2007.

Internet resources: <www.dominicana.com.do>.

1 metric ton = about 1.1 short tons; 1 kilometer = 0.6 mi (statute); 1 metric ton-km cargo = about 0.68 short ton-mi cargo; c.i.f.: cost, insurance, and freight; f.o.b.: free on board

East Timor

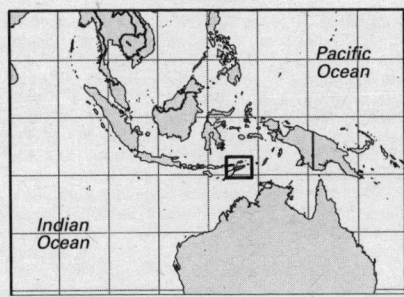

Official name: Repúblika Demokrátika Timor Lorosa'e (Tetum); República Democrática de Timor-Leste (Portuguese) (Democratic Republic of Timor-Leste). **Form of government:** republic with one legislative body (National Parliament [88]). **Chief of State:** President José Ramos-Horta (from 2007). **Head of government:** Prime Minister Xanana Gusmão (from 2007). **Capital:** Dili. **Official languages:** Tetum and Portuguese; Indonesian and English are "working" languages. **Official religion:** none. **Monetary unit:** 1 US dollar ($) = 100 centavos (minor currency coins introduced in November 2003 at par with US coins).

Demography

Area: 5,639 sq mi, 14,604 sq km. **Population** (2006): 1,032,000. **Density** (2006): persons per sq mi 183.0, persons per sq km 70.7. **Urban** (2001): 24.0%. **Sex distribution** (2003): male 50.94%; female 49.06%. **Age breakdown** (2003): under 15, 38.7%; 15–29, 26.9%; 30–44, 19.0%; 45–59, 10.6%; 60–74, 4.0%; 75 and over, 0.7%. **Ethnic composition** (1999): East Timorese 80%; other (nearly all Indonesian, and particularly West Timorese) 20%. **Religious affiliation** (2000): Roman Catholic 87%; Protestant 5%; Muslim 3%; traditional beliefs 3%; other 2%. **Major cities** (2000): Dili 48,200; Dare 17,100; Baucau 14,200; Maliana 12,300; Ermera 12,000. **Location:** southeast Asia, eastern end of the island of Timor plus an enclave on the western end, bordering the Timor Sea and Indonesia.

Vital statistics

Birth rate per 1,000 population (2003): 27.7 (world avg. 21.3). **Death rate** per 1,000 population (2003): 6.4 (world avg. 9.1). **Natural increase rate** per 1,000 population (2003): 21.3 (world avg. 12.2). **Total fertility rate** (avg. births per childbearing woman; 2003): 3.8. **Marriage rate** per 1,000 population (1997–98): 0.4. **Divorce rate** per 1,000 population (1997–98): 0.1. **Life expectancy** at birth (2003): male 63.0 years; female 67.0 years.

National economy

Budget (2002–03). *Revenue:* $77,100,000 (tax revenue 52.0%, grants 42.8%; nontax revenue 5.2%). *Expenditures:* $70,500,000 (education 24.3%, economic affairs 23.3%, general public services 17.0%, public order 13.9%, health 10.5%, defense 7.0%). **Production** (metric tons except as noted). *Agriculture,*

forestry, fishing (2003): corn (maize) 70,200, rice 65,400, cassava 41,500; livestock (number of live animals; 2003) 345,000 pigs, 170,000 cattle, 1,300,000 chickens; fish catch (2001) 356. *Mining and quarrying* (2001): commercial quantities of marble are exported. *Manufacturing* (2001): principally the production of textiles, garments, handicrafts, bottled water, and processed coffee. *Energy production (consumption):* electricity (kW-hr; 1998) 40,000,000 (n.a.). **Households.** Average household size (1995) 4.9. **Population economically active** (2001): total 232,000; activity rate of total population 28% (participation rates: ages 15–64, 57%). **Gross national product** (2003): $351,000,000 ($430 per capita). **Tourism:** available beds for tourists (1998) 580. **Land use** as % of total land area (2000): in temporary crops 4.7%, in permanent crops 0.7%, in pasture 10.1%; overall forest area 34.3%.

Foreign trade

Imports (1998): $135,000,000 (foodstuffs 26%, of which rice 10%; construction materials 15%; petroleum products 10%; unspecified 49%). *Major import sources* (2003): Australia 44.0%, Indonesia 16.8%, Singapore 12.9%, Japan 7.3%, Portugal 4.3%. **Exports** (1998): $55,000,000 (agricultural products 93%, of which nonfood crops [nearly all coffee] 51%, livestock 22%, food crops 15%; garments, bottled water, handicrafts, and other manufactured goods 5%). *Major export destination:* Indonesia 96%.

Transport and communications

Transport. *Roads* (December 1999): total length 1,414 km (57% of paved roads were in poor or damaged condition in late 1999; gravel roads were not usable for most vehicles). *Vehicles* (1998): passenger cars 3,156; trucks and buses 7,140. *Air transport:* airports (2001) with scheduled flights 2. **Communications,** in total units (units per 1,000 persons). Daily newspaper circulation (2002): 1,500 (1.8); telephone main lines (1996): 6,600 (8).

Education and health

Educational attainment (2001). Percentage of adult population having: no formal education 57%, primary education 23%, secondary 18%, higher 1.4%. **Literacy** (2001): total population age 15 and over literate 203,000 (48%). **Health:** physicians (1996–97) 122 (1 per 6,590 persons); hospital beds (1999) 560 (1 per 1,277 persons); infant mortality rate per 1,000 live births (2003) 50.5.

Military

Total active duty personnel (2003): 650 (army 94.3%, naval element 5.7%); UN peacekeeping troops (August 2004) 425; UN presence slated to end in May 2005 per May 2004 announcement.

Background

The Portuguese first settled on the island of Timor in 1520 and were granted rule over Timor's eastern half in 1860. The Timor political party Fretilin declared East Timor independent in 1975 after Portugal withdrew its troops. It was invaded by Indonesian forces and was incorporated as a province of Indonesia in 1976. The takeover, which resulted in thousands of

East Timorese deaths during the next two decades, was disputed by the UN. In 1999 an independence referendum won overwhelmingly; civilian militias, armed by the military and led by local supporters of integration, then rampaged through the province, killing 1,000–2,000 people. The Indonesian parliament rescinded Indonesia's annexation of the territory, and East Timor was returned to its preannexation status as a non-self-governing territory, though this time under UN supervision. Preparation for independence got under way in 2001, with East Timorese voting by universal suffrage in August for a Constituent Assembly of 88 members. Independence was declared on 20 May 2002 and was followed by the swearing in of Xanana Gusmão as the first president of the country.

Recent Developments

East Timor was accepted as the 25th member of the Association of Southeast Asian Nations (ASEAN) Regional Forum in July 2005. There was still instability in the country, however. In August 2006 the UN Integrated Mission in Timor-Leste, the third UN mission in the country since independence in 2002, was authorized, and in September it took over policing duties from the Australian-led multinational force already in place.

Internet resources: <www.gov.east-timor.org>.

Ecuador

Official name: República del Ecuador (Republic of Ecuador). **Form of government:** unitary multiparty republic with one legislative house (National Congress [125]). **Head of state and government:** President Rafael Correa (from 2007). **Capital:** Quito. **Official language:** Spanish (Quechua and Shuar are also official languages for the indigenous peoples). **Official religion:** none. **Monetary unit:** the US dollar ($) was formally adopted as the national currency on 9 Sep 2000; the pegged value of the sucre (S/.), the former national currency, was US$1 = S/. 25,000.

Demography

Area: 105,037 sq mi, 272,045 sq km (includes 884 sq mi [2,289 sq km] in nondelimited areas). **Population** (2006): 13,419,000. **Density** (2006): persons per sq mi 127.8, persons per sq km 49.3. **Urban** (2003): 61.8%. **Sex distribution** (2003): male 49.99%; female 50.01%. **Age breakdown** (2003): under 15, 34.4%; 15–29, 28.6%; 30–44, 19.1%; 45–59, 10.9%; 60–74, 5.1%; 75 and over, 1.9%. **Ethnic composition** (2000): mestizo 42.0%; Amerindian 40.8%; white 10.6%; black 5.0%; other 1.6%. **Religious affiliation** (2000): Roman Catholic 94.1%; Protestant 1.9%; other 4.0%. **Major cities** (2001): Guayaquil 1,985,379; Quito 1,399,378; Cuenca 277,374; Machala 204,578; Santo Domingo de los Colorados 200,421. **Location:** northwestern South America, bordering Colombia, Peru, and the Pacific Ocean.

Vital statistics

Birth rate per 1,000 population (2003): 23.7 (world avg. 21.3; excludes nomadic Indian tribes). **Death rate** per 1,000 population (2003): 4.3 (world avg. 9.1; excludes nomadic Indian tribes). **Natural increase rate** per 1,000 population (2003): 19.4 (world avg. 12.2; excludes nomadic Indian tribes). **Total fertility rate** (avg. births per childbearing woman; 2003): 2.8. **Life expectancy** at birth (2003): male 73.0 years; female 78.8 years.

National economy

Budget (2002). *Revenue:* $4,526,000,000 (nonpetroleum revenue 72.4%, of which value-added tax 33.8%, income tax 14.8%; petroleum revenue 27.6%). *Expenditures:* $4,694,000,000 (current expenditure 73.9%; capital expenditure 26.1%). **Public debt** (external, outstanding; 2002): $13,828,-000,000. **Production** (metric tons except as noted). *Agriculture, forestry, fishing* (2002): sugarcane 5,690,895, bananas 5,609,460, fruit palm oil 1,450,000; livestock (live animals) 4,794,000 cattle, 3,007,000 pigs, 142,000,000 chickens; roundwood (2001) 10,919,709 cu m; fish catch (2001) 654,539. *Mining and quarrying* (2000): limestone 3,147,000; gold 2,823 kg. *Manufacturing* (value added in $'000,000; 1999): food products 497; refined petroleum 413; beverages 223. *Energy production (consumption):* electricity (kW-hr; 2000) 10,607,000,000 (10,607,000,000); crude petroleum (barrels; 2001) 146,200,000 ([2000] 61,026,-000); petroleum products (2000) 7,567,000 (5,723,000); natural gas (cu m; 2000) 569,500,000 (569,500,000). **Household income and expenditure.** Average household size (2001) 4.1; average annual income per household (1995) S/. 9,825,610; sources of income (1995): self-employment 70.9%, wages 16.0%, transfer payments 6.7%, other 6.4%; expenditure (1995): food and tobacco 37.9%, transportation and communications 15.0%, clothing 9.2%, household furnishings 6.5%. **Population economically active** (2001): total 4,124,185; activity rate of total population 49.6% (participation rates: ages 15 and over, 72.8%; female 42.3%; unemployed 13.3%). **Gross national product** (2003): $23,347,000,000 ($1,790 per capita). **Land use** as % of total land area

---

1 metric ton = about 1.1 short tons;   1 kilometer = 0.6 mi (statute);   1 metric ton-km cargo = about 0.68 short ton-mi cargo;   c.i.f.: cost, insurance, and freight;   f.o.b.: free on board

(2000): in temporary crops 5.8%, in permanent crops 4.9%, in pasture 18.4%; overall forest area 38.1%. **Tourism** (2002): receipts $447,000,000; expenditures $364,000,000.

Foreign trade

Imports (2000-f.o.b. in balance of trade and c.i.f. for commodities and trading partners): $3,446,000,000 (chemicals and chemical products 23.5%; machinery and apparatus 21.1%; mineral fuels and lubricants 8.2%; food and live animals 7.6%). *Major import sources* (2001): US 29.4%; Colombia 10.3%; Japan 8.2%; Venezuela 4.7%; Chile 4.5%. **Exports** (2000): $4,822,000,000 (mineral fuels and lubricants 50.7%, of which crude petroleum 44.5%; food 35.7%, of which bananas 17.0%, fish and crustaceans 11.8%; cut flowers 3.2%). *Major export destinations* (2001): US 36.2%; Colombia 5.0%; South Korea 4.6%; Germany 4.3%; Japan 4.0%.

Transport and communications

Transport. *Railroads* (2000): route length 956 km; passenger-km 5,000,000; metric ton-km cargo, less than 500,000. *Roads* (1999): total length 43,197 km (paved 19%). *Vehicles* (1999): passenger cars 322,300; trucks and buses 272,000. *Air transport* (2001; Ecuatoviana and TAME airlines): passenger-km 901,000,000; metric ton-km cargo 14,344,000. **Communications**, in total units (units per 1,000 persons). Daily newspaper circulation (1996): 820,000 (70); radios (2001): 5,130,000 (422); televisions (2002): 3,034,000 (237); telephone main lines (2003): 1,549,000 (119); cellular telephone subscribers (2003): 2,394,400 (184); personal computers (2002): 403,000 (31); Internet users (2003): 569,700 (44).

Education and health

Educational attainment (1990). Percentage of population age 25 and over having: no formal schooling 2.2%; incomplete primary 54.3%; primary 28.0%; postsecondary 15.5%. **Literacy** (2001): total population age 15 and over literate 91.0%; males 92.3%; females 89.7%. **Health** (2000): physicians 18,335 (1 per 456 persons); hospital beds 19,564 (1 per 427 persons); infant mortality rate per 1,000 live births (2003) 25.4. **Food** (2001): daily per capita caloric intake 2,333 (vegetable products 86%, animal products 14%); 103% of FAO recommended minimum.

Military

Total active duty personnel (2003): 59,500 (army 84.0%, navy 9.3%, air force 6.7%). **Military expenditure as percentage of GNP** (1999): 3.7% (world 2.4%); per capita expenditure $38.

Background

Ecuador was conquered by the Incas in AD 1450 and came under Spanish control in 1534. Under the Spaniards it was a part of the viceroyalty of Peru until 1740, when it became a part of the viceroyalty of New Granada. It gained its independence from Spain in 1822 as part of the republic of Gran Colombia, and in 1830 it became a sovereign state. A succession of authoritarian governments ruled into the mid-20th century, and economic hardship and social unrest

prompted the military to take a strong role. Border disputes led to war between Peru and Ecuador in 1941; the two fought periodically until agreeing to a final demarcation in 1998. The economy, booming in the 1970s with petroleum profits, was depressed in the 1980s by reduced oil prices and earthquake damage. A new constitution was adopted in 1979. In the 1990s social unrest caused political instability and several changes of heads of state. In a controversial move to help stabilize the economy, the US dollar replaced the sucre as the national currency in 2000.

Recent Developments

Rafael Correa Delgado won the nation's presidential election in November 2006. Correa, an economist and self-described admirer of populist Venezuelan Pres. Hugo Chávez, threatened a moratorium on "illegitimate" foreign-debt payments and promised to strengthen state control over the country's extensive oil resources. Violent protests in February and March by residents of the oil-producing Amazon Basin had forced repeated pipeline shutdowns and a brief suspension of exports. In May the government canceled its operating contract with American multinational Occidental Petroleum, which pumped nearly one-fifth of Ecuador's crude, seized its assets, and turned them over to state-owned Petroecuador. The US retaliated by breaking off free-trade talks. Strong world oil prices cushioned the effect of political turmoil on the economy, but poverty continued to drive Ecuadorans to seek their fortunes abroad.

Internet resources: <www.ecuador.com>.

Egypt

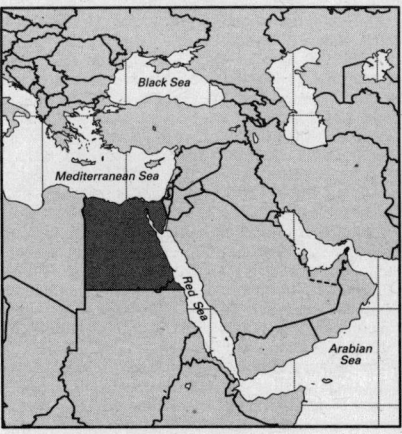

Official name: Jumhuriah Misr al-'Arabiyah (Arab Republic of Egypt). **Form of government:** republic with one legislative house (People's Assembly [454, including 10 nonelective seats]). **Chief of state:** President Hosni Mubarak (from 1981). **Head of government:** Prime Minister Ahmed Nazif (from 2004). **Capital:** Cairo. **Official language:** Arabic. **Official religion:** Islam. **Monetary unit:** 1 Egyptian pound (£E) = 100 piastres; valuation (1 Jul 2007) US$1 = £E 5.69.

Demography

Area: 385,229 sq mi, 997,739 sq km. **Population** (2006): 72,034,000. **Density** (2006): persons per sq mi 187.0, persons per sq km 72.2. **Urban** (2002): 45.0%. **Sex distribution** (2003): male 50.46%; female 49.54%. **Age breakdown** (2003): under 15, 33.9%; 15–29, 28.1%; 30–44, 19.4%; 45–59, 12.0%; 60–74, 5.5%; 75 and over, 1.1%. **Ethnic composition** (2000): Egyptian Arab 84.1%; Sudanese Arab 5.5%; Arabized Berber 2.0%; Bedouin 2.0%; Rom (Gypsy) 1.6%; other 4.8%. **Religious affiliation** (2000): Muslim 84.4% (nearly all Sunni); Christian 15.1%, of which Orthodox 13.6%, Protestant 0.8%, Roman Catholic 0.3%; nonreligious 0.5%. **Major cities** ('000; 1996): Cairo 6,789 (10,834; 2003 urban agglomeration); Alexandria 3,328; Al-Jizah 2,222; Shubra al-Khaymah 871; Port Said 470. **Location:** northern Africa, bordering the Mediterranean Sea, the Gaza Strip, Israel, the Red Sea, The Sudan, and Libya.

Vital statistics

Birth rate per 1,000 population (2003): 24.4 (world avg. 21.3). **Death rate** per 1,000 population (2003): 5.4 (world avg. 9.1). **Natural increase rate** per 1,000 population (2003): 19.0 (world avg. 12.2). **Total fertility rate** (avg. births per childbearing woman; 2003): 3.0. **Life expectancy** at birth (2003): male 67.9 years; female 73.0 years.

National economy

Budget (2000–01). *Revenue:* £E 97,938,000,000 (income and profits taxes 28.4%, sales taxes 18.4%, customs duties 13.3%, oil revenue 4.7%, Suez Canal fees 3.6%). *Expenditures:* £E 111,669,000,000 (current expenditure 76.7%; capital expenditure 23.3%). **Public debt** (external, outstanding; 2002): $26,624,000,-000. **Population economically active** (1999–2000): total 18,818,000; activity rate 29.7% (participation rates [1998]: ages 15–64, 45.9%; female 21.4%; unemployed 8.1%). **Production** ('000; metric tons except as noted). *Agriculture, forestry, fishing* (2003): sugarcane 12,000, corn (maize) 6,400, tomatoes 6,350; livestock ('000; number of live animals) 4,672 sheep, 3,810 cattle, 3,560 buffalo; roundwood (2003) 16,905,059 cu m; fish catch (2001) 772. *Mining and quarrying* (1999–2000): gypsum 3,027; iron ore 2,932; salt 1,990. *Manufacturing* (value added in $'000,000; 1998): chemicals (all forms) 1,535; food products 958; textiles 828. *Energy production (consumption):* electricity ('000,000 kW-hr; 2000) 76,282 (76,282); coal (2000) none (458); crude petroleum ('000 barrels; 2001) 243,400 ([2000] 239,400); petroleum products (2000) 28,815 (21,512); natural gas ('000,000 cu m; 2000) 21,000 (21,000). **Gross national product** (2003): $93,850,000,000 ($1,390 per capita). **Land use** as % of total land area (2000): in temporary crops 2.8%, in permanent crops 0.5%; overall forest area 0.1%. **Households.** Average household size (2000) 4.7. **Tourism** (2002): receipts $3,764,000,-000; expenditures $1,278,000,000.

Foreign trade

Imports (1999-c.i.f.): US$15,962,000,000 (machinery and apparatus 22.6%; food 18.3%, of which cereals 8.1%; chemicals and chemical products 11.5%; iron and steel 5.6%). *Major import sources* (2001): US 18.6%; Italy 6.6%; Germany 6.5%; France 4.9%; China 4.4%. **Exports** (1999-f.o.b.): US$3,501,000,-000 (crude petroleum 27.4%; refined petroleum 8.4%; food 7.9%; wearing apparel 7.9%; raw cotton 6.8%). *Major export destinations* (2001): Italy 15.0%; US 14.4%; UK 9.3%; France 4.7%; Germany 4.1%.

Transport and communications

Transport. *Railroads* (1999): length 4,810 km; passenger-km (1998) 56,667,000,000; metric ton-km cargo (1996) 4,117,000,000. *Roads* (1999): length 64,000 km (paved 78%). *Vehicles* (1998): passenger cars 1,154,753; trucks and buses 510,766. *Inland water* (2000): Suez Canal, number of transits 14,141; metric ton cargo 438,962,000. *Air transport* (2001): passenger-km 8,892,000,000; metric ton-km cargo 239,040,000; airports (1998) 11. **Communications,** in total units (units per 1,000 persons). Daily newspaper circulation (2000): 2,780,000 (43); radios (2000): 21,900,000 (418); televisions (2002): 15,206,000 (229); telephone main lines (2003): 8,735,700 (127); cellular telephone subscribers (2003): 5,797,500 (85); personal computers (2003): 1,500,000 (22); Internet users (2003): 2,700,000 (39).

Education and health

Literacy (2000): total population age 15 and over literate 55.3%; males 66.6%; females 43.8%. **Health** (2002–03): physicians 145,000 (1 per 464 persons); hospital beds 143,100 (1 per 470 persons); infant mortality rate per 1,000 live births (2003) 35.3. **Food** (2001): daily per capita caloric intake 3,385 (vegetable products 92%, animal products 8%); 133% of FAO recommended minimum.

Military

Total active duty personnel (2003): 450,000 (army 71.1%, navy 4.4%, air force [including air defense] 24.5%). **Military expenditure as percentage of GNP** (1999): 2.7% (world 2.4%); per capita expenditure $36.

Background

Egypt is home to one of the world's oldest continuous civilizations. Upper and Lower Egypt were united c. 3000 BC, beginning a period of cultural achievement and a line of native rulers that lasted nearly 3,000 years. Egypt's ancient history is divided into the Old, Middle, and New Kingdoms, spanning 31 dynasties and lasting to 332 BC. The pyramids date from the Old Kingdom; the cult of Osiris and the refinement of sculpture, from the Middle Kingdom; and the era of empire and the Exodus of the Jews, from the New Kingdom. An Assyrian invasion occurred in the 7th century BC, and the Persian Achaemenids established a dynasty in 525 BC. The invasion by Alexander the Great in 332 BC inaugurated the Macedonian Ptolemaic period and the ascendancy of Alexandria. The Romans held Egypt from 30 BC to AD 395; later it was placed under the control of Constantinople. Constantine's granting of tolerance in 313 to the Christians began the development of a formal Egyptian (Coptic) church. Egypt came under Arab control in 642 and ultimately was

---

1 metric ton = about 1.1 short tons;　1 kilometer = 0.6 mi (statute);　1 metric ton-km cargo = about 0.68 short ton-mi cargo;　c.i.f.: cost, insurance, and freight;　f.o.b.: free on board

transformed into an Arabic-speaking state, with Islam as the dominant religion. Held by the Umayyad and Abbasid dynasties, in 969 it became the center of the Fatimid dynasty. In 1250 the Mamluks established a dynasty that lasted until 1517, when Egypt fell to the Ottoman Turks. An economic decline ensued, and with it a decline in Egyptian culture. Egypt became a British protectorate in 1914 and received nominal independence in 1922, when a constitutional monarchy was established. A coup overthrew the monarchy in 1952, with Gamal Abdel Nasser taking power. Following three wars with Israel, Egypt, under Nasser's successor, Anwar al-Sadat, ultimately played a leading role in Middle East peace talks. Sadat was succeeded by Hosni Mubarak, who followed Sadat's peace initiatives and in 1982 regained Egyptian sovereignty (lost in 1967) over the Sinai Peninsula. Although Egypt took part in the coalition against Iraq during the Persian Gulf War (1991), it later made peace overtures to Iraq and other countries in the region.

Recent Developments

In April 2006 three suicide bombers believed to be linked to al-Qaeda attacked the Red Sea resort area of Dahab, killing 30. In May the conviction of Ayman Nour, the leader of Egypt's al-Ghad ("Tomorrow") Party who was incarcerated on charges that he had falsified documents when he petitioned to establish the party, was upheld by the Court of Cassation, suggesting to some that the Egyptian judiciary was controlled by government directives. Nour and his liberal supporters were seen by many as a political alternative to the authoritarian regime of Pres. Hosni Mubarak, and Nour's imprisonment seemed calculated to prevent him from challenging Mubarak's son Gamal, who was being groomed to run in the next presidential elections.

Internet resources: <www.touregypt.net>.

El Salvador

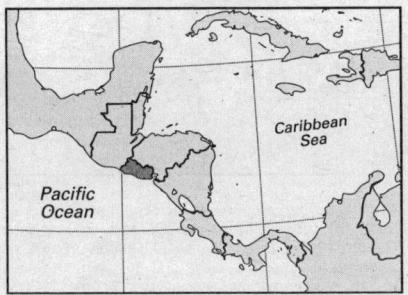

Official name: República de El Salvador (Republic of El Salvador). **Form of government:** republic with one legislative house (Legislative Assembly [84]). **Chief of state and government:** President Antonio Saca (from 2004). **Capital:** San Salvador. **Official language:** Spanish. **Official religion:** none (Roman Catholicism, although not official, enjoys special recognition in the constitution). **Monetary units:** 1 colón (₡) = 100 centavos; valuation (1 Jul 2007; pegged rate) US$1 = ₡8.91 (colón rarely in use; the US dollar has also been legal tender since 1 Jan 2001).

Demography

Area: 8,124 sq mi, 21,041 sq km. **Population** (2006): 6,991,000. **Density** (2006): persons per sq mi 860.5, persons per sq km 332.3. **Urban** (2003): 59.6%. **Sex distribution** (2002): male 48.67%; female 51.33%. **Age breakdown** (2002): under 15, 37.1%; 15–29, 28.7%; 30–44, 17.2%; 45–59, 9.8%; 60–74, 5.0%; 75 and over 2.2%. **Ethnic composition** (2000): mestizo 88.3%; Amerindian 9.1%, of which Pipil 4.0%; white 1.6%; other/unknown 1.0%. **Religious affiliation** (1995): Roman Catholic 78.2%; Protestant 17.1%, of which Pentecostal 13.3%; other Christian 1.9%; other 2.8%. **Major cities** (2000): San Salvador 479,600 (urban agglomeration 1,959,036); Soyapango 285,300 (within San Salvador urban agglomeration); Mejicanos 172,500 (within San Salvador urban agglomeration); Santa Ana 164,500; San Miguel 159,700. **Location:** Central America, bordering Guatemala, Honduras, and the North Pacific Ocean.

Vital statistics

Birth rate per 1,000 population (2003): 27.9 (world avg. 21.3); (1998) legitimate 27.2%. **Death rate** per 1,000 population (2003): 6.0 (world avg. 9.1). **Natural increase rate** per 1,000 population (2003): 21.9 (world avg. 12.2). **Total fertility rate** (avg. births per childbearing woman; 2003): 3.2. **Marriage rate** per 1,000 population (2001): 4.6. **Life expectancy** at birth (2003): male 67.0 years; female 74.4 years.

National economy

Budget. Revenue (2001): US$1,499,400,000 (sales taxes 57.2%, corporate taxes 13.1%, individual income taxes 11.4%, import duties 9.7%). *Expenditures:* US$1,968,600,000 (education 23.3%, police 15.7%, economic services 14.7%, social services 12.7%, health 11.1%, defense 6.6%). **Public debt** (external, outstanding; 2002): $4,712,000,000. **Production** (metric tons except as noted). *Agriculture, forestry, fishing* (2002): sugarcane 4,933,000, corn (maize) 637,000, sorghum 139,000; livestock (number of live animals) 1,392,000 cattle, 153,000 pigs; roundwood (2001) 5,200,000 cu m; fish catch (2001) 18,142. *Mining and quarrying* (2002): limestone 3,200,000. *Manufacturing* (value added in $'000,000; 1998): food products 306; wearing apparel 249; drugs and medicines 128. *Energy production (consumption):* electricity (kW-hr; 2000) 3,546,000,000 (4,242,000,000); crude petroleum (barrels; 2000) none (7,147,000); petroleum products (2000) 901,000 (1,723,000). **Household income and expenditure.** Average household size (2000) 4.5; average income per household (1992–93) ₡22,930; expenditure (1990–91): food and beverages 37.0%, housing 12.1%, transportation and communications 10.2%, clothing and footwear 6.7%. **Land use** as % of total land area (2000): in temporary crops 30.9%, in permanent crops 12.1%, in pasture 38.3%; overall forest area 5.8%. **Population economically active** (1999): total 2,444,900; activity rate of total population 40.1% (participation rates: ages 15–64 (1995) 62.9%; female 40.7%; unemployed 7.0%). **Gross national product** (2003): US$14,387,000,000 (US$2,200 per capita). **Tourism** (2002): receipts US$342,000,000; expenditures US$229,000,000.

Foreign trade

Imports (2000-c.i.f.): $4,947,000,000 (Imports for re-export 23.3%; machinery and apparatus 15.5%; chemicals and chemical products 11.2%; food 10.4%; petroleum [all forms] 10.3%). *Major import sources* (2002): US 49.6%; Guatemala 8.1%; Honduras 3.0%; Costa Rica 2.9%; unspecified 30.4%. **Exports** (2000-f.o.b.): $2,941,000,000 (reexports [mostly clothing] 54.4%; coffee 10.1%; paper and paper products 2.8%; yarn, fabrics, made-up articles 2.7%). *Major export destinations:* US 67.0%; Guatemala 11.5%; Honduras 5.9%; Nicaragua 3.8%; unspecified 6.9%.

Transport and communications

Transport. *Railroads* (2001): operational route length 283 km; (1999) passenger-km 8,000,000; metric ton-km cargo 19,000,000. *Roads* (1999): total length 10,029 km (paved 20%). *Vehicles* (2000): passenger cars 148,000; trucks and buses 250,800. *Air transport* (2001; TACA International Airlines only): passenger-km 6,150,000,000; metric ton-km cargo 379,000; airports (2001) with scheduled flights 1. **Communications,** in total units (units per 1,000 persons). Daily newspaper circulation (2000): 217,000 (35); radios (2000): 2,970,000 (478); televisions (2000): 1,250,000 (201); telephone main lines (2003): 752,600 (116); cellular telephone subscribers (2003): 1,149,800 (177); personal computers (2002): 163,000 (25); Internet users (2003): 550,000 (84).

Education and health

Educational attainment (1992). Percentage of population over age 25 having: no formal schooling 34.7%; incomplete primary education 37.6%; complete primary (through ninth grade) 10.8%; secondary 9.4%; higher technical 2.4%; incomplete undergraduate 1.1%; complete undergraduate 2.9%; other/unknown 1.1%. **Literacy** (1999): total population age 15 and over literate 78.3%; males literate 81.3%; females literate 75.6%. **Health** (2002): physicians 8,212 (1 per 794 persons); hospital beds 4,562 (1 per 1,429 persons); infant mortality rate per 1,000 live births (2003) 26.8. **Food** (2002): daily per capita caloric intake 2,584 (vegetable products 87%, animal products 13%); 113% of FAO recommended minimum.

Military

Total active duty personnel (2003): 15,500 (army 89.4%, navy 4.5%, air force 6.1%). **Military expenditure as percentage of GNP** (1999): 0.9% (world 2.4%); per capita expenditure $18.

Background

The Spanish arrived in the area in 1524 and subjugated the Pipil Indian kingdom of Cuzcatlán by 1539. The country was divided into two districts, San Salvador and Sonsonate, both attached to Guatemala. When independence came in 1821, San Salvador was incorporated into the Mexican Empire; upon its collapse in 1823, Sonsonate and San Salvador combined to form the new state of El Salvador within the United Provinces of Central America. From its founding, El Salvador experienced a high degree of political turmoil and was under military rule from 1931 to 1979, when the government was ousted in a coup. Elections held in 1982 set up a new government, and in 1983 a new constitution was adopted, but civil war continued through the 1980s. An accord in 1992 brought an uneasy truce.

Recent Developments

In March 2006 El Salvador became the first Central American state to implement the Central America–Dominican Republic Free Trade Agreement (CAFTA–DR) with the United States, amid fear that U.S. agricultural imports would further impoverish Salvadoran peasants. That month El Salvador also concluded a deal with Venezuelan Pres. Hugo Chávez that provided cheaper petroleum for Salvadoran consumers. Poverty continued to lead many Salvadorans to migrate to the US, and they sent back remittances of about $2.8 billion annually. Meanwhile, though El Salvador remained the only Latin American nation with troops still in Iraq, U.S. Pres. George W. Bush proposed cutting U.S. aid.

Internet resources: <www.elsalvadorturismo.gob.sv>.

Equatorial Guinea

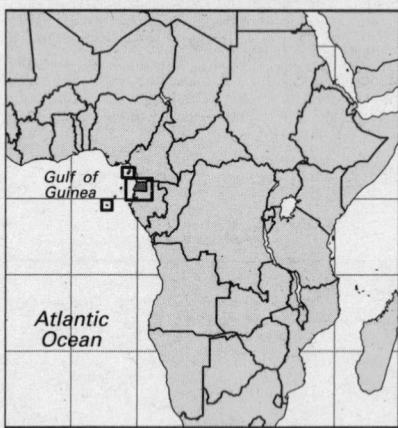

Official name: República de Guinea Ecuatorial (Spanish); République du Guinée Équatoriale (French) (Republic of Equatorial Guinea). **Form of government:** republic with one legislative house (House of Representatives of the People [100]). **Chief of state:** President Teodoro Obiang Nguema Mbasogo (from 1979). **Head of government:** Prime Minister Ricardo Mangue Obama Nfubea (from 2006). **Capital:** Malabo. **Official languages:** Spanish; French. **Official religion:** none. **Monetary unit:** 1 CFA franc (CFAF) = 100 centimes; valuation (1 Jul 2007) US$1 = CFAF 485.18; the CFAF is pegged to the euro (€) at €1 = CFAF 655.96 from 1 Jan 2002.

---

1 metric ton = about 1.1 short tons;   1 kilometer = 0.6 mi (statute);   1 metric ton-km cargo = about 0.68 short ton-mi cargo;   c.i.f.: cost, insurance, and freight;   f.o.b.: free on board

Demography

Area: 10,831 sq mi, 28,051 sq km. **Population** (2006): 515,000. **Density** (2006): persons per sq mi 47.5, persons per sq km 18.4. **Urban** (2003): 48.1%. **Sex distribution** (2002): male 48.77%; female 51.23%. **Age breakdown** (2002): under 15, 42.4%; 15–29, 27.0%; 30–44, 16.2%; 45–59, 8.3%; 60–74, 4.8%; 75 and over, 1.3%. **Ethnic composition** (1995): Fang 82.9%; Bubi 9.6%; other 7.5%. **Religious affiliation** (2000): Roman Catholic 80.1%; Muslim 4.0%; African Christian 3.7%; Protestant 3.1%; other 9.1%. **Major cities** (2003): Malabo 92,900; Bata 66,800; Mbini 11,600; Ebebiyin 9,100; Luba 6,800. **Location:** western Africa, the mainland portion bordering Cameroon, Gabon, and the Bight of Biafra (inlet of the Atlantic Ocean).

Vital statistics

Birth rate per 1,000 population (2003): 36.9 (world avg. 21.3). **Death rate** per 1,000 population (2003): 12.5 (world avg. 9.1). **Natural increase rate** per 1,000 population (2003): 24.4 (world avg. 12.2). **Total fertility rate** (avg. births per childbearing woman; 2003): 4.7. **Life expectancy** at birth (2003): male 52.6 years; female 56.9 years.

National economy

Budget (2002). *Revenue:* CFAF 414,484,000,000 (oil revenue 81.6%, of which royalties 41.5%; tax revenue 15.3%; nontax revenue 3.1%). *Expenditures:* CFAF 227,236,000,000 (capital expenditure 55.7%; current expenditure 44.3%). **Public debt** (external, outstanding; 2002): $209,100,000. **Gross national product** (at current market prices; 2003): $2,200,-000,000 ($4,400 per capita). **Production** (metric tons except as noted). *Agriculture, forestry, fishing* (2002): roots and tubers 105,000 (of which cassava 45,000, sweet potatoes 36,000), palm oil 35,000, bananas 20,000; livestock (number of live animals) 38,000 sheep, 9,000 goats, 6,100 pigs; roundwood (2003) 811,000 cu m, of which saw logs and veneer logs 364,000; fish catch (2001) 3,500. *Mining and quarrying:* gold (2002) 500 kg. *Manufacturing:* methanol (2002) 719,000. *Energy production (consumption):* electricity (kW-hr; 2000) 23,000,000 (23,000,000); crude petroleum (barrels; 2003) 97,601,000 ([2000] 102,600); petroleum products (2000) none (53,000); natural gas (2002) 1,050,-,000,000 (n.a.). **Population economically active** (1997): total 177,000; activity rate of total population 40.0% (participation rates: ages 15–64, 74.7%; female 35.4%). **Household income and expenditure.** Sources of income (1988): wages and salaries 57.0%, business income 42.0%, other 1.0%; expenditure (2000): food and beverages 60.4%; clothing 14.7%; household furnishings 8.6%. **Tourism:** tourism is a government priority but remains undeveloped. **Land use** as % of total land area (2000): in temporary crops 4.6%, in permanent crops 3.6%, in pasture 3.7%; overall forest area 62.5%.

Foreign trade

Imports (2001-c.i.f.): CFAF 593,400,000,000 (for petroleum sector 80.8%; other machinery and apparatus 11.6%; petroleum products 4.8%). *Major import sources* (1999): US 60%; France 12%; Spain 8%; Italy 6%; Cameroon 3%. **Exports** (2001-f.o.b.): CFAF 1,346,700,000,000 (crude petroleum 91.6%; methanol 4.5%; wood 2.9%; cocoa beans 0.1%). *Major export destinations* (1999): Spain 46%; China 24%; Japan 7%; US 7%; Chile 5%.

Transport and communications

Transport. *Roads* (1999): total length 2,880 km (paved 13%). *Vehicles* (1994): passenger cars 6,500; trucks and buses 4,000. *Air transport* (1998): passenger-km 4,000,000; airports (2003) with scheduled flights 3. **Communications,** in total units (units per 1,000 persons). Daily newspaper circulation (1996): 2,000 (4.9); radios (1997): 180,000 (428); televisions (1997): 4,000 (9.8); telephone main lines (2003): 9,600 (18); cellular telephone units (2003): 41,500 (76); personal computers (2002): 4,000 (6.9); Internet users (2002): 1,800 (3.6).

Education and health

Educational attainment (1983). Percentage of population age 15 and over having: no schooling 35.4%; some primary education 46.6%; primary 13.0%; secondary 2.3%; postsecondary 1.1%; not specified 1.6%. **Literacy** (2000): percentage of total population age 15 and over literate 83.2%; males literate 92.5%; females literate 74.4%. **Health:** physicians (1996) 106 (1 per 4,065 persons); hospital beds (1990) 992 (1 per 350 persons); infant mortality rate per 1,000 live births (2003) 89.0.

Military

Total active duty personnel (2003): 1,320 (army 83.3%, navy 9.1%, air force 7.6%). **Military expenditure as percentage of GNP** (1999): 3.2% (world 2.4%); per capita expenditure $40.

Background

The first inhabitants of the mainland region appear to have been Pygmies. The now-prominent Fang and Bubi reached the mainland region in the 17th-century Bantu migrations. Equatorial Guinea was ceded by the Portuguese to the Spanish in the late 18th century; it was frequented by slave traders, as well as by British, German, Dutch, and French merchants. Bioko was administered by British authorities (1827–58) before the official takeover by the Spanish. The mainland (Río Muni) was not effectively occupied by the Spanish until 1926. Independence was declared in 1968, followed by a reign of terror and economic chaos under the dictatorial president Macías Nguema, who was overthrown by a military coup in 1979 and later executed. A new constitution was adopted in 1982, but political unrest persisted.

Recent Developments

The production of crude petroleum was economically the most important development perhaps in the entire history of Equatorial Guinea. With world prices soaring, oil revenues poured into the country. In 2005 economic growth of up to 50% was predicted as petroleum production reached 380,000 barrels a day. By 2006 Equatorial Guinea had become sub-Saharan Africa's third largest petroleum producer, behind only Nigeria and Angola. US foreign direct investment topped $10 billion in that year, the fourth most in sub-Saharan Africa. While most of the country's citizens did not receive any of the oil wealth, however, many living on as little as one dollar a day, in 2006 Pres. Teodoro Obiang Nguema's son Teodorin was sued for debt after having apparently spent nearly $8 million in South Africa on cars and homes. In February 2006 the government agreed to settle a territorial dispute with Gabon over three small islands in potentially oil-rich offshore waters in the Gulf of Guinea.

Internet resources:
<www.cia.gov/cia/publications/factbook/geos/ek.html>.

Eritrea

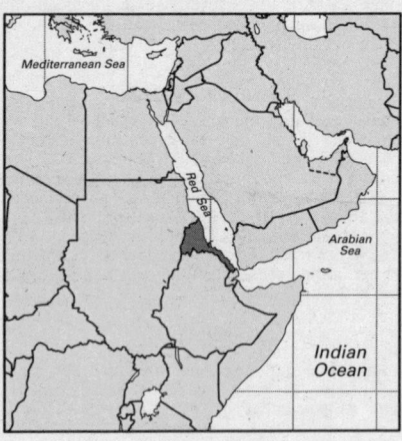

Official name: State of Eritrea. **Form of government:** transitional regime with one interim legislative body (Transitional National Assembly [150]). Constitution adopted in May 1997 was still not implemented in mid-2005. **Head of state and government:** President Isaias Afwerki (from 1993). **Capital:** Asmara. **Official language:** none. **Official religion:** none. **Monetary unit:** 1 nakfa (Nfa) = 100 cents; valuation (1 Jul 2007) US$1 = Nfa 15.00.

Demography

Area: 46,774 sq mi, 121,144 sq km. **Population** (2006): 4,787,000. **Density** (2006; based on land area only): persons per sq mi 122.7, persons per sq km 47.4. **Urban** (2003): 19.9%. **Sex distribution** (2003): male 49.75%; female 50.25%. **Age breakdown** (2003): under 15, 44.7%; 15–29, 27.2%; 30–44, 14.1%; 45–59, 8.7%; 60–74, 4.3%; 75 and over, 1.0%. **Ethnolinguistic composition** (2000): Tigrinya (Tigray) 51.8%; Tigré 17.9%; Afar 8.1%; Saho 4.3%; Kunama 4.1%; other 13.8%. **Religious affiliation** (2000): Christian 50.5%, of which Eritrean Orthodox 46.1%; Muslim 44.7%; other 4.8%. **Major cities** (2000): Asmara (2001) 503,000; Keren 70,000; Mendefera 65,000; Asseb (2003) 56,300; Massawa 35,000. **Location:** the Horn of eastern Africa, bordering The Sudan, the Red Sea, Djibouti, and Ethiopia.

Vital statistics

Birth rate per 1,000 population (2003): 39.4 (world avg. 21.3). **Death rate** per 1,000 population (2003): 13.2 (world avg. 9.1). **Natural increase rate** per 1,000 population (2003): 26.2 (world avg. 12.2). **Total fertility rate** (avg. births per childbearing woman; 2003): 5.7. **Marriage rate** per 1,000 population (1992): 6.8. **Life expectancy** at birth (2003): male 51.5 years; female 54.9 years.

National economy

Budget (2001). *Revenue:* Nfa 3,361,900,000 (grants 40.9%; tax revenue 38.0%, of which direct taxes 17.0%, import duties 12.2%; nontax revenue 15.9%; extraordinary revenue 5.2%). *Expenditures:* Nfa 4,545,300,000 (current expenditure 72.3%; capital expenditure 27.7%). **Production** (metric tons except as noted). *Agriculture, forestry, fishing* (2003): roots and tubers 85,000, sorghum 64,000, potatoes 33,000; livestock (number of live animals; 2003) 2,100,000 sheep, 1,927,500 cattle, 1,700,000 goats; roundwood (2003) 2,366,117; fish catch (2001) 8,820. *Mining and quarrying* (2001): salt 200,000; marble and granite are quarried, as are sand and aggregate (gravel) for construction. *Manufacturing* (value added in $'000,000; 2001): beverages 17; food products 6; tobacco products 5. *Energy production (consumption):* electricity (kW-hr; 2002) 249,117,000 (194,161,000); petroleum products (2000) n.a. (191,000). **Gross national product** (at current market prices; 2002): $850,000,000 ($190 per capita). **Public debt** (external, outstanding; 2002): $496,400,000. **Households.** Average household size (2000) 5.3. **Population economically active** (1996): 1,649,000; activity rate of total population 41.4%. **Tourism** (2002): receipts from visitors $73,000,000. **Land use** as % of total land area (2000): in temporary crops 5.0%, in permanent crops 0.03%, in pasture 69.0%; overall forest area 13.5%.

Foreign trade

Imports (2002-c.i.f.): $538,000,000 (food and live animals 28.4%, of which cereals [all forms] 13.6%, raw sugar 7.9%; machinery and apparatus 17.5%; road vehicles 11.5%; chemicals and chemical products 6.6%; iron and steel 6.2%). *Major import sources* (2001): Italy 18.7%; Saudi Arabia 16.6%; UAE 15.3%; US 4.8%. **Exports** (2002-f.o.b.): $52,000,000 (raw sugar 60.8%; synthetic woven fabrics 4.4%; vegetables and fruits 3.3%; fish 2.9%; sesame 2.7%). *Major export destinations* (2001): The Sudan 48.9%; Italy 8.2%; Germany 3.5%.

Transport and communications

Transport. *Railroads* (2001): part of the 306-km rail line that formerly connected Massawa and Agordat is under reconstruction; the 118-km section between Massawa and Asmara was reopened in 2003. *Roads* (1999): total length 4,010 km (paved 22%). *Vehicles* (1996): automobiles 5,940. *Air transport* (2001; Asmara airport only): passenger arrivals 39,266, passenger departures 46,448; freight loaded 202 metric tons, freight unloaded 1,548 metric tons; airports (2000) with scheduled flights 2. **Communications,** in

1 metric ton = about 1.1 short tons;   1 kilometer = 0.6 mi (statute);   1 metric ton-km cargo = about 0.68 short ton-mi cargo;   c.i.f.: cost, insurance, and freight;   f.o.b.: free on board

total units (units per 1,000 persons). Daily newspaper circulation (2000): 104,000 (28); radios (2001): 1,763,000 (464); televisions (2002): 215,000 (50); telephone main lines (2003): 38,100 (9.2); personal computers (2003): 12,000 (2.9); Internet users (2003): 9,500 (2.3).

Education and health

Literacy (2003): total population age 15 and over literate, 58.6%; males 69.9%; females 47.6%. **Health** (2000): physicians 173 (1 per 21,457 persons); hospital beds: 3,126 (1 per 1,187 persons); infant mortality rate per 1,000 live births (2003) 76.3. **Food** (2001): daily per capita caloric intake 1,690 (vegetable 94%, animal products 6%); 76% of FAO recommended minimum.

Military

Total active duty personnel (2002): 172,200 (army 98.7%, navy 0.8%, air force 0.5%). UN peacekeeping force along Eritrean-Ethiopian border (September 2004) 3,900. **Military expenditure as percentage of GNP** (1999): 27.4% (world 2.4%); per capita expenditure $52.

Did you know? The Eritrean cities of Massawa and Asmara are notable for their rich Italianate architecture and urban design, legacies of the Italian occupation of the region from the 1880s until 1941. After the end of the war of independence from Ethiopia in the 1990s, restoration returned the cities to their earlier grandeur.

Background

As the site of the main ports of the Aksumite empire, Eritrea was linked to the beginnings of the Ethiopian kingdom, but it retained much of its independence until it came under Ottoman rule in the 16th century. In the 17th and 19th centuries, control of the territory was disputed among Ethiopia, the Ottomans, the kingdom of Tigray, Egypt, and Italy; it became an Italian colony in 1890. Eritrea was used as the main base for the Italian invasions of Ethiopia (1896 and 1935–36) and in 1936 became part of Italian East Africa. It was captured by the British in 1941, federated to Ethiopia in 1952, and made a province of Ethiopia in 1962. Thirty years of guerrilla warfare by Eritrean secessionist groups ensued. A provisional Eritrean government was established in 1991 after the overthrow of the Ethiopian government, and independence came in 1993. A new constitution was ratified in 1997.

Recent Developments

The economy of Eritrea, one of the world's poorest nations, remained in deficit in 2006, and its external debt exceeded $500 million, up from $75 million in 1997. The diplomatic stalemate between Eritrea and Ethiopia, who had fought a bloody war between 1998 and 2000, continued for the sixth year. In October Eritrea spurned calls by the UN Security Council to remove its 1,500 troops and 14 tanks from a postwar buffer zone. The government continued to deny Eritreans political and press freedoms. Among the victims of the harsh regime were 15 journalists who spent their fifth year in jail notwithstanding pleas for their freedom from supporters overseas.

Internet resources: <http://allafrica.com/eritrea>.

Estonia

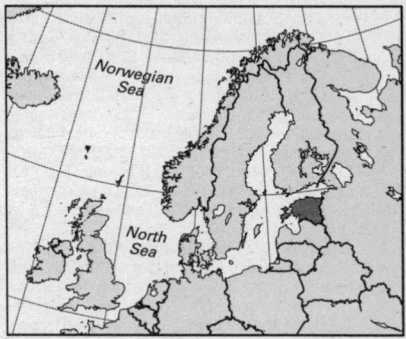

Official name: Eesti Vabariik (Republic of Estonia). **Form of government:** unitary multiparty republic with a single legislative body (Riilgikogu [101]). **Chief of state:** President Toomas Hendrik Ilves (from 2006). **Head of government:** Prime Minister Andrus Ansip (from 2005). **Capital:** Tallinn. **Official language:** Estonian. **Official religion:** none. **Monetary unit:** 1 kroon (EEK) = 100 senti; valuation (1 Jul 2007) US$1 = EEK 11.57.

Demography

Area: 17,462 sq mi, 45,227 sq km. **Population** (2006): 1,343,000. **Density** (2004): persons per sq mi 76.9, persons per sq km 29.7. **Urban** (2002): 69.4%. **Sex distribution** (2003): male 46.09%; female 53.91%. **Age breakdown** (2002): under 15, 15.8%; 15–29, 22.7%; 30–44, 21.5%; 45–59, 19.1%; 60–74, 14.9%; 75 and over, 6.0%. **Ethnic composition** (2000): Estonian 67.9%; Russian 25.6%; Ukrainian 2.1%; Belarusian 1.3%; Finnish 0.9%; other 2.2%. **Religious affiliation** (1995): Christian 38.1%, of which Orthodox 20.4%, Evangelical Lutheran 13.7%; other (mostly nonreligious) 61.9%. **Major cities** (2003): Tallinn 400,378; Tartu 101,169; Narva 67,752; Kohtla-Jarve 46,765; Pärnu 44,781. **Location:** eastern Europe, bordering the Gulf of Finland, Russia, Latvia, the Gulf of Riga, and the Baltic Sea.

Vital statistics

Birth rate per 1,000 population (2002): 9.6 (world avg. 21.3); legitimate 43.7%. **Death rate** per 1,000 population (2002): 13.5 (world avg. 9.1). **Natural increase rate** per 1,000 population (2002): –3.9 (world avg. 12.2). **Total fertility rate** (avg. births per childbearing woman; 2002): 1.4. **Marriage rate** per 1,000 population (2002): 4.3. **Divorce rate** per 1,000 population (2002): 3.0. **Life expectancy** at birth (2002): male 64.4 years; female 76.6 years.

National economy

Budget (2001). *Revenue:* EEK 36,881,000,000 (social security contributions 31.2%, value-added taxes

23.4%, personal income taxes 19.2%, excise taxes 9.3%). *Expenditures:* EEK 36,548,000,000 (social security and welfare 31.5%, health 16.3%, education 7.3%, police 7.2%, defense 5.0%). **Public debt** (external, outstanding; 2002): $482,000,000. **Production** (metric tons except as noted). *Agriculture, forestry, fishing* (2002): barley 249,400, potatoes 210,900, wheat 74,400; livestock (number of live animals) 345,000 pigs, 260,500 cattle; roundwood (2001) 10,200,000 cu m; fish catch (2001) 105,634. *Mining and quarrying* (2002): oil shale 12,400,000; peat 1,518,600. *Manufacturing* (value of production in EEK '000,000; 2001): food products 9,282; wood products (excluding furniture) 7,321; fabricated metal products 4,251. *Energy production (consumption):* electricity (kW-hr; 2002) 8,527,000,000 (5,686,000,000); hard coal (2002) none (60,000); lignite (2000) 11,727,000 (13,232,000); petroleum products (2000) none (736,000,000); natural gas (cu m; 2002) none (743,000,000). **Tourism** (2002): receipts $555,000,000; expenditures $231,000,000. **Population economically active** (2002): total 652,700; activity rate of total population 48.0% (participation rates: ages 15–74, 62.3%; female 48.9%; unemployed 10.3%). **Household income and expenditure** (2002). Average household size (2000) 2.2; average disposable income per household (1998) EEK 53,049; sources of income: wages and salaries 64.5%, transfers 25.0%, self-employment 5.2%, other 5.3%; expenditure: food and beverages 32.6%, housing 15.7%, transportation and communications 13.1%, clothing and footwear 6.2%. **Gross national product** (2003): $6,699,000,000 ($4,960 per capita). **Land use** as % of total land area (2000): in temporary crops 26.5%, in permanent crops 0.3%, in pasture 7.1%; overall forest area 48.7%.

Foreign trade

Imports (2001-c.i.f.): EEK 75,073,000,000 (electrical and nonelectrical machinery 33.5%, textiles and apparel 10.3%, foodstuffs 9.4%, transport equipment 8.9%). *Major import sources:* Finland 29.9%; Germany 11.2%; Sweden 10.0%; Russia 7.8%; Latvia 4.0%. **Exports** (2001-f.o.b.): EEK 57,832,000,000 (electrical and nonelectrical machinery 33.1%, wood and paper products 15.2%, textiles and apparel 14.0%). *Major export destinations:* Finland 33.9%; Sweden 14.0%; Germany 6.9%; Latvia 6.9%; UK 4.2%.

Transport and communications

Transport. *Railroads* (2002): route length 963 km; passenger-km 177,000,000; metric ton-km cargo 9,697,000,000. *Roads* (2000): total length 16,430 km (paved 51%). *Vehicles* (2002): passenger cars 400,700; trucks and buses 85,700. *Air transport* (2002; Estonian Air): passenger-km 355,000,000; metric ton-km cargo 5,000,000; airports (2001) 1. **Communications**, in total units (units per 1,000 persons). Daily newspaper circulation (1996): 255,000 (174); radios (2001): 1,590,000 (1,136); televisions (2002): 702,000 (502); telephone main lines (2003): 464,000 (343); cellular telephone subscribers (2003): 1,050,200 (776); personal computers (2002): 285,000 (210); Internet users (2002): 444,000 (328).

Health and nutrition

Health (2002): physicians 4,190 (1 per 324 persons); hospital beds 8,088 (1 per 168 persons); infant mortality rate per 1,000 live births (2002) 5.7. **Food** (2001): daily per capita caloric intake 3,048 (vegetable products 75%, animal products 25%); 119% of FAO recommended minimum.

Military

Total active duty personnel (2003): 5,510 (army 88.0%, navy 8.0%, air force 4.0%). **Military expenditure as a percentage of GNP** (1999): 1.5% (world 2.4%); per capita expenditure $120.

Background

The lands on the eastern shores of the Baltic Sea were invaded by Vikings in the 9th century AD and later by Danes, Swedes, and Russians, but the Estonians were able to withstand the assaults until the Danes took control in 1219. In 1346 the Danes sold their sovereignty to the Teutonic Order, which was then in possession of Livonia (southern Estonia and Latvia). In the mid-16th century Estonia was once again divided, with northern Estonia capitulating to Sweden and Poland gaining Livonia, which it surrendered to Sweden in 1629. Russia acquired Livonia and Estonia in 1721. Nearly a century later, serfdom was abolished, and from 1881 Estonia underwent intensive Russification. In 1918 Estonia obtained independence from Russia, which lasted until the Soviet Union occupied the country in 1940 and forcibly incorporated it into the USSR. Germany held the region (1941–44) during World War II, but the Soviet regime was restored in 1944, after which Estonia's economy was collectivized and integrated into that of the Soviet Union. In 1991, along with other parts of the former USSR, it proclaimed its independence and subsequently held elections. Estonia continued negotiations with Russia to settle their common border.

Recent Developments

Estonia joined both the EU and NATO in 2004. Since then its economy has boomed, growing by 11.5% in 2006. Unemployment dropped to 5.9% in 2006 from 10.3% the year before Estonia joined the international organizations. The IMF predicted in 2006 that inflation, one of the obstacles to Estonia's adoption of the euro, could fall below 4% in 2007.

Internet resources: <http://visitestonia.com>.

Ethiopia

Official name: Federal Democratic Republic of Ethiopia. **Form of government:** federal republic with two legislative houses (Federal Council [108]; Council of People's Representatives [546]). **Chief of state:** President Girma Wolde-Giorgis (from 2001). **Head of government:** Prime Minister Meles Zenawi (from 1995). **Capital:** Addis Ababa. **Official language:** none (Amharic is the "working" language). **Official religion:**

---

1 metric ton = about 1.1 short tons;   1 kilometer = 0.6 mi (statute);   1 metric ton-km cargo = about 0.68 short ton-mi cargo;   c.i.f.: cost, insurance, and freight;   f.o.b.: free on board

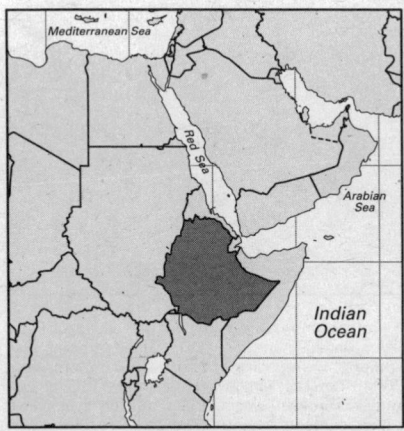

none. **Monetary unit:** 1 birr (Br) = 100 cents; valuation (1 Jul 2007) US$1 = Br 9.21.

Demography

Area: 435,186 sq mi, 1,127,127 sq km. **Population** (2006): 74,778,000. **Density** (2006): persons per sq mi 171.8, persons per sq km 66.3. **Urban** (2002): 15.6%. **Sex distribution** (2002): male 50.14%; female 49.86%. **Age breakdown** (2002): under 15, 44.9%; 15–29, 28.0%; 30–44, 14.5%; 45–59, 8.2%; 60–74, 3.7%; 75 and over, 0.7%. **Ethnolinguistic composition** (1994): Oromo 31.8%; Amharic 29.3%; Somali 6.2%; Tigrinya 5.9%; Walaita 4.6%; Gurage 4.2%; Sidamo 3.4%; Afar 1.9%; Hadya-Libide 1.7%; other 11.0%. **Religious affiliation** (1994): Ethiopian Orthodox 50.3%; Muslim 32.9%; Protestant 10.1%; traditional beliefs 4.8%; Roman Catholic 0.6%; other 1.3%. **Major cities** (1994): Addis Ababa 2,112,737; Dire Dawa 164,851; Nazret 127,842; Gonder 112,249; Dese 97,314. **Location:** the Horn of eastern Africa, bordering Eritrea, Djibouti, Somalia, Kenya, and The Sudan.

Vital statistics

Birth rate per 1,000 population (2003): 39.9 (world avg. 21.3). **Death rate** per 1,000 population (2003): 15.5 (world avg. 9.1). **Natural increase rate** per 1,000 population (2003): 24.4 (world avg. 12.2). **Total fertility rate** (avg. births per childbearing woman; 2003): 5.6. **Life expectancy** at birth (2003): male 47.3 years; female 49.7 years. **Adult population** (ages 15–49) **living with HIV** (beginning of 2004): 4.4% (world avg. 1.1%).

National economy

Budget (1999–2000). *Revenue:* Br 11,222,000,000 (tax revenue 57.8%, of which import duties 22.5%, income and profit tax 19.3%, sales tax 12.8%, export duties 1.3%; nontax revenue 26.9%; grants 15.3%). *Expenditures:* Br 17,184,000,000 (current expenditure 80.0%, of which defense 39.8%, wages 20.5%, education and health 12.2%, debt payment 6.5%; capital expenditure 20.0%). **Public debt** (external, outstanding; 2002): $6,313,000,000. **Tourism** (2002): receipts $77,000,000; expenditures $45,-

000,000. **Gross national product** (2003): $6,325,-000,000 ($90 per capita). **Production** (metric tons except as noted). *Agriculture, forestry, fishing* (2002): corn (maize) 2,600,000, sugarcane 2,500,000, sorghum 1,820,000; livestock (number of live animals) 35,500,000 cattle, 11,438,000 sheep, 9,622,-000 goats; roundwood (2001) 91,283,000 cu m; fish catch (2001) 15,390. *Mining and quarrying* (2001–02): rock salt 61,000; tantalum 37,000 kg; niobium 6,100 kg. *Manufacturing* (value added in $'000,000; 2001): food products 143; beverages 95; nonmetallic mineral products 38. *Energy production (consumption):* electricity (kW-hr; 2000) 1,700,-000,000 (1,700,000,000); crude petroleum (barrels; 2000) none (5,498,000); petroleum products (2000) 611,000 (1,508,000). **Land use** as % of total land area (2000): in temporary crops 10.0%, in permanent crops 0.7%, in pasture 20.0%; overall forest area 4.2%. **Population economically active** (2000): total 27,781,000; activity rate of total population 44.3% (participation rates [1999]: ages over 15, 80.5%; female [1999] 45.5%). **Households.** Average household size (2000) 5.2.

Foreign trade

Imports (2000-f.o.b. in balance of trade and c.i.f. for commodities and trading partners): $1,260,000,000 (machinery and apparatus 19.8%, refined petroleum 19.6%, road vehicles 12.0%, chemicals and chemical products 11.3%, iron and steel 5.6%). *Major import sources:* Yemen 19.1%; Italy 8.9%; Japan 8.2%; China 7.7%; India 5.2%; Germany 5.2%. **Exports** (2000): $482,000,000 (coffee 53.0%, leather 8.5%, nonmonetary gold 5.7%, sesame seeds 4.6%). *Major export destinations:* Germany 19.6%; Japan 11.7%; Djibouti 10.7%; Saudi Arabia 8.1%; Italy 6.7%; Somalia 6.1%.

Transport and communications

Transport. *Railroads* (2001): length 681 km (length of Ethiopian segment of Addis Ababa–Djibouti railroad); (1998–99) passenger-km 151,000,000 (includes Djibouti part of Addis Ababa–Djibouti railroad); (1998–99) metric ton-km cargo 90,000,000 (includes Djibouti part of Addis Ababa–Djibouti railroad). *Roads* (2001): total length 29,799 km (paved 13%). *Vehicles* (1999): passenger cars 54,240; trucks and buses 34,333. *Air transport* (2003; Ethiopian Airlines only): passenger-km 3,573,-000,000; metric ton-km cargo 93,000,000; airports (1997) 31. **Communications,** in total units (units per 1,000 persons). Daily newspaper circulation (1997): 86,000 (1.5); radios (2000): 11,800,000 (189); televisions (2000): 376,000 (6); telephone main lines (2003): 435,000 (6.3); cellular telephone subscribers (2003): 97,800 (1.4); personal computers (2003): 150,000 (2.2); Internet users (2003): 75,000 (1.1).

Education and health

Literacy (2000): total population age 15 and over literate 39.1%; males 47.2%; females 30.9%. **Health** (2001–02): physicians 1,833 (1 per 35,604 persons); hospital beds 11,367 (1 per 5,740 persons); infant mortality rate per 1,000 live births (2003) 98.6. **Food** (2002): daily per capita caloric intake 1,857 (vegetable products 95%, animal products 5%); 80% of FAO recommended minimum.

Military

Total active duty personnel (2003): 162,500 (army 98.5%, air force 1.5%); UN peacekeeping personnel along Ethiopian-Eritrean border (August 2004) 3,900. **Military expenditure as percentage of GNP** (1999): 8.8% (world 2.4%); per capita expenditure $9.

Background

Ethiopia, the Biblical land of Cush, was inhabited from earliest antiquity and was once under ancient Egyptian rule. Geez-speaking agriculturalists established the kingdom of Daamat in the 2nd millennium BC. After 300 BC they were superseded by the kingdom of Aksum, whose King Menilek I, according to legend, was the son of King Solomon and the Queen of Sheba. Christianity was introduced in the 4th century AD and became widespread. Ethiopia's prosperous Mediterranean trade was cut off by the Muslim Arabs in the 7th and 8th centuries, and the area's interests were directed eastward. Contact with Europe resumed in the late 15th century with the arrival of the Portuguese. Modern Ethiopia began with the reign of Tewodros II, who began the consolidation of the country. In the wake of European encroachment, the coastal region was made an Italian colony in 1890, but under Emperor Menilek II the Italians were defeated and ousted in 1896. Ethiopia prospered under his rule, and his modernization programs were continued by Emperor Haile Selassie in the 1930s. In 1936 Italy again gained control of the country, and it was held as part of Italian East Africa until 1941, when it was liberated by the British. Ethiopia incorporated Eritrea in 1952. In 1974 Haile Selassie was deposed, and a Marxist government, plagued by civil wars and famine, controlled the country until 1991. In 1993 Eritrea gained its independence, but border conflicts with Ethiopia and neighboring Somalia continued in the 1990s.

Recent Developments

The Ethiopian economy grew at a rate of 10.6% in 2006, the second straight year with growth above 10%, and roughly 80% of its exports were agricultural. The border dispute with Eritrea continued throughout 2006, and the UN Mission in Ethiopia and Eritrea was extended through July 2007. Ethiopia's increasingly visible involvement in the situation in Somalia resulted in the escalation of a war of words between Ethiopia and Eritrea. In December Ethiopia—a supporter of the Transitional Federal Government of Somalia—launched a coordinated air and ground war into Somalia. The military action, which had tacit US support, succeeded in driving the ruling Union of Islamic Courts from power.

Internet resources: <www.ethiopians.com>.

Faroe Islands

Official name: Føroyar (Faroese); Færøerne (Danish) (Faroe Islands; English-language alternative spelling is Faeroe Islands). **Political status:** self-governing region of the Danish realm with a single legislative body (Lagting [32]). **Chief of state:** Danish Queen Margrethe

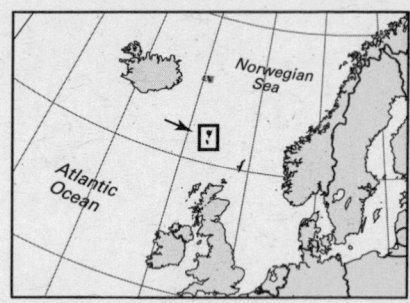

II (from 1972), represented by High Commissioner Søren Christensen (from 2005). **Head of home government:** Prime Minister Jóannes Eidesgaard (from 2004). **Capital:** Tórshavn (Thorshavn). **Official languages:** Faroese; Danish. **Official religion:** Evangelical Lutheran. **Monetary unit:** 1 Danish krone (Dkr) = 100 øre; valuation (1 Jul 2007) US$1 = Dkr 5.49. The local currency, the Faroese króna (Fkr), is equivalent to the Danish krone. Banknotes used are Faroese or Danish; coins are Danish.

Demography

Area: 540.1 sq mi, 1,398.8 sq km. **Population** (2006): 48,100. **Density** (2006): persons per sq mi 89.1, persons per sq km 34.4. **Urban** (2003): 38.6%. **Sex distribution** (2003): male 51.90%; female 48.10%. **Age breakdown** (2003): under 15, 23.6%; 15–29, 19.4%; 30–44, 20.9%; 45–59, 18.4%; 60–74, 11.3%; 75 and over, 6.4%. **Ethnic composition** (2000): Faroese 97.0%; Danish 2.5%; other Scandinavian 0.4%; other 0.1%. **Religious affiliation** (1995): Evangelical Lutheran Church of Denmark 80.8%; Plymouth Brethren 10.1%; Roman Catholic 0.2%; other (mostly nonreligious) 8.9%. **Major towns** (2003): Tórshavn 18,420; Klaksvík 4,794; Runavík 2,557; Tvøroyri 1,867. **Location:** island group north of the British Isles between the Norwegian Sea and the North Atlantic Ocean.

Vital statistics

Birth rate per 1,000 population (2002): 15.0 (world avg. 21.3); (1998) legitimate 62.0%. **Death rate** per 1,000 population (2002): 8.3 (world avg. 9.1). **Natural increase rate** per 1,000 population (2002): 6.7 (world avg. 12.2). **Total fertility rate** (avg. births per childbearing woman; 2002): 2.5. **Marriage rate** per 1,000 population (2002): 5.2. **Divorce rate** per 1,000 population (2002): 1.1. **Life expectancy** at birth (2003): male 75.4 years; female 82.4 years.

National economy

Budget (2002). *Revenue:* Dkr 3,762,060,000 (income taxes 44.5%, customs and excise duties 32.9%, transfers from the Danish government 16.7%). *Expenditures:* Dkr 3,586,220,000 (health and social welfare 46.6%, education 17.6%, debt service 10.5%, agriculture, fishing, and commerce 4.1%). **Gross national product** (at current market prices; 2002): $1,290,000,000 ($27,270 per capita). **Production**

1 metric ton = about 1.1 short tons;   1 kilometer = 0.6 mi (statute);   1 metric ton-km cargo = about 0.68 short ton-mi cargo;   c.i.f.: cost, insurance, and freight;   f.o.b.: free on board

(metric tons except as noted). *Agriculture, forestry, fishing* (2002): potatoes 1,500, other vegetables, grass, hay, and silage are produced; livestock (number of live animals) 70,000 sheep, 2,398 cattle; fish catch (2001) 524,837 (of which blue whiting 259,761, saithe 45,792, cod 38,706, herring 35,172, capelin 32,110, mackerel 24,005, prawns, shrimps, and other crustaceans 20,239). *Mining and quarrying*: negligible (the maritime boundary demarcation agreement between the Shetland Islands [UK] and the Faroes in May 1999 allowed for the exploration of deep-sea petroleum). *Manufacturing* (value added in Dkr '000,000; 1999): processed fish 393; all other manufacturing 351; important products include handicrafts and woolen textiles and clothing. *Energy production (consumption):* electricity (kW-hr; 2002) 239,644,000 ([2001] 223,000,000); petroleum products (2001) none (285,603). **Population economically active** (2002): total 29,540; activity rate of total population 62% (participation rates: female [1997] 46%; unemployed 3%). **Public debt** (to Denmark; end of 2001): none. **Households**. Expenditure (1998): food and beverages 25.1%, transportation and communications 17.7%, housing 12.5%, recreation 11.9%, energy 7.7%. **Land use** as % of total land area (1997): in temporary crops 2%, in pasture 93%; overall forest area, negligible.

Foreign trade

Imports (2002): Dkr 3,896,000,000 (goods for household consumption 28.3%, machinery and transport equipment 21.3%, goods for industries 19.0%). *Major import sources:* Denmark 31.4%; Norway 18.7%; Germany 7.6%; Sweden 6.5%; UK 4.6%. **Exports** (2002): Dkr 4,107,000,000 (chilled and frozen fish [excluding salmon] 50.4%, salted fish 16.3%, salmon 14.8%, prawns 5.7%, fish meal and fish oil 4.8%, trout 3.2%). *Major export destinations:* UK 24.4%; Denmark 20.5%; Spain 11.7%; France 8.2%; Germany 6.9%; Norway 6.5%.

Transport and communications

Transport. *Roads* (2001): total length 464 km. *Vehicles* (2001): passenger cars 15,615; trucks, vans, and buses 3,698. *Air transport* (2001): airports with scheduled flights 1. **Communications**, in total units (units per 1,000 persons). Daily newspaper circulation (1996): 6,000 (136); radios (2000): 102,000 (2,222); televisions (2000): 46,800 (1,022); telephone main lines (2002): 23,000 (482); cellular telephone subscribers (2002): 30,700 (644); Internet users (2002): 25,000 (524).

Health

(2001): physicians 90 (1 per 518 persons); hospital beds (2002) 290 (1 per 163 persons); infant mortality rate per 1,000 live births (2003) 6.5.

Military

Defense responsibility lies with Denmark.

Background

First settled by Irish monks (c. 700), the islands were colonized by the Vikings (c. 800) and were ruled by Norway from the 11th century until 1380, when they passed to Denmark. They unsuccessfully sought independence in 1946 but received self-government in 1948.

Recent Developments

In February 2007 the Faroe Islands and Iceland signed an agreement that defined the maritime boundary between the two countries, resolving a dispute that had lasted more than three decades. This officially established the valuable fishing rights of both and the limits of each country's continental shelf claim, which would prove extremely important in the event of the future discovery of offshore petroleum fields.

Internet resources: <www.tourist.fo>.

Fiji

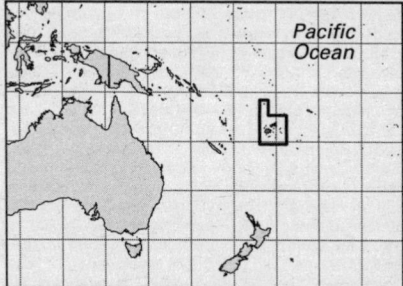

Official name: Republic of the Fiji Islands; Kai Vakarairai ni Fiji (Fijian). **Form of government:** multiparty republic with two legislative houses (Senate [32; all seats are nonelected]; House of Representatives [72]). **Chief of state:** President Ratu Josefa Iloilo (from 2000). **Head of government:** Prime Minister Voreqe Bainimarama (from 2007). **Capital:** Suva. **Official languages:** English, Fijian, and Hindustani have equal status per constitution. **Official religion:** none. **Monetary unit:** 1 Fiji dollar (F$) = 100 cents; valuation (1 Jul 2007) US$1 = F$1.59.

Demography

Area: 7,055 sq mi, 18,272 sq km. **Population** (2006): 855,000. **Density** (2006): persons per sq mi 121.2, persons per sq km 46.8. **Urban** (2003): 51.7%. **Sex distribution** (2003): male 50.21%; female 49.79%. **Age breakdown** (2003): under 15, 32.1%; 15–29, 28.8%; 30–44, 19.9%; 45–59, 12.8%; 60–74, 5.6%; 75 and over, 0.8%. **Ethnic composition** (2000): Fijian 52.0%; Indian 41.5%; other 6.5%. **Religious affiliation** (2000): Christian 56.8%, of which Protestant 37.1%, independent Christian 8.5%, Roman Catholic 8.4%; Hindu 33.3%; Muslim 6.9%; nonreligious 1.3%; Sikh 0.7%; other 1.0%. **Major cities** (1996; "urban centers"): Suva 167,421; Lautoka 42,917; Nadi 30,791; Labasa 24,187; Nausori 21,645. **Location:** archipelago in the South Pacific Ocean, between Hawaii (US) and New Zealand.

Vital statistics

Birth rate per 1,000 population (2003): 23.1 (world avg. 21.3). **Death rate** per 1,000 population (2003): 5.7 (world avg. 9.1). **Natural increase rate** per 1,000 population (2003): 17.4 (world avg. 12.2). **Total fertility rate** (avg. births per childbearing woman; 2003): 2.8. **Life expectancy** at birth (2003): male 66.4 years; female 71.4 years.

National economy

Budget (2002). *Revenue:* F$949,388,000 (customs duties 54.9%, income and estate taxes 29.0%, fees and royalties 5.6%). *Expenditures:* F$1,345,300,000 (goods and services 42.5%, debt redemption 14.2%, education 12.5%, defense 4.2%). **Production** (metric tons except as noted). *Agriculture, forestry, fishing* (2003): sugarcane 3,300,000, coconuts 170,000, taro 38,000; livestock (number of live animals) 320,000 cattle, 248,000 goats, 139,000 pigs; roundwood (2003) 383,000 cu m; fish catch (2001) 44,689. *Mining and quarrying* (2003): gold 3,517 kg; silver 1,247 kg. *Manufacturing* (2002): raw sugar 317,000; cement 102,000; flour 59,000. *Energy production (consumption):* electricity (kW-hr; 2000) 545,000,000 (545,000,000); coal (2000) none (18,000); petroleum products (2000) none (205,000). **Tourism:** receipts from visitors (2002) US$261,000,000; expenditures by nationals abroad (2000) US$78,000,000. **Land use** as % of total land area (2000): in temporary crops 10.9%, in permanent crops 4.7%, in pasture 9.6%; overall forest area 44.6%. **Population economically active** (1996): total 297,770; activity rate of total population 38.4% (participation rates: ages 15–64, 60.6%; female 32.8%; unemployed [2000] 12.2%). **Gross national product** (2003): US$1,969,000,000 (US$2,360 per capita). **Public debt** (external, outstanding; 2002): US$165,400,000. **Households.** Average household size (2000) 6.1; expenditure (1991): food, beverages, and tobacco 41.5%, housing and energy 21.4%, transportation and communications 12.9%, household durable goods 6.5%.

Foreign trade

Imports (2003-c.i.f.): F$2,215,000,000 (transport equipment 16.1%, mineral fuels 15.0%, machinery and apparatus 13.8%, textiles and wearing apparel 10.7%, live animals and animal products 6.2%). *Major import sources:* Australia 37.5%; New Zealand 18.8%; US 9.2%; Singapore 6.4%; Japan 5.4%. **Exports** (2003-f.o.b.): F$1,273,000,000 (reexports [mostly petroleum products] 26.0%, clothing 19.8%, sugar 18.1%, fish 6.7%, gold 6.0%). *Major export destinations:* Australia 27.4%; US 24.5%; UK 19.5%; New Zealand 5.6%; Japan 4.5%.

Transport and communications

Transport. *Railroads* (1999): length 595 km. *Roads* (1999): total length 3,440 km (paved 49%). *Vehicles* (2000): passenger cars 50,005; trucks and buses 35,038. *Air transport* (2003; Air Pacific only): passenger-km 2,190,000,000; metric ton-km cargo 62,692,000; airports (1997) with scheduled flights 13. **Communications,** in total units (units per 1,000 persons). Daily newspaper circulation (2001): 49,000 (60); radios (1997): 500,000 (636); televisions (2000): 92,000 (114); telephone main lines (2003): 102,000 (124); cellular telephone subscribers (2003): 109,900 (133); personal computers (2002): 40,000 (49); Internet users (2003): 55,000 (67).

Education and health

Educational attainment (1996): Percentage of population age 25 and over having: no formal schooling 4.4%; some education 22.3%; incomplete secondary 47.7%; complete secondary 17.0%; some higher 6.7%; university degree 1.9%. **Literacy** (2001): total population age 15 and over literate 93.2%; males 95.2%; females 91.2%. **Health** (2003): physicians 373 (1 per 2,229 persons); hospital beds (1999) 2,097 (1 per 385 persons); infant mortality rate per 1,000 live births 13.4. **Food** (2002): daily per capita caloric intake 2,894 (vegetable products 84%, animal products 16%); 127% of FAO recommended minimum.

Military

Total active duty personnel (2003): 3,500 (army 91.4%, navy 8.6%). **Military expenditure as percentage of GNP** (1999): 2.0% (world 2.4%); per capita expenditure US$42.

The Fijian flag features the Union Jack, reflecting its history as a British colony, and includes Fiji's coat of arms. The arms includes a white shield bearing symbols of England, the Cross of St. George and a lion. Local symbols also appear: sugar cane, coconuts, bananas, and a dove are featured, and the lion holds a coconut.

Background

Archaeological evidence shows that the islands of Fiji were occupied in the late 2nd millennium BC and that the inhabitants had developed pottery by c. 1300 BC. The first European sighting was by the Dutch in the 17th century; in 1774 the islands were visited by Capt. James Cook, who found a mixed Melanesian-Polynesian population with a complex society. Traders and the first missionaries arrived in 1835. In 1857 a British consul was appointed, and in 1874 Fiji was proclaimed a crown colony. It became independent as a member of the Commonwealth in 1970 and was declared a republic in 1987 following a military coup. Elections in 1992 restored civilian rule. A new constitution was approved in 1997.

Recent Developments

Despite the election of a new parliament in May 2006 and the establishment of a multiparty cabinet under Prime Minister Laisenia Qarase, the political situation in Fiji was uneasy. In December the head of the military, Commodore Voreque Bainimarama, initiated the fourth coup in Fiji in 20 years. He declared himself to be the acting head of state and replaced Qarase with Jona Senilagakali, a military doctor. The coup triggered widespread condemnation, and the Commonwealth suspended Fiji's membership. The economy faced the loss of preferential trade agreements for Fiji's two major exports, sugar and clothing, and the accompanying job losses.

Internet resources: <www.fiji.org.nz>.

---

1 metric ton = about 1.1 short tons; 1 kilometer = 0.6 mi (statute); 1 metric ton-km cargo = about 0.68 short ton-mi cargo; c.i.f.: cost, insurance, and freight; f.o.b.: free on board

Finland

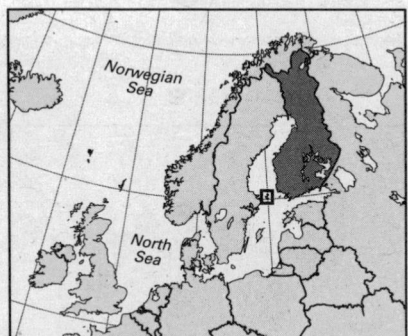

Official names: Suomen Tasavalta (Finnish); Republiken Finland (Swedish) (Republic of Finland). **Form of government:** multiparty republic with one legislative house (Parliament [200]). **Chief of state:** President Tarja Halonen (from 2000). **Head of government:** Prime Minister Matti Vanhanen (from 2003). **Capital:** Helsinki. **Official languages:** none (Finnish and Swedish are national languages). **Official religion:** none. **Monetary unit:** 1 euro (€) = 100 cents; valuation (1 Jul 2007) US$1 = €0.74; at conversion on 1 Jan 2002, €1 = 5.95 Finnish markka (Fmk).

Demography

Area (includes inland water area of 13,001 sq mi [33,672 sq km]): 130,559 sq mi; 338,145 sq km. **Population** (2006): 5,265,000. **Density** (2006; based on land area only): persons per sq mi 44.8, persons per sq km 17.3. **Urban** (2003): 83.3%. **Sex distribution** (2003): male 48.88%; female 51.12%. **Age breakdown** (2003): under 15, 17.8%; 15–29, 18.6%; 30–44, 20.6%; 45–59, 22.5%; 60–74, 13.6%; 75 and over, 6.9%. **Ethnic composition** (2000): Finnish 91.9%; Swedish 5.9%; Karelian 0.8%; Russian 0.2%; other 1.2%. **Religious affiliation** (2002): Evangelical Lutheran 84.9%; Finnish (Greek) Orthodox 1.1%; nonreligious 12.9%; other 1.1%. **Major cities** (2003): Helsinki 559,716 (urban agglomeration 1,075,000); Espoo 221,097 (within Helsinki urban agglomeration); Tampere 199,823; Vantaa 181,890 (within Helsinki urban agglomeration); Turku 174,618. **Location:** northern Europe, bordering Norway, Russia, the Gulf of Finland, the Baltic Sea, the Gulf of Bothnia, and Sweden.

Vital statistics

Birth rate per 1,000 population (2002): 10.7 (world avg. 21.3); (2000) legitimate 60.8%. **Death rate** per 1,000 population (2002): 9.5 (world avg. 9.1). **Natural increase rate** per 1,000 population (2002): 1.2 (world avg. 12.2). **Total fertility rate** (avg. births per childbearing woman; 2002): 1.7. **Marriage rate** per 1,000 population (2002): 5.3. **Divorce rate** per 1,000 population (2002): 2.6. **Life expectancy** at birth (2002): male 74.6 years; female 81.6 years.

National economy

Budget (2003). *Revenue:* €35,755,000,000 (income and property taxes 36.6%, value-added taxes 27.4%, excise duties 13.7%). *Expenditures:* €35,755,000,000 (social security and health 23.8%, education 16.4%, interest on state debt 9.6%, agriculture and forestry 7.2%, defense 5.5%). **Production** (metric tons except as noted). *Agriculture, forestry, fishing* (2002): silage 6,842,500, barley 1,738,700, oats 1,507,800; livestock (number of live animals; 2002) 1,315,000 pigs, 1,025,400 cattle, 200,000 reindeer; roundwood (2002) 52,210,000 cu m; fish catch (2001) 165,835. *Mining and quarrying* (2002): chromite (concentrate) 340,000; zinc (metal content) 61,580; gold 4,666 kg. *Manufacturing* (value added in €'000,000; 2000): radio, television, and communications equipment 6,289; wood pulp, paper, and paper products 5,472; nonelectrical machinery and equipment 3,183. *Energy production (consumption):* electricity (kW-hr; 2001) 71,229,000,000 (81,188,000,000); coal (2000) none (5,131,000); crude petroleum (barrels; 2000) none (78,409,000); petroleum products (2000) 12,131,000 (9,305,000); natural gas (cu m; 2000) none (4,079,844,000). **Population economically active** (2002): total 2,610,000; activity rate of total population 50.2% (participation rates: ages 15–64, 74.5%; female 47.9%; unemployed 9.1%). **Household income and expenditure** (2001). Average household size 2.2; disposable income per household €28,807; sources of gross income (2000): wages and salaries 55.4%, transfer payments 24.3%, other 20.3%; expenditure: housing and energy 28.7%, transportation and communications 18.0%, food, beverages, and tobacco 16.0%. **Gross national product** (2003): $140,755,000,000 ($27,020 per capita). **Public debt** (2001): $52,850,000,000. **Tourism** (in $'000,000; 2002): receipts 1,573; expenditures 2,002. **Land use** as % of total land area (2000): in temporary crops 7.2%, in permanent crops 0.03%, in pasture 0.07%; overall forest area 72.0%.

Foreign trade

Imports (2001-c.i.f.): €35,891,000,000 (electrical machinery and apparatus 18.2%; nonelectrical machinery and apparatus 13.8%; mineral fuels 11.6%; automobiles 7.0%). *Major import sources:* Germany 14.5%; Sweden 10.2%; Russia 9.5%; US 6.8%; UK 6.4%; France 4.5%. **Exports** (2001-f.o.b.): €47,800,000,000 (electrical machinery and apparatus 24.3%; paper and paper products 18.8%; nonelectrical machinery and apparatus 11.6%; wood and wood products [excluding furniture] 5.1%). *Major export destinations:* Germany 12.3%; US 9.7%; UK 9.6%; Sweden 8.4%; Russia 5.9%; France 4.6%.

Transport and communications

Transport. Railroads: route length (2002) 5,850 km; passenger-km 3,305,000,000; metric ton-km cargo 9,664,000,000. *Roads* (2002; excludes Åland Islands): total length 78,137 km (paved 64%). *Vehicles* (2002): passenger cars 2,194,683; trucks and buses 319,699. *Air transport* (2003; Finnair): passenger-km 12,971,000,000; metric ton-km cargo 314,500,000; airports (2001) 27. **Communications**, in total units (units per 1,000 persons). Daily newspaper circulation (2000): 2,360,000 (456); radios (2000): 8,400,000 (1,623); televisions (2000): 3,580,000 (692); telephone main lines (2002): 2,850,000 (547); cellular telephone subscribers (2002): 4,400,000 (845); personal computers (2002): 2,300,000 (442); Internet users (2002): 2,650,000 (509).

Education and health

Educational attainment (end of 2000). Percentage of population age 25 and over having: incomplete upper-secondary education 38.6%; complete upper secondary or vocational 34.5%; higher 26.9%. **Literacy**: virtually 100%. **Health** (2002): physicians 16,446 (1 per 316 persons); hospital beds 38,025 (1 per 137 persons); infant mortality rate per 1,000 live births 3.6. **Food** (2001): daily per capita caloric intake 3,202 (vegetable products 64.3%, animal products 35.7%); 118% of FAO recommended minimum.

Military

Total active duty personnel (2003): 27,000 (army 71.1%, navy 18.5%, air force 10.4%). **Military expenditure as percentage of GNP** (1999): 1.4% (world 2.4%); per capita expenditure $344.

Did you know? The *Kalevala*, Finland's national epic, was compiled from oral sources in the early 19th century. Kalevala, the dwelling place of the poem's chief characters, is a poetic name for Finland, meaning "land of heroes."

Background

Recent archaeological discoveries have led some to suggest that human habitation in Finland dates back at least 100,000 years. Ancestors of the Sami apparently were present in Finland by about 7000 BC. The ancestors of the present-day Finns came from the southern shore of the Gulf of Finland in the 1st millennium BC. The area was gradually Christianized from the 11th century. From the 12th century Sweden and Russia contested for supremacy in Finland, but by 1323 Sweden ruled most of the country. Russia was ceded part of Finnish territory in 1721; in 1808 Alexander I of Russia invaded Finland, which in 1809 was formally ceded to Russia. The subsequent period saw the growth of Finnish nationalism. Russia's losses in World War I and the Russian Revolution of 1917 set the stage for Finland's independence in 1917. It was defeated by the Soviet Union in the Russo-Finnish War (1939–40) but then sided with Nazi Germany against the Soviets during World War II and regained the territory it had lost. Facing defeat again by the advancing Soviets in 1944, it reached a peace agreement with the USSR, ceding territory and paying reparations. Finland's economy recovered after World War II. It joined the EU in 1995.

Recent Developments

In January 2006 Pres. Tarja Halonen, the country's first woman head of state, was reelected for a second six-year term. Finnish cellular-phone giant Nokia and its German rival Siemens announced in June that they would unite their network operations. In August Russia paid Finland €222 million (€1 = about $1.27) and agreed to provide another €25–30 million in goods and services to cancel the last of its debts to the country. These stemmed from Russia assuming responsi-bility for the debts incurred by the former Soviet Union, which had owed Finland more than €1 billion.

Internet resources: <www.finland-tourism.com>.

France

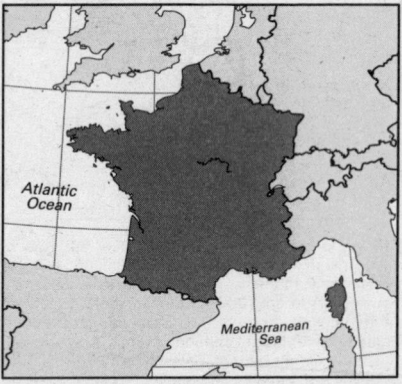

Official name: République Française (French Republic). **Form of government:** republic with two legislative houses (Parliament; Senate [321], National Assembly [577]). **Chief of state:** President Nicolas Sarkozy (from 2007). **Head of government:** Prime Minister François Fillon (from 2007). **Capital:** Paris. **Official language:** French. **Official religion:** none. **Monetary unit:** 1 euro (€) = 100 cents; valuation (1 Jul 2007) US$1 = €0.74; at conversion on 1 Jan 2002, €1 = 6.56 French francs (F).

Demography

Area: 210,026 sq mi, 543,965 sq km. **Population** (2006): 61,114,000. **Density** (2006): persons per sq mi 291.0, persons per sq km 112.3. **Urban** (2003): 76.3%. **Sex distribution** (2003): male 48.77%; female 51.23%. **Age breakdown** (2003): under 15, 18.6%; 15–29, 19.4%; 30–44, 21.6%; 45–59, 19.8%; 60–74, 12.8%; 75 and over, 7.8%. **Ethnic composition** (2000): French 76.9%; Algerian and Moroccan Berber 2.2%; Italian 1.9%; Portuguese 1.5%; Moroccan Arab 1.5%; Fleming 1.4%; Algerian Arab 1.3%; Basque 1.3%; Jewish 1.2%; German 1.2%; Vietnamese 1.0%; Catalan 0.5%; other 8.1%. **Religious affiliation** (2000): Roman Catholic 82.3%; Muslim 7.1%; atheist 4.4%; Protestant 3.7%; Orthodox 1.1%; Jewish 1.0%; other 0.4%. **Major cities** (1999): Paris 2,125,246 (metropolitan area 9,644,507); Marseille 798,430 (1,349,772); Lyon 445,452 (1,348,832); Toulouse 390,350 (761,090); Nice 342,738 (888,784); Nantes 270,251 (544,932); Strasbourg 264,115 (427,245); Montpellier 225,392 (287,981); Bordeaux 215,363 (753,931); Rennes 206,229 (272,263); Le Havre 190,905 (248,547); Reims 187,206 (215,581); Lille 184,493 (1,000,900); Saint-Étienne 180,210 (291,960); Toulon 160,639 (519,640). **Location:** western Europe, bordering the North Atlantic Ocean,

---

1 metric ton = about 1.1 short tons; 1 kilometer = 0.6 mi (statute); 1 metric ton-km cargo = about 0.68 short ton-mi cargo; c.i.f.: cost, insurance, and freight; f.o.b.: free on board

Belgium, Luxembourg, Germany, Switzerland, Italy, the Mediterranean Sea, Spain, and Andorra. **Dependent territories:** French Guiana, French Polynesia, Guadeloupe, Martinique, Mayotte, New Caledonia, Réunion, Saint Pierre and Miquelon, and Wallis and Futuna. **Mobility** (1990). Population living in same residence as in 1982: 51.4%; same region 89.0%; different region 8.8%; different country 2.2%. **Households** (1999). Average household size 2.4; 1 person 31.0%, 2 persons 31.1%, 3 persons 16.2%, 4 persons 13.8%, 5 persons or more 7.9%. Family households (1999): 15,942,369 (67.0%); nonfamily 7,865,703 (33.0%). **Immigration** (2000): immigrants admitted 53,879 (from Africa 56.0%, of which Algerian 16.9%; from Europe 23.1%; from Asia 12.4%).

Vital statistics

Birth rate per 1,000 population (2003): 12.5 (world avg. 21.3); (2002) legitimate 54.8%; illegitimate 45.2%. **Death rate** per 1,000 population (2003): 9.1 (world avg. 9.1). **Natural increase rate** per 1,000 population (2003): 3.4 (world avg. 12.2). **Total fertility rate** (avg. births per childbearing woman; 2003): 1.9. **Marriage rate** per 1,000 population (2002): 4.7. **Divorce rate** per 1,000 population (2002): 2.2. **Life expectancy** at birth (2003): male 75.6 years; female 83.1 years.

Social indicators

Quality of working life. Average workweek (2001): 38.4 hours. Annual rate per 100,000 workers for (1999): injury or accident 4,432 (deaths 0.1%); accidents in transit to work (1994) 708 (deaths 68.3). Average days lost to labor stoppages per 1,000 workers (1994): 21.0. Trade union membership (2003): 1,900,000 (8% of labor force). **Access to services** (1992). Proportion of dwellings having: central heating 86.0%; piped water 97.0%; indoor plumbing 95.8%. **Social participation.** Eligible voters participating in last (June 2002) national election: 64.4%. Population over 15 years of age participating in voluntary associations (1997): 28.0%. **Social deviance.** Offense rate per 100,000 population (1998) for: murder 1.6, rape 13.4, other assault 583.8; theft (including burglary and housebreaking) 6,107.6. Incidence per 100,000 in general population of: homicide (2000) 0.9; suicide (2000) 16.8. **Material well-being** (2002). Households possessing: automobile 79%; color television 94%; VCR (2001) 70%; microcomputer 37%; washing machine 91%; microwave 68%; dishwasher (2001) 39%.

National economy

Gross national product (2003): US$1,523,025,-000,000 (US$24,770 per capita). **Budget** (2001). *Revenue:* €244,846,800,000 (value-added taxes 55.7%, personal income tax 21.8%, corporate income tax 20.1%). *Expenditures:* €268,669,600,000 (current expenditure 89.9%, of which public debt 14.9%, pensions 11.3%, social services 11.3%; development expenditure 10.1%). **Public debt** (2001): $756,080,000,000. **Production** (metric tons except as noted). *Agriculture, forestry, fishing* (2003): corn (maize) 59,170,000, wheat 30,582,000, sugar beets 29,238,000, barley 9,818,000, potatoes 6,235,000, grapes 6,178,000, rapeseed 3,341,000, apples 2,402,000, dry peas 1,617,000, sunflower seeds

1,494,000, triticale 1,291,000, tomatoes 834,000, carrots 682,000, oats 555,000, lettuce 426,000, green peas 396,000, dry onions 393,000, cauliflower 390,000, string beans 373,000; livestock (number of live animals) 19,517,000 cattle, 15,058,000 pigs, 9,204,000 sheep, 220,000,000 chickens; roundwood 36,850,000 cu m; fish catch 877,995. *Mining and quarrying* (2001): gypsum 4,500,000; kaolin 375,000; potash 257,000; gold 80,700 troy oz. *Manufacturing* (value added in $'000,000; 2000; data unavailable for production of food, beverages, and tobacco products): motor vehicles, trailers, and motor vehicle parts 17,157; pharmaceuticals, soaps, and paints 16,360; fabricated metal products 12,996; general purpose machinery 7,064; basic chemicals 6,378; aircraft and spacecraft 6,045; plastic products 6,014; publishing 5,184; medical, measuring, and testing appliances 4,765; telecommunications equipment 4,615. *Energy production* (consumption; consumption data includes Monaco): electricity (kW-hr; 2001) 520,000,-000,000 ([2000] 477,288,000,000); hard coal (2001; last coal-producing mine closed in April 2004) 2,400,000 ([2000] 21,090,000); lignite (2000) 296,000 (335,000); crude petroleum (barrels; 2001) 11,027,000 ([1999] 608,200,000); petroleum products (2000) 76,665,000 (71,631,000); natural gas (cu m; 2001) 1,982,000,000 ([2000] 43,555,-000,000). **Population economically active** (2001): total 27,812,600; activity rate of total population 47.0% (participation rates: ages 15–64 [1994] 67.6%; female [2001] 47.9%; unemployed 12.1%). **Household income and expenditure.** Average household size (1999) 2.5; average disposable income per household (2001) €26,570; sources of income (1995): wages and salaries 70.0%, self-employment 24.4%, social security 5.6%; expenditure (2001): housing and energy 23.4%, transportation 15.2%, food and nonalcoholic beverages 14.4%, recreation 8.9%, restaurants and hotels 7.6%. **Tourism** (in $'000,000; 2002): receipts $32,329; expenditures $19,460. **Land use** as % of total land area (2000): in temporary crops 33.5%, in permanent crops 2.1%, in pasture 18.4%; overall forest area 27.9%.

Foreign trade

Imports (2002-c.i.f.; includes Monaco): US$303,800,000,000 (machinery and apparatus 24.2%; transport equipment 13.5%; chemicals and chemical products 12.9%; petroleum [all forms] 9.2%; food 7.0%). *Major import sources:* Germany 17.2%; Italy 9.0%; US 8.0%; UK 7.3%; Spain 7.2%; Belgium 6.6%; The Netherlands 4.7%; China 3.5%; Japan 3.2%; Switzerland 2.2%; Ireland 2.0%. **Exports** (2002-f.o.b.; includes Monaco): US$304,900,000,-000 (machinery and apparatus 23.2%; transport equipment 20.5%, of which road vehicles 14.0%, aircraft and spacecraft 5.6%; chemicals and chemical products 14.9%, of which pharmaceuticals 4.9%; food 7.9%; iron and steel 3.2%; perfumes, cosmetics, and toiletries 2.9%). *Major export destinations:* Germany 14.5%; UK 10.3%; Spain 9.7%; Italy 9.1%; US 8.1%; Belgium 7.2%; The Netherlands 4.0%; Switzerland 3.2%; Japan 1.7%; Portugal 1.5%.

Transport and communications

Transport. *Railroads* (2002): route length 32,008 km; (2000) passenger-km 69,870,000,000; metric ton-km cargo 55,370,000,000. *Roads* (1999): total length 893,300 km (paved 100%). *Vehicles* (2000): passenger cars 28,060,000; trucks and buses 5,673,000. *Air transport* (2003; Air France only): passenger-km 99,122,000,000; metric ton-km cargo 4,875,000,000; airports (1996) 61. **Communications**, in total units (units per 1,000 persons). Daily newspaper circulation (2000): 11,800,000 (201); radios (2000): 55,900,000 (950); televisions (2000): 37,000,000 (628); telephone main lines (2003): 33,905,400 (566); cellular telephone subscribers (2003): 41,683,100 (696); personal computers (2002): 20,700,000 (347); Internet users (2003): 21,900,000 (366).

Education and health

Educational attainment (2001). Percentage of population age 25–64 with at least upper secondary education 63.2%. **Health:** physicians (2002) 199,000 (1 per 301 persons); hospital beds (2001) 477,000 (1 per 126 persons); infant mortality rate (2003) 4.4. **Food** (2001): daily per capita caloric intake 3,629 (vegetable products 63%, animal products 37%); 129% of FAO recommended minimum.

Military

Total active duty personnel (2003): 259,050 (army 52.9%, navy 17.1%, air force 24.7%, unallocated 5.3%). **Military expenditure as percentage of GNP** (1999): 2.7% (world 2.4%); per capita expenditure $658.

 **Did you know?** The Loire is the longest river in France, rising in the southern Massif Central and flowing north and west for 634 mi (1,020 km) to the Atlantic Ocean, which it enters south of the Bretagne (Brittany) peninsula.

Background

Archaeological excavations in France indicate continuous settlement from Paleolithic times. About 1200 BC the Gauls migrated into the area, and in 600 BC Ionian Greeks established several settlements, including one at Marseille. Julius Caesar completed the Roman conquest of Gaul in 50 BC. During the 6th century AD the Salian Franks ruled; by the 8th century power had passed to the Carolingians, the greatest of whom was Charlemagne. The Hundred Years' War (1337–1453) resulted in the return to France of land that had been held by the British; by the end of the 15th century, France approximated its modern boundaries. The 16th century was marked by the Wars of Religion between Protestants (Huguenots) and Roman Catholics. Henry IV's Edict of Nantes (1598) granted substantial religious toleration, but this was revoked in 1685 by Louis XIV, who helped to raise monarchical absolutism to new heights. In 1789 the French Revolution proclaimed the rights of the individual and destroyed the ancient regime. Napoleon ruled from 1799 to 1814, after which a limited monarchy was restored until 1871, when the Third Republic was created. World War I (1914–18) ravaged the northern part of France. After Nazi Germany's invasion during World War II, the collaborationist Vichy regime governed. Liberated by Allied and Free French forces in 1944, France restored parliamentary democracy under the Fourth Republic. A costly war in Indochina and rising nationalism in French colonies during the 1950s overwhelmed the Fourth Republic. The Fifth Republic was established in 1958 under Charles de Gaulle, who presided over the dissolution of most of France's overseas colonies. In 1981 François Mitterrand became France's first elected Socialist president. During the 1990s the French government, balancing right- and left-wing forces, moved toward solidifying European unity.

Recent Developments

France in 2006 was affected by a crisis over the First Job Contract (CPE) law. In February, in order to tackle France's problem with unemployment among the young, Prime Minister Dominique de Villepin introduced this law, which would allow employers to dismiss workers under 26 years old during the first two-year "trial period" of their employment without having to state the cause or go through a time-consuming labor tribunal. Opposition among French students built steadily, and by early April demonstrations around the country had grown to include over a million people. That month the government announced that it would replace the CPE law with a return to the previous policy of subsidizing companies that employed French youth. Politics were dominated by the 2007 election to succeed Pres. Jacques Chirac. It resulted in a runoff contested by Nicolas Sarkozy, the leader of the ruling party, and the Socialist Party's Ségolène Royal. Sarkozy won and was sworn in in May 2007. French diplomacy came to the fore as the international community struggled to halt the fighting between Israel and Hezbollah in Lebanon, in which France had a close interest because of its historic ties. At the UN France and the US succeeded in achieving a cease-fire and a UN peacekeeping force to police it. France dismayed many in August when it announced that while it would command the UN force, it would contribute only an extra 200 troops toward the projected 15,000 total. Evidently stung by international criticism, and possibly shamed by Italy's prompt offer of 3,000 troops, France agreed later to provide another 1,600 troops. Europe's complex relationship with Turkey was further complicated in October when France's National Assembly passed a bill making it a crime to deny the genocide in 1915 of Armenians at the hands of the Ottoman Turks. The move convinced many that the French government was determined to keep Turkey out of the European Union.

Internet resources: <www.franceguide.com>.

French Guiana

Official name: Département de la Guyane française (Department of French Guiana). **Political status:** overseas department of France with two legislative houses (General Council [19]; Regional Council [31]).

---

1 metric ton = about 1.1 short tons;   1 kilometer = 0.6 mi (statute);   1 metric ton-km cargo = about 0.68 short ton-mi cargo;   c.i.f.: cost, insurance, and freight;   f.o.b.: free on board

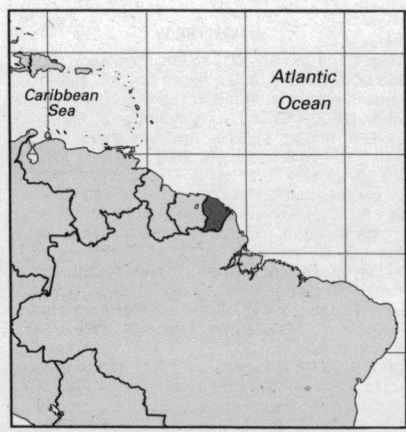

Caribbean Sea
Atlantic Ocean

Chief of state: President Nicolas Sarkozy of France (from 2007). **Heads of government:** Prefect Jean-Pierre Laflaquière (from 2006), President Pierre Désert of the General Council (from 2004), and President Antoine Karam of the Regional Council (from 1992). **Capital:** Cayenne. **Official language:** French. **Official religion:** none. **Monetary unit:** 1 euro (€) = 100 cents; valuation (1 Jul 2007) US$1 = €0.74; at conversion on 1 Jan 2002, €1 = 6.56 French francs (F).

Demography

Area: 32,253 sq mi, 83,534 sq km. **Population** (2006): 199,000. **Density** (2006): persons per sq mi 6.2, persons per sq km 2.4. **Urban** (2003): 75.4%. **Sex distribution** (1999): male 50.36%; female 49.64%. **Age breakdown** (1999): under 15, 34.0%; 15–29, 24.2%; 30–44, 23.3%; 45–59, 12.5%; 60–74, 4.3%; 75 and over, 1.7%. **Ethnic composition** (2000): Guianese Mulatto 37.9%; French 8.0%; Haitian 8.0%; Surinamese 6.0%; Antillean 5.0%; Chinese 5.0%; Brazilian 4.9%; East Indian 4.0%; other (other West Indian, Hmong, other South American) 21.2%. **Religious affiliation** (2000): Christian 84.6%, of which Roman Catholic 80.0%, Protestant 3.9%; Chinese folk-religionist 3.6%; Spiritist 3.5%; nonreligious/atheist 3.0%; traditional beliefs 1.9%; Hindu 1.6%; Muslim 0.9%; other 0.9%. **Major cities** (1999 [commune pop.]): Cayenne 50,594 (urban agglomeration 84,181); Saint-Laurent-du-Maroni 19,211; Kourou 19,107; Matoury 18,032 (within Cayenne urban agglomeration); Rémire-Montjoly 15,555 (within Cayenne urban agglomeration). **Location:** northern South America, bordering the Atlantic Ocean, Brazil, and Suriname.

Vital statistics

Birth rate per 1,000 population (2003): 21.3 (world avg. 21.3); (2000) legitimate 17.6%. **Death rate** per 1,000 population (2003): 4.8 (world avg. 9.1). **Natural increase rate** per 1,000 population (2003): 16.5 (world avg. 12.2). **Total fertility rate** (avg. births per childbearing woman; 2003): 3.1. **Marriage rate** per 1,000 population (1999): 3.5. **Divorce rate** per 1,000 population (1998): 1.0. **Life expectancy** at birth (2003): male 73.4 years; female 80.2 years.

National economy

Budget (2000). *Revenue:* €141,000,000 (direct taxes 32.6%, indirect taxes 29.8%, revenue from French central government 17.7%, development receipts 15.6%). *Expenditures:* €141,000,000 (current expenditures 83.0%, capital expenditures 17.0%). **Production** (metric tons except as noted). *Agriculture, forestry, fishing* (2002): rice 19,900, cassava 10,375, cabbages 6,350; livestock (number of live animals) 10,500 pigs, 9,200 cattle; roundwood (2001) 139,000 cu m; fish catch (2001) 5,231. *Mining and quarrying* (2001): stone, sand, and gravel 1,500; gold 127,671 troy oz. *Manufacturing* (2001): pork 1,245; chicken meat 560; finished wood products (1996) 3,172 cu m. *Number of satellites launched from the Kourou Space Center* (2002): 12. *Energy production (consumption):* electricity (kW-hr; 2000) 455,000,000 (455,000,000); petroleum products (2000) none (292,000). **Household income and expenditure.** Average household size (1999) 3.3; income per household (1997) €31,203; sources of income (1997): wages and salaries and self-employed 72.9%, transfer payments 20.2%; expenditure (1994): food and beverages 28.7%, housing 11.7%, energy 9.0%, clothing and footwear 6.4%, health 2.7%, other 41.5%. **Land use** as % of total land area (2000): in temporary crops 0.14%, in permanent crops 0.05%, in pasture 0.08%; overall forest area 89.9%. **Gross national product** (2000): $2,360,000,000 ($14,370 per capita). **Population economically active** (1999): total 62,634; activity rate of total population 39.4% (participation rates: age 15 and over 60.5%; female 43.8%; unemployed [March 2003] 22.8%). **Tourism** (2002): receipts $45,000,000.

Foreign trade

Imports (2002): €643,000,000 (food products 21.8%, road vehicles 12.8%, refined petroleum 9.0%, nonelectrical machinery 8.6%). *Major import sources:* France 51.5%; Trinidad and Tobago 8.7%; The Netherlands 2.5%; Germany 2.5%; Japan 2.5%. **Exports** (2002): €129,000,000 (nonferrous metals [nearly all gold] 70.5%, food products [mostly fish, shrimp, and rice] 12.5%, parts for air and space vehicles 3.1%). *Major export destinations:* France 62.8%; Belgium 10.1%; Switzerland 9.3%; Brazil 3.9%; Guadeloupe 3.1%.

Transport and communications

Transport. *Roads* (1996): total length 1,245 km. *Vehicles* (1999): passenger cars 32,900; trucks and buses 11,900. *Air transport* (2002): passenger arrivals 186,920; passenger departures 192,764; cargo unloaded 4,569 metric tons, cargo loaded 2,119 metric tons; airports (2001) with scheduled flights 1. **Communications,** in total units (units per 1,000 persons). Daily newspaper circulation (1996): 2,000 (14); radios (1997): 104,000 (702); televisions (1998): 37,000 (202); telephone main lines (1999): 49,000 (308); cellular telephone subscribers (2002): 138,200 (781); personal computers (1999): 23,000 (145); Internet users (2001): 3,200 (17).

Education and health

Educational attainment (1990). Percentage of population age 25 and over having: incomplete primary education or no declaration 61.7%; completed primary

5.3%; some secondary 15.9%; completed secondary 8.2%; some higher 4.9%; completed higher 4.0%. **Health** (2000): physicians 219 (1 per 737 persons); hospital beds 750 (1 per 215 persons); infant mortality rate per 1,000 live births (2003) 12.8. **Food** (1992): daily per capita caloric intake 2,900 (vegetable products 70%, animal products 30%); 128% of FAO recommended minimum.

Military

Total active duty personnel (2003): French troops 3,100.

Background

Originally settled by the Spanish, French, and Dutch, the territory of French Guiana was awarded to France in 1667, and the inhabitants were made French citizens after 1877. By 1852 the French began using the territory as a penal colony with one locale, on Devils Island, being especially notorious. It became an overseas territory of France in 1946; the penal colonies were closed by 1939.

Recent Developments

The European Space Agency has regularly launched communication satellites from French Guiana, and the space center near Kourou, completed in 1968, is a major factor in the local economy. In February 2007 a ceremony was held marking the beginning of construction of a launch base for Roscosmos, the Russian Federal Space Agency.

Internet resources:
<www.countryreports.org/french.htm>.

French Polynesia

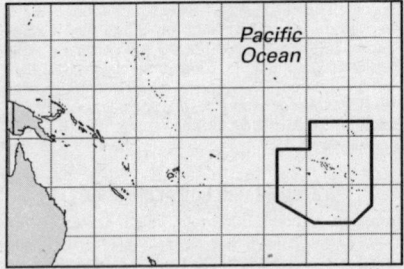

Pacific Ocean

Official name: Polynésie française (French); Polynesia Farani (Tahitian) (French Polynesia). **Political status:** overseas country of France with one legislative house (Assembly [57]). **Chief of state:** President Nicolas Sarkozy of France (from 2007). **Head of government:** President Gaston Tong Sang (from 2006). **Capital:** Papeete. **Official languages:** French; Tahitian. **Official religion:** none. **Monetary unit:** 1 Franc de la Comptoirs française du pacifique (CFPF) = 100 centimes; valuation (1 Jul 2007) US$1 = CFPF 88.26; the CFPF is pegged to the euro (€) at €1 = CFPF 119.25 from 1 Jan 2002.

Demography

Area: 1,544 sq mi, 4,000 sq km. **Population** (2006): 258,000. **Density** (2006; based on land area only): persons per sq mi 189.8, persons per sq km 73.3. **Urban** (2002): 52.1%. **Sex distribution** (2002): male 51.39%; female 48.61%. **Age breakdown** (2002): under 15, 29.9%; 15–29, 26.0%; 30–44, 23.5%; 45–59, 13.3%; 60–74, 5.9%; 75 and over, 1.4%. **Ethnic composition** (1996): Polynesian and part-Polynesian 82.8%; European (mostly French) 11.9%; Asian (mostly Chinese) 4.7%; other 0.6%. **Religious affiliation** (1995): Protestant 50.2%, of which Evangelical Church of French Polynesia (Presbyterian) 46.1%; Roman Catholic 39.5%; other Christian 9.9%, of which Mormon 5.9%; other 0.4%. **Major communes** (2002): Faaa 28,339 (part of Papeete urban agglomeration); Papeete 26,181 (urban agglomeration [2002] 124,864); Punaauia 23,706 (part of Papeete urban agglomeration); Moorea-Maiao 14,550; Pirae 14,499 (part of Papeete urban agglomeration). **Location:** Oceania, an archipelago in the South Pacific Ocean, about midway between South America and Australia.

Vital statistics

Birth rate per 1,000 population (2002): 19.6 (world avg. 21.3); (1996) legitimate 35.4%. **Death rate** per 1,000 population (2002): 4.5 (world avg. 9.1). **Natural increase rate** per 1,000 population (2002): 15.1 (world avg. 12.2). **Total fertility rate** (avg. births per childbearing woman; 2003): 2.1. **Marriage rate** per 1,000 population (2000): 4.6. **Life expectancy** at birth (2003): male 73.1 years; female 77.9 years.

National economy

Budget (2001). *Revenue:* CFPF 108,036,000,000 (indirect taxes 55.1%, direct taxes and nontax revenue 44.9%). *Expenditures:* CFPF 140,709,000,000 (current expenditure 68.1%, capital expenditure 31.9%). **Public debt** (external, outstanding; 1999): $542,000,000. **Production** (metric tons except as noted). *Agriculture, forestry, fishing* (2002): coconuts 88,000, copra 9,416, cassava 6,000; livestock (number of live animals) 34,000 pigs, 16,500 goats, 10,800 cattle; fish catch (2001) 15,470; export production of black pearls (1998) 6,050 kg. *Mining and quarrying:* estimated annual production of phosphates ranges from 1,000,000 to 1,200,000 tons. *Manufacturing* (1999): coconut oil 6,386; other manufactures include monoï oil (primarily refined coconut and sandalwood oils), beer, printed cloth, and sandals. *Energy production (consumption):* electricity (kW-hr; 2001) 495,000,000 (495,000,000); petroleum products (2000) none (177,000). **Population economically active** (1996): total 87,121; activity rate of total population 39.7% (participation rates: ages 14 and over, 68.3%; female 38.7%; unemployed 13.2%). **Tourism** (1999): receipts from visitors $394,000,000. **Gross national product** (at current market prices; 2001): $4,100,000,000 ($17,290 per capita). **Household income and expenditure** (1986). Average household size (1996) 4.3; average annual income per household CFPF 2,153,112; sources of income (1993): salaries 61.9%, self-employment 21.5%, transfer payments 16.6%; expendi-

---

1 metric ton = about 1.1 short tons;   1 kilometer = 0.6 mi (statute);   1 metric ton-km cargo = about 0.68 short ton-mi cargo;   c.i.f.: cost, insurance, and freight;   f.o.b.: free on board

ture: food and beverages 32.1%, household furnishings 12.3%, transportation 12.2%, energy 8.1%, recreation and education 6.9%, clothing 6.3%. **Land use** as % of total land area (2000): in temporary crops 0.8%, in permanent crops 5.5%, in pasture 5.5%; overall forest area 28.7%.

Foreign trade

Imports (2001-c.i.f.): CFPF 135,569,000,000 (machinery and apparatus 19.7%; consumer goods 16.0%; mineral fuels 8.5%). *Major import sources* (2000): France 35.9%; US 13.9%; Australia 9.3%; New Zealand 7.4%; Germany 4.8%. **Exports** (2001-f.o.b.): CFPF 18,677,000,000 (pearl products 80.0%, of which black cultured pearls 76.1%; fish 7.3%; *nono* fruit 4.6%; coconut oil 1.6%; *monoï* oil 0.8%). *Major export destinations* (2000): Japan 36.9%; Hong Kong 20.9%; France 14.5%; US 12.1%; New Caledonia 5.0%.

Transport and communications

Transport. *Roads* (1996): total length 884 km (paved 44%). *Motor vehicles:* passenger cars (1996) 47,300; trucks and buses (1993) 15,300. *Air transport* (2001): passengers carried 1,453,513; freight handled 9,834 metric tons; airports (1994) with scheduled flights 17. **Communications,** in total units (units per 1,000 persons). Daily newspaper circulation (1996): 24,000 (110); radios (1997): 128,000 (574); televisions (2000): 44,500 (189); telephone main lines (2002): 52,000 (219); cellular telephone subscribers (2002): 90,000 (375); personal computers (2002): 70,000 (292); Internet users (2002): 35,000 (146).

Education and health

Educational attainment (1996). Percentage of population age 15 and over having: no formal schooling 4.9%; primary education 37.4%; secondary 49.0%; higher 8.7%. **Literacy** (2000): total population age 15 and over literate, almost 100%. **Health** (2002): physicians 429 (1 per 568 persons); hospital beds (2003) 971 (1 per 256 persons); infant mortality rate per 1,000 live births 9.0. **Food** (2001): daily per capita caloric intake 2,889 (vegetable products 72%, animal products 28%); 127% of FAO recommended minimum.

Military

Total active duty personnel (2003): 2,400 French military personnel.

Background

European contact with the islands of French Polynesia was gradual. Portuguese navigator Ferdinand Magellan sighted Pukapuka in the Tuamotu group in 1521. The southern Marquesas Islands were discovered in 1595. Dutch explorer Jacob Roggeveen in 1722 discovered Makatea, Bora-Bora, and Maupiti. Captain Samuel Wallis in 1767 discovered Tahiti, Moorea, and Maiao Iti. The Society Islands were named after the Royal Society, which had sponsored the expedition under Capt. James Cook that observed from Tahiti the 1769 transit of the planet Venus. Tubuai was discovered on Cook's last voyage, in 1777. The islands became French protectorates in

the 1840s, and in the 1880s the French colony of Oceania was established. French Polynesia became an overseas territory of France after World War II and was granted partial autonomy in 1977.

Recent Developments

Effective 2 Mar 2004, the status of French Polynesia changed from that of a French overseas territory to that of a French overseas country that "governs itself freely and democratically through its elected representatives and by way of local referendum." In July 2005 the legislature established a committee to investigate the French aboveground nuclear testing in 1966–74. In February 2006 the committee issued its report, which contained allegations of intentional misinformation and the hiding of civilian radiation exposure by the French military. New Caledonia's economy benefited from strong nickel prices as well as a stable tourism market.

Internet resources:
<www.polynesianislands.com/fp>.

Gabon

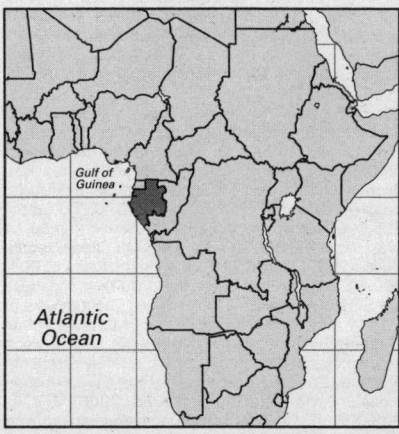

Official name: République Gabonaise (Gabonese Republic). **Form of government:** unitary multiparty republic with a Parliament comprising two legislative houses (Senate [91]; National Assembly [120]). **Chief of state:** President Omar Bongo Ondimba (from 1967). **Head of government:** Prime Minister Jean Eyeghe Ndong (from 2006). **Capital:** Libreville. **Official language:** French. **Official religion:** none. **Monetary unit:** 1 CFA franc (CFAF) = 100 centimes; valuation (1 Jul 2007) US$1 = CFAF 485.18; the CFAF is pegged to the euro (€) at €1 = 655.96 from 1 Jan 2002.

Demography

Area: 103,347 sq mi, 267,667 sq km. **Population** (2006): 1,406,000. **Density** (2006): persons per sq mi 13.6, persons per sq km 5.3. **Urban** (2003): 83.8%. **Sex distribution** (2003): male 49.59%; female 50.41%. **Age breakdown** (2003): under 15, 42.3%; 15–29, 26.3%; 30–44, 16.6%; 45–59, 8.7%; 60–74, 4.8%; 75 and over, 1.3%. **Ethnic composition**

(2000): Fang 28.6%; Punu 10.2%; Nzebi 8.9%; French 6.7%; Mpongwe 4.1%. **Religious affiliation** (2000): Christian 90.6%, of which Roman Catholic 56.6%, Protestant 17.7%; Muslim 3.1%; traditional beliefs 1.7%. **Major cities** (2003): Libreville 420,000; Port-Gentil 88,000; Franceville (1993) 30,246; Oyem 23,000; Moanda (1993) 21,921. **Location:** western Africa, bordering Cameroon, Republic of the Congo, the South Atlantic Ocean, and Equatorial Guinea.

Vital statistics

Birth rate per 1,000 population (2003): 36.5 (world avg. 21.3). **Death rate** per 1,000 population (2003): 11.2 (world avg. 9.1). **Natural increase rate** per 1,000 population (2003): 25.3 (world avg. 12.2). **Total fertility rate** (avg. births per childbearing woman; 2003): 4.8. **Life expectancy** at birth (2003): male 55.5 years; female 58.8 years. **Adult population** (ages 15–49) **living with HIV** (2004): 8.1% (world avg. 1.1%).

National economy

Budget (2001). *Revenue:* CFAF 1,190,100,000,000 (oil revenues 65.7%; taxes on international trade 17.7%; income tax 8.3%; value-added tax 5.1%; other revenues 3.2%). *Expenditures:* CFAF 976,200,000,000 (current expenditure 81.0%, of which service on public debt 31.0%, wages and salaries 21.9%, transfers 14.3%; capital expenditure 19.0%). **Public debt** (external, outstanding; 2002): $3,231,000,000. **Tourism:** receipts from visitors (2001) $7,000,000; expenditures by nationals abroad (2002) $219,000,000. **Gross national product** (2003): $4,813,000,000 ($3,580 per capita). **Production** (metric tons except as noted). *Agriculture, forestry, fishing* (2003): plantains 170,000, yams 155,000, sugarcane 135,000; livestock (number of live animals) 212,000 pigs, 195,000 sheep; roundwood (2003) 3,106,710 cu m; fish catch (2001) 40,559. *Mining and quarrying* (2002): manganese ore 1,816,000; gold 70 kg (excludes about 400 kg of illegally mined gold smuggled out of Gabon). *Manufacturing* (value added in $'000,000; 1995): wood products (excluding furniture) 44; refined petroleum products 25; food products 22. *Energy production (consumption):* electricity (kW-hr; 2000) 1,354,000,000 (1,354,000,000); crude petroleum (barrels; 2002) 108,000,000 ([2000] 5,610,000); petroleum products (2000) 593,400 (590,000); natural gas (cu m; 2000) 810,000,000 (810,000,000). **Population economically active** (2000): total 555,000; activity rate of total population 44.1% (participation rates [1985] ages 15–64, 68.2%; female 44.5%; unemployed [1996] 20%). **Households.** Average household size (2000) 6.1. **Land use** as % of total land area (2000): in temporary crops 1.3%, in permanent crops 0.7%, in pasture 18.1%; overall forest area 84.7%.

Foreign trade

Imports (2003): CFAF 602,000,000,000 (for petroleum sector 27.9%, other unspecified 72.1%). *Major import sources* (2000): France 44%; US 11%; The Netherlands 5%; Germany 3%; Spain 3%. **Exports** (2003): CFAF 1,842,000,000,000 (crude petroleum and petroleum products 80.5%, wood 10.2%, manganese ore and concentrate 4.8%). *Major export destinations* (2000): US 63%; China 7%; Australia 6%; France 4%; South Korea 4%.

Transport and communications

Transport. *Railroads* (2002): route length 814 km; (2002) passenger-km 97,500,000; (2002) metric ton-km cargo carried 1,553,000,000. *Roads* (1996): total length 7,670 km (paved 8%). *Vehicles* (1997): passenger cars 24,750; trucks and buses 16,490. *Air transport* (2000): passenger-km 1,204,000,000; airports (1997) 17. **Communications**, in total units (units per 1,000 persons). Daily newspaper circulation (1997): 33,000 (30); radios (2000) 630,000 (501); televisions (2002): 400,000 (308); telephone main lines (2003): 38,400 (29); cellular telephone subscribers (2003): 300,000 (224); personal computers (2003): 30,000 (22); Internet users (2003): 35,000 (26).

Education and health

Educational attainment of economically active population (1993): no formal schooling and incomplete primary education 37.7%; complete primary 32.1%; complete secondary 16.4%; postsecondary certificate or degree 13.8%. **Literacy** (2000): total population age 15 and over literate 71%; males literate 80%; females literate 62%. **Health:** physicians (1995) 321 (1 per 3,455 persons); hospital beds (1995) 4,631 (1 per 240 persons); infant mortality rate per 1,000 live births (2003) 55.1. **Food** (2001): daily per capita caloric intake 2,602 (vegetable products 87%, animal products 13%); 111% of FAO recommended minimum.

Military

Total active duty personnel (2003): 4,700 (army 68.1%, navy 10.6%, air force 21.3%); French troops (2003) 800. **Military expenditure as percentage of GNP** (1999): 2.4% (world 2.4%); per capita expenditure $78.

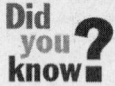

Did you know? The top green stripe on Gabon's flag represents the extensive forests in the country. The yellow stripe in the center symbolizes the equator, which bisects the country, and the bottom blue stripe symbolizes the Atlantic Ocean.

Background

Artifacts dating from late Paleolithic and early Neolithic times have been found in Gabon, but it is not known when the Bantu speakers who established Gabon's ethnic composition arrived. Pygmies were probably the original inhabitants. The Fang arrived in the late 18th century and were followed by the Portuguese and by French, Dutch, and English traders. The slave trade dominated commerce in the 18th and much of the 19th century. The French then took control, and Gabon was administered (1843–86) with

1 metric ton = about 1.1 short tons;   1 kilometer = 0.6 mi (statute);   1 metric ton-km cargo = about 0.68 short ton-mi cargo;   c.i.f.: cost, insurance, and freight;   f.o.b.: free on board

French West Africa. In 1886 the colony of French Congo was established to include both Gabon and the Congo; in 1910 Gabon became a separate colony within French Equatorial Africa. An overseas territory of France from 1946, it became an autonomous republic within the French Community in 1958 and declared its independence in 1960. Rule by a sole political party was established in the 1960s, but discontent with it led to riots in Libreville in 1990. Legalization of opposition parties led to new elections in 1990. Peace negotiations with Chadian rebels and with the Republic of the Congo were ongoing in the 1990s.

Recent Developments

Gabon benefited from soaring worldwide oil prices in 2005 and 2006, and record revenues poured in. The prevailing thought was that the country's reserves were dwindling, however, and in 2005 the IMF recommended that the government set aside a portion of the revenues for debt payment and future needs. In 2006 the UN estimated that two-thirds of the people of Gabon lived below the poverty line, surviving on less than $1 a day.

Internet resources: <www.gabonnews.com>.

The Gambia

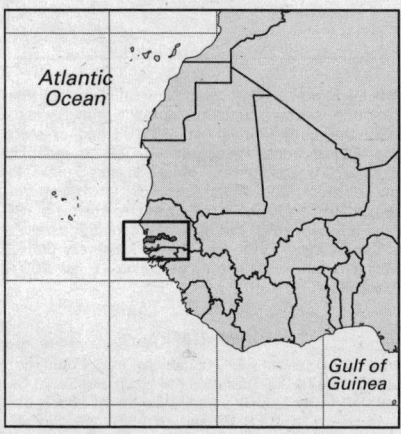

Official name: The Republic of The Gambia. Form of government: multiparty republic with one legislative house (National Assembly [53, including 5 nonelective seats]). Head of state and government: President Col. Yahya Jammeh (from 1994). Capital: Banjul. Official language: English. Official religion: none. Monetary unit: 1 dalasi (D) = 100 butut; valuation (1 Jul 2007) US$1 = D 27.36.

Demography

Area (including inland water area of 802 sq mi [2,077 sq km]): 4,127 sq mi, 10,689 sq km. Population (2006): 1,556,000. Density (2006; based on land area only): persons per sq mi 468.0, persons per sq km 180.7. Urban (2003): 26.1%. Sex distribution (2003): male 49.59%; female 50.41%. Age breakdown (2003): under 15, 44.9%; 15–29, 26.4%;

30–44, 15.5%; 45–59, 8.8%; 60–74, 3.6%; 75 and over, 0.8%. Ethnic composition (1993): Malinke 34.1%; Fulani 16.2%; Wolof 12.6%; Diola 9.2%; Soninke 7.7%; other 20.2%. Religious affiliation (1993): Muslim 95.0%; Christian 4.1%; traditional beliefs and other 0.9%. Major cities/urban areas (2003): Kanifing 322,410 (Kanifing includes the urban areas of Serekunda and Bakau); Brikama 63,000; Banjul 34,828 (Greater Banjul 523,589 [Kanifing and Banjul make up most of Greater Banjul]). Location: western Africa, bordering Senegal on three sides and the North Atlantic Ocean.

Vital statistics

Birth rate per 1,000 population (2003): 40.8 (world avg. 21.3). Death rate per 1,000 population (2003): 12.4 (world avg. 9.1). Natural increase rate per 1,000 population (2003): 28.4 (world avg. 12.2). Total fertility rate (avg. births per childbearing woman; 2002): 5.5. Life expectancy at birth (2003): male 52.4 years; female 56.4 years.

National economy

Budget (2002). Revenue: D 1,528,700,000 (tax revenue 68.0%, of which taxes on international trade 39.1%, corporate taxes 11.6%; grants 21.4%; nontax revenue 10.6%). Expenditures: D 1,870,700,000 (current expenditure 70.5%, of which interest payments 19.8%; capital expenditure 29.5%). Production (metric tons except as noted). Agriculture, forestry, fishing (2002): millet 84,618, peanuts (groundnuts) 71,526, paddy rice 20,452; livestock (number of live animals) 327,000 cattle, 262,000 goats, 146,000 sheep; roundwood (2001) 724,000 cu m; fish catch (2001) 34,527, of which Atlantic Ocean 32,037, inland water 2,490. Mining and quarrying: sand, clay, and gravel are excavated for local use. Manufacturing (value added in $; 1995): food products and beverages 6,000,000; textiles, clothing, and footwear 750,000; wood products 550,000. Energy production (consumption): electricity (kW-hr; 2001) 134,000,000 (134,000,000); petroleum products (2000) none (88,000). Population economically active (1998): total 575,140; activity rate of total population 47.3% (participation rates: ages 15–64, 86.6%; female 40.0%). Tourism (2000): receipts from visitors $48,000,000; expenditures by nationals abroad (1997) $16,000,000. Households. Average household size (2000) 7.9; expenditure (1991; low-income population in Banjul and Kanifing only): food and beverages 58.0%, clothing and footwear 17.5%, energy and water 5.4%, housing 5.1%, education, health, transportation and communications, recreation, and other 14.0%. Public debt (external, outstanding; 2002): $503,600,000. Gross national product (at current market prices; 2003): $442,000,000 ($310 per capita). Land use as % of total land area (2000): in temporary crops 23.0%, in permanent crops 0.5%, in pasture 45.9%; overall forest area 48.1%.

Foreign trade

Imports (2002-c.i.f.): $160,100,000 (imports for reexport comprise 36.0% of total; food and live animals 23.5%; machinery and transport equipment 17.0%; petroleum products 10.6%). Major import sources: EU 31.0%; China 22.3%; Senegal 9.2%. Exports (2002-f.o.b.): $111,000,000 (reexports 70.4%;

peanuts [groundnuts] 21.6%; fruits and vegetables 3.7%; fish and fish products 2.6%). *Major export destinations:* EU 76.6%; Asian countries 16.7%.

Transport and communications

Transport. *Roads* (1999): total length 2,700 km (paved 35%). *Vehicles* (1997): passenger cars 7,267; trucks and buses (1996) 9,000. *Air transport* (2001; Yumdum International Airport at Banjul): passenger arrivals 300,000, passenger departures 300,000; cargo loaded and unloaded 2,700 metric tons; airports (2000) with scheduled flights 1. **Communications,** in total units (units per 1,000 persons). Daily newspaper circulation (2000): 39,400 (30); radios (2000): 520,000 (396); televisions (2000): 3,940 (3); telephone main lines (2002): 38,400 (29); cellular telephone subscribers (2002): 100,000 (75); personal computers (2002): 19,000 (14); Internet users (2002): 25,000 (19).

Education and health

Literacy (1998): total population age 15 and over literate 34.6%; males literate 41.9%; females literate 27.5%. **Health** (2000): physicians 105 (1 per 12,977 persons); hospital beds 1,140 (1 per 1,199 persons); infant mortality rate per 1,000 live births (2003) 74.9. **Food** (2002): daily per capita caloric intake 2,273 (vegetable products 94%, animal products 6%); 96% of FAO recommended minimum.

Military

Total active duty personnel (2003): 800 (army 100%). **Military expenditure as percentage of GNP** (1999): 1.3% (world 2.4%); per capita expenditure $12.

Background

Beginning about the 13th century AD, the Wolof, Malinke, and Fulani peoples settled in different parts of what is now The Gambia and established villages and then kingdoms in the region. European exploration began when the Portuguese sighted the Gambia River in 1455. Britain and France both settled in the area in the 17th century. The British Fort James, on an island about 20 mi (32 km) from the river's mouth, was an important collection point for the slave trade. In 1783 the Treaty of Versailles reserved the Gambia River for Britain. After the British abolished slavery in 1807, they built a fort at the mouth of the river to block the continuing slave trade. In 1889 The Gambia's boundaries were agreed upon by Britain and France; the British declared a protectorate over the area in 1894. Independence was proclaimed in 1965, and The Gambia became a republic within the Commonwealth in 1970. It formed a limited confederation with Senegal in 1982 that was dissolved in 1989. During the 1990s the government was in turmoil.

Recent Developments

Freedom of the press had been severely limited by laws passed in December 2004. A leading editor and opponent of these laws was murdered in that month, and another editor was jailed and his paper closed after he tried to report a coup attempt in 2006. In September 2006 the government issued licenses to a Canadian company for the exploration and development of petroleum fields in two offshore blocks.

Internet resources: <www.visitthegambia.gm>.

Georgia

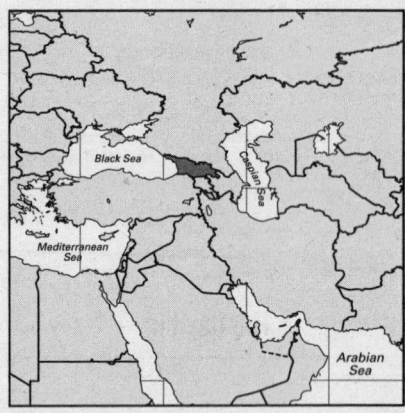

Official name: Sak'art'velo (Georgia). **Form of government:** unitary multiparty republic with a single legislative body (Parliament [235]). **Head of state and government:** President Mikheil Saakashvili (from 2004), assisted by Prime Minister Zurab Nogaideli (from 2005). **Capital:** Tbilisi. **Official language:** Georgian (locally Abkhazian, in Abkhazia). **Official religion:** none; but special recognition is given to the Georgian Orthodox Church. **Monetary unit:** 1 Georgian lari = 100 tetri; valuation (1 Jul 2007) US$1 = 1.77 lari.

Demography

Area: 27,086 sq mi, 70,152 sq km. **Population** (2006): 4,474,000 (includes Abkhazia and South Ossetia). **Density** (2006): persons per sq mi 165.2, persons per sq km 63.8. **Urban** (2002): 52.3%. **Sex distribution** (2002): male 47.16%; female 52.84%. **Age breakdown** (2002): under 15, 21.0%; 15–29, 22.8%; 30–44, 21.9%; 45–59, 15.6%; 60–74, 14.6%; 75 and over, 4.1%. **Ethnic composition** (2000): Georgian 57.9%; Mingrelian 9.1%; Armenian 8.1%; Russian 6.3%; Azerbaijani 5.7%; Ossetian 3.0%; Greek 1.9%; Abkhazian 1.8%; other 6.2%. **Religious affiliation** (1995): Christian 46.2%, of which Georgian Orthodox 36.7%, Armenian Apostolic 5.6%, Russian Orthodox 2.7%, other Christian 1.2%; Sunni Muslim 11.0%; other (mostly nonreligious) 42.8%. **Major cities** (2002): Tbilisi 1,081,679; K'ut'aisi 185,965; Bat'umi 121,806; Rust'avi 116,348; Sokhumi (1994) 112,000. **Location:** Caucasus region of southwestern Asia, bordering Russia, Azerbaijan, Armenia, Turkey, and the Black Sea.

---

1 metric ton = about 1.1 short tons;   1 kilometer = 0.6 mi (statute);   1 metric ton-km cargo = about 0.68 short ton-mi cargo;   c.i.f.: cost, insurance, and freight;   f.o.b.: free on board

Vital statistics

Birth rate per 1,000 population (2003): 10.0 (world avg. 21.3). **Death rate** per 1,000 population (2003): 8.9 (world avg. 9.1). **Natural increase rate** per 1,000 population (2003): 1.1 (world avg. 12.2). **Total fertility rate** (avg. births per childbearing woman; 2003): 1.4. **Marriage rate** per 1,000 population (2001): 2.7. **Divorce rate** per 1,000 population (2001): 0.4. **Life expectancy** at birth (2003): male 72.1 years; female 79.2 years.

National economy

Budget (2002). *Revenue:* 928,600,000 lari (tax revenue 83.1%, of which value-added tax 40.4%, social security tax 17.4%, excise tax 11.3%; nontax revenue 8.5%; grants 8.4%). *Expenditures:* 920,500,000 lari (current expenditure 99.7%, of which social security and welfare 30.0%, public order 9.1%, health 4.5%, defense 4.4%, education 4.1%; capital expenditure 0.3%). **Public debt** (external, outstanding; 2002): $1,444,000,000. **Population economically active** (2000): total 1,748,800 (excludes informal sector, which was about 750,000 persons in 1998); activity rate of total population 35.1% (participation rates [1993]: ages 16–65 [male], 16–60 [female] 55.6%; female 47.8%; unemployed [2000] 12.0%). **Production** (metric tons except as noted). *Agriculture, forestry, fishing* (2002): potatoes 414,000, wheat 306,000, corn (maize) 290,000; livestock (number of live animals) 1,180,000 cattle, 568,000 sheep; fish catch (2001) 1,910. *Mining and quarrying* (2001): manganese ore 98,300. *Manufacturing* (value of production in $'000,000; 2001; excludes Abkhazia and South Ossetia): food products 139.6, basic metals 36.5, transport equipment 27.0. *Energy production (consumption):* electricity (kW-hr; 2001) 5,700,000,-000 (5,700,000,000); coal (2000) 7,000 (27,000); crude petroleum (barrels; 2001) 719,000 (719,000); petroleum products (2000) 10,600 (1,305,000); natural gas (cu m; 2000) 59,019,000 (1,002,000,000). **Gross national product** (2003): $3,780,000,000 ($830 per capita). **Household income and expenditure.** Average household size (2000) 4.6; sources of income (1993): wages and salaries 34.5%, benefits 21.9%, agricultural income 21.6%, other 22.0%; expenditure (1993): taxes 42.5%, retail goods 32.3%, savings 16.4%, transportation 4.2%. **Tourism** ($'000,000; 2002): receipts 472; expenditures 174. **Land use** as % of total land area (2000): in temporary crops 11.4%, in permanent crops 3.9%, in pasture 27.9%; overall forest area 43.7%.

Foreign trade

Imports (2001-c.i.f.): $684,000,000 (food [all forms] 23.8%; mineral fuels 22.7%; machinery and apparatus 18.3%; transport equipment 7.1%). *Major import sources:* Turkey 15.4%; Russia 13.3%; Azerbaijan 10.7%; Germany 10.1%; Ukraine 7.2%. **Exports** (2001-f.o.b.): $320,000,000 (beverages [including wine] 16.7%; iron and steel 15.9%; aircraft and parts 11.3%; food [all forms] 8.8%; mineral fuels 8.6%). *Major export destinations:* Russia 23.0%; Turkey 21.5%; Turkmenistan 9.0%; UK 7.2%; Switzerland 4.9%.

Transport and communications

Transport. *Railroads* (2001): 1,546 km; passenger-km 398,000,000; metric ton-km cargo 4,473,000,-000. *Roads* (2001): 20,215 km (paved 93.5%). *Vehicles* (1999): passenger cars 247,872; trucks and buses 43,421. *Air transport* (2001): passenger-km 241,000,000; metric ton-km cargo 3,000,000; airports with scheduled flights 1. **Communications,** in total units (units per 1,000 persons). Radios (2000): 2,790,000 (556); televisions (2002): 1,856,000 (357); telephone main lines (2003): 650,500 (133); cellular telephone subscribers (2003): 522,300 (107); personal computers (2002): 156,000 (31); Internet users (2003): 150,500 (31).

Health and nutrition

Health (2001): physicians 22,000 (1 per 213 persons); hospital beds 24,520 (1 per 208 persons); infant mortality rate per 1,000 live births (2002) 23.3. **Food** (2002): daily per capita caloric intake 2,354 (vegetable products 82%, animal products 18%); 92% of FAO recommended minimum.

Military

Total active duty personnel (2003): 17,500 (army 49.3%, air force 7.1%, navy 10.5%, paramilitary 33.1%). About 3,000 Russian troops acting as a buffer force between Georgians and Abkhazians were in Abkhazia in August 2004 along with about 125 UN peacekeeping troops. **Military expenditure as percentage of GNP** (1999): 1.2% (world 2.4%); per capita expenditure $33.

 **Did you know?** The world's deepest known cave is Krubera, in the Georgian republic of Abkhazia. In October 2004 a Ukrainian spelelogical expedition descended to more than 2,000 m (6,560 ft). South African gold miners, however, routinely descend below 3,400 m (11,000 ft).

Background

Ancient Georgia was the site of the kingdoms of Iberia and Colchis, whose fabled wealth was known to the ancient Greeks. The area was part of the Roman empire by 65 BC and became Christian in AD 337. For the next three centuries it was involved in the conflicts between the Byzantine and Persian empires; after 654 it was controlled by Arab caliphs, who established an emirate in Tbilisi. It was controlled by the Bagratids from the 8th to the 12th century, and the zenith of Georgia's power was reached in the reign of Queen Tamara, whose realm stretched from Azerbaijan to Circassia, forming a pan-Caucasian empire. Invasions by Mongols and Turks in the 13th and 14th centuries disintegrated the kingdom, and the fall of Constantinople (now Istanbul) to the Ottoman Turks in 1453 isolated it from western Christendom. The next three centuries saw repeated invasions by the Armenians, Turks, and Persians. Georgia sought Russian protection in 1783, and in 1801 it was annexed to Russia. After the Russian Revolution of 1917, the area was briefly independent; in 1921 a Soviet regime was installed, and in 1936 Georgia became the Georgian SSR, a full member of the Soviet Union. In 1990 a noncommunist coalition came to power in the first free elections ever held in Soviet Georgia, and in 1991 Georgia declared independence. In the 1990s, while Pres. Eduard Shevardnadze tried to steer a middle course, internal dissension resulted in conflicts with the northwestern republic of Abkhazia, and external distrust of Russian motives in the area grew. In 1992 Abkhazia reinstated its 1925 constitution and declared independence, which Georgia refused to recognize.

Recent Developments

Relations with Russia were strained in 2006. Georgian Pres. Mikheil Saakashvili publicly blamed Russia for a January explosion that disrupted Russian natural gas imports, and in late March the Russian government imposed a ban on imports of Georgian wine and mineral water. Georgia in turn threatened to block Russia's entry into the World Trade Organization. The Georgian parliament in July demanded the withdrawal of Russian peacekeeping forces from Abkhazia and from South Ossetia. In October Moscow imposed a transport blockade on Georgia and began deporting Georgian nationals in retaliation for the September arrest of four Russian servicemen on suspicion of espionage. Russia's Gazprom announced that in 2007 it would more than double the price it charged Georgia for natural gas in 2007 (though the new price would still fall below average world prices).

Internet resources:
<www.parliament.ge/gotoGeorgia.htm>.

Germany

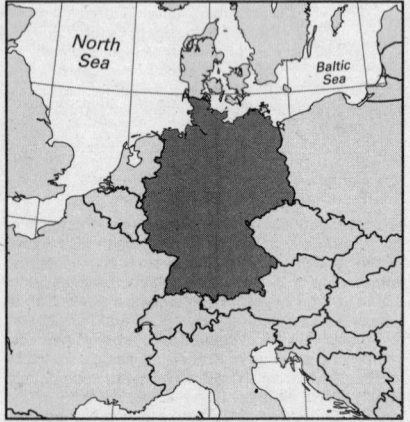

Official name: Bundesrepublik Deutschland (Federal Republic of Germany). **Form of government:** federal multiparty republic with two legislative houses (Federal Council [69]; Federal Diet [603]). **Chief of state:** President Horst Köhler (from 2004). **Head of government:** Chancellor Angela Merkel (from 2005). **Capital:** Berlin; some ministries remain in Bonn. **Official language:** German. **Official religion:** none. **Monetary unit:** 1 euro (€) = 100 cents; valuation (1 Jul 2007) US$1 = €0.74; at conversion on 1 Jan 2002, €1= 1.96 Deutsche Marks (DM).

Demography

Area: 137,847 sq mi, 357,023 sq km. **Population** (2006): 82,442,000. **Density** (2006): persons per sq mi 598.1, persons per sq km 230.9. **Urban** (2003): 88.1%. **Major cities** (2002; urban agglomerations [2000]): Berlin 3,388,434 (city population coextensive with urban agglomeration); Hamburg 1,726,363 (2,664,000); Munich 1,227,958 (2,291,000); Cologne 967,940 (3,050,000); Frankfurt am Main 641,076 (3,681,000); Essen 591,889 (6,531,000; part of the Rhine-Ruhr North urban agglomeration); Dortmund 589,240 (6,531,000); part of the Rhine-Ruhr North urban agglomeration); Stuttgart 587,152 (2,672,000); Düsseldorf 570,765 (3,233,000); Bremen 540,950 (880,000); Hannover 516,415 (1,283,000); Duisburg 512,030 (6,531,000; part of the Rhine-Ruhr North urban agglomeration); Leipzig 493,052; Nuremberg (Nürnberg) 491,307 (1,189,-000). **Location:** central Europe, bordering Denmark, the Baltic Sea, Poland, the Czech Republic, Austria, Switzerland, France, Luxembourg, Belgium, The Netherlands, and the North Sea. **Sex distribution** (2003): male 48.78%; female 51.22%. **Ethnic composition** (by nationality; 2000): German 88.2%; Turkish 3.4% (including Kurdish 0.7%); Italian 1.0%; Greek 0.7%; Serb 0.6%; Russian 0.6%; Polish 0.4%; other 5.1%. **Age breakdown** (2003): under 15, 14.9%; 15–29, 17.0%; 30–44, 24.3%; 45–59, 19.3%; 60–74, 16.9%; 75 and over, 7.6%. **Religious affiliation** (2000): Christian 75.8%, of which Protestant 35.6% (including Lutheran 33.9%), Roman Catholic 33.5%, Orthodox 0.9%, independent Christian 0.9%, other Christian 4.9%; Muslim 4.4%; Jewish 0.1%; nonreligious 17.2%; atheist 2.2%; other 0.3%. **Households** (2000). Number of households 38,124,000; average household size 2.2; 1 person 36.0%, 2 persons 33.4%, 3 persons 14.7%, 4 persons 11.5%, 5 or more persons 4.4%.

Vital statistics

Birth rate per 1,000 population (2003): 8.6 (world avg. 21.3); legitimate 73.0%; illegitimate 27.0%. **Death rate** per 1,000 population (2003): 10.3 (world avg. 9.1). **Natural increase rate** per 1,000 population (2003): –1.7 (world avg. 12.2). **Total fertility rate** (avg. births per childbearing woman; 2003): 1.4. **Marriage rate** per 1,000 population (2003): 4.6. **Divorce rate** per 1,000 population (2003): 2.6. **Life expectancy** at birth (2003): male 75.5 years; female 81.6 years.

Social indicators

Quality of working life. Average workweek (2002): 37.9 hours. Annual rate per 100,000 workers (1993) for: injuries or accidents at work 4,808; deaths, including commuting accidents, 6.7. Proportion of labor force insured for damages of income loss resulting from: injury, virtually 100%; permanent disability, virtually 100%; death, virtually 100%. Average days lost to labor stoppages per 1,000 workers (2000): 0.3. **Access to services.** Proportion of dwellings (2002) having: electricity, virtually 100%; piped water supply, virtually 100%; flush sewage disposal (1993) 98.4%; public fire protection, virtually 100%. **Social participation.** Eligible voters participating in last (September

1 metric ton = about 1.1 short tons;   1 kilometer = 0.6 mi (statute);   1 metric ton-km cargo = about 0.68 short ton-mi cargo;   c.i.f.: cost, insurance, and freight;   f.o.b.: free on board

2002) national election 79.1%. Trade union membership in total workforce (2003): c. 18%. Practicing religious population (1994): 5% of Protestants and 25% of Roman Catholics "regularly" attend religious services. **Social deviance** (2000). Offense rate per 100,000 population for: murder and manslaughter 3.8; sexual abuse 37.0, of which rape and forcible sexual assault 11.7, child molestation 10.2; assault and battery 153.2; theft 754.2. **Material well-being** (2001; median income). Households possessing: automobile 75.1%; telephone 96.4%; mobile telephone 55.7%; color television 95.9%; washing machine 95.1%; clothes dryer 33.3%; personal computer 53.4%; dishwasher 51.3%; high-speed Internet access 12.0%.

National economy

Budget (2001). *Revenue:* €922,472,000,000 (taxes 87.9%, loan interest 2.7%, other 9.4%). *Expenditures:* €972,104,000,000 (current expenditure 66.1%, of which purchase of current goods and services 22.2%, personnel costs 18.6%; capital expenditure 33.9%). **Total public debt** (2001): $1,109,680,-000,000. **Production** (value of production in € except as noted; 2002). *Agriculture, forestry, fishing:* cereal grains 4,265,000,000, fodder plants 4,148,-000,000, flowers and ornamental plants 2,797,-000,000, vegetables 1,334,000,000, sugar beets 1,267,000,000, potatoes 939,000,000, grapes for wine 929,000,000, oilseeds 876,000,000, fruits 628,000,000; livestock (number of live animals; 2003) 26,251,000 pigs, 13,732,000 cattle, 2,658,-000 sheep, 110,000,000 chickens; roundwood 42,380,000 cu m; fish catch (metric tons; 2001) 266,000. *Mining and quarrying* (metric tons; 2001): potash (potassium oxide content) 3,549,000; feldspar 500,000. *Manufacturing* (value added in $'000,000; 2000): motor vehicles 72,300; nonelectrical machinery and apparatus 71,800; chemicals (including pharmaceuticals) 62,900; food and beverages 44,700; electrical machinery and apparatus [excluding telecommunications, electronics] 38,600; fabricated metal products 37,000; petroleum products and coal derivatives 28,200; printing and publishing 25,400; rubber products and plastic products 23,700; base metals 22,100. *Energy production (consumption):* electricity (kW-hr; 2001) 565,284,-000,000 ([2000] 583,415,000,000); hard coal (2002) 26,364,000 ([2000] 64,357,000); lignite (2002) 181,416,000 ([2000] 169,942,000); crude petroleum (barrels; 2003) 30,003,000 ([2000] 775,820,000); petroleum products (2000) 98,024,-000 (104,149,000); natural gas (cu m; 2002) 24,158,000,000 ([2000] 109,387,000,000). **Gross national product** (at current market prices; 2003): $2,084,631,000,000 ($25,250 per capita). **Household income and expenditure.** Average annual income per household (1998) DM 75,144 ($42,702); sources of take-home income (1997): wages 77.6%, self-employment 12.0%, transfer payments 10.4%; expenditure (2001): housing and energy 24.5%, transportation 14.2%, food and nonalcoholic beverages 12.3%, recreation and culture 9.7%, household furnishings 7.1%, clothing and footwear 6.4%, restaurants and hotels 4.9%. **Tourism** (2002): receipts $19,158,000,000; expenditures $53,196,000,000. **Population economically active** (2002): total 40,607,000; activity rate of total population 49.3% (participation rates: ages 15–64 [2001] 71.5%; female 44.3%; unemployed 10.0%). **Land use** as % of total land area (2000): in temporary crops 33.8%, in permanent crops 0.6%, in pasture 14.5%; overall forest area 30.7%.

Foreign trade

Imports (2002-c.i.f.): €522,062,000,000 (machinery and equipment 22.6%, of which televisions, telecommunications equipment, and electronic components 6.0%, office machinery and computers 5.3%; transport equipment 14.3%, of which road vehicles 10.2%; chemicals and chemical products 10.6%; crude petroleum and natural gas 6.0%; food products and beverages 5.0%; base metals 4.8%; wearing apparel 3.1%). *Major import sources:* France 9.5%; The Netherlands 8.3%; US 7.7%; UK 6.4%; Italy 6.4%; Belgium 5.2%; Austria 4.1%; China 4.0%; Switzerland 3.7%; Japan 3.6%. **Exports** (2002-f.o.b.): €648,306,000,000 (machinery and equipment 26.3%, of which nonelectrical machinery 14.1%, televisions, telecommunications equipment, and electronic components 4.8%; transport equipment 23.4%, of which road vehicles 19.1%; chemicals and chemical products 11.8%; base metals 4.5%; medical and precision instruments and watches and clocks 4.0%). *Major export destinations:* France 10.8%; US 10.3%; UK 8.4%; Italy 7.3%; The Netherlands 6.1%; Austria 5.1%; Belgium 4.8%; Spain 4.6%; Switzerland 4.1%; Poland 2.5%.

Transport and communications

Transport. *Railroads* (2001): length 85,653 km; (2002) passenger-km 70,814,000,000; (2002) metric ton-km cargo 72,014,000,000. *Roads* (2002): total length 230,800 km (paved 99%). *Vehicles* (2002): passenger cars 44,383,300; trucks and buses 2,735,600. *Air transport* (2003; Lufthansa Group, Condor, and Eurowings only): passenger-km 112,089,000,000; metric ton-km cargo 7,088,600,000; airports (1997) 35. **Communications**, in total units (units per 1,000 persons). Daily newspaper circulation (2000): 25,100,000 (305); radios (2000): 77,900,000 (948); televisions (2002): 54,533,000 (661); telephone main lines (2003): 54,350,000 (658); cellular telephone subscribers (2003): 64,800,000 (785); personal computers (2002): 35,921,000 (435); Internet users (2003): 39,000,000 (473).

Education and health

Educational attainment (2000). Percentage of population age 25 and over having: primary and lower secondary 50.6%; intermediate secondary 17.9%; vocational secondary 8.7%; postsecondary and higher (all levels) 22.8%. **Health:** physicians (2001) 298,000 (1 per 276 persons); hospital beds (2001) 552,680 (1 per 150 persons); infant mortality rate per 1,000 live births (2002) 4.2. **Food** (2001): daily per capita caloric intake 3,567 (vegetable products 71%, animal products 29%); 134% of FAO recommended minimum.

Military

Total active duty personnel (2003): 284,500 (army 67.3%, navy 9.0%, air force 23.7%); German peacekeeping troops abroad (May 2004) 7,700; US troops in Germany (August 2004) 75,600. **Military expenditure as percentage of GNP** (1999): 1.6% (world 2.4%); per capita expenditure $395.

Background

Germanic tribes entered the region about the 2nd century BC, displacing the Celts. The Romans failed to conquer the region, which became a political entity only with the division of the Carolingian Empire in the 9th century AD. The monarchy's control was weak, and power increasingly devolved upon the nobility, organized in feudal states. The monarchy was restored under Saxon rule in the 10th century, and the Holy Roman Empire, centering on Germany and northern Italy, was revived. Continuing conflict between the Holy Roman emperors and the Roman Catholic popes undermined the empire, and its dissolution was accelerated by Martin Luther's revolt in 1517, which divided Germany, and ultimately Europe, into Protestant and Roman Catholic camps, culminating in the Thirty Years' War (1618–48). Germany's population and borders were greatly reduced, and its numerous feudal princes gained virtually full sovereignty. In 1862 Otto von Bismarck came to power in Prussia and over the next decade reunited Germany in the German Empire. It was dissolved in 1918 after the German defeat in World War I. Germany was stripped of much of its territory and all of its colonies. In 1933 Adolf Hitler became chancellor and established a totalitarian state, the Third Reich, dominated by the Nazi Party. Hitler's invasion of Poland in 1939 plunged the world into World War II. Following its defeat in 1945, Germany was divided by the Allied Powers into four zones of occupation. Disagreement with the USSR over the reunification of the zones led to the creation in 1949 of the Federal Republic of Germany (West Germany) and the German Democratic Republic (East Germany). Berlin, the former capital, remained divided. West Germany became a prosperous parliamentary democracy, East Germany a one-party state under Soviet control. The East German Communist government was brought down peacefully in 1989, and Germany was reunited in 1990. After the initial euphoria over unity, the former West Germany sought to incorporate the former East Germany both politically and economically, resulting in heavy financial burdens for the wealthier western Germans. The country continued to move toward deeper political and economic integration with Western Europe through its membership in the European Union (EU).

Recent Developments

Attention in the political sphere in 2006 focused on the reform attempts of the government. A number of measures were agreed upon, among them a federal reform package, a reform of the corporate tax system, and an increase in tax rates for Germany's highest earners. In 2006 the German military embarked on two new overseas deployments, still a deeply controversial issue in Germany. The first mission was to head the EU's rapid-reaction force deployed to the Democratic Republic of the Congo and Gabon to assist the 17,000-strong UN peacekeeping force there. In September the German navy sent eight ships and two helicopters to patrol the Lebanese coast following the cessation of hostilities between Israel and the Hezbollah militia—the first German deployment to the Middle East since World War II—raising the possibility,

however slight, of German forces firing upon Israelis. The controversy over this demonstrated that the legacy of World War II continued to influence the debate over Germany's global role.

Internet resources: <www.germany-tourism.de>.

Ghana

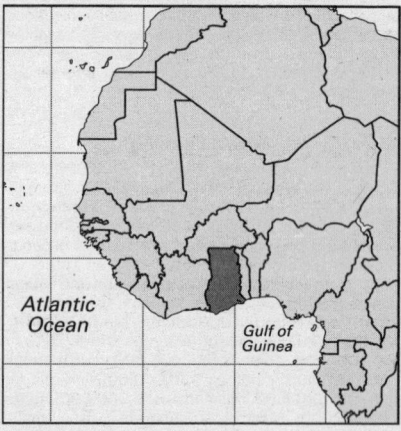

Atlantic Ocean

Gulf of Guinea

Official name: Republic of Ghana. **Form of government:** unitary multiparty republic with one legislative house (House of Parliament [230]). **Head of state and government:** President John Agyekum Kufuor (from 2001). **Capital:** Accra. **Official language:** English. **Official religion:** none. **Monetary unit:** 1 cedi (₵) = 100 pesewas; valuation (1 Jul 2007) US$1 = ₵9,438.

Demography

Area: 92,098 sq mi, 238,533 sq km. **Population** (2006): 22,410,000. **Density** (2006): persons per sq mi 243.3, persons per sq km 93.9. **Urban** (2003): 45.4%. **Sex distribution** (2000): male 49.46%; female 50.54%. **Age breakdown** (2000): under 15, 41.2%; 15–29, 28.3%; 30–44, 17.3%; 45–59, 7.9%; 60–74, 4.3%; 75 and over, 1.0%. **Ethnic composition** (2000): Akan 41.6%; Mossi 23.0%; Ewe 10.0%; Ga-Adangme 7.2%; Gurma 3.4%; Nzima 1.8%; Yoruba 1.6%; other 11.4%. **Religious affiliation** (2000): Christian 55.4%, of which Protestant 16.6%, African Christian 14.4%, Roman Catholic 9.5%; traditional beliefs 24.4%; Muslim 19.7%; other 0.5%. **Major cities** (2002): Accra 1,605,400; Kumasi 627,600; Tamale 269,200; Tema 237,700; Obuasi 122,600. **Location:** western Africa, bordering Burkina Faso, Togo, the Atlantic Ocean, and Côte d'Ivoire.

Vital statistics

Birth rate per 1,000 population (2003): 25.8 (world avg. 21.3). **Death rate** per 1,000 population (2003): 10.5 (world avg. 9.1). **Natural increase rate** per 1,000 population (2003): 15.3 (world avg. 12.2).

1 metric ton = about 1.1 short tons;   1 kilometer = 0.6 mi (statute);   1 metric ton-km cargo = about 0.68 short ton-mi cargo;   c.i.f.: cost, insurance, and freight;   f.o.b.: free on board

Total fertility rate (avg. births per childbearing woman; 2003): 3.3. Life expectancy at birth (2003): male 55.7 years; female 57.4 years.

National economy

Budget (2000). Revenue: ₵5,385,000,000,000 (tax revenue 82.0%, of which indirect taxes 37.5%, direct taxes 26.2%, trade taxes 18.3%; grants 10.7%; non-tax revenue 7.3%). Expenditures: ₵7,525,100,-000,000 (current expenditure 66.9%, capital expenditure 33.1%). Public debt (external, outstanding; 2002): $6,129,000,000. Households. Average household size (1999) 4.3. Gross national product (2003): $6,563,000,000 ($320 per capita). Production (metric tons except as noted). Agriculture, forestry, fishing (2002): roots and tubers 15,491,000 (of which cassava 9,731,000, yams 3,900,000, taro 1,860,000), bananas and plantains 2,291,000, cereals 2,162,000 (of which corn [maize] 1,407,000, sorghum 316,000, rice 280,000, millet 159,000); livestock (number of live animals) 3,410,000 goats, 2,970,000 sheep, 22,000,000 chickens; roundwood (2001) 21,979,000 cu m; fish catch (2001) 459,000. Mining and quarrying (2002): manganese (metal content) 363,000; bauxite 684,000; gold 2,241,000 troy oz. Manufacturing (value added in ₵; 1993): tobacco 71,474,700,000; footwear 60,350,600,000; chemical products 40,347,600,000. Energy production (consumption): electricity (kW-hr; 2001) 8,321,-000,000 (8,029,000,000); coal (2000) none (3,000); crude petroleum (barrels; 2000) 87,000 (8,210,000); petroleum products (2000) 1,062,000 (1,567,000). Population economically active (1999): total 11,590,000; activity rate of total population 60.5% (participation rates: over age 15 [1984] 82.5%; female 51.1%.). Tourism (2002): receipts $358,000,-000; expenditures $120,000,000. Land use as % of total land area (2000): in temporary crops 15.9%, in permanent crops 9.7%, in pasture 36.7%; overall forest area 27.8%.

Foreign trade

Imports (2000-f.o.b. in balance of trade and c.i.f. for commodities and trading partners): $2,933,000,000 (crude and refined petroleum 18.9%, machinery and apparatus 18.8%, road vehicles 11.6%, food 10.9%). Major import sources: Nigeria 10.9%; UK 9.2%; US 7.5%; Germany 7.1%; The Netherlands 6.3%; Italy 5.0%. Exports (2000): $1,671,000,000 (gold 36.7%, cocoa beans 15.5%, aluminum 9.1%, sawn wood 4.9%). Major export destinations: Switzerland 23.5%; UK 18.9%; The Netherlands 11.2%; US 5.9%; Germany 5.4%.

Transport and communications

Transport. Railroads (2000): route length 953 km; (1996) passenger-km 209,000,000; (1996) metric ton-km cargo 160,000,000. Roads (1996): total length 38,700 km (paved 40%). Vehicles (1999): passenger cars 90,400; trucks and buses 119,900. Air transport (2003; Ghana Airways only): passenger-km 906,000,000; metric ton-km cargo 16,630,000; airports (1996) with scheduled flights 1. Communications, in total units (units per 1,000 persons). Daily newspaper circulation (2000): 273,000 (14); radios (2000): 13,900,000 (710); televisions (2000): 2,300,000 (118); telephone main lines (2003): 302,300 (14); cellular telephone subscribers (2003):

799,900 (36); personal computers (2002): 82,000 (3.8); Internet users (2002): 170,000 (7.8).

Education and health

Educational attainment (1984). Percentage of population age 25 and over having: no formal schooling 60.4%; primary education 7.1%; middle school 25.4%; secondary 3.5%; vocational and other post-secondary 2.9%; higher 0.6%. Literacy (2000): total population age 15 and over literate 8,070,000 (70.2%); males literate 4,520,000 (79.8%); females literate 3,550,000 (61.2%). Health: physicians (1996) 1,058 (1 per 16,129 persons); hospital beds (1998) 26,991 (1 per 667 persons); infant mortality rate per 1,000 live births (2003) 53.0. Food (2002): daily per capita caloric intake 2,667 (vegetable products 95%, animal products 5%); 116% of FAO recommended minimum.

Military

Total active duty personnel (2003): 7,000 (army 71.4%, navy 14.3%, air force 14.3%). Military expenditure as percentage of GNP (1999): 0.8% (world 2.4%); per capita expenditure $3.

Background

The modern state of Ghana is named after the ancient Ghana empire that flourished until the 13th century AD in the western Sudan, about 500 mi (800 km) northwest of the modern state. The Akan peoples then founded their first states in modern Ghana. Gold-seeking Mande traders arrived by the 14th century, and Hausa merchants arrived by the 16th century. During the 15th century the Mande founded the states of Dagomba and Mamprussi in the northern half of the region. The Ashanti, an Akan people, originated in the central forest region and formed a strongly centralized empire that was at its height in the 18th and 19th centuries. European exploration of the region began early in the 15th century, when the Portuguese landed on the Gold Coast; they later established a settlement at Elmina as headquarters for the slave trade. By the mid-18th century the Gold Coast was dominated by numerous forts controlled by Dutch, British, and Danish merchants. Britain made the Gold Coast a crown colony in 1874, and British protectorates over the Ashanti and the northern territories were established in 1901. In 1957 the Gold Coast became the independent state of Ghana.

Recent Developments

Considered a model of African economic recovery and political reform, Ghana received attention from the international community in 2006. In May Japanese Prime Minister Junichiro Koizumi headed a trade delegation to Accra; a visit by Chinese Prime Minister Wen Jiabao followed the next month. In August a delegation of South Korean engineers studied plans for the redevelopment of a railroad that Ghana hoped would make it a gateway to West Africa. That month Ghana signed a $547 million aid package with the US Millennium Challenge Corporation for agriculture, transportation, and poverty-alleviation projects.

Internet resources:
<www.africaonline.com.gh/Tourism>.

Greece

Official name: Elliniki Dhimokratia (Hellenic Republic). **Form of government:** unitary multiparty republic with one legislative house (Greek Chamber of Deputies [300]). **Chief of state:** President Karolos Papoulias (from 2005). **Head of government:** Prime Minister Konstantinos (Kostas) Karamanlis (from 2004). **Capital:** Athens. **Official language:** Greek. **Official religion:** Eastern Orthodox. **Monetary unit:** 1 euro (€) = 100 cents; valuation (1 Jul 2007) US$1 = €0.74; at conversion on 1 Jan 2002, €1= 340.75 Greek drachma (Dr).

Demography

Area: 50,949 sq mi, 131,957 sq km. **Population** (2006): 11,130,000. **Density** (2006): persons per sq mi 218.5, persons per sq km 84.3. **Urban** (2002): 60.3%. **Sex distribution** (2001): male 49.49%; female 50.51%. **Age breakdown** (2002): under 15, 15.2%; 15–29, 22.0%; 30–44, 22.3%; 45–59, 18.0%; 60–74, 16.5%; 75 and over, 6.0%. **Ethnic composition** (2000): Greek 90.4%; Macedonian 1.8%; Albanian 1.5%; Turkish 1.4%; Pomak 0.9%; Roma (Gypsy) 0.8%; other 3.2%. **Religious affiliation** (1995): Christian 95.2%, of which Eastern Orthodox 94.0%, Roman Catholic 0.5%; Muslim 1.3%; other 3.5%. **Major cities** (2001): Athens 745,514 (urban agglomeration 3,120,000); Thessaloniki 363,987 (urban agglomeration [2000] 789,000); Piraeus (Piraievs) 175,697 (within Athens urban agglomeration); Patrai 163,446; Peristerion 137,918 (within Athens urban agglomeration); Iraklion 137,711. **Location:** southern Europe, bordering Albania, Macedonia, Bulgaria, Turkey, and the Mediterranean Sea.

Vital statistics

Birth rate per 1,000 population (2003): 9.7 (world avg. 21.3); (2001) legitimate 95.7%. **Death rate** per 1,000 population (2003): 10.0 (world avg. 9.1). **Natural increase rate** per 1,000 population (2003): –0.3 (world avg. 12.2). **Total fertility rate** (avg. births per childbearing woman; 2002): 1.3. **Marriage rate** per 1,000 population (2001): 5.7. **Life expectancy** at birth (2003): male 76.3 years; female 81.4 years.

National economy

Budget (2001). *Revenue:* Dr 20,596,049,000,000 (indirect taxes 31.9%; direct taxes 22.5%; nontax

revenue 28.9%; other 16.7%). *Expenditures:* Dr 20,596,049,000,000 (current expenditure 86.9%, of which health and social insurance 10.3%, education and culture 6.8%, defense 6.8%; capital expenditure 13.1%). **Public debt** (2001): $116,870,000,000. **Production** (metric tons except as noted). *Agriculture, forestry, fishing* (2002): sugar beets 2,780,000, wheat 2,033,000, corn (maize) 2,014,000; livestock (number of live animals) 9,205,000 sheep, 5,023,000 goats, 938,000 pigs; roundwood (2001) 1,915,930 cu m; fish catch (2001) 192,190. *Mining and quarrying:* bauxite (2001) 1,931,000; crude magnesite 483,000; marble 200,000 cu m. *Manufacturing* (value added in Dr '000,000,000; 1999): food 573; paints, soaps, varnishes, drugs, and medicines 371; electrical machinery 287. *Energy production (consumption):* electricity (kW-hr; 2000) 49,296,000,000 (49,285,000,000); hard coal (2000) none (1,121,000); lignite (2000) 63,887,000 (64,564,000); crude petroleum (barrels; 2000) 183,800 (138,800,000); petroleum products (2000) 20,265,000 (16,667,000); natural gas (cu m; 2000) 49,280,000 (2,030,900,000). **Land use** as % of total land area (2000): in temporary crops 21.3%, in permanent crops 8.6%, in pasture 36.3%; overall forest area 27.9%. **Household income and expenditure.** Average household size (2000) 3.0; income per family (1998–99) Dr 6,429,000; sources of income (1998–99): wages and salaries 35.7%, transfer payments 16.7%, self-employment 14.9%, other 32.7%; expenditure (1999): food and beverages 24.9%, transportation and communications 14.3%, cafe/hotel expenditures 9.4%, housing 8.1%, household furnishings 7.3%. **Gross national product** (2003): $146,563,000,000 ($13,720 per capita). **Population economically active** (2001): total 4,362,300; activity rate of total population 42.1% (participation rates: ages 15–64, 56.9%; female 40.2%; unemployed 10.2%). **Tourism** (2002): receipts $9,741,000,000; expenditures $2,450,000,000.

Foreign trade

Imports (2000-c.i.f.): $29,816,000,000 (machinery and apparatus 18.6%, chemicals and chemical products 11.5%, crude petroleum 10.1%, road vehicles 9.5%, food products 9.1%, ships and boats 5.2%). *Major import sources:* Italy 12.9%; Germany 12.8%; France 7.2%; The Netherlands 5.8%; UK 5.0%. **Exports** (2000-f.o.b.): $10,964,000,000 (food 14.6%, of which fruits and nuts 6.0%; clothing and apparel 12.8%; refined petroleum 12.5%; machinery and apparatus 9.8%; aluminum 4.2%). *Major export destinations:* Germany 12.3%; Italy 9.2%; UK 6.3%; US 5.8%; Turkey 5.0%.

Transport and communications

Transport. *Railroads* (2000): route length 2,299 km; passenger-km 1,629,000,000; metric ton-km cargo 427,000,000. *Roads* (1999): total length 117,000 km (paved 92%). *Vehicles* (2001): passenger cars 3,423,704; trucks and buses 1,112,926. *Air transport* (2003; Olympic Airways): passenger-km 6,240,000,000; metric ton-km cargo 55,800,000; airports (1997) 36. **Communications,** in total units (units per 1,000 persons). Daily newspaper circulation (2000): 1,530,000 (140); radios (2000): 5,220,000 (478); televisions (2000): 5,330,000

---

1 metric ton = about 1.1 short tons;   1 kilometer = 0.6 mi (statute);   1 metric ton-km cargo = about 0.68 short ton-mi cargo;   c.i.f.: cost, insurance, and freight;   f.o.b.: free on board

(488); telephone main lines (2003): 5,205,100 (454); cellular telephone subscribers (2003): 8,936,200 (785); personal computers (2002): 900,000 (82); Internet users (2003): 1,718,400 (150).

Education and health

Educational attainment (2001). Percentage of population age 25 and over having: no formal schooling/preprimary 12.7%; primary education 34.3%; lower secondary 8.5%; upper secondary 25.7%; postsecondary 3.4%; incomplete and complete higher 15.4%. **Literacy** (2000): total population age 15 and over literate 97.2%; males 98.6%; females 96.0%. **Health:** physicians (2001) 46,325 (1 per 221 persons); hospital beds (2000) 49,804 (1 per 205 persons); infant mortality rate per 1,000 live births (2003) 5.7. **Food** (2001): daily per capita caloric intake 3,754 (vegetable products 78%, animal products 22%); 150% of FAO recommended minimum.

Military

Total active duty personnel (2003): 177,600 (army 70.7%, navy 10.7%, air force 18.6%). **Military expenditure as percentage of GNP** (1999): 4.7% (world 2.4%); per capita expenditure $573.

Did you know? Rhodes is the major city of the island of Rhodes and capital of the *nomos* (department) of Dhodhekanisos (in the Dodecanese islands), Greece. In Classical history, Rhodes was a maritime power and the site of the Colossus of Rhodes, a statue that was purportedly more than 100 ft (32 m) tall.

Background

The earliest urban society in Greece was the palace-centered Minoan civilization, which reached its height on Crete c. 2000 BC. It was succeeded by the mainland Mycenaean civilization, which arose c. 1600 BC following a wave of Indo-European invasions. About 1200 BC a second wave of invasions destroyed the Bronze Age cultures, and a dark age followed, known mostly through the epics of Homer. At the end of this time, classical Greece began to emerge (c. 750 BC) as a collection of independent city-states, including Sparta in the Peloponnese and Athens in Attica. The civilization reached its zenith after repelling the Persians at the beginning of the 5th century BC and began to decline after the civil strife of the Peloponnesian War at the century's end. In 338 BC the Greek city-states were taken over by Philip II of Macedon, and Greek culture was spread by Philip's son Alexander the Great throughout his empire. The Romans, themselves heavily influenced by Greek culture, conquered the Greek states in the 2nd century BC. After the fall of Rome, Greece remained part of the Byzantine empire until the mid-15th century, when it became part of the expanding Ottoman Empire; it gained its independence in 1832. It was occupied by Nazi Germany during World War II. Civil war followed and lasted until 1949, when communist forces were defeated. In 1952 Greece joined NATO. A military junta ruled the country from 1967 to 1974, when democracy was restored and a referendum declared an end to the Greek monarchy. In 1981 Greece joined the European Community, the first Eastern European country to do so. Upheavals in the Balkans in the 1990s strained Greece's relations with some neighboring states, notably the former Yugoslav entity that took the name Republic of Macedonia.

Recent Developments

Scandals rocked Greece during 2006. In early February news broke that some 100 mobile phones, including that of Prime Minister Kostantinos (Kostas) Karamanlis, had been tapped for about a year in 2004–05, and in December Vodafone, the mobile-phone service provider in question, was fined €76 million (€1 = about $1.33). A former judge was sentenced in August to 25 years' imprisonment in the first of several trial-fixing cases. The director of the Hellenic Competition Commission was arrested in September on charges of attempting to extract a €2.5 million bribe from a major dairy firm. In September Karamanlis, Russian Pres. Vladimir Putin, and Bulgarian Pres. Georgi Purvanov announced that they would build an oil pipeline from the Bulgarian port of Burgas to Alexandroupolis, Greece.

Internet resources: <www.gnto.gr>.

Greenland

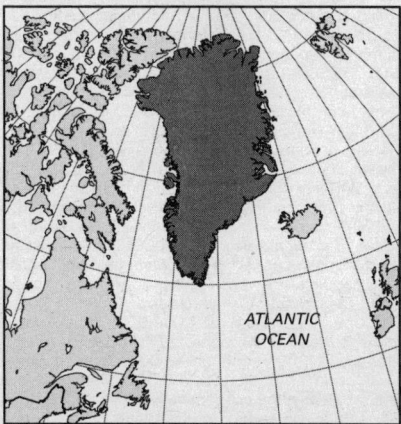

Official name: Kalaallit Nunaat (Greenlandic); Grønland (Danish) (Greenland). **Political status:** integral part of the Danish realm with one legislative house (Parliament [31]). **Chief of state:** Danish monarch Queen Margrethe II (from 1972). **Heads of government:** High Commissioner (for Denmark) Søren Hald Møller (from 2005); Prime Minister (for Greenland) Hans Enoksen (from 2002). **Capital:** Nuuk (Godthåb). **Official languages:** Greenlandic; Danish. **Official religion:** Evangelical Lutheran (Lutheran Church of Greenland). **Monetary unit:** 1 Danish krone (Dkr) = 100 øre; valuation (1 Jul 2007) US$1 = Dkr 5.49.

Demography

Area: 836,330 sq mi, 2,166,086 sq km. **Population** (2006): 57,200. **Density** (2006; ice-free areas only): persons per sq mi 0.36, persons per sq km 0.14.

Urban (2003): 82.2%. **Sex distribution** (2003): male 53.37%; female 46.63%. **Age breakdown** (2003): under 15, 26.2%; 15–29, 19.7%; 30–44, 27.9%; 45–59; 17.4%; 60–74, 7.5%; 75 and over, 1.3%. **Ethnic composition** (2000): Greenland Eskimo 79.1%; Danish 13.6%; other 7.3%. **Religious affiliation** (2000): Protestant 69.2%, of which Evangelical Lutheran 64.2%, Pentecostal 2.8%; other Christian 27.4%; other/nonreligious 3.4%. **Major towns** (2003): Nuuk (Godthåb) 13,884; Sisimiut (Holsteinsborg) 5,263; Ilulissat (Jakobshavn) 4,525. **Location:** North Atlantic Ocean, east of northern Canada.

Vital statistics

Birth rate per 1,000 population (2003): 16.1 (world avg. 21.3); (1993) legitimate 29.2%. **Death rate** per 1,000 population (2003): 7.7 (world avg. 9.1). **Natural increase rate** per 1,000 population (2003): 8.4 (world avg. 12.2). **Total fertility rate** (avg. births per childbearing woman; 2003): 2.4. **Marriage rate** per 1,000 population (1993): 7.1. **Life expectancy** at birth (2003): male 65.4 years; female 72.7 years.

National economy

Budget (2001). *Revenue:* Dkr 7,648,000,000 (block grant from Danish government 37.9%; income tax 30.5%; import duties 8.8%). *Expenditures* (2001): Dkr 7,069,000,000 (current expenditure 92.1%, of which social welfare 24.1%, culture and education 21.1%, health 11.9%, defense 3.7%; capital [development] expenditure 7.9%). **Public debt** (2000): $53,000,000. **Tourism** (2002): number of overnight stays at hotels 179,349, of which visitors from within Greenland 94,552, from Denmark 55,602, from the US 6,227. **Production** (metric tons except as noted). *Fishing, animal products:* fish catch (2001) 292,000 (by local boats 143,000, of which prawn 85,800, halibut 20,700, crab 14,200; by foreign boats 149,000); livestock (number of live animals; 2002) 18,967 sheep, 3,100 reindeer; animal products (value of external sales in Dkr '000; 1998) sealskins 31,044, polar bear skins 579. *Manufacturing:* principally handicrafts and fish processing. *Energy production (consumption):* electricity (kW-hr; 2002) 311,000,000 ([2001] 284,000,000); crude petroleum (barrels; 1999) none (1,307,000); petroleum products (2000) none (181,000). **Gross national product** (1998): $1,150,000,000 ($20,500 per capita). **Population economically active** (2002): total 31,506; activity rate of total population 55.7% (participation rates: ages 15–62, 82.9%; female [1987] 43.4%; unemployed [2002] 6.5%). **Households.** Average household size (1998): 2.6; income per person (1997): Dkr 144,700; expenditure (1994): food, beverages, and tobacco 41.6%; housing and energy 22.4%; transportation and communications 10.2%; recreation 6.4%. **Land use** as % of total land area (2000): in temporary crops, negligible, in pasture 0.6%; overall forest area, negligible.

Foreign trade

Imports (2002): Dkr 2,891,000,000 (goods for trades and industries 19.8%; food, beverages, and tobacco products 16.4%; goods for construction industry 14.8%; mineral fuels 8.9%; machinery 6.8%;

transport equipment 3.1%). *Major import sources:* Denmark 70%; Norway 8%. **Exports** (2002): Dkr 2,140,000,000 (marine products 88.4%, of which shrimp 55.7%, fish 20.6%, crab 10.1%). *Major export destinations:* Denmark 88%; US 4%; UK 2%.

Transport and communications

Transport. *Roads* (1998): total length 150 km (paved 60%). *Vehicles* (2001): passenger cars 2,485; trucks and buses 1,483. *Air transport* (2001; Air Greenland A/S only): passenger-km 211,000,000; metric ton-km cargo 24,000,000; airports (1998) with scheduled flights 18. **Communications,** in total units (units per 1,000 persons). Daily newspaper circulation (1996): 1,000 (18); radios (1997): 27,000 (482); televisions (1997): 22,000 (393); telephone main lines (2002): 25,300 (447); cellular telephone subscribers (2002): 17,700 (313); Internet users (2002): 9,100 (161).

Education and health

Literacy (1999): total population age 15 and over literate: virtually 100%. **Health** (2001): physicians 89 (1 per 634 persons); hospital beds 406 (1 per 139 persons); infant mortality rate per 1,000 live births (2003) 16.8.

Military

Total active duty personnel. Denmark is responsible for Greenland's defense. Greenlanders are not liable for military service.

 **Did you know?** Greenland is the world's largest island, covering 840,000 sq mi (2,175,600 sq km) and lying in the North Atlantic Ocean. Its deeply indented coastline is 24,430 mi (39,330 km) long, a distance roughly equivalent to the Earth's circumference at the Equator.

Background

The Inuit probably crossed to northwestern Greenland from North America, along the islands of the Canadian Arctic, from 4000 BC to AD 1000. The Norwegian Erik the Red visited Greenland in 982; his son, Leif Eriksson, introduced Christianity in the 11th century. Greenland came under joint Danish-Norwegian rule in the late 14th century. The original Norse settlements became extinct in the 15th century, but Greenland was recolonized by Denmark in 1721. In 1776 Denmark closed the Greenland coast to foreign trade; it was not reopened until 1950. Greenland became part of the kingdom of Denmark in 1953. Home rule was established in 1979.

Recent Developments

The effects of global warming were clearly visible in Greenland in recent years. A study in 2006 showed that Greenland's ice sheet was melting at a rate of 239 cu km (57 cu mi) annually and that the rate was

---

1 metric ton = about 1.1 short tons;   1 kilometer = 0.6 mi (statute);   1 metric ton-km cargo = about 0.68 short ton-mi cargo;   c.i.f.: cost, insurance, and freight;   f.o.b.: free on board

increasing. In 2007 explorers continued studying an island in Greenland, long thought to be a peninsula, that had been discovered in September 2005 after melting ice revealed that it was not connected to the mainland.

Internet resources: <www.greenland.com>.

Grenada

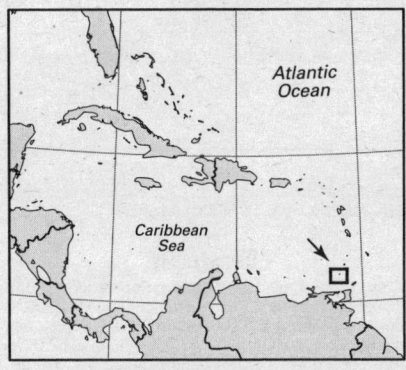

Atlantic Ocean

Caribbean Sea

Official name: Grenada. Form of government: constitutional monarchy with two legislative houses (Senate [13]; House of Representatives [15, excluding the speaker]). Chief of state: Queen Elizabeth II (from 1952), represented by Governor-General Sir Daniel Williams (from 1996). Head of government: Prime Minister Keith Mitchell (from 1995). Capital: St. George's. Official language: English. Official religion: none. Monetary unit: 1 East Caribbean dollar (EC$) = 100 cents; valuation (1 Jul 2007) US$1 = EC$2.67.

Demography

Area: 133 sq mi, 344 sq km. Population (2006): 107,000. Density (2006): persons per sq mi 804.5, persons per sq km 311.0. Urban (2001): 38.4%. Sex distribution (2001): male 49.55%; female 50.45%. Age breakdown (2001): under 15, 35.1%; 15–29, 28.1%; 30–44, 17.6%; 45–59, 9.0%; 60 and over, 10.2%. Ethnic composition (2000): black 51.7%; mixed 40.0%; Indo-Pakistani 4.0%; white 0.9%; other 3.4%. Religious affiliation (1995): Roman Catholic 57.8%; Protestant 37.6%, of which Anglican 14.4%, Pentecostal 8.3%, Seventh-day Adventist 7.0%; other 4.6%, of which Rastafarian c. 3.0%. Major localities (2001): St. George's 3,908 (urban agglomeration 35,559); Gouyave (1991) 3,100; Grenville 2,300. Location: island between the Caribbean Sea and the Atlantic Ocean, north of Trinidad and Tobago.

Vital statistics

Birth rate per 1,000 population (2003): 22.9 (world avg. 21.3). Death rate per 1,000 population (2003): 7.5 (world avg. 9.1). Natural increase rate per 1,000 population (2003): 15.4 (world avg. 12.2). Total fertility rate (avg. births per childbearing woman; 2003): 2.5. Marriage rate per 1,000 population (2001): 5.0.

Divorce rate per 1,000 population (2001): 1.1. Life expectancy at birth (2003): male 62.7 years; female 66.3 years.

National economy

Budget (2000). Revenue: EC$297,900,000 (tax revenue 89.1%, of which tax on international trade 51.3%, general sales taxes 17.1%, income taxes 17.5%; grants from abroad 10.9%). Expenditures: EC$365,700,000 (current expenditure 63.0%, of which wages 31.3%, transfers 13.2%, debt 11.3%; capital expenditure 37.0%). Public debt (external, outstanding; 2002): US$268,700,000. Tourism (2002): receipts from visitors US$84,000,000; expenditures by nationals abroad US$8,000,000. Gross national product (at current market prices; 2003): US$396,000,000 (US $3,790 per capita). Production (metric tons except as noted). Agriculture, forestry, fishing (2002): sugarcane 7,200, coconuts 6,800, bananas 4,100; livestock (number of live animals) 13,100 sheep, 7,100 goats, 5,850 pigs; fish catch (2001) 2,247. Mining and quarrying: excavation of limestone, sand, and gravel for local use. Manufacturing (value of production in EC$'000; 1997): wheat flour 13,390; soft drinks 9,798; beer 7,072. Energy production (consumption): electricity (kW-hr; 2000) 118,000,000 (118,000,000); petroleum products (2000) none (69,000). Household income and expenditure. Average household size (1991) 3.7; income per household (1988) EC$7,097; expenditure (1987): food, beverages, and tobacco 40.7%, household furnishings and operations 13.7%, housing 11.9%, transportation 9.1%. Population economically active (1998): total 41,015; activity rate of total population 46% (participation rate: ages 15–64, 78%; female 43.5%; unemployed 15.2%). Land use as % of total land area (2000): in temporary crops 3%, in permanent crops 29%, in pasture 3%; overall forest area 15%.

Foreign trade

Imports (2002-f.o.b. in balance of trade and c.i.f. for commodities and trading partners): US$233,-200,000 (machinery and transport equipment 27.4%; food 16.6%; chemicals and chemical products 11.1%; mineral fuels 9.8%). Major import sources: US 45.8%; Caricom 25.6%; EU 12.5%, of which UK 6.0%; Venezuela 4.6%. Exports (2002): US$59,700,000 (domestic exports 92.1%, of which electronic components 39.2%, nutmeg 21.4%, fish 7.4%, paper products 2.5%, cocoa beans 2.3%; reexports 7.9%). Major export destinations: US 38.9%; EU 34.5%, of which UK 1.2%; Caricom 22.2%.

Transport and communications

Transport. Roads (1999): total length 1,040 km (paved 61%). Vehicles (1991): passenger cars 4,739; trucks and buses 3,068. Air transport (2001; Point Salines airport): passengers 331,000; cargo 2,747 metric tons; airports (1998) with scheduled flights 2. Communications, in total units (units per 1,000 persons). Radios (1997): 57,000 (615); televisions (1997): 33,000 (353); telephone main lines (2002): 33,500 (317); cellular telephone subscribers (2002): 7,600 (71); personal computers (2002): 14,000 (132); Internet users (2002): 15,000 (142).

Education and health

Educational attainment (1991). Percentage of population age 25 and over having: no formal schooling 1.8%; primary education 74.9%; secondary 15.5%; higher 4.7%, of which university 2.8%; other/unknown 3.1%. Literacy (1995): total population age 15 and over literate 50,000 (85.0%). Health (1999): physicians 81 (1 per 1,233 persons); hospital beds (2000) 623 (1 per 161 persons); infant mortality rate per 1,000 live births (2003) 14.6. Food (2002): daily per capita caloric intake 2,932 (vegetable products 74%, animal products 26%); 121% of FAO recommended minimum.

Military

Total active duty personnel (1997): a 730-member police force includes an 80-member paramilitary unit and a 30-member coast guard unit.

Background

The warlike Carib Indians dominated Grenada when Christopher Columbus sighted the island in 1498 and named it Concepción; they ruled it for the next 150 years. In 1674 it became subject to the French crown and remained so until 1762, when British forces captured it. In 1833 the island's black slaves were freed. Grenada was the headquarters of the government of the British Windward Islands 1885–1958 and a member of the West Indies Federation 1958–62. It became a self-governing state in association with Britain in 1967 and gained its independence in 1974. In 1979 a left-wing government took control in a bloodless coup. Relations with its US-oriented Latin American neighbors became strained as Grenada leaned toward Cuba and the Soviet bloc. In order to counteract this trend, the US invaded the island in 1983; democratic self-government was reestablished in 1984. Its relations with Cuba, once suspended, were restored in 1997.

Recent Developments

In January 2005 Grenada established diplomatic relations with China, severing ties with Taiwan in the process. China responded by offering in March of that year to rebuild the national stadium damaged in September 2004 by Hurricane Ivan.

Internet resources: <www.grenadagrenadines.com>.

Guadeloupe

Official name: Département de la Guadeloupe (Department of Guadeloupe). Political status: overseas department (France) with two legislative houses (General Council [42]; Regional Council [41]). Chief of state: President Nicolas Sarkozy of France (from 2007). Heads of government: Prefect Jean-Jacques Brot (from 2006); President of the General Council Jacques Gillot (from 2001); President of the Regional Council Victorin Lurel (from 2004). Capital: Basse-Terre. Official language: French. Official religion: none. Monetary unit: 1 euro (€) = 100 cents; valua-

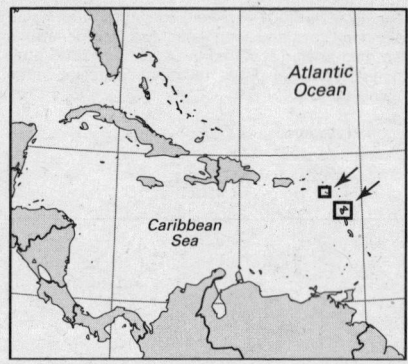

tion (1 Jul 2007) US$1 = €0.74; at conversion on 1 Jan 2002, €1 = 6.56 French francs (F).

Demography

Area: 658 sq mi, 1,705 sq km. Population (2006): 458,000. Density (2006): persons per sq mi 696.0, persons per sq km 268.6. Urban (2001): 99.6%. Sex distribution (2002): male 47.93%; female 52.07%. Age breakdown (1999): under 15, 23.6%; 15–29, 22.4%; 30–44, 24.3%; 45–59, 15.7%; 60–74, 9.3%; 75 and over, 4.7%. Ethnic composition (2000): Creole (mulatto) 76.7%; black 10.0%; Guadeloupe mestizo (French–East Asian) 10.0%; white 2.0%; other 1.3%. Religious affiliation (1995): Roman Catholic 81.1%; Jehovah's Witness 4.8%; Protestant 4.7%; other 9.4%. Major communes (1999): Les Abymes 63,054 (within Pointe-à-Pitre urban agglomeration); Saint-Martin (Marigot) 29,078; Le Gosier 25,360 (within Pointe-à-Pitre urban agglomeration); Pointe-à-Pitre 20,948 (urban agglomeration 171,773); Basse-Terre 12,410 (urban agglomeration 54,076). Location: islands in the eastern Caribbean Sea, southeast of Puerto Rico.

Vital statistics

Birth rate per 1,000 population (2003): 16.2 (world avg. 21.3); (1997) legitimate 37.0%. Death rate per 1,000 population (2003): 6.0 (world avg. 9.1). Natural increase rate per 1,000 population (2003): 10.2 (world avg. 12.2). Total fertility rate (avg. births per childbearing woman; 2003): 1.9. Marriage rate per 1,000 population (2002): 4.1. Divorce rate per 1,000 population (1997): 1.3. Life expectancy at birth (2003): male 74.4 years; female 80.8 years.

National economy

Budget (1998). Revenue: F 4,227,000,000 (tax revenues 69.0%, of which direct taxes 42.5%, value-added taxes 25.1%; advances, loans, and transfers 26.8%). Expenditures: F 7,874,000,000 (current expenditures 70.6%, capital [development] expenditures 10.6%; advances and loans 18.8%). Production (metric tons except as noted). Agriculture, forestry, fishing (2002): sugarcane 798,072, bananas 135,000, yams 10,032; livestock (number of

1 metric ton = about 1.1 short tons;   1 kilometer = 0.6 mi (statute);   1 metric ton-km cargo = about 0.68 short ton-mi cargo;   c.i.f.: cost, insurance, and freight;   f.o.b.: free on board

live animals) 85,000 cattle, 28,000 goats; round-wood (2001) 15,300 cu m; fish catch (2001) 10,114. *Mining and quarrying* (2000): pumice 210,000. *Manufacturing* (2002): cement 284,000; raw sugar 51,726; rum 67,151 hectoliters. *Energy production (consumption)*: electricity (kW-hr; 2000) 1,220,000,000 (1,220,000,000); petroleum products (2000) none (497,000). **Land use** as % of total land area (2000): in temporary crops 11%, in permanent crops 4%, in pasture 14%; overall forest area 48%. **Population economically active** (1999): total 191,362; activity rate of total population 45.3% (participation rates: ages 15–64 [1995] 73.2%; female 49.1%; unemployed [2003] 24.1%). **Gross national product** (2000): $6,148,000,000 ($14,370 per capita). **Household income and expenditure.** Average household size (1999) 2.9; disposable income per household (1999) €26,938; sources of income (1988): wages and salaries 78.9%, self-employment 12.7%, transfer payments 8.4%; expenditure (1994–95): housing 26.2%, food and beverages 21.4%, transportation and communications 14.1%, household durables 6.0%, culture and leisure 4.2%. **Tourism** (2000): receipts from visitors $418,000,000.

Foreign trade

Imports (2001): €1,835,000,000 (food and agriculture products 19.8%, consumer goods 18.6%, machinery and equipment 15.8%). *Major import sources* (1998): France 63.4%; Germany 4.4%; Italy 3.5%; Martinique 3.4%; US 2.9%. **Exports** (2001): €169,000,000 (food and agricultural products 58.4% [including bananas, sugar, rum, melons, eggplant, and flowers]). *Major export destinations* (1998): France 68.5%; Martinique 9.4%; Italy 4.8%; Belgium-Luxembourg 3.3%; French Guiana 3.0%.

Transport and communications

Transport. *Roads* (1998): total length 3,415 km (paved [1986] 80%). *Vehicles* (1999): passenger cars 117,700; trucks and buses 31,400. *Air transport* (2002): passenger arrivals and departures 1,807,400; cargo handled 16,179 metric tons, cargo unloaded 5,204 metric tons; airports (1997) with scheduled flights 7. **Communications,** in total units (units per 1,000 persons). Daily newspaper circulation (1995): 35,000 (81); radios (1997): 113,000 (258); televisions (1999): 118,000 (262); telephone main lines (2001): 210,000 (457); cellular telephone subscribers (2002): 323,500 (697); personal computers (2001): 100,000 (217); Internet users (2001): 20,000 (43).

Education and health

Educational attainment (1990). Percentage of population age 25 and over having: incomplete primary, or no declaration 59.8%; primary education 14.5%; secondary 19.0%; higher 6.7%. **Literacy** (1992): total population age 15 and over literate 225,400 (90.1%); males literate 108,700 (89.7%); females literate 116,700 (90.5%). **Health** (2001): physicians 835 (1 per 515 persons); hospital beds 2,435 (1 per 177 persons); infant mortality rate per 1,000 live births (2003) 9.1. **Food** (1995): daily per capita caloric intake 2,732 (vegetable products 75%, animal products 25%); 129% of FAO recommended minimum.

Military

Total active duty personnel (2003): French troops in Antilles (Guadeloupe and Martinique) 4,100.

Background

The Carib Indians held off the Spanish and French for a number of years before the islands of Guadeloupe became part of France in 1674. The British occupied Guadeloupe for short periods in the 18th and 19th centuries; the islands became officially French in 1816. In 1946 Guadeloupe was made an overseas territory of France. Tourism has benefited the economy in recent decades.

Recent Developments

Until a 2003 referendum, Guadeloupe administered Saint-Martin (the French part of the island of Saint Martin; Dutch Sint Maarten occupies the other part) and Saint-Barthélemy. The vote was in favor of separate status with France, as distinct from being subprefectures of Guadeloupe. Meanwhile, Guadeloupe and Martinique rejected Paris's proposed merger of their regional and general councils.

Internet resources: <www.guadeloupe-info.com>.

Guam

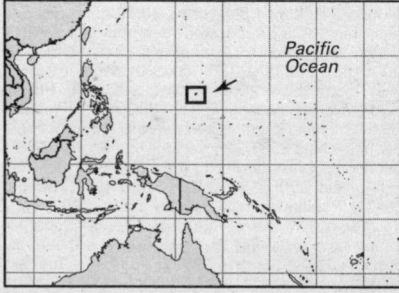

Pacific Ocean

Official name: Teritorion Guam (Chamorro); Territory of Guam (English). **Political status:** self-governing, organized, unincorporated territory of the US with one legislative house (Guam Legislature [15]). **Chief of state:** President of the US George W. Bush (from 2001). **Head of government:** Governor Felix Camacho (from 2003). **Capital:** Hagåtña (Agana). **Official languages:** Chamorro; English. **Official religion:** none. **Monetary unit:** 1 US dollar (US$) = 100 cents.

Demography

Area: 209 sq mi, 541 sq km. **Population** (2006): 172,000. **Density** (2006; based on land area): persons per sq mi 823.0, persons per sq km 317.9. **Urban** (2003): 93.7%. **Sex distribution** (2000): male 51.15%; female 48.85%. **Age breakdown** (2000): under 15, 30.5%; 15–29, 24.1%; 30–44, 23.3%; 45–59, 13.9%; 60–74, 6.7%; 75 and over, 1.5%. **Ethnic composition** (2000): Pacific Islander 44.6%, of which Chamorro 37.0%; Asian 32.5%, of which Filipino 26.3%, Korean 2.5%; white 6.8%; black 1.0%; mixed 13.9%; other 1.2%. **Religious affiliation**

(1995): Roman Catholic 74.7%; Protestant 12.8%; other Christian 2.4%; other 10.1%. **Major populated places** (2000): Tamuning 10,833; Mangilao 7,794; Yigo 6,391; Astumbo 5,207; Hagåtña 1,122. **Location:** Oceania, island in the North Pacific Ocean, south of the Northern Mariana Islands.

Vital statistics

Birth rate per 1,000 population (2003): 19.7 (world avg. 21.3); (2000) legitimate 45.4%. **Death rate** per 1,000 population (2003): 4.3 (world avg. 9.1). **Natural increase rate** per 1,000 population (2002): 15.4 (world avg. 12.2). **Total fertility rate** (avg. births per childbearing woman; 2003): 2.6. **Marriage rate** per 1,000 population (2000): 9.7. **Divorce rate** per 1,000 population (2000): 4.0. **Life expectancy** at birth (2003): male 74.8 years; female 81.0 years.

National economy

Budget (2001). *Revenue:* $662,994,000 (local taxes 63.6%, federal contributions 27.4%, other 9.0%). *Expenditures:* $518,433,000 (current expenditures 91.6%, capital expenditures 8.4%). **Production**. *Agriculture, forestry, fishing* (value of production in $'000; 2000): long beans 234, cucumbers 166, watermelons 106; livestock (number of live animals [2002]) 200,000 poultry, 5,000 pigs, 680 goats; fish catch (metric tons; 2001) 507, value of aquaculture production (1996) $1,442,000. *Mining and quarrying:* sand and gravel. *Manufacturing* (value of sales in $'000; 2002): food processing 26,733; printing and publishing 7,382; fabricated metal products 4,052. *Energy production (consumption):* electricity (kW-hr; 2000) 830,000,000 (830,000,000); petroleum products (metric tons; 2000) none (1,327,000). **Households.** Average household size (2000) 3.9 (excludes US military and dependents); average annual income per household $38,983 (excludes US military and dependents). **Gross domestic product** (at current market prices; 2000): $3,419,920,000 ($22,120 per capita). **Population economically active** (2001): total 64,800; activity rate of total population 42% (participation rates: over age 15, 55.8%; female 45.1%; unemployed [September 2001] 13.5%). **Tourism** (1999): receipts from visitors $1,908,000,000. **Land use** as % of total land area (2000): in temporary crops 9%, in permanent crops 16%, in pasture 15%; overall forest area 38%.

Foreign trade

Imports (2001): $503,000,000 (food products and nonalcoholic beverages 32%; leather products including footwear 20%; motor vehicles and parts 12%; clothing 8%). *Major import sources:* significantly US and Japan. **Exports** (2001): $60,800,000 (food products 52.2%, of which fish 51.4%; petroleum and natural gas products 6.2%; perfumes and colognes 6.0%; tobacco products 5.8%). *Major export destinations:* Japan 50.0%; Palau 9.4%; Federated States of Micronesia 9.1%; Hong Kong 7.4%; Taiwan 4.7%.

Transport and communications

Transport. *Roads* (1999): total length 885 km (paved 76%). *Vehicles* (2001): passenger cars 64,018; trucks and buses 28,322. *Air transport* (2003; Continental Micronesia only): passenger-km 3,697,000,000; metric ton-km cargo 61,256,000; airports with scheduled flights 1. **Communications,** in total units (units per 1,000 persons). Daily newspaper circulation (1996): 28,000 (178); radios (1997): 221,000 (1,400); televisions (1997): 106,000 (668); telephone main lines (2002): 76,425 (478); cellular telephone subscribers (2001): 32,600 (207); Internet users (2002): 50,000 (313).

Education and health

Educational attainment (2000). Percentage of population age 25 and over having: no formal schooling to some secondary education 23.7%; completed secondary 31.9%; some higher 24.5%; undergraduate 15.3%; advanced degree 4.6%. **Literacy:** virtually 100%. **Health** (1999): physicians 130 (1 per 1,169 persons); hospital beds 192 (1 per 792 persons); infant mortality rate per 1,000 live births (2003) 7.4.

Military

Total active duty US personnel (2003): 3,293 (army 1.2%; navy 45.5%; air force 53.3%).

Background

Possibly visited by Ferdinand Magellan in 1521, Guam was formally claimed by Spain in 1565. It remained Spanish until it was ceded to the US after the Spanish-American War in 1898. During World War II the Japanese occupied the island (1941–44). It subsequently became a major US air and naval base. In 1950 it was made a US territory.

Recent Developments

It was announced in 2005 that the US and Japan had reached an agreement to transfer about 8,000 Marines and 10,000 of their dependents from the Japanese island of Okinawa to Guam between 2006 and 2014. In addition, the military planned to spend $15 billion on new infrastructure in Guam in support of this move.

Internet resources: <http://ns.gov.gu>.

Guatemala

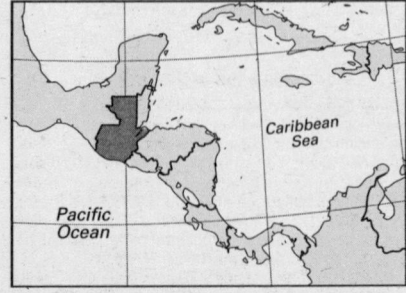

---

1 metric ton = about 1.1 short tons;   1 kilometer = 0.6 mi (statute);   1 metric ton-km cargo = about 0.68 short ton-mi cargo;   c.i.f.: cost, insurance, and freight;   f.o.b.: free on board

Official name: República de Guatemala (Republic of Guatemala). **Form of government:** republic with one legislative house (Congress of the Republic [158]). **Head of state and government:** President Óscar Berger Perdomo (from 2004). **Capital:** Guatemala City. **Official language:** Spanish. **Official religion:** none. **Monetary unit:** 1 quetzal (Q) = 100 centavos; valuation (1 Jul 2007) US$1 = Q 7.85.

Demography

Area: 42,130 sq mi, 109,117 sq km. **Population** (2006): 13,019,000. **Density** (2006): persons per sq mi 309.0, persons per sq km 119.3. **Urban** (2003): 46.3%. **Sex distribution** (2003): male 50.67%; female 49.33%. **Age breakdown** (2003): under 15, 42.9%; 15–29, 27.8%; 30–44, 15.6%; 45–59, 8.7%; 60–74, 4.0%; 75 and over, 1.0%. **Ethnic composition** (2000): mestizo 63.7%; Amerindian 33.1%; black 2.0%; white 1.0%; other 0.2%. **Religious affiliation** (1995): Roman Catholic 75.9%, of which Catholic/traditional syncretist 25.0%; Protestant 21.8%; other 2.3%. **Major cities** (2002): Guatemala City 942,348 (urban agglomeration [2001] 3,366,000); Mixco 277,400 (within Guatemala City urban agglomeration); Villa Nueva 187,700 (within Guatemala City urban agglomeration); Quetzaltenango 106,700; Escuintla 65,400. **Location:** Central America, bordering Mexico, Belize, the Caribbean Sea, Honduras, El Salvador, and the Pacific Ocean.

Vital statistics

Birth rate per 1,000 population (2003): 35.1 (world avg. 21.3). **Death rate** per 1,000 population (2003): 6.8 (world avg. 9.1). **Natural increase rate** per 1,000 population (2003): 28.3 (world avg. 12.2). **Total fertility rate** (avg. births per childbearing woman; 2003): 4.7. **Marriage rate** per 1,000 population (1999): 5.5. **Life expectancy** at birth (2003): male 64.3 years; female 66.2 years.

National economy

Budget (2000). *Revenue:* Q 15,554,320,000 (tax revenue 96.9%, of which VAT 45.2%, income tax 23.7%; grants 2.2%; nontax revenue 0.9%). *Expenditures:* Q 18,220,750,000 (current expenditures 80.6%; capital expenditures 19.4%). **Public debt** (external, outstanding; 2002): $2,972,000,000. **Tourism** (2002): receipts from visitors $612,000,000; expenditures by nationals abroad $267,000,000. **Production** (metric tons except as noted). *Agriculture, forestry, fishing* (2003): sugarcane 17,500,000, corn (maize) 1,053,560, bananas 1,000,000; livestock (number of live animals) 2,540,000 cattle, 780,000 pigs, 27,000,000 chickens; roundwood (2001) 16,069,873 cu m; fish catch (2001) 14,300. *Mining and quarrying* (2001): gypsum 100,000; gold 4,500 kg; marble 3,800 cu m. *Manufacturing* (value added in Q '000,000; 1998): food and beverage products 298; clothing and textiles 119; machinery and metal products 55. *Energy production (consumption):* electricity (kW-hr; 2000) 6,048,000,000 (5,344,000,000); crude petroleum (barrels; 2000) 7,500,000 (6,600,-000); petroleum products (2000) 820,000 (2,859,-000); natural gas (cu m; 2000) 11,020,000 (11,020,000). **Household income and expenditure.** Average household size (2000) 4.5; income per household (1989) Q 4,306; expenditure (1981): food 64.4%, housing and energy 16.0%, transportation

and communications 7.0%, household furnishings 5.0%, clothing 3.1%. **Gross national product** (at current market prices; 2003): $23,486,000,000 ($1,910 per capita). **Population economically active** (1998–99): total 4,207,946; activity rate of total population 38.9% (participation rates: ages 15–64, 53.4%; female 36.2%; unemployed [1995] 1.4%). **Land use** as % of total land area (2000): in temporary crops 12.5%, in permanent crops 5.0%, in pasture 24.0%; overall forest area 26.3%.

Foreign trade

Imports (2000-f.o.b. in balance of trade and c.i.f. for commodities and trading partners): $4,882,000,000 (machinery and apparatus 22.1%, chemicals and chemical products 16.0%, crude and refined petroleum 11.0%, road vehicles 10.2%). *Major import sources:* US 39.7%; Mexico 11.7%; El Salvador 6.4%; Venezuela 5.4%; Costa Rica 4.1%. **Exports** (2000): $2,699,000,000 (agricultural products 52.1%, of which coffee 21.3%, sugar 7.1%, bananas 6.6%, spices 3.0%; crude petroleum 5.9%). *Major export destinations:* US 36.1%; El Salvador 12.6%; Honduras 8.6%; Costa Rica 4.7%; Mexico 4.5%.

Transport and communications

Transport. *Railroads* (2003): route length 784 km (mostly inoperable in 2003; no passenger service). *Roads* (1999): total length 14,118 km (paved 35%). *Vehicles* (1999): passenger cars 578,733; trucks and buses 53,236. *Air transport* (1998; Aviateca Airlines only): passenger-km 480,000,000; metric ton-km cargo 50,000,000; airports (1996) 2. **Communications,** in total units (units per 1,000 persons). Daily newspaper circulation (2000): 377,000 (33); radios (2000): 902,000 (79); televisions (2000): 697,000 (61); telephone main lines (2002): 846,000 (71); cellular telephone subscribers (2002): 1,577,100 (132); personal computers (2002): 173,000 (14); Internet users (2002): 400,000 (33).

Education and health

Educational attainment (1994). Percentage of population age 25 and over having: no formal schooling 45.2%; incomplete primary education 20.8%; complete primary 18.0%; some secondary 4.8%; secondary 7.2%; higher 4.0%. **Literacy** (2002): total population age 15 and over literate 69.9%; males literate 77.3%; females literate 62.5%. **Health** (2003): physicians 11,700 (1 per 1,053 persons); hospital beds (2002) 6,000 (1 per 2,000 persons); infant mortality rate per 1,000 live births 37.9. **Food** (2001): daily per capita caloric intake 2,203 (vegetable products 91%, animal products 9%); 101% of FAO recommended minimum.

Military

Total active duty personnel (2003): 31,400 (army 93.0%, navy 4.8%, air force 2.2%). **Military expenditure as percentage of GNP** (1999): 0.7% (world 2.4%); per capita expenditure $10.

Background

From simple farming villages dating to 2500 BC, the Maya of Guatemala and the Yucatan developed an impressive civilization. The civilization of the Maya declined after AD 900, and the Spanish began the subjugation of their descendants in 1523. The Central American colonies declared independence from Spain in Guatemala City in 1821, and Guatemala became part of the Mexican Empire until its collapse in 1823. In 1839 Guatemala became an independent republic under the first of a series of dictators who held power almost continuously for the next century. In 1945 a liberal-democratic coalition came to power and instituted sweeping reforms. Attempts to expropriate land belonging to US business interests prompted the US government in 1954 to sponsor an invasion. In the following years Guatemala's social revolution came to an end and most of the reforms were reversed. Chronic political instability and violence thenceforth marked Guatemalan politics; most of the 200,000 deaths that resulted were blamed on government forces. In 1991 the country abandoned its long-standing claims of sovereignty over Belize, and the two established diplomatic relations. It continued to experience violence as guerrillas sought to seize power. A peace treaty was signed in 1996, and the country started slowly to recover from its civil war.

Recent Developments

In March 2005 Guatemala ratified the Central America–Dominican Republic Free Trade Agreement (CAFTA–DR) despite continued protests against it. The country, with the firm backing of the US, challenged Venezuela for a rotating seat on the UN Security Council in October 2006. Neither country could gain the required two-thirds of the votes of the UN General Assembly, so both countries withdrew their candidacy, and the seat went to Panama in November. In March 2007 US Pres. George W. Bush was greeted with protests during a visit to Guatemala over his refusal to halt the deportation of illegal Guatemalan immigrants.

Internet resources: <www.terra.com.gt/turismogt>.

Guernsey

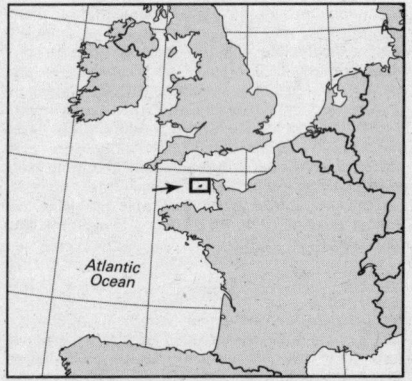

Atlantic
Ocean

Data exclude Guernsey dependencies (particularly Alderney and Sark) unless otherwise indicated. **Official**

name: Bailiwick of Guernsey. **Political status:** crown dependency (UK) with one legislative house (States of Deliberation [51; includes ex officio members and two representatives from Alderney]); Alderney and Sark have their own parliaments. **Chief of state:** Queen Elizabeth II (from 1952), represented by Lieutenant Governor Sir Fabian Malbon (from 2005). **Head of government:** Chief Minister Mike Torode. **Capital:** St. Peter Port. **Official language:** English. **Monetary unit:** 1 Guernsey pound (equivalent to pound sterling) = 100 pence; valuation (1 Jul 2007) US$1 = 0.50 Guernsey pound.

Demography

Area: 30.2 sq mi, 78.1 sq km (including areas of Guernsey dependencies, of which Alderney 3.1 sq mi [7.9 sq km], Sark 1.6 sq mi [4.2 sq km], others 1.2 sq mi [3.0 sq km]). **Population** (2006; includes Alderney, Sark, and other dependencies): 63,700. **Density** (2006; includes Alderney, Sark, and other dependencies): persons per sq mi 2,123.3, persons per sq km 816.7. **Urban** (2003; includes Jersey): 30.5%. **Sex distribution** (2001): male 48.72%; female 51.28%. **Age breakdown** (2001): under 15, 17.2%; 15–29, 18.8%; 30–44, 23.2%; 45–59, 20.0%; 60–74, 13.4%; 75 and over, 7.4%. **Population by place of birth** (2001): Guernsey 64.3%; UK 27.4%; Portugal 1.9%; Jersey 0.7%; Ireland 0.7%; Alderney 0.2%; Sark 0.1%; other Europe 3.2%; other 1.5%. **Religious affiliation** (1990): Anglican 65.2%; other 34.8%. **Major cities** (2001; pop. of parish): St. Peter Port 16,488; Vale 9,573; Castel 8,975; St. Sampson 8,592; St. Martin 6,267. **Location:** western Europe, island in the English Channel, northwest of France.

Vital statistics

Birth rate per 1,000 population (2003): 9.4 (world avg. 21.3); (2000) legitimate 65.2%. **Death rate** per 1,000 population (2003): 9.8 (world avg. 9.1). **Natural increase rate** per 1,000 population (2002): –0.4 (world avg. 12.2). **Total fertility rate** (avg. births per childbearing woman; 2003): 1.4. **Marriage rate** per 1,000 population (2000): 5.7. **Divorce rate** per 1,000 population (2000): 2.9. **Life expectancy** at birth (2003): male 77.0 years; female 83.1 years.

National economy

Budget (1999). *Revenue:* £306,991,000 (income tax 79.7%, customs duties and excise taxes 5.7%, document duties 2.7%, corporation taxes 2.1%, automobile taxes 1.9%). *Expenditures:* £244,418,000 (welfare 31.1%, health 26.2%, education 15.9%, administrative services 6.7%, law and order 4.9%, community services 4.1%). **Gross national product** (at current market prices; 2002): $2,116,833,000 ($33,650 per capita). **Production** (metric tons except as noted). *Agriculture, forestry, fishing* (1999): tomatoes (1998) 2,449, flowers 1,154,000 boxes, of which roses 288,000 boxes, freesia 184,000 boxes, carnations 161,000 boxes; livestock (number of live animals) 3,262 cattle; fish catch (2001; includes Jersey): 4,414, of which crustaceans 2,169 (sea spiders and crabs 1,988), mollusks 1,456 (abalones, winkles, and conch 523), marine fish 789. *Manufacturing* (1999): milk 98,830 hectoliters. *Energy*

1 metric ton = about 1.1 short tons;   1 kilometer = 0.6 mi (statute);   1 metric ton-km cargo = about 0.68 short ton-mi cargo;   c.i.f.: cost, insurance, and freight;   f.o.b.: free on board

production (consumption): electricity (kW-hr; 1999–2000), n.a. (273,013,000). **Households.** Average household size (2001) 2.6; expenditure (1996): housing 21.6%, food 12.7%, household goods and services 11.2%, recreation services 9.2%, transportation 8.5%, clothing and footwear 5.6%, personal goods 4.9%, energy 4.1%. **Population economically active** (2001): total 32,293; activity rate of total population 51.5% (participation rates: ages 15–64, 80.4%; female 45.3%). **Tourism** (1996): receipts $275,000,000. **Land use** as % of total land area (1999): in pasture 37%; overall forest area 3%.

Foreign trade

Imports (1998): petroleum products are important. *Major import sources* (1998): mostly UK. **Exports** (1998): £93,000,000 (manufactured goods 51%, of which electronic components 18%, printed products 10%; agricultural products 42%, of which flowers 25%, plants 10%; fish, crustaceans, and mollusks 7%). *Major export destinations* (1998): mostly UK.

Transport and communications

Transport. *Vehicles* (2000): passenger cars 37,598; trucks and buses 7,338. *Air transport* (2001; Guernsey airport): passenger arrivals 429,076, passenger departures 430,254; cargo loaded 969 metric tons, cargo unloaded 3,557 metric tons; airports (1999) with scheduled flights 2 (includes one airport on Alderney). **Communications,** in total units (units per 1,000 persons). Daily newspaper circulation (1998): 15,784 (260); telephone main lines (2001): 55,000 (877); cellular telephone subscribers (2001): 31,500 (502); Internet users (2000): 20,000 (320).

Education and health

Literacy (2002): virtually 100%. **Health** (1999): physicians 93 (1 per 654 persons); infant mortality rate per 1,000 live births (2003) 4.9. *Food* (2002; data for the UK): daily per capita caloric intake 3,412 (vegetable products 69%, animal products 31%); 135% of FAO recommended minimum.

Military

Total active duty personnel: The UK is responsible for defense.

Guinea

Official name: République de Guinée (Republic of Guinea). **Form of government:** unitary multiparty republic with one legislative house (National Assembly [114 seats]). **Head of state and government:** President Lansana Conté (from 1984), assisted by Prime Minister Lansana Kouyaté (from 2007). **Capital:** Conakry. **Official language:** French. **Official religion:** none. **Monetary unit:** 1 Guinean franc (GF) = 100 cauris; valuation (1 Jul 2007) US$1 = GF 3,511.

Demography

Area: 94,919 sq mi, 245,836 sq km. **Population** (2006): 9,603,000. **Density** (2006): persons per sq mi 101.2, persons per sq km 39.1. **Urban** (2003): 34.9%. **Sex distribution** (2003): male 49.95%; female

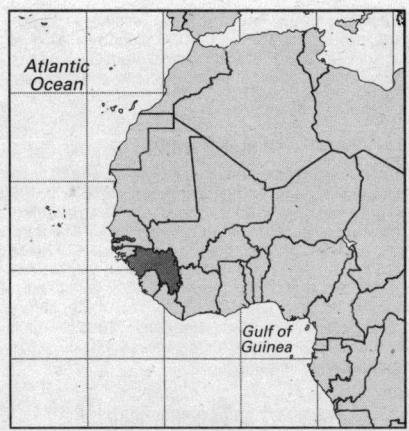

50.05%. **Age breakdown** (2003): under 15, 44.5%; 15–29, 26.4%; 30–44, 15.4%; 45–59, 8.7%; 60–74, 4.1%; 75 and over, 0.9%. **Ethnic composition** (1996): Fulani 38.6%; Malinke 23.2%; Susu 11.0%; Kissi 6.0%; Kpelle 4.6%; other 16.6%. **Religious affiliation** (1996): Muslim 85.0%; Christian 10.0%; other 5.0%. **Major cities** (2001): Conakry 1,565,200; Kankan 88,800; Labé 64,500; Kindia 56,000; Nzérékoré 55,000. **Location:** western Africa, bordering Guinea-Bissau, Senegal, Mali, Côte d'Ivoire, Liberia, Sierra Leone, and the North Atlantic Ocean.

Vital statistics

Birth rate per 1,000 population (2003): 42.5 (world avg. 21.3). **Death rate** per 1,000 population (2003): 15.7 (world avg. 9.1). **Natural increase rate** per 1,000 population (2003): 26.8 (world avg. 12.2). **Total fertility rate** (avg. births per childbearing woman; 2003): 5.9. **Life expectancy** at birth (2003): male 48.3 years; female 50.8 years.

National economy

Budget (2002). *Revenue:* GF 909,700,000,000 (tax revenue 76.2%, of which value-added tax 20.3%, mining sector 16.0%, tax on trade 15.3%, income tax 10.4%; grants 16.0%; nontax revenue 7.8%). *Expenditures:* GF 1,281,800,000 (current expenditure 61.5%, of which defense 14.4%, interest 8.2%; capital expenditure 38.5%). **Production** (metric tons except as noted). *Agriculture, forestry, fishing* (2003): cassava 1,150,000, rice 845,000, oil palm fruit 830,000; livestock (number of live animals) 3,285,000 cattle, 1,201,000 goats, 13,500,000 chickens; roundwood 12,236,000 cu m; fish catch (2001) 90,000. *Mining and quarrying* (2001): bauxite 17,950,000; alumina 550,000; gold 13,000 kg. *Manufacturing* (2001): cement 300,000. *Energy production (consumption):* electricity (kW-hr; 2000) 569,000,000 (569,000,000); petroleum products (2000) none (373,000). **Households.** Average household size (2000) 4.0; expenditure (1985): food 61.5%, health 11.2%, clothing 7.9%, housing 7.3%. **Gross national product** (2003): $3,372,000,000 ($430 per capita). **Public debt** (external, outstanding; 2002): $2,972,000,000. **Population economically active** (2000): total 4,047,000; activity rate of total population 49.9%. **Tourism** (2002): receipts $43,000,-000; expenditures $31,000,000. **Land use** as % of total land area (2000): in temporary crops 3.6%, in permanent crops 2.4%, in pasture 43.5%; overall forest area 28.2%.

Foreign trade

Imports (2000-f.o.b. in balance of trade and c.i.f. for commodities and trading partners): $612,400,000 (refined petroleum 24.8%, food 18.0%, machinery and apparatus 10.0%, road vehicles 8.7%). *Major import sources* (2000): Côte d'Ivoire 21.4%; France 19.8%; US 7.9%; Belgium 7.7%; Japan 5.6%. **Exports** (2002): $700,400,000 (bauxite 43.6%, gold 20.5%, alumina 18.3%, diamonds 4.9%, fish 4.0%, coffee 2.5%). *Major export destinations* (2002): Spain 10.5%; Belgium 10.1%; Cameroon 10.1%; US 9.6%; France 7.4%; Germany 5.0%.

Transport and communications

Transport. *Railroads* (2000): route length of operational lines for cargo (mostly bauxite) transport 274 km; metric ton-km cargo (1993) 710,000,000. *Roads* (1999): total length 30,500 km (paved 16.5%). *Vehicles* (1996): passenger cars 14,100; trucks and buses 21,000. *Air transport* (1998): passenger-km 50,000,000; metric ton-km cargo 5,000,000; airports (2000) 1. **Communications,** in total units (units per 1,000 persons). Daily newspaper circulation (1988): 13,000 (2); radios (2000): 422,000 (52); televisions (2000): 357,000 (44); telephone main lines (2003): 26,200 (3.4); cellular telephone subscribers (2003): 111,500 (14); personal computers (2003): 43,000 (5.5); Internet users (2003): 40,000 (5.2).

Education and health

Educational attainment of those age 6 and over having attended school (1983): primary 55.2%; secondary 32.7%; vocational 3.4%; higher 8.7%. **Literacy** (2000): percentage of total population age 15 and over literate 41.0%; males literate 55.0%; females literate 27.0%. **Health:** physicians (1995) 920 (1 per 7,693 persons); hospital beds (1990) 3,700 (1 per 1,667 persons); infant mortality rate (2003) 93.3. **Food** (2001): daily per capita caloric intake 2,362 (vegetable products 96%, animal products 4%); 102% of FAO recommended minimum.

Military

Total active duty personnel (2003): 9,700 (army 87.7%, navy 4.1%, air force 8.2%). **Military expenditure as percentage of GNP** (1999): 1.6% (world 2.4%); per capita expenditure $7.

Did you know? Guinea's flag features three vertical stripes echoing France's red-white-blue *Tricouleur*, but with red, yellow, and green, the pan-African colors. Other African flags featuring these colors include Burkina Faso, Cameroon, Ethiopia, Ghana, Guinea-Bissau, and Mali.

Background

About AD 900 successive migrations of the Susu swept down from the desert and pushed the original inhabitants of Guinea, the Baga, to the Atlantic coast. Small kingdoms of the Susu rose in importance in the 13th century and later extended their rule to the coast. In the mid-15th century the Portuguese visited the coast and developed a slave trade. In the 16th century the Fulani established domination over the Fouta Djallon region; they ruled into the 19th century. In the early 19th century the French arrived and in 1849 proclaimed the coastal region a French protectorate. In 1895 French Guinea became part of the federation of French West Africa. In 1946 it was made an overseas territory of France, and in 1958 it achieved independence. Following a military coup in 1984, Guinea began implementing Westernized government systems. A new constitution was adopted in 1991, and the first multiparty elections were held in 1993. During the 1990s Guinea accommodated several hundred thousand war refugees from neighboring Liberia and Sierra Leone.

Recent Developments

Social unrest roiled Guinea. In June 2005 and February 2006 unions called strikes to protest the prices of foodstuffs, which had in some cases doubled in recent months. Protesters also demanded the ouster of the president, who had promised to name a prime minister with significant powers but had appointed a close political ally to the post. Clashes between protesters and government forces in early 2007 left at least 100 dead.

Internet resources: <www.mirinet.net.gn/ont>.

Guinea-Bissau

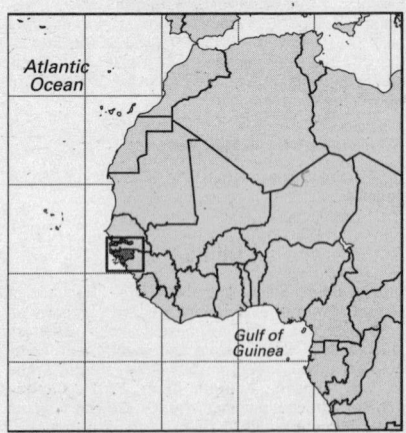

Atlantic Ocean

Gulf of Guinea

Official name: República da Guiné-Bissau (Republic of Guinea-Bissau). **Form of government:** multiparty republic (reestablished as of March 2004 legislative elections) (National People's Assembly [102]). **Chief**

---

1 metric ton = about 1.1 short tons;   1 kilometer = 0.6 mi (statute);   1 metric ton-km cargo = about 0.68 short ton-mi cargo;   c.i.f.: cost, insurance, and freight;   f.o.b.: free on board

of state: President João Bernardo Vieira (from 2005). **Head of government:** Prime Minister Martinho Ndafa Kabi (from 2007). **Capital:** Bissau. **Official language:** Portuguese. **Official religion:** none. **Monetary unit:** 1 CFA franc (CFAF) = 100 centimes; valuation (1 Jul 2007) US$1 = CFAF 485.18 (formerly pegged to the French franc and since 1 Jan 2002 to the euro at €1 = CFAF 655.96).

Demography

Area: 13,948 sq mi, 36,125 sq km; area figures include water area of about 3,089 sq mi (8,000 sq km). **Population** (2006): 1,442,000. **Density** (2006; based on land area only): persons per sq mi 132.8, persons per sq km 51.3. **Urban** (2003): 34.0%. **Sex distribution** (2003): male 48.52%; female 51.48%. **Age breakdown** (2003): under 15, 41.9%; 15–29, 28.1%; 30–44, 15.9%; 45–59, 9.4%; 60–74, 4.0%; 75 and over, 0.7%. **Ethnic composition** (1996): Balante 30%; Fulani 20%; Mandyako 14%; Malinke 13%; Pepel 7%; nonindigenous Cape Verdean mulatto 2%; other 14%. **Religious affiliation** (2000): traditional beliefs 45.2%; Muslim 39.9%; Christian 13.2%, of which Roman Catholic 9.9%; other 1.7%. **Major cities** (1997): Bissau 200,000 (urban agglomeration [2003] 336,000); Bafatá 15,000; Cacheu 14,000; Gabú 10,000. **Location:** western Africa, bordering Senegal, Guinea, and the North Atlantic Ocean.

Vital statistics

Birth rate per 1,000 population (2003): 38.4 (world avg. 21.3). **Death rate** per 1,000 population (2003): 16.6 (world avg. 9.1). **Natural increase rate** per 1,000 population (2003): 21.8 (world avg. 12.2). **Total fertility rate** (avg. births per childbearing woman; 2003): 5.1. **Life expectancy** at birth (2003): male 45.1 years; female 48.9 years.

National economy

Budget (2001). *Revenue:* CFAF 47,530,000,000 (foreign grants 40.0%; tax revenue 31.0%, of which taxes on international trade 13.6%, general sales tax 7.3%; nontax revenue 29.0%, of which fishing licenses 15.6%). *Expenditures:* CFAF 63,162,000,000 (current expenditures 65.7%, of which scheduled external interest payments 19.4%; capital expenditures 34.3%). **Public debt** (external, outstanding; 2002): $662,100,000. **Production** (metric tons except as noted). *Agriculture, forestry, fishing* (2002): cashew nuts 80,000, oil palm fruit 80,000, rice 79,900; livestock (number of live animals) 515,000 cattle, 350,000 pigs, 325,000 goats; roundwood (1999) 592,000 cu m; fish catch (2001) 5,000. *Mining and quarrying:* extraction of construction materials only. *Manufacturing* (2000): processed wood 11,200; wood products 4,400; dried and smoked fish 3,500. *Energy production (consumption):* electricity (kW-hr; 2000) 58,000,000 (58,000,000); petroleum products (2000) none (88,000). **Population economically active** (1992): total 471,000; activity rate of total population 46.9% (participation rates [1991]: over age 10, 67.1%; female 40.5%). **Households.** Average household size (1996) 6.9. **Gross national product** (at current market prices; 2003): $202,000,000 ($140 per capita). **Land use** as % of total land area (2000): in temporary crops 10.7%, in permanent crops 8.8%, in pasture 38.4%; overall forest area 60.5%.

Foreign trade

Imports (2001-c.i.f.): $96,700,000 (foodstuffs 18.7%, of which rice 6.6%; transport equipment 13.2%; equipment and machinery 7.7%; fuel and lubricants 6.2%; unspecified 39.3%). *Major import sources:* Portugal 30.9%; Senegal 28.3%; China 11.3%; The Netherlands 6.8%; Japan 5.8%. **Exports** (2001-f.o.b.): $47,200,000 (cashews 95.6%; cotton 2.3%; logs 1.5%). *Major export destinations:* India 85.6%; Portugal 3.8%; Senegal 2.5%; France 1.7%.

Transport and communications

Transport. *Roads* (1999): total length 4,400 km (paved 10%). *Vehicles* (1996): passenger cars 7,120; trucks and buses 5,640. *Air transport* (1998): passenger-km 10,000,000; airports (1997) with scheduled flights 2. **Communications**, in total units (units per 1,000 persons). Daily newspaper circulation (2000): 6,390 (5); radios (2001): 56,200 (178); telephone main lines (2002): 10,600 (8.2); cellular telephone subscribers (2003): 1,300 (1); Internet users (2003): 19,000 (15).

Education and health

Literacy (1995): total population age 15 and over literate 54.9%; males literate 68.0%; females literate 42.5%. **Health:** physicians (1996) 193 (1 per 6,024 persons); hospital beds (1998) 1,832 (1 per 667 persons); infant mortality rate per 1,000 live births (2003) 110.3. **Food** (2002): daily per capita caloric intake 2,024 (vegetable products 93%, animal products 7%); 88% of FAO recommended minimum.

Military

Total active duty personnel (2003): 9,250 (army 73.5%, navy 3.8%, air force 1.1%, paramilitary [gendarmerie] 21.6%). **Military expenditure as percentage of GNP** (1999): 2.7% (world 2.4%); per capita expenditure $4.

Background

More than 1,000 years ago the coast of Guinea-Bissau was occupied by iron-using agriculturists. They grew irrigated and dry rice and were also the major suppliers of marine salt to the western Sudan. At about the same time, the region came under the influence of the Mali empire and became a tributary kingdom known as Gabú. After 1546 Gabú was virtually autonomous; vestiges of the kingdom lasted until 1867. The earliest overseas contacts came in the 15th century with the Portuguese, who imported slaves from the Guinea area to the offshore Cape Verde Islands. Portuguese control of Guinea-Bissau was marginal despite claims to sovereignty there. The end of the slave trade forced the Portuguese inland in search of new profits. Their subjugation of the interior was slow and sometimes violent; it was not effectively achieved until 1915, though sporadic resistance continued until 1936. Guerrilla warfare in the 1960s led to the country's independence in 1974, but political turmoil continued and the government was overthrown by a military coup in 1980. A new constitution was adopted in 1984, and the first multiparty elections were held in 1994. A destructive civil war in 1998 was followed by a military coup in 1999 and another in 2003.

Recent Developments

Elections were held in June and July 2005 to choose the first elected president since the coup of 2003. No candidate secured enough votes to win outright, and a runoff was held 24 July. This was won by former president João Bernardo Vieira, who had ruled from 1980 to 1999. Prime Minister Carlos Gomes refused to recognize the president, and in October 2005 he was dismissed by Vieira, which decision the Supreme Court upheld in January 2006. In July of that year the Community of Portuguese-Speaking Countries elected Vieira as their chairman.

Internet resources: <www.bissau.com>.

Guyana

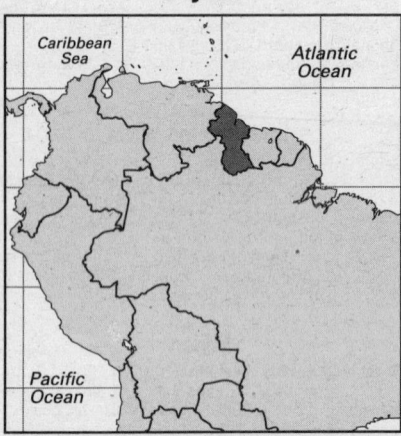

Official name: Co-operative Republic of Guyana. Form of government: unitary multiparty republic with one legislative house (National Assembly [65]). Chief of state: President Bharrat Jagdeo (from 1999). Head of government: Prime Minister Sam Hinds (from 1999). Capital: Georgetown. Official language: English. Official religion: none. Monetary unit: 1 Guyana dollar (G$) = 100 cents; valuation (1 Jul 2007) US$1 = G$190.01.

Demography

Area: 83,012 sq mi, 214,999 sq km (includes inland water area of c. 7,000 sq mi [18,000 sq km]). Population (2006): 756,000. Density (2006; based on land area only): persons per sq mi 9.9, persons per sq km 4.0. Urban (2003): 37.6%. Sex distribution (2002): male 49.30%; female 50.70%. Age breakdown (2002): under 15, 27.6%; 15–29, 31.0%; 30–44, 21.3%; 45–59, 12.8%; 60–74, 5.4%; 75 and over, 1.9%. Ethnic composition (1992–93): East Indian 49.4%; black (African Negro and Bush Negro) 35.6%; Amerindian 6.8%; Portuguese 0.7%; Chinese 0.4%; mixed 7.1%. Religious affiliation (1995): Christian 40.9%, of which Protestant 27.5% (including Anglican 8.6%), Roman Catholic 11.5%, Ethiopian Orthodox 1.1%; Hindu 34.0%; Muslim 9.0%; other 16.1%. Major cities (2002): Georgetown 137,330 (urban agglomeration [2003] 231,000); Linden 29,572; New Amsterdam (1997) 25,000; Corriverton (1997) 24,000. Location: northern South America, bordering the North Atlantic Ocean, Suriname, Brazil, and Venezuela.

Vital statistics

Birth rate per 1,000 population (2003): 18.7 (world avg. 21.3). Death rate per 1,000 population (2003): 8.5 (world avg. 9.1). Natural increase rate per 1,000 population (2003): 10.2 (world avg. 12.2). Total fertility rate (avg. births per childbearing woman; 2003): 2.1. Life expectancy at birth (2003): male 62.1 years; female 67.3 years.

National economy

Budget (1999): Revenue: G$36,544,000,000 (tax revenue 91.6%, of which consumption taxes 32.0%, income taxes on companies 22.2%, personal income taxes 15.5%, import duties 11.4%; nontax revenue 8.2%). Expenditures: G$41,983,000,000 (current expenditure 71.2%, of which debt charges 13.8%; development expenditure 28.8%). Production (metric tons except as noted). Agriculture, forestry, fishing (2002): rice 450,000, raw sugar (2001) 284,000, coconuts 45,000; livestock (number of live animals) 130,000 sheep, 100,000 cattle, 12,500,000 chickens; roundwood (2001) 1,188,000 cu m; fish catch (2003) 56,307, of which shrimps and prawns 22,584. Mining and quarrying (2003): bauxite 1,716,000; gold 357,000 troy oz; diamonds 413,000 carats. Manufacturing (2002): flour 36,570; rum 145,900 hectoliters; beer and stout 108,500 hectoliters. Energy production (consumption): electricity (kW-hr; 2000) 894,000,000 (894,000,000); petroleum products (2000) none (521,000). Population economically active (1997): total 263,807; activity rate of total population 33.9% (participation rates: ages 15–64 [1992] 59.5%; female 35.2%; unemployed 9.1%). Gross national product (2003): US$689,000,000 (US$900 per capita). Public debt (external, outstanding; 2003): US$1,084,000,000. Households. Average household size (2002) 4.0. Tourism (2002): receipts from visitors US$49,000,000; expenditures by nationals abroad US$38,000,000. Land use as % of total land area (2000): in temporary crops 2.4%, in permanent crops 0.2%, in pasture 6.2%; overall forest area 78.5%.

Foreign trade

Imports (2002-f.o.b. in balance of trade and commodities and c.i.f. for trading partners): US$563,-100,000 (consumer goods 28.0%, fuels and lubricants 22.3%, capital goods 20.1%). Major import sources (2001): US 24%; Netherlands Antilles 17%; Chile 16%; Trinidad and Tobago 13%; UK 6%. Exports (2002): US$494,900,000 (gold 27.5%, sugar 24.1%, shrimp 10.6%, rice 9.2%, timber 7.2%, bauxite 7.1%). Major export destinations (2001): US 22%; Canada 20%; UK 12%; Netherlands Antilles 12%; Belgium 5%.

1 metric ton = about 1.1 short tons;   1 kilometer = 0.6 mi (statute);   1 metric ton-km cargo = about 0.68 short ton-mi cargo;   c.i.f.: cost, insurance, and freight;   f.o.b.: free on board

Transport and communications

Transport. *Roads* (1999): total length 7,970 km (paved 7%). *Vehicles* (1995): passenger cars 24,000; trucks and buses 9,000. *Air transport* (1999; scheduled flights only): passenger-km 276,600,000; metric ton-km cargo 2,200,000; airports (2000) with scheduled international flights 1. **Communications,** in total units (units per 1,000 persons). Daily newspaper circulation (1996): 42,000 (54); radios (1997): 420,-000 (539); televisions (1999): 60,000 (77); telephone main lines (2002): 80,400 (92); cellular telephone subscribers (2002): 87,300 (99); personal computers (2002): 24,000 (27); Internet users (2002): 125,000 (142).

Education and health

Educational attainment (1980). Percentage of population age 25 and over having: no formal schooling 8.1%; primary education 72.8%; secondary 17.3%; higher 1.8%. **Literacy** (2002): total population age 15 and over literate 98.7%; males literate 99.0%; females literate 98.3%. **Health:** physicians (1999) 203 (1 per 3,846 persons); hospital beds (2002) 3,274 (1 per 229 persons); infant mortality rate per 1,000 live births (2003) 35.1. **Food** (2002): daily per capita caloric intake 2,692 (vegetable products 84%, animal products 16%); 119% of FAO recommended minimum.

Military

Total active duty personnel (2003): 1,600 (army 87.5%, navy 6.3%, air force 6.2%). **Military expenditure as percentage of GNP** (1999): 0.8% (world 2.4%); per capita expenditure $7.

Background

Guyana was colonized by the Dutch in the 17th century. During the Napoleonic Wars the British occupied the territory and afterward purchased the colonies of Demerara, Berbice, and Essequibo, united in 1831 as British Guiana. The slave trade was abolished in 1807, but emancipation of the 100,000 slaves in the colonies was not completed until 1838. From the 1840s East Indian and Chinese indentured servants were brought to work the plantations; by 1917 almost 240,000 East Indians had migrated to British Guiana. It was made a crown colony in 1928 and granted home rule in 1953. Political parties began to emerge, developing on racial lines as the People's Progressive Party (largely East Indian) and the People's National Congress (largely black). The PNC formed a coalition government and led the country into independence as Guyana in 1966. In 1970 Guyana became a republic within the Commonwealth; in 1980 it adopted a new constitution. Venezuela has long claimed land west of the Essequibo River, and the UN has continued to arbitrate the issue.

Recent Developments

Several petroleum companies held talks with Guyanese officials ahead of an expected ruling by the arbitration panel of the UN Convention on the Law of the Sea on a maritime border dispute with Suriname over the potentially lucrative oil deposits in the offshore Corentyne region.

Internet resources: <www.guyana.org>.

Haiti

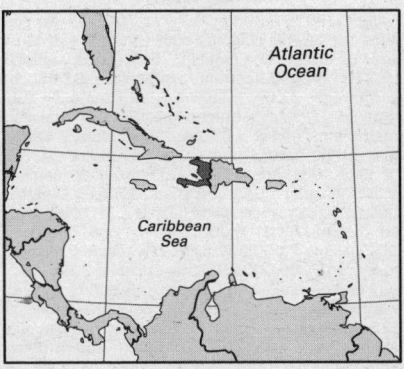

Official name: Repiblik Dayti (Haitian Creole); République d'Haïti (French) (Republic of Haiti). **Form of government:** republic with two legislative houses (Senate [30]; Chamber of Deputies [99]). **Chief of state:** President René Préval (from 2006). **Head of government:** Prime Minister Jacques Édouard Alexis (from 2006). **Capital:** Port-au-Prince. **Official languages:** Haitian Creole; French. **Official religions:** Roman Catholicism has special recognition per concordat with the Vatican; voodoo became officially sanctioned per governmental decree of April 2003. **Monetary unit:** 1 gourde (G) = 100 centimes; valuation (1 Jul 2007) US$1 = G 35.59.

Demography

Area: 10,695 sq mi, 27,700 sq km. **Population** (2006): 8,808,000. **Density** (2006): persons per sq mi 823.6, persons per sq km 318.0. **Urban** (2003): 37.5%. **Sex distribution** (2003): male 48.35%; female 51.65%. **Age breakdown** (2003): under 15, 42.7%; 15–29, 29.3%; 30–44, 14.2%; 45–59, 8.2%; 60–74, 4.5%; 75 and over, 1.1%. **Ethnic composition** (2000): black 94.2%; mulatto 5.4%; other 0.4%. **Religious affiliation** (1995): Roman Catholic 68.5% (about 80% of all Roman Catholics also practice voodoo); Protestant 24.1%, of which Baptist 5.9%, Pentecostal 5.3%, Seventh-day Adventist 4.6%; other 7.4%. **Major cities** (1999): Port-au-Prince 990,558 (metropolitan area [2003] 1,977,036); Carrefour 336,222 (within Port-au-Prince metropolitan area); Delmas 284,079 (within Port-au-Prince metropolitan area); Cap-Haïtien 113,555; Pétion-Ville (1997) 76,155 (within Port-au-Prince metropolitan area). **Location:** western third of the island of Hispaniola, between the North Atlantic Ocean and the Caribbean Sea.

Vital statistics

Birth rate per 1,000 population (2003): 36.7 (world avg. 21.3). **Death rate** per 1,000 population (2003): 12.7 (world avg. 9.1). **Natural increase rate** per 1,000 population (2003): 24.0 (world avg. 12.2). **Total fertility rate** (avg. births per childbearing woman; 2003): 5.2. **Life expectancy** at birth (2003): male 51.0 years; female 53.7 years. **Adult population** (ages 15–49) **living with HIV** (2004): 5.6% (world avg. 1.1%).

National economy

Budget (2002). *Revenue:* G 7,721,700,000 (general sales tax 31.3%; customs duties 26.8%; individual taxes on income and profits 20.5%). *Expenditures:* G 10,376,700,000 (current expenditure 81.6%, of which wages 33.6%, transfers 4.8%, interest on public debt 1.2%; capital expenditure 18.4%). **Production** (metric tons except as noted). *Agriculture, forestry, fishing* (2002): sugarcane 1,010,000, cassava (manioc) 335,000, bananas 295,000; livestock (number of live animals) 1,943,000 goats, 1,450,000 cattle, 1,001,000 pigs; roundwood (2001) 2,210,000 cu m; fish catch (2001) 5,000. *Mining and quarrying* (2001): sand 2,000,000 cu m. *Manufacturing* (value added in G '000,000; 2001 [at prices of 1986–87]): food and beverages 467.1; textiles, wearing apparel, and footwear 202.4; chemical and rubber products 62.8. *Energy production (consumption):* electricity (kW-hr; 2000) 635,000,000 (635,000,000); petroleum products (2000) none (463,000). **Land use** as % of total land area (2000): in temporary crops 28.3%, in permanent crops 11.6%, in pasture 17.8%; overall forest area 3.2%. **Population economically active** (2002): total 4,100,000; activity rate of total population 55% (participation rates: ages 15–64 [1990] 64.8%; female [1996] 43.0%; unemployed unofficially [1996] 60%). **Household income and expenditure.** Average household size (1982) 4.4; average annual income of urban wage earners (1984): G 1,545; expenditure (1996): food, beverages, and tobacco 49.4%, housing and energy 9.1%, transportation 8.7%, clothing and footwear 8.5%. **Public debt** (external, outstanding; 2002): $1,063,000,000. **Gross national product** (at current market prices; 2003): $3,214,000,000 ($380 per capita). **Tourism** (2001): receipts from visitors $54,000,000; expenditures by nationals abroad (1998) $37,000,000.

Foreign trade

Imports (2002-f.o.b. in balance of trade and c.i.f. in commodities and trading partners): $1,054,200,000 (food and live animals 22.4%, basic manufactures 19.9%, machinery and transport equipment 15.2%, petroleum and derivatives 14.9%). *Major import sources* (1999): US 60%; Dominican Republic 4%; Japan 3%; France 3%; Canada 3%. **Exports** (2002): $274,400,000 (reexports to US 80.8%, of which clothing and apparel 79.1%; mangoes 2.6%; cacao 2.0%; essential oils 1.5%; leather goods 1.1%). *Major export destinations* (1999): US 90%; Canada 3%; Belgium 2%; France 2%.

Transport and communications

Transport. *Roads* (1999): total length 4,160 km (paved 24%). *Vehicles* (1996): passenger cars 32,000; trucks and buses 21,000. *Air transport* (2000; Port-au-Prince Airport only): passenger arrivals and departures 924,000; cargo unloaded and loaded 15,300 metric tons; airports (1997) with scheduled flights 2. **Communications**, in total units (units per 1,000 persons). Daily newspaper circulation (2000): 21,500 (3); radios (2000): 395,000 (55); televisions (2000): 35,900 (5); telephone main lines (2002): 130,000 (16); cellular telephone subscribers (2002): 140,000 (17); Internet users (2002): 80,000 (9.6).

Education and health

Educational attainment (1986–87). Percentage of population age 25 and over having: no formal schooling 59.5%; primary education 30.5%; secondary 8.6%; vocational and teacher training 0.7%; higher 0.7%. **Literacy** (1995): total population age 15 and over literate 1,930,000 (45.0%); males literate 992,000 (48.0%); females literate 938,000 (42.2%). **Health:** physicians (1999) 1,910 (1 per 4,000 persons); hospital beds (1996) 5,241 (1 per 1,242 persons); infant mortality rate per 1,000 live births (2003) 77.0. **Food** (2002): daily per capita caloric intake 2,086 (vegetable products 93%, animal products 7%); 92% of FAO recommended minimum.

Military

Total active duty personnel: The Haitian army was disbanded in 1995. The national police force had 5,300 personnel in 2003; UN peacekeeping troops (October 2004) 3,092.

Background

Haiti gained its independence when the former slaves of the island, initially led by Toussaint-Louverture, and later by Jean-Jacques Dessalines, rebelled against French rule in 1791–1804. The new republic encompassed the entire island of Hispaniola, but the eastern portion was restored to Spain in 1809. The island was reunited under Haitian Pres. Jean-Pierre Boyer (1818–43); after his overthrow the eastern portion revolted and formed the Dominican Republic. Haiti's government was marked by instability, with frequent coups and assassinations. It was occupied by the US in 1915–34. In 1957 the dictator François ("Papa Doc") Duvalier came to power. Despite an economic decline and civil unrest, Duvalier ruled until his death in 1971. He was succeeded by his son, Jean-Claude ("Baby Doc") Duvalier, who was forced into exile in 1986. Haiti's first free presidential elections, held in 1990, were won by Jean-Bertrand Aristide. He was deposed by a military coup in 1991, after which tens of thousands of Haitians attempted to flee to the US in small boats. The military government stepped down in 1994, and Aristide returned from exile and resumed the presidency.

Recent Developments

The most prominent event in Haiti in 2006 came in February, when polls were held to elect a president and a national legislature. The internationally monitored elections ended two difficult years of interim rule by officials appointed following the ouster of former president Jean-Bertrand Aristide. René Préval, the country's president from 1996 to 2001, garnered overwhelming support from Haiti's poor and easily defeated 33 opponents to earn a six-year term. Political progress was matched by increased international support and engagement. In July international donors pledged $750 million over the next fiscal year toward Haiti's recovery efforts. In August the UN Security Council unanimously extended its Stabilization Mission in Haiti through February 2007 (it was later extended again into October). The Caribbean Community restored Haiti's suspended membership. The

---

1 metric ton = about 1.1 short tons;   1 kilometer = 0.6 mi (statute);   1 metric ton-km cargo = about 0.68 short ton-mi cargo;   c.i.f.: cost, insurance, and freight;   f.o.b.: free on board

Haiti Hemispheric Opportunity Through Partnership Encouragement (HOPE) act, a trade bill to create 20,000 assembly jobs in Haiti, was passed by the US Congress in December. Haitians living overseas sent back some $1 billion in remittances, which represented roughly 20% of the country's GDP.

Internet resources: <www.haiti.org>.

Honduras

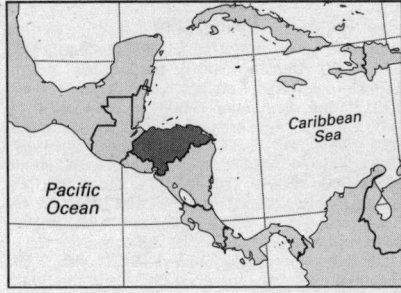

Official name: República de Honduras (Republic of Honduras). **Form of government:** multiparty republic with one legislative house (National Assembly [128]). **Head of state and government:** President Manuel Zelaya (from 2006). **Capital:** Tegucigalpa. **Official language:** Spanish. **Official religion:** none. **Monetary unit:** 1 Honduran lempira (L) = 100 centavos; valuation (1 Jul 2007) US$1 = L 19.23.

Demography

Area: 43,433 sq mi, 112,492 sq km. **Population** (2006): 7,329,000. **Density** (2006): persons per sq mi 168.7, persons per sq km 65.2. **Urban** (2003): 47.5%. **Sex distribution** (2002): male 50.09%; female 49.91%. **Age breakdown** (2002): under 15, 41.9%; 15–29, 29.1%; 30–44, 15.3%; 45–59, 8.3%; 60–74, 4.1%; 75 and over, 1.3%. **Ethnic composition** (2000): mestizo 86.6%; Amerindian 5.5%; black (including Black Carib) 4.3%; white 2.3%; other 1.3%. **Religious affiliation** (1995): Roman Catholic 86.7%; Protestant 10.4%, of which Pentecostal 5.7%; other 2.9%. **Major cities** (2001): Tegucigalpa 769,061; San Pedro Sula 439,086; La Ceiba 114,584; El Progreso 90,475; Choluteca 75,600. **Location:** Central America, bordering the Caribbean Sea, Nicaragua, the North Pacific Ocean, El Salvador, and Guatemala.

Vital statistics

Birth rate per 1,000 population (2002): 32.3 (world avg. 21.3). **Death rate** per 1,000 population (2002): 6.3 (world avg. 9.1). **Natural increase rate** per 1,000 population (2002): 26.0 (world avg. 12.2). **Total fertility rate** (avg. births per childbearing woman; 2002): 4.2. **Life expectancy** at birth (2002): male 65.2 years; female 68.7 years.

National economy

Budget (1999). *Revenue:* L 14,621,500,000 (tax revenue 92.6%, of which indirect taxes 72.8%, direct taxes 19.8%; nontax revenue 5.1%; transfers 2.3%).

Expenditures: L 18,197,700,000 (current expenditure 67.9%; capital expenditure 32.1%). **Public debt** (external, outstanding; 2002): $4,211,000,000. **Production** (metric tons except as noted). *Agriculture, forestry, fishing* (2002): sugarcane 4,300,000, bananas 965,066, oil palm fruit 735,802; livestock (number of live animals) 1,859,737 cattle, 538,033 pigs, 18,648,000 chickens; roundwood (2001) 9,531,959 cu m; fish catch (2001) 16,451. *Mining and quarrying* (2001): gypsum 59,500; zinc (metal content) 48,485; silver 35,000 kg. *Manufacturing* (value added in L '000,000; 1996): food products 1,937; wearing apparel 1,266; beverages 700. *Energy production (consumption):* electricity (kW-hr; 2001) 4,191,600,000 (4,191,600,000); petroleum products (2000) none (1,382,000). **Tourism** (2002): receipts from visitors $342,000,000; expenditures by nationals abroad $185,000,000. **Population economically active** (2001): total 2,438,000; activity rate of total population 38.5% (participation rates: ages 15–64, 64.5%; female 35.7%; unemployed 4.2%). **Gross national product** (at current market prices; 2003): $6,760,000,000 ($970 per capita). **Household income and expenditure.** Average household size (2000) 5.1; sources of income (1985): wages and salaries 58.8%, transfer payments 1.8%, other 39.4%; expenditure (1986): food 44.4%, utilities and housing 22.4%, clothing and footwear 9.0%, household furnishings 8.3%. **Land use** as % of total land area (2000): in temporary crops 9.5%, in permanent crops 3.2%, in pasture 13.5%; overall forest area 48.1%.

Foreign trade

Imports (2001-c.i.f.): $2,984,000,000 (food products and live animals 18.3%, machinery and electrical equipment 15.1%, chemicals and chemical products 14.1%, mineral fuels and lubricants 13.2%). *Major import sources:* US 46.2%; Guatemala 9.9%; El Salvador 6.2%; Mexico 4.7%; Costa Rica 3.5%. **Exports** (2001-f.o.b.): $1,329,000,000 (bananas 15.4%, shrimp 13.3%, coffee 12.1%, nontraditional exports [including African palm oil, decorative plants, and mangoes] 42.2%). *Major export destinations:* US 45.7%; El Salvador 10.2%; Guatemala 9.7%; Belgium 4.7%; Germany 4.3%.

Transport and communications

Transport. *Railroads* (2000): serviceable lines 205 km; most tracks are out of use but not dismantled. *Roads* (2001): total length 13,603 km (paved 20%). *Vehicles* (1999): passenger cars 326,541; trucks and buses 59,322. *Air transport* (1995): passenger-km 341,000,000; metric ton-km cargo 33,000,000; airports (1996) with scheduled flights 8. **Communications,** in total units (units per 1,000 persons). Daily newspaper circulation (2000): 349,000 (55); radios (2000): 2,620,000 (412); televisions (2002): 809,000 (119); telephone main lines (2003): 334,400 (49); cellular telephone subscribers (2002): 326,500 (49); personal computers (2002): 91,000 (14); Internet users (2003): 185,416 (27).

Education and health

Educational attainment (1988). Percentage of population age 10 and over having: no formal schooling 33.4%; primary education 50.1%; secondary education 13.4%; higher 3.1%. **Literacy** (2000): total population age 15 and over literate 74.6%; males literate

74.7%; females literate 74.5%. **Health:** physicians (2000) 5,287 (1 per 1,201 persons); hospital beds (2003) 5,069 (1 per 1,353 persons); infant mortality rate per 1,000 live births (2002) 30.9. **Food** (2001): daily per capita caloric intake 2,405 (vegetable products 85%, animal products 15%); 106% of FAO recommended minimum.

Military

Total active duty personnel (2003): 12,000 (army 69.2%, navy 11.7%, air force 19.1%); US troops (August 2003) 390. **Military expenditure as percentage of GNP** (1999): 0.7% (world 2.4%); per capita expenditure $6.

Background

Early residents of Honduras were part of the Maya civilization that flourished in the 1st millennium AD. Christopher Columbus reached Honduras in 1502, and permanent settlement followed. A major war between the Spanish and the Indians broke out in 1537, culminating in the decimation of the Indian population through disease and enslavement. After 1570 Honduras was part of the captaincy general of Guatemala until Central American independence in 1821. Part of the United Provinces of Central America, Honduras withdrew in 1838 and declared its independence. In the 20th century, under military rule, there was constant civil war and some intervention by the US. A civilian government assumed office in 1982. The military remained in the background, however, as the activity of leftist guerrillas increased.

Recent Developments

In March 2005 Honduras ratified the Central America–Dominican Republic Free Trade Agreement (CAFTA–DR), which allows the duty-free import of many Honduran products into the US from 2008. The country took control of foreign-owned oil storage facilities in January 2007, a controversial move that would save Honduras an estimated $66 million annually.

Internet resources: <www.honduras.com>.

Hong Kong

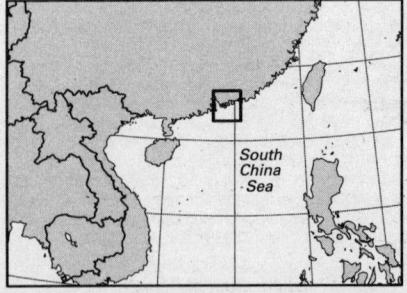

South
China
Sea

Official name: Xianggang Tebie Xingzhengqu (Chinese); Hong Kong Special Administrative Region (English). **Political status:** special administrative region (People's Republic of China) with one legislative house (Legislative Council [60; 30 seats are directly elected by ordinary voters, and the remaining 30 are elected by special interest groups]). **Chief of state:** President Hu Jintao of China (from 2003). **Head of government:** Chief Executive Donald Tsang (from 2005). **Official languages:** Chinese; English. **Official religion:** none. **Monetary unit:** 1 Hong Kong dollar (HK$) = 100 cents; valuation (1 Jul 2007) US$1 = HK$7.82.

Demography

Area: 426 sq mi, 1,104 sq km. **Population** (2006): 6,997,000. **Density** (2006): persons per sq mi 16,425, persons per sq km 6,338. **Urban** (2003): 100.0%. **Sex distribution** (2003): male 48.42%; female 51.58%. **Age breakdown** (2002): under 15, 16.1%; 15–29, 20.6%; 30–44, 28.9%; 45–59, 19.4%; 60–74, 10.4%; 75 and over, 4.6%. **Ethnic composition** (2003): Chinese 95%; other 5%. **Religious affiliation** (1994): Buddhist and Taoist 73.8%; Christian 8.4%, of which Protestant 4.3%, Roman Catholic 4.1%; New Religionist 3.2%; Muslim 0.8%; Hindu 0.2%; nonreligious/atheist 13.5%; other 0.1%. **Location:** east Asia, bordering China and the South China Sea.

Vital statistics

Birth rate per 1,000 population (2003): 6.8 (world avg. 21.3). **Death rate** per 1,000 population (2003): 5.4 (world avg. 9.1). **Natural increase rate** per 1,000 population (2003): 1.4 (world avg. 12.2). **Total fertility rate** (avg. births per childbearing woman; 2003): 1.3. **Marriage rate** per 1,000 population (2003): 5.2. **Life expectancy** at birth (2003): male 78.6 years; female 84.3 years.

National economy

Budget (2002–03). *Revenue:* HK$173,345,000,000 (earnings and profits taxes 41.2%; indirect taxes 22.6%, of which property taxes 5.1%; capital revenue 12.8%). *Expenditures:* HK$273,055,000,000 (education 14.7%; social welfare 11.9%; housing 10.6%; health 9.1%; police 7.5%; economic services 5.4%). **Gross domestic product** (2003): US$173,306,-000,000 (US$25,430 per capita). **Production** (metric tons except as noted). *Agriculture, forestry, fishing* (2000): vegetables 42,500, fruits and nuts 2,022, field crops 508; livestock (2002; number of live animals) 100,000 pigs, 25,000 cattle, 3,000,000 chickens; fish catch (2001) 179,600. *Manufacturing* (value added in HK$'000,000; 2001): publishing and printed materials 12,309; electronic parts and components 9,945; textiles 6,874. *Energy production (consumption):* electricity (kW-hr; 2000) 31,329,-000,000 (40,351,000,000); coal (2000) none (6,057,000); petroleum products (2000) none (5,070,000). **Population economically active** (2003): total 3,487,800; activity rate of total population 51.3% (participation rates: over age 15, 61.1%; female 43.9%; unemployed 7.3%). **Household income and expenditure.** Average household size (2003) 3.1; annual income per household (1996) HK$210,000; expenditure (2001): housing and energy 22.2%, clothing and footwear 15.2%, food and nonalcoholic beverages 13.5%, household furnishings 12.6%, transportation 11.0%. **Tourism** (2001): receipts US$8,241,000,000; expenditures US$12,494,000,-000. **Land use** as % of total land area (2000): in temporary and permanent crops 5.4%, in pasture 29.3%; overall forest area 18.0%.

Foreign trade

Imports (2003-c.i.f.): HK$1,805,800,000,000 (consumer goods 31.9%, capital goods 26.7%, foodstuffs 3.2%, mineral fuels and lubricants 2.0%). *Major import sources:* China 43.5%; Japan 11.9%; Taiwan 6.9%; US 5.5%; Singapore 5.0%. **Exports** (2003-f.o.b.): HK$1,742,400,000,000 (reexports 93.0%, of which consumer goods 35.4%, capital goods 26.0%; domestic exports 7.0%, of which clothing accessories and apparel 3.7%). *Major export destinations:* China 42.6%; US 18.6%; Japan 5.2%; UK 3.3%; Germany 3.2%.

Transport and communications

Transport. *Railroads* (2003): route length 64 km (combined length of East Rail and West Rail; West Rail was inaugurated in December 2003); (2002) passenger-km 4,540,000,000 (East Rail only). *Roads* (2003): total length 1,924 km (paved 100%). *Vehicles* (2003): passenger cars 357,000; trucks and buses 137,000. *Air transport* (2003; Cathay Pacific and Dragonair only): passenger-km 46,523,000,000; metric ton-km cargo 6,057,000,000; airports (2003) with scheduled flights 1. **Communications,** in total units (units per 1,000 persons). Daily newspaper circulation (2000): 5,280,000 (792); radios (2000): 4,560,000 (684); televisions (2000): 3,290,000 (493); telephone main lines (2003): 3,820,000 (561); cellular telephone subscribers (2004): 7,625,700 (1,114); personal computers (2002): 2,864,000 (422); Internet users (2003): 3,212,800 (469).

Education and health

Educational attainment (2003). Percentage of population age 15 and over having: no formal schooling 6.9%; primary education 20.4%; secondary 46.2%; matriculation 5.3%; nondegree higher 7.8%; higher degree 13.4%. **Literacy** (2000): total population age 15 and over literate 93.5%; males literate 96.5%; females literate 90.2%. **Health** (2003): physicians 10,884 (1 per 625 persons); hospital beds 35,378 (1 per 192 persons); infant mortality rate per 1,000 live births (2003) 2.3. **Food** (2001): daily per capita caloric intake 3,104 (vegetable products 68%, animal products 32%); 136% of FAO recommended minimum.

Military

Total active duty personnel (2003): 4,000 troops of Chinese army to intervene in local matters only at the request of the Hong Kong government.

Did you know? Hong Kong ("fragrant harbor" in Chinese) developed initially on the basis of its excellent natural harbor and lucrative trade opportunities, particularly opium dealing. It is located to the east of the Pearl River (Zhu Jiang) estuary on the south coast of China.

Background

The island of Hong Kong and adjacent islets were ceded by China to the British in 1842, and the Kowloon Peninsula and the New Territories were later leased by the British from China for 99 years (1898–1997). A joint Chinese-British declaration, signed on 19 Dec 1984, paved the way for the entire territory to be returned to China, which occurred on 1 Jul 1997.

Recent Developments

The Hong Kong legislature passed a controversial Interception of Communications and Surveillance Ordinance, which allowed authorities to obtain a judge's permission to monitor private communications with telephone wiretaps, e-mail scans, and other covert techniques. Critics feared an erosion of civic freedoms, even though there was a precedent: the Police Special Branch had monitored suspected communists in Hong Kong under British rule during the 1960s and 1970s.

Internet resources: <www.discoverhongkong.com>.

Hungary

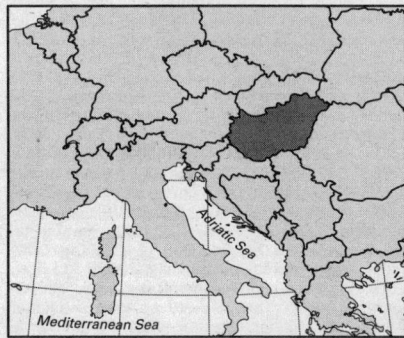

Official name: Magyar Köztársaság (Republic of Hungary). **Form of government:** unitary multiparty republic with one legislative house (National Assembly [386]). **Chief of state:** President László Sólyom (from 2005). **Head of government:** Prime Minister Ferenc Gyurcsány (from 2004). **Capital:** Budapest. **Official language:** Hungarian. **Official religion:** none. **Monetary unit:** 1 forint (Ft) = 100 filler; valuation (1 Jul 2007) US$1 = Ft 181.92.

Demography

Area: 35,919 sq mi, 93,030 sq km. **Population** (2006): 10,064,000. **Density** (2006): persons per sq mi 280.2, persons per sq km 108.2. **Urban** (2004): 64.8%. **Sex distribution** (2004): male 47.49%; female 52.51%. **Age breakdown** (2004): under 15, 15.9%; 15–29, 21.9%; 30–44, 19.8%; 45–59, 21.4%; 60–74, 14.5%; 75 and over, 6.5%. **Ethnic composition** (2000): Hungarian 84.4%; Rom (Gypsy) 5.3%; Ruthenian 2.9%; German 2.4%; Romanian 1.0%; Slovak 0.9%; Jewish 0.6%; other 2.5%. **Religious affiliation** (1998): Roman Catholic 57.8%; Reformed 17.7%;

Lutheran 3.9%; Jewish 0.2%; nonreligious 18.5%; other/unknown 1.9%. **Major cities** (2004): Budapest 1,708,000; Debrecen 205,000; Miskolc 178,000; Szeged 163,000; Pécs 158,000. **Location:** central Europe, bordering Slovakia, Ukraine, Romania, Serbia and Montenegro, Croatia, Slovenia, and Austria.

Vital statistics

Birth rate per 1,000 population (2003): 9.3 (world avg. 21.3); (2002) legitimate 68.7%. **Death rate** per 1,000 population (2003): 13.4 (world avg. 9.1). **Natural increase rate** per 1,000 population (2003): –4.1 (world avg. 12.2). **Total fertility rate** (avg. births per childbearing woman; 2003): 1.3. **Marriage rate** per 1,000 population (2003): 4.5. **Life expectancy** at birth (2002): male 68.3 years; female 76.6 years.

National economy

Budget (2002). *Revenue:* Ft 6,338,100,000,000 (social contributions 34.1%, taxes on goods and services 32.1%, personal income taxes 15.1%). *Expenditures:* Ft 7,781,600,000,000 (social protection 30.2%, public debt 8.8%, transport 8.1%, health 5.8%, education 5.2%, defense 3.0%). **Production** (metric tons except as noted). *Agriculture, forestry, fishing* (2003): corn (maize) 4,534,000, wheat 2,920,000, sugar beets 1,802,000; livestock (number of live animals) 4,658,000 pigs, 1,281,000 sheep, 714,000 cattle; roundwood (2002) 5,637,000 cu m; fish catch (2001) 19,694. *Mining and quarrying* (2002): bauxite 720,000. *Manufacturing* (value added in $'000,000; 2000): electrical machinery and apparatus 1,309; motor vehicles and parts 1,105; food products 1,001. *Energy production (consumption):* electricity (kW-hr; 2003) 34,282,000,000 (43,188,000,000); hard coal (2003) 672,000 ([2000] 1,280,000); lignite (2003) 11,984,000 (14,619,000); crude petroleum (barrels; 2003) 7,586,000 ([2000] 45,853,000); petroleum products (2000) 6,202,000 (5,817,000); natural gas (cu m; 2003) 3,087,000,000 (14,558,000,000). **Public debt** (external, outstanding; 2002): $13,551,000,000. **Population economically active** (2003): total 4,166,400; activity rate of total population 41.1% (participation rates: ages 15–74, 53.8%; female [2002] 44.5%; unemployed 5.9%). **Tourism** ($'000,000; 2002): receipts 3,273; expenditures 1,722. **Gross national product** (2003): $64,028,000,000 ($6,330 per capita). **Household income and expenditure.** Average household size (2002) 2.5; income per household (2001) Ft 2,898,000; sources of income (2001): wages 48.3%, transfers 25.7%, self-employment 16.3%; expenditure (2002): food products 28.8%, housing and energy 17.6%, transportation and communications 16.5%, recreation 7.0%. **Land use** as % of total land area (2000): in temporary crops 50.0%, in permanent crops 2.2%, in pasture 11.4%; overall forest area 19.9%.

Foreign trade

Imports (2002-c.i.f.): Ft 9,704,000,000,000 (electrical machinery 17.0%, nonelectrical machinery 14.6%, road vehicles 8.1%, mineral fuels 7.0%, telecommunications equipment 6.2%). *Major import sources:* Germany 24.3%; Italy 7.5%; Austria 6.9%; Russia 6.1%; China 5.5%. **Exports** (2002-f.o.b.): Ft 8,874,000,000,000 (telecommunications equipment 15.5%, electrical machinery 11.2%, power-generating machinery 10.9%, road vehicles 8.7%, office machines and computers 7.1%). *Major export destinations:* Germany 35.5%; Austria 7.1%; Italy 5.8%; France 5.7%; UK 4.7%.

Transport and communications

Transport. *Railroads* (2003): route length 7,898 km; passenger-km (2002) 10,408,000,000; metric ton-km cargo 7,980,000,000. *Roads* (1999): total length 188,203 km (paved 43%). *Vehicles* (2003): passenger cars 2,777,000; trucks and buses 395,000. *Air transport* (2003): passenger-km 3,130,400,000; metric ton-km cargo 46,000,000; airports with scheduled flights 1. **Communications,** in total units (units per 1,000 persons). Daily newspaper circulation (1996): 1,895,000 (186); radios (2000): 7,050,000 (690); televisions (2000): 4,460,000 (437); telephone main lines (2002): 3,666,400 (361); cellular telephone subscribers (2002): 6,862,800 (676); personal computers (2002): 1,100,000 (108); Internet users (2002): 1,600,000 (158).

Education and health

Educational attainment (1990). Population age 25 and over having: no formal schooling 1.3%; primary education 57.9%; secondary 30.7%; higher 10.1%. **Health** (2002): physicians 32,452 (1 per 313 persons); hospital beds 80,340 (1 per 126 persons); infant mortality rate per 1,000 live births (2003) 7.3. **Food** (2001): daily per capita caloric intake 3,520 (vegetable products 69%, animal products 31%); 134% of FAO recommended minimum.

Military

Total active duty personnel (2003): 33,400 (army 70.7%, air force 23.1%, headquarters staff 6.2%). **Military expenditure as percentage of GNP** (1999): 1.7% (world 2.4%); per capita expenditures $185.

Background

The western part of Hungary was incorporated into the Roman Empire in 14 BC. The Magyars, a nomadic people, occupied the middle basin of the Danube River in the late 9th century AD. Stephen I, crowned in 1000, Christianized the country and organized it into a strong and independent state. Invasions by the Mongols in the 13th century and by the Ottoman Turks in the 14th century devastated the country, and by 1568 the territory of modern Hungary had been divided into three parts: Royal Hungary went to the Habsburgs; Transylvania gained autonomy in 1566 under the Turks; and the central plain remained under Turkish control until the late 17th century, when the Austrian Habsburgs took over. Hungary declared its independence from Austria in 1849, and in 1867 the dual monarchy of Austria-Hungary was established. Its defeat in World War I resulted in the dismemberment of Hungary, leaving it only those areas in which Magyars predominated. In an attempt to regain some of this lost territory, Hungary cooperated with the Germans against the Soviet Union during World War II. After the war, a pro-Soviet provisional

1 metric ton = about 1.1 short tons;   1 kilometer = 0.6 mi (statute);   1 metric ton-km cargo = about 0.68 short ton-mi cargo;   c.i.f.: cost, insurance, and freight;   f.o.b.: free on board

government was established, and in 1949 the Hungarian People's Republic was formed. Opposition to this Stalinist regime broke out in 1956 but was suppressed. Nevertheless, from 1956 to 1988 communist Hungary grew to become the most tolerant of the Soviet-bloc nations of Eastern Europe. It gained its independence in 1989 and soon attracted the largest amount of direct foreign investment in east-central Europe. In 1999 it joined NATO and in 2004 the European Union.

Recent Developments

In 2006, for the first time in Hungary's postcommunist history, voters renewed the mandate of the incumbent government coalition. Its biggest challenge was to strengthen the economy. In July plans to adopt the euro by a target date of 2010 were abandoned as it became clear that Hungary would fail to reduce deficits enough to meet the EU rules. Subsequently, the government finalized an unpopular reform package, which included a substantial tax increase, cuts in welfare spending, and reductions in energy consumption subsidies, as well as a partial reform of the public-administration sector. Also for the first time in Hungary's democratic history, municipal elections failed to reaffirm support for the incumbents.

Internet resources: <www.hungary.com>.

Iceland

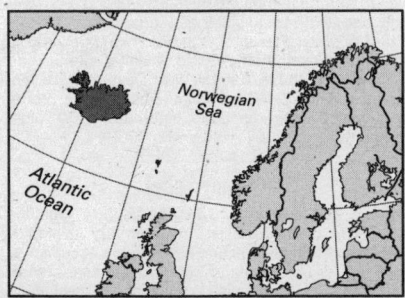

Official name: Lýdhveldidh Ísland (Republic of Iceland). **Form of government:** unitary multiparty republic with one legislative house (Althingi [63]). **Chief of state:** President Ólafur Ragnar Grímsson (from 1996). **Head of government:** Prime Minister Geir H. Haarde (from 2006). **Capital:** Reykjavík. **Official language:** Icelandic. **Official religion:** Evangelical Lutheran. **Monetary unit:** 1 króna (ISK) = 100 aurar; valuation (1 Jul 2007) US$1 = ISK 62.09.

Demography

Area: 39,741 sq mi, 102,928 sq km. **Population** (2006): 302,000. **Density** (2006; calculated with reference to 9,191 sq mi [23,805 sq km] area free of glaciers [comprising 4,603 sq mi {11,922 sq km}], lava fields or wasteland [comprising 24,918 sq mi {64,538 sq km}], and lakes [comprising 1,064 sq mi {2,757 sq km}]): persons per sq mi 32.9, persons per sq km 12.7. **Urban** (2003): 93.8%. **Sex distribution** (2003): male 50.02%; female 49.98%. **Age breakdown** (2003): under 15, 22.9%; 15–29, 22.1%;

30–44, 21.9%; 45–59, 17.8%; 60–74, 9.9%; 75 and over, 5.4%. **Ethnic composition** (2003; by citizenship): Icelandic 96.5%; European 2.5%, of which Nordic 0.6%; Asian 0.6%; other 0.4%. **Religious affiliation** (2001): Protestant 92.2%, of which Evangelical Lutheran 87.1%, other Lutheran 4.1%; Roman Catholic 1.7%; other and not specified 6.1%. **Major cities** (2003): Reykjavík 112,554 (urban area 179,992); Kópavogur 25,016 (within Reykjavík urban area); Hafnarfjördhur 20,720 (within Reykjavík urban area); Akureyri 15,867; Gardhabær 8,695 (within Reykjavík urban area). **Location:** northern Europe, an island between the Greenland Sea, the Norwegian Sea, and the North Atlantic Ocean.

Vital statistics

Birth rate per 1,000 population (2002): 14.1 (world avg. 21.3); (2001) legitimate 36.7%. **Death rate** per 1,000 population (2002): 6.3 (world avg. 9.1). **Natural increase rate** per 1,000 population (2002): 7.8 (world avg. 12.2). **Total fertility rate** (avg. births per childbearing woman; 2002): 1.9. **Marriage rate** per 1,000 population (2002): 5.6. **Divorce rate** per 1,000 population (2002): 1.8. **Life expectancy** at birth (2001–02): male 78.4 years; female 82.6 years.

National economy

Budget (2004). *Revenue:* ISK 279,425,000,000 (tax revenue 90.3%, of which value-added tax 30.8%, individual income tax 26.4%, social security contribution 10.4%; nontax revenue 9.7%). *Expenditures:* ISK 273,035,000,000 (social security and health 40.4%, education 11.8%, social affairs 8.4%, interest payment 5.5%). **Public debt** (2003): $3,333,000,000. **Production** (metric tons except as noted). *Agriculture, forestry, fishing* (2002): potatoes 8,800, cereals 4,400, tomatoes 948; livestock (number of live animals) 469,657 sheep, 71,267 horses, 67,225 cattle; fish catch (value in ISK '000,000; 2002) 77,075, of which cod 28,655, redfish 5,918, herring 4,319, halibut 4,129, shrimp 4,110. *Mining and quarrying* (2002): diatomite 31,000. *Manufacturing* (value added in ISK '000,000; 1996): preserved and processed fish 18,114; other food products 10,848; printing and publishing 6,914. *Energy production (consumption):* electricity (kW-hr; 2002) 8,409,000,000 (8,409,000,000); coal (2000) none (101,000); petroleum products (2000) none (560,000). **Land use** as % of total land area (2000): in temporary crops 0.07%, in pasture 22.7%; overall forest area 0.3%. **Population economically active** (2004): total 162,400; activity rate of total population 55.9% (participation rates: ages 16–74, 81.5%; female (2002) 46.9%; unemployed 2.6%). **Gross national product** (2003): $8,813,000,000 ($30,810 per capita). **Household income and expenditure.** Average household size (2002) 2.8; annual employment income per household (2002) ISK 2,330,000; sources of income (2001): wages and salaries 78.6%, pension 10.3%, self-employment 2.0%, other 9.1%; expenditure (2003): housing and energy 20.3%, food, beverages, and tobacco 19.9%, transportation and communications 18.7%, recreation and culture 13.9%, household goods 6.1%. **Tourism** (2002): receipts $250,000,000; expenditures $365,000,000.

Foreign trade

Imports (2002-f.o.b. in balance of trade and c.i.f. in commodities and trading partners): ISK

207,609,000,000 (machinery and apparatus 20.4%; transport equipment 11.9%; food products 9.5%; crude petroleum and petroleum products 7.9%; clothing and footwear 4.4%). *Major import sources:* US 11.1%; Germany 10.7%; Denmark 8.5%; Norway 8.0%; UK 7.4%; The Netherlands 6.0%. **Exports** (2002): ISK 203,394,000,000 (marine products 62.8%, of which cod 23.9%, shrimp 6.3%, redfish 5.3%, haddock 4.0%; aluminum 18.9%; medicinal products 3.0%). *Major export destinations:* Germany 18.5%; UK 17.6%; US 10.8%; The Netherlands 10.8%; Spain 5.3%.

Transport and communications

Transport. *Roads* (2002): total length 12,955 km (paved 33%). *Vehicles* (2003): passenger cars 161,721; trucks and buses 21,977. *Air transport* (2003; Icelandair only): passenger-km 2,999,800,-000; metric ton-km cargo 95,500,000; airports (1996) with scheduled flights 24. **Communications,** in total units (units per 1,000 persons). Daily newspaper circulation (2000): 100,000 (347); radios (2000): 270,000 (960); televisions (2000): 143,000 (509); telephone main lines (2003): 190,700 (660); cellular telephone subscribers (2003): 279,100 (966); personal computers (2002): 130,000 (451); Internet users (2003): 195,000 (675).

Education and health

Educational attainment (2002): Percentage of population ages 25–64 having: primary and some secondary education 34.4%; secondary 45.7%; higher 19.9%. **Literacy:** virtually 100%. **Health:** physicians (2002) 1,029 (1 per 280 persons); hospital beds 2,432 (1 per 118 persons); infant mortality rate per 1,000 live births (2002) 2.2. **Food** (2001): daily per capita caloric intake 3,313 (vegetable products 59%, animal products 41%); 121% of FAO recommended minimum.

Military

Total active duty personnel (2003): 120 coast guard personnel; NATO-sponsored US-manned Iceland Defense Force (August 2004): 1,800. **Military expenditure as percentage of GNP** (1999): none (world average 2.4%).

Background

Iceland was settled by Norwegian seafarers in the 9th century and was Christianized by 1000. Its legislature, the Althing, was founded in 930, making it one of the oldest legislative assemblies in the world. Iceland united with Norway in 1262. It became an independent state of Denmark in 1918 but severed those ties to become an independent republic in 1944. Vigdís Finnbogadóttir became the world's first female elected president in 1980.

Recent Developments

Iceland's economy grew an estimated 4.5% in 2006, following two years of 7.5% annual growth. The healthy gain was largely due to investment in a 690-MW hy-dropower project at Kárahnjúkar and an aluminum

plant being built by Alcoa at Reyðarfjörður. These two projects cost $3–3.5 billion and were to be completed in 2007. In September the US government closed its military base at Keflavík, which had been in operation since 1951. In defiance of an international ban, Iceland resumed whaling in October, after a two-decade halt.

Internet resources: <www.icetourist.is>.

India

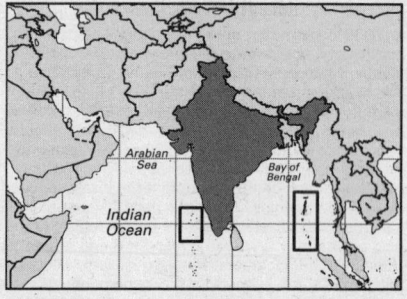

Official name: Bharat (Hindi); Republic of India (English). **Form of government:** multiparty federal republic with two legislative houses (Council of States [245; can have a maximum of 250 members, up to 12 of whom may be nominated by the president], House of the People [545, including 2 nonelective seats]). **Chief of state:** President Pratibha Patil (from 2007). **Head of government:** Prime Minister Manmohan Singh (from 2004). **Capital:** New Delhi. **Official languages:** Hindi; English. **Official religion:** none. **Monetary unit:** 1 Indian rupee (Re, plural Rs) = 100 paise; valuation (1 Jul 2007) US$1 = Rs 40.75.

Demography

Area: 1,222,559 sq mi, 3,166,414 sq km (excludes 46,660 sq mi [120,849 sq km] of territory claimed by India as part of Jammu and Kashmir but occupied by Pakistan or China; inland water constitutes 9.6% of total area of India [including all of Indian-claimed Jammu and Kashmir]). **Population** (2006): 1,119,-538,000. **Density** (2006): persons per sq mi 915.7, persons per sq km 353.6. **Urban** (2001): 27.8%. **Sex distribution** (2001): male 51.74%; female 48.26%. **Age breakdown** (2001): under 15, 35.3%; 15–29, 26.6%; 30–44, 19.5%; 45–59, 10.9%; 60–74, 6.0%; 75 and over, 1.4%; unknown 0.3%. **Major cities** (2001; urban agglomerations, 2001): Greater Mumbai (Greater Bombay) 11,914,398 (16,368,084); Delhi 9,817,439 (12,791,458); Kolkata (Calcutta) 4,580,-544 (13,216,546); Bangalore 4,292,223 (5,686,-844); Chennai (Madras) 4,216,268 (6,424,624); Ahmadabad 3,515,361 (4,519,278); Hyderabad 3,449,878 (5,533,640); Pune (Poona) 2,540,069 (3,755,525); Kanpur 2,532,138 (2,690,486); Surat 2,433,787 (2,811,466); Jaipur 2,324,319 (2,324,-319); New Delhi (within Delhi urban agglomeration) 294,783. **Location:** southern Asia, bordering Pakistan, China, Nepal, Bhutan, Myanmar, Bangladesh, and the Indian Ocean. **Linguistic composition** (1991;

---

1 metric ton = about 1.1 short tons;   *1 kilometer = 0.6 mi (statute);*   *1 metric ton-km cargo = about 0.68 short ton-mi cargo;*   *c.i.f.: cost, insurance, and freight;*   *f.o.b.: free on board*

mother tongue except as noted): Hindi 27.58% (including associated languages and dialects, 38.58%); Bengali 8.22%; Telugu 7.80%; Marathi 7.38%; Tamil 6.26%; Urdu 5.13%; Gujarati 4.81%; Kannada 3.87%; Malayalam 3.59%; Oriya 3.32%; Punjabi 2.76%; Assamese 1.55%; Bhili/Bhilodi 0.66%; Santhali 0.62%; Kashmiri 0.47% (1981); Gondi 0.25%; Sindhi 0.25%; Nepali 0.25%; Konkani 0.21%; Tulu 0.18%; Kurukh 0.17%; Manipuri 0.15%; Bodo 0.14%; Khandeshi 0.12%; other 3.26%. Hindi (66.00%) and English (19.00%) are also spoken as lingua francas (second languages). **Religious affiliation** (2000): Hindu 73.72%; Muslim 11.96%, of which Sunni 8.97%, Shi'i 2.99%; Christian 6.08%, of which Independent 2.99%, Protestant 1.47%, Roman Catholic 1.35%, Orthodox 0.27%; traditional beliefs 3.39%; Sikh 2.16%; Buddhist 0.71%; Jain 0.40%; Baha'i 0.12%; Zoroastrian (Parsi) 0.02%; other 1.44%. **Households** (2001). Total number of households 191,963,935. Average household size 5.4. Type of household: permanent 51.8%; semipermanent 30.0%; temporary 18.2%. Average number of rooms per household 2.2; 1 room 38.4%, 2 rooms 30.0%, 3 rooms 14.3%, 4 rooms 7.5%, 5 rooms 2.9%, 6 or more rooms 3.7%, unspecified number of rooms 3.2%.

Vital statistics

Birth rate per 1,000 population (2003): 23.3 (world avg. 21.3). **Death rate** per 1,000 population (2003): 8.5 (world avg. 9.1). **Natural increase rate** per 1,000 population (2003): 14.8 (world avg. 12.2). **Total fertility rate** (avg. births per childbearing woman; 2003): 2.9. **Life expectancy** at birth (2003): male 62.9 years; female 64.4 years.

Social indicators

Educational attainment (1991; excludes Jammu and Kashmir; no formal schooling: males 43.3%, females 72.8%; complete secondary or higher education: males 10.6%, females 3.7%. Percentage of population age 25 and over having: no formal schooling 57.5%, incomplete primary education 28.0%; complete primary or some secondary 7.2%; complete secondary or higher 7.3%. **Quality of working life** (the first two statistics apply to the workers employed in the "organized sector" only [27.8 million in 2001, of which 19.1 million were employed in the public sector and 8.7 million were employed in the private sector]); few legal protections exist for the more than 370 million workers in the "unorganized sector"). Average workweek (2001): 46 hours. Rate of fatal injuries per 100,000 employees (2001) 36. Agricultural workers in servitude to creditors (early 1990s) 10–20%. **Access to services** (2001). Percentage of total (urban, rural) households having access to: electricity for lighting purposes 55.8% (87.6%, 43.5%); kerosene for lighting purposes 43.3% (11.6%, 55.6%), water closets 18.0% (46.1%, 7.1%), pit latrines 11.5% (14.6%, 10.3%), no latrines 63.6% (26.3%, 78.1%), closed drainage for waste water 12.5% (34.5%, 3.9%), open drainage for waste water 33.9% (43.4%, 30.3%), no drainage for waste water 53.6% (22.1%, 65.8%). Type of fuel used for cooking in households: firewood 52.5% (22.7%, 64.1%), LPG (liquefied petroleum gas) 17.5% (48.0%, 5.7%), kerosene 6.5% (19.2%, 1.6%), crop residue 10.0% (2.1%, 13.1%), cow dung 9.8% (2.0%, 12.8%), electricity 0.2% (0.3%, 0.1%). Source of drinking water: hand pump or tube well 41.3% (21.3%, 48.9%), piped water 36.7% (68.7%, 24.3%), well

18.2% (7.7%, 22.2%), river, canal, spring, public tank, pond, or lake 2.7% (0.7%, 3.5%). **Social participation.** Eligible voters participating in April/May 2004 national election: 58.1%. Trade union membership (1998): c. 16,000,000 (primarily in the public sector). **Social deviance** (1990). Offense rate per 100,000 population for: murder 4.1; dacoity (gang robbery) 1.3; theft and housebreaking 56.6; riots 12.0. Rate of suicide per 100,000 population (1991): 9.0. **Material well-being** (2001). Total (urban, rural) households possessing: televisions 31.6% (64.3%, 18.9%), telephones 9.1% (23.0%, 3.8%), scooters, motorcycles, or mopeds 11.7% (24.7%, 6.7%), cars, jeeps, or vans 2.5% (5.6%, 1.3%). Households availing banking services 35.5% (49.5%, 30.1%).

National economy

Gross national product (2003): $567,604,000,000 ($530 per capita). **Budget** (2002). Revenue (central government only): Rs 3,088,200,000,000 (tax revenue 76.4%, of which excise taxes 29.5%, taxes on income and profits 29.4%; nontax revenue 23.1%; other 0.5%). *Expenditures:* Rs 4,239,100,000,000 (general public services 61.0%, of which public debt payments 26.8%; economic affairs 15.3%; defense 15.2%; education 2.5%; health 1.7%). **Public debt** (external, outstanding; 2002): $88,271,000,000. **Production** (in '000 metric tons except as noted). *Agriculture, forestry, fishing* (2002): cereals 491,174 (of which rice 116,580, wheat 71,814, corn [maize] 10,570, sorghum 7,060, millet 6,150), sugarcane 279,000, fruits 34,720 (of which bananas 16,450, mangoes 11,400, oranges 2,980, apples 1,420, lemons and limes 1,370, pineapples 1,100), oilseeds 16,750 (of which peanuts [groundnuts] 5,400, rapeseed 5,040, soybeans 4,270, sunflower seeds 870, castor beans 590, sesame 580), pulses 10,760 (of which chickpeas 5,320, dry beans 3,000, pigeon peas 2,440), coconuts 9,300, eggplants 8,800, seed cotton 5,580, jute 1,789, tea 826, natural rubber 650, tobacco 575, garlic 497, cashews 460, betel 330, coffee 317, ginger 275, pepper 51; livestock (number of live animals; 2002) 221,-900,000 cattle, 124,000,000 goats, 95,100,000 water buffalo, 58,800,000 sheep, 18,000,000 pigs, 900,000 camels; roundwood 319,418,047 cu m, of which fuelwood 300,564,000 cu m, industrial roundwood 18,854,000; fish catch (2001) 5,965,230, of which freshwater fish 2,950,003, marine fish 2,301,609, crustaceans 498,827. *Mining and quarrying* (2002–03): limestone 136,224; iron ore 54,432 (approximate metal content); bauxite 9,439; manganese 617 (approximate metal content); chromium (2001–02) 543 (approximate metal content); zinc 299 (approximate metal content); lead 40.6 (approximate metal content); copper 38 (approximate metal content); gold 2,873 kg; gem diamonds (2002) 17,000 carats. *Manufacturing* (value added in $'000,000; 2000): industrial chemicals 4,274; food products 3,723; paints, soaps, varnishes, drugs, and medicines 3,500; textiles 3,498; iron and steel 2,989; nonelectrical machinery and apparatus 2,457; cements, bricks, and tiles 1,988; refined petroleum 1,870; motor vehicles and parts 1,744. *Energy production (consumption):* electricity (kW-hr; 2002) 529,692,000,000 (529,698,000,-000); hard coal (2003) 348,432,000 ([2000] 315,583,000); lignite (2003) 26,004,000 ([2000] 22,704,000); crude petroleum (barrels; 2002) 248,520,000 ([2000] 579,300,000); petroleum products (2000) 75,409,000 (79,876,000); natural gas (cu m; 2002) 29,495,000,000 ([2000] 24,315,-000,000). **Land use** as % of total land area (2000): in temporary crops 54.4%, in permanent crops 2.7%, in pasture 3.7%; overall forest area 21.6%. **Population economically active** (2001): total 402,512,190; activity rate of total population 39.2% (female 36.5%; unemployed 10.4%). **Household income and expenditure.** Average household size (2002) 5.4; sources of income (1984–85): salaries and wages 42.2%, self-employed 39.7%, interest 8.6%, profits and dividends 6.0%, rent 3.5%; expenditure (1998–99): food, beverages, and tobacco 52.1%, transportation and communications 13.7%, housing and energy 10.2%, clothing and footwear 5.2%, health 4.4%. **Service enterprises** (net value added in Rs '000,000,000; 1998–99): wholesale and retail trade 1,562; finance, real estate, and insurance 1,310; transport and storage 804; community, social, and personal services 763; construction 545. **Tourism** (2002): receipts from visitors $2,923,000,000; expenditures by nationals abroad $3,449,000,000.

Foreign trade

Imports (2003–04): $77,032,000,000 (crude petroleum and refined petroleum 26.7%; electronic goods [including computer software] 10.2%; precious and semiprecious stones 9.3%; gold and silver 8.8%; non-electrical machinery and apparatus 6.1%; organic and inorganic chemicals 5.2%). *Major import sources* (2002–03): US 7.2%; Belgium 6.0%; UK 4.5%; China 4.5%; Germany 3.9%; Switzerland 3.8%; South Africa 3.4%; Japan 3.0%; Malaysia 2.4%; Singapore 2.2%. **Exports** (2003–04): $63,454,000,000 (engineering goods 19.2%; cut and polished diamonds and jewelry 16.6%; chemicals and chemical products 14.5%; food and agricultural products 11.7%; cotton ready-made garments 9.6%; petroleum products 5.5%; cotton yarn, fabrics, and thread 5.2%). *Major export destinations* (2002–03): US 20.7%; UAE 6.3%; Hong Kong 5.0%; UK 4.7%; Germany 4.0%; China 3.7%; Japan 3.5%; Belgium 3.2%; Italy 2.5%; Bangladesh 2.2%.

Transport and communications

Transport. *Railroads* (2002): route length 144,647 km; passenger-km 936,037,000,000 (includes Indian Railways and 15 regional railways); metric ton-km cargo 541,783,000,000 (includes Indian Railways and 9 regional railways). *Roads* (2002): total length 3,319,644 km (paved 46%). *Vehicles* (2001): passenger cars 7,058,000; trucks and buses 3,582,000. *Air transport* (2002–03): passenger-km 28,561,922,-000; metric ton-km cargo 567,272,000; airports (2002) with scheduled flights 96. **Communications,** in total units (units per 1,000 persons). Daily newspaper circulation (2000): 61,000,000 (60); radios (2000): 123,000,000 (121); televisions (2000): 79,000,000 (78); telephone main lines (2003): 48,917,000 (46); cellular telephone subscribers (2003): 26,154,400 (24); personal computers (2002): 7,500,000 (7.2); Internet users (2003): 18,481,000 (17).

Education and health

Literacy (2001): percentage of total population age 15 and over literate 64.8%; males literate 75.3%;

females literate 53.7%. **Health** (1999): physicians 519,000 (1 per 1,923 persons); hospital beds 918,000 (1 per 1,087 persons); infant mortality rate per 1,000 live births (2003) 59.6. **Food** (2001): daily per capita caloric intake 2,487 (vegetable products 92%, animal products 8%); 113% of FAO recommended minimum.

Military

Total active duty personnel (2003): 1,325,000 (army 83.0%, navy 4.2%, air force 12.8%); personnel in paramilitary forces 1,089,700. **Military expenditure as percentage of GNP** (1999): 2.5% (world 2.4%); per capita expenditure $11.

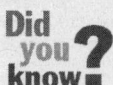

Did you know? The city of Simla is the capital of Himachal Pradesh state, northwestern India. It was built by the British on land they retained after the Gurkha War of 1814–16 and was used for resting troops. It gained popularity as a summer resort because of its cool climate and scenic setting, and from 1865 to 1939 it served as India's summer capital.

Background

India has been inhabited for thousands of years. Agriculture dates back to at least the 7th millennium BC, and an urban civilization, that of the Indus Valley, was established by 2600 BC. Buddhism and Jainism arose in the 6th century BC in reaction to the caste-based society created by the Vedic religion and its successor, Hinduism. Muslim invasions began c. AD 1000, establishing the long-lived Delhi sultanate in 1206 and the Mughal dynasty in 1526. Vasco da Gama's voyage to India in 1498 initiated several centuries of commercial rivalry among the Portuguese, Dutch, English, and French. British conquests in the 18th and 19th centuries led to the rule of the British East India Co., and direct administration by the British Empire began in 1858. After Mohandas K. Gandhi helped end British rule in 1947, Jawaharlal Nehru became India's first prime minister and he, his daughter, Indira Gandhi, and his grandson Rajiv Gandhi guided the nation's destiny for all but a few years until 1989. The subcontinent was partitioned into two countries—India, with a Hindu majority, and Pakistan, with a Muslim majority—in 1947. A later clash with Pakistan resulted in the creation of Bangladesh in 1971. In the 1980s and '90s, Sikhs sought to establish an independent state in Punjab, and ethnic and religious conflicts took place in other parts of the country as well.

Recent Developments

In 2006 India registered 8% growth in national income for the fourth successive year. Foreign direct investment increased sharply in 2005–06, and as much as $320 billion in foreign direct investment for the country's infrastructure was expected in 2007–12. Despite a sharp increase in international oil prices, the rate of inflation was in check and moderate, at about 5%. The government responded to continued high rates of suicides by deeply indebted

1 metric ton = about 1.1 short tons;   1 kilometer = 0.6 mi (statute);   1 metric ton-km cargo = about 0.68 short ton-mi cargo;   c.i.f.: cost, insurance, and freight;   f.o.b.: free on board

farmers by lowering the rate of interest for farm loans and increasing financial support. US Pres. George W. Bush's visit to India in March concluded with an agreement on cooperation regarding India's civilian nuclear-energy capability that allowed US sales of nuclear fuel and technology (the first since 1974). Prime Minister Manmohan Singh traveled to Brazil to launch the India–Brazil–South Africa trilateral forum. Earlier in the year, in a speech in which Singh launched a bus service across the border with Pakistan, he proposed a treaty offering peace and security to Pakistan. In November Chinese Pres. Hu Jintao visited India (the first in 10 years by a Chinese leader), and the two countries agreed to double trade to $40 billion annually and to continue efforts to resolve border issues.

Internet resources: <www.tourismofindia.com>.

Indonesia

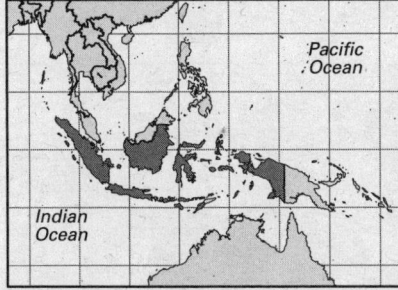

Official name: Republik Indonesia (Republic of Indonesia). Form of government: unitary multiparty republic with two legislative houses (Regional Representatives Council [128]; House of Representatives [500]). Head of state and government: President Susilo Bambang Yudhoyono (from 2004). Capital: Jakarta. Official language: Indonesian (Bahasa Indonesia). Official religion: monotheism. Monetary unit: 1 Indonesian rupiah (Rp) = 100 sen; valuation (1 Jul 2007) US$1 = Rp 9,042.

Demography

Area: 730,024 sq mi, 1,890,754 sq km. Population (2006): 222,731,000. Density (2006): persons per sq mi 305.1, persons per sq km 117.8. Urban (2003): 45.6%. Sex distribution (2000): male 50.14%; female 49.86%. Age breakdown (2000): under 15, 30.4%; 15–29, 29.3%; 30–44, 21.8%; 45–59, 11.3%; 60–74, 5.8%; 75 and over, 1.4%. Ethnic composition (2000): Javanese 36.4%; Sundanese 13.7%; Malay 9.4%; Madurese 7.2%; Han Chinese 4.0%; Minangkabau 3.6%. Religious affiliation (2000): Muslim 76.5%; Christian 13.1%, of which Protestant 5.7%, independent Christian 4.0%, Roman Catholic 2.7%; Hindu 3.4%; traditional beliefs 2.5%; nonreligious 1.9%; other 2.6%. Major cities (2000): Jakarta 8,347,083 (urban agglomeration [2003] 12,300,000); Surabaya 2,599,796; Bandung 2,136,260; Medan 1,904,273; Bekasi 1,663,802. Location: archipelago in southeast Asia, bordering Malaysia, the Pacific Ocean, Papua New Guinea, and the Indian Ocean.

Vital statistics

Birth rate per 1,000 population (2003): 21.5 (world avg. 21.3). Death rate per 1,000 population (2003): 6.3 (world avg. 9.1). Total fertility rate (avg. births per childbearing woman; 2003): 2.5. Marriage rate per 1,000 population (2001; Muslim population only): 8.7. Life expectancy at birth (2003): male 66.5 years; female 71.5 years.

National economy

Budget (2002). Revenue: Rp 300,190,000,000,000 (tax revenue 70.3%, of which income tax 33.9%, VAT 21.9%; nontax revenue 29.7%, of which revenue from petroleum 15.9%). Expenditures: Rp 327,860,-000,000,000 (current expenditure 57.7%; development expenditure 12.3%; expenditure 30.0%). Public debt (external, outstanding; 2002): $70,011,-000,000. Population economically active (2001): total 98,812,448; activity rate 46.1% (participation rates: over age 15 [2000] 67.8%; unemployed 8.1%). Households. Average household size (2000) 3.9. Production (metric tons except as noted). Agriculture, forestry, fishing (2002): rice 51,604,000, palm fruit oil 40,000,000, sugarcane 23,400,000; livestock (number of live animals) 12,400,000 goats, 11,200,000 cattle, 7,350,000 sheep; roundwood (2001) 119,209,000 cu m; fish catch (2001) 5,068,000. Mining and quarrying (2002): bauxite 1,283,000; copper (metal content) 1,172,000; nickel (metal content) 123,000. Manufacturing (value added in Rp '000,000,000; 2000): machinery and transport equipment 57,296; food products 44,736; chemicals and plastics 39,168. Energy production (consumption): electricity (kW-hr; 2000) 99,511,-000,000 (99,511,000,000); coal (2001) 90,648,000 ([2000] 19,668,000); crude petroleum (barrels; 2003) 452,000,000 ([2000] 385,600,000); petroleum products (2000) 48,518,000 (50,136,000); natural gas (cu m; 2002) 86,400,000,000 ([2000] 21,500,000,000). Gross national product (2003): $172,733,000,000 ($810 per capita). Tourism (2002): receipts $4,306,000,000; expenditures $3,368,000,000. Land use as % of total land area (2000): in temporary crops 11.3%, in permanent crops 7.2%, in pasture 6.2%; overall forest area 58.0%.

Foreign trade

Imports (2000-c.i.f.): $33,515,000,000 (machinery and apparatus 18.8%, refined petroleum 10.6%, food and live animals 8.3%, crude petroleum 7.8%, organic chemicals 7.3%). Major import sources: Japan 16.0%; Singapore 11.3%; US 10.1%; South Korea 6.2%; China 6.0%. Exports (2000-f.o.b.): $62,124,000,000 (natural gas 10.7%, crude petroleum 9.8%, garments 7.7%, telecommunications equipment 5.6%, wood products 5.2%, computers and parts 4.9%). Major export destinations: Japan 23.2%; US 13.7%; Singapore 10.6%; South Korea 7.0%; China 4.5%.

Transport and communications

Transport. Railroads (2000): route length 6,458 km; passenger-km 19,228,000,000; metric ton-km cargo 4,997,000,000. Roads (1999): length 355,951 km (paved 57%). Vehicles (2000): passenger cars 3,038,913; trucks and buses 2,373,414. Air transport (1999): passenger-km (2002) 19,690,000,000;

metric ton-km cargo 340,932,000; airports (1996) 81. **Communications,** in total units (units per 1,000 persons). Daily newspaper circulation (2000): 4,870,-000 (23); radios (2000): 33,200,000 (157); televisions (2000): 31,500,000 (149); telephone main lines (2002): 7,750,000 (37); cellular telephone subscribers (2002): 11,700,000 (55); personal computers (2002): 2,519,000 (12); Internet users (2002): 8,000,000 (38).

Education and health

Educational attainment (2000). Percentage of population age 15 and over having: no schooling or incomplete primary 23.9%; primary and some secondary 53.8%; complete secondary 17.9%; some higher 2.2%; complete higher 2.2%. **Literacy** (2000): total population age 15 and over literate 86.9%; males literate 91.8%; females literate 82.0%. **Health** (1999): physicians 31,603 (1 per 6,605 persons); hospital beds 124,834 (1 per 1,671 persons); infant mortality rate per 1,000 live births (2003) 38.1. **Food** (2002): daily per capita caloric intake 2,904 (vegetable products 96%, animal products 4%); 134% of FAO recommended minimum.

Military

Total active duty personnel (2003): 302,000 (army 76.2%, navy 14.9%, air force 8.9%). **Military expenditure as percentage of GNP** (1999): 1.1% (world 2.4%); per capita expenditure $7.

Background

Proto-Malay peoples migrated to Indonesia from mainland Asia before 1000 BC. Commercial relations were established with China in about the 5th century AD, and Hindu and Buddhist cultural influences from India began to take hold. Arab traders brought Islam to the islands in the 13th century; the religion took hold throughout the islands, except for Bali, which retained its Hindu religion and culture. European influence began in the 16th century, and the Dutch ruled Indonesia from the late 17th century until 1942, when the Japanese invaded. Independence leader Sukarno declared Indonesia's independence in 1945, which the Dutch granted, with nominal union to The Netherlands, in 1949; Indonesia dissolved this union in 1954. The suppression of an alleged coup attempt in 1965 resulted in the deaths of more than 300,000 people the government claimed to be communists, and by 1968 Gen. Suharto had taken power. His government forcibly incorporated East Timor into Indonesia in 1975–76, with much loss of life. In the 1990s the country was beset by political, economic, and environmental problems, and Suharto was deposed in 1998.

Recent Developments

Several government policies won widespread support during 2006. The first was the progress toward local elections in the strife-torn province of Aceh, where separatist conflict over the past three decades had cost thousands of lives and immense economic disruption. In 2006 the government steered through the parliament a complex new law that enabled elections and governance reforms in the province and, among other things, allowed for the integration of former separatists into the local political system. These local elections were held in December. Successes in the anticorruption drive were another positive outcome, though corruption remained pervasive in Indonesia. During the year more than 300 national and regional political leaders and officials were tried and found guilty of corruption. Most prominent among these were the religious affairs minister in the previous government and four members of the national election commission. The government's economic policy was also successful. By midyear quarterly economic growth had risen to 5.22%, making Indonesia one of the better-performing economies in Southeast Asia, though figures showed that Indonesia had 11.6 million unemployed, a substantial increase over the previous two years. During the year Indonesia took further steps toward consolidating its democracy by holding nationwide direct elections for governors and district heads.

Internet resources: <www.budpar.go.id>.

Iran

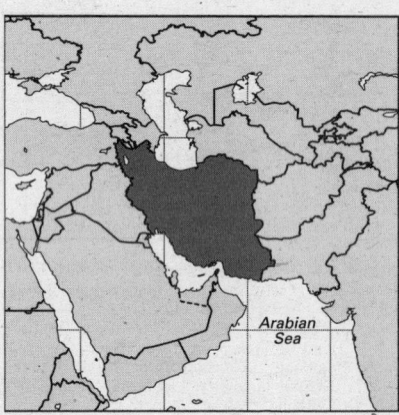

Arabian Sea

Official name: Jomhuri-ye Eslami-ye Iran (Islamic Republic of Iran). **Form of government:** unitary Islamic republic with one legislative house (Islamic Consultative Assembly [290]). **Supreme political/religious authority:** *Rahbar* (Spiritual Leader; not required to be a supreme theological authority) Ayatollah Sayyed Ali Khamenei (from 1989). **Head of state and government:** President Mahmoud Ahmadinejad (from 2005). **Capital:** Tehran. **Official language:** Farsi (Persian). **Official religion:** Islam. **Monetary unit:** 1 rial (Rls); valuation (1 Jul 2007) US$1 = Rls 9,262.

Demography

Area (land area only): 628,789 sq mi, 1,628,554 sq km. **Population** (2006; based on total area of 636,374 sq mi [1,648,200 sq km]): 69,341,000. **Density** (2006): persons per sq mi 109.0, persons per sq km 42.1. **Urban** (2003): 66.7%. **Sex distribution** (2003): male 50.99%; female 49.01%. **Age**

1 metric ton = about 1.1 short tons;   1 kilometer = 0.6 mi (statute);   1 metric ton-km cargo = about 0.68 short ton-mi cargo;   c.i.f.: cost, insurance, and freight;   f.o.b.: free on board

breakdown (2003): under 15, 29.4%; 15–29, 34.5%; 30–44, 19.4%; 45–59, 10.0%; 60–74, 5.1%; 75 and over, 1.6%. **Ethnic composition** (2000): Persian 34.9%; Azerbaijani 15.9%; Kurd 13.0%; Luri 7.2%; Gilaki 5.1%; Mazandarani 5.1%; Afghan 2.8%; Arab 2.5%; other 13.5%. **Religious affiliation** (2000): Muslim 95.6% (Shi'i 90.1%; Sunni 5.5%); Zoroastrian 2.8%; Christian 0.5%; other 1.1%. **Major cities** (1996): Tehran 6,758,845; Mashhad 1,887,405; Esfahan 1,266,072; Tabriz 1,191,043; Shiraz 1,053,025. **Location:** Middle East, bordering the Caspian Sea, Turkmenistan, Afghanistan, Pakistan, the Gulf of Oman, the Persian Gulf, Iraq, Turkey, Azerbaijan, and Armenia.

Vital statistics

Birth rate per 1,000 population (2003): 17.2 (world avg. 21.3). **Death rate** per 1,000 population (2003): 5.6 (world avg. 9.1). **Natural increase rate** per 1,000 population (2003): 11.6 (world avg. 12.2). **Total fertility rate** (avg. births per childbearing woman; 2003): 1.9. **Marriage rate** per 1,000 population (2002–03): 9.9. **Life expectancy** at birth (2003): male 68.0 years; female 70.7 years.

National economy

Budget (2001–02). *Revenue:* Rls 180,975,-000,000,000 (petroleum and natural gas revenue 57.0%; taxes 23.0%, of which corporate 6.8%, import duties 6.5%; other 20.0%). *Expenditures:* Rls 168,992,000,000,000 (current expenditure 66.6%; development expenditures 15.1%; other 18.3%). **Public debt** (external, outstanding; 2002): $6,578,-,000,000. **Tourism** (2002): receipts $1,249,-000,000; expenditures $2,514,000,000. **Gross national product** (2003): $132,896,000,000 ($2,000 per capita). **Production** (metric tons except as noted). *Agriculture, forestry, fishing* (2003): wheat 12,900,000, sugar beets 5,300,000, sugarcane 3,650,000; livestock (number of live animals) 53,900,000 sheep, 9,000,000 cattle; roundwood (2003) 1,310,751 cu m; fish catch (2001–02) 399,000. *Mining and quarrying* (metal content; 2001): iron ore 5,400,000; copper ore 120,000; manganese 105,000. *Manufacturing* (value added in $'000,000; 2000): basic chemicals 5,871; motor vehicles and parts 5,091; iron and steel 4,199. *Energy production (consumption):* electricity (kW-hr; 2003–04) 146,923,000,000 ([2002–03] 136,231,000,000); coal (2000) 1,394,000 (2,094,-000); crude petroleum (barrels; 2003–04) 1,364,000,000 ([2000] 470,000,000); petroleum products (2000) 68,687,000 (54,319,000); natural gas (cu m; 2001–02) 86,300,000,000 (66,-600,000,000). **Population economically active** (2002–03): total 19,819,000; activity rate 30.0% (participation rates: over age 15 [1996] 44.0%; female [1996] 12.7%; unemployed [2002–03] 15.7%). **Household income and expenditure.** Average household size (2000) 4.6; annual average income per urban household (1998–99) Rls 15,151,894; sources of urban income (1998–99): wages 32.8%, self-employment 29.6%, other 37.6%; expenditure (1997–98): food, beverages, and tobacco 32.5%, housing and energy 27.0%, transportation 11.4%. **Land use** as % of total land area (2000): in temporary crops 8.8%, in permanent crops 1.2%, in pasture 26.9%; overall forest area 4.5%.

Foreign trade

Imports (2002-f.o.b. in balance of trade and c.i.f. in commodities and trading partners): $20,336,-000,000 (nonelectrical machinery and apparatus 22.1%, road vehicles 15.4%, chemicals and chemical products 11.1%, iron and steel 8.0%, food products 7.2%, gold 7.1%). *Major import sources* (2002): Germany 17.1%; Switzerland 9.3%; UAE 9.0%; France 5.9%; Italy 5.8%. **Exports** (2002): $28,356,000,000 (crude and refined petroleum 85.4%, carpets 1.9%, nuts 1.7%). *Major export destinations* (2003): Japan 23.0%; China 10.2%; Italy 6.6%; Taiwan 6.4%; South Korea 5.0%.

Transport and communications

Transport. *Railroads* (2002–03): route length 7,265 km; (2001–02) passenger-km 8,043,000,000; (2001–02) metric ton-km cargo 14,613,000,000. *Roads* (2001–02): length 80,720 km (paved 100%). *Vehicles* (2000–01): passenger cars 1,351,800; trucks and buses 384,900. *Air transport* (2003; Iran Air): passenger-km 7,658,000,000; metric ton-km cargo 99,050,000; airports (1996) 19. **Communications,** in total units (units per 1,000 persons). Daily newspaper circulation (2000): 1,780,000 (28); radios (2000): 17,900,000 (281); televisions (2002): 11,331,500 (173); telephone main lines (2003): 14,571,100 (220); cellular telephone subscribers (2003): 3,376,500 (51); personal computers (2002): 4,900,000 (75); Internet users (2003): 4,300,000 (65).

Education and health

Literacy (2002): total population age 15 and over literate 77.1%; males literate 83.5%; females literate 70.4%. **Health** (2002–03): physicians 17,975 (1 per 3,726 persons; excludes private sector physicians); hospital beds 110,797 (1 per 604 persons); infant mortality rate per 1,000 live births (2003) 44.2. **Food** (2001): daily per capita caloric intake 2,931 (vegetable products 90%, animal products 10%); 122% of FAO recommended minimum.

Military

Total active duty personnel (2003): 540,000 (revolutionary guard corps 22.2%, army 64.9%, navy 3.3%, air force 9.6%). **Military expenditure as percentage of GNP** (1999): 2.9% (world 2.4%); per capita expenditure $106.

Did you know? Shiraz is the capital of Fars province in south-central Iran, lying at an elevation of 4,875 ft. (1,486 m). Famous for its wine, it is notable for its gardens, shrines, and mosques. Shiraz is the birthplace of the Persian poets Sa'di and Hafez, whose garden tombs, both resplendently renovated, lie on the northern outskirts.

Background

Habitation in Iran dates to c. 100,000 BC, but recorded history began with the Elamites c. 3000 BC. The Medes flourished from c. 728 BC but were overthrown (550 BC) by the Persians, who were in turn conquered by Alexander the Great in the 4th century BC. The Parthians created a Greek-speaking empire that lasted from 247 BC to AD 226, when control passed to the Sasanians. Arab Muslims conquered them in 640 and ruled Iran for 850 years. In 1502 the Safavids established a dynasty that lasted until 1736. The Qajars ruled from 1779, but in the 19th century the country was controlled economically by the Russian and British empires. Reza Khan seized power in a coup (1921). His son Mohammad Reza Shah Pahlavi alienated religious leaders with a program of modernization and Westernization and was overthrown in 1979; Shi'ite cleric Ruhollah Khomeini then set up a fundamentalist Islamic republic, and Western influence was suppressed. The destructive Iran-Iraq War of the 1980s ended in a stalemate. During the 1990s the government gradually moved to a more liberal conduct of state affairs.

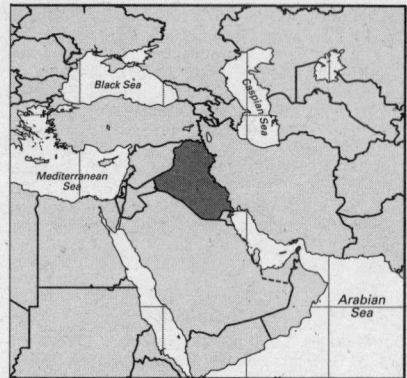

Recent Developments

Perhaps the most important development for Iran in 2006 was the continuing confrontation with the International Atomic Energy Agency (IAEA) and the Western world, which demanded that Iran eschew development of uranium enrichment in its nuclear program. The situation deteriorated in January when Iran ended its moratorium on uranium enrichment, which it claimed was for peaceful purposes. Pres. Mahmoud Ahmadinejad announced in April that Iran had successfully enriched uranium. In May US Secretary of State Condoleezza Rice indicated the US's willingness to participate with the European Union (EU) in direct negotiations with the Iranian government. Iran responded positively to the offer, but the UN Security Council deadline of the end of August for Iran to have ceased uranium enrichment was ignored. The nuclear crisis quickly became a wider debate on overall Iran-US relations. Iran was convinced that the US was enmeshed in a deteriorating situation in Iraq and an extended commitment to Afghanistan and therefore would not contemplate opening a front against Iran. In December the Security Council imposed sanctions on goods and technology related to Iran's uranium-enrichment and ballistic-missile programs in response to the continued research activities. In March 2007 further UN sanctions, including an arms embargo, were imposed by the Security Council.

Internet resources: <www.itto.org>.

Iraq

Official name: Al-Jumhuriyah al-Iraqiyah (Republic of Iraq). **Form of government:** multiparty republic with one legislative house (Council of Representatives [275]). **Head of state:** President Jalal Talabani (from 2005). **Head of government:** Prime Minister Nuri al-Maliki (from 2006). **Capital:** Baghdad. **Official languages:** Arabic; Kurdish. **Official religion:** Islam. **Monetary unit:** 1 (new) Iraqi dinar (ID); valuation (1 Jul 2007) US$1 = ID 1,247.

Demography

Area: 167,618 sq mi, 434,128 sq km. **Population** (2006): 28,513,000. **Density** (2006): persons per sq mi 166.0, persons per sq km 64.1. **Urban** (2000): 67.5%. **Sex distribution** (2001): male 50.57%; female 49.43%. **Age breakdown** (2000): under 15, 42.1%; 15–29, 30.4%; 30–44, 15.6%; 45–59, 7.4%; 60–74, 3.5%; 75 and over, 1.0%. **Ethnic composition** (2000): Arab 64.7%; Kurd 23.0%; Azerbaijani 5.6%; Turkmen 1.2%; Persian 1.1%; other 4.4%. **Religious affiliation** (2000): Shi'i Muslim 62.0%; Sunni Muslim 34.0%; Christian (primarily Chaldean rite and Syrian rite Catholic and Nestorian) 3.2%; other (primarily Yazidi syncretist) 0.8%. **Major cities** (2003): Baghdad 5,750,000; Mosul 1,800,000; Al-Basrah 1,400,000; Irbil 850,000; Karkuk 750,000. **Location:** Middle East, bordering Turkey, Iran, the Persian Gulf, Kuwait, Saudi Arabia, Jordan, and Syria.

Vital statistics

Birth rate per 1,000 population (2003): 33.7 (world avg. 21.3). **Death rate** per 1,000 population (2003): 5.8 (world avg. 9.1). **Natural increase rate** per 1,000 population (2003): 27.9 (world avg. 12.2). **Total fertility rate** (avg. births per childbearing woman; 2003): 4.5. **Marriage rate** per 1,000 population (2000): 7.3. **Divorce rate** per 1,000 population (1997): 1.3. **Life expectancy** at birth (2003): male 66.7 years; female 69.0 years.

National economy

Budget (2003). *Revenue:* ID 4,596,000,000,000 (petroleum revenue 89%; other 11%). *Expenditures:* ID 9,233,000,000,000 (current expenditure 79.7%; development expenditure 20.3%). **Production** (metric tons except as noted). *Agriculture, forestry, fishing* (2002): wheat 800,000, dates 650,000, potatoes 625,000; livestock (number of live animals) 6,200,-000 sheep, 1,400,000 cattle; roundwood (2001) 111,294 cu m; fish catch (2001) 22,800. *Mining and quarrying* (2002): phosphate rock 100,000. *Manufacturing* (value added in $'000,000; 1995): refined petroleum 143; bricks, tiles, and cement 103; food products 59. *Energy production (consumption):* electricity (kW-hr; 2000) 30,521,000,000 (30,521,000,000); crude petroleum (barrels; 2003) 485,400,000 ([2000] 180,793,000); petroleum products (2000) 20,589,000 (18,644,000); natural gas (cu m; 2002)

---

1 metric ton = about 1.1 short tons; 1 kilometer = 0.6 mi (statute); 1 metric ton-km cargo = about 0.68 short ton-mi cargo; c.i.f.: cost, insurance, and freight; f.o.b.: free on board

2,900,000,000 ([2000] 3,737,000,000). **Household income and expenditure** (1988). Average household size 8.9; sources of income: self-employment 33.9%, wages and salaries 23.9%, transfers 23.0%, rent 18.6%; expenditure (1993): food 62%, housing 12%, clothing 10%. **Gross domestic product** (2003): $19,110,000,000 ($770 per capita). **Public debt** (external, outstanding; 1999): $23,000,000,000. **Population economically active** (1996): total 5,573,000; activity rate of total population 27.6% (participation rates: ages 15–64, 45.7%; female 25.0%). **Tourism** (2001): receipts $14,500,000; expenditures $30,600,000. **Land use** as % of total land area (2000): in temporary crops 12.5%, in permanent crops 0.8%, in pasture 9.1%; overall forest area 1.8%.

Foreign trade

Imports (2003-c.i.f.): $9,933,000,000 (UN oil-for-food program 65.7%, capital goods 17.0%, consumer goods 11.4%). *Major import sources:* EU 36.4%; Asia (excluding Middle East) 25.7%; Arab countries 19.9%. **Exports** (2003-f.o.b.): $10,086,000,000 (crude petroleum 82.8%; food and live animals 5.0%). *Major export destinations:* Western Hemisphere (mostly US) 71.2%; EU 13.3%; Arab countries 8.8%.

Transport and communications

Transport. *Railroads* (1999): route length 2,603 km; passenger-km 499,600,000; metric ton-km cargo 830,200,000. *Roads* (1999): total length 45,550 km (paved 84%). *Vehicles* (1998): passenger cars 735,521; trucks and buses 349,202. *Air transport:* Iraqi Airways resumed international flights in September 2004 after 14 years of being grounded by war and sanctions. **Communications,** in total units (units per 1,000 persons). Daily newspaper circulation (2000): 431,000 (19); radios (2000): 5,030,000 (222); televisions (2000): 1,880,000 (83); telephone main lines (2002): 675,000 (28); cellular telephone subscribers (2002): 20,000 (1); Internet users (2002): 25,000 (1).

Education and health

Educational attainment (1987). Percentage of population age 10 and over having: no formal schooling 52.8%; primary education 21.5%; secondary 11.6%; higher 4.1%; unknown 10.0%. **Literacy** (1995): total population age 15 and over literate 58.0%; males literate 70.7%; females literate 45.0%. **Health:** physicians (1998) 11,046 (1 per 1,937 persons); hospital beds (1999) 26,961 (1 per 817 persons); infant mortality rate per 1,000 live births (2003) 55.2. **Food** (2000): daily per capita caloric intake 2,197 (vegetable products 96%, animal products 4%); 91% of FAO recommended minimum.

Military

Total active duty personnel: US/allied coalition forces (November 2004): 138,000/24,000. **Military expenditure as percentage of GDP** (1999): 5.5% (world 2.4%); per capita expenditure $57.

Background

Called Mesopotamia in classical times, the region gave rise to the world's earliest civilizations, including those of Sumer, Akkad, and Babylon. Conquered by Alexander the Great in 330 BC, the area later became a battleground between Romans and Parthians, then between Sasanians and Byzantines. Arab Muslims conquered it in the 7th century AD and ruled until the Mongols took over in 1258. The Ottomans took control in the 16th century and ruled until 1917. The British occupied the country during World War I and created the kingdom of Iraq in 1921. The British occupied Iraq again during World War II. A king was restored following the war, but a revolution ended the monarchy in 1958. Following a series of military coups, the socialist Ba'th Party, led by Saddam Hussein, took control and established totalitarian rule in 1968. The Iran-Iraq War of the 1980s and the Persian Gulf War (precipitated by the Iraqi invasion of Kuwait in 1990) brought heavy casualties and disrupted the economy. The 1990s were dominated by economic and political turmoil. In response to increasingly willful and autocratic behavior by Saddam Hussein and the contention that Iraq was in possession of weapons of mass destruction (none were ever found), on 19 March 2003 air attacks on Baghdad began, and soon afterward US and British ground forces invaded southern Iraq from Kuwait; within a month most of the country was under the control of coalition forces. Saddam was taken into custody in December. In July US authorities established an Iraqi Governing Council, and a new interim constitution was agreed upon in late February 2004. Almost immediately after the occupation began, however, various forms of Iraqi opposition arose, and resistance attacks grew in frequency and violence in the years that followed.

Recent Developments

Political life in Iraq in 2006 was influenced by the results of the general elections of December 2005, in which the United Iraqi Alliance of Shi'ite religious parties captured 128 of 278 seats in the parliament, while Sunni and Kurdish blocs finished second and third. The National Assembly met in April and reelected Jalal al-Talabani to be president of the country for the next four years. Talabani nominated Nuri Kamal al-Maliki of the Islamic Da'wah (Shi'ite) Party as prime minister, and the Assembly approved the selection. Maliki's national unity cabinet, which included Shi'ite, Sunni, and Kurdish ministers, was sworn in in May.

The year was marked by a substantial increase in violence in Iraq, notably between the Arab Sunni and Shi'ite communities, which led to the deaths of tens of thousands of people (in November the Iraqi minister of health estimated that some 150,000 Iraqi civilians had been killed since the invasion in 2003). The major armed militias of the Shi'ite were Jaysh al-Mahdi, the military force of the anti-American cleric Muqtada al-Sadr, and the Firqat-Badr militia of the Supreme Council for the Islamic Revolution in Iraq. These two militias were able to infiltrate the police force and organize death squads, which carried out violence and retaliation against Sunnis. The Sunni militants were mainly armed terrorist groups, such as al-Qaeda, that fought alongside secular Sunni nationalist contingents, such as former Ba'thists. Hundreds of thousands of Sunni and Shi'ites fled to safer areas, both inside the country and in neighboring Syria and Jordan (in May 2007 it was estimated that there were more than 2 million Iraqis living in these two countries). The Sunni accused Iran of intervening to help the Shi‘ites, who in turn accused Syria and some Arab Gulf countries of helping Sunni insurgents and radical Muslims.

The al-Qaeda network in Iraq suffered an important loss in June 2006 when an American air raid killed their leader, the Jordanian-born Iraqi Abu Musab al-Zarqawi. On 30 December former president Saddam Hussein was executed for having had 148 people killed for an alleged attempt in 1982 to assassinate him. In October the National Assembly adopted by a very thin margin a law that would allow the establishment of federal regions in Iraq. While one of the major Shi‘ite parties and the Kurds supported this law, Sunni leaders and a number of Shi‘ite deputies opposed it bitterly, saying it would lead to more violence in the country and weaken the authority of the central government. The Kurdish community in the north, which remained more stable than the rest of the country, continued building up its own institutions and enacting legislation to create a semiautonomous region.

Internet resources:
<www.iraqigovernment.org/index_en.htm >.

Ireland

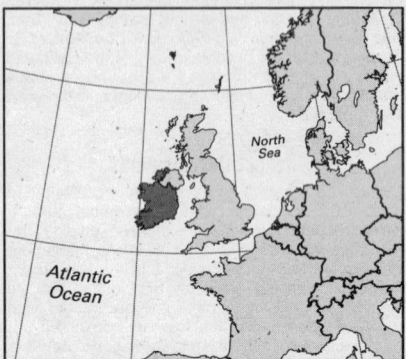

North Sea

Atlantic Ocean

Official name: Éire (Irish); Ireland (English). **Form of government:** unitary multiparty republic with two legislative houses (Senate [60, including 11 nonelective seats]; House of Representatives [166]). **Chief of state:** President Mary McAleese (from 1997). **Head of government:** Prime Minister Bertie Ahern (from 1997). **Capital:** Dublin. **Official languages:** Irish; English. **Official religion:** none. **Monetary unit:** 1 euro (€) = 100 cents; valuation (1 Jul 2007) US$1 = €0.74; at conversion on 1 Jan 2002, €1= 0.79 Irish pound (£Ir).

Demography

Area: 27,133 sq mi, 70,273 sq km. **Population** (2006): 4,250,000. **Density** (2006): persons per sq mi 156.6, persons per sq km 60.5. **Urban** (2002): 59.6%. **Sex distribution** (2003): male 49.68%; female 50.32%. **Age breakdown** (2003): under 15, 21.0%; 15–29, 24.1%; 30–44, 22.3%; 45–59, 17.4%; 60–74, 10.3%; 75 and over, 4.9%. **Ethnic composi-**

tion (2000): Irish 95.0%; British 1.7%, of which English 1.4%; Ulster Irish 1.0%; US white 0.8%; other 1.5%. **Religious affiliation** (2002): Roman Catholic 88.4%; Church of Ireland (Anglican) 3.0%; other Christian 1.6%; nonreligious 3.5%; other 3.5%. **Major cities** (2002): Dublin 495,781 (urban agglomeration 1,004,600); Cork 123,062; Galway 65,832; Limerick 54,023; Waterford 44,594. **Location:** western Europe, bordering the UK (Northern Ireland), the Irish Sea, the Celtic Sea, and the North Atlantic Ocean.

Vital statistics

Birth rate per 1,000 population (2003): 15.5 (world avg. 21.3). **Death rate** per 1,000 population (2003): 7.2 (world avg. 9.1). **Natural increase rate** per 1,000 population (2003): 8.3 (world avg. 12.2). **Marriage rate** per 1,000 population (2003): 5.1. **Total fertility rate** (avg. births per childbearing woman; 2003): 2.0. **Life expectancy** at birth (2002): male 75.1 years; female 80.3 years.

National economy

Budget (2000). *Revenue:* £Ir 21,741,000,000 (income taxes 33.0%, value-added tax 27.0%, excise taxes 15.4%). *Expenditures:* £Ir 19,297,000,000 (social welfare 27.9%, health 20.9%, education 14.9%, debt service 10.5%). **Total public debt** (2001): $37,837,410,000. **Gross national product** (2003): $105,160,000,000 ($26,960 per capita). **Tourism** (2002): receipts $3,768,000,000; expenditures $3,741,000,000. **Production** (metric tons except as noted). *Agriculture, forestry, fishing* (2002): sugar beets 1,313,000, barley 963,000, wheat 867,000; livestock (number of live animals) 6,408,000 cattle, 4,807,000 sheep, 1,763,000 pigs; roundwood (2001) 2,455,000 cu m; fish catch (2001) 417,244. *Mining and quarrying* (metal content; 2002): zinc ore 252,700; lead ore 32,500. *Manufacturing* (gross value added in €'000,000; 2001): chemicals and chemical products 12,370; electrical and optical equipment 7,293; food and beverages 6,902. *Energy production (consumption):* electricity (kW-hr; 2000) 23,750,000,000 (23,848,000,000); coal (2000) none (2,828,000); crude petroleum (barrels; 2000) none (24,540,000); petroleum products (2000) 3,197,000 (7,708,000); natural gas (cu m; 2000) 1,120,800,000 (4,019,000,000). **Population economically active** (2002): total 1,827,100; activity rate 46.6% (participation rates: ages 15–64 [2000] 68%; female [2000] 40.3%; unemployed 4.3%). **Household income and expenditure.** Average household size (2002) 2.9; income per household (1994–95): £Ir 16,224; expenditure (1996): food and beverages 35.4%, transportation 13.9%, rent/household goods 11.6%. **Land use** as % of total land area (2000): in temporary crops 15.2%, in permanent crops 0.03%, in pasture 48.6%; overall forest area 9.6%.

Foreign trade

Imports (2000-c.i.f.): €54,858,000,000 (machinery and apparatus 43.4%, of which computers and parts 20.5%, electronic microcircuits 5.1%; chemicals and chemical products 10.8%; road vehicles 7.3%; food 5.1%). *Major import sources:* UK 31.3%; US 16.6%; Germany 5.8%; Japan 4.8%; France 4.7%. **Exports**

---

1 metric ton = about 1.1 short tons;   1 kilometer = 0.6 mi (statute);   1 metric ton-km cargo = about 0.68 short ton-mi cargo;   c.i.f.: cost, insurance, and freight;   f.o.b.: free on board

(2000-f.o.b.): €82,562,000,000 (computers and parts 23.5%; organic chemicals 20.2%; food 7.1%; electronic microcircuits 5.3%; sound-recording devices 5.0%; telecommunications equipment 4.2%). *Major export destinations:* UK 21.8%; US 17.2%; Germany 11.3%; France 7.6%; The Netherlands 5.6%.

Transport and communications

Transport. *Railroads* (2001): route length 1,947 km; passenger-km 1,515,303,000; metric ton-km cargo 515,754,000. *Roads* (1999): length 92,500 km (paved 94%). *Vehicles* (2000): passenger cars 1,269,245; trucks and buses 188,814. *Air transport* (2001; Aer Lingus only): passenger-km 8,901,000-,000; metric ton-km cargo 146,530,000; airports (1996) 9. **Communications,** in total units (units per 1,000 persons). Daily newspaper circulation (2000): 574,000 (150); radios (2000): 2,660,000 (695); televisions (2002): 2,707,000 (694); telephone main lines (2003): 1,955,000 (486); cellular telephone subscribers (2003): 3,400,000 (845); personal computers (2002): 1,654,000 (421); Internet users (2003): 1,260,000 (313).

Education and health

Educational attainment (1999). Percentage of population ages 25–64 and over having: no formal schooling through lower secondary 49%; upper secondary 30%; higher 21%, of which university 11%. **Health:** physicians (1998) 8,114 (1 per 457 persons); hospital beds (2002) 13,020 (1 per 306 persons); infant mortality rate per 1,000 live births (2000) 5.6. **Food** (2001): daily per capita caloric intake 3,666 (vegetable products 69%, animal products 31%); 146% of FAO recommended minimum.

Military

Total active duty personnel (2003): 10,460 (army 81.3%, navy 10.5%, air force 8.2%). **Military expenditure as percentage of GNP** (1999): 1.0% (world 2.4%); per capita expenditure $208.

Did you know? Waterford glass is a heavy cut glassware produced in Waterford, Ireland, since 1729. Waterford glass, is characterized by thick walls, deeply incised geometric cutting, and brilliant polish. The smoky, bluish gray color of early Waterford glass was considered a drawback, and a clear crystal was produced after 1830.

Background

Human settlement in Ireland began c. 6000 BC, and Celtic migration dates from c. 300 BC. St. Patrick is credited with Christianizing the country in the 5th century AD. Norse domination began in 795 and ended in 1014, when the Norse were defeated by Brian Boru. Gaelic Ireland's independence ended in 1171 when English King Henry II proclaimed himself overlord of the island. Beginning in the 16th century, Irish Catholic landowners fled religious persecution by the English and were replaced by English and Scottish Protestant migrants. The United Kingdom of Great Britain and Ireland was established in 1801. The Great Famine of the 1840s led over two million

people to emigrate and built momentum for Irish Home Rule. The Easter Rising (1916) was followed by civil war (1919–21) between the Catholic majority in southern Ireland, who favored complete independence, and the Protestant majority in the north, who preferred continued union with Britain. Southern Ireland was granted dominion status and became the Irish Free State in 1921, and in 1937 it adopted the name Éire and became a sovereign independent nation. It remained neutral during World War II. Britain recognized the status of Ireland in 1949 but declared that cession of the northern six counties could not occur without the consent of the Parliament of Northern Ireland. In 1973 Ireland joined the European Economic Community (later the European Community) and is now a member of the EU. The late 20th century was dominated by sectarian hostilities between the island's Catholics and Protestants.

Recent Developments

Some unfavorable signs started to appear in Ireland's economic landscape, after more than a decade of exceptional growth, as 2006 drew to a close. GNP growth rates of 6–8% had been achieved in the period 2003–05, but the most credible estimates for 2006 were in the region of 5% and perhaps 3–4% for 2007. Other disturbing signals were a rising rate of inflation and some faltering in consumer confidence in the latter half of the year. The government continued to focus its energy on developments in Northern Ireland. With the ending of the Irish Republican Army's campaign of violence came hope for a political solution, and in March 2007 the political parties in Northern Ireland agreed on a historic power-sharing arrangement in the assembly and executive there.

Internet resources: <www.ireland.ie>.

Isle of Man

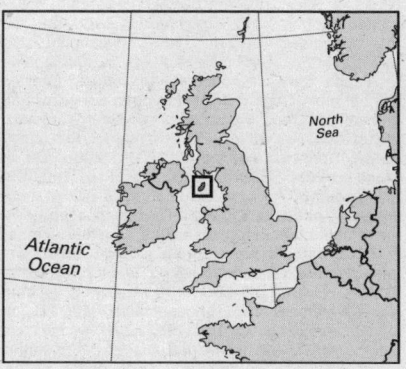

Official name: Isle of Man (Manx Gaelic: Ellan Vannin). **Political status:** crown dependency (UK) with two legislative bodies (collectively named Tynwald; Legislative Council [11, including 3 nonelective seats]; House of Keys [24]). **Chief of state:** Queen Elizabeth II (from 1952), represented by Lieutenant Governor Sir Paul Haddacks (from 2005). **Head of government:**

Chief Minister Tony Brown (from 2006). **Capital:** Douglas. **Official language:** English. **Official religion:** none. **Monetary unit:** 1 Manx pound (£M) = 100 new pence; valuation (1 Jul 2007) US$1 = £M 0.50; the Manx pound is equivalent in value to the pound sterling (£).

Demography

Area: 220.9 sq mi, 572.0 km. **Population** (2006): 78,400. **Density** (2006): persons per sq mi 354.8, persons per sq km 137.1. **Urban** (2001): 72.6%. **Sex distribution** (2001): male 48.97%; female 51.03%. **Age breakdown** (2001): under 15, 17.9%; 15–29, 17.5%; 30–44, 22.6%; 45–59, 20.1%; 60–74, 13.6%; 75 and over, 8.3%. **Population by place of birth** (2001): Isle of Man 48.0%; UK 45.2%, of which England 38.2%, Scotland 3.5%, Northern Ireland 2.3%, Wales 1.2%; Ireland 2.3%; other Europe 1.0%; other 3.5%. **Religious affiliation** (2000): Christian 63.7%, of which Anglican 40.5%, Methodist 9.9%, Roman Catholic 8.2%; other (mostly nonreligious) 36.3%. **Major towns** (2001): Douglas 25,347; Onchan 8,803; Ramsey 7,322; Peel 3,785; Port Erin 3,369. **Location:** Irish Sea, midway between Ireland and Great Britain.

Vital statistics

Birth rate per 1,000 population (2003): 11.1 (world avg. 21.3); (2002) legitimate 64.6%. **Death rate** per 1,000 population (2003): 11.0 (world avg. 9.1). **Natural increase rate** per 1,000 population (2003): 0.1 (world avg. 12.2). **Total fertility rate** (avg. births per childbearing woman; 1999): 1.6. **Marriage rate** per 1,000 population (2002): 5.6. **Divorce rate** per 1,000 population (2000): 3.6. **Life expectancy** at birth (1999): male 73.9 years; female 80.8 years.

National economy

Budget (2001–02). *Revenue:* £466,177,000 (customs duties and excise taxes 64.3%; income taxes 34.8%, of which resident 30.5%, nonresident 4.3%; nontax revenue 0.9%). *Expenditures:* £360,499,000 (health and social security 39.8%; education 19.1%; transportation 6.8%; home affairs 6.0%; tourism and recreation 5.8%). **Production.** *Agriculture, forestry, fishing:* main crops include hay, oats, barley, wheat, and orchard crops; livestock (number of live animals; 2002) 171,000 sheep, 34,000 cattle; fish catch (value of principal catch in £; 2001): 2,200,000, of which scallops 1,600,000, queen scallops 600,000. *Mining and quarrying:* sand and gravel. *Manufacturing* (value added in $; 1996–97): electrical and nonelectrical machinery/apparatus, textiles, other 103,700,000; food and beverages 18,600,000. *Energy production (consumption):* electricity (kW-hr; 2001–02), n.a. (345,000,000). **Household income and expenditure.** Average household size (2001) 2.4; income per household (1981–82) £7,479; sources of income (1981– 82): wages and salaries 64.1%, transfer payments 16.9%, interest and dividends 11.2%, self-employment 6.6%; expenditure (1981–82): food and beverages 31.0%, transportation 14.9%, energy 11.0%, housing 7.9%, clothing and footwear 7.0%. **Gross national product** (at current market prices; 2001–02): $1,770,000,000 ($23,000 per capita).

Population economically active (2001): total 39,685; activity rate of total population 52.0% (participation rates: ages 16 and over 64.2%; female 45.4%; unemployed 1.6%). **Tourism:** receipts from visitors (1999) $90,600,000; number of tourists (2001) 201,300. **Land use** as % of total land area (2000): in temporary crops 8.1%, in permanent crops 0.7%, in pasture 71.5%.

Foreign trade

Imports: n.a. *Major import sources:* mostly the UK. **Exports:** traditional exports include scallops, herring, beef, lambs, and tweeds. *Major export destinations:* mostly the UK.

Transport and communications

Transport. *Railroads* (2001): route length 61 km. *Roads* (2001): total length, more than 805 km. *Vehicles* (2001): passenger cars 45,195; trucks and buses 4,635. *Air transport* (1998; Manx Airlines): passenger-km 846,775,000; metric ton-km cargo 168,000; airports (2001) with scheduled flights 1. **Communications,** in total units (units per 1,000 persons). Newspaper circulation (2001): 2 weekly newspapers and 1 biweekly newspaper (n.a.); televisions (2000): 28,600 (355); telephone main lines (2001): 56,000 (741); cellular telephone subscribers (2001): 32,000 (424).

Health

Physicians (2003) 143 (1 per 540 persons); hospital beds (1998) 505 (1 per 143 persons); infant mortality rate per 1,000 live births (2002) 3.0. **Food** (2002): daily per capita caloric intake 3,412 (vegetable products 69%, animal products 31%); 135% of FAO recommended minimum.

Military

Total active duty personnel: the UK is responsible for defense.

Israel

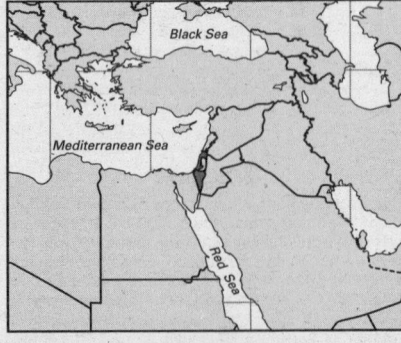

Official name: Medinat Yisrael (Hebrew); Israil (Arabic) (State of Israel). **Form of government:** multiparty

---

1 metric ton = about 1.1 short tons; 1 kilometer = 0.6 mi (statute); 1 metric ton-km cargo = about 0.68 short ton-mi cargo; c.i.f.: cost, insurance, and freight; f.o.b.: free on board

republic with one legislative house (Knesset [120]). **Chief of state:** President Shimon Peres (from 2007). **Head of government:** Prime Minister Ehud Olmert (from 2006). **Capital:** Jerusalem is the proclaimed capital of Israel and the actual seat of government, but recognition of its status as capital by the international community has largely been withheld. **Official languages:** Hebrew; Arabic. **Official religion:** none. **Monetary unit:** 1 New (Israeli) sheqel (NIS) = 100 agorot; valuation (1 Jul 2007) US$1 = NIS 4.25.

Demography

Area: 8,357 sq mi, 21,643 sq km (excludes the West Bank and the Gaza Strip; includes the Golan Heights and East Jerusalem). **Population** (2006): 6,801,000. **Density** (2006): persons per sq mi 813.8, persons per sq km 314.2. **Urban** (2002): 91.6%. **Sex distribution** (2000): male 49.33%; female 50.67%. **Age breakdown** (2000): under 15, 28.6%; 15–29, 25.1%; 30–44, 18.7%; 45–59, 14.5%; 60–74, 8.8%; 75 and over, 4.3%. **Ethnic composition** (2004): Jewish 76.2%; Arab and other 23.8%. **Religious affiliation** (2004): Jewish 76.2%; Muslim (mostly Sunni) 15.7%; Christian 2.1%; Druze 1.6%; other 4.4%. **Major cities** (2003): Jerusalem 680,400; Tel Aviv–Yafo 360,400; Haifa 270,800; Rishon LeZiyyon 211,600; Ashdod 187,500. **Location:** Middle East, bordering Lebanon, Syria, Jordan, the West Bank, Egypt, the Gaza Strip, and the Mediterranean Sea.

Vital statistics

Birth rate per 1,000 population (2002): 21.0 (world avg. 21.3); (2000; Jewish population only) legitimate 97.2%. **Death rate** per 1,000 population (2002): 5.8 (world avg. 9.1). **Natural increase rate** per 1,000 population (2002): 15.2 (world avg. 12.2). **Total fertility rate** (avg. births per childbearing woman; 2002): 2.9. **Marriage rate** per 1,000 population (2001): 5.9. **Divorce rate** per 1,000 population (2001): 1.7. **Life expectancy** at birth (2001): male 77.3 years; female 81.2 years.

National economy

Budget (2003). *Revenue:* NIS 205,703,000,000 (tax revenue 75.4%, of which income tax 35.4%, value-added tax 27.7%; nontax revenue 18.0%; grants 6.6%). *Expenditures:* NIS 220,903,000,000 (defense 21.2%; social security and welfare 19.5%; interest on loans 15.1%; education 14.6%; health 7.2%). **Public debt** (2001): $111,658,000,000. **Gross national product** (2003): $105,160,000,000 ($16,020 per capita). **Production** (metric tons except as noted). *Agriculture, forestry, fishing* (2002): potatoes 375,000, tomatoes 352,000, grapefruit and pomelos 255,000; livestock (number of live animals) 392,000 sheep, 390,000 cattle; roundwood (2002) 27,000 cu m; fish catch (2001) 25,100. *Mining and quarrying* (2001): phosphate rock 3,511,000, potash 1,774,000. *Manufacturing* (value added in $'000,-000; 2000): electronic components 2,243; medical, measuring, and testing appliances 2,103; fabricated metals 1,686. *Energy production (consumption):* electricity (kW-hr; 2001) 43,838,000,000 ([2000] 41,459,000,000); hard coal (2000) none (10,257,-000); lignite (2000) 888,000 (888,000); crude petroleum (barrels; 2000) 29,000 (75,800,000); petroleum products (2000) 9,244,000 (10,428,000); natural gas (cu m; 2000) 8,779,000 (8,779,000).

Population economically active (2003): total 2,601,000; activity rate 40.2% (participation rates: over age 15, 54.3%; female 46.0%; unemployed 10.7%). **Household income and expenditure** (2002). Average household size 3.4; net annual income per household (2001) NIS 136,332; sources of income (2000): salaries and wages 67.5%, self-employment 11.5%; expenditure (2001): housing 22.6%, transport and communications 20.1%, food and beverages 17.0%, education 13.4%, health 4.9%. **Tourism** (2002): receipts $1,197,000,000; expenditures $2,547,000,000. **Land use** as % of total land area (2000): in temporary crops 16.4%, in permanent crops 4.2%, in pasture 6.9%; overall forest area 6.4%.

Foreign trade

Imports (2002-f.o.b. in balance of trade and c.i.f. in commodities and trading partners; balance of trade data excludes the Gaza Strip and the West Bank): $33,106,000,000 (machinery and apparatus 23.7%; diamonds 21.7%; chemicals and chemical products 9.6%; crude petroleum and refined petroleum 7.7%; road vehicles 5.7%). *Major import sources:* US 18.5%; Belgium 9.1%; Germany 7.1%; UK 6.7%; Switzerland 6.3%. **Exports** (2002): $29,511,000,000 (cut diamonds 28.2%; telecommunications equipment 9.2%; rough diamonds 6.5%; organic chemicals 3.9%; electronic microcircuits 3.6%; aircraft parts 3.6%; pharmaceuticals 3.1%). *Major export destinations:* US 40.2%; Belgium 6.3%; Hong Kong 4.7%; UK 3.9%; Germany 3.5%.

Transport and communications

Transport. *Railroads* (2002): route length 678 km; passenger-km 1,116,000,000, metric ton-km cargo 1,102,000,000. *Roads* (2002): total length 16,903 km (paved 100%). *Vehicles* (2002): passenger cars 1,496,878; trucks and buses 347,566. *Air transport* (2003; El Al only): passenger-km 12,126,000,000; metric ton-km cargo 1,091,342,000; airports (1999) with scheduled flights 7. **Communications,** in total units (units per 1,000 persons). Daily newspaper circulation (2000): 1,770,000 (290); radios (2000): 3,210,000 (526); televisions (2000): 2,040,000 (335); telephone main lines (2002): 3,006,000 (453); cellular telephone subscribers (2002): 6,334,000 (954); personal computers (2002): 1,610,000 (243); Internet users (2002): 2,000,000 (301).

Education and health

Educational attainment (2001). Percentage of population age 15 and over having: no formal schooling 3.1%; primary 1.7%; secondary 56.7%; postsecondary, vocational, and higher 38.5%. **Literacy** (2001): 96.9%. **Health** (2002): physicians 21,800 (1 per 291 persons); hospital beds 40,116 (1 per 158 persons); infant mortality rate per 1,000 live births 11.3. **Food** (2001): daily per capita caloric intake 3,512 (vegetable products 81.1%, animal products 18.9%); 137% of FAO recommended minimum.

Military

Total active duty personnel (2003): 167,600 (army 74.6%, navy 4.5%, air force 20.9%). **Military expenditure as percentage of GNP** (1999): 8.8% (world 2.4%); per capita expenditure $1,510.

Background

The record of human habitation in Israel is at least 100,000 years old. Efforts by Jews to establish a national state there began in the late 19th century. Britain supported Zionism and in 1922 assumed political responsibility for what was Palestine. Migration of Jews there during Nazi persecution led to deteriorating relations with Arabs. In 1947 the UN voted to partition the region into separate Jewish and Arab states, a decision opposed by neighboring Arab countries. The State of Israel was proclaimed in 1948, and Egypt, Transjordan, Syria, Lebanon, and Iraq immediately declared war on it. Israel won this war as well as the 1967 Six-Day War, in which it claimed the West Bank from Jordan and the Gaza Strip from Egypt. Another war with its Arab neighbors followed in 1973, but the Camp David Accords led to the signing of a peace treaty between Israel and Egypt in 1979. Israel invaded Lebanon to quell the Palestine Liberation Organization (PLO) in 1982, and in the late 1980s a Palestinian resistance movement arose in the occupied territories. Peace negotiations between Israel and the Arab states and Palestinians began in 1991. Israel and the PLO agreed in 1993 upon a five-year extension of self-government to the Palestinians of the West Bank and the Gaza Strip. Israel signed a full peace treaty with Jordan in 1994. Israeli soldiers and Lebanon's Hezbollah forces clashed in 1997. Following numerous contentious talks between Israel and Lebanon, Israeli troops abruptly withdrew from Lebanon in 2000.

Recent Developments

A 34-day war with the Iranian-backed Hezbollah in Lebanon broke out in July 2006, after a border skirmish in which eight Israeli soldiers were killed and two abducted by Hezbollah militiamen. Israel launched a massive air operation, bombing Hezbollah positions and strategic targets such as the Beirut airport, roads, and bridges. Many criticized Israel for a "lack of proportionality" in its response. Israel, however, saw Hezbollah's actions in the context of Iran's nuclear weapons drive—Hezbollah's prime purpose, in Israel's view, was to threaten it with devastating rocket attacks if it took preemptive military action against Iran. In just 39 minutes the Israeli air force destroyed most of Hezbollah's Iranian-made Zilzal long-range rockets. The strikes also caused hundreds of civilian deaths, however. UN Security Council Resolution 1701, which ended the fighting in August, called for an embargo on arms to Hezbollah, removal of the militiamen from southern Lebanon, and the deployment in the south of the Lebanese army, backed by a large multinational UN force. The war caused losses estimated at $7–15 billion to Lebanon and $1.6–3 billion to Israel, while 163 Israelis and more than 1,000 Lebanese died. The war diverted attention from the Israeli-Palestinian conflict, which had escalated significantly after the kidnapping of an Israeli soldier in June. As Palestinian militiamen in Gaza continued to fire Qassam rockets at nearby Israeli settlements, Israeli forces stepped up their cross-border raids, killing hundreds of Palestinian fighters and arresting many more. The radical group Hamas won a landslide victory in Palestinian parliamentary elections in January, and this seemed likely

to further erode prospects for peace between the two. (Hamas's charter rules out negotiations with Israel and calls for the establishment of Islamic control over all Palestinian land, including Israel.) Most of the international community cut off direct funding to the Palestinian government after Hamas refused to recognize Israel, accept previous Israeli-Palestinian agreements, and renounce terrorism.

Internet Resources: <www.goisrael.com>.

Italy

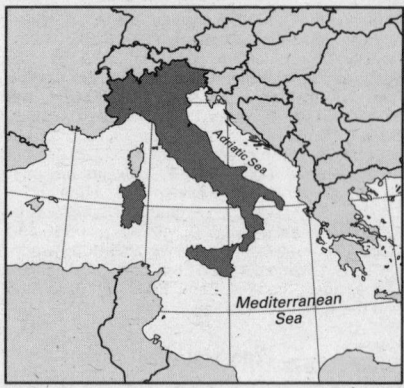

Official name: Repubblica Italiana (Italian Republic). **Form of government:** republic with two legislative houses (Senate [321, including 6 nonelective seats]; Chamber of Deputies [630]). **Chief of state:** President Giorgio Napolitano (from 2006). **Head of government:** Prime Minister Romano Prodi (from 2006). **Capital:** Rome. **Official language:** Italian. **Official religion:** none. **Monetary unit:** 1 euro (€) = 100 cents; valuation (1 Jul 2007) US$1 = €0.74; at conversion on 1 Jan 2002, €1= 1,936.27 Italian lire (Lit).

Demography

Area: 116,346 sq mi, 301,336 sq km. **Population** (2006): 58,888,000. **Density** (2006): persons per sq mi 506.1, persons per sq km 195.4. **Urban** (2003): 67.4%. **Sex distribution** (2003): male 48.44%; female 51.56%. **Age breakdown** (2003): under 15, 14.2%; 15–29, 18.0%; 30–44, 23.5%; 45–59, 19.3%; 60–74, 16.3%; 75 and over, 8.7%. **Ethnolinguistic composition** (2000): Italian 96.0%; North African Arab 0.9%; Italo-Albanian 0.8%; Albanian 0.5%; German 0.4%; Austrian 0.4%; other 1.0%. **Religious affiliation** (2000): Roman Catholic 79.6%; nonreligious 13.2%; Muslim 1.2%; other 6.0%. **Major cities and urban agglomerations** (major city populations are 2001 preliminary census figures; urban agglomeration populations are 2000 estimates by the UN): Rome 2,459,776 (2,649,000); Milan 1,182,693 (4,251,000); Naples 993,386 (3,012,000); Turin 857,433 (1,294,000); Palermo 652,640; Genoa 603,560 (890,000); Bologna 369,955; Florence 352,227 (778,000); Bari 312,452; Catania 306,464; Venice 266,181; Verona

---

1 metric ton = about 1.1 short tons;   1 kilometer = 0.6 mi (statute);   1 metric ton-km cargo = about 0.68 short ton-mi cargo;   c.i.f.: cost, insurance, and freight;   f.o.b.: free on board

243,474; Messina 236,621; Trieste 209,520. **Location:** southern Europe, bordering Switzerland, Austria, Slovenia, the Mediterranean Sea, and France. **National origin** (1991): Italian 99.3%; foreign-born 0.7%, of which European 0.3%, African 0.2%, Asian 0.1%, other 0.1%. **Households.** Average household size (2000) 2.6; composition of households: 1 person 23.3%, 2 persons 26.1%, 3 persons 23.0%, 4 persons 20.2%, 5 or more persons 7.4%. Family households (1991): 15,538,335 (73.8%); nonfamily 5,527,105 (26.2%), of which 1-person 19.5%. **Immigration** (1997): immigrants 162,857, from Europe 41.1%, of which EU countries 14.2%; Africa 25.5%; Asia 19.0%; Western Hemisphere 14.0%.

Vital statistics

Birth rate per 1,000 population (2003): 9.2 (world avg. 21.3); (2000) legitimate 89.8%; illegitimate 10.2%. **Death rate** per 1,000 population (2003): 10.1 (world avg. 9.1). **Natural increase rate** per 1,000 population (2003): –0.9 (world avg. 12.2). **Total fertility rate** (avg. births per childbearing woman; 2002): 1.3. **Marriage rate** per 1,000 population (2001): 4.7. **Divorce rate** per 1,000 population (2000): 0.7. **Life expectancy** at birth (2003): male 76.5 years; female 82.5 years.

Social indicators

Quality of working life. Average workweek (2001): 39.3 hours. Annual rate per 100,000 workers (2000) for: nonfatal injury 4,030; fatal injury 7. Percentage of labor force insured for damages or income loss (1992) resulting from: injury 100%; permanent disability 100%; death 100%. Number of working days lost to labor stoppages per 1,000 workers (1996): 97. **Material well-being.** Rate per 1,000 of population possessing (1995): telephone 434; automobile 550; television 436. **Social participation.** Eligible voters participating in last national election (13 May 2001): 81.2%. Trade union membership in total workforce (2000): c. 35%. **Social deviance** (2000). Offense rate per 100,000 population for: murder 1.3; rape 4.1; assault 210.4 (1995); theft, including burglary and housebreaking 2,466; drug trafficking 61.1; suicide 6.3 (1996). **Access to services** (2002). Nearly 100% of dwellings have access to electricity, a safe water supply, and toilet facilities. **Leisure** (1998). Favorite leisure activities (as percentage of household spending on culture): cinema 21.8%; sporting events 14.6%; theater 13.8%.

National economy

Gross national product (at current market prices; 2003): $1,242,978,000,000 ($21,560 per capita). **Budget** (2000). *Revenue:* €444,502,000,000 (social security contributions 32.5%, individual-income taxes 28.6%, taxes on goods and services 15.9%, corporate income tax 5.9%). *Expenditures:* €462,352,-000,000 (social benefits 41.9%, interest payments 16.0%, grants to general government units 14.9%). **Tourism** (2002): receipts $26,915,000,000; expenditures $16,935,000,000. **Production** (metric tons except as noted). *Agriculture, forestry, fishing* (2003): corn (maize) 8,978,000, sugar beets 8,300,000, grapes 7,484,000, tomatoes 6,634,000, wheat 6,243,000, olives 3,150,000, oranges 1,962,000, apples 1,945,000, potatoes 1,604,000, rice 1,360,000, peaches and nectarines 1,357,000, bar-

ley 1,026,000, lettuce 914,000, pears 822,000; livestock (number of live animals) 10,950,000 sheep, 9,111,000 pigs, 6,430,000 cattle, 100,000,000 chickens; roundwood (2002) 7,789,000 cu m; fish catch (2001) 528,666. *Mining and quarrying* (2001): loam rock 13,973,000; rock salt 3,281,300; feldspar 3,092,400; barite 10,800; lead 4,000. *Manufacturing* (value added in $'000,000; 2000): nonelectrical machinery and apparatus 25,935; fabricated metal products 22,934; food products 13,468; paints, soaps, pharmaceuticals 10,594; bricks, cement, ceramics 8,418; textiles 8,165; wearing apparel 7,524; motor vehicles and parts 7,254; plastic products 6,627; furniture 5,924; footwear and leather products 5,592; telecommunications equipment 5,374. *Energy production (consumption):* electricity (kW-hr; 2003) 292,632,000,000 ([2000] 320,986,000,-000); hard coal (2000) negligible (18,013,000); lignite (2000) 114,000 (130,000); crude petroleum (barrels; 2001) 27,714,000 ([2000] 599,600,000); petroleum products (2000) 84,900,000 (81,700,-000); natural gas (cu m; 2003) 13,456,000,000 ([2000] 70,770,000,000). **Population economically active** (2001): total 23,901,000; activity rate of total population 42.4% (participation rates: ages 15–64, 63.0%; female 38.7%; unemployed 9.6%). **Household income and expenditure** (2000). Average household size 2.6; sources of income (1996): salaries and wages 38.8%, property income and self-employment 38.5%, transfer payments 22.0%; expenditure (2001): housing 34.9%, food and beverages 18.9%, transportation and communications 16.7%, leisure 6.3%, other 16.2%. **Land use** as % of total land area (2000): in temporary crops 28.2%, in permanent crops 9.7%, in pasture 15.1%; overall forest area 34.0%. **Public debt** (2002): $1,333,669,000,000.

Foreign trade

Imports (2000-c.i.f.): $235,859,000,000 (machinery 20.5%, chemicals 12.0%, road vehicles 11.0%, crude petroleum 7.2%, food 6.9%, iron and steel 3.6%). *Major import sources:* Germany 17.5%; France 11.2%; The Netherlands 5.7%; UK 5.4%; US 5.3%; Spain 4.1%; Belgium 4.0%; Switzerland 3.0%. **Exports** (2000-f.o.b.): $237,640,000,000 (machinery and apparatus 27.7%, chemicals and chemical products 9.1%, road vehicles 8.1%, apparel and clothing accessories 5.6%, textile yarn and fabrics 5.1%, food 4.3%). *Major export destinations:* Germany 15.0%; France 12.5%; US 10.3%; UK 6.8%; Spain 6.2%; Switzerland 3.3%; Belgium 2.7%; The Netherlands 2.6%.

Transport and communications

Transport. *Railroads:* (2002) length 19,786 km; (2001) passenger-km 46,675,000,000; (2001) metric ton-km cargo 24,995,000,000. *Roads* (1997): total length 654,676 km (paved 100%). *Vehicles* (2001): passenger cars 33,129,300; trucks and buses 3,749,200. *Air transport* (2003: Alitalia and Air One only): passenger-km 30,736,000,000; metric ton-km cargo 1,355,000,000; airports (1997) 34. **Communications,** in total units (units per 1,000 persons). Daily newspaper circulation (2000): 5,920,-000 (104); radios (2000): 50,000,000 (878); televisions (2000): 28,100,000 (494); telephone main lines (2003): 26,596,000 (453); cellular telephone subscribers (2003): 55,918,000 (1,018); personal computers (2002): 13,025,000 (231); Internet users (2003): 18,500,000 (337).

Education and health

Educational attainment (1995). Percentage of labor force age 15 and over having: basic literacy or primary education 40.4%; secondary 30.5%; postsecondary technical training 5.1%; some college 19.2%; college degree 4.3%. **Literacy** (2000): total population age 15 and over literate 48,100,000 (98.4%); males literate 23,800,000 (98.9%); females literate 24,300,000 (98.0%). **Health:** physicians (2001) 348,862 (1 per 164 persons); hospital beds (2001) 254,663 (1 per 224 persons); infant mortality rate (2003) 6.2. **Food** (2001): daily per capita caloric intake 3,680 (vegetable products 75%, animal products 25%); 146% of FAO recommended minimum.

Military

Total active duty personnel (2003): 200,000 (army 58.0%, navy 18.0%, air force 24.0%); US military forces (2004) 13,400. **Military expenditure as percentage of GNP** (1999): 2.0% (world 2.4%); per capita expenditure $412.

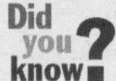

Did you know? The first degree of doctor of civil law was awarded by the University of Bologna in the second half of the 12th century.

Background

The Etruscan civilization arose in the 9th century BC and was overthrown by the Romans in the 4th–3rd centuries BC. Barbarian invasions of the 4th and 5th centuries AD destroyed the western Roman empire. Italy's political fragmentation lasted for centuries but did not diminish its impact on European culture, notably during the Renaissance. From the 15th to the 18th century, Italian lands were ruled by France, the Holy Roman Empire, Spain, and Austria. When Napoleonic rule ended in 1815, Italy was again a grouping of independent states. The Risorgimento successfully united most of Italy, including Sicily and Sardinia, by 1861, and the unification of peninsular Italy was completed by 1870. Italy joined the Allies during World War I, but social unrest in the 1920s brought to power the Fascist movement of Benito Mussolini, and Italy allied itself with Nazi Germany in World War II. Defeated by the Allies in 1943, Italy proclaimed itself a republic in 1946. It was a charter member of NATO (1949) and of the European Community. It completed the process of setting up regional legislatures with limited autonomy in the 1970s. Since World War II it has experienced rapid changes of government but has remained socially stable. It worked with other European countries to establish the European Union.

Recent Developments

In 2006 Italy experienced a huge association football (soccer) scandal, which deflated some of the excitement generated in July when the national team defeated France to capture the Fédération Internationale de Football Association World Cup. Tapes of conversations between referees and Luciano Moggi,

general manager of the Turin team Juventus, were released, and Moggi was overheard giving instructions as to which match officials he wanted assigned to certain games. The scandal grew to involve match-fixing, transfer-fixing, false accounting, and betting, with officials, referees, linesmen, and players implicated. Half of the players on the team that had just taken home the World Cup were from affected clubs, including captain Fabio Cannavaro. Signs of strain appeared over Italy's peacekeeping force in Afghanistan and the dispatch in late August of a 2,500-strong ground and naval force to Lebanon, though Italy announced the withdrawal by year's end of all Italian troops in Iraq.

Internet resources: <www.italyemb.org>.

Jamaica

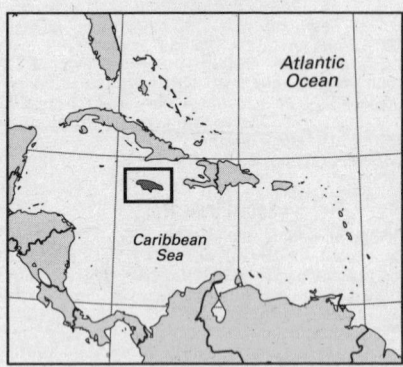

Official name: Jamaica. **Form of government:** constitutional monarchy with two legislative houses (Senate [21]; House of Representatives [60]). Jamaica is to become a republic by 2007 per announcement of prime minister in September 2003. **Chief of state:** Queen Elizabeth II (from 1952), represented by Governor-General Kenneth Hall (from 2006). **Head of government:** Prime Minister Bruce Golding (from 2007). **Capital:** Kingston. **Official language:** English. **Official religion:** none. **Monetary unit:** 1 Jamaica dollar (J$) = 100 cents; valuation (1 Jul 2007) US$1 = J$68.42.

Demography

Area: 4,244 sq mi, 10,991 sq km. **Population** (2006): 2,667,000. **Density** (2006): persons per sq mi 628.4, persons per sq km 242.7. **Urban** (2001): 52.0%. **Sex distribution** (2001): male 49.22%; female 50.78%. **Age breakdown** (2002): under 15, 32.3%; 15–29, 25.9%; 30–44, 20.6%; 45–59, 11.0%; 60–74, 6.8%; 75 and over, 3.4%. **Ethnic composition** (2001): black 91.6%; mixed race 6.2%; East Indian 0.9%; Chinese 0.2%; white 0.2%; other/unknown 0.9%. **Religious affiliation** (2001): Protestant 61.2%, of which Church of God 23.8%, Seventh-day Adventist 10.8%, Pentecostal 9.5%; Roman Catholic 2.6%; other Christian 1.7%; Rastafarian 0.9%; nonreligious 20.9%; other/unknown 12.7%. **Major cities**

(2001): Kingston 96,052 (metro area 579,137); Portmore 161,658; Spanish Town 131,515; Montego Bay 96,488; May Pen 57,334. **Location:** island in the Caribbean Sea south of Cuba.

Vital statistics

Birth rate per 1,000 population (2003): 19.3 (world avg. 21.3). **Death rate** per 1,000 population (2003): 6.4 (world avg. 9.1). **Natural increase rate** per 1,000 population (2003): 12.9 (world avg. 12.2). **Total fertility rate** (avg. births per childbearing woman; 2003): 2.0. **Marriage rate** per 1,000 population (1999): 10.4. **Divorce rate** per 1,000 population (1999): 0.4. **Life expectancy** at birth (2003): male 73.8 years; female 78.0 years.

National economy

Budget (2000–01). *Revenue:* J$101,018,000,000 (tax revenue 86.2%, of which income taxes 35.1%, consumption taxes 26.4%, custom duties 8.4%; nontax revenue 7.7%; bauxite levy 2.7%; capital revenue 1.7%; grants 1.7%). *Expenditures:* J$104,171,000,-000 (current expenditure 91.0%, of which debt interest 41.2%, wages 33.8%; capital expenditure 9.0%). **Production** (metric tons except as noted). *Agriculture, forestry, fishing* (2002): sugarcane 2,400,000, citrus fruits 221,000, vegetables and melons 197,000; livestock (number of live animals) 440,000 goats, 400,000 cattle, 180,000 pigs; roundwood (2002) 867,000 cu m; fish catch (2001) 10,212. *Mining and quarrying* (2003): bauxite 13,443,000; alumina 3,844,000; gypsum 162,000. *Manufacturing* (2001): cement 595,000; animal feeds 385,000; sugar 205,000. *Energy production (consumption):* electricity (kW-hr; 2000) 6,631,000,000 (6,631,000,000); coal (2000) none (72,000); crude petroleum (barrels; 2000) none (7,762,000); petroleum products (2000) 998,000 (3,326,000). **Population economically active** (April 2001): total 1,105,800; activity rate of total population 42.4% (participation rates: ages 14 and over 63.0%; female 43.9%; unemployed 14.8%). **Gross national product** (2003): US$7,285,000,000 (US$2,760 per capita). **Public debt** (external, outstanding; 2002): US$4,592,000,000. **Household income and expenditure.** Average household size (2001) 3.5; average annual income per household (1988) J$8,356; sources of income (1989): wages and salaries 66.1%, self-employment 19.3%, transfers 14.6%; expenditure (1988): food and beverages 55.6%, housing 7.9%, fuel and other household supplies 7.4%, health care 7.0%, transportation 6.4%. **Tourism:** receipts (2002) US$1,200,000,000; expenditures US$258,000,000. **Land use** as % of total land area (2000): in temporary crops 16.1%, in permanent crops 10.2%, in pasture 21.1%; overall forest area 30.0%.

Foreign trade

Imports (2001-c.i.f.): US$3,365,000,000 (consumer goods 29.4%, capital goods 16.8%, refined petroleum and other fuels and lubricants 12.4%, crude petroleum 5.0%). *Major import sources* (2001): US 44.8%; Caricom 12.7%; Latin American countries 10.5%; EU 9.3%, of which UK 3.0%. **Exports** (2001-f.o.b.): US$1,225,000,000 (alumina 52.5%, bauxite 7.7%, wearing apparel 7.2%, refined sugar 5.8%, coffee 2.5%, rum 2.4%). *Major export destinations:* US 31.1%; Canada 15.6%; UK 12.8%; Norway 7.5%.

Transport and communications

Transport. *Railroads* (2003): route length 201 km (inoperable since 1992 except for 92-km section leased to a mining operator). *Roads* (1999): total length 18,700 km (paved 70%). *Vehicles* (2000–01): passenger cars 168,179, trucks and buses 62,634. *Air transport* (2003; Air Jamaica only): passenger-km 5,005,000,000; metric ton-km cargo 48,859,000; airports (2000) with scheduled flights 4. **Communications,** in total units (units per 1,000 persons). Daily newspaper circulation (2000): 161,-000 (62); radios (2000): 2,030,000 (784); televisions (2000): 502,000 (194); telephone main lines (2002): 444,400 (169); cellular telephone subscribers (2002): 1,400,000 (533); personal computers (2002): 141,000 (54); Internet users (2002): 600,000 (228).

Education and health

Educational attainment (2001). Percentage of population age 15 and over having: no formal schooling 0.9%; primary education 25.5%; secondary 55.5%; higher 12.3%, of which university 4.2%; other/unknown 5.8%. **Literacy** (2000): total population age 15 and over literate 88%; males literate 83%; females literate 91%. **Health** (2000): physicians 435 (1 per 5,988 persons); hospital beds (2001) 3,795 (1 per 686 persons); infant mortality rate per 1,000 live births (2003) 13.3. **Food** (2002): daily per capita caloric intake 2,685 (vegetable products 85%, animal products 15%); 120% of FAO recommended minimum.

Military

Total active duty personnel (2003): 2,830 (army 88.3%, coast guard 6.7%, air force 5.0%). **Military expenditure as percentage of GNP** (1999): 0.8% (world 2.4%); per capita expenditure US$19.

Background

The island of Jamaica was settled by Arawak Indians c. AD 600. It was sighted by Christopher Columbus in 1494; Spain colonized it in the early 16th century but neglected it because it lacked gold reserves. Britain gained control in 1655, and by the end of the 18th century Jamaica had become a prized colonial possession due to the volume of sugar produced by slave laborers. Slavery was abolished in the late 1830s, and the plantation system collapsed. Jamaica gained full internal self-government in 1959 and became an independent country within the British Commonwealth in 1962.

Recent Developments

Jamaica was a signatory to the PetroCaribe agreement of 2005, through which Venezuela offered Caribbean countries fuels on a deferred-payment plan. In March 2007 an agreement was signed under which, starting in 2009, Jamaica would purchase from Venezuela 2.5 million metric tons of liquified natural gas annually to replace more expensive petroleum in the bauxite/alumina and electricity-generating industries.

Internet Resources: <www.visitjamaica.com>.

Japan

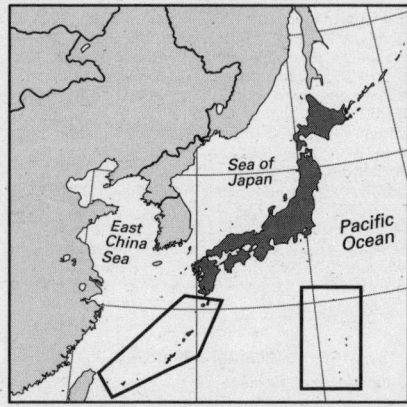

Official name: Nihon (Japan). **Form of government:** constitutional monarchy with a national Diet consisting of two legislative houses (House of Councillors [247]; House of Representatives [480]). **Symbol of state:** Emperor Akihito (from 1989). **Head of government:** Prime Minister Shinzo Abe (from 2006). **Capital:** Tokyo. **Official language:** Japanese. **Official religion:** none. **Monetary unit:** 1 yen (¥) = 100 sen; valuation (1 Jul 2007) US$1 = ¥123.18.

Demography

Area: 145,908 sq mi, 377,889 sq km. **Population** (2006): 127,716,000. **Density** (2006): persons per sq mi 875.3, persons per sq km 338.0. **Urban** (2001): 78.9%. **Sex distribution** (2003): male 48.85%; female 51.15%. **Age breakdown** (2003): under 15, 14.1%; 15–29, 18.6%; 30–44, 20.3%; 45–59, 21.3%; 60–74, 17.4%; 75 and over, 8.3%. **Composition** by nationality (2002): Japanese 98.7%; Korean 0.5%; Chinese 0.3%; other 0.5%. **Immigration** (2000): permanent immigrants/registered aliens admitted 1,686,444, from North and South Korea 37.7%, Taiwan, Hong Kong, and China 19.9%, Brazil 15.1%, Philippines 8.6%, Peru 2.7%, US 2.6%, Thailand 1.7%, Indonesia 1.1%, UK 1.0%, Vietnam 0.6%, Canada 0.6%, India 0.6%, Pakistan 0.4%, other 7.4%. **Major cities** (2002): Tokyo 8,025,538; Yokohama 3,433,612; Osaka 2,484,326; Nagoya 2,109,681; Sapporo 1,822,992; Kobe 1,478,380; Kyoto 1,387,264; Fukuoka 1,302,454; Kawasaki 1,245,780; Hiroshima 1,113,786; Saitama (created in 2001 with the merger of the cities of Urawa, Omiya, and Yono) 1,029,327; Kita-Kyushu 999,806; Sendai 986,713. **Location:** eastern Asia; island chain between the North Pacific Ocean and the Sea of Japan. **Religious affiliation** (1995): Shinto and related religions 93.1% (many Japanese practice both Shintoism and Buddhism); Buddhism 69.6%; Christian 1.2%; other 8.1%. **Households** (2000). Total households 46,782,000; average household size 2.7; composition of households 1 person 27.6%, 2 persons 25.1%, 3 persons 18.8%, 4 persons 16.9%, 5 persons 6.8%, 6 or more persons 4.8%. Family households 33,769,000

(72.2%); nonfamily 13,013,000 (27.8%). **Mobility** (2002). Percentage of total population moving: within a prefecture 2.5%; between prefectures 2.1%.

Vital statistics

Birth rate per 1,000 population (2003): 8.9 (world avg. 21.3). **Death rate** per 1,000 population (2003): 8.0 (world avg. 9.1). **Natural increase rate** per 1,000 population (2003): 0.9 (world avg. 12.2). **Total fertility rate** (avg. births per childbearing woman; 2003): 1.3. **Marriage rate** per 1,000 population (2003): 5.9; average age at first marriage (2003) men 29.4 years, women 27.4 years. **Divorce rate** per 1,000 population (2003): 2.3. **Life expectancy** at birth (2003): male 78.4 years; female 85.3 years.

Social indicators

Quality of working life. Average hours worked per month (2002): 153.1. Annual rate of industrial deaths per 100,000 workers (2001): 2.7. Proportion of labor force insured for damages or income loss resulting from injury, permanent disability, and death (2001): 65.4%. Average man-days lost to labor stoppages per 1,000,000 workdays (1998): 6.8. Average duration of journey to work (1996): 19.0 minutes. Rate per 1,000 workers of discouraged workers (unemployed no longer seeking work: 1997): 89.4. **Access to services** (1989). Proportion of households having access to: gas supply 64.6%; safe public water supply 94.0%; public sewage collection 89.4%. **Social participation.** Eligible voters participating in last national election (November 2003): 52%. Population 15 years and over participating in social-service activities on a voluntary basis (1991): 26.3%. Trade union membership in total workforce (2002): 20.2%. **Social deviance** (2001). Offense rate per 100,000 population for: homicide 0.6; robbery 1.2; larceny and theft 14.2. Incidence in general population of drug and substance abuse per 100,000 population, 0.1. Rate of suicide per 100,000 population: 23.1. **Material well-being** (2001). Households possessing: automobile 84.4%; telephone, virtually 100%; color television 99.3%; refrigerator 98.4%; air conditioner 87.2%; washing machine 99.3%; vacuum cleaner 98.2%; videocassette recorder 79.6%; camera 86.8%; microwave oven 96.2%; compact disc player 60.5%; personal computer 57.2%; cellular phone 78.6%.

National economy

Gross national product (at current market prices; 2003): $4,389,791,000,000 ($34,510 per capita). **Budget** (2002–03). *Revenue:* ¥81,230,000,000,000 (government bonds 36.9%; income tax 19.5%; corporation tax 13.8%; value-added tax 12.1%; stamp and customs duties 3.9%). *Expenditures:* ¥81,230,000,000,000 (social security 22.5%; debt service 20.5%; public works 10.3%; national defense 6.1%). **Public debt** (March 2004): $6,740,000,000,000. **Population economically active** (2002): total 66,890,000; activity rate of total population 52.5% (participation rates: age 15 and over, 63.9%; female 40.9%; unemployed 5.4%). **Household income and expenditure** (2002). Average household size 2.7; average annual income per household ¥6,338,000; sources of income (1994): wages and salaries 59.0%, transfer payments 20.5%, self-employment 12.8%, other 7.3%; expenditure (2002): food 23.3%, transportation and communications 12.0%, recreation 10.1%, fuel, light, and water charges 6.9%, housing 6.5%, clothing and footwear 4.7%, education 4.2%, medical care 3.8%, furniture and household utensils 3.4%. **Tourism** (2002): receipts from visitors $3,499,000,000; expenditures by nationals abroad $26,681,000,000. **Production** (metric tons except as noted). *Agriculture, forestry, fishing* (2002): rice 11,111,000, sugar beets 4,098,000, potatoes 2,980,000, cabbages 2,500,000, sugarcane 1,400,000, onions 1,270,000, sweet potatoes 1,030,000, apples 911,000, wheat 827,800, tomatoes 800,000, cucumbers 740,000, carrots 700,000, watermelons 570,000, lettuce 560,000, eggplant 450,000, pears 375,500, spinach 320,000, cantaloupes 305,000, soybeans 270,200, persimmons 269,300, grapes 231,700, pumpkins 220,000, taro 218,000, barley 217,000, strawberries 210,000, yams 200,000, peaches 175,100, peppers 171,000, cauliflower 115,000, plums 112,700; livestock (number of live animals) 9,612,000 pigs, 4,564,000 cattle, 283,102,000 chickens; roundwood (2001) 16,236,538 cu m; fish catch (2000) 5,752,178, of which squid 671,100, scallops 515,000, cod 398,900, crabs 42,000. *Mining and quarrying* (2001): limestone 182,255,000; silica stone 14,213,000; dolomite 3,389,000; pyrophyllite 403,000; zinc 44,519; lead 4,997; copper 744; silver 80,397 kg; gold 7,815 kg. *Energy production (consumption)*: electricity (kW-hr; 2000) 1,091,499,000,000 (1,091,499,000,000); coal (2000) 3,127,000 (147,891,000); crude petroleum (barrels; 2000) 2,500,000 (1,535,900,000); petroleum products (2000) 182,429,000, of which (by volume [1998]) diesel 32.8%, heavy fuel oil 21.7%, gasoline 21.7%, kerosene and jet fuel 12.0% (190,196,000), natural gas (cu m; 2000) 2,452,600,000 (73,485,300,000). Composition of energy supply by source (1998): crude oil and petroleum products 50.9%, coal 17.0%, nuclear power 14.2%, natural gas 12.8%, hydroelectric power 4.1%, other 1.0%. Domestic energy demand by end use (1998): mining and manufacturing 46.3%, residential and commercial 26.3%, transportation 25.2%, other 2.2%. *Manufacturing* (2001): crude steel 102,866,000; steel products 78,927,000; pig iron 78,836,000; cement 76,550,000; sulfuric acid 6,727,000; plastic products 6,300,000; fertilizers 4,200,000; newsprint 3,210,000; cotton fabrics 710,000,000 sq m; synthetic fabrics 1,920,000 sq m; finished products (in number of units) 420,000,000 watches and clocks, 51,062,000 industrial robots, 46,072,000 cellular phones, 12,421,000 air conditioners, 11,350,000 computers, 9,777,000 passenger cars, 9,112,000 cameras, 8,993,000 video cameras, 5,446,000 vacuum cleaners, 4,184,000 bicycles, 4,059,000 automatic washing machines, 3,875,000 electric refrigerators, 3,130,000 color televisions, 2,675,000 microwave ovens, 2,398,000 photocopy machines, 2,328,000 motorcycles, 1,916,000 facsimile machines, 1,185,000 videocassette recorders. **Land use** as % of total land area (2000): in temporary crops 12.3%, in permanent crops 1.0%, in pasture 1.1%; overall forest area 64.0%.

Foreign trade

Imports (2001-c.i.f.): ¥42,415,500,000,000 (machinery and apparatus 28.5%, of which computers and office machinery 6.5%; crude and refined petroleum 13.3%; food products 12.4%, chemicals and chemical products 7.3%, apparel and clothing accessories 5.5%). *Major import sources:* US 18.1%; China 16.6%; South Korea 4.9%; Indonesia 4.3%; Australia 4.1%; Taiwan 4.1%; Malaysia 3.7%; UAE 3.7%; Germany 3.6%; Saudi Arabia 3.5%. **Exports** (2001-f.o.b.): ¥48,979,200,000,000 (machinery and apparatus 44.4%, of which electronic microcircuits 7.4%, computers and office machinery 5.8%; road vehicles and parts 18.6%; base and fabricated metals 5.9%; precision instruments 5.4%). *Major export destinations:* US 30.0%; China 7.7%; South Korea 6.3%; Taiwan 6.0%; Hong Kong 5.8%; Germany 3.9%; Singapore 3.6%; UK 3.0%; Thailand 2.9%; The Netherlands 2.8%.

Transport and communications

Transport. *Railroads* (2001): length 23,654 km; rolling stock—(1995) locomotives 1,787, (1995) passenger cars 25,973, (1995) freight cars 12,688; passengers carried 21,700,000,000; passenger-km 385,421,000,000; metric ton-km cargo 22,193,000,000. *Roads* (2002): total length 1,232,000 km (paved 82%). *Vehicles* (2002): passenger cars 42,655,000; trucks and buses 18,200,000. *Air transport* (2000): passengers carried 205,106,000; passenger-km 256,428,000,000; metric ton-km cargo 9,800,000,000; airports (1996) with scheduled flights 73. *Urban transport* (2000; Tokyo, Nagoya, and Osaka metropolis traffic range only): passengers carried 57,719,000, of which by rail 34,020,000, by road 19,466,000, by subway 4,233,000. **Communications**, in total units (units per 1,000 persons). Daily newspaper circulation (2000): 73,300,000 (578); radios (2000): 121,000,000 (956); televisions (2002): 99,852,000 (785); telephone main lines (2002): 71,149,000 (558); cellular telephone subscribers (2003): 86,659,000 (680); personal computers (2002): 48,700,000 (383); Internet users (2002): 57,200,000 (449). *Radio and television broadcasting* (2001): total radio stations 1,586, of which commercial 707; total television stations 15,088, of which commercial 8,299. Commercial broadcasting hours (by percentage of programs; 2001): reports—radio 12.6%, television 21.4%; education—radio 2.4%, television 12.1%; culture—radio 13.5%, television 24.8%; entertainment—radio 69.0%, television 39.2%. Advertisements (daily average; 2001): radio 158, television 431.

Education and health

Educational attainment (1998). Percentage of population ages 25–64 having: no formal schooling through complete primary education 2.4%; incomplete through complete secondary 79.9%; postsecondary 17.7%. **Literacy:** total population age 15 and over literate, virtually 100%. **Health** (2002): physicians 260,500 (1 per 489 persons); dentists 91,783 (1 per 1,388 persons); nurses 1,096,967 (1 per 116 persons); pharmacists 212,720 (1 per 583 persons); midwives (2000) 24,511 (1 per 5,176 persons); hospital beds 1,642,593 (1 per 78 persons); infant mortality rate per 1,000 live births (2003) 3.0. **Food** (2001): daily per capita caloric intake 2,768 (vegetable products 79%, animal products 21%); 118% of FAO recommended minimum.

Military

Total active duty personnel (2003): 239,900 (army 61.8%, navy 18.5%, air force 19.0%); US troops (August 2004) 40,000. **Military expenditure as percentage of GNP** (1999): 1.0% (world 2.4%); per capita expenditure $342.

Did you know? The last eruption of Mount Fuji took place in 1707. Mount Fuji is the highest mountain in Japan, rising to 12,388 ft (3,776 m) near the Pacific coast in central Honshu, about 60 mi (100 km) west of Tokyo. Although the volcano has been dormant since 1707, it is still generally classified as active.

Background

Japan's history began with the accession of the legendary first emperor, Jimmu, in 660 BC. The Yamato court established the first unified Japanese state in the 4th–5th century AD; during this period Buddhism arrived in Japan by way of Korea. For centuries Japan borrowed heavily from Chinese culture, but it began to sever its links with the mainland by the 9th century. In 1192 Minamoto Yoritomo established Japan's first *bakufu*, or shogunate. Unification was achieved in the late 1500s under the leadership of Oda Nobunaga, Toyotomi Hideyoshi, and Tokugawa Ieyasu. During the Tokugawa shogunate, beginning in 1603, the government imposed a policy of isolation. Under the leadership of Emperor Meiji (1868–1912), it adopted a constitution (1889) and began a program of modernization and Westernization. Japanese imperialism led to war with China (1894–95) and Russia (1904–05) as well as to the annexation of Korea (1910) and Manchuria (1931). During World War II Japan attacked US forces in Hawaii and the Philippines (December 1941) and occupied European colonial possessions in South Asia. In 1945 the US dropped atomic bombs on Hiroshima and Nagasaki, and Japan surrendered to the Allied powers. US postwar occupation of Japan led to a new democratic constitution in 1947. In rebuilding Japan's ruined industrial plant, new technology was used in every major industry. A tremendous economic recovery followed, and it was able to maintain a favorable balance of trade into the 1990s.

Recent Developments

The greatest military threat Japan had faced since the end of the Cold War emerged in October 2006 as North Korea set off its first nuclear explosion. Months earlier it had demonstrated a new accuracy in test launchings of its short- and medium-range missiles capable of reaching targets, including US bases, on all four of Japan's main islands and Okinawa. After the missile firings, Chief Cabinet Secretary Shinzo Abe, who was to become prime minister two months later, joined Foreign Minister Taro Aso and Defense Director Fukushiro Nukaga in declaring that Japan should study developing the capability to carry out preemptive strikes against launching sites in North Korea. Fearful that North Korea's nuclear explosion might induce Japan to build its own nuclear arsenal, US Secretary of State Condoleezza Rice visited Tokyo and declared that the US retained "the will and capability to meet the full range—and I underscore, the full range—of its deterrent and security commitments to Japan." The upshot was the end to a six-decade taboo in Japan on debating nuclear weapons, though opponents vastly outnumbered those supporters who dared to speak out in favor of nuclear weapons in the only country to suffer nuclear attacks. North Korea also ignored Japan's demand for a full explanation of what had happened to 13 Japanese citizens whom in 2002 North Korean leader Kim Jong Il had admitted abducting from Japan beginning in the 1970s. Forty thousand US troops were stationed in Japan in 2006. In May Kyodo News Agency reported that the Japanese government estimated its costs for a proposed realignment of US bases at ¥1.1 trillion (about $9.3 billion), in addition to the officially announced $6 billion it would give the US to defray the costs of removing from Okinawa to Guam 17,000 American Marines and dependents. Japan brought home the 600 ground troops who had been in Iraq since January 2004 for reconstruction and water-purification efforts. Japan agreed, however, to expand its air-force transportation and cargo services to US and coalition forces in Iraq and extend fueling services that its ships in the Indian Ocean had been providing to the navies of allied forces engaged in Afghanistan.

Japan's closely watched population statistics showed a slight upturn in 2006. January–July births rose for the first time in six years, and marriages increased for the first time in five years. (In 2005, for the first time, Japan's overall population had declined.) A record period of economic growth—58 months—was reached in November, though this yielded only a 10% increase in GDP.

Internet Resources: <www.jnto.go.jp>.

Jersey

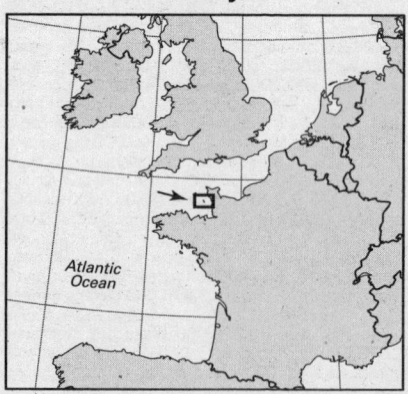

Official name: Bailiwick of Jersey. **Political status:** crown dependency (UK) with one legislative house (States of Jersey [58, including 53 elected officials

---

1 metric ton = about 1.1 short tons;   1 kilometer = 0.6 mi (statute);   1 metric ton-km cargo = about 0.68 short ton-mi cargo;   c.i.f.: cost, insurance, and freight;   f.o.b.: free on board

and 5 ex officio members with limited legislative rights]). **Chief of state:** British Monarch Queen Elizabeth II (from 1952), represented by Lieutenant Governor Andrew Ridgway (from 2006). **Head of government:** Chief Minister Frank Walker (from 2005). **Capital:** Saint Helier. **Official language:** English (until the 1960s French was an official language of Jersey and is still used by the court and legal professions; Jèrriais, a Norman-French dialect, is spoken by a small number of residents). **Official religion:** none. **Monetary unit:** 1 Jersey pound (£J) = 100 pence; valuation (1 Jul 2007) US$1 = £J0.50; at par with the British pound (£).

Demography

Area: 45.6 sq mi, 118.2 sq km. **Population** (2006): 88,300. **Density** (2006): persons per sq mi 1,919.6, persons per sq km 748.3. **Urban** (2001; includes Guernsey): 28.9%. **Sex distribution** (2001): male 48.73%; female 51.27%. **Age breakdown** (2001): under 15, 16.9%; 15–29, 18.4%; 30–44, 25.9%; 45–59, 19.7%; 60–74, 12.6%; 75 and over, 6.5%. **Population by place of birth** (2001): Jersey 52.6%; UK, Guernsey, or Isle of Man 35.8%; Portugal 5.9%; France 1.2%; other 4.5%. **Religious affiliation** (2000; includes Guernsey): Christian 86.0%, of which Anglican 44.1%, Roman Catholic 14.6%, other Protestant 6.9%, unaffiliated Christian 20.1%; nonreligious/atheist 13.4%; other 0.6%. **Major cities** (2001; population of parishes): St. Helier 28,310; St. Saviour 12,491; St. Brelade 10,134. **Location:** western Europe, island in the English Channel.

Vital statistics

Birth rate per 1,000 population (2003): 10.4 (world avg. 21.3). **Death rate** per 1,000 population (2003): 9.2 (world avg. 9.1). **Natural increase rate** per 1,000 population (2003): 1.2 (world avg. 12.2). **Total fertility rate** (avg. births per childbearing woman; 2003): 1.6. **Marriage rate** per 1,000 population (2001): 7.6. **Divorce rate** per 1,000 population (2001): 3.2. **Life expectancy** at birth (2003): male 76.5 years; female 81.6 years.

National economy

Budget (2001). *Revenue:* £400,085,000 (income tax 86.8%, import duties 8.7%, interest payment 1.5%, other 3.0%). *Expenditures:* £369,138,000 (current expenditure 79.3%, of which health 25.7%, education 19.0%, social security 18.2%, public services 5.1%; capital expenditure 20.7%). **Production.** *Agriculture, forestry, fishing:* fruits and vegetables, mostly potatoes and greenhouse tomatoes; greenhouse flowers are important export crops; livestock (number of live animals; 2001) 4,552 mature dairy cattle; fish catch (value of catch in £'000; 2002): 6,053, of which crustaceans (including lobsters and crabs) 3,695, scallops 758, marine fish 713, oysters 607. *Manufacturing:* light industry, mainly electrical goods, textiles and clothing. *Energy production (consumption):* electricity (kW-hr; 2001) 153,000,000 (567,000,000). **Gross national product** (at current market prices; 2003): $4,805,000,000 ($54,810 per capita). **Household income and expenditure.** Average household size (2001) 2.4; average annual income of workers (2001) £22,700; expenditure (1998–99): housing 20.1%, recreation 16.5%, transportation 12.8%, household furnishings 11.6%, food

11.5%, alcoholic beverages 6.0%, clothing and footwear 5.5%. **Population economically active** (2003): total 46,620; activity rate of total population 53.2% (participation rates [2001]: ages 15–64, 81.7%; female 45.5%; unemployed [June 2004] 0.9%). **Tourism** (1996): receipts $429,000,000; number of visitors for at least one night (2001) 470,000. **Land use** as % of total land area (1997): in temporary and permanent crops 29%, in pasture 22%; overall forest area 6%.

Foreign trade

Customs ceased recording imports and exports·as of 1980. *Major import sources* (2001): mostly the UK. **Exports:** agricultural and marine exports (2001): £40,626,000 (potatoes 67.4%, greenhouse tomatoes 19.1%, flowers 3.3%, zucchini 3.0%, crustaceans 2.0%, mollusks 2.0%). *Major export destinations:* mostly the UK.

Transport and communications

Transport. *Roads* (1995): total length 557 km (paved 100%). *Vehicles* (2002): passenger cars 74,007; trucks and buses 12,957. *Air transport* (1999; Jersey European Airways): passenger-km 890,438,000; metric ton-km cargo 923,000; airports (2002) with scheduled flights 1. **Communications,** in total units (units per 1,000 persons). Daily newspaper circulation (2002): 22,897 (262); telephone main lines (2002): 74,300 (851); cellular telephone subscribers (2002): 72,000 (824); Internet users (2001): 8,000 (92).

Education and health

Educational attainment (2001). Percentage of male population (16–64), female population (16–59) having: no formal degree 34.1%; undergraduate 7.1%; graduate (advanced degree) 4.1%. **Literacy** (2002): 100.0%. **Health:** physicians (2001) 174 (1 per 500 persons); hospital beds (1995) 651 (1 per 130 persons); infant mortality rate per 1,000 live births (2003) 5.4.

Military

Total active duty personnel (2003): none; defense is the responsibility of the UK.

Jordan

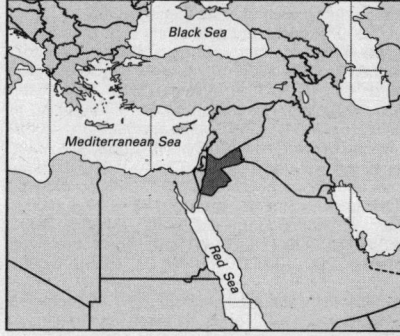

Official name: Al-Mamlakah al-Urdunniyah al-Hashimiyah (Al-Urdun) (Hashemite Kingdom of Jordan). Form of government: constitutional monarchy with two legislative houses (Senate [55; all members are appointed by the king]; House of Representatives [110]). Head of state and government: King Abdullah II (from 1999), assisted by Prime Minister Marouf al-Bakhit (from 2005). Capital: Amman. Official language: Arabic. Official religion: Islam. Monetary unit: 1 Jordan dinar (JD) = 1,000 fils; valuation (1 Jul 2007) US$1 = JD 0.71.

Demography

Area: 34,495 sq mi, 89,342 sq km. Population (2006): 5,505,000. Density (2006): persons per sq mi 159.6, persons per sq km 61.6. Urban (2003): 78.7%. Sex distribution (2003): male 52.30%; female 47.70%. Age breakdown (2002): under 15, 36.6%; 15–29, 30.4%; 30–44, 19.8%; 45–59, 8.0%; 60–74, 4.3%; 75 and over, 0.9%. Ethnic composition (2000): Arab 97.8%, of which Jordanian 32.4%, Palestinian 32.2%, Iraqi 14.0%, Bedouin 12.8%; Circassian 1.2%; other 1.0%. Religious affiliation (2000): Sunni Muslim 93.5%; Christian 4.1%; other 2.4%. Major cities (1994): Amman 969,598; Az-Zarqa 350,849; Irbid 208,329; Ar-Rusayfah 137,247; Wadi Essier 89,104. Location: the Middle East, bordering Syria, Iraq, Saudi Arabia, the Gulf of Aqaba, Israel, and parts of the Emerging Palestinian Autonomous Areas.

Vital statistics

Birth rate per 1,000 population (2003): 27.4 (world avg. 21.3). Death rate per 1,000 population (2003): 3.1 (world avg. 9.1). Natural increase rate per 1,000 population (2003): 24.3 (world avg. 12.2). Total fertility rate (avg. births per childbearing woman; 2003): 3.7. Marriage rate per 1,000 population (2003): 9.0. Divorce rate per 1,000 population (2003): 1.7. Life expectancy at birth (2003): male 70.6 years; female 72.4 years.

National economy

Budget (2003). Revenue: JD 2,511,000,000 (tax revenue 43.1%, of which sales tax 23.7%, custom duties 8.0%, income and profits taxes 7.8%; nontax revenue 32.9%, of which licenses and fees 11.2%; foreign grants 24.0%). Expenditures: JD 2,678,000,000 (current expenditure 76.8%, of which defense 23.5%, social security and other transfers 21.7%, wages 15.6%, interest payments 10.1%; capital expenditure 23.2%). Public debt (external, outstanding; 2002): $7,076,000,000. Production (metric tons except as noted). Agriculture, forestry, fishing (2002): tomatoes 359,830, olives 180,900, cucumbers 150,000; livestock (number of live animals) 1,457,910 sheep, 557,260 goats; roundwood (2001) 233,544 cu m; fish catch (2001) 1,060. Mining and quarrying (2002): phosphate ore 7,107,200; potash 1,956,200. Manufacturing (value added in $'000,000; 2000): chemicals and chemical products 236; tobacco products 184; bricks, cement, ceramics 168. Energy production (consumption): electricity (kW-hr; 2003) 7,341,000,000 (7,341,000,000); crude petroleum (barrels; 2002) 14,600 ([2000] 27,789,000); petroleum products (2002) 3,627,000 ([2000] 4,481,000); natural gas (cu m; 2002) 269,000,000 ([2000] 283,000,000). Land use as % of total land area (2000): in temporary crops 2.7%, in permanent crops 1.8%, in pasture 8.9%; overall forest area 1.0%. Tourism (2002): receipts $786,000,000; expenditures $416,000,000. Population economically active (2001): total 1,293,000; activity rate of total population 23.6% (participation rates: over age 15, 40.2%; female 14.9%; unemployed 14.5%). Gross national product (2003): $9,800,000,000 ($1,850 per capita). Household income and expenditure. Average household size (2003) 5.7; income per household (1997) JD 5,464; sources of income (1997): wages and salaries 52.4%, rent and property income 24.5%, transfer payments 12.8%, self-employment 10.3%; expenditure (1997): food and beverages 44.3%, housing and energy 23.5%, transportation 8.2%, clothing and footwear 6.2%, education 4.5%, health care 2.5%.

Foreign trade

Imports (2003-c.i.f.): JD 4,072,000,000 (food products 15.5%; machinery and apparatus 13.4%; crude petroleum 11.5%; chemicals and chemical products 10.9%; transport equipment 9.2%). Major import sources: Saudi Arabia 11.3%; Germany 7.9%; China 7.9%; US 6.8%; Iraq 6.5%. Exports (2003-f.o.b.): JD 2,185,000,000 (domestic exports 76.7%, of which clothing 20.5%, chemicals and chemical products 17.8% [including medicines and pharmaceuticals 6.0%], potash 6.6%, vegetables 4.6%, phosphates 4.2%; reexports 23.3%). Major export destinations: US 29.0%; Iraq 13.4%; India 8.4%; Saudi Arabia 6.5%; Israel 4.1%.

Transport and communications

Transport. Railroads (2003): length 788 km; passenger-km 2,100,000; metric ton-km cargo 348,000,000. Roads (2000): total length 7,245 km (paved 69%). Vehicles (2001): passenger cars 245,357; trucks and buses 110,920. Air transport (2003; Royal Jordanian airlines only): passenger-km 4,553,000,000; metric ton-km cargo 200,728,000; airports (1999) 3. Communications, in total units (units per 1,000 persons). Daily newspaper circulation (2000): 383,000 (77); radios (2000): 1,850,000 (372); televisions (2002): 138,900 (177); telephone main lines (2003): 622,600 (113); cellular telephone subscribers (2003): 1,325,300 (242); personal computers (2002): 200,000 (38); Internet users (2003): 457,000 (45).

Education and health

Educational attainment (2003). Percentage of population age 15 and over having: no formal schooling 9.9%; primary education 54.8%; secondary 17.8%; postsecondary and vocational 8.1%; higher 9.4%. Literacy (2003): percentage of population age 15 and over literate 90.1%; males literate 94.9%; females literate 85.1%. Health: physicians (2000) 9,493 (1 per 523 persons); hospital beds (2001) 8,982 (1 per 575 persons); infant mortality rate per 1,000 live births (2003) 22.0. Food (2001): daily per capita caloric intake 2,769 (vegetable products 89%, animal products 11%); 113% of FAO recommended minimum.

1 metric ton = about 1.1 short tons;   1 kilometer = 0.6 mi (statute);   1 metric ton-km cargo = about 0.68 short ton-mi cargo;   c.i.f.: cost, insurance, and freight;   f.o.b.: free on board

Military

Total active duty personnel (2003): 100,500 (army 84.6%, navy 0.5%, air force 14.9%). Military expenditure as percentage of GDP (1999): 9.2% (world 2.4%); per capita expenditure $150.

Did you know? The Dead Sea, actually a landlocked salt lake, lies between Jordan and Israel. Its extreme salinity excludes all animal or vegetable life, allowing only bacteria.

Background

Jordan shares much of its history with Israel, since both occupied the area known historically as Palestine. Much of present-day eastern Jordan was incorporated into Israel under Kings David and Solomon c. 1000 BC. It fell to the Seleucids in 330 BC and to Muslim Arabs in the 7th century AD. The Crusaders extended the kingdom of Jerusalem east of the Jordan River in 1099. Jordan submitted to Ottoman Turkish rule during the 16th century. In 1920 the area comprising Jordan (then known as the Transjordan) was established within the British mandate of Palestine. Transjordan became an independent state in 1927, although the British mandate did not end until 1948. After hostilities with the new state of Israel ceased in 1949, Jordan annexed the West Bank of the Jordan River, administering the territory until Israel gained control of it in the Six-Day War of 1967. In 1970–71 Jordan was wracked by fighting between the government and guerrillas of the Palestine Liberation Organization (PLO), a struggle that ended in the expulsion of the PLO from Jordan. In 1988 King Hussein renounced all Jordanian claims to the West Bank in favor of the PLO. In 1994 Jordan and Israel signed a full peace agreement. Upon the death of King Hussein in 1999, his son Abdullah took over the throne.

Recent Developments

In 2006 King Abdullah II actively pursued regional peace, including the revival of the peace process between Israel and the Palestinians. He stressed the importance of negotiation and met several times with Palestinian Pres. Mahmoud Abbas. He warned of impending civil wars in Iraq, the Palestinian territories, and Lebanon, and joined the leaders of Egypt and Saudi Arabia in supporting the democratically elected Lebanese government. He also strongly condemned Hezbollah's abduction in July of two Israeli soldiers, which triggered a 34-day war. Abdullah invited several Iraqi leaders to discuss ways to end the sectarian conflict in Iraq.

Internet resources: <www.seejordan.org>.

Kazakhstan

Official name: Qazaqstan Respublikasy (Republic of Kazakhstan). Form of government: unitary republic with a parliament consisting of two chambers (Senate [39, including 7 nonelective seats] and Assembly [77]). Head of state and government: President Nursultan Nazarbayev (from 1991), assisted by Prime Minister Karim Masimov (from 2007). Capital: As-

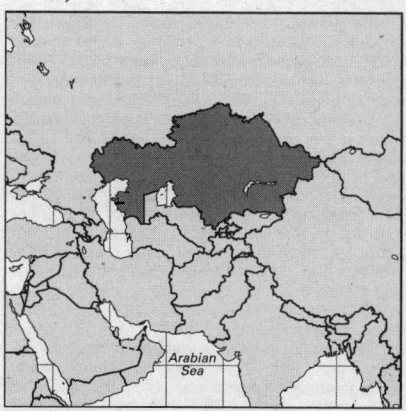

tana. Official language: Kazakh (Russian commands equal status at state-owned organizations and local government bodies). Official religion: none. Monetary unit: 1 tenge (T) = 100 tiyn; valuation (1 Jul 2007) US$1 = 124.02 tenge.

Demography

Area: 1,052,100 sq mi, 2,724,900 sq km. Population (2006): 15,242,000. Density (2006): persons per sq mi 14.5, persons per sq km 5.6. Urban (2001): 55.8%. Sex distribution (2003): male 48.35%; female 51.65%. Age breakdown (2003): under 15, 25.3%; 15–29, 27.8%; 30–44, 21.3%; 45–59, 14.4%; 60–74, 8.9%; 75 and over, 2.3%. Ethnic composition (1999): Kazakh 53.4%; Russian 30.0%; Ukrainian 3.7%; Uzbek 2.5%; German 2.4%; Tatar 1.7%; other 6.3%. Religious affiliation (1995): Muslim (mostly Sunni) 47.0%; Russian Orthodox 8.2%; Protestant 2.1%; other (mostly nonreligious) 42.7%. Major cities (1999): Almaty 1,130,068; Qaraghandy (Karaganda) 436,900; Shymkent (Chimkent) 360,100; Taraz 330,100; Astana 319,318. Location: central Asia, bordering Russia, China, Kyrgyzstan, Uzbekistan, the Aral Sea, Turkmenistan, and the Caspian Sea.

Vital statistics

Birth rate per 1,000 population (2003): 15.3 (world avg. 21.3); (2000) legitimate 76.1%. Death rate per 1,000 population (2003): 9.7 (world avg. 9.1). Natural increase rate per 1,000 population (2003): 5.6 (world avg. 12.2). Total fertility rate (avg. births per childbearing woman; 2003): 1.9. Life expectancy at birth (2003): male 65.6 years; female 71.3 years.

National economy

Budget (2001). Revenue: 743,550,000,000 tenge (tax revenue 91.1%, of which income and profits taxes 34.8%, sales tax 29.3%, social security 17.5%; nontax revenue 8.9%). Expenditures: 749,092,-000,000 tenge (social security 24.9%; education 14.0%; health 8.3%; debt 6.7%; defense 4.3%). Population economically active (2001): total 7,479,100; activity rate of total population 50.4% (participation rates: ages 16–59 [male], 16–54 [female] 73.6%; female 46.0%; unemployed 12.8%). Production (metric tons except as noted). Agriculture, forestry, fishing

(2003): wheat 11,519,000, potatoes 2,320,000, barley 2,220,000; livestock (number of live animals) 9,920,200 sheep, 4,559,500 cattle, 23,600,000 chickens; fish catch (2001) 31,071. *Mining and quarrying* (2000): iron ore 13,828,000; bauxite 3,730,000; chromite 2,607,000. *Manufacturing* (value of production in '000,000 tenge; 2002): metallurgy 396,000; food 307,000; oil and nuclear energy 149,000. *Energy production (consumption):* electricity (kW-hr; 2002) 58,464,000,000 ([2000] 54,616,000,000); hard coal (2002) 70,608,000 ([2000] 45,503,000); lignite (2002) 2,616,000 ([2000] 2,235,000); crude petroleum (barrels; 2002) 348,224,000 ([2000] 18,800,000); petroleum products (2000) 5,961,000 (5,592,000); natural gas (cu m; 2002) 9,112,000,000 ([2000] 11,001,800,000). **Gross national product** (2003): $26,535,000,000 ($1,780 per capita). **Public debt** (external, outstanding; 2002): $3,209,000,000. **Household income and expenditure**. Average household size (1999) 3.6; sources of income (2001): salaries and wages 72.1%, social benefits 9.2%; expenditure (2001): food and beverages 56.0%, housing 11.7%. **Land use** as % of total land area (2000): in temporary crops 8.0%, in permanent crops 0.05%, in pasture 68.6%; overall forest area 4.5%. **Tourism** (2002): receipts $621,000,000; expenditures $756,000,000.

Foreign trade

Imports (2000-c.i.f.): $5,052,000,000 (machinery and apparatus 27.4%; mineral fuels and lubricants 11.5%; chemicals and chemical products 11.4%; transport equipment 11.1%). *Major import sources:* Russia 48.7%; Germany 6.6%; US 5.5%; UK 4.3%; Italy 3.1%. **Exports** (2000-f.o.b.): $9,139,000,000 (crude petroleum 49.4%; nonferrous metals 13.7%, of which copper 7.5%; iron and steel 12.0%; cereals 6.0%). *Major export destinations:* Russia 19.5%; Bermuda 14.9%; British Virgin Islands 11.6%; Italy 9.8%; China 7.3%.

Transport and communications

Transport. *Railroads* (2001): route length 13,500 km; passenger-km 10,384,000,000; metric ton-km cargo 135,653,000,000. *Roads* (1999): total length 109,445 km (paved 90%). *Vehicles* (2001): passenger cars 1,000,298; trucks and buses 278,711. *Air transport* (2001): passenger-km 1,901,100,000; metric ton-km cargo 44,000,000; airports (1999) with scheduled flights 20. **Communications,** in total units (units per 1,000 persons). Radios (2000): 6,270,000 (422); televisions (2000): 3,580,000 (241); telephone main lines (2002): 2,081,900 (130); cellular telephone subscribers (2002): 1,027,000 (64); Internet users (2002): 250,000 (16).

Education and health

Educational attainment (1999). Population age 25 and over having: no formal schooling or some primary education 9.1%; primary education 23.1%; secondary and some postsecondary 57.8%; higher 10.0%. **Literacy** (2002): percentage of total population age 15 and over literate 99.4%; males literate 99.7%; females literate 99.2%. **Health** (2002): physicians 55,800 (1 per 277 persons); hospital beds 108,300

(1 per 143 persons); infant mortality rate per 1,000 live births (2003) 31.9. **Food** (2001): daily per capita caloric intake 2,477 (vegetable products 73%, animal products 27%); 97% of FAO recommended minimum.

Military

Total active duty personnel (2003): 65,800 (army 71.1%, air force 28.9%). **Military expenditure as percentage of GNP** (1999): 0.9% (world avg. 2.4%); per capita expenditure $40.

Background

Named for its earliest inhabitants, the Kazakhs, the area came under Mongol rule in the 13th century. The Kazakhs consolidated a nomadic empire in the 15th–16th centuries. Under Russian rule by the mid-19th century, it became part of the Kirgiz Autonomous Republic formed by the Soviets in 1920, and in 1925 its name was changed to the Kazakh Autonomous Soviet Socialist Republic. Kazakhstan obtained its independence in 1991, and during the 1990s it attempted to stabilize its economy.

Recent Developments

Economic ties with Russia were strengthened in 2006 by an agreement on the joint development of a huge gas field in Kazakhstan. Oil started flowing through the pipeline from central Kazakhstan to China. In June Kazakhstan signed an agreement to ship oil through the newly opened Baku–Tbilisi–Ceyhan pipeline, which directly linked the Caspian Sea with the Mediterranean Sea. There were setbacks in Kazakhstan's efforts to commit to democratization. In April two opposition politicians were prevented from leaving the country to address the European Parliament, and in June the Kazakh parliament adopted a law restricting media outlets.

Internet resources: <www.president.kz>.

Kenya

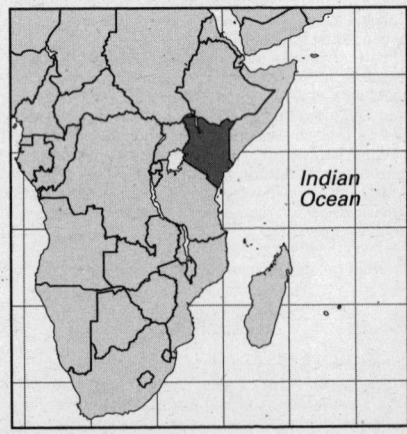

Indian Ocean

---

1 metric ton = about 1.1 short tons;   1 kilometer = 0.6 mi (statute);   1 metric ton-km cargo = about 0.68 short ton-mi cargo;   c.i.f.: cost, insurance, and freight;   f.o.b.: free on board

Official name: Jamhuri ya Kenya (Swahili); Republic of Kenya (English). **Form of government:** unitary multiparty republic with one legislative house (National Assembly [224, including 14 nonelective seats]). **Head of state and government:** President Mwai Kibaki (from 2002). **Capital:** Nairobi. **Official languages:** Swahili; English. **Official religion:** none. **Monetary unit:** 1 Kenya shilling (K Sh) = 100 cents; valuation (1 Jul 2007) US$1 = K Sh 66.58.

Demography

Area: 224,961 sq mi, 582,646 sq km. **Population** (2006): 34,059,000. **Density** (2006): persons per sq mi 151.4, persons per sq km 58.5. **Urban** (2003): 39.4%. **Sex distribution** (2003): male 50.11%; female 49.89%. **Age breakdown** (2003): under 15, 42.4%; 15–29, 31.5%; 30–44, 15.1%; 45–59, 7.3%; 60–74, 3.0%; 75 and over, 0.7%. **Ethnic composition** (1989): Kikuyu 17.7%; Luhya 12.4%; Luo 10.6%; Kalenjin 9.8%; Kamba 9.8%; other 39.7%. **Religious affiliation** (2000): Christian 79.3%, of which Roman Catholic 22.0%, African Christian 20.8%, Protestant 20.1%; Muslim 7.3%; other 13.4%. **Major cities** (1999; pop. of urban core[s]): Nairobi 2,143,354; Mombasa 665,018; Kisumu 322,734; Nakuru 219,366; Eldoret 167,016. **Location:** eastern Africa, bordering Ethiopia, Somalia, the Indian Ocean, Tanzania, Uganda, and The Sudan.

Vital statistics

Birth rate per 1,000 population (2003): 40.2 (world avg. 21.3). **Death rate** per 1,000 population (2003): 15.6 (world avg. 9.1). **Natural increase rate** per 1,000 population (2003): 24.6 (world avg. 12.2). **Total fertility rate** (avg. births per childbearing woman; 2003): 5.0. **Life expectancy** at birth (2003): male 47.4 years; female 45.7 years. **Adult population** (ages 15–49) **living with HIV** (2004): 6.7% (world avg. 1.1%).

National economy

Budget (2001–02). *Revenue:* K Sh 206,665,-600,000 (tax revenue 86.6%, of which income and profit taxes 29.0%, value-added tax 27.2%, import duties 15.3%; nontax revenue 13.4%). *Expenditures:* K Sh 235,832,000,000 (recurrent expenditure 80.4%, of which administration 29.7%, education 22.2%, defense 6.1%, health 6.0%; development expenditure 19.6%). **Public debt** (external, outstanding; 2002): $5,139,000,000. **Production** (metric tons except as noted). *Agriculture, forestry, fishing* (2003): sugarcane 4,500,000, corn (maize) 2,300,000, potatoes 900,000; livestock (number of live animals) 11,500,000 cattle, 11,000,000 goats, 7,700,000 sheep; roundwood (2002) 1,704,250 cu m; fish catch (2001) 165,160, of which freshwater fish 95.5%. *Mining and quarrying* (2000): soda ash 238,200; fluorite 100,100; salt 16,400. *Manufacturing* (value added in K£'000 [Kenya pound (K£) as a unit of account equals 20 K Sh]; 1995): food products 847,000; beverages and tobacco 249,000; machinery and transport equipment 226,000. *Energy production (consumption):* electricity (kW-hr; 2001) 4,338,400,000 (3,654,800,000); coal (2000) none (98,000); crude petroleum (barrels; 2000) none (18,000,000); petroleum products (2001) 1,695,-600 (2,385,200). **Households.** Average household size (1998) 3.4; expenditure (1993–94): food 42.4%,

housing and energy 24.1%, clothing and footwear 9.1%, transportation 6.4%, other 18.0%. **Population economically active** (2001): total 12,952,000; activity rate of total population 42.1% (participation rates [1985]: ages 15–64, 76.2%; female [1997] 46.1%). **Gross national product** (2003): $12,604,000,000 ($390 per capita). **Tourism** (2002): receipts from visitors $297,000,000; expenditures by nationals abroad (2001) $143,000,000. **Land use** as % of total land area (2000): in temporary crops 7.9%, in permanent crops 1.0%, in pasture 37.4%; overall forest area 30.0%.

Foreign trade

Imports (2002-c.i.f.): K Sh 277,275,000,000 (crude petroleum and petroleum products 22.8%, machinery and transport equipment 19.3%, chemicals and chemical products 14.1%). *Major import sources* (2001): US 16.4%; UAE 10.7%; Saudi Arabia 7.8%; South Africa 7.1%; UK 7.1%. **Exports** (2002): K Sh 158,600,000,000 (tea 21.4%, horticultural products [mostly cut flowers] 13.8%, petroleum products 7.6%, coffee 4.1%, other [including nontraditional fruits and vegetables, iron and steel, and fish] 53.1%). *Major export destinations* (2001): Uganda 17.4%; UK 12.5%; The Netherlands 6.5%; Pakistan 6.1%; US 5.6%.

Transport and communications

Transport. *Railroads* (2000): route length 2,700 km; passenger-km 302,000,000; metric ton-km cargo 1,557,000,000. *Roads* (1999): total length 63,800 km (paved 14%). *Vehicles* (2000): passenger cars 244,836; trucks and buses 96,726. *Air transport* (1998): passenger-km 2,091,000,000; metric ton-km cargo 243,000,000; airports (1997) with scheduled flights 11. **Communications**, in total units (units per 1,000 persons). Daily newspaper circulation (2000): 303,000 (10); radios (2001): 6,801,000 (221); televisions (2000): 758,000 (25); telephone main lines (2003): 328,400 (10); cellular telephone subscribers (2003): 1,590,800 (50); personal computers (2002): 204,000 (6.5); Internet users (2002): 400,000 (13).

Education and health

Literacy (2002): total population over age 15 literate 84.3%; males literate 90.0%; females literate 78.5%. **Health** (2002): physicians 4,740 (1 per 6,623 persons); hospital beds 60,657 (1 per 515 persons); infant mortality rate per 1,000 live births (2003): 65.6. **Food** (2001): daily per capita caloric intake 2,058 (vegetable products 88%, animal products 12%); 89% of FAO recommended minimum.

Military

Total active duty personnel (2003): 24,120 (army 82.9%, navy 6.7%, air force 10.4%). **Military expenditure as percentage of GNP** (1999): 1.9% (world 2.4%); per capita expenditure $7.

Background

The coastal region of East Africa was dominated by Arabs until it was seized by the Portuguese in the 16th century. The Masai people held sway in the north and moved into central Kenya in the 18th century, while the Kikuyu expanded from their home region in south-central Kenya. The interior was explored by European missionaries in the 19th century. After the British took control, Kenya was established as a British protectorate (1890) and a crown colony (1920). The Mau Mau rebellion of the 1950s was directed against European colonialism. In 1963 the country became fully independent, and a year later a republican government under Jomo Kenyatta was elected. In 1992 Kenyan Pres. Daniel arap Moi allowed the country's first multiparty elections in three decades, though the balloting was marred by violence and fraud. Political turmoil occurred over the following years.

Recent Developments

The government continued to face allegations of corruption in 2006. In February, Pres. Mwai Kibaki ordered the publication of a report on the long-running Goldenberg financial scandal, which had cost the government hundreds of millions of dollars. The report implicated former president Daniel arap Moi and six of his aides. A few days later Finance Minister David Mwiraria resigned, protesting that corruption allegations made against him were false. His resignation was followed by that of two other cabinet members. The IMF then announced that promised aid of 23.5 billion Kenya shillings (about $325 million) would be withheld because of the ongoing corruption charges, while the World Bank added press freedom to the conditions the government would have to meet before its freeze on credits amounting to 19 billion Kenya shillings (about $260 million) was lifted.

Internet resources: <www.magicalkenya.com>.

Kiribati

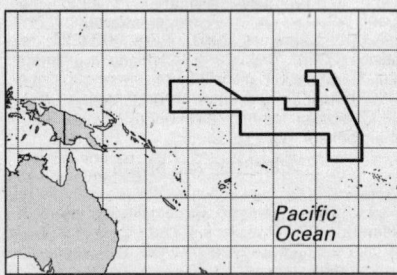

Pacific Ocean

Official name: Republic of Kiribati. **Form of government:** unitary republic with a unicameral legislature (House of Assembly [42, including two nonelective members]). **Head of state and government:** President Anote Tong (from 2003). **Capital:** Bairiki, on Tarawa Atoll. **Official language:** English. **Official religion:** none. **Monetary unit:** 1 Australian dollar ($A) = 100 cents; valuation (1 Jul 2007) US$1 = $A 1.18.

Demography

Area: 312.9 sq mi, 810.5 sq km (including uninhabited islands). **Population** (2004): 89,100. **Density** (2006; based on inhabited island areas [280 sq mi (726 sq km)] only): persons per sq mi 334.3, persons

per sq km 128.9. **Urban** (2003): 47.3%. **Sex distribution** (2003): male 49.65%; female 50.35%. **Age breakdown** (2003): under 15, 39.7%; 15–29, 26.3%; 30–44, 18.8%; 45–59, 10.1%; 60–74, 4.3%; 75 and over, 0.9%. **Ethnic composition** (2000): Micronesian 98.8%; Polynesian 0.7%; European 0.2%; other 0.3%. **Religious affiliation** (2000): Roman Catholic 54.6%; Kiribati Protestant (Congregational) 37.0%; Mormon 2.7%; Baha'i 2.4%; other Protestant 2.3%; other/nonreligious 1.0%. **Major city** (2000): Tarawa (urban area) 36,717. **Location:** western Pacific Ocean, south of the Hawaiian Islands (US).

Vital statistics

Birth rate per 1,000 population (2003): 31.2 (world avg. 21.3). **Death rate** per 1,000 population (2003): 8.6 (world avg. 9.1). **Total fertility rate** (avg. births per childbearing woman; 2003): 4.3. **Natural increase rate** per 1,000 population (2003): 22.6 (world avg. 12.2). **Marriage rate** per 1,000 population (1988): 5.2. **Life expectancy** at birth (2003): male 58.0 years; female 64.0 years.

National economy

Budget (2000). *Revenue:* $A 107,800,000 (nontax revenue 59.5%, tax revenue 22.9%, grants 17.6%). *Expenditures:* $A 90,000,000 (current expenditures 87.2%, capital expenditures 12.8%). **Public debt** (external, outstanding; 1999): $9,500,000. **Tourism:** receipts from visitors (2001) US$3,200,000; expenditures by nationals abroad (1999) US$2,000,000. **Land use** as % of total land area (2000): in temporary crops 3%, in permanent crops 51%; overall forest area 38%. **Production** (metric tons except as noted). *Agriculture, forestry, fishing* (2003): coconuts 99,000, roots and tubers 7,300 (of which taro 1,900), fresh vegetables 5,800; livestock (number of live animals) 12,000 pigs, 450,000 chickens; fish catch (2001) 32,393. *Manufacturing* (1996): processed copra 9,321; other important products are processed fish, baked goods, clothing, and handicrafts. *Energy production (consumption):* electricity (kW-hr; 2000) 7,000,000 (7,000,000); petroleum products (2000) none (8,000). **Gross national product** (2003): US$84,000,000 (US$880 per capita). **Population economically active** (1995): total 38,407; activity rate of total population 49.5% (participation rates: over age 15, 84.0%; female 47.8%; unemployed [2000] 1.5%). **Households.** Average household size (1995) 6.5; expenditure (1996): food 45.0%, nonalcoholic beverages 10.0%, transportation 8.0%, energy 8.0%, education 8.0%.

Foreign trade

Imports (1999): $A 63,700,000 (food and live animals 28.3%; machinery and transport equipment 22.6%; mineral fuels 10.3%; beverages and tobacco products 7.7%). *Major import sources* (2001): Australia 26.5%; Poland 15.7%; Fiji 14.8%; US 9.5%; Japan 8.0%. **Exports** (1999): $A 14,000,000 (domestic exports 92.6%, of which copra 63.9%, seaweed 5.1%, other [including fish for food and pet fish] 23.6%; reexports 7.4%). *Major export destinations* (2001): Japan 45.8%; Thailand 24.8%; South Korea 10.7%; Bangladesh 5.5%; Brazil 3.0%.

1 metric ton = about 1.1 short tons;   1 kilometer = 0.6 mi (statute);   1 metric ton-km cargo = about 0.68 short ton-mi cargo;   c.i.f.: cost, insurance, and freight;   f.o.b.: free on board

Transport and communications

Transport. *Roads* (1996): total length 670 km (paved 5%). *Vehicles* (2000; registered vehicles in South Tarawa only): passenger cars 477; trucks and buses 277. *Air transport* (1996): passenger-km 7,000,000; metric ton-km cargo 1,000,000; airports 9. **Communications,** in total units (units per 1,000 persons). Radios (2000): 32,600 (386); televisions (2000): 3,030 (36); telephone main lines (2002): 4,500 (51); cellular telephone subscribers (2002): 500 (5.7); personal computers (2001): 2,000 (25); Internet users (2002): 2,000 (23).

Education and health

Educational attainment (1995). Percentage of population age 25 and over having: no schooling 7.8%; primary education 68.5%; secondary or higher 23.7%. **Literacy** (1998): population age 15 and over literate 92%; males literate 94%; females literate 91%. **Health:** physicians (1998) 26 (1 per 3,378 persons); hospital beds (1990) 306 (1 per 233 persons); infant mortality rate per 1,000 live births (2003) 51.3. **Food** (2001): daily per capita caloric intake 2,922 (vegetable products 88%, animal products 12%); 128% of FAO recommended minimum.

Background

The islands were settled by Austronesian-speaking peoples before the 1st century AD. In 1765 the British discovered the island of Nikunau; the first permanent European settlers arrived in 1837. In 1916 the Gilbert and Ellice islands and Banaba became a crown colony of Britain; they were later joined by the Phoenix and Line islands. In 1979 the colony became the nation of Kiribati.

Did you know? The remote Kiritimati Atoll, part of the Pacific nation Kiribati, is the world's oldest and one of the largest coral formations in the world. Kiritimati was used for British nuclear testing in the 1950s; it now has a large coconut plantation and fish farms.

Recent Developments

Kiribati joined the International Whaling Commission (IWC) in 2005. At the IWC's June 2006 annual meeting Kiribati voted in favor of the St. Kitts and Nevis Declaration, a document calling in general terms for an end to the moratorium on commercial whaling. This motion passed by one vote, though it required a larger majority to be acted upon, and many of its opponents claimed that Kiribati's vote had been purchased with the promise of development aid by whaling countries.

Internet Resources: <www.kiribati.spto.org>.

North Korea

Official name: Choson Minjujuui In'min Konghwaguk (Democratic People's Republic of Korea). **Form of**

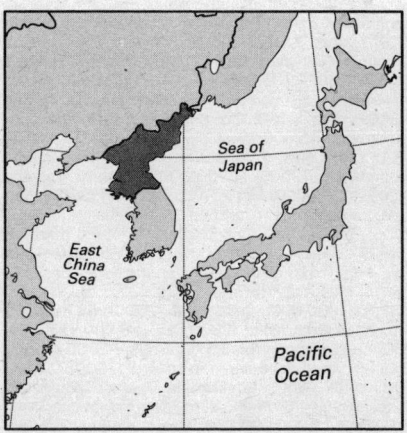

government: unitary single-party republic with one legislative house (Supreme People's Assembly [687]). **Head of state and government:** Chairman of the National Defense Commission Kim Jong Il (from 1998). **Capital:** P'yongyang. **Official language:** Korean. **Official religion:** none. **Monetary unit:** 1 won = 100 chon; valuation (1 Jul 2007) US$1 = 2.20 won.

Demography

Area: 47,399 sq mi, 122,762 sq km. **Population** (2006): 22,583,000. **Density** (2006): persons per sq mi 476.4, persons per sq km 184.0. **Urban** (2003): 61.1%. **Sex distribution** (2000): male 48.48%; female 51.52%. **Age breakdown** (2000): under 15, 25.6%; 15–29, 24.5%; 30–44, 24.7%; 45–59, 14.4%; 60–74, 9.0%; 75 and over, 1.8%. **Ethnic composition** (1999): Korean 99.8%; Chinese 0.2%. **Religious affiliation** (2000): nonreligious 55.6%; atheist 15.6%; Ch'ondogyo 12.9%; traditional beliefs 12.3%; Christian 2.1%; Buddhist 1.5%. **Major cities** (1993): P'yongyang (2001) 3,164,000 (urban agglomeration); Namp'o (2000) 1,022,000 (urban agglomeration); Hamhung 709,730; Ch'ongjin 582,480; Kaesong 334,433. **Location:** eastern Asia, bordering China, Russia, the Sea of Japan (East Sea), South Korea, and the Yellow Sea.

Vital statistics

Birth rate per 1,000 population (2003): 17.6 (world avg. 21.3). **Death rate** per 1,000 population (2003): 6.9 (world avg. 9.1). **Natural increase rate** per 1,000 population (2003): 10.7 (world avg. 12.2). **Total fertility rate** (avg. births per childbearing woman; 2003): 2.3. **Marriage rate** per 1,000 population (1987): 9.3. **Divorce rate** per 1,000 population (1987): 0.2. **Life expectancy** at birth (2003): male 68.1 years; female 73.6 years.

National economy

Budget (1999). *Revenue:* 19,801,000,000 won (turnover tax and profits from state enterprises). *Expenditures:* 20,018,200,000 won (1994; national economy 67.8%, social and cultural affairs 19.0%, defense 11.6%). **Population economically active** (1997): total 11,898,000; activity rate of total population 55.8% (participation rates [1988–93]: ages 15–64, 49.5%; female 46.0%). **Production** (metric tons except as noted). *Agriculture, forestry, fishing* (2002): rice 2,190,000, potatoes 1,884,000, corn (maize) 1,651,000; livestock (number of live animals) 3,152,000 pigs, 2,693,000 goats, 575,000 cattle; roundwood (2000) 4,900,000 cu m; fish catch (2001): 264,000. *Mining and quarrying* (2002): iron ore (metal content) 1,150,000; magnesite 1,000,-000; phosphate rock 300,000. *Manufacturing* (1999): cement 16,000,000; crude steel 8,100,000; pig iron 6,600,000. *Energy production (consumption):* electricity (kW-hr; 2000) 32,815,000,000 (32,815,000,000); hard coal (2000) 53,873,000 (55,540,000); lignite (2000) 15,728,000 (15,728,-000); crude petroleum (barrels; 2000) none (18,000,000); petroleum products (2000) 2,654,-000 (4,063,000). **Households.** Average household size (1999) 4.6. **Public debt** (external, outstanding; 1999): $12,000,000,000. **Gross national product** (1999): $9,912,000,000 ($457 per capita). **Land use** as % of total land area (2000): in temporary crops 20.8%, in permanent crops 2.5%, in pasture 0.4%; overall forest area 68.2%.

Foreign trade

Imports (2001): $1,847,000,000 (excludes trade with South Korea; food, beverages, and other agricultural products 23.7%, machinery and apparatus 15.0%, mineral fuels and lubricants 14.3%, textiles and clothing 12.6%). *Major import sources:* China 31.0%; Japan 13.5%; South Korea 12.3%; India 8.4%; Singapore 6.1%. **Exports** (2001): $826,000,-000 (excludes trade with South Korea; live animals and agricultural products 30.2%, textiles and wearing apparel 21.6%, machinery and apparatus 15.1%, base and fabricated metals 9.3%). *Major export destinations:* Japan 27.3%; South Korea 21.3%; China 20.2%; Hong Kong 4.6%; Thailand 3.0%.

Transport and communications

Transport. *Railroads* (1999): length 8,533 km. *Roads* (1998): total length 23,407 km (paved 8%). *Vehicles* (1990): passenger cars 248,000. *Air transport* (1997): passenger-km 286,000,000; short ton-mi cargo 18,600,000; metric ton-km cargo 30,000,000; airports (2001) with scheduled flights 1. **Communications,** in total units (units per 1,000 persons). Daily newspaper circulation (2000): 4,500,000 (208); radios (2000): 3,330,000 (154); televisions (2000): 1,170,000 (54); telephone main lines (1999): 1,100,000 (46).

Education and health

Educational attainment (1987–88). Percentage of population age 16 and over having attended or graduated from postsecondary-level school: 13.7%. **Literacy** (1997): 95%. **Health** (1995): physicians 64,039 (1 per 337 persons); hospital beds 293,457 (1 per 73 persons); infant mortality rate (2003) 25.7. **Food** (2002): daily per capita caloric intake 2,142 (vegetable products 94%, animal products 6%); 92% of FAO recommended minimum.

Military

Total active duty personnel (2003): 1,082,000 (army 87.8%, navy 4.3%, air force 7.9%). **Military expenditure as percentage of GNP** (1999): 18.8% (world 2.4%); per capita expenditure $199.

Background

According to tradition, the ancient kingdom of Choson was established in the northern part of the Korean Peninsula, probably by peoples from northern China, in the 3rd millennium BC and was conquered by China in 108 BC. The kingdom was ruled by the Yi dynasty from 1392 to 1910. That year Korea was formally annexed by Japan. It was freed from Japanese control in 1945, at which time the USSR occupied the area north of latitude 38° N and the US occupied the area south of it. The Democratic People's Republic of Korea (DPRK) was established as a communist state in 1948. North Korea launched an invasion of South Korea in 1950, initiating the Korean War, which ended with an armistice in 1953. Under Kim Il-sung, North Korea became one of the most harshly regimented societies in the world, with a state-owned economy that failed to produce adequate food. In the late 1990s, under Kim Il-sung's successor, Kim Jong Il, the country endured a serious famine; as many as a million Koreans may have died.

Recent Developments

In 2006 North Korea captured the world's attention with a series of missile launches in July and the successful test of a nuclear weapon in October. Condemnation was nearly universal—two critical UN Security Council resolutions were unanimously passed within days of each act. The nuclear test called into question the viability of the so-called six-party nuclear talks, between North Korea, the US, China, South Korea, Japan, and Russia, designed to halt North Korea's nuclear ambitions. These talks reconvened in February 2007, however, resulting in historic agreements. North Korea agreed to abandon its nuclear programs, relinquish all weapons-grade nuclear material, and allow international inspectors unfettered access to its nuclear sites. The US and Japan were to normalize relations with North Korea, and the US agreed to take the DPRK off its list of state sponsors of terrorism. The international community would restore frozen funds and resume delivery of energy and food aid to the impoverished nation. At the resumption of talks in March, however, disagreements led to an apparent suspension of these progressive steps.

Internet resources: <www.kcna.co.jp/index-e.htm>.

South Korea

Official name: Taehan Min'guk (Republic of Korea). **Form of government:** unitary multiparty republic with one legislative house (National Assembly [299]). **Head of state and government:** President Roh Moo Hyun (from 2003), assisted by Prime Minister Han Duck Soo (from 2007). **Capital:** Seoul. **Official language:** Korean. **Official religion:** none. **Monetary unit:** 1 won (W) = 100 chon; valuation (1 Jul 2007) US$1 = W 923.36.

1 metric ton = about 1.1 short tons;   1 kilometer = 0.6 mi (statute);   1 metric ton-km cargo = about 0.68 short ton-mi cargo;   c.i.f.: cost, insurance, and freight;   f.o.b.: free on board

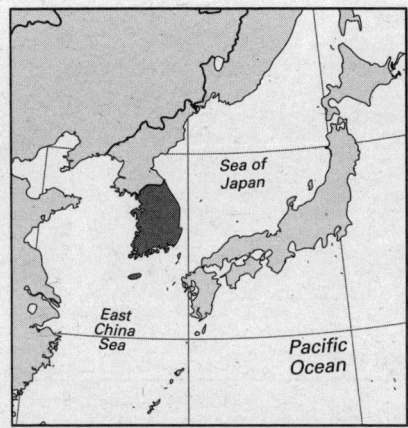

Sea of Japan

East China Sea

Pacific Ocean

Demography

Area: 38,474 sq mi, 99,646 sq km. **Population** (2006): 47,983,000. **Density** (2006): persons per sq mi 1,247, persons per sq km 481.5. **Urban** (2003): 80.3%. **Sex distribution** (2003): male 50.30%; female 49.70%. **Age breakdown** (2003): under 15, 20.2%; 15–29, 23.6%; 30–44, 26.8%; 45–59, 17.5%; 60–74, 9.4%; 75 and over, 2.5%. **Ethnic composition** (2000): Korean 97.7%; Japanese 2.0%; US white 0.1%; Han Chinese 0.1%; other 0.1%. **Religious affiliation** (1995): religious 50.7%, of which Buddhist 23.2%, Protestant 19.7%, Roman Catholic 6.6%, Confucian 0.5%, Wonbulgyo 0.2%, Ch'ondogyo 0.1%, other 0.4%; nonreligious 49.3%. **Major cities** (2003): Seoul 10,280,523; Pusan 3,747,369; Inch'on 2,596,102; Taegu 2,540,647; Taejon 1,424,844. **Location:** northeast Asia, bordering North Korea, the Sea of Japan (East Sea), and the Yellow Sea; Cheju Island lies off the southern coast in the East China Sea.

Vital statistics

Birth rate per 1,000 population (2003): 10.3 (world avg. 21.3). **Death rate** per 1,000 population (2003): 6.0 (world avg. 9.1). **Natural increase rate** per 1,000 population (2003): 4.3 (world avg. 12.2). **Total fertility rate** (avg. births per childbearing woman; 2003): 1.2. **Marriage rate** per 1,000 population (2002): 6.3. **Divorce rate** per 1,000 population (2002): 3.0. **Life expectancy** at birth (2003): male 71.7 years; female 79.3 years.

National economy

Budget (2002). *Revenue:* W 105,876,700,000,000 (tax revenue 88.6%, of which income and profits taxes 34.3%, value-added tax 30.2%; nontax revenue 11.4%). *Expenditures:* W 105,876,700,000,000 (economic services 25.9%, education 17.4%, defense 16.2%, social services 13.1%). **Public debt** (external, outstanding; 2001): $33,742,000,000. **Production** (metric tons except as noted). *Agriculture, forestry, fishing* (2003): rice 6,068,000, cabbages 2,576,000, onions 933,000; livestock (number of live animals) 8,912,000 pigs, 1,935,000 cattle, 98,000,000 chickens; roundwood (2002) 4,062,638 cu m; fish catch (2001) 2,282,486. *Mining and quarrying* (2001): iron

ore 195,000. *Manufacturing* (units; 2001): transistors 21,126,000,000; mobile phones 89,834,000; color television receivers 15,914,000. *Energy production (consumption):* electricity (kW-hr; 2000) 295,156,000,000 (295,156,000,000); coal (2000) 4,150,000 (66,525,000); crude petroleum (barrels; 2000) none (891,500,000); petroleum products (2000) 97,275,000 (63,447,000); natural gas (cu m; 2000) none (19,833,700,000). **Household income and expenditure** (2001). Average household size 3.5; annual income per household W 31,501,200; sources of income: wages 84.2%, other 15.8%; expenditure: food and beverages 26.3%, transportation and communications 16.3%, education 11.3%. **Gross national product** (at current market prices; 2003): $576,426,000,000 ($12,030 per capita). **Population economically active** (2001): total 22,181,000; activity rate 46.9% (participation rates: ages 15–64, 64.6%; female 41.3%; unemployed [2002] 3.1%). **Tourism** (2002): receipts $5,919,000,000; expenditures $9,036,000,000. **Land use** as % of total land area (2000): in temporary crops 17.4%, in permanent crops 2.0%, in pasture 0.5%; overall forest area 63.3%.

Foreign trade

Imports (2001-c.i.f.): $141,098,000,000 (electric and electronic products 19.4%, crude petroleum 15.1%, nonelectrical machinery and transport equipment 14.5%, chemicals and chemical products 9.2%, food and live animals 4.8%). *Major import sources:* Japan 18.9%; US 15.9%; China 9.4%; Saudi Arabia 5.7%; Australia 3.9%. **Exports** (2001-f.o.b.): $150,439,000,000 (electric and electronic products 25.0%, transport equipment 17.0%, nonelectrical machinery and apparatus 15.6%, chemicals and chemical products 8.3%). *Major export destinations:* US 20.7%; China 12.1%; Japan 11.0%; Hong Kong 6.3%; Taiwan 3.9%.

Transport and communications

Transport. *Railroads* (2001): length 6,819 km; passenger-km 29,172,000,000; metric ton-km cargo 10,492,000,000. *Roads* (2001): total length 91,396 km (paved 77%). *Vehicles* (2001): passenger cars 8,889,000; trucks and buses 3,768,000. *Air transport* (2002; scheduled flights of Asiana and Korean Air only): passenger-km 48,325,000,000; metric ton-km cargo 4,590,000,000; airports (1996) with scheduled flights 14. **Communications**, in total units (units per 1,000 persons). Daily newspaper circulation (2000): 18,500,000 (393); radios (2000): 48,600,000 (1,033); televisions (2000): 17,100,000 (364); telephone main lines (2003): 22,877,000 (472); cellular telephone subscribers (2003): 33,592,000 (694); personal computers (2003): 26,700,000 (551); Internet users (2003): 29,220,000 (603).

Education and health

Educational attainment (1995). Percentage of population age 25 and over having: no formal schooling 8.5%; primary education or less 17.7%; some secondary and secondary 53.1%; postsecondary 20.6%. **Literacy** (2001): total population age 15 and over literate 97.9%; males literate 99.2%; females literate 96.6%. **Health** (2002): physicians 78,592 (1 per 606 persons); hospital beds 316,015 (1 per 151 persons); infant mortality rate per 1,000 live births (2003) 7.3. **Food** (2001): daily per capita caloric intake 3,055 (vegetable products 85%, animal products 15%); 130% of FAO recommended minimum.

Military

Total active duty personnel (2003): 686,000 (army 81.6%, navy 9.2%, air force 9.2%); US military forces (2004): 40,258. **Military expenditure as percentage of GNP** (1999): 2.9% (world 2.4%); per capita expenditure $246.

Background

Civilization in the Korean Peninsula dates to the 3rd millennium BC (see background of Democratic People's Republic of Korea, above). The Republic of Korea was established in 1948 in the southern portion of the Korean peninsula. In 1950 North Korean troops invaded South Korea, precipitating the Korean War. UN forces intervened on the side of South Korea, while Chinese troops backed North Korea in the war, which ended with an armistice in 1953. The devastated country was rebuilt with US aid, and South Korea prospered in the postwar era, developing a strong export-oriented economy. It experienced an economic downturn in the mid-1990s that affected many economies in the area.

Recent Developments

South Korea in 2006 faced political, economic, and diplomatic uncertainty, with presidential elections slated for December 2007, growing anxieties about the economy, and North Korea's nuclear test in October. Despite solid economic growth of 5% and an unemployment rate of 4%, there were fears of an overheated housing market and frustrations with the education system that led a growing number of the affluent to educate their children abroad. The value of exports broke the $300 billion mark in 2006, however, which placed South Korea 11th in the world among exporters. On the diplomatic front, South Korea's key bilateral relationships deteriorated. North-South relations almost collapsed after a missile launch by North Korea in July. Relations with the US continued to show signs of friction over issues such as divergent policies toward North Korea and differences over the future role that the US would play in defending South Korea. Relations were already bad with Japan, but a territorial dispute over two rocks in the sea between the two countries nearly turned into a military clash in the spring. Relations with China also deteriorated, with disputes over whether an early kingdom was Korean or Chinese and over a reef that could be seen only at low tide.

Internet resources: <www.korea.net>.

Kuwait

Official name: Dawlat al-Kuwayt (State of Kuwait). **Form of government:** constitutional monarchy with one legislative body (National Assembly [50, excluding cabinet ministers not elected to National Assembly serving ex officio]). **Head of state and government:** Emir Sheikh Sabah al-Ahmad al-Jabir al-Sabah (from 2006), assisted by Prime Minister Sheikh Nas-

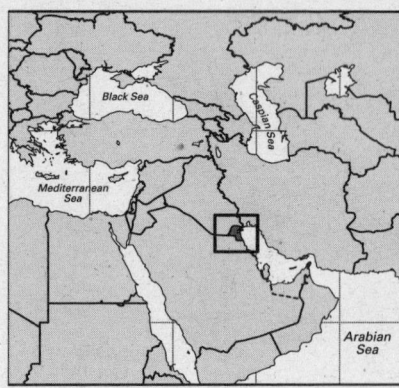

sar Muhammad al-Ahmad al-Sabah (from 2006). **Capital:** Kuwait (city). **Official language:** Arabic. **Official religion:** Islam. **Monetary unit:** 1 Kuwaiti dinar (KD) = 1,000 fils; valuation (1 Jul 2007) US$1 = KD 0.29.

Demography

Area: 6,880 sq mi, 17,818 sq km. **Population** (2006): 3,084,000. **Density** (2006): persons per sq mi 448.3, persons per sq km 173.1. **Urban** (2001): 96.1%. **Sex distribution** (2003): male 60.31%; female 39.69%. **Age breakdown** (2003): under 15, 27.9%; 15–29, 31.8%; 30–44, 23.9%; 45–59, 12.1%; 60–74, 3.7%; 75 and over, 0.6%. **Ethnic composition** (2000): Arab 74%, of which Kuwaiti 30%, Palestinian 17%, Jordanian 10%, Bedouin 9%; Kurd 10%; Indo-Pakistani 8%; Persian 4%; other 4%. **Religious affiliation** (1995): Muslim 85%, of which Sunni 45%, Shi'i 30%, other Muslim 10%; other (mostly Christian and Hindu) 15%. **Major cities** (1995): As-Salimiyah 130,215; Qalib ash-Shuyukh 102,178; Hawalli 82,238; Kuwait (city) 28,859 (urban agglomeration [2003] 1,222,000). **Location:** the Middle East, bordering Iraq, the Persian Gulf, and Saudi Arabia.

Vital statistics

Birth rate per 1,000 population (2003): 21.8 (world avg. 21.3). **Death rate** per 1,000 population (2003): 2.5 (world avg. 9.1). **Natural increase rate** per 1,000 population (2003): 19.3 (world avg. 12.2). **Total fertility rate** (avg. births per childbearing woman; 2003): 3.1. **Marriage rate** per 1,000 population (2000): 4.9. **Divorce rate** per 1,000 population (2000): 1.7. **Life expectancy** at birth (2003): male 75.7 years; female 77.6 years.

National economy

Budget (2003–04). *Revenue:* KD 3,397,000,000 (oil revenue 87.5%). *Expenditures:* KD 5,666,000,000 (wages 32.4%, defense 18.5%, social security and welfare 14.8%, health 14.8%, economic development 8.5%, education 6.0%). **Tourism** (2002): receipts from visitors $119,000,000; expenditures by nationals abroad $3,021,000,000. **Gross national product** (2003): $38,037,000,000 ($16,340 per capita). **Pro-**

duction (metric tons except as noted). *Agriculture, forestry, fishing* (2002): tomatoes 35,127, cucumbers and gherkins 33,004, eggplants 12,002; livestock (number of live animals) 800,000 sheep, 130,000 goats, 18,000 cattle; fish catch (2001) 6,041. *Mining and quarrying* (2001): sulfur 524,000; lime 40,000. *Manufacturing* (value added in $'000,-000; 1999): refined petroleum products 2,481; food products 170; nonmetallic mineral products 158. *Energy production (consumption):* electricity (kW-hr; 2000) 32,853,000,000 (32,853,000,000); crude petroleum (barrels; 2002) 680,000,000 ([2000] 274,129,000); petroleum products (2000) 33,410,-000 (8,583,000); natural gas (cu m; 2002) 8,297,-000,000 ([2000] 9,177,000,000). **Population economically active** (2003): total 1,466,092, of which Kuwaiti 19.1%, non-Kuwaiti 80.9%; activity rate of total population 57.6% (participation rates: ages 15–59, 73.8%; female [1995] 26.1%; unemployed 1.2%). **Household income and expenditure.** Average household size (2002) 5.0; sources of income (1986): wages and salaries 53.8%, self-employment 20.8%, other 25.4%; expenditure (2000): housing energy 26.7%, food 18.3%, transportation and communications 16.1%, household furnishings 14.7%, clothing and footwear 8.9%. **Land use** as % of total land area (2000): in temporary crops 0.6%, in permanent crops 0.1%, in pasture 7.6%; overall forest area 0.3%.

Foreign trade

Imports (2003-c.i.f.): KD 3,217,000,000 (machinery and apparatus 24.0%, transport equipment 20.5%, food 14.0%, chemicals and chemical products 8.7%). *Major import sources:* US 11.1%; Japan 10.7%; Germany 9.5%; Saudi Arabia 6.6%; Italy 5.5%; China 5.3%. **Exports** (2003-f.o.b.): KD 6,162,000,000 (crude petroleum and petroleum products 91.9%, ethylene products 3.0%, reexports 2.5%). *Major export destinations:* Japan 22.1%; South Korea 13.1%; US 12.0%; Taiwan 10.7%; Singapore 10.2%.

Transport and communications

Transport. *Roads* (1999): total length 4,450 km (paved 81%). *Vehicles* (2001): passenger cars 715,000; trucks and buses 226,000. *Air transport* (2003): passenger-km 6,714,693,000; metric ton-km cargo 219,428,000; airports (2003) with scheduled flights 1. **Communications,** in total units (units per 1,000 persons). Daily newspaper circulation (2000): 836,000 (374); radios (2000): 1,400,000 (624); televisions (2000): 1,090,000 (486); telephone main lines (2003): 486,900 (198); cellular telephone subscribers (2003): 1,420,000 (578); personal computers (2002): 285,000 (121); Internet users (2003): 567,000 (231).

Education and health

Educational attainment (1988). Percentage of population age 25 and over having: no formal schooling 44.8%; primary education 8.6%; some secondary 15.1%; complete secondary 15.1%; higher 16.4%. **Literacy** (2001): total population age 15 and over literate 82.4%; males literate 84.3%; females literate 80.3%. **Health** (2002): physicians 3,780 (1 per 625 persons); hospital beds 5,200 (1 per 455 persons); infant mortality rate per 1,000 live births (2003) 10.7. **Food** (2001): daily per capita caloric intake 3,170 (vegetable products 78%, animal products 22%); 131% of FAO recommended minimum.

Military

Total active duty personnel (2003): 15,500 (army [including central staff] 71.0%, navy 12.9%, air force 16.1%); US and coalition troops (March 2004) 26,000. **Military expenditure as percentage of GNP** (1999): 7.7% (world 2.4%); per capita expenditure $1,410.

Background

Faylakah Island, in Kuwait Bay, had a civilization dating back to the 3rd millennium BC that flourished until 1200 BC. Greek colonists resettled the island in the 4th century BC. Abd Rahim of the Sabah dynasty became sheikh in 1756, the first of a family that continues to rule Kuwait. In 1899, to thwart German and Ottoman influences, Kuwait gave Britain control of its foreign affairs. Following the outbreak of war in 1914, Britain established a protectorate there. In 1961, after Kuwait became independent, Iraq laid claim to it. British troops defended Kuwait, the Arab League recognized its independence, and Iraq dropped its claim. Iraqi forces invaded and occupied Kuwait in 1990, and a US-led military coalition drove them out in 1991. The destruction of many of Kuwait's oil wells complicated reconstruction efforts.

Recent Developments

The emir of Kuwait, Sheikh Jabir al-Ahmad al-Jabir al-Sabah, died on 15 Jan 2006. In accordance with the constitution, he was immediately replaced by Crown Prince Sheikh Saad al-Abdullah al-Salim al-Sabah. This led to an open power struggle with Prime Minister Sheikh Sabah al-Ahmad al-Jabir al-Sabah. The cabinet moved swiftly to nominate the prime minister as the next emir of Kuwait, and the parliament unanimously elected him. The change in leadership helped to assert the powers and importance of the parliament and the cabinet. Disagreements stemming from demands by lawmakers for democratic reforms and electoral redistricting led the emir to dissolve the parliament and call for new elections. The elections took place in June, with the opposition winning 33 of the 50 elected seats. For the first time in any Kuwaiti parliamentary election, women voted.

Internet resources: <www.kuwait-info.org>.

Kyrgyzstan

Official name: Kyrgyz Respublikasy (Kyrgyz); Respublika Kirgizstan (Russian) (Kyrgyz Republic). **Form of government:** unitary multiparty republic with two legislative houses (Assembly of People's Representatives [45]; Legislative Assembly [60]). **Head of state:** President Kurmanbek Bakiyev (from 2005). **Head of government:** Prime Minister Almazbek Atambayev (from 2007). **Capital:** Bishkek. **Official languages:** Kyrgyz; Russian. **Official religion:** none. **Monetary unit:** 1 som (K.S.) = 100 tyiyn; valuation (1 Jul 2007) US$1 = K.S. 41.45.

Demography

Area: 76,641 sq mi, 198,500 sq km. **Population** (2006): 5,192,000. **Density** (2006): persons per sq mi 67.7, persons per sq km 26.2. **Urban** (2003): 33.9%. **Sex distribution** (2001): male 48.84%; female

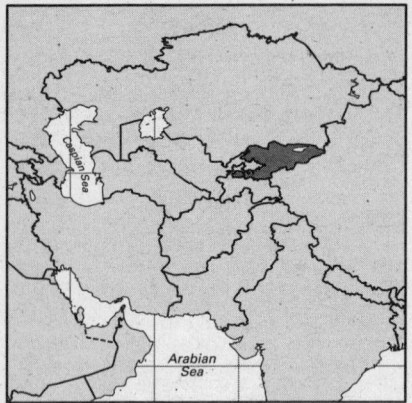

horses; roundwood (2001) 26,000 cu m; fish catch (2001) 201. *Mining and quarrying* (2002): mercury 300; antimony 200; gold (2001) 24,600 kg. *Manufacturing* (value of production in '000,000 som; 2001): ferrous metals 21,268; nonferrous metals 21,243; flour 3,914. *Energy production (consumption):* electricity (kW-hr; 2001) 13,667,000,000 (11,503,000,000); hard coal (1999) 97,000 (878,-000); lignite (2000) 321,000 (339,000); crude petroleum (barrels; 2001) 553,000 (553,000); petroleum products (2001) 131,000 (387,000); natural gas (cu m; 2001) 32,800,000 (655,700,000). **Household income and expenditure.** Average household size (1999) 4.3; income per household (1994) 4,359 som; sources of income (1999): wages and salaries 29.2%, self-employment 25.6%, other 45.2%; expenditure (1990): food and clothing 48.0%, health care 13.1%, housing 5.9%. **Gross national product** (2003): $1,649,000,000 ($330 per capita). **Tourism** (2002): receipts from visitors, $36,000,000; expenditures by nationals abroad, $10,000,000.

51.16%. **Age breakdown** (2001): under 15, 35.0%; 15–29, 28.1%; 30–44, 18.6%; 45–59, 9.2%; 60–74, 7.0%; 75 and over, 2.1%. **Ethnic composition** (1999): Kyrgyz 64.9%; Uzbek 13.8%; Russian 12.5%; Hui 1.1%; Ukrainian 1.0%; Uighur 1.0%; other 5.7%. **Religious affiliation** (1997): Muslim (mostly Sunni) 75.0%; Christian 6.7%, of which Russian Orthodox 5.6%; other (mostly nonreligious) 18.3%. **Major cities** (1999): Bishkek (Frunze) 750,327; Osh 208,520; Jalal-Abad 70,401; Tokmok 59,409; Kara-Köl 47,159. **Location:** central Asia, bordering Kazakhstan, China, Tajikistan, and Uzbekistan.

Vital statistics

Birth rate per 1,000 population (2003): 21.9 (world avg. 21.3); (1994) legitimate 83.2%. **Death rate** per 1,000 population (2003): 7.3 (world avg. 9.1). **Natural increase rate** per 1,000 population (2003): 14.6 (world avg. 12.2). **Total fertility rate** (avg. births per childbearing woman; 2001): 2.5. **Marriage rate** per 1,000 population (1999): 5.6. **Divorce rate** per 1,000 population (1999): 4.6. **Life expectancy** at birth (2003): male 63.5 years; female 71.7 years.

National economy

Budget (2001). *Revenue:* K.S. 12,544,000,000 (tax revenue 73.2%, of which VAT 33.6%, taxes on income 16.0%, excise taxes 8.8%, other taxes 14.8%; nontax revenue 21.3%; grants 5.5%). *Expenditures:* K.S. 13,133,000,000 (education 21.7%; general public services 16.0%; social security 10.8%; health 10.5%; defense 7.5%). **Public debt** (external, outstanding; 2002): $1,394,000,000. **Land use** as % of total land area (2000): in temporary crops 7.1%, in permanent crops 0.3%, in pasture 48.4%; overall forest area 5.2%. **Population economically active** (2001): total 1,939,000; activity rate of total population 39.2% (participation rates [2000]: ages 16–59 [male], 16–54 [female] 62.0%; female (1999) 44.9%; unemployed [2001] 7.8%. **Production** (metric tons except as noted). *Agriculture, forestry, fishing* (2002): mixed grasses and legumes 2,900,000, wheat 1,306,000, potatoes 1,244,000; livestock (number of live animals) 3,104,000 sheep, 988,000 cattle, 350,000

Foreign trade

Imports (2001-f.o.b. in balance of trade and c.i.f. for commodities and trading partners): $467,200,000 (petroleum and natural gas 22.6%, machinery and apparatus 21.0%, food products 11.7%, chemicals and chemical products 9.5%). *Major import sources:* Russia 18.2%; Kazakhstan 17.5%; Uzbekistan 14.3%; China 10.4%; US 5.7%. **Exports** (2001): $476,-200,000 (nonferrous metals [significantly gold] 51.7%, machinery and apparatus 12.0%, electricity 9.8%, agricultural products [significantly tobacco] 9.5%). *Major export destinations:* Switzerland 26.1%; Germany 19.8%; Russia 13.5%; Uzbekistan 10.1%; Kazakhstan 8.2%.

Transport and communications

Transport. *Railroads* (2000): length 424 km; passenger-km 44,000,000; metric ton-km cargo 348,000,-000. *Roads* (1999): total length 18,500 km (paved 91%). *Vehicles* (2000): passenger cars 187,322. *Air transport* (1999): passenger-km 532,000,000; metric ton-km cargo 56,000,000; airports with scheduled flights 2. **Communications**, in total units (units per 1,000 persons). Daily newspaper circulation (2000): 73,000 (15); radios (2000): 542,000 (111); televisions (2000): 239,000 (49); telephone main lines (2002): 394,800 (79); cellular telephone subscribers (2002): 53,100 (10); personal computers (2002): 65,000 (13); Internet users (2002): 152,000 (30).

Education and health

Educational attainment (1999). Percentage of population age 15 and over having: primary education 6.3%; some secondary 18.3%; completed secondary 50.0%; some postsecondary 14.9%; higher 10.5%. **Literacy** (1999): total population age 15 and over literate 97.5%; males literate 98.5%; females literate 96.5%. **Health** (1997): physicians 15,100 (1 per 307 persons); hospital beds 40,700 (1 per 114 persons); infant mortality rate per 1,000 live births (2003) 38.0. **Food** (2001): daily per capita caloric intake 2,882 (vegetable products 81%, animal products 19%); 111% of FAO recommended minimum.

1 metric ton = about 1.1 short tons;   1 kilometer = 0.6 mi (statute);   1 metric ton-km cargo = about 0.68 short ton-mi cargo;   c.i.f.: cost, insurance, and freight;   f.o.b.: free on board

Military

Total active duty personnel (2003): 10,900 (army 78.0%, air force 22.0%); US troops (July 2004) 1,200. A Russian air base opened in Kyrgyzstan in October 2003. Military expenditure as percentage of GNP (1999): 2.4% (world 2.4%); per capita expenditure $62.

Background

The Kyrgyz, a nomadic people of Central Asia, settled in the Tian Shan region in ancient times. They were conquered by Genghis Khan's son Jochi in 1207. The area became part of the Qing empire of China in the mid-18th century. The region came under Russian control in the 19th century, and its rebellion against Russia in 1916 resulted in a long period of brutal repression. Kirgiziya became an autonomous province of the USSR in 1924 and was made the Kirghiz Soviet Socialist Republic in 1936. Kyrgyzstan gained independence in 1991. In the 1990s it struggled with its democratization process and with establishing a thriving economy.

Recent Developments

An antiterrorist operation by Kyrgyz and Uzbek special forces in August 2006 resulted in the death of a prominent religious figure, which caused the opposition to warn that antigovernment sentiment among the Uzbek minority of southern Kyrgyzstan was rising. Kyrgyzstan's relations with the United States were worsened by a disagreement over the amount of compensation the US was to pay for use of the military air base near Bishkek, which provided support to antiterrorism coalition forces in Afghanistan. After several demands thought by some observers to be attempts to force the US military out of the region, an agreement was reached on an annual payment of $150 million in aid and monetary compensation.

Internet resources: <www.kyrgyzstan.org>.

Laos

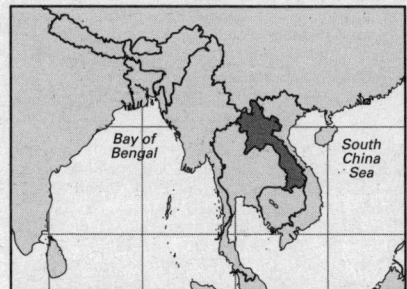

Official name: Sathalanalat Paxathipatai Paxaxon Lao (Lao People's Democratic Republic). Form of government: unitary single-party people's republic with one legislative house (National Assembly [109]). Chief of state: President Choummaly Sayasone (from 2006). Head of government: Prime Minister Bouasone Bouphavanh (from 2006). Capital: Vientiane (Viangchan). Official language: Lao. Official religion: none. Monetary unit: 1 kip (KN) = 100 at; valuation (1 Jul 2007) US$1 = KN 9,773.

Demography

Area: 91,429 sq mi, 236,800 sq km. Population (2006): 5,751,000. Density (2006): persons per sq mi 62.9, persons per sq km 24.3. Urban (2002): 25.0%. Sex distribution (2002): male 49.97%; female 50.03%. Age breakdown (2000): under 15, 42.8%; 15–29, 27.0%; 30–44, 16.3%; 45–59, 8.3%; 60–74, 4.6%; 75 and over, 1.0%. Ethnic composition (2000): Lao-Lum (Lao) 53.0%; Lao-Theung (Mon-Khmer) 23.0%; Lao-Tai (Tai) 13.0%; Lao-Soung (Miao [Hmong] and Man [Yao]) 10.0%; other (ethnic Chinese or Vietnamese) 1.0%. Religious affiliation (2000): Buddhist 48.8%; traditional beliefs 41.7%; nonreligious 4.3%; Christian 2.1%; other 3.1%. Major cities (2003): Vientiane 194,200 (urban agglomeration [2001] 663,-000); Savannakhét 58,200; Pakxé 50,100; Xam Nua 40,700; Muang Khammouan 27,300. Location: southeastern Asia, bordering China, Vietnam, Cambodia, Thailand, and Myanmar (Burma).

Vital statistics

Birth rate per 1,000 population (2003): 36.9 (world avg. 21.3). Death rate per 1,000 population (2004): 12.4 (world avg. 9.1). Natural increase rate per 1,000 population (2003): 24.5 (world avg. 12.2). Total fertility rate (avg. births per childbearing woman; 2003): 4.9. Life expectancy at birth (2003): male 52.3 years; female 56.3 years.

National economy

Budget (2001–02). Revenue: KN 2,481,000,000,-000 (tax revenue 82.3%; nontax revenue 17.7%). Expenditures: KN 3,614,000,000,000 (capital expenditure 59.9%, of which foreign-financed 34.8%; current expenditure 40.1%). Public debt (external, outstanding; 2002): $2,620,000,000. Tourism (2002): receipts from visitors $113,000,000; expenditures by nationals abroad (2000) $8,000,000. Population economically active (2000): total 2,625,000; activity rate of total population 50% (participation rates: female 47%; unemployed [1994] 2.6%). Production (metric tons except as noted). Agriculture, forestry, fishing (2002): rice 2,410,000, sugarcane 210,000, corn (maize) 113,000; livestock (number of live animals) 1,425,900 pigs, 1,150,000 cattle, 15,000,-000 chickens; roundwood (2001) 6,455,000 cu m; fish catch (2001) 80,000. Mining and quarrying (2002): gypsum 130,000; tin (metal content) 350; gold (2003) 115,000 troy oz. Manufacturing (1998): plastic products 3,225; tobacco 1,000; detergent 912. Energy production (consumption): electricity (kW-hr; 2000) 1,225,000,000 (497,000,000); coal (2000) 1,000 (1,000); petroleum products (2000) none (119,000). Gross national product (2003): $1,821,000,000 ($320 per capita). Households. Average household size (1995) 6.1; average annual income per household KN 3,710. Land use as % of total land area (2000): in temporary crops 3.8%, in permanent crops 0.4%, in pasture 3.8%; overall forest area 54.4%.

Foreign trade

Imports (2000-c.i.f.): $569,000,000 (consumption goods 50.6%, mineral fuels 13.9%, materials for garment assembly 10.6%, construction and electrical equipment 7.6%). *Major import sources* (2001): Thailand 52.0%; Vietnam 26.5%; China 5.7%; Singapore 3.3%; Japan 1.5%. **Exports** (2000-f.o.b.): $351,000,-000 (electricity 32.0%, garments 26.1%, wood products [mostly logs and timber] 24.8%, motorcycles 6.3%). *Major export destinations* (2001): Vietnam 41.5%; Thailand 14.8%; France 6.1%; Germany 4.6%; Belgium 2.2%.

Transport and communications

Transport. *Roads* (1999): total length 21,716 km (paved [1995] 45%). *Vehicles* (1996): passenger cars 16,320; trucks and buses 4,200. *Air transport* (1997): passenger-km 48,000,000; metric ton-km cargo 5,000,000; airports (1996) with scheduled flights 11. **Communications,** in total units (units per 1,000 persons). Daily newspaper circulation (2000): 21,100 (4); radios (2000): 781,000 (148); televisions (2000): 52,800 (10); telephone main lines (2002): 61,900 (11); cellular telephone subscribers (2002): 55,200 (10); personal computers (2002): 15,000 (2.7); Internet users (2002): 18,000 (3.3).

Education and health

Educational attainment (1985). Percentage of population age 6 and over having: no schooling 49.3%; primary 41.2%; secondary 9.1%; higher 0.4%. **Literacy** (1995): total population age 15 and over literate 56.6%; males literate 69.4%; females literate 44.4%. **Health:** physicians (1996) 1,167 (1 per 4,115 persons); hospital beds (1990) 10,364 (1 per 402 persons); infant mortality rate per 1,000 live births (2003) 88.9. **Food** (2001): daily per capita caloric intake 2,309 (vegetable products 93%, animal products 7%); (2001) 108% of FAO recommended minimum.

Military

Total active duty personnel (2003): 29,100 (army 88.0%, air force 12.0%). **Military expenditure as percentage of GNP** (1999): 2.0% (world 2.4%); per capita expenditure $5.

Background

The Lao people migrated into Laos from southern China after the 8th century AD, displacing indigenous tribes. In the 14th century Fa Ngum founded the first Laotian state, Lan Xang. Except for a period of rule by Burma (1574–1637), the Lan Xang kingdom ruled Laos until 1713, when it split into three kingdoms. France gained control of the region in 1893. In 1945 Japan seized it and declared Laos independent. The area reverted to French rule after World War II. The Geneva Conference of 1954 unified and granted independence to Laos. Communist forces took control in 1975, establishing the Lao People's Democratic Republic. Laos held its first election in 1989 and promulgated a new constitution in 1991. Although its economy was adversely affected by the mid-1990s Asian monetary crises, it realized a longtime goal in 1997 when it joined the Association of Southeast Asian Nations.

Recent Developments

Plans for the increasing of mining revenue and the generation and sale of hydroelectricity took shape in Laos in 2005 and 2006. Copper production began at an Australian-owned mine in early 2005, and the government expected mining revenues to double in the next 15 years. Construction began at the end of 2005 on the $1.2-billion Nam Theun II dam in central Laos, which would produce 1,070 MW of hydroelectricity annually upon completion in 2009, though protests against the environmental and social effects of the massive project continued. Financial and construction agreements between the governments of Laos and Thailand signed in May 2006 marked the beginning of the Nam Ngum II hydroelectricity project. It would annually generate 615 MW of power for sale to Thailand upon completion in 2013.

Internet resources: <www.visit-laos.com>.

Latvia

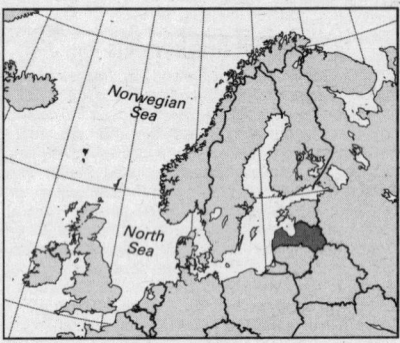

Official name: Latvijas Republika (Republic of Latvia). **Form of government:** unitary multiparty republic with a single legislative body (Parliament, or Saeima [100]). **Chief of state:** President Valdis Zatlers (from 2007). **Head of government:** Prime Minister Aigars Kalvitis (from 2004). **Capital:** Riga. **Official language:** Latvian. **Official religion:** none. **Monetary unit:** 1 lats (Ls; plural lati) = 100 santimi; valuation (1 Jul 2007) US$1 = 0.52 lats.

Demography

Area: 24,938 sq mi, 64,589 sq km. **Population** (2006): 2,287,000. **Density** (2006): persons per sq mi 91.7, persons per sq km 35.4. **Urban** (2002): 67.8%. **Sex distribution** (2002): male 46.03%; female 53.97%. **Age breakdown** (2000): under 15, 18.1%; 15–29, 21.2%; 30–44, 21.4%; 45–59, 18.3%; 60–74, 15.7%; 75 and over, 5.3%. **Ethnic composition** (2002): Latvian 58,2%; Russian 29.2%; Belarusian 4.0%; Ukrainian 2.6%; Polish 2.5%; Lithuanian 1.4%; other 2.1%. **Religious affiliation** (1995): Christian 39.6%, of which Protestant 16.7% (of which Lutheran 14.6%), Roman Catholic 14.9%, Orthodox 8.0%; Jewish 0,6%; other (mostly nonreligious) 59.8%. **Major cities** (2002): Riga 747,157;

---

1 metric ton = about 1.1 short tons;   1 kilometer = 0.6 mi (statute);   1 metric ton-km cargo = about 0.68 short ton-mi cargo;   c.i.f.: cost, insurance, and freight;   f.o.b.: free on board

Daugavpils 113,409; Liepaja 87,505; Jelgava 65,927; Jurmala 55,328. **Location:** eastern Europe, bordering Estonia, Russia, Belarus, Lithuania, and the Baltic Sea.

Vital statistics

Birth rate per 1,000 population (2002): 8.6 (world avg. 21.3); (1998) legitimate 62.9%. **Death rate** per 1,000 population (2002): 13.9 (world avg. 9.1). **Natural increase rate** per 1,000 population (2002): –5.3 (world avg. 12.2). **Total fertility rate** (avg. births per childbearing woman; 2002): 1.2. **Marriage rate** per 1,000 population (2002): 4.2. **Divorce rate** per 1,000 population (2002): 2.5. **Life expectancy** at birth (2002): male 65.4 years; female 76.8 years.

National economy

Budget (2001). *Revenue:* Ls 1,244,100,000 (social security contributions 35.3%, value-added taxes 28.2%, income taxes 14.3%, excises 13.0%, nontax revenue 9.2%). *Expenditures:* Ls 1,399,800,000 (social security and welfare 40.7%, health 11.0%, police 7.0%, education 6.3%, defense 3.1%). **Public debt** (external, outstanding; 2002): $1,124,-000,000. **Production** (metric tons except as noted). *Agriculture, forestry, fishing* (2002): grasses for forage and silage 14,000,000, potatoes 768,000, sugar beets 622,000; livestock (number of live animals) 453,000 pigs, 388,000 cattle; roundwood (2001) 14,037,000 cu m; fish catch (2002) 105,000. *Mining and quarrying* (2001): peat 555,-000. *Manufacturing* (value added in Ls '000,000; 1998): alcoholic beverages 79.4; sawn wood 64.4; veneer/plywood 37.6. *Energy production (consumption):* electricity (kW-hr; 2001) 4,236,000,000 ([2002] 6,323,000,000); coal (2002) none (102,-000); petroleum products (2002) none (1,084,000); natural gas (cu m; 2002) none (1,610,000,000). **Household income and expenditure.** Average household size (2000) 2.7; annual disposable income per household (2002) Ls 2,076; sources of income (1998): wages and salaries 55.8%, pensions and transfers 25.7%; expenditure (2001–02): food, beverages, and tobacco 40.0%, transportation and communications 15.0%, housing and energy 14.0%. **Tourism** (in $'000,000; 2002): receipts 161; expenditures 230. **Gross national product** (2003): $9,441,000,000 ($4,070 per capita). **Population economically active** (2002): total 1,123,000; activity rate of total population 48.1% (participation rates: ages 15–64 [2000] 67.5%; female [2000] 48.5%; unemployed 12.0%). **Land use** as % of total land area (2000): in temporary crops 29.7%, in permanent crops 0.5%, in pasture 9.8%; overall forest area 47.1%.

Foreign trade

Imports (2002-c.i.f.): Ls 2,497,000,000 (machinery and apparatus 21.3%, chemicals and chemical products 10.5%, transport vehicles 9.8%, mineral fuels 9.7%). *Major import sources:* Germany 17.2%; Lithuania 9.8%; Russia 8.8%; Finland 8.0%; Sweden 6.4%. **Exports** (2002-f.o.b.): Ls 1,409,000,000 (wood and wood products [mostly sawn wood] 33.6%, base and fabricated metals [mostly iron and steel] 13.2%, textiles and clothing 12.8%). *Major export destinations:* Germany 15.5%; UK 14.6%; Sweden 10.5%; Lithuania 8.4%; Estonia 6.0%.

Transport and communications

Transport. *Railroads* (2002): length 2,270 km; passenger-km (2000) 715,000,000; metric-km cargo 15,020,000,000. *Roads* (1999): total length 73,227 km (paved 39%). *Vehicles* (2002): passenger cars 552,200; trucks and buses 113,900. *Air transport* (1999): passenger-km 238,000,000; metric ton-km cargo 10,000,000; airports with scheduled flights (2001) 2. **Communications,** in total units (units per 1,000 persons). Daily newspaper circulation (2000): 586,000 (247); radios (2000): 1,650,000 (695); televisions (2002): 1,955,000 (850); telephone main lines (2003): 653,900 (283); cellular telephone subscribers (2003): 1,219,600 (529); personal computers (2002): 400,000 (171); Internet users (2003): 936,000 (406).

Education and health

Educational attainment (2000). Percentage of population age 15 and over having: some and complete primary education 8.5%; lower secondary 26.5%; upper secondary 51.1%; higher 13.9%. **Literacy** (2000): 99.8%. **Health** (2002): physicians 7,900 (1 per 295 persons); hospital beds 18,200 (1 per 128 persons); infant mortality rate per 1,000 live births (2002) 9.9. **Food** (2001): daily per capita caloric intake 2,809 (vegetable products 72%, animal products 28%); 110% of FAO recommended minimum.

Military

Total active duty personnel (2003): 4,880, excluding 3,200 border guards classified as paramilitary (army 82.0%, navy 12.7%, air force 5.3%). **Military expenditure as percentage of GNP** (1999): 0.9% (world 2.4%); per capita expenditure $59.

Background

Latvia was settled by the Balts in ancient times. It was conquered by the Vikings in the 9th century and later dominated by its German-speaking neighbors, who Christianized the people in the 12th–13th centuries. By 1230 German rule was established. From the mid-16th to the early 18th century, the region was split between Poland and Sweden, but by the end of the 18th century all of Latvia had been annexed by Russia. Latvia declared its independence after the Russian Revolution of 1917, but in 1940 the Soviet Red Army invaded. Held by Nazi Germany in 1941–44, the country was recaptured by the Soviets and incorporated into the Soviet Union. Latvia gained its independence in 1991 with the breakup of the Soviet Union; throughout the 1990s it sought to privatize the economy and build ties with Western Europe.

Recent Developments

In joining NATO on 29 March and the EU on 1 May, Latvia in 2004 achieved its main foreign-policy goals since regaining independence. Riga contributed to international missions in Iraq, Afghanistan, and the Balkans in 2005 and 2006 and generally maintained good relations with the rest of the world. The country opened an embassy in Turkey in 2005 and in Japan in 2006. Relations with Russia, strained following years of Soviet domination, thawed somewhat, as Latvia's president accepted an invitation to Moscow in May 2005 to commemorate the 60th anniversary of the end of World War II in Europe. Latvia's economy grew by over 10% in both 2005 and 2006, though inflation remained high.

Internet resources: <www.latviatourism.lv>.

Lebanon

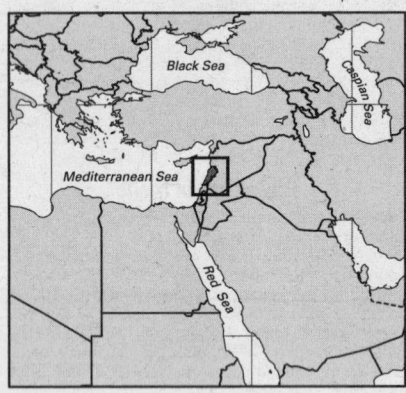

Official name: Al-Jumhuriyah al-Lubnaniyah (Lebanese Republic). Form of government: unitary multiparty republic with one legislative house (National Assembly [128]). Chief of state: President Émile Lahoud (from 1998). Head of government: Prime Minister Fouad Siniora (from 2005). Capital: Beirut. Official language: Arabic. Official religion: none. Monetary unit: 1 Lebanese pound (£L) = 100 piastres; valuation (1 Jul 2007) US$1 = £L 1,503.

Demography

Area: 4,016 sq mi, 10,400 sq km. Population (2006): 3,834,000 (excludes about 400,000 unnaturalized Palestinian refugees). Density (2006): persons per sq mi 954.7, persons per sq km 368.7. Urban (2001): 90.1%. Sex distribution (2002): male 48.48%; female 51.52%. Age breakdown (2002): under 15, 27.4%; 15–29, 32.2%; 30–44, 21.0%; 45–59, 10.1%; 60–74, 7.1%; 75 and over, 2.2%. Ethnic composition (2000): Arab 84.5%, of which Lebanese 71.2%, Palestinian 12.1%; Armenian 6.8%; Kurd 6.1%; other 2.6%. Religious affiliation (1995): Muslim 55.3%, of which Shi'i 34.0%, Sunni 21.3%; Christian 37.6%, of which Catholic 25.1% (Maronite 19.0%, Greek Catholic or Melchite 4.6%), Orthodox 11.7% (Greek Orthodox 6.0%, Armenian Apostolic 5.2%), Protestant 0.5%; Druze 7.1%. Major cities (1998): Beirut 1,100,000 (urban agglomeration 2,115,000 [2001]); Tripoli 200,000; Sidon 140,000; Tyre (Sur) 110,000; An-Nabatiyah 84,000. Location: the Middle East, bordering Syria, Israel, and the Mediterranean Sea.

Vital statistics

Birth rate per 1,000 population (2003): 19.7 (world avg. 21.3). Death rate per 1,000 population (2003): 6.3 (world avg. 9.1). Natural increase rate per 1,000 population (2003): 13.4 (world avg. 12.2). Total fertility rate (avg. births per childbearing woman; 2003): 1.9. Life expectancy at birth (2003): male 69.6 years; female 74.6 years.

National economy

Budget (2000). Revenue: £L 4,091,435,000,000 (1998; tax revenue 74.6%, of which customs revenues 44.1%, income tax 9.0%, taxes on goods and services 8.4%, property tax 8.4%, miscellaneous taxes and fees 2.1%; nontax revenue 25.4%). Expenditures: £L 8,190,034,000,000 (current expenditures 81.1%, of which debt service 40.0%, public services 13.3%, defense 9.7%, education 8.3%, social security 6.4%, health 2.6%; capital expenditures 18.9%). Production (metric tons except as noted). Agriculture, forestry, fishing (2002): potatoes 257,000, tomatoes 247,-000, cucumbers and gherkins 161,000; livestock (number of live animals) 385,000 goats, 350,000 sheep, 33,000,000 chickens; roundwood (2001) 89,426 cu m; fish catch (2001) 3,970. Mining and quarrying (1996): lime 16,000; salt 4,000; gypsum 2,000. Manufacturing (2001): cement 2,727,000; flour 420,000; olive oil 7,000. Energy production (consumption): electricity (kW-hr; 2001) 10,452,000,000 ([2000] 10,633,000,000); coal, n.a. (117,000); crude petroleum (barrels; 1998) none (1,358,000); petroleum products (2001) none (4,784,000). Gross national product (2003): $18,187,000,000 ($4,040 per capita). Population economically active (1997): total 1,362,000; activity rate of total population 39.7% (unemployed 8.5%). Public debt (external, outstanding; 2002): $13,829,000,000. Households. Average household size (2000) 4.5; average annual income per household (1994; ESCWA estimate for Beirut only) £L 2,400,000. Tourism (2002): receipts from visitors $956,000,000. Land use as % of total land area (2000): in temporary crops 18.6%, in permanent crops 13.9%, in pasture 1.6%; overall forest area 3.5%.

Foreign trade

Imports (2002-c.i.f.): $6,445,000,000 (mineral products 15.1%, machinery and apparatus 13.4%, food and live animals 13.3%, chemicals and chemical products 9.8%). Major import sources: Italy 10.8%; Germany 9.0%; France 8.0%; US 7.2%; China 6.7%. Exports (2002): $1,046,000,000 (precious metal [significantly gold] jewelry 20.5%, machinery and apparatus 11.4%, chemicals and chemical products 10.3%, food and beverages 9.8%, paper and paper products 9.4%). Major export destinations: Switzerland 12.6%; Saudi Arabia 9.2%; UAE 9.1%; Syria 7.2%; Iraq 6.8%.

Transport and communications

Transport. Roads (1996): total length 6,350 km (paved 95%). Vehicles (1997): passenger cars 1,299,398; trucks and buses 85,242. Air transport (2001; Middle East Airlines and Trans-Mediterranean Airways): passenger-km 1,661,000,000; metric ton-km cargo 216,700,000; airports (1999) 1. Communications, in total units (units per 1,000 persons). Daily newspaper circulation (2000): 383,000 (107); radios (2000): 2,460,000 (687); televisions (2000): 1,200,000

1 metric ton = about 1.1 short tons;   1 kilometer = 0.6 mi (statute);   1 metric ton-km cargo = about 0.68 short ton-mi cargo;   c.i.f.: cost, insurance, and freight;   f.o.b.: free on board

(335); telephone main lines (2002): 678,800 (198); cellular telephone subscribers (2002): 775,100 (227); personal computers (2002): 275,000 (81); Internet users (2002): 400,000 (117).

Education and health

Literacy (2000): total population age 15 and over literate 87.4%; males literate 93.1%; females literate 82.2%. **Health** (1997): physicians 7,203 (1 per 476 persons); hospital beds (1995) 11,596 (1 per 319 persons); infant mortality rate per 1,000 live births (2003) 26.4. **Food** (2001): daily per capita caloric intake 3,184 (vegetable products 85%, animal products 15%); 128% of FAO recommended minimum.

Military

Total active duty personnel (2003): Lebanese national armed forces 72,100 (army 97.1%, navy 1.5%, air force 1.4%). External regular military forces include: UN peacekeeping force in Lebanon (August 2004) 2,000; Syrian army (September 2004) 14,000. **Military expenditure as percentage of GNP** (1999): 4.0% (world 2.4%); per capita expenditure $185.

Background

Much of present-day Lebanon corresponds to ancient Phoenicia, which was settled c. 3000 BC. In the 6th century AD, Christians fleeing Syrian persecution settled in what is now northern Lebanon and founded the Maronite Church. Arab tribesmen settled in southern Lebanon and by the 11th century had founded the Druze faith. Lebanon was later ruled by the Mamluks. In 1516 the Ottoman Turks seized control; the Turks ended the local rule of the Druze Shihab princes in 1842. After the massacre of Maronites by Druze in 1860, France forced the Ottomans to form an autonomous province for the Christian area, known as Mount Lebanon. Following World War I, it was administered by the French military, but by late 1946 it was fully independent. After the Arab-Israeli War of 1948–49, Palestinian refugees settled in southern Lebanon. In 1970 the Palestine Liberation Organization (PLO) moved its headquarters there and began raids into northern Israel. The Christian-dominated Lebanese government tried to curb them, and in response the PLO sided with Lebanon's Muslims in their conflict with Christians, sparking a civil war by 1975. In 1982 Israeli forces invaded in an effort to drive Palestinian forces out of southern Lebanon. Israeli troops withdrew from most of Lebanon in 1985, leaving the conflict unresolved, but later returned. A cease-fire, agreed to in 1996, was broken in 1997 when Israeli soldiers and Lebanon's Hezbollah forces clashed.

Recent Developments

In July 2006 Hezbollah paramilitary forces launched a military operation into Israel, killing a number of Israeli soldiers and taking two as prisoners of war. This action led Israel to launch a major military offensive against Hezbollah. Hezbollah's use of new weapons and tactics prolonged the confrontation. In August the UN Security Council brokered a cease-fire and put forth Resolution 1701 in an effort to curtail hostilities. Both sides stopped fighting that month. The resolution accepted the government's pledge to deploy 15,000 Lebanese army troops along the southern borders, called for the Israelis to withdraw from Lebanese territory, and promised the formation of a United Nations Interim Force in Lebanon (UNIFIL) headed by France that had the right to stop Lebanese armed elements from operating south of the Litani River. UNIFIL would also assist in securing Lebanese borders to prevent the entry of arms to paramilitary groups. The 34-day war and the political stalemate had a very negative impact on the Lebanese economy. GDP was predicted to decline 5% in 2006, and the treasury deficit increased in the first eight months of the year to 32%, compared with about 25% in all of 2005. Though whole areas in the south of the country and parts of Beirut needed to be rebuilt, Lebanon received generous monetary assistance from Arab Gulf states and the European Union.

Internet resources: <www.presidency.gov.lb>.

Lesotho

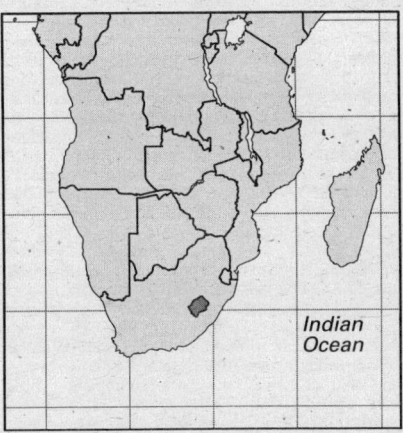

Indian
Ocean

Official name: Lesotho (Sotho); Kingdom of Lesotho (English). **Form of government:** constitutional monarchy with 2 legislative houses (Senate [33]; National Assembly [120]). **Chief of state:** King Letsie III (from 1996). **Head of government:** Prime Minister Bethuel Pakalitha Mosisili (from 1998). **Capital:** Maseru. **Official languages:** Sotho; English. **Official religion:** Christianity. **Monetary unit:** 1 loti (plural maloti [M]) = 100 lisente; valuation (1 Jul 2007) US$1 = M 7.09.

Demography

Area: 11,720 sq mi, 30,355 sq km. **Population** (2006): 2,022,000. **Density** (2006; de facto): persons per sq mi 172.5, persons per sq km 66.6. **Urban** (2001; de jure figure including absentee miners working in South Africa): 13.4%. **Sex distribution** (2001; de jure figure including absentee miners working in South Africa): male 50.62%; female 49.38%. **Age breakdown** (2001; de jure figure including absentee miners working in South Africa): under 15, 35.3%; 15–29, 31.4%; 30–44, 14.8%; 45–59, 10.0%; 60–74, 5.9%; 75 and over, 2.6%. **Ethnic composition** (2000): Sotho 80.3%; Zulu 14.4%; other 5.3%. **Religious affiliation** (2000): Christian 91.0%, of which

Roman Catholic 37.5%, Protestant (mostly Presbyterian) 13.0%, African Christian 11.8%; other (mostly traditional beliefs) 9.0%. **Major urban centers** (1996): Maseru 137,837 (urban agglomeration [2001] 271,000); Teyateyaneng 48,869; Maputsoe 27,951; Hlotse 23,122; Mafeteng 20,804. **Location:** southern Africa, surrounded by South Africa.

Vital statistics

Birth rate per 1,000 population (2003): 27.3 (world avg. 21.3). **Death rate** per 1,000 population (2003): 24.6 (world avg. 9.1). **Natural increase rate** per 1,000 population (2003): 2.7 (world avg. 12.2). **Total fertility rate** (avg. births per childbearing woman; 2003): 3.5. **Life expectancy** at birth (2003): male 36.8 years; female 37.1 years. **Adult population** (ages 15–49) living with HIV (2004): 28.9% (world avg. 1.1%).

National economy

Budget (2000–01). *Revenue:* M 2,752,200,000 (customs receipts 40.9%, grants and nontax revenue 29.4%, income tax 11.4%, sales tax 10.2%). *Expenditures:* M 2,897,900,000 (personal emoluments 31.8%, capital expenditure 17.8%, subsidies and transfers 9.6%, interest payments 9.0%). **Public debt** (external, outstanding; 2002): $611,000,000. **Production** (metric tons except as noted). *Agriculture, forestry, fishing* (2002): corn (maize) 300,000, potatoes 90,000, wheat 51,000; livestock (number of live animals) 850,000 sheep, 650,000 goats, 540,000 cattle; roundwood (2001) 2,028,134 cu m; fish catch (2001) 32. *Mining and quarrying* (2001): diamonds 1,140 carats. *Manufacturing* (value added in $'000,000; 1995): food products 58; beverages 38; textiles 14. *Energy production (consumption):* data for Lesotho included with South Africa. **Tourism** (2002): receipts from visitors $20,000,000; expenditures by nationals abroad $14,000,000. **Population economically active** (1993): total 617,871; activity rate of total population 45.1% (participation rates: ages 15–64 [1986] 79.8%; female 23.7%; unemployed [2001] 40%). **Households.** Average household size (2000) 5.0; expenditure (1989): food 48.0%, clothing 16.4%, household durable goods 11.9%, housing and energy 10.1%, transportation 4.7%. **Gross national product** (at current market prices; 2003): $1,049,000,000 ($590 per capita). **Land use** as % of total land area (2000): in temporary crops 10.9%, in permanent crops 0.1%, in pasture 65.9%; overall forest area 0.5%.

Foreign trade

Imports (2001-f.o.b. in balance of trade and c.i.f. in commodities and trading partners): M 5,824,-000,000 (1999; food products 15.3%, unspecified commodities 84.7%). *Major import sources* (2001): Customs Union of Southern Africa (mostly South Africa) 82.8%; Asian countries 14.9%. **Exports** (2001): M 2,426,000,000 (manufactured goods [mostly clothing] 74.7%, machinery and transport equipment 10.5%, beverages 3.6%, wool 2.5%). *Major export destinations:* North America (mostly the US) 62.8%; Customs Union of Southern Africa (mostly South Africa) 37.0%.

Transport and communications

Transport. *Railroads* (2001): length 2.6 km. *Roads* (1999): total length 5,940 km (paved 18%). *Vehicles* (1996): passenger cars 12,610; trucks and buses 25,000. *Air transport* (1999): passenger-km, negligible (less than 500,000); metric ton-km cargo, negligible; airports (1997) with scheduled flights 1. **Communications,** in total units (units per 1,000 persons). Daily newspaper circulation (2000): 14,300 (8); radios (2000): 94,600 (53); televisions (2002): 63,000 (35); telephone main lines (2002): 28,600 (13); cellular telephone subscribers (2002): 96,800 (45); Internet users (2002): 21,000 (9.7).

Education and health

Educational attainment (1986–87). Percentage of population age 10 and over having: no formal education 22.9%; primary 52.8%; secondary 23.2%; higher 0.6%. **Literacy** (2000–04): total population age 15 and over literate 81.4%; males literate 73.7%; females literate 90.3%. **Health:** physicians (1995) 105 (1 per 18,527 persons); hospital beds (1992) 2,400 (1 per 765 persons); infant mortality rate per 1,000 live births (2003) 86.2. **Food** (2001): daily per capita caloric intake 2,320 (vegetable products 97%, animal products 3%); 102% of FAO recommended minimum.

Military

Total active duty personnel (2003): 2,000 (Royal Lesotho Defence Force). **Military expenditure as percentage of GNP** (1999): 2.6% (world 2.4%); per capita expenditure $14.

Background

Bantu-speaking farmers began to settle the area in the 16th century, and a number of chiefdoms arose. The most powerful organized the Basotho in 1824 and obtained British protection in 1843, as tension between the Basotho and the South African Boers increased. The area became a British territory in 1868 and was annexed to the Cape Colony in 1871. The colony's effort to disarm the Basotho resulted in revolt in 1880, and four years later it separated from the colony and became a British High Commission Territory. In 1966 it declared its independence. A new constitution (1993) ended seven years of military rule. In the late 20th century, Lesotho suffered from internal political problems and a deteriorating economy.

Recent Developments

Some 265,000 people in Lesotho, and 23% of the adult population, were living with HIV/AIDS in 2005. In early 2005 the ending of worldwide textile quotas caused the closing of textile factories, a key factor in Lesotho's economy, and the feared loss of 56,000 jobs. The industry rebounded in 2006, however, because low labor costs made Lesotho textiles competitive and the government appealed for overseas buyers to purchase goods from Lesotho on ethical grounds.

Internet resources: <www.lesotho.gov.ls>.

1 metric ton = about 1.1 short tons;   1 kilometer = 0.6 mi (statute);   1 metric ton-km cargo = about 0.68 short ton-mi cargo;   c.i.f.: cost, insurance, and freight;   f.o.b.: free on board

Liberia

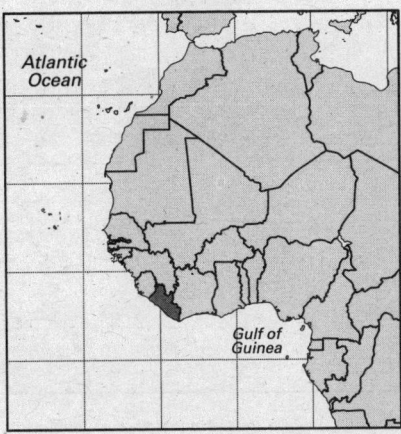

Official name: Republic of Liberia. **Form of government:** multiparty republic with two legislative bodies (Senate [30]; House of Representatives [64]). **Head of state and government:** President Ellen Johnson-Sirleaf (from 2006). **Capital:** Monrovia. **Official language:** English. **Official religion:** none. **Monetary unit:** 1 Liberian dollar (L$) = 100 cents; valuation (1 Jul 2007) US$1 = L$57.50 (par value rate to US$ ineffective from January 1998; the independent free market exchange rate was roughly US$1 = L$60 in August 2001).

Demography

Area: 37,743 sq mi, 97,754 sq km. **Population** (2006): 3,042,000. **Density** (2006): persons per sq mi 80.6, persons per sq km 31.1. **Urban** (2001): 45.5%. **Sex distribution** (2002): male 49.47%; female 50.53%. **Age breakdown** (2001): under 15, 43.2%; 15–29, 27.0%; 30–44, 15.1%; 45–59, 9.4%; 60–74, 4.2%; 75 and over, 1.1%. **Ethnic composition** (2000): Kpelle 18.9%; Bassa 13.1%; Grebo 10.3%; Gio (Dan) 7.4%; Kru 6.9%; Mano 6.1%; Loma 5.3%; Kissi 3.8%; Krahn 3.7%; Americo-Liberians 2.4% (descendants of freed US slaves); other 22.1%. **Religious affiliation** (1995): traditional beliefs 63.0%; Christian 21.0%, of which Protestant 13.5%, African Christian 5.1%, Roman Catholic 2.4%; Muslim 16.0%. **Major cities** (2002): Monrovia 543,000; Zwedru 33,800; Buchanan 27,000; Yekepa 22,500; Harper 19,600. **Location:** western Africa, bordering Guinea, Côte d'Ivoire, the North Atlantic Ocean, and Sierra Leone.

Vital statistics

Birth rate per 1,000 population (2003): 45.3 (world avg. 21.3). **Death rate** per 1,000 population (2003): 17.8 (world avg. 9.1). **Natural increase rate** per 1,000 population (2003): 27.5 (world avg. 12.2). **Total fertility rate** (avg. births per childbearing woman; 2003): 6.2. **Life expectancy** at birth (2003): male 47.0 years; female 49.3 years. **Adult population** (ages 15–49) **living with HIV** (2004): 5.9% (world avg. 1.1%).

National economy

Budget (2002). *Revenue:* US$72,700,000 (tax revenue 96.7%, of which import duties 23.1%, income and profit taxes 19.8%, maritime revenue 18.4%, stamps and land rental 17.9%, petroleum sales tax 8.3%; nontax revenue 3.3%). *Expenditures:* US$80,100,000 (development expenditures [including national security] 67.5%; current expenditures 32.5%, of which wages 16.7%, interest on debt 7.9%, goods and services 7.4%). **Population economically active** (1997): total 1,183,000; activity rate 51.4% (participation rates: ages 10–64 [1994] 64.0%; female 39.5%; unemployed [1996] 95%). **Production** (metric tons except as noted). *Agriculture, forestry, fishing* (2002): cassava 445,000, natural rubber 220,000, rice 187,000; livestock (number of live animals) 220,000 goats, 210,000 sheep, 5,000,000 chickens; roundwood (2001) 5,261,930 cu m; fish catch 11,514. *Mining and quarrying* (2001): diamonds 170,000 carats; gold 1,000 kg. *Manufacturing* (2000): palm oil 42,000; cement 15,000; cigarettes 22,000,000 units (1992). International maritime licensing (fees earned; 2002): more than US$13,000,000. *Energy production (consumption):* electricity (kW-hr; 2000) 524,000,000 (524,000,000); petroleum products (2000) none (128,000). **Public debt** (external, outstanding; 2002): US$1,065,000,000. **Households.** Average household size (1983) 4.3; expenditure (1998): food 34.4%, housing 14.9%, clothing 13.8%, household furnishings 6.1%, beverages and tobacco 5.7%, energy 5.0%. **Gross national product** (2003): US$445,000,000 (US$130 per capita). **Land use** as % of total land area (2000): in temporary crops 3.9%, in permanent crops 2.2%, in pasture 20.8%; overall forest area 31.3%.

Foreign trade

Imports (2001): US$196,900,000 (food and live animals 31.1%, of which rice 14.0%; petroleum and petroleum products 20.7%; machinery and transport equipment 18.0%). *Major import sources* (1999): South Korea 27%; Japan 25%; Germany 14%; Singapore 7%; Croatia 5%. **Exports** (2001): US$127,900,000 (logs and timber 54.1%, rubber 42.2%). *Major export destinations* (2001): Norway 24%; Germany 11%; US 9%; France 8%; Singapore 7%.

Transport and communications

Transport. *Railroads* (2001): route length 490 km; (1998) metric ton-km cargo 860,000,000. *Roads* (1999): total length 10,600 km (paved 6%). *Vehicles* (1996): passenger cars 9,400; trucks and buses 25,000. *Air transport* (1992): passenger-km 7,000,000; metric ton-km cargo 1,000,000; airports (2000) with scheduled flights 2. **Communications,** in total units (units per 1,000 persons). Daily newspaper circulation (2000): 37,800 (12); radios (2000): 863,000 (274); televisions (2000): 78,700 (25); telephone main lines (1999): 6,600 (2.2).

Education and health

Literacy (2000): total population age 15 and over literate 54.0%. **Health:** physicians (1992) 257 (1 per 8,333 persons); infant mortality rate per 1,000 live births (2002) 133.8. **Food** (2001): daily per capita caloric intake 1,946 (vegetable products 97%, animal products 3%); 84% of FAO recommended minimum.

Military

Total active duty personnel: UN peacekeeping troops (September 2004) 14,700; 18,000 of 40,000 former combatants were disarmed by April 2004. **Military expenditure as percentage of GNP** (1999): 1.2% (world 2.4%); per capita expenditure US$2.

Did you know? In 1847 a committee of Liberian women had the task of choosing a flag for the new nation. Their design echoed the US flag, but with a single white star in the blue canton symbolizing Liberia's status as the only free, Westernized state in Africa. The 11 stripes represent 11 men who signed the Liberian Declaration of Independence.

Background

Africa's oldest republic, Liberia was established as a home for freed US slaves under the American Colonization Society, which founded a colony at Cape Mesurado in 1821. In 1822 Jehudi Ashmun, a Methodist minister, became the director of the settlement and Liberia's real founder. Joseph Jenkins Roberts, Liberia's first nonwhite governor, proclaimed Liberian independence in 1847 and expanded its boundaries, which were officially established in 1892. In 1980 a coup led by Samuel K. Doe marked the end of the Americo-Liberians' long political dominance over the descendents of indigenous Africans. A rebellion in 1989 escalated into a destructive civil war in the 1990s. A peace agreement was reached in 1996, and elections were held in 1997.

Recent Developments

Liberia made history in November 2005 by choosing Africa's first female president, Ellen Johnson-Sirleaf, in elections deemed fair and transparent by international observers. Her administration set up a Truth and Reconciliation Commission, much like the one in post-apartheid South Africa, to investigate allegations of human-rights abuses in the country between 1979 and the end of civil war in 2003; dismissed the entire staff of the Ministry of Finance in an anticorruption operation; and announced a new program to expand female education. In March 2006 former Liberian leader Charles Taylor was arrested in Nigeria, where he had been living in exile, and sent to Sierra Leone to stand trial for crimes against humanity in Liberia and Sierra Leone. The trial, which was moved to the International Criminal Court in The Netherlands, was scheduled to begin in April 2007.

Internet resources: <www.liberianews.com>.

Libya

Official name: Al-Jamahiriyah al-'Arabiyah al-Libiyah al-Sha'biyah al-Ishtirakiyah al-'Uzma (Socialist People's Libyan Arab Jamahiriya). **Form of government:** socialist state with one policy-making body (General People's Congress [760]). **Chief of state:** Muammar al-Qaddafi (de facto; from 1969); Secretary of General

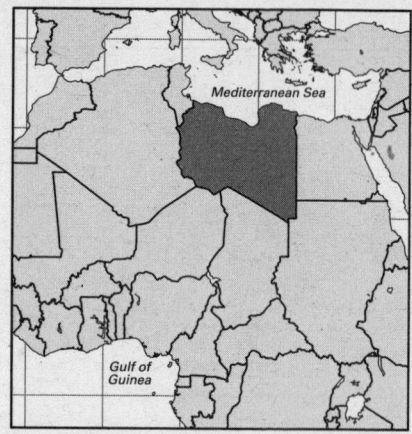

People's Congress Zentani Muhammad al-Zentani (de jure; from 1992). **Head of government:** Secretary of the General People's Committee (Prime Minister) Al-Baghdadi Ali al-Mahmudi (from 2006). **Capital:** Tripoli. **Official language:** Arabic. **Official religion:** Islam. **Monetary unit:** 1 Libyan dinar (LD) = 1,000 dirhams; valuation (1 Jul 2007) US$1 = LD 1.29.

Demography

Area: 679,362 sq mi, 1,759,540 sq km. **Population** (2006): 5,968,000. **Density** (2006): persons per sq mi 8.6, persons per sq km 3.3. **Urban** (2001): 88.0%. **Sex distribution** (2001): male 51.41%; female 48.59%. **Age breakdown** (2001): under 15, 35.4%; 15–29, 31.7%; 30–44, 19.1%; 45–59, 8.0%; 60–74, 4.5%; 75 and over, 1.3%. **Ethnic composition** (2000): Arab 87.1%, of which Libyan 57.2%, Bedouin 13.8%, Egyptian 7.7%, Sudanese 3.5%, Tunisian 2.9%; Berber 6.8%, of which Arabized 4.2%; other 6.1%. **Religious affiliation** (1995): Sunni Muslim 96.1%; other 3.9%. **Major cities** (1995): Tripoli 1,140,000 (urban agglomeration [2001] 1,776,000); Banghazi 650,-000 (urban agglomeration [2000] 829,000); Misratah 280,000; Surt 150,000. **Location:** northern Africa, bordering the Mediterranean Sea, Egypt, The Sudan, Chad, Niger, Algeria, and Tunisia.

Vital statistics

Birth rate per 1,000 population (2003): 27.4 (world avg. 21.3). **Death rate** per 1,000 population (2003): 3.5 (world avg. 9.1). **Natural increase rate** per 1,000 population (2003): 23.9 (world avg. 12.2). **Total fertility rate** (avg. births per childbearing woman; 2003): 3.5. **Life expectancy** at birth (2003): male 73.9 years; female 78.3 years.

National economy

Budget (2001). *Revenue:* LD 5,998,800,000 (oil revenues 60.1%, other 39.9%). *Expenditures:* LD 5,625,600,000 (current expenditures 63.9%, development expenditures 27.3%, extraordinary expenditures 8.8%). **Public debt** (2001): $2,359,000,000.

1 metric ton = about 1.1 short tons;   1 kilometer = 0.6 mi (statute);   1 metric ton-km cargo = about 0.68 short ton-mi cargo;   c.i.f.: cost, insurance, and freight;   f.o.b.: free on board

Production (metric tons except as noted). *Agriculture, forestry, fishing* (2002): watermelons 218,000, potatoes 195,000, dry onions 182,000; livestock (number of live animals; 2001) 4,130,000 sheep, 1,265,000 goats, 25,000,000 chickens; roundwood (2001) 652,000 cu m; fish catch (2001) 33,339. *Mining and quarrying* (2001): lime 250,000; gypsum 150,000; salt 40,000. *Manufacturing* (value of production in LD '000,000; 1996): base metals 212, electrical equipment 208, petrochemicals 175. *Energy production (consumption):* electricity (kW-hr; 2001) 20,180,000,000 (18,770,000,000); coal (2000) none (5,000); crude petroleum (barrels; 2002) 482,000,000 ([2000] 157,000,000); petroleum products (2001) 15,070,700 (6,629,200); natural gas (cu m; 2001) 6,174,000,000 (4,265,-100,000). **Households**. Average household size (2000) 6.3. **Tourism** (2002): receipts $75,000,000; expenditures $548,000,000. **Population economically active** (1996): total 1,224,000; activity rate of total population 26.1% (participation rates [1993]: ages 10 and over, 35.2%; female 9.8%; unemployed [2000] 30.0%). **Gross domestic product** (2000): $38,000,000,000 ($6,200 per capita). **Land use** as % of total land area (2000): in temporary crops 1.0%, in permanent crops 0.2%, in pasture 7.6%; overall forest area 0.2%.

Foreign trade

Imports (2001): $8,700,000,000 (1997; machinery 25.9%, food products 20.0%, road vehicles 10.1%, chemical products 7.5%). *Major import sources* (2001): Italy 28.5%; Germany 12.1%; UK 6.6%; Tunisia 6.0%; France 5.9%. **Exports** (2001): $7,500,000,000 (crude petroleum 85%, refined petroleum 11%, natural gas 2%). *Major export destinations:* Italy 39.8%; Germany 15.6%; Spain 14.1%; Turkey 6.4%; France 5.5%.

Transport and communications

Transport. *Roads* (1999): total length 83,200 km (paved 57%). *Vehicles* (1996): passenger cars 809,514; trucks and buses 357,528. *Air transport* (2001): passenger-km 410,000,000; metric ton-km cargo 259,000. **Communications**, in total units (units per 1,000 persons). Daily newspaper circulation (2000): 78,600 (14); radios (2000): 1,430,000 (259); televisions (2000): 717,000 (133); telephone main lines (2003): 750,000 (136); cellular telephone subscribers (2003): 100,000 (18); personal computers (2002): 130,000 (23); Internet users (2003): 160,000 (29).

Education and health

Educational attainment (1984). Percentage of population age 25 and over having: no formal schooling (illiterate) 59.7%; incomplete primary education 15.4%; complete primary 8.5%; some secondary 5.2%; secondary 8.5%; higher 2.7%. **Literacy** (1998): percentage of total population age 15 and over literate 78.1%; males literate 89.6%; females literate 65.4%. **Health**: physicians (1997) 6,092 (1 per 781 persons); hospital beds (1998) 18,100 (1 per 312 persons; includes beds in clinics); infant mortality rate per 1,000 live births (2003) 26.8. **Food** (2001): daily per capita caloric intake 3,333 (vegetable products 89%, animal products 11%); 141% of FAO recommended minimum.

Military

Total active duty personnel (2003): 76,000 (army 59.2%, navy 10.5%, air force 30.3%). **Military expenditure as percentage of GNP** (1995): 6.1% (world 2.4%); per capita expenditure $342.

Background

Greeks and Phoenicians settled the area in the 7th century BC. It was conquered by Rome in the 1st century BC and by Arabs in the 7th century AD. In the 16th century the Ottoman Turks combined Libya's three regions under one regency in Tripoli. In 1911 Italy claimed control of Libya, and by the outbreak of World War II, 150,000 Italians lived there. It became an independent state in 1951. The discovery of oil in 1959 brought wealth to Libya. A decade later a group of army officers led by Muammar al-Qaddafi deposed the king and made the country an Islamic republic. Under Qaddafi's rule it supported the Palestinian Liberation Organization and terrorist groups, bringing protests from many countries, particularly the US. Intermittent warfare with Chad during the 1970s and '80s ended with Chad's defeat of Libya in 1987. International relations in the 1990s were dominated by the consequences of the 1988 bombing of an American airliner over Lockerbie, Scotland; the US accused Libyan nationalists of the deed and imposed a trade embargo on Libya, endorsed by the UN in 1992.

Recent Developments

Following 25 years of estrangement between the two countries, in 2006 the US removed Libya from the list of state sponsors of terrorism and restored full diplomatic relations. US Secretary of State Condoleezza Rice met with Libya's foreign minister in September in New York City. A US decision to lift the embargo on aircraft exports to Libya and an agreement providing for British support to Libya through the UN Security Council against any aggression were additional indicators of the country's reintegration in the international fold. The UK also offered Libya assistance to convert its weapons-of-mass-destruction facilities into civilian production plants. In domestic affairs both Libyan leader Muammar al-Qaddafi and his son Saif ul-Islam called for the acceleration of reforms, including continued privatization of public corporations; modernization and diversification of the economy; the release of political prisoners; investigations into cases of torture and human rights abuse; and the drafting of a permanent constitution. With massive estimated oil reserves, Libya planned to increase daily production from 1.6 million to 2 million barrels by mid-2007 and to invest $30 billion over the next 10 years in oil development. In September the National Oil Company provided 41 of the 250 remaining oil and gas concessions to international corporations.

Internet resources: <www.arab.net/libya>.

Liechtenstein

Official name: Fürstentum Liechtenstein (Principality of Liechtenstein). **Form of government:** constitutional monarchy with one legislative house (Diet [25]). **Chief of state:** Prince Hans Adam II (from 1989); Regent, Prince Alois (from 2004). **Head of government:** Otmar Hasler (from 2001). **Capital:** Vaduz. **Official language:**

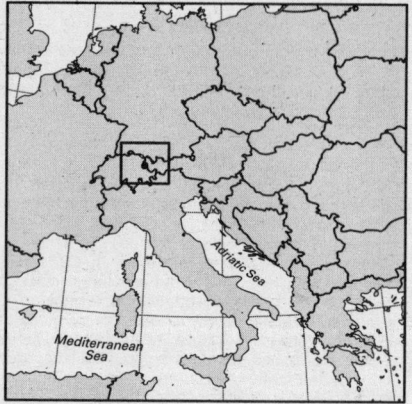

German. **Official religion:** none. **Monetary unit:** 1 Swiss franc (Sw F) = 100 centimes; valuation (1 Jul 2007) US$1 = Sw F 1.22.

Demography

Area: 61.8 sq mi, 160.0 sq km. **Population** (2006): 35,100. **Density** (2006): persons per sq mi 566.1, persons per sq km 219.4. **Urban** (2003): 21.6%. **Sex distribution** (2003): male 49.11%; female 50.89%. **Age breakdown** (2003): under 15, 17.0%; 15–29, 20.2%; 30–44, 25.9%; 45–59, 21.2%; 60–74, 10.8%; 75 and over, 4.9%. **Ethnic composition** (2002): Liechtensteiner 65.8%; Swiss 10.9%; Austrian 5.9%; German 3.4%; Italian 3.3%; other 10.7%. **Religious affiliation** (1998): Roman Catholic 80.0%; Protestant 7.5%; Muslim 3.3%; Eastern Orthodox 0.7%; atheist 0.6%; other 7.9%. **Major cities** (2002): Schaan 5,556; Vaduz 4,949. **Location:** central Europe, between Austria and Switzerland.

Vital statistics

Birth rate per 1,000 population (2003): 10.9 (world avg. 21.3); (1997) legitimate 86.0%. **Death rate** per 1,000 population (2003): 6.8 (world avg. 9.1). **Natural increase rate** per 1,000 population (2003): 4.1 (world avg. 12.2). **Total fertility rate** (avg. births per childbearing woman; 2002): 1.5. **Marriage rate** per 1,000 population (2001): 11.5. **Divorce rate** per 1,000 population (1994): 1.4. **Life expectancy** at birth (2003): male 75.6 years; female 82.9 years.

National economy

Budget (2001). *Revenue:* Sw F 804,100,000 (taxes and duties 85.8%, investment income 5.5%, charges and fees 5.0%, real estate capital-gains taxes and death and estate taxes 3.7%). *Expenditures:* Sw F 751,400,000 (financial affairs 34.8%, social welfare 19.5%, education 14.1%, general administration 10.2%, public safety 5.5%, transportation 4.8%). **Tourism** (2001): 123,273 tourist overnight stays. **Population economically active** (2002): total 17,011; activity rate of total population 50.7% (participation rates: ages 15–64, 71.4%;

female 40.4%; unemployed 2.1%). **Households.** Average household size (1990) 2.7. **Production** (metric tons except as noted). *Agriculture and forestry* (2002): significantly market gardening, other crops include cereals and apples; livestock (number of live animals) 6,000 cattle, 3,000 pigs, 2,900 sheep; commercial timber (1999) 22,000 cu m. *Manufacturing* (2000): small-scale precision manufacturing includes optical lenses, electron microscopes, electronic equipment, and high-vacuum pumps; metal manufacturing, construction machinery, and ceramics are important; dairy products and wine are also produced. *Energy production (consumption):* electricity (kW-hr; 2001) 93,282,000 (313,450,000); coal (2000) none (24); petroleum products (2000) none (47,100). **Gross national product** (1999): $2,664,000,000 ($63,550 per capita). **Land use** as % of total land area (2000): in temporary crops 25%, in permanent crops 1%, in pasture 31%; overall forest area 47%.

Foreign trade

Data exclude trade with Switzerland and transshipments through Switzerland. Liechtenstein has formed a customs union with Switzerland since 1923. **Imports** (2000): Sw F 1,456,000,000 (machinery and apparatus 30.4%, glass [all forms] and ceramics 11.0%, fabricated metals 10.0%, iron and steel 5.7%, transport equipment 5.7%). *Major import sources:* Germany 34.6%; Austria 31.8%; Italy 7.9%; US 6.1%; France 3.5%. **Exports** (2000): Sw F 3,032,000,000 (machinery and apparatus [mostly electronic products and precision tools] 35.1%, fabricated metals 15.2%, glass and ceramic products [including lead crystal and specialized dental products] 9.9%, food products 5.3%). *Major export destinations:* Germany 25.8%; US 20.0%; Austria 8.4%; France 7.8%; Italy 6.5%.

Transport and communications

Transport. *Railroads* (1998): length 18.5 km. *Roads* (1999): total length 323 km. *Vehicles* (2002): passenger cars 23,265; trucks and buses 2,824. *Air transport:* the nearest scheduled airport service is through Zürich, Switzerland. **Communications,** in total units (units per 1,000 persons). Daily newspaper circulation (1998): 17,900 (565); radios (1997): 21,000 (658); televisions (1997): 12,000 (364); telephone main lines (2002): 19,900 (583); cellular telephone subscribers (2002): 11,400 (333); Internet users (2002): 20,000 (585).

Education and health

Educational attainment (1990). Percentage of population not of preschool age or in compulsory education having: no formal schooling 0.3%; primary and lower secondary education 39.3%; higher secondary and vocational 47.6%; some postsecondary 7.4%; university 4.2%; other and unknown 1.1%. **Literacy:** virtually 100%. **Health:** physicians (2000) 46 (1 per 714 persons); hospital beds (1997) 108 (1 per 288 persons); infant mortality rate per 1,000 live births (2003) 4.9. **Food** (1999; figures are derived from statistics for Switzerland and Austria): daily per capita caloric intake 3,600 (vegetable products 65%, animal products 35%); 134% of FAO recommended minimum.

1 metric ton = about 1.1 short tons;   1 kilometer = 0.6 mi (statute);   1 metric ton-km cargo = about 0.68 short ton-mi cargo;   c.i.f.: cost, insurance, and freight;   f.o.b.: free on board

Military

Total active duty personnel: Liechtenstein has had no standing army since 1868.

Background

The Rhine plain was occupied for centuries by two independent lordships of the Holy Roman Empire, Vaduz and Schellenberg. The principality of Liechtenstein, consisting of these two lordships, was founded in 1719 and remained part of the Holy Roman Empire. It was included in the German Confederation (1815–66). In 1866 it became independent, recognizing Vaduz and Schellenberg as unique regions forming separate electoral districts. An almost 60-year ruling coalition dissolved in 1997, and the prince urged adoption of constitutional reforms.

Recent Developments

In 2005 the International Court of Justice ruled against Liechtenstein in its suit demanding damages from Germany for having given artworks and other valuables from Liechtenstein to Czechoslovakia as war reparations following World War II. A commission formed in 2001 cleared Liechtenstein and its financial institutions in April 2005 of most serious claims that they had profited from Nazi associations or activities during that war.

Internet resources: <www.tourismus.li>.

Lithuania

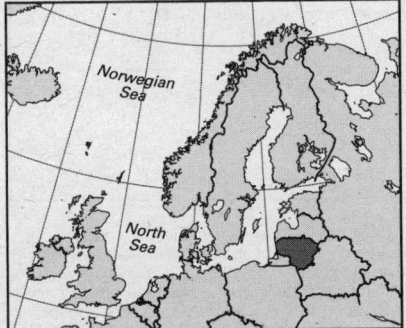

Official name: Lietuvos Respublika (Republic of Lithuania). **Form of government:** unitary multiparty republic with a single legislative body, the Seimas (141). **Head of state:** President Valdas Adamkus (from 2004). **Head of government:** Prime Minister Gediminas Kirkilas (from 2006). **Capital:** Vilnius. **Official language:** Lithuanian. **Official religion:** none. **Monetary unit:** 1 litas (LTL) = 100 centai; valuation (1 Jul 2007) US$1 = LTL 2.55.

Demography

Area: 25,212 sq mi, 65,300 sq km. **Population** (2006): 3,392,000. **Density** (2006): persons per sq mi 134.5, persons per sq km 51.9. **Urban** (2003): 66.8%. **Sex distribution** (2003): male 46.70%; female 53.30%. **Age breakdown** (2004): under 15, 17.7%; 15–29, 21.9%; 30–44, 22.4%; 45–59, 17.8%; 60–74, 14.2%; 75 and over, 6.0%. **Ethnic composition** (2001): Lithuanian 83.5%; Polish 6.7%; Russian 6.3%; Belarusian 1.2%; Ukrainian 0.7%; other 1.6%. **Religious affiliation** (2001): Roman Catholic 79.0%; nonreligious 9.5%; Orthodox 4.8%, of which Old Believers 0.8%; Protestant 1.0%; unknown 5.4%; other 0.3%. **Major cities** (2004): Vilnius 553,038; Kaunas 368,917; Klaipeda 190,098; Siauliai 131,184; Panevezys 117,606. **Location:** eastern Europe, bordering Latvia, Belarus, Poland, Russia, and the Baltic Sea.

Vital statistics

Birth rate per 1,000 population (2003): 8.9 (world avg. 21.3); (2001) legitimate 74.6%. **Death rate** per 1,000 population (2003): 11.9 (world avg. 9.1). **Natural increase rate** per 1,000 population (2003): –3.0 (world avg. 12.2). **Total fertility rate** (avg. births per childbearing woman; 2003): 1.3. **Marriage rate** per 1,000 population (2003): 4.9. **Divorce rate** per 1,000 population (2003): 3.1. **Life expectancy** at birth (2003): male 66.5 years; female 77.9 years.

National economy

Budget (2002). *Revenue:* LTL 15,112,000,000 (tax revenue 92.5%, of which value-added tax 25.2%, individual income tax 23.6%, social security tax 22.7%, excise tax 10.6%; nontax revenue 7.5%). *Expenditures:* LTL 15,907,000,000 (current expenditure 90.0%, of which social security and welfare 28.0%, wages 23.2%; capital expenditure 10.0%). **Gross national product** (2003): $15,509,000,000 ($4,490 per capita). **Production** (metric tons except as noted). *Agriculture, forestry, fishing* (2002): hay 2,500,000, potatoes 1,531,300, wheat 1,165,100; livestock (number of live animals) 1,010,800 pigs, 751,500 cattle; roundwood (2001) 5,700,000 cu m; fish catch (2001) 153,932. *Mining and quarrying* (2002): limestone 857,500; peat 262,700. *Manufacturing* (value of production in LTL '000,000; 2000): food and beverages 4,952; refined petroleum products 4,303; wearing apparel 2,034. *Energy production (consumption):* electricity (kW-hr; 2000) 11,424,000,000 (10,088,000,000); coal (2000) none (131,000); crude petroleum (barrels; 2000) 2,316,000 (34,766,000); petroleum products (2002) 6,543,500 (2,756,000); natural gas (cu m; 2000) none (2,462,000,000). **Public debt** (external, outstanding; 2002): $2,486,000,000. **Population economically active** (2001): total 1,745,300; activity rate of total population 50.2% (participation rates: ages 15–64, 69.3%; female 49.8%; registered unemployed 12.7%). **Household income and expenditure.** Average household size (2000) 2.7; average annual household disposable income (1997): LTL 12,914; sources of income (2001): wages and salaries 53.6%, transfers 24.2%, self-employment 11.3%; expenditure (2001): food and beverages 42.4%, housing and energy 13.6%, transportation and communications 11.8%, clothing and footwear 6.5%. **Land use** as % of total land area (2000): in temporary crops 45.3%, in permanent crops 0.9%, in pasture 7.7%; overall forest area 31.9%. **Tourism** (2001): receipts from visitors $513,000,000; expenditures by nationals abroad $341,000,000.

Foreign trade

Imports (2002-c.i.f.): LTL 28,220,000,000 (mineral fuels [mostly crude petroleum] 17.8%, machinery and apparatus 17.5%, transport equipment 16.4%, chemicals and chemical products 8.7%, textiles and clothing 7.9%). *Major import sources:* Russia 21.4%; Germany 17.2%; Italy 4.9%; Poland 4.8%; France 3.9%. **Exports** (2002-f.o.b.): LTL 20,280,000,000 (mineral fuels [mostly refined petroleum] 19.0%, transport equipment [mostly auto components] 15.9%, textiles and clothing 15.0%, agricultural and food products 10.8%, machinery and apparatus 9.9%). *Major export destinations:* UK 13.5%; Russia 12.1%; Germany 10.3%; Latvia 9.6%; Denmark 5.0%.

Transport and communications

Transport. *Railroads* (2001): route length 1,696 km; passenger-km 533,000,000; metric ton-km cargo 7,741,000,000. *Roads* (2002): total length 76,573 km (paved 91%). *Vehicles* (2002): passenger cars 1,133,477; trucks and buses 104,544. *Air transport* (2001): passenger-km 484,000,000; metric ton-km cargo 3,000,000; airports with scheduled flights (2001) 3. **Communications,** in total units (units per 1,000 persons). Daily newspaper circulation (1996): 344,000 (93); radios (2000): 1,750,000 (500); televisions (2002): 1,704,500 (487); telephone main lines (2003): 824,200 (253); cellular telephone subscribers (2003): 2,169,900 (666); personal computers (2003): 380,000 (110); Internet users (2003): 695,700 (213).

Education and health

Educational attainment (2001). Percentage of population age 10 and over having: no schooling and incomplete primary education 5.1%; complete primary 20.8%; incomplete and complete secondary 42.2%; postsecondary 31.9%, of which university 12.6%. **Literacy** (2000): total population age 15 and over literate 99.6%. **Health** (2004): physicians 13,682 (1 per 252 persons); hospital beds 29,990 (1 per 115 persons); infant mortality rate per 1,000 live births (2003) 6.7. **Food** (2001): daily per capita caloric intake 3,384 (vegetable products 76%, animal products 24%); 132% of FAO recommended minimum.

Military

Total active duty personnel (2003): 12,700 (excludes 13,850 in paramilitary; army 62.6%, navy 5.1%, air force 9.1%, volunteer national defense force 13.5%, centrally controlled staff 9.7%). **Military expenditure as percentage of GNP** (1999): 1.3% (world 2.4%); per capita expenditure $87.

Background

Lithuanian tribes united in the mid-13th century to oppose the Teutonic knights. Gediminas, one of the grand dukes, expanded Lithuania into an empire that dominated much of Eastern Europe in the 14th through 16th centuries. In 1386 the Lithuanian grand duke became the king of Poland, and the two countries remained closely associated until Lithuania was acquired by Russia in the Third Partition of Poland in 1795. Occupied by Germany during World War I, it declared its independence in 1918. In 1940 the Red Army gained control of Lithuania. Germany

occupied it again in 1941–44, but the USSR regained control in 1944. With the breakup of the USSR, Lithuania became independent in 1991. It signed a border treaty with Russia in 1997, and it joined the European Union and NATO in 2004.

Recent Developments

Lithuania's economic situation since joining the EU was very positive. Foreign direct investment reached $6.1 billion by midyear 2005 and $8.6 billion by midyear 2006, and the GDP grew by 8.8% in the first quarter of 2006. In July 2006 Russia halted the flow of oil to Lithuania's refinery (the only one in the Baltic States), ostensibly to fix a leak in the pipeline, after a 30% share in the refinery was sold to a Polish company. Lithuania considered blocking talks on a cooperation treaty between the EU and Russia in February 2007 as the oil flow had not begun again.

Internet resources: <www.tourism.lt>.

Luxembourg

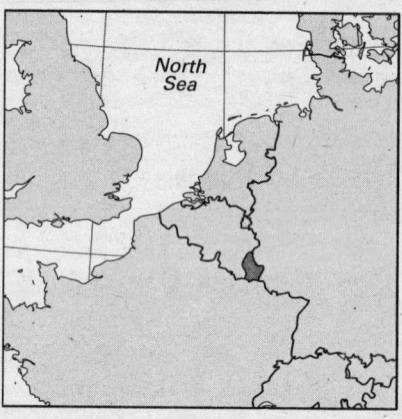

North Sea

Official name: Groussherzogtum Lëtzebuerg (Luxemburgian); Grand-Duché de Luxembourg (French); Grossherzogtum Luxemburg (German) (Grand Duchy of Luxembourg). **Form of government:** constitutional monarchy with two legislative houses (Council of State [21]; Chamber of Deputies [60]). **Chief of state:** Grand Duke Henri (from 2000). **Head of government:** Prime Minister Jean-Claude Juncker (from 1995). **Capital:** Luxembourg. **Official language:** none; Luxemburgian (national); French (used for most official purposes); German (lingua franca). **Official religion:** none. **Monetary unit:** 1 euro (€) = 100 cents; valuation (1 Jul 2007) US$1 = €0.74; at conversion on 1 Jan 2002, €1= 40.3 Luxembourg franc (Lux F).

Demography

Area: 999 sq mi, 2,586 sq km. **Population** (2006): 461,000. **Density** (2006): persons per sq mi 461.5, persons per sq km 178.3. **Urban** (2003): 91.9%. **Sex distribution** (2003): male 49.30%; female 50.70%.

---

1 metric ton = about 1.1 short tons;   1 kilometer = 0.6 mi (statute);   1 metric ton-km cargo = about 0.68 short ton-mi cargo;   c.i.f.: cost, insurance, and freight;   f.o.b.: free on board

Age breakdown (2003): under 15, 18.9%; 15–29, 18.6%; 30–44, 25.5%; 45–59, 18.4%; 60–74, 12.9%; 75 and over, 5.7%. Ethnic composition (nationality; 2003): Luxemburger 61.9%; Portuguese 13.5%; French 4.8%; Italian 4.2%; Belgian 3.5%; German 2.3%; English 1.0%; other 8.8%. Religious affiliation (2000): Roman Catholic 90.6%; Protestant 2.1%; other Christian 1.1%; Muslim 1.0%; nonreligious 3.7%; other 1.5%. Major cities (2001; pops. of localities): Luxembourg 76,688; Esch-sur-Alzette 27,146; Dudelange 17,320; Schifflange 7,849; Bettembourg 7,157. Location: western Europe, bordering Belgium, Germany, and France.

Vital statistics

Birth rate per 1,000 population (2003): 11.8 (world avg. 21.3); (2002) legitimate 76.8%. Death rate per 1,000 population (2003): 9.0 (world avg. 9.1). Natural increase rate per 1,000 population (2003): 2.8 (world avg. 12.2). Total fertility rate (avg. births per childbearing woman; 2003): 1.6. Marriage rate per 1,000 population (2003): 4.5. Divorce rate per 1,000 population (2003): 2.3. Life expectancy at birth (2000–02): male 74.9 years; female 81.0 years.

National economy

Budget (2002). Revenue: €5,977,200,000 (direct taxes 47.4%, indirect taxes 38.5%, other 14.1%). Expenditures: €5,976,100,000 (current expenditure 85.7%, development expenditure 14.3%). Public debt (2001): $1,080,000,000. Production (metric tons except as noted). Agriculture and forestry (2002): corn (maize) 139,000, wheat 67,126, barley 65,000; livestock (number of live animals; 2000) 205,000 cattle, 80,141 pigs; roundwood (2001) 142,000 cu m. Mining and quarrying (2002): limited quantities of limestone and slate. Manufacturing (2002): rolled steel 4,467,000; crude steel 2,736,000; cement 800,-000. Energy production (consumption): electricity (kW-hr; 2000) 1,228,000,000 (6,950,000,000); coal (2000) none (171,000); petroleum products (2000) none (1,906,000); natural gas (cu m; 2000) none (782,000,000). Household income and expenditure. Average household size (2000) 2.5; income per household (2002) €61,800; sources of income (1992): wages and salaries 67.1%, transfer payments 28.1%, self-employment 4.8%; expenditure (2002): food, beverages, and tobacco 21.0%, housing 20.7%, transportation and communications 19.3%, entertainment and education 8.6%, household goods and furniture 8.3%, clothing and footwear 5.3%. Gross national product (2003): $15,509,-000,000 ($43,940 per capita). Population economically active (2002): total 285,700; activity rate of total population 63.9% (participation rates: ages 15–64 [2001] 64.4%; female [2001] 40.2%; unemployed [2002] 3.0%). Tourism (2002): receipts from visitors $2,186,000,000; expenditures $1,896,-000,000. Land use as % of total land area (2000): in temporary crops 23.6%, in permanent crops 0.5%, in pasture 25.2%; overall forest area 34.3%.

Foreign trade

Imports (2001-c.i.f.): €12,335,000,000 (machinery and apparatus 21.5%, transport equipment 15.2%, base and fabricated metals 11.3%, chemicals and chemical products 10.1%). Major import sources: Belgium 34.3%; Germany 25.1%; France 12.8%; The Netherlands 5.8%; US 5.1%. Exports (2001-f.o.b.): €9,082,000,000 (base and fabricated metals [mostly iron and steel] 28.1%, machinery and apparatus 24.0%, chemicals and chemical products 6.3%, transport equipment 4.3%, food products 4.2%). Major export destinations: Germany 24.6%; France 19.6%; Belgium 12.3%; UK 8.2%; Italy 6.2%.

Transport and communications

Transport. Railroads (2002): route length 274 km; passenger-km 268,000,000; metric ton-km cargo 613,000,000. Roads (1999): total length 5,166 km (paved 100%). Vehicles (2003): passenger cars 287,245; trucks and buses 22,691. Air transport (2002): passengers carried 1,517,000; cargo 578,-944 metric tons; airports with scheduled flights 1. Communications, in total units (units per 1,000 persons). Daily newspaper circulation (1996): 135,000 (325); radios (2000): 300,000 (685); televisions (2000): 170,000 (391); telephone main lines (2002): 355,400 (797); cellular telephone subscribers (2002): 473,000 (1,061); personal computers (2002): 265,000 (594); Internet users (2002): 165,000 (370).

Education and health

Literacy (2001): virtually 100% literate. Health (2002): physicians 1,137 (1 per 393 persons); hospital beds 3,035 (1 per 147 persons); infant mortality rate per 1,000 live births (2003) 5.0. Food (1995): daily per capita caloric intake 3,530 (vegetable products 68%, animal products 32%); 134% of FAO recommended minimum.

Military

Total active duty personnel (2003): 900 (army 100%). Military expenditure as percentage of GNP (1999): 0.8% (world 2.4%); per capita expenditure $326.

Background

At the time of Roman conquest (57–50 BC), Luxembourg was inhabited by a Belgic tribe. After AD 400, Germanic tribes invaded the region. Made a duchy in 1354, it was ceded to the house of Burgundy in 1443 and to the Habsburgs in 1477. In the mid-16th century it became part of the Spanish Netherlands. It was made a grand duchy in 1815. After an uprising in 1830, its western portion became part of Belgium, while the remainder was held by The Netherlands. In 1867 the European powers guaranteed the neutrality and independence of Luxembourg. In the late 19th century it exploited its extensive iron-ore deposits. It was invaded and occupied by Germany in both world wars. It abandoned its neutrality by joining NATO in 1949; it had joined the Benelux Economic Union in 1944. A member of the European Union, its economy has continued to expand. On 7 Oct 2000, Grand Duke Jean abdicated power in favor of his son, Crown Prince Henri, after 36 years on the throne.

Recent Developments

Luxembourg's Grand Duke Henri paid a weeklong state visit to China at the invitation of Chinese Pres. Hu Jintao to exchange ideas on bilateral relations and international areas of concern. In an analysis of more than 150 selected countries, the International

Monetary Fund reported that in 2005 Luxembourg led the world with a GDP per capita of nearly $69,800.

Internet resources: <www.ont.lu>.

Macau

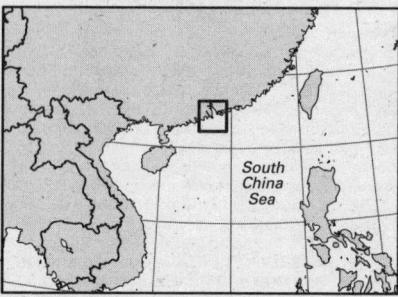

South China Sea

Official name: Aomen Tebie Xingzhengqu (Chinese); Região Administrativa Especial de Macau (Portuguese) (Macau Special Administrative Region). **Political status:** special administrative region (China) with one legislative house (Legislative Council [27, including 10 directly elected seats, 7 seats appointed by the chief executive, and 10 seats appointed by special-interest groups]). **Chief of state:** President Hu Jintao of China (from 2003). **Head of government:** Chief Executive Edmund Ho Hau-wah (from 1999). **Capital:** Macau. **Official languages:** Chinese; Portuguese. **Official religion:** none. **Monetary unit:** 1 pataca (MOP) = 100 avos; valuation (1 Jul 2007) US$1 = MOP 8.13.

Demography

Area: 10.9 sq mi, 28.2 sq km. **Population** (2006): 505,000. **Density** (2006): persons per sq mi 46,330.3, persons per sq km 17,907.8. **Urban** (2004): virtually 100% (about 0.5% of Macau's population live on sampans and other vessels). **Sex distribution** (2003): male 48.07%; female 51.93%. **Age breakdown** (2003): under 15, 18.7%; 15–29, 22.8%; 30–44, 27.3%; 45–59, 21.0%; 60–74, 6.7%; 75 and over, 3.5%. **Nationality** (2001; resident pop.): Chinese 95.2%; Portuguese 2.0%; Filipino 1.2%; other 1.6%. **Religious affiliation** (1998): nonreligious 60.8%; Buddhist 16.7%; other 22.5%. **Major city** (2000 est.): Macau 437,900. **Location:** eastern Asia, bordering China and the South China Sea.

Vital statistics

Birth rate per 1,000 population (2003): 7.2 (world avg. 21.3). **Death rate** per 1,000 population (2003): 3.3 (world avg. 9.1). **Natural increase rate** per 1,000 population (2003): 3.9 (world avg. 12.2). **Total fertility rate** (avg. births per childbearing woman; 2002): 1.1. **Marriage rate** per 1,000 population (2003): 2.9. **Divorce rate** per 1,000 population (2003): 1.0. **Life expectancy** at birth (2002): male 77.0 years; female 82.0 years.

National economy

Budget (1998). *Revenue:* MOP 14,831,099,000 (recurrent receipts 69.1%, autonomous agency receipts 21.4%, capital receipts 2.2%). *Expenditures:* MOP 14,831,099,000 (recurrent payments 61.1%, autonomous agency expenditures 21.4%, capital payments 17.5%). **Production** (metric tons except as noted). *Agriculture and fishing* (1999): eggs 650; livestock (number of live animals) 500,000 chickens; fish catch (2000) 1,500. *Quarrying* (value added in MOP '000,000; 1997): 13. *Manufacturing* (value added in MOP '000,000; 2001): wearing apparel 2,090; textiles 522; printing and publishing 95. *Energy production (consumption):* electricity (kW-hr; 2000) 1,571,000,000 (1,766,000,000); petroleum products (2000) none (500,000). **Public debt** (long-term, external; 1999): $706,000,000. **Population economically active** (2001): total 231,266; activity rate of total population 53.1% (participation rates: over age 14, 66.1%; female 46.5%; unemployed 7.0%). **Household income and expenditure.** Average household size (2001) 3.1; annual income per household MOP 181,884; expenditure (1987–88): food 38.3%, housing 19.7%, education, health, and other services 12.1%, transportation 7.4%, clothing and footwear 6.8%, energy 4.0%, household durable goods 3.7%, other goods 8.0%. **Gross domestic product** (at current market prices; 2002): $6,731,246,000 ($15,320 per capita). **Tourism:** receipts from visitors (2002) $4,415,000,000; expenditures by nationals abroad (1999) $131,000,000. **Land use** as % of total land area (2000): "green area" 22.4%.

Foreign trade

Imports (2002): MOP 20,323,000,000 (textile materials 32.3%; capital goods 13.8%; clothing and footwear 13.3%; food, beverages, and tobacco 11.4%). *Major import sources:* China 41.7%; Hong Kong 14.5%; Taiwan 6.7%; Japan 6.7%; France 4.3%. **Exports** (2002): MOP 18,925,000,000 (domestic exports 78.1%, of which machine-knitted clothing 42.1%, machine-woven clothing 27.4%, footwear 3.6%; reexports 21.9%). *Major export destinations:* US 48.4%; China 15.6%; Germany 7.5%; Hong Kong 5.8%; UK 5.4%.

Transport and communications

Transport. *Roads* (2003): total length 345 km (paved 100%). *Vehicles* (1999): passenger cars 47,776; trucks and buses 5,812. *Air transport* (2001; Air Macau only): passenger-km 1,907,988,000; metric ton-km cargo 22,616,000. **Communications,** in total units (units per 1,000 persons). Daily newspaper circulation (2000): 210,100 (488); radios (2000): 215,300 (500); televisions (2000): 123,100 (286); telephone main lines (2003): 174,600 (391); cellular telephone subscribers (2003): 364,000 (815); personal computers (2002): 92,000 (208); Internet users (2003): 120,000 (269).

Education and health

Educational attainment (2001). Population age 25 and over having: no formal schooling 7.6%; incomplete primary education 13.6%; completed primary

---

1 metric ton = about 1.1 short tons;   1 kilometer = 0.6 mi (statute);   1 metric ton-km cargo = about 0.68 short ton-mi cargo;   c.i.f.: cost, insurance, and freight;   f.o.b.: free on board

26.6%; some secondary 23.9%; completed secondary and post-secondary 28.3%. **Literacy** (2001): percentage of population age 15 and over literate 91.3%; males literate 95.3%; females literate 87.8%. **Health** (2002): physicians 915 (1 per 480 persons); hospital beds 990 (1 per 444 persons); infant mortality rate per 1,000 live births (2003) 0.6. **Food** (1998): daily per capita caloric intake 2,471 (vegetable products 76%, animal products 24%); 108% of FAO recommended minimum.

Military

Total active duty personnel: Chinese troops (2001) 500.

Did you know? Macau's flag features a white lotus flower, its 3 petals symbolizing Macau's 3 areas; 5 yellow stars refer to Chinese rule. The water and bridge below the lotus and the green field suggest the region's geography and fertile land.

Background

Portuguese traders first arrived in Macau in 1513, and it soon became the chief market center for the trade between China and Japan. It was declared a Portuguese colony in 1849 and an overseas territory in 1951. In December 1999 Portugal returned Macau to Chinese rule.

Recent Developments

Vigorous new development in the gaming industry boosted revenue and employment in Macau. In 2006 Macau surpassed Las Vegas in terms of total gambling revenue with just under $7 billion, as 22 million people, most from mainland China, visited. Revenues were predicted to grow by up to 20% annually.

Internet resources: <www.macautourism.gov.mo>.

Macedonia

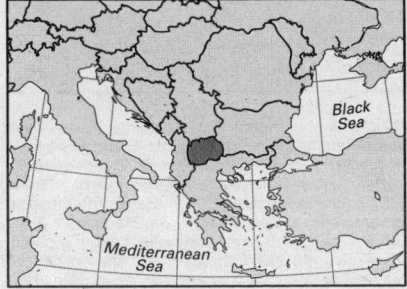

Official name: Republika Makedonija (Macedonian); Republika e Maqedonisë (Albanian) (Republic of Macedonia [member of the UN under the name The Former Yugoslav Republic of Macedonia]). **Form of government:** unitary multiparty republic with a unicameral legislative (Assembly [120]). **Head of state:** President Branko Crvenkovski (from 2004). **Head of**

government: Prime Minister Nikola Gruevski (from 2006). **Capital:** Skopje. **Official languages:** Macedonian; Albanian. **Official religion:** none. **Monetary unit:** denar; valuation (1 Jul 2007) US$1 = 46.52 denar.

Demography

Area: 9,928 sq mi, 25,713 sq km (including inland water area). **Population** (2006): 2,041,000. **Density** (2006): persons per sq mi 205.6, persons per sq km 79.4. **Urban** (2003): 59.5%. **Sex distribution** (2002): male 50.20%; female 49.80%. **Age breakdown** (2002): under 15, 21.1%; 15–29, 23.8%; 30–44, 22.0%; 45–59, 18.1%; 60–64, 11.2%; 65 and over, 3.3%. **Ethnic composition** (2002): Macedonian 64.2%; Albanian 25.2%; Turkish 3.9%; Rom (Gypsy) 2.7%; Serbian 1.8%; Bosniac 0.8%; other 1.5%. **Religious affiliation** (2000): Orthodox 59.3%; Sunni Muslim 28.3%; Roman Catholic 3.5%; nonreligious 6.6%; other 2.3%. **Major cities** (1994): Skopje 440,577; Bitola 75,386; Prilep 67,371; Kumanovo 66,237; Tetovo 50,376. **Location:** southeastern Europe, bordering Serbia and Montenegro, Bulgaria, Greece, and Albania.

Vital statistics

Birth rate per 1,000 population (2003): 11.9 (world avg. 21.3); legitimate (2000) 90.2%. **Death rate** per 1,000 population (2003): 8.8 (world avg. 9.1). **Natural increase rate** per 1,000 population (2003): 3.1 (world avg. 12.2). **Total fertility rate** (avg. births per childbearing woman; 2003): 1.6. **Marriage rate** per 1,000 population (2000): 7.0. **Life expectancy** at birth (2003): male 70.8 years; female 75.8 years.

National economy

Budget (2002). *Revenue:* 53,089,000,000 denar (tax. revenue 94.2%, of which value-added tax 33.7%, excise taxes 20.6%, income and profit tax 19.6%, import duties 10.0%; nontax revenue 5.8%). *Expenditure:* 59,979,000,000 denar (wages and salaries 29.5%, pensions 26.1%, goods and services 20.0%, interest 6.1%). **External debt** (2002): $1,262,000,000. **Production** (metric tons except as noted). *Agriculture, forestry, fishing* (2002): wheat 267,100, potatoes 183,000, corn (maize) 140,200; livestock (number of live animals) 1,233,800 sheep, 259,000 cattle; roundwood (2001) 740,000 cu m; fish catch (2001) 1,181. *Mining and quarrying* (2001; contained metal of ore): lead 11,000; copper 7,000; silver 15,000 kg. *Manufacturing* (1998): cement 461,195; steel sheets 276,464; detergents 21,990. *Energy production (consumption):* electricity (kW-hr; 2000) 6,811,000,000 (6,923,000,000); hard coal (2000) none (155,000); lignite (2000) 7,516,000 (7,702,000); crude petroleum (barrels; 2000) none (5,886,000); petroleum products (2000) 775,000 (838,000); natural gas (cu m; 2000) none (64,503,000). **Household income and expenditure.** Average household size (2002) 3.6; income per household (2000) $3,798; sources of income (2000): wages and salaries 54.2%, transfer payments 22.6%, savings 3.2%, other 20.0%; expenditure: food 38.4%, transportation and communications 9.7%, fuel and lighting 8.2%, beverages and tobacco 7.6%. **Gross national product** (at current market prices; 2003): $4,058,000,000 ($1,980 per capita). **Population economically active** (2000): total 811,000; activity rate 39.9% (participation rates:

ages 15–64, 52.9%; female 38.5%; unemployed [2002] 31.9%). **Land use** as % of total land area (2000): in temporary crops 21.8%, in permanent crops 1.7%, in pasture 25.0%; overall forest area 35.6%. **Tourism** (2002): receipts from visitors $39,000,000; expenditures by nationals abroad $45,000,000.

Foreign trade

Imports (2001-c.i.f.): $1,688,000,000 (mineral fuels 13.9%, machinery and apparatus 13.0%, food and live animals 11.5%, chemicals and chemical products 10.2%). *Major import sources* (2002): Germany 14.3%; Greece 12.1%; Yugoslavia 9.4%; Slovenia 6.6%; Bulgaria 6.5%; Italy 6.0%. **Exports** (2001-f.o.b.): $1,155,000,000 (clothing 27.7%, iron and steel 16.9%, tobacco [all forms] 6.5%, nonferrous base metals 6.4%, beverages 4.0%). *Major export destinations* (2002): Yugoslavia 22.1%; Germany 21.0%; Greece 10.4%; Italy 7.1%; US 7.0%.

Transport and communications

Transport. *Railroads* (2002): route length 699 km; passenger-km 98,000,000; metric ton-km cargo 334,000,000. *Roads* (2000): length 12,522 km (paved 58%). *Vehicles* (2002): passenger cars 307,600; trucks and buses 33,000. *Air transport* (2003; Macedonian Airline): passenger-km 294,000,000; metric ton-km cargo 141,000; airports (2002) with scheduled flights 2. **Communications,** in total units (units per 1,000 persons). Daily newspaper circulation (2000): 89,400 (44); radios (2000): 415,000 (205); televisions (2000): 571,000 (282); telephone main lines (2002): 560,000 (271); cellular telephone subscribers (2002): 365,300 (177); Internet users (2002): 100,000 (48).

Education and health

Educational attainment (1994). Percentage of population age 15 and over having: less than full primary education 25.0%; primary 33.4%; secondary 32.3%; postsecondary and higher 8.7%; unknown 0.6%. **Literacy** (1998): 94.6%. **Health** (2000): physicians 4,455 (1 per 454 persons); hospital beds 10,248 (1 per 198 persons); infant mortality rate per 1,000 live births (2003) 10.7. **Food** (2001): daily per capita caloric intake 2,552 (vegetable products 80%, animal products 20%); 100% of FAO recommended minimum.

Military

Total active duty personnel (2003): 12,850 (army 90.7%, headquarters staff 9.3%). **Military expenditure as percentage of GNP** (1999): 2.5% (world 2.4%); per capita expenditure $112.

Background

Macedonia has been inhabited since before 7000 BC. Part of it was incorporated into a Roman province in AD 29. It was settled by Slavic tribes by the mid-6th century AD. Seized by the Bulgarians in 1185, it was ruled by the Ottoman Empire from 1371 to 1912. The north and center of the region were annexed by Ser-

bia in 1913 and in 1918 became part of what was later known as Yugoslavia. When Yugoslavia was partitioned by the Axis powers in 1941, Yugoslav Macedonia was occupied principally by Bulgaria. Macedonia again became part of Yugoslavia in 1946. After Croatia and Slovenia seceded from Yugoslavia, fear of Serbian dominance drove Macedonia to declare its independence in 1991. Because of Greek objections to the new state using the name of an ancient Greek province, it entered the UN as "the Former Yugoslav Republic of Macedonia."

Recent Developments

Parliamentary elections were held in Macedonia in July 2006. Representatives of the international community had previously named free and fair elections as a key condition for Macedonia's accession to NATO and the European Union. The elections were widely assessed as free and fair. Macedonia's economy continued to make slow progress in 2006, with GDP growth of 4%. The main economic issue remained an extremely high unemployment rate of 37–38%. The disagreement with Greece over Macedonia's name remained unresolved.

Internet resources: <www.sinf.gov.mk>.

Madagascar

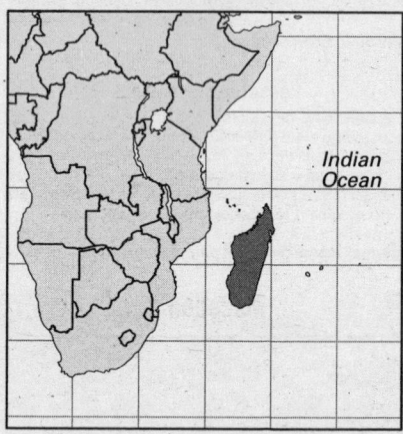

Indian Ocean

Official name: Repoblikan'i Madagasikara (Malagasy); République de Madagascar (French) (Republic of Madagascar). **Form of government:** federal multiparty republic with two legislative houses (Senate [90]; National Assembly [160]). **Heads of state and government:** President Marc Ravalomanana (from 2002), assisted by Prime Minister Charles Rabemananjara (from 2007). **Capital:** Antananarivo. **Official languages:** none; Malagasy is the national language and French is widely spoken; the two versions of the constitution are in Malagasy and French. **Official religion:** none. **Monetary unit:** 1 ariary (MGA) = 100 centimes; valuation (1 Jul 2007) US$1 = MGA 1,882. The ariary (MGA), the precolonial currency of Madagascar, replaced the Malagasy franc (FMG) in July 2003 at a rate of 1 MGA = FMG 5.

Demography

Area: 226,658 sq mi, 587,041 sq km. **Population** (2006): 19,105,000. **Density** (2006): persons per sq mi 84.3, persons per sq km 32.5. **Urban** (2001): 30.1%. **Sex distribution** (2000): male 49.70%; female 50.30%. **Age breakdown** (2000): under 15, 45.0%; 15–29, 26.5%; 30–44, 15.8%; 45–59, 7.9%; 60–74, 3.8%; 75 and over, 1.0%. **Ethnic composition** (2000): Malagasy 95.9%, of which Merina 24.0%, Betsi-misaraka 13.4%, Betsileo 11.3%, Tsimihety 7.0%, Sakalava 5.9%; Makua 1.1%; French 0.6%; Comorian 0.5%; Reunionese 0.4%; other 1.5%. **Religious affiliation** (2000): Christian 49.5%, of which Protestant 22.7%, Roman Catholic 20.3%; traditional beliefs 48.0%; Muslim 1.9%; other 0.6%. **Major cities** (2001): Antananarivo 1,403,449; Toamasina 179,-045; Antsirabe 160,356; Fianarantsoa 144,225; Mahajanga 135,660. **Location:** island in the Indian Ocean, east of the mainland of southern Africa.

Vital statistics

Birth rate per 1,000 population (2003): 42.2 (world avg. 21.3). **Death rate** per 1,000 population (2003): 11.9 (world avg. 9.1). **Natural increase rate** per 1,000 population (2003): 30.3 (world avg. 12.2). **Total fertility rate** (avg. births per childbearing woman; 2003): 5.7. **Life expectancy** at birth (2003): male 53.8 years; female 58.5 years.

National economy

Budget (2000). *Revenue:* FMG 3,068,000,000,000 (taxes 96.9%, of which duties on trade 51.9%, value-added tax 16.7%, income tax 15.2%; nontax receipts 3.1%). *Expenditures:* FMG 4,168,600,000,000 (current expenditure 57.6%, of which general administration 21.1%, debt service 14.7%, education 13.3%, defense 7.7%, health 4.4%, agriculture 2.0%; capital expenditure 42.4%). **Public debt** (external, outstanding; 2002): $4,137,000,000. **Production** (metric tons except as noted). *Agriculture, forestry, fishing* (2002): paddy rice 2,671,000, cassava 2,510,000, sugarcane 2,223,000; *livestock* (number of live animals) 11,000,000 cattle, 1,600,000 pigs, 1,350,000 goats; roundwood (2001) 10,012,542 cu m; fish catch (2001) 143,000, of which crustaceans (2001) 18,881. *Mining and quarrying* (2002): chromite ore 15,600; graphite 1,300; gold, none (illegally smuggled, c. 3,500 kg). *Manufacturing* (2000): refined sugar 62,487; cement 50,938; soap 15,385. *Energy production (consumption):* electricity (kW-hr; 2000) 807,000,000 (807,000,000); coal (2000) none (10,000); crude petroleum (barrels; 2000) none (3,379,000); petroleum products (2000) 311,000 (568,000). **Population economically active** (1993): total 5,914,000; activity rate of total population 48.9% (participation rates [1995]: over age 10, 59.4%; female 38.4%). **Gross national product** (at current market prices; 2003): $4,848,000,000 ($290 per capita). **Household income and expenditure.** Average household size (1993; Malagasy households only) 4.6; expenditure (1983; Antananarivo only; excludes housing): food 60.4%, fuel and light 9.1%, clothing and footwear 8.6%, household goods and utensils 2.4%. **Land use** as % of total land area (2000): in temporary crops 5.0%, in permanent crops

1.0%, in pasture 41.3%; overall forest area 20.2%. **Tourism** (2002): receipts from visitors $36,000,000; expenditures by nationals abroad $91,000,000.

Foreign trade

Imports (2001-f.o.b. in balance of trade and c.i.f. for commodities and trading partners): FMG 7,363,-000,000,000 (petroleum [all forms] 15.0%, machinery and apparatus 14.7%, consumer goods 11.8%, other [mostly imports for export-processing zones] 39.3%). *Major import sources:* France 21.5%; China 9.1%; South Africa 5.5%; Japan 4.4%; US 4.2%. **Exports** (2001): FMG 6,356,000,000,000 (export-processing zones exports [mostly textiles and clothing] 35.3%, vanilla 17.0%, cloves 9.9%, shellfish 9.6%). *Major export destinations:* France 29.7%; US 13.9%; Mauritius 2.6%; unspecified countries 34.7%.

Transport and communications

Transport. *Railroads:* route length (2003) 901 km; passenger-km (2000) 24,471,000; metric ton-km cargo (2000) 27,200,000. *Roads* (1999): total length 49,827 km (paved 12%). *Vehicles* (1998): passenger cars 64,000; trucks and buses 9,100. *Air transport* (2003; Air Madagascar): passenger-km 715,920,-000; metric ton-km cargo 9,740,000; airports (1994) with scheduled flights 44. **Communications**, in total units (units per 1,000 persons). Daily newspaper circulation (2000): 77,500 (5); radios (2000): 3,350,-000 (216); televisions (2002): 410,000 (25); telephone main lines (2003): 59,600 (3.6); cellular telephone subscribers (2003): 279,500 (17); personal computer users (2003): 80,000 (4.9); Internet users (2003): 70,500 (4.3).

Education and health

Literacy (2000): percentage of total population age 15 and over literate 66.5%; males literate 73.6%; females literate 59.7%. **Health** (2000): physicians 1,428 (1 per 10,859 persons); hospital beds (total number of regional and provincial hospital beds) 7,043 (1 per 2,202 persons); infant mortality rate per 1,000 live births (2002) 81.9. **Food** (2001): daily per capita caloric intake 2,072 (vegetable products 91%, animal products 9%); 91% of FAO recommended minimum.

Military

Total active duty personnel (2003): 13,500 (army 92.6%, navy 3.7%, air force 3.7%). **Military expenditure as percentage of GNP** (1999): 1.2% (world 2.4%); per capita expenditure $3.

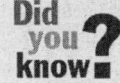 **Did you know?** Madagascar is the world's fourth largest island, after Greenland, New Guinea, and Borneo. Many zoologically primitive primates have survived and evolved into unique forms.

Background

Indonesians migrated to Madagascar about AD 700. The first European to visit the island was Portuguese navigator Diogo Dias in 1500. Trade in arms and slaves allowed the development of Malagasy kingdoms at the beginning of the 17th century. The Merina kingdom became dominant in the 18th century and in 1868 signed a treaty granting France control over the northwestern coast. In 1895 French troops took the island, and Madagascar became a French overseas territory in 1946. As the Malagasy Republic, it gained independence in 1960. It severed ties with France in the 1970s, taking its present name in 1975. A new constitution was adopted in 1992. The country has since been both politically and economically unstable.

Recent Developments

Although Pres. Marc Ravalomanana's investor-friendly policies had brought the country over 5% economic growth and $100 million of foreign investment in the previous year, in 2006 much of the population continued to earn only $1 a day. Madagascar was the first country to win large funds from the U.S.'s Millennium Challenge Account, which imposed strict conditions on the award of grants, and the International Monetary Fund granted it substantial debt relief. Potentially the biggest news for the island state was the discovery of offshore oil fields estimated to hold some five billion barrels of oil.

Internet resources:
<www.embassy.org/madagascar>.

Malawi

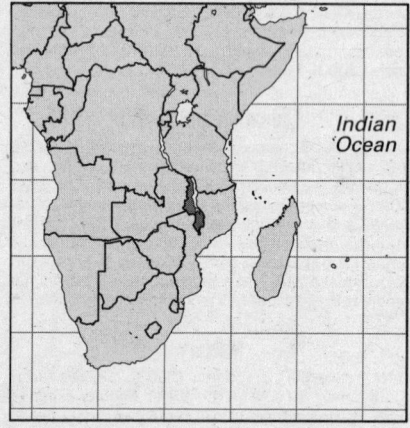

Indian Ocean

Official name: Republic of Malawi. **Form of government:** multiparty republic with one legislative house (National Assembly [193]). **Head of state and government:** President Bingu wa Mutharika (from 2004). **Capital:** Lilongwe (the judiciary meets in Blantyre). **Official language:** none. **Official religion:** none. **Monetary unit:** 1 Malawi kwacha (MK) = 100 tambala; valuation (1 Jul 2007) US$1 = MK 143.24.

Demography

Area: 45,747 sq mi, 118,484 sq km. **Population** (2006): 13,014,000. **Density** (2006): persons per sq mi 284.5, persons per sq km 109.8. **Urban** (2002): 15.1%. **Sex distribution** (2001): male 49.39%; female 50.61%. **Age breakdown** (2001): under 15, 44.4%; 15–29, 30.4%; 30–44, 13.5%; 45–59, 7.2%; 60–74, 3.7%; 75 and over, 0.8%. **Ethnic composition** (2000): Chewa 34.7%; Maravi 12.2%; Ngoni 9.0%; Yao 7.9%; Tumbuka 7.9%; Lomwe 7.7%; Ngonde 3.5%; other 17.1%. **Religious affiliation** (2000): Protestant 38.5%; Roman Catholic 24.7%; Muslim 14.8%; traditional beliefs 7.8%; other 14.2%. **Major cities** (1998): Blantyre 502,053; Lilongwe 440,471; Mzuzu 86,980; Zomba 65,915; Karonga 27,811. **Location:** southeastern Africa, bordering Tanzania, Mozambique, and Zambia.

Vital statistics

Birth rate per 1,000 population (2003): 44.7 (world avg. 21.3). **Death rate** per 1,000 population (2003): 22.6 (world avg. 9.1). **Natural increase rate** per 1,000 population (2003): 22.1 (world avg. 12.2). **Total fertility rate** (avg. births per childbearing woman; 2003): 6.1. **Life expectancy** at birth (2003): male 37.6 years; female 38.4 years. **Adult population** (ages 15–49) **living with HIV** (2004): 14.2% (world avg. 1.1%).

National economy

Budget (2001–02). *Revenue:* MK 22,853,200,000 (tax revenue 72.5%, of which surtax 21.5%, income and profit tax 17.1%, import tax 8.4%; grants 19.8%; nontax revenue 7.7%). *Expenditures:* MK 30,476,300,000 (current expenditure 86.7%; capital expenditure 9.9%; other 3.4%). **Public debt** (external, outstanding; 2002): $2,688,000,000. **Production** (metric tons except as noted). *Agriculture* (2002): sugarcane 1,900,000, corn (maize) 1,603,000, cassava 1,540,000; livestock (number of live animals) 1,700,000 goats, 750,000 cattle, 456,000 pigs; roundwood (2001) 5,515,659 cu m; fish catch (2001) 41,187. *Mining and quarrying* (2002): limestone 175,000; gemstones 16,500 kg. *Manufacturing* (value added in $'000,000; 2001): food products 62; beverages 28; chemicals and chemical products 11. *Energy production (consumption):* electricity (kW-hr; 2002) 1,156,000,000 ([2000] 884,000,000); hard coal (2002) 41,900 ([2000] 17,000); petroleum products (2000) none (209,000). **Land use** as % of total land area (2000): in temporary crops 22.3%, in permanent crops 1.5%, in pasture 19.7%; overall forest area 27.2%. **Population economically active** (1998): total 4,509,290; activity rate 45.4% (participation rates: ages 10 and over 66.9%; female 50.2%). **Gross national product** (2003): $1,832,000,000 ($170 per capita). **Households.** Average household size (1998) 4.3; expenditure (2001): food 55.5%, clothing and footwear 11.7%, housing 9.6%, household goods 8.4%. **Tourism:** receipts (2002) $125,000,000; expenditures (1994) $78,000,000.

Foreign trade

Imports (2001-c.i.f.): MK 39,480,000,000 (1998): food 16.4%, of which cereals 13.1%; machinery and apparatus 15.3%; chemicals and chemical products 13.2%; road vehicles 11.6%; mineral fuels 9.6%). *Major import sources* (2001): South Africa 39.7%;

1 metric ton = about 1.1 short tons;   1 kilometer = 0.6 mi (statute);   1 metric ton-km cargo = about 0.68 short ton-mi cargo;   c.i.f.: cost, insurance, and freight;   f.o.b.: free on board

Zimbabwe 16.0%; Zambia 10.9%; India 3.2%; Germany 2.7%. **Exports** (2001-f.o.b.): MK 31,816,-000,000 (tobacco 57.7%; sugar 12.5%; tea 7.7%; apparel 1.7%; coffee 1.4%). *Major export destinations:* South Africa 19.1%; US 15.4%; Germany 11.2%; Japan 7.6%; The Netherlands 5.4%.

Transport and communications

Transport. *Railroads* (1999–2000): route length 797 km; passenger-km 19,000,000; metric ton-km cargo 62,000,000. *Roads* (1998): total length 16,451 km (paved 19%). *Vehicles* (2001): passenger cars 22,500; trucks and buses 57,600. *Air transport* (2003; Air Malawi only): passenger-km 146,900,000; metric ton-km cargo 1,176,000; airports (1998) 5. **Communications,** in total units (units per 1,000 persons). Daily newspaper circulation (1996; circulation for one newspaper only): 22,000 (2.3); radios (2000): 5,426,000 (499); televisions (2000): 32,600 (3); telephone main lines (2003): 85,000 (8.1); cellular telephone subscribers (2003): 135,100 (13); personal computers (2003): 16,000 (1.5); Internet users (2003): 36,000 (3.4).

Education and health

Educational attainment (1998). Percentage of population age 25 and over having: no formal education 40.9%; primary education 48.7%; secondary 9.7%; university 0.7%. **Literacy** (2000): total population age 15 and over literate 60.1%; males literate 74.5%; females literate 46.5%. **Health:** physicians (1989) 186 (1 per 47,634 persons); hospital beds (1998) 14,200 (1 per 746 persons); infant mortality rate per 1,000 live births (2003) 105.2. **Food** (2001): daily per capita caloric intake 2,168 (vegetable products 97%, animal products 3%); 93% of FAO recommended minimum.

Military

Total active duty personnel (2003): 5,300 (army 100%; navy, none; air force, none). **Military expenditure as percentage of GNP** (1999): 0.6% (world 2.4%); per capita expenditure $1.

Background

Inhabited since at least 8000 BC, the region was settled by Bantu-speaking peoples between the 1st and the 4th century AD. About 1480 they founded the Maravi Confederacy, which encompassed most of central and southern Malawi. In northern Malawi the Ngonde people established a kingdom about 1600. The slave trade flourished during the 18th–19th centuries. Britain established colonial authority in 1891, and the area became known as Nyasaland in 1907. The colonies of Northern and Southern Rhodesia and Nyasaland formed a federation (1951–53), which was dissolved in 1963. The next year Malawi achieved independence. In 1966 it became a republic, with Hastings Banda as president. In 1971 Banda was designated president for life, and he ruled until he was defeated in multiparty elections in 1994. A new constitution was adopted in 1995.

Recent Developments

Political instability and infighting continued to plague Malawi. In January 2005 Pres. Bingu wa Mutharika accused his predecessor and fellow party member, Bakili Muluzi, of plotting to murder him, and in February Mutharika quit the United Democratic Front, which then tried unsuccessfully to impeach him. In February 2006 Mutharika attempted to remove his vice president, Cassim Chilumpha. He was reinstated, but in April he, too, was charged with plotting to assassinate the president and was arrested. His trial began in early 2007.

Internet resources: <www.malawi.gov.mw>.

Malaysia

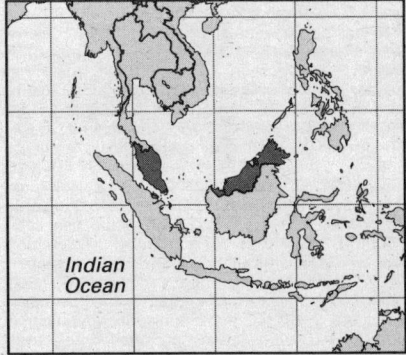

Official name: Malaysia. **Form of government:** federal constitutional monarchy with two legislative houses (Senate [70, including 44 appointees of the Paramount Ruler; the remaining 26 are indirectly elected]; House of Representatives [219]). **Chief of state:** Yang di-Pertuan Agong (Paramount Ruler) Tuanku Mizan Zainal Abidin ibni al-Marhum Sultan Mahmud (from 2006). **Head of government:** Prime Minister Datuk Seri Abdullah Ahmad Badawi (from 2003). **Capital:** transferring from Kuala Lumpur to Putrajaya between 1999 and 2012. **Official language:** Malay. **Official religion:** Islam. **Monetary unit:** 1 ringgit, or Malaysian dollar (RM) = 100 cents; pegged since 6 Oct 2000 to the US dollar at the rate of US$1 = RM 3.80.

Demography

Area: 127,366 sq mi, 329,876 sq km. **Population** (2006): 26,640,000. **Density** (2006): persons per sq mi 209.2, persons per sq km 80.8. **Urban** (2002): 59.0%. **Sex distribution** (2000): male 50.93%; female 49.07%. **Age breakdown** (2000): under 15, 33.0%; 15–29, 28.3%; 30–44, 21.0%; 45–59, 11.6%; 60–74, 4.9%; 75 and over, 1.2%. **Ethnic composition** (2000): Malay and other indigenous 61.3%; Chinese 24.5%; Indian 7.2%; other nonindigenous 1.1%; noncitizen 5.9%. **Religious affiliation** (2000): Muslim 60.4%; Buddhist 19.2%; Christian 9.1%; Hindu 6.3%; Chinese folk religionist 2.6%; other 2.4%. **Major cities** (2000): Kuala Lumpur 1,297,526; Ipoh 566,211; Klang 563,173; Petaling Jaya 438,084; Johor Bahru 384,613. **Location:** southeastern Asia, on the Malay Peninsula and the northern third of the island of Borneo, bordering Thailand, the South China Sea, Brunei, and Indonesia.

Vital statistics

Birth rate per 1,000 population (2003): 21.9 (world avg. 21.3). **Death rate** per 1,000 population (2003): 4.7 (world avg. 9.1). **Natural increase rate** per 1,000 population (2003): 17.2 (world avg. 12.2). **Total fertility rate** (avg. births per childbearing woman; 2003): 3.1. **Life expectancy** at birth (2003): male 71.0 years; female 75.5 years.

National economy

Budget (2001). *Revenue:* RM 79,567,000,000 (income tax 52.9%, nontax revenue 25.1%, taxes on goods and services 16.9%, taxes on international trade 5.1%). *Expenditures:* RM 63,757,000,000 (education 22.6%, interest payments 15.1%, defense and internal security 13.0%, social security 8.7%, health 7.3%, transport 2.1%, agriculture 2.1%). **Population economically active** (1999): total 9,010,000; activity rate 39.7% (participation rates: ages 15–64, 60.6%; female [2000] 34.7%; unemployed 3.0%). **Production** (metric tons except as noted). *Agriculture, forestry, fishing* (2002): palm fruit oil 67,400,000, rice 2,091,000, coconuts 700,000; livestock (number of live animals) 1,824,000 pigs, 748,000 cattle; roundwood (2001) 16,347,000 cu m; fish catch (2001) 1,393,000. *Mining and quarrying* (2001): iron ore 376,000; struverite 9,657; tin (metal content) 4,973. *Manufacturing* (value added in $'000,000; 2000): electronic products 4,962; refined petroleum products 2,492; telecommunications equipment 2,062. *Energy production (consumption):* electricity (kW-hr; 2003; excludes Sabah and Sarawak) 84,024,000,000 ([2000] 69,268,000,000); coal (2003) 168,000 ([2000] 3,761,000,000); crude petroleum (barrels; 2003; Sabah and Sarawak only) 268,300,000 ([2000] 155,548,000); petroleum products (2000) 19,386,000 (20,495,000); natural gas (cu m; 2003) 51,808,000,000 ([2000] 29,454,000,000). **Gross national product** (2003): $93,683,000,000 ($3,780 per capita). **Public debt** (external, outstanding; 2002): $26,200,000,000. **Household income and expenditure.** Average household size (2000) 4.5; annual income per household (1999) RM 32,784; expenditure (1998–99): food at home 22.2%, housing and energy 21%, food away from home 10.9%. **Tourism** (2002): receipts $6,785,-000,000; expenditures $2,618,000,000. **Land use** as % of total land area (2000): in temporary crops 5.5%, in permanent crops 17.6%, in pasture 0.9%; overall forest area 58.7%.

Foreign trade

Imports (2002-c.i.f.): RM 303,510,000,000 (microcircuits, transistors, and valves 29.2%; computers/office machines 6.9%; telecommunications equipment 4.3%; other electrical machinery 6.6%). *Major import sources:* Japan 17.8%; US 16.4%; Singapore 12.0%; China 7.8%; Taiwan 5.6%. **Exports** (2002-f.o.b.): RM 354,480,000,000 (microcircuits, transistors, and valves 20.5%; computers/office machines 18.4%; telecommunications equipment 5.4%; fixed vegetable oils 3.9%; crude petroleum 3.3%). *Major export destinations:* US 20.2%; Singapore 17.1%; Japan 11.2%; Hong Kong 5.7%; China 5.6%.

Transport and communications

Transport. *Railroads* (2000): route length 2,227 km; passenger-km 1,241,000,000 (peninsular Malaysia and Singapore); metric ton-km cargo 918,000,000 (peninsular Malaysia and Singapore). *Roads* (2000): total length 66,445 km (paved 76%). *Vehicles* (2000): passenger cars 4,212,567; trucks and buses 713,946. *Air transport* (2003; Malaysian airline only): passenger-km 36,797,000,000; metric ton-km cargo 2,176,000,000; airports (1997) 39. **Communications,** in total units (units per 1,000 persons). Daily newspaper circulation (2000): 3,672,000 (158); radios (2000): 9,762,000 (420); televisions (2002): 5,103,000 (210); telephone main lines (2003): 4,571,600 (182); cellular telephone subscribers (2003): 11,124,100 (442); personal computers (2002): 3,600,000 (147); Internet users (2003): 8,692,100 (345).

Education and health

Educational attainment (1996). Percentage of population age 25 and over having: no formal schooling 16.7%; primary education 33.7%; secondary 42.8%; higher 6.8%. **Literacy** (2000): total population age 15 and over literate 87.5%; males literate 91.4%; females literate 83.4%. **Health** (2002): physicians 17,442 (1 per 1,406 persons); hospital beds (2001) 41,927 (1 per 570 persons); infant mortality rate per 1,000 live births 7.9. **Food** (2001): daily per capita caloric intake 2,927 (vegetable products 82%, animal products 18%); 131% of FAO recommended minimum.

Military

Total active duty personnel (2003): 104,000 (army 77.0%, navy 13.5%, air force 9.5%). **Military expenditure as percentage of GDP** (1999): 2.3% (world 2.4%); per capita expenditure $78.

Did you know? Kuala Lumpur International Airport, one of the largest airports in the world, is located in the city's Gateway Park, a development that includes a major hotel, golf course, and amusement park.

Background

Malaya has been inhabited for 6,000–8,000 years, and small kingdoms existed in the 2nd–3rd century AD, when adventurers from India first arrived. Sumatran exiles founded the city-state of Malacca about 1400, and it flourished as a trading and Islamic religious center until its capture by the Portuguese in 1511. Malacca passed to the Dutch in 1641. The British founded a settlement on Singapore Island in 1819, and by 1867 they had established the Straits Settlements, including Malacca, Singapore, and Penang. During the late 19th century the Chinese began to migrate to Malaya. Japan invaded in 1941. Opposition to British rule led to the creation of the United Malays National Organization (UNMO) in 1946, and in 1948 the peninsula was federated with Penang. Malaya gained independence in 1957, and

---

the federation of Malaysia was established in 1963. Its economy expanded greatly from the late 1970s, but it suffered from the economic slump that struck the area in the mid-1990s.

Recent Developments

Long considered a model of ethnic and religious tolerance, Malaysia showed signs in 2006 of tensions between conservative Muslims and their non-Muslim countrymen. In April a crowd of Muslims destroyed a 19th-century Hindu temple in Kuala Lumpur. Some local governments enacted bans on couples' kissing and holding hands in public and on owning dogs (considered unclean by conservative Muslims), while a coalition of organizations called on the government to enforce constitutional guarantees of religious equality and freedom of worship. US-based Dell and Intel expanded their operations in the country, the German chip maker Infineon Technologies opened a state-of-the-art semiconductor factory, and Singapore-based electronics manufacturer Flextronics began construction of another factory. Malaysia sought to establish itself as a major hub in the burgeoning biotechnology industry by opening the manufacturing facility of a new government-owned drug and biotech company, creating a $200 million fund to support biotech initiatives, and launching a new technology park near the capital.

Internet resources:
<www.geographia.com/malaysia>.

Maldives

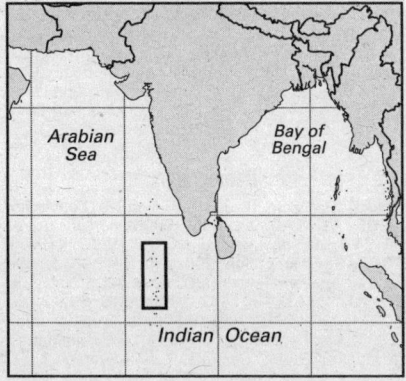

Arabian Sea

Bay of Bengal

Indian Ocean

Official name: Divehi Jumhuriyya (Republic of Maldives). **Form of government:** republic with one legislative house (Majlis [42; excludes eight nonelective seats]). **Head of state and government:** President Maumoon Abdul Gayoom (from 1978). **Capital:** Male. **Official language:** Divehi. **Official religion:** Islam. **Monetary unit:** 1 Maldivian rufiyaa (Rf) = 100 laari; valuation (1 Jul 2007) US$1 = Rf 12.92.

Demography

Area: 115 sq mi, 298 sq km. **Population** (2006): 300,000. **Density** (2006): persons per sq mi 6,652, persons per sq km 2,568 (based on areas of inhabited island only). **Urban** (2002): 27.0%. **Sex distribu-** tion (2003): male 50.73%; female 49.27%. **Age breakdown** (2003): under 15, 36.1%; 15–29, 31.7%; 30–44, 18.0%; 45–59, 7.9%; 60–74, 5.2%; 75 and over, 1.1%. **Ethnic composition** (2000): Maldivian 98.5%; Sinhalese 0.7%; other 0.8%. **Religious affiliation:** virtually 100% Sunni Muslim. **Major city** (2000): Male 74,069. **Location:** islands in the Indian Ocean, south of India.

Vital statistics

Birth rate per 1,000 population (2003): 35.7 (world avg. 21.3). **Death rate** per 1,000 population (2003): 6.0 (world avg. 9.1). **Natural increase rate** per 1,000 population (2003): 29.7 (world avg. 12.2). **Total fertility rate** (avg. births per childbearing woman; 2003): 5.3. **Marriage rate** per 1,000 population (2001): 11.6. **Divorce rate** per 1,000 population (2001): 5.5. **Life expectancy** at birth (2003): male 62.0 years; female 64.6 years.

National economy

Budget (2001). *Revenue:* Rf 2,513,200,000 (nontax revenue 50.8%; taxation 41.4%; foreign aid 7.3%). *Expenditures:* Rf 2,886,200,000 (general public services 42.1%, of which defense 15.2%; education 18.5%; health 10.4%; transportation and communications 8.9%; transfer payments 2.3%). **Public debt** (external, outstanding; 2002): $221,700,000. **Production** (metric tons except as noted). *Agriculture, forestry, fishing* (2001): vegetables and melons 28,000, coconuts 15,000, fruits (excluding melons) 9,000; fish catch 125,814. *Mining and quarrying:* coral for construction materials. *Manufacturing:* details, n.a.; however, major industries include boat building and repairing, coir yarn and mat weaving, coconut and fish processing, lacquerwork, garment manufacturing, and handicrafts. *Energy production (consumption):* electricity (kW-hr; 2000) 104,000,000 (104,000,000); petroleum products (2000) none (163,000). **Tourism** (2002): receipts from visitors $318,000,000; expenditures by nationals abroad $46,000,000. **Population economically active** (2000): total 87,987; activity rate of total population 32.6% (participation rates: ages 15–64, 58.5%; female 33.8%; unemployed 2.0%). **Household income and expenditure.** Average household size (2000) 6.8; annual income per household (1990) Rf 2,616; expenditure (1995): food, beverages and tobacco 36.9%, housing and energy 14.9%, transportation and communications 11.1%, clothing and footwear 9.8%, education 8.6%, household furnishings 8.3%. **Gross national product** (2003): $674,000,000 ($2,300 per capita). **Land use** as % of total land area (2000): in temporary crops 13%, in permanent crops 17%, in pasture 3%; overall forest area 3%.

Foreign trade

Imports (2001-c.i.f.): $395,400,000 (food products 36.9%; petroleum products 12.1%; transport equipment 10.5%; construction-related goods 10.2%). *Major import sources:* Asian countries 69%, of which Singapore 25%, Sri Lanka 13%, India 10%, Malaysia 9%; European countries 14%. **Exports** (2001-f.o.b.): $110,200,000 (domestic exports 69.1%, of which fish 32.5%, garments 29.3%, live tropical fish 2.8%; reexports 30.9%, of which jet fuel 25.6%). *Major export destinations:* US 39%; Sri Lanka 21%; European countries 15%.

The Maldive Islands are a series of coral atolls built up from the crowns of a submerged ancient volcanic mountain range. All the islands are low-lying, none rising to more than 6 ft (1.8 m) above sea level.

Transport and communications

Transport. *Vehicles* (2002): passenger cars 2,594; trucks and buses 644. *Air transport* (2001): passenger-km 385,000,000; airports (1997) with scheduled flights 5. **Communications**, in total units (units per 1,000 persons). Daily newspaper circulation (1996): 5,000 (19); radios (1997): 34,000 (129); televisions (2000): 10,900 (40); telephone main lines (2002): 28,700 (102); cellular telephone subscribers (2002): 41,900 (149); personal computers (2002): 20,000 (71); Internet users (2002): 15,000 (53).

Education and health

Educational attainment (2000). Population age 25 and over 71,937; percentage with university education 0.4%. **Literacy** (1995): total population age 15 and over literate 93.2%; males literate 93.0%; females literate 93.3%. **Health** (2003): physicians 314 (1 per 905 persons); hospital beds 643 (1 per 443 persons); infant mortality rate per 1,000 live births (2002) 38.0. **Food** (2001): daily per capita caloric intake 2,587 (vegetable products 75%, animal products 25%); 117% of FAO recommended minimum.

Military

Total active duty personnel: combined army/police force 700–1,000. **Military expenditure as percentage of GDP** (2002): 6.2%; per capita expenditure $103.

Background

The archipelago was settled in the 5th century BC by Buddhists from Sri Lanka and southern India, and Islam was adopted there in 1153. The Portuguese held sway in Male in 1558–73. The islands were a sultanate under the Dutch rulers of Ceylon (now Sri Lanka) during the 17th century. After the British gained control of Ceylon in 1796, the area became a British protectorate, a status formalized in 1887. The islands won full independence from Britain in 1965, and in 1968 a republic was founded. During the 1990s its economy gradually developed.

Recent Developments

The tsunami that had devastated the Maldives in December 2004 exacted a tremendous toll on the economy as well as on the lives of the country's residents. In 2005 GDP contracted 5.5%, ending 20 years of 8% average annual growth, and the Maldives required an estimated $1.5 billion in aid. Pres. Maumoon Abdul Gayoom announced a plan for democratization that included a revision of the constitution by June 2007 and the country's first multiparty elections in 2008 (political parties had begun registering

in June 2005). In March 2007, however, it was announced that the date for this election had been pushed back to 2010.

Internet resources: <www.visitmaldives.com>.

Mali

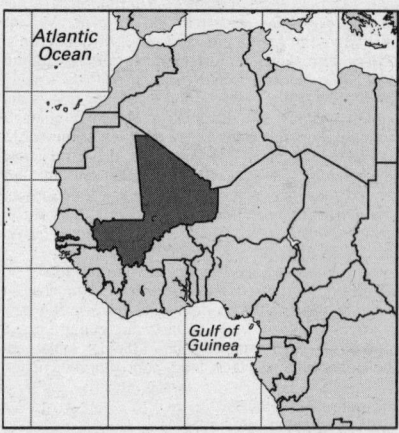

Official name: République du Mali (Republic of Mali). **Form of government:** multiparty republic with one legislative house (National Assembly [147]). **Chief of state:** President Amadou Toumani Touré (from 2002). **Head of government:** Prime Minister Ousmane Issoufi Maïga (from 2004). **Capital:** Bamako. **Official language:** French. **Official religion:** none. **Monetary unit:** 1 CFA franc (CFAF) = 100 centimes; valuation (1 Jul 2007) US$1 = CFAF 485.18; the CFAF is pegged to the euro (€) at €1 = 655.96 from 1 Jan 2002.

Demography

Area: 482,077 sq mi, 1,248,574 sq km. **Population** (2006): 11,717,000. **Density** (2006): persons per sq mi 24.3, persons per sq km 9.4. **Urban** (1998): 28.7%. **Sex distribution** (2001): male 48.9%; female 51.1%. **Age breakdown** (2001): under 15, 47.2%; 15–29, 26.8%; 30–44, 13.3%; 45–59, 7.9%; 60–74, 4.0%; 75 and over, 0.8%. **Ethnic composition** (2000): Bambara 30.6%; Senufo 10.5%; Fula Macina (Niafunke) 9.6%; Soninke 7.4%; Tuareg 7.0%; Maninka 6.6%; Songhai 6.3%; Dogon 4.3%; Bobo 3.5%; other 14.2%. **Religious affiliation** (2000): Muslim 82%; traditional beliefs 16%; Christian 2%. **Major cities** (1998): Bamako 1,016,167; Sikasso 113,803; Ségou 90,898; Mopti 79,840; Gao 54,903. **Location:** western Africa, bordering Algeria, Niger, Burkina Faso, Côte d'Ivoire, Guinea, Senegal, and Mauritania.

Vital statistics

Birth rate per 1,000 population (2003): 47.8 (world avg. 21.3). **Death rate** per 1,000 population (2003): 19.2 (world avg. 9.1). **Natural increase rate** per 1,000 population (2003): 28.6 (world avg. 12.2).

1 metric ton = about 1.1 short tons; 1 kilometer = 0.6 mi (statute); 1 metric ton-km cargo = about 0.68 short ton-mi cargo; c.i.f.: cost, insurance, and freight; f.o.b.: free on board

Total fertility rate (avg. births per childbearing woman; 2003): 6.7. Life expectancy at birth (2003): male 44.7 years; female 46.2 years.

National economy

Budget (2002). Revenue: CFAF 379,400,000,000 (tax revenue 82.7%, nontax revenue 17.3%). Expenditures: CFAF 601,500,000,000 (current expenditure 46.7%, of which wages and salaries 14.9%, education 4.9%, interest on public debt 3.5%; capital expenditure 53.3%). Public debt (external, outstanding; 2002): $2,487,000,000. Tourism (2000): receipts from visitors $71,000,000; expenditures by nationals abroad $41,000,000. Population economically active (2001): total 5,895,000; activity rate of total population 53.7%. Production (metric tons except as noted). Agriculture, forestry, fishing (2002): millet 1,034,211, sorghum 951,417, rice 926,497; livestock (number of live animals) 15,000,000 goats and sheep, 6,818,000 cattle, 700,000 asses; roundwood (2001) 5,200,428 cu m; fish catch (2001) 100,035. Mining and quarrying (1997): limestone 20,000; phosphate 3,000; iron oxide 708. Manufacturing (2000): cement 40,000; sugar 28,000; soap (1995) 10,097. Energy production (consumption): electricity (kW-hr; 2000) 412,000,000 (412,000,000); petroleum products (2000) none (161,000). Gross national product (2003): $3,428,000,000 ($290 per capita). Households. Average household size (2000) 5.6. Land use as % of total land area (2000): in temporary crops 3.8%, in permanent crops, negligible, in pasture 24.6%; overall forest area 10.8%.

Foreign trade

Imports (2001): CFAF 532,900,000,000 (machinery and apparatus 46.0%, petroleum products 25.9%, food products 13.0%). Major import sources (1999): African countries 51%, of which Côte d'Ivoire 20%; France 18%; Germany 3%; Hong Kong 3%. Exports (2001): CFAF 530,500,000,000 (gold 66.7%, raw cotton and cotton products 15.7%, live animals 8.5%). Major export destinations (1999): Italy 12%; Taiwan 10%; Thailand 10%; South Korea 9%; Canada 8%; Portugal 5%.

Transport and communications

Transport. Railroads (1999): route length 729 km; passenger-km 210,000,000; metric ton-km cargo 241,000,000. Roads (1996): total length 15,100 km (paved 12%). Vehicles (1996): passenger cars 26,190; trucks and buses 18,240. Air transport (1999; represents 1/11 of the traffic of Air Afrique, which was operated by 11 West African states and was declared bankrupt in February 2002): passenger-km 235,000,000; metric ton-km cargo 36,000,000; airports (1999) 9. Communications, in total units (units per 1,000 persons). Daily newspaper circulation (1997): 45,000 (4.6); radios (2001): 1,976,000 (180); televisions (2002): 376,200 (33); telephone main lines (2002): 56,600 (5.3); cellular phone subscribers (2002): 250,000 (23); personal computers (2002): 15,000 (1.5); Internet users (2002): 25,000 (2.3).

Education and health

Literacy (2000): percentage of total population age 15 and over literate 41.5%; males literate 48.9%; females literate 34.4%. Health: physicians (1993) 483 (1 per 18,376 persons); hospital beds (1998) 2,412 (1 per 4,168 persons); infant mortality rate per 1,000 live births (2003) 119.2. Food (2001): daily per capita caloric intake 2,376 (vegetable products 91%, animal products 9%); 101% of FAO recommended minimum.

Military

Total active duty personnel (2003): 7,350 (army 100%). Military expenditure as percentage of GNP (1999): 2.3% (world 2.4%); per capita expenditure $6.

Background

Inhabited since prehistoric times, the region was situated on a caravan route across the Sahara. In the 12th century the Malinke empire of Mali was founded on the Upper and Middle Niger. In the 15th century the Songhai empire in the Timbuktu-Gao region gained control. In 1591 Morocco invaded the area, and Timbuktu remained under the Moors for two centuries. In the mid-19th century the French conquered the area, which became a part of French West Africa known as the French Sudan. In 1946 it became an overseas territory of the French Union. It was proclaimed the Sudanese Republic in 1958, briefly joined with Senegal (1959–60) to form the Mali Federation, and became the Republic of Mali in 1960. The government was overthrown by military coups in 1968 and 1991. Elections were held in 1992 and 1997, but political instability continued.

Recent Developments

Mali continued to reel from natural and economic disasters. A locust plague in 2004 was followed by drought in 2005, both of which added to a sharp rise in the price of food. In 2005 an estimated 70% of the population lived on less than $1 a day. In June 2005 the Group of Eight countries canceled about $2 billion of Mali's debt.

Internet resources:
<www.oxfam.org.uk/coolplanet/ontheline/explore/journey/mali/malindex.htm>.

Malta

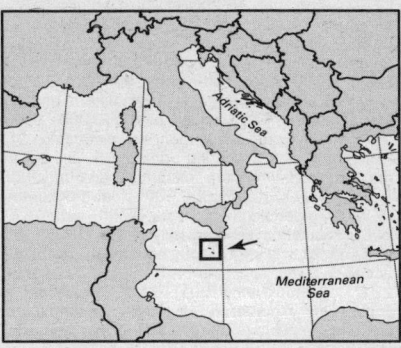

Official name: Repubblikka ta' Malta (Maltese); Republic of Malta (English). Form of government: unitary multiparty republic with one legislative house (House of Representatives [65]). **Chief of state:** President Eddie Fenech Adami (from 2004). **Head of government:** Prime Minister Lawrence Gonzi (from 2004). **Capital:** Valletta. **Official languages:** Maltese; English. **Official religion:** Roman Catholicism. **Monetary unit:** 1 Maltese lira (Lm) = 100 cents = 1,000 mils; valuation (1 Jul 2007) US$1 = Lm 0.32.

Demography

Area: 121.7 sq mi, 315.1 sq km. **Population** (2006): 405,000. **Density** (2006): persons per sq mi 3,319.7, persons per sq km 1,285.7. **Urban** (2000): 90.5%. **Sex distribution** (2004): male 49.54%; female 50.46%. **Age breakdown** (2004): under 15, 18.2%; 15–29, 22.1%; 30–44, 20.0%; 45–59, 22.3%; 60–74, 12.1%; 75 and over, 5.3%. **Ethnic composition** (2000): Maltese 93.8%; British 2.1%; Arab 2.0%; Italian 1.5%; other 0.6%. **Religious affiliation** (2000): Roman Catholic 94.5%; unaffiliated Christian 2.7%; Protestant 0.8%; Muslim 0.5%; nonreligious 1.0%; other 0.5%. **Major localities** (2004): Birkirkara 22,435; Qormi 18,547; Mosta 18,070; Zabbar 15,134; Valletta 7,137 (urban agglomeration [2003] 83,000). **Location:** islands in the Mediterranean Sea, south of Sicily (Italy).

Vital statistics

Birth rate per 1,000 population (2003): 10.1 (world avg. 21.3); legitimate 83.2%. **Death rate** per 1,000 population (2003): 7.9 (world avg. 9.1). **Natural increase rate** per 1,000 population (2003): 2.2 (world avg. 12.2). **Total fertility rate** (avg. births per childbearing woman; 2003): 1.5. **Marriage rate** per 1,000 population (2003): 6.1. **Life expectancy** at birth (2003): male 76.3 years; female 80.8 years.

National economy

Budget (2001). *Revenue:* Lm 797,400,000 (social security 22.5%; income tax 20.9%; value-added tax 14.4%; grants and loans 13.6%). *Expenditures:* Lm 766,700,000 (recurrent expenditures 80.2%, of which social security 24.1%, education 6.1%; capital expenditure 10.5%; public debt service 9.3%). **Public debt** (2001): $616,000,000. **Production** (metric tons except where noted). *Agriculture, forestry, fishing* (2002): vegetables 49,200 (of which melons 12,800, tomatoes 7,400, onions 4,392, cabbage 3,900, garlic 551), potatoes 27,500, wheat 9,600; livestock (number of live animals; 2002) 79,300 pigs, 18,000 cattle, 6,600 sheep; fish catch (2003) 1,070. *Quarrying* (2002): small quantities of limestone and salt. *Manufacturing* (value added in $'000,000; 1998): telecommunications equipment and electronics 149; food products 69; wearing apparel 63. *Energy production (consumption):* electricity (kW-hr; 2000) 1,875,000,000 (1,875,000,000); coal (2000) none (325,000); petroleum products (2000) none (677,-000). **Population economically active** (1998): total 144,824; activity rate of total population 38.4% (participation rates: ages 15–64 [1985] 45.9%; female 27.6%; unemployed [2001] 6.1%). **Household income and expenditure.** Average household size (2001) 3.1; average annual income per household (1982) Lm 4,736; sources of income (1993): wages

and salaries 63.8%, professional and unincorporated enterprises 19.3%, rents, dividends, and interest 16.9%; expenditure (2000): food and beverages 36.6%, transportation and communications 23.4%, recreation, entertainment, and education 9.4%, household furnishings and operations 7.6%. **Tourism** (2002): receipts from visitors $568,000,000; expenditures by nationals abroad $153,000,000. **Gross national product** (2003): $3,678,000,000 ($9,260 per capita). **Land use** as % of total land area (2000): in temporary crops 25%, in permanent crops 3%; overall forest area, negligible.

Foreign trade

Imports (2000-c.i.f.): Lm 1,492,400,000 (electronic microcircuits 37.3%, refined petroleum 7.0%, chemicals and chemical products 6.9%, food 6.0%). *Major import sources* (2001): Italy 17.3%; France 10.3%; Singapore 8.3%; Japan 7.6%; UK 7.5%. **Exports** (2000-f.o.b.): Lm 1,072,400,000 (electronic microcircuits 62.1%, apparel and clothing accessories 5.9%, refined petroleum 4.4%, children's toys and games 4.3%). *Major export destinations* (2001): US 15.2%; Germany 13.4%; Singapore 11.6%; France 8.9%; UK 8.7%.

Transport and communications

Transport. *Roads* (1997): total length 1,961 km (paved 94%). *Vehicles* (2000): passenger cars 202,883; trucks and buses 52,604. *Air transport* (2001): passenger-km 2,364,000,000; (2000) metric ton-km cargo 14,292,000; airports (1999) with scheduled flights 1. **Communications,** in total units (units per 1,000 persons). Daily newspaper circulation (1996): 54,000 (145); radios (1997): 255,000 (680); televisions (2000): 217,000 (556); telephone main lines (2003): 208,300 (521); cellular telephone subscribers (2003): 290,000 (725); personal computers (2002): 101,000 (255); Internet users (2002): 120,000 (303).

Education and health

Educational attainment (2001). Percentage of population age 15 and over having: no formal schooling 4.3%; primary education 34.4%; general secondary 37.6%; vocational secondary 5.7%; some postsecondary 11.8%; undergraduate 5.4%; graduate 0.8%. **Literacy** (2000): total population age 15 and over literate 279,000 (92.1%). **Health** (1996): physicians 925 (1 per 403 persons); hospital beds 2,140 (1 per 174 persons); infant mortality rate per 1,000 live births (2003) 4.0. **Food** (2001): daily per capita caloric intake 3,495 (vegetable products 73%, animal products 27%); 141% of FAO recommended minimum.

Military

Total active duty personnel (2003): 2,140 (army 100%). **Military expenditure as percentage of GNP** (1999): 0.8% (world 2.4%); per capita expenditure $73.

Background

Inhabited as early as 3800 BC, Malta was ruled by the Carthaginians from the 6th century BC until it came

---

1 metric ton = about 1.1 short tons;   1 kilometer = 0.6 mi (statute);   1 metric ton-km cargo = about 0.68 short ton-mi cargo;   c.i.f.: cost, insurance, and freight;   f.o.b.: free on board

under Roman control in 218 BC. In AD 60 the apostle Paul converted the inhabitants to Christianity. It was under Byzantine rule until the Arabs seized control in 870. In 1091 the Normans defeated the Arabs, and Malta was ruled by feudal lords until it came under the Knights of Malta in 1530. Napoleon seized control in 1798, the British took it in 1800, and it was returned to the knights in 1802. The Maltese protested and acknowledged the British as sovereign, an arrangement ratified in 1814. It became self-governing in 1921 but reverted to a colonial regime in 1936. Malta was severely bombed by Germany and Italy during World War II, and in 1942 it received the George Cross, Britain's highest civilian decoration. In 1964 it gained independence within the Commonwealth, and in 1974 became a republic. When its alliance with Britain ended in 1979, Malta proclaimed its neutral status.

Recent Developments

Malta's membership in the EU added to its problem of illegal immigration from Africa, mostly from Libya. Meetings between five European and five African countries were held in Malta in 2005 and 2006 to discuss the issue. Joint naval patrols by EU countries began in late 2006 but were not allowed into Libyan waters. Conditions for immigrants were poor in the small Maltese detention centers, leading to protests and at least two breakouts in 2006.

Internet resources: <www.mol.net.mt>.

Marshall Islands

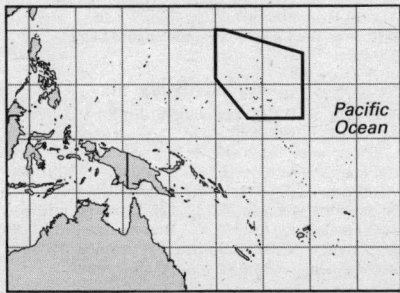

Official name: Majol (Marshallese); Republic of the Marshall Islands (English). **Form of government:** unitary republic with two legislative houses (Council of Iroij [12; advisory body only]; Nitijela [33]). **Head of state and government:** President Kessai Note (from 2000). **Capital:** Majuro (Rita). **Official languages:** Marshallese (Kajin-Majol); English. **Official religion:** none. **Monetary unit:** 1 US dollar (US$) = 100 cents.

Demography

Area: 70.05 sq mi, 181.43 sq km. **Population** (2006): 60,400. **Density** (2006): persons per sq mi 862.9, persons per sq km 333.7. **Urban** (2004): 65.0%. **Sex distribution** (2003): male 51.07%; female 48.93%. **Age breakdown** (2003): under 15, 39.2%; 15–29, 30.7%; 30–44, 16.4%; 45–59, 9.6%; 60–74, 3.1%; 75 and over, 1.0%. **Ethnic composition** (nationality; 2000): Marshallese 88.5%; US white

6.5%; other Pacific islanders and East Asians 5.0%. **Religious affiliation** (1995): Protestant 62.8%; Roman Catholic 7.1%; Mormon 3.1%; Jehovah's Witness 1.0%; other 26.0%. **Major towns** (1999): Majuro (Rita) 19,300; Ebeye 9,300; Laura 2,300; Ajeltake 1,200; Enewetak 820. **Location:** Oceania, group of atolls and reefs in the North Pacific Ocean, halfway between Hawaii and Papua New Guinea.

Vital statistics

Birth rate per 1,000 population (2003): 34.2 (world avg. 21.3). **Death rate** per 1,000 population (2003): 5.0 (world avg. 9.1). **Natural increase rate** per 1,000 population (2003): 29.2 (world avg. 12.2). **Total fertility rate** (avg. births per childbearing woman; 2003): 4.1. **Life expectancy** at birth (2003): male 67.4 years; female 71.4 years.

National economy

Budget (2002). *Revenue:* $83,600,000 (US government grants 70.3%, tax revenue 22.2%, nontax revenue 7.5%). *Expenditures:* $74,000,000 (current expenditure 79.3%, capital expenditure 20.7%). **Public debt** (external, outstanding; 1996–97): $124,900,-000. **Production** (metric tons except as noted). *Agriculture, forestry, fishing* (value of production for household consumption in $'000; 1999): fish 3,920; pork 1,496; breadfruit 646; fish catch (2002) 38,242, of which skipjack 37,057. *Mining and quarrying:* for local construction only. *Manufacturing* (2002): copra 2,653; coconut oil and processed (chilled or frozen) fish are important products; the manufacture of handicrafts and personal items (clothing, mats, boats, etc.) by individuals is also significant. *Energy production (consumption):* electricity (kW-hr; 2002) 79,764,000 (79,764,000). **Household income and expenditure.** Average household size (2000) 7.8; annual median income per household (1999) $6,840; expenditure (2003): food 35.9%, housing and energy 17.1%, transportation 13.7%, education and communication 6.6%, clothing 4.3%. **Gross national product** (2003): $143,000,000 ($2,710 per capita). **Population economically active** (1999): total 14,677; activity rate of total population 28.9% (participation rates: over age 15, 51.1%; female 34.1%; unemployed 30.9%). **Tourism** (2002): receipts $4,000,000. **Land use** as % of total land area (2000): in temporary crops 17%, in permanent crops 39%, in pasture 22%.

Foreign trade

Imports (2000-c.i.f.): $68,200,000 (mineral fuels and lubricants 43.6%; machinery and transport equipment 16.9%; food, beverages, and tobacco 10.9%). *Major import sources:* US 61.4%; Japan 5.1%; Australia 2.0%; Hong Kong 1.9%; Taiwan 1.3%. **Exports** (2000-f.o.b.): $7,300,000 (copra cake 16.2%; crude coconut oil 14.7%; aquarium fish 6.2%). *Major export destinations:* US 71%; other 29%.

Transport and communications

Transport. *Roads:* only Majuro and Kwajalein have paved roads. *Vehicles* (2002): passenger cars 1,910; trucks and buses 193. *Air transport* (2001; Air Marshall Islands only): passenger-km 24,972,000; metric ton-km cargo 183,000; airports (2002) 32. **Communications**, in total units (units per 1,000 persons).

Telephone main lines (2003): 4,500 (83); cellular telephone subscribers (2003): 600 (11); personal computers (2002): 3,000 (56); Internet users (2003): 1,400 (26).

Education and health

Educational attainment (1999). Percentage of population age 25 and over having: no formal schooling 3.1%; elementary education 35.5%; secondary 46.5%; some higher 12.3%; undergraduate degree 1.7%; advanced degree 0.9%. Literacy (latest): total population age 15 and over literate 19,377 (91.2%); males literate 9,993 (92.4%); females literate 9,384 (90.0%). Health: physicians (1997) 34 (1 per 1,452 persons); hospital beds (2002) 140 (1 per 380 persons); infant mortality rate per 1,000 live births (2003) 31.6.

Military

The US provides for the defense of the Republic of the Marshall Islands under the 1984 and 2003 compacts of free association.

Background

The islands were sighted in 1529 by the Spanish navigator Álvaro Saavedra. Germany purchased them from Spain in 1899, and Japan seized them in 1914. During World War II the US took Kwajalein and Enewetak, and the Marshall Islands were made part of a UN trust territory under US jurisdiction in 1947. Bikini and Enewetak atolls served as testing grounds for US nuclear weapons from 1946 to 1958. The country became an internally self-governing republic in 1979. In 1986 it became fully self-governing when it entered into a Compact of Free Association with the US, which was renewed in 2003.

Recent Developments

The Marshall Islands was one of six Pacific countries that continued to recognize Taiwan in 2006; the country received an $800,000 Taiwanese grant in that year to establish a microcredit facility. A Chinese company, meanwhile, began new construction in 2007 at a tuna-processing plant that had previously employed 600 people.

Internet resources: <http://marshall.csu.edu.au>.

Martinique

Official name: Département de la Martinique (Department of Martinique). Political status: overseas department (France) with two legislative houses (General Council [45]; Regional Council [41]). Chief of state: President Nicolas Sarkozy of France (from 2007). Head of government: Prefect (for France) Yves Dassonville (from 2004); President of the General Council (for Martinique) Claude Lise (from 1992). Capital: Fort-de-France. Official language: French. Official religion: none. Monetary unit: 1 euro (€) = 100 cents; valuation (1 Jul 2007) US$1 = €0.74; at conversion on 1 Jan 2002, €1 = 6.56 French francs (F).

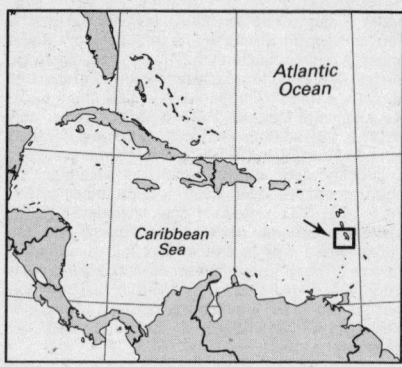

Demography

Area: 436 sq mi, 1,128 sq km. Population (2006): 400,000. Density (2006): persons per sq mi 917.4, persons per sq km 354.6. Urban (2001): 95.2%. Sex distribution (2001): male 49.47%; female 50.53%. Age breakdown (2001): under 15, 23.1%; 15–29, 23.3%; 30–44, 26.3%; 45–59, 13.8%; 60–74, 9.1%; 75 and over, 4.4%. Ethnic composition (2000): mixed race (black/white/Asian) 93.4%; French (metropolitan and Martinique white) 3.0%; East Indian 1.9%; other 1.7%. Religious affiliation (1995): Roman Catholic 86.5%; Protestant 8.0% (mostly Seventh-day Adventist); Jehovah's Witness 1.6%; other 3.9%, including Hindu, syncretist, and nonreligious. Major communes (1999): Fort-de-France 94,049; Le Lamentin 35,460; Le Robert 21,201; Schoelcher 20,845; Sainte-Marie 20,058. Location: island in Atlantic Ocean and the Caribbean Sea, between Dominica and Saint Lucia.

Vital statistics

Birth rate per 1,000 population (2003): 15.0 (world avg. 21.3); (1997) legitimate 31.8%. Death rate per 1,000 population (2003): 6.4 (world avg. 9.1). Natural increase rate per 1,000 population (2003): 8.6 (world avg. 12.2). Total fertility rate (avg. births per childbearing woman; 2003): 1.8. Marriage rate per 1,000 population (1999): 4.2. Divorce rate per 1,000 population (1999): 0.9. Life expectancy at birth (2003): male 79.3 years; female 78.2 years.

National economy

Budget (1999). Revenue: F 1,298,000,000 (general receipts from French central government and local administrative bodies 45.0%; tax receipts 34.0%, of which indirect taxes 19.5%, direct taxes 14.5%). Expenditures: F 1,298,000,000 (health and social assistance 42.0%; wages and salaries 16.7%; other administrative services 7.2%; debt amortization 5.0%). Public debt (1994): $186,700,000. Production (metric tons except as noted). Agriculture, forestry, fishing (2002): bananas 303,800, sugarcane 207,000, pineapples 18,000; livestock (number of live animals) 35,000 pigs, 34,000 sheep, 25,000 cattle; roundwood (2001) 12,000 cu m; fish catch (2001) 6,251. Mining and quarrying (2001): salt 200,000, pumice 130,000. Manufacturing (2002): cement

1 metric ton = about 1.1 short tons; 1 kilometer = 0.6 mi (statute); 1 metric ton-km cargo = about 0.68 short ton-mi cargo; c.i.f.: cost, insurance, and freight; f.o.b.: free on board

(2001) 220,000; sugar 5,340; rum 91,629 hecto-liters. *Energy production (consumption):* electricity (kW-hr; 2000) 1,085,000,000 (1,085,000,000); crude petroleum (barrels; 2000) none (6,000,000); petroleum products (2000) 751,000 (575,000). **Household income and expenditure.** Average household size (1999) 3.0; annual net income per household (1997) €29,516; sources of income (1997): wages and salaries 49.0%, inheritance or endowment 16.4%, self-employment 14.7%, other 19.9%; expenditure (1993): food and beverages 32.1%, transportation and communications 20.7%, housing and energy 10.6%, household durable goods 9.4%, clothing and footwear 8.0%. **Tourism** (2001): receipts from visitors $237,000,000; number of visitors 654,000. **Gross domestic product** (2000): $5,064,-000,000 ($13,160 per capita). **Population economically active** (1998): total 165,900; activity rate of total population 43.7% (participation rates: ages 15–64, 70.7%; female 45.9%; unemployed [March 2003] 22.2%). **Land use** as % of total land area (2000): in temporary crops 10%, in permanent crops 9%, in pasture 11%; overall forest area 44%.

Foreign trade

Imports (2001-c.i.f.): €1,878,000,000 (consumer goods 20%, processed foods, beverages, and tobacco 18%, automobiles 12%). *Major import sources* (2000): France 63.5%; Venezuela 5.8%; Germany 3.9%; Italy 3.1%; Netherlands Antilles 2.3%. **Exports** (2001-f.o.b.): €274,000,000 (bananas 35%, processed foods and beverages [significantly rum] 21%, machinery and apparatus 15%, refined petroleum 9%). *Major export destinations* (2000): France 57.8%; Guadeloupe 21.4%; French Guiana 3.7%; UK 3.4%; Belgium 2.7%.

Transport and communications

Transport. *Roads* (1994): total length 2,077 km (paved [1988] 75%). *Vehicles* (1998): passenger cars 147,589; trucks and buses 35,615. *Air transport* (2001): passenger arrivals 706,929, passenger departures 701,597; cargo loaded 5,656 metric tons; cargo unloaded 9,303 metric tons; airports (2000) 1. **Communications,** in total units (units per 1,000 persons). Daily newspaper circulation (1996): 32,000 (83); radios (1997): 82,000 (213); televisions (1999): 66,000 (168); telephone main lines (2001): 172,192 (417); cellular telephone subscribers (2002): 319,900 (790); personal computers (2001): 52,000 (130); Internet users (2001): 40,000 (100).

Education and health

Educational attainment (1990). Percentage of population age 25 and over having: incomplete primary, or no declaration 54.3%; primary education 18.0%; secondary 20.0%; higher 7.7%. **Health** (2000): physicians 762 (1 per 507 persons); hospital beds 2,674 (1 per 144 persons); infant mortality rate per 1,000 live births (2003) 7.4. **Food** (1998): daily per capita caloric intake 2,865 (vegetable products 75%, animal products 25%); 118% of FAO recommended minimum.

Military

Total active duty personnel (2004): 4,100 French troops.

Background

Carib Indians, who had ousted earlier Arawak inhabitants, resided on the island when Christopher Columbus visited it in 1502. In 1635 the French established a colony there. The British captured and held the island in 1762–63 and again during the Napoleonic Wars, but each time it was returned to France. Made a department of France in 1946, Martinique remains under French rule despite a 1970s independence movement.

Recent Developments

Martinique in September 2006 was the scene of demonstrations by nationals of neighboring Saint Lucia, who were protesting new French immigration laws that, they claimed, targeted them unfairly. The protesters alleged that Saint Lucians who had lived in Martinique for as many as 30 years were being denied extensions to their resident visas.

Internet resources: <www.martinique.org>.

Mauritania

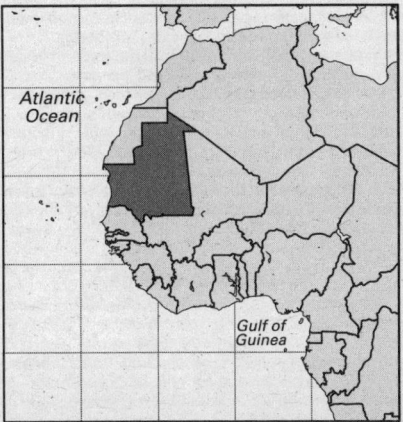

Official name: Al-Jumhuriyah al-Islamiyah al-Muritaniyah (Islamic Republic of Mauritania). **Form of government:** unitary multiparty republic with two legislative houses (Senate [56]; National Assembly [81]). **Head of state and government:** President Sidi Muhammad Ould Cheikh Abdallahi (from 2007), assisted by Prime Minister Zeine Ould Zeidane (from 2007). **Capital:** Nouakchott. **Official language:** Arabic (Arabic, Fulani, Soninke, and Wolof are national languages). **Official religion:** Islam. **Monetary unit:** 1 ouguiya (UM) = 5 khoums; valuation (1 Jul 2007) US$1 = UM 266.91.

Demography

Area: 398,000 sq mi, 1,030,700 sq km. **Population** (2006): 3,158,000. **Density** (2006): persons per sq mi 7.9, persons per sq km 3.1. **Urban** (2000): 57.7%. **Sex distribution** (2000): male 49.51%; female 50.49%. **Age breakdown** (2000): under 15, 43.9%; 15–29, 27.0%; 30–44, 15.9%; 45–59, 7.7%; 60–74, 4.3%; 75 and over, 1.2%. **Ethnic composition**

(1993): Moor 70% (of which about 40% "black" Moor [Haratin, or African Sudanic] and about 30% "white" Moor [Bidan, or Arab-Berber]); other black African 30% (mostly Wolof, Tukulor, Soninke, and Fulani). **Religious affiliation** (2000): Sunni Muslim 99.1%; traditional beliefs 0.5%; Christian 0.3%; other 0.1%. **Major cities** (2000): Nouakchott 558,195; Nouadhibou 72,337; Rosso 48,922; Boghé 37,531; Adel Bagrou 36,007. **Location:** northern Africa, bordering Western Sahara (annexed by Morocco), Algeria, Mali, Senegal, and the North Atlantic Ocean.

Vital statistics

Birth rate per 1,000 population (2003): 42.1 (world avg. 21.3). **Death rate** per 1,000 population (2003): 13.0 (world avg. 9.1). **Natural increase rate** per 1,000 population (2003): 29.1 (world avg. 12.2). **Total fertility rate** (avg. births per childbearing woman; 2003): 6.1. **Life expectancy** at birth (2003): male 49.7 years; female 54.1 years.

National economy

Budget (2002). *Revenue:* UM 101,000,000,000 (fishing royalties 51.2%; tax revenue 38.7%, of which taxes on goods and services 19.3%, income taxes 12.0%, import taxes 6.2%; revenue from public enterprises 4.8%; capital revenue 2.3%; other 3.0%). *Expenditures:* UM 84,400,000,000 (current expenditure 62.1%, of which goods and services 25.6%, wages and salaries 15.4%, interest on public debt 9.8%, defense 5.8%; capital expenditure 37.9%). **Land use** as % of total land area (2000): in temporary crops 0.5%, in permanent crops 0.01%, in pasture 38.3%; overall forest area 0.3%. **Production** (metric tons except as noted). *Agriculture, forestry, fishing* (2002): rice 67,900, millet 51,500, sorghum 25,405; livestock (number of live animals) 7,600,000 sheep, 5,100,000 goats, 1,500,000 cattle; roundwood (2001) 1,470,448 cu m; fish catch (2001) 83,596, of which octopuses 20,308. *Mining and quarrying* (gross weight; 2002): iron ore 9,553,000; gypsum 100,000. *Manufacturing* (value added in $'000,000; 1997): food, beverages, and tobacco products 5.2; machinery, transport equipment, and fabricated metals 3.8; bricks, tiles, and cement 1.6. *Energy production (consumption):* electricity (kW-hr; 2002) 263,972,000 (191,893,000); coal (2000) none (6,000); crude petroleum (barrels; 2000) none (7,147,000); petroleum products (2000) 860,000 (961,000). **Population economically active** (2001): total 786,000; activity rate of total population 30.9% (participation rates: over age 10 [1991] 45.5%; female [1994] 22.9%; unemployed [1999] 21.0%). **Households.** Average household size (2000): 5.3; expenditure (1990): food and beverages 73.1%, clothing and footwear 8.1%, energy and water 7.7%, transportation and communications 2.0%. **Gross national product** (2003): $1,163,000,000 ($430 per capita). **Public debt** (external, outstanding; 2002): $1,984,-000,000. **Tourism** (1999): receipts $28,000,000; expenditures $55,000,000.

Foreign trade

Imports (2002): $418,000,000 (capital goods 26.0%; petroleum products 25.8%; food products 12.8%; vehicles and parts 9.3%; construction materials 9.1%). *Major import sources:* France 20.8%; Belgium-Luxembourg 8.8%; Spain 6.7%; Germany 5.6%; Italy 4.2%. **Exports** (2002): $330,300,000 (iron ore 55.6%; fish 43.4%, of which cephalopods 29.0%). *Major export destinations:* Italy 14.8%; France 14.4%; Spain 12.1%; Germany 10.8%; Belgium-Luxembourg 10.3%; Japan 6.4%.

Transport and communications

Transport. *Railroads* (2000): route length 717 km; passenger-km, negligible; (2000) metric ton-km cargo 7,766,000,000. *Roads* (1999): total length 7,891 km (paved 26%). *Vehicles* (1999): passenger cars 9,900; trucks and buses 17,300. *Air transport* (1999; data represent ¹/₁₁ of the total scheduled traffic of Air Afrique; Air Afrique was declared bankrupt in February 2002): passenger-km 290,000,000; metric ton-km cargo (1998) 13,524,000; airports (1997) with scheduled flights 9. **Communications,** in total units (units per 1,000 persons). Daily newspaper circulation (1996): 1,000 (0.4); radios (1997): 360,000 (147); televisions (1999): 247,000 (100); telephone main lines (2002): 31,500 (12); cellular telephone subscribers (2003): 300,000 (109); personal computers (2002): 29,000 (11); Internet users (2002): 10,000 (3.7).

Education and health

Educational attainment (2000). Percentage of population age 6 and over having: no formal schooling 43.9%; no formal schooling but literate 2.5%; Islamic schooling 18.4%; primary education 37.3%; lower secondary 5.3%; upper secondary 4.6%; higher technical 0.4%; higher 1.7%. **Literacy** (2000): percentage of total population age 10 and over literate 52.5%; males literate 60.1%; females literate 45.3%. **Health:** physicians (1994) 200 (1 per 11,085 persons); hospital beds (1988) 1,556 (1 per 1,217 persons); infant mortality rate per 1,000 live births (2003) 73.8. **Food** (2001): daily per capita caloric intake 2,764 (vegetable products 84%, animal products 16%); 120% of FAO recommended minimum.

Military

Total active duty personnel (2003): 15,750 (army 95.2%, navy 3.2%, air force 1.6%). **Military expenditure as percentage of GNP** (1999): 4.0% (world 2.4%); per capita expenditure $14.

Background

Inhabited in ancient times by Sanhadja Berbers, in the 11th and 12th centuries Mauritania was the center of the Berber Almoravid movement, which imposed Islam. Arab tribes arrived in the 15th century and formed powerful confederations; the Portuguese also arrived then. France gained control of the coast in 1817 and in 1903 made the territory a protectorate. In 1904 it was added to French West Africa, and later it became a colony. In 1960 Mauritania achieved independence. Its first president was ousted in a 1978 military coup. After a series of military rulers, in 1991 a new constitution was adopted, and multiparty elections were held in 1992. During

---

1 metric ton = about 1.1 short tons;   1 kilometer = 0.6 mi (statute);   1 metric ton-km cargo = about 0.68 short ton-mi cargo;   c.i.f.: cost, insurance, and freight;   f.o.b.: free on board

the 1990s relations between the government and opposition groups deteriorated, even as there was some success in liberalizing the economy.

Recent Developments

Dissident Mauritanian army officers staged a bloodless coup on 3 Aug 2005, with Col. Ely Ould Mohamed Vall emerging as the country's leader. He proposed a referendum on constitutional reforms, including shortening presidents' terms and imposing presidential age limits, that were supported by 96% of voters in 2006. Vall pledged to step down after elections in 2007. In February 2006 the country began pumping oil from offshore fields. More oil discoveries were expected.

Internet resources: <www.ami.mr/fr/defaultfr.htm>.

Mauritius

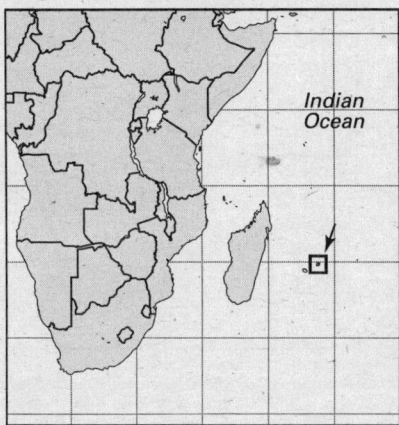

Indian
Ocean

Official name: Republic of Mauritius. **Form of government:** republic with one legislative house (National Assembly [70, including 8 "bonus" seats allocated to minor parties]). **Chief of state:** President Sir Anerood Jugnauth (from 2003). **Head of government:** Prime Minister Navin Ramgoolam (from 2005). **Capital:** Port Louis. **Official language:** English. **Official religion:** none. **Monetary unit:** 1 Mauritian rupee (Mau Re; plural Mau Rs) = 100 cents; valuation (1 Jul 2007) US$1 = Mau Rs 31.53.

Demography

Area: 788 sq mi, 2,040 sq km. **Population** (2006): 1,255,000. **Density** (2006): persons per sq mi 1,592.6, persons per sq km 615.2. **Urban** (2002): 42.5%. **Sex distribution** (2003): male 49.49%; female 50.51%. **Age breakdown** (2000): under 15, 25.2%; 15–29, 26.0%; 30–44, 24.8%; 45–59, 14.9%; 60–74, 6.8%; 75 and over, 2.3%. **Ethnic composition** (2000): Indo-Pakistani 67.0%; Creole (mixed Caucasian, Indo-Pakistani, and African) 27.4%; Chinese 3.0%; other 2.6%. **Religious affiliation** (2000): Hindu 49.6%; Christian 32.2%, of which Roman Catholic 23.6%; Muslim 16.6%; Buddhist 0.4%; other 1.2%. **Major urban areas** (2000): Port Louis

144,303; Beau Bassin-Rose Hill 103,872; Vacoas-Phoenix 100,066; Curepipe 78,920; Quatre Bornes 75,884. **Location:** island in the Indian Ocean, east of Madagascar.

Vital statistics

Data from 2003 exclude Agalega. **Birth rate** per 1,000 population (2003): 16.3 (world avg. 21.3). **Death rate** per 1,000 population (2003): 6.7 (world avg. 9.1). **Natural increase rate** per 1,000 population (2003): 9.6 (world avg. 12.2). **Total fertility rate** (avg. births per childbearing woman; 2003): 1.9. **Marriage rate** per 1,000 population (2003): 8.5. **Divorce rate** per 1,000 population (2003): 0.9. **Life expectancy** at birth (2003): male 68.6 years; female 75.5 years.

National economy

Budget (2001–02). *Revenue:* Mau Rs 28,319,-500,000 (tax revenue 82.2%, of which taxes on goods and services 39.2%, import duties 20.8%, income tax 12.6%; nontax revenue 16.2%; grants 1.1%). *Expenditures:* Mau Rs 33,385,800,000 (social security 21.8%; government services 18.1%; education 15.4%; economic services 12.3%; interest on debt 10.6%; health 8.7%). **Tourism** (2001): receipts from visitors $612,000,000; expenditures by nationals abroad $204,000,000. **Public debt** (external, outstanding; 2002): $832,000,000. **Gross national product** (2003): $5,012,000,000 ($4,090 per capita). **Production** (metric tons except as noted). *Agriculture, forestry, fishing* (2002): sugarcane 4,874,000, vegetables 21,000, roots and tubers 15,000; livestock (number of live animals) 93,000 goats, 28,000 cattle, 14,000 pigs; roundwood (2001) 17,000 cu m; fish catch (2001) 10,753. *Manufacturing* (value added in Mau Rs '000,000; 2001): apparel 9,651; food products 2,757; beverages and tobacco 1,717. *Energy production (consumption):* electricity (kW-hr; 2000) 1,777,000,000 (1,777,-000,000); coal (2000) none (254,000); petroleum products (2000) none (724,000). **Population economically active** (2002): total 541,100; activity rate of total population 44.7% (participation rates: ages 15 and over, 59.8%; female 34.6%; unemployed 9.7%). **Household income and expenditure.** Average household size (2000) 4.2; annual income per household (2001–02) Mau Rs 170,784; sources of income (1990): salaries and wages 48.4%, entrepreneurial income 41.2%, transfer payments 10.4%; expenditure (2001–02): food and nonalcoholic beverages 31.9%, transportation 12.7%, housing and energy 9.4%, alcoholic beverages and tobacco products 9.1%, clothing and footwear 6.4%. **Land use** as % of total land area (2000): in temporary crops 49%, in permanent crops 3%, in pasture 3%; overall forest area 8%.

Foreign trade

Imports (2001-c.i.f.): Mau Rs 57,940,000,000 (fabrics and yarn 18.3%; food and live animals 14.3%; machinery and apparatus 14.3%; refined petroleum 9.5%; transport equipment 8.1%). *Major import sources:* South Africa 13.9%; France 9.3%; India 7.9%; China 7.1%; Germany 5.4%. **Exports** (2001-f.o.b.): Mau Rs 47,511,000,000 (domestic exports 91.8%, of which clothing 54.4%, sugar 18.0%, fabric, yarn, and made-up articles 4.7%; reexports 4.1%; ships' stores and bunkers 4.1%). *Major export destinations:* UK

31.3%; US 20.3%; France 18.7%; Madagascar 6.1%; Italy 3.8%.

Transport and communications

Transport. *Roads* (1998): total length 1,905 km (paved 93%). *Vehicles* (2002): passenger cars 61,885; trucks and buses 13,892. *Air transport* (2003; Air Mauritius only): passenger-km 5,213,-000,000; metric ton-km cargo 194,510,000; airports (1998) with scheduled flights 1. **Communications,** in total units (units per 1,000 persons). Daily newspaper circulation (2000): 84,300 (71); radios (2000): 450,000 (379); televisions (2000): 318,000 (268); telephone main lines (2003): 348,200 (285); cellular telephone subscribers (2003): 462,400 (379); personal computers (2002): 180,000 (149); Internet users (2003): 150,000 (123).

Education and health

Educational attainment (2000). Percentage of population age 25 and over having: no formal education 12.3%; primary 44.1%; lower secondary 23.2%; upper secondary/some higher 17.3%; complete higher 2.6%; unknown 0.5%. **Literacy** (2000): percentage of total population age 12 and over literate 85.1%; males literate 88.7%; females literate 81.6%. **Health** (2003): physicians 1,172 (1 per 1,043 persons); hospital beds 3,827 (1 per 320 persons); infant mortality rate per 1,000 live births 13.2. **Food** (2001): daily per capita caloric intake 2,995 (vegetable products 86%, animal products 14%); 132% of FAO recommended minimum.

Military

Total active duty personnel (2003): none; however, a special 2,000-person paramilitary force ensures internal security. **Military expenditure as percentage of GNP** (1999): 0.2% (world 2.4%); per capita expenditure $7.

Did you know? In early 2005, Mauritius launched an initiative to make it the first country in the world to achieve complete wireless broadband access.

Background

The island was visited by the Portuguese in the early 16th century. The Dutch took possession in 1598 and made attempts to settle it (1638–58 and 1664–1710) before abandoning it to pirates. The French East India Company occupied Mauritius in 1721 and administered it until the French government took over in 1767. Sugar production allowed the colony to prosper. The British captured the island in 1810 and were granted formal control in 1814. In the late 19th century, competition from beet sugar and the opening of the Suez Canal caused an economic decline. After World War II, Mauritius adopted political and economic reforms, and in 1968 it became an independent state within the Commonwealth. In 1992 it became a republic. It experienced political unrest during the 1990s.

Recent Developments

Pres. Anerood Jugnauth threatened in 2007 to pull Mauritius out of the Commonwealth over the question of the sovereignty of the Chagos Archipelago (British Indian Ocean Territory), which included Diego Garcia, an atoll that the British had cleared of all inhabitants (the Ilois) after having purchased the islands from Mauritius in 1965 and leased to the US for a naval support base. Many of the Ilois lived in poverty in Mauritius. A ruling in 2006 held that they had the right to return.

Internet resources: <www.mauritius.net>.

Mayotte

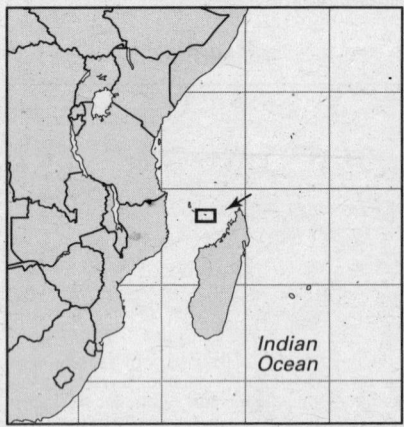

Indian Ocean

Official name: Collectivité Départementale de Mayotte (Departmental Collectivity of Mayotte); known as Mahoré or Maore in Shimaoré, the local Swahili-based language. **Political status:** overseas dependency of France with one legislative house (General Council [19]); claimed by Comoros since 1975. **Chief of state:** President of France Nicolas Sarkozy (from 2007). **Head of government:** President of the General Council Said Omar Oili (from 2004). **Capital:** Mamoudzou. **Official language:** French. **Official religion:** none. **Monetary unit:** 1 euro (€) = 100 cents; valuation (1 Jul 2007) US$1 = €0.74; at conversion on 1 Jan 2002, €1 = 6.56 French francs (F).

Demography

Area: 144.1 sq mi, 373.3 sq km. **Population** (2006): 188,000. **Density** (2006): persons per sq mi 1,305.6, persons per sq km 502.7. **Sex distribution** (2002): male 50.10%; female 49.90%. **Age breakdown** (2002): under 15, 42.0%; 15–29, 29.0%; 30–44, 17.0%; 45–59, 7.0%; 60 and over, 5.0%. **Place of birth** (2002): Mayotte (including 2–4% for metropolitan France) 65.6% (nearly all ethnic Comorian); nearby islands of the Comoros 33.1% (nearly all ethnic Comorian); other 1.3%. **Ethnic composition** (2000): Comorian (Mauri, Mahorais; a mixture of

---

1 metric ton = about 1.1 short tons;   1 kilometer = 0.6 mi (statute);   1 metric ton-km cargo = about 0.68 short ton-mi cargo;   c.i.f.: cost, insurance, and freight;   f.o.b.: free on board

Bantu, Arab, and Malagasy peoples) 92.3%; Swahili 3.2%; white (French) 1.8%; Makua 1.0%; other 1.7%. **Religious affiliation** (2000): Sunni Muslim 96.5%; Christian, principally Roman Catholic, 2.2%; other 1.3%. **Major communes** (2002): Mamoudzou 45,485; Koungou 15,383; Dzaoudzi 12,308. **Location:** island in the Indian Ocean, between the northern tip of Madagascar and the African mainland.

Vital statistics

Birth rate per 1,000 population (2003): 42.9 (world avg. 21.3). **Death rate** per 1,000 population (2003): 8.3 (world avg. 9.1). **Natural increase rate** per 1,000 population (2003): 34.6 (world avg. 12.2). **Total fertility rate** (avg. births per childbearing woman; 2003): 6.1. **Life expectancy** at birth (2003): male 58.5; female 62.8.

National economy

Budget (1997). *Revenue:* F 1,022,400,000 (1993; current revenue 68.8%, of which subsidies 40.0%, indirect taxes 16.8%, direct taxes 4.9%; development revenue 31.2%, of which loans 11.6%, subsidies 7.9%). *Expenditures:* F 964,200,000 (current expenditure 75.2%; development expenditure 24.8%). **Production** (metric tons except as noted). *Agriculture, forestry, fishing* (1997): bananas 30,200, cassava 10,000, cinnamon 27,533 kg; livestock (number of live animals; 1997) 25,000 goats, 17,000 cattle, 2,000 sheep; fish catch (1999) 1,502. *Manufacturing:* mostly processing of agricultural products and materials used in housing construction (including siding and roofing materials, joinery, and latticework). *Energy production (consumption):* electricity (kW-hr; 2002) 107,056,000 (107,056,000). **Tourism** (number of visitors; 2001): 35,000; receipts (1999) $10,000,000. **Population economically active** (1997): total 42,896; activity rate of total population 32.7% (participation rates: ages 15–64, 58.6%; female 43.4%; unemployed 41.5%). **Gross national product** (2000): $398,000,000 ($2,700 per capita). **Households.** Average household size (1997) 4.6; expenditure (1991): food 42.2%, clothing and footwear 31.5%, household furnishings 8.8%, energy and water 6.8%, transportation 5.1%.

Foreign trade

Imports (2002): €181,800,000 (food products 27.0%; machinery and apparatus 18.9%; transport equipment 16.1%; chemicals 8.7%; metals and metal products 7.4%). *Major import sources* (1997): France 66.0%; South Africa 14.0%; Asia 11.0%. **Exports** (2002): €6,300,000 (ylang-ylang 11.1%; vanilla 3.2%; unspecified commodities 85.7%). *Major export destinations* (1997): France 80.0%; Comoros 15.0%.

Transport and communications

Transport. *Roads* (1998): total length 233 km (paved 77%). *Vehicles* (1998): 8,213. *Air transport* (2002): passenger arrivals and departures 133,686; cargo unloaded and loaded 1,048 metric tons; airports (2002) with scheduled flights 1. **Communications,** in total units (units per 1,000 persons). Radios (1996): 50,000 (427); televisions (1999): 3,500 (30); telephone main lines (2001): 10,000 (70); cellular telephone subscribers (2002): 21,700 (147).

Education and health

Educational attainment (2002). Percentage of population age 15 and over having: no formal education 46%; primary education 25%; lower secondary 16%; upper secondary 8%; higher 5%. **Literacy** (1997): total population age 15 and over literate 63,053 (86.1%). **Health:** physicians (1997) 57 (1 per 2,304 persons); hospital beds 186 (1 per 706 persons); infant mortality rate per 1,000 live births (2003) 65.9.

Military

Total active duty personnel (2003): 3,600 French troops are assigned to Mayotte and Réunion.

Background

Originally inhabited by descendants of Bantu and Malayo-Indonesian peoples, Mayotte was converted to Islam by Arab invaders in the 15th century. Taken by a Malagasy tribe from Madagascar at the end of the 18th century, it came under French control in 1843. Together with the other Comoros islands and Madagascar, it became part of a single French overseas territory in the early 20th century. It has been administered separately since 1975, when the three northernmost islands of the Comoros declared independence.

Recent Developments

Illegal immigration, mostly from the nearby Comoros, continued to be one of the major problems facing Mayotte. It was estimated that one-third of the island's residents were illegal. In 2005 France threatened measures including withdrawing the right of French nationality based on birth—the single maternity ward on Mayotte was the busiest in all of France, as pregnant women risked their lives to give birth on French territory to French citizens.

Internet resources: <www.mayotte-tourisme.com>.

Mexico

Official name: Estados Unidos Mexicanos (United Mexican States). **Form of government:** federal republic with two legislative houses (Senate [128]; Chamber of Deputies [500]). **Head of state and government:** President Felipe Calderón Hinojosa (from 2006). **Capital:** Mexico City. **Official language:** Spanish. **Official religion:** none. **Monetary unit:** 1 Mexican peso (Mex$) = 100 centavos; valuation (1 Jul 2007) US$1 = Mex$10.79.

Demography

Area: 758,450 sq mi, 1,964,375 sq km. **Population** (2006): 104,038,000. **Density** (2006): persons per sq mi 137.2, persons per sq km 53.0. **Urban** (2002): 74.6%. **Sex distribution** (2002): male 48.82%; female 51.18%. **Age breakdown** (2000): under 15, 34.3%; 15–29, 28.5%; 30–44, 19.5%; 45–59, 10.5%; 60–74, 5.3%; 75 and over, 1.9%. **Ethnic composition** (2000): mestizo 64.3%; Amerindian 18.0%, of which detribalized 10.5%; Mexican white 15.0%; Arab 1.0%; Mexican black 0.5%; Spaniard 0.3%; US white 0.2%; other 0.7%. **Religious affiliation** (2000):

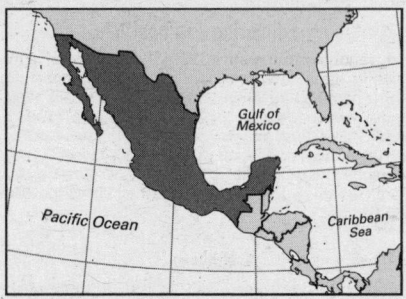

Roman Catholic 90.4%; Protestant (including Evangelical) 3.8%; other 5.8%. **Major cities** (2000): Mexico City 8,605,239 (urban agglomeration [2001] 18,268,000); Guadalajara 1,646,183 (urban agglomeration 3,697,000); Puebla 1,271,673 (urban agglomeration 1,888,000); Ciudad Netzahualcóyotl 1,225,083; Juárez 1,187,275; Tijuana 1,148,681; Monterrey 1,110,909 (urban agglomeration 3,267,-000); León 1,020,818; Mérida 662,530; Chihuahua 657,876. **Location:** middle America, bordering the US, the Gulf of Mexico, the Caribbean Sea, Belize, Guatemala, and the North Pacific Ocean. **Place of birth** (1990): 93.1% native-born; 6.9% foreign-born and unknown. **Households.** Total households (2000) 21,954,733; distribution by size (2000): 1 person 6.0%, 2 persons 12.3%, 3 persons 17.2%, 4 persons 21.8%, 5 persons 17.7%, 6 persons 10.9%, 7 or more persons 14.1%. **Emigration** (2000): legal immigrants into the US 173,900.

Vital statistics

Birth rate per 1,000 population (2003): 21.9 (world avg. 21.3). **Death rate** per 1,000 population (2003): 4.7 (world avg. 9.1). **Natural increase rate** per 1,000 population (2003): 17.2 (world avg. 12.2). **Total fertility rate** (avg. births per childbearing woman; 2002): 2.3. **Marriage rate** per 1,000 population (2001): 6.6. **Divorce rate** per 1,000 population (2001): 0.6. **Life expectancy** at birth (2003): male 71.9 years; female 77.6 years.

Social indicators

Access to services (2000). Proportion of dwellings having: electricity 94.8%; piped water supply 83.3%; drained sewage 76.2%. **Quality of working life.** Average workweek (1999): 44.4 hours (manufacturing only). Annual rate (1992) per 100,000 insured workers for: temporary disability 6,426; indemnification for permanent injury 239; death 18. Labor stoppages (2001): 35, involving 23,234 workers. **Social participation.** Eligible voters participating in last national election (July 2003): 41.7%. Practicing religious population in total affiliated population: national average of weekly attendance (1993) 11%. **Social deviance** (1991). Criminal cases tried by local authorities per 100,000 population for: murder 60.3; rape 22.4; other assault 301.0; theft 703.8. Incidence per 100,000 in general population of: alcoholism (2000) 7.6; drug and substance abuse 26.6; suicide (2001) 3.1.

National economy

Gross national product (2003): US$637,159,000,-000 (US$6,230 per capita). **Budget** (2001). *Revenue:* Mex$939,114,500,000 (income tax 30.4%, VAT 22.2%, royalties 21.7%, excise tax 11.8%, import duties 3.1%, other 10.8%). *Expenditures:* Mex$996,950,-600,000 (current expenditure 63.4%, of which social security and welfare 41.8%, interest on public debt 16.7%; capital expenditure 36.6%). **Public debt** (external, outstanding; 2002): US$76,327,000,000. **Tourism** (2002): receipts from visitors US$8,858,-000,000; expenditures by nationals abroad US$6,-060,000,000. **Production** (metric tons except as noted). *Agriculture, forestry, fishing* (2002): sugarcane 46,000,000, corn (maize) 17,500,000, sorghum 5,800,000, oranges 3,844,000, wheat 3,273,000, tomatoes 2,084,000, bananas 2,077,000, chilies and green peppers 1,756,000, lemons and limes 1,680,-000, dry beans 1,648,000, mangoes 1,413,000, watermelons 1,226,000, coconuts 959,000, avocados 897,000, barley 839,000, papayas 689,000, pineapples 585,000, grapes 446,000, carrots 379,000, coffee (green) 320,000, cauliflower 200,000; livestock (number of live animals) 30,600,000 cattle, 17,000,000 pigs, 9,400,000 goats, 8,100,000 ducks, 6,700,000 sheep, 6,255,000 horses, 5,850,000 turkeys, 3,280,000 mules, 3,260,000 asses, 520,-800,000 chickens; roundwood (2001) 45,156,000 cu m; fish catch (2001) 1,475,000. *Mining and quarrying* (2002): bismuth 1,126 (metal content; world rank: 1); celestite 94,015 (world rank: 1); silver 2,747,000 kg (metal content; world rank: 1); fluorite 622,000 (world rank: 2); cadmium 1,609 (metal content; world rank: 4); lead 138,700 (metal content; world rank: 5); gypsum 6,740,000 (world rank: 6); zinc 446,100 (metal content; world rank: 6); sulfur 1,460,000 (world rank: 9); copper 329,900 (metal content; world rank: 12); gold 21,324 kg (world rank: 19); iron ore 5,965,000 (metal content). *Manufacturing* (value added in US$'000,000; 2000): motor vehicles and parts 10,718; food products 8,883; paints, soaps, pharmaceuticals 7,044; beverages 5,422; bricks, cement, ceramics 3,580; iron and steel 2,891; paper and paper products 2,243; basic chemicals 1,682; fabricated metal products 1,518. *Energy production (consumption):* electricity (kW-hr; 2003) 263,488,000,000 ([2000] 229,747,000,000); hard coal (2000) 2,214,-000 (2,724,000); lignite (2000) 9,130,000 (9,570,-000); crude petroleum (barrels; 2003) 1,244,000,000 ([2000] 467,393,000); petroleum products (2000) 73,045,000 (87,048,000); natural gas (cu m; 2003) 47,377,000,000 ([2000] 36,953,000,000). **Household income and expenditure.** Average household size (2000) 4.4; income per household (2000) Mex$15,-762; sources of income (2000): wages and salaries 63.4%, property and entrepreneurship 23.6%, transfer payments 10.0%, other 2.9%; expenditure (2000): food, beverages, and tobacco 29.9%, transportation and communications 17.8%, education 17.3%, housing (includes household furnishings) 16.5%, clothing and footwear 5.8%. **Population economically active** (2001): total 39,682,800; activity rate of total population 39.9% (participation rates: ages 15–64 [1999] 63.4%; female 29.9%; unemployed [2002] 4.4%). **Land use** as % of total land area (2000): in temporary crops 13.0%, in permanent crops 1.3%, in pasture 41.9%; overall forest area 28.9%.

1 metric ton = about 1.1 short tons;   1 kilometer = 0.6 mi (statute);   1 metric ton-km cargo = about 0.68 short ton-mi cargo;   c.i.f.: cost, insurance, and freight;   f.o.b.: free on board

Foreign trade

Imports (2002): US$168,679,000,000 (non-maquiladora sector 64.8%, of which machinery and apparatus 18.9%, transport and communications equipment 13.0%, chemicals and chemical products 7.4%, processed food, beverages, and tobacco 3.7%; maquiladora sector 35.2%, of which electrical machinery, apparatus, and electronics 15.9%, non-electrical machinery and apparatus 5.4%, textiles and clothing 3.3%, rubber and plastic products 3.0%). *Major import sources:* US 63.2%; Japan 5.5%; China 3.7%; Germany 3.6%; Canada 2.7%; Taiwan 2.5%; South Korea 2.3%. **Exports** (2002): US$160,682,000,000 (non-maquiladora sector 51.4%, of which road vehicles and parts 16.0%, machinery and apparatus 8.9%, crude petroleum 8.2%; maquiladora sector 48.6%, of which electrical machinery, apparatus, and electronics 24.2%, nonelectrical machinery and apparatus 10.2%, textiles and clothing 4.3%). *Major export destinations:* US 89.0%; Canada 1.7%; South America 1.5%; Caribbean countries 1.4%; Central America 1.1%; Germany 0.9%; Spain 0.8%.

Transport and communications

Transport. *Railroads* (2003): route length 26,655 km; passenger-km 67,000,000; metric ton-km cargo 54,813,000,000. *Roads* (2003): total length 348,529 km (paved 33%). *Vehicles* (1999): passenger cars 9,842,006; trucks and buses 4,749,789. *Air transport* (2003; AeroMexico and Mexicana only): passenger-km 25,409,000,000; metric ton-km cargo 145,351,000,000; airports (2001) 85. **Communications,** in total units (units per 1,000 persons). Daily newspaper circulation (2000): 9,580,000 (98); radios (2000): 32,330,000 (330); televisions (2000): 27,700,000 (283); telephone main lines (2002): 14,941,600 (147); cellular telephone subscribers (2002): 25,928,000 (254); personal computers (2002): 8,353,000 (83); Internet users (2002): 10,033,000 (98).

Education and health

Educational attainment (2000). Population age 15 and over having: no primary education 10.3%; some primary 18.1%; completed primary 19.4%; incomplete secondary 5.3%; complete secondary 19.1%; some higher 16.8%; higher 11.0%. Literacy (2000): total population age 15 and over literate 91.4%; males literate 93.4%; females literate 89.5%. **Health** (2002): physicians 140,286 (1 per 734 persons); hospital beds 76,529 (1 per 1,346 persons); infant mortality rate per 1,000 live births (2002) 17.4. **Food** (2001): daily per capita caloric intake 3,160 (vegetable products 82%, animal products 18%); 136% of FAO recommended minimum.

Military

Total active duty personnel (2003): 192,770 (army 74.7%, navy 19.2%, air force 6.1%). **Military expenditure as percentage of GNP** (1999): 0.6% (world 2.4%); per capita expenditure $27.

Background

Inhabited for more than 20,000 years, Mexico produced great civilizations in AD 100–900, including the Olmec, Toltec, Mayan, and Aztec. The Aztec were conquered in 1521 by Spanish explorer Hernán Cortés, who established Mexico City on the site of the Aztec capital, Tenochtitlán. Francisco de Montejo conquered the remnants of Maya civilization in the mid-16th century, and Mexico became part of the viceroyalty of New Spain. In 1821 rebels negotiated a status quo independence from Spain, and in 1823 a new congress declared Mexico a republic. In 1845 the US voted to annex Texas, initiating the Mexican War. Under the Treaty of Guadalupe Hidalgo in 1848, Mexico ceded a vast territory in what is now the western and southwestern US. The Mexican government endured several rebellions and civil wars in the late 19th and early 20th centuries. During World War II it declared war on the Axis powers (1942), and in the postwar era it was a founding member of the UN (1945) and the Organization of American States (1948). In 1993 it ratified the North American Free Trade Agreement. The election of Vicente Fox to the presidency in 2000 ended 71 years of rule by the Institutional Revolutionary Party.

Recent Developments

The July presidential election was the focus of public debate in Mexico during 2006. Five candidates competed for the presidency, but the campaign centered on the bitter rivalry between Andrés Manuel López Obrador (Alliance for the Good of All), a popular former head of the Federal District government and the candidate who led in the public-opinion polls during much of the race, and Felipe Calderón, representing the incumbent center-right PAN (National Action Party). Calderón charged that López Obrador was "a danger for Mexico" and a Hugo Chávez-style populist whose social-justice programs would endanger the country's hard-won financial stability. Calderón sought to benefit from outgoing Pres. Vicente Fox's personal popularity by advocating continuity in economic policy. Although balloting occurred without major disruptions, the extremely close vote totals for Calderón and López Obrador quickly led to controversy. The Federal Electoral Institute announced that it would not release results of its national exit poll because the difference between the two leading candidates was within the sample's statistical margin of error, and first López Obrador and then Calderón claimed victory. A district-level tally several days later confirmed an extremely narrow lead for Calderón, but López Obrador demanded a ballot-by-ballot recount. At the same time, he announced a national campaign of peaceful civic resistance to bring public pressure on electoral authorities, and at the end of July his supporters blockaded one of Mexico City's main boulevards and occupied the public plaza facing the National Palace. In early September Calderón was declared president-elect after a final count gave him 36.7% of valid votes, compared with López Obrador's 36.1%. López Obrador refused to accept the decision. The prolonged controversy did not impact the Mexican stock market or overall economic performance. Gross domestic product grew by 4.7% in inflation-adjusted terms during the year, and consumer prices rose by only 3.6%. Mexico, the world's fifth largest oil producer, also continued to benefit from high international petroleum prices.

Internet resources: <www.visitmexico.com>.

Micronesia

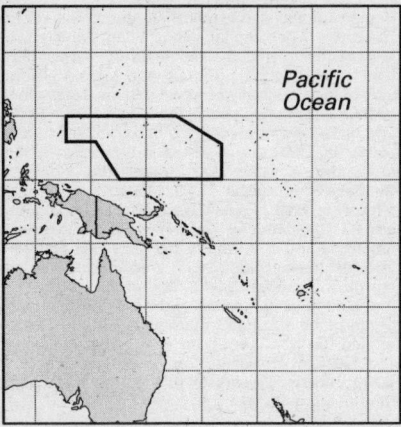

Pacific
Ocean

Official name: Federated States of Micronesia. **Form of government:** federal nonparty republic in free association with the US with one legislative house (Congress [14]). **Head of state and government:** President Emanuel Mori (from 2007). **Capital:** Palikir, on Pohnpei. **Official language:** none. **Official religion:** none. **Monetary unit:** 1 US dollar (US$) = 100 cents.

Demography

Area: 270.8 sq mi, 701.4 sq km. **Population** (2006): 108,000. **Density** (2006): persons per sq mi 398.5; persons per sq km 154.1. **Urban** (2000): 28.5%. **Sex distribution** (2000): male 50.64%; female 49.36%. **Age breakdown** (2000): under 15, 40.3%; 15–29, 28.4%; 30–44, 16.9%; 45–59, 9.1%; 60–74, 3.9%; 75 and over, 1.4%. **Ethnic composition** (2000): Chuukese/Mortlockese 33.6%; Pohnpeian 24.9%; Yapese 10.6%; Kosraean 5.2%; US white 4.5%; Asian 1.3%; other 19.9%. **Religious affiliation** (2000): Roman Catholic 52.7%; Protestant 41.7%, of which Congregational 40.1%; Mormon 1.0%; other/unknown 4.6%. **Major towns** (2000): Weno, in Chuuk state 13,900; Tol, in Chuuk state 9,500; Palikir, on Pohnpei 6,227; Kolonia, on Pohnpei 5,681; Colonia, on Yap 3,350. **Location:** Oceania, island group in the North Pacific Ocean, northeast of New Guinea.

Vital statistics

Birth rate per 1,000 population (2003): 26.5 (world avg. 21.3). **Death rate** per 1,000 population (2003): 5.1 (world avg. 9.1). **Natural increase rate** per 1,000 population (2003): 21.4 (world avg. 12.2). **Total fertility rate** (avg. births per childbearing woman; 2003): 3.5. **Life expectancy** at birth (2003): male 67.4 years; female 71.0 years.

National economy

Budget (2001–02). *Revenue:* $160,400,000 (external grants 71.2%, tax revenue 17.7%, nontax revenue [including fishing rights fees] 11.1%). *Expendi-*

tures: $154,800,000 (current expenditures 83.4%, capital expenditure 16.6%). **Public debt** (external, outstanding; 2000): $85,700,000. **Population economically active** (2000): total 37,414; activity rate of total population 35.0% (participation rates: ages 15–64, 61.7%; female 42.9%; unemployed 22.0%). **Production** (metric tons except as noted). *Agriculture, fishing* (2002): coconuts 140,000, cassava 11,800, sweet potatoes 3,000; livestock (number of live animals) 32,000 pigs, 13,900 cattle, 4,000 goats; fish catch (2001) 18,100, of which skipjack tuna 10,300, yellowfin tuna 5,300. *Mining and quarrying:* quarrying of sand and aggregate for local construction only. *Manufacturing:* n.a.; however, copra and coconut oil, traditionally important products, are being displaced by garment production; the manufacture of handicrafts and personal items (clothing, mats, boats, etc.) by individuals is also important. *Energy production (consumption):* electricity (kW-hr; 1997) 100,333,000 (100,333,000); petroleum products (1992) none (77,000). **Household income and expenditure.** Average household size (2000) 6.7; annual income per household $8,944 (median income: $4,618); sources of income (1994): wages and salaries 51.8%, operating surplus 23.0%, social security 2.1%; expenditure (1985): food and beverages 73.5%. **Land use** as % of total land area (2000): in temporary crops 6%, in permanent crops 46%, in pasture 16%; overall forest area 22%. **Gross national product** (at current market prices; 2003): $261,000,000 ($2,090 per capita). **Tourism** (2001): receipts from visitors $13,000,000.

Foreign trade

Imports (1999): $12,328,000 (food and live animals 24.8%, mineral fuels 20.3%, machinery and transport equipment 19.5%, beverages and tobacco products 6.0%). *Major import sources* (2000): US 43.9%; Australia 19.8%; Japan 12.5%. **Exports** (1999): $2,128,000 (fish 92.0%, bananas 1.2%). *Major export destinations* (1996): Japan 79.0%; US 18.3%.

Transport and communications

Transport. *Roads* (1990): total length 226 km (paved 17%). *Vehicles* (1998): passenger cars 2,044; trucks and buses 354. *Air transport:* airports (1997) with scheduled flights 4. **Communications,** in total units (units per 1,000 persons). Radios (1996): 70,000 (667); televisions (1999): 2,400 (21); telephone main lines (2001): 10,000 (93); cellular telephone subscribers (2002): 1,800 (150); Internet users (2000): 6,000 (51).

Education and health

Educational attainment (2000). Percentage of population age 25 and over having: no formal schooling 12.3%; primary education 37.0%; some secondary 18.3%; secondary 12.9%; some college 18.4%. **Literacy** (2000): total population age 10 and over literate 72,140 (92.4%); males literate 36,528 (92.9%); females literate 35,612 (91.9%). **Health** (1998): physicians 68 (1 per 1,677 persons); hospital beds (1997) 260 (1 per 447 persons); infant mortality rate per 1,000 live births (2003) 32.4.

1 metric ton = about 1.1 short tons;   1 kilometer = 0.6 mi (statute);   1 metric ton-km cargo = about 0.68 short ton-mi cargo;   c.i.f.: cost, insurance, and freight;   f.o.b.: free on board

Military

External security is provided by the US.

Background

The islands of Micronesia were probably settled by people from eastern Melanesia some 3,500 years ago. Europeans first landed on the islands in the 16th century. Spain took control of the islands in 1886, then sold them to Germany in 1899. The islands came under Japanese rule after World War I. They were captured by US forces during World War II, and in 1947 they became a UN trust territory administered by the US. The group of islands centered on the Caroline Islands became an internally self-governing federation in 1979. In 1986 Micronesia entered into a Compact of Free Association with the US, which was amended in 2003. In the late 1990s the republic was struggling to solve its economic difficulties.

Recent Developments

The Federated States of Micronesia (FSM) signed the Pacific Island Countries Trade Agreement at the first China–Pacific Island Countries Economic Development and Cooperation Forum in April 2006. This action, intended to lessen the FSM's reliance on its Compact of Free Association with the US, made the country the 11th signatory to the agreement. At the forum China announced grants in the amount of $2.5 million to the FSM as well as the country's inclusion on China's official list of approved tourist destinations.

Internet resources: <www.fsmgov.org>.

Moldova

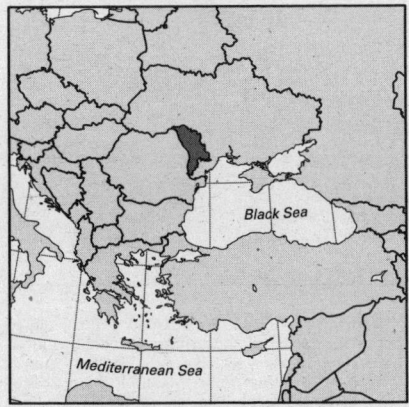

Black Sea

Mediterranean Sea

Official name: Republica Moldova (Republic of Moldova). **Form of government:** unitary parliamentary republic with a single legislative body (Parliament [101]). **Head of state:** President Vladimir Voronin (from 2001). **Head of government:** Prime Minister Vasile Tarlev (from 2001). **Capital:** Chisinau. **Official language:** Romanian (constitutionally designated as Moldovan). **Official religion:** none. **Monetary unit:** 1

Moldovan leu (plural lei) = 100 bani; valuation (1 Jul 2007) free rate, US$1 = 12.37 Moldovan lei.

Demography

Area: 13,067 sq mi, 33,843 sq km. **Population** (2006): 4,192,000 (includes Moldovans working abroad). **Density** (2006): persons per sq mi 320.8, persons per sq km 123.9. **Urban** (2002): 45.3%. **Sex distribution** (2002): male 47.84%; female 52.16%. **Age breakdown** (2001): under 15, 22.4%; 15–29, 25.5%; 30–44, 21.1%; 45–59, 16.6%; 60–74, 11.0%; 75 and over, 3.4%. **Ethnic composition** (2000): Moldovan 48.2%; Ukrainian 13.8%; Russian 12.9%; Bulgarian 8.2%; Rom (Gypsy) 6.2%; Gagauz 4.2%; other 6.5%. **Religious affiliation** (1995): Orthodox 46.0%, of which Romanian Orthodox 35.0%, Russian Orthodox 9.5%; Muslim 5.5%; Catholic 1.8%, of which Roman Catholic 0.6%; Protestant 1.7%; Jewish 0.9%; other (mostly nonreligious) 44.1%. **Major cities** (2003; includes Moldovans working abroad): Chisinau 662,400; Tiraspol 185,000; Balti 145,900; Tighina 125,000; Râbnita 62,000. **Location:** eastern Europe, bordering Ukraine and Romania.

Vital statistics

Birth rate per 1,000 population (2002): 9.9 (world avg. 21.3); (1995) legitimate 87.7%. **Death rate** per 1,000 population (2002): 11.5 (world avg. 9.1). **Natural increase rate** per 1,000 population (2002): –1.6 (world avg. 12.2). **Total fertility rate** (avg. births per childbearing woman; 2002): 1.7. **Marriage rate** per 1,000 population (2002): 6.0. **Life expectancy** at birth (2002): male 60.6 years; female 69.4 years.

National economy

Budget (2002). *Revenue:* 6,611,000,000 lei (value-added tax 30.8%; social fund contributions 24.9%; excise taxes 9.9%; personal income tax 7.1%; profits tax 6.5%; duties and customs taxes 5.0%). *Expenditures:* 7,057,000,000 lei (current expenditures 95.3%, of which social fund expenditures 26.9%, education 17.6%, interest payments 6.9%, health care 11.2%; capital expenditure 4.7%). **Production** (metric tons except as noted). *Agriculture, forestry, fishing* (2002): corn (maize) 1,192,770, wheat 1,122,270, sugar beets 1,116,034; livestock (number of live animals) 834,870 sheep, 448,898 pigs, 404,845 cattle; roundwood (2001) 56,800 cu m; fish catch (2001) 1,576. *Mining and quarrying* (2000): sand and gravel 277,000; gypsum 32,100. *Manufacturing* (value of production in $'000,000; 1998; excludes Transnistria [Stonga Nistruli]): food products 299; beverages 194; tobacco products 44. *Energy production (consumption):* electricity (kW-hr; 2000) 3,110,000,000 (5,095,000,000); coal (2000) none (180,000); petroleum products (2000) none (409,000); natural gas (cu m; 2000) none (2,519,000,000). **Population economically active** (2003): total 1,473,580; activity rate of total population 34.8% (participation rates: female [2001] 50.1%; unemployed 7.9%). **Gross national product** (2003): $2,137,000,000 ($590 per capita). **Public debt** (external, outstanding; 2002): $846,000,000. **Tourism** (2002): receipts from visitors $47,000,000; expenditures by nationals abroad $86,000,000. **Household income and expenditure.** Average household size (2002) 3.3; annual average income per household

(2002) $1,200; sources of income (1994): wages and salaries 41.2%, social benefits 15.3%, agricultural income 10.4%, other 33.1%; expenditure (2001): food and drink 40.4%, housing 13.5%, utilities 10.5%, transportation 8.9%, clothing 7.6%, health 3.9%. **Land use** as % of total land area (2000): in temporary crops 55.1%, in permanent crops 10.7%, in pasture 11.7%; overall forest area 9.9%.

Foreign trade

Imports (2002): $1,103,000,000 (mineral products 21.7%; machinery and apparatus 14.0%; chemicals and chemical products 10.7%; textiles 10.0%). *Major import sources:* Ukraine 20.4%; Russia 15.3%; Romania 11.4%; Germany 9.2%; Italy 7.5%. **Exports** (2002): $710,000,000 (processed food, beverages [significantly wine], and tobacco products 37.8%; textiles and wearing apparel 16.7%; vegetables, fruits, seeds, and nuts 15.0%). *Major export destinations:* Russia 35.4%; Ukraine 9.1%; Italy 9.1%; Romania 8.4%; Germany 7.4%.

Transport and communications

Transport. *Railroads* (2000): length 2,710 km; passenger-km 315,000,000; metric ton-km cargo 1,513,000,000. *Roads* (2000): total length 12,691 km (paved 86%). *Vehicles* (2001): passenger cars 256,500. *Air transport* (2003; Air Moldova only): passenger-km 238,000,000; metric ton-km cargo 540,-000; airports (2001) 1. **Communications,** in total units (units per 1,000 persons). Daily newspaper circulation (2000): 660,000 (154); radios (2000): 3,250,000 (758); televisions (2000): 1,270,000 (297); telephone main lines (2002): 706,900 (161); cellular telephone subscribers (2002): 338,200 (77); personal computers (2002): 77,000 (18); Internet users (2002): 150,000 (34).

Education and health

Literacy (2000): total population age 15 and over literate 98.9%; males literate 99.5%; females literate 98.3%. **Health** (2001): physicians 12,800 (1 per 334 persons); hospital beds 25,000 (1 per 171 persons); infant mortality rate per 1,000 live births (2002) 41.6. **Food** (2001): daily per capita caloric intake 2,766 (vegetable products 86%, animal products 14%); 108% of FAO recommended minimum.

Military

Total active duty personnel (2003): 6,910 (army 84.1%, air force 15.9%). Opposition forces in Transnistria (excluding militia; 2003) c. 9,500. **Military expenditure as percentage of GNP** (1999): 1.6% (world 2.4%); per capita expenditure $10.

Background

Moldova, once part of the principality of Moldavia, was founded by the Vlachs in the 14th century. In the mid-16th century it was under Ottoman rule. In 1774 it came under Russian control and lost portions of its territory. In 1859 it joined with the principality of Walachia to form the state of Romania, and in 1918 some of the territory it had ceded earlier also joined Romania. Romania was compelled to cede some of the Moldavian area to Russia in 1940, and that area combined with what Russia already controlled to become the Moldavian SSR. In 1991 Moldavia declared independence from the Soviet Union. It adopted the Romanian spelling of Moldova after having legitimized (1989) the use of the Roman rather than the Cyrillic alphabet. During the 1990s the country struggled to find economic equilibrium.

Recent Developments

In 2006 Moldovan Pres. Vladimir Voronin continued his pro-Western foreign policy. Russia, which had imported 80% of Moldova's wine, the country's chief export, reacted by imposing a total ban on such trade in March. In the first six months of 2006, Russia also doubled the price of natural gas sold to Moldova. Russia continued to station troops in the breakaway Transnistria, where much of the country's industry was located. In September Transnistrian authorities carried out a referendum in which 97.1% of those voting backed independence, though Western observers drew attention to irregularities in the poll. An improvement in relations with Russia seemed likely after Moldova signed an agreement in late December that removed one of the last hurdles to Russia's joining the World Trade Organization.

Internet resources: <www.turism.md>.

Monaco

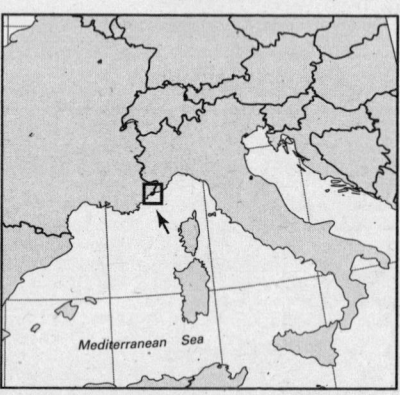

Official name: Principauté de Monaco (Principality of Monaco). **Form of government:** constitutional monarchy with one legislative body (National Council [24]). **Chief of state:** Prince Albert II (from 2005). **Head of government:** Minister of State Jean-Paul Proust (from 2005). **Capital:** no separate area is distinguished as such. **Official language:** French. **Official religion:** Roman Catholicism. **Monetary unit:** 1 euro (€) = 100 centimes; valuation (1 Jul 2007) US$1 = €0.74; at conversion on 1 Jan 2002, €1 = 6.56 French francs (F).

---

1 metric ton = about 1.1 short tons;   1 kilometer = 0.6 mi (statute);   1 metric ton-km cargo = about 0.68 short ton-mi cargo;   c.i.f.: cost, insurance, and freight;   f.o.b.: free on board

Demography

Area: 0.76 sq mi, 1.97 sq km. **Population** (2006): 32,800. **Density** (2006): persons per sq mi 43,157.9, persons per sq km 16,649.7. **Urban** (2000): 100%. **Sex distribution** (2000): male 48.54%; female 51.4%. **Age breakdown** (2000): under 15, 13.2%; 15–29, 13.4%; 30–44, 22.1%; 45–59, 22.4%; 60–74, 17.4%; 75 and over, 11.5%. **Ethnic composition** (2000): French 45.8%; Ligurian (Genoan) 17.2%; Monegasque 16.9%; British 4.5%; Jewish 1.7%; other 13.9%. **Religious affiliation** (2000): Christian 93.2%, of which Roman Catholic 89.3%; Jewish 1.7%; nonreligious and other 5.1%. **Location:** western Europe, bordering the Mediterranean Sea and France.

Vital statistics

Birth rate per 1,000 population (2003): 9.5 (world avg. 21.3). **Death rate** per 1,000 population (2003): 12.8 (world avg. 9.1). **Natural increase rate** per 1,000 population (2003): –3.3 (world avg. 12.2). **Total fertility rate** (avg. births per childbearing woman; 2003): 1.8. **Marriage rate** per 1,000 population (2002): 5.4. **Divorce rate** per 1,000 population (2002): 2.1. **Life expectancy** at birth (2003): male 75.4 years; female 83.4 years.

National economy

Budget (2001). *Revenue:* €624,254,804 (value-added taxes 50%, state-run monopolies 20%). *Expenditures:* €621,041,725 (current expenditure 65.5%, capital expenditure 34.5%). **Production**. *Agriculture, forestry, fishing:* some horticulture and greenhouse cultivation; no agriculture as such. *Manufacturing* (value of export sales in €'000,000; 2001): chemicals, cosmetics, perfumery, and pharmaceuticals 347; plastic products 179; light electronics and precision instruments 81. *Energy production (consumption):* electricity (kW-hr; 2001), n.a. (475,000,000 [imported from France]). **Gross national product** (2002): $849,000,000 ($26,300 per capita). **Population economically active** (2001): total 39,543, of which Monegasque 3,471, foreign workers 36,072; female participation in labor force 42.4%. **Households.** Average household size (1998) 2.2. **Tourism** (2002): 2,191 hotel rooms; 263,000 overnight stays; 3 casinos run by the state attract 400,000 visitors annually. **Land use** as % of total land area (2000): public gardens 20%.

Foreign trade

Data exclude trade with France; Monaco has participated in a customs union with France since 1963. **Imports** (2001): €394,000,000 (consumer goods and parts for industrial production [including pharmaceuticals, perfumes, clothing, publishing] 23.8%, food products 22.6%, transport equipment and parts 20.0%). *Major import sources:* EEC 64.0%; US, Japan, Switzerland, and Norway 11.6%; African countries 8.8%. **Exports** (2001): €403,000,000 (rubber and plastic products, glass, construction materials, organic chemicals, and paper and paper products 31.4%, products of automobile industry 21.4%, consumer goods 17.0%). *Major export destinations:* EEC 63.5%; US, Japan, Switzerland, and Norway 10.6%; African countries 8.6%.

Transport and communications

Transport. *Railroads* (2001): length 1.7 km; passengers 2,171,100; cargo 3,357 tons. *Roads* (2001): total length 50 km (paved 100%). *Vehicles* (1997): passenger cars 21,120; trucks and buses 2,770. *Air transport:* airports with scheduled flights, none; fixed-wing service is provided at Nice, France; helicopter service is available at Fontvieille. **Communications,** in total units (units per 1,000 persons). Daily newspaper circulation (1999): 10,000 (300); radios (1997): 34,000 (1,030); televisions (1997): 25,000 (758); telephone main lines (2002): 33,700 (1,040); cellular telephone subscribers (2002): 19,300 (596); Internet users (2002): 16,000 (494).

Education and health

Literacy: virtually 100%. **Health** (2002): physicians 156 (1 per 207 persons); hospital beds 521 (1 per 62 persons); infant mortality rate per 1,000 live births (2003) 5.6. **Food:** daily per capita caloric intake, n.a.; assuming consumption patterns similar to France (2000) 3,591 (vegetable products 62%, animal products 38%); 143% of FAO recommended minimum.

Military

Defense responsibility lies with France according to the terms of the Versailles Treaty of 1919.

 **Did you know?**

Monaco is the second smallest country in the world and the smallest country in the United Nations. Its area covers only two square kilometers.

Background

Inhabited since prehistoric times, Monaco was known to the Phoenicians, Greeks, Carthaginians, and Romans. In 1191 the Genoese took possession of it; in 1297 the reign of the Grimaldi family began. The Grimaldis allied themselves with France except for the period 1524–1641, when they were under the protection of Spain. France annexed Monaco in 1793, and it remained under French control until the fall of Napoleon, when the Grimaldis returned. In 1815 it was put under the protection of Sardinia. A treaty in 1861 called for the sale of the towns of Menton and Roquebrune to France and the establishment of Monaco's independence. Monaco is one of Europe's most luxurious resorts. In 1997 the 700-year rule of the Grimaldis, then under Prince Rainier III, was celebrated.

Recent Developments

In 2006 Monaco focused on environmental issues, especially global warming. In February it ratified the Kyoto Protocol on climate change. Following the successful reclamation of land from the sea some years earlier, a new project envisioned building an island off Monte Carlo.

Internet Resources: <www.visitmonaco.com>.

Mongolia

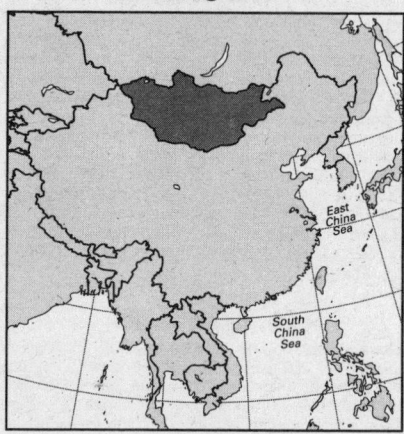

Official name: Mongol Uls (Mongolia). **Form of government:** unitary multiparty republic with one legislative house (State Great Hural [76]). **Chief of state:** President Nambaryn Enkhbayar (from 2005). **Head of government:** Prime Minister Miyeegombo Enkhbold (from 2006). **Capital:** Ulaanbaatar (Ulan Bator). **Official language:** Khalkha Mongolian. **Official religion:** none. **Monetary unit:** 1 tugrik (Tug) = 100 mongo; valuation (1 Jul 2007) US$1 = Tug 1,164.

Demography

Area: 603,930 sq mi, 1,564,160 sq km. **Population** (2006): 2,580,000. **Density** (2006): persons per sq mi 4.3, persons per sq km 1.6. **Urban** (2002): 56.4%. **Sex distribution** (2002): male 49.53%; female 50.47%. **Age breakdown** (2002): under 15, 32.7%; 15–29, 31.4%; 30–44, 21.2%; 45–59, 9.2%; 60–69, 3.4%; 70 and over, 2.1%. **Ethnic composition** (2000): Khalkha Mongol 81.5%; Kazakh 4.3%; Dörbed Mongol 2.8%; Bayad 2.1%; Buryat Mongol 1.7%; Dariganga Mongol 1.3%; Zakhchin 1.3%; Tuvan (Uriankhai) 1.1%; other 3.9%. **Religious affiliation** (1995): Tantric Buddhist (Lamaism) 96.0%; Muslim 4.0%. **Major cities** (2000): Ulaanbaatar (Ulan Bator) 760,077; Erdenet 68,310; Darhan 65,791; Choybalsan 41,714; Ulaangom 26,319. **Location:** north-central Asia, bordering Russia and China.

Vital statistics

Birth rate per 1,000 population (2003): 21.4 (world avg. 21.3); legitimate 82.2%. **Death rate** per 1,000 population (2003): 7.2 (world avg. 9.1). **Natural increase rate** per 1,000 population (2003): 14.2 (world avg. 12.2). **Total fertility rate** (avg. births per childbearing woman; 2003): 2.3. **Marriage rate** per 1,000 population (2001): 5.1. **Divorce rate** per 1,000 population (2001): 1.5. **Life expectancy** at birth (2003): male 61.6 years; female 66.1 years.

National economy

Budget (2002). *Revenue:* Tug 466,527,000,000 (taxes 76.4%, of which VAT 25.2%, income tax 15.2%, social security contributions 11.4%, customs duties 11.2%; nontax revenue 23.6%). *Expenditures:* Tug 536,549,300,000 (education, health, social services 52.3%; wages 19.6%; capital investment 11.9%; interest 3.3%; other 12.9%). **Public debt** (external; 2002): $950,400,000. **Tourism** (2002): receipts $167,000,000; expenditures $119,000,000. **Population economically active** (2002): total 872,600; activity rate of total population 35.7% (participation rates: ages 15 and over 62.2%; female 49.8%; unemployed 4.6%). **Production** (metric tons except as noted). *Agriculture, forestry, fishing* (2002): wheat 149,336, potatoes 65,560, vegetables and melons 45,000; livestock (number of live animals) 11,937,300 sheep, 8,858,000 goats, 3,100,000 horses; roundwood (2001) 631,000 cu m; fish catch (2001) 117. *Mining and quarrying* (2002): copper 376,300; fluorspar concentrate 159,800; molybdenum 3,384. *Manufacturing* (value added by manufacturing in Tug '000,000; 2001): textiles 82,486; food and beverages 81,319; clothing and apparel 23,007. *Energy production (consumption):* electricity (kW-hr; 2001) 3,017,000,000 (3,213,000,000); hard coal (2000) 833,000 (876,000); lignite (2000) 4,178,000 (4,177,000); petroleum products (2000) none (420,000). **Gross national product** (2003): $1,188,000,000 ($480 per capita). **Household income and expenditure** (2001): Average household size 4.4; annual income per household Tug 1,226,000; sources of income: wages 29.2%, self-employment 28.6%, transfer payments 8.0%, other 34.2%; expenditure: food 42.5%, clothing 16.2%, transportation and communications 7.8%, education 7.1%, housing 6.8%, health care 1.7%. **Land use** as % of total land area (2000): in temporary crops 0.7%, in permanent crops, negligible, in pasture 82.5%; overall forest area 6.8%.

Foreign trade

Imports (2002): $659,000,000 (machinery and apparatus 19.5%, food and agricultural products 19.0%, mineral fuels 18.6%, textiles and clothing 12.7%). *Major import sources:* Russia 34.1%; China 24.4%; South Korea 12.2%; Japan 6.2%; Germany 4.5%. **Exports** (2002): $500,900,000 (2001; copper concentrate 28.1%, gold 14.3%, cashmere [all forms] 13.4%, fluorspar 3.8%). *Major export destinations* (2002): China 42.4%; US 31.6%; Russia 8.6%; South Korea 4.4%; Australia 3.5%.

Transport and communications

Transport. *Railroads* (2001): length 1,815 km; passenger-km (2001): 1,062,200,000; metric ton-km cargo 5,287,900,000. *Roads* (2001): total length 49,250 km (paved 4%). *Vehicles* (2001): passenger cars 53,200; trucks and buses 36,600. *Air transport* (2001): passenger-km 538,900,000; metric ton-km cargo 9,500,000; airports with scheduled flights 1. **Communications,** in total units (units per 1,000 persons). Daily newspaper circulation (1996): 68,000 (27); radios (2000): 368,000 (154); televisions (2002): 189,600 (79); telephone main lines

(2002): 128,000 (53); cellular telephone subscribers (2002): 216,000 (89); personal computers (2002): 69,000 (21); Internet users (2002): 50,000 (28).

Education and health

Educational attainment (2000). Percentage of population age 10 and over having: no formal education 11.6%; primary education 23.5%; secondary 46.1%; vocational secondary 11.2%; higher 7.6%. **Literacy** (2000): percentage of total population age 15 and over literate 98.9%; males literate 99.1%; females literate 98.8%. **Health** (2001): physicians 6,639 (1 per 365 persons); hospital beds 18,100 (1 per 135 persons); infant mortality rate per 1,000 live births (2003) 23.8. **Food** (2001): daily per capita caloric intake 1,974 (vegetable products 60%, animal products 40%); 81% of FAO recommended minimum.

Military

Total active duty personnel (2003): 8,600 (army 87.2%, air force 12.8%). **Military expenditure as percentage of GNP** (1999): 2.1% (world 2.4%); per capita expenditure $5.

Did you know? The Gobi ("waterless place" in Mongolian) is a great desert and semidesert region of Central Asia. Much of the Gobi is not sandy desert but bare rock. Cars may drive over this surface for long distances in any direction.

Background

In Neolithic times Mongolia was inhabited by small groups of nomads. During the 3rd century BC it became the center of the Xiongnu empire. Turkic-speaking peoples held sway in the 4th–10th centuries AD. In the early 13th century Genghis Khan united the Mongol tribes and conquered central Asia. His successor, Ogodei, conquered the Chin dynasty of China in 1234. Kublai Khan established the Yuan, or Mongol, dynasty in China in 1279. After the 14th century the Ming dynasty of China confined the Mongols to their homeland in the steppes; later they became part of the Chinese Ch'ing dynasty. Inner Mongolia was incorporated into China in 1644. After the fall of the Ch'ing dynasty in 1911, Mongol princes declared Mongolia's independence from China, and in 1921 Russian forces helped drive off the Chinese. The Mongolian People's Republic was established in 1924 and recognized by China in 1946. The nation adopted a new constitution in 1992 and shortened its name to Mongolia.

Recent Developments

Mongolia's government was voted out of office in early January 2006, and Mongolian People's Revolutionary Party Chairman Miyeegombo Enkhbold was elected prime minister. Draft amendments to the 1997 Minerals Law, introduced in the Great Hural in December 2005, caused disquiet among foreign investors in Mongolia's mining industry and also sections of the public. A new redaction of the law,

adopted in July, gave the government the right to acquire up to 50% of the resources of deposits discovered with the help of state funds and gave local people in proposed mining areas more powers over exploitation licenses.

Internet resources: <www.mongoliatourism.gov.mn>.

Montenegro

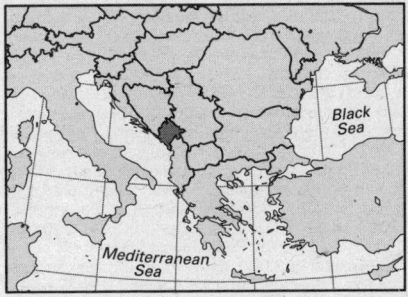

Official name: Republika Crna Gora (Republic of Montenegro). **Form of government:** multiparty republic with one legislative house (Parliament [81, including 5 seats reserved for the Albanian community]). **Chief of state:** President Filip Vujanovic (from 2003). **Head of government:** Prime Minister Zeljko Sturanovic (from 2006). **Capital:** Cetinje. **Administrative center:** Podgorica. **Official language:** Montenegro Serbian (of the iekavian dialect). **Official religion:** none. **Monetary unit:** 1 euro (€) = 100 cents; valuation (1 Jul 2007) US$1 = €0.74; Montenegro uses the euro as its official currency, even though it is not a member of the EU.

Demography

Area: 5,333 sq mi, 13,812 sq km. **Population** (2006): 624,000. **Density** (2006): persons per sq mi 117.0, persons per sq km 45.2. **Urban** (2003): 56.1%. **Sex distribution** (2003): male 49.22%; female 50.78%. **Age breakdown** (2003): under 15, 20.6%; 15–29, 23.1%; 30–44, 20.5%; 45–59, 18.2%; 60–74, 12.8%; 75 and over, 3.9%; unknown 0.9%. **Ethnic composition** (2003): Montenegrin 43.2%; Serb 32.0%; Bosniac/Muslim 11.8%; Albanian 5.0%; undeclared 4.0%; other 4.0%. **Religious affiliation** (2000): Eastern Orthodox c. 45%; Muslim c. 16%; Roman Catholic c. 5%; Protestant/independent Christian c. 5%; nonreligious/atheist c. 16%; unknown c. 13%. **Major cities** (2003): Podgorica 136,473; Niksic 58,212; Pljevlja 21,377; Bijelo Polje 15,883; Cetinje 15,137. **Location:** southeastern Europe, bordering Croatia, Bosnia and Herzegovina, Serbia, Albania, and the Mediterranean Sea.

Vital statistics

Birth rate per 1,000 population (2004): 12.6 (world avg. 21.1). **Death rate** per 1,000 population (2004): 9.2 (world avg. 9.0). **Natural increase rate** per 1,000 population (2004): 3.4 (world avg. 12.1). **Total fertility rate** (avg. births per childbearing woman; 2003): 1.82. **Life expectancy** at birth (2003; Serbia and Montenegro): male 70.0 years; female 75.2 years.

National economy

Budget (2005). *Revenue:* €581,034,440 (tax revenue 67.9%, of which VAT and excise taxes 44.6%, income tax 11.5%, taxes on international trade 7.1%; nontax revenue 32.1%). *Expenditures:* €543,420,-083 (wages and salaries 28.7%; transfers 22.3%; debt service 21.3%). **Public debt** (external, outstanding; January 2006): $605,639,000. **Production** (metric tons except as noted). *Agriculture, forestry, fishing* (2005): potatoes 132,830, grapes 36,960, tomatoes (2004) 22,818; livestock (number of live animals) 254,000 sheep, 169,000 cattle, 27,000 pigs; roundwood (2004; state forests only) 184,200 cu m; fisheries production 1,236. *Mining and quarrying* (2005): bauxite 672,345; sea salt 15,000. *Manufacturing* (value added in €'000; 2002): base metals and fabricated metal products (mostly of aluminum) 61,170; food products, beverages, and tobacco 40,648; paper products, publishing, and printing 8,090. *Energy production (consumption):* electricity (kW-hr; 2005) 2,864,000,000 (n.a.); hard coal (2004) n.a. (63,900); lignite (2005) 1,290,000 ([2004] 1,420,000). **Population economically active** (2004): total 259,092; activity rate 41.1% (participation rates: over age 15, 51.7%; female 43.1%; unemployed [2005] 27.7%). **Household** (2005). Average household size 3.4; average annual income per household €5,511 ($6,854); sources of income: wages and salaries 59.6%, transfer payments 20.9%, agriculture 8.7%; expenditure: food 42.3%, housing 12.1%, transportation 8.6%, clothing and footwear 7.0%, communications 5.7%, household furnishings 4.9%. **Tourism** (2005): receipts $267,529,000; expenditures $12,781,000. **Land use** as % of total land area (2002): in temporary crops 3.3%, in permanent crops 1.0%, in pasture 33.0%; overall forest area 39.5%.

Foreign trade

Imports (2005): €940,344,000 (machinery and transportation equipment 22.3%, of which motor vehicles 6.1%; mineral fuels and lubricants 15.6%; food and live animals 15.6%; household equipment 15.1%; chemicals and chemical products 8.7%; beverages and tobacco 3.6%). *Major import sources:* Serbia (including Kosovo) 34.8%; Italy 9.2%; Slovenia 7.1%; Croatia 7.0%; Greece 5.6%; Germany 4.9%. **Exports** (2005): €434,458,000 (aluminum 42.9%; machinery and transportation equipment 11.7%; food and live animals 8.3%; beverages and tobacco 7.1%; wood and wood products 4.1%; chemicals and chemical products 2.7%; mineral fuels and lubricants 2.1%). *Major export destinations:* Serbia (including Kosovo) 36.8%; Italy 27.3%; Greece 9.1%; Slovenia 6.8%; Bosnia and Herzegovina 5.3%).

Transport and communications

Transport. *Railroads* (2005): length 250 km; passenger-km 122,920,000; metric ton-km cargo 132,782,000. *Roads* (2005): total length 7,353 km (paved 58%). *Air transport* (2005): passengers 697,740. **Communications,** in total units (units per 1,000 persons). Daily newspaper circulation (2004): 73,000 (118); telephone main lines (2005):

177,663 (285); cellular telephone subscribers (2005): 543,220 (873); Internet users (2004): 50,000 (81).

Education and health

Educational attainment (2003). Percentage of population age 15 and over having: no formal education/unknown 6.4%; incomplete primary education 9.6%; complete primary 23.0%; secondary 21.5%; vocational/technical 26.9%; higher 12.6%. **Literacy** (2003): total population age 20 and over literate 97.3%; males literate 99.2%; females literate 95.5%. **Health** (2004): physicians 1,239 (1 per 501 persons); hospital beds 4,079 (1 per 152 persons); infant mortality rate per 1,000 live births 7.8. **Food** (2004; Serbia and Montenegro): daily per capita caloric intake 2,776 (vegetable products 67%, animal products 33%); 109% of FAO recommended minimum.

Military

Total active duty personnel (2006): n.a. **Military expenditure as percentage of GDP** (2005): n.a.; per capita expenditure, n.a.

Background

The Kingdom of the Serbs, Croats, and Slovenes was created after the collapse of Austria-Hungary at the end of World War I. The country signed treaties with Czechoslovakia and Romania in 1920–21, marking the beginning of the Little Entente. In 1929 an absolute monarchy was established, the country's name was changed to Yugoslavia, and it was divided into regions without regard to ethnic boundaries. Axis powers invaded Yugoslavia in 1941, and German, Italian, Hungarian, and Bulgarian troops occupied it for the rest of World War II. In 1945 the Socialist Federal Republic of Yugoslavia was established; it included the republics of Bosnia and Herzegovina, Croatia, Macedonia, Montenegro, Serbia, and Slovenia. Its independent form of communism under Josip Broz Tito's leadership provoked the USSR. Internal ethnic tensions flared up in the 1980s, causing the country's ultimate collapse. In 1991–92 independence was declared by Croatia, Slovenia, Macedonia, and Bosnia and Herzegovina; the new Federal Republic of Yugoslavia (containing roughly 45% of the population and 40% of the area of its predecessor) was proclaimed by Serbia and Montenegro. Still fueled by long-standing ethnic tensions, hostilities continued into the 1990s. Despite the approval of the Dayton Peace Accords (1995), sporadic fighting continued and was followed in 1998–99 by Serbian repression and expulsion of ethnic populations in Kosovo. In September–October 2000, the battered nation of Yugoslavia ended the autocratic rule of Pres. Slobodan Milosevic. In April 2001 he was arrested and in June extradited to The Hague to stand trial for war crimes, genocide, and crimes against humanity committed during the fighting in Kosovo. In February 2003 both houses of the Yugoslav federal legislature voted to accept a new state charter and change the name of the country from Yugoslavia to Serbia and Montenegro. Henceforth, defense, international political and economic relations, and human rights matters would be handled centrally, while all other func-

---

1 metric ton = about 1.1 short tons;   1 kilometer = 0.6 mi (statute);   1 metric ton-km cargo = about 0.68 short ton-mi cargo;   c.i.f.: cost, insurance, and freight;   f.o.b.: free on board

tions would be run from the republican capitals, Belgrade and Podgorica, respectively. A provision was included for both states to vote on independence after three years, and in June 2006 Montenegro's Parliament declared the republic's independence, severing some 88 years of union with Serbia.

Recent Developments

In 2006 Serbia, along with 83 other countries, officially recognized Montenegro, which became the 192nd member state of the United Nations and joined a number of other international organizations, including the NATO Partnership for Peace program. In early November Zeljko Sturanoyic was elected prime minister by Parliament, and his government began the daunting task of leading Montenegro toward European integration by implementing comprehensive institutional, political, and economic reforms and, in particular, by adopting a new constitution in line with European political standards. Montenegro's economy showed signs of growth. Inflation had been held to 1.8% a year since the introduction of the euro in 2000. Monthly wages averaged only €230 euro (€1 = about $1.25) but were up from €150 in 2002. Unemployment was about 15.7%, though it had decreased from 18.6% in 2005, and the rate among 18–24-year-olds was nearly 60%. In the first half of 2006, GDP grew by 6.5% and industrial production by 2.9%.

Internet resources: <www.monstat.cg.yu/EngPrva.htm>

Morocco

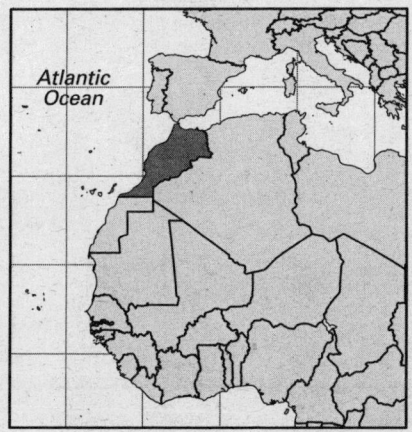

Atlantic Ocean

Official name: Al-Mamlakah al-Maghribiyah (Kingdom of Morocco). **Form of government:** constitutional monarchy with two legislative houses (House of Councillors [270 {indirectly elected seats}]; House of Representatives [325]). **Chief of state and head of government:** King Muhammad VI (from 1999), assisted by Prime Minister Driss Jettou (from 2002). **Capital:** Rabat. **Official language:** Arabic. **Official religion:** Islam. **Monetary unit:** 1 Moroccan dirham (DH) = 100 Moroccan francs; valuation (1 Jul 2007) US$1 = DH 8.26.

Demography

Area (includes Western Sahara): 274,461 sq mi, 710,850 sq km. **Population** (2006; includes Western Sahara, annexure of Morocco whose unresolved political status [from 1991] is to be eventually decided by an internationally sponsored referendum; Western Sahara area: 97,344 sq mi, 252,120 sq km; Western Sahara population [2006] 372,000): 30,646,000. **Density** (2006): persons per sq mi 111.7, persons per sq km 43.1. **Urban** (2002): 56.6%. **Sex distribution** (2002): male 49.75%; female 50.25%. **Age breakdown** (2002): under 15, 30.9%; 15–29, 30.3%; 30–44, 20.4%; 45–59, 10.9%; 60–74, 5.9%; 75 and over, 1.6%. **Ethnic composition** (2000): Berber 45%, of which Arabized 24%; Arab 44%; Moors originally from Mauritania 10%; other 1%. **Religious affiliation** (2000): Muslim (mostly Sunni) 98.3%; Christian 0.6%; other 1.1%. **Major urban areas** (2003): Casablanca 3,353,000; Rabat-Salé (2000) 1,616,000; Fès 1,053,000; Marrakech (2000) 822,000; Tangier 681,444. **Location:** northern Africa, bordering the Mediterranean Sea, Algeria, the Spanish exclaves of Ceuta and Melilla, and the North Atlantic Ocean.

Vital statistics

Birth rate per 1,000 population (2002): 21.0 (world avg. 21.3). **Death rate** per 1,000 population (2002): 5.6 (world avg. 9.1). **Natural increase rate** per 1,000 population (2002): 15.4 (world avg. 12.2). **Total fertility rate** (avg. births per childbearing woman; 2002): 3.0. **Life expectancy** at birth (2002): male 67.5 years; female 72.1 years.

National economy

Budget. *Revenue* (2003): DH 102,482,000,000 (value-added tax 25.5%; individual income tax 17.2%; excise taxes 15.2%; corporate taxes 14.2%; international trade 12.2%; stamp tax 5.2%). *Expenditures* (2003): DH 128,113,000,000 (current expenditure 76.8%, of which wages 42.1%, debt payment 13.5%; capital expenditure 17.1%; transfers to local governments 6.1%). **Public debt** (external, outstanding; 2002): $15,001,000,000. **Population economically active** (2001): total 10,230,000; activity rate 35.4% (unemployed [2002] 11.6%). **Production** (metric tons except as noted). *Agriculture, forestry, fishing* (2002): wheat 3,356,000, sugar beets 2,985,900, barley 1,669,000; livestock (number of live animals) 16,335,000 sheep, 5,090,000 goats, 2,669,000 cattle; roundwood (2001) 971,000 cu m; fish catch (2001) 1,083,000, of which sardines 763,000, octopuses 113,000. *Mining and quarrying* (2002): phosphate rock 21,808,000; barite 469,900; zinc (metal content) 178,400. *Manufacturing* (value added in $'000,000; 2001): food products 778; tobacco products 635; wearing apparel 565. *Energy production (consumption):* electricity (kW-hr; 2002) 15,539,-300,000 (14,085,000,000); coal (2001) 135,000 ([2000] 4,029,000); crude petroleum (barrels; 2002) 97,000 ([2000] 52,288,000); petroleum products (2002) 6,339,500 ([2000] 6,553,000); natural gas (cu m; 2002) 48,700,000 ([2000] 49,900,000). **Gross national product** (2003): $39,661,000,000 ($1,320 per capita). **Tourism** (2002): receipts $2,046,000,000; expenditures $444,000,000. **Households.** Average household size (2002) 5.5; expenditure (1994): food 45.2%, housing 12.5%, transportation 7.6%. **Land use** as % of total land area

(2000): in temporary crops 19.6%, in permanent crops 2.2%, in pasture 47.1%; overall forest area 6.8%.

Foreign trade

Imports (2002-c.i.f.): DH 129,346,000,000 (machinery and apparatus 19.3%; mineral fuels 15.6%, of which crude petroleum 10.0%; food, beverages, and tobacco 11.8%; cotton fabric and fibers 6.4%). *Major import sources* (2001): France 24.1%; Spain 10.3%; UK 6.2%; Italy 5.0%; Germany 5.0%. **Exports** (2002-f.o.b.; cannabis is an important illegal export): DH 85,653,000,000 (garments 21.4%; food, beverages, and tobacco 20.5%, of which crustaceans and mollusks 6.6%; knitwear 10.4%; phosphoric acid 6.8%; machinery and apparatus 6.6%; phosphates 5.2%). *Major export destinations* (2001): France 32.8%; Spain 15.3%; UK 8.6%; Italy 5.7%; Germany 4.2%.

Transport and communications

Transport. *Railroads* (2002): route length 1,907 km; passenger-km 2,145,000,000; metric ton-km cargo 4,974,000,000. *Roads* (2001): total length 57,226 km (paved 56%). *Vehicles* (2000): passenger cars 1,211,100; trucks and buses 415,700. *Air transport* (2002; Royal Air Maroc only): passenger-km 6,044,800,000; metric ton-km cargo 51,285,000; airports (2002) 15. **Communications**, in total units (units per 1,000 persons). Daily newspaper circulation (2000): 740,000 (26); radios (2000): 6,920,000 (243); televisions (2000): 4,720,000 (166); telephone main lines (2003): 1,219,200 (41); cellular telephone subscribers (2003): 7,332,800 (243); personal computers (2003): 600,000 (20); Internet users (2003): 800,000 (27).

Education and health

Literacy (2000): total population over age 15 literate 48.9%; males literate 61.1%; females literate 35.1%. **Health** (2002): physicians 13,955 (1 per 2,123 persons); hospital beds (1998) 26,153 (1 per 1,062 persons); infant mortality rate per 1,000 live births (2002) 44.0. **Food** (2001): daily per capita caloric intake 3,046 (vegetable products 93%, animal products 7%); 126% of FAO recommended minimum.

Military

Total active duty personnel (2003): 196,300 (army 89.1%, navy 4.0%, air force 6.9%). **Military expenditure as percentage of GNP** (1999): 4.3% (world 2.4%); per capita expenditure $49.

Background

The Berbers entered Morocco near the end of the 2nd millennium BC. Phoenicians established trading posts along the Mediterranean during the 12th century BC, and Carthage had settlements along the Atlantic in the 5th century BC. After the fall of Carthage, Morocco became a loyal ally of Rome, and in AD 42 it was annexed by Rome as part of the province of Mauretania. It was invaded by Muslims in the 7th century. Beginning in the mid-11th century, the Almoravids, Almohads, and Marinids ruled successively. After the fall of the Marinids in the mid-15th century, the

Sa'dis ruled for a century after 1550. The French fought Morocco over the Algerian boundary in the 1840s, and the Spanish seized part of Moroccan territory in 1859. It was a French protectorate from 1912 until its independence in 1956. In the mid-1970s it reasserted claim to the Western Sahara, and in 1976 Spanish troops left there. Conflicts with Mauritania and Algeria over the region continued into the 1990s. As the decade wore on, the UN tried to solve the dispute. King Hassan II died in July 1999 after 38 years on the throne and was succeeded by his eldest son, Sidi Muhammad, who took the name Muhammad VI.

Recent Developments

Morocco's free-trade agreement (FTA) with the United States came into force in January 2006, while a long-delayed FTA was signed with Egypt, Tunisia, and Jordan in July. In April UN Secretary-General Kofi Annan reluctantly abandoned his support for a referendum for self-determination in the Western Sahara and proposed instead direct negotiations between Morocco and the separatist Polisario Front. Morocco repeated its offer of autonomy status for the territory but rejected independence. Economic indicators were encouraging. Real GDP growth was set at 7.3% and inflation at 3.7%, owing partially to high oil prices.

Internet resources: <www.mincom.gov.ma>.

Mozambique

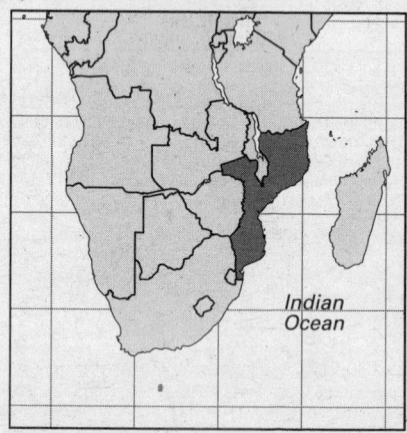

Official name: República de Moçambique (Republic of Mozambique). **Form of government:** multiparty republic with a single legislative house (Assembly of the Republic [250]). **Head of state and government:** President Armando Guebuza (from 2005) assisted by Prime Minister Luisa Diogo (from 2004). **Capital:** Maputo. **Official language:** Portuguese. **Official religion:** none. **Monetary unit:** 1 metical (Mt; plural meticais) = 100 centavos; valuation (1 Jul 2007) US$1 = Mt 25,870.

---

1 metric ton = about 1.1 short tons;   1 kilometer = 0.6 mi (statute);   1 metric ton-km cargo = about 0.68 short ton-mi cargo;   c.i.f.: cost, insurance, and freight;   f.o.b.: free on board

Demography

Area: 308,642 sq mi, 799,379 sq km. **Population** (2006): 19,687,000. **Density** (2006): persons per sq mi 63.8, persons per sq km 24.6. **Urban** (2001): 33.3%. **Sex distribution** (2003): male 49.27%; female 50.73%. **Age breakdown** (2003): under 15, 43.8%; 15–29, 26.5%; 30–44, 16.2%; 45–59, 8.9%; 60–74, 3.8%; 75 and over, 0.7%. **Ethnic composition** (2000): Makuana 15.3%; Makua 14.5%; Tsonga 8.6%; Sena 8.0%; Lomwe 7.1%; Tswa 5.7%; Chwabo 5.5%; other 35.3%. **Linguistic composition** (1997): Makua 26.3%; Tsonga 11.4%; Lomwe 7.6%; Sena 7.0%; Portuguese 6.5%; Chuaba 6.3%; other Bantu languages 33.0%; other 1.9%. **Religious affiliation** (2000): traditional beliefs 50.4%; Christian 38.4%, of which Roman Catholic 15.8%, Protestant 8.9%; Muslim 10.5%. **Major cities** (1997): Maputo 989,386; Matola 440,927; Beira 412,588; Nampula 314,965; Chimoio 177,608. **Location:** southern Africa, bordering Tanzania, the Indian Ocean, South Africa, Swaziland, Zimbabwe, Zambia, and Malawi.

Vital statistics

Birth rate per 1,000 population (2003): 36.9 (world avg. 21.3). **Death rate** per 1,000 population (2003): 23.0 (world avg. 9.1). **Natural increase rate** per 1,000 population (2003): 13.9 (world avg. 12.2). **Total fertility rate** (avg. births per childbearing woman; 2003): 5.0. **Life expectancy** at birth (2003): male 38.9 years; female 37.4 years. **Adult population** (ages 15–49) **living with HIV** (2004): 12.2% (world avg. 1.1%).

National economy

Budget (2002). *Revenue:* Mt 22,077,000,000,000 (tax revenue 48.1%, of which VAT 20.8%, taxes on international trade 8.4%, personal income tax 5.9%; grants 45.1%; nontax revenue 6.8%). *Expenditures:* Mt 29,032,000,000,000 (current expenditures 46.4%; capital expenditures 41.8%; net lending 11.8%). **Public debt** (external, outstanding; 2002): $2,526,000,000. **Production** (metric tons except as noted). *Agriculture, forestry, fishing* (2003): cassava 6,149,897, corn (maize) 1,248,000, sugarcane 400,000; livestock (number of live animals) 1,320,000 cattle, 392,000 goats, 28,000,000 chickens; roundwood (2002) 18,043,000 cu m; fish catch (2001) 32,512. *Mining and quarrying* (2002): tantalite 46,900 kg; gold 17 kg (official figures; unofficial artisanal production is 360–480 kg per year). *Manufacturing* (value added in Mt '000,000,000; 2002): aluminum 13,547; beverages 2,130; food products 1,789. *Energy production (consumption):* electricity (kW-hr; 2000) 6,974,000,000 (1,562,000,000); coal (2001) 17,700 (n.a.); petroleum products (2000) none (334,000); natural gas (cu m; 2000) 563,800 (563,800). **Household income and expenditure.** Average family size (1997) 4.1; source of income (1992–93; city of Maputo only): wages and salaries 51.6%, self-employment 12.5%, barter 11.5%, private farming 7.7%; expenditure (1992–93; city of Maputo only): food, beverages, and tobacco 74.6%, housing and energy 11.7%, transportation and communications 4.7%, clothing and footwear 3.7%, education and recreation 1.4%, health 0.8%. **Tourism** (2002): receipts from visitors $144,000,000; expenditures by nationals abroad $298,000,000. **Population economically active** (2002): total 9,696,000; ac-

tivity rate 55.3%. **Gross national product** (2003): $3,897,000,000 ($210 per capita). **Land use** as % of total land area (2000): in temporary crops 5.0%, in permanent crops 0.3%, in pasture 56.1%; overall forest area 39.0%.

Foreign trade

Imports (2001-f.o.b. in balance of trade and c.i.f. for commodities and trading partners): $1,063,000,000 (machinery and apparatus 14.9%; refined petroleum 12.5%; food products 11.8%, of which cereals 8.0%; transport equipment 7.0%; unspecified commodities 21.9%). *Major import sources:* South Africa 42%; Australia 7%; Spain 4%; unspecified 23%. **Exports** (2001): $703,000,000 (aluminum 54.5%; food products 20.1%, of which crustaceans and mollusks 13.4%; electricity 8.1%; cotton 2.3%). *Major export destinations:* Belgium 35%; Zimbabwe 10%; Germany 7%; The Netherlands 7%; Spain 5%.

Transport and communications

Transport. *Railroads* (2002): route length 3,123 km; (2001) passenger-km 142,000,000; (2001) metric ton-km cargo 774,500,000. *Roads* (1996): total length 30,400 km (paved 19%). *Vehicles* (1999): passenger cars 78,600; trucks and buses 46,900. *Air transport:* (2001) passenger-km 272,400,000; metric ton-km cargo 6,700,000; airports (1997) with scheduled flights 7. **Communications,** in total units (units per 1,000 persons). Daily newspaper circulation (2000): 53,000 (3); radios (2000): 778,000 (44); televisions (2002): 257,600 (14); telephone main lines (2002): 83,700 (4.6); cellular telephone subscribers (2003): 428,900 (23); personal computers (2002): 82,000 (4.5); Internet users (2002): 50,000 (2.8).

Education and health

Educational attainment (1997). Percentage of population 15 and over having: no formal schooling 78.4%; primary education 18.4%; secondary 2.0%; technical 0.4%; higher 0.2%; other/unknown 0.6%. **Literacy** (2000): percentage of total population age 15 and over literate 43.8%; males literate 59.9%; females literate 28.4%. **Health:** physicians (2003) 500 (1 per 37,000 persons); hospital beds (1997) 12,630 (1 per 1,210 persons); infant mortality rate per 1,000 live births (2003) 137.8. **Food** (2001): daily per capita caloric intake 1,980 (vegetable products 98%, animal products 2%); 85% of FAO recommended minimum.

Military

Total active duty personnel (2003): 8,200 (army 85.4%, navy 2.4%, air force 12.2%). **Military expenditure as percentage of GNP** (1999): 2.5% (world 2.4%); per capita expenditure $5.

Background

Inhabited in prehistoric times, Mozambique was settled by Bantu peoples about the 3rd century AD. Arab traders occupied the coastal region from the 14th century, and the Portuguese controlled the area from the early 16th century. The slave trade later became an important part of the economy. In the late 19th century private trading companies began to administer parts of the inland areas. It became an overseas province of Portugal in 1951. After years of war beginning in the 1960s, the country was granted independence in 1975. It was wracked by civil war in the 1970s and '80s. In 1990 a new constitution was promulgated, and a peace treaty was signed with the rebels in 1992.

Recent Developments

Mozambique's economic situation brightened somewhat with the announcement in January 2005 that the country's $154 million debt to the UK was canceled. In September of that year the World Bank approved a $120 million credit to help finance the country's antipoverty campaign. Drought in late 2005 that created acute food shortages, however, was followed in early 2006 by flooding that left thousands homeless and an earthquake that caused extensive property damage.

Internet resources: <www.mozambique.mz>.

Myanmar (Burma)

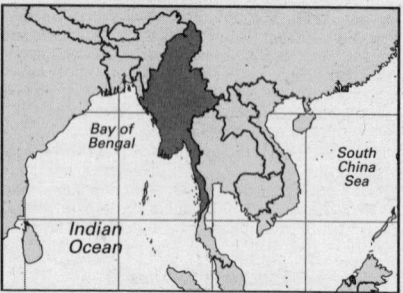

Bay of Bengal

South China Sea

Indian Ocean

Official name: Pyidaungzu Myanma Naingngandaw (Union of Myanmar). Form of government: military regime. Head of state and government: Chairman of the State Peace and Development Council Gen. Than Shwe (from 1997), assisted by Prime Minister Lieut. Gen. Soe Win (from 2004). Capital: Naypyidaw. Official language: Burmese. Official religion: none. Monetary unit: 1 Myanmar kyat (K) = 100 pyas; valuation (1 Jul 2007) US$1 = K 6.53 (rate pegged to the Special Drawing Right of the International Monetary Fund).

Demography

Area: 261,228 sq mi, 676,577 sq km. Population (2006): 47,383,000. Density (2006): persons per sq mi 181.4, persons per sq km 70.0. Urban (2002): 29.0%. Sex distribution (2002): male 49.81%; female 50.19%. Age breakdown (2002): under 15, 28.5%; 15–29, 30.8%; 30–44, 22.0%; 45–59, 11.4%; 60 and over, 5.7%. Ethnic composition (2000): Burman 55.9%; Karen 9.5%; Shan 6.5%; Han Chinese 2.5%; Mon 2.3%; Yangbye 2.2%; Kachin 1.5%; other 19.6%. Religious affiliation (2000): Buddhist 72.7%; Christian 8.3%; Muslim 2.4%; Hindu 2.0%; traditional beliefs 12.6%; other 2.0%. Major cities (2004 est.): Yangon (Rangoon) 4,455,500;

Mandalay 1,176,900; Moulmein (Mawlamyine) 405,800; Bassein (Pathein) 215,600; Pegu (Bago) 200,900. Location: southeastern Asia, bordering China, Laos, Thailand, the Andaman Sea, the Bay of Bengal, Bangladesh, and India.

Vital statistics

Birth rate per 1,000 population (2003): 23.7 (world avg. 21.3). Death rate per 1,000 population (2003): 11.2 (world avg. 9.1). Natural increase rate per 1,000 population (2003): 12.5 (world avg. 12.2). Total fertility rate (avg. births per childbearing woman; 2003): 2.2. Life expectancy at birth (2002): male 54.1 years; female 57.6 years.

National economy

Budget (2000–01). Revenue: K 134,550,000,000 (revenue from taxes 56.4%, of which taxes on goods and services 32.8%, taxes on income 19.4%; nontax revenue 43.4%; foreign grants 0.2%). Expenditures: K 221,255,000,000 (defense 28.7%; agriculture and forestry 17.4%; education 14.2%; public works and housing 9.2%). Public debt (external, outstanding; 2002): $5,391,000,000. Tourism (2001): receipts from visitors $45,000,000; expenditures by nationals abroad $27,000,000. Production (metric tons except as noted). Agriculture, forestry, fishing (2002): rice 21,900,000, sugarcane 6,333,000, dry beans 1,467,330; livestock (number of live animals) 11,551,000 cattle, 4,498,680 pigs, 2,252,020 buffalo; roundwood (2001) 39,365,000 cu m; fish catch (2001) 1,288,134. Mining and quarrying (2001): copper (metal content) 26,300; jade 1,700,000 kg; rubies, sapphires, and spinel 8,630,000 carats. Manufacturing (2001): cement 384,000; refined sugar 101,000; fertilizers 60,100. Energy production (consumption): electricity (kW-hr; 2000) 5,076,000,000 (5,076,000,000); hard coal (2000) 51,000 (43,000); lignite (2000) 524,000 (524,000); crude petroleum (barrels; 2001) 3,300,000 ([2000] 7,339,000); petroleum products (2000) 820,000 (1,625,000); natural gas (cu m; 2001) 6,800,300,000 ([2000] 1,427,000,000). Households. Average household size (2000) 4.8; expenditure (1994; Yangon only): food and beverages 67.1%, fuel and lighting 6.6%, transportation 4.0%, charitable contributions 3.1%, medical care 3.1%. Gross national product (1996): $119,334,000,000 ($2,610 per capita). Population economically active (1999): total 23,700,000; activity rate of total population 57.1% (unemployed 4.1%). Land use as % of total land area (2000): in temporary crops 15.1%, in permanent crops 0.9%, in pasture 0.5%; overall forest area 52.3%.

Foreign trade

Imports (2000–01-c.i.f.): K 14,900,000,000 (machinery and transport equipment 25.2%, chemicals and chemical products 12.9%, mineral fuels 7.7%, food and live animals 3.9%). Major import sources (2001): China 21.8%; Singapore 16.6%; Thailand 13.9%; South Korea 9.1%; Malaysia 8.0%; Japan 7.1%. Exports (2000–01-f.o.b.): K 12,262,000,000 (domestic exports 68.6%, of which food 26.1% [including pulses 13.5%], min-

1 metric ton = about 1.1 short tons;   1 kilometer = 0.6 mi (statute);   1 metric ton-km cargo = about 0.68 short ton-mi cargo;   c.i.f.: cost, insurance, and freight;   f.o.b.: free on board

eral fuels [significantly natural gas] 9.6%, teak and other hardwood 6.5%; reexports [significantly garments] 31.4%). *Major export destinations* (2001): Thailand 26.0%; US 16.2%; India 10.2%; China 5.0%; Singapore 3.6%.

Transport and communications

Transport. *Railroads* (2000): route length 3,955 km; passenger-km 4,451,000,000; metric ton-km cargo 1,222,000,000. *Roads* (1996): total length 28,200 km (paved 12%). *Vehicles* (1999): passenger cars 171,300; trucks and buses 83,400. *Air transport* (1999): passenger-km 355,000,000; metric ton-km cargo 40,000,000; airports (1996) 19. **Communications,** in total units (units per 1,000 persons). Daily newspaper circulation (2000): 376,000 (9); radios (2001): 2,772,000 (66); televisions (2002): 390,400 (8); telephone main lines (2003): 357,300 (7.2); cellular telephone subscribers (2003): 66,500 (1.3); personal computers (2002): 250,000 (5.1); Internet users (2003): 28,000 (0.5).

Education and health

Literacy (2000): total population age 15 and over literate 84.7%; males literate 89.0%; females literate 80.5%. **Health** (1999): physicians 14,622 (1 per 2,838 persons); hospital beds (1997) 28,943 (1 per 1,433 persons); infant mortality rate per 1,000 live births (2003) 83.0. **Food** (2001): daily per capita caloric intake 2,822 (vegetable products 96%, animal products 4%); 132% of FAO recommended minimum.

Military

Total active duty personnel (2003): 488,000 (army 93.6%, navy 3.3%, air force 3.1%). **Military expenditure as percentage of GNP** (1999): 7.8% (world 2.4%); per capita expenditure $112.

Background

Myanmar, until 1989 known as Burma, has long been inhabited, with the Mon and Pyu states dominant between the 1st century BC and the 9th century AD. It was united in the 11th century under a Burmese dynasty that was overthrown by the Mongols in the 13th century. The Portuguese, Dutch, and English traded there in the 16th–17th centuries. The modern Burmese state was founded in the 18th century. It fell to the British in 1885 and became a province of India. It was occupied by Japan in World War II and became independent in 1948. A military coup took power in 1962 and nationalized major economic sectors. Civilian unrest in the 1980s led to antigovernment rioting. In 1990 opposition parties won in national elections, but the army remained in control. Trying to negotiate for a freer government amid the unrest, Aung San Suu Kyi, the National League for Democracy (NLD) leader, was awarded the Nobel Peace Prize in 1991. She spent extended periods of the 1990s under house arrest.

Recent Developments

After Myanmar's ruling junta, the State Peace and Development Council, extended the house arrest of the National League for Democracy leader Aung San Suu Kyi (who had spent 11 of the past 17 years under house arrest), US Pres. George W. Bush responded by renewing economic sanctions against Myanmar for three more years. In September the UN Security Council added Myanmar to its list of countries considered a threat to international peace and security. Myanmar approved a Sino-Myanmarese oil pipeline linking the deepwater port of Sittwe with China, however, and ties with India and North Korea were upgraded.

Internet resources: <www.myanmar-tourism.com>.

Namibia

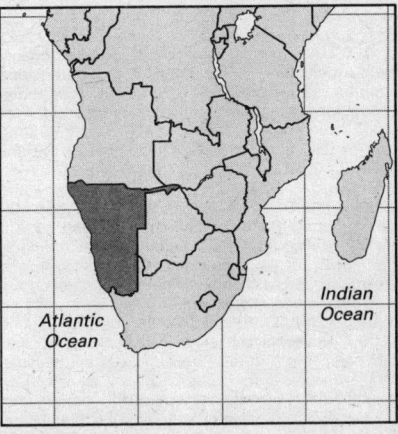

Official name: Republic of Namibia. **Form of government:** republic with two legislative houses (National Council [26]; National Assembly [72 elected and up to 6 appointed members]). **Head of state and government:** President Hifikepunye Pohamba (from 2005), assisted by Prime Minister Nahas Angula (from 2005). **Capital:** Windhoek. **Official language:** English. **Official religion:** none. **Monetary unit:** 1 Namibian dollar (N$) = 100 cents; valuation (1 Jul 2007) US$1 = N$7.18.

Demography

Area: 318,193 sq mi, 824,116 sq km. **Population** (2006): 1,959,000. **Density** (2006): persons per sq mi 6.2, persons per sq km 2.4. **Urban** (2001): 31.4%. **Sex distribution** (2001): male 48.73%; female 51.27%. **Age breakdown** (1999): under 15, 43.2%; 15–29, 28.6%; 30–44, 15.1%; 45–59, 7.7%; 60–74, 4.0%; 75 and over, 1.4%. **Ethnic composition** (2000): Ovambo 34.4%; mixed race (black/white) 14.5%; Kavango 9.1%; Afrikaner 8.1%; San (Bushmen) and Bergdama 7.0%; Herero 5.5%; Nama 4.4%; Kwambi 3.7%; German 2.8%; other 10.5%. **Religious affiliation** (2000): Protestant (mostly Lutheran) 47.5%; Roman Catholic 17.7%; African Christian 10.8%; traditional beliefs 6.0%; other 18.0%. **Major cities** (2001): Windhoek 216,000 (urban agglomeration); Walvis Bay 40,849; Swakopmund 25,442 (population of constituency [second-order administrative subdivision]); Rehoboth 21,782; Rundu 19,597. **Location:** southwestern Africa, bordering Angola, Zambia, Botswana, South Africa, and the Atlantic Ocean.

Vital statistics

Birth rate per 1,000 population (2003): 27.4 (world avg. 21.3). **Death rate** per 1,000 population (2003): 16.7 (world avg. 9.1). **Natural increase rate** per 1,000 population (2003): 10.7 (world avg. 12.2). **Total fertility rate** (avg. births per childbearing woman; 2003): 3.5. **Life expectancy** at birth (2003): male 46.0 years; female 46.1 years. **Adult population** (ages 15–49) living with HIV (2004): 21.3% (world avg. 1.1%).

National economy

Budget (2002–03). *Revenue:* N$10,256,000,000 (taxes on income and profits 38.5%; taxes on international trade 25.3%; taxes on goods and services 23.6%; nontax revenue 9.7%). *Expenditures:* N$12,257,000,000 (current expenditure 84.3%; development expenditure 15.7%). **Public debt** (external, outstanding; 1998): US$747,700,000. **Production** (metric tons except as noted). *Agriculture and fishing* (2002): roots and tubers 270,000, millet 65,000, corn (maize) 27,700; livestock (number of live animals) 2,509,000 cattle, 2,370,000 sheep, 1,769,000 goats; fish catch (2001) 547,542. *Mining and quarrying* (2001): gem diamonds (2002) 1,550,000 carats; fluorite 81,200; zinc (metal content) 31,803 *Manufacturing:* products include cut gems (primarily diamonds), fur products (from Karakul sheep), and processed foods (fish, meats, and dairy products). *Energy production (consumption):* electricity (kW-hr; 2001) 27,000,000 (603,000,000); coal (2000) none (3,000). **Households.** Average household size (2001) 5.1; sources of income (1992): wages and salaries 69.0%, income from property 25.6%, transfer payments 5.4%. **Population economically active:** total (1991) 493,580; activity rate of total population, 34.9% (participation rates: ages 15–64, 61.3%; female 43.5%; unemployed 20.1%). **Gross national product** (2003): US$3,771,000,000 (US$1,870 per capita). **Tourism** (2002): receipts US$219,000,000; expenditures (1998) US$56,000,000. **Land use** as % of total land area (2000): in temporary crops 1.0%, in permanent crops, negligible, in pasture 46.2%; overall forest area 9.8%.

Foreign trade

Imports (1997-f.o.b. in balance of trade and c.i.f. for commodities and trading partners): N$7,718,000,000 (food, beverages, and tobacco 24.1%; machinery and apparatus 15.0%; transport equipment 14.7%; base and fabricated metals 7.5%). *Major import sources* (2000): South Africa 86.4%; Germany 2.0%; UK 2.0%; US 1.3%. **Exports** (2001): N$8,901,000,000 (diamonds 45.4%; metals 18.6%, of which gold 2.3%, zinc 1.5%, other [mostly uranium and copper] 14.8%; fish 10.4%; meat [mostly beef] 7.0%). *Major export destinations* (1998): UK 43%; South Africa 26%; Spain 14%; France 8%.

Transport and communications

Transport. *Railroads:* route length (1999) 2,382 km; (1995–96) passenger-km 48,300,000; (1995–96) metric ton-km 1,082,000,000. *Roads* (2000): total length 66,467 km (paved 7%). *Vehicles:* passenger cars (1996) 74,875; trucks and buses (1995)

66,500. *Air transport* (2001; Air Namibia only): passenger-km 624,000,000; metric ton-km cargo 72,575,000; airports (1997) 11. **Communications,** in total units (units per 1,000 persons). Daily newspaper circulation (2000): 34,700 (19); radios (2000): 258,000 (141); televisions (2000): 69,400 (38); telephone main lines (2003): 127,400 (66); cellular telephone subscribers (2003): 223,700 (116); personal computers (2003): 191,000 (99); Internet users (2003): 65,000 (34).

Education and health

Educational attainment (1991). Percentage of population age 25 and over having: no formal schooling 35.1%; primary education 31.9%; secondary 28.5%; higher 4.5%. **Literacy** (2000): total population age 15 and over literate 830,200 (82.1%); males literate 416,000 (82.9%); females literate 414,200 (81.2%). **Health** (2000; public sector only): physicians 244 (1 per 7,500 persons); hospital beds 6,739 (1 per 271 persons); infant mortality rate per 1,000 live births (2003) 50.7. **Food** (2001): daily per capita caloric intake 2,745 (vegetable products 85%, animal products 15%); 120% of FAO recommended minimum.

Military

Total active duty personnel (2003): 9,000 (army 100.0%). **Military expenditure as percentage of GNP** (1999): 2.9% (world 2.4%); per capita expenditure $53.

Did you know? A cool, coastal desert, the Namib Desert extends for 1,200 mi (1,900 km) along the entire Atlantic coast of Namibia. It reaches inland 80 to 100 m (130 to 160 km) to the foot of the Great Escarpment. Its name is derived from the Nama language, implying "an area where there is nothing."

Background

Long inhabited by indigenous peoples, Namibia was explored by the Portuguese in the late 15th century. In 1884 it was annexed by Germany as German South West Africa. It was captured in World War I by South Africa, which received it as a mandate from the League of Nations in 1920 and refused to give it up after World War II. A UN resolution in 1966 ending the mandate was challenged by South Africa in the 1970s and '80s. Through long negotiations involving many factions and interests, Namibia achieved independence in 1990.

Recent Developments

Namibia ranked 125th on the UN's Human Development Report of 177 countries in 2005—an estimated 40% of the population lived below the poverty line. Some 230,000 people were HIV-positive in Namibia in 2005, and that year the UN gave the country a $44.7 million grant to combat HIV/AIDS. The development of the Kudu offshore natural gas field continued in 2006. The country

---

1 metric ton = about 1.1 short tons;   1 kilometer = 0.6 mi (statute);   1 metric ton-km cargo = about 0.68 short ton-mi cargo;   c.i.f.: cost, insurance, and freight;   f.o.b.: free on board

was almost completely dependent on South Africa for its electricity, and it was hoped that the development of the Kudu field, along with unexplored offshore fields and the controversial Epupa hydroelectric project on the Kunene River, would reduce this dependence.

Internet resources: <www.namibiatourism.com.na>.

Nauru

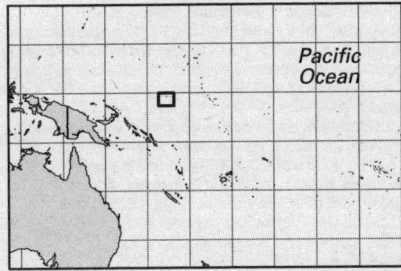

Official name: Naoero (Republic of Nauru). Form of government: republic with one legislative house (Parliament [18]). Head of state and government: President Ludwig Scotty (from 2004). Capital: government offices are located in Yaren district. Official language: none; Nauruan is the national language; English is the language of business and government. Official religion: none. Monetary unit: 1 Australian dollar ($A) = 100 cents; valuation (1 Jul 2007) US$1 = $A 1.18.

Demography

Area: 8.2 sq mi, 21.2 sq km. Population (2006): 10,100. Density (2006): persons per sq mi 1,232, persons per sq km 476.4. Urban (2001): 100%. Sex distribution (2001): male 50.50%; female 49.50%. Age breakdown (2001): under 15, 40.3%; 15–29, 26.8%; 30–44, 19.0%; 45–59, 10.7%; 60–74, 3.0%; 75 and over, 0.2%. Ethnic composition (1992): Nauruan 68.9%; other Pacific Islander 23.7%, of which Kiribati 12.8%, Tuvaluan 8.7%; Asian 5.9%, of which Filipino 2.5%, Chinese 2.3%; other 1.5%. Religious affiliation (1995): Protestant 53.5%, of which Congregational 35.3%, Pentecostal 4.8%; Roman Catholic 27.5%; other 19.0%. Major cities: none; population of Yaren district (1996) 700. Location: western Pacific Ocean, near the equator east of Papua New Guinea.

Vital statistics

Birth rate per 1,000 population (2002): 21.8 (world avg. 21.3). Death rate per 1,000 population (2002): 7.5 (world avg. 9.1). Natural increase rate per 1,000 population (2002): 14.3 (world avg. 12.2). Total fertility rate (avg. births per childbearing woman; 2003): 3.4. Marriage rate per 1,000 population (1995): 5.3. Life expectancy at birth (2003): male 58.4 years; female 65.7 years.

National economy

Budget (1999). Revenue: $A 38,700,000. Expenditures: $A 37,200,000. Public debt (external, outstanding; beginning of 1996): US$150,000,000.

Tourism: receipts from visitors, virtually none. Gross national product (at current market prices; 1997): US$128,000,000 (US$11,538 per capita). Production (metric tons except as noted). Agriculture and fishing (2002): coconuts 1,600, vegetables 450, tropical fruit (including mangoes) 275; livestock (number of live animals) 2,800 pigs; fish catch (2001) 400. Mining and quarrying (2001): phosphate rock (gross weight) 400,000. Manufacturing: none; virtually all consumer manufactures are imported. Energy production (consumption): electricity (kW-hr; 2000) 33,000,000 (33,000,000); petroleum products (2000) none (44,000). Population economically active (1992): 2,453 (Nauruan only); activity rate of total population 35.9% (unemployed 18.2%). Households. Average household size (1992; employed only) 10.0.

Foreign trade

Imports (1999): US$20,000,000 (agricultural products 65.0%, of which food 45.0%; remainder 35.0%). Major import sources (2001): Australia 49.4%; US 16.9%; Indonesia 7.9%; India 4.8%; UK 4.6%. Exports (1999): US$40,000,000 (phosphate, virtually 100%). Major export destinations (2001): New Zealand 28.6%; Australia 23.6%; Thailand 14.7%; South Korea 11.5%; Japan 9.6%.

Transport and communications

Transport. Railroads (2001): length 5 km. Roads (2001): total length 30 km (paved 79%). Vehicles (1989): passenger cars, trucks, and buses 1,448. Air transport (1996): passenger-km 243,000,000; metric ton-km cargo 24,000,000; airports (2001) with scheduled flights 1. Communications, in total units (units per 1,000 persons). Radios (1997): 7,000 (609); televisions (1997): 500 (48); telephone main lines (2001): 1,900 (160); cellular telephone subscribers (2001): 1,500 (130); Internet users (2001): 300 (26).

Education and health

Educational attainment (1992; Nauruan only). Percentage of population age 5 and over having: primary education or less 77.4%; secondary education 12.9%; higher 4.1%; not stated 5.6%. Literacy (1999): total population age 15 and over literate 99%. Health (2003): physicians 5 (1 per 2,016 persons); hospital beds 60 (1 per 168 persons); infant mortality rate per 1,000 live births 10.3. Food (2002; data for Oceania): daily per capita caloric intake 2,952 (vegetable products 70%, animal products 30%); 129% of FAO recommended minimum.

Military

Total active duty personnel (2003): Nauru does not have any military establishment. The defense is assured by Australia, but no formal agreement exists.

Background

Nauru was inhabited by Pacific islanders when British explorers arrived in 1798 and named it Pleasant Island for the friendly welcome they received. Annexed by Germany in 1888, it was occupied by Australia at the start of World War I, and in 1919 it was placed under a joint mandate of Britain, Australia, and New Zealand. During World War II it was occupied by the Japanese. Made a UN trust territory under Australian administration in 1947, it gained independence in 1968. During the mid-1990s Nauru suffered political unrest.

Recent Developments

Nauru and Australia continued to experience friction over the so-called "Pacific solution," Australia's decision to house asylum seekers, many of them Afghans and Iraqis, in a detention center on Nauru. Nauru imposed a fine on Australia in 2006 for every asylum application that had been unresolved for more than a year. In September 2006 Pres. Ludwig Scotty addressed the UN General Assembly to protest Taiwan's exclusion from that body. Nauru received a large portion of its foreign aid from Taiwan.

Internet resources:
<www.cia.gov/cia/publications/factbook/geos/nr.html>.

Nepal

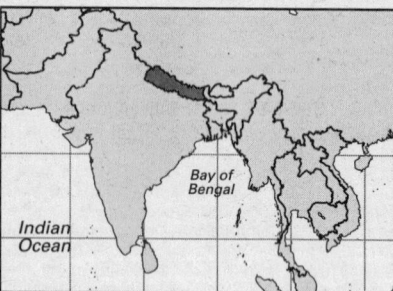

Official name: Nepal Adhirajya (Kingdom of Nepal). **Form of government:** constitutional monarchy. **Chief of state:** King Gyanendra Bir Bikram Shah Deva (from 2001). **Head of government:** Prime Minister Girija Prasad Koirala (from 2006). **Capital:** Kathmandu. **Official language:** Nepali. **Official religion:** Hinduism. **Monetary unit:** 1 Nepalese rupee (NRs) = 100 paisa (pice); valuation (1 Jul 2007) US$1 = NRs 66.09.

Demography

Area: 56,827 sq mi, 147,181 sq km. **Population** (2006): 27,678,000. **Density** (2006): persons per sq mi 487.1, persons per sq km 188.1. **Urban** (2002): 13.0%. **Sex distribution** (2001): male 49.95%; female 50.05%. **Age breakdown** (2001): under 15, 39.3%; 15–29, 27.0%; 30–44, 17.1%; 45–59, 10.1%; 60–74, 5.2%; 75 and over, 1.3%. **Ethnic composition** (2000): Nepalese 55.8%; Maithili 10.8%; Bhojpuri 7.9%; Tharu 4.4%; Tamang 3.6%; Newar 3.0%; Awadhi 2.7%; Magar 2.5%; Gurkha 1.7%; other 7.6%. **Religious affiliation** (2001): Hindu 80.6%; Buddhist 10.7%; Muslim 4.2%; Kirat (local traditional belief) 3.6%; Christian 0.5%; other 0.4%. **Major cities** (2001): Kathmandu 671,846; Biratnagar 166,674; Lalitpur 162,991; Pokhara 156,312; Birganj 112,484. **Location:** south-central Asia, bordering China and India.

Vital statistics

Birth rate per 1,000 population (2003): 32.5 (world avg. 21.3). **Death rate** per 1,000 population (2003): 9.8 (world avg. 9.1). **Natural increase rate** per 1,000 population (2002): 22.7 (world avg. 12.2). **Total fertility rate** (avg. births per childbearing woman; 2003): 4.4. **Life expectancy** at birth (2003): male 59.4 years; female 58.6 years.

National economy

Budget (2001). *Revenue:* NRs 48,596,000,000 (taxes on goods and services 34.1%, taxes on international trade 28.1%, income taxes 19.0%, state property revenues 1.9%, other 16.9%). *Expenditures:* NRs 74,289,000,000 (current expenditure 59.3%, of which education 14.0%, defense 7.8%, health 2.8%; development expenditure 40.7%, of which economic services 25.7%). **Public debt** (external, outstanding; 2002): $2,913,000,000. **Production** (metric tons except as noted). *Agriculture, forestry, fishing* (2002): rice 4,130,000, sugarcane 2,248,000, corn (maize) 1,511,000; livestock (number of live animals) 6,979,000 cattle, 6,607,000 goats, 3,701,000 buffalo; roundwood (2002) 13,988,000 cu m; fish catch (2002) 33,270. *Mining and quarrying* (2001): limestone 280,000; talc 6,000; salt 2,000. *Manufacturing* (value added in $'000,000; 1996): textiles 99; tobacco products 46; beverages 35. *Energy production (consumption):* electricity (kW-hr; 2000) 1,425,000,000 (1,525,000,000); coal (2000) 18,000 (435,000); petroleum products (2000) none (684,000). **Tourism** (2002): receipts from visitors $107,000,000; expenditures by nationals abroad (2001) $80,000,000. **Population economically active** (2001): total 11,138,000; activity rate of total population 48% (participation rates: ages 10 years and over, 58.2%; female [1991] 45.5%; unemployed 5.1%). **Household income and expenditure** (1984–85). Average household size (2001) 5.4; income per household NRs 14,796; sources of income: self-employment 63.4%, wages and salaries 25.1%, rent 7.5%, other 4.0%; expenditure: food and beverages 61.2%, housing 17.3%, clothing 11.7%, health care 3.7%, education and recreation 2.9%, transportation and communications 1.2%. **Gross national product** (at current market prices; 2003): $5,824,000,000 ($240 per capita). **Land use** as % of total land area (2000): in temporary crops 21.3%, in permanent crops 0.6%, in pasture 12.3%; overall forest area 27.3%.

Foreign trade

Imports (2000–01-c.i.f.): NRs 115,687,000,000 (basic manufactures [including fabrics, yarns, and made-up articles] 35.6%, machinery and transport equipment 19.9%, chemicals and chemical products 11.2%, mineral fuels [mostly refined petroleum] 9.7%). *Major import sources* (2001): India 36.7%; Argentina 15.5%; China 15.3%; UAE 5.8%; Singapore 5.1%. **Exports** (2000–01-f.o.b.): NRs 55,654,000,000 (ready-made garments 23.6%, carpets 15.4%, pashmina shawls 12.4%, vegetable ghee 6.4%). *Major export destinations* (2001): US 30.7%; India 30.2%; Germany 11.6%; Argentina 7.4%; Japan 2.3%.

1 metric ton = about 1.1 short tons; 1 kilometer = 0.6 mi (statute); 1 metric ton-km cargo = about 0.68 short ton-mi cargo; c.i.f.: cost, insurance, and freight; f.o.b.: free on board

Transport and communications

Transport. *Railroads* (2002): route length 59 km; passengers carried 1,600,000; freight handled 22,000 metric tons. *Roads* (1997): total length 7,700 km (paved 42%). *Vehicles* (2000): passenger cars 53,073; trucks and buses 32,065. *Air transport* (2000): passenger-km 1,023,000,000; metric ton-km cargo 108,000,000; airports (1996) with scheduled flights 24. **Communications**, in total units (units per 1,000 persons). Daily newspaper circulation (1996): 250,000 (11); radios (2000): 883,000 (39); televisions (2000): 159,000 (7); telephone main lines (2003): 371,800 (16); cellular telephone subscribers (2003): 50,400 (2.1); personal computers (2002): 85,000 (3.7); Internet users (2002): 80,000 (3.4).

Education and health

Educational attainment (2001). Percentage of population age 6 and over having: no formal schooling 8.7%; primary education 41.9%; incomplete secondary 30.6%; complete secondary and higher 17.6%; unknown 1.2%. **Literacy** (2001): total population age 15 and over literate 53%; males literate 60%; females literate 43%. **Health** (1999): physicians 1,259 (1 per 17,589 persons); hospital beds 5,190 (1 per 4,267 persons); infant mortality rate per 1,000 live births (2003) 70.6. **Food** (2001): daily per capita caloric intake 2,459 (vegetable products 94%, animal products 6%); 112% of FAO recommended minimum.

Military

Total active duty personnel (2003): 63,000 (army 100%). **Military expenditure as percentage of GNP** (1999): 0.8% (world 2.4%); per capita expenditure $2.

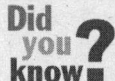

Junko Tabei of Japan, with Ang Tsering Sherpa of Nepal, was the first woman to reach the summit of Mount Everest (16 May 1975).

Background

Nepal developed under early Buddhist influence, and dynastic rule dates from about the 4th century AD. It was formed into a single kingdom in 1769 and fought border wars with China, Tibet, and British India in the 18th–19th centuries. Its independence was recognized by Britain in 1923. A new constitution in 1990 restricted royal authority and accepted a democratically elected parliamentary government. The Maoist Communist Party of Nepal began an armed insurgency in 1996. Nepal signed trade agreements with India in 1997. On 1 Jun 2001, King Birendra, the queen, and seven other members of the royal family were fatally shot by Crown Prince Dipendra, who then turned the gun on himself.

Recent Developments

Nepal witnessed historic political changes in 2006. King Gyanendra was forced to relinquish power following protests by the opposition in April during which 23 people were killed and 5,000 injured. The House of Representatives, which had been dissolved in 2002, was restored, and in May it brought the army under civilian control, dissolved the royal privy council, and declared Nepal a secular state. In November the Maoist rebels who had waged a decadelong bloody insurgency signed a comprehensive peace accord with the government, and in January 2007 they joined a transitional government. Economic growth for 2006 was less than 2%.

Internet resources: <www.welcomenepal.com>.

The Netherlands

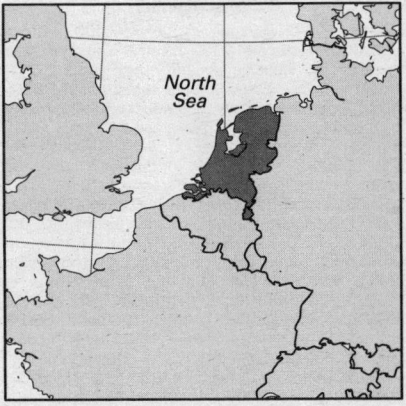

North Sea

Official name: Koninkrijk der Nederlanden (Kingdom of The Netherlands). **Form of government:** constitutional monarchy with a parliament (States General) comprising two legislative houses (First Chamber [75]; Second Chamber [150]). **Chief of state:** Queen Beatrix (from 1980). **Head of government:** Prime Minister Jan Peter Balkenende (from 2002). **Seat of government:** The Hague. **Capital:** Amsterdam. **Official language:** Dutch. **Official religion:** none. **Monetary unit:** 1 euro (€) = 100 cents; valuation (1 Jul 2007) US$1 = €0.74; at conversion on 1 Jan 2002, €1 = 2.20 Netherlands guilders (f.).

Demography

Area: 16,034 sq mi, 41,528 sq km (including inland and coastal water area totaling 2,990 sq mi [7,745 sq km]). **Population** (2006): 16,343,000. **Density** (2006; based on land area only): persons per sq mi 1,253, persons per sq km 483.8. **Urban** (2001): 89.6%. **Sex distribution** (2003): male 49.50%; female 50.50%. **Age breakdown** (2000): under 15, 18.6%; 15–29, 19.3%; 30–44, 24.2%; 45–59, 19.8%; 60–74, 12.1%; 75 and over, 6.0%. **Ethnic composition** (by place of origin [including 2nd generation] 2002): Netherlander 81.6%; Indonesian 2.5%; German 2.5%; Turkish 2.1%; Surinamese 2.0%; Moroccan 1.8%; Netherlands Antillean/Aruban 0.8%; other 6.7%. **Religious affiliation** (1999): Roman Catholic 31.0%; Reformed (NHK) 14.0%; other Reformed 7.0%; Muslim 4.5%; Hindu 0.5%; nonreligious and other 43.0%. **Major urban agglomerations** (2000): Amsterdam 1,002,868; Rotterdam 989,956; The Hague 610,245; Utrecht 366,186; Eindhoven

302,274. **Location:** northwestern Europe, bordering the North Sea, Germany, and Belgium.

Vital statistics

Birth rate per 1,000 population (2003): 12.4 (world avg. 21.3); legitimate 72.8%. **Death rate** per 1,000 population (2003): 8.7 (world avg. 9.1). **Natural increase rate** per 1,000 population (2003): 3.0 (world avg. 12.2). **Total fertility rate** (avg. births per childbearing woman; 2003): 1.7. **Marriage rate** per 1,000 population (2000): 5.3. **Life expectancy** at birth (2003): male 76.2 years; female 80.9 years.

National economy

Budget (1997). *Revenue:* f. 324,360,000,000 (social security taxes 41.1%, income and corporate taxes 24.8%, value-added and excise taxes 22.7%, property taxes 3.0%). *Expenditures:* f. 337,620,-000,000 (social security and welfare 37.4%, health 14.8%, education 10.0%, interest payments 9.1%, defense 3.9%, transportation 3.5%). **Public debt** (2002): $240,951,000,000. **Production** (metric tons except as noted). *Agriculture, forestry, fishing* (2002): potatoes 7,363,000, sugar beets 6,250,000, wheat 1,057,000; livestock (number of live animals; 2002) 11,648,000 pigs, 3,858,000 cattle, 1,186,000 sheep; roundwood (2002) 839,000 cu m; fish catch (2001) 570,226. *Manufacturing* (value added in €'000,000; 2000): food, beverages, and tobacco 11,625; chemicals and chemical products 8,314; electric/electronic machinery 6,429. *Energy production (consumption):* electricity (kW-hr; 2000) 92,110,000,000 (111,025,000,000); coal (2000) negligible (12,972,000); crude petroleum (barrels; 2000) 9,889,000 (377,450,000); petroleum products (2000) 63,322,000 (34,027,000); natural gas (cu m; 2000) 76,741,000,000 (51,469,000,000). **Household income and expenditure.** Average household size (2003) 2.3; disposable income per household (2000) €26,653; sources of income (1996): wages 48.4%, transfers 28.5%, self-employment 11.3%; expenditure (2000): housing and energy 23.2%, food and beverages 14.2%, transportation and communications 11.7%, textiles and clothing 6.4%. **Gross national product** (2003): $426,641,-000,000 ($26,310 per capita). **Population economically active** (1998): total 7,735,000; activity rate of total population 49.3% (participation rates: ages 15–64, 72.9%; female 42.5%; unemployed [February 2001–January 2002] 2.0%). **Tourism** (2002): receipts $7,706,000,000; expenditures $12,919,-000,000. **Land use** as % of total land area (2000): in temporary crops 26.9%, in permanent crops 1.0%, in pasture 29.9%; overall forest area 11.1%.

Foreign trade

Imports (2001-c.i.f.): €217,151,000,000 (computers and related equipment 11.9%, chemicals and chemical products 11.4%, mineral fuels 10.1%, food 8.2%, road vehicles 7.0%). *Major import sources:* Germany 18.5%; US 9.8%; Belgium-Luxembourg 9.3%; UK 8.9%; France 5.7%. **Exports** (2001-f.o.b.): €240,833,000,000 (chemicals and chemical products 15.4%, food 12.3%, computers and related equipment 11.7%, mineral fuels 9.2%).

Major export destinations: Germany 25.6%; Belgium-Luxembourg 11.9%; UK 11.2%; France 10.3%; Italy 6.2%.

Transport and communications

Transport. *Railroads* (2001): length 2,809 km; passenger-km 14,392,000,000; metric ton-km cargo 4,293,000,000. *Roads* (1999): total length 116,500 km (paved 90%). *Vehicles* (2002): passenger cars 6,711,000; trucks and buses 997,000. *Air transport* (2001; KLM only): passenger-km 57,848,000,000; metric ton-km cargo 4,464,000,000; airports (1996) 6. **Communications,** in total units (units per 1,000 persons). Daily newspaper circulation (2000): 4,870,000 (306); radios (2000): 15,600,000 (980); televisions (2000): 8,570,000 (538); telephone main lines (2003): 10,004,000 (614); cellular telephone subscribers (2003): 12,500,000 (768); personal computers (2002): 7,557,000 (467); Internet users (2003): 8,500,000 (822).

Education and health

Educational attainment (2001). Percentage of population ages 15–64 having: primary education 14.1%; lower secondary 9.3%; upper secondary/vocational 54.3%; tertiary vocational 15.1%; university 6.9%; unknown 0.3%. **Health** (2000): physicians 27,161 (1 per 586 persons); hospital beds 90,747 (1 per 175 persons); infant mortality rate per 1,000 live births (2003) 5.2. **Food** (2001): daily per capita caloric intake 3,282 (vegetable products 64%, animal products 36%); 117% of FAO recommended minimum.

Military

Total active duty personnel (2003): 53,130 (army 43.6%, navy 22.8%, air force 20.8%, paramilitary 12.8%). **Military expenditure as percentage of GNP** (1999): 1.8% (world 2.4%); per capita expenditure $445.

Background

Celtic and Germanic tribes inhabited The Netherlands at the time of the Roman conquest. Under the Romans, trade and industry flourished, but by the mid-3rd century AD Roman power had waned, eroded by resurgent German tribes and the encroachment of the sea. A Germanic invasion (406–07) ended Roman control. The Merovingian dynasty followed the Romans but was supplanted in the 7th century by the Carolingian dynasty, which converted the area to Christianity. After Charlemagne's death in 814, the area was increasingly the target of Viking attacks. It became part of the kingdom of Lotharingia, which established an Imperial Church. In the 12th–14th centuries dike building occurred on a large scale. The dukes of Burgundy gained control in the late 14th century. By the early 16th century the Low Countries were ruled by the Spanish Habsburgs. In 1581 the seven northern provinces, led by Calvinists, declared their independence from Spain, and in 1648, following the Thirty Years' War, Spain recognized Dutch independence. The 17th century was the golden age of Dutch civilization. The Dutch East

---

1 metric ton = about 1.1 short tons;   1 kilometer = 0.6 mi (statute);   1 metric ton-km cargo = about 0.68 short ton-mi cargo;   c.i.f.: cost, insurance, and freight;   f.o.b.: free on board

India Company secured Asian colonies, and the country's standard of living soared. In the 18th century the region was conquered by the French and became the kingdom of Holland under Napoleon (1806). It remained neutral in World War I and declared neutrality in World War II but was occupied by Germany. It joined NATO in 1949, was a founding member of what is now the European Community, and is part of the EU.

Recent Developments

The procedures for the assessment of the decision process leading to physician-assisted suicide and voluntary euthanasia—which were tolerated in The Netherlands under well-defined restraints—were altered in 2006 in an effort to increase openness; all reviews of reported cases (stripped of personally identifying information) were to be published on the Internet. Tougher immigration policies were introduced in 2006 in light of evidence that new citizens and other immigrants who had resided in The Netherlands for many years had not integrated as successfully as had been hoped. Applicants in some cases would be required to undergo examination in advance to establish a basic knowledge of Dutch society and language. Immigration Minister Rita Verdonk developed strict policies and attempted to enforce them consistently, resulting in criticism from those who challenged her judgments and demanded more flexibility. In May Verdonk publicly questioned the legality of the Dutch citizenship of Ayaan Hirsi Ali, a Somali-born member of the parliament. Hirsi Ali had admitted that in 1992 she had given erroneous information when she sought political asylum in The Netherlands. She retained her Dutch citizenship but took a job at the American Enterprise Institute in Washington DC, while in December the parliament stripped Verdonk of her immigration responsibilities.

Internet resources: <www.holland.com>.

Netherlands Antilles

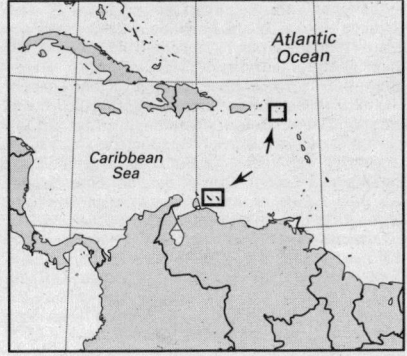

Atlantic Ocean

Caribbean Sea

Official name: Nederlandse Antillen (Netherlands Antilles). **Political status:** nonmetropolitan territory of The Netherlands with one legislative house (States of the Netherlands Antilles [22]). **Chief of state:** Queen Beatrix (from 1980), represented by Governor Frits Goedgedrag (from 2002). **Head of government:** Prime Minister Emily de Jongh-Elhage (from 2006). **Capital:** Willemstad. **Official language:** Dutch. **Official religion:** none. **Monetary unit:** 1 Netherlands Antillean guilder (NA f.) = 100 cents; valuation (1 Jul 2007) US$1 = NA f. 1.80.

Demography

Area: 308 sq mi, 800 sq km. **Population** (2006): 189,000. **Density** (2006): persons per sq mi 613.6, persons per sq km 236.3. **Urban** (2001): 69.6%. **Sex distribution** (2003): male 46.81%; female 53.19%. **Age breakdown** (2001): under 15, 24.2%; 15–29, 18.2%; 30–44, 25.5%; 45–59, 19.0%; 60–74, 9.4%; 75 and over, 3.7%. **Ethnic composition** (2000): local black-other (Antillean Creole) 81.1%; Dutch 5.3%; Surinamese 2.9%; other (significantly West Indian black) 10.7%. **Religious affiliation** (2001): Roman Catholic 72.0%; Protestant 16.0%; Spiritist 0.9%; Buddhist 0.5%; Jewish 0.4%; Baha'i 0.3%; Hindu 0.2%; Muslim 0.2%; other/unknown 9.5%. **Major cities** (2001): Willemstad (urban agglomeration) 125,000; Kralendijk 7,900; Philipsburg 6,300. **Location:** two separate island groups in the Caribbean Sea, one just north of Venezuela, the other east of Puerto Rico.

Vital statistics

Birth rate per 1,000 population (2001): 13.6 (world avg. 21.3); (1988) legitimate 51.6%. **Death rate** per 1,000 population (2001): 6.4 (world avg. 9.1). **Natural increase rate** per 1,000 population (2001): 7.2 (world avg. 12.2). **Total fertility rate** (avg. births per childbearing woman; 2003): 2.0. **Marriage rate** per 1,000 population (2003): 4.2. **Divorce rate** per 1,000 population (1999): 2.6. **Life expectancy** at birth (2003): male 73.2 years; female 77.7 years.

National economy

Budget (2002). *Revenue:* NA f. 616,500,000 (tax revenue 86.5%, of which sales tax 40.6%, import duties 20.6%, excise on gasoline 12.7%; nontax revenue 11.7%; grants 1.8%). *Expenditures:* NA f. 669,000,-000 (current expenditures 94.7%, of which transfers 32.0%, wages 31.1%, interest payments 16.1%, goods and services 12.9%; development expenditures 5.3%). **Production** (metric tons except as noted). *Agriculture and fishing:* mostly tomatoes, beans, cucumbers, gherkins, melons, and lettuce grown on hydroponic farms; aloes grown for export, divi-divi pods, and sour orange fruit are nonhydroponic crops; livestock (number of live animals; 2002) 13,000 goats, 7,300 sheep, 135,000 chickens; fish catch (2001) 955. *Mining and quarrying* (2001): salt 500,000, sulfur by-product 30,000. *Manufacturing* (2000): residual fuel oil 5,112,000; gas-diesel oils 2,525,000; other manufactures include electronic parts, cigarettes, textiles, rum, and Curaçao liqueur. *Energy production (consumption):* electricity (kW-hr; 2000) 1,120,500,000 (1,120,000,000); crude petroleum (barrels; 2000) none (107,000,000); petroleum products (2000) 10,459,000 (2,052,000). **Land use** as % of total land area (2000): in temporary crops 10.0%; overall forest area 1%. **Tourism** (2001): receipts from visitors $746,000,000; expenditures by nationals abroad (2000) $339,000,000. **Households.** Average household size (2001) 2.9; expenditure (1996; Curaçao only): housing 26.5%, transportation and communications 19.9%, food 14.7%, household furnishings 8.8%, recreation and education 8.2%, clothing and footwear 7.5%. **Gross domestic product** (at current market prices; 2001): $2,546,000,000 ($14,720 per capita). **Population economically active** (2001): total 81,558; activity rate of total population 46.4% (participation rates: ages 15–64, 68.7%; female 49.0%; unemployed [2002] 14.2%). **Public debt** (2003): $2,458,-000,000.

Foreign trade

Imports (2001): NA f. 2,850,000,000 (nonpetroleum domestic imports 67.8%, crude petroleum and petroleum products 17.6%, imports of Curaçao free zone 14.6%). *Major import sources* (2000): US 25.8%; Mexico 20.7%; Gabon 6.6%; Italy 5.8%; The Netherlands 5.5%. **Exports** (2001): NA f. 984,000,000 (goods procured in ports for ships' bunkers 37.7%, re-exports of Curaçao free zone 30.9%, nonpetroleum domestic exports 18.3%). *Major export destinations* (2000): US 35.9%; Guatemala 9.4%; Venezuela 8.7%; France 5.4%; Singapore 2.8%.

Transport and communications

Transport. *Roads* (1992): total length 590 km (paved 51%). *Vehicles* (1999): passenger cars 74,840; trucks and buses 17,415. *Air transport* (2001; Curaçao and Sint Maarten airports): passenger arrivals and departures 2,131,000; freight loaded and unloaded 18,900 metric tons; airports (2000) with scheduled flights 5. **Communications**, in total units (units per 1,000 persons). Daily newspaper circulation (1996): 70,000 (341); radios (1997): 217,000 (1,039); televisions (1997): 69,000 (330); telephone main lines (2001): 81,000 (372); cellular telephone subscribers (1998): 16,000 (77); Internet users (1999): 2,000 (9.3).

Education and health

Educational attainment (2001). Percentage of population 25 and over having: no formal schooling 0.8%; primary education 24.2%; lower secondary 42.8%; upper secondary 16.8%; higher 11.4%; unknown 4.0%. **Literacy** (1995): total population age 15 and over literate 194,900 (96.6%); males literate 93,300 (96.6%); females literate 101,600 (96.6%). **Health** (2001): physicians 333 (1 per 520 persons); hospital beds 1,343 (1 per 129 persons); infant mortality rate per 1,000 live births (2003) 10.7. **Food** (2001): daily per capita caloric intake 2,565 (vegetable products 72%, animal products 28%); 106% of FAO recommended minimum.

Military

Total active duty personnel (2004): 1,000 Dutch naval personnel in Netherlands Antilles and Aruba.

Background

The islands of the Netherlands Antilles were sighted by Christopher Columbus in 1493 and claimed for Spain. In the 17th century the Dutch gained control,

and in 1845 the islands became the Netherlands Antilles. In 1954 they became an integral part of The Netherlands, with full autonomy in domestic affairs. Aruba seceded from the group in 1986.

Recent Developments

According to an agreement signed in November 2005, the Netherlands Antilles would break up on 1 July 2007, with Sint Maarten and Curaçao becoming "countries" of The Netherlands while the small islands of Bonaire, Saba, and Sint Eustatius became "overseas municipalities." In February 2007, however, it was announced that the date for dissolution had been delayed until 15 Dec 2008.

Internet resources:
<www.cia.gov/cia/publications/factbook/geos/nt.html>.

New Caledonia

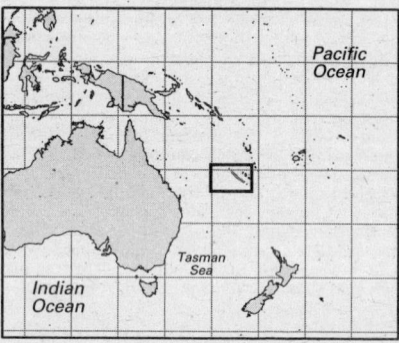

Pacific Ocean

Tasman Sea

Indian Ocean

Official name: Nouvelle-Calédonie (New Caledonia). **Political status:** overseas collectivity (France) with one legislative house (Congress [54]; operates in association with 3 provincial assemblies). The Nouméa Accord of 1998 granted New Caledonia limited autonomy with likely independence by 2013. **Chief of state:** President of France Nicolas Sarkozy (from 2007), represented by High Commissioner Michel Mathieu (from 2005). **Head of government:** President Marie-Noëlle Thémereau (from 2004). **Capital:** Nouméa. **Official language:** none; Kanak languages and French have special recognition per the Nouméa Accord. **Official religion:** none. **Monetary unit:** 1 franc of the Comptoirs français du Pacifique (CFPF) = 100 centimes; valuation (1 Jul 2007) US$1 = CFPF 88.26; the CFPF is pegged to the euro (€) at €1 = CFPF 119.25 from 1 Jan 2002.

Demography

Area: 7,172 sq mi, 18,575 sq km. **Population** (2006): 238,000. **Density** (2006): persons per sq mi 33.2, persons per sq km 12.8. **Urban** (2002): 79.0%. **Sex distribution** (2003): male 50.33%; female

1 metric ton = about 1.1 short tons;   1 kilometer = 0.6 mi (statute);   1 metric ton-km cargo = about 0.68 short ton-mi cargo;   c.i.f.: cost, insurance, and freight;   f.o.b.: free on board

49.67%. **Age breakdown** (2003): under 15, 29.7%; 15–29, 25.4%; 30–44, 21.6%; 45–59, 13.9%; 60–74, 7.5%; 75 and over, 1.9%. **Ethnic composition** (1996): Melanesian 45.3%, of which local (Kanak) 44.1%, Vanuatuan 1.2%; European 34.1%; Wallisian or Futunan 9.0%; Indonesian 2.6%; Tahitian 2.6%; Vietnamese 1.4%; other 5.0%. **Religious affiliation** (2000): Roman Catholic 54.2%; Protestant 14.0%; Muslim 2.7%; other Christian 2.1%; other 27.0%. **Major cities** (1996): Nouméa 76,293 (urban agglomeration 118,823); Mont-Dore 20,780 (within Nouméa urban agglomeration); Dumbéa 13,888 (within Nouméa urban agglomeration). **Location:** South Pacific Ocean, about 1,100 mi (1,800 km) east of Queensland, Australia.

Vital statistics

Birth rate per 1,000 population (2003): 18.6 (world avg. 21.3); (1996) legitimate 36.4%. **Death rate** per 1,000 population (2003): 5.1 (world avg. 9.1). **Natural increase rate** per 1,000 population (2003): 13.5 (world avg. 12.2). **Total fertility rate** (avg. births per childbearing woman; 2003): 2.4. **Marriage rate** per 1,000 population (2001): 4.3. **Divorce rate** per 1,000 population (1999): 0.8. **Life expectancy** at birth (2003): male 70.6 years; female 76.6 years.

National economy

Budget (2001). *Revenue:* $A 1,184,000,000 (tax revenue 74.7%, nontax revenue 25.3%). *Expenditures:* $A 1,156,000,000 (current expenditure 90.1%, development expenditure 9.9%). **Production** (metric tons except as noted). *Agriculture, forestry, fishing* (2003): coconuts 16,000, yams 11,222, vegetables 3,900; livestock (number of live animals) 110,000 cattle, 25,500 pigs, 510,000 poultry; roundwood (2002) 4,800 cu m; fish catch (2001) 5,197, of which shrimp 1,870, tuna 1,008, sea cucumbers 489. *Mining and quarrying:* nickel ore (2003) 6,625,000, of which nickel content (2002) 59,867; cobalt (2002) 900 (recovered). *Manufacturing* (2003): cement (2002) 100,080; ferronickel (metal content) 50,666; nickel matte (metal content) 10,857. *Energy production (consumption):* electricity (kW-hr; 2002) 1,758,000,000 (1,758,000,000); coal (2000) none (160,000); petroleum products (2000) none (405,000). **Population economically active** (1996): total 80,589; activity rate of total population 40.9% (participation rates: over age 14, 57.3%; female 39.7%; unemployed 18.6%). **Public debt** (external, outstanding; 1999): $746,000,000. **Gross national product** (at current market prices; 2001): $3,200,000,000 ($15,060 per capita). **Household income and expenditure.** Average household size (2002) 3.9; average annual income per household (1991) CFPF 3,361,233; sources of income (1991): wages and salaries 68.2%, transfer payments 13.7%, other 18.1%; expenditure (1991): food and beverages 25.9%, housing 20.4%, transportation and communications 16.1%, recreation 4.8%. **Tourism:** receipts from visitors (2001) $93,000,000. **Land use** as % of total land area (2000): in temporary crops 0.4%, in permanent crops 0.3%, in pasture 11.8%; overall forest area 20.4%.

Foreign trade

Imports (2002-c.i.f.): CFPF 127,123,000,000 (machinery and apparatus 18.2%, food 15.6%, transportation equipment 15.2%, mineral products [mostly coal and refined petroleum] 13.4%, chemicals and chemical products 8.4%). *Major import sources* (2003): France 50.0%; Singapore 10.4%; Australia 10.2%; New Zealand 4.1%; Germany 3.8%. **Exports** (2002-f.o.b.): CFPF 59,101,000,000 (ferronickel 64.2%, nickel matte 13.0%, nickel ore 12.3%, shrimp 2.3%). *Major export destinations* (2003): France 26.0%; Japan 21.4%; Taiwan 16.6%; Spain 8.8%; Australia 6.4%.

Transport and communications

Transport. *Roads* (2000): total length 5,432 km (paved [1993] 52%). *Vehicles:* passenger cars (2001) 85,500; trucks and buses (1997) 23,000. *Air transport* (2003; Air Calédonie only): passenger-km 46,000,000, metric ton-km cargo 4,115,000; airports (2004) with scheduled flights 11. **Communications,** in total units (units per 1,000 persons). Daily newspaper circulation (1996): 24,000 (121); radios (1997): 107,000 (533); televisions (1999): 101,000 (480); telephone main lines (2002): 52,000 (232); cellular telephone subscribers (2002): 80,000 (357); Internet users (2003): 60,000 (262).

Education and health

Educational attainment (1996). Percentage of population age 14 and over having: no formal schooling 5.7%; primary education 28.9%; lower secondary 30.2%; upper secondary 24.6%; higher 10.5%. **Health** (1999): physicians 418 (1 per 497 persons); hospital beds 838 (1 per 248 persons); infant mortality rate per 1,000 live births (2003) 8.1. **Food** (2001): daily per capita caloric intake 2,770 (vegetable products 76%, animal products 24%); 120% of FAO recommended minimum.

Military

Total active duty personnel (2003): 2,700 French troops.

Background

Excavations indicate an Austronesian presence in New Caledonia about 2000–1000 BC. The islands were visited by James Cook in 1774 and by various navigators and traders in the 18th–19th centuries. They were occupied by France in 1853 and were a penal colony from 1864 to 1897. During World War II the islands were the site of Allied bases. They became a French overseas territory in 1946. In 1987 residents voted by referendum to remain part of France.

Recent Developments

New nickel mines were developed in New Caledonia in 2006, despite opposition on political and environmental grounds and labor unrest over the hiring of 2,500 Filipino workers to build the mine complexes. The government aimed to attract some $4 billion in investment to reduce New Caledonia's dependence on French aid (which equaled approximately $1 billion a year).

Internet resources:
<www.newcaledoniatourism-south.com>.

New Zealand

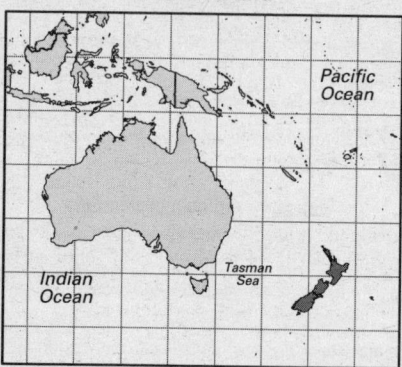

Official name: New Zealand (English); Aotearoa (Maori). **Form of government:** constitutional monarchy with one legislative house (House of Representatives [120, including seven elective seats allocated to Maoris]). **Chief of state:** Queen Elizabeth II (from 1952), represented by Governor-General Anand Satyanand (from 2006). **Head of government:** Prime Minister Helen Clark (from 1999). **Capital:** Wellington. **Official languages:** English; Maori. **Official religion:** none. **Monetary unit:** 1 New Zealand dollar ($NZ) = 100 cents; valuation (1 Jul 2007) US$1 = $NZ 1.29.

Demography

Area: 104,515 sq mi, 270,692 sq km. **Population** (2006): 4,141,000. **Density** (2006): persons per sq mi 39.6, persons per sq km 15.3. **Urban** (2002): 86.0%. **Sex distribution** (2001): male 49.07%; female 50.93%. **Age breakdown** (2001): under 15, 22.5%; 15–29, 20.4%; 30–44, 23.0%; 45–59, 18.0%; 60–74, 10.7%; 75 and over, 5.4%. **Ethnic composition** (2001): European 73.8%; Maori (local Polynesian) 13.5%; Asian 6.1%; other Pacific Peoples (mostly other Polynesian) 6.0%; other 0.6%. **Religious affiliation** (2001): Christian 55.2%, of which Anglican 15.3%, Roman Catholic 12.7%, Presbyterian 11.3%; nonreligious 26.9%; Buddhist 1.1%; Hindu 1.0%; other religions/not specified 15.8%. **Major urban areas** (2001): Auckland 1,074,513; Wellington 339,750; Christchurch 334,107; Hamilton 166,128; Dunedin 107,088. **Location:** between the South Pacific Ocean and the Tasman Sea, southeast of Australia.

Vital statistics

Birth rate per 1,000 population (2003): 14.1 (world avg. 21.3); (2001) legitimate 56.3%. **Death rate** per 1,000 population (2003): 7.5 (world avg. 9.1). **Natural increase rate** per 1,000 population (2003): 6.6 (world avg. 12.2). **Total fertility rate** (avg. births per childbearing woman; 2003): 1.8. **Marriage rate** per 1,000 population (2001): 5.1. **Life expectancy** at birth (2003): male 75.3 years; female 81.4 years.

National economy

Budget (2000–01). *Revenue:* $NZ 37,156,000,000 (income taxes 59.4%, taxes on goods and services 34.4%, nontax revenue 6.2%). *Expenditures:* $NZ 37,019,000,000 (social welfare 37.0%, health 19.0%, education 17.6%). **Production** (metric tons except as noted). *Agriculture, forestry, fishing* (2002): apples 537,000, barley 406,000, wheat 355,000; livestock (number of live animals) 43,142,000 sheep, 9,633,000 cattle, 358,000 pigs; roundwood (2000) 20,523,000 cu m; fish catch (2001) 637,000. *Mining and quarrying* (2001): limestone 4,746,000; iron ore and sand concentrate 1,636,000; gold 9,850 kg. *Manufacturing* (1999): wood pulp 1,572,000; chemical fertilizers 1,365,-000; wool yarn 23,500. *Energy production (consumption):* electricity (kW-hr; 2000) 39,010,000,000 (39,010,000,000); hard coal (2000) 3,355,000 (1,755,000); lignite (2000) 213,000 (261,000); crude petroleum (barrels; 2000) 13,068,000 (40,-001,000); petroleum products (2000) 5,038,000 (5,365,000); natural gas (cu m; 2000) 5,445,-000,000 (5,444,000,000). **Household income and expenditure.** Average household size (1998) 2.8; annual gross income per household (2000–01) $NZ 53,076; sources of income (1998): wages and salaries 65.8%, transfer payments 15.2%, self-employment 9.8%, other 9.2%; expenditure (2000–01): housing 23.9%, food 16.5%, transportation 15.9%, household goods 12.8%, clothing 3.2%. **Tourism** (2002): receipts US$2,918,000,000; expenditures US$1,480,000,000. **Gross national product** (2003): US$63,608,000,000 (US$15,870 per capita). **Population economically active** (2000): total 1,923,700; activity rate 50.1% (participation rates: over age 15, 66.2%; female 45.3%; unemployed 5.7%). **Land use** as % of total land area (2000): in temporary crops 5.6%, in permanent crops 6.9%, in pasture 51.7%; overall forest area 29.7%.

Foreign trade

Imports (2001–02-f.o.b. in balance of trade and c.i.f. in commodities and trading partners): $NZ 32,165,000,000 (machinery and apparatus 21.4%, crude and refined petroleum 13.7%, vehicles 13.4%, plastics 3.7%). *Major import sources:* Australia 21.4%; US 13.7%; Japan 10.8%; China 7.2%; Germany 4.7%. **Exports** (2001–02): $NZ 31,676,-000,000 (domestic exports 96.2%, of which dairy products 20.6%, beef and sheep meat 12.7%, wood and paper products 10.8%, machinery and apparatus 6.1%, fruits and nuts 3.7%; reexports 3.8%). *Major export destinations:* Australia 19.9%; US 15.3%; Japan 11.5%; UK 4.9%; South Korea 4.5%; China 4.5%.

Transport and communications

Transport. *Railroads* (1999): route length 3,912 km; passengers carried (2001–02) 14,330,000; metric ton-km cargo (1998) 3,960,000,000. *Roads* (1999): total length 92,075 km (paved 62%). *Vehicles* (2002): passenger cars 1,960,503; trucks and buses 374,005. *Air transport* (1999; Air New Zealand only): passenger-km 19,879,000,000; met-

---

1 metric ton = about 1.1 short tons;   1 kilometer = 0.6 mi (statute);   1 metric ton-km cargo = about 0.68 short ton-mi cargo;   c.i.f.: cost, insurance, and freight;   f.o.b.: free on board

ric ton-km cargo 851,744,000; airports (1997) 36. **Communications,** in total units (units per 1,000 persons). Daily newspaper circulation (2000): 799,000 (207); radios (2000): 3,850,000 (997); televisions (2000): 2,010,000 (522); telephone main lines (2002): 1,765,000 (448); cellular telephone subscribers (2003): 2,599,000 (648); personal computers (2002): 1,630,000 (414); Internet users (2003): 2,110,000 (526).

Education and health

Educational attainment (2001). Percentage of population ages 25–64 having: no formal schooling to incomplete secondary 26%; secondary 36%; vocational and some undergraduate 24%; completed undergraduate 14%. **Literacy:** virtually 100%. **Health** (2002): physicians 8,403 (1 per 469 persons); hospital beds 23,825 (1 per 165 persons); infant mortality rate per 1,000 live births (2003) 6.1. **Food** (2001): daily per capita caloric intake 3,235 (vegetable products 67%, animal products 33%); 123% of FAO recommended minimum.

Military

Total active duty personnel (2003): 8,610 (army 51.5%, air force 23.0%, navy 25.6%). **Military expenditure as percentage of GNP** (1999): 1.2% (world 2.4%); per capita expenditure $156.

Background

Polynesian occupation of New Zealand dates to about AD 1000. First sighted by Dutch explorer Abel Janszoon Tasman in 1642, the main islands were charted by Capt. James Cook in 1769. Named a British crown colony in 1840, the area was the scene of warfare between colonists and native Maori through the 1860s. In 1907 the colony became the Dominion of New Zealand. It administered Western Samoa during 1919–62 and participated in both world wars. When Britain joined what is now the European Union in the early 1970s, its influence led New Zealand to expand its export markets and diversify its economy.

Recent Developments

The state budget projected an operating surplus of $NZ 8.5 billion in 2005–06 and $NZ 5.6 billion in 2006–07. An extra $NZ 1.3 billion on new roads over five years included moves to ease Auckland's traffic gridlock and accelerate highway projects in Auckland and Christchurch. New Zealand's deployment of 120 military personnel for reconstruction work in Afghanistan was extended to September 2007. An additional 55 troops and police were dispatched in April to the Solomon Islands to supplement 82 personnel helping to curb civil unrest in the capital, Honiara, and another 120 defense personnel were committed to the international effort to avert civil war in East Timor. Stab-resistant body armor was issued in February to 6,500 police in response to an increase in slashing and stabbing assaults on officers. In September frontline police were controversially issued with Taser stun guns for a 12-month trial. In August former trial judge and parliamentary ombudsman Anand Satyanand, of Indo-Fi-

jian parentage, became New Zealand's first governor-general of Asian descent.

Internet resources: <www.newzealand.com>.

Nicaragua

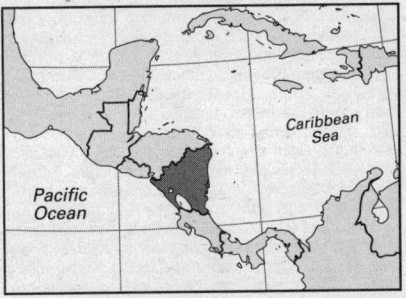

Official name: República de Nicaragua (Republic of Nicaragua). **Form of government:** unitary multiparty republic with one legislative house (National Assembly [92, including two unsuccessful 2001 presidential candidates meeting constitutional requirements for seating]). **Head of state and government:** President Daniel Ortega (from 2007). **Capital:** Managua. **Official language:** Spanish. **Official religion:** none. **Monetary unit:** 1 córdoba oro (C$) = 100 centavos; valuation (1 Jul 2007) US$1 = C$18.78.

Demography

Area: 50,337 sq mi, 130,373 sq km; land area alone equals 46,464 sq mi, 120,340 sq km. **Population** (2006): 5,233,000. **Density** (2006; based on land area): persons per sq mi 112.6; persons per sq km 43.5. **Urban** (2001): 56.5%. **Sex distribution** (2003): male 50.01%; female 49.99%. **Age breakdown** (2003): under 15, 38.8%; 15–29, 30.4%; 30–44, 17.5%; 45–59, 8.6%; 60–74, 3.7%; 75 and over, 0.9%. **Ethnic composition** (2000): mestizo (Spanish/Indian) 63.1%; white 14.0%; black 8.0%; multiple ethnicities 5.0%; other 9.9%. **Religious affiliation** (1995): Roman Catholic 85.1%; Protestant 11.6%, of which Evangelical 8.8%; nonreligious 1.3%; other 2.0%. **Major cities** (1995): Managua (urban agglomeration, 2003) 1,098,000; León 123,865; Chinandega 97,387; Masaya 88,971; Granada 71,783. **Location:** Central America, bordering Honduras, the Caribbean Sea, Costa Rica, and the North Pacific Ocean.

Vital statistics

Birth rate per 1,000 population (2003): 26.1 (world avg. 21.3). **Death rate** per 1,000 population (2003): 4.6 (world avg. 9.1). **Natural increase rate** per 1,000 population (2003): 21.5 (world avg. 12.2). **Total fertility rate** (avg. births per childbearing woman; 2003): 3.0. **Life expectancy** at birth (2003): male 67.7 years; female 71.8 years.

National economy

Budget (2002). *Revenue:* C$8,592,400,000 (tax revenue 94.7%, of which sales tax 42.2%, import duties

29.2%, tax on income and profits 18.8%; nontax revenue 5.3%). *Expenditures:* C$11,905,000,000 (current expenditure 67.2%, development expenditure 32.8%). **Public debt** (external, outstanding; 2002): US$5,576,000,000. **Production** (metric tons except as noted). *Agriculture, forestry, fishing* (2002): sugarcane 3,389,000, corn (maize) 483,330, rice 264,-000; livestock (number of live animals) 3,350,000 cattle, 420,000 pigs; roundwood 5,920,000 cu m; fish catch (2001) 28,520, of which crustaceans 15,486. *Mining and quarrying* (2001): gold 117,350 troy oz. *Manufacturing* (value added in C$'000,000; 2002 [at 1980 prices]): food 1,975; beverages 1,349; cement, bricks, tiles 576; refined petroleum 222; chemical products 206. *Energy production (consumption):* electricity (kW-hr; 2002) 2,620,000,000 ([2000] 2,403,000,000); crude petroleum (barrels; 2000) none (6,069,000); petroleum products (2000) 785,000 (1,138,000). **Tourism** (2002): receipts from visitors US$110,000,000; expenditures by nationals abroad US$69,000,000. **Land use** as % of total land area (2000): in temporary crops 15.9%, in permanent crops 1.9%, in pasture 39.7%; overall forest area 27.0%. **Population economically active** (2001): total 1,900,400; activity rate of total population 37.7% (participation rates: ages 15–64 [2000] 64.1%; female [2000] 29.5%; unemployed 10.5%). **Gross national product** (2003): US$3,989,000,000 (US$730 per capita). **Households.** Average household size (2002) 5.6; expenditure (1999): food and beverages 41.8%, education 9.8%, housing 9.8%, transportation 8.5%.

Foreign trade

Imports (2003-f.o.b. in balance of trade and c.i.f. in commodities and trading partners): US$1,887,-000,000 (nondurable consumer goods 25.9%; mineral fuels 17.4%; capital goods for industry 11.8%; durable consumer goods 7.5%). *Major import sources:* US 24.7%; Venezuela 9.7%; Costa Rica 9.0%; Mexico 8.4%; Guatemala 7.3%. **Exports** (2003): US$605,000,000 (non-marine food products 44.6%, of which coffee 14.1%, meat 13.5%; lobster 6.0%; gold 5.8%; shrimp 5.5%). *Major export destinations:* US 33.4%; El Salvador 17.3%; Costa Rica 8.1%; Honduras 7.2%; Mexico 4.6%.

Transport and communications

Transport. *Roads* (2002): total length 18,709 km (paved 11%). *Vehicles* (2002): passenger cars 83,168; trucks and buses 121,796. *Air transport* (2000): passenger-km 72,000,000; metric ton-km cargo 600,000; airports (1997) with scheduled flights 10. **Communications,** in total units (units per 1,000 persons). Daily newspaper circulation (2000): 152,000 (30); radios (2000): 1,370,000 (270); televisions (2000): 350,000 (69); telephone main lines (2002): 171,600 (32); cellular telephone subscribers (2002): 202,800 (38); personal computers (2002): 90,000 (17); Internet users (2002): 150,000 (28).

Education and health

Educational attainment (1995). Percentage of population age 25 and over having: no formal schooling 30.6%; no formal schooling (literate) 3.9%; primary

education 39.2%; secondary 17.0%; technical 3.1%; incomplete undergraduate 2.2%; complete undergraduate 4.0%. **Literacy** (2000): total population age 15 and over literate 66.5%; males literate 66.3%; females literate 66.8%. **Health:** physicians (2002) 2,066 (1 per 2,491 persons); hospital beds 5,031 (1 per 1,023 persons); infant mortality rate per 1,000 live births (2003) 31.2. **Food** (2001): daily per capita caloric intake 2,256 (vegetable products 92%, animal products 8%); 99% of FAO recommended minimum.

Military

Total active duty personnel (2003): 14,000 (army 85.7%, navy 5.7%, air force 8.6%). **Military expenditure as percentage of GNP** (1999): 1.2% (world 2.4%); per capita expenditure US$5.

Background

Nicaragua has been inhabited for thousands of years, most notably by the Maya. Christopher Columbus arrived in 1502, and Spanish explorers discovered Lake Nicaragua soon thereafter. Nicaragua was governed by Spain until 1821, when it declared its independence. It was part of Mexico and then the United Provinces of Central America until 1838, when full independence was achieved. The US intervened in political affairs by maintaining troops there in 1912–33. Ruled by the dictatorial Somoza dynasty from 1936 to 1979, it was taken over by the Sandinistas after a popular revolt. They were opposed by armed insurgents, the US-backed contras, from 1981. The Sandinista government nationalized several sectors of the economy but lost the national elections in 1990. The new government returned many economic activities to private control, but unrest continued through the 1990s.

Recent Developments

Political fighting over constitutional reforms limiting the powers of the president ended with an agreement to delay the changes until after Pres. Enrique Bolaños stepped down in January 2007. The election of November 2006 brought former president and antagonist of the US Daniel Ortega back to power, aided by a new election rule that allowed a candidate to declare victory with only 35% of the vote after the first round (Ortega gained 38%). The Central America–Dominican Republic Free Trade Agreement (CAFTA–DR), ratified by Nicaragua in October 2005, went into effect in April 2006. The Heavily Indebted Poor Countries and Multilateral Debt Relief initiatives canceled more than $1.1 billion of Nicaragua's foreign debt in 2006, but 80% of the country still lived on less than $2 a day.

Internet resources: <www.intur.gob.ni>.

Niger

Official name: République du Niger (Republic of Niger). **Form of government:** multiparty republic with one legislative house (National Assembly [113]). **Head of state and government:** President Mamadou Tandja (from

1 metric ton = about 1.1 short tons;   1 kilometer = 0.6 mi (statute);   1 metric ton-km cargo = about 0.68 short ton-mi cargo;   c.i.f.: cost, insurance, and freight;   f.o.b.: free on board

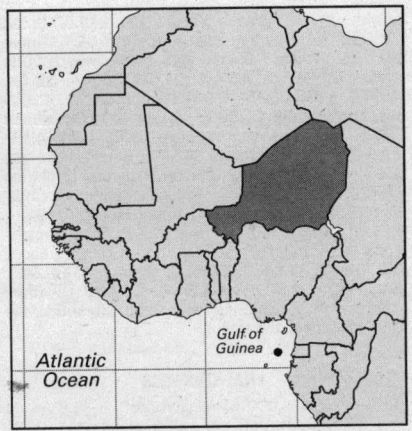

Gulf of Guinea

Atlantic Ocean

1999), assisted by Prime Minister Seyni Oumarou (from 2007). **Capital:** Niamey. **Official language:** French. **Official religion:** none. **Monetary unit:** 1 CFA franc (CFAF) = 100 centimes; valuation (1 Jul 2007) US$1 = CFAF 485.18 (earlier pegged to the French franc, after 1 Jan 2002 the CFAF was pegged at 655.96 to the euro).

Demography

Area: 459,286 sq mi, 1,189,546 sq km. **Population** (2006): 12,841,000. **Density** (2006): persons per sq mi 28.0, persons per sq km 10.8. **Urban** (2001): 16.2%. **Sex distribution** (2001): male 49.86%; female 50.14%. **Age breakdown** (2001): under 15, 48.0%; 15–29, 26.3%; 30–44, 14.1%; 45–59, 7.8%; 60–74, 3.2%; 75 and over, 0.6%. **Ethnolinguistic composition** (2000): Zerma- (Djerma-) Songhai 25.7%; Tazarawa 14.9%; Fulani (Peul) 11.1%; Hausa 6.6%; other 41.7%. **Religious affiliation** (2000): Sunni Muslim 90.7%; traditional beliefs 8.7%; Christian 0.5%; other 0.1%. **Major cities** (2001): Niamey 674,950 (urban agglomeration [2003] 890,000); Zinder 170,574; Maradi 147,038; Agadez 76,957; Tahoua 72,446. **Location:** western Africa, bordering Algeria, Libya, Chad, Nigeria, Benin, Burkina Faso, and Mali.

Vital statistics

Birth rate per 1,000 population (2003): 49.5 (world avg. 21.3). **Death rate** per 1,000 population (2003): 21.7 (world avg. 9.1). **Natural increase rate** per 1,000 population (2003): 27.8 (world avg. 12.2). **Total fertility rate** (avg. births per childbearing woman; 2003): 6.9. **Life expectancy** at birth (2003): male 42.3 years; female 42.1 years.

National economy

Budget (2003). *Revenue:* CFAF 221,281,000,000 (taxes 69.3%, external aid and gifts 29.2%, nontax revenue 1.5%). *Expenditures:* CFAF 272,200,-000,000 (current expenditures 57.6%, of which education 10.9%, defense and public order 8.4%, interest 6.4%, health 3.8%; development expenditures 42.4%). **Public debt** (external, outstanding; 2002): $1,604,000,000. **Tourism** (2002): receipts from visi-tors $28,000,000; expenditures by nationals abroad $16,000,000. **Gross national product** (2003): $2,361,000,000 ($200 per capita). **Production** (metric tons except as noted). *Agriculture, forestry, fishing* (2003): millet 2,567,200, sorghum 669,700, cowpeas 654,200; livestock (number of live animals) 6,900,000 goats, 4,500,000 sheep, 2,260,000 cattle; roundwood (2002) 8,601;400 cu m; fish catch (2001) 20,821. *Mining and quarrying* (2003): uranium 3,143; salt 3,000. *Manufacturing* (value added in CFAF '000,000; 1998): paper and products 3,171; food 1,697; soaps and other chemical products 1,547. *Energy production (consumption):* electricity (kW-hr; 2000) 238,000,000 (451,000,000); coal (2000) 175,000 (175,000); petroleum products (2001) none (138,300). **Population economically active** (1988; excludes nomadic population): total 2,315,694; activity rate of total population 31.9% (participation rates: ages 15–64, 55.2%; female 20.4%). **Households.** Average household size (2002) 6.4; expenditure (1996): food, beverages, and tobacco products 45.1%, housing and energy 13.9%, transportation 12.1%, household furnishings 7.7%, clothing and footwear 5.8%. **Land use** as % of total land area (2000): in temporary crops 3.5%, in permanent crops 0.01%, in pasture 9.5%; overall forest area 1.0%.

Foreign trade

Imports (2003): CFAF 275,700,000,000 (food products 28.6%, capital goods 26.3%, petroleum products 11.5%, intermediate goods 6.7%). *Major import sources:* France 17.1%; Côte d'Ivoire 15.0%; Nigeria 8.1%; Japan 4.6%. **Exports** (2003): CFAF 203,300,-000,000 (uranium 32.2%, reexports 17.9%, cattle 17.5%, onions 7.7%, cowpeas 5.3%). *Major export destinations:* France 37.1%; Nigeria 33.6%; Japan 17.2%; Spain 3.8%.

Transport and communications

Transport. *Roads* (2000): total length 14,000 km (paved 26%). *Vehicles* (1999): passenger cars; 26,000, trucks and buses 35,600. *Air transport* (2000; represents $^1/_{11}$ of the traffic of Air Afrique; Air Afrique, an airline jointly owned by 11 African countries [including Niger], was declared bankrupt in 2002): passenger-km 216,000,000; airports (1999) with scheduled flights 6. **Communications,** in total units (units per 1,000 persons). Daily newspaper circulation (1996): 2,000 (0.2); radios (2000): 1,270,000 (121); televisions (2000): 388,000 (37); telephone main lines (2002): 22,400 (1.9); cellular telephone subscribers (2003): 24,000 (2); personal computers (2002): 7,000 (0.6); Internet users (2002): 15,000 (1.3).

Education and health

Educational attainment (1988). Percentage of population age 25 and over having: no formal schooling 85.0%; Koranic education 11.2%; primary education 2.5%; secondary 1.1%; higher 0.2%. **Literacy** (2001): total population age 15 and over literate 16.5%; males literate 24.4%; females literate 8.9%. **Health:** physicians (1997) 324 (1 per 28,171 persons); infant mortality rate per 1,000 live births (2003) 123.6. **Food** (2001): daily per capita caloric intake 2,118 (vegetable products 94%, animal products 6%); 90% of FAO recommended minimum.

Military

Total active duty personnel (2003): 5,300 (army 98.1%, air force 1.9%). **Military expenditure as percentage of GNP** (1999): 1.2% (world 2.4%); per capita expenditure $2.

Background

On the territory of Niger, there is evidence of Neolithic culture, and several kingdoms existed there before the colonialists arrived. First explored by Europeans in the late 18th century, it became a French colony in 1922. It became an overseas territory of France in 1946 and gained independence in 1960. The first multiparty elections were held in 1993.

Recent Developments

A locust infestation in 2004 and years of drought brought about a food crisis in Niger. In June 2006 the UN called for $3 million for emergency food aid. Recent studies, however, showed that over the past 30 years almost 3 million ha (7.5 million ac) of land in Niger had been covered with trees by poor farmers, leading to an estimated 600,000 new acres of arable land.

Internet resources: <www.nigerembassyusa.org>.

Nigeria

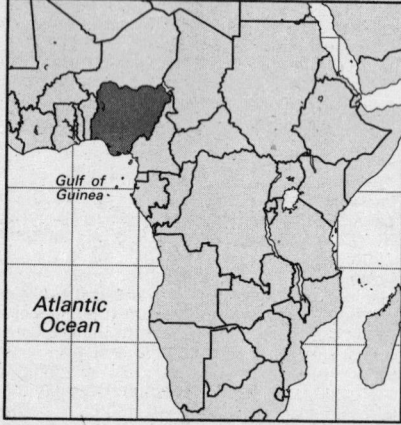

Gulf of Guinea

Atlantic Ocean

Official name: Federal Republic of Nigeria. **Form of government:** federal republic with two legislative bodies (Senate [109]; House of Representatives [360]). **Head of state and government:** President Umaru Yar'Adua (from 2007). **Capital:** Abuja. **Official language:** English. **Official religion:** none. **Monetary unit:** 1 Nigerian naira (N) = 100 kobo; valuation (1 Jul 2007) US$1 = N129.14.

Demography

Area: 356,669 sq mi, 923,768 sq km. **Population** (2006): 134,375,000. **Density** (2006): persons per sq mi 376.7, persons per sq km 145.5. **Urban** (2002): 44.9%. **Sex distribution** (2003): male 50.59%; female 49.41%. **Age breakdown** (2003): under 15, 43.6%; 15–29, 27.9%; 30–44, 15.4%; 45–59, 8.5%; 60–74, 3.9%; 75 and over, 0.7%. **Ethnic composition** (2000): Yoruba 17.5%; Hausa 17.2%; Igbo (Ibo) 13.3%; Fulani 10.7%; Ibibio 4.1%; Kanuri 3.6%; Egba 2.9%; Tiv 2.6%; Bura 1.1%; Nupe 1.0%; Edo 1.0%; other 25.0%. **Religious affiliation** (2000): Christian 45.9%, of which independent Christian 15.0%, Anglican 13.0%, other Protestant 9.0%, Roman Catholic 8.0%; Muslim 43.9%; African indigenous 9.8%; other 0.4%. **Major cities** (2002): Lagos 8,030,000; Kano 3,250,000; Ibadan 3,080,000; Kaduna 1,460,000; Benin City 1,050,000. **Location:** western Africa, bordering Niger, Chad, Cameroon, the Gulf of Guinea, and Benin.

Vital statistics

Birth rate per 1,000 population (2003): 38.8 (world avg. 21.3). **Death rate** per 1,000 population (2003): 13.8 (world avg. 9.1). **Natural increase rate** per 1,000 population (2003): 25.0 (world avg. 12.2). **Total fertility rate** (avg. births per childbearing woman; 2003): 5.4. **Life expectancy** at birth (2003): male 50.9 years; female 51.1 years. **Adult population** (ages 15–49) **living with HIV** (2004): 5.4% (world avg. 1.1%).

National economy

Budget (2003). *Revenue:* N 2,752,107,000,000 (nontax revenue 62.6%, of which crude oil export proceeds 35.1%, crude oil sales to domestic refineries 14.0%; tax revenue 37.4%, of which oil profits tax 15.9%, tax on international trade 8.5%). *Expenditures:* N 2,853,918,000,000 (state and local governments 40.5%, current expenditure 32.0%, Nigerian National Petroleum Corporation [NNPC] 15.8%, capital expenditure 8.8%). **Production** (metric tons except as noted). *Agriculture, forestry, fishing* (2003): cassava 40,927,000, yams 30,439,000, millet 9,974,000; livestock 27,000,000 goats, 22,500,000 sheep, 15,163,700 cattle; roundwood (2002) 69,482,328 cu m; fish catch (2001) 476,544. *Mining and quarrying* (2002): limestone 3,400,000; marble 130,000. *Manufacturing* (value added in N'000,000; 1995): food and beverages 25,415; textiles 16,193; chemical products 11,181. *Energy production (consumption):* electricity (kW-hr; 2000) 17,757,000,000 (17,757,000,000); coal (2000) 61,000 (61,000); crude petroleum (barrels; 2003) 899,300,000 ([2001] 106,580,000); petroleum products (2000) 4,500,000 (10,199,000); natural gas (cu m; 2000) 12,539,000 (7,123,000). **Households.** Average household size (2002) 4.9; annual income per household (1992–93) N 15,000. **Gross national product** (2003): $42,984,000,000 ($320 per capita). **Public debt** (external, outstanding; 2002): $28,057,000,000. **Population economically active** (1993–94): total 29,000,000; activity rate 31.0% (participation rates: ages 15–59, 64.4%; female 44.0%). **Tourism** (2002): receipts $263,000,000; expenditures $950,000,000. **Land use** as % of total land area (2000): in temporary crops 31.0%, in permanent crops 2.9%, in pasture 43.0%; overall forest area 14.8%.

---

1 metric ton = about 1.1 short tons;   1 kilometer = 0.6 mi (statute);   1 metric ton-km cargo = about 0.68 short ton-mi cargo;   c.i.f.: cost, insurance, and freight;   f.o.b.: free on board

Foreign trade

Imports (2003-c.i.f.): $10,853,000,000 ([2000] machinery and apparatus 21.1%; chemicals and chemical products 20.1%; food 18.9%, of which cereals 7.1%; road vehicles 10.4%; iron and steel 6.2%). *Major import sources* (2003): China 13.6%; UK 9.3%; France 8.0%; US 7.8%; The Netherlands 6.5%; Germany 5.9%; South Korea 5.8%. **Exports** (2003-f.o.b.): $19,887,000,000 (crude petroleum 99.7%, remainder 0.3%). *Major export destinations* (2003): US 40.2%; Spain 8.3%; Brazil 5.3%; France 5.0%; Indonesia 4.6%; Japan 4.1%; India 4.0%.

Transport and communications

Transport. *Railroads* (2000): length 3,505 km; passenger-km 179,000,000 (1997); metric ton-km cargo 120,000,000 (1997). *Roads* (1999): total length 62,598 km (paved 19%). *Vehicles* (1996): passenger cars 773,000. *Air transport* (2002; Nigeria Airways only): passenger-km 892,720,000; metric ton-km cargo 10,783,000; airports (1998) 12. **Communications,** in total units (units per 1,000 persons). Daily newspaper circulation (2000): 2,770,000 (24); radios (2000): 23,000,000 (200); televisions (2000): 7,840,000 (68); telephone main lines (2003): 853,100 (6.9); cellular telephone subscribers (2003): 3,149,500 (26); personal computers (2002): 853,000 (7.1); Internet users (2003): 750,000 (6.1).

Education and health

Literacy (2002): total population age 15 and over literate 40,700,000 (64.1%); males literate 22,600,000 (62.3%); females literate 18,100,000 (56.2%). **Health** (2002): physicians 25,914 (1 per 4,722 persons); hospital beds 54,872 (1 per 2,230 persons); infant mortality rate per 1,000 live births (2003) 71.3. **Food** (2001): daily per capita caloric intake 2,747 (vegetable products 97%, animal products 3%); 116% of FAO recommended minimum.

Military

Total active duty personnel (2003): 78,500 (army 79.0%, navy 8.9%, air force 12.1%). **Military expenditure as percentage of GNP** (1999): 1.7% (world 2.4%); per capita expenditure $13.

Background

Inhabited for thousands of years, Nigeria was the center of the Nok culture from 500 BC to AD 200 and of several precolonial empires, including the state of Kanem-Bornu and the Songhai, Hausa, and Fulani kingdoms. Visited in the 15th century by Europeans, it became a center for the slave trade. The area began to come under British control in 1861; by 1903 British rule was total. Nigeria gained independence in 1960 and became a republic in 1963. Ethnic strife soon led to military coups, and military groups ruled the country from 1966 to 1979 and from 1983 to 1999. A civil war between the central government and the former Eastern Region—which seceded and called itself Biafra—began in 1967 and ended in 1970 with Biafra's surrender after widespread starvation and civilian deaths. In 1991 the capital was moved from Lagos to Abuja. The government's execution of environmental activist Ken Saro-Wiwa in 1995 led to international sanctions, and civil-

ian rule was finally reestablished in 1999. By far the most populous nation in Africa, Nigeria suffers from rapid population increase, political instability, foreign debt, slow economic growth, a high rate of violent crime, and rampant government corruption.

Recent Developments

Debt repayment formed the basis of Pres. Olusegun Obasanjo's economic-reform plan, and record crude oil prices in 2006 helped Nigeria to become the first African state to pay off its debt to the Paris Club of lenders. The government's anticorruption campaign reached high up the ranks of Nigeria's political elite. In September it was announced that indictments were being prepared against 24 state governors, and the majority party suspended Vice Pres. Atiku Abubakar for three months over corruption allegations, disqualifying him from running in the 2007 presidential election. An upsurge in violence was seen in 2006 in the oil-producing communities of the Niger delta over demands by the area's inhabitants for greater control over the region's oil wealth. Militants carried out a wave of attacks on pipelines and other oil facilities, including kidnappings of foreign oil workers, and production was slashed by a fifth. In August President Obasanjo ordered the military to crack down on delta militias, but violence erupted again early in October, which allegedly resulted in the death of 17 soldiers. Nigeria was a model for other African Union countries in its observance of international law. In March it arrested Charles Taylor, the former president of Liberia, and handed him over to Sierra Leonean authorities for trial on charges of war crimes. In August Nigeria ended a drawn-out conflict by ceding the disputed oil-rich Bakassi peninsula to Cameroon in accordance with a 2002 International Court of Justice ruling.

Internet resources: <www.nigeriatourism.net>.

Northern Mariana Islands

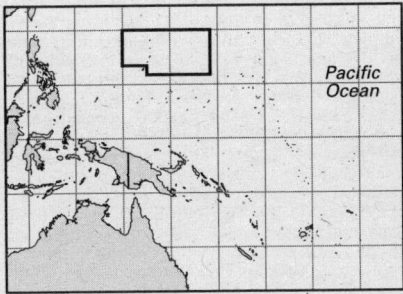

Official name: Commonwealth of the Northern Mariana Islands. **Political status:** self-governing commonwealth in association with the US, having two legislative houses (Senate [9]; House of Representatives [18]; residents elect a nonvoting representative to the US Congress. **Chief of state:** President of the US George W. Bush (from 2001). **Head of government:** Governor Benigno R. Fitial (from 2006). **Seat of government:** on Saipan. **Official languages:** Chamorro, Carolinian, and English. **Official religion:** none. **Monetary unit:** 1 US dollar (US$) = 100 cents.

Demography

Area: 176.5 sq mi, 457.1 sq km. **Population** (2006): 76,200. **Density** (2006): persons per sq mi 431.7, persons per sq km 166.7. **Urban** (2002; all of Saipan was designated an urban area in 2002): 90.0%. **Sex distribution** (2000): male 46.21%; female 53.79%. **Age breakdown** (2000): under 15, 22.5%; 15–29, 31.8%; 30–44, 32.3%; 45–59, 10.7%; 60–74, 2.3%; 75 and over, 0.4%. **Ethnic composition** (2000; includes aliens): Filipino 26.2%; Chinese 22.1%; Chamorro 21.3%; Carolinian 3.8%; other Asian 7.5%; other Pacific Islander 6.6%; white 1.8%; multiethnic and other 10.7%. **Religious affiliation** (1995): Roman Catholic 59.6%; Protestant 18.7%; other Christian 1.4%; other 20.3%. **Major villages** (2000): San Antonio 4,741; Garapan 3,588; Susupe 2,083. **Location:** Oceania, islands in the North Pacific Ocean, between Hawaii (US) and the Philippines.

Vital statistics

Birth rate per 1,000 population (2002): 20.0 (world avg. 21.3). **Death rate** per 1,000 population (2002): 2.4 (world avg. 9.1). **Natural increase rate** per 1,000 population (2002): 17.6 (world avg. 12.2). **Total fertility rate** (avg. births per childbearing woman; 2002): 1.4. **Life expectancy** at birth (2002): male 72.9 years; female 79.2 years.

National economy

Budget (2002). *Revenue:* $199,713,000 (tax revenue 83.5%, of which income tax 28.5%, corporate tax 24.3%, excise tax 9.4%; nontax revenue 16.5%). *Expenditures:* $212,089,000 (2001; health 20.4%, education 20.1%, general government 15.0%, social services 12.0%, public safety 9.3%). **Public debt** (external, outstanding; 1999): $146,000,000. **Gross national product** (1999): $664,600,000 ($9,600 per capita). **Production** (metric tons except as noted). *Agriculture and fishing* (1998): cucumbers 175, bananas 174, watermelons 134; livestock (number of live animals; 1998) 1,789 cattle, 831 pigs, 29,409 chickens; fish catch (2001) 197. *Mining and quarrying:* negligible amount of quarrying for building material. *Manufacturing* (value of sales in $'000,000; 2002): garments 639; bricks, tiles, and cement 12; printing and related activities 5. **Tourism** (1998): receipts from visitors $394,000,000. **Population economically active** (2000): total 44,471; activity rate of total population 64.2% (participation rates: ages 16 and over, 84.1%; female 49.9%; unemployed 3.9%). **Households.** Average household size (2000) 3.7; average income per household (2000) $37,015; sources of income (1994): wages 83.9%, interest and rental 7.2%, self-employment 7.2%, transfer payments 1.7%. **Land use** as % of total land area (2000): in temporary crops 13%, in permanent crops 4%, in pasture 11%; overall forest area 30%.

Foreign trade

Imports (1997): $836,200,000 (clothing and accessories 37.0%, foodstuffs 9.6%, petroleum and petroleum products 8.2%, transport equipment and parts 5.0%, construction materials 4.2%). *Major import sources:* Guam 35.6%, Hong Kong 24.0%, Japan 14.1%, South Korea 9.6%, US 7.6%. **Exports** (2002): $817,000,000 (garments and accessories 99.8%, of which cotton garments 69.8%; remainder 0.2%). *Major export destinations:* nearly all to the US.

Transport and communications

Transport. *Roads* (1998): total length 360 km (paved, nearly 100%). *Vehicles* (2001): passenger cars 11,019; trucks and buses 4,928. *Air transport* (1999; Saipan International Airport only): aircraft landings 23,853; boarding passengers 562,364; airports (2002) with scheduled flights 2 (international flights are regularly scheduled at Saipan and at Rota; Tinian has nonscheduled domestic service. Additional domestic airports mainly handle charter flights). **Communications,** in total units (units per 1,000 persons). Radios (1999): 10,500 (152); televisions (1999): 4,100 (59); telephone main lines (2000): 20,990 (309); cellular telephone subscribers (2000): 3,000 (57).

Education and health

Educational attainment (2000). Percentage of population age 25 and over having: primary education 14.1%; some secondary 17.5%; completed secondary 35.8%; some postsecondary 12.0%; completed undergraduate or higher 20.6%. **Literacy** (2000): 100%. **Health:** physicians (1999) 31 (1 per 2,170 persons); hospital beds (1998) 74 (1 per 877 persons); infant mortality rate per 1,000 live births (2002): 7.5.

Military

The US is responsible for military defense; headquarters of the US Pacific Command are in Hawaii.

Background

The Northern Mariana Islands were discovered by Ferdinand Magellan in 1521 and colonized by Spain in 1668. Sold to Germany in 1899, they were occupied by Japan in 1914 and became a Japanese mandate from the League of Nations after 1919. They were the scene of fierce fighting in World War II; Tinian was the base for the US planes that dropped atomic bombs on Hiroshima and Nagasaki. They were granted to the US in 1947 as a UN trust territory, became self-governing in 1978, and became a commonwealth under US sovereignty in 1986, when its residents became US citizens. The UN trusteeship ended in 1986.

Recent Developments

The Northern Mariana Islands suffered from economic difficulties in recent years. The country experienced a $100 million deficit in 2005, much of it a result of shortfalls in the funding of retirement for government employees. After Japan Airlines suspended its flights from Tokyo that year, the number of tourist arrivals dropped by 20%, though by early 2007 the situation was improving slightly with an increase in Chinese and Korean visitors.

Internet resources: <www.mymarianas.com>.

---

1 metric ton = about 1.1 short tons; 1 kilometer = 0.6 mi (statute); 1 metric ton-km cargo = about 0.68 short ton-mi cargo; c.i.f.: cost, insurance, and freight; f.o.b.: free on board

Norway

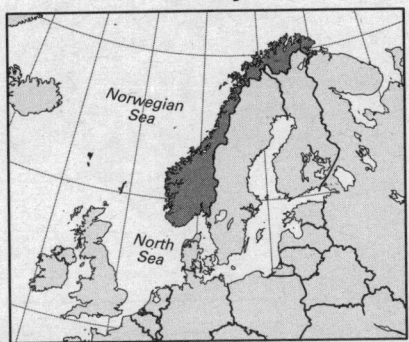

Official name: Kongeriket Norge (Kingdom of Norway). **Form of government:** constitutional monarchy with one legislative house (Parliament [165]). **Chief of state:** King Harald V (from 1991). **Head of government:** Prime Minister Jens Stoltenberg (from 2005). **Capital:** Oslo. **Official language:** Norwegian. **Official religion:** Evangelical Lutheran. **Monetary unit:** 1 Norwegian krone (NKr) = 100 øre; valuation (1 Jul 2007) US$1 = NKr 5.90.

Demography

Area: 148,726 sq mi, 385,199 sq km (includes Svalbard and Jan Mayen). **Population** (2006): 4,659,000. **Density** (2004): persons per sq mi 36.7, persons per sq km 14.2. **Urban** (2003): 78.6%. **Sex distribution** (2003): male 49.56%; female 50.44%. **Age breakdown** (2003): under 15, 20.0%; 15–29, 18.7%; 30–44, 22.4%; 45–59, 19.7%; 60–74, 11.4%; 75 and over, 7.8%. **Ethnic composition** (2000): Norwegian 93.8%; Vietnamese 2.4%; Swedish 0.5%; Punjabi 0.4%; Urdu 0.3%; US white 0.3%; Lapp 0.3%; Danish 0.3%; other 1.7%. **Major cities** (2003): Oslo 517,401 (urban agglomeration [2003] 795,000); Bergen 235,423; Trondheim 152,699; Stavanger 111,007; Bærum 102,529. **Location:** northern Europe, bordering the Barents Sea, Russia, Finland, Sweden, the North Sea, and the Norwegian Sea.

Vital statistics

Birth rate per 1,000 population (2003): 12.4 (world avg. 21.3); legitimate 50.0%. **Death rate** per 1,000 population (2003): 9.3 (world avg. 9.1). **Natural increase rate** per 1,000 population (2003): 3.1 (world avg. 12.2). **Total fertility rate** (avg. births per childbearing woman; 2003): 1.8. **Marriage rate** per 1,000 population (2001): 5.1. **Divorce rate** per 1,000 population (2001): 2.3. **Life expectancy** at birth (2003): male 77.0 years; female 81.9 years.

National economy

Budget (2001). *Revenue:* NKr 829,345,000,000 (value-added taxes 30.7%, tax on income 28.6%, social security taxes 20.2%). *Expenditures:* NKr 617,372,000,000 (social security and welfare 37.8%, health 15.9%, education 13.6%, debt service 4.6%). **Public debt** (December 2002): $60,900,000,000. **Production** (metric tons except as noted). *Agriculture, forestry, fishing* (2002): barley 601,000, potatoes 389,000, oats 312,000; livestock (number of live animals) 2,396,000 sheep, 967,200 cattle; roundwood (2002) 8,649,000 cu m; fish catch (2003) 2,544,692, of which herring 561,858, capelin 249,124, cod 217,462, pollock 212,209. *Mining and quarrying* (2001): ilmenite concentrate 600,000, iron ore (metal content) 340,000, cobalt 3,134. *Manufacturing* (value added in $'000,000; 2001): food products 2,353; ship/boat construction and repair 1,543; nonelectrical machinery 1,257. *Energy production (consumption):* electricity (kW-hr; 2003) 107,268,000,000 ([2000] 123,985,000,000); coal (2000) 632,000 (1,035,000); crude petroleum (barrels; 2001) 1,275,000,000 ([2000] 119,000,000); petroleum products (2000) 17,338,000 (11,321,000); natural gas (cu m; 2001) 57,848,000,000 ([2000] 4,167,500). **Household income and expenditure.** Average household size (2001) 2.3; annual income (excluding taxes) per household (2002) NKr 333,500; expenditure (2001–03): housing 20.1%, transportation 17.3%, recreation and culture 12.6%, food 10.3%, household furnishings 7.0%. **Land use** as % of total land area (2000): in temporary crops 2.9%, in pasture 0.5%; overall forest area 28.9%. **Gross national product** (2003): $197,658,000,000 ($43,350 per capita). **Population economically active** (2001): total 2,362,000; activity rate of total population 52.3% (participation rates: ages 15–64, 80.3%; female 46.6%; unemployed [2001] 3.9%). **Tourism** (2002): receipts $2,738,000,000; expenditures $5,814,000,000.

Foreign trade

Imports (2001-c.i.f.): NKr 296,161,000,000 (machinery and transport equipment 42.1%, of which road vehicles 8.7%; ships 3.4%; chemicals and chemical products 9.5%; metals and metal products 7.7%; food products 6.7%; petroleum products 3.0%). *Major import sources:* Sweden 15.2%; Germany 12.6%; UK 7.9%; Denmark 7.1%; US 7.1%. **Exports** (2001-f.o.b.): NKr 529,966,000,000 (crude petroleum 44.3%; natural gas 11.5%; machinery and transport equipment 11.4%; metals and metal products 7.9%; fish 5.6%). *Major export destinations:* UK 19.6%; Germany 12.2%; The Netherlands 10.4%; France 9.4%; Sweden 8.0%.

Transport and communications

Transport. *Railroads* (2001): route length 4,178 km; passenger-km 2,536,000,000; metric ton-km cargo 2,451,000,000. *Roads* (2002): total length 91,545 km (paved [1998] 74%). *Vehicles* (2001): passenger cars 1,872,862; trucks and buses 444,626. *Air transport* (2002; principally SAS and Braathens ASA): passenger-km 11,549,000,000; metric ton-km cargo 190,500,000; airports (1996) 50. **Communications,** in total units (units per 1,000 persons). Daily newspaper circulation (2000): 2,620,000 (585); radios (2000): 4,110,000 (915); televisions (2000): 3,000,000 (669); telephone main lines (2002): 3,343,000 (734); cellular telephone subscribers (2003): 4,163,400 (909); personal computers (2002): 2,405,000 (528); Internet users (2002): 2,288,000 (503).

Education and health

Educational attainment (2000). Percentage of population age 16 and over having: primary and lower secondary education 21.5%; higher secondary 55.0%; higher 21.3%; unknown 2.2%. **Literacy** (2000): virtually 100% literate. **Health:** physicians (2003) 12,322 (1 per 370 persons); hospital beds (2003) 22,662 (1 per 201 persons); infant mortality rate per 1,000 live births (2003) 3.4. **Food** (2001): daily per capita caloric intake 3,382 (vegetable products 67%, animal products 33%); 126% of FAO recommended minimum.

Military

Total active duty personnel (2003): 26,600 (army 58.3%, navy 22.9%, air force 18.8%). **Military expenditure as percentage of GNP** (1999): 2.2% (world avg. 2.4%); per capita expenditure $742.

Background

Several principalities were united into the kingdom of Norway in the 11th century. From 1380 it had the same king as Denmark until it was ceded to Sweden in 1814. The union with Sweden was dissolved in 1905, and Norway's economy grew rapidly. The country remained neutral during World War I, although its shipping industry played a vital role in the conflict. It declared its neutrality in World War II but was invaded and occupied by German troops. Norway is a member of NATO but turned down membership in the EU in 1994. Its economy grew consistently during the 1990s.

Did you know? Norway's capital, Oslo, was formerly Christiania (1624-1877) and Kristiania (1877-1925). The city was founded by King Harald Hardraade about 1050. After the city was destroyed by fire in 1624, Christian IV of Denmark-Norway built a new town and called it Christiania.

Recent Developments

The Norwegian economy remained strong in 2006. With average unemployment in Norway of 3.6%, workers from Sweden and Eastern European countries were welcomed. One of the most serious problems facing the country was the question of pollution in the energy industries. Huge energy projects such as Langaled, the world's longest undersea pipeline, from the western coast of Norway to Great Britain, required considerable amounts of power, and provisions for future energy needs appeared to be seriously inadequate. The prospects of a coming energy crisis during the winter of 2006–07 moved the government to start up highly polluting natural-gas production before the development of cleaning technology to reduce carbon-dioxide levels.

Internet resources: <www.norway.org>.

Oman

Official name: Saltanat 'Uman (Sultanate of Oman). **Form of government:** monarchy with two advisory bodies (Council of State [57; all seats are nonelected]; Consultative Council [83]). **Head of state and government:** Sultan (from 1970) and Prime Minister (from 1972) Qabus ibn Sa'id. **Capital:** Muscat. **Official language:** Arabic. **Official religion:** Islam. **Monetary unit:**

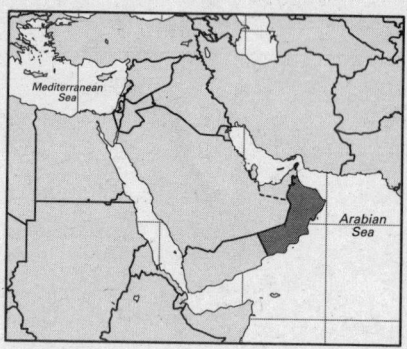

1 rial Omani (RO) = 1,000 baizas; valuation (1 Jul 2007) US$1 = RO 0.38.

Demography

Area: 119,500 sq mi, 309,500 sq km. **Population** (2006): 2,416,000. **Density** (2006): persons per sq mi 21.1, persons per sq km 8.1. **Urban** (2001): 76.5%. **Sex distribution** (2002): male 56.9%; female 43.1%. **Age breakdown** (2002): under 15, 33.7%; 15–29, 32.3%; 30–44, 22.5%; 45–59, 7.7%; 60–74, 3.0%; 75 and over 0.8%. **Ethnic composition** (2000): Omani Arab 48.1%; Indo-Pakistani 31.7%, of which Balochi 15.0%, Bengali 4.4%, Tamil 2.5%; other Arab 7.2%; Persian 2.8%; Zanzibari (blacks originally from Zanzibar) 2.5%; other 7.7%. **Religious affiliation** (2000): Muslim 87.4%, of which Ibadiyah Muslim 75% (principal minorities are Sunni Muslim and Shi'i Muslim); Hindu 5.7%; Christian 4.9%; Buddhist 0.8%; other 1.2%. **Major cities** (2003): As-Sib 223,267 (within Muscat urban agglomeration); Salalah 156,587; Matrah 154,316 (within Muscat urban agglomeration); Bawshar 149,506 (within Muscat urban agglomeration); Suhar 104,057. **Location:** the Middle East, bordering the Gulf of Oman, the Arabian Sea, Yemen, Saudi Arabia, and the UAE; the Ru'us al-Jibal enclave occupies the northern tip of the Musandam Peninsula and borders the UAE, the Persian Gulf, and the Strait of Hormuz.

Vital statistics

Birth rate per 1,000 population (2003): 37.5 (world avg. 21.3). **Death rate** per 1,000 population (2003): 4.0 (world avg. 9.1). **Natural increase rate** per 1,000 population (2003): 33.5 (world avg. 12.2). **Total fertility rate** (avg. births per childbearing woman; 2003): 5.9. **Life expectancy** at birth (2003): male 70.4 years; female 74.9 years.

National economy

Budget (2004). *Revenue:* RO 2,925,000,000 (oil revenue 72.8%; other 27.2%). *Expenditures:* RO 3,425,000,000 (current expenditure 71.3%, of which civil ministries 36.7%, defense 28.4%, interest paid on loans 2.3%; capital expenditure 26.6%; other 2.1%). **Public debt** (external, outstanding; 2002): $1,979,000,000. **Gross national product** (2003): $19,877,000,000 ($7,830 per capita). **Tourism** (2002): receipts

1 metric ton = about 1.1 short tons; 1 kilometer = 0.6 mi (statute); 1 metric ton-km cargo = about 0.68 short ton-mi cargo; c.i.f.: cost, insurance, and freight; f.o.b.: free on board

$242,000,000; expenditures $771,000,000. **Households**. Average household size (2002) 6.7; expenditure (1995): housing and utilities 27.9%, food, beverages, and tobacco 26.4%, transportation 19.8%, clothing and shoes 7.9%, household goods and furniture 6.2%, education, health services, entertainment, and other 11.8%. **Production** (metric tons except as noted). *Agriculture and fishing* (2002): dates 248,458, bananas 33,680, watermelons 29,914; livestock (number of live animals) 998,000 goats, 354,000 sheep, 314,000 cattle; fish catch (2001) 128,544. *Mining and quarrying* (2002): marble 136,000; chromite (gross weight) 23,975; gold 301 kg. *Manufacturing* (value added in $'000,000; 2001): petroleum products 1,012; nonmetallic mineral products 124; food products 106. *Energy production (consumption):* electricity (kW-hr; 2002) 10,331,000,000 (10,331,000,000); crude petroleum (barrels; 2003) 299,000,000 (20,000,000); petroleum products (2000) 4,134,000 (3,176,000); natural gas (cu m; 2001) 9,100,000,000 (6,300,000,000). **Population economically active** (2003; employed only; includes 579,643 expatriate workers in private sector and 123,045 government employees, of which 80.5% are Omani): total 702,688; activity rate of total population 30.1% (participation rates: over age 15, 60.9%; female 9.7%; unemployed [1996] 20%). **Land use** as % of total land area (2000): in temporary crops 0.1%, in permanent crops 0.1%, in pasture 3.2%; overall forest area, negligible.

Foreign trade

Imports (2003-f.o.b. in balance of trade and c.i.f. for commodities and trading partners): RO 2,527,-000,000 (machinery and apparatus 28.4%; manufactured goods 15.4%; motor vehicles and parts 13.4%; food and live animals 11.4%; chemicals and chemical products 7.5%). *Major import sources:* UAE 21.6%; Japan 17.1%; US 6.2%; UK 5.7%; Germany 4.4%; India 4.4%. **Exports** (2003): RO 4,487,-000,000 (domestic exports 86.6%, of which crude and refined petroleum 66.5%, natural gas 13.3%, live animals and animal products 1.4%, base and fabricated [mostly copper] metals 0.9%; reexports 13.4%, of which motor vehicles and parts 7.5%, beverages and tobacco products 1.8%). *Major export destinations* (excludes petroleum and natural gas; includes reexports): UAE 32.7%; Iran 18.3%; Saudi Arabia 8.4%; US 3.6%; Yemen 2.6%.

Transport and communications

Transport. *Roads* (1999): total length 33,020 km (paved 24%). *Vehicles* (2001): passenger cars 309,217; trucks and buses 132,290. *Air transport* (2002; Oman Air only): passenger-km 1,189,-300,000; metric ton-km cargo 9,230,000; airports (1999) with scheduled flights 6. **Communications**, in total units (units per 1,000 persons). Daily newspaper circulation (1996): 63,000 (28); radios (2000): 1,490,000 (621); televisions (2002): 1,382,500 (553); telephone main lines (2002): 233,900 (92); cellular telephone subscribers (2002): 464,900 (183); personal computers (2002): 95,000 (37); Internet users (2002): 180,000 (71).

Education and health

Educational attainment (1993). Percentage of population age 15 and over having: no formal schooling (illiterate) 41.2%; no formal schooling (literate) 14.9%; primary 18.9%; secondary 21.1%; higher technical 2.0%; higher undergraduate 1.5%; higher graduate 0.1%; other 0.3%. **Literacy** (2003): percentage of total population age 15 and over literate 75.8%; males literate 83.0%; females literate 67.2%. **Health** (2002): physicians 3,536 (1 per 713 persons); hospital beds 5,168 (1 per 488 persons); infant mortality rate per 1,000 live births (2003) 21.0.

Military

Total active duty personnel (2003): 41,700 (army 60.0%, navy 10.1%, air force 9.8%, royal household 20.1%). **Military expenditure as percentage of GNP** (1999): 15.3% (world 2.4%); per capita expenditure $726.

Background

Oman has been inhabited for at least 10,000 years. Arabs began migrating there in the 9th century BC. Tribal warfare was endemic until the conversion to Islam in the 7th century AD. It was ruled by Ibadi imams until 1154, when a royal dynasty was established. The Portuguese controlled the coastal areas from about 1507 to 1650, when they were expelled. The Al Bu Sa'id dynasty, founded in the mid-18th century, still rules Oman. Oil was discovered in 1964. In 1970 the sultan was deposed by his son, who began a policy of modernization, and under him the country joined the Arab League and the UN. In the Persian Gulf War, Oman cooperated with the allied forces against Iraq. In the 1990s it continued to expand its foreign relations.

Recent Developments

Oman's economic outlook was strong in recent years. Dramatically higher oil and gas prices led to a projected 16% GDP growth in 2006. In September 2006 the US signed into law a free trade agreement between the two countries that Oman had signed in 2005. Four new oil fields were discovered in 2006, and that year the country's third mega-gas plant began production, raising Oman's annual output of liquefied natural gas to 10 million tons.

Internet resources: <www.omantourism.gov.om>.

Pakistan

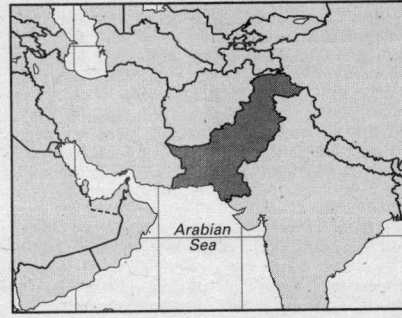

Official name: Islam-i Jamhuriya-e Pakistan (Islamic Republic of Pakistan). **Form of government:** military-backed constitutional regime with two legislative houses (Senate [100]; National Assembly [342]). **Chiefs of state and government:** President Pervez Musharraf (from 2001), assisted by Prime Minister Shaukat Aziz (from 2004). **Capital:** Islamabad. **Official language:** Urdu. **Official religion:** Islam. **Monetary unit:** 1 Pakistan rupee (PRs) = 100 paisa; valuation (1 Jul 2007) US$1 = PRs 60.52.

Demography

Demographic information, except ethnic and religious data, excludes Afghan refugees (2004; 1,100,000) and the 2004 populations of Azad Kashmir (3,175,000) and the Northern Areas (1,075,000); also excludes 32,494-sq-mi (84,159-sq-km) area of Pakistani-administered Jammu and Kashmir (comprising both Azad Kashmir and the Northern Areas). **Area:** 307,374 sq mi, 796,096 sq km. **Population** (2004): 151,600,000. **Density** (2003): persons per sq mi 493.2, persons per sq km 190.4. **Urban** (2002): 38.0%. **Sex distribution** (2002): male 51.92%; female 48.08%. **Age breakdown** (1998): under 15, 43.2%; 15–29, 26.9%; 30–44, 15.6%; 45–59, 8.8%; 60–74, 4.3%; 75 and over, 1.2%. **Ethnic composition** (2000): Punjabi 52.6%; Pashtun 13.2%; Sindhi 11.7%; Urdu-speaking muhajirs 7.5%; Balochi 4.3%; other 10.7%. **Religious affiliation** (2000): Muslim 96.1% (mostly Sunni, with Shi'i comprising about 17%); Christian 2.5%; Hindu 1.2%; others (including Ahmadiyah) 0.2%. **Major cities** (1998): Karachi 9,269,000; Lahore 5,063,000; Faisalabad 1,977,000; Rawalpindi 1,406,000; Multan 1,182,-000. **Location:** southern Asia, bordering China, India, the Arabian Sea, Iran, and Afghanistan.

Vital statistics

Birth rate per 1,000 population (2003): 32.0 (world avg. 21.3). **Death rate** per 1,000 population (2003): 8.9 (world avg. 9.1). **Natural increase** per 1,000 population (2003): 23.1 (world avg. 12.2). **Total fertility rate** (avg. births per childbearing woman; 2003): 4.4. **Life expectancy** at birth (2003): male 61.3 years; female 63.1 years.

National economy

Budget (2001–02). *Revenue:* PRs 632,799,000,000 (sales tax 26.9%, nontax receipts 26.0%, income taxes 22.4%, customs duties 8.0%, excise taxes 7.4%). *Expenditures:* PRs 773,289,000,000 (public-debt service 41.4%, defense 19.6%, development 16.1%, general administration 6.6%, grants and subsidies 3.3%). **Public debt** (external, outstanding; 2002): $28,102,-000,000. **Production** (metric tons except as noted). *Agriculture, forestry, fishing* (2002): sugarcane 48,041,600, wheat 18,226,100, rice 6,343,000; livestock (number of live animals) 50,900,000 goats, 24,398,000 sheep, 153,000,000 chickens; roundwood (2002) 27,691,679 cu m; fish catch (2001) 623,425. *Mining and quarrying* (2001–02): limestone 9,805,000; rock salt 1,359,000; gypsum 328,000. *Manufacturing* (2001–02): cement 9,935,000; urea 4,216,200; refined sugar 3,246,600. *Energy production (consumption):* electricity (kW-hr; 2001)

67,704,000,000 (67,704,000,000); coal (2000) 3,168,000 (4,125,000); crude petroleum (barrels; 2000–01) 21,100,000 ([2000] 51,188,000); petroleum products (2000) 6,123,000 (17,856,000); natural gas (cu m; 2000–01) 24,800,000,000 ([2000] 21,036,000,000). **Population economically active** (2002): total 41,540,000; activity rate of total population 28.5% (participation rates: ages 15–64 [1999] 43.1%; female [1996–97] 14.4%; unemployed 7.8%). **Gross national product** (2003): $69,236,000,000 ($470 per capita). **Household income and expenditure** (1998–99). Average household size 6.8; income per household PRs 81,444; sources of income: self-employment 40.9%, wages and salaries 32.3%, transfer payments 11.3%, other 15.5%; expenditure: food 49.1%, housing 20.9%, clothing and footwear 7.8%, education 3.6%, transportation and communications 3.3%, recreation 0.2%. **Tourism** (2002): receipts $105,000,000; expenditures $179,000,000. **Land use** as % of total land area (2000): in temporary crops 27.6%, in permanent crops 0.9%, in pasture 6.5%; overall forest area 3.1%.

Foreign trade

Imports (2001–02-f.o.b. in balance of trade and c.i.f. for commodities and trading partners): $10,339,-000,000 (machinery and apparatus 15.6%; refined petroleum 15.2%; chemicals and chemical products 14.4%; crude petroleum 11.9%; food 8.0%; transport equipment 4.8%). *Major import sources* (2000–01): UAE 12.5%; Saudi Arabia 11.7%; Kuwait 8.9%; Japan 5.4%; US 5.2%; China 4.9%. **Exports** (2001–02): $9,135,000,000 (textiles 63.6%, of which cotton yarn and fabric 22.6%, bedding 10.1%, ready-made garments 9.6%, knitwear 9.3%; leather and leather products 7.4%; rice 4.9%; sporting goods 3.3%; carpets 2.7%). *Major export destinations:* EU 27.4%, of which UK 7.2%, Germany 4.9%; US 24.7%; UAE 7.9%; Hong Kong 4.8%.

Transport and communications

Transport. *Railroads* (2000–01): route length 7,791 km; passenger-km 19,590,000,000; metric ton-km cargo 4,520,000,000. *Roads* (2001–02): total length 251,661 km (paved 59%). *Vehicles* (2001): passenger cars 758,600; trucks and buses 253,100. *Air transport* (2000–01): passenger-km 9,739,-000,000; (1999) metric ton-km cargo 329,832,000; airports (1997) 35. **Communications,** in total units (units per 1,000 persons). Daily newspaper circulation (2000): 4,190,000 (30); radios (2000): 14,700,-000 (121); televisions (2000): 18,300,000 (131); telephone main lines (2003): 3,982,800 (27); cellular telephone subscribers (2003): 2,624,800 (18); personal computers (2001): 600,000 (4.1); Internet users (2002): 1,500,000 (10).

Education and health

Educational attainment (1990). Percentage of population age 25 and over having: no formal schooling 73.8%; some primary education 9.7%; secondary 14.0%; postsecondary 2.5%. **Literacy** (2000): total population age 15 and over literate 43.2%; males literate 57.5%; females literate 27.9%. **Health** (2001): physicians 96,248 (1 per 1,516 persons); hospital

1 metric ton = about 1.1 short tons;   1 kilometer = 0.6 mi (statute);   1 metric ton-km cargo = about 0.68 short ton-mi cargo;   c.i.f.: cost, insurance, and freight;   f.o.b.: free on board

beds 97,945 (1 per 1,490 persons); infant mortality rate per 1,000 live births (2003) 76.6. **Food** (2001): daily per capita caloric intake 2,457 (vegetable products 81%, animal products 19%); 106% of FAO recommended minimum.

Military

Total active duty personnel (2003): 620,000 (army 88.7%, navy 4.0%, air force 7.3%). **Military expenditure as percentage of GNP** (1999): 5.9% (world 2.4%); per capita expenditure $25.

Background

Pakistan has been inhabited since about 3500 BC. From the 3rd century BC to the 2nd century AD, it was part of the Mauryan and Kushan kingdoms. The first Muslim conquests were in the 8th century AD. The British East India Company subdued the reigning Mughal dynasty in 1757. During the period of British colonial rule, what is now Pakistan was part of India. When the British withdrew in 1947, the new state of Pakistan came into existence by act of the British Parliament. Kashmir remained a disputed territory between Pakistan and India, resulting in military clashes and full-scale war in 1965. Civil war between East Pakistan (now Bangladesh) and West Pakistan resulted in independence for Bangladesh in 1971. Many Afghan refugees migrated to Pakistan during the Soviet-Afghan War in the 1980s. Pakistan elected Benazir Bhutto, the first woman to head a modern Islamic state, in 1988. She was ousted in 1990 on charges of corruption and incompetence. During the 1990s border flare-ups with India continued, and Pakistan conducted nuclear tests.

Recent Developments

In 2006 Pakistan was affected by a continuing insurrection campaign of sabotage and assassination in Balochistan and the failure to root out renascent al-Qaeda and Taliban forces, most notably in South and North Waziristan. Afghan Pres. Hamid Karzai accused Pres. Pervez Musharraf of not doing enough to challenge the insurgents said to be based in Pakistan's tribal areas. In December Islamabad announced that the army would fence and mine key mountain routes used by insurgents on the Pakistan-Afghanistan border. Some progress was made against terrorism suspects. In April a man wanted by the US for his involvement in the 1998 bombings of the US embassies in Kenya and Tanzania was killed in North Waziristan. The interception of a telephone call made in August from Pakistan to Britain, reportedly urging plotters to proceed with attacks on US-bound jetliners, led to the apprehension of more than a score of alleged suicide bombers. Pres. George W. Bush visited Pakistan in March, followed by Secretary of State Condoleezza Rice in June. Pakistan and US naval units participated in a joint counterterrorism exercise in September, and in October Pakistan agreed to purchase F-16 aircraft and other US weapons valued at $5 billion. Relations with India were strained. In July, Lashkar-e Tayyiba, a banned Pakistani-based terrorist organization, was deemed responsible for commuter-train bombings in Mumbai (Bombay). New Delhi postponed peace talks with Islamabad and threatened "hot pursuit" of terrorists across international frontiers.

Internet resources: <www.infopak.gov.pk>.

Palau

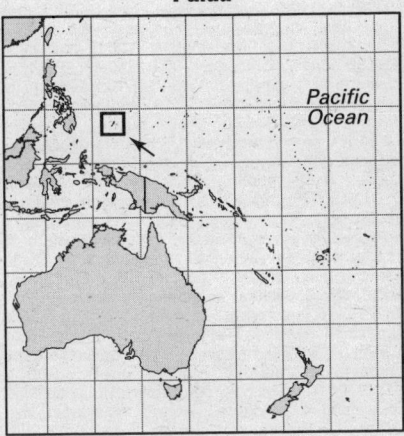

Pacific Ocean

Official name: Belu'u er a Belau (Palauan); Republic of Palau (English). **Form of government:** unitary republic with a national congress composed of two legislative houses (Senate [9]; House of Delegates [16]). **Head of state and government:** President Tommy Remengesau, Jr. (from 2001). **Capital:** Melekeok, on Babelthuap (the main island of Palau). **Official languages:** Palauan; English; Sonsorolese-Tobian. **Official religion:** none. **Monetary unit:** 1 US dollar (US$) = 100 cents.

Demography

Area: 188 sq mi, 488 sq km. **Population** (2006): 20,100. **Density** (2006): persons per sq mi 106.9, persons per sq km 41.2. **Urban** (2002): 73.0%. **Sex distribution** (2000): male 54.63%; female 45.37%. **Age breakdown** (2000): under 15, 23.9%; 15–29, 24.2%; 30–44, 29.9%; 45–59, 14.2%; 60–74, 5.5%; 75 and over 2.3%. **Ethnic composition** (2000): Palauan 69.9%; Asian 25.5%; other Micronesian 2.5%; other 2.1%. **Religious affiliation** (2000): Roman Catholic 41.6%; Protestant 23.3%; Modekngei (marginal Christian sect) 8.8%; other Christian 6.8%; other 19.5%. **Major city** (2000): Koror 13,303. **Location:** island group in the North Pacific Ocean, east of the Philippines.

Vital statistics

Birth rate per 1,000 population (2003): 19.0 (world avg. 21.3). **Death rate** per 1,000 population (2003): 7.0 (world avg. 9.1). **Natural increase rate** per 1,000 population (2003): 12.0 (world avg. 12.2). **Total fertility rate** (avg. births per childbearing woman; 2003): 2.5. **Life expectancy** at birth (2003): male 66.4 years; female 72.8 years.

National economy

Budget (2002). *Revenue:* $70,058,000 (grants from the US 49.4%; tax revenue 36.0%; nontax revenue 14.6%). *Expenditures:* $79,691,000 (current expenditure 74.6%, of which wages and salaries 38.1%; capital expenditure 25.4%). **Public debt** (external, outstanding; 2000): $20,000,000. **Production.** *Agri-*

culture and fishing (value of sales in $; 1998): eggs (1999) 609,626, fruit and vegetables 97,225, root crops (taro, cassava, sweet potatoes) 6,566; livestock (number of live animals; 2001) 702 pigs, 21,189 poultry; fish catch (2001; pounds) 593,473, of which sturgeon and unicorn fish 101,613, parrot fish 57,516, rabbit fish 25,613, groupers 23,835, emperor fish 20,586, crabs 17,347, wrasses 14,315, tuna and mackerel 13,366. *Manufacturing:* includes handicrafts and small items. *Energy production (consumption):* electricity (kW-hr; 2000) 210,000,000 (210,000,000); petroleum products (metric tons; 2000), none (79,000). *Tourism* (2002): receipts from visitors $59,000,000. **Land use** as % of total land area (2000): in temporary crops 9%, in permanent crops 4%, in pasture 7%; overall forest area 76%. **Population economically active** (2000): total 9,845; activity rate of total population 51.5% (participation rates: over age 15, 67.6%; female [1995] 39.6%; unemployed 2.3%). **Gross national product** (at current market prices; 2003): $150,000,000 ($7,500 per capita). **Household income and expenditure.** Average household size (2000) 5.7; income per household (1989) $8,882; sources of income (1989): wages 63.7%, social security 12.0%, self-employment 7.4%, retirement 5.5%, interest, dividend, or net rental 4.3%, remittance 4.1%, public assistance 1.0%, other 2.0%; expenditure (1997): food 42.2%, beverages and tobacco 14.8%, entertainment 13.1%, transportation 6.4%, clothing 5.7%, household goods 2.7%, other 15.1%.

Foreign trade

Imports (2001): $95,700,000 (machinery and transport equipment 24.2%; food and live animals 15.2%; mineral fuels and lubricants 10.4%; beverages and tobacco products 8.3%; chemicals and chemical products 7.4%). *Major import sources:* US 39.3%; Guam 14.0%; Japan 10.2%; Singapore 7.7%; South Korea 6.4%; Taiwan 5.3. **Exports** (2001): $9,000,000 (mostly high-grade tuna and garments). *Major export destinations:* mostly US, Japan, and Taiwan.

Transport and communications

Transport. *Roads* (1993): total length 64 km (paved 59%). *Vehicles* (2001): passenger cars and trucks 4,452. *Air transport* (2001): passenger arrivals 64,143, passenger departures 61,472; airports (1997) with scheduled flights 1. **Communications,** in total units (units per 1,000 persons). Radios (1997): 12,000 (663); televisions (1997): 11,000 (606); telephone main lines (1994): 2,615 (160).

Education and health

Educational attainment (2000). Percentage of population age 25 and over having: no formal schooling 3.1%; completed primary 11.5%; some secondary 7.9%; completed secondary 48.9%; some postsecondary 18.6%; higher 10.0%. **Literacy** (1997): total population age 15 and over literate 99.9%. **Health:** physicians (1998) 20 (1 per 906 persons); hospital beds (1990) 70 (1 per 200 persons); infant mortality rate per 1,000 live births (2003) 6.4.

Military

The US is responsible for the external security of Palau, as specified in the Compact of Free Association of 1 Oct 1994.

Background

Palau's inhabitants began arriving 3,000 years ago in successive waves from the Indonesian and Philippine archipelagos and from Polynesia. The islands had been under nominal Spanish ownership for more than three centuries when they were sold to Germany in 1899. They were seized by Japan in 1914 and taken by Allied forces in 1944 during World War II. Palau became part of the UN Trust Territory of the Pacific Islands in 1947 and became a sovereign state in 1994; the US provides economic assistance and maintains a military presence in the islands.

Recent Developments

Palau remained one of six Pacific countries to recognize Taiwan. In September 2005 Pres. Tommy Remengesau, Jr., urged the UN to admit Taiwan as a member, and in September 2006 his country hosted the first Taiwan–Pacific Allies Summit.

Internet resources: <www.visit-palau.com>.

Panama

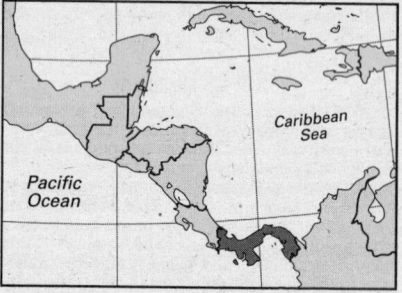

Official name: República de Panamá (Republic of Panama). **Form of government:** multiparty republic with one legislative house (Legislative Assembly [78]). **Head of state and government:** President Martín Torrijos (from 2004). **Capital:** Panama City. **Official language:** Spanish. **Official religion:** none. **Monetary unit:** 1 balboa (B) = 100 cents; valuation (1 Jul 2007) US$1 = B 1.02.

Demography

Area: 28,973 sq mi, 75,040 sq km. **Population** (2006): 3,191,000. **Density** (2006): persons per sq mi 110.1, persons per sq km 42.5. **Urban** (2000): 56.3%. **Sex distribution** (2002): male 50.48%; female 49.52%. **Age breakdown** (2002): under 15, 31.3%; 15–29, 26.9%; 30–44, 21.4%; 45–59, 12.2%; 60–74, 6.1%; 75 and over, 2.1%. **Ethnic composition**

---

1 metric ton = about 1.1 short tons;   1 kilometer = 0.6 mi (statute);   1 metric ton-km cargo = about 0.68 short ton-mi cargo;   c.i.f.: cost, insurance, and freight;   f.o.b.: free on board

(2000): mestizo 58.1%; black and mulatto 14.0%; white 8.6%; Amerindian 6.7%; Asian 5.5%; other 7.1%. **Religious affiliation** (1995): Roman Catholic 82.2%; unaffiliated Christian 12.9%; other (mostly ethnoreligionist) 4.9%. **Major cities** (2000): Panama City 415,964 (urban agglomeration [2001] 1,202,000); San Miguelito 293,745 (district adjacent to Panama City within Panama City urban agglomeration); David 77,734 (pop. of *cabecera*); Arraiján 63,753 (pop. of *cabecera*); La Chorrera 55,871. **Location:** Central America, bordering the Caribbean Sea, Colombia, the North Pacific Ocean, and Costa Rica.

Vital statistics

Birth rate per 1,000 population (2003): 19.5 (world avg. 21.3); legitimate 19.7%. **Death rate** per 1,000 population (2003): 6.3 (world avg. 9.1). **Natural increase rate** per 1,000 population (2003): 13.2 (world avg. 12.2). **Total fertility rate** (avg. births per child-bearing woman; 2003): 2.5. **Marriage rate** per 1,000 population (2001): 3.6. **Divorce rate** per 1,000 population (2001): 0.9. **Life expectancy** at birth (2003): male 70.0 years; female 74.8 years.

National economy

Budget (2000). *Revenue:* B 2,688,400,000 (tax revenue 62.6%, of which income taxes 12.6%, social security contributions 18.5%, corporate tax 5.8%; nontax revenue 37.4%, of which entrepreneurial and property income 21.1%). *Expenditures:* B 2,803,900,-000 (social security and welfare 20.9%; health 17.2%; education 16.6%; defense 7.1%; economic affairs 7.0%). **Public debt** (external, outstanding; 2002): $6,408,000,000. **Production** (metric tons except as noted). *Agriculture, forestry, fishing* (2002): sugarcane 1,441,000, bananas 600,000, rice 320,000; livestock (number of live animals) 1,533,000 cattle, 280,000 pigs, 170,000 horses; roundwood 1,321,-000 cu m; fish catch (2001) 237,394. *Mining and quarrying* (2001): limestone 270,000; gold 48,600 troy oz. *Manufacturing* (value of production in B '000,000; 1998): food products 1,203, of which meat 341, dairy products 144; refined petroleum 299; beverages 176. *Energy production (consumption):* electricity (kW-hr; 2001) 4,858,000,000 ([2000] 4,953,-000,000); coal (2000) none (70,000); crude petroleum (barrels; 2000) none (16,251,000); petroleum products (2000) 2,066,000 (2,258,000); natural gas (cu m; 2000) none (61,505,000). **Tourism** (2002): receipts from visitors $679,000,000; expenditures by nationals abroad $178,000,000. **Households.** Average household size (2000) 4.2; average annual income per household (1990) B 5,450 ($5,450). **Population economically active** (1998; excludes indigenous population): total 1,083,580; activity rate of total population 42.2% (participation rates: ages 15–69 [1997] 64.3%, female [1997] 35.6%, unemployed 13.6%). **Gross national product** (2003): $12,681,000,000 ($4,250 per capita). **Land use** as % of total land area (2000): in temporary crops 7.3%, in permanent crops 2.0%, in pasture 20.2%; overall forest area 38.6%.

Foreign trade

Data exclude Colón Free Zone. **Imports** (2001-c.i.f.): B 2,964,000,000 (mineral fuels 21.0%, of which crude petroleum 14.4%; machinery and apparatus 19.1%; chemicals and chemical products 11.2%; transport equipment 8.7%). *Major import sources:* US 32.5%; Colón Free Zone 11.9%; Ecuador 8.0%; Colombia 5.7%; Venezuela 5.2%. **Exports** (2001-f.o.b.): B 809,000,000 (bananas 15.1%; fish 11.9%; shrimps 8.7%; petroleum products 7.1%; unspecified 38.6%). *Major export destinations:* US 48.1%; Nicaragua 5.1%; Costa Rica 4.8%; Belgium 4.5%; Sweden 3.7%.

Transport and communications

Transport. *Railroads* (2000): route length 354 km. *Roads* (1997): total length 11,301 km (paved 33%). *Vehicles:* passenger cars (1998) 228,722; trucks and buses 84,020. Panama Canal traffic (2000–01): oceangoing transits 12,197; cargo 196,242,000 metric tons. *Air transport* (2001; COPA only): passenger-km 3,004,000,000; metric ton-km cargo 25,235,000; airports (1996) 10. **Communications,** in total units (units per 1,000 persons). Daily newspaper circulation (2000): 183,000 (62); radios (2000): 884,000 (300); televisions (2002): 553,900 (191); telephone main lines (2002): 386,900 (129); cellular telephone subscribers (2003): 834,000 (268); personal computers (2002): 115,000 (38); Internet users (2001): 120,000 (41).

Education and health

Educational attainment (1990). Percentage of population age 25 and over having: no formal schooling 11.6%; primary 41.6%; secondary 28.7%; undergraduate 12.4%; graduate 0.7%; other/unknown 5.0%. **Literacy** (2000): total population age 15 and over literate 91.3%; males 92.5%; females 91.3%. **Health** (2000): physicians 3,798 (1 per 776 persons); hospital beds 7,553 (1 per 390 persons); infant mortality rate per 1,000 live births (2003) 21.4. **Food** (2001): daily per capita caloric intake 2,386 (vegetable products 76%, animal products 24%); 103% of FAO recommended minimum.

Military

Total active duty personnel (2003): none; Panama has an 11,800-member national police force. **Military expenditure as percentage of GNP** (1999): 1.4% (world avg. 2.4%); per capita expenditure $45.

Background

Panama was inhabited by Native Americans when the Spanish arrived in 1501. The first successful Spanish settlement was founded by Vasco Núñez de Balboa in 1510. Panama was part of the viceroyalty of New Granada until it declared its independence from Spain in 1821 to join the Gran Colombia union. In 1903 it revolted against Colombia and was recognized by the US, to which it ceded the Canal Zone. The completed Panama Canal was opened in 1914; its jurisdiction reverted from the US to Panama in 1999. An invasion by US troops in 1989 overthrew the de facto ruler, Gen. Manuel Noriega.

Recent Developments

In 2006 a referendum to expand the capacity of the Panama Canal was held. The proposal, estimated to cost $5.25 billion and take seven to eight years to conclude, called for building two new three-chamber locks in the canal and creating a third lane of traffic capable of handling large container ships that the canal was currently unable to accommodate. Opponents contended that the project was based on uncertain projections about maritime trade and that it would cost much more than had been budgeted. In October 78% of voters supported the proposed expansion.

Internet resources: <www.visitpanama.com>.

Papua New Guinea

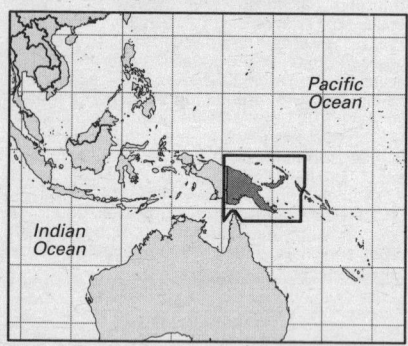

Official name: Independent State of Papua New Guinea. Form of government: constitutional monarchy with one legislative house (National Parliament [109]). Chief of state: Queen Elizabeth II (from 1952), represented by Governor-General Sir Paulias Matane (from 2004). Head of government: Prime Minister Sir Michael Somare (from 2002). Capital: Port Moresby. Official language: English; English, Motu, and Tok Pisin (English Creole) are national languages. Official religion: none. Monetary unit: 1 Papua New Guinea kina (K) = 100 toea; valuation (1 Jul 2007) US$1 = K 3.02.

Demography

Area: 178,704 sq mi, 462,840 sq km. Population (2006): 6,001,000. Density (2006): persons per sq mi 33.6, persons per sq km 13.0. Urban (2001): 17.6%. Sex distribution (2000): male 51.87%; female 48.13%. Age breakdown (2000): under 15, 38.8%; 15–29, 28.7%; 30–44, 17.1%; 45–59, 9.7%; 60–74, 4.7%; 75 and over, 1.0%. Ethnic composition (1983; PNG has several thousand separate communities, most with only a few hundred people): New Guinea Papuan 84.0%; New Guinea Melanesian 15.0%; other 1.0%. Religious affiliation (2000): Christian 95.1%, of which non-Anglican Protestant 56.6%, Roman Catholic 30.0%, Anglican 6.7%; traditional beliefs 3.6%; Baha'i 0.8%; other 0.5%. Major cities (2000): Port Moresby 254,158; Lae 78,038; Madang 27,394; Wewak 19,724; Goroka 18,618. Location: group of islands, including the eastern half of the island of New Guinea, in the South Pacific Ocean near the Equator, bordering Indonesia and to the north of Australia.

Vital statistics

Birth rate per 1,000 population (2003): 31.1 (world avg. 21.3). Death rate per 1,000 population (2003): 7.6 (world avg. 9.1). Natural increase rate per 1,000 population (2003): 23.5 (world avg. 12.2). Total fertility rate (avg. births per childbearing woman; 2003): 4.1. Life expectancy at birth (2003): male 62.1 years; female 66.4 years.

National economy

Budget (2001). Revenue: K 2,859,000,000 (tax revenue 86.6%, of which value-added tax 27.0%, corporate tax 24.2%, income tax 22.7%, excise tax 6.5%; nontax revenue ◄3.4%). Expenditures (2000): K 3,081,800,000 (current expenditure 70.8%, of which transfer to provincial governments 16.8%, interest payments 12.4%; development expenditure 29.2%). Public debt (external, outstanding; 2002): $1,488,000,000. Production (metric tons except as noted). Agriculture, forestry, fishing (2002): oil palm fruit 1,250,000, bananas 725,000, coconuts 513,000; livestock (number of live animals) 1,650,000 pigs, 3,800,000 chickens; roundwood (2002) 8,597,000 cu m; fish catch (2001) 53,763. Mining and quarrying (2000): copper (metal content) 200,900; gold 74,300 kg; silver 73,200 kg. Manufacturing (1998): palm oil 241,485; copra 124,349; wood products (excluding furniture) 3,054,000 cu m. Energy production (consumption): electricity (kW-hr; 2000) 2,180,000,000 (2,180,000,000); coal (2000) none (1,000); crude petroleum (barrels; 2000) 28,807,000 (513,100); natural gas (cu m; 2000) 83,544,000 (83,544,000); petroleum products (2000) 49,000 (717,000). Land use as % of total land area (2000): in temporary crops 0.5%, in permanent crops 1.4%, in pasture 0.4%; overall forest area 67.6%. Gross national product (2003): $2,823,000,000 ($510 per capita). Population economically active (1990; citizens of PNG over age 10 involved in "money-raising" activities only): total 1,715,330; activity rate 36.9% (participation rates: female 41.5%; unemployed 7.7%). Tourism (2001): receipts $101,000,000; expenditures $38,000,000.

Foreign trade

Imports (2000-c.i.f.): $1,035,000,000 (petroleum products 22%; food 16%; transport equipment 14%; nonelectrical machinery 12%; chemicals and chemical products 7%). Major import sources (2000): Australia 55.8%; Japan 11.3%; US 6.5%; Singapore 5.4%; New Zealand 3.5%. Exports (2002-f.o.b.): $1,638,000,000 (gold 36.0%; crude petroleum 22.5%; copper 16.0%; logs 5.7%; palm oil 5.1%). Major export destinations (2002): Australia 49.3%; Singapore 18.8%; New Zealand 4.4%; Japan 4.2%; Malaysia 2.8%.

Transport and communications

Transport. Roads (1996): total length 19,600 km (paved 4%). Vehicles (1998): passenger cars 21,700; trucks and buses 89,700. Air transport (1999): passenger-km 641,000,000; metric ton-km cargo 80,000,000; airports (1999) with scheduled flights 42. Communications, in total units (units per 1,000 persons). Daily newspaper circulation (2000): 72,600 (14); radios (2000): 446,000 (86); televisions (2000): 88,200 (17); telephone main lines (2002): 62,000 (11); cellular telephone subscribers

---

1 metric ton = about 1.1 short tons;   1 kilometer = 0.6 mi (statute);   1 metric ton-km cargo = about 0.68 short ton-mi cargo;   c.i.f.: cost, insurance, and freight;   f.o.b.: free on board

(2002): 15,000 (2.7); personal computers (2002): 321,000 (59); Internet users (2002): 75,000 (14).

Education and health

Educational attainment (1990). Percentage of population age 25 and over having: no formal schooling 82.6%; some primary education 8.2%; completed primary 5.0%; some secondary 4.2%. **Literacy** (2000): total population age 15 and over literate 63.9%; males literate 70.6%; females literate 56.8%. **Health**: physicians (1998) 342 (1 per 13,708 persons); hospital beds (1993) 14,119 (1 per 294 persons); infant mortality rate per 1,000 live births (2003) 54.8. **Food** (2001): daily per capita caloric intake 2,193 (vegetable products 91%, animal products 9%); 96% of FAO recommended minimum.

Military

Total active duty personnel (2004): 3,100 (army 80.6%, navy 12.9%, air force 6.5%). **Military expenditure as percentage of GNP** (1999): 1.1% (world 2.4%); per capita expenditure $7.

Background

Papua New Guinea has been inhabited since prehistoric times. The Portuguese sighted the coast in 1512, and in 1545 the Spanish claimed the island. The first colony was founded in 1793 by the British. In 1828 the Dutch claimed the western half as part of the Dutch East Indies. In 1884 Britain annexed the southeastern part and Germany took over the northeastern sector. The British part became the Territory of Papua in 1906 and passed to Australia, which also governed the German sector after World War I. After World War II, Australia governed both sectors as the Territory of Papua and New Guinea. Dutch New Guinea was annexed to Indonesia in 1969. Papua New Guinea achieved independence in 1975 and joined the British Commonwealth. It moved to resolve its war with Bougainville independence fighters in 1997. The decadelong war on the island of Bougainville ended when final terms for peace were negotiated on 1 Jun 2001.

Recent Developments

Disagreement with regional ally Australia marked the past several years for Papua New Guinea. In 2005 an Australian aid program worth $750 million was scrapped. In 2006 the government refused to allow Australia to use Manus Island as an offshore detention facility for asylum seekers, and in 2007 plans for a multibillion-dollar natural gas pipeline between the two countries fell through.

Internet resources: <www.pngembassy.org>.

Paraguay

Official name: República del Paraguay (Spanish); Tetä Paraguáype (Guaraní) (Republic of Paraguay). **Form of government:** multiparty republic with two legislative houses (Senate [45]; Chamber of Deputies [80]). **Head of state and government:** President Nicanor Duarte Frutos (from 2003). **Capital:** Asunción. **Official languages:** Spanish; Guaraní. **Official religion:** none, although Roman Catholicism enjoys

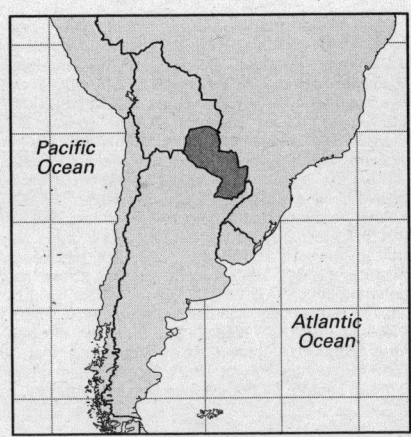

special recognition in the 1992 constitution. **Monetary unit:** 1 Paraguayan Guaraní (₲) = 100 céntimos; valuation (1 Jul 2007) US$1 = ₲ 5,228.

Demography

Area: 157,048 sq mi, 406,752 sq km. **Population** (2006): 5,993,000. **Density** (2006): persons per sq mi 38.2, persons per sq km 14.7. **Urban** (2002): 56.7%. **Sex distribution** (2002): male 50.70%; female 49.30%. **Age breakdown** (2003): under 15, 38.4%; 15–29, 26.1%; 30–44, 17.8%; 45–59, 10.8%; 60–74, 5.2%; 75 and over, 1.7%. **Ethnic composition** (2000): mixed (white/Amerindian) 85.6%; white 9.3%, of which German 4.4%, Latin American 3.4%; Amerindian 1.8%; other 3.3%. **Religious affiliation** (2000): Roman Catholic 90.1%; Protestant 5.2%; nonreligious/atheist 1.3%; other 3.4%. **Major urban areas** (2002): Asunción 513,399 (2003 urban agglomeration population equals 1,639,000); Ciudad del Este 223,350; Encarnación 69,769; Pedro Juan Caballero 64,153; Caaguazú 50,329. **Location:** central South America, bordering Brazil, Argentina, and Bolivia.

Vital statistics

Birth rate per 1,000 population (2003): 30.1 (world avg. 21.3). **Death rate** per 1,000 population (2003): 4.6 (world avg. 9.1). **Natural increase rate** per 1,000 population (2003): 25.5 (world avg. 12.2). **Total fertility rate** (avg. births per childbearing woman; 2002): 4.1. **Marriage rate** per 1,000 population (2002; Civil Registry records only): 3.0. **Life expectancy** at birth (2003): male 71.9 years; female 77.0 years.

National economy

Budget (2002). *Revenue:* ₲5,048,300,000,000 (tax revenue 64.2%, of which taxes on goods and services 38.9%, customs duties 10.3%, income taxes 8.9%, social security 6.1%; nontax revenue including grants 35.8%). *Expenditures:* ₲6,072,900,000,000 (current expenditure 78.6%; capital expenditure 21.4%). **Public debt** (external, outstanding; 2002): $2,064,000,000. **Population economically active** (2000): total 2,560,608; activity rate 48.5% (participation rates: ages 15 and over, 81.0%; female 38.6%; unemployed [2001] 15.3%). **Production** (metric tons except as noted). *Agriculture, forestry, fishing* (2002): cassava 4,142,000, soybeans 3,276,000, sugarcane 3,210,000; livestock (number of live animals) 9,900,000 cattle, 2,750,000 pigs, 15,500,000 chickens; roundwood 9,787,000 cu m; fish catch (2001) 25,000. *Mining and quarrying* (2002): hydraulic cement 650,000; kaolin 66,700; gypsum 4,300. *Manufacturing* (value added in constant prices of 1982, 6'000,000; 2001): food products 61,056; wood products (excluding furniture) 21,695; beverages 18,589. *Energy production (consumption):* electricity (kW-hr; 2000) 53,521,000,000 (6,136,000,000); crude petroleum (barrels; 2000) none (777,000); petroleum products (2000) 102,000 (1,076,000). **Gross national product** (2003): $6,213,000,000 ($1,100 per capita). **Households.** Average household size (2000) 4.4. **Tourism** (2002): receipts $62,000,000; expenditures $65,000,000. **Land use** as % of total land area (2000): in temporary crops 7.2%, in permanent crops 0.2%, in pasture 54.6%; overall forest area 58.8%.

Foreign trade

Imports (2002-f.o.b. in balance of trade and c.i.f. in commodities and trading partners): $1,672,000,000 (machinery and apparatus 21.6%, chemicals and chemical products 17.4%, refined petroleum 14.3%, transport equipment 6.0%, food products 5.6%). *Major import sources:* Brazil 30.6%; Argentina 20.6%; China 12.6%; US 5.0%; Japan 4.0%. **Exports** (2002): $951,000,000 (excludes value of hydroelectricity exports to Brazil and Argentina; soybeans 35.8%, processed meats 7.6%, soybean oil 7.5%, leather and leather products 6.1%, wood manufactures 5.9%). *Major export destinations:* Brazil 37.1%; Uruguay 17.4%; Cayman Islands 8.2%; Chile 5.2%; US 3.9%.

Transport and communications

Transport. *Railroads* (1998): route length 441 km; passenger-km 3,000,000; metric ton-km cargo 5,500,000. *Roads* (1999): total length 29,500 km (paved 51%). *Vehicles* (2002): passenger cars 274,186; trucks 189,115. *Air transport* (2000): passenger-km 270,503,000; metric ton-km cargo 24,346,000; airports (1998) 5. **Communications,** in total units (units per 1,000 persons). Daily newspaper circulation (2000): 227,000 (43); radios (2000): 961,000 (182); televisions (2000): 1,150,000 (218); telephone main lines (2003): 273,200 (46); cellular telephone subscribers (2003): 1,770,300 (299); personal computers (2002): 200,000 (35); Internet users (2003): 120,000 (20).

Education and health

Educational attainment (2002). Percentage of population age 15 and over having: no formal schooling 5.0%; primary education 55.0%; secondary 33.5%; higher 5.3%; not stated 1.2%. **Literacy** (2002): percentage of total population age 15 and over literate 92.9%; males literate 93.9%; females literate 91.9%. **Health:** physicians (1995) 3,730 (1 per 1,294 persons); hospital beds (2002) 5,834 (1 per 945 persons); infant mortality rate per 1,000 live births (2003) 27.7. **Food** (2001): daily per capita caloric intake 2,576 (vegetable products 78%, animal products 22%); 112% of FAO recommended minimum.

Military

Total active duty personnel (2003): 18,600 (army 80.1%, navy 10.8%, air force 9.1%). **Military expenditure as percentage of GNP** (1999): 1.1% (world 2.4%); per capita expenditure $15.

Paraguay has a distinctive musical tradition, especially of songs and ballads. Typical music for dancing includes polkas and languid *guaranías,* played on the native harp. Perhaps the most famous dance is the *galopa,* a variant of which is the bottle dance, in which dancers balance bottles on their heads.

Background

Seminomadic tribes speaking Guaraní were in Paraguay long before it was settled by Spain in the 16th and 17th centuries. Paraguay was part of the viceroyalty of Río de la Plata until it became independent in 1811. It suffered from dictatorial governments in the 19th century and from the 1865 war with Brazil, Argentina, and Uruguay. The Chaco War with Bolivia over disputed territory was settled primarily in Paraguay's favor by the peace treaty of 1938. Military governments, including that of Alfredo Stroessner, predominated in the mid-20th century until the election of a civilian president, Juan Carlos Wasmosy, in 1993. Paraguay suffered a financial crisis in the late 1990s, and democratic government was in jeopardy.

Recent Developments

Legal and personal problems involving former Paraguayan political figures were prominent in recent years. Gen. Lino Oviedo, who had been charged with having masterminded the 1999 assassination of Vice Pres. Luis María Argaña and had been convicted on charges surrounding an attempted coup in 1996, returned in June 2004 from exile in Brazil and was promptly clapped in prison to serve out a 10-year sentence. In January 2005 he was acquitted of the charge from 1999. He hoped to stand in the presidential election scheduled for 2008. In February 2005 the body of Cecilia Cubas, the kidnapped daughter of former president Raúl Cubas, was discovered outside of Asunción. In December 2006, 15 people from the extremist group Free Fatherland were convicted of the crime. Former president Luiz González Macchi's conviction in 2000 on embezzlement charges was overturned in September 2006, but in December he was convicted of having concealed a $1 million Swiss bank account and sentenced to eight years in prison.

Internet resources: <www.senatur.gov.py>.

Peru

Official name: República del Perú (Spanish) (Republic of Peru). **Form of government:** unitary multiparty republic with one legislative house (Congress [120]).

1 metric ton = about 1.1 short tons;   1 kilometer = 0.6 mi (statute);   1 metric ton-km cargo = about 0.68 short ton-mi cargo;   c.i.f.: cost, insurance, and freight;   f.o.b.: free on board

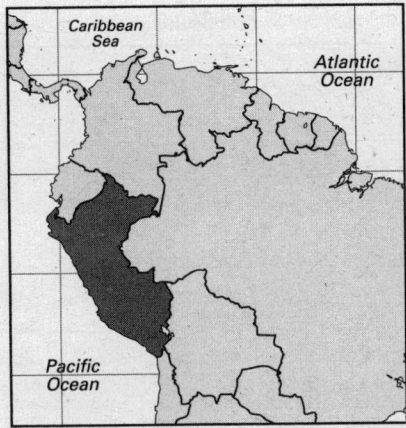

Caribbean Sea

Atlantic Ocean

Pacific Ocean

Head of state and government: President Alan García (from 2006), assisted by Prime Minister Jorge del Castillo (from 2006). **Capital:** Lima. **Official languages:** Spanish; Quechua; Aymara. **Official religion:** Roman Catholicism. **Monetary unit:** 1 nuevo sol (S/.) = 100 céntimos; valuation (1 Jul 2007) US$1 = S/. 3.16.

Demography

Area: 496,218 sq mi, 1,285,198 sq km. **Population** (2006): 27,515,000. **Density** (2006): persons per sq mi 55.4, persons per sq km 21.4. **Urban** (2003): 73.5%. **Sex distribution** (2003): male 50.35%; female 49.65%. **Age breakdown** (2003): under 15, 32.6%; 15–29, 27.2%; 30–44, 20.8%; 45–59, 11.9%; 60–74, 6.0%; 75 and over, 1.5%. **Ethnic composition** (2000): Quechua 47.0%; mestizo 31.9%; white 12.0%; Aymara 5.4%; Japanese 0.5%; other 3.2%. **Religious affiliation** (2000): Roman Catholic 95.7%; other (of which mostly Protestant) 4.3%. **Major cities** (2000): metropolitan Lima 7,496,831; Arequipa 762,000; Trujillo 652,000; Chiclayo 517,000; Iquitos 367,000. **Location:** western South America, bordering Ecuador, Colombia, Brazil, Bolivia, Chile, and the South Pacific Ocean.

Vital statistics

Birth rate per 1,000 population (2003): 22.6 (world avg. 21.3). **Death rate** per 1,000 population (2003): 6.2 (world avg. 9.1). **Natural increase rate** per 1,000 population (2003): 16.4 (world avg. 12.2). **Total fertility rate** (avg. births per childbearing woman; 2003): 2.7. **Life expectancy** at birth (2003): male 67.2 years; female 70.7 years.

National economy

Budget (2001). *Revenue:* S/. 27,039,000,000 (VAT 43.7%, income taxes 20.8%, nontax revenue 15.1%, import duties 10.1%, payroll tax 3.1%), other taxes 7.2%. *Expenditures:* S/. 32,378,000,000 (current expenditure 73.7%, capital expenditure 13.8%, interest payments 12.5%). **Public debt** (external, outstanding; 2002): $20,477,000,000. **Production** (metric tons except as noted). *Agriculture, forestry, fishing* (2002): sugarcane 8,422,000, potatoes 3,299,000, rice 2,124,000; livestock (number of live animals) 14,300,000 sheep, 4,950,000 cattle, 90,000,000 chickens; roundwood 9,928,385 cu m; fish catch (2001) 7,995,500. *Mining and quarrying* (2003): iron ore 3,540,700 (metal content); zinc 1,171,000 (metal content); copper 625,300 (metal content). *Manufacturing* (value in S/. '000,000 [at market prices]; 1996): processed foods 275.1; base metal products 188.6; textiles and leather products 129.5. *Energy production (consumption):* electricity (kW-hr; 2000) 19,912,000,000 (19,912,000,000); coal (2000) 12,000 (528,000); crude petroleum (barrels; 2002) 35,661,000 ([2001] 70,800,000); petroleum products (2000) 7,503,000 (7,620,000); natural gas (cu m; 2000) 820,932,000 (820,932,000). **Population economically active** (1998): total 7,407,280; activity rate of total population 45.7% (participation rates: over age 15, 66.9%; female 43.8%; urban unemployed [2001] 7.9%). **Gross national product** (at current market prices; 2003): $58,458,000,000 ($2,150 per capita). **Household income and expenditure.** Average household size (2001) 4.5; income per household (1988) $2,173; sources of income (1991): self-employment 67.1%, wages 23.3%, transfers 7.6%; expenditure (1990): food 29.4%, recreation and education 13.2%, household durables 10.1%. **Tourism** (2002): receipts $801,000,000; expenditures $616,000,000. **Land use** as % of total land area (2000): in temporary crops 2.9%, in permanent crops 0.4%, in pasture 21.2%; overall forest area 50.9%.

Foreign trade

Imports (2001-f.o.b. in balance of trade and c.i.f. in commodities and trading partners): $7,316,000,000 (machinery and apparatus 25.0%, chemicals and chemical products 16.1%, crude and refined petroleum 11.9%, food 11.0%). *Major import sources:* US 23.1%; Argentina 6.2%; Japan 5.9%; Chile 5.9%; Colombia 5.2%. **Exports** (2001): $6,826,000,000 (gold 17.1%, fish foodstuffs for animals 12.3%, refined copper and copper products 11.7%, apparel and clothing accessories 7.4%, crude and refined petroleum 6.1%, zinc ores and concentrates 5.2%). *Major export destinations:* US 24.8%; UK 13.5%; China 6.2%; Japan 5.6%; Switzerland 4.5%.

Transport and communications

Transport. *Railroads* (2000): route length 1,608 km; (1999) passenger-km 144,000,000; metric ton-km cargo 891,000,000. *Roads* (1999): total length 78,128 km (paved 13%). *Vehicles* (1999): passenger cars 684,533; trucks and buses 403,652. *Air transport* (2002; Total for 5 national airlines): passenger-km 2,214,000,000; metric ton-km cargo 99,000,000; airports (1996) 27. **Communications,** in total units (units per 1,000 persons). Daily newspaper circulation (1996): 2,000,000 (84); radios (1997): 7,080,000 (273); televisions (2002): 4,592,400 (172); telephone main lines (2003): 1,839,200 (67); cellular telephone subscribers (2003): 2,908,800 (106); personal computers (2002): 1,149,000 (43); Internet users (2003): 2,850,000 (104).

Education and health

Educational attainment (1993). Percentage of population age 15 and over having: no formal schooling 12.3%; less than primary education 0.3%; primary

31.5%; secondary 35.5%; higher 20.4%. **Literacy** (2000): total population age 15 and over literate 89.9%; males literate 94.7%; females literate 85.3%. **Health** (2002): physicians 32,619 (1 per 821 persons); hospital beds 43,074 (1 per 621 persons); infant mortality rate per 1,000 live births (2003) 34.0. **Food** (2001): daily per capita caloric intake 2,610 (vegetable products 87%, animal products 13%); 111% of FAO recommended minimum.

Military

Total active duty personnel (2003): 100,000 (army 60.0%, navy 25.0%, air force 15.0%). **Military expenditure as percentage of GNP** (1999): 2.4% (world 2.4%); per capita expenditure $45.

Background

Peru was the center of the Inca empire, which was established about 1230 with its capital at Cuzco. In 1533 it was conquered by Francisco Pizarro, and it was dominated by Spain for almost 300 years as the viceroyalty of Peru. It declared its independence in 1821, and freedom was achieved in 1824. Peru was defeated in the War of the Pacific with Chile (1879–83). A boundary dispute with Ecuador erupted into war in 1941 and gave Peru control over a larger part of the Amazon basin; further disputes ensued until the border was demarcated again in 1998. The government was overthrown by a military junta in 1968, and civilian rule was restored in 1980. The government of Alberto Fujimori dissolved the legislature in 1992 and promulgated a new constitution the following year. It later successfully combated the Sendero Luminoso (Shining Path) and Tupac Amarú rebel movements. Fujimori won a second term in 1995 and a controversial third term in 2000, but he left office and the country late that year amid allegations of corruption.

Recent Developments

The presidential election dominated life in Peru during the first half of 2006. Alan García, a former president (1985–90) and head of the American Popular Revolutionary Alliance (APRA) party, won 53% of the vote in a June run-off election. His first term had been widely viewed as a failure; his policy mistakes had plunged the country into economic free fall, and the Shining Path insurgent movement had grown increasingly strong. However, Peru was in far better shape economically than it had been in 1985. GNP growth was over 6%, and inflation was virtually nonexistent. The value of the country's exports approached $23 billion, a 30% increase over 2005, and resulted in a record-level trade surplus. Peru's principal exports—copper, zinc, and gold—were in high demand worldwide and commanded high prices. A significant disconnect still existed between those positive signs and job creation, however. The central and southern highlands were Peru's poorest regions, and bringing even modest prosperity to them would be a major challenge. Peru and the US negotiated a free-trade agreement that in June 2007 still had not been approved by the US Congress.

Internet resources: <www.peru.info>.

Philippines

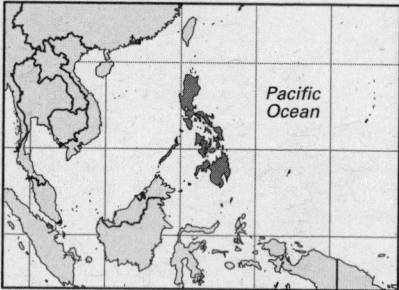

Pacific Ocean

Official name: Republika ng Pilipinas (Pilipino); Republic of the Philippines (English). **Form of government:** unitary republic with two legislative houses (Senate [24]; House of Representatives [236]). **Chief of state and head of government:** President Gloria Macapagal Arroyo (from 2001). **Capital:** Quezon City/Manila; additional offices/ministries are located in other suburbs of Metro Manila. **Official languages:** Pilipino; English. **Official religion:** none. **Monetary unit:** 1 Philippine peso (P) = 100 centavos; valuation (1 Jul 2007) US$1 = P 46.19.

Demography

Area: 122,121 sq mi, 316,294 sq km (sum of regional areas; actual total may be different). **Population** (2006): 85,563,000. **Density** (2006): persons per sq mi 738.7, persons per sq km 285.2. **Urban** (2003): 61.0%. **Sex distribution** (2002): male 50.37%; female 49.63%. **Age breakdown** (2002): under 15, 35.1%; 15–29, 28.1%; 30–44, 19.3%; 45–59, 11.2%; 60–74, 5.0%; 75 and over, 1.3%. **Ethnolinguistic composition** (by mother tongue of households; 1995): Pilipino (Tagalog) 29.3%; Cebuano 23.3%; Ilocano 9.3%; Hiligaynon Ilongo 9.1%; Bicol 5.7%; Waray 3.8%; Pampango 3.0%; Pangasinan 1.8%; other 14.7%. **Religious affiliation** (2000): Roman Catholic 81.0%; Protestant 6.6%; Muslim 5.1%; indigenous Christian 4.3%; other Christian 0.7%; traditional beliefs 0.2%; other/unknown 2.1%. **Major cities** (2000): Quezon City 2,173,831; Manila 1,581,082 (Metro Manila, 9,932,560); Caloocan 1,177,604; Davao 1,147,116; Cebu 718,821. **Location:** southeastern Asia, archipelago between the Philippine Sea and the South China Sea, east of Vietnam.

Vital statistics

Birth rate per 1,000 population (2003): 25.1 (world avg. 21.3). **Death rate** per 1,000 population (2003): 5.1 (world avg. 9.1). **Natural increase rate** per 1,000 population (2003): 20.0 (world avg. 12.2). **Total fertility rate** (avg. births per childbearing woman; 2003): 3.1. **Life expectancy** at birth (2003): male 67.2 years; female 72.5 years.

National economy

Budget (2001). *Revenue:* P 563,732,000,000 (income taxes 39.6%, international duties 17.1%, sales

---

1 metric ton = about 1.1 short tons;   1 kilometer = 0.6 mi (statute);   1 metric ton-km cargo = about 0.68 short ton-mi cargo;   c.i.f.: cost, insurance, and freight;   f.o.b.: free on board

tax 15.4%, nontax revenues 12.8%). *Expenditures:* P 706,327,000,000 (debt service 24.6%, education 17.2%, economic affairs 12.9%, public order 6.8%, defense 4.6%). **Public debt** (external, outstanding; 2002): $32,967,000,000. **Production** (metric tons except as noted). *Agriculture, forestry, fishing* (2002): sugarcane 25,835,000, coconuts 13,682,560, rice 13,270,653; livestock (number of live animals) 11,652,700 pigs, 6,250,000 goats, 125,730,000 chickens; roundwood (2001) 16,013,084 cu m; fish catch (2001) 2,280,512. *Mining and quarrying* (2002): nickel 26,532 (metal content); copper 18,364 (metal content); chromite 2,000. *Manufacturing* (gross value added in P '000,000; 2001): food products 361,217; electrical machinery 95,592; petroleum and coal products 73,280. *Energy production (consumption):* electricity (kW-hr; 2002) 48,180,000,000 ([2001] 47,049,000,000); hard coal (2002) 1,644,000 ([2000] 8,599,000); crude petroleum (barrels; 2000) 401,000 (117,700,000); petroleum products (2000) 13,913,000 (15,003,000); natural gas (cu m; 2000) 10,276,000 (10,276,000). **Household income and expenditure** (2000). Average household size (2002) 5.0; income per family P 144,506; sources of income: wages 52.1%, entrepreneurial income 25.1%, receipts from abroad 11.1%; expenditure: food, beverages, and tobacco 45.4%, housing 14.2%, transportation 6.8%. **Gross national product** (at current market prices; 2003): $87,771,000,000 ($1,080 per capita). **Population economically active** (2002): total 35,421,000; activity rate 42.8% (participation rates: ages 15 and over [2003] 67.1%; female [2001] 38.6%; unemployed [2003] 11.4%). **Tourism** (2002): receipts $1,741,000,000; expenditures $871,000,000. **Land use** as % of total land area (2000): in temporary crops 18.9%, in permanent crops 16.8%, in pasture 4.3%; overall forest area 19.4%.

Foreign trade

Imports (2001-c.i.f.): $29,551,000,000 (electronic components 16.0%, computer parts 9.3%, crude petroleum 9.0%, chemicals and chemical products 8.5%, food 7.4%, telecommunications equipment 5.8%). *Major import sources:* Japan 20.6%; US 16.9%; South Korea 6.6%; Singapore 6.1%; Taiwan 5.4%; Hong Kong 4.3%. **Exports** (2001-f.o.b.): $32,150,000,000 (electronic microcircuits 34.4%, computers and computer parts 21.9%, apparel and clothing accessories 7.5%, food 4.0%). *Major export destinations:* US 27.5%; Japan 15.7%; The Netherlands 9.3%; Singapore 7.2%; Taiwan 6.6%; Hong Kong 4.9%.

Transport and communications

Transport. *Railroads* (2000): route length 897 km; passenger-km 12,000,000; metric ton-km cargo 660,000,000. *Roads* (2000): total length 201,994 km (paved 39%). *Vehicles* (2001): passenger cars 729,350; trucks and buses 285,282. *Air transport* (2002; Philippines Airlines only): passenger-km 13,956,270,000; metric ton-km cargo 266,913,000; airports (1996) with scheduled flights 21. **Communications,** in total units (units per 1,000 persons). Daily newspaper circulation (2000): 6,300,000 (82); radios (2000): 12,400,000 (161); televisions (2002): 14,542,000 (182); telephone main lines (2002): 3,310,900 (42); cellular telephone subscribers (2002): 15,201,000 (191); personal computers

(2002): 2,200,000 (28); Internet users (2002): 3,500,000 (44).

Education and health

Educational attainment (2000). Percentage of population age 25 and over having: no formal schooling 3.8%; primary education 38.5%; incomplete secondary 12.5%; complete secondary 17.2%; technical 5.9%; incomplete undergraduate 11.8%; complete undergraduate 7.3%; graduate 0.7%; unknown 2.3%. **Literacy** (2001): total population age 15 and over literate 95.1%. **Health** (2002): physicians 91,408 (1 per 872 persons); hospital beds 85,166 (1 per 936 persons); infant mortality rate per 1,000 live births (2003) 25.0. **Food** (2001): daily per capita caloric intake 2,372 (vegetable products 85%, animal products 15%); 105% of FAO recommended minimum.

Military

Total active duty personnel (2003): 106,000 (army 62.3%, navy 22.6%, air force 15.1%). **Military expenditure as percentage of GNP** (1999): 1.4% (world 2.4%); per capita expenditure $14.

Did you know? Cadiz is a chartered city and port in northern Negros Island, Philippines. It is one of five chartered cities and one of the principal ports on the island, where most of the country's sugar is grown and refined and where fishing is a major industry.

Background

In ancient times, the inhabitants of the Philippines were a diverse agglomeration of peoples who arrived in various waves of immigrants from the Asian mainland. Ferdinand Magellan arrived in 1521. The islands were colonized by the Spanish, who retained control until the islands were ceded to the US in 1898 following the Spanish-American War. The Commonwealth of the Philippines was established in 1935 to prepare the country for political and economic independence, which was delayed by World War II and the Japanese invasion. The islands were liberated by US forces during 1944–45, and the Republic of the Philippines was proclaimed in 1946, with a government patterned on that of the US. In 1965 Ferdinand Marcos was elected president. He declared martial law in 1972, and it lasted until 1981. After 20 years of dictatorial rule, he was driven from power in 1986. Corazon Aquino became president and instituted a period of democratic rule that continued with the 1992 election of Fidel Ramos. Through the 1990s the government tried to come to terms with independence fighters in the southern islands.

Recent Developments

In February 2006 military officials in the Philippines announced that they had blocked a coup to overthrow Pres. Gloria Macapagal Arroyo. Thousands of people, led by former president Corazon Aquino, marched through the financial district of Manila calling for Arroyo to resign over questions about the legitimacy of her 2004 reelection. The New People's Army (NPA), a communist guerrilla group that had been trying to overthrow the government since 1969, resulting in some 40,000 deaths, became increasingly active. The army redeployed some troops that had been opposing another guerrilla army, the Moro Islamic Liberation Front (MILF), who fought for greater autonomy for Muslims in southern islands of the predominately Roman Catholic country. A scandal developed in August with the revelation that some candidates for nursing degrees had obtained advance copies of their examinations. Among the many Filipinos going to work abroad because of widespread unemployment at home, nurses were in particular demand, especially in the United States. Heavy rain in February triggered a landslide that buried the village of Guinsaugon. Disaster workers aided by US Marines dug 139 bodies from the deep mud, but more than 1,000 people were never found.

Internet resources: <www.gov.ph>.

Poland

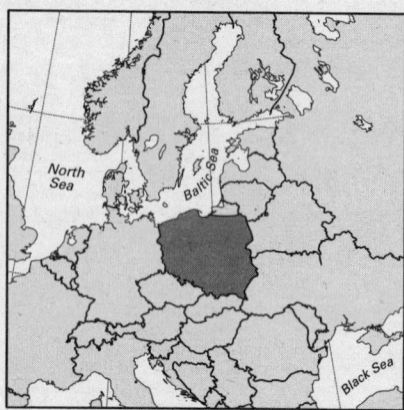

Official name: Rzeczpospolita Polska (Republic of Poland). **Form of government:** unitary multiparty republic with two legislative houses (Senate [100]; Diet [460]). **Chief of state:** President Lech Kaczynski (from 2005). **Head of government:** Prime Minister Jaroslaw Kaczynski (from 2006). **Capital:** Warsaw. **Official language:** Polish. **Official religion:** none (Roman Catholicism has special recognition per 1997 concordat with Vatican City). **Monetary unit:** 1 zloty (Zl) = 100 groszy; valuation (1 Jul 2007) US$1 = Zl 2.78.

Demography

Area: 120,728 sq mi, 312,685 sq km. **Population** (2006): 38,136,000. **Density** (2006): persons per sq mi 315.9, persons per sq km 122.0. **Urban** (2002): 61.8%. **Sex distribution** (2002): male 48.43%; female 51.57%. **Age breakdown** (2002): under 15, 18.3%; 15–29, 24.6%; 30–44, 20.6%; 45–59, 20.1%; 60–74, 11.5%; 75 and over, 4.5%. **Ethnolinguistic composition** (1997): Polish 94.2%; Ukrainian 3.9%; German 1.3%; Belarusian 0.6%. **Religious affiliation** (1995): Roman Catholic 90.7%; Ukrainian Catholic 1.4%; Polish Orthodox 1.4%; Protestant 0.5%; Jehovah's Witness 0.5%;

other (mostly nonreligious) 5.5%. **Major cities** (2002): Warsaw 1,671,670 (urban agglomeration; 2001) 2,282,000; Lódz 789,318; Kraków 758,544; Wroclaw 640,367; Poznan 578,886. **Location:** central Europe, bordering the Baltic Sea, Russia (exclave of Kaliningrad), Lithuania, Belarus, Ukraine, Slovakia, Czech Republic, and Germany.

Vital statistics

Birth rate per 1,000 population (2003): 10.5 (world avg. 21.3); (2000) legitimate 87.9%. **Death rate** per 1,000 population (2003): 10.0 (world avg. 9.1). **Natural increase rate** per 1,000 population (2003): 0.5 (world avg. 12.2). **Total fertility rate** (avg. births per childbearing woman; 2003): 1.4. **Marriage rate** per 1,000 population (2002): 5.0. **Divorce rate** per 1,000 population (2002): 1.2. **Life expectancy** at birth (2003): male 69.8 years; female 78.3 years.

National economy

Budget (2002). *Revenue:* Zl 143,022,000,000 (value-added tax 40.0%, income tax 27.3%, excise tax 21.9%, nontax revenue 10.8%). *Expenditures:* Zl 182,922,-000,000 (social security and welfare 25.2%, public debt 13.1%, education 12.2%, defense 5.1%). **Gross national product** (2003): $201,389,000,000 ($5,270 per capita). **Production** (metric tons except as noted). *Agriculture, forestry, fishing* (1999): (gross value of production in Zl '000,000) potatoes 4,066, wheat 3,747, fruit 3,578; livestock (number of live animals) 18,538,000 pigs, 6,555,000 cattle; roundwood (2001) 21,170,000 cu m; fish catch (2001) 261,376. *Mining and quarrying* (2000): sulfur 1,369,000; copper ore (metal content) 390,700; silver (recoverable metal content) 1,144. *Manufacturing* (value added in Zl '000,000; 1999): food products 13,764; beverages 13,582; transport equipment 10,596. *Energy production (consumption):* electricity ('000,000 kW-hr; 2002) 140,880 ([2000] 138,810); hard coal (2002) 104,112,000 ([2000] 83,390,000); lignite (2002) 58,212,000 ([2000] 59,500,000); crude petroleum (barrels; 2000) 4,844,000 (134,125,000); petroleum products (2000) 16,417,000 (16,668,000); natural gas (cu m; 2002) 5,255,000,000 ([2000] 14,760,-000,000). **Public debt** (external, outstanding; 2002): $29,374,000,000. **Population economically active** (2002): total 17,785,700; activity rate of total population 46.0% (participation rates: 15 and over, 55.0%; female 45.7%; unemployed 17.5%). **Household income and expenditure.** Average household size (2002) 2.9; average annual income (2002) Zl 25,600; sources of income (2001): wages 46.7%, transfers 33.8%, self-employment 13.9%; expenditure (2001): food, beverages, and tobacco 28.0%, housing and energy 25.6%, transportation and communications 14.6%, recreation 6.6%. **Tourism** (2002): receipts $4,500,-000,000; expenditures $3,200,000,000. **Land use** as % of total land area (2000): in temporary crops 46.0%, in permanent crops 1.1%, in pasture 13.4%; overall forest area 29.7%.

Foreign trade

Imports (2001-c.i.f.): Zl 206,253,000,000 (machinery and apparatus 26.1%, chemicals and chemical products 13.9%, road vehicles 7.8%, crude petroleum

1 metric ton = about 1.1 short tons;   1 kilometer = 0.6 mi (statute);   1 metric ton-km cargo = about 0.68 short ton-mi cargo;   c.i.f.: cost, insurance, and freight;   f.o.b.: free on board

5.7%, food 5.3%, textile yarn and fabrics 5.2%). *Major import sources:* Germany 24.0%; Russia 8.8%; Italy 8.3%; France 6.8%; UK 4.2%. **Exports** (2001-f.o.b.): Zl 148,115,000,000 (machinery and apparatus 20.4%, road vehicles 8.9%, food 7.1%, furniture and furniture parts 6.9%, chemicals and chemical products 5.9%, apparel and clothing accessories 5.4%, ships and boats 5.2%). *Major export destinations:* Germany 34.4%; Italy 5.4%; France 5.4%; UK 5.0%; The Netherlands 4.7%.

Transport and communications

Transport. *Railroads* (2002): length 22,981 km; passenger-km 20,809,000,000; metric ton-km cargo 47,756,000. *Roads* (1999): total length 381,046 km (paved 66%). *Vehicles* (2001): passenger cars 9,991,260; trucks and buses 1,783,008. *Air transport* (2002; LOT only): passenger-km 6,672,000,000; metric ton-km cargo 80,000,000; airports (1997) 8. **Communications,** in total units (units per 1,000 persons). Daily newspaper circulation (2000): 4,170,-000 (108); radios (2000): 20,200,000 (523); televisions (2000): 15,500,000 (400); telephone main lines (2003): 12,300,000 (319); cellular telephone subscribers (2003): 17,400,000 (451); personal computers (2002): 4,079,000 (106); Internet users (2003): 8,970,000 (232).

Education and health

Educational attainment (2002). Percentage of population age 13 and over having: no formal schooling/incomplete primary education 5.6%; complete primary 29.8%; secondary/vocational 51.5%; postsecondary 3.2%; university 9.9%, of which doctorate 0.3%. **Literacy** (2000): 99.8%. **Health** (2002): physicians 86,608 (1 per 446 persons); hospital beds 188,038 (1 per 205 persons); infant mortality rate per 1,000 live births (2003) 9.0. **Food** (2001): daily per capita caloric intake 3,397 (vegetable products 75%, animal products 25%); 130% of FAO recommended minimum.

Military

Total active duty personnel (2003): 163,000 (army 63.8%, navy 8.8%, air force 22.4%, other 5.0%). **Military expenditure as percentage of GNP** (1999): 2.1% (world 2.4%); per capita expenditure $173.

Background

Established as a kingdom in 922 under Mieszko I, Poland was united with Lithuania in 1386 under the Jagiellon Dynasty (1386–1572) to become the dominant power in east-central Europe. In 1466 it wrested western and eastern Prussia from the Teutonic Order, and its lands eventually stretched to the Black Sea. Wars with Sweden and Russia in the late 17th century led to the loss of considerable territory. In 1697 the electors of Saxony became kings of Poland, virtually ending Polish independence. In the late 18th century Poland was divided among Prussia, Russia, and Austria and ceased to exist. After 1815 the former Polish lands came under Russian domination, and from 1863 Poland was a Russian province. After World War I an independent Poland was established by the Allies. The invasion of Poland in 1939 by the USSR and Germany precipitated World War II, during which the Nazis sought to purge its culture and its

large Jewish population. Reoccupied by Soviet forces in 1945, it was controlled by a Soviet-dominated government from 1947. In the 1980s the Solidarity labor movement achieved major political reforms, and free elections were held in 1989. An economic austerity program instituted in 1990 sped the transition to a market economy. In 2004 Poland joined the European Union (EU).

Recent Developments

In 2006 the Polish government focused on reducing Poland's dependence on Russian energy supplies by diversifying energy sources and investing heavily in the modernization of the domestic energy sector. As a staunch ally of the United States, Poland pledged to maintain its troops—though in reduced numbers—in Iraq through the end of 2007 and to send 1,000 troops to Afghanistan by early 2007. Poland's economy was strong, with GDP growth estimated at 5.2%, an increase of 16.9% in exports, a 13.0% rise in imports, and easy passage of the 2007 draft budget. The unemployment rate dropped to 15.2% but was still the highest in the EU. Thanks in part to its EU accession, Poland was classified among the most attractive investment destinations.

Internet resources: <www.polandtour.org>.

Portugal

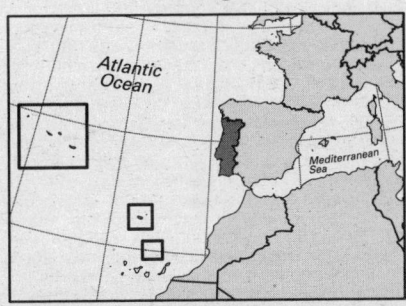

Official name: República Portuguesa (Portuguese Republic). **Form of government:** republic with one legislative house (Assembly of the Republic [230]). **Chief of state:** President Aníbal Cavaco Silva (from 2006). **Head of government:** Prime Minister José Sócrates (from 2005). **Capital:** Lisbon. **Official language:** Portuguese. **Official religion:** none. **Monetary unit:** 1 euro (€) = 100 cents; valuation (1 Jul 2007) US$1 = €0.74; at conversion on 1 Jan 2002, € 1= 200.482 Portuguese escudos (Esc).

Demography

Area: 35,567 sq mi, 92,118 sq km. **Population** (2006): 10,605,000. **Density** (2006): persons per sq mi 298.2, persons per sq km 115.1. **Urban** (2001): 65.8%. **Sex distribution** (2001): male 48.34%; female 51.66%. **Age breakdown** (2000): under 15, 17.1%; 15–29, 23.0%; 30–44, 21.5%; 45–59, 17.8%; 60–74, 14.5%; 75 and over, 6.1%. **Ethnic composition** (2000): Portuguese 91.9%; mixed-race people from Angola, Mozambique, and Cape Verde 1.6%; Brazilian 1.4%; Marrano 1.2%; other European

1.2%; Han Chinese 0.9%; other 1.8%. **Religious affiliation** (2000): Christian 92.4%, of which Roman Catholic 87.4%, independent Christian 2.7%, Protestant 1.3%, other Christian 1.0%; nonreligious/atheist 6.5%; Buddhist 0.6%; other 0.5%. **Major cities** (2001): Lisbon 564,657 (urban agglomeration 3,447,173); Porto 263,131; Amadora 175,872; Braga 164,192; Coimbra 148,443. **Location:** southwestern Europe, bordering Spain and the North Atlantic Ocean.

Vital statistics

Birth rate per 1,000 population (2003): 11.0 (world avg. 21.3). **Death rate** per 1,000 population (2003): 10.3 (world avg. 9.1). **Natural increase rate** per 1,000 population (2003): 0.7 (world avg. 12.2). **Total fertility rate** (avg. births per childbearing woman; 2003): 1.5. **Marriage rate** per 1,000 population (2002): 5.4. **Divorce rate** per 1,000 population (2001): 1.8. **Life expectancy** at birth (2003): male 73.9 years; females 80.7 years.

National economy

Budget (2001). *Revenue:* Esc 5,793,400,000,000 (taxes on goods and services 52.0%, income taxes 39.5%). *Expenditures:* Esc 6,616,800,000,000 (current expenditure 89.2%, development expenditure 10.8%). **Public debt** (2001): $61,224,180,000. **Production** (metric tons except as noted). *Agriculture, forestry, fishing* (2002): potatoes 1,200,000, tomatoes 994,000, grapes 900,000; livestock (number of live animals) 5,478,000 sheep, 2,389,000 pigs, 1,399,000 cattle; roundwood (2002) 8,742,000 cu m; fish catch (2001) 199,000. *Mining and quarrying* (2001): marble 1,000,000; copper (metal content) 83,000; tin (metal content) 1,200. *Manufacturing* (value added in Esc '000,000; 1998): machinery and transport equipment 606,000, of which transport equipment 232,000; petroleum refining 517,000; wearing apparel and footwear 307,000. *Energy production (consumption):* electricity (kW-hr; 2000) 47,459,000,000 (48,390,000,000); coal (2000) negligible (6,154,000); crude petroleum (barrels; 2000) none (85,200,000); petroleum products (2000) 10,170,000 (12,200,000); natural gas (cu m; 2000) none (2,424,600,000). **Tourism** (2002): receipts $5,919,000,000; expenditures $2,276,000,000. **Population economically active** (2001): total 5,211,300; activity rate of total population 51.3% (participation rates: ages 15–64 [1997], 68.5%; female 45.6%; unemployed 4.1%). **Gross national product** (at current market prices; 2003): $123,664,000,000 ($12,130 per capita). **Household income and expenditure.** Average household size (1999) 3.1; sources of income (1995): wages and salaries 44.4%, self-employment 23.4%, transfers 22.2%; expenditure (1994–95): food 23.9%, housing 20.6%, transportation and communications 18.9%. **Land use** as % of total land area (2000): in temporary crops 21.7%, in permanent crops 7.8%, in pasture 15.7%; overall forest area 40.1%.

Foreign trade

Imports (2000-c.i.f.): €43,358,000,000 (road vehicles 14.1%; nonelectrical machinery and apparatus 11.4%; mineral fuels and lubricants 10.3%; electrical machinery and telecommunications equipment 9.9%; food products 9.3%; chemicals and chemical products 9.1%). *Major import sources* (2001): Spain 26.5%; Germany 13.9%; France 10.3%; Italy 6.7%; UK 5.0%. **Exports** (2000-f.o.b.): €26,446,000,000 (machinery and apparatus 19.7%, of which telecommunications equipment 4.2%; road vehicles 13.5%; apparel and clothing accessories 11.6%; footwear 5.7%; chemicals and chemical products 5.5%; fabrics 4.7%). *Major export destinations* (2001): Germany 19.2%; Spain 18.6%; France 12.6%; UK 10.3%; US 5.8%.

Transport and communications

Transport. *Railroads* (1999): route length 3,579 km; passenger-km 4,380,000,000; metric ton-km cargo 2,560,000,000. *Roads* (1999): total length 68,732 km (paved 86%). *Vehicles* (1998): passenger cars 3,200,000; trucks and buses 1,097,000. *Air transport* (2001): passenger-km 10,457,000,000; metric ton-km cargo 53,865,000; airports (2000) 16. **Communications,** in total units (units per 1,000 persons). Daily newspaper circulation (2000): 324,000 (32); radios (2000): 3,080,000 (304); televisions (2000): 6,380,000 (630); telephone main lines (2003): 4,279,000 (414); cellular telephone subscribers (2003): 9,341,000 (904); personal computers (2002): 1,394,000 (134); Internet users (2002): 2,000,000 (194).

Education and health

Educational attainment (1991). Percentage of population age 25 and over having: no formal schooling 16.1%; some primary education 61.5%; some secondary 10.6%; postsecondary 3.5%. **Literacy** (2000): total population age 15 and over literate 92.2%; males literate 94.8%; females literate 90.0%. **Health** (2001): physicians 33,536 (1 per 310 persons); hospital beds 38,802 (1 per 268 persons); infant mortality rate per 1,000 live births (2003) 5.2. **Food** (2002): daily per capita caloric intake 3,741 (vegetable products 71%, animal products 29%); 153% of FAO recommended minimum.

Military

Total active duty personnel (2003): 44,900 (army 59.5%, navy 24.4%, air force 16.1%). **Military expenditure as percentage of GNP** (1999): 2.1% (world 2.4%); per capita expenditure $240.

Did you know? Portugal is home to a third of the world's cork trees, which produce more than half of the world's annual supply of cork stoppers for wine.

Background

Celtic peoples settled the Iberian peninsula in the 1st millennium BC. They were conquered about 140 BC by the Romans, who ruled until the 5th century AD, when the area was invaded by Germanic tribes. A Muslim invasion in 711 left only the northern part of Portugal

---

1 metric ton = about 1.1 short tons;   1 kilometer = 0.6 mi (statute);   1 metric ton-km cargo = about 0.68 short ton-mi cargo;   c.i.f.: cost, insurance, and freight;   f.o.b.: free on board

in Christian hands. In 1139 it became the kingdom of Portugal and expanded as it reconquered the Muslim-held sectors. The boundaries of modern continental Portugal were completed in 1270 under King Afonso III. In the 15th and 16th centuries the monarchy encouraged exploration that took Portuguese navigators to Africa, India, Indonesia, China, the Middle East, and South America, where colonies were established. António de Oliveira Salazar ruled Portugal as a dictator in the mid-20th century; he died in office in 1970, and his successor was ousted in a coup in 1974. A new constitution was adopted in 1976 (revised 1982), and civilian rule resumed. Portugal was a charter member of NATO and is a member of the European Union.

Recent Developments

The early part of 2006 in Portugal was dominated by the January election to replace Socialist Pres. Jorge Sampaio. Two Socialist candidates split the vote on the left, handing former center-right prime minister Aníbal Cavaco Silva a solid first-round win with 51% of the vote. Following his inauguration Cavaco Silva helped to craft a bipartisan pact to reform the country's justice system and called for a greater effort to crack down on corruption after Portugal ranked an embarrassing 16th in Transparency International's 2006 Bribe Payers' Index. Overall the economy looked rosier than in recent years. Unemployment fell to near 7%, and GDP grew 1.3% in 2006, higher than the roughly 1% initially expected, thanks in large part to burgeoning export growth. The government, led by Socialist Prime Minister José Sócrates, moved forward with a number of long-awaited reform plans, including efforts to reduce public-sector spending and cut through bureaucratic red tape. Improved tax collection, as well as reigned-in spending, was expected to cut the country's budget deficit to about 4.8% of GDP in 2006, down from more than 6% in 2005.

Internet resources: <www.portugal.org>.

Puerto Rico

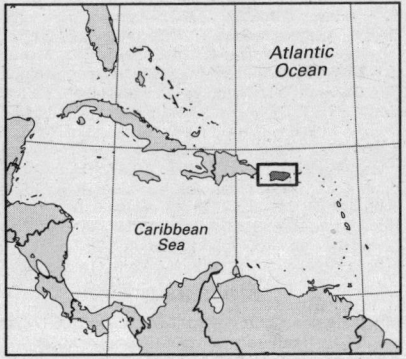

Atlantic Ocean

Caribbean Sea

Official name: Estado Libre Asociado de Puerto Rico; Commonwealth of Puerto Rico. **Political status:** self-governing commonwealth in association with the US, having two legislative houses (Senate [27]; House of Representatives [51]). **Chief of state:** President of the US George W. Bush (from 2001). **Head of government:** Governor Aníbal Acevedo Vilá (from 2005). **Capital:** San Juan. **Official languages:** Spanish; English. **Monetary unit:** 1 US dollar (US$) = 100 cents.

Demography

Area: 3,515 sq mi, 9,104 sq km. **Population** (2006): 3,927,000. **Density** (2006): persons per sq mi 1,117, persons per sq km 431.3. **Urban** (2001): 75.6%. **Sex distribution** (2002): male 48.09%; female 51.91%. **Age breakdown** (2000): under 15, 23.8%; 15–29, 23.3%; 30–44, 20.4%; 45–59, 17.1%; 60–74, 10.6%; 75 and over, 4.8%. **Ethnic composition** (2000): local white 72.1%; black 15.0%; mulatto 10.0%; US white 2.2%; other 0.7%. **Religious affiliation** (2000): Roman Catholic 75.0%; Protestant 19.5%; other 5.5%. **Location:** island in the Caribbean Sea, east of Cuba.

Vital statistics

Birth rate per 1,000 population (2003): 14.3 (world avg. 21.3). **Death rate** per 1,000 population (2003): 7.7 (world avg. 9.1). **Natural increase rate** per 1,000 population (2003): 6.6 (world avg. 12.2). **Total fertility rate** (avg. births per childbearing woman; 2003): 1.9. **Marriage rate** per 1,000 population (2001): 6.9. **Divorce rate** per 1,000 population (2001): 3.8. **Life expectancy** at birth (2003): male 73.3 years; female 81.6 years.

National economy

Budget. Revenue (2002): $10,556,400,000 (tax revenue 62.6%, of which income taxes 46.5%, excise taxes 14.1%; federal grants 19.0%; nontax revenue 18.4%). *Expenditures:* $10,556,400,000 (2001; welfare 22.3%; education 22.3%; public safety and protection 15.7%; debt service 9.8%; health 9.2%). **Public debt** (outstanding; 1999): $22,678,200,000. **Production** (in metric tons except as noted). *Agriculture and fishing* (2002): sugarcane 320,000, plantains 82,000, bananas 50,000; livestock (number of live animals) 390,000 cattle, 118,000 pigs; fish catch (2001) 3,952. *Mining* (value of production in $'000; 2002): crushed stone 38. *Manufacturing* (value added in $'000,000; 2001): chemicals, pharmaceuticals, and allied products 17,365; nonelectrical machinery 3,320; professional and scientific equipment 1,874. *Energy production (consumption):* electricity (kW-hr; 2003) 23,700,000,000 (23,700,-000,000); coal (2001) none (172,000); crude petroleum (barrels; 2001) none (58,400,000); petroleum products (2000) 2,478,000 (4,641,000). **Gross national product** (2003): $47,400,000,000 ($12,240 per capita). **Population economically active** (July 2004): total 1,400,400; activity rate 35.9% (participation rates: ages 16 and over, 46.3%; female (2002) 40.1%; unemployed 12.2%). **Household income and expenditure** (2002). Average family size 3.6; income per family $27,017; sources of income: wages and salaries 56.3%, transfers 29.5%, self-employment 6.4%, rent 5.2%, other 2.6%; expenditure (1999): food and beverages 18.8%, health care 17.8%, transportation 12.8%, housing 12.1%, household furnishings 11.6%, clothing 7.9%, recreation 7.7%. **Tourism** (2002): receipts $2,486,000,000; expenditures $928,000,000. **Land use** as % of total land area (2000): in temporary crops 3.9%, in permanent crops 5.5%, in pasture 23.7%; overall forest area 25.8%.

Foreign trade

Imports (2002–03): $33,800,000,000 (chemicals 44.8%, electronics 10.2%, transport equipment 7.0%, food and beverages 6.7%, refined petroleum 6.0%). *Major import sources:* US 48.9%; Ireland 20.7%; Japan 3.9%. **Exports** (2002–03): $55,200,000,000 (pharmaceutical and chemical products 71.8%, electronic and electrical products 12.5%). *Major export destinations:* US 86.4%; The Netherlands 2.1%; Belgium 2.0%.

Transport and communications

Transport. *Railroads* (2002; privately owned railway for sugarcane transport only): length 96 km. *Roads* (2003): total length 24,431 km (paved 94%). *Vehicles:* passenger cars (2001) 2,064,100; trucks and buses (1999) 306,600. *Air transport* (1998): passenger arrivals and departures 9,285,000; cargo loaded and unloaded 275,500 metric tons (handled by the Luis Muñoz Marín International Airport only); airports (1998) with scheduled flights 7. **Communications,** in total units (units per 1,000 persons). Daily newspaper circulation (2000): 481,000 (126); radios (2000): 2,830,000 (742); televisions (2000): 1,260,000 (330); telephone main lines (2001): 1,330,000 (336); cellular telephone subscribers (2001): 1,211,000 (307); Internet users (2001): 600,000 (152).

Education and health

Educational attainment (2000). Percentage of population age 25 and over having: no formal schooling to secondary education 25.4%; some upper secondary to some higher 56.3%; undergraduate or graduate degree 18.3%. **Literacy** (2001): total population age 15 and over literate 93.8%. **Health:** physicians (1999) 6,650 (1 per 571 persons); hospital beds (2001) 12,669 (1 per 303 persons); infant mortality rate (2003) 8.5.

Military

Total active duty personnel (2004): The US naval base at Ceiba was closed in March 2004.

Background

Puerto Rico was inhabited by Arawak Indians when it was settled by the Spanish in the early 16th century. It remained largely undeveloped economically until the late 18th century. After 1830 it gradually developed a plantation economy based on the export crops of sugarcane, coffee, and tobacco. The independence movement began in the late 19th century, and Spain ceded the island to the US in 1898, after the Spanish-American War. In 1917 Puerto Ricans were granted US citizenship, and in 1952 the island became a commonwealth with autonomy in internal affairs. The question of Puerto Rican statehood has been a political issue, with commonwealth status approved by voters in 1967, 1993, and 1998.

Recent Developments

In May 2006 the treasury ran out of funds to pay public servants, and public services came to a partial standstill. A new sales tax, which took effect in November, was intended to help alleviate the commonwealth's debt.

Internet resources: <www.gotopuertorico.com>.

Qatar

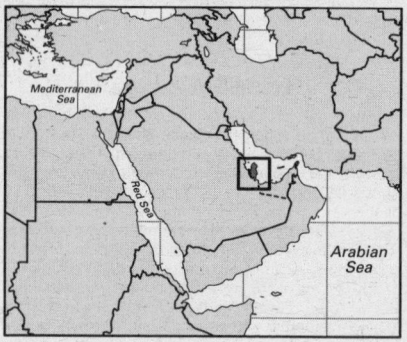

Official name: Dawlat Qatar (State of Qatar). **Form of government:** monarchy (emirate); Islamic law is the basis of legislation in the state. **Heads of state and government:** Emir Sheikh Hamad ibn Khalifah al-Thani (from 1995), assisted by Prime Minister Sheikh Hamad ibn Jassim ibn Jabr al-Thani (from 2007). **Capital:** Doha. **Official language:** Arabic. **Official religion:** Islam. **Monetary unit:** 1 riyal (QR) = 100 dirhams; valuation (1 Jul 2007) US$1 = QR 3.63.

Demography

Area: 4,184 sq mi, 10,836 sq km. **Population** (2006): 838,065. **Density** (2006): persons per sq mi 200.3, persons per sq km 77.3. **Urban** (2001): 92.9%. **Sex distribution** (2003): male 65.5%; female 34.5%. **Age breakdown** (2003): under 15, 24.7%; 15–29, 23.5%; 30–44, 24.3%; 45–59, 21.8%; 60–74, 5.1%; 75 and over, 0.6%. **Ethnic composition** (2000): Arab 52.5%, of which Palestinian 13.4%, Qatari 13.3%, Lebanese 10.4%, Syrian 9.4%; Persian 16.5%; Indo-Pakistani 15.2%; black African 9.5%; other 6.3%. **Religious affiliation** (2000): Muslim (mostly Sunni) 82.7%; Christian 10.4%; Hindu 2.5%; other 4.4%. **Major cities** (2004): Ad-Dawhah (Doha) 338,760; Ar-Rayyan 272,583; Al-Wakrah 20,205; Umm Salal 15,935. **Location:** the Middle East, bordering the Persian Gulf and Saudi Arabia.

Vital statistics

Birth rate per 1,000 population (2004): 15.6 (world avg. 21.3). **Death rate** per 1,000 population (2004): 4.5 (world avg. 9.1). **Natural increase rate** per 1,000 population (2004): 11.1 (world avg. 12.2). **Total fertility rate** (avg. births per childbearing woman; 2003):

---

1 metric ton = about 1.1 short tons;   1 kilometer = 0.6 mi (statute);   1 metric ton-km cargo = about 0.68 short ton-mi cargo;   c.i.f.: cost, insurance, and freight;   f.o.b.: free on board

3.1. **Marriage rate** per 1,000 population (2002): 3.9. **Divorce rate** per 1,000 population (2002): 1.2. **Life expectancy** at birth (2003): male 70.7 years; female 75.8 years.

National economy

Budget (2003–04). *Revenue:* QR 29,155,000,000 (oil and natural gas revenue 67.5%, investment income 23.5%, other 9.0%). *Expenditures:* QR 23,212,-000,000 (current expenditure 73.6%, of which wages and salaries 26.0%; capital expenditure 26.4%). **Production** (metric tons except as noted). *Agriculture and fishing* (2002): dates 16,500, tomatoes 11,000, pumpkin and squash 8,500; livestock (number of live animals; 2002) 200,000 sheep, 179,000 goats, 50,000 camels; fish catch (2001) 7,142. *Mining and quarrying* (2002): limestone 900,000; sulfur 221,000; gypsum, sand and gravel, and clay are also produced. *Manufacturing* (value added in $'000,000; 2000): iron and steel 210; refined petroleum 144; industrial chemicals 133. *Energy production (consumption):* electricity (kW-hr; 2001) 9,951,100,000 (9,951,100,000); crude petroleum (barrels; 2001) 243,788,000 ([2000] 27,200,000); petroleum products (2000) 8,265,000 (1,974,000); natural gas (cu m; 2000) 29,558,-000,000 (15,993,000,000). **Population economically active** (2001): total 317,000; activity rate of total population 53.1% (participation rates [1997]: ages 15–64, 59.7%; female 21.0%). **Gross national product** (2001): $7,200,000,000 ($12,000 per capita). **Households.** Average household size (2002) 7.1; expenditure (2001): housing 17.8%, food 16.5%, transportation 15.8%, household furnishings 8.6%, clothing and footwear 7.1%, education 5.5%, communications 5.5%. **Tourism** (2002): total number of tourists staying in hotels 586,645. **Land use** as % of total land area (2000): in temporary crops 1.6%, in permanent crops 0.3%, in pasture 4.5%; overall forest area 0.1%.

Foreign trade

Imports (2002-c.i.f.): $4,052,000,000 (machinery and apparatus 30.7%, of which general industrial machinery 9.0%, specialized machinery 6.4%; road vehicles 13.3%; food and live animals 10.4%; chemicals and chemical products 6.8%). *Major import sources:* US 13.0%; Japan 10.5%; Italy 9.0%; UK 7.6%; Germany 7.0%; UAE 7.0%; Saudi Arabia 6.2%. **Exports** (2002-f.o.b.): $8,231,000,000 (liquefied natural gas 42.6%; crude petroleum 35.0%; refined petroleum 6.7%; iron and steel 2.8%). *Major export destinations:* Japan 28.9%; South Korea 21.1%; Singapore 12.4%; UAE 5.3%; Thailand 4.6%.

Transport and communications

Transport. *Roads* (1996): total length 1,230 km (paved 90%). *Vehicles* (2000): passenger cars 199,600; trucks and buses 92,900. *Air transport* (2002; Qatar Airways): passenger-km 5,664,301,000; metric ton-km cargo 178,710,000; airports (2002) with scheduled flights 1. **Communications,** in total units (units per 1,000 persons). Daily newspaper circulation (1995): 90,000 (161); radios (1997): 250,000 (432); televisions (1998): 490,000 (846); telephone main lines (2003): 184,500 (289); cellular telephone subscribers (2003): 376,500 (590); personal computers (2002): 110,000 (178); Internet users (2003): 126,000 (197).

Education and health

Educational attainment (1986). Percentage of population age 25 and over having: no formal education 53.3%, of which illiterate 24.3%; primary 9.8%; preparatory (lower secondary) 10.1%; secondary 13.3%; postsecondary 13.3%; other 0.2%. **Literacy** (2001): total population age 15 and over literate 81.7%; males literate 80.8%; females literate 83.7%. **Health** (2002): physicians 1,518 (1 per 399 persons); hospital beds 1,357 (1 per 447 persons); infant mortality rate per 1,000 live births (2002) 20.3.

Military

Total active duty personnel (2003): 12,400 (army 68.5%, navy 14.5%, air force 16.9%; US troops (August 2004) 3,400. **Military expenditure as percentage of GNP** (1999): 10.0% (world 2.4%); per capita expenditure $1,470.

Background

Qatar was partly controlled by Bahrain in the 18th and 19th centuries and was nominally part of the Ottoman Empire until World War I. In 1916 it became a British protectorate. Oil was discovered in 1939, and the country rapidly modernized. Qatar declared independence in 1971, when the British protectorate ended. In 1991 it served as a base for air strikes against Iraq in the Persian Gulf War.

Recent Developments

Qatar's energy industry, especially its liquefied natural gas (LNG) and gas-to-liquids (GTL) sectors, continued its phenomenal growth in 2006. Progress was also ongoing in the country's long-planned Dolphin Gas Project to deliver substantial quantities of gas to the neighboring United Arab Emirates via an undersea pipeline. In addition, the government announced plans to spend $15 billion to increase the number of the country's tanker fleet to further expand its already substantial exports of LNG. The country showed progress toward its goal of becoming the world's largest LNG supplier.

Internet resources: <www.experienceqatar.com>.

Réunion

Official name: Département de la Réunion (Department of Réunion). **Political status:** overseas department (France) with two legislative houses (General Council [49]; Regional Council [45]). **Chief of state:** President of France Nicolas Sarkozy (from 2007). **Head of government:** Prefect Pierre-Henry Maccioni (from 2006). **Capital:** Saint-Denis. **Official language:** French. **Official religion:** none. **Monetary unit:** 1 euro (€) = 100 cents; valuation (1 Jul 2007) US$1 = €0.74 (1 French franc [F] = 100 centimes; at conversion on 1 Jan 2002, €1 = 6.56 French francs [F]).

Demography

Area: 968 sq mi, 2,507 sq km (excludes the French overseas territory of French Southern and Antarctic

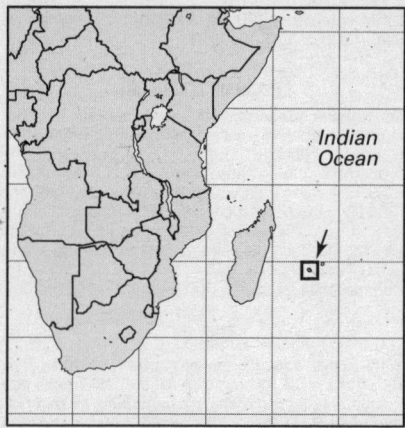

Indian
Ocean

Territories). **Population** (2006): 791,000. **Density** (2006): persons per sq mi 817.1, persons per sq km 315.5. **Urban** (1999): 82.7%. **Sex distribution** (1999): male 49.15%; female 50.85%. **Age breakdown** (1999): under 15, 27.0%; 15–29, 24.8%; 30–44, 24.4%; 45–59, 13.8%; 60–74, 7.2%; 75 and over, 2.8%. **Ethnic composition** (2000): mixed race (black-white-South Asian) 42.6%; local white 25.6%; South Asian 23.0%, of which Tamil 20.0%; Chinese 3.4%; East African 3.4%; Malagasy 1.4%; other 0.6%. **Religious affiliation** (1995): Roman Catholic 89.4%; Pentecostal 2.7%; other Christian 1.8%; other (mostly Muslim) 6.1%. **Major cities** (1999): Saint-Denis 131,557 (pop. of commune; agglomeration 158,139); Saint-Paul 87,712 (pop. of commune); Saint-Pierre 68,915 (pop. of commune; agglomeration 129,238); Le Tampon 60,323 (pop. of commune; within Saint-Pierre agglomeration); Saint-Louis 43,519 (pop. of commune). **Location:** island in the western Indian Ocean, east of Madagascar and near Mauritius.

Vital statistics

Birth rate per 1,000 population (2003): 20.2 (world avg. 21.3); (1997) legitimate 41.5%. **Death rate** per 1,000 population (2003): 5.5 (world avg. 9.1). **Natural increase rate** per 1,000 population (2003): 14.7 (world avg. 12.2). **Total fertility rate** (avg. births per childbearing woman; 2003): 2.5. **Marriage rate** per 1,000 population (1998): 4.8. **Divorce rate** per 1,000 population (1997): 1.3. **Life expectancy** at birth (2003): male 70.0 years; female 77.0 years.

National economy

Budget (1998). *Revenue:* F 4,624,000,000 (receipts from the French central government and local administrative bodies 52.7%, tax receipts 20.2%, loans 8.9%). *Expenditures:* F 4,300,000,000 (current expenditures 68.7%, development expenditures 31.3%). **Tourism** (2002): receipts $284,000,000. **Gross national product** (1998): $5,070,000,000 ($7,270 per capita). **Production** (metric tons except as noted). *Agriculture, forestry, fishing* (2001): sugarcane 1,850,000, corn (maize) 17,000, bananas

10,200; livestock (number of live animals) 78,000 pigs, 37,000 goats, 30,000 cattle; roundwood (2002) 36,100 cu m; fish catch (2002) 3,635. *Mining and quarrying*: gravel and sand for local use. *Manufacturing* (value added in F '000,000; 1997): food and beverages 1,019, of which meat and milk products 268; construction materials (mostly cement) 394; fabricated metals 258; printing and publishing 192. *Energy production (consumption):* electricity (kW-hr; 2000) 1,575,000,000 (1,575,000,000); petroleum products (2000) none (741,000). **Population economically active** (1998): total 288,760; activity rate of total population 41.2% (participation rates: ages 15–64, 57.5%; female 44.3%; unemployed [2000] 36.5%). **Household income and expenditure.** Average household size (1999) 3.3; average annual income per household (1997) F 136,800; sources of income (1997): wages and salaries and self-employment 41.8%, transfer payments 41.3%, other 16.9%; expenditure (1994–95): food and beverages 22.0%, transportation and communications 19.0%, housing and energy 10.0%, household furnishings 8.0%, recreation 6.0%. **Land use** as % of total land area (2000): in temporary crops 14%, in permanent crops 2%, in pasture 5%; overall forest area 28%.

Foreign trade

Imports (2002): €2,966,000,000 (food and agricultural products 18.2%, automobiles 12.9%, electrical machinery and electronics 9.0%, pharmaceuticals and medicines 8.4%, clothing and footwear 7.9%). *Major import sources* (1998): France 66.0%; EC 14.0%. **Exports** (1998): €185,700,000 (sugar 58.9%, machinery, apparatus, and transport equipment 17.5%, rum 2.5%, lobster 1.7%). *Major export destinations* (1998): France 70.0%; EC 9.0%; Madagascar 4.5%; Mauritius 2.3%.

Transport and communications

Transport. *Roads* (1994): total length 2,754 km (paved [1991] 79%). *Vehicles* (1999): passenger cars 190,300; trucks and buses 44,300. *Air transport* (2001; Saint-Denis airport only): passenger arrivals 747,044, passenger departures 744,788; cargo unloaded 17,945 metric tons, cargo loaded 8,881 metric tons; airports (2001) with scheduled flights 2. **Communications,** in total units (units per 1,000 persons). Daily newspaper circulation (1996): 83,000 (123); radios (1997): 173,000 (252); televisions (1998): 130,000 (186); telephone main lines (2001): 300,000 (410); cellular telephone subscribers (2002): 489,800 (659); personal computers (1999): 32,000 (45); Internet users (2002): 150,000 (202).

Education and health

Educational attainment (1986–87). Percentage of population age 25 and over having: no formal schooling 18.8%; primary education 44.3%; lower secondary 21.6%; upper secondary 11.0%; higher 4.3%. **Literacy** (1996): total population age 16–66 literate 373,487 (91.3%); males literate 179,154 (89.9%); females literate 194,333 (92.7%). **Health** (2002): physicians 1,137 (1 per 449 persons); hospital beds (2000) 2,124 (1 per 337 persons); infant mortality rate per 1,000 live births (2003) 8.3.

---

1 metric ton = about 1.1 short tons;   1 kilometer = 0.6 mi (statute);   1 metric ton-km cargo = about 0.68 short ton-mi cargo;   c.i.f.: cost, insurance, and freight;   f.o.b.: free on board

Military

Total active duty personnel (2003): 3,600 French troops (includes troops stationed on Mayotte).

Background

The island of Réunion was settled in the 17th century by the French, who brought slaves from eastern Africa to work on coffee and sugar plantations there. It was a French colony until 1946, when it became an overseas territory of France. Its economy is based almost entirely on the export of sugar.

Recent Developments

Réunion was· seriously affected by an outbreak of chikungunya, a usually nonfatal viral disease spread by mosquitoes, in 2006. Tourism was badly hit, and France was forced to step in and inject €76 million (about $91 million) into the economy.

Internet resources: <www.la-reunion-tourisme.com>.

Romania

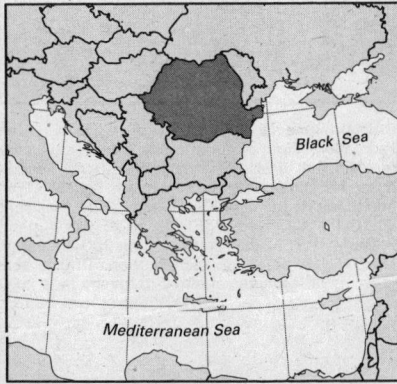

Black Sea

Mediterranean Sea

Official name: Romania. Form of government: unitary republic with two legislative houses (Senate [137]; Assembly of Deputies [332, including 18 nonelective seats]). Chief of state: President Traian Basescu (from 2004). Head of government: Prime Minister Calin Popescu Tariceanu (from 2004). Capital: Bucharest. Official language: Romanian. Official religion: none. Monetary unit: 1 Romanian new leu (plural lei) = 100 bani; valuation (1 Jul 2007) US$1 = 2.31 new lei.

Demography

Area: 92,043 sq mi, 238,391 sq km. Population (2006): 21,577,000. Density (2006): persons per sq mi 234.4, persons per sq km 90.5. Urban (2002): 52.7%. Sex distribution (2002): male 48.75%; female 51.25%. Age breakdown (2002): under 15, 17.6%; 15–29, 23.4%; 30–44, 21.0%; 45–59, 18.7%; 60–74, 14.4%; 75 and over, 4.9%. Ethnic composition (2002): Romanian 89.5%; Hungarian 6.6%; Roma (Gypsy) 2.5%; other 1.4%. Religious affiliation (2002): Romanian Orthodox 86.7%; Protestant 6.4%; Roman Catholic 4.7%; Greek Orthodox 0.9%; Muslim 0.3%; other 1.0%. Major cities (2002): Bucharest 1,921,751; Iasi 321,580; Cluj-Napoca 318,027; Timisoara 317,651; Constanta 310,526. Location: southeastern Europe, bordering Ukraine, Moldova, the Black Sea, Bulgaria, Serbia and Montenegro, and Hungary.

Vital statistics

Birth rate per 1,000 population (2002): 9.7 (world avg. 21.3). Death rate per 1,000 population (2002): 12.4 (world avg. 9.1). Natural increase rate per 1,000 population (2002): –2.7 (world avg. 12.2). Total fertility rate (avg. births per childbearing woman; 2002): 1.3. Marriage rate per 1,000 population (1995): 6.8. Life expectancy at birth (2002): male 67.4 years; female 74.8 years.

National economy

Budget ('000,000 lei; 2000). Revenue: 119,763,500 (value-added tax 42.1%, excise tax 17.2%, personal income tax 16.6%, nontax revenue 4.5%). Expenditures: 105,923,100 (economic affairs 23.0%, education 19.0%, defense 13.3%, public order 13.2%). Public debt (external, outstanding; 2002): $8,112,000,000. Production (metric tons except as noted). Agriculture, forestry, and fishing (2002): corn (maize) 8,500,000, wheat 4,380,000, potatoes 4,000,000; livestock (number of live animals) 7,251,000 sheep, 4,446,-800 pigs, 2,799,800 cattle; roundwood (2002) 15,154,000 cu m; fish catch (2001) 18,455. Mining (2000): iron (metal content) 55,000; bauxite 135,000; zinc (metal content of concentrate) 27,455. Manufacturing (value-added in '000,000,000 lei; 1996): food products 5.8; beverages 3.0; iron and steel 1.6. Energy production (consumption): electricity (kW-hr; 2001) 53,640,000,000 ([2000] 51,241,-000,000); hard coal (2000) 281,000 (2,649,000); lignite (2001) 29,431,000 ([2000] 29,313,000); crude petroleum (barrels; 2001) 45,164,000 ([2000] 80,419,000); petroleum products (2001) 9,192,000 (8,230,000); natural gas (cu m; 2001) 12,172,-000,000 ([2000] 16,000,000,000). Population economically active (2001): total 11,446,900; activity rate 52.6% (participation rates: ages 15–64, 74.5%; female 46.2%; unemployed 6.6%). Households. Average household size (2000) 3.1. Gross national product (2003): $51,194,000,000 ($2,310 per capita). Tourism (2002): receipts $612,000,000; expenditures $396,000,000. Land use as % of total land area (2000): in temporary crops 40.7%, in permanent crops 2.3%, in pasture 21.5%; overall forest area 28.0%.

Foreign trade

Imports (2001-f.o.b. in balance of trade and c.i.f. in commodities and trading partners): $15,552,-000,000 (nonelectrical machinery and apparatus 11.9%, fabrics 11.6%, electrical machinery and telecommunications equipment 10.9%, chemicals and chemical products 9.3%, crude and refined petroleum 8.7%). Major import sources: Italy 20.0%; Germany 15.2%; Russia 7.6%; France 6.3%; Hungary 3.9%. Exports (2001): $11,385,000,000 (apparel and clothing accessories 24.4%, electrical machinery and telecommunications equipment 8.0%, iron and steel 7.2%, nonelectrical machinery and apparatus 6.7%, footwear 5.6%, refined petroleum 5.3%). Major *export destinations:* Italy 25.1%; Germany 15.6%; France 8.1%; UK 5.2%; Turkey 4.0%.

Transport and communications

Transport. *Railroads* (2000): length 11,385 km; passenger-km 11,632,000,000; metric ton-km cargo 17,982,000,000. *Roads* (2001): length 198,603 km (paved 64%). *Vehicles* (2000): cars 3,128,782; trucks and buses 461,635. *Air transport* (2002): passenger-km 1,908,000,000; metric ton-km cargo 8,664,000; airports (2001) 8. **Communications,** in total units (units per 1,000 persons). Daily newspaper circulation (2000): 6,560,000 (300); radios (2000): 7,310,000 (334); televisions (2000): 8,340,000 (381); telephone main lines (2003): 4,300,000 (205); cellular telephone subscribers (2003): 6,900,000 (329); personal computers (2002): 1,800,000 (83); Internet users (2003): 4,000,000 (191).

Education and health

Educational attainment (1992). Percentage of population age 25 and over having: no schooling 5.4%; some primary education 24.4%; some secondary 63.2%; postsecondary 6.9%. **Literacy** (2000): total population age 15 and over literate 98.1%; males literate 99.0%; females literate 97.3%. **Health:** physicians (2002) 41,300 (1 per 525 persons); hospital beds (2002) 161,500 (1 per 135 persons); infant mortality rate per 1,000 live births (2002) 17.3. **Food** (2001): daily per capita caloric intake 3,407 (vegetable products 80%, animal products 20%); 125% of FAO recommended minimum.

Military

Total active duty personnel (2004): 97,200 (army 67.9%, navy 7.4%, air force 14.4%, other 10.3%). **Military expenditure as percentage of GNP** (2001): 1.6% (world 2.4%); per capita expenditure $97.

Background

Romania was formed in 1862 by the unification of the principalities Moldavia and Walachia, which had once been part of the ancient country of Dacia. During World War I, Romania sided with the Allies and doubled its territory in 1918 with the addition of Transylvania, Bukovina, and Bessarabia. Allied with Germany in World War II, it was occupied by Soviet troops in 1944 and became a satellite country of the USSR in 1948. During the 1960s Romania's foreign policy was frequently independent of the Soviet Union's. The communist regime of Nicolae Ceausescu was overthrown in 1989, and free elections were held in 1990. Throughout the 1990s Romania struggled with rampant corruption and organized crime as it tried to stabilize its economy.

Recent Developments

Romania became a member of the European Union (EU) on 1 Jan 2007. It was one of the poorest countries in the EU, with a GDP only one-third of the EU average, but in 2006 the country had experienced GDP growth of 7%, and further growth was expected with the trade benefits of membership. Billions of dollars in aid would be withheld by the EU, however, if Romania did not take steps to eliminate political corruption and regulate its borders. EU membership caused a flood of applications for work visas and citizenship from Moldovans. Romania granted citizenship to Moldovans whose parents or grandparents had been Romanian citizens before 1940, when Moldova was a part of Romania, but Pres. Traian Basescu promised to stop the practice after he estimated that as many as 800,000 citizenship applications could be filed.

Internet resources: <www.romaniatourism.com>.

Russia

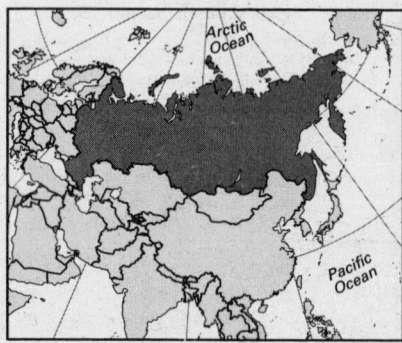

Official name: Rossiyskaya Federatsiya (Russian Federation). **Form of government:** federal multiparty republic with a bicameral legislative body (Federal Assembly comprising the Federation Council [178] and the State Duma [450]). **Head of state:** President Vladimir Putin (from 1999). **Head of government:** Prime Minister Mikhail Fradkov (from 2004). **Capital:** Moscow. **Official language:** Russian. **Official religion:** none. **Monetary unit:** 1 ruble (Rub) = 100 kopecks; valuation (1 Jul 2007) market rate, US$1 = Rub 25.82.

Demography

Area: 6,592,800 sq mi, 17,075,400 sq km. **Population** (2006): 142,394,000. **Density** (2006): persons per sq mi 21.6, persons per sq km 8.3. **Urban** (2003): 73.3%. **Sex distribution** (2002): male 46.60%; female 53.40%. **Age breakdown** (2002): under 15, 16.7%; 15–29, 23.4%; 30–44, 22.4%; 45–59, 18.7%; 60–74, 14.0%; 75 and over, 4.8%. **Ethnic composition** (2002): Russian 79.82%; Tatar 3.83%; Ukrainian 2.03%; Bashkir 1.15%; Chuvash 1.13%; Chechen 0.94%; Armenian 0.78%; Mordvin 0.58%; Belarusian 0.56%; Avar 0.52%; Kazakh 0.45%; Udmurt 0.44%; Azerbaijani 0.43%; Mari 0.42%; German 0.41%; Kabardinian 0.36%; Ossetian 0.35%; other 5.80%. **Religious affiliation** (2000): Christian 57.4%, of which Orthodox 49.7%, Protestant 6.2%, Roman Catholic 1.0%, other Christian 0.5%; Muslim 7.6%; traditional beliefs 0.8%; Jewish 0.7%; Hindu 0.5%; Buddhist 0.4%; nonreligious 27.4%; atheist 5.2%. **Major cities** (2002): Moscow 10,101,500; St. Petersburg 4,669,400; Novosibirsk 1,425,600; Nizhny Nov-

---

1 metric ton = about 1.1 short tons;   1 kilometer = 0.6 mi (statute);   1 metric ton-km cargo = about 0.68 short ton-mi cargo;   c.i.f.: cost, insurance, and freight;   f.o.b.: free on board

gorod 1,311,200; Yekaterinburg 1,293,000; Samara 1,158,100; Omsk 1,133,900; Kazan 1,105,300; Chelyabinsk 1,078,300; Rostov-na-Donu 1,070,200; Ufa 1,042,400; Volgograd 1,012,800. **Location:** eastern Europe and northern Asia, bordering the Arctic Ocean, the Pacific Ocean, North Korea, China, Mongolia, Kazakhstan, the Caspian Sea, Azerbaijan, Georgia, the Black Sea, Ukraine, Belarus, Latvia, Estonia, Finland, and Norway; the exclave of Kaliningrad on the Baltic Sea borders Lithuania and Poland. **Migration** (2002): immigrants 184,612; emigrants 106,685. **Refugees** (2002): 828,784, of which from Kazakhstan 301,137, Uzbekistan 106,299, Tajikistan 86,041, Georgia 62,868. **Households** (1999). Total households 52,116,000; average household size 2.8; distribution by size (1995): 1 person 19.2%; 2 persons 26.2%; 3 persons 22.6%; 4 persons 20.5%; 5 persons or more 11.5%.

Vital statistics

Birth rate per 1,000 population (2002): 9.6 (world avg. 21.3); (2001) legitimate 70.5%; illegitimate 29.5%. **Death rate** per 1,000 population (2002): 16.3 (world avg. 9.1). **Natural increase rate** per 1,000 population (2002): –6.5 (world avg. 12.2). **Total fertility rate** (avg. births per childbearing woman; 2002): 1.3. **Marriage rate** per 1,000 population (2002): 7.1. **Divorce rate** per 1,000 population (2002): 6.0. **Life expectancy** at birth (2002): male 58.5 years; female 71.9 years.

Social indicators

Quality of working life (2002). Average workweek: 40 hours. Annual rate per 100,000 workers of: injury or accident 460; industrial illness 22.2; death 13.8. Average days lost to labor strikes per 1,000 employees (1999): 35.7. **Social participation.** Trade union membership in total workforce (2000; state enterprises only): 100%. **Social deviance.** Offense rate per 100,000 population (2002) for: murder 22.5; rape 5.6; serious injury 40.7; larceny-theft 761.5. Incidence per 100,000 population (2000) of: alcoholism (1992) 1,727.5; substance abuse 25.6; suicide 39.2. **Material well-being** (2002). Durable goods possessed per 100 households: automobiles 27; personal computers 7; televisions 126; refrigerators and freezers 113; washing machines 93; VCRs 50; motorcycles 26; bicycles 71.

National economy

Public debt (external, outstanding; 2002): $96,223,000,000. **Budget** (2001). *Revenue:* Rub 2,438,105,000,000 (tax revenue 83.3%, of which value-added tax 26.2%, social security tax 25.4%, individual income tax 9.0%, excise tax 8.5%; nontax revenue 16.7%). *Expenditures:* Rub 2,202,868,-000,000 (current expenditure 91.3%, of which social security 33.7%, defense 12.6%, public services 8.2%, law enforcement 5.9%; capital expenditure 8.7%). **Gross national product** (2003): $374,937,000,000 ($2,160 per capita). **Production** (metric tons except as noted). *Agriculture, forestry, fishing* (2002): wheat 50,557,000, potatoes 31,900,000, barley 18,688,-000, sugar beets 15,500,000, vegetables (other than potatoes) 13,800,000, rye 7,139,000, oats 5,700,000, sunflower seeds 3,600,000, apples 1,800,000, peas 1,578,000, corn (maize) 1,541,-000, rice 483,000, buckwheat 304,000; livestock

(number of live animals) 27,106,000 cattle, 16,048,000 pigs, 13,035,000 sheep; roundwood (2002) 176,900,000 cu m; fish catch (2001) 3,718,000. *Mining and quarrying* (2001): iron ore 82,800,000; copper (metal content) 600,000; nickel (metal content) 325,000; zinc (metal content) 124,000; chrome ore (marketable) 69,926; platinum 35,000; vanadium 9,000; antimony (metal content) 4,500; molybdenum 2,600; silver 380,000 kg; gold 152,500 kg; gem diamonds 11,600,000 carats. *Manufacturing* (value added in $'000,000; 2001): food products 5,090; nonferrous base metals 4,282; iron and steel 3,083; motor vehicles and parts 2,547; bricks, cement, ceramics 2,254; special purpose machinery 2,213; basic chemicals 2,037; general purpose machinery 2,024; fabricated metal products 1,794; beverages 1,780; refined petroleum products 1,761; paper and paper products 1,294; paints, soaps, pharmaceuticals 1,252; tobacco products 754; wood and wood products (excluding furniture) 753; electricity distribution and control apparatus 561. *Energy production (consumption):* electricity (kW-hr; 2003) 913,900,000,000 ([2000] 863,700,-000,000); hard coal (2003) 195,900,000 ([2000] 142,224,000); lignite (2003) 79,000,000 ([2000] 91,700,000); crude petroleum (barrels; 2003) 3,019,000,000 ([2000] 1,312,000,000); petroleum products (2000) 159,281,000 (96,990,000); natural gas (cu m; 2003) 526,000,000,000 ([2000] 318,-000,000,000). **Population economically active** (2002): total 71,919,000; activity rate of total population 50.0% (participation rates: ages over 15, 82.6%; female 48.6%; unemployed 8.6%). **Land use** as % of total land area (2000): in temporary crops 7.4%, in permanent crops 0.1%, in pasture 5.4%; overall forest area 50.4%. **Household income and expenditure.** Average household size (2002) 2.8; income per household: Rub 52,400; sources of income (2002): wages 66.2%, pensions and stipends 14.9%, income from entrepreneurial activities 12.0%, property income 4.9%, other 2.0%; expenditure (2002): food 41.7%, clothing 13.3%, housing 6.2%, furniture and household appliances 5.7%, alcohol and tobacco 3.2%, transportation 2.7%. **Tourism** (2002): receipts $4,188,000,000; expenditures $12,005,000,000.

Foreign trade

Imports (2001-c.i.f.): $41,528,000,000 (machinery and apparatus 21.8%, of which general industrial machinery 5.9%; food and live animals 16.1%; chemicals and chemical products 12.1%; road vehicles 4.5%; iron and steel 3.5%). *Major import sources* (2002): Germany 14.3%; Belarus 8.8%; Ukraine 7.0%; US 6.4%; China 5.2%; Italy 4.8%; Kazakhstan 4.2%; France 4.1%. **Exports** (2001-f.o.b.): $99,198,-000,000 (fuels and lubricants 53.9%, of which crude petroleum 24.8%, natural gas 18.0%, refined petroleum 9.5%; nonferrous metals 6.8%; iron and steel 5.6%; chemicals and chemical products 4.8%; machinery and apparatus 4.6%; special transactions 11.6%). *Major export destinations* (2002): Germany 7.6%; Italy 7.0%; The Netherlands 6.8%; China 6.4%; Belarus 5.5%; Ukraine 5.5%; Switzerland 5.1%; US 3.8%; UK 3.6%; Poland 3.5%.

Transport and communications

Transport. *Railroads* (2002): length 139,000 km; passenger-km 152,900,000,000; metric ton-km cargo 1,510,000,000. *Roads* (2002): total length 593,000 km (paved 91%). *Vehicles* (2000): passenger cars 20,247,800; trucks and buses (1999) 5,021,000. *Air transport* (2002): passenger-km 64,700,000,000; metric ton-km cargo 2,700,000,000; airports (1998) 75. **Communications,** in total units (units per 1,000 persons). Daily newspaper circulation (2000): 15,300,000 (105); radios (2000): 61,100,000 (418); televisions (2000): 61,500,000 (421); telephone main lines (2002): 35,500,000 (242); cellular telephone subscribers (2002): 17,608,800 (120); personal computers (2002): 13,000,000 (89); Internet users (2002): 6,000,000 (41).

Education and health

Educational attainment (2002). Percentage of population age 15 and over having: no formal schooling 2.1%; primary education 7.7%; some secondary 18.1%; complete secondary/basic vocational 53.0%; incomplete higher 3.1%; complete higher 16.0%, of which advanced degrees 0.3%. **Health** (2002): physicians 678,000 (1 per 212 persons); hospital beds 1,653,000 (1 per 87 persons); infant mortality rate per 1,000 live births (2002) 13.3. **Food** (2001): daily per capita caloric intake 3,014 (vegetable products 78%, animal products 22%); 115% of FAO recommended minimum.

Military

Total active duty personnel (2004): 1,212,700 (army 29.7%, navy 12.8%, air force 15.2%, strategic deterrent forces 8.2%, paramilitary [includes railway troops, special construction troops, federal border guards, interior troops, and other federal guard units] 34.1%). **Military expenditure as percentage of GNP** (1999): 5.6% (world 2.4%); per capita expenditure $239.

Background

The region between the Dniester and Volga rivers was inhabited from ancient times by various peoples, including the Slavs. The area was overrun from the 8th century BC to the 6th century AD by successive nomadic peoples, including the Sythians, Sarmatians, Goths, Huns, and Avars. Kievan Rus, a confederation of principalities ruled from Kiev, emerged c. the 10th century. It lost supremacy in the 11th and 12th centuries to independent principalities, including Novgorod and Vladimir. Novgorod ascended in the north and was the only Russian principality to escape the domination of the Mongol Golden Horde in the 13th century. In the 14th–15th centuries the princes of Moscow gradually overthrew the Mongols. Under Ivan IV, Russia began to expand. The Romanov dynasty arose in 1613. Expansion continued under Peter I (the Great) and Catherine II (the Great). The area was invaded by Napoleon in 1812; after his defeat, Russia received most of the grand duchy of Warsaw (1815). Russia annexed Georgia, Armenia, and Caucasus territories in the 19th century. The Russian southward advance against the Ottoman Empire was of key importance to Europe. Russia was defeated in the Crimean War. It sold Alaska to the US in 1867. Russia's defeat in the Russo-Japanese War led to an unsuccessful uprising in 1905. In World War I it fought against the Central Powers.

The Russian Revolution that overthrew the czarist regime in 1917 marked the beginning of a government of soviets ("councils"). The Bolsheviks brought the main part of the former empire under communist control and organized it as the Russian Soviet Federated Socialist Republic (RSFSR; coextensive with present-day Russia). The Russian SFSR joined other soviet republics in 1922 to form the USSR. Although it fought with the Allies in World War II, after the war tensions with the West led to the decades-long Cold War.

Upon the dissolution of the USSR in 1991, the Russian SFSR was renamed Russia and became the leading member of the Commonwealth of Independent States. It adopted a new constitution in 1993. During the 1990s it struggled on several fronts, beset with economic difficulties, political corruption, and independence movements. Vladimir Putin was elected president in 2000, with economic reform, governmental reorganization, cutbacks in the military, and rooting out corruption and favoritism as his chief goals.

Recent Developments

The situation in Chechnya appeared to be gradually stabilizing as a result of Moscow's policy of "Chechenization," which saw the federal authorities devolve responsibility for the everyday running of affairs to the Chechens themselves. The pro-Moscow Chechen forces gained the upper hand, and in March Ramzan Kadyrov, son of the republic's pro-Moscow president assassinated in 2004, was appointed prime minister. He worked hard to rebuild Chechnya's war-wrecked infrastructure and to revive traditional Islamic customs. Instability continued to spread through the area, however, most notably in Ingushetia and Dagestan.

The Russian economy grew by 6.5% in 2006, assisted by high oil prices. Foreign reserves exceeded $270 billion, and inflation was held below 10%, which made 2006 the first year of single-digit inflation since the collapse of the USSR. In September Russia cleared its debts to the Paris Club of creditor nations.

In pursuing the concept of Russia as an "energy superpower," the state increased its direct ownership of the oil industry to about 34% of production and its share of the gas industry to close to 90%. Russia's state-controlled gas giant, Gazprom, cut gas supplies to Ukraine over a price dispute and by year's end raised the gas prices to most of the other former Soviet countries. Western governments expressed concern over the interest shown by several Russian state-owned companies in acquiring foreign assets, notably Gazprom's pursuit of gas-distribution companies in Western Europe, since it did not reciprocate by allowing Western companies access to its own Russian pipelines.

Russia concentrated on building new strategic relationships with members of the nonaligned movement, including China, India, and Venezuela. In July Putin held a trilateral summit with Chinese Pres. Hu Jintao and Indian Prime Minister Manmohan Singh—the first such meeting between the three countries. Despite international fears that Tehran might be seeking to produce nuclear weapons under its cover, Russia agreed to open the nuclear power plant that it was helping to build in Iran in September 2007.

Internet resources: <www.russiatourism.ru>.

---

1 metric ton = about 1.1 short tons; 1 kilometer = 0.6 mi (statute); 1 metric ton-km cargo = about 0.68 short.
ton-mi cargo; c.i.f.: cost, insurance, and freight; f.o.b.: free on board

Rwanda

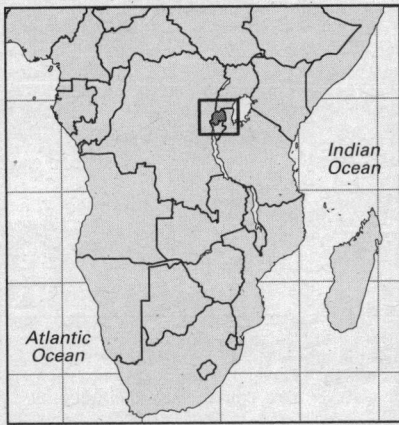

Indian Ocean

Atlantic Ocean

Official name: Repubulika y'u Rwanda (Rwanda); République Rwandaise (French); Republic of Rwanda (English). **Form of government:** multiparty republic with two legislative bodies (Senate [26]; Chamber of Deputies [80]). **Head of state and government:** President Maj. Gen. Paul Kagame (from 2000), assisted by Prime Minister Bernard Makuza (from 2000). **Capital:** Kigali. **Official languages:** Rwanda; French; English. **Official religion:** none. **Monetary unit:** 1 Rwanda franc (RF); valuation (1 Jul 2007) US$1 = RF 556.54.

Demography

Area: 9,758 sq mi, 25,273 sq km (land area only). **Population** (2006): 8,771,000. **Density** (2006): persons per sq mi 898.9, persons per sq km 347.1. **Urban** (2002): 16.7%. **Sex distribution** (2002): male 47.71%; female 52.29%. **Age breakdown** (2002): under 15, 42.7%; 15–29, 30.7%; 30–44, 14.9%; 45–59, 7.6%; 60–74, 3.3%; 75 and over, 0.8%. **Ethnic composition** (2002): Hutu 85%; Tutsi 14%; Twa 1%. **Religious affiliation** (2000): Roman Catholic 51.0%; Protestant 28.8%; traditional beliefs 9.0%; Muslim 7.9%; independent Christian 2.1%; other 1.2%. **Major cities** (2002): Kigali 608,141; Gitarama 84,669; Butare 77,449; Ruhengeri 70,525; Gisenyi 67,192. **Location:** east-central Africa, bordering Uganda, Tanzania, Burundi, and the Democratic Republic of the Congo.

Vital statistics

Birth rate per 1,000 population (2003): 40.8 (world avg. 21.3). **Death rate** per 1,000 population (2003): 16.8 (world avg. 9.1). **Natural increase rate** per 1,000 population (2003): 24.0 (world avg. 12.2). **Total fertility rate** (avg. births per childbearing woman; 2003): 5.6. **Life expectancy** at birth (2003): male 45.3 years; female 47.4 years. **Adult population** (ages 15–49) **living with HIV** (2004): 5.1% (world avg. 1.1%).

National economy

Budget (2001). *Revenue:* RF 149,500,000,000 (grants 42.3%; taxes on goods and services 27.4%;

income tax 16.0%; import and export duties 7.4%; nontax revenue 6.9%). *Expenditures:* RF 189,200,000,000 (current expenditures 56.8%, of which wages 28.4%, education 15.8%, defense 15.1%, health 2.7%, debt payment 1.5%; capital expenditure 43.2%). **Production** (metric tons except as noted). *Agriculture, forestry, fishing* (2002): plantains 2,784,870, sweet potatoes 1,292,361, potatoes 1,038,931; livestock (number of live animals) 815,000 cattle, 760,000 goats, 260,000 sheep; roundwood (2002) 7,836,000 cu m; fish catch (2001) 7,263. *Mining and quarrying* (2002): cassiterite (tin content) 197; niobium 43; tantalum 24. *Manufacturing* (value added in RF '000,000; 2000): food and nonalcoholic beverages 37,981; nonmetallic products 3,109; metal products 1,087. *Energy production (consumption):* electricity (kW-hr; 2000) 169,000,000 (182,000,000); petroleum products (2000) none (174,000); natural gas (cu m; 2000) 250,300 (250,300). **Population economically active** (1996): total 3,021,000; activity rate of total population 50.8% (participation rates: ages 14 and over, 86.0%; female 49.0%). **Land use** as % of total land area (2000): in temporary crops 36.5%, in permanent crops 10.1%, in pasture 22.1%; overall forest area 12.4%. **Households.** Average household size (1991) 4.7. **Gross national product** (2002): $1,826,000,000 ($220 per capita). **Public debt** (external, outstanding; 2002): $1,305,000,000. **Tourism:** receipts (2002) $31,000,000; expenditures $24,000,000.

Foreign trade

Imports (2000): $239,800,000 (capital goods 22.1%, food 19.4%, energy products 18.7%, intermediate goods 18.1%). *Major import sources* (2002): Kenya 21.9%; Germany 8.4%; Belgium 7.9%; Israel 4.3%; US 3.5%. **Exports** (2001): $90,400,000 (niobium and tantalum 45.2%, tea 25.6%, coffee 20.1%). *Major export destinations* (2002): Indonesia 30.8%; Germany 14.6%; Hong Kong 8.9%; South Africa 5.5%.

Transport and communications

Transport. *Roads* (1999): total length 12,000 km (paved 8%). *Vehicles* (1996): passenger cars 13,000; trucks 17,100. *Air transport* (2000; Kigali airport only): passengers embarked and disembarked 101,000; cargo loaded and unloaded 4,300 metric tons; airports (2002) with scheduled flights 2. **Communications,** in total units (units per 1,000 persons). Daily newspaper circulation (1995): 500 (0.1); radios (1997): 601,000 (101); telephone main lines (2002): 23,200 (2.8); cellular telephone subscribers (2003): 134,000 (16); Internet users (2002): 25,000 (3).

Education and health

Literacy (2000): percentage of total population age 15 and over literate 66.8%; males literate 73.7%; females literate 60.2%. **Health:** physicians (1992) 150 (1 per 50,000 persons); hospital beds (1990) 12,152 (1 per 588 persons); infant mortality rate per 1,000 live births (2003) 94.3. **Food** (2001): daily per capita caloric intake 2,086 (vegetable products 97%, animal products 3%); 90% of FAO recommended minimum.

Military

Total active duty personnel (2003): 51,000 (army 78.4%, navy 2.0%, national police 19.6%). **Military**

expenditure as percentage of GNP (1999): 4.5% (world 2.4%); per capita expenditure $12.

Background

Originally inhabited by the Twa, a Pygmy people, Rwanda became home to the Hutu, who were well established there when the Tutsi appeared in the 14th century. The Tutsi conquered the Hutu and in the 15th century founded a kingdom near Kigali. The Belgians occupied Rwanda in 1916, and the League of Nations created Ruanda-Urundi as a Belgian mandate in 1923. The Tutsi retained their dominance until shortly before Rwanda reached independence in 1962, when the Hutu took control of the government and stripped the Tutsi of much of their land. Many Tutsi fled Rwanda, and the Hutu dominated the country's political system, waging sporadic civil wars until mid-1994, when the death of the country's leader in a plane crash—apparently shot down—led to massive violence. The Tutsi-led Rwandan Patriotic Front (RPF) took over the country by force after the massacre of almost 500,000 Tutsi by Hutu. Two million refugees, mostly Hutu, fled to neighboring countries after the RPF's victory.

Recent Developments

In 2006 the Rwandan government replaced its 12 provinces with 5 larger, multiethnic zones to weaken ethnic conflict and promote power sharing. The World Bank granted the country 100% debt relief from 1 July. In April negotiations began in Tanzania toward the integration of Rwanda into the East African Community. Meanwhile, genocide trials dragged on. Because some European countries had refused to extradite suspected perpetrators of genocide on the grounds that Rwanda still had the death penalty, the government drafted legislation to abolish capital punishment. Pres. Paul Kagame castigated the International Criminal Tribunal for Rwanda for its slow, expensive proceedings, which would cost an estimated $1 billion by the end of 2007 and had delivered fewer than 40 verdicts.

Internet resources: <www.rwandatourism.com>.

Saint Kitts and Nevis

Official name: Federation of Saint Kitts and Nevis. **Form of government:** constitutional monarchy with one legislative house (National Assembly [15, including 4 nonelective seats]). **Chief of state:** British Monarch Queen Elizabeth II (from 1952), represented by Governor-General Sir Cuthbert Sebastian (from 1996). **Head of government:** Prime Minister Denzil Douglas (from 1995). **Capital:** Basseterre. **Official language:** English. **Official religion:** none. **Monetary unit:** 1 Eastern Caribbean dollar (EC$) = 100 cents; valuation (1 Jul 2007) US$1 = EC$2.67.

Demography

Area: 104.0 sq mi, 269.4 sq km. **Population** (2006): 49,100. **Density** (2006): persons per sq mi 472.1, persons per sq km 182.3. **Urban** (2000): 34.2%. **Sex distribution** (2001): male 49.70%; female 50.30%.

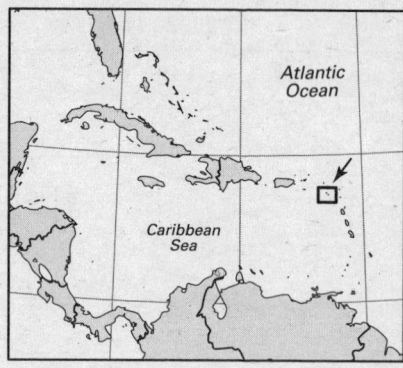

Atlantic Ocean

Caribbean Sea

Age breakdown (2000): under 15, 30.3%; 15–29, 24.9%; 30–44, 22.2%; 45–59, 11.2%; 60–74, 7.1%; 75 and over, 4.3%. **Ethnic composition** (2000): black 90.4%; mulatto 5.0%; Indo-Pakistani 3.0%; white 1.0%; other/unspecified 0.6%. **Religious affiliation** (1995): Protestant 84.6%, of which Anglican 25.2%, Methodist 25.2%, Pentecostal 8.4%, Moravian 7.6%; Roman Catholic 6.7%; Hindu 1.5%; other 7.2%. **Major towns** (2001): Basseterre 13,033; Charlestown (1994) 1,411. **Location:** islands in the Caribbean Sea, between Puerto Rico and Trinidad and Tobago.

Vital statistics

Birth rate per 1,000 population (2003): 18.5 (world avg. 21.3); (1983) legitimate 19.2%. **Death rate** per 1,000 population (2003): 8.9 (world avg. 9.1). **Natural increase rate** per 1,000 population (2001): 9.6 (world avg. 12.2). **Total fertility rate** (avg. births per childbearing woman; 2003): 2.4. **Marriage rate** per 1,000 population (2001): 7.1. **Divorce rate** per 1,000 population (2002): 0.5. **Life expectancy** at birth (2003): male 68.8 years; female 74.6 years.

National economy

Budget (2001). *Revenue:* EC$270,100,000 (tax revenue 72.8%, of which import duties 34.0%, taxes on income and profits 21.4%, taxes on domestic goods and services 14.1%; nontax revenue 27.2%). *Expenditures:* EC$406,000,000 (current expenditure 75.6%; development expenditure 24.4%). **Production** (metric tons except as noted). *Agriculture and fishing* (2002): sugarcane 191,400, tropical fruit 1,300, coconuts 1,000; livestock (number of live animals) 14,400 goats, 14,000 sheep, 4,300 cattle; fish catch (2001) 291. *Mining and quarrying:* excavation of sand for local use. *Manufacturing* (2001): raw sugar 20,193; carbonated beverages (1995) 45,000 hectoliters; beer 20,000 hectoliters. *Energy production (consumption):* electricity (kW-hr; 2000) 100,000,-000 (100,000,000); petroleum products (2000) none (33,000). **Gross national product** (2003): US$321,000,000 (US$6,880 per capita). **Household income and expenditure.** Average household size (2001) 2.9; average annual income per wage earner (1994) EC$9,940; expenditure (1978): food, beverages, and tobacco 55.6%, household furnishings

1 metric ton = about 1.1 short tons;   1 kilometer = 0.6 mi (statute);   1 metric ton-km cargo = about 0.68 short ton-mi cargo;   c.i.f.: cost, insurance, and freight;   f.o.b.: free on board

9.4%, housing 7.6%, clothing and footwear 7.5%, fuel and light 6.6%, transportation 4.3%, other 9.0%. **Public debt** (external, outstanding; 2002): US$252,-200,000. **Population economically active** (1980): total 17,125; activity rate of total population 39.5% (participation rates: ages 15–64, 69.5%; female 41.0%; unemployed [1997] 4.5%). **Land use** as % of total land area (2000): in temporary crops 19%, in permanent crops 3%, in pasture 6%; overall forest area 11%. **Tourism:** receipts from visitors (2002) US$57,000,000; expenditures by nationals abroad (2001) US$8,000,000.

Foreign trade

Imports (2001-c.i.f.): US$189,200,000 (machinery and apparatus 22.4%; food 14.4%; fabricated metals 7.9%; chemicals and chemical products 6.9%; refined petroleum 6.4%). *Major import sources* (2002): US 41.5%; Trinidad and Tobago 16.2%; Canada 9.8%; UK 6.9%; Japan 4.0%. **Exports** (2001-f.o.b.): US$31,-000,000 (electrical switches, relays, and fuses 56.1%; raw sugar 21.0%; telecommunications equipment [parts] 3.2%). *Major export destinations* (2002): US 66.6%; UK 7.6%; Canada 6.8%; Portugal 6.0%; Germany 2.9%.

Transport and communications

Transport. *Railroads* (2000; light railway serving the sugar industry on Saint Kitts): length 58 km. *Roads* (2001): total length 318 km (paved 44%). *Vehicles* (2001): passenger cars 5,826; trucks and buses 2,989. *Air transport* (2001; Saint Kitts airport only): passenger arrivals 135,237; passenger departures 134,937; cargo handled 1,802; airports (1998) with scheduled flights 2. **Communications,** in total units (units per 1,000 persons). Radios (1997): 28,000 (701); televisions (1997): 10,000 (264); telephone main lines (2002): 23,500 (500); cellular telephones (2002): 5,000 (106); personal computers (2002): 9,000 (191); Internet users (2002): 10,000 (213).

Education and health

Educational attainment (1991). Percentage of population age 25 and over having: no formal schooling 1.6%; primary education 45.9%; secondary 38.4%; higher 8.9%; other or not stated 5.2%. **Literacy** (1990): total population age 15 and over literate 25,500 (90.0%); males literate 13,100 (90.0%); females literate 12,400 (90.0%). **Health** (2001): physicians 49 (1 per 936 persons); hospital beds 178 (1 per 258 persons); infant mortality rate per 1,000 live births (2003) 15.4. **Food** (2001): daily per capita caloric intake 2,997 (vegetable products 74%, animal products 26%); 124% of FAO recommended minimum.

Military

Total active duty personnel: in July 1997 the National Assembly approved a bill creating a 50-member army. **Military expenditure as percentage of GNP** (1998; includes expenditure for police): 3.5%; per capita expenditure US$226.

Background

Saint Kitts became the first British colony in the West Indies in 1623. Anglo-French rivalry grew in the 17th century and lasted more than a century. In 1783, by the Treaty of Versailles, the islands became wholly British possessions. They were united with Anguilla from 1882 to 1980 but became an independent federation within the British Commonwealth in 1983. In 1997 Nevis considered becoming independent.

Recent Developments

After European subsidies were cut over several years, the commercial sugar harvests that had sustained Saint Kitts and Nevis for close to 400 years came to an end in 2005. The country continued to recognize Taiwan, which donated $12 million to build a stadium for the Cricket World Cup in March 2007.

Internet resources: <www.stkittsnevis.net>.

Saint Lucia

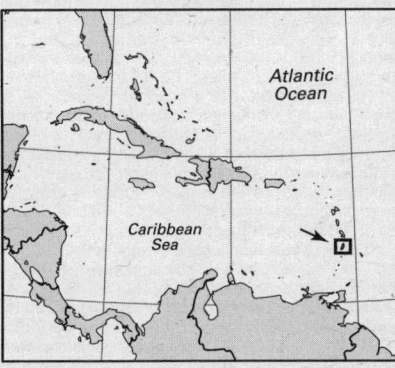

Official name: Saint Lucia. **Form of government:** constitutional monarchy with a parliament consisting of two legislative chambers (Senate [11]; House of Assembly [17 {elected seats only}]). **Chief of state:** Queen Elizabeth II (from 1952), represented by Governor-General Dame Pearlette Louisy (from 1997). **Head of government:** Prime Minister Stephenson King (from 2007). **Capital:** Castries. **Official language:** English. **Official religion:** none. **Monetary unit:** 1 Eastern Caribbean dollar (EC$) = 100 cents; valuation (1 Jul 2007) US$1 = EC$2.67.

Demography

Area: 238 sq mi, 617 sq km. **Population** (2006): 165,000. **Density** (2006): persons per sq mi 693.3, persons per sq km 267.4. **Urban** (2001): 38.0%. **Sex distribution** (2001): male 48.92%; female 51.08%. **Age breakdown** (2001): under 15, 31.2%; 15–29, 27.4%; 30–44, 20.6%; 45–59, 10.7%; 60 and over, 10.1%. **Ethnic composition** (2000): black 50%; mulatto 44%; East Indian 3%; white 1%; other 2%. **Religious affiliation** (2001): Roman Catholic 67.5%; Protestant 22.0%, of which Seventh-day Adventist 8.4%, Pentecostal 5.6%; Rastafarian 2.1%; nonreligious 4.5%; other/unknown 3.9%. **Major urban area** (2001): Castries 37,549. **Location:** island between the Caribbean Sea and North Atlantic Ocean, north of Trinidad and Tobago.

Vital statistics

Birth rate per 1,000 population (2003): 20.9 (world avg. 21.3); (2000) legitimate 14.3%. **Death rate** per 1,000 population (2003): 5.2 (world avg. 9.1). **Natural increase rate** per 1,000 population (2003): 15.7 (world avg. 12.2). **Total fertility rate** (avg. births per childbearing woman; 2003): 2.3. **Marriage rate** per 1,000 population (2001): 2.8. **Divorce rate** per 1,000 population (2001): 0.4. **Life expectancy** at birth (2003): male 69.5 years; female 76.9 years.

National economy

Budget (2002). *Revenue:* EC$505,700,000 (tax revenue 81.6%, of which consumption duties on imported goods 42.5%, taxes on income and profits 21.3%, goods and services 16.5%; nontax revenue 12.7%; grants 5.7%). *Expenditures:* EC$543,600,000 (current expenditures 74.6%; development expenditures and net lending 25.4%). **Public debt** (external, outstanding; 2002): US$210,700,000. **Production** (metric tons except as noted). *Agriculture and fishing* (2002): bananas 92,000, mangoes 28,000, coconuts 14,000; *livestock* (number of live animals) 14,950 pigs, 12,500 sheep, 12,400 cattle; *fish catch* (2001) 1,984. *Mining and quarrying:* excavation of sand for local construction and pumice. *Manufacturing* (value of production in EC$'000; 1998): alcoholic beverages and tobacco 31,120; paper products and cardboard boxes 28,747; electrical and electronic components 16,245. *Energy production (consumption):* electricity (kW-hr; 2000) 375,000,000 (375,000,000); petroleum products (2000) none (110,000). **Population economically active** (2002): total 74,949; activity rate of total population 47.0% (participation rates: ages 15 and over 66.8%; female [2000] 47.2%; unemployed 16.2%). **Gross national product** (at current market prices; 2003): US$650,000,000 (US$4,050 per capita). **Households.** Average household size (2001) 3.2. **Land use** as % of total land area (2000): in temporary crops 7%, in permanent crops 23%, in pasture 3%; overall forest area 15%. **Tourism:** receipts from visitors (2002) US$218,000,000; expenditures by nationals abroad (2001) US$32,000,000.

Foreign trade

Imports (2002): US$277,100,000 (food and beverages 26.2%; machinery and apparatus 23.5%; manufactured goods 17.3%; chemicals and chemical products 9.0%; refined petroleum 8.7%). *Major import sources:* US 38.0%; Trinidad and Tobago 14.6%; UK 9.5%; Japan 3.3%; Canada 3.1%. **Exports** (2002): US$54,900,000 (bananas 49.9%; beer and ale 15.9%; clothing 3.2%; electrical and electronic components 3.2%). *Major export destinations:* UK 37.6%; US 20.3%; Trinidad and Tobago 11.8%; Barbados 9.7%; Dominica 5.3%.

Transport and communications

Transport. *Roads* (1999): total length 1,210 km (paved 5%). *Vehicles* (2001): passenger cars 22,453; trucks and buses 8,972. *Air transport* (2001; combined data for both Castries and Vieux Fort airports): passenger arrivals and departures 679,000; cargo unloaded and loaded 3,500 metric tons; airports (2000) with scheduled flights 2. **Communications, in** total units (units per 1,000 persons). Radios (1997): 100,000 (668); televisions (1997): 40,000 (267); telephone main lines (2002): 51,100 (320); cellular telephone subscribers (2002): 14,300 (90); personal computers (2002): 24,000 (150); Internet users (2001): 13,000 (82).

Education and health

Educational attainment (2000). Percentage of population age 15 and over having: no formal schooling 6.5%; primary education 56.2%; secondary 27.5%; higher vocational 4.5%; university 2.7%; other/unknown 2.6%. **Literacy** (2000): 90.2%. **Health** (2002): physicians 92 (1 per 1,740 persons); hospital beds 285 (1 per 562 persons); infant mortality rate per 1,000 live births (2003) 15.4. **Food** (2001): daily per capita caloric intake 2,849 (vegetable products 72%, animal products 28%); 118% of FAO recommended minimum.

Military

Total active duty personnel (2000): the 300-member police force includes a specially trained paramilitary unit and a coast guard unit.

Did you know? The landmark twin mountain peaks of the Pitons on St. Lucia were added to the list of UNESCO World Heritage sites in 2004. The Pitons are volcanic spires rising to 2,526 ft. (770 m) and 2,438 ft. (743 m), and the site includes hot springs, a significant coral reef, and richly varied flora and fauna.

Background

Caribs replaced early Arawak inhabitants on the island c. AD 800–1300. Settled by the French in 1650, it was ceded to Great Britain in 1814 and became one of the Windward Islands in 1871. It became fully independent in 1979. The economy is based on agriculture and tourism.

Recent Developments

A commission was formed in June 2005 to review and suggest changes to Saint Lucia's 25-year-old constitution. The country requested seven UK police officers in April 2006 to help with its growing crime problem, and in August it set up a special unit to protect tourists. That same month the country appointed environmental consultants to study climate change and the potential rise in sea level that would threaten the island country.

Internet resources: <www.stlucia.org>.

Saint Vincent and the Grenadines

Official name: Saint Vincent and the Grenadines. **Form of government:** constitutional monarchy with one legislative house (House of Assembly [21, includ-

1 metric ton = about 1.1 short tons;   1 kilometer = 0.6 mi (statute);   1 metric ton-km cargo = about 0.68 short ton-mi cargo;   c.i.f.: cost, insurance, and freight;   f.o.b.: free on board

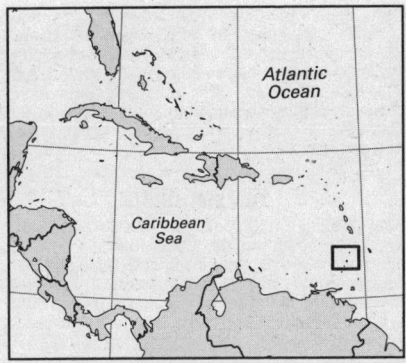

ing 6 nonelective seats and excluding speaker, who may be elected from within or from outside the House of Assembly membership]). **Chief of state:** British Monarch Queen Elizabeth II (from 1952), represented by Governor-General Sir Frederick Ballantyne (from 2002). **Head of government:** Prime Minister Ralph Gonsalves (from 2001). **Capital:** Kingstown. **Official language:** English. **Official religion:** none. **Monetary unit:** 1 Eastern Caribbean dollar (EC$) = 100 cents; valuation (1 Jul 2007) US$1 = EC$2.67.

Demography

Area: 150.3 sq mi, 389.3 sq km. **Population** (2006): 96,800. **Density** (2006): persons per sq mi 644.0, persons per sq km 248.7. **Urban** (2000): 54.4%. **Sex distribution** (2000): male 49.90%; female 50.10%. **Age breakdown** (1999): under 15, 31.3%; 15–29, 31.2%; 30–44, 19.6%; 45–59, 9.4%; 60–74, 5.9%; 75 and over, 2.6%. **Ethnic composition** (1999): black 65.5%; mulatto 23.5%; Indo-Pakistani 5.5%; white 3.5%; black-Amerindian 2.0%. **Religious affiliation** (1995): Protestant 57.6%; unaffiliated Christian 20.6%; Roman Catholic 10.7%; Hindu 3.3%; Muslim 1.5%; other/nonreligious 6.3%. **Major city** (2000): Kingstown 16,209. **Location:** islands in the Caribbean Sea, north of Trinidad and Tobago.

Vital statistics

Birth rate per 1,000 population (2002): 17.6 (world avg. 21.3); (1999) legitimate 17.9%. **Death rate** per 1,000 population (2002): 6.9 (world avg. 9.1). **Natural increase rate** per 1,000 population (2002): 10.7 (world avg. 12.2). **Total fertility rate** (avg. births per childbearing woman; 2003): 2.0. **Marriage rate** per 1,000 population (2002): 4.5. **Divorce rate** per 1,000 population (2002): 0.4. **Life expectancy** at birth (2003): male 71.3 years; female 74.9 years.

National economy

Budget (2002). *Revenue:* EC$312,000,000 (current revenue 80.8%, of which taxes on international trade and transactions 38.8%, income tax 25.6%, taxes on goods and services 15.7%; grants 5.1%; nontax revenue 13.8%; capital revenue 0.3%). *Expenditures:* EC$348,000,000 (current expenditure 81.3%, development expenditure 18.7%). **Public debt** (external, outstanding; 2002): US$173,-700,000. **Production** (metric tons except as noted):

Agriculture and fishing (2000): bananas 45,951, coconuts 23,700, eddoes and dasheens 4,400; livestock (number of live animals) 13,000 sheep, 9,500 pigs, 6,200 cattle; fish catch (2002) 643. *Mining and quarrying:* sand and gravel for local use. *Manufacturing* (value added in EC$'000,000; 2000): beverages and tobacco products 17.4; food 15.6; paper products and publishing 3.6. *Energy production (consumption):* electricity (kW-hr; 2000) 85,000,000 (85,000,000); petroleum products (2000) none (53,000). **Tourism:** receipts from visitors (2002) US$81,000,000; expenditures by nationals abroad (2001) US$10,000,000. **Land use** as % of total land area (2000): in temporary crops 18%, in permanent crops 18%, in pasture 5%; overall forest area 15%. **Gross national product** (2003): US$361,000,000 (US$3,300 per capita). **Population economically active** (1991): total 41,682; activity rate of total population 39.1% (participation rates: ages 15–64, 67.5%; female 35.9%; unemployed [1996] more than 30%). **Households.** Average household size (1991) 3.9; income per household (1988) EC$4,579.

Foreign trade

Imports (2001-c.i.f.): US$186,500,000 (food products 20.4%; machinery and transport equipment 19.0%; chemicals and chemical products 9.8%; fuels 9.0%). *Major import sources:* US 34.5%; Caricom countries 31.2%, of which Trinidad and Tobago 19.9%; UK 9.8%; Japan 3.5%. **Exports** (2001-f.o.b.): US$45,700,000 (domestic exports 86.9%, of which bananas 28.4%, packaged flour 13.2%, packaged rice 9.2%, eddoes and dasheens 3.4%; reexports 13.1%). *Major export destinations:* Caricom countries 53.7%, of which Trinidad and Tobago 17.0%, Barbados 9.8%, St. Lucia 7.9%; UK 36.8%.

Transport and communications

Transport. *Roads* (1999): total length 1,040 km (paved 31%). *Vehicles* (1999): passenger cars 7,989; trucks and buses 3,920. *Air transport* (2000): passenger arrivals 132,445; passenger departures 134,012; airports (1998) with scheduled flights 5. **Communications,** in total units (units per 1,000 persons). Radios (1995): 65,000 (591); televisions (1995): 17,700 (161); telephone main lines (2002): 27,300 (234); cellular telephone subscribers (2002): 10,000 (85); personal computers (2002): 14,000 (192); Internet users (2002): 7,000 (60).

Education and health

Educational attainment (1980). Percentage of population age 25 and over having: no formal schooling 2.4%; primary education 88.0%; secondary 8.2%; higher 1.4%. **Literacy** (1991): total population age 15 and over literate 64,000 (96.0%). **Health** (1998): physicians 59 (1 per 1,883 persons); hospital beds (2000) 209 (1 per 535 persons); infant mortality rate per 1,000 live births (2002) 18.1. **Food** (2001): daily per capita caloric intake 2,609 (vegetable products 83%, animal products 17%); 108% of FAO recommended minimum.

Military

Total active duty personnel (1992): 634-member police force includes a coast guard and paramilitary unit.

Background

The French and the British contested for control of Saint Vincent and the Grenadines until 1763, when it was ceded to England by the Treaty of Paris. The original inhabitants, the Caribs, recognized British sovereignty but revolted in 1795. Most of the Caribs were deported; many who remained were killed in volcanic eruptions in 1812 and 1902. In 1969 Saint Vincent and the Grenadines became a self-governing state in association with the United Kingdom, and in 1979 it achieved full independence.

Recent Developments

The government announced in September 2005 that offshore exploration for oil was planned. Saint Vincent and the Grenadines continued to be one of the few Caribbean countries that recognized Taiwan. In 2006 Taiwan offered $25 million in grants and loans to construct an international airport for the country.

Internet resources: <www.svgtourism.com>.

Samoa

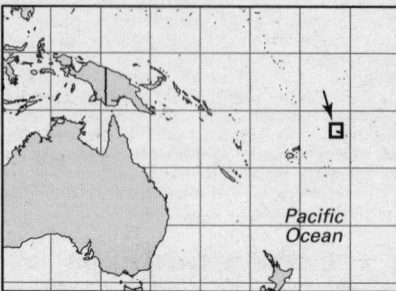

Pacific Ocean

Official name: Malo Sa'oloto Tuto'atasi o Samoa (Samoan); Independent State of Samoa (English). Form of government: constitutional monarchy with one legislative house (Legislative Assembly [49]). Chief of state: Head of State Tuiatua Tupua Tamasese Efi (from 2007). Head of government: Prime Minister Tuila'epa Sa'ilele Malielegaoi (from 1998). Capital: Apia. Official languages: Samoan; English. Official religion: none. Monetary unit: 1 tala (SA$ [WS$ prior to July 1997], plural tala) = 100 sene; valuation (1 Jul 2007) US$1 = SA$2.92.

Demography

Area: 1,093 sq mi, 2,831 sq km. Population (2006): 183,000. Density (2006): persons per sq mi 167.4, persons per sq km 64.6. Urban (2002): 22.0%. Sex distribution (2001): male 52.09%; female 47.91%. Age breakdown (2001): under 15, 40.8%; 15–29, 25.6%; 30–44, 17.9%; 45–59, 9.2%; 60–74, 5.0%; 75 and over, 1.5%. Ethnic composition (1997): Samoan (Polynesian) 92.6%; Euronesian (European and Polynesian) 7.0%; European 0.4%. Religious affiliation (1995): Mormon 25.8%; Congregational 24.6%; Roman Catholic 21.3%; Methodist 12.2%;

Pentecostal 8.0%; Seventh-day Adventist 3.9%; other Christian 1.7%; other 2.5%. Major towns (2001): Apia 38,836 (urban agglomeration 60,734); Vaitele 5,200 (within Apia urban agglomeration); Faleasi'u 3,209; Vailele 3,175 (within Apia urban agglomeration); Le'auva'a 2,828. Location: group of islands in the South Pacific Ocean, about halfway between Hawaii (US) and New Zealand.

Vital statistics

Birth rate per 1,000 population (2003): 28.6 (world avg. 21.3). Death rate per 1,000 population (2003): 5.5 (world avg. 9.1). Natural increase rate per 1,000 population (2003): 23.1 (world avg. 12.2). Total fertility rate (avg. births per childbearing woman; 2003): 4.1. Life expectancy at birth (2003): male 67.4 years; female 73.0 years.

National economy

Budget (2000–01). Revenue: SA$262,400,000 (tax revenue 66.6%, grants 24.8%, nontax revenue 8.6%). Expenditures: SA$281,700,000 (current expenditure 58.4%, development expenditure 36.6%, net lending 5.0%). Public debt (external, outstanding; 2002): US$156,800,000. Production (metric tons except as noted). Agriculture, forestry, fishing (2002): coconuts 140,000, bananas 21,500, taro 17,000; livestock (number of live animals) 201,000 pigs, 28,000 cattle, 450,000 chickens; roundwood (2001) 131,000 cu m; fish catch (2001) 12,966. Manufacturing (in WS$'000; 1990): beer 8,708; cigarettes 6,551; coconut cream 5,576. Energy production (consumption): electricity (kW-hr; 2000) 66,000,000 (66,000,-000); petroleum products (2000) none (45,000). Households. Average household size (2001) 7.7. Population economically active (2001): total 50,000; activity rate of total population 28.3% (female [1991] 32.0%). Gross national product (at current market prices; 2003): US$284,000,000 (US$1,600 per capita). Tourism: receipts from visitors (2002) US$46,-000,000; expenditures by nationals abroad (1999) US$4,000,000. Land use as % of total land area (2000): in temporary crops 20.8%, in permanent crops 24.0%, in pasture 0.7%; overall forest area 37.2%.

Foreign trade

Imports (2001–02-c.i.f.): SA$465,000,000 (petroleum products 10.2%, imports for government 5.2%, unspecified 84.6%). Major import sources: New Zealand 34.4%; Australia 26.6%; US 11.8%; Fiji 8.7%; Japan 6.6%. Exports (2001–02-f.o.b.): SA$49,500,-000 (fresh fish 66.9%, garments 11.5%, beer 6.7%, coconut cream 6.6%). Major export destinations: American Samoa 52.3%; US 32.2%; New Zealand 6.8%; Germany 3.4%; Australia 2.7%.

Transport and communications

Transport. Roads (1996): total length 790 km (paved 42%). Vehicles (1995): passenger cars 1,068; trucks and buses 1,169. Air transport (1999): passenger-km 244,000,000; metric ton-km cargo 23,000,000; airports (1997) with scheduled flights 3. Communications, in total units (units per 1,000 persons). Radios (1997): 178,000 (1,035);

1 metric ton = about 1.1 short tons;   1 kilometer = 0.6 mi (statute);   1 metric ton-km cargo = about 0.68 short ton-mi cargo;   c.i.f.: cost, insurance, and freight;   f.o.b.: free on board

televisions (1998): 9,000 (52); telephone main lines (2002): 11,800 (65); cellular telephone subscribers (2002): 2,700 (15); personal computers (2002): 1,000 (6.7); Internet users (2002): 4,000 (22).

Education and health

Literacy (2000): total population over age 15 literate 80.2%; males literate 81.2%; females literate 79.0%. **Health:** physicians (1996) 62 (1 per 2,919 persons); hospital beds (1991) 863 (1 per 255 persons); infant mortality rate per 1,000 live births (2003) 26.0. **Food** (1992): daily per capita caloric intake 2,828 (vegetable products 74%, animal products 26%); 124% of FAO recommended minimum.

Military

No military forces are maintained; New Zealand is responsible for defense.

Background

Polynesians inhabited the islands of the Samoan archipelago for thousands of years before they were visited by Europeans in the 18th century. Control of the islands was contested by the US, Britain, and Germany until 1899, when they were divided between the US and Germany. In 1914 Western Samoa was occupied by New Zealand, which received it as a League of Nations mandate in 1920. After World War II, it became a UN trust territory administered by New Zealand, and it achieved independence in 1962. In 1997 the word Western was dropped from the country's name.

Recent Developments

Friction between Samoa and American Samoa marked 2005. Claiming that Samoans were overstaying their 14-day permits, American Samoa tightened its border controls. Samoa in return introduced a similar system. The World Bank estimated in 2006 that remittances from abroad represented 40% of Samoa's GDP and that an equal amount in unofficial remittances went unreported. New construction took place with Chinese assistance as Samoa prepared to host the XIII South Pacific Games in August and September 2007.

Internet resources: <www.visitsamoa.ws>.

San Marino

Official name: Serenissima Repubblica di San Marino (Most Serene Republic of San Marino). **Form of government:** unitary multiparty republic with one legislative house (Great and General Council [60]). **Heads of state and government:** two captains-regent who serve six-month terms beginning in April and October. **Capital:** San Marino. **Official language:** Italian. **Official religion:** none. **Monetary unit:** 1 euro (€) = 100 cents; valuation (1 Jul 2007) US$1 = €0.74; at conversion on 1 Jan 2002, €1= 1,936.27 Italian lire (Lit).

Demography

Area: 23.63 sq mi, 61.20 sq km. **Population** (2006): 30,200. **Density** (2006): persons per sq mi 1,278, persons per sq km 493.5. **Urban** (2003): 88.7%. **Sex distribution** (2003): male 48.94%; female 51.06%.

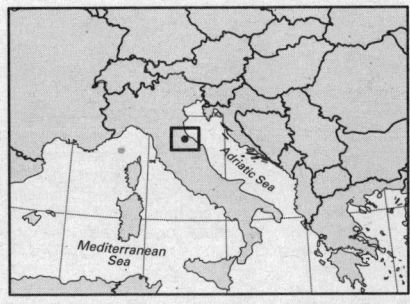

Age breakdown (2003): under 15, 14.1%; 15–29, 16.6%; 30–44, 27.3%; 45–59, 19.7%; 60–74, 14.2%; 75 and over, 8.1%. **Ethnic composition** (2003): Sammarinesi 85.7%; Italian 13.0%; other 1.3%. **Religious affiliation** (2000): Roman Catholic 88.7%; Pentecostal 1.8%; other 9.5%. **Major cities** (2000): Serravalle/Dogano 8,547; San Marino 4,439; Borgo Maggiore (1997) 2,394; Murata (1997) 1,549; Domagnano (1997) 1,048. **Location:** southern Europe, completely surrounded by Italy.

Vital statistics

Birth rate per 1,000 population (2002): 10.4 (world avg. 21.3). **Death rate** per 1,000 population (2002): 7.1 (world avg. 9.1). **Natural increase rate** per 1,000 population (2002): 3.3 (world avg. 12.2). **Total fertility rate** (avg. births per childbearing woman; 2002): 1.3. **Marriage rate** per 1,000 population (2002): 7.3. **Divorce rate** per 1,000 population (1998–2000): 1.6. **Life expectancy** at birth (2000): male 77.6 years; female 85.0 years.

National economy

Budget (2003). *Revenue:* €288,000,000 (direct taxes 34.7%; import taxes 33.0%; nontax revenue 22.0%). *Expenditures:* €272,400,000 (current expenditures 92.0%; capital expenditures 8.0%). **Public debt** (2003): $52,900,000. **Tourism:** number of tourist arrivals (2002) 3,102,453; receipts from visitors (1994) $252,500,000. **Population economically active** (2003): total 20,236; activity rate of total population 69.3% (participation rates: ages 15–64 [2002] 72.1%; female 41.5%; unemployed [2004] 3.9%). **Households.** Total number of households (2003) 11,723; average household size (2003) 2.5; expenditure (1991): food, beverages, and tobacco 22.1%, housing, fuel, and electrical energy 20.9%, transportation and communications 17.6%, clothing and footwear 8.0%, furniture, appliances, and goods and services for the home 7.2%, education 7.1%, health and sanitary services 2.6%, other goods and services 14.5%. **Production** (metric tons except as noted). *Agriculture* (early 1980s): wheat 4,400, grapes 700, barley 500; livestock (number of live animals; 1998) 831 cattle, 748 pigs. *Manufacturing* (1998): processed meats 324,073 kg, of which beef 226,570 kg, pork 87,764 kg, veal 7,803 kg; cheese 61,563 kg; butter 12,658 kg. *Energy production (consumption):* all electrical power is imported via electrical grid from Italy ([2001] 193,371,696); natural gas, none ([2001] 50,641,790). **Gross national product** (at current market prices; 2002): $836,000,000 ($29,360 per capita). **Land use** as % of total land area (2000): in temporary crops, permanent crops, pasture, or forest 65%.

Foreign trade

A customs union with Italy has existed since 1862. **Imports** (2002): $1,657,000,000 (manufactured goods of all kinds, petroleum products, electricity, and gold). *Major import source:* Italy. **Exports** (2002): $1,566,000,000 (goods include electronics, postage stamps, leather products, ceramics, wine, wood products, and building stone). *Major export destination:* Italy (in the late 1990s Italy accounted for 87% of all foreign trade).

Transport and communications

Transport. *Roads* (2001): total length 252 km. *Vehicles* (2002): passenger cars 28,470; trucks and buses 2,748. *Air transport:* airports with scheduled flights, none; there is, however, a heliport that provides passenger and cargo service between San Marino and Rimini, Italy, during the summer months. **Communications,** in total units (units per 1,000 persons). Daily newspaper circulation (1996): 2,000 (72); radios (1998): 16,000 (610); televisions (1998): 9,055 (358); telephone main lines (2002): 20,601 (716); cellular telephone subscribers (2002): 16,759 (583); Internet users (2002): 14,300 (531).

Education and health

Educational attainment (2003). Percentage of population age 14 and over having: basic literacy or primary education 41.0%; some secondary 25.0%; secondary 27.0%; higher degree 7.0%. **Literacy** (2001): total population age 15 and over literate 98.7%; males literate 98.9%; females literate 98.4%. **Health** (2002): physicians 117 (1 per 230 persons); hospital beds 134 (1 per 191 persons); infant mortality rate per 1,000 live births (2002) 6.8. **Food** (2000; figures are for Italy): daily per capita caloric intake 3,661 (vegetable products 74%, animal products 26%); 146% of FAO recommended minimum.

Military

Total active duty personnel (2003): none; defense is provided by a public security force of about 50. **Military expenditure as percentage of national budget** (1992): 1.0% (world 3.6%); per capita expenditure (1987) $155.

Did you know? Tourism is the sector of greatest expansion in San Marino, and it makes a major contribution to the inhabitants' income. Alongside traditional excursion tourism, a convention-type tourism, based on the development of modern hotel facilities, and residential tourism are growing.

Background

According to tradition, San Marino was founded in the early 4th century AD by St. Marinus. By the 12th century it had developed into a commune and remained independent despite challenges from neighboring rulers, including the Malatesta family in nearby Rimini, Italy. San Marino survived the Renaissance as a relic of the self-governing Italian city-state and remained an independent republic after the unification of Italy in 1861. It is one of the smallest republics in the world, and it may be the oldest one in Europe.

Recent Developments

San Marino continued to be an economic oasis on the turbulent Italian peninsula. The country's interest in interacting more with the world economy was evident. It was weighing the benefits of applying for membership in the European Union. Efforts to increase transparency and security were made in 2006, chief among them joining Interpol in September.

Internet resources:
<http://www.visitsanmarino.com>.

São Tomé and Príncipe

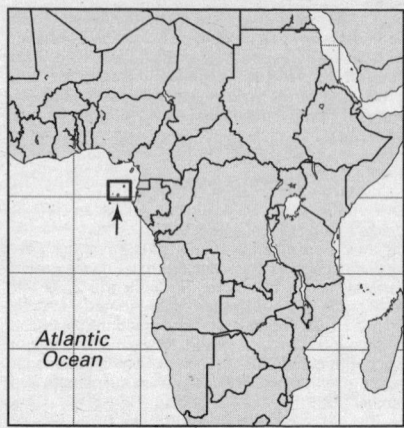

Atlantic Ocean

Official name: República democrática de São Tomé e Príncipe (Democratic Republic of São Tomé and Príncipe). **Form of government:** multiparty republic with one legislative house (National Assembly [55]). **Chief of state:** President Fradique de Menezes (from 2003). **Head of government:** Prime Minister Tomé Vera Cruz (from 2006). **Capital:** São Tomé. **Official language:** Portuguese. **Official religion:** none. **Monetary unit:** 1 dobra (Db) = 100 cêntimos; valuation (1 Jul 2007) US$1 = Db 13,734.

Demography

Area: 386 sq mi, 1,001 sq km. **Population** (2006): 152,000. **Density** (2006): persons per sq mi 393.8, persons per sq km 151.8. **Urban** (2001): 47.7%. **Sex distribution** (2001): male 49.59%, female 50.41%. **Age breakdown** (2001): under 15, 47.7%; 15–29,

---

1 metric ton = about 1.1 short tons;   1 kilometer = 0.6 mi (statute);   1 metric ton-km cargo = about 0.68 short ton-mi cargo;   c.i.f.: cost, insurance, and freight;   f.o.b.: free on board

27.5%; 30–44, 12.6%; 45–59, 6.3%; 60–74, 4.5%; 75 and over, 1.4%. **Ethnic composition** (2000): black-white admixture 79.5%; Fang 10.0%; angolares (descendants of former Angolan slaves) 7.6%; Portuguese 1.9%; other 1.0%. **Religious affiliation** (1995): Roman Catholic, about 89.5%; remainder mostly Protestant, predominantly Seventh-day Adventist and an indigenous Evangelical Church. **Major cities** (2001): São Tomé 51,886; Neves 6,700; Santana 6,300; Trindade 6,000; Santo António 1,040. **Location:** islands in the Gulf of Guinea, straddling the Equator west of Gabon.

Vital statistics

Birth rate per 1,000 population (2003): 41.9 (world avg. 21.3). **Death rate** per 1,000 population (2003): 7.1 (world avg. 9.1). **Natural increase rate** per 1,000 population (2003): 34.8 (world avg. 12.2). **Total fertility rate** (avg. births per childbearing woman; 2003): 5.8. **Life expectancy** at birth (2003): male 64.8 years; female 67.8 years.

National economy

Budget (2000). *Revenue:* Db 183,400,000,000 (grants 56.4%; taxes 32.4%, of which sales taxes 10.9%, import taxes 9.8%, income and profit taxes 9.1%; nontax revenue 11.2%). *Expenditures:* Db 244,400,000,000 (capital expenditure 63.3%; recurrent expenditure 36.7%, of which personnel costs 11.8%, debt service 10.0%, goods and services 6.2%, transfers 3.0%, defense 0.5%). **Public debt** (external, outstanding; 2002): $307,900,000. **Production** (metric tons except as noted). *Agriculture, forestry, fishing* (2002): oil palm fruit 40,000, bananas 35,000, coconuts 26,600; livestock (number of live animals) 4,800 goats, 4,100 cattle, 2,600 sheep; roundwood (2001) 9,000 cu m; fish catch (2001) 3,500, principally marine fish and shellfish. *Mining and quarrying:* some quarrying to support local construction industry. *Manufacturing* (value in Db; 1995): beer 880,000; clothing 679,000; lumber 369,000. *Energy production (consumption):* electricity (kW-hr; 2000) 18,000,-000 (18,000,000); petroleum products (2000) none (29,000). **Households.** Average household size (1981) 4.0; expenditure (1995): food 71.9%, housing and energy 10.2%, transportation and communications 6.4%, clothing and other items 5.3%, household durable goods 2.8%, education and health 1.7%. **Tourism** (2002): receipts from visitors $10,000,000; expenditures by nationals abroad $1,000,000. **Population economically active** (1994): total 51,789; activity rate of total population 40.8% (participation rates: ages 15–64 [1981] 61.1%; female [1991] 32.4%; unemployed [1994] 29.0%). **Gross national product** (2003): $50,000,000 ($320 per capita). **Land use** as % of total land area (2000): in temporary crops 6.3%, in permanent crops 46.9%, in pasture 1.0%; overall forest area 28.3%.

Foreign trade

Imports (2002): $24,800,000 (investment goods 52.9%, food and other agricultural products 20.2%, petroleum products 17.9%). *Major import sources:* Portugal 38.9%; US 22.2%; UK 9.3%. **Exports** (2002): $5,500,000 (cocoa beans 80.0%; other exports include copra, coffee, and palm oil). *Major export des-*

tinations: The Netherlands 27.3%; Portugal 18.2%; Canada 9.1%.

Transport and communications

Transport. *Roads* (1999): total length 320 km (paved 68%). *Vehicles* (1996): passenger cars 4,040; trucks and buses 1,540. *Air transport* (1998): passenger-km 9,000,000; short ton-km cargo 1,000,000; airports (2000) 2. **Communications,** in total units (units per 1,000 persons). Radios (1997): 38,000 (272); televisions (1997): 23,000 (163); telephone main lines (2003): 7,000 (46); cellular telephone subscribers (2003): 4,800 (32); Internet users (2003): 15,000 (97).

Education and health

Literacy (1991): total population age 15 and over literate 73.0%; males literate 85.0%; females literate 62.0%. **Health:** physicians (1996) 61 (1 per 2,147 persons); hospital beds (1983) 640 (1 per 158 persons); infant mortality rate per 1,000 live births (2003) 46.0. **Food** (2001): daily per capita caloric intake 2,567 (vegetable products 96%, animal products 4%); 109% of FAO recommended minimum.

Military

Total active duty personnel (1995): 600 (a 5-member crew of the Portuguese air force is stationed in São Tomé and Príncipe to provide humanitarian assistance). **Military expenditure as percentage of GNP** (1999): 1.0% (world 2.4%); per capita expenditure $3.

Did you know? An Italian agronomist has revived production of cocoa from an ancient species on the island of Príncipe. Some of the plants date to 1820, when they were first introduced, and the flavor associated with chocolate produced from these plants is notably pure.

Background

First visited by European navigators in the 1470s, the islands of São Tomé and Príncipe were colonized by the Portuguese in the 16th century and were used in the trade and transshipment of slaves. Sugarcane and cacao were the main cash crops. The islands became an overseas province of Portugal in 1951 and achieved independence in 1975. During recent decades the country's economy was heavily dependent on international assistance.

Recent Developments

São Tomé and Príncipe was thought to be surrounded by huge oil reserves. In May 2006 the first oil strike was confirmed, though it was announced in January 2007 that this oil was not of commercial quality. By February 2007, companies had paid at least $237 million for oil exploration rights. In March of that year the country reached the completion point of the Enhanced Heavily Indebted Poor Countries Initiative of the World Bank and the IMF. This led to debt relief and aid amounting to some $314 million.

Internet resources: <www.saotome.st>.

Saudi Arabia

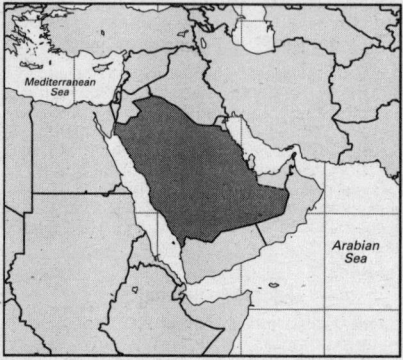

Official name: Al-Mamlakah al-'Arabiyah al-Sa'udiyah (Kingdom of Saudi Arabia). **Form of government:** monarchy (assisted by the Consultative Council consisting of 120 appointed members). **Head of state and government:** King Abdullah (from 2005). **Capital:** Riyadh. **Official language:** Arabic. **Official religion:** Islam. **Monetary unit:** 1 Saudi riyal (SRIs) = 100 halalah; valuation (1 Jul 2007) US$1 = SRIs 3.75.

Demography

Area: 830,000 sq mi, 2,149,690 sq km. **Population** (2006): 23,687,000 (expatriates constitute 27% total population). **Density** (2006): persons per sq mi 28.5, persons per sq km 11.0. **Urban** (2001): 86.7%. **Sex distribution** (2003): male 54.90%; female 45.10%. **Age breakdown** (2003): under 15, 39.7%; 15–29, 26.9%; 30–44, 21.7%; 45–59, 8.0%; 60–74, 2.9%; 75 and over, 0.8%. **Ethnic composition** (2000): Arab 88.1%, of which Saudi Arab 74.2%, Bedouin 3.9%, Gulf Arab 3.0%; Indo-Pakistani 5.5%; African black 1.5%; Filipino 1.0%; other 3.9%. **Religious affiliation** (2000): Muslim 94%, of which Sunni 84%, Shi'i 10%; Christian 3.5%, of which Roman Catholic 3%; Hindu 1%; nonreligious/other 1.5%. **Major urban agglomerations** (2000): Riyadh 4,549,000; Jiddah 3,192,000; Mecca 1,335,000; Medina 891,000; Al-Dammam 764,000. **Location:** the Middle East, bordering Iraq, Kuwait, the Persian Gulf, Qatar, UAE, Oman, Yemen, the Red Sea, the Gulf of Aqaba, and Jordan.

Vital statistics

Birth rate per 1,000 population (2002): 37.3 (world avg. 21.3). **Death rate** per 1,000 population (2002): 5.9 (world avg. 9.1). **Natural increase rate** per 1,000 population (2002): 31.4 (world avg. 12.2). **Total fertility rate** (avg. births per childbearing woman; 2002): 6.2. **Life expectancy** at birth (2002): male 66.7 years; female 70.2 years.

National economy

Budget (2002). *Revenue:* SRIs 157,000,000,000 (oil revenues 78.9%). *Expenditures:* SRIs 202,000,000,-

000 (defense and security 34.3%, human resource development 23.3%, public administration, municipal transfers, and subsidies 22.4%, health and social development 9.4%). **Production** (metric tons except as noted). *Agriculture and fishing* (2002): alfalfa 2,000,000, wheat 1,800,000, dates 783,000; livestock (number of live animals) 8,000,000 sheep, 4,650,000 goats, 415,000 camels; fish catch (2001) 57,385. *Mining and quarrying* (2002): gypsum 450,000; silver 14,000 kg; gold 5,000 kg. *Manufacturing* (value added in $'000,000; 1998): industrial chemicals 3,349; refined petroleum 1,806; cement, bricks, and tiles 1,505. *Energy production (consumption):* electricity (kW-hr; 2002) 138,200,000,000 ([2000] 126,441,000,000); crude petroleum (barrels; 2002) 2,589,000,000 ([2000] 658,800,000); petroleum products (2000) 100,994,000 (52,045,000); natural gas (cu m; 2002) 62,014,000,000 ([2000] 49,808,300,000). **Population economically active** (2003): total 7,437,400, of which 3,833,000 foreign workers and 3,604,400 Saudi nationals; activity rate of total population 31.0% (participation rates: ages 15–64, 56.2%; unemployed [2002] 11.0%). **Gross national product** (2003): $186,776,000,000 ($8,530 per capita). **Households.** Average household size (2002) 6.1; expenditure (1998–99): food and nonalcoholic beverages 37.3%, transportation 18.9%, housing and energy 15.7%, household furnishings 9.7%. **Tourism** (in $'000,000; 2002): receipts 3,420; expenditures 7,356. **Land use** as % of total land area (2000): in temporary crops 1.7%, in permanent crops 0.1%, in pasture 79.1%; overall forest area 0.7%.

Foreign trade

Imports (2001-c.i.f.): SRIs 116,930,000,000 (transport equipment 21.3%, of which road vehicles 16.5%; machinery and apparatus 20.6%, of which general industrial machinery 5.7%; food and live animals 13.5%; chemicals and chemical products 9.6%; iron and steel 4.0%). *Major import sources* (2003): US 15.0%; Japan 10.3%; Germany 8.9%; UK 5.9%; China 5.9%. **Exports** (2001-f.o.b.): SRIs 274,085,000,000 (crude petroleum 72.8%; refined petroleum 16.0%; organic chemicals 3.6%; polyethylene 1.6%). *Major export destinations* (2002): US 19.7%; Japan 14.3%; South Korea 9.5%; Singapore 5.4%; India 5.1%.

Transport and communications

Transport. *Railroads* (2003): route length 1,392 km; (2001) passenger-km 222,000,000; (2001) metric ton-km cargo 856,000,000. *Roads* (2003): total length 167,857 km (paved 100%). *Vehicles* (1996): passenger cars 1,744,000; trucks and buses 1,192,000. *Air transport* (2003; Saudi Arabian Airlines only): passenger-km 23,372,000,000; metric ton-km cargo 85,451,000; airports (2002) with scheduled flights 25. **Communications,** in total units (units per 1,000 persons). Daily newspaper circulation (1996): 1,105,000 (59); radios (2000): 7,180,000 (326); televisions (2002): 5,803,500 (265); telephone main lines (2003): 3,502,600 (155); cellular telephone subscribers (2003): 7,238,200 (321); personal computers (2002): 3,003,000 (137); Internet users (2003): 1,500,000 (67).

1 metric ton = about 1.1 short tons;   1 kilometer = 0.6 mi (statute);   1 metric ton-km cargo = about 0.68 short ton-mi cargo;   c.i.f.: cost, insurance, and freight;   f.o.b.: free on board

Education and health

Educational attainment (2000). Percentage of Saudi (non-Saudi) population age 10 and over who: are illiterate 19.9% (12.1%), are literate/have primary education 39.5% (40.6%), have some/completed secondary education 34.2% (36.0%), have at least begun university education 6.4% (11.3%). **Health** (2001): physicians 31,983 (1 per 709 persons); hospital beds 46,622 (1 per 485 persons); infant mortality rate per 1,000 live births (2002) 49.6. **Food** (2001): daily per capita caloric intake 2,841 (vegetable products 85%, animal products 15%); 119% of FAO recommended minimum.

Military

Total active duty personnel (2003): 124,500 (army 60.2%, navy 12.4%, air force 27.4%); most US military withdrew in 2003. **Military expenditure as percentage of GNP** (1999): 14.9% (world 2.4%); per capita expenditure $996.

Background

Saudi Arabia is the historical home of Islam, founded by Muhammad in Medina in 622. During medieval times, local and foreign rulers fought for control of the Arabian Peninsula; in 1517 the Ottomans prevailed. In the 18th–19th centuries Islamic leaders supporting religious reform struggled to regain Saudi territory, all of which was restored by 1904. The British held Saudi lands as a protectorate from 1915 to 1927; then they acknowledged the sovereignty of the Kingdom of the Hejaz and Najd. The two kingdoms were unified as the Kingdom of Saudi Arabia in 1932. Since World War II, it has supported the Palestinian cause in the Middle East and maintained close ties with the US.

Recent Developments

King Abdullah's strategic visit to China, India, Malaysia, and Pakistan and the signing of a number of agreements to build joint refineries and petrochemical plants signaled a possible shift in Saudi economic outlook away from partnerships with the US and Europe. The Saudis were reportedly looking to boost relations with countries that did not have an interest in Saudi internal affairs. The economic situation remained robust, helped by the international increase in crude oil prices. Although Russia overtook Saudi Arabia as the main global oil producer, Riyadh was still the main global oil exporter. Some fundamentalist Muslims were unhappy about Riyadh's proclamation that it would make major changes to the Saudi educational system in an effort to emphasize the spirit of modernity, nonviolence, and cooperation with non-Muslims that was dictated by Muslim teachings. Rising tensions between Tehran and Washington and European capitals over the nuclear issue in Iran caused Saudi Arabia to exert pressure on Syria to sever its alliance with Iran and to discourage the pro-Iranian Hezbollah in Lebanon from attacking Israeli posts in southern Lebanon.

Internet resources: <www.sauditourism.gov.sa>.

Senegal

Official name: République du Sénégal (Republic of Senegal). **Form of government:** multiparty republic

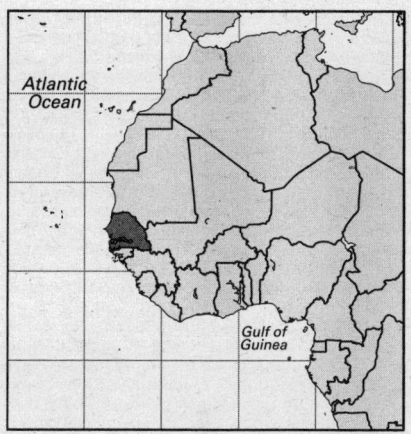

with one legislative house (National Assembly [150]). **Head of state and government:** President Abdoulaye Wade (from 2000), assisted by Prime Minister Cheikh Hadjibou Soumaré (from 2007). **Capital:** Dakar. **Official language:** French. **Official religion:** none. **Monetary unit:** 1 CFA franc (CFAF) = 100 centimes; valuation (1 Jul 2007) US$1 = CFAF 485.18; the CFAF is pegged to the euro (€) at €1 = CFAF 656.96 from 1 Jan 2002.

Demography

Area: 75,955 sq mi, 196,722 sq km. **Population** (2006): 10,961,000. **Density** (2006): persons per sq mi 144.3, persons per sq km 55.7. **Urban** (2000): 47.4%. **Sex distribution** (2003): male 49.09%; female 50.91%. **Age breakdown** (2003): under 15, 43.7%; 15–29, 28.1%; 30–44, 15.7%; 45–59, 8.0%; 60–74, 3.6%; 75 and over, 0.9%. **Ethnic composition** (2000): Wolof 34.6%; Peul (Fulani) and Tukulor 27.1%; Serer 12.0%; Malinke (Mandingo) 9.7%; other 16.6%. **Religious affiliation** (2000): Muslim 87.6%; traditional beliefs 6.2%; Christian 5.5%, of which Roman Catholic 4.7%; other 0.7%. **Major cities** (2002): Dakar 1,983,093 (includes urban departments of Pikine [768,826] and Guédiawaye [pop. 258,370], adjacent to Dakar department [955,897]); Thiès 237,849; Kaolack 172,305; Saint-Louis 154,555; Mbour 153,503. **Location:** western Africa, bordering Mauritania, Mali, Guinea, Guinea-Bissau, the North Atlantic Ocean, and The Gambia.

Vital statistics

Birth rate per 1,000 population (2003): 36.2 (world avg. 21.3). **Death rate** per 1,000 population (2003): 11.0 (world avg. 9.1). **Natural increase rate** per 1,000 population (2003): 25.2 (world avg. 12.2). **Total fertility rate** (avg. births per childbearing woman; 2003): 4.9. **Life expectancy** at birth (2003): male 54.8 years; female 58.0 years.

National economy

Budget (2002). *Revenue:* CFAF 713,900,000,000 (tax revenue 85.7%; grants 9.6%; nontax revenue 4.7%). *Expenditures:* CFAF 738,100,000,000 (current expenditures 62.6%, of which wages 27.0%, education 21.2%, health 5.7%, interest payment 3.8%;

development expenditure 37.4%). **Public debt** (external, outstanding; 2002): $3,339,000,000. **Production** (metric tons except as noted). *Agriculture, forestry, fishing* (2002): sugarcane 890,000, peanuts (groundnuts) 501,298, millet 414,687; livestock (number of live animals) 4,900,000 sheep, 4,000,000 goats, 3,230,000 cattle; roundwood (2002) 5,971,559 cu m; fish catch (2001) 405,409, of which crustaceans and mollusks 22,288. *Mining and quarrying* (2003): phosphate 1,918,900; salt (2002) 141,000. *Manufacturing* ($'000,000; 2000): food products 81; transport equipment 74, of which ships and boats 39; printing and publishing 63. *Energy production (consumption):* electricity (kW-hr; 2001) 1,651,200,000 (1,651,200,000); crude petroleum (barrels; 2000) none (6,707,000); petroleum products (2000) 979,000 (1,243,000); natural gas (cu m; 2000) 538,000 (538,000). **Population economically active** (2001): total 4,294,000; activity rate of total population 44.6%. **Households.** Average household size (2002) 8.7. **Tourism** (2000): receipts $140,000,000; expenditures (1999) $54,000,000. **Gross national product** (at current market prices; 2003): $5,563,000,000 ($550 per capita). **Land use** as % of total land area (2000): in temporary crops 12.3%, in permanent crops 0.2%, in pasture 29.3%; overall forest area 32.2%.

Foreign trade

Imports (2001-f.o.b. in balance of trade and c.i.f. in commodities and trading partners): $1,730,000,000 (food and live animals 22.3%, of which cereals 13.2%, rice 8.2%; mineral fuels and lubricants 16.8%, of which crude petroleum 9.8%; machinery and apparatus 15.1%; chemicals and chemical products 11.1%). *Major import sources:* France 27.8%; Nigeria 9.8%; Thailand 7.7%; Germany 4.8%; US 4.2%. **Exports** (2001): $785,000,000 (fresh fish 16.1%; refined petroleum 15.5%; fresh crustaceans and mollusks 12.0%; bunkers and ships' stores 12.0%; phosphorous pentoxide and phosphoric acids 9.5%; peanut [groundnut] oil 9.1%). *Major export destinations:* France 16.7%; India 12.4%; Greece 7.3%; Mali 6.9%; Italy 6.0%.

Transport and communications

Transport. *Railroads* (2002): route length 906 km; passenger-km 105,000,000; metric ton-km cargo 345,000,000. *Roads* (1999): total length 14,576 km (paved 29%). *Vehicles* (2001): passenger cars 193,000; trucks and buses 79,000. *Air transport* (2001; Air Afrique, an airline jointly owned by 11 African countries [including Senegal], was declared bankrupt in February 2002): passenger-km 304,000,000; airports (1996) with scheduled flights 7. **Communications**, in total units (units per 1,000 persons). Daily newspaper circulation (2000): 47,000 (5); radios (2001): 1,254,400 (128); televisions (2000): 376,000 (40); telephone main lines (2003): 228,800 (22); cellular telephone subscribers (2003): 575,900 (56); personal computers (2003): 220,000 (21); Internet users (2003): 225,000 (22).

Education and health

Literacy (2000): percentage of total population age 15 and over literate 38.3%; males literate 48.1%;

females literate 28.7%. **Health:** physicians (1996) 649 (1 per 13,162 persons); hospital beds (1998) 3,582 (1 per 2,500 persons); infant mortality rate per 1,000 live births (2003): 57.6. **Food** (2001): daily per capita caloric intake 2,277 (vegetable products 91%, animal products 9%); 95% of FAO recommended minimum.

Military

Total active duty personnel (2004): 13,620 (army 87.4%, navy 7.0%, air force 5.6%); French troops (August 2004) 1,100. **Military expenditure as percentage of GNP** (1999): 1.7% (world 2.4%); per capita expenditure $8.

Background

Links between the peoples of Senegal and North Africa were established in the 10th century AD. Islam was introduced in the 11th century, although animism retained a hold on the country into the 19th century. The Portuguese explored the coast in 1445, and in 1638 the French established a trading post at the mouth of the Senegal River. Throughout the 17th and 18th centuries, Europeans exported slaves, ivory, and gold from Senegal. The French gained control over the coast in the early 19th century and moved inland, checking the expansion of the Tukulor empire; in 1895 Senegal became part of French West Africa. Its inhabitants were made French citizens in 1946, and it became an overseas territory of France. It became an autonomous republic in 1958 and was federated with Mali in 1959–60. It became an independent state in 1960. In 1982 it entered a confederation with The Gambia, called Senegambia, which was dissolved in 1989.

Recent Developments

The flow of illegal migrants from Senegal attempting to reach Europe through the Canary Islands increased dramatically in 2006 after Morocco and Mauritania initiated stricter border and coastal patrols. The Spanish government halted the repatriation of Senegalese migrants in June after protests against their treatment led Senegal's government to suspend cooperation with the program. After negotiations between the two governments, the deportations resumed in mid-September.

Internet resources: <www.senegal-tourism.com>.

Serbia

Official name: Republika Srbija (Republic of Serbia). **Form of government:** republic with National Assembly (250). **Chief of state:** President Boris Tadic (from 2004). **Head of government:** Prime Minister Vojislav Kostunica (from 2004). **Capital:** Belgrade. **Official language:** Serbian. **Official religion:** none. **Monetary unit:** 1 Serbian dinar (CSD) = 100 paras; valuation (1 Jun 2007) $1 = 69.57 Serbian dinars; the Serbian dinar replaced Yugoslav new dinar on 4 Feb 2003, at rate of 1 to 1. Kosovo uses the euro adopted on 1 Jan 2002; valuation (1 Jul 2007) US$1 = €0.74.

1 metric ton = about 1.1 short tons; 1 kilometer = 0.6 mi (statute); 1 metric ton-km cargo = about 0.68 short ton-mi cargo; c.i.f.: cost, insurance, and freight; f.o.b.: free on board

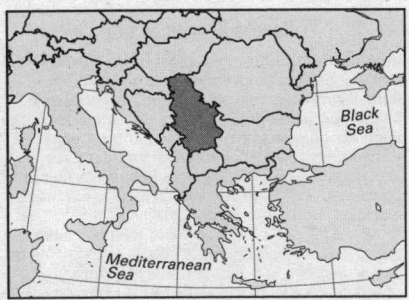

Demography

Area: 34,128 sq mi, 88,391 sq km. **Population** (2006; excludes Kosovo, whose 2006 population estimate per a Kosovar' source is 2,532,000): 7,495,000. **Density** (2006; excludes Kosovo, the area of which is 4,203 sq mi [10,887 sq km]): persons per sq mi 250.5, persons per sq km 96.7. **Urban** (2002; excludes Kosovo): 56.4%. **Sex distribution** (2002; excludes Kosovo): male 48.63%; female 51.37%. **Age breakdown** (2002; excludes Kosovo): under 15, 15.7%; 15–29, 20.2%; 30–44, 19.9%; 45–59, 21.1%; 60–74, 17.2%; 75–84, 4.7%; 85 and over, 0.6%; unknown 0.6%. **Ethnic composition** (2002; excludes Kosovo): Serb 82.9%; Hungarian 3.9%; Bosniac 1.8%; Rom (Gypsy) 1.4%; Yugoslav 1.1%; Croat 0.9%; Montenegrin 0.9%; other 7.1%. **Religious affiliation** (2000; Serbia and Montenegro): Christian 67.9%, of which Orthodox 56.8%, Roman Catholic 5.1%; Muslim 16.2%; nonreligious/atheist 15.9%. **Major cities** (2002): Belgrade 1,120,092; Novi Sad 191,405; Nis 173,724; Pristina (in Kosovo; 2003 est.) 165,844; Kragujevac 146,373. **Location:** southeastern Europe, bordering Romania, Bulgaria, Macedonia, Albania, Montenegro, Bosnia and Herzegovina, Croatia, and Hungary.

Vital statistics

Birth rate per 1,000 population (2005; excludes Kosovo): 10.4 (world avg. 21.1); (2004) legitimate 77.8%. **Death rate** per 1,000 population (2005; excludes Kosovo): 14.3 (world avg. 9.0). **Total fertility rate** (avg. births per childbearing woman; 2004; excludes Kosovo): 1.60. **Life expectancy** at birth (2004; excludes Kosovo): male 69.9 years; female 75.4 years.

National economy

Budget (2005). *Revenue:* CSD 701,200,000,000 (tax revenue 91.2%, of which VAT 30.8%, excises and customs duties 15.7%, personal and corporate income tax 14.9%; nontax revenue 8.8%). *Expenditures:* CSD 669,600,000,000 (current expenditure 95.1%; capital expenditure 4.9%). **Population economically active** (2005; includes Kosovo): total 3,453,293; activity rate of total population 45.6% (participation rates: over age 15, 53.5%; female 43.1%; unemployed [August 2005–July 2006; excludes Kosovo] 33.0%). **Production** (metric tons except as noted). *Agriculture, forestry, fishing* (2005): corn (maize) 7,085,666, sugar beets 3,101,176, wheat 2,007,060; livestock (number of live animals) 3,165,000 pigs, 1,576,000 sheep, 1,079,000 cattle; roundwood (2004) 2,562,000 cu m; fisheries production (2004; Serbia and Montenegro) 5,390 (from aquaculture 75%). *Mining and quarrying* (2004; Serbia and Montenegro): bauxite 486,000; copper (metal content) 25,000; lead (metal content) 2,000. *Manufacturing* (value added in CSD '000,000 [constant 2002 prices]; 2004): food products and beverages 48,970; chemicals and chemical products 21,862; cement, bricks, and ceramics 11,445. *Energy production (consumption)* (excludes Kosovo): electricity (kW-hr; 2004) 33,874,000,000 (22,911,000,000); coal (2004) 424,000 (303,000); lignite (2004) 34,400,000 (30,900,000); crude petroleum (barrels; 2004) 4,840,000 ([2003; Serbia and Montenegro] 27,300,000); petroleum products (2004; Serbia and Montenegro) 2,300,000 ([2003; Serbia and Montenegro] 2,824,000); natural gas (cu m; 2004) 317,000,000 (794,000,000). **Gross national product** (2003): $17,359,000,000 ($2,310 per capita). **Public debt** (external, outstanding; June 2006): $15,463,600,000. **Households.** Average household size (2006; excludes Kosovo) 3.2; average annual income per household CSD 394,740 ($5,620); sources of income: wages and salaries 47.7%, transfers 26.5%, self-employment 5.5%; expenditure: food and nonalcoholic beverages 35.1%, housing and energy 18.9%, transportation 11.2%, clothing and footwear 6.8%. **Tourism** (2004): receipts $220,000,000. **Remittances** (2005): receipts $2,400,000,000. **Land use** as % of total land area (2002; excludes Kosovo): in temporary crops 43.3%, in permanent crops 4.1%, in pasture 18.2%; overall forest area 25.2%.

Foreign trade

Imports (2005-f.o.b. in balance of trade and c.i.f. in commodities and trading partners): $10,575,-700,000 (mineral fuels 18.9%; chemicals and chemical products 13.6%; machinery and apparatus 10.3%; transportation equipment 8.2%; base metals 7.6%; textiles and wearing apparel 4.4%; food and food products 4.0%; paper and paper products 3.2%). *Major import sources:* Russia 15.9%; Germany 10.3%; Italy 8.6%; China 4.8%; US 3.6%. **Exports** (2005): $4,553,400,000 (base metals 15.4%; food and food products 14.7%; chemicals and chemical products 8.8%; rubber and plastic products 6.4%; machinery and apparatus 4.9%). *Major export destinations:* Bosnia and Herzegovina 16.4%; Italy 14.4%; Germany 9.8%; Macedonia 5.8%; Russia 5.0%.

Transport and communications

Transport. *Railroads* (2005): route length 3,809 km; passenger-km 715,000,000; metric ton-km cargo 3,481,000,000. *Roads* (2004): total length 38,507 km (paved 62%). *Vehicles* (2005): passenger cars 1,497,418; trucks and buses 257,642. *Air transport* (2005): passenger-km 1,218,000,000; metric ton-km cargo 5,940,000. **Communications,** in total units (units per 1,000 persons). Daily newspaper circulation (2002; Serbia and Montenegro): 1,015,000 (95); televisions (2000; Serbia and Montenegro): 2,980,000 (279); telephone main lines (2005): 2,672,700 (356); cellular telephone subscribers (2005): 5,222,100 (696); personal computers (2004; Serbia and Montenegro): 389,000 (36); Internet users (2005): 1,400,000 (186).

Education and health

Educational attainment (2002). Percentage of population age 15 and over having: no formal education/unknown 7.8%; incomplete primary education 16.2%; complete primary 23.9%; secondary 41.1%; higher 11.0%. **Literacy** (2002): total population age 10 and over literate 96.6%. **Health** (2004): physicians (2003) 19,900 (1 per 379 persons); hospital beds 45,283 (1 per 166 persons); infant mortality rate (2005; excludes Kosovo) 6.7. **Food** (2004; Serbia and Montenegro): daily per capita caloric intake 2,776 (vegetable products 67%, animal products 33%); 109% of FAO recommended minimum.

Background

The Kingdom of the Serbs, Croats, and Slovenes was created after the collapse of Austria-Hungary at the end of World War I. The country signed treaties with Czechoslovakia and Romania in 1920–21, marking the beginning of the Little Entente. In 1929 an absolute monarchy was established, the country's name was changed to Yugoslavia, and it was divided into regions without regard to ethnic boundaries. Axis powers invaded Yugoslavia in 1941, and German, Italian, Hungarian, and Bulgarian troops occupied it for the rest of World War II. In 1945 the Socialist Federal Republic of Yugoslavia was established; it included the republics of Bosnia and Herzegovina, Croatia, Macedonia, Montenegro, Serbia, and Slovenia. Its independent form of communism under Josip Broz Tito's leadership provoked the USSR. Internal ethnic tensions flared up in the 1980s, causing the country's ultimate collapse. In 1991–92 independence was declared by Croatia, Slovenia, Macedonia, and Bosnia and Herzegovina; the new Federal Republic of Yugoslavia (containing roughly 45% of the population and 40% of the area of its predecessor) was proclaimed by Serbia and Montenegro. Still fueled by long-standing ethnic tensions, hostilities continued into the 1990s. Despite the approval of the Dayton Peace Accords (1995), sporadic fighting continued and was followed in 1998–99 by Serbian repression and expulsion of ethnic populations in Kosovo. In September–October 2000, the battered nation of Yugoslavia ended the autocratic rule of Pres. Slobodan Milosevic. In April 2001 he was arrested and in June extradited to The Hague to stand trial for war crimes, genocide, and crimes against humanity committed during the fighting in Kosovo. In February 2003 both houses of the Yugoslav federal legislature voted to accept a new state charter and change the name of the country from Yugoslavia to Serbia and Montenegro. Henceforth, defense, international political and economic relations, and human rights matters would be handled centrally, while all other functions would be run from the republican capitals, Belgrade and Podgorica, respectively. The move was seen as an acknowledgment that Serbia and Montenegro had little in common, and a provision was included for both states to vote on independence after three years, and Serbia declared its independence in June 2006, shortly after Montenegro severed its federal union with Serbia.

Recent Developments

In November 2006 a new constitution was adopted that supporters said would help pave the way for Serbia's membership in the European Union (EU). There was increasing pressure on Serbia from the International Criminal Tribunal for the Former Yugoslavia to extradite indicted Bosnian Serb war criminal Ratko Mladic to face trial. Belgrade's failure to do so resulted in the suspension of talks on the Stabilization and Association Agreement, the first step to EU membership. A decision in the near future on the status of Kosovo was expected—negotiations between Serbian and Kosovar representatives of the UN-administered province began in February. Belgrade insisted that Kosovo remain an integral part of Serbia, while Kosovo's ethnic Albanian majority demanded full independence. GDP grew by 6.7% in the first half of 2006, and foreign investment continued to expand, though unemployment remained high at 27%.

Internet resources: <www.serbia-tourism.org>; <http://webrzs.statserb.sr.gov.yu/axd/en/index.php>.

Seychelles

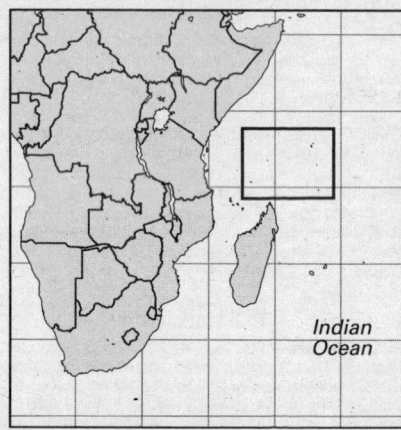

Indian Ocean

Official name: Repiblik Sesel (Creole); Republic of Seychelles (English); République des Seychelles (French). **Form of government:** multiparty republic with one legislative house (National Assembly [34]). **Head of state and government:** President James Michel (from 2004). **Capital:** Victoria. **Official languages:** none; Creole, English, and French are national languages. **Official religion:** none. **Monetary unit:** 1 Seychelles rupee (SR) = 100 cents; valuation (1 Jul 2007) US$1 = SR 6.34.

Demography

Area: 176 sq mi, 455 sq km. **Population** (2006): 83,200. **Density** (2006): persons per sq mi 427.7, persons per sq km 182.9. **Urban** (2002): 64.6%. **Sex distribution** (2002): male 49.81%; female 50.19%.

1 metric ton = about 1.1 short tons;   1 kilometer = 0.6 mi (statute);   1 metric ton-km cargo = about 0.68 short ton-mi cargo;   c.i.f.: cost, insurance, and freight;   f.o.b.: free on board

Age breakdown (2003): under 15, 27.3%; 15–29, 28.2%; 30–44, 26.4%; 45–59, 9.9%; 60–74, 5.5%; 75 and over, 2.7%. **Ethnic composition** (2000): Seychellois Creole (mixture of Asian, African, and European) 93.2%; British 3.0%; French 1.8%; Chinese 0.5%; Indian 0.3%; other unspecified 1.2%. **Religious affiliation** (2000): Roman Catholic 90.4%; Anglican 6.7%; Hindu 0.6%; other (mostly nonreligious) 2.3%. **Major city** (2004): Victoria 25,500. **Location**: group of islands in the Indian Ocean, northeast of Madagascar.

Vital statistics

Birth rate per 1,000 population (2002): 18.3 (world avg. 21.3); (1998) legitimate 24.7%. **Death rate** per 1,000 population (2002): 8.0 (world avg. 9.1). **Natural increase rate** per 1,000 population (2002): 10.3 (world avg. 12.2). **Total fertility rate** (avg. births per childbearing woman; 2002): 2.0. **Marriage rate** per 1,000 population (2002): 5.3. **Divorce rate** per 1,000 population (2002): 1.4. **Life expectancy** at birth (2002): male 66.6 years; female 75.8 years.

National economy

Budget (2002). *Revenue:* SR 1,487,000,000 (tax revenue 70.0%, of which customs taxes and duties 23.7%, sales tax 18.9%, tax on income and profit 16.9%; nontax revenue 28.3%; grants 1.7%). *Expenditures:* SR 2,061,000,000 (current expenditure 82.0%, of which debt service 15.4%, education 7.6%, health 6.7%; capital expenditure 16.0%; net lending 2.0%). **Tourism** (2002): receipts from visitors $130,000,000; expenditures by nationals abroad $32,000,000. **Land use** as % of total land area (2000): in temporary crops 2%, in permanent crops 13%; overall forest area 67%. **Gross national product** (2003): $626,000,000 ($7,480 per capita). *Production* (metric tons except as noted). *Agriculture and fishing* (2003): coconuts 3,200, bananas 1,970, cinnamon 230; livestock (number of live animals) 18,500 pigs, 5,150 goats, 520,000 chickens; fish catch (2002) 48,960. *Mining and quarrying* (1998): guano 5,000. *Manufacturing* (2002): canned tuna 34,503; animal feed 18,565; copra 262. *Energy production (consumption):* electricity (kW-hr; 2002) 218,800,000 (182,400,000,000); petroleum products (2000) none (74,000). **Population economically active** (2002): total 34,017; activity rate of total population 41.9% (participation rates [2000]: ages 15–64, 81.5%; female [2000] 43.0%; unemployed [1999] 11.5%). **Public debt** (external, outstanding; 2002): $149,300,000. **Household income and expenditure**. Average household size (2002) 4.0; sources of income (1997): wages and salaries 77.2%, self-employment 3.8%, transfer payments 3.2%; expenditure (2001): food 25.5%, housing and energy 14.8%, beverages 13.3% (of which alcoholic 10.7%), clothing and footwear 6.7%, transportation 5.8%, recreation 5.5%.

Foreign trade

Imports (2003-c.i.f.): SR 2,231,000,000 (food and beverages 31.0%, of which fish, crustaceans, and mollusks 16.1%; mineral fuels 16.1%; machinery 12.3%; base and fabricated metals 8.1%; transport equipment 5.7%). *Major import sources:* Saudi Arabia 15.7%; South Africa 12.6%; Italy 10.6%; France 10.4%; Spain 10.4%; UK 7.7%. **Exports** (2003-f.o.b.): SR 1,484,000,000 (domestic exports 76.9%, of which canned tuna 69.0%, other processed fish 1.8%, fresh and frozen fish 1.9%; reexports 23.1%, of which petroleum products 19.8%). *Major export destinations* (2002): UK 39.2%; France 32.0%; Italy 14.5%; Germany 7.5%.

Transport and communications

Transport. *Roads* (2002): total length 456 km (paved 96%). *Vehicles* (2002): passenger cars 6,923; trucks and buses 2,551. *Air transport* (2002; Air Seychelles only): passenger-km 1,397,000,000; metric ton-km cargo 28,000,000; airports (2002) with scheduled flights 2. **Communications**, in total units (units per 1,000 persons). Daily newspaper circulation (1996): 3,000 (46); radios (1997): 42,000 (560); televisions (2000): 16,000 (203); telephone main lines (2002): 21,700 (269); cellular telephone subscribers (2003): 54,500 (682); personal computers (2002): 13,000 (157); Internet users (2002): 11,700 (145).

Education and health

Educational attainment (2003). Percentage of population age 12 and over having: less than primary or primary education 23.2%; secondary 73.4%; higher 3.4%. **Literacy** (2002): total population age 12 and over literate 91.0%; males literate 90.0%; females literate 92.0%. **Health** (2002): physicians 103 (1 per 792 persons); hospital beds 438 (1 per 185 persons); infant mortality rate per 1,000 live births (2002) 17.6. **Food** (2001): daily per capita caloric intake 2,461 (vegetable products 81%, animal products 19%); 105% of FAO recommended minimum.

Military

Total active duty personnel (2003): 450. **Military expenditure as percentage of GNP** (1997): 3.8% (world 2.6%); per capita expenditure $194.

Did you know? The five rays on the Seychelles flag symbolize the sky and sea (blue); the life-giving sun (yellow); the people and their work for unity and love (red); social justice and harmony (white); and the land (green).

Background

The first recorded landing on the uninhabited Seychelles was made in 1609 by an expedition of the British East India Co. The archipelago was claimed by the French in 1756 and surrendered to the British in 1810. Seychelles became a British crown colony in 1903 and a republic within the Commonwealth in 1976. A one-party socialist state since 1979, Seychelles began moving toward democracy in the 1990s; it adopted a new constitution in 1993.

Recent Developments

Seychelles sustained some $30 million in damage as a result of the Indian Ocean tsunami of 26 Dec 2004. The Paris Club of creditor nations froze debt repayments for Seychelles through 2005. In 2006 new hotels and other tourism facilities valued at $475 million were planned or under construction.

Internet resources: <www.seychelles.com>.

Sierra Leone

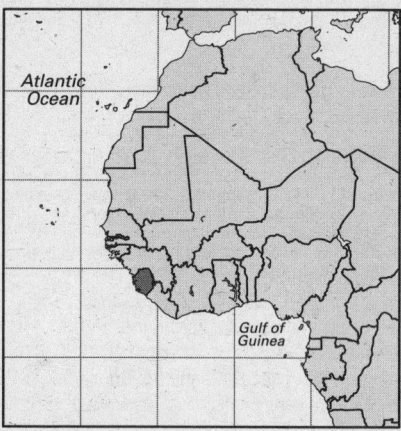

Official name: Republic of Sierra Leone. **Form of government:** republic with one legislative body (Parliament [124, including 12 paramount chiefs]). **Head of state and government:** President Ahmad Tejan Kabbah (from 1998). **Capital:** Freetown. **Official language:** English. **Official religion:** none. **Monetary unit:** 1 leone (Le) = 100 cents; valuation (1 Jul 2007) US$1 = Le 3,014.

Demography

Area: 27,699 sq mi, 71,740 sq km. **Population** (2006): 5,124,000. **Density** (2006): persons per sq mi 185.0, persons per sq km 71.4. **Urban** (2000): 36.6%. **Sex distribution** (2003): male 48.31%; female 51.69%. **Age breakdown** (2003): under 15, 44.8%; 15–29, 26.1%; 30–44, 15.3%; 45–59, 8.5%; 60–74, 4.4%; 75 and over, 0.8%. **Ethnic composition** (2000): Mende 26.0%; Temne 24.6%; Limba 7.1%; Kuranko 5.5%; Kono 4.2%; Fulani 3.8%; Bullom-Sherbro 3.5%; other 25.3%. **Religious affiliation** (2000): Sunni Muslim 45.9%; traditional beliefs 40.4%; Christian 11.4%; other 2.3%. **Major cities** (2003): Freetown (urban agglomeration; 2001) 837,000; Koidu 113,700; Makeni 110,700; Bo 82,400; Kenema 72,400. **Location:** western Africa, bordering Guinea, Liberia, and the North Atlantic Ocean.

Vital statistics

Birth rate per 1,000 population (2003): 43.9 (world avg. 21.3). **Death rate** per 1,000 population (2003): 20.7 (world avg. 9.1). **Natural increase rate** per 1,000 population (2003): 23.2 (world avg. 12.2). **Total fertility rate** (avg. births per childbearing woman; 2003): 5.9. **Life expectancy** at birth (2003): male 40.3 years; female 45.4 years.

National economy

Budget (2002). *Revenue:* Le 239,425,000,000 (customs duties and excise taxes 64.0%, income tax 25.1%, other 10.9%). *Expenditures:* Le 701,834,000,000 (re-

current expenditures 65.1%, of which wages and salaries 18.8%, goods and services 12.9%, defense and security 12.9%, debt service 9.4%; capital expenditures 34.9%). **Gross national product** (2003): $808,000,000 ($150 per capita). **Production** (metric tons except as noted). *Agriculture, forestry, fishing* (2002): cassava 260,000, rice 250,000, oil palm fruit 180,000; livestock (number of live animals) 400,000 cattle, 370,000 sheep, 220,000 goats; roundwood (2002) 5,497,220 cu m; fish catch (2003) 82,923. *Mining and quarrying* (2002): rutile, none (production at world's richest deposit was halted between 1995 and August 2004 because of the civil war and its lasting effects); diamonds 351,860 carats (does not include smuggled artisanal production, which was estimated to be 600,000 carats between 1999 and 2001); gold 30 kg. *Manufacturing* (value added in Le '000,000; 1993): food 36,117; chemicals 10,560; earthenware 1,844. *Energy production (consumption):* electricity (kW-hr; 2000) 246,000,000 (246,000,000); crude petroleum (barrels; 2000) none (1,796,000); petroleum products (2000) 183,000 (145,000). **Households.** Average household size (2002) 6.6. **Public debt** (external, outstanding; 2002): $1,262,000,000. **Population economically active** (2002): total 1,771,000; activity rate of total population 36.7% (participation rates [1991]: ages 10–64, 53.3%; female [2001] 32.4%; unemployed [registered; 1992] 10.6%). **Tourism** (1999): receipts $8,000,000; expenditures $4,000,000. **Land use** as % of total land area (2000): in temporary crops 6.8%, in permanent crops 0.8%, in pasture 30.7%; overall forest area 14.7%.

Foreign trade

Imports (2002-c.i.f.): Le 554,837,500,000 (food and live animals 26.7%; fuels 19.6%; machinery and transport equipment 18.9%; chemicals and chemical products 6.9%). *Major import sources* (2001): UK 25.3%; The Netherlands 10.1%; US 7.9%; Germany 6.3%; Italy 5.6%. **Exports** (2002-f.o.b.): Le 102,011,-900,000 (diamonds 85.7%; cacao 2.5%; rutile, none; reexports 4.8%). *Major export destinations* (2001): Belgium 40.6%; US 9.1%; UK 8.5%; Germany 7.8%; Japan 5.6%.

Transport and communications

Transport. *Railroads* (2002; Marampa Mineral Railway; there are no passenger railways): length 84 km. *Roads* (1999): total length 11,700 km (paved 11%). *Vehicles* (2003): passenger cars 17,439; trucks and buses 12,428. *Air transport* (2000): passenger-km 93,000,000; airports (2003) with scheduled flights 1. **Communications,** in total units (units per 1,000 persons). Daily newspaper circulation (2000): 17,700 (4); radios (2000): 1,140,000 (259); televisions (2000): 57,400 (13); telephone main lines (2002): 24,000 (4.8); cellular telephone subscribers (2002): 67,000 (14); personal computers (1999): 100 (n.a.); Internet users (2002): 8,000 (1.6).

Education and health

Educational attainment (1985). Percentage of population age 5 and over having: no formal schooling 64.1%; primary education 18.7%; secondary 9.7%; higher 1.5%. **Literacy** (1995): total population age 15

1 metric ton = about 1.1 short tons;   1 kilometer = 0.6 mi (statute);   1 metric ton-km cargo = about 0.68 short ton-mi cargo;   c.i.f.: cost, insurance, and freight;   f.o.b.: free on board

May 2007, Jamestown VA: Queen Elizabeth II visited the US to observe the 400th anniversary of the founding of the Jamestown colony, the first permanent British settlement in America. Above, she visits a replica of the *Susan Constant* with Philip Emerson, director of the Jamestown-Yorktown Foundation.

9 Jun 2007, Baghdad: A US soldier searches a house in the Rasheed neighborhood of the capital. As polls showed sharply declining public support for the four-year-old US intervention in Iraq, Pres. George W. Bush named a counterinsurgency expert, US Army General David Petraeus, as the new military commander in Iraq. In January 2007 the White House initiated a new military strategy, a "surge" in troop strength that sent an additional 30,000 troops to the troubled nation. By July, US troop strength was at a new high of 160,000 and US deaths had passed the 3,600 mark. Democrats who took power in both the House and Senate in the 2006 elections attempted to pass legislation calling for a specific timetable for the withdrawal of US troops but had not done so as of midsummer.

10 Jul 2007, Islamabad: *(below)* Soldiers take shelter after religious militants occupied a women's religious school within Pakistan's historic Red Mosque complex. After a siege that lasted nine days, they were evicted by government troops who raided the complex in fighting that left at least 70 militants and nine soldiers dead.

27 Jun 2007, Tehran: After Iran's government announced it would begin rationing gasoline in the face of a shortage, citizens looted and destroyed a number of gas stations in Tehran and around the nation.

13 Jun 2007, Gaza City, Gaza Strip: A Hamas militant runs to avoid sniper fire during an eight-day clash between members of the radical Hamas and centrist Fatah factions. After days of fighting, Hamas took complete control of the Gaza Strip, while Fatah leaders fled to their stronghold in the West Bank. The crisis in the Palestinian territories complicated the position of embattled Israeli PM Ehud Olmert, above.

30 Jun 2007, Glasgow, Scotland: Two British Muslims crashed an SUV carrying a car bomb into Glasgow's airport; no one died. Police said the crash was related to two failed car bombings in London the day before. Six other Muslims were arrested in the plot.

1 Jul 2007, Kennebunkport ME: *(center right)* Russia's President, Vladimir Putin, joined US President Bush for two days of summit talks.

6 Jun 2007, Paris: *(bottom right)* New French President Nicolas Sarkozy, left, walks with outgoing President Jacques Chirac. The rightist Sarkozy defeated Socialist Ségolène Royal in May.

27 Jun 2007, London: *(below)* Gordon Brown took over as Britain's Prime Minister after longtime PM Tony Blair stepped down.

17 Apr 2007, Blacksburg VA:
Students at Virginia Tech
University attend a memorial
vigil after a crazed student
gunman, Cho Seung-Hui, 23,
went on a shooting rampage
that left 32 people dead, then
committed suicide. It was the
deadliest shooting incident in
recent US history.

1 Aug 2007, Minneapolis:
Cars and trucks teeter over the
Mississippi River shortly after
the eight-lane Interstate 35
(I-35W) bridge collapsed during
a Wednesday afternoon rush
hour. Rescue teams recovered
the bodies of 5 victims in the
first days after the tragedy, but
8 people were still missing and
presumed dead as of 6 August;
scores of people were injured.
The bridge, which is estimated
to have been used by as many
as 144,000 cars each day, had
been cited as having structural
problems as early as 1990
and had been scheduled to be
replaced by 2025 at the latest.

5 Jun 2007, Manchester NH: With no clear heir apparent to George W. Bush as leader of the Republican Party, the race for the party's 2008 presidential nomination was regarded as the most wide-open campaign in recent years. GOP hopefuls at an early debate included, from left, Tom Tancredo, Tommy Thompson, Sam Brownback, Mitt Romney, Rudy Giuliani, John McCain, Mike Huckabee, Duncan Hunter, Jim Gilmore, Ron Paul.

3 June 2007, Manchester NH: The race for the Democratic Party nomination also featured an exceptionally large number of prospective candidates early in the campaign season: from left, Mike Gravel, Christopher Dodd, John Edwards, Hillary Clinton, Barack Obama, Bill Richardson, Joseph Biden, Dennis Kucinich.

1 May 2007, Phoenix:
Demonstrators marched as Congress began deliberating a major bipartisan bill that sought to overhaul US immigration policy. The bill failed to pass; critics denounced it as a form of amnesty for illegal immigrants.

19 Apr 2007, Washington:
Attorney General Alberto Gonzales testifies before the Senate Judiciary Committee as controversy raged over the 2006 dismissals of eight US district attorneys.

4 Jan 2007, Washington: Rep. Nancy Pelosi (Dem.-CA) made history by becoming the first woman Speaker of the US House of Representatives.

6 Mar 2007, Washington: I. Lewis (Scooter) Libby, a former top White House aide, was convicted on four of five charges in a CIA leak case and was sentenced to 30 months in prison. In July President Bush commuted his sentence.

Sweet

10 Nov 2006, San Bruno CA: YouTube co-founders Steven Chen, left, and Chad Hurley are all smiles shortly before Internet search giant Google bought their do-it-yourself video website for $1.65 billion. Noting the new era of interactive websites, TIME named "You" the Person of the Year 2006.

11 Jun 2007, San Francisco: Apple co-founder and master pitchman Steve Jobs touts the year's hottest high-tech introduction, the multifunction, sleekly designed iPhone that debuted amid enormous interest later in June.

14 Nov 2006, Toronto: An enthusiast tries out Nintendo's new Wii system as major video-game companies Sony, Nintendo, and Microsoft continued to introduce improved game systems. Nintendo, long in third place, enjoyed success with the Wii system, whose revolutionary wireless system responds to the player's movements. The Wii proved more popular than Sony's new, more expensive PlayStation 3 system.

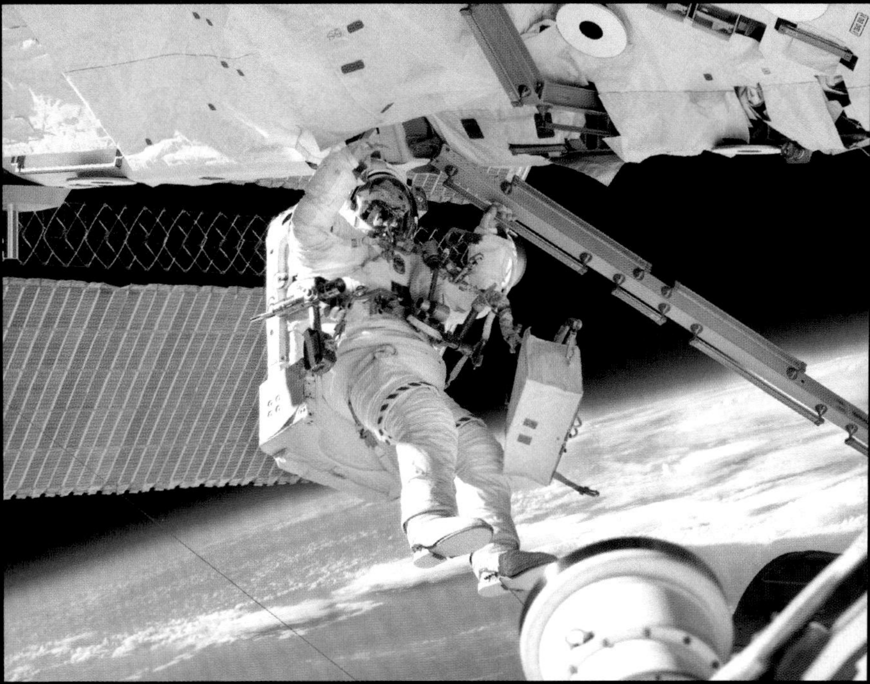

NASA/AP Images

13 Jun 2007, Earth orbit: US astronaut Steven Swanson works on a solar-power array outside the International Space Station. Swanson and felllow astronauts aboard the space shuttle *Atlantis* visited the station to install new support trusses and solar arrays on the growing orbiting laboratory.

Institute of Vertebrate Paleontology & Paleoanthropology, Beijing—AP Images

13 Jun 2007, Beijing: Chinese scientists announced the discovery of an enormous dinosaur with several birdlike qualities, including feathered arms; above, an artist's concept. The beast, christened *Giganto-raptor erlianensis*, was roughly the size of famed predator *Tyrannosaurus rex*, at some 26 ft. in length.

8 Feb 2007, Jakarta: Residents battled severe floods as massive rainfall left some 400,000 people homeless in Indonesia. A United Nations report issued in February 2007 linked the increasing frequency of extreme weather conditions to the warming climate of the planet. The UN report cited "very high confidence" that man-made hydrocarbon emissions have contributed significantly to global warming.

7 Jun 2007, Heiligendamm, Germany: Leaders of major world nations, including, from left, Tony Blair (UK), George W. Bush (US), Angela Merkel (Germany), and Vladimir Putin (Russia), convened for their annual G-8 summit. Before the conference, President Bush called for voluntary national caps on hydrocarbon emisssions; he rejected mandatory caps proposed by Merkel and other leaders at the summit.

22 Jan 2007, Westlake Village CA: Firefighters battle a wildfire threatening homes. As the planet's climate heats up, experts predict, wildfires will become both more frequent and more intense.

7 Aug 2007, San Francisco: Slugger Barry Bonds of the Giants smacks home run No. 756 to top Hank Aaron on the total career homers list. Bonds, believed by some to have used steroids in the past, strongly denies having done so and remains a highly controversial figure.

14 Jun 2007, Cleveland: *(below)* Peter Holt, owner of the San Antonio Spurs, lofts the NBA championship trophy after the Spurs swept the Cleveland Cavaliers and their superstar LeBron James in four games to win the team's fourth NBA title in nine years. Led by forward Tim Duncan, the Spurs cemented their claim to being one of the game's great dynasties.

8 Jul 2007, London: Tying a record held by Björn Borg, Swiss ace Roger Federer beat Spain's Rafael Nadal to win his fifth Wimbledon tournament in a row.

7 Jul 2007, London: Venus Williams beat Marion Bartoli to win her fourth Wimbledon singles title.

27 Jun 2007, Valencia, Spain: *(above)* Crew members scramble aloft to trim sails as yachts representing Switzerland, left, and New Zealand compete for the America's Cup. The Swiss team won the trophy.

10 Jun 2007, Paris: *(left)* The colorful Rafael Nadal reacts as he defeats Roger Federer to win the French Open tennis championship, played on a clay surface. The Nadal-Federer matchup is fast becoming one of the game's classic rivalries.

11 Jul 2007: *Harry Potter and the Order of the Phoenix,* the fifth film in the highly popular series, was released ten days before the long-awaited final book in J.K. Rowling's set of seven novels of teenage wizardry appeared. From left, Daniel Radcliffe (Harry), Rupert Grint (Ron), and Emma Watson (Hermione

10 Jun 2007, New York City: The cast of rock musical *Spring Awakening* performs at the Tony Awards. The show, based on

25 May 2007: In a summer movie season filled with sequels and "threequels," Keira Knightley and Johnny Depp reprised their roles as a sassy heroine and woozy

Will Hart—HBO

0 Jun 2007: *The Sopranos*, HBO's award-winning, highly popular series based on the lives of a New ersey Mafia family, ended its eight-year run with an enigmatic, inconclusive final scene that many fans nd critics declared unsatisfying. Above, stars James Gandolfini, Edie Falco, and Robert Iler.

Jul 2007, London: Fergie (Stacy Ann Ferguson) of the US hip-hop group Black Eyed Peas performs at he Live Earth concert at Wembley Stadium. The Live Earth concerts, designed to raise awareness of lobal warming as an international issue, were staged in 11 locations on a single day and featured some 50 performers. The various shows were watched by an international television and Internet audience

Lady Bird Johnson: The former First Lady, a life-long counselor to her husband Lyndon and an effective advocate for beautifying the nation, died at 94.

Jerry Falwell: The Baptist minister, who helped found the Moral Majority in 1979 and was a strong spokesman for the religious right, died at 73.

Boris Yeltsin: The former president of Russia, who helped turn back a communist coup in 1991 but later became highly unpopular, died at 76.

Beverly Sills: Opera's beloved, down-to-earth soprano, who also led New York City's Lincoln Center arts complex, died at 78.

Kurt Vonnegut, Jr.: The novelist of darkly satiric visions, a World War II veteran, died at 84.

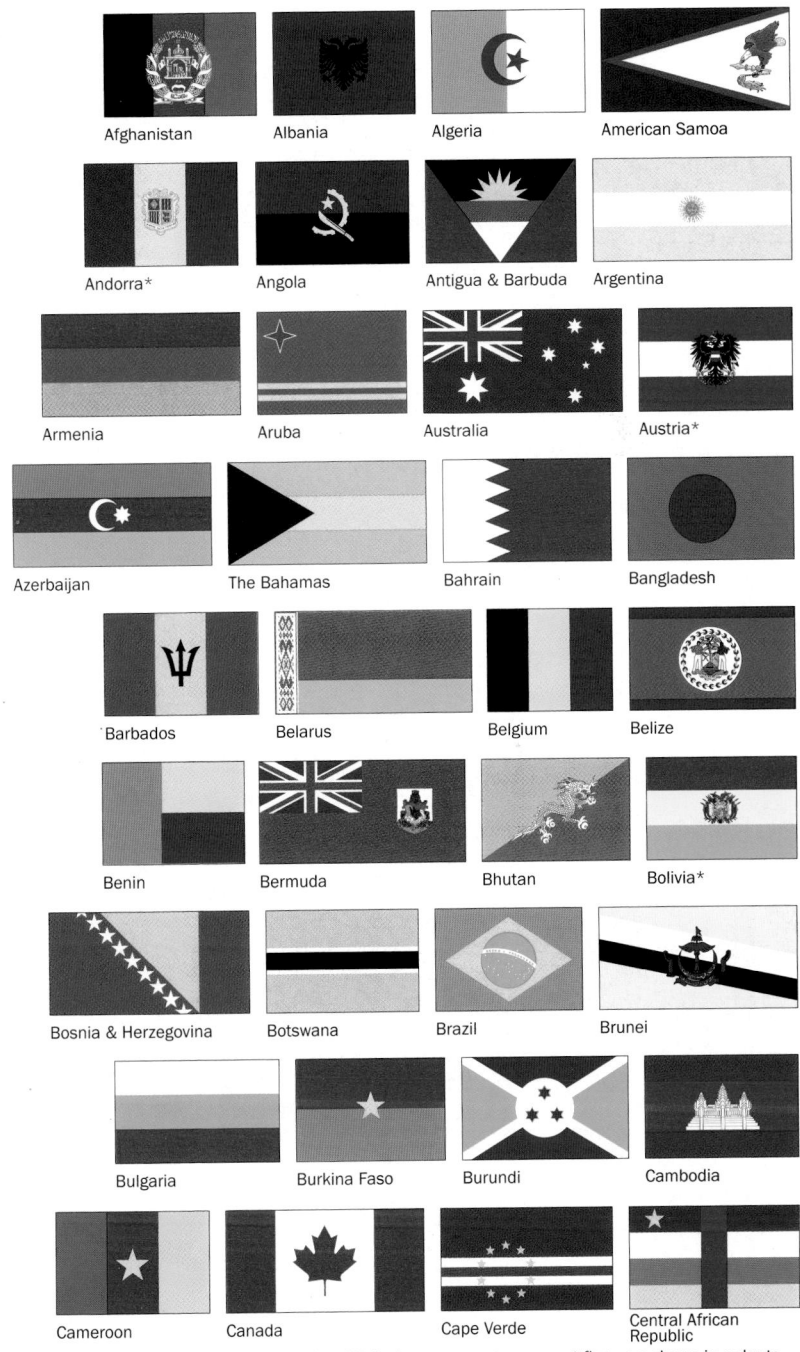

Afghanistan Albania Algeria American Samoa

Andorra* Angola Antigua & Barbuda Argentina

Armenia Aruba Australia Austria*

Azerbaijan The Bahamas Bahrain Bangladesh

Barbados Belarus Belgium Belize

Benin Bermuda Bhutan Bolivia*

Bosnia & Herzegovina Botswana Brazil Brunei

Bulgaria Burkina Faso Burundi Cambodia

Cameroon Canada Cape Verde Central African Republic

Civil flags are shown except where marked thus (*); in these cases, government flags are shown in order to illustrate emblems. Both styles are official national flags.

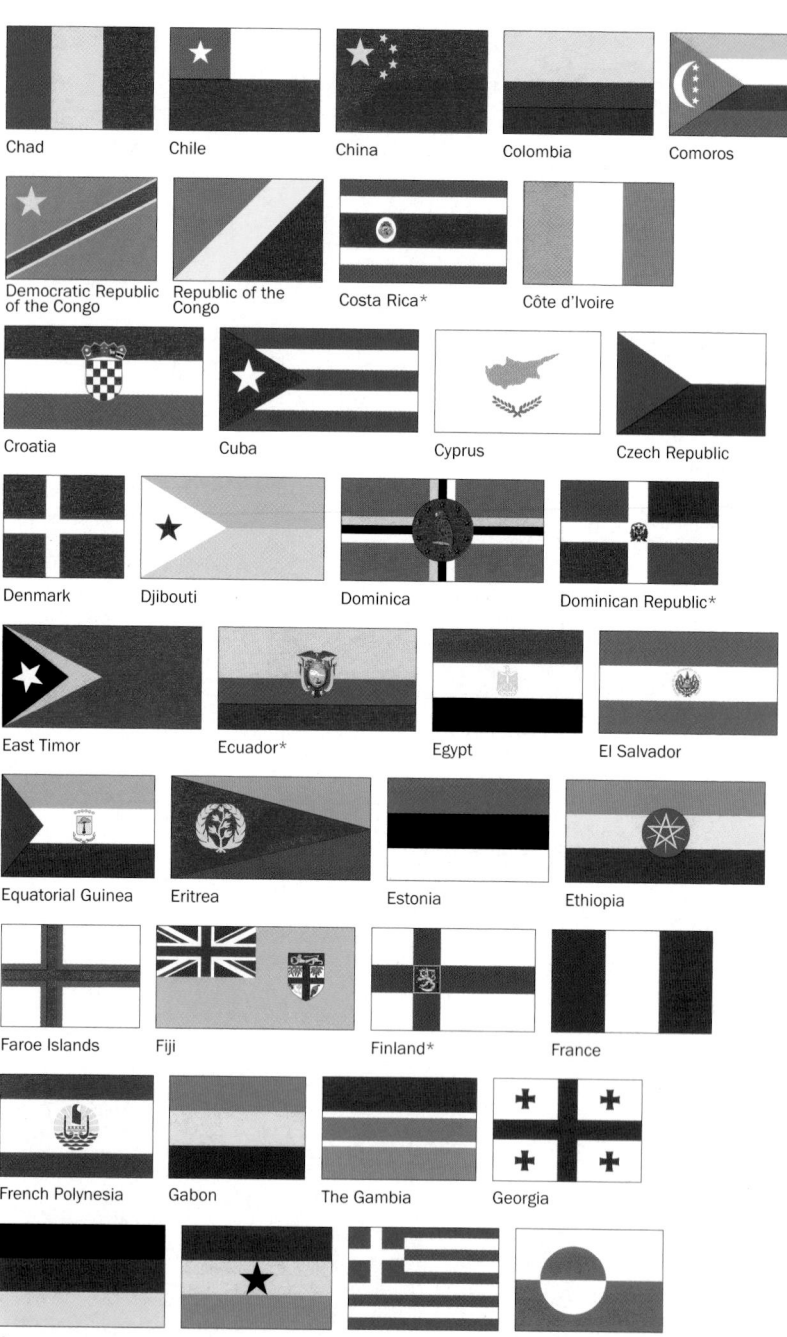

Chad

Chile

China

Colombia

Comoros

Democratic Republic of the Congo

Republic of the Congo

Costa Rica*

Côte d'Ivoire

Croatia

Cuba

Cyprus

Czech Republic

Denmark

Djibouti

Dominica

Dominican Republic*

East Timor

Ecuador*

Egypt

El Salvador

Equatorial Guinea

Eritrea

Estonia

Ethiopia

Faroe Islands

Fiji

Finland*

France

French Polynesia

Gabon

The Gambia

Georgia

Germany

Ghana

Greece

Greenland

Civil flags are shown except where marked thus (*); in these cases, government flags are shown in order to illustrate emblems. Both styles are official national flags.

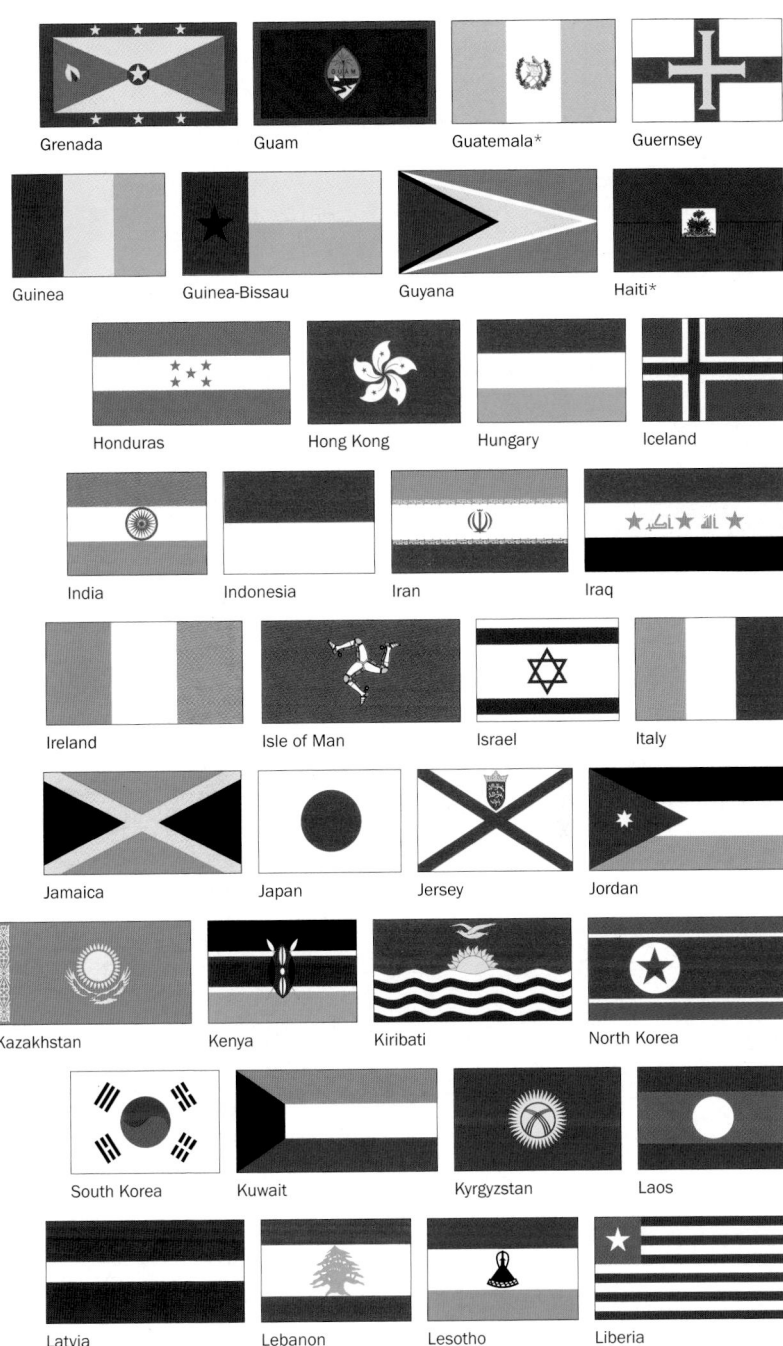

Grenada · Guam · Guatemala* · Guernsey

Guinea · Guinea-Bissau · Guyana · Haiti*

Honduras · Hong Kong · Hungary · Iceland

India · Indonesia · Iran · Iraq

Ireland · Isle of Man · Israel · Italy

Jamaica · Japan · Jersey · Jordan

Kazakhstan · Kenya · Kiribati · North Korea

South Korea · Kuwait · Kyrgyzstan · Laos

Latvia · Lebanon · Lesotho · Liberia

Civil flags are shown except where marked thus (*); in these cases, government flags are shown in order to illustrate emblems. Both styles are official national flags.

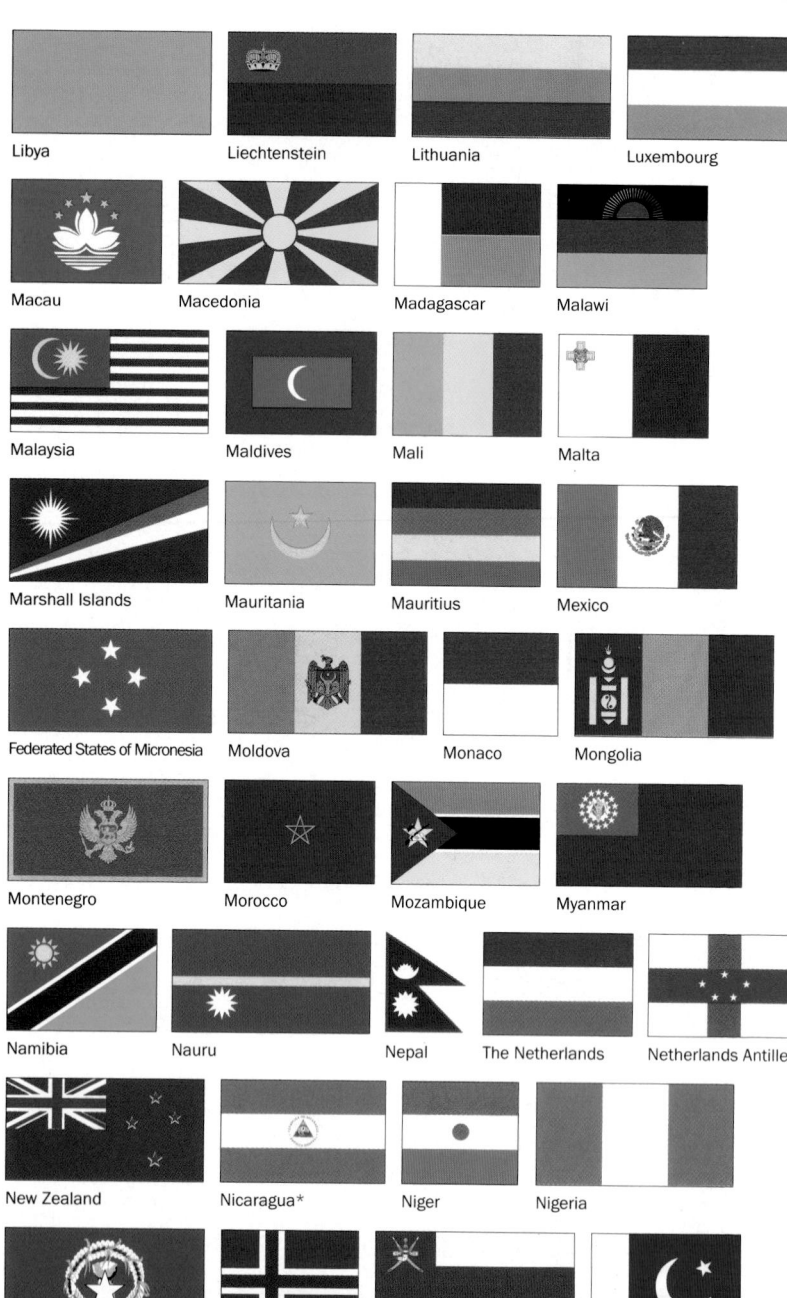

Libya   Liechtenstein   Lithuania   Luxembourg

Macau   Macedonia   Madagascar   Malawi

Malaysia   Maldives   Mali   Malta

Marshall Islands   Mauritania   Mauritius   Mexico

Federated States of Micronesia   Moldova   Monaco   Mongolia

Montenegro   Morocco   Mozambique   Myanmar

Namibia   Nauru   Nepal   The Netherlands   Netherlands Antilles

New Zealand   Nicaragua*   Niger   Nigeria

Northern Mariana Islands   Norway   Oman   Pakistan

Civil flags are shown except where marked thus (*); in these cases, government flags are shown in order to illustrate emblems. Both styles are official national flags.

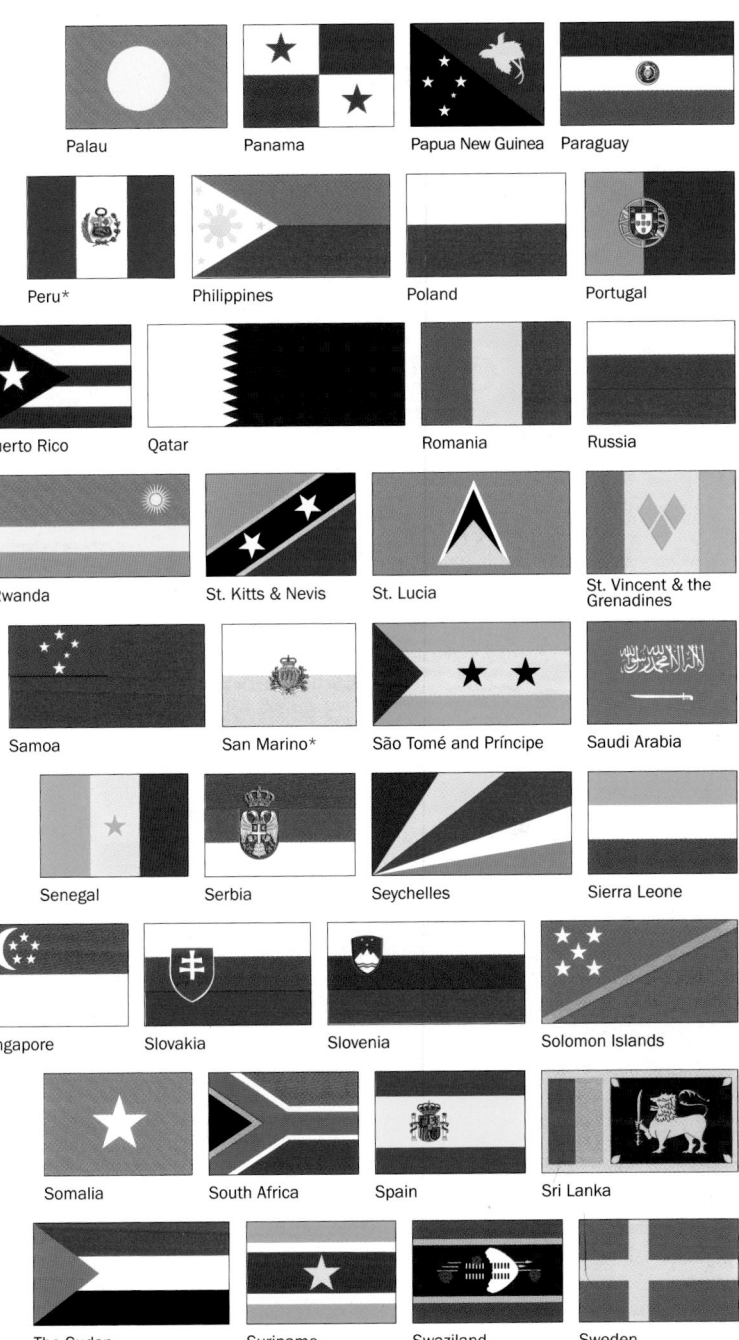

Palau   Panama   Papua New Guinea   Paraguay

Peru*   Philippines   Poland   Portugal

Puerto Rico   Qatar   Romania   Russia

Rwanda   St. Kitts & Nevis   St. Lucia   St. Vincent & the Grenadines

Samoa   San Marino*   São Tomé and Príncipe   Saudi Arabia

Senegal   Serbia   Seychelles   Sierra Leone

Singapore   Slovakia   Slovenia   Solomon Islands

Somalia   South Africa   Spain   Sri Lanka

The Sudan   Suriname   Swaziland   Sweden

Civil flags are shown except where marked thus (*); in these cases, government flags are shown in order to illustrate emblems. Both styles are official national flags.

Switzerland    Syria    Taiwan    Tajikistan

Tanzania    Thailand    Togo    Tonga

Trinidad & Tobago    Tunisia    Turkey    Turkmenistan

Tuvalu    Uganda   Ukraine    United Arab Emirates

United Kingdom    United States    Uruguay

Uzbekistan    Vanuatu    Vatican City    Venezuela*

Vietnam    Virgin Islands (US)   Yemen    Zambia

Zimbabwe

Civil flags are shown except where marked thus (*); in these cases, government flags are shown in order to illustrate emblems. Both styles are official national flags.

World Religions

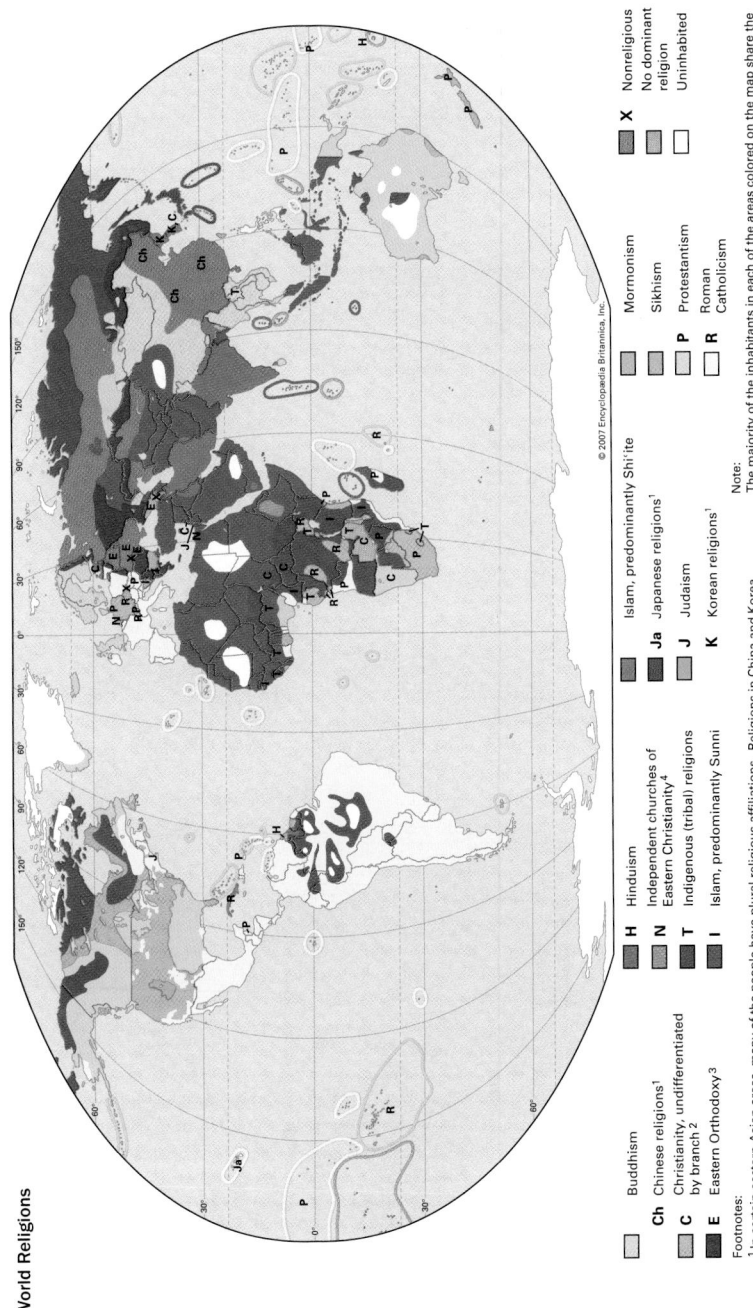

© 2007 Encyclopædia Britannica, Inc.

Buddhism

Ch Chinese religions[1]

C Christianity, undifferentiated by branch[2]

E Eastern Orthodoxy[3]

H Hinduism

N Independent churches of Eastern Christianity[4]

T Indigenous (tribal) religions

I Islam, predominantly Sunni

Islam, predominantly Shi'ite

Ja Japanese religions[1]

J Judaism

K Korean religions[1]

Mormonism

Sikhism

P Protestantism

R Roman Catholicism

X Nonreligious

No dominant religion

Uninhabited

Note:
The majority of the inhabitants in each of the areas colored on the map share the religious tradition indicated. Letter symbols show religious traditions shared by at least 25 percent of the inhabitants within areas no smaller than 1,000 square miles. Therefore minority religions of city dwellers have generally not been represented.

Footnotes:
[1] In certain eastern Asian areas, many of the people have plural religious affiliations. Religions in China and Korea include Buddhism, Taoism, Confucianism, and folk cults. The Japanese religions include Shinto and Buddhism.
[2] Chiefly mingled Protestantism and Roman Catholicism, neither predominant.
[3] Including Greek and Russian Orthodox Christianity.
[4] Including Armenian, Coptic, Ethiopian, East and West Syrian.

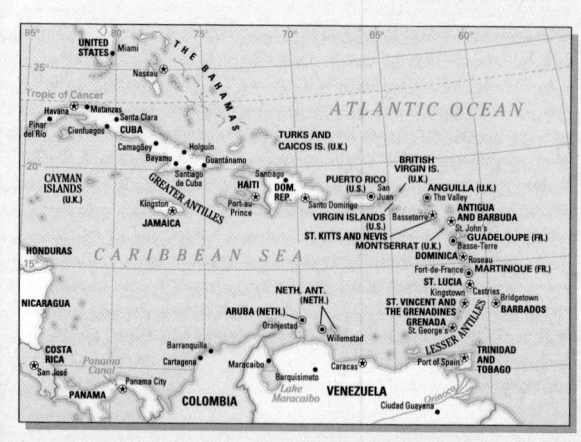
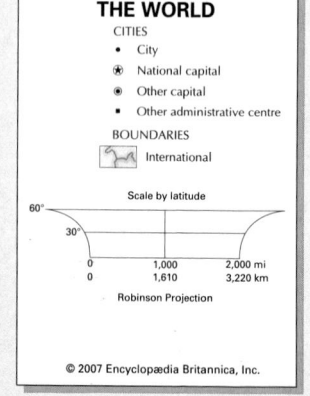

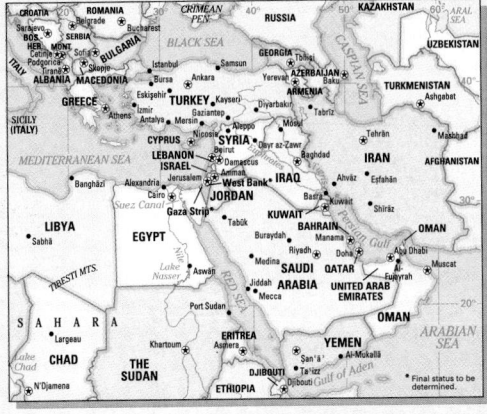

Africa

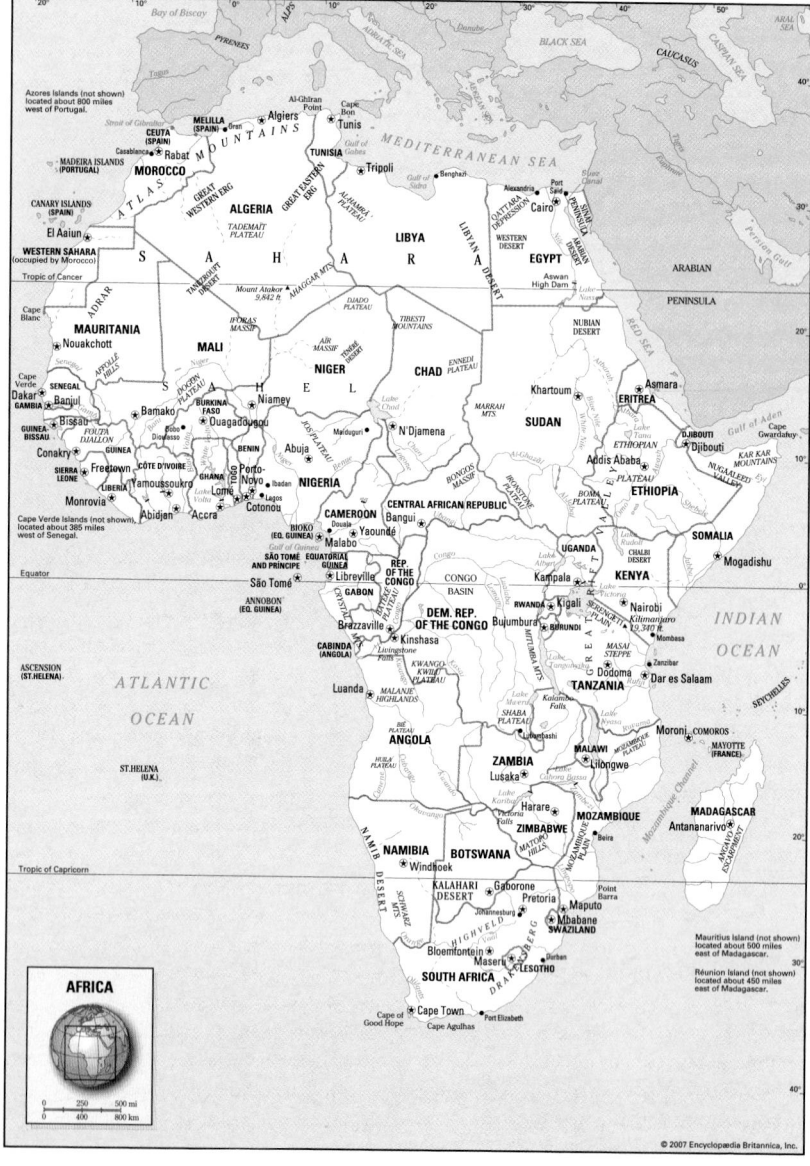

© 2007 Encyclopædia Britannica, Inc.

Asia

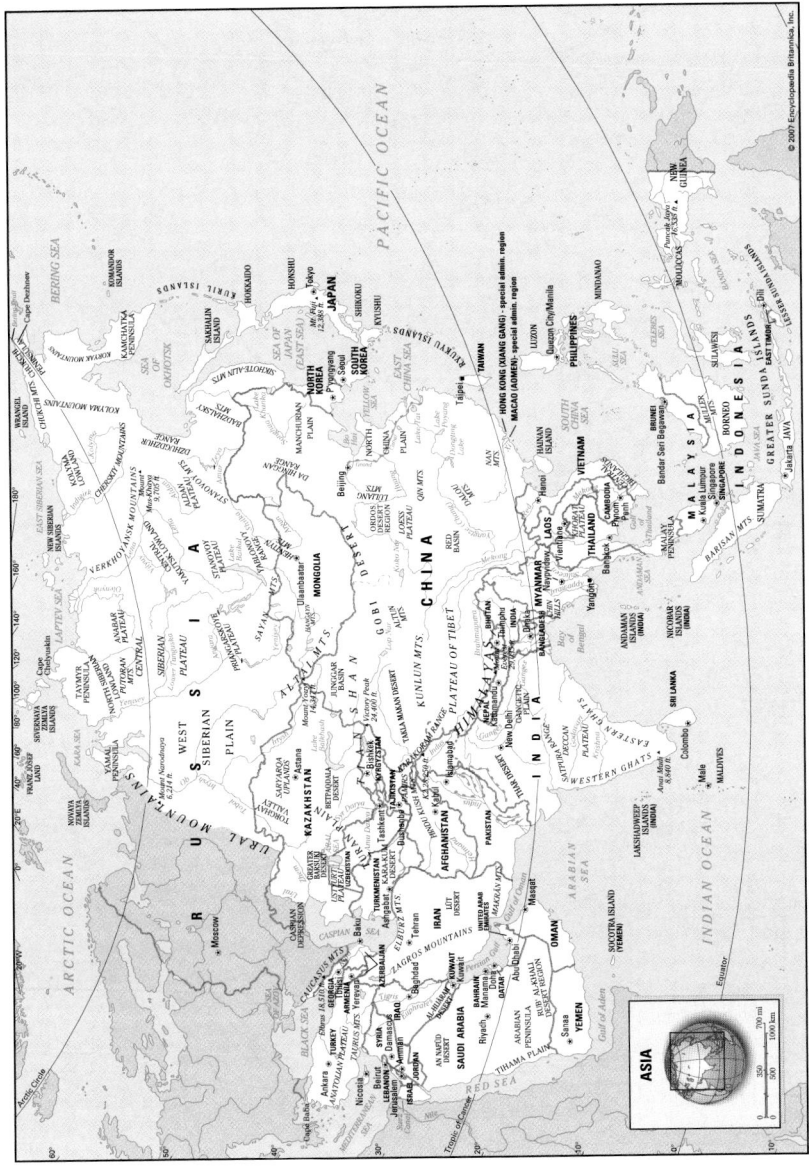

© 2007 Encyclopædia Britannica, Inc.

Europe

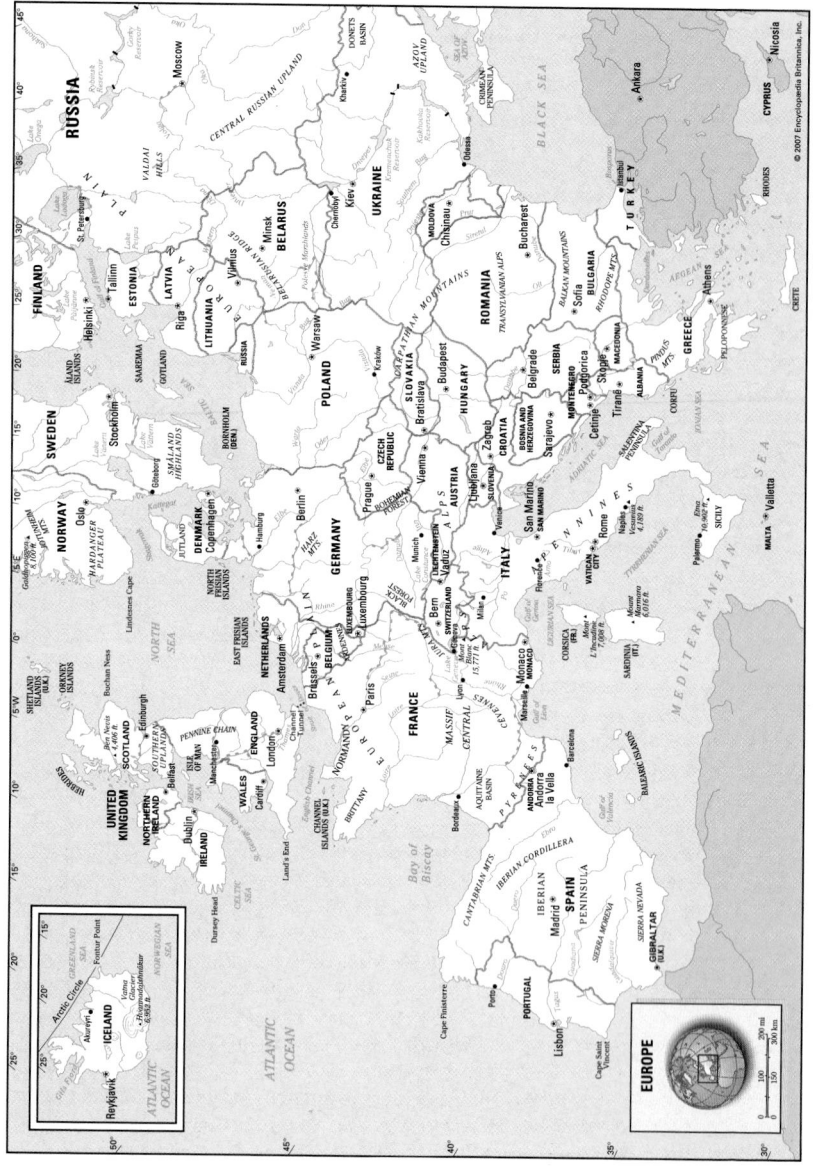

North America

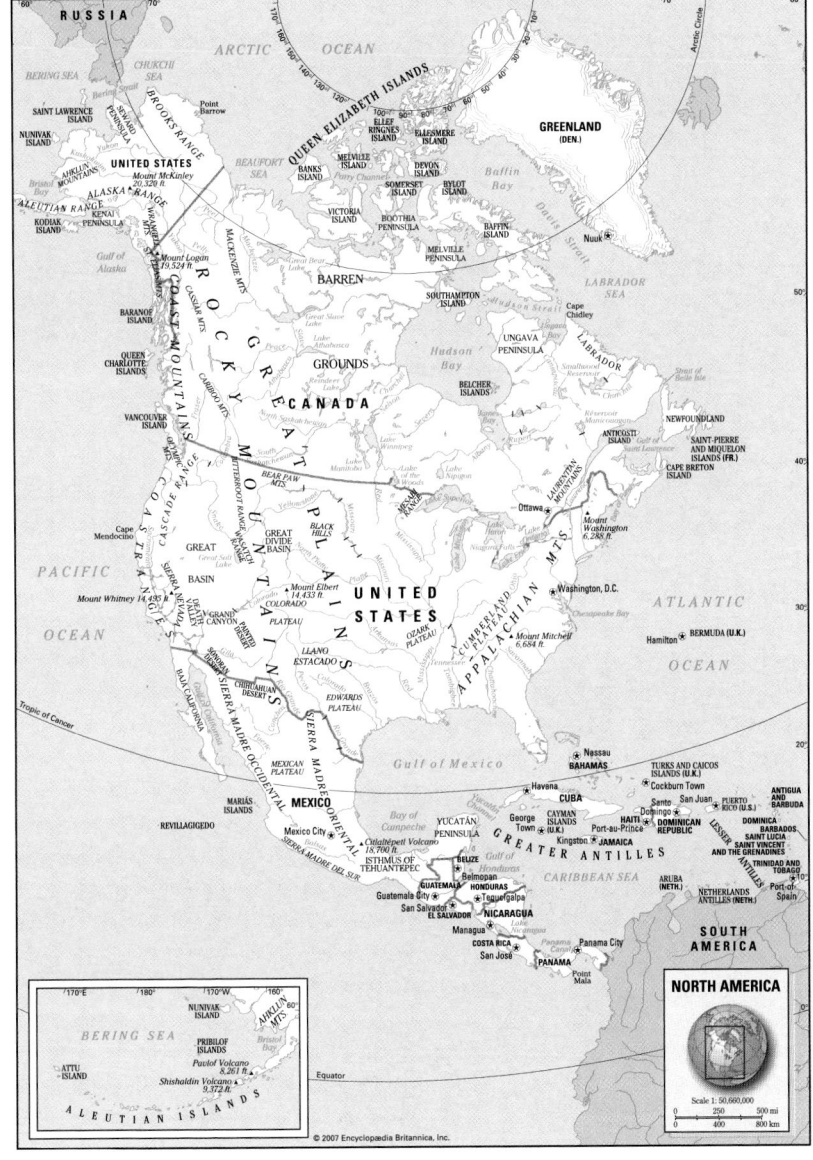

NORTH AMERICA

Scale 1: 50,660,000

© 2007 Encyclopædia Britannica, Inc.

South America

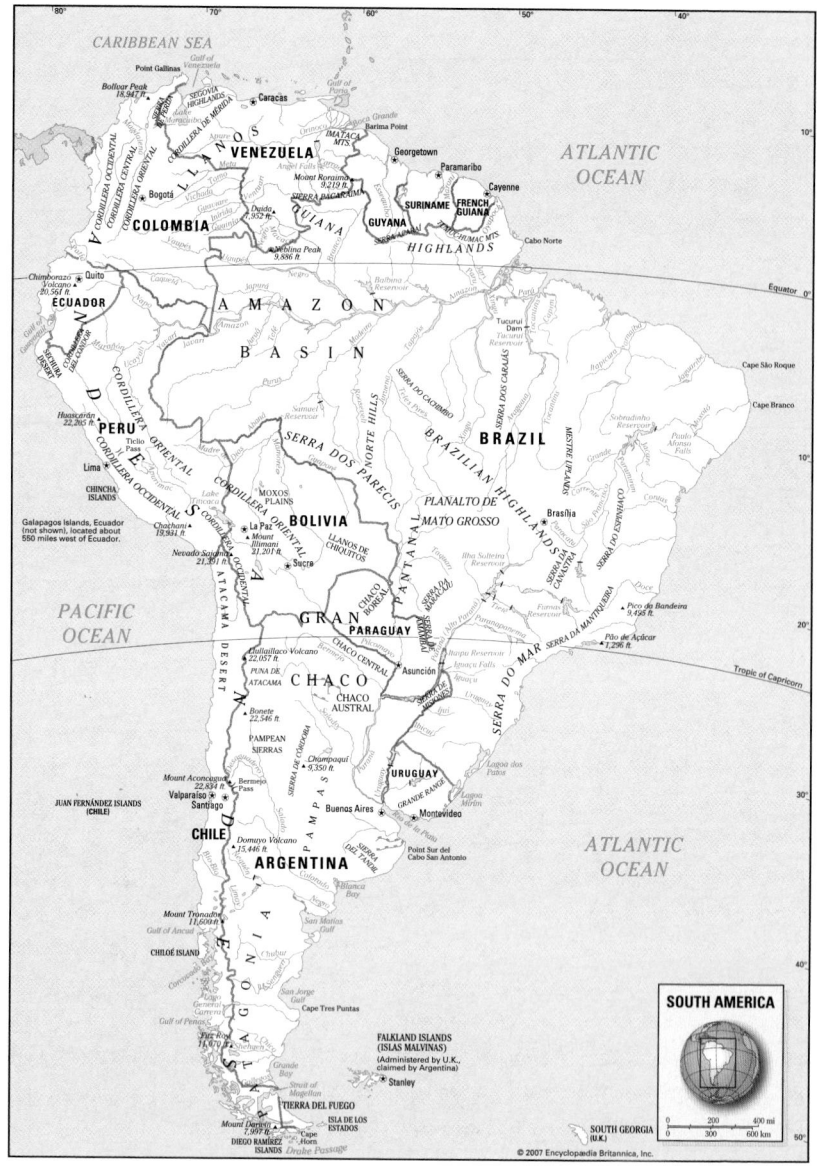

Australia

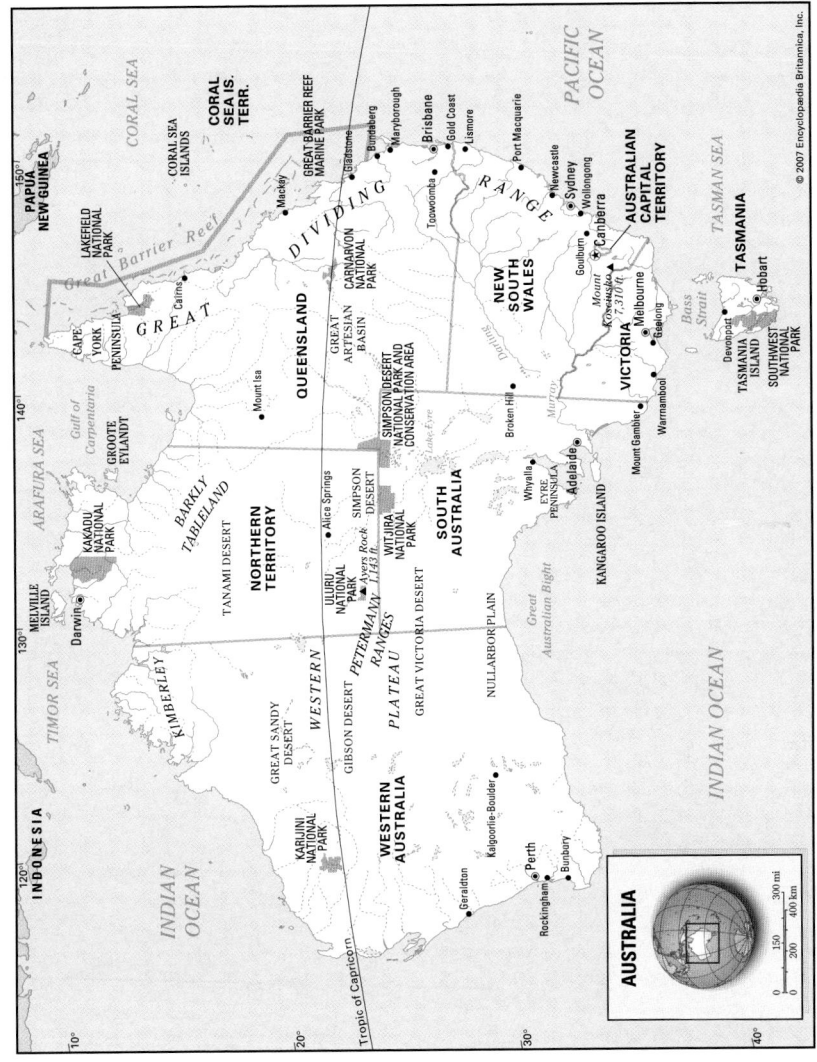

© 2007 Encyclopædia Britannica, Inc.

Oceania/Pacific Islands

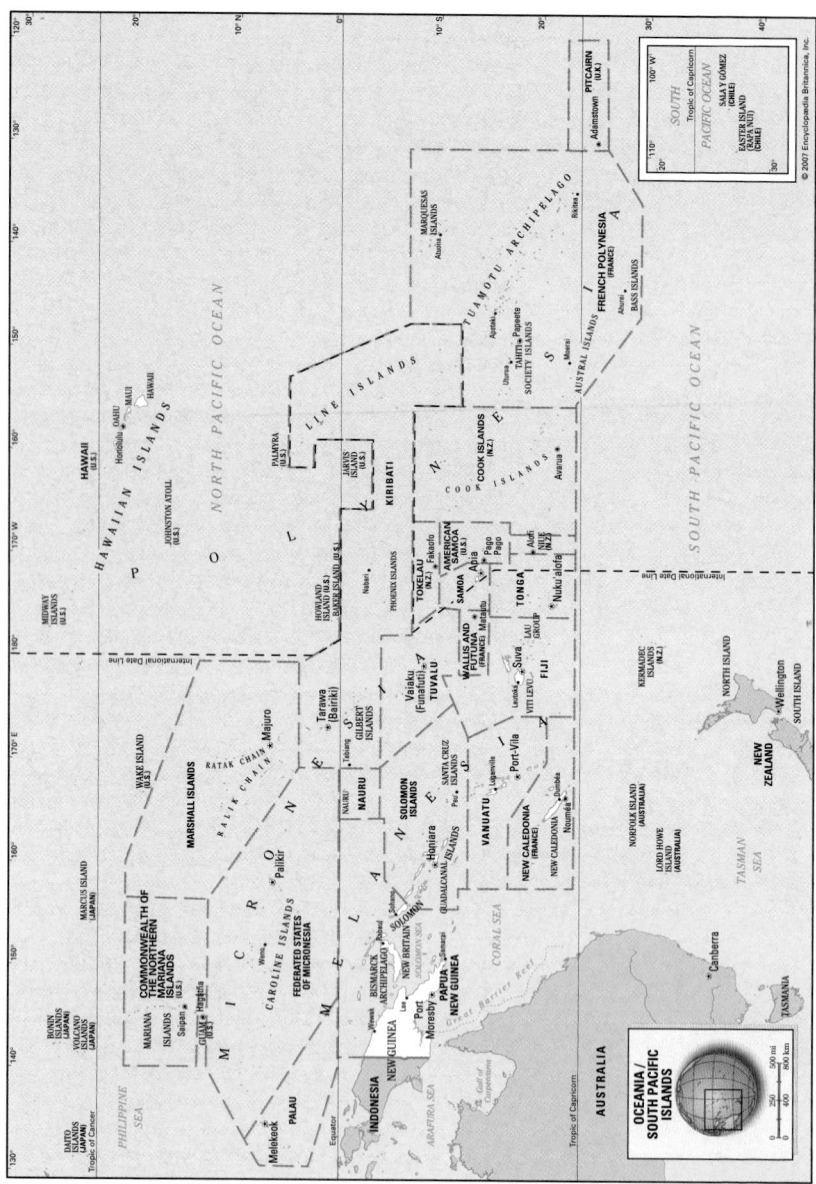

and over literate 791,000 (31.4%); males literate 555,000 (45.4%); females literate 236,000 (18.2%). **Health:** physicians (1996) 339 (1 per 13,696 persons); hospital beds (1998) 3,364 (1 per 1,250 persons); infant mortality rate per 1,000 live births (2003) 146.9. **Food** (2001): daily per capita caloric intake 1,874 (vegetable products 97%, animal products 3%); 81% of FAO recommended minimum.

Military

Total active duty personnel (2003): 14,000 (army 98.6%, navy 1.4%, air force, none); UN peacekeeping troops (September 2004) 8,500. **Military expenditure as percentage of GNP** (1999): 3.0% (world 2.4%); per capita expenditure $4.

Background

The earliest inhabitants of Sierra Leone were probably the Buloms; the Mende and Temne peoples arrived in the 15th century. The coastal region was visited by the Portuguese in the 15th century, and by 1495 there was a Portuguese fort on the site of modern Freetown. European ships visited the coast regularly to trade for slaves and ivory, and the English built trading posts on offshore islands in the 17th century. British abolitionists and philanthropists founded Freetown in 1787 as a private venture for freed and runaway slaves. In 1808 the coastal settlement became a British colony. The region became a British protectorate in 1896. It achieved independence in 1961 and became a republic in 1971. It was marked by political and economic turmoil in the late 20th century as successive military regimes tried to assume power. UN peacekeeping forces were stationed there but were ineffectual in preventing bloodletting and atrocities.

Recent Developments

Sierra Leone continued to recover from the effects of the 11-year civil war that ended in 2002. In December 2005 the UN Mission in Sierra Leone left the country, having completed its mandate. That year the Group of Eight countries canceled the debt of the country, which had the lowest GDP per capita in the world in 2004. In April 2006 former Liberian leader Charles Taylor was transported to Sierra Leone, where he was charged with 17 counts of crimes against humanity for his actions during the civil war.

Internet resources: <www.sierra-leone.org>.

Singapore

Official name: Hsin-chia-p'o Kung-ho-kuo (Mandarin Chinese); Republik Singapura (Malay); Singapore Kudiyarasu (Tamil); Republic of Singapore (English). **Form of government:** unitary multiparty republic with one legislative house (Parliament [90, including 6 nonelective seats]). **Head of state:** President Sellapan Rama (S.R.) Nathan (from 1999). **Head of state government:** Prime Minister Lee Hsien Loong (from 2004). **Capital:** Singapore. **Official languages:** Chinese; Malay; Tamil; English. **Official religion:** none. **Monetary unit:** 1 Singapore dollar (S$) = 100 cents; valuation (1 Jul 2007) US$1 = S$1.53.

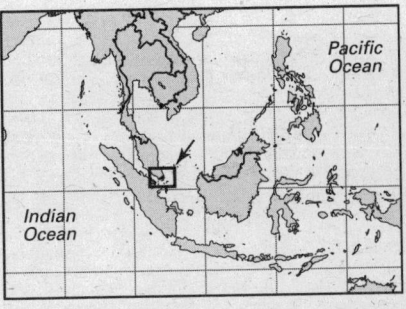

Demography

Area: 270.0 sq mi, 699.4 sq km. **Population** (2006): 4,408,000. **Density** (2006): persons per sq mi 16,326, persons per sq km 6,303. **Urban:** 100%. **Sex distribution** (2003): male 49.75%; female 50.25%. **Age breakdown** (2003): under 15, 20.8%; 15–29, 20.2%; 30–44, 27.4%; 45–59, 20.4%; 60–74, 8.5%; 75 and over, 2.7%. **Ethnic composition** (2003): Chinese 76.3%; Malay 13.8%; Indian 8.3%; other 1.6%. **Religious affiliation** (2000): Buddhist 42.5%; Muslim 14.9%; Christian 14.6%; Taoist 8.5%; Hindu 4.0%; traditional beliefs 0.6%; nonreligious 14.9%. **Location:** southeastern Asia, islands between Malaysia and Indonesia.

Vital statistics

Birth rate per 1,000 population (2003): 10.4 (world avg. 21.3). **Death rate** per 1,000 population (2003): 4.4 (world avg. 9.1). **Natural increase rate** per 1,000 population (2003): 6.0 (world avg. 12.2). **Total fertility rate** (avg. births per childbearing woman; 2003): 1.3. **Marriage rate** per 1,000 population (2003): 6.4. **Life expectancy** at birth (2003): male 76.9 years; female 80.9 years.

National economy

Budget (2003). *Revenue:* S$24,659,200,000 (income tax 42.2%, nontax revenue 14.6%, goods and services tax 11.0%, customs and excise duties 7.3%, motor vehicle taxes 5.3%). *Expenditures:* S$27,189,-300,000 (security 34.0%, development expenditure 29.3%, education 17.9%, health 6.1%, trade and industry 1.9%). **Production** (metric tons except as noted). *Agriculture and fishing* (2003): vegetables and fruits 5,010; livestock (number of live animals) 250,000 pigs, 2,000,000 chickens; fish catch (2001) 8,704. *Mining and quarrying* (value of output in S$; 1994): granite 75,800,000. *Manufacturing* (value added in US$'000,000; 2001): office, accounting, and computer equipment 5,576; electronic valves and tubes 4,829; chemicals and chemical products 4,209. *Energy production (consumption):* electricity (kW-hr; 2000) 31,665,000,000 (31,665,000,000); crude petroleum (barrels; 2000) none (306,629,000); petroleum products (2000) 27,613,000 (10,790,000); natural gas (cu m; 2000) none (1,411,000,000). **Household income and expenditure.** Average household size (2002) 4.2; income per household (2000) S$59,316; expenditure (1998): food 23.7%, transportation and communications 22.8%, housing costs and furnishings 21.6%, education 6.9%, clothing and footwear 4.1%, health 3.3%, other 17.6%. **Tourism**

(2002): receipts from visitors US$4,932,000,000; expenditures by nationals abroad US$5,213,000,000. **Gross national product** (2003): US$90,228,000,000 (US$21,230 per capita). **Population economically active** (2003): total 2,150,100; activity rate of total population 62.6% (participation rates: ages 15 and over, 64.2%; female 53.9%; unemployed 4.6%). **Land use** as % of total land area (2000): in temporary and permanent crops 1.4%; overall forest area 3.3%.

Foreign trade

Imports (2003-c.i.f.): S$222,811,000,000 (electronic valves [including integrated circuits and semiconductors] 21.7%; crude and refined petroleum 13.5%; computers and related parts 11.2%; chemicals and chemical products 6.7%; telecommunications equipment 4.0%). *Major import sources:* Malaysia 16.8%; US 13.9%; Japan 12.0%; China 8.7%; Taiwan 5.1%; Thailand 4.3%. **Exports** (2003-f.o.b.): S$251,096,-000,000 (electronic valves 20.9%; computers and related parts 17.9%; chemicals and chemical products 11.8%, of which organic chemicals 6.4%; crude and refined petroleum 10.9%; telecommunications equipment 4.6%). *Major export destinations:* Malaysia 15.8%; US 13.3%; Hong Kong 10.0%; China 7.0%; Japan 6.7%; Taiwan 4.8%; Thailand 4.3%.

Transport and communications

Transport. *Railroads* (2003): length 131 km. *Roads* (2003): total length 3,144 km (paved 99%). *Vehicles* (2003): passenger cars 424,712; trucks and buses 138,538. *Air transport* (2003): passenger-km 65,376,000,000; metric ton-km cargo 6,683,000,-000; airports (2003) 1. **Communications,** in total units (units per 1,000 persons). Daily newspaper circulation (2000): 1,197,301 (298); radios (2000): 2,700,000 (672); televisions (2000): 1,220,000 (304); telephone main lines (2002): 1,927,200 (463); cellular telephone subscribers (2002): 3,312,600 (795); personal computers (2002): 2,590,000 (622); Internet users (2002): 2,100,000 (504).

Education and health

Educational attainment (2000). Percentage of population age 15 and over having: no schooling 19.6%; primary education 23.1%; secondary 39.5%; postsecondary 17.8%. **Literacy** (2003): total population age 15 and over literate 94.2%. **Health** (2003): physicians 6,292 (1 per 670 persons); hospital beds 11,855 (1 per 290 persons); infant mortality rate per 1,000 live births 2.2. **Food** (1988–90): daily per capita caloric intake 3,121 (vegetable products 76%, animal products 24%); 136% of FAO recommended minimum.

Military

Total active duty personnel (2003): 72,500 (army 69.0%, navy 12.4%, air force 18.6%). **Military expenditure as percentage of GNP** (1999): 4.8% (world 2.4%); per capita expenditure US$1,100.

Background

Long inhabited by fishermen and pirates, Singapore was an outpost of the Sumatran empire of Srivijaya until the 14th century, when it passed to Java and then Siam. It became part of the Malacca empire in the 15th century. In the 16th century the Portuguese controlled the area; they were followed by the Dutch in the 17th century. In 1819 Singapore was ceded to the British East India Co., becoming part of the Straits Settlements and the center of British colonial activity in southeast Asia. The Japanese occupied the islands in 1942–45. In 1946 it became a crown colony. It achieved full internal self-government in 1959, became a part of Malaysia in 1963, and gained independence in 1965. It is influential in the affairs of the Association of Southeast Asian Nations. The country's dominant voice in politics for 30 years after independence was Lee Kuan Yew.

Recent Developments

Singapore hosted a series of World Bank–IMF meetings, which drew to a close in January 2006. The event was the biggest international conference ever organized by Singapore. The government, eager for all to go well, barred 27 nongovernmental organization activists. The decision generated controversy, and eventually Singapore allowed all but five to attend. Official sanction was given for casinos in Singapore. Plans were made for two major casino resorts to open within the next five years, one in the downtown Marina Bay area, to be run by Las Vegas Sands, and the other on the resort island of Sentosa.

Internet resources: <www.sg>.

Slovakia

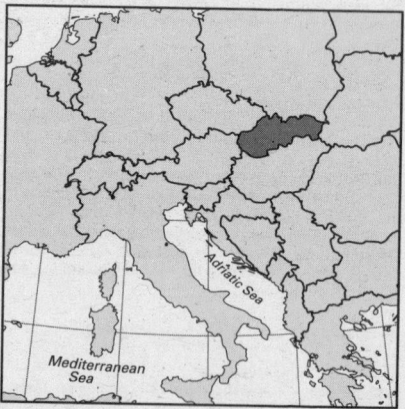

Official name: Slovenska Republika (Slovak Republic). **Form of government:** unitary multiparty republic with one legislative house (National Council [150]). **Chief of state:** President Ivan Gasparovic (from 2004). **Head of government:** Prime Minister Robert Fico (since 2006). **Capital:** Bratislava. **Official language:** Slovak. **Official religion:** none. **Monetary unit:** 1 Slovak koruna (Sk) = 100 halura; valuation (1 Jul 2007) US$1 = Sk 24.80.

---

1 metric ton = about 1.1 short tons; 1 kilometer = 0.6 mi (statute); 1 metric ton-km cargo = about 0.68 short ton-mi cargo; c.i.f.: cost, insurance, and freight; f.o.b.: free on board

Demography

Area: 18,933 sq mi, 49,035 sq km. **Population** (2006): 5,391,000. **Density** (2006): persons per sq mi 284.7, persons per sq km 109.9. **Urban** (2002): 57.6%. **Sex distribution** (2004): male 48.53%; female 51.47%. **Age breakdown** (2001): under 15, 18.9%; 15–29, 25.1%; 30–44, 21.5%; 45–59, 18.9%; 60–74, 11.0%; 75 and over, 4.6%. **Ethnic composition** (2001): Slovak 85.8%; Hungarian 9.7%; Rom (Gypsy) 1.7%; Czech 0.8%; Ruthenian and Ukrainian 0.7%; other 1.3%. **Religious affiliation** (2001): Roman Catholic 68.9%; Protestant 9.2%, of which Slovak Evangelical 6.9%, Reformed Christian 2.0%; Greek Catholic 4.1%; Eastern Orthodox 0.9%; nonreligious and other 16.9%. **Major cities** (2001): Bratislava 428,672; Kosice 236,093; Presov 92,786; Nitra 87,285; Zilina 85,400. **Location:** central Europe, bordering Poland, Ukraine, Hungary, Austria, and the Czech Republic.

Vital statistics

Birth rate per 1,000 population (2003): 9.6 (world avg. 21.3); (2001) legitimate 80.2%. **Death rate** per 1,000 population (2003): 9.7 (world avg. 9.1). **Natural increase rate** per 1,000 population (2003): −0.1 (world avg. 12.2). **Total fertility rate** (avg. births per childbearing woman; 2002): 1.3. **Marriage rate** per 1,000 population (2003): 4.8. **Divorce rate** per 1,000 population (2003): 2.0. **Life expectancy** at birth (2002): male 69.6 years; female 77.7 years.

National economy

Budget (2002). *Revenue:* Sk 391,800,000,000 (tax revenue 88.1%, of which social security contribution 35.6%, value-added tax 21.0%, income tax 11.9%; nontax revenue 11.9%). *Expenditures:* Sk 459,300,-000,000 (current expenditures 88.9%, of which social welfare 26.5%, wages 14.4%, health 11.7%, debt service 8.3%; investment 11.1%). **Production** (metric tons except as noted). *Agriculture, forestry, fishing* (2002): wheat 1,554,000, sugar beets 1,340,000, corn (maize) 754,000; livestock (number of live animals) 1,554,000 pigs, 608,000 cattle, 316,000 sheep; roundwood (2002) 5,765,400 cu m; fish catch (2001) 3,142. *Mining and quarrying* (2001): iron ore (metal content) 300,000; gold 157 kg. *Manufacturing* (value added in $'000,000; 1998): food products 289; nonelectrical machinery 280; iron and steel 232. *Energy production (consumption):* electricity (kW-hr; 2002) 32,436,-000,000 ([2000] 29,297,000,000); hard coal (2000) none (4,656,000); lignite (2001) 3,424,000 ([2000] 4,213,000); crude petroleum (barrels; 2001) 400,000 ([2000] 42,822,000); petroleum products (2000) 4,181,000 (1,777,000); natural gas (cu m; 2001) 212,000,000 ([2000] 6,886,-000,000). **Population economically active** (2001): total 2,665,837; activity rate of total population 49.6% (participation rates: ages 15–64, 79.6%; female 47.7%; unemployed 18.0%). **Household income and expenditure.** Average household size (2002) 3.2; gross income per household (2001) Sk 89,352; sources of income (2001): wages and salaries 67.1%, transfer payments 15.8%; expenditure (2001): food, beverages, and tobacco 27.4%, housing and energy 17.2%, transportation and communications 13.7%, clothing and footwear 8.6%. **Public debt** (external, outstanding; 2002): $4,295,-000,000. **Gross national product** (2003): $26,483,-000,000 ($4,920 per capita). **Tourism:** receipts from visitors (2002) $724,000,000; expenditure by nationals abroad $442,000,000. **Land use** as % of total land area (2000): in temporary crops 30.2%, in permanent crops 2.6%, in pasture 18.0%; overall forest area 45.3%.

Foreign trade

Imports (2002): $16,502,000,000 (machinery and apparatus 25.6%, mineral fuels 14.6%, transport equipment 12.8%, base and fabricated metals 8.9%). *Major import sources:* Germany 22.6%; Czech Republic 15.2%; Russia 12.5%; Italy 6.9%; France 4.4%. **Exports** (2002): $14,385,000,000 (transport equipment [mostly road vehicles] 21.2%, machinery and apparatus 18.8%, base and fabricated metals [mostly iron and steel] 14.3%, mineral fuels 7.2%). *Major export destinations:* Germany 26.0%; Czech Republic 15.2%; Italy 10.7%; Austria 7.7%; Hungary 5.5%; Poland 5.3%.

Transport and communications

Transport. *Railroads* (2001): length 3,665 km; passenger-km 2,805,000,000; metric ton-km cargo 10,929,000,000. *Roads* (2001): total length 17,735 km. *Vehicles* (2003): passenger cars 1,327,000; trucks and buses 141,000. *Air transport* (2003; Slovak Airlines only): passenger-km 41,003,000; metric ton-km cargo 308,000; airports (2002) with scheduled flights 2. **Communications,** in total units (units per 1,000 persons). Daily newspaper circulation (2000): 938,000 (174); radios (2000): 5,200,000 (965); televisions (2000): 2,190,000 (407); telephone main lines (2002): 1,294,700 (241); cellular telephone subscribers (2003): 3,678,800 (684); personal computers (2002): 970,000 (180); Internet users (2003): 1,375,800 (256).

Education and health

Educational attainment (1991). Percentage of adult population having: incomplete primary education 0.7%; primary and incomplete secondary 37.9%; complete secondary 50.9%; higher 9.5%; unknown 1.0%. **Literacy** (2001): total population age 15 and over literate 100%. **Health** (2001): physicians 20,430 (1 per 263 persons); hospital beds 54,759 (1 per 98 persons); infant mortality rate per 1,000 live births (2002) 8.1. **Food** (2000): daily per capita caloric intake 3,133 (vegetable products 75%, animal products 25%); 127% of FAO recommended minimum.

Military

Total active duty personnel (2003): 22,000 (army 62.3%, air force 31.8%, headquarters staff 5.9%). **Military expenditure as percentage of GNP** (1999): 1.8% (world 2.4%); per capita expenditure $187.

Did you know? The city of Bratislava is the capital of Zapadni Slovensko *kraj* (region) and the capital of Slovakia. It lies in the extreme southwestern part of the country, along the Danube. Vienna, Austria, is only 35 mi (56 km) to the west.

Background

Slovakia was inhabited in the first centuries AD by Il-lyrian, Celtic, and Germanic tribes. Slovaks settled there around the 6th century. It became part of Great Moravia in the 9th century but was conquered by the Magyars c. 907. It remained in the kingdom of Hungary until the end of World War I, when the Slovaks joined the Czechs to form the new state of Czechoslovakia in 1918. In 1938 Slovakia was declared an autonomous unit within Czechoslovakia; it was nominally independent under German protection in 1939–45. After the expulsion of the Germans, Slovakia joined a reconstituted Czechoslovakia, which came under Soviet domination in 1948. In 1969 a partnership between the Czechs and Slovaks established the Slovak Socialist Republic. The fall of the communist regime in 1989 led to a revival of interest in autonomy, and Slovakia became an independent nation in 1993.

Recent Developments

In 2004 Slovakia acceded to both NATO and the European Union (EU) and won international praise as a reform leader. In May 2005 the country became the seventh EU member to ratify the EU constitution. Earlier that year Slovakia had hosted US Pres. George W. Bush, the first sitting US president to visit the country, and Russian Pres. Vladimir Putin. In October 2005 it was elected for the first time as a rotating member of the UN Security Council. The country's economy was one of the strongest in the EU, with growth of 8.3% in 2006 and projected growth of 8.8% for 2007. Inflation in 2006 stood at 3.7%. The country was poised to adopt the euro on schedule in January 2009.

Internet resources: <www.slovakiatourism.sk>.

Slovenia

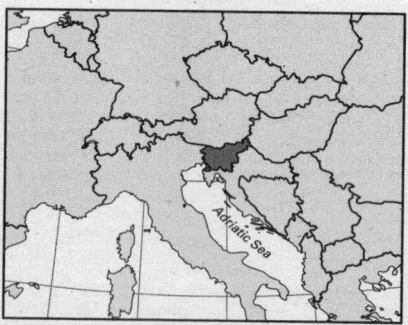

Official name: Republika Slovenija (Republic of Slovenia). **Form of government:** unitary multiparty republic with two legislative houses (National Council [40]; National Assembly [90]). **Head of state:** President Janez Drnovsek (from 2002). **Head of government:** Prime Minister Janez Jansa (from 2004). **Capital:** Ljubljana. **Official language:** Slovene. **Official religion:** none.

Monetary unit: 1 euro (€) = 100 cents; valuation (1 Jul 2007) US$1 = €0.74; at conversion on 1 Jan 2007, €1 = 239,640 Slovene tolarjev (SIT).

Demography

Area: 7,827 sq mi, 20,273 sq km. **Population** (2006): 2,006,000. **Density** (2006): persons per sq mi 256.3, persons per sq km 98.9. **Urban** (2002): 50.8%. **Sex distribution** (2003): male 48.95%; female 51.05%. **Age breakdown** (2002): under 15, 15.3%; 15–29, 21.5%; 30–44, 22.7%; 45–59, 20.5%; 60–74, 14.4%; 75 and over, 5.6%. **Ethnic composition** (2002): Slovene 91.2%; Serb 2.2%; Croat 2.0%; Bosniac (ethnic Muslim) 1.8%; other 2.8%. **Religious affiliation** (2000): Christian 92.1%, of which Roman Catholic 83.5%, unaffiliated Christian 4.7%, Protestant 1.6%, Orthodox 0.6%; nonreligious/atheist 7.8%; other 0.1%. **Major cities** (2002): Ljubljana 258,873; Maribor 93,847; Celje 37,834; Kranj 35,587; Velenje 26,742. **Location:** southeastern Europe, bordering Austria, Hungary, Croatia, the Adriatic Sea, and Italy.

Vital statistics

Birth rate per 1,000 population (2002): 8.8 (world avg. 21.3); legitimate 59.8%. **Death rate** per 1,000 population (2002): 9.4 (world avg. 9.1). **Natural increase rate** per 1,000 population (2002): –0.6 (world avg. 12.2). **Total fertility rate** (avg. births per childbearing woman; 2002): 1.2. **Marriage rate** per 1,000 population (2002): 3.5. **Divorce rate** per 1,000 population (2002): 1.2. **Life expectancy** at birth (2002): male 72.3 years; female 79.9 years.

National economy

Budget (2003). *Revenue:* SIT 2,376,000,000,000 (2002; tax revenue 91.7%, of which social security contributions 32.7%, taxes on goods and services 32.3%, personal income tax 19.0%; nontax revenue 8.3%). *Expenditures:* SIT 2,454,000,000,000 (2002; current expenditures 90.8%, of which wages 45.9%, transfers 44.9%; development expenditures 9.2%). **Public debt** (external, outstanding; 2001): $2,700,-000,000. **Production** (metric tons except as noted). *Agriculture, forestry, fishing* (2002): silage 1,085,-000, corn (maize) 255,000, sugar beets 190,000; livestock (number of live animals) 599,895 pigs, 477,075 cattle; roundwood (2001) 2,283,000 cu m; fish catch (2001) 3,040. *Mining and quarrying* (2002): dimension stone 105,000. *Manufacturing* (value added in $'000,000; 2001): base and fabricated metals 771; nonelectrical machinery and professional equipment 573; chemicals and chemical products 473. *Energy production (consumption):* electricity (kW-hr; 2003) 13,064,000,000 (12,588,-000,000); hard coal (2000) none (446,000); lignite (2003) 4,854,000 (5,358,000); crude petroleum (barrels; 2000) 7,330 (1,165,000); petroleum products (2000) 133,000 (2,214,000); natural gas (cu m; 2003) 4,900,000 (1,114,000,000). **Land use** as % of total land area (2000): in temporary crops 8.6%, in permanent crops 1.5%, in pasture 15.6%; overall forest area 55.0%. **Household income and expenditure** (2001). Average household size (2002) 2.8; income per household SIT 3,090,000; sources of income:

---

1 metric ton = about 1.1 short tons;   1 kilometer = 0.6 mi (statute);   1 metric ton-km cargo = about 0.68 short ton-mi cargo;   c.i.f.: cost, insurance, and freight;   f.o.b.: free on board

wages 60.0%, transfers 26.6%; expenditure: transportation and communications 25.8%, food and beverages 17.8%, housing 10.4%, recreation 9.3%. **Gross national product** (at current market prices; 2003): $23,229,000,000 ($11,830 per capita). **Population economically active** (2003): total 959,000; activity rate 48.0% (participation rates: ages 15 and over 56.5%; female 45.9%; unemployed 10.9%). **Tourism** (2002): receipts from visitors $1,083,000,000; expenditures by nationals abroad $614,000,000.

Foreign trade

Imports (2003-c.i.f.): €12,237,000,000 (machinery and transport equipment 34.4%, of which road vehicles 11.1%; chemicals and chemical products 13.3%; mineral fuels 7.7%; food products 5.1%). *Major import sources:* Germany 19.3%; Italy 18.3%; France 10.1%; Austria 8.6%; Croatia 3.6%. **Exports** (2003-f.o.b.): €11,285,000,000 (machinery and transport equipment 36.5%, of which electrical machinery and apparatus 11.6%; road vehicles 11.4%; chemicals and chemical products 13.8%, of which medicines and pharmaceuticals 7.0%; furniture and parts 6.9%). *Major export destinations:* Germany 23.1%; Italy 13.1%; Croatia 8.9%; Austria 7.3%; France 5.7%.

Transport and communications

Transport. *Railroads* (2003): length 1,229 km; passenger-km 778,000,000; metric ton-km cargo 3,274,000,000. *Roads* (2003): total length 20,155 km (paved 81%). *Vehicles:* passenger cars (2003) 889,580; trucks and buses 69,363. *Air transport* (2003): passenger-km 837,000,000; metric ton-km cargo 3,538,000; airports (2003) with scheduled flights 3. **Communications,** in total units (units per 1,000 persons). Daily newspaper circulation (2000): 334,000 (171); radios (2000): 792,000 (405); televisions (2002): 732,000 (366); telephone main lines (2003): 812,300 (407); cellular telephone subscribers (2003): 1,739,100 (871); personal computers (2002): 600,000 (301); Internet users (2002): 750,000 (376).

Education and health

Educational attainment (2002). Percentage of population age 15 and over having: no formal schooling 0.7%; incomplete and complete primary education 32.2%; secondary 54.1%; some higher 5.1%; undergraduate 6.9%; advanced degree 1.0%. **Literacy** (2001): 99.6%. **Health** (2002): physicians 4,636 (1 per 430 persons); hospital beds 10,147 (1 per 197 persons); infant mortality rate per 1,000 live births 3.8.

Military

Total active duty personnel (2003): 6,550 (army 100%). **Military expenditure as percentage of GNP** (1999): 1.4% (world 2.4%); per capita expenditure $227.

Background

The Slovenes settled the region in the 6th century AD. In the 8th century it was incorporated into the Frankish empire of Charlemagne, and in the 10th century it came under Germany as part of the Holy Roman Empire. Except for 1809–14, when Napoleon ruled the area, most of the lands belonged to Austria until the formation of the Kingdom of Serbs, Croats, and Slovenes in 1918. It became a constituent republic of Yugoslavia in 1946 and received a section of the former Italian Adriatic coastline in 1947. In 1990 Slovenia held the first contested multiparty elections in Yugoslavia since before World War II. In 1991 it seceded from Yugoslavia; its independence was internationally recognized in 1992.

Recent Developments

In 2004 Slovenia joined both NATO and the European Union (EU). Slovenia's relations with Croatia, its southern neighbor, remained strained, owing primarily to the still-unresolved demarcation of the sea and land border between them. Nonetheless, Slovenia continued to support Croatia's candidacy for membership in the EU, the constitution of which Slovenia ratified in February 2005. In 2006 the country's unemployment rate was the lowest since independence in 1991. On 1 Jan 2007 Slovenia adopted the euro, becoming the first of the 10 countries that had joined in 2004 to do so and the 13th country overall.

Internet resources: <www.slovenia-tourism.si>.

Solomon Islands

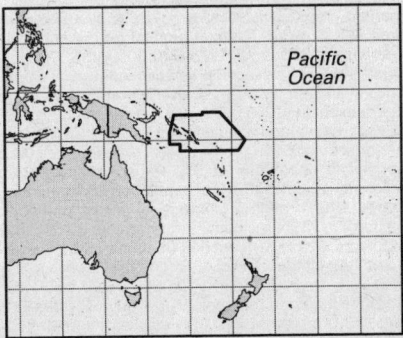

Official name: Solomon Islands. **Form of government:** constitutional monarchy with one legislative house (National Parliament [50]). **Chief of state:** Queen Elizabeth II (from 1952), represented by Governor-General Sir Nathaniel Waena (from 2004). **Head of government:** Prime Minister Manasseh Sogavare (from 2006). **Capital:** Honiara. **Official language:** English. **Official religion:** none. **Monetary unit:** 1 Solomon Islands dollar (SI$) = 100 cents; valuation (1 Jul 2007) US$1 = SI$7.63.

Demography

Area: 10,954 sq mi, 28,370 sq km. **Population** (2006): 482,000. **Density** (2006): persons per sq mi 44.0, persons per sq km 17.0. **Urban** (2002): 21.0%. **Sex distribution** (2004): male 51.64%; female 48.36%. **Age breakdown** (2003): under 15, 42.9%; 15–29, 29.2%; 30–44, 15.5%; 45–59, 7.6%; 60–74, 3.8%; 75 and over, 1.0%. **Ethnic composition** (2002):

Melanesian 93.0%; Polynesian 4.0%; Micronesian 1.5%; other 1.5%. **Religious affiliation** (2000): Christian 90.8%, of which Protestant 74.0% (including Church of Melanesia [Anglican] 38.2%, Roman Catholic 10.8%; traditional beliefs 3.1%; other 6.1%. **Major cities** (1999): Honiara 49,107 (urban agglomeration [2001] 78,000); Noro 3,482; Gizo 2,960; Auki 1,606; Tulagi 1,333. **Location:** southwestern Pacific Ocean, east of Papua New Guinea.

Vital statistics

Birth rate per 1,000 population (2003): 32.5 (world avg. 21.3). **Death rate** per 1,000 population (2003): 4.1 (world avg. 9.1). **Natural increase rate** per 1,000 population (2003): 28.4 (world avg. 12.2). **Total fertility rate** (avg. births per childbearing woman; 2003): 4.5. **Life expectancy** at birth (2003): male 69.6 years; female 74.7 years.

National economy

Budget (2003). *Revenue:* SI$681,300,000 (tax revenue 48.9%, of which international trade tax 19.3%, sales tax 16.4%, income tax 13.2%; grants 45.4%; nontax revenue 5.7%). *Expenditures:* SI$670,900,000 (current expenditure 60.2%, of which wages 24.4%, goods and services 13.2%, interest 7.4%; capital expenditure 39.8%). **Tourism** (2002): receipts from visitors US$1,000,000; expenditures by nationals abroad US$6,000,000. **Land use** as % of total land area (2000): in temporary crops 0.6%, in permanent crops 2.0%, in pasture 1.4%; overall forest area 88.8%. **Gross national product** (at current market prices; 2003): US$273,000,000 (US$600 per capita). **Household income and expenditure.** Average household size (2002) 6.6; average annual income per household (1991) US$2,387; sources of income (1983): wages and salaries 74.1%, other 25.9%; expenditure (1992): food 46.8%, housing 11.0%, household operations 10.9%, transportation 9.9%, recreation and health 7.9%. **Population economically active** (1999): total 85,124; activity rate of total population 21.0% (participation rates: female 32.2%; unemployed 32.5%). **Production** (metric tons except as noted). *Agriculture, forestry, fishing* (2002): coconuts 330,000, palm oil fruit 140,000, sweet potatoes 84,000; livestock (number of live animals) 68,000 pigs, 13,000 cattle, 220,000 chickens; roundwood (2002) 692,000 cu m; fish catch (2001) 30,075. *Manufacturing* (2002): vegetable oils and fats 50,000, palm oil 35,000, coconut oil 15,000. *Energy production (consumption):* electricity (kW-hr; 2002) 57,061,000 (57,061,000); petroleum products (2000) none (54,000). **Public debt** (external, outstanding; 2002): US$150,200,000.

Foreign trade

Imports (2003-c.i.f.): SI$639,500,000 (food, beverages, and tobacco 23.6%, crude petroleum 17.3%, machinery and transport equipment 12.7%, construction materials 10.7%, unspecified 32.9%). *Major import sources:* Australia 28.0%; Singapore 23.2%; New Zealand 5.2%; Fiji 4.6%; Papua New Guinea 4.4%. **Exports** (2003-f.o.b.): SI$557,000,000 (timber 66.6%, fish products 16.7%, cacao beans 9.6%). *Major export destinations:* China 25.8%;

Japan 17.9%; South Korea 15.2%; Philippines 9.9%; Thailand 6.2%; Singapore 5.6%.

Transport and communications

Transport. *Roads* (1996): total length 1,360 km (paved 2.5%). *Vehicles* (1993): passenger cars 2,052; trucks and buses 2,574. *Air transport* (1999): passenger-km 47,278,000; metric ton-km cargo 1,250,000; airports (1997) with scheduled flights 21. **Communications,** in total units (units per 1,000 persons). Radios (1997): 57,000 (141); televisions (2000): 9,570 (23); telephone main lines (2002): 6,600 (15); cellular telephone subscribers (2002): 1,000 (2.2); personal computers (2002): 18,000 (41); Internet users (2002): 2,200 (5).

Education and health

Educational attainment (1986; indigenous population only). Percentage of population age 25 and over having: no schooling 44.4%; primary education 46.2%; secondary 6.8%; higher 2.6%. **Literacy** (1999): total population age 15 and over literate 181,000 (76%); males literate 102,500 (83%); females literate 78,500 (68%). **Health:** physicians (2003) 53 (1 per 8,491 persons); hospital beds (1999) 881 (1 per 459 persons); infant mortality rate per 1,000 live births (2003) 22.9. **Food** (2001): daily per capita caloric intake 2,272 (vegetable products 92%, animal products 8%); 100% of FAO recommended minimum.

Military

Total active duty personnel (2003): none; multinational regional intervention force (from mid-2003; primarily Australian) for combating violence and lawlessness withdrew in 2004 except for police forces.

Background

The Solomon Islands were probably settled c. 2000 BC by Austronesian people. Visited by the Spanish in 1568, the islands were subsequently explored and charted by the Dutch, French, and British. They came under British protection in 1893 and became the British Solomon Islands. During World War II, the Japanese invasion of 1942 ignited three years of the most bitter fighting in the Pacific, particularly on Guadalcanal. The protectorate became self-governing in 1975 and fully independent in 1978. (Another island group named Solomon Islands, which includes Bougainville, is part of Papua New Guinea.)

Recent Developments

The Regional Assistance Mission to Solomon Islands (RAMSI), an Australian-led police and military force in the country since 2003, continued to try to impose order. In September 2006 Julian Moti, an Australian citizen, was selected to become attorney general, but a month later he was arrested by RAMSI and local police on child-sex charges. In April 2007 a tsunami crashed into the Solomon Islands, killing at least 43 and leaving thousands homeless.

Internet resources: <www.visitsolomons.com.sb>.

1 metric ton = about 1.1 short tons; 1 kilometer = 0.6 mi (statute); 1 metric ton-km cargo = about 0.68 short ton-mi cargo; c.i.f.: cost, insurance, and freight; f.o.b.: free on board

Somalia

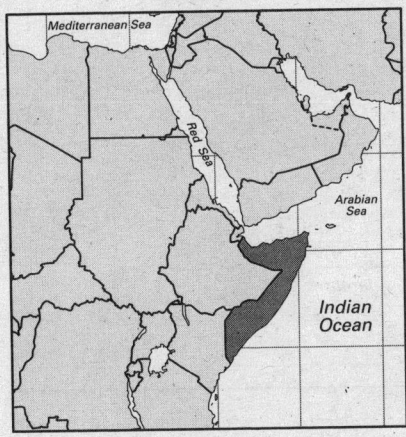

Official name: Soomaaliya (Somali); Al-Sumal (Arabic) (Somalia). **Form of government:** transitional regime (the "new transitional government" from October 2004 lacked effective control in July 2007) with one legislative body (Transitional Federal Assembly [216 planned; 194 members were sworn in on 22 Aug 2004]). At present Somalia is divided into three autonomous regions: Somaliland in the northwest, Puntland in the northeast, and Somalia in the south. **Head of state and government:** President Abdullahi Yusuf Ahmed (from 2004), assisted by Prime Minister Ali Muhammad Ghedi (from 2004). **Capital:** Mogadishu. **Official languages:** Somali; Arabic. **Official religion:** Islam. **Monetary unit:** 1 Somali shilling (So.Sh.) = 100 cents; valuation (1 Jul 2007) US$1 = So.Sh. 1,382 (in the fall of 2003 the black-market value was about 18,000 So.Sh. = $1).

Demography

Area: 246,000 sq mi, 637,000 sq km. **Population** (2006): 8,496,000. **Density** (2006): persons per sq mi 34.5, persons per sq km 13.3. **Urban** (2002): 34%. **Sex distribution** (2002): male 51.47%; female 48.53%. **Age breakdown** (2002): under 15, 46.4%; 15–29, 26.4%; 30–44, 16.3%; 45–59, 8.1%; 60–74, 2.4%; 75 and over, 0.4%. **Ethnic composition** (2000): Somali 92.4%; Arab 2.2%; Afar 1.3%; other 4.1%. **Religious affiliation** (1995): Sunni Muslim 99.9%; other 0.1%. **Major cities** (1990): Mogadishu 1,212,000 (estimated urban agglomeration, 2003); Hargeysa 90,000; Kismaayo 90,000; Berbera 70,000; Marka 62,000. **Location:** eastern Africa, bordering Djibouti, the Gulf of Aden, the Indian Ocean, Kenya, and Ethiopia.

Vital statistics

Birth rate per 1,000 population (2003): 46.4 (world avg. 21.3). **Death rate** per 1,000 population (2003): 17.6 (world avg. 9.1). **Natural increase rate** per 1,000 population (2003): 28.8 (world avg. 12.2). **Total fertility rate** (avg. births per childbearing woman; 2003): 7.0. **Life expectancy** at birth (2003): male 45.7 years; female 49.1 years.

National economy

Budget (1991). *Revenue:* So.Sh. 151,453,000,000 (domestic revenue sources, principally indirect taxes and import duties 60.4%; external grants and transfers 39.6%). *Expenditures:* So.Sh. 141,141,000,000 (general services 46.9%; economic and social services 31.2%; debt service 7.0%). **Production** (metric tons except as noted). *Agriculture, forestry, fishing* (2002): fruits (excluding melons) 220,000, sugarcane 210,000, corn (maize) 210,000; livestock (number of live animals) 13,100,000 sheep, 12,700,000 goats, 6,200,000 camels; roundwood (2001) 9,936,520 cu m; fish catch (2001) 20,000. *Mining and quarrying* (2001): gypsum 1,500; salt 1,000. *Manufacturing* (value added in So.Sh. '000,000; 1988): food 794; cigarettes and matches 562; hides and skins 420. *Energy production (consumption):* electricity (kW-hr; 2000) 282,000,000 (282,000,000); crude petroleum (barrels; 1991) none (806,000); petroleum products (1991) none (59,000). **Household income and expenditure.** Average household size (2002) 5.2; income per household (2002): $226; sources of income (2002): self-employment 50%, remittances 22.5%, wages 14%, rent/aid 13.5%; expenditure (1983; Mogadishu only): food and tobacco 62.3%, housing 15.3%, clothing 5.6%, energy 4.3%, other 12.5%. **Population economically active** (2001): total 3,906,000; activity rate of total population 52.2% (participation rates: ages 15–64 [2002] 56.4%; unemployed [2002] 47.5%). **Gross domestic product** (2001): $1,000,000,000 ($110 per capita). **Public debt** (external, outstanding; 2002): $1,860,000,000. **Land use** as % of total land area (2000): in temporary crops 1.7%, in permanent crops 0.04%, in pasture 68.5%; overall forest area 12.0%.

Foreign trade

Imports (2002-c.i.f.): $354,000,000 (agricultural products 32.9%, of which raw sugar 20.0%, cereals 5.1%; unspecified 67.1%). *Major import sources* (2003): Djibouti 32%; Kenya 15%; Brazil 11%; UAE 5%; Thailand 4%. **Exports** (2002-f.o.b.): $97,000,000 (agricultural products 85.4%, of which goats and sheep 56.9%, bovines 17.5%, camels 10.0%; unspecified 14.6%). *Major export destinations* (2003): UAE 39%; Yemen 24%; Oman 11%; China 6%; Kuwait 4%.

Transport and communications

Transport. *Roads* (1999): total length 22,100 km (paved 12%). *Vehicles* (1996): passenger cars 1,020; trucks and buses 6,440. *Air transport* (1991): passenger-km 131,000,000; metric ton-km cargo 5,000,000; airports (2002) with scheduled flights 1. **Communications,** in total units (units per 1,000 persons). Daily newspaper circulation (2000): 7,250 (1); radios (2002): 760,000 (98); televisions (2002): 28,700 (3.7); telephones (2002; includes cellular telephones): 116,000 (15); personal computers (2002): 6,200 (0.8).

Education and health

Literacy (2002): percentage of total population age 15 and over literate 19.2%; males literate 25.1%; females literate 13.1%. **Health** (1997): physicians 265 (1 per 25,032 persons); hospital beds 2,786 (1 per 2,381 persons); infant mortality rate per 1,000 live births (2003) 120.3. **Food** (2000): daily per capita caloric intake 1,628 (vegetable products 62%, animal products 38%); 70% of FAO recommended minimum.

Military

Total active duty personnel: no national army from 1991. **Military expenditure as percentage of GNP** (1990): 0.9% (world 4.3%); per capita expenditure $1.

Background

Muslim Arabs and Persians first established trading posts along the coasts of Somalia in the 7th–10th centuries. By the 10th century Somali nomads occupied the area inland from the Gulf of Aden, and the south and west were inhabited by various groups of pastoral Oromo peoples. Intensive European exploration began after the British occupation of Aden in 1839, and in the late 19th century Britain and Italy set up protectorates in the region. During World War II the Italians invaded British Somaliland (1940); a year later British troops retook the area, and Britain administered the region until 1950, when Italian Somaliland became a UN trust territory. In 1960 it was united with the former British Somaliland, and the two became the independent Republic of Somalia. Since then it has suffered political and civil strife, including military dictatorship, civil war, drought, and famine. In the 1990s no effective central government existed. In 1991 a proclamation of a Republic of Somaliland, on territory corresponding to the former British Somaliland, was issued by a breakaway group, but it did not receive international recognition. A multinational force intervened from 1992 to 1994 in an unsuccessful attempt to stabilize the region. The country remained in turmoil.

Recent Developments

The dramatic rise and fall of a coalition of fundamentalist Muslims, the Islamic Courts Union (ICU), took place in 2006. A series of battles between the ICU and an American-backed alliance of militia leaders and businessmen ended in complete victory for the ICU, which came to control much of the country. Ethiopia was antagonized by Eritrean military assistance to the ICU and increased its support of the Transitional Federal Government (TFG), based in Baidoa, threatening to transform the Somali power struggle into a proxy war. The ICU rejected American allegations that senior al-Qaeda operatives operated in areas under its control. In December Ethiopian forces invaded Somalia in support of the TFG, routing the ICU fighters. As of July 2007 fierce fighting still took place in parts of the country.

Internet resources: <www.unsomalia.net>.

South Africa

Official name: Republic of South Africa. **Form of government:** multiparty republic with two legislative houses (National Council of Provinces [90]; National Assembly [400]). **Head of state and government:** President Thabo Mbeki (from 1999). **Capitals** (de facto): Pretoria/Tshwane (executive); Bloem-

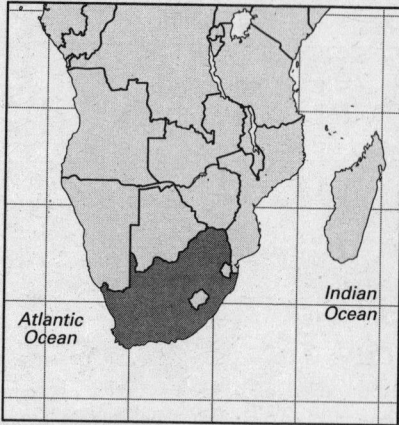

fontein/Mangaung (judicial); Cape Town (legislative). **Official languages:** Afrikaans; English; Ndebele; Pedi; Sotho; Swazi; Tsonga; Tswana; Venda; Xhosa; Zulu. **Official religion:** none. **Monetary unit:** 1 rand (R) = 100 cents; valuation (1 Jul 2007) US$1 = R 7.05.

Demography

Area: 470,693 sq mi, 1,219,090 sq km. **Population** (2006): 47,391,000. **Density** (2006): persons per sq mi 100.6, persons per sq km 38.8. **Urban** (2002): 57.7%. **Sex distribution** (2001): male 47.82%; female 52.18%. **Age breakdown** (2001): under 15, 32.0%; 15–29, 29.5%; 30–44, 20.2%; 45–59, 11.0%; 60–74, 5.5%; 75 and over, 1.8%. **Ethnic composition** (2001): black 78.4%, of which Zulu 23.8%, Xhosa 17.6%, Pedi 9.4%, Tswana 8.2%, Sotho 7.9%, Tsonga 4.4%, Swazi 2.7%, other black 4.4%; white 9.6%; Coloured 8.9%; Asian 2.5%; other 0.6%. **Religious affiliation** (2000): Christian 83.1%, of which black independent churches 39.1%, Protestant 31.8%, Roman Catholic 7.1%; traditional beliefs 8.4%; Hindu 2.4%; Muslim 2.4%; nonreligious 2.4%; other 1.3%. **Major cities** (2003): Cape Town 2,733,000; Durban 2,396,100; Johannesburg 1,675,200; Pretoria 1,249,700; Port Elizabeth 848,400. **Location:** southern Africa, bordering Namibia, Botswana, Zimbabwe, Mozambique, Swaziland, and the southern Atlantic and western Indian Oceans; wholly contained within South Africa is the country of Lesotho.

Vital statistics

Birth rate per 1,000 population (2003): 19.7 (world avg. 21.3). **Death rate** per 1,000 population (2003): 19.3 (world avg. 9.1). **Natural increase rate** per 1,000 population (2003): 0.4 (world avg. 12.2). **Marriage rate** per 1,000 population (2000): 3.2. **Divorce rate** per 1,000 population (2000): 0.8. **Total fertility rate** (avg. births per childbearing woman; 2003): 2.4. **Life expectancy** at birth (2003): male 44.6 years; female 46.0 years. **Adult population** (ages 15–49) living with HIV (2004): 21.5% (world avg. 1.1%).

1 metric ton = about 1.1 short tons;   1 kilometer = 0.6 mi (statute);   1 metric ton-km cargo = about 0.68 short ton-mi cargo;   c.i.f.: cost, insurance, and freight;   f.o.b.: free on board

National economy

Budget (2001–02). *Revenue:* R 248,447,200,000 (personal income taxes 36.6%, value-added taxes 23.6%, company income taxes 17.7%, other 22.1%). *Expenditures:* R 262,589,800,000 (transfer to provinces 46.2%, interest on public debt 18.1%, police and prisons 9.2%, defense 6.1%). **Public debt** (external, outstanding; 2002): $9,427,000,000. **Production** (in R '000,000 except as noted). *Agriculture, forestry, fishing* (in value of production; 2000): poultry 8,270, corn (maize) 5,654, beef 3,904; roundwood (2001) 30,616,000 cu m; fish catch (2001) 760,000 metric tons. *Mining and quarrying* (in value of sales; 2002): gold 41,386; platinum-group metals 34,829; coal 31,140. *Manufacturing* (value added in $'000,000; 1999): food products 2,225; iron and steel 2,225; transport equipment 2,100. *Energy production (consumption):* electricity (kW-hr; 2002) 217,704,000,000 ([2001] 182,565,000,000); coal (metric tons; 2002) 222,456,000 ([2000] 156,248,000); crude petroleum (barrels; 2000) 6,027,000 (193,255,000); includes Botswana, Lesotho, Namibia, and Swaziland); petroleum products (metric tons; 2000; includes Botswana, Lesotho, Namibia, and Swaziland) 24,653,000 (17,645,000); natural gas (cu m; 2000) 1,666,000,000 (1,666,000,000). **Population economically active** (2001): total 15,358,000; activity rate of total population 34.5% (participation rates: over age 15, 50.7%; female 46.7%; unemployed [2001] 29.5%). **Household income and expenditure.** Average household size (2001) 3.8; average annual disposable income per household (1996) R 47,600; expenditure (1998): food, beverages, and tobacco 31.3%; transportation 14.3%; housing 9.3%; household furnishings and operation 8.9%. **Gross national product** (2003): $125,971,000,000 ($2,780 per capita). **Tourism** (2002): receipts $2,728,000,000; expenditures $1,804,000,000. **Land use** as % of total land area (2000): in temporary crops 12.1%, in permanent crops 0.8%, in pasture 68.7%; overall forest area 7.3%.

Foreign trade

Imports (2001): $24,188,000,000 (nonelectrical machinery 18.0%, crude petroleum 12.9%, chemicals and chemical products 11.9%, electrical machinery 11.5%). *Major import sources* (2001): US 11.0%; Germany 10.5%; UK 7.4%; Japan 5.5%; China 4.4%; unspecified 17.1%. **Exports** (2001): $27,928,000,000 (diamonds 18.6%, gold 12.6%, iron and steel 7.8%, food 6.5%, nonelectrical machinery 6.3%, industrial chemicals 6.2%, road vehicles 5.6%, coal 5.2%). *Major export destinations* (2002): UK 12.9%; US 12.8%; Germany 9.1%; Japan 8.9%; Italy 5.8%.

Transport and communications

Transport. *Railroads:* route length (2001) 20,384 km; passenger-km 3,930,000,000; metric ton-km cargo 106,786,000,000. *Roads* (1999): length 331,265 km (paved 41%). *Vehicles* (2002): passenger cars 4,135,037; trucks and buses 2,202,032. *Air transport* (2000; SAA only): passenger-km 19,320,000,000; metric ton-km cargo 677,048,000; airports (1996) 24. **Communications,** in total units (units per 1,000 persons). Daily newspaper circulation (2000): 1,590,000 (32); radios (2000): 16,800,000 (338); televisions (2002) 8,018,000 (177); telephone main lines (2002): 4,844,000 (107); cellular telephone subscribers (2003): 16,860,000 (364); personal computers (2002): 3,300,000 (73); Internet users (2002): 3,100,000 (68).

Education and health

Educational attainment (2000). Percentage of population age 20 and over having: no formal schooling 17.9%; some primary education 16.0%; complete primary/some secondary 37.2%; complete secondary 20.4%; higher 8.5%. **Literacy** (2000): total population age 15 and over literate 85.3%; males literate 86.0%; females literate 84.6%. **Health:** physicians (2000) 29,788 (1 per 1,453 persons); hospital beds (1998) 144,363 (1 per 290 persons); infant mortality rate per 1,000 live births (2003) 63.7. **Food** (2001): daily per capita caloric intake 2,889 (vegetable products 87%, animal products 13%); 114% of FAO recommended minimum.

Military

Total active duty personnel (2003): 55,750 (army 64.6%, navy 8.1%, air force 16.6%, intraservice medical service 10.7%). **Military expenditure as percentage of GNP** (1999): 1.5% (world 2.4%); per capita expenditure $45.

Did you know? The Cape of Good Hope is a rocky promontory at the southern end of the Cape Peninsula in South Africa. The Portuguese navigator Bartolomeu Dias first sighted it in 1488, and its discovery was considered a good omen that India could be reached by sea from Europe.

Background

San and Khoikhoi peoples roamed southern Africa as hunters and gatherers in the Stone Age, and the latter had developed a pastoralist culture by the time of European contact. By the 14th century, Bantu-speaking peoples had settled in the area and developed gold and copper mining and an active East African trade. In 1652 the Dutch established a colony at the Cape of Good Hope; the Dutch settlers became known as Boers and later as Afrikaners, after their Afrikaans language. In 1795 British forces captured the Cape, and in the 1830s, to escape British rule, Dutch settlers began the Great Trek northward and established the independent Boer republics of Orange Free State and the South African Republic (later the Transvaal region), which the British annexed as colonies by 1902 after the 30-month-long Boer War. In 1910 the British colonies of Cape Colony, Transvaal, Natal, and Orange River were unified into the new Union of South Africa. It became independent and withdrew from the Commonwealth in 1961. Throughout the 20th century South African politics were dominated by the issue of maintaining white supremacy over the country's black majority, and in 1948 South Africa formally instituted apartheid. Faced by increasing worldwide condemnation, it began dismantling the policy in the 1980s and ended it in 1990. In free elections in 1994, Nelson Mandela became the country's first black president. South Africa also rejoined the Commonwealth in 1994.

Recent Developments

The South African government's AIDS policy was criticized at the International AIDS Conference in Toronto in 2006, where the special UN envoy for AIDS in Africa said that South Africa propounded "theories more worthy of a lunatic fringe than of a concerned and compassionate state." In the first three quarters of 2006 the economic growth rate was 5.1%, the highest in 22 years. This was based on high commodity prices and consumer spending encouraged by low interest rates. Manufacturing benefited from the weakening of the rand against the dollar. The unemployment rate remained high, at 25.6%, but was at a six-year low. The first India–Brazil–South Africa summit was held in Brazil in September.

Internet resources: <www.southafrica.net>.

Spain

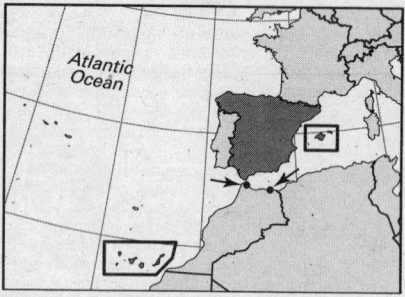

Official name: Reino de España (Kingdom of Spain). **Form of government:** constitutional monarchy with two legislative houses (Senate [259, including 51 indirectly elected]; Congress of Deputies [350]). **Chief of state:** King Juan Carlos I (from 1975). **Head of government:** Prime Minister José Luis Rodríguez Zapatero (from 2004). **Capital:** Madrid. **Official language:** Castilian Spanish; per constitution, Euskera [Basque], Catalan, Galician, and all other Spanish languages are also official in their Autonomous Communities). **Official religion:** none. **Monetary unit:** 1 euro (€) = 100 cents; valuation (1 Jul 2007) US$1 = €0.74; at conversion on 1 Jan 2002, €1 = 166.386 pesetas (Ptas).

Demography

Area: 194,845 sq mi, 504,645 sq km. **Population** (2006): 44,561,000. **Density** (2006): persons per sq mi 228.7, persons per sq km 88.3. **Urban** (2002): 77.8%. **Sex distribution** (2002): male 48.95%; female 51.05%. **Age breakdown** (2002): under 15, 14.6%; 15–29, 21.7%; 30–44, 24.0%; 45–59, 18.0%; 60–74, 14.2%; 75 and over, 7.5%. **Ethnic composition** (2000): Spaniard 44.9%; Catalonian 28.0%; Galician 8.2%; Basque 5.5%; Aragonese 5.0%; Rom (Gypsy) 2.0%; other 6.4%. **Religious affiliation** (2000): Roman Catholic 92.0%; Muslim 0.5%; Protestant 0.3%; other 7.2%. **Major cities** (2001): Madrid 2,938,723; Barcelona 1,503,884; Valencia 738,441; Seville 684,633; Zaragoza 614,905. **Location:** southwestern Europe, bordering France, Andorra, the Mediterranean Sea, Gibraltar, the Atlantic Ocean, and Portugal; the North African exclaves of Ceuta and Melilla border Morocco.

Vital statistics

Birth rate per 1,000 population (2003): 10.1 (world avg. 21.3). **Death rate** per 1,000 population (2003): 8.8 (world avg. 9.1). **Total fertility rate** (avg. births per childbearing woman; 2003): 1.3. **Life expectancy** at birth (2002): male 75.7 years; female 83.1 years.

National economy

Budget (2002). *Revenue:* €108,824,300,000 (direct taxes 46.6%, of which income tax 27.2%; indirect taxes 41.8%, of which value-added tax on products 27.8%; other taxes 11.6%). *Expenditures:* €112,586,900,000 (public debt 15.7%; health 9.8%; pensions 5.7%; defense 5.6%; public works 4.4%). **Tourism** (2002): receipts $33,609,000,000; expenditures $6,638,000,000. **Gross national product** (2003): $698,208,000,000 ($16,990 per capita). **Land use** as % of total land area (2000): in temporary crops 26.5%, in permanent crops 9.9%, in pasture 22.9%; overall forest area 28.8%. **Production** (metric tons except as noted). *Agriculture, forestry, fishing* (2002): barley 8,332,900, sugar beets 7,877,000, wheat 6,782,000; livestock (number of live animals) 24,300,624 sheep, 23,857,776 pigs, 6,411,000 cattle; roundwood (2001) 15,839,000 cu m; fish catch (2001) 1,289,081. *Mining and quarrying* (metal content in metric tons; 2001): zinc 164,900; lead 49,500. *Manufacturing* (value added in €'000,000; 2001): transport equipment 35,774; petroleum products 26,242; food products 14,771. *Energy production (consumption):* electricity (kW-hr; 2002) 229,000,000,000 (218,400,000,000); hard coal (2001) 10,491,000 ([2000] 32,804,000); lignite (2000) 12,154,000 (12,850,000); crude petroleum (barrels; 2003) 2,701,000 ([2000] 429,000,000); petroleum products (2000) 50,071,000 (50,840,000); natural gas (cu m; 2002) 509,700,000 ([2000] 17,752,000,000). **Public debt** (2001): $334,240,000,000. **Population economically active** (2001): total 17,814,600; activity rate of total population 43.7% (participation rates: ages [1995] 16–64, 60.7%; female 39.2%; unemployed 10.5%). **Household income and expenditure.** Average household size (2000) 3.2; income per household (2000) Ptas 3,205,693; expenditure (1995): housing 26.0%, food 24.0%, transportation 12.8%, clothing/footwear 7.4%.

Foreign trade

Imports (2001-f.o.b. in balance of trade): $154,993,000,000 (road vehicles 15.6%, nonelectrical machinery 13.3%, chemicals and chemical products 11.2%, electrical machinery 8.7%, crude and refined petroleum 8.6%). *Major import sources* (2002): France 16.9%; Germany 16.5%; Italy 8.6%; UK 6.4%; The Netherlands 4.8%. **Exports** (2001): $116,149,000,000 (road vehicles 23.0%; machinery 16.0%; food 12.0%, of which fruits and vegetables 6.3%; chemicals and chemical products 9.7%). *Major ex-*

port destinations (2002): France 18.9%; Germany 11.4%; Portugal 9.5%; UK 9.5%; Italy 9.3%.

Transport and communications

Transport. *Railroads* (2001): route length 13,832 km; passenger-km 19,190,000,000; metric ton-km cargo 12,216,000,000. *Roads* (1999): length 346,548 km (paved 99%). *Vehicles* (2001): cars 18,151,000; trucks and buses 4,005,000. *Air transport* (2003; combined total of Iberia, Air Europa, Air Nostrum, Binter Canarias, and Spanair): passenger-km 61,674,-000,000; metric ton-km cargo 820,963,000; airports (1997) with scheduled flights 25. **Communications,** in total units (units per 1,000 persons). Daily newspaper circulation (2000): 4,060,000 (100); radios (2000): 13,500,000 (333); televisions (2000): 24,000,000 (591); telephone main lines (2003): 17,567,500 (429); cellular telephone subscribers (2003): 37,507,000 (916); personal computers (2002): 7,972,000 (196); Internet users (2003): 9,789,000 (239).

Education and health

Educational attainment (2001). Percentage of population age 16 and over having: no formal schooling 15.4%; primary education 23.1%; secondary 48.0%; undergraduate degree 6.6%; graduate degree 6.9%. **Literacy** (2001): total population age 15 and over literate 97.7%; males literate 96.9%; females literate 98.6%. **Health:** physicians (2000) 179,033 (1 per 227 persons); hospital beds (2001) 160,815 (1 per 254 persons); infant mortality rate per 1,000 live births (2003) 3.6. **Food** (2000): daily per capita caloric intake 3,352 (vegetable products 73%, animal products 27%); 136% of FAO recommended minimum.

Military

Total active duty personnel (2003): 150,700 (army 63.4%, navy 15.2%, air force 15.1%, other 6.3%). **Military expenditure as percentage of GNP** (1999): 1.3% (world 2.4%); per capita expenditure $192.

Background

Remains of Stone Age populations dating back some 35,000 years have been found in Spain. Celtic peoples arrived in the 9th century BC, followed by the Romans, who dominated Spain from c. 200 BC until the Visigoth invasion in the early 5th century. In the early 8th century most of the peninsula fell to Muslims (Moors) from North Africa and remained under their control until it was gradually reconquered by the Christian kingdoms of Castile, Aragon, and Portugal. Spain was reunited in 1479 following the marriage of Ferdinand II (of Aragon) and Isabella I (of Castile). The last Muslim kingdom, Granada, was reconquered in 1492, and around this time Spain also established a colonial empire in the Americas. In 1516 the throne passed to the Habsburgs, whose rule ended in 1700 when Philip V became the first Bourbon king of Spain. His ascendancy caused the War of the Spanish Succession, which resulted in the loss of numerous European possessions and sparked revolution in most of Spain's American colonies. Spain lost its remaining overseas possessions to the US in the Spanish-American War (1898). It became a republic in 1931. The Spanish Civil War (1936–39) ended in victory for the Nationalists under Gen. Francisco Franco, who ruled

as dictator until his death in 1975. His successor as head of state, King Juan Carlos I, restored the monarchy; a new constitution in 1978 established a parliamentary monarchy. Spain joined NATO in 1982 and the European Community in 1986.

Recent Developments

In March 2006 the Basque separatist organization ETA (Euzkadi Ta Askatasuna) declared the first "permanent cease-fire" in its 40-year armed struggle against Spain. Coming after three years without any fatalities (the campaign had claimed more than 800 victims), the announcement raised hopes of an end to the conflict. Doubts about ETA's intentions were reinforced by the refusal of Batasuna, ETA's banned political wing, to condemn violence, as well as the announcement in November that French police had suspected the organization in the theft of 350 pistols. At the end of December, an ETA bomb exploded at the Madrid airport and caused two deaths and many injuries. Catalonia, Spain's other historically nationalist region, acquired a new autonomy statute, approved by 74% of voters in a June referendum. Officials in the Canary Islands were overwhelmed by a huge increase in the number of sub-Saharan African refugees. This humanitarian crisis fueled considerable public alarm at the scale and impact of immigration, both legal and illegal. The government responded with intensified calls for a common European immigration policy as well as high-level diplomacy with the African countries to help to stem the exodus and to dispatch navy boats to patrol their shores. Spain reinforced its contingent in the NATO mission in Afghanistan and committed more than 1,000 troops to the UN peacekeeping mission in Lebanon.

Internet resources: <www.tourspain.es>.

Sri Lanka

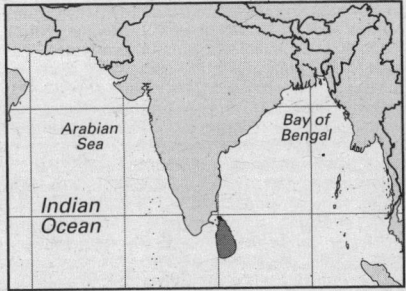

Official name: Sri Lanka Prajatantrika Samajavadi Janarajaya (Sinhala); Ilangai Jananayaka Socialisa Kudiarasu (Tamil) (Democratic Socialist Republic of Sri Lanka). **Form of government:** unitary multiparty republic with one legislative house (Parliament [225]). **Head of state and government:** President Mahinda Rajapakse (from 2005), assisted by Prime Minister Ratnasiri Wickremanayake (from 2005). **Capitals:** Colombo (executive); Sri Jayewardenepura Kotte (Colombo suburb; legislative and judicial). **Official languages:** Sinhala; Tamil. **Official religion:** none. **Monetary unit:** 1 Sri Lanka rupee (SL Rs) = 100 cents; valuation (1 Jul 2007) US$1 = SL Rs 111.36.

Demography

Area: 25,332 sq mi, 65,610 sq km. **Population** (2006): 19,879,000. **Density** (2006): persons per sq mi 784.7, persons per sq km 303.0. **Urban** (2002): 25.0%. **Sex distribution** (2001): male 49.47%; female 50.53%. **Age breakdown** (2001): under 15, 27.9%; 15–29, 27.1%; 30–44, 22.7%; 45–59, 13.6%; 60–74, 7.0%; 75 and over, 1.7%. **Ethnic composition** (2000): Sinhalese 72.4%; Tamil 17.8%; Sri Lankan Moor 7.4%; other 2.4%. **Religious affiliation** (2001): Buddhist 76.7%; Muslim 8.5%; Hindu 7.9%; Christian 6.8%; other 0.1%. **Major cities** (2001; provisional figures [except for 7 districts experiencing civil war]): Colombo 642,163; Dehiwala–Mount Lavinia 209,787; Moratuwa 177,190; Negombo 121,933; Sri Jayewardenepura Kotte 115,826. **Location:** island in the northern Indian Ocean, lying southeast of India.

Vital statistics

Birth rate per 1,000 population (2003): 16.1 (world avg. 21.3). **Death rate** per 1,000 population (2003): 6.5 (world avg. 9.1). **Natural increase rate** per 1,000 population (2003): 11.1 (world avg. 12.2). **Total fertility rate** (avg. births per childbearing woman; 2003): 1.9. **Marriage rate** per 1,000 population (1997): 8.9. **Life expectancy** at birth (2003): male 70.1 years; female 75.3 years.

National economy

Budget (2001). *Revenue:* SL Rs 231,463,000,000 (sales tax 19.7%, excise taxes 19.4%, income taxes 15.0%, nontax revenue 11.6%). *Expenditures:* SL Rs 383,686,000,000 (interest payments 24.6%, defense 17.8%, social welfare 13.4%). **Public debt** (external, outstanding; 2002): $8,455,000,000. **Production** (metric tons except as noted). *Agriculture, forestry, fishing* (2002): rice 2,794,000, coconuts 1,900,000, sugarcane 1,050,000; livestock (number of live animals) 1,565,000 cattle, 661,200 buffalo; roundwood (2001) 6,468,369 cu m; fish catch (2001) 288,010. *Mining and quarrying* (2001): graphite 6,585; sapphires 453,800 carats. *Manufacturing* (value added, in $'000,000; 1995): food, beverages, and tobacco 601; textiles and apparel 391; petrochemicals 116. *Energy production (consumption):* electricity (kW-hr; 2001) 6,520,000,000 (6,520,000,000); coal (2000) none (negligible); crude petroleum (barrels; 2000) none (16,712,000); petroleum products (2000) 2,062,000 (3,215,000). **Gross national product** (2003): $17,846,000,000 ($930 per capita). **Land use** as % of total land area (2000): in temporary crops 13.8%, in permanent crops 15.7%, in pasture 6.8%; overall forest area 30.0%. **Population economically active:** total (2001) 6,729,700 (excludes 7 districts experiencing civil war); activity rate 40% (participation rates: ages 10 and over, 48.3%; female 33.3%; unemployed 7.8%). **Household income and expenditure** (1992). Average household size (2000; excludes 7 districts experiencing civil war) 4.6; income per household SL Rs 116,100; sources of income: wages 48.5%, property income and self-employment 41.8%, transfers 9.7%; expenditure: food 58.6%, transportation 16.0%, clothing 8.4%. **Tourism** (2002): receipts $253,000,000; expenditures $253,000,000.

Foreign trade

Imports (2002-c.i.f.): SL Rs 584,491,000,000 (textiles [mostly yarns and fabrics] 21.6%; petroleum and natural gas 12.9%; foods 11.4%; machinery and equipment 10.5%). *Major import sources:* India 13.9%; Hong Kong 8.2%; Singapore 7.2%; Japan 5.9%; South Korea 5.0%; Taiwan 4.8%. **Exports** (2002-f.o.b.): SL Rs 449,850,000,000 (clothing and accessories 51.6%; tea 13.5%; precious and semi-precious stones 5.9%; rubber products 3.9%). *Major export destinations:* US 38.9%; UK 13.0%; Belgium-Luxembourg 5.7%; Germany 4.4%; India 3.8%.

Transport and communications

Transport. *Railroads* (2001): route length 1,449 km; (1998) passenger-km 3,264,000,000; (1998) metric ton-km cargo 132,000,000. *Roads* (1996): total length 99,200 km (paved 40%). *Vehicles* (2001): passenger cars 353,701; trucks and buses 244,166. *Air transport* (2001): passenger-km 4,126,000,000; metric ton-km cargo 224,000,000; airports (2001) 1. **Communications,** in total units (units per 1,000 persons). Daily newspaper circulation (2000): 539,000 (29); radios (2000): 3,870,000 (208); televisions (2000): 2,060,000 (111); telephone main lines (2002): 881,400 (47); cellular telephone subscribers (2002): 931,600 (49); personal computers (2002): 250,000 (13); Internet users (2002): 200,000 (11).

Education and health

Literacy (2000): percentage of population age 15 and over literate 91.6%; males literate 94.4%; females literate 89.0%. **Health** (1999): physicians 6,938 (1 per 2,740 persons); hospital beds (2001) 57,946 (1 per 324 persons); infant mortality rate per 1,000 live births (2003) 15.2. **Food** (2001): daily per capita caloric intake 2,274 (vegetable products 93%, animal products 7%); 102% of FAO recommended minimum.

Military

Total active duty personnel (2003): 152,300 (army 77.5%, navy 9.8%, air force 12.7%). **Military expenditure as percentage of GNP** (1999): 4.7% (world 2.4%); per capita expenditure $38.

Background

The Sinhalese people of Sri Lanka (Ceylon) probably originated with the blending of aboriginal inhabitants and migrating Indo-Aryans from India c. 5th century BC. The Tamils were later immigrants from Dravidian India, migrating over a period from the early centuries AD to c. 1200. Buddhism was introduced during the 3rd century BC. As Buddhism spread, the Sinhalese kingdom extended its political control over Ceylon but lost it to invaders from southern India in the 10th century AD. Between 1200 and 1505 Sinhalese power gravitated to southwestern Ceylon, while a southern Indian dynasty seized power in the north and established the Tamil kingdom in the 14th century. Foreign invasions from India, China, and Malaya occurred in the 13th–15th centuries. In 1505 the Portuguese arrived, and by 1619 they controlled most of the island. The Sinhalese enlisted the Dutch to help oust the Por-

---

1 metric ton = about 1.1 short tons;   1 kilometer = 0.6 mi (statute);   1 metric ton-km cargo = about 0.68 short ton-mi cargo;   c.i.f.: cost, insurance, and freight;   f.o.b.: free on board

tuguese and eventually came under the control of the Dutch East India Co., which relinquished power in 1796 to the British. In 1802 Ceylon became a crown colony, gaining independence in 1948. It became the Republic of Sri Lanka in 1972 and was renamed the Democratic Socialist Republic of Sri Lanka in 1978. Civil strife between Tamil and Sinhalese groups has beset the country in recent years, with the Tamils demanding a separate autonomous state in northern Sri Lanka.

Recent Developments

Pres. Mahinda Rajapakse attempted in 2006 to restart progress toward a settlement of the dispute with the Liberation Tigers of Tamil Eelam (LTTE), a conflict that had plagued Sri Lanka since 1983. Meetings held in February reportedly went well, but later suicide bombings targeted high-ranking officers, and government convoys and gunboats were attacked. International monitors blamed government troops for the deaths of 17 aid workers, mostly ethnic Tamils. Although neither side formally renounced the cease-fire agreed to in 2002, observers deemed that it was dead. In May the European Union declared the LTTE a terrorist organization, a step taken earlier by the US, Canada, India, and the UK.

Internet resources: <www.priu.gov.lk>.

The Sudan

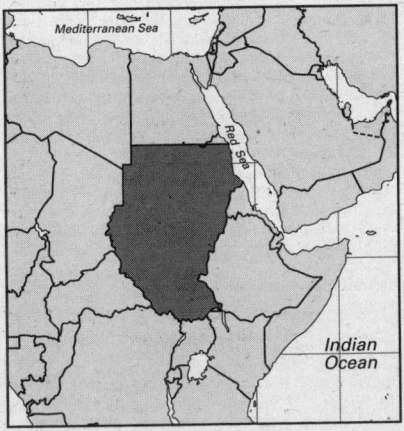

Official name: Jumhuriyat al-Sudan (Republic of the Sudan). **Form of government:** federal republic with one legislative body (National Assembly [360, including 90 seats not elected directly]). **Head of state and government:** President Omar Hassan Ahmad al-Bashir (from 1989). **Capitals:** Khartoum (executive); Omdurman (legislative). **Official language:** Arabic; English has been designated the "principal" language in southern Sudan. **Official religion:** Islamic law and custom are sources of national law per 1998 constitution. **Monetary unit:** 1 Sudanese dinar (Sd); valuation (1 Jul 2007) US$1 = Sd 200.22 (the Sudanese dinar [Sd], introduced May 1992 at a value equal to 10 Sudanese pounds [LSd], officially replaced the Sudanese pound on March 1, 1999).

Demography

Area: 967,499 sq mi, 2,505,810 sq km (includes about 129,810 sq km of inland water). **Population** (2006): 36,992,000. **Density** (2006): persons per sq mi 38.2, persons per sq km 14.8. **Urban** (2002): 37.1%. **Sex distribution** (2001): male 50.64%; female 49.36%. **Age breakdown** (2001): under 15, 44.6%; 15–29, 27.6%; 30–44, 15.6%; 45–59, 8.4%; 60–74, 3.3%; 75 and over, 0.5%. **Ethnic composition** (1983): Sudanese Arab 49.1%; Dinka 11.5%; Nuba 8.1%; Beja 6.4%, Nuer 4.9%; Zande 2.7%; Bari 2.5%; Fur 2.1%; other 12.7%. **Religious affiliation** (2000): Sunni Muslim 70.3%; Christian 16.7%, of which Roman Catholic 8%, Anglican 6%; traditional beliefs 11.9%; other 1.1%. **Major cities** (1993): Omdurman 1,271,403; Khartoum 947,483; Khartoum North 700,887; Port Sudan 308,195; Kassala 234,622. **Location:** northeastern Africa, bordering Egypt, the Red Sea, Eritrea, Ethiopia, Kenya, Uganda, Democratic Republic of the Congo, Central African Republic, Chad, and Libya.

Vital statistics

Birth rate per 1,000 population (2003): 36.5 (world avg. 21.3). **Death rate** per 1,000 population (2003): 9.6 (world avg. 9.1). **Natural increase rate** per 1,000 population (2003): 26.9 (world avg. 12.2). **Total fertility rate** (avg. births per childbearing woman; 2003): 5.1. **Life expectancy** at birth (2003): male 56.6 years; female 58.9 years.

National economy

Budget (2001). *Revenue:* Sd 365,200,000,000 (tax revenue 51.5%, of which custom duties 21.3%, VAT 10.3%; nontax revenue 48.5%). *Expenditures:* Sd 418,800,000,000 (current expenditure 81.9%, of which wages 31.4%; development expenditure 18.1%). **Public debt** (external, outstanding; 2002): $9,043,000,000. **Production** (metric tons except as noted). *Agriculture, forestry, fishing* (2002): sugarcane 5,000,000, sorghum 2,800,000, peanuts (groundnuts) 945,000; livestock (number of live animals) 47,043,000 sheep, 40,000,000 goats, 38,325,000 cattle; roundwood (2002) 19,241,332 cu m; fish catch (2001) 59,000. *Mining and quarrying* (2001): salt 120,000; gold 6,800 kg. *Manufacturing* (2001): raw sugar 689,000; flour (2000) 600,000; cement 190,000. *Energy production (consumption):* electricity (kW-hr; 2000) 2,264,000,000 (2,264,000,000); crude petroleum (barrels; 2001) 145,100,000 ([2000] 14,609,000); petroleum products (2001) 2,674,700 ([2000] 1,876,000). **Gross national product** (2003): $15,372,000,000 ($460 per capita). **Population economically active** (2000): total 12,207,000; activity rate of total population 37.8% (female 29.9%). **Households.** Average household size (2000): 6.1. **Tourism** (2002): receipts from visitors $62,000,000; expenditures by nationals abroad $91,000,000. **Land use** as % of total land area (2000): in temporary crops 6.8%, in permanent crops 0.2%, in pasture 49.3%; overall forest area 25.9%.

Foreign trade

Imports (2001-c.i.f.): $1,586,000,000 (machinery and equipment 27.9%; foodstuffs 16.4%, of which wheat and wheat flour 8.7%; transport equipment 12.8%; chemicals and chemical products 7.8%).

Major import sources (2002): China 19.8%; Saudi Arabia 6.9%; India 5.5%; Germany 5.5%; UK 5.4%. **Exports** (2001-f.o.b.): $1,699,000,000 (crude petroleum 74.7%; refined petroleum 6.3%; sesame seeds 6.2%; gold 2.6%; cotton 2.6%). *Major export destinations* (2002): China 55.3%; Japan 13.9%; Saudi Arabia 5.4%; South Korea 3.8%; Egypt 3.3%.

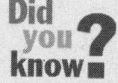

Did you know? The Nile, called "the father of African rivers," is the longest river in the world. The Nile River basin covers about one-tenth of the area of the African continent.

Transport and communications

Transport. *Railroads:* route length (2000) 5,901 km; (2001) passenger-km 78,000,000; metric ton-km cargo 1,250,000,000. *Roads* (1999): total length 11,900 km (paved 36%). *Vehicles* (1996): passenger cars 285,000; trucks and buses 53,000. *Air transport* (2001): passenger-km 803,000,000; metric ton-km cargo 54,542,000; airports (1997) with scheduled flights 3. **Communications**, in total units (units per 1,000 persons). Daily newspaper circulation (2000): 912,000 (26); radios (2001): 16,642,000 (461); televisions (2002): 12,661,000 (386); telephone main lines (2003): 900,000 (27); cellular telephone subscribers (2003): 650,000 (20); personal computers (2002): 200,000 (6.1); Internet users (2003): 300,000 (2.6).

Education and health

Literacy (2000): total population age 15 and over literate 55.8%; males literate 69.5%; females literate 46.3%. **Health:** physicians (1997) 3,423 (1 per 9,395 persons); hospital beds (1998) 36,419 (1 per 909 persons); infant mortality rate per 1,000 live births (2003) 65.6. **Food** (2001): daily per capita caloric intake 2,288 (vegetable products 80%, animal products 20%); 97% of FAO recommended minimum.

Military

Total active duty personnel (2004): 104,800 (army 95.4%, navy 1.7%, air force 2.9%); main opposition force in southern Sudan (Sudanese People's Liberation Army) between 20,000 and 30,000 (a permanent cease-fire between the central government and the main opposition force in southern Sudan was signed on 31 Dec 2004; a comprehensive peace plan was implemented in January 2005. African Union peacekeeping troops in Darfur (October 2004): 400; authorized 3,300. **Military expenditure as percentage of GNP** (1999): 4.8% (world 2.4%); per capita expenditure $33.

Background

From the end of the 4th millennium BC Nubia (now the northern Sudan) periodically came under Egyptian rule, and it was part of the kingdom of Cush from the 11th century BC to the 4th century AD. Christian missionaries converted The Sudan's three principal kingdoms during the 6th century AD; these black Christian kingdoms coexisted with their Muslim Arab neighbors in Egypt for centuries, until the influx of Arab immigrants brought about their collapse in the 13th–15th centuries. Egypt had conquered all of The Sudan by 1874 and encouraged British interference in the region; this aroused Muslim opposition and led to the revolt of al-Mahdi, who captured Khartoum in 1885 and established a Muslim theocracy in The Sudan that lasted until 1898, when his forces were defeated by the British. The British ruled the country, generally in partnership with Egypt, until The Sudan achieved independence in 1956. Since then the country has fluctuated between ineffective parliamentary government and unstable military rule. The non-Muslim population of the south has engaged in ongoing rebellion against the Muslim-controlled government of the north, leading to famines and the displacement of some four million people. Arab militias known as Janjaweed responded by killing as many as 400,000 people since 2003 and causing a massive humanitarian disaster.

Recent Developments

In July 2006 the secretary-general of the Southern Sudan People's Liberation Army reaffirmed his government's commitment to the terms of the Comprehensive Peace Agreement signed in January 2005. The African Union (AU) was reluctant to retain its Darfur peacekeeping force (AMIS) in the face of mounting attacks and casualties, but it eventually extended the force's mandate until the end of June 2007 to give time for an agreement to be reached between the Sudanese government and the Darfur rebels and for a UN peacekeeping force to take over. In May 2006 a peace treaty was signed in Abuja, Nigeria, that appeared to offer significant concessions to both sides, but two of the three rebel groups refused to sign it. In August the UN Security Council proposed the creation of a 22,000-strong joint UN/AU force. The Sudanese government, which had accepted the presence of AMIS only with reluctance and had consistently opposed the intervention of a UN force on the grounds that it was an infringement of the country's sovereignty, formally agreed in April 2007 to permit at least elements of this force into the area.

Internet resources: <www.sudan.net>.

Suriname

Official name: Republiek Suriname (Republic of Suriname). **Form of government:** multiparty republic with one legislative house (National Assembly [51]). **Head of state and government:** President Ronald Venetiaan (from 2000), assisted by Vice President Ram Sardjoe (from 2005). **Capital:** Paramaribo. **Official language:** Dutch. **Official religion:** none. **Monetary unit:** 1 Suriname dollar (SRD) = 100 cents; valuation (1 Jul 2007) US$1 = SRD 2.78. In January 2004 the Suriname dollar (SRD) replaced the Suriname guilder (Sf); Sf 1,000 = SRD 1.

Demography

Area: 63,251 sq mi, 163,820 sq km. **Population** (2006): 502,000. **Density** (2006): persons per sq mi

---

1 metric ton = about 1.1 short tons;   *1 kilometer = 0.6 mi (statute);*   *1 metric ton-km cargo = about 0.68 short ton-mi cargo;*   *c.i.f.: cost, insurance, and freight;*   *f.o.b.: free on board*

7.9, persons per sq km 3.1. **Urban** (2001): 74.8%. **Sex distribution** (2000): male 50.77%; female 49.23%. **Age breakdown** (2000): under 15, 32.1%; 15–29, 27.2%; 30–44, 22.7%; 45–59, 9.9%; 60–74, 6.4%; 75 and over, 1.7%. **Ethnic composition** (1999): Indo-Pakistani 37.0%; Suriname Creole 31.0%; Javanese 15.0%; Bush Negro 10.0%; Amerindian 2.5%; Chinese 2.0%; white 1.0%; other 1.5%. **Religious affiliation** (2000): Christian 50.4%, of which Roman Catholic 22.3%, Protestant (mostly Moravian) 17.1%, unaffiliated/other Christian 11.0%; Hindu 17.8%; Muslim 13.9%; nonreligious 4.8%; Spiritists (including followers of Voodoo) 3.5%; traditional beliefs 1.9%; other 7.7%. **Major cities** (1996/1997): Paramaribo 222,800 (urban agglomeration 289,000); Lelydorp 15,600; Nieuw Nickerie 11,100; Mungo (Moengo) 6,800; Meerzorg 6,600. **Location:** northern South America, bordering the North Atlantic Ocean, French Guiana, Brazil, and Guyana.

Vital statistics

Birth rate per 1,000 population (2003): 19.4 (world avg. 21.3). **Death rate** per 1,000 population (2003): 6.8 (world avg. 9.1). **Natural increase rate** per 1,000 population (2003): 12.6 (world avg. 12.2). **Total fertility rate** (avg. births per childbearing woman; 2003): 2.4. **Marriage rate** per 1,000 population (2000): 5.3. **Divorce rate** per 1,000 population (2000): 0.9. **Life expectancy** at birth (2003): male 66.8 years; female 71.8 years.

National economy

Budget (1998). *Revenue:* Sf 137,200,000,000 (indirect taxes 40.4%; direct taxes 36.2%; bauxite levy 10.9%; grants 12.5%). *Expenditures:* Sf 188,000,-000,000 (current expenditures 90.2%, of which wages and salaries 39.1%, transfers 11.7%, debt service 1.3%; capital expenditures 9.8%). **Public debt** (external, outstanding; 1996): $216,500,000. **Production** (metric tons except as noted). *Agriculture, forestry, fishing* (2002): rice 192,000, sugarcane 120,000, bananas 43,000; livestock (number of live animals) 136,000 cattle, 24,000 pigs, 2,200,000 chickens; roundwood (2002) 200,000 cu m; fish catch (2001) 18,915, of which shrimp 7,390. *Mining and quarrying* (2001): bauxite 4,512,000; alumina 1,900,000; gold 300 kg (recorded production; unrecorded production may be as high as 30,000 kg). *Manufacturing* (value of production at factor cost in Sf; 1993): food products 992,000,000; beverages 558,000,000; tobacco 369,000,000. *Energy production (consumption):* electricity (kW-hr; 2000) 1,648,000,000 (1,648,000,000); crude petroleum (barrels; 2001) 5,000,000 ([2000] 3,000,000); petroleum products (2000; production of petroleum products began in 2000; data not available) none (478,000). **Population economically active** (1999): total 84,646; activity rate of total population 19.8% (participation rates: [1992; districts of Wanica and Paramaribo only] ages 15–64, 56.0%; female 34.4%; unemployed 14.0%). **Gross national product** (2003): $841,000,000 ($1,940 per capita). **Households.** Average household size (1998) 4.8. **Tourism** (2002): receipts from visitors $3,000,000; expenditures by nationals abroad $10,000,000. **Land use** as % of total land area (2000): in temporary crops 0.4%, in permanent crops 0.06%, in pasture 0.1%; overall forest area 90.5%.

Foreign trade

Imports (2000-c.i.f.): $526,500,000 (nonelectrical machinery 22.5%, food products 13.4%, road vehicles 13.2%, chemicals and chemical products 10.2%, refined petroleum 5.8%). *Major import sources* (2001): US 34%; The Netherlands 17%; Trinidad and Tobago 13%; Netherlands Antilles 8%; Japan 5%. **Exports** (2000-f.o.b.): $514,000,000 (alumina 62.1%, gold 11.4%, crustaceans and mollusks 7.0%, crude petroleum 4.3%, refined petroleum 2.3%, rice 2.2%). *Major export destinations* (2001): US 26%; Norway 16%; France 10%; The Netherlands 9%; Canada 7%.

Transport and communications

Transport. *Railroads* (1997; all private): length 301 km; passengers, not applicable. *Roads* (1996): total length 4,530 km (paved 26%). *Vehicles* (2000): passenger cars 61,365; trucks and buses 23,220. *Air transport* (1998): passenger-km 1,072,000,000; metric ton-km cargo 127,000,000; airports with scheduled flights 1. **Communications,** in total units (units per 1,000 persons). Daily newspaper circulation (1996): 50,000 (122); radios (1997): 300,000 (728); televisions (2000): 109,000 (253); telephone main lines (2003): 79,800 (152); cellular telephone subscribers (2003): 168,100 (320); personal computers (2001): 20,000 (45); Internet users (2002): 20,000 (42).

Education and health

Literacy (2001): total population age 15 and over literate 92.2%; males literate 93.6%; females literate 90.7%. **Health:** physicians (1999) 213 (1 per 2,000 persons); hospital beds (1998) 1,449 (1 per 288 persons); infant mortality rate per 1,000 live births (2003) 24.7. **Food** (2001): daily per capita caloric intake 2,643 (vegetable products 86%, animal products 14%); 117% of FAO recommended minimum.

Military

Total active duty personnel (2003): 1,840 (army 76.1%, navy 13.0%, air force 10.9%). **Military expenditure as percentage of GNP** (1999): 1.8% (world 2.4%); per capita expenditure $33.

Background

Suriname was inhabited by various native peoples prior to European settlement. Spanish explorers claimed it in 1593, but the Dutch began to settle there in 1602, followed by the English in 1651. It was ceded to the Dutch in 1667, and in 1682 the Dutch West India Co. introduced coffee and sugarcane plantations and African slaves to cultivate them. Slavery was abolished in 1863, and indentured servants were brought from China, Java, and India to work the plantations, adding to the population mix. Except for brief interludes of British rule (1799–1802, 1804–15), it remained a Dutch colony. It gained internal autonomy in 1954 and independence in 1975. A military coup in 1980 ended civilian control until the electorate approved a new constitution in 1987. Military control resumed after a coup in 1990. Elections were held in 1991, followed by a resumption of democratic government.

Recent Developments

Suriname's economy seemed to be strengthening. Inflation in 2005 was 10%, down from 99% in 1999. In 2006 GDP growth was estimated to be 5%. The country hoped for the resolution of a long-standing border dispute with Guyana in 2007. At stake were fishing and mineral rights in potentially oil-rich waters offshore and in the Courantyne River.

Internet resources: <www.parbo.com/tourism>.

Swaziland

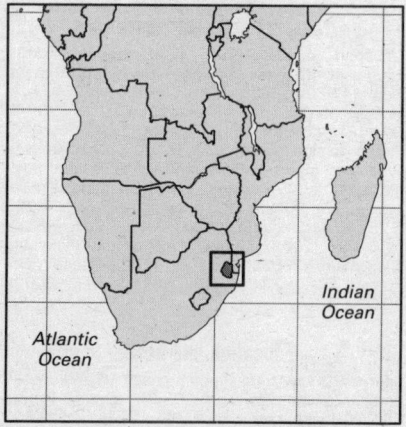

Indian Ocean

Atlantic Ocean

Official name: Umbuso weSwatini (Swazi); Kingdom of Swaziland (English). **Form of government:** constitutional monarchy with two legislative houses (Senate [30; includes 20 nonelective seats]; House of Assembly [65; includes 10 nonelective seats]). **Head of state and government:** King Mswati III (from 1986), assisted by Prime Minister Absalom Themba Dlamini (from 2003). **Capitals:** Mbabane (administrative and judicial); Lozitha and Ludzidzini (royal); Lobamba (legislative). **Official languages:** Swati (Swazi); English. **Official religion:** none. **Monetary unit:** 1 lilangeni (plural emalangeni [E]; at par with the South African rand) = 100 cents; valuation (1 Jul 2007) US$1 = E 7.05.

Demography

Area: 6,704 sq mi, 17,364 sq km. **Population** (2006): 1,029,000. **Density** (2006): persons per sq mi 153.5; persons per sq km 59.3. **Urban** (2003): 23.5%. **Sex distribution** (2003): male 49.80%; female 50.20%. **Age breakdown** (2003): under 15, 41.4%; 15–29, 30.7%; 30–44, 14.7%; 45–59, 7.9%; 60–74, 4.3%; 75 and over, 1.0%. **Ethnic composition** (2000): Swazi 82.3%; Zulu 9.6%; Tsonga 2.3%; Afrikaner 1.4%; mixed (black-white) 1.0%; other 3.4%. **Religious affiliation** (2000): Christian 67.5%, of which African indigenous 45.6%, Protestant 15.2%, Roman Catholic 5.4%; traditional beliefs 12.2%; other (mostly unaffiliated Christian) 20.3%. **Major cities** (1997): Mbabane 57,992; Manzini 25,571 (urban agglomeration 78,734); Big Bend 9,374; Mhlume 7,661; Malkerns 7,400. **Location:** southern Africa, bordering South Africa and Mozambique.

Vital statistics

Birth rate per 1,000 population (2003): 28.6 (world avg. 21.3). **Death rate** per 1,000 population (2003): 23.1 (world avg. 9.1). **Natural increase rate** per 1,000 population (2003): 5.5 (world avg. 12.2). **Total fertility rate** (avg. births per childbearing woman; 2003): 3.8. **Life expectancy** at birth (2003): male 41.0 years; female 38.9 years. **Adult population** (ages 15–49) **living with HIV** (2004): 38.8% (world avg. 1.1%).

National economy

Budget (2001–02). *Revenue:* E 3,094,000,000 (receipts from Customs Union of Southern Africa 48.6%; tax on income and profits 23.4%; sales tax 13.2%; foreign-aid grants 3.9%). *Expenditures:* E 3,409,000,000 (current expenditure 74.4%; development expenditure 25.4%; net lending 0.2%). **Gross national product** (2003): $1,492,000,000 ($1,350 per capita). **Population economically active** (2001): total 392,000; activity rate of total population 39.3% (unemployed 31.6%). **Public debt** (external, outstanding; 2002): $273,700,000. **Land use** as % of total land area (2000): in temporary crops 10.3%, in permanent crops 0.7%, in pasture 69.8%; overall forest area 30.3%. **Production** (metric tons except as noted). *Agriculture, forestry, fishing* (2002): sugarcane 4,000,000, corn (maize) 85,000, grapefruit and pomelo 37,000; livestock (number of live animals) 615,000 cattle, 422,000 goats; roundwood (2002) 890,000 cu m; fish catch (2001) 142. *Mining and quarrying* (2001): stone 350,000 cu m. *Manufacturing* (value added in $'000; 1994): food and beverages 244,000, of which beverage processing 153,000; paper and paper products 35,000; textiles 19,000. *Energy production (consumption):* electricity (kW-hr; 2000) 265,000,000 (702,000,000); coal (2001) 380,000 (n.a.). **Household income and expenditure.** Average household size (1986) 5.7; annual income per household (1985) E 332; sources of income (1985): wages and salaries 44.4%, self-employment 22.2%, transfers 12.2%, other 21.2%; expenditure (1985): food and beverages 33.5%, rent and fuel 13.4%, household durable goods 12.8%, transportation and communications 8.8%, clothing and footwear 6.0%, recreation 3.3%. **Tourism** (2002): receipts $26,000,000; expenditures $33,000,000.

Foreign trade

Imports (2001-f.o.b. in balance of trade and c.i.f. in commodities and trading partners): $832,000,000 (food and live animals 15.6%; machinery and apparatus 13.6%; chemicals and chemical products 13.2%; road vehicles 9.5%; refined petroleum 9.2%). *Major import sources:* South Africa 94.5%; Hong Kong 1.0%; Japan 0.9%. **Exports** (2001): $678,000,-000 (soft drink [including sugar and fruit juice] concentrates 38%; sugar 14%; apparel and clothing accessories 12%; wood pulp 9%). *Major export destinations:* South Africa 78.0%; Mozambique 4.6%; US 4.0%.

Transport and communications

Transport. *Railroads* (2001; scheduled passenger train service was terminated in January 2001): route length 301 km; metric ton-km cargo 700,000,000. *Roads* (1996): total length 3,810 km (paved 29%). *Vehicles* (1998): passenger cars 34,064; trucks and buses 35,030. *Air transport:* (1998) passenger-km 43,000,000; (1995) metric ton-km cargo 127,000; airports (1997) with scheduled flights 1. **Communications,** in total units (units per 1,000 persons). Daily newspaper circulation (2000): 27,100 (26); radios (2000): 169,000 (162); televisions (2000): 124,000 (110); telephone main lines (2003): 46,200 (44); cellular telephone subscribers (2003): 88,000 (84); personal computers (2003): 30,000 (29); Internet users (2003): 27,000 (26).

Education and health

Educational attainment (1986). Percentage of population age 25 and over having: no formal schooling 42.1%; some primary education 23.9%; complete primary 10.5%; some secondary 19.2%; complete secondary and higher 4.3%. **Literacy** (2000): total population age 15 and over literate 79.6%; males literate 80.8%; females literate 78.6%. **Health:** physicians (1996) 148 (1 per 6,663 persons); hospital beds (2000; excludes National Psychiatric Hospital) 1,570 (1 per 665 persons); infant mortality rate per 1,000 live births (2003) 67.4. **Food** (2001): daily per capita caloric intake 2,593 (vegetable products 85%, animal products 15%); 112% of FAO recommended minimum.

Military

Total active duty personnel (2003): 3,500 troops. **Military expenditure as percentage of GNP** (1999): 1.5% (world 2.4%); per capita expenditure $20.

Background

Stone tools and rock paintings indicate prehistoric habitation in the region, but it was not settled until the Bantu-speaking Swazi people migrated there in the 18th century and established the nucleus of the Swazi nation. The British gained control in the 19th century after the Swazi king sought their aid against the Zulus.

Following the South African War, the British governor of Transvaal administered Swaziland; his powers were transferred to the British high commissioner in 1906. In 1949 the British rejected the Union of South Africa's request to control Swaziland. The country gained limited self-government in 1963 and achieved independence in 1968. In the 1970s new constitutions were framed based on the supreme authority of the king and traditional tribal government. During the 1990s forces demanding democracy arose, but the kingdom remained in place. In 2005 a new constitution was signed that contained a bill of rights, but it retained the ban on opposition political parties.

Recent Developments

In 2005 local and international attention focused on the dreadful statistics that defined life for the people of Swaziland: 70% of the population living on an income of less than $1 a day; at 42.6%, the highest rate of HIV/AIDS infection in the world; 69,000 children orphaned by HIV/AIDS and a further 60,000 vulnerable with sick parents or caregivers; and 300,000 people dependent on food aid. Taiwan invested large sums in Swaziland's textile industry in 2006, but employment in the factories actually dropped, from 40,000 to 22,000.

Internet resources: <www.mintour.gov.sz>.

Sweden

Official name: Konungariket Sverige (Kingdom of Sweden). **Form of government:** constitutional monarchy and parliamentary state with one legislative house (Parliament [349]). **Chief of state:** King Carl XVI Gustaf (from 1973). **Head of government:** Prime Minister Fredrik Reinfeldt (from 2006). **Capital:** Stockholm. **Official language:** Swedish. **Official religion:** none. **Monetary unit:** 1 Swedish krona (SKr) = 100 ore; valuation (1 Jul 2007) US$1 = SKr 6.85.

Demography

Area: 173,860 sq mi, 450,295 sq km. **Population** (2006): 9,082,000. **Density** (2006): persons per sq mi 52.2, persons per sq km 20.2. **Urban** (2001): 81.2%. **Sex distribution** (2002): male 49.52%; female 50.48%. **Age breakdown** (2002): under 15, 18.2%; 15–29, 18.1%; 30–44, 20.8%; 45–59, 20.6%; 60–74, 13.4%; 75 and over, 8.9%. **Ethnic composition** (2002; by place of birth): Swedish

88.5%; other European 6.9%, of which Finnish 2.2%, Serb/Montenegrin 0.8%, Bosniac 0.6%; Asian 3.0%, of which Iranian 0.6%; African 0.6%; other 1.0%. **Religious affiliation** (1999): Church of Sweden 86.5% (about 30% nonpracticing); Muslim 2.3%; Roman Catholic 1.8%; Pentecostal 1.1%; other 8.3%. **Major cities** (2003): Stockholm 758,148; Göteborg 474,921; Malmö 265,481; Uppsala 179,673; Linköping 135,066. **Location:** northern Europe, bordering Finland, the Gulf of Bothnia, the Baltic Sea, and Norway.

Vital statistics

Birth rate per 1,000 population (2002): 10.7 (world avg. 21.3); legitimate (2001) 44.5%. **Death rate** per 1,000 population (2002): 10.6 (world avg. 9.1). **Natural increase rate** per 1,000 population (2002): 0.1 (world avg. 12.2). **Total fertility rate** (avg. births per childbearing woman; 2002): 1.6. **Marriage rate** per 1,000 population (2002): 4.3. **Divorce rate** per 1,000 population (2002): 2.4. **Life expectancy** at birth (2003): male 78.1 years; female 82.5 years.

National economy

Budget (2001). *Revenue:* SKr 755,126,000,000 (value-added and excise taxes 36.0%, social security 31.6%, income and capital gains taxes 17.9%, property taxes 5.3%). *Expenditures:* SKr 716,379,000,000 (health and social affairs 30.6%, debt service 11.3%, defense 6.3%, education 5.7%). **Public debt** (2004): $170,915,000,000. **Production** (metric tons except as noted). *Agriculture, forestry, fishing* (2002): sugar beets 2,800,000, wheat 2,117,000, barley 1,778,500; livestock (number of live animals) 1,882,000 pigs, 1,637,000 cattle, 427,000 sheep; roundwood (2002) 67,500,000 cu m; fish catch (2001) 318,600. *Mining and quarrying* (2001): iron ore 19,486,000; zinc (metal content) 156,300; copper (metal content) 74,300. *Manufacturing* (value added in $'000,000; 1999): telecommunications equipment, electronics 9,200; nonelectrical machinery and apparatus 6,100; road vehicles 6,000. *Energy production (consumption):* electricity (kW-hr; 2002) 143,136,000,000 ([2000] 152,193,000,000); coal (2000) none (3,057,000); crude petroleum (barrels; 2000) none (149,000,000); petroleum products (2000) 18,985,000 ·(12,227,000); natural gas (cu m; 2000) none (833,083,000). **Household income and expenditure.** Average household size (2000) 2.2; average annual disposable income per household (2000) SKr 239,000; sources of income (1996): wages and salaries 59.2%, transfer payments 26.1%, other 14.7%; expenditure (1996): housing 27.6%, transportation and communications 17.1%, food and beverages 16.5%, recreation 9.1%, energy 5.8%. **Tourism** (2002): receipts $4,233,000,000; expenditures $6,816,000,000. **Gross national product** (at current market prices; 2003): $258,319,000,000 ($28,840 per capita). **Population economically active** (2001): total 4,414,000; activity rate of total population 49.5% (participation rates: ages 16–64 [2000] 77.9%; female 47.8%; unemployed 4.0%). **Land use** as % of total land area (2000): in temporary crops 6.6%, in permanent crops 0.01%, in pasture 10.9%; overall forest area 65.9%.

Foreign trade

Imports (2001-c.i.f.): SKr 656,200,000,000 (nonelectrical machinery and apparatus 16.6%; electrical machinery and apparatus 14.0%; chemicals and chemical products 10.8%; road vehicles 9.3%; crude and refined petroleum 7.8%). *Major import sources* (2002): Germany 18.5%; Denmark 8.8%; UK 8.6%; Norway 8.2%; The Netherlands 6.7%. **Exports** (2001-f.o.b.): SKr 783,500,000,000 (nonelectrical machinery and apparatus 16.9%; road vehicles 12.1%; telecommunications equipment, electronics 9.3%; paper and paper products 8.5%; medicines and pharmaceuticals 5.5%; iron and steel 5.0%). *Major export destinations* (2002): US 11.6%; Germany 10.1%; Norway 9.0%; UK 8.2%; Denmark 5.9%.

Transport and communications

Transport. *Railroads* (2001): length 11,255 km; (2000) passenger-km 8,251,000,000; metric ton-km cargo 20,088,000,000. *Roads* (2002): total length 422,000 km (public 50.2%). *Vehicles* (2001): passenger cars 4,019,000; trucks and buses 410,000. *Air transport* (2002; includes SAS international and domestic traffic applicable to Sweden): passenger-km 10,896,000; metric ton-km cargo 266,676,000; airports (2001) 49. **Communications,** in total units (units per 1,000 persons). Daily newspaper circulation (2000): 3,830,000 (432); radios (2000): 8,270,000 (932); televisions (2000): 5,090,000 (574); telephone main lines (2002): 6,579,000 (736); cellular telephone subscribers (2002): 7,949,000 (889); personal computers (2002): 5,556,000 (621); Internet users (2002): 5,125,000 (573).

Education and health

Educational attainment (2002). Percentage of population age 16–74 having: lower secondary education 27%; incomplete or complete upper secondary education 45%; up to 3 years postsecondary 12%; 3 years or more postsecondary 14%; unknown 2%. **Literacy** (2002): virtually 100%. **Health** (2001): physicians 25,200 (1 per 354 persons); hospital beds 29,122 (1 per 306 persons); infant mortality rate per 1,000 live births (2002) 3.3. **Food** (2001): daily per capita caloric intake 3,164 (vegetable 70%, animal 30%); 118% of FAO recommended minimum.

Military

Total active duty personnel (2003): 27,600 (army 50.0%, navy 28.6%, air force 21.4%). **Military expenditure as percentage of GNP** (1999): 2.3% (world 2.4%); per capita expenditure $601.

Background

The first inhabitants of Sweden were apparently hunters who crossed the land bridge from Europe c. 9000 BC. During the Viking era (9th–10th centuries) the Swedes controlled river trade in eastern Europe between the Baltic Sea and the Black Sea and also raided western European lands. Sweden was loosely united and Christianized in the 11th–12th centuries. It conquered the Finns in the 12th century and in the

---

1 metric ton = about 1.1 short tons;   1 kilometer = 0.6 mi (statute);   1 metric ton-km cargo = about 0.68 short ton-mi cargo;   c.i.f.: cost, insurance, and freight;   f.o.b.: free on board

14th united with Norway and Denmark under a single monarchy. It broke away in 1523 under Gustav I Vasa. In the 17th century it emerged as a great European power in the Baltic region, but its dominance declined after its defeat in the Second Northern War (1700–21). Sweden became a constitutional monarchy in 1809 and united with Norway 1814–1905; it acknowledged Norwegian independence in 1905. It maintained its neutrality during both world wars. It was a charter member of the UN but abstained from membership in the European Union (EU) until the 1990s and in NATO altogether. A new constitution drafted in 1975 reduced the monarch's role to that of ceremonial head of state. In 1997 it decided to begin the controversial shutdown of its nuclear power industry.

Recent Developments

The elections in September 2006 ended 12 years of socialist rule in Sweden, producing a new center-right government under Prime Minister Fredrik Reinfeldt. The former government was hurt by alleged mismanagement after the 2004 Indian Ocean tsunami, in which nearly 550 Swedish tourists were killed. The economic growth rate was more than 4%, public and government finances were balanced, and higher dividends to shareholders fueled a stock market that had risen for three years in a row.

Internet resources: <www.visit-sweden.com>.

Switzerland

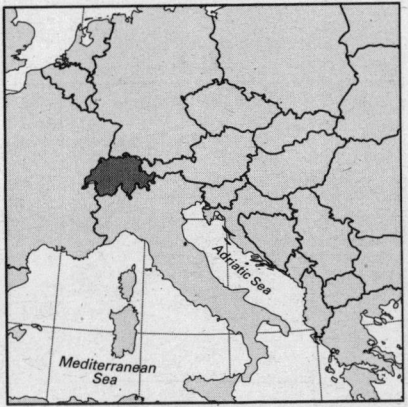

Official name: Confédération Suisse (French); Schweizerische Eidgenossenschaft (German); Confederazione Svizzera (Italian); Confederaziun Svizra (Romansh) (Swiss Confederation). **Form of government:** federal state with two legislative houses (Council of States [46]; National Council [200]). **Head of state and government:** President Micheline Calmy-Rey (from 2007). **Capitals:** Bern (administrative); Lausanne (judicial). **Official languages:** French; German; Italian; Romansh (locally). **Official religion:** none. **Monetary unit:** 1 Swiss Franc (Sw F) = 100 centimes; valuation (1 Jul 2007) US$1 = Sw F 1.22.

Demography

Area: 15,940 sq mi, 41,284 sq km. **Population** (2006): 7,533,000. **Density** (2006): persons per sq mi 472.6, persons per sq km 182.5. **Urban** (2002): 67.8%. **Sex distribution** (2003): male 48.90%; female 51.10%. **Age breakdown** (2003): under 15, 16.9%; 15–29, 18.0%; 30–44, 24.2%; 45–59, 20.2%; 60–74, 13.3%; 75 and over, 7.4%. **National composition** (2001): Swiss 80.2%; Yugoslav 4.8%; Italian 4.5%; Portuguese 1.9%; German 1.5%; Spanish 1.2%; other 5.9%. **Religious affiliation** (2000): Roman Catholic 41.8%; Protestant 35.2%; Muslim 4.3%; Orthodox 1.8%; Jewish 0.2%; nonreligious 11.1%; other 5.6%. **Major urban agglomerations** (2003): Zürich 978,300; Geneva 476,100; Basel 403,800; Bern 321,600; Lausanne 294,500. **Location:** central Europe, bordering Germany, Austria, Liechtenstein, Italy, and France.

Vital statistics

Birth rate per 1,000 population (2003): 9.8 (world avg. 21.3); legitimate 87.6%. **Death rate** per 1,000 population (2003): 8.6 (world avg. 9.1). **Natural increase rate** per 1,000 population (2003): 1.2 (world avg. 12.2). **Total fertility rate** (avg. births per childbearing woman; 2002): 1.4. **Marriage rate** per 1,000 population (2003): 5.5. **Divorce rate** per 1,000 population (2003): 2.2. **Life expectancy** at birth (2003): male 77.7 years; female 83.0 years.

National economy

Budget (2002). *Revenue:* Sw F 130,595,000,000 (1999; taxes on income and profits 51.1%, taxes on goods and services 20.1%, property taxes 1.5%). *Expenditures:* Sw F 132,989,000,000 (1999; social security 19.4%, education 18.4%, economic affairs 14.0%, health 12.6%, interest 8.4%, defense 4.5%). **National debt** (end of year; 2002): Sw F 122,366,000,000. **Tourism** (2002): receipts from visitors $7,628,000,000; expenditures by nationals abroad $6,427,000,000. **Production** (metric tons except as noted). *Agriculture, forestry, fishing* (2002): sugar beets 1,100,000, cow's milk (2001) 626,000, wheat 584,000; livestock (number of live animals) 1,593,000 cattle, 1,536,000 pigs; roundwood (2002) 4,344,000 cu m; fish catch (2001) 2,850. *Mining* (2003): salt 300,000; cut and polished diamond exports (1998): $1,340,000,000. *Manufacturing* (value added in $'000,000; 2001): chemicals and chemical products 7,363; nonelectrical machinery 7,067; professional and scientific equipment 6,233. *Energy production (consumption):* electricity (kW-hr; 2002) 65,011,000,000 (60,503,000,000); coal (2000) none (156,000); crude petroleum (barrels; 2000) none (33,900,000); petroleum products (2000) 4,861,000 (10,181,000); natural gas (cu m; 2000) negligible (2,971,000,000). **Gross national product** (2003): $292,892,000,000 ($39,880 per capita). **Population economically active** (2002): total 4,177,000 (includes 1,058,000 foreign workers); activity rate of total population 56.2% (participation rates: ages 15 and over, 68.7%; female 44.5%; unemployed 2.5%). **Household income and expenditure** (2000). Average household size 2.4; average gross income per household Sw F 104,352; sources of income (2000): work 72.4%, transfers 22.3%; expenditure (2001): housing and energy 27.5%, food and nonalcoholic beverages 13.5%, transportation

11.0%, recreation 10.5%, hotels and cafes 10.0%. **Land use** as % of total land area (2000): in temporary crops 10.4%, in permanent crops 0.6%, in pasture 28.9%; overall forest area 30.3%.

Foreign trade

Imports (2002-c.i.f.): Sw F 123,125,000,000 (chemical products 22.1%, machinery 21.1%, vehicles 10.4%, food products 8.0%). *Major import sources* (2003): Germany 33.3%; Italy 11.1%; France 11.1%; US 4.4%; UK 4.0%. **Exports** (2002-f.o.b.): Sw F 130,380,000,000 (chemicals and chemical products 34.4%, machinery 24.3%, precision instruments, watches, jewelry 17.3%, fabricated metals 7.5%). *Major export destinations* (2003): Germany 21.2%; US 10.6%; France 8.8%; Italy 8.4%; UK 4.8%; Japan 3.9%.

Transport and communications

Transport. *Railroads:* length (2000) 5,062 km; passenger-km 14,665,000,000; metric ton-km cargo 9,112,000,000. *Roads* (2002): total length 71,192 km. *Vehicles* (2003): passenger cars 3,753,890; trucks and buses 292,329. *Air transport* (2003; Swiss airlines only): passenger-km 24,083,000,000; metric ton-km cargo 1,305,000,000; airports (1996) with scheduled flights 5. **Communications**, in total units (units per 1,000 persons). Daily newspaper circulation (2000): 2,650,000 (369); radios (2000): 7,200,000 (1,002); televisions (2000): 3,940,000 (548); telephone main lines (2002): 5,419,000 (744); cellular telephone subscribers (2003): 6,172,000 (843); personal computers (2002): 5,160,000 (709); Internet users (2002): 2,556,000 (351).

Education and health

Educational attainment (2000). Percentage of resident Swiss and resident alien population age 25–64 having: compulsory education 19.0%; secondary 56.8%; higher 24.2%. **Health** (2002): physicians 25,921 (1 per 281 persons); hospital beds (2001) 44,316 (1 per 163 persons); infant mortality rate per 1,000 live births 4.5. **Food** (2001): daily per capita caloric intake 3,440 (vegetable products 66%, animal products 34%); 129% of FAO recommended minimum.

Military

Total active duty personnel (2003): 3,300 (excludes 351,000 reservists). **Military expenditure as percentage of GNP** (1999): 1.2% (world 2.4%); per capita expenditure $469.

Background

The original inhabitants of Switzerland were the Helvetians, who were conquered by the Romans in the 1st century BC. Germanic tribes penetrated the region from the 3rd to the 6th century AD, and Muslim and Magyar raiders ventured in during the 10th century. It came under the Holy Roman Empire in the 11th century. In 1291 three cantons formed an anti-Habsburg league that became the nucleus of the Swiss Confederation. It was a center of the Reformation, which divided the confederation and led to a period of polit-ical and religious conflict. The French organized Switzerland as the Helvetic Republic in 1798. In 1815 the Congress of Vienna recognized Swiss independence and guaranteed its neutrality. A new federal state was formed in 1848 with Bern as the capital. It remained neutral in both world wars and continued to guard this stance. With the formation of the European Union (EU), it took steps toward provisional association with the European economic area.

Recent Developments

The Swiss GDP in 2006 was expected to grow at 2.7% (compared with the 2.5% forecast for the euro zone), with unemployment at 3.3%. While opening its doors to more EU citizens, Switzerland ratified new immigration and asylum laws that effectively blocked unskilled labor from outside Europe and clamped down on refugees. Critics condemned the new law as one of Europe's strictest and protested that an identity-papers rule was particularly unfair because genuine victims of persecution and war often had no documents. The Swiss finally approved a 2002 US request to provide details of any bank accounts suspected of being used for terrorist funding. The Federal Prosecutor's Office revealed in June that intelligence officials had thwarted a plan by an Algerian group with reported links to al-Qaeda to shoot down an Israeli passenger flight taking off from Geneva. The impact of global warming was tangible in July when about 600,000 cu m (20 million cu ft) of rock fell from the Eiger peak, highlighting previous warnings that three-quarters of Switzerland's glaciers were at risk of melting by 2050.

Internet resources: <www.myswitzerland.com>.

Syria

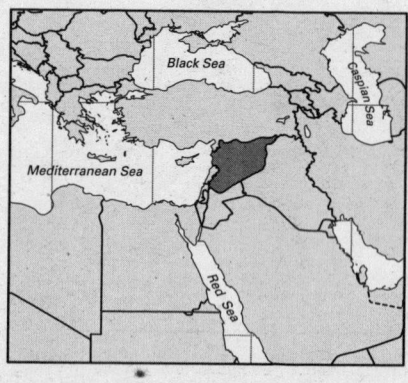

Official name: Al-Jumhuriyah al-'Arabiyah al-Suriyah (Syrian Arab Republic). **Form of government:** unitary multiparty republic with one legislative house (People's Council [250]). **Head of state and government:** President Bashar al-Assad (from 2000), assisted by Prime Minister Muhammad Naji al-Otari (from 2003). **Capital:** Damascus. **Official language:** Arabic. **Official religion:** none, although Islam is the required religion

1 metric ton = about 1.1 short tons;   1 kilometer = 0.6 mi (statute);   1 metric ton-km cargo = about 0.68 short ton-mi cargo;   c.i.f.: cost, insurance, and freight;   f.o.b.: free on board

of the head of state and is the basis of the legal system. **Monetary unit:** 1 Syrian pound (LS) = 100 piastres; valuation (1 Jul 2007) US$1 = LS 53.17.

Demography

Area (includes territory in the Golan Heights recognized internationally as part of Syria): 71,498 sq mi, 185,180 sq km. **Population** (2006): 18,542,000 (excludes 800,000 Iraqi refugees). **Density** (2006): persons per sq mi 259.3, persons per sq km 100.1. **Urban** (2001): 51.8%. **Sex distribution** (2001): male 51.15%; female 48.85%. **Age breakdown** (2001): under 15, 40.4%; 15–29, 30.1%; 30–44, 15.6%; 45–59, 8.8%; 60 and over, 5.1%. **Ethnic composition** (2000): Syrian Arab 74.9%; Bedouin Arab 7.4%; Kurd 7.3%; Palestinian Arab 3.9%; Armenian 2.7%; other 3.8%. **Religious affiliation** (1992): Muslim 86.0%, of which Sunni 74.0%, 'Alawite (Shi'i) 12.0%; Christian 5.5%; Druze 3.0%; other 5.5%. **Major cities:** Aleppo (2000) 2,229,000 (urban agglomeration); Damascus (2001) 2,195,000 (urban agglomeration); Homs (Hims) (2000) 811,000 (urban agglomeration); Latakia (1994) 306,535; Hamah (1994) 229,000. **Location:** the Middle East, bordering Turkey, Iraq, Jordan, Israel, Lebanon, and the Mediterranean Sea.

Vital statistics

Birth rate per 1,000 population (2003): 29.5 (world avg. 21.3). **Death rate** per 1,000 population (2003): 5.0 (world avg. 9.1). **Natural increase rate** per 1,000 population (2003): 24.5 (world avg. 12.2). **Total fertility rate** (avg. births per childbearing woman; 2003): 3.7. **Marriage rate** per 1,000 population (2000; Syrian Arabs only): 8.6. **Divorce rate** per 1,000 population (2000; Syrian Arabs only): 0.7. **Life expectancy** at birth (2003): male 68.2 years; female 70.7 years.

National economy

Budget (2000). *Revenue:* LS 275,400,000,000 (taxes 31.2%, revenue from loans 13.4%, transit duties 8.0%, other 47.4%). *Expenditures:* LS 275,400,-000,000 (current expenditures 52.1%, capital [development] expenditures 47.9%). **Public debt** (external, outstanding; 2002): $15,849,000,000. **Gross national product** (2003): $20,211,000,000 ($1,160 per capita). **Production** (metric tons except as noted). *Agriculture, forestry, fishing* (2002): wheat 4,755,000, sugar beets 1,481,000, olives 999,000; livestock (number of live animals) 13,497,000 sheep, 932,000 goats, 867,000 cattle; roundwood (2001) 50,400 cu m; fish catch (2001) 14,171. *Mining and quarrying* (2001): phosphate rock 2,043,000; gypsum 345,000; salt 106,000. *Manufacturing* (2000): cement 4,631,000; fertilizers 453,000; cottonseed cake 288,000. *Energy production (consumption):* electricity (kW-hr; 2000) 22,626,000,000 (23,946,-000,000); crude petroleum (barrels; 2002) 191,900,-000 ([2000] 88,342,000); petroleum products (2000) 11,351,000 (11,020,000); natural gas (cu m; 2001) 5,833,000,000 (5,833,000,000). **Population economically active** (2000): total 4,937,000; activity rate of total population 30.3% (participation rates: ages 15 and over, 50.9%; female 19.8%; unemployed 9.5%). **Households.** Average household size (2000): 6.0. **Tourism** (2002): receipts $1,366,000,000; expenditures (2001) $610,000,000. **Land use** as % of total land area (2000): in temporary crops 24.7%, in permanent crops 4.4%, in pasture 45.5%; overall forest area 2.5%.

Foreign trade

Imports (2000-c.i.f.): $3,815,000,000 (food 14.6%, of which cereals 4.9%; chemicals and chemical products 12.9%; nonelectrical machinery and equipment 10.9%; iron and steel 10.7%; textile yarn 7.5%). *Major import sources:* Germany 6.8%; US 6.8%; Italy 6.2%; Ukraine 6.2%; China 5.3%; Turkey 5.0%; South Korea 5.0%. **Exports** (2000-f.o.b.): $4,634,000,000 (crude petroleum 69.1%; refined petroleum 7.0%; raw cotton 4.1%; vegetables 2.9%; apparel and clothing accessories 2.8%). *Major export destinations:* Italy 32.0%; France 22.5%; Turkey 10.4%; Saudi Arabia 5.9%; Lebanon 4.1%.

Transport and communications

Transport. *Railroads* (2001; excludes length of Syrian part of railway opened in August 2000 linking Aleppo, Syria, and Mosul, Iraq): route length 2,676 km; passenger-km 304,000,000; metric ton-km cargo 1,491,-000,000. *Roads* (2000): total length 44,575 km (paved 21%). *Vehicles* (2000): passenger cars 138,-823; trucks and buses (1998) 282,664. *Air transport* (2001): passenger-km 1,626,950; metric ton-km cargo 15,357,000; airports with scheduled flights 5. **Communications,** in total units (units per 1,000 persons). Daily newspaper circulation (2000): 326,000 (20); radios (2000): 4,500,000 (276); televisions (2002): 3,094,000 (182); telephone main lines (2002): 2,099,300 (123); cellular telephone units (2002): 400,000 (24); personal computers (2002): 330,000 (19); Internet users (2002): 220,000 (13).

Education and health

Literacy (2000): percentage of population age 15 and over literate 74.4%; males literate 88.3%; females literate 60.5%. **Health** (2003): physicians 25,147 (1 per 699 persons); hospital beds 26,202 (1 per 671 persons); infant mortality rate per 1,000 live births (2003) 31.7. **Food** (2001): daily per capita caloric intake 3,038 (vegetable products 88%, animal products 12%); 123% of FAO recommended minimum.

Military

Total active duty personnel (2003): 319,000 (army 67.4%, navy 1.3%, air force 12.5%, air defense 18.8%); troops stationed in Lebanon (October 2003) 20,000. **Military expenditure as percentage of GNP** (1999): 7.0% (world 2.4%); per capita expenditure $280.

Did you know? Many scholars believe that Syria's capital, Damascus (colloquially al-Sham, "the northern" in relation to Arabia), may be the oldest continuously inhabited city in the world.

Background

Syria has been inhabited for several thousand years. From the 3rd millennium BC it was under the control variously of Sumerians, Akkadians, Amorites, Egyptians, Hittites, Assyrians, and Babylonians. In the 6th century BC it became part of the Persian Achaemenian dynasty, which fell to Alexander the Great in 330 BC. Seleucid rulers governed it from 301 BC to c. 164 BC; then Parthians and Nabataean Arabs divided the region. It flourished as a Roman province (64 BC–AD 300) and as part of the Byzantine Empire (300–634) until Muslims invaded and established control. It came under the Ottoman Empire in 1516, which held it, except for brief rules by Egypt, until the British invaded in World War I. After the war it became a French mandate; it achieved independence in 1945. It united with Egypt in the United Arab Republic (1958–61). During the Six-Day War (1967), it lost the Golan Heights to Israel. Syrian troops frequently clashed with Israeli troops in Lebanon during the 1980s and '90s. Hafez al-Assad's long and harsh regime was marked also by antagonism toward Syria's neighbors Turkey and Iraq.

Recent Developments

Foreign affairs dominated Syria's agenda throughout 2006. Syria's preeminent position in Lebanon, which had been severely undermined by the withdrawal of Syrian military and security forces in 2005, steadily deteriorated, and Damascus increased material support for a collection of radical Palestinian organizations operating there. Damascus also strengthened ties to Tehran and Moscow. Syria and Iran signed a mutual-defense pact in June. This defense agreement coincided with reports of an arrangement that authorized the Russian Black Sea Fleet to use two Syrian ports. Syria condemned Israel's large-scale incursion into southern Lebanon in mid-July and threatened to intervene if Israeli forces advanced toward Syrian territory. Tens of thousands of refugees poured across the border to escape the fighting. During a meeting of Arab foreign ministers in Beirut in August, Syria's foreign minister suggested that Arab countries cut off oil supplies to world markets; he was rebuked by his Saudi and Libyan counterparts. Cartoons published in a Danish newspaper that depicted the Prophet Muhammad, a practice forbidden in Islam, sparked violent demonstrations in early February outside the Danish, Norwegian, and French embassies. In March Najah al-Attar was appointed a vice president and became the first woman and first non-Ba'th Party member to hold the post.

Internet resources: <www.syriatourism.org>.

Taiwan

Official name: Chung-hua Min-kuo (Republic of China) Form of government: multiparty republic with a Legislature (Legislative Yuan [225]). Chief of state: President Chen Shui-bian (from 2000). Head of government: Premier Chang Chun-hsiung (from 2007). Administrative center: Taipei. Official language: Mandarin Chinese. Official religion: none. Monetary unit: 1 New Taiwan dollar (NT$) = 100 cents; valuation (1 Jul 2007) US$1 = NT$32.84.

Demography

Area: 13,972 sq mi, 36,188 sq km. Population (2006; includes Quemoy and Matsu groups): 22,815,000. Density (2006; includes Quemoy and

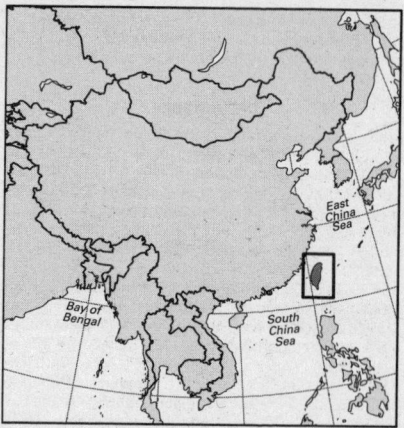

Matsu groups): persons per sq mi 1,633, persons per sq km 630.5. Urban (1991; excludes Quemoy and Matsu groups): 74.7%. Sex distribution (2003; includes Quemoy and Matsu groups): male 50.98%; female 49.02%. Age breakdown (2002; includes Quemoy and Matsu groups): under 15, 20.8%; 15–29, 24.9%; 30–44, 25.3%; 45–59, 16.7%; 60–74, 9.1%; 75 and over, 3.2%. Ethnic composition (1997): Han Chinese, Chinese mainland minorities, and others 98.2%; indigenous tribal peoples 1.8%, of which Ami 0.6%. Religious affiliation (1997): Buddhism 22.4%; Taoism 20.7%; I-kuan Tao 4.3%; Protestant 1.6%; Roman Catholic 1.4%; other Christian 0.3%; Muslim 0.2%; Baha'i 0.1%; other (mostly Christian folk-religionists) 49.0%. Major cities (2003): Taipei 2,638,065; Kao-hsiung 1,508,917; T'ai-chung 999,476; T'ai-nan 746,287; Chi-lung 391,657. Location: island between the East China Sea, the Philippine Sea, and the South China Sea north of the Philippines and southeast of mainland China.

Vital statistics

Birth rate per 1,000 population (2003): 10.1 (world avg. 21.3). Death rate per 1,000 population (2003): 5.8 (world avg. 9.1). Natural increase rate per 1,000 population (2003): 4.3 (world avg. 12.2). Total fertility rate (avg. births per childbearing woman; 2003): 1.2. Marriage rate per 1,000 population (2003): 7.6. Divorce rate per 1,000 population (2003): 2.9. Life expectancy at birth (2003): male 73.4 years; female 79.1 years.

National economy

Budget (1999). Revenue: NT$3,391,948,000,000 (income taxes 18.0%, business tax 9.1%, commodity tax 6.5%, land tax 6.4%, customs duties 4.6%). Expenditures: NT$3,371,702,000,000 (administration and defense 24.5%, education 19.4%). Population economically active (May 2003): total 10,022,000; activity rate of total population 44.4% (participation rates: over age 15 [December 2002], 57%; female [May 2003] 40.4%; unemployed [May 2003] 5.0%). Production (metric tons except as noted). Agriculture,

1 metric ton = about 1.1 short tons;   1 kilometer = 0.6 mi (statute);   1 metric ton-km cargo = about 0.68 short ton-mi cargo;   c.i.f.: cost, insurance, and freight;   f.o.b.: free on board

forestry, fishing (2000): sugarcane 2,894,000, rice 1,559,000, citrus fruits 440,382; livestock (number of live animals) 7,494,954 pigs, 202,491 goats, 161,700 cattle; timber 21,134 cu m; fish catch (2003) 1,498,983. *Mining and quarrying* (2000): marble 17,800,000. *Manufacturing* (2002): cement 19,228,026; steel ingots 18,240,256; paperboard 3,274,932. *Energy production (consumption):* electricity (kW-hr; 2002) 165,901,000,000 (151,193,-000,000); coal (2001) none (48,000,000); crude petroleum (barrels; 2002) 349,000 (360,000,000); natural gas (cu m; 2001) 918,000,000 (8,264,000,-000). **Tourism** (2002): receipts from visitors US$4,584,000,000; expenditures by nationals abroad US$6,956,000,000. **Gross national product** (2002): US$283,375,000,000 (US$12,570 per capita). **Household income and expenditure** (1999). Average household size (2003) 3.2; income per household NT$1,181,082; expenditure: food, beverages, and tobacco 25.1%, rent, fuel, and power 24.9%, education and recreation 13.0%, transportation 11.1%, health care 11.0%, clothing 4.1%. **Land use** as % of total land area (2001): in temporary crops 16.1%, in permanent crops 6.6%, in pasture 0.3%; overall forest area 58.1%.

Foreign trade

Imports (2002-c.i.f.): US$112,591,000,000 (electronic machinery 28.5%, nonelectrical machinery 16.0%, minerals 11.2%, chemicals 10.1%, metals and metal products 8.2%, precision instruments, clocks, watches, and musical instruments 5.8%). *Major import sources:* Japan 24.2%; US 16.1%; South Korea 6.8%; Germany 3.9%; Malaysia 3.7%. **Exports** (2002-f.o.b.): US$130,641,000,000 (nonelectrical machinery, electrical machinery, and electronics 57.4%, textile products 10.0%, plastic articles 5.9%, transportation equipment 3.7%). *Major export destinations:* Hong Kong 23.6%; US 20.5%; Japan 9.2%; Singapore 3.2%; Germany 2.9%.

Transport and communications

Transport. *Railroads* (2002; Taiwan Railway Administration only): route length 1,119 km; passenger-km 9,666,000,000, metric ton-km cargo 919,000,000. *Roads* (2002): total length 20,816 km (excludes urban). *Vehicles* (2002): passenger cars 4,989,000; trucks and buses 882,000. *Air transport* (1998): passenger-km 39,218,000,000; metric ton-km cargo 4,129,300,000; airports (1996) 13. **Communications**, in total units (units per 1,000 persons). Radios (1996): 8,620,000 (402); televisions (1999): 9,200,000 (418); telephone main lines (2003): 13,355,000 (590); cellular telephone subscribers (2003): 25,089,600 (1,108); personal computers (2002): 8,887,000 (396); Internet users (2003): 8,830,000 (390).

Education and health

Educational attainment (1999). Percentage of population age 25 and over having: no formal schooling 7.0%; less than complete primary education 6.3%; primary 21.3%; incomplete secondary 25.7%; secondary 21.8%; some college 10.4%; higher 7.5%. **Literacy** (1999): population age 15 and over literate 16,414,896 (94.6%); males literate 8,641,549 (97.6%); females literate 7,773,347 (91.4%). **Health** (2001): physicians 30,562 (1 per 731 persons); hospital beds 127,676 (1 per 175 persons); infant mortality rate per 1,000 live births (2003) 5.3.

Military

Total active duty personnel (2002): 290,000 (army 69.0%, navy 15.5%, air force 15.5%). **Military expenditure as percentage of GNP** (1999): 5.2% (world 2.4%); per capita expenditure US$690.

Background

Known to the Chinese as early as the 7th century, Taiwan was widely settled by them early in the 17th century. In 1646 the Dutch seized control of the island, only to be ousted in 1661 by a large influx of Chinese refugees from the Ming Dynasty. Taiwan fell to the Manchus in 1683 and was not open to Europeans again until 1858. In 1895 it was ceded to Japan following the Sino-Japanese War. A Japanese military center in World War II, it was frequently bombed by US planes. After Japan's defeat it was returned to China, which was then governed by the Nationalists. When the Communists took over mainland China in 1949, the Nationalist government fled to Taiwan and made it their seat of government, with Gen. Chiang Kai-shek as president. In 1954 he and the US signed a mutual defense treaty, and Taiwan received US support for almost three decades, developing its economy in spectacular fashion. It was recognized by many noncommunist countries as the representative of all China until 1971, when it was replaced in the UN by the People's Republic of China. Martial law was lifted in Taiwan in 1987 and travel restrictions with mainland China in 1988. In 1989 opposition parties were legalized. The relationship with the mainland became increasingly close in the 1990s.

Recent Developments

Taiwan was shocked by allegations of corruption against Pres. Chen Shui-bian in 2006. His son-in-law, Chao Chien-ming, was indicted on insider-trading charges in the summer; first lady Wu Shu-chen was charged with having misused a secret diplomatic fund under the president's control; and Chen himself was accused of having used state funds slated for national affairs on personal expenditures and of having falsified receipts. Tens of thousands of people protested against corruption and the Chen administration. Chen was also accused of having risked Taiwanese lives for his own political prestige by provoking the mainland on independence issues. Waves of demonstrations continued throughout the year, including a student hunger strike and a sit-in by more than 100 professors. In August the most serious effort to remove Chen from office rallied more than a million participants in a series of marches. Taiwan's relationship with the US was strained. In February Chen dismantled a government committee responsible for overseeing an eventual reunification with China. The US insisted that Taiwan not change the status quo across the Taiwan Strait and aborted talks on sales of US military aircraft to Taiwan. In 2006 Taiwan's GDP grew by 4.6%, and its trade with China continued to enjoy a surplus of tens of billions of dollars. Over 70% of Taiwan's offshore investments went to China. Taiwan also attracted sizable direct investment from the US, Japan, South Korea, and Sweden.

Internet resources: <www.tbroc.gov.tw>.

Tajikistan

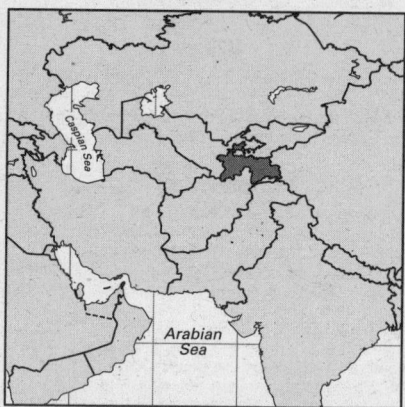

Official name: Jumhurii Tojikistan (Republic of Tajikistan). **Form of government:** parliamentary republic with two legislative houses (National Assembly [33, including 8 members appointed by the president]; Assembly of Representatives [63]). **Chief of state:** President Imomali Rakhmon (from 1994). **Head of government:** Prime Minister Akil Akilov (from 1999). **Capital:** Dushanbe. **Official language:** Tajik (Tojik). **Official religion:** none. **Monetary unit:** 1 somoni = 100 dinars; valuation (1 Jul 2007) US$1 = 3.45 somoni. The somoni (equal to 1,000 Tajik rubles) was introduced on 30 Oct 2000.

Demography

Area: 55,300 sq mi, 143,100 sq km (includes c. 400 sq mi [c. 1,035 sq km] ceded to China in May 2002). **Population** (2006): 7,063,000. **Density** (2006): persons per sq mi 127.7, persons per sq km 49.4. **Urban** (2000): 26.6%. **Sex distribution** (2000): male 50.30%; female 49.70%. **Age breakdown** (2000): under 15, 39.4%; 15–29, 27.7%; 30–44, 18.4%; 45–59, 7.6%; 60–74, 5.4%; 75 and over, 1.5%. **Ethnic composition** (2000): Tajik 80.0%; Uzbek 15.3%; Russian 1.1%; Tatar 0.3%; other 3.3%. **Religious affiliation** (1995): Sunni Muslim 80.0%; Shi'i Muslim 5.0%; Russian Orthodox 1.5%; Jewish 0.1%; other (mostly nonreligious) 13.4%. **Major cities** (2002): Dushanbe 575,900; Khujand 147,400; Kulyab 79,500; Kurgan-Tyube 61,200; Ura-Tyube 51,700. **Location:** central Asia, bordering Kyrgyzstan, China, Afghanistan, and Uzbekistan.

Vital statistics

Birth rate per 1,000 population (2003): 24.3 (world avg. 21.3); (1994) legitimate 90.8%. **Death rate** per 1,000 population (2003): 6.0 (world avg. 9.1). **Natural increase rate** per 1,000 population (2003): 18.3 (world avg. 12.2). **Total fertility rate** (avg. births per childbearing woman; 2003): 3.0. **Marriage rate** per 1,000 population (2001): 4.6. **Divorce rate** per 1,000 population (1994): 0.8. **Life expectancy** at birth (2003): male 61.4 years; female 67.5 years.

National economy

Budget (2001). *Revenue:* 342,316,000 somoni (tax revenue 91.6%, of which value-added tax 25.1%, taxes on aluminum and cotton 18.3%, customs duties 15.1%, income and profit taxes 13.8%, excise taxes 4.5%; nontax revenue 8.4%). *Expenditures:* 338,418,000 somoni (current expenditures 77.5%, of which state authorities 19.7%, education 18.9%, state bodies and administration 11.7%, defense 8.7%, health 7.3%, law enforcement 4.1%, debt payment 4.1%; capital expenditures 22.5%). **Production** (metric tons except as noted). *Agriculture, forestry, fishing* (2002): raw seed cotton 515,000, potatoes 400,000, wheat 361,000; livestock (number of live animals) 1,490,000 sheep, 1,091,000 cattle, 779,000 goats; fish catch (2001) 236. *Mining and quarrying* (2000): antimony (metal content) 2,000; gold 2,700 kg. *Manufacturing* (value of production in '000,000 somoni at 1998 constant prices; 2001): nonferrous metals 442,000 (aluminum production by weight in 2001 equaled 289,100 metric tons); food 138,000; textiles 104,000. *Energy production (consumption):* electricity (kW-hr; 2001) 14,400,000,000 (13,500,000,000); coal (2001) 24,900 (122,000); crude petroleum (barrels; 2000) 132,000 (95,000); petroleum products (2000) none (753,000); natural gas (cu m; 2000) 38,594,000 (748,500,000). **Tourism** (2002): receipts from visitors $2,000,000; expenditures by nationals abroad $2,000,000. **Population economically active** (2002): total 1,829,000; activity rate of total population 29.6% (participation rates: ages 15–59 [male], 15–54 [female] 55.1%; female [1996] 46.5%; unemployed 2.3%). **Gross national product** (2003): $1,221,000,000 ($190 per capita). **Public debt** (external, outstanding; 2002): $912,000,000. **Land use** as % of total land area (2000): in temporary crops 6.6%, in permanent crops 0.9%, in pasture 24.9%; overall forest area 2.8%. **Household income and expenditure.** Average household size (2000) 5.9; (1995) income per household 18,744 Tajik rubles; sources of income (1995): wages and salaries 34.5%, self-employment 34.0%, borrowing 2.4%, pension 2.0%, other 27.1%; expenditure: food 81.5%, clothing 10.2%, transport 2.5%, fuel 2.1%, other 3.7%.

Foreign trade

Imports (2001): $773,000,000 (alumina 23.9%, petroleum products and natural gas 12.9%, electricity 12.7%, grain and flour 8.0%). *Major import sources* (2000): Uzbekistan 28.8%; Russia 16.1%; Ukraine 13.1%; Kazakhstan 12.8%; Azerbaijan 9.8%. **Exports** (2001): $652,000,000 (aluminum 61.0%, electricity 12.1%, cotton fiber 10.9%). *Major export destinations* (2000): Russia 37.4%; The Netherlands 25.7%; Uzbekistan 14.1%; Switzerland 10.4%; Italy 2.8%.

Transport and communications

Transport. *Railroads* (2001): length 482 km; passenger-km 32,000,000; metric ton-km cargo 1,248,000,000. *Roads* (1996): total length 13,747 km (paved 83%). *Vehicles* (1996): passenger cars 680,000; trucks and buses 8,190. *Air transport* (2001; Tajikistan Airlines only): passenger-km 605,000,000; metric ton-km cargo 4,841,000; airports (2002) 2. **Communications,** in total units (units per 1,000 persons). Daily newspaper circulation (2000): 123,000 (20); radios (2000): 870,000 (141); televisions (2000): 2,010,000 (326); telephone main lines (2003): 242,100 (37); cellular phone subscribers (2003): 47,600 (7.3); Internet users (2003): 4,100 (0.6).

Education and health

Educational attainment (1989). Percentage of population age 25 and over having: primary education or no formal schooling 16.3%; some secondary 21.1%; completed secondary and some postsecondary 55.1%; higher 7.5%. **Literacy** (2001): percentage of total population age 15 and over literate 99.3%; males literate 98.9%; females literate 99.6%. **Health** (2002): physicians 13,393 (1 per 472 persons); hospital beds 40,387 (1 per 157 persons); infant mortality rate per 1,000 live births (2003) 50.0. **Food** (2001): daily per capita caloric intake 1,662 (vegetable products 92%, animal products 8%); 65% of FAO recommended minimum.

Military

Total active duty personnel (2003): 6,000 (army 100%); Russian troops (2004) 20,000, including 9,-000 along the Tajik-Afghan border; US troops (2004) 3,000. **Military expenditure as percentage of GNP** (1999): 1.3% (world 2.4%); per capita expenditure $13.

Background

Settled by the Persians c. the 6th century BC, Tajikistan was part of the empires of the Persians and of Alexander the Great and his successors. In the 7th–8th centuries AD it was conquered by the Arabs, who introduced Islam. The Uzbeks controlled the region in the 15th–18th centuries. In the 1860s Russia took over much of Tajikistan. In 1924 it became an autonomous republic under the administration of the Uzbek Soviet Socialist Republic, and it gained republic status in 1929. It achieved independence with the collapse of the Soviet Union in 1991. Civil war raged through much of the 1990s between government forces and an opposition of mostly Islamic forces. Peace was reached in 1997.

Recent Developments

Issues of economic development dominated public life in Tajikistan throughout 2006. Construction proceeded on two large hydropower installations on the Vakhsh River, but a disagreement over the height of the dam at Rogun held up the most important of the projects. In mid-March the International Monetary Fund confirmed its write-off of $99 million of Tajikistan's external debt. Lack of employment opportunities at home drove hundreds of thousands of men of working age—possibly a million or more—to go abroad, mostly to Russia, to find work. Law-enforcement officials repeatedly expressed concern that extremist groups, particularly the Islamic Movement of Uzbekistan and Hizb ut-Tahrir, were becoming more active and more violent in 2006.

Internet resources: <www.tajiktour.tajnet.com>.

Tanzania

Official name: Jamhuri ya Muungano wa Tanzania (Swahili); United Republic of Tanzania (English). **Form**

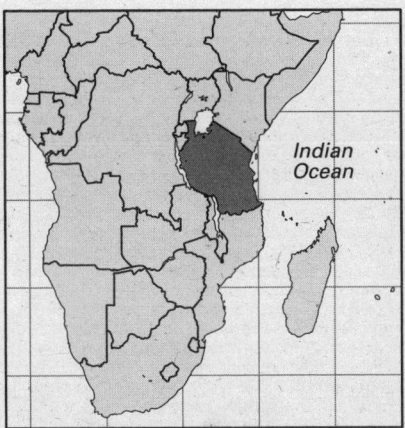

Indian Ocean

of government: unitary multiparty republic with one legislative house (National Assembly [274]). **Head of state and government:** President Jakaya Kikwete (from 2005), assisted by Prime Minister Edward Lowassa (from 2005). **Capital:** Dar es Salaam (capital designate, Dodoma). **Official languages:** Swahili; English. **Official religion:** none. **Monetary unit:** 1 Tanzania shilling (T Sh) = 100 cents; valuation (1 Jul 2007) US$1 = T Sh 1,263.

Demography

Area: 364,901 sq mi, 945,090 sq km. **Population** (2006): 37,445,000. **Density** (2006): persons per sq mi 109.7, persons per sq km 42.4. **Urban** (2002): 23.0%. **Sex distribution** (2002): male 48.92%; female 51.08%. **Age breakdown** (2002): under 15, 44.3%; 15–29, 27.7%; 30–44, 15.3%; 45–59, 7.1%; 60–74, 4.1%; 75 and over, 1.5%. **Ethnolinguistic composition** (2000): Sukuma 9.5%; Hehet and Bena 4.5%; Gogo 4.4%; Haya 4.2%; Nyamwezi 3.6%; Makonde 3.3%; Chagga 3.0%; Ha 2.9%; other 64.6%. **Religious affiliation** (2000): Christian 46.9%; Muslim 31.8%; ethnoreligionist 16.1%. **Major urban areas** (2002): Dar es Salaam 2,336,055; Arusha 270,485; Mbeya 230,-318; Mwanza 209,806; Morogoro 206,868. **Location:** eastern Africa, bordering Kenya, the Indian Ocean, Mozambique, Malawi, Zambia, the Democratic Republic of the Congo, Burundi, Rwanda, and Uganda.

Vital statistics

Birth rate per 1,000 population (2003): 39.5 (world avg. 21.3). **Death rate** per 1,000 population (2003): 17.4 (world avg. 9.1). **Natural increase rate** per 1,000 population (2003): 22.1 (world avg. 12.2). **Total fertility rate** (avg. births per childbearing woman; 2003): 5.3. **Life expectancy** at birth (2003): male 43.3 years; female 45.8 years. **Adult population** (ages 15–49) **living with HIV** (2004): 8.8% (world avg. 1.1%).

National economy

Budget (2003–04). *Revenue:* T Sh 1,447,500,000,-000 (VAT 34.2%, income tax 24.9%, excise tax 15.0%, import duties 9.0%). *Expenditures:* T Sh 2,-531,500,000 (current expenditure 74.5%, of which wages 18.3%, education 17.7%, health 8.4%, interest payments on debt 4.8%; capital expenditure 25.5%). **Tourism** (2002): receipts from visitors $694,000,000; expenditures by nationals abroad $337,000,000. **Land use** as % of total land area (2000): in temporary crops 4.5%, in permanent crops 1.1%, in pasture 39.6%; overall forest area 43.9%. **Gross national product** (2002; mainland Tanzania only): $10,201,-000,000 ($290 per capita). **Public debt** (external, outstanding; 2002): $6,201,000,000. **Production** (metric tons except as noted). *Agriculture, forestry, fishing* (2002): cassava 6,880,000, corn (maize) 2,700,500, sweet potatoes 950,100; livestock (number of live animals) 17,700,000 cattle, 11,650,000 goats, 3,550,-000 sheep; roundwood 23,438,758 cu m; fish catch (2001) 336,200. *Mining and quarrying* (2002): gold 37,000 kg; garnets 23,000 kg; tanzanites 4,800 kg. *Manufacturing* (value added in $'000,000; 1999): beverages 39; food products 33; tobacco products 28. *Energy production (consumption):* electricity (kW-hr; 2000) 2,603,000,000 (2,548,000,000); coal (2000) 79,000 (79,000); crude petroleum (barrels; 2000) none (3,738,000); petroleum products (2000) 475,-000 (1,170,000). **Population economically active** (2002): total 18,525,000; activity rate 53.8% (participation rates [1991]: over age 10, 87.8%; female [1991] 40.0%). **Households.** Average household size (2002) 4.9; expenditure (1994): food 64.2%, clothing 9.9%, housing 8.3%, energy 7.6%, transportation 4.1%.

Foreign trade

Imports (2002-f.o.b. in balance of trade and c.i.f. in commodities and trading partners): T Sh 1,601,000,-000,000 (consumer goods 31.0%, of which food products 8.8%; machinery and apparatus 22.2%; transport equipment 13.2%; crude and refined petroleum 11.8%). *Major import sources:* South Africa 11.4%; Japan 8.4%; India 6.5%; Russia 6.1%; UAE 5.9%; UK 5.7%; Kenya 5.7%. **Exports** (2002): T Sh 846,000,000,000 (minerals [mostly gold, significantly diamonds and other gemstones] 42.4%; cashews 5.8%; tobacco 5.6%; coffee 4.0%; tea 3.4%; other [significantly fish products] 38.8%). *Major export destinations:* UK 18.5%; France 17.4%; Japan 11.0%; India 7.3%; The Netherlands 6.2%.

Transport and communications

Transport. *Railroads* (2001): length 3,690 km; passenger-km 471,000,000 (Tanzanian Railways only); metric ton-km cargo 1,380,000,000 (Tanzanian Railways only). *Roads* (1999): length 88,200 km (paved 4.2%). *Vehicles* (1999): passenger cars 33,900; trucks and buses 98,800. *Air transport* (2003; Air Tanzania only): passenger-km 151,332,000; metric ton-km 1,796,000; airports (1999) with scheduled flights 11. **Communications,** in total units (units per 1,000 persons). Daily newspaper circulation (2000): 130,000 (4); radios (2000): 9,130,000 (281); televisions (2000): 650,000 (20); telephone main lines (2003): 149,100 (4.2); cellular telephone subscribers (2003): 891,200 (25); personal computers (2003): 200,000 (5.7); Internet users (2003): 250,000 (7.1).

Education and health

Literacy (2001): percentage of population age 15 and over literate 76.0%; males literate 84.5%; fe-

males literate 67.9%. **Health:** physicians (1995) 1,-277 (1 per 22,030 persons); hospital beds (1993) 26,820 (1 per 1,000 persons); infant mortality rate (2003) 103.7. **Food** (2001): daily per capita caloric intake 1,997 (vegetable products 94%, animal products 6%); 86% of FAO recommended minimum.

Military

Total active duty personnel (2003): 27,000 (army 85.2%, navy 3.7%, air force 11.1%). **Military expenditure as percentage of GNP** (1999): 1.4% (world 2.4%); per capita expenditure $4.

Background

Inhabited from the 1st millennium BC, Tanzania was occupied by Arab and Indian traders and Bantu-speaking peoples by the 10th century AD. The Portuguese gained control of the coastline in the late 15th century, but they were driven out by the Arabs of Oman and Zanzibar in the late 18th century. German colonists entered the area in the 1880s, and in 1891 the Germans declared the region a protectorate as German East Africa. In World War I Britain captured the German holdings, which became a British mandate (1920) under the name Tanganyika. Britain retained control of the region after World War II when it became a UN trust territory (1947). Tanganyika gained independence in 1961 and became a republic in 1962. In 1964 it united with Zanzibar under the name Tanzania.

Did you know? Lake Victoria, also called Victoria Nyanza, having an area of 26,828 sq mi (69,484 sq km), is the largest lake in Africa and the chief reservoir of the Nile River.

Recent Developments

In 2006 Pres. Jakaya Mrisho Kikwete named a record number of women as ministers and as deputy ministers, including to the important portfolios of finance, foreign affairs, justice, and education. Kikwete promised to root out poverty and raise standards of living and to improve opportunities for education. He faced a range of problems in semiautonomous Zanzibar, however, and had to deal with corruption in the mainland public services. The budget for 2006–07 contained increased funds to reduce poverty and to make it easier for small farmers and businessmen to get credit from lenders. Steps were taken in April to protect the environment and water resources by banning the export of timber and by evicting livestock owners from riverbeds. That month a group from Zanzibar filed a case, later dismissed, seeking the annulment of the union with mainland Tanzania.

Internet resources: <www.tanzania.go.tz>.

Thailand

Official name: Muang Thai, or Prathet Thai (Kingdom of Thailand). **Form of government:** constitutional

---

1 metric ton = about 1.1 short tons;   1 kilometer = 0.6 mi (statute);   1 metric ton-km cargo = about 0.68 short ton-mi cargo;   c.i.f.: cost, insurance, and freight;   f.o.b.: free on board

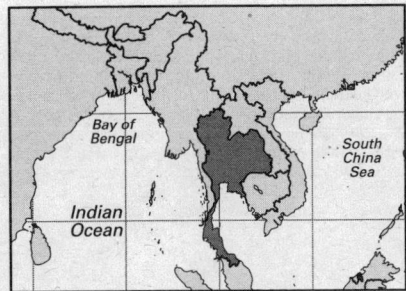

monarchy with two legislative houses (Senate [200]; House of Representatives [500]). **Chief of state:** King Bhumibol Adulyadej (from 1946). **Head of government:** Prime Minister Surayud Chulanont (from 2006). **Capital:** Bangkok. **Official language:** Thai. **Official religion:** Buddhism. **Monetary unit:** 1 Thai baht (B) = 100 stangs; valuation (1 Jul 2007) US$1 = B 31.62.

Demography

Area: 198,117 sq mi, 513,120 sq km. **Population** (2006): 64,632,000. **Density** (2006): persons per sq mi 326.2, persons per sq km 126.0. **Urban** (2001): 28.6%. **Sex distribution** (2000): male 49.24%; female 50.76%. **Age breakdown** (2003): under 15, 24.5%; 15–29, 26.5%; 30–44, 23.7%; 45–59, 15.7%; 60–74, 7.8%; 75 and over, 1.8%. **Ethnic composition** (2000): Tai peoples 81.4%, of which Thai (Siamese) 34.9%, Lao 26.5%; Han Chinese 10.6%; Malay 3.7%; Khmer 1.9%; other 2.4%. **Religious affiliation** (2000): Buddhist 94.2%; Muslim 4.6%; Christian and other 1.2%. **Major cities** (2000): Bangkok 6,320,174; Samut Prakan 378,694; Nonthaburi 291,307; Udon Thani 220,493; Nakhon Ratchasima 204,391. **Location:** southeastern Asia, bordering Laos, Cambodia, the Gulf of Thailand, Malaysia, and Myanmar (Burma).

Vital statistics

Birth rate per 1,000 population (2002): 14.0 (world avg. 21.3). **Death rate** per 1,000 population (2002): 6.0 (world avg. 9.1). **Natural increase rate** per 1,000 population (2002): 8.0 (world avg. 12.2). **Total fertility rate** (avg. births per childbearing woman; 2002): 1.8. **Marriage rate** per 1,000 population (2000): 5.4. **Divorce rate** per 1,000 population (2000): 1.1. **Life expectancy** at birth (2002): male 69.9 years; female 74.9 years.

National economy

Budget (2001–02). *Revenue:* B 903,550,000,000 (tax revenue 90.3%, of which income taxes 28.7%, VAT 26.1%, taxes on international trade 11.5%, consumption tax 10.8%; nontax revenue 9.7%). *Expenditures:* B 1,023,000,000,000 (education 21.8%; defense 7.5%; agriculture 7.4%; health 7.1%; social security 6.9%; public order 5.5%). **Public debt** (external, outstanding; 2002): $22,-628,000,000. **Production** (metric tons except as noted). *Agriculture, forestry, fishing* (2002): sugarcane 62,350,000, rice 25,945,000, cassava 16,-870,000; livestock (number of live animals)

6,688,904 pigs, 4,640,355 cattle, 121,000,000 chickens; roundwood (2001) 27,351,000 cu m; fish catch (2001) 3,605,544, of which mollusks 224,222. *Mining and quarrying* (2001): gypsum 6,191,000; dolomite 871,300; feldspar 710,500. *Manufacturing* (2001): cement 27,913,000; refined sugar 4,865,000; crude steel 2,127,000. *Energy production (consumption):* electricity (kW-hr; 2002) 108,418,000,000 (105,182,000,000); hard coal (2000) negligible (4,098,000); lignite (2001) 19,619,000 ([2000] 17,586,000); crude petroleum (barrels; 2001) 22,600,000 ([2000] 252,000,000); petroleum products (2000) 34,968,000 (30,468,000); natural gas (cu m; 2001) 20,633,000,000 ([2000] 19,338,400,000). **Tourism** (2002): receipts from visitors $7,902,-000,000; expenditures by nationals abroad $3,-303,000,000. **Population economically active** (2001): total 33,920,000; activity rate of total population 53.9% (participation rates: over age 14, 72.1%; female [2000] 45.0%; unemployed 3.2%). **Gross national product** (2001): $136,063,000,000 ($2,190 per capita). **Household income and expenditure** (1998). Average household size (2000) 3.9; average annual income per household B 149,904; sources of income: wages and salaries 40.1%, self-employment 29.8%, transfer payments 7.9%, other 22.2%; expenditure: food, tobacco, and beverages 37.7%, housing 21.4%, transportation and communications 13.3%, medical and personal care 5.1%, clothing 3.5%, education 2.3%. **Land use** as % of total land area (2000): in temporary crops 29.4%, in permanent crops 6.5%, in pasture 1.6%; overall forest area 28.9%.

Foreign trade

Imports (2001-f.o.b. in balance of trade and c.i.f. for commodities and trading partners): $62,057,-000,000 (electrical machinery 22.1%, of which electronic components and parts 10.9%; nonelectrical machinery 17.4%, of which computers and parts 6.3%; chemicals and chemical products 10.3%; crude petroleum 9.3%). *Major import sources* (2002): Japan 23.0%; US 9.6%; China 7.6%; Malaysia 5.6%; Singapore 4.5%. **Exports** (2001): $65,113,000,000 (food products 14.9%, of which fish, crustaceans, and mollusks 6.2%; computers and parts 12.3%; microcircuits and other electronics 7.2%; chemicals and chemical products 5.7%; garments and clothing accessories 5.6%). *Major export destinations* (2002): US 19.6%; Japan 14.5%; Singapore 8.1%; Hong Kong 5.4%; China 5.2%.

Transport and communications

Transport. *Railroads* (2000): route length 4,041 km; passenger-km 10,040,000,000; metric ton-km cargo 3,347,000,000. *Roads* (2001): total length 53,436 km (paved 98%). *Vehicles* (2002): passenger cars 2,281,000; trucks and buses 4,145,000. *Air transport* (1999): passenger-km 38,345,195,000; metric ton-km cargo 1,670,717,000; airports (1996) 25. **Communications,** in total units (units per 1,000 persons). Daily newspaper circulation (2000): 3,990,-000 (64); radios (2000): 14,700,000 (235); televisions (2000): 17,700,000 (284); telephone main lines (2003): 6,600,000 (106); cellular telephone subscribers (2002): 16,117,000 (260); personal computers (2002): 2,461,000 (40); Internet users (2003): 6,031,300 (96).

Education and health

Educational attainment (2000). Percentage of population age 6 and over having: no formal schooling 8.5%; primary education 59.0%; lower secondary 12.5%; upper secondary 11.2%; some higher 2.2%; undergraduate 5.2%; advanced degree 0.4%; other/unknown 1.0%. **Literacy** (2000): 95.5%. **Health** (2001): physicians 18,531 (1 per 3,395 persons); hospital beds 141,380 (1 per 445 persons); infant mortality rate per 1,000 live births (2002) 20.0. **Food** (2001): daily per capita caloric intake 2,486 (vegetable products 88%, animal products 12%); 112% of FAO recommended minimum.

Military

Total active duty personnel (2003): 314,200 (army 60.5%, navy 25.2%, air force 14.3%). **Military expenditure as percentage of GNP** (1999): 1.7% (world 2.4%); per capita expenditure $34.

Background

The region of Thailand has been occupied continuously for 20,000 years. It was part of the Mon and Khmer kingdoms from the 9th century AD. Thai-speaking peoples emigrated from China c. the 10th century. During the 13th century two Thai states emerged: the Sukhothai kingdom, founded c. 1220 after a successful revolt against the Khmer, and Chiang Mai, founded in 1296 after the defeat of the Mon. In 1350 the Thai kingdom of Ayutthaya succeeded Sukhothai. The Burmese were its most powerful rivals, occupying it briefly in the 16th century and destroying the kingdom in 1767. The Chakri dynasty came to power in 1782, moving the capital to Bangkok and extending the empire along the Malay Peninsula and into Laos and Cambodia. The country was named Siam in 1856. Though Western influence increased during the 19th century, Siam's rulers avoided colonization by granting concessions to European countries; it was the only southeast Asian nation able to do so. In 1917 it entered World War I on the side of the Allies. It became a constitutional monarchy following a military coup in 1932 and was officially renamed Thailand in 1939. It was occupied by Japan in World War II. It participated in the Korean War as a UN forces member and was allied with South Vietnam in the Vietnam War. Along with other Southeast Asian nations, it suffered from the 1990s regional financial crisis.

Recent Developments

In January 2006 Prime Minister Thaksin Shinawatra, a telecommunications tycoon, sold assets in his family-owned Shin Corp. to Singapore's Temasek Holdings, earning his family $1.9 billion in tax-free revenue. The deal fueled discontent that had been mounting during his rule, and mass protests took place in Bangkok to demand his resignation. In September, however, the military, led by Gen. Sonthi Boonyaratkalin, overthrew Thaksin in a bloodless coup while he was attending a meeting of the UN General Assembly. Sonthi abolished the constitution and installed Gen. Surayud Chulanont, a retired army chief widely respected for his integrity, as interim prime minister, while promising an election in October 2007. The coup leaders justified their action by citing Thaksin's corruption and his heavy-handed crackdown on persistent Muslim insurgency in the south. While most middle-class Bangkokians approved of it for having ousted a corrupt, undemocratic leader, the majority of the poor in the countryside, Thaksin's main support base, and the international community saw the coup, the first since 1991, as a setback for democracy.

Internet resources: <www.tourismthailand.org>.

Togo

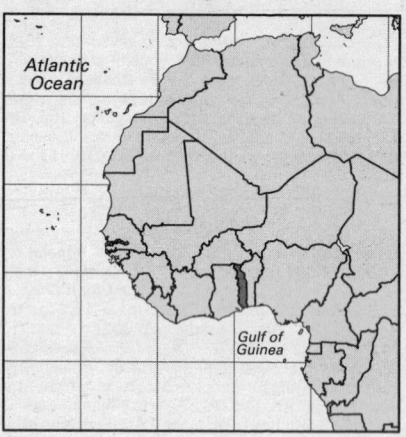

Official name: République Togolaise (Togolese Republic). **Form of government:** multiparty republic with one legislative body (National Assembly [81]). **Chief of state:** President Faure Gnassingbé (from 2005). **Head of government:** Prime Minister Yawovi Agboyibo (from 2006). **Capital:** Lomé. **Official language:** French. **Official religion:** none. **Monetary unit:** 1 CFA franc (CFAF) = 100 centimes; valuation (1 Jul 2007) US$1 = CFAF 485.18; the CFAF is pegged to the euro (€) at €1 = CFAF 655.96 from 1 Jan 2002.

Demography

Area: 21,925 sq mi, 56,785 sq km. **Population** (2006): 5,549,000. **Density** (2006): persons per sq mi 253.1, persons per sq km 97.7. **Urban** (2002): 33.9%. **Sex distribution** (2004): male 49.55%; female 50.45%. **Age breakdown** (2001): under 15, 45.6%; 15–29, 28.1%; 30–44, 14.8%; 45–59, 7.5%; 60–74, 3.3%; 75 and over, 0.7%. **Ethnic composition** (2000): Ewe 22.2%; Kabre 13.4%; Wachi 10.0%; Mina 5.6%; Kotokoli 5.6%; Bimoba 5.2%; Losso 4.0%; Gurma 3.4%; Lamba 3.2%; Adja 3.0%; other 24.4%. **Religious affiliation** (2000): Christian 37.8%, of which Roman Catholic 24.3%; traditional beliefs 37.7%; Muslim 18.9%; other 5.6%. **Major cities** (2003): Lomé 676,400 (urban agglomeration 749,700); Sokodé 84,200; Kpalimé 75,200; Atakpamé 64,300; Kara 49,800. **Location:** western Africa, bordering Burkina Faso, Benin, the Bight of Benin, and Ghana.

---

1 metric ton = about 1.1 short tons;   1 kilometer = 0.6 mi (statute);   1 metric ton-km cargo = about 0.68 short ton-mi cargo;   c.i.f.: cost, insurance, and freight;   f.o.b.: free on board

Vital statistics

Birth rate per 1,000 population (2003): 35.2 (world avg. 21.3). **Death rate** per 1,000 population (2003): 11.5 (world avg. 9.1). **Natural increase rate** per 1,000 population (2003): 23.7 (world avg. 12.2). **Total fertility rate** (avg. births per childbearing woman; 2003): 5.0. **Life expectancy** at birth (2003): male 52.0 years; female 54.0 years. **Adult population** (ages 15–49) **living with HIV** (2004): 4.1% (world avg. 1.1%).

National economy

Budget (2002). *Revenue:* CFAF 128,300,000,000 (tax revenue 92.5%, nontax revenue 4.8%, grants 2.7%). *Expenditures:* CFAF 135,300,000,000 (current expenditure 89.4%, capital expenditure 10.6%). **Public debt** (external, outstanding; 2002): $1,337,000,000. **Production** (metric tons except as noted). *Agriculture, forestry, fishing:* cassava 651,530, yams 549,070, corn (maize) 463,930; livestock (number of live animals) 1,700,000 sheep, 1,460,000 goats, 300,000 pigs; roundwood 5,-835,447 cu m; fish catch (2001) 23,283. *Mining and quarrying:* limestone (2001) 2,400,000; phosphate rock (2002) 1,380,000. *Manufacturing* (value added in CFAF '000,000; 1998): food products, beverages, and tobacco manufactures 41,400; metallic goods 12,000; nonmetallic manufactures 8,500. *Energy production (consumption):* electricity (kW-hr; 2000) 68,000,000 (580,000,000); petroleum products (2000) none (471,000). **Population economically active** (2000): total 1,913,000; activity rate of total population 38.1% (participation rates: over age 15, 70.7%; female 39.9%; unemployed [1994] 16–18%). **Gross national product** (at current market prices; 2003): $1,492,000,000 ($310 per capita). **Households.** Average household size (1999) 6.0; expenditure (1987): food and beverages 45.9%, services 20.5%, household durable goods 13.9%, clothing 11.4%, housing 5.9%. **Land use** as % of total land area (2000): in temporary crops 46.1%, in permanent crops 2.2%, in pasture 18.4%; overall forest area 9.4%. **Tourism** (2002): receipts $9,000,000; expenditures $4,000,000.

Foreign trade

Imports (2001-c.i.f. [except in 2002 balance of trade]): $355,000,000 (food 18.2%, of which cereals 9.4%; refined petroleum 15.7%; chemicals and chemical products 10.4%; machinery and apparatus 9.8%; cement 8.8%; iron and steel 8.8%). *Major import sources:* France 19.1%; Canada 6.5%; Italy 6.1%; Côte d'Ivoire 5.7%; Germany 4.5%. **Exports** (2001): $220,200,000 (cement 29.4%, phosphates 20.3%, cotton 10.1%, iron and steel 8.6%). *Major export destinations:* Ghana 22.4%; Benin 16.9%; Burkina Faso 10.4%; Philippines 6.3%; Niger 4.5%.

Transport and communications

Transport. *Railroads* (1999): route length 395 km; (1998) passenger-km 35,200,000; metric ton-km cargo 758,700,000. *Roads* (1999): total length 7,520 km (paved 32%). *Vehicles* (1996): passenger cars 79,200; trucks and buses 34,240. *Air transport* (Air Afrique, an airline jointly owned by 11 African countries [including Togo], was declared bankrupt in February 2002): airports (1998) 2. **Communications,** in total units (units per 1,000 persons). Daily newspaper circulation (2000): 20,100 (4); radios (2000): 1,330,000 (265); televisions (2002): 590,000 (123); telephone main lines (2003): 60,600 (12); cellular telephone subscribers (2003): 220,000 (44); personal computers (2003): 160,000 (32); Internet users (2003): 210,000 (42).

Education and health

Educational attainment (1981). Percentage of population age 25 and over having: no formal schooling 76.5%; primary education 13.5%; secondary 8.7%; higher 1.3%. **Literacy** (2000): total population age 15 and over literate 57.1%; males 72.4%; females 42.5%. **Health:** physicians (1995) 320 (1 per 13,158 persons); hospital beds (1990) 5,307 (1 per 694 persons); infant mortality rate per 1,000 live births (2003) 80.0. **Food** (2001): daily per capita caloric intake 2,287 (vegetable products 97%, animal products 3%); 99% of FAO recommended minimum.

Military

Total active duty personnel (2003): 8,550 (army 94.7%, navy 2.3%, air force 3.0%). **Military expenditure as percentage of GNP** (1999): 1.8% (world 2.4%); per capita expenditure $5.

Background

Until 1884 what is now Togo was an intermediate zone between the black African military states of Ashanti and Dahomey, and its various ethnic groups lived in isolation from each other. In 1884 it became part of the Togoland German protectorate, which was occupied by British and French forces in 1914. In 1922 the League of Nations assigned eastern Togoland to France and the western portion to Britain. In 1946 the British and French governments placed the territories under UN trusteeship. Ten years later British Togoland was incorporated into the Gold Coast, and French Togoland became an autonomous republic within the French Union. Togo gained independence in 1960. It suspended its constitution 1967–80. A multiparty constitution was approved in 1992, but the political situation remained unstable.

Recent Developments

The death on 5 Feb 2005 of Gnassingbé Eyadéma, who had led Togo for 38 years, catalyzed a political crisis. Prompted by the military, the legislature hastily rewrote the constitution and installed in office Eyadéma's son, Faure Gnassingbé. This coup was loudly protested by Togolese and international observers alike. Weeks of demonstrations and a national strike ensued until, on 25 February, Gnassingbé stepped down and the deputy head of parliament took over as acting president, pending elections in 60 days' time. Gnassingbé, however, won the April elections (which international observers reported as flawed), setting off another round of violent protests; human rights organizations estimated that some 800 people had died in Togo since February. Fearing reprisals from the government, as many as 40,000 people had fled and lived in exile in neighboring countries in 2006.

Internet resources:
<www.republicoftogo.com/fr/home.asp>.

Tonga

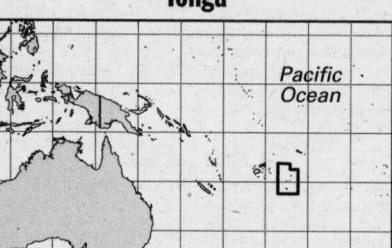

Pacific
Ocean

Official name: Pule'anga Fakatu'i 'o Tonga (Tongan); Kingdom of Tonga (English). **Form of government:** constitutional monarchy with one legislative house (Legislative Assembly [30; includes 12 nonelective seats and 9 nobles elected by the 33 hereditary nobles of Tonga]). **Head of state and government:** King Siaosi (George) Tupou V (from 2006), assisted by Prime Minister of the Privy Council Feleti Sevele (from 2006). **Capital:** Nuku'alofa. **Official languages:** Tongan; English. **Official religion:** none. **Monetary unit:** 1 pa'anga (T$) = 100 seniti; valuation (1 Jul 2007) US$1 = T$2.07.

Demography

Area: 289.5 sq mi, 749.9 sq km, of which land area equals 278.1 sq mi, 720.3 sq km. **Population** (2006): 102,000. **Density** (2006; based on land area): persons per sq mi 366.8, persons per sq km 141.6. **Urban** (2002): 39.0%. **Sex distribution** (2002): male 50.93%; female 49.07%. **Age breakdown** (1996): under 15, 39.1%; 15–29, 28.0%; 30–44, 15.1%; 45–59, 10.0%; 60–74, 6.0%; 75 and over, 1.8%. **Ethnic composition** (1996): Tongan and part Tongan 98.2%; other 1.8%. **Religious affiliation** (1998): Free Wesleyan 41.2%; Roman Catholic 15.8%; Mormon 13.6%; other (mostly other Protestant) 29.4%. **Major cities** (1986): Nuku'alofa (1996) 22,400 (urban agglomeration [2001] 33,000); Neiafu 3,879; Haveluloto 3,070. **Location:** archipelago in the South Pacific Ocean between Hawaii and New Zealand.

Vital statistics

Birth rate per 1,000 population (2003): 24.5 (world avg. 21.3). **Death rate** per 1,000 population (2003): 5.5 (world avg. 9.1). **Natural increase rate** per 1,000 population (2003): 19.0 (world avg. 12.2). **Total fertility rate** (avg. births per childbearing woman; 2003): 3.0. **Marriage rate** per 1,000 population (1994): 7.7. **Divorce rate** per 1,000 population (1994): 0.8. **Life expectancy** at birth (2003): male 66.4 years; female 71.4 years.

National economy

Budget(2002). *Revenue:* T$93,200,000 (foreign-trade taxes 52.0%, government services revenue 13.7%, income tax 16.7%, sales taxes 8.2%). *Expenditures:*

T$99,400,000 (2001; general administration 20.9%, education 14.0%, health 10.2%, social security 6.7%, agriculture 6.5%, law and order 5.7%, defense 4.6%). **Public debt** (external, outstanding; 2002): US$72,-600,000. **Production** (metric tons except as noted). *Agriculture, forestry, fishing* (2002): coconuts 57,700, pumpkins, squash, and gourds 17,000, cassava 9,000; livestock (number of live animals) 80,853 pigs, 12,500 goats, 300,000 chickens; roundwood 2,100 cu m; fish catch (2001) 4,673. *Mining and quarrying:* coral and sand for local use. *Manufacturing* (output in T$'000,000; 1996): food products and beverages 8,203; paper products 1,055; chemical products 964. *Energy production (consumption):* electricity (kW-hr; 2002) 36,176,000 (36,176,000); petroleum products (2000) n.a. (39,000). **Tourism:** receipts (2002) US$9,000,000; expenditures (2001) US$3,000,000. **Gross national product** (2003): US$152,000,000 (US$1,490 per capita). **Population economically active** (1996): total 33,908; activity rate 34.7% (participation rates: ages 15 and over 57.0%; female 36.0%; unemployed 13.3%). **Households.** Average household size (1996) 6.0; expenditure (1991–92): food 43.2%, transportation 15.5%, household 14.2%, housing 6.4%, tobacco and beverages 5.4%, clothing and footwear 4.2%. **Land use** as % of total land area (2000): in temporary crops 24%, in permanent crops 43%, in pasture 6%; overall forest area 5%.

Foreign trade

Imports (2000–01-f.o.b. in balance of trade and c.i.f. in commodities and trading partners): US$70,100,-000 (food and live animals 32.3%, mineral fuels and chemical products 25.6%, machinery and transport equipment 11.2%). *Major import sources* (2002): New Zealand 30.8%; Fiji 20.7%; US 14.3%; Australia 13.2%; China 6.2%. **Exports** (2000–01): US$6,700,-000 (squash 40.8%, fish 27.7%, root crops 15.4%, kava 2.3%, vanilla beans 2.3%). *Major export destinations* (2002): Japan 43.3%; US 41.0%; Greece 3.8%; New Zealand 3.6%; Taiwan 2.7%.

Transport and communications

Transport. *Roads* (1996): total length 680 km (paved 27%). *Vehicles* (1998): passenger cars 6,419, commercial vehicles 9,189. *Air transport* (1999): passenger-km 19,000,000; metric ton-km cargo 2,000,000; airports (1996) with scheduled flights 6. **Communications,** in total units (units per 1,000 persons). Daily newspaper circulation (2000): 12,300 (123); radios (1997): 61,000 (619); televisions (1997): 2,000 (21); telephone main lines (2002): 11,200 (113); cellular telephone subscribers (2002): 3,400 (34); personal computers (2002): 2,000 (20); Internet users (2002): 2,900 (29).

Education and health

Educational attainment (1996). Percentage of population age 25 and over having: primary education 26%; lower secondary 58%; upper secondary 8%; higher 6%; not stated 2%. **Literacy** (1996): 98.5%. **Health:** physicians (2002; government only) 32 (1 per 3,057 persons); hospital beds (1992) 307 (1 per 320 persons); infant mortality rate per 1,000 live births (2003) 13.4. **Food** (1992): daily per capita caloric in-

---

1 metric ton = about 1.1 short tons;   1 kilometer = 0.6 mi (statute);   1 metric ton-km cargo = about 0.68 short ton-mi cargo;   c.i.f.: cost, insurance, and freight;   f.o.b.: free on board

take 2,946 (vegetable products 82%, animal products 18%); 129% of FAO recommended minimum.

Military

Total active duty personnel (1999): 125-member naval force; an air force was created in 1996.

Background

Tonga was inhabited at least 3,000 years ago by people of the Lapita culture. The Tongans developed a stratified social system headed by a paramount ruler whose dominion by the 13th century extended as far as the Hawaiian Islands. The Dutch visited the islands in the 17th century; in 1773 Capt. James Cook arrived and named the archipelago the Friendly Islands. The modern kingdom was established during the reign (1845–93) of King George Tupou I. It became a British protectorate in 1900. This was dissolved in 1970, when Tonga, the only ancient kingdom surviving from the pre-European period in Polynesia, achieved complete independence within the Commonwealth.

Recent Developments

King Taufa'ahau Tupou IV died in September 2006 and was succeeded by his eldest son, who became King Siaosi (George) Tupou V. In November 2006 the National Committee for Political Reform presented a report that included the suggestion that members of parliament be popularly elected. When the recommendations were not implemented, a large crowd rioted, razing 80% of the capital's business district. The new king indicated his support of the recommendations in 2007.

Internet resources: <www.tongatapu.net.to>.

Trinidad and Tobago

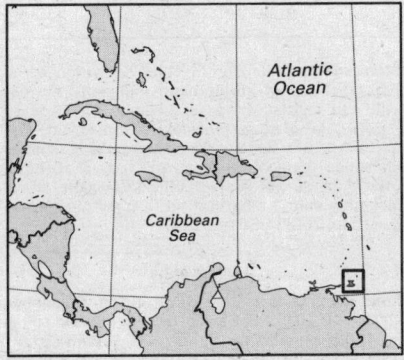

Official name: Republic of Trinidad and Tobago. Form of government: multiparty republic with two legislative houses (Senate [31]; House of Representatives [36; excludes speaker]). Chief of state: President Maxwell Richards (from 2003). Head of government: Prime Minister Patrick Manning (from 2001). Capital: Port of Spain. Official language: English. Official religion: none. Monetary unit: 1 Trinidad and Tobago dollar (TT$) = 100 cents; valuation (1 Jul 2007) US$1 = TT$6.32.

Demography

Area: 1,980 sq mi, 5,127 sq km. Population (2006): 1,301,000. Density (2006): persons per sq mi. 657.1, persons per sq km 253.8. Urban (2002): 74.5%. Sex distribution (2001): male 51.22%; female 48.78%. Age breakdown (2001): under 15, 24.3%; 15–29, 27.1%; 30–44, 22.5%; 45–59, 15.5%; 60–74, 7.7%; 75 and over, 2.9%. Ethnic composition (2000): black 39.2%; East Indian 38.6%; mixed 16.3%; Chinese 1.6%; white 1.0%; other/not stated 3.3%. Religious affiliation (1990): six largest Protestant bodies 29.7%; Roman Catholic 29.4%; Hindu 23.7%; Muslim 5.9%; other 11.3%. Major cities (2000): Chaguanas 67,433; San Fernando 55,149; Port of Spain 49,031; Arima 32,278; Point Fortin 19,056. Location: islands northeast of Venezuela between the North Atlantic Ocean and the Caribbean Sea.

Vital statistics

Birth rate per 1,000 population (2003): 12.7 (world avg. 21.3). Death rate per 1,000 population (2003): 8.7 (world avg. 9.1). Natural increase rate per 1,000 population (2003): 4.0 (world avg. 12.2). Total fertility rate (avg. births per childbearing woman; 2003): 1.8. Marriage rate per 1,000 population (1998): 6.2. Divorce rate per 1,000 population (1998): 1.1. Life expectancy at birth (2003): male 67.1 years; female 72.2 years.

National economy

Budget (2001–02). Revenue: TT$14,672,000,000 (income taxes 31.5%; petroleum sector 29.0%; sales tax 23.7%; taxes on international trade 5.7%; other 10.1%). Expenditures: TT$13,861,000,000 (current expenditures 90.4%, of which transfers and subsidies 33.9%, wages 30.9%, interest payment 16.8%, other 8.8%; development expenditures 9.6%). Production (metric tons except as noted). Agriculture, forestry, fishing (2002): sugarcane 1,050,000, coconuts 24,000, oranges 4,987; livestock (number of live animals) 60,500 goats, 31,600 cattle, 25,000,000 chickens; roundwood (2000) 116,500 cu m; fish catch (2001) 11,415. Mining and quarrying (2000): natural asphalt 9,900. Manufacturing (2000): anhydrous ammonia and urea 3,719,000; methanol 2,480,000; steel billets 744,000. Energy production (consumption): electricity (kW-hr; 2000) 5,460,-000,000 (5,460,000,000); crude petroleum (barrels; 2000) 43,786,000 (59,102,000); petroleum products (2000) 8,037,000 (1,055,000); natural gas (cu m; 2000) 10,448,000,000 (10,448,000,000). Households. Average household size (2000) 3.7; expenditure (1993): food, beverages, and tobacco 25.5%, housing 21.6%, transportation 15.2%, household furnishings 14.3%, clothing and footwear 10.4%. Tourism (2002): receipts from visitors US$224,-000,000; expenditures by nationals abroad (2001) US$151,000,000. Land use as % of total land area (2000): in temporary crops 14.6%, in permanent crops 9.2%, in pasture 2.1%; overall forest area 50.5%. Gross national product (at current market prices; 2003): US$9,538,000,000 (US$7,260 per capita). Population economically active (2001): total 576,900; activity rate of total population 45.5% (participation rates: ages 15 and over 60.7%; female 36.6%; unemployed 10.9%). Public debt (external, outstanding; 2002): US$1,697,000,000.

Foreign trade

Imports (2001-c.i.f.): TT$24,510,000,000 (crude petroleum 19.3%, general industrial machinery 16.1%, floating docks 9.3%, food products 7.5%, refined petroleum 4.1%). *Major import sources:* US 34.4%; Venezuela 11.1%; Brazil 5.1%; UK 4.9%; Panama 4.6%. **Exports** (2001-f.o.b.): TT$31,873,000,000 (refined petroleum 29.4%, floating docks 12.6%, crude petroleum 9.3%, anhydrous ammonia 8.5%, iron and steel 5.7%, methanol 5.0%). *Major export destinations:* US 42.3%; Mexico 7.4%; Jamaica 7.0%; Barbados 5.5%; France 3.9%.

Transport and communications

Transport. *Roads* (1999): total length 7,900 km (paved 51%). *Vehicles* (1996): passenger cars 122,000; trucks and buses 24,000. *Air transport* (2001; BWIA only): passenger-km 2,496,000,000; metric ton-km cargo 56,236,000; airports (2000) with scheduled flights 2. **Communications,** in total units (units per 1,000 persons). Daily newspaper circulation (2000): 155,000 (123); radios (2000): 672,000 (532); televisions (2000): 429,000 (340); telephone main lines (2002): 325,100 (250); cellular telephone subscribers (2002): 361,900 (278); personal computers (2002): 104,000 (80); Internet users (2002): 138,000 (106).

Education and health

Educational attainment (1990). Percentage of population age 25 and over having: no formal schooling 4.5%; primary education 56.4%; secondary 32.1%; higher 3.4%; other/not stated 3.6%. **Literacy** (2000): total population age 15 and over literate 93.8%; males literate 95.5%; females literate 92.1%. **Health:** physicians (1999) 1,171 (1 per 1,076 persons); hospital beds 4,384 (1 per 287 persons); infant mortality rate per 1,000 live births (2003) 25.0. **Food** (2001): daily per capita caloric intake 2,756 (vegetable products 84%, animal products 16%); 114% of FAO recommended minimum.

Military

Total active duty personnel (2003): 2,700 (army 74.1%, coast guard 25.9%). **Military expenditure as percentage of GNP** (1999): 1.4% (world 2.4%); per capita expenditure US$78.

Background

When Christopher Columbus visited Trinidad in 1498, it was inhabited by the Arawak Indians; Caribs inhabited Tobago. The islands were settled by the Spanish in the 16th century. In the 17th and 18th centuries African slaves were imported for plantation labor to replace the original Indian population, which had been worked to death by the Spanish. Trinidad was surrendered to the British in 1797. The British attempted to settle Tobago in 1721, but the French captured the island in 1781 and transformed it into a sugar-producing colony; the British acquired it in 1802. After slavery ended in the islands in 1834–38, immigrants from India were brought in to work the plantations. The islands of Trinidad and Tobago were administratively combined in 1889. Granted limited self-government in 1925, the islands became an independent state within the Commonwealth in 1962 and a republic in 1976. Political unrest was followed in 1990 by an attempted Muslim fundamentalist coup against the government.

Recent Developments

Trinidad and Tobago's rapid pace of heavy industrial development continued, especially in the field of mineral fuels. A South Korean company won a contract in late 2006 to construct a $180 million refinery to produce high-octane gas. A German firm announced in February 2007 that it would build a $1.1 billion petrochemicals complex in Trinidad and Tobago.

Internet resources: <www.visittnt.com>.

Tunisia

Official name: Al-Jumhuriyah al-Tunisiyah (Republic of Tunisia). **Form of government:** multiparty republic with one legislative house (Chamber of Deputies [189]). **Chief of state:** President Zine al-Abidine Ben Ali (from 1987). **Head of government:** Prime Minister Mohamed Ghannouchi (from 1999). **Capital:** Tunis. **Official language:** Arabic. **Official religion:** Islam. **Monetary unit:** 1 dinar (D) = 1,000 millimes; valuation (1 Jul 2007) US$1= D 1.30.

Demography

Area: 63,170 sq mi, 163,610 sq km. **Population** (2006): 10,141,000. **Density** (2006): persons per sq mi 160.5, persons per sq km 62.0. **Urban** (2002): 63.4%. **Sex distribution** (2002): male 50.30%; female 49.70%. **Age breakdown** (2002): under 15, 27.9%; 15–29, 30.6%; 30–44, 21.6%; 45–59, 10.8%; 60–74, 7.8%; 75 and over, 1.3%. **Ethnic composition** (2000): Tunisian Arab 67.2%; Bedouin Arab 26.6%; Algerian Arab 2.4%; Berber 1.4%; other 2.4%. **Religious affiliation** (2000): Sunni Muslim 98.9%; Christian 0.5%; other 0.6%. **Major cities** (2003): Tunis

---

1 metric ton = about 1.1 short tons;   1 kilometer = 0.6 mi (statute);   1 metric ton-km cargo = about 0.68 short ton-mi cargo;   c.i.f.: cost, insurance, and freight;   f.o.b.: free on board

699,700 (urban agglomeration [2001] 1,927,000); Safaqis 270,700; Al-Arianah 217,100 (within Tunis urban agglomeration); Ettadhamen 188,700 (within Tunis urban agglomeration); Susah 155,900. **Location:** northern Africa, bordering the Mediterranean Sea, Libya, and Algeria.

Vital statistics

Birth rate per 1,000 population (2003): 16.0 (world avg. 21.3). **Death rate** per 1,000 population (2003): 5.0 (world avg. 9.1). **Natural increase rate** per 1,000 population (2003): 11.0 (world avg. 12.2). **Total fertility rate** (avg. births per childbearing woman; 2003): 1.8. **Marriage rate** per 1,000 population (2001): 6.4. **Divorce rate** per 1,000 population (1999): 0.1. **Life expectancy** at birth (2003): male 72.8 years; female 76.2 years.

National economy

Budget (2002). *Revenue:* D 11,533,000,000 (tax revenue 91.5%, of which goods and services 34.4%, income tax 22.1%, social security 18.9%, import duties 9.9%; nontax revenue 8.5%). *Expenditures:* D 11,533,000,000 (current expenditure 79.8%, of which interest on public debt 8.5%; development expenditure 20.2%). **Public debt** (external, outstanding; 2002): $10,641,000,000. **Production** (metric tons except as noted). *Agriculture, forestry, fishing* (2002): olives 1,500,000, tomatoes 810,000, cereals 538,000; livestock (number of live animals) 6,850,000 sheep, 1,450,000 goats, 760,000 cattle; roundwood (2002) 2,329,000 cu m; fish catch (2001) 100,000. *Mining and quarrying* (2002): phosphate rock 8,144,000; iron ore 198,000; zinc (metal content) 35,692. *Manufacturing* (2002): cement 6,022,000; phosphoric acid 1,219,000; lime 471,000. *Energy production (consumption):* electricity (kW-hr; 2001) 9,787,000,000 ([2000] 9,944,000,000); coal (2000) none (1,000); crude petroleum (barrels; 2001) 25,712,000 (13,625,000); petroleum products (2000) 1,889,000 (3,649,000); natural gas (cu m; 2001) 2,143,100,000 ([2000] 1,923,000,000). **Household income and expenditure.** Average household size (2000) 4.7; income per household D 6,450; expenditure (2000): food and beverages 38.0%, housing and energy 21.5%, household durables 11.1%, health and personal care 10.0%, transportation 9.7%, recreation 8.7%, other 1.0%. **Gross national product** (2003): $22,211,000,000 ($2,240 per capita). **Population economically active** (2002): total 3,375,700; activity rate of total population 34.5% (participation rates: age 15 and over 48.0%; female 24.3%; unemployed 14.9%). **Tourism** (2002): receipts $1,422,000,000; expenditures $260,000,000. **Land use** as % of total land area (2000): in temporary crops 18.4%, in permanent crops 13.7%, in pasture 26.3%; overall forest area 3.1%.

Foreign trade

Imports (2002-c.i.f.): D 13,511,000,000 (nonelectrical machinery and equipment 19.6%, fabric 12.7%, food products 10.5%, electrical machinery and equipment 10.0%, crude and refined petroleum 8.3%). *Major import sources:* France 25.6%; Italy 19.5%; Germany 8.9%; Spain 5.0%; US 3.2%. **Exports** (2002-f.o.b.): D 9,749,000,000 (clothing 30.4%, knitwear 8.4%, crude petroleum 7.3%, phosphates and phosphate derivatives 6.8%, electrical cable and wire

4.7%). *Major export destinations:* France 31.3%; Italy 21.6%; Germany 11.5%; Spain 4.8%; Libya 4.6%.

Transport and communications

Transport. *Railroads* (2001): route length 2,169 km; passenger-km 1,283,500,000; metric ton-km cargo 2,286,100,000. *Roads* (1997): total length 23,100 km (paved 79%). *Vehicles* (2000): passenger cars 482,700; trucks and buses 250,300. *Air transport* (2001; Tunis Air only): passenger-km 2,696,313,000; metric ton-km cargo 20,104,000; airports (1998) 5. **Communications,** in total units (units per 1,000 persons). Daily newspaper circulation (1996): 280,000 (31); radios (1997): 2,060,000 (224); televisions (1999): 1,800,000 (190); telephone main lines (2003): 1,163,800 (118); cellular telephone subscribers (2003): 1,899,900 (192); personal computers (2003): 400,000 (41); Internet users (2003): 630,000 (64).

Education and health

Literacy (2000): total population age 10 and over literate 74.4%; males literate 83.5%; females literate 65.3%. **Health** (2002): physicians 8,463 (1 per 1,156 persons); hospital beds 16,682 (1 per 586 persons); infant mortality rate per 1,000 live births (2003) 26.8. **Food** (2001): daily per capita caloric intake 3,293 (vegetable products 89%, animal products 11%); 138% of FAO recommended minimum.

Military

Total active duty personnel (2003): 35,000 (army 77.1%, navy 12.9%, air force 10.0%). **Military expenditure as percentage of GNP** (1999): 1.8% (world 2.4%); per capita expenditure $38.

Background

From the 12th century BC the Phoenicians had a series of trading posts on the northern African coast. By the 6th century BC the Carthaginian kingdom encompassed most of present-day Tunisia. The Romans ruled from 146 BC until the Muslim Arab invasions in the mid-7th century AD. The area was fought over, won, and lost by many, including the Abbasids, the Almohads, the Spanish, and the Ottoman Turks, who finally conquered it in 1574 and held it until the late 19th century. For a time it maintained autonomy as the French, British, and Italians contended for the region. In 1881 Tunisia became a French protectorate. In World War II US and British forces captured it (1943) to end a brief German occupation. In 1956 France granted it full independence; Habib Bourguiba assumed power and remained in office until 1987.

Recent Developments

In 2006 the Tunisian government refused to alter its repressive policies toward dissent, evidenced by the hunger strike of Mohammed Abbou, a lawyer and activist who had been imprisoned in March 2005 for criticizing the Tunisian regime, and attacks on Neila Charchour Hachicha, a blogger and the founder of the Parti Libéral Méditerranéen, and activist and writer Naziha Regiba (Um Ziad). Nevertheless, US Secretary of Defense Donald Rumsfeld made it clear during a visit in February that the US regarded Tunisia as an essential ally in the struggle against transnational terrorism. Tunisia's external debt stood at $18.64 billion, about 62.1% of GDP. The IMF expected that figure to fall to 49.5% of GDP by 2011, given that GDP growth in 2006 was estimated to have reached 5.3%.

Internet resources: <www.tourismtunisia.com>.

Turkey

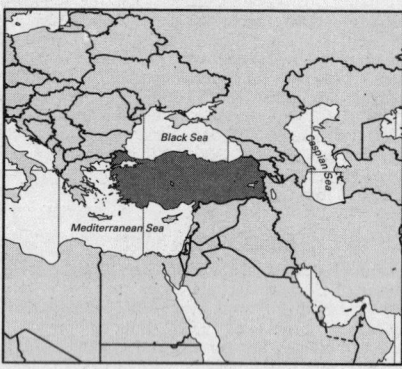

Official name: Turkiye Cumhuriyeti (Republic of Turkey). **Form of government:** multiparty republic with one legislative house (Turkish Grand National Assembly [550]). **Chief of state:** President Abdullah Gul (from 2007). **Head of government:** Prime Minister Recep Tayyip Erdogan (from 2003). **Capital:** Ankara. **Official language:** Turkish. **Official religion:** none. **Monetary unit:** 1 Turkish New lira (TRY) = 100 kurush; valuation (1 Jul 2007) US$1 = TRY 1.31.

Demography

Area: 302,535 sq mi, 783,562 sq km. **Population** (2006): 72,932,000. **Density** (2006): persons per sq mi 241.1, persons per sq km 93.1. **Urban** (2004): 61.2%. **Sex distribution** (2000): male 50.57%; female 49.43%. **Age breakdown** (2000): under 15, 29.1%; 15–29, 28.8%; 30–44, 21.5%; 45–59, 11.8%; 60–74, 6.8%; 75 and over, 2.0%. **Ethnic composition** (2000): Turk 65.1%; Kurd 18.9%; Crimean Tatar 7.2%; Arab 1.8%; Azerbaijani 1.0%; Yoruk 1.0%; other 5.0%. **Religious affiliation** (2000): Muslim 97.2%, of which Sunni 67%, Shi'i 30% (including nonorthodox Alevi 26%); Christian (mostly Eastern Orthodox) 0.6%; other 2.2%. **Major urban agglomerations** (2001): Istanbul 10,243,000; Ankara 4,611,000; Izmir 3,437,000; Bursa (2000) 1,166,000; Adana (2000) 1,091,000. **Location:** southwestern Asia and a small part in southeastern Europe, bordering the Black Sea, Georgia, Armenia, Azerbaijan, Iran, Iraq, Syria, the Mediterranean Sea, Greece, and Bulgaria.

Vital statistics

Birth rate per 1,000 population (2003): 20.9 (world avg. 21.3). **Death rate** per 1,000 population (2003): 7.0 (world avg. 9.1). **Natural increase rate** per 1,000

population (2003): 13.9 (world avg. 12.2). **Total fertility rate** (avg. births per childbearing woman; 2003): 2.4. **Marriage rate** per 1,000 population (2000): 7.1. **Divorce rate** per 1,000 population (2000): 0.5. **Life expectancy** at birth (2003): male 66.4 years; female 71.0 years.

National economy

Budget (2003). *Revenue:* TL 100,238,122,000,000,000 (tax revenue 84.1%, of which tax on income 27.7%; nontax revenue 14.0%; grants 1.9%). *Expenditures:* TL 140,053,981,000,000,000 (interest payments 41.8%; personnel 21.6%; investments 5.1%). **Public debt** (external, outstanding; 2002): $61,823,000,000. **Production** (in '000 metric tons except as noted). *Agriculture, forestry, fishing* (2003): wheat 19,000, sugar beets 13,090, tomatoes 9,750; livestock (number of live animals) 27,000,000 sheep, 10,400,000 cattle, (2000) 373,000 angora goats; roundwood (2002) 18,465,000 cu m; fish catch (2001) 595,000. *Mining* (2002): refined borates 436,000; chromite 313,637; copper ore (metal content) 48,253. *Manufacturing* (value added in $'000,000; 2000): textiles 16,289; refined petroleum 4,839; food products 4,111. *Energy production (consumption):* electricity (kW-hr; 2003) 139,700,000,000 ([2000] 117,709,000,000); hard coal (2003) 2,996,000 ([2000] 15,393,000); lignite (2003) 43,536,000 ([2000] 64,406,000); crude petroleum (barrels; 2003) 16,988,000 ([2000] 172,115,000); petroleum products (2003) 19,723,000 (26,108,000); natural gas (cu m; 2000) 630,102,000 (15,762,000,000). **Tourism** (2002): receipts from visitors $11,901,000,000; expenditures by nationals abroad $1,880,000,000. **Population economically active** (2004): total 24,457,000; activity rate of total population 34.1% (participation rates: over age 14, 49.2%; female 26.6%; unemployed 9.3%). **Gross national product** (2003): $197,220,000,000 ($2,790 per capita). **Household income and expenditure** (1994). Average household size (2002) 4.5; income per household TL 165,089,000; expenditure: food, tobacco, and café expenditures 38.5%, housing 22.8%, clothing 9.0%. **Land use** as % of total land area (2000): in temporary crops 31.4%, in permanent crops 3.3%, in pasture 16.1%; overall forest area 13.3%.

Foreign trade

Imports (2003-c.i.f.): $68,734,000,000 (chemicals and chemical products 16.2%; nonelectrical machinery 11.9%; crude petroleum and natural gas 11.3%; motor vehicles 9.3%; electrical machinery 9.1%; iron and steel 6.8%). *Major import sources:* Germany 13.7%; Italy 7.9%; Russia 7.9%; France 6.0%; US 5.0%; UK 5.0%. **Exports** (2003-f.o.b.): $46,878,000,000 (textiles, apparel, and clothing accessories 20.3%; vehicles 11.2%; electrical and electronic machinery 7.4%; nonelectrical machinery 6.3%; iron and steel 6.2%; raw and prepared fruits and vegetables 5.3%). *Major export destinations:* Germany 15.9%; US 8.0%; UK 7.8%; Italy 6.8%; France 6.0%.

Transport and communications

Transport. *Railroads* (2003): length 8,671 km; passenger-km 5,893,000,000; metric ton-km cargo

1 metric ton = about 1.1 short tons;   1 kilometer = 0.6 mi (statute);   1 metric ton-km cargo = about 0.68 short ton-mi cargo;   c.i.f.: cost, insurance, and freight;   f.o.b.: free on board

8,271,000,000. *Roads* (2000): total length 383,636 km (paved [1997] 25%). *Vehicles* (2003): passenger cars 4,677,765; trucks and buses 1,713,605. *Air transport* (2003; Turkish Airlines only): passenger-km 16,113,000; metric ton-km cargo 369,199,000; airports (1996) 26. **Communications,** in total units (units per 1,000 persons). Daily newspaper circulation (2000): 7,480,000 (111); radios (2001): 32,195,000 (470); televisions (2002): 29,440,000 (423); telephone main lines (2003): 18,916,700 (277); cellular telephone subscribers (2003): 27,887,500 (408); personal computers (2002): 3,000,000 (45); Internet users (2003): 5,500,000 (81).

Education and health

Educational attainment (1993). Percentage of population age 25 and over having: no formal schooling 30.5%; incomplete primary education 6.6%; complete primary 40.4%; incomplete secondary 3.1%; complete secondary or higher 19.1%; unknown 0.3%. **Literacy** (2003): total population age 15 and over literate 88.3%; males literate 95.3%; females literate 79.9%. **Health:** physicians (2001) 82,920 (1 per 826 persons); hospital beds (2000) 156,549 (1 per 431 persons); infant mortality rate per 1,000 live births (2003) 38.3. **Food** (2000): daily per capita caloric intake 3,343 (vegetable products 90%, animal products 10%); 133% of FAO recommended minimum.

Military

Total active duty personnel (2003): 514,850 (army 78.1%, navy 10.2%, air force 11.7%). **Military expenditure as percentage of GNP** (1999): 5.3% (world 2.4%); per capita expenditure $154.

 The seaport city of Istanbul, originally Byzantium and later Constantinople, is the largest city in Turkey. It was formerly the capital of the Byzantine Empire, of the Ottoman Empire, and—until 1923—of the Turkish Republic. The old, walled city of Istanbul stands on a triangular peninsula between Europe and Asia.

Background

Turkey's early history corresponds to that of Asia Minor, the Byzantine Empire, and the Ottoman Empire. Byzantine rule emerged when Constantine the Great made Constantinople (now Istanbul) his capital. The Ottoman Empire, begun in the 12th century, dominated for more than 600 years; it ended in 1918 after the Young Turk revolt precipitated its demise. Under the leadership of Mustafa Kemal Ataturk, a republic was proclaimed in 1923, and the caliphate was abolished in 1924. Turkey remained neutral throughout most of World War II, siding with the Allies in 1945. Since the war it has alternated between civil and military governments and has had several conflicts with Greece and over Cyprus. The 1990s saw political and civic turmoil between fundamentalist Muslims and secularists.

Recent Developments

The negotiation of Turkey's accession to the European Union (EU) advanced at a snail's pace in 2006. A preliminary EU report showed that Turkish laws were largely compatible with EU norms. Progress was held up, however, by Turkey's refusal to open its harbors and air space to (Greek) Cypriot shipping and aircraft until such time as Turkish Cypriots were allowed to establish direct communications with the outside world, without having to go through Turkey. The EU Commission welcomed the approval by the Turkish parliament in October of the ninth package of liberal reforms but did not find them sufficient. It was particularly critical of article 301 of the penal code, which punishes insults to the Turkish state and Turkish identity. In the southeastern provinces more than 180 members of the security forces and 70 civilians were killed by PKK (Kurdistan Workers' Party) snipers and land mines in 18 months to the end of June. Turkey agreed to send troops to assist in providing humanitarian relief to Lebanon in the enlarged UNIFIL, the UN peacekeeping force there. The Turkish economy continued to perform strongly. GNP rose by 5.5%, exports increased by 16%, and imports rose by 18% in the year.

Internet resources: <www.turizm.gov.tr>.

Turkmenistan

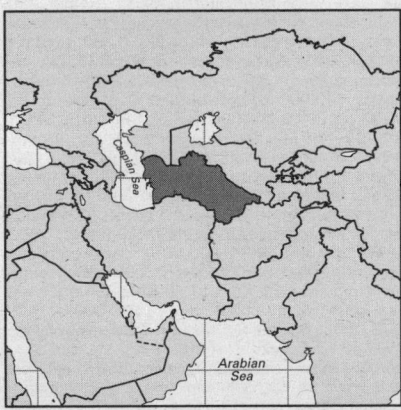

Official name: Turkmenistan. **Form of government:** unitary republic with one legislative body (Majlis [Parliament; 50]). **Head of state and government:** President Gurbanguly Berdymukhammedov (from 2006). **Capital:** Ashgabat. **Official language:** Turkmen. **Official religion:** none. **Monetary unit:** manat; valuation (1 Jul 2007) US$1 = 5,200 manat.

Demography

Area: 188,500 sq mi, 488,100 sq km. **Population** (2006): 4,899,000. **Density** (2006): persons per sq mi 26.0, persons per sq km 10.0. **Urban** (2002): 44.9%. **Sex distribution** (2001): male 49.44%; female 50.56%. **Age breakdown** (2001): under 15, 37.9%; 15–29, 27.9%; 30–44, 23.7%; 45–59, 6.5%; 60–74, 3.5%; 75 and over, 0.5%. **Ethnic composition** (1997): Turkmen 77.0%; Uzbek 9.2%; Russian 6.7%; Kazakh 2.0%; Tatar 0.8%; other 4.3%. **Religious affiliation** (1995): Muslim (mostly Sunni) 87.0%; Russian

Orthodox 2.4%; other (mostly nonreligious) 10.6%. **Major cities** (1999): Ashgabat (2002) 743,000; Turkmenabat 203,000; Dasoguz 165,000; Mary 123,000; Balkanabat 108,000. **Location:** central Asia, bordering Kazakhstan, Uzbekistan, Afghanistan, Iran, and the Caspian Sea.

Vital statistics

Birth rate per 1,000 population (2003): 28.0 (world avg. 21.3); (1998) legitimate 96.2%. **Death rate** per 1,000 population (2003): 8.9 (world avg. 9.1). **Natural increase rate** per 1,000 population (2003): 19.1 (world avg. 12.2). **Total fertility rate** (avg. births per childbearing woman; 2003): 3.5. **Marriage rate** per 1,000 population (1998): 5.4. **Divorce rate** per 1,000 population (1994): 1.5. **Life expectancy** at birth (2003): male 57.7 years; female 64.8 years.

National economy

Budget (1999). *Revenue:* 3,693,100,000,000 manat (value-added tax 25.6%, pension and social security fund 22.5%, repayments of scheduled gas 13.0%, excise tax 10.2%, personal income tax 6.1%). *Expenditures:* 3,894,300,000,000 manat (education 26.9%, pension and social security 15.6%, defense and security 14.9%, health 14.1%, agriculture 5.7%). **Public debt** (external, outstanding; 2000): $1,731,000,000. **Production** (metric tons except as noted). *Agriculture, forestry, fishing* (2002): wheat 2,033,000, seed cotton 600,000, vegetables and melons 327,000; livestock (number of live animals) 6,375,000 sheep and goats, 860,000 cattle, 4,800,000 poultry; roundwood (2000) 2,000,000 cu m; fish catch (2001) 12,792. *Mining and quarrying* (2000): gypsum 100,000, sodium sulfate 60,000, sulfur 9,000. *Manufacturing* (value of production in '000,000 manat; 1994): ferrous and nonferrous metals 278; machinery and metalworks 223; food products 129. *Energy production (consumption):* electricity (kW-hr; 2000) 9,845,000,000 (8,777,000,000); crude petroleum (barrels; 2001) 58,000,000 (19,000,000); petroleum products (2000) 6,113,000 (2,354,000); natural gas (cu m; 2001) 46,439,000,000 (7,362,000,000). **Household income and expenditure.** Average household size (2000) 4.7; sources of income (1998): wages and salaries 70.6%, pensions and grants 20.9%, self-employment (mainly agricultural income) 2.3%, nonwage income of workers 1.1%; expenditure (1998): food 45.2%, clothing and footwear 16.8%, furniture 13.3%, transportation 7.6%, health 7.0%. **Population economically active** (2000): total 1,950,000; activity rate of total population 42.0% (participation rates [1996]: ages 16–59 [male], 16–54 [female] 73.0%; female 42.7%). **Gross national product** (2003): $5,400,000,000 ($1,120 per capita). **Tourism:** receipts from visitors (1998) $192,000,000; expenditures (1997) $125,000,000. **Land use** as % of total land area (2000): in temporary crops 3.7%, in permanent crops 0.1%, in pasture 65.3%; overall forest area 8.0%.

Foreign trade

Imports (2002 data in balance of trade is c.i.f.): $2,119,000,000 (machinery and transport equipment 40.5%, basic manufactures 18.6%, chemicals and chemical products 9.9%, food products 5.4%). *Major import sources* (2002): Ukraine 17.9%; Germany 12.1%; UAE 11.7%; Russia 10.6%; Turkey 8.8%; Iran 7.3%. **Exports** (2002): $2,856,000,000 (natural gas 57.5%, petrochemicals 14.2%, crude petroleum 11.9%, cotton yarn and fabrics 2.8%, raw cotton 1.7%). *Major export destinations* (2000): Russia 41.1%; Germany 16.2%; Iran 9.7%; Turkey 7.4%; Ukraine 6.6%.

Transport and communications

Transport. *Railroads* (1999): length 2,313 km; passenger-km 701,000,000; metric ton-km cargo 7,337,000,000. *Roads* (1999): total length 24,000 km (paved 81%). *Vehicles* (1995): passenger cars 220,000; trucks and buses 58,200. *Air transport* (2001; Turkmenavia only): passenger-km 1,631,000,000; metric ton-km cargo 35,000,000; airports (2002) with scheduled flights 1. **Communications,** in total units (units per 1,000 persons). Radios (2000): 1,190,000 (256); televisions (2000): 911,000 (196); telephone main lines (2002): 374,000 (77); cellular phone subscribers (2002): 8,200 (1.7); Internet users (2001): 8,000 (1.6).

Education and health

Literacy (1999): total population age 15 and over literate 98.0%. **Health** (1995): physicians 13,500 (1 per 330 persons); hospital beds 46,000 (1 per 97 persons); infant mortality rate per 1,000 live births (2003) 73.2. **Food** (2001): daily per capita caloric intake 2,738 (vegetable products 97%, animal products 3%); 107% of FAO recommended minimum.

Military

Total active duty personnel (2003): 29,000 (army 86.3%, navy 3.4%, air force 10.3%). **Military expenditure as percentage of GNP** (1999): 3.4% (world 2.4%); per capita expenditure $122.

Background

The earliest traces of human settlement in central Asia, dating back to Paleolithic times, have been found in Turkmenistan. The nomadic, tribal Turkmen probably entered the area in the 11th century AD. They were conquered by the Russians in the early 1880s, and the region became part of Russian Turkistan. It was organized as the Turkmen Soviet Socialist Republic in 1924 and became a constituent republic of the USSR in 1925. The country gained full independence from the USSR in 1991 under the name Turkmenistan. From 1990 to 2006 the country was ruled by the ever more autocratic and mercurial strongman Saparmurad Niyazov.

Recent Developments

Prominent members of the opposition in exile announced immediately after Pres. Saparmurad Niyazov's death in late December 2006 that they would return to Turkmenistan to promote the democratization of the country, but the Turkmen security services warned that any opposition leader who tried to enter the country would be arrested. There were in-

---

1 metric ton = about 1.1 short tons;   1 kilometer = 0.6 mi (statute);   1 metric ton-km cargo = about 0.68 short ton-mi cargo;   c.i.f.: cost, insurance, and freight;   f.o.b.: free on board

dications throughout the year that mismanagement of the gas-rich country's economy was affecting the national income. Through much of the year, a tug-of-war continued with the Russian firm Gazprom and other customers over the future price of Turkmen gas. At the end of June, Turkmenistan threatened to cut off gas supplies to Russia in October if an agreement was not reached; in September Gazprom acceded to the Turkmen demand for $100 per 1,000 cu m—a 54% increase over the previously agreed price—in return for an increased export volume in 2007–09.

Internet resources:
<www.turkmenistanembassy.org>.

Tuvalu

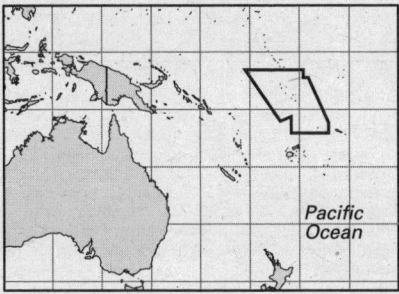

Pacific Ocean

Official name: Tuvalu. **Form of government:** constitutional monarchy with one legislative house (Parliament [12]). **Chief of state:** British Queen Elizabeth II (from 1952), represented by Governor-General Filoimea Telito (from 2005). **Head of government:** Prime Minister Apisai Ielemia (from 2006). **Capital:** government offices are at Vaiaku, Fongafale islet, on Funafuti atoll. **Official language:** none. **Official religion:** none. **Monetary units:** 1 Tuvalu dollar = 1 Australian dollar ($T = $A) = 100 Tuvalu and Australian cents; valuation (1 Jul 2007) US$1 = $A 1.18.

Demography

Area: 9.90 sq mi, 25.63 sq km. **Population (2006):** 10,600. **Density (2006):** persons per sq mi 1,071, persons per sq km 413.6. **Urban (2002):** 47.0%. **Sex distribution (2002):** male 49.46%; female 50.54%. **Age breakdown (2002):** under 15, 36.2%; 15–29, 21.2%; 30–44, 20.2%; 45–59, 13.8%; 60–74, 6.8%; 75 and over, 1.8%. **Ethnic composition (2000):** Tuvaluan (Polynesian) 96.3%; mixed (Pacific Islander/European/Asian) 1.0%; Micronesian 1.0%; European 0.5%; other 1.2%. **Religious affiliation (1995):** Church of Tuvalu (Congregational) 85.4%; Seventh-day Adventist 3.6%; Roman Catholic 1.4%; Jehovah's Witness 1.1%; Baha'i 1.0%; other 7.5%. **Major locality (2002):** Fongafale, on Funafuti atoll, 4,492. **Location:** western Pacific Ocean, lying east of Papua New Guinea near the equator.

Vital statistics

Birth rate per 1,000 population (2002): 27.1 (world avg. 21.3). **Death rate** per 1,000 population (2002): 9.9 (world avg. 9.1). **Natural increase rate** per 1,000 population (2002): 17.2 (world avg. 12.2). **Total fertility rate** (avg. births per childbearing woman; 2002): 3.7. **Life expectancy** at birth (2002): male 61.7 years; female 65.1 years.

National economy

Budget (2001). *Revenue:* $A 33,519,000. *Expenditures:* $A 24,091,000. **Gross national product** (1998): US$14,700,000 (US$1,400 per capita). **Production** (metric tons except as noted). *Agriculture and fishing* (2002): coconuts 1,000, tropical fruit 400, vegetables 380,; livestock (number of live animals) 13,200 pigs, 10,000 ducks, 40,000 chickens; fish catch (2001) 500. *Manufacturing:* tiny amounts of copra, handicrafts, and garments. Overseas employment (2000) of Tuvaluan seafarers contributes about US$5,000,000 annually to the Tuvalu economy. *Energy production (consumption):* electricity (kW-hr; 1992) 1,300,000 (1,300,000). **Tourism** (1998): receipts from visitors US$200,000. **Population economically active** (1991): total 5,910; activity rate of total population 65.3% (participation rates: ages 15–64, 85.5%; female [1979] 51.3%; unemployed [1979] 4.0%). **Household income and expenditure.** Average household size (1994): Funafuti 7.0, other islands 5.8; average annual gross income per household (1994): Funafuti $A 12,012, other islands $A 3,536; sources of income (1987): agriculture and other 45.0%, cash economy only 38.0%, overseas remittances 17.0%; expenditure (1992): food 45.5%, housing and household operations 11.5%, transportation 10.5%, alcohol and tobacco 10.5%, clothing 7.5%, other 14.5%. **Land use** as % of total land area (2000): coconut trees occupy c. 77% of land area.

Foreign trade

Imports (2002): $A 20,362,000 (food products including live animals 23.5%, mineral fuels 13.8%, machinery and apparatus 12.4%, base and fabricated metals 8.8%, transport equipment 7.3%). *Major import sources:* Australia 34.7%; Fiji 29.4%; New Zealand 13.9%; Japan 10.3%; China 3.7%. **Exports** (2002): $A 252,000 (primarily copra, stamps, and handicrafts). *Major export destinations:* Fiji 58.9%; Australia 22.3%; New Zealand 11.4%; Japan 5.7%.

Transport and communications

Transport. *Roads* (2000): total length 28 km (paved, none). *Air transport:* airports (2001) 1. **Communications,** in total units (units per 1,000 persons). Radios (1997): 4,000 (384); televisions (1996): 100 (13); telephone main lines (2002): 1,300 (125).

Education and health

Educational attainment (mid-1990s). Percentage of population age 15 and over (on Funafuti) having: no formal schooling through completed primary education 31.9%; some secondary 46.6%; completed secondary to some higher 18.6%; completed higher 2.9%. **Literacy** (1990): total population literate in Tuvaluan 8,593 (95.0%); literacy in English estimated at 45.0%. **Health** (1999): physicians 8 (1 per 1,375 persons); hospital beds (1990) 30 (1 per 302 persons); infant mortality rate per 1,000 live births (2002): 35.0.

Military

Total active duty personnel: none; Tuvalu relies on Australian-trained volunteers from Fiji and Papua New Guinea.

Background

The original Polynesian settlers of Tuvalu probably came mainly from Samoa or Tonga. The islands were sighted by the Spanish in the 16th century. Europeans settled there in the 19th century and intermarried with Tuvaluans. During this period Peruvian slave traders, known as "blackbirders," decimated the population. In 1856 the US claimed the four southern islands for guano mining. Missionaries from Europe arrived in 1865 and rapidly converted the islanders to Christianity. In 1892 Tuvalu joined the British Gilbert Islands, a protectorate that became the Gilbert and Ellice Islands Colony in 1916. Tuvaluans voted in 1974 for separation from the Gilberts (now Kiribati), whose people are Micronesian. Tuvalu gained independence in 1978, and in 1979 the US relinquished its claims. Elections were held in 1981, and a revised constitution was adopted in 1986. In recent decades, the government has tried to find overseas job opportunities for its citizens.

Recent Developments

Tuvalu, comprising low coral atolls and reef islands vulnerable to rising sea levels, urged a UN summit in November 2006 to make the reduction of greenhouse gases a priority. Tuvalu voted in favor of a Japanese proposal to allow the resumption of commercial whaling at the International Whaling Commission meeting in 2006 but denied that it had done so because of Japan's promises to build a new desalination plant, a deepwater wharf, and a power plant.

Internet resources: <www.timelesstuvalu.com>.

Uganda

Official name: Republic of Uganda. **Form of government:** nonparty republic with one legislative house (Parliament [305, including 10 nonelected members]). **Head of state and government:** President Yoweri Museveni (from 1986), assisted by Prime Minister Apolo Nsibambi (from 1999). **Capital:** Kampala. **Official language:** English. **Official religion:** none. **Monetary unit:** 1 Uganda shilling (U Sh) = 100 cents; valuation (1 Jul 2007) US$1 = U Sh 1,701.

Demography

Area: 93,263 sq mi, 241,551 sq km (includes 16,984 sq mi [43,989 sq km] water area). **Population** (2006): 28,196,000. **Density** (2006; based on land area only): persons per sq mi 369.6, persons per sq km 142.7. **Urban** (2002): 12.2%. **Sex distribution** (2002): male 48.99%; female 51.01%. **Age breakdown** (2002): under 15, 50.9%; 15–29, 26.4%; 30–44, 13.4%; 45–59, 5.6%; 60–74, 3.0%; 75 and over, 0.7%. **Ethnolinguistic composition** (1991): Ganda 18.1%; Nkole 10.7%; Kiga 8.4%;

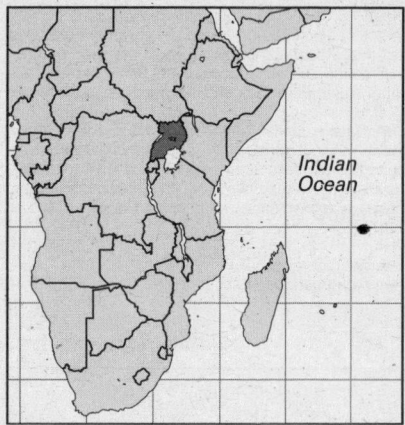

Soga 8.2%; Lango 5.9%; Lugbara 4.7%; Gisu 4.5%; Acholi 4.4%. **Religious affiliation** (1995): Christian 66%, of which Roman Catholic 33%, Protestant 33% (of which mostly Anglican); traditional beliefs 18%; Muslim 16%. **Major cities** (2002): Kampala urban agglomeration 1,208,544; Gulu 113,144; Lira 89,871; Jinja 86,520; Mbale 70,437. **Location:** eastern Africa, bordering The Sudan, Kenya, Lake Victoria, Tanzania, Rwanda, and the Democratic Republic of the Congo.

Vital statistics

Birth rate per 1,000 population (2003): 46.6 (world avg. 21.3). **Death rate** per 1,000 population (2003): 17.0 (world avg. 9.1). **Natural increase rate** per 1,000 population (2003): 29.6 (world avg. 12.2). **Total fertility rate** (avg. births per childbearing woman; 2003): 6.7. **Life expectancy** at birth (2003): male 43.4 years; female 46.4 years. **Adult population** (ages 15–49) **living with HIV** (2004): 4.1% (world avg. 1.1%).

National economy

Budget (2001–02). *Revenue:* U Sh 1,977,500,000,-000 (tax revenue 58.4%, of which VAT 19.9%, excise taxes 18.3%, income taxes 14.4%, tax on international trade 5.9%; grants 36.6%; nontax revenue 5.0%). *Expenditures:* U Sh 2,565,000,000,000 (current expenditures 55.8%, of which public administration 14.3%, education 14.1%, defense 8.2%, health 6.4%, public order 4.5%; capital expenditures 44.2%). **Production** (metric tons except as noted). *Agriculture, forestry, fishing* (2002): plantains 9,600,000, cassava 5,300,000, sweet potatoes 2,515,000; livestock (number of live animals) 5,900,000 cattle, 5,600,000 goats, 25,500,000 chickens; roundwood 38,316,824 cu m; fish catch (2001) 356,032. *Mining and quarrying* (2002): cobalt 450; columbite-tantalite (ore and concentrate) 6,463 kg. *Manufacturing* (2001): cement 431,084; sugar 130,326; soap 90,807. *Energy production (consumption):* electricity (kW-hr; 2001) 1,534,-700,000 (1,534,700,000); petroleum products

1 metric ton = about 1.1 short tons;   1 kilometer = 0.6 mi (statute);   1 metric ton-km cargo = about 0.68 short ton-mi cargo;   c.i.f.: cost, insurance, and freight;   f.o.b.: free on board

(2000) none (436,000). **Tourism** (2002): receipts from visitors $185,000,000; expenditures by nationals abroad (1999) $141,000,000. **Gross national product** (2003): $6,173,000,000 ($240 per capita). **Population economically active** (2002): total 11,995,000; activity rate of total population 48.5% (participation rates [2001]: ages 15–64, 78.9%; female [2001] 35.2%). **Public debt** (external, outstanding; 2002): $3,690,000,000. **Household income and expenditure** (1999–2000). Average household size (2002) 4.7; income per household U Sh 141,000; sources of income: wages and self-employment 78.0%, transfers 13.0%, rent 9.0%; expenditure: food and beverages 51.0%, rent, energy, and services 17.0%, education 7.0%, household durable goods 6.0%, transportation 5.0%, health 4.0%. **Land use** as % of total land area (2000): in temporary crops 25.7%, in permanent crops 10.7%, in pasture 25.9%; overall forest area 21.0%.

Foreign trade

Imports (2001–02-c.i.f.): $1,084,900,000 (machinery and apparatus 28.3%, refined petroleum 16.1%, food and live animals 15.9%, road vehicles 15.8%, pharmaceuticals 4.9%). *Major import sources* (2002): Kenya 45.1%; South Africa 6.7%; India 5.6%; UK 5.5%; France 3.4%. **Exports** (2001–02-f.o.b.): $475,500,000 (unroasted coffee 21.6%, fish products 17.0%, tea 5.7%, cereal 2.8%, cotton 2.8%). *Major export destinations* (2002): Belgium 16.2%; The Netherlands 13.7%; Germany 7.5%; Spain 5.5%; Hong Kong 4.9%.

Transport and communications

Transport. *Railroads* (2000): route length 1,241 km; metric ton-km cargo (2001) 220,000,000. *Roads* (1996): total length 26,800 km (paved 7.7%). *Vehicles* (2000): passenger cars 49,016; trucks and buses 55,683. *Air transport* (2000): passenger-km 215,000,000; airports (2002) 1. **Communications,** in total units (units per 1,000 persons). Daily newspaper circulation (2000): 45,900 (2); radios (2000): 2,920,000 (127); televisions (2002): 442,800 (18); telephone main lines (2003): 61,000 (2.4); cellular telephone subscribers (2003): 776,200 (30); personal computers (2003): 103,000 (4); Internet users (2003): 125,000 (4.9).

Education and health

Educational attainment (1991). Percentage of population age 25 and over having: no formal schooling or less than one full year 46.9%; primary education 42.1%; secondary 10.5%; higher 0.5%. **Literacy** (2001): population age 10 and over literate 68.0%; males literate 78.1%; females literate 58.0%. **Health:** physicians (1993) 840 (1 per 22,399 persons); hospital beds (1996) 22,788 (1 per 880 persons); infant mortality rate per 1,000 live births (2003) 87.9. **Food** (2001): daily per capita caloric intake 2,398 (vegetable products 94%, animal products 6%); 103% of FAO recommended minimum.

Military

Total active duty personnel (2003): 60,000 (army 100%). **Military expenditure as percentage of GNP** (1999): 2.3% (world 2.4%); per capita military expenditure $6.

Background

By the 19th century the region around Uganda comprised several separate kingdoms inhabited by various peoples, including Bantu- and Nilotic-speaking tribes. Arab traders reached the area in the 1840s. The native kingdom of Buganda was visited by the first European explorers in 1862. Protestant and Roman Catholic missionaries arrived in the 1870s, and the development of religious factions led to persecution and civil strife. In 1894 Buganda was formally proclaimed a British protectorate. As Uganda, it gained its independence in 1962, and in 1967 it adopted a republican constitution. The civilian government was overthrown in 1971 and replaced by a military regime under Idi Amin. His invasion of Tanzania in late 1978 resulted in the collapse of his regime. In 1985 the civilian government was again deposed by the military, which in turn was overthrown in 1986. A constituent assembly enacted a new constitution in 1995.

Recent Developments

After his reelection in February 2006, Pres. Yoweri Museveni said his government's emphasis would be on the expansion of the country's infrastructure, the encouragement of subsistence agriculture and commercial farming, the building up of local industry, and the political unification under one president of the three East African states—Uganda, Kenya, and Tanzania. In May the government launched a new plan to deal with the long-running civil war in the north, though Museveni firmly rejected any negotiated settlement with the rebel Lord's Resistance Army (LRA), whose leader, Joseph Kony, had, at the government's request, been indicted by the International Criminal Court for war crimes. Kony's offer to talk with the government was nonetheless accepted, and the government of Southern Sudan offered to act as mediator. In July the Ugandan government proposed the granting of a total amnesty to the rebels if they renounced the rebellion. After Raska Lukwiya, a prominent leader in the LRA, was killed, Kony demanded a general ceasefire, which was signed in August and renewed for a month in November to allow the LRA forces to assemble at two sites in Southern Sudan. Peace talks continued into May 2007, however, with claims and counterclaims of violations and without tangible success.

Internet resources: <www.visituganda.com>.

Ukraine

Official name: Ukrayina (Ukraine). **Form of government:** unitary multiparty republic with a single legislative body (Supreme Council [450]). **Head of state:** President Viktor Yushchenko (from 2005). **Head of government:** Prime Minister Viktor Yanukovych (from 2006). **Capital:** Kiev (Kyyiv). **Official language:** Ukrainian. **Official religion:** none. **Monetary unit:** hryvnya (pl. hryvnyas); valuation (1 Jul 2007) US$1 = 5.10 hryvnyas.

Demography

Area: 233,062 sq mi, 603,628 sq km. **Population** (2006): 46,757,000. **Density** (2006): persons per sq mi 200.6, persons per sq km 77.5. **Urban** (2004): 67.6%. **Sex distribution** (2004): male 46.22%; female

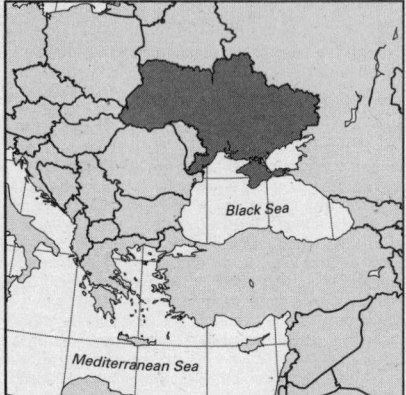

53.78%. **Age breakdown** (2003): under 15, 16.3%; 15–29, 22.6%; 30–44, 21.7%; 45–59, 18.7%; 60–74, 15.0%; 75 and over, 5.7%. **Ethnic composition** (2001): Ukrainian 77.8%; Russian 17.3%; Belarusian 0.6%; Moldovan 0.5%; Crimean Tatar 0.5%; other 3.3%. **Religious affiliation** (1995): Ukrainian Orthodox (Russian patriarchy) 19.5%; Ukrainian Orthodox (Kiev patriarchy) 9.7%; Ukrainian Catholic (Uniate) 7.0%; Protestant 3.6%; other Orthodox 1.6%; Roman Catholic 1.2%; Jewish 0.9%; other (mostly nonreligious) 56.5%. **Major cities** (2001): Kiev 2,621,700 (2003); Kharkiv 1,470,000; Dnipropetrovsk 1,064,000; Odessa 1,029,000; Donetsk 1,016,000. **Location:** eastern Europe, bordering Belarus, Russia, the Black Sea, Romania, Moldova, Hungary, Slovakia, and Poland.

Vital statistics

Birth rate per 1,000 population (2003): 8.6 (world avg. 21.3); legitimate 80.1%. **Death rate** per 1,000 population (2003): 16.1 (world avg. 9.1). **Natural increase rate** per 1,000 population (2003): –7.5 (world avg. 12.2). **Total fertility rate** (avg. births per childbearing woman; 2003): 1.3. **Life expectancy** at birth (2003): male 61.1 years; female 72.2 years.

National economy

Budget (2003). *Revenue:* 54,986,700,000 hryvnas (tax revenue 64.9%, of which tax on profits of enterprises 23.8%, VAT 22.9%, excise tax 9.3%; nontax revenue 28.6%; other 6.5%). *Expenditures:* 56,010,-900,000 hryvnas (2001; social security 43.2%; economy 8.2%; debt payment 6.7%; education 6.2%; public order 6.1%; defense 5.8%; health 1.9%). **Production** (metric tons except as noted). *Agriculture, forestry, fishing* (2002): wheat 20,550,000, potatoes 16,100,000, sugar beets 14,400,000; livestock (number of live animals) 9,421,000 cattle, 8,370,000 pigs, 1,875,000 sheep and goats; roundwood (2002) 9,859,300 cu m; fish catch (2001) 382,300. *Mining and quarrying* (2001): iron ore (2003) 62,952,000; manganese (metal content) 930,000; ilmenite concentrate 600,000. *Manufacturing* (value of production in '000,000 hryvnas;

1998): iron and steel 14,525; food and beverages 12,974; nonelectrical machinery 3,838. *Energy production (consumption):* electricity (kW-hr; 2002) 172,800,000,000 ([2000] 167,596,000,000); hard coal (2003) 75,792,000 ([2000] 84,209,000); lignite (2003) 648,000 ([2000] 1,058,000); crude petroleum (barrels; 2003) 29,027,000 ([2000] 70,265,000); petroleum products (barrels; 2000) 8,822,000 (9,999,000); natural gas (cu m; 2003) 16,346,000,000 (76,089,500,000). **Population economically active** (2002): total 22,701,700; activity rate of total population 47.2% (participation rates: ages 16–59 [male], 15–64 [female] 56.6%; female 48.9%; unemployed 10.1% [registered 5.8%]). **Public debt** (external; 2002): $8,349,000,000. **Gross national product** (2003): $46,739,000,000 ($970 per capita). **Tourism** (2002): receipts $2,992,000,000; expenditures $2,087,000,000. **Household income and expenditure.** Average household size (2002): 2.7; income per household (2003) 8,800 hryvnyas; sources of income (2003): wages and salaries 43.4%, subsidies and pensions 35.2%, profit and mixed income 16.4%, property income 5.0%; expenditures (2003): food and beverages 62.7%, consumer goods 30.6%, housing 6.7%. **Land use** as % of total land area (2000): in temporary crops 56.2%, in permanent crops 1.6%, in pasture 13.7%; overall forest area 16.5%.

Foreign trade

Imports (2002): $17,959,000,000 (machinery 22.4%, natural gas 19.6%, crude petroleum 13.5%, chemicals and chemical products 13.1%, food and raw materials 6.6%). *Major import sources* (2003): Russia 32.9%; Germany 13.5%; Turkmenistan 9.6%; Italy 4.6%; China 4.3%. **Exports** (2002): $18,669,-000,000 (ferrous and nonferrous metals 39.3%, wood and wood products 14.5%, food and raw materials 13.2%, machinery 11.5%, chemicals and chemical products 10.0%). *Major export destinations* (2003): Russia 17.6%; Turkey 7.3%; Italy 6.0%; China 5.3%; Germany 3.6%.

Transport and communications

Transport. *Railroads* (2001): length 22,218 km; passenger-km 52,661,000,000; metric ton-km cargo 177,465,000,000. *Roads* (2003): total length 169,739 km (paved 97%). *Vehicles* (2001): passenger cars 5,313,000. *Air transport* (2003): passenger-km 2,352,000,000; metric ton-km cargo 13,536,000; airports (1999) with scheduled flights 12. **Communications,** in total units (units per 1,000 persons). Daily newspaper circulation (2000): 4,970,000 (101); radios (2000): 43,800,000 (889); televisions (2000): 22,500,000 (456); telephone main lines (2002): 10,833,200 (216); cellular telephone subscribers (2002): 4,200,000 (84); personal computers (2002): 951,000 (19); Internet users (2002): 900,000 (18).

Education and health

Literacy (1999): percentage of total population age 15 and over literate 99.6%; males literate 99.7%; females literate 99.5%. **Health** (2003): physicians 223,000 (1 per 214 persons); hospital beds

1 metric ton = about 1.1 short tons;   1 kilometer = 0.6 mi (statute);   1 metric ton-km cargo = about 0.68 short ton-mi cargo;   c.i.f.: cost, insurance, and freight;   f.o.b.: free on board

458,000 (1 per 104 persons); infant mortality rate per 1,000 live births (2003) 20.8. **Food** (2001): daily per capita caloric intake 3,008 (vegetable products 80%, animal products 20%); 118% of FAO recommended minimum.

Military

Total active duty personnel (2003): 295,500 (army 50.1%, air force 16.6%, navy 4.6%, headquarters 14.2%, paramilitary 14.5%). **Military expenditure as percentage of GNP** (1999): 3.0% (world 2.4%); per capita expenditure $103.

Background

The area around Ukraine was invaded and occupied in the first millennium BC by the Cimmerians, Scythians, and Sarmatians and in the first millennium AD by the Goths, Huns, Bulgars, Avars, Khazars, and Magyars. Slavic tribes settled there after the 4th century. Kiev was the chief town of Kievan Rus. The Mongol conquest in the mid-13th century decisively ended Kievan power. Ruled by Lithuania in the 14th century and Poland in the 16th century, it fell to Russian rule in the 18th century. The Ukrainian National Republic, established in 1917, declared its independence from Soviet Russia in 1918 but was reconquered in 1919; it was made the Ukrainian Soviet Socialist Republic of the USSR in 1922. The northwestern region was held by Poland from 1919 to 1939. Ukraine suffered a severe famine in 1932–33 under Soviet leader Joseph Stalin; over five million Ukrainians died of starvation in an unprecedented peacetime catastrophe. Overrun by Axis armies in 1941 in World War II, it was further devastated before being retaken by the Soviets in 1944. It was the site of the 1986 accident in Chernobyl, at a Soviet-built nuclear power plant. Ukraine declared independence in 1991. In recent years it has struggled economically as well as politically.

Recent Developments

The year 2006 saw dramatic changes in the political landscape of Ukraine, beginning with the dismissal by the parliament of Prime Minister Yury Yekhanurov's cabinet in January and culminating with a victory in the parliamentary elections by the Party of Regions, led by Viktor Yanukovych, in March. The results were a serious setback for Pres. Viktor Yushchenko. The balloting was widely considered to be the most democratic in the brief history of independent Ukraine. Negotiations for the formation of a ruling coalition led to Yushchenko agreeing to nominate Yanukovych to the prime minister's post after he agreed to be bound by the regime's commitment to join European structures and the World Trade Organization (WTO) and to hold a referendum on joining NATO. The coalition lasted barely 11 weeks. The key dilemma for Ukraine was the ambiguity of the revised constitution, particularly whether control of foreign policy was vested in the president or the prime minister. It was announced in May 2007 that early elections would be held to try to resolve the issue. Natural gas from Russia, 90% of which passes through Ukraine to supply about 25% of Europe's natural-gas needs, was temporarily cut off in early January. The dispute was resolved under an agreement by which Russia's energy company Gazprom agreed to sell gas at a price of $230 per

1,000 cu m to a joint-venture company, which in turn would sell the gas to Ukraine for $95 per 1,000 cu m.

Internet resources: <www.ukremb.com>.

United Arab Emirates

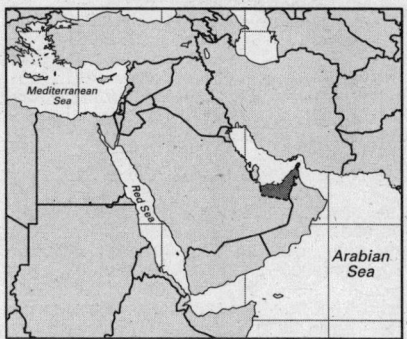

Official name: Al-Imarat al-'Arabiyah al-Muttahidah (United Arab Emirates). **Form of government:** federation of seven emirates with one advisory body (Federal National Council [40; all appointed seats]). **Chief of state:** President Sheikh Khalifah ibn Zayid al-Nahyan (from 2004). **Head of government:** Prime Minister Sheikh Muhammad ibn Rashid al-Maktum (from 2006). **Capital:** Abu Dhabi. **Official language:** Arabic. **Official religion:** Islam. **Monetary unit:** 1 UAE dirham (Dh) = 100 fils; valuation (1 Jul 2007) US$1 = Dh 3.67.

Demography

Area: 32,280 sq mi, 83,600 sq km. **Population** (2006): 4,214,000. **Density** (2006): persons per sq mi 130.5, persons per sq km 50.4. **Urban** (2001): 87.2%. **Sex distribution** (2001): male 67.63%; female 32.37%. **Age breakdown** (2001): under 15, 26.2%; 15–29, 29.2%; 30–44, 33.4%; 45–59, 9.6%; 60–74, 1.4%; 75 and over, 0.2%. **Ethnic composition** (2000): Arab 48.1%, of which UAE Arab 12.2%, UAE Bedouin 9.4%, Egyptian Arab 6.2%, Omani Arab 4.1%, Saudi Arab 4.0%; South Asian 35.7%, of which Pashtun 7.1%, Balochi 7.1%, Malayali 7.1%; Persian 5.0%; Filipino 3.4%; white 2.4%; other 5.4%. **Religious affiliation** (1995): Muslim 96.0% (Sunni 80.0%, Shi'i 16.0%); other (mostly Christian and Hindu) 4.0%. **Major cities** (2003): Dubai 1,171,000; Abu Dhabi 552,000; Sharjah 519,000; Al-'Ayn 348,000; 'Ajman 225,000. **Location:** the Middle East, bordering the Persian Gulf, the Gulf of Oman, Oman, and Saudi Arabia.

Vital statistics

Birth rate per 1,000 population (2003): 15.1 (world avg. 21.3). **Death rate** per 1,000 population (2003): 1.5 (world avg. 9.1). **Natural increase rate** per 1,000 population (2003): 13.6 (world avg. 12.2). **Total fertility rate** (avg. births per childbearing woman; 2003): 2.5. **Marriage rate** per 1,000 population (2003): 3.0. **Divorce rate** per 1,000 population (2003): 0.8. **Life expectancy** at birth (2003): male 72.3 years; female 77.4 years.

National economy

Budget (2001). *Revenue:* Dh 82,480,000,000 (oil revenue 58.5%, non-oil revenue 41.5%). *Expenditures:* Dh 96,083,000,000 (current expenditures 80.5%, capital [development] expenditure 19.5%). **Gross national product** (2001): $69,568,000,000 ($19,945 per capita). **Tourism** (2002): receipts $1,328,000,000. **Production** (metric tons except as noted). *Agriculture, forestry, fishing* (2002): dates 760,000, spinach 620,000, tomatoes 400,000; livestock (number of live animals) 1,300,000 goats, 510,000 sheep, 220,000 camels; fish catch (2001) 117,607. *Mining and quarrying* (2001): aluminum 500,000; gypsum 90,000; lime 50,000. *Manufacturing* (value of production in Dh '000,000; 1998): chemical products (including refined petroleum) 10,096; textiles and wearing apparel 2,397; fabricated metal products 1,999. *Energy production (consumption):* electricity (kW-hr; 2000) 31,890,000,000 (31,890,000,000); crude petroleum (barrels; 2001) 740,000,000 ([2000] 152,801,000); petroleum products (2000) 26,137,000 (6,028,000); natural gas (cu m; 2001) 41,300,000,000 ([2000] 16,469,000,000). **Population economically active** (2001): total 1,853,000; activity rate of total population 53.1% (participation rates [1995]: over age 15, 55.4%; female 11.7%; unemployed [2001] 1.8%). **Households.** Average household size (2000) 5.0; expenditure (1996): rent, fuel, and light 36.1%, transportation and communications 14.9%, food 14.4%, education, recreation, and entertainment 10.3%, durable household goods 7.4%, clothing 6.7%. **Land use** as % of total land area (2000): in temporary crops 0.7%, in permanent crops 2.2%, in pasture 3.6%; overall forest area 3.8%.

Foreign trade

Imports (2001): Dh 120,600,000,000 (for emirates of Abu Dhabi, Dubai, and Sharjah only; machinery and transport equipment 37.6%, food 23.2%, textiles 13.9%, basic manufactures 8.4%, chemicals 6.3%, optical and medical equipment 2.8%). *Major import sources:* Japan 10.2%; US 9.6%; UK 8.8%; China 8.6%; Germany 6.7%; India 6.7%; Italy 6.2%; South Korea 5.3%. **Exports** (2001): Dh 176,900,000,000 (domestic exports 71.1%, of which crude petroleum 36.7%, natural gas 7.1%, refined petroleum products 4.6%, nonmonetary gold 4.4%; reexports 28.9%). *Major export destinations:* Japan 36.4%; India 7.5%; South Korea 7.1%; Singapore 6.3%; Iran 3.8%; Oman 3.4%.

Transport and communications

Transport. *Roads* (1999): total length 3,791 km (paved 100%). *Vehicles* (1996): passenger cars 201,000; trucks and buses 56,950. *Air transport* (2002; Emirates Air only): passenger-km 30,170,000,000; metric ton-km cargo 1,960,764,000; airports (2001) with scheduled flights 6. **Communications,** in total units (units per 1,000 persons). Daily newspaper circulation (2000): 507,000 (156); radios (2000): 1,030,000 (318); televisions (2000): 948,000 (292); telephone main lines (2003): 1,135,800 (281); cellular telephone subscribers (2003): 2,972,300 (736); personal computers (2002): 450,000 (141); Internet users (2003): 1,110,200 (275).

Education and health

Educational attainment (1995). Percentage of population age 10 and over having: no formal schooling 47.6%; primary education 27.8%; secondary 16.0%; higher 8.6%. **Literacy** (2000): total population age 15 and over literate 76.3%; males literate 75.0%; females literate 79.3%. **Health** (1999): physicians 6,059 (1 per 485 persons); hospital beds 7,448 (1 per 394 persons); infant mortality rate per 1,000 live births (2003) 8.0. **Food** (2001): daily per capita caloric intake 3,192 (vegetable products 75%, animal products 25%); 132% of FAO recommended minimum.

Military

Total active duty personnel (2003): 50,500 (army 87.1%, navy 5.0%, air force 7.9%). **Military expenditure as percentage of GDP** (1999): 4.1% (world 2.4%); per capita expenditure $935.

Did you know? For many centuries the oyster beds of the Persian Gulf produced some of the world's finest pearls. Since the Great Depression of the 1930s, however, the trade has declined continuously, mostly due to the competition of cheaper cultured pearls from Japan and elsewhere.

Background

The Persian Gulf was the location of important trading centers as early as Sumerian times. Its people converted to Islam in Muhammad's lifetime. The Portuguese entered the region in the early 16th century, and the British East India Company arrived about 100 years later. In 1820 the British exacted a peace treaty with local rulers along the coast of the eastern Arabian Peninsula. The area formerly called the Pirate Coast became known as the Trucial Coast. In 1892 the rulers agreed to restrict foreign relations to Britain. Though the British administered the region from 1853, they never assumed sovereignty; each state maintained full internal control. The states formed the Trucial States Council in 1960. In 1971 the sheikhs terminated defense treaties with Britain and established the six-member federation. Ras al-Khaymah joined it in 1972. The UAE aided coalition forces against Iraq in the Persian Gulf War (1991).

Recent Developments

Attention in 2006 was focused on the country's first elections, in December, in which half of the advisory Federal National Council was chosen by a representative Electoral Commission. Although the government enacted legislation that permitted construction workers—most of whom were noncitizens from Asian countries—to unionize and pursue collective bargaining, laws were passed obliging UAE companies to hire only citizens for managerial and secretarial positions. The economy of the UAE grew 11.5% in 2006, but the IMF warned that growth would slow dramatically in 2007 and the stock market fell by 30%.

Internet resources: <www.uae.org.ae>.

1 metric ton = about 1.1 short tons; 1 kilometer = 0.6 mi (statute); 1 metric ton-km cargo = about 0.68 short ton-mi cargo; c.i.f.: cost, insurance, and freight; f.o.b.: free on board

United Kingdom

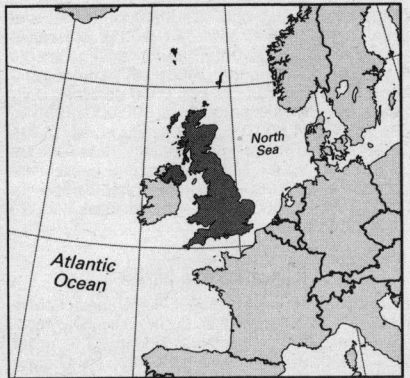

North Sea

Atlantic Ocean

Official name: United Kingdom of Great Britain and Northern Ireland. **Form of government:** constitutional monarchy with two legislative houses (House of Lords [688]; House of Commons [659]). **Chief of state:** Queen Elizabeth II (from 1952). **Head of government:** Prime Minister Gordon Brown (from 2007). **Capital:** London. **Official language:** English. **Official religion:** Churches of England and Scotland "established" (protected by the state, but not "official") in their respective countries; no established church in Northern Ireland or Wales. **Monetary unit:** 1 pound sterling (£) = 100 new pence; valuation (1 Jul 2007) US$1 = £0.50.

Demography

Area: 93,628 sq mi, 242,495 sq km, of which England 50,301 sq mi, 130,279 sq km; Wales 8,005 sq mi, 20,733 sq km; Scotland 30,080 sq mi, 77,907 sq km; Northern Ireland 5,242 sq mi, 13,576 sq km. **Population** (2006): 60,501,000. **Density** (2006): persons per sq mi 646.1, persons per sq km 249.5. **Urban** (2003): 89.1%. **Age breakdown** (2001): under 15, 18.9%; 15–29, 18.8%; 30–44, 22.6%; 45–59, 18.9%; 60–74, 13.3%; 75 and over, 7.5%. **Ethnic composition** (2001): white 92.1%; black 2.0%, of which Caribbean origin 1.0%, African origin 0.8%; Asian Indian 1.8%; Pakistani 1.3%; Bangladeshi 0.5%; Chinese 0.4%; other and not stated 1.9%. **Sex distribution** (2001): male 48.62%; female 51.38%. **Religious affiliation** (2001): Christian 71.6%, of which Anglican 29.0%, Roman Catholic 11.0%; Muslim 2.7%; Hindu 1.0%; Sikh 0.6%; Jewish 0.5%; nonreligious 15.5%; other 8.1%. **Major cities** (2001; urban agglomeration [2000]): Greater London 7,172,091; Manchester 392,819 ([2001] 2,482,328); Birmingham 977,087 (2,272,000); Leeds 715,402 (1,433,000); Newcastle 259,536 (1,026,000); Liverpool 439,473 (951,000); Glasgow 629,501; Sheffield 513,234; Bradford 467,665; Edinburgh 452,194; Bristol 380,615; Wakefield 315,172; Cardiff 305,353; Coventry 300,848; Doncaster 286,865; Sunderland 280,807; Belfast 277,391. **Location:** western Europe, bordering the North Sea, the English Channel, the Celtic Sea, the Irish Sea, and Ireland. **Dependencies:** Anguilla, Bermuda, British Virgin Islands, Cayman Islands, Falkland Islands, Gibraltar, Guernsey, Isle of Man, Jersey, Montserrat, Pitcairn Island, Saint Helena and Dependencies,

and Turks and Caicos Islands. **Mobility** (1991; Great Britain only). Population living in the same residence as 1990: 90.1%; different residence, same country (of Great Britain) 8.1%; different residence, different country of Great Britain 1.2%; from outside Great Britain 0.6%. **Households** (2002; Great Britain only). Average household size 2.4; 1 person 29%, couple 29%, couple with 1–2 children 19%, couple with 3 or more children 10%, single parent with children 9%, other 4%. **Immigration** (2001): permanent residents 372,000, from Australia 13.4%, Bangladesh, India, and Sri Lanka 6.2%, South Africa 4.8%, New Zealand 4.3%, Pakistan 3.5%, US 3.2%, Canada 1.6%, other 63.0%, of which EU 22.3%.

Vital statistics

Birth rate per 1,000 population (2003): 11.7 (world avg. 21.3); (2002; Great Britain only) legitimate 59.4%. **Death rate** per 1,000 population (2003): 10.3 (world avg. 9.1). **Natural increase rate** per 1,000 population (2003): 1.4 (world avg. 12.2). **Total fertility rate** (avg. births per childbearing woman; 2003): 1.7. **Marriage rate** per 1,000 population (2001): 4.9. **Divorce rate** per 1,000 population (2002): 2.7. **Life expectancy** at birth (2002): male 75.7 years; female 80.4 years.

Social indicators

Quality of working life (2002). Average full-time workweek (hours): male 39.6, female 34.4. Annual rate per 100,000 workers for (2000–01; Great Britain only): injury or accident 2,778.6; death 5.0. Proportion of labor force (employed persons) insured for damages or income loss resulting from: injury 100%; permanent disability 100%; death 100%. Average days lost to labor stoppages per 1,000 employee workdays (2001): 20. **Access to services** (2000). Proportion of households having access to: bath or shower 100%; toilet 100%. **Social participation.** Eligible voters participating in last national election (June 2001): 59.4%. Population age 16 and over participating in voluntary work (2001; Great Britain only): 39%. Trade union membership in total workforce (2001) 29.1%. **Social deviance** (2001–02; England and Wales only). Offense rate per 100,000 population for: theft and handling stolen goods 3,856.2; vandalism 1,809.9; burglary 1,296.2; violence against the person 1,105.6; fraud and forgery 539.2; robbery 205.8; sexual offense 69.7. **Leisure** (1994). Favorite leisure activities (hours weekly): watching television 17.1; listening to radio 10.3; reading 8.8, of which books 3.8, newspapers 3.3; gardening 2.1. **Material well-being** (2001). Households possessing: automobile 74.0%, telephone 94.0%, television receiver (2000) 98.3%, refrigerator/freezer 95.0%, washing machine 93.0%, central heating 92.0%, video recorder 90.0%.

National economy

Budget (2001–02). *Revenue:* £388,357,000,000 (production and import taxes 35.5%, income tax 28.1%, social security contributions 16.3%). *Expenditures:* £380,867,000,000 (social protection 41.8%, health 16.1%, education 12.3%, defense 7.3%). **Gross national product** (2003): $1,680,300,000,000 ($28,350 per capita). **Total national debt** (31 Mar 2000): £426,239,200,000 ($679,894,200,000). **Land use** as % of total land area (2000): in temporary crops 24.4%, in permanent crops 0.2%, in pasture 45.8%; overall forest area 11.6%. **Tourism** (2002): receipts from visitors $17,591,000,000; expenditures by nationals abroad $40,409,000,000. **Production** (value of production in £'000,000). *Agriculture, forestry, fishing* (2001): wheat 1,322, vegetables 970, barley 726, potatoes 600, rapeseed 275, sugar beets 255, fruit 243, oats 64; livestock (number of live animals) 36,716,000 sheep, 10,602,000 cattle, 5,845,000 pigs; roundwood (2002) 7,577,000 cu m; fish catch (2001) 530,000 tons. *Mining and quarrying* (2000): limestone and dolomite 662; sand and gravel 619; china clay (kaolin) 234. *Manufacturing* (value added in £'000,000; 2000): electrical and optical equipment 21,137; food and beverages 20,628; paper, printing, and publishing 19,575; metal manufacturing 16,275; transport equipment 15,968; chemicals and chemical products 14,918; machinery and equipment 12,319; textiles and leather products 7,159. *Energy production (consumption):* electricity (kW-hr; 2001) 352,985,000,000 ([2000] 391,093,-000,000); hard coal (metric tons; 2000) 30,600,000 (58,440,000); crude petroleum (barrels; 2000) 880,107,000 (605,657,000); petroleum products (metric tons; 2000) 80,410,000 (72,458,000); natural gas (cu m; 2000) 127,197,000,000 (113,807,-600,000). **Population economically active** (2002): total 29,183,000; activity rate of total population 59.6% (participation rates: ages 16–64, 74.4%; female 45.9%; unemployed 5.2%). **Household income and expenditure** (2000–01). Average household size (2002) 2.4; average annual disposable income per household £21,242; sources of income: wages and salaries 67.0%, social security benefits 12.0%, income from self-employment 8.9%, dividends and interest 4.0%; expenditure: housing 16.6%, food and beverages 16.0%, transport and vehicles 14.3%, household goods 8.5%, clothing 5.7%.

Foreign trade

Imports (2002): £220,242,000,000 (machinery and apparatus 27.3%, of which radios, televisions, and electronics 6.7%, computers 6.1%; transport equipment 19.8%, of which motor vehicles and parts 13.7%, aircraft 5.4%; chemicals and chemical products 10.7%, of which pharmaceuticals 3.9%, basic chemicals 3.8%; food products 5.1%; wearing apparel 3.5%). *Major import sources:* Germany 13.7%; US 11.3%; France 8.5%; The Netherlands 6.8%; Belgium-Luxembourg 5.9%; Italy 4.7%; Ireland 4.2%; Japan 3.7%; Spain 3.7%; China 3.0%. **Exports** (2002): £185,848,000,000 (machinery and apparatus 32.5%, of which radios, televisions, and electronics 10.6%, nonelectrical machinery 8.5%, computers 5.6%; transport equipment 16.8%, of which motor vehicles and parts 10.1%, aircraft 6.2%; chemicals and chemical products 15.4%, of which pharmaceuticals 5.7%; crude petroleum and natural gas 5.8%; base metals 3.5%). *Major export destinations:* US 15.1%; Germany 11.8%; France 10.0%; Ireland 8.3%; The Netherlands 7.5%; Belgium-Luxembourg 5.7%; Italy 4.6%; Spain 4.5%; Sweden 2.1%; Japan 1.9%.

Transport and communications

Transport. *Railroads* (2001–02; Great Britain only): length 32,000 km; passenger-km 39,104,000,000;

metric ton-km cargo 19,700,000,000. *Roads* (2001): total length 392,408 km (paved 100%). *Vehicles* (2001): passenger cars 23,899,000, trucks and buses 2,544,000. *Air transport* (2001): passenger-km 249,000,000,000; metric ton-km cargo 5,196,000,000; airports (2001) 150. **Communications,** in total units (units per 1,000 persons). Daily newspaper circulation (2000): 19,300,000 (329); radios (2000): 84,500,000 (1,432); televisions (1999): 38,800,000 (652); telephone main lines (2002): 34,898,000 (591); cellular telephone subscribers (2002): 49,677,000 (841); personal computers (2002): 23,972,000 (406); Internet users (2002): 25,000,000 (423).

Education and health

Educational attainment (1999). Percentage of population age 25–64 having: up to lower secondary education only 38%; completed secondary 37%; higher 25%, of which at least some university 17%. **Literacy** (2002): total population literate, virtually 100%. **Health:** physicians (2001; Great Britain only) 71,107 (1 per 826 persons); hospital beds (2000) 242,671 (1 per 246 persons); infant mortality rate per 1,000 live births (2003) 4.7. **Food** (2001): daily per capita caloric intake 3,368 (vegetable products 70%, animal products 30%); 134% of FAO recommended minimum.

Military

Total active duty personnel (2003): 212,660 (army 54.9%, navy 19.9%, air force 25.2%); US troops (2004) 11,800. **Military expenditure as percentage of GNP** (1999): 2.5% (world 2.4%); per capita expenditure $615.

Background

The early pre-Roman inhabitants of Britain were Celtic-speaking peoples, including the Brythonic people of Wales, the Picts of Scotland, and the Britons of Britain. Celts also settled in Ireland c. 500 BC. Julius Caesar invaded and took control of the area in 55–54 BC. The Roman province of Britannia endured until the 5th century and included present-day England and Wales. In the 5th century Nordic tribes of Angles, Saxons, and Jutes invaded Britain. The invasions had little effect on the Celtic peoples of Wales and Scotland.

Christianity began to flourish in the 6th century. During the 8th–9th centuries, Vikings, particularly Danes, raided the coasts of Britain. In the late 9th century Alfred the Great repelled a Danish invasion, which helped bring about the unification of England under Athelstan. The Scots attained dominance in Scotland, which was finally unified under Malcolm II (1005–34).

William of Normandy took England in 1066. The Norman kings established a strong central government and feudal state. The French language of the Norman rulers eventually merged with the Anglo-Saxon of the common people to form the English language. From the 11th century, Scotland came under the influence of the English throne. Henry II conquered Ireland in the late 12th century. His sons, kings Richard I and John, had conflicts with the clergy and nobles, and eventually John was forced to grant

---

1 metric ton = about 1.1 short tons;   1 kilometer = 0.6 mi (statute);   1 metric ton-km cargo = about 0.68 short ton-mi cargo;   c.i.f.: cost, insurance, and freight;   f.o.b.: free on board

the nobles concessions in Magna Carta (1215). The concept of community of the realm developed during the 13th century, providing the foundation for parliamentary government. During the reign of Edward I, statute law developed to supplement English common law, and the first Parliament was convened. In 1314 Robert Bruce won independence for Scotland. The Tudors became the ruling family of England following the Wars of the Roses (1455–85). Henry VIII established the Church of England and made Wales part of his realm. The reign of Elizabeth I began a period of colonial expansion; 1588 brought the defeat of the Spanish Armada. In 1603 James VI of Scotland ascended to the English throne, becoming James I, and established a personal union of the two kingdoms.

The English Civil Wars erupted in 1642 between Royalists and Parliamentarians, ending in the execution of Charles I (1649). After 11 years of Puritan rule under Oliver Cromwell and his son (1649–60), the monarchy was restored with Charles II. In 1707 England and Scotland assented to the Act of Union, forming the kingdom of Great Britain. The Hanoverians ascended to the English throne in 1714, when George Louis, elector of Hanover, became George I of Great Britain. During the reign of George III, Great Britain's American colonies won independence (1783). This was followed by a period of war with revolutionary France and later with the empire of Napoleon (1789–1815).

In 1801 legislation united Great Britain with Ireland to create the United Kingdom of Great Britain and Ireland. Britain was the birthplace of the Industrial Revolution in the late 18th century, and it remained the world's foremost economic power until the late 19th century. During the reign of Queen Victoria, Britain's colonial expansion reached its zenith, though the older dominions, including Canada and Australia, were granted independence (1867 and 1901, respectively).

The UK entered World War I allied with France and Russia in 1914. Following the war, revolutionary disorder erupted in Ireland, and in 1921 the Irish Free State was granted dominion status. The six counties of Ulster, however, remained in the UK as Northern Ireland. The UK entered World War II in 1939. Following the war the Irish Free State became the Irish Republic and left the Commonwealth. India gained independence from the UK in 1947.

Throughout the postwar period and into the 1970s, the UK continued to grant independence to its overseas colonies and dependencies. With UN forces, it participated in the Korean War (1950–53). In 1956 it intervened militarily in Egypt during the Suez Crisis. In 1982 it defeated Argentina in the Falkland Islands War. As a result of continuing social strife in Northern Ireland, it joined with Ireland in several peace initiatives, which eventually resulted in an agreement to establish an assembly in Northern Ireland. In 1997 referenda approved in Scotland and Wales devolved power to both countries, though both remained part of the UK.

Recent Developments

In September 2006 British Prime Minister Tony Blair, the first Labour Party leader to win three successive general election victories, announced that he would step down within 12 months. By the summer of 2006 Labour's support in the opinion polls had fallen to 32–33%, and the party performed badly in parliamentary and local elections. The main beneficiary of Labour's weakness was the Conservative Party. David Cameron, elected Conservative leader in De-

cember 2005, spent the year seeking to shed his party's right-wing image, emphasizing economic stability, strong public services, civil liberties, and climate change. Britain's third party, the Liberal Democrats, had a more troubled year. In January Charles Kennedy, the party leader, admitted to having had a drinking problem and resigned. One of the party's leading MPs, Mark Oaten, then resigned after evidence was produced that he had had sex with "rent boys" (young male prostitutes). Nevertheless, the Liberal Democrats did well in by-elections, as voters wanted to register their disapproval with both Labour and the Conservatives.

In August, 24 people suspected of plotting to destroy up to 10 aircraft flying from London's Heathrow Airport to the US with liquid explosives were arrested. The number of work permits issued to people from Poland and other Eastern European countries that had joined the European Union (EU) in 2004 (predicted to be some 13,000 permits a year but actually numbering no fewer than 427,095 in less than three years) had generated controversy, and in October Britain responded by announcing restrictions on Bulgarians and Romanians coming to work in the UK after the two countries joined the EU in 2007. The UK's economic growth rate rose to about 2.6% in 2006. Employment reached a record of 29 million, but the labor force grew even faster, partly as a result of immigration from Eastern Europe, so the rate of unemployment also increased, to 5.5%.

British troops continued to play a significant role in Iraq and Afghanistan. Britain had 7,200 troops in Iraq at midyear. The number of British troops in Afghanistan increased substantially, reaching 5,600 in Kabul and in the southern province of Helmand in November. This was a matter of domestic contention; polls showed that a large majority of British voters believed that victories were not attainable and that the troops should be brought home quickly.

Blair and Irish Prime Minister Bertie Ahern brought Northern Ireland's leading politicians together in October at St. Andrews, Scotland, and announced a plan for reviving devolution. The two main requirements were that all parties accept the police and courts and that all agree to power sharing. The leaders agreed, and after elections in March 2007, the Northern Ireland Assembly, which had been suspended in October 2002, was restored in May.

Internet resources: <www.visitbritain.com>.

United States

Official name: United States of America. **Form of government:** federal republic with two legislative houses (Senate [100]; House of Representatives [435, excluding 4 nonvoting delegates from the District of Columbia, the US Virgin Islands, American Samoa, and Guam; a nonvoting resident commissioner from Puerto Rico; and a nonvoting resident representative from the Northern Mariana Islands]). **Head of state and government:** President George W. Bush (from 2001). **Capital:** Washington DC. **Official language:** none. **Official religion:** none. **Monetary unit:** 1 dollar (US$) = 100 cents.

Demography

Area: 3,676,487 sq mi, 9,522,058 sq km (total area per 2000 computer-based survey equals 3,676,487

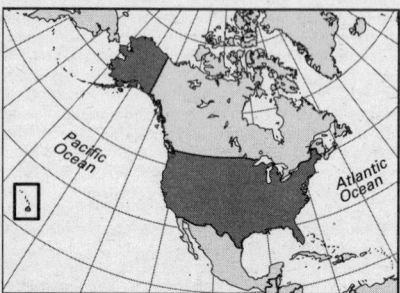

sq mi [9,522,058 sq km], of which land area equals 3,537,439 sq mi [9,161,925 sq km], inland water area equals 78,797 sq mi [204,083 sq km], and Great Lakes water area equals 60,251 sq mi [156,049 sq km]). **Population** (2006): 299,330,000. **Density** (2006; based on land area only): persons per sq mi 84.6, persons per sq km 32.7. **Urban** (2000): 79.0%. **Sex distribution** (2003): male 49.19%; female 50.81%. **Age breakdown** (2003): under 15, 20.9%; 15–29, 20.8%; 30–44, 22.4%; 45–59, 19.4%; 60–74, 10.5%; 75 and over, 6.0%. **Population by race and Hispanic origin** (2002; persons of Hispanic origin may be of any race): non-Hispanic white 68.5%; Hispanic 13.5%; non-Hispanic black 12.8%; Asian and Pacific Islander 4.2%; American Indian and Eskimo 1.0%. **Religious affiliation** (2000): Christian 84.7%, of which Protestant 45.7%, Roman Catholic 18.2%, unaffiliated Christian 15.8%, Orthodox 1.8%, other Christian (primarily Mormon and Jehovah's Witness) 3.2%; Jewish 2.0%; Muslim 1.5%; Buddhist 0.9%; Hindu 0.4%; nonreligious 9.0%; atheist 0.8%; other 0.7%. **Mobility** (2000). Population living in the same residence as in 1999: 84.0%; different residence, same county 9.0%; different county, same state 3.0%; different state 3.0%; moved from abroad 1.0%. **Households** (2002). Total households 109,297,000 (married-couple families 56,747,000 [51.9%]). Average household size (2002) 2.6; 1 person 26.4%, 2 persons 33.1%, 3 persons 16.2%, 4 persons 14.5%, 5 or more persons 9.8%. Family households: 74,329,000 (68.0%); nonfamily 34,968,000 (32.0%), of which 1-person 82.3%. **Place of birth** (2000): native-born 245,708,000 (89.6%); foreign-born 28,379,000 (10.4%), of which Mexico 7,841,000, the Philippines 1,222,000, China and Hong Kong 1,067,000, India 1,007,000, Cuba 952,000, Vietnam 863,000, El Salvador 765,000, South Korea 701,000. **Major cities** (2003): New York 8,085,742; Los Angeles 3,819,951; Chicago 2,869,121; Houston 2,009,690; Philadelphia 1,479,339; Phoenix 1,388,416; San Diego 1,266,753; San Antonio 1,214,725; Dallas 1,208,318; Detroit 911,402. **Location:** North America, bordering Canada, the Atlantic Ocean, the Gulf of Mexico, Mexico, and the Pacific Ocean. Outlying state of Alaska nearly touches eastern Russia and borders the Arctic Ocean and the Pacific Ocean; Hawaii is an island group in the Pacific Ocean. **Dependencies:** American Samoa, Guam, Northern Mariana Islands, Puerto Rico, and Virgin Islands (of the US). **Immigration** (2001): permanent immigrants admitted 1,064,318, from Mexico 19.2%, India 6.2%, former USSR 5.2%, China 4.8%, the Philippines 4.8%, Africa 4.7%, Viet-

nam 3.3%, El Salvador 2.9%, Canada 2.8%, Cuba 2.4%, Haiti 2.1%, Dominican Republic 2.0%, South Korea 1.9%, Jamaica 1.4%, other 36.3%. Refugees (end of 2003) 452,548. Asylum seekers (end of 2000) 386,330.

Vital statistics

Birth rate per 1,000 population (2001): 14.5 (world avg. 21.3); legitimate 66.5%; illegitimate 33.5%. **Death rate** per 1,000 population (2001): 8.5 (world avg. 9.1). **Natural increase rate** per 1,000 population (2001): 6.0 (world avg. 12.2). **Marriage rate** per 1,000 population (2001): 8.4; median age at first marriage (1991): men 26.3 years, women 24.1 years. **Divorce rate** per 1,000 population (2001): 4.0. **Total fertility rate** (avg. births per childbearing woman; 2001): 2.1. **Life expectancy** at birth (2001): white male 75.0 years, black and other male (1996) 68.9 years; white female 80.2 years, black and other female (1996) 76.1 years.

Social indicators

Quality of working life (2001). Average workweek: 39.2 hours. Annual death rate per 100,000 workers (2000): 4.5; leading causes of occupational deaths (1999): transportation incidents 43.4%, contact with objects/equipment 17.1%, assaults/violent acts 14.8%. Average days per 1,000 workdays lost to labor stoppages (2000): 1.8. Average duration of journey to work (2000): 20.7 minutes (private automobile 87.9%, of which drive alone 75.7%, carpool 12.2%; take public transportation 4.7%; walk 2.9%; work at home 3.3%; other 1.2%). Rate per 1,000 employed workers of discouraged workers (unemployed no longer seeking work; 2000): 1.8. **Access to services** (1995). Proportion of occupied dwellings having access to: electricity, virtually 100.0%; safe public water supply 99.4% (12.6% from wells); public sewage collection 77.0%; septic tanks 22.8%. **Social participation.** Eligible voters participating in last presidential election (2004): 60.7%. Population age 18 and over participating in voluntary work (1999): 66.0%. Trade-union membership in total workforce (2000): 14.9%. **Social deviance** (2002). Offense rate per 100,000 population for: murder 6.0; rape 33.9; robbery 158.6; aggravated assault 326.4; motor-vehicle theft 464.3; burglary and housebreaking 774.7; larceny-theft 2,540.1; drug-abuse violation 587.1; drunkenness 149.1. Estimated drug and substance users (population age 12 and over; 1999): cigarettes 57,296,000; binge alcohol 44,486,000; marijuana 11,476,000; other illicit drugs 6,645,000. Rate per 100,000 population of suicide (1999): 10.7. **Leisure** (2002). Favorite leisure activities (percentage of total population age 18 and over that undertook activity at least once in the previous year): movie 60.0%, exercise program 55.0%, gardening 47.0%, home improvement 42.0%, amusement park 42.0%, sports events 35.0%, playing sports 30.0%, charity work 29.0%. **Material well-being** (2001). Occupied dwellings with householder possessing: automobile 95.6%; telephone 94.6%; radio receiver 99.0%; television receiver 98.9%; videocassette recorder and DVD players 89.8%; washing machine 78.6%; air conditioner 75.5%; clothers dryer 73.6%; cable television

1 metric ton = about 1.1 short tons;   1 kilometer = 0.6 mi (statute);   1 metric ton-km cargo = about 0.68 short ton-mi cargo;   c.i.f.: cost, insurance, and freight;   f.o.b.: free on board

68.0%. **Recreational expenditures** (2001): $593,-900,000,000 (television and radio receivers, computers, and video equipment 17.8%; golfing, bowling, and other participatory activities 12.3%; nondurable toys and sports equipment 11.2%; sports supplies 10.2%; magazines and newspapers 5.9%; books and maps 5.9%; spectator amusements 4.9%, of which theater and opera 1.7%, spectator sports 1.7%, movies 1.5%; flowers, seeds, and potted plants 3.1%; other 28.7%).

National economy

Budget (2001). *Revenue:* $2,136,900,000,000 (individual income tax 48.8%, social-insurance taxes and contributions 36.4%, corporation income tax 10.4%, excise taxes 3.4%, customs duties 1,0%). *Expenditures:* $1,856,200,000,000 (social security and medicare 37.5%, defense 16.1%, interest on debt 11.1%, other 35.3%). **Total outstanding national debt** (mid-November 2004): $7,443,900,000,000. **Gross national product** (2003): $10,945,792,000,000 ($37,610 per capita). **Business activity** (1997): number of businesses 23,645,000 (sole proprietorships 72.6%, active corporations 19.9%, active partnerships 7.5%), of which services 10,114,000, wholesaling and retailing 4,455,000; business receipts $18,057,000,000,000 (active corporations 88.0%, sole proprietorships 4.8%, active partnerships 7.2%), of which wholesaling and retailing $5,136,000,-000,000, services $2,130,000,000,000; net profit $1,270,000,000,000 (active corporations 72.0%, sole proprietorships 14.7%, partnerships 13.3%), of which services $203,000,000,000, wholesaling and retailing $10,000,000,000. New business starts and business failures (1995): total number of new business starts 168,158; total failures 71,194, of which commercial service 21,850, retail trade 12,952; failure rate per 10,000 concerns 90.0; current liabilities of failed concerns $37,507,000,000; average liability $526,830. Business expenditures for new plant and equipment (1995): total $594,465,000,000, of which trade, services, and communications $244,-829,000,000, manufacturing businesses $172,-308,000,000 (durable goods 53.0%, nondurable goods 47.0%), public utilities $42,816,000,000, transportation $37,021,000,000, mining and construction $35,985,000. **Production.** *Agriculture, forestry, fishing* (value of production/catch in $'000,000 except as noted; 2002): corn (maize) 21,213, soybeans 14,755, wheat 5,863, cotton lint 3,394, potatoes 3,151, grapes 2,853, oranges 1,834, tobacco 1,726, apples 1,571, head lettuce 1,456, tomatoes 1,171, almonds 1,049, sorghum 884, rice 841, onions 716, cottonseed 638, barley 597, peanuts (groundnuts) 594, broccoli 551, carrots 551, sweet corn 531, dry beans 519, peaches 507, bell peppers 499, cantaloupes 404, avocados 362, lemons 341, watermelons 329, sunflower seeds 317, cabbage 301, pears 297, grapefruit 286, sweet cherries 274, cauliflower 241, pecans 169, strawberries 121; livestock (number of live animals) 97,277,000 cattle, 58,943,000 pigs, 6,685,000 sheep, 5,300,000 horses, 1,940,000 chickens; roundwood 500,434,000 cu m; fish and shellfish catch 3,467, of which fish 1,558 (including salmon 359, Alaska pollack 163), shellfish 1,909 (including shrimp 560, crabs 521). *Mining* (metal content in metric tons except as noted; 2001): iron 37,800,000; copper 1,340,000; zinc 830,000; lead 420,000; molybdenum 38,300; vanadium 2,700; mercury 550; silver 1,800,000 kg; gold 350,000 kg; helium 101,000,000 cu m. *Quarrying* (metric tons; 2000): crushed stone 1,300,000,000; sand and gravel 1,139,000,000; cement 75,000,000; common salt 45,000,000; clay 40,700,000; phosphate rock 34,200,000; lime 20,000,000; gypsum 18,800,000. *Manufacturing* (value added in $'000,000; 1999): transportation equipment 268,511, of which motor vehicle parts 86,310, motor vehicles 80,134, aerospace products and parts 73,897; computers and electronic products 265,442, of which semiconductors and related components 102,003; chemicals and chemical products 229,284, of which pharmaceuticals and medicine 74,108; food 177,659; fabricated metal products 142,451; nonelectrical machinery 138,798; paper and paper products 74,602; plastics 72,183; base metals 66,733; printing 62,428; electrical machinery 60,458. *Energy production (consumption):* electricity (kW-hr; 2001) 3,778,500,000,000 ([2000] 4,159,039,000); hard coal (metric tons; 2000) 895,189,000 (893,343,-000); lignite (metric tons; 2000) 80,505,000 (77,151,000); crude petroleum (barrels; 2001) 2,163,000,000 ([2000] 5,664,000,000); petroleum products (metric tons; 2000) 767,065,000 (767,-031,000); natural gas (cu m; 2001) 549,557,000,-000 ([2000] 660,039,000,000). Domestic production of energy by source (2001): coal 32.7%, natural gas 27.7%, crude petroleum 17.3%, nuclear power 11.2%, renewable energy 7.7%, other 3.4%. *Energy consumption by source* (2000): petroleum and petroleum products 40.5%, natural gas 24.2%, coal 23.8%, nuclear electric power 8.3%, hydroelectric and thermal 3.2%; by end use: industrial 38.9%, residential and commercial 33.7%, transportation 27.4%. **Household income and expenditure.** Average household size (2002) 2.6; median annual income per household (2001) $42,228, of which median Asian and Pacific Islander household $53,635, median white household $44,517, median non-Hispanic household $46,305, median Hispanic household $33,565, median black (including Hispanic) household $29,470; sources of personal income (2000): wages and salaries 57.6%, self-employment 8.6%, transfer payments 8.5%, other 25.3%; expenditure (1999): transportation 18.9%, housing 18.9%, food at home 7.9%, household furnishings 7.2%, fuel and utilities 6.4%, food away from home 5.7%, recreation 5.5%, health 5.3%, wearing apparel 4.7%, education 1.7%, other 17.8%. **Average annual expenditure** of "consumer units" (households, plus individuals sharing households or budgets; 2001): total $39,518, of which housing $13,011, transportation $7,633, food $5,321, pensions and social security $3,326, health care $2,182, clothing $1,743, other $6,302. **Selected household characteristics** (2002). Total number of households 109,297,000, of which (family households by race) white 83.0%, black 12.2%, other 4.8%; in central cities 31.4% (1994), in suburbs 46.3% (1994), outside metropolitan areas 22.3% (1994); (by tenure; 1994) owned 74,399,000 (68.1%), rented 34,897,000 (31.9%); family households 74,329,000, of which married couple 76.4%, female head with own children (includes adoptees and stepchildren) under age 18, 10.8%, female head without own children (includes adoptees and stepchildren) under 18, 6.9%; nonfamily households 34,969,000, of which female living alone 48.0%, male living alone 34.3%, other 17.7%. **Population economically active** (2002): total 144,863,000; activity rate of total population 50.1% (participation rates: age 16 and over 66.6%; female 46.5%; unemployed [October 2004] 5.5%). **Tourism** (2002): receipts from visitors $66,547,000,000; expenditures by nationals abroad $58,044,000,000; number of foreign visitors 41,892,000,000 ([2000] 14,594,000 from Canada, 10,322,000 from Mexico, 11,597,000 from Europe); number of nationals traveling abroad 56,359,000 ([2000] 18,849,000 to Mexico, 15,114,-000 to Canada). Land use as % of total land area (2000): in temporary crops 19.3%, in permanent crops 0.2%, in pasture 25.5%; overall forest area 24.7%.

Foreign trade

Imports (2002): $1,161,400,000,000 (motor vehicles and parts 14.5%, electrical machinery [excluding televisions and electronic components] 7.0%, crude petroleum 6.8%, computers and office equipment 6.6%, chemicals and chemical products 6.5%, televisions and electronic components 5.7%, wearing apparel 5.5%, general industrial machinery 3.0%, power generating machinery 2.9%). *Major import sources:* Canada 18.0%; Mexico 11.6%; China 10.8%; Japan 10.5%; Germany 5.4%; UK 3.5%; South Korea 3.1%; Taiwan 2.8%; France 2.4%; Italy 2.1%; Malaysia 2.1%; Ireland 1.9%. **Exports** (2002): $693,100,000,000 (electrical machinery [excluding televisions and electronic components] 9.7%, chemicals and related products 8.9%, motor vehicles 8.3%, agricultural commodities 7.7%, power generating machinery 4.7%, computers and office equipment 4.4%, general industrial machinery 4.3%, airplanes 3.9%, scientific and precision equipment 3.9%, specialized industrial machinery 3.4%). *Major export destinations:* Canada 23.2%; Mexico 14.1%; Japan 7.4%; UK 4.8%; Germany 3.8%; South Korea 3.3%; China 3.2%; Taiwan 2.7%; France 2.7%; The Netherlands 2.6%; Singapore 2.3%; Belgium 1.9%.

Transport and communications

Transport. *Railroads* (1998): length 212,433 km; (1999) passenger-km 21,568,000,000; metric ton-km cargo (1997) 2,075,000,000. *Roads* (2001): total length 6,354,231 km (paved 91%). *Vehicles* (2001): passenger cars 137,633,000; trucks and buses 92,795,000. *Air transport* (2002): passenger-km 1,598,000,000,000; metric ton-km cargo 87,390,000,000; localities (1996) with scheduled flights 834 (includes 292 localities in Alaska). Certified route passenger/cargo air carriers (1992) 77; operating revenue ($'000,000; 1991) 74,942, of which domestic 56,119, international 18,823; operating expenses 76,669, of which domestic 56,596, international 20,073. **Communications,** in total units (units per 1,000 persons). Daily newspaper circulation (2000): 55,773,000 (198); radios (2000): 598,000,000 (2,118); televisions (2000): 241,000,000 (854); telephone main lines (2003): 181,599,900 (621); cellular telephone subscribers (2003): 158,722,000 (543); personal computers (2002): 190,000,000 (659); Internet users (2002): 159,000,000 (551).

Education and health

Educational attainment (2000). Percentage of population age 25 and over having: primary and incomplete

secondary 15.9%; secondary 33.1%; some postsecondary 25.4%; 4-year higher degree 17.0%; advanced degree 8.6%. Number of earned degrees (2000): bachelor's degree 1,237,875; master's degree 457,056; doctor's degree 44,808; first-professional degrees (in fields such as medicine, theology, and law) 80,057. **Food** (2001): daily per capita caloric intake 3,776 (vegetable products 73%, animal products 27%); 143% of FAO recommended minimum. Per capita consumption of major food groups (kilograms annually; 2001): milk 256.6; fresh vegetables 124.5; cereal products 116.9; fresh fruits 113.4; red meat 72.5; potatoes 64.4; poultry products 47.8; sugar 32.6; fats and oils 32.5; fish and shellfish 21.2. **Health:** doctors of medicine (2001) 836,200 (1 per 346 persons), of which office-based practice 514,000 (including specialties in internal medicine 18.4%, general and family practice 13.6%, pediatrics 8.7%, other specialty 8.6%, obstetrics and gynecology 6.3%, anesthesiology 5.6%, psychiatry 5.0%, general surgery 5.0%, orthopedic surgery 3.5%, cardiovascular diseases 3.3%, ophthalmology 3.1%, emergency medicine 3.1%, diagnostic radiology 3.0%); doctors of osteopathy 47,000; nurses (2002) 2,311,000 (1 per 125 persons); dentists (2002) 180,000 (1 per 1,603 persons); hospital beds (2001) 987,000 (1 per 289 persons), of which nonfederal 94.7% (community hospitals 83.7%, psychiatric 9.0%, long-term general and special 1.9%), federal 5.3%; infant mortality rate per 1,000 live births (2001) 7.0.

Military

Total active duty personnel (2003): 1,427,000 (army 34.0%, navy 28.0%, air force 25.8%, marines 12.2%). **Military expenditure as percentage of GNP** (1999): 3.0% (world 2.4%); per capita expenditure $1,030. **Security assistance to the world** (2002): $7,209,-000,000, for underwriting the purchase of US weapons 50.6%, of which Israel 28.3%, Egypt 18.0%, Jordan 1.0%; for economic support 30.5%, of which Israel 10.0%, Egypt 9.1%, Jordan 2.1%; for the Andean Counterdrug Initiative 9.2%; for nonproliferation, antiterrorism, and de-mining 4.3%; for international narcotics and law enforcement 3.0%; for peacekeeping operations 1.9%.

Background

The territory that is now the US was originally inhabited for several thousand years by numerous American Indian peoples who had probably emigrated from Asia. European exploration and settlement from the 16th century began displacement of the Indians. The first permanent European settlement, by the Spanish, was at St. Augustine FL, in 1565; the British settled Jamestown VA (1607), Plymouth MA (1620), Maryland (1632), and Pennsylvania (1681). They took New York, New Jersey, and Delaware from the Dutch in 1664, a year after the Carolinas had been granted to British noblemen. The British defeat of the French in 1763 ensured British political control over the 13 colonies.

Political unrest caused by British colonial policy culminated in the American Revolution (1775–83) and the Declaration of Independence (1776). The US was first organized under the Articles of Confederation

---

1 metric ton = about 1.1 short tons; 1 kilometer = 0.6 mi (statute); 1 metric ton-km cargo = about 0.68 short ton-mi cargo; c.i.f.: cost, insurance, and freight; f.o.b.: free on board

(1781), then finally under the Constitution (1787) as a federal republic. Boundaries extended west to the Mississippi River, excluding Spanish Florida. Land acquired from France by the Louisiana Purchase (1803) nearly doubled the country's territory. The US fought the War of 1812 with the British and acquired Florida from Spain in 1819. In 1830 it legalized removal of American Indians to lands west of the Mississippi River. Settlement expanded to the West Coast in the mid-19th century, especially after the discovery of gold in California in 1848. Victory in the Mexican War (1846–48) brought the territory of seven more future states (including California and Texas) into US hands. The northwestern boundary was established by treaty with Great Britain in 1846. The US acquired southern Arizona by the Gadsden Purchase (1853). It suffered disunity during the conflict between the slavery-based plantation economy in the South and the free industrial and agricultural economy in the North, culminating in the American Civil War and the abolition of slavery under the 13th Amendment.

After Reconstruction (1865–77), the US experienced rapid growth, urbanization, industrial development, and European immigration. In 1877 it authorized allotment of Indian reservation land to individual tribesmen, resulting in widespread loss of land to whites. By the beginning of the 20th century, it had acquired outlying territories, including Alaska, the Midway Islands, the Hawaiian Islands, the Philippines, Puerto Rico, Guam, Wake Island, American Samoa, the Panama Canal Zone, and the Virgin Islands.

The US participated in World War I during 1917–18. It granted suffrage to women in 1920 and citizenship to American Indians in 1924. The stock market crash of 1929 led to the Great Depression. The US entered World War II after the Japanese bombing of Pearl Harbor (7 Dec 1941). The explosion of the first atomic bomb on Hiroshima, Japan (6 Aug 1945), brought about the end of the war and set the US apart as a military power. After the war the US was involved in the reconstruction of Europe and Japan and embroiled in a rivalry with the Soviet Union that became known as the Cold War. It participated in the Korean War. In 1952 it granted autonomous commonwealth status to Puerto Rico.

Racial segregation in schools was declared unconstitutional in 1954. Alaska and Hawaii were made states in 1959, bringing the total to 50. In 1964 Congress passed the Civil Rights Act and authorized full-scale intervention in the Vietnam War. The mid- to late 1960s were marked by widespread civil disorder, including race riots and antiwar demonstrations. The US accomplished the first manned lunar landing in 1969. All US troops were withdrawn from Vietnam by 1973. The US led a coalition of forces against Iraq in the Persian Gulf War (1991), sent troops to Somalia (1992) to aid starving populations, and participated in NATO air strikes against Serb forces in the former Yugoslavia in 1995 and 1999. Administration of the Panama Canal was turned over to Panama in 1999.

Recent Developments

In 2006, for the third consecutive year, more than 800 US soldiers died in Iraq (by May 2007 more than 3,375 had died since the conflict began in 2003). As thousands of Iraqis were killed and US troop losses mounted, domestic support for Pres. George W. Bush and his Iraq policy fell rapidly, and even loyal Republicans began to break with the president, many decrying the absence of a strategy to win in Iraq. A bipartisan Iraq Study Group cochaired by former secretary of state James A. Baker III and former congressman Lee H. Hamilton issued a report calling for increased regional diplomacy and phased withdrawal of the overstretched US military from Iraq. At year's end, however, Bush instead enacted a "surge," or temporary escalation in US forces, led by aggressive new field commanders. In April 2007 it was reported that this "short-term" escalation was going to be extended.

In a rebuke to Bush and his party, voters decisively endorsed Democrats in 2006 congressional and state elections. The Republicans' 12-year control of Congress was ended as Democrats captured 31 new seats in the House of Representatives, for a prospective 233–202 advantage there. More surprisingly, Democrats effectively gained 6 Senate seats, turning a 55–45 deficit into narrow 51–49 control. The election led to the naming of the first female speaker of the house, Nancy Pelosi of California. Democrats also made substantial gains in 2006 state elections, winning 20 of 36 governorships at stake, for a total of 28 Democratic governors, and establishing a clear advantage in state legislatures. A series of serious ethical controversies roiled the Republican party during the year, allowing Democrats to decry "a culture of corruption" in Washington. Perhaps most significant among these, investigations of officials who dealt with convicted Republican lobbyist Jack Abramoff led to the resignation of Tom DeLay, a senior Texas congressman. One controversial bill, which authorized dramatically expanded funding for embryonic-stem-cell research, was vetoed by Bush in July 2006, using his first veto in more than five years in office. In May 2007 he vetoed his second bill, the Democrat-crafted Iraq war-funding bill, which was tied to a timetable for the withdrawal of American troops. Among the other bills passed by the new Congress, some of which drew threats of further vetoes, were ones enacting all of the recommendations of the 9/11 Commission and raising the federal minimum wage.

Despite a slowdown in key auto and housing sectors, the US economy expanded for the fifth consecutive year. Some 1.8 million new payroll jobs were created, and the jobless rate fell from 5% to 4.5%, even as tens of thousands of undocumented workers from abroad joined the workforce. Inflation dropped to the lowest rate in three years. The S&P 500 finished the year up 13.6%, and the Dow Jones Industrial Average gained 16.3%. Rapid growth in government revenues slashed the US budget deficit for fiscal 2006 to $248 billion. The country's trade deficit set another record during the year, and the US dollar dropped more than 10% against the euro.

Control of security in Afghanistan was turned over to NATO during the year. Taliban rebels continued to stage a violent resurgence, making 2006 the country's bloodiest year since the Taliban was ousted from power in 2001. The Afghan drug trade flourished as security deteriorated. About half of the 40,000 troops in the country belonged to the US, and in response to repeated calls for assistance, the UK announced in February 2007 that it was sending 1,400 additional troops, while in April Australia announced plans to double its commitment, to over 1,000 soldiers. In July 2006 North Korea test-fired seven missiles, including a long-range version that some analysts said was capable of hitting the western United States. The missile failed almost immediately, but not before the US had activated still-unproven interceptor-missile systems in Alaska and California. North Korea then shocked even its closest ally, China, by detonating a nuclear device in October. North Korea ultimately agreed to resume international talks, and in February 2007 the parties reached an agreement under which North Korea would give up its nuclear weapons and allow international inspections of its facilities in exchange for, among other things, energy and food aid and normalized relations with Japan and the US. Korea missed a key deadline in April, however. The year 2006 produced a record US trade deficit with China of more than $215 billion, as the Chinese economy continued its tremendous growth. The US moved notably closer to India during the year. A treaty granting technological assistance to India's civilian nuclear-power program was approved in December. Venezuelan Pres. Hugo Chávez led an effort to counter US economic and political influence in the hemisphere. In early 2007 he decreed the government assumption of majority control of the remaining foreign-owned oil operations, including several American ones, in Venezuela.

Internet resources: <www.seeamerica.org>.

Uruguay

Atlantic
Ocean

Official name: República Oriental del Uruguay (Oriental Republic of Uruguay). **Form of government:** republic with two legislative houses (Senate [31, includes the vice president, who serves as ex officio presiding officer]; Chamber of Representatives [99]). **Head of state and government:** President Tabaré Ramón Vázquez Rosas (from 2005). **Capital:** Montevideo. **Official language:** Spanish. **Official religion:** none. **Monetary unit:** 1 peso uruguayo ($U) = 100 centesimos; valuation (1 Jul 2007) US$1 = $U 24.18.

Demography

Area: 68,679 sq mi, 177,879 sq km. **Population** (2006): 3,266,000. **Density** (2006): persons per sq mi 47.6, persons per sq km 18.4. **Urban** (2002):

92.5%. **Sex distribution** (2003): male 48.40%; female 51.60%. **Age breakdown** (2003): under 15, 24.2%; 15–29, 22.9%; 30–44, 19.7%; 45–59, 15.8%; 60–74, 11.6%; 75 and over, 5.8%. **Ethnic composition** (2000): white (mostly Spanish, Italian, or mixed Spanish-Italian) 94.5%; mestizo 3.1%; mulatto 2.0%; other 0.4%. **Religious affiliation** (2000): Roman Catholic 78.2% (about 30–40% of Roman Catholics are estimated to be nonreligious); Protestant 3.3%; other Christian 5.3%; Jewish 1.2%; atheist 6.3%; other 5.7%. **Major cities** (1996): Montevideo (2004) 1,383,416; Salto 93,113; Paysandú 74,568; Las Piedras 66,584; Rivera 62,859. **Location:** southern South America, bordering Brazil, the South Atlantic Ocean, and Argentina.

Vital statistics

Birth rate per 1,000 population (2003): 15.9 (world avg. 21.3). **Death rate** per 1,000 population (2003): 9.4 (world avg. 9.1). **Natural increase rate** per 1,000 population (2003): 6.5 (world avg. 12.2). **Total fertility rate** (avg. births per childbearing woman; 2003): 2.2. **Marriage rate** per 1,000 population (2003): 4.2. **Divorce rate** per 1,000 population (2003): 2.0. **Life expectancy** at birth (2003): male 71.3 years; female 79.2 years.

National economy

Budget (2002). *Revenue:* $U 55,949,000,000 (tax revenue 81.9%, of which taxes on goods and services 42.7%, income and profit taxes 20.7%, import tax 2.4%, nontax revenue 9.6%; grants 8.1%; other 0.4%). *Expenditures:* $U 68,851,000,000 (social security and welfare 42.2%, general public services 11.2%, education 8.9%, health 6.3%, defense 4.4%). **Public debt** (external, outstanding; 2002): US$6,-851,000,000. **Production** (metric tons except as noted). *Agriculture, forestry, fishing* (2002): rice 939,489, wheat 270,000, sugarcane 170,000; livestock (number of live animals) 11,667,000 cattle, 11,250,000 sheep; roundwood 5,674,646 cu m; fish catch (2001) 105,051. *Mining and quarrying* (2002): limestone 1,300,000; gypsum 183,000; gold 66,841 troy oz. *Manufacturing* (value added in US$'000,000; 2000): refined petroleum products 563; food products 505; chemicals and chemical products 186. *Energy production (consumption):* electricity (kW-hr; 2000) 7,588,000,000 (7,974,000,000); coal (2000) none (1,000); crude petroleum (barrels; 2000) none (14,088,000); petroleum products (2000) 1,793,-000 (1,640,000). **Households.** Avg. household size (2002) 3.4. **Population economically active** (2003): total 1,240,500 (from urban areas only); activity rate 48.3% (participation rates: ages 14 and over, 58.2%; female 45.0%; unemployed 16.8%). **Gross national product** (at current market prices; 2003): US$12,-904,000,000 (US$3,820 per capita). **Tourism** (2002): receipts US$318,000,000; expenditures US$178,000,000. **Land use** as % of total land area (2000): in temporary crops 7.4%, in permanent crops 0.2%, in pasture 77.4%; overall forest area 7.4%.

Foreign trade

Imports (2002-c.i.f.): US$1,964,000,000 (chemicals and chemical products 17.4%; machinery and

---

1 metric ton = about 1.1 short tons;   1 kilometer = 0.6 mi (statute);   1 metric ton-km cargo = about 0.68 short ton-mi cargo;   c.i.f.: cost, insurance, and freight;   f.o.b.: free on board

appliances 15.1%; crude and refined petroleum 15.0%; food, beverages, and tobacco 14.4%; plastic products 5.9%). *Major import sources:* Argentina 27.5%; Brazil 19.8%; US 8.4%; Russia 5.7%; Germany 4.1%. **Exports** (2002): US$1,861,000,000 (hides and leather goods 13.5%; beef 13.5%; textiles and wearing apparel 11.9%; dairy products and eggs 7.6%; rice 7.5%; fish and crustaceans 5.3%). *Major export destinations:* Brazil 23.2%; US 7.4%; Argentina 6.1%; Germany 5.8%; China 5.6%.

Transport and communications

Transport. *Railroads* (1998): track length 3,002 km; passenger-km 14,000,000; metric ton-km cargo 244,000,000. *Roads* (1997): length 8,683 km (excludes streets under local control; paved 30%). *Vehicles* (2002): passenger cars 617,028; trucks and buses 53,915. *Air transport* (2000): passenger-km 747,000,000; airports (1997) 1. **Communications**, in total units (units per 1,000 persons). Daily newspaper circulation (2000): 973,000 (293); radios (2000): 2,000,000 (603); televisions (2000): 1,760,000 (536); telephone main lines (2002): 946,500 (280); cellular telephone subscribers (2002): 652,000 (193); personal computers (2001): 370,000 (110); Internet users (2001): 400,000 (119).

Education and health

Educational attainment (2002). Percentage of population age 25 and over having: incomplete primary education 9.8%; primary 33.6%; some secondary 17.2%; complete secondary 22.2%; higher 17.2%. **Literacy** (2001 est.): population age 15 and over literate 97.6%; males 97.2%; females 98.1%. **Health** (2002): physicians 12,905 (1 per 261 persons); hospital beds 6,695 (1 per 502 persons); infant mortality rate per 1,000 live births (2002) 13.6. **Food** (2001): daily per capita caloric intake 2,848 (vegetable products 65%, animal products 35%); 107% of FAO recommended minimum.

Military

Total active duty personnel (2003): 24,000 (army 63.3%, navy 23.8%, air force 12.9%). **Military expenditure as percentage of GNP** (1999): 1.3% (world 2.4%); per capita expenditure US$83.

Background

The Spanish navigator Juan Díaz de Solís sailed into the Río de la Plata in 1516. The Portuguese established Colonia in 1680. Subsequently, the Spanish established Montevideo in 1726, driving the Portuguese from their settlement; 50 years later Uruguay became part of the viceroyalty of Río de la Plata. It gained independence from Spain in 1811. The Portuguese regained it in 1821, incorporating it into Brazil as a province. A revolt against Brazil in 1825 led to its being recognized as an independent state in 1828. It battled Paraguay 1865–70. For much of World War II Uruguay remained neutral. The presidential office was abolished in 1951 and replaced with a nine-member council. The country adopted a new constitution and restored the presidential system in 1966. A military coup occurred in 1973, but the country returned to civilian rule in 1985. The 1990s brought a general upturn in the economy.

Recent Developments

The Uruguayan economy grew more than 5% in 2006, marking the third straight year of significant expansion, though unemployment was still running over 10%. Pres. Tabaré Vázquez made it clear early in the year that the pursuit of a free trade agreement with the United States was of the highest priority. The more radical sectors of the government coalition became increasingly upset with this possibility, however. As the debate heated up, Vázquez abruptly announced that Uruguay would not pursue the agreement. In a conflict with Argentina over the building of two large paper-pulp plants on the Uruguayan side of the Río Uruguay, Argentine environmental groups cut the highway routes between the two countries. The resulting trade and tourism loss to Uruguay was estimated in the hundreds of millions of dollars. Argentina took Uruguay to the World Court in its effort to stop the construction of the plants and lost.

Internet resources: <www.turismo.gub.uy>.

Uzbekistan

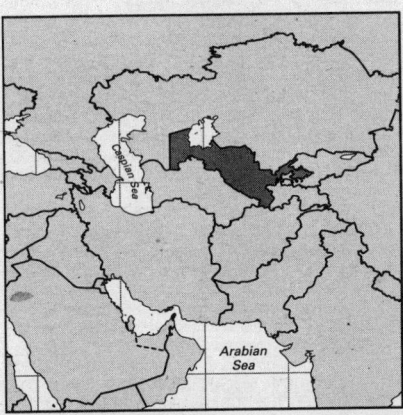

Official name: Uzbekiston Respublikasi (Republic of Uzbekistan). **Form of government:** multiparty republic with a single legislative body (Supreme Assembly [250]). **Heads of state and government:** President Islam Karimov (from 1990), assisted by Prime Minister Shavkat Mirziyayev (from 2003). **Capital:** Tashkent (Toshkent). **Official language:** Uzbek. **Official religion:** none. **Monetary unit:** sum (plural sumy); valuation (1 Jul 2007) US$1 = 1,266 sumy.

Demography

Area: 172,700 sq mi, 447,400 sq km. **Population** (2006): 26,383,000. **Density** (2006): persons per sq mi 152.8, persons per sq km 59.0. **Urban** (2002): 36.6%. **Sex distribution** (2001): male 49.55%; female 50.45%. **Age breakdown** (2001): under 15, 36.4%; 15–29, 28.6%; 30–44, 19.6%; 45–59, 8.5%; 60–74, 5.4%; 75 and over, 1.5%. **Ethnic composition** (1998): Uzbek 75.8%; Russian 6.0%; Tajik 4.8%; Kazakh 4.1%; Tatar 1.6%; other 7.7%. **Religious affiliation** (2000): Muslim (mostly Sunni) 76.2%; nonreligious 18.1%; Russian Orthodox 0.8%; Jewish 0.2%;

other 4.7%. **Major cities** (1999): Tashkent 2,142,-700; Namangan 376,600; Samarkand 362,300; Andijon 323,900; Bukhara 237,900. **Location:** Central Asia, bordering Kazakhstan, Kyrgyzstan, Tajikistan, Afghanistan, and Turkmenistan.

Vital statistics

Birth rate per 1,000 population (2003): 21.6 (world avg. 21.3). **Death rate** per 1,000 population (2003): 5.8 (world avg. 9.1). **Natural increase rate** per 1,000 population (2003): 15.8 (world avg. 12.2). **Total fertility rate** (avg. births per childbearing woman; 2003): 2.4. **Marriage rate** per 1,000 population (1999): 7.1. **Life expectancy** at birth (2003): male 67.0 years; female 73.0 years.

National economy

Budget (1999). *Revenue:* 611,897,000,000 sumy (taxes on income and profits 30.5%, value-added tax 27.3%, excise taxes 22.8%, property and land taxes 12.1%, other 7.3%). *Expenditures:* 654,259,000,000 sumy (social and cultural affairs 36.7%, investments 18.7%, national economy 10.4%, transfers 10.4%, administration 2.2%, interest on debt 1.9%, other 19.2%). **Household income and expenditure** (1995). Average household size (2000) 5.5; income per household 35,165 sumy; sources of income: wages and salaries 63.0%, subsidies, grants, and nonwage income 34.9%, other 2.1%; expenditure: food and beverages 71%, clothing and footwear 14%, recreation 6%, household durables 4%, housing 3%. **Public debt** (external, outstanding; 2002): $3,901,000,000. **Tourism** (2002): receipts $68,000,000. **Production** (metric tons except as noted). *Agriculture, forestry, fishing* (2002): wheat 4,956,000, seed cotton 3,200,000, vegetables 2,300,000; livestock (number of live animals) 8,220,000 sheep, 5,400,000 cattle, 14,500,000 chickens; roundwood (2001) 24,980 cu m; fish catch (2001) 8,152. *Mining and quarrying* (2000): copper (metal content) 91,800; gold 62,276 kg. *Manufacturing* (1998): cement 3,358,000; cotton fiber 1,138,000; mineral fertilizer 897,000. *Energy production (consumption):* electricity (kW-hr; 2001) 47,961,000,000 (48,455,000,000); hard coal (2000) 69,000 (69,000); lignite (1999) 2,901,000 (2,829,000); crude petroleum (barrels; 2000) 30,412,000 (30,412,000); petroleum products (2000) 5,991,000 (5,695,000); natural gas (cu m; 2002) 58,429,000,000 (50,630,000,000). **Gross national product** (2003): $10,779,000,000 ($420 per capita). **Population economically active** (2001): total 9,136,000; activity rate of total population 36.5% (participation rates: ages 16–59 [male], 16–54 [female] 70.4%; female [1994] 43.0%; unemployed [official rate] 0.4%). **Land use** as % of total land area (2000): in temporary crops 10.8%, in permanent crops 0.8%, in pasture 55.0%; overall forest area 4.8%.

Foreign trade

Imports (2002-c.i.f.): $2,712,000,000 (machinery and metalworking products 48.9%, food products 21.3%, other 29.8%). *Major import sources:* Russia 20.5%; South Korea 17.4%; Germany 8.9%; Kazakhstan 7.5%; US 6.4%; Ukraine 6.3%. **Exports** (2002-f.o.b.): $2,988,400,000 ([2000] cotton fiber 27.5%,

energy products [including natural gas and crude petroleum] 10.3%, base metals [significantly] gold 6.6%, food products 5.4%). *Major export destinations* (2002): Russia 17.3%; Ukraine 10.2%; Italy 8.3%; Tajikistan 7.8%; South Korea 7.1%; Poland 4.7%.

Transport and communications

Transport. *Railroads* (2000): length 3,950 km; (1999) passenger-km 1,900,000,000; (1999) metric ton-km cargo 13,900,000,000. *Roads* (1997): total length 84,400 km (paved 87%). *Vehicles* (1994): passenger cars 865,300; buses 14,500. *Air transport* (2000; Uzbekistan Airways): passenger-km 3,732,000,000; metric ton-km cargo 76,600,000; airports (1998) with scheduled flights 9. **Communications,** in total units (units per 1,000 persons). Daily newspaper circulation (2000): 74,200 (3); televisions (2000): 6,830,000 (276); telephone main lines (2003): 1,717,100 (67); cellular telephone subscribers (2003): 320,800 (13); Internet users (2003): 492,000 (19).

Education and health

Literacy (2000): percentage of total population age 15 and over literate 99.2%; males literate 99.6%; females literate 98.8%. **Health** (1995): physicians 76,200 (1 per 302 persons); hospital beds 192,000 (1 per 120 persons); infant mortality rate per 1,000 live births (2003) 36.0. **Food** (2001): daily per capita caloric intake 2,379 (vegetable products 82%, animal products 18%); 93% of FAO recommended minimum.

Military

Total active duty personnel (2003): 55,000 (army 72.7%, air force 27.3%). **Military expenditure as percentage of GNP** (1999): 1.7% (world 2.4%); per capita expenditure $38.

Background

Genghis Khan's grandson Shibaqan received the territory of Uzbekistan as his inheritance in the 13th century AD. His Mongols ruled over nearly 100 mainly Turkic tribes, who would eventually intermarry with the Mongols to form the Uzbeks and other Turkic peoples of central Asia. In the early 16th century, a federation of Mongol-Uzbeks invaded and occupied settled regions, including an area called Transoxania that would become the Uzbeks' permanent homeland. By the early 19th century the region was dominated by the khanates of Khiva, Bukhara, and Quqon, all of which eventually succumbed to Russian domination. The Uzbek Soviet Socialist Republic was created in 1924. In June 1990 Uzbekistan became the first Central Asian republic to declare sovereignty. It achieved full independence from the USSR in 1991. During the 1990s its economy was considered the strongest in Central Asia, though its political system was deemed harsh.

Recent Developments

In 2006 Uzbekistan continued a political reorientation toward Russia. In January the country joined the Eurasian Economic Community, a group consisting of Russia, Belarus, Kazakhstan, Kyrgyzstan, and Tajik-

---

1 metric ton = about 1.1 short tons;   1 kilometer = 0.6 mi (statute);   1 metric ton-km cargo = about 0.68 short ton-mi cargo;   c.i.f.: cost, insurance, and freight;   f.o.b.: free on board

istan. Later in the year Uzbekistan initiated moves to join the Russian-dominated Collective Security Treaty Organization. Repression of political oppositionists, human rights activists, and religious communities continued. In March Tashkent published a resolution restricting the work of foreign journalists. That month leaders of the Sunshine Coalition, a political opposition group promoting democratization, were sentenced to lengthy jail terms. (By mid-June at least 11 human rights activists had been jailed, according to Human Rights Watch.) Also in March the World Bank suspended new loans to Uzbekistan, and Uzbek authorities closed the local office of the United Nations High Commissioner for Refugees (UNHCR). The move was interpreted abroad as having been motivated by official Uzbek irritation that the UNHCR had arranged for more than 400 Uzbek refugees, who had fled to Kyrgyzstan after violence in Andijan in 2005, to move to third countries rather than being repatriated against their will.

Internet resources: <www.uzbektourism.uz>.

Vanuatu

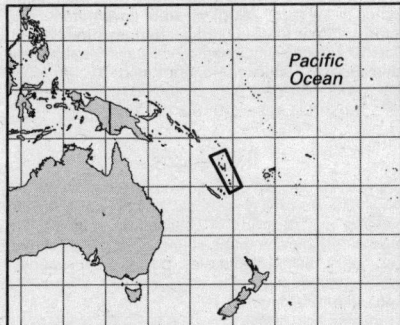

Pacific Ocean

Official name: Ripablik blong Vanuatu (Bislama); République de Vanuatu (French); Republic of Vanuatu (English). Form of government: republic with a single legislative house (Parliament [52]). Chief of state: President Kalkot Mataskelekele (from 2004). Head of government: Prime Minister Ham Lini (from 2004). Capital: Port-Vila. Official languages: Bislama; French; English. Official religion: none. Monetary unit: vatu (VT); valuation (1 Jul 2007) US$1 = VT 108.10.

Demography

Area: 4,707 sq mi, 12,190 sq km. Population (2006): 215,000. Density (2006): persons per sq mi 45.7, persons per sq km 17.6. Urban (2002): 21.0%. Sex distribution (1999): male 51.46%; female 48.54%. Age breakdown (1999): under 15, 37.8%; 15–29, 29.4%; 30–44, 18.2%; 45–59, 9.7%; 60–74, 4.0%; 75 and over, 0.9%. Ethnic composition (1999): Ni-Vanuatu 98.7%; European and other Pacific Islanders 1.3%. Religious affiliation (2000): Christian 89.3%, of which Protestant 53.7%, Anglican 18.2%, Roman Catholic 15.5%; Custom (traditional beliefs) 3.5%; Baha'i 2.9%; other 4.3%. Major towns (1999): Vila (Port-Vila) 30,139; Luganville 11,360. Location: island group in Oceania, between the South Pacific Ocean and the Coral Sea.

Vital statistics

Birth rate per 1,000 population (2003): 24.3 (world avg. 21.3). Death rate per 1,000 population (2003): 8.1 (world avg. 9.1). Natural increase rate per 1,000 population (2003): 16.2 (world avg. 12.2). Total fertility rate (avg. births per childbearing woman; 2003): 3.0. Life expectancy at birth (2003): male 60.3 years; female 63.2 years.

National economy

Budget (2001). Revenue: VT 6,887,000,000 (tax revenue 84.0%, of which taxes on goods and services 48.4%, tax on import duties 33.2%; foreign grants 6.4%; nontax revenue 9.4%). Expenditures: VT 7,885,000,000 (wages and salary 47.4%; goods and services 23.3%; transfers 10.1%; interest payments 3.1%; other [including technical assistance] 16.0%). Public debt (external, outstanding; 2002): $69,700,-000. Production (metric tons except as noted). Agriculture, forestry, fishing (2002): coconuts 200,000, roots and tubers 45,000, bananas 13,000; livestock (number of live animals) 151,000 cattle, 62,000 pigs, 340,000 chickens; roundwood 119,000 cu m; fish catch (2001) 26,690. Mining and quarrying: small quantities of coral-reef limestone, crushed stone, sand, and gravel. Manufacturing (value added in VT '000,000; 1995): food, beverages, and tobacco 645; wood products 423; fabricated metal products 377. Energy production (consumption): electricity (kW-hr; 2000) 38,000,000 (38,000,000); petroleum products (2000) none (26,000). Land use as % of total land area (2000): in temporary crops 2.5%, in permanent crops 7.4%, in pasture 3.4%; overall forest area 36.7%. Population economically active (1999): total 76,370; activity rate of total population 40.9% (participation rates: ages 15–64, 78.2%; female 49.6%). Gross national product (2003): $248,-000,000 ($1,180 per capita). Household income and expenditure (1985; Vila and Luganville only). Average household size (1989) 5.1; income per household $11,299; sources of income: wages and salaries 59.0%, self-employment 33.7%; expenditure (1990; Vila and Luganville only): food and nonalcoholic beverages 30.5%, housing 20.7%, transportation 13.2%, health and recreation 12.3%, tobacco and alcohol 10.4%. Tourism (2001): receipts from visitors $46,000,000; expenditures by nationals abroad $8,000,000.

Foreign trade

Imports (2002-c.i.f.): VT 12,433,000,000 (machinery and transport equipment 22.9%, food and live animals 17.2%, chemicals and chemical products 12.1%, mineral fuels 11.2%). Major import sources: Australia 39.3%; New Zealand 17.6%; Fiji 8.3%; France 5.3%; New Caledonia 4.0%. Exports (2002-f.o.b.): VT 2,793,000,000 (domestic exports 76.3%, of which coconut oil 16.9%, kava 15.6%, timber 7.1%, beef 6.9%, copra 6.2%; reexports 23.7%). Major export destinations (domestic exports only): Australia 29.2%; EC 10.8%; Japan 10.7%; New Caledonia 9.0%; Bangladesh 4.9%.

Transport and communications

Transport. Roads (1996): total length 1,070 km (paved 24%). Vehicles (1996): passenger cars 4,000; trucks and buses 2,600. Air transport (2001;

Air Vanuatu only): passenger-km 212,039,000; metric ton-km 1,899,000; airports (1996) with scheduled flights 29. **Communications,** in total units (units per 1,000 persons). Radios (1997): 62,000 (350); televisions (2000): 2,280 (12); telephone main lines (2003): 6,500 (32); cellular telephone subscribers (2003): 7,800 (38); personal computers (2002): 3,000 (15); Internet users (2003): 7,500 (36).

Education and health

Educational attainment (1999). Percentage of population age 15 and over having: no formal schooling 18.0%; incomplete primary education 20.6%; completed primary 35.5%; some secondary 12.2%; completed secondary 8.5%; higher 5.2%, of which university 1.3%. **Literacy** (1998): total population age 15 and over literate 64%. **Health** (1997): physicians 21 (1 per 8,524 persons); hospital beds 573 (1 per 312 persons); infant mortality rate per 1,000 live births (2003) 58.1. **Food** (2001): daily per capita caloric intake 2,565 (vegetable products 87%, animal products 13%); 113% of FAO recommended minimum.

Military

Total active duty personnel: Vanuatu has a paramilitary force of about 300.

Background

The islands of Vanuatu were inhabited for at least 3,000 years by Melanesian peoples before being discovered in 1606 by the Portuguese. They were rediscovered by French navigator Louis-Antoine de Bougainville in 1768, then explored by English mariner Capt. James Cook in 1774 and named the New Hebrides. Sandalwood merchants and European missionaries arrived in the mid-19th century; they were followed by British and French cotton planters. Control of the islands was sought by both the French and British, who agreed in 1906 to form a condominium government. During World War II a major Allied naval base was on Espíritu Santo; the island group escaped Japanese invasion. The New Hebrides became the independent Republic of Vanuatu in 1980. Much of the nation's housing was ravaged by a hurricane in 1987.

Recent Developments

The economy of Vanuatu was relatively strong in recent years, growing by 7% in 2005 and an estimated 5.5% in 2006, while inflation dropped to 1.5%. Tourism, which in 2006 represented 16% of the country's GDP, received a boost from the inauguration in November of a Solomon Airlines flight that originated in Australia. Vanuatu in 2006 became the first Pacific island country to receive funding from the US Millennium Challenge Account Program when it signed an agreement for a grant of more than $65 million for infrastructure projects to be dispersed over five years. A goal of the program was to increase average per capita income by $200.

Internet resources: <www.vanuatutourism.com>.

Vatican City State

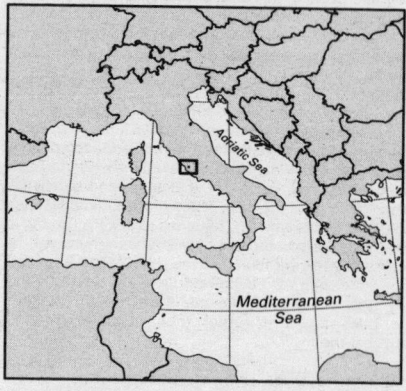

In full: State of the Vatican City (Holy See). **Form of government:** ecclesiastical. **Chief of state:** Pope Benedict XVI (from 2005). **Head of government:** Secretary of State Tarcisio Cardinal Bertone (from 2006). **Capital:** Vatican City. **Languages:** Italian, Latin. **Religion:** Roman Catholic. **Monetary unit:** 1 euro (€) = 100 cents; US$1 = €0.74 (1 Jul 2007); at conversion on 1 Jan 2002, €1 = 1,936.3 lira (Lit).

Demography

Area: 0.44 sq km, 0.17 sq mi. **Population:** (2004 est.): 780. **Density:** (2004): persons per sq mi 4,588, persons per sq km 1,772. **Location:** southern Europe, within the commune of Rome, Italy. **Annual budget:** $209 million. **Industries:** banking and finance; printing; production of a small amount of mosaics and uniforms; tourism.

Background

Vatican City, the independent papal state, is the smallest independent state in the world. Its medieval and Renaissance walls form its boundaries except on the southeast, at St. Peter's Square. Within the walls is a miniature nation, with its own diplomatic missions, newspaper, post office, radio station, banking system, army of more than 100 Swiss Guards, and publishing house. Extraterritoriality of the state extends to Castel Gandolfo, summer home of the Pope, and to several churches and palaces in Rome proper. Its independent sovereignty was recognized in the Lateran Treaty of 1929. The pope has absolute executive, legislative, and judicial powers within the city. He appoints the members of the Vatican's government organs, which are separate from those of the Holy See. The state's many imposing buildings include St. Peter's Basilica, the Vatican Palace, and the Vatican Museums. Frescoes by Michelangelo and Pinturicchio in the Sistine Chapel and Raphael's Stanze are also there. The Vatican Library contains a priceless collection of manuscripts from the pre-Christian and Christian eras.

---

1 metric ton = about 1.1 short tons;   1 kilometer = 0.6 mi (statute);   1 metric ton-km cargo = about 0.68 short ton-mi cargo;   c.i.f.: cost, insurance, and freight;   f.o.b.: free on board

Recent Developments

On 2 Apr 2005 Pope John Paul II died in Vatican City. The beloved pope, the first ever from Poland, had been in office for 26 years, the third longest tenure of any pontiff. A German cardinal, Joseph Ratzinger, who had held the post of prefect of the Sacred Congregation for the Doctrine of Faith and had been the chief theological adviser to John Paul for two decades, was elected to succeed John Paul II. He chose the papal name Benedict XVI. One of the primary goals of Vatican City in 2007 was the restoration of ties with China.

Internet resources: <www.vatican.va>.

Venezuela

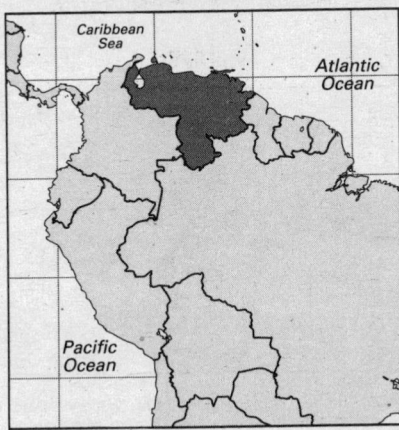

Official name: República Bolivariana de Venezuela (Bolivarian Republic of Venezuela). **Form of government:** federal multiparty republic with a unicameral legislature (National Assembly [165]). **Head of state and government:** President Hugo Chávez Frias (from 2002). **Capital:** Caracas. **Official language:** Spanish; 31 indigenous Indian languages were made official in May 2002. **Official religion:** none. **Monetary unit:** 1 bolívar (B, plural Bs) = 100 céntimos; valuation (1 Jul 2007) US$1 = Bs 2,147.

Demography

Area: 353,841 sq mi, 916,445 sq km. **Population** (2006): 27,216,000. **Density** (2006): persons per sq mi 76.9, persons per sq km 29.7. **Urban** (2003 est.): 87.7%. **Sex distribution** (2001): male 49.56%; female 50.44%. **Age breakdown** (2001): under 15, 33.1%; 15–29, 27.5%; 30–44, 20.7%; 45–59, 11.7%; 60–74, 5.1%; 75 and over, 1.9%. **Ethnic composition** (1993): mestizo 67%; white 21%; black 10%; Indian 2%. **Religious affiliation** (2000): Roman Catholic 89.5%; Protestant 2.0%; other Christian 1.4%; Spiritist 1.1%; nonreligious/atheist 2.2%; other 3.8%. **Major cities** (2001; preliminary unadjusted census results): Caracas 1,836,000 (urban agglomeration 3,177,000); Maracaibo 1,609,000; Valencia 1,196,000; Barquisimeto 811,000; Ciudad Guayana 629,000. **Location:** northern South America, bordering the Caribbean Sea, the North Atlantic Ocean, Guyana, Brazil, and Colombia.

Vital statistics

Birth rate per 1,000 population (2003): 22.6 (world avg. 21.3). **Death rate** per 1,000 population (2003): 5.1 (world avg. 9.1). **Total fertility rate** (avg. births per childbearing woman; 2003): 2.7. **Marriage rate** per 1,000 population (2003): 2.9. **Life expectancy** at birth (2002): male 70.8 years; female 76.6 years.

National economy

Budget (2000). *Revenue:* Bs 14,664,587,000,000 (oil revenues 59.2%, value-added tax 17.3%, income tax 9.0%, import duties 7.3%). *Expenditures:* Bs 17,238,854,000,000 (subsidies 50.5%, wages and salaries 19.1%, capital expenditure 14.5%, debt service 11.6%, goods and services 2.7%). **Public debt** (external, outstanding; 2002): $23,265,000,000. **Production** (metric tons except as noted). *Agriculture, forestry, fishing* (2002): sugarcane 6,909,000, corn (maize) 1,805,000, rice 790,000; livestock (number of live animals) 14,500,000 cattle, 5,655,000 pigs, 115,000,000 chickens; roundwood (2002) 4,667,000 cu m; fish catch (2001) 435,000. *Mining and quarrying* (2001): iron ore 16,902,000; bauxite 4,526,000; gold 9,076 kg. *Manufacturing* (value added in 1984 Bs '000,000; 1997): ferrous and nonferrous metals 16,355; food products 13,277; chemicals 10,004. *Energy production (consumption):* electricity (kW-hr; 2000) 85,211,000,000 (85,211,000,000); coal (2000) 7,885,000 (180,000); crude petroleum (barrels; 2001) 972,000,000 ([2000] 382,000,000); petroleum products (2000) 53,937,000 (19,530,000); natural gas (cu m; 2000) 28,382,700,000 (28,382,700,000). **Tourism** (2002): receipts $468,000,000; expenditures $1,041,000,000. **Land use** as % of total land area (2000): in temporary crops 2.9%, in permanent crops 0.9%, in pasture 20.7%; overall forest area 56.1%. **Gross national product** (2003): $89,150,000,000 ($3,490 per capita). **Population economically active** (1997): total 9,507,125; activity rate 41.7% (participation rates: over age 15, 64.6%; female 35.9%; unemployed 10.6%). **Household income and expenditure.** Average household size (1990) 5.1; average annual income per household (1981) Bs 42,492; expenditure (1995): food 40.6%, housing 13.8%, transportation and communications 8.6%, clothing 5.3%, health 3.1%, education and recreation 2.9%.

Foreign trade

Imports (2001-f.o.b. in balance of trade): $16,435,000,000 (nonelectrical machinery 16.5%, chemicals and chemical products 14.1%, road vehicles 14.0%, electrical machinery 9.8%). *Major import sources:* US 33.9%; Colombia 8.7%; Brazil 5.9%; Mexico 4.7%; Japan 4.6%. **Exports** (2001-f.o.b. in balance of trade): $25,304,000,000 (crude petroleum 58.3%, refined petroleum 23.6%, iron and steel 3.1%, aluminum 3.0%). *Major export destinations* (2002): US 56.4%; Netherlands Antilles 6.1%; Colombia 2.9%; Dominican Republic 2.8%; Brazil 2.7%.

Transport and communications

Transport. *Railroads* (1996): length (1994) 627 km; passenger-km 149,905; metric ton-km cargo 54,474,000. *Roads* (1999): total length 96,155 km (paved 34%). *Vehicles* (1997): passenger cars 1,505,000; trucks and buses 542,000. *Air transport* (1998): passenger-km 3,133,000,000; metric ton-km cargo 332,000,000; airports (1997) with scheduled flights 20. **Communications**, in total units (units per 1,000 persons). Daily newspaper circulation (2000): 5,000,000 (206); radios (2000): 7,140,000 (294); televisions (2000): 4,490,000 (185); telephone main lines (2002): 2,841,800 (112); cellular telephone subscribers (2002): 6,463,600 (256); personal computers (2002): 1,536,000 (61); Internet users (2002): 1,274,400 (51).

Education and health

Educational attainment (1993). Percentage of population age 25 and over having: no formal schooling 8.0%; primary education or less 43.7%; some secondary and secondary education 38.3%; postsecondary 10.0%. **Literacy** (1995 est.): total population age 15 and over literate 91.1%; males 91.8%; females 90.3%. **Health** (1999): physicians 46,886 (1 per 508 persons); public hospital beds (2000) 40,675 (1 per 620 persons); infant mortality rate per 1,000 live births (2003) 17.2. **Food** (2002): daily per capita caloric intake 2,337 (vegetable products 83%, animal products 17%); 95% of FAO recommended minimum.

Military

Total active duty personnel (2003): 82,300 (army 69.3%, navy 22.2%, air force 8.5%). **Military expenditure as percentage of GNP** (1999): 1.4% (world 2.4%); per capita expenditure $61.

Background

In 1498 Christopher Columbus sighted Venezuela; in 1499 the navigators Alonso de Ojeda, Amerigo Vespucci, and Juan de la Cosa traced the coast. A Spanish missionary established the first European settlement at Cumaná c. 1520. In 1718 it was included in the viceroyalty of New Granada and was made a captaincy general in 1731. Venezuelan Creoles led by Francisco de Miranda and Simón Bolívar spearheaded the South American independence movement, and though Venezuela declared independence from Spain in 1811, that status was not assured until 1821. Military dictators generally ruled the country from 1830 until the overthrow of Marcos Pérez Jiménez in 1958. A new constitution adopted in 1961 marked the beginning of democracy. As a founding member of OPEC, it enjoyed relative economic prosperity from oil production during the 1970s, and its economy has remained dependent on the world petroleum market. The leftist president Hugo Chávez Frías promulgated a new constitution in 1999, and he was reelected in 2002; a period of great political and economic tumult ensued.

Recent Developments

Venezuelans elected Hugo Chávez to a second consecutive six-year presidential term in December 2006. He announced his intention to draft a new socialist constitution to replace the constitution of 1999, with priority given to protecting minority rights, private property, and political pluralism. Increased in-

come from petroleum (in 2006 the price of Maracaibo crude approached an all-time high of $70 a barrel before stabilizing at just under $60) provided additional resources for the Venezuelan government "missions" that focused on alleviating poverty and building support for the government. Chávez boasted of having pumped $16 billion of oil profits into three dozen countries, mostly in Latin America, since taking power in 1999. Venezuela had a positive trade balance that was 37% higher than in 2005 and foreign reserves that surpassed $30 billion. Chávez intensified his campaign during 2006 to create a confederation of South American states that would counter US influence in the Western Hemisphere. In May 2007 Chávez seized majority control of the last remaining foreign-owned oil projects in Venezuela, valued at some $30 billion.

Internet resources: <www.venezuelatuya.com>.

Vietnam

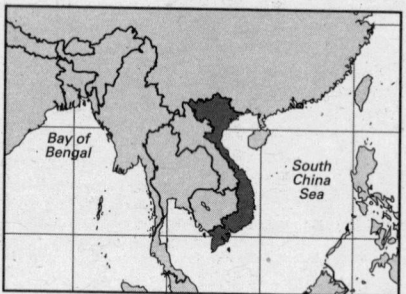

Official name: Cong Hoa Xa Hoi Chu Nghia Viet Nam (Socialist Republic of Vietnam). **Form of government:** socialist republic with one legislative house (National Assembly [493]). **Head of state:** President Nguyen Minh Triet (from 2006). **Head of government:** Prime Minister Nguyen Tan Dung (from 2006). **Capital:** Hanoi. **Official language:** Vietnamese. **Official religion:** none. **Monetary unit:** 1 dong (D) = 10 hao = 100 xu; valuation (1 Jul 2007) US$1 = D 16,110.

Demography

Area: 127,149 sq mi, 329,315 sq km. **Population** (2006): 83,458,000. **Density** (2006): persons per sq mi 656.4, persons per sq km 253.4. **Urban** (2002): 25.1%. **Sex distribution** (2002): male 49.20%, female 50.80%. **Age breakdown** (2003): under 15, 30.2%; 15–29, 29.4%; 30–44, 21.8%; 45–59, 10.8%; 60–74, 5.7%; 75 and over, 2.0%. **Ethnic composition** (2000): Vietnamese 85.0%; Han Chinese 3.5%; Montagnards 1.9%; Tho (Tay) 1.6%; Tai 1.5%; Muong 1.4%; Khmer 1.2%; Nung 1.0%; other 2.9%. **Religious affiliation** (1995): Buddhist 66.7%; Christian 8.7%, of which Roman Catholic 7.7%, Protestant 1.0%; Cao Dai (a New-Religionist group) 3.5%; Hoa Hao (a New-Religionist group) 2.1%; other 19.0%. **Major cities** (1992): Ho Chi Minh City 5,479,000 (2002); Hanoi 2,931,400 (2002); Haiphong 783,133; Da Nang 382,674; Buon Ma Thuot

282,095. **Location:** southeastern Asia, bordering China, the Gulf of Tonkin, the South China Sea, the Gulf of Thailand, Cambodia, and Laos.

Vital statistics

Birth rate per 1,000 population (2003): 20.1 (world avg. 21.3). **Death rate** per 1,000 population (2003): 6.4 (world avg. 9.1). **Natural increase rate** per 1,000 population (2003): 13.7 (world avg. 12.2). **Total fertility rate** (avg. births per childbearing woman; 2003): 2.3. **Life expectancy** at birth (2003): male 67.0 years; female 72.0 years.

National economy

Budget (2003). *Revenue:* D 123,700,000,000,000 (tax revenue 77.9%, of which corporate income taxes 24.6%, VAT 23.2%, taxes on trade 18.7%; nontax revenues 20.5%; grants 1.6%). *Expenditures:* D 148,400,000,000,000 (current expenditures 64.6%, of which social services 27.9%, economic services 5.3%, interest payment 4.5%; capital expenditures 35.4%). **Public debt** (external, outstanding; 2002): $12,181,000,000. **Gross national product** (2003): $38,786,000,000 ($480 per capita). **Tourism** (1998): receipts from visitors $86,000,000. **Production** (metric tons except as noted). *Agriculture, forestry, fishing* (2002): rice 34,064,000, sugarcane 16,824,000, cassava 4,158,000; livestock (number of live animals) 60,000,000 ducks, 23,170,000 pigs, 4,063,000 cattle; roundwood (2002) 30,730,000 cu m, of which fuelwood 26,547,000 cu m, industrial roundwood 4,183,000 cu m; fish catch (2001) 1,491,000, of which marine fish 1,321,000. *Mining and quarrying* (2002): phosphate rock (gross weight) 770,000; tin (metal content) 4,000. *Manufacturing* (gross value of production in $'000,000; 2000): food products 736; cement, bricks and pottery 418; wearing apparel 376. *Energy production (consumption):* electricity (kW-hr; 2001) 29,800,000,000 ([2000] 26,594,000,000); coal (2002) 15,900,000 ([2000] 7,978,000); crude petroleum (barrels; 2002) 136,700,000 ([2000] negligible); petroleum products (2000) 154,000 (8,969,000); natural gas (cu m; 2002) 2,260,000,000 ([2000] 1,355,000,000). **Population economically active** (2002): total 38,715,000; activity rate 48.9% (participation rates [2001]: ages 15 and over 70.5%; unemployed 6.0%). **Household income and expenditure.** Average household size (2002) 5.0; income per household (1990; wage workers and government officials only) D 577,008; expenditure (1990): food 62.4%, clothing 5.0%, household goods 4.6%, education 2.9%, housing 2.5%. **Land use** as % of total land area (2000): in temporary crops 18.7%, in permanent crops 5.4%, in pasture 2.0%; overall forest area 30.2%.

Foreign trade

Imports (2002-f.o.b. in balance of trade and c.i.f. in commodities and trading partners): $19,733,-000,000 (machinery equipment [including aircraft] 19.2%; petroleum products 10.2%; garment material and leather 8.7%; iron and steel 6.8%; fertilizers 2.7%; motorcycles 2.1%). *Major import sources:* Taiwan 12.9%; Singapore 12.8%; Japan 12.7%; South Korea 11.6%; China 10.9%. **Exports** (2002): $16,706,000,000 (crude petroleum 19.6%; garments 16.5%; fish, crustaceans, and mollusks 12.1%;

footwear 11.2%; rice 4.3%; electronic products 2.9%). *Major export destinations:* Japan 14.6%; US 14.5%; China 9.0%; Australia 8.0%; Singapore 5.8%; Taiwan 4.9%.

Transport and communications

Transport. *Railroads* (2001): route length 3,142 km; passenger-km 3,428,000,000; metric ton-km cargo 2,054,400,000. *Roads* (1999): total length 93,300 km (paved 25%). *Vehicles* (2003): passenger cars, trucks, and buses 600,000. *Air transport* (2002; Vietnam Airlines only): passenger-km 2,963,000,000; metric ton-km cargo 81,000,000; airports (1997) with scheduled flights 12. **Communications**, in total units (units per 1,000 persons). Daily newspaper circulation (2000): 313,000 (4); radios (2000): 8,520,000 (109); televisions (2000): 14,500,000 (185); telephone main lines (2003): 4,402,000 (54); cellular telephone subscribers (2003): 2,742,000 (34); personal computers (2002): 800,000 (10); Internet users (2003): 3,500,000 (43).

Education and health

Educational attainment (1989). Percentage of population age 25 and over having: no formal education (illiterate) 16.6%; incomplete and complete primary 69.8%; incomplete and complete secondary 10.6%; higher 2.6%; unknown 0.4%. **Literacy** (2001): percentage of population age 15 and over literate 92.7%; males 94.5%; females 90.9%. **Health** (2002): physicians 45,073 (1 per 1,769 persons); hospital beds 178,385 (1 per 447 persons); infant mortality rate per 1,000 live births (2003) 30.8. **Food** (2001): daily per capita caloric intake 2,533 (vegetable products 89%, animal products 11%); 117% of FAO recommended minimum.

Military

Total active duty personnel (2003): 484,000 (army 85.1%, navy 8.7%, air force 6.2%). **Military expenditure as percentage of GNP** (1997): 2.4% (world 2.5%); per capita expenditure $44.

Background

A distinct Vietnamese group began to emerge c. 200 BC in the independent kingdom of Nam Viet, which was annexed to China in the 1st century BC. The Vietnamese were under continuous Chinese control until the 10th century AD. The southern region was gradually overrun by Vietnamese from the north in the late 15th century. The area was divided into two parts in the early 17th century, with the northern part known as Tonkin, and the southern part as Cochin China. In 1802 the northern and southern parts of Vietnam were unified under a single dynasty.

Following several years of attempted French colonial expansion in the region, the French captured Saigon in 1859 and later the rest of the area, controlling it until World War II. The Japanese occupied Vietnam 1940–45 and declared it independent at the end of World War II, a move the French opposed. The French and Vietnamese fought the First Indochina War until French forces with US financial backing were defeated at Dien Bien Phu in 1954; evacuation of French troops ensued.

Following an international conference at Geneva, Vietnam was partitioned along the 17th parallel, with the northern part under Ho Chi Minh and the southern part under Bao Dai; the partition was to be temporary, but the reunification elections scheduled for 1956 were never held. Bao Dai declared the independence of South Vietnam (Republic of Vietnam), while the Communists established North Vietnam (Democratic Republic of Vietnam). The activities of North Vietnamese guerrillas and pro-communist rebels in South Vietnam led to US intervention and the Vietnam War. A cease-fire agreement was signed in 1973, and US troops were withdrawn. The civil war soon resumed, and in 1975 North Vietnam invaded South Vietnam and the South Vietnamese government collapsed. In 1976 the two Vietnams were united as the Socialist Republic of Vietnam. From the mid-1980s the government enacted a series of economic reforms and began to open up to Asian and Western nations. During the 1990s the US moved to normalize relations with it.

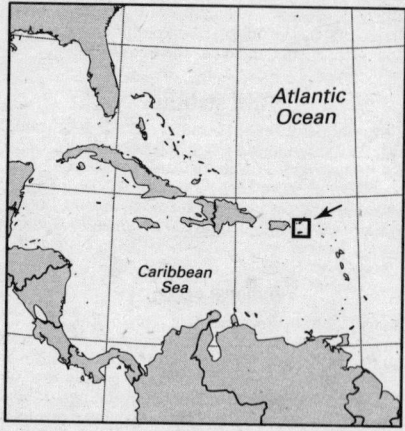

Recent Developments

The year 2006 marked the 20th anniversary of Vietnam's adoption of its economic-reform program known as *doi moi* ("renovation") and the convening of the 10th National Congress of the Vietnam Communist Party. The Congress, held in April, adopted a socioeconomic-development plan for 2006–10 with the objective of maintaining annual GDP growth rates of 7.5–8%, lowering urban unemployment to less than 5%, and reducing poverty. Vietnam and China inaugurated joint naval patrols in the Gulf of Tonkin in April and in August agreed to demarcate the border by 2008 and cooperate in developing energy resources. In July Vietnam was visited by US warships for the fourth time since the Vietnam War. It hosted four heads of state, including US Pres. George W. Bush and Chinese Pres. Hu Jintao, in November. In January 2007 Vietnam was admitted as the 150th member of the World Trade Organization.

Internet resources: <www.vietnamtourism.com>.

Virgin Islands (US)

Official name: Virgin Islands of the United States. **Political status:** organized unincorporated territory of the US with one legislative house (Senate [15]). **Chief of state:** President of the US George W. Bush (from 2001). **Head of government:** Governor John deJongh, Jr. (from 2007). **Capital:** Charlotte Amalie. **Official language:** English. **Official religion:** none. **Monetary unit:** 1 US dollar (US$) = 100 cents.

Demography

Area: 136 sq mi, 353 sq km. **Population** (2006): 113,000. **Density** (2006): persons per sq mi 830.9, persons per sq km 320.1. **Urban** (2000): 92.6%. **Sex distribution** (2000): male 47.75%; female 52.25%. **Age breakdown** (2000): under 15, 26.1%; 15–29, 19.4%; 30–44, 21.2%; 45–59, 20.5%; 60–74, 9.8%; 75 and over, 3.0%. **Ethnic composition** (2000): black 61.1%; US white 15.0%; Puerto Rican 12.0%; French Creole (from Martinique and Guadeloupe) 9.0%; British 1.0%; other 1.9%. **Religious affiliation** (2000): Christian 96.3%, of which Protestant 51.0% (including Anglican 13.0%), Roman Catholic 27.5%, independent Christian 12.2%; nonreligious 2.2%; other 1.5%. **Major towns** (2000): Charlotte Amalie 11,004 (urban agglomeration 18,914); Christiansted 2,637; Frederiksted 732. **Location:** northeastern Caribbean, islands between the Caribbean Sea and the North Atlantic Ocean.

Vital statistics

Birth rate per 1,000 population (2003): 15.0 (world avg. 21.3); (1998) legitimate 30.2%. **Death rate** per 1,000 population (2003): 5.7 (world avg. 9.1). **Natural increase rate** per 1,000 population (2003): 9.3 (world avg. 12.2). **Total fertility rate** (avg. births per childbearing woman; 2003): 2.2. **Marriage rate** per 1,000 population (1993): 35.1. **Divorce rate** per 1,000 population (1993): 4.5. **Life expectancy** at birth (2003): male 74.7 years; female 82.7 years.

National economy

Budget (2002). *Revenue:* $580,200,000 (personal income tax 54.7%, gross receipts tax 16.5%, property tax 7.9%). *Expenditures:* $573,000,000 (direct federal expenditures 100.0%). **Production.** *Agriculture, forestry, fishing* (value of sales in $'000; 1998): milk 1,263, livestock and livestock products 655 (of which cattle and calves 439, hogs and pigs 46), ornamental plants and other nursery products 364; livestock (number of live animals: 2002) 8,000 cattle, 4,000 goats, 3,500 chickens; fish catch (2001) 300 metric tons. *Mining and quarrying:* sand and crushed stone for local use. *Manufacturing* (value of sales in $'000; 1997): food and food products 31,949; stone, clay, and glass products 21,897; printing and publishing 21,127. *Energy production (consumption):* electricity (kW-hr; 2000) 1,090,000,000 (1,090,000,000); coal (metric tons; 2000) none (257,000); crude petroleum (barrels; 2000) none (124,700,000); petroleum products (metric tons; 2000) 15,385,000 (2,470,000). **Tourism** (2002): receipts from visitors $1,240,-000,000. **Household income and expenditure.** Average household size (2000) 2.6; average annual in-

---

1 metric ton = about 1.1 short tons;   1 kilometer = 0.6 mi (statute);   1 metric ton-km cargo = about 0.68 short ton-mi cargo;   c.i.f.: cost, insurance, and freight;   f.o.b.: free on board

come per household (2000) $34,991; expenditures (2001): housing 38.8%, food and beverages 12.5%, transportation 11.1%, education and communications 7.1%, health 5.8%. **Population economically active** (2002; excludes armed forces): total 49,440; activity rate of total population 45.4% (participation rates: ages 16–64, 72.5% [1990]; female 47.8% [1990]; unemployed 8.7%). **Gross domestic product** (at current market prices; 2002): $2,479,000,000 ($22,530 per capita). **Public debt** (1999): $1,200,000,000. **Land use** as % of total land area (2000): in temporary crops 12%, in permanent crops 3%, in pasture 15%; overall forest area 41%.

Foreign trade

Imports (2002): $4,213,200,000 (foreign crude petroleum 75.8%, other [significantly manufactured goods] 24.2%). *Major import sources* (2001): US 13.8%; Puerto Rico 2.0%; other countries 84.2%. **Exports** (2002): $3,876,300,000 (refined petroleum 83.4%, unspecified 16.6%). *Major export destinations* (2001): US 74.8%; Puerto Rico 18.7%; other countries 6.5%.

Transport and communications

Transport. *Roads* (1996): total length 856 km. *Vehicles* (1993): passenger cars 51,000; trucks and buses 13,300. Cruise ships (2003): passenger arrivals 1,773,948. *Air transport* (2003; St. Croix and St. Thomas airports): passenger arrivals 598,907; airports (1999) with scheduled flights 2. **Communications,** in total units (units per 1,000 persons). Daily newspaper circulation (2000): 43,000 (364); radios (1996): 107,000 (927); televisions (2000): 64,700 (594); telephone main lines (2001): 69,040 (635); cellular telephone subscribers (2001): 41,000 (375); Internet users (2002): 30,000 (273).

Education and health

Educational attainment (2000). Percentage of population age 25 and over having: no formal schooling through lower secondary education 18.5%; incomplete upper secondary 21.0%; completed secondary 26.0%; incomplete undergraduate degree 17.8%; completed undergraduate degree 10.4%; graduate degree 6.3%. **Health** (2002): physicians 161 (1 per 675 persons); infant mortality rate per 1,000 live births (2003) 8.4.

Military

Total active duty personnel: no domestic military force is maintained; the US is responsible for defense and external security.

Background

The Virgin Islands of the US probably were originally settled by Arawak Indians, but they were inhabited by the Caribs when Christopher Columbus landed on St. Croix in 1493. St. Croix was occupied by the Dutch, English, French, and Spanish and was at one time owned by the Knights of Malta. Denmark occupied St. Thomas, St. John, and St. Croix and established them as a Danish colony in 1754. The US purchased the Danish West Indies in 1917 for $25 million and changed the name to the Virgin Islands. They were administered by the US Department of the Interior from 1931. In 1954 the Organic Act of the Virgin Islands created the current governmental structure, and in 1970 the first popularly elected governor took office. The area suffered extensive damage by hurricanes in 1995.

Recent Developments

Lack of transparency and political corruption were problems facing the territory. A US government audit in April 2005 criticized the US Virgin Islands Port Authority for having mismanaged millions of dollars in contract bids for government projects. In June 2006 charges were filed against a prominent government employee and two others for having tendered for government contracts worth some $1.4 million with a fictitious company.

Internet resources: <www.usvitourism.vi>.

Yemen

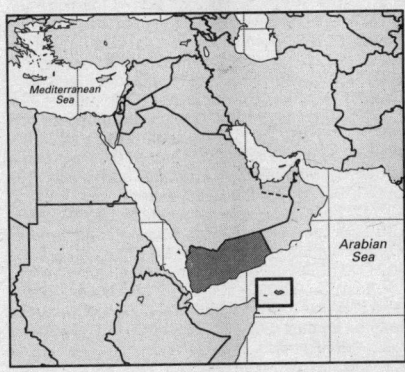

Official name: Al-Jumhuriyah al-Yamaniyah (Republic of Yemen). **Form of government:** multiparty republic with two legislative houses (Consultative Council [111 nonelected seats]; House of Representatives [301]). **Head of state:** President Major General 'Ali 'Abdallah Salih (from 1990). **Head of government:** Prime Minister 'Ali Muhammad Mujawar (from 2007). **Capital:** Sanaa. **Official language:** Arabic. **Official religion:** Islam. **Monetary unit:** 1 Yemeni Rial (YRls) = 100 fils; valuation (1 Jul 2007): US$1 = YRls 198.95.

Demography

Area: 214,300 sq mi, 555,000 sq km. **Population** (2006): 20,676,000. **Density** (2006): persons per sq mi 96.5, persons per sq km 37.3. **Urban** (2001): 25.0%. **Sex distribution** (2003): male 50.91%; female 49.09%. **Age breakdown** (2003): under 15, 46.8%; 15–29, 29.0%; 30–44, 12.8%; 45–59, 7.3%; 60–74, 3.1%; 75 and over, 1.0%. **Ethnic composition** (2000): Arab 92.8%; Somali 3.7%; black 1.1%; Indo-Pakistani 1.0%; other 1.4%. **Religious affiliation** (2000): Muslim 98.9%, of which Sunni 60%, Shi'i 40%; Hindu 0.7%; Christian 0.2%; other 0.2%. **Major cities** (2001): Sanaa 1,590,624; Aden 509,886; Ta'izz 450,000; Al-Hudaydah 425,000; Al-Mukalla 165,000. **Location:** the Middle East, bordering Oman, the Arabian Sea, the Gulf of Aden, the Red Sea, and Saudi Arabia.

Vital statistics

Birth rate per 1,000 population (2003): 41.4 (world avg. 21.3). **Death rate** per 1,000 population (2003): 8.8 (world avg. 9.1). **Natural increase rate** per 1,000 population (2003): 32.6 (world avg. 12.2). **Total fertility rate** (avg. births per childbearing woman; 2003): 6.8. **Life expectancy** at birth (2003): male 59.2 years; female 62.9 years.

National economy

Budget (2002). *Revenue:* YRls 570,100,000,000 (tax revenue 91.9%, of which oil revenue 68.7%, indirect taxes 12.1%, direct taxes 11.1%; nontax revenue 6.5%; grants 1.6%). *Expenditures:* YRls 587,600,-000,000 (wages and salaries 22.9%; defense 21.9%; transfers and subsidies 20.8%; economic development 18.1%; interest on debt 6.0%). **Public debt** (external, outstanding; 2002): $4,563,000,000. **Population economically active** (1999): total 4,090,680; activity rate of total population 23.5% (participation rates: age 15 and over, 45.9%; female 23.7%; unemployed 11.5%). **Production** (metric tons except as noted). *Agriculture, forestry, fishing* (2002): sorghum 360,000, tomatoes 261,692, potatoes 208,597; livestock (number of live animals) 5,028,968 sheep, 4,452,540 goats, 34,800,000 chickens; roundwood (2002) 326,262 cu m; fish catch (2001) 142,200. *Mining and quarrying* (2002): salt 150,000; gypsum 100,000. *Manufacturing* (value added in YRls '000,000; 2002): food, beverages, and tobacco 42,342; nonmetallic mineral products 13,209; chemicals and chemical products 9,884. *Energy production (consumption):* electricity (kW-hr; 2002) 3,100,-000,000 (2,960,000,000); crude petroleum (barrels; 2003) 163,600,000 ([2000] 29,600,000); petroleum products (2000) 3,956,000 (2,635,000). **Gross national product** (2003): $9,894,000,000 ($520 per capita). **Households.** Average household size (2002) 7.1; income per household (1998) YRls 29,035. **Tourism** (2002): receipts $38,000,000; expenditures $78,000,000. **Land use** as % of total land area (2000): in temporary crops 2.9%, in permanent crops 0.2%, in pasture 30.4%; overall forest area 0.9%.

Foreign trade

Imports (2001-c.i.f. in balance of trade and f.o.b. in commodities and trading partners): $2,466,000,000 (food and live animals 29.0%, of which cereals and related products 13.3%; machinery and apparatus 15.6%; petroleum products 12.0%; chemicals and chemical products 9.2%). *Major import sources:* UAE 12.5%; Saudi Arabia 12.4%; India 5.5%; Kuwait 5.2%; US 4.9%. **Exports** (2001): $3,373,000,000 (crude petroleum 86.3%; refined petroleum 7.4%; fish and fish products 1.7%; vegetables and fruits 0.7%). *Major export destinations:* India 18.3%; Thailand 18.0%; South Korea 13.2%; China 9.6%; Singapore 9.4%.

Transport and communications

Transport. *Roads* (2001; excludes unimproved roads and all roads in 'Adan governorate): total length 17,973 km (paved 54%). *Vehicles* (2001): passenger cars 354,048; trucks and buses (2000)

454,584. *Air transport* (2000): passenger-km 1,574,000,000; metric ton-km cargo 32,000,000; airports (1998) with scheduled flights 12. **Communications**, in total units (units per 1,000 persons). Daily newspaper circulation (2000): 270,000 (15); radios (2000): 1,170,000 (65); televisions (2000): 5,100,000 (283); telephone main lines (2002): 542,200 (28); cellular telephone subscribers (2002): 411,100 (21); personal computers (2002): 145,000 (7.4); Internet users (2002): 100,000 (5.1).

Education and health

Educational attainment (1998). Percentage of population age 10 and over having: no formal schooling 49.5%; reading and writing ability 32.2%; primary education 11.0%; secondary education 4.6%; higher 2.7%. **Literacy** (2003): percentage of total population age 15 and over literate 50.3%; males literate 70.5%; females literate 30.1%. **Health:** physicians (2000) 3,491 (1 per 5,161 persons); hospital beds (2001) 9,802 (1 per 1,903 persons); infant mortality rate per 1,000 live births (2003) 65.0. **Food** (2001): daily per capita caloric intake 2,050 (vegetable products 94%, animal products 6%); 85% of FAO recommended minimum.

Military

Total active duty personnel (2003): 66,700 (army 90.0%, navy 2.5%, air force 7.5%). **Military expenditure as percentage of GNP** (1999): 6.1% (world 2.4%); per capita expenditure $22.

Background

Yemen was the home of ancient Minaean, Sabaean, and Himyarite kingdoms. The Romans invaded the region in the 1st century AD. In the 6th century it was conquered by Ethiopians and Persians. Following conversion to Islam in the 7th century, it was ruled nominally under a caliphate. The Egyptian Ayyubid dynasty ruled there from 1173 to 1229, after which the region passed to the Rasulids. From 1517 through 1918, the Ottoman Empire maintained varying degrees of control, especially in the northwestern section. A boundary agreement was reached in 1934 between the northwestern imam-controlled territory, which subsequently became the Yemen Arab Republic (North Yemen), and the southeastern British-controlled territory, which subsequently became the People's Democratic Republic of Yemen (South Yemen). Relations between the two Yemens remained tense and were marked by conflict throughout the 1970s and 1980s. Reaching an accord, the two officially united as the Republic of Yemen in 1990. Its 1993 elections were the first free, multiparty general elections held in the Arabian Peninsula, and they were the first in which women participated. In 1994, after a two-month civil war, a new constitution was approved.

Recent Developments

Reversing an earlier decision to step down in June, Pres. Maj. Gen. 'Ali 'Abdallah Salih extended his 28-year presidency by winning another 7-year term in

---

1 metric ton = about 1.1 short tons;   1 kilometer = 0.6 mi (statute);   1 metric ton-km cargo = about 0.68 short ton-mi cargo;   c.i.f.: cost, insurance, and freight;   f.o.b.: free on board

Yemen's democratic elections in September 2006. One of his goals was to attract international aid to Yemen, which remained one of the poorest countries in the world; international aid amounted to a minimal $13 per capita. The Yemeni government continued to be a close ally of the US in its "war on terrorism." In 2006 a number of European tourists and diplomats were abducted by tribal groups and used to bargain for the release of prisoners. In an effort to discourage these abductions, which damaged the country's international reputation and economy, at least two convicted kidnappers were executed in 2006.

Internet resources: <www.yementourism.com>.

Zambia

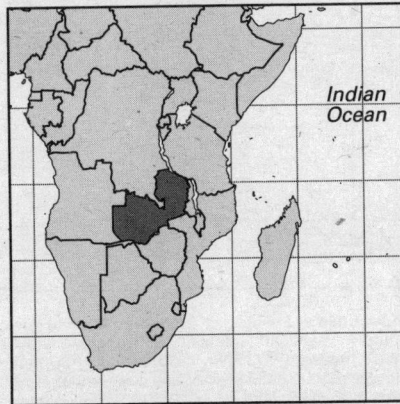

Indian Ocean

Official name: Republic of Zambia. Form of government: multiparty republic with one legislative house (National Assembly [158, including 8 nonelective seats]). Head of state and government: President Levy Mwanawasa (from 2002). Capital: Lusaka. Official language: English. Official religion: none; however, in 1996 Zambia was declared a Christian nation per the preamble of a constitutional amendment. Monetary unit: 1 Zambian kwacha (K) = 100 ngwee; valuation (1 Jul 2007) US$1 = K 3,743.

Demography

Area: 290,585 sq mi, 752,612 sq km. Population (2006): 11,288,000. Density (2006): persons per sq mi 38.8, persons per sq km 15.0. Urban (2000): 34.7%. Sex distribution (2000): male 50.04%; female 49.96%. Age breakdown (2000): under 15, 47.0%; 15–29, 30.0%; 30–44, 12.9%; 45–59, 5.9%; 60–74, 3.4%; 75 and over, 0.8%. Ethnic composition (2000): Bemba 18.0%; Tonga 12.7%; Chewa 7.2%; Lozi 5.6%; Tumbuka 4.2%; other 52.3%. Religious affiliation (1995): Christian 47.8%, of which Protestant 22.9%, Roman Catholic 16.9%, African Christian 5.6%; traditional beliefs 27.0%; Muslim 1.0%; other 24.2%. Major cities (2000): Lusaka 1,084,703 (urban agglomeration [2003] 1,394,000); Ndola 374,757; Kitwe 363,734; Kabwe 176,758; Chingola 147,448. Location: southern Africa, bordering Tanzania, Malawi, Mozambique, Zimbabwe, Botswana, Namibia, Angola, and the Democratic Republic of the Congo.

Vital statistics

Birth rate per 1,000 population (2003): 39.5 (world avg. 21.3). Death rate per 1,000 population (2003): 24.3 (world avg. 9.1). Natural increase rate per 1,000 population (2003): 15.2 (world avg. 12.2). Total fertility rate (avg. births per childbearing woman; 2003): 5.2. Life expectancy at birth (2003): male 38.8 years; female 39.3 years. Adult population (ages 15–49) living with HIV (2004): 16.5% (world avg. 1.1%).

National economy

Budget (2003). Revenue: K 5,104,000,000,000 (tax revenue 69.5%, of which income tax 31.5%, value-added tax 28.3%, excise taxes 9.4%; grants 27.9%; nontax revenue 2.6%). Expenditures: K 6,338,000,-000,000 (current expenditures 63.2%, of which wages 27.3%, interest payment 12.5%, transfers 10.2%; capital expenditures 36.8%). Public debt (external, outstanding; 2002): $4,737,000,000. Production (metric tons except as noted). Agriculture, forestry, fishing (2002): sugarcane 1,800,000, cassava 950,000, corn (maize) 900,000; livestock (number of live animals) 2,600,000 cattle, 1,270,000 goats, 30,000,000 chickens; roundwood (2001) 8,053,000 cu m; fish catch (2001) 70,911. Mining and quarrying (2002): copper (metal content) 330,000; cobalt (metal content) 6,144; amethyst 1,065,000 kg. Manufacturing (value added in $'000,000; 1995): food products 86; beverages 77; paints, soaps, and pharmaceuticals 47. Energy production (consumption): electricity (kW-hr; 2000) 7,797,000,000 (6,023,000,000); coal (2000) 194,000 (128,000); crude petroleum (barrels; 2000) none (1,830,000); petroleum products (2000) 22,000 (438,000). Households. Average household size (2002) 5.1. Tourism (2002): receipts from visitors $134,000,000; expenditures by nationals abroad $67,000,000. Population economically active (1996): total 3,454,000; activity rate of total population 38.2% (participation rates [1991]: over age 10, 52.6%; female 29.6%). Gross national product (at current market prices; 2003): $3,946,000,000 ($520 per capita). Land use as % of total land area (2000): in temporary crops 7.1%, in permanent crops 0.03%, in pasture 40.4%; overall forest area 42.0%.

Foreign trade

Imports (2002): $1,253,000,000 (nonelectrical machinery and equipment 21.6%, chemicals and chemical products 14.9%, printed matter 11.3%, road vehicles 8.8%, cereals [all forms] 8.0%). Major import sources: South Africa 51.2%; UK 12.3%; Zimbabwe 7.8%; India 3.6%; Japan 3.2%. Exports (2002): $930,000,000 (refined copper 50.0%, other base metals [including cobalt] 8.9%, food and live animals 7.3%, manufactures of base metals 5.8%). Major export destinations: UK 42.3%; South Africa 23.0%; Tanzania 7.6%; Switzerland 6.1%; Democratic Republic of the Congo 4.3%.

Transport and communications

Transport. Railroads (2003; Zambia Railways Limited only): length 1,266 km; (1997) passenger-km 267,-000,000; (1998) metric ton-km cargo 702,000,000. Roads (1999): total length 38,898 km (paved 18%).

Vehicles (1996): passenger cars 157,000; trucks and buses 81,000. *Air transport* (2003; Zambian Airways Limited only): passenger-km 14,217,000; airports (1998) 4. **Communications,** in total units (units per 1,000 persons). Daily newspaper circulation (2000): 125,000 (12); radios (2000): 1,510,000 (145); televisions (2000): 1,400,000 (134); telephone main lines (2003): 88,400 (7.9); cellular telephone subscribers (2003): 241,000 (22); personal computers (2003): 95,000 (8.5); Internet users (2003): 68,200 (6.1).

Education and health

Educational attainment (1993). Percentage of population age 14 and over having: no formal schooling 18.6%; some primary education 54.8%; some secondary 25.1%; higher 1.5%. **Literacy** (2000): population age 15 and over literate 78.1%; males literate 85.2%; females literate 71.5%. **Health:** physicians (1995) 647 (1 per 14,492 persons); hospital beds (1989) 22,461 (1 per 349 persons); infant mortality rate per 1,000 live births (2003) 99.3. **Food** (2001): daily per capita caloric intake 1,885 (vegetable products 95%, animal products 5%); 82% of FAO recommended minimum.

Military

Total active duty personnel (2003): 18,100 (army 91.2%; air force 8.8%). **Military expenditure as percentage of GNP** (1999): 1.0% (world 2.4%); per capita expenditure $3.

Background

Archaeological evidence suggests that early humans roamed present-day Zambia one to two million years ago. Ancestors of the modern Tonga tribe reached the region early in the 2nd millennium BC, but other modern peoples from Congo and Angola reached the country only in the 17th and 18th centuries. Portuguese trading missions were established early in the 18th century. Emissaries of Cecil Rhodes and the British South Africa Co. concluded treaties with most of the Zambian chiefs during the 1890s. The company administered the region known as Northern Rhodesia until 1924, when it became a British protectorate. It was part of the Central African Federation of Rhodesia and Nyasaland in 1953–63. In 1964 Northern Rhodesia became the independent republic of Zambia. A constitutional amendment was passed in 1990 allowing opposition parties; the following years were filled with political tension.

Recent Developments

In late 2006 China canceled $211 million of Zambia's debt, and in February 2007 Chinese Pres. Hu Jintao, on a two-day tour of the country, promised $800 million in investments over the next three years. He also inaugurated the first of five economic zones funded by China in Africa, with a $200 million copper smelter anchoring the development. This zone was expected to provide 50,000 new jobs by 2010 in addition to the estimated 10,000 already created by recent Chinese invest-

ment. Residents, however, claimed that the actual number of new jobs being created for Zambians, rather than Chinese workers, was much smaller and that the jobs themselves were dangerous and inadequately supervised and paid well below the minimum wage.

Internet resources: <www.zambia.co.zm>.

Zimbabwe

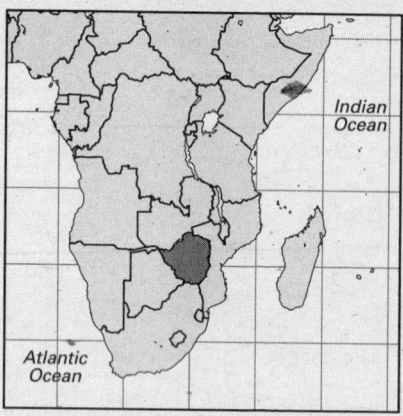

Official name: Republic of Zimbabwe. **Form of government:** multiparty republic with one legislative house (House of Assembly [150, including 30 non-elective seats]). **Head of state and government:** President Robert Mugabe (from 1987). **Capital:** Harare. **Official language:** English. **Official religion:** none. **Monetary unit:** 1 Zimbabwe dollar (Z$) = 100 cents; valuation (1 Jul 2007) US$1 = Z$254.53.

Demography

Area: 150,872 sq mi, 390,757 sq km. **Population** (2006): 12,237,000 (includes 3–4 million Zimbabweans outside of the country). **Density** (2006): persons per sq mi 81.1, persons per sq km 31.3. **Urban** (2001): 36.0%. **Sex distribution** (2003): male 49.57%; female 50.43%. **Age breakdown** (2003): under 15, 39.7%; 15–29, 32.6%; 30–44, 15.1%; 45–59, 7.3%; 60–74, 4.1%; 75 and over, 1.2%. **Ethnic composition** (2000): Shona 67.1%; Ndebele 13.0%; Chewa 4.9%; British 3.5%; other 11.5%. **Religious affiliation** (1995): Christian 45.4%, of which Protestant (including Anglican) 23.5%, African indigenous 13.5%, Roman Catholic 7.0%; animist 40.5%; other 14.1%. **Major cities** (2002): Harare 1,444,534; Bulawayo 676,787; Chitungwiza 321,782; Mutare (1992) 131,808; Gweru (1992) 124,735. **Location:** southern Africa, bordering Mozambique, South Africa, Botswana, Namibia, and Zambia.

Vital statistics

Birth rate per 1,000 population (2003): 30.3 (world avg. 21.3). **Death rate** per 1,000 population (2003):

---

1 metric ton = about 1.1 short tons;   1 kilometer = 0.6 mi (statute);   1 metric ton-km cargo = about 0.68 short ton-mi cargo;   c.i.f.: cost, insurance, and freight;   f.o.b.: free on board

22.0 (world avg. 9.1). **Natural increase rate** per 1,000 population (2003): 8.3 (world avg. 12.2). **Total fertility rate** (avg. births per childbearing woman; 2003): 3.7. **Life expectancy** at birth (2002): male 41.6 years; female 38.8 years. **Adult population** (ages 15–49) **living with HIV** (2004): 24.6% (world avg. 1.1%).

National economy

Budget (2002). *Revenue:* Z$300,385,000,000 (tax revenue 93.5%, of which income tax 53.0%, sales tax 24.1%, customs duties 9.0%, excise tax 6.2%; nontax revenue 6.5%). *Expenditures:* Z$351,-321,000,000 (current expenditures 91.3%, of which goods and services 61.5%, transfer payments 15.7%, interest payments 14.1%; development expenditure 7.2%; net lending 1.5%). **Population economically active** (1992): total 3,600,000; activity rate of total population 34.6% (participation rates: over age 15, 63.4%; female 39.8%). **Production** (metric tons except as noted). *Agriculture, forestry, fishing* (2002): sugarcane 4,700,000, corn (maize) 499,000, seed cotton 200,400; livestock (number of live animals) 5,753,000 cattle, 2,970,000 goats, 605,000 pigs; roundwood 9,107,600 cu m; fish catch (2001) 13,200. *Mining and quarrying* (value of production in Z$'000,000; 2000): gold 8,521; asbestos 2,776; coal 2,690. *Manufacturing* (value added in US$'000,000; 1998): beverages 171; foodstuffs 148; textiles 99. *Energy production (consumption):* electricity (kW-hr; 2000) 6,996,000,000 ([2000] 12,110,000,000); coal (2000) 4,400,000 (4,437,000); petroleum products (2000) none (1,072,000). **Public debt** (external, outstanding; 2002): US$3,123,000,000. **Household income and expenditure.** Average household size (2002) 4.4; income per household (1992) Z$1,689; expenditure (1995): food 33.6%, housing 17.3%, beverages and tobacco 16.0%, household durable goods 7.5%, clothing and footwear 6.9%, transportation 6.6%, education 4.5%. **Gross national product** (2002): US$6,165,000,000 (US$480 per capita). **Tourism:** receipts (2002) US$76,000,000; expenditures (1998) US$131,000,000. **Land use** as % of total land area (2000): in temporary crops 8.3%, in permanent crops 0.3%, in pasture 44.5%; overall forest area 49.2%.

Foreign trade

Imports (2001): US$1,779,000,000 (machinery and transport equipment 28.1%, chemicals and chemical products 22.9%, petroleum products 15.7%, food 3.8%, electricity 3.1%). *Major import sources* (2002): South Africa 47.7%; Democratic Republic of the Congo 5.7%; Mozambique 5.3%; Germany 3.1%; UK 3.1%. **Exports** (2001): US$1,609,000,000 (tobacco 36.9%, gold 14.0%, horticultural products [including cut flowers] 7.4%, ferroalloys 5.1%, cotton lint 5.1%, sugar 4.4%). *Major export destinations* (2001): South Africa 17.7%; UK 12.6%; Germany 8.3%; China 7.1%; Japan 6.6%.

Transport and communications

Transport. *Railroads* (2001): route length 3,077 km; (1998) passenger-km 408,223,000; (2000) metric ton-km cargo 3,326,000. *Roads* (1996): total length 18,338 km (paved 47%). *Vehicles* (2000): passenger cars 573,000; trucks and

buses 39,000. *Air transport* (2003; Air Zimbabwe only): passenger-km 436,530,000; metric ton-km cargo 18,494,000; airports (1997) with scheduled flights 7. **Communications,** in total units (units per 1,000 persons). Daily newspaper circulation (2000): 205,000 (18); radios (2000): 4,110,000 (362); televisions (1999): 2,074,000 (183); telephone main lines (2003): 300,900 (26); cellular telephone subscribers (2003): 379,100 (32); personal computers (2003): 620,000 (53); Internet users (2002): 500,000 (43).

Education and health

Educational attainment (1992). Percentage of population age 25 and over having: no formal schooling 22.3%; primary 54.3%; secondary 13.1%; higher 3.4%. **Literacy** (2001): percentage of total population age 15 and over literate 89.3%; males literate 93.3%; females literate 85.5%. **Health:** physicians (1996) 1,603 (1 per 6,904 persons); hospital beds (1996) 22,975 (1 per 501 persons); infant mortality rate per 1,000 live births (2003) 65.5. **Food** (2001): daily per capita caloric intake 2,133 (vegetable products 92%, animal products 8%); 89% of FAO recommended minimum.

Military

Total active duty personnel (2003): 29,000 (army 86.2%, air force 13.8%). **Military expenditure as percentage of GNP** (1999): 5.0% (world 2.4%); per capita expenditure US$23.

Background

Remains of Stone Age cultures dating back 500,000 years have been found in the Zimbabwe area. The first Bantu-speaking peoples reached it during the 5th–10th centuries AD, driving the San (Bushmen) inhabitants into the desert. A second migration of Bantu-speakers began c. 1830. During this period the British and Afrikaners moved up from the south, and the area came under the administration of the British South Africa Co. 1889–1923. Called Southern Rhodesia (1911–64), it became a self-governing British colony in 1923. The colony united in 1953 with Nyasaland (Malawi) and Northern Rhodesia (Zambia) to form the Central African Federation of Rhodesia and Nyasaland. The federation dissolved in 1963, and Southern Rhodesia reverted to its former colonial status. In 1965 it issued a unilateral declaration of independence considered illegal by the British government, which led to economic sanctions against it. The country proclaimed itself a republic in 1970 and called itself Rhodesia 1964–79. In 1979 it instituted limited majority rule and changed its name to Zimbabwe Rhodesia. It was granted independence by Britain in 1980 and became Zimbabwe. Robert Mugabe, Zimbabwe's first prime minister, became president in 1987. Although a multiparty system was established in 1990, Mugabe's rule became more and more autocratic.

Recent Developments

Zimbabwe's international status remained controversial. In late May 2005 the government pursued "Operation Drive Out Trash" to uproot what it called illegal slums and black-market vendors by bulldozing the kiosks, homes, and subsistence gardens of the country's poorest, many of whom supported the op-position. Hundreds of thousands of people were turned out into the winter cold and another 30,000 arrested, and many thousands more fled the country. The economy was close to ruin. Doctors and nurses went on strike in late 2006, causing the non-emergency health-care system essentially to come to a halt. They were joined by electricity workers in January, leading to disruption of the capital's power supply, and teachers and professors in February. They were protesting the fact that their salaries had not kept up with inflation, which in March reached an annual rate of 1,700%, the highest in the world. That month members of the opposition were arrested and brutally beaten by security forces, with opposition leader Morgan Tsvangirai receiving a fractured skull.

Internet resources: <www.gta.gov.zw>.

Antarctica

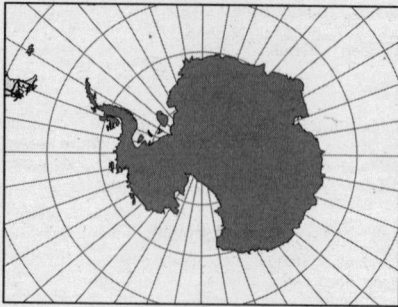

Background

The Russian F.G. von Bellingshausen (1778–1852), the Englishman Edward Bransfield (1795?–1852), and the American Nathaniel Palmer (1799–1877) all claimed first sightings of the continent in 1820. The period from the 1760s to c. 1900 was dominated by the exploration of Antarctic and subantarctic seas. In the early 20th century, the "heroic era" of Antarctic exploration, Robert Scott and, later, Ernest Shackleton made expeditions deep into the interior. Roald Amundsen reached the South Pole in December 1911, and Scott followed in 1912. The first half of the 20th century was also Antarctica's colonial period. Seven nations claimed sectors of the continent, while many other nations carried out explorations. In 1957–58, 12 nations established over 50 stations on the continent for cooperative study. In 1961 the Antarctic Treaty, which reserved Antarctica for free and nonpolitical scientific study, was enacted. A 1991 agreement imposed a permanent ban on mineral exploitation.

Recent Developments

Antarctic tourism quadrupled in the last decade; in 2005–06 there were more than 30,000 visitors during the austral summer. In June 2005 representa-tives at the Antarctic Treaty Consultative Meeting approved a protocol that would impose financial liability on any Antarctic operator that failed to respond to any environmental emergency it had caused. British and American scientists announced in 2005 that 87% of 244 marine glacial fronts had retreated in the past 61 years. It was also reported that on 24 Sept 2006 the hole in the ozone layer over Antarctica matched the largest ever recorded, with an area of 29.5 million sq km (11.4 million sq mi). The European Project for Ice Coring in 2005 retrieved an ice core 3,270 m (10,729 ft) in length that covered some 900,000 years of Antarctic history and contained the oldest ice ever retrieved.

Internet resources: <www.antarctica.org>.

Arctic Regions

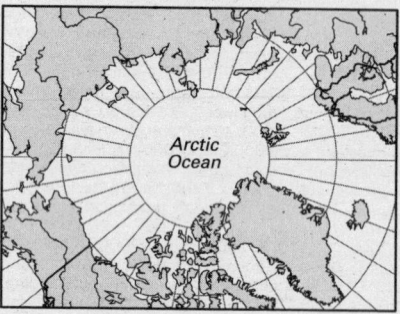

The Arctic regions may be defined in physical terms (astronomical [north of the Arctic Circle, latitude 66° 30′ N], climatic [above the 10 °C (50 °F) July isotherm], or vegetational [above the northern limit of the tree line]) or in human terms (the territory inhabited by the circumpolar cultures—Inuit [Eskimo] and Aleut in North America and Russia, Sami [Lapp] in northern Scandinavia and Russia, and 29 other peoples of the Russian North, Siberia, and East Asia). No single national sovereignty or treaty regime governs the region, which includes portions of eight countries: Canada, the United States, Russia, Finland, Sweden, Norway, Iceland, and Greenland (part of Denmark). The Arctic Ocean, 14.09 million sq km (5.44 million sq mi) in area, constitutes about two-thirds of the region. The land area consists of permanent ice cap, tundra, or taiga. The population (2006 est.) of peoples belonging to the circumpolar cultures is about 475,000 (Aleuts [in Russia and Alaska], more than 4,000; Athabascans [North America], 40,000; Inuits [or Eskimos, in Russian Chukhotka, North America, and Greenland], 155,000; Sami [Northern Europe], 70,000; and 31 indigenous peoples of the Russian North, totaling more than 200,000). International organizations concerned with the Arctic include the Arctic Council, the Barents Euro-Arctic Council, the Inuit Circumpolar Conference, and the Indigenous Peoples' Secretariat. International scientific cooperation in the Arctic is the focus of the International Arctic Research Center of the University of Alaska at Fairbanks.

1 metric ton = about 1.1 short tons;   1 kilometer = 0.6 mi (statute);   1 metric ton-km cargo = about 0.68 short ton-mi cargo;   c.i.f.: cost, insurance, and freight;   f.o.b.: free on board

Membership in International Organizations

African Union (AU; formerly [until 2002] Organization for African Unity)
Founded: 1963. Members: 53 countries of Africa (all except Morocco).
Web site: <www.africa-union.org>.

Andean Community
Founded: 1969. Members: Bolivia, Colombia, Ecuador, Peru.
Web site: <www.comunidadandina.org>.

Asia-Pacific Economic Cooperation (APEC)
Founded: 1989. Members: Australia, Brunei, Canada, Chile, China, Hong Kong, Indonesia, Japan, Malaysia, Mexico, New Zealand, Papua New Guinea, Peru, the Philippines, Russia, Singapore, South Korea, Taiwan, Thailand, US, Vietnam.
Web site: <www.apec.org>.

Association of Southeast Asian Nations (ASEAN)
Founded: 1967. Members: Brunei, Cambodia, Indonesia, Laos, Malaysia, Myanmar (Burma), the Philippines, Singapore, Thailand, Vietnam.
Web site: <www.aseansec.org>.

Caribbean Community and Common Market (CARICOM)
Founded: 1973. Members: Antigua and Barbuda, the Bahamas (Community member only), Barbados, Belize, Dominica, Grenada, Guyana, Haiti, Jamaica, Montserrat, St. Kitts and Nevis, St. Lucia, St. Vincent and the Grenadines, Suriname, Trinidad and Tobago; also 5 associate members.
Web site: <www.caricom.org>.

Common Market for Eastern and Southern Africa (COMESA)
Founded: 1994. Members: Angola, Burundi, Comoros, Democratic Republic of the Congo, Djibouti, Egypt, Eritrea, Ethiopia, Kenya, Libya, Madagascar, Malawi, Mauritius, Rwanda, Seychelles, The Sudan, Swaziland, Uganda, Zambia, Zimbabwe.
Web site: <www.comesa.int>.

Commonwealth (also called Commonwealth of Nations)
Founded: 1931. Members: United Kingdom and 52 other countries, all of which were once under British rule or administratively connected to another member country (Fiji suspended in December 2006); Nauru is a Special Member.
Web site: <www.thecommonwealth.org>.

Commonwealth of Independent States (CIS)
Founded: 1991. Members: Armenia, Azerbaijan, Belarus, Georgia, Kazakhstan, Kyrgyzstan, Moldova, Russia, Tajikistan, Turkmenistan, Uzbekistan, Ukraine.
Web site: <www.cisstat.com>.

Community of Portuguese Language Countries (CPLP)
Founded: 1996. Members: Angola, Brazil, Cape Verde, East Timor, Guinea-Bissau, Mozambique, Portugal, São Tomé and Príncipe.
Web site: <www.cplp.org>.

Council of Europe
Founded: 1949. Members: 46 European and former Soviet countries; 2 candidates for membership; 5 observer states.
Web site: <www.coe.int>.

Economic Community of West African States (ECOWAS)
Founded: 1975. Members: Benin, Burkina Faso, Cape Verde, Côte d'Ivoire, The Gambia, Ghana, Guinea, Guinea-Bissau, Liberia, Mali, Niger, Nigeria, Senegal, Sierra Leone, Togo.
Web site: <www.ecowas.int>.

European Free Trade Association (EFTA)
Founded: 1960. Members: Iceland, Liechtenstein, Norway, Switzerland.
Web site: <www.efta.int>.

European Union (EU)
Founded: 1950. Members: Austria, Belgium, Bulgaria, Cyprus, Czech Republic, Denmark, Estonia, Finland, France, Germany, Greece, Hungary, Ireland, Italy, Latvia, Lithuania, Luxembourg, Malta, The Netherlands, Poland, Portugal, Romania, Slovakia, Slovenia, Spain, Sweden, UK; in mid-2007, 3 additional countries in southeastern Europe were undergoing membership preparations.
Web site: <www.europa.eu.int>.

Group of Eight (G-8)
Founded: 1975. Members: Canada, France, Germany, Italy, Japan, Russia, UK, US, European Union.
Web site: <www.g8.utoronto.ca>.

Gulf Cooperation Council (GCC)
Founded: 1981. Members: Bahrain, Kuwait, Oman, Qatar, Saudi Arabia, United Arab Emirates.
Web site: <www.gcc-sg.org/index_e.html>.

Latin American Integration Association (ALADI)
Founded: 1980. Members: Argentina, Bolivia, Brazil, Chile, Colombia, Cuba, Ecuador, Mexico, Paraguay, Peru, Uruguay, Venezuela.
Web site: <www.aladi.org>.

League of Arab States (Arab League)
Founded: 1945. Members: Algeria, Bahrain, Comoros, Djibouti, Egypt, Iraq, Jordan, Kuwait, Lebanon, Libya, Mauritania, Morocco, Oman, Palestinian Authority, Qatar, Saudi Arabia, Somalia, The Sudan, Syria, Tunisia, United Arab Emirates, Yemen; Eritrea is an observer.
Web site: <www.arableagueonline.org>.

Nordic Council of Ministers
Founded: 1971. Members: Denmark, Finland, Iceland, Norway, Sweden; autonomous regions of Greenland, Faroe Islands, Åland Islands.
Web site: <www.norden.org>.

North Atlantic Treaty Organization (NATO)
Founded: 1949. Members: Belgium, Bulgaria, Canada, Czech Republic, Denmark, Estonia, France, Germany, Greece, Hungary, Iceland, Italy, Latvia, Lithuania, Luxembourg, The Netherlands, Norway, Poland, Portugal, Romania, Slovakia, Slovenia, Spain, Turkey, UK, US.
Web site: <www.nato.int>.

Organisation for Economic Co-operation and Development (OECD)
Founded: 1960. Members: Australia, Austria, Belgium, Canada, Czech Republic, Denmark, Finland, France, Germany, Greece, Hungary, Iceland, Ireland, Italy, Japan, Luxembourg, Mexico, The Netherlands, New Zealand, Norway, Poland, Portugal, Slovak Republic, South Korea, Spain, Sweden, Switzerland, Turkey, UK, US.
Web site: <www.oecd.org>.

Organization for Security and Co-operation in Europe (OSCE)
Founded: 1973. Members: 54 countries of Europe and Central Asia, plus Canada and the US.
Web site: <www.osce.org>.

Organization of American States (OAS)
Founded: 1948. Members: all 35 independent countries of the Western Hemisphere (Cuba's participation has been denied since 1962).
Web site: <www.oas.org>.

Organization of the Petroleum Exporting Countries (OPEC)
Founded: 1960. Members: Algeria, Angola, Indonesia, Iran, Iraq, Kuwait, Libya, Nigeria, Qatar, Saudi Arabia, United Arab Emirates, Venezuela.
Web site: <www.opec.org>.

Organization of the Islamic Conference (OIC)
Founded: 1969. Members: 57 Islamic countries (mainly in Africa and Asia), Palestinian Authority; 5 observer countries.
Web site: <www.oic-oci.org>.

Pacific Islands Forum (PIF; formerly [until 2000] South Pacific Forum)
Founded: 1971. Members: Australia, Cook Islands, Fiji, Kiribati, Marshall Islands, Federated States of Micronesia, Nauru, New Zealand, Niue, Palau, Papua New Guinea, Samoa, Solomon Islands, Tonga, Tuvalu, Vanuatu.
Web site: <www.forumsec.org>.

Secretariat of the Pacific Community (SPC; formerly South Pacific Commission)
Founded: 1947. Members: American Samoa, Australia, Cook Islands, Fiji Islands, France, French Polynesia, Guam, Kiribati, Federated States of Micronesia, Marshall Islands, Nauru, New Caledonia, New Zealand, Niue, Northern Mariana Islands, Palau, Papua New Guinea, Pitcairn Islands, Samoa, Solomon Islands, Tokelau, Tonga, Tuvalu, US, Vanuatu, Wallis and Futuna.
Web site: <www.spc.int/>.

Union of South American Nations (UNASUR/UNASUL)
Founded: 2004. Members: Argentina, Bolivia, Brazil, Chile, Colombia, Ecuador, Guyana, Paraguay, Peru, Suriname, Uruguay, Venezuela.
Web site: <www.comunidadandina.org>.

South Asian Association for Regional Cooperation (SAARC)
Founded: 1985. Members: Bangladesh, Bhutan, India, Maldives, Nepal, Pakistan, Sri Lanka.
Web site: <www.saarc-sec.org>.

Southern African Development Community (SADC)
Founded: 1980. Members: Angola, Botswana, Democratic Republic of the Congo, Lesotho, Malawi, Mauritius, Mozambique, Namibia, South Africa, Swaziland, Tanzania, Zambia, Zimbabwe.
Web site: <www.sadc.int>.

Southern Common Market (MERCOSUL/MERCOSUR)
Founded: 1991. Members: Argentina, Brazil, Paraguay, Uruguay, Venezuela; associate members Chile, Bolivia, Mexico, Peru.
Web site: <www.mercosur.int/msweb>.

United Nations (UN)
Founded: 1945. Members: 192 countries (the Vatican and Taiwan are not members).
Web site: <www.un.org>.

World Trade Organization (WTO)
Founded: 1995. Members: 150 member countries worldwide; 31 observer states as of January 2007.
Web site: <www.wto.org>.

Secretaries-General of the United Nations

The UN General Assembly appoints the Secretary-General to a five-year term on the recommendation of the 15-member Security Council; permanent members of the Security Council have veto power over nominees. The Secretary-General balances diverse and sometimes conflicting duties in the various roles of diplomat, advocate, administrator, and civil servant. The Secretary-General has a broad mandate, being able to marshal resources and advocacy on issues as various as peace efforts around the globe and disease prevention and treatment. Internet resource: <www.un.org>.

SECRETARY GENERAL	TERM	COMMENTS
Sir Gladwyn Jebb (acting) (UK)	1945–1946	
Trygve Lie (Norway)	1946–1952	resigned in November 1952
Dag Hammarskjöld (Sweden)	1953–1961	died in September 1961
U Thant (Burma, now Myanmar)	1961–1971	acting Secretary-General November 1961; elected 1962
Kurt Waldheim (Austria)	1972–1981	China vetoed a third term
Javier Pérez de Cuéllar (Peru)	1982–1991	
Boutros Boutros-Ghali (Egypt)	1992–1996	US vetoed a second term
Kofi Annan (Ghana)	1997–2006	
Ban Ki-moon (South Korea)	2007–	

The International Criminal Court

The International Criminal Court (ICC) was established by the Rome Statute of the International Criminal Court on 17 Jul 1998. Although the ICC is not yet fully operational, the statute that created it went into force on 1 Jul 2002. As of June 2007, the ICC has 104 member countries.

President
Philippe Kirsch (Canada)

First Vice President
Akua Kuenyehia (Ghana)

Second Vice President
René Blattmann (Bolivia)

Chief Prosecutor
Luis Moreno-Ocampo (Argentina)

Judges
List A—elected as experts in criminal law and procedure
Karl T. Hudson-Phillips (Trinidad and Tobago)
Claude Jorda (France)
Georghios M. Pikis (Cyprus)
Elizabeth Odio Benito (Costa Rica)
Song Sang-Hyun (Republic of Korea)

Judges (continued)
Fatoumata Dembele Diarra (Mali)
Sir Adrian Fulford (United Kingdom)
Sylvia Steiner (Brazil)
Ekaterina Trendafilova (Bulgaria)

List B—elected as experts in international law and human rights law
Navanethem Pillay (South Africa)
Hans-Peter Kaul (Germany)
Mauro Politi (Italy)
Akua Kuenyehia (Ghana)
Philippe Kirsch (Canada)
René Blattmann (Bolivia)
Erkki Kourula (Finland)
Anita Usacka (Latvia)

Registrar
Bruno Cathala (France)

United Nations Membership by Date of Admission

COUNTRY	DATE OF ADMISSION	COUNTRY	DATE OF ADMISSION	COUNTRY	DATE OF ADMISSION
Argentina	24 Oct 1945	Venezuela	15 Nov 1945	Malaysia	17 Sep 1957
Belarus	24 Oct 1945	Guatemala	21 Nov 1945	Guinea	12 Dec 1958
Brazil	24 Oct 1945	Norway	27 Nov 1945	Benin	20 Sep 1960
Chile	24 Oct 1945	The Netherlands	10 Dec 1945	Burkina Faso	20 Sep 1960
China[1]	24 Oct 1945	Honduras	17 Dec 1945	Cameroon	20 Sep 1960
Cuba	24 Oct 1945	Uruguay	18 Dec 1945	Central African Rep.	20 Sep 1960
Denmark	24 Oct 1945	Ecuador	21 Dec 1945	Chad	20 Sep 1960
Dominican Rep.	24 Oct 1945	Iraq	21 Dec 1945	Dem. Rep. of the	20 Sep 1960
Egypt	24 Oct 1945	Belgium	27 Dec 1945	Congo	
El Salvador	24 Oct 1945	Afghanistan	19 Nov 1946	Rep. of the Congo	20 Sep 1960
France	24 Oct 1945	Iceland	19 Nov 1946	Côte d'Ivoire	20 Sep 1960
Haiti	24 Oct 1945	Sweden	19 Nov 1946	Cyprus	20 Sep 1960
Iran	24 Oct 1945	Thailand	16 Dec 1946	Gabon	20 Sep 1960
Lebanon	24 Oct 1945	Pakistan	30 Sep 1947	Madagascar	20 Sep 1960
Luxembourg	24 Oct 1945	Yemen	30 Sep 1947	Niger	20 Sep 1960
New Zealand	24 Oct 1945	Myanmar	19 Apr 1948	Somalia	20 Sep 1960
Nicaragua	24 Oct 1945	Israel	11 May 1949	Togo	20 Sep 1960
Paraguay	24 Oct 1945	Indonesia	28 Sep 1950	Mali	28 Sep 1960
Philippines	24 Oct 1945	Albania	14 Dec 1955	Senegal	28 Sep 1960
Poland	24 Oct 1945	Austria	14 Dec 1955	Nigeria	7 Oct 1960
USSR (later Russia)	24 Oct 1945	Bulgaria	14 Dec 1955	Sierra Leone	27 Sep 1961
Saudi Arabia	24 Oct 1945	Cambodia	14 Dec 1955	Mauritania	27 Oct 1961
Syria	24 Oct 1945	Finland	14 Dec 1955	Mongolia	27 Oct 1961
Turkey	24 Oct 1945	Hungary	14 Dec 1955	Tanzania	14 Dec 1961
Ukraine	24 Oct 1945	Ireland	14 Dec 1955	Burundi	18 Sep 1962
UK	24 Oct 1945	Italy	14 Dec 1955	Jamaica	18 Sep 1962
US	24 Oct 1945	Jersey	14 Dec 1955	Rwanda	18 Sep 1962
Greece	25 Oct 1945	Jordan	14 Dec 1955	Trinidad and Tobago	18 Sep 1962
India	30 Oct 1945	Laos	14 Dec 1955	Algeria	8 Oct 1962
Peru	31 Oct 1945	Libya	14 Dec 1955	Uganda	25 Oct 1962
Australia	1 Nov 1945	Nepal	14 Dec 1955	Kuwait	14 May 1963
Costa Rica	2 Nov 1945	Portugal	14 Dec 1955	Kenya	16 Dec 1963
Liberia	2 Nov 1945	Romania	14 Dec 1955	Malawi	1 Dec 1964
Colombia	5 Nov 1945	Spain	14 Dec 1955	Malta	1 Dec 1964
Mexico	7 Nov 1945	Sri Lanka	14 Dec 1955	Zambia	1 Dec 1964
South Africa	7 Nov 1945	Morocco	12 Nov 1956	The Gambia	21 Sep 1965
Canada	9 Nov 1945	The Sudan	12 Nov 1956	Maldives	21 Sep 1965
Ethiopia	13 Nov 1945	Tunisia	12 Nov 1956	Singapore	21 Sep 1965
Panama	13 Nov 1945	Japan	18 Dec 1956	Guyana	20 Sep 1966
Bolivia	14 Nov 1945	Ghana	8 Mar 1957	Lesotho	17 Oct 1966

United Nations Membership by Date of Admission (continued)

COUNTRY	DATE OF ADMISSION	COUNTRY	DATE OF ADMISSION	COUNTRY	DATE OF ADMISSION
Botswana	17 Oct 1966	Djibouti	20 Sep 1977	Kyrgyzstan	2 Mar 1992
Barbados	9 Dec 1966	Vietnam	20 Sep 1977	Moldova	2 Mar 1992
Mauritius	24 Apr 1968	Solomon Islands	19 Sep 1978	San Marino	2 Mar 1992
Swaziland	24 Sep 1968	Dominica	18 Dec 1978	Tajikistan	2 Mar 1992
Equatorial Guinea	12 Nov 1968	St. Lucia	18 Sep 1979	Turkmenistan	2 Mar 1992
Fiji	13 Oct 1970	Zimbabwe	25 Aug 1980	Uzbekistan	2 Mar 1992
Bahrain	21 Sep 1971	St. Vincent and	16 Sep 1980	Bosnia and	22 May 1992
Bhutan	21 Sep 1971	the Grenadines		Herzegovina	
Qatar	21 Sep 1971	Vanuatu	15 Sep 1981	Croatia	22 May 1992
Oman	7 Oct 1971	Belize	25 Sep 1981	Slovenia	22 May 1992
United Arab	9 Dec 1971	Antigua and	11 Nov 1981	Georgia	31 Jul 1992
Emirates		Barbuda		Czech Republic	19 Jan 1993
The Bahamas	18 Sep 1973	St. Kitts and Nevis	23 Sep 1983	Slovakia	19 Jan 1993
Germany	18 Sep 1973	Brunei	21 Sep 1984	Macedonia[2]	8 Apr 1993
Bangladesh	17 Sep 1974	Namibia	23 Apr 1990	Eritrea	28 May 1993
Grenada	17 Sep 1974	Liechtenstein	18 Sep 1990	Monaco	28 May 1993
Guinea-Bissau	17 Sep 1974	Estonia	17 Sep 1991	Andorra	28 Jul 1993
Cape Verde	16 Sep 1975	North Korea	17 Sep 1991	Palau	15 Dec 1994
Mozambique	16 Sep 1975	South Korea	17 Sep 1991	Kiribati	14 Sep 1999
São Tomé	16 Sep 1975	Latvia	17 Sep 1991	Nauru	14 Sep 1999
and Príncipe		Lithuania	17 Sep 1991	Tonga	14 Sep 1999
Papua New Guinea	10 Oct 1975	Marshall Islands	17 Sep 1991	Tuvalu	5 Sep 2000
Comoros	12 Nov 1975	Federated States	17 Sep 1991	Serbia	1 Nov 2000
Suriname	4 Dec 1975	of Micronesia		Switzerland	10 Sep 2002
Seychelles	21 Sep 1976	Armenia	2 Mar 1992	East Timor	27 Sep 2002
Angola	1 Dec 1976	Azerbaijan	2 Mar 1992	(Timor-Leste)	
Samoa	15 Dec 1976	Kazakhstan	2 Mar 1992	Montenegro	28 Jun 2006

[1]The Republic of China (Taiwan) held the seat until 25 Oct 1971, when UN Res. 2758 gave the membership and a seat on the Security Council to the People's Republic of China. [2]Macedonia is known in the UN as The Former Yugoslav Republic of Macedonia.

Rulers and Regimes
Europe
Roman Emperors

Overlapping reigns denote corulers. Diocletian (284–305) laid the foundation for the Byzantine Empire in the East when he appointed Maximian (286–305) to rule over the Western portion of the empire. Rome thus remained a unified state but was divided administratively. Theodosius I (379–395) was the last emperor to rule over a unified Roman Empire. When he died, Rome split into Eastern and Western empires. For a complete list of the Eastern emperors after the fall of Rome, see "Byzantine Empire."

REIGN	BYNAME	FULL NAME
27 BC–AD 14	Augustus	Caesar Augustus
14–37	Tiberius	Tiberius Caesar Augustus
37–41	Caligula	Gaius Caesar Augustus Germanicus
41–54	Claudius	Tiberius Claudius Caesar Augustus Germanicus
54–68	Nero	Nero Claudius Caesar Augustus Germanicus
68–69	Galba	Servius Galba Caesar Augustus
69	Otho	Marcus Otho Caesar Augustus
69	Vitellius	Aulus Vitellius Germanicus
69–79	Vespasian	Caesar Vespasianus Augustus
79–81	Titus	Titus Vespasianus Augustus
81–96	Domitian	Caesar Domitianus Augustus
96–98	Nerva	Nerva Caesar Augustus
98–117	Trajan	Caesar Nerva Traianus Augustus
117–138	Hadrian	Caesar Traianus Hadrianus Augustus
138–161	Antoninus Pius	Caesar Titus Aelius Hadrianus Antoninus Augustus Pius
161–180	Marcus Aurelius	Marcus Aurelius Antoninus
161–169	Lucius Verus	Lucius Aurelius Verus
177–192	Commodus	Lucius Aelius Aurelius Commodus
193	Pertinax	Publius Helvius Pertinax
193	Didius Julianus	Marcus Didius Severus Julianus

Roman Emperors (continued)

REIGN	BYNAME	FULL NAME
193–211	Septimius Severus	Lucius Septimius Severus Pertinax
198–217	Caracalla	Marcus Aurelius Severus Antoninus
209–212	Geta	Publius Septimius Geta
217–218	Macrinus	Marcus Opellius Severus Macrinus
218–222	Elagabalus	Sacerdos dei invicti solis Elagabali Marcus Aurelius Antoninus
222–235	Alexander Severus	Marcus Aurelius Severus Alexander
235–238	Maximin	Gaius Julius Verus Maximinus
238	Gordian I	Marcus Antonius Gordianus Sempronianus Romanus Africanus
238	Gordian II	Marcus Antonius Gordianus Sempronianus Romanus Africanus
238	Maximus	Marcus Clodius Pupienus Maximus
238	Balbinus	Decius Caelius Calvinus Balbinus
238–244	Gordian III	Marcus Antonius Gordianus
244–249	Philip	
249–251	Decius	Galus Messius Quintus Trianus Decius
251	Hostilian	Gaius Valens Hostilianus Messius Quintus
251–253	Gallus	Gaius Vibius Trebonianus Gallus
253	Aemilian	Marcus Aemilius Aemilianus
253–260	Valerian	Publius Licinius Valerianus
253–268	Gallienus	Publius Licinius Egnatius Gallienus
268–270	Claudius II Gothicus	Marcus Aurelius Valerius Claudius
269–270	Quintillus	Marcus Aurelius Claudius Quintillus
270–275	Aurelian	Lucius Domitius Aurelianus
275–276	Tacitus	Marcus Claudius Tacitus
276	Florian	Marcus Annius Florianus
276–282	Probus	Marcus Aurelius Probus
282–283	Carus	Marcus Aurelius Carus
283–285	Carinus	Marcus Aurelius Carinus
283–284	Numerian	Marcus Aurelius Numerius Numerianus
284–305[1]	Diocletian	Gaius Aurelius Valerius Diocletianus
286–305[2]	Maximian	Marcus Aurelius Valerius Maximianus Heraclius
305–311[1]	Galerius	Gaius Galerius Valerius Maximianus
305–306[2]	Constantius I Chlorus	Flavius Valerius Constantius
306–307[2]	Severus	Flavius Valerius Severus
306–312[2]	Maxentius	Marcus Aurelius Valerius Maxentius
308–324[1]	Licinius	Valerius Licinianus Licinius
312–337[2]	Constantine I	Flavius Valerius Constantinus
337–340[2]	Constantine II	Flavius Claudius [or Julius] Constantinus
337–350[2]	Constans I	Flavius Julius Constans
337–361[2]	Constantius II	Flavius Julius [or Valerius] Constantius
350–353[2]	Magnentius	Flavius Magnus Magnentius
361–363[2]	Julian	Flavius Claudius Julianus
363–364[2]	Jovian	Flavius Jovianus
364–375[2]	Valentinian I	Flavius Valentinianus
364–378[1]	Valens	Flavius Valens
365–366[1]	Procopius	
375–383[2]	Gratian	Flavius Gratianus Augustus
375–392[2]	Valentinian II	Flavius Valentinianus
379–395[2]	Theodosius I	Flavius Theodosius
395–408[1]	Arcadius	Flavius Arcadius
395–423[2]	Honorius	Flavius Honorius
408–450[1]	Theodosius II	
421[2]	Constantius III	
425–455[2]	Valentinian III	Flavius Placidius Valentinianus
450–457[1]	Marcian	Marcianus
455[2]	Petronius Maximus	Flavius Ancius Petronius Maximus
455–456[2]	Avitus	Flavius Maccilius Eparchus Avitus
457–474[1]	Leo I	Leo Thrax Magnus
457–461[2]	Majorian	Julius Valerius Majorianus
461–467[2]	Libius Severus	Libius Severianus Severus
467–472[2]	Anthemius	Procopius Anthemius
472[2]	Olybrius	Anicius Olybrius
473–474[2]	Glycerius	
474–475[2]	Julius Nepos	
474[1]	Leo II	
474–491[1]	Zeno	
475–476[2]	Romulus Augustulus	Flavius Momyllus Romulus Augustulus

[1]Ruled in the East only. [2]Ruled in the West only.

Sovereigns of Britain

SOVEREIGN	DYNASTY OR HOUSE	REIGN
Kings of Wessex (West Saxons)		
Egbert	Saxon	802–839
Aethelwulf (Ethelwulf)	Saxon	839–856/858
Aethelbald (Ethelbald)	Saxon	855/856–860
Aethelberht (Ethelbert)	Saxon	860–865/866
Aethelred I (Ethelred)	Saxon	865/866–871
Alfred the Great	Saxon	871–899
Edward the Elder	Saxon	899–924
Sovereigns of England		
Athelstan[1]	Saxon	925–939
Edmund I	Saxon	939–946
Eadred (Edred)	Saxon	946–955
Eadwig (Edwy)	Saxon	955–959
Edgar	Saxon	959–975
Edward the Martyr	Saxon	975–978
Ethelred II the Unready (Aethelred)	Saxon	978–1013
Sweyn Forkbeard	Danish	1013–14
Ethelred II the Unready (restored)	Saxon	1014–16
Edmund II Ironside	Saxon	1016
Canute	Danish	1016–35
Harold I Harefoot	Danish	1035–40
Hardecanute	Danish	1040–42
Edward the Confessor	Saxon	1042–66
Harold II	Saxon	1066
William I the Conqueror	Norman	1066–87
William II	Norman	1087–1100
Henry I	Norman	1100–35
Stephen	Blois	1135–54
Henry II	Plantagenet	1154–89
Richard I	Plantagenet	1189–99
John	Plantagenet	1199–1216
Henry III	Plantagenet	1216–72
Edward I	Plantagenet	1272–1307
Edward II	Plantagenet	1307–27
Edward III	Plantagenet	1327–77
Richard II	Plantagenet	1377–99
Henry IV	Plantagenet: Lancaster	1399–1413
Henry V	Plantagenet: Lancaster	1413–22
Henry VI	Plantagenet: Lancaster	1422–61
Edward IV	Plantagenet: York	1461–70

SOVEREIGN	DYNASTY OR HOUSE	REIGN
Sovereigns of England (continued)		
Henry VI (restored)	Plantagenet: Lancaster	1470–71
Edward IV (restored)	Plantagenet: York	1471–83
Edward V	Plantagenet: York	1483
Richard III	Plantagenet: York	1483–85
Henry VII	Tudor	1483–1509
Henry VIII	Tudor	1509–47
Edward VI	Tudor	1547–53
Mary I	Tudor	1553–58
Elizabeth I	Tudor	1558–1603
Sovereigns of Great Britain and the United Kingdom[2, 3]		
James I (VI of Scotland)[2]	Stuart	1603–25
Charles I	Stuart	1625–49
Commonwealth		
Oliver Cromwell, Lord Protector		1653–58
Richard Cromwell, Lord Protector		1658–59
Sovereigns of Great Britain and the United Kingdom (restored)		
Charles II	Stuart	1660–85
James II	Stuart	1685–88
William III and Mary II[4]	Orange/ Stuart	1689–1702
Anne	Stuart	1702–14
George I	Hanover	1714–27
George II	Hanover	1727–60
George III[3]	Hanover	1760–1820
George IV[5]	Hanover	1820–30
William IV	Hanover	1830–37
Victoria	Hanover	1837–1901
Edward VII	Saxe-Coburg-Gotha	1901–10
George V[6]	Windsor	1910–36
Edward VIII[7]	Windsor	1936
George VI	Windsor	1936–52
Elizabeth II	Windsor	1952–

[1]Athelstan was king of Wessex and the first king of all England.   [2]James VI of Scotland became also James I of England in 1603. Upon accession to the English throne he styled himself "King of Great Britain" and was so proclaimed. Legally, however, he and his successors held separate English and Scottish kingships until the Act of Union of 1707, when the two kingdoms were united as the Kingdom of Great Britain.   [3]The United Kingdom was formed on 1 Jan 1801, with the union of Great Britain and Ireland. After 1801 George III was styled "King of the United Kingdom of Great Britain and Ireland."   [4]William and Mary, as husband and wife, reigned jointly until Mary's death in 1694. William then reigned alone until his own death in 1702.   [5]George IV was regent from 5 Feb 1811.   [6]In 1917, during World War I, George V changed the name of his house from Saxe-Coburg-Gotha to Windsor.   [7]Edward VIII succeeded upon the death of his father, George V, on 20 Jan 1936, but abdicated on 11 Dec 1936, before coronation.

Rulers of Scotland

Knowledge about the early Scottish kings (until Malcolm II) is slim and is partly based on traditional lists. The dating of reigns is thus inexact.

RULER	REIGN	RULER	REIGN
Kenneth I MacAlpin	843–858	Aed (Aodh)	877–878
Donald I	858–862	Eochaid (Eocha) and Giric (Ciric)[1]	878–889
Constantine I	862–877	Donald II	889–900

Rulers of Scotland (continued)

RULER	REIGN	RULER	REIGN
Constantine II	900–943	Alexander III	1249–86
Malcolm I	943–954	Margaret, Maid of Norway	1286–90
Indulf	954–962		
Dub	962–966	Interregnum	1290–92
Culen	966–971		
Kenneth II	971–995	John de Balliol	1292–96
Constantine III	995–997		
Kenneth III	997–1005	Interregnum	1296–1306
Malcolm II	1005–34		
Duncan I	1034–40	Robert I the Bruce	1306–29
Macbeth	1040–57	David II	1329–71
Lulach	1057–58		
Malcolm III Canmore	1058–93	House of Stewart (Stuart)[2]	
Donald Bane (Donalbane)	1093–94	Robert II	1371–90
Duncan II	1093–94	Robert III	1390–1406
Donald Bane (restored)	1094–97	James I	1406–37
Edgar	1097–1107	James II	1437–60
Alexander I	1107–24	James III	1460–88
David I	1124–53	James IV	1488–1513
Malcolm IV	1153–65	James V	1513–42
William I the Lion	1165–1214	Mary, Queen of Scots	1542–67
Alexander II	1214–49	James VI[3]	1567–1625

[1]*Eochaid may have been a minor and Giric his guardian, or Giric may have been a usurper. Both appear in the lists of kings for the period.* [2]*"Stewart" was the original spelling for the Scottish family, but during the 16th century French influence led to the adoption of the spelling Stuart (or Steuart), owing to the absence of the letter "w" in the French alphabet.* [3]*James VI of Scotland became also James I of England in 1603. Upon accession to the English throne he styled himself "King of Great Britain" and was so proclaimed. Legally, however, he and his successors held separate English and Scottish kingships until the Act of Union of 1707, when the two kingdoms were united as the Kingdom of Great Britain.*

British Prime Ministers

The origin of the term prime minister and the question of to whom it should originally be applied have long been issues of scholarly and political debate. Although the term was used as early as the reign of Queen Anne (1702–14), it acquired wider currency during the reign of George II (1727–60), when it began to be used as a term of reproach toward Robert Walpole. The title prime minister did not become official until 1905, to refer to the leader of a government.

Before the development of the Conservative and Liberal parties in the mid-19th century, parties in Britain were, for the most part, simply alliances of prominent groups or aristocratic families. The designations Whig and Tory tend often to be approximate. In all cases, the party designation is that of the prime minister; he or she might lead a coalition government, as did David Lloyd George and Winston Churchill (in his first term).

PRIME MINISTER	PARTY	TERM	PRIME MINISTER	PARTY	TERM
Robert Walpole	Whig	1721–42	William Henry Cavendish-Bentinck	Whig	1807–09
Spencer Compton	Whig	1742–43			
Henry Pelham	Whig	1743–54	Spencer Perceval	Tory	1809–12
Thomas Pelham-Holles	Whig	1754–56	Robert Banks Jenkinson	Tory	1812–27
William Cavendish	Whig	1756–57	George Canning	Tory	1827
Thomas Pelham-Holles	Whig	1757–62	Frederick John Robinson	Tory	1827–28
John Stuart		1762–63	Arthur Wellesley	Tory	1828–30
George Grenville		1763–65	Charles Grey	Whig	1830–34
Charles Watson Wentworth	Whig	1765–66	William Lamb	Whig	1834
			Arthur Wellesley	Tory	1834
William Pitt		1766–68	Robert Peel	Tory	1834–35
Augustus Henry Fitzroy		1768–70	William Lamb	Whig	1835–41
Frederick North		1770–82	Robert Peel	Conservative	1841–46
Charles Watson Wentworth	Whig	1782	John Russell	Whig-Liberal	1846–52
			Edward Geoffrey Stanley	Conservative	1852
William Petty-Fitzmaurice		1782–83	George Hamilton-Gordon		1852–55
William Henry Cavendish-Bentinck	Whig	1783	Henry John Temple	Liberal	1855–58
			Edward Geoffrey Stanley	Conservative	1858–59
William Pitt	Tory	1783–1801	Henry John Temple	Liberal	1859–65
Henry Addington	Tory	1801–04	John Russell	Liberal	1865–66
William Pitt	Tory	1804–06	Edward Geoffrey Stanley	Conservative	1866–68
William Wyndham Grenville		1806–07	Benjamin Disraeli	Conservative	1868
			William Ewart Gladstone	Liberal	1868–74

British Prime Ministers (continued)

PRIME MINISTER	PARTY	TERM	PRIME MINISTER	PARTY	TERM
Benjamin Disraeli	Conservative	1874–80	Ramsay Macdonald	Labour	1929–35
William Ewart Gladstone	Liberal	1880–85	Stanley Baldwin	Conservative	1935–37
Robert Cecil	Conservative	1885–86	Neville Chamberlain	Conservative	1937–40
William Ewart Gladstone	Liberal	1886	Winston Churchill	Conservative	1940–45
Robert Cecil	Conservative	1886–92	Clement Attlee	Labour	1945–51
William Ewart Gladstone	Liberal	1892–94	Winston Churchill	Conservative	1951–55
Archibald Philip Primrose	Liberal	1894–95	Anthony Eden	Conservative	1955–57
Robert Cecil	Conservative	1895–1902	Harold Macmillan	Conservative	1957–63
Arthur James Balfour	Conservative	1902–05	Alec Douglas-Home	Conservative	1963–64
Henry Campbell-Banner-man	Liberal	1905–08	Harold Wilson	Labour	1964–70
			Edward Heath	Conservative	1970–74
H.H. Asquith	Liberal	1908–16	Harold Wilson	Labour	1974–76
David Lloyd George	Liberal	1916–22	James Callaghan	Labour	1976–79
Bonar Law	Conservative	1922–23	Margaret Thatcher	Conservative	1979–90
Stanley Baldwin	Conservative	1923–24	John Major	Conservative	1990–97
Ramsay Macdonald	Labour	1924	Tony Blair	Labour	1997–2007
Stanley Baldwin	Conservative	1924–29	Gordon Brown	Labour	2007–

Rulers of France

RULER	REIGN	RULER	REIGN
Carolingian dynasty		**Valois dynasty**	
Pippin III the Short	751–768	Philip VI (Philippe)	1328–50
Charles I (Charlemagne, Kingdom of the Franks)	768–814	John II (Jean)	1350–64
		Charles V	1364–80
Louis I (Kingdom of the Franks)	814–840	Charles VI	1380–1422
civil war	840–843	Charles VII	1422–61
Charles II (Kingdom of the West Franks)	843–877	Louis XI	1461–83
Louis II (Kingdom of the West Franks)	877–879	Charles VIII	1483–98
Louis III (Kingdom of the West Franks)	879–882		
Carloman (Kingdom of the West Franks)	879–884	**Valois dynasty (Orléans branch)**	
Charles (III) (Charles III, Holy Roman Empire)	884–887	Louis XII	1498–1515
		Valois dynasty (Angoulême branch)	
Robertian (Capetian) dynasty		Francis I (François)	1515–47
Eudes	888–898	Henry II (Henri)	1547–59
		Francis II (François)	1559–60
Carolingian dynasty		Charles IX	1560–74
Charles III	893/898–923	Henry III (Henri)	1574–89
Robertian (Capetian) dynasty		**House of Bourbon**	
Robert I	922–923	Henry IV (Henri)	1589–1610
Rudolf (Raoul, or Rodolphe)	923–936	Louis XIII	1610–43
		Louis XIV	1643–1715
Carolingian dynasty		Louis XV	1715–74
Louis IV	936–954	Louis XVI	1774–92
Lothair (Lothaire)	954–986	Louis (XVII)	1793–95
Louis V	986–987		
		First Republic	
Capetian dynasty		National Convention	1792–95
Hugh Capet (Hugues Capet)	987–996	Directorate	1795–99
Robert II	996–1031	Consulate (Napoléon Bonaparte)	1799–1804
Henry I (Henri)	1031–60		
Philip I (Philippe)	1060–1108	**First Empire (emperors)**	
Louis VI	1108–37	Napoleon I (Napoléon Bonaparte)	1804–14, 1815
Louis VII	1137–80	Napoleon (II)	1815
Philip II (Philippe)	1180–1223		
Louis VIII	1223–26	**House of Bourbon**	
Louis IX (Saint Louis)	1226–70	Louis XVIII	1814–24
Philip III (Philippe)	1270–85	Charles X	1824–30
Philip IV (Philippe)	1285–1314		
Louis X	1314–16	**House of Orléans**	
John I (Jean)	1316	Louis-Philippe	1830–48
Philip V (Philippe)	1316–22		
Charles IV	1322–28	**Second Republic (president)**	
		Louis-Napoléon Bonaparte	1848–52

Rulers of France (continued)

RULER	REIGN	RULER	REIGN
Second Empire (emperor)		**Third Republic (presidents) (continued)**	
Napoleon III (Louis-Napoléon Bonaparte)	1852–70	Albert Lebrun	1932–40
Third Republic (presidents)		**French State (État Français, or Vichy France)**	
Adolphe Thiers	1871–73	Philippe Pétain	1940–44
Marie-Edmé-Patrice-Maurice, comte de	1873–79		
Mac-Mahon, duc de Magenta		**Provisional government**	1944–47
Jules Grévy	1879–87		
Sadi Carnot	1887–94	**Fourth Republic (presidents)**	
Jean Casimir-Périer	1894–95	Vincent Auriol	1947–54
Félix Faure	1895–99	René Coty	1954–59
Émile Loubet	1899–1906		
Armand Fallières	1906–13	**Fifth Republic (presidents)**	
Raymond Poincaré	1913–20	Charles de Gaulle	1959–69
Paul Deschanel	1920	Georges Pompidou	1969–74
Alexandre Millerand	1920–24	Valéry Giscard d'Estaing	1974–81
Gaston Doumergue	1924–31	François Mitterrand	1981–95
Paul Doumer	1931–32	Jacques Chirac	1995–2007
		Nicolas Sarkozy	2007–

Rulers of Spain

RULER	REIGN	RULER	REIGN
House of Habsburg		**House of Bourbon (Borbón) continued**	
Charles I (Carlos)	1516–56	Isabella II (Isabel)	1833–68
Philip II (Felipe)	1556–98		
Philip III (Felipe)	1598–1621	**Interregnum**	1868–70
Philip IV (Felipe)	1621–65		
Charles II (Carlos)	1665–1700	**House of Savoy**	
		Amadeus I (Amadeo)	1870–73
House of Bourbon (Borbón)			
Philip V (Felipe)	1700–24	**Republic**	1873–74
Louis (Luis)	1724		
Philip V (2nd time)	1724–46	**House of Bourbon (Borbón)**	
Ferdinand VI (Fernando)	1746–59	Alfonso XII	1874–85
Charles III (Carlos)	1759–88	Alfonso XIII	1886–1931
Charles IV (Carlos)	1788–1808		
Ferdinand VII (Fernando)	1808	**Republic**	1931–39
House of Bonaparte		**Nationalist Regime**	
Joseph (José)	1808–13	Francisco Franco	1939–75
House of Bourbon (Borbón)		**House of Bourbon (Borbón)**	
Ferdinand VII (2nd time)	1814–33	Juan Carlos	1975–

Rulers of Germany

On 25 Jul 1806 the Confederation of the Rhine was founded, with Karl Theodor von Dalberg as prince primate (1806–13). After the dissolution of the Rhine Confederation, there was no true central power until 1815, when the German Confederation was founded. In 1867 the governing structure became the North German Confederation, and in 1871 the German Reich. For rulers of Germany before the Confederation of the Rhine, see Holy Roman Emperors.

RULER	REIGN OR TERM	RULER	REIGN OR TERM
Emperors		**Presidents (continued)**	
Hohenzollern dynasty		Walter Simons (acting)	1925
Wilhelm I	1871–88	Paul von Hindenburg	1925–34
Friedrich III	1888	Adolf Hitler (Führer)	1934–45
Wilhelm II	1888–1918	Karl Dönitz	1945
Presidents		**Chancellors**	
Richard Müller	1918	Otto Fürst von Bismarck	1871–90
Robert Leinert	1918–19	Leo Graf von Caprivi	1890–94
Wilhelm Pfannkuch	1919	Chlodwig Fürst zu Hohenlohe-	1894–1900
Eduard David	1919	Schillingsfürst	
Friedrich Ebert	1919–25	Bernhard Graf Fürst von Bülow	1900–09
Hans Luther (acting)	1925	Theobald von Bethmann Hollweg	1909–17

Rulers of Germany (continued)

RULER	REIGN OR TERM	RULER	REIGN OR TERM
Chancellors (continued)		**Chancellors (continued)**	
Georg Michaelis	1917	Wilhelm Marx	1923–24
Georg Graf von Hertling	1917–18	Hans Luther	1925–26
Maximilian Prinz von Baden	1918	Wilhelm Marx	1926–28
Friedrich Ebert	1918	Hermann Müller	1928–30
Philipp Scheidemann	1919	Heinrich Brüning	1930–32
Gustav Bauer	1919–20	Franz von Papen	1932
Wolfgang Kapp (in rebellion)	1920	Kurt von Schleicher	1932–33
Hermann Müller	1920	Adolf Hitler	1933–45
Konstantin Fehrenbach	1920–21	Joseph Goebbels	1945
Joseph Wirth	1921–22	Lutz Graf Schwerin von Krosigk	1945
Wilhelm Cuno	1922–23	(chairman of interim government)	
Gustav Stresemann	1923		

Allied occupation   1945–49

German Democratic Republic (East Germany)[1]

Presidents		**Chairmen of the Council of State (continued)**	
Johannes Dieckmann (acting)	1949	Willi Stoph	1973–76
Wilhelm Pieck	1949–60	Erich Honecker	1976–89
Johannes Dieckmann (acting)	1960	Egon Krenz	1989
		Manfred Gerlach (acting)	1989–90
Chairmen of the Council of State		Sabine Bergmann-Pohl	1990
Walter Ulbricht	1960–73		
Friedrich Ebert (acting)	1973		

Federal Republic of Germany (West Germany)[1]

Presidents		**Chancellors**	
Karl Arnold (acting)	1949	Konrad Adenauer	1949–63
Theodor Heuss	1949–59	Ludwig Erhard	1963–66
Heinrich Lübke	1959–69	Kurt Georg Kiesinger	1966–69
Gustav Heinemann	1969–74	Willy Brandt	1969–74
Walter Scheel	1974–79	Walter Scheel (acting)	1974
Karl Carstens	1979–84	Helmut Schmidt	1974–82
Richard von Weizsäcker	1984–94	Helmut Kohl	1982–98
Roman Herzog	1994–99	Gerhard Schröder	1998–2005
Johannes Rau	1999–2004	Angela Merkel	2005–
Horst Köhler	2004–		

[1]After WWII, Germany was split into four occupational zones, governed by the French, British, American, and Soviet powers. The Western zones were merged and, on 23 May 1949, became the independent Federal Republic of Germany. On 7 October of the same year, the Soviet zone was proclaimed the German Democratic Republic. On 3 Oct 1990, the latter was incorporated into the Federal Republic of Germany.

Holy Roman Emperors

The Holy Roman Empire encompassed a varying complex of lands in Western and Central Europe. Ruled over by Frankish and then German kings, the empire officially dissolved on 6 Aug 1806, when Francis II resigned his title.

EMPEROR	REIGN	EMPEROR	REIGN
Carolingian dynasty		**House of Franconia**	
Charlemagne (Charles I)	800–814	Conrad I	911–918
Louis I	814–840		
Civil War	840–843	**Carolingian dynasty**	
Lothair I	843–855	Berengar	915–924
Louis II	855–875		
Charles II	875–877	**House of Saxony (Liudolfings)**	
Interregnum	877–881	Henry I	919–936
Charles III	881–887	Otto I	936–973
Interregnum	887–891	Otto II	973–983
		Otto III	983–1002
House of Spoleto		Henry II	1002–24
Guy	891–894		
Lambert	894–898	**Salian dynasty**	
		Conrad II	1024–39
Carolingian dynasty		Henry III	1039–56
Arnulf	896–899		
Louis III	901–905		

Holy Roman Emperors (continued)

EMPEROR	REIGN
Salian dynasty (continued)	
Henry IV	1056–1106
Rival claimants:	
Rudolf	1077–80
Hermann	1081–93
Conrad	1093–1101
Henry V	1105/06–25
House of Supplinburg	
Lothair II	1125–37
House of Hohenstaufen	
Conrad III	1138–52
Frederick I (Barbarossa)	1152–90
Henry VI	1190–97
Philip	1198–1208
Welf dynasty	
Otto IV	1198–1214
House of Hohenstaufen	
Frederick II	1215–50
Rival claimants:	
Henry (VII)	1220–35
Henry Raspe	1246–47
Wiliam of Holland	1247–56
Conrad IV	1250–54
Great Interregnum	1254–73
Richard	1257–72
Alfonso (Alfonso X of Castile)	1257–75
House of Habsburg	
Rudolf I	1273–91
House of Nassau	
Adolf	1292–98
House of Habsburg	
Albert I	1298–1308
House of Luxembourg	
Henry VII	1308–13

EMPEROR	REIGN
House of Habsburg	
Frederick (III)	1314–26
House of Wittelsbach	
Louis IV	1314–46
House of Luxembourg	
Charles IV	1346–78
Wenceslas	1378–1400
House of Wittelsbach	
Rupert	1400–10
House of Luxembourg	
Jobst	1410–11
Sigismund	1410–37
House of Habsburg	
Albert II	1438–39
Frederick III	1440–93
Maximilian I	1493–1519
Charles V	1519–56
Ferdinand I	1556–64
Maximilian II	1564–76
Rudolf II	1576–1612
Matthias	1612–19
Ferdinand II	1619–37
Ferdinand III	1637–57
Leopold I	1658–1705
Joseph I	1705–11
Charles VI	1711–40
House of Wittelsbach	
Charles VII	1742–45
House of Habsburg	
Francis I	1745–65
Joseph II	1765–90
Leopold II	1790–92
Francis II	1792–1806

Rulers of Russia[1]

RULER	REIGN
Princes and Grand Princes of Moscow (Muscovy): Danilovich dynasty[2]	
Daniel (son of Alexander Nevsky)	c. 1276–1303
Yury	1303–25
Ivan I	1325–40
Semyon (Simeon)	1340–53
Ivan II	1353–59
Dmitry Donskoy	1359–89
Vasily I	1389–1425
Vasily II	1425–62
Ivan III	1462–1505
Vasily III	1505–33
Ivan IV	1533–47
Tsars of Russia: Danilovich dynasty	
Ivan IV	1547–84
Fyodor I	1584–98
Tsars of Russia: Time of Troubles	
Boris Godunov	1598–1605
Fyodor II	1605

RULER	REIGN
Tsars of Russia: Time of Troubles (continued)	
False Dmitry	1605–06
Vasily (IV)	1606–10
Interregnum	1610–12
Tsars and Empresses of Russia and the Russian Empire: Romanov dynasty[3]	
Michael III	1613–45
Alexis	1645–76
Fyodor III	1676–82
Peter I (Ivan V coruler 1682–96)	1682–1725
Catherine I	1725–27
Peter II	1727–30
Anna	1730–40
Ivan VI	1740–41
Elizabeth	1741–61 (O.S.)
Peter III[4]	1761–62 (O.S.)
Catherine II	1762–96
Paul	1796–1801
Alexander I	1801–25

Rulers of Russia[1] (continued)

RULER	REIGN	RULER	REIGN
Tsars and Empresses of Russia and the Russian Empire: Romanov dynasty[3] (continued)		**Chairmen (or First Secretaries) of the Communist Party of the Soviet Union (continued)**	
Nicholas I	1825–55	Georgy Malenkov	1953
Alexander II	1855–81	Nikita Khrushchev	1953–64
Alexander III	1881–94	Leonid Brezhnev	1964–82
Nicholas II	1894–1917	Yury Andropov	1982–84
		Konstantin Chernenko	1984–85
Provisional government	1917	Mikhail Gorbachev	1985–91
Chairmen (or First Secretaries) of the Communist Party of the Soviet Union		**Presidents of Russia**	
		Boris Yeltsin	1990–99
Vladimir Lenin	1917–24	Vladimir Putin	2000–
Joseph Stalin	1924–53		

[1]This table includes leaders of Muscovy, Russia, the Russian Empire, and the Soviet Union.   [2]The Danilovich dynasty is a late branch of the Rurik dynasty, named after its progenitor, Daniel.   [3]On 22 (O.S.) Oct 1721, Peter I the Great took the title of "emperor." However, despite the official titling, conventional usage took an odd turn. Every male sovereign continued usually to be called tsar, but every female sovereign was conventionally called empress.   [4]The direct line of the Romanov dynasty came to an end in 1761 with the death of Elizabeth, daughter of Peter I, but subsequent rulers of the "Holstein-Gottorp dynasty" (the first, Peter III, was son of Charles Frederick, duke of Holstein-Gottorp, and Anna, daughter of Peter I) took the family name of Romanov.

Middle East

Byzantine Emperors

The Byzantine Empire comprised what was previously the eastern half of the Roman Empire. It survived for nearly 1,000 years after the western half had crumbled into various feudal kingdoms; it finally fell to Ottoman Turkish onslaughts in 1453. For emperors of the Eastern Roman Empire (at Constantinople) before the fall of Rome, see "Roman Emperors."

EMPEROR	REIGN	EMPEROR	REIGN
Zeno	474–491	Alexander	912–913
Anastasius I	491–518	Constantine VII Porphyrogenitus	913–959
Justin I	518–527	Romanus I Lecapenus	920–944
Justinian I	527–565	Romanus II	959–963
Justin II	565–578	Nicephorus II Phocas	963–969
Tiberius II Constantine	578–582	John I Tzimisces	969–976
Maurice Tiberius	582–602	Basil II Bulgaroctonus	976–1025
Phocas	602–610	Constantine VIII	1025–28
Heraclius	610–641	Romanus III Argyrus	1028–34
Heraclius Constantine	641	Michael IV	1034–41
Heraclonas (or Heraclius)	641	Michael V Calaphates	1041–42
Constans II (Constantine Pogonatus)	641–668	Zoe (empress)	1042–56
Constantine IV	668–685	Constantine IX Monomachus	1042–55
Justinian II Rhinotmetus	685–695	Theodora (empress)	1055–56
Leontius	695–698	Michael VI Stratioticus	1056–57
Tiberius III	698–705	Isaac I Comnenus	1057–59
Justinian II Rhinotmetus (restored)	705–711	Constantine X Ducas	1059–67
Philippicus	711–713	Romanus IV Diogenes	1067–71
Anastasius II	713–715	Michael VII Ducas	1071–78
Theodosius III	715–717	Nicephorus III Botaniates	1078–81
Leo III	717–741	Alexius I Comnenus	1081–1118
Constantine V Copronymus	741–775	John II Comnenus	1118–43
Leo IV	775–780	Manuel I Comnenus	1143–80
Constantine VI	780–797	Alexius II Comnenus	1180–83
Irene (empress)	797–802	Andronicus I Comnenus	1183–85
Nicephorus I	802–811	Isaac II Angelus	1185–95
Stauracius	811	Alexius III Angelus	1195–1203
Michael I Rhangabe	811–813	Isaac II Angelus (restored) and Alexius IV Angelus (joint ruler)	1203–04
Leo V	813–820	Alexius V Ducas Murtzuphlus	1204
Michael II Balbus	820–829		
Theophilus	829–842		
Michael III	842–867	**Latin emperors**	
Basil I	867–886	Baldwin I	1204–06
Leo VI	886–912	Henry	1206–16

Byzantine Emperors (continued)

EMPEROR	REIGN	EMPEROR	REIGN
Latin emperors (continued)		**Greek emperors restored**	
Peter	1217	Michael VIII Palaeologus	1261–82
Yolande (empress)	1217–19	Andronicus II Palaeologus	1282–1328
Robert	1221–28	Andronicus III Palaeologus	1328–41
Baldwin II	1228–61	John V Palaeologus	1341–76
John	1231–37	John VI Cantacuzenus	1347–54
		Andronicus IV Palaeologus	1376–79
		John V Palaeologus (restored)	1379–90
Nicaean emperors		John VII Palaeologus	1390
Constantine (XI) Lascaris	1204–05?	John V Palaeologus (restored)	1390–91
Theodore I Lascaris	1205?–22	Manuel II Palaeologus	1391–1425
John III Ducas Vatatzes	1222–54	John VIII Palaeologus	1421–48
Theodore II Lascaris	1254–58	Constantine XI Palaeologus	1449–53
John IV Lascaris	1258–61		

Caliphs

When Muhammad died on 8 Jun 632, Abu Bakr, his father-in-law, succeeded to his political and administrative functions. He and his three immediate successors are known as the "perfect" or "rightly guided" caliphs. After them, the title was borne by the 14 Umayyad caliphs of Damascus (from 661–750) and subsequently by the 38 'Abbasid caliphs of Baghdad (both are named after their clans of origin). The empire of the caliphate grew rapidly through conquest during its first two centuries to include most of southwestern Asia, North Africa, and Spain. 'Abbasid power ended in 945,

when the Buyids took Baghdad under their rule. They retained the 'Abbasid caliphs as figureheads; other dynasties in Central Asia and the Ganges River basin acknowledged the 'Abbasid caliphs as spiritual leaders. The Fatimids, however, proclaimed a new caliphate in 920 in their capital of al-Mahdiyah in Tunisia; it lasted until 1171, by which time opposition within the sect caused it to disintegrate. 'Abbasid authority was partially restored in the 12th century, but the caliphate ceased to exist with the Mongol destruction of Baghdad in 1258. Some principal caliphs are listed below.

CALIPH	REIGN	CALIPH	REIGN
"Perfect" caliphs		**Fatimid caliphs (al-Mahdiyah)**	
Abu Bakr	632–634	al-Mahdi	909–934
'Umar I	634–644	al-Qa'im	934–946
'Uthman ibn 'Affan	644–656	al-Mansur	946–953
'Ali	656–661	al-Mu'izz	953–975
		al-Hakim	996–1021
Umayyad caliphs (Damascus)		al-Mustansir	1036–94
Mu'awiyah I	661–680	al-Musta'li	1094–1101
'Abd al-Malik	685–705		
al-Walid	705–715	**'Abbasid caliph (Baghdad)**	
Hisham	724–743	al-Nasir	1180–1225
Marwan II	744–750		
'Abbasid caliphs (Baghdad)			
as-Saffah	749–754		
Harun	786–809		
al-Ma'mun	813–833		

Sultans of the Ottoman Empire

One of the most powerful states in the world during the 15th and 16th centuries, the Ottoman empire was created by Turkish tribes in Anatolia and spanned more than 600 years. It came to an end in 1922, when it was replaced by the Turkish Republic and various successor states in southeastern Europe and the Middle East. At its height

the empire included most of southeastern Europe, the Middle East as far east as Iraq, North Africa as far west as Algeria, and most of the Arabian Peninsula. The term Ottoman is a dynastic appellation derived from Osman (Arabic: 'Uthman), the nomadic Turkmen chief who founded both the dynasty and the empire.

SULTAN	REIGN	SULTAN	REIGN
Osman I	c. 1300–1324	Murad II (second reign)	1446–1451
Orhan	1324–1360	Mehmed II (second reign)	1451–1481
Murad I	1360–1389	Bayezid II	1481–1512
Bayezid I	1389–1402	Selim I	1512–1520
Mehmed I	1413–1421	Suleyman I	1520–1566
Murad II	1421–1444	Selim II	1566–1574
Mehmed II	1444–1446	Murad III	1574–1595

Sultans of the Ottoman Empire (continued)

SULTAN	REIGN	SULTAN	REIGN
Mehmed III	1595–1603	Osman III	1754–1757
Ahmed I	1603–1617	Mustafa III	1757–1774
Mustafa I	1617–1618	Abdulhamid I	1774–1789
Osman II	1618–1622	Selim III	1789–1807
Mustafa I (second reign)	1622–1623	Mustafa IV	1807–1808
Murad IV	1623–1640	Mahmud II	1808–1839
Ibrahim	1640–1648	Abdulmecid I	1839–1861
Mehmed IV	1648–1687	Abdulaziz	1861–1876
Suleyman II	1687–1691	Murad V	1876
Ahmed II	1691–1695	Abdulhamid II	1876–1909
Mustafa II	1695–1703	Mehmed V	1909–1918
Ahmed III	1703–1730	Mehmed VI	1918–1922
Mahmud I	1730–1754		

Persian Dynasties

Dates given are approximate and may overlap.

DYNASTY/KINGDOM	PERIOD	DYNASTY/KINGDOM	PERIOD
Median	728–550 BC	Seljuqs	1038–1157
Achaemenian	559–330 BC	Mongols[4]	1220–1335
Hellenistic period of Alexander and the Seleucids[1]	330 BC–247 BC	Timurids and Ottoman Turks	1380–1501
Parthian period (Arsacid dynasty)[2]	247 BC–AD 224	Safavid	1502–1736
Sasanian	224–651	Afghan interlude	1723–36
Arab invasion and the advent of Islam	640–829	Nader Shah	1736–47
		Zand	1750–79
Iranian intermezzo[3]	821–1055	Qajars	1794–1925
		Pahlavi	1925–79

[1]Dates from the death of Darius III, the last Achaemenian king, and the invasion of Alexander the Great. [2]Dates from the year in which the Parnian chief Arsaces first battled the Seleucids. [3]Includes the Tahirid, Samanid, Ghaznavids, and Buyid dynasties. [4]Mainly the Il-Khanid dynasty (1256–1353).

Asia

Indian Dynasties

Dates given are approximations.

DYNASTY	LOCATION	DATES	DYNASTY	LOCATION	DATES
Nanda	Ganges Valley	400 BC	Pala	Bengal	800–1100
Maurya	India, barring the area south of Mysore (Karnataka)	400–200 BC	Pratihara	western India and upper Ganges Valley	900–1100
			Rastrakuta	western and central Deccan	800–1100
Indo-Greeks	northern India	200–100 BC			
Sunga	Ganges Valley and parts of central India	200–100 BC	Cola	Tamil Nadu	900–1300
			Candella	Bundelkhand	1000–1200
			Cauhan	Rajasthan	1000–1200
Satavahana	northern Deccan	100 BC–AD 300	Caulukya	Gujarat	1000–1300
Saka	western India	100 BC–AD 400	Paramara	western and central India	1000–1100
Kusana	northern India and Central Asia	AD 100–300			
			Later Calukya	western and central Deccan	1000–1200
Gupta	northern India	400–600			
Harsa	northern India	700	Hoysala	central and southern Deccan	1200–1400
Pallava	Tamil Nadu	400–900			
Calukya	western and central Deccan	600–800	Yadava	northern Deccan	1200–1300
			Pandya	Tamil Nadu	1300–1400

Japanese Historical Periods and Rulers

PERIOD	DATES	PERIOD	DATES
Asuka	552–710	Muromachi (or Ashikaga)	1338–1573
Nara	710–784	Azuchi-Momoyama	1574–1600
Heian	794–1185	Edo (or Tokugawa)	1603–1867
Kamakura	1192–1333	Meiji	1868–1912

Japanese Historical Periods and Rulers (continued)

Reign dates for the first 28 sovereigns (Jimmu through Senka) are taken from the *Nihon shoki* ("Chronicles of Japan"). The first 14 sovereigns are considered legendary, and while the next 14 are known to have existed, their exact reign dates have not been verified historically. When the year of actual accession and year of formal coronation are different, the latter is placed in parentheses after the former. If the two events took place in the same year, no special notation is used. If only the coronation year is known, it is placed in parentheses.

EMPEROR	REIGN
Jimmu	(660)–585 BC
Suizei	(581)–549 BC
Annei	549–511 BC
Itoku	(510)–477 BC
Kosho	(475)–393 BC
Koan	(392)–291 BC
Korei	(290)–215 BC
Kogen	(214)–158 BC
Kaika	158–98 BC
Sujin	(97)–30 BC
Suinin	(29 BC)–AD 70
Keiko	(71)–130
Seimu	(131)–190
Chuai	(192)–200
Jingu Kogo (regent)	201–269
Ojin	(270)–310
Nintoku	(313)–399
Richu	(400)–405
Hanzei	(406)–410
Ingyo	(412)–453
Anko	453–456
Yuryaku	456–479
Seinei	(480)–484
Kenzo	(485)–487
Ninken	(488)–498
Buretsu	498–506
Keitai	(507)–531
Ankan	531 (534)–535
Senka	535–539
Kimmei	539–571
Bidatsu	(572)–585
Yomei	585–587
Sushun	587–592
Suiko (empress regnant)	593–628
Jomei	(629)–641
Kogyoku (empress regnant)	(642)–645
Kotoku	645–654
Saimei (empress regnant: Kogyoku rethroned)	(655)–661
Tenji	661 (668)–672
Kobun	672
Temmu	672 (673)–686
Jito (empress regnant)	686 (690)–697
Mommu	697–707
Gemmei (empress regnant)	707–715
Gensho (empress regnant)	715–724
Shomu	724–749
Koken (empress regnant)	749–758
Junnin	758–764
Shotoku (empress regnant: Koken rethroned)	764 (765)–770
Konin	770–781
Kammu	781–806
Heizei	806–809
Saga	809–823
Junna	823–833
Nimmyo	833–850
Montoku	850–858
Seiwa	858–876
Yozei	876 (877)–884
Koko	884–887

EMPEROR	REIGN
Uda	887–897
Daigo	897–930
Suzaku	930–946
Murakami	946–967
Reizei	967–969
En'yu	969–984
Kazan	984–986
Ichijo	986–1011
Sanjo	1011–16
Go–Ichijo	1016–36
Go–Suzaku	1036–45
Go–Reizei	1045–68
Go–Sanjo	1068–72
Shirakawa	1072–86
Horikawa	1086–1107
Toba	1107–23
Sutoku	1123–41
Konoe	1141–55
Go–Shirakawa	1155–58
Nijo	1158–65
Rokujo	1165–68
Takakura	1168–80
Antoku	1180–85[1]
Go–Toba	1183 (1184)–98
Tsuchimikado	1198–1210
Juntoku	1210 (1211)–21
Chukyo	1221
Goshirakawa	1221 (1222)–32
Shijo	1232 (1233)–42
Go–Saga	1242–46
Go–Fukakusa	1246–59/60
Kameyama	1259/60–74
Gouda	1274–87
Fushimi	1287 (1288)–98
Go–Fushimi	1298–1301
Go–Nijo	1301–08
Hanazono	1308–18
Go–Daigo	1318–39
Go–Murakami	1339–68
Chokei	1368–83
Go–Kameyama	1383–92

The Northern court[2]

EMPEROR	REIGN
Kogon	1331 (1332)–33
Komyo	1336 (1337/38)–48
Suko	1348 (1349/50)–51
Go–Kogon	1351 (1353/54)–71
Go–Enyu	1371 (1374/75)–82
Go–Komatsu	1382–92
Go–Komatsu	1392–1412
Shoko	1412 (1414)–28
Go–Hanazono	1428 (1429/30)–64
Go–Tsuchimikado	1464 (1465/66)–1500
Go–Kashiwabara	1500 (1521)–26
Go–Nara	1526 (1536)–57
Ogimachi	1557 (1560)–86
Go–Yozei	1586 (1587)–1611
Go–Mizunoo	1611–29
Meisho (empress regnant)	1629 (1630)–43
Go–Komyo	1643–54
Go–Sai	1654/55 (1656)–63

Japanese Historical Periods and Rulers (continued)

EMPEROR The Northern court[2] (continued)	REIGN	EMPEROR The Northern court[2] (continued)	REIGN
Reigen	1663–87	Ninko	1817–46
Higashiyama	1687–1709	Komei	1846 (1847)–66
Nakamikado	1709 (1710)–35	Meiji (personal name: Mutsuhito; era name: Meiji)	1867 (1868)–1912
Sakuramachi	1735–47		
Momozono	1747–62	Taisho (personal name: Yoshihito; era name: Taisho)	1912 (1915)–26
Go-Sakuramachi (empress regnant)	1762 (1763)–71		
Go-Momozono	1771–79	Hirohito (era name: Showa)	1926 (1928)–1989
Kokaku	1780–1817	Akihito (era name: Heisei)	1989 (1990)–

[1]Antoku's reign overlaps that of Go-Toba. Go-Toba was placed on the throne by the Minamoto clan after the rival Taira clan had fled Kyoto with Antoku.   [2]From 1336 until 1392 Japan witnessed the spectacle of two contending Imperial courts—the Southern court of Go-Daigo and his descendants, whose sphere of influence was restricted to the immediate vicinity of the Yoshino Mountains, and the Northern court of Kogon and his descendants, which was under the domination of the Ashikaga family.

Chinese Dynasties

Dates given for early dynasties are approximate and may overlap.

DYNASTY	ALTERNATE NAME	DATES	DYNASTY	ALTERNATE NAME	DATES
Hsia[1]	Xia	c. 2205–1766 BC	Six Dynasties[2] (continued)		
Shang		c. 1760–1030 BC	Southern Qi		479–502
Western Zhou	Chou	c. 1050–771 BC	Southern Liang		502–57
Eastern Zhou	Chou	c. 771–255 BC	Southern Chen		557–89
Qin	Ch'in	221–206 BC	Sui		581–618
Han		206 BC–AD 220	T'ang	Tang	618–907
Western Jin	Chin	265–317	Five Dynasties[3]	Ten Kingdoms[3]	907–960
Eastern Jin[2]	Chin	317–420	Sung	Song	960–1279
Six Dynasties[2]		220–589	Yüan	Yuan, Mongol	1206–1368
Wu		222–80	Ming		1368–1644
Eastern Jin[2]		317–420	Ch'ing	Qing, Manchu	1644–1911/12
Liusong		420–79			

[1]The Hsia Dynasty is mentioned in legends but is of undetermined historicity.   [2]Between the fall of the Han and the establishment of the Sui, China was divided into two societies, northern and southern. The Six Dynasties had their capital at Nanjing in the south. The Eastern Jin is considered one of these six dynasties and so is listed twice.   [3]Period of time between the fall of the T'ang dynasty and the founding of the Sung dynasty, when five would-be dynasties followed one another in quick succession in North China. The era is also known as the period of the Ten Kingdoms because 10 regimes dominated separate regions of South China during the same period.

Leaders of the People's Republic of China Since 1949

Chinese Communist Party leaders

NAME	TITLE	DATES
Mao Zedong	CCP chairman	1949–1976
Hua Guofeng	CCP chairman	1976–1981
Hu Yaobang	CCP chairman; after September 1982, general secretary of the CCP	1981–1987
Zhao Ziyang	CCP general secretary	1987–1989
Jiang Zemin	CCP general secretary	1989–2002
Hu Jintao	CCP general secretary	2002–

premiers

NAME	DATES
Zhou Enlai	1949–1976
Hua Guofeng	1976–1980
Zhao Ziyang	1980–1987
Li Peng	1987–1998
Zhu Rongji	1998–2003
Wen Jiabao	2003–

Note: although he held no top party or state position, Deng Xiaoping was de facto leader of China from 1977 to 1997.

Dalai Lamas

The Dalai Lama is the head of the dominant Dge-lugs-pa (Yellow Hat) order of Tibetan Buddhists and, until 1959, was both spiritual and temporal ruler of Tibet. In accordance with the belief in reincarnate lamas, which began to develop in the 14th century, the successors of the first Dalai Lama were considered his rebirths and came to be regarded as physical manifestations of the compassionate bodhisattva ("buddha-to-be"), Avalokitesvara.

Dalai Lamas (continued)

DALAI LAMA	NAME	LIVED	DALAI LAMA	NAME	LIVED
first	Dge-'dun-grub-pa	1391–1475	eighth	'Jam-dpal-rgya-mtsho	1758–1804
second	Dge-'dun-rgya-mtsho	1475–1542	ninth	Lung-rtogs-rgya-mtsho	1806–1815[1]
third	Bsod-nams-rgya-mtsho	1543–1588	tenth	Tshul-khrims-rgya-mtsho	1816–1837[1]
fourth	Yon-tan-rgya-mtsho	1589–1617	eleventh	Mkhas-grub-rgya-mtsho	1838–1856[1]
fifth	Ngag-dbang-rgya-mtsho	1617–1682	twelfth	'Phrin-las-rgya-mtsho	1856–1875[1]
sixth	Tshangs-dbyangs-rgya-mtsho	1683–1706	thirteenth	Thub-bstan-rgya-mtsho	1875–1933[2]
seventh	Bskal-bzang-rgya-mtsho	1708–1757	fourteenth	Bstan-'dzin-rgya-mtsho	1935–[3]

[1]Dalai Lamas 9–12 all died young, and the country was ruled by regencies.   [2]Reigned as head of a sovereign state from 1912.   [3]Ruled from exile in Dharmsala, India, from 1960.

The Americas

Pre-Columbian Civilizations

Various aboriginal American Indian cultures evolved in Meso-America (part of Mexico and Central America) and the Andean region (western South America) prior to Spanish exploration and conquest in the 16th century. These pre-Columbian civilizations were extraordinary developments in human society and culture, characterized by kingdoms and empires, great monuments and cities, and refinements in the arts, metallurgy, and writing. Dates given below are approximations.

CULTURE	LOCATION	DATES
Meso-American civilizations		
Olmec	Gulf coast of southern Mexico	1150 BC–800 BC
Zapotec	Oaxaca, particularly Monte Albán	500 BC–AD 900
Totonac	east-central Mexico	500 BC–AD 900
Teotihuacán	Teotihuacán, in the Valley of Mexico	AD 400–600
Maya	southern Mexico and Guatemala	250–900
Toltec	central Mexico	900–1200
Aztec	central and southern Mexico	1400–early 1500s
Andean civilizations		
Nazca	southern coast of Peru	200 BC–AD 600
Recuay	northern highlands of Peru	200 BC–AD 600
Tiwanaku	Lake Titicaca, Bolivia	200 BC–AD 1000
Moche (Mochica)	northern coast of Peru	AD 1–700
Inca	Pacific coast of South America	1100–1532

Africa

Historic Sub-Saharan African States

STATE	LOCATION IN PRESENT-DAY COUNTRIES	FLOURISHED
Aksumite kingdom	Ethiopia, Sudan	1st–10th centuries
Asante empire	Ghana	18th–19th centuries
Basuto kingdom	Lesotho	19th century
Benin kingdom	Nigeria	12th–19th centuries
kingdom of Buganda	Uganda	14th–20th centuries
kingdom of Bunyoro	Uganda	15th–19th centuries
kingdom of Burundi	Burundi	17th–20th centuries
kingdom of Dahomey	Benin	17th–19th centuries
Darfur	Sudan	17th–19th centuries
kingdom of Dongola	Sudan	7th–14th centuries
Fulani empire	Cameroon, Niger, Nigeria	19th–20th centuries
Ghana empire	Mali, Mauritania	4th–13th centuries
Hausa states	Nigeria	14th–19th centuries
Kanem-Bornu	Nigeria, Chad, Cameroon, Niger, Libya	9th–19th centuries
Kongo kingdom	Angola, Dem. Rep. of Congo	14th–17th centuries
Kuba kingdom	Dem. Rep. of Congo	17th–19th centuries
kingdom of Kush	Egypt, Sudan	c. 850 BC–c. AD 325
Luba empire	Dem Rep. of Congo	16th–19th centuries
Lunda empire	Dem. Rep. of Congo, Angola, Zambia	17th–19th centuries
Mali empire	Mali, Mauritania, Senegal, Gambia, Guinea-Bissau	13th–16th centuries

Historic Sub-Saharan African States (continued)

STATE	LOCATION IN PRESENT-DAY COUNTRIES	FLOURISHED
Ndongo kingdom	Angola	14th–17th centuries
kingdom of Nubia	Egypt, Sudan	4th–7th centuries
Oyo empire	Nigeria	16th–19th centuries
Rozwi empire	Zimbabwe, Botswana	17th–19th centuries
Shewa empire	Ethiopia	15th–19th centuries
Songhai empire	Nigeria, Niger	6th–17th centuries
Tukulor empire	Mali	19th century
Wolof empire	Senegal	14th–19th centuries
Zeng empire	Somalia, Kenya, Tanzania, Mozambique	10th–16th centuries
Zulu kingdom	South Africa	19th century

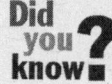

Did you know? One of Africa's least-explored regions, the northern part of the Republic of the Congo, an area of huge swamps and nearly impenetrable forests, was traversed by foot in 1999. Dr. Michael Fay, an ecologist with the Wildlife Conservation Society, and a team of 12 others undertook a 1,200-mi (1,900-km) survey of this area as well as similar areas in neighboring Gabon. The team concluded that this wilderness is seriously threatened.

Populations

Largest Urban Agglomerations

Agglomerations include a central city and associated neighboring communities.
Source: United Nations, World Urbanization Prospects: The 2005 Revision.

RANK	AGGLOMERATION	COUNTRY	POPULATION (2005)	RANK	AGGLOMERATION	COUNTRY	POPULATION (2005)
1	Tokyo	Japan	35,197,000	15	Osaka-Kobe	Japan	11,268,000
2	Mexico City	Mexico	19,411,000	16	Cairo	Egypt	11,128,000
3	New York City–Newark	US	18,718,000	17	Lagos	Nigeria	10,886,000
				18	Beijing	China	10,717,000
4	São Paulo	Brazil	18,333,000	19	Manila	Philippines	10,686,000
5	Mumbai (Bombay)	India	18,196,000	20	Moscow	Russia	10,654,000
6	Delhi	India	15,048,000	21	Paris	France	9,820,000
7	Shanghai	China	14,503,000	22	Istanbul	Turkey	9,712,000
8	Calcutta (Kolkata)	India	14,277,000	23	Seoul	Rep. of Korea	9,645,000
9	Jakarta	Indonesia	13,215,000	24	Chicago	US	8,814,000
10	Buenos Aires	Argentina	12,550,000	25	London	UK	8,505,000
11	Dhaka	Bangladesh	12,430,000	26	Guangzhou	China	8,425,000
12	Los Angeles–Long Beach–Santa Ana	US	12,298,000	27	Bogotá	Colombia	7,747,000
				28	Tehran	Iran	7,314,000
13	Karachi	Pakistan	11,608,000	29	Shenzhen	China	7,233,000
14	Rio de Janeiro	Brazil	11,469,000	30	Lima	Peru	7,186,000

Migration of Foreigners into Selected Countries

Percentages of foreign or foreign-born populations in selected Organisation for Economic Co-operation and Development countries. Source: <www.oecd.org>.

COUNTRY	FOREIGNERS AS % OF TOTAL POPULATION 2000	2004	COUNTRY	FOREIGNERS AS % OF TOTAL POPULATION 2000	2004
Luxembourg[1]	37.3	39.0	Denmark[1]	4.8	4.9
Australia[2]	23.0	23.6	UK[1]	4.0	4.9
Switzerland[1]	19.3	20.2	Norway[1]	4.0	4.6
New Zealand[2]	17.2	18.8	Spain[1]	2.2	4.6
Canada[2]	17.4	18.4	The Netherlands[1]	4.2	4.3
US[2]	11.0	12.8	Portugal[1]	2.1	4.3
Austria[1]	8.8	9.5	Czech Republic[1]	1.9	2.5
Germany[1]	8.9	8.9	Japan[1]	1.3	1.5
Belgium[1]	8.4	8.4	South Korea[1]	0.4	0.9
Ireland[1]	3.3	5.5	Italy[1]	2.4	N/A
Sweden[1]	5.4	5.1	Mexico[2]	0.5	N/A

N/A indicates data not available. [1]*Indicates foreign population.* [2]*Indicates foreign-born population.*

Persons of Concern Worldwide

The Office of the UN High Commissioner for Refugees (UNHCR) attempts to ease the plight of various "persons of concern," including refugees and asylum seekers. Sources: UNHCR Refugees by Numbers; UNHCR 2004 Global Refugee Trends; Global IDP Project.

Persons of Concern to UNHCR by Category (17 Jun 2005)

REGION	REFUGEES	ASYLUM SEEKERS	RETURNED REFUGEES	INTERNALLY DISPLACED PERSONS[1]	STATELESS AND OTHER	TOTAL
Asia and Pacific	836,725	20,247	10,263	386,104	341,414	1,594,753
Africa	2,748,365	198,848	329,710	1,233,927	34,758	4,548,308
Europe	2,317,817	285,030	18,971	1,767,199	1,152,899	5,541,916
North America	562,252	291,000	—	—	—	853,252
Latin America and Caribbean	36,190	8,109	89	2,000,000	26,350	2,070,738
Total	9,236,521	839,107	1,494,610	5,574,170	2,053,029	19,197,437

Total Number of Refugees (1 Jan of each year)

YEAR	REFUGEES	YEAR	REFUGEES
1996	14,860,600	2001	12,062,500
1997	13,317,400	2002	12,029,900
1998	11,966,200	2003	10,389,600
1999	11,429,700	2004	9,671,800
2000	11,625,700	2005	9,236,500

Origin of Major Refugee Populations[2] (1 Jan 2005)

COUNTRY OF ORIGIN	TOTAL	COUNTRY OF ORIGIN	TOTAL
Afghanistan	2,084,900	Vietnam	349,780
The Sudan	730,600	Iraq	311,800
Burundi	485,800	Azerbaijan	250,579
Dem. Rep. of the Congo	462,200	Serbia and Montenegro	236,999
Somalia	389,300	Bosnia and Herzegovina	229,339
Liberia	353,467	Angola	228,838

Destination of Major Refugee Populations[1] (estimates as of 1 Jan 2004)

COUNTRY OF ASYLUM	TOTAL	COUNTRY OF ASYLUM	TOTAL
Iran	1,045,976	China	299,375
Pakistan	960,617	United Kingdom	289,054
Germany	876,622	Serbia and Montenegro	276,683
Tanzania	602,088	Chad	259,880
United States	420,854	Uganda	250,482

Internally Displaced Persons (IDPs)

COUNTRY	TOTAL NUMBER	RECEIVING UNHCR ASSISTANCE
The Sudan	6,000,000	662,302
Colombia	1,580,396–3,410,041	2,000,000
Angola	40,000–340,000	—
Dem. Rep. of the Congo	2,330,000	—
Iraq	1,000,000+	—
Myanmar (Burma)	526,000	—
Indonesia	342,000–600,000	—
Turkey	350,000–1,000,000+	—
Afghanistan	167,000–200,000	159,549
Uganda	1,400,000	—
Côte d'Ivoire	500,000	38,039
India	600,000+	—
Azerbaijan	578,545	578,545
Sri Lanka	352,374	352,374
Burundi	170,000	—
Russia	339,000	334,796
Bosnia and Herzegovina	309,240	309,240

[1]Data include only those IDPs to whom UNHCR extends protection and/or assistance. [2]A separate mandate of the UN Relief and Works Agency for Palestine Refugees in the Near East (UNWRA) covers more than 4 million Palestinians. Palestinians outside of the UNWRA, such as those in Iraq and Libya, number 427,800.

Languages of the World

Most Widely Spoken Languages

Listing the languages spoken by more than 1% of humankind, this table enumerates speakers of each tongue as a primary or secondary language. Figures based on data from Linguasphere 2000. For more information visit <www.linguasphere.org>.

LANGUAGE	NUMBER OF SPEAKERS (MILLIONS)	% OF WORLD POPULATION (APPROXIMATE)	LANGUAGE FAMILY
English	1,000	16	Indo-European (Germanic)
Mandarin	1,000	16	Sino-Tibetan (Chinese)
Hindi/Urdu[1]	900	15	Indo-European (Indo-Aryan)
Spanish	450	7	Indo-European (Romance)
Russian/Belarusian	320	5	Indo-European (Slavic)
Arabic	250	4	Afro-Asiatic (Semitic)
Bengali/Sylhetti	250	4	Indo-European (Indo-Aryan)
Malay/Indonesian	200	3	Austronesian (Malayo-Polynesian)
Portuguese	200	3	Indo-European (Romance)
Japanese	130	2	isolated language
French	125	2	Indo-European (Romance)
German	125	2	Indo-European (Germanic)
Thai/Lao	90	1	Tai
Punjabi	85	1	Indo-European (Indo-Aryan)
Wu	85	1	Sino-Tibetan (Chinese)
Javanese	80	1	Austronesian (Malayo-Polynesian)
Marathi	80	1	Indo-European (Indo-Aryan)
Turkish/Azeri/Turkmen	80	1	Altaic (Turkic)
Korean	75	1	isolated language
Vietnamese	75	1	Mon-Khmer (Vietic)
Cantonese	70	1	Sino-Tibetan (Chinese)
Italian	70	1	Indo-European (Romance)
Tamil	70	1	Dravidian
Telugu	70	1	Dravidian
Ukrainian	65	1	Indo-European (Slavic)
Bhojpuri/Maithili	60	1	Indo-European (Indo-Aryan)
Persian/Tajik	60	1	Indo-European (Iranian)
Swahili	60	1	Afro-Asiatic (Niger-Congo)
Tagalog	60	1	Austronesian (Malayo-Polynesian)

[1]*Although Hindi and Urdu use different writing systems, these languages are branches of Hindustani and are orally mutually intelligible.*

English Neologisms

New entries from Merriam-Webster's Collegiate® Dictionary, Eleventh Edition (© 2007). The date in parentheses is the date of the word's earliest recorded use in English of the sense that the date precedes (not necessarily of the word's very earliest meaning in English).

agnolotti (1953): a pasta in the form of semicircular cases containing a filling (as of meat, cheese, or vegetables)

Bollywood (1976): the motion-picture industry in India

chaebol (1984): a family-controlled industrial conglomerate in South Korea

crunk (2000): a style of Southern rap music featuring repetitive chants and rapid dance rhythms

DVR (abbreviation): digital video recorder

flex-cuff (1981): a plastic strip that can be fastened as a restraint around a person's wrists or ankles

ginormous (c. 1948): extremely large: humongous

gray literature (1975): written material (as a report) that is not published commercially or is not generally accessible

hardscape (1984): structures (as fountains, benches, or gazebos) that are incorporated into a landscape

IED (abbreviation): improvised explosive device

microgreen (1998): a shoot of a standard salad plant (as celery or arugula)

nocebo (1961): a harmless substance that when taken by a patient is associated with harmful effects due to negative expectations or the psychological condition of the patient

perfect storm (1936): a critical or disastrous situation created by a powerful concurrence of factors

RPG (abbreviation): rocket-propelled grenade

smackdown (1997): 1: the act of knocking down or bringing down an opponent. 2: a contest in entertainment wrestling. 3: a decisive defeat. 4: a confrontation between rivals or competitors

snowboardcross (1997): a snowboard race that includes jumps and turns

speed dating (2000): an event at which each participant converses individually with all the prospective partners for a few minutes in order to select those with whom dates are desired

English Neologisms (continued)

sudoku (2004): a puzzle in which several numbers are to be filled into a 9×9 grid of squares so that every row, every column, and every 3×3 box contains the numbers 1 through 9

telenovela (1976): a soap opera produced in and televised in or from many Latin American countries

viewshed (1981): the natural environment that is visible from one or more viewing points

Scholarship

National Libraries of the World

The national libraries listed below are generally open to the public. National libraries are usually the primary repository for a nation's printed works. Sources: "National Libraries of the World: An Address List," IFLA Publications; *International Dictionary of Library Histories,* 2001, Fitzroy Dearborn Publishers.

LIBRARY	LOCATION	YEAR FOUNDED[1]	SPECIAL COLLECTIONS, ARCHIVES, PAPERS
Biblioteca Nacional de España	Madrid, Spain	1836	manuscripts, Miguel de Cervantes
Biblioteca Nacional de la República Argentina	Buenos Aires	1810	Arturo Frondizi
Biblioteca Nacional de México	Mexico City	1867	Jesuit works, early Mexican printing
Biblioteca Nacional de Portugal	Lisbon	1796	Luís de Camões, Desiderius Erasmus
Biblioteca Nacional de Venezuela	Caracas	1833	politics and diplomacy, Simón Bolívar
Biblioteca Nazionale Centrale di Firenze	Florence, Italy	1861	Reformation, Galileo Galilei
Biblioteca Nazionale Centrale di Roma	Rome, Italy	1876	Jesuit collections, Gabriele D'Annunzio
Biblioteka Narodowa	Warsaw, Poland	1928	engravings, music
Bibliothèque et Archives Nationales du Québec	Montreal, QC, Canada	2004	artists' books, maps
Bibliothèque Nationale de France	Paris	1461	Denis Diderot, Jean-Paul Sartre
British Library	London	1973[2]	Charles Dickens, George B. Shaw
Deutsche Nationalbibliothek Frankfurt am Main	Germany	2006	bibliographies, exile literature (1933–45)
Deutsche Nationalbibliothek Leipzig	Germany	2006	socialism, Anne-Frank-Shoah-Bibliothek
Fundação Biblioteca Nacional	Rio de Janeiro, Brazil	1810	botany, Latin American music
Jewish National and University Library	Jerusalem, Israel	1892	world Jewish history, Albert Einstein
Koninklijke Bibliotheek	The Hague, Netherlands	1798	Hugo Grotius, Constantijn Huygens
Library and Archives Canada	Ottawa	2004	hockey, portraits of Canadians
Library of Congress	Washington DC	1800	Americana, folk music, early motion pictures
National Agricultural Library	Beltsville MD	1962	research reports
National Diet Library[3]	Tokyo, Japan	1948	Japanese culture, Allied occupation
National Library of Australia	Canberra	1960	Asian and Pacific area
National Library of China[4]	Beijing	1909	art, early communism
National Library of Education	Washington DC	1994	research reports
National Library of India	Kolkata (Calcutta)	1903	rare journals of vernacular languages
National Library of Ireland	Dublin	1877	biography, Gaelic manuscripts
National Library of Medicine	Bethesda MD	1956	history of medicine
National Library of New Zealand[5]	Wellington	1965	European exploration, missionary activity
National Library of Pakistan	Islamabad	1993	manuscripts, censuses
National Library of the Philippines	Manila	1901	presidential papers
National Library of Russia[6]	St. Petersburg	1795	rare books, Russian history
National Library of Scotland	Edinburgh	1925	mountaineering, witchcraft

National Libraries of the World (continued)

LIBRARY	LOCATION	YEAR FOUNDED	SPECIAL COLLECTIONS, ARCHIVES, PAPERS
National Library of South Africa	Pretoria; Cape Town	1999	Africana, cookery
National Library of Wales	Aberystwyth	1907	publications of overseas Welsh settlements

[1]In present institutional form.   [2]Originally founded in 1753 as the British Museum Library.   [3]Kokuritsu Kokkai Toshokan.   [4]Zhongguo Guojia Tushuguan.   [5]Te Puna Matauranga o Aotearoa.   [6]Rossyskaya Natsionalnaya Biblioteka.

World Education Profile

This table provides comparative data about the education systems in 30 selected countries. Definitions as well as information gathering and reporting methods vary widely from country to country, so the statistics presented here are not always exactly comparable.

Compulsory education = the number of years of education and ages of pupils required by the system; **net enrollment ratio** = the actual number of children attending primary school or secondary school as a percentage of all children in the primary school or secondary school age group as defined by the country (number may exceed 100%); **gross enrollment ratio** for higher education = total enrollment in higher education, regardless of age, as a percentage of all persons of school-leaving age to five years thereafter; **student/teacher ratio** = number of pupils or students per teacher at each level; **expenditure** = total public expenditure on education as a percentage of GDP.

Sources: Britannica World Data, 2004; UNESCO Statistical Yearbook, 2004.

COUNTRY	YEAR	% LITERACY RATE OF THOSE 15 AND OLDER			COMPULSORY EDUCATION		ENROLLMENT RATIO (2001–02)			STUDENT/TEACHER RATIO (2001–02)			EXPENDITURE
		TOTAL	M	F	# YEARS	AGES	NET PRI.	NET SEC.	GROSS HIGHER	PRI.	SEC.	HIGHER[1]	
Africa													
Egypt	2000	55.3	66.6	43.8	8	6-13	90	81	—	22	17	—	—
Kenya	1999	81.5	88.3	74.8	8	6-13	70	24	3	32	—	—	6.2
Senegal	2000	37.3	47.3	27.6	6	7-12	58	—	—	49	27	25.0[2]	3.2
South Africa	2000	85.3	86.0	84.6	9	7-15	90	62[4]	15	37	30	22.8[3]	—
Asia													
China	2000	90.9	95.1	86.5	9	6-14	93[4]	—	13[4]	20[4]	—	7.8	—
India	2000	57.2	68.4	45.4	9	6-14	83[4]	—	11[4]	40[4]	—	17.5	4.1
Indonesia	2000	86.9	91.8	82.0	9	7-15	92	—	15	21	14	15.0	1.3
Iran	2000	76.3	83.2	69.3	5	6-10	87	—	20	24	29	14.3	5.0
Israel	2000	96.7	—	—	11	5-15	100	89	58	12	8	19.0	7.3
Japan	2002	100.0	100.0	100.0	10	6-15	100	100	49	20	14	18.9	3.6
Philippines	2000	95.3	95.1	95.5	7	6-12	93	56	31	35	38	—	3.2
Saudi Arabia	2000	80.1[5]	84.1	67.2	6	6-11	59	53	22	12	13	18.4	—
Thailand	2000	95.5	—	—	9	6-14	86	—	37	19	—	19.1	5.0
Turkey	2000	85.1	93.5	76.5	9	6-14	88	—	25	—	—	22.7	3.7
Europe													
France	1995	98.8	98.9	98.7	11	6-16	100[4]	92[4]	54[4]	19[4]	—	39.6	5.8
Germany	1998	100.0	100.0	100.0	13	6-18	83	88	48	14	14	11.2	4.6
Greece	2000	97.2	98.6	96.0	10	6-15	95[4]	85[4]	61[4]	13[4]	—	22.6	3.8
Italy	2000	98.4	98.9	98.1	9	6-14	100[4]	—	50[4]	11[4]	—	32.0	4.7
Poland	2000	99.8	99.8	99.8	9	7-15	98	91	58	15	17	14.9	5.4
Russia	1999	99.4	—	—	10	6-15	—	—	70	17	—	12.7	3.1
Sweden	2000	100.0	100.0	100.0	10	7-16	100	99	76	11	13	8.2	7.7
United Kingdom	1997	100.0[6]	100.0	100.0	12	5-16	100[4]	95[4]	59[4]	18[4]	—	20.4	—
Latin America													
Argentina	1999	96.7	96.8	96.7	10	5-14	100	81	56	20	12	—	4.6
Brazil	2000	86.7	85.5	85.3	8	7-14	97	72	18	23	19	11.2	4.0
Cuba	2000	96.4	96.9	96.8	9	6-14	96	83	27	14	12	5.3[6]	9.0
Mexico	2000	91.4	93.4	89.5	10	6-15	99	60	21	27	17	9.4	5.1
Peru	2000	89.9	94.7	85.3	11	6-16	100	66[4]	32	29	—	14.2	—
North America													
Canada	2002	100.0	—	—	11	6-16	100[4]	98[4]	59[4]	17[4]	—	14.4	5.2
United States	1998	95.5	95.7	95.3	12	6-17	93	85	81	15[4]	—	15.3	5.6
Oceania													
Australia	1998	99.5	—	—	10	6-15	96	88	65	—	—	20.6	4.6

[1]Latest data.   [2]Universities only.   [3]1994 data.   [4]2000–01.   [5]10 and over; non-Saudi population literate: 87.9%.   [6]Total population.

Religion

World Religions

At the beginning of the 21st century, one-third of the world's population is Christian, another one-fifth is Muslim, about one-eighth is Hindu, and one-eighth is nonreligious. Most people living in Europe and the Americas are Christian, while the vast majority of Muslims and Hindus are found in Asia. The plurality of Christians are Roman Catholics, of Muslims are Sunni, and of Hindus are Vaishnavites. Africa hosts slightly more Christians than Muslims, with much of the rest of the population listed as ethnic religionists, which describes followers of local, tribal, animistic, or shamanistic religions.

In addition to the predominant world religions (Christianity, Islam, Hinduism), there are small but noticeable percentages of Chinese folk religionists, Buddhists, other ethnic religionists, atheists, and new-religionists. Among the remaining distinct religions, Sikhs, Spiritists, Jews, Baha'is, Confucianists, Jains, Shintoists, Taoists, and Zoroastrians each make up less than one-half of one percent of religious adherents.

Christianity

Christianity traces its origins to the 1st century AD and to Jesus of Nazareth, whom it affirms to be the chosen one (Christ) of God. Geographically the most widely diffused of all faiths, it has a constituency of more than two billion people. Its largest groups are the Roman Catholic Church, the Eastern Orthodox churches, and the Protestant churches; in addition, there are several independent churches of Eastern Christianity as well as numerous sects throughout the world.

Christianity's sacred scripture is the Bible, particularly the New Testament. Its principal tenets are that Jesus is the son of God (the second person of the Holy Trinity), that God's love for the world is the essential component of his being, and that Jesus died to redeem humankind.

Christianity was originally a movement of Jews who accepted Jesus as the messiah, but the movement quickly became predominantly Gentile. Nearly all Christian churches have an ordained clergy, which lead group worship services and are viewed as intermediaries between the laity and the divine in some churches. Most Christian churches administer at least two sacraments: baptism and the Lord's Supper.

Islam

Islam is a religion that originated in the Middle East and was promulgated by the Prophet Muhammad in Arabia in the 7th century AD. The Arabic term islam, literally "surrender," illuminates the fundamental religious idea of Islam—that the believer (called a Muslim, from the active particle of islam) accepts "surrender to the will of Allah (Arabic: God)." Allah's will is made known through the sacred scriptures, the Qur'an (Koran), which Allah revealed to his messenger, Muhammad. In Islam, Muhammad is considered the last of a series of prophets (including Adam, Noah, Jesus, and others), and his message simultaneously consummates and abrogates the "revelations" attributed to earlier prophets.

The religious obligations of all Muslims are summed up in the Five Pillars of Islam. The fundamental concept in Islam is the Shari'ah, or Law, which embraces the total way of life commanded by God. Observant Muslims pray five times a day and join in community worship on Fridays at the mosque, where worship is led by an imam. Every believer is required to make a pilgrimage to Mecca, the holiest city, at least once in a lifetime, barring poverty or physical incapacity. The month of Ramadan is set aside for fasting. Jihad, considered a sixth pillar by some sects, is not accepted by most of the Islamic community as a call to wage physical war against unbelievers.

Divisions occurred early in Islam, brought about by disputes over the succession to the caliphate, resulting in various sects (Sunni, Shi'ite, Ismaili, Sufi). From the 19th century, the concept of the Islamic community inspired Muslim peoples to cast off Western colonial rule, and in the late 20th century fundamentalist movements toppled a number of secular Middle Eastern governments. A movement of African American Muslims emerged in the 20th century in the US.

Hinduism

Hinduism is the oldest of the world's major religions, dating back more than 3,000 years, though its present forms are of more recent origin. It evolved from Vedism, the religion of the Indo-European peoples who settled in India at the end of the 2nd millennium BC. The vast majority of the world's Hindus live in India, though significant minorities may be found in Pakistan and Sri Lanka, and smaller numbers live in Myanmar, South Africa, Trinidad, Europe, and the US.

Though the various Hindu sects each rely on their own set of scriptures, they all revere the ancient Vedas, which were brought to India by Aryan invaders after 1200 BC. The philosophical Vedic texts called the Upanishads explored the search for knowledge that would allow mankind to escape the cycle of reincarnation. Fundamental to Hinduism is the belief in a cosmic principle of ultimate reality called brahman, and its identity with the individual soul, or atman. All creatures go through a cycle of rebirth, or samsara, which can be broken only by spiritual self-realization, after which liberation, or moksha, is attained. The principle of karma determines a being's status within the cycle of rebirth.

The greatest Hindu deities are Brahma, Vishnu, and Shiva. The major sources of classical mythology are the Mahabharata (which includes the Bhagavadgita, the most important religious text of Hinduism), the Ramayana, and the Puranas. The hierarchical social structure of the caste system is important in Hinduism; it is supported by the principle of dharma. During the 20th century Hinduism was blended with Indian nationalism to become a potent political force.

Other major religions

Buddhism, a religion concentrated in Asia with some representation in North America, was founded by the Buddha (Siddhartha Gautama, or Gotama) in northeast India in the 5th century BC. By adhering to the Buddha's teachings, the believer can alleviate suffering through an understanding of the transitory nature of existence, in the hopes of achieving enlightenment. Distinct from Buddhism, **Shinto** is the
(continued on page 603)

The 2007 Annual Megacensus of Religions

David B. Barrett, Todd M. Johnson, and Peter F. Crossing

Each year since 1750, churches and religions around the world have generated increasing volumes of new statistical data. Much of this is uncovered in decennial governmental censuses: half the countries of the world have long asked their populations to state their religions, if any, and still do today. The other major source of data each year consists of the decentralized censuses undertaken by many religious headquarters. Almost all Christian denominations ask and answer each year statistical

Worldwide Adherents of All Religions, mid-2007

	AFRICA	ASIA	EUROPE	LATIN AMERICA
Christians	441,184,000	359,614,000	565,254,700	533,386,000
Affiliated Christians	415,932,000	353,986,000	540,826,000	527,382,000
Roman Catholics	155,246,000	127,074,000	274,865,000	472,317,000
Independents	96,011,000	189,463,000	24,252,000	46,013,000
Protestants	125,152,000	59,201,000	70,345,000	58,130,000
Orthodox	40,651,000	13,700,000	170,468,000	973,000
Anglicans	47,036,000	845,000	26,070,000	853,000
Marginal Christians	3,615,000	3,310,000	4,523,000	11,526,000
Doubly affiliated	−51,779,000	−39,607,000	−29,697,000	−62,430,000
Unaffiliated Christians	25,252,000	5,628,000	24,428,700	6,004,000
Muslims	378,135,700	961,961,000	39,691,800	1,777,000
Hindus	2,757,000	868,348,000	1,680,000	760,000
Chinese universists	37,500	384,206,000	309,000	183,000
Buddhists	158,000	379,080,000	1,775,000	743,000
Ethnoreligionists	113,605,000	145,997,000	1,152,000	3,733,000
Neoreligionists	123,000	103,548,000	380,000	800,000
Sikhs	62,900	21,701,000	478,000	6,600
Jews	129,000	5,718,000	1,840,000	971,000
Spiritists	3,200	2,000	139,000	13,193,000
Baha'is	2,135,000	3,677,000	139,000	891,000
Confucianists	300	6,373,000	18,000	800
Jains	82,400	5,173,000	0	0
Taoists	0	3,392,000	0	0
Shintoists	0	2,732,000	0	7,600
Zoroastrians	1,000	152,000	5,500	0
Other religionists	80,000	75,000	260,000	110,000
Nonreligious	6,246,000	615,877,000	94,750,000	17,092,000
Atheists	606,000	128,048,000	19,787,000	2,829,000
Total population	**945,346,000**	**3,995,674,000**	**727,659,000**	**576,483,000**

Continents. These follow current UN demographic terminology, which now divides the world into the six major areas shown above. See United Nations, *World Population Prospects: The 2004 Revision* (New York: UN, 2005), with populations of all continents, regions, and countries covering the period 1950–2050, with 100 variables for every country each year. Note that "Asia" includes the former Soviet Central Asian states, and "Europe" includes all of Russia eastward to the Pacific.

Countries. The last column enumerates sovereign and nonsovereign countries in which each religion or religious grouping has a numerically significant and organized following.

Adherents. As defined in the 1948 Universal Declaration of Human Rights, a person's religion is what he or she professes, confesses, or states that it is. Totals are enumerated for each of the world's 239 countries following the methodology of the *World Christian Encyclopedia*, 2nd ed. (2001), and *World Christian Trends* (2001), using recent censuses, polls, surveys, yearbooks, reports, Web sites, literature, and other data. See the World Christian Database <www.worldchristiandatabase.org> for more detail. Religions are ranked in order of worldwide size in mid-2007.

Alphabetical listing of religions

Atheists. Persons professing atheism, skepticism, disbelief, or irreligion, including the militantly antireligious (opposed to all religion). In the past two years, a flurry of books (Dawkins, Dennett, Harris, Hitchens, et al.) have outlined the Western philosophical and scientific basis for atheism. Ironically, the vast majority of atheists today are found in Asia (primarily Chinese communists).

Buddhists. 56% Mahayana, 38% Theravada (Hinayana), 6% Tantrayana (Lamaism).

Chinese universists. Followers of a unique complex of beliefs and practices that may include universism (yin/yang cosmology with dualities earth/heaven, evil/good, darkness/light), ancestor cult, Confucian ethics, divination, festivals, folk religion, goddess worship, household gods, local deities, mediums, metaphysics, monasteries, neo-Confucianism, popular religion, sacrifices, shamans, spirit writing, and Taoist and Buddhist elements.

Christians. Followers of Jesus Christ, enumerated here under **Affiliated Christians**, those affiliated with churches (church members, with names written on church rolls, usually total number of baptized persons including chil-

questions on major religious subjects. A third annual source is the total of 27,000 new books on the religious situation in each single country, as well as some 9,000 printed annual yearbooks or official handbooks. Together, these three major sources of data constitute a massive annual megacensus, though decentralized and uncoordinated. The two tables below combine all these data around religious affiliation. The first table summarizes worldwide adherents by reli-gion. The second goes into more detail for the United States of America. What might be surprising in these tables, especially in the highly secularized Western world, is the resiliency of religion around the world. Atheists and nonreligious, whom many predicted would dominate in the 21st century, are only 14% of the world's population—declining annually as a percentage. Details may not add to total given because of rounding.

NORTHERN AMERICA	OCEANIA	WORLD	%	NUMBER OF COUNTRIES
273,388,400	26,990,300	2,199,817,400	33.3	239
219,451,000	22,741,000	2,080,318,000	31.4	239
83,377,000	8,637,000	1,121,516,000	17.0	236
75,627,000	1,730,000	433,096,000	6.5	222
61,077,000	7,906,000	381,811,000	5.8	233
6,524,000	830,000	233,146,000	3.5	136
2,836,000	4,946,000	82,586,000	1.2	165
11,755,000	692,000	35,421,000	0.5	215
−21,745,000	−2,000,000	−207,258,000	−3.1	181
53,937,400	4,249,300	119,499,400	1.8	232
5,450,600	438,400	1,387,454,500	21.0	210
1,715,000	466,000	875,726,000	13.2	126
740,000	146,000	385,621,500	5.8	96
3,288,000	565,000	385,609,000	5.8	136
1,579,000	339,000	266,405,000	4.0	145
1,594,000	88,300	106,533,300	1.6	107
630,000	49,000	22,927,500	0.3	44
6,191,000	107,000	14,956,000	0.2	135
164,000	7,400	13,508,600	0.2	56
718,000	137,000	7,697,000	0.1	219
0	52,200	6,444,300	0.1	15
8,400	700	5,264,500	0.1	11
12,200	0	3,404,200	0.1	5
61,800	0	2,801,400	0.0	8
20,600	1,700	180,800	0.0	24
670,000	10,000	1,205,000	0.0	79
38,821,000	4,040,000	776,826,000	11.7	238
1,779,000	416,000	153,465,000	2.3	220
336,831,000	33,854,000	6,615,847,000	100.0	239

dren baptized, dedicated, or undedicated): total in 2007 being 2,080,318,000, shown above divided among the six standardized ecclesiastical blocs and with (negative and italicized) figures for those **Doubly affiliated** persons (all who are baptized members of two denominations); and **Unaffiliated Christians,** who are persons professing or confessing in censuses or polls to be Christians though not so affiliated. **Independents.** This term here denotes members of Christian churches and networks who regard themselves as postdenominationalist and neo-apostolic and thus independent of historic, mainstream, organized, institutionalized, confessional, denominationalist Christianity. **Marginal Christians.** Members of denominations who define themselves as Christians but who are on the margins of organized mainstream Christianity (e.g., Unitarians, Mormons, Jehovah's Witnesses, Christian Scientists, and Religious Scientists).

Confucianists. Non-Chinese followers of Confucius and Confucianism, mostly Koreans in Korea.

Ethnoreligionists. Followers of local, tribal, animistic, or shamanistic religions, with members restricted to one ethnic group.

Hindus. 68% Vaishnavites, 27% Shaivites, 2% neo-Hindus and reform Hindus.

Jews. Adherents of Judaism. For detailed data on "core" Jewish population, see the annual "World Jewish Populations" article in the American Jewish Committee's *American Jewish Year Book*.

Muslims. 84% Sunnites, 14% Shi'ites, 2% other schools.

Neoreligionists. Followers of Asian 20th-century neoreligions, neoreligious movements, radical new crisis religions, and non-Christian syncretistic mass religions.

Nonreligious. Persons professing no religion, nonbelievers, agnostics, freethinkers, uninterested, or dereligionized secularists indifferent to all religion but not militantly so.

Other religionists. Including a handful of religions, quasi-religions, pseudoreligions, parareligions, religious or mystic systems, and religious and semireligious brotherhoods of numerous varieties.

Total population. UN medium variant figures for mid-2007, as given in *World Population Prospects: The 2004 Revision*.

Religious Adherents in the United States of America, 1900–2005

For categories not described below, see notes to Worldwide Adherents of All Religions, pp. 600–601.

	1900	%	MID-1970	%	MID-1990	%
Christians	73,260,000	96.4	190,723,000	90.8	218,162,000	85.4
Affiliated Christians	54,425,000	71.6	152,874,000	72.8	175,327,000	68.6
Independents	5,850,000	7.7	35,666,000	17.0	66,900,000	26.2
Roman Catholics	10,775,000	14.2	48,305,000	23.0	56,500,000	22.1
Protestants	35,000,000	46.1	58,568,000	27.9	60,216,000	23.6
Marginal Christians	800,000	1.1	6,126,000	2.9	8,940,000	3.5
Orthodox	400,000	0.5	4,189,000	2.0	5,150,000	2.0
Anglicans	1,600,000	2.1	3,196,000	1.5	2,450,000	1.0
Doubly affiliated	*0*	*0.0*	*−3,176,000*	*−1.5*	*−24,829,000*	*−9.7*
Evangelicals	*32,068,000*	*42.2*	*35,248,000*	*16.8*	*38,400,000*	*15.0*
evangelicals	*11,000,000*	*14.5*	*45,500,000*	*21.7*	*90,656,000*	*35.5*
Unaffiliated Christians	18,835,000	24.8	37,849,000	18.0	42,835,000	16.8
Jews	1,500,000	2.0	6,700,000	3.2	5,535,000	2.2
Muslims	10,000	0.0	800,000	0.4	3,499,600	1.4
Black Muslims	0	0.0	200,000	0.1	1,250,000	0.5
Buddhists	30,000	0.0	200,000	0.1	1,880,000	0.7
Neoreligionists	10,000	0.0	560,000	0.3	1,155,000	0.5
Ethnoreligionists	100,000	0.1	70,000	0.0	780,000	0.3
Hindus	1,000	0.0	100,000	0.0	750,000	0.3
Baha'is	2,800	0.0	138,000	0.1	600,000	0.2
Sikhs	0	0.0	10,000	0.0	160,000	0.1
Spiritists	0	0.0	0	0.0	120,000	0.0
Chinese universists	70,000	0.1	90,000	0.0	76,000	0.0
Shintoists	0	0.0	0	0.0	50,000	0.0
Zoroastrians	0	0.0	0	0.0	14,400	0.0
Taoists	0	0.0	0	0.0	10,000	0.0
Jains	0	0.0	0	0.0	5,000	0.0
Other religionists	10,200	0.0	450,000	0.2	530,000	0.2
Nonreligious	1,000,000	1.3	10,070,000	4.8	21,442,000	8.4
Atheists	1,000	0.0	200,000	0.1	770,000	0.3
US population	**75,995,000**	**100.0**	**210,111,000**	**100.0**	**255,539,000**	**100.0**

Methodology. This table extracts and analyzes a microcosm of the world religion table. It depicts the United States, the country with the largest number of adherents to Christianity, the world's largest religion. Statistics at five points in time from 1900 to 2005 are presented. Each religion's **Annual Change** for 1990–2000 is also analyzed by **Natural** increase (births minus deaths, plus immigrants minus emigrants) per year and **Conversion** increase (new converts minus new defectors) per year, which together constitute the **Total** increase per year. **Rate** increase is then computed as a percentage per year.

Structure. Vertically the table lists 30 major religious categories (including nonreligious) in the US are listed with the largest (Christians) first. Indented names of groups in the "Adherents" column are subcategories of the groups above them and are also counted in these unindented totals, so they should not be added twice into the column total. Figures in italics draw adherents from all categories of Christians above and so cannot be added together with them. Figures for Christians are built upon detailed head counts by churches, often to the last digit. Totals are then rounded to the nearest 1,000. Because of rounding, the corresponding percentage figures may sometimes not total exactly 100%. Religions are ranked in order of size in 2005.

Christians. This means all persons who profess publicly to follow Jesus Christ as God and Savior. This category is subdivided into **Affiliated Christians** (church members) and **Unaffiliated** (nominal) **Christians** (professing Christians not affiliated with any church). See also the note on Christians to the world religion table. The first six lines under "Affiliated Christians" are ranked by size in 2005 of each of the 6 megablocs (Anglican, Independent, Marginal Christian, Orthodox, Protestant, and Roman Catholic).

Evangelicals/evangelicals. These two designations—italicized and enumerated separately here—cut across all of the six Christian traditions or ecclesiastical blocs listed above and should be considered separately from them. The **Evangelicals** (capital *E*) are mainly Protestant churches, agencies, and individuals that call themselves by this term (for example, members of the National Association of Evangelicals); they usually emphasize 5 or more of 7, 9, or 21 fundamental doctrines (salvation by faith, personal acceptance, verbal inspiration of Scripture, depravity of man, Virgin Birth, miracles of Christ, atonement, evangelism, Second Advent, et al.). The **evangelicals** (lowercase e) are Christians of evangelical conviction from all traditions who are committed to the evangel (gospel) and involved in personal witness and mission in the world.

Jews. Core Jewish population relating to Judaism, excluding Jewish persons professing a different religion.
Other categories. Definitions are as given under the world religion table.

MID-2000	%	MID-2005	%	ANNUAL CHANGE, 1990–2000			
				NATURAL	CONVERSION	TOTAL	RATE (%)
234,666,700	82.6	243,422,700	81.6	2,322,100	−570,900	1,751,200	0.74
187,706,000	66.1	194,828,000	65.3	1,857,400	−433,000	1,424,400	0.75
68,606,000	24.1	72,441,000	24.3	678,900	88,100	767,000	1.09
62,970,000	22.2	67,902,000	22.8	623,100	363,300	986,400	1.52
57,697,000	20.3	57,498,000	19.3	570,900	−610,700	−39,800	−0.07
10,197,000	3.6	10,908,000	3.7	100,900	41,300	142,200	1.36
5,266,000	1.9	5,612,000	1.9	52,100	17,100	69,200	1.28
2,300,000	0.8	2,248,000	0.8	22,800	−33,200	−10,400	−0.46
−19,330,000	−6.8	−21,781,000	−7.3	−191,300	−298,900	−490,200	2.42
40,325,000	14.2	41,105,000	13.8	399,000	−243,000	156,000	0.38
95,900,000	33.7	101,034,000	33.9	949,000	77,800	1,026,800	1.05
46,960,700	16.5	48,594,700	16.3	464,700	−137,900	326,800	0.69
5,642,000	2.0	5,729,000	1.9	55,800	−38,400	17,400	0.31
4,322,000	1.5	4,760,200	1.6	42,800	44,800	87,600	1.95
1,650,000	0.6	1,850,000	0.6	16,300	23,700	40,000	2.31
2,587,000	0.9	2,795,000	0.9	25,600	16,000	41,600	1.56
1,414,000	0.5	1,490,000	0.5	14,000	1,200	15,200	1.05
1,333,000	0.5	1,416,000	0.5	13,200	3,400	16,600	1.22
1,235,000	0.4	1,330,000	0.4	12,200	6,800	19,000	1.49
625,000	0.2	669,000	0.2	6,200	2,600	8,800	1.37
239,000	0.1	268,000	0.1	2,400	3,400	5,800	2.32
141,000	0.0	148,000	0.0	1,400	0	1,400	0.97
80,000	0.0	86,200	0.0	800	400	1,200	1.50
57,400	0.0	60,200	0.0	600	0	600	0.96
16,100	0.0	16,900	0.0	200	0	200	0.97
11,400	0.0	11,900	0.0	100	0	100	0.86
7,400	0.0	7,900	0.0	100	0	100	1.32
577,000	0.2	600,000	0.2	5,700	−1,100	4,600	0.78
30,055,000	10.6	34,242,000	11.5	297,400	540,000	837,400	2.64
1,145,000	0.4	1,160,000	0.4	11,300	−8,300	3,000	0.26
284,154,000	**100.0**	**298,213,000**	**100.0**	**2,812,000**	**0**	**2,812,000**	**0.97**

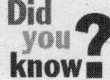

Did you know? The first sale of a military airplane was made on 8 Feb 1908, when Orville and Wilbur Wright contracted to supply one Wright Model A flyer to the US Army Signal Corps, plus a $5,000 bonus should it exceed the speed requirement of 40 miles (65 km) per hour. The next year the plane completed its trial flights and met the condition for the bonus.

World Religions (continued)

(continued from page 599)
indigenous religion of Japan and has no founder, sacred scriptures, or fixed dogmas. Also based in Asia, **Chinese folk religionists** are followers of local deities and engage in ancestor worship and divination. They also adhere to Confucian ethics, though statistically **Confucianists** are categorized as non-Chinese (mostly Korean) followers of Confucius, a Chinese philosopher of the 6th century BC. Confucianism is not an organized religion as much as it is a political and social ideology. Also in the Confucian tradition, a **Taoist** seeks the correct path of human conduct and an understanding of the Absolute Tao.

Zoroastrianism is an ancient pre-Islamic religion of Iran that survives there and in India. It was founded by the Iranian prophet Zoroaster in the 6th century BC and has both monotheistic and dualistic features. Also founded in Iran is the **Baha'i** faith, created as a universal religion in the mid-19th century AD for the worship of Baha' Ullah and his forerunner, the Bab; it has no priesthood or formal sacraments and is chiefly concerned with social ethics.

Jainism was founded in India in the 6th century BC by Vardhamana, or Mahavira, a monastic reformer in the Vedic, or early Hindu, tradition. Jainism emphasizes a path to spiritual purity and enlightenment through a disciplined mode of life founded upon the tradition of ahimsa, nonviolence to all living creatures.

Sikhism is a monotheistic religion founded in the late 15th century AD in India, historically associated with the Punjab region, though it includes representation in Europe and North America.

Judaism, like Christianity and Islam, is monotheistic and maintains the manifestation of God in human events, particularly through Moses in the Torah at Mount Sinai in the 13th century BCE. Jews, who come together in both religious and ethnic communities, have worldwide representation, with the greatest concentration in North America and the Middle East.

New-Religionists are followers of New Religious movements and non-Christian syncretistic mass religions.

Chronological List of Popes

According to Roman Catholic doctrine, the pope is the successor of **St. Peter**, who was head of the Apostles. The pope thus is seen to have full and supreme power of jurisdiction over the universal church in matters of faith and morals, as well as in church discipline and government. Until the 4th century, the popes were usually known only as bishops of Rome. From 1309–77, the popes' seat was at Avignon, France. In the table, **antipopes**, who opposed the legitimately elected bishop of Rome and endeavored to secure the papal throne, are listed in italics. The elections of several antipopes are greatly obscured by incomplete or biased records, and at times even their contemporaries could not decide who was the true pope. It is impossible, therefore, to establish an absolutely definitive list of antipopes.

POPE	REIGN	POPE	REIGN	POPE	REIGN
Peter	?–c. 64	Anastasius II	496–498	Valentine	827
Linus	c. 67–76/79	Symmachus	498–514	Gregory IV	827–844
Anacletus	76–88 or 79–91	*Laurentius*	498, 501– c. 505/507	*John*	844
Clement I	88–97 or 92–101	Hormisdas	514–523	Sergius II	844–847
Evaristus	c. 97–c. 107	John I	523–526	Leo IV	847–855
Alexander I	105–115 or 109–119	Felix IV (or III)[1]	526–530	Benedict III	855–858
Sixtus I	c. 115–c. 125	*Dioscorus*	530	*Anastasius*	855
Telesphorus	c. 125–c. 136	Boniface II	530–532	*(Anastasius the Librarian)*	
Hyginus	c. 136–c. 140	John II	533–535	Nicholas I	858–867
Pius I	c. 140–155	Agapetus I	535–536	Adrian II	867–872
Anicetus	c. 155–c. 166	Silverius	536–537	John VIII	872–882
Soter	c. 166–c. 175	Vigilius	537–555	Marinus I	882–884
Eleutherius	c. 175–189	Pelagius I	556–561	Adrian III	884–885
Victor I	c. 189–199	John III	561–574	Stephen V (or VI)[2]	885–891
Zephyrinus	c. 199–217	Benedict I	575–579	Formosus	891–896
Calixtus I (Callistus)	217?–222	Pelagius II	579–590	Boniface VI	896
Hippolytus	217, 218–235	Gregory I	590–604	Stephen VI (or VII)[2]	896
Urban I	222–230	Sabinian	604–606	Romanus	897
Pontian	230–235	Boniface III	604	Theodore II	897
Anterus	235–236	Boniface IV	608–615	John IX	898–900
Fabian	236–250	Deusdedit (Adeodatus I)	615–618	Benedict IV	900
Cornelius	251–253	Boniface V	619–625	Leo V	903
Novatian	251	Honorius I	625–638	*Christopher*	903–904
Lucius I	253–254	Severinus	640	Sergius III	904–911
Stephen I	254–257	John IV	640–642	Anastasius III	911–913
Sixtus II	257–258	Theodore I	642–649	Lando	913–914
Dionysius	259–268	Martin I	649–655	John X	914–928
Felix I	269–274	Eugenius I	654–657	Leo VI	928
Eutychian	275–283	Vitalian	657–672	Stephen VII (or VIII)[2]	929–931
Gaius	283–296	Adeodatus II	672–676	John XI	931–935
Marcellinus	291/296–304	Donus	676–678	Leo VII	936–939
Marcellus I	308–309	Agatho	678–681	Stephen VIII (or IX)[2]	939–942
Eusebius	309/310	Leo II	682–683	Marinus II	942–946
Miltiades (Melchiades)	311–314	Benedict II	684–685	Agapetus II	946–955
Sylvester I	314–335	John V	685–686	John XII	955–964
Mark	336	Conon	686–687	Leo VIII[3]	963–965
Julius I	337–352	Sergius I	687–701	Benedict V[3]	964–966?
Liberius	352–366	*Theodore*	687	John XIII	965–972
Felix (II)	355–358	*Paschal*	687	Benedict VI	973–974
Damasus I	366–384	John VI	701–705	*Boniface VII (1st time)*	974
Ursinus	366–367	John VII	705–707	Benedict VII	974–983
Siricius	384–399	Sisinnius	708	John XIV	983–984
Anastasius I	399–401	Constantine	708–715	*Boniface VII (2nd time)*	984–985
Innocent I	401–417	Gregory II	715–731	John XV (or XVI)[4]	985–996
Zosimus	417–418	Gregory III	731–741	Gregory V	996–999
Boniface I	418–422	Zacharias (Zachary)	741–752	*John XVI (or XVII)[4]*	997–998
Eulalius	418–419	Stephen (II)[2]	752	Sylvester II	999–1003
Celestine I	422–432	Stephen II (or III)[2]	752–757	John XVII (or XVIII)[4]	1003
Sixtus III	432–440	Paul I	757–767	John XVIII (or XIX)[4]	1004–09
Leo I	440–461	*Constantine (II)*	767–768	Sergius IV	1009–12
Hilary	461–468	*Philip*	768	*Gregory (VI)*	1012
Simplicius	468–483	Stephen III (or IV)[2]	768–772	Benedict VIII	1012–24
Felix III (or II)[1]	483–492	Adrian I	772–795	John XIX (or XX)[4]	1024–32
Gelasius I	492–496	Leo III	795–816	Benedict IX (1st time)	1032–44
		Stephen IV (or V)[2]	816–817	Sylvester III	1045
		Paschal I	817–824		
		Eugenius II	824–827		

Chronological List of Popes (continued)

POPE	REIGN	POPE	REIGN	POPE	REIGN
Benedict IX	1045	Clement IV	1265–68	Innocent VIII	1484–92
(2nd time)		Gregory X	1271–76	Alexander VI	1492–1503
Gregory VI	1045–46	Innocent V	1276	Pius III	1503
Clement II	1046–47	Adrian V	1276	Julius II	1503–13
Benedict IX	1047–48	John XXI[4]	1276–77	Leo X	1513–21
(3rd time)		Nicholas III	1277–80	Adrian VI	1522–23
Damasus II	1048	Martin IV[5]	1281–85	Clement VII	1523–34
Leo IX	1049–54	Honorius IV	1285–87	Paul III	1534–49
Victor II	1055–57	Nicholas IV	1288–92	Julius III	1550–55
Stephen IX (or X)[2]	1057–58	Celestine V	1294	Marcellus II	1555
Benedict X	1058–59	Boniface VIII	1294–1303	Paul IV	1555–59
Nicholas II	1059–61	Benedict XI	1303–04	Pius IV	1559–65
Alexander II	1061–73	Clement V (at	1305–14	Pius V	1566–72
Honorius (II)	1061–72	Avignon from		Gregory XIII	1572–85
Gregory VII	1073–85	1309)		Sixtus V	1585–90
Clement (III)	1080–1100	John XXII[4]	1316–34	Urban VII	1590
Victor III	1086–87	(at Avignon)		Gregory XIV	1590–91
Urban II	1088–99	Nicholas (V)	1328–30	Innocent IX	1591
Paschal II	1099–1118	(at Rome)		Clement VIII	1592–1605
Theodoric	1100–02	Benedict XII	1334–42	Leo XI	1605
Albert (Aleric)	1102	(at Avignon)		Paul V	1605–21
Sylvester (IV)	1105–11	Clement VI	1342–52	Gregory XV	1621–23
Gelasius II	1118–19	(at Avignon)		Urban VIII	1623–44
Gregory (VIII)	1118–21	Innocent VI	1352–62	Innocent X	1644–55
Calixtus II	1119–24	(at Avignon)		Alexander VII	1655–67
(Callistus)		Urban V	1362–70	Clement IX	1667–69
Honorius II	1124–30	(at Avignon)		Clement X	1670–76
Celestine (II)	1124	Gregory XI	1370–78	Innocent XI	1676–89
Innocent II	1130–43	(at Avignon, then		Alexander VIII	1689–91
Anacletus (II)	1130–38	Rome from 1377)		Innocent XII	1691–1700
Victor (IV)	1138	Urban VI	1378–89	Clement XI	1700–21
Celestine II	1143–44	Clement (VII)	1378–94	Innocent XIII	1721–24
Lucius II	1144–45	(at Avignon)		Benedict XIII	1724–30
Eugenius III	1145–53	Boniface IX	1389–1404	Clement XII	1730–40
Anastasius IV	1153–54	Benedict (XIII)	1394–1423	Benedict XIV	1740–58
Adrian IV	1154–59	(at Avignon)		Clement XIII	1758–69
Alexander III	1159–81	Innocent VII	1404–06	Clement XIV	1769–74
Victor (IV)	1159–64	Gregory XII	1406–15	Pius VI	1775–99
Paschal (III)	1164–68	Alexander (V)	1409–10	Pius VII	1800–23
Calixtus (III)	1168–78	(at Bologna)		Leo XII	1823–29
Innocent (III)	1179–80	John (XXIII)	1410–15	Pius VIII	1829–30
Lucius II	1181–85	(at Bologna)		Gregory XVI	1831–46
Urban III	1185–87	Martin V[5]	1417–31	Pius IX	1846–78
Gregory VIII	1187	Clement (VIII)	1423–29	Leo XIII	1878–1903
Clement III	1187–91	Eugenius IV	1431–47	Pius X	1903–14
Celestine III	1191–98	Felix (V) (Amadeus	1439–49	Benedict XV	1914–22
Innocent III	1198–1216	VIII of Savoy)		Pius XI	1922–39
Honorius III	1216–27	Nicholas V	1447–55	Pius XII	1939–58
Gregory IX	1227–41	Calixtus III	1455–58	John XXIII	1958–63
Celestine IV	1241	(Callistus)		Paul VI	1963–78
Innocent IV	1243–54	Pius II	1458–64	John Paul I	1978
Alexander IV	1254–61	Paul II	1464–71	John Paul II	1978–2005
Urban IV	1261–64	Sixtus IV	1471–84	Benedict XVI	2005–

[1]The higher number is used if Felix (II), who reigned from 355 to 358 and is ordinarily classed as an antipope, is counted as a pope. [2]Though elected on 23 Mar 752, Stephen (II) died two days later before he could be consecrated and thus is ordinarily not counted. The issue has made the numbering of subsequent Stephens somewhat irregular. [3]Either Leo VIII or Benedict V may be considered an antipope. [4]A confusion in the numbering of popes named John after John XIV (reigned 983–984) resulted because some 11th-century historians mistakenly believed that there had been a pope named John between antipope Boniface VII and the true John XV (reigned 985–996). Therefore they mistakenly numbered the real popes John XV to XIX as John XVI to XX. These popes have since customarily been renumbered XV to XIX, but John XXI and John XXII continue to bear numbers that they themselves formally adopted on the assumption that there had indeed been 20 Johns before them. In current numbering there thus exists no pope by the name of John XX. [5]In the 13th century the papal chancery misread the names of the two popes Marinus as Martin, and as a result of this error Simon de Brie in 1281 assumed the name of Pope Martin IV instead of Martin II. The enumeration has not been corrected, and thus there exist no Martin II and Martin III.

Law & Crime

International Terrorist Organizations

"Terrorism" is a subjective term. The list of organizations included here is that of the US Department of State, issued on 11 Oct 2005. The list is updated periodically.

Abu Nidal Organization (ANO) (Fatah Revolutionary Council, Arab Revolutionary Brigades, Black September, Revolutionary Organization of Socialist Muslims)
  Founded in 1974 as splinter group from PLO; led by Sabri al-Banna.
  country or region of operation: Middle East, primarily Iraq and Lebanon; has also operated in Asia and Europe
  primary goals: elimination of Israel, establishment of Palestinian state
Abu Sayyaf Group (ASG)
  Founded in early 1990s as splinter group from Moro National Liberation Front by Abdurajak Abubakar Janjalani; mainly made up of semiautonomous factions.
  country or region of operation: the Philippines, Malaysia
  primary goals: establishment of independent Islamic state in southern Philippines
Ansar al-Islam (Partisans of Islam)
  Founded in 2001, an offshoot of the Islamic Movement in Iraqi Kurdistan; led by Najmeddin Faraj Ahmed, aka Mullah Krekar (currently in custody in Norway awaiting deportation to Iraq).
  country or region of operation: Iraq
  primary goals: establishment of an Islamic state in the Kurdish areas of northern Iraq, expulsion of Operation Iraqi Freedom (OIF) coalition from Iraq
al-Aqsa Martyrs Brigades
  Founded in 2000 as an offshoot of Fatah; diffuse cell-based leadership structure.
  country or region of operation: Gaza Strip, West Bank, Israel
  primary goals: drive Israeli forces out of the West Bank and Gaza Strip, establish a Palestinian state with Jerusalem as its capital
Armed Islamic Group (GIA)
  Founded in 1992; leadership uncertain; fewer than 50 active members thought to be at large.
  country or region of operation: Algeria
  primary goals: replacement of secular Algerian government with an Islamic state
Asbat al-Ansar
  Founded in the late 1980s, a splinter faction of Muslim fighters in Lebanon's civil war; led by Abou Mahjan, aka Abdel Karim as-Saadi.
  country or region of operation: Lebanon
  primary goals: replacement of secular Lebanese government with an Islamic state based on the ancient caliphate system of government
Aum Shinrikyo (Aum Supreme Truth, Aleph)
  Founded in 1987 by Shoko Asahara; led by Fumihiro Joyu.
  country or region of operation: Japan
  primary goals: takeover of Japan and the world
Basque Fatherland and Liberty (ETA) (Euzkadi Ta Askatasuna)
  Founded in 1959; allegedly led by Mikel Albizu Iriarte, aka Mikel Antza.
  country or region of operation: Basque autonomous regions of northern Spain and southwestern France
  primary goals: establishment of independent Basque state based on Marxism
Communist Party of the Philippines/New People's Army (CPP/NPA)
  Founded in 1969 as a Maoist successor to the pro-Soviet Partido Komunista Pilipinas; led from exile by José María Sisón.
  country or region of operation: the Philippines
  primary goals: overthrow of the Philippine government
Continuity Irish Republican Army (CIRA)
  Founded in 1994 as a splinter group of Irish Republican Army (IRA) after the latter declared its first cease-fire.
  country or region of operation: Northern Ireland, Irish Republic
  primary goals: removal of British forces from Northern Ireland
Hamas (Islamic Resistance Movement)
  Founded in 1987 by Sheikh Ahmed Yasin as offshoot of Muslim Brotherhood; led by Khalid Meshal.
  country or region of operation: Gaza Strip, West Bank, Israel; also present throughout Middle East
  primary goals: elimination of Israel, establishment of Islamic Palestinian state
Harakat ul-Mujahidin (HUM) (Movement of Holy Warriors)
  Founded in mid-1980s or early 1990s; led by Farooq Kashmiri.
  country or region of operation: the Kashmir region of Pakistan and India
  primary goals: to make Kashmir part of an Islamic state
Hezbollah (Party of God) (Islamic Jihad, Revolutionary Justice Organization, Organization of the Oppressed on Earth, Islamic Jihad for the Liberation of Palestine)
  Founded in 1982; governed by the Majlis al-Shura (Consultative Council) led by Hassan Nasrallah; spiritual leader Sheikh Muhammad Hussein Fadlallah.
  country or region of operation: Lebanon; also has cells worldwide

International Terrorist Organizations (continued)

primary goals: establishment of Islamic rule in Lebanon, elimination of Israel, liberation of occupied Arab lands

Islamic Jihad Group (IJG)
Founded in 2004; offshoot of Islamic Movement of Uzbekistan (IMU).
country or region of operation: Central Asia
primary goals: replacement of secular Uzbekistan government with an Islamic state

Islamic Movement of Uzbekistan (IMU)
Founded in 1996; led by Tohir Yoldashev.
country or region of operation: Central and South Asia, primarily Uzbekistan, Tajikistan, Kyrgyzstan, Afghanistan, Iran, and Pakistan
primary goals: replacement of secular Uzbekistan government with an Islamic state

Jaish-e-Mohammed (Army of Muhammad)
Founded in 2000 as a spin-off from Harakat ul-Mujahidin; led by Maulana Masood Azhar.
country or region of operation: South Asia, primarily Pakistan and India
primary goals: establishment of Pakistani control over India-administered Kashmir

al-Jamaʻa al-Islamiya (Islamic Group, IG)
Founded late 1970s; loosely organized in two factions led by Mustafa Hamza (currently in custody in Egypt) and Rifai Taha Musa; spiritual leader Sheikh Umar Abd al-Rahman.
country or region of operation: Egypt; also operates in several countries worldwide
primary goals: replacement of Egyptian government with an Islamic state

Jemaah Islamiya (JI)
Founded in the mid-1990s as a successor to Darul Islam; led by Abu Bakar Baasyir.
country or region of operation: Southeast Asia, particularly Indonesia, Singapore, and Malaysia
primary goals: establishment of a pan-Islamic state in Southeast Asia

al-Jihad (Egyptian Islamic Jihad, Jihad Group, Islamic Jihad)
Founded late 1970s by Ayman al-Zawahiri; merged with al-Qaeda in 2001.
country or region of operation: Egypt and other countries, including Yemen, Afghanistan, Pakistan, Lebanon, and Great Britain; activities now centered mainly outside Egypt
primary goals: replacement of Egyptian government with an Islamic state, attacks on US and Israeli interests

Kahane Chai (Kach)
Kach founded in 1971 by Meir Kahane; Kahane Chai founded as follow-up group by Binyamin Kahane after Meir's assassination in 1990; Binyamin Kahane assassinated in 2000.
country or region of operation: Israel, West Bank
primary goals: expansion of Israel, removal of Palestinians

Kongra-Gel (KGK, formerly Kurdistan Workers Party, PKK, KADEK)
Founded in 1974; led by Abdullah Ocalan (imprisoned since 1999).
country or region of operation: Turkey; also operates in Europe and the Middle East
primary goals: establishment of independent Kurdish state

Lashkar-e Tayyiba (LT, Army of the Righteous)
Founded in 1990 as the military arm of Markaz-ud-Dawa-wal-Irshad (MDI), a Pakistani-based Islamic fundamentalist organization; led by Abdul Wahid Kashmiri.
country or region of operation: South Asia, primarily Pakistan and India
primary goals: establishment of Pakistani control over India-administered Kashmir, creation of a pan-Islamic state in Central Asia

Lashkar I Jhangvi
Founded in 1996 as an offshoot of the Sipah-e Sahaba (the Army of Muhammad's Companions); decentralized leadership structure.
country or region of operation: Pakistan
primary goals: replacement of the Pakistani government with an Islamic state

Liberation Tigers of Tamil Eelam (LTTE)
Founded in 1976; led by Velupillai Prabhakaran.
country or region of operation: Sri Lanka
primary goals: establishment of an independent Tamil state

Libyan Islamic Fighting Group (LIFG)
Founded in 1995 among Libyans who had fought against Soviet forces in Afghanistan; led by Anas Sebai.
country or region of operation: Libya, various Middle Eastern and European countries
primary goals: overthrow of the government of Libyan leader Muammar al-Qaddafi

Moroccan Islamic Combatant Group (GICM)
Founded in the 1990s as an offshoot of the Moroccan organization Shabiba Islamiya (Islamic Youth).
country or region of operation: Afghanistan, Belgium, Denmark, Egypt, France, Morocco, Spain, Turkey, United Kingdom
primary goals: creation of an Islamic state in Morocco

Mujahedin-e Khalq Organization (MEK) (National Liberation Army of Iran [NLA, the militant wing], People's Mujahidin of Iran [PMOI], National Council of Resistance [NCR], Muslim Iranian Student's Society [front organization to garner financial support])
Founded 1960s; led by Maryam and Masud Rajavi.
country or region of operation: Iran, Iraq
primary goals: establishment of secular government in Iran

International Terrorist Organizations (continued)

National Liberation Army (ELN)
Founded in 1965; led by Nicolas Rodríguez Bautista.
country or region of operation: Colombia
primary goals: replacement of ruling Colombian government with Marxist state

Palestine Liberation Front (PLF)
Founded in mid-1970s as splinter group from PFLP–GC.
country or region of operation: Israel, Iraq
primary goals: elimination of Israel, establishment of Palestinian state

Palestinian Islamic Jihad (PIJ)
Founded in 1970s; most active faction led by Ramadan Shallah.
country or region of operation: Israel, West Bank, Gaza Strip; also elsewhere in Middle East, primarily Lebanon and Syria
primary goals: elimination of Israel, establishment of Islamic Palestinian state

Popular Front for the Liberation of Palestine (PFLP)
Founded as part of PLO in 1967 by George Habash (discontinued PLO participation in 1993); led by Ahmed Sadat (imprisoned by the Palestinian Authority since 2002).
country or region of operation: Syria, Lebanon, Israel, West Bank, Gaza Strip
primary goals: promotion of national unity and revitalization of PLO, opposition to peace negotiations with Israel

Popular Front for the Liberation of Palestine–General Command (PFLP–GC)
Founded in 1968 as splinter group from PFLP; led by Ahmad Jabril.
country or region of operation: Syria, Lebanon, Israel, West Bank, Gaza Strip
primary goals: opposition to PLO and to peace negotiations with Israel

al-Qaeda
Founded in late 1980s; established and led by Osama bin Laden.
country or region of operation: worldwide
primary goals: establishment of worldwide Islamic rule, overthrow of non-Islamic governments, expulsion of Western influences from Muslim states, killing of US citizens

al-Qaeda Organization in the Islamic Maghreb (formerly Salafist Group for Call and Combat, GSPC)
Founded in 1996 as a splinter of the Armed Islamic Group; led by Abou Mossaab Abdelouadoud.
country or region of operation: primarily Algeria, with significant activity elsewhere in North Africa and in Europe
primary goals: replacement of the Algerian government with an Islamic state

Real IRA (True IRA)
Founded in 1998 as splinter group of Irish Republican Army (IRA); led by Michael "Mickey" McKevitt (imprisoned since 2001).
country or region of operation: Northern Ireland; also elsewhere in Great Britain and in Ireland
primary goals: removal of British forces from Northern Ireland, unification of Ireland

Revolutionary Armed Forces of Colombia (FARC)
Founded in 1964 as military branch of Colombian Communist Party; governed by group led by Manuel Marulanda and including Jorge Briceno and five others.
country or region of operation: Colombia; also some operations in Venezuela, Ecuador, and Panama
primary goals: replacement of ruling Colombian government with Marxist state

Revolutionary Nuclei (Revolutionary Cells)
Founded in 1995 as offshoot of or successor to Revolutionary People's Struggle (ELA).
country or region of operation: Greece, primarily Athens
primary goals: elimination of US military bases in Greece, opposition to capitalism and NATO/EU membership

Revolutionary Organization 17 November
Founded in 1975; relatively small group operating secretly, allegedly led by Alexandros Giotopoulos (imprisoned in Greece since 2002).
country or region of operation: Greece, primarily Athens
primary goals: elimination of US military bases in Greece, removal of Turkish forces from Cyprus, opposition to capitalism and NATO/EU membership

Revolutionary People's Liberation Party/Front (DHKP/C) (Devrimci Sol, Revolutionary Left, Dev Sol)
Founded in 1978 as splinter group from Turkish People's Liberation Party/Front; led by Dursun Karatas.
country or region of operation: Turkey, primarily Istanbul
primary goals: promotion of Marxism, opposition to US and NATO

Shining Path (Sendero Luminoso, SL)
Founded late 1960s by Abimael Guzman; led by Macario Ala.
country or region of operation: Peru, primarily rural areas
primary goals: replacement of Peruvian government with communist state, opposition to influence by foreign governments

Tanzim Qaidat al-Jihad fi Bilad al-Rafidayn (QJBR) (al-Qaeda in Iraq) (formerly Jamaat al-Tawhid waal-Jihad, JTJ, al-Zarqawi Network)
Founded April 2004 by Abu Musab al-Zarqawi shortly after the commencement of OIF; adopted current name October 2004 after merging with Osama bin Laden's al-Qaeda.
country or region of operation: Iraq
primary goals: expulsion of OIF coalition from Iraq, establishment of Islamic state in Iraq

International Terrorist Organizations (continued)

United Self-Defense Forces of Colombia (Autodefensas Unidas de Colombia, AUC)
Founded in 1997 as umbrella organization of paramilitary groups; led by Carlos Castaño.
country or region of operation: Colombia
primary goals: opposition to and defense against leftist guerrilla groups

Did you know? The Kiwi is the national bird and symbol of New Zealand. It is the best-known of four flightless birds that are native to that country. The kiwi as a symbol first appeared in military badges of New Zealand soldiers sent overseas in the late 19th century. It became a household term internationally after the Kiwi Shoe Polish was launched in the early 20th century.

Military Affairs

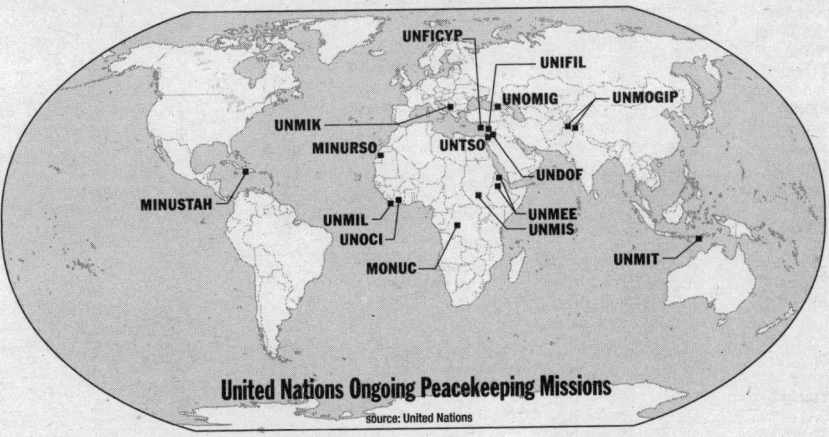

United Nations Ongoing Peacekeeping Missions

source: United Nations

MINURSO	United Nations Mission for the Referendum in Western Sahara—since April 1991 (226)[1]
MINUSTAH	United Nations Stabilization Mission in Haiti—since June 2004 (7,050)[2]
MONUC	United Nations Organization Mission in the Democratic Republic of the Congo—since November 1999 (17,321)[3]
UNDOF	United Nations Disengagement Observer Force (in the Golan Heights)—since May 1974 (1,103)
UNFICYP	United Nations Peacekeeping Force in Cyprus—since March 1964 (852)[4]
UNIFIL	United Nations Interim Force in Lebanon—since March 1978 (13,225)
UNMEE	United Nations Mission in Ethiopia and Eritrea—since July 2000 (1,681)
UNMIK	United Nations Interim Administration Mission in Kosovo—since June 1999 (37)[5]
UNMIL	United Nations Mission in Liberia—since September 2003 (14,138)[6]
UNMIS	United Nations Mission in the Sudan—since March 2005 (9,397)[7,8]
UNMIT	United Nations Integrated Mission in Timor-Leste—since August 2006 (33)[9]
UNMOGIP	United Nations Military Observer Group in India and Pakistan—since January 1949 (44)
UNOCI	United Nations Operation in Côte d'Ivoire—since April 2004 (8,043)[10]
UNOMIG	United Nations Observer Mission in Georgia—since August 1993 (130)[11]
UNTSO	United Nations Truce Supervision Organization (in Jerusalem)—since May 1948 (150)

Parenthetical figures indicate military personnel as of 31 May 2007. [1]6 police officers are also assigned to MINURSO. [2]1,760 police officers are also assigned to MINUSTAH. [3]1,036 police officers are also assigned to MONUC. [4]65 police officers are also assigned to UNFICYP. [5]2,050 civilian police are also assigned to UNMIK. [6]1,158 police officers are also assigned to UNMIL. [7]625 police officers are also assigned to UNMIS. [8]Although the change was not immediately implemented, on 31 Aug 2006 the UN expanded the mandate of UNMIS to include a contribution to a joint African Union/UN force in the Darfur region. [9]1,626 police officers are also assigned to UNMIT. [10]1,162 police officers are also assigned to UNOCI. [11]12 police officers are also assigned to UNOMIG.

Nations with Largest Armed Forces

Countries with a military strength of at least 125,000 active personnel. Personnel numbers are in thousands ('000) and reflect 2006 data; spending totals are from 2006 budgets. Dollars refer to US currency. Source: The International Institute of Strategic Studies, The Military Balance, 2007.

COUNTRY	MILITARY PERSONNEL ACTIVE	MILITARY PERSONNEL RESERVES	DEFENSE SPENDING ($ BILLIONS)	ARMY MAIN BATTLE TANKS	NAVY MAJOR WARSHIPS/ CARRIERS	NAVY SUB-MARINES	AIR FORCE COMBAT AIRCRAFT	STRATEGIC NUCLEAR WEAPONS
China	2,255.0	800.0	35.3	7,580+	76/0	58	2,643	yes
United States	1,506.8	973.7	582.0[1]	7,620+	106/12	68	2,658	yes
India	1,316.0	1,155.0	22.3	3,978	58/1	16	849	yes
Korea, North	1,106.0	4,700.0	2.3	3,500+	8/0	63	590	yes
Russia	1,027.0	20,000.0	32.1[1]	22,831+	71/1	53	3,252	yes
Korea, South	687.0	4,500.0	23.7	2,330	43/0	20	518	
Pakistan	619.0	302.0[2]	4.1	2,461+	6/0	8	352	yes
Iran	545.0	350.0	6.6	1,613+	5/0	3	286	
Turkey	514.9	378.7	8.1	4,205	26/0	12	445	
Egypt	468.5	479.0	2.9	3,855	11/0	4	471	
Vietnam	455.0	5,000.0	3.4	1,315	11/0	2	221	
Myanmar (Burma)	375.0	107.3[2]	6.2[3]	150	3/0	0	125	
Syria	307.6	354.0	1.4	4,950	2/0	0	584	
Thailand	306.6	200.0	2.1	333	20/1	0	165	
Indonesia	302.0	400.0	2.6	0	28/0	2	94	
Taiwan	290.0	1,657.0	9.5[1]	926+	33/0	4	479	
Brazil	287.9	1,340.0	16.4	219	15/1	5	276	
France	254.9	21.7	49.3[1]	926	35/2	10	307	yes
Germany	245.7	161.8	38.8[1]	2,035	16/0	13	295	
Japan	240.4	41.8	41.1	980	53/0	16	280	
Mexico	237.8	39.9	3.2	0	7/0	0	84	
Iraq	227.0	0.0	—	—	0/0	0	0	
Saudi Arabia	224.5	15.5[2]	25.4[3]	910	11/0	0	278	
Colombia	208.6	61.9	3.8	0	4/0	4	90	
Eritrea	201.8	120.0	0.1[3]	150	0/0	0	8	
Morocco	200.8	150.0	2.2	540	3/0	0	89	
Italy	191.2	56.5	17.0[1]	320	26/2	7	258	
United Kingdom	191.0	199.3	60.5[1]	386	28/3	15	278	yes
Ukraine	187.6	1,000.0	1.9[1]	3,784	5/0	1	373	
Israel	168.0	408.0	7.7	3,657	3/0	3	402	[4]
Ethiopia	152.5	0.0	0.3	250+	0/0	0	48	
Sri Lanka	150.9	5.5	0.7	62	0/0	0	18	
Spain	147.3	319.0	9.1	323	12/1	4	182	
Greece	147.1	288.5	4.8	1,434	17/0	9	278	
Poland	141.5	234.0	5.8	947	8/0	5	187	
Algeria	137.5	150.0	3.0	920	9/0	2	204	
Bangladesh	126.5	63.2[2]	0.8	180	5/0	0	62	

[1]Spending estimate based on 2007 budget. [2]Paramilitary forces. [3]Spending based on 2005 budget. [4]Although believed by many to possess the world's sixth largest arsenal of nuclear weapons, Israel has never declared a nuclear capability nor has one been proven to exist.

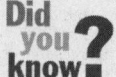

Did you know? One of the most famous airplanes ever built was Howard Hughes's HK-1 Hercules. Crafted of laminated birch wood and popularly known as the "Spruce Goose," the plane was designed during World War II in an effort to build a troop-and-cargo transport plane that did not rely on precious wartime materials in its construction. After some five years and numerous design changes, the plane made its public debut on 2 Nov 1947, when Hughes piloted the aircraft for its first and only flight, which lasted for roughly a mile. At the time the Spruce Goose (a nickname Hughes always hated) was three times larger than any plane ever built, and it still holds the record for the largest wingspan of any aircraft. After its test flight, the plane was put in its hangar and kept in flight-ready condition for nearly 30 years, as per Hughes's orders. It is now on permanent display at the Evergreen Aviation Educational Center in McMinnville OR.

United States

American History: Jamestown at 400

by Richard Brookhiser for TIME

They thought they were lost. The *Susan Constant,* the *Godspeed,* and the *Discovery* had sailed from London on 20 Dec 1606, carrying 144 passengers and crew, bound for Virginia. Howling winds pinned them to the coast of England for six weeks. After crossing the Atlantic by a southerly route and re-provisioning in the West Indies, they headed north, expecting landfall in the third week of April 1607. Instead they found a tempest. For four days they sounded, seeking offshore shallows in vain. Then, at 4 AM on 26 April, they saw land. The three ships sailed into Chesapeake Bay and found, in the words of one voyager, "fair meadows and goodly tall trees, with such fresh waters running through the woods, as I was almost ravished at the first sight thereof." They picked an island in a river for a fortified outpost and named it after their king, James.

In May 2007, Jamestown celebrated its 400th birthday, and Queen Elizabeth II, King James I's great-great-great-great-great-great-great-great-great-great-granddaughter, was present to observe the occasion. But it's worth remembering that Jamestown was a giant gamble. The trials were severe, the errors numerous, the losses colossal, the gains, eventually, great. Life in Jamestown was a three-way tug-of-war between daily survival, the settlers' own preconceptions, and the need to adapt to a new world.

Jamestown did not invent America, but in its will to survive, its quest for democracy, its exploitation of both Indians and slaves, it created the template for so many of the struggles—and achievements—that have made us who we are. It contained in embryo the same contradictions that still resonate in America today—the tension between freedom and authority, between public purpose and private initiative, between our hopes and our fears.

Jamestown spawned four centuries of myths. The wreck of a reinforcement expedition in Bermuda inspired Shakespeare's play *The Tempest* (1611), complete with Caliban, a savage aboriginal; a passage in one of John Smith's many promotional tracts inspired a verse in Peggy Lee's song "Fever" (1958)—"Captain Smith and Pocahontas had a very mad affair."

In reality, Jamestown was a hardheaded business proposition. The 104 English settlers who stayed when the ships went home—gentlemen, soldiers, privateers, artisans, laborers, boys (no women yet)—were late entrants in the New World sweepstakes. Spain had conquered Mexico by 1521, Peru by 1534. The mines disgorged silver, and by the end of the 16th century, Mexico City and Lima had universities, printing presses, and tens of thousands of inhabitants. The Portuguese were harvesting dyewood in Brazil, and the French were trading for furs in Canada. Even the somewhat overlooked Chesapeake had seen European passersby: the Native Americans were not unused to strangers with pale skins and sailing ships.

But anyone's venture is special to him. And the England of James I and his predecessor, Elizabeth I, suffered from overpopulation and poverty. Pushing people into other lands could solve both problems and even have a side benefit. As the Rev. Richard Hakluyt, England's premier geographer, put it, "Valiant youths rusting [from] lack of employment" would flourish in America and produce goods and crops that would enrich their homeland. The notion was so prevalent that it inspired a blowhard character in the 1605 play *Eastward Ho!* to declare that all Virginia colonists had chamber pots of "pure gold."

That would have surprised the Jamestown settlers, who faced an array of challenges, all of them together crushing. It was a project of the London Co., a group of merchants with a royal patent: imagine that Congress gave Wal-Mart and General Electric permission to colonize Mars. But of necessity, the day-to-day decisions were made in Jamestown, and its leaders were always fighting. Leaders who were incompetent or unpopular—sometimes the most competent were the least popular—were deposed on the spot. The typical 17th-century account of Jamestown argues that everything would have gone well if everyone besides the author had not done wrong. Smith, for instance, described his fellow colonists as "ten times more fit to spoil a commonwealth than...to begin one."

Many things did go wrong. The most pressing problem was sustenance. The first year, the settlers drank from the James River, succumbing to typhoid, dysentery and salt poisoning. Once they had dug a well they were able to drink safely, but what would they eat? Gardening and farming were fiendishly difficult. Studies of tree rings show that the Chesapeake was baked by drought during the first seven years of the colony. This meant they were dependent on bartering or seizing supplies from local Indians, whose own stores were depleted. The settlers who died of disease or starvation had to be replaced by new settlers from England, who arrived once or twice a year (their ranks increasingly included women).

The London Co. expected a return on its outlay, but it was slow in coming. It's not that the settlers weren't capable of working hard. One month after they landed, they realized they needed a log palisade to protect them from Indian arrows. As archaeologist William M. Kelso points out (in *Jamestown: The Buried Truth*), in 19 days and in a June swelter they cut and split more than 600 trees weighing 200 to 400 kg (400 to 800 lb) each and set them in a triangular trench three football fields long and 0.75 m (2.5 ft) deep. In 2004 New Line Cinema built a replica of the fort for its film *The New World* and did it in about the same amount of time—with power tools.

But forts cannot be exported. The Rev. Hakluyt had imagined that the colonies "would yield unto us all the commodities of Europe, Africa, and Asia." Perhaps the settlers would discover gold. All they found were a small number of semiprecious stones—garnets, amethysts, quartz crystals. Perhaps they could manufacture glass. One resupply ship brought eight German and Polish craftsmen. Most of them ran off to live with the Indians.

The Red and the White. Relations between white and red men were the most variable factor in Jamestown's early history. The western Chesapeake was ruled by Wahunsonacock, chief of the Powhatan. He was an expansionist, no less than the English, having brought 30 local tribes under his sway, an empire of 15,000 people. In December 1607, Smith described his royal state: "He sat covered with a great robe, made of raccoon skins, and all the tails hanging by," flanked by "two rows of men, and behind them as many women, with all their heads and shoulders painted red." The settlers hoped to make the chief a tributary to James I; he hoped to make them allies of his. Sometimes they fought; sometimes they traded. Wahunsonacock wanted the copper the settlers offered in exchange for food, and he very much wanted their swords and firearms.

But when the Indians refused to trade for food, the colonists died horribly. The winter of 1609 became the "starving time." The colonists ate horses, dogs, cats, vermin, even (it was said) corpses. In June 1610 the survivors staggered onto their ships and sailed into the bay, either looking for help or intending to sail home. Help came with the arrival of three ships from England and new settlers. The shattered colony was put under strict martial law. The penalties for running away included shooting, hanging, burning, and being broken on the wheel.

Military discipline was a stopgap; serious reform, with long-reaching consequences, was already under way. The London Co. had reorganized itself as the Virginia Co. of London in 1609, and over the next dozen years settlers and backers alike realized the colony could not be run as an overseas mining company or an armed camp. Success would depend on large numbers of people and the steady production of exportable goods. That meant the incentives for living in Jamestown had to be modified.

One prophetic idea was to recruit religious outcasts —Englishmen who longed to put an ocean between them and the established Anglican church. Some radical Protestants, known as Dissenters, had already fled to Holland. The Virginia Co. lured some Dissenters over and opened negotiations with others. One boatload of Pilgrims, blown north, landed in Plymouth (now in Massachusetts), in 1620. Religious pluralism in British North America would suffer many backtracks and false starts (Virginia would develop its own Anglican establishment as time passed), but the first step was taken in Jamestown.

The White and the Black. Jamestown also was the first place to find a cash cow and an economic system for exploiting it. The Powhatan smoked a crude indigenous species of tobacco. But in 1612, John Rolfe imported seeds of *Nicotiana tabacum*, the Spanish-American weed that was already a craze in England. By 1620 the colony had shipped almost 23,000 kg (50,000 lb) home. Fifty years later, Virginia and Maryland would ship 6.8 million kg (15 million lb). Tobacco and foodstuffs were grown on privately owned farms. Beginning in 1618, old settlers were offered 100 acres of land, and newcomers who paid their way were given 50 acres, plus 50 more for every additional person they brought.

Many of those additional people were indentured servants who, in return for their transatlantic passage, bound themselves to labor for seven years. In 1619 the *White Lion*, a privateer, brought a new labor source—"20 and odd negroes" from Angola. Our original sin was not very original—Spain and Portugal had already brought 200,000 African slaves to the Americas—and the colony was slow to exploit the practice. Slaves did not outnumber indentured servants in Virginia until the 1670s. Once acquired, however, the habit of bondage would prove addicting— economic and social nicotine.

But the need to keep these newly successful tobacco growers in line led to Jamestown's most far-reaching innovation, representative government. In 1618 the Virginia Co. created a general assembly to advise the governor—including "burgesses," or representatives, elected by property owners, on the theory that "every man will more willingly obey laws to which he has yielded his consent."

The general assembly first met for five days in the summer of 1619. It discussed Indian relations, church attendance, gambling, drunkenness, and the price of tobacco. It sounds like today's Iowa caucuses: war and peace, social issues, bread and butter. From this seed would grow the House of Burgesses, the elective house of Virginia's colonial legislature and the political academy of George Washington and Thomas Jefferson. In their rough-and-ready way, the Jamestown settlers had planted the seeds of a dynamic system, democratic capitalism, along with an institution that would pervert it, chattel slavery, and a force that would supply the cure, the goal of liberty.

As the colony flourished, its Powhatan neighbors became alarmed. Trading posts were one thing, permanent farms another. On 22 March 1622, the new leader of the Powhatan, Opechancanough, launched dawn raids on 28 plantations and settlements along the James River, killing 347 colonists, a quarter of the total population. Jamestown itself escaped, warned by an Indian boy who had converted to Christianity. Dispirited and disorganized, hundreds more of the colonists died the following winter, the second "starving time."

The attack was a brilliant tactical stroke, but it sealed the fate of the attackers. The survivors responded with all-out war. In July 1624, some 800 Indian warriors risked a two-day battle with 60 armored and well-armed colonists and lost. Twenty years later, Opechancanough, nearly a century old, was captured and shot in the back in a Jamestown jail. This too set a pattern: of conflict and expulsion, which lasted until the last Indians were beaten and settled on reservations in the late 19th century.

Back home, the Virginia Co. sputtered in wrath at the imprudence of the colonists in allowing themselves to be killed. A royal commission found the colony to be "weak and miserable," and the company's charter was revoked in 1624. From then on, its governors would be appointed by the king.

Jamestown left a record of spite, want, and death, to say nothing of the long-range problems, from racism to lung cancer, of which the colonists were unaware. Yet they survived. Key aspects of the Jamestown template—chiefly the lures of religious liberty, private ownership, and a measure of self-rule —guaranteed that British North America would be populous enough to withstand challenges from France and Holland and, finally, the power grabs of the mother country.

The settlers came with ideas they had to junk. Some of their brightest hopes were false. They worked hard and got other people to do their work for them. They were foolish, fierce, and surprisingly stubborn. When one thing failed, they tried another. We are their descendants.

United States History

United States Chronology

1492 Christopher Columbus, sailing under the Spanish flag, discovers America, 12 October.

1497 John Cabot, representing England, explores the Atlantic coast of what is now Canada.

1513 Ponce de León of Spain lands in Florida and gives that region its name.

1519–22 Ferdinand Magellan's Spanish ship—the *Vittoria*—is the first to sail around the world.

1534 France sends Jacques Cartier to find a route to the Far East; he explores along the St. Lawrence River, and France lays claim to part of North America.

1541 Hernando de Soto of Spain discovers the Mississippi River near the site of Memphis.

1565 St. Augustine, the oldest permanent settlement in the US, is founded by Spaniards.

1587 A party under John White lands at Roanoke Island (now in North Carolina); when White returns three years later, the entire settlement has disappeared.

1607 The English make the first permanent settlement in the New World at Jamestown; Virginia becomes the first of the 13 English colonies.

1619 The first representative assembly in America, the House of Burgesses, meets in Virginia; the first blacks land in Virginia.

1620 Pilgrims from the ship *Mayflower* found a settlement at Plymouth.

1649 The Act Concerning Religion passed by Maryland's legislature is the first law of religious toleration in the English colonies.

1682 The Sieur de La Salle explores the lower Mississippi valley and claims the entire region for France.

1733 Georgia, the 13th and last of the English colonies in America, is founded.

1754 Both England and the colonies reject the Albany Plan of Union to unite the colonies. The French and Indian War between France and England begins in America.

1763 The Treaty of Paris ends the French and Indian War; Britain wins control of the New World; Louisiana is ceded to Spain, Florida to Britain.

1765 The Quartering Act and the Stamp Act anger Americans; nine colonies are represented at the Stamp Act Congress.

1770 British troops fire on a crowd, killing five people in the so-called Boston Massacre.

1772 Committees of Correspondence are organized in almost all of the colonies.

1773 The Boston Tea Party, the first action in a chain leading to war with Britain, takes place.

1774 The First Continental Congress meets at Philadelphia PA and protests the five Intolerable Acts.

1775 The battles of Lexington and Concord and Bunker Hill occur; the Second Continental Congress meets.

1776 The Declaration of Independence is adopted. George Washington crosses the Delaware River to fight at Trenton NJ.

1777 Americans capture Gen. John Burgoyne and a large British force at Saratoga NY.

1778–79 Gen. George Rogers Clark leads a victorious expedition into the Northwest Territory.

1781 Washington accepts the surrender of Charles Cornwallis at Yorktown VA. The Articles of Confederation become the government of the US.

1783 A treaty of peace with Great Britain is signed at Paris, formally ending the Revolutionary War.

1786–87 Shays's Rebellion in Massachusetts shows weaknesses of the Confederation government.

1787 The Northwest Territory is organized by Congress. A convention meets to draft a new constitution.

1788 The US Constitution is ratified by the necessary nine states to ensure adoption.

1789 The new US government goes into effect; Washington is inaugurated president; the first Congress meets in New York City.

1791 The Bill of Rights is added to the Constitution. Vermont is the first new state admitted to the Union.

1793 Eli Whitney invents the cotton gin, which leads to large-scale cotton growing in the South.

1800 The national capital is moved from Philadelphia PA to Washington DC.

1803 Louisiana is purchased from France. The Supreme Court makes its *Marbury* v. *Madison* decision; Congress halts the importation of slaves into the US after 1807.

1804–06 Meriwether Lewis and William Clark blaze an overland trail to the Pacific and return.

1807 Robert Fulton's steamboat makes a successful journey from New York City to Albany NY.

1812–14 The US maintains its independence in a conflict with Britain, the War of 1812.

1818 The US and Canada settle a boundary dispute and agree on an open border between the countries.

1820 The Missouri Compromise settles the problem of slavery in new states for the next 30 years.

1823 The Monroe Doctrine warns European nations that the US will protect the Americas.

1825 The Erie Canal, from the Hudson River to the Great Lakes, becomes a great water highway to the Middle West.

1829 The inauguration of Pres. Andrew Jackson introduces the era of Jacksonian Democracy.

1836 Texas wins its independence from Mexico.

1843 The first migration begins on the Oregon Trail.

1845 Texas is annexed and admitted as a state.

1846 The Oregon boundary dispute is settled with Britain. The Mexican War begins.

1847 Brigham Young leads a party of Mormons into the Salt Lake valley, Utah.

1848 The Mexican War ends; the US gains possession of the California and New Mexico regions.

1849 The gold rush to California begins.

1850 The Compromise of 1850 admits California as a free state and postpones war between the North and South.

1853 The Gadsden Purchase adds 117,935 sq km (45,535 sq mi) to what is now the southwestern US.

1854 The Kansas-Nebraska Act reopens the slavery issue and leads to the organization of the Republican party.

1857 The Dred Scott decision of the Supreme Court declares that the Missouri Compromise is illegal.

1860 Abraham Lincoln is elected president; South Carolina secedes from the Union.

1861 The Confederate States of America is formed; the Civil War begins; Union forces are routed at Bull Run, Virginia. Telegraph links New York City with San Francisco CA.

1862 Gen. Ulysses S. Grant launches a Union attack in the West; the Confederate invasion of Maryland is halted at Antietam. The Homestead Act grants 160 acres to each settler.

1863 Federal forces win decisive battles at Gettysburg PA, Vicksburg MS, and Chattanooga TN. The Emancipation Proclamation takes effect.

1864 Gen. William Tecumseh Sherman captures Atlanta and marches across Georgia; Grant closes in on Richmond VA.

1865 Gen. Robert E. Lee surrenders to Grant at Appomattox Court House VA, ending the Civil War. Lincoln is assassinated.

1867 Reconstruction acts impose military rule on the South. Alaska is purchased from Russia.

1869 The first transcontinental railroad is completed as two lines meet at Promontory UT.

1876 The telephone is invented. The Centennial Exposition in Philadelphia PA celebrates the 100th birthday of the US.

1877 The withdrawal of the last federal troops from the South ends the Reconstruction period. Railroad workers begin the first nationwide strike.

1879 The first practical electric light is invented by Thomas A. Edison.

1883 The Pendleton Civil Service Act provides for examinations as the basis of appointment to some government positions.

1884–85 The first skyscraper, the Home Insurance Building, is erected in Chicago.

1886 The American Federation of Labor (AFL) is organized; its first president is Samuel Gompers.

1887 The Interstate Commerce Act is adopted to control railroads that cross state lines.

1889–90 The first pan-American conference is held in Washington DC.

1890 The Sherman Anti-Trust Act is passed in an effort to curb the growth of monopolies.

1896 Henry Ford's first car is driven on the streets of Detroit MI.

1898 The US wins the Spanish-American War and gains the Philippines, Puerto Rico, and Guam.

1903 The air age begins with the successful airplane flight by the Wright brothers.

1906 The Federal Food and Drug Act is passed to protect the public from impure food and drugs.

1912 New Mexico and Arizona, the 47th and 48th states, are admitted to the Union.

1913 Federal income tax is authorized by the 16th Amendment; the 17th Amendment provides for the popular election of US senators.

1914 The Panama Canal is opened. World War I breaks out in Europe; Pres. Woodrow Wilson appeals for neutrality in the US.

1915 A German submarine sinks the *Lusitania* with the loss of 124 American lives. A telephone line is established coast to coast.

1917 Germany begins open submarine warfare; the US declares war against Germany.

1918 Pres. Wilson proposes "Fourteen Points" as the basis for peace; Americans fight at Chateau-Thierry, Belleau Wood, Saint-Mihiel, and Argonne Forest; an armistice ends the war.

1918–19 Pres. Wilson attends the Paris Peace Conference of victorious nations.

1919 The US Senate rejects the League of Nations. Navy pilots make the first flight across the Atlantic. Prohibition is established by the 18th Amendment.

1920 The right to vote is given to women by the 19th Amendment. Pittsburgh PA radio station KDKA begins broadcasting.

1921 National immigration quotas are introduced.

1921–22 The Washington Conference restricts warship construction among the chief naval powers.

1924 The army plane *Chicago* makes the first flight around the world.

1927 Charles A. Lindbergh makes the first nonstop solo flight across the Atlantic.

1928 The Kellogg-Briand Pact outlaws war.

1929 The stock market reaches a new high, then crashes; the panic marks the beginning of the Great Depression; millions of workers are unemployed.

1932 Franklin Delano Roosevelt is elected president.

1933 The New Deal is launched; the gold standard is suspended; the National Recovery Act is passed; bank deposits are insured; the Tennessee Valley Authority is organized. The 21st Amendment repeals prohibition.

1934 Congress tightens control over securities, passes the first Reciprocal Trade Agreement Act, and launches the federal housing program.

1935 The National Labor Relations (Wagner) Act guarantees collective bargaining to labor; the Congress of Industrial Organizations (CIO) is founded. The Social Security Act is passed.

1936 The Hoover Dam (Boulder Dam) is completed across the Colorado River.

1938 The Fair Labor Standards Act provides a federal yardstick for wages and hours of workers.

1939 Germany invades Poland to start World War II; the US declares neutrality.

1940 The US begins a huge rearmament program; the first peacetime draft takes effect. Roosevelt defies tradition and accepts the presidential nomination for a third term.

1941 The Lend-Lease Act is passed; the Atlantic Charter is signed; the Japanese attack on Pearl Harbor, Hawaii, brings the US into World War II.

1942 Americans launch a counteroffensive in the Pacific; the Allies invade North Africa.

1943 The Allied invasion of Italy is the first landing on the European continent.

1944 The Allies launch the greatest sea-to-land assault in history in the invasion of France; the Allies invade the Philippines; the "GI Bill of Rights" is passed.

1945 Germany surrenders, 8 May; an atomic bomb is dropped on Hiroshima, 6 August; Japan surrenders, 2 September. The Cold War begins between the US and the Soviet Union. The United Nations (UN) is formally launched on 24 October.

1946 The Philippines is granted independence by the US. The Atomic Energy Commission is created.

1947 The Senate passes the Truman Doctrine. The Taft-Hartley labor law is enacted. The Department of Defense consolidates the army, navy, and air force.

1948 The European Recovery Program is enacted. Harry S. Truman is elected president.

1949 The Fair Deal program is announced. The US and its allies force the Soviet Union to lift the Berlin blockade. The North Atlantic Treaty Organization (NATO) is founded.

1950 The US and several other members of the UN send military forces to the aid of the Republic of Korea; bitter war develops.

1951 A two-term limit is put on the presidency by ratification of the 22nd Amendment to the Constitution.

1952 The US and its allies end the occupation of West Germany. The election of Dwight D. Eisenhower ends 20 years of Democratic governance.

1953 The Korean War ends. The Department of Health, Education, and Welfare becomes the 10th cabinet post.

1954 Racial segregation of public schools is declared illegal by the Supreme Court. The Southeast Asia Treaty Organization (SEATO) is founded.

1955 The two largest labor organizations merge into one group—the AFL-CIO. The Salk poliomyelitis vaccine is proved successful.

1956 Eisenhower is reelected president; Democrats win control of Congress.

1957 The Eisenhower Doctrine to strengthen the US position in the Middle East is adopted.

1958 The first US artificial Earth satellite is launched. The US joins the International Atomic Energy Agency.

1959 Alaska becomes the 49th state, Hawaii the 50th.

1960 A US reconnaissance plane is shot down over the Soviet Union.

1961 The CIA is involved in an unsuccessful invasion of Cuba at the Bay of Pigs. The 23rd Amendment to the Constitution gives Washington DC residents the right to vote in presidential elections. The first American makes spaceflight. American troops are sent to defend West Berlin.

1962 The Cuban missile crisis erupts; the Soviets remove missiles from Cuba on US urging.

1963 The March on Washington for Jobs and Freedom takes place. Pres. John F. Kennedy is assassinated in Dallas TX. A nuclear test-ban treaty is signed.

1964 The 24th Amendment to the Constitution bans poll taxes in federal elections. The civil rights bill is passed. The Supreme Court allows reapportionment.

1965 US combat forces fight in Vietnam. The voting-rights bill and the Medicare Act are signed. The Department of Housing and Urban Development becomes the 11th cabinet post.

1966 The Department of Transportation becomes the 12th cabinet post.

1967 The 25th Amendment to the Constitution provides for presidential succession.

1968 The assassinations of Martin Luther King, Jr., and Robert F. Kennedy provoke race riots.

1969 US astronauts land on the Moon.

1970 Four students at Kent State University in Ohio are killed by National Guard soldiers during anti-Vietnam War protests.

1971 The 26th Amendment to the Constitution gives 18-year-olds the right to vote in all elections.

1972 Pres. Richard M. Nixon visits China and the Soviet Union.

1973 The US withdraws its troops from Vietnam. Vice-Pres. Spiro T. Agnew resigns. OPEC raises the price of petroleum 400%.

1974 The Watergate scandal and the threat of impeachment force Nixon to resign.

1977 The Department of Energy becomes a new cabinet post. A treaty is signed to return the Panama Canal to Panama by the year 2000.

1978 Pres. Jimmy Carter hosts the Camp David talks between Israel's Menachem Begin and Egypt's Anwar el-Sadat.

1979 The second Strategic Arms Limitation Talks (SALT II) treaty is signed by the US and the Soviet Union. Militants seize 66 American hostages in a takeover of the US embassy in Iran.

1980 The Department of Health, Education, and Welfare is separated into the Department of Health and Human Services and the Department of Education.

1981 Pres. Ronald Reagan is wounded in an assassination attempt. A major tax cut and increased defense spending pass Congress. Sandra Day O'Connor is appointed the first woman Supreme Court justice.

1983 Reagan announces the Star Wars missile-defense program. The US invades Grenada.

1985 A summit between Reagan and Soviet leader Mikhail Gorbachev is held in Geneva, Switzerland.

1986 The space shuttle *Challenger* explodes shortly after liftoff. The US bombs targets in Libya. The Iran-contra affair is revealed.

1987 The Iran-contra hearings are held. The stock market collapses. Reagan and Gorbachev sign the Intermediate-Range Nuclear Forces (INF) treaty.

1988 The Department of Veterans Affairs is approved as a cabinet post.

1989 The *Exxon Valdez* supertanker spills 10 million gallons of crude oil off the Alaskan coast. The US invades Panama. The Berlin Wall ceases to divide the two Germanys, signaling the end of the Cold War.

1990 Troops are sent to Saudi Arabia in response to Iraq's invasion of Kuwait.

1991 An air and ground war leads to the Iraqi surrender and withdrawal from Kuwait. The Soviet Union comes apart.

1992 The 27th Amendment to the Constitution bars Congress from giving itself a midterm pay raise. Riots erupt in Los Angeles after a jury acquits white policemen accused of beating African American Rodney King. The North American Free Trade Agreement (NAFTA) is signed by the US, Canada, and Mexico.

1993 Janet Reno becomes the first woman attorney general. The World Trade Center in New York City is bombed.

1995 Timothy McVeigh detonates a bomb in a terrorist attack on the Alfred P. Murrah Federal Building in Oklahoma City OK, killing 168 people.

1998 Pres. Bill Clinton is impeached for perjury and obstruction of justice; he is acquitted by the Senate the following year.

2000 The results of the presidential election are challenged by Vice Pres. Al Gore; the US Supreme Court overrules the Florida Supreme Court's order for a statewide manual recount of ballots; George W. Bush wins the presidency.

2001 On 11 September, two hijacked airplanes demolish the World Trade Center in New York City, another crashes into the Pentagon outside Washington DC, and a fourth crashes in the southern Pennsylvania countryside. Pres. Bush calls for a global "war on terror" and sends US troops into Afghanistan, eventually displacing the Taliban regime.

2002 Republicans take control of both houses of Congress, holding both the legislative and executive branches of government for the first time since 1952.

2003 The US launches a war to depose the Saddam Hussein regime in Iraq and takes control of the country after just weeks of fighting. Congress passes a $350 billion tax cut.

2004 Scandal erupts with the publication of photos of prisoner abuse at Abu Ghraib prison in Iraq. The independent 9/11 Commission finds no credible evidence of a connection between Iraq and al-Qaeda's attacks of 11 Sep 2001. Bush is reelected president.

2005 The US lags among donor nations in debt forgiveness for developing nations and disaster aid. Hurricane Katrina strikes the Gulf Coast, destroying much of New Orleans and killing 1,833 people.

2006 Conservative lawyer John G. Roberts, Jr., is appointed to the Supreme Court as chief justice. Former vice president Al Gore's documentary film, *An Inconvenient Truth*, convinces many people that global warming is a danger to the environment (it will win an Academy Award in 2007). As the Iraq War continues, Democrats gain control of both houses of Congress.

2007 In an effort to quell a persistent insurrection against the US-backed government of Iraq, Pres. Bush orders a "surge" of 20,000 additional US troops.

Important Documents in US History

Mayflower Compact

On 21 Nov 1620 (11 November, Old Style), 41 male passengers on the Mayflower signed the following compact prior to their landing at Plymouth (now Massachusetts). The compact resulted from the fear that some members of the company might leave the group and settle on their own. The Mayflower Compact bound the signers into a body politic for the purpose of forming a government and pledged them to abide by any laws and regulations that would later by established. The document was not a constitution but rather an adaptation of the usual church covenant to a civil situation. It became the foundation of Plymouth's government.

In the name of God, Amen.

We whose names are underwritten, the loyal subjects of our dread sovereign Lord, King James, by the grace of God, of Great Britain, France and Ireland king, defender of the faith, etc., having undertaken, for the glory of God, and advancement of the Christian faith, and honor of our king and country, a voyage to plant the first colony in the Northern parts of Virginia, do by these presents solemnly and mutually in the presence of God, and one of another, covenant and combine ourselves together into a civil body politic, for our better ordering and preservation and furtherance of the ends aforesaid; and by virtue hereof to enact, constitute, and frame such just and equal laws, ordinances, acts, constitutions, and offices, from time to time, as shall be thought most meet and convenient for the general good of the colony, unto which we promise all due submission and obedience.

In witness whereof we have hereunder subscribed our names at Cape-Cod the 11 of November, in the year of the reign of our sovereign lord, King James, of England, France, and Ireland the eighteenth, and of Scotland the fifty-fourth. Anno Domine 1620.

Declaration of Independence

On 4 Jul 1776 the Continental Congress officially adopted the Declaration of Independence. Two days before, the Congress had "unanimously" voted (with New York abstaining) to be free and independent from Britain. The Declaration of Independence was written largely by Thomas Jefferson. After modifications by the Congress, the document was prepared and voted upon. New York delegates voted to accept it on 15 July, and on 19 July the Congress ordered the document to be engrossed as "The Unanimous Declaration of the Thirteen United States of America." It was accordingly put on parchment, and members of the Congress present on 2 August affixed their signatures to this parchment copy on that day, and others later. The last signer was Thomas McKean of Delaware, whose name was not placed on the document before 1777.

The Unanimous Declaration of the Thirteen United States of America

When in the Course of human events, it becomes necessary for one people to dissolve the political bands which have connected them with another, and to assume among the powers of the earth, the separate and equal station to which the Laws of Nature and of Nature's God entitle them, a decent respect to the opinions of mankind requires that they should declare the causes which impel them to the separation.—We hold these truths to be self-evident, that all men are created equal, that they are endowed by their Creator with certain unalienable Rights, that among these are Life, Liberty and the pursuit of Happiness.—That to secure these rights, Governments are instituted among Men, deriving their just powers from the consent of the governed,—That whenever any Form of Government becomes destructive of these ends, it is the Right of the People to alter or to abolish it, and to institute new Government, laying its foundation on such principles and organizing its powers in such form, as to them shall seem most likely to effect their Safety and Happiness. Prudence, indeed, will dictate that Governments long established should not be changed for light and transient causes; and accordingly all experience hath shown, that mankind are more disposed to suffer, while evils are sufferable, than to right themselves by abolishing the forms to which they are accustomed. But when a long train of abuses and usurpations, pursuing invariably the same Object evinces a design to reduce them under absolute Despotism, it is their right, it is their duty, to throw off such Government, and to provide new Guards for their future security.—Such has been the patient sufferance of these Colonies; and such is now the necessity which constrains them to alter their former Systems of Government. The history of the present King of Great Britain is a history of repeated injuries and usurpations, all having in direct object the establishment of an absolute Tyranny over these States.

To prove this, let Facts be submitted to a candid world.—He has refused his Assent to Laws, the most wholesome and necessary for the public good.—He has forbidden his Governors to pass Laws of immediate and pressing importance, unless suspended in their operation till his Assent should be obtained; and when so suspended, he has utterly neglected to attend to them.—He has refused to pass other Laws for the accommodation of large districts of people, unless those people would relinquish the right of Representation in the Legislature, a right inestimable to them and formidable to tyrants only.—He has called together legislative bodies at places unusual, uncomfortable, and distant from the depository of their public Records, for the sole purpose of fatiguing them into compliance with his measures.—He has dissolved Representative Houses repeatedly, for opposing with manly firmness his invasions on the rights of the people.—He has refused for a long time, after such dissolutions, to cause others to be elected; whereby the Legislative powers, incapable of Annihilation, have returned to the People at large for their exercise; the State remaining in the mean time exposed to all the dangers of invasion from without, and convulsions within.—He has endeavoured to prevent the population of these States; for that purpose obstructing the Laws for Naturalization of Foreigners; refusing to pass others to encourage their migration hither, and raising the conditions of new Appropriations of Lands.—He has obstructed the Administration of Justice, by refusing his Assent to Laws for establishing Judiciary powers.—He has made judges dependent on his Will alone, for the tenure of their offices, and the amount and payment of their salaries.—He has erected a multitude of New Offices, and sent hither swarms of Officers to harrass our people, and eat out their substance.—He has kept among us, in times of peace, Standing Armies, without the Consent of our legislatures.—He has affected to render the Military independent of and superior to the Civil power.—He has combined with others to subject us to a jurisdiction foreign to our constitution, and unacknowledged by our laws; giving his Assent to their Acts of pretended Legislation:—For quartering large bodies of armed troops among us:—For protecting them, by a mock Trial, from punishment for any Murders which they should commit on the Inhabitants of these States:—For cutting off our Trade with all parts of the world:—For imposing Taxes on us without our Consent:—For depriving us in many cases, of the benefits of Trial by Jury:—For transporting us beyond Seas to be tried for pretended offences:—For abolishing the free System of English Laws in a neighbouring Province, establishing therein an Arbitrary government, and enlarging its Boundaries so as to render it at once an example and fit instrument for introducing the same absolute rule into these Colonies:—For taking away our Charters, abolishing our most valuable Laws, and altering fundamentally the Forms of our Governments:—For suspending our own Legislatures, and declaring themselves invested with power to legislate for us in all cases whatsoever.—He has abdicated Government here, by declaring us out of his Protection and waging War against us.—He has plundered our seas, ravaged our Coasts, burnt our towns, and destroyed the lives of our people.—He is at this time transporting large Armies of foreign Mercenaries to compleat the works of death, desolation and tyranny, already begun with circumstances of Cruelty & perfidy scarcely paralleled in the most barbarous ages, and totally unworthy the Head of a civilized nation.—He

has constrained our fellow Citizens taken Captive on the high Seas to bear Arms against their Country, to become the executioners of their friends and Brethren, or to fall themselves by their Hands.—He has excited domestic insurrections amongst us, and has endeavoured to bring on the inhabitants of our frontiers, the merciless Indian Savages, whose known rule of warfare, is an undistinguished destruction of all ages, sexes and conditions. In every stage of these Oppressions We have Petitioned for Redress in the most humble terms: Our repeated Petitions have been answered only by repeated injury. A Prince, whose character is thus marked by every act which may define a Tyrant, is unfit to be the ruler of a free people. Nor have We been wanting in attentions to our Brittish brethren. We have warned them from time to time of attempts by their legislature to extend an unwarrantable jurisdiction over us. We have reminded them of the circumstances of our emigration and settlement here. We have appealed to their native justice and magnanimity, and we have conjured them by the ties of our common kindred to disavow these usurpations, which, would inevitably interrupt our connections and correspondence. They too have been deaf to the voice of justice and of consanguinity. We must, therefore, acquiesce in the necessity, which denounces our Separation, and hold them, as we hold the rest of mankind, Enemies in War, in Peace Friends.—

We, therefore, the Representatives of the United States of America, in General Congress, Assembled, appealing to the Supreme Judge of the world for the rectitude of our intentions, do, in the Name, and by Authority of the good People of these Colonies, solemnly publish and declare, That these United Colonies are, and of Right ought to be Free and Independent States; that they are Absolved from all Allegiance to the British Crown, and that all political connection between them and the State of Great Britain, is and ought to be totally dissolved; and that as Free and Independent States, they have full Power to levy War, conclude Peace, contract Alliances, establish Commerce, and to do all other Acts and Things which Independent States may of right do.—And for the support of this Declaration, with a firm reliance on the protection of Divine Providence, we mutually pledge to each other our Lives, our Fortunes and our sacred Honor.

Signers of the Declaration of Independence

	BIRTHPLACE	OCCUPATION
Connecticut		
Samuel Huntington (1731–1796)	Windham CT	lawyer, judge
Roger Sherman (1721–1793)	Newton MA	cobbler, surveyor, lawyer, judge
William Williams (1731–1811)	Lebanon CT	merchant, judge
Oliver Wolcott (1726–1797)	Windsor CT	soldier, sheriff, judge
Delaware		
Thomas McKean (1734–1817)	New London PA	lawyer, judge
George Read (1733–1798)	North East MD	lawyer, judge
Caesar Rodney (1728–1784)	Dover DE	judge
Georgia		
Button Gwinnett (c. 1735–1777)	bapt. Gloucester, England	merchant
Lyman Hall (1724–1790)	Wallingford CT	physician
George Walton (c. 1741–1804)	Farmville VA	lawyer, judge

Signers of the Declaration of Independence (continued)

	BIRTHPLACE	OCCUPATION
Maryland		
Charles Carroll of Carrollton (1737–1832)	Annapolis MD	lawyer
Samuel Chase (1741–1811)	Somerset county MD	lawyer, judge
William Paca (1740–1799)	Abingdon MD	lawyer, judge
Thomas Stone (1743–1787)	Charles county MD	lawyer
Massachusetts		
John Adams (1735–1826)	Braintree (Quincy) MA	lawyer
Samuel Adams (1722–1803)	Boston MA	politician
Elbridge Gerry (1744–1814)	Marblehead MA	merchant
John Hancock (1737–1793)	Braintree (Quincy) MA	merchant
Robert Treat Paine (1731–1814)	Boston MA	lawyer, judge
New Hampshire		
Josiah Bartlett (1729–1795)	Amesbury MA	physician, judge
Matthew Thornton (c. 1714–1803)	Ireland	physician
William Whipple (1730–1785)	Kittery ME	merchant, soldier, judge
New Jersey		
Abraham Clark (1726–1794)	Elizabethtown NJ	surveyor, lawyer, sheriff
John Hart (c. 1711–1779)	Stonington CT	farmer, judge
Francis Hopkinson (1737–1791)	Philadelphia PA	lawyer, judge, author
Richard Stockton (1730–1781)	near Princeton NJ	lawyer
John Witherspoon (1723–1794)	Gifford, Scotland	clergyman, author, educator
New York		
William Floyd (1734–1821)	Brookhaven NY	soldier
Francis Lewis (1713–1802)	Llandaff, Wales	merchant
Philip Livingston (1716–1778)	Albany NY	merchant
Lewis Morris (1726–1798)	Morrisania (Bronx county) NY	farmer, soldier, judge
North Carolina		
Joseph Hewes (1730–1779)	Kingston NJ	merchant
William Hooper (1742–1790)	Boston MA	lawyer, judge
John Penn (1741–1788)	near Port Royal VA	lawyer
Pennsylvania		
George Clymer (1739–1813)	Philadelphia PA	merchant
Benjamin Franklin (1706–1790)	Boston MA	printer, publisher, author, scientist
Robert Morris (1734–1806)	Lancashire, England	merchant
John Morton (1724–1777)	Ridley PA	judge
George Ross (1730–1779)	New Castle DE	lawyer, judge
Benjamin Rush (1746–1813)	Byberry PA	physician
James Smith (c. 1719–1806)	Dublin, Ireland	lawyer
George Taylor (1716–1781)	Ireland	ironmaster
James Wilson (1742–1798)	Fife, Scotland	lawyer, judge
Rhode Island		
William Ellery (1727–1820)	Newport RI	lawyer, judge
Stephen Hopkins (1707–1785)	Providence RI	judge, educator
South Carolina		
Thomas Heyward, Jr. (1746–1809)	St. Helena's (now St. Luke's) parish SC	lawyer, judge
Thomas Lynch, Jr. (1749–1779)	Winyah SC	lawyer
Arthur Middleton (1742–1787)	near Charleston SC	planter, legislator
Edward Rutledge (1749–1800)	Charleston SC	lawyer
Virginia		
Carter Braxton (1736–1797)	Newington Plantation VA	planter
Thomas Jefferson (1743–1826)	Shadwell VA	lawyer, author, educator
Benjamin Harrison (c. 1726–1791)	Berkeley VA	planter, politician
Francis Lightfoot Lee (1734–1797)	Westmoreland county VA	farmer
Richard Henry Lee (1732–1794)	Westmoreland county VA	planter, judge
Thomas Nelson, Jr. (1738–1789)	Yorktown VA	planter
George Wythe (1726–1806)	Elizabeth City county (Hampton) VA	lawyer, educator

The Constitution of the United States

The Constitution was written during the summer of 1787 in Philadelphia by 55 delegates to a Constitutional Convention that was called ostensibly to amend the Articles of Confederation. It was submitted for ratification to the 13 states on 28 Sep 1787. In June 1788, after the Constitution had been ratified by nine states (as required by Article VII), Congress set 4 Mar 1789 as the date for the new government to commence proceedings.

Preamble

We the People of the United States, in Order to form a more perfect Union, establish Justice, insure domestic Tranquility, provide for common defence, promote the general Welfare, and secure the Blessings of Liberty to ourselves and our Posterity, do ordain and establish this Constitution for the United States of America.

Article I

Section 1—

All legislative Powers herein granted shall be vested in a Congress of the United States, which shall consist of a Senate and House of Representatives.

Section 2—

The House of Representatives shall be composed of Members chosen every second Year by the People of the several States, and the Electors in each State shall have the Qualifications requisite for Electors of the most numerous Branch of the State Legislature.

No Person shall be a Representative who shall not have attained to the Age of twenty five Years, and been seven Years a Citizen of the United States, and who shall not, when elected, be an Inhabitant of that State in which he shall be chosen.

Representatives and direct Taxes shall be apportioned among the several States which may be included within this Union, according to their respective Numbers, which shall be determined by adding to the whole Number of free Persons, including those bound to Service for a Term of Years, and excluding Indians not taxed, three fifths of all other Persons. The actual Enumeration shall be made within three Years after the first Meeting of the Congress of the United States, and within every subsequent Term of ten Years, in such Manner as they shall by Law direct. The Number of Representatives shall not exceed one for every thirty Thousand, but each State shall have at Least one Representative; and until such enumeration shall be made, the State of New Hampshire shall be entitled to chuse three, Massachusetts eight, Rhode-Island and Providence Plantations one, Connecticut five, New-York six, New Jersey four, Pennsylvania eight, Delaware one, Maryland six, Virginia ten, North Carolina five, South Carolina five, and Georgia three.

When vacancies happen in the Representation from any State, the Executive Authority thereof shall issue Writs of Election to fill such Vacancies.

The House of Representatives shall chuse their speaker and other Officers; and shall have the sole Power of Impeachment.

Section 3—

The Senate of the United States shall be composed of two Senators from each State, chosen by the Legislature thereof for six Years; and each Senator shall have one Vote.

Immediately after they shall be assembled in Consequence of the first Election, they shall be divided as equally as may be into three Classes. The Seats of the Senators of the first Class shall be vacated at the Expiration of the second Year, of the second Class at the Expiration of the fourth Year, and of the third Class at the Expiration of the sixth Year, so that one third may be chosen every second Year; and if Vacancies happen by Resignation, or otherwise, during the Recess of the Legislature of any State, the Executive thereof may make temporary Appointments until the next Meeting of the Legislature, which shall then fill such Vacancies.

No Person shall be a Senator who shall not have attained to the Age of thirty Years, and been nine Years a Citizen of the United States, and who shall not, when elected, be an Inhabitant of that State for which he shall be chosen.

The Vice President of the United States shall be President of the Senate, but shall have no Vote, unless they be equally divided.

The Senate shall chuse their other Officers, and also a President pro tempore, in the Absence of the Vice President, or when he shall exercise the Office of President of the United States.

The Senate shall have the sole Power to try all Impeachments. When sitting for that Purpose, they shall be on Oath or Affirmation. When the President of the United States is tried, the Chief Justice shall preside: And no Person shall be convicted without the concurrence of two thirds of the Members present. Judgment in Cases of Impeachment shall not extend further than to removal from Office, and disqualification to hold and enjoy any Office of honor, Trust or Profit under the United States: but the Party convicted shall nevertheless be liable and subject to Indictment, Trial, Judgment and Punishment, according to law.

Section 4—

The Times, Places and Manner of holding Elections for Senators and Representatives, shall be prescribed in each State by the Legislature thereof; but the Congress may at any time by Law make or alter such Regulations, except as to the Places of chusing Senators.

The Congress shall assemble at least once in every Year, and such Meeting shall be on the first Monday in December, unless they shall by Law appoint a different Day.

Section 5—

Each House shall be the Judge of the Elections, Returns and Qualifications of its own Members, and a Majority of each shall constitute a Quorum to do business; but a smaller Number may adjourn from day to day, and may be authorized to compel the Attendance of absent Members, in such Manner, and under such Penalties as each House may provide.

Each House may determine the Rules of its Proceedings, punish its Members for disorderly Behaviour, and, with the Concurrence of two thirds, expel a Member.

Each House shall keep a journal of its Proceedings, and from time to time publish the same, excepting such Parts as may in their Judgment require Secrecy; and the yeas and Nays of the Members of either House on any question shall, at the Desire of one fifth of those Present, be entered on the journal.

Neither House, during the Session of Congress, shall, without the Consent of the other, adjourn for more than three days, nor to any other place than that in which the two Houses shall be sitting.

Section 6—
The Senators and Representatives shall receive a Compensation for their Services, to be ascertained by Law, and paid out of the Treasury of the United States. They shall in all Cases, except Treason, Felony and Breach of the Peace, be privileged from Arrest during their Attendance at the Session of their respective Houses, and in going to and returning from the same; and for any Speech or Debate in either House, they shall not be questioned in any other Place.

No Senator or Representative shall, during the Time for which he was elected, be appointed to any civil Office under the Authority of the United States, which shall have been created, or the Emoluments whereof shall have been encreased during such time; and no Person holding any Office under the United States, shall be a Member of either House during his Continuance in Office.

Section 7—
All Bills for raising Revenue shall originate in the House of Representatives; but the Senate may propose or concur with Amendments as on other Bills.

Every Bill which shall have passed the House of Representatives and the Senate, shall, before it become a Law, be presented to the President of the United States; If he approve he shall sign it, but if not he shall return it, with his Objections to that House in which it shall have originated, who shall enter the Objections at large on their Journal, and proceed to reconsider it. If after such Reconsideration two thirds of that House shall agree to pass the Bill, it shall be sent, together with the Objections, to the other House, by which it shall likewise be reconsidered, and if approved by two thirds of that House, it shall become a Law. But in all such Cases the Votes of both Houses shall be determined by yeas and Nays, and the Names of the Persons voting for and against the Bill shall be entered on the Journal of each House respectively. If any Bill shall not be returned by the President within ten Days (Sundays excepted) after it shall have been presented to him, the Same shall be a Law, in like Manner as if he had signed it, unless the Congress by their Adjournment prevent its Return, in which Case it shall not be a Law.

Every Order, Resolution, or Vote to which the Concurrence of the Senate and House of Representatives may be necessary (except on a question of Adjournment) shall be presented to the President of the United States; and before the Same shall take Effect, shall be approved by him, or being disapproved by him, shall be repassed by two thirds of the Senate and House of Representatives, according to the Rules and Limitations prescribed in the Case of a Bill.

Section 8—
The Congress shall have Power To lay and collect Taxes, Duties, Imposts and Excises, to pay the Debts and provide for the common Defence and general Welfare of the United States; but all Duties, Imposts and Excises shall be uniform throughout the United States;

To borrow Money on the credit of the United States;

To regulate Commerce with foreign Nations, and among the several States, and with the Indian Tribes;

To establish an uniform Rule of Naturalization, and uniform Laws on the subject of Bankruptcies throughout the United States;

To coin Money, regulate the Value thereof, and of foreign Coin, and fix the Standard of Weights and Measures;

To provide for the Punishment of counterfeiting the Securities and current Coin of the United States;

To establish Post Offices and post Roads;

To promote the Progress of Science and useful Arts, by securing for limited Times to Authors and Inventors the exclusive Right to their respective Writings and Discoveries;

To constitute Tribunals inferior to the supreme Court;

To define and punish Piracies and Felonies committed on the high Seas, and Offences against the Law of Nations;

To declare War, grant Letters of Marque and Reprisal, and make rules concerning Captures on Land and Water;

To raise and support Armies, but no Appropriation of Money to that Use shall be for a longer Term than two Years;

To provide and maintain a Navy;

To make Rules for the Government and Regulation of the land and naval Forces;

To provide for calling forth the Militia to execute the Laws of the Union, suppress Insurrections and repel Invasions;

To provide for organizing, arming, and disciplining, the Militia, and for governing such Part of them as may be employed in the Service of the United States, reserving to the States respectively, the Appointment of the Officers, and the Authority of training the Militia according to the discipline prescribed by Congress;

To exercise exclusive Legislation in all Cases whatsoever, over such District (not exceeding ten Miles square), as may, by Cession of particular States, and the Acceptance of Congress, become the Seat of the Government of the United States, and to exercise like Authority over all Places purchased by the Consent of the Legislature of the State in which the Same shall be for the Erection of Forts, Magazines, Arsenals, dock-Yards, and other needful Buildings; — And

To make all Laws which shall be necessary and proper for carrying into Execution the foregoing Powers, and all other Powers vested by this Constitution in the Government of the United States, or in any Department or Officer thereof.

Section 9—
The Migration or Importation of such Persons as any of the States now existing shall think proper to admit, shall not be prohibited by the Congress prior to the Year one thousand eight hundred and eight, but a Tax or duty may be imposed on such Importation, not exceeding ten dollars for each Person.

The Privilege of the Writ of Habeas Corpus shall not be suspended, unless when in Cases of Rebellion or Invasion the public Safety may require it.

No Bill of Attainder or ex post facto Law shall be passed.

No Capitation, or other direct, Tax shall be laid, unless in Proportion to the Census or Enumeration herein before directed to be taken.

No Tax or Duty shall be laid on Articles exported from any State.

No Preference shall be given by any Regulation of Commerce or Revenue to the Ports of one State over those of another; nor shall Vessels bound to, or from, one State, be obliged to enter, clear or pay Duties in another.

No money shall be drawn from the Treasury, but in Consequence of Appropriations made by Law; and a regular Statement and Account of the Receipts and Expenditures of all public Money shall be published from time to time.

No Title of Nobility shall be granted by the United States: And no Person holding any Office of Profit or Trust under them, shall, without the Consent of the Congress, accept of any present, Emolument, Office, or Title, of any kind whatever, from any King, Prince, or foreign State.

Section 10—

No State shall enter into any Treaty, Alliance, or Confederation; grant Letters of Marque and Reprisal; coin Money; emit Bills of Credit; make any Thing but gold and silver Coin a Tender in Payment of Debts; pass any Bill of Attainder, ex post facto Law, or Law impairing the Obligation of Contracts, or grant any Title of Nobility.

No State shall, without the Consent of the Congress, lay any Imposts or Duties on Imports or Exports, except what may be absolutely necessary for executing it's inspection Laws: and the net Produce of all Duties and Imposts, laid by any State on Imports or Exports, shall be for the Use of the Treasury of the United States; and all such Laws shall be subject to the Revision and Controul of the Congress.

No State shall, without the Consent of Congress, lay any Duty of Tonnage, keep Troops, or Ships of War in time of Peace, enter into any Agreement or Compact with another State, or with a foreign Power, or engage in War, unless actually invaded, or in such imminent Danger as will not admit of delay.

Article II

Section 1—

The executive Power shall be vested in a President of the United States of America. He shall hold his Office during the Term of four Years, and, together with the Vice President, chosen for the same Term, be elected, as follows

Each State shall appoint, in such Manner as the Legislature thereof may direct, a Number of Electors, equal to the whole Number of Senators and Representatives to which the State may be entitled in the Congress: but no Senator or Representative, or Person holding an Office of Trust or Profit under the United States, shall be appointed an Elector.

The Electors shall meet in their respective States, and vote by Ballot for two Persons, of whom one at least shall not be an Inhabitant of the same State with themselves. And they shall make a List of all the Persons voted for, and of the Number of Votes for each; which List they shall sign and certify, and transmit sealed to the Seat of the Government of the United States, directed to the President of the Senate. The President of the Senate shall, in the Presence of the Senate and House of Representatives, open all the Certificates, and the Votes shall then be counted. The Person having the greatest Number of Votes shall be the President, if such Number be a Majority of the whole Number of Electors appointed; and if there be more than one who have such Majority, and have an equal Number of Votes, then the House of Representatives shall immediately chuse by Ballot one of them for President: and if no Person have a Majority, then from the five

highest on the List the said House shall in like Manner chuse the President. But in chusing the President, the Votes shall be taken by States, the Representation from each State having one Vote; A quorum for this Purpose shall consist of a Member or Members from two thirds of the States, and a Majority of all the States shall be necessary to a Choice. In every Case, after the Choice of the President, the Person having the greatest Number of Votes of the Electors shall be the Vice President. But if there should remain two or more who have equal Votes, the Senate shall chuse from them by Ballot the Vice President.

The Congress may determine the Time of chusing the Electors, and the Day on which they shall give their Votes; which Day shall be the same throughout the United States.

No Person except a natural born Citizen, or a Citizen of the United States, at the time of the Adoption of this Constitution, shall be eligible to the Office of President; neither shall any Person be eligible to that Office who shall not have attained to the Age of thirty five Years, and been fourteen Years a Resident within the United States.

In Case of the Removal of the President from Office, or of his Death, Resignation, or Inability to discharge the Powers and Duties of the said Office, the Same shall devolve on the Vice President, and the Congress may by Law provide for the Case of Removal, Death, Resignation or Inability, both of the President and Vice President, declaring what Officer shall then act as President, and such Officer shall act accordingly, until the Disability be removed, or a President shall be elected.

The President shall, at stated Times, receive for his Services, a Compensation, which shall neither be encreased nor diminished during the Period for which he shall have been elected, and he shall not receive within that Period any other Emolument from the United States, or any of them.

Before he enter on the Execution of his Office, he shall take the following Oath or Affirmation: "I do solemnly swear (or affirm) that I will faithfully execute the Office of President of the United States, and will to the best of my Ability, preserve, protect and defend the Constitution of the United States."

Section 2—

The President shall be Commander in Chief of the Army and Navy of the United States, and of the Militia of the several States, when called into the actual Service of the United States; he may require the Opinion, in writing, of the principal Officer in each of the executive Departments, upon any Subject relating to the Duties of their respective Offices, and he shall have Power to grant Reprieves and Pardons for Offences against the United States, except in Cases of Impeachment.

He shall have Power, by and with the Advice and Consent of the Senate, to make Treaties, provided two thirds of the Senators present concur; and he shall nominate, and by and with the Advice and Consent of the Senate, shall appoint Ambassadors, other public Ministers and Consuls, Judges of the supreme Court, and all other Officers of the United States, whose Appointments are not herein otherwise provided for, and which shall be established by Law: but the Congress may by Law vest the Appointment of such inferior Officers, as they think proper, in the President alone, in the Courts of Law, or in the Heads of Departments.

The President shall have Power to fill up all Vacancies that may happen during the Recess of the Senate, by granting Commissions which shall expire at the End of their next Session.

Section 3—

He shall from time to time give to the Congress Information of the State of the Union, and recommend to their Consideration such Measures as he shall judge necessary and expedient; he may, on extraordinary Occasions, convene both Houses, or either of them, and in Case of Disagreement between them, with Respect to the Time of Adjournment, he may adjourn them to such Time as he shall think proper; he shall receive Ambassadors and other public Ministers; he shall take Care that the Laws be faithfully executed, and shall Commission all the Officers of the United States.

Section 4—

The President, Vice President and all civil Officers of the United States, shall be removed from Office on Impeachment for, and Conviction of, Treason, Bribery, or other High Crimes and Misdemeanors.

Article III

Section 1—

The judicial Power of the United States, shall be vested in one supreme Court, and in such inferior Courts as the Congress may from time to time ordain and establish. The Judges, both of the supreme and inferior Courts, shall hold their Offices during good Behaviour, and shall, at stated Times, receive for their Services, a Compensation, which shall not be diminished during their Continuance in Office.

Section 2—

The judicial Power shall extend to all Cases, in Law and Equity, arising under this Constitution, the Laws of the United States, and Treaties made, or which shall be made, under their Authority; — to all Cases affecting Ambassadors, other public Ministers and Consuls; — to all Cases of admiralty and maritime jurisdiction; — to Controversies to which the United States shall be a Party; — to Controversies between two or more States;-between a State and Citizens of another State; — between Citizens of different States; — between Citizens of the same State claiming Lands under Grants of different States, and between a State, or the Citizens thereof, and foreign States, Citizens or Subjects.

In all Cases affecting Ambassadors, other public Ministers and Consuls, and those in which a State shall be Party, the supreme Court shall have original Jurisdiction. In all the other Cases before mentioned, the supreme Court shall have appellate Jurisdiction, both as to Law and Fact, with such Exceptions, and under such Regulations as the Congress shall make.

The Trial of all Crimes, except in Cases of Impeachment, shall be by Jury; and such Trial shall be held in the State where the said Crimes shall have been committed; but when not committed within any State, the Trial shall be at such Place or Places as the Congress may by Law have directed.

Section 3—

Treason against the United States, shall consist only in levying War against them, or in adhering to their Enemies, giving them Aid and Comfort. No Person shall be convicted of Treason unless on the Testimony of two Witnesses to the same overt Act, or on Confession in open Court.

The Congress shall have Power to declare the Punishment of Treason, but no Attainder of Treason shall work Corruption of Blood, or Forfeiture except during the Life of the Person attainted.

Article IV

Section 1—

Full Faith and Credit shall be given in each State to the public Acts, Records, and judicial Proceedings of every other State. And the Congress may by general Laws prescribe the Manner in which such Acts, Records and Proceedings shall be proved, and the Effect thereof.

Section 2—

The Citizens of each State shall be entitled to all Privileges and Immunities of Citizens in the several States.

A person charged in any State with Treason, Felony, or other Crime, who shall flee from justice, and be found in another State, shall on Demand of the executive Authority of the State from which he fled, be delivered up, to be removed to the State having Jurisdiction of the Crime.

No Person held to Service or Labour in one State, under the Laws thereof, escaping into another, shall in Consequence of any Law or Regulation therein, be discharged from such Service or Labour, but shall be delivered upon on Claim of the Party to whom such Service or Labour may be due.

Section 3—

New States may be admitted by the Congress into this Union; but no new State shall be formed or erected within the Jurisdiction of any other State; nor any State be formed by the Junction of two or more States, or Parts of States, without the Consent of the Legislatures of the States concerned as well as of the Congress.

The Congress shall have Power to dispose of and make all needful Rules and Regulations respecting the Territory or other Property belonging to the United States; and nothing in this Constitution shall be so construed as to Prejudice any Claims of the United States, or of any particular State.

Section 4—

The United States shall guarantee to every State in this Union a Republican Form of Government, and shall protect each of them against Invasion; and on Application of the Legislature, or of the Executive (when the Legislature cannot be convened) against domestic Violence.

Article V

The Congress, whenever two thirds of both Houses shall deem it necessary, shall propose Amendments to this Constitution, or, on the Application of the Legislatures of two thirds of the several States, shall call a Convention for proposing Amendments, which, in either Case, shall be valid to all Intents and Purposes, as Part of this Constitution, when ratified by the Legislatures of three fourths of the several States, or by Conventions in three fourths thereof, as the one or the other Mode of Ratification may be proposed by the Congress; Provided that no Amendment which may be made prior to the Year One thousand eight hundred and eight shall in any Manner affect the first and fourth Clauses in the Ninth Section of the first

Article; and that no State, without its Consent, shall be deprived of its equal Suffrage in the Senate.

Article VI
All Debts contracted and Engagements entered into, before the Adoption of this Constitution, shall be as valid against the United States under this Constitution, as under the Confederation.

This Constitution, and the Laws of the United States which shall be made in Pursuance thereof; and all Treaties made, or which shall be made, under the Authority of the United States, shall be the supreme Law of the Land; and the Judges in every State shall be bound thereby, any Thing in the Constitution or Laws of any State to the Contrary notwithstanding.

The Senators and Representatives before mentioned, and the Members of the several State Legislatures, and all executive and judicial Officers, both of the United States and of the several States, shall be bound by Oath or Affirmation, to support this Constitution; but no religious Test shall ever be required as a Qualification to any Office or public Trust under the United States.

Article VII
The Ratification of the Conventions of nine States, shall be sufficient for the Establishment of this Constitution between the States so ratifying the Same.

Done in Convention by the Unanimous Consent of the States present the Seventeenth Day of September in the Year of our Lord one thousand seven hundred and Eighty seven and of the Independence of the United States of America the Twelfth
IN WITNESS whereof We have hereunto subscribed our Names,

G⁰ Washington—
Presid^t. and deputy from Virginia

New Hampshire
John Langdon
Nicholas Gilman

Massachusetts
Nathaniel Gorham
Rufus King

Connecticut
Wm. Saml. Johnson
Roger Sherman

New York
Alexander Hamilton

New Jersey
Wil: Livingston
David Brearley
Wm. Paterson
Jona: Dayton

Pennsylvania
B. Franklin
Thomas Mifflin
Robt Morris
Geo. Clymer
Thos. FitzSimons
Jared Ingersoll
James Wilson
Gouv Morris

Delaware
Geo: Read
Gunning Bedford jun
John Dickinson
Richard Bassett
Jaco: Broom

Maryland
James McHenry
Dan of St Thos. Jenifer
Danl Carroll

Virginia
John Blair—
James Madison Jr.

North Carolina
Wm. Blount
Rich'd Dobbs Spaight
Hu Williamson

South Carolina
J. Rutledge
Charles Cotesworth Pinckney
Charles Pinckney
Pierce Butler

Georgia
William Few
Abr Baldwin

Attest:
William Jackson, *Secretary*

[*Rhode Island and the Providence Plantations*
Rhode Island did not send delegates to the Constitutional Convention.]

Bill of Rights

The first 10 amendments to the Constitution were adopted as a single unit on 15 Dec 1791. Together, they constitute a collection of mutually reinforcing guarantees of individual rights and of limitations on federal and state governments.

Amendment I
Congress shall make no law respecting an establishment of religion, or prohibiting the free exercise thereof; or abridging the freedom of speech, or of the press; or the right of the people peaceably to assemble, and to petition the Government for a redress of grievances.

Amendment II
A well regulated Militia, being necessary to the security of a free State, the right of the people to keep and bear Arms, shall not be infringed.

Amendment III
No Soldier shall, in time of peace be quartered in any house, without the consent of the Owner, nor in time of war, but in a manner to be prescribed by law.

Amendment IV
The right of the People to be secure in their persons,

houses, papers, and effects, against unreasonable searches and seizures, shall not be violated, and no Warrants shall issue, but upon probable cause, supported by Oath or affirmation, and particularity describing the place to be searched, and the persons or things to be seized.

Amendment V

No person shall be held to answer for a capital, or otherwise infamous crime, unless on a presentment or indictment of a Grand Jury, except in cases arising in the land or naval forces, or in the Militia, when in actual service in time of War or public danger; nor shall any person be subject for the same offence to be twice put in jeopardy of life or limb; nor shall be compelled in any criminal case to be a witness against himself, nor be deprived of life, liberty, or property, without due process of law; nor shall private property be taken for public use, without just compensation.

Amendment VI

In all criminal prosecutions, the accused shall enjoy the right to a speedy and public trial, by an impartial jury of the State and district wherein the crime shall have been committed, which district shall have been previously ascertained by law, and to be informed of the nature and cause of the accusation; to be confronted with the witnesses against him; to have compulsory process for obtaining witnesses in his favor, and to have Assistance of Counsel for his defence.

Amendment VII

In Suits at common law, where the value in controversy shall exceed twenty dollars, the right of trial by jury shall be preserved, and no fact tried by a jury, shall be otherwise re-examined in any Court of the United States, than according to the rules of the common law.

Amendment VIII

Excessive bail shall not be required, nor excessive fines imposed, nor cruel and unusual punishments inflicted.

Amendment IX

The enumeration in the Constitution, of certain rights, shall not be construed to deny or disparage others retained by the people.

Amendment X

The powers not delegated to the United States by the Constitution, nor prohibited by it to the States, are reserved to the States respectively, or to the people.

Further Amendments

Amendment XI
(ratified 7 Feb 1795)

The Judicial power of the United States shall not be construed to extend to any suit in law or equity, commenced or prosecuted against one of the United States by Citizens of another State, or by Citizens or Subjects of any Foreign State.

Amendment XII
(ratified 15 Jun 1804)

The Electors shall meet in their respective states and vote by ballot for President and Vice-President, one of whom, at least, shall not be an inhabitant of the same state with themselves; they shall name in their ballots the person voted for as President, and in distinct ballots the person voted for as Vice-President, and they shall make distinct lists of all persons voted for as President, and of all persons voted for as Vice-President, and of the number of votes for each, which lists they shall sign and certify, and transmit sealed to the seat of the government of the United States, directed to the President of the Senate; — The President of the Senate shall, in the presence of the Senate and House of Representatives, open all the certificates and the votes shall then be counted; — The person having the greatest number of votes for President, shall be the President, if such number be a majority of the whole number of Electors appointed; and if no person have such majority, then from the persons having the highest numbers not exceeding three on the list of those voted for as President, the House of Representatives shall choose immediately, by ballot, the President. But in choosing the President, the votes shall be taken by states, the representation from each state having one vote; a quorum for this purpose shall consist of a member or members from two-thirds of the states, and a majority of all the states shall be necessary to a choice. And if the House of Representatives shall not choose a President whenever the right of choice shall devolve upon then, before the fourth day of March next following, then the Vice-President shall act as President, as in the case of the death or other constitutional disability of the President. — The person having the greatest number of votes as Vice-President, shall be the Vice-President, if such number be a majority of the whole number of Electors appointed, and if no person have a majority, then from the two highest numbers on the list, the Senate shall choose the Vice-President; a quorum for the purpose shall consist of two-thirds of the whole number of Senators, and a majority of the whole number shall be necessary to a choice. But no person constitutionally ineligible to the office of President shall be eligible to that of Vice-President of the United States.

Amendment XIII
(ratified 6 Dec 1865)

Section 1—
Neither slavery nor involuntary servitude, except as a punishment for crime whereof the party shall have been duly convicted, shall exist within the United States, or any place subject to their jurisdiction.

Section 2—
Congress shall have power to enforce this article by appropriate legislation.

Amendment XIV
(ratified 9 Jul 1868)

Section 1—
All persons born or naturalized in the United States, and subject to the jurisdiction thereof, are citizens of the United States and of the State wherein they reside. No State shall make or enforce any law which shall abridge the privileges or immunities of citizens of the United States; nor shall any State deprive any person of life, liberty, or property, without due process of law; nor deny to any person within its jurisdiction the equal protection of the laws.

Section 2—

Representatives shall be apportioned among the several States according to their respective numbers, counting the whole number of persons in each State, excluding Indians not taxed. But when the right to vote at any election for the choice of electors for President and Vice President of the United States, Representatives in Congress, the Executive and Judicial officers of a State, or the members of the Legislature thereof, is denied to any of the male inhabitants of such State, being twenty-one years of age, and citizens of the United States, or in any way abridged, except for participation in rebellion, or other crime, the basis of representation therein shall be reduced in the proportion which the number of such male citizens shall bear to the whole number of male citizens twenty-one years of age in such State.

Section 3—

No person shall be a Senator or Representative in Congress, or elector of President and Vice President, or hold any office, civil or military, under the United States, or under any State, who, having previously taken an oath, as a member of Congress, or as an officer of the United States, or as a member of any State legislature, or as an executive or judicial officer of any State, to support the Constitution of the United States, shall have engaged in insurrection or rebellion against the same, or given aid or comfort to the enemies thereof. But Congress may by a vote of two-thirds of each House, remove such disability.

Section 4—

The validity of the public debt of the United States, authorized by law, including debts incurred for payment of pensions and bounties for services in suppressing insurrection or rebellion, shall not be questioned. But neither the United States nor any State shall assume or pay any debt or obligation incurred in aid of insurrection or rebellion against the United States, or any claim for the loss or emancipation of any slave; but all such debts, obligations and claims shall be held illegal and void.

Section 5—

The Congress shall have power to enforce, by appropriate legislation, the provisions of this article.

Amendment XV
(ratified 8 Feb 1870)

Section 1—

The right of citizens of the United States to vote shall not be denied or abridged by the United States or by any State on account of race, color, or previous condition of servitude.

Section 2—

The Congress shall have power to enforce this article by appropriate legislation.

Amendment XVI
(ratified 3 Feb 1913)

The Congress shall have power to lay and collect taxes on incomes, from whatever source derived, without apportionment among the several States, and without regard to any census or enumeration.

Amendment XVII
(ratified 13 Feb 1913)

The Senate of the United States shall be composed of two Senators from each State, elected by the people thereof for six years; and each Senator shall have one vote. The electors in each State shall have the qualifications requisite for electors of the most numerous branch of the State legislatures.

When vacancies happen in the representation of any State in the Senate, the executive authority of such State shall issue writs of election to fill such vacancies: Provided, That the legislature of any State may empower the executive thereof to make temporary appointments until the people fill the vacancies by election as the legislature may direct.

This amendment shall not be so construed as to affect the election or term of any Senator chosen before it becomes valid as part of the Constitution.

Amendment XVIII
(ratified 16 Jan 1919; repealed 5 Dec 1933 by Amendment XXI)

Section 1—

After one year from the ratification of this article the manufacture, sale, or transportation of intoxicating liquors within, the importation thereof into, or the exportation thereof from the United States and all territory subject to the jurisdiction thereof for beverage purposes is hereby prohibited.

Section 2—

The Congress and the several States shall have concurrent power to enforce this article by appropriate legislation.

Section 3—

This article shall be inoperative unless it shall have been ratified as an amendment to the Constitution by the legislatures of the several States as provided in the Constitution, within seven years from the date of the submission hereof to the States by the Congress.

Amendment XIX
(ratified 18 Aug 1920)

The right of citizens of the United States to vote shall not be denied or abridged by the United States or by any State on account of sex.

Congress shall have power to enforce this article by appropriate legislation.

Amendment XX
(ratified 23 Jan 1933)

Section 1—

The terms of the President and Vice President shall end at noon on the 20th day of January, and the terms of Senators and Representatives at noon on the 3d day of January, of the years in which such terms would have ended if this article had not been ratified; and the terms of their successors shall then begin.

Section 2—

The Congress shall assemble at least once in every year, and such meeting shall begin at noon on the 3d day of January, unless they shall by law appoint a different day.

Section 3—

If, at the time fixed for the beginning of the term of the President, the President elect shall have died, the Vice President elect shall become President. If a President shall not have been chosen before the time fixed for the beginning of his term, or if the President elect shall have failed to qualify, then the Vice President elect shall act as President until a President shall have qualified; and the Congress may by law provide for the case wherein neither a President elect nor a Vice President elect shall have qualified, declaring who shall then act as President, or the manner in which one who is to act shall be selected, and such person shall act accordingly until a President or Vice President shall have qualified.

Section 4—
The Congress may by law provide for the case of the death of any of the persons from whom the House of Representatives may choose a President whenever the right of choice shall have devolved upon them, and for the case of the death of any of the persons from whom the Senate may choose a Vice President whenever the right of choice shall have devolved upon them.

Section 5—
Sections 1 and 2 shall take effect on the 15th day of October following the ratification of this article.

Section 6—
This article shall be inoperative unless it shall have been ratified as an amendment to the Constitution by the legislatures of three-fourths of the several States within seven years from the date of its submission.

Amendment XXI
(ratified 5 Dec 1933)

Section 1—
The eighteenth article of amendment to the Constitution of the United States is hereby repealed.

Section 2—
The transportation or importation into any State, Territory, or possession of the United States for delivery or use therein of intoxicating liquors, in violation of the laws thereof, is hereby prohibited.

Section 3—
This article shall be inoperative unless it shall have been ratified as an amendment to the Constitution by conventions in the several States, as provided in the Constitution, within seven years from the date of the submission hereof to the States by the Congress.

Amendment XXII
(ratified 27 Feb 1951)

Section 1—
No person shall be elected to the office of the President more than twice, and no person who has held the office of President, or acted as President, for more than two years of a term to which some other person was elected President shall be elected to the office of the President more than once. But this Article shall not apply to any person holding the office of President when this Article was proposed by the Congress, and shall not prevent any person who may be holding the office of President, or acting as President, during the term within which this Article becomes operative from holding the office of President or acting as President during the remainder of such term.

Section 2—
This Article shall be inoperative unless it shall have been ratified as an amendment to the Constitution by the legislatures of three-fourths of the several States within seven years from the date of its submission to the States by the Congress.

Amendment XXIII
(ratified 29 Mar 1961)

Section 1—
The District constituting the seat of Government of the United States shall appoint in such manner as the Congress may direct:

A number of electors of President and Vice President equal to the whole number of Senators and Representatives in Congress to which the District would be entitled if it were a State, but in no event more than the least populous State; they shall be in addition to those appointed by the States, but they shall be considered, for the purposes of the election of President and Vice President, to be electors appointed by a State; and they shall meet in the District and perform such duties as provided by the twelfth article of amendment.

Section 2—
The Congress shall have power to enforce this article by appropriate legislation.

Amendment XXIV
(ratified 23 Jan 1964)

Section 1—
The right of citizens of the United States to vote in any primary or other election for President or Vice President, for electors for President or Vice President, or for Senator or Representative in Congress, shall not be denied or abridged by the United States or any State by reason of failure to pay any poll tax or other tax.

Section 2—
The Congress shall have power to enforce this article by appropriate legislation.

Amendment XXV
(ratified 23 Jan 1967)

Section 1—
In case of the removal of the President from office or of his death or resignation, the Vice President shall become President.

Section 2—
Whenever there is a vacancy in the office of the Vice President, the President shall nominate a Vice President who shall take office upon confirmation by a majority vote of both Houses of Congress.

Section 3—
Whenever the President transmits to the President pro tempore of the Senate and the Speaker of the House of Representatives his written declaration that he is unable to discharge the powers and duties of his office, and until he transmits to them a written declaration to the contrary, such powers and duties shall be discharged by the Vice President as Acting President.

Section 4—
Whenever the Vice president and a majority of either the principal officers of the executive departments or of such other body as Congress may by law provide, transmit to the President pro tempore of the Senate and the Speaker of the House of Representatives their written declaration that the President is unable to discharge the powers and duties of his office, the Vice President shall immediately assume the powers and duties of the office as Acting President.

Thereafter, when the President transmits to the President pro tempore of the Senate and the Speaker of the House of Representatives his written declaration that no inability exists, he shall resume the powers and duties of his office unless the Vice President and a majority of either the principal officers of the executive department or of such other body as Congress may by law provide, transmit within four days to the President pro tempore of the Senate and the Speaker of the House of Representatives their written declaration that the President is unable to discharge the powers and duties of his office. Thereupon Congress shall decide the issue, assembling within forty-eight hours for that purpose if not in session. If the Congress, within twenty-one days after receipt of the latter written declaration, or, if Congress is not in session, within twenty-one days after Congress is required to assemble, determines by two-thirds vote of both Houses that the President is unable to discharge the powers and duties of his office, the Vice President shall continue to discharge the same as Acting President; otherwise, the President shall resume the powers and duties of his office.

Amendment XXVI
(ratified 1 Jul 1971)

Section 1—
The right of citizens of the United States, who are eighteen years of age or older, to vote shall not be denied or abridged by the United States or by any State on account of age.

Section 2—
The Congress shall have power to enforce this article by appropriate legislation.

Amendment XXVII
(ratified 7 May 1992)

No law, varying the compensation for the services of the Senators and Representatives, shall take effect, until an election of representatives shall have intervened.

Confederate States and Secession Dates

In the months following Abraham Lincoln's election as president in 1860, seven states of the Deep South held conventions and approved secession, thus precipitating the Civil War. After the attack on Fort Sumter SC on 12 Apr 1861, Virginia, Arkansas, North Carolina, and Tennessee also seceded (Tennessee was the only state to hold a popular referendum without a convention on secession). The Confederacy operated as a separate government, with Jefferson Davis as president and Alexander H. Stephens as vice president. Its principal goals were the preservation of states' rights and the institution of slavery. Although it enjoyed a series of military victories in the first two years of fighting, the surrender at Appomattox VA by Gen. Robert E. Lee on 9 Apr 1865 signaled its dissolution.

STATE	DATE	STATE	DATE	STATE	DATE
South Carolina	20 Dec 1860	Georgia	19 Jan 1861	Arkansas	6 May 1861
Mississippi	9 Jan 1861	Louisiana	26 Jan 1861	North Carolina	20 May 1861
Florida	10 Jan 1861	Texas	1 Feb 1861	Tennessee	8 Jun 1861
Alabama	11 Jan 1861	Virginia	17 Apr 1861		

Emancipation Proclamation

The Emancipation Proclamation was issued by Pres. Abraham Lincoln and freed the slaves of the Confederate states in rebellion against the Union. After the Battle of Antietam (17 Sep 1862), Lincoln issued his proclamation calling on the revolted states to return to their allegiance before the next year, otherwise their slaves would be declared free men. No state returned, and the threatened declaration was issued on 1 Jan 1863.

By the President of the United States of America:

A Proclamation.

Whereas, on the twenty-second day of September, in the year of our Lord one thousand eight hundred and sixty-two, a proclamation was issued by the President of the United States, containing, among other things, the following, to wit:

"That on the first day of January, in the year of our Lord one thousand eight hundred and sixty-three, all persons held as slaves within any State or designated part of a State, the people whereof shall then be in rebellion against the United States, shall be then, thenceforward, and forever free; and the Executive Government of the United States, including the military and naval authority thereof, will recognize and maintain the freedom of such persons, and will do no act or acts to repress such persons, or any of them, in any efforts they may make for their actual freedom.

"That the Executive will, on the first day of January

aforesaid, by proclamation, designate the States and parts of States, if any, in which the people thereof, respectively, shall then be in rebellion against the United States; and the fact that any State, or the people thereof, shall on that day be, in good faith, represented in the Congress of the United States by members chosen thereto at elections wherein a majority of the qualified voters of such State shall have participated, shall, in the absence of strong countervailing testimony, be deemed conclusive evidence that such State, and the people thereof, are not then in rebellion against the United States."

Now, therefore I, Abraham Lincoln, President of the United States, by virtue of the power in me vested as Commander-in-Chief, of the Army and Navy of the United States in time of actual armed rebellion against the authority and government of the United States, and as a fit and necessary war measure for suppressing said rebellion, do, on this first day of January, in the year of our Lord one thousand eight hundred and sixty-three, and in accordance with my purpose so to do publicly proclaimed for the full period of one hundred days, from the day first above mentioned, order and designate as the States and parts of States wherein the people thereof respectively, are this day in rebellion against the United States, the following, to wit:

Arkansas, Texas, Louisiana, (except the Parishes of St. Bernard, Plaquemines, Jefferson, St. John, St. Charles, St. James Ascension, Assumption, Terrebonne, Lafourche, St. Mary, St. Martin, and Orleans, including the City of New Orleans) Mississippi, Alabama, Florida, Georgia, South Carolina, North Carolina, and Virginia, (except the forty-eight counties designated as West Virginia, and also the counties of Berkley, Accomac, Northampton, Elizabeth City, York, Princess Ann, and Norfolk, including the cities of Norfolk and Portsmouth[]], and which excepted parts, are for the present, left precisely as if this proclamation were not issued.

And by virtue of the power, and for the purpose aforesaid, I do order and declare that all persons held as slaves within said designated States, and parts of States, are, and henceforward shall be free; and that the Executive government of the United States, including the military and naval authorities thereof, will recognize and maintain the freedom of said persons.

And I hereby enjoin upon the people so declared to be free to abstain from all violence, unless in necessary self-defence; and I recommend to them that, in all cases when allowed, they labor faithfully for reasonable wages.

And I further declare and make known, that such persons of suitable condition, will be received into the armed service of the United States to garrison forts, positions, stations, and other places, and to man vessels of all sorts in said service.

And upon this act, sincerely believed to be an act of justice, warranted by the Constitution, upon military necessity, I invoke the considerate judgment of mankind, and the gracious favor of Almighty God.

In witness whereof, I have hereunto set my hand and caused the seal of the United States to be affixed.

Done at the City of Washington, this first day of January, in the year of our Lord one thousand eight hundred and sixty three, and of the Independence of the United States of America the eighty-seventh.

By the President: Abraham Lincoln.
William H. Seward, Secretary of State.

Gettysburg Address

On 19 Nov 1863 Pres. Abraham Lincoln delivered this speech at the consecration of the National Cemetery at Gettysburg PA, the site of one of the most decisive battles of the American Civil War. The main address at the dedication ceremony was one of two hours, delivered by Edward Everett, the best-known orator of the time. It is Lincoln's short speech, however, which is remembered, not only as a memorial to those who gave their lives on the battlefield, but as a statement of the ideals on which the nation was founded.

Four score and seven years ago our fathers brought forth on this continent a new nation, conceived in Liberty, and dedicated to the proposition that all men are created equal. Now we are engaged in a great civil war, testing whether that nation or any nation so conceived and so dedicated, can long endure. We are met on a great battle-field of that war. We have come to dedicate a portion of that field, as a final resting place for those who here gave their lives that that nation might live. It is altogether fitting and proper that we should do this. But, in a larger sense, we can not dedicate—we can not consecrate—we can not hallow—this ground. The brave men, living and dead, who struggled here, have consecrated it, far above our poor power to add or detract. The world will little note, nor long remember what we say here, but it can never forget what they did here. It is for us the living, rather, to be dedicated here to the unfinished work which they who fought here have thus far so nobly advanced. It is rather for us to be here dedicated to the great task remaining before us—that from these honored dead we take increased devotion to that cause for which they gave the last full measure of devotion—that we here highly resolve that these dead shall not have died in vain—that this nation, under God, shall have a new birth of freedom—and that government of the people, by the people, for the people, shall not perish from the earth.

United States Government

The Presidency at a Glance

	PRESIDENCY	POLITICAL PARTY	TIME IN OFFICE	VICE PRESIDENT
1	George Washington	Federalist	1789–1797	John Adams
2	John Adams	Federalist	1797–1801	Thomas Jefferson
3	Thomas Jefferson	Jeffersonian Republican	1801–1809	Aaron Burr George Clinton
4	James Madison	Jeffersonian Republican	1809–1817	George Clinton Elbridge Gerry
5	James Monroe	Jeffersonian Republican	1817–1825	Daniel D. Tompkins

The Presidency at a Glance (continued)

	PRESIDENCY	POLITICAL PARTY	TIME IN OFFICE	VICE PRESIDENT
6	John Quincy Adams	National Republican	1825–1829	John C. Calhoun
7	Andrew Jackson	Democratic	1829–1837	John C. Calhoun
				Martin Van Buren
8	Martin Van Buren	Democratic	1837–1841	Richard M. Johnson
9	William Henry Harrison*	Whig	4 Mar–4 Apr 1841	John Tyler
10	John Tyler	Whig	1841–1845	none
11	James K. Polk	Democratic	1845–1849	George Mifflin Dallas
12	Zachary Taylor*	Whig	1849–1850	Millard Fillmore
13	Millard Fillmore	Whig	1850–1853	none
14	Franklin Pierce	Democratic	1853–1857	William Rufus de Vane King
15	James Buchanan	Democratic	1857–1861	John C. Breckinridge
16	Abraham Lincoln*†	Republican	1861–1865	Hannibal Hamlin
				Andrew Johnson
17	Andrew Johnson	Democratic (Union)	1865–1869	none
18	Ulysses S. Grant	Republican	1869–1877	Schuyler Colfax
				Henry Wilson
19	Rutherford B. Hayes	Republican	1877–1881	William A. Wheeler
20	James A. Garfield*†	Republican	4 Mar–19 Sep 1881	Chester A. Arthur
21	Chester A. Arthur	Republican	1881–1885	none
22	Grover Cleveland	Democratic	1885–1889	Thomas A. Hendricks
23	Benjamin Harrison	Republican	1889–1893	Levi Parons Morton
24	Grover Cleveland	Democratic	1893–1897	Adlai E. Stevenson
25	William McKinley*†	Republican	1897–1901	Garret A. Hobart
				Theodore Roosevelt
26	Theodore Roosevelt	Republican	1901–1909	Charles Warren Fairbanks
27	William Howard Taft	Republican	1909–1913	James Schoolcraft Sherman
28	Woodrow Wilson	Democratic	1913–1921	Thomas R. Marshall
29	Warren G. Harding*	Republican	1921–1923	Calvin Coolidge
30	Calvin Coolidge	Republican	1923–1929	Charles G. Dawes
31	Herbert Hoover	Republican	1929–1933	Charles Curtis
32	Franklin D. Roosevelt*	Democratic	1933–1945	John Nance Garner
				Henry A. Wallace
				Harry S. Truman
33	Harry S. Truman	Democratic	1945–1953	Alben W. Barkley
34	Dwight D. Eisenhower	Republican	1953–1961	Richard M. Nixon
35	John F. Kennedy*†	Democratic	1961–1963	Lyndon B. Johnson
36	Lyndon B. Johnson	Democratic	1963–1969	Hubert H. Humphrey
37	Richard M. Nixon**	Republican	1969–1974	Spiro T. Agnew
				Gerald R. Ford
38	Gerald R. Ford	Republican	1974–1977	Nelson A. Rockefeller
39	Jimmy Carter	Democratic	1977–1981	Walter F. Mondale
40	Ronald Reagan	Republican	1981–1989	George H.W. Bush
41	George H.W. Bush	Republican	1989–1993	Dan Quayle
42	William J. Clinton	Democratic	1993–2001	Albert Gore
43	George W. Bush	Republican	2001–	Richard B. Cheney

*Died in office.   **Resigned from office.   †Assassinated.*

Presidential Biographies

George Washington (22 Feb [11 Feb, Old Style] 1732, Westmoreland county VA–14 Dec 1799, Mt. Vernon, in Fairfax county VA), American Revolutionary commander-in-chief (1775–83) and first president of the US (1789–97). Born into a wealthy family, he was educated privately and worked as a surveyor from age 14. In 1752 he inherited his brother's estate at Mount Vernon, including 18 slaves whose ranks grew to 49 by 1760, though he disapproved of slavery. In the French and Indian War he was commissioned a colonel and sent to the Ohio Territory. After Edward Braddock was killed, Washington became commander of all Virginia forces, entrusted with defending the western frontier (1755–58). He resigned to manage his estate and in 1759 married Martha Dandridge Custis (1731–1802), a widow. He served in the House of Burgesses 1759–74, where he supported the colonists' cause, and in the Continental Congress 1774–75. In 1775 he was elected to command the Continental Army. In the ensuing American Revolution, he proved a brilliant commander and stalwart leader despite several defeats. With the war effectively ended by the capture of Yorktown (1781), he resigned his commission and returned to Mount Vernon (1783). He was a delegate to and presiding officer of the Constitutional Convention (1787) and helped secure ratification of the Constitution in Virginia. When the state electors met to select the first president

(1789), Washington was the unanimous choice. He formed a cabinet to balance sectional and political differences but was committed to a strong central government. Elected to a second term, he followed a middle course between the political factions that became the Federalist Party and Democratic Party. He proclaimed a policy of neutrality in the war between Britain and France (1793) and sent troops to suppress the Whiskey Rebellion (1794). He declined to serve a third term, setting a 144-year precedent, and retired in 1797 after delivering his "Farewell Address." Known as the "father of his country," he is regarded as one of the greatest figures in US history.

John Adams (30 Oct [19 Oct, Old Style] 1735, Braintree [now in Quincy] MA—4 Jul 1826, Quincy MA), first vice president (1789–97) and second president (1797–1801) of the US. He practiced law in Boston and in 1764 married Abigail Smith. Active in the American independence movement, he was elected to the Massachusetts legislature and served as a delegate to the Continental Congress (1774–78), where he was appointed to several committees, including one with Thomas Jefferson and others to draft the Declaration of Independence. He served as a diplomat in France, The Netherlands, and England (1778–88). In the first US presidential election, he received the second largest number of votes and became vice president under George Washington. Adams's term as president was marked by controversy over his signing the Alien and Sedition Acts in 1798 and by his alliance with the conservative Federalist Party. In 1800 he was defeated for reelection by Jefferson and retired to live a secluded life in Massachusetts. In 1812 he was reconciled with Jefferson, with whom he began an illuminating correspondence. Both men died on 4 Jul 1826, the Declaration's 50th anniversary. Pres. John Quincy Adams was his son.

Thomas Jefferson (13 Apr [2 Apr, Old Style] 1743, Shadwell VA—4 Jul 1826, Monticello VA), third president of the US (1801–9). He was a planter and lawyer from 1767, as well as a slaveholder who opposed slavery. While a member of the House of Burgesses (1769–75), he initiated the Committee of Correspondence (1773) with Richard Henry Lee and Patrick Henry. In 1774 he wrote the influential *Summary View of the Rights of British America*, stating that the British Parliament had no authority to legislate for the colonies. A delegate to the second Continental Congress, he was appointed to the committee to draft the Declaration of Independence and became its primary author. He was elected governor of Virginia (1779–81) but was unable to organize effective opposition when British forces invaded the colony (1780–81). Criticized for his conduct, he retired, vowing to remain a private citizen. Again a member of the Continental Congress (1783–85), he proposed territorial provisions later incorporated in the Northwest Ordinances. He traveled in Europe on diplomatic missions and became minister to France (1785–89). George Washington made him secretary of state (1790–93). He soon became embroiled in conflict with Alexander Hamilton over their opposing interpretations of the Constitution. This led to the rise of factions and political parties, with Jefferson representing the Democratic-Republicans. He served as vice president (1797–1801) but opposed the Alien and Sedition Acts enacted under Pres. John Adams. As part of this opposition, Jefferson drafted one of the Virginia and Kentucky Resolutions. In 1801 he became president after an electoral-vote tie with Aaron Burr was settled by the House of Representatives. Jefferson initiated frugal fiscal policies and simplicity in the ceremonial role of the president. He oversaw the Louisiana Purchase and authorized the Lewis and Clark Expedition. He sought to avoid involvement in the Napoleonic Wars by signing the Embargo Act. He retired to his plantation, Monticello, where he pursued his many interests in science, philosophy, and architecture. He served as president of the American Philosophical Society 1797–1815, and in 1819 he founded and designed the University of Virginia. In January 2000, the Thomas Jefferson Memorial Foundation accepted the conclusion, supported by DNA evidence, that Jefferson had fathered at least one, and perhaps as many as six, children with Sally Hemings, one of his house slaves. After a long estrangement, he and Adams became reconciled in 1813 and exchanged views on national issues. They both died on July 4, 1826, the 50th anniversary of the signing of the Declaration of Independence.

James Madison (16 Mar [5 Mar, Old Style] 1751, Port Conway VA—28 Jun 1836, Montpelier VA), fourth president of the US (1809–17). He served in the state legislature (1776–80, 1784–86). At the Constitutional Convention (1787), his active participation and his careful notes on the debates earned him the title "father of the Constitution." To promote ratification, he collaborated with Alexander Hamilton and John Jay on *The Federalist*. In the House of Representatives (1789–97), he sponsored the Bill of Rights, was a leading Jeffersonian Republican, and split with Hamilton over funding state war debts. In reaction to the Alien and Sedition Acts, he drafted one of the Virginia and Kentucky Resolutions (1798). He was appointed secretary of state (1801–9) by Thomas Jefferson, with whom he developed US foreign policy. Elected president in 1808, he was occupied by the trade and shipping embargo problems caused by France and Britain that led to the War of 1812. He was reelected in 1812; his second term was marked principally by the war, during which he reinvigorated the Army and also saw approval of the charter of the Second Bank of the US and the first US protective tariff. He retired to his Virginia estate, Montpelier, with his wife, Dolley (1768–1849), whose political acumen he had long prized. He continued to write articles and letters and served as rector of the University of Virginia (1826–36).

James Monroe (28 Apr 1758, Westmoreland county VA—4 Jul 1831, New York NY), fifth president of the US (1817–25). He fought in the American Revolution and studied law under Thomas Jefferson. He served in the Congress (1783–86) and Senate (1790–94), where he opposed George Washington's administration. He nevertheless became minister to France (1794–96), where he misled the French about US politics and was recalled. He served as governor of Virginia 1799–1802. President Jefferson sent him to France, where he helped negotiate the Louisiana Purchase (1803), then named him minister to Britain (1803–7). He returned to Virginia and became governor (1811), but he resigned to become US secretary of state (1811–17) and secretary of war (1814–15). He served two terms as president, presiding in a period that became known as the Era of Good Feelings. He oversaw the Seminole War (1817–18) and the acquisition of the Floridas (1819–21) and signed the Missouri Compromise (1820). With secretary of state John Quincy Adams, he developed the principles of US foreign policy later called the Monroe Doctrine.

John Quincy Adams (11 Jul 1767, Braintree [now in Quincy] MA–23 Feb 1848, Washington DC), sixth president of the US (1825–29). He was the eldest son of Pres. John Adams and Abigail. He accompanied his father to Europe on diplomatic missions (1778–80) and was later appointed minister to The Netherlands (1794) and Prussia (1797). In 1801 he returned to Massachusetts and served in the Senate (1803–8). Resuming his diplomatic service, he became minister to Russia (1809–11) and Britain (1815–17). Appointed secretary of state (1817–24), he was instrumental in acquiring Florida from Spain and in drafting the Monroe Doctrine. He was one of three candidates in the 1824 presidential election, in which none received a majority of the electoral votes, though Andrew Jackson received a plurality. The decision went to the House of Representatives, where Adams received crucial support from Henry Clay and the electoral votes necessary to elect him president. He appointed Clay secretary of state, which further angered Jackson. Adams's presidency was unsuccessful; when he ran for reelection, Jackson defeated him. In 1830 he was elected to the House of Representatives, where he served until his death. He was outspoken in his opposition to slavery and in 1839 proposed a constitutional amendment forbidding slavery in any new state admitted to the Union. Southern congressmen prevented discussion of antislavery petitions by passing gag rules (repealed in 1844 as a result of Adams's persistence). In 1841 he successfully defended the slaves in the *Amistad* mutiny case.

Andrew Jackson (15 Mar 1767, Waxhaws region SC– 8 Jun 1845, the Hermitage, near Nashville TN), seventh president of the US (1829–37). He fought briefly in the American Revolution near his frontier home, where his family was killed. He studied law and in 1788 was appointed prosecuting attorney for western North Carolina. When the region became the state of Tennessee, he was elected to the House of Representatives (1796–97) and Senate (1797–98). He served on the state supreme court (1798–1804) and in 1802 was elected major general of the Tennessee militia. When the War of 1812 began, he offered the US the services of his 50,000-volunteer militia. He was sent to fight the Creek Indians allied with the British in Mississippi Territory. After a lengthy battle (1813–14), he defeated them at the Battle of Horseshoe Bend. After capturing Pensacola FL from the British-allied Spanish, he marched overland to engage the British in Louisiana. A decisive victory at the Battle of New Orleans made him a national hero, dubbed "Old Hickory" by the press. After US acquisition of Florida, he was named governor of the territory (1821). One of four candidates in the 1824 presidential election, he won an electoral-votes plurality but the House gave the election to John Quincy Adams. In 1828 Jackson defeated Adams after a fierce campaign and became the first president elected from west of the Appalachian Mountains. His election was considered a triumph of political democracy. He replaced many federal officeholders with his supporters, a process that became known

as the spoils system. He pursued a policy of moving Native Americans westward with the Indian Removal Acts. He split with his vice president, John C. Calhoun, over the nullification movement. His reelection in 1832 was due in part to support for his anticapitalistic fiscal policies and a controversial veto that affected the Bank of the US. His popularity continued to build throughout his presidency. During his tenure a strong Democratic Party developed that led to a vigorous two-party system.

Martin Van Buren (5 Dec 1782, Kinderhook NY–24 Jul 1862, Kinderhook NY), eighth president of the US (1837–41). He practiced law and served in the NY state senate (1812–20) and as state attorney general (1816–19). He became the leader of an informal group of political supporters, called the Albany Regency because they dominated state politics even while Van Buren was in Washington. He was elected to the US Senate (1821–28), where he supported states' rights and opposed a strong central government. After John Quincy Adams became president, he joined with Andrew Jackson and others to form a group that later became the Democratic Party. He was elected governor of New York (1828) but resigned to become US secretary of state (1829–31). He was nominated for vice president at the first Democratic Party convention (1832) and served under Jackson (1833–37). As Jackson's chosen successor, he defeated William H. Harrison to win the 1836 election. His presidency was marked by an economic depression, the Maine-Canada border dispute, the Seminole War in Florida, and debate over the annexation of Texas. He was defeated in his bid for reelection and failed to win the Democratic nomination in 1844 because of his antislavery views. In 1848 he was nominated for president by the Free Soil Party but failed to win the election and retired.

William Henry Harrison (9 Feb 1773, Charles City county VA–4 Apr 1841, Washington DC), ninth president of the US (1841). Born into a political family, he enlisted in the army at 18 and served under Anthony Wayne at the Battle of Fallen Timbers. In 1798 he became secretary of the Northwest Territories, and in 1800 governor of the new Indiana Territory. In response to pressure from white settlers, he negotiated treaties with the Native Americans that ceded millions of acres of additional land to the US. When Tecumseh organized an uprising in 1811, Harrison led a US force to defeat the Indians at the Battle of Tippecanoe, a victory that largely established his reputation in the public mind. In the War of 1812 he was made a brigadier general and defeated the British and their Indian allies at the Battle of the Thames in Ontario. After the war he moved to Ohio, where he became prominent in the Whig Party. He served in the House of Representatives (1816–19) and Senate (1825–28). As the Whig candidate in the 1836 presidential election, he lost narrowly. In 1840 he and his running mate, John Tyler, won election with a slogan emphasizing Harrison's frontier triumph: "Tippecanoe and Tyler too!" The 68-year-old Harrison delivered his inaugural speech without a hat or overcoat in a cold drizzle, contracted pneumonia, and died one month later, the first president to die in office.

John Tyler (29 Mar 1790, Charles City county VA–18 Jan 1862, Richmond VA), 10th president of the US (1841–45). He practiced law before serving in the state legislature (1811–16, 1823–25, 1839) and as governor of Virginia (1825–27). In the House of Representatives (1817–21) and Senate (1827–36), he was a states-rights supporter. Though a slaveholder, he sought to prohibit the slave trade in the District of Columbia, provided Maryland and Virginia concurred. He resigned from the Senate rather than acquiesce to state instructions to change his vote on a censure of Pres. Andrew Jackson. After breaking with the Democratic Party, he was nominated by the Whig Party for vice president under William H. Harrison. They won the 1840 election, carefully avoiding the issues and stressing party loyalty and the slogan "Tippecanoe and Tyler too!" Harrison died a month after taking office, and Tyler became the first to attain the presidency "by accident." He vetoed a national bank bill supported by the Whigs, and all but one member of the cabinet resigned, leaving him without party support. Nonetheless, he reorganized the navy, settled the second of the Seminole Wars in Florida, and oversaw the annexation of Texas. He was nominated for reelection but withdrew in favor of James Polk and retired to his Virginia plantation. Committed to states' rights but opposed to secession, he organized the Washington Peace Conference (1861) to resolve sectional differences. When the Senate rejected a proposed compromise, Tyler urged Virginia to secede.

James Knox Polk (2 Nov 1795, Mecklenburg county NC–15 Jun 1849, Nashville TN), 11th president of the US (1845–49). He became a lawyer in Tennessee and a friend and supporter of Andrew Jackson, who helped Polk win election to the House of Representatives (1825–39). He left the House to become governor of Tennessee (1839–41). At the deadlocked 1844 Democratic convention Polk was nominated as the compromise candidate; he is considered the first dark-horse presidential candidate. A proponent of western expansion, he campaigned with the slogan "Fifty-four Forty or Fight," to bring a solution to the Oregon Question. Elected at 49, the youngest president to that time, he successfully concluded the Oregon border dispute with Britain (1846) and secured passage of the Walker Tariff Act (1846), which lowered import duties and helped foreign trade. He led the prosecution of the Mexican War, which resulted in large territorial gains but reopened the debate over the extension of slavery. His administration also established the Department of the Interior, the US Naval Academy, and the Smithsonian Institution, oversaw revision of the treasury system, and proclaimed the validity of the Monroe Doctrine. Though an efficient and competent president, deft in his handling of Congress, he was exhausted by his efforts and did not seek reelection; he died three months after leaving office.

Zachary Taylor (24 Nov 1784, Montebello VA–9 Jul 1850, Washington DC), 12th president of the US (1849–50). Born in Virginia, he grew up on the Kentucky frontier. He fought in the War of 1812, the Black Hawk War (1832), and the Seminole War in Florida (1835–42), earning the nickname "Old Rough-and-Ready" for his indifference to hardship. Sent to Texas in anticipation of war with Mexico, he defeated the Mexican invaders at the battles of Palo Alto and Resaca de la Palma (1846). After the Mexican War formally began, he captured Monterrey and granted the Mexican army an eight-week armistice. Displeased, Pres. James Polk moved Taylor's best troops to serve under Winfield Scott in the invasion of Veracruz. Taylor ignored orders to remain in Monterrey and marched south to defeat a large Mexican force at the Battle of Buena Vista (1847). He became a national hero and was nominated as the Whig candidate for president (1848). He defeated Lewis Cass to win the election. His brief term was marked by a controversy over the new territories that produced the Compromise of 1850 as well as by a scandal involving members of his cabinet. He died, probably of cholera, after only 16 months in office and was succeeded by Millard Fillmore.

Millard Fillmore (7 Jan 1800, Locke Township, NY–8 Mar 1874, Buffalo NY), 13th president of the US (1850–53). Born into poverty, he became an indentured apprentice at 15. He studied law with a local judge and began to practice in Buffalo in 1823. Initially identified with the Anti-Masonic Party (1828–34), he followed his political mentor, Thurlow Weed, to the Whigs and was soon a leader of the party's northern wing. He served in the House of Representatives (1833–35, 1837–43), where he became a follower of Henry Clay. In 1848 the Whigs nominated Fillmore as vice president, and he was elected with Zachary Taylor. He became president on Taylor's death in 1850. Though he abhorred slavery, he supported the Compromise of 1850 and insisted on federal enforcement of the Fugitive Slave Act. His stand, which alienated the North, led to his defeat by Winfield Scott at the Whigs' nominating convention in 1852 and effectively led to the death of the party. Throughout his career he advocated US internal development and was an early champion of expansion in the Pacific. In 1853 he sent Matthew Perry with a US fleet to Japan, forcing its isolationist government to enter into trade and diplomatic relations. He returned to Buffalo and was nominated for president by the third-party Know-Nothing Party in 1856, but he was defeated by Democrat James Buchanan.

Franklin Pierce (23 Nov 1804, Hillsboro NH–8 Oct 1869, Concord NH), 14th president of the US (1853–57). He practiced law and served in the House of Representatives (1833–37) and Senate (1837–42). He returned to his law practice, serving briefly in the Mexican War. At the deadlocked Democratic convention of 1852, he was nominated as the compromise candidate; though largely unknown nationally, he unexpectedly trounced Winfield Scott in the general election. For the sake of harmony and business prosperity, he was inclined to oppose antislavery agitation so as to placate Southern opinion. He promoted US territorial expansion, resulting in the diplomatic controversy of the Ostend Manifesto. He reorganized the diplomatic and consular service and created the Court of Claims. He encouraged plans for a transcontinental railroad and approved the Gadsden Purchase. To promote northwestern migration and conciliate sectional demands, he approved the Kansas-Nebraska Act but was unable to settle the resultant problems. Defeated for renomination by James Buchanan in 1856, he retired from politics.

James Buchanan (23 Apr 1791, near Mercersburg PA–1 Jun 1868, near Lancaster PA), 15th president of the US (1857–61). He became a lawyer and member of the Pennsylvania legislature before serving in the House of Representatives (1821–31), as minister to Russia (1832–34), and in the Senate (1834–45). He was secretary of state in James Polk's cabinet (1845–49). As minister to Britain (1853–56), he helped draft the Ostend

Manifesto. In 1856 he secured the Democratic nomination and election as president, defeating John C. Fremont. Though experienced in government and law, he lacked the moral courage to deal effectively with the slavery crisis and equivocated on the question of Kansas's status as a slaveholding state. The ensuing split within his party allowed Abraham Lincoln to win the election of 1860. He denounced the secession of South Carolina following the election and sent reinforcements to Fort Sumter, but he failed to respond further to the mounting crisis.

Abraham Lincoln (12 Feb 1809, near Hodgenville KY—15 Apr 1865, Washington DC), 16th president of the US (1861–65). Born in a Kentucky log cabin, he moved to Indiana in 1816 and to Illinois in 1830. He worked as a storekeeper, rail-splitter, postmaster, and surveyor, then enlisted as a volunteer in the Black Hawk War and became a captain. Though largely self-taught, he practiced law in Springfield IL and served in the state legislature (1834–40). He was elected as a Whig to the House of Representatives (1847–49). As a circuit-riding lawyer from 1849, he became one of the state's most successful lawyers, noted for his shrewdness, common sense, and honesty (earning him the nickname "Honest Abe"). In 1856 he joined the Republican Party, which nominated him as its candidate in the 1858 Senate election. In a series of seven debates with Stephen A. Douglas (the Lincoln-Douglas Debates), he argued against the extension of slavery into the territories, though not against slavery itself. Although morally opposed to slavery, he was not an abolitionist. During the campaign, he attempted to rebut Douglas's charge that he was a dangerous radical by reassuring audiences that he did not favor political equality for blacks. Despite his loss in the election, the debates brought him national attention. He again ran against Douglas in the 1860 presidential election, which he won by a large margin. But the South opposed his position on slavery in the territories, and before his inauguration seven Southern states had seceded from the Union. The ensuing American Civil War completely consumed Lincoln's administration. He excelled as a wartime leader, creating a high command for directing all the country's energies and resources toward the war effort and combining statecraft and overall command of the armies with what some have called military genius. However, his abrogation of some civil liberties, especially the writ of habeas corpus, and the closing of several newspapers by his generals disturbed both Democrats and Republicans, including some members of his own cabinet. To unite the North and influence foreign opinion, he issued the Emancipation Proclamation (1863); his Gettysburg Address (1863) further ennobled the war's purpose. The continuing war affected some Northerners' resolve and his reelection was not assured, but strategic battle victories turned the tide and he easily defeated George B. McClellan in 1864. His platform included passage of the 13th Amendment outlawing slavery (ratified 1865). At his second inaugural, with victory in sight, he spoke of moderation in reconstructing the South and building a harmonious Union. On 14 Apr, five days after the war ended, he was shot by John Wilkes Booth and soon after died.

Andrew Johnson (29 Dec 1808, Raleigh NC—31 Jul 1875, near Carter Station TN), 17th president of the US (1865–69). Born in North Carolina and reared in Tennessee, he was self-educated and initially worked as a tailor. He organized a workingman's party and was elected to the state legislature (1835–43), where he became a spokesman for small farmers. He served in the House of Representatives (1843–53) and as governor of Tennessee (1853–57). Elected to the Senate (1857–62), he opposed antislavery agitation, but in 1860 he opposed Southern secession, even after Tennessee seceded in 1861, and during the Civil War he was the only Southern senator who refused to join the Confederacy. In 1862 he was appointed military governor of Tennessee, then under Union control. In 1864 he was selected to run for vice president with Pres. Abraham Lincoln; he assumed the presidency after Lincoln's assassination. During Reconstruction he favored a moderate policy that readmitted former Confederate states to the Union with few provisions for reform or civil rights for freedmen. In 1867 the Radical Republicans in Congress passed civil rights legislation and established the Freedmen's Bureau. His veto angered Congress, which passed the Tenure of Office Act. In 1868 in defiance of the act, Johnson dismissed secretary of war Edwin M. Stanton, an ally of the Radicals. The House responded by impeaching the president for the first time in US history. In the subsequent Senate trial, the charges proved weak and the necessary two-thirds vote needed for conviction failed by one vote. Johnson remained in office until 1869, but his effectiveness had ended. He returned to Tennessee, where he won reelection to the Senate shortly before he died.

Ulysses S. Grant (Hiram Ulysses Grant) (27 Apr 1822, Point Pleasant OH—23 Jul 1885, Mount McGregor NY), 18th president of the US (1869–77). He served in the Mexican War under Zachary Taylor; he resigned his commission in 1854 when he could not afford to bring his family west. Allegations that he became a drunkard in the lonely years in the West and in later life, though never proved, would affect his reputation. He worked unsuccessfully at farming in Missouri and at his family's leather business in Illinois. When the Civil War began (1861), he was appointed brigadier general; his 1862 attack on Fort Donelson TN, produced the first major Union victory. He drove off a Confederate attack at Shiloh but was criticized for heavy Union losses. He devised the campaign to take the stronghold of Vicksburg MS, in 1863, cutting the Confederacy in half from east to west. Following his victory at the Battle of Chattanooga in 1864, he was appointed commander of the Union army. While William T. Sherman made his famous march across Georgia, Grant attacked Robert E. Lee's forces in Virginia, bringing the war to an end in 1865. Grant's administrative ability and innovative strategies were largely responsible for the Union victory. His successful Republican presidential campaign made him, at 46, the youngest man yet elected president. His two terms were marred by administrative inaction and political scandal involving members of his cabinet, including the Crédit Mobilier scandal and the Whiskey Ring operation. He was more successful in foreign affairs, in which he was aided by his secretary of state, Hamilton Fish. He supported amnesty for Confederate leaders and protection for black civil rights. His veto of a bill to increase the amount of legal tender (1874) diminished the currency crisis in the next 25 years.

In 1881 he moved to New York; when a partner defrauded an investment firm co-owned by his son, the family was impoverished. His memoirs were published by his friend Mark Twain.

Rutherford Birchard Hayes (4 Oct 1822, Delaware OH—17 Jan 1893, Fremont OH), 19th president of the US (1877–81). He practiced law in Cincinnati, representing defendants in several fugitive-slave cases and becoming associated with the new Republican Party. After fighting in the Union army, he served in the House of Representatives (1865–67). As governor of Ohio (1868–72, 1875–76), he advocated a sound currency backed by gold. In 1876 he won the Republican nomination for president. His opponent, Samuel Tilden, won a larger popular vote, but Hayes's managers contested the electoral-vote returns in four states, and a special Electoral Commission awarded the election to Hayes. As part of a secret compromise reached with Southerners, he withdrew the remaining federal troops from the South, ending Reconstruction, and promised not to interfere with elections there, ensuring the return of white Democratic supremacy. He introduced civil-service reform based on merit, incurring a dispute with Roscoe Conkling and the conservative "stalwart" Republicans. At the request of state governors, he used federal troops against strikers in the railroad strikes of 1877. Declining to run for a second term, he retired to work for humanitarian causes.

James Abram Garfield (19 Nov 1831, near Orange [in Cuyahoga county] OH—19 Sep 1881, Elberon [now in Long Branch] NJ), 20th president of the US (1881). He graduated from Williams College, then returned to Ohio to teach and head an academy that became Hiram College. In the Civil War he led the 42nd Ohio Volunteers and fought at Shiloh and Chickamauga. He resigned as a major general to serve in the House of Representatives (1863–80). A Radical Republican during Reconstruction, he served on the Electoral Commission in the 1876 election and was the House Republican leader from 1876 to 1880, when he was elected to the Senate. At the 1880 Republican nominating convention, the delegates supporting Ulysses S. Grant and James Blaine became deadlocked. On the 36th ballot Garfield was nominated as a compromise presidential candidate, with Chester Arthur as vice president, and won by a narrow margin. His brief term, less than 150 days, was marked by a dispute with Sen. Roscoe Conkling over patronage. On July 2 he was shot at Washington's railroad station by Charles J. Guiteau, an Arthur supporter. He died on September 19 after 11 weeks of public debate over the ambiguous constitutional conditions for presidential succession (later clarified by the 20th and 25th Amendments).

Chester Alan Arthur (5 Oct 1829, North Fairfield VT—18 Nov 1886, New York NY), 21st president of the US (1881–85). He practiced law in New York City from 1854. He became active in local Republican politics and a close associate of party leader Roscoe Conkling, and was appointed customs collector for the port of New York (1871–78), an office long known for its employment of the spoils system. He conducted the business of the office with integrity but continued to pad its payroll with Conkling loyalists. At the Republican national convention in 1880, Arthur became the compromise choice for vice president on the ticket with James Garfield, and he became president upon Garfield's assassi-

nation. As president, Arthur displayed unexpected independence by vetoing measures that rewarded political patronage. He also signed the Pendleton Act, which created a civil-service system based on merit. He recommended the appropriations that initiated the rebuilding of the Navy toward the strength it later achieved in the Spanish-American War (1898). He failed to win his party's nomination for a second term.

(Stephen) Grover Cleveland (18 Mar 1837, Caldwell NJ—24 Jun 1908, Princeton NJ), 22nd and 24th president of the US (1885–89, 1893–97). He practiced law in Buffalo NY from 1859, where he entered Democratic Party politics. As mayor of Buffalo (1881–82), he was known as a foe of corruption. As governor of New York (1883–85), he earned the hostility of Tammany Hall with his independence, but in 1884 he won the Democratic nomination for president. The first Democratic president since 1856, he supported civil-service reform and opposed high protective tariffs, which became an issue in the 1888 election, when he was narrowly defeated by Benjamin Harrison. In 1892 he was re-elected by a huge popular plurality. In 1893 he attributed the US's severe economic depression to the Sherman Silver Purchase Act of 1890 and strongly urged Congress to repeal the act. The economic unrest resulted in the Pullman Strike in 1894. An isolationist, he opposed territorial expansion. In 1895 he invoked the Monroe Doctrine in the border dispute between Britain and Venezuela. By 1896 supporters of the Free Silver Movement controlled the Democratic Party, which nominated William Jennings Bryan instead of Cleveland for president. He retired to New Jersey, where he lectured at Princeton University.

Benjamin Harrison (20 Aug 1833, North Bend OH—13 Mar 1901, Indianapolis IN), 23rd president of the US (1889–93). The grandson of Pres. William H. Harrison, he practiced law in Indianapolis from the mid-1850s. He served in the Union army in the Civil War, rising to brigadier general. He served a term in the Senate (1881–87) and, even though he lost reelection, was nominated for president by the Republicans. He went on to defeat the incumbent, Grover Cleveland, who lost despite winning more of the popular vote. As president, his domestic policy was marked by passage of the Sherman Antitrust Act. His foreign policy expanded US influence abroad. His secretary of state, James Blaine, presided at the conference that led to the establishment of the Pan-American Union, resisted pressure to abandon US interests in the Samoan Islands (1889), and negotiated a treaty with Britain in the Bering Sea Dispute (1891). Defeated for reelection by Cleveland in 1892, he returned to Indianapolis to practice law. In 1898–99 he was the leading counsel for Venezuela in its boundary dispute with Britain.

William McKinley (29 Jan 1843, Niles OH—14 Sep 1901, Buffalo NY), 25th president of the US (1897–1901). He served in the Civil War as an aide to Col. Rutherford B. Hayes, who later encouraged his political career. He was elected to the House of Representatives (1877–91), where he favored protective tariffs and sponsored the McKinley Tariff of 1890. With the support of Mark Hanna, he was elected governor (1892–96). In 1896 he won the Republican presidential nomination and the general election, defeating William Jennings Bryan. He called a special session of Congress to increase customs duties, but was soon embroiled in events in Cuba and responses to the sinking of the USS *Maine*, which led to the Spanish-American War. At the war's end, he advocated US dependency status for the Philippines, Puerto Rico, and other former Spanish territories. He again defeated Bryan by a large majority in 1900 and began a tour to urge control of trusts and commercial reciprocity to boost foreign trade, issues neglected during the war. In Buffalo NY on 6 Sep 1901, he was fatally shot by an anarchist, Leon Czolgosz. He was succeeded by Theodore Roosevelt.

Theodore Roosevelt (27 Oct 1858, New York NY—6 Jan 1919, Oyster Bay NY), 26th president of the US (1901–9). He was elected to the New York legislature in 1882, where he became a Republican leader opposed to the Democratic political machine. After political defeats and the death of his wife, he went to the Dakota Territory to ranch. He returned to New York to serve on the US Civil Service Commission (1889–95) and as head of the city's board of police commissioners (1895–97). A supporter of William McKinley, he served as assistant secretary of the navy (1897–98). When the Spanish-American War was declared, he resigned to organize a cavalry unit, the Rough Riders. He returned to New York a hero and was elected governor in 1899. As the Republican vice-presidential nominee, he took office when McKinley was reelected, and he became president on McKinley's assassination in 1901. One of his early initiatives was to urge enforcement of the Sherman Antitrust Act against business monopolies. He won election in his own right in 1904, defeating Alton Parker. At his urging, Congress regulated railroad rates and passed the Pure Food and Drug Act and Meat Inspection Act (1906) to provide new consumer protections. He set aside national forests, parks, and mineral, oil, and coal lands for conservation. He and secretary of state Elihu Root announced the Roosevelt corollary to the Monroe Doctrine, which reinforced the US position as defender of the Western Hemisphere. For mediating an end to the Russo-Japanese War, he received the 1906 Nobel Peace Prize. He secured a treaty with Panama for construction of a trans-isthmus canal. Declining to seek reelection, he secured the nomination for William H. Taft. After traveling in Africa and Europe, he tried to win the Republican presidential nomination in 1912; when he was rejected, he organized the Bull Moose Party and ran on a policy of New Nationalism, but he failed to win the election. Throughout his life he continued to write, publishing extensively on history, politics, travel, and nature.

William Howard Taft (15 Sep 1857, Cincinnati OH—8 Mar 1930, Washington DC), 27th president of the US (1909–13). He served on the state superior court (1887–90), as US solicitor general (1890–92), and as US appellate judge (1892–1900). He was appointed head of the Philippine Commission to set up a civilian government in the islands and was its first civilian governor (1901–4). He served as US secretary of war (1904–8) under Pres. Theodore Roosevelt, who supported Taft's nomination for president in 1908. He won the election but became allied with the conservative Republicans, causing a rift with party progressives. He was again the nominee in 1912, but the split with Roosevelt and the Bull Moose Party resulted in the electoral victory of Woodrow Wilson. Taft later taught law at Yale University (1913–21), served on the National War Labor Board (1918), and was a supporter of the League of Nations. As chief justice of the Supreme Court (1921–30), he introduced reforms that made it more efficient. He secured passage of the Judges Act of 1925, which gave the Court wider discretion in accepting cases. His important opinion in *Myers* v. *US* (1926) upheld the president's authority to remove federal officials. In poor health, he resigned in 1930.

(Thomas) Woodrow Wilson (28 Dec 1856, Staunton VA—3 Feb 1924, Washington DC), 28th president of the US (1913–21). He earned a law degree and later received his doctorate from Johns Hopkins University. He taught political science at Princeton University (1890–1902), and as its president (1902–10), he introduced various reforms. With the support of progressives, he was elected governor of New Jersey. His reform measures attracted national attention, and he became the Democratic presidential nominee in 1912. His campaign emphasized the progressive measures of his New Freedom policy, and he defeated Theodore Roosevelt and William H. Taft to win the presidency. As president, he approved legislation that lowered tariffs, created the Federal Reserve System, established the Federal Trade Commission, and strengthened labor unions. In foreign affairs he promoted self-government for the Philippines and sought to contain the Mexican civil war. From 1914 he maintained US neutrality in World War I, offering to mediate a settlement and initiate peace negotiations. After the sinking of the *Lusitania* (1915) and other unarmed ships, he obtained a pledge from Germany to stop its submarine campaign. Campaigning on the theme that he had "kept us out of war," he was narrowly reelected in 1916, defeating Charles Evans Hughes. Germany's renewed submarine attacks on unarmed passenger ships caused Wilson to ask for a declaration of war in April 1917. In a continuing effort to negotiate a peace agreement, he presented the Fourteen Points (1918). He led the US delegation to the Paris Peace Conference, where he attempted to stand on his original principles but was forced to compromise by the demands of various countries. The Treaty of Versailles faced opposition in the Senate from the Republican majority led by Henry C. Lodge. In search of popular support for the treaty and its League of Nations, Wilson began a cross-country speaking tour, but he collapsed and returned to Washington DC (Sep 1919), where a stroke left him partially paralyzed. He rejected any attempts to compromise his version of the League of Nations and urged his Senate followers to vote against ratification of the treaty, which was defeated in 1920. He was awarded the 1919 Nobel Peace Prize for his work on the League of Nations.

Warren Gamaliel Harding (2 Nov 1865, Caledonia (now Blooming Grove) OH—2 Aug 1923, San Francisco CA), 29th president of the US (1921–23). He became a newspaper publisher in Marion OH, where he was allied with the Republican Party's political machine. He served successively as state senator (1899–1902), lieutenant governor (1903–04), and US senator (1915–21), supporting conservative policies. At the deadlocked 1920 Republican presidential convention, he was chosen as the compromise candidate. Pledging a "return to normalcy" after World War I, he defeated James Cox with over 60% of the popular vote, the largest margin to that time. On his recommendation, Congress established a budget system for the federal government, passed a high protective tariff, revised wartime taxes, and restricted immigration. His administration convened the Washington Conference (1921–22). His ill-advised cabinet and patronage appointments, including Albert Fall, led to the Teapot Dome scandal and characterized his administration as corrupt. While in Alaska, he received word of the corruption about to be exposed and headed back. He arrived in San Francisco exhausted, reportedly suffering from food poisoning and other ills, and died there under unclear circumstances. He was succeeded by his vice president, Calvin Coolidge.

(John) Calvin Coolidge (4 Jul 1872, Plymouth VT—5 Jan 1933, Northampton MA), 30th president of the US (1923–29). He practiced law in Massachusetts from 1897 and served as lieutenant governor before being elected governor in 1918. He gained national attention by calling out the state guard during the Boston police strike in 1919. At the 1920 Republican convention, "Silent Cal" was nominated for vice president on Warren G. Harding's winning ticket. When Harding died in office in 1923, Coolidge became president. He restored confidence in an administration discredited by scandals and won the presidential election in 1924, defeating Robert La Follette. He vetoed measures to provide farm relief and bonuses to World War I veterans. His presidency was marked by apparent prosperity. Congress maintained a high protective tariff and instituted tax reductions that favored capital. Coolidge declined to run for a second term. His conservative policies of domestic and international inaction have come to symbolize the era between World War I and the Great Depression.

Herbert Clark Hoover (10 Aug 1874, West Branch IA—20 Oct 1964, New York NY), 31st president of the US (1929–33). As a mining engineer, he administered engineering projects on four continents (1895–1913). He then headed Allied relief operations in England and Belgium prior to World War I, at which time he was appointed national food administrator (1917–19) and instituted programs that furnished food to the Allies and famine-stricken areas of Europe. Appointed secretary of commerce (1921–27), he reorganized the department, creating divisions to regulate broadcasting and aviation. He oversaw commissions to build Boulder (later Hoover) Dam and the St. Lawrence Seaway. In 1928, as the Republican presidential candidate, he soundly defeated Alfred E. Smith. His hopes for a "New Day" program were quickly overwhelmed by the Great Depression. As a believer in individual freedom, he vetoed bills to create a federal unemployment agency and to fund public-works projects, instead favoring private charity. In 1932 he finally allowed relief to farmers through the Reconstruction Finance Corp. He was overwhelmingly defeated in 1932 by Franklin Roosevelt. He continued to speak out against relief measures and criticized New Deal programs. After World War II he participated in famine-relief work in Europe and was appointed head of the Hoover Commission.

Franklin Delano Roosevelt (30 Jan 1882, Hyde Park NY—12 Apr 1945, Warm Springs GA), 32nd president of the US (1933–45). He was attracted to politics as an admirer of his cousin Pres. Theodore Roosevelt and became active in the Democratic Party. In 1905 he married distant cousin Eleanor Roosevelt, who would become a valued adviser in future years. He served in the state senate (1910–13) and as assistant secretary of the navy (1913–20). In 1920 he was nominated for vice president. The next year he was stricken with polio; though unable to walk, he remained active in politics. As governor of New York (1929–33), he set up the first state relief agency in the US. In 1932 he won the Democratic presidential nomination with the help of James Farley and easily defeated Pres. Herbert Hoover. In his inaugural address to a nation of more than 13 million unemployed, he pronounced that "the only thing we have to fear is fear itself." Congress passed most of the changes he sought in his New Deal program in the first hundred days of his term. He was overwhelmingly reelected in 1936 over Alf Landon. To solve legal challenges to the New Deal, he proposed enlarging the Supreme Court, but his "court-packing" plan aroused strong opposition and had to be abandoned. By the late 1930s economic recovery had slowed, but Roosevelt was more concerned with the growing threat of war. In 1940 he was reelected to an unprecedented third term, defeating Wendell Willkie. He maintained US neutrality toward the war in Europe but approved the principle of lend-lease and in 1941 met with Winston Churchill to draft the Atlantic Charter. With US entry into World War II, he mobilized industry for military production and formed an alliance with Britain and the Soviet Union; he met with Churchill and Joseph Stalin to form war policy at Tehran (1943) and Yalta (1945). Despite declining health, he won reelection for a fourth term against Thomas Dewey (1944) but served only briefly before his death. His presidency is well regarded in US history.

Harry S. Truman (8 May 1884, Lamar MO—26 Dec 1972, Kansas City MO), 33rd president of the US (1945–53). He worked at various jobs before serving with distinction in World War I. He became a partner in a Kansas City haberdashery; when the business failed, he entered Democratic Party politics with the help of Thomas Pendergast. He was elected county judge (1922–24), and later became presiding judge of the county court (1926–34). His reputation for honesty and good management gained him bipartisan support. In the Senate (1935–45), he led a committee that exposed fraud in defense production. In 1944 he was chosen to replace the incumbent Henry Wallace as vice-presidential nominee and was elected with Pres. Franklin Roosevelt. After only 82 days as vice president, he became president on Roosevelt's death (April 1945). He quickly made final arrangements for the San Francisco charter-writing meeting of the UN; helped arrange Germany's unconditional surrender on 8 May, which ended World War II in Europe; and in July attended the Potsdam Conference. The Pacific war ended officially on 2 Sep, after he ordered atomic bombs dropped on Hiroshima and Nagasaki; his justification was a report that 500,000 US troops would be lost in a conventional invasion of Japan. He announced the Truman Doctrine to aid Greece and Turkey (1947), established the Central Intelligence Agency, and pressed for passage of the Marshall Plan to aid European countries. In 1948 he defeated Thomas Dewey despite widespread expectation of his own defeat. He initiated a foreign policy of containment to restrict the Soviet Union's sphere of influence, pursued his

Point Four Program, and initiated the Berlin airlift and the NATO pact of 1949. In the Korean War he sent troops under Gen. Douglas MacArthur to head the United Nations forces. Problems of pursuing the war occupied his administration until he retired. Though he was often criticized during his presidency, Truman's reputation grew steadily in later years.

Dwight David Eisenhower (14 Oct 1890, Denison TX— 28 Mar 1969, Washington DC), 34th president of the US (1953–61). He graduated from West Point (1915), then served in the Panama Canal Zone (1922–24) and in the Philippines under Douglas MacArthur (1935–39). In World War II Gen. George Marshall appointed him to the army's war-plans division (1941), then chose him to command US forces in Europe (1942). After planning the invasions of North Africa, Sicily, and Italy, he was appointed supreme commander of Allied forces (1943). He planned the Normandy Campaign (1944) and the conduct of the war in Europe until the German surrender (1945). He was promoted to five-star general (1944) and was named army chief of staff in 1945. He served as president of Columbia University from 1948 until being appointed supreme commander of NATO in 1951. Both Democrats and Republicans courted Eisenhower as a presidential candidate; in 1952, as the Republican candidate, he defeated Adlai Stevenson with the largest popular vote up to that time. He defeated Stevenson again in 1956 in an even larger landslide. His achievements included efforts to contain Communism with the Eisenhower Doctrine. He sent federal troops to Little Rock AR to enforce integration of a city high school (1957). When the Soviet Union launched Sputnik I (1957), he was criticized for failing to develop the US space program and responded by creating NASA (1958). In his last weeks in office the US broke diplomatic relations with Cuba.

John Fitzgerald Kennedy (29 May 1917, Brookline MA—22 Nov 1963, Dallas TX), 35th president of the US (1961–63). The son of Joseph P. Kennedy, he graduated from Harvard University and joined the Navy in World War II, where he earned medals for heroism. Elected to the House of Representatives (1947–53) and the Senate (1953–60), he supported social legislation and became increasingly committed to civil rights legislation. He supported the policies of Harry Truman but accused the State Department of trying to force Chiang Kai-shek into a coalition with Mao Zedong. In 1960 he won the Democratic nomination for president; after a vigorous campaign, managed by his brother Robert F. Kennedy and aided financially by his father, he narrowly defeated Richard Nixon. He was the youngest person and the first Roman Catholic elected president. In his inaugural address he called on Americans to "ask not what your country can do for you, ask what you can do for your country." He proposed tax-reform and civil rights legislation but received little congressional support. He established the Peace Corps and the Alliance for Progress. His foreign policy began with the abortive Bay of Pigs invasion (1961), which emboldened the Soviet Union to move missiles to Cuba, sparking the Cuban missile crisis. In 1963 he successfully concluded the Nuclear Test-Ban Treaty. In November 1963 he was assassinated while riding in a motorcade in Dallas by a sniper, allegedly Lee Harvey Oswald. The killing is considered the most notorious political murder of

the 20th century. Kennedy's youth, energy, and charming family brought him world adulation and sparked the idealism of a generation, for whom the Kennedy White House became known as "Camelot." Details about his powerful family and personal life, especially concerning his extramarital affairs, tainted his image in later years.

Lyndon Baines Johnson (27 Aug 1908, Gillespie county TX—22 Jan 1973, San Antonio TX), 36th president of the US (1963–69). He taught school in Houston before going to Washington DC in 1932 as a congressional aide. There he was befriended by Sam Rayburn and his political career blossomed. He won a seat in the House of Representatives (1937–49) as the New Deal was under conservative attack. His loyalty impressed Pres. Franklin Roosevelt, who made Johnson a protégé. He won election to the Senate in 1949 in a vicious campaign that saw fraud on both sides. As Democratic whip (1951–55) and majority leader (1955–61), he developed a talent for consensus building among dissident factions with methods both tactful and ruthless. He was largely responsible for passage of the civil rights bills of 1957 and 1960, the first in the 20th century. In 1960 he was elected vice president; he became president after the assassination of John F. Kennedy. In his first few months in office he won from Congress passage of a huge quantity of important civil rights, tax-reduction, antipoverty, and conservation legislation. He defeated Barry Goldwater in the 1964 election by the largest popular majority to that time and announced his Great Society program. He was diverted from overseeing its enactment by the escalation of US involvement in the Vietnam War, beginning with the Gulf of Tonkin Resolution. His approval ratings diminished markedly and led to his decision not to seek reelection in 1968. He retired to his Texas ranch.

Richard Milhous Nixon (9 Jan 1913, Yorba·Linda CA— 22 Apr 1994, New York NY), 37th president of the US (1969–74). He studied law at Duke University and practiced in California 1937–42. After serving in World War II, he was elected to the House of Representatives in 1947, employing harsh campaign tactics. He came to national attention with the Alger Hiss case and was elected to the Senate in 1951, again following a bitter campaign. He won the vice presidency in 1952 on a ticket with Dwight D. Eisenhower; they were reelected easily in 1956. As presidential candidate in 1960, he lost narrowly to John F. Kennedy. After failing to win the 1962 California gubernatorial race, he retired from politics and moved to New York to practice law. He reentered politics by running for president in 1968, and he defeated Hubert H. Humphrey with his "Southern strategy" of seeking votes from Southern and Western conservatives in both parties. As president, he began to gradually withdraw US military forces in an effort to end the Vietnam War while ordering the secret bombing of North Vietnamese military centers in Laos and Cambodia. Attacks on North Vietnamese sanctuaries in Cambodia drew widespread protest. Economic problems caused by inflation made the US budget deficit the largest to date, and in 1971 Nixon established unprecedented peacetime controls on wages and prices. He won reelection in 1972 with a landslide victory over George McGovern. Assisted by Henry A. Kissinger, he concluded the Vietnam War. He reopened communications with Communist China and made a state visit there. On his visit to the Soviet Union, the first by a US president, he signed the bilateral SALT agreements. The Watergate scandal overshadowed his second term; his complicity in efforts to cover up his involvement and the likelihood of impeachment led to his becoming, in August 1974, the first president to resign from office. Though never convicted of wrongdoing, he was pardoned by his successor, Gerald Ford. He retired to write his memoirs and books on foreign policy.

Gerald Rudolph Ford, Jr. (Leslie Lynch King, Jr.; 14 Jul 1913, Omaha NE—26 Dec 2006, Rancho Mirage CA), 38th president of the US (1974–77). He was an infant when his parents divorced, and his mother later married Gerald R. Ford. He attended the University of Michigan and Yale Law School, and practiced law in Michigan after World War II. He served in the House of Representative 1948–73, becoming minority leader in 1965. After Spiro Agnew resigned as vice president in 1973, Richard Nixon nominated Ford to fill the vacant post. When the Watergate scandal forced Nixon's departure, Ford became the first president who had not been elected to either the vice presidency or the presidency. A month later he pardoned Nixon; to counter widespread outrage, he voluntarily appeared before a House subcommittee to explain his action. His administration gradually lowered the high inflation rate it inherited. Ford's relations with the Democratic-controlled Congress were typified by his more than 50 vetoes, of which more than 40 were sustained. In the final days of the Vietnam War in 1975, he ordered an airlift of 237,000 anti-Communist Vietnamese refugees, most of whom came to the US. Reaction against Watergate contributed to his defeat by James Earl Carter, Jr., in 1976.

James Earl Carter, Jr. (1 Oct 1924, Plains GA), 39th president of the US (1977–81). He graduated from the US Naval Academy and served in the navy until 1953, when he left to manage the family peanut business. He served in the state senate 1962–66. Elected governor (1971–75), he opened Georgia's government offices to blacks and women and introduced stricter budgeting procedures for state agencies. In 1976, though lacking a national political base or major backing, he won the Democratic nomination and the presidency, defeating the sitting president, Gerald Ford. As president, Carter helped negotiate a peace treaty between Egypt and Israel, signed a treaty with Panama to make the Panama Canal a neutral zone after 1999, and established full diplomatic relations with China. In 1979–80 the Iran hostage crisis became a major political liability. He responded more forcefully to the USSR's invasion of Afghanistan in 1979, embargoing the shipment of US grain to that country and leading a boycott of the 1980 Summer Olympics in Moscow. Hampered by high inflation and a recession engineered to tame it, he lost his bid for reelection to Ronald Reagan. He subsequently became involved in international diplomatic negotiations and helped oversee elections in countries with insecure democratic traditions. Carter was awarded the Nobel Peace Prize in 2002.

Ronald Wilson Reagan (6 Feb 1911, Tampico IL–5 Jun 2004, Bel Air CA), 40th president of the US (1981–89). He attended Eureka College and worked as a radio sports announcer before going to Hollywood in 1937. In his career as a movie actor, he had roles in 50 films and was twice president of the Screen Actors Guild (1947–52, 1959–60). Reagan became a spokesman for the General Electric Co. and hosted its television theater program 1954–62. Having gradually changed his political affiliation from liberal Democrat to conservative Republican, he was elected governor of California and served 1967–74. In 1980 he defeated incumbent Pres. James Earl Carter, Jr., to become president. Shortly after taking office, he was wounded in an assassination attempt. Reagan adopted supply-side economics to promote rapid economic growth and reduce the federal deficit. Congress approved most of his proposals (1981), which succeeded in lowering inflation but doubled the national debt by 1986. He began the largest peacetime military buildup in US history and in 1983 proposed construction of the Strategic Defense Initiative. His foreign policy included the INF Treaty to restrict intermediate-range nuclear weapons and the invasion of Grenada. In 1984 Reagan defeated Walter Mondale in a landslide for reelection. Details of his administration's involvement in the Iran-Contra Affair emerged in 1986 and significantly weakened his popularity and authority. Though his intellectual capacity for governing was often disparaged, his artful communication skills enabled him to pursue numerous conservative policies with conspicuous success. In 1994 he revealed that he had Alzheimer disease.

George Herbert Walker Bush (12 Jun 1924, Milton MA), 41st president of the US (1989–93). The son of Prescott Bush, later a Connecticut senator, he served in World War II, graduated from Yale University, and started an oil business in Texas. He served in the House of Representatives 1966–70 as a Republican. He then served as ambassador to the UN (1971–72), chief liaison to China (1974–76), and head of the CIA (1976–77). In 1980 he ran for president but lost the nomination to Ronald Reagan. Bush served as vice president with Reagan (1981–88), whom he succeeded as president, defeating Michael Dukakis. He made no dramatic departures from Reagan's policies. In 1989 he ordered a brief military invasion of Panama, which toppled that country's leader, Gen. Manuel Noriega. He helped impose a UN-approved embargo against Iraq in 1990 to force its withdrawal from Kuwait. When Iraq refused, he authorized a US-led air offensive that began the Persian Gulf War. Despite general approval of his foreign policy, an economic recession led to his defeat by William Jefferson Clinton in 1992. His son George W. Bush was elected president in 2000 and reelected in 2004. In the aftermath of the 26 Dec 2004 tsunami, Bush joined fellow former president Bill Clinton as leader of a fundraising effort to aid victims of the disaster.

William Jefferson Clinton (William Jefferson Blythe III; 19 Aug 1946, Hope AR), 42nd president of the US (1993–2001). He was adopted, after his father's death in a car crash, by his mother's second husband, Roger Clinton. He attended Georgetown University, Oxford University (as a Rhodes Scholar), and Yale Law School, then taught at the University of Arkansas School of Law. He served as state attorney general (1977–79) and served several terms as governor (1979–81, 1983–92), during which he reformed Arkansas's educational system and encouraged the growth of industry through favorable tax policies. He won the Democratic presidential nomination in 1992, after withstanding charges of personal impropriety, and defeated the incumbent, George H.W. Bush. As president, he obtained approval of the North American Free Trade Agreement in 1993. He and his wife, Hillary Rodham Clinton, strongly advocated their plan to overhaul the US health care system, but Congress rejected it. He committed US forces to a peacekeeping initiative in Bosnia and Herzegovina. In 1994 the Democrats lost control of Congress for the first time since 1954. Clinton defeated Robert Dole to win reelection in 1996. He faced renewed charges of personal impropriety, this time involving Monica Lewinsky, and as a result, in 1998 he became the second president in history to be impeached. Charged with perjury and obstruction of justice, he was acquitted at his Senate trial in 1999. His two terms saw sustained economic growth and successive budget surpluses, the first in three decades. In the aftermath of the 26 Dec 2004 tsunami, Clinton joined fellow former president George H.W. Bush as leader of a fundraising effort to aid victims of the disaster.

George Walker Bush (6 Jul 1946, New Haven CT), 43rd president of the US (from 2001). The eldest child of Pres. George H.W. Bush, he attended Yale University and Harvard Business School. After spending a decade in the oil business with mixed success, he served as managing general partner of the Texas Rangers baseball franchise. In 1994 he was elected governor of Texas (1995–2000). Despite losing the national popular vote to Vice President Al Gore by more than 500,000 votes, he gained the presidency when a Supreme Court ruling effectively ended a recount of ballots in Florida. His response to the terrorist attacks on 11 Sep 2001 gave shape to his administration. The invasion of Iraq by US-led forces in March 2003 was followed by a problematic occupation during which a burgeoning insurgency threatened Iraqi efforts to stabilize a democratically elected government. Bush won reelection in 2004. The loss of Republican control of Congress in elections in November 2006 limited his power to steer legislation to passage at the end of his time in the White House.

Presidents' Wives and Children

Maiden names of the presidents' wives appear in small capital letters.

DATE OF MARRIAGE | **PRESIDENTS, WIVES, AND CHILDREN**

George Washington
6 Jan 1759 — **Martha DANDRIDGE Custis** (2 Jun 1731–22 May 1802)
no children

John Adams
25 Oct 1764 — **Abigail SMITH** (22 Nov 1744–28 Oct 1818)
▸ Abigail Amelia Adams (1765–1813), ▸ John Quincy Adams (1767–1848), ▸ Susanna Adams (1768–1770), ▸ Charles Adams (1770–1800), ▸ Thomas Boylston Adams (1772–1832)

Thomas Jefferson
1 Jan 1772 — **Martha WAYLES Skelton** (30 Oct 1748–6 Sep 1782)
▸ Martha Washington Jefferson (1772–1836), ▸ Jane Randolph Jefferson (1774–1775), ▸ infant son (1777–1777), ▸ Mary Jefferson (1778–1804), ▸ Lucy Elizabeth Jefferson (1780–1781), ▸ Lucy Elizabeth Jefferson (1782–1785)

James Madison
15 Sep 1794 — **Dolley Dandridge PAYNE Todd** (20 May 1768–12 Jul 1849)
no children

James Monroe
16 Feb 1786 — **Elizabeth KORTRIGHT** (30 Jun 1768–23 Sep 1830)
▸ Eliza Kortright Monroe (1786–1835?), ▸ James Spence Monroe (1799–1800), ▸ Maria Hester Monroe (1803–1850)

John Quincy Adams
26 Jul 1797 — **Louisa Catherine JOHNSON** (12 Feb 1775–15 May 1852)
▸ George Washington Adams (1801–1829), ▸ John Adams (1803–1834), ▸ Charles Francis Adams (1807–1886), ▸ Louisa Catherine Adams (1811–1812)

Andrew Jackson
Aug 1791 — **Rachel DONELSON Robards** (15? Jun 1767–22 Dec 1828)
no children

Martin Van Buren
21 Feb 1807 — **Hannah HOES** (8 Mar 1783–5 Feb 1819)
▸ Abraham Van Buren (1807–1873), ▸ John Van Buren (1810–1866), ▸ Martin Van Buren (1812–1855), ▸ Smith Thompson Van Buren (1817–1876)

William Henry Harrison
25 Nov 1795 — **Anna Tuthill SYMMES** (25 Jul 1775–25 Feb 1864)
▸ Elizabeth Bassett Harrison (1796–1846), ▸ John Cleves Symmes Harrison (1798–1830), ▸ Lucy Singleton Harrison (1800–1826), ▸ William Henry Harrison (1802–1838), ▸ John Scott Harrison (1804–1878), ▸ Benjamin Harrison (1806–1840), ▸ Mary Symmes Harrison (1809–1842), ▸ Carter Bassett Harrison (1811–1839), ▸ Anna Tuthill Harrison (1813–1865), ▸ James Findlay Harrison (1814–1817)

Presidents' Wives and Children (continued)

DATE OF MARRIAGE	PRESIDENTS, WIVES, AND CHILDREN

John Tyler

29 Mar 1813 — **Letitia CHRISTIAN** (12 Nov 1790–10 Sep 1842)
▶ Mary Tyler (1815–1848), ▶ Robert Tyler (1816–1877), ▶ John Tyler (1819–1896), ▶ Letitia Tyler (1821–1907), ▶ Anne Contesse Tyler (1825–1825), ▶ Alice Tyler (1827–1854), ▶ Tazewell Tyler (1830–1874)

26 Jun 1844 — **Julia GARDINER** (4 May 1820–10 Jul 1889)
▶ David Gardiner Tyler (1846–1927), ▶ John Alexander Tyler (1848–1883), ▶ Julia Gardiner Tyler (1849?–1871), ▶ Lachlan Tyler (1851–1902), ▶ Lyon Gardiner Tyler (1853–1935), ▶ Robert Fitzwalter Tyler (1856–1927), ▶ Pearl Tyler (1860–1947)

James K. Polk

1 Jan 1824 — **Sarah CHILDRESS** (4 Sep 1803–14 Aug 1891)
no children

Zachary Taylor

21 Jun 1810 — **Margaret Mackall SMITH** (21 Sep 1788–14 Aug 1852)
▶ Anne Margaret Mackall Taylor (1811–1875), ▶ Sarah Knox Taylor (1814–1835), ▶ Octavia Pannel Taylor (1816–1820), ▶ Margaret Smith Taylor (1819–1820), ▶ Mary Elizabeth Taylor (1824–1909), ▶ Richard Taylor (1826–1879)

Millard Fillmore

5 Feb 1826 — **Abigail POWERS** (13 Mar 1798–30 Mar 1853)
▶ Millard Powers Fillmore (1828–1889), ▶ Mary Abigail Fillmore (1832–1854)

10 Feb 1858 — **Caroline CARMICHAEL McIntosh** (21 Oct 1813–11 Aug 1881)
no children

Franklin Pierce

10 Nov 1834 — **Jane Means APPLETON** (12 Mar 1806–2 Dec 1863)
▶ Franklin Pierce (1836–1836), ▶ Frank Robert Pierce (1839–1843), ▶ Benjamin Pierce (1841–1853)

James Buchanan

never married

Abraham Lincoln

4 Nov 1842 — **Mary Ann TODD** (13 Dec 1818–16 Jul 1882)
▶ Robert Todd Lincoln (1843–1926), ▶ Edward Baker Lincoln (1846–1850), ▶ William Wallace Lincoln (1850–1862), ▶ Thomas Lincoln (1853–1871)

Andrew Johnson

17 May 1827 — **Eliza McCARDLE** (4 Oct 1810–15 Jan 1876)
▶ Martha Johnson (1828–1901), ▶ Charles Johnson (1830–1863), ▶ Mary Johnson (1832–1883), ▶ Robert Johnson (1834–1869), ▶ Andrew Johnson (1852–1879)

Ulysses S. Grant

22 Aug 1848 — **Julia Boggs DENT** (26 Jan 1826–14 Dec 1902)
▶ Frederick Dent Grant (1850–1912), ▶ Ulysses Simpson Grant (1852–1929), ▶ Ellen Wrenshall Grant (1855–1922), ▶ Jesse Root Grant (1858–1934)

Rutherford B. Hayes

30 Dec 1852 — **Lucy Ware WEBB** (28 Aug 1831–25 Jun 1889)
▶ Birchard Austin Hayes (1853–1926), ▶ James Webb Cook Hayes (1856–1934), ▶ Rutherford Platt Hayes (1858–1927), ▶ Joseph Thompson Hayes (1861–1863), ▶ George Crook Hayes (1864–1866), ▶ Fanny Hayes (1867–1950), ▶ Scott Russell Hayes (1871–1923), ▶ Manning Force Hayes (1873–1874)

James A. Garfield

11 Nov 1858 — **Lucretia RUDOLPH** (19 Apr 1832–13 Mar 1918)
▶ Eliza Arabella Garfield (1860–1863), ▶ Harry Augustus Garfield (1863–1942), ▶ James Rudolph Garfield (1865–1950), ▶ Mary Garfield (1867–1947), ▶ Irvin McDowell Garfield (1870–1951), ▶ Abram Garfield (1872–1958), ▶ Edward Garfield (1874–1876)

Chester A. Arthur

25 Oct 1859 — **Ellen Lewis HERNDON** (30 Aug 1837–12 Jan 1880)
▶ William Lewis Herndon Arthur (1860–1863), ▶ Chester Alan Arthur (1864–1937), ▶ Ellen Herndon Arthur (1871–1915)

Presidents' Wives and Children (continued)

DATE OF MARRIAGE	PRESIDENTS, WIVES, AND CHILDREN

Grover Cleveland

2 Jun 1886 **Frances FOLSOM** (21 Jul 1864–29 Oct 1947)
▶ Ruth Cleveland (1891–1904), ▶ Esther Cleveland (1893–1980), ▶ Marion Cleveland (1895–1977), ▶ Richard Folsom Cleveland (1897–1974), ▶ Francis Grover Cleveland (1903–1995)

Benjamin Harrison

20 Oct 1853 **Caroline Lavinia SCOTT** (1 Oct 1832–25 Oct 1892)
▶ Russell Benjamin Harrison (1854–1936), ▶ Mary Scott Harrison (1858–1930)

6 Apr 1896 **Mary Scott LORD Dimmick** (30 Apr 1858–5 Jan 1948)
▶ Elizabeth Harrison (1897–1955)

William McKinley

25 Jan 1871 **Ida SAXTON** (8 Jun 1847–26 May 1907)
▶ Katherine McKinley (1871–1875), ▶ Ida McKinley (1873–1873)

Theodore Roosevelt

27 Oct 1880 **Alice Hathaway LEE** (29 Jul 1861–14 Feb 1884)
▶ Alice Lee Roosevelt (1884–1980)

2 Dec 1886 **Edith Kermit CAROW** (6 Aug 1861–30 Sep 1948)
▶ Theodore Roosevelt (1887–1944), ▶ Kermit Roosevelt (1889–1943), ▶ Ethel Carow Roosevelt (1891–1977), ▶ Archibald Bulloch Roosevelt (1894–1979), ▶ Quentin Roosevelt (1897–1918)

William Howard Taft

19 Jun 1886 **Helen HERRON** (2 Jun 1861–22 May 1943)
▶ Robert Alphonso Taft (1889–1953), ▶ Helen Herron Taft (1891–1987), ▶ Charles Phelps Taft (1897–1983)

Woodrow Wilson

24 Jun 1885 **Ellen Louise AXSON** (15 May 1860–6 Aug 1914)
▶ Margaret Woodrow Wilson (1886–1944), ▶ Jessie Woodrow Wilson (1887–1933), ▶ Eleanor Randolph Wilson (1889–1967)

18 Dec 1915 **Edith BOLLING Galt** (15 Oct 1872–28 Dec 1961)
no children

Warren G. Harding

8 Jul 1891 **Florence Mabel KLING De Wolf** (15 Aug 1860–21 Nov 1924)
no children

Calvin Coolidge

4 Oct 1905 **Grace Anna GOODHUE** (3 Jan 1879–8 Jul 1957)
▶ John Coolidge (1906–2000), ▶ Calvin Coolidge (1908–1924)

Herbert Hoover

10 Feb 1899 **Lou HENRY** (29 Mar 1874–7 Jan 1944)
▶ Herbert Clark Hoover (1903–1969), ▶ Allan Henry Hoover (1907–1993)

Franklin D. Roosevelt

17 Mar 1905 **(Anna) Eleanor ROOSEVELT** (11 Oct 1884–7 Nov 1962)
▶ Anna Eleanor Roosevelt (1906–1975), ▶ James Roosevelt (1907–1991), ▶ Franklin Roosevelt (1909–1909), ▶ Elliott Roosevelt (1910–1990), ▶ Franklin Delano Roosevelt (1914–1988), ▶ John Aspinwall Roosevelt (1916–1981)

Harry S. Truman

28 Jun 1919 **Elizabeth Virginia (Bess) WALLACE** (13 Feb 1885–18 Oct 1982)
▶ Margaret (Mary) Truman (1924–   )

Dwight D. Eisenhower

1 Jul 1916 **Marie (Mamie) Geneva DOUD** (14 Nov 1896–1 Nov 1979)
▶ Doud Dwight Eisenhower (1917–1921), ▶ John Sheldon Doud Eisenhower (1922–   )

John F. Kennedy

12 Sep 1953 **Jacqueline Lee BOUVIER** (28 Jul 1929–19 May 1994)
▶ Caroline Bouvier Kennedy (1957–   ), ▶ John Fitzgerald Kennedy (1960–1999), Patrick Bouvier Kennedy (1963–1963)

Presidents' Wives and Children (continued)

DATE OF MARRIAGE	PRESIDENTS, WIVES, AND CHILDREN
	Lyndon B. Johnson
17 Nov 1934	**Claudia Alta (Lady Bird) Taylor** (22 Dec 1912–11 Jul 2007) ▸ Lynda Bird Johnson (1944–), ▸ Luci Baines Johnson (1947–)
	Richard M. Nixon
21 Jun 1940	**Thelma Catherine (Patricia) Ryan** (16 Mar 1912–22 Jun 1993) ▸ Patricia Nixon (1946–), ▸ Julie Nixon (1948–)
	Gerald R. Ford
15 Oct 1948	**Elizabeth Ann (Betty) Bloomer Warren** (8 Apr 1918–) ▸ Michael Gerald Ford (1950–), ▸ John Gardner Ford (1952–), ▸ Steven Meigs Ford (1956–), ▸ Susan Elizabeth Ford (1957–)
	Jimmy Carter
7 Jul 1946	**(Eleanor) Rosalynn Smith** (18 Aug 1927–) ▸ John William Carter (1947–), ▸ James Earl Carter (1950–), ▸ Donnel Jeffrey Carter (1952–), ▸ Amy Lynn Carter (1967–)
	Ronald Reagan
24 Jan 1940	**Jane Wyman (née Sarah Jane Fulks)** (4 Jan 1914–) ▸ Maureen Elizabeth Reagan (1941–2001), ▸ Michael Edward Reagan (1945–), ▸ Christine Reagan (1947–1947)
4 Mar 1952	**Nancy Davis (née Anne Frances Robbins)** (6 Jul 1921–) ▸ Patricia Ann Reagan (1952–), ▸ Ronald Prescott Reagan (1958–)
	George H.W. Bush
6 Jan 1945	**Barbara Pierce** (8 Jun 1925–) ▸ George Walker Bush (1946–), ▸ Robin Bush (1949–1953), ▸ John Ellis (Jeb) Bush (1953–), ▸ Neil Mallon Bush (1955–), ▸ Marvin Pierce Bush (1956–), ▸ Dorothy Walker Bush (1959–)
	William J. Clinton
11 Oct 1975	**Hillary Diane Rodham** (26 Oct 1947–) ▸ Chelsea Clinton (1980–)
	George W. Bush
5 Nov 1977	**Laura Lane Welch** (4 Nov 1946–) ▸ Barbara Bush (1981–), ▸ Jenna Bush (1981–)

Presidential Succession

The president is the chief executive of the US. In contrast to the parliamentary form of government, under which the head of state is mainly ceremonial, the presidential system, such as that in the US, vests the president with great authority. The role of the president—including the process of presidential succession—is outlined in Article II of the Constitution of 1787, the fundamental law of the US federal system of government. Presidential nomination procedures are often recognized as constitutional elements, though they are outside the letter of the Constitution.

The Presidential Succession Act of 1792 established the stages of succession: from the president to the vice president, then to the Senate president pro tempore and next to the speaker of the House of Representatives. In 1886 new legislation removed the latter two from succession, replacing them with cabinet officers. The pattern of presidential succession was again changed in 1947, when the the speaker of the House was placed next in line after the vice president, followed by the Senate president pro tempore, the secretary of state, and, finally, the remaining cabinet officers in the order that their departments were first formed.

History

The administration of the first president, George Washington, set the customary precedent of serving only two terms, a tradition maintained until Pres. Franklin D. Roosevelt was elected to a third and fourth term in the 1940s. Congress adopted the 22nd Amendment in 1951, which limits presidents to two terms in office.

In 1841 William Henry Harrison became the first president to die in office and was succeeded by his vice president, John Tyler. In 1850, when Zachary Taylor died after only 16 months in office, he was succeeded by Millard Fillmore. In the same manner, vice president Andrew Johnson assumed the presidency after Pres. Abraham Lincoln's assassination.

When Pres. James Garfield was shot on 2 Jul 1881, he became incapacitated, raising serious constitutional questions over who should perform the functions of the presidency. For 80 days the president lay ill, and it was generally agreed that, in such cases, the vice president (Chester Arthur) was empowered by the Constitution to assume the powers and duties of the office of president. But should Arthur be only acting president until Garfield recovered, or would he receive the office itself and thus displace his predecessor?

Because of an ambiguity in the Constitution, opinion was divided, and, because Congress was not in session, the problem could not be debated there. No further action was taken before the death of the president, the result of slow blood poisoning, on 19 September. This ambiguity over succession was later clarified by the 20th (1933) and 25th (1967) Amendments. Other vice presidents who succeeded upon the death of presidents included Theodore Roosevelt in 1901; Calvin Coolidge in 1923; Harry S. Truman in 1945; and Lyndon B. Johnson in 1963.

In the 2000 presidential election, Republican George W. Bush lost the popular vote but narrowly defeated Democratic Vice President Al Gore after a divided Supreme Court intervened to halt the manual recounting of disputed ballots in Florida, thereby giving Bush enough electoral votes to capture the presidency.

Please visit <www.britannica.com/presidents> for information about all previous presidential elections.

Vice Presidents

	NAME	DATES OF BIRTH/DEATH	BIRTHPLACE	TIME IN OFFICE	PRESIDENT
1	John Adams	30 Oct 1735–4 Jul 1826	Braintree (now Quincy) MA	1789–97	George Washington
2	Thomas Jefferson	13 Apr 1743–4 Jul 1826	Shadwell VA	1797–1801	John Adams
3	Aaron Burr	6 Feb 1756–14 Sep 1836	Newark NJ	1801–05	Thomas Jefferson
4	George Clinton[1]	26 Jul 1739–20 Apr 1812	Little Britain NY	1805–09 1809–12	Thomas Jefferson James Madison
5	Elbridge Gerry	17 Jul 1744–23 Nov 1814	Marblehead MA	1813–14	James Madison
6	Daniel D. Tompkins	21 Jun 1774–11 Jun 1825	Scarsdale NY	1817–25	James Monroe
7	John C. Calhoun[2]	18 Mar 1782–31 Mar 1850	Abbeville district SC	1825–29 1829–32	John Quincy Adams Andrew Jackson
8	Martin Van Buren	5 Dec 1782–24 Jul 1862	Kinderhook NY	1833–37	Andrew Jackson
9	Richard M. Johnson	17 Oct 1781–19 Nov 1850	Beargrass VA (now Louisville KY)	1837–41	Martin Van Buren
10	John Tyler	29 Mar 1790–18 Jan 1862	Charles City county VA	1841	William Henry Harrison[1]
11	George Mifflin Dallas	10 Jul 1792–31 Dec 1864	Philadelphia PA	1845–49	James K. Polk
12	Millard Fillmore	7 Jan 1800–8 Mar 1874	Locke township NY	1849–50	Zachary Taylor[1]
13	William Rufus de Vane King[1]	7 Apr 1786–18 Apr 1853	Sampson county NC	4 Mar– 18 Apr 1853	Franklin Pierce
14	John C. Breckinridge	21 Jan 1821–17 May 1875	near Lexington KY	1857–61	James Buchanan
15	Hannibal Hamlin	27 Aug 1809–4 Jul 1891	Paris Hill ME	1861–65	Abraham Lincoln[1]
16	Andrew Johnson	29 Dec 1808–31 Jul 1875	Raleigh NC	1865	
17	Schuyler Colfax	23 Mar 1823–13 Jan 1885	New York NY	1869–73	Ulysses S. Grant
18	Henry Wilson[1]	16 Feb 1812–22 Nov 1875	Farmington NH	1873–75	Ulysses S. Grant
19	William A. Wheeler	30 Jun 1819–4 Jun 1887	Malone NY	1877–81	Rutherford B. Hayes
20	Chester A. Arthur	5 Oct 1829–18 Nov 1886	North Fairfield VT	1881	James A. Garfield[1]
21	Thomas A. Hendricks[1]	7 Sep 1819–25 Nov 1885	Zanesville OH	4 Mar– 25 Nov 1885	Grover Cleveland
22	Levi Parsons Morton	16 May 1824–16 May 1920	Shoreham VT	1889–93	Benjamin Harrison
23	Adlai E. Stevenson	23 Oct 1835–14 Jun 1914	Christian county KY	1893–97	Grover Cleveland
24	Garret A. Hobart[1]	3 Jun 1844–21 Nov 1899	Long Branch NJ	1897–99	William McKinley
25	Theodore Roosevelt	27 Oct 1858–6 Jan 1919	New York NY	1901	William McKinley[1]
26	Charles Warren Fairbanks	11 May 1852–4 Jun 1918	Union county OH	1905–09	Theodore Roosevelt
27	James Schoolcraft Sherman[1]	24 Oct 1855–30 Oct 1912	Utica NY	1909–12	William Howard Taft
28	Thomas R. Marshall	14 Mar 1854–1 Jun 1925	North Manchester IN	1913–21	Woodrow Wilson
29	Calvin Coolidge	4 Jul 1872–5 Jan 1933	Plymouth VT	1921–23	Warren G. Harding[1]
30	Charles G. Dawes	27 Aug 1865–23 Apr 1851	Marietta OH	1925–29	Calvin Coolidge
31	Charles Curtis	25 Jan 1860–8 Feb 1936	Kansas Territory	1929–33	Herbert Hoover

Vice Presidents (continued)

	NAME	DATES OF BIRTH/DEATH	BIRTHPLACE	TIME IN OFFICE	PRESIDENT
32	John Nance Garner	22 Nov 1868–7 Nov 1967	Red River county TX	1933–41	Franklin D. Roosevelt
33	Henry A. Wallace	7 Oct 1888–18 Nov 1965	Adair county IA	1941–45	Franklin D. Roosevelt
34	Harry S. Truman	8 May 1884–26 Dec 1972	Lamar MO	1945	Franklin D. Roosevelt[1]
35	Alben W. Barkley	24 Nov 1877–30 Apr 1956	Graves county KY	1949–53	Harry S. Truman
36	Richard M. Nixon	9 Jan 1913–22 Apr 1994	Yorba Linda CA	1953–61	Dwight D. Eisenhower
37	Lyndon B. Johnson	27 Aug 1908–22 Jan 1973	Gillespie county TX	1961–63	John F. Kennedy[1]
38	Hubert H. Humphrey	27 May 1911–13 Jan 1978	Wallace SD	1965–69	Lyndon B. Johnson
39	Spiro T. Agnew[2]	9 Nov 1918–17 Sep 1996	Baltimore MD	1969–73	Richard M. Nixon
40	Gerald R. Ford	14 Jul 1913	Omaha NE	1973–74	Richard M. Nixon[2]
41	Nelson A. Rockefeller	8 Jul 1908–26 Jan 1979	Bar Harbor ME	1974–77	Gerald R. Ford
42	Walter F. Mondale	5 Jan 1928	Ceylon MN	1977–81	Jimmy Carter
43	George H.W. Bush	12 Jun 1924	Milton MA	1981–89	Ronald Reagan
44	Dan Quayle	4 Feb 1947	Indianapolis IN	1989–93	George H.W. Bush
45	Albert Gore	31 Mar 1948	Washington DC	1993–2001	William J. Clinton
46	Richard B. Cheney	30 Jan 1941	Lincoln NE	2001–	George W. Bush

[1]Died in office.
[2]Resigned from office.

US Presidential Cabinets

The cabinet is composed of the heads of executive departments chosen by the president with the consent of the Senate. Cabinet officials do not hold seats in Congress and are not regulated by the US Constitution, which makes no mention of such a body. The existence of the cabinet is a matter of custom dating back to George Washington, who consulted regularly with his department heads as a group. Original dates of service are given for officials appointed midterm and for newly created posts. Ad interim officials are not listed. Presidencies and new positions are indicated in bold.

George Washington

30 APR 1789–3 MARCH 1793 (TERM 1)

State	Thomas Jefferson
Treasury	Alexander Hamilton
War	Henry Knox
Attorney General	Edmund Randolph

4 MAR 1793–3 MAR 1797 (TERM 2)

State	Thomas Jefferson; Edmund Randolph (2 Jan 1794); Timothy Pickering (20 Aug 1795)
Treasury	Alexander Hamilton; Oliver Wolcott, Jr. (2 Feb 1795)
War	Henry Knox; Timothy Pickering (2 Jan 1795); James McHenry (6 Feb 1796)
Attorney General	Edmund Randolph; William Bradford (29 Jan 1794); Charles Lee (10 Dec 1795)

John Adams

4 MAR 1797–3 MAR 1801

State	Timothy Pickering; John Marshall (6 Jun 1800)
Treasury	Oliver Wolcott, Jr.; Samuel Dexter (1 Jan 1801)
War	James McHenry; Samuel Dexter (12 Jun 1800)
Navy	Benjamin Stoddert (18 Jun 1798)
Attorney General	Charles Lee

Thomas Jefferson

4 MAR 1801–3 MAR 1805 (TERM 1)

State	James Madison
Treasury	Samuel Dexter; Albert Gallatin (14 May 1801)
War	Henry Dearborn
Navy	Benjamin Stoddert; Robert Smith (27 Jul 1801)
Attorney General	Levi Lincoln

US Presidential Cabinets (continued)

Thomas Jefferson (continued)

4 MAR 1805–3 MAR 1809 (TERM 2)

State	James Madison
Treasury	Albert Gallatin
War	Henry Dearborn
Navy	Robert Smith
Attorney General	John Breckenridge; Caesar Augustus Rodney (20 Jan 1807)

James Madison

4 MAR 1809–3 MAR 1813 (TERM 1)

State	Robert Smith
Treasury	Albert Gallatin
War	John Smith; William Eustis (8 Apr 1809); John Armstrong (5 Feb 1813)
Navy	Robert Smith; Paul Hamilton (15 May 1809); William Jones (19 Jan 1813)
Attorney General	Caesar Augustus Rodney; William Pinkney (6 Jan 1812)

4 MAR 1813–3 MAR 1817 (TERM 2)

State	James Monroe
Treasury	Albert Gallatin; George Washington Campbell (9 Feb 1814); Alexander James Dallas (14 Oct 1814); William Harris Crawford (22 Oct 1816)
War	John Armstrong; James Monroe (1 Oct 1814); William Harris Crawford (8 Aug 1815)
Navy	William Jones; Benjamin Williams Crowninshield (16 Jan 1815)
Attorney General	William Pinkney; Richard Rush (11 Feb 1814)

James Monroe

4 MAR 1817–3 MAR 1821 (TERM 1)

State	John Quincy Adams
Treasury	William Harris Crawford
War	John C. Calhoun
Navy	Benjamin Williams Crowninshield; Smith Thompson (1 Jan 1819)
Attorney General	Richard Rush; William Wirt (15 Nov 1817)

4 MAR 1821–3 MAR 1825 (TERM 2)

State	John Quincy Adams
Treasury	William Harris Crawford
War	John C. Calhoun
Navy	Smith Thompson; Samuel Lewis Southard (16 Sep 1823)
Attorney General	William Wirt

John Quincy Adams

4 MAR 1825–3 MAR 1829

State	Henry Clay
Treasury	Richard Rush
War	James Barbour; Peter Buell Porter (21 Jun 1828)
Navy	Samuel Lewis Southard
Attorney General	William Wirt

Andrew Jackson

4 MAR 1829–3 MAR 1833 (TERM 1)

State	Martin Van Buren; Edward Livingston (24 May 1831)
Treasury	Samuel Delucenna Ingham; Louis McLane (8 Aug 1831)
War	John Henry Eaton; Lewis Cass (8 Aug 1831)
Navy	John Branch; Levi Woodbury (23 May 1831)
Attorney General	John Macpherson Berrien; Roger Brooke Taney (20 Jul 1831)

4 MAR 1833–3 MAR 1837 (TERM 2)

State	Edward Livingston; Louis McLane (29 May 1833); John Forsyth (1 Jul 1834)
Treasury	Louis McLane; William John Duane (1 Jun 1833); Roger Brooke Taney (23 Sep 1833); Levi Woodbury (1 Jul 1834)
War	Lewis Cass
Navy	Levi Woodbury; Mahlon Dickerson (30 Jun 1834)
Attorney General	Roger Brooke Taney; Benjamin Franklin Butler (18 Nov 1833)

US Presidential Cabinets (continued)

Martin Van Buren

4 MAR 1837–3 MAR 1841

State	John Forsyth
Treasury	Levi Woodbury
War	Joel Roberts Poinsett
Navy	Mahlon Dickerson; James Kirke Paulding (1 Jul 1838)
Attorney General	Benjamin Franklin Butler; Felix Grundy (1 Sep 1838); Henry Dilworth Gilpin (11 Jan 1840)

William Henry Harrison

4 MAR 1841–4 APR 1841

State	Daniel Webster
Treasury	Thomas Ewing
War	John Bell
Navy	George Edmund Badger
Attorney General	John Jordan Crittenden

John Tyler

6 APR 1841–3 MAR 1845

State	Daniel Webster; Abel Parker Upshur (24 Jul 1843); John C. Calhoun (1 Apr 1844)
Treasury	Thomas Ewing; Walter Forward (13 Sep 1841); John Canfield Spencer (8 Mar 1843); George Mortimer Bibb (4 Jul 1844)
War	John Bell; John Canfield Spencer (12 Oct 1841); James Madison Porter (8 Mar 1843); William Wilkins (20 Feb 1844)
Navy	George Edmund Badger; Abel Parker Upshur (11 Oct 1841); David Henshaw (24 Jul 1843); Thomas Walker Gilmer (19 Feb 1844); John Young Mason (26 Mar 1844)
Attorney General	John Jordan Crittenden; Hugh Swinton Legaré (20 Sep 1841); John Nelson (1 Jul 1843)

James K. Polk

4 MAR 1845–3 MAR 1849

State	James Buchanan
Treasury	Robert James Walker
War	William Learned Marcy
Navy	George Bancroft; John Young Mason (9 Sep 1846)
Attorney General	John Young Mason; Nathan Clifford (17 Oct 1846); Isaac Toucey (29 Jun 1848)

Zachary Taylor

4 MAR 1849–9 JUL 1850

State	John Middleton Clayton
Treasury	William Morris Meredith
War	George Washington Crawford
Navy	William Ballard Preston
Attorney General	Reverdy Johnson
Interior	Thomas Ewing (8 Mar 1849)

Millard Fillmore

10 JUL 1850–3 MAR 1853

State	Daniel Webster; Edward Everett (6 Nov 1852)
Treasury	Thomas Corwin
War	George Washington Crawford; Charles Magill Conrad (15 Aug 1850)
Navy	William Alexander Graham; John Pendleton Kennedy (26 Jul 1852)
Attorney General	Reverdy Johnson; John Jordan Crittenden (14 Aug 1850)
Interior	Thomas Ewing; Thomas McKean Thompson McKennan (15 Aug 1850); Alexander Hugh Holmes Stuart (16 Sep 1850)

Franklin Pierce

4 MAR 1853–3 MAR 1857

State	William Learned Marcy
Treasury	James Guthrie
War	Jefferson Davis
Navy	James Cochran Dobbin
Attorney General	Caleb Cushing
Interior	Robert McClelland

US Presidential Cabinets (continued)

James Buchanan

4 MAR 1857–3 MAR 1861

State	Lewis Cass; Jeremiah Sullivan Black (17 Dec 1860)
Treasury	Howell Cobb; Philip Francis Thomas (12 Dec 1860); John Adams Dix (15 Jan 1861)
War	John Buchanan Floyd
Navy	Isaac Toucey
Attorney General	Jeremiah Sullivan Black; Edwin McMasters Stanton (22 Dec 1860)
Interior	Jacob Thompson

Abraham Lincoln

4 MAR 1861–3 MAR 1865 (TERM 1)

State	William Henry Seward
Treasury	Salmon Portland Chase; William Pitt Fessenden (5 Jul 1864)
War	Simon Cameron; Edwin McMasters Stanton (20 Jun 1862)
Navy	Gideon Welles
Attorney General	Edward Bates; James Speed (5 Dec 1864)
Interior	Caleb Blood Smith; John Palmer Usher (8 Jan 1863)

4 MAR 1865–15 APR 1865 (TERM 2)

State	William Henry Seward
Treasury	Hugh McCulloch
War	Edwin McMasters Stanton
Navy	Gideon Welles
Attorney General	James Speed
Interior	John Palmer Usher

Andrew Johnson

15 APR 1865–3 MAR 1869

State	William Henry Seward
Treasury	Hugh McCulloch
War	Edwin McMasters Stanton; John McAllister Schofield (1 Jun 1868)
Navy	Gideon Welles
Attorney General	James Speed; Henry Stanbery (23 Jul 1866); William Maxwell Evarts (20 Jul 1868)
Interior	John Palmer Usher; James Harlan (15 May 1865); Orville Hickman Browning (1 Sep 1866)

Ulysses S. Grant

4 MAR 1869–3 MAR 1873 (TERM 1)

State	Elihu Benjamin Washburne; Hamilton Fish (17 Mar 1869)
Treasury	George Sewall Boutwell
War	John Aaron Rawlins; William Tecumseh Sherman (11 Sep 1869); William Worth Belknap (1 Nov 1869)
Navy	Adolph Edward Borie; George Maxwell Robeson (25 Jun 1869)
Attorney General	Ebenezer Rockwood Hoar; Amos Tappan Akerman (8 Jul 1870); George Henry Williams (10 Jan 1872)
Interior	Jacob Dolson Cox; Columbus Delano (1 Nov 1870)

4 MAR 1873–3 MAR 1877 (TERM 2)

State	Hamilton Fish
Treasury	William Adams Richardson; Benjamin Helm Bristow (4 Jun 1874); Lot Myrick Morrill (7 Jul 1876)
War	William Worth Belknap; Alphonso Taft (11 Mar 1876); James Donald Cameron (1 Jun 1876)
Navy	George Maxwell Robeson
Attorney General	George Henry Williams; Edward Pierrepont (15 May 1875); Alphonso Taft (1 Jun 1876)
Interior	Columbus Delano; Zachariah Chandler (19 Oct 1875)

Rutherford B. Hayes

4 MAR 1877–3 MAR 1881

State	William Maxwell Evarts
Treasury	John Sherman
War	George Washington McCrary; Alexander Ramsey (12 Dec 1879)
Navy	Richard Wigginton Thompson; Nathan Goff, Jr. (6 Jan 1881)
Attorney General	Charles Devens
Interior	Carl Schurz

US Presidential Cabinets (continued)

James A. Garfield

4 MAR 1881–19 SEP 1881

State	James Gillespie Blaine
Treasury	William Windom
War	Robert Todd Lincoln
Attorney General	(Isaac) Wayne MacVeagh
Navy	William Henry Hunt
Interior	Samuel Jordan Kirkwood

Chester A. Arthur

20 SEP 1881–3 MAR 1885

State	James Gillespie Blaine; Frederick Theodore Frelinghuysen (19 Dec 1881)
Treasury	William Windom; Charles James Folger (14 Nov 1881); Walter Quintin Gresham (24 Sep 1884); Hugh McCulloch (31 Oct 1884)
War	Robert Todd Lincoln
Navy	William Henry Hunt; William Eaton Chandler (17 Apr 1882)
Attorney General	(Isaac) Wayne MacVeagh; Benjamin Harris Brewster (3 Jan 1882)
Interior	Samuel Jordan Kirkwood; Henry Moore Teller (17 Apr 1882)

Grover Cleveland

4 MAR 1885–3 MAR 1889

State	Thomas Francis Bayard
Treasury	Daniel Manning; Charles Stebbins Fairchild (1 Apr 1887)
War	William Crowninshield Endicott
Navy	William Collins Whitney
Attorney General	Augustus Hill Garland
Interior	Lucius Quintus Cincinnatus Lamar; William Freeman Vilas (16 Jan 1888)
Agriculture	Norman Jay Colman (13 Feb 1889)

Benjamin Harrison

4 MAR 1889–3 MAR 1893

State	James Gillespie Blaine; John Watson Foster (29 Jun 1892)
Treasury	William Windom; Charles Foster (24 Feb 1891)
War	Redfield Proctor; Stephen Benton Elkins (24 Dec 1891)
Navy	Benjamin Franklin Tracy
Attorney General	William Henry Harrison Miller
Interior	John Willock Noble
Agriculture	Jeremiah McLain Rusk

Grover Cleveland

4 MAR 1893–3 MAR 1897

State	Walter Quintin Gresham; Richard Olney (10 Jun 1895)
Treasury	John Griffin Carlisle
War	Daniel Scott Lamont
Navy	Hilary Abner Herbert
Attorney General	Richard Olney; Judson Harmon (11 Jun 1895)
Interior	Hoke Smith; David Rowland Francis (4 Sep 1896)
Agriculture	Julius Sterling Morton

William McKinley

4 MAR 1897–3 MAR 1901 (TERM 1)

State	John Sherman; William Rufus Day (28 Apr 1898); John Hay (30 Sep 1898)
Treasury	Lyman Judson
War	Russell Alexander Alger; Elihu Root (1 Aug 1899)
Navy	John Davis Long
Attorney General	Joseph McKenna; John William Griggs (1 Feb 1898)
Interior	Cornelius Newton Bliss; Ethan Allen Hitchcock (20 Feb 1899)
Agriculture	James Wilson

4 MAR 1901–14 SEP 1901 (TERM 2)

State	John Hay
Treasury	Lyman Judson Gage
War	Elihu Root
Navy	John Davis Long
Attorney General	John William Griggs; Philander Chase Knox (10 Apr 1901)
Interior	Ethan Allen Hitchcock
Agriculture	James Wilson

US Presidential Cabinets (continued)

Theodore Roosevelt

14 SEP 1901–3 MAR 1905 (TERM 1)

State	John Hay
Treasury	Lyman Judson Gage; Leslie Mortier Shaw (1 Feb 1902)
War	Elihu Root; William Howard Taft (1 Feb 1904)
Navy	John Davis Long; William Henry Moody (1 May 1902); Paul Morton (1 Jul 1904)
Attorney General	Philander Chase Knox; William Henry Moody (1 Jul 1904)
Interior	Ethan Allen Hitchcock
Agriculture	James Wilson
Commerce and Labor	George Bruce Cortelyou (16 Feb 1903); Victor Howard Metcalf (1 Jul 1904)

4 MAR 1905–3 MAR 1909 (TERM 2)

State	John Hay; Elihu Root (19 Jul 1905); Robert Bacon (27 Jan 1909)
Treasury	Leslie Mortier Shaw; George Bruce Cortelyou (4 Mar 1907)
War	William Howard Taft; Luke Edward Wright (1 Jul 1908)
Navy	Paul Morton; Charles Joseph Bonaparte (1 Jul 1905); Victor Howard Metcalf (17 Dec 1906); Truman Handy Newberry (1 Dec 1908)
Attorney General	William Henry Moody; Charles Joseph Bonaparte (17 Dec 1906)
Interior	Ethan Allen Hitchcock; James Rudolph Garfield (4 Mar 1907)
Agriculture	James Wilson
Commerce and Labor	Victor Howard Metcalf; Oscar Solomon Straus (17 Dec 1906)

William Howard Taft

4 MAR 1909–3 MAR 1913

State	Philander Chase Knox
Treasury	Franklin MacVeagh
War	Jacob McGavock Dickinson; Henry Lewis Stimson (22 May 1911)
Navy	George von Lengerke Meyer
Attorney General	George Woodward Wickersham
Interior	Richard Achilles Ballinger; Walter Lowrie Fisher (7 Mar 1911)
Agriculture	James Wilson
Commerce and Labor	Charles Nagel

Woodrow Wilson

4 MAR 1913–3 MAR 1917 (TERM 1)

State	William Jennings Bryan; Robert Lansing (23 Jun 1915)
Treasury	William Gibbs McAdoo
War	Lindley Miller Garrison; Newton Diehl Baker (9 Mar 1916)
Navy	Josephus Daniels
Attorney General	James Clark McReynolds; Thomas Watt Gregory (3 Sep 1914)
Interior	Franklin Knight Lane
Agriculture	David Franklin Houston
Commerce	William Cox Redfield (5 Mar 1913)
Labor	William Bauchop Wilson (5 Mar 1913)

4 MAR 1917–3 MAR 1921 (TERM 2)

State	Robert Lansing; Bainbridge Colby (23 Mar 1920)
Treasury	William Gibbs McAdoo; Carter Glass (16 Dec 1918); David Franklin Houston (2 Feb 1920)
War	Newton Diehl Baker
Navy	Josephus Daniels
Attorney General	Thomas Watt Gregory; Alexander Mitchell Palmer (5 Mar 1919)
Interior	Franklin Knight Lane; John Barton Payne (13 Mar 1920)
Agriculture	David Franklin Houston; Edwin Thomas Meredith (2 Feb 1920)
Commerce	William Cox Redfield; Joshua Willis Alexander (16 Dec 1919)
Labor	William Bauchop Wilson

Warren G. Harding

4 MAR 1921–2 AUG 1923

State	Charles Evans Hughes
Treasury	Andrew William Mellon
War	John Wingate Weeks
Navy	Edwin Denby
Attorney General	Harry Micajah Daugherty

US Presidential Cabinets (continued)

Warren G. Harding (continued)

4 MAR 1921–2 AUG 1923 (CONTINUED)

Interior	Albert Bacon Fall; Hubert Work (5 Mar 1923)
Agriculture	Henry Cantwell Wallace
Commerce	Herbert Hoover
Labor	James John Davis

Calvin Coolidge

3 AUG 1923–3 MAR 1925 (TERM 1)

State	Charles Evans Hughes
Treasury	Andrew William Mellon
War	John Wingate Weeks
Navy	Edwin Denby; Curtis Dwight Wilbur (18 Mar 1924)
Attorney General	Harry Micajah Daugherty; Harlan Fiske Stone (9 Apr 1924)
Interior	Hubert Work
Agriculture	Henry Cantwell Wallace; Howard Mason Gore (21 Nov 1924)
Commerce	Herbert Hoover
Labor	James John Davis

4 MAR 1925–3 MAR 1929 (TERM 2)

State	Frank Billings Kellogg
Treasury	Andrew William Mellon
War	John Wingate Weeks; Dwight Filley Davis (14 Oct 1925)
Navy	Curtis Dwight Wilbur
Attorney General	John Garibaldi Sargent
Interior	Hubert Work; Roy Owen West (21 Jan 1929)
Agriculture	William Marion Jardine
Commerce	Herbert Hoover; William Fairfield Whiting (11 Dec 1928)
Labor	James John Davis

Herbert Hoover

4 MAR 1929–3 MAR 1933

State	Henry Lewis Stimson
Treasury	Andrew William Mellon; Ogden Livingston Mills (13 Feb 1932)
War	James William Good; Patrick Jay Hurley (9 Dec 1929)
Navy	Charles Francis Adams
Attorney General	William De Witt Mitchell
Interior	Ray Lyman Wilbur
Agriculture	Arthur Mastick Hyde
Commerce	Robert Patterson Lamont; Roy Dikeman Chapin (14 Dec 1932)
Labor	James John Davis; William Nuckles Doak (9 Dec 1930)

Franklin D. Roosevelt

4 MAR 1933–20 JAN 1937 (TERM 1)

State	Cordell Hull
Treasury	William Hartman Woodin; Henry Morgenthau, Jr. (8 Jan 1934)
War	George Henry Dern
Navy	Claude Augustus Swanson
Attorney General	Homer Stille Cummings
Interior	Harold Le Claire Ickes
Agriculture	Henry Agard Wallace
Commerce	Daniel Calhoun Roper
Labor	Frances Perkins

20 JAN 1937–20 JAN 1941 (TERM 2)

State	Cordell Hull
Treasury	Henry Morgenthau, Jr.
War	Harry Hines Woodring; Henry Lewis Stimson (10 Jul 1940)
Attorney General	Homer Stille Cummings; Frank Murphy (17 Jan 1939); Robert Houghwout Jackson (18 Jan 1940)
Navy	Claude Augustus Swanson; Charles Edison (11 Jan 1940); Frank Knox (10 Jul 1940)
Interior	Harold Le Claire Ickes
Agriculture	Henry Agard Wallace; Claude Raymond Wickard (5 Sep 1940)
Commerce	Daniel Calhoun Roper; Harry Lloyd Hopkins (23 Jan 1939); Jesse Holman Jones (19 Sep 1940)
Labor	Frances Perkins

US Presidential Cabinets (continued)

Franklin D. Roosevelt (continued)

20 JAN 1941–20 JAN 1945 (TERM 3)

State	Cordell Hull; Edward Reilly Stettinius (1 Dec 1944)
Treasury	Henry Morgenthau, Jr.
War	Henry Lewis Stimson
Navy	Frank Knox; James Vincent Forrestal (18 May 1944)
Attorney General	Robert Houghwout Jackson; Francis Biddle (5 Sep 1941)
Interior	Harold Le Claire Ickes
Agriculture	Claude Raymond Wickard
Commerce	Jesse Holman Jones
Labor	Frances Perkins

20 JAN 1945–12 APR 1945 (TERM 4)

State	Edward Reilly Stettinius
Treasury	Henry Morgenthau, Jr.
War	Henry Lewis Stimson
Navy	James Vincent Forrestal
Attorney General	Francis Biddle
Interior	Harold Le Claire Ickes
Agriculture	Claude Raymond Wickard
Commerce	Jesse Holman Jones; Henry Agard Wallace (2 Mar 1945)
Labor	Frances Perkins

Harry S. Truman

12 APR 1945–20 JAN 1949 (TERM 1)

State	Edward Reilly Stettinius; James Francis Byrnes (3 Jul 1945); George Catlett Marshall (21 Jan 1947)
Treasury	Henry Morgenthau, Jr.; Frederick Moore (23 Jul 1945); John Wesley Snyder (25 Jun 1946)
War	Henry Lewis Stimson; Robert Porter Patterson (27 Sep 1945); Kenneth Clairborne Royall (25 Jul 1947)
Defense	James Vincent Forrestal (17 Sep 1947)
Navy	James Vincent Forrestal
Attorney General	Francis Biddle; Thomas Campbell Clark (1 Jul 1945)
Interior	Harold Le Claire Ickes; Julius Albert Krug (18 Mar 1946)
Agriculture	Claude Raymond Wickard; Clinton Presba Anderson (30 Jun 1945); Charles Franklin Brannan (2 Jun 1948)
Commerce	Henry Agard Wallace; William Averell Harriman (28 Jan 1947); Charles Sawyer (6 May 1948)
Labor	Frances Perkins; Lewis Baxter Schwellenbach (1 Jul 1945)

20 JAN 1949–20 JAN 1953 (TERM 2)

State	Dean Gooderham Acheson
Treasury	John Wesley Snyder
Defense	James Vincent Forrestal; Louis Arthur Johnson (28 Mar 1949); George Catlett Marshall (21 Sep 1950); Robert Abercrombie Lovett (17 Sep 1951)
Attorney General	Thomas Campbell Clark; James Howard McGrath (24 Aug 1949)
Interior	Julius Albert Krug; Oscar Littleton Chapman (19 Jan 1950)
Agriculture	Charles Franklin Brannan
Commerce	Charles Sawyer
Labor	Maurice Joseph Tobin

Dwight D. Eisenhower

20 JAN 1953–20 JAN 1957 (TERM 1)

State	John Foster Dulles
Treasury	George Magoffin Humphrey
Defense	Charles Erwin Wilson
Attorney General	Herbert Brownell
Interior	Douglas McKay; Frederick Andrew Seaton (8 Jun 1956)
Agriculture	Ezra Taft Benson
Commerce	Sinclair Weeks
Labor	Martin Patrick Durkin; James Paul Mitchell (9 Oct 1953)
Health, Education, and Welfare	Oveta Culp Hobby (11 Apr 1953); Marion Bayard Folson (1 Aug 1955)

20 JAN 1957–20 JAN 1961 (TERM 2)

State	John Foster Dulles; Christian Archibald Herter (22 Apr 1959)
Treasury	George Magoffin Humphrey; Robert Bernerd Anderson (29 Jul 1957)

US Presidential Cabinets (continued)

Dwight D. Eisenhower (continued)

20 JAN 1957–20 JAN 1961 (TERM 2) (CONTINUED)

Defense	Charles Erwin Wilson; Neil Hosler McElroy (9 Oct 1957); Thomas Sovereign Gates, Jr. (2 Dec 1959)
Attorney General	Herbert Brownell, Jr.; William Pierce Rogers (27 Jan 1958)
Interior	Frederick Andrew Seaton
Agriculture	Ezra Taft Benson
Commerce	Sinclair Weeks; Frederick Henry Mueller (10 Aug 1959)
Labor	James Paul Mitchell
Health, Education, and Welfare	Marion Bayard Folsom; Arthur Sherwood Flemming (1 Aug 1958)

John F. Kennedy

20 JAN 1961–22 NOV 1963

State	(David) Dean Rusk
Treasury	C. (Clarence) Douglas Dillon
Defense	Robert Strange McNamara
Attorney General	Robert F. Kennedy
Interior	Stewart Lee Udall
Agriculture	Orville Lothrop Freeman
Commerce	Luther Hartwell Hodges
Labor	Arthur Joseph Goldberg; W. (William) Willard Wirtz (25 Sep 1962)
Health, Education, and Welfare	Abraham Alexander Ribicoff; Anthony Joseph Celebrezze (31 Jul 1962)

Lyndon B. Johnson

22 NOV 1963–20 JAN 1965 (TERM 1)

State	(David) Dean Rusk
Treasury	C. (Clarence) Douglas Dillon
Defense	Robert Strange McNamara
Attorney General	Robert F. Kennedy
Interior	Stewart Lee Udall
Agriculture	Orville Lothrop Freeman
Commerce	Luther Hartwell Hodges
Labor	W. (William) Willard Wirtz
Health, Education, and Welfare	Anthony Joseph Celebrezze

20 JAN 1965–20 JAN 1969 (TERM 2)

State	(David) Dean Rusk
Treasury	C. (Clarence) Douglas Dillon; Henry Hamill Fowler (1 Apr 1965); Joseph Walker Barr (23 Dec 1968)
Defense	Robert Strange McNamara; Clark McAdams Clifford (1 Mar 1968)
Attorney General	Nicholas deBelleville Katzenbach; William Ramsey Clark (10 Mar 1967)
Interior	Stewart Lee Udall
Agriculture	Orville Lothrop Freeman
Commerce	John Thomas Connor; Alexander Buel Trowbridge (14 Jun 1967); Cyrus Rowlett Smith (6 Mar 1968)
Labor	W. (William) Willard Wirtz
Health, Education, and Welfare	Anthony Joseph Celebrezze; John William Gardner (18 Aug 1965); Wilbur Joseph Cohen (9 May 1968)
Housing and Urban Development	Robert Clifton Weaver (18 Jan 1966); Robert Coldwell Wood (7 Jan 1969)
Transportation	Alan Stephenson Boyd (16 Jan 1967)

Richard Nixon

20 JAN 1969–20 JAN 1973 (TERM 1)

State	William Pierce Rogers
Treasury	David Matthew Kennedy; John Bowden Connally, Jr. (11 Feb 1971); George Pratt Shultz (12 Jun 1972)
Defense	Melvin Robert Laird
Attorney General	John Newton Mitchell; Richard Gordon Kleindienst (12 Jun 1972)
Interior	Walter Joseph Hickel; Rogers Clark Ballard Morton (29 Jan 1971)
Agriculture	Clifford Morris Hardin; Earl Lauer Butz (2 Dec 1971)
Commerce	Maurice Hubert Stans; Peter George Peterson (21 Feb 1972)
Labor	George Pratt Shultz; James Day Hodgson (2 Jul 1970)
Health, Education, and Welfare	Robert Hutchinson Finch; Elliot Lee Richardson (24 Jun 1970)
Housing and Urban Development	George Wilcken Romney
Transportation	John Anthony Volpe

20 JAN 1973–9 AUG 1974 (TERM 2)

State	William Pierce Rogers; Henry Alfred Kissinger (22 Sep 1973)
Treasury	George Pratt Shultz; William Edward Simon (8 May 1974)

US Presidential Cabinets (continued)

Richard Nixon (continued)

20 JAN 1973–9 AUG 1974 (TERM 2) (CONTINUED)

Defense	Elliot Lee Richardson; James Rodney Schlesinger (2 Jul 1973)
Attorney General	Richard Gordon Kleindienst; Elliot Lee Richardson (25 May 1973); William Bart Saxbe (4 Jan 1974)
Interior	Rogers Clark Ballard Morton
Agriculture	Earl Lauer Butz
Commerce	Frederick Baily Dent
Labor	Peter Joseph Brennan
Health, Education, and Welfare	Caspar Willard Weinberger
Housing and Urban Development	James Thomas Lynn
Transportation	Claude Stout Brinegar

Gerald Ford

9 AUG 1974–20 JAN 1977

State	Henry Alfred Kissinger
Treasury	William Edward Simon
Defense	James Rodney Schlesinger; Donald Henry Rumsfeld (20 Nov 1975)
Attorney General	William Bart Saxbe; Edward Hirsch Levi (7 Feb 1975)
Interior	Rogers Clark Ballard Morton; Stanley Knapp Hathaway (13 Jun 1975); Thomas Savig Kleppe (17 Oct 1975)
Agriculture	Earl Lauer Butz; John Albert Knebel (4 Nov 1976)
Commerce	Frederick Baily Dent; Rogers Clark Ballard Morton, Jr. (1 May 1975); Elliot Lee Richardson (2 Feb 1976)
Labor	Peter Joseph Brennan; John Thomas Dunlop (18 Mar 1975); Willie Julian Usery, Jr. (10 Feb 1976)
Health, Education, and Welfare	Caspar Willard Weinberger; Forrest David Matthews (8 Aug 1975)
Housing and Urban Development	James Thomas Lynn; Carla Anderson Hills (10 Mar 1975)
Transportation	Claude Stout Brinegar; William Thaddeus Coleman, Jr. (7 Mar 1975)

Jimmy Carter

20 JAN 1977–20 JAN 1981

State	Cyrus Vance; Edmund Sixtus Muskie (8 May 1980)
Treasury	Werner Michael Blumenthal; George William Miller (6 Aug 1979)
Defense	Harold Brown
Attorney General	Griffin Boyette Bell; Benjamin Richard Civiletti (16 Aug 1979)
Interior	Cecil Dale Andrus
Agriculture	Robert Selmer Bergland
Commerce	Juanita Morris Kreps; Philip Morris Klutznick (9 Jan 1980)
Labor	Fred Ray Marshall
Health, Education, and Welfare	Joseph Anthony Califano, Jr.; Patricia Roberts Harris (3 Aug 1979)
Health and Human Services	Patricia Roberts Harris (27 Sep 1979)
Housing and Urban Development	Patricia Roberts Harris; Moon Landrieu (24 Sep 1979)
Transportation	Brockman Adams; Neil Edward Goldschmidt (24 Sep 1979)
Energy	James Rodney Schlesinger (1 Oct 1977); Charles William Duncan, Jr. (24 Aug 1979)
Education	Shirley Mount Hufstedler (6 Dec 1979)

Ronald Reagan

20 JAN 1981–20 JAN 1985 (TERM 1)

State	Alexander Meigs Haig, Jr.; George Pratt Shultz (16 Jul 1982)
Treasury	Donald Thomas Regan
Defense	Caspar Willard Weinberger
Attorney General	William French Smith
Interior	James Gaius Watt; William Patrick Clark (21 Nov 1983)
Agriculture	John Rusling Block
Commerce	Malcolm Baldrige
Labor	Raymond Joseph Donovan
Health and Human Services	Richard Schultz Schweiker; Margaret Mary O'Shaughnessy Heckler (9 Mar 1983)
Housing and Urban Development	Samuel Riley Pierce, Jr.
Transportation	Drew (Andrew) Lindsay Lewis, Jr.; Elizabeth Hanford Dole (7 Feb 1983)
Energy	James Burrows Edwards; Donald Paul Hodel (8 Dec 1982)
Education	Terrel Howard Bell

20 JAN 1985–20 JAN 1989 (TERM 2)

State	George Pratt Shultz
Treasury	Donald Thomas Regan; James Addison Baker III (25 Feb 1985); Nicholas Frederick Brady (18 Aug 1988)

US Presidential Cabinets (continued)

Ronald Reagan (continued)

20 JAN 1985–20 JAN 1989 (TERM 2) (CONTINUED)

Defense	Caspar Willard Weinberger; Frank Charles Carlucci III (21 Nov 1987)
Attorney General	William French Smith; Edwin Meese III (25 Feb 1985); Richard Lewis (Dick) Thornburgh (11 Aug 1988)
Interior	Donald Paul Hodel
Agriculture	John Rusling Block; Richard Edmund Lyng (7 Mar 1986)
Commerce	Malcolm Baldrige; Calvin William Verity, Jr. (19 Oct 1987)
Labor	Raymond James Donovan; William Emerson (Bill) Brock III (29 Apr 1985); Ann Dore McLaughlin (17 Dec 1987)
Health and Human Services	Margaret Mary O'Shaughnessy Heckler; Otis Ray Bowen (13 Dec 1985)
Housing and Urban Development	Samuel Riley Pierce, Jr.
Transportation	Elizabeth Hanford Dole; James Horace Burnley IV (3 Dec 1987)
Energy	John Stewart Herrington
Education	Terrel Howard Bell; William John Bennett (7 Feb 1985); Lauro Fred Cavazos, Jr. (20 Sep 1988)

George H.W. Bush

20 JAN 1989–20 JAN 1993

State	James Addison Baker III
Treasury	Nicholas Frederick Brady
Attorney General	Richard Lewis (Dick) Thornburgh; William P. Barr (20 Nov 1991)
Interior	Manuel Lujan, Jr.
Agriculture	Clayton Keith Yeutter; Edward Madigan (7 Mar 1991)
Commerce	Robert Adam Mosbacher
Labor	Elizabeth Hanford Dole
Defense	Richard (Dick) Cheney
Health and Human Services	Louis Wade Sullivan
Housing and Urban Development	Jack F. Kemp
Transportation	Samuel K. Skinner; Andrew H. Card (22 Jan 1992)
Energy	James David Watkins
Education	Lauro Fred Cavazos, Jr.; Lamar Alexander (14 Mar 1991)
Veterans Affairs	Edward Joseph Derwinski (15 Mar 1989)

William J. Clinton

20 JAN 1993–20 JAN 1997 (TERM 1)

State	Warren M. Christopher
Treasury	Lloyd Bentsen, Jr.; Robert E. Rubin (10 Jan 1995)
Attorney General	Janet Reno
Interior	Bruce Babbitt
Agriculture	Mike Espy; Dan Glickman (30 Mar 1995)
Commerce	Ronald H. Brown; Mickey Kantor (12 Apr 1996)
Labor	Robert B. Reich
Defense	Les Aspin; William J. Perry (3 Feb 1994)
Health and Human Services	Donna E. Shalala
Housing and Urban Development	Henry G. Cisneros
Transportation	Federico Peña
Energy	Hazel R. O'Leary
Education	Richard W. Riley
Veterans Affairs	Jesse Brown

20 JAN 1997–20 JAN 2001 (TERM 2)

State	Madeleine Albright
Treasury	Robert E. Rubin; Lawrence H. Summers (2 Jul 1999)
Attorney General	Janet Reno
Interior	Bruce Babbitt
Agriculture	Dan Glickman
Commerce	William M. Daley; Norman Mineta (21 Jul 2000)
Labor	Alexis M. Herman
Defense	William Cohen
Health and Human Services	Donna E. Shalala
Housing and Urban Development	Andrew M. Cuomo
Transportation	Rodney Slater
Energy	Federico Peña; Bill Richardson (18 Aug 1998)
Education	Richard W. Riley
Veterans Affairs	Togo D. West, Jr.; Hershel W. Gober (25 Jul 2000)

US Presidential Cabinets (continued)

George W. Bush

20 JAN 2001–20 JAN 2005 (TERM 1)

State	Colin Powell
Treasury	Paul O'Neill; John Snow (7 Feb 2003)
Attorney General	John Ashcroft
Interior	Gale Norton
Agriculture	Ann M. Veneman
Commerce	Don Evans
Labor	Elaine Chao
Defense	Donald Rumsfeld
Health and Human Services	Tommy Thompson
Housing and Urban Development	Mel Martinez; Alphonso Jackson (31 Mar 2004)
Transportation	Norman Mineta
Energy	Spencer Abraham
Education	Rod Paige
Veterans Affairs	Anthony Principi
Homeland Security	Tom Ridge (8 Oct 2001)

20 JAN 2005– (TERM 2)

		WEB SITE
State	Condoleezza Rice	<www.state.gov>
Treasury	John Snow; Henry M. Paulson, Jr. (19 Jun 2006)	<www.ustreas.gov>
Attorney General	Alberto Gonzales	<www.usdoj.gov>
Interior	Gale Norton; Dirk Kempthorne (26 May 2006)	<www.doi.gov>
Agriculture	Mike Johanns	<www.usda.gov>
Commerce	Carlos Gutierrez	<www.commerce.gov>
Labor	Elaine Chao	<www.dol.gov>
Defense	Donald Rumsfeld; Robert M. Gates (18 Dec 2006)	<www.defenselink.mil>
Health and Human Services	Michael O. Leavitt	<www.hhs.gov>
Housing and Urban Development	Alphonso Jackson	<www.hud.gov>
Transportation	Norman Mineta; Mary E. Peters (30 Sep 2006)	<www.dot.gov>
Energy	Samuel W. Bodman	<www.energy.gov>
Education	Margaret Spellings	<www.ed.gov>
Veterans Affairs	Jim Nicholson	<www.va.gov>
Homeland Security	Michael Chertoff	<www.dhs.gov>

Additionally, the White House lists the following as cabinet-rank members: Vice President Richard (Dick) B. Cheney, Chief of Staff Joshua B. Bolten, Environmental Protection Agency Administrator Stephen Johnson, US Trade Representative Susan Schwab, Office of Management and Budget Director Rob Portman, and Office of National Drug Control Policy Director John Walters.

 **Did you know?** The Great Red Spot, the most conspicuous feature on the planet Jupiter, is an enormous storm system that has been raging for more than 300 years. It is about 26,000 km (16,200 mi) long and 14,000 km (8,700 mi) wide—large enough to engulf two Earth-sized planets side by side.

Impeachment

The American federal impeachment process is rooted in Article II, Section 4, of the US Constitution. Impeachment has rarely been employed, largely because it is such a cumbersome process. It can occupy Congress for a lengthy period of time, fill thousands of pages of testimony, and involve conflicting and troublesome political pressures. Repeated attempts in the US Congress to amend the procedure, however, have been unsuccessful, partly because impeachment is regarded as an integral part of the system of checks and balances in the US government.

Andrew Johnson was the first US president ever impeached. In 1868 he was charged with attempting to remove, contrary to statute, the secretary of war, Edwin M. Stanton, with inducing a general of the army to violate an act of Congress, and with contempt of Congress. Johnson was acquitted by a margin of a single vote. In 1974 the Judiciary Committee of the House of Representatives voted three articles of impeachment against Pres. Richard M. Nixon, but he resigned before impeachment proceedings in the full House could begin. In December 1998 the House of Representatives voted to impeach Pres. William J. Clinton, charging him with perjury and obstruction of justice in investigations of his relationship with a White House intern, Monica Lewinsky. In the trial, the Senate voted not guilty on the perjury charge (55–45) and not guilty on the obstruction of justice charge (50–50); since 67 guilty votes are needed for a conviction, President Clinton was acquitted.

Every US state except Oregon provides for the removal of executive and judicial officers by impeachment. Exact procedures vary somewhat from state to state, but they are all similar to federal impeachment.

Supreme Court

Justices of the Supreme Court of the United States

Listed under presidents who made appointments (bold). Chief justices' names appear in italics.

NAME	TERM OF SERVICE[1]
George Washington	
John Jay	1789–95
James Wilson	1789–98
John Rutledge	1790–91
William Cushing	1790–1810
John Blair	1790–96
James Iredell	1790–99
Thomas Johnson	1792–93
William Paterson	1793–1806
John Rutledge[2]	1795
Samuel Chase	1796–1811
Oliver Ellsworth	1796–1800
John Adams	
Bushrod Washington	1799–1829
Alfred Moore	1800–04
John Marshall	1801–35
Thomas Jefferson	
William Johnson	1804–34
Brockholst Livingston	1807–23
Thomas Todd	1807–26
James Madison	
Gabriel Duvall	1811–35
Joseph Story	1812–45
James Monroe	
Smith Thompson	1823–43
John Quincy Adams	
Robert Trimble	1826–28
Andrew Jackson	
John McLean	1830–61
Henry Baldwin	1830–44
James M. Wayne	1835–67
Roger Brooke Taney	1836–64
Philip P. Barbour	1836–41
Martin Van Buren	
John Catron	1837–65
John McKinley	1838–52
Peter V. Daniel	1842–60
John Tyler	
Samuel Nelson	1845–72
James Polk	
Levi Woodbury	1845–51
Robert C. Grier	1846–70
Millard Fillmore	
Benjamin R. Curtis	1851–57
Franklin Pierce	
John Archibald Campbell	1853–61
James Buchanan	
Nathan Clifford	1858–81
Abraham Lincoln	
Noah H. Swayne	1862–81
Samuel Freeman Miller	1862–90
David Davis	1862–77
Stephen Johnson Field	1863–97
Salmon P. Chase	1864–73

NAME	TERM OF SERVICE[1]
Ulysses S. Grant	
William Strong	1870–80
Joseph P. Bradley	1870–92
Ward Hunt	1873–82
Morrison Remick Waite	1874–88
Rutherford B. Hayes	
John Marshall Harlan	1877–1911
William B. Woods	1881–87
James Garfield	
Stanley Matthews	1881–89
Chester A. Arthur	
Horace Gray	1882–1902
Samuel Blatchford	1882–93
Grover Cleveland	
Lucius Q.C. Lamar	1888–93
Melville Weston Fuller	1888–1910
Benjamin Harrison	
David J. Brewer	1890–1910
Henry B. Brown	1891–1906
George Shiras, Jr.	1892–1903
Howell E. Jackson	1893–95
Grover Cleveland	
Edward Douglass White	1894–1910
Rufus Wheeler Peckham	1896–1909
William McKinley	
Joseph McKenna	1898–1925
Theodore Roosevelt	
Oliver Wendell Holmes	1902–32
William R. Day	1903–22
William H. Moody	1906–10
William H. Taft	
Horace H. Lurton	1910–14
Charles Evans Hughes	1910–16
Willis Van Devanter	1911–37
Joseph R. Lamar	1911–16
Edward Douglass White	1910–21
Mahlon Pitney	1912–22
Woodrow Wilson	
James C. McReynolds	1914–41
Louis Brandeis	1916–39
John H. Clarke	1916–22
Warren G. Harding	
William Howard Taft	1921–30
George Sutherland	1922–38
Pierce Butler	1923–39
Edward T. Sanford	1923–30
Calvin Coolidge	
Harlan Fiske Stone	1925–41
Herbert Hoover	
Charles Evans Hughes	1930–41
Owen Roberts	1930–45
Benjamin N. Cardozo	1932–38

NAME	TERM OF SERVICE[1]
Franklin D. Roosevelt	
Hugo L. Black	1937–71
Stanley F. Reed	1938–57
Felix Frankfurter	1939–62
William O. Douglas	1939–75
Frank Murphy	1940–49
Harlan Fiske Stone	1941–46
James F. Byrnes	1941–42
Robert H. Jackson	1941–54
Wiley B. Rutledge	1943–49
Harry S. Truman	
Harold H. Burton	1945–58
Fred M. Vinson	1946–53
Tom C. Clark	1949–67
Sherman Minton	1949–56
Dwight D. Eisenhower	
Earl Warren	1953–69
John Marshall Harlan	1955–71
William J. Brennan, Jr.	1956–90
Charles E. Whittaker	1957–62
Potter Stewart	1958–81
John F. Kennedy	
Byron R. White	1962–93
Arthur J. Goldberg	1962–65
Lyndon B. Johnson	
Abe Fortas	1965–69
Thurgood Marshall	1967–91
Richard M. Nixon	
Warren E. Burger	1969–86
Harry A. Blackmun	1970–94
Lewis F. Powell, Jr.	1972–87
William H. Rehnquist	1972–86
Gerald Ford	
John Paul Stevens	1975–
Ronald Reagan	
Sandra Day O'Connor	1981–2006
William H. Rehnquist	1986–2005
Antonin Scalia	1986–
Anthony M. Kennedy	1988–
George H.W. Bush	
David H. Souter	1990–
Clarence Thomas	1991–
Bill Clinton	
Ruth Bader Ginsburg	1993–
Stephen G. Breyer	1994–
George W. Bush	
John G. Roberts	2005–
Samuel Anthony Alito, Jr.	2006–

[1]The year the justice took the judicial oath is here used as the beginning date of service, for until that oath is taken the justice is not vested with the prerogatives of the office. Justices, however, receive their commissions ("letters patent") before taking their oaths—in some instances, in the preceding year.   [2]John Rutledge was acting chief justice; the US Senate refused to confirm him.

Milestones of US Supreme Court Jurisprudence

Information includes cases' short names, citation, year of release, and a short description of the Supreme Court's findings and importance for US law.

Marbury v. Madison, 5 U.S. 137 (1803): the first instance in which the high court declared an act of Congress (the Judiciary Act of 1789, which in part authorized the court to compel action by the executive branch) to be unconstitutional, thus establishing the doctrine of judicial review.

Martin v. Hunter's Lessee, 14 U.S. 304 (1816): asserted the US Supreme Court's power of appellate review of state Supreme Court decisions.

McCulloch v. Maryland, 17 U.S. 316 (1819): affirmed the constitutional doctrine of the "implied powers" of Congress, determining that Congress had not only the powers expressly conferred upon it by the Constitution but also all authority "appropriate" to carry out such powers.

Dred Scott v. Sandford, 60 U.S. 393 (1857): ruled that blacks, free or enslaved, were not citizens under the Constitution, and further determined that only states, and not Congress or territorial governments, had the power to prohibit slavery, thus overturning the Missouri Compromise of 1820 and legalizing slavery in all US territories. The citizenship of all races was affirmed with the ratification of the Fourteenth Amendment in 1868.

Santa Clara County v. Southern Pacific Railroad Co., 118 U.S. 394 (1886): established that corporations are "persons" within the meaning of the Fourteenth Amendment, extending to them the rights of due process and equal protection.

Plessy v. Ferguson, 163 U.S. 537 (1896): permitted racial segregation in "separate but equal" public facilities.

Lochner v. New York, 198 U.S. 45 (1905): found that a state labor law limiting the number of hours in the work week violated due process because the "right of contract between the employer and employees" is protected under the Fourteenth Amendment.

Standard Oil Co. of New Jersey et al. v. United States, 221 U.S. 1 (1911): ruled that the activities of the Standard Oil Company of New Jersey, a holding company that through its subsidiaries controlled most of the US petroleum industry, constituted an undue restraint of trade and ordered the company's dissolution under the Sherman Antitrust Act.

Schenck v. United States, 249 U.S. 47 (1919): found, in the case of an American socialist convicted of espionage for distributing antidraft leaflets during wartime, that First Amendment freedom of expression is limited when there exists a "clear and present danger that [the speech] will bring about the substantive evils that Congress has a right to prevent."

Brown v. Board of Education of Topeka, 349 U.S. 294 (1954): ruled that racial segregation in public schools violated the Fourteenth Amendment, overturning the doctrine of "separate but equal" facilities reached in Plessy v. Ferguson.

Mapp v. Ohio, 367 U.S. 643 (1961): found that the Fourth Amendment prohibition of unreasonable search and seizure, and the inadmissibility of evidence obtained in violation of it, applied to state as well as to federal government.

Baker v. Carr, 369 U.S. 186 (1962): ruled that, under the equal protection clause of the Fourteenth Amendment, issues relating to the apportionment of congressional districts could be resolved in federal courts.

Gideon v. Wainwright, 372 U.S. 335 (1963): declared that the Sixth Amendment right to counsel applies to defendants in state as well as federal courts.

New York Times Co. v. Sullivan, 376 U.S. 254 (1964): protected the press from the prospects of large damage awards in libel cases by requiring that "actual malice" be demonstrated; public officials who sue for damages must prove that a falsehood had been issued with knowledge that it was false or in reckless disregard of whether it was false or not.

Heart of Atlanta Motel v. United States, 379 U.S. 241; Katzenbach v. McClung, 379 U.S. 294 (1964): upheld Title II of the Civil Rights Act of 1964 (which prohibits segregation or discrimination in places of public accommodation involved in interstate commerce) in the cases of an Atlanta motel and a Birmingham AL restaurant, both of which discriminated against blacks. The court ruled that both engaged in transactions affecting interstate commerce, and thus were within the purview of congressional regulation, and that the Civil Rights Act itself was constitutional.

Griswold v. Connecticut, 381 U.S. 479 (1965): ruled that a state law prohibiting the use of contraceptives (including providing information, advice, or prescriptions for them) violated "the right of marital privacy" implied within the Bill of Rights.

Miranda v. Arizona, 384 U.S. 436 (1966): ruled that the prosecution may not use statements made by a person in police custody unless minimum procedural safeguards were followed and established guidelines to guarantee arrested persons' Fifth Amendment right not to be compelled to incriminate themselves. These guidelines included informing arrestees prior to questioning that they have the right to remain silent, that anything they say may be used against them as evidence, and that they have the right to the counsel of an attorney.

Loving v. Virginia, 388 U.S. 1 (1967): declared that antimiscegenation laws (prohibitions of interracial marriage) have no legitimate purpose outside of racial discrimination and thus violate the Fourteenth Amendment.

New York Times Co. v. United States, 403 U.S. 713 (1971): in what was known as the "Pentagon Papers" case, the court vacated a US Justice Department injunction that restrained the New York Times and Washington Post from publishing excerpts of a top-secret report on the Vietnam War, ruling that such prior restraint of the press was subject to a "heavy burden of . . . justification," which the government failed to meet.

Wisconsin v. Yoder, 406 U.S. 205 (1972): in the case of members of an Old Order Amish community who refused on religious grounds to keep their children in school past the eighth grade, found that the right to free exercise of religion outweighed the state's interest in universal education.

Roe v. Wade, 410 U.S. 113 (1973): held that overly restrictive state regulation of abortion is unconstitutional. In balancing the "compelling state interest[s]" in protecting the health of pregnant women and the potential life of fetuses, the court ruled that regulation of abortion could begin no sooner than about the end of the first trimester, with increasing regulation permissible in the second and third trimesters;

the state's interest in protecting the fetus was found to increase with the fetus's "capability for meaningful life outside the mother's womb."

Gregg v. *Georgia*, 428 U.S. 153; *Proffitt* v. *Florida*, 428 U.S. 242; *Jurek* v. *Texas*, 428 U.S. 262 (1976): ruled that the death penalty, in and of itself, does not violate the Eighth Amendment if applied under certain guidelines in first-degree murder cases.

Cruzan by Cruzan v. *Director, Missouri Department of Health*, 497 U.S. 261 (1990): found that, in the absence of "clear and convincing evidence" of a person's desire to refuse medical treatment or not to live on life support, a state could require that such treatment continue. When such evidence exists, however, a patient's wishes must be respected.

Rust v. *Sullivan*, 500 U.S. 173 (1991): ruled that Congress could prohibit recipients of family-planning funds from providing or discussing abortion as a family planning option. The court held that this did not violate the First Amendment because clinics were still free to provide such counseling as a "financially and physically" separate activity.

Planned Parenthood of Southeastern Pennsylvania v. *Casey*, 505 U.S. 833 (1992): softened the ruling in *Roe* v. *Wade* by finding that some state regulation of abortion prior to fetal viability, including a 24-hour waiting period, mandatory counseling, and a parental-consent requirement for minors, is permissible as long as the regulations do not place an "undue burden" on the woman.

Romer v. *Evans*, 517 U.S. 620 (1996): invalidated a Colorado referendum passed by popular vote that prohibited conferral of protected status on the basis of sexual orientation; the court ruled that the referendum was overbroad, bore little relationship to legimate state interests, and violated the Fourteenth Amendment of the US Constitution.

Oncale v. *Sundowner Offshore Services, Inc., et al.*, 523 U.S. 75 (1998): found that Title VII's prohibition of workplace sexual discrimination applied equally in cases when the harasser and victim are of the same sex.

Boy Scouts of America v. *Dale*, 530 U.S. 640 (2000): ruled that the Boy Scouts, because it is a private organization, was within its rights when it dismissed a scoutmaster expressly because of his avowed homosexuality. The court reasoned that a state statute banning discrimination on the basis of sexual orientation in places of public accommodation was outweighed by the Scouts' First Amendment right to freedom of association.

Stenberg v. *Carhart*, 530 U.S. 914 (2000): ruled that a state law criminalizing the performance of dilation and extraction—or "partial-birth"—abortions violated the Constitution (following the same reasoning as in *Roe* v. *Wade*) because it allowed no consideration of the health of the woman in choosing the procedure.

Bush v. *Gore*, 531 U.S. 98 (2000): stopped the manual recounts, then under way in certain Florida counties at the demand of Al Gore, of disputed ballots from the November 2000 presidential election on the grounds that inconsistent vote-counting standards among the several counties involved amounted to a violation of the Fourteenth Amendment's equal protection clause. Because George W. Bush at the time led Al Gore in the number of officially recognized Florida votes, the decision meant that he would win the state and thus the general election, despite having lost the popular vote.

Atkins v. *Virginia*, 536 U.S. 304 (2002): ruled that the death penalty, when applied to mentally retarded individuals, constitutes a "cruel and unusual punishment" prohibited by the Eighth Amendment.

Eldred v. *Ashcroft*, 537 U.S. 186 (2003): upheld a 1998 federal statute that granted a 20-year extension to all existing copyrights.

Lockyer v. *Andrade*, 538 U.S. 63; *Ewing* v. *California*, 538 U.S. 11 (2003): upheld a "three-strikes" law that imposes long prison sentences for a third offense, even nonviolent crimes.

State Farm Mutual Auto Insurance Co. v. *Campbell*, 538 U.S. 408 (2003): placed limits on "irrational and arbitrary" punitive damages and established new guidelines that generally bar consideration of a defendant's wealth or conduct outside the state's borders and lower the ratio of punitive to compensatory damages.

Brown v. *Legal Foundation of Washington*, 538 U.S. 216 (2003): held that channeling interest on short-term deposits by lawyers on accounts held in trust for their clients to legal assistance programs for the poor is not an unconstitutional taking of property.

Nevada Department of Human Resources v. *Hibbs*, 538 U.S. 721 (2003): held that state governments may be sued by their employees for failing to honor the federally guaranteed right to take time off from work for family emergencies.

United States v. *American Library Association*, 539 U.S. 194 (2003): upheld the Children's Internet Protection Act, which conditions access to federal grants and subsidies upon the installation of antipornography filters on all Internet-connected computers.

Grutter v. *Bollinger*, 539 U.S. 306 (2003); *Gratz* v. *Bollinger*, 539 U.S. 244 (2003): in a pair of decisions addressing affirmative action in admissions at the University of Michigan, the court endorsed *Regents of the University of California* v. *Bakke*'s articulation of diversity as a compelling interest, so long as the admissions program's operation is "holistic" and "individualized," and upheld Michigan's law school admissions program. In *Gratz*, the court struck down Michigan's undergraduate admissions program because reserving spaces for underrepresented minorities was the "functional equivalent of a quota."

Georgia v. *Ashcroft*, 539 U.S. 461 (2003): ruled that race-sensitive redistricting could consider more general minority influence in the political process when drawing particular district lines rather than addressing only the actual number of minority voters present.

Lawrence v. *Texas*, 539 U.S. 558 (2003): explicitly overruling *Bowers* v. *Hardwick*, 478 U.S. 186 (1986), the court declared that gay men and lesbians are "entitled to respect for their private lives" under the due process clause of the Fourteenth Amendment and rendered unconstitutional state statutes outlawing sex between adults of the same gender.

Elk Grove Unified School District v. *Newdow*, 542 U.S. 1 (2004): sidestepping the question of whether the inclusion of the phrase "under God" was an unconstitutional endorsement by a public school of a religious viewpoint, the court ruled that Michael Newdow, who filed suit on behalf of his daughter, lacked standing to file on her behalf because he was not the custodial parent.

Blakely v. *Washington*, 542 U.S. 296 (2004): held that the Washington state system permitting judges to make independent findings that increase a convicted defendant's sentence beyond the ordinary range for the crime violated the Sixth Amendment guarantee of a right to trial by jury and to a higher standard of proof.

Cheney v. *US District Court*, 542 U.S. 367 (2004): sent the Sierra Club and Judicial Watch back to the lower court in a dispute over the level of executive privilege the vice president's energy policy task force exercises in the face of discovery orders. The court held that "[s]pecial considerations control when the Executive's interests in maintaining its autonomy and safeguarding its communications' confidentiality are implicated."

Hamdi v. *Rumsfeld*, 542 U.S. 507; *Rasul* v. *Bush*, 542 U.S. 466 (2004): ruled that while the Congress may empower the executive branch to detain even US citizens as enemy combatants, any enemy combatant in US custody may challenge detention as illegal in federal court with the assistance of counsel. The court declared that "a state of war is not a blank check for the president when it comes to the rights of the nation's citizens."

United States v. *Booker* and *United States* v. *Fanfan*, 543 U.S. 220 (2005): ruled that mandatory federal sentencing guidelines violated defendants' Sixth Amendment right to jury trials because the guidelines require judges to make decisions of fact affecting prison time.

Roper v. *Simmons*, 543 U.S. 551 (2005): held that the execution of a felon who had committed a capital crime while a juvenile violates the Eighth Amendment prohibition of cruel and unusual punishment, that "the State cannot extinguish [the juvenile defendant's] life and his potential to attain a mature understanding of his own humanity."

Gonzales v. *Raich*, 545 U.S. 1 (2005): ruled that doctors may not prescribe marijuana to ease the symptoms patients and sufferers of other serious illnesses experience. The Court held that the federal Controlled Substances Act, which bars medical use of marijuana, overrides state legislation allowing such use.

Kelo v. *City of New London*, 545 U.S. 469 (2005): found that governmental entities may exercise the power of eminent domain over private property and cede the property to private developers to promote economic growth, so long as a carefully formulated plan to provide significant benefits to the community provides a rational basis for the taking.

Gonzales v. *Oregon*, 546 U.S. 243 (2006): ruled that an Oregon law permitting physicians to provide lethal drugs to terminally ill patients did not violate the Controlled Substances Act.

Hamdan v. *Rumsfeld*, 548 U.S. ___ (2006): ruled that the government's special military commissions were not lawful courts. The commissions were to have tried some of the prisoners who had been captured in the "global war on terror."

Gonzales v. *Carhart*, 550 U.S. ___ (2007): held that a federal law banning "partial-birth" abortion was not unconstitutional.

Parents Involved in Community Schools v. *Seattle School District No. 1*, 551 U.S. ___ (2007): held that using a student's race in determining the availability of a spot at a desired school, even for the purpose of preventing resegregation, violated the 14th Amendment.

Hein v. *Freedom from Religion Foundation*, 551 U.S. ___ (2007): ruled that taxpayers had no standing to challenge the use of federal money to support the Office of Faith-Based and Community Initiatives, despite questions about the separation of church and state.

Federal Election Commission v. *Wisconsin Right to Life*, 551 U.S. ___ (2007): held that a restriction on union- and corporate-sponsored advertising from a 2002 campaign-finance law threatened free speech.

United States Congress

The Senate, 110th Congress

According to Article I, Section 3, of the US Constitution, a US senator must be at least 30 years old, must reside in the state he or she represents at the time of the election, and must have been a citizen of the United States for 9 years. Voters elect two senators from each state; terms are for 6 years and begin on 3 January. Senators originally made $6.00 per day; each current senator's salary is $165,200 per year. The majority and minority leaders and the president pro tempore receive $183,500 per year.

US Senate Web site: <www.senate.gov>.

Senate leadership

president:	Richard Cheney
president pro tempore:	Robert C. Byrd
majority leader:	Harry Reid
minority leader:	Mitch McConnell
asst. majority leader (majority whip):	Dick Durbin
asst. minority leader (minority whip):	Trent Lott

STATE	NAME AND PARTY	SERVICE BEGAN	TERM ENDS
Alabama	Richard Shelby (R)	1987	2011
	Jeff Sessions (R)	1997	2009
Alaska	Ted Stevens (R)	1968[1]	2009
	Lisa Murkowski (R)	2002	2011
Arizona	John McCain (R)	1987	2011
	Jon Kyl (R)	1995	2013
Arkansas	Blanche Lincoln (D)	1999	2011
	Mark Pryor (D)	2003	2009
California	Dianne Feinstein (D)	1992[2]	2013
	Barbara Boxer (D)	1993	2011
Colorado	Wayne Allard (R)	1997	2009
	Ken Salazar (D)	2005	2011

The Senate, 110th Congress (continued)

STATE	NAME AND PARTY	SERVICE BEGAN	TERM ENDS
Connecticut	Chris Dodd (D)	1981	2011
	Joe Lieberman (ID)	1989	2013
Delaware	Joseph R. Biden, Jr. (D)	1973	2009
	Tom Carper (D)	2001	2013
Florida	Bill Nelson (D)	2001	2013
	Mel Martinez (R)	2005	2011
Georgia	Saxby Chambliss (R)	2003	2009
	Johnny Isakson (R)	2005	2011
Hawaii	Daniel K. Inouye (D)	1963	2011
	Daniel Kahikina Akaka (D)	1990[3]	2013
Idaho	Larry Craig (R)	1991	2009
	Mike Crapo (R)	1999	2011
Illinois	Dick Durbin (D)	1997	2009
	Barack Obama (D)	2005	2011
Indiana	Richard G. Lugar (R)	1977	2013
	Evan Bayh (D)	1999	2011
Iowa	Chuck Grassley (R)	1981	2011
	Tom Harkin (D)	1985	2009
Kansas	Sam Brownback (R)	1996[4]	2011
	Pat Roberts (R)	1997	2009
Kentucky	Mitch McConnell (R)	1985	2009
	Jim Bunning (R)	1999	2011
Louisiana	Mary L. Landrieu (D)	1997	2009
	David Vitter (R)	2005	2011
Maine	Olympia J. Snowe (R)	1995	2013
	Susan Collins (R)	1997	2009
Maryland	Benjamin L. Cardin (D)	2007	2013
	Barbara Mikulski (D)	1987	2011
Massachusetts	Edward M. Kennedy (D)	1962	2013
	John Kerry (D)	1985	2009
Michigan	Carl Levin (D)	1979	2009
	Debbie Stabenow (D)	2001	2013
Minnesota	Amy Klobuchar (D)	2007	2013
	Norm Coleman (R)	2003	2009
Mississippi	Thad Cochran (R)	1979	2009
	Trent Lott (R)	1989	2013
Missouri	Kit Bond (R)	1987	2011
	Claire McCaskill (D)	2007	2013
Montana	Max Baucus (D)	1979	2009
	Jon Tester (D)	2007	2013
Nebraska	Chuck Hagel (R)	1997	2009
	Ben Nelson (D)	2001	2013
Nevada	Harry Reid (D)	1987	2011
	John Ensign (R)	2001	2013
New Hampshire	Judd Gregg (R)	1993	2011
	John E. Sununu (R)	2003	2009
New Jersey	Robert Menendez (D)	2006[5]	2013
	Frank R. Lautenberg (D)	2003	2009
New Mexico	Pete V. Domenici (R)	1973	2009
	Jeff Bingaman (D)	1983	2013
New York	Charles E. Schumer (D)	1999	2011
	Hillary Rodham Clinton (D)	2001	2013
North Carolina	Elizabeth Dole (R)	2003	2009
	Richard Burr (R)	2005	2011
North Dakota	Kent Conrad (D)	1987	2013
	Byron L. Dorgan (D)	1993	2011
Ohio	Sherrod Brown (D)	2007	2013
	George V. Voinovich (R)	1999	2011
Oklahoma	James M. Inhofe (R)	1994[6]	2009
	Tom Coburn (R)	2005	2011
Oregon	Ron Wyden (D)	1996[7]	2011
	Gordon Smith (R)	1997	2009
Pennsylvania	Arlen Specter (R)	1981	2011
	Robert P. Casey (D)	2007	2013
Rhode Island	Jack Reed (D)	1997	2009
	Sheldon Whitehouse (D)	2007	2013
South Carolina	Lindsey Graham (R)	2003	2009
	Jim DeMint (R)	2005	2011

The Senate, 110th Congress (continued)

STATE	NAME AND PARTY	SERVICE BEGAN	TERM ENDS
South Dakota	Tim Johnson (D)	1997	2009
	John Thune (R)	2005	2011
Tennessee	Bob Corker (R)	2007	2013
	Lamar Alexander (R)	2003	2009
Texas	Kay Bailey Hutchison (R)	1993[8]	2013
	John Cornyn (R)	2002	2009
Utah	Orrin G. Hatch (R)	1977	2013
	Bob Bennett (R)	1993	2011
Vermont	Patrick Leahy (D)	1975	2011
	Bernie Sanders (I)	2007	2013
Virginia	John Warner (R)	1979	2009
	Jim Webb (D)	2007	2013
Washington	Patty Murray (D)	1993	2011
	Maria Cantwell (D)	2001	2013
West Virginia	Robert C. Byrd (D)	1959	2013
	Jay Rockefeller (D)	1985	2009
Wisconsin	Herb Kohl (D)	1989	2013
	Russ Feingold (D)	1993	2011
Wyoming	John Barrasso (R)	2007[9]	2009
	Mike Enzi (R)	1997	2009

Republicans: 49; Democrats: 49; Independents: 1; Independent Democrats: 1

[1]Ted Stevens was appointed in December 1968 to fill the vacancy caused by the death of Edward Lewis (Bob) Bartlett. [2]Dianne Feinstein was elected in November 1992 to complete the term of Pete Wilson, who resigned in 1991 to become California's governor. [3]Daniel Kahikina Akaka was appointed in April 1990 after winning a special election to fill the vacancy caused by the death of Spark M. Matsunaga. [4]Sam Brownback was elected in November 1996 to complete the term of Bob Dole, who resigned to campaign for the presidency. [5]Robert Menendez was appointed in January 2006 to fill the vacancy caused by the resignation of Jon S. Corzine. [6]James M. Inhofe was elected in November 1994 to complete the term of David Boren, who resigned to become president of the University of Oklahoma. [7]Ron Wyden was elected in January 1996 to complete the term of Bob Packwood, who resigned in 1995. [8]Kay Bailey Hutchison was elected in June 1993 to complete the term of Lloyd Bentsen, Jr., who resigned to become secretary of the treasury. [9]John Barrasso was appointed in June 2007 to fill the vacancy caused by the death of Craig Thomas.

Senate Standing Committees

COMMITTEE	CHAIRMAN (PARTY–STATE)	RANKING MINORITY MEMBER (PARTY–STATE)	NUMBER OF MEMBERS MAJORITY	NUMBER OF MEMBERS MINORITY	NUMBER OF SUBCOMMITTEES
Agriculture, Nutrition, and Forestry	Tom Harkin (D-IA)	Saxby Chambliss (R-GA)	11	10	5
Appropriations	Robert C. Byrd (D-WV)	Thad Cochran (R-MS)	15	14	12
Armed Services	Carl Levin (D-MI)	John McCain (R-AZ)	13	12	6
Banking, Housing, and Urban Affairs	Chris Dodd (D-CT)	Richard Shelby (R-AL)	11	10	5
Budget	Kent Conrad (D-ND)	Judd Gregg (R-NH)	12[1]	11	none
Commerce, Science, and Transportation	Daniel K. Inouye (D-HI)	Ted Stevens (R-AK)	12	11	7
Energy and Natural Resources	Jeff Bingaman (D-NM)	Pete V. Domenici (R-NM)	12[1]	11	4
Environment and Public Works	Barbara Boxer (D-CA)	James M. Imhofe (R-OK)	10[1]	9	6
Finance	Max Baucus (D-MT)	Chuck Grassley (R-IA)	11	10	5
Foreign Relations	Joseph R. Biden, Jr. (D-DE)	Richard G. Lugar (R-IN)	11	10	7
Health, Education, Labor, and Pensions	Edward M. Kennedy (D-MA)	Mike Enzi (R-WY)	11[1]	10	3
Homeland Security and Governmental Affairs	Joe Lieberman (ID-CT)	Susan Collins (R-ME)	9	8	3
Judiciary	Patrick Leahy (D-VT)	Arlen Specter (R-PA)	10	9	7
Rules and Administration	Dianne Feinstein (D-CA)	Bob Bennett (R-UT)	10	9	none
Small Business and Entrepreneurship	John Kerry (D-MA)	Olympia J. Snowe (R-ME)	10	9	none
Veterans Affairs	Daniel K. Akaka (D-HI)	Larry Craig (R-ID)	8[1]	7	none

[1]Bernie Sanders is an Independent but caucuses with the Democratic Party.

Senate Special, Select, and Other Committees

COMMITTEE	CHAIRMAN (PARTY–STATE)	RANKING MINORITY MEMBER (PARTY–STATE)	NUMBER OF MEMBERS MAJORITY	NUMBER OF MEMBERS MINORITY
Special Committee on Aging	Herb Kohl (D-WI)	Gordon Smith (R-OR)	11	10
Select Committee on Ethics	Barbara Boxer (D-CA)	John Cornyn (R-TX)	3	3
Committee on Indian Affairs	Byron L. Dorgan (D-ND)	Lisa Murkowski (R-AK)	8	7
Select Committee on Intelligence	Jay Rockefeller (D-WV)	Kit Bond (R-MO)	8	7

Joint Committees of Congress

The joint committees of Congress include members from both the Senate and the House of Representatives. They function as overseeing entities but do not have the power to approve appropriations or legislation. Chairmanship of the Joint Economic Committee is determined by seniority and alternates between the Senate and the House every Congress. The Joint Committee on the Library of Congress is evenly made up of members from the House Administration Committee and the Senate Rules and Administration Committee. Chairmanship and vice chairmanship of the Joint Committee on Printing alternates between the House and the Senate every Congress. The Joint Committee on Taxation is composed of five members from the Senate Committee on Finance and five members from the House Committee on Ways and Means (three majority and two minority members from each).

COMMITTEE	CHAIRMAN (PARTY-STATE)	VICE CHAIRMAN (PARTY-STATE)	NUMBER OF MEMBERS DEMOCRATS	NUMBER OF MEMBERS REPUBLICANS
Economic	Sen. Charles E. Schumer (D-NY)	Rep. Carolyn B. Maloney (D-NY)	12	8
Library	Sen. Dianne Feinstein (D-CA)	Robert A. Brady (D-PA)	5	4
Printing	Rep. Robert A. Brady (D-PA)	Sen. Dianne Feinstein (D-CA)	5	4
Taxation	Rep. Charles B. Rangel (D-NY)	Sen. Max Baucus (D-MT)	6	4

The House of Representatives, 110th Congress

Parties: Democrat (D); Republican (R); Independent (I).
Party totals: Democrats 232; Republicans 201; vacancies 2.

According to Article I, Section 2, of the US Constitution, a US representative must be at least 25 years old, must reside in the state he or she represents at the time of the election, and must have been a citizen of the United States for seven years. Each state is entitled to at least one representative, with additional seats apportioned based on population. Each congressperson originally represented 30,000 people; the range in 2005 was from 509,294 (Wyoming) to 935,670 (Montana) persons per representative. Terms are for 2 years and begin on 3 January (unless otherwise noted). The current representative's salary is $165,200 per year. The majority and minority leaders receive $183,500 per year; the speaker of the house receives $212,100 per year.

American Samoa, the District of Columbia, Guam, and the Virgin Islands elect delegates; Puerto Rico elects a resident commissioner. Their formal duties are the same, but the resident commissioner serves a four-year term. They may participate in debate and serve on committees but are not permitted to vote. US House Web site: <www.house.gov>.

Numbers preceding the names refer to districts. Certain states gained (+) or lost (−) districts by reapportionment since the 107th Congress.

House leadership

Speaker of the house:	Nancy Pelosi (D-CA)
Majority leader:	Steny H. Hoyer (D-MD)
Minority leader:	John A. Boehner (R-OH)
Majority whip:	James E. Clyburn (D-SC)
Minority whip:	Roy Blunt (R-MO)

STATE	REPRESENTATIVES	SERVICE BEGAN
Alabama	1. Jo Bonner (R)	Jan 2003
	2. Terry Everett (R)	Jan 1993
	3. Mike Rogers (R)	Jan 2003
	4. Robert B. Aderholt (R)	Jan 1997
	5. Robert E. (Bud) Cramer, Jr. (D)	Jan 1991
	6. Spencer Bachus (R)	Jan 1993
	7. Artur Davis (D)	Jan 2003
Alaska	Don Young (R)	Mar 1973
Arizona (+2)	1. Rick Renzi (R)	Jan 2003
	2. Trent Franks (R)	Jan 2003
	3. John B. Shadegg (R)	Jan 1995
	4. Ed Pastor (D)	Sep 1991
	5. Harry E. Mitchell (D)	Jan 2007
	6. Jeff Flake (R)	Jan 2001

STATE	REPRESENTATIVES	SERVICE BEGAN
Arizona (cont.)	7. Raúl M. Grijalva (D)	Jan 2003
	8. Gabrielle Giffords (D)	Jan 2007
Arkansas	1. Marion Berry (D)	Jan 1997
	2. Vic Snyder (D)	Jan 1997
	3. John Boozman (R)[1]	Nov 2001
	4. Mike Ross (D)	Jan 2001
California (+1)	1. Mike Thompson (D)	Jan 1999
	2. Wally Herger (R)	Jan 1987
	3. Daniel E. Lungren (R)	Jan 2005
	4. John T. Doolittle (R)	Jan 1991
	5. Doris O. Matsui (D)[2]	Mar 2005
	6. Lynn C. Woolsey (D)	Jan 1993
	7. George Miller (D)	Jan 1975
	8. Nancy Pelosi (D)	Jun 1987

The House of Representatives, 110th Congress (continued)

STATE	REPRESENTATIVES	SERVICE BEGAN
California (cont.)	9. Barbara Lee (D)	Apr 1998
	10. Ellen O. Tauscher (D)	Jan 1997
	11. Jerry McNerney (D)	Jan 2007
	12. Tom Lantos (D)	Jan 1981
	13. Fortney "Pete" Stark (D)	Jan 1973
	14. Anna G. Eshoo (D)	Jan 1993
	15. Michael M. Honda (D)	Jan 2001
	16. Zoe Lofgren (D)	Jan 1995
	17. Sam Farr (D)	Jun 1993
	18. Dennis A. Cardoza (D)	Jan 2003
	19. George Radanovich (R)	Jan 1995
	20. Jim Costa (D)	Jan 2005
	21. Devin Nunes (R)	Jan 2003
	22. Kevin McCarthy (R)	Jan 2007
	23. Lois Capps (D)	Mar 1998
	24. Elton Gallegly (R)	Jan 1987
	25. Howard P. "Buck" McKeon (R)	Jan 1993
	26. David Dreier (R)	Jan 1981
	27. Brad Sherman (D)	Jan 1997
	28. Howard L. Berman (D)	Jan 1983
	29. Adam B. Schiff (D)	Jan 2001
	30. Henry A. Waxman (D)	Jan 1975
	31. Xavier Becerra (D)	Jan 1993
	32. Hilda L. Solis (D)	Jan 2001
	33. Diane E. Watson (D)[3]	Jun 2001
	34. Lucille Roybal-Allard (D)	Jan 1993
	35. Maxine Waters (D)	Jan 1991
	36. Jane F. Harman (D)[4]	Jan 1993
	37. Laura Richardson (D)[5]	Sep 2007
	38. Grace F. Napolitano (D)	Jan 1999
	39. Linda T. Sánchez (D)	Jan 2003
	40. Edward R. Royce (R)	Jan 1993
	41. Jerry Lewis (R)	Jan 1979
	42. Gary G. Miller (R)	Jan 1999
	43. Joe Baca (D)	Nov 1999
	44. Ken Calvert (R)	Jan 1993
	45. Mary Bono (R)	Apr 1998
	46. Dana Rohrabacher (R)	Jan 1989
	47. Loretta Sanchez (D)	Jan 1997
	48. John Campbell (R)[6]	Dec 2005
	49. Darrell E. Issa (R)	Jan 2001
	50. Brian P. Bilbray (R)[7]	Jan 1995
	51. Bob Filner (D)	Jan 1993
	52. Duncan Hunter (R)	Jan 1981
	53. Susan A. Davis (D)	Jan 2001
Colorado (+1)	1. Diana DeGette (D)	Jan 1997
	2. Mark Udall (D)	Jan 1999
	3. John T. Salazar (D)	Jan 2005
	4. Marilyn N. Musgrave (R)	Jan 2003
	5. Doug Lamborn (R)	Jan 2007
	6. Thomas G. Tancredo (R)	Jan 1999
	7. Ed Perlmutter (D)	Jan 2007
Connecticut (−1)	1. John B. Larson (D)	Jan 1999
	2. Joe Courtney (D)	Jan 2007
	3. Rosa L. DeLauro (D)	Jan 1991
	4. Christopher Shays (R)	Aug 1987
	5. Christopher S. Murphy (D)	Jan 2007
Delaware	Michael N. Castle (R)	Jan 1993
Florida (+2)	1. Jeff Miller (R)[8]	Oct 2001
	2. Allen Boyd (D)	Jan 1997
	3. Corrine Brown (D)	Jan 1993

STATE	REPRESENTATIVES	SERVICE BEGAN
Florida (cont.)	4. Ander Crenshaw (R)	Jan 2001
	5. Ginny Brown-Waite (R)	Jan 2003
	6. Cliff Stearns (R)	Jan 1989
	7. John L. Mica (R)	Jan 1993
	8. Ric Keller (R)	Jan 2001
	9. Michael Bilirakis (R)	Jan 1983
	10. C.W. Bill Young (R)	Jan 1971
	11. Kathy Castor (D)	Jan 2007
	12. Adam H. Putnam (R)	Jan 2001
	13. Vern Buchanan (R)	Jan 2007
	14. Connie Mack (R)	Jan 2005
	15. Dave Weldon (R)	Jan 1995
	16. Tim Mahoney (D)	Jan 2007
	17. Kendrick B. Meek (D)	Jan 2003
	18. Ileana Ros-Lehtinen (R)	Aug 1989
	19. Robert Wexler (R)	Jan 1997
	20. Debbie Wasserman Schultz (D)	Jan 2005
	21. Lincoln Diaz-Balart (R)	Jan 1993
	22. Ron Klein (D)	Jan 2007
	23. Alcee L. Hastings (D)	Jan 1993
	24. Tom Feeney (R)	Jan 2003
	25. Mario Diaz-Balart (R)	Jan 2003
Georgia (+2)	1. Jack Kingston (R)	Jan 1993
	2. Sanford D. Bishop, Jr. (D)	Jan 1993
	3. Lynn A. Westmoreland (R)	Jan 2005
	4. Henry C. Johnson (D)	Jan 2007
	5. John Lewis (D)	Jan 1987
	6. Tom Price (R)	Feb 2005
	7. John Linder (R)	Jan 1993
	8. Jim Marshall (D)	Jan 2003
	9. Nathan Deal (R)	Jan 1993
	10. Paul Broun (R)[9]	Jul 2007
	11. Phil Gingrey (R)	Jan 2003
	12. John Barrow (D)	Jan 2005
	13. David Scott (D)	Jan 2003
Hawaii	1. Neil Abercrombie (D)[10]	Sep 1986
	2. Mazie K. Hirono (D)	Jan 2007
Idaho	1. Bill Sali (R)	Jan 2007
	2. Michael K. Simpson (R)	Jan 1999
Illinois (−1)	1. Bobby L. Rush (D)	Jan 1993
	2. Jesse L. Jackson, Jr. (D)	Dec 1995
	3. Daniel Lipinski (D)	Jan 2005
	4. Luis V. Gutierrez (D)	Jan 1993
	5. Rahm Emanuel (D)	Jan 2003
	6. Peter J. Roskam (R)	Jan 2007
	7. Danny K. Davis (D)	Jan 1997
	8. Melissa L. Bean (D)	Jan 2005
	9. Janice D. Schakowsky (D)	Jan 1999
	10. Mark Steven Kirk (R)	Jan 2001
	11. Jerry Weller (R)	Jan 1995
	12. Jerry F. Costello (D)	Aug 1988
	13. Judy Biggert (R)	Jan 1999
	14. J. Dennis Hastert (R)	Jan 1987
	15. Timothy V. Johnson (R)	Jan 2001
	16. Donald A. Manzullo (R)	Jan 1993
	17. Phil Hare (D)	Jan 2007
	18. Ray LaHood (R)	Jan 1995
	19. John Shimkus (R)	Jan 1997
Indiana (−1)	1. Peter J. Visclosky (D)	Jan 1985
	2. Joe Donnelly (D)	Jan 2007
	3. Mark E. Souder (R)	Jan 1995

The House of Representatives, 110th Congress (continued)

STATE	REPRESENTATIVES	SERVICE BEGAN
Indiana (cont.)	4. Steve Buyer (R)	Jan 1993
	5. Dan Burton (R)	Jan 1983
	6. Mike Pence (R)	Jan 2001
	7. Julia Carson (D)	Jan 1997
	8. Brad Ellsworth (D)	Jan 2007
	9. Baron P. Hill (D)[11]	Jan 1999
Iowa	1. Bruce L. Braley (D)	Jan 2007
	2. David Loebsack (D)	Jan 2007
	3. Leonard L. Boswell (D)	Jan 1997
	4. Tom Latham (R)	Jan 1995
	5. Steve King (R)	Jan 2003
Kansas	1. Jerry Moran (R)	Jan 1997
	2. Nancy E. Boyda (D)	Jan 2007
	3. Dennis Moore (D)	Jan 1999
	4. Todd Tiahrt (R)	Jan 1995
Kentucky	1. Ed Whitfield (R)	Jan 1995
	2. Ron Lewis (R)	May 1994
	3. John A. Yarmuth (D)	Jan 2007
	4. Geoff Davis (R)	Jan 2005
	5. Harold Rogers (R)	Jan 1981
	6. Ben Chandler (D)[12]	Feb 2004
Louisiana	1. Bobby Jindal (R)	Jan 2005
	2. William J. Jefferson (D)	Jan 1991
	3. Charlie Melancon (D)	Jan 2005
	4. Jim McCrery (R)	Apr 1988
	5. Rodney Alexander (R)	Jan 2003
	6. Richard H. Baker (R)	Jan 1987
	7. Charles W. Boustany, Jr. (R)	Jan 2005
Maine	1. Thomas H. Allen (D)	Jan 1997
	2. Michael H. Michaud (D)	Jan 2003
Maryland	1. Wayne T. Gilchrest (R)	Jan 1991
	2. C.A. "Dutch" Ruppersberger (D)	Jan 2003
	3. John P. Sarbanes (D)	Jan 2007
	4. Albert Russell Wynn (D)	Jan 1993
	5. Steny H. Hoyer (D)	May 1981
	6. Roscoe G. Bartlett (R)	Jan 1993
	7. Elijah E. Cummings (D)	Apr 1996
	8. Chris Van Hollen (D)	Jan 2003
Massachusetts	1. John W. Olver (D)	Jun 1991
	2. Richard E. Neal (D)	Jan 1989
	3. James P. McGovern (D)	Jan 1997
	4. Barney Frank (D)	Jan 1981
	5. vacant	
	6. John F. Tierney (D)	Jan 1997
	7. Edward J. Markey (D)	Nov 1976
	8. Michael E. Capuano (D)	Jan 1999
	9. Stephen F. Lynch (D)[13]	Oct 2001
	10. William D. Delahunt (D)	Jan 1997
Michigan (−1)	1. Bart Stupak (D)	Jan 1993
	2. Peter Hoekstra (R)	Jan 1993
	3. Vernon J. Ehlers (R)	Dec 1993
	4. Dave Camp (R)	Jan 1991
	5. Dale E. Kildee (D)	Jan 1977
	6. Fred Upton (R)	Jan 1987
	7. Tim Walberg (R)	Jan 2007
	8. Mike Rogers (R)	Jan 2001
	9. Joe Knollenberg (R)	Jan 1993

STATE	REPRESENTATIVES	SERVICE BEGAN
Michigan (cont.)	10. Candice S. Miller (R)	Jan 2003
	11. Thaddeus G. McCotter (R)	Jan 2003
	12. Sander M. Levin (D)	Jan 1983
	13. Carolyn C. Kilpatrick (D)	Jan 1997
	14. John Conyers, Jr. (D)	Jan 1965
	15. John D. Dingell (D)	Dec 1955
Minnesota	1. Timothy J. Walz (D)	Jan 2007
	2. John Kline (R)	Jan 2003
	3. Jim Ramstad (R)	Jan 1991
	4. Betty McCollum (D)	Jan 2001
	5. Keith Ellison (D)	Jan 2007
	6. Michele Bachmann (R)	Jan 2007
	7. Collin C. Peterson (D)	Jan 1991
	8. James L. Oberstar (D)	Jan 1975
Mississippi (−1)	1. Roger F. Wicker (R)	Jan 1995
	2. Bennie G. Thompson (D)	Apr 1993
	3. Charles W. "Chip" Pickering (R)	Jan 1997
	4. Gene Taylor (D)	Oct 1989
Missouri	1. William Lacy Clay (D)	Jan 2001
	2. W. Todd Akin (R)	Jan 2001
	3. Russ Carnahan (D)	Jan 2005
	4. Ike Skelton (D)	Jan 1977
	5. Emanuel Cleaver (D)	Jan 2005
	6. Sam Graves (R)	Jan 2001
	7. Roy Blunt (R)	Jan 1997
	8. Jo Ann Emerson (R)	Nov 1996
	9. Kenny C. Hulshof (R)	Jan 1997
Montana	Dennis R. Rehberg (R)	Jan 2001
Nebraska	1. Jeff Fortenberry (R)	Jan 2005
	2. Lee Terry (R)	Jan 1999
	3. Adrian Smith (R)	Jan 2007
Nevada (+1)	1. Shelley Berkley (D)	Jan 1999
	2. Dean Heller (R)	Jan 2007
	3. Jon C. Porter (R)	Jan 2003
New Hampshire	1. Carol Shea-Porter (D)	Jan 2007
	2. Paul W. Hodes (D)	Jan 2007
New Jersey	1. Robert E. Andrews (D)	Nov 1990
	2. Frank A. LoBiondo (R)	Jan 1995
	3. Jim Saxton (R)	Nov 1984
	4. Christopher H. Smith (R)	Jan 1981
	5. Scott Garrett (R)	Jan 2003
	6. Frank Pallone, Jr. (D)	Nov 1988
	7. Mike Ferguson (R)	Jan 2001
	8. Bill Pascrell, Jr. (D)	Jan 1997
	9. Steven R. Rothman (D)	Jan 1997
	10. Donald M. Payne (D)	Jan 1989
	11. Rodney P. Frelinghuysen (R)	Jan 1995
	12. Rush D. Holt (D)	Jan 1999
	13. Albio Sires (D)[14]	Nov 2006
New Mexico	1. Heather Wilson (R)	Jun 1998
	2. Steve Pearce (R)	Jan 2003
	3. Tom Udall (D)	Jan 1999
New York (−2)	1. Timothy H. Bishop (D)	Jan 2003
	2. Steve Israel (D)	Jan 2001

The House of Representatives, 110th Congress (continued)

STATE	REPRESENTATIVES	SERVICE BEGAN
New York (cont.)	3. Peter T. King (R)	Jan 1993
	4. Carolyn McCarthy (D)	Jan 1997
	5. Gary L. Ackerman (D)	Mar 1983
	6. Gregory W. Meeks (D)	Feb 1998
	7. Joseph Crowley (D)	Jan 1999
	8. Jerrold Nadler (D)	Nov 1992
	9. Anthony D. Weiner (D)	Jan 1999
	10. Edolphus Towns (D)	Jan 1983
	11. Yvette D. Clarke (D)	Jan 2007
	12. Nydia M. Velázquez (D)	Jan 1993
	13. Vito Fossella (R)	Nov 1997
	14. Carolyn B. Maloney (D)	Jan 1993
	15. Charles B. Rangel (D)	Jan 1971
	16. José E. Serrano (D)	Mar 1990
	17. Eliot L. Engel (D)	Jan 1989
	18. Nita M. Lowey (D)	Jan 1989
	19. John J. Hall (D)	Jan 2007
	20. Kirsten E. Gillibrand (D)	Jan 2007
	21. Michael R. McNulty (D)	Jan 1989
	22. Maurice D. Hinchey (D)	Jan 1993
	23. John M. McHugh (R)	Jan 1993
	24. Michael A. Arcuri (D)	Jan 2007
	25. James T. Walsh (R)	Jan 1989
	26. Thomas M. Reynolds (R)	Jan 1999
	27. Brian Higgins (D)	Jan 2005
	28. Louise McIntosh Slaughter (D)	Jan 1987
	29. John R. "Randy" Kuhl, Jr. (R)	Jan 2005
North Carolina (+1)	1. G.K. Butterfield (D)	Jan 2005
	2. Bob Etheridge (D)	Jan 1997
	3. Walter B. Jones (R)	Jan 1995
	4. David E. Price (D)	Jan 1997
	5. Virginia Foxx (R)	Jan 2005
	6. Howard Coble (R)	Jan 1985
	7. Mike McIntyre (D)	Jan 1997
	8. Robin Hayes (R)	Jan 1999
	9. Sue Wilkins Myrick (R)	Jan 1995
	10. Patrick T. McHenry(R)	Jan 2005
	11. Heath Shuler (D)	Jan 2007
	12. Melvin L. Watt (D)	Jan 1993
	13. Brad Miller (D)	Jan 2003
North Dakota	Earl Pomeroy (D)	Jan 1993
Ohio (−1)	1. Steve Chabot (R)	Jan 1995
	2. Jean Schmidt (R)	Sep 2005
	3. Michael R. Turner (R)	Jan 2003
	4. Jim Jordan (R)	Jan 2007
	5. vacant	
	6. Charles A. Wilson (D)	Jan 2007
	7. David L. Hobson (R)	Jan 1991
	8. John A. Boehner (R)	Jan 1991
	9. Marcy Kaptur (D)	Jan 1983
	10. Dennis J. Kucinich (D)	Jan 1997
	11. Stephanie Tubbs Jones (D)	Jan 1999
	12. Patrick J. Tiberi (R)	Jan 2001
	13. Betty Sutton (D)	Jan 2007
	14. Steven C. LaTourette (R)	Jan 1995
	15. Deborah Pryce (R)	Jan 1993
	16. Ralph Regula (R)	Jan 1973
	17. Tim Ryan (D)	Jan 2003
	18. Zachary T. Space (D)	Jan 2007

STATE	REPRESENTATIVES	SERVICE BEGAN
Oklahoma (−1)	1. John Sullivan (R)[15]	Feb 2002
	2. Dan Boren (D)	Jan 2005
	3. Frank D. Lucas (R)	May 1994
	4. Tom Cole (R)	Jan 2003
	5. Mary Fallin (R)	Jan 2007
Oregon	1. David Wu (D)	Jan 1999
	2. Greg Walden (R)	Jan 1999
	3. Earl Blumenauer (D)	May 1996
	4. Peter A. DeFazio (D)	Jan 1987
	5. Darlene Hooley (D)	Jan 1997
Pennsylvania (−2)	1. Robert A. Brady (D)	May 1998
	2. Chaka Fattah (D)	Jan 1995
	3. Phil English (R)	Jan 1995
	4. Jason Altmire (D)	Jan 2007
	5. John E. Peterson (R)	Jan 1997
	6. Jim Gerlach (R)	Jan 2003
	7. Joe Sestak (D)	Jan 2007
	8. Patrick J. Murphy (D)	Jan 2007
	9. Bill Shuster (R)	May 2001
	10. Christopher P. Carney (D)	Jan 2007
	11. Paul E. Kanjorski (D)	Jan 1985
	12. John P. Murtha (D)	Feb 1974
	13. Allyson Y. Schwartz (D)	Jan 2005
	14. Michael F. Doyle (D)	Jan 1995
	15. Charles W. Dent (R)	Jan 2005
	16. Joseph R. Pitts (R)	Jan 1997
	17. Tim Holden (D)	Jan 1993
	18. Tim Murphy (R)	Jan 2003
	19. Todd Russell Platts (R)	Jan 2001
Rhode Island	1. Patrick J. Kennedy (D)	Jan 1995
	2. James R. Langevin (D)	Jan 2001
South Carolina	1. Henry E. Brown, Jr. (R)	Jan 2001
	2. Joe Wilson (R)[16]	Dec 2001
	3. J. Gresham Barrett (R)	Jan 2003
	4. Bob Inglis (R)	Jan 2005
	5. John M. Spratt, Jr. (D)	Jan 1983
	6. James E. Clyburn (D)	Jan 1993
South Dakota	Stephanie Herseth Sandlin (D)[17]	Jun 2004
Tennessee	1. David Davis (R)	Jan 2007
	2. John J. Duncan, Jr., (R)	Nov 1988
	3. Zach Wamp (R)	Jan 1995
	4. Lincoln Davis (D)	Jan 2003
	5. Jim Cooper (D)[18]	Jan 1983
	6. Bart Gordon (D)	Jan 1985
	7. Marsha Blackburn (R)	Jan 2003
	8. John S. Tanner (D)	Jan 1989
	9. Steve Cohen (D)	Jan 2007
Texas (+2)	1. Louie Gohmert (R)	Jan 2005
	2. Ted Poe (R)	Jan 2005
	3. Sam Johnson (R)	May 1991
	4. Ralph M. Hall (R)[19]	Jan 1981
	5. Jeb Hensarling (R)	Jan 2003
	6. Joe Barton (R)	Jan 1985
	7. John Abney Culberson (R)	Jan 2001
	8. Kevin Brady (R)	Jan 1997
	9. Al Green (D)	Jan 2005
	10. Michael T. McCaul (R)	Jan 2005

The House of Representatives, 110th Congress (continued)

STATE	REPRESENTATIVES	SERVICE BEGAN
Texas (cont.)	11. K. Michael Conaway (R)	Jan 2005
	12. Kay Granger (R)	Jan 1997
	13. Mac Thornberry (R)	Jan 1995
	14. Ron Paul (R)	Jan 1997
	15. Rubén Hinojosa (D)	Jan 1997
	16. Silvestre Reyes (D)	Jan 1997
	17. Chet Edwards (D)	Jan 2005
	18. Sheila Jackson-Lee (D)	Jan 1995
	19. Randy Neugebauer (R)[20]	Jun 2003
	20. Charles A. Gonzalez (D)	Jan 1999
	21. Lamar S. Smith (R)	Jan 1987
	22. Nick Lampson (D)[21]	Jan 1997
	23. Ciro D. Rodriguez (D)[22]	Apr 1997
	24. Kenny Marchant (R)	Jan 2005
	25. Lloyd Doggett (D)	Jan 2005
	26. Michael C. Burgess (R)	Jan 2003
	27. Solomon P. Ortiz (D)	Jan 1983
	28. Henry Cuellar (D)	Jan 2005
	29. Gene Green (D)	Jan 1993
	30. Eddie Bernice Johnson (D)	Jan 1993
	31. John R. Carter (R)	Jan 2003
	32. Pete Sessions (R)	Jan 1997
Utah	1. Rob Bishop (R)	Jan 2003
	2. Jim Matheson (D)	Jan 2001
	3. Chris Cannon (R)	Jan 1997
Vermont	Peter Welch (D)	Jan 2007
Virginia	1. Jo Ann Davis (R)	Jan 2001
	2. Thelma D. Drake (R)	Jan 2005
	3. Robert C. Scott (D)	Jan 1993
	4. J. Randy Forbes (R)[23]	Jun 2001
	5. Virgil H. Goode, Jr. (R)	Jan 1997
	6. Bob Goodlatte (R)	Jan 1993
	7. Eric Cantor (R)	Jan 2001
	8. James P. Moran (D)	Jan 1991
	9. Rick Boucher (D)	Jan 1983

STATE	REPRESENTATIVES	SERVICE BEGAN
Virginia (cont.)	10. Frank R. Wolf (R)	Jan 1981
	11. Tom Davis (R)	Jan 1995
Washington	1. Jay Inslee (D)[24]	Jan 1993
	2. Rick Larsen (D)	Jan 2001
	3. Brian Baird (D)	Jan 1999
	4. Doc Hastings (R)	Jan 1995
	5. Cathy McMorris Rodgers (R)	Jan 2005
	6. Norman D. Dicks (D)	Jan 1977
	7. Jim McDermott (D)	Jan 1989
	8. David G. Reichert (R)	Jan 2005
	9. Adam Smith (D)	Jan 1997
West Virginia	1. Alan B. Mollohan (D)	Jan 1983
	2. Shelley Moore Capito (R)	Jan 2001
	3. Nick J. Rahall II (D)	Jan 1977
Wisconsin (−1)	1. Paul Ryan (R)	Jan 1999
	2. Tammy Baldwin (D)	Jan 1999
	3. Ron Kind (D)	Jan 1997
	4. Gwen Moore (D)	Jan 2005
	5. F. James Sensen-brenner, Jr. (R)	Jan 1979
	6. Thomas E. Petri (R)	Apr 1979
	7. David R. Obey (D)	Apr 1969
	8. Steve Kagen (D)	Jan 2007
Wyoming	Barbara Cubin (R)	Jan 1995

JURISDICTION	REPRESENTATIVES	SERVICE BEGAN
American Samoa	(Delegate) Eni F.H. Faleomavaega (D)	Jan 1989
District of Columbia	(Delegate) Eleanor Holmes Norton (D)	Jan 1991
Guam	(Delegate) Madeleine Bordallo (D)	Jan 2003
Puerto Rico	(Resident Commissioner) Luis G. Fortuño (R)	Jan 2005
US Virgin Islands	(Delegate) Donna M. Christensen (D)	Jan 1997

[1]John Boozman was elected 20 Nov 2001 following the resignation of Asa Hutchinson. [2]Doris O. Matsui was elected 8 Mar 2005 following the death of Robert T. Matsui. [3]Diane E. Watson was elected 5 Jun 2001 following the death of Julian C. Dixon. [4]Jane F. Harman did not serve 3 Jan 1999–3 Jan 2001. [5]Laura Richardson was elected 21 Aug 2007 following the death of Juanita Millender-McDonald. [6]John Campbell took office 6 Dec 2005 following the resignation of Christopher Cox. [7]Brian P. Bilbray did not serve 3 Jan 2001–6 Jun 2005. He took office 6 June 2005 following the resignation of Randall (Duke) Cunningham. [8]Jeff Miller was elected 16 Oct 2001 following the resignation of Joe Scarborough. [9]Paul Broun was elected 17 Jul 2007 following the death of Charlie Norwood. [10]Neil Abercrombie did not serve 3 Jan 1987–3 Jan 1991. [11]Baron P. Hill did not serve 3 Jan 2005–3 Jan 2007. [12]Ben Chandler was elected 17 Feb 2004 following the resignation of Ernie Fletcher. [13]Stephen F. Lynch was elected 16 Oct 2001 following the death of John Joseph Moakley. [14]Albio Sires took office 13 Nov 2006 following the resignation of Robert Menendez. [15]John Sullivan was elected 8 Jan 2002 following the resignation of Steve Largent. [16]Joe Wilson was elected 18 Dec 2001 following the death of Floyd Spence. [17]Stephanie Herseth Sandlin was elected 1 Jun 2004 following the resignation of William Janklow. [18]Jim Cooper did not serve 3 Jan 1995–3 Jan 2003. [19]Ralph M. Hall defected to the Republican Party on 5 Jan 2004. [20]Randy Neugebauer was elected 3 June 2003 following the resignation of Larry Combest. [21]Nick Lampson did not serve 3 Jan 2005–3 Jan 2007. [22]Ciro D. Rodriguez took office 12 Apr 1997 following the death of Frank Tejada. He did not serve 3 Jan 2005–3 Jan 2007. [23]J. Randy Forbes was elected 19 Jun 2001 following the death of Norman Sisisky. [24]Jay Inslee did not serve 3 Jan 1995–3 Jan 1999.

House of Representatives Standing Committees

COMMITTEE	CHAIRMAN (PARTY-STATE)	RANKING MINORITY MEMBER (PARTY-STATE)	NUMBER OF MEMBERS MAJORITY	NUMBER OF MEMBERS MINORITY	NUMBER OF SUBCOM-MITTEES
Agriculture	Collin C. Peterson (D-MN)	Bob Goodlatte (R-VA)	25	21	6
Appropriations	David R. Obey (D-WI)	Jerry Lewis (R-CA)	37	29	12
Armed Services	Ike Skelton (D-MO)	Duncan Hunter (R-CA)	34	28	7
Budget	John M. Spratt, Jr. (D-SC)	Paul Ryan (R-WI)	22	17	none
Education and Labor	George Miller (D-CA)	Howard P. "Buck" McKeon (R-CA)	27	22	5
Energy and Commerce	John D. Dingell (D-MI)	Joe Barton (R-TX)	31	26	6
Financial Services	Barney Frank (D-MA)	Spencer Bachus (R-AL)	37	33	5
Foreign Affairs	Tom Lantos (D-CA)	Ileana Ros-Lehtinen (R-FL)	27	23	7
Homeland Security	Bennie G. Thompson (D-MS)	Peter T. King (R-NY)	19	15	6
House Administration	Robert A. Brady (D-PA)	Vernon J. Ehlers (R-MI)	6	3	2
Judiciary	John Conyers, Jr. (D-MI)	Lamar S. Smith (R-TX)	23	17	5
Natural Resources	Nick J. Rahall II (D-WV)	Don Young (R-AK)	27	22	5
Oversight and Government Reform	Henry A. Waxman (D-CA)	Tom Davis (R-VA)	23	18	5
Rules	Louise McIntosh Slaughter (D-NY)	David Dreier (R-CA)	9	4	2
Science and Technology	Bart Gordon (D-TN)	Ralph M. Hall (R-TX)	24	20	5
Small Business	Nydia M. Velázquez (D-NY)	Steve Chabot (R-OH)	18	15	5
Standards of Official Conduct	Stephanie Tubbs Jones (D-OH)	Doc Hastings (R-WA)	5	5	none
Transportation and Infrastructure	James L. Oberstar (D-MN)	John L. Mica (R-FL)	41	34	6
Veterans' Affairs	Bob Filner (D-CA)	Steve Buyer (R-IN)	16	13	4
Ways and Means	Charles B. Rangel (D-NY)	Jim McCrery (R-LA)	24	17	6
Permanent Select Committee on Intelligence	Silvestre Reyes (D-TX)	Peter Hoekstra (R-MI)	12	9	4
Select Committee on Energy Independence and Global Warming	Edward J. Markey (D-MA)	F. James Sensenbrenner, Jr. (R-WI)	9	6	none

---

Did you know? Henri Matisse's painting *Le Bateau* (*The Boat*) was accidentally hung upside down in New York's Museum of Modern Art for 47 days in 1961. During that time 116,000 visitors saw it, but it wasn't until stockbroker Genevieve Habert called the *New York Times* about the mistake that the director of exhibitions was notified and the work was rehung properly.

Electoral Votes by State

Each state receives one electoral vote for each of its representatives and one for each of its two senators, ensuring at least three votes for each state, as the Constitution guarantees at least one representative regardless of population. Allocations are based on the 2000 census and are applicable for subsequent elections.

Total: 538; Majority needed to elect president and vice president: 270

STATE	NUMBER OF VOTES	STATE	NUMBER OF VOTES	STATE	NUMBER OF VOTES
Alabama	9	Kentucky	8	North Dakota	3
Alaska	3	Louisiana	9	Ohio	20
Arizona	10	Maine	4	Oklahoma	7
Arkansas	6	Maryland	10	Oregon	7
California	55	Massachusetts	12	Pennsylvania	21
Colorado	9	Michigan	17	Rhode Island	4
Connecticut	7	Minnesota	10	South Carolina	8
Delaware	3	Mississippi	6	South Dakota	3
District of Columbia	3	Missouri	11	Tennessee	11
Florida	27	Montana	3	Texas	34
Georgia	15	Nebraska	5	Utah	5
Hawaii	4	Nevada	5	Vermont	3
Idaho	4	New Hampshire	4	Virginia	13
Illinois	21	New Jersey	15	Washington	11
Indiana	11	New Mexico	5	West Virginia	5
Iowa	7	New York	31	Wisconsin	10
Kansas	6	North Carolina	15	Wyoming	3

Congressional Apportionment

The US Constitution requires a decennial census to determine the apportionment of representatives for each state in the House of Representatives. There was no reapportionment based on 1920 census figures.

STATE	representatives										
	1790	1800	1810	1820	1830	1840	1850	1860	1870	1880	1890
Alabama	NA	NA	1[1]	3	5	7	7	6	8	8	9
Alaska	NA	NA	NA	NA	NA	NA	NA	NA	NA	NA	NA
Arizona	NA	NA	NA	NA	NA	NA	NA	NA	NA	NA	NA
Arkansas	NA	NA	NA	NA	1[1]	1	2	3	4	5	6
California	NA	NA	NA	NA	NA	2[1]	2	3	4	6	7
Colorado	NA	NA	NA	NA	NA	NA	NA	NA	1[1]	1	2
Connecticut	7	7	7	6	6	4	4	4	4	4	4
Delaware	1	1	2	1	1	1	1	1	1	1	1
Florida	NA	NA	NA	NA	NA	1[1]	1	1	2	2	2
Georgia	2	4	6	7	9	8	8	7	9	10	11
Hawaii	NA	NA	NA	NA	NA	NA	NA	NA	NA	NA	NA
Idaho	NA	NA	NA	NA	NA	NA	NA	NA	NA	1[1]	1
Illinois	NA	NA	1[1]	1	3	7	9	14	19	20	22
Indiana	NA	NA	1[1]	3	7	10	11	11	13	13	13
Iowa	NA	NA	NA	NA	NA	2[1]	2	6	9	11	11
Kansas	NA	NA	NA	NA	NA	NA	NA	1	3	7	8
Kentucky	2	6	10	12	13	10	10	9	10	11	11
Louisiana	NA	NA	1[1]	3	3	4	4	5	6	6	6
Maine	NA	NA	NA	7	8	7	6	5	5	4	4
Maryland	8	9	9	9	8	6	6	5	6	6	6
Massachusetts	14	17	20	13	12	10	11	10	11	12	13
Michigan	NA	NA	NA	NA	1[1]	3	4	6	9	11	12
Minnesota	NA	NA	NA	NA	NA	NA	2[1]	2	3	5	7
Mississippi	NA	NA	1[1]	1	2	4	5	5	6	7	7
Missouri	NA	NA	NA	1	2	5	7	9	13	14	15
Montana	NA	NA	NA	NA	NA	NA	NA	NA	NA	1[1]	1
Nebraska	NA	NA	NA	NA	NA	NA	NA	1[1]	1	3	6
Nevada	NA	NA	NA	NA	NA	NA	NA	1[1]	1	1	1
New Hampshire	4	5	6	6	5	4	3	3	3	2	2
New Jersey	5	6	6	6	6	5	5	5	7	7	8
New Mexico	NA	NA	NA	NA	NA	NA	NA	NA	NA	NA	NA
New York	10	17	27	34	40	34	33	31	33	34	34
North Carolina	10	12	13	13	13	9	8	7	8	9	9
North Dakota	NA	NA	NA	NA	NA	NA	NA	NA	NA	1[1]	1
Ohio	NA	1[1]	6	14	19	21	21	19	20	21	21
Oklahoma	NA	NA	NA	NA	NA	NA	NA	NA	NA	NA	NA
Oregon	NA	NA	NA	NA	NA	NA	1[1]	1	1	1	2
Pennsylvania	13	18	23	26	28	24	25	24	27	28	30
Rhode Island	2	2	2	2	2	2	2	2	2	2	2
South Carolina	6	8	9	9	9	7	6	4	5	7	7
South Dakota	NA	NA	NA	NA	NA	NA	NA	NA	NA	2[1]	2
Tennessee	1[1]	3	6	9	13	11	10	8	10	10	10
Texas	NA	NA	NA	NA	NA	2[1]	2	4	6	11	13
Utah	NA	NA	NA	NA	NA	NA	NA	NA	NA	NA	1[1]
Vermont	2	4	6	5	5	4	3	3	3	2	2
Virginia	19	22	23	22	21	15	13	11	9	10	10
Washington	NA	NA	NA	NA	NA	NA	NA	NA	NA	1[1]	2
West Virginia	NA	NA	NA	NA	NA	NA	NA	NA	3	4	4
Wisconsin	NA	NA	NA	NA	NA	2[1]	3	6	8	9	10
Wyoming	NA	NA	NA	NA	NA	NA	NA	NA	NA	1[1]	1
Total	106	142	186	213	242	232	237	243	293	332	357

Congressional Apportionment (continued)

STATE	representatives									
	1900	1910	1930	1940	1950	1960	1970	1980	1990	2000
Alabama	9	10	9	9	9	8	7	7	7	7
Alaska	NA	NA	NA	NA	1¹	1	1	1	1	1
Arizona	NA	1²	1	2	2	3	4	5	6	8
Arkansas	7	7	7	7	6	4	4	4	4	4
California	8	11	20	23	30	38	43	45	52	53
Colorado	3	4	4	4	4	4	5	6	6	7
Connecticut	5	5	6	6	6	6	6	6	6	5
Delaware	1	1	1	1	1	1	1	1	1	1
Florida	3	4	5	6	8	12	15	19	23	25
Georgia	11	12	10	10	10	10	10	10	11	13
Hawaii	NA	NA	NA	NA	1¹	2	2	2	2	2
Idaho	1	2	2	2	2	2	2	2	2	2
Illinois	25	27	27	26	25	24	24	22	20	19
Indiana	13	13	12	11	11	11	11	10	10	9
Iowa	11	11	9	8	8	7	6	6	5	5
Kansas	8	8	7	6	6	5	5	5	4	4
Kentucky	11	11	9	9	8	7	7	7	6	6
Louisiana	7	8	8	8	8	8	8	8	7	7
Maine	4	4	3	3	3	2	2	2	2	2
Maryland	6	6	6	6	7	8	8	8	8	8
Massachusetts	14	16	15	14	14	12	12	11	10	10
Michigan	12	13	17	17	18	19	19	18	16	15
Minnesota	9	10	9	9	9	8	8	8	8	8
Mississippi	8	8	7	7	6	5	5	5	5	4
Missouri	16	16	13	13	11	10	10	9	9	9
Montana	1	2	2	2	2	2	2	2	1	1
Nebraska	6	6	5	4	4	3	3	3	3	3
Nevada	1	1	1	1	1	1	1	2	2	3
New Hampshire	2	2	2	2	2	2	2	2	2	2
New Jersey	10	12	14	14	14	15	15	14	13	13
New Mexico	NA	1²	1	2	2	2	2	3	3	3
New York	37	43	45	45	43	41	39	34	31	29
North Carolina	10	10	11	12	12	11	11	11	12	13
North Dakota	2	3	2	2	2	2	1	1	1	1
Ohio	21	22	24	23	23	24	23	21	19	18
Oklahoma	5¹	8	9	8	6	6	6	6	6	5
Oregon	2	3	3	4	4	4	4	5	5	5
Pennsylvania	32	36	34	33	30	27	25	23	21	19
Rhode Island	2	3	2	2	2	2	2	2	2	2
South Carolina	7	7	6	6	6	6	6	6	6	6
South Dakota	2	3	2	2	2	2	2	1	1	1
Tennessee	10	10	9	10	9	9	8	9	9	9
Texas	16	18	21	21	22	23	24	27	30	32
Utah	1	2	2	2	2	2	2	3	3	3
Vermont	2	2	1	1	1	1	1	1	1	1
Virginia	10	10	9	9	10	10	10	10	11	11
Washington	3	5	6	6	7	7	7	8	9	9
West Virginia	5	6	6	6	6	5	4	4	3	3
Wisconsin	11	11	10	10	10	10	9	9	9	8
Wyoming	1	1	1	1	1	1	1	1	1	1
Total	391	435	435	435	437	435	435	435	435	435

NA: Not applicable.   ¹Number assigned after apportionment.   ²Included in anticipation of statehood.

Military Affairs

US Military Leadership

President, Commander in Chief:	George W. Bush (20 Jan 2001)
Secretary of Defense:	Robert M. Gates (18 Dec 2006)
Chairman, Joint Chiefs of Staff:	Peter Pace (30 Sep 2005)
Vice Chairman, Joint Chiefs of Staff:	Edmund P. Giambastiani, Jr. (12 Aug 2005)

RANK/POSITION	NAME (DATE ASSUMED POST)
Army	
Chief of Staff	George W. Casey, Jr. (10 Apr 2007)
Vice Chief of Staff	Richard A. Cody (24 Jun 2004)
Sergeant Major	Kenneth O. Preston (15 Jan 2004)
Sec. of the Army (acting)	Pete Geren (9 Mar 2007)
Under Sec. of the Army	Pete Geren (21 Feb 2006)
Navy	
Chief of Naval Operations	Michael Mullen (July 2005)
Vice Chief of Naval Operations	Robert F. Willard (17 Feb 2005)
Master Chief Petty Officer	Joe R. Campa, Jr. (10 Jul 2006)
Sec. of the Navy	Donald C. Winter (3 Jan 2006)
Under Sec. of the Navy	*vacant*

RANK/POSITION	NAME (DATE ASSUMED POST)
Air Force	
Chief of Staff	T. Michael Moseley (2 Sep 2005)
Vice Chief of Staff	John D.W. Corley (2 Sep 2005)
Chief Master Sergeant	Rodney J. McKinley (30 Jun 2006)
Sec. of the Air Force	Michael W. Wynne (3 Nov 2005)
Under Sec. of the Air Force	Ronald M. Sega (4 Aug 2005)
Marine Corps	
Commandant	James T. Conway (13 Nov 2006)
Asst. Commandant	Robert Magnus (8 Sep 2005)
Sergeant Major	John L. Estrada (27 Jun 2003)
Coast Guard	
Commandant	Thad W. Allen (25 May 2006)
Vice Commandant	Vivien S. Crea (5 Jun 2006)
Chief of Staff	Robert J. Papp, Jr. (21 Apr 2006)
Master Chief Petty Officer	Charles W. Bowen (14 Jun 2006)

Unified Combatant Commands

The Unified Combatant Commands provide operational control of US combat forces and are organized geographically to a significant extent. Unified Commanders receive orders through the chairman of the Joint Chiefs of Staff. Its structure is flexible, changing to accommodate evolving US security needs. Although the number of commands may vary, each command must be composed of forces from at least two of the armed services. Information is current as of April 2007.

COMMAND	HEADQUARTERS	COMMANDER IN CHIEF
US European Command	Stuttgart-Vaihingen, Germany	Gen. Bantz John Craddock, USA
US Pacific Command	Honolulu HI	Adm. Timothy J. Keating, USN
US Joint Forces Command	Norfolk VA	Gen. Lance Smith, USAF
US Southern Command	Miami FL	Adm. James Stavridis, USN
US Central Command	MacDill Air Force Base, Florida	Adm. William J. Fallon, USN
US Northern Command	Peterson Air Force Base, Colorado	Gen. Victor E. Renuart, Jr., USAF
US Special Operations Command	MacDill Air Force Base, Florida	Gen. Bryan D. Brown, USA
US Transportation Command	Scott Air Force Base, Illinois	Gen. Norton A. Schwartz, USAF
US Strategic Command	Offutt Air Force Base, Nebraska	Gen. James E. Cartwright, USMC

North Atlantic Treaty Organization (NATO) International Commands

The NATO military command structure comprises two main strategic commands, Allied Command for Operations (ACO) and Allied Command Transformation (ACT, which works closely with the US Joint Forces Command). Their subordinate centers, also listed, change as their security measures evolve.

ALLIED COMMAND OPERATIONS (ACO)
Headquarters (SHAPE) Casteau, Belgium
Supreme Allied Commander, Europe (SACEUR)
  Gen. Bantz John Craddock (USA) (Dec 2006–)

SUBORDINATE OPERATIONAL COMMANDS
Joint Force Command Brunssum,
  JFC HQ Brunssum, Netherlands
Commander in Chief: Gen. Egon Ramms
  (Army, Germany) (26 Jan 2007–)

Joint Force Command Naples,
  JFC HQ Naples, Italy
Commander in Chief: Adm. H.G. Ulrich III (USN) (23 May 2005–)

Joint Command Lisbon,
  JC HQ Oeiras, Portugal
Commander in Chief: Vice Adm. John Stufflebeem
  (USN) (15 Jun 2005–)

NATO International Commands (continued)

ALLIED COMMAND TRANSFORMATION (ACT)
Headquarters Norfolk VA
Supreme Allied Commander, Transformation: Gen.
Lance L. Smith (USAF) (7 Nov 2005–)

SUBORDINATE CENTERS AND SCHOOLS
Joint Analysis and Lessons Learned Centre (JALLC),
Lisbon, Portugal
Joint Force Training Centre (JFTC), Bydgoszcz, Poland
Joint Warfare Centre (JWC), Stavanger, Norway

NATO Communications and Information Systems
School (NCISS), Latina, Italy
NATO Defense College (NDC), Rome, Italy
NATO School, Oberammergau, Germany
NATO Undersea Research Centre (NURC), La Spezia,
Italy

Chairmen of the Joint Chiefs of Staff, 1949–2007

The 1949 amendments to the National Security Act of 1947 created the position of chairman of the Joint Chiefs of Staff, the principal military adviser to the president, the secretary of defense, and the National Security Council. The president appoints the chairman for a two-year term with the advice and consent of the Senate. In 1986 the chairman's eligibility for service increased from two to three reappointments (there is no limit on reappointment during wartime). The Joint Chiefs of Staff consist of the chairman, a vice chairman, the chief of staff of the Army, the chief of staff of the Air Force, the chief of naval operations, and the commandant of the Marine Corps.

NAME	MILITARY BRANCH	DATES OF SERVICE
Gen. of the Army Omar N. Bradley	US Army	16 Aug 1949–15 Aug 1953
Adm. Arthur W. Radford	US Navy	15 Aug 1953–15 Aug 1957
Gen. Nathan F. Twining	US Air Force	15 Aug 1957–30 Sep 1960
Gen. Lyman L. Lemnitzer	US Army	1 Oct 1960–30 Sep 1962
Gen. Maxwell D. Taylor	US Army	1 Oct 1962–1 Jul 1964
Gen. Earle G. Wheeler	US Army	3 Jul 1964–2 Jul 1970
Adm. Thomas H. Moorer	US Navy	2 Jul 1970–1 Jul 1974
Gen. George S. Brown	US Air Force	1 Jul 1974–20 Jun 1978
Gen. David C. Jones	US Air Force	21 Jun 1978–18 Jun 1982
Gen. John W. Vessey, Jr.	US Army	18 Jun 1982–30 Sep 1985
Adm. William J. Crowe, Jr.	US Navy	1 Oct 1985–30 Sep 1989
Gen. Colin L. Powell	US Army	1 Oct 1989–30 Sep 1993
Adm. David E. Jeremiah (acting)	US Navy	1 Oct 1993–24 Oct 1993
Gen. John M. Shalikashvili	US Army	25 Oct 1993–30 Sep 1997
Gen. Harry Shelton	US Army	1 Oct 1997–1 Oct 2001
Gen. Richard B. Myers	US Air Force	1 Oct 2001–30 Sep 2005
Gen. Peter Pace	US Marine Corps	30 Sep 2005–

Worldwide Deployment of the US Military

Deployments of active duty military personnel as of 30 Sep 2006. Regional totals include countries and areas not shown in the table. N/A means not available. Source: US Department of Defense.

COUNTRY/REGIONAL AREA	TOTAL	ARMY	NAVY	MARINE CORPS	AIR FORCE
US and territories					
continental US[1]	897,011	390,153	135,652	104,327	266,879
Alaska	20,363	11,183	69	32	9,079
Hawaii[1]	34,935	18,687	6,080	5,050	5,118
Guam[1]	2,867	42	1,149	3	1,673
Puerto Rico[1]	146	54	39	0	28
transients	45,537	6,356	9,771	24,103	5,307
afloat	99,110	0	99,110	0	0
total ashore and afloat	**1,099,969**	**426,496**	**251,873**	**133,542**	**288,090**
Europe					
Belgium	1,361	784	76	0	461
Bosnia and Herzegovina	232	190	15	7	20
Germany[1]	64,319	48,583	282	269	15,185
Greece	395	9	333	11	42
Iceland	133	0	119	0	14
Italy[1]	10,449	2,880	3,259	53	4,257
The Netherlands	591	294	24	16	257
Portugal	922	25	36	8	853

Worldwide Deployment of the US Military (continued)

COUNTRY/REGIONAL AREA	TOTAL	ARMY	NAVY	MARINE CORPS	AIR FORCE
Europe (continued)					
Serbia (including Kosovo)	1,721	1,655	0	1	65
Spain	1,521	94	913	193	321
Turkey[1]	1,810	63	8	20	1,719
United Kingdom[1]	10,331	397	584	70	9,280
afloat	1,715	0	·1,715	0	0
total ashore and afloat	96,119	55,060	7,404	913	32,742
East Asia and Pacific					
Japan[1]	33,453	1,965	3,742	14,424	13,322
South Korea[1]	29,086	19,755	274	242	8,815
afloat	11,117	0	11,117	0	0
total ashore and afloat	74,530	21,833	·15,297	15,109	22,291
North Africa, Near East, and South Asia					
Afghanistan[2]	21,500	15,900	700	200	4,700
Iraq (Operation Iraqi Freedom)[2]	185,500	119,500	20,200	25,600	20,200
Bahrain	1,357	25	1,122	186	24
Qatar	446	184	4	67	191
afloat	2,510	0	356	2,154	0
total ashore and afloat (excluding Iraq and Afghanistan)	5,452	736	1,635	2,586	495
Western Hemisphere					
total ashore and afloat	2,059	711	617	370	361
all foreign countries (excluding Iraq and Afghanistan)					
ashore	262,586	78,906	78,097	44,720	60,863
afloat	22,381	0	20,227	2,154	0
total ashore and afloat	284,967	78,906	98,324	46,874	60,863
worldwide (excluding Iraq and Afghanistan)					
ashore	1,263,470	505,402	230,860	178,262	348,953
afloat	121,491	0	119,337	2,154	0
total ashore and afloat	1,384,960	505,402	350,197	180,416	348,953

[1]Service members deployed to Operation Iraqi Freedom are included in these country figures.
[2]Includes deployed Reserve/National Guard.

Military Ranks and Monthly Pay

Pay given in dollars as of 1 Apr 2007.

Enlisted personnel					
	E-1	E-2	E-3	E-4	E-5
Army	private	private	private first class	corporal	sergeant
Navy	seaman recruit	seaman apprentice	seaman	petty officer third class	petty officer second class
Air Force	airman basic	airman	airman first class	senior airman	staff sergeant
Marine Corps	private	private first class	lance corporal	corporal	sergeant
0–6 years	1,204–1,301	1,459	1,534–1,729	1,700–1,979	1,854–2,171
6–12 years				2,063	2,324–2,614
12–18 years					2,630
18–24 years					
over 24 years					

	E-6	E-7	E-8	E-9
Army	staff sergeant	sergeant first class	master sergeant, first sergeant	sergeant major
Navy	petty officer first class	chief petty officer	senior chief petty officer	master chief petty officer
Air Force	technical sergeant	master sergeant, first sergeant	senior master sergeant, first sergeant	chief master sergeant
Marine Corps	staff sergeant	gunnery sergeant	master sergeant, first sergeant	master gunnery sergeant, sergeant major

Military Ranks and Monthly Pay (continued)

Enlisted personnel (continued)

0–6 years	2,023–2,420	2,339–2,781		
6–12 years	2,519–2,831	2,882–3,153	3,365–3,514	4,111
12–18 years	3,000–3,090	3,327–3,570	3,606–3,836	4,204–4,460
18–24 years	3,134	3,674–3,852	4,052–4,347	4,598–5,010
over 24 years		3,925–4,204	4,451–4,799	5,209–6,382

Warrant officers

	W-1	W-2	W-3	W-4	W-5
Army	warrant officer	chief warrant officer	chief warrant officer	chief warrant officer	chief warrant officer
Navy	"	"	"	"	"
Marine Corps	"	"	"	"	"

	W-1	W-2	W-3	W-4	W-5
0–6 years	2,413–2,891	2,749–3,145	3,107–3,413	3,402–3,869	
6–12 years	3,065–3,442	3,323–3,737	3,552–4,111	4,046–4,401	
12–18 years	3,610–3,905	3,872–4,167	4,245–4,560	4,669–5,128	
18–24 years	4,025–4,170	4,284–4,516	4,848–5,159	5,311–5,752	6,050–6,356
over 24 years		4,589	5,282–5,450	5,968–6,338	6,585–7,916

Officers (with more than 4 years served as an enlisted or warrant member of the armed services)

	O-1E	O-2E	O-3E
Army	second lieutenant	first lieutenant	captain
Navy	ensign	lieutenant, jr. grade	lieutenant
Air Force	second lieutenant	first lieutenant	captain
Marine Corps	second lieutenant	first lieutenant	captain

0–6 years	3,107	3,857	4,392
6–12 years	3,318–3,566	3,937–4,274	4,602–4,983
12–18 years	3,689–3,857	4,437–4,559	5,228–5,554
18–24 years			5,716
over 24 years			

Officers

	O-1	O-2	O-3	O-4	O-5
Army	second lieutenant	first lieutenant	captain	major	lieutenant colonel
Navy	ensign	lieutenant, jr. grade	lieutenant	lieutenant commander	commander
Air Force	second lieutenant	first lieutenant	captain	major	lieutenant colonel
Marine Corps	second lieutenant	first lieutenant	captain	major	lieutenant colonel

	O-1	O-2	O-3	O-4	O-5
0–6 years	2,469–3;107	2,844–3,731	3,292–4,392	3,745–4,688	4,340–5,291
6–12 years		3,937	4,602–4,983	4,957–5,603	5,502–5,906
12–18 years			5,228–5,356	5,882–6,188	6,110–6,776
18–24 years				6,252	6,968–7,373
over 24 years					

	O-6	O-7	O-8	O-9	O-10
Army	colonel	brigadier general	major general	lieutenant general	general
Navy	captain	rear admiral (lower half)	rear admiral (upper half)	vice admiral	admiral
Air Force	colonel	brigadier general	major general	lieutenant general	general
Marine Corps	colonel	brigadier general	major general	lieutenant general	general

	O-6	O-7	O-8	O-9	O-10
0–6 years	5,206–6,095	7,024–7,621	8,453–8,965		
6–12 years	6,118–6,415	7,838–8,301	9,194–9,666		
12–18 years	6,415–7,424	8,549–9,577	10,030–10,448		
18–24 years	7,802–8,395	10,236	10,901–11,598	11,947–12,119	13,659–13,726
over 24 years	8,613–9,216	10,236–10,494	11,598–12,186	12,367–14,819	14,011–16,796

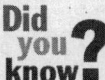

Did you know? Communications satellites comprising a network or system are nearly always launched to a distance of 35,890 km (22,300 mi) above the Earth. At this altitude the motion of a satellite becomes synchronized with the Earth's rotation, causing the craft to remain fixed over a single location. If properly positioned, three communications satellites traveling in such a synchronous orbit can relay signals between stations around the world.

Number of Living Veterans[1]

Source: Statistical Abstract of the US: 2007.

AGE IN YEARS	KOREAN CONFLICT	VIETNAM ERA	GULF WAR[2]	TOTAL WARTIME[3,4]	TOTAL PEACETIME	TOTAL VETERANS[4]
Under 35	—	—	1,940,000	1,940,000	27,000	1,966,000
35-39	—	—	886,000	886,000	431,000	1,317,000
40-44	—	—	573,000	573,000	1,106,000	1,679,000
45-49	—	191,000	422,000	595,000	1,291,000	1,886,000
50-54	—	1,448,000	294,000	1,609,000	425,000	2,034,000
55-59	—	3,309,000	178,000	3,360,000	124,000	3,484,000
60-64	—	2,091,000	59,000	2,102,000	571,000	2,673,000
65 and over	3,257,000	1,015,000	27,000	7,091,000	2,257,000	9,348,000
Female, total	77,000	260,000	688,000	1,153,000	559,000	1,712,000
Total[5]	3,257,000	8,055,000	4,378,000	18,156,000	6,231,000	24,387,000

[1]As of 30 Sep 2005. Includes those living outside of the US. Estimated. [2]Service from 2 Aug 1990 to the present. [3]Veterans who served in more than one wartime period are counted only once. [4]Includes an estimate of 3,526,000 veterans of World War II, all 65 or over, of which 164,000 are female. [5]Details may not add to totals given because of rounding.

Veterans Receiving Compensation

Numbers of veterans receiving compensation for service-related disabilities and low-income veterans receiving pensions who have permanent and total mostly non-service-related disabilities or are age 65 or older. N/A means not applicable.

TIME OF SERVICE	1980	1990	2000	2001	2002	2003	2004	2005
World War I	198,000	18,000	—[1]	—[1]	—[1]	—[1]	—[1]	—[1]
World War II	1,849,000	1,294,000	676,000	624,000	583,000	546,000	506,000	466,000
Korean conflict[2]	317,000	305,000	255,000	246,000	243,000	241,000	237,000	231,000
Vietnam era[3]	569,000	685,000	848,000	862,000	922,000	983,000	1,028,000	1,068,000
Gulf War[4]	N/A	N/A	326,000	368,000	421,000	479,000	540,000	617,000
Peacetime	262,000	444,000	567,000	569,000	575,000	583,000	587,000	591,000
Total	3,195,000	2,746,000	2,672,000	2,669,000	2,744,000	2,832,000	2,898,000	2,973,000

[1]Fewer than 500. [2]Service from 27 Jun 1950–31 Jan 1955. [3]Service from 5 Aug 1964–7 May 1975. [4]Service from 2 Aug 1990 to the present.

US Casualties of War

Data prior to World War I are based on incomplete records. Casualty data exclude personnel captured or missing in action. N/A means not available or unknown. Sources: US Department of Defense and US Coast Guard.

WAR	SERVICE BRANCH	NUMBER OF COMBATANTS	WOUNDED[1]	CASUALTIES BATTLE DEATHS	OTHER DEATHS	TOTAL DEATHS
Revolutionary War (1775–83)	Army	N/A	6,004	4,044	N/A	N/A
	Navy	N/A	114	342	N/A	N/A
	Marines	N/A	70	49	N/A	N/A
	total	184,000–250,000[2]	6,188	4,435	20,000[2]	24,435
War of 1812 (1812–15)	Army	N/A	4,000	1,950	N/A	N/A
	Navy	N/A	439	265	N/A	N/A
	Marines	N/A	66	45	N/A	N/A
	Coast Guard	100	N/A	0	N/A	N/A
	total	286,830	4,505	2,260	N/A	N/A
Indian Wars (about 1817–98)	total	106,000[2]	N/A	1,000[2]	N/A	N/A
Mexican-American War (1846–48)	Army	N/A	4,102	1,721	11,550	13,271
	Navy	N/A	3	1	N/A	N/A
	Marines	N/A	47	11	N/A	N/A
	Coast Guard	71	N/A	N/A	N/A	N/A
	total	78,789	4,152[4]	1,733[4]	N/A	N/A
Civil War (1861–65) Union	Army	2,128,948	280,040	138,154	221,374	359,528
	Navy	N/A	1,710	2,112	2,411	4,523
	Marines	84,415	131	148	312	460

US Casualties of War (continued)

WAR	SERVICE BRANCH	NUMBER OF COMBATANTS	WOUNDED[1]	CASUALTIES BATTLE DEATHS	OTHER DEATHS	TOTAL DEATHS
Civil War (1861–65)	Coast Guard	219	N/A	1	N/A	N/A
Union (continued)	total	N/A	281,881[4]	140,415	224,097[4]	364,512[4]
Confederate[3]	total	600,000–1,500,000	137,000[2]	74,524	124,000[2]	198,524
Spanish-American War	Army	280,564	1,594	369	2,061	2,430
(1898)	Navy	22,875	47	10	N/A	N/A
	Marines	3,321	21	6	N/A	N/A
	Coast Guard	660	N/A	0	N/A	0
	total	307,420	1,662	385	2,061	N/A
World War I	Army[4]	4,057,101	193,663	50,510	55,868	106,378
(1917–18)	Navy	599,051	819	431	6,856	7,287
	Marines	78,839	9,520	2,461	390	2,851
	Coast Guard	8,835	N/A	111	81	192
	total	4,743,826	204,002[4]	53,513	63,195	116,708
World War II	Army[4]	11,260,000	565,861	234,874	83,400	318,274
(1941–46)	Navy	4,183,466	37,778	36,950	25,664	62,614
	Marines	669,100	68,207	19,733	4,778	24,511
	Coast Guard	241,093	N/A	574	1,343	1,917
	total	16,353,659	671,846[4]	292,131	115,185	407,316
Korean War	Army	2,834,000	77,596	27,731	2,125	29,856
(1950–53)	Navy	1,177,000	1,576	506	154	660
	Marines	424,000	23,744	4,266	242	4,508
	Air Force	1,285,000	368	1,238	314	1,552
	Coast Guard	8,500[5]	0	0	0	0
	total	5,764,143	103,284	33,741	2,835	36,576
Vietnam War[5]	Army	4,368,000	96,802	30,952	7,261	38,213
(1964–73)	Navy	1,842,000	4,178	1,628	934	2,562
	Marines	794,000	51,392	13,091	1,749	14,840
	Air Force	1,740,000	931	1,744	841	2,585
	Coast Guard	8,000	60	7	N/A	7
	total	8,752,000	153,363[6]	47,422	10,785[4]	58,207[4]
Persian Gulf War[7]	Army	338,636	354	98	126	224
(1990–91)	Navy	152,419	12[8]	5[8]	50[8]	55[8]
	Marines	97,878	92	24	44	68
	Air Force	76,543	9	20	15	35
	Coast Guard	400	N/A	N/A	N/A	N/A
	total	665,876	467	147	235	382
War on Terrorism[9]	Army	N/A	973	161	115	276
(2001–)	Navy	N/A	10	16	15	31
	Marines	N/A	92	10	27	37
	Air Force	N/A	66	9	16	25
	Coast Guard	N/A	N/A	N/A	N/A	N/A
	total	N/A	1,141	196	173	369
Iraq War[10]	Army	N/A	15,746	1,767	449	2,216
(2003–)	Navy	N/A	539	46	25	71
	Marines	N/A	7,753	775	134	909
	Air Force	N/A	276	18	13	31
	Coast Guard	N/A	N/A	1	0	1
	total	N/A	24,314	2,607	621	3,228

other[11]

[1]Data in this column account for the total number of wounds. Marine Corps data for World War II, the Spanish-American War, and earlier wars represent the number of combatants wounded. [2]Estimate. [3]US service members only. [4]Excluding unavailable Coast Guard data. [5]Number eligible for Korean Service Medal. [6]Excludes 150,332 wounded that did not require hospital care. [7]Data for military personnel serving in the theater of operation. [8]Includes Coast Guard. [9]Data for 7 Oct 2001–24 Mar 2007. [10]Data through 24 Mar 2007. [11]US casualties of other recent military operations: in Grenada (1983) 119 wounded, 19 battle deaths; in Panama (1989) 324 wounded, 23 battle deaths; in Somalia (1992–94) 153 wounded, 43 battle deaths.

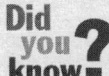

Did you know?

Ouroboros was the emblematic serpent of ancient Egypt and Greece, represented with its tail in its mouth as continually devouring itself and being reborn. It represented the eternal cycle of destruction and re-creation. In the 19th century, a vision of Ouroboros gave the German chemist Friedrich August Kekule von Stradonitz the idea of linked carbon atoms forming the benzene ring.

Leading Department of Defense Contractors

Top 75 Department of Defense contractors listed according to net value of prime contract awards, fiscal year 2005. Source: <www.defenselink.mil/pubs>.

RANK	CONTRACTOR	AMOUNT (US$)	RANK	CONTRACTOR	AMOUNT (US$)
1	Lockheed Martin	19,447,130,633	37	Washington Group International	879,146,162
2	Boeing	18,317,886,797			
3	Northrop Grumman	13,512,356,291	38	Engineered Support Systems	769,274,209
4	General Dynamics	10,640,762,393	39	Cardinal Health	765,862,546
5	Raytheon	9,109,329,221	40	CACI International	764,655,418
6	Halliburton	5,827,623,078	41	Rockwell Collins	759,010,311
7	BAE Systems	5,582,580,591	42	Harris	736,700,728
8	United Technologies	5,021,702,617	43	McKesson	686,451,339
9	L-3 Communications Holding	4,713,813,503	44	Mass. Institute of Technology	611,330,360
			45	Aerospace	611,298,284
10	Computer Sciences	2,827,726,732	46	Mitre	585,391,425
11	Science Applications International	2,795,942,100	47	Dell	583,605,853
			48	General Atomic Technologies	573,641,426
12	ITT Industries	2,493,318,283	49	A.P. Møller Gruppen	572,382,572
13	Humana	2,260,685,194	50	Valero Energy	564,413,358
14	General Electric	2,196,664,311	51	Shaw Group	560,732,461
15	Health Net	2,031,991,411	52	Government of Canada	553,293,195
16	Triwest Healthcare Alliance	1,803,645,659	53	Johnson Controls	553,110,924
			54	IAP Worldwide Services	525,358,171
17	Textron	1,599,948,596	55	Worldcom	516,210,073
18	URS	1,522,958,486	56	Rolls-Royce Group	514,161,982
19	GM GDLS Defense Group	1,513,312,459	57	Chugach Alaska	504,624,025
20	Honeywell International	1,504,768,268	58	Arinc	486,216,121
21	BP	1,502,105,956	59	Thales	481,641,138
22	Bechtel Group	1,486,859,510	60	Jacobs Engineering Group	477,477,591
23	Oshkosh Truck	1,473,875,526	61	Parsons	469,149,873
24	Electronic Data Systems	1,450,518,021	62	United Industrial	468,951,882
25	Public Warehousing	1,425,343,056	63	Unicor/Federal Prison Industries	460,112,883
26	Renco Group	1,406,264,190	64	Environmental Chemical	455,224,069
27	FedEx	1,369,725,116	65	American Body Armor and Equipment	419,951,585
28	Stewart & Stevenson Services	1,295,813,335			
			66	Government of the US	413,319,818
29	Alliant Techsystems	1,274,541,046	67	DRS Technologies	409,913,756
30	Bell Boeing Joint Program	1,204,289,914	68	Mantech International	404,357,230
31	Booz Allen Hamilton	1,162,989,915	69	Hensel Phelps Construction	395,597,704
32	N.V. Koninklijke Nederlandsche	1,069,504,184	70	Johns Hopkins University	394,216,813
			71	IBM	382,408,117
33	Exxon Mobil	1,046,077,242	72	Bahrain Petroleum	380,370,300
34	Amerisourcebergen	1,020,843,133	73	Altria Group	377,038,990
35	Evergreen International Airlines	985,088,202	74	Raytheon/Lockheed Martin Javelin	365,922,948
36	Anteon International	938,637,452	75	Battelle Memorial Institute	358,128,214

CIA Directors

The National Security Act of 26 Jul 1947 established the CIA on 18 Sep 1947. By authority of a presidential directive of 22 Jan 1946, the director of central intelligence serves as a member of the National Intelligence Authority and as head of the Central Intelligence Group. The director coordinates the nation's intelligence activities and informs the president on issues of national security.

NAME	DATES OF SERVICE
Rear Adm. Sidney W. Souers, USNR	23 Jan 1946–10 Jun 1946
Lt. Gen. Hoyt S. Vandenberg, USA	10 Jun 1946–1 May 1947
Rear Adm. Roscoe H. Hillenkoetter, USN	1 May 1947–7 Oct 1950
Gen. Walter Bedell Smith, USA	7 Oct 1950–9 Feb 1953
Allen W. Dulles	26 Feb 1953–29 Nov 1961
John A. McCone	29 Nov 1961–28 Apr 1965
Vice Adm. William F. Raborn, Jr., USN (Ret.)	28 Apr 1965–30 Jun 1966
Richard M. Helms	30 Jun 1966–2 Feb 1973
James R. Schlesinger	2 Feb 1973–2 Jul 1973

NAME	DATES OF SERVICE
William E. Colby	4 Sep 1973–30 Jan 1976
George H.W. Bush	30 Jan 1976–20 Jan 1977
Adm. Stansfield Turner, USN (Ret.)	9 Mar 1977–20 Jan 1981
William J. Casey	28 Jan 1981–29 Jan 1987
William H. Webster	26 May 1987–31 Aug 1991
Robert M. Gates	6 Nov 1991–20 Jan 1993
R. James Woolsey	5 Feb 1993–10 Jan 1995
John M. Deutch	10 May 1995–15 Dec 1996
George J. Tenet	11 Jul 1997–11 Jul 2004
John E. McLaughlin	12 Jul 2004–20 Apr 2005
Porter J. Goss	21 Apr 2005–29 May 2006
Gen. Michael V. Hayden, USAF	30 May 2006–

The National Security Council (NSC)

The National Security Act of 1947 established the NSC to advise the president on policies relating to national security. In addition to regular attendees, the chief of staff to the president, counsel to the presi-dent, and assistant to the president for economic pol-icy are invited to attend all meetings. The attorney general and the director of the Office of Management and Budget are also invited to attend when needed.

chair	George W. Bush (president)
regular attendees	Richard B. Cheney (vice president)
	Condoleezza Rice (secretary of state)
	Henry M. Paulson, Jr. (secretary of the treasury)
	Robert M. Gates (secretary of defense)
	Stephen Hadley (assistant to the president for national security affairs)
military adviser	Peter Pace (chairman of the joint chiefs of staff)
intelligence adviser	Michael V. Hayden (director of the CIA)
additional participants	Joshua B. Bolten (chief of staff)
	Fred Fielding (counsel to the president)
	Allan Hubbard (assistant to the president for economic policy)
	Alberto Gonzales (attorney general)
	Rob Portman (director of the Office of Management and Budget)

On 23 Mar 1953 Pres. Dwight D. Eisenhower estab-lished the office of assistant to the president for na-tional security affairs (commonly referred to as the national security advisor). Holders of this office are listed below.

NAME	DATES OF SERVICE	NAME	DATES OF SERVICE
Robert Cutler	23 Mar 1953–2 Apr 1955	William P. Clark	4 Jan 1982–17 Oct 1983
Dillon Anderson	2 Apr 1955–1 Sep 1956	Robert C. McFarlane	17 Oct 1983–4 Dec 1985
Robert Cutler	7 Jan 1957–24 Jun 1958	John M. Poindexter	4 Dec 1985– 25 Nov 1986
Gordon Gray	24 Jun 1958–13 Jan 1961	Frank C. Carlucci	2 Dec 1986–23 Nov 1987
McGeorge Bundy	20 Jan 1961–28 Feb 1966	Colin L. Powell	23 Nov 1987–20 Jan 1989
Walt W. Rostow	1 Apr 1966–2 Dec 1968	Brent Scrowcroft	20 Jan 1989–20 Jan 1993
Henry A. Kissinger	2 Dec 1968–3 Nov 1975[1]	W. Anthony Lake	20 Jan 1993–14 Mar 1997
Brent Scowcroft	3 Nov 1975–20 Jan 1977	Samuel R. Berger	14 Mar 1997–20 Jan 2001
Zbigniew Brzezinski	20 Jan 1977–21 Jan 1981	Condoleezza Rice	26 Jan 2001–26 Jan 2005
Richard V. Allen	21 Jan 1981–4 Jan 1982	Stephen Hadley	26 Jan 2005–

[1]Henry A. Kissinger served concurrently as secretary of state from 21 Sep 1973.

United States Population

The Changing Face of America

The population of the United States increased by 32.7 million people between the censuses of 1990 and 2000. That increase represented the largest population growth in census history. Census 2000 revealed a nation with more ethnic and racial diversity. During the 1990s the Hispanic population (Hispanics may be of any race) increased by 58%, the Asian population by 48%. The immigration of these groups accounted for about 13.3 million of the country's total population—a number not equaled in American history. The second largest number of immigrants recorded—10.1 million people—occurred between 1905 and 1914. Of the 281.4 million people residing in the United States on census day, non-Hispanic whites accounted for 69.1% of the population; Hispanics, 12.5%; blacks, 12.3%; and Asians, 3.6%.

The changing face of the United States was reflected in cities, suburbs, and rural areas. For the first time, nearly half of the nation's 100 largest cities were home to more African Americans, Hispanics, Asians, and other minorities than to non-Hispanic whites. While the population of the country's fastest-growing cities, such as Las Vegas and Phoenix, increased in all racial and ethnic categories, 71 of the top 100 cities lost non-Hispanic white residents to the suburbs and beyond. The nation's largest cities gained 3.8 million Hispanic residents, a 43% increase from a decade ago. Many cities, including Boston, Los Angeles, and Dallas, would have lost population in the 1990s were it not for large gains in the number of Hispanics.

Even with the arrival of a record number of immigrants (who tend to be relatively young), the United States continued to age as a nation. The median age of the country's population in 2000 was 35.3—five years older than the median age in 1950. (The median age splits the population in half: 50% are over the median age, 50% under it.) This increase in median age was tied to the graying of the post-World War II "baby boom" generation. Born from 1946 through 1964, baby boomers between 36 and 54 years of age represented 28% of the country's total population. The median age for non-Hispanic whites was 38.6, Asians 32.7, blacks 30.2, and Hispanics 25.8. Census 2000 revealed that the country's population was 50.9% female and 49.1% male. There were 37.1 million males under the age of 18 as compared with 35.2 million females. By the age of 36, however, there were more females than males. Female senior citizens 65 years and older outnumbered males 20.6 million to 14.4 million.

The Northeast and Midwest regions had the country's oldest populations. Median ages for those regions were 36.8 and 35.6, respectively. In contrast, the West had the population with the youngest median age, 33.8.

State Populations, 1790–2006

Resident population of the states and the District of Columbia. Numbers are in thousands ('000)[1].
Source: US Census Bureau.

STATE	1790	1800	1810	1820	1830	1840	1850	1860	1870	1880	1890	1900
AL		1	9	128	310	591	772	964	997	1,263	1,513	1,829
AK										33	32	64
AZ									10	40	88	123
AR			1	14	30	98	210	435	484	803	1,128	1,312
CA							93	380	560	865	1,213	1,485
CO								34	40	194	413	540
CT	238	251	262	275	298	310	371	460	537	623	746	908
DE	59	64	73	73	77	78	92	112	125	147	168	185
DC		8	15	23	30	34	52	75	132	178	230	279
FL					35	54	87	140	188	269	391	529
GA	83	163	252	341	517	691	906	1,057	1,184	1,542	1,837	2,216
HI												154
ID									15	33	89	162
IL			12	55	157	476	851	1,712	2,540	3,078	3,826	4,822
IN		6	25	147	343	686	988	1,350	1,681	1,978	2,192	2,516
IA						43	192	675	1,194	1,625	1,912	2,232
KS								107	364	996	1,428	1,470
KY	74	221	407	564	688	780	982	1,156	1,321	1,649	1,859	2,147
LA			77	153	216	352	518	708	727	940	1,119	1,382
ME	97	152	229	298	399	502	583	628	627	649	661	694
MD	320	342	381	407	447	470	583	687	781	935	1,042	1,188
MA	379	423	472	523	610	738	995	1,231	1,457	1,783	2,239	2,805
MI			5	9	32	212	398	749	1,184	1,637	2,094	2,421
MN							6	172	440	781	1,310	1,751
MS		8	31	75	137	376	607	791	828	1,132	1,290	1,551
MO			20	67	140	384	682	1,182	1,721	2,168	2,679	3,107
MT									21	39	143	243
NE								29	123	452	1,063	1,066
NV								7	42	62	47	42
NH	142	184	214	244	269	285	318	326	318	347	377	412
NJ	184	211	246	278	321	373	490	672	906	1,131	1,445	1,884
NM								62	92	120	160	195
NY	340	589	959	1,373	1,919	2,429	3,097	3,881	4,383	5,083	6,003	7,269
NC	394	478	556	639	738	753	869	993	1,071	1,400	1,618	1,894
ND									5	2	37	191	319
OH		45	231	581	938	1,519	1,980	2,340	2,665	3,198	3,672	4,158
OK											259	790
OR							12	52	91	175	318	414
PA	434	602	810	1,049	1,348	1,724	2,312	2,906	3,522	4,283	5,258	6,302
RI	69	69	77	83	97	109	148	175	217	277	346	429
SC	249	346	415	503	581	594	669	704	706	996	1,151	1,340
SD									12	98	349	402
TN	36	106	262	423	682	829	1,003	1,110	1,259	1,542	1,768	2,021
TX							213	604	819	1,592	2,236	3,049
UT							11	40	87	144	211	277
VT	85	154	218	236	281	292	314	315	331	332	332	344
VA	692	808	878	938	1,044	1,025	1,119	1,220	1,225	1,513	1,656	1,854
WA								1	12	24	75	357	518
WV	56	79	105	137	177	225	302	377	442	618	763	959
WI						31	305	776	1,055	1,315	1,693	2,069
WY									9	21	63	93
US total[2]	3,929	5,308	7,240	9,638	12,866	17,069	23,192	31,443	39,818[3]	50,156	62,948	75,995

[1]Details may not add to totals given because of rounding. [2]Alaska and Hawaii are not included in the US total until

State Populations, 1790–2006 (continued)

1910	1920	1930	1940	1950	1960	1970	1980	1990	2000	2006 EST.
2,138	2,348	2,646	2,833	3,062	3,267	3,444	3,894	4,040	4,447	4,599
64	55	59	73	129	226	300	402	550	627	670
204	334	436	499	750	1,302	1,771	2,718	3,665	5,131	6,166
1,574	1,752	1,854	1,949	1,910	1,786	1,923	2,286	2,351	2,673	2,811
2,378	3,427	5,677	6,907	10,586	15,717	19,953	23,668	29,811	33,872	36,458
799	940	1,036	1,123	1,325	1,754	2,207	2,890	3,294	4,301	4,753
1,115	1,381	1,607	1,709	2,007	2,535	3,032	3,108	3,287	3,406	3,505
202	223	238	267	318	446	548	594	666	784	853
331	438	487	663	802	764	757	638	607	572	582
753	968	1,468	1,897	2,771	4,952	6,789	9,746	12,938	15,982	18,090
2,609	2,896	2,909	3,124	3,445	3,943	4,590	5,463	6,478	8,186	9,364
192	256	368	423	500	633	769	965	1,108	1,212	1,285
326	432	445	525	589	667	713	944	1,007	1,294	1,466
5,639	6,485	7,631	7,897	8,712	10,081	11,114	11,427	11,431	12,419	12,832
2,701	2,930	3,239	3,428	3,934	4,662	5,194	5,490	5,544	6,080	6,314
2,225	2,404	2,471	2,538	2,621	2,758	2,824	2,914	2,777	2,926	2,982
1,691	1,769	1,881	1,801	1,905	2,179	2,247	2,364	2,478	2,688	2,764
2,290	2,417	2,615	2,846	2,945	3,038	3,219	3,661	3,687	4,042	4,206
1,656	1,799	2,102	2,364	2,684	3,257	3,641	4,206	4,222	4,469	4,288
742	768	797	847	914	969	992	1,125	1,228	1,275	1,322
1,295	1,450	1,632	1,821	2,343	3,101	3,922	4,217	4,781	5,296	5,616
3,366	3,852	4,250	4,317	4,691	5,149	5,689	5,737	6,016	6,349	6,437
2,810	3,668	4,842	5,256	6,372	7,823	8,875	9,262	9,295	9,938	10,096
2,076	2,387	2,564	2,792	2,982	3,414	3,805	4,076	4,376	4,919	5,167
1,797	1,791	2,010	2,184	2,179	2,178	2,217	2,521	2,575	2,845	2,911
3,293	3,404	3,629	3,785	3,955	4,320	4,677	4,917	5,117	5,595	5,843
376	549	538	559	591	675	694	787	799	902	945
1,192	1,296	1,378	1,316	1,326	1,411	1,483	1,570	1,578	1,711	1,768
82	77	91	110	160	285	489	800	1,202	1,998	2,496
431	443	465	492	533	607	738	921	1,109	1,236	1,315
2,537	3,156	4,041	4,160	4,835	6,067	7,168	7,365	7,748	8,414	8,725
327	360	423	532	681	951	1,016	1,303	1,515	1,819	1,955
9,114	10,385	12,588	13,479	14,830	16,782	18,237	17,558	17,991	18,976	19,306
2,206	2,559	3,170	3,572	4,062	4,556	5,082	5,882	6,632	8,049	8,857
577	647	681	642	620	632	618	653	639	642	636
4,767	5,759	6,647	6,908	7,947	9,706	10,652	10,798	10,847	11,353	11,478
1,657	2,028	2,396	2,336	2,233	2,328	2,559	3,025	3,146	3,451	3,579
673	783	954	1,090	1,521	1,769	2,091	2,633	2,842	3,421	3,701
7,665	8,720	9,631	9,900	10,498	11,319	11,794	11,864	11,883	12,281	12,441
543	604	687	713	792	859	947	947	1,003	1,048	1,068
1,515	1,684	1,739	1,900	2,117	2,383	2,591	3,122	3,486	4,012	4,321
584	637	693	643	653	681	666	691	696	755	782
2,185	2,338	2,617	2,916	3,292	3,567	3,924	4,591	4,877	5,689	6,039
3,897	4,663	5,825	6,415	7,711	9,580	11,197	14,229	16,986	20,852	23,508
373	449	508	550	689	891	1,059	1,461	1,723	2,233	2,550
356	352	360	359	378	390	444	511	563	609	624
2,062	2,309	2,422	2,678	3,319	3,967	4,648	5,347	6,189	7,079	7,643
1,142	1,357	1,563	1,736	2,379	2,853	3,409	4,132	4,867	5,894	6,396
1,221	1,464	1,729	1,902	2,006	1,860	1,744	1,950	1,793	1,808	1,818
2,334	2,632	2,939	3,138	3,435	3,952	4,418	4,706	4,892	5,364	5,557
146	194	226	251	291	330	332	470	454	494	515
91,972	105,711	122,775	131,669	150,697	179,323	203,302[3]	226,546[3]	248,791[3]	281,422	299,398

1960, the year after both achieved statehood. [3]Figures were revised by the Census Bureau after the census.

Total US Population and Area, 1790–2000

The total land/water area numbers from 1790 to 1970 were recalculated for the 1980 census. Information for Alaska and Hawaii is included in all censuses after 1940. Source: US Census Bureau.

CENSUS	POPULATION	POPULATION GROWTH (%)	TOTAL LAND/WATER AREA (SQ MI)	LAND AREA (SQ MI)	PEOPLE/ SQ MI OF LAND AREA
1790	3,929,214	—	891,364	864,746	4.5
1800	5,308,483	35.1	891,364	864,746	6.1
1810	7,239,881	36.4	1,722,685	1,681,828	4.3
1820	9,638,453	33.1	1,792,552	1,749,462	5.5
1830	12,866,020	33.5	1,792,552	1,749,462	7.4
1840	17,069,453	32.7	1,792,552	1,749,462	9.8
1850	23,191,876	35.9	2,991,655	2,940,042	7.9
1860	31,443,321	35.6	3,021,295	2,969,640	10.6
1870	39,818,449	26.6	3,612,299	3,540,705	11.2
1880	50,189,209	26.0	3,612,299	3,540,705	14.2
1890	62,979,766	25.5	3,612,299	3,540,705	17.8
1900	76,212,168	21.0	3,618,770	3,547,314	21.5
1910	92,228,496	21.0	3,618,770	3,547,045	26.0
1920	106,021,537	15.0	3,618,770	3,546,931	29.9
1930	123,202,624	16.2	3,618,770	3,551,608	34.7
1940	132,164,569	7.3	3,618,770	3,551,608	37.2
1950	151,325,798	14.5	3,618,770	3,552,206	42.6
1960	179,323,175	18.5	3,618,770	3,540,911	50.6
1970	203,302,031	13.4	3,618,770	3,536,855	57.5
1980	226,542,199	11.4	3,618,770	3,539,289	64.0
1990	248,718,302	9.8	3,717,796	3,536,278	70.3
2000	281,422,509	13.1	3,794,083	3,537,439	79.6

US Population by Race, Sex, Median Age, and Residence

Numbers are in thousands ('000) except for the median age figures and the residency percentages. N/A means not available. Source: US Census Bureau.

YEAR	RACE			SEX		MEDIAN AGE	RESIDENCE[2]	
	WHITE	BLACK	OTHER[1]	MALE	FEMALE		URBAN (%)	RURAL (%)
1790	3,172	757	N/A	N/A	N/A	N/A	5.1	94.9
1800	4,306	1,002	N/A	N/A	N/A	N/A	6.1	93.9
1810	5,862	1,378	N/A	N/A	N/A	N/A	7.3	92.7
1820	7,867	1,772	N/A	4,897	4,742	16.7	7.2	92.8
1830	10,537	2,329	N/A	6,532	6,334	17.2	8.8	91.2
1840	14,196	2,874	N/A	8,689	8,381	17.8	10.8	89.2
1850	19,553	3,639	N/A	11,838	11,354	18.9	15.4	84.6
1860	26,923	4,442	79	16,085	15,358	19.4	19.8	80.2
1870	34,337	5,392	89	19,494	19,065	20.2	25.7	74.3
1880	43,403	6,581	172	25,519	24,637	20.9	28.2	71.8
1890	55,101	7,489	358	32,237	30,711	22.0	35.1	64.9
1900	66,809	8,834	351	38,816	37,178	22.9	39.6	60.4
1910	81,732	9,828	413	47,332	44,640	24.1	45.6	54.4
1920	94,821	10,463	427	53,900	51,810	25.3	51.2	48.8
1930	110,287	11,891	597	62,137	60,638	26.4	56.1	43.9
1940	118,215	12,866	589	66,062	65,608	29.0	56.5	43.5
1950	134,942	15,042	713	74,833	75,864	30.2	64.0	36.0
1960	158,832	18,872	1,620	88,331	90,992	29.5	69.9	30.1
1970	178,098	22,581	2,557	98,926	104,309	28.0	73.6	26.3
1980	194,713	26,683	5,150	110,053	116,493	30.0	73.7	26.3
1990	199,686	29,986	9,233	121,271	127,494	32.8	78.0	22.0
2000	211,461	34,658	13,118	138,054	143,368	35.3	79.0	21.0
2005	237,855	37,909	20,646	146,000	150,411	36.2	N/A	N/A

[1]*"Other" refers to Asians, Pacific Islanders, American Indians, Alaska Natives, and those belonging to two or more races. Alaska and Hawaii are excluded from the population numbers until 1960, the first census after they became states in 1959.*   [2]*The census definitions for urban and rural areas have changed through the decades.*

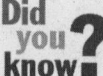

Did you know? Historically, Guinea-Bissau was the center of the Portuguese West African slave trade. Military posts at Cacheu from the early 17th century and at Bissau from the 18th century served as collection points. Slaves were often transported from Guinea-Bissau to the slave trading center of Cape Verde.

US Population by Race and Hispanic Origin

Census 2000 was the first US census in which individuals could report themselves as being of more than one race. For the comparison with the 1990 census results, this table uses the 2000 census information for the population indicating one race. Hispanic or Latino people may be of any race.

Source: US Census Bureau.

RACE	1990 CENSUS NUMBER	%	2000 CENSUS NUMBER	%	% INCREASE FROM 1990 TO 2000
White	199,686,070	80.3	211,460,626	75.1	+5.9
Black or African American	29,986,060	12.1	34,658,190	12.3	+15.6
American Indian or Alaska Native	1,959,234	0.8	2,475,956	0.9	+26.4
Asian	6,908,638	2.8	10,242,998	3.6	+48.3
Native Hawaiian/other Pacific Islander	365,024	0.1	398,835	0.1	+9.3
Some other race	9,804,847	3.9	15,359,073	5.5	+56.6
Two or more races	N/A[1]	N/A	6,826,228	2.4	N/A
Total population	**248,709,873**	**100.0**	**281,421,906**	**100.0[2]**	**+13.2**

HISPANIC OR LATINO POPULATION	1990 CENSUS NUMBER	%	2000 CENSUS NUMBER	%	% DIFFERENCE 1990/2000
Hispanic or Latino (of any race)	22,354,059	9.0	35,305,818	12.5	+57.9
Not Hispanic or Latino	226,355,814	91.0	246,116,088	87.5	+8.7
Total population	**248,709,873**	**100.0**	**281,421,906**	**100.0**	**+13.2**

[1]N/A: not available.   [2]Totals may not equal 100% due to rounding.

Foreign-Born Population in the US, 1850–2005

The foreign-born population consists of persons born outside the United States to parents who were not US citizens. Information from 1950 to 1990 was taken from sample data. Year 2000 information was an estimate derived before the decennial census was conducted. Populations of Alaska and Hawaii were included starting in 1960. In 1850 and 1860, information on nativity was not collected for slaves. The data in the table include the slave population as part of the native-born population.

Source: Statistical Abstract of the United States: 2007.

YEAR	POPULATION TOTAL	FOREIGN-BORN	% OF TOTAL	YEAR	POPULATION TOTAL	FOREIGN-BORN	% OF TOTAL
1850	23,191,876	2,244,602	9.7	1940	131,669,275	11,594,896	8.8
1860	31,443,321	4,138,697	13.2	1950	150,216,110	10,347,395	6.9
1870	38,558,371	5,567,229	14.4	1960	179,325,671	9,738,091	5.4
1880	50,155,783	6,679,943	13.3	1970	203,210,158	9,619,302	4.7
1890	62,622,250	9,249,547	14.8	1980	226,545,805	14,079,906	6.2
1900	75,994,575	10,341,276	13.6	1990	248,709,873	19,767,316	7.9
1910	91,972,266	13,515,886	14.7	2000	274,087,000	28,379,000	10.4
1920	105,710,620	13,920,692	13.2	2004	288,280,000	34,244,000	11.9
1930	122,775,046	14,204,149	11.6	2005	291,155,000	35,157,000	12.1

Total Immigrants Admitted to the US, 1901–2006

Numbers shown include only immigrant aliens admitted for permanent residence and are for fiscal years. Currently the fiscal year begins 1 October and ends 30 September. Prior to 1976, the fiscal year began 1 July and ended 30 June.

YEAR	NUMBER	YEAR	NUMBER	YEAR	NUMBER	YEAR	NUMBER
1901	487,918	1911	878,587	1921	805,228	1931	97,139
1902	648,743	1912	838,172	1922	309,556	1932	35,576
1903	857,046	1913	1,197,892	1923	522,919	1933	23,068
1904	812,870	1914	1,218,480	1924	706,896	1934	29,470
1905	1,026,499	1915	326,700	1925	294,314	1935	34,956
1906	1,100,735	1916	298,826	1926	304,488	1936	36,329
1907	1,285,349	1917	295,403	1927	335,175	1937	50,244
1908	782,870	1918	110,618	1928	307,255	1938	67,895
1909	751,786	1919	141,132	1929	279,678	1939	82,998
1910	1,041,570	1920	430,001	1930	241,700	1940	70,756
Totals 1901–10	8,795,386	1911–20	5,735,811	1921–30	4,107,209	1931–40	528,431

Total Immigrants Admitted to the US, 1901–2006 (continued)

YEAR	NUMBER	YEAR	NUMBER	YEAR	NUMBER	YEAR	NUMBER
1941	51,776	1951	205,717	1961	271,344	1971	370,478
1942	28,781	1952	265,520	1962	283,763	1972	384,685
1943	23,725	1953	170,434	1963	306,260	1973	398,515
1944	28,551	1954	208,177	1964	292,248	1974	393,919
1945	38,119	1955	237,790	1965	296,697	1975	385,378
1946	108,721	1956	321,625	1966	323,040	1976[1]	499,093
1947	147,292	1957	326,867	1967	361,972	1977	458,755
1948	170,570	1958	253,265	1968	454,448	1978	589,810
1949	188,317	1959	260,686	1969	358,579	1979	394,244
1950	249,187	1960	265,398	1970	373,326	1980	524,295
Totals 1941–50	1,035,039	1951–60	2,515,479	1961–70	3,321,677	1971–80	4,399,172

YEAR	NUMBER	YEAR	NUMBER	YEAR	NUMBER
1981	595,014	1991	1,826,595	2001	1,058,902
1982	533,624	1992	973,445	2002	1,059,356
1983	550,052	1993	903,916	2003	703,542
1984	541,811	1994	803,993	2004	957,883
1985	568,149	1995	720,177	2005	1,122,373
1986	600,027	1996	915,560	2006	1,266,264
1987	599,889	1997	797,847		
1988	641,346	1998	653,206		
1989	1,090,172	1999	644,787		
1990	1,535,872	2000	841,002		
Totals 1981–90	7,255,956	1991–2000	9,080,528	2001–06	6,168,320

Totals 1901–2006: 52,943,008

[1]Includes the 15 months from 1 Jul 1975 through 30 Sep 1976.

Immigrants Admitted to the US by Country of Birth and State of Residence

Fiscal Year 2005. Korea used to designate North and South Korea. Source: <www.dhs.gov>.

STATE OF RESIDENCE	TOTAL IMMIGRANTS	TOP FIVE COUNTRIES OF BIRTH (NUMBER OF IMMIGRANTS)
Alabama	4,200	Mexico (569), India (431), China (328), Korea (203), Canada (196)
Alaska	1,525	Philippines (435), Russia (115), Mexico (96), China (92), Ukraine (92)
Arizona	18,988	Mexico (8,373), Canada (769), India (739), Philippines (636), China (543)
Arkansas	2,698	Mexico (870), India (215), China (202), El Salvador (139), Philippines (132)
California	232,023	Mexico (63,092), Philippines (23,993), China (17,668), India (14,724), Vietnam (12,047)
Colorado	11,977	Mexico (2,891), China (765), India (516), Vietnam (452), Canada (432)
Connecticut	15,335	India (1,571), Jamaica (901), China (894), Poland (796), Brazil (743)
Delaware	2,992	India (439), Mexico (357), China (279), Korea (178), Philippines (114)
District of Columbia	2,457	El Salvador (311), Ethiopia (310), China (113), Nigeria (112), Philippines (98)
Florida	122,918	Cuba (30,624), Colombia (9,821), Haiti (7,378), Venezuela (6,182), Jamaica (5,270)
Georgia	31,535	India (3,671), Mexico (3,377), Korea (1,622), China (1,376), Vietnam (1,308)
Hawaii	6,480	Philippines (3,447), China (625), Japan (559), Korea (280), Vietnam (207)
Idaho	2,768	Mexico (992), Bosnia and Herzegovina (353), China (126), Canada (94), Philippines (76)
Illinois	52,419	Mexico (9,838), India (5,978), Poland (5,626), Philippines (2,989), China (2,571)
Indiana	6,915	Mexico (941), India (621), China (541), Philippines (424), Canada (209)
Iowa	4,536	Bosnia and Herzegovina (685), Mexico (647), India (315), Vietnam (275), China (249)
Kansas	4,514	Mexico (955), India (460), Vietnam (352), China (278), Kenya (149)
Kentucky	5,267	Bosnia and Herzegovina (567), India (511), China (393), Cuba (318), Mexico (288)
Louisiana	3,777	Vietnam (342), India (318), China (285), Honduras (231), Mexico (214)
Maine	1,908	Somalia (202), Canada (182), China (124), The Sudan (121), India (108)
Maryland	22,870	India (1,785), China (1,600), El Salvador (1,432), Philippines (1,180), Korea (1,070)

Immigrants Admitted to the US by Country of Birth and State of Residence (continued)

STATE OF RESIDENCE	TOTAL IMMIGRANTS	TOP FIVE COUNTRIES OF BIRTH (NUMBER OF IMMIGRANTS)
Massachusetts	34,236	Brazil (3,588), India (3,100), China (3,000), Dominican Republic (1,946), Haiti (1,221)
Michigan	23,597	India (3,595), Iraq (1,475), China (1,293), Mexico (1,189), Canada (946)
Minnesota	15,546	Somalia (2,223), Ethiopia (1,303), India (830), Liberia (713), Mexico (696)
Mississippi	1,831	Mexico (256), India (224), Philippines (154), China (147), Vietnam (107)
Missouri	8,744	Bosnia and Herzegovina (1,688), India (786), Mexico (535), China (530), Vietnam (343)
Montana	589	Canada (81), Philippines (65), China (41), United Kingdom (36), Russia (33)
Nebraska	2,997	Mexico (538), The Sudan (261), Vietnam (189), India (168), China (141)
Nevada	9,823	Mexico (2,424), Philippines (1,725), China (518), Cuba (416), El Salvador (346)
New Hampshire	3,298	India (459), Bosnia and Herzegovina (277), China (221), Brazil (207), Canada (197)
New Jersey	56,180	India (9,624), Dominican Republic (3,688), Philippines (3,354), Colombia (2,558), China (2,539)
New Mexico	3,513	Mexico (1,828), China (176), India (150), Cuba (128), Vietnam (110)
New York	136,828	China (14,505), Dominican Republic (14,226), India (6,693), Jamaica (6,437), Guyana (6,433)
North Carolina	16,715	Mexico (1,901), India (1,774), China (1,112), Vietnam (1,245), Canada (742)
North Dakota	864	Bosnia and Herzegovina (165), Canada (72), India (49), The Sudan (47), China (43), Germany (43), Philippines (43)
Ohio	16,897	India (1,984), China (1,271), Somalia (764), Ukraine (717), Mexico (700)
Oklahoma	4,702	Mexico (1,238), India (373), Vietnam (351), China (257), Philippines (204)
Oregon	9,623	Mexico (1,632), Ukraine (1,409), China (823), Vietnam (464), Russia (421)
Pennsylvania	28,908	India (3,362), China (2,359), Mexico (1,222), Ukraine (1,176), Korea (1,163)
Rhode Island	3,852	Dominican Republic (639), Guatemala (273), Colombia (250), Liberia (238), Cape Verde (229)
South Carolina	5,029	India (529), Mexico (448), China (315), Canada (261), Philippines (257)
South Dakota	881	The Sudan (113), Ethiopia (81), Bosnia and Herzegovina (63), Philippines (57), China (51)
Tennessee	8,962	Mexico (1,093), India (900), China (637), Philippines (521), Egypt (385)
Texas	95,958	Mexico (38,040), India (7,139), China (4,139), Vietnam (3,919), Philippines (3,353)
Utah	5,082	Mexico (922), Bosnia and Herzegovina (279), China (217), Brazil (184), Canada (170)
Vermont	1,042	Bosnia and Herzegovina (133), Canada (123), India (74), China (50), United Kingdom (43)
Virginia	27,100	India (2,776), El Salvador (1,562), Philippines (1,420), China (1,327), Korea (1,265)
Washington	26,482	Ukraine (4,079), Mexico (2,330), India (1,747), Philippines (1,670), China (1,508)
West Virginia	847	India (133), China (101), Philippines (39), United Kingdom (36), Guatemala (32)
Wisconsin	7,909	Mexico (1,054), India (876), China (593), Canada (303), Bosnia and Herzegovina (273)
Wyoming	321	Mexico (75), Canada (28), China (28), Philippines (23), Russia (13)

Americans 65 and Older, 1900–2007

Data for Hawaii and Alaska are included after 1950. Source: US Census Bureau.

CENSUS YEAR	NUMBER OF PEOPLE 65 AND OLDER	% OF TOTAL POPULATION	CENSUS YEAR	NUMBER OF PEOPLE 65 AND OLDER	% OF TOTAL POPULATION
1900	3,080,498	4.1	1960	16,559,580	9.2
1910	3,949,524	4.3	1970	20,065,502	9.8
1920	4,933,215	4.7	1980	25,549,427	11.3
1930	6,633,805	5.4	1990	31,241,831	12.6
1940	9,019,314	6.8	2000	34,991,753	12.4
1950	12,269,537	8.1	2007	37,849,672	12.6

Poverty Level by State

Source: US Census Bureau. Totals may vary due to rounding.

STATE	% OF PEOPLE IN POVERTY			NUMBER OF PEOPLE IN POVERTY ('000)		
	1980	1990	2005	1980	1990	2005
Alabama	21.2	19.2	16.7	810	779	750
Alaska	9.6	11.4	10.0	36	57	66
Arizona	12.8	13.7	15.2	354	484	917
Arkansas	21.5	19.6	13.9	484	472	382
California	11.0	13.9	13.2	2,619	4,128	4,716
Colorado	8.6	13.7	11.4	247	461	530
Connecticut	8.3	6.0	9.4	255	196	326
Delaware	11.8	6.9	9.3	68	48	78
District of Columbia	20.9	21.1	21.3	131	120	115
Florida	16.7	14.4	11.1	1,692	1,896	1,975
Georgia	13.9	15.8	14.4	727	1,001	1,298
Hawaii	8.5	11.0	8.6	81	121	110
Idaho	14.7	14.9	9.9	138	157	143
Illinois	12.3	13.7	11.5	1,386	1,606	1,441
Indiana	11.8	13.0	12.6	645	714	774
Iowa	10.8	10.4	11.3	311	289	327
Kansas	9.4	10.3	12.5	215	259	337
Kentucky	19.3	17.3	14.8	701	628	599
Louisiana	20.3	23.6	18.3	868	952	748
Maine	14.6	13.1	12.6	158	162	166
Maryland	9.5	9.9	9.7	389	468	542
Massachusetts	9.5	10.7	10.1	542	626	641
Michigan	12.9	14.3	12.0	1,194	1,315	1,196
Minnesota	8.7	12.0	8.1	342	524	412
Mississippi	24.3	25.7	20.1	591	684	571
Missouri	13.0	13.4	11.6	625	700	659
Montana	13.2	16.3	13.8	102	134	128
Nebraska	13.0	10.3	9.5	199	167	167
Nevada	8.3	9.8	10.6	70	119	260
New Hampshire	7.0	6.3	5.6	63	68	73
New Jersey	9.0	9.2	6.8	659	711	592
New Mexico	20.6	20.9	17.9	268	319	347
New York	13.8	14.3	14.5	2,391	2,571	2,760
North Carolina	15.0	13.0	13.1	877	829	1,115
North Dakota	15.5	13.7	11.2	99	87	70
Ohio	9.8	11.5	12.3	1,046	1,256	1,392
Oklahoma	13.9	15.6	15.6	406	481	543
Oregon	11.5	9.2	12.0	309	267	436
Pennsylvania	9.8	11.0	11.2	1,142	1,328	1,372
Rhode Island	10.7	7.5	12.1	97	71	127
South Carolina	16.8	16.2	15.0	534	548	626
South Dakota	18.8	13.3	11.8	127	93	90
Tennessee	19.6	16.9	14.9	884	833	872
Texas	15.7	15.9	16.2	2,247	2,684	3,681
Utah	10.0	8.2	9.2	148	143	232
Vermont	12.0	10.9	7.6	62	61	47
Virginia	12.4	11.1	9.2	647	705	684
Washington	12.7	8.9	10.2	538	434	636
West Virginia	15.2	18.1	15.4	297	328	276
Wisconsin	8.5	9.3	10.2	403	448	553
Wyoming	10.4	11.0	10.6	49	51	54
All US	**13.0**	**13.5**	**12.6**	**29,272**	**33,585**	**36,950**

Population of US Territories

Total midyear population. Source: US Census Bureau.

YEAR	PUERTO RICO	GUAM	VIRGIN ISLANDS	AMERICAN SAMOA	NORTHERN MARIANA ISLANDS
1970	2,721,754	86,470	63,476	27,267	12,359
1975	2,935,124	102,110	94,484	29,640	14,938
1980	3,209,648	106,869	99,636	32,418	16,890
1985	3,382,106	120,615	100,760	38,633	21,386
1990	3,536,910	134,110	104,235	47,199	44,037
1995	3,731,006	143,856	113,896	56,911	58,128
2000	3,915,798	154,623	120,917	65,446	71,912
2007	3,944,259	173,456	108,448	57,663	84,546

States and Other Areas of the United States

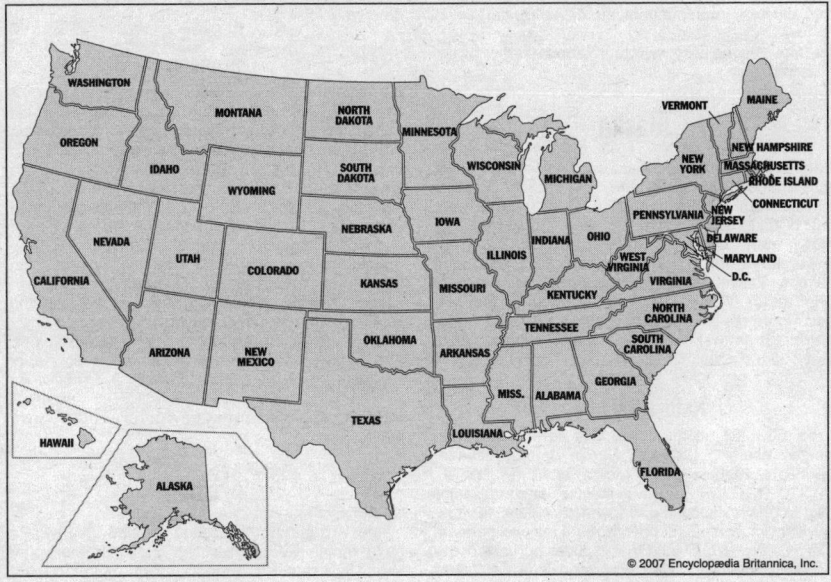

© 2007 Encyclopædia Britannica, Inc.

Alabama

Name: Alabama, from the Choctaw language, meaning "thicket clearers." **Nickname:** Heart of Dixie. **Capital:** Montgomery. **Rank:** population: 23rd; area: 28th; pop. density: 26th. **Motto:** *Audemus Jura Nostra Defendere* (We Dare Defend Our Rights). **Song:** "Alabama," words by Julia S. Tutwiler and music by Edna Gockel Gussen. **Amphibian:** Red Hills salamander. **Bird:** yellowhammer. **Fish:** largemouth bass (freshwater); tarpon (saltwater). **Flower:** camellia. **Fossil:** *Basilosaurus cetoides.* **Gemstone:** star blue quartz. **Insect:** monarch butterfly. **Mineral:** hematite. **Reptile:** Alabama red-bellied turtle. **Rock:** marble. **Tree:** southern longleaf pine.

Natural features

Area: 52,419 sq mi, 135,765 sq km. **Mountain ranges:** Appalachians, Raccoon, Lookout. **Highest point:** Cheaha Mountain, 2,407 ft (734 m). **Largest lake:** Lake Guntersville. **Major rivers:** Mobile, Alabama, Tombigbee, Tennessee, Chattahoochee, Conecuh, Pea, Tensaw, Tallapoosa. **Natural regions:** the Appalachian Plateaus, extending across the north central region; interior low plateaus, far north; valley and ridge province and small portion of the Piedmont Province, covering the east; coastal plain, covering the southern half of the state. **Location:** South, bordering Tennessee, Georgia, Florida, Mississippi. **Climate:** temperate, with mild winters and hot, humid summers; temperatures mellowed by altitude in the northern counties and relatively higher in the southern counties; summer heat is often alleviated by winds blowing in from the Gulf of Mexico. **Land use:** forested, 67.5%; agricultural, 13.8%; pasture, 5.7%; other, 13.0%.

People

Population (2003): 4,501,000; 88.7 persons per sq mi (34.2 persons per sq km) (land area only). **Vital statistics** (2001; per 1,000 population): birth rate, 13.7; death rate, 10.1; marriage rate, 9.6; divorce rate, 5.3. **Major cities:** Birmingham, 239,000; Montgomery, 201,000; Mobile, 195,000; Huntsville, 163,000.

Government

Statehood: entered the Union on 14 Dec 1819 as the 22nd state. **State constitution:** adopted 1901. **Representation in US Congress:** 2 senators; 7 representatives. **Electoral college:** 9 votes (in the 2004 general elections based on the 2000 census). **Political divisions:** 67 counties.

Economy

Employment: services, 25.2%; trade, 21.6%; manufacturing, 16.9%; government, 16.4%; construction, 6.2%; finance, insurance, real estate, 4.9%; transportation, public utilities, 4.6%; agriculture, forestry, fishing, 3.5%; mining, 0.5%. **Production:** manufacturing, 19.0%; services, 16.9%; trade, 16.9%; government, 15.8%; finance, insurance, real estate, 14.7%; transportation, utilities, 8.7%; construction, 4.7%; agriculture, forestry, fisheries, 2.0%; mining, 1.3%. **Chief agricultural products:** *Crops:* cotton, corn, soybeans, peanuts (groundnuts), potatoes, sweet potatoes, peaches, pecans, fruits and vegetables, winter wheat, hay, honey. *Livestock:* cattle, poultry, hogs. *Fish catch:* marine fish, including red snapper; freshwater fish, including catfish; marine crustaceans, including shrimp, crab; marine mollusks, including mussels, oysters. **Chief manufactured products:** food products, meat products, poultry processing, textiles, apparel, wood products, mobile homes, paper and paperboard, petroleum products, plastics and rubber products, iron and steel, aluminum products, semiconductors, electronic components, motor vehicle parts.

Internet resources: <www.touralabama.org>; <www.alabama.gov>.

Alaska

Name: Alaska, from the Aleut word *Alyeska,* meaning "great land." **Nickname:** The Last Frontier. **Capital:** Juneau. **Rank:** population: 47th; area: 1st; pop. density: 50th. **Motto:** North to the Future. **Song:** "Alaska's Flag," words by Marie Drake and music by Elinor Dusenbury. **Bird:** willow ptarmigan. **Fish:** giant king salmon. **Flower:** forget-me-not. **Fossil:** *Mammuthus primigenius* (woolly mammoth). **Gemstone:** jade. **Insect:** four spot skimmer dragonfly. **Mammal:** moose. **Marine mammal:** bowhead whale. **Mineral:** gold. **Tree:** sitka spruce.

Natural features

Area: 663,267 sq mi, 1,717,854 sq km. **Mountain ranges:** Wrangell, Chugach, Alaska, Brooks, Aleutian, Boundary. **Highest point:** Mount McKinley (Denali), 20,320 ft (6,194 m). **Largest lake:** Iliamna. **Major rivers:** Yukon, Porcupine, Tanana, Koyukuk, Noatak, Kuskokwim, Susitna, Copper. **Natural regions:** panhandle, a narrow strip of land that includes portions of the Coast Mountains; coastal archipelago and the Gulf of Alaska islands; the Alaska Peninsula and Aleutian island chain that separates the North Pacific from the Bering Sea; the Alaska Range, extending across the south-central region; the Interior Plateau, including the basin of the Yukon River, and the central plains and tablelands of the interior, the Seward Peninsula to the west, and the Brooks Range, sometimes called the North Slope, to the north; the Arctic Coastal Plain, a treeless region of tundra lying at the northernmost edge of the state; tundra-covered islands of the Bering Sea. **Location:** bordered by Canada. **Climate:** temperate with much regional variation in temperature and precipitation; *southern coastal and southeastern region, Gulf of Alaska and Aleutian islands:* cool summers and moderate winters, with high precipitation; *interior basin:* moderate summers and very cold winters, with low to moderate precipitation; *islands and coast of the Bering Sea:* cool summers and very cold winters; *central plains and uplands:* moderate summers and frigid winters; *North Slope:* moderate summers and frigid winters, though not as severe as interior regions. **Land use:** forested, 24.1 (24)%; pasture, 0.0%; other, 75.6 (76)%.

People

Population (2003): 649,000; 1.1 persons per sq mi (0.4 person per sq km) (land area only). **Vital statistics** (2001; per 1,000 population): birth rate, 16.0; death rate, 4.7; marriage rate, 8.2; divorce rate, 4.1. **Major cities:** Anchorage, 269,000; Juneau (metropolitan area; 2001 est.), 30,558; College, 11,402 (2000); Sitka, 8,716 (2001 est.).

Government

Statehood: entered the Union on 3 Jan 1959 as the 49th state. **State constitution:** adopted 1956. **Representation in US Congress:** 2 senators; 1 representative. **Electoral college:** 3 votes. **Political divisions:** 16 boroughs.

Economy

Employment: services, 26.9%; government, 24.4%; trade, 18.7%; transportation, public utilities, 7.7%; finance, insurance, real estate, 5.3%; construction, 5.1%; manufacturing, 4.8%; agriculture, forestry, fishing, 4.1%; mining, 3.0%. **Production:** mining, 20.1%; government, 19.4%; transportation, utilities, 16.7%; services, 13.0%; trade, 10.1%; finance, insurance, real estate, 10.1%; construction, 4.6%; manufacturing, 4.2%; agriculture, forestry, fishing, 1.7%. **Chief agricultural products:** *Crops:* hay, milk, potatoes, timber. *Livestock:* cattle, pigs. *Fish catch:* marine fish, salmon, herring, groundfish, shellfish, crab, shrimp. **Chief manufactured products:** processed fish and seafood (fresh, frozen, canned, and cured), lumber and wood products, paper products, transportation products.

Internet resources: <www.travelalaska.com>; <www.alaska.gov>.

Arizona

Name: Arizona, from *arizonac,* derived from two Papago Indian words meaning "place of the young spring." **Nickname:** Grand Canyon State. **Capital:** Phoenix. **Rank:** population: 18th; area: 6th; pop. density: 36th. **Motto:** *Ditat Deus* (God Enriches). **Song:** "Arizona March Song," words by Margaret Rowe Clifford and music by Maurice Blumenthal. **Amphibian:** Arizona treefrog. **Bird:** cactus wren. **Fish:** Arizona trout. **Flower:** saguaro blossom. **Fossil:** petrified wood. **Gemstone:** turquoise. **Mammal:** ringtail. **Reptile:** Arizona ridgenose rattlesnake. **Tree:** palo verde.

Natural features

Area: 113,998 sq mi, 295,254 sq km. **Mountain ranges:** Black, Gila Bend, Chuska, Hualapai, San Francisco, White. **Highest point:** Humphreys Peak, 12,633 ft (3,851 m). **Largest lake:** Lake Roosevelt. **Major rivers:** Colorado, Little Colorado, Verde, Salt, Gila. **Natural regions:** the Colorado Plateaus, northeast third of the state, include Grand Canyon and Painted Desert; the basin and range province, south, east, central, and northwest, includes Sonoran Desert in the southwest corner and part of the Great Basin Desert to the northwest. **Location:** Southwest, bordering Utah, Colorado, New Mexico, California, and Nevada; international border with Mexico. **Climate:** varies with location; half of Arizona is semiarid, one-third is arid, and the remainder is humid; *basin and range region:* arid and semiarid to subtropical climate; *Colorado Plateaus:* cool to cold winters and a semiarid climate; *Transition Zone:* climate ranges widely, from arid to humid. **Land use:** pasture, 55.7%; forested, 22.4%; agricultural, 1.7%; other, 20.2%.

People

Population (2003): 5,581,000; 49.1 persons per sq mi (19.0 persons per sq km) (land area only). **Vital statistics (2001; per 1,000 population): birth rate, 17.1; death rate, 7.7; marriage rate, 8.0; divorce rate, 4.2. **Major cities:** Phoenix, 1,372,000; Tucson, 503,000; Mesa, 427,000; Glendale, 231,000; Scottsdale, 216,000; Chandler, 202,000; Tempe, 160,000.

Government

Statehood: entered the Union on 14 Feb 1912 as the 48th state. **State constitution:** adopted 1911. **Representation in US Congress:** 2 senators; 6 representatives. **Electoral college:** 10 votes (in the 2004 general elections based on the 2000 census). **Political divisions:** 15 counties.

Economy

Employment: services, 32.5%; trade, 22.7%; government, 13.4%; manufacturing, 8.8%; finance, insurance, real estate, 8.3%; construction, 6.6%; transportation, public utilities, 4.5%; agriculture, forestry, fishing, 2.6%; mining, 0.6%. **Production:** services, 22.0%; finance, insurance, real estate, 18.7%; trade, 17.4%; manufacturing, 14.4%; government, 12.1%; transportation, public utilities, 7.3%; construction, 5.8%; agriculture, forestry, fishing, 1.5%; mining, 0.8%. **Chief agricultural products:** *Crops:* cotton and cottonseed, wheat, sorghum, hay, barley, corn (maize), potatoes, grapes, apples, vegetables and melons, dairy products, lettuce. *Livestock:* cattle and calves, hogs and pigs, sheep and lambs, angora goats. **Chief manufactured products:** semiconductors, communications equipment, electric and electronic equipment, transportation equipment, soap products, nonferrous metal products.

Internet resources: <www.arizonaguide.com>; <www.az.gov>.

Arkansas

Name: Arkansas, from an unknown Native American word describing the Quapaw tribe (also known as the Arkansaw), meaning "people who live downstream." **Nickname:** The Natural State. **Capital:** Little Rock. **Rank:** population: 32nd; area: 27th; pop. density: 34th. **Motto:** *Regnat Populus* (The People Rule). **Song:** "Arkansas," words and music by Eva Ware Barnett. **Bird:** mockingbird. **Flower:** apple blossom. **Gemstone:** diamond. **Insect:** honeybee. **Mammal:** white-tailed deer. **Mineral:** quartz crystal. **Rock:** bauxite. **Tree:** pine tree.

Natural features

Area: 53,179 sq mi, 137,732 sq km. **Mountain ranges:** Ozark, Ouachita. **Highest point:** Mount Magazine, 2,753 ft (839 m). **Largest lake:** Lake Chicot. **Major rivers:** Arkansas, Red, Ouachita, White. **Natural regions:** the Ozark Plateaus, including the Boston Mountains, north and northwest regions; the Ouachita Province, including the Arkansas valley and the Ouachita Mountains, central region; Coastal Plain, extends from southwest to northeast. **Location:** South, bordering Missouri, Tennessee, Mississippi, Louisiana, Texas, and Oklahoma. **Climate:** temperate, with mild winters and hot summers. **Land use:** forested, 55.2%; agricultural, 30.3%; pasture, 6.0%; other, 8.5%,

People

Population (2003): 2,726,000; 52.4 persons per sq mi (20.2 persons per sq km) (land area only). **Vital statistics** (2001; per 1,000 population): birth rate, 14.3; death rate, 10.3; marriage rate, 14.8; divorce rate, 6.6. **Major cities** (2000): Little Rock, 184,000 (2002); Fort Smith, 80,268; North Little Rock, 60,433; Fayetteville, 58,047; Jonesboro, 55,515.

Government

Statehood: entered the Union on 15 Jun 1836 as the 25th state. **State constitution:** adopted 1874. **Representation in US Congress:** 2 senators; 4 representatives. **Electoral college:** 6 votes (in the 2004 general elections based on the 2000 census). **Political divisions:** 75 counties.

Economy

Employment: services, 24.4%; trade, 21.3%; manufacturing, 18.3%; government, 13.9%; agriculture, forestry, fishing, 6.6%; construction, 5.8%; transportation, public utilities, 5.5%; finance, insurance, real estate, 4.8%; mining, 0.4%. **Production:** manufacturing, 22.5%; trade, 18.4%; services, 15.6%; government, 12.3%; finance, insurance, real estate, 11.6%; transportation, public utilities, 10.5%; construction, 4.6%; agriculture, forestry, fisheries, 3.7%; mining, 0.8%. **Chief agricultural products:** *Crops:* corn (maize), cotton, hay, rice, sorghum, soybeans, wheat, apples, blueberries, grapes, peaches, pecans, strawberries, tomatoes, watermelon. *Livestock:* cattle and calves, hogs and pigs, poultry. *Aquaculture:* catfish. **Chief manufactured products:** food products, meatpacking, poultry processing, lumber, paper and paper products, refined petroleum, chemical products, plastic and rubber products, iron and steel manufacturing, fabricated metal products, machinery, transportation products.

Internet resources: <www.arkansas.com>; <www.arkansas.gov>.

California

Nickname: Golden State. **Capital:** Sacramento. **Rank:** population: 1st; area: 3rd; pop. density: 12th. **Motto:** *Eureka* (I. Have Found It). **Song:** "I Love You, California," words by F.B. Silverwood and music by A.F. Frankenstein. **Bird:** California quail. **Fish:** golden trout (freshwater); garibaldi (saltwater). **Flower:** California poppy. **Fossil:** saber-tooth cat. **Gemstone:** benitoite. **Insect:** California dogface butterfly. **Mammal:** California grizzly bear. **Marine mammal:** California gray whale. **Mineral:** gold. **Reptile:** desert tortoise. **Rock:** serpentine. **Tree:** California redwood.

Natural features

Area: 163,696 sq mi, 423,970 sq km. **Mountain ranges:** Coast Range, Sierra Nevada, Santa Lucia, Cascade Range, Klamath Mountains, Tehachapi Mountains, San Gabriel Mountains, San Bernadino Mountains. **Highest point:** Mount Whitney, 14,494 ft (4,417 m). **Largest lake:** Lake Tahoe. **Major rivers:** Colorado, Sacramento, Pit, San Joaquin. **Natural regions:** Basin and Range Province, northeast corner, also eastern border with Arizona and southern Nevada; Cascade-Sierra Mountains, running from north to south along the east-central region; Pacific Border Province, west, including the Coast Ranges to the west, the Klamath Mountains to the north, the Los Angeles Ranges to the south, and the California Trough (commonly referred to as the Central Valley) to the east; Lower Californian Province, southwest tip. **Location:** West, bordering Oregon, Nevada, and Arizona; international border with Mexico. **Climate:** Mediterranean climate, with moderate temperatures, warm, dry summers, and cool, rainy winters. **Land use:** forested, 32.6%; pasture, 22.4%; agricultural, 10.6%; other, 34.4%.

People

Population (2003): 35,484,000; 227.5 persons per sq mi (87.8 persons per sq km) (land area only). **Vital statistics** (2001; per 1,000 population): birth rate, 15.5; death rate, 6.8; marriage rate, 6.6; divorce rate, 6.6. **Major cities:** Los Angeles, 3,799,000; San Diego, 1,260,000; San Jose, 900,000; San Francisco, 764,000; Long Beach, 472,000; Fresno, 445,000; Sacramento, 435,000; Oakland, 403,000.

Government

Statehood: entered the Union on 9 Sep 1850 as the 31st state. **State constitution:** adopted 1879. **Representation in US Congress:** 2 senators; 52 representatives. **Electoral college:** 55 votes (in the 2004 general elections based on the 2000 census). **Political divisions:** 58 counties.

Economy

Employment: services, 33.8%; trade, 20.7%; government, 13.3%; manufacturing, 11.2%; finance, insurance, real estate, 8.0%; construction, 4.6%; transportation, public utilities, 4.5%; agriculture, forestry, fishing, 3.7%; mining, 0.2%. **Production:** services, 23.4%; finance, insurance, real estate, 21.7%; trade, 15.9%; manufacturing, 14.6%; government, 10.7%; transportation, utilities, 7.3%; construction, 3.8%; agriculture, forestry, fishing, 1.9%; mining, 0.6%. **Chief agricultural products:** *Crops:* wheat, oats, rice, grains, apples, apricots, cherries, grapes, olives, peaches, pears, citrus fruits, strawberries, onions, lima beans, artichokes, broccoli, snap beans, vegetables, dairy products, eggs. *Livestock:* cattle and calves, sheep and lambs. *Fish catch:* bonito, halibut, mackerel, groundfish, rockfish (commonly called Pacific red snapper), sablefish (also called black cod), soles and sanddabs, sardines, white seabass, shark, swordfish, tuna, crab, California spiny lobster, Pacific Ocean (pink) shrimp, prawns, squid. *Extractive products:* timber. **Chief manufactured products:** food products, meat and poultry processing, soft drink products, beer and wine, textiles, apparel, lumber and wood products, paper and paper products, printing, refined petroleum, asphalt, chemical products, pharmaceuticals, plastic and rubber products, glass and glass products, construction materials, steel products, metal products, machinery, communications equipment, semiconductors and computers, electronics, transportation equipment, furniture, medical equipment, sporting goods.

Internet resources: <www.gocalif.com>; <www.ca.gov>.

Colorado

Name: Colorado, from a Spanish word meaning "red." **Nickname:** Centennial State. **Capital:** Denver. **Rank:** population: 22nd; area: 8th; pop. density: 37th. **Motto:** *Nil Sine Numine* (Nothing Without Providence). **Song:** "Where the Columbines Grow," words and music by A.J. Flynn. **Bird:** lark bunting. **Fish:** greenback cutthroat trout. **Flower:** white and lavender columbine. **Fossil:** stegosaurus. **Gemstone:** aquamarine. **Insect:** Colorado hairstreak butterfly. **Mammal:** Rocky Mountain bighorn sheep. **Tree:** Colorado blue spruce.

Natural features

Area: 104,094 sq mi, 269,601 sq km. **Mountain ranges:** Rocky Mountains, Front, Medicine Bow, Park, Rabbit Ears, San Juan Mountains, Sangre de Cristo Range, Sawatch. **Highest point:** Mount Elbert, 14,433 ft (4,399 m). **Largest lakes:** Blue Mesa Reservoir (man-made); Grand Lake (natural). **Major rivers:** Colorado, Arkansas, South Platte, Rio Grande. **Natural regions:** the Great Plains Province, eastern half of state, includes the High Plains to the east, Colorado Piedmont to the west, and Raton Section to the south; Southern Rocky Mountains, running down the middle of the state; Middle Rocky Mountains and Wyoming Basin, northwest corner; Colorado Plateaus, western and southwestern border, include the Uinta Basin to the north, the Canyon Lands in the middle, and the Navajo Section to the south. **Location:** West, bordering Wyoming, Nebraska, Kansas, Oklahoma, New Mexico, and Utah. **Climate:** *Eastern plains:* with hot summers and dry, cold, windy, and generally harsh winters; *piedmont:* similar to eastern plains, also experiences the Chinook wind, a dry, descending winter airstream from the high mountains that is warmed by compression as it descends; *mountains and high plateaus:* cool summers, cold winters and much increased precipitation; snow may fall during any month of the year, with amounts ranging from about 20 to 50 inches. **Land use:** pasture, 42.0%; forest, 28.3%; agricultural, 17.2%; other, 12.5%.

People

Population (2003): 4,551,000; 43.9 persons per sq mi (16.9 persons per sq km) (land area only). **Vital statistics** (2001; per 1,000 population): birth rate, 15.9; death rate, 6.4; marriage rate, 8.7; divorce rate, N/A. **Major cities:** Denver, 560,000; Colorado Springs, 371,000; Aurora, 286,000; Lakewood, 144,000; Fort Collins, 125,000.

Government

Statehood: entered the Union on 1 Aug 1876 as the 38th state. **State constitution:** adopted 1876. **Representation in US Congress:** 2 senators; 6 representatives. **Electoral college:** 9 votes (in the 2004 general elections based on the 2000 census). **Political divisions:** 63 counties.

Economy

Employment: services, 32.3%; trade, 22.0%; government, 13.5%; finance, insurance, real estate, 8.4%; manufacturing, 8.2%; construction, 6.5%; transportation, public utilities, 5.4%; agriculture, forestry, fishing, 2.8%; mining, 0.9%. **Production:** services, 23.1%; finance, insurance, real estate, 17.5%; trade, 16.1%; transportation, utilities, 12.2%; government, 11.9%; manufacturing, 10.2%; construction, 6.0%; mining, 1.6%; agriculture, 1.5%. **Chief agricultural products:** *Crops:* millet, corn (maize), hay, potatoes, onions, sugar beets, sunflowers, wheat, dairy products, eggs, greenhouse products. *Livestock:* cattle and calves, hogs and pigs, sheep and lambs. **Chief manufactured products:** meat products, beverages, printing, semiconductors, computer and electronic products.

Internet resources: <www.colorado.com>; <www.colorado.gov>.

Connecticut

Name: Connecticut, from the Mohegan word *Quinnehtukqut,* meaning "long river place" or "beside the long tidal river." **Nickname:** Constitution State. **Capital:** Hartford. **Rank:** population: 29th; area: 48th; pop. density: 4th. **Motto:** *Qui Transtulit Sustinet* (He Who Transplanted Still Sustains). **Song:** "Yankee Doodle," words from folk tradition, melody from an English tune, "The World Turned Upside Down." **Bird:** robin. **Flower:** mountain laurel. **Fossil:** *Eubrontes giganteus.* **Insect:** praying mantis. **Mammal:** sperm whale. **Mineral:** garnet. **Shellfish:** eastern oyster. **Tree:** white oak.

Natural features

Area: 5,543 sq mi, 14,357 sq km. **Mountain range:** Berkshire Hills. **Highest point:** Mount Frissell, 2,380 ft (725 m). **Largest lake:** Candlewood Lake. **Major rivers:** Connecticut, Housatonic, Thames. **Natural regions:** the New England Province covers the state, divided into the Western Upland, Central Lowland (Connecticut Valley), and Eastern Upland. **Location:** New England, bordering Massachusetts, Rhode Island, and New York. **Climate:** moderate temperate climate; coastal portions have somewhat warmer winters and cooler summers than does the interior; northwestern uplands have cooler and longer winters with heavier falls of snow; occasional hurricanes cause flooding and damage, particularly along the coastline. **Land use:** forest, 54.2%; agricultural, 5.4%; pasture, 1.0%; other, 39.4%.

People

Population (2003): 3,483,000; 718.9 persons per sq mi (277.6 persons per sq km) (land area only). **Vital statistics** (2001; per 1,000 population): birth rate, 12.9; death rate, 8.7; marriage rate, 5.6; divorce rate, 2.9. **Major cities:** Bridgeport, 140,000; Hartford, 125,000; New Haven, 124,000; Stamford, 120,000.

Government

Statehood: entered the Union on 9 Jan 1788 as the 5th state. **State constitution:** adopted 1965. **Representation in US Congress:** 2 senators; 6 representatives. **Electoral college:** 7 votes (in the 2004 general elections based on the 2000 census). **Political divisions:** 8 counties.

Economy

Employment: services, 34.3%; trade, 20.2%; manufacturing, 14.0%; government, 11.2%; finance, insurance, real estate, 9.5%; construction, 4.8%; trans-

portation, public utilities, 4.2%; agriculture, forestry, fishing, 1.5%; mining, 0.1%. **Production:** finance, insurance, real estate, 28.7%; services, 22.0%; manufacturing, 16.5%; trade, 14.5%; government, 8.3%; transportation, utilities, 5.9%; construction, 3.3%; agriculture, 0.7%; mining, 0.1%. **Chief agricultural products:** *Crops:* corn (maize), silage, hay, tobacco, apples, pears, dairy products, eggs. *Livestock:* poultry, cattle, sheep, horses. *Fish catch:* lobster, clams, oysters, shad, marine fish. **Chief manufactured products:** printing, pharmaceutical products, soap and cleaning products, plastics, metal products, machinery, communications equipment, electronics, aerospace products, aircraft engines.

Internet resources: <www.ctbound.org>; <www.ct.gov>.

Delaware

Name: Delaware, from Delaware River and Bay; named in turn for Sir Thomas West, Baron De La Warr. **Nickname:** First State. **Capital:** Dover. **Rank:** population: 45th; area: 49th; pop. density: 6th. **Motto:** Liberty and Independence. **Song:** "Our Delaware," words by George B. Hynson and music by Will M.S. Brown. **Bird:** Blue Hen Chicken. **Fish:** weakfish. **Flower:** peach blossom. **Insect:** ladybug. **Mineral:** sillimanite. **Tree:** American holly.

Natural features

Area: 2,489 sq mi, 6,447 sq km. **Highest point:** Ebright Road, New Castle County, 442 ft (135 m). **Largest lake:** Red Mill Pond. **Major rivers:** Delaware, Nanticoke, Pocomoke. **Natural regions:** the Piedmont Province, including the Piedmont Upland, covers the northernmost tip of the state; the remainder consists of the Coastal Plain. **Location:** East Coast, bordering Pennsylvania, New Jersey, and Maryland. **Climate:** temperate, with high humidity, hot summers and cold winters. **Land use:** agricultural, 36.1%; forest, 30.1%; pasture, 0.6%; other, 33.3%.

People

Population (2003): 817,000; 418.1 persons per sq mi (161.5 persons per sq km) (land area only). **Vital statistics** (2001; per 1,000 population): birth rate, 13.9; death rate, 8.9; marriage rate, 6.7; divorce rate, 4.0. **Major cities** (2000): Wilmington, 72,664; Dover, 32,135; Newark, 28,547.

Government

Statehood: entered the Union on 7 Dec 1787 as the 1st state. **State constitution:** adopted 1897. **Representation in US Congress:** 2 senators; 1 representative. **Electoral college:** 3 votes. **Political divisions:** 3 counties.

Economy

Employment: services, 28.6%; trade, 20.6%; government, 13.5%; finance, insurance, real estate, 12.8%; manufacturing, 12.6%; construction, 6.1%; transportation, public utilities, 3.8%; agriculture, forestry, fishing, 1.9%. **Production:** finance, insurance, real estate, 39.8%; services, 15.5%; manufacturing, 14.2%; trade, 11.1%; government, 9.2%; transportation, utilities, 5.1%; construction, 4.3%; agriculture, 0.8%. **Chief agricultural products:** *Crops:* corn, soybeans, wheat, barley, peas, vegetables, dairy products. *Livestock:* poultry, cattle, hogs. *Fish catch:* crustaceans, crab, clams. **Chief manufactured products:** chemicals, food products, paper products, rubber and plastics products, metal products, printed materials.

Internet resources: <www.visitdelaware.net>; <www. delaware.gov>.

District of Columbia

Motto: *Justitia Omnibus* (Justice for All). **Bird:** woodthrush. **Flower:** American Beauty rose. **Tree:** scarlet oak.

Natural features

Area: 68 sq mi, 177 sq km. **Major river:** Potomac. **Location:** Atlantic seaboard, bordered by Maryland and Virginia. **Climate:** humid, subtropical climate.

People

Population (2003): 563,000; 9,229.5 persons per sq mi (3,540.9 persons per sq km) (land area only). **Vital statistics:** (2001; per 1,000 population): birth rate, 14.8; death rate, 10.4; marriage rate, 6.8; divorce rate, 2.3.

Government

Representation in US Congress: 1 congressional delegate. **Political divisions:** 8 wards.

Economy

Employment (1997): services, 43.5%; government, 36.0%; trade, 7.3%; finance, insurance, real estate, 5.2%; transportation, public utilities, 3.0%; manufacturing, 1.9%; construction, 1.5%; agricultural service, forestry, fishing, 1.4%. **Production** (2000): services, 38.3%; government, 36.6%; finance, insurance, real estate, 13.5%; transportation, utilities, 5.0%; trade, 4.0%; manufacturing, 1.4%; construction, 1.0%; others, 0.2%. **Chief manufactured products:** printing and publishing products.

Internet resources: <www.dc.gov>.

Florida

Name: Florida, in honor of *Pascua florida* ("feast of the flowers"), Spain's Easter celebration. **Nickname:** Sunshine State. **Capital:** Tallahassee. **Rank:** population: 4th; area: 26th; pop. density: 8th. **Motto:** In God We Trust. **Song:** "Old Folks at Home" ("Swanee River"), words and music by Stephen Foster. **Bird:** mockingbird. **Butterfly:** zebra longwing. **Fish:** sailfish (saltwater); largemouth bass (freshwater). **Flower:** orange blossom. **Gemstone:** moonstone. **Mammal:** Florida panther. **Marine mammal:** manatee. **Saltwater mammal:** porpoise. **Reptile:** alligator. **Rock:** agatized coral. **Tree:** sabal palm.

Natural features

Area: 65,755 sq mi, 170,304 sq km. **Highest point:** 345 ft (105 m), in Walton County. **Largest lake:** Lake Okeechobee. **Major rivers:** Kissimmee, Suwannee, St. Johns, Caloosahatchee, Indian, Withlacoochee, Apalachicola, Perdido, St. Marys. **Natural regions:** Western Highlands, a region at the westernmost end of the panhandle; Marianna Lowlands, east of the Western Highlands; Tallahassee Hills, covering the northern border with Georgia; Central Highlands, extending down the middle two-thirds of the peninsula; Coastal Lowlands, curving along the east, south, and west coasts of the peninsula; the Everglades, far southern quarter of the peninsula. **Location:** Southeast, bordering Georgia and Alabama. **Climate:** tropical south of a west–east line drawn from Bradenton along the south shore of Lake Okeechobee to Vero Beach, and subtropical north of this line; hot, humid summers and mild, pleasant winters; hurricane season from June to November. **Land use:** forest, 42.3%; pasture, 15.8%; agricultural, 10.6%; other, 31.4%.

People

Population (2003): 17,019,000; 315.6 persons per sq mi (121.9 persons per sq km) (land area only). **Vital statistics** (2001; per 1,000 population): birth rate, 13.2; death rate, 10.2; marriage rate, 9.7; divorce rate, 5.4. **Major cities:** Jacksonville, 762,000; Miami, 375,000; Tampa, 315,000; St. Petersburg, 249,000; Hialeah, 228,000; Orlando, 194,000; Fort Lauderdale, 158,000; Tallahassee, 155,000.

Government

Statehood: entered the Union on 3 Mar 1845 as the 27th state. **State constitution:** adopted 1968. **Representation in US Congress:** 2 senators; 23 representatives. **Electoral college:** 27 votes (in the 2004 general elections based on the 2000 census). **Political divisions:** 67 counties.

Economy

Employment: services, 35.3%; trade, 23.2%; government, 13.1%; finance, insurance, real estate, 8.2%; manufacturing, 6.4%; construction, 5.7%; transportation, public utilities, 4.8%; agriculture, forestry, fishing, 3.0%; mining, 0.1%. **Production:** services, 24.4%; finance, insurance, real estate, 21.5%; trade, 19.1%; government, 12.2%; transportation, utilities, 8.6%; manufacturing, 7.2%; construction, 5.1%; agriculture, 1.8%; mining, 0.2%. **Chief agricultural products:** *Crops:* citrus fruit, fruits and vegetables, corn (maize), cotton, peanuts (groundnuts), soybeans, sugarcane, tobacco, honey, dairy products, eggs, nursery plants and flowers. *Livestock:* cattle and calves, poultry, hogs and pigs. *Aquaculture:* catfish. *Fish catch:* marine fish, crab, shrimp, oyster. **Chief manufactured products:** food products, meatpacking, soft drinks, apparel, paper products, pesticides and fertilizers, agricultural chemicals, plastics, construction materials, fabricated metal products, machinery, communications equipment, semiconductors, electronics, aerospace products, airplane engines, ships and boats, medical and surgical equipment.

Internet resources: <www.flausa.com>.

For details about state governments, see pages 714–719; for energy data, see pages 737–738.

Georgia

Name: Georgia, named for George II, king of England at the time the colony of Georgia was founded. **Nickname:** Empire State of the South; Peach State. **Capital:** Atlanta. **Rank:** population: 9th; area: 21st; pop. density: 18th. **Mottos:** Wisdom, Justice, and Moderation; Agriculture and Commerce, 1776. **Song:** "Georgia on My Mind," words by Stuart Gorrell and music by Hoagy Carmichael. **Bird:** brown thrasher. **Fish:** largemouth bass. **Flower:** cherokee rose. **Fossil:** shark tooth. **Gemstone:** quartz. **Insect:** honeybee. **Marine mammal:** right whale. **Mineral:** staurolite. **Reptile:** gopher tortoise. **Tree:** live oak.

Natural features

Area: 59,425 sq mi, 153,909 sq km. **Mountain range:** Blue Ridge Mountains. **Highest point:** Brasstown Bald, 4,784 ft (1,458 m). **Largest lake:** Lanier. **Major rivers:** Chattahoochee, Flint, Apalachicola, Ocmulgee, Oconee, Altamaha, Savannah. **Natural regions:** Blue Ridge Province, north-central edge; Valley and Ridge Province, northwest corner; Piedmont Province, northern half of state; Coastal Plain, southern half of state, divided into the Sea Island Section (southeast) and the East Gulf Coastal Plain (southwest). **Location:** South, bordering North Carolina, South Carolina, Florida, Alabama, and Tennessee. **Climate:** temperate, though maritime tropical air masses dominate the climate in summer; generally hot summers and cool winters; precipitation somewhat evenly distributed throughout the seasons in the north, whereas the southern and coastal areas have more summer rains; snow seldom occurs outside the mountainous northern counties. **Land use:** forest, 62.1%; agricultural, 19.8%; pasture, 3.6%; other, 14.6%.

People

Population (2003): 8,685,000; 150.0 persons per sq mi (57.9 persons per sq km) (land area only). **Vital statistics** (2001; per 1,000 population): birth rate, 16.5; death rate, 7.7; marriage rate, 6.3; divorce rate, 3.8. **Major cities:** Atlanta, 425,000; Columbus, 186,000; Savannah, 128,000.

Government

Statehood: entered the Union on 2 Jan 1788 as the 4th state. **State constitution:** adopted 1982. **Representation in US Congress:** 2 senators; 11 representatives. **Electoral college:** 15 votes (in the 2004 general elections based on the 2000 census). **Political divisions:** 159 counties.

Economy

Employment: services, 27.7%; trade, 23.1%; government, 14.9%; manufacturing, 13.5%; finance, insurance, real estate, 6.7%; transportation, public utilities, 5.8%; construction, 5.7%; agriculture, forestry, fishing, 2.5%; mining, 0.2%. **Production:** services, 19.2%; trade, 18.4%; manufacturing, 17.0%; finance, insurance, real estate, 15.3%; government, 11.9%; transportation, utilities, 11.4%; construction, 5.0%; agriculture, 1.3%; mining, 0.5%. **Chief agricultural products:** *Crops:* peanuts (groundnuts), pecans, rye, corn (maize), cotton, cottonseed, hay, oats, sorghum, soybeans, tobacco, wheat, peaches, apples, onions, watermelon, snap beans, cabbage, cucumbers, blueberries, grapes, honey, dairy products. *Livestock:* poultry, pigs, cattle. *Aquaculture:* catfish, trout. *Extractive products:* timber. **Chief manufactured products:** food products, soft drinks, textiles, wood products, paper products, chemical products, transportation equipment.

Internet resources: <www.georgia.org>; <www.georgia.gov>.

Hawaii

Nickname: Aloha State. **Capital:** Honolulu. **Rank:** population: 42nd; area: 47th; pop. density: 13th. **Motto:** *Ua Mau ke Ea o ka Aina i ka Pono* (The Life of the Land Is Perpetuated in Righteousness). **Song:** *"Hawaii Ponoi"* ("Our Hawaii"). **Bird:** nēnē, or Hawaiian goose. **Fish:** rectangular triggerfish (in Hawaiian, *humuhumunukunuku apua'a*). **Flower:** yellow hibiscus (in Hawaiian, *pua ma'o hau hele*). **Gemstone:** black coral. **Marine mammal:** humpback whale. **Tree:** kukui, or candlenut.

Natural features

Area: Total area,10,931 sq mi, 29,311 sq km; the eight largest islands are: *Hawaii:* 4,028 sq mi, 10,433 sq km; *Maui:* 728 sq mi, 1,886 sq km; *Oahu:* 607 sq mi, 1,574 sq km; *Kauai:* 552 sq mi, 1,430 sq km; *Molokai:* 280 sq mi, 725 sq km; *Lanai:* 140 sq mi, 363 sq km; *Niihau:* 72 sq mi, 186 sq km; *Kahoolawe:* 45 sq mi, 117 sq km. **Highest point:** Mauna Kea, Hawaii, 13,796 ft (4,205 m). **Major rivers:** *Hawaii:* Wailuku; *Kauai:* Waimea, Hanalei. **Natural regions:** The eight major islands at the eastern end of the 1,500-mile-long chain of islands are, from west to east, Niihau, Kauai, Oahu, Molokai, Lanai, Kahoolawe, Maui, and Hawaii; each island contains regions of mountains, deeps, ridges, and wide beaches; active volcanoes are found on the island of Hawaii. **Location:** islands surrounded by the Pacific Ocean. **Climate:** tropical; rainfall variations throughout the state are dramatic, ranging from 8.7 inches (220 mm) a year at Kawaihae on the island of Hawaii, to roughly 444 inches (11,280 mm) at Mount Waialeale on the island of Kauai. **Land use:** forest, 28.9%; pasture, 23.4%; agricultural, 7.1%; other, 40.6%.

People

Population (2003): Total, 1,258,000; 195.9 persons per sq mi (75.6 persons per sq km) (land area only). Populations by county (2001 estimates): *Kaui County:* 59,223; *Honolulu County:* 881,295; *Maui County:* 131,662; *Hawaii County:* 152,083. **Vital statistics** (2001; per 1,000 population): birth rate, 14.5; death rate, 6.8; marriage rate, 20.4; divorce rate, 3.8. **Major cities** (2000): Honolulu, 378,000 (2002); Hilo, 40,759; Kailua, 36,513; Kaneohe, 34,970; Waipahu, 33,108.

Government

Statehood: entered the Union on 21 Aug 1959 as the 50th state. **State constitution:** adopted 1950. **Representation in US Congress:** 2 senators; 2 representatives. **Electoral college:** 4 votes. **Political divisions:** 5 counties.

Economy

Employment: services, 31.3%; government, 22.3%; trade, 22.0%; finance, insurance, real estate, 8.4%; transportation, public utilities, 6.3%; construction, 4.2%; agriculture, forestry, fishing, 2.8%; manufacturing, 2.7%; mining, 0.1%. **Production:** finance, insurance, real estate, 23.2%; services, 22.1%; government, 21.8%; trade, 14.7%; transportation, utilities, 10.4%; construction, 4.0%; manufacturing, 2.5%; agriculture, 1.2%; mining, 0.1%. **Chief agricultural products:** *Crops:* pineapples, sugarcane, flowers, macadamia nuts, coffee, milk, eggs. *Livestock:* cattle. *Aquaculture:* fish, shellfish. **Chief manufactured products:** food products, processed sugar, canned pineapple, preserved fruits and vegetables, apparel and textile products, printing and publishing.

Internet resources: <www.gohawaii.com>; <www.hawaii.gov>.

Idaho

Nickname: Gem State. **Capital:** Boise. **Rank:** population: 39th; area: 11th; pop. density: 44th. **Motto:** *Esto Perpetua* (It Is Forever). **Song:** "Here We Have Idaho," words by McKinley Helm and Albert J. Tompkins, music by Sallie Hume Douglas. **Bird:** mountain bluebird. **Fish:** cutthroat trout. **Flower:** syringa. **Fossil:** Hagerman horse fossil (*Equus simplicidens*). **Gemstone:** star garnet. **Horse:** Appaloosa. **Insect:** monarch butterfly. **Tree:** western white pine.

Natural features

Area: 83,570 sq mi, 216,446 sq km. **Mountain ranges:** Northern Rocky Mountains, Middle Rocky Mountains, Sawtooth, Pioneer, Continental Divide, Beaverhead, Clearwater, Bitterroot, Salmon River, Lost River Range, Lemhi Range. **Highest point:** Borah Peak, 12,662 ft (3,859 m). **Largest lake:** Lake Pend Oreille. **Major rivers:** Snake, Salmon. **Natural regions:** Northern Rocky Mountains, covering most of the northern half of the state; Columbia Plateaus, extending across the south-central and southwestern regions; Great Basin region of the Basin and Range Province, southeast; Middle Rocky Mountains, extreme southeast tip. **Location:** Northwest, bordering Montana, Wyoming, Utah, Nevada, Oregon, and Washington; international border with Canada. **Climate:** continental, with warm wet summers and cold dry winters, but regionally diverse: in general, precipitation increases and mean temperatures drop with increases in altitude. **Land use:** pasture, 40.0%; forest, 32.3%; agricultural, 10.9%; other, 16.8%.

People

Population (2003): 1,366,000; 16.5 persons per sq mi (6.4 persons per sq km) (land area only). **Vital statistics** (2001; per 1,000 population): birth rate, 16.0; death rate, 7.4; marriage rate, 11.4; divorce rate, 5.6. **Major cities** (2000): Boise, 190,000 (2002); Nampa, 51,867; Pocatello, 51,466; Idaho Falls, 50,730; Meridian, 34,919.

Government

Statehood: entered the Union on 3 Jul 1890 as the 43rd state. **State constitution:** adopted 1889. **Representation in US Congress:** 2 senators; 2 representatives. **Electoral college:** 4 votes. **Political divisions:** 44 counties.

Economy

Employment: services, 26.1%; trade, 22.7%; government, 15.0%; manufacturing, 11.4%; agriculture, forestry, fishing, 7.5%; construction, 7.1%; finance, insurance, real estate, 5.4%; transportation, public utilities, 4.4%; mining, 0.5%. **Production:** manufacturing, 21.6%; trade, 16.6%; services, 16.3%; government, 13.4%; finance, insurance, real estate, 11.8%; transportation, utilities, 7.8%; construction, 6.6%; agriculture, 5.2%; mining, 0.6%. **Chief agricultural products:** *Crops:* potatoes, wheat, hay, sugar beets, barley, alfalfa seed, Kentucky Blue Grass seed, hops, beans, onions, lentils, peas, honey, dairy products. *Livestock:* cattle, calves, sheep, lambs. *Extractive products:* timber, trout. **Chief manufactured products:** food processing, lumber and wood products, paper, printing, chemicals, plastics and rubber products, nonmetallic mineral products, fabricated metal products, machinery, computers and electronic products, transportation equipment, furniture.

Internet resources: <www.visitid.org>; <www.idaho.gov>.

Illinois

Name: Illinois, from a Native American word meaning "tribe of superior men." **Nickname:** Prairie State. **Capital:** Springfield. **Rank:** population: 5th; area: 24th; pop. density: 11th. **Motto:** State Sovereignty, National Union. **Slogan:** Land of Lincoln. **Song:** "Illinois," words by Charles H. Chamberlain and music by Archibald Johnston. **Bird:** cardinal. **Fish:** bluegill. **Flower:** violet. **Fossil:** tully monster. **Insect:** monarch butterfly. **Mammal:** white-tailed deer. **Mineral:** fluorite. **Tree:** white oak.

Natural features

Area: 57,914 sq mi, 149,998 sq km. **Highest point:** Charles Mound, 1,235 ft (376 m). **Largest lake:** Carlyle Lake. **Major rivers:** Mississippi, Ohio, Wabash. **Natural regions:** central Lowland, a region of sloping hills and broad, shallow river valleys covering almost the entire state; Ozark Plateaus, extreme southwest; Interior Low Plateaus and Coastal Plain, extreme southeastern tip. **Location:** Midwest, bordering Wisconsin, Indiana, Kentucky, Missouri, and Iowa. **Climate:** continental, with hot summers and cold, snowy winters; wide seasonal and regional variations. **Land use:** agricultural, 70.1%; forest, 11.4%; pasture, 4.4%; other, 14.2%.

People

Population (2003): 12,654,000; 227.7 persons per sq mi (87.9 persons per sq km) (land area only). **Vital statistics** (2001; per 1,000 population): birth rate, 15.0; death rate, 8.4; marriage rate, 7.3; divorce rate, 3.2.

For details about state governments, see pages 714–719; for energy data, see pages 737–738.

Major cities: Chicago, 2,886,000; Aurora, 157,000; Rockford, 151,000; Naperville, 135,000; Joliet, 118,000; Peoria, 113,000; Springfield, 112,000.

Government

Statehood: entered the Union on 3 Dec 1818 as the 21st state. State constitution: adopted 1970. Representation in US Congress: 2 senators; 20 representatives. Electoral college: 21 votes (in the 2004 general elections based on the 2000 census). Political divisions: 102 counties.

Economy

Employment: services, 30.9%; trade, 21.2%; manufacturing, 14.0%; government, 12.2%; finance, insurance, real estate, 9.0%; transportation, public utilities, 5.5%; construction, 4.7%; agriculture, forestry, fishing, 2.3%; mining, 0.3%. Production: services, 22.6%; finance, insurance, real estate, 20.4%; manufacturing, 16.3%; trade, 16.2%; government, 9.9%; transportation, utilities, 9.2%; construction, 4.5%; agriculture, 0.8%; mining, 0.3%. Chief agricultural products: Crops: corn (maize), soybeans, wheat, hay, oats, sorghum, apples, peaches, snap beans, sweet corn, potatoes, cabbage, dairy products, eggs. Livestock: pigs, cattle, calves, horses, poultry. Chief manufactured products: food products, beverages, textiles, leather goods, apparel, wood products, paper products, printing, petroleum and coal products, asphalt paving, chemicals, pharmaceuticals, plastics and rubber products, nonmetallic mineral products, iron and steel products, fabricated metals, machinery, computers and electronics, appliances, and transportation equipment.

Internet resources: <www.enjoyillinois.com>; <www.illinois.gov>.

Indiana

Name: Indiana, generally thought to mean "land of the Indians." Nickname: Hoosier State. Capital: Indianapolis. Rank: population: 14th; area: 38th; pop. density: 16th. Motto: The Crossroads of America. Song: "On the Banks of the Wabash, Far Away," words and music by Paul Dresser. Bird: cardinal. Flower: peony. Rock: limestone. Tree: tulip tree (yellow poplar).

Natural features

Area: 36,418 sq mi, 94,321 sq km. Highest point: 1,257 ft (383 m), near Fountain City. Largest lake: Lake Monroe. Major rivers: Wabash, Ohio. Natural regions: Central Lowland comprises most of the state and includes the Eastern Lake section to the north, and the Till Plains in the center; Interior Low Plateaus, including the Highland Rim section, cover the southern quarter of the state. Location: Midwest, bordering Michigan, Ohio, Kentucky, and Illinois. Climate: continental, with four distinct seasons; hot summers, cold winters, mild spring and fall, with increased risk of tornadoes in spring. Land use: agricultural, 59.6%; forest, 18.9%; pasture, 5.0%; other, 16.4%.

People

Population (2003): 6,196,000; 172.7 persons per sq mi (66.7 persons per sq km) (land area only). Vital statistics (2001; per 1,000 population): birth rate,

14.4; death rate, 9.0; marriage rate, 5.7; divorce rate, N/A. Major cities: Indianapolis, 784,000; Fort Wayne, 210,000; Evansville, 119,000; South Bend, 107,000; Gary, 101,000.

Government

Statehood: entered the Union on 11 Dec 1816 as the 19th state. State constitution: adopted 1851. Representation in US Congress: 2 senators; 10 representatives. Electoral college: 11 votes (in the 2004 general elections based on the 2000 census). Political divisions: 92 counties.

Economy

Employment: services, 26.2%; trade, 22.7%; manufacturing, 19.7%; government, 11.7%; finance, insurance, real estate, 6.0%; construction, 5.8%; transportation, public utilities, 4.8%; agriculture, forestry, fishing, 3.0%; mining, 0.3%. Production: manufacturing, 30.9%; services, 16.6%; trade, 15.4%; finance, insurance, real estate, 13.0%; government, 10.0%; transportation, utilities, 7.6%; construction, 5.1%; agriculture, 1.0%; mining, 0.4%. Chief agricultural products: Crops: corn (maize), soybeans, wheat, hay, popcorn, tobacco, tomatoes, peppermint, spearmint, watermelon, blueberries, snap beans, cucumbers, apples, milk, eggs. Livestock: pigs, cattle, calves, poultry. Chief manufactured products: iron and steel, metal products, motor vehicle parts, machinery, food products, dairy products, soft drinks, wood products, paper products, mobile homes, asphalt.

Internet resources: <www.enjoyindiana.com>; <www.in.gov>.

Iowa

Name: Iowa, named for the Iowa (or Ioway) Indians who once inhabited the area. Nickname: Hawkeye State. Capital: Des Moines. Rank: population: 30th; area: 23rd; pop. density: 33rd. Motto: Our Liberties We Prize and Our Rights We Will Maintain. Song: "The Song of Iowa," words by S.H.M. Byers, to the tune of "O Tannenbaum." Bird: eastern goldfinch. Flower: wild rose. Rock: geode. Tree: oak.

Natural features

Area: 56,272 sq mi, 145,743 sq km. Highest point: near Sibley, 1,670 ft (509 m). Largest lake: Spirit Lake. Major rivers: Des Moines, Mississippi, Missouri, Big Sioux. Natural regions: overall, Central Lowland, including the Western Lake section, north and central regions; Dissected Till Plains, south; Wisconsin Driftless Section, northeast corner. Location: Midwest, bordering Minnesota, Wisconsin, Illinois, Missouri, Nebraska, and South Dakota. Climate: continental, with hot summers and cold, snowy winters. Land use: agricultural, 78.1%; forest, 5.4%; pasture, 4.1%; other, 12.4%.

People

Population (2003): 2,944,000; 52.7 persons per sq mi (20.3 persons per sq km) (land area only). Vital statistics (2001; per 1,000 population): birth rate, 13.0; death rate, 9.5; marriage rate, 7.2; divorce rate, 3.2. Major cities: Des Moines, 198,000; Cedar

Rapids, 123,000; Davenport, 98,359 (2000); Sioux City, 85,013 (2000); Waterloo, 68,747 (2000).

Government

Statehood: entered the Union on 28 Dec 1846 as the 29th state. **State constitution:** adopted 1857. **Representation in US Congress:** 2 senators, 5 representatives. **Electoral college:** 7 votes. **Political divisions:** 99 counties.

Economy

Employment: services, 26.8%; trade, 22.4%; manufacturing, 14.0%; government, 13.2%; agriculture, forestry, fishing, 7.7%; finance, insurance, real estate, 6.2%; construction, 5.1%; transportation, public utilities, 4.4%; mining, 0.1%. **Production:** manufacturing, 22.4%; services, 17.0%; trade, 16.9%; finance, insurance, real estate, 15.1%; government, 12.0%; transportation, utilities, 8.5%; construction, 4.4%; agriculture, 3.5%; mining, 0.3%. **Chief agricultural products:** *Crops:* corn (maize), soybeans, hay, oats, grain, milk, eggs, butter, honey, popcorn, sorghum. *Livestock:* poultry, hogs and pigs, beef cattle, sheep. **Chief manufactured products:** food products, dairy products, meatpacking, pesticide, fertilizer, and other agricultural chemicals, farm machinery, construction machinery, household appliances, motor vehicle parts.

Internet resources: <www.traveliowa.com>; <www.iowa.gov>.

Kansas

Name: Kansas, from the Sioux word *kansa* ("people of the south wind") for the Native Americans who lived in the region. **Nickname:** Sunflower State. **Capital:** Topeka. **Rank:** population: 33rd; area: 13th; pop. density: 40th. **Motto:** *Ad Astra Per Aspera* (To the Stars Through Difficulties). **Song:** "Home on the Range," words by Brewster Higley and music by Dan Kelly. **Amphibian:** barred tiger salamander. **Bird:** western meadowlark. **Flower:** wild native sunflower. **Insect:** honeybee. **Mammal:** American buffalo. **Reptile:** ornate box turtle. **Tree:** cottonwood.

Natural features

Area: 82,277 sq mi, 213,096 sq km. **Highest point:** Mount Sunflower, 4,039 ft (1,231 m). **Largest lake:** Milford Lake. **Major rivers:** Kansas, Arkansas, Big Blue, Republican, Solomon, Saline, Smoky Hill, Cimarron, Verdigris, Neosho (Grand). **Natural regions:** the Great Plains Province, covering the western half of the state, consists of the High Plains to the west and the Plains Border to the east; the Central Lowland covers the eastern half of the state and consists of the Dissected Till Plains to the north and the Osage Plains to the south. **Location:** Midwest, bordering Nebraska, Missouri, Oklahoma, and Colorado. **Climate:** temperate but continental, with great extremes between summer and winter temperatures but few long periods of extreme hot or cold. **Land use:** agricultural, 64.4%; pasture, 24.0%; forest, 2.8%; other, 8.8%.

People

Population (2003): 2,724,000; 33.3 persons per sq mi (12.9 persons per sq km) (land area only). **Vital statistics** (2001; per 1,000 population): birth rate, 14.5; death rate, 9.1; marriage rate, 7.6; divorce rate, 3.2. **Major cities:** Wichita, 355,000; Overland Park, 158,000; Kansas City, 147,000; Topeka, 122,000; Olathe, 101,000.

Government

Statehood: entered the Union on 29 Jan 1861 as the 34th state. **State constitution:** adopted 1859. **Representation in US Congress:** 2 senators; 4 representatives. **Electoral college:** 6 votes. **Political divisions:** 105 counties.

Economy

Employment: services, 26.5%; trade, 22.2%; government, 16.0%; manufacturing, 12.6%; agriculture, forestry, fishing, 5.9%; finance, insurance, real estate, 5.7%; construction, 5.2%; transportation, public utilities, 4.9%; mining, 1.2%. **Production:** trade, 18.2%; services, 17.4%; manufacturing, 16.8%; government, 13.5%; finance, insurance, real estate, 12.9%; transportation, utilities, 12.5%; construction, 4.6%; agriculture, 2.9%; mining, 1.3%. **Chief agricultural products:** *Crops:* wheat, corn (maize), sorghum, hay, soybeans, sunflower seed and oil, apples, peaches, pecans. *Livestock:* beef cattle and calves, hogs, lambs, sheep, dairy cows, horses and other equines. **Chief manufactured products:** food products, grain and oilseed milling, meat products, printing, refined petroleum, soap and cleaning products, plastic products, aerospace products and parts, aircraft.

Internet resources: <www.travelks.com>; <www.accesskansas.org>.

Kentucky

Name: Kentucky, possibly from the Iroquois word for "prairie." **Nickname:** Bluegrass State. **Capital:** Frankfort. **Rank:** population: 26th; area: 36th; pop. density: 22nd. **Motto:** United We Stand, Divided We Fall. **Song:** "My Old Kentucky Home," words and music by Stephen Foster. **Bird:** cardinal. **Butterfly:** viceroy butterfly. **Fish:** Kentucky bass. **Flower:** goldenrod. **Horse:** Thoroughbred. **Tree:** tulip poplar. **Wild animal:** gray squirrel.

Natural features

Area: 40,409 sq mi, 104,659 sq km. **Mountain ranges:** Cumberland, Pine. **Highest point:** Black Mountain, 4,145 ft (1,263 m). **Largest lake:** Kentucky Lake. **Major rivers:** Mississippi, Ohio, Big Sandy, Licking, Kentucky, Salt, Green, Tradewater, Cumberland, Tennessee. **Natural regions:** Appalachian Plateaus, eastern third of the state; Interior Low Plateaus, including the Highland Rim section and the Lexington Plain, cover the remainder, with the exception of the Coastal Plain, which covers the extreme southwest tip. **Location:** Midwest, bordering Indiana, Ohio, West Virginia, Virginia, Tennessee, Missouri, and Illinois. **Climate:** temperate continental climate,

For details about state governments, see pages 714–719; for energy data, see pages 737–738.

with hot, humid summers and cold winters. **Land use:** forest, 48.6%; agricultural, 34.8%; pasture, 5.9%; other, 10.7%.

People

Population (2003): 4,118,000; 103.7 persons per sq mi (40.0 persons per sq km) (land area only). **Vital statistics** (2001; per 1,000 population): birth rate, 13.6; death rate, 9.8; marriage rate, 9.1; divorce rate, 5.5. **Major cities** (2000): Lexington-Fayette, 264,000 (2002); Louisville, 251,000 (2002); Owensboro, 54,067; Bowling Green, 49,296; Covington, 43,370.

Government

Statehood: entered the Union on 1 Jun 1792 as the 15th state. **State constitution:** adopted 1891. **Representation in US Congress:** 2 senators; 6 representatives. **Electoral college:** 8 votes. **Political divisions:** 120 counties.

Economy

Employment: services, 25.4%; trade, 21.7%; government, 14.9%; manufacturing, 14.9%; agriculture, forestry, fishing, 6.4%; construction, 5.8%; transportation, public utilities, 5.2%; finance, insurance, real estate, 4.5%; mining, 1.2%. **Production:** manufacturing, 27.5%; services, 16.0%; trade, 15.7%; government, 13.5%; finance, insurance, real estate, 10.9%; transportation, utilities, 8.0%; construction, 4.5%; mining, 2.1%; agriculture, 1.8%. **Chief agricultural products:** *Crops:* tobacco, soybeans, corn (maize), wheat, hay, sorghum, eggs, dairy products. *Livestock:* racing and show horses, beef and dairy cattle, hogs, poultry, sheep. **Chief manufactured products:** food products, meat packing, beverages, tobacco, apparel, paper products, printing, chemical products, paint, resin and synthetic rubber products, plastic products, iron and steel, aluminum, fabricated metal products, machinery, appliances, motor vehicles.

Internet resources: <www.kentuckytourism.com>; <www.kentucky.gov>.

Louisiana

Name: Louisiana, named for Louis XIV, king of France. **Nickname:** Pelican State. **Capital:** Baton Rouge. **Rank:** population: 24th; area: 33rd; pop. density: 23rd. **Motto:** Union, Justice and Confidence. **Songs:** "Give Me Louisiana," words and music by Doralice Fontane, arranged by John W. Schaum; "You Are My Sunshine," words and music by Jimmy H. Davis and Charles Mitchell. **Amphibian:** green tree frog. **Bird:** brown pelican. **Crustacean:** crawfish. **Freshwater fish:** white perch. **Flower:** magnolia. **Fossil:** petrified palmwood. **Gemstone:** agate. **Insect:** honeybee. **Mammal:** black bear. **Reptile:** alligator. **Tree:** bald cypress.

Natural features

Area: 51,840 sq mi, 134,264 sq km. **Highest point:** Driskill Mountain, 535 ft (163 m). **Largest lake:** Lake Ponchartrain. **Major rivers:** Mississippi, Red, Sabine. **Natural regions:** the entire state consists of the Coastal Plain and is divided into the West Gulf Coastal Plain to the west, the Mississippi Alluvial Plain to the northeast, and the East Gulf Coastal Plain in the southeast. **Location:** South, bordering Arkansas, Mississippi, and Texas. **Climate:** subtropical, with hot, humid summers, tempered by frequent afternoon thunder showers, alternating with mild winters; subject to tropical storms: the hurricane season extends for six months, from June through November. **Land use:** forest, 49.1%; agricultural, 19.7%; pasture, 5.7%; other, 25.6%.

People

Population (2003): 4,496,000; 103.2 persons per sq mi (39.8 persons per sq km) (land area only). **Vital statistics** (2001; per 1,000 population): birth rate, 14.9; death rate, 9.3; marriage rate, 8.6; divorce rate, N/A. **Major cities:** New Orleans, 474,000; Baton Rouge, 226,000; Shreveport, 199,000; Lafayette, 111,000.

Government

Statehood: entered the Union on 30 Apr 1812 as the 18th state. **State constitution:** adopted 1974. **Representation in US Congress:** 2 senators; 7 representatives. **Electoral college:** 9 votes. **Political divisions:** 64 parishes.

Economy

Employment: services, 29.2%; trade, 21.6%; government, 17.4%; manufacturing, 8.7%; construction, 6.8%; transportation, public utilities, 5.6%; finance, insurance, real estate, 5.3%; agriculture, forestry, fishing, 2.8%; mining, 2.7%. **Production:** services, 17.6%; manufacturing, 15.2%; trade, 15.1%; finance, insurance, real estate, 13.0%; government, 12.3%; mining, 11.7%; transportation, utilities, 9.2%; construction, 4.9%; agriculture, 1.0%. **Chief agricultural products:** *Crops:* soybeans, cotton, corn (maize), sorghum, hay, sugarcane, rice, wheat, sweet potatoes, pecans, strawberries, peaches, milk, eggs. *Livestock:* cattle, chickens, hogs. *Aquaculture:* catfish, crawfish. *Fish catch:* shrimp, oysters, marine fish, freshwater fish. *Extractive products:* timber. **Chief manufactured products:** industrial chemicals, agricultural chemicals, plastics materials and resins, petroleum refining, cane sugar products, beverages, food products, paper, metal products, wood products, communications equipment, ships and boats.

Internet resources: <www.louisianatravel.com>; <www.louisiana.gov>.

Maine

Name: Maine, possibly named for the former French province of Maine, or used to distinguish the mainland portion of the territory from offshore islands. **Nickname:** Pine Tree State. **Capital:** Augusta. **Rank:** population: 40th; area: 39th; pop. density: 38th. **Motto:** *Dirigo* (I Direct). **Song:** "State of Maine Song," words and music by Roger Vinton Snow. **Bird:** chickadee. **Fish:** landlocked salmon. **Flower:** white pine cone and tassel. **Fossil:** *Pertica quadrifaria.* **Gemstone:** tourmaline. **Insect:** honeybee. **Mammal:** moose. **Tree:** white pine.

Natural features

Area: 35,385 sq mi, 91,646 sq km. **Mountain ranges:** Appalachians, Longfellow. **Highest point:** Mount Katahdin, 5,268 ft (1,606 m). **Largest lake:** Moosehead Lake. **Major rivers:** Saco, Androscoggin, Kennebec, Penobscot, St. John's, St. Croix, Allagash. **Natural regions:** entire state is part of the larger New England Province, subdivided into the White Mountain section (southwest), Seaboard Lowland Section (southeast coastline), and New England Upland Section (north and central regions). **Location:** New England, bordering New Hampshire; international border with Canada. **Climate:** cool maritime climate, with coldest temperatures and greatest snowfall occurring in northern regions. **Land use:** forest, 85.8%; agricultural, 2.4%; pasture, 0.2%; other 11.6%.

People

Population (2003): 1,306,000; 42.3 persons per sq mi (16.3 persons per sq km) (land area only). **Vital statistics** (2001; per 1,000 population): birth rate, 10.9; death rate, 9.7; marriage rate, 9.0; divorce rate, 3.9. **Major cities** (2000): Portland, 64,249; Lewiston, 35,690; Bangor, 31,473; South Portland, 23,324; Auburn, 23,203.

Government

Statehood: entered the Union on 15 Mar 1820 as the 23rd state. **State constitution:** adopted 1819. **Representation in US Congress:** 2 senators; 2 representatives. **Electoral college:** 4 votes. **Political divisions:** 16 counties.

Economy

Employment: services, 30.2%; trade, 23.0%; government, 13.7%; manufacturing, 13.1%; construction, 6.3%; finance, insurance, real estate, 5.9%; transportation, public utilities, 4.1%; agriculture, forestry, fishing, 3.7%. **Production:** services, 20.1%; finance, insurance, real estate, 18.8%; trade, 18.0%; manufacturing, 15.4%; government, 14.0%; transportation, utilities, 7.0%; construction, 4.6%; agriculture, forestry, fishing 2.0%. **Chief agricultural products:** *Crops:* potatoes, blueberries, hay, apples, cranberries, oats, honey, corn (maize), dairy products, eggs. *Livestock:* poultry, cattle, sheep. *Aquaculture:* salmon, rainbow trout. *Fish catch:* marine fish, lobster, shrimp, crab, clams, haddock, cod, mackerel. *Extractive industries:* timber. **Chief manufactured products:** paper, leather, lumber and wood products, food products, semiconductors, apparel, printing and publishing, plastic products, ships and boats.

Internet resources: <www.visitmaine.com>; <www.maine.gov>.

Maryland

Name: Maryland, in honor of Henrietta Maria (queen of Charles I of England). **Nickname:** Old Line State. **Capital:** Annapolis. **Rank:** population: 19th; area: 42nd; pop. density: 5th. **Motto:** *Fatti Maschii, Parole Femine* (Manly Deeds, Womanly Words). **Song:** "Maryland, My Maryland," words by James Ryder Randall, to the tune of "Lauriger Horatius." **Bird:** Baltimore oriole. **Crustacean:** Maryland blue crab. **Dinosaur:** *Astrodon johnstoni.* **Fish:** rockfish (striped bass). **Flower:** black-eyed Susan. **Insect:** Baltimore checkerspot. **Reptile:** diamondback terrapin. **Tree:** white oak.

Natural features

Area: 12,407 sq mi, 32,133 sq km. **Mountain ranges:** Allegheny Mountains, Appalachians. **Highest point:** Backbone Mountain, 3,360 ft (1,024 m). **Largest lake:** Deep Creek Lake. **Major rivers:** Potomac, Patuxent, Susquehanna. **Natural regions:** Coastal Plain, eastern half of the state, includes the Embayed Section near the southwest corner of the peninsula; Piedmont Province, central, and including the Piedmont Upland to the north and the Piedmont Lowlands to the west; Blue Ridge Province, northwest; Valley and Ridge Province, part of western neck; Appalachian Plateau, extreme western neck. **Location:** East coast, bordering Pennsylvania, Delaware, District of Columbia, Virginia, and West Virginia. **Climate:** continental in the west, but a humid, subtropical climate prevails in the east; hurricanes often bring much rain to eastern regions. **Land use:** forest, 38.7%; agricultural, 24.9%; pasture, 3.3%; other, 33.1%.

People

Population (2003): 5,509,000; 563.6 persons per sq mi (217.6 persons per sq km) (land area only). **Vital statistics** (2001; per 1,000 population): birth rate, 13.9; death rate, 8.1; marriage rate, 7.1; divorce rate, 3.0. **Major cities** (2000): Baltimore, 639,000 (2002); Frederick, 52,767; Gaithersburg, 52,613; Bowie, 50,269; Rockville, 47,388.

Government

Statehood: entered the Union on 28 Apr 1788 as the 7th state. **State constitution:** adopted 1867. **Representation in US Congress:** 2 senators; 8 representatives. **Electoral college:** 10 votes. **Political divisions:** 23 counties.

Economy

Employment: services, 34.4%; trade, 21.1%; government, 17.3%; finance, insurance, real estate, 8.3%; manufacturing, 6.4%; construction, 6.3%; transportation, public utilities, 4.4%; agriculture, forestry, fishing, 1.8%; mining, 0.1%. **Production:** services, 24.2%; finance, insurance, real estate, 21.3%; government, 17.5%; trade, 15.2%; manufacturing, 8.1%; transportation, utilities, 7.5%; construction, 5.4%; agriculture, 0.8%; mining, 0.1%. **Chief agricultural products:** *Crops:* corn (maize), soybeans, wheat, vegetables, potatoes, tobacco, dairy products, eggs. *Livestock:* cattle, pigs, poultry. *Aquaculture:* hybrid striped bass, catfish, tilapia, trout, oysters. *Fish catch:* blue crab, other crustaceans, oysters, mollusks, marine fish. **Chief manufactured products:** primary metals, ships and boats, food products, motor vehicles, chemical products, paper and printing, plastics and rubber, fabricated metal products, machinery, computers and electronics, transportation equipment.

For details about state governments, see pages 714–719; for energy data, see pages 737–738.

Internet resources: <www.mdisfun.org>; <www.maryland.gov>.

Massachusetts

Name: Massachusetts, named for the Massachusett tribe of Native Americans who lived in the Great Blue Hill region south of Boston; the word *Massachusett* means "at or about the great hill." Nickname: Bay State. Capital: Boston. Rank: population: 13th; area: 45th; pop. density: 3rd. Motto: *Ense Petit Placidam Sub Libertate Quietem* (By the Sword We Seek Peace, but Peace Only Under Liberty). Song: "All Hail to Massachusetts," words and music by Arthur J. Marsh. Bird: black-capped chickadee. Fish: cod. Flower: mayflower. Fossil: theropod dinosaur tracks. Gemstone: rhodonite. Insect: ladybug. Marine mammal: right whale. Mineral: babingtonite. Rock: Roxbury puddingstone. Tree: American elm.

Natural features

Area: 10,555 sq mi, 27,336 sq km. Mountain ranges: Berkshire Mountains, Hoosac Range, Taconic Range. Highest point: Mount Greylock, 3,491 ft (1,064 m). Largest lake: Webster Lake. Major rivers: Connecticut, Charles, Merrimack, Housatonic, Taunton. Natural regions: the New England Province, comprising most of the state, subdivided into the Taconic Section along the west, the New England Upland Section in the central region, and the Seaboard Lowland Section covering the eastern third of the state; Coastal Plain, comprising the peninsula region. Location: New England, bordering New Hampshire, Rhode Island, Connecticut, New York, and Vermont. Climate: temperate continental climate, with cold snowy winters and warm, humid summers; climate is colder but drier in western Massachusetts, although its winter snowfalls may be more severe. Land use: forest, 53.3%; agricultural, 4.2%; pasture, 0.7%; other, 41.8%.

People

Population (2003): 6,433,000; 820.5 persons per sq mi (316.8 persons per sq km) (land area only). Vital statistics (2001; per 1,000 population): birth rate, 13.0; death rate, 8.9; marriage rate, 6.4; divorce rate, 2.4. Major cities: Boston, 589,000; Worcester, 175,000; Springfield, 152,000; Lowell, 105,000; Cambridge, 102,000.

Government

Statehood: entered the Union on 6 Feb 1788 as the 6th state. State constitution: adopted 1780. Representation in US Congress: 2 senators; 10 representatives. Electoral college: 12 votes. Political divisions: 14 counties.

Economy

Employment: services, 38.2%; trade, 20.6%; manufacturing, 11.9%; government, 11.2%; finance, insurance, real estate, 8.2%; construction, 4.6%; transportation, public utilities, 4.1%; agriculture, forestry, fishing, 1.3%; mining, 0.1%. Production: services, 26.8%; finance, insurance, real estate, 24.5%; trade, 15.3%; manufacturing, 13.9%; government, 9.1%; transportation, utilities, 5.6%; construction, 4.1%;

agriculture, 0.5%. Chief agricultural products: *Crops:* tobacco, cranberries, hay, potatoes, sweet corn, dairy products, eggs. *Livestock:* cattle, poultry. *Fish catch:* marine fish, lobster, crab, mollusks. *Aquaculture:* oysters, quahogs, soft-shelled clams, scallops. Chief manufactured products: Food products, dairy products, soft drinks, textiles, paper products, printing, pharmaceuticals, plastic products, nonferrous metal products, fabricated metal products, machinery, communications equipment, semiconductors and electronics, electrical equipment, software, aerospace equipment, aircraft engines, surgical and medical equipment.

Internet resources: <www.mass-vacation.com>; <www.mass.gov>.

Michigan

Name: Michigan, from Native American word *Michigana* meaning "great, or, large lake." Nicknames: Wolverine State and Great Lake State. Capital: Lansing. Rank: population: 8th; area: 22nd; pop. density: 15th. Motto: *Si Quaeris Peninsulam Amoenam, Circumspice* (If You Seek a Pleasant Peninsula, Look Around You). Song: "Michigan, My Michigan," words by Giles Kavanagh and music by H.J. O'Reilly Clint. Bird: robin. Fish: brook trout. Flower: apple blossom. Gemstone: chlorastrolite. Mammal: white-tailed deer (game mammal). Reptile: painted turtle. Rock: Petoskey stone. Tree: white pine.

Natural features

Area: 96,716 sq mi, 250,494 sq km. Highest point: Mount Arvon, 1,980 ft (604 m). Largest lake: Houghton Lake. Major rivers: Montreal, Brule, Menominee, St. Clair. Natural regions: the Central Lowland, Eastern Lake Section, covers all of Lower Michigan and part of the Upper Peninsula region; the western half of the Upper Peninsula consists of Superior Upland, as do two small areas at the eastern end. Location: Midwest, bordering Ohio, Indiana, and Wisconsin; international border with Canada. Climate: continental; the Great Lakes cool the hot winds of summer and warm the cold winds of winter, giving Michigan a milder climate than some other north-central states, although the Upper Peninsula is relatively cooler; very high snowfall along the coast of Lake Michigan. Land use: forest, 51.3%; agricultural, 22.8%; pasture, 4.4%; other, 21.4%.

People

Population (2003): 10,080,000; 177.5 persons per sq mi (68.5 persons per sq km) (land area only). Vital statistics (2001; per 1,000 population): birth rate, 13.4; death rate, 8.6; marriage rate, 6.7; divorce rate, 3.9. Major cities: Detroit, 925,000; Grand Rapids, 197,000; Warren, 138,000; Flint, 122,000; Sterling Heights, 126,000; Lansing, 119,000; Ann Arbor, 115,000; Livonia, 100,000.

Government

Statehood: entered the Union on 26 Jan 1837 as the 26th state. State constitution: adopted 1963. Representation in US Congress: 2 senators; 16 representatives. Electoral college: 17 votes (in the 2004 general elections based on the 2000 census). **Political divisions:** 83 counties.

Economy

Employment: services, 29.2%; trade, 22.2%; manufacturing, 18.4%; government, 12.1%; finance, insurance, real estate, 6.9%; construction, 4.9%; transportation, public utilities, 3.8%; agriculture, forestry, fishing, 2.3%; mining, 0.2%. **Production:** manufacturing, 26.2%; services, 19.6%; trade, 17.1%; finance, insurance, real estate, 14.1%; government, 10.3%; transportation, utilities, 6.6%; construction, 4.8%; agriculture, 0.9%; mining, 0.3%. **Chief agricultural products:** *Crops:* apples, asparagus, beans, blueberries, carrots, celery, cherries, corn (maize), flowers, grapes and wine, honey, wool, maple syrup, mint, onions, peaches, plums, potatoes, dairy products, eggs, strawberries, sugar, soybeans. *Livestock:* beef and dairy cattle and calves, pigs, poultry, sheep and lambs. *Aquaculture:* Rainbow, brook and brown trout, yellow perch, catfish. *Extractive industries:* Christmas trees. **Chief manufactured products:** Motor vehicles, salt, plastics, pharmaceuticals, soaps and cleansers, milled grain, dry cereals, agricultural machinery, office furniture, dairy products, preserved fruits and vegetables, printed matter, electrical equipment, construction materials, measuring and control devices.

Internet resources: <www.michigan.org>; <www.michigan.gov>.

Minnesota

Name: Minnesota, from a Dakota word meaning "sky-tinted water." **Nickname:** North Star State. **Capital:** St. Paul. **Rank:** population: 21st; area: 14th; pop. density: 31st. **Motto:** *L'Étoile du Nord* (The Star of the North). **Song:** "Hail! Minnesota," first verse and music by Truman E. Rickard, second verse by Arthur E. Upson. **Bird:** common loon. **Fish:** walleye pike. **Flower:** pink and white lady slipper. **Gemstone:** Lake Superior agate. **Insect:** monarch butterfly. **Tree:** Norway pine.

Natural features

Area: 86,939 sq mi, 225,171 sq km. **Mountain ranges:** Mesabi, Vermillion, Cuyuna. **Highest point:** Eagle Mountain, 2,301 ft (701 m). **Largest lake:** Red Lake. **Major rivers:** Minnesota, St. Croix, Mississippi. **Natural regions:** Superior Upland, northeast corner; Central Lowland, covering most of the state; Western Lake Section, center; Dissected Till Plains, extreme southwest corner and south-central edge; Wisconsin Driftless Section, extreme southeast. **Location:** North central, bordering Wisconsin, Iowa, South Dakota, and North Dakota; international border with Canada. **Climate:** continental, with very cold winters and warm summers. **Land use:** agricultural, 44.8 (45)%; forest, 29.1 (29)%; pasture, 3.0%; other, 23.1 (23)%.

People

Population (2003): 5,059,000; 63.5 persons per sq mi (24.5 persons per sq km) (land area only). **Vital statistics** (2001; per 1,000 population): birth rate, 13.8; death rate, 7.6; marriage rate, 6.8; divorce rate, 3.3 **Major cities** (2000) Minneapolis, 376,000

(2002); St. Paul, 284,000 (2002); Duluth, 86,918; Rochester, 85,806; Bloomington, 85,172.

Government

Statehood: entered the Union on 11 May 1858 as the 32nd state. **State constitution:** adopted 1857. **Representation in US Congress:** 2 senators; 8 representatives. **Electoral college:** 10 votes. **Political divisions:** 87 counties.

Economy

Employment: services, 30.3%; trade, 22.0%; manufacturing, 14.3%; government, 12.0%; finance, insurance, real estate, 7.6%; transportation, public utilities, 4.7%; construction, 4.6%; agriculture, forestry, fishing, 4.2%; mining, 0.3%. **Production:** services, 20.8%; finance, insurance, real estate, 18.5%; manufacturing, 18.1%; trade, 17.6%; government, 10.2%; transportation, utilities, 7.6%; construction, 5.0%; agriculture, 1.7%; mining, 0.5%. **Chief agricultural products:** *Crops:* corn (maize), green peas, dry beans, onions, carrots, apples, oats, hay, spring wheat, barley, soybeans, potatoes, sugar beets, flaxseed, dairy products, eggs. *Livestock:* pigs, cattle and calves, poultry, sheep and lambs. **Chief manufactured products:** food processing, beer and malt beverages, dairy products, meatpacking, industrial machinery, computers and office machines, electronics and electric equipment, precision instruments, printing and publishing, call centers and communications, information technology, forest products, medical manufacturing, plastics manufacturing.

Internet resources: <www.exploreminnesota.com>; <www.state.mn.us>.

Mississippi

Name: Mississippi, from a Native American word meaning "great waters" or "father of waters." **Nickname:** Magnolia State. **Capital:** Jackson. **Rank:** population: 31st; area: 31st; pop. density: 32nd. **Motto:** *Virtute et Armis* (By Valor and Arms). **Song:** "Go, Mississippi," words and music by Houston Davis. **Bird:** mockingbird. **Fish:** largemouth bass. **Flower:** magnolia. **Fossil:** prehistoric whale. **Insect:** honeybee. **Mammal:** white-tailed deer. **Marine mammal:** bottle-nosed dolphin (porpoise). **Rock:** petrified wood. **Tree:** magnolia tree.

Natural features

Area: 48,430 sq mi, 125,434 sq km. **Highest point:** Woodall Mountain, 806 ft (246 m). **Major rivers:** Mississippi, Pearl, Big Black, Yazoo, Tombigbee, Pascagoula, Tennessee. **Natural regions:** the entire state consists of the Coastal Plain, subdivided into the Mississippi Alluvial Plain in the west, and the East Gulf Coastal Plain comprising the central and eastern regions. **Location:** South, bordering Tennessee, Alabama, Louisiana, and Arkansas. **Climate:** mild, with hot, humid summers and mild winters; coastal area is subject to hurricanes from June to October. **Land use:** forest, 61.9%; agricultural, 21.5%; pasture, 6.5%; other, 10.1%.

For details about state governments, see pages 714–719; for energy data, see pages 737–738.

People

Population (2003): 2,881,000; 61.4 persons per sq mi (23.7 persons per sq km) (land area only). **Vital statistics** (2001; per 1,000 population): birth rate, 15.1; death rate, 9.9; marriage rate, 6.7; divorce rate, 5.4. **Major cities** (2000): Jackson, 181,000 (2002); Gulfport, 71,127; Biloxi, 50,644; Hattiesburg, 44,779; Greenville, 41,633.

Government

Statehood: entered the Union on 10 Dec 1817 as the 20th state. **State constitution:** adopted 1890. **Representation in US Congress:** 2 senators; 5 representatives. **Electoral college:** 6 votes (in the 2004 general elections based on the 2000 census). **Political divisions:** 82 counties.

Economy

Employment: services, 24.5%; trade, 19.7%; government, 17.8%; manufacturing, 17.5%; construction, 5.5%; agriculture, forestry, fishing, 5.2%; finance, insurance, real estate, 4.7%; transportation, public utilities, 4.5%; mining, 0.6%. **Production:** manufacturing, 20.6%; services, 17.4%; trade, 16.8%; government, 16.0%; finance, insurance, real estate, 11.4%; transportation, utilities, 9.5%; construction, 4.7%; agriculture, 2.6%; mining, 1.0%. **Chief agricultural products:** *Crops:* cotton, soybeans, rice, wheat, corn, greenhouse and nursery plants, sweet potatoes, pecans, eggs. *Livestock:* poultry, cattle. *Aquaculture:* catfish, pearl farming. *Fish catch:* marine fish, freshwater fish, shrimp, oysters, crustaceans. *Extractive industries:* timber. **Chief manufactured products:** food products, transportation equipment, apparel, textiles, paper, electrical equipment, rubber products, primary metal products.

Internet resources: <www.visitmississippi.org>; <www.mississippi.gov>.

Missouri

Name: Missouri, named for Native American tribe that lived in the region; the name means "town of the large canoes." **Nickname:** Show Me State. **Capital:** Jefferson City. **Rank:** population: 17th; area: 18th; pop. density: 28th. **Motto:** *Salus Populi Suprema Lex Esto* (The Welfare of the People Shall Be the Supreme Law). **Song:** "Missouri Waltz," words by J.R. Shannon and music by John Valentine Eppel, arrangement by Frederick Knight Logan. **Aquatic animal:** paddlefish. **Bird:** bluebird. **Fish:** channel catfish. **Flower:** white hawthorn blossom. **Fossil:** crinoid. **Insect:** honeybee. **Mammal:** Missouri mule. **Mineral:** galena. **Rock:** mozarkite. **Tree:** flowering dogwood.

Natural features

Area: 69,704 sq mi, 180,533 sq km. **Mountain ranges:** Ozark Plateau, St. Francois Mountains. **Highest point:** Taum Sauk Mountain, 1,772 ft (540 m). **Largest lake:** Truman Lake. **Major rivers:** Missouri, Mississippi, Des Plaines. **Natural regions:** the Central Lowland, northwestern, subdivided into the Dissected Till Plains to the north and the Osage Plains to the west; Ozark Plateaus, including the Springfield-Salem Plateaus, southeast; Coastal Plain, including the Mississippi Alluvial Plain, extreme southeast tip. **Location:**

Midwest, bordering Iowa, Illinois, Kentucky, Tennessee, Arkansas, Oklahoma, Kansas, and Nebraska. **Climate:** continental, with hot, humid summers and cold winters; lies in "Tornado Alley," the zone of maximum tornado occurrence, and has an average of 27 tornadoes annually. **Land use:** agricultural, 45.4%; forest, 30.4%; pasture, 13.6%; other, 10.6%.

People

Population (2003): 5,704,000; 82.8 persons per sq mi (32.0 persons per sq km) (land area only). **Vital statistics** (2001; per 1,000 population): birth rate, 13.6; death rate, 9.8; marriage rate, 7.6; divorce rate, 4.3. **Major cities:** Kansas City, 443,000; St. Louis, 338,000; Springfield, 152,000; Independence, 113,000.

Government

Statehood: entered the Union on 10 Aug 1821 as the 24th state. **State constitution:** adopted 1945. **Representation in US Congress:** 2 senators; 9 representatives. **Electoral college:** 11 votes. **Political divisions:** 114 counties.

Economy

Employment: services, 29.3%; trade, 21.8%; government, 13.3%; manufacturing, 12.9%; finance, insurance, real estate, 6.8%; transportation, public utilities, 5.8%; construction, 5.5%; agriculture, forestry, fishing, 4.5%; mining, 0.2%. **Production:** services, 20.5%; manufacturing, 19.3%; trade, 17.1%; finance, insurance, real estate, 15.3%; government, 11.4%; transportation, utilities, 10.1%; construction, 4.9%; agriculture, 1.1%; mining, 0.3%. **Chief agricultural products:** *Crops:* soybeans, corn (maize), cotton, rice, grain sorghum, hay, wheat, fruits and vegetables, dairy products. *Livestock:* cattle, pigs, sheep, poultry. *Extractive industries:* timber. **Chief manufactured products:** industrial machinery, transportation equipment, food processing, malt beverages, soft drinks, meat and poultry products, preserved fruits and vegetables, soaps and detergents, agricultural chemicals, pharmaceuticals, printing and publishing, primary metals, nonelectrical machinery, fabricated metals, petroleum and coal products, electrical equipment, stone, clay and glass products.

Internet resources: <www.missouritourism.org>; <www.missouri.gov>.

Montana

Name: Montana, from the Spanish word *montaña* ("mountain," or "mountainous region"). **Nickname:** Treasure State. **Capital:** Helena. **Rank:** population: 44th; area: 4th; pop. density: 48th. **Motto:** *Oro y Plata* (Gold and Silver). **Song:** "Montana," words by Charles C. Cohan and music by Joseph E. Howard. **Bird:** western meadowlark. **Fish:** cutthroat trout. **Flower:** bitterroot. **Fossil:** *Maiasaura*. **Gemstones:** agate and sapphire. **Mammal:** grizzly bear. **Tree:** ponderosa pine.

Natural features

Area: 147,042 sq mi, 380,838 sq km. **Mountain ranges:** Rocky Mountains, Grand Tetons. **Highest**

point: Granite Peak, 12,799 ft (3,901 m). **Largest lake:** Flathead Lake. **Major rivers:** Kootenai, Clark Fork, Flathead, Missouri, Yellowstone. **Natural regions:** Northern Rocky Mountains, western two-fifths of the state; Middle Rocky Mountains, small area along the south-central border; Missouri Plateau region of the Great Plains Province, eastern three-fifths of the state. **Location:** Northwest, bordering North Dakota, South Dakota, Wyoming, and Idaho; international border with Canada. **Climate:** continental; most of Great Plains region is semiarid, with warm summers and cold winters; west of the Rocky Mountains the climate is milder. **Land use:** pasture, 49.4%; forest, 20.6%; agricultural, 19.9%; other, 10.1%.

People

Population (2003): 918,000; 6.3 persons per sq mi (2.4 persons per sq km) (land area only). **Vital statistics** (2001; per 1,000 population): birth rate, 12.3; death rate, 9.1; marriage rate, 7.2; divorce rate, 2.6. **Major cities** (2000): Billings, 89,847; Missoula, 57,053; Great Falls, 56,690; Butte-Silver Bow, 34,606; Bozeman, 27,509; Helena, 25,780.

Government

Statehood: entered the Union on 8 Nov 1889 as the 41st state. **State constitution:** adopted 1972. **Representation in US Congress:** 2 senators; 1 representative. **Electoral college:** 3 votes. **Political divisions:** 56 counties.

Economy

Employment: services, 30.4%; trade, 23.4%; government, 15.5%; agriculture, forestry, fishing, 6.7%; finance, insurance, real estate, 6.1%; construction, 6.1%; manufacturing, 5.6%; transportation, public utilities, 5.0%; mining, 1.3%. **Production:** services, 20.3%; trade, 16.9%; government, 16.4%; finance, insurance, real estate, 13.7%; transportation, utilities, 11.9%; manufacturing, 7.5%; construction, 5.6%; agriculture, 4.0%; mining, 3.7%. **Chief agricultural products:** *Crops:* wheat, barley, hay, oats, safflowers, sunflowers, mustard, sugar beets, dry beans, grapes, garlic, oil seeds, corn (maize), potatoes, honey, cherries, dairy products. *Livestock:* beef and dairy cattle and calves, sheep and lambs, poultry, horses, llamas. *Extractive industries:* timber, Christmas trees. **Chief manufactured products:** food processing, lumber and wood products, metal processing, petroleum products, chemical manufacturing, cement and concrete products, fabricated metal products, machinery.

Internet resources: <www.visitmt.com>; <www.mt.gov>.

Nebraska

Name: Nebraska, from a Native American word meaning "flat water," a reference to the Platte River. **Nickname:** Cornhusker State. **Capital:** Lincoln. **Rank:** population: 38th; area: 15th; pop. density: 42nd. **Motto:** Equality Before the Law. **Song:** "Beautiful Nebraska," words and music by Jim Fras. **Bird:** western meadowlark. **Fish:** channel catfish. **Flower:** goldenrod. **Fossil:** mammoth. **Gemstone:** blue agate. **Insect:**

honeybee. **Mammal:** white-tailed deer. **Rock:** prairie agate. **Tree:** cottonwood.

Natural features

Area: 77,354 sq mi, 200,345 sq km. **Highest point:** 5,424 ft (1,653 m), in Johnson Township, southwestern part of Kimball County. **Largest lake:** Lake McConaughy. **Major rivers:** Missouri, Platte, Elkhorn, Loup, Republican, Big Blue, Niobrara. **Natural regions:** Great Plains Province, western three-quarters of the state; Missouri Plateau at the northern corners; High Plains, central and north central; Plains Border, south border; Central Lowland, including the Dissected Till Plains, eastern quarter of the state. **Location:** Central, bordering South Dakota, Iowa, Missouri, Kansas, Colorado, and Wyoming. **Climate:** continental, with hot summers and very cold winters; blizzards are not uncommon in winter; western half of state is semiarid. **Land use:** agricultural, 47.9%; pasture, 44.4%; forest, 1.6%; other, 6.1%.

People

Population (2003): 1,739,000; 22.6 persons per sq mi (8.7 persons per sq km) (land area only). **Vital statistics** (2001; per 1,000 population): birth rate, 14.8; death rate, 8.8; marriage rate, 8.1; divorce rate, 3.7. **Major cities** (2000): Omaha, 399,000 (2002); Lincoln, 232,000 (2002); Bellevue, 44,382; Grand Island, 42,940; Kearney, 27,431.

Government

Statehood: entered the Union on 1 Mar 1867 as the 37th state. **State constitution:** adopted 1875. **Representation in US Congress:** 2 senators; 3 representatives. **Electoral college:** 5 votes. **Political divisions:** 93 counties.

Economy

Employment: services, 28.1%; trade, 22.2%; government, 14.1%; manufacturing, 10.4%; agriculture, forestry, fishing, 7.3%; finance, insurance, real estate, 7.2%; transportation, public utilities, 5.5%; construction, 5.0%; mining, 0.2%. **Production:** services, 19.1%; trade, 16.7%; finance, insurance, real estate, 15.5%; government, 14.1%; manufacturing, 14.0%; transportation, utilities, 10.8%; agriculture, 4.8%; construction, 4.8%; mining, 0.1%. **Chief agricultural products:** *Crops:* corn (maize), soybeans, hay, wheat, sorghum, dry edible beans, sugar beets. *Livestock:* beef and dairy cattle, pigs, sheep, poultry. **Chief manufactured products:** meatpacking, canned and frozen fruits and vegetables, flour, cereal, grain products, beverages, dairy products, livestock feeds, transportation equipment, motorcycles, small commercial vehicles, printing and publishing, rubber and plastic goods, fabricated metals, primary metals.

Internet resources: <www.visitnebraska.org>; <www.nebraska.gov>.

Nevada

Name: Nevada, from the Spanish *nevada* ("snow clad"), a reference to the high mountain scenery of the

Sierra Nevada on the southwestern border with California. **Nicknames:** Sagebrush State and Silver State. **Capital:** Carson City. **Rank:** population: 35th; area: 7th; pop. density: 43rd. **Motto:** All for Our Country. **Song:** "Home Means Nevada," words and music by Bertha Raffeto. **Bird:** mountain bluebird. **Fish:** Lahontan cutthroat trout. **Flower:** sagebrush. **Fossil:** ichthyosaur. **Gemstones:** fire opal, turquoise. **Mammal:** desert bighorn sheep. **Metal:** silver. **Reptile:** desert tortoise. **Rock:** sandstone. **Trees:** single-leaf piñon and bristlecone pine.

Natural features

Area: 110,561 sq mi, 286,351 sq km. **Mountain ranges:** Snake, Schell Creek, Monitor, Toiyabe, Shoshone, Humboldt, Santa Rosa. **Highest point:** Boundary Peak, 13,140 ft (4,005 m). **Largest lakes:** Pyramid Lake (natural), Lake Mead (artificial). **Major rivers:** Humboldt, Truckee, Carson, Walker, Muddy, Virgin. **Natural regions:** Basin and Range Province covers all of the state, except for the southwestern corner, which consists of the Cascade-Sierra Mountains, and the northeastern corner, which comprises part of the Columbia Plateau. **Location:** West, bordering Idaho, Utah, Arizona, California, and Oregon. **Climate:** semiarid but with regional variation: northern and eastern areas have long, cold winters and short, relatively hot summers, whereas in southern Nevada the summers are long and hot and the winters brief and mild. **Land use:** pasture, 65.9%; forest, 11.7%; agricultural, 1.2%; other, 21.2%.

People

Population (2003): 2,241,000; 20.4 persons per sq mi (7.9 persons per sq km) (land area only). **Vital statistics** (2001; per 1,000 population): birth rate, 16.1; death rate, 7.8; marriage rate, 75.0; divorce rate, 6.8. **Major cities:** Las Vegas, 509,000; Reno, 190,000; Henderson, 206,000; North Las Vegas, 136,000; Sparks, 66,346 (2000).

Government

Statehood: entered the Union on 31 Oct 1864 as the 36th state. **State constitution:** adopted 1864. **Representation in US Congress:** 2 senators; 2 representatives. **Electoral college:** 5 votes (in the 2004 general elections based on the 2000 census). **Political divisions:** 16 counties; 1 independent city.

Economy

Employment: services, 42.2%; trade, 19.5%; government, 10.7%; construction, 8.9%; finance, insurance, real estate, 7.0%; transportation, public utilities, 4.7%; manufacturing, 4.1%; agriculture, forestry, fishing, 1.5%; mining, 1.5%. **Production:** services, 32.5%; finance, insurance, real estate, 16.9%; trade, 15.0%; government, 10.3%; construction, 10.2%; transportation, utilities, 8.0%; manufacturing, 4.1%; mining, 2.2%; agriculture, 0.7%. **Chief agricultural products:** *Crops:* hay, wheat, corn (maize), potatoes, rye, oats, alfalfa, barley, vegetables, dairy products, some fruits. *Livestock:* cattle, horses, sheep, hogs, poultry. **Chief manufactured products:** food processing, candy, frozen desserts, dairy products, soft drinks, paper products, chemical products, plastics, construction materials, industrial machinery, printing and publishing.

Internet resources: <www.travelnevada.com>; <www.nevada.gov>.

New Hampshire

Name: New Hampshire, named for Hampshire, England, by Captain John Mason. **Nickname:** Granite State. **Capital:** Concord. **Rank:** population: 41st; area: 44th; pop. density: 19th. **Motto:** Live Free or Die. **Songs:** "Old New Hampshire," words by John F. Holmes and music by Maurice Hoffmann; "New Hampshire, My New Hampshire," words by Julius Richelson and music by Walter P. Smith. **Amphibian:** red-spotted newt. **Bird:** purple finch. **Fish:** brook trout (freshwater); striped bass (saltwater). **Flower:** purple lilac. **Gemstone:** smokey quartz. **Insect:** ladybug. **Mammal:** white-tailed deer. **Mineral:** beryl. **Rock:** granite. **Tree:** white birch.

Natural features

Area: 9,350 sq mi, 24,216 sq km. **Mountain ranges:** White Mountains, Ossipee, Sandwich Range, Presidential Range. **Highest point:** Mount Washington, 6,288 ft (1,917 m). **Largest lake:** Lake Winnipesaukee. **Major rivers:** Merrimack, Salmon Falls, Connecticut, Saco, Piscataqua, Androscoggin. **Natural regions:** the New England Province covers the entire state, and is subdivided into the White Mountain Section occupying the northern third, the New England Upland Section in the south-central region, and the Seaboard Lowland Section in the southeast corner. **Location:** New England, bordering Maine, Massachusetts, and Vermont; international border with Canada. **Climate:** temperate, but highly varied: winter temperatures may drop below 0 °F (−18 °C) for days at a time; summers are relatively cool, and precipitation is rather evenly distributed over the four seasons. **Land use:** forest, 79.3%; agricultural, 2.0%; pasture, 0.7%; other, 18.1%.

People

Population (2003): 1,288,000; 143.6 persons per sq mi (55.5 persons per sq km) (land area only). **Vital statistics** (2001; per 1,000 population): birth rate, 11.9; death rate, 7.8; marriage rate, 8.6; divorce rate, 5.0. **Major cities** (2000): Manchester, 108,000 (2002); Nashua, 86,605; Concord, 40,687; Derry, 34,021; Rochester, 28,461.

Government

Statehood: entered the Union on 21 Jun 1788 as the 9th state. **State constitution:** adopted 1784. **Representation in US Congress:** 2 senators; 2 representatives. **Electoral college:** 4 votes. **Political divisions:** 10 counties.

Economy

Employment: services, 31.5%; trade, 24.0%; manufacturing, 15.5%; government, 10.9%; finance, insurance, real estate, 6.9%; construction, 6.0%; transportation, public utilities, 3.5%; agriculture, forestry, fishing, 1.6%; mining, 0.1%. **Production:** finance, insurance, real estate, 23.2%; manufacturing, 22.1%; services, 19.6%; trade, 16.5%; government, 7.8%; transportation, utilities, 5.8%; construction, 4.1%; agriculture, 0.7%; mining, 0.1%. **Chief agricultural**

products: *Crops:* apples, honey, fruits and vegetables, ornamental horticulture, Christmas trees, dairy products, eggs, herbs, maple syrup, wool. *Livestock:* horses, dairy cattle, sheep. *Fish catch:* marine fish, seafood. *Extractive products:* timber. **Chief manufactured products:** industrial machinery, computers and software, electrical equipment, semiconductors, processed foods, precision instruments, medical and surgical instruments, fabricated metal products, rubber and plastic products, printing and publishing, paper products.

Internet resources: <www.visitnh.gov>; <www.state. nh.us>.

New Jersey

Name: New Jersey, named for the island of Jersey in the English Channel. **Nickname:** Garden State. **Capital:** Trenton. **Rank:** population: 10th; area: 46th; pop. density: 1st. **Motto:** Liberty and Prosperity. **Bird:** eastern goldfinch. **Fish:** brook trout. **Flower:** violet. **Fossil:** *Hadrosaurus foulkii.* **Insect:** honeybee. **Mammal:** horse. **Tree:** red oak.

Natural features

Area: 8,721 sq mi, 21,588 sq km. **Mountain range:** Appalachians. **Highest point:** Kittatinny Mountain, 1,803 ft (550 m). **Largest lake:** Lake Hopatcong. **Major rivers:** Delaware, Hudson, Passaic, Hackensack, Raritan. **Natural regions:** the Valley and Ridge Province, Middle Section, northwest corner; the New England Province, consisting of the New England Upland Section, located east of the Valley and Ridge area; Piedmont Province, including the Piedmont Lowlands, extending from the northeast corner to part of the border with Pennsylvania; the southern half of the state consists of the Coastal Plain, Embayed Section. **Location:** Northeast, bordering New York, Delaware, and Pennsylvania. **Climate:** continental; relatively colder winters in northwest, milder conditions in the south, and hot summers throughout the state. **Land use:** forest, 31.7%; agricultural, 13.4%; pasture, 0.6%; other, 54.3%.

People

Population (2003): 8,638,000; 1,164.6 persons per sq mi (449.6 persons per sq km) (land area only). **Vital statistics** (2001; per 1,000 population): birth rate, 14.0; death rate, 8.8; marriage rate, 6.6; divorce rate, 3.5. **Major cities:** Newark, 277,000; Jersey City, 240,000; Paterson, 151,000; Elizabeth, 123,000; Trenton, 85,403 (2000).

Government

Statehood: entered the Union on 18 Dec 1787 as the 3rd state. **State constitution:** adopted 1947. **Representation in US Congress:** 2 senators; 13 representatives. **Electoral college:** 15 votes. **Political divisions:** 21 counties.

Economy

Employment: services, 32.8%; trade, 21.6%; government, 13.0%; manufacturing, 11.0%; finance, insurance, real estate, 9.7%; transportation, public utili-

ties, 6.3%; construction, 4.3%; agriculture, forestry, fishing, 1.2%; mining, 0.1%. **Production:** finance, insurance, real estate, 23.7%; services, 23.5%; trade, 17.0%; manufacturing, 11.9%; government, 10.1%; transportation, utilities, 9.5%; construction, 3.8%; agriculture, 0.5%; mining, 0.1%. **Chief agricultural products:** *Crops:* cranberries, blueberries, peaches, asparagus, bell peppers, spinach, lettuce, cucumbers, sweet corn, tomatoes, snap beans, cabbage, escarole and endive, eggplants, nursery and greenhouse products, dairy products, eggs. *Livestock:* horses, cattle, poultry. *Fish catch:* bluefish, tilefish, flounder, hake, shellfish. **Chief manufactured products:** chemical products, pharmaceuticals, electronic and electrical equipment, communications equipment, semiconductors, industrial equipment, petroleum products, fabricated metal products, clay products, food products.

Internet resources:
<www.visitnj.org>; <www.newjersey.gov>.

New Mexico

Name: New Mexico, named for the country of Mexico. **Nickname:** Land of Enchantment. **Capital:** Santa Fe. **Rank:** population: 36th; area: 5th; pop. density: 45th. **Motto:** *Crescit Eundo* (It Grows as It Goes). **Songs:** "O, Fair New Mexico," words and music by Elizabeth Garrett; *"Así es Nuevo Mexico,"* words and music by Amadeo Lucero. **Bird:** roadrunner. **Fish:** New Mexico cutthroat trout. **Flower:** yucca. **Fossil:** coelophysis. **Gemstone:** turquoise. **Insect:** tarantula hawk wasp. **Tree:** piñon pine.

Natural features

Area: 121,590 sq mi, 314,915 sq km. **Mountain ranges:** Rocky Mountains, Sangre de Cristo Range. **Highest point:** Wheeler Peak, 13,160 ft (4,011 m). **Largest lake:** Elephant Butte Reservoir. **Major rivers:** Rio Grande, Pecos, Canadian, San Juan, Gila. **Natural regions:** eastern third of the state consists of the Great Plains Province, subdivided into the Raton Section to the north, the High Plains along the eastern edge, and the Pecos Valley to the west; Southern Rocky Mountains, north-central region; Colorado Plateau, including the Navajo Section and Datil Section, northwest corner; Basin and Range Province, central region and southwest corner, with the Sacramento Section to the east and the Mexican Highland to the south. **Location:** Southwest, bordering Colorado, Oklahoma, Texas, and Arizona; international border with Mexico. **Climate:** arid; moderate temperatures but great variation by altitude; temperatures drop dramatically after dark. **Land use:** pasture, 67.2%; forest, 18.1%; agricultural, 3.1%; other, 11.6%.

People

Population (2003): 1,875,000; 15.5 persons per sq mi (6.0 persons per sq km). **Vital statistics** (2001; per 1,000 population). Birth rate, 15.4; death rate, 7.7; marriage rate, 7.9; divorce rate, 5.1. **Major cities** (2000): Albuquerque, 464,000 (2002); Las Cruces, 74,267; Santa Fe, 62,203; Rio Rancho, 51,765; Roswell, 45,293.

For details about state governments, see pages 714–719; for energy data, see pages 737–738.

Government

Statehood: entered the Union on 6 Jan 1912 as the 47th state. **State constitution:** adopted 1911. **Representation in US Congress:** 2 senators; 3 representatives. **Electoral college:** 5 votes. **Political divisions:** 33 counties.

Economy

Employment: services, 29.7%; trade, 21.9%; government, 20.4%; construction, 6.4%; finance, insurance, real estate, 6.0%; manufacturing, 5.7%; transportation, public utilities, 4.2%; agriculture, forestry, fishing, 3.6%; mining, 2.1%. **Production:** services, 18.0%; government, 16.8%; manufacturing, 16.7%; trade, 13.6%; finance, insurance, real estate, 13.1%; mining, 8.4%; transportation, utilities, 7.4%; construction, 4.0%; agriculture, 2.1%. **Chief agricultural products:** *Crops:* pecans, apples, potatoes, onions, dry beans, chile, peanuts (groundnuts), hay, sorghum, corn (maize), wheat, eggs, dairy products, wool. *Livestock:* dairy and beef cattle, poultry, sheep and lambs. *Extractive industries:* timber. **Chief manufactured products:** electronic equipment, semiconductors, printing and publishing, processed foods.

Internet resources: <www.newmexico.org>; <www.state.nm.us>.

New York

Name: New York, named in honor of the English Duke of York. **Nickname:** Empire State. **Capital:** Albany. **Rank:** population: 3rd; area: 30th; pop. density: 7th. **Motto:** *Excelsior* (Ever Upward). **Song:** "I Love New York," words and music by Steve Karmen. **Bird:** bluebird. **Fish:** brook trout. **Flower:** rose. **Fossil:** *Eurypterus remipes.* **Gemstone:** garnet. **Mammal:** beaver. **Tree:** sugar maple.

Natural features

Area: 54,556 sq mi, 141,299 sq km. **Mountain ranges:** Adirondack, Catskill, Shawangunk, Taconic. **Highest point:** Mount Marcy, 5,344 ft (1,629 m). **Largest lake:** Oneida Lake. **Major rivers:** Hudson, Mohawk, Genesee, Oswego, Delaware, Susquehanna, Allegheny. **Natural regions:** the Central Lowland, Eastern Lake Section, extends along the northern coast of Lake Ontario; St. Lawrence Valley, Northern Section, extends along the northern border with Canada; Adirondack Province, northeast; Appalachian Plateaus, including the Mohawks, Southern New York, and Catskill Sections, extend along southern border with Pennsylvania and up halfway through the state; Valley and Ridge Province, southeastern edge bordering Connecticut and Massachusetts; Coastal Plain, Embayed Section, covering the islands of Manhattan and Long Island. **Location:** Northeast, bordering Vermont, Massachusetts, Connecticut, New Jersey, and Pennsylvania; international border with Canada. **Climate:** temperate continental, with hot, humid summers and cold, dry, snowy winters. **Land use:** forest, 56.4%; agricultural, 17.4%; pasture, 8.7%; other, 17.5%.

People

Population (2003): 19,190,000; 406.4 persons per sq mi (156.9 persons per sq km) (land area only). **Vital statistics** (1999; per 1,000 population): birth rate, 13.9; death rate, 8.3; marriage rate, 7.9; divorce rate, 3.0. **Major cities:** New York, 8,084,000; Buffalo, 288,000; Rochester, 217,000; Yonkers, 197,000; Syracuse, 145,000; Albany, 95,658 (2000).

Government

Statehood: entered the Union on 26 Jul 1788 as the 11th state. **State constitution:** adopted 1894. **Representation in US Congress:** 2 senators; 31 representatives. **Electoral college:** 31 votes (in the 2004 general elections based on the 2000 census). **Political divisions:** 62 counties.

Economy

Employment: services, 35.9%; trade, 19.0%; government, 14.1%; finance, insurance, real estate, 11.1%; manufacturing, 9.7%; transportation, public utilities, 4.9%; construction, 3.9%; agriculture, forestry, fishing, 1.3%; mining, 0.1%. **Production:** finance, insurance, real estate, 32.8%; services, 23.0%; trade, 12.9%; manufacturing, 10.3%; government, 10.2%; transportation, utilities, 7.3%; construction, 3.0%; agriculture, 0.4%; mining, 0.1%. **Chief agricultural products:** *Crops:* apples, cabbage, corn (maize), potatoes, onions, grapes, snap beans, dry beans, grain, hay, cherries, strawberries, maple syrup, horticulture products, milk, eggs, dairy products. *Livestock:* cattle and calves, chickens. **Chief manufactured products:** food processing, chemical products, apparel, primary metals, industrial machinery, computers and software, scientific and measuring instruments, transportation equipment, electric and electronic equipment, industrial machinery, printing and publishing, biotechnology.

Internet resources: <www.iloveny.com>; <www.state.ny.us>.

North Carolina

Name: North Carolina, named in honor of Charles I of England. **Nickname:** The Old North State. **Capital:** Raleigh. **Rank:** population: 11th; area: 29th; pop. density: 17th. **Motto:** *Esse Quam Videri* (To Be Rather Than to Seem). **Song:** "The Old North State," words by William Gaston to a German tune. **Bird:** cardinal. **Fish:** channel bass. **Flower:** dogwood. **Gemstone:** emerald. **Insect:** honeybee. **Mammal:** gray squirrel. **Reptile:** eastern box turtle. **Rock:** granite. **Tree:** pine.

Natural features

Area: 53,819 sq mi, 139,389 sq km. **Mountain ranges:** Appalachian, Great Smoky, Blue Ridge. **Highest point:** Mount Mitchell, 6,684 ft (2,037 m). **Largest lake:** Lake Mattamuskeet. **Major rivers:** Roanoke, Yadkin, Pee Dee. **Natural regions:** Valley and Ridge Province, far western edge; Piedmont Province, consisting of the Piedmont Upland, extends in a southwest to northeast direction through the center of the state; Coastal Plain comprises the eastern third, divided into the Sea Island Section to the south and the Embayed Section to the north. **Location:** East coast, bordering Virginia, South Carolina, Georgia, and Tennessee. **Climate:** ranges from medium continental conditions in the mountain region (though summers are cooler and rainfall heavier) to the subtropical conditions of the state's southeastern corner;

hurricanes occasionally occur along the coast, and there have been tornadoes inland. **Land use:** forest, 60%; agricultural, 19%; pasture, 3%; other, 19%.

People

Population (2003): 8,407,000; 172.6 persons per sq mi (66.6 persons per sq km) (land area only). **Vital statistics** (2001; per 1,000 population): birth rate, 15.1; death rate, 8.6; marriage rate, 7.8; divorce rate, 4.5. **Major cities:** Charlotte, 581,000; Raleigh, 307,000; Greensboro, 228,000; Durham, 196,000; Winston-Salem, 189,000; Fayetteville, 124,000.

Government

Statehood: entered the Union on 21 Nov 1789 as the 12th state. **State constitution:** adopted 1970. **Representation in US Congress:** 2 senators, 12 representatives. **Electoral college:** 15 votes (in the 2004 general elections based on the 2000 census). **Political divisions:** 100 counties.

Economy

Employment: services, 25.1%; trade, 21.2%; manufacturing, 18.5%; government, 15.2%; construction, 6.6%; finance, insurance, real estate, 5.9%; transportation, public utilities, 4.3%; agriculture, forestry, fishing, 3.1%; mining, 0.1%. **Production:** manufacturing, 24.1%; finance, insurance, real estate, 18.3%; services, 16.4%; trade, 15.0%; government, 12.5%; transportation, utilities, 7.1%; construction, 4.9%; agriculture, 1.5%; mining, 0.2%. **Chief agricultural products:** *Crops:* tobacco, corn (maize), barley, potatoes, peanuts (groundnuts), apples, blueberries, grapes, peaches, pecans, strawberries, tomatoes, cabbages, watermelons, cucumbers, sweet potatoes, horticultural products, Christmas trees, dairy products, eggs. *Livestock:* cattle, chickens, pigs, horses. *Aquaculture:* catfish, trout. *Extractive industries:* timber. **Chief manufactured products:** textiles, cotton and synthetic fibers, yarns, threads, knitted goods, cigarettes and tobacco products, chemical products, pharmaceuticals, electronic and electrical equipment, furniture, lumber, paper products, processed foods.

Internet resources: <www.visitnc.com>; <www.northcarolina.gov>.

North Dakota

Name: North Dakota, from the Dakota division of the Sioux, the Native American tribe that inhabited the plains before the arrival of Europeans; *dakota* is the Sioux word for "friend." **Nickname:** Peace Garden State. **Capital:** Bismarck. **Rank:** population: 48th; area: 17th; pop. density: 47th. **Motto:** Liberty and Union Now and Forever, One and Inseparable. **Song:** "North Dakota Hymn," words by James W. Foley and music by C.S. Putnam. **Bird:** western meadowlark. **Fish:** northern pike. **Flower:** wild prairie rose. **Fossil:** teredo petrified wood. **Tree:** American elm.

Natural features

Area: 70,700 sq mi, 183,112 sq km. **Highest point:** White Butte, 3,506 ft (1,069 m). **Largest lake:** Devils

Lake. **Major rivers:** Red, Souris, Missouri, Little Missouri, James. **Natural regions:** central Lowland covers eastern half of the state, with the Western Lake Section lying in the east-central region; Great Plains Province, western half of the state, includes sections of the Missouri Plateau to the north and south. **Location:** North central, bordering Minnesota, South Dakota, and Montana; international border with Canada. **Climate:** continental, with hot summers and cold winters, warm days and cool nights in summer, low humidity and low precipitation, and much wind and sunshine. **Land use:** agricultural, 65.3%; pasture, 25.7%; forest, 1.0%; other, 8.1%.

People

Population (2003): 634,000; 9.2 persons per sq mi (3.5 persons per sq km) (land area only). **Vital statistics** (2001; per 1,000 population): birth rate, 12.2; death rate, 9.5; marriage rate, 6.6; divorce rate, 2.7. **Major cities** (2000) Fargo, 90,599; Bismarck, 55,532; Grand Forks, 49,321; Minot, 36,567.

Government

Statehood: entered the Union on 2 Nov 1889 as the 39th state. **State constitution:** adopted 1889. **Representation in US Congress:** 2 senators; 1 representative. **Electoral college:** 3 votes. **Political divisions:** 53 counties.

Economy

Employment: services, 28.5%; trade, 22.5%; government, 16.4%; agriculture, forestry, fishing, 9.7%; manufacturing, 5.7%; finance, insurance, real estate, 5.6%; transportation, public utilities, 5.3%; construction, 5.2%; mining, 1.1%; **Production:** trade, 19.5%; services, 19.4%; government, 14.4%; finance, insurance, real estate, 14.1%; transportation, utilities, 10.3%; manufacturing, 9.0%; construction, 5.5%; agriculture, 4.1%; mining, 3.6%. **Chief agricultural products:** *Crops:* hard red spring wheat, durum wheat, flaxseed, canola, dry beans, sunflowers, barley, honey, potatoes, dairy products, wool. *Livestock:* cattle, sheep, pigs. *Extractive industries:* timber. **Chief manufactured products:** food processing, wood products, petroleum products, transportation equipment, machinery.

Internet resources: <www.ndtourism.com>; <www.northdakota.gov>.

Ohio

Name: Ohio, from an Iroquois word meaning "great river." **Nickname:** Buckeye State. **Capital:** Columbus. **Rank:** population: 7th; area: 35th; pop. density: 9th. **Motto:** With God, All Things Are Possible. **Song:** "Beautiful Ohio," words by Ballad MacDonald and music by Mary Earl. **Bird:** cardinal. **Flower:** red carnation. **Fossil:** *Trilobite isotelus.* **Gemstone:** flint. **Insect:** ladybug. **Mammal:** white-tailed deer. **Reptile:** black racer snake. **Tree:** Ohio buckeye.

Natural features

Area: 44,825 sq mi, 116,096 sq km. **Highest point:** Campbell Hill, 1,550 ft (472 m). **Largest lake:** Grand

Lake St. Marys. **Major rivers:** Ohio, Maumee, Cuyahoga, Miami, Scioto, Muskingum. **Natural regions:** the Appalachian Plateau, eastern half of the state, includes the Southern New York Section to the north, and the Kanawha Section to the east; the Central Lowlands, western half of the state, includes the Eastern Lake Section in the northwest corner, the Till Plains in the central region, and the Lexington Plain in the southwest. **Location:** Midwest, bordering Michigan, Pennsylvania, West Virginia, Kentucky, and Indiana. **Climate:** continental, with hot, humid summers and cold, dry winters. **Land use:** agricultural, 45.9%; forest, 28.9%; pasture, 5.3%; other, 20.0%.

People

Population (2003): 11,436,000; 279.3 persons per sq mi (107.8 persons per sq km) (land area only). **Vital statistics** (2001; per 1,000 population): birth rate, 13.4; death rate, 9.5; marriage rate, 7.3; divorce rate, 4.0. **Major cities:** Columbus, 725,000; Cleveland, 468,000; Cincinnati, 324,000; Toledo, 309,000; Akron, 214,000; Dayton, 163,000.

Government

Statehood: entered the Union on 1 Mar 1803 as the 17th state. **State constitution:** adopted 1851. **Representation in US Congress:** 2 senators; 19 representatives. **Electoral college:** 20 votes (in the 2004 general elections based on the 2000 census). **Political divisions:** 88 counties.

Economy

Employment: services, 29.0%; trade, 22.8%; manufacturing, 17.0%; government, 12.1%; finance, insurance, real estate, 7.2%; construction, 5.1%; transportation, public utilities, 4.3%; agriculture, forestry, fishing, 2.3%; mining, 0.3%. **Production:** manufacturing, 25.8%; services, 18.2%; trade, 16.8%; finance, insurance, real estate, 15.5%; government, 10.7%; transportation, utilities, 7.4%; construction, 4.3%; agriculture, 0.8%; mining, 0.4%. **Chief agricultural products:** *Crops:* corn (maize), soybeans, grapes, apples, vegetables, tobacco, winter wheat, dairy products, eggs, greenhouse and nursery products. *Livestock:* cattle, hogs, poultry, goats. *Extractive industries:* timber. **Chief manufactured products:** industrial machinery, non-electrical machinery, food processing, transportation equipment, fabricated metals, iron and steel, chemical products and pharmaceuticals, rubber products.

Internet resources: <www.discoverohio.com>; <www.ohio.gov>.

Oklahoma

Name: Oklahoma, from two Choctaw words: *okla* meaning "people" and *humma* meaning "red." **Nickname:** Sooner State. **Capital:** Oklahoma City. **Rank:** population: 28th; area: 19th; pop. density: 35th. **Motto:** *Labor Omnia Vincit* (Labor Conquers All Things). **Song:** "Oklahoma," words by Richard Rodgers and music by Oscar Hammerstein. **Bird:** scissor-tailed flycatcher. **Fish:** white, or sand, bass. **Flower:** mistletoe. **Insect:** honeybee. **Mammal:** bison. **Reptile:** collared lizard (also know as the mountain boomer). **Rock:** rose rock. **Tree:** redbud.

Natural features

Area: 69,898 sq mi, 181,036 sq km. **Mountain ranges:** Ouachita, Arbuckle, Wichita, Sandstone Hills. **Highest point:** Black Mesa, 4,978 ft (1,517 m). **Largest lake:** Lake Eufaula. **Major rivers:** Arkansas, Red, Canadian. **Natural regions:** Great Plains Province, panhandle region, includes the High Plains to the west and the Plains Border to the east; Central Lowland, covers most of the state, includes the Osage Plains in the central region; West Gulf Coastal Plain, southeastern corner; Ouachita Province, east-central region, includes the Arkansas Valley in the center and the Ouachita Mountains to the south; Ozark Plateaus, northeast corner, includes the Boston Mountains and Springfield-Salem Plateaus. **Location:** South central, bordering Kansas, Missouri, Arkansas, Texas, New Mexico, and Colorado. **Climate:** variable by region: the southern humid belt merges with a colder northern continental one and humid eastern and dry western zones that cut through the state; no region is free from heavy wind; typical sudden rises and falls in temperature cause many heavy thunderstorms, blizzards, and tornadoes. **Land use:** pasture, 39.4%; agricultural, 37.2%; forest, 14.2%; other, 9.3%.

People

Population (2003): 3,512,000; 51.1 persons per sq mi (19.7 persons per sq km) (land area only). **Vital statistics** (2001; per 1,000 population): birth rate, 14.8; death rate, 10.0; marriage rate, 4.9; divorce rate, 3.4. **Major cities** (2000): Oklahoma City, 519,000 (2002); Tulsa, 392,000 (2002); Norman, 95,694; Lawton, 92,757; Broken Arrow, 74,859.

Government

Statehood: entered the Union on 16 Nov 1907 as the 46th state. **State constitution:** adopted 1907. **Representation in US Congress:** 2 senators; 6 representatives. **Electoral college:** 7 votes (in the 2004 general elections based on the 2000 census). **Political divisions:** 77 counties.

Economy

Employment: services, 28.3%; trade, 20.9%; government, 16.6%; manufacturing, 10.0%; finance, insurance, real estate, 5.8%; agriculture, forestry, fishing, 5.6%; transportation, public utilities, 5.1%; construction, 4.8%; mining, 3.0%. **Production:** services, 18.2%; manufacturing, 16.9%; trade, 16.5%; government, 15.9%; finance, insurance, real estate, 12.2%; transportation, utilities, 9.2%; mining, 4.9%; construction, 3.8%; agriculture, 2.3%. **Chief agricultural products:** *Crops:* wheat, hay, sorghum, soybeans, cotton, dairy products. *Livestock:* cattle and calves, poultry, hogs and pigs. **Chief manufactured products:** electronics and electrical equipment, communications equipment, transportation equipment, food processing, petroleum products.

Internet resources: <www.travelok.com>; <www.ok.gov>.

Oregon

Nickname: Beaver State. **Capital:** Salem. **Rank:** population: 27th; area: 10th; pop. density: 39th. **Motto:** *Alis Volat Propiis* (She Flies with Her Own Wings). **Song:** "Oregon, My Oregon," words by J.A. Buchanan and music by Henry B. Murtagh. **Bird:** western meadowlark. **Fish:** Chinook salmon. **Flower:** Oregon grape. **Gemstone:** Oregon sunstone. **Insect:** Oregon swallowtail. **Mammal:** beaver. **Rock:** thunderegg. **Tree:** Douglas fir.

Natural features

Area: 98,381 sq mi, 254,805 sq km. **Mountain ranges:** Coast Range, Klamath Mountains, Cascade Range, Blue Mountains, Wallowa Mountains. **Highest point:** Mount Hood, 11,235 ft (3,424 m). **Largest lake:** Upper Klamath Lake. **Major rivers:** Snake, Owyhee, Columbia, Coquille. **Natural regions:** northern Rocky Mountains, northeastern corner, includes the Blue Mountain Section; Columbia Plateaus, north and north-central region, includes the Walla Walla Plateau in the central section, Harney Section to the south, and Payette Section to the southeast; Basin and Range Province, south-central border, includes the Great Basin; Cascade Sierra Mountains, includes the Middle and Southern Cascades, west central; Pacific Border Province, western coast, with the Klamath Mountains to the south, the Oregon Coast Range in the center and north, and the Puget Trough to the east. **Location:** Northwest, bordering Washington, Idaho, Nevada, and California. **Climate:** ranges from equable, mild, marine conditions on the coast to continental conditions of dryness and extreme temperature in the interior. **Land use:** forest, 43.4%; pasture, 36.4%; agricultural, 8.7%; other, 11.5%.

People

Population (2003): 3,560,000; 37.1 persons per sq mi (14.3 persons per sq km) (land area only). **Vital statistics** (2001; per 1,000 population): birth rate, 13.5; death rate, 8.7; marriage rate, 7.7; divorce rate, 4.9. **Major cities:** Portland, 539,000; Eugene, 140,000; Salem, 141,000; Gresham, 90,205 (2000); Beaverton, 76,129 (2000).

Government

Statehood: entered the Union on 14 Feb 1859 as the 33rd state. **State constitution:** adopted 1857. **Representation in US Congress:** 2 senators; 5 representatives. **Electoral college:** 7 votes. **Political divisions:** 36 counties.

Economy

Employment: services, 29.4%; trade, 22.8%; manufacturing, 13.1%; government, 12.6%; finance, insurance, real estate, 6.6%; construction, 5.7%; agriculture, forestry, fishing, 5.1%; transportation, public utilities, 4.5%; mining, 0.2%. **Production:** manufacturing, 24.8%; services, 17.6%; trade, 16.1%; finance, insurance, real estate, 14.4%; government, 11.8%; transportation, utilities, 7.1%; construction, 5.3%; agriculture, 2.8%; mining, 0.1%. **Chief agricultural products:** *Crops:* horticulture and nursery products, Christmas trees, berries, pears, cherries, ap-

ples, hazelnuts, snap beans, peas, onions, carrots, wheat, hay, potatoes, barley, dry beans, mint, hops, corn (maize), sugar beets, dairy products. *Livestock:* cattle and calves, horses, mink, poultry, sheep and lambs. *Fish catch:* marine fish, tuna, salmon, shellfish, crab, shrimp. *Extractive industries:* timber. **Chief manufactured products:** lumber and wood products, food processing, aircraft and spacecraft, electronics, semiconductors, computers.

Internet resources: <www.traveloregon.com>; <www.oregon.gov>.

Pennsylvania

Name: Pennsylvania, named for Admiral Sir William Penn, father of the territory's founder, William Penn, and including also the term *sylvania* ("woodlands"). **Nickname:** Keystone State. **Capital:** Harrisburg. **Rank:** population: 6th; area: 32nd; pop. density: 10th. **Motto:** Virtue, Liberty, and Independence. **Song:** "Pennsylvania," written and composed by Eddie Khoury and Ronnie Bonner. **Bird:** ruffled grouse. **Fish:** brook trout. **Flower:** mountain laurel. **Fossil:** *Phacops rana.* **Insect:** firefly. **Mammal:** white-tailed deer. **Tree:** hemlock.

Natural features

Area: 46,055 sq mi, 119,283 sq km. **Mountain ranges:** Appalachian, Allegheny. **Highest point:** Mount Davis, 3,213 ft (979 m). **Largest lake:** Raystown Lake. **Major rivers:** Delaware, Lehigh, Schuylkill, Susquehanna, Ohio. **Natural regions:** central Lowland, Eastern Lake Section, extreme northwestern edge; Appalachian Plateaus, including the Southern New York, Allegheny Mountain, and Kanawha Sections, western half of state; Valley and Ridge Province, central region, includes portions of the Appalachian Mountains; Piedmont Province, comprising the Piedmont Lowlands and Upland, southeast corner; Coastal Plain, extreme southeast edge; New England Province, with the New England Upland Section, east-central border. **Location:** Northeast, bordering New York, New Jersey, Delaware, Maryland, West Virginia, Ohio. **Climate:** continental, with warm humid summers and cold snowy winters in general, but with wide fluctuations in seasonal temperatures. **Land use:** forest, 55.3%; agricultural, 18.1%; pasture, 3.2%; other, 23.5%.

People

Population (2003): 12,365,000; 275.9 persons per sq mi (106.5 persons per sq km) (land area only). **Vital statistics** (2001; per 1,000 population): birth rate, 12.0; death rate, 10.5; marriage rate, 6.0; divorce rate, 3.2. **Major cities:** Philadelphia, 1,492,000; Pittsburgh, 328,000; Allentown, 106,000; Erie, 102,000; Reading, 81,207 (2000).

Government

Statehood: entered the Union on 12 Dec 1787 as the 2nd state. **State constitution:** adopted 1968. **Representation in US Congress:** 2 senators, 21 representatives. **Electoral college:** 21 votes (in the 2004 general elections based on the 2000 census). **Political divisions:** 67 counties.

For details about state governments, see pages 714–719; for energy data, see pages 737–738.

Economy

Employment: services, 32.7%; trade, 21.5%; manufacturing, 14.5%; government, 11.4%; finance, insurance, real estate, 7.7%; construction, 5.0%; transportation, public utilities, 4.9%; agriculture, forestry, fishing, 2.0%; mining, 0.4%. **Production:** services, 22.4%; manufacturing, 19.4%; finance, insurance, real estate, 18.4%; trade, 15.2%; government, 10.2%; transportation, utilities, 8.6%; construction, 4.2%; agriculture, 0.9%; mining, 0.7%. **Chief agricultural products:** *Crops:* mushrooms, apples, tobacco, grapes, peaches, cut flowers, dairy products. *Livestock:* cattle, poultry, pigs, horses. **Chief manufactured products:** electronic equipment, communications systems, semiconductors, chemical and pharmaceutical products, food processing, iron and steel, industrial machinery, transportation equipment, paper products, printing and publishing.

Internet resources: <www.visitpa.com>; <www.state.pa.us>.

Rhode Island

Name: Rhode Island, from the Greek island of Rhodes. **Nicknames:** Little Rhody and Ocean State. **Capital:** Providence. **Rank:** population: 43rd; area: 50th; pop. density: 2nd. **Motto:** Hope. **Song:** "Rhode Island," words and music by T. Clarke Brown. **Bird:** Rhode Island red. **Flower:** violet. **Mineral:** bowenite. **Rock:** cumberlandite.

Natural features

Area: 1,545 sq mi, 4,002 sq km, including 168 sq mi, 435 sq km of water surface. **Highest point:** Jerimoth Hill, 812 ft (247 m). **Largest lake:** Scituate Reservoir. **Major rivers:** Blackstone, Pawtuxet, Pawcatuck. **Natural regions:** the entire state is part of the New England Province, subdivided into the New England Upland (western two-thirds) and the Seaboard Lowland (eastern third). **Location:** New England, bordering Connecticut and Massachusetts. **Climate:** humid continental climate; marine influences are discernible in differences between coastal and inland location; extreme weather conditions including tropical storms, ice storms, and heavy snow. **Land use:** forest, 53.2%; agricultural, 4.5%; pasture, 0.4%; other, 41.9%.

People

Population (2003): 1,076,000; 1,029.7 persons per sq mi (397.6 persons per sq km) (land area only). **Vital statistics** (2001; per 1,000 population): birth rate, 12.7; death rate, 9.5; marriage rate, 8.6; divorce rate, 3.3. **Major cities** (2000) Providence, 176,000 (2002); Warwick, 85,808; Cranston, 79,269; Pawtucket, 72,958; East Providence, 48,688.

Government

Statehood: entered the Union on 29 May 1790 as the 13th state. **State constitution:** adopted 1986. **Representation in US Congress:** 2 senators; 2 representatives. **Electoral college:** 4 votes. **Political divisions:** 5 counties.

Economy

Employment: services, 34.7%; trade, 20.3%; manufacturing, 14.8%; government, 13.4%; finance, insurance, real estate, 7.6%; construction, 4.4%; transportation, public utilities, 3.4%; agriculture, forestry, fishing, 1.3%; mining, 0.1%. **Production:** finance, insurance, real estate, 26.7%; services, 21.7%; trade, 14.3%; manufacturing, 12.6%; government, 12.0%; transportation, utilities, 6.7%; construction, 5.3%; agriculture, 0.7%. **Chief agricultural products:** *Crops:* hay, corn (maize), apples, peaches, dairy products, eggs, potatoes. *Livestock:* poultry, cattle, sheep. *Fish catch:* marine fish, shellfish. **Chief manufactured products:** jewelry, silverware, textiles, fabricated metal products, electrical equipment, machinery, surgical and navigation instruments, plastic goods, printing and publishing, primary metals, food processing.

Internet resources: <www.visitrhodeisland.com>; <www.ri.gov>.

South Carolina

Name: South Carolina, named in honor of Charles I of England. **Nickname:** Palmetto State. **Capital:** Columbia. **Rank:** population: 25th; area: 40th; pop. density: 21st. **Mottoes:** *Animis Opibusque Parati* (Prepared in Mind and Resources); *Dum Spiro Spero* (While I Breathe, I Hope). **Songs:** "Carolina," words by Henry Timrod and music by Anne Custis Burgess; "South Carolina on My Mind," words and music by Hank Martin and Buzz Arledge. **Amphibian:** spotted salamander. **Bird:** Carolina wren. **Fish:** striped bass. **Flower:** Carolina jessamine. **Gemstone:** amethyst. **Insect:** Carolina mantid. **Mammal:** white-tailed deer. **Reptile:** loggerhead turtle. **Rock:** blue granite. **Tree:** palmetto.

Natural features

Area: 32,020 sq mi, 82,932 sq km. **Mountain range:** Blue Ridge Mountains. **Highest point:** Sassafras Mountain, 3,560 ft (1,085 m). **Largest lake:** Lake Marion. **Major rivers:** Pee Dee, Savannah, Ashley, Combahee, Edisto. **Natural regions:** Coastal Plain covers the eastern two-thirds of the state and includes the Sea Island Section in the central region; Piedmont Province extends across the central and western region, includes the Piedmont Upland; Blue Ridge Province, Southern Section, far northwestern corner. **Location:** Southeast, bordering North Carolina and Georgia. **Climate:** subtropical, with hot, humid summers and generally mild winters; an average of 10 tornadoes a year, usually occurring during the spring; hurricanes are less frequent, but they do in some years cause damage to the coast. **Land use:** forest, 64.4%; agricultural, 13.1%; pasture, 2.4%; other, 20.0%.

People

Population (2003): 4,147,000; 137.7 persons per sq mi (53.2 persons per sq km) (land area only). **Vital statistics** (2001; per 1,000 population): birth rate, 14.1; death rate, 9.0; marriage rate, 9.3; divorce rate, 3.5. **Major cities** (2000): Columbia, 117,000 (2002); Charleston, 96,650; North Charleston, 79,641; Greenville, 56,002; Rock Hill, 49,765.

Government

Statehood: entered the Union on 23 May 1788 as the 8th state. **State constitution:** adopted 1895. **Representation in US Congress:** 2 senators; 6 representatives. **Electoral college:** 8 votes. **Political divisions:** 46 counties.

Economy

Employment: services, 24.7%; trade, 22.4%; manufacturing, 17.3%; government, 16.7%; construction, 6.4%; finance, insurance, real estate, 5.9%; transportation, public utilities, 4.1%; agriculture, forestry, fishing, 2.4%; mining, 0.1%. **Production:** manufacturing, 21.4%; trade, 17.4%; services, 16.4%; government, 15.1%; finance, insurance, real estate, 13.7%; transportation, utilities, 8.9%; construction, 5.9%; agriculture, 1.1%; mining, 0.2%. **Chief agricultural products:** *Crops:* tobacco, cotton, barley, corn (maize), peanuts, oats, grains, peaches, apples, pecans, watermelons, sweet potatoes, tomatoes, snap beans, cucumbers, dairy products, eggs. *Livestock:* cattle and calves, chickens, pigs. **Chief extractive products:** timber, marine fish, oysters, clams, shrimp. **Chief manufactured products:** Chemical products, industrial chemicals, pharmaceuticals, and agricultural fertilizers, textiles, apparel, industrial machinery, plastic and rubber products, paper and paperboard, electronics and electrical equipment, motor vehicle parts and accessories, lumber.

Internet resources: <www.discoversouthcarolina.com>.

South Dakota

Name: South Dakota, from the Dakota division of the Sioux, the Native American tribe that inhabited the plains before the arrival of Europeans; *dakota* is the Sioux word for "friend." **Nickname:** Mount Rushmore State. **Capital:** Pierre. **Rank:** population: 46th; area: 16th; pop. density: 46th. **Motto:** Under God the People Rule. **Song:** "Hail! South Dakota," words and music by Deecort Hammitt. **Bird:** Chinese ring-necked pheasant. **Fish:** walleye. **Flower:** pasque. **Fossil:** triceratops. **Gemstone:** Fairburn agate. **Insect:** honeybee. **Mammal:** coyote. **Mineral:** rose quartz. **Tree:** Black Hills spruce.

Natural features

Area: 77,117 sq mi, 199,731 sq km. **Mountain range:** Black Hills. **Highest point:** Harney Peak, 7,242 ft (2,207 m). **Largest lake:** Lake Thompson. **Major rivers:** Big Sioux, Vermillion, James, Grand, Moreau, Cheyenne, Bad, White. **Natural regions:** the Central Lowland, eastern third of the state, includes the Dissected Till Plains along the eastern edge and the Western Lake Section at the center; the Great Plains Province, western two-thirds of the state; Black Hills, far west; High Plains, southern border; Missouri Plateau, west. **Location:** North central, bordering North Dakota, Minnesota, Iowa, Nebraska, Wyoming, and Montana. **Climate:** characterized by extremes in temperature, low precipitation, and relatively low humidity; cyclonic storms occur frequently in the east-river section during the spring and summer. **Land use:** pasture, 46.5%; agricultural, 44.8%; forest, 3.3%; other, 5.4%.

People

Population (2003): 764,000; 10.1 persons per sq mi (3.9 persons per sq km) (land area only). **Vital statistics (2001; per 1,000 population):** birth rate, 14.1; death rate, 9.1; marriage rate, 9.1; divorce rate, 3.4. **Major cities (2000):** Sioux Falls, 130,000 (2002); Rapid City, 59,607; Aberdeen, 24,658.

Government

Statehood: entered the Union on 2 Nov 1889 as the 40th state. **State constitution:** adopted 1889. **Representation in US Congress:** 2 senators; 1 representative. **Electoral college:** 3 votes. **Political divisions:** 66 counties.

Economy

Employment: services, 27.5%; trade, 22.3%; government, 13.7%; manufacturing, 10.3%; agriculture, forestry, fishing, 9.1%; finance, insurance, real estate, 7.2%; construction, 5.0%; transportation, public utilities, 4.5%; mining, 0.5%. **Production:** finance, insurance, real estate, 18.1%; trade, 17.7%; services, 17.6%; manufacturing, 14.0%; government, 12.6%; transportation, utilities, 8.2%; agriculture, 6.9%; construction, 4.1%; mining, 0.6%. **Chief agricultural products:** *Crops:* corn (maize), hay, wheat, sunflowers, dairy products, eggs, flaxseed, barley, wool, rye, sorghum, soybeans. *Livestock:* cattle and calves, pigs, sheep. **Chief manufactured products:** industrial machinery, office machines, computers, food products, electronics, printing and publishing, lumber mills, fabricated metal products, medical instruments, truck-trailer manufactures, jewelry.

Internet resources: <www.travelsd.com>; <www.state.sd.us>.

Tennessee

Name: Tennessee, from Cherokee village name. **Nickname:** Volunteer State. **Capital:** Nashville. **Rank:** population: 16th; area: 34th; pop. density: 20th. **Motto:** Agriculture and Commerce. **Songs:** "My Homeland, Tennessee," by Nell Grayson Taylor and Roy Lamont Smith; "When It's Iris Time in Tennessee," by Willa Mae Waid; "My Tennessee,". by Francis Hannah Tranum; "The Tennessee Waltz," by Redd Stewart and Pee Wee King; "Rocky Top," by Boudleaux and Felice Bryant. **Amphibian:** cave salamander. **Bird:** mockingbird. **Fish:** largemouth bass, channel catfish. **Flower:** iris. **Gemstone:** river pearl. **Insects:** firefly, ladybug. **Mammal:** raccoon. **Reptile:** box turtle. **Rocks:** limestone, agate. **Tree:** tulip poplar.

Natural features

Area: 42,143 sq mi, 109,151 sq km. **Mountain ranges:** Unaka Mountains, Great Smoky Mountains. **Highest point:** Clingmans Dome, 6,642 ft (2,024 m). **Largest lake:** Reelfoot. **Major rivers:** Tennessee, Cumberland, Mississippi. **Natural regions:** Blue Ridge Province, eastern border; Valley and Ridge Province, extends from southwest to northeast; Appalachian Plateau, central, running from south to north, includes the Cumberland Plateau Section in the center

For details about state governments, see pages 714–719; for energy data, see pages 737–738.

and the Cumberland Mountain Section at the northern end; Interior Low Plateau, west central, includes the Nashville Basin and Highland Rim Section. **Location:** South, bordering Kentucky, Virginia, North Carolina, Georgia, Alabama, Mississippi, Arkansas, and Missouri. **Climate:** moderate continental climate, with cool, but not cold, winters and warm summers. **Land use:** forest, 50.3%; agricultural, 28.4%; pasture, 4.3%; other, 17.1%.

People

Population (2003): 5,842,000; 141.7 persons per sq mi (54.7 persons per sq km) (land area only). **Vital statistics** (2001; per 1,000 population): birth rate, 14.0; death rate, 9.6; marriage rate, 13.9; divorce rate, 5.2. **Major cities:** Memphis, 649,000; Nashville-Davidson, 546,000; Knoxville, 174,000; Chattanooga, 155,000; Clarksville, 106,000.

Government

Statehood: entered the Union on 1 Jun 1796 as the 16th state. **State constitution:** adopted 1870. **Representation in US Congress:** 2 senators; 9 representatives. **Electoral college:** 11 votes. **Political divisions:** 95 counties.

Economy

Employment: services, 27.8%; trade, 21.8%; manufacturing, 16.2%; government, 12.1%; finance, insurance, real estate, 6.7%; construction, 5.9%; transportation, public utilities, 5.4%; agriculture, forestry, fishing, 3.8%; mining, 0.2%. **Production:** manufacturing, 20.8%; services, 20.6%; trade, 19.1%; finance, insurance, real estate, 14.1%; government, 11.5%; transportation, utilities, 8.3%; construction, 4.4%; agriculture, 0.9%; mining, 0.3%. **Chief agricultural products:** *Crops:* cotton, tobacco, peaches, apples, tomatoes, snap beans, honey, dairy products, eggs, wool, hay, corn (maize), wheat, sorghum. *Livestock:* cattle, poultry, hogs, sheep. *Aquaculture:* catfish, trout. *Extractive products:* timber. **Chief manufactured products:** transportation equipment, motor vehicles, aircraft parts, boats, chemical and pharmaceutical products, printing and publishing, electronics, lumber, paper, apparel, surgical appliances and supplies.

Internet resources: <www.tennessee.gov>.

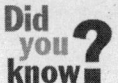 **Did you know?** During the War of 1812, thousands of men from Tennessee enlisted to serve in the army, including such notable figures as Andrew Jackson, Davey Crockett, and Sam Houston.

Texas

Name: Texas, from the Caddo Indian word *teysha*, or *tejas*, which means "hello friend." **Nickname:** Lone Star State. **Capital:** Austin. **Rank:** population: 2nd; area: 2nd; pop. density: 27th. **Motto:** Friendship. **Song:** "Texas, Our Texas," by William J. Marsh and Gladys Yoakum Wright. **Bird:** mockingbird. **Fish:** Guadalupe bass. **Flower:** bluebonnet. **Fossil:** pleurocoelus. **Gemstone:** Texas blue topaz. **Insect:** monarch butterfly. **Mammal:** Mexican free-tailed bat (flying); longhorn (large); armadillo (small). **Reptile:** horned lizard. **Rock:** petrified palmwood. **Tree:** pecan.

Natural features

Area: 268,581 sq mi, 695,621 sq km. **Mountain ranges:** Rocky Mountains, Guadalupe Mountains. **Highest point:** Guadalupe Peak, 8,751 ft (2,667 m). **Largest lake:** Caddo Lake. **Major rivers:** Red, Trinity, Brazos, Colorado, Rio Grande. **Natural regions:** Coastal Plain, southern and eastern regions, includes the West Gulf Coastal Plain near the east-central coast; Central Lowland, north central, includes the Osage Plains; Great Plains Province, extends from the panhandle across most of central and western Texas, includes the Edwards Plateau to the south, Pecos Valley to the west, High Plains to the north, and Central Texas Section; Basin and Range Province, extreme western region, comprising the Mexican Highland to the south and the Sacramento Section to the north. **Location:** Southwest, bordering Oklahoma, Arkansas, Louisiana, and New Mexico; international border with Mexico. **Climate:** varies by region, though summers are generally very hot and winters are somewhat mild; East Texas is considerably wetter than the very dry West Texas region; tornadoes are a frequent threat between April and November. **Land use:** pasture, 58.5%; agricultural, 23.9%; forest, 7.0%; other, 10.6%.

People

Population (2003): 22,119,000; 84.5 persons per sq mi (32.6 persons per sq km) (land area only). **Vital statistics** (2001; per 1,000 population): birth rate, 17.6; death rate, 7.1; marriage rate, 9.4; divorce rate, 4.1. **Major cities:** Houston, 2,010,000; Dallas, 1,211,000; San Antonio, 1,194,000; Austin, 672,000; El Paso, 577,000; Fort Worth, 568,000; Arlington, 350,000; Corpus Christi, 279,000; Plano, 238,000; Garland, 220,000.

Government

Statehood: entered the Union on 29 Dec 1845 as the 28th state. **State constitution:** adopted 1876. **Representation in US Congress:** 2 senators; 30 representatives. **Electoral college:** 34 votes (in the 2004 general elections based on the 2000 census). **Political divisions:** 254 counties.

Economy

Employment: services, 29.1%; trade, 21.6%; government, 14.5%; manufacturing, 10.1%; finance, insurance, real estate, 7.5%; construction, 6.1%; transportation, public utilities, 5.4%; agriculture, forestry, fishing, 3.5%; mining, 2.2%. **Production:** services, 19.9%; trade, 17.6%; finance, insurance, real estate, 14.7%; manufacturing, 14.0%; government, 11.2%; transportation, utilities, 10.9%; mining, 5.7%; construction, 4.7%; agriculture, 1.3%. **Chief agricultural products:** *Crops:* cotton, apples, greenhouse and nursery products, corn (maize), sorghum, wheat, dairy products, eggs, rice. *Livestock:* cattle, pigs, chickens. *Extractive products:* timber, shrimp. **Chief manufactured products:** Refined petroleum, petroleum products, food products, computers and electronics, chemicals and plastics, apparel, wood and paper products, nonelectrical machinery, fabricated metal products, aerospace products and parts, aircraft parts, motor vehicle parts.

Internet resources: <www.traveltex.com>; <www.texas.gov>.

Utah

Name: Utah, named for the Ute tribe; the word *ute* means "people of the mountains." **Nickname:** Beehive State. **Capital:** Salt Lake City. **Rank:** population: 34th; area: 12th; pop. density: 41st. **Motto:** Industry. **Song:** "Utah, We Love Thee," by Evan Stephens. **Bird:** California seagull. **Fish:** Bonneville cutthroat trout. **Flower:** sego lily. **Fossil:** allosaurus. **Gemstone:** topaz. **Insect:** honeybee. **Mammal:** Rocky Mountain elk. **Mineral:** copper. **Rock:** coal. **Tree:** blue spruce.

Natural features

Area: 84,899 sq mi, 219,887 sq km. **Mountain ranges:** Uinta Mountains, Wasatch Range, Rocky Mountains. **Highest point:** Kings Peak, 13,528 ft (4,123 m). **Largest lake:** Great Salt Lake. **Major rivers:** Colorado, Green, Sevier. **Natural regions:** Basin and Range Province, western half of the state, includes the Great Salt Lake Desert and Bonneville Salt Flats to the north and the Great Basin to the south; Middle Rocky Mountains, northeast; Colorado Plateaus, east-central and southeast regions, includes the Grand Canyon Section to the south, the High Plateaus of Utah and Canyon Lands in the center, the Navajo Section in the extreme southeast corner, and the Uinta Basin to the north. **Location:** West, bordering Idaho, Wyoming, Colorado, Arizona, and Nevada. **Climate:** primarily arid; southwest has a warm, almost dry, subtropical climate, while the southern part of the Colorado Plateau has cool, dry winters and wet summers. **Land use:** pasture, 45.1%; forest, 26.3%; agricultural, 3.9%; other, 24.7%.

People

Population (2003): 2,351,000; 28.6 persons per sq mi (11.0 persons per sq km) (land area only). **Vital statistics** (2001; per 1,000 population): birth rate, 21.8; death rate, 5.6; marriage rate, 10.6; divorce rate, 4.4. **Major cities:** Salt Lake City, 181,000; West Valley City, 111,000; Provo, 105,000; Sandy, 88,418 (2000); Orem, 84,324 (2000).

Government

Statehood: entered the Union on 4 Jan 1896 as the 45th state. **State constitution:** adopted 1895. **Representation in US Congress:** 2 senators; 3 representatives. **Electoral college:** 5 votes. **Political divisions:** 29 counties.

Economy

Employment: services, 29.7%; trade, 22.0%; government, 14.6%; manufacturing, 10.9%; finance, insurance, real estate, 7.8%; construction, 7.0%; transportation, public utilities, 4.9%; agriculture, forestry, fishing, 2.4%; mining, 0.7%. **Production:** services, 20.6%; trade, 16.9%; finance, insurance, real estate, 16.4%; government, 14.4%; manufacturing, 13.3%; transportation, utilities, 8.8%; construction, 6.5%; mining, 1.8%; agriculture, 1.1%. **Chief agricultural products:** *Crops:* hay, grains, peaches, cherries, onions, dairy products. *Livestock:* cattle, sheep, mink, poultry. *Aquaculture:* trout. **Chief manufactured products:** industrial machinery, computers, office equipment, transportation equipment, aerospace products, missile parts, motor vehicle parts, surgical tools, electromedical equipment, food processing.

Internet resources: <www.utah.com>; <www.utah.gov>.

Vermont

Name: Vermont, from the French *vert mont,* meaning "green mountain." **Nickname:** Green Mountain State. **Capital:** Montpelier. **Rank:** population: 49th; area: 43rd; pop. density: 30th. **Motto:** Freedom and Unity. **Song:** "These Green Mountains," by Diane Martin and Rita Burgess Gluck. **Bird:** hermit thrush. **Flower:** red clover. **Insect:** honeybee. **Mammal:** Morgan horse. **Tree:** sugar maple.

Natural features

Area: 9,614 sq mi, 24,901 sq km. **Mountain ranges:** Green Mountains, Appalachian Mountains, Hoosac Range, Taconic Range. **Highest point:** Mount Mansfield, 4,393 ft (1,339 m). **Largest lake:** Lake Champlain. **Major rivers:** Lamoille, Winooski, Otter Creek, Poultney, White, Missisquoi. **Natural regions:** the New England Province, eastern two-thirds of the state, includes the Taconic Section to the south, the Green Mountain Section in the center, New England Upland Section along the east-central edge, and the White Mountain Section in the far northeast corner; the St. Lawrence Valley, western edge of the state, with the Champlain Section in the central portion; the Valley and Ridge Province, with the Hudson Valley, small section along the west-central edge. **Location:** New England, bordering New Hampshire, Massachusetts, and New York; international border with Canada. **Climate:** cool continental, with very cold, snowy winters and warm, mild summers. **Land use:** forest, 75.4%; agricultural, 8.2%; pasture, 3.6%; other, 12.9%.

People

Population (2003): 619,000; 66.9 persons per sq mi (25.8 persons per sq km) (land area only). **Vital statistics** (2001; per 1,000 population): birth rate, 10.6; death rate, 8.5; marriage rate, 9.9; divorce rate, 4.0. **Major city:** Burlington, 38,889 (2000).

Government

Statehood: entered the Union on 4 Mar 1791 as the 14th state. **State constitution:** adopted 1793. **Representation in US Congress:** 2 senators; 1 representative. **Electoral college:** 3 votes. **Political divisions:** 14 counties.

Economy

Employment: services, 32.4%; trade, 21.0%; manufacturing, 13.7%; government, 12.8%; construction, 6.5%; finance, insurance, real estate, 5.7%; transportation, public utilities, 4.0%; agriculture, forestry,

For details about state governments, see pages 714–719; for energy data, see pages 737–738.

fishing, 3.7%; mining, 0.2%. **Production:** services, 22.3%; finance, insurance, real estate, 17.7%; manufacturing, 17.5%; trade, 15.7%; government, 12.4%; transportation, utilities, 7.6%; construction, 4.4%; agriculture, 2.2%; mining, 0.3%. **Chief agricultural products:** Crops: apples, honey, corn (maize), hay, greenhouse and nursery products, Christmas trees, maple syrup, fruits and vegetables, dairy products, eggs, wool. Livestock: cattle and calves, chickens, turkeys, sheep, horses. Extractive products: timber. **Chief manufactured products:** electrical and electronic equipment, fabricated metal products, nonelectrical machinery, paper and allied products, printing and publishing, food products, transportation equipment, lumber and wood products.

Internet resources: <www.travel-vermont.com>; <www.vermont.gov>.

Virginia

Name: Virginia, named in honor of Elizabeth I of England, known as the "Virgin Queen." **Nickname:** Old Dominion. **Capital:** Richmond. **Rank:** population: 12th; area: 37th; pop. density: 14th. **Motto:** Sic Semper Tyrannis (Thus Ever to Tyrants). **Song:** "Carry Me Back to Old Virginia," words and music by James B. Bland. **Bird:** cardinal. **Fish:** brook trout. **Flower:** dogwood. **Fossil:** Chesapecten jeffersonius. **Insect:** tiger swallowtail butterfly. **Tree:** dogwood.

Natural features

Area: 42,774 sq mi, 109,151 sq km. **Mountain ranges:** Blue Ridge, Appalachian Mountains. **Highest point:** Mount Rogers, 5,729 ft (1,746 m). **Largest lake:** Smith Mountain Lake. **Major rivers:** Potomac, Shenandoah, James, Roanoke. **Natural regions:** Coastal Plain, eastern region below the Potomac River; Piedmont Province extends from the south-central border up to the border with Maryland, includes the Piedmont Upland and Piedmont Lowlands; Blue Ridge Province, west of the Piedmont Province; Valley and Ridge region, covers most of western Virginia, includes the Shenandoah Valley and Allegheny, Shenandoah, and Appalachian Mountains; Appalachian Plateau, extreme western tip of the state, includes the Cumberland Mountain and Kanawha Sections. **Location:** East coast, bordering Maryland, North Carolina, Tennessee, Kentucky, and West Virginia. **Climate:** generally mild and equable but varies according to elevation and proximity to Chesapeake Bay and the Atlantic. **Land use:** forest, 60.5%; agricultural, 17.1%; pasture, 6.0%; other, 16.3%.

People

Population (2003): 7,386,000; 186.5 persons per sq mi (72.0 persons per sq km) (land area only). **Vital statistics** (2001; per 1,000 population): birth rate, 14.0; death rate, 7.8; marriage rate, 9.0; divorce rate, 4.3. **Major cities:** Virginia Beach, 434,000; Norfolk, 239,000; Chesapeake, 207,000; Richmond, 197,000; Newport News, 180,000; Hampton, 146,000; Alexandria, 131,000; Portsmouth, 100,565 (2000); Roanoke, 94,911 (2000).

Government

Statehood: entered the Union on 26 Jun 1788 as the 10th state. **State constitution:** adopted 1970. **Representation in US Congress:** 2 senators; 11 representatives. **Electoral college:** 13 votes. **Political divisions:** 95 counties.

Economy

Employment: services, 30.1%; trade, 20.1%; government, 18.9%; manufacturing, 10.2%; finance, insurance, real estate, 6.9%; construction, 6.2%; transportation, public utilities, 4.7%; agriculture, forestry, fishing, 2.5%; mining, 0.3%. **Production:** services, 22.6%; government, 17.8%; finance, insurance, real estate, 17.3%; trade, 14.4%; manufacturing, 13.1%; transportation, utilities, 9.0%; construction, 4.6%; agriculture, 0.8%; mining, 0.4%. **Chief agricultural products:** Crops: tobacco, soybeans, corn (maize), peanuts (groundnuts), cotton, apples, tomatoes, wheat, hay, potatoes, honey. Livestock: chickens, turkeys, pigs, cattle, sheep. Aquaculture: clams, softshell crabs, oysters, trout, catfish, hybrid striped bass. Extractive products: timber, blue crab. **Chief manufactured products:** electronics and electrical equipment, paper products, tobacco products, plastic materials, pharmaceutical and chemical products, food products, printing and publishing.

Internet resources: <www.virginia.org>; <www.virginia.gov>.

Washington

Name: Washington, named in honor of George Washington. **Nickname:** Evergreen State. **Capital:** Olympia. **Rank:** population: 15th; area: 20th; pop. density: 25th. **Motto:** Alki (By and By). **Song:** "Washington My Home," words and music by Helen Davis. **Bird:** willow goldfinch. **Fish:** steelhead trout. **Flower:** coast rhododendron. **Fossil:** Columbian mammoth. **Gemstone:** petrified wood. **Insect:** green darner dragonfly. **Tree:** western hemlock.

Natural features

Area: 71,300 sq mi, 184,665 sq km. **Mountain ranges:** Olympic Mountains, Cascade Range, Blue Mountains. **Highest point:** Mount Rainier, 14,410 ft (4,392 m). **Largest lake:** Moses Lake. **Major rivers:** Columbia, Pend Oreille, Snake, Yakima. **Natural regions:** Pacific Border Province, western quarter of the state, includes the Olympic Mountains to the west and the Puget Trough to the east; Cascade-Sierra Mountains, running north to south down center of state, include the Northern and Middle Cascades; Northern Rocky Mountains, northeast corner; Columbia Plateaus, eastern, central, and southern regions, include the Walla Walla Plateau in the center and the Blue Mountain Section in the southeast corner. **Location:** Northwest, bordering Idaho and Oregon; international border with Canada. **Climate:** moderate winters and cool summers west of the Cascades; east of the Cascade Range seasonal temperature variations are greater, with cold winters and warm, mild summers; throughout the state precipitation is greatest in the cooler months, with frequent cyclonic storms, some with gale-force winds. **Land use:** forest, 40.9%; agricultural, 19.7%; pasture, 17.4%; other, 22.0%.

People

Population (2003): 6,131,000; 92.1 persons per sq mi (35.6 persons per sq km) (land area only). **Vital statistics** (2001; per 1,000 population): birth rate, 13.6; death rate, 7.4; marriage rate, 7.2; divorce rate, 4.5. **Major cities:** Seattle, 570,000; Spokane, 196,000; Tacoma, 198,000; Vancouver, 150,000; Bellevue, 113,000; Everett, 91,488 (2000).

Government

Statehood: entered the Union on 11 Nov 1889 as the 42nd state. **State constitution:** adopted 1889. **Representation in US Congress:** 2 senators; 9 representatives. **Electoral college:** 11 votes. **Political divisions:** 39 counties.

Economy

Employment: services, 28.7%; trade, 21.9%; government, 15.7%; manufacturing, 11.8%; finance, insurance, real estate, 7.3%; construction, 5.6%; transportation, public utilities, 4.6%; agriculture, forestry, fishing, 4.2%; mining, 0.2%. **Production:** services, 25.0%; finance, insurance, real estate, 17.4%; trade, 16.8%; government, 13.2%; manufacturing, 12.6%; transportation, utilities, 7.9%; construction, 4.9%; agriculture, 2.1%; mining, 0.2%. **Chief agricultural products:** *Crops:* apples, peaches, pears, cherries, grapes, apricots, raspberries, dried peas, lentils, asparagus, carrots, sweet corn, green peas, potatoes, mint oil, hops, wheat, hay. *Livestock:* cattle and calves, poultry, horses. *Extractive products:* oysters, clams, mussels, crab, shrimp, geoduck, sea cucumbers, marine fish, salmon, timber. **Chief manufactured products:** aerospace equipment, food processing, forest products, advanced medical and technology products, aluminum products, fish processing.

Internet resources: <www.experiencewashington. com>; <www.access.wa.gov>.

West Virginia

Name: West Virginia, named in honor of Elizabeth I of England, who was also known as the "Virgin Queen." **Nickname:** Mountain State. **Capital:** Charleston. **Rank:** population: 37th; area: 41st; pop. density: 29th. **Motto:** *Montani Semper Liberi* (Mountaineers Are Always Free). **Song:** "This Is My West Virginia," words and music by Iris Bell; "West Virginia, My Home Sweet Home," words and music by Julian G. Hearne, Jr.; "The West Virginia Hills," words by David King and music by H.E. Engle. **Bird:** cardinal. **Fish:** brook trout. **Flower:** rhododendron. **Gemstone:** West Virginia fossil coral. **Insect:** monarch butterfly. **Mammal:** black bear. **Tree:** sugar maple.

Natural features

Area: 24,230 sq mi, 62,755 sq km. **Mountain ranges:** Appalachian Mountains, Allegheny Mountains. **Highest point:** Spruce Knob, 4,862 ft (1,482 m). **Largest lake:** Summersville Lake. **Major rivers:** Ohio, Big Sandy, Guyandotte, Great Kanawha, Little Kanawha, Monongahela, Potomac. **Natural regions:** Valley and

Ridge Province, eastern edge of the state, includes portions of the Shenandoah Mountains; the remainder of the state consists of the Appalachian Plateaus and includes the Kanawha Section to the south, the Allegheny Mountains, and the Allegheny Mountains in the northeast. **Location:** East, bordering Pennsylvania, Maryland, Virginia, Kentucky, and Ohio. **Climate:** humid continental, except for a marine modification in the lower panhandle. **Land use:** forest, 77.2%; agricultural, 9.2%; pasture, 3.1%; other, 10.5%.

People

Population (2003): 1,810,000; 75.2 persons per sq mi (29.0 persons per sq km) (land area only). **Vital statistics** (2001; per 1,000 population): birth rate, 11.4; death rate, 11.6; marriage rate, 7.9; divorce rate, 5.2. **Major cities** (2000): Charleston, 53,421; Huntington, 51,475; Parkersburg, 33,099; Wheeling, 31,419; Morgantown, 26,809.

Government

Statehood: entered the Union on 20 Jun 1863 as the 35th state. **State constitution:** adopted 1872. **Representation in US Congress:** 2 senators; 3 representatives. **Electoral college:** 5 votes. **Political divisions:** 55 counties.

Economy

Employment: services, 28.1%; trade, 22.2%; government, 17.1%; manufacturing, 9.9%; construction, 5.9%; transportation, public utilities, 5.2%; finance, insurance, real estate, 4.8%; agriculture, forestry, fishing, 3.3%; mining, 3.3%. **Production:** services, 17.9%; manufacturing, 16.0%; government, 15.5%; trade, 15.5%; finance, insurance, real estate, 11.3%; transportation, utilities, 11.3%; mining, 7.3%; construction, 4.6%; agriculture, 0.6%. **Chief agricultural products:** *Crops:* hay, apples, corn (maize), tobacco, peaches, dairy products. *Livestock:* cattle, sheep, poultry. *Extractive products:* timber. **Chief manufactured products:** chemical products, automobile parts, primary metal and fabricated metal products, glassware, computer software, wood products, electrical equipment, industrial machinery, pharmaceuticals.

Internet resources: <www.wvtourism.com>; <www.wv.gov>.

Wisconsin

Name: Wisconsin, an anglicized version of a French rendering of a Native American name said to mean "the place where we live." **Nickname:** Badger State. **Capital:** Madison. **Rank:** population: 20th; area: 25th; pop. density: 24th. **Motto:** Forward. **Song:** "On, Wisconsin," words and music by William T. Purdy. **Bird:** robin. **Fish:** muskellunge (muskie). **Flower:** wood violet. **Fossil:** trilobite. **Insect:** honeybee. **Mammal:** badger. **Mineral:** galena. **Rock:** red granite. **Tree:** sugar maple.

Natural features

Area: 65,498 sq mi, 169,639 sq km. **Mountain ranges:** Baraboo Range, Rib Mountain, Gogebic Range. **Highest point:** Timms Hill, 1,953 ft (595 m).

For details about state governments, see pages 714–719; for energy data, see pages 737–738.

Largest lake: Lake Winnebago. **Major rivers:** Wisconsin, St. Croix, Rock, Mississippi, Namekagon, Wolf, Pine-Popple, Brule, Pike. **Natural regions:** Superior Upland, divided into highland and lowland sections, northern half of the state; Central Lowland, southern half of the state, divided into the Wisconsin Driftless Section to the west and the Eastern Lake Section to the east, with a section of the Till Plains occupying a small area at the southern border. **Location:** Midwest, bordering Michigan, Illinois, Iowa, and Minnesota. **Climate:** continental, with long, cold winters and warm, but relatively short, summers. **Land use:** forest, 45.2%; agricultural, 27.5%; pasture, 5.3%; other, 22.0%.

People

Population (2003): 5,472,000; 100.8 persons per sq mi (38.9 persons per sq km). **Vital statistics** (2001; per 1,000 population): birth rate, 12.9; death rate, 8.6; marriage rate, 6.5; divorce rate, 3.2. **Major cities:** Milwaukee, 591,000; Madison, 215,000; Green Bay, 102,000; Kenosha, 90,352 (2000); Racine, 81,855 (2000).

Government

Statehood: entered the Union on 29 May 1848 as the 30th state. **State constitution:** adopted 1848. **Representation in US Congress:** 2 senators; 9 representatives. **Electoral college:** 10 votes (in the 2004 general elections based on the 2000 census). **Political divisions:** 72 counties.

Economy

Employment: services, 26.7%; trade, 21.8%; manufacturing, 19.2%; government, 11.9%; finance, insurance, real estate, 6.8%; construction, 4.8%; transportation, public utilities, 4.4%; agriculture, forestry, fishing, 4.2%; mining, 0.1%. **Production:** manufacturing, 26.3%; services, 17.8%; trade, 15.8%; finance, insurance, real estate, 15.6%; government, 10.6%; transportation, utilities, 7.1%; construction, 4.7%; agriculture, 1.9%; mining, 0.1%. **Chief agricultural products:** *Crops:* Dairy products, corn (maize), honey, maple syrup, oats, hay, snap and green beans, potatoes, strawberries, tart cherries, cranberries, Christmas trees, mint for oil, beets, cabbage, carrots, green peas, cucumbers. *Livestock:* cattle and calves, hogs, mink. *Extractive products:* freshwater fish. **Chief manufactured products:** processed foods, beer, industrial machinery, paper and paper products, fabricated metal products, transportation equipment, household appliances.

Internet resources: <www.travelwisconsin.com>; <www.wisconsin.gov>.

Wyoming

Name: Wyoming, from the Delaware Indian word, meaning "mountains and valleys alternating." **Nicknames:** Equality State and Cowboy State. **Capital:** Cheyenne. **Rank:** population: 50th; area: 9th; pop. density: 49th. **Motto:** Equal Rights. **Song:** "Wyoming," words by Charles E. Winter and music by George E. Knapp. **Bird:** meadowlark. **Fish:** cutthroat trout. **Flower:** Indian paintbrush. **Fossil:** knightia. **Gemstone:** jade. **Mammal:** bison. **Reptile:** horned toad. **Tree:** plains cottonwood.

Natural features

Area: 97,814 sq mi, 253,336 sq km. **Mountain ranges:** Rocky Mountains, Big Horn, Grand Tetons, Wind River Range, Continental Divide, Sierra Madre Range, Washakie Mountains. **Highest point:** Gannett Peak, 13,804 ft (4,207 m). **Largest lake:** Yellowstone Lake. **Major rivers:** Snake, Colorado, Green, Columbia. **Natural regions:** Great Plains Province, eastern third of the state, includes the Black Hills in the northeast corner, the High Plains in the southwest corner, and the Missouri Plateau in the center; Wyoming Basin, central and southern regions; Southern Rocky Mountains, southern border; the Middle Rocky Mountains, northwest third of the state, also cover a small area on the southern border; Northern Rocky Mountains, extreme northwest tip of the state. **Location:** West, bordering Montana, South Dakota, Nebraska, Colorado, Utah, and Idaho. **Climate:** semiarid continental, with long, cold winters and relatively short, warm summers. **Land use:** pasture, 72.2%; forest, 8.2%; agricultural, 5.0%; other, 14.7%.

People

Population (2003): 501,000; 5.2 persons per sq mi (2.0 persons per sq km) (land area only). **Vital statistics** (2001; per 1,000 population): birth rate, 12.7; death rate, 8.2; marriage rate, 10.3; divorce rate, 6.1. **Major cities** (2000): Cheyenne, 53,011; Casper, 49,644; Laramie, 27,204.

Government

Statehood: entered the Union on 10 Jul 1890 as the 44th state. **State constitution:** adopted 1889. **Representation in US Congress:** 2 senators; 1 representative. **Electoral college:** 3 votes. **Political divisions:** 23 counties.

Economy

Employment: services, 25.0%; trade, 21.3%; government, 19.5%; construction, 6.9%; finance, insurance, real estate, 6.6%; mining, 5.9%; transportation, public utilities, 5.4%; agriculture, forestry, fishing, 5.3%; manufacturing, 4.1%. **Production:** mining, 22.0%; transportation, utilities, 14.8%; government, 14.1%; trade, 11.8%; services, 11.6%; finance, insurance, real estate, 11.3%; manufacturing, 6.6%; construction, 5.4%; agriculture, 2.5%. **Chief agricultural products:** *Crops:* hay, wheat, barley, sugar beets and sugar, corn (maize), wool. *Livestock:* cattle and calves, sheep and lambs. **Chief manufactured products:** refined petroleum, lumber and wood products, food products, fabricated metal products.

Internet resources: <www.wyomingtourism.org>; <www.wyoming.gov>.

 **Did you know?** The United States has the largest known reserves of coal in the world, and roughly half of the coal it produces comes from Wyoming, while one-third of the coal that is consumed in the nation is taken from that state's Powder River Basin.

State Government

Governors of US States and Territories

Governors of New Hampshire and Vermont serve two-year terms; all others serve four-year terms. Parties: Democrat (D); Republican (R); Popular Democrat (PD); Covenant (C). Sources: National Governors Association; Council of State Governments.

STATE	GOVERNOR	IN OFFICE SINCE	PRESENT TERM EXPIRES
Alabama	Bob Riley (R)	January 2003	January 2011
Alaska	Sarah Palin (R)	December 2006	December 2010*
Arizona	Janet Napolitano (D)	January 2003	January 2011
Arkansas	Mike Beebe (D)	January 2007	January 2011*
California	Arnold Schwarzenegger (R)[1]	November 2003	January 2011
Colorado	Bill Ritter (D)	January 2007	January 2011*
Connecticut	M. Jodi Rell (R)[2]	July 2004	January 2011*
Delaware	Ruth Ann Minner (D)	January 2001	January 2009
Florida	Charlie Crist (R)	January 2007	January 2011*
Georgia	Sonny Perdue (R)	January 2003	January 2011
Hawaii	Linda Lingle (R)	December 2002	December 2010
Idaho	C.L. "Butch" Otter (R)	January 2007	January 2011*
Illinois	Rod Blagojevich (D)	January 2003	January 2011*
Indiana	Mitch Daniels (R)	January 2005	January 2009*
Iowa	Chet Culver (D)	January 2007	January 2011*
Kansas	Kathleen Sebelius (D)	January 2003	January 2011
Kentucky	Ernie Fletcher (R)	December 2003	December 2007*
Louisiana	Kathleen Babineaux Blanco (D)	January 2004	January 2008*
Maine	John Baldacci (D)	January 2003	January 2011
Maryland	Martin O'Malley (D)	January 2007	January 2011*
Massachusetts	Deval Patrick (D)	January 2007	January 2011*
Michigan	Jennifer Granholm (D)	January 2003	January 2011
Minnesota	Tim Pawlenty (R)	January 2003	January 2011*
Mississippi	Haley Barbour (R)	January 2004	January 2008*
Missouri	Matt Blunt (R)	January 2005	January 2009*
Montana	Brian Schweitzer (D)	January 2005	January 2009*
Nebraska	Dave Heineman (R)[3]	January 2005	January 2011
Nevada	Jim Gibbons (R)	January 2007	January 2011*
New Hampshire	John Lynch (D)	January 2005	January 2009*
New Jersey	Jon Corzine (D)	January 2006	January 2010*
New Mexico	Bill Richardson (D)	January 2003	January 2011
New York	Eliot Spitzer (D)	January 2007	January 2011*
North Carolina	Michael F. Easley (D)	January 2001	January 2009
North Dakota	John Hoeven (R)	December 2000	December 2008*
Ohio	Ted Strickland (D)	January 2007	January 2011*
Oklahoma	Brad Henry (D)	January 2003	January 2011
Oregon	Ted Kulongoski (D)	January 2003	January 2011
Pennsylvania	Edward G. Rendell (D)	January 2003	January 2011
Rhode Island	Don Carcieri (R)	January 2003	January 2011
South Carolina	Mark Sanford (R)	January 2003	January 2011
South Dakota	Mike Rounds (R)	January 2003	January 2011
Tennessee	Phil Bredesen (D)	January 2003	January 2011
Texas	Rick Perry (R)[4]	December 2000	January 2011*
Utah	Jon Huntsman, Jr. (R)	January 2005	January 2009*
Vermont	Jim Douglas (R)	January 2005	January 2009*
Virginia	Tim Kaine (D)	January 2006	January 2010
Washington	Chris Gregoire (D)	January 2005	January 2009*
West Virginia	Joe Manchin III (D)	January 2005	January 2009*
Wisconsin	Jim Doyle (D)	January 2003	January 2011*
Wyoming	Dave Freudenthal (D)	January 2003	January 2011

TERRITORY	GOVERNOR	IN OFFICE SINCE	PRESENT TERM EXPIRES
American Samoa	Togiola T.A. Tulafono (D)[5]	April 2003	January 2009
Guam	Felix Perez Camacho (R)	January 2003	January 2011
Northern Mariana Islands	Benígno Fitial (C)	January 2006	January 2010*
Puerto Rico	Aníbal Acevedo Vilá (PD)	January 2005	January 2009*
Virgin Islands	John deJongh, Jr. (D)	January 2007	January 2011*

Governors of US States and Territories (continued)

*Present governor is eligible for reelection. [1]*Arnold Schwarzenegger was elected in October 2003 following the recall of former governor Gray Davis. Gov. Schwarzenegger was elected to a full term in November 2006.* [2]*Lt. Gov. M. Jodi Rell became governor on 1 Jul 2004 following John G. Rowland's resignation. Gov. Rell was elected to a full term in November 2006.* [3]*Lt. Gov. Dave Heineman became governor on 21 Jan 2005 following Mike Johanns's appointment to the office of US secretary of agriculture. Gov. Heineman was elected to a full term in November 2006.* [4]*Lt. Gov. Rick Perry became governor in December 2000 following George W. Bush's election as president of the United States. Gov. Perry was elected to a full term in November 2002.* [5]*Lt. Gov. Togiola T.A. Tulafono became governor in April 2003 following the death of Gov. Tauese Sunia. Gov. Tulafono was elected to a full term in November 2004.*

Did you know?

The deepest continental body of water on Earth is Lake Baikal in southern Siberia, Russia. It reaches a maximum depth of 5,314 feet (1,620 meters). Plant and animal life in the lake is rich and varied, and about three-quarters of the species are peculiar to Baikal. Approximately 600 plant species live on or near the surface of the water, and there are more than 1,200 animal species at different depths, including one mammal, the Baikal seal.

State Officers and Legislatures

Sources: *Web sites from the individual states;* The Book of the States, *vol. 38; and the* CSG State Directory, *published by the Council of State Governments. Legislature figures are as of January 2007.*

STATE/OFFICE	OFFICEHOLDER	PAY[1]
Alabama		
Governor	Bob Riley (R)	$96,361
Lt. Gov.	Jim Folsom, Jr. (D)	$48,966
Sec. of State	Beth Chapman (R)	$71,500
Atty. Gen.	Troy King (R)	$153,927
Treasurer	Kay Ivey (R)	$71,500
Legislature		
Senate	Dem: 23; Rep: 12	
House	Dem: 61; Rep: 43; vacant: 1	
Alaska		
Governor	Sarah Palin (R)	$125,000
Lt. Gov.	Sean R. Parnell (R)	$100,000
Sec. of State[2]		
Atty. Gen.	Talis J. Colberg (R)	$124,752
Treasurer[3]	Brian Andrews (Deputy Treasury Commissioner)(R)	$100,476
Legislature		
Senate	Dem: 9; Rep: 11	
House	Dem: 17; Rep: 23	
Arizona		
Governor	Janet Napolitano (D)	$95,000
Lt. Gov.[4]		
Sec. of State	Jan Brewer (R)	$70,000
Atty. Gen.	Terry Goddard (D)	$90,000
Treasurer	Dean Martin (R)	$70,000
Legislature		
Senate	Dem: 13; Rep: 17	
House	Dem: 27; Rep: 33	
Arkansas		
Governor	Mike Beebe (D)	$77,028
Lt. Gov.	Bill Halter (D)	$37,229
Sec. of State	Charlie Daniels (D)	$48,182
Atty. Gen.	Dustin McDaniel (D)	$64,189
Treasurer	Martha A. Shoffner (D)	$48,182
General Assembly		
Senate	Dem: 27; Rep: 8	
House	Dem: 75; Rep: 25	
California		
Governor	Arnold Schwarzenegger (R)	$175,000
Lt. Gov.	John Garamendi (D)	$131,250
Sec. of State	Debra Bowen (D)	$131,250
Atty. Gen.	Edmund G. Brown, Jr. (D)	$148,750
Treasurer	Bill Lockyer (D)	$140,000
Legislature		
Senate	Dem: 25; Rep: 15	
Assembly	Dem: 48; Rep: 32	
Colorado		
Governor	Bill Ritter (D)	$90,000
Lt. Gov.	Barbara O'Brien (D)	$68,500
Sec. of State	Mike Coffman (R)	$68,500
Atty. Gen.	John W. Suthers (R)	$80,000
Treasurer	Cary Kennedy (D)	$68,500
General Assembly		
Senate	Dem: 20; Rep: 15	
House	Dem: 39; Rep: 26	
Connecticut		
Governor	M. Jodi Rell (R)	$150,000
Lt. Gov.	Michael C. Fedele (R)	$110,000
Sec. of State	Susan Bysiewicz (D)	$110,000
Atty. Gen.	Richard Blumenthal (D)	$110,000
Treasurer	Denise L. Nappier (D)	$110,000
General Assembly		
Senate	Dem: 24; Rep: 12	
House	Dem: 107; Rep: 44	
Delaware		
Governor	Ruth Ann Minner (D)	$132,500
Lt. Gov.	John Carney, Jr. (D)	$73,100
Sec. of State	Harriet Smith Windsor (D)	$119,700
Atty. Gen.	Joseph Biden III (D)	$136,600
Treasurer	Jack Markell (D)	$106,200
General Assembly		
Senate	Dem: 13; Rep: 8	
House	Dem: 18; Rep: 23	

State Officers and Legislatures (continued)

STATE/OFFICE	OFFICEHOLDER	PAY[1]
Florida		
Governor	Charlie Crist (R)	$129,060
Lt. Gov.	Jeffrey D. Kottkamp (R)	$123,688
Sec. of State	Kurt Browning (R)	$119,000
Atty. Gen.	Bill McCollum (R)	$127,771
Treasurer[3]	Alex Sink (Chief Financial Officer) (D)	$127,771
Legislature		
Senate	Dem: 14; Rep: 26	
House	Dem: 41; Rep: 78; vacant: 1	
Georgia		
Governor	Sonny Perdue (R)	$131,481
Lt. Gov.	Casey Cagle (R)	$86,442
Sec. of State	Karen Handel (R)	$116,664
Atty. Gen.	Thurbert E. Baker (D)	$130,020
Treasurer[3]	W. Daniel Ebersole (Dir., Office of Treasury and Fiscal Services) (R)	$121,882
General Assembly		
Senate	Dem: 22; Rep: 34	
House	Dem: 75; Rep: 105	
Hawaii		
Governor	Linda Lingle (R)	$94,780
Lt. Gov.	James R. Aiona, Jr. (R)	$90,041
Sec. of State[2]		
Atty. Gen.	Mark J. Bennett (R)	$107,100
Treasurer[3]	Georgina K. Kawamura (Director of Finance) (R)	$102,000
Legislature		
Senate	Dem: 20; Rep: 5	
House	Dem: 43; Rep: 8	
Idaho		
Governor	C.L. "Butch" Otter (R)	$98,500
Lt. Gov.	Jim Risch (R)	$26,750
Sec. of State	Ben Ysursa (R)	$82,500
Atty. Gen.	Lawrence Wasden (R)	$91,500
Treasurer	Ron G. Crane (R)	$82,500
Legislature		
Senate	Dem: 7; Rep: 28	
House	Dem: 19; Rep: 51	
Illinois		
Governor	Rod Blagojevich (D)	$154,100
Lt. Gov.	Pat Quinn (D)	$117,800
Sec. of State	Jesse White (D)	$135,900
Atty. Gen.	Lisa Madigan (D)	$135,900
Treasurer	Alexi Giannoulias (D)	$117,800
General Assembly		
Senate	Dem: 37; Rep: 22	
House	Dem: 66; Rep: 52	
Indiana		
Governor	Mitch Daniels (R)	$95,000
Lt. Gov.	Becky Skillman (R)	$76,000
Sec. of State	Todd Rokita (R)	$66,000
Atty. Gen.	Steve Carter (R)	$79,400
Treasurer	Richard E. Mourdock (R)	$66,000
General Assembly		
Senate	Dem: 17; Rep: 33	
House	Dem: 51; Rep: 49	
Iowa		
Governor	Chet Culver (D)	$130,000
Lt. Gov.	Patty Judge (D)	$103,212
Sec. of State	Michael A. Mauro (D)	$103,212

STATE/OFFICE	OFFICEHOLDER	PAY[1]
Iowa (continued)		
Atty. Gen.	Tom Miller (D)	$123,669
Treasurer	Michael L. Fitzgerald (D)	$103,212
General Assembly		
Senate	Dem: 30; Rep: 20	
House	Dem: 54; Rep: 46	
Kansas		
Governor	Kathleen Sebelius (D)	$98,331
Lt. Gov.	Mark V. Parkinson (D)	$111,523
Sec. of State	Ron Thornburgh (R)	$76,389
Atty. Gen.	Paul Morrison (D)	$76,389
Treasurer	Lynn Jenkins (R)	$76,389
Legislature		
Senate	Dem: 10; Rep: 30	
House	Dem: 46; Rep: 79	
Kentucky		
Governor	Ernie Fletcher (R)	$130,705
Lt. Gov.	Steve Pence (R)	$95,815
Sec. of State	Trey Grayson (R)	$95,815
Atty. Gen.	Gregory D. Stumbo (D)	$95,815
Treasurer	Jonathan Miller (D)	$95,815
General Assembly		
Senate	Dem: 16; Rep: 21; Ind: 1	
House	Dem: 61; Rep: 39	
Louisiana		
Governor	Kathleen Babineaux Blanco (D)	$95,000
Lt. Gov.	Mitch Landrieu (D)	$85,008
Sec. of State	Jay Dardenne (R)	$85,000
Atty. Gen.	Charles C. Foti, Jr. (D)	$85,000
Treasurer	John Kennedy (D)	$85,000
Legislature		
Senate	Dem: 24; Rep: 15	
House	Dem: 60; Rep: 41; Ind: 1; vacant: 3	
Maine		
Governor	John Baldacci (D)	$70,000
Lt. Gov.[5]		
Sec. of State	Matthew Dunlap (D)	N/A
Atty. Gen.	G. Steven Rowe (D)	$78,062
Treasurer	David G. Lemoine (D)	$71,032
Legislature		
Senate	Dem: 18; Rep: 17	
House	Dem: 89; Rep: 60; Unenrolled: 2	
Maryland		
Governor	Martin O'Malley (D)	$150,000
Lt. Gov.	Anthony G. Brown (D)	$125,000
Sec. of State	Dennis Schnepfe (D)	$87,500
Atty. Gen.	Douglas F. Gansler (D)	$125,000
Treasurer	Nancy K. Kopp (D)	$125,000
General Assembly		
Senate	Dem: 33; Rep: 14	
House	Dem: 104; Rep: 37	
Massachusetts		
Governor	Deval Patrick (D)	$135,000
Lt. Gov.	Timothy Murray (D)	$120,000
Sec. of State	William Francis Galvin (D)	$120,000
Atty. Gen.	Martha Coakley (D)	$122,500
Treasurer	Timothy Cahill (D)	$120,000
General Court (legislature)		
Senate	Dem: 35; Rep: 5	
House	Dem: 141; Rep: 19	

State Officers and Legislatures (continued)

STATE/OFFICE	OFFICEHOLDER	PAY[1]
Michigan		
Governor	Jennifer Granholm (D)	$177,000
Lt. Gov.	John D. Cherry, Jr. (D)	$123,900
Sec. of State	Terri Lynn Land (R)	$124,900
Atty. Gen.	Mike Cox (R)	$124,900
Treasurer	Robert J. Kleine (D)	$118,616
Legislature		
Senate	Dem: 17; Rep: 21	
House	Dem: 58; Rep: 52	
Minnesota		
Governor	Tim Pawlenty (R)	$120,303
Lt. Gov.	Carol Molnau (R)	$78,197
Sec. of State	Mark Ritchie (D)	$90,227
Atty. Gen.	Lori Swanson (D)	$114,288
Treasurer[3]	Tom J. Hanson	$108,388
	(Commissioner of Finance) (R)	
Legislature		
Senate	Dem: 44; Rep: 23	
House	Dem: 85; Rep: 49	
Mississippi		
Governor	Haley Barbour (R)	$122,160
Lt. Gov.	Amy Tuck (R)	$60,000
Sec. of State	Eric Clark (D)	$90,000
Atty. Gen.	Jim Hood (D)	$108,960
Treasurer	Tate Reeves (R)	$90,000
Legislature		
Senate	Dem: 27; Rep: 25	
House	Dem: 74; Rep: 47; vacant: 1	
Missouri		
Governor	Matt Blunt (R)	$120,087
Lt. Gov.	Peter Kinder (R)	$77,184
Sec. of State	Robin Carnahan (D)	$96,455
Atty. Gen.	Jay Nixon (D)	$104,332
Treasurer	Sarah Steelman (R)	$96,455
General Assembly		
Senate	Dem: 13; Rep: 21	
House	Dem: 71; Rep: 92	
Montana		
Governor	Brian Schweitzer (D)	$96,462
Lt. Gov.	John Bohlinger (R)	$74,173
Sec. of State	Brad Johnson (R)	$76,539
Atty. Gen.	Mike McGrath (D)	$85,762
Treasurer[3]	Janet Kelly (Dir.,	$86,870
	Department of	
	Administration) (D)	
Legislature		
Senate	Dem: 26; Rep: 24	
House	Dem: 49; Rep: 50; Constitution: 1	
Nebraska		
Governor	Dave Heineman (R)	$85,000
Lt. Gov.	Rick Sheehy (R)	$60,000
Sec. of State	John A. Gale (R)	$65,000
Atty. Gen.	Jon Bruning (R)	$75,000
Treasurer	Shane Osborn (R)	$60,000
Legislature (unicameral)		
Senate	49 nonpartisan members	
Nevada		
Governor	Jim Gibbons (R)	$117,000
Lt. Gov.	Brian K. Krolicki (R)	$50,000
Sec. of State	Ross Miller (D)	$80,000
Atty. Gen.	Catherine Cortez Masto(D)	$110,000
Treasurer	Kate Marshall (D)	$80,000

STATE/OFFICE	OFFICEHOLDER	PAY[1]
Nevada (continued)		
Legislature		
Senate	Dem: 10; Rep: 11	
Assembly	Dem: 27; Rep: 15	
New Hampshire		
Governor	John Lynch (D)	$102,704
Lt. Gov.[5]		
Sec. of State	William Gardner (D)	$89,128
Atty. Gen.	Kelly Ayotte (R)	$99,317
Treasurer	Catherine Provencher (I)	$89,128
General Court (legislature)		
Senate	Dem: 14; Rep: 10	
House	Dem: 239; Rep: 161	
New Jersey		
Governor	Jon Corzine (D)	$175,000
Lt. Gov.[5]		
Sec. of State	Nina Mitchell Wells (D)	$141,000
Atty. Gen.	Anne Milgram (D)	$141,000
Treasurer	Bradley I. Abelow (D)	$141,000
Legislature		
Senate	Dem: 22; Rep: 18	
General Assembly	Dem: 49; Rep: 31	
New Mexico		
Governor	Bill Richardson (D)	$110,000
Lt. Gov.	Diane Denish (D)	$85,000
Sec. of State	Mary Herrera (D)	$85,000
Atty. Gen.	Gary K. King (D)	$95,000
Treasurer	James B. Lewis (D)	$85,000
Legislature		
Senate	Dem: 24; Rep: 18	
House	Dem: 42; Rep: 28	
New York		
Governor	Eliot Spitzer (D)	$179,000
Lt. Gov.	David A. Paterson (D)	$151,500
Sec. of State	Lorraine Cortés-Vázquez (D)	$120,800
Atty. Gen.	Andrew M. Cuomo (D)	$151,500
Treasurer	Aida Brewer	$109,190
Legislature		
Senate	Dem: 28; Rep: 34	
Assembly	Dem: 105; Rep: 45	
North Carolina		
Governor	Michael F. Easley (D)	$123,819
Lt. Gov.	Beverly Perdue (D)	$109,279
Sec. of State	Elaine F. Marshall (D)	$109,279
Atty. Gen.	Roy Cooper (D)	$109,279
Treasurer	Richard H. Moore (D)	$109,279
General Assembly		
Senate	Dem: 31; Rep: 19	
House	Dem: 68; Rep: 52	
North Dakota		
Governor	John Hoeven (R)	$88,926
Lt. Gov.	Jack Dalrymple (R)	$69,035
Sec. of State	Alvin A. Jaeger (R)	$70,739
Atty. Gen.	Wayne Stenehjem (R)	$77,655
Treasurer	Kelly Schmidt (R)	$66,805
Legislative Assembly		
Senate	Dem: 21; Rep: 26	
House	Dem: 33; Rep: 61	

State Officers and Legislatures (continued)

STATE/OFFICE	OFFICEHOLDER	PAY[1]
Ohio		
Governor	Ted Strickland (D)	$130,291
Lt. Gov.	Lee Fisher (D)	$130,020
Sec. of State	Jennifer Brunner (D)	$105,185
Atty. Gen.	Marc Dann (D)	$105,185
Treasurer	Richard Cordray (D)	$105,185
General Assembly		
Senate	Dem: 12; Rep: 21	
House	Dem: 46; Rep: 52	
Oklahoma		
Governor	Brad Henry (D)	$110,299
Lt. Gov.	Jari Askins (D)	$85,500
Sec. of State	M. Susan Savage (D)	$90,000
Atty. Gen.	W.A. Drew Edmondson (D)	$103,109
Treasurer	Scott Meacham (D)	$87,875
Legislature		
Senate	Dem: 24; Rep: 24	
House	Dem: 44; Rep: 57	
Oregon		
Governor	Ted Kulongoski (D)	$93,600
Lt. Gov.[4]		
Sec. of State	Bill Bradbury (D)	$72,000
Atty. Gen.	Hardy Myers (D)	$77,200
Treasurer	Randall Edwards (D)	$72,000
Legislative Assembly		
Senate	Dem: 18; Rep: 12	
House	Dem: 31; Rep: 29	
Pennsylvania		
Governor	Edward G. Rendell (D)	$161,173
Lt. Gov.	Catherine Baker Knoll (D)	$135,383
Sec. of State	Pedro A. Cortés (D)	$116,045
Atty. Gen.	Tom Corbett (R)	$134,096
Treasurer	Robin L. Wiessmann (D)	$134,096
General Assembly		
Senate	Dem: 21; Rep: 29	
House	Dem: 102; Rep: 101	
Rhode Island		
Governor	Don Carcieri (R)	$105,194
Lt. Gov.	Elizabeth H. Roberts (D)	$88,584
Sec. of State	A. Ralph Mollis (D)	$88,584
Atty. Gen.	Patrick C. Lynch (D)	$94,121
Treasurer	Frank T. Caprio (D)	$88,584
General Assembly		
Senate	Dem: 33; Rep: 5	
House	Dem: 62; Rep: 13	
South Carolina		
Governor	Mark Sanford (R)	$106,078
Lt. Gov.	André Bauer (R)	$46,545
Sec. of State	Mark Hammond (R)	$92,007
Atty. Gen.	Henry McMaster (R)	$92,007
Treasurer	Ken Wingate (R) (interim)	$92,007
General Assembly		
Senate	Dem: 20; Rep: 26	
House	Dem: 51; Rep: 73	
South Dakota		
Governor	Mike Rounds (R)	$105,544
Lt. Gov.	Dennis Daugaard (R)	$14,399
Sec. of State	Chris Nelson (R)	$71,713
Atty. Gen.	Larry Long (R)	$89,618
Treasurer	Vernon L. Larson (R)	$71,713

STATE/OFFICE	OFFICEHOLDER	PAY[1]
South Dakota (continued)		
Legislature		
Senate	Dem: 15; Rep: 20	
House	Dem: 20; Rep: 50	
Tennessee		
Governor	Phil Bredesen (D)	$85,000
Lt. Gov.[6]	Ron Ramsey (R)	$49,500
Sec. of State	Riley Darnell (D)	$139,116
Atty. Gen.	Robert E. Cooper, Jr. (D)	$129,948
Treasurer	Dale Sims (D)	$139,116
General Assembly		
Senate	Dem: 16; Rep: 17	
House	Dem: 53; Rep: 46	
Texas		
Governor	Rick Perry (R)	$115,345
Lt. Gov.	David Dewhurst (R)	$115,345
Sec. of State	Roger Williams (R)	$117,546
Atty. Gen.	Greg Abbott (R)	$125,000
Treasurer[3]	Susan Combs (Comptroller) (R)	$92,217
Legislature		
Senate	Dem: 11; Rep: 20	
House	Dem: 69; Rep: 81	
Utah		
Governor	Jon Huntsman, Jr. (R)	$104,100
Lt. Gov.	Gary R. Herbert (R)	$81,000
Sec. of State[2]		
Atty. Gen.	Mark Shurtleff (R)	$98,895
Treasurer	Edward T. Alter (R)	$81,000
Legislature		
Senate	Dem: 8; Rep: 21	
House	Dem: 20; Rep: 55	
Vermont		
Governor	Jim Douglas (R)	$138,465
Lt. Gov.	Brian Dubie (R)	$58,760
Sec. of State	Deborah L. Markowitz (D)	$87,796
Atty. Gen.	William H. Sorrell (D)	$105,102
Treasurer	Jeb Spaulding (D)	$87,796
General Assembly		
Senate	Dem: 23; Rep: 7	
House	Dem: 93; Rep: 49; Ind: 2; Progressive: 6	
Virginia		
Governor	Tim Kaine (D)	$124,855
Lt. Gov.	Bill Bolling (R)	$36,321
Sec. of State	Katherine K. Hanley (D)	$135,311
Atty. Gen.	Robert F. McDonnell (R)	$110,667
Treasurer	J. Braxton Powell (D)	$118,644
General Assembly		
Senate	Dem: 17; Rep: 23	
House	Dem: 40; Rep: 57; Ind: 3	
Washington		
Governor	Chris Gregoire (D)	$148,035
Lt. Gov.	Brad Owen (D)	$77,382
Sec. of State	Sam Reed (R)	$103,736
Atty. Gen.	Rob McKenna (R)	$134,577
Treasurer	Michael J. Murphy (D)	$103,736
Legislature		
Senate	Dem: 32; Rep: 17	
House	Dem: 62; Rep: 36	

State Officers and Legislatures (continued)

STATE/OFFICE	OFFICEHOLDER	PAY[1]
West Virginia		
Governor	Joe Manchin III (D)	$95,000
Lt. Gov.[7]	Earl Ray Tomblin (D)	—
Sec. of State	Betty Ireland (R)	$70,000
Atty. Gen.	Darrell V. McGraw, Jr. (D)	$85,000
Treasurer	John D. Perdue (D)	$75,000
Legislature		
Senate	Dem: 23; Rep: 11	
House	Dem: 72; Rep: 28	
Wisconsin		
Governor	Jim Doyle (D)	$131,768
Lt. Gov.	Barbara Lawton (D)	$69,579
Sec. of State	Douglas La Follette (D)	$62,549
Atty. Gen.	J.B. Van Hollen (R)	$127,868

STATE/OFFICE	OFFICEHOLDER	PAY[1]
Wisconsin (continued)		
Treasurer	Dawn Marie Sass (D)	$62,549
Legislature		
Senate	Dem: 18; Rep: 15	
Assembly	Dem: 47; Rep: 52	
Wyoming		
Governor	Dave Freudenthal (D)	$105,000
Lt. Gov.[4]		
Sec. of State	Max Maxfield (R)	$92,000
Atty. Gen.	Patrick J. Crank (D)	$100,776
Treasurer	Joseph B. Meyer (R)	$92,000
Legislature		
Senate	Dem: 7; Rep: 23	
House	Dem: 17; Rep: 43	

[1]The salary rates are from January 2005 or January 2006. [2]Lieutenant governor serves as secretary of state. [3]No official state treasurer; official in charge of general treasury performs duties. [4]Secretary of state assumes duties of lieutenant governor. [5]No official lieutenant governor; president of the Senate succeeds the governor. [6]In Tennessee speaker of the Senate and lieutenant governor are one and the same. [7]In West Virginia president of the Senate and lieutenant governor are one and the same.

Cities of the United States

US Urban Growth, 1850–2005

Source: US Census Bureau.

RANK	CITY	1850	1900	1950	1980	1990	2005
1	New York NY[1]	515,547	3,437,202	7,891,957	7,071,639	7,322,564	8,143,197
2	Los Angeles CA	1,610	102,479	1,970,358	2,966,850	3,485,398	3,844,829
3	Chicago IL	29,963	1,698,575	3,620,962	3,005,072	2,783,726	2,842,518
4	Houston TX	2,396	44,633	596,163	1,595,138	1,630,553	2,016,582
5	Philadelphia PA[1]	121,376	1,293,697	2,071,605	1,688,210	1,585,577	1,463,281
6	Phoenix AZ		5,544	106,818	789,704	983,403	1,461,575
7	San Antonio TX	3,488	53,321	408,442	785,880	935,933	1,256,509
8	San Diego CA		17,700	334,387	875,538	1,110,549	1,255,540
9	Dallas TX		42,638	434,462	904,078	1,006,877	1,213,825
10	San Jose CA		21,500	95,280	629,442	782,248	912,332
11	Detroit MI	21,019	285,704	1,849,568	1,203,339	1,027,974	886,671
12	Indianapolis IN	8,091	169,164	427,173	700,807	741,952	784,118
13	Jacksonville FL	1,045	28,429	204,517	540,920	635,230	782,623
14	San Francisco CA[1]	34,776	342,782	775,357	678,974	723,959	739,426
15	Columbus OH	17,882	125,560	375,901	564,871	632,910	730,657
16	Austin TX	629	22,258	132,459	345,496	465,622	690,252
17	Memphis TN	8,841	102,320	396,000	646,356	610,337	672,277
18	Baltimore MD	169,054	508,957	949,708	786,775	736,014	635,815
19	Fort Worth TX		26,688	278,778	385,164	447,619	624,067
20	Charlotte NC	1,065	18,091	134,042	314,447	395,934	610,949
21	El Paso TX		15,906	130,485	425,259	515,342	598,590
22	Milwaukee WI	20,061	285,315	637,392	636,212	628,088	578,887
23	Seattle WA		80,671	467,591	493,846	516,259	573,911
24	Boston MA	136,881	560,892	801,444	562,994	574,283	559,034
25	Denver CO[1]		133,859	415,786	492,365	467,610	557,917
26	Louisville KY[1]	43,194	204,731	369,129	298,451	269,063	556,429
27	Washington DC[1]	40,001	278,718	802,178	638,333	606,900	550,521
28	Nashville TN[1]	10,165	80,865	174,307	455,651	510,784	549,110
29	Las Vegas NV			24,624	164,674	258,295	545,147
30	Portland OR		90,426	373,628	366,383	437,319	533,427

[1]Cities with boundaries contiguous with their respective counties: New York, Philadelphia, San Francisco, Denver, Louisville (Jefferson county), Washington (District of Columbia), and Nashville (Davidson county).

Fifteen Fastest-Growing Cities in the US

Based on a population of 250,000 or more. Source: US Census Bureau.

	POPULATION		
CITY	1 APR 2000	1 JUL 2005	CHANGE (%)
Bakersfield CA	243,213	295,536	+21.5
Raleigh NC	284,800	341,530	+19.9
Stockton CA	244,011	286,926	+17.6
Fort Worth TX	541,339	624,067	+15.3
Riverside CA	255,193	290,086	+13.7
Las Vegas NV	480,044	545,147	+13.6
Atlanta GA	416,425	470,688	+13.0
Plano TX	222,000	250,096	+12.7
Sacramento CA	407,018	456,441	+12.1
Mesa AZ	397,770	442,780	+11.3
Phoenix AZ	1,321,627	1,461,575	+10.6
Albuquerque NM	448,354	494,236	+10.2
San Antonio TX	1,151,447	1,256,509	+9.1
Arlington TX	333,202	362,805	+8.9
Charlotte NC	561,973	610,949	+8.7

Fifteen Cities with the Greatest Population Losses in the US

Based on a population of 250,000 or more. Source: US Census Bureau.

		POPULATION				POPULATION	
CITY	CHANGE (%)	1 APR 2000	1 JUL 2005	CITY	CHANGE (%)	1 APR 2000	1 JUL 2005
Detroit MI	-6.8	951,270	886,671	Washington DC	-3.8	572,059	550,521
Cincinnati OH	-6.8	331,283	308,728	Philadelphia PA	-3.6	1,517,550	1,463,280
New Orleans LA[1]	-6.2	484,674	454,863	Milwaukee WI	-3.0	596,988	578,887
Cleveland OH	-5.3	477,472	452,208	Tulsa OK	-2.7	393,120	382,457
Pittsburgh PA	-5.3	334,563	316,718	Minneapolis MN	-2.6	382,747	372,811
Boston MA	-5.1	589,141	559,034				
San Francisco CA	-4.8	776,773	739,426				
Buffalo NY	-4.4	292,648	279,745				
St. Paul MN	-4.1	286,788	275,150				
Toledo OH	-4.0	313,782	301,285				

[1]New Orleans population change -53.9% (-261,286) between 1 Apr 2000 and 1 Jul 2006 due to Hurricane Katrina.

Racial Makeup of the Fifteen Largest US Cities

Information is given in percent of the total population. The Hispanic or Latino category is listed for comparative purposes even though Hispanic or Latino people may be of any race; thus, the rows of racial percentages will not add up to 100 if the Hispanic or Latino entries are included. Excludes population living in institutions. Source: US Census Bureau, American Community Survey, 2005 Data Profiles.

CITY	WHITE	BLACK OR AFRICAN AMERICAN	AMERICAN INDIAN AND ALASKA NATIVE	ASIAN	NATIVE HAWAIIAN AND OTHER PACIFIC ISLANDER	SOME OTHER RACE	TWO OR MORE RACES	HISPANIC OR LATINO	TOTAL POPULATION
New York NY	44.0	25.3	0.4	11.6	—	17.0	1.6	27.9	7,956,113
Los Angeles CA	49.1	9.9	0.4	11.1	0.3	26.9	2.4	48.9	3,731,437
Chicago IL	38.6	34.9	0.2	4.8	0.1	19.9	1.6	28.8	2,701,926
Houston TX	56.7	23.5	0.3	5.8	0.1	12.5	1.1	42.3	1,941,430
Philadelphia PA	42.1	44.7	0.2	5.2	—	6.3	1.5	10.4	1,406,415
Phoenix AZ	73.7	5.1	2.1	2.0	0.1	15.0	2.1	41.8	1,377,980
San Diego CA	63.2	6.8	0.5	15.8	0.5	9.7	3.5	25.9	1,208,331
San Antonio TX	64.0	6.1	0.7	1.8	0.1	24.1	3.2	61.2	1,202,223
Dallas TX	56.9	23.7	0.5	2.8	—	15.0	1.2	42.1	1,144,946
San Jose CA	50.4	3.3	0.4	30.6	0.3	12.1	2.8	31.5	887,330
Detroit MI	11.1	82.1	0.4	1.1	—	3.7	1.5	5.6	836,056
Jacksonville FL	61.4	30.7	0.3	3.7	—	2.4	1.5	5.4	768,537
Indianapolis IN	66.3	25.5	0.3	1.6	—	3.8	2.4	6.2	765,310
San Francisco CA	53.2	6.5	0.3	33.1	0.4	3.8	2.7	13.8	719,077
Columbus OH	65.5	26.2	0.2	3.9	—	1.5	2.6	3.5	693,983

— Less than 0.05 percent.
Details may not add to 100% because of rounding.

Area and Zip Codes Web Sites

US telephone area codes and postal codes change frequently to accommodate telecommunications user patterns and expansions and shifts in patterns of business and residential development. With regard to telephone area codes, in some cases, an area receives an entirely new area code; in others, a new area code "overlays" the preceding one. Check local listings to determine whether to dial "1" before dialing outside of the area code or to dial the area code as well as the telephone number when dialing within the area code.

Area codes: <www.nanpa.com>.
Zip codes: <http://zip4.usps.com/zip4/welcome.jsp>.

Law and Crime

US Crime Trends, 2006

The crime trends shown below represent the percent change in crimes reported to police for the first six months of 2006 as compared to the same time period in the year 2005. A negative number indicates that crime has declined. Details may not add to totals given due to rounding.

Source: Federal Bureau of Investigation, *Preliminary Semiannual Uniform Crime Report, January–June 2006.*

POPULATION GROUP AND AREA	NUMBER OF AGENCIES[1]	POPULATION ('000)	VIOLENT CRIME[2]	PROPERTY CRIME[3]	MURDER
cities					
1,000,000 and over	10	24,886	+1.6	−3.6	+6.7
500,000 to 999,999	20	13,503	+4.5	−2.8	+8.4
250,000 to 499,999	35	12,627	+6.8	−4.0	+1.3
100,000 to 249,999	175	26,265	+5.0	−3.2	+2.5
50,000 to 99,999	353	24,094	+5.2	−1.7	−8.1
25,000 to 49,999	630	21,694	+5.7	−0.7	−9.4
10,000 to 24,999	1,412	22,315	+4.3	−2.7	+7.5
under 10,000	5,624	18,353	+2.4	−1.8	−11.9
counties					
metropolitan[4]	1,332	50,760	+3.0	−1.8	+3.1
nonmetropolitan[5]	1,944	21,410	−5.9	−3.5	−13.1
total	**11,535**	**235,906**	**+3.7**	**−2.6**	**+1.4**

POPULATION GROUP AND AREA	FORCIBLE RAPE	ROBBERY	AGGRAVATED ASSAULT	BURGLARY	LARCENY/ THEFT	CAR THEFT	ARSON
cities							
1,000,000 and over	+2.3	+6.2	−2.1	−1.5	−4.7	−1.8	+9.2
500,000 to 999,999	−2.4	+10.9	+0.8	+4.1	−5.6	−1.8	+4.7
250,000 to 499,999	+1.2	+11.7	+4.6	+2.4	−6.4	−2.7	−1.3
100,000 to 249,999	+2.7	+12.5	+1.2	+0.4	−4.3	−3.0	+3.6
50,000 to 99,999	−0.7	+11.7	+3.1	+1.5	−2.8	−0.2	+20.0
25,000 to 49,999	+0.6	+11.0	+4.4	+2.6	−1.6	−0.3	+7.2
10,000 to 24,999	+0.0	+12.8	+2.1	+0.3	−3.4	−2.4	+11.9
under 10,000	−2.6	+6.8	+2.2	+0.6	−2.2	−3.2	+20.0
counties							
metropolitan[4]	−0.8	+8.4	+1.8	+3.1	−3.2	−4.0	+3.1
nonmetropolitan[5]	−8.1	−0.3	−5.8	−3.7	−3.3	−3.9	−0.9
total	[6]	**+9.7**	**+1.2**	**+1.2**	**−3.8**	**−2.3**	**+6.8**

[1]*Law enforcement agencies.* [2]*Includes murder, forcible rape, robbery, and aggravated assault.* [3]*Includes burglary, larceny/theft, and car theft, but excludes data for arson.* [4]*Includes crimes reported to sheriffs' departments, county police departments, and state police within Metropolitan Statistical Areas.* [5]*Includes crimes reported to sheriffs' departments, county police departments, and state police outside Metropolitan Statistical Areas.* [6]*Negligible.*

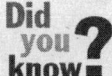

Did you know? The movement of people from a city to suburbs and the surrounding countryside creates a larger metropolitan area, and the metropolitan areas tend to merge into even larger urban agglomerations, the megalopolises. The biggest in the US is "Boswash," which stretches from Boston MA to Washington DC.

State Crime Rates, 2000–05
Crimes reported to the police per 100,000 population.

STATE	2000 TOTAL	2001[1] TOTAL	2002 TOTAL	2003 TOTAL	2004 TOTAL	2005 TOTAL
AL	4,546	4,319	4,465	4,475	4,452	4,324
AK	4,249	4,236	4,310	4,360	4,018	4,244
AZ	5,830	6,077	6,386	6,147	5,845	5,351
AR	4,115	4,134	4,158	4,088	4,512	4,585
CA	3,740	3,903	3,944	4,006	3,971	3,849
CO	3,983	4,219	4,348	4,299	4,293	4,436
CT	3,233	3,118	2,997	2,984	2,913	2,833
DE[2]	4,478	4,053	3,939	4,090	3,732	3,744
DC[3]	7,277	7,710	8,022	7,489	6,230	6,206
FL	5,695	5,570	5,421	5,188	4,891	4,716
GA	4,751	4,646	4,507	4,715	4,722	4,621
HI	5,199	5,386	6,044	5,547	5,047	5,048
ID	3,186	3,133	3,173	3,175	3,039	2,955
IL[4]	4,286	4,098	4,016	3,844	3,729	3,632
IN	3,752	3,831	3,750	3,708	3,723	3,780
IA	3,234	3,301	3,448	3,254	3,176	3,125
KS[5]	4,409	4,321	4,087	4,408	4,349	4,174
KY[6]	2,960	2,938	2,903	2,759	2,783	2,797
LA	5,423	5,338	5,098	4,948	5,049	4,278
ME	2,620	2,688	2,656	2,559	2,514	2,525
MD	4,816	4,867	4,747	4,503	4,341	4,247
MA	3,026	3,099	3,094	3,036	2,919	2,821
MI	4,110	4,082	3,874	3,790	3,548	3,643
MN	3,488	3,584	3,535	3,376	3,309	3,381
MS	4,004	4,185	4,159	4,031	3,774	3,539
MO	4,528	4,776	4,602	4,575	4,395	4,453
MT[5]	3,533	3,689	3,513	3,461	3,230	3,424
NE	4,096	4,330	4,257	4,046	3,830	3,710
NV	4,269	4,266	4,498	4,903	4,823	4,848
NH	2,433	2,322	2,220	2,203	2,207	1,928
NJ	3,161	3,225	3,024	2,914	2,785	2,688
NM	5,519	5,324	5,078	4,756	4,885	4,851
NY	3,100	2,925	2,804	2,715	2,641	2,554
NC	4,919	4,938	4,721	4,725	4,608	4,543
ND	2,288	2,418	2,406	2,190	1,996	2,076
OH	4,042	4,178	4,107	3,984	4,015	4,014
OK	4,559	4,607	4,743	4,818	4,743	4,551
OR	4,845	5,044	4,868	5,061	4,929	4,687
PA	2,995	2,961	2,841	2,828	2,826	2,842
RI	3,476	3,685	3,589	3,281	3,131	2,970
SC	5,221	4,753	5,297	5,328	5,289	5,101
SD	2,320	2,332	2,279	2,177	2,106	1,952
TN	4,890	5,153	5,019	5,080	5,002	5,028
TX	4,956	5,153	5,190	5,153	5,035	4,862
UT	4,476	4,243	4,452	4,505	4,322	4,096
VT	2,987	2,769	2,530	2,343	2,420	2,400
VA	3,028	3,178	3,140	3,000	2,953	2,921
WA	5,106	5,152	5,107	5,102	5,193	5,239
WV	2,603	2,560	2,515	2,594	2,777	2,898
WI	3,209	3,321	3,253	3,101	2,873	2,902
WY	3,298	3,518	3,581	3,578	3,564	3,385
US crime rate	**4,125**	**4,161**	**4,119**	**4,067**	**3,983**	**3,899**

2005 CRIME RATES IN DETAIL

	VIOLENT CRIMES					PROPERTY CRIMES			
STATE	MURDER[7]	FORCIBLE RAPE	AGGRAVATED ASSAULT	ROBBERY	TOTAL[7]	BURGLARY	LARCENY/ THEFT	MOTOR VEHICLE THEFT	TOTAL
AL	8.2	34.3	248	141	432	954	2,650	288	3,892
AK	4.8	81.1	465	80.9	632	623	2,599	391	3,613
AZ	7.5	33.8	327	144	513	948	2,965	924	4,838

State Crime Rates, 2000–05 (continued)

2005 CRIME RATES IN DETAIL (CONTINUED)

STATE	VIOLENT CRIMES					PROPERTY CRIMES			
	MURDER[7]	FORCIBLE RAPE	AGGRAVATED ASSAULT	ROBBERY	TOTAL[7]	BURGLARY	LARCENY/ THEFT	MOTOR VEHICLE THEFT	TOTAL
AR	6.7	42.9	387	91.1	528	1,085	2,711	262	4,058
CA	6.9	26.0	317	176	526	693	1,917	713	3,323
CO	3.7	43.4	265	84.6	397	745	2,735	560	4,040
CT	2.9	20.0	139	113	275	437	1,824	297	2,558
DE[2]	4.4	44.7	428	155	632	689	2,144	279	3,111
DC[3]	35.4	30.2	721	672	1,459	650	2,695	1,402	4,747
FL	5.0	37.1	497	169	708	926	2,658	423	4,008
GA	6.2	23.6	264	155	449	931	2,751	490	4,172
HI	1.9	26.9	148	78.5	255	768	3,308	716	4,793
ID	2.4	40.4	195	18.6	257	564	1,932	202	2,698
IL[4]	6.0	33.7	330	182	552	607	2,165	309	3,080
IN	5.7	29.6	180	109	324	698	2,412	347	3,456
IA	1.3	27.9	223	38.9	291	606	2,043	185	2,834
KS[5]	3.7	38.4	280	65.3	387	689	2,758	340	3,787
KY[6]	4.6	34.0	140	88.4	267	634	1,686	211	2,531
LA	9.9	31.4	435	118	594	871	2,495	318	3,683
ME	1.4	24.7	61.7	24.4	112	479	1,833	102	2,413
MD	9.9	22.6	414	257	703	641	2,294	608	3,544
MA	2.7	27.1	308	119	457	541	1,527	295	2,364
MI	6.1	51.3	363	132	552	697	1,918	477	3,091
MN	2.2	44.0	159	92.0	297	579	2,227	278	3,084
MS	7.3	39.3	149	82.3	278	920	2,084	257	3,260
MO	6.9	28.0	366	124	525	738	2,746	443	3,928
MT	1.9	32.2	229	18.9	282	389	2,543	211	3,143
NE	2.5	32.9	193	59.1	287	532	2,574	317	3,423
NV	8.5	42.1	362	195	607	972	2,154	1,115	4,242
NH	1.4	30.9	72.3	27.4	132	317	1,377	102	1,796
NJ	4.8	13.9	184	152	355	447	1,568	318	2,333
NM	7.4	54.1	542	98.7	702	1,094	2,640	415	4,148
NY	4.5	18.9	240	183	446	353	1,570	186	2,109
NC	6.7	26.5	289	146	468	1,201	2,546	328	4,075
ND	1.1	24.2	65.5	7.4	98.2	312	1,500	166	1,978
OH	5.1	39.8	143	163	351	873	2,429	361	3,663
OK	5.3	41.7	371	91.0	509	1,006	2,644	392	4,042
OR	2.2	34.8	182	68.1	287	759	3,112	529	4,400
PA	6.1	28.9	235	155	425	452	1,729	237	2,417
RI	3.2	29.8	146	72.1	251	494	1,816	409	2,719
SC	7.4	42.5	579	132	761	1,001	2,954	384	4,339
SD	2.3	46.7	108	18.6	176	324	1,344	108	1,776
TN	7.2	36.4	542	167	753	1,027	2,828	421	4,276
TX	6.2	37.2	330	157	530	962	2,962	409	4,332
UT	2.3	37.3	143	44.3	227	606	2,919	344	3,869
VT	1.3	23.3	83.5	11.7	120	492	1,686	103	2,281
VA	6.1	22.7	155	99.2	283	392	2,035	211	2,638
WA	3.3	44.7	206	92.1	346	960	3,150	784	4,893
WV	4.4	17.7	206	44.6	273	621	1,794	210	2,625
WI	3.5	20.6	135	82.2	242	441	1,993	227	2,660
WY	2.7	24.0	188	15.3	230	476	2,534	145	3,155
Total US	**5.6**	**31.7**	**291**	**141**	**469**	**727**	**2,286**	**417**	**3,430**

[1]This table does not include the murder and nonnegligent homicides that occurred because of the terrorist attacks of 11 Sep 2001. [2]Forcible rape count estimated for 2000. [3]Includes reported offenses at the National Zoo and offenses reported by the Metro Transit Police. [4]Data for Illinois are estimated or incomplete. [5]Crime counts estimated for 2000. [6]Data for Kentucky are limited or estimated between 2000 and 2002. [7]Includes nonnegligent manslaughter.

Sources: Statistical Abstract of the United States: 2007; US Bureau of Justice Statistics <http://bjsdata.ojp.usdoj.gov/dataonline>.

Crime in the US, 1983–2005

This table presents the number of crimes reported in the seven categories that, with arson, are known as Part I crimes and are used by the Federal Bureau of Investigation to assess trends in criminality in the country.

Source: Federal Bureau of Investigation.

| YEAR | VIOLENT CRIME | | | | PROPERTY CRIME | | |
	MURDER[1]	FORCIBLE RAPE	ROBBERY	AGGRAVATED ASSAULT	BURGLARY	LARCENY/ THEFT	MOTOR VEHICLE THEFT
1983	19,308	78,918	506,567	653,294	3,129,851	6,712,759	1,007,933
1984	18,692	84,233	485,008	685,349	2,984,434	6,591,874	1,032,165
1985	18,976	87,671	497,874	723,246	3,073,348	6,926,380	1,102,862
1986	20,613	91,459	542,775	834,322	3,241,410	7,257,153	1,224,137
1987	20,096	91,111	517,704	855,088	3,236,184	7,499,851	1,288,674
1988	20,675	92,486	542,968	910,092	3,218,077	7,705,872	1,432,916
1989	21,500	94,504	578,326	951,707	3,168,170	7,872,442	1,564,800
1990	23,438	102,555	639,271	1,054,863	3,073,909	7,945,670	1,635,907
1991	24,703	106,593	687,732	1,092,739	3,157,150	8,142,228	1,661,738
1992	23,760	109,062	672,478	1,126,974	2,979,884	7,915,199	1,610,834
1993	24,526	106,014	659,870	1,135,607	2,834,808	7,820,909	1,563,060
1994	23,326	102,216	618,949	1,113,179	2,712,774	7,879,812	1,539,287
1995	21,606	97,470	580,509	1,099,207	2,593,784	7,997,710	1,472,441
1996	19,645	96,252	535,594	1,037,049	2,506,400	7,904,685	1,394,238
1997	18,208	96,153	498,534	1,023,201	2,460,526	7,743,760	1,354,189
1998	16,974	93,144	447,186	976,583	2,332,735	7,376,311	1,242,781
1999	15,522	89,411	409,371	911,740	2,100,739	6,955,520	1,152,075
2000	15,586	90,178	408,016	911,706	2,050,992	6,971,590	1,160,002
2001	16,037	90,863	423,557	909,023	2,116,531	7,092,267	1,228,391
2002	16,204	95,136	420,637	894,348	2,151,875	7,052,922	1,246,096
2003	16,528	93,883	414,235	859,030	2,154,834	7,026,802	1,261,226
2004	16,148	95,089	401,470	847,381	2,144,446	6,937,089	1,237,851
2005	16,692	93,934	417,122	862,947	2,154,126	6,776,807	1,235,226

Crime trends: percent change in number of offenses[2]

| YEARS COMPARED | VIOLENT CRIME | | | | PROPERTY CRIME | | |
	MURDER[1]	FORCIBLE RAPE	ROBBERY	AGGRAVATED ASSAULT	BURGLARY	LARCENY/ THEFT	MOTOR VEHICLE THEFT
2005/2004	+3.4	−1.2	+3.9	+1.8	+0.5	−2.3	−0.2
2005/2001	+4.1	+3.4	−1.5	−5.1	+1.8	−4.4	+0.6
2005/1996	−24.0	−2.4	−22.1	−16.8	−14.1	−14.3	−11.4

[1]Includes the crime of nonnegligent manslaughter.   [2]A minus sign indicates a decrease in crime; a plus sign indicates an increase.

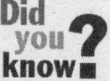

Did you know? Actual names of US towns: Embarrass, Wisconsin; Goofy Ridge, Illinois; French Lick, Indiana; Intercourse, Alabama; Bumble Bee, Arizona; Toad Suck, Arkansas; Truth or Consequences, New Mexico; Hellhole Palms, California; Uncertain, Texas; and Unalaska, Alaska.

US Cities with Highest and Lowest Crime Rates

This table ranks cities by the number of violent and property crimes—the crime index total—reported during 2003. All cities listed have a population of 100,000 or more. The information in the table is derived from preliminary data provided by the Federal Bureau of Investigation.

CITIES	CRIME INDEX TOTAL[1]	MURDER	FORCIBLE RAPE	ROBBERY	AGGRAVATED ASSAULT	BURGLARY	LARCENY/ THEFT	CAR THEFT
Highest Crime Rates								
New York NY	236,215	597	1,609	25,989	31,253	28,293	124,846	23,628
Los Angeles CA	184,605	515	1,226	16,577	30,506	25,115	77,111	33,555
Chicago IL[2]	182,306	598	N/A	17,302	19,784	25,064	96,779	22,779
Houston TX	143,993	278	768	10,985	11,957	26,522	72,032	21,451
Dallas TX	114,765	226	601	7,963	8,075	21,927	58,554	17,419
Phoenix AZ	107,545	241	526	3,676	5,279	17,104	55,068	25,651
San Antonio TX	90,252	85	537	2,060	4,570	14,619	62,179	6,202
Philadelphia PA	83,074	348	1,004	9,617	9,651	10,656	37,864	13,934

US Cities with Highest and Lowest Crime Rates (continued)

CITIES	CRIME INDEX TOTAL[1]	MURDER	FORCIBLE RAPE	ROBBERY	AGGRAVATED ASSAULT	BURGLARY	LARCENY/ THEFT	CAR THEFT
Lowest Crime Rates								
Detroit MI	83,533	366	814	5,817	11,727	14,100	25,353	25,356
Memphis TN	65,853	126	449	4,299	5,438	16,908	30,099	8,534
Thousand Oaks CA	1,986	1	12	38	150	332	1,311	142
Simi Valley CA	2,046	2	16	45	101	466	1,211	205
Amherst Town NY	2,097	1	5	40	74	176	1,735	66
Cary NC	2,353	0	17	36	56	397	1,717	130
Stamford CT	2,438	2	11	135	123	319	1,595	253
Centennial CO	2,502	1	28	22	133	415	1,693	210
Daly City CA	2,516	0	24	154	166	242	1,490	440
Naperville IL[2]	2,555	0	N/A	23	61	291	2,096	84
Livonia MI	2,691	0	13	56	116	389	1,846	271
Edison Township NJ	2,918	1	11	115	158	465	1,755	413

N/A stands for not available. [1]*Includes murder, forcible rape, robbery, aggravated assault, burglary, larceny/theft, and car theft.* [2]*Total excludes the crime of forcible rape.*

Total Arrests in the US

Estimates for the year 2005. Source: Federal Bureau of Investigation, Crime in the United States, 2005.

TYPE OF CRIME	NUMBER OF ARRESTS	TYPE OF CRIME	NUMBER OF ARRESTS
violent crime		**other crime types (continued)**	
aggravated assault	331,469	drunkenness	412,930
robbery	85,309	fraud	231,721
forcible rape	18,733	vandalism	206,351
murder and nonnegligent manslaughter	10,335	weapons (carrying, possessing, etc.)	142,878
violent crime total	**445,846**	curfew and loitering law violations	104,054
		stolen property (buying, receiving, possessing)	99,173
property crime		offenses against the family and children	93,172
larceny/theft	854,856	forgery and counterfeiting	87,346
burglary	220,391	runaways	81,222
motor vehicle theft	108,301	sex offenses (except forcible rape and prostitution)	67,072
arson	12,012		
property crime total	**1,195,560**	prostitution and commercialized vice	62,663
		vagrancy	24,372
other crime types		embezzlement	14,097
drug abuse violations	1,357,841	gambling	8,101
driving under the influence	997,338	suspicion (not included in total)	2,747
other assaults	958,477	all other offenses (except traffic)	2,837,806
disorderly conduct	501,129	**total arrests**	**10,367,072**
liquor laws	437,923		

US State and Federal Prison Population

Source: US Bureau of Justice Statistics.

STATE	NUMBER OF PRISONERS 31 DEC 1980	31 DEC 1990	31 DEC 2004	31 DEC 2005	% CHANGE (31 DEC 2004 TO 31 DEC 2005)
Alabama	6,543	15,665	25,887	27,888	+7.7
Alaska[1]	822	2,622	4,554	4,812	+5.7
Arizona[2]	4,372	14,261	32,515	33,471	+2.9
Arkansas	2,911	7,322	13,807	13,511	-2.1
California	24,569	97,309	166,556	170,676	+2.5
Colorado	2,629	7,671	20,293	21,456	+5.7
Connecticut[1]	4,308	10,500	19,497	19,442	-0.3
Delaware[1]	1,474	3,471	6,927	6,944	+0.2
Florida	20,735	44,387	85,533	89,768	+5.0
Georgia[2]	12,178	22,411	51,104	48,749	-4.6
Hawaii[1]	985	2,533	5,960	6,146	+3.1
Idaho	817	1,961	6,375	6,818	+6.9
Illinois	11,899	27,516	44,054	44,919	+2.0
Indiana	6,683	12,736	24,008	24,455	+1.9
Iowa[2]	2,481	3,967	8,525	8,737	+2.5
Kansas	2,494	5,775	8,966	9,068	+1.1

US State and Federal Prison Population (continued)

STATE	NUMBER OF PRISONERS 31 DEC 1980	31 DEC 1990	31 DEC 2004	31 DEC 2005	% CHANGE (31 DEC 2004 TO 31 DEC 2005)
Kentucky	3,588	9,023	17,814	19,662	+10.4
Louisiana	8,889	18,599	36,939	36,083	−2.3
Maine	814	1,523	2,024	2,023	[3]
Maryland	7,731	17,848	23,285	22,737	−2.4
Massachusetts	3,185	8,345	10,144	10,701	+5.5
Michigan	15,124	34,267	48,883	49,546	+1.4
Minnesota	2,001	3,176	8,758	9,281	+6.0
Mississippi	3,902	8,375	20,983	20,515	−2.2
Missouri	5,726	14,943	31,081	30,823	−0.8
Montana	739	1,425	3,164	3,509	+10.9
Nebraska	1,446	2,403	4,130	4,455	+7.9
Nevada	1,839	5,322	11,365	11,782	+3.7
New Hampshire	326	1,342	2,448	2,530	+3.3
New Jersey	5,884	21,128	26,757	27,359	+2.2
New Mexico	1,279	3,187	6,379	6,571	+3.0
New York	21,815	54,895	63,751	62,743	−1.6
North Carolina	15,513	18,411	35,434	36,365	+2.6
North Dakota	253	483	1,327	1,385	+4.4
Ohio	13,489	31,822	44,806	45,854	+2.3
Oklahoma	4,796	12,285	24,508	24,826	+1.3
Oregon	3,177	6,492	13,183	13,411	+1.7
Pennsylvania	8,171	22,290	40,963	42,380	+3.5
Rhode Island[1]	813	2,392	3,430	3,654	+6.5
South Carolina	7,862	17,319	23,428	23,160	−1.1
South Dakota	635	1,341	3,095	3,463	+11.9
Tennessee	7,022	10,388	25,884	26,369	+1.9
Texas	29,892	50,042	168,105	169,003	+0.5
Utah	932	2,496	5,991	6,373	+6.4
Vermont[1]	480	1,049	1,968	2,078	+5.6
Virginia	8,920	17,593	35,564	35,344	−0.6
Washington	4,399	7,995	16,614	17,382	+4.6
West Virginia	1,257	1,565	5,067	5,312	+4.8
Wisconsin	3,980	7,465	22,959	22,720	−1.0
Wyoming	534	1,110	1,980	2,047	+3.4
state	305,458	708,393	1,316,772	1,338,306	+1.6
federal[4]	24,363	65,526	180,328	187,618	+4.0
US total	329,821	773,919	1,497,100	1,525,924	+1.9

[1]Jails and prisons are part of an integrated system. Data include total jail and prison population.   [2]Population figures are based on custody counts.   [3]Negligible.   [4]As of 31 Dec 2001, the transfer of responsibility for sentenced felons from the District of Columbia to the Federal Bureau of Prisons was completed, so the District of Columbia no longer operates a prison system and has been excluded from these statistics.

Death Penalty Sentences in the US

This table excludes military and federal sentences and executions. Sources: US Bureau of Justice Statistics; Death Penalty Information Center; NAACP Legal Defense and Educational Fund, Inc.

STATE	EXECUTIONS 1976–PRESENT[1]	2006	PRISONERS UNDER DEATH SENTENCE (AS OF 1 JAN 2007)[2]	SOME DEATH-PENALTY CRIMES
Alabama	35	1	191	intentional murder[3]
Alaska	—	—	—	no death penalty
Arizona	22	0	124	1st-degree murder[3]
Arkansas	27	0	37	capital murder[3]; treason
California	13	1	660	1st-degree murder[3]; treason; train wrecking
Colorado	1	0	2	1st-degree murder[3]; treason
Connecticut	1	0	8	capital felony (8 types of aggravated murder)
Delaware	14	0	18	1st-degree murder[3]
District of Columbia	—	—	—	no death penalty
Florida	64	4	397	1st-degree murder; felonious murder; capital drug trafficking; capital sexual battery
Georgia	39	0	107	murder; treason; aircraft hijacking; kidnapping[4]
Hawaii	—	—	—	no death penalty
Idaho	1	0	20	1st-degree murder[3]; aggravated kidnapping
Illinois	12	0	11	1st-degree murder[3]
Indiana	17	1	23	murder[3]

Death Penalty Sentences in the US (continued)

STATE	EXECUTIONS 1976-PRESENT[1]	2006	PRISONERS UNDER DEATH SENTENCE (AS OF 1 JAN 2007)[2]	SOME DEATH-PENALTY CRIMES
Iowa	—	—	—	no death penalty
Kansas	0	0	9	capital murder[3]
Kentucky	2	0	41	murder[3]; aggravated kidnapping
Louisiana	27	0	88	1st-degree murder; treason; rape[5]
Maine	—	—	—	no death penalty
Maryland	5	0	8	1st-degree murder[5]
Massachusetts	—	—	—	no death penalty
Michigan	—	—	—	no death penalty
Minnesota	—	—	—	no death penalty
Mississippi	8	1	66	capital murder; aircraft hijacking
Missouri	66	0	51	1st-degree murder
Montana	3	1	2	capital murder[3]; capital sexual assault
Nebraska	3	0	9	1st-degree murder[3]
Nevada	12	1	80	1st-degree murder[3]
New Hampshire	0	0	0	capital murder (6 types)
New Jersey	0	0	11	murder by one's own conduct; contract murder; solicitation[7]
New Mexico	1	0	2	1st-degree murder[3]
New York	0	0	1	1st-degree murder[3,8]
North Carolina	43	4	185	1st-degree murder
North Dakota	—	—	—	no death penalty
Ohio	24	5	192	murder[3]
Oklahoma	84	4	88	1st-degree murder[3]
Oregon	2	0	33	murder[3]
Pennsylvania	3	0	226	1st-degree murder[3]
Rhode Island	—	—	—	no death penalty
South Carolina	36	1	67	murder[3]
South Dakota	0	0	4	1st-degree murder[3]; aggravated kidnapping
Tennessee	2	1	107	1st-degree murder[3]
Texas	391	24	393	criminal homicide[3]
Utah	6	0	9	murder[3]
Vermont	—	—	—	no death penalty
Virginia	98	4	20	1st-degree murder[3]
Washington	4	0	9	1st-degree murder[3]
West Virginia	—	—	—	no death penalty
Wisconsin	—	—	—	no death penalty
Wyoming	1	0	2	1st-degree murder
totals	**1,070**	**53**	**3,350**	

[1]In 1976 the US Supreme Court ruled that capital punishment was not unconstitutional. [2]In mid-2002 the Supreme Court ruled that juries, not judges, must make decisions determining death penalty cases and that it was unconstitutional to execute mentally retarded offenders. These two decisions could reduce the number of people sentenced to death. [3]With aggravating factors or circumstances. [4]With bodily injury or ransom when the victim dies. [5]Aggravated rape of a victim under 12. [6]Premeditated or committed during the act of a felony and meeting certain death penalty requirements. [7]By command or threat in the act of a narcotics conspiracy. [8]In 2004 the New York death penalty statute was declared unconstitutional.

Directors of the Federal Bureau of Investigation (FBI)

The FBI evolved from an unnamed force appointed by Attorney General Charles J. Bonaparte on 26 Jul 1908. It is the unit of the Department of Justice responsible for investigating foreign intelligence and terrorist activities and violations of federal criminal law. The president appoints the director of the FBI with confirmation from the Senate. Since Hoover's tenure, a director's term may not exceed 10 years.

NAME	DATES OF SERVICE
Stanley Finch	26 Jul 1908–30 Apr 1912
Alexander Bruce Bielaski	30 Apr 1912–10 Feb 1919
William E. Allen (acting)	10 Feb 1919–30 Jun 1919
William J. Flynn	1 Jul 1919–21 Aug 1921
William J. Burns	22 Aug 1921–14 Jun 1924
J. Edgar Hoover	10 May 1924–2 May 1972
L. Patrick Gray (acting)	3 May 1972–27 Apr 1973
William D. Ruckelshaus (acting)	30 Apr 1973–9 Jul 1973
Clarence M. Kelley	9 Jul 1973–15 Feb 1978
William H. Webster	23 Feb 1978–25 May 1987
John Otto (acting)	26 May 1987–2 Nov 1987
William S. Sessions	2 Nov 1987–19 Jul 1993
Floyd I. Clarke (acting)	19 Jul 1993–1 Sep 1993
Louis J. Freeh	1 Sep 1993–25 Jun 2001
Thomas J. Pickard (acting)	25 Jun 2001–4 Sep 2001
Robert S. Mueller, III	4 Sep 2001–

Society

Family

Average Family Size, 1950–2005
Source: US Census Bureau.

YEAR	NUMBER OF FAMILIES ('000)	PEOPLE PER FAMILY (AVERAGE)	YEAR	NUMBER OF FAMILIES ('000)	PEOPLE PER FAMILY (AVERAGE)	YEAR	NUMBER OF FAMILIES ('000)	PEOPLE PER FAMILY (AVERAGE)
1950	39,303	3.54	1970	51,586	3.58	1990	66,090	3.17
1955	41,951	3.59	1975	55,712	3.42	1995	69,305	3.19
1960	45,111	3.67	1980	59,550	3.29	2000	72,025	3.17
1965	47,956	3.70	1985	62,706	3.23	2005	74,341	3.18

US Population by Age
Numbers are in thousands ('000). Source: US Census Bureau midyear 2007 estimate. Details may not add to total given because of rounding.

AGE	POPULATION NUMBER	(%)	AGE	POPULATION NUMBER	(%)
under 5 years	20,817	6.9	65 to 74 years	19,368	6.4
5 to 9 years	19,873	6.6	75 to 84 years	12,925	4.3
10 to 14 years	20,240	6.7	85 years and over	5,557	1.8
15 to 19 years	21,666	7.2	total population	301,140	100.0
20 to 24 years	21,034	7.0			
25 to 34 years	40,193	13.3	under 20 years	82,596	27.4
35 to 44 years	42,929	14.3	20 years and over	218,544	72.6
45 to 54 years	43,840	14.6	65 years and over	37,850	12.6
55 to 64 years	32,698	10.9			

Living Arrangements of Children Under 18 in the US
Children under 18 years of age, 2004. Numbers in thousands ('000). Source: US Census Bureau.

LIVING IN HOUSEHOLD WITH:	UNDER 6	6–11	12–17	UNDER 18
both parents	16,110	16,136	16,436	48,682
mother only	4,036	4,802	5,339	14,176
father only	939	914	1,097	2,950
neither parent	3	18	38	60
totals	23,793	24,106	25,307	73,205

Children Living Below the Poverty Level

This table covers children under the age of 18 (as of March of the following year). Hispanics may be of any race. All numbers are in thousands ('000). Statistics that are not available are noted N/A. Source: US Census Bureau. For the definition of the poverty level, see <www.census.gov/hhes/poverty/povdef.html>.

YEAR	% OF CHILDREN BELOW THE POVERTY LEVEL ALL[1]	WHITE[2]	BLACK	ASIAN/ PACIFIC ISLANDER	HISPANIC	NUMBER OF CHILDREN BELOW THE POVERTY LEVEL ALL[1]	WHITE[2]	BLACK	ASIAN/ PACIFIC ISLANDER	HISPANIC
1982	21.9	14.4	47.6	N/A	39.5	13,647	6,566	4,472	N/A	2,181
1983	22.3	14.8	46.7	N/A	38.1	13,911	6,649	4,398	N/A	2,312
1984	21.5	13.7	46.6	N/A	39.2	13,420	6,156	4,413	N/A	2,376
1985	20.7	12.8	43.6	N/A	40.3	13,010	5,745	4,157	N/A	2,606
1986	20.5	13.0	43.1	N/A	37.7	12,876	5,789	4,148	N/A	2,507
1987	20.3	11.8	45.1	23.5	39.3	12,843	5,230	4,385	455	2,670
1988	19.5	11.0	43.5	24.1	37.6	12,455	4,888	4,296	474	2,631
1989	19.6	11.5	43.7	19.8	36.2	12,590	5,110	4,375	392	2,603
1990	20.6	12.3	44.8	17.6	38.4	13,431	5,532	4,550	374	2,865
1991	21.8	13.1	45.9	17.5	40.4	14,341	5,918	4,755	360	3,094
1992	22.3	13.2	46.6	16.4	40.0	15,294	6,017	5,106	363	3,637
1993	22.7	13.6	46.1	18.2	40.9	15,727	6,255	5,125	375	3,873
1994	21.8	12.5	43.8	18.3	41.5	15,289	5,823	4,906	318	4,075
1995	20.8	11.2	41.9	19.5	40.0	14,665	5,115	4,761	564	4,080
1996	20.5	11.1	39.9	19.5	40.3	14,463	5,072	4,519	571	4,237

Children Living Below the Poverty Level (continued)

	% OF CHILDREN BELOW THE POVERTY LEVEL					NUMBER OF CHILDREN BELOW THE POVERTY LEVEL				
YEAR	ALL[1]	WHITE[2]	BLACK	ASIAN/ PACIFIC ISLANDER	HISPANIC	ALL[1]	WHITE[2]	BLACK	ASIAN/ PACIFIC ISLANDER	HISPANIC
1997	19.9	11.4	37.2	20.3	36.8	14,113	5,204	4,225	628	3,972
1998	18.9	10.6	36.7	18.0	34.4	13,467	4,822	4,151	564	3,837
1999	16.9	9.4	33.2	11.9	30.3	12,280	4,155	3,813	381	3,693
2000	16.2	9.1	31.2	12.7	28.4	11,587	4,018	3,581	420	3,522
2001	16.3	9.5	30.2	11.5	28.0	11,733	4,194	3,492	369	3,570
2002	16.7	9.4	32.3	11.7[3]	28.6	12,133	4,090	3,645	315[3]	3,782
2003	17.6	9.8	34.1	12.5[3]	29.7	12,866	4,233	3,877	344[3]	4,077
2004	17.8	10.5	33.7	9.8[3]	28.9	13,041	4,519	3,788	281[3]	4,098
2005	17.6	10.0	34.5	11.0[3]	28.3	12,896	4,254	3,841	317[3]	4,143

[1]Includes other and unclassified. [2]Excludes Hispanic population. [3]Excludes Pacific Islanders.

Child Care Arrangements in the US

This table is based on sample surveys of households with children 3–5 years old who were not yet in kindergarten. Day care centers, Head Start programs, preschools, prekindergarten, and nursery schools were included as center-based programs. The columns do not add to 100% because some children participated in more than one type of nonparental arrangement. Detail may not add to totals due to rounding. Although complete statistics from the 2001 survey were not available before press time, 56.4% of children ages 3–5 were enrolled in center-based programs in 2001, down 3.3% from 1999. Source: US National Center for Education Statistics.

YEAR OF SURVEY	CHILDREN NUMBER	(%)	UNDER PARENTAL CARE (%)	UNDER A RELATIVE'S CARE (%)	UNDER A NONRELATIVE'S CARE (%)	IN A CENTER-BASED PROGRAM (%)
1991	8,428,000	100.0	31.0	16.9	14.8	52.8
1995	9,232,000	100.0	25.9	19.4	16.9	55.1
1999	8,525,000	100.0	23.1	22.8	16.1	59.7

		details from the 1999 survey				
FEATURE	CHILDREN NUMBER	(%)	UNDER PARENTAL CARE (%)	UNDER A RELATIVE'S CARE (%)	UNDER A NONRELATIVE'S CARE (%)	IN A CENTER-BASED PROGRAM (%)
age						
3 years old	3,814,000	44.7	30.8	24.4	16.2	45.7
4 years old	3,705,000	43.5	17.7	22.0	15.9	69.6
5 years old	1,006,000	11.8	13.5	20.2	16.1	76.5
race/ethnic group						
white, non-Hispanic	5,389,000	63.2	23.2	18.8	19.4	60.0
black, non-Hispanic	1,214,000	14.2	13.7	33.4	7.4	73.2
Hispanic	1,376,000	16.1	33.4	26.5	12.7	44.2
other	547,000	6.4	16.6	30.2	10.4	66.1
household income						
less than $10,001	1,064,000	12.5	27.5	27.5	13.2	55.9
$10,001–20,000	1,342,000	15.7	27.7	29.4	13.7	51.1
$20,001–30,000	1,333,000	15.6	29.8	27.1	12.5	51.4
$30,001–40,000	1,098,000	12.9	24.8	22.5	14.7	55.4
$40,001–50,000	848,000	9.9	23.1	21.3	13.6	60.2
$50,001–75,000	1,397,000	16.4	17.8	17.3	21.0	66.6
more than $75,000	1,443,000	16.9	13.1	15.9	21.3	74.6

Children in the US Living with Nonparents

Children under 18 years of age, March 2002. Numbers in thousands ('000). Source: US Census Bureau.

LIVING ARRANGEMENT	YEARS OF AGE			
	UNDER 6	6–11	12–17	UNDER 18
with grandparent	635	462	476	1,273
with other relative	192	224	386	802
in foster home	62	81	92	235
with other nonrelative	137	171	268	575
with opposite-sex unmarried adults (children under 15 only)	62	83	40	186

US Adoptions of Foreign-Born Children

Adoptions of foreign children by US citizens are tracked by the number of immigrant visas issued to orphans entering the US. Source: US Department of State.

TOP 10 COUNTRIES OF ORIGIN	ADOPTIONS FISCAL YEAR		TOP 10 COUNTRIES OF ORIGIN	ADOPTIONS FISCAL YEAR		TOTAL FOREIGN ADOPTIONS FISCAL YEAR	
	2005	2006		2005	2006		
1. China	7,906	6,493	6. Kazakhstan	755	587	2000	17,718
2. Guatemala	3,783	4,135	7. Ukraine	821	460	2001	19,237
3. Russia	4,639	3,706	8. Liberia	183	353	2002	20,099
4. South Korea	1,630	1,376	9. Colombia	291	344	2003	21,616
5. Ethiopia	441	732	10. India	323	320	2004	22,884
						2005	22,728
						2006	20,679

US Nursing Home Population

The data in this table were gathered in 1999 through interviews conducted by the National Nursing Home Survey. Residents of more than one race were recorded in the "black and other" category. Numbers may not add to totals because of rounding. N/A indicates that reliable numbers were not available.

Source: US National Center for Health Statistics.

AGE AT INTERVIEW	TOTAL RESIDENTS	%	MALE	GENDER %	FEMALE	%
under 65	158,700	9.8	80,000	17.5	78,700	6.7
65–74	194,800	12.0	84,100	18.4	110,700	9.5
75–84	517,600	31.8	149,500	32.7	368,100	31.5
85 and older	757,100	46.5	144,200	31.5	612,900	52.4
total	1,628,300	100.0	457,900	100.0	1,170,400	100.0

	WHITE	%	BLACK AND OTHER	RACE %	BLACK	%	UNKNOWN
under 65	115,400	8.3	39,300	18.2	32,800	18.4	N/A
65–74	157,300	11.3	35,800	16.6	30,300	17.0	N/A
75–84	440,600	31.6	71,100	32.9	58,700	32.8	N/A
85 and older	681,700	48.9	69,700	32.3	56,900	31.8	N/A
total	1,394,400	100.0	215,900	100.0	178,700	100.0	17,400

	NORTHWEST	%	MIDWEST	RESIDENT LOCATION %	SOUTH	%	WEST	%
under 65	34,200	8.9	45,000	9.0	51,300	9.7	28,200	13.1
65–74	46,400	12.1	58,900	11.8	63,400	11.9	26,100	12.1
75–84	118,500	30.9	153,200	30.8	179,100	33.7	66,800	31.1
85 and older	184,300	48.1	241,100	48.4	237,700	44.7	94,000	43.7
total	383,400	100.0	498,200	100.0	531,500	100.0	215,200	100.0

Unmarried-Couple Households in the US

Data based on Current Population Survey except for census years of 1960 and 1970. Census 2000 data shown separately. Numbers in thousands ('000). Source: US Census Bureau.

YEAR	TOTAL US HOUSEHOLDS	UNMARRIED-COUPLE HOUSEHOLDS (OPPOSITE SEX)	% OF TOTAL HOUSEHOLDS	NO CHILDREN UNDER 15	WITH CHILDREN UNDER 15
1960 census	52,799	439	0.8	242	197
1970 census	63,401	523	0.8	327	196
1980	80,776	1,589	2.0	1,159	431
1985	86,789	1,983	2.3	1,380	603
1990	93,347	2,856	3.1	1,966	891
1995	98,990	3,668	3.7	2,349	1,319
2000	104,705	4,736	4.5	3,061	1,675

UNMARRIED-COUPLE HOUSEHOLDS	2000 CENSUS
male householder/female partner	2,615
male householder/male partner	301
female householder/female partner	293
female householder/male partner	2,266
unmarried-couple households	5,475
total households	105,480

Marital Status of Population by Sex, 1950–2003

The data in this table are taken from surveys of individuals 18 or over conducted by the US Census Bureau and exclude members of the armed forces ex-cept those living off post or with their families on post. Data exclude Alaska and Hawaii prior to 1960. Source: US Census Bureau.

	TOTAL						
	1950	1960	1970	1980	1990	2000	2003
Total individuals surveyed in hundred thousands ('000,000)	111.7	125.5	132.5	159.5	181.8	201.8	212.4
Percentage of individuals never married	22.8	22.0	16.2	20.3	22.2	23.9	24.4
Percentage of individuals married	67.0	67.3	71.7	65.5	61.9	59.5	56.6
Percentage of individuals widowed	8.3	8.4	8.9	8.0	7.6	6.8	6.6
Percentage of individuals divorced	1.9	2.3	3.2	6.2	8.3	9.8	10.2
Percentage of males never married	26.2	25.3	18.9	23.8	25.8	27.0	27.9
Percentage of males married	68.0	69.1	75.3	68.4	64.3	61.5	58.9
Percentage of males widowed	4.2	3.7	3.3	2.6	2.7	2.7	2.6
Percentage of males divorced	1.7	1.9	2.5	5.2	7.2	8.8	8.8
Percentage of females never married	11.1	12.3	13.7	17.1	18.9	21.1	21.2
Percentage of females married	37.6	42.6	68.5	63.0	59.7	57.6	54.5
Percentage of females widowed	7.0	8.3	13.9	12.8	12.1	10.5	10.3
Percentage of females divorced	1.2	1.7	3.9	7.1	9.3	10.8	11.5

United States Education

Educational Attainment by Gender and Race

For people 25 years old and older. Percentage rates for 1960, 1970, and 1980 are based on sample data from the decennial censuses. Rates for 1990, 2000, and 2002 are based on the Current Population Survey.
Source: US Census Bureau.

Percentage who had graduated from high school[1]

	ALL RACES[2]		WHITE		BLACK		HISPANIC[3]		ASIAN/PACIFIC ISLANDER	
CENSUS	MALE	FEMALE	MALE	FEMALE	MALE	FEMALE	MALE	FEMALE	MALE	FEMALE
1960	39.5	42.5	41.6	44.7	18.2	21.8	N/A	N/A	N/A	N/A
1970	51.9	52.8	54.0	55.0	30.1	32.5	37.9	34.2	N/A	N/A
1980	67.3	65.8	69.6	68.1	50.8	51.5	67.3	65.8	N/A	N/A
1990	77.7	77.5	79.1	79.0	65.8	66.5	50.3	51.3	84.0	77.2
2000	84.2	84.0	84.8	85.0	78.7	78.3	56.6	57.5	88.2	83.4
2002	83.8	84.4	84.3	85.2	78.5	78.9	56.1	57.9	89.5	85.5

Percentage who had graduated from college[4]

	ALL RACES[2]		WHITE		BLACK		HISPANIC[3]		ASIAN/PACIFIC ISLANDER	
CENSUS	MALE	FEMALE	MALE	FEMALE	MALE	FEMALE	MALE	FEMALE	MALE	FEMALE
1960	9.7	5.8	10.3	6.0	2.8	3.3	N/A	N/A	N/A	N/A
1970	13.5	8.1	14.4	8.4	4.2	4.6	7.8	4.3	N/A	N/A
1980	20.1	12.8	21.3	13.3	8.4	8.3	9.4	6.0	N/A	N/A
1990	24.4	18.4	25.3	19.0	11.9	10.8	9.8	8.7	44.9	35.4
2000	27.8	23.6	28.5	23.9	16.3	16.7	10.7	10.6	47.6	40.7
2002	28.5	25.1	29.1	25.4	16.4	17.5	11.0	11.2	50.9	43.8

N/A means not available. [1]Through 1990, finished four years or more of high school. [2]Includes races not shown separately in the table. [3]Hispanics may be of any race. [4]Through 1990, finished four years or more of college.

Did you know? The original color of the US president's residence was the pale grey of the sandstone from which it was built, but it was called the "White House" as early as 1809 because the light sandstone contrasted sharply with the red brick of nearby buildings. It was not until 1902, however, that the building was officially renamed the "White House" by Pres. Theodore Roosevelt.

National Spelling Bee

A spelling bee is a contest or game in which players attempt to spell correctly and aloud words assigned them by an impartial judge. Competition may be individual, with players eliminated when they misspell a word and the last remaining player being the winner, or between teams, the winner being the team with the most players remaining at the close of the contest. The spelling bee is an old custom that was revived in schools in the United States in the late 19th century and enjoyed a great vogue there and in Great Britain. In the US, local, regional, and national competitions continue to be held annually. The US National Spelling Bee was begun by the *Louisville Courier-Journal* newspaper in 1925, and it was taken over by Scripps Howard, Inc., in 1941. The National Spelling Bee was not held in 1943–45. To qualify, spellers must meet nine requirements, including that they have neither reached their 16th birthday nor passed beyond the eighth grade. National Spelling Bee Web site: <www.spellingbee.com>.

YEAR	CHAMPION & SPONSOR	WINNING WORD
1953	Elizabeth Hess, *Arizona Republic* (Phoenix AZ)	soubrette
1954	William Cashore, *Norristown Times Herald* (Pennsylvania)	transept
1955	Sandra Sloss, *St. Louis Globe-Democrat* (Missouri)	crustaceology
1956	Melody Sachko, *Pittsburgh Press* (Pennsylvania)	condominium
1957	Sandra Owen, *Canton Repository* (Ohio)	
	Dana Bennett, *Rocky Mountain News* (Denver CO)	schappe
1958	Jolitta Schlehuber, *Topeka Daily Capital* (Kansas)	syllepsis
1959	Joel Montgomery, *Rocky Mountain News* (Denver CO)	catamaran
1960	Henry Feldman, *Knoxville News-Sentinel* (Tennessee)	eudaemonic
1961	John Capehart, *Tulsa Tribune* (Oklahoma)	smaragdine
1962	Nettie Crawford, *El Paso Herald-Post* (Texas)	
	Michael Day, *St. Louis Globe-Democrat* (Missouri)	esquamulose
1963	Glen Van Slyke III, *Knoxville News-Sentinel* (Tennessee)	equipage
1964	William Kerek, *Akron Beacon Journal* (Ohio)	sycophant
1965	Michael Kerpan, Jr., *Tulsa Tribune* (Oklahoma)	eczema
1966	Robert A. Wake, *Houston Chronicle* (Texas)	ratoon
1967	Jennifer Reinke, *Omaha World-Herald* (Nebraska)	chihuahua
1968	Robert L. Walters, *Topeka Daily Capital* (Kansas)	abalone
1969	Susan Yoachum, *Dallas Morning News* (Texas)	interlocutory
1970	Libby Childress, *Winston-Salem Journal & Sentinel* (North Carolina)	croissant
1971	Jonathan Knisely, *Philadelphia Bulletin* (Pennsylvania)	shalloon
1972	Robin Kral, *Lubbock Avalanche-Journal* (Texas)	macerate
1973	Barrie Trinkle, *Fort Worth Press* (Texas)	vouchsafe
1974	Julie Ann Junkin, *Birmingham Post-Herald* (Alabama)	hydrophyte
1975	Hugh Tosteson, *San Juan Star* (Puerto Rico)	incisor
1976	Tim Kneale, *Syracuse Herald Journal-American* (New York)	narcolepsy
1977	John Paola, *Pittsburgh Press* (Pennsylvania)	cambist
1978	Peg McCarthy, *Topeka Capital-Journal* (Kansas)	deification
1979	Katie Kerwin, *Rocky Mountain News* (Denver CO)	maculature
1980	Jacques Bailly, *Rocky Mountain News* (Denver CO)	elucubrate
1981	Paige Pipkin, *El Paso Herald-Post* (Texas)	sarcophagus
1982	Molly Dieveney, *Rocky Mountain News* (Denver CO)	psoriasis
1983	Blake Giddens, *El Paso Herald-Post* (Texas)	purim
1984	Daniel Greenblatt, *Loudoun Times-Mirror* (Virginia)	luge
1985	Balu Natarajan, *Chicago Tribune* (Illinois)	milieu
1986	Jon Pennington, *Patriot News* (Harrisburg PA)	odontalgia
1987	Stephanie Petit, *Pittsburgh Press* (Pennsylvania)	staphylococci
1988	Rageshree Ramachandran, *Sacramento Bee* (California)	elegiacal
1989	Scott Isaacs, *Rocky Mountain News* (Denver CO)	spoliator
1990	Amy Marie Dimak, *Seattle Times* (Washington)	fibranne
1991	Joanne Lagatta, *Wisconsin State Journal* (Madison WI)	antipyretic
1992	Amanda Goad, *Richmond News Leader* (Virginia)	lyceum
1993	Geoff Hooper, *Commercial Appeal* (Memphis TN)	kamikaze
1994	Ned G. Andrews, *Knoxville News-Sentinel* (Tennessee)	antediluvian
1995	Justin Tyler Carroll, *Commercial Appeal* (Memphis TN)	xanthosis
1996	Wendy Guey, *Palm Beach Post* (Florida)	vivisepulture
1997	Rebecca Sealfon, *Daily News* (New York NY)	euonym
1998	Jody-Anne Maxwell, Phillips & Phillips Stationery Suppliers, Ltd. (Kingston, Jamaica)	chiaroscurist
1999	Nupur Lala, *Tampa Tribune* (Florida)	logorrhea
2000	George Abraham Thampy, *St. Louis Post-Dispatch* (Missouri)	demarche
2001	Sean Conley, *Aitkin Independent Age* (Minnesota)	succedaneum
2002	Pratyush Buddiga, *Rocky Mountain News* (Denver CO)	prospicience
2003	Sai Gunturi, *Dallas Morning News* (Texas)	pococurante
2004	David Tidmarsh, *South Bend Tribune* (Indiana)	autochthonous
2005	Anurag Kashyap, *San Diego Union-Tribune* (California)	appoggiatura
2006	Kerry Close, *Asbury Park Press* (New Jersey)	ursprache
2007	Evan M. O'Dorney, *Contra Costa Times* (California)	serrefine

Business

World Economy: India, Inc.

by Michael Elliott and Alex Perry, TIME

Even if you have never gone to India—never wrapped your food in a piping-hot naan or had your eyeballs singed by one of Bollywood's spectacular movies—there is a good chance you encounter some piece of the nation and its culture every day of your life. It might be the place you eat (although you don't know it) if your luggage is lost on a connecting flight or the guys to whom your company has outsourced its data processing. Every night, young radiologists in Bangalore read CT scans e-mailed to them by emergency-room doctors in the US. Few modern Americans are surprised to find that their dentist or lawyer is of Indian origin or are shocked to hear how vital Indians have been to California's high-tech industry. In ways big and small, Indians are changing the world.

That's possible because India—the second most populous nation in the world and projected to be by 2015 the most populous—is itself being transformed. Writers like to attach catchy tags to nations, which is why you have read plenty about the rise of Asian tigers and the Chinese dragon. Now here comes the elephant.

India's economy is growing more than 8% a year, and the country is modernizing so fast that old friends are bewildered by the changes that occurred between visits. The economic boom is taking place at a time when the US and India are forging new ties. During the Cold War, relations between New Delhi and Washington were frosty at best, as India cozied up to the Soviet Union and successive US administrations armed and supported India's regional rival, Pakistan. But in a breathtaking shift, the Bush administration in 2004 declared India a strategic partner and proposed a bilateral deal to share nuclear know-how. After decades when it hardly registered in the political or public consciousness, India is finally on the US mental map.

The Subcontinent Wakes. Among policymakers in Washington, the new approach can be explained simply: India is the un-China. One Asian giant is run by a Communist Party that increasingly appeals to nationalism as a way of legitimating its power. The other is the largest democracy the world has ever seen. The US will always have to deal with China, but it has learned that doing so is never easy: China bristles too much with old resentments at the hands of the West. India is no pushover either (try suggesting in New Delhi that outsiders might usefully broker a deal with Pakistan about Kashmir, the disputed territory over which the two countries have fought three wars), but democrats are easier to talk to than communist apparatchiks. Making friends with India is a good way for the US to hedge its Asia bet.

Democracy aside, there is a second way in which India is the un-China—and it's not to India's credit. In most measures of modernization, China is way ahead. In 2005 per capita income in India was US$3,300; in China it was US$6,800. Prosperity and progress haven't touched many of the nearly 650,000 villages where more than two-thirds of India's population lives. Backbreaking, empty-stomach poverty, which China has been tackling successfully for decades, is still all too common in India.

Education for women, which was the critical driver of China's rise to become the workshop of the world, lags terribly in India. The nation has more people with HIV/AIDS than any other in the world, but until recently the Indian government was in a disgraceful state of denial about the extent of the epidemic. Transportation networks and electrical grids, which are crucial to industrial development and job creation, are so dilapidated that it will take many years to modernize them.

Yet the litany of India's comparative shortcomings omits a fundamental truth: China started first. China's key economic reforms took shape in the late 1970s, India's not until the early 1990s. But India is younger and freer than China. Many of its companies are already innovative world beaters. India is playing catch-up, for sure, but it has the skills, the people, and the sort of hustle and dynamism that Americans respect, to do so. It deserves the new notice it has got in the US. We're all about to discover: this elephant can dance.

Bombay, India's Driving Wheel. If you want to catch a glimpse of the new India, with all its dizzying promise and turbocharged ambition, then head to its biggest, messiest, sexiest city—Bombay. Home to 18.4 million people and counting, the city, formally known as Mumbai, is projected by 2015 to be the planet's second most populous metropolis, after Tokyo. But it's already a world of its own. Walk down its teeming streets, and you'll encounter crime lords and Bollywood stars, sprawling slums and Manhattan-priced condos, and jam-packed bars where DJs play the music of the Punjab, bhangra—a pulsating sound track familiar to clubgoers in London and New York City.

Bombay is where Wall Street gets equities analyzed, where Kellogg, Brown & Root sources kitchen staff for the US Army in Iraq, and where your credit-card details may be stored—or stolen. It's where a phone operator who calls herself Mary (but is really Meenakshi) sells Texans on two-week vacations that include the Taj Mahal and cut-rate heart surgery. Chances are those medical tourists will touch down in Bombay, since 40% of international flights to India land here, delivering thousands of new visitors every day—an increasing number of whom are staying for good. The reason is simple: to know Bombay is to know modern India. It's the channel for a billion ambitions and an emblem of globalization you can reach out and touch, a giant city where change is pouring in and rippling out around the world.

City of Squalor. But if India's biggest city is its great hope, Bombay also embodies many of the country's staggering problems. The obstacles hampering India's progress—poor infrastructure, weak government, searing inequality, corruption, and crime—converge in Bombay. Although India boasts more billionaires than China, 81% of its population lives on US$2 a day or less, compared with 47% of Chinese, according to the 2005 UN Population Reference Bureau Report.

The nation's class divide is starkest in cities like Bombay, where million-dollar apartments overlook million-population slums. For all its glitz, Bombay remains a temple to inefficiency. In 2003 it had one bus for every 1,300 people, two public parking spots for every 1,000 cars, 17 public toilets for every million people, and one civic hospital for 7.2 million people in the northern slums, according to a report prepared for the state government by McKinsey & Co. At least one-third of the country's population lacks clean drinking water, and two million of its people do not have access to a toilet.

Whether Bombay's entrepreneurial energy can be directed toward lifting more of its people out of despair will help define the nation's future. The country's pro-growth prime minister, Manmohan Singh, has said he dreams that Bombay will someday make people "forget Shanghai"—China's financial capital, whose modern gleam is a reminder of the gap between India and its rip-roaring eastern rival. Right now it's not much of a contest. India's GDP (gross domestic product) growth was 8.4% in 2005 versus 10% for China, while foreign investment in India was an estimated US$8.4 billion, compared with US$72.4 billion in China.

City of Strivers. But India does possess one indispensable asset, which has sustained its democracy and catapulted it to the cusp of global power: the ingenuity of its citizens. And nowhere is that essential commodity in greater supply than in Bombay. "Things just happen here," says Sanjay Bhandarkar, managing director of investment bank Rothschild's India. "Because people have to make things work themselves."

The rise of China has been the product of methodical state planning, but India's newfound energy is all about private hustle, a trait that Americans can appreciate. Rakesh Jhunjhunwala, a billionaire trader in Bombay, says initiative represents Bombay's—and India's—advantage over its competitors. "It's people who make countries," he says, "not governments."

Bombay has brimmed with cocky entrepreneurs since the Portuguese took possession of seven malarial islands off the western Indian coast in 1534 and called them Good Bay, or Bom Baia. Big talk attracts big crowds, and five centuries of migration have made Bombay the largest commercial center between Europe and East Asia. Nobody actually comes from Bombay. Even families who have lived there for generations still refer to an ancestral village 1,000 miles away as home.

That sense of a place apart is reinforced by geography and architecture. You cross the sea or an estuary to reach downtown Bombay. And once there, you find a tropical British city of Victorian railway stations, Art Deco apartment blocks, and Edwardian office buildings. Christabelle Noronha, a PR executive who has lived in the city all her life, says the sense of being in a foreign land gives Bombay an uninhibited air. "If everyone is a stranger, then everyone is free," she says.

As the subcontinent's New York City, Bombay is built not on tradition but on drive. "Pull anyone out of any part of India, and put them in Bombay," says Rothschild's Bhandarkar, "and he'll acquire that sense of purpose." India's great industrialists—the Tatas, the Ambanis, the Godrejs—all began in Bombay. The city's stock exchanges account for 92% of the country's total share turnover, and the nation's central bank and hundreds of brokerages and investors have set up their Indian headquarters there, including such global powerhouses as HSBC, JPMorgan Chase, and Bank of America.

Bombay's port handles half of India's trade, and its southern business district is one of the centers of the global outsourcing boom. India's music industry and much of its media are based in Bombay, as is Bollywood, the Hindi film industry. Such a concentration of business activity breeds a sophisticated, cosmopolitan outlook—hence Bombay has the best hotels, bars, restaurants, and nightclubs to be found in India. And every day, according to the official census, hundreds move to the city to seek their fortune in its streets.

City of Dreams. To migrants from India's poor states, the metropolis is known as Mayanagri, the City of Dreams. To its slums come people from India's villages, hitching rides and dodging train fares, prepared to sell spicy peanuts at traffic lights for a few cents a day and pay US$1 a month to live in a tin hut. For some of them, the principal opportunity the city offers is a life of crime—running bootlegging operations or gambling dens—or renting out the hovels in which millions of Bombay's inhabitants live. Just as for Bombay's gilded elite, the city is the place to be. "I came from nothing," says a Bombay gangster who grew up in Bihar, India's poorest state, and now owns 30,000 huts in four slums. "Now I have money, phones, cars, houses, a wife, and two girlfriends. If you were me, you'd love Bombay too."

That's not to say it's easy to love. If you judge Bombay by governance, it sounds as though the city is falling apart. In a calamity in July 2005 that was mercifully forgotten with the advent of Hurricane Katrina weeks later, heavy monsoon rains flooded Bombay for a week as the city's 150-year-old drains and sewers collapsed. At least 435 people died.

The infrastructure bears other scars of neglect. Consider the city's small and ancient stock of trains: each is crammed with an average of 4,500 people aboard, although most have a capacity of 1,750. As a result, passenger groups say, an astonishing 3,500 travelers die every year on the tracks, hundreds simply falling from the trains. City rent controls have kept the price of its swankiest apartments almost unchanged since 1940, encouraging landlords to let them crumble—as several blocks do, fatally, every year.

Visitors to the most prestigious offices in the country in southern Bombay run a gauntlet of homeless people outside. Movie director Shekhar Kapur, who returned after years in London and Los Angeles, says living in Bombay means confronting the class divide daily: "This must be one of the few places on earth where the rich try to work off a few pounds in the gym, step outside, and are confronted by a barefoot child of skin and bones begging for something to eat."

India's great hope runs on hope itself. Everyone who arrives there chasing a rainbow has a stake in keeping Bombay going. One day all those millions of expectations will have to be satisfied. But for now, the City of Dreams is living up to its name.

US Economy

The US Mint

The US Mint, the world's largest producer of coins and medals, was established by Congress on 2 Apr 1792. It is a bureau of the US Department of the Treasury. The mint manufactures and distributes coins, protects the country's gold and silver assets, and creates medals, commemorative coins, and coin proof sets for purchase by the public. In 2006 it produced 15.5 billion pennies, nickels, dimes, quarters, half dollars, and golden dollars. The director of the mint is appointed by the president and serves a five-year term; in mid-2007 the director was Edmund C. Foy.

From its Washington DC headquarters, the mint operates facilities in Philadelphia PA, Denver CO, San Francisco CA, and West Point NY. All engraving of coins is done at the Philadelphia site (established 1792), where general circulation coins, medals, and coin dies are also produced. Denver (1863) manufactures general circulation coins and coin dies and provides storage for gold and silver bullion. San Francisco (1854) produces only commemorative coins and proof sets; West Point (1937) manufactures uncirculated and proof sets of gold, silver, and platinum coins and stores these metals. The mint is also responsible for the storage and protection of more than 145 million ounces of gold bullion at Fort Knox KY.

Although general circulation coins were once made from gold, silver, and copper, this is no longer the case. Gold coin production was discontinued in 1933, and in 1966 silver ceased to be used in dimes and quarters. Currently, pennies are composed of copper-plated zinc, golden dollar coins of manganese brass, and all other general circulation coins of cupronickel, an alloy of copper and nickel. In early 2000 the mint began circulating the golden dollar coin, intended to replace the older Susan B. Anthony dollar coin. The new coin featured the image of Sacagawea, the Shoshone Indian woman who traveled as a guide with the Lewis and Clark Expedition in 1804–06. In 1999 the mint began issuing a series of quarters featuring the 50 states. Five quarters were to be issued annually, about 10 weeks apart, each featuring one state's design. State quarters were released in order of the states' ratification of the US Constitution. Introduced in 2007 were Idaho, Montana, Utah, Washington, and Wyoming; scheduled for 2008 are Alaska, Arizona, Hawaii, New Mexico, and Oklahoma. Nickels commemorating the Lewis and Clark Expedition were released in 2004 and 2005; those issued in 2005 featured a slightly different portrait of Thomas Jefferson. Dollar coins commemorating the US presidents were issued beginning in 2007, with subjects released in the order that they served. The coins are the same size, weight, and metal composition as the Sacagawea golden dollar and have an image of the Statue of Liberty on the back. Only deceased presidents are planned subjects, and currently the schedule of production runs through 2016.

US Mint Web site: <www.usmint.gov>.

Denominations of US Currency

VALUE	PORTRAIT ON FRONT	DESIGN ON BACK	WHEN CIRCULATED
		PAPER MONEY	
$1	George Washington	Great Seal of US	1929–
$2	Thomas Jefferson	Monticello	1929–75
$2	Thomas Jefferson	John Trumbull's *Signing of the Declaration of Independence*	1976–
$5[1]	Abraham Lincoln	Lincoln Memorial	2000–
$10[1]	Alexander Hamilton	US Treasury	2000–
$20[1]	Andrew Jackson	White House	1998–
$50[1]	Ulysses S. Grant	US Capitol	1997–
$100[1]	Benjamin Franklin	Independence Hall	1996–
$500[2]	William McKinley	ornate figure of value	1929–69
$1,000[2]	Grover Cleveland	ornate figure of value	1929–69
$5,000[2]	James Madison	ornate figure of value	1929–69
$10,000[2]	Salmon P. Chase	ornate figure of value	1929–69
$100,000[3]	Woodrow Wilson	ornate figure of value	—

[1]Earlier versions issued starting 1929 had same subjects as current version. [2]Last printed in 1945. [3]Printed 1934–35 but never issued to public.

VALUE	PORTRAIT ON FRONT	DESIGN ON BACK	WHEN CIRCULATED
		COINS	
1¢	Abraham Lincoln	"one cent" and wheat	1909–58
1¢	Abraham Lincoln	Lincoln Memorial	1959–
5¢	Thomas Jefferson	Monticello	1938–2003; 2006–
5¢	Thomas Jefferson	"Westward Journey" designs	2004–05
10¢	Franklin D. Roosevelt	torch	1946–
25¢	George Washington	eagle	1932–74; 1977–98
25¢	George Washington	colonial drummer	1975–76[1]
25¢	George Washington	50 state designs	1999–2008

[1]All 25¢, 50¢, and $1 coins issued in 1975 and 1976 carried the double date 1776–1976.

Denominations of US Currency (continued)

COINS (CONTINUED)

VALUE	PORTRAIT ON FRONT	DESIGN ON BACK	WHEN CIRCULATED
50¢	John F. Kennedy	presidential seal	1964–74; 1977–
50¢	John F. Kennedy	Independence Hall	1975–76[1]
$1	Dwight D. Eisenhower	eagle	1971–74; 1977–78
$1	Dwight D. Eisenhower	Liberty Bell and Moon	1975–76[1]
$1	Susan B. Anthony	eagle	1979–80; 1999
$1	Sacagawea	eagle	2000–06
$1	presidential portraits	Statue of Liberty	2007–16

[1]All 25¢, 50¢, and $1 coins issued in 1975 and 1976 carried the double date 1776–1976.

50 STATE QUARTERS PROGRAM

STATE	WHEN ISSUED	STATE	WHEN ISSUED	STATE	WHEN ISSUED
Alabama	2003	Louisiana	2002	Ohio	2002
Alaska	2008	Maine	2003	Oklahoma	2008
Arizona	2008	Maryland	2000	Oregon	2005
Arkansas	2003	Massachusetts	2000	Pennsylvania	1999
California	2005	Michigan	2004	Rhode Island	2001
Colorado	2006	Minnesota	2005	South Carolina	2000
Connecticut	1999	Mississippi	2002	South Dakota	2006
Delaware	1999	Missouri	2003	Tennessee	2002
Florida	2004	Montana	2007	Texas	2004
Georgia	1999	Nebraska	2006	Utah	2007
Hawaii	2008	Nevada	2006	Vermont	2001
Idaho	2007	New Hampshire	2000	Virginia	2000
Illinois	2003	New Jersey	1999	Washington	2007
Indiana	2002	New Mexico	2008	West Virginia	2005
Iowa	2004	New York	2001	Wisconsin	2004
Kansas	2005	North Carolina	2001	Wyoming	2007
Kentucky	2001	North Dakota	2006		

PRESIDENTIAL $1 COINS PROGRAM

2007   George Washington, John Adams, Thomas Jefferson, James Madison
2008   James Monroe, John Quincy Adams, Andrew Jackson, Martin Van Buren

US Currency and Coins in Circulation

Currency and coins outstanding and currency in circulation by denomination, 31 Dec 2006. Source: Treasury Bulletin, March 2007.

	TOTAL CURRENCY AND COINS	CURRENCY	COINS[1]
amounts in circulation	$820,144,768,198	$783,497,237,540	$36,647,530,658
less amounts held by:			
US Treasury	278,873,778	20,447,234	258,426,544
Federal Reserve Banks	176,461,778,445	175,661,179,744	800,598,701
total amounts outstanding	996,885,420,421	959,178,864,518	37,706,555,903

DENOMINATION	TOTAL CURRENCY IN CIRCULATION	FEDERAL RESERVE NOTES[2]	US NOTES	CURRENCY NO LONGER ISSUED
$1	$ 9,049,316,340	$ 8,905,529,500	$ 143,503	$143,643,337
$2	1,532,419,520	1,400,212,626	132,194,318	12,576
$5	10,492,843,480	10,356,036,390	109,055,410	27,751,680
$10	15,986,791,460	15,965,549,690	6,300	21,235,470
$20	119,219,518,240	119,199,409,800	3,840	20,104,600
$50	62,790,638,100	62,779,137,750	500	11,499,850
$100	564,112,426,800	564,079,692,200	10,740,900	21,993,700
$500	142,383,000	142,189,000	5,500	188,500
$1,000	165,675,000	165,462,000	5,000	208,000
$5,000	1,765,000	1,710,000	—	55,000
$10,000	3,460,000	3,360,000	—	100,000
fractional notes[3]	600	—	90	510
total currency	783,497,237,540	782,998,288,956	252,155,361	246,793,223

[1]Excludes coins sold to collectors at premium prices.   [2]Issued on or after 1 Jul 1929.   [3]Represents value of certain partial denominations not presented for redemption.

Energy

Energy Consumption by State and Sector

Figures represent '000,000,000,000 BTU for the year 2001. Sources: Energy Information Administration, <www.eia.doe.gov>; US Census Bureau.

	TOTAL	RESIDENTIAL	COMMERCIAL	INDUSTRIAL	TRANS-PORTATION	PER CAPITA ('000,000 BTU)
Alabama	1,943	380	254	863	446	435
Alaska	737	53	65	413	206	1,165
Arizona	1,353	344	312	221	476	255
Arkansas	1,106	219	148	462	278	411
California	7,853	1,446	1,509	1,928	2,971	227
Colorado	1,270	303	287	294	386	287
Connecticut	853	267	215	134	238	248
Delaware	293	62	52	113	66	368
District of Columbia	168	34	104	4	26	295
Florida	4,135	1,193	958	598	1,386	253
Georgia	2,881	642	503	876	860	343
Hawaii	282	35	39	77	132	231
Idaho	501	105	95	180	122	379
Illinois	3,870	928	829	1,173	939	309
Indiana	2,802	504	397	1,296	604	457
Iowa	1,151	229	179	472	270	393
Kansas	1,044	215	192	385	252	386
Kentucky	1,880	339	246	846	449	462
Louisiana	3,500	348	264	2,135	753	783
Maine	491	111	74	199	107	381
Maryland	1,420	391	372	252	405	264
Massachusetts	1,549	461	379	261	447	242
Michigan	3,120	790	598	928	804	312
Minnesota	1,745	381	336	526	502	350
Mississippi	1,173	234	163	427	349	410
Missouri	1,815	496	389	374	559	322
Montana	366	70	60	128	108	403
Nebraska	627	152	130	182	163	365
Nevada	629	147	108	169	205	300
New Hampshire	322	87	65	68	102	256
New Jersey	2,500	573	554	491	882	294
New Mexico	679	107	122	220	230	371
New York	4,135	1,194	1,303	667	970	217
North Carolina	2,591	641	513	743	694	316
North Dakota	407	61	56	203	88	639
Ohio	3,982	892	682	1,429	979	350
Oklahoma	1,540	298	233	544	466	444
Oregon	1,064	252	208	298	307	306
Pennsylvania	3,923	931	709	1,286	997	319
Rhode Island	227	73	63	26	66	215
South Carolina	1,549	322	235	609	383	381
South Dakota	248	60	50	54	83	327
Tennessee	2,195	500	369	746	581	382
Texas	12,029	1,570	1,356	6,426	2,677	564
Utah	725	140	140	233	213	318
Vermont	164	48	33	31	52	267
Virginia	2,315	549	534	547	685	322
Washington	2,034	471	377	586	600	339
West Virginia	762	157	111	311	183	423
Wisconsin	1,863	401	313	729	422	345
Wyoming	439	39	51	238	111	889
total	**96,275**	**20,241**	**17,332**	**32,431**	**26,272**	**338**

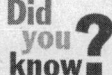

Did you know? The platypus's sensitive snout has been shown by researchers to contain electroreceptors, which enable it to detect the electrical field produced by the moving muscles of its prey. The platypus finds its food chiefly in underwater mud, and each day it consumes nearly its own weight in crustaceans, fishes, frogs, mollusks, tadpoles, and earthworms.

Energy Consumption by Source

Figures represent '000,000,000,000 BTU. Source: US Energy Information Administration, <www.eia.doe.gov>.

	PETROLEUM	NATURAL GAS	COAL	HYDROELECTRIC POWER	NUCLEAR ELECTRIC POWER
Alabama	539.6	342.3	845.6	85.0	317.2
Alaska	292.2	413.1	15.9	13.7	0.0
Arizona	524.2	245.2	424.1	80.4	300.1
Arkansas	378.6	231.6	274.0	25.9	154.4
California	3,604.4	2,513.9	67.9	256.3	347.1
Colorado	461.8	385.0	400.3	12.7	0.0
Conneticut	438.7	149.4	40.0	2.9	161.2
Delaware	146.5	51.8	38.3	0.0	0.0
District of Columbia	33.5	30.6	0.7	0.0	0.0
Florida	1,989.7	569.8	726.1	1.5	330.0
Georgia	1,034.0	362.7	772.0	20.6	351.9
Hawaii	239.8	2.9	17.6	1.0	0.0
Idaho	155.3	81.8	11.2	73.5	0.0
Illinois	1,304.1	970.7	993.6	1.5	965.0
Indiana	837.3	513.7	1,567.1	5.8	0.0
Iowa	400.9	225.2	444.9	8.6	40.3
Kansas	391.0	273.8	354.6	0.3	108.1
Kentucky	704.3	216.7	1,010.7	39.2	0.0
Louisiana	1,491.4	1,339.5	240.0	7.4	181.1
Maine	233.4	101.2	7.9	26.9	0.0
Maryland	568.1	191.4	317.3	12.0	142.7
Massachusetts	762.4	364.1	109.0	−0.1[1]	53.7
Michigan	1,041.7	928.7	796.5	4.4	279.1
Minnesota	673.5	345.0	353.1	8.5	123.2
Mississippi	485.5	340.8	198.3	0.0	103.7
Missouri	718.8	288.6	716.1	8.5	87.6
Montana	168.0	66.5	184.3	67.3	0.0
Nebraska	217.8	124.1	227.5	11.4	91.2
Nevada	250.2	181.3	188.6	25.6	0.0
New Hampshire	178.3	24.8	40.1	10.1	90.8
New Jersey	1,246.3	585.8	112.2	−1.3[1]	318.3
New Mexico	251.0	262.1	297.1	2.4	0.0
New York	1,712.5	1,205.9	315.0	225.4	422.0
North Carolina	949.6	215.6	756.5	26.4	394.7
North Dakota	138.0	62.6	419.8	13.6	0.0
Ohio	1,305.2	835.7	1,343.0	5.2	161.6
Oklahoma	588.4	548.4	376.8	22.5	0.0
Oregon	368.2	235.5	43.4	291.4	0.0
Pennsylvania	1,454.4	669.1	1,378.5	10.5	770.3
Rhode Island	99.8	98.6	0.1	<0.05	0.0
South Carolina	469.5	147.2	414.4	1.9	521.0
South Dakota	111.9	37.0	44.3	34.9	0.0
Tennessee	708.2	265.4	688.0	63.2	298.6
Texas	5,521.0	4,434.6	1,493.4	12.2	398.7
Utah	261.4	168.1	398.6	5.2	0.0
Vermont	88.9	8.0	0.1	9.0	43.6
Virginia	911.2	246.7	482.4	−12.5[1]	269.1
Washington	842.5	323.1	99.5	556.9	86.2
West Virginia	215.0	152.2	872.3	9.7	0.0
Wisconsin	668.4	363.0	494.7	20.9	120.2
Wyoming	157.0	104.0	500.2	8.9	0.0
total	38,333.3	22,844.5	21,904.7	2,117.6	8,032.7

[1]*Results from pumped storage expending more electricity to meet demand during peak periods than is created.*

Travel and Tourism

Passports, Visas, and Immunizations

With certain exceptions, a passport is required by law for all US citizens, including infants, to travel outside the United States and its territories. The exceptions of travel without passport to Mexico, Canada, Bermuda, and countries in the Caribbean were eliminated in 2007 by implementation of the Western Hemisphere Travel Initiative. Passports can be applied for at 9,000 passport acceptance facilities nationwide, including most government facilities. State Department passport agencies accept applications only by appointment, usually from those in need of expedited service (two weeks or less). Passport agencies are located in Aurora CO, Boston MA, Chicago IL, Honolulu HI, Houston TX, Los Angeles CA, Miami FL, New Orleans LA, New York City NY, Norwalk CT, Philadelphia PA, San Francisco CA, Seattle WA, and Washington DC. Everyone must apply in person for his or her first passport; those issued to persons aged 16 and older may be renewed by mail if the person's expiring passport is undamaged and in his or her possession and was issued no more than 15 years previously. Applicants should submit the appropriate paperwork several months in advance of planned travel to allow for processing. New passport fees total $97 for persons age 16 and up ($55 passport fee, $30 execution fee, $12 security surcharge) and $82 for those under 16 ($40 passport fee, $30 execution fee, $12 security surcharge); expedited service is an additional $60. Renewal fees are $67 for all ages. Passports are mailed to applicants in about six weeks or about two weeks for rush service. The status of a passport application may be checked online at <http://passportstatus.state.gov/opss/OPSS_Status_i.asp> or by contacting the National Passport Information Center at 1-877-487-2778 (toll-free; automated information; representatives available weekdays 6 am to 12 am ET, except federal holidays).

To apply in person for a passport requires submission of an application form; proof of US citizenship, such as a certified birth certificate; proof of identity, such as a driver's license; two identical recent 2×2-inch photographs; a social security number; and all applicable fees. Options for proving identity or citizenship are listed on the State Department Web site. A passport is valid for 10 years, or 5 years if issued to a person age 15 or younger. To renew by mail requires submission of an application form, the most recent passport, two identical photographs, and applicable fees. Frequent travelers may request a passport with extra pages. A passport that is lost or stolen in a foreign country must be immediately reported to local police and the nearest US embassy or consulate, to allow for the citizen's reentry into the US. Replacing a lost or stolen passport requires completion of a form reporting the loss or theft and an application for a new passport, as well as the usual documentation, photographs, and fees.

Visas. A visa is usually a stamp placed on a US passport by a foreign country's officials allowing the passport owner to visit that country. It is the traveler's responsibility to check visa regulations and obtain visas where necessary before traveling to a foreign country. Visas may be acquired from the embassy or consulate of the intended destination and can be applied for by mail. Processing fees vary among countries.

Immunizations. Under regulations adopted by the World Health Organization, some countries require International Certificates of Vaccination against yellow fever. Other immunizations, such as those for tetanus and polio, should also be up-to-date. Preventive measures for malaria are recommended for some destinations. There are no immunization requirements for returning to the United States. Many countries require HIV/AIDS testing for work, study, or residence permits or for long-term stays.

For passport information, forms, and office locations, access the State Department Web site at <http://travel.state.gov/passport>. Entry requirements for foreign countries, including necessity of visas, immunizations, and HIV testing, are available at <http://www.travel.state.gov/travel/tips/brochures/brochures_1229.html>. Additional information on required or recommended health-care measures can be obtained from the Centers for Disease Control and Prevention (CDC) at <www.cdc.gov/travel> or by calling 1-877-FYI-TRIP; also helpful are local health departments and the Government Printing Office publication *Health Information for International Travel*, available at the CDC Web site.

Travelers to and from the US

Data for 2002 showed that overseas travel to the US dropped significantly during 2002, primarily as a response to the terrorist attacks of 11 Sep 2001. Since then, however, travel has rebounded at varying levels. 2006 data for all US resident travel to specific overseas countries are not available, but data for air travel to the various regions, as well as Mexico and Canada, are presented below. Source: US Department of Commerce, International Trade Administration, Office of Travel and Tourism Industries.

TOP COUNTRIES OF ORIGIN FOR VISITORS TO THE US (2006)

		% CHANGE FROM 2005
UK	4,176,211	−4
Japan	3,672,584	−5
Germany	1,385,520	−2
France	789,815	−10
South Korea	757,721	+7
Australia	603,275	+4
Italy	532,829	−2
Brazil	525,271	+8
China[1]	457,728	+13
The Netherlands	446,785	—
total overseas	**21,668,290**	**—**
Canada	15,995,000	+8
Mexico	13,400,000	+6
total worldwide	**46,077,257**	**+4**

REGIONAL DESTINATION OF US AIR TRAVELERS ABROAD (2006)

		% CHANGE FROM 2005
Europe	12,995,893	+4
Caribbean	5,780,787	+7
Asia	5,207,977	+8
Central America	2,371,223	+3
South America	2,317,921	+6
Oceania	828,799	+6
Middle East	478,282	−14
Africa	167,490	−18
total overseas	**30,148,372**	**+5**
Mexico	5,747,999	+1
Canada	3,861,639	−1
total worldwide	**39,758,010**	**+4**

Travelers to and from the US (continued)

TOP 10 STATES AND CITIES VISITED BY OVERSEAS VISITORS (2005)[2]

STATE	VISITORS/ IN THOUSANDS ('000)	% CHANGE FROM 2004	CITY	VISITORS/ IN THOUSANDS ('000)	% CHANGE FROM 2004
New York	6,092	+12	New York NY	5,810	+13
California	4,791	+14	Los Angeles CA	2,580	+13
Florida	4,379	−1	San Francisco CA	2,124	+14
Hawaii	2,255	+2	Miami FL	2,081	−5
Nevada	1,821	+12	Orlando FL	2,016	+3
Illinois	1,149	+18	Oahu/Honolulu HI	1,821	−3
Guam[3]	1,127	+9	Las Vegas NV	1,778	+14
New Jersey	997	+20	Washington DC	1,106	+5
Texas	954	+9	Chicago IL	1,084	+16
Massachusetts	867	−7	Boston MA	802	−4

[1]Data for China include Hong Kong.   [2]Excludes Canadian and Mexican visitors to the US.   [3]Guam is a US territory. If Guam were excluded, Georgia would rank 10th on the list with about 650,000 overseas visitors.

Customs Exemptions

Upon returning to the US from a foreign country, travelers must pay duty on items acquired outside the US. If the value of the items is greater than the allowable exemption, duty must be paid on the excess amount. The general exemption is $800 per person, but it can also be $200 or $1,600 in certain situations. Exemptions apply if the items are in the traveler's possession, are for the traveler's own use, and are declared to Customs. The traveler must also have been out of the country for at least 48 hours (unless returning from Mexico or the US Virgin Islands) and must not have used any part of the exemption within the past 30 days; if one or both of these requirements does not apply, the allowable exemption drops to $200 per person and includes additional restrictions. The general exemption of $800 includes no more than 200 previously exported cigarettes, 100 cigars, and no more than one liter of alcoholic beverages. Cuban tobacco products are prohibited unless purchased in Cuba on authorized travel. Family members may combine their total exemptions in a joint declaration. The $800 exemption also applies to travelers returning from any of 28 countries and dependencies in the Caribbean Basin or Andean Region but may include two liters of alcoholic beverages, as long as one of the liters was produced in one of these. The 28 countries and dependencies are Antigua and Barbuda, Aruba, The Bahamas, Barbados, Belize, Bolivia, the British Virgin Islands, Colombia, Costa Rica, Dominica, the Dominican Republic, Ecuador, El Salvador, Grenada, Guatemala, Guyana, Haiti, Honduras, Jamaica, Montserrat, the Netherlands Antilles, Nicaragua, Panama, Peru, St. Kitts and Nevis, St. Lucia, St. Vincent and the Grenadines, and Trinidad and Tobago. A $1,600 exemption applies to travelers returning from a trip that included the US Virgin Islands, American Samoa, or Guam, and includes 1,000 cigarettes and five liters of alcoholic beverages; of this amount, 800 cigarettes and one liter of alcohol must be from one of the US islands. The $1,600 exemption also applies to multi-country travel (such as a cruise) to a US possession and any of the 28 Caribbean Basin and Andean Region countries and dependencies, as long as no more than $800 worth of goods was purchased in those locations.

Gifts valued at $100 or less ($200 or less for gifts sent from American Samoa, Guam, or the US Virgin Islands) may be sent to the US without duty as long as no single person receives more than this value within a single day. Alcoholic beverages may not be sent by mail; tobacco and alcohol-based perfumes worth more than $5 are not included in the exemption. Travelers may ship goods home for personal use without duty if the value of the goods is $200 or less and no single person receives more than this value within a single day. This personal exemption increases to $1,600 for goods purchased and shipped from American Samoa, Guam, or the US Virgin Islands.

Customs information is available from the Customs and Border Protection Web site at <www.cbp.gov/xp/cgov/travel>.

US State Department Travel Warnings

The State Department issues Travel Warnings when it is believed best for Americans to avoid certain countries in the interests of safety. It also releases Public Announcements of more short-term hazards, such as terrorist threats or political coups, that may endanger American travelers; these include an expiration date when the announcement need no longer be heeded. The department also makes available Consular Information Sheets for all countries, which may discuss safety conditions in that country not severe enough to require a travel warning. Current information can be found at <http://travel.state.gov> or by phone at 1-202-647-5225.

Travel Warnings were in effect on 12 Jul 2007 for the following: Afghanistan, Algeria, Burundi, the Central African Republic, Chad, Colombia, the Democratic Republic of the Congo, Côte d'Ivoire, East Timor, Eritrea, Indonesia, Iran, Iraq, Israel (including the West Bank and Gaza Strip), Kenya, Lebanon, Nepal, Nigeria, Pakistan, the Philippines, Saudi Arabia, Somalia, Sri Lanka, The Sudan, Syria, Uzbekistan, and Yemen.

Public Announcements in effect on the same day and set to expire on various dates in May–November included advisories for Central Asia, Fiji, Guinea, Laos, Mexico, the Middle East and North Africa, Paraguay, and Zimbabwe, as well as a worldwide caution.

Employment

US Employment by Gender and Occupation

Numbers may not add up to totals due to rounding. Source: US Bureau of Labor Statistics.

| OCCUPATION | WORKERS 16 YEARS AND OLDER (NUMBERS IN '000) | | | | | |
| | TOTAL | | MEN | | WOMEN | |
	2003	2004	2003	2004	2003	2004
management, professional, and related occupations	47,929	48,532	23,735	24,136	24,194	24,396
management, business, and financial operations occupations	19,934	20,235	11,534	11,718	8,400	8,517
management occupations	14,468	14,555	9,094	9,210	5,374	5,344
business and financial operations occupations	5,465	5,680	2,440	2,508	3,026	3,172
professional and related occupations	27,995	28,297	12,201	12,418	15,794	15,879
computer and mathematical occupations	3,122	3,140	2,223	2,292	900	848
architecture and engineering occupations	2,727	2,760	2,343	2,380	384	380
life, physical, and social science occupations	1,375	1,365	783	777	592	588
community and social services occupations	2,184	2,170	862	845	1,323	1,325
legal occupations	1,508	1,554	811	795	697	759
education, training, and library occupations	7,768	7,900	2,038	2,104	5,730	5,796
arts, design, entertainment, sports, and media occupations	2,663	2,687	1,395	1,425	1,267	1,262
health care practitioner and technical occupations	6,648	6,721	1,746	1,799	4,902	4,922
service occupations	22,086	22,720	9,460	9,826	12,626	12,894
health care support occupations	2,926	2,921	311	311	2,616	2,609
protective service occupations	2,727	2,847	2,164	2,230	563	616
food preparation and serving-related occupations	7,254	7,279	3,151	3,196	4,104	4,084
building and grounds cleaning and maintenance occupations	4,947	5,185	2,920	3,085	2,027	2,100
personal care and service occupations	4,232	4,488	915	1,004	3,316	3,484
sales and office occupations	35,496	35,464	12,851	12,805	22,645	22,660
sales and related occupations	15,960	15,983	8,137	8,105	7,823	7,878
office and administrative support occupations	19,536	19,481	4,714	4,700	14,823	14,781
natural resources, construction, and maintenance occupations	14,205	14,582	13,541	13,930	665	652
farming, fishing, and forestry occupations	1,050	991	819	786	231	204
construction and extraction occupations	8,114	8,522	7,891	8,306	223	216
installation, maintenance, and repair occupations	5,041	5,069	4,830	4,838	211	231
production, transportation, and material moving occupations	18,020	17,954	13,745	13,827	4,274	4,126
production occupations	9,700	9,462	6,696	6,587	3,004	2,875
transportation and material moving occupations	8,320	8,491	7,049	7,240	1,270	1,251
total	137,736	139,252	73,332	74,524	64,404	64,728

US Workers Earning the Minimum Wage

This table refers to wage and salary workers who are paid hourly rates. It excludes the incorporated self-employed. The prevailing federal minimum wage was $5.15/hour in 2006. Workers earning less than $5.15/hour may have been working in jobs that are exempted from the minimum wage provision of the Fair Labor Standards Act. Numbers in thousands ('000). Source: US Bureau of Labor Statistics.

WORKER CHARACTERISTICS	TOTAL NUMBER OF WORKERS	BELOW $5.15/HR	AT $5.15/HR	TOTAL NUMBER OF WORKERS AT OR BELOW $5.15/HR	
				NUMBER	%
age					
16–24 years	16,649	619	247	866	5.2
25 years and over	59,865	664	162	826	1.4
total (16 years and over)	76,514	1,283	409	1,692	2.2
men					
16–24 years	8,583	198	98	296	3.4
25 years and over	29,609	224	49	273	0.9
16 years and over	38,193	422	146	569	1.5
women					
16–24 years	8,065	421	149	570	7.1
25 years and over	30,256	440	114	553	1.8
16 years and over	38,321	861	263	1,124	2.9
race and Hispanic or Latino ethnicity[1]					
white (16 years and over)	61,907	1,105	329	1,435	2.3
black (16 years and over)	9,903	111	62	173	1.8
Asian (16 years and over)	2,654	30	8	38	1.4
Hispanic or Latino (16 years and over)	13,121	155	68	223	1.7
full- and part-time workers[2]					
full-time	58,452	554	99	653	1.1
part-time	17,930	724	310	1,034	5.8

[1]Data for racial groups other than those listed are not included. Hispanics may be of any race and are included in both white and black population groups. For these reasons, data for the race/ethnic group category will not add up to total. [2]Full- and part-time workers are distinguished by the number of hours worked. These data do not add up to total because of a small number of multiple jobholders whose status on the principal job is unknown.

Comparative Hourly Compensation Costs

The table shows private-industry employer compensation costs per hour worked by an employee in March 2005. Sums may not add to totals due to rounding. Source: US Bureau of Labor Statistics.

COMPENSATION	ALL WORKERS		GOODS-PRODUCING WORKERS[1]		SERVICE WORKERS[2]	
	COST ($)	(%)	COST ($)	(%)	COST ($)	(%)
wages and salaries	17.15	71	18.66	65.5	16.78	72.6
paid leave	1.54	6.4	1.72	6.0	1.5	6.5
vacation	0.76	3.2	0.89	3.1	0.73	3.2
holiday	0.53	2.2	0.63	2.2	0.51	2.2
sick	0.19	0.8	0.13	0.5	0.2	0.9
other	0.06	0.3	0.07	0.3	0.06	0.3
supplemental pay	0.68	2.8	1.24	4.4	0.54	2.3
premium[3]	0.24	1.0	0.59	2.1	0.16	0.7
shift differentials	0.06	0.2	0.08	0.3	0.05	0.2
nonproduction bonuses	0.38	1.6	0.57	2.0	0.33	1.4
insurance	1.76	7.3	2.45	8.6	1.59	6.9
life	0.04	0.2	0.06	0.2	0.04	0.2
health	1.64	6.8	2.28	8.0	1.48	6.4
short-term disability	0.05	0.2	0.08	0.3	0.04	0.2
long-term disability	0.03	0.1	0.03	0.1	0.03	0.1
retirement and savings	0.9	3.7	1.59	5.6	0.73	3.1
defined benefit	0.45	1.9	1.08	3.8	0.3	1.3
defined contribution	0.45	1.8	0.51	1.8	0.43	1.9

Comparative Hourly Compensation Costs (continued)

COMPENSATION	ALL WORKERS COST ($)	(%)	GOODS-PRODUCING WORKERS[1] COST ($)	(%)	SERVICE WORKERS[2] COST ($)	(%)
legally required benefits	2.10	8.7	2.73	9.6	1.95	8.4
Social Security[4]	1.43	5.9	1.61	5.6	1.39	6.0
Old-Age, Survivors, and Disability Insurance (OASDI)	1.15	4.8	1.29	4.5	1.12	4.8
Medicare	0.28	1.2	0.31	1.1	0.28	1.2
federal unemployment insurance	0.03	0.1	0.03	0.1	0.03	0.1
state unemployment insurance	0.16	0.7	0.2	0.7	0.15	0.6
workers' compensation	0.48	2.0	0.89	3.1	0.37	1.6
other benefits[5]	0.04	0.2	0.08	0.3	0.03	0.1
total benefits	7.02	29.0	9.82	34.5	6.34	27.4
total compensation	24.17	100	28.48	100	23.11	100

[1]Includes mining, construction, and manufacturing. [2]Includes transportation, communication, and public utilities; wholesale and retail trade; finance, insurance, and real estate; and service industries. [3]Pay for overtime, weekends, and holidays. [4]The total employer cost for Social Security comprises an OASDI portion and a Medicare portion. [5]Includes severance pay and supplemental unemployment benefits.

Median Income by Educational and Social Variables

Table refers to people who worked full-time throughout the year and are 15 years and over as of March of the following year. Median income dollar amounts are not adjusted for inflation. N/A means not available. Source: US Census Bureau.

	median income ($) males				median income ($) females			
	1980	1990	2000	2003	1980	1990	2000	2003
full-time workers	19,173	28,979	38,891	41,503	11,591	20,591	29,123	31,653
educational level[1]								
less than 9th grade	N/A	10,319	14,131	15,461	N/A	6,268	8,546	9,296
9th to 12th grade (no diploma)	N/A	14,736	18,915	18,990	N/A	7,055	10,063	10,786
high school graduate	N/A	21,546	27,480	28,763	N/A	10,818	15,153	15,962
some college, no degree	N/A	26,591	33,319	35,073	N/A	13,963	20,166	21,007
associate degree	N/A	29,358	38,026	39,015	N/A	17,364	23,124	24,808
bachelor's degree	N/A	36,067	49,080	50,916	N/A	20,967	30,418	31,309
master's degree	N/A	43,125	59,732	61,698	N/A	29,747	40,619	41,334
professional degree	N/A	63,741	83,701	88,530	N/A	34,064	46,084	48,536
doctorate degree	N/A	51,845	71,271	73,853	N/A	37,242	51,460	53,003
race and origin[2,3]								
white	13,328	21,170	29,797	30,732	4,947	10,317	16,079	17,422
white (non-Hispanic)	13,681	21,958	31,508	32,331	4,980	10,581	16,665	18,301
black	8,009	12,868	21,343	21,986	4,580	8,328	15,881	16,581
Hispanic origin	9,659	13,470	19,498	21,053	4,405	7,532	12,248	13,642
age[2]								
15 to 24 years	4,597	6,319	9,546	9,961	3,124	4,902	7,360	7,435
25 to 34 years	15,580	21,393	30,254	30,562	6,973	12,589	21,049	21,992
35 to 44 years	20,037	29,773	37,922	39,195	6,465	14,504	22,077	23,472
45 to 54 years	19,974	31,007	41,039	42,079	6,403	14,230	23,732	25,866
55 to 64 years	15,914	24,804	34,189	38,915	4,926	9,400	16,920	20,368
65 years and over	7,339	14,183	19,411	20,363	4,226	8,044	11,023	11,845
all workers over age 14	12,530	20,293	28,343	29,931	4,920	10,070	16,063	17,259

[1]The income figures for the various educational levels are for workers 25 years old and over. Before 1991, the level of education categories used by the US Census Bureau differed from the categories presented in this table. Because of this, the 1980 figures for the median income by educational level are not completely comparable with the figures for later years. The figures presented in the 1990 column for educational levels are actually for 1991, the first year the educational categories listed in this table were used by the US Census Bureau. [2]Figures for the 1980 sections covering "race and origin" and "age" are for civilian workers only. [3]Hispanic people may be of any race.

The 20 US Metropolitan Areas with the Highest Average Annual Salaries

Includes workers covered by two programs, Unemployment Insurance and Unemployment Compensation for Federal Employees. A minus sign indicates a decrease in the average annual salary. Source: US Bureau of Labor Statistics.

METROPOLITAN AREA	ANNUAL SALARY ($) 2001	2002	SALARY CHANGE (%)	METROPOLITAN AREA	ANNUAL SALARY ($) 2001	2002	SALARY CHANGE (%)
San Jose, CA	65,931	63,056	-4.4	Seattle-Bellevue-Everett, WA	45,299	46,093	1.8
New York, NY	59,097	57,708	-2.4	Boston, MA[4]	45,766	45,685	-0.2
San Francisco, CA	59,654	56,602	-5.1	Bergen-Passaic, NJ	44,701	45,185	1.1
New Haven, CT[1]	52,198	51,170	-2.0	Hartford, CT	43,880	44,387	1.2
Middlesex, NJ[2]	49,950	50,457	1.0	Boulder-Longmont, CO	44,310	44,037	-0.6
Jersey City, NJ	47,638	49,562	4.0	Wilmington-Newark, DE-MD[5]	42,177	43,401	2.9
Newark, NJ	47,715	48,781	2.2	Chicago, IL	42,685	43,239	1.3
Washington, DC[3]	47,589	48,430	1.8	Detroit, MI	42,704	43,224	1.2
Trenton, NJ	46,831	47,969	2.4	Dallas, TX	42,706	43,000	0.7
Oakland, CA	45,920	46,877	2.1	Houston, TX	42,784	42,712	-0.2

[1]New Haven area includes Bridgeport, Stamford, Waterbury, and Danbury. [2]Middlesex area includes Somerset and Hunterdon. [3]Washington DC area includes areas in Maryland, Virginia, and West Virginia. [4]Boston area includes Worcester, Lawrence, Lowell, and Brockton. [5]Wilmington-Newark area includes parts of Maryland.

US Federal Minimum Wage Rates

The table shows the actual minimum wage for the year in question (since 1951) and the value of that minimum wage adjusted for inflation in the year 2007. Source: US Bureau of Labor Statistics.

YEAR	minimum wage DOLLARS	2007 DOLLARS	YEAR	minimum wage DOLLARS	2007 DOLLARS	YEAR	minimum wage DOLLARS	2007 DOLLARS
1951	0.75	5.92	1970	1.60	8.47	1989	3.35	5.55
1952	0.75	5.81	1971	1.60	8.11	1990	3.80	5.97
1953	0.75	5.77	1972	1.60	7.86	1991	4.25	6.41
1954	0.75	5.73	1973	1.60	7.40	1992	4.25	6.22
1955	0.75	5.75	1974	2.00	8.33	1993	4.25	6.04
1956	1.00	7.55	1975	2.10	8.02	1994	4.25	5.89
1957	1.00	7.31	1976	2.30	8.30	1995	4.25	5.73
1958	1.00	7.11	1977	2.30	7.79	1996	4.75	5.56
1959	1.00	7.06	1978	2.65	8.35	1997	5.15	6.59
1960	1.00	6.94	1979	2.90	8.20	1998	5.15	6.49
1961	1.15	7.90	1980	3.10	7.73	1999	5.15	6.35
1962	1.15	7.82	1981	3.35	7.57	2000	5.15	6.14
1963	1.25	8.39	1982	3.35	7.13	2001	5.15	5.97
1964	1.25	8.28	1983	3.35	6.91	2002	5.15	5.88
1965	1.25	8.15	1984	3.35	6.62	2003	5.15	5.75
1966	1.25	7.92	1985	3.35	6.39	2004	5.15	5.60
1967	1.40	8.61	1986	3.35	6.28	2005	5.15	5.42
1968	1.60	9.44	1987	3.35	6.06	2006	5.15	5.25
1969	1.60	8.95	1988	3.35	5.82	2007	5.85	5.85

US Civilian Federal Employment

Sources: US Office of Personnel Management; Statistical Abstract of the United States (2004–2005).

AGENCIES[1]	1970	1980	1990	2000	2003
legislative branch	29,939	39,710	37,495	31,157	31,297
judicial branch	6,879	15,178	23,605	32,186	34,472
departments of the executive branch	1,772,363	1,716,970	2,065,542	1,592,200	1,687,158
State	40,042	23,497	25,288	27,983	31,402
Treasury	90,683	124,663	158,655	143,508	134,302
Defense	1,169,173	960,116	1,034,152	676,268	669,096
Justice	40,075	56,327	83,932	125,970	115,259
Interior	71,671	77,357	77,679	73,818	74,818
Agriculture	114,309	129,139	122,594	104,466	107,204
Commerce	36,124	48,563	69,920	47,652	37,330
Labor	10,928	23,400	17,727	16,040	16,296
Health & Human Services (HHS)	110,186	155,662	123,959	62,605	67,240
Housing & Urban Development	15,046	16,964	13,596	10,319	10,660
Transportation	66,970	72,361	67,364	63,598	89,262
Energy	7,156	21,557	17,731	15,692	15,823
Education	0	7,364	4,771	4,734	4,593

US Civilian Federal Employment (continued)

AGENCIES[1]	1970	1980	1990	2000	2003
departments of the executive branch (continued)					
Veterans Affairs	169,241	228,285	248,174	219,547	226,171
independent agencies[2]	N/A	N/A	999,894	1,050,900	988,434
Board of Governors of the Federal Reserve System	N/A	N/A	1,525	1,644	1,761
Commodity Futures Trading Commission	N/A	N/A	542	574	534
Consumer Product Safety Commission	N/A	N/A	520	479	482
Environmental Protection Agency	0	14,715	17,123	18,036	18,126
Equal Employment Opportunity Commission	797	3,515	2,880	2,780	2,669
Federal Communications Commission	N/A	N/A	1,778	1,965	2,058
Federal Deposit Insurance Corporation	2,462	3,520	17,641	6,958	5,502
Federal Emergency Management Agency (FEMA)	0	3,427	3,137	4,813	6,191
Federal Trade Commission	N/A	N/A	988	1,019	1,076
General Services Administration[3]	37,661	37,654	20,277	14,334	13,615
National Aeronautics & Space Administration	30,674	23,714	24,872	18,819	18,908
National Archives & Records Administration	N/A	N/A	3,120	2,702	3,027
National Labor Relations Board	N/A	N/A	2,263	2,054	1,932
National Science Foundation	N/A	N/A	1,318	1,247	1,327
Nuclear Regulatory Commission	0	3,283	3,353	2,858	3,034
Office of Personnel Management	5,513	8,280	6,636	3,780	3,410
Peace Corps	N/A	N/A	1,178	1,065	1,118
Securities & Exchange Commission	N/A	N/A	2,302	2,955	3,132
Small Business Administration	4,397	5,804	5,128	4,150	3,824
Smithsonian Institution	2,547	4,403	5,092	5,065	5,133
Social Security Administration	N/A	N/A	N/A	64,474	64,414
Tennessee Valley Authority	23,785	51,714	28,392	13,145	13,379
US Information Agency	10,156	8,138	8,555	2,436	2,362
US Postal Service	721,183	660,014	816,886	860,726	801,552
total, all agencies	2,866,313	2,875,866	3,128,267	2,798,101	2,743,063

N/A means not available. [1]Includes other branches or agencies not shown separately. The Office of Homeland Security was created by an executive order of Pres. George W. Bush after the terrorist attacks of 11 Sep 2001. On 24 Jan 2003 the Department of Homeland Security, a cabinet-level agency within the executive branch of government, replaced the Office of Homeland Security. In the largest US governmental reorganization since World War II, the new department acquired 22 security-related agencies. Prior to this reorganization, the agencies had been administered by other governmental entities or, in FEMA's case, had been an independent agency. [2]The Defense Intelligence Agency was excluded as of November 1984, the National Imagery and Mapping Agency as of October 1996. Entries for 1990, 2000, and 2001 exclude the Central Intelligence Agency and the National Security Agency. [3]Entry for 1980 includes the National Archives and Records Administration, which became an independent agency in 1985.

Older Americans in the Workforce

All numbers are in thousands ('000). Figures are from March 2002 and may not add up to totals due to rounding. Source: US Census Bureau.

	WORKFORCE BY AGE							
	55 AND OVER		55–59		60–64		65 AND OLDER	
GENDER AND OCCUPATION TYPE	NUMBER	%	NUMBER	%	NUMBER	%	NUMBER	%
men and women								
managerial and professional	6,561	33.4	3,590	36.3	1,731	32	1,241	28.6
technical, sales, and administrative support	5,668	28.9	2,720	27.5	1,608	29.7	1,340	30.9
service occupations	2,525	12.9	1,130	11.4	733	13.6	662	15.3
precision production, craft, and repair	1,820	9.3	1,044	10.6	488	9	288	6.6
operators, fabricators, and laborers	2,344	11.9	1,163	11.8	680	12.6	501	11.6
farming, forestry, and fishing	700	3.6	233	2.4	169	3.1	299	6.9
total	19,618	100	9,878	100	5,408	100	4,331	100
men								
managerial and professional	3,701	34.9	1,868	35.7	1,025	35.8	808	32.3
technical, sales, and administrative support	2,072	19.5	984	18.8	541	18.9	546	21.9
service occupations	938	8.9	387	7.4	273	9.5	278	11.1

Older Americans in the Workforce (continued)

	WORKFORCE BY AGE							
GENDER AND OCCUPATION TYPE	55 AND OVER		55–59		60–64		65 AND OLDER	
	NUMBER	%	NUMBER	%	NUMBER	%	NUMBER	%
men (continued)								
precision production, craft, and repair	1,633	15.4	956	18.3	427	14.9	250	10
operators, fabricators, and laborers	1,731	16.3	859	16.4	477	16.7	395	15.8
farming, forestry, and fishing	523	4.9	183	3.5	118	4.1	221	8.9
total	10,598	100	5,237	100	2,861	100	2,499	100
women								
managerial and professional	2,860	31.7	1,722	37.1	705	27.7	432	23.6
technical, sales, and administrative support	3,596	39.9	1,736	37.4	1,066	41.9	794	43.3
service occupations	1,587	17.6	743	16	461	18.1	384	20.9
precision production, craft, and repair	187	2.1	87	1.9	61	2.4	38	2.1
operators, fabricators, and laborers	613	6.8	304	6.5	203	8	107	5.8
farming, forestry, and fishing	177	2	49	1.1	51	2	78	4.2
total	9,020	100	4,641	100	2,547	100	1,832	100

Strikes and Lockouts in the US

Strikes and lockouts are referred to as work stoppages by the Bureau of Labor Statistics. This table covers work stoppages since 1950 involving 1,000 workers or more. The number of workers and stoppages are for stoppages begun during that year. The number of days out from work pertains to all strikes or lockouts in effect during the year, whether they began in that year or not. The heading for estimated working time includes all workers except those employed in private households, forestry, or fisheries. Source: US Bureau of Labor Statistics.

	strikes and lockouts		work time lost			strikes and lockouts		work time lost	
		WORKERS INVOLVED	DAYS LOST	% OF WORKING			WORKERS INVOLVED	DAYS LOST	% OF WORKING
YEAR	NUMBER	('000)	('000)	TIME	YEAR	NUMBER	('000)	('000)	TIME
1950	424	1,698	30,390	0.26	1979	235	1,021	20,409	0.09
1951	415	1,462	15,070	0.12	1980	187	795	20,844	0.09
1952	470	2,746	48,820	0.38	1981	145	729	16,908	0.07
1953	437	1,623	18,130	0.14	1982	96	656	9,061	0.04
1954	265	1,075	16,630	0.13	1983	81	909	17,461	0.08
1955	363	2,055	21,180	0.16	1984	62	376	8,499	0.04
1956	287	1,370	26,840	0.20	1985	54	324	7,079	0.03
1957	279	887	10,340	0.07	1986	69	533	11,861	0.05
1958	332	1,587	17,900	0.13	1987	46	174	4,481	0.02
1959	245	1,381	60,850	0.43	1988	40	118	4,381	0.02
1960	222	896	13,260	0.09	1989	51	452	16,996	0.07
1961	195	1,031	10,140	0.07	1990	44	185	5,926	0.02
1962	211	793	11,760	0.08	1991	40	392	4,584	0.02
1963	181	512	10,020	0.07	1992	35	364	3,989	0.01
1964	246	1,183	16,220	0.11	1993	35	182	3,981	0.01
1965	268	999	15,140	0.10	1994	45	322	5,021	0.02
1966	321	1,300	16,000	0.10	1995	31	192	5,771	0.02
1967	381	2,192	31,320	0.18	1996	37	273	4,889	0.02
1968	392	1,855	35,367	0.20	1997	29	339	4,497	0.01
1969	412	1,576	29,397	0.16	1998	34	387	5,116	0.02
1970	381	2,468	52,761	0.29	1999	17	73	1,996	0.01
1971	298	2,516	35,538	0.19	2000	39	394	20,419	0.06
1972	250	975	16,764	0.09	2001	29	99	1,151	0.00
1973	317	1,400	16,260	0.08	2002	19	46	660	0.00
1974	424	1,796	31,809	0.16	2003	14	129	4,091	0.01
1975	235	965	17,563	0.09	2004	17	171	3,344	0.01
1976	231	1,519	23,962	0.12	2005	22	100	1,736	0.01
1977	298	1,212	21,258	0.10	2006	20	70	2,688	0.01
1978	219	1,006	23,774	0.11					

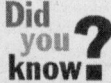

Did you know?   In the Great Depression, during the decade of the 1930's, unemployment in the US averaged over 18%, and in the worst year, 1933, it topped 25%. Only in 1941 did the rate fall to 10%, and the US has not had double-digit unemployment in any year since.

US Trade Union Membership

Numbers are in thousands ('000). N/A means not available. Source: US Bureau of Labor Statistics.

YEAR	NUMBER OF UNION MEMBERS	% OF TOTAL LABOR FORCE	YEAR	NUMBER OF UNION MEMBERS	% OF TOTAL LABOR FORCE	YEAR	NUMBER OF UNION MEMBERS	% OF TOTAL LABOR FORCE
1900[1]	791	N/A	1940	8,717	26.9	1980	20,095	23.0
1905	1,918	N/A	1945	14,322	35.5	1985	16,996	18.0
1910	2,116	N/A	1950	14,300[3]	31.5	1990	16,740	16.1
1915	2,560	N/A	1955	16,802	33.2	1995	16,360	14.9
1920	5,034	N/A	1960	17,049	31.4	2000	16,258	13.5
1925	3,566	N/A	1965	17,299	28.4	2004	15,472	12.5
1930[2]	3,401	11.6	1970	19,381	27.4	2005	15,685	12.5
1935	3,584	13.2	1977[4]	19,335	23.8	2006	15,359	12.0

[1]Data from 1900 to 1925 include Canadian members whose union headquarters were in the US. [2]Agricultural workers were not included as part of the total labor force for the years from 1930 to 1970. [3]Rounded to nearest hundred thousand. [4]Data for 1975 were not available. Data for 1977 on include only employed union members.

US Unemployment Rates

Unemployment rates of the civilian labor force 16 years and older. Source: US Bureau of Labor Statistics.

YEAR	UNEMPLOYMENT RATE (%)	YEAR	UNEMPLOYMENT RATE (%)	YEAR	UNEMPLOYMENT RATE (%)	YEAR	UNEMPLOYMENT RATE (%)
1947	3.9	1962	5.5	1977	7.1	1992	7.5
1948	3.8	1963	5.7	1978	6.1	1993	6.9
1949	5.9	1964	5.2	1979	5.8	1994	6.1
1950	5.3	1965	4.5	1980	7.1	1995	5.6
1951	3.3	1966	3.8	1981	7.6	1996	5.4
1952	3.0	1967	3.8	1982	9.7	1997	4.9
1953	2.9	1968	3.6	1983	9.6	1998	4.5
1954	5.5	1969	3.5	1984	7.5	1999	4.2
1955	4.4	1970	4.9	1985	7.2	2000	4.0
1956	4.1	1971	5.9	1986	7.0	2001	4.7
1957	4.3	1972	5.6	1987	6.2	2002	5.8
1958	6.8	1973	4.9	1988	5.5	2003	6.0
1959	5.5	1974	5.6	1989	5.3	2004	5.5
1960	5.5	1975	8.5	1990	5.6	2005	5.1
1961	6.7	1976	7.7	1991	6.8	2006	4.6

Social Characteristics of the Unemployed in the US

Unemployment as a % of the civilian labor force. N/A means not available. Source: US Bureau of Labor Statistics.

SOCIAL CHARACTERISTICS	UNEMPLOYMENT RATES BY YEAR (%)									
	1975	1980	1985	1990	1995	2000	2001	2002	2003	2004
age (both sexes)										
16–19[3]	19.9	17.8	18.6	15.5	17.3	13.1	14.7	16.5	17.4	17.0
25 and over	6.0	5.1	5.6	4.4	4.3	3.0	3.7	4.6	5.0	4.3
sex (20 years and older)										
men[3]	6.8	5.9	6.2	5.0	4.8	3.3	4.2	5.3	5.7	5.0
women[3]	8.0	6.4	6.6	4.9	4.9	3.6	4.1	5.1	5.1	4.9
race/ethnicity										
white[3]	7.8	6.3	6.2	4.8	4.9	3.5	4.2	5.1	5.2	4.8
black[3]	14.8	14.3	15.1	11.4	10.4	7.6	8.6	10.2	10.8	10.4
Hispanic[1, 3]	12.2	10.1	10.5	8.2	9.3	5.7	6.6	7.5	7.7	7.0
family										
women maintaining families	10.0	9.2	10.4	8.3	8.0	5.9	6.6	N/A	N/A	N/A
married men, spouse present	5.1	4.2	4.3	3.4	3.3	2.0	2.7	3.6	3.8	3.1[4]
overall unemployment[3]	8.5	7.1	7.2	5.6	5.6	4.0	4.7	5.8	6.0	5.5

[1]Hispanics may be of any race and are included in both the white and black racial categories in this table. [2]25 and over (2004): quarterly average. [3]2003 and 2004 figures are averages of monthly figures of the given year. [4]Average of June–December 2004 figures.

US Unemployment by Occupation

Unemployment rates are for the civilian noninstitutional population aged 16 years and older. Rates represent unemployment as a percent of the labor force for each occupational group. The unemployment rate totals include people without previous work experience and those whose last job was in the military. 2004 data reflect revised population controls used in the survey. Source: US Bureau of Labor Statistics.

OCCUPATION	THOUSANDS OF PERSONS		TOTAL (%)	
	2003	2004	2003	2004
Management, professional, and related occupations	**1,556**	**1,346**	**3.1**	**2.7**
Management, business, and financial operations occupations	627	544	3.1	2.6
Management occupations	430	369	2.9	2.5
Business and financial operations occupations	198	175	3.5	3.0
Professional and related occupations	929	801	3.2	2.8
Computer and mathematical occupations	181	136	5.5	4.2
Architecture and engineering occupations	124	80	4.4	2.8
Life, physical, and social science occupations	48	35	3.3	2.5
Community and social services occupations	57	65	2.5	2.9
Legal occupations	35	31	2.3	1.9
Education, training, and library occupations	225	207	2.8	2.5
Arts, design, entertainment, sports, and media occupations	171	157	6.0	5.5
Health care practitioner and technical occupations	88	90	1.3	1.3
Service occupations	**1,681**	**1,617**	**7.1**	**6.6**
Health care support occupations	171	169	5.5	5.5
Protective service occupations	129	113	4.5	3.8
Food preparation and serving related occupations	683	656	8.6	8.3
Building and grounds cleaning and maintenance occupations	447	421	8.3	7.5
Personal care and service occupations	250	257	5.6	5.4
Sales and office occupations	**2,070**	**1,937**	**5.5**	**5.2**
Sales and related occupations	995	912	5.9	5.4
Office and administrative support occupations	1,076	1,025	5.2	5.0
Natural resources, construction, and maintenance occupations	**1,244**	**1,440**	**8.1**	**7.3**
Farming, fishing, and forestry occupations	136	132	11.4	11.8
Construction and extraction occupations	814	786	9.1	8.4
Installation, maintenance, and repair occupations	295	222	5.5	4.2
Production, transportation, and material moving occupations	**1,555**	**1,393**	**7.9**	**7.2**
Production occupations	807	714	7.7	7.0
Transportation and material moving occupations	748	679	8.2	7.4
Total, 16 years and over	**8,774**	**8,149**	**6.0**	**5.5**

Occupational Illnesses and Injuries in the US

This table displays the number of nonfatal work injuries and illnesses recorded in 2005. The injuries and illnesses resulted in days away from work in the private industries listed. Numbers may not add to totals because of rounding and nonclassifiable responses. Numbers are in thousands ('000). N/A means not available. Source: US Bureau of Labor Statistics.

CHARACTERISTIC	PRIVATE INDUSTRY[1]	GOODS-PRODUCING INDUSTRIES		
		NATURAL RESOURCES AND MINING[1,2]	CONSTRUCTION	MANUFACTURING
injury or illness				
sprains, strains	503.5	8.6	54.5	74.2
bruises, contusions	107.8	3.6	11.2	16.7
cuts, lacerations	101.7	2.4	17.8	21.5
fractures	95.8	3.6	18.1	17.1
heat burns	17.2	0.3	1.2	3.5
carpal tunnel syndrome	16.5	0.1	0.6	5.4
tendinitis	5.7	0.1	0.6	1.9
chemical burns	6.4	0.2	0.8	1.8
amputations	8.5	0.4	1.3	3.8
multiple traumatic injuries	50.1	1.4	6.7	7.7
body part affected by injury or illness				
head	81.1	2.4	12.9	16.0
eye	34.7	1.2	6.4	9.7
neck	18.5	0.3	2.4	2.3
trunk	428.5	8.7	48.4	68.4
shoulder	77.8	1.6	8.0	15.2
back	270.9	4.7	30.2	38.6

Occupational Illnesses and Injuries in the US (continued)

CHARACTERISTIC	PRIVATE INDUSTRY[1]	GOODS-PRODUCING INDUSTRIES		
		NATURAL RESOURCES AND MINING[1,2]	CONSTRUCTION	MANU-FACTURING
body part affected by injury or illness (continued)				
upper extremities	284.8	6.4	37.6	68.1
wrist	56.3	0.8	5.1	12.7
hand, except finger	47.0	0.9	7.2	10.9
finger	111.1	3.2	15.7	30.8
lower extremities	271.7	6.9	39.2	37.8
knee	100.6	2.4	12.6	13.4
foot, except toe	43.8	0.9	7.0	7.6
toe	12.9	0.3	1.6	2.2
body systems	18.0	0.5	1.7	2.5
multiple parts	121.0	2.5	13.7	12.9
source of injury or illness				
chemicals and chemical products	18.4	1.1	1.6	4.5
containers	151.7	2.0	6.8	24.3
furniture and fixtures	46.8	0.3	2.9	6.1
machinery	80.5	2.9	9.7	26.9
parts and materials	128.7	3.3	36.7	36.8
worker motion or position	181.8	2.9	20.8	37.4
floors, walkways, ground surfaces	234.4	4.9	32.0	24.5
tools, instruments, and equipment	80.3	1.9	16.7	14.3
vehicles	109.6	2.7	8.4	11.6
health care patient	54.5	—	[3]	[3]
exposure or event leading to injury or illness				
contact with objects and equipment	338.1	11.2	55.6	76.9
struck by object	167.7	5.7	30.6	31.8
struck against object	85.5	2.3	12.6	16.3
caught in equipment or object	54.6	2.4	6.0	21.4
fall to lower level	79.3	2.2	21.8	7.8
fall on same level	167.2	2.7	12.4	18.3
slip, trip, loss of balance—without fall	36.2	0.6	4.9	5.4
overexertion	298.1	4.5	28.5	47.9
overexertion in lifting	160.0	2.0	15.7	24.7
repetitive motion	43.8	0.3	2.5	15.2
exposure to harmful substances	51.9	1.4	5.5	10.4
transportation accidents	61.2	1.5	6.2	4.7
fires and explosions	2.6	0.1	0.4	0.7
assaults and violent acts by person	14.6	0.1	0.2	0.3
total cases	**1,234.7**	**27.9**	**157.1**	**209.1**

CHARACTERISTIC	SERVICE-PRODUCING INDUSTRIES			
	TRADE, TRANSPORTATION, AND UTILITIES[2]	FINANCIAL SERVICES	HOTELS AND RESTAURANTS	OTHER SERVICES
injury or illness				
sprains, strains	172.4	48.5	30.6	114.8
bruises, contusions	36.3	10.2	8.4	21.4
cuts, lacerations	27.0	9.8	14.3	8.8
fractures	26.9	9.8	6.9	13.4
heat burns	2.8	1.0	6.1	2.2
carpal tunnel syndrome	3.6	3.3	1.0	2.5
tendinitis	1.3	0.6	0.3	1.1
chemical burns	1.7	0.7	0.5	0.7
amputations	1.7	0.7	0.5	0.3
multiple traumatic injuries	15.1	5.7	3.8	9.7
body part affected by injury or illness				
head	24.3	8.6	4.8	12.1
eye	8.5	3.2	1.6	4.1
neck	6.3	2.3	0.6	4.3
trunk	142.3	40.2	27.3	93.2
shoulder	27.2	6.6	4.9	14.4
back	88.0	26.3	17.5	65.6

Occupational Illnesses and Injuries in the US (continued)

| | SERVICE-PRODUCING INDUSTRIES | | | |
	TRADE, TRANSPORTATION, AND UTILITIES[2]	FINANCIAL SERVICES	HOTELS AND RESTAURANTS	OTHER SERVICES
CHARACTERISTIC				
body part affected by injury or illness (continued)				
upper extremities	74.3	26.9	29.9	41.3
wrist	15.7	6.8	4.0	11.0
hand, except finger	11.4	4.3	6.2	6.2
finger	27.0	9.3	13.3	11.8
lower extremities	91.0	30.3	19.6	47.0
knee	34.2	10.8	7.7	19.5
foot, except toe	15.1	4.5	2.6	6.2
toe	4.8	1.4	0.7	2.0
body systems	3.8	3.6	1.5	4.3
multiple parts	36.1	15.7	8.2	31.9
source of injury or illness				
chemicals and chemical products	4.1	2.4	1.4	3.2
containers	78.7	12.6	12.5	14.8
furniture and fixtures	15.5	6.6	4.9	10.5
machinery	20.1	7.3	6.3	7.3
parts and materials	34.1	7.8	3.1	6.8
worker motion or position	54.8	21.5	12.8	31.5
floors, walkways, ground surfaces	67.8	28.8	23.6	53.0
tools, instruments, and equipment	18.2	7.7	8.2	13.2
vehicles	51.5	14.6	5.5	15.5
health care patient	0.1	0.6	3	53.8
exposure or event leading to injury or illness				
contact with objects and equipment	99.1	30.2	28.0	37.1
struck by object	51.7	14.7	14.6	18.7
struck against object	26.0	6.3	9.5	10.5
caught in equipment or object	14.1	3.6	2.3	4.8
fall to lower level	24.0	9.3	4.1	10.1
fall on same level	47.9	21.1	20.4	44.4
slip, trip, loss of balance—without fall	11.1	3.6	3.6	7.0
overexertion	105.0	23.7	13.0	75.6
overexertion in lifting	59.8	14.0	7.3	36.5
repetitive motion	10.3	6.4	2.6	6.5
exposure to harmful substances	9.7	6.2	8.7	10.0
transportation accidents	25.5	10.0	3.0	10.3
fires and explosions	0.9	0.3	3	0.2
assaults and violent acts by person	2.1	1.1	0.7	10.1
total cases	380.1	130.1	93.9	235.9

[1]Excludes farms with fewer than 11 employees.   [2]The Mine Safety and Health Administration provided data for mining; the Federal Railroad Administration provided railroad transportation data. The mining category excludes independent mining contractors.   [3]Fewer than 50 cases.

US Work-Related Fatalities by Cause

Totals for major categories may include some smaller categories not listed in the table. Percentages may not add up to totals because of rounding. Source: US Bureau of Labor Statistics.

| | 2000–04 | 2005 | |
	NUMBER (AVG.)	NUMBER	(%)
CAUSE OF FATALITY			
transportation incidents	**2,467**	**2,480**	**43**
highway	1,380	1,428	25
collision between vehicles, mobile equipment	682	716	13
moving in same direction	143	175	3
moving in opposite directions, oncoming	249	263	5
moving in intersection	141	133	2
vehicle struck stationary object or equipment	318	369	7
noncollision	342	314	6
jackknifed or overturned—no collision	281	272	5
nonhighway (farm, industrial premises)	347	340	6
overturned	181	183	3

US Work-Related Fatalities by Cause (continued)

CAUSE OF FATALITY	2000–04 NUMBER (AVG.)	2005 NUMBER	2005 (%)
transportation incidents (continued)			
worker struck by a vehicle	365	390	7
water vehicle	81	86	2
rail vehicle	58	84	1
aircraft	233	147	3
assaults and violent acts	**878**	**.787**	**14**
homicides	624	564	10
shooting	484	439	8
stabbing	62	60	1
self-inflicted injury	215	177	3
contact with objects and equipment	**952**	**1,001**	**18**
struck by object	552	604	11
struck by falling object	340	383	7
struck by flying object	52	52	1
caught in or compressed by equipment or objects	260	277	5
caught in running equipment or machinery	135	121	2
caught in or crushed in collapsing materials	121	109	2
falls	**756**	**767**	**13**
fall to lower level	668	662	12
fall from ladder	122	129	2
fall from roof	152	160	3
fall from scaffold, staging	88	82	1
fall on same level	67	83	1
exposure to harmful substances or environments	**494**	**496**	**9**
contact with electric current	266	250	4
contact with overhead power lines	121	110	2
contact with temperature extremes	39	55	1
exposure to caustic, noxious, or allergenic substances	107	132	2
inhalation of substance	53	65	1
oxygen deficiency	81	59	1
drowning, submersion	59	48	1
fires and explosions	**177**	**158**	**3**
total	**5,742**	**5,702**	**100**

Consumer Prices

US Consumer Price Index, 1913–2006

This table presents the annual change in the Consumer Price Index (CPI) since 1913. The CPI is used as an indicator of price changes in the goods and services purchased by US consumers. The information provided is based on the purchases of a specific group of urban consumers who serve as a sample population representing more than 80% of the total US population. Each annual CPI is compared with the average index level of 100, which is a base number that represents the average price level for the 36-month period covering the years 1982, 1983, and 1984. A minus sign indicates a decrease.

Source: US Bureau of Labor Statistics.

YEAR	ANNUAL CPI	% ANNUAL CHANGE IN CPI	YEAR	ANNUAL CPI	% ANNUAL CHANGE IN CPI	YEAR	ANNUAL CPI	% ANNUAL CHANGE IN CPI
1913	9.9		1921	17.9	-10.5	1929	17.1	0.0
1914	10.0	1.0	1922	16.8	-6.1	1930	16.7	-2.3
1915	10.1	1.0	1923	17.1	1.8	1931	15.2	-9.0
1916	10.9	7.9	1924	17.1	0.0	1932	13.7	-9.9
1917	12.8	17.4	1925	17.5	2.3	1933	13.0	-5.1
1918	15.1	18.0	1926	17.7	1.1	1934	13.4	3.1
1919	17.3	14.6	1927	17.4	-1.7	1935	13.7	2.2
1920	20.0	15.6	1928	17.1	-1.7	1936	13.9	1.5

US Consumer Price Index, 1913–2006 (continued)

YEAR	ANNUAL CPI	% ANNUAL CHANGE IN CPI	YEAR	ANNUAL CPI	% ANNUAL CHANGE IN CPI	YEAR	ANNUAL CPI	% ANNUAL CHANGE IN CPI
1937	14.4	3.6	1961	29.9	1.0	1985	107.6	3.6
1939	13.9	-1.4	1962	30.2	1.0	1986	109.6	1.9
1938	14.1	-2.1	1963	30.6	1.3	1987	113.6	3.6
1940	14.0	0.7	1964	31.0	1.3	1988	118.3	4.1
1941	14.7	5.0	1965	31.5	1.6	1989	124.0	4.8
1942	16.3	10.9	1966	32.4	2.9	1990	130.7	5.4
1943	17.3	6.1	1967	33.4	3.1	1991	136.2	4.2
1944	17.6	1.7	1968	34.8	4.2	1992	140.3	3.0
1945	18.0	2.3	1969	36.7	5.5	1993	144.5	3.0
1946	19.5	8.3	1970	38.8	5.7	1994	148.2	2.6
1947	22.3	14.4	1971	40.5	4.4	1995	152.4	2.8
1948	24.1	8.1	1972	41.8	3.2	1996	156.9	3.0
1949	23.8	-1.2	1973	44.4	6.2	1997	160.5	2.3
1950	24.1	1.3	1974	49.3	11.0	1998	163.0	1.6
1951	26.0	7.9	1975	53.8	9.1	1999	166.6	2.2
1952	26.5	1.9	1976	56.9	5.8	2000	172.2	3.4
1953	26.7	0.8	1977	60.6	6.5	2001	177.1	2.8
1954	26.9	0.7	1978	65.2	7.6	2002	179.9	1.6
1955	26.8	-0.4	1979	72.6	11.3	2003	184.0	2.3
1956	27.2	1.5	1980	82.4	13.5	2004	188.9	2.7
1957	28.1	3.3	1981	90.9	10.3	2005	195.3	3.4
1958	28.9	2.8	1982	96.5	6.2	2006	201.6	3.0
1959	29.1	0.7	1983	99.6	3.2			
1960	29.6	1.7	1984	103.9	4.3			

US Consumer Price Indexes by Item Group, 1975–2006

The information provided is based on the purchases of a specific group of urban consumers who serve as a sample population representing more than 80% of the total US population. Each annual CPI is compared with the average index level of 100, which is a base number that represents the average price level for the 36-month period covering the years 1982, 1983, and 1984. Source: US Bureau of Labor Statistics.

ITEM GROUP	1975	1980	1985	1990	1995	2000	2004	2005	2006
					CONSUMER PRICE INDEX				
all items	53.8	82.4	107.6	130.7	152.4	172.2	188.9	195.3	201.6
commodities	58.2	86.0	105.4	122.8	136.4	149.2	154.7	160.2	164.0
energy	42.1	86.0	101.6	102.1	105.2	124.6	151.4	177.1	196.9
food	59.8	86.8	105.6	132.4	148.4	167.8	186.2	190.7	195.2
shelter	48.8	81.0	109.8	140.0	165.7	193.4	218.8	224.4	232.1
transportation	50.1	83.1	106.4	120.5	139.1	153.3	163.1	173.9	180.9
medical care	47.5	74.9	113.5	162.8	220.5	260.8	310.1	323.2	336.2
apparel	72.5	90.9	105.0	124.1	132.0	129.6	120.4	119.5	119.5

ITEM GROUP	1975	1980	1985	1990	1995	2000	2004	2005	2006
					% CHANGE IN CPI[1]				
all items	9.1	13.5	3.6	5.4	2.8	3.4	2.7	3.4	3.2
commodities	8.8	12.3	2.1	5.2	1.9	3.3	2.3	3.6	2.4
energy	10.5	30.9	0.7	8.3	0.6	16.9	10.9	17.0	11.2
food	8.5	8.6	2.3	5.8	2.8	2.3	3.4	2.4	2.4
shelter	9.9	17.6	5.6	5.4	3.2	3.3	2.7	2.6	3.4
transportation	9.4	17.9	2.6	5.6	3.6	6.2	3.5	6.6	4.0
medical care	12.0	11.0	6.3	9.0	4.5	4.1	4.4	4.2	4.0
apparel	4.5	7.1	2.8	4.6	-1.0	-1.3	-0.4	-0.7	0.0

[1]Annual percent change from the preceding year.

Sample US Consumer Price Indexes by Region, 2005–2006

This table presents the regional annual averages of the Consumer Price Index (CPI) for 2006 and the percent change of those averages from 2005 to 2006. The information provided is based on the purchases of a specific group of urban consumers who serve as a sample population representing more than 80% of the total US population. Each annual CPI is compared with the average index level of 100, which is a base number that represents the average price level for the 36-month period covering the years 1982, 1983, and 1984. A minus sign indicates a decrease in price from 2005. Source: US Bureau of Labor Statistics.

Sample US Consumer Price Indexes by Region, 2005–2006 (continued)

ITEM GROUP	NORTHEAST 2006 CPI	NORTHEAST % CHANGE FROM 2005	MIDWEST 2006 CPI	MIDWEST % CHANGE FROM 2005	SOUTH 2006 CPI	SOUTH % CHANGE FROM 2005	WEST 2006 CPI	WEST % CHANGE FROM 2005
all items	215.0	3.6	193.0	2.4	194.7	3.4	205.7	3.4
commodities	167.9	2.7	159.3	2.0	165.0	2.4	163.9	2.4
energy	198.5	12.1	191.3	9.0	189.8	11.8	215.5	11.5
food	199.1	2.8	188.8	2.1	193.3	2.4	199.8	1.9
shelter	270.1	4.2	216.4	1.8	205.5	3.6	237.1	3.8
transportation	180.5	3.8	180.9	4.3	178.9	3.8	183.3	4.0
medical care	357.2	4.3	336.2	4.4	322.2	3.3	337.1	4.4
apparel	119.3	−1.2	110.2	−2.7	132.3	0.8	112.1	2.1

US Budget

US Public Debt

In order to fund governmental operations while the federal budget is running at a deficit, the Department of the Treasury borrows money by selling Treasury bills, US savings bonds, and other securities to the public. The money borrowed by the Treasury is referred to as the public debt. A broader measure of the federal debt is known as the gross federal debt. It consists of the public debt plus money borrowed by federal agencies. The GDP is the gross domestic product. Source: US Office of Management and Budget.

END OF FISCAL YEAR	PUBLIC DEBT (IN $ MILLIONS)	% OF GDP	GROSS FEDERAL DEBT (IN $ MILLIONS)	% OF GDP	END OF FISCAL YEAR	PUBLIC DEBT (IN $ MILLIONS)	% OF GDP	GROSS FEDERAL DEBT (IN $ MILLIONS)	% OF GDP
1940	42,772	44.2	50,696	52.4	1990	2,411,558	42.0	3,206,290	55.9
1950	219,023	80.1	256,853	93.9	2000	3,409,804	35.1	5,628,700	58.0
1960	236,840	45.6	290,525	56.0	2005	4,592,213	37.4	7,905,300	64.4
1970	283,198	28.0	380,921	37.6	2006	4,828,973	37.0	8,451,351	64.7
1980	711,923	26.1	909,041	33.3					

US Governmental Spending, 1800–2006

Entries for the years prior to 1933 are based on the administrative budget concept rather than on the unified budget concept. For a discussion of the unified budget concept, see <www.whitehouse.gov/omb/budget/fy2008/pdf/hist.pdf>. The figures are in thousands ('000). A minus sign indicates a deficit.

Source: US Office of Management and Budget.

YEAR[1]	FEDERAL INCOME	FEDERAL SPENDING	SURPLUS OR DEFICIT	YEAR[1]	FEDERAL INCOME	FEDERAL SPENDING	SURPLUS OR DEFICIT
1800	10,849	10,786	63	1824	19,381	20,327	−945
1801	12,935	9,395	3,541	1825	21,841	15,857	5,984
1802	14,996	7,862	7,134	1826	25,260	17,036	8,225
1803	11,064	7,852	3,212	1827	22,966	16,139	6,827
1804	11,826	8,719	3,107	1828	24,764	16,395	8,369
1805	13,561	10,506	3,054	1829	24,828	15,203	9,624
1806	15,560	9,804	5,756	1830	24,844	15,143	9,701
1807	16,398	8,354	8,044	1831	28,527	15,248	13,279
1808	17,061	9,932	7,128	1832	31,866	17,289	14,577
1809	7,773	10,281	−2,507	1833	33,948	23,018	10,931
1810	9,384	8,157	1,228	1834	21,792	18,628	3,164
1811	14,424	8,058	6,365	1835	35,430	17,573	17,857
1812	9,801	20,281	−10,480	1836	50,827	30,868	19,959
1813	14,340	31,682	−17,341	1837	24,954	37,243	−12,289
1814	11,182	34,721	−23,539	1838	26,303	33,865	−7,562
1815	15,729	32,708	−16,979	1839	31,483	26,899	4,584
1816	47,678	30,587	17,091	1840	19,480	24,318	−4,837
1817	33,099	21,844	11,255	1841	16,860	26,566	−9,706
1818	21,585	19,825	1,760	1842	19,976	25,206	−5,230
1819	24,603	21,464	3,140	1843	8,303	11,858	−3,555
1820	17,881	18,261	−380	1844	29,321	22,338	6,984
1821	14,573	15,811	−1,237	1845	29,970	22,937	7,033
1822	20,232	15,000	5,232	1846	29,700	27,767	1,933
1823	20,541	14,707	5,834	1847	26,496	57,281	−30,786

US Governmental Spending, 1800–2006 (continued)

YEAR[1]	FEDERAL INCOME	FEDERAL SPENDING	SURPLUS OR DEFICIT	YEAR[1]	FEDERAL INCOME	FEDERAL SPENDING	SURPLUS OR DEFICIT
1848	35,736	45,377	-9,641	1914	725,117	725,525	-408
1849	31,208	45,052	-13,844	1915	683,417	746,093	-62,676
1850	43,603	39,543	4,060	1916	761,445	712,967	48,478
1851	52,559	47,709	4,850	1917	1,100,500	1,953,857	-853,357
1852	49,847	44,195	5,652	1918	3,645,240	12,677,359	-9,032,120
1853	61,587	48,184	13,403	1919	5,130,042	18,492,665	-13,362,623
1854	73,800	58,045	15,755	1920	6,648,898	6,357,677	291,222
1855	65,351	59,743	5,608	1921	5,570,790	5,061,785	509,005
1856	74,057	69,571	4,486	1922	4,025,901	3,289,404	736,496
1857	68,965	67,796	1,170	1923	3,852,795	3,140,287	712,508
1858	46,655	74,185	-27,530	1924	3,871,214	2,907,847	963,367
1859	53,486	69,071	-15,585	1925	3,640,805	2,923,762	717,043
1860	56,065	63,131	-7,066	1926	3,795,108	2,929,964	865,144
1861	41,510	66,547	-25,037	1927	4,012,794	2,857,429	1,155,365
1862	51,987	474,762	-422,774	1928	3,900,329	2,961,245	939,083
1863	112,697	714,741	-602,043	1929	3,861,589	3,127,199	734,391
1864	264,627	865,323	-600,696	1930	4,057,884	3,320,211	737,673
1865	333,715	1,297,555	-963,841	1931	3,115,557	3,577,434	-461,877
1866	.558,033	520,809	37,223	1932	1,923,892	4,659,182	-2,735,290
1867	490,634	357,543	133,091	1933	1,996,844	4,598,496	-2,601,652
1868	405,638	377,340	28,298	1934	2,955,000	6,541,000	-3,586,000
1869	370,944	322,865	48,078	1935	3,609,000	6,412,000	-2,803,000
1870	411,255	309,654	101,602	1936	3,923,000	8,228,000	-4,304,000
1871	383,324	292,177	91,147	1937	5,387,000	7,580,000	-2,193,000
1872	374,107	277,518	96,589	1938	6,751,000	6,840,000	-89,000
1873	333,738	290,345	43,393	1939	6,295,000	9,141,000	-2,846,000
1874	304,979	302,634	2,345	1940	6,548,000	9,468,000	-2,920,000
1875	288,000	274,623	13,377	1941	8,712,000	13,653,000	-4,941,000
1876	294,096	265,101	28,995	1942	14,634,000	35,137,000	-20,503,000
1877	281,406	241,334	40,072	1943	24,001,000	78,555,000	-54,554,000
1878	257,764	236,964	20,800	1944	43,747,000	91,304,000	-47,557,000
1879	273,827	266,948	6,879	1945	45,159,000	92,712,000	-47,553,000
1880	333,527	267,643	65,884	1946	39,296,000	55,232,000	-15,936,000
1881	360,782	260,713	100,069	1947	38,514,000	34,496,000	4,018,000
1882	403,525	257,981	145,544	1948	41,560,000	29,764,000	11,796,000
1883	398,288	265,408	132,879	1949	39,415,000	38,835,000	580,000
1884	348,520	244,126	104,394	1950	39,443,000	42,562,000	-3,119,000
1885	323,691	260,227	63,464	1951	51,616,000	45,514,000	6,102,000
1886	336,440	242,483	93,957	1952	66,167,000	67,686,000	-1,519,000
1887	371,403	267,932	103,471	1953	69,608,000	76,101,000	-6,493,000
1888	379,266	267,925	111,341	1954	69,701,000	70,855,000	-1,154,000
1889	387,050	299,289	87,761	1955	65,451,000	68,444,000	-2,993,000
1890	403,081	318,041	85,040	1956	74,587,000	70,640,000	3,947,000
1891	392,612	365,774	26,839	1957	79,990,000	76,578,000	3,412,000
1892	354,938	345,023	9,914	1958	79,636,000	82,405,000	-2,769,000
1893	385,820	383,478	2,342	1959	79,249,000	92,098,000	-12,849,000
1894	306,355	367,525	-61,170	1960	92,492,000	92,191,000	301,000
1895	324,729	356,195	-31,466	1961	94,388,000	97,723,000	-3,335,000
1896	338,142	352,179	-14,037	1962	99,676,000	106,821,000	-7,146,000
1897	347,722	365,774	-18,052	1963	106,560,000	111,316,000	-4,756,000
1898	405,321	443,369	-38,047	1964	112,613,000	118,528,000	-5,915,000
1899	515,961	605,072	-89,112	1965	116,817,000	118,228,000	-1,411,000
1900	567,241	520,861	46,380	1966	130,835,000	134,532,000	-3,698,000
1901	587,685	524,617	63,068	1967	148,822,000	157,464,000	-8,643,000
1902	562,478	485,234	77,244	1968	152,973,000	178,134,000	-25,161,000
1903	561,881	517,006	44,875	1969	186,882,000	183,640,000	3,242,000
1904	541,087	583,660	-42,573	1970	192,807,000	195,649,000	-2,842,000
1905	544,275	567,279	-23,004	1971	187,139,000	210,172,000	-23,033,000
1906	594,984	570,202	24,782	1972	207,309,000	230,681,000	-23,373,000
1907	665,860	579,129	86,732	1973	230,799,000	245,707,000	-14,908,000
1908	601,862	659,196	-57,334	1974	263,224,000	269,359,000	-6,135,000
1909	604,320	693,744	-89,423	1975	279,090,000	332,332,000	-53,242,000
1910	675,512	693,617	-18,105	1976	298,060,000	371,792,000	-73,732,000
1911	701,833	691,202	10,631	TQ	81,232,000	95,975,000	-14,744,000
1912	692,609	689,881	2,728	1977	355,559,000	409,218,000	-53,659,000
1913	714,463	714,864	-401	1978	399,561,000	458,746,000	-59,185,000

US Governmental Spending, 1800–2006 (continued)

YEAR[1]	FEDERAL INCOME	FEDERAL SPENDING	SURPLUS OR DEFICIT
1979	463,302,000	504,028,000	−40,726,000
1980	517,112,000	590,941,000	−73,830,000
1981	599,272,000	678,241,000	−78,968,000
1982	617,766,000	745,743,000	−127,977,000
1983	600,562,000	808,364,000	−207,802,000
1984	666,486,000	851,853,000	−185,367,000
1985	734,088,000	946,396,000	−212,308,000
1986	769,215,000	990,430,000	−221,215,000
1987	854,353,000	1,004,082,000	−149,728,000
1988	909,303,000	1,064,455,000	−155,152,000
1989	991,190,000	1,143,646,000	−152,456,000
1990	1,031,969,000	1,253,165,000	−221,195,000
1991	1,055,041,000	1,324,369,000	−269,328,000
1992	1,091,279,000	1,381,655,000	−290,376,000
1993	1,154,401,000	1,409,489,000	−255,087,000
1994	1,258,627,000	1,461,877,000	−203,250,000
1995	1,351,830,000	1,515,802,000	−163,972,000
1996	1,453,062,000	1,560,535,000	−107,473,000
1997	1,579,292,000	1,601,250,000	−21,958,000
1998	1,721,798,000	1,652,585,000	69,213,000
1999	1,827,454,000	1,701,891,000	125,563,000
2000	2,025,218,000	1,788,773,000	236,445,000
2001	1,991,194,000	1,863,770,000	127,424,000
2002	1,853,173,000	2,010,970,000	−157,797,000
2003	1,782,342,000	2,157,637,000	−375,295,000
2004	1,880,071,000	2,292,215,000	−412,144,000
2005	2,153,859,000	2,472,205,000	−318,346,000
2006	2,407,254,000	2,655,435,000	−248,181,000

[1]The fiscal year ended on 31 December for the budgets from 1800 to 1842. It ended on 30 June for the budgets from 1844 through 1976 and on 30 September from fiscal year 1977. The budget figures for 1843 are for the period from 1 January to 30 June. The third quarter of 1976 was budgeted separately because of the change in the fiscal year calendar. It is referred to as the Transition Quarter (TQ).

Annual National Average Terms on Conventional Single-Family Mortgages, 1977–2005

Source: Federal Housing Finance Board Monthly Interest Rate Survey.

YEAR	CONTRACT INTEREST RATE (%)	INITIAL FEES AND CHARGES (%)	EFFECTIVE INTEREST RATE (%)	TERM TO MATURITY (YEARS)	MORTGAGE AMOUNT ($'000)	PURCHASE PRICE ($'000)	LOAN TO PRICE RATIO (%)
1977	8.82	1.22	9.02	26.3	36.3	49.6	75.0
1978	9.37	1.30	9.59	26.7	41.4	57.1	74.6
1979	10.59	1.50	10.85	27.4	48.2	67.7	73.5
1980	12.46	1.97	12.84	27.2	51.7	73.4	72.9
1981	14.39	2.39	14.91	26.4	53.7	76.3	73.1
1982	14.73	2.65	15.31	25.6	55.0	78.4	72.9
1983	12.26	2.39	12.73	26.0	59.9	83.1	74.5
1984	11.99	2.57	12.48	26.8	64.5	86.6	77.0
1985	11.17	2.51	11.64	25.9	70.2	96.1	75.8
1986	9.79	2.21	10.18	25.6	79.3	110.6	74.1
1987	8.95	2.08	9.30	26.8	89.1	121.8	75.2
1988	8.98	1.96	9.30	27.7	97.4	131.6	76.0
1989	9.81	1.87	10.13	27.7	104.5	142.8	74.8
1990	9.74	1.79	10.05	27.0	104.0	142.6	74.7
1991	9.07	1.58	9.34	26.5	106.3	146.7	74.4
1992	7.83	1.58	8.11	25.4	108.7	146.4	76.6
1993	6.93	1.20	7.13	25.5	107.0	143.1	77.2
1994	7.31	1.10	7.49	27.1	109.9	142.0	79.9
1995	7.69	0.97	7.85	27.4	110.4	142.8	79.9
1996	7.58	0.97	7.74	26.9	118.7	155.1	79.0
1997	7.52	0.98	7.68	27.5	126.6	164.5	79.4
1998	6.97	0.85	7.10	27.8	131.8	173.4	78.9
1999	7.14	0.74	7.25	28.2	139.3	184.2	78.5
2000	7.86	0.67	7.96	28.7	148.3	198.9	77.8

Annual National Average Terms on Conventional Single-Family Mortgages, 1977–2005 (cont.)

YEAR	CONTRACT INTEREST RATE (%)	INITIAL FEES AND CHARGES (%)	EFFECTIVE INTEREST RATE (%)	TERM TO MATURITY (YEARS)	MORTGAGE AMOUNT ($'000)	PURCHASE PRICE ($'000)	LOAN TO PRICE RATIO (%)
2001	6.94	0.53	7.03	27.6	155.7	215.5	76.2
2002	6.44	0.46	6.51	27.3	163.4	231.2	75.1
2003	5.67	0.37	5.73	26.8	167.9	243.4	73.5
2004	5.68	0.40	5.74	27.9	185.5	262.0	74.9
2005	5.85	0.38	5.90	28.5	211.9	299.8	74.7

US Bankruptcy Filings, 1980–2006

This table shows the number of business and nonbusiness (consumer) bankruptcy filings in the US since 1980. Bankruptcy is intended to give debtors a fresh start in managing their resources by cancelling many of their debts through a court order called a "discharge." It is also meant to give creditors a fair share of the money that the debtors can afford to pay back.

Businesses may file for bankruptcy under chapter 11 of the IRS Code. Chapter 11 offers protection from creditor demands to a business in debt so that its officers and managers have time to reorganize in order to fulfill obligations to creditors. In some instances, creditors may receive dollar-for-dollar what the business owes them, plus interest. In others, the creditor may only receive pennies on the owed dollar.

Individuals may file for bankruptcy under either chapter 7 of the IRS Code (under which debtors may liquidate assets with the supervision of a trustee in order to receive a nearly immediate discharge of debts) or chapter 13 (under which the debtor enters into a payment plan to repay debt out of future earnings over a three-to-five-year period, with the oversight of a trustee). Source: American Bankruptcy Institute.

YEAR	TOTAL FILINGS	BUSINESS FILINGS	NONBUSINESS FILINGS	CONSUMER FILINGS AS A PERCENTAGE OF TOTAL FILINGS
1980	331,264	43,694	287,570	86.81%
1981	363,943	48,125	315,818	86.78%
1982	380,251	69,300	310,951	81.78%
1983	348,880	62,436	286,444	82.10%
1984	348,521	64,004	284,517	81.64%
1985	412,510	71,277	341,233	82.72%
1986	530,438	81,235	449,203	84.69%
1987	577,999	82,446	495,553	85.74%
1988	613,465	63,853	549,612	89.59%
1989	679,461	63,235	616,226	90.69%
1990	782,960	64,853	718,107	91.72%
1991	943,987	71,549	872,438	92.42%
1992	971,517	70,643	900,874	92.73%
1993	875,202	62,304	812,898	92.88%
1994	832,829	52,374	780,455	93.71%
1995	926,601	51,959	874,642	94.39%
1996	1,178,555	53,549	1,125,006	95.46%
1997	1,404,145	54,027	1,350,118	96.15%
1998	1,442,549	44,367	1,398,182	96.92%
1999	1,319,465	37,884	1,281,581	97.12%
2000	1,253,444	35,472	1,217,972	97.17%
2001	1,492,129	40,099	1,452,030	97.31%
2002	1,577,651	38,540	1,539,111	97.56%
2003	1,660,245	35,037	1,625,208	97.89%
2004	1,597,462	34,317	1,563,145	97.85%
2005	2,078,415	39,201	2,039,214	98.11%
2006	617,660	19,695	597,965	96.81%

US Taxes

US Federal Taxation Structure

This table shows the range of income taxes for various types of households in each tax bracket. In 2007 the standard deductions are $5,350 for those submitting returns under status "single" and status "married filing separately"; $7,850 for those filing under status "head of household"; and $10,700 for those submitting returns under status "married filing jointly" or "qualifying widows and widowers with a dependent child." Source: US Department of the Treasury, Internal Revenue Service.

US Federal Taxation Structure (continued)

Single — Schedule X

IF TAXABLE INCOME

IS OVER	BUT NOT OVER	THEN THE TAX IS	PLUS	OF THE AMOUNT OVER
$0	$7,825	—	10%	$0
$7,825	$31,850	$782.50	15%	$7,825
$31,850	$77,100	$4,386.25	25%	$31,850
$77,100	$160,850	$15,698.75	28%	$77,100
$160,850	$349,700	$39,148.75	33%	$160,850
$349,700	—	$101,469.25	35%	$349,700

Married Filing Jointly or Qualifying Widow(er) — Schedule Y-1

IF TAXABLE INCOME

IS OVER	BUT NOT OVER	THEN THE TAX IS	PLUS	OF THE AMOUNT OVER
$0	$15,650	—	10%	$0
$15,650	$63,700	$1,565.00	15%	$15,650
$63,700	$128,500	$8,772.50	25%	$63,700
$128,500	$195,850	$24,972.50	28%	$128,500
$195,850	$349,700	$43,830.50	33%	$195,850
$349,700	—	$94,601.00	35%	$349,700

Married Filing Separately — Schedule Y-2

IF TAXABLE INCOME

IS OVER	BUT NOT OVER	THEN THE TAX IS	PLUS	OF THE AMOUNT OVER
$0	$7,825	—	10%	$0
$7,825	$31,850	$782.50	15%	$7,825
$31,850	$64,250	$4,386.25	25%	$31,850
$64,250	$97,250	$12,486.25	28%	$64,250
$97,250	$174,850	$21,915.25	33%	$97,250
$174,850	—	$47,300.50	35%	$174,850

Head of Household — Schedule Z

IF TAXABLE INCOME

IS OVER	BUT NOT OVER	THEN THE TAX IS	PLUS	OF THE AMOUNT OVER
$0	$11,200	—	10%	$0
$11,200	$42,650	$1,120.00	15%	$11,200
$42,650	$110,100	$5,837.50	25%	$42,650
$110,100	$178,350	$22,700.00	28%	$110,100
$178,350	$349,700	$41,810.00	33%	$178,350
$349,700	—	$98,355.50	35%	$349,700

Individual Income Taxes by State

This table shows tax rates as of 1 Jan 2007 for tax year 2007. Source: The Federation of Tax Administrators, <www.taxadmin.org/fta/rate/ind_inc.html>.

STATE	TAX RATES LOW	TAX RATES HIGH	NUMBER OF BRACKETS	INCOME BRACKETS LOW	INCOME BRACKETS HIGH	PERSONAL EXEMPTION SINGLE	PERSONAL EXEMPTION MARRIED	PERSONAL EXEMPTION CHILDREN	FEDERAL TAX DEDUCTIBLE
AL	2.0	5.0	3	500[1]	3,000[1]	1,500	3,000	300	Yes
AK	No state income tax								
AZ	2.59	4.57	5	10,000[1]	150,000[1]	2,100	4,200	2,300	
AR[2]	1.0	7.0[3]	6	3,599	30,100	22[4]	44[4]	22[4]	
CA[2]	1.0	9.3[5]	6	6,622[1]	43,468[1]	91[4]	182[4]	285[4]	
CO	4.63		1	Flat rate		None			
CT	3.0	5.0	2	10,000[1]	10,000[1]	12,750[6]	24,500[6]	0	
DE	2.2	5.95	6	5,000	60,000	110[4]	220[4]	110[4]	
DC	4.5	8.7	3	10,000	40,000	2,400	4,800	2,400	
FL	No state income tax								
GA	1.0	6.0	6	750[7]	7,000[7]	2,700	5,400	3,000	
HI	1.4	8.25	9	2,400[1]	48,000[1]	1,040	2,080	1,040	
ID[2]	1.6	7.8	8	1,198[8]	23,964[8]	3,400[9]	6,800[9]	3,400[9]	
IL	3.0		1	Flat rate		2,000	4,000	2,000	
IN	3.4		1	Flat rate		1,000	2,000	1,000	
IA[2]	0.36	8.98	9	1,343	60,436	40[4]	80[4]	40[4]	Yes
KS	3.5	6.45	3	15,000[1]	30,000[1]	2,250	4,500	2,250	
KY	2.0	6.0	6	3,000	75,000	20[4]	40[4]	20[4]	
LA	2.0	6.0	3	12,500[1]	25,000[1]	4,500[10]	9,000[10]	1,000[10]	Yes
ME[2]	2.0	8.5	4	4,550[1]	18,250[1]	2,850	5,700	2,850	
MD	2.0	4.75	4	1,000	3,000	2,400	4,800	2,400	
MA[2]	5.3		1	Flat rate		4,125	8,250	1,000	

Individual Income Taxes by State (continued)

STATE	TAX RATES		NUMBER OF BRACKETS	INCOME BRACKETS		PERSONAL EXEMPTION			FEDERAL TAX DEDUCTIBLE
	LOW	HIGH		LOW	HIGH	SINGLE	MARRIED	CHILDREN	
MI[2]	3.9		1	Flat rate		3,300	6,600	3,300	
MN[2]	5.35	7.85	3	21,310[11]	69,991[11]	3,400[9]	6,800[9]	3,400[9]	
MS	3.0	5.0	3	5,000	10,000	6,000	12,000	1,500	
MO	1.5	6.0	10	1,000	9,000	2,100	4,200	1,200	
MT[2]	1.0	6.9	7	2,300	14,500	1,980	3,960	1,980	Yes[12]
NE[2]	2.56	6.84	4	2,400[13]	27,001[13]	106[4]	212[4]	106[4]	Yes[12]
NV	No state income tax								
NH	State income tax is limited to dividends and interest income only								
NJ	1.4	8.97	6	20,000[14]	500,000[14]	1,000	2,000	1,500	
NM	1.7	5.3	4	5,500[15]	16,000[15]	3,400[9]	6,800[9]	3,400[9]	
NY	4.0	6.85	5	8,000[1]	20,000[1]	0	0	1,000	
NC[16]	6.0	8.0	4	12,750[16]	120,000[16]	3,400[9]	6,800[9]	3,400[9]	
ND[2]	2.1	5.54[17]	5	30,650[17]	336,550[17]	3,400[9]	6,800[9]	3,400[9]	
OH[2]	0.649	6.555	9	5,000	200,000	1,400[18]	2,800[18]	1,400[18]	
OK	0.5	5.65[19]	7	1,000[1]	10,000[1]	1,000	2,000	1,000	Yes[19]
OR[2]	5.0	9.0	3	2,750[1]	6,851[1]	159[4]	318[4]	159[4]	Yes[12]
PA	3.07		1	Flat rate		None			
RI	25.0% federal tax liability[20]								
SC[2]	2.5	7.0	6	2,570	12,850	3,400[9]	6,800[9]	3,400[9]	
SD	No state income tax								
TN	State income tax is limited to dividends and interest income only								
TX	No state income tax								
UT	2.3	6.98[21]	6	1,000[1]	5,501[1]	2,550[9]	5,100[9]	2,550[9]	Yes[21]
VT[2]	3.6	9.5	5	30,650[22]	336,551[22]	3,400[9]	6,800[9]	3,400[9]	
VA	2.0	5.75	4	3,000	17,000	900	1,800	900	
WA	No state income tax								
WV	3.0	6.5	5	10,000	60,000	2,000	4,000	2,000	
WI[2]	4.6	6.75	4	9,160[23]	137,411[23]	700	1,400	700	
WY	No state income tax								

[1]For joint returns, the taxes are twice the tax imposed on half the income. [2]Sixteen states have statutory provision for automatic adjustment of tax brackets, personal exemption, or standard deductions to the rate of inflation. Massachusetts, Michigan, Nebraska, and Ohio index the personal exemption amounts only. [3]A special tax table is available for low-income taxpayers reducing their tax payments. [4]Tax credits. [5]An additional 1.0% tax is imposed on taxable income over $1 million. [6]Combined personal exemptions and standard deduction. An additional tax credit is allowed ranging from 75% to 0% based on state adjusted gross income. Exemption amounts are phased out for higher-income taxpayers until they are eliminated for households earning over $56,500. [7]The tax brackets reported are for single individuals. For married households filing separately, the same rates apply to income brackets ranging from $500 to $5,000; the income brackets range from $1,000 to $10,000 for joint filers. [8]For joint returns, the tax is twice the tax imposed on half the income. A $10 filing tax is charged for each return, and a $15 credit is allowed for each exemption. [9]These states allow personal exemption or standard deductions as provided in the Internal Revenue Code. Utah allows a personal exemption equal to three-fourths the federal exemptions. [10]Combined personal exemption and standard deduction. [11]The tax brackets reported are for single individuals. For married couples filing jointly, the same rates apply for income under $31,150 to over $123,751. A 6.4% alternative minimum tax rate is also applicable. [12]Deduction is limited to $10,000 for joint returns and $5,000 for individuals in Missouri and Montana and to $5,000 in Oregon. [13]The tax brackets reported are for single individuals. For married couples filing jointly, the same rates apply for income under $4,000 to over $50,001. [14]The tax brackets reported are for single individuals. For married couples filing jointly, the tax rates range from 1.4% to 8.97%, applying to seven income brackets between $20,000 to over $500,000. [15]The tax brackets reported are for single individuals. For married couples filing jointly, the same rates apply for income under $8,000 to over $24,000. Married households filing separately pay the tax imposed on half the income. [16]The tax brackets reported are for single individuals. For married taxpayers, the same rates apply to income brackets ranging from $21,250 to $200,000. Lower exemption amounts are allowed for high-income taxpayers. Tax rates are scheduled to decrease after tax year 2007. [17]The tax brackets reported are for single individuals. For married taxpayers, the same rates apply to income brackets ranging from $51,200 to $336,551. An additional $300 personal exemption is allowed for joint returns or unmarried heads of households. [18]Plus an additional $20 per exemption tax credit. [19]The rate range reported is for single persons not deducting federal income tax. For married persons filing jointly, the same rates apply to income brackets ranging from $2,000 to $15,000. Separate schedules, with rates ranging from 0.5% to 10%, apply to taxpayers deducting federal income taxes. [20]Federal tax liability prior to the enactment of the Economic Growth and Tax Relief Act of 2001. [21]One-half of the federal income taxes are deductible. The taxpayer has an option of using the standard brackets and rates with all deductions or paying a flat 5.35% of income with limited deductions. [22]The tax brackets reported are for single individuals. For married couples filing jointly, the same rates apply for income under $51,200 to over $336,551. [23]The tax brackets reported are for single individuals. For married taxpayers, the same rates apply to income brackets ranging from $12,210 to $183,211. An additional $250 exemption is provided for each taxpayer or spouse age 65 or over.

Arts, Entertainment, & Leisure

Theater: Girls, Girls, Girls

by Richard Zoglin, TIME

"What's the story, morning glory? / What's the word, hummingbird?" That was Broadway teen talk back in the early '60s, when the high school kids in *Bye Bye Birdie* gossiped about their friends in a game of telephone tag. More than 40 years later, another band of gossip girls is peeking out of another set of windows on a Broadway stage. How far have we advanced? Well, the kids are in a college sorority now, and the squeals of excitement—and the title of the show's opening song—have evolved into dumbed-down Valley-speak: "Omigod You Guys!"

The show is *Legally Blonde: The Musical,* based on the 2001 movie starring Reese Witherspoon as Elle Woods, a bubbleheaded campus queen who goes to Harvard Law School and proves she can hold her own with the eggheads. Perky, pretty in pink, and packaged with the requisite mix of campy condescension and you-go-girl inspiration, the show opened on 29 Apr 2007 and became a hit, largely thanks to the theater's hot audience of the moment: tween and teen girls.

You've heard of them. They're the ones who are making TV shows like *Ugly Betty* into surprise hits and keeping Beyoncé and Avril Lavigne at the top of the pop charts. Hollywood, oddly, has been ignoring them lately, as romantic comedies have taken a backseat to guy films like *300* and *Wild Hogs,* superhero sequels and slasher films. But Broadway, long worried about its graying audience, is in hot pursuit.

A good deal of the credit for this nascent relationship goes to possibly the least-appreciated breakthrough hit of the past decade: *Wicked.* The musical prequel to *The Wizard of Oz,* told from the witches' point of view, was dismissed by most critics when it opened in the fall of 2003. But more than three years later, *Wicked* is regularly the highest-grossing show on Broadway, with three more companies setting box-office records around the country. And the show's most avid fans are tween girls, who have connected with its themes of friendship, prejudice, and self-realization—identifying with Elphaba, the "wicked" witch who's actually just misunderstood.

The girl appeal, however, is something of a sore subject for the producers of *Wicked.* They commissioned an audience survey that found the demographic breakdown of people who see *Wicked* is in line with that of most Broadway shows: more of its audience is over 35 than under 35. "Yes, girls come. They're enthusiastic. They're at the stage door," says David Stone, one of the show's producers. "But they're not all that's coming."

True, but with preteen girls snapping up Glinda earrings and DEFY GRAVITY shirts at the Ozdust boutique, they're the crowd the show has really grabbed. "I liked Elphaba because she was different," says Jami, a 10-year-old in Buffalo Grove IL, who has virtu-ally memorized the script from reading the US$40 coffee-table companion book and recently acted out the entire show with two friends in her bedroom. "It made me feel that it's good to be different."

She may have a point—and not just because she's my niece. *Wicked* has tapped into a theme that seems to crop up in a lot of Broadway shows these days: stories of misfits or underdogs who prove their worth in spite of the odds. *Hairspray* revolves around a zaftig high-school dance whiz who fights for racial integration and fat-girl power in 1962 Baltimore. *The Color Purple* is the uplifting story of an African American girl's journey from abused teen to empowered adult. Even in shows in which the gender balance is more equal, such as *Spring Awakening* and *The 25th Annual Putnam County Spelling Bee,* the emotional core seems to reside in the females.

Broadway is getting shrewder about courting all kids, but particularly girls. Stars from TV's *American Idol* have turned up in musicals—Frenchie Davis in *Rent,* Diana DeGarmo in *Hairspray,* and Fantasia Barrino in *The Color Purple* (since she joined the cast, the show has set a house attendance record). Disney, which introduced a new family audience to the theater with shows like *The Lion King,* will soon bring *The Little Mermaid* to the stage. And coming in the fall of 2007 to London: a musical version of *Desperately Seeking Susan,* the 1985 movie about a housewife who's sucked into the punk underworld of downtown Manhattan, set to Blondie music.

Of course, Broadway musicals, from *The King and I* to *Annie,* have long been partial to girl-centered stories. More than 62% of the Broadway audience is made up of women, and they tend to make the decisions about what the whole family sees. Even so, no producer wants his or her musical pigeonholed as a young-girl show; niche audiences don't make hits. Yet the influx of young theatergoers to shows like *Wicked* is a trend producers can't afford to ignore. "We've talked about how we lost a generation who didn't think it was cool to go to the theater," says *Wicked*'s Stone. "A lot of us have started to get that audience back. Younger people are coming back to the theater—and yet older people aren't leaving."

That was *Legally Blonde*'s marketing challenge: to get the girls without turning off their parents or the boys. Producer Hal Luftig sees Elle as a "great heroine who learns something about herself"—but hopes guys will see a message in the show's love story too: "If you treat a girl with respect, you might just get her."

Well, OK. But the merchandise in the theater lobby—pink-lettered baseball Ts, sweatpants with OMIGOD! on the rear—suggests that producers already know which sex will be filling most of the seats. And if they don't, the perky young women onstage won't be the only ones crying "Omigod!"

Cinema: Boys Who Like Toys

by Rebecca Winters Keegan, TIME

He's one of the most powerful tastemakers in Hollywood, the guy behind the record-breaking success of *300*, the hit status of NBC's *Heroes*, and the reign of the the Xbox 360 gaming console. He enjoys invitations to the Skywalker Ranch and hangs out with guys like Nicolas Cage and Quentin Tarantino at conventions. He's zealously loyal, notoriously finicky, and often aggressive with those who dare to disagree with him. Oh, and occasionally he likes to dress up as Spider-Man.

He is the fanboy, the typically geeky 16-to-34-year-old male (though there are some fangirls) whose slavish devotion to a pop-culture subject, like a comic-book character or a video game, drives him to blog, podcast, chat, share YouTube videos, go to comic-book conventions, and, once in a while, see a movie on the subject of his obsession. And he's having his way with Hollywood.

Exhibit A is *Transformers*, the summer of 2007's big hit in which the hero is played by Peter Cullen, a Canadian voice actor familiar to the teensiest fraction of moviegoers. With Steven Spielberg producing and Michael Bay directing this US$150 million extravaganza about dueling alien robot races, the protagonist could have been Will Smith or magazine-cover bait like Justin Timberlake. But Cullen was the voice of the character Optimus Prime in the *Transformers* TV show, a treasured part of the canon for true fans. (If the phrase "robots in disguise" sets your toes atappin', you may be one of them.)

These alpha fans are enjoying an unprecedented era of influence, through blogs, podcasts, and movie-news sites that have become trusted sources of movie information for millions of filmgoers. And not just on casting decisions. "They're the new tastemakers," says Avi Arad, a producer behind *Spider-Man 3* and *Fantastic Four: Rise of the Silver Surfer*. "Hardcore fans represent a small piece of the viewing public, but they influence geek culture, journalists, Wall Street. You don't want them to trash your project." If these fans embrace a project, as they did *300* and *Heroes*, they can kick-start a hit.

Who are they? Typically they're like John Campea, 35, of Toronto, who founded The Movie Blog as a hobby in 2003 while working at a visual-effects company, or Josh Tyler, 30, a design engineer from Dallas who has built an audience of one million for his site Cinemablend by being one of the more cleverly critical fanboys. Or they're like Berge Garabedian, 33, of Montreal, who put his JoBlo.com after critics trashed *Armageddon*, a movie he and all of his friends loved. They're guys who love—obsessively—certain types of movies.

"There are a lot more people who identify with me, a film fan, than a film expert," says Campea. "I'm the guy who stands at the watercooler with everybody." The watercooler is getting crowded. Now Campea has so much traffic on his site that income from Google ads pays a decent salary for him and two other writers.

The fanboy phenomenon started long, long ago (1977) in a galaxy far, far away (San Diego) when a then little-known director named George Lucas attended an intimate comic-book convention to promote a movie called *Star Wars*. Lucas's films have since become a gateway drug for a generation of movie addicts. And Comic-Con, the San Diego convention of genre buffs, has become a Hollywood must-attend event, albeit one where dressing to impress means dry cleaning your Darth Vader costume.

It's significant that this fanboy Christmas happens not in Hollywood but two hours south. The appeal of the species is that they're outsiders to the movie industry and are therefore able to retain a sense of awe about it. At the same time, they're outsiders in the real world, caring passionately about subjects most people shrug off—like who will play Spock in the 2008 *Star Trek* prequel. In search of kindred souls, they turn to the Web.

Comic-Con remains a force, especially for movies like 300, the computer-graphics-heavy update of the battle of Thermopylae, which shocked the industry by grossing more than US$450 million worldwide. Most mainstream-media critics trounced it, but 60% of the males who bought tickets on opening weekend said they were drawn by seeing references to the movie on the Web, where readers of sites like Garabedian's were frenetically discussing it.

No one is really sure how many alpha fans there are. As the first movie-fan website to get a toehold, Ain't It Cool News (AICN) has more traffic than the websites of established media like *Entertainment Weekly* or *Variety*. The top eight movie-fan websites have a total of six million to eight million unique users a month. Many movie-news sites are weekday coffee-break reads, but the fan sites' traffic peaks on weekends, when visitors are deciding what movies to see. The writer-director Kevin Smith, who has a top-rated podcast, believes fanboys deserve all the credit for the US$26 million that *Clerks II* earned at the box office in 2006, five times what the film cost.

Other fanboys who have gone on to work in the business include *Spider-Man* director Sam Raimi; the two *Transformers* writers, Alex Kurtzman and Roberto Orci; and David Arquette, who showed up for a screening of the horror film he wrote and directed, *The Tripper*, in a fake-blood-spattered suit. "I can relate more to people at a horror convention than I can to most Hollywood executives," says Arquette. "They're more passionate."

Of course, another movie that fanboys were panting about at Comic-Con was the summer of 2006's *Snakes on a Plane*, which New Line Cinema pumped to the Web audience but declined to screen for mainstream critics; it tanked. The fanboys are outsiders for a reason: the rest of the world doesn't always share their taste. The poor performance of 2007's *Grindhouse*, the double feature from two fanboy deities, directors Quentin Tarantino and Robert Rodriguez, shows that fanboy love can get you only so far.

Although studios are courting the top fanboys now, it wasn't always thus. AICN created a sport of snagging scoops—reviews from test screenings of unfinished films, scripts, artwork—that put Hollywood on the defensive. All that's over now. Indeed, the kind of insider status some enjoy may threaten the fanboys' biggest asset: the fact that they're just movie-obsessed nerds like their readers. But you can't put the genie back into the bottle. The lads have become such objects of fascination for the industry that it has paid the group its ultimate compliment. The movie *Fanboys* opens in early 2008.

Motion Pictures

Academy Awards (Oscars), 2006

The Academy of Motion Picture Arts and Sciences was formed in 1927 and first awarded the Academy Awards of Merit in May 1929. The honored categories have varied over the years, but best picture, actor, actress, and director have been awarded since the beginning. Awards for supporting actor and actress were added for the films of 1936 and best foreign-language film for 1947. The ceremony is generally held in the early spring of the year following the release of films under consideration; the latest Oscars were awarded 25 Feb 2007 in Los Angeles. Award: gold-plated statuette of a man with a sword.

Academy of Motion Picture Arts and Sciences Web site: <www.oscars.org>.

CATEGORY	WINNER
Motion picture of the year	*The Departed* (US/Hong Kong; Graham King, producer)
Director	Martin Scorsese (*The Departed*, US/Hong Kong)
Actor	Forest Whitaker (*The Last King of Scotland*, UK)
Actress	Helen Mirren (*The Queen*, UK/France/Italy)
Supporting actor	Alan Arkin (*Little Miss Sunshine*, US)
Supporting actress	Jennifer Hudson (*Dreamgirls*, US)
Foreign-language film	*The Lives of Others* (Germany; Florian Henckel von Donnersmarck, director)
Animated feature	*Happy Feet* (Australia/US; George Miller, director)
Animated short	*The Danish Poet* (Norway/Canada; Torill Kove, director)
Live-action short	*West Bank Story* (US; Ari Sandel, director)
Documentary feature	*An Inconvenient Truth* (US; Davis Guggenheim, director)
Documentary short	*The Blood of Yingzhou District* (China/US; Ruby Yang and Thomas Lennon, directors)
Cinematography	Guillermo Navarro (*Pan's Labyrinth*, Mexico/Spain/US)
Art direction	Eugenio Caballero, art direction; Pilar Revuelta, set decoration (*Pan's Labyrinth*, Mexico/Spain/US)
Film editing	Thelma Schoonmaker (*The Departed*, US/Hong Kong)
Costume design	Milena Canonero (*Marie Antoinette*, Japan/France/US)
Makeup	David Martí and Montse Ribé (*Pan's Labyrinth*, Mexico/Spain/US)
Original score	Gustavo Santaolalla (*Babel*, France/US/Mexico)
Original song	"I Need To Wake Up," Melissa Etheridge (*An Inconvenient Truth*, US)
Sound mixing	Michael Minkler, Bob Beemer, and Willie Burton (*Dreamgirls*, US)
Sound editing	Alan Robert Murray and Bub Asman (*Letters from Iwo Jima*, US)
Visual effects	John Knoll, Hal Hickel, Charles Gibson, and Allen Hall (*Pirates of the Caribbean: Dead Man's Chest*, US)
Screenplay, adaptation	William Monahan (*The Departed*, US/Hong Kong)
Screenplay, original	Michael Arndt (*Little Miss Sunshine*, US)

Academy Awards (Oscars), 1928–2006

2007 awards ceremony scheduled to be held 24 Feb 2008 in Los Angeles.

BEST PICTURE

1928 *Wings*
1929 *The Broadway Melody*
1930 *All Quiet on the Western Front*
1931 *Cimarron*
1932 *Grand Hotel*
1933 *Cavalcade*
1934 *It Happened One Night*
1935 *Mutiny on the Bounty*
1936 *The Great Ziegfeld*
1937 *The Life of Emile Zola*
1938 *You Can't Take It with You*
1939 *Gone with the Wind*
1940 *Rebecca*
1941 *How Green Was My Valley*
1942 *Mrs. Miniver*
1943 *Casablanca*
1944 *Going My Way*
1945 *The Lost Weekend*
1946 *The Best Years of Our Lives*
1947 *Gentleman's Agreement*
1948 *Hamlet*
1949 *All the King's Men*

BEST PICTURE (CONTINUED)

1950 *All About Eve*
1951 *An American in Paris*
1952 *The Greatest Show on Earth*
1953 *From Here to Eternity*
1954 *On the Waterfront*
1955 *Marty*
1956 *Around the World in 80 Days*
1957 *The Bridge on the River Kwai*
1958 *Gigi*
1959 *Ben-Hur*
1960 *The Apartment*
1961 *West Side Story*
1962 *Lawrence of Arabia*
1963 *Tom Jones*
1964 *My Fair Lady*
1965 *The Sound of Music*
1966 *A Man for All Seasons*
1967 *In the Heat of the Night*
1968 *Oliver!*
1969 *Midnight Cowboy*

BEST PICTURE (CONTINUED)

1970 *Patton*
1971 *The French Connection*
1972 *The Godfather*
1973 *The Sting*
1974 *The Godfather Part II*
1975 *One Flew Over the Cuckoo's Nest*
1976 *Rocky*
1977 *Annie Hall*
1978 *The Deer Hunter*
1979 *Kramer vs. Kramer*
1980 *Ordinary People*
1981 *Chariots of Fire*
1982 *Gandhi*
1983 *Terms of Endearment*
1984 *Amadeus*
1985 *Out of Africa*
1986 *Platoon*
1987 *The Last Emperor*
1988 *Rain Man*
1989 *Driving Miss Daisy*
1990 *Dances with Wolves*
1991 *The Silence of the Lambs*

Academy Awards (Oscars), 1928–2006 (continued)

BEST PICTURE (CONTINUED)
1992 Unforgiven
1993 Schindler's List
1994 Forrest Gump
1995 Braveheart
1996 The English Patient
1997 Titanic

BEST PICTURE (CONTINUED)
1998 Shakespeare in Love
1999 American Beauty
2000 Gladiator
2001 A Beautiful Mind
2002 Chicago

BEST PICTURE (CONTINUED)
2003 The Lord of the Rings:
       The Return of the King
2004 Million Dollar Baby
2005 Crash
2006 The Departed

BEST ACTOR
1928 Emil Jannings (The Last Command; The Way of All Flesh)
1929 Warner Baxter (In Old Arizona)
1930 George Arliss (Disraeli)
1931 Lionel Barrymore (A Free Soul)
1932 Wallace Beery (The Champ), Fredric March (Dr. Jekyll and Mr. Hyde)
1933 Charles Laughton (The Private Life of Henry VIII)
1934 Clark Gable (It Happened One Night)
1935 Victor McLaglen (The Informer)
1936 Paul Muni (The Story of Louis Pasteur)
1937 Spencer Tracy (Captains Courageous)
1938 Spencer Tracy (Boys Town)
1939 Robert Donat (Goodbye, Mr. Chips)
1940 James Stewart (The Philadelphia Story)
1941 Gary Cooper (Sergeant York)
1942 James Cagney (Yankee Doodle Dandy)
1943 Paul Lukas (Watch on the Rhine)
1944 Bing Crosby (Going My Way)
1945 Ray Milland (The Lost Weekend)
1946 Fredric March (The Best Years of Our Lives)
1947 Ronald Colman (A Double Life)
1948 Laurence Olivier (Hamlet)
1949 Broderick Crawford (All the King's Men)
1950 José Ferrer (Cyrano de Bergerac)
1951 Humphrey Bogart (The African Queen)
1952 Gary Cooper (High Noon)
1953 William Holden (Stalag 17)
1954 Marlon Brando (On the Waterfront)
1955 Ernest Borgnine (Marty)
1956 Yul Brynner (The King and I)
1957 Alec Guinness (The Bridge on the River Kwai)
1958 David Niven (Separate Tables)
1959 Charlton Heston (Ben-Hur)
1960 Burt Lancaster (Elmer Gantry)
1961 Maximilian Schell (Judgment at Nuremberg)
1962 Gregory Peck (To Kill a Mockingbird)
1963 Sidney Poitier (Lilies of the Field)
1964 Rex Harrison (My Fair Lady)
1965 Lee Marvin (Cat Ballou)
1966 Paul Scofield (A Man for All Seasons)
1967 Rod Steiger (In the Heat of the Night)
1968 Cliff Robertson (Charly)
1969 John Wayne (True Grit)
1970 George C. Scott (Patton) (refused)
1971 Gene Hackman (The French Connection)
1972 Marlon Brando (The Godfather)
1973 Jack Lemmon (Save the Tiger)
1974 Art Carney (Harry and Tonto)
1975 Jack Nicholson (One Flew Over the Cuckoo's Nest)
1976 Peter Finch (Network) (posthumous)
1977 Richard Dreyfuss (The Goodbye Girl)
1978 Jon Voight (Coming Home)
1979 Dustin Hoffman (Kramer vs. Kramer)
1980 Robert De Niro (Raging Bull)
1981 Henry Fonda (On Golden Pond)
1982 Ben Kingsley (Gandhi)

BEST ACTOR (CONTINUED)
1983 Robert Duvall (Tender Mercies)
1984 F. Murray Abraham (Amadeus)
1985 William Hurt (Kiss of the Spider Woman)
1986 Paul Newman (The Color of Money)
1987 Michael Douglas (Wall Street)
1988 Dustin Hoffman (Rain Man)
1989 Daniel Day-Lewis (My Left Foot)
1990 Jeremy Irons (Reversal of Fortune)
1991 Anthony Hopkins (The Silence of the Lambs)
1992 Al Pacino (Scent of a Woman)
1993 Tom Hanks (Philadelphia)
1994 Tom Hanks (Forrest Gump)
1995 Nicolas Cage (Leaving Las Vegas)
1996 Geoffrey Rush (Shine)
1997 Jack Nicholson (As Good as It Gets)
1998 Roberto Benigni (Life Is Beautiful)
1999 Kevin Spacey (American Beauty)
2000 Russell Crowe (Gladiator)
2001 Denzel Washington (Training Day)
2002 Adrien Brody (The Pianist)
2003 Sean Penn (Mystic River)
2004 Jamie Foxx (Ray)
2005 Philip Seymour Hoffman (Capote)
2006 Forest Whitaker (The Last King of Scotland)

BEST ACTRESS
1928 Janet Gaynor (7th Heaven; Street Angel; Sunrise)
1929 Mary Pickford (Coquette)
1930 Norma Shearer (The Divorcee)
1931 Marie Dressler (Min and Bill)
1932 Helen Hayes (The Sin of Madelon Claudet)
1933 Katharine Hepburn (Morning Glory)
1934 Claudette Colbert (It Happened One Night)
1935 Bette Davis (Dangerous)
1936 Luise Rainer (The Great Ziegfeld)
1937 Luise Rainer (The Good Earth)
1938 Bette Davis (Jezebel)
1939 Vivien Leigh (Gone with the Wind)
1940 Ginger Rogers (Kitty Foyle)
1941 Joan Fontaine (Suspicion)
1942 Greer Garson (Mrs. Miniver)
1943 Jennifer Jones (The Song of Bernadette)
1944 Ingrid Bergman (Gaslight)
1945 Joan Crawford (Mildred Pierce)
1946 Olivia de Havilland (To Each His Own)
1947 Loretta Young (The Farmer's Daughter)
1948 Jane Wyman (Johnny Belinda)
1949 Olivia de Havilland (The Heiress)
1950 Judy Holliday (Born Yesterday)
1951 Vivien Leigh (A Streetcar Named Desire)
1952 Shirley Booth (Come Back, Little Sheba)
1953 Audrey Hepburn (Roman Holiday)
1954 Grace Kelly (The Country Girl)
1955 Anna Magnani (The Rose Tattoo)
1956 Ingrid Bergman (Anastasia)
1957 Joanne Woodward (The Three Faces of Eve)
1958 Susan Hayward (I Want to Live!)
1959 Simone Signoret (Room at the Top)

Academy Awards (Oscars), 1928–2006 (continued)

1960 Elizabeth Taylor (*Butterfield 8*)
1961 Sophia Loren (*Two Women*)
1962 Anne Bancroft (*The Miracle Worker*)
1963 Patricia Neal (*Hud*)
1964 Julie Andrews (*Mary Poppins*)
1965 Julie Christie (*Darling*)
1966 Elizabeth Taylor (*Who's Afraid of Virginia Woolf?*)
1967 Katharine Hepburn (*Guess Who's Coming to Dinner*)
1968 Katharine Hepburn (*The Lion in Winter*), Barbra Streisand (*Funny Girl*)
1969 Maggie Smith (*The Prime of Miss Jean Brodie*)
1970 Glenda Jackson (*Women in Love*)
1971 Jane Fonda (*Klute*)
1972 Liza Minnelli (*Cabaret*)
1973 Glenda Jackson (*A Touch of Class*)
1974 Ellen Burstyn (*Alice Doesn't Live Here Anymore*)
1975 Louise Fletcher (*One Flew Over the Cuckoo's Nest*)
1976 Faye Dunaway (*Network*)
1977 Diane Keaton (*Annie Hall*)
1978 Jane Fonda (*Coming Home*)
1979 Sally Field (*Norma Rae*)
1980 Sissy Spacek (*Coal Miner's Daughter*)
1981 Katharine Hepburn (*On Golden Pond*)
1982 Meryl Streep (*Sophie's Choice*)
1983 Shirley MacLaine (*Terms of Endearment*)
1984 Sally Field (*Places in the Heart*)
1985 Geraldine Page (*The Trip to Bountiful*)
1986 Marlee Matlin (*Children of a Lesser God*)
1987 Cher (*Moonstruck*)
1988 Jodie Foster (*The Accused*)
1989 Jessica Tandy (*Driving Miss Daisy*)
1990 Kathy Bates (*Misery*)
1991 Jodie Foster (*The Silence of the Lambs*)
1992 Emma Thompson (*Howards End*)
1993 Holly Hunter (*The Piano*)
1994 Jessica Lange (*Blue Sky*)
1995 Susan Sarandon (*Dead Man Walking*)
1996 Frances McDormand (*Fargo*)
1997 Helen Hunt (*As Good as It Gets*)
1998 Gwyneth Paltrow (*Shakespeare in Love*)
1999 Hilary Swank (*Boys Don't Cry*)
2000 Julia Roberts (*Erin Brockovich*)
2001 Halle Berry (*Monster's Ball*)
2002 Nicole Kidman (*The Hours*)
2003 Charlize Theron (*Monster*)
2004 Hilary Swank (*Million Dollar Baby*)
2005 Reese Witherspoon (*Walk the Line*)
2006 Helen Mirren (*The Queen*)

BEST SUPPORTING ACTOR

1936 Walter Brennan (*Come and Get It*)
1937 Joseph Schildkraut (*The Life of Emile Zola*)
1938 Walter Brennan (*Kentucky*)
1939 Thomas Mitchell (*Stagecoach*)
1940 Walter Brennan (*The Westerner*)
1941 Donald Crisp (*How Green Was My Valley*)
1942 Van Heflin (*Johnny Eager*)
1943 Charles Coburn (*The More the Merrier*)
1944 Barry Fitzgerald (*Going My Way*)
1945 James Dunn (*A Tree Grows in Brooklyn*)
1946 Harold Russell (*The Best Years of Our Lives*)
1947 Edmund Gwenn (*Miracle on 34th Street*)
1948 Walter Huston (*The Treasure of the Sierra Madre*)

BEST SUPPORTING ACTOR (CONTINUED)

1949 Dean Jagger (*Twelve O'Clock High*)
1950 George Sanders (*All About Eve*)
1951 Karl Malden (*A Streetcar Named Desire*)
1952 Anthony Quinn (*Viva Zapata!*)
1953 Frank Sinatra (*From Here to Eternity*)
1954 Edmond O'Brien (*The Barefoot Contessa*)
1955 Jack Lemmon (*Mister Roberts*)
1956 Anthony Quinn (*Lust for Life*)
1957 Red Buttons (*Sayonara*)
1958 Burl Ives (*The Big Country*)
1959 Hugh Griffith (*Ben-Hur*)
1960 Peter Ustinov (*Spartacus*)
1961 George Chakiris (*West Side Story*)
1962 Ed Begley (*Sweet Bird of Youth*)
1963 Melvyn Douglas (*Hud*)
1964 Peter Ustinov (*Topkapi*)
1965 Martin Balsam (*A Thousand Clowns*)
1966 Walter Matthau (*The Fortune Cookie*)
1967 George Kennedy (*Cool Hand Luke*)
1968 Jack Albertson (*The Subject Was Roses*)
1969 Gig Young (*They Shoot Horses, Don't They?*)
1970 John Mills (*Ryan's Daughter*)
1971 Ben Johnson (*The Last Picture Show*)
1972 Joel Grey (*Cabaret*)
1973 John Houseman (*The Paper Chase*)
1974 Robert De Niro (*The Godfather Part II*)
1975 George Burns (*The Sunshine Boys*)
1976 Jason Robards (*All the President's Men*)
1977 Jason Robards (*Julia*)
1978 Christopher Walken (*The Deer Hunter*)
1979 Melvyn Douglas (*Being There*)
1980 Timothy Hutton (*Ordinary People*)
1981 John Gielgud (*Arthur*)
1982 Louis Gossett, Jr. (*An Officer and a Gentleman*)
1983 Jack Nicholson (*Terms of Endearment*)
1984 Haing S. Ngor (*The Killing Fields*)
1985 Don Ameche (*Cocoon*)
1986 Michael Caine (*Hannah and Her Sisters*)
1987 Sean Connery (*The Untouchables*)
1988 Kevin Kline (*A Fish Called Wanda*)
1989 Denzel Washington (*Glory*)
1990 Joe Pesci (*Goodfellas*)
1991 Jack Palance (*City Slickers*)
1992 Gene Hackman (*Unforgiven*)
1993 Tommy Lee Jones (*The Fugitive*)
1994 Martin Landau (*Ed Wood*)
1995 Kevin Spacey (*The Usual Suspects*)
1996 Cuba Gooding, Jr. (*Jerry Maguire*)
1997 Robin Williams (*Good Will Hunting*)
1998 James Coburn (*Affliction*)
1999 Michael Caine (*The Cider House Rules*)
2000 Benicio Del Toro (*Traffic*)
2001 Jim Broadbent (*Iris*)
2002 Chris Cooper (*Adaptation*)
2003 Tim Robbins (*Mystic River*)
2004 Morgan Freeman (*Million Dollar Baby*)
2005 George Clooney (*Syriana*)
2006 Alan Arkin (*Little Miss Sunshine*)

BEST SUPPORTING ACTRESS

1936 Gale Sondergaard (*Anthony Adverse*)
1937 Alice Brady (*In Old Chicago*)
1938 Fay Bainter (*Jezebel*)
1939 Hattie McDaniel (*Gone with the Wind*)
1940 Jane Darwell (*The Grapes of Wrath*)
1941 Mary Astor (*The Great Lie*)
1942 Teresa Wright (*Mrs. Miniver*)

Academy Awards (Oscars), 1928–2006 (continued)

BEST SUPPORTING ACTRESS (CONTINUED)

1943 Katina Paxinou (*For Whom the Bell Tolls*)
1944 Ethel Barrymore (*None but the Lonely Heart*)
1945 Anne Revere (*National Velvet*)
1946 Anne Baxter (*The Razor's Edge*)
1947 Celeste Holm (*Gentleman's Agreement*)
1948 Claire Trevor (*Key Largo*)
1949 Mercedes McCambridge (*All the King's Men*)
1950 Josephine Hull (*Harvey*)
1951 Kim Hunter (*A Streetcar Named Desire*)
1952 Gloria Grahame (*The Bad and the Beautiful*)
1953 Donna Reed (*From Here to Eternity*)
1954 Eva Marie Saint (*On the Waterfront*)
1955 Jo Van Fleet (*East of Eden*)
1956 Dorothy Malone (*Written on the Wind*)
1957 Miyoshi Umeki (*Sayonara*)
1958 Wendy Hiller (*Separate Tables*)
1959 Shelley Winters (*The Diary of Anne Frank*)
1960 Shirley Jones (*Elmer Gantry*)
1961 Rita Moreno (*West Side Story*)
1962 Patty Duke (*The Miracle Worker*)
1963 Margaret Rutherford (*The V.I.P.s*)
1964 Lila Kedrova (*Zorba the Greek*)
1965 Shelley Winters (*A Patch of Blue*)
1966 Sandy Dennis (*Who's Afraid of
       Virginia Woolf?*)
1967 Estelle Parsons (*Bonnie and Clyde*)
1968 Ruth Gordon (*Rosemary's Baby*)
1969 Goldie Hawn (*Cactus Flower*)
1970 Helen Hayes (*Airport*)
1971 Cloris Leachman (*The Last Picture Show*)
1972 Eileen Heckart (*Butterflies Are Free*)
1973 Tatum O'Neal (*Paper Moon*)
1974 Ingrid Bergman (*Murder on the Orient
       Express*)
1975 Lee Grant (*Shampoo*)
1976 Beatrice Straight (*Network*)
1977 Vanessa Redgrave (*Julia*)
1978 Maggie Smith (*California Suite*)
1979 Meryl Streep (*Kramer vs. Kramer*)
1980 Mary Steenburgen (*Melvin and Howard*)
1981 Maureen Stapleton (*Reds*)
1982 Jessica Lange (*Tootsie*)
1983 Linda Hunt (*The Year of
       Living Dangerously*)
1984 Peggy Ashcroft (*A Passage to India*)
1985 Anjelica Huston (*Prizzi's Honor*)
1986 Dianne Wiest (*Hannah and Her Sisters*)
1987 Olympia Dukakis (*Moonstruck*)
1988 Geena Davis (*The Accidental Tourist*)
1989 Brenda Fricker (*My Left Foot*)
1990 Whoopi Goldberg (*Ghost*)
1991 Mercedes Ruehl (*The Fisher King*)
1992 Marisa Tomei (*My Cousin Vinny*)
1993 Anna Paquin (*The Piano*)
1994 Dianne Wiest (*Bullets over Broadway*)
1995 Mira Sorvino (*Mighty Aphrodite*)
1996 Juliette Binoche (*The English Patient*)
1997 Kim Basinger (*L.A. Confidential*)
1998 Judi Dench (*Shakespeare in Love*)
1999 Angelina Jolie (*Girl, Interrupted*)
2000 Marcia Gay Harden (*Pollock*)
2001 Jennifer Connelly (*A Beautiful Mind*)
2002 Catherine Zeta-Jones (*Chicago*)
2003 Renée Zellweger (*Cold Mountain*)
2004 Cate Blanchett (*The Aviator*)
2005 Rachel Weisz (*The Constant Gardener*)
2006 Jennifer Hudson (*Dreamgirls*)

FOREIGN LANGUAGE FILM (AMERICAN TITLES)

1947 *Shoe-Shine* (Italy)
1948 *Monsieur Vincent* (France)
1949 *The Bicycle Thief* (Italy)
1950 *The Walls of Malapaga* (France/Italy)
1951 *Rashomon* (Japan)
1952 *Forbidden Games* (France)
1953 not awarded
1954 *Gate of Hell* (Japan)
1955 *Samurai, the Legend of Musashi* (Japan)
1956 *La Strada* (Italy)
1957 *The Nights of Cabiria* (Italy)
1958 *My Uncle* (France)
1959 *Black Orpheus* (France)
1960 *The Virgin Spring* (Sweden)
1961 *Through a Glass Darkly* (Sweden)
1962 *Sundays and Cybele* (France)
1963 *8½* (Italy)
1964 *Yesterday, Today, and Tomorrow* (Italy)
1965 *The Shop on Main Street*
       (Czechoslovakia)
1966 *A Man and a Woman* (France)
1967 *Closely Watched Trains* (Czechoslovakia)
1968 *War and Peace* (USSR)
1969 *Z* (Algeria)
1970 *Investigation of a Citizen Above Suspicion*
       (Italy)
1971 *The Garden of the Finzi Continis* (Italy)
1972 *The Discreet Charm of the Bourgeoisie*
       (France)
1973 *Day for Night* (France)
1974 *Amarcord* (Italy)
1975 *Dersu Uzala* (USSR)
1976 *Black and White in Color* (Ivory Coast)
1977 *Madame Rosa* (France)
1978 *Get Out Your Handkerchiefs* (France)
1979 *The Tin Drum* (West Germany)
1980 *Moscow Does Not Believe
       in Tears* (USSR)
1981 *Mephisto* (Hungary)
1982 *To Begin Again* (Spain)
1983 *Fanny & Alexander* (Sweden)
1984 *Dangerous Moves* (Switzerland)
1985 *The Official Story* (Argentina)
1986 *The Assault* (The Netherlands)
1987 *Babette's Feast* (Denmark)
1988 *Pelle the Conqueror* (Denmark)
1989 *Cinema Paradiso* (Italy)
1990 *Journey of Hope* (Switzerland)
1991 *Mediterraneo* (Italy)
1992 *Indochine* (France)
1993 *Belle Epoque* (Spain)
1994 *Burnt by the Sun* (Russia)
1995 *Antonia's Line* (The Netherlands)
1996 *Kolya* (Czech Republic)
1997 *Character* (The Netherlands)
1998 *Life Is Beautiful* (Italy)
1999 *All About My Mother* (Spain)
2000 *Crouching Tiger, Hidden Dragon*
       (Taiwan)
2001 *No Man's Land* (Bosnia and
       Herzegovina)
2002 *Nowhere in Africa* (Germany)
2003 *The Barbarian Invasions* (Canada)
2004 *The Sea Inside* (Spain)
2005 *Tsotsi* (South Africa)
2006 *The Lives of Others* (Germany)

Academy Awards (Oscars), 1928–2006 (continued)

DIRECTING

1928 Lewis Milestone (*Two Arabian Knights*), Frank Borzage (*7th Heaven*)
1929 Frank Lloyd (*The Divine Lady*)
1930 Lewis Milestone (*All Quiet on the Western Front*)
1931 Norman Taurog (*Skippy*)
1932 Frank Borzage (*Bad Girl*)
1933 Frank Lloyd (*Cavalcade*)
1934 Frank Capra (*It Happened One Night*)
1935 John Ford (*The Informer*)
1936 Frank Capra (*Mr. Deeds Goes to Town*)
1937 Leo McCarey (*The Awful Truth*)
1938 Frank Capra (*You Can't Take It with You*)
1939 Victor Fleming (*Gone with the Wind*)
1940 John Ford (*The Grapes of Wrath*)
1941 John Ford (*How Green Was My Valley*)
1942 William Wyler (*Mrs. Miniver*)
1943 Michael Curtiz (*Casablanca*)
1944 Leo McCarey (*Going My Way*)
1945 Billy Wilder (*The Lost Weekend*)
1946 William Wyler (*The Best Years of Our Lives*)
1947 Elia Kazan (*Gentleman's Agreement*)
1948 John Huston (*The Treasure of the Sierra Madre*)
1949 Joseph L. Mankiewicz (*A Letter to Three Wives*)
1950 Joseph L. Mankiewicz (*All About Eve*)
1951 George Stevens (*A Place in the Sun*)
1952 John Ford (*The Quiet Man*)
1953 Fred Zinnemann (*From Here to Eternity*)
1954 Elia Kazan (*On the Waterfront*)
1955 Delbert Mann (*Marty*)
1956 George Stevens (*Giant*)
1957 David Lean (*The Bridge on the River Kwai*)
1958 Vincente Minnelli (*Gigi*)
1959 William Wyler (*Ben-Hur*)
1960 Billy Wilder (*The Apartment*)
1961 Robert Wise, Jerome Robbins (*West Side Story*)
1962 David Lean (*Lawrence of Arabia*)
1963 Tony Richardson (*Tom Jones*)
1964 George Cukor (*My Fair Lady*)
1965 Robert Wise (*The Sound of Music*)
1966 Fred Zinnemann (*A Man for All Seasons*)
1967 Mike Nichols (*The Graduate*)
1968 Carol Reed (*Oliver!*)
1969 John Schlesinger (*Midnight Cowboy*)
1970 Franklin J. Schaffner (*Patton*)
1971 William Friedkin (*The French Connection*)
1972 Bob Fosse (*Cabaret*)
1973 George Roy Hill (*The Sting*)
1974 Francis Ford Coppola (*The Godfather Part II*)
1975 Milos Forman (*One Flew Over the Cuckoo's Nest*)
1976 John G. Avildsen (*Rocky*)
1977 Woody Allen (*Annie Hall*)
1978 Michael Cimino (*The Deer Hunter*)
1979 Robert Benton (*Kramer vs. Kramer*)
1980 Robert Redford (*Ordinary People*)
1981 Warren Beatty (*Reds*)
1982 Richard Attenborough (*Gandhi*)
1983 James L. Brooks (*Terms of Endearment*)
1984 Milos Forman (*Amadeus*)
1985 Sydney Pollack (*Out of Africa*)
1986 Oliver Stone (*Platoon*)
1987 Bernardo Bertolucci (*The Last Emperor*)
1988 Barry Levinson (*Rain Man*)

DIRECTING (CONTINUED)

1989 Oliver Stone (*Born on the Fourth of July*)
1990 Kevin Costner (*Dances with Wolves*)
1991 Jonathan Demme (*The Silence of the Lambs*)
1992 Clint Eastwood (*Unforgiven*)
1993 Steven Spielberg (*Schindler's List*)
1994 Robert Zemeckis (*Forrest Gump*)
1995 Mel Gibson (*Braveheart*)
1996 Anthony Minghella (*The English Patient*)
1997 James Cameron (*Titanic*)
1998 Steven Spielberg (*Saving Private Ryan*)
1999 Sam Mendes (*American Beauty*)
2000 Steven Soderbergh (*Traffic*)
2001 Ron Howard (*A Beautiful Mind*)
2002 Roman Polanski (*The Pianist*)
2003 Peter Jackson (*The Lord of the Rings: The Return of the King*)
2004 Clint Eastwood (*Million Dollar Baby*)
2005 Ang Lee (*Brokeback Mountain*)
2006 Martin Scorsese (*The Departed*)

SCREENPLAY, ADAPTATION[1]

1928 Benjamin Glazer (*7th Heaven*)
1931 Howard Estabrook (*Cimarron*)
1932 Edwin Burke (*Bad Girl*)
1933 Victor Heerman, Sarah Y. Mason (*Little Women*)
1934 Robert Riskin (*It Happened One Night*)
1935 Dudley Nichols (*The Informer*)[2]
1936 Pierre Collings, Sheridan Gibney (*The Story of Louis Pasteur*)[2]
1937 Norman Reilly Raine, Heinz Herald, Geza Herczeg (*The Life of Emile Zola*)[2]
1938 George Bernard Shaw, W.P. Lipscomb, Cecil Lewis, Ian Dalrymple (*Pygmalion*)[2]
1939 Sidney Howard (*Gone with the Wind*)[2]
1940 Donald Ogden Stewart (*The Philadelphia Story*)[2]
1941 Sidney Buchman, Seton I. Miller (*Here Comes Mr. Jordan*)[2]
1942 George Froeschel, James Hilton, Claudine West, Arthur Wimperis (*Mrs. Miniver*)[2]
1943 Julius J. Epstein, Philip G. Epstein, Howard Koch (*Casablanca*)[2]
1944 Frank Butler, Frank Cavett (*Going My Way*)[2]
1945 Charles Brackett, Billy Wilder (*The Lost Weekend*)[2]
1946 Robert E. Sherwood (*The Best Years of Our Lives*)[2]
1947 George Seaton (*Miracle on 34th Street*)[2]
1948 John Huston (*The Treasure of the Sierra Madre*)[2]
1949 Joseph L. Mankiewicz (*A Letter to Three Wives*)[2]
1950 Joseph L. Mankiewicz (*All About Eve*)[2]
1951 Michael Wilson, Harry Brown (*A Place in the Sun*)[2]
1952 Charles Schnee (*The Bad and the Beautiful*)[2]
1953 Daniel Taradash (*From Here to Eternity*)[2]
1954 George Seaton (*The Country Girl*)[2]
1955 Paddy Chayefsky (*Marty*)[2]
1956 James Poe, John Farrow, S.J. Perelman (*Around the World in 80 Days*)
1957 Pierre Boulle, Michael Wilson, Carl Foreman (*The Bridge on the River Kwai*)
1958 Alan Jay Lerner (*Gigi*)
1959 Neil Paterson (*Room at the Top*)
1960 Richard Brooks (*Elmer Gantry*)
1961 Abby Mann (*Judgment at Nuremberg*)

Academy Awards (Oscars), 1928–2006 (continued)

SCREENPLAY, ADAPTATION[1] (CONTINUED)

1962 Horton Foote (To Kill a Mockingbird)
1963 John Osborne (Tom Jones)
1964 Edward Anhalt (Becket)
1965 Robert Bolt (Doctor Zhivago)
1966 Robert Bolt (A Man for All Seasons)
1967 Stirling Silliphant (In the Heat of the Night)
1968 James Goldman (The Lion in Winter)
1969 Waldo Salt (Midnight Cowboy)
1970 Ring Lardner, Jr. (M*A*S*H)
1971 Ernest Tidyman (The French Connection)
1972 Mario Puzo, Francis Ford Coppola (The Godfather)
1973 William Peter Blatty (The Exorcist)
1974 Francis Ford Coppola, Mario Puzo (The Godfather Part II)
1975 Lawrence Hauben, Bo Goldman (One Flew Over the Cuckoo's Nest)
1976 William Goldman (All the President's Men)
1977 Alvin Sargent (Julia)
1978 Oliver Stone (Midnight Express)
1979 Robert Benton (Kramer vs. Kramer)
1980 Alvin Sargent (Ordinary People)
1981 Ernest Thompson (On Golden Pond)
1982 Costa-Gavras, Donald Stewart (Missing)
1983 James L. Brooks (Terms of Endearment)
1984 Peter Shaffer (Amadeus)
1985 Kurt Luedtke (Out of Africa)
1986 Ruth Prawer Jhabvala (A Room with a View)
1987 Mark Peploe, Bernardo Bertolucci (The Last Emperor)
1988 Christopher Hampton (Dangerous Liaisons)
1989 Alfred Uhry (Driving Miss Daisy)
1990 Michael Blake (Dances with Wolves)
1991 Ted Tally (The Silence of the Lambs)
1992 Ruth Prawer Jhabvala (Howards End)
1993 Steven Zaillian (Schindler's List)
1994 Eric Roth (Forrest Gump)
1995 Emma Thompson (Sense and Sensibility)
1996 Billy Bob Thornton (Sling Blade)
1997 Brian Helgeland, Curtis Hanson (L.A. Confidential)
1998 Bill Condon (Gods and Monsters)
1999 John Irving (The Cider House Rules)
2000 Stephen Gaghan (Traffic)
2001 Akiva Goldsman (A Beautiful Mind)
2002 Ronald Harwood (The Pianist)
2003 Fran Walsh, Philippa Boyens, Peter Jackson (The Lord of the Rings: The Return of the King)
2004 Alexander Payne, Jim Taylor (Sideways)
2005 Larry McMurtry, Diana Ossana (Brokeback Mountain)
2006 William Monahan (The Departed)

SCREENPLAY, ORIGINAL[1]

1928 Ben Hecht (Underworld)[4], Joseph Farnham (The Fair Co-Ed; Laugh, Clown, Laugh; Telling the World [title writing])
1929 Hans Kräly (The Patriot)
1930 Frances Marion (The Big House)
1931 John Monk Saunders (The Dawn Patrol)[4]
1932 Frances Marion (The Champ)[4]
1933 Robert Lord (One Way Passage)[4]
1934 Arthur Caesar (Manhattan Melodrama)[4]
1935 Ben Hecht, Charles MacArthur (The Scoundrel)[4]

SCREENPLAY, ORIGINAL[1] (CONTINUED)

1936 Pierre Collings, Sheridan Gibney (The Story of Louis Pasteur)[4]
1937 William A. Wellman, Robert Carson (A Star Is Born)[4]
1938 Eleanore Griffin, Dore Schary (Boys Town)[4]
1939 Lewis R. Foster (Mr. Smith Goes to Washington)[4]
1940 Preston Sturges (The Great McGinty)[3], Benjamin Glazer, John S. Toldy (Arise, My Love)[4]
1941 Herman J. Mankiewicz, Orson Welles (Citizen Kane)[3], Harry Segall (Here Comes Mr. Jordan)[4]
1942 Michael Kanin, Ring Lardner, Jr. (Woman of the Year)[3], Emeric Pressburger (Forty-Ninth Parallel)[4]
1943 Norman Krasna (Princess O'Rourke)[3], William Saroyan (The Human Comedy)[4]
1944 Lamar Trotti (Wilson)[3], Leo McCarey (Going My Way)[4]
1945 Richard Schweizer (Marie-Louise)[3], Charles G. Booth (The House on 92nd Street)[4]
1946 Muriel Box, Sydney Box (The Seventh Veil)[3], Clemence Dane (Vacation from Marriage)[4]
1947 Sidney Sheldon (The Bachelor and the Bobby-Soxer)[3], Valentine Davies (Miracle on 34th Street)[4]
1948 Richard Schweizer, David Wechsler (The Search)[4]
1949 Robert Pirosh (Battleground)[3], Douglas Morrow (The Stratton Story)[4]
1950 Charles Brackett, Billy Wilder, D.M. Marshman, Jr. (Sunset Boulevard)[3], Edna Anhalt, Edward Anhalt (Panic in the Streets)[4]
1951 Alan Jay Lerner (An American in Paris)[3], Paul Dehn, James Bernard (Seven Days to Noon)[4]
1952 T.E.B. Clarke (The Lavender Hill Mob)[3], Fredric M. Frank, Theodore St. John, Frank Cavett (The Greatest Show on Earth)[4]
1953 Charles Brackett, Walter Reisch, Richard L. Breen (Titanic)[3], Dalton Trumbo[5] (as Ian McLellan Hunter, Roman Holiday)[4]
1954 Budd Schulberg (On the Waterfront)[3], Philip Yordan (Broken Lance)[4]
1955 William Ludwig, Sonya Levien (Interrupted Melody)[3], Daniel Fuchs (Love Me or Leave Me)[4]
1956 Albert Lamorisse (The Red Balloon)[3], Dalton Trumbo[5] (as Robert Rich, The Brave One)[4]
1957 George Wells (Designing Woman)
1958 Nedrick Young[5] (as Nathan E. Douglas), Harold Jacob Smith (The Defiant Ones)
1959 Russell Rouse, Clarence Greene, Stanley Shapiro, Maurice Richlin (Pillow Talk)
1960 Billy Wilder, I.A.L. Diamond (The Apartment)
1961 William Inge (Splendor in the Grass)
1962 Ennio de Concini, Alfredo Giannetti, Pietro Germi (Divorce—Italian Style)
1963 James R. Webb (How the West Was Won)
1964 S.H. Barnett, Peter Stone, Frank Tarloff (Father Goose)
1965 Frederic Raphael (Darling)
1966 Claude Lelouch, Pierre Uytterhoeven (A Man and a Woman)
1967 William Rose (Guess Who's Coming to Dinner)
1968 Mel Brooks (The Producers)

Academy Awards (Oscars), 1928–2006 (continued)

1969 William Goldman (*Butch Cassidy and the Sundance Kid*)
1970 Francis Ford Coppola, Edmund H. North (*Patton*)
1971 Paddy Chayefsky (*The Hospital*)
1972 Jeremy Larner (*The Candidate*)
1973 David S. Ward (*The Sting*)
1974 Robert Towne (*Chinatown*)
1975 Frank Pierson (*Dog Day Afternoon*)
1976 Paddy Chayefsky (*Network*)
1977 Woody Allen, Marshall Brickman (*Annie Hall*)
1978 Nancy Dowd, Waldo Salt, Robert C. Jones (*Coming Home*)
1979 Steve Tesich (*Breaking Away*)
1980 Bo Goldman (*Melvin and Howard*)
1981 Colin Welland (*Chariots of Fire*)
1982 John Briley (*Gandhi*)
1983 Horton Foote (*Tender Mercies*)
1984 Robert Benton (*Places in the Heart*)
1985 Earl W. Wallace, William Kelley, Pamela Wallace (*Witness*)
1986 Woody Allen (*Hannah and Her Sisters*)
1987 John Patrick Shanley (*Moonstruck*)
1988 Ronald Bass, Barry Morrow (*Rain Man*)
1989 Tom Schulman (*Dead Poets Society*)
1990 Bruce Joel Rubin (*Ghost*)
1991 Callie Khouri (*Thelma & Louise*)
1992 Neil Jordan (*The Crying Game*)
1993 Jane Campion (*The Piano*)
1994 Quentin Tarantino, Roger Avary (*Pulp Fiction*)
1995 Christopher McQuarrie (*The Usual Suspects*)
1996 Joel Coen, Ethan Coen (*Fargo*)
1997 Ben Affleck, Matt Damon (*Good Will Hunting*)
1998 Marc Norman, Tom Stoppard (*Shakespeare in Love*)
1999 Alan Ball (*American Beauty*)
2000 Cameron Crowe (*Almost Famous*)
2001 Julian Fellowes (*Gosford Park*)
2002 Pedro Almodóvar (*Talk to Her*)
2003 Sofia Coppola (*Lost in Translation*)
2004 Charlie Kaufman (*Eternal Sunshine of the Spotless Mind*)
2005 Paul Haggis, Bobby Moresco (*Crash*)
2006 Michael Arndt (*Little Miss Sunshine*)

CINEMATOGRAPHY

1928 Charles Rosher, Karl Struss (*Sunrise*)
1929 Clyde De Vinna (*White Shadows in the South Seas*)
1930 Joseph T. Rucker, Willard Van Der Veer (*With Byrd at the South Pole*)
1931 Floyd Crosby (*Tabu*)
1932 Lee Garmes (*Shanghai Express*)
1933 Charles Bryant Lang, Jr. (*A Farewell to Arms*)
1934 Victor Milner (*Cleopatra*)
1935 Hal Mohr (*A Midsummer Night's Dream*)
1936 Gaetano Gaudio (*Anthony Adverse*)
1937 Karl Freund (*The Good Earth*)
1938 Joseph Ruttenberg (*The Great Waltz*)
1939 Gregg Toland (*Wuthering Heights*)[6], Ernest Haller, Ray Rennahan (*Gone with the Wind*)[7]
1940 George Barnes (*Rebecca*)[6], Georges Perinal (*The Thief of Bagdad*)[7]
1941 Arthur Miller (*How Green Was My Valley*)[6], Ernest Palmer, Ray Rennahan (*Blood and Sand*)[7]
1942 Joseph Ruttenberg (*Mrs. Miniver*)[6], Leon Shamroy (*The Black Swan*)[7]

CINEMATOGRAPHY (CONTINUED)

1943 Arthur Miller (*The Song of Bernadette*)[6], Hal Mohr, W. Howard Greene (*The Phantom of the Opera*)[7]
1944 Joseph LaShelle (*Laura*)[6], Leon Shamroy (*Wilson*)[7]
1945 Harry Stradling (*The Picture of Dorian Gray*)[6], Leon Shamroy (*Leave Her to Heaven*)[7]
1946 Arthur Miller (*Anna and the King of Siam*)[6], Charles Rosher, Leonard Smith, Arthur Arling (*The Yearling*)[7]
1947 Guy Green (*Great Expectations*)[6], Jack Cardiff (*Black Narcissus*)[7]
1948 William Daniels (*The Naked City*)[6], Joseph Valentine, William V. Skall, Winton Hoch (*Joan of Arc*)[7]
1949 Paul C. Vogel (*Battleground*)[6], Winton Hoch (*She Wore a Yellow Ribbon*)[7]
1950 Robert Krasker (*The Third Man*)[6], Robert Surtees (*King Solomon's Mines*)[7]
1951 William C. Mellor (*A Place in the Sun*)[6], Alfred Gilks, John Alton (*An American in Paris*)[7]
1952 Robert Surtees (*The Bad and the Beautiful*)[6], Winton C. Hoch, Archie Stout (*The Quiet Man*)[7]
1953 Burnett Guffey (*From Here to Eternity*)[6], Loyal Griggs (*Shane*)[7]
1954 Boris Kaufman (*On the Waterfront*)[6], Milton Krasner (*Three Coins in the Fountain*)[7]
1955 James Wong Howe (*The Rose Tattoo*)[6], Robert Burks (*To Catch a Thief*)[7]
1956 Joseph Ruttenberg (*Somebody Up There Likes Me*)[6], Lionel Lindon (*Around the World in 80 Days*)[7]
1957 Jack Hildyard (*The Bridge on the River Kwai*)
1958 Sam Leavitt (*The Defiant Ones*)[6], Joseph Ruttenberg (*Gigi*)[7]
1959 William C. Mellor (*The Diary of Anne Frank*)[6], Robert L. Surtees (*Ben-Hur*)[7]
1960 Freddie Francis (*Sons and Lovers*)[6], Russell Metty (*Spartacus*)[7]
1961 Eugen Shuftan (*The Hustler*)[6], Daniel L. Fapp (*West Side Story*)[7]
1962 Jean Bourgoin, Walter Wottitz (*The Longest Day*)[6], Fred A. Young (*Lawrence of Arabia*)[7]
1963 James Wong Howe (*Hud*)[6], Leon Shamroy (*Cleopatra*)[7]
1964 Walter Lassally (*Zorba the Greek*)[6], Harry Stradling (*My Fair Lady*)[7]
1965 Ernest Laszlo (*Ship of Fools*)[6], Freddie Young (*Doctor Zhivago*)[7]
1966 Haskell Wexler (*Who's Afraid of Virginia Woolf?*)[6], Ted Moore (*A Man for All Seasons*)[7]
1967 Burnett Guffey (*Bonnie and Clyde*)
1968 Pasqualino De Santis (*Romeo and Juliet*)
1969 Conrad Hall (*Butch Cassidy and the Sundance Kid*)
1970 Freddie Young (*Ryan's Daughter*)
1971 Oswald Morris (*Fiddler on the Roof*)
1972 Geoffrey Unsworth (*Cabaret*)
1973 Sven Nykvist (*Cries and Whispers*)
1974 Fred Koenekamp, Joseph Biroc (*The Towering Inferno*)
1975 John Alcott (*Barry Lyndon*)
1976 Haskell Wexler (*Bound for Glory*)
1977 Vilmos Zsigmond (*Close Encounters of the Third Kind*)
1978 Nestor Almendros (*Days of Heaven*)

Academy Awards (Oscars), 1928–2006 (continued)

CINEMATOGRAPHY (CONTINUED)

1979 Vittorio Storaro (*Apocalypse Now*)
1980 Geoffrey Unsworth, Ghislain Cloquet (*Tess*)
1981 Vittorio Storaro (*Reds*)
1982 Billy Williams, Ronnie Taylor (*Gandhi*)
1983 Sven Nykvist (*Fanny & Alexander*)
1984 Chris Menges (*The Killing Fields*)
1985 David Watkin (*Out of Africa*)
1986 Chris Menges (*The Mission*)
1987 Vittorio Storaro (*The Last Emperor*)
1988 Peter Biziou (*Mississippi Burning*)
1989 Freddie Francis (*Glory*)
1990 Dean Semler (*Dances with Wolves*)
1991 Robert Richardson (*JFK*)
1992 Philippe Rousselot (*A River Runs Through It*)
1993 Janusz Kaminski (*Schindler's List*)
1994 John Toll (*Legends of the Fall*)
1995 John Toll (*Braveheart*)
1996 John Seale (*The English Patient*)
1997 Russell Carpenter (*Titanic*)
1998 Janusz Kaminski (*Saving Private Ryan*)
1999 Conrad L. Hall (*American Beauty*)
2000 Peter Pau (*Crouching Tiger, Hidden Dragon*)
2001 Andrew Lesnie (*The Lord of the Rings: The Fellowship of the Ring*)
2002 Conrad L. Hall (*Road to Perdition*)
2003 Russell Boyd (*Master and Commander: The Far Side of the World*)
2004 Robert Richardson (*The Aviator*)
2005 Dion Beebe (*Memoirs of a Geisha*)
2006 Guillermo Navarro (*Pan's Labyrinth*)

VISUAL EFFECTS[B]

1939 E.H. Hansen (*The Rains Came*)
1940 Lawrence Butler (*The Thief of Bagdad*)
1941 Farciot Edouart, Gordon Jennings (*I Wanted Wings*)
1942 Farciot Edouart, Gordon Jennings, William L. Pereira (*Reap the Wild Wind*)
1943 Fred Sersen (*Crash Dive*)
1944 A. Arnold Gillespie, Donald Jahraus, Warren Newcombe (*Thirty Seconds Over Tokyo*)
1945 John P. Fulton (*Wonder Man*)
1946 Thomas Howard (*Blithe Spirit*)
1947 A. Arnold Gillespie, Warren Newcombe (*Green Dolphin Street*)
1948 Paul Eagler, J. McMillan Johnson, Russell Shearman, Clarence Slifer (*Portrait of Jennie*)
1949 *Mighty Joe Young*
1950 *Destination Moon*
1951 *When Worlds Collide*
1952 *Plymouth Adventure*
1953 *The War of the Worlds*
1954 *20,000 Leagues Under the Sea*
1955 *The Bridges at Toko-Ri*
1956 John Fulton (*The Ten Commandments*)
1958 Tom Howard (*tom thumb*)
1959 A. Arnold Gillespie, Robert MacDonald (*Ben-Hur*)
1960 Gene Warren, Tim Baar (*The Time Machine*)
1961 Bill Warrington (*The Guns of Navarone*)
1962 Robert MacDonald (*The Longest Day*)
1963 Emil Kosa, Jr. (*Cleopatra*)
1964 Peter Ellenshaw, Hamilton Luske, Eustace Lycett (*Mary Poppins*)
1965 John Stears (*Thunderball*)
1966 Art Cruickshank (*Fantastic Voyage*)

VISUAL EFFECTS[B] **(CONTINUED)**

1967 L.B. Abbott (*Doctor Dolittle*)
1968 Stanley Kubrick (*2001: A Space Odyssey*)
1969 Robbie Robertson (*Marooned*)
1970 A.D. Flowers, L.B. Abbott (*Tora! Tora! Tora!*)
1971 Alan Maley, Eustace Lycett, Danny Lee (*Bedknobs and Broomsticks*)
1972 L.B. Abbott, A.D. Flowers (*The Poseidon Adventure*)
1974 Frank Brendel, Glen Robinson, Albert Whitlock (*Earthquake*)
1975 Albert Whitlock, Glen Robinson (*The Hindenburg*)
1976 Carlo Rambaldi, Glen Robinson, Frank Van der Veer (*King Kong*), L.B. Abbott, Glen Robinson, Matthew Yuricich (*Logan's Run*)
1977 John Stears, John Dykstra, Richard Edlund, Grant McCune, Robert Blalack (*Star Wars*)
1978 Les Bowie, Colin Chilvers, Denys Coop, Roy Field, Derek Meddings, Zoran Perisic (*Superman*)
1979 H.R. Giger, Carlo Rambaldi, Brian Johnson, Nick Allder, Denys Ayling (*Alien*)
1980 Brian Johnson, Richard Edlund, Dennis Muren, Bruce Nicholson (*The Empire Strikes Back*)
1981 Richard Edlund, Kit West, Bruce Nicholson, Joe Johnston (*Raiders of the Lost Ark*)
1982 Carlo Rambaldi, Dennis Muren, Kenneth F. Smith (*E.T.: The Extra-Terrestrial*)
1983 Richard Edlund, Dennis Muren, Ken Ralston, Phil Tippet (*Return of the Jedi*)
1984 Dennis Muren, Michael McAlister, Lorne Peterson, George Gibbs (*Indiana Jones and the Temple of Doom*)
1985 Ken Ralston, Ralph McQuarrie, Scott Farrar, David Berry (*Cocoon*)
1986 Robert Skotak, Stan Winston, John Richardson, Suzanne Benson (*Aliens*)
1987 Dennis Muren, William George, Harley Jessup, Kenneth Smith (*Innerspace*)
1988 Ken Ralston, Richard Williams, Edward Jones, George Gibbs (*Who Framed Roger Rabbit*)
1989 John Bruno, Dennis Muren, Hoyt Yeatman, Dennis Skotak (*The Abyss*)
1990 Eric Brevig, Rob Bottin, Tim McGovern, Alex Funke (*Total Recall*)
1991 Robert Skotak (*Terminator 2: Judgment Day*)
1992 Ken Ralston, Doug Chiang, Doug Smythe, Tom Woodruff, Jr. (*Death Becomes Her*)
1993 Dennis Muren, Stan Winston, Phil Tippett, Michael Lantieri (*Jurassic Park*)
1994 Ken Ralston, George Murphy, Stephen Rosenbaum, Allen Hall (*Forrest Gump*)
1995 Scott E. Anderson, Charles Gibson, Neal Scanlan, John Cox (*Babe*)
1996 Volker Engel, Douglas Smith, Clay Pinney, Joseph Viskocil (*Independence Day*)
1997 Robert Legato, Mark Lasoff, Thomas L. Fisher, Michael Kanfer (*Titanic*)
1998 Joel Hynek, Nicholas Brooks, Stuart Robertson, Kevin Mack (*What Dreams May Come*)
1999 John Gaeta, Janek Sirrs, Steve Courtley, Jon Thum (*The Matrix*)
2000 John Nelson, Neil Corbould, Tim Burke, Rob Harvey (*Gladiator*)

Academy Awards (Oscars), 1928–2006 (continued)

VISUAL EFFECTS[8] (CONTINUED)

2001 Jim Rygiel, Randall William Cook, Richard Taylor, Mark Stetson (*The Lord of the Rings: The Fellowship of the Ring*)

2002 Jim Rygiel, Joe Letteri, Randall William Cook, Alex Funke (*The Lord of the Rings: The Two Towers*)

2003 Jim Rygiel, Joe Letteri, Randall William Cook, Alex Funke (*The Lord of the Rings: The Return of the King*)

2004 John Dykstra, Scott Stokdyk, Anthony LaMolinara, John Frazier (*Spider-Man 2*)

2005 Joe Letteri, Brian Van't Hul, Christian Rivers, Richard Taylor (*King Kong*)

2006 John Knoll, Hal Hickel, Charles Gibson, Allen Hall (*Pirates of the Caribbean: Dead Man's Chest*)

MAKEUP

1981 Rick Baker (*An American Werewolf in London*)

1982 Sarah Monzani, Michele Burke (*Quest for Fire*)

1984 Paul LeBlanc, Dick Smith (*Amadeus*)

1985 Michael Westmore, Zoltan Elek (*Mask*)

1986 Chris Walas, Stephan Dupuis (*The Fly*)

1987 Rick Baker (*Harry and the Hendersons*)

1988 Ve Neill, Steve La Porte, Robert Short (*Beetlejuice*)

1989 Manlio Rocchetti, Lynn Barber, Kevin Haney (*Driving Miss Daisy*)

1990 John Caglione, Jr., Doug Drexler (*Dick Tracy*)

1991 Stan Winston, Jeff Dawn (*Terminator 2: Judgment Day*)

1992 Greg Cannom, Michele Burke, Matthew W. Mungle (*Bram Stoker's Dracula*)

1993 Greg Cannom, Ve Neill, Yolanda Toussieng (*Mrs. Doubtfire*)

1994 Rick Baker, Ve Neill, Yolanda Toussieng (*Ed Wood*)

1995 Peter Frampton, Paul Pattison, Lois Burwell (*Braveheart*)

1996 Rick Baker, David LeRoy Anderson (*The Nutty Professor*)

1997 Rick Baker, David LeRoy Anderson (*Men in Black*)

1998 Jenny Shircore (*Elizabeth*)

1999 Christine Blundell, Trefor Proud (*Topsy-Turvy*)

2000 Rick Baker, Gail Ryan (*Dr. Seuss' How the Grinch Stole Christmas*)

2001 Peter Owen, Richard Taylor (*The Lord of the Rings: The Fellowship of the Ring*)

2002 John Jackson, Beatrice Alba (*Frida*)

2003 Richard Taylor, Peter King (*The Lord of the Rings: The Return of the King*)

2004 Valli O'Reilly, Bill Corso (*Lemony Snicket's A Series of Unfortunate Events*)

2005 Howard Berger, Tami Lane (*The Chronicles of Narnia: The Lion, the Witch, and the Wardrobe*)

2006 David Martí, Montse Ribé (*Pan's Labyrinth*)

ORIGINAL SCORE

1938 Erich Wolfgang Korngold (*The Adventures of Robin Hood*)

1939 Herbert Stothart (*The Wizard of Oz*)

1940 Leigh Harline, Paul J. Smith, Ned Washington (*Pinocchio*)

ORIGINAL SCORE (CONTINUED)

1941 Bernard Herrmann (*All That Money Can Buy*)

1942 Max Steiner (*Now, Voyager*)

1943 Alfred Newman (*The Song of Bernadette*)

1944 Max Steiner (*Since You Went Away*)

1945 Miklos Rozsa (*Spellbound*)

1946 Hugo Friedhofer (*The Best Years of Our Lives*)

1947 Dr. Miklos Rozsa (*A Double Life*)

1948 Brian Easdale (*The Red Shoes*)

1949 Aaron Copland (*The Heiress*)

1950 Franz Waxman (*Sunset Blvd.*)

1951 Franz Waxman (*A Place in the Sun*)

1952 Dimitri Tiomkin (*High Noon*)

1953 Bronislau Kaper (*Lili*)

1954 Dimitri Tiomkin (*The High and Mighty*)

1955 Alfred Newman (*Love Is a Many-Splendored Thing*)

1956 Victor Young (*Around the World in 80 Days*)

1957 Malcolm Arnold (*The Bridge on the River Kwai*)[9]

1958 Dimitri Tiomkin (*The Old Man and The Sea*)

1959 Miklos Rozsa (*Ben-Hur*)

1960 Ernest Gold (*Exodus*)

1961 Henry Mancini (*Breakfast at Tiffany's*)

1962 Maurice Jarre (*Lawrence of Arabia*)

1963 John Addison (*Tom Jones*)

1964 Richard M. Sherman, Robert B. Sherman (*Mary Poppins*)

1965 Maurice Jarre (*Doctor Zhivago*)

1966 John Barry (*Born Free*)

1967 Elmer Bernstein (*Thoroughly Modern Millie*)

1968 John Barry (*The Lion in Winter*)[10], John Green (*Oliver!*)[11]

1969 Burt Bacharach (*Butch Cassidy and the Sundance Kid*)[10], Lennie Hayton, Lionel Newman (*Hello, Dolly!*)[11]

1970 Francis Lai (*Love Story*), The Beatles (*Let It Be*)[12]

1971 Michel Legrand (*Summer of '42*)

1972 Charles Chaplin, Raymond Rasch, Larry Russell (*Limelight*)

1973 Marvin Hamlisch (*The Way We Were*)

1974 Nino Rota, Carmine Coppola (*The Godfather Part II*)

1975 John Williams (*Jaws*)

1976 Jerry Goldsmith (*The Omen*)

1977 John Williams (*Star Wars*)

1978 Giorgio Moroder (*Midnight Express*)

1979 Georges Delerue (*A Little Romance*)

1980 Michael Gore (*Fame*)

1981 Vangelis (*Chariots of Fire*)

1982 John Williams (*E.T.: The Extra-Terrestrial*), Henry Mancini, Leslie Bricusse (*Victor/Victoria*)[12]

1983 Bill Conti (*The Right Stuff*), Michel Legrand, Alan Bergman, Marilyn Bergman (*Yentl*)[12]

1984 Maurice Jarre (*A Passage to India*), Prince (*Purple Rain*)[12]

1985 John Barry (*Out of Africa*)

1986 Herbie Hancock (*'Round Midnight*)

1987 Ryuichi Sakamoto, David Byrne, Cong Su (*The Last Emperor*)

1988 Dave Grusin (*The Milagro Beanfield War*)

1989 Alan Menken (*The Little Mermaid*)

1990 John Barry (*Dances with Wolves*)

Academy Awards (Oscars), 1928–2006 (continued)

ORIGINAL SCORE (CONTINUED)

1991   Alan Menken (*Beauty and the Beast*)
1992   Alan Menken (*Aladdin*)
1993   John Williams (*Schindler's List*)
1994   Hans Zimmer (*The Lion King*)
1995   Luis Enrique Bacalov (*The Postman [Il Postino]*)[10], Alan Menken, Stephen Schwartz (*Pocahontas*)[13]
1996   Gabriel Yared (*The English Patient*)[10], Rachel Portman (*Emma*)[13]
1997   James Horner (*Titanic*)[10], Anne Dudley (*The Full Monty*)[13]
1998   Nicola Piovani (*Life Is Beautiful*)[10], Stephen Warbeck (*Shakespeare in Love*)[13]
1999   John Corigliano (*The Red Violin*)
2000   Tan Dun (*Crouching Tiger, Hidden Dragon*)
2001   Howard Shore (*The Lord of the Rings: The Fellowship of the Ring*)
2002   Elliot Goldenthal (*Frida*)
2003   Howard Shore (*The Lord of the Rings: The Return of the King*)
2004   Jan A.P. Kaczmarek (*Finding Neverland*)
2005   Gustavo Santaolalla (*Brokeback Mountain*)
2006   Gustavo Santaolalla (*Babel*)

ORIGINAL SONG

1934   Con Conrad, Herb Magidson, "The Continental" from *The Gay Divorcee*
1935   Harry Warren, Al Dubin, "Lullaby of Broadway" from *Gold Diggers of 1935*
1936   Jerome Kern, Dorothy Fields, "The Way You Look Tonight" from *Swing Time*
1937   Harry Owens, "Sweet Leilani" from *Waikiki Wedding*
1938   Ralph Rainger, Leo Robin, "Thanks for the Memory" from *The Big Broadcast of 1938*
1939   Harold Arlen, E. Y. Harburg, "Over the Rainbow" from *The Wizard of Oz*
1940   Leigh Harline, Ned Washington, "When You Wish Upon a Star" from *Pinocchio*
1941   Jerome Kern, Oscar Hammerstein II, "The Last Time I Saw Paris" from *Lady Be Good*
1942   Irving Berlin, "White Christmas" from *Holiday Inn*
1943   Harry Warren, Mack Gordon, "You'll Never Know" from *Hello, Frisco, Hello*
1944   James Van Heusen, Johnny Burke, "Swinging on a Star" from *Going My Way*
1945   Richard Rodgers, Oscar Hammerstein, "It Might As Well Be Spring" from *State Fair*
1946   Harry Warren, Johnny Mercer, "On the Atchison, Topeka and the Santa Fe" from *The Harvey Girls*
1947   Allie Wrubel, Ray Gilbert, "Zip-a-dee-doo-dah" from *Song of the South*
1948   Jay Livingston, Ray Evans, "Buttons and Bows" from *The Paleface*
1949   Frank Loesser, "Baby, It's Cold Outside" from *Neptune's Daughter*
1950   Ray Evans, Jay Livingston, "Mona Lisa" from *Captain Carey, U.S.A.*
1951   Hoagy Carmichael, Johnny Mercer, "In the Cool, Cool, Cool of the Evening" from *Here Comes the Groom*
1952   Dimitri Tiomkin, Ned Washington, "High Noon (Do Not Forsake Me, Oh My Darlin')" from *High Noon*
1953   Sammy Fain, Paul Francis Webster, "Secret Love" from *Calamity Jane*

ORIGINAL SONG (CONTINUED)

1954   Jule Styne, Sammy Cahn, "Three Coins in the Fountain" from *Three Coins in the Fountain*
1955   Sammy Fain, Paul Francis Webster, "Love Is a Many-Splendored Thing" from *Love Is a Many-Splendored Thing*
1956   Jay Livingston, Ray Evans, "Whatever Will Be, Will Be (Que Sera, Sera)" from *The Man Who Knew Too Much*
1957   James Van Heusen, Sammy Cahn, "All the Way" from *The Joker is Wild*
1958   Frederick Loewe, Alan Jay Lerner, "Gigi" from *Gigi*
1959   James Van Heusen, Sammy Cahn, "High Hopes" from *A Hole in the Head*
1960   Manos Hadjidakis, "Never on Sunday" from *Never on Sunday*
1961   Henry Mancini, Johnny Mercer, "Moon River" from *Breakfast at Tiffany's*
1962   Henry Mancini, Johnny Mercer, "Days of Wine and Roses" from *Days of Wine and Roses*
1963   James Van Heusen, Sammy Cahn, "Call Me Irresponsible" from *Papa's Delicate Condition*
1964   Richard M. Sherman, Robert B. Sherman, "Chim Chim Cher-ee" from *Mary Poppins*
1965   Johnny Mandel, Paul Francis Webster, "The Shadow of Your Smile" from *The Sandpiper*
1966   John Barry, Don Black, "Born Free" from *Born Free*
1967   Leslie Bricusse, "Talk to the Animals" from *Doctor Doolittle*
1968   Michel Legrand, Alan Bergman, Marilyn Bergman, "The Windmills of Your Mind" from *The Thomas Crown Affair*
1969   Burt Bacharach, Hal David, "Raindrops Keep Fallin' On My Head" from *Butch Cassidy and the Sundance Kid*
1970   Fred Karlin, Robb Royer [aka Robb Wilson], James Griffin [aka Arthur James], "For All We Know" from *Lovers and Other Strangers*
1971   Isaac Hayes, "Theme from Shaft" from *Shaft*
1972   Al Kasha, Joel Hirschhorn, "The Morning After" from *The Poseidon Adventure*
1973   Marvin Hamlisch, Alan Bergman, Marilyn Bergman, "The Way We Were" from *The Way We Were*
1974   Al Kasha, Joel Hirschhorn, "We May Never Love Like This Again" from *The Towering Inferno*
1975   Keith Carradine, "I'm Easy" from *Nashville*
1976   Barbra Streisand, Paul Williams, "Evergreen (Love Theme from A Star is Born)" from *A Star is Born*
1977   Joseph Brooks, "You Light Up My Life" from *You Light Up My Life*
1978   Paul Jabara, "Last Dance" from *Thank God It's Friday*
1979   David Shire, Norman Gimbel, "It Goes Like It Goes" from *Norma Rae*
1980   Michael Gore, Dean Pitchford, "Fame" from *Fame*
1981   Burt Bacharach, Carole Bayer Sager, Christopher Cross, Peter Allen, "Arthur's Theme (Best That You Can Do)" from *Arthur*
1982   Jack Nitzsche, Buffy Sainte-Marie, Will Jennings, "Up Where We Belong" from *An Officer and a Gentleman*

Academy Awards (Oscars), 1928–2006 (continued)

ORIGINAL SONG (CONTINUED)

1983 Giorgio Moroder, Keith Forsey, Irene Cara, "Flashdance...What a Feeling" from *Flashdance*

1984 Stevie Wonder, "I Just Called to Say I Love You" from *The Woman in Red*

1985 Lionel Richie, "Say You, Say Me" from *White Nights*

1986 Giorgio Moroder, Tom Whitlock, "Take My Breath Away" from *Top Gun*

1987 Franke Previte, John DeNicola, Donald Markowitz, "(I've Had) The Time of My Life" from *Dirty Dancing*

1988 Carly Simon, "Let the River Run" from *Working Girl*

1989 Alan Menken, Howard Ashman, "Under the Sea" from *The Little Mermaid*

1990 Stephen Sondheim, "Sooner or Later (I Always Get My Man)" from *Dick Tracy*

1991 Alan Menken, Howard Ashman, "Beauty and the Beast" from *Beauty and the Beast*

1992 Alan Menken, Tim Rice, "A Whole New World" from *Aladdin*

1993 Bruce Springsteen, "Streets of Philadelphia" from *Philadelphia*

1994 Elton John, Tim Rice, "Can You Feel the Love Tonight" from *The Lion King*

ORIGINAL SONG (CONTINUED)

1995 Alan Menken, Stephen Schwartz, "Colors of the Wind" from *Pocahontas*

1996 Andrew Lloyd Webber, Tim Rice, "You Must Love Me" from *Evita*

1997 James Horner, Will Jennings, "My Heart Will Go On" from *Titanic*

1998 Stephen Schwartz, "When You Believe" from *The Prince of Egypt*

1999 Phil Collins, "You'll Be in My Heart" from *Tarzan*

2000 Bob Dylan, "Things Have Changed" from *Wonder Boys*

2001 Randy Newman, "If I Didn't Have You" from *Monsters, Inc.*

2002 Eminem, Jeff Bass, Luis Resto, "Lose Yourself" from *8 Mile*

2003 Fran Walsh, Howard Shore, Annie Lennox, "Into the West," from *The Lord of the Rings: The Return of the King*

2004 Jorge Drexler, "Al otro lado del río," from *The Motorcycle Diaries*

2005 Jordan Houston, Cedric Coleman, Paul Beauregard, "It's Hard Out Here for a Pimp" from *Hustle & Flow*

2006 Melissa Etheridge, "I Need To Wake Up," from *An Inconvenient Truth*

[1]The current screenplay categories were adopted for the 1957 awards. Until then, various separate writing awards were given for silent-film title writing, screenplay, story and screenplay, and motion picture story. [2]Screenplay (for script only).   [3]Story and screenplay (for narrative and script; also called original screenplay).   [4]Motion picture story (for narrative only; also called original story).   [5]Actual winner was blacklisted at the time of the award and the honored work was attributed to another name or person; pseudonym or nominal winner listed in parentheses.   [6]Black and white.   [7]Color.   [8]Until 1963, both visual and sound effects were honored as special effects. Only those awards for visual effects are listed here.   [9]Scoring. [10]Drama or not a musical.   [11]Musical   [12]Song score.   [13]Musical or comedy.

Sundance Film Festival, 2007

Founded as the Utah/US Film Festival in Salt Lake City in 1978, the exhibition has traditionally focused on documentary and dramatic works from outside the Hollywood mainstream. It came under the auspices of actor Robert Redford's Sundance Institute in 1985 and is held every January in Park City UT.

Sundance Institute Web site: <www.sundance.org>.

American Grand Jury Prize, drama	*Padre Nuestro* (*Our Father*; US; director, Christopher Zalla)
American Grand Jury Prize, documentary	*Manda Bala* (*Send a Bullet*; US/Brazil; director, Jason Kohn)
World Grand Jury Prize, drama	*Adama Meshugaat* (*Sweet Mud*; Israel; director, Dror Shaul)
World Grand Jury Prize, documentary	*Vores Lykkes Fjender* (*Enemies of Happiness*; Denmark; directors, Eva Mulvad and Anja Al Erhayem)
Audience Award, drama	*Grace Is Gone* (US; director, James C. Strouse)
Audience Award, documentary	*Hear and Now* (US; director, Irene Taylor Brodsky)
Audience Award, world cinema, drama	*Once* (Ireland; director, John Carney)
Audience Award, world cinema, documentary	*In the Shadow of the Moon* (UK; director, David Sington)
Best director, drama	Jeffrey Blitz (*Rocket Science*, US)
Best director, documentary	Sean Fine and Andrea Nix Fine (*War Dance*, US)
Cinematography, drama	Benoit Debie (*Joshua*, US)
Cinematography, documentary	Heloisa Passos (*Manda Bala* [*Send a Bullet*], US/Brazil)
Waldo Salt Screenwriting Award	James C. Strouse, (*Grace Is Gone*, US)
Special Jury Prize, documentary	*No End in Sight* (US; director, Charles Ferguson)
Special Jury Prize, world cinema, documentary	*Hot House* (Israel; director, Shimon Dotan)
Special Jury Prize, drama (acting)	Jess Weixler (*Teeth*, US); Tamara Podemski (*Four Sheets to the Wind*, US)
Special Jury Prize, drama (singularity of vision)	Chris Smith (*The Pool*, US)

Sundance Film Festival, 2007 (continued)

Special Jury Prize, world cinema, drama	*L'Heritage* (*The Legacy*; France; directors, Géla Babluani and Temur Babluani
Jury Prize, short filmmaking	*Everything Will Be Okay* (US; director, Don Hertzfeldt); *The Tube with a Hat* (Romania; director, Radu Jude)
Sundance/NHK International Filmmakers Award	*Agnus Dei* (Argentina; director, Lucía Cedrón); *Bury Me Standing* (US; director, Caran Hartsfield); *Two by the River* (Japan; director, Tomoko Kana); and *The Good Heart* (Iceland; director, Dagur Kári)
Alfred P. Sloan Prize	*Dark Matter* (US; director, Chen Shi-Zhen)

Golden Globes, 2007

The Hollywood Foreign Press Association, a group of non-US film critics working in Hollywood, began awarding prizes for outstanding American motion pictures and acting in 1944 and created the Golden Globe Award in 1945. Over the years the prizes have expanded from recognizing only motion pictures and actors and actresses to include direction (1946),

screenwriting and film music (1947), foreign-language film (1950), and television (1955), as well as a number of other categories of achievement. Prize: globe encircled by a strip of motion picture film, in gold.

Golden Globes/Hollywood Foreign Press Association Web site: <www.hfpa.org>.

Film

Drama	*Babel* (director, Alejandro González Iñárritu)
Musical/comedy	*Dreamgirls* (director, Bill Condon)
Director	Martin Scorsese (*The Departed*)
Actress, drama	Helen Mirren (*The Queen*)
Actor, drama	Forest Whitaker (*The Last King of Scotland*)
Actress, musical/comedy	Meryl Streep (*The Devil Wears Prada*)
Actor, musical/comedy	Sacha Baron Cohen (*Borat: Cultural Learnings of America for Make Benefit Glorious Nation of Kazakhstan*)
Best foreign-language film	*Letters from Iwo Jima* (Japan/US; director, Clint Eastwood)
Supporting actress	Jennifer Hudson (*Dreamgirls*)
Supporting actor	Eddie Murphy (*Dreamgirls*)
Screenplay	Peter Morgan (*The Queen*)
Original score	Alexandre Desplat (*The Painted Veil*)
Original song	"The Song of the Heart" (*Happy Feet*), music and lyrics, Prince Rogers Nelson

Television

Drama series	*Grey's Anatomy*, Touchstone Television
Actress, drama series	Kyra Sedgwick (*The Closer*)
Actor, drama series	Hugh Laurie (*House*)
Musical/comedy series	*Ugly Betty*, Touchstone Television
Actress, musical/comedy series	America Ferrera (*Ugly Betty*)
Actor, musical/comedy series	Alec Baldwin (*30 Rock*)
Miniseries/movie for TV	*Elizabeth I*, Company Pictures/channel 4/HBO Films
Actress, miniseries/movie for TV	Helen Mirren (*Elizabeth I*)
Actor, miniseries/movie for TV	Bill Nighy (*Gideon's Daughter*)
Supporting actress, series/miniseries/movie	Emily Blunt (*Gideon's Daughter*)
Supporting actor, series/miniseries/movie	Jeremy Irons (*Elizabeth I*)

Toronto International Film Festival, 2006

Founded in 1976, the Toronto International Film Festival is one of North America's best-attended exhibitions and a frequent forum for the premiere of major feature films. The festival, held in September, awards

seven prizes, three of which are for Canadian films.

Toronto International Film Festival Web site: <www.e.bell.ca/filmfest>.

Canadian feature film	*Manufactured Landscapes* (director, Jennifer Baichwal)
Canadian first feature	*Sur la trace d'Igor Rizzi* (director, Noël Mitrani)
Canadian short	*Les Jours* (director, Maxime Giroux)
FIPRESCI Prize	*Death of a President* (UK; director, Gabriel Range)
People's Choice Award	*Bella* (USA; director, Alejandro Gómez Monteverde
Discovery Award	*Reprise* (Norway; director, Joachim Trier)
Cultural Innovation Award	*Tavka: A Man's Fear of God* (Turkey/Germany; director, Ozer Kiziltan)

Cannes International Film Festival, 2007

Established in 1946, the Cannes International Film Festival is among the best known and most influential film exhibitions in the world. Some 50 feature films and 30 short films are chosen for several categories of the Official Selection each year, with a majority of those competing for the festival's various prizes. A nine-member feature-film jury and a four-member short-film and Cinéfondation jury give awards to the best film (Palme d'Or) and other outstanding films (special jury prizes) in their respective categories. The Grand Prix goes to the feature film judged the most original, and the feature jury also chooses the winners of the performance, direction, and screenplay awards. The Caméra d'Or, for best first film, draws on feature films from the Official Selection and from two parallel exhibitions, the Directors' Fortnight and the International Critics' Week, and is awarded by a jury comprising film industry professionals and members of the moviegoing public. The Cinéfondation awards are for works of one hour or less by film-school students.

Cannes International Film Festival Web site: <www.festival-cannes.com>.

feature films ▸ **Palme d'Or:** 4 luni, 3 saptamini, si 2 zile (4 Months, 3 Weeks, and 2 Days) (Romania; director, Cristian Mungiu); ▸ **Grand Prix:** Mogari no mori (The Mourning Forest) (Japan/France; director, Naomi Kawase); ▸ **Best actress:** Jeon Do Yeon (Secret Sunshine, South Korea); ▸ **Best actor:** Konstantin Lavronenko (Izgnanie [The Banishment], Russia); ▸ **Best direction:** Julian Schnabel (Le Scaphandre et le papillon [The Diving Bell and the Butterfly], France/US); ▸ **Best screenplay:** Fatih Akin (Auf der anderen seite [The Edge of Heaven], Germany/Turkey); ▸ **Special jury award:** Persepolis (France; directors, Marjane Satrapi and Vincent Paronnaud); Stellet Licht (Silent Light) (Mexico/France/The Netherlands; director, Carlos Reygadas); ▸ **Caméra d'Or:** Meduzot (France/Israel; directors, Etgar Keret and Shira Geffen)

short films ▸ **Palme d'Or:** Ver llover (Watching It Rain) (Mexico; director, Elisa Miller); ▸ **Special distinction:** Ah ma (Grandma) (Singapore; director, Anthony Chen); Run (New Zealand; director, Mark Albiston)

Cinéfondation ▸ **1st prize:** Ahora todos parecen contentos (Argentina; director, Gonzalo Tobal); ▸ **2nd prize:** Ru dao (Way Out) (China; director, Chen Tao); ▸ **3rd prize:** A Reunion (South Korea; director, Hong Sung Hoon); Minus (Serbia/Montenegro; director, Pavle Vuckovic)

Berlin International Film Festival, 2007

The Berlin International Film Festival (Internationale Filmfestspiele Berlin), held annually since its founding in West Berlin in 1951, comprises some 20 separate competitions and juries emphasizing aspects of both worldwide and German cinema, each with their own prizes. The International Jury, made up of film-industry figures from across the globe, selects the winners of the Golden and Silver Berlin Bears, the festival's top awards.

Berlin International Film Festival Web site: <www.berlinale.de>.

Golden Berlin Bear	Tu ya de hun shi (China; director, Wang Quan'an)
Jury Grand Prize (Silver Bear)	El otro (The Other) (Argentina/France/Germany; director, Ariel Rotter)
Silver Berlin Bear, director	Joseph Cedar (Beaufort, Israel)
Silver Berlin Bear, actress	Nina Hoss (Yella, Germany)
Silver Berlin Bear, actor	Julio Chavez (El otro [The Other], Argentina/France/Germany)
Silver Berlin Bear, artistic contribution	Ensemble cast (The Good Shepherd, US)
Silver Berlin Bear, film music	David Mackenzie (Hallam Foe, UK)
Alfred Bauer Prize for a work of particular innovation	Sai bo gu ji man gwen chan a (I'm a Cyborg, but That's OK, South Korea; director, Park Chan-wook)
Ecumenical Jury Prizes	Competition: Tu ya de hun shi (Tuya's Marriage; China; director, Wang Quan'an); Panorama: Luo Ye Gui Gen (Getting Home; Hong Kong; director, Zhang Yang); Forum: Chrigu (Switzerland; directors, Jan Gassmann and Christian Ziörjen)
FIPRESCI Awards	Competition: Obsluhoval jsem anglického krále (I Served the King of England; Czech Republic; director, Jiri Menzel); Panorama: Takva—A Man's Fear of God (Turkey; director, Ozer Kiziltan); Forum: Jagdhunde (Hounds; Germany; director, Ann-Kristin Reyels)

US National Film Registry

The US Library of Congress established the National Film Preservation Board in 1988 with the goal of identifying "culturally, historically, or aesthetically important" American films. The board selects 25 films to add to the National Film Registry every year.

National Film Registry Web site: <www.loc.gov/film/>.

US National Film Registry (continued)

Abbott and Costello Meet
   Frankenstein (1948)
Adam's Rib (1949)
The Adventures of Robin Hood
   (1938)
The African Queen (1951)
Alien (1979)
All About Eve (1950)
All My Babies (1953)
All Quiet on the Western Front
   (1930)
All That Heaven Allows (1955)
All That Jazz (1979)
All the King's Men (1949)
America, America (1963)
American Graffiti (1973)
An American in Paris (1951)
Annie Hall (1977)
Antonia: A Portrait of the
   Woman (1974)
The Apartment (1960)
Apocalypse Now (1979)
Applause (1929)
Atlantic City (1980)
The Awful Truth (1937)
Baby Face (1933)
The Bad and the Beautiful (1953)
Badlands (1973)
The Band Wagon (1953)
The Bank Dick (1940)
The Battle of San Pietro (1945)
Beauty and the Beast (1991)
Ben-Hur (1926)
Ben-Hur (1959)
The Best Years of Our Lives (1946)
Big Business (1929)
The Big Parade (1925)
The Big Trail (1930)
The Big Sleep (1946)
The Birth of a Nation (1915)
The Black Pirate (1926)
The Black Stallion (1979)
Blacksmith Scene (1893)
Blade Runner (1982)
Blazing Saddles (1974)
The Blood of Jesus (1941)
The Blue Bird (1918)
Bonnie and Clyde (1967)
Boyz n the Hood (1991)
Bride of Frankenstein (1935)
The Bridge on the River Kwai
   (1957)
Bringing Up Baby (1938)
Broken Blossoms (1919)
A Bronx Morning (1931)
The Buffalo Creek Flood: An Act
   of Man (1975)
Butch Cassidy and the
   Sundance Kid (1969)
Cabaret (1972)
The Cameraman (1928)
Carmen Jones (1954)
Casablanca (1942)
Castro Street (1966)
Cat People (1942)
Chan Is Missing (1982)
The Cheat (1915)
The Chechahcos (1924)
Chinatown (1974)

Chulas Fronteras (1976)
Citizen Kane (1941)
The City (1939)
City Lights (1931)
Civilization (1916)
Clash of the Wolves (1925)
Cologne: From the Diary of Ray
   and Esther (1939)
Commandment Keeper Church,
   Beaufort, South Carolina, May
   1940 (1940)
The Conversation (1974)
Cool Hand Luke (1967)
The Cool World (1963)
Cops (1922)
A Corner in Wheat (1909)
The Court Jester (1956)
The Crowd (1928)
The Curse of Quon Gwon
   (1916–17)
Czechoslovakia 1968 (1969)
Daughter of Shanghai (1937)
Daughters of the Dust (1991)
David Holzman's Diary (1968)
The Day the Earth Stood Still
   (1951)
Dead Birds (1964)
The Deer Hunter (1978)
Destry Rides Again (1939)
Detour (1946)
Dickson Experimental Sound
   Film (1894–95)
D.O.A. (1950)
Do the Right Thing (1989)
The Docks of New York (1928)
Dodsworth (1936)
Dog Star Man: Part IV (1964)
Don't Look Back (1967)
Double Indemnity (1944)
Dr. Strangelove or: How I
   Learned To Stop Worrying and
   Love the Bomb (1964)
Dracula (1931)
Drums of Winter (1988)
Duck Amuck (1953)
Duck and Cover (1951)
Duck Soup (1933)
E.T.: The Extra-Terrestrial (1982)
Early Abstractions #1–5, 7, 10
   (1939–56)
Easy Rider (1969)
Eaux d'Artifice (1953)
El Norte (1983)
Empire (1964)
The Emperor Jones (1933)
The Endless Summer (1966)
Enter the Dragon (1973)
Eraserhead (1977)
Evidence of the Film (1913)
The Exploits of Elaine (1914)
The Fall of the House of
   Usher (1928)
Fantasia (1940)
Fargo (1996)
Fast Times at Ridgemont High
   (1982)
Fatty's Tintype Tangle (1915)
Film Portrait (1970)
Five Easy Pieces (1970)

Flash Gordon (series) (1936)
Flesh and the Devil (1927)
Footlight Parade (1933)
Force of Evil (1948)
The Forgotten Frontier (1931)
42nd Street (1933)
The Four Horsemen of
   the Apocalypse (1921)
Fox Movietone News: Jenkins
   Orphanage Band (1928)
Frank Film (1973)
Frankenstein (1931)
Freaks (1932)
The French Connection (1971)
The Freshman (1925)
From Here to Eternity (1953)
From Stump to Ship (1930)
From the Manger to the
   Cross (1912)
Fuji (1974)
Fury (1936)
Garlic Is As Good As Ten
   Mothers (1980)
The General (1927)
Gerald McBoing-Boing (1950)
Gertie the Dinosaur (1914)
Giant (1956)
Gigi (1958)
The Godfather (1972)
The Godfather, Part II (1974)
Going My Way (1944)
Gold Diggers of 1933 (1933)
The Gold Rush (1925)
Gone with the Wind (1939)
Goodfellas (1990)
The Graduate (1967)
The Grapes of Wrath (1940)
Grass: A Nation's Battle for
   Life (1925)
The Great Dictator (1940)
The Great Train Robbery
   (1903)
Greed (1924)
Groundhog Day (1993)
Gun Crazy (1949)
Gunga Din (1939)
H2O (1929)
Halloween (1978)
Hands Up (1929)
Harlan County, U.S.A. (1976)
Harold and Maude (1971)
The Heiress (1949)
Hell's Hinges (1916)
High Noon (1952)
High School (1968)
Hindenburg Disaster Newsreel
   Footage (1937)
His Girl Friday (1940)
The Hitch-Hiker (1953)
Hoop Dreams (1994)
Hoosiers (1986)
Hospital (1970)
The Hospital (1971)
The House in the Middle (1954)
House of Usher (1960)
How Green Was My Valley (1941)
How the West Was Won (1962)
The Hunters (1957)
The Hustler (1961)

US National Film Registry (continued)

I Am a Fugitive from a Chain Gang (1932)
The Immigrant (1917)
Imitation of Life (1934)
In the Heat of the Night (1967)
In the Land of the Head Hunters (1914)
In the Street (1948–52)
Intolerance (1916)
Invasion of the Body Snatchers (1956)
It (1927)
It Happened One Night (1934)
The Italian (1915)
It's a Wonderful Life (1946)
Jailhouse Rock (1957)
Jam Session (1942)
Jammin' the Blues (1944)
Jaws (1975)
Jazz on a Summer's Day (1959)
The Jazz Singer (1927)
Jeffries-Johnson World's Championship Boxing Contest (1910)
Kannapolis, NC (1941)
Killer of Sheep (1977)
King: A Filmed Record... Montgomery to Memphis (1970)
King Kong (1933)
The Kiss (1896)
Kiss Me Deadly (1955)
Knute Rockne, All American (1940)
Koyaanisqatsi (1983)
The Lady Eve (1941)
Lady Helen's Escapade (1909)
Lady Windermere's Fan (1925)
Lambchops (1929)
The Land Beyond the Sunset (1912)
Lassie Come Home (1943)
The Last Command (1928)
The Last of the Mohicans (1920)
The Last Picture Show (1971)
Laura (1944)
Lawrence of Arabia (1962)
The Learning Tree (1969)
Let's All Go to the Lobby (1957)
Letter from an Unknown Woman (1948)
The Life and Death of 9413: A Hollywood Extra (1928)
The Life and Times of Rosie the Riveter (1980)
The Life of Emile Zola (1937)
Little Caesar (1930)
Little Fugitive (1953)
Little Miss Marker (1934)
The Living Desert (1953)
The Lost World (1925)
Louisiana Story (1948)
Love Finds Andy Hardy (1938)
Love Me Tonight (1932)
Magical Maestro (1952)
The Magnificent Ambersons (1942)
The Making of an American (1920)
The Maltese Falcon (1941)
The Manchurian Candidate (1962)

Manhatta (1921)
Manhattan (1979)
March of Time: Inside Nazi Germany (1938)
Marian Anderson: The Lincoln Memorial Concert (1939)
Marty (1955)
M*A*S*H (1970)
Master Hands (1936)
Matrimony's Speed Limit (1913)
Mean Streets (1973)
Medium Cool (1969)
Meet Me in St. Louis (1944)
Melody Ranch (1940)
The Memphis Belle: A Story of a Flying Fortress (1944)
Meshes of the Afternoon (1943)
Midnight Cowboy (1969)
Mildred Pierce (1945)
The Miracle of Morgan's Creek (1944)
Miracle on 34th Street (1947)
Miss Lulu Bett (1921)
Modern Times (1936)
Modesta (1956)
Mom and Dad (1944)
Morocco (1930)
Motion Painting No. 1 (1947)
A Movie (1958)
Mr. Smith Goes to Washington (1939)
Multiple Sidosis (1970)
The Music Box (1932)
The Music Man (1962)
My Darling Clementine (1946)
My Man Godfrey (1936)
The Naked Spur (1953)
Nanook of the North (1922)
Nashville (1975)
National Lampoon's Animal House (1978)
National Velvet (1944)
Naughty Marietta (1935)
Network (1976)
A Night at the Opera (1935)
The Night of the Hunter (1955)
Night of the Living Dead (1968)
Ninotchka (1939)
North by Northwest (1959)
Nostalgia (1971)
Nothing but a Man (1964)
Notorious (1946)
The Nutty Professor (1963)
OffOn (1968)
On the Waterfront (1954)
One Flew over the Cuckoo's Nest (1975)
One Froggy Evening (1955)
Out of the Past (1947)
The Outlaw Josey Wales (1976)
The Ox-Bow Incident (1943)
Pass the Gravy (1928)
Paths of Glory (1957)
Patton (1970)
The Pearl (1948)
Peter Pan (1924)
The Phantom of the Opera (1925)
The Philadelphia Story (1940)
Pinocchio (1940)

A Place in the Sun (1951)
Planet of the Apes (1968)
The Plow That Broke the Plains (1936)
Point of Order (1964)
The Poor Little Rich Girl (1917)
Popeye the Sailor Meets Sindbad the Sailor (1936)
Porky in Wackyland (1938)
Power of the Press (1928)
Powers of Ten (1978)
President McKinley Inauguration Footage (1901)
Primary (1960)
Princess Nicotine; or, The Smoke Fairy (1909)
The Prisoner of Zenda (1937)
The Producers (1968)
Psycho (1960)
The Public Enemy (1931)
Pull My Daisy (1958)
Punch Drunks (1934)
Pups Is Pups (Our Gang) (1930)
Raging Bull (1980)
Raiders of the Lost Ark (1981)
A Raisin in the Sun (1961)
Rear Window (1954)
Rebel Without a Cause (1955)
Red Dust (1932)
Red River (1948)
Regeneration (1915)
Reminiscences of a Journey to Lithuania (1971–72)
Republic Steel Strike Riot Newsreel Footage (1937)
Return of the Secaucus 7 (1980)
Ride the High Country (1962)
Rip Van Winkle (1896)
The River (1937)
Road to Morocco (1942)
Rocky (1976)
The Rocky Horror Picture Show (1975)
Roman Holiday (1953)
Rose Hobart (1936)
Sabrina (1954)
Safety Last (1923)
Salesman (1969)
Salome (1922)
Salt of the Earth (1954)
San Francisco Earthquake and Fire, April 18, 1906 (1906)
Scarface (1932)
Schindler's List (1993)
The Searchers (1956)
Serene Velocity (1970)
Sex, Lies, and Videotape (1989)
Seven Brides for Seven Brothers (1954)
Seventh Heaven (1927)
Shadow of a Doubt (1943)
Shadows (1959)
Shaft (1971)
Shane (1953)
She Done Him Wrong (1933)
Sherlock, Jr. (1924)
Sherman's March (1986)
Shock Corridor (1963)

US National Film Registry (continued)

The Shop Around the
  Corner (1940)
Show Boat (1936)
Show People (1928)
Siege (1940)
Singin' in the Rain (1952)
Sky High (1922)
Snow White (1933)
Snow White and the
  Seven Dwarfs (1937)
Some Like It Hot (1959)
The Son of the Sheik (1926)
The Sound of Music (1965)
St. Louis Blues (1929)
Stagecoach (1939)
A Star Is Born (1954)
Star Theatre (1901)
Star Wars (1977)
Steamboat Willie (1928)
The Sting (1973)
Stormy Weather (1943)
Stranger Than Paradise (1984)
A Streetcar Named Desire (1951)
Sullivan's Travels (1941)
Sunrise (1927)
Sunset Boulevard (1950)
Sweet Smell of Success (1957)
Swing Time (1936)
The T.A.M.I. Show (1964)
Tabu (1931)
Tacoma Narrows Bridge
  Collapse (1940)
The Tall T (1957)
Tarzan and His Mate (1934)
Taxi Driver (1976)
The Tell-Tale Heart (1953)

The Ten Commandments (1956)
Tess of the Storm Country (1914)
Tevye (1939)
Theodore Case Sound Test:
  Gus Visser and His Singing
  Duck (1925)
There It Is (1928)
The Thief of Bagdad (1924)
The Thin Blue Line (1988)
The Thin Man (1934)
The Thing from Another
  World (1951)
Think of Me First as a Person
  (1960-75)
This Js Cinerama (1952)
This Is Spinal Tap (1984)
Through Navajo Eyes
  (series) (1966)
A Time for Burning (1966)
A Time out of War (1954)
Tin Toy (1988)
To Be or Not To Be (1942)
To Fly (1976)
To Kill a Mockingbird (1962)
Tootsie (1982)
Top Hat (1935)
Topaz (1945)
Touch of Evil (1958)
Toy Story (1995)
Traffic in Souls (1913)
Trance and Dance in Bali (1952)
The Treasure of the Sierra
  Madre (1948)
Trouble in Paradise (1932)
Tulips Shall Grow (1942)
Twelve O'Clock High (1949)

2001: A Space Odyssey (1968)
Unforgiven (1992)
Verbena Tragica (1939)
Vertigo (1958)
The Wedding March (1928)
West Side Story (1961)
Westinghouse Works (1904)
What's Opera, Doc? (1957)
Where Are My Children? (1916)
White Heat (1949)
Why Man Creates (1968)
Why We Fight (series) (1943-45)
Wild and Woolly (1917)
The Wild Bunch (1969)
Wild River (1960)
Will Success Spoil Rock
  Hunter? (1957)
The Wind (1928)
Wings (1927)
Within Our Gates (1920)
The Wizard of Oz (1939)
Woman of the Year (1942)
A Woman Under the
  Influence (1974)
Woodstock (1970)
Yankee Doodle Dandy (1942)
Young Frankenstein (1974)
Young Mr. Lincoln (1939)
Zapruder Film of Kennedy
  Assassination (1963)

Worldwide Top-Grossing Films (Actual Dollars)

As of 5 Aug 2007. Includes reissues. Source: Exhibitor Relations Co., Inc.

1	Titanic	1997
2	The Lord of the Rings: The Return of the King	2003
3	Pirates of the Caribbean: Dead Man's Chest	2006
4	Harry Potter and the Sorcerer's Stone	2001
5	Pirates of the Caribbean: At World's End	2007
6	The Lord of the Rings: The Two Towers	2002
7	Star Wars: The Phantom Menace	1999
8	Shrek 2	2004
9	Jurassic Park	1993
10	Harry Potter and the Goblet of Fire	2005
11	Spider-Man 3	2007
12	Harry Potter and the Chamber of Secrets	2002
13	The Lord of the Rings: The Fellowship of the Ring	2001
14	Finding Nemo	2003
15	Star Wars: Revenge of the Sith	2005
16	Spider-Man	2002
17	Independence Day	1996
18	E.T.: The Extra-Terrestrial	1982
19	Harry Potter and the Prisoner of Azkaban	2004
20	The Lion King	1994
21	Spider-Man 2	2004
22	Star Wars	1977
23	Harry Potter and the Order of the Phoenix	2007
24	The Da Vinci Code	2006
25	The Chronicles of Narnia: The Lion, the Witch, and the Wardrobe	2005

Top US Video Rentals and Sales, 2006

Data reflect DVD rentals and sales.
Source: Video Business. Web site: <www.videobusiness.com>.

	RENTALS	SALES
1	Flightplan	Pirates of the Caribbean: Dead Man's Chest
2	Wedding Crashers	Cars

Top US Video Rentals and Sales, 2006 (continued)

	RENTALS	SALES
3	Walk the Line	The Chronicles of Narnia: The Lion, the Witch, and the Wardrobe
4	Failure To Launch	Harry Potter and the Goblet of Fire
5	Fun with Dick and Jane	Over the Hedge
6	Click	King Kong
7	Inside Man	Ice Age: The Meltdown
8	King Kong	Wedding Crashers
9	RV	Walk the Line
10	Lord of War	The Little Mermaid
11	The Benchwarmers	Chicken Little
12	Rumor Has It...	The Da Vinci Code
13	The Break-Up	Lady and the Tramp
14	The Family Stone	X-Men: The Last Stand
15	The Chronicles of Narnia: The Lion, the Witch, and the Wardrobe	Talladega Nights: The Ballad of Ricky Bobby
16	Derailed	High School Musical
17	Jarhead	Superman Returns
18	The Lake House	Bambi II
19	Firewall	The Devil Wears Prada
20	A History of Violence	Grey's Anatomy (Season 2)

US Top-Grossing Films in Constant US Dollars (Estimated)

Admissions—the number of tickets sold to a movie—tell a different story from the raw dollars earned. While recent films have made hundreds of millions of dollars, only 2 of the top 10 films in terms of attendance were released after 1980. Includes reissues. Source: Exhibitor Relations Co., Inc.

		ADMISSIONS	2007 US DOLLARS	ACTUAL US DOLLARS
1	Gone with the Wind (1939)	202,044,600	1,329,453,600	198,676,459
2	Star Wars (1977)	178,119,600	1,172,026,900	460,998,007
3	The Sound of Music (1965)	142,415,400	937,093,200	158,671,368
4	E.T. the Extra-Terrestrial (1982)	141,854,300	933,401,500	434,949,459
5	The Ten Commandments (1956)	131,000,000	861,980,000	65,500,000
6	Titanic (1997)	128,345,900	844,515,900	600,788,188
7	Jaws (1975)	128,078,800	842,758,600	260,000,000
8	Doctor Zhivago (1965)	124,135,500	816,811,300	111,721,910
9	The Exorcist (1973)	110,568,700	727,541,800	232,671,011
10	Snow White and the Seven Dwarfs (1937)	109,000,000	717,220,000	184,925,486

US Top-Grossing Film Openings

As of 29 Jul 2007. Table lists the largest box-office receipts over the first three days of theatrical release in the United States. Source: Exhibitor Relations Co., Inc.

		ACTUAL US DOLLARS			ACTUAL US DOLLARS
1	Spider-Man 3 (2007)	151,116,516	13	Harry Potter and the Chamber of Secrets (2002)	88,357,488
2	Pirates of the Caribbean: Dead Man's Chest (2006)	135,634,554	14	Spider-Man 2 (2004)	88,156,227
3	Shrek the Third (2007)	121,629,270	15	X2: X-Men United (2003)	85,558,731
4	Spider-Man (2002)	114,844,116	16	The Passion of the Christ (2004)	83,848,082
5	Pirates of the Caribbean: At World's End (2007)	114,732,820	17	Star Wars: Attack of the Clones (2002)	80,027,814
6	Star Wars: Revenge of the Sith (2005)	108,435,841	18	Harry Potter and the Order of the Phoenix	77,108,414
7	Shrek 2 (2004)	108,037,878	19	The Da Vinci Code (2006)	77,073,388
8	X-Men: The Last Stand (2006)	102,750,665	20	The Simpsons Movie	74,036,787
9	Harry Potter and the Goblet of Fire (2005)	102,335,066	21	Austin Powers in Goldmember (2002)	73,071,188
10	Harry Potter and the Prisoner of Azkaban (2004)	93,687,367	22	Lord of the Rings: The Return of the King (2003)	72,629,713
11	The Matrix Reloaded (2003)	91,774,413	23	The Lost World: Jurassic Park (1997)	72,132,785
12	Harry Potter and the Sorcerer's Stone (2001)	90,294,621	24	300 (2007)	70,885,301
			25	Transformers (2007)	70,502,384

Television

Emmy Award-winning Television Series, 1948–2006

1948
Most popular program: *Pantomime Quiz*, KTLA
TV film: "The Necklace," *Your Show Time*

1949
Live show: *The Ed Wynn Show*, KTTV
Kinescope show: *The Texaco Star Theater*, KNBH (NBC)
TV film: *The Life of Riley*, KNBH
Pub. svc./cultural/educ.: *Crusade in Europe*, KECA-TV/KTTV (ABC)
Children's: *Time for Beany*, KTLA

1950
Variety: *The Alan Young Show*, KTTV (CBS)
Drama: *Pulitzer Prize Playhouse*, KECA-TV (ABC)
Game/audience particip.: *Truth or Consequences*, KTTV (CBS)
Children's: *Time for Beany*, KTLA
Educational: *KFI-TV University*, KFI-TV
Cultural: *Campus Chorus and Orchestra*, KTSL

1951
Variety: *Your Show of Shows* (NBC)
Comedy: *The Red Skelton Show* (NBC)
Drama: *Studio One* (CBS)

1952
Variety: *Your Show of Shows* (NBC)
Comedy: *I Love Lucy* (CBS)
Drama: *Robert Montgomery Presents* (NBC)
Mystery/action/adventure: *Dragnet* (NBC)
Public affairs: *See It Now* (CBS)
Aud. particip./quiz/panel: *What's My Line?* (CBS)
Children's: *Time for Beany* (syndicated)

1953
Variety: *Omnibus* (CBS)
Comedy: *I Love Lucy* (CBS)
Drama: *The U.S. Steel Hour* (ABC)
Mystery/action/adventure: *Dragnet* (NBC)
Public affairs: *Victory at Sea* (NBC)
Aud. particip./quiz/panel: *This Is Your Life* (NBC); *What's My Line?* (CBS)
Children's: *Kukla, Fran, and Ollie* (NBC)

1954
Variety: *Disneyland* (ABC)
Comedy: *Make Room for Daddy* (ABC)
Drama: *The United States Steel Hour* (ABC)
Mystery/intrigue: *Dragnet* (NBC)
Western/adventure: *Stories of the Century* (syndicated)
Cultural/relig./educ.: *Omnibus* (CBS)
Aud. particip./quiz/panel: *This Is Your Life* (NBC)
Children's: *Lassie* (CBS)

1955
Variety: *The Ed Sullivan Show* (CBS)
Comedy: *The Phil Silvers Show: You'll Never Get Rich* (CBS)
Drama: *Producers' Showcase* (NBC)
Action/adventure: *Disneyland* (ABC)
Music: *Your Hit Parade* (NBC)
Documentary: *Omnibus* (CBS)
Aud. particip.: *The $64,000 Question* (CBS)
Children's: *Lassie* (CBS)

1956
Series (½ hr. or less): *The Phil Silvers Show: You'll Never Get Rich* (CBS) •
Series (1 hr. or more): *Caesar's Hour* (NBC)
New series: *Playhouse 90* (CBS)

1957
Mus./var./aud. par./quiz: *The Dinah Shore Chevy Show* (NBC)
Comedy: *The Phil Silvers Show: You'll Never Get Rich* (CBS)
Drama, continuing: *Gunsmoke* (CBS)
Drama, anthology: *Playhouse 90* (CBS)
New series: *The Seven Lively Arts* (CBS)
Public service: *Omnibus* (ABC/NBC)

1959[1]
Musical/variety: *The Dinah Shore Chevy Show* (NBC)
Comedy: *The Jack Benny Show* (CBS)
Drama (<1 hr.): *Alcoa-Goodyear Playhouse* (NBC)
Drama (1 hr.+): *Playhouse 90* (CBS)
Western: *Maverick* (ABC)
News reporting: *The Huntley-Brinkley Report* (NBC)
Public service: *Omnibus* (NBC)
Panel/quiz/aud. particip.: *What's My Line?* (CBS)

1960
Variety: "The Fabulous Fifties" (CBS)
Humor: "Art Carney Special" (NBC)
Drama: *Playhouse 90* (CBS)
News: *The Huntley-Brinkley Report* (NBC)
Public affairs/education: *The Twentieth Century* (CBS)
Children's: *Huckleberry Hound* (syndicated)

1961
Variety: *Astaire Time* (NBC)
Humor: *The Jack Benny Show* (CBS)
Drama: "Macbeth," *Hallmark Hall of Fame* (NBC)
News: *The Huntley-Brinkley Report* (NBC)
Public affairs/education: *The Twentieth Century* (CBS)
Children's: "Aaron Copland's Birthday Party," *Young People's Concert* (CBS)
Program of the year: "Macbeth," *Hallmark Hall of Fame* (NBC)

1962
Variety: *The Garry Moore Show* (CBS)
Humor: *The Bob Newhart Show* (NBC)
Drama: *The Defenders* (CBS)
News: *The Huntley-Brinkley Report* (NBC)
Educational/public affairs: *David Brinkley's Journal* (NBC)
Children's: "New York Philharmonic Young People's Concert with Leonard Bernstein" (CBS)
Program of the year: "Victoria Regina," *Hallmark Hall of Fame* (NBC)

1963
Variety: *The Andy Williams Show* (NBC)
Humor: *The Dick Van Dyke Show* (CBS)
Drama: *The Defenders* (CBS)
News: *The Huntley-Brinkley Report* (NBC)
Commentary/public affairs: *David Brinkley's Journal* (NBC)
Documentary: "The Tunnel" (NBC)
Panel/quiz/aud. particip.: *G-E College Bowl* (CBS)

Emmy Award-winning Television Series, 1948–2006 (continued)

1963 (continued)
Children's: *Walt Disney's Wonderful World of Color* (NBC)
Program of the year: "The Tunnel" (NBC)

1964
Variety: *The Danny Kaye Show* (CBS)
Comedy: *The Dick Van Dyke Show* (CBS)
Drama: *The Defenders* (CBS)
News reports: *The Huntley-Brinkley Report* (NBC)
Commentary/public affairs: "Cuba—Part I: The Bay of Pigs," "Cuba—Part II: The Missile Crisis," *NBC White Paper* (NBC)
Documentary: "The Making of the President 1960" (ABC)
Children's: *Discovery '63–'64* (ABC)
Program of the year: "The Making of the President 1960" (ABC)

1965[2]
Entertainment: *The Dick Van Dyke Show* (CBS); "The Magnificent Yankee," *Hallmark Hall of Fame* (NBC); "My Name Is Barbra" (CBS); "What Is Sonata Form?," *New York Philharmonic Young People's Concerts with Leonard Bernstein* (CBS)
News/docu./info./sports: "I, Leonardo da Vinci," *Saga of Western Man* (ABC); "The Louvre" (NBC)

1966
Variety: *The Andy Williams Show* (NBC)
Comedy: *The Dick Van Dyke Show* (CBS)
Drama: *The Fugitive* (ABC)

1967
Variety: *The Andy Williams Show* (NBC)
Comedy: *The Monkees* (NBC)
Drama: *Mission: Impossible* (CBS)

1968
Musical/variety: *Rowan and Martin's Laugh-In* (NBC)
Comedy: *Get Smart* (NBC)
Drama: *Mission: Impossible* (CBS)

1969
Musical/variety: *Rowan and Martin's Laugh-In* (NBC)
Comedy: *Get Smart* (NBC)
Drama: *NET Playhouse* (NET)

1970
Variety/musical: *The David Frost Show* (syndicated)
Comedy: *My World and Welcome to It* (NBC)
Drama: *Marcus Welby, M.D.* (ABC)

1971
Comedy: *All in the Family* (CBS)
Drama: *The Senator* (segment), *The Bold Ones* (NBC)
Variety, musical: *The Flip Wilson Show* (NBC)
Variety, talk: *The David Frost Show* (syndicated)
New series: *All in the Family* (CBS)

1972
Comedy: *All in the Family* (CBS)
Drama: "Elizabeth R," *Masterpiece Theatre* (PBS)
Variety, musical: *The Carol Burnett Show* (CBS)
Variety, talk: *The Dick Cavett Show* (ABC)
New series: "Elizabeth R," *Masterpiece Theatre* (PBS)

1973
Comedy: *All in the Family* (CBS)

1973 (continued)
Drama (continuing): *The Waltons* (CBS)
Drama/comedy (limited): "Tom Brown's Schooldays," *Masterpiece Theatre* (PBS)
Variety, musical: *The Julie Andrews Hour* (ABC)
New series: *America* (NBC)

1974
Comedy: *M*A*S*H* (CBS)
Drama: "Upstairs, Downstairs," *Masterpiece Theatre* (PBS)
Limited series: *Columbo* (NBC)
Music/variety: *The Carol Burnett Show* (CBS)

1975
Comedy: *The Mary Tyler Moore Show* (CBS)
Drama: "Upstairs, Downstairs," *Masterpiece Theatre* (PBS)
Limited series: "Benjamin Franklin" (CBS)
Comedy-variety/music: *The Carol Burnett Show* (CBS)

1976
Comedy: *The Mary Tyler Moore Show* (CBS)
Drama: *Police Story* (NBC)
Limited series: "Upstairs, Downstairs," *Masterpiece Theatre* (PBS)
Comedy-variety/music: *NBC's Saturday Night* (NBC)

1977
Comedy: *The Mary Tyler Moore Show* (CBS)
Drama: "Upstairs, Downstairs," *Masterpiece Theatre* (PBS)
Limited series: *Roots* (ABC)
Comedy-variety/music: *Van Dyke and Company* (NBC)

1978
Comedy: *All in the Family* (CBS)
Drama: *The Rockford Files* (NBC)
Limited series: *Holocaust* (NBC)
Comedy-variety/music: *The Muppet Show* (syndicated)
Informational: *The Body Human* (CBS)

1979
Comedy: *Taxi* (ABC)
Drama: *Lou Grant* (CBS)
Limited series: *Roots: The Next Generations* (ABC)
Comedy-variety/music: "Steve & Eydie Celebrate Irving Berlin" (NBC)

1980
Comedy: *Taxi* (ABC)
Drama: *Lou Grant* (CBS)
Limited series: *Edward & Mrs. Simpson* (syndicated)
Variety/music: *IBM Presents Baryshnikov on Broadway* (ABC)

1981
Comedy: *Taxi* (ABC)
Drama: *Hill Street Blues* (NBC)
Limited series: *Shogun* (NBC)
Informational: *Steve Allen's Meeting of Minds* (PBS)

1982
Comedy: *Barney Miller* (ABC)
Drama: *Hill Street Blues* (NBC)
Limited series: *Marco Polo* (NBC)
Informational: *Creativity with Bill Moyers* (PBS)

Emmy Award-winning Television Series, 1948–2006 (continued)

1983
Comedy: *Cheers* (NBC)
Drama: *Hill Street Blues* (NBC)
Limited series: *Nicholas Nickleby* (syndicated)
Informational: *The Barbara Walters Specials* (ABC)

1984
Comedy: *Cheers* (NBC)
Drama: *Hill Street Blues* (NBC)
Limited series: "Concealed Enemies," *American Playhouse* (PBS)
Informational: *A Walk Through the 20th Century with Bill Moyers* (PBS)

1985
Comedy: *The Cosby Show* (NBC)
Drama: *Cagney & Lacey* (CBS)
Limited series: "The Jewel in the Crown," *Masterpiece Theatre* (PBS)
Informational: *The Living Planet: A Portrait of the Earth* (PBS)

1986
Comedy: *The Golden Girls* (NBC)
Drama: *Cagney & Lacey* (CBS)
Miniseries: *Peter the Great* (NBC)
Informational: "Laurence Olivier—A Life," *Great Performances* (PBS); *Planet Earth* (PBS)

1987
Comedy: *The Golden Girls* (NBC)
Drama: *L.A. Law* (NBC)
Miniseries: *A Year in the Life* (NBC)
Informational: *Smithsonian World* (PBS); "Unknown Chaplin," *American Masters* (PBS)

1988
Comedy: *The Wonder Years* (ABC)
Drama: *thirtysomething* (ABC)
Miniseries: *The Murder of Mary Phagan* (NBC)
Informational: "Buster Keaton: A Hard Act to Follow," *American Masters* (PBS); *Nature* (PBS)

1989
Comedy: *Cheers* (NBC)
Drama: *L.A. Law* (NBC)
Miniseries: *War and Remembrance* (ABC)
Variety/music/comedy: *The Tracy Ullman Show* (Fox)
Informational: *Nature* (PBS)

1990
Comedy: *Murphy Brown* (CBS)
Drama: *L.A. Law* (NBC)
Miniseries: *Drug Wars: The Camarena Story* (NBC)
Variety/music/comedy: *In Living Color* (Fox)
Informational: *Smithsonian World* (PBS)

1991
Comedy: *Cheers* (NBC)
Drama: *L.A. Law* (NBC)
Miniseries: *Separate But Equal* (ABC)
Informational: *The Civil War* (PBS)

1992
Comedy: *Murphy Brown* (CBS)
Drama: *Northern Exposure* (CBS)
Miniseries: *A Woman Named Jackie* (NBC)
Variety/music/comedy: *The Tonight Show Starring Johnny Carson* (NBC)

1992 (continued)
Informational: *MGM: When the Lion Roars* (TNT)

1993
Comedy: *Seinfeld* (NBC)
Drama: *Picket Fences* (CBS)
Miniseries: *Prime Suspect 2* (PBS)
Variety/music/comedy: *Saturday Night Live* (NBC)
Informational: *Healing and the Mind with Bill Moyers* (PBS)

1994
Comedy: *Frasier* (NBC)
Drama: *Picket Fences* (CBS)
Miniseries: *Prime Suspect 3* (PBS)
Variety/music/comedy: *Late Show with David Letterman* (CBS)
Informational: *Later with Bob Costas* (NBC)

1995
Comedy: *Frasier* (NBC)
Drama: *NYPD Blue* (ABC)
Miniseries: *Joseph* (TNT)
Variety/music/comedy: *The Tonight Show with Jay Leno* (NBC)
Informational: *Baseball* (PBS); *TV Nation* (NBC)

1996
Comedy: *Frasier* (NBC)
Drama: *ER* (NBC)
Miniseries: *Gulliver's Travels* (NBC)
Variety/music/comedy: *Dennis Miller Live* (HBO)
Informational: *Lost Civilizations* (NBC)

1997
Comedy: *Frasier* (NBC)
Drama: *Law & Order* (NBC)
Miniseries: *Prime Suspect 5: Errors of Judgment* (PBS)
Variety/music/comedy: *Tracey Takes On . . .* (HBO)
Informational: *Biography* (A&E); *The Great War and the Shaping of the 20th Century* (PBS)

1998
Comedy: *Frasier* (NBC)
Drama: *The Practice* (ABC)
Miniseries: *From the Earth to the Moon* (HBO)
Variety/music/comedy: *Late Show with David Letterman* (CBS)
Nonfiction: *The American Experience* (PBS)

1999
Comedy: *Ally McBeal* (Fox)
Drama: *The Practice* (ABC)
Miniseries: *Horatio Hornblower: The Even Chance* (A&E)
Variety/music/comedy: *Late Show with David Letterman* (CBS)
Nonfiction: *The American Experience* (PBS); *American Masters* (PBS)

2000
Comedy: *Will & Grace* (NBC)
Drama: *The West Wing* (NBC)
Miniseries: *The Corner* (HBO)
Variety/music/comedy: *Late Show with David Letterman* (CBS)
Nonfiction: "Hitchcock, Selznick, and the End of Hollywood," *American Masters* (PBS)

Emmy Award-winning Television Series, 1948–2006 (continued)

2001
Comedy: *Sex and the City* (HBO)
Drama: *The West Wing* (NBC)
Miniseries: *Anne Frank* (ABC)
Variety/music/comedy: *Late Show with David Letterman* (CBS)
Nonfiction: "Lucille Ball: Finding Lucy," *American Masters* (PBS)

2002
Comedy: *Friends* (NBC)
Drama: *The West Wing* (NBC)
Miniseries: *Band of Brothers* (HBO)
Variety/music/comedy: *Late Show with David Letterman* (CBS)
Nonfiction special: *9/11* (CBS)

2003
Comedy: *Everybody Loves Raymond* (CBS)
Drama: *The West Wing* (NBC)
Miniseries: *Steven Spielberg Presents Taken* (Sci Fi)
Variety/music/comedy: *The Daily Show with Jon Stewart* (Comedy Central)
Nonfiction special: *Benjamin Franklin* (PBS); *American Masters* (PBS)

2004
Comedy: *Arrested Development* (Fox)
Drama: *The Sopranos* (HBO)

2004 (continued)
Miniseries: *Angels in America* (HBO)
Variety/music/comedy: *The Daily Show with Jon Stewart* (Comedy Central)
Nonfiction special: *The Forgetting: A Portrait of Alzheimer's* (PBS)

2005
Comedy: *Everybody Loves Raymond* (CBS)
Drama: *Lost* (ABC)
Miniseries: "The Lost Prince," *Masterpiece Theatre* (PBS)
Variety/music/comedy: *The Daily Show with Jon Stewart* (Comedy Central)
Nonfiction special: *Unforgivable Blackness: The Rise and Fall of Jack Johnson* (PBS)

2006
Comedy: *The Office* (NBC)
Drama: *24* (Fox)
Miniseries: *Elizabeth I* (HBO)
Variety/music/comedy: *The Daily Show with Jon Stewart* (Comedy Central)
Nonfiction special: *Rome: Engineering an Empire* (The History Channel)

[1]*Because of a change in the eligibility period, no awards were given in 1958; the 1959 awards included all of calendar year 1958 and part of 1959.*   [2]*Programs this year were classified only so far as "Entertainment" and "News, Documentaries, Information and Sports," with several winners in each classification.*

Theater

Tony Award Winners, 2007

The American Theatre Wing, a philanthropic and educational organization established in 1939, created the Tony Awards in 1947 to recognize distinguished achievement in the theater arts as presented on Broadway. The award is named for Antoinette Perry, a former director of the American Theatre Wing; since 1967 it has been presented in conjunction with the League of American Theatres and Producers, a Broadway trade association. A 15–30-member nominating committee selects nominees each May from among the year's new or newly revived Broadway shows; a body of some 750 current and former theater professionals, critics, and agents votes for the winners. The awards are presented in New York City in early June. Prize: silver medallion, set in a base, depicting on one face the masks of tragedy and comedy and on the other the profile of Antoinette Perry.

Tony Awards Web site: <www.tonyawards.com>.

▸ **musical:** *Spring Awakening* (book and lyrics, Steven Sater; music, Duncan Sheik); ▸ **play:** *The Coast of Utopia* (playwright, Tom Stoppard); ▸ **revival of a musical:** *Company* (book, George Furth; music and lyrics, Stephen Sondheim); ▸ **revival of a play:** *Journey's End* (playwright, R.C. Sherriff); ▸ **book, musical:** Steven Sater (*Spring Awakening*); ▸ **score:** Steven Sater and Duncan Sheik (*Spring Awakening*); ▸ **leading actress, musical:** Christine Ebersol (*Grey Gardens*); ▸ **leading actor, musical:** David Hyde Pierce (*Curtains*); ▸ **leading actress, play:** Julie White (*The Little Dog Laughed*); ▸ **leading actor, play:** Frank Langella (*Frost/Nixon*); ▸ **featured actress, musical:** Mary Louise Wilson (*Grey Gardens*); ▸ **featured actor, musical:** John Gallagher, Jr. (*Spring Awakening*); ▸ **featured actress, play:** Jennifer Ehle (*The Coast of Utopia*); ▸ **featured actor, play:** Billy Crudup (*The Coast of Utopia*); ▸ **direction, musical:** Michael Mayer (*Spring Awakening*); ▸ **direction, play:** Jack O'Brien (*The Coast of Utopia*); ▸ **costume design, musical:** William Ivey Long (*Grey Gardens*); ▸ **costume design, play:** Catherine Zuber (*The Coast of Utopia*); ▸ **lighting design, musical:** Kevin Adams (*Spring Awakening*); ▸ **lighting design, play:** Brian MacDevitt, Kenneth Posner, and Natasha Katz (*The Coast of Utopia*); ▸ **scenic design, musical:** Bob Crowley (*Mary Poppins*); ▸ **scenic design, play:** Bob Crowley and Scott Pask (*The Coast of Utopia*); ▸ **orchestrations:** Duncan Sheik (*Spring Awakening*); ▸ **choreography:** Bill T. Jones (*Spring Awakening*); ▸ **regional theater award:** Alliance Theatre, Atlanta GA.

Tony Awards, 1947–2007

YEAR	BEST MUSICAL	BEST PLAY
1947	*not awarded*	*All My Sons* (Arthur Miller)[1]
1948	*not awarded*	*Mister Roberts* (Thomas Heggen and Joshua Logan)
1949	*Kiss Me, Kate* (book, Bella Spewack and Samuel Spewack; music and lyrics, Cole Porter)	*Death of a Salesman* (Arthur Miller)
1950	*South Pacific* (book, Oscar Hammerstein II and Joshua Logan; music, Richard Rodgers; lyrics, Oscar Hammerstein II)	*The Cocktail Party* (T.S. Eliot)
1951	*Guys and Dolls* (book, Jo Swerling and Abe Burrows; music and lyrics, Frank Loesser)	*The Rose Tattoo* (Tennessee Williams)
1952	*The King and I* (book and lyrics, Oscar Hammerstein II; music, Richard Rodgers)	*The Fourposter* (Jan de Hartog)
1953	*Wonderful Town* (book, Joseph Fields and Jerome Chodorov; music, Leonard Bernstein; lyrics, Betty Comden and Adolph Green)	*The Crucible* (Arthur Miller)
1954	*Kismet* (book, Charles Lederer and Luther Davis; music, Alexander Borodin; adaptation and lyrics, Robert Wright and George Forrest)	*The Teahouse of the August Moon* (John Patrick)
1955	*The Pajama Game* (book, George Abbott and Richard Bissell; music and lyrics, Richard Adler and Jerry Ross)	*The Desperate Hours* (Joseph Hayes)
1956	*Damn Yankees* (book, George Abbott and Douglass Wallop; music and lyrics, Richard Adler and Jerry Ross)	*The Diary of Anne Frank* (Frances Goodrich and Albert Hackett)
1957	*My Fair Lady* (book and lyrics, Alan Jay Lerner; music, Frederick Loewe)	*Long Day's Journey into Night* (Eugene O'Neill)
1958	*The Music Man* (book, Meredith Willson and Franklin Lacey; music and lyrics, Meredith Willson)	*Sunrise at Campobello* (Dore Schary)
1959	*Redhead* (book, Herbert Fields, Dorothy Fields, Sidney Sheldon, and David Shaw; music, Albert Hague; lyrics, Dorothy Fields)	*J.B.* (Archibald MacLeish)
1960 (tie)	*The Sound of Music* (book, Howard Lindsay and Russel Crouse; music, Richard Rodgers; lyrics, Oscar Hammerstein II); *Fiorello!* (book, Jerome Weidman and George Abbott; music, Jerry Brock; lyrics, Sheldon Harnick)	*The Miracle Worker* (William Gibson)
1961	*Bye Bye Birdie* (book, Michael Stewart; music, Charles Strouse; lyrics, Lee Adams)	*Beckett* (Jean Anouilh, translated by Lucienne Hill)
1962	*How To Succeed in Business Without Really Trying* (book, Abe Burrows, Jack Weinstock, and Willie Gilbert; music and lyrics, Frank Loesser)	*A Man for All Seasons* (Robert Bolt)
1963	*A Funny Thing Happened on the Way to the Forum* (book, Burt Shevelove and Larry Gelbart; music and lyrics, Stephen Sondheim)	*Who's Afraid of Virginia Woolf?* (Edward Albee)
1964	*Hello, Dolly!* (book, Michael Stewart; music and lyrics, Jerry Herman)	*Luther* (John Osborne)
1965	*Fiddler on the Roof* (book, Joseph Stein; music, Jerry Bock; lyrics, Sheldon Harnick)	*The Subject Was Roses* (Frank Gilroy)
1966	*Man of La Mancha* (book, Dale Wasserman; music, Mitch Leigh; lyrics, Joe Darion)	*Marat/Sade* (Peter Weiss, translated by Geoffrey Skelton)
1967	*Cabaret* (book, Joe Masteroff; music, John Kander; lyrics, Fred Ebb)	*The Homecoming* (Harold Pinter)
1968	*Hallelujah, Baby!* (book, Arthur Laurents; music, Jule Styne; lyrics, Betty Comden and Adolph Green)	*Rosencrantz and Guildenstern Are Dead* (Tom Stoppard)
1969	*1776* (book, Peter Stone; music and lyrics, Sherman Edwards)	*The Great White Hope* (Howard Sackler)
1970	*Applause* (book, Betty Comden and Adolph Greene; music, Charles Strouse; lyrics, Lee Adams)	*Borstal Boy* (Frank McMahon)
1971	*Company* (book, George Furth; music and lyrics, Stephen Sondheim)	*Sleuth* (Anthony Shaffer)
1972	*Two Gentlemen of Verona* (book, John Guare and Mel Shapiro; music, Galt MacDermot; lyrics, John Guare)	*Sticks and Bones* (David Rabe)
1973	*A Little Night Music* (book, Hugh Wheeler; music and lyrics, Stephen Sondheim)	*That Championship Season* (Jason Miller)
1974	*Raisin* (book, Robert Nemiroff and Charlotte Zaltzberg; music, Judd Woldin; lyrics, Robert Brittan)	*The River Niger* (Joseph A. Walker)
1975	*The Wiz* (book, William F. Brown; music and lyrics, Charlie Smalls)	*Equus* (Peter Shaffer)
1976	*A Chorus Line* (book, James Kirkwood and Nicholas Dante; music, Marvin Hamlisch; lyrics, Edward Kleban)	*Travesties* (Tom Stoppard)
1977	*Annie* (book, Thomas Meehan; music, Charles Strouse; lyrics, Martin Charnin)	*The Shadow Box* (Michael Christofer)
1978	*Ain't Misbehavin'* (book, Murray Horwitz and Richard Maltby, Jr.; music, Fats Waller; lyrics, Fats Waller and many others)	*Da* (Hugh Leonard)
1979	*Sweeney Todd* (book, Hugh Wheeler; music and lyrics, Stephen Sondheim)	*The Elephant Man* (Bernard Pomerance)
1980	*Evita* (book and lyrics, Tim Rice; music, Andrew Lloyd Webber)	*Children of a Lesser God* (Mark Medoff)
1981	*42nd Street* (book, Michael Stewart and Mark Bramble; music, Harry Warren; lyrics, Al Dubin)	*Amadeus* (Peter Shaffer)

Tony Awards, 1947–2007 (continued)

YEAR	BEST MUSICAL	BEST PLAY
1982	Nine (book, Arthur Kopit; music and lyrics, Maury Yeston)	The Life and Adventures of Nicholas Nickleby (David Edgar)
1983	Cats (book and lyrics, T.S. Eliot; music, Andrew Lloyd Webber)	Torch Song Trilogy (Harvey Fierstein)
1984	La Cage aux Folles (book, Harvey Fierstein; music and lyrics, Jerry Herman)	The Real Thing (Tom Stoppard)
1985	Big River (book, William Hauptman; music and lyrics, Roger Miller)	Biloxi Blues (Neil Simon)
1986	The Mystery of Edwin Drood (book, music, and lyrics, Rupert Holmes)	I'm Not Rappaport (Herb Gardner)
1987	Les Misérables (book, Alain Boublil and Claude-Michel Schönberg; music, Claude-Michel Schönberg; lyrics, Herbert Kretzmer and Alain Boublil)	Fences (August Wilson)
1988	The Phantom of the Opera (book, Richard Stilgoe and Andrew Lloyd Webber; music, Andrew Lloyd Webber; lyrics, Charles Hart and Richard Stilgoe)	M. Butterfly (David Henry Hwang)
1989	Jerome Robbins' Broadway (compilation)	The Heidi Chronicles (Wendy Wasserstein)
1990	City of Angels (book, Larry Gelbart; music, Cy Coleman; lyrics, David Zippel)	The Grapes of Wrath (Frank Galati)
1991	The Will Rogers Follies (book, Peter Stone; music, Cy Coleman; lyrics, Betty Comden and Adolph Green)	Lost in Yonkers (Neil Simon)
1992	Crazy for You (book, Ken Ludwig; music and lyrics, George Gershwin and Ira Gershwin)	Dancing at Lughnasa (Brian Friel)
1993	Kiss of the Spider Woman (book, Terrence McNally; music, John Kander; lyrics, Fred Ebb)	Angels in America: Millennium Approaches (Tony Kushner)
1994	Passion (book, James Lapine; music and lyrics, Stephen Sondheim)	Angels in America: Perestroika (Tony Kushner)
1995	Sunset Boulevard (book and lyrics, Don Black and Christopher Hampton; music, Andrew Lloyd Webber)	Love! Valour! Compassion! (Terrence McNally)
1996	Rent (book, music, and lyrics, Jonathan Larson)	Master Class (Terrence McNally)
1997	Titanic (book, Peter Stone; music and lyrics, Maury Yeston)	The Last Night of Ballyhoo (Alfred Uhry)
1998	The Lion King (book, Roger Allers and Irene Mecchi; music and lyrics, Elton John, Tim Rice, and others)	Art (Yasmina Reza)
1999	Fosse (compilation)	Side Man (Warren Leight)
2000	Contact (book, John Weidman; music and lyrics, various artists)	Copenhagen (Michael Frayn)
2001	The Producers (book, Mel Brooks and Thomas Meehan; music and lyrics, Mel Brooks)	Proof (David Auburn)
2002	Thoroughly Modern Millie (book, Richard Morris and Dick Scanlan; music, Jeanine Tesori; lyrics, Dick Scanlan)	The Goat, or Who Is Sylvia? (Edward Albee)
2003	Hairspray (book, Mark O'Donnell and Thomas Meehan; music, Marc Shaiman; lyrics, Scott Wittman and Marc Shaiman)	Take Me Out (Richard Greenberg)
2004	Avenue Q (book, Jeff Whitty; music and lyrics, Robert Lopez and Jeff Marx)	I Am My Own Wife (Doug Wright)
2005	Monty Python's Spamalot (book, Eric Idle; music and lyrics, John Du Prez and Eric Idle)	Doubt (John Patrick Shanley)
2006	Jersey Boys (book, Marshall Brickman and Rick Elice; music, Bob Gaudio; lyrics, Bob Crewe)	The History Boys (Alan Bennett)
2007	Spring Awakening (book and lyrics, Steven Sater; music, Duncan Sheik)	The Coast of Utopia (Tom Stoppard)

[1]Awarded to playwright.

Longest-Running Broadway Shows

As of 11 Jun 2007. Source: Internet Broadway Database, <www.ibdb.com>.

	SHOW	RUN	TOTAL PERFORMANCES		SHOW	RUN	TOTAL PERFORMANCES
1	The Phantom of the Opera	1988–	8,077	9	Miss Saigon	1991–2001	4,092
				10	The Lion King	1997–	3,987
2	Cats	1982–2000	7,485	11	42nd Street	1980–89	3,486
3	Les Misérables	1987–2003	6,680	12	Grease	1972–80	3,388
4	A Chorus Line	1975–90	6,137	13	Fiddler on the Roof	1964–72	3,242
5	Oh! Calcutta! [revival]	1976–89	5,959	14	Life with Father	1939–47	3,224
				15	Tobacco Road	1933–41	3,182
6	Beauty and the Beast	1994–	5,405	16	Hello, Dolly!	1964–70	2,844
				17	My Fair Lady	1956–62	2,717
7	Rent	1996–	4,625	18	The Producers	2001–07	2,502
8	Chicago [revival]	1996–	4,402	19	Annie	1977–83	2,377

Longest-Running Broadway Shows (continued)

SHOW	RUN	TOTAL PERFORMANCES	SHOW	RUN	TOTAL PERFORMANCES
20 Cabaret	1998–2004	2,377	23 Abie's Irish Rose	1922–27	2,327
21 Mamma Mia!	2001–	2,350	24 Oklahoma!	1943–48	2,212
22 Man of La Mancha	1965–71	2,328	25 Smokey Joe's Cafe	1995–2000	2,036

Encyclopædia Britannica's 25 Notable US Theater Companies

COMPANY	LOCATION	ARTISTIC DIRECTOR (2007)
The Acting Company	New York NY	Margot Harley
Actors Theatre of Louisville	Louisville KY	Marc Masterson
Alley Theatre	Houston TX	Gregory Boyd
American Conservatory Theater	San Francisco CA	Carey Perloff
American Repertory Theatre	Cambridge MA	Robert Woodruff
Arena Stage	Washington DC	Molly Smith
Center Theatre Group	Los Angeles CA	Michael Ritchie
Chicago Shakespeare Theater	Chicago IL	Barbara Gaines
Circle in the Square	New York NY	Theodore Mann
Cincinnati Playhouse in the Park	Cincinnati OH	Edward Stern
Cleveland Public Theatre	Cleveland OH	Raymond Bobgan
Colony Theatre Company	Burbank CA	Barbara Beckley
El Teatro Campesino	San Juan Bautista CA	Luis Valdez
Ford's Theatre	Washington DC	Paul R. Tetreault
Goodman Theatre	Chicago IL	Robert Falls
Guthrie Theater	Minneapolis MN	Joe Dowling
La Jolla Playhouse	La Jolla CA	Christopher Ashley
Long Wharf Theatre	New Haven CT	Gordon Edelstein
Pasadena Playhouse	Pasadena CA	Sheldon Epps
The Public Theater	New York NY	Oskar Eustis
Seattle Repertory Theatre	Seattle WA	David Esbjornson
Steppenwolf Theatre Company	Chicago IL	Martha Lavey
Studio Arena Theatre	Buffalo NY	Kathleen Gaffney
Victory Gardens Theater	Chicago IL	Dennis Zacek
Yale Repertory Theatre	New Haven CT	James Bundy

Music

Grammy Awards 2006

The National Academy of Recording Arts and Sciences was established in 1957 as a professional organization for musicians, producers, technicians, and executives in the US recording industry. The Grammys, first awarded in 1958, recognize excellence in the recording industry without regard to record sales or chart position. Nominees and winners are selected by the Academy's individual members according to the members' areas of expertise. In addition to the four general categories (record, album, and song of the year, and best new artist) for which all members are eligible to vote, for 2006 there were 108 categories in 31 fields, of which Academy members were permitted to vote in no more than 8 fields. Prizes for works released 1 Oct 2005–30 Sep 2006 were awarded in Los Angeles on 13 Feb 2007. Prize: gold miniature phonograph.

Grammy Award Web site: <www.grammy.com>.

category: winner (performer in parentheses for songwriting/production awards)

record (single) of the year: "Not Ready To Make Nice,"Dixie Chicks; ▸ album of the year: Taking the Long Way, Dixie Chicks; ▸ song of the year: "Not Ready To Make Nice," Dixie Chicks; ▸ new artist: Carrie Underwood; ▸ pop vocal performance, female: "Ain't No Other Man," Christina Aguilera; ▸ pop vocal performance, male: "Waiting On the World To Change," John Mayer; ▸ pop vocal performance, duo/group: "My Humps," Black Eyed Peas; ▸ pop vocal album: Continuum, John Mayer; ▸ pop vocal album, traditional: Duets: An American Classic, Tony Bennett; ▸ rock vocal performance, solo: "Someday Baby," Bob Dylan; ▸ rock vocal performance, duo/group: "Dani California," Red Hot Chili Peppers; ▸ hard rock performance: "Woman," Wolfmother; ▸ metal performance: "Eyes of the Insane," Slayer; ▸ rock song: "Dani California," Anthony Kiedis, Chad Smith, Flea, and John Frusciante, songwriters (Red Hot Chili Peppers); ▸ rock album: Stadium Arcadium, Red Hot Chili Peppers; ▸ alternative music album: St. Elsewhere, Gnarls Barkley; ▸ R&B vocal performance, female: "Be Without You," Mary J. Blige; ▸ R&B vocal performance, male: "Heaven," John Legend; ▸ R&B vocal performance, duo/group: "Family Affair," John Legend, Joss Stone, and Van Hunt; ▸ R&B song: "Be

Grammy Awards 2006 (continued)

Without You," Bryan Michael Cox, Jason Perry, Johnta Austin, and Mary J. Blige, songwriters (Mary J. Blige); ▶ R&B album: The Breakthrough, Mary J. Blige; ▶ R&B album, contemporary: B'Day, Beyoncé ▶ rap performance, solo: "What You Know," T.I.; ▶ rap performance, duo/group: "Ridin'," Chamillionaire and Krayzie Bone; ▶ rap song: "Money Maker," Ludacris and Pharrell Williams, songwriters (Ludacris); ▶ rap album: Release Therapy, Ludacris; ▶ country vocal performance, female: "Jesus, Take the Wheel," Carrie Underwood; ▶ country vocal performance, male: "The Reason Why," Vince Gill; ▶ country vocal performance, duo/group: "Not Ready To Make Nice," Dixie Chicks; ▶ country song: "Jesus, Take the Wheel," Brett James, Gordie Sampson, and Hillary Lindsey, songwriters (Carrie Underwood); ▶ country album: Taking the Long Way, Dixie Chicks; ▶ bluegrass album: Instrumentals, Ricky Skaggs and Kentucky Thunder; ▶ new age album: Amarantine, Enya; ▶ jazz album, contemporary: The Hidden Land, Béla Fleck and the Flecktones; ▶ jazz album, vocal: Turned to Blue, Nancy Wilson; ▶ jazz instrumental solo: Michael Brecker (Some Skunk Funk); ▶ jazz album, instrumental: The Ultimate Adventure, Chick Corea; ▶ jazz album, large ensemble: Some Skunk Funk, Randy Brecker/Michael Brecker; ▶ jazz album, Latin: Simpático, Brian Lynch and Eddie Palmieri, Sr.; ▶ gospel song: "Imagine Me," Kirk Franklin, songwriter (Kirk Franklin); ▶ gospel album, rock/rap: Turn Around, Jonny Lang; ▶ gospel album, pop/contemporary: Wherever You Are, Third Day; ▶ gospel album, Southern/country/bluegrass: Glory Train, Randy Travis; ▶ gospel album, traditional: Alive in South Africa, Israel and New Breed; ▶ gospel album, contemporary R&B: Hero, Kirk Franklin); ▶ Latin album, pop: Limón y sal, Julieta Venegas; and Adentro, Ricardo Arjona Morales (tie); ▶ Latin album, rock/alternative/urban: Amar es combatir, Mana; ▶ Latin album, tropical: Directo al corazón, Gilberto Santa Rosa; ▶ Mexican/Mexican-American album: Historias de mi tierra, Pepe Aguilar; ▶ Tejano album: Sigue el Taconazo, Chente Barrera y Taconazo; ▶ blues album, traditional: Risin' with the Blues, Ike Turner; ▶ blues album, contemporary: After the Rain, Irma Thomas; ▶ folk album, traditional: We Shall Overcome: The Seeger Sessions, Bruce Springsteen; ▶ folk album, contemporary/Americana: Modern Times, Bob Dylan; ▶ Native American music album: Dance with the Wind, Mary Youngblood; ▶ Hawaiian music album: Legends of Hawaiian Slack Key Guitar: Live from Maui, Daniel Ho, George Kahumoku, Jr., Paul Konwiser, and Wayne Wong, producers; ▶ reggae album: Love Is My Religion, Ziggy Marley; ▶ world music album, traditional: Blessed, Soweto Gospel Choir; ▶ world music album, contemporary: Wonder Wheel, The Klezmatics; ▶ polka album: Polka in Paradise, Jimmy Sturr and His Orchestra; ▶ spoken word album: Our Endangered Values: America's Moral Crisis, Jimmy Carter; and With Ossie and Ruby: In This Life Together, Ossie Davis and Ruby Dee (tie); ▶ comedy album: The Carnegie Hall Performance, Lewis Black; ▶ producer, non-classical: Rick Rubin; ▶ producer, classical: Elaine L. Martone; ▶ classical album: Mahler: Symphony No. 7; Michael Tilson Thomas, conductor; Andreas Neubronner, producer (San Francisco Symphony); ▶ orchestral performance: Mahler: Symphony No. 7; Michael Tilson Thomas, conductor; Andreas Neubronner, producer (San Francisco Symphony); ▶ opera recording: Osvaldo Golijov: Ainadamar (Fountain of Tears), Robert Spano, conductor; Sid McLauchlan and Valerie Gross, producers (Dawn Upshaw, Jessica Rivera, and Kelley O'Connor, soloists); ▶ chamber music performance: Intimate Voices, Emerson String Quartet; ▶ classical vocal performance: Rilke Songs, Lorraine Hunt Lieberson, soloist; ▶ contemporary classical composition: Osvaldo Golijov: Ainadamar (Fountain of Tears), Osvaldo Golijov, composer; ▶ short-form music video: "Here It Goes Again," Andy Ross, Damian Kulash, Jr., Dan Konopka, Timothy Nordwind, and Trish Sie, directors; Andy Ross, Damian Kulash, Jr., Dan Konopka, Timothy Nordwind, and Trish Sie, producers (OK Go)

Grammy Awards Top Winners, 1958–2006

The year denotes the period for which the winning work or artist was recognized; the prizes were generally awarded during the following year.

YEAR	RECORD (SINGLE) OF THE YEAR	ALBUM OF THE YEAR	BEST NEW ARTIST
1958	"Nel Blu Dipinto Di Blu (Volare)," Domenico Modugno	The Music from Peter Gunn, Henry Mancini	not awarded
1959	"Mack the Knife," Bobby Darin	Come Dance with Me, Frank Sinatra	Bobby Darin
1960	"Theme from A Summer Place," Percy Faith	The Button-Down Mind of Bob Newhart, Bob Newhart	Bob Newhart
1961	"Moon River," Henry Mancini	Judy at Carnegie Hall, Judy Garland	Peter Nero
1962	"I Left My Heart in San Francisco," Tony Bennett	The First Family, Vaughn Meader	Robert Goulet
1963	"The Days of Wine and Roses," Henry Mancini	The Barbra Streisand Album, Barbra Streisand	Ward Swingle (The Swingle Singers)
1964	"The Girl from Ipanema," Stan Getz & Astrud Gilberto	Getz/Gilberto, Stan Getz & João Gilberto	The Beatles
1965	"A Taste of Honey," Herb Alpert	September of My Years, Frank Sinatra	Tom Jones

Grammy Awards Top Winners, 1958–2006 (continued)

YEAR	RECORD (SINGLE) OF THE YEAR	ALBUM OF THE YEAR	BEST NEW ARTIST
1966	"Strangers in the Night," Frank Sinatra	*A Man and His Music*, Frank Sinatra	*not awarded*
1967	"Up, Up, and Away," The 5th Dimension	*Sgt. Pepper's Lonely Hearts Club Band*, The Beatles	Bobbie Gentry
1968	"Mrs. Robinson," Simon & Garfunkel	*By the Time I Get to Phoenix*, Glen Campbell	José Feliciano
1969	"Aquarius/Let the Sunshine In," The 5th Dimension	*Blood, Sweat & Tears*, Blood, Sweat & Tears	Crosby, Stills & Nash
1970	"Bridge over Troubled Water," Simon & Garfunkel	*Bridge over Troubled Water*, Simon & Garfunkel	The Carpenters
1971	"It's Too Late," Carole King	*Tapestry*, Carole King	Carly Simon
1972	"The First Time Ever I Saw Your Face," Roberta Flack	*The Concert for Bangla Desh*, George Harrison and Friends	America
1973	"Killing Me Softly with His Song," Roberta Flack	*Innervisions*, Stevie Wonder	Bette Midler
1974	"I Honestly Love You," Olivia Newton-John	*Fulfillingness' First Finale*, Stevie Wonder	Marvin Hamlisch
1975	"Love Will Keep Us Together," Captain & Tennille	*Still Crazy After All These Years*, Paul Simon	Natalie Cole
1976	"This Masquerade," George Benson	*Songs in the Key of Life*, Stevie Wonder	Starland Vocal Band
1977	"Hotel California," The Eagles	*Rumours*, Fleetwood Mac	Debby Boone
1978	"Just the Way You Are," Billy Joel	*Saturday Night Fever*, The Bee Gees	A Taste of Honey
1979	"What a Fool Believes," The Doobie Brothers	*52nd Steet*, Billy Joel	Rickie Lee Jones
1980	"Sailing," Christopher Cross	*Christopher Cross*, Christopher Cross	Christopher Cross
1981	"Bette Davis Eyes," Kim Carnes	*Double Fantasy*, John Lennon & Yoko Ono	Sheena Easton
1982	"Rosanna," Toto	*Toto IV*, Toto	Men at Work
1983	"Beat It," Michael Jackson	*Thriller*, Michael Jackson	Culture Club
1984	"What's Love Got to Do with It," Tina Turner	*Can't Slow Down*, Lionel Richie	Cyndi Lauper
1985	"We Are the World," USA for Africa	*No Jacket Required*, Phil Collins	Sade
1986	"Higher Love," Steve Winwood	*Graceland*, Paul Simon	Bruce Hornsby and the Range
1987	"Graceland," Paul Simon	*The Joshua Tree*, U2	Jody Watley
1988	"Don't Worry, Be Happy," Bobby McFerrin	*Faith*, George Michael	Tracy Chapman
1989	"Wind Beneath My Wings," Bette Midler	*Nick of Time*, Bonnie Raitt	Milli Vanilli [revoked]
1990	"Another Day in Paradise," Phil Collins	*Back on the Block*, Quincy Jones	Mariah Carey
1991	"Unforgettable," Natalie Cole with Nat King Cole	*Unforgettable: With Love*, Natalie Cole	Marc Cohn
1992	"Tears in Heaven," Eric Clapton	*Unplugged*, Eric Clapton	Arrested Development
1993	"I Will Always Love You," Whitney Houston	*The Bodyguard*, Whitney Houston	Toni Braxton
1994	"All I Wanna Do," Sheryl Crow	*MTV Unplugged*, Tony Bennett	Sheryl Crow
1995	"Kiss from a Rose," Seal	*Jagged Little Pill*, Alanis Morissette	Hootie and the Blowfish
1996	"Change the World," Eric Clapton	*Falling into You*, Celine Dion	LeAnn Rimes
1997	"Sunny Came Home," Shawn Colvin	*Time Out of Mind*, Bob Dylan	Paula Cole
1998	"My Heart Will Go On," Celine Dion	*The Miseducation of Lauryn Hill*, Lauryn Hill	Lauryn Hill
1999	"Smooth," Santana featuring Rob Thomas	*Supernatural*, Santana	Christina Aguilera
2000	"Beautiful Day,"U2	*Two Against Nature*, Steely Dan	Shelby Lynne
2001	"Walk On,"U2	*O Brother, Where Art Thou?*, various artists	Alicia Keys
2002	"Don't Know Why," Norah Jones	*Come Away with Me*, Norah Jones	Norah Jones
2003	"Clocks," Coldplay	*Speakerboxxx/The Love Below*, OutKast	Evanescence
2004	"Here We Go Again," Ray Charles and Norah Jones	*Genius Loves Company*, Ray Charles and various artists	Maroon 5
2005	"Boulevard of Broken Dreams," Green Day	*How To Dismantle an Atomic Bomb*, U2	John Legend

Grammy Awards Top Winners, 1958–2006 (continued)

YEAR	RECORD (SINGLE) OF THE YEAR	ALBUM OF THE YEAR	BEST NEW ARTIST
2006	"Not Ready To Make Nice," Dixie Chicks	*Taking the Long Way,* Dixie Chicks	Carrie Underwood
2007	to be held in February 2008		

Eurovision Song Contest, 1956–2007

The European Broadcasting Union (EBU), an association of national television and radio companies from Europe and the Mediterranean, began the Eurovision Song Contest in 1956 to promote European pop-music composers and performers. Each EBU member country, along with several provisional participants, can nominate one original song per year, in any language, with a maximum length of three minutes. The overall winner is selected through a point scheme based on call-in votes from viewers and juries in each participating country. Eurovision Song Contest Web site: <www.eurovision.tv>.

YEAR SONG, SONGWRITER(S) (PERFORMER, COUNTRY)
1956 "Refrain," Emile Gardaz, Géo Voumard (Lys Assia, Switzerland)
1957 "Net als toen," Willy van Hemert, Guus Jansen (Corry Brokken, The Netherlands)
1958 "Dors mon amour," Pierre Delanoe, Hubert Giraud (André Clavaeu, France)
1959 "Een beetje," Willy van Hemert, Dick Schallies (Teddy Scholten, The Netherlands)
1960 "Tom Pillibi," Pierre Cour, André Popp (Jacqueline Boyer, France)
1961 "Nous les amoureux," Jacques Datin, Maurice Vidalin (Jean-Claude Pascal, Luxembourg)
1962 "Un Premier amour," Rolande Valade, Claude Henri Vic (Isabelle Aubret, France)
1963 "Dansevise," Sejr Volmer Sorensen, Otto Francker (Grethe and Jorgen Ingmann, Denmark)
1964 "Non ho l'étà," Nicola Salerno (Gigliola Cinquetti, Italy)
1965 "Poupée de cire, poupée de son," Serge Gainsbourg (France Gall, Luxembourg)
1966 "Merci chérie," Udo Jürgens, Thomas Horbiger (Udo Jürgens, Austria)
1967 "Puppet on a String," Bill Martin, Phil Coulter (Sandie Shaw, United Kingdom)
1968 "La, la, la," Ramon Arcusa, Manuel de la Calva (Massiel, Spain)
1969 "Vivo cantando," A. Alcaide, Maria José de Cerato (Salomé, Spain); "Boom Bang-a-Bang," Peter Warne, Alan Moorhouse (Lulu, United Kingdom); "De troubadour," Lennie Kuhr, David Hartsena (Lennie Kuhr, The Netherlands); "Un Jour, un enfant," Eddy Marnay, Emile Stern (Frida Boccara, France) (four-way tie)
1970 "All Kinds of Everything," Derry Lindsay, Jackie Smith (Dana, Ireland)
1971 "Un Banc, un arbre, une rue," Yves Dessca, Jean-Pierre Bourtayre (Séverine, Monaco)
1972 "Après toi," Klaus Munro, Yves Dessca, Mario Panas (Vicky Leandros, Luxembourg)
1973 "Tu te reconnaîtras," Vline Buggy, Claude Morgan (Anne-Marie David, Luxembourg)
1974 "Waterloo," Stikkan Anderson, Benny Andersson, Björn Ulvaeus (ABBA, Sweden)
1975 "Ding dinge dong," Wil Luikinga, Eddy Owens, Dick Bakker (Teach-In, The Netherlands)
1976 "Save Your Kisses for Me," Tony Hiller, Lee Sheriden, Martin Lee (Brotherhood of Man, United Kingdom)
1977 "L'Oiseau et l'enfant," José Gracy, Jean-Paul Cara (Marie Myriam, France)
1978 "A-Ba-Ni-Bi," Ehud Manor, Nurit Hirsh (Izhar Cohen and the Alphabeta, Israel)
1979 "Hallelujah," Shimrit Orr, Kobi Oshrat (Gali Atari and Milk and Honey, Israel)
1980 "What's Another Year," Shay Healy (Johnny Logan, Ireland)
1981 "Making Your Mind Up," Andy Hill, John Danter (Bucks Fizz, United Kingdom)
1982 "Ein bisschen Frieden," Bernd Meinunger, Ralph Siegel (Nicole, West Germany)
1983 "Si la vie est cadeau," Alain Garcia, Jean-Pierre Millers (Corinne Hermes, Luxembourg)
1984 "Diggi-loo diggi-ley," Britt Lindeborg, Torgny Soederberg (Herrey's, Sweden)
1985 "La det swinge," Rolg Loevland (Bobbysocks, Norway)
1986 "J'aime la vie," Marino Atria, J.P. Furnemont, A. Crisci (Sandra Kim, Belgium)
1987 "Hold Me Now," Sean Sherrard (Johnny Logan, Ireland)
1988 "Ne partez pas sans moi," Nella Martinetti, Atila Sereftug (Céline Dion, Switzerland)
1989 "Rock Me," Stevo Cvikich, Rajko Dujmich (Riva, Yugoslavia)
1990 "Insieme: 1992," Toto Cutugno (Toto Cutugno, Italy)
1991 "Fångad av en stormvind," Stephan Berg (Carola, Sweden)
1992 "Why Me," Sean Sherrard (Linda Martin, Ireland)
1993 "In Your Eyes," Jimmy Walsh (Niamh Kavanagh, Ireland)
1994 "Rock 'n' Roll Kids," Brendan Graham (Paul Harrington and Charlie McGettigan, Ireland)
1995 "Nocturne," Petter Skavlan, Rolf Lovland (Secret Garden, Norway)
1996 "The Voice," Brendan Graham (Eimear Quinn, Ireland)
1997 "Love Shine a Light," Kimberley Rew (Katrina and the Waves, United Kingdom)
1998 "Diva," Yoav Ginay (Dana International, Israel)
1999 "Take Me to Your Heaven," Gert Lengstrand (Charlotte Nilsson, Sweden)
2000 "Fly on the Wings of Love," Jørgen Olsen (Olsen Brothers, Denmark)
2001 "Everybody," Maian-Anna Käarmas, Ivar Must (Tanel Padar, Dave Benton, and 2XL, Estonia)
2002 "I Wanna," Marija Naumova, Marats Samauskis (Marie N, Latvia)
2003 "Every Way That I Can," Demir Demirkan, Sertab Erener (Sertab Erener, Turkey)
2004 "Wild Dances," Ruslana Lyzhichko, Aleksandr Ksenofontov (Ruslana, Ukraine)
2005 "My Number One," Christos Dantis, Natalia Germanou (Elena Paparizou, Greece)
2006 "Hard Rock Hallelujah," LORDI (LORDI, Finland)
2007 "Molitva," Sasa Milosevic Mare (Marija Serifovic, Serbia)

Brit Awards, 2007

The British Phonographic Industry, a trade association of record companies, established the Brit Awards In 1977 to recognize pop acts from Great Britain and abroad. Prize: statuette. Web site: <www.brits.co.uk>.

BRITISH CATEGORIES
Male solo artist: James Morrison
Female solo artist: Amy Winehouse
Group: Arctic Monkeys
MasterCard Album: Arctic Monkeys, *Whatever People Say I Am, That's What I'm Not*
Breakthrough artist: The Fratellis
Single: Take That, "Patience"
Live act: Muse

INTERNATIONAL CATEGORIES
Male solo artist: Justin Timberlake
Female solo artist: Nelly Furtado
Group: The Killers
Album: The Killers, *Sam's Town*
Breakthrough artist: Orson

ADDITIONAL CATEGORY
Outstanding contribution: Oasis

Country Music Association Awards, 2006

The Country Music Association, founded in 1958 as a trade organization for the country and western music industry, began its annual awards ceremony in 1967 and made it the first nationally televised music awards show the following year. Ceremonies are held in November. Prize: hand-blown crystal statuette. Country Music Association Awards Web site: <www.cmaawards.com>

▸ **entertainer of the year:** Kenny Chesney; ▸ **female vocalist of the year:** Carrie Underwood; ▸ **male vocalist of the year:** Keith Urban; ▸ **Horizon Award:** Carrie Underwood; ▸ **vocal duo of the year:** Brooks & Dunn; ▸ **vocal group of the year:** Rascal Flatts; ▸ **album of the year:** *Time Well Wasted,* Brad Paisley; Chris DuBois, Frank Rogers, producers; ▸ **song of the year:** "Believe," Craig Wiseman, Ronnie Dunn, songwriters; ▸ **single of the year:** "Believe," Brooks & Dunn; Tony Brown, Kix Brokks, Ronnie Dunn, producers; ▸ **music video of the year:** "Believe," Robert Deaton, George J. Flanigen IV, directors (Brooks & Dunn); ▸ **musical event of the year:** "When I Get Where I'm Going," Brad Paisley with Dolly Parton; ▸ **musician of the year:** Randy Scruggs (guitar)

The All-Time Top 50 Best-Selling Albums in the United States

As of June 2007. Album sales are given only to the nearest million copies, and in the case of a tie albums are listed alphabetically by artist. Source: Recording Industry Association of America (RIAA), <www.riaa.com>.

	ALBUM	ARTIST	YEAR		ALBUM	ARTIST	YEAR
1	Their Greatest Hits (1971–1975)	The Eagles	1976	25	Born in the U.S.A.	Bruce Springsteen	1984
2	Thriller	Michael Jackson	1982	26	Backstreet Boys	Backstreet Boys	1997
3	Untitled ("Led Zeppelin IV")	Led Zeppelin	1971	27	Ropin' the Wind	Garth Brooks	1991
4	The Wall	Pink Floyd	1979	28	Greatest Hits	Journey	1988
5	Back in Black	AC/DC	1980	29	Bat out of Hell	Meat Loaf	1977
6	Greatest Hits, Volume I & Volume II	Billy Joel	1985	30	Metallica	Metallica	1991
7	Double Live	Garth Brooks	1998	31	Simon & Garfunkel's Greatest Hits	Simon & Garfunkel	1972
8	Come on Over	Shania Twain	1997	32	...Baby One More Time	Britney Spears	1999
9	The Beatles ("The White Album")	The Beatles	1968	33	Millennium	Backstreet Boys	1999
10	Rumours	Fleetwood Mac	1977	34	Whitney Houston	Whitney Houston	1985
11	Boston	Boston	1976	35	Greatest Hits 1974–1978	Steve Miller Band	1978
12	The Bodyguard (soundtrack)	Whitney Houston & various artists	1992	36	Purple Rain (soundtrack)	Prince and the Revolution	1984
13	1967–70	The Beatles	1973	37	Live/1975–85	Bruce Springsteen & the E Street Band	1986
14	No Fences	Garth Brooks	1990	38	Abbey Road	The Beatles	1969
15	Hotel California	The Eagles	1976	39	Slippery When Wet	Bon Jovi	1986
16	Cracked Rear View	Hootie & the Blowfish	1994	40	II	Boyz II Men	1994
17	Greatest Hits	Elton John	1974	41	No Jacket Required	Phil Collins	1985
18	Physical Graffiti	Led Zeppelin	1975	42	Hysteria	Def Leppard	1987
19	Jagged Little Pill	Alanis Morissette	1995	43	Wide Open Spaces	Dixie Chicks	1998
20	1962–66	The Beatles	1973	44	Pieces of You	Jewel	1995
21	Saturday Night Fever (soundtrack)	The Bee Gees & various artists	1977	45	Breathless	Kenny G	1992
22	Appetite for Destruction	Guns N' Roses	1987	46	Led Zeppelin II	Led Zeppelin	1969
23	Dark Side of the Moon	Pink Floyd	1973	47	Yourself or Someone Like You	Matchbox 20	1996
24	Supernatural	Santana	1999	48	Ten	Pearl Jam	1991
				49	Kenny Rogers' Greatest Hits	Kenny Rogers	1980
				50	Hot Rocks 1964–1971	The Rolling Stones	1972

Rock and Roll Hall of Fame Inductees

Music-industry professionals established the Rock and Roll Hall of Fame Foundation in 1983 in order to "recognize the contributions of those who have had a significant impact on the evolution, development, and perpetuation of rock and roll." Performers are eligible for induction 25 years after the release of their first record. The foundation's nominating committee compiles an annual list of eligible artists and distributes this list to about 1,000 rock experts throughout the world. Those performers receiving the highest number of votes, as well as at least 50% of the vote, are inducted. Special committees select inductees in other categories. Those elected to membership receive a statuette depicting an abstract human figure holding aloft a gold record. 2007 inductees appear in **boldface**.

Web site: <www.rockhall.com>.

NAME (YEAR OF INDUCTION)
AC/DC (2003)
Paul Ackerman[1] (1995)
Aerosmith (2001)
The Allman Brothers Band (1995)
Herb Alpert and Jerry Moss[2] (2006)
The Animals (1994)
Louis Armstrong[3] (1990)
Chet Atkins[4] (2002)
LaVern Baker (1991)
Hank Ballard (1990)
The Band (1994)
Dave Bartholomew[1] (1991)
Frank Barsalona[2] (2005)
Ralph Bass[1] (1991)
The Beach Boys (1988)
The Beatles (1988)
The Bee Gees (1997)
Benny Benjamin[4] (2003)
Chuck Berry (1986)
Black Sabbath (2006)
Chris Blackwell[1] (2001)
Hal Blaine[4] (2000)
Bobby "Blue" Bland (1992)
Blondie (2006)
Booker T. and the MG's (1992)
David Bowie (1996)
Charles Brown[3] (1999)
James Brown (1986)
Ruth Brown (1993)
Jackson Browne (2004)
Buffalo Springfield (1997)
Solomon Burke (2001)
James Burton[4] (2001)
The Byrds (1991)
Johnny Cash (1992)
Ray Charles (1986)
Leonard Chess[1] (1987)
Charlie Christian[3] (1990)
Eric Clapton (2000)
Dick Clark[1] (1993)
The Clash (2003)
The Coasters (1987)
Eddie Cochran (1987)
Nat King Cole[3] (2000)
Sam Cooke (1986)
Elvis Costello & the Attractions (2003)
Floyd Cramer[4] (2003)
Cream (1993)
Creedence Clearwater Revival (1993)
Crosby, Stills & Nash (1997)
Bobby Darin (1990)
Clive Davis[1] (2000)
Miles Davis (2006)
The Dells (2004)

NAME (YEAR OF INDUCTION)
Bo Diddley (1987)
Dion (1989)
Willie Dixon[3] (1994)
Fats Domino (1986)
Tom Donahue[1] (1996)
The Doors (1993)
Steve Douglas[4] (2003)
The Drifters (1988)
Bob Dylan (1988)
The Eagles (1998)
Earth, Wind & Fire (2000)
Duane Eddy (1994)
Ahmet Ertegun[1] (1987)
Nesuhi Ertegun[2] (1991)
The Everly Brothers (1986)
Leo Fender[1] (1992)
The Flamingos (2001)
Fleetwood Mac (1998)
The Four Seasons (1990)
The Four Tops (1990)
Aretha Franklin (1987)
Alan Freed[1] (1986)
Milt Gabler[1] (1993)
Marvin Gaye (1987)
Gerry Goffin and Carole King[1] (1990)
Berry Gordy, Jr.[1] (1988)
Bill Graham[1] (1992)
Grandmaster Flash and the Furious Five (2007)
The Grateful Dead (1994)
Al Green (1995)
Woody Guthrie[3] (1988)
Buddy Guy (2005)
Bill Haley (1987)
John Hammond[2] (1986)
George Harrison (2004)
Isaac Hayes (2002)
The Jimi Hendrix Experience (1992)
Billie Holiday[3] (2000)
Holland, Dozier, and Holland[1] (1990)
Buddy Holly (1986)
John Lee Hooker (1991)
Howlin' Wolf[3] (1991)
The Impressions (1991)
The Inkspots[3] (1989)
The Isley Brothers (1992)
Mahalia Jackson[3] (1997)
Michael Jackson (2001)
The Jackson Five (1997)
James Jamerson[4] (2000)
Elmore James[3] (1992)
Etta James (1993)
Jefferson Airplane (1996)
Billy Joel (1999)

NAME (YEAR OF INDUCTION)
Elton John (1994)
Little Willie John (1996)
Johnnie Johnson[4] (2001)
Robert Johnson[3] (1986)
Janis Joplin (1995)
Louis Jordan[3] (1987)
B.B. King (1987)
King Curtis[4] (2000)
The Kinks (1990)
Gladys Knight and the Pips (1996)
Leadbelly[3] (1988)
Led Zeppelin (1995)
Brenda Lee (2002)
Jerry Leiber and Mike Stoller[1] (1987)
John Lennon (1994)
Jerry Lee Lewis (1986)
Little Richard (1986)
The Lovin' Spoonful (2000)
Frankie Lymon and the Teenagers (1993)
Lynyrd Skynyrd (2006)
The Mamas and the Papas (1998)
Bob Marley (1994)
Martha and the Vandellas (1995)
George Martin[1] (1999)
Curtis Mayfield (1999)
Paul McCartney (1999)
Clyde McPhatter (1987)
Joni Mitchell (1997)
Bill Monroe[3] (1997)
The Moonglows (2000)
Scotty Moore[4] (2000)
Van Morrison (1993)
Jelly Roll Morton[3] (1998)
Syd Nathan[1] (1997)
Ricky Nelson (1987)
The O'Jays (2005)
Roy Orbison (1987)
The Orioles[3] (1995)
Mo Ostin[1] (2003)
Johnny Otis[1] (1994)
Earl Palmer[4] (2000)
Parliament-Funkadelic (1997)
Les Paul[3] (1988)
Carl Perkins (1987)
Tom Petty and the Heartbreakers (2002)
Sam Phillips[1] (1986)
Wilson Pickett (1991)
Pink Floyd (1996)
Gene Pitney (2002)
The Platters (1990)
The Police (2003)
Doc Pomus[1] (1992)

Rock and Roll Hall of Fame Inductees (continued)

NAME (YEAR OF INDUCTION)
Elvis Presley (1986)
The Pretenders (2005)
Lloyd Price (1998)
Prince (2004)
Professor Longhair[3] (1992)
Queen (2001)
R.E.M. (2007)
Ma Rainey[3] (1990)
Bonnie Raitt (2000)
The Ramones (2002)
Otis Redding (1989)
Jimmy Reed (1991)
The Righteous Brothers (2003)
Smokey Robinson (1987)
Jimmie Rodgers[3] (1986)
The Rolling Stones (1989)
The Ronettes (2007)
Sam and Dave (1992)
Santana (1998)
Pete Seeger[3] (1996)
Bob Seger (2004)
The Sex Pistols (2006)
Del Shannon (1999)
The Shirelles (1996)
Paul Simon (2001)
Simon & Garfunkel (1990)
Percy Sledge (2005)
Sly and the Family Stone (1993)
Bessie Smith[3] (1989)

NAME (YEAR OF INDUCTION)
Patti Smith (2007)
The Soul Stirrers[3] (1989)
Phil Spector[1] (1989)
Dusty Springfield (1999)
Bruce Springsteen (1999)
The Staple Singers (1999)
Steely Dan (2001)
Seymour Stein[2] (2005)
Jim Stewart[1] (2002)
Rod Stewart (1994)
The Supremes (1988)
Talking Heads (2002)
James Taylor (2000)
The Temptations (1989)
Allen Toussaint[1] (1998)
Traffic (2004)
Big Joe Turner (1987)
Ike and Tina Turner (1991)
U2 (2005)
Ritchie Valens (2001)
Van Halen (2007)
The Velvet Underground (1996)
Gene Vincent (1998)
T-Bone Walker[3] (1987)
Dinah Washington[3] (1993)
Muddy Waters (1987)
Jann S. Wenner[2] (2004)
Jerry Wexler[1] (1987)
The Who (1990)

NAME (YEAR OF INDUCTION)
Hank Williams[3] (1987)
Bob Wills and His Texas Playboys[3] (1999)
Jackie Wilson (1987)
Stevie Wonder (1989)
Jimmy Yancey[3] (1986)
The Yardbirds (1992)
Neil Young (1995)
The (Young) Rascals (1997)
Frank Zappa (1995)
ZZ Top (2004)

[1]*Nonperformers.* [2]*Lifetime Achievement.* [3]*Early Influences.* [4]*Sidemen.*

Encyclopædia Britannica's 25 World-Class Orchestras

ORCHESTRA	LOCATION	FOUNDED	MUSIC DIRECTOR OR CONDUCTOR (2007)
Berlin Philharmonic Orchestra	Berlin, Germany	1882	Sir Simon Rattle
Boston Symphony Orchestra	Boston MA	1881	James Levine
Chicago Symphony Orchestra	Chicago IL	1891	Bernard Haitink[1]
Cleveland Orchestra	Cleveland OH	1918	Franz Welser-Möst
Gewandhaus Orchestra	Leipzig, Germany	1743	Riccardo Chailly
Israel Philharmonic Orchestra	Tel Aviv, Israel	1936	Zubin Mehta
London Philharmonic Orchestra	London, England	1932	Kurt Masur
London Symphony Orchestra	London, England	1904	Valery Gergiev
Los Angeles Philharmonic	Los Angeles CA	1919	Esa-Pekka Salonen[2]
Montreal Symphony Orchestra	Montreal, QC, Canada	1934	Kent Nagano
New York Philharmonic	New York NY	1842	Lorin Maazel[3]
NHK Symphony Orchestra	Tokyo, Japan	1926	Vladimir Ashkenazy
Orchestre de la Suisse Romande	Geneva, Switzerland	1918	Marek Janowski
Orchestre de Paris	Paris, France	1967	Christoph Eschenbach[4]
Orchestre National de France	Paris, France	1934	Kurt Masur
Oslo Philharmonic Orchestra	Oslo, Norway	1919	Jukka-Pekka Saraste
Philadelphia Orchestra	Philadelphia PA	1900	Christoph Eschenbach
Philharmonia Orchestra	London, England	1945	Christoph von Dohnányi
Pittsburgh Symphony Orchestra	Pittsburgh PA	1896	Sir Andrew Davis[5]
Royal Concertgebouw Orchestra	Amsterdam, Netherlands	1888	Mariss Jansons
Royal Philharmonic Orchestra	London, England	1946	Daniele Gatti
Saint Louis Symphony Orchestra	St. Louis MO	1880	David Robertson
St. Petersburg State Symphony Orchestra	St. Petersburg, Russia	1988	Aleksandr Kantorov
San Francisco Symphony	San Francisco CA	1911	Michael Tilson Thomas
Vienna Philharmonic Orchestra	Vienna, Austria	1842	guest conductors

[1]*Principal conductor. The search for a music director is ongoing in 2007.* [2]*Gustavo Dudamel will assume the musical directorship of the Los Angeles Philharmonic in September 2009.* [3]*Alan Gilbert will assume the musical directorship of the New York Philharmonic in 2009.* [4]*Paavo Järvi will assume the musical directorship of the Orchestre de Paris in September 2010.* [5]*Artistic advisor. Manfred Honeck will assume the musical directorship of the Pittsburgh Symphony Orchestra in September 2008.*

Encyclopædia Britannica's Top 25 Opera Companies

COMPANY	LOCATION	FOUNDED	GENERAL OR ARTISTIC DIRECTOR (2007)
Arena di Verona[1]	Verona, Italy	1913	Claudio Orazi
Bayerische Staatsoper (Bavarian State Opera)	Munich, Germany	1653	Kent Nagano[2]
Bolshoi Opera	Moscow, Russia	1776	Makvala Kasrashvili
Canadian Opera Company	Toronto, ON, Canada	1950	Richard Bradshaw
Grand Théâtre de Genève	Geneva, Switzerland	1962	Jean-Marie Blanchard
Los Angeles Opera	Los Angeles CA	1986	Plácido Domingo
Lyric Opera of Chicago	Chicago IL	1954	William Mason
Magyar Állami Opera (Hungarian State Opera)	Budapest, Hungary	1884	Lajos Vass
Mariinsky Opera Company	St. Petersburg, Russia	1783	Valery Gergiev
Metropolitan Opera	New York NY	1883	Peter Gelb
Opera Australia	Sydney, NSW, and Melbourne, VIC, Australia	1956	Richard Hickox[3]
Opera Cleveland	Cleveland OH	2007	Leon Major
Opéra National de Paris	Paris, France	1669	Gerard Mortier
Royal Opera	London, England	1732	Antonio Pappano[3]
San Francisco Opera	San Francisco CA	1923	David Gockley
Staatsoper Unter den Linden (Berlin State Opera)	Berlin, Germany	1742	Peter Mussbach
Suomen Kansallisooppera (Finnish National Opera)	Helsinki, Finland	1873	Erkki Korhonen
Teatro alla Scala (La Scala)	Milan, Italy	1778	Stéphane Lissner
Teatro dell'Opera di Roma	Rome, Italy	1880	Mauro Trombetta
Teatro di San Carlo	Naples, Italy	1737	Alessio Vlad
Teatro Massimo	Palermo, Italy	1897	Lorenzo Mariani
Théâtre du Châtelet	Paris, France	1862	Jean-Luc Choplin
Vancouver Opera	Vancouver, BC, Canada	1958	James W. Wright
Washington National Opera	Washington DC	1956	Plácido Domingo
Wiener Staatsoper (Vienna State Opera)	Vienna, Austria	1869	Ioan Holender

[1]The Arena di Verona was built in the first century AD; it has been primarily an opera venue since 1913. [2]Bavarian general music director. Klaus Bachler will assume the post of general manager of the Bayerische Staatsoper in 2008. [3]Music director. The position of general or artistic director does not exist.

Did you know? It has been speculated that when King James I of England hired 54 of the best writers and scholars in the country for a new English version of the Bible in 1611, William Shakespeare might have been among them. Although there is no conclusive evidence for the Bard's participation in the project, it is nevertheless intriguing that the 46th word of the 46th Psalm is "shake," and the 46th word from the end of the Psalm is "spear." Shakespeare, who was fond of cryptograms, was 46 years old at the time.

Pageants

Miss America Winners, 1921–2007

The Miss America Pageant was founded in 1921 as an Atlantic City NJ tourist attraction. Purely a beauty contest in its early years, the competition added a talent category in 1935 and began awarding scholarships a decade later. After 1989 the pageant required evidence of community service, and by 2001 contestants were judged on the basis of talent, community service, leadership, knowledge and understanding, and appearance in swimsuits and eveningwear. Prize: $50,000 college scholarship. Miss America Contest Web site: <www.missamerica.org>.

YEAR	WINNER (HOMETOWN)	YEAR	WINNER (HOMETOWN)
1921	Margaret Gorman (Washington DC)	1934	*not held*
1922	Mary Katherine Campbell (Columbus OH)	1935	Henrietta Leaver (Pittsburgh PA)
1923	Mary Katherine Campbell (Columbus OH)	1936	Rose Coyle (Philadelphia PA)
1924	Ruth Malcomson (Philadelphia PA)	1937	Bette Cooper (Bertrand Island NJ)
1925	Fay Lanphier (Oakland CA)	1938	Marilyn Meseke (Marion OH)
1926	Norma Smallwood (Tulsa OK)	1939	Patricia Donnelly (Detroit MI)
1927	Lois Delander (Joliet IL)	1940	Frances Burke (Philadelphia PA)
1928–32	*not held*	1941	Rosemary LaPlanche (Los Angeles CA)
1933	Marian Bergeron (West Haven CT)	1942	Jo-Carroll Dennison (Tyler TX)

Miss America Winners, 1921–2007 (continued)

YEAR	WINNER (HOMETOWN)	YEAR	WINNER (HOMETOWN)
1943	Jean Bartel (Los Angeles CA)	1976	Tawny Godin (Saratoga Springs NY)
1944	Venus Ramey (Washington DC)	1977	Dorothy Benham (Edina MN)
1945	Bess Myerson (New York NY)	1978	Susan Perkins (Columbus OH)
1946	Marilyn Buferd (Los Angeles CA)	1979	Kylene Barker (Roanoke VA)
1947	Barbara Walker (Memphis TN)	1980	Cheryl Prewitt (Ackerman MS)
1948	BeBe Shopp (Hopkins MN)	1981	Susan Powell (Elk City OK)
1949	Jacque Mercer (Litchfield AZ)	1982	Elizabeth Ward (Russellville AR)
1950[1]		1983	Debra Maffett (Anaheim CA)
1951	Yolande Betbeze (Mobile AL)	1984	Suzette Charles (Mays Landing NJ)[2]
1952	Colleen Hutchins (Salt Lake City UT)	1985	Sharlene Wells (Salt Lake City UT)
1953	Neva Langley (Macon GA)	1986	Susan Akin (Meridian MS)
1954	Evelyn Ay (Ephrata PA)	1987	Kellye Cash (Memphis TN)
1955	Lee Meriwether (San Francisco CA)	1988	Kaye Lani Rae Rafko (Monroe MI)
1956	Sharon Ritchie (Denver CO)	1989	Gretchen Carlson (Anoka MN)
1957	Marian McKnight (Manning SC)	1990	Debbye Turner (Columbia MO)
1958	Marilyn Van Derbur (Denver CO)	1991	Marjorie Vincent (Oak Park IL)
1959	Mary Ann Mobley (Brandon MS)	1992	Carolyn Sapp (Honolulu HI)
1960	Lynda Mead (Natchez MS)	1993	Leanza Cornett (Jacksonville FL)
1961	Nancy Fleming (Montague MI)	1994	Kimberly Aiken (Columbia SC)
1962	Maria Fletcher (Asheville NC)	1995	Heather Whitestone (Birmingham AL)
1963	Jacquelyn Mayer (Sandusky OH)	1996	Shawntel Smith (Muldrow OK)
1964	Donna Axum (El Dorado AR)	1997	Tara Dawn Holland (Overland Park KS)
1965	Vonda Van Dyke (Phoenix AZ)	1998	Kate Shindle (Evanston IL)
1966	Deborah Bryant (Overland Park KS)	1999	Nicole Johnson (Virginia Beach VA)
1967	Jane Jayroe (Laverne OK)	2000	Heather French (Maysville KY)
1968	Debra Barnes (Pittsburg KS)	2001	Angela Perez Baraquio (Honolulu HI)
1969	Judith Ford (Belvidere IL)	2002	Katie Harman (Gresham OR)
1970	Pam Eldred (Bloomfield MI)	2003	Erika Harold (Urbana IL)
1971	Phyllis George (Denton TX)	2004	Ericka Dunlap (Orlando FL)
1972	Laurel Schaefer (Bexley OH)	2005	Deirdre Downs (Birmingham AL)
1973	Terry Meeuwsen (De Pere WI)	2006	Jennifer Berry (Tulsa OK)
1974	Rebecca King (Denver CO)	2007	Lauren Nelson (Lawton OK)
1975	Shirley Cothran (Denton TX)		

[1]Until the 1950 competition, winners were given the title for the year in which they won; thereafter, they were given the title for the following year, during which most of their reign took place. As a result no Miss America 1950 was named. [2]Runner-up, crowned after resignation of Vanessa Williams (Millwood NY).

Miss Universe Winners, 1952–2007

The Miss Universe contest originated in 1952 as a swimwear competition in Long Beach CA in conjunction with the Miss USA pageant. The two pageants were held concurrently until 1965. Women aged 18–27 from some 80 countries and dependencies participate in the competition annually, and the contest is broadcast across the globe. Judging is based on an interview and appearances in swimwear and evening wear. Though it remains primarily a beauty contest, the competition's organizers emphasize a message of cross-cultural harmony and opportunity for women, and winners work with the UN and other organizations to promote HIV/AIDS awareness and women's health and reproductive initiatives. Prize: one-year employment contract, cash, products, and services. Miss Universe contest Web site: <www.miss universe.com>.

YEAR	WINNER (COUNTRY)	YEAR	WINNER (COUNTRY)
1952	Armi Kuusela (Finland)	1967	Sylvia Louise Hitchcock (US)
1953	Christiane Martel (France)	1968	Martha Vasconcellos (Brazil)
1954	Miriam Stevenson (US)	1969	Gloria Diaz (Philippines)
1955	Hillevi Rombin (Sweden)	1970	Marisol Malaret (Puerto Rico)
1956	Carol Morris (US)	1971	Georgina Rizk (Lebanon)
1957	Gladys Zender (Peru)	1972	Kerry Anne Wells (Australia)
1958	Luz Marina Zuluaga (Colombia)	1973	Margarita Moran (Philippines)
1959	Akiko Kojima (Japan)	1974	Amparo Muñoz (Spain)
1960	Linda Bement (US)	1975	Anne Marie Pohtamo (Finland)
1961	Marlene Schmidt (West Germany)	1976	Rina Messinger (Israel)
1962	Norma Nolan (Argentina)	1977	Janelle Commissiong (Trinidad and Tobago)
1963	Ieda Maria Vargas (Brazil)	1978	Margaret Gardiner (South Africa)
1964	Kiriaki Corinna Tsopei (Greece)	1979	Maritza Sayalero (Venezuela)
1965	Apasra Hongsakula (Thailand)	1980	Shawn Nichols Weatherly (US)
1966	Margareta Arvidsson (Sweden)	1981	Mona Irene Lailan Sáez Conde (Venezuela)

Miss Universe Winners, 1952–2007 (continued)

YEAR	WINNER (COUNTRY)	YEAR	WINNER (COUNTRY)
1982	Karen Diane Baldwin (Canada)	1996	Joseph Alicia Machado Fajardo (Venezuela)
1983	Lorraine Downes (New Zealand)	1997	Brook Antoinette Mahealani Lee (US)
1984	Yvonne Ryding (Sweden)	1998	Wendy Fitzwilliam (Trinidad and Tobago)
1985	Deborah Carthy-Deu (Puerto Rico)	1999	Mpule Kwelagobe (Botswana)
1986	Bárbara Palacios Teyde (Venezuela)	2000	Lara Dutta (India)
1987	Cecilia Carolina Bolocco Fonck (Chile)	2001	Denise M. Quiñones August (Puerto Rico)
1988	Porntip Nakhirunkanok (Thailand)	2002	Justine Pasek (Panama)[1]
1989	Angela Visser (The Netherlands)	2003	Amelia Vega (Dominican Republic)
1990	Mona Grudt (Norway)	2004	Jennifer Hawkins (Australia)
1991	Lupita Jones (Mexico)	2005	Natalie Glebova (Canada)
1992	Michelle McLean (Namibia)	2006	Zuleyka Rivera (Puerto Rico)
1993	Dayanara Torres (Puerto Rico)	2007	Riyo Mori (Japan)
1994	Sushmita Sen (India)		
1995	Chelsi Smith (US)		

[1]Oksana Fyodorova (Russia) was dismissed for breach of contract on 23 Sep 2002.

Arts and Letters Awards

Pulitzer Prizes, 2007

The Pulitzer Prizes are awarded annually by Columbia University, New York City, based on recommendations from the Pulitzer Prize Board. The prizes, originally endowed by newspaper editor Joseph Pulitzer, were first awarded in 1917. Over the years categories have been added, and 21 prizes are now presented. All prizes include a $10,000 cash award; the exception is the prize for public service in journalism, which is a gold medal.

Pulitzer Prize Web site: <www.pulitzer.org>.

Journalism

CATEGORY AND DESCRIPTION	WINNER	PUBLICATION	SUBJECT
Public Service: awarded to a newspaper for notable public service	staff	The Wall Street Journal	probe of controversial back-dating of stock options for business executives
Breaking News Reporting: awarded for local reporting of breaking news	staff	Oregonian, Portland OR	coverage of the tragic story of the search for a family missing in the mountains of Oregon
Investigative Reporting: awarded to an individual or team for an investigative article or series	Brett Blackledge	Birmingham News, Birmingham AL	investigation exposing the cronyism and corruption in Alabama's two-year college system
Explanatory Reporting: awarded for clarification of a difficult subject through clear communication of in-depth knowledge	Kenneth R. Weiss, Usha Lee McFarling, and Rick Loomis	Los Angeles Times	scientific coverage of the state of the Earth's distressed oceans
Local Reporting: awarded for consistent, intelligent coverage of a particular topic	Debbie Cenziper	Miami Herald	reports on waste, favoritism, and lack of oversight at the Miami housing agency
National Reporting: awarded for coverage of national news	Charlie Savage	Boston Globe	reporting on President George W. Bush's controversial use of "signing statements" to by-pass provisions of new laws
International Reporting: awarded for coverage of international news	staff	The Wall Street Journal	coverage of the negative social and environmental impact of China's booming capitalism
Feature Writing	Andrea Elliott	New York Times	portrait of an immigrant imam in America
Commentary	Cynthia Tucker	Atlanta Journal-Constitution	columns that evince a strong sense of morality and community awareness
Criticism	Jonathan Gold	LA Weekly	restaurant reviews
Editorial Writing: awarded for ability to sway public opinion through solid reasoning, clear style, and "moral purpose"	Arthur Browne, Beverly Weintraub, and Heidi Evans	New York Daily News	editorials on behalf of workers at "ground zero" now experiencing health problems

Journalism (continued)

CATEGORY AND DESCRIPTION	WINNER	PUBLICATION	SUBJECT
Editorial Cartooning: awarded for a cartoon or group of cartoons displaying creativity, superior drawing, and editorial effectiveness	Walt Handelsman	*Newsday,* Long Island NY	
Breaking News Photography: awarded for color or black-and-white photographs of breaking news, individually or as a group	Oded Balilty	Associated Press	coverage of the removal of illegal settlers in the West Bank by the Israelis
Feature Photography: awarded for color or black-and-white feature photographs, individually or as a group	Renée C. Byer	*Sacramento Bee*	photo essay on a single mother and her young son's battle against cancer

Letters, Drama, and Music

Fiction
Awarded for a work of fiction, preferably about American life, by an American author.

YEAR	TITLE	AUTHOR	YEAR	TITLE	AUTHOR
1917	no award		1952	*The Caine Mutiny*	Herman Wouk
1918	*His Family*	Ernest Poole	1953	*The Old Man and the Sea*	Ernest Hemingway
1919	*The Magnificent Ambersons*	Booth Tarkington	1954	no award	
1920	no award		1955	*A Fable*	William Faulkner
1921	*The Age of Innocence*	Edith Wharton	1956	*Andersonville*	MacKinlay Kantor
1922	*Alice Adams*	Booth Tarkington	1957	no award	
1923	*One of Ours*	Willa Cather	1958	*A Death in the Family*[1]	James Agee
1924	*The Able McLaughlins*	Margaret Wilson	1959	*The Travels of Jaimie McPheeters*	Robert Lewis Taylor
1925	*So Big*	Edna Ferber			
1926	*Arrowsmith*	Sinclair Lewis	1960	*Advise and Consent*	Allen Drury
1927	*Early Autumn*	Louis Bromfield	1961	*To Kill a Mockingbird*	Harper Lee
1928	*The Bridge of San Luis Rey*	Thornton Wilder	1962	*The Edge of Sadness*	Edwin O'Connor
			1963	*The Reivers*	William Faulkner
1929	*Scarlet Sister Mary*	Julia Peterkin	1964	no award	
1930	*Laughing Boy*	Oliver Lafarge	1965	*The Keepers of the House*	Shirley Ann Grau
1931	*Years of Grace*	Margaret Ayer Barnes			
1932	*The Good Earth*	Pearl S. Buck	1966	*Collected Stories*	Katherine Anne Porter
1933	*The Store*	T.S. Stribling	1967	*The Fixer*	Bernard Malamud
1934	*Lamb in His Bosom*	Caroline Miller	1968	*The Confessions of Nat Turner*	William Styron
1935	*Now in November*	Josephine Winslow Johnson	1969	*House Made of Dawn*	N. Scott Momaday
1936	*Honey in the Horn*	Harold L. Davis	1970	*Collected Stories*	Jean Stafford
1937	*Gone with the Wind*	Margaret Mitchell	1971	no award	
1938	*The Late George Apley*	John Phillips Marquand	1972	*Angle of Repose*	Wallace Stegner
			1973	*The Optimist's Daughter*	Eudora Welty
1939	*The Yearling*	Marjorie Kinnan Rawlings	1974	no award	
			1975	*The Killer Angels*	Michael Shaara
1940	*The Grapes of Wrath*	John Steinbeck	1976	*Humboldt's Gift*	Saul Bellow
1941	no award		1977	no award	
1942	*In This Our Life*	Ellen Glasgow	1978	*Elbow Room*	James Alan McPherson
1943	*Dragon's Teeth*	Upton Sinclair			
1944	*Journey in the Dark*	Martin Flavin	1979	*The Stories of John Cheever*	John Cheever
1945	*A Bell for Adano*	John Hersey			
1946	no award		1980	*The Executioner's Song*	Norman Mailer
1947	*All the King's Men*	Robert Penn Warren	1981	*A Confederacy of Dunces*[1]	John Kennedy Toole
1948	*Tales of the South Pacific*	James A. Michener	1982	*Rabbit Is Rich*	John Updike
			1983	*The Color Purple*	Alice Walker
1949	*Guard of Honor*	James Gould Cozzens	1984	*Ironweed*	William Kennedy
			1985	*Foreign Affairs*	Alison Lurie
1950	*The Way West*	A.B. Guthrie, Jr.	1986	*Lonesome Dove*	Larry McMurtry
1951	*The Town*	Conrad Richter	1987	*A Summons to Memphis*	Peter Taylor

Letters, Drama, and Music (continued)

Fiction (continued)

YEAR	TITLE	AUTHOR	YEAR	TITLE	AUTHOR
1988	Beloved	Toni Morrison	1998	American Pastoral	Philip Roth
1989	Breathing Lessons	Anne Tyler	1999	The Hours	Michael Cunningham
1990	The Mambo Kings Play Songs of Love	Oscar Hijuelos	2000	Interpreter of Maladies	Jhumpa Lahiri
1991	Rabbit at Rest	John Updike	2001	The Amazing Adventures of Kavalier and Clay	Michael Chabon
1992	A Thousand Acres	Jane Smiley	2002	Empire Falls	Richard Russo
1993	A Good Scent from a Strange Mountain	Robert Olen Butler	2003	Middlesex	Jeffrey Eugenides
1994	The Shipping News	E. Annie Proulx	2004	The Known World	Edward P. Jones
1995	The Stone Diaries	Carol Shields	2005	Gilead	Marilynne Robinson
1996	Independence Day	Richard Ford	2006	March	Geraldine Brooks
1997	Martin Dressler: The Tale of an American Dreamer	Steven Millhauser	2007	The Road	Cormac McCarthy

[1]Work published and prize awarded posthumously.

Drama
Awarded for a play, preferably about American life, by an American author.

YEAR	TITLE	AUTHOR	YEAR	TITLE	AUTHOR
1917	no award		1951	no award	
1918	Why Marry?	Jesse Lynch Williams	1952	The Shrike	Joseph Kramm
			1953	Picnic	William Inge
1919	no award		1954	The Teahouse of the August Moon	John Patrick
1920	Beyond the Horizon	Eugene O'Neill			
1921	Miss Lulu Bett	Zona Gale	1955	Cat on a Hot Tin Roof	Tennessee Williams
1922	Anna Christie	Eugene O'Neill			
1923	Icebound	Owen Davis	1956	The Diary of Anne Frank	Albert Hackett, Frances Goodrich
1924	Hell-Bent fer Heaven	Hatcher Hughes			
1925	They Knew What They Wanted	Sidney Howard	1957	Long Day's Journey into Night	Eugene O'Neill
1926	Craig's Wife	George Kelly	1958	Look Homeward, Angel	Ketti Frings
1927	In Abraham's Bosom	Paul Green	1959	J.B.	Archibald MacLeish
1928	Strange Interlude	Eugene O'Neill	1960	Fiorello!	Jerome Weidman, George Abbott, Jerry Bock, Sheldon Harnick
1929	Street Scene	Elmer L. Rice			
1930	The Green Pastures	Marc Connelly			
1931	Alison's House	Susan Glaspell			
1932	Of Thee I Sing	George S. Kaufman, Morrie Ryskind, Ira Gershwin	1961	All the Way Home	Tad Mosel
			1962	How To Succeed in Business Without Really Trying	Frank Loesser, Abe Burrows
1933	Both Your Houses	Maxwell Anderson			
1934	Men in White	Sidney Kingsley			
1935	The Old Maid	Zoe Akins	1963	no award	
1936	Idiot's Delight	Robert E. Sherwood	1964	no award	
1937	You Can't Take It with You	Moss Hart, George S. Kaufman	1965	The Subject Was Roses	Frank D. Gilroy
			1966	no award	
1938	Our Town	Thornton Wilder	1967	A Delicate Balance	Edward Albee
1939	Abe Lincoln in Illinois	Robert E. Sherwood	1968	no award	
1940	The Time of Your Life	William Saroyan	1969	The Great White Hope	Howard Sackler
1941	There Shall Be No Night	Robert E. Sherwood	1970	No Place To Be Somebody	Charles Gordone
1942	no award				
1943	The Skin of Our Teeth	Thornton Wilder	1971	The Effect of Gamma Rays on Man-in-the-Moon Marigolds	Paul Zindel
1944	no award				
1945	Harvey	Mary Chase			
1946	State of the Union	Russel Crouse, Howard Lindsay	1972	no award	
			1973	That Championship Season	Jason Miller
1947	no award				
1948	A Streetcar Named Desire	Tennessee Williams	1974	no award	
			1975	Seascape	Edward Albee
1949	Death of a Salesman	Arthur Miller	1976	A Chorus Line	Michael Bennett, James Kirkwood, Nicholas Dante, Marvin Hamlisch, Edward Kleban
1950	South Pacific	Richard Rodgers, Oscar Hammerstein II, Joshua Logan			

Letters, Drama, and Music (continued)

Drama (continued)

YEAR	TITLE	AUTHOR	YEAR	TITLE	AUTHOR
1977	The Shadow Box	Michael Cristofer	1993	Angels in America: Millennium Approaches	Tony Kushner
1978	The Gin Game	Donald L. Coburn			
1979	Buried Child	Sam Shepard	1994	Three Tall Women	Edward Albee
1980	Talley's Folly	Lanford Wilson	1995	The Young Man from Atlanta	Horton Foote
1981	Crimes of the Heart	Beth Henley			
1982	A Soldier's Play	Charles Fuller	1996	Rent[1]	Jonathan Larson
1983	'Night, Mother	Marsha Norman	1997	no award	
1984	Glengarry Glen Ross	David Mamet	1998	How I Learned To Drive	Paula Vogel
1985	Sunday in the Park with George	Stephen Sondheim, James Lapine	1999	Wit	Margaret Edson
			2000	Dinner with Friends	Donald Margulies
			2001	Proof	David Auburn
1986	no award		2002	Topdog/Underdog	Suzan-Lori Parks
1987	Fences	August Wilson	2003	Anna in the Tropics	Nilo Cruz
1988	Driving Miss Daisy	Alfred Uhry	2004	I Am My Own Wife	Doug Wright
1989	The Heidi Chronicles	Wendy Wasserstein	2005	Doubt: A Parable	John Patrick Shanley
1990	The Piano Lesson	August Wilson			
1991	Lost in Yonkers	Neil Simon	2006	no award	
1992	The Kentucky Cycle	Robert Schenkkan	2007	Rabbit Hole	David Lindsay-Abaire

[1] Awarded posthumously.

History

Awarded for a work on the subject of American history.

YEAR	TITLE	AUTHOR	YEAR	TITLE	AUTHOR
1917	With Americans of Past and Present Days	J.J. Jusserand	1933	The Significance of Sections in American History	Frederick J. Turner
1918	A History of the Civil War, 1861–1865	James Ford Rhodes	1934	The People's Choice	Herbert Agar
1919	no award		1935	The Colonial Period of American History	Charles McLean Andrews
1920	The War with Mexico, 2 vols.	Justin H. Smith	1936	A Constitutional History of the United States	Andrew C. McLaughlin
1921	The Victory at Sea	William Sowden Sims, Burton Jesse Hendrick	1937	The Flowering of New England, 1815–1865	Van Wyck Brooks
1922	The Founding of New England	James Truslow Adams	1938	The Road to Reunion, 1865–1900	Paul Herman Buck
1923	The Supreme Court in United States History	Charles Warren	1939	A History of American Magazines	Frank Luther Mott
1924	The American Revolution: A Constitutional Interpretation	Charles Howard McIlwain	1940	Abraham Lincoln: The War Years	Carl Sandburg
			1941	The Atlantic Migration, 1607–1860	Marcus Lee Hansen
1925	History of the American Frontier	Frederic L. Paxson	1942	Reveille in Washington, 1860–1865	Margaret Leech
1926	A History of the United States	Edward Channing	1943	Paul Revere and the World He Lived in	Esther Forbes
1927	Pinckney's Treaty	Samuel Flagg Bemis	1944	The Growth of American Thought	Merle Curti
1928	Main Currents in American Thought, 2 vols.	Vernon Louis Parrington	1945	Unfinished Business	Stephen Bonsal
			1946	The Age of Jackson	Arthur M. Schlesinger, Jr.
1929	The Organization and Administration of the Union Army, 1861–1865	Fred Albert Shannon	1947	Scientists Against Time	James Phinney Baxter III
			1948	Across the Wide Missouri	Bernard De Voto
1930	The War of Independence	Claude H. Van Tyne	1949	The Disruption of American Democracy	Roy Franklin Nichols
1931	The Coming of the War, 1914	Bernadotte E. Schmitt	1950	Art and Life in America	Oliver W. Larkin
1932	My Experiences in the World War	John J. Pershing	1951	The Old Northwest: Pioneer Period, 1815–1840	R. Carlyle Buley

Letters, Drama, and Music (continued)

History (continued)

YEAR	TITLE	AUTHOR
1952	The Uprooted	Oscar Handlin
1953	The Era of Good Feelings	George Dangerfield
1954	A Stillness at Appomattox	Bruce Catton
1955	Great River: The Rio Grande in North American History	Paul Horgan
1956	The Age of Reform	Richard Hofstadter
1957	Russia Leaves the War: Soviet-American Relations, 1917–1920	George F. Kennan
1958	Banks and Politics in America	Bray Hammond
1959	The Republican Era: 1869–1901	Leonard D. White, Jean Schneider
1960	In the Days of McKinley	Margaret Leech
1961	Between War and Peace: The Potsdam Conference	Herbert Feis
1962	The Triumphant Empire: Thunder-Clouds Gather in the West, 1763–1766	Lawrence H. Gipson
1963	Washington, Village and Capital, 1800–1878	Constance McLaughlin Green
1964	Puritan Village: The Formation of a New England Town	Sumner Chilton Powell
1965	The Greenback Era	Irwin Unger
1966	The Life of the Mind in America[1]	Perry Miller
1967	Exploration and Empire: The Explorer and the Scientist in the Winning of the American West	William H. Goetzmann
1968	The Ideological Origins of the American Revolution	Bernard Bailyn
1969	Origins of the Fifth Amendment	Leonard W. Levy
1970	Present at the Creation: My Years in the State Department	Dean Acheson
1971	Roosevelt: The Soldier of Freedom	James MacGregor Burns
1972	Neither Black nor White	Carl N. Degler
1973	People of Paradox: An Inquiry Concerning the Origins of American Civilization	Michael Kammen
1974	The Americans: The Democratic Experience	Daniel J. Boorstin
1975	Jefferson and His Time, vols. 1–5	Dumas Malone
1976	Lamy of Santa Fe	Paul Horgan
1977	The Impending Crisis, 1841–1867[2]	David M. Potter, Don E. Fehrenbacher
1978	The Visible Hand: The Managerial Revolution in American Business	Alfred D. Chandler, Jr.
1979	The Dred Scott Case	Don E. Fehrenbacher
1980	Been in the Storm So Long	Leon F. Litwack
1981	American Education: The National Experience, 1783–1876	Lawrence A. Cremin
1982	Mary Chesnut's Civil War	C. Vann Woodward[3]
1983	The Transformation of Virginia, 1740–1790	Rhys L. Isaac
1984	no award	
1985	Prophets of Regulation	Thomas K. McCraw
1986	The Heavens and the Earth: A Political History of the Space Age	Walter A. McDougall
1987	Voyagers to the West: A Passage in the Peopling of America on the Eve of the Revolution	Bernard Bailyn
1988	The Launching of Modern American Science, 1846–1876	Robert V. Bruce
1989	Battle Cry of Freedom: The Civil War Era	James M. McPherson
1989	Parting the Waters: America in the King Years, 1954–1963	Taylor Branch
1990	In Our Image: America's Empire in the Philippines	Stanley Karnow
1991	A Midwife's Tale	Laurel Thatcher Ulrich
1992	The Fate of Liberty: Abraham Lincoln and Civil Liberties	Mark E. Neely, Jr.
1993	The Radicalism of the American Revolution	Gordon S. Wood
1994	no award	
1995	No Ordinary Time: Franklin and Eleanor Roosevelt: The Home Front in World War II	Doris Kearns Goodwin
1996	William Cooper's Town: Power and Persuasion on the Frontier of the Early American Republic	Alan Taylor
1997	Original Meanings: Politics and Ideas in the Making of the Constitution	Jack N. Rakove
1998	Summer for the Gods: The Scopes Trial and America's Continuing Debate over Science and Religion	Edward J. Larson
1999	Gotham: A History of New York City to 1898	Edwin G. Burrows, Mike Wallace
2000	Freedom from Fear: The American People in Depression and War, 1929–1945	David M. Kennedy
2001	Founding Brothers: The Revolutionary Generation	Joseph J. Ellis

Letters, Drama, and Music (continued)

History (continued)

YEAR	TITLE	AUTHOR
2002	The Metaphysical Club: A Story of Ideas in America	Louis Menand
2003	An Army at Dawn: The War in North Africa, 1942–1943	Rick Atkinson
2004	A Nation Under Our Feet: Black Political Struggles in the Rural South from Slavery to the Great Migration	Steven Hahn

YEAR	TITLE	AUTHOR
2005	Washington's Crossing	David Hackett Fischer
2006	Polio: An American Story	David M. Oshinsky
2007	The Race Beat: The Press, the Civil Rights Struggle, and the Awakening of a Nation	Gene Roberts, Hank Klibanoff

[1]Awarded posthumously.   [2]Potter died before completing the work; Fehrenbacher wrote the final chapters and edited it.   [3]Editor.

Biography or Autobiography
Awarded for a biography or autobiography by an American author.

YEAR	TITLE	AUTHOR
1917	Julia Ward Howe	Laura Elizabeth Howe Richards, Maude Howe Elliott; assisted by Florence Howe Hall
1918	Benjamin Franklin, Self-Revealed	William Cabell Bruce
1919	The Education of Henry Adams	Henry Adams
1920	The Life of John Marshall, 4 vols.	Albert J. Beveridge
1921	The Americanization of Edward Bok	Edward Bok
1922	A Daughter of the Middle Border	Hamlin Garland
1923	The Life and Letters of Walter H. Page	Burton J. Hendrick
1924	From Immigrant to Inventor	Michael Idvorsky Pupin
1925	Barrett Wendell and His Letters	M.A. De Wolfe Howe
1926	The Life of Sir William Osler, 2 vols.	Harvey Cushing
1927	Whitman	Emory Holloway
1928	The American Orchestra and Theodore Thomas	Charles Edward Russell
1929	The Training of an American: The Earlier Life and Letters of Walter H. Page	Burton J. Hendrick
1930	The Raven	Marquis James
1931	Charles W. Eliot	Henry James
1932	Theodore Roosevelt	Henry F. Pringle
1933	Grover Cleveland	Allan Nevins
1934	John Hay	Tyler Dennett
1935	R.E. Lee	Douglas S. Freeman
1936	The Thought and Character of William James	Ralph Barton Perry
1937	Hamilton Fish	Allan Nevins
1938	Andrew Jackson, 2 vols.	Marquis James
1938	Pedlar's Progress	Odell Shepard
1939	Benjamin Franklin	Carl Van Doren

YEAR	TITLE	AUTHOR
1940	Woodrow Wilson, Life and Letters, vols. 7 and 8	Ray Stannard Baker
1941	Jonathan Edward	Ola Elizabeth Winslow
1942	Crusader in Crinoline	Forrest Wilson
1943	Admiral of the Ocean Sea	Samuel Eliot Morison
1944	The American Leonardo: The Life of Samuel F.B. Morse	Carleton Mabee
1945	George Bancroft: Brahmin Rebel	Russell Blaine Nye
1946	Son of the Wilderness	Linnie Marsh Wolfe
1947	The Autobiography of William Allen White	William Allen White
1948	Forgotten First Citizen: John Bigelow	Margaret Clapp
1949	Roosevelt and Hopkins	Robert E. Sherwood
1950	John Quincy Adams and the Foundations of American Foreign Policy	Samuel Flagg Bemis
1951	John C. Calhoun: American Portrait	Margaret Louise Coit
1952	Charles Evans Hughes	Merlo J. Pusey
1953	Edmund Pendleton, 1721–1803	David J. Mays
1954	The Spirit of St. Louis	Charles A. Lindbergh
1955	The Taft Story	William S. White
1956	Benjamin Henry Latrobe	Talbot Faulkner Hamlin
1957	Profiles in Courage	John F. Kennedy
1958	George Washington, vols. 1–7[1]	Douglas Southall Freeman, John Alexander Carroll, Mary Wells Ashworth
1959	Woodrow Wilson, American Prophet	Arthur Walworth
1960	John Paul Jones	Samuel Eliot Morison

Letters, Drama, and Music (continued)

Biography or Autobiography (continued)

YEAR	TITLE	AUTHOR
1961	Charles Sumner and the Coming of the Civil War	David Donald
1962	no award	
1963	Henry James	Leon Edel
1964	John Keats	Walter Jackson Bate
1965	Henry Adams, 3 vols.	Ernest Samuels
1966	A Thousand Days	Arthur M. Schlesinger, Jr.
1967	Mr. Clemens and Mark Twain	Justin Kaplan
1968	Memoirs	George E. Kennan
1969	The Man from New York: John Quinn and His Friends	Benjamin Lawrence Reid
1970	Huey Long	T. Harry Williams
1971	Robert Frost: The Years of Triumph, 1915–1938	Lawrance Thompson
1972	Eleanor and Franklin	Joseph P. Lash
1973	Luce and His Empire	W.A. Swanberg
1974	O'Neill, Son and Artist	Louis Sheaffer
1975	The Power Broker: Robert Moses and the Fall of New York	Robert A. Caro
1976	Edith Wharton: A Biography	R.W.B. Lewis
1977	A Prince of Our Disorder: The Life of T.E. Lawrence	John E. Mack
1978	Samuel Johnson	Walter Jackson Bate
1979	Days of Sorrow and Pain: Leo Baeck and the Berlin Jews	Leonard Baker
1980	The Rise of Theodore Roosevelt	Edmund Morris
1981	Peter the Great: His Life and World	Robert K. Massie
1982	Grant: A Biography	William McFeely
1983	Growing Up	Russell Baker
1984	Booker T. Washington: The Wizard of Tuskegee, 1901–1915	Louis R. Harlan
1985	The Life and Times of Cotton Mather	Kenneth Silverman
1986	Louise Bogan: A Portrait	Elizabeth Frank
1987	Bearing the Cross: Martin Luther King, Jr., and the Southern Christian Leadership Conference	David J. Garrow
1988	Look Homeward: A Life of Thomas Wolfe	David Herbert Donald
1989	Oscar Wilde[2]	Richard Ellmann
1990	Machiavelli in Hell	Sebastian de Grazia
1991	Jackson Pollock	Steven Naifeh, Gregory White Smith
1992	Fortunate Son: The Healing of a Vietnam Vet	Lewis B. Puller, Jr.
1993	Truman	David McCullough
1994	W.E.B. Du Bois: Biography of a Race 1868–1919	David Levering Lewis
1995	Harriet Beecher Stowe: A Life	Joan D. Hedrick
1996	God: A Biography	Jack Miles
1997	Angela's Ashes: A Memoir	Frank McCourt
1998	Personal History	Katharine Graham
1999	Lindbergh	A. Scott Berg
2000	Vera (Mrs. Vladimir Nabokov)	Stacy Schiff
2001	W.E.B. Du Bois: The Fight for Equality and the American Century, 1919–1963	David Levering Lewis
2002	John Adams	David McCullough
2003	Master of the Senate	Robert A. Caro
2004	Khrushchev: The Man and His Era	William Taubman
2005	De Kooning: An American Master	Mark Stevens and Annalyn Swan
2006	American Prometheus: The Triumph and Tragedy	Kai Bird, Martin J. Sherwin
2007	The Most Famous Man in America: The Biography of Henry Ward Beecher	Debby Applegate

[1]Freeman died in 1953 after completing vols. 1–6; Carroll and Ashworth continued his work with vol. 7.
[2]Awarded posthumously.

Poetry
Awarded for a collection of original verse by an American author.

YEAR	TITLE	AUTHOR
1922	Collected Poems	Edwin Arlington Robinson
1923	The Ballad of the Harp-Weaver; A Few Figs from Thistles; Eight Sonnets in American Poetry, 1922: A Miscellany	Edna St. Vincent Millay
1924	New Hampshire: A Poem with Notes and Grace Notes	Robert Frost
1925	The Man Who Died Twice	Edwin Arlington Robinson
1926	What's O'Clock[1]	Amy Lowell
1927	Fiddler's Farewell	Leonora Speyer

Letters, Drama, and Music (continued)

Poetry (continued)

YEAR	TITLE	AUTHOR
1928	Tristram	Edwin Arlington Robinson
1929	John Brown's Body	Stephen Vincent Benét
1930	Selected Poems	Conrad Aiken
1931	Collected Poems	Robert Frost
1932	The Flowering Stone	George Dillon
1933	Conquistador	Archibald MacLeish
1934	Collected Verse	Robert Hillyer
1935	Bright Ambush	Audrey Wurdemann
1936	Strange Holiness	Robert P. Tristram Coffin
1937	A Further Range	Robert Frost
1938	Cold Morning Sky	Marya Zaturenska
1939	Selected Poems	John Gould Fletcher
1940	Collected Poems	Mark Van Doren
1941	Sunderland Capture	Leonard Bacon
1942	The Dust Which Is God	William Rose Benét
1943	A Witness Tree	Robert Frost
1944	Western Star[1]	Stephen Vincent Benét
1945	V-Letter and Other Poems	Karl Shapiro
1946	no award	
1947	Lord Weary's Castle	Robert Lowell
1948	The Age of Anxiety	W.H. Auden
1949	Terror and Decorum	Peter Viereck
1950	Annie Allen	Gwendolyn Brooks
1951	Complete Poems	Carl Sandburg
1952	Collected Poems	Marianne Moore
1953	Collected Poems, 1917–1952	Archibald MacLeish
1954	The Waking	Theodore Roethke
1955	Collected Poems	Wallace Stevens
1956	Poems: North & South	Elizabeth Bishop
1957	Things of This World	Richard Wilbur
1958	Promises: Poems 1954–1956	Robert Penn Warren
1959	Selected Poems, 1928–1958	Stanley Kunitz
1960	Heart's Needle	W.D. Snodgrass
1961	Times Three: Selected Verse from Three Decades	Phyllis McGinley
1962	Poems	Alan Dugan
1963	Pictures from Breughel[1]	William Carlos Williams
1964	At the End of the Open Road	Louis Simpson

YEAR	TITLE	AUTHOR
1965	77 Dream Songs	John Berryman
1966	Selected Poems	Richard Eberhart
1967	Live or Die	Anne Sexton
1968	The Hard Hours	Anthony Hecht
1969	Of Being Numerous	George Oppen
1970	Untitled Subjects	Richard Howard
1971	The Carrier of Ladders	William S. Merwin
1972	Collected Poems	James Wright
1973	Up Country	Maxine Kumin
1974	The Dolphin	Robert Lowell
1975	Turtle Island	Gary Snyder
1976	Self-Portrait in a Convex Mirror	John Ashbery
1977	Divine Comedies	James Merrill
1978	Collected Poems	Howard Nemerov
1979	Now and Then	Robert Penn Warren
1980	Selected Poems	Donald Justice
1981	The Morning of the Poem	James Schuyler
1982	The Collected Poems[2]	Sylvia Plath
1983	Selected Poems	Galway Kinnell
1984	American Primitive	Mary Oliver
1985	Yin	Carolyn Kizer
1986	The Flying Change	Henry Taylor
1987	Thomas and Beulah	Rita Dove
1988	Partial Accounts: New and Selected Poems	William Meredith
1989	New and Collected Poems	Richard Wilbur
1990	The World Doesn't End	Charles Simic
1991	Near Changes	Mona Van Duyn
1992	Selected Poems	James Tate
1993	The Wild Iris	Louise Glück
1994	Neon Vernacular: New and Selected Poems	Yusef Komunyakaa
1995	The Simple Truth	Philip Levine
1996	The Dream of the Unified Field	Jorie Graham
1997	Alive Together: New and Selected Poems	Lisel Mueller
1998	Black Zodiac	Charles Wright
1999	Blizzard of One	Mark Strand
2000	Repair	C.K. Williams
2001	Different Hours	Stephen Dunn
2002	Practical Gods	Carl Dennis
2003	Moy Sand and Gravel	Paul Muldoon
2004	Walking to Martha's Vineyard	Franz Wright
2005	Delights & Shadows	Ted Kooser
2006	Late Wife	Claudia Emerson
2007	Native Guard	Natasha Trethewey

[1]Awarded posthumously.   [2]Work published and prize awarded posthumously.

General Nonfiction

Awarded for a work of nonfiction, ineligible for any other category, by an American author.

YEAR	TITLE	AUTHOR
1962	The Making of the President, 1960	Theodore H. White
1963	The Guns of August	Barbara W. Tuchman
1964	Anti-intellectualism in American Life	Richard Hofstadter

YEAR	TITLE	AUTHOR
1965	O Strange New World	Howard Mumford Jones
1966	Wandering Through Winter	Edwin Way Teale
1967	The Problem of Slavery in Western Culture	David Brion Davis

Letters, Drama, and Music (continued)

General nonfiction (continued)

YEAR	TITLE	AUTHOR
1968	Rousseau and Revolution: A History of Civilization in France, England, and Germany from 1756 and in the Remainder of Europe from 1715 to 1789	Will and Ariel Durant
1969	The Armies of the Night	Norman Mailer
1969	So Human an Animal	Rene Jules Dubos
1970	Gandhi's Truth	Erik H. Erikson
1971	The Rising Sun	John Toland
1972	Stilwell and the American Experience in China, 1911–1945	Barbara W. Tuchman
1973	Fire in the Lake: The Vietnamese and the Americans in Vietnam	Frances Fitzgerald
1973	Children of Crisis, vols. 2 and 3	Robert Coles
1974	The Denial of Death[1]	Ernest Becker
1975	Pilgrim at Tinker Creek	Annie Dillard
1976	Why Survive?: Being Old in America	Robert N. Butler
1977	Beautiful Swimmers	William W. Warner
1978	The Dragons of Eden	Carl Sagan
1979	On Human Nature	Edward O. Wilson
1980	Gödel, Escher, Bach: An Eternal Golden Braid	Douglas R. Hofstadter
1981	Fin-de-Siècle Vienna: Politics and Culture	Carl E. Schorske
1982	The Soul of a New Machine	Tracy Kidder
1983	Is There No Place on Earth for Me?	Susan Sheehan
1984	The Social Transformation of American Medicine	Paul Starr
1985	The Good War: An Oral History of World War Two	Studs Terkel
1986	Common Ground: A Turbulent Decade in the Lives of Three American Families	J. Anthony Lukas
1986	Move Your Shadow: South Africa, Black and White	Joseph Lelyveld
1987	Arab and Jew: Wounded Spirits in a Promised Land	David K. Shipler
1988	The Making of the Atomic Bomb	Richard Rhodes
1989	A Bright Shining Lie: John Paul Vann and America in Vietnam	Neil Sheehan
1990	And Their Children After Them	Dale Maharidge, Michael Williamson
1991	The Ants	Bert Holldobler, Edward O. Wilson
1992	The Prize: The Epic Quest for Oil, Money, and Power	Daniel Yergin
1993	Lincoln at Gettysburg: The Words That Remade America	Garry Wills
1994	Lenin's Tomb: The Last Days of the Soviet Empire	David Remnick
1995	The Beak of the Finch: A Story of Evolution in Our Time	Jonathan Weiner
1996	The Haunted Land: Facing Europe's Ghosts After Communism	Tina Rosenberg
1997	Ashes to Ashes: America's Hundred-Year Cigarette War, the Public Health, and the Unabashed Triumph of Philip Morris	Richard Kluger
1998	Guns, Germs, and Steel: The Fates of Human Societies	Jared Diamond
1999	Annals of the Former World	John McPhee
2000	Embracing Defeat: Japan in the Wake of World War II	John W. Dower
2001	Hirohito and the Making of Modern Japan	Herbert P. Bix
2002	Carry Me Home: Birmingham, Alabama, the Climactic Battle of the Civil Rights Revolution	Diane McWhorter
2003	"A Problem from Hell": America and the Age of Genocide	Samantha Power
2004	Gulag: A History	Anne Applebaum
2005	Ghost Wars	Steve Coll
2006	Imperial Reckoning: The Untold Story of Britain's Gulag in Kenya	Caroline Elkins
2007	The Looming Tower: Al-Qaeda and the Road to 9/11	Lawrence Wright

[1]Awarded posthumously.

Music
Awarded for a musical piece of "significant dimension" composed by an American and first performed or recorded in the United States during the year.

YEAR	TITLE	AUTHOR
1943	Secular Cantata No. 2: A Free Song	William Schuman
1944	Symphony No. 4, Opus 34	Howard Hanson

Letters, Drama, and Music (continued)

Music (continued)

YEAR	TITLE	COMPOSER	YEAR	TITLE	COMPOSER
1945	Appalachian Spring	Aaron Copland	1981	no award	
1946	The Canticle of the Sun	Leo Sowerby	1982	Concerto for Orchestra	Roger Sessions
1947	Symphony No. 3	Charles Ives	1983	Symphony No. 1 (Three	Ellen Taaffe Zwilich
1948	Symphony No. 3	Walter Piston		Movements for	
1949	Music for the film	Virgil Thomson		Orchestra)	
	Louisiana Story		1984	"Canti del sole" for Tenor	Bernard Rands
1950	The Consul	Gian Carlo Menotti		and Orchestra	
1951	Giants in the Earth	Douglas S. Moore	1985	Symphony RiverRun	Stephen Albert
1952	Symphony Concertante	Gail Kubik	1986	Wind Quintet IV	George Perle
1953	no award		1987	The Flight into Egypt	John Harbison
1954	Concerto for Two	Quincy Porter	1988	12 New Etudes for	William Bolcom
	Pianos and Orchestra			Piano	
1955	The Saint of Bleecker	Gian Carlo Menotti	1989	Whispers out of Time	Roger Reynolds
	Street		1990	"Duplicates": A Concerto	Mel Powell
1956	Symphony No. 3	Ernst Toch		for Two Pianos and	
1957	Meditation on	Norman Dello Joio		Orchestra	
	Ecclesiastics		1991	Symphony	Shulamit Ran
1958	Vanessa	Samuel Barber	1992	The Face of the Night,	Wayne Peterson
1959	Concerto for Piano and	John LaMontaine		The Heart of the	
	Orchestra			Dark	
1960	Second String Quartet	Elliott Carter	1993	Trombone Concerto	Christopher
1961	Symphony No. 7	Walter Piston			Rouse
1962	The Crucible	Robert Ward	1994	Of Reminiscences and	Gunther Schuller
1963	Piano Concerto No. 1	Samuel Barber		Reflections	
1964	no award		1995	Stringmusic	Morton Gould
1965	no award		1996	Lilacs, for Voice and	George Walker
1966	Variations for Orchestra	Leslie Bassett		Orchestra	
1967	Quartet No. 3	Leon Kirchner	1997	Blood on the Fields	Wynton Marsalis
1968	Echoes of Time and	George Crumb	1998	String Quartet No. 2	Aaron Jay Kernis
	the River			(Musica	
1969	String Quartet No. 3	Karel Husa		Instrumentalis)	
1970	Time's Encomium	Charles Wuorinen	1999	Concerto for Flute,	Melinda Wagner
1971	Synchronisms No. 6 for	Mario Davidovsky		Strings, and	
	Piano and Electronic			Percussion	
	Sound		2000	Life Is a Dream, Opera	Lewis Spratlan
1972	Windows	Jacob Druckman		in Three Acts: Act II,	
1973	String Quartet No. 3	Elliott Carter		Concert Version	
1974	Notturno	Donald Martino	2001	Symphony No. 2 for	John Corigliano
1975	From the Diary of	Dominick Argento		String Orchestra	
	Virginia Woolf		2002	Ice Field	Henry Brant
1976	Air Music	Ned Rorem	2003	On the Transmigration	John Adams
1977	Visions of Terror and	Richard Wernick		of Souls	
	Wonder		2004	Tempest Fantasy	Paul Moravec
1978	Deja Vu for Percussion	Michael Colgrass	2005	Second Concerto for	Steven Stucky
	Quartet and Orchestra			Orchestra	
1979	Aftertones of Infinity	Joseph	2006	Piano Concerto: "Chiavi	Yehudi Wyner
		Schwantner		in mano"	
1980	In Memory of a Summer	David Del Tredici	2007	Sound Grammar	Ornette Coleman
	Day				

Special Awards and Citations[1]

YEAR	RECIPIENT	FOR	YEAR	RECIPIENT	FOR
1992	Art Spiegelman	graphic novel Maus	2006	Edmund S. Morgan	commemoration of his
1996	Herb Caen	contributions as a voice			life's work as an
		of San Francisco			American historian
1998	George Gershwin[2]	centennial		Thelonious Monk[2]	commemoration of his
		commemoration of his			contributions to jazz
		birth, celebrating his	2007	Ray Bradbury	commemoration of his
		life's work in music			contributions to science
1999	Duke Ellington[2]	centennial			fiction and fantasy
		commemoration of his		John Coltrane[2]	commemoration of his
		birth, celebrating his			contributions to jazz
		life's work in music			

[1]For the past 20 years.   [2]Awarded posthumously.

National Book Awards

In 1950 a consortium of publishing groups established the National Book Awards. The goals were to bring exceptional books written by Americans to the public's attention and to encourage reading in general. Award categories have varied from the inaugural 3 to as many as 28 in 1980. Today, the awards recognize achievements in four genres: fiction, nonfiction, poetry, and young people's literature. A five-member, independent judging panel chooses a winner for each genre. Award: $10,000 cash and a bronze sculpture.

Fiction

YEAR	TITLE	AUTHOR
1950	The Man with the Golden Arm	Nelson Algren
1951	The Collected Stories of William Faulkner	William Faulkner
1952	From Here to Eternity	James Jones
1953	Invisible Man	Ralph Ellison
1954	The Adventures of Augie March	Saul Bellow
1955	A Fable	William Faulkner
1956	Ten North Frederick	John O'Hara
1957	The Field of Vision	Wright Morris
1958	The Wapshot Chronicle	John Cheever
1959	The Magic Barrel	Bernard Malamud
1960	Goodbye, Columbus	Philip Roth
1961	The Waters of Kronos	Conrad Richter
1962	The Moviegoer	Walker Percy
1963	Morte d'Urban	J.F. Powers
1964	The Centaur	John Updike
1965	Herzog	Saul Bellow
1966	The Collected Stories of Katherine Anne Porter	Katherine Anne Porter
1967	The Fixer	Bernard Malamud
1968	The Eighth Day	Thornton Wilder
1969	Steps	Jerzy Kosinski
1970	Them	Joyce Carol Oates
1971	Mr. Sammler's Planet	Saul Bellow
1972	The Complete Stories	Flannery O'Connor
1973	Augustus	John Williams
1973	Chimera	John Barth
1974	A Crown of Feathers and Other Stories	Isaac Bashevis Singer
1974	Gravity's Rainbow	Thomas Pynchon
1975	Dog Soldiers: A Novel	Robert Stone

Fiction (continued)

YEAR	TITLE	AUTHOR
1975	The Hair of Harold Roux	Thomas Williams
1976	J.R.	William Gaddis
1977	The Spectator Bird	Wallace Stegner
1978	Blood Tie	Mary Lee Settle
1979	Going After Cacciato	Tim O'Brien
1980	Sophie's Choice[1]	William Styron
1981	Plains Song[1]	Wright Morris
1982	Rabbit Is Rich[1]	John Updike
1983	The Color Purple[1]	Alice Walker
1984	Victory over Japan: A Book of Stories	Ellen Gilchrist
1985	White Noise	Don DeLillo
1986	World's Fair	E.L. Doctorow
1987	Paco's Story	Larry Heinemann
1988	Paris Trout	Pete Dexter
1989	Spartina	John Casey
1990	Middle Passage	Charles Johnson
1991	Mating	Norman Rush
1992	All the Pretty Horses	Cormac McCarthy
1993	The Shipping News	E. Annie Proulx
1994	A Frolic of His Own	William Gaddis
1995	Sabbath's Theater	Philip Roth
1996	Ship Fever	Andrea Barrett
1997	Cold Mountain	Charles Frazier
1998	Charming Billy	Alice McDermott
1999	Waiting	Ha Jin
2000	In America	Susan Sontag
2001	The Corrections	Jonathan Franzen
2002	Three Junes	Julia Glass
2003	The Great Fire	Shirley Hazzard
2004	The News From Paraguay	Lily Tuck
2005	Europe Central	William T. Vollmann
2006	The Echo Maker	Richard Powers

Nonfiction

YEAR	TITLE	AUTHOR
1950	The Life of Ralph Waldo Emerson	Ralph L. Rusk
1951	Herman Melville	Newton Arvin
1952	The Sea Around Us	Rachel Carson
1953	The Course of Empire	Bernard A. De Voto
1954	A Stillness at Appomattox	Bruce Catton
1955	The Measure of Man: On Freedom, Human Values, Survival, and the Modern Temper	Joseph Wood Krutch
1956	American in Italy	Herbert Kubly
1957	Russia Leaves the War	George F. Kennan
1958	The Lion and the Throne: The Life and Times of Sir Edward Coke (1552–1634)	Catherine Drinker Bowen
1959	Mistress to an Age: A Life of Madame de Staël	J. Christopher Herold
1960	James Joyce	Richard Ellmann
1961	The Rise and Fall of the Third Reich: A History of Nazi Germany	William L. Shirer
1962	The City in History: Its Origins, Its Transformations, and Its Prospects	Lewis Mumford
1963	Henry James, Vol. II: The Conquest of London (1870–1881); Vol. III: The Middle Years (1882–1895)	Leon Edel
1964	The Rise of the West: A History of the Human Community[2]	William H. McNeill
1965	The Life of Lenin[2]	Louis Fischer
1966	A Thousand Days: John F. Kennedy in the White House[2]	Arthur M. Schlesinger, Jr.
1967	The Enlightenment: An Interpretation, Vol. I[2]	Peter Gay
1968	Memoirs: 1925–1950[2]	George F. Kennan
1969	White over Black: American Attitudes Toward the Negro, 1550–1812[2]	Winthrop D. Jordan
1970	Huey Long[2]	T. Harry Williams

National Book Awards (continued)

Nonfiction (continued)

YEAR	TITLE	AUTHOR
1971	Roosevelt: The Soldier of Freedom[2]	James MacGregor Burns
1972	Eleanor and Franklin: The Story of Their Relationship, Based on Eleanor Roosevelt's Private Papers[3]	Joseph P. Lash
1973	George Washington, Vol. IV: Anguish and Farewell, 1793–1799[3]	James Thomas Flexner
1974	Macaulay: The Shaping of the Historian[4]	John Clive
1975	The Life of Emily Dickinson[3]	Richard B. Sewall
1976	The Problem of Slavery in the Age of Revolution, 1770–1823[2]	David Brion Davis
1977	Norman Thomas: The Last Idealist[5]	W.A. Swanberg
1978	Samuel Johnson[5]	W. Jackson Bate
1979	Robert Kennedy and His Times[5]	Arthur M. Schlesinger, Jr.
1980	The Right Stuff[6]	Tom Wolfe
1981	China Men[6]	Maxine Hong Kingston
1982	The Soul of a New Machine[6]	Tracy Kidder
1983	China: Alive in the Bitter Sea[6]	Fox Butterfield
1984	Andrew Jackson and the Course of American Democracy, 1833–1845	Robert V. Remini
1985	Common Ground: A Turbulent Decade in the Lives of Three American Families	J. Anthony Lukas
1986	Arctic Dreams	Barry Lopez
1987	The Making of the Atomic Bomb	Richard Rhodes
1988	A Bright Shining Lie: John Paul Vann and America in Vietnam	Neil Sheehan
1989	From Beirut to Jerusalem	Thomas L. Friedman
1990	The House of Morgan: An American Banking Dynasty and the Rise of Modern Finance	Ron Chernow
1991	Freedom	Orlando Patterson
1992	Becoming a Man: Half a Life Story	Paul Monette
1993	United States: Essays, 1952–1992	Gore Vidal
1994	How We Die: Reflections on Life's Final Chapter	Sherwin B. Nuland
1995	The Haunted Land: Facing Europe's Ghosts After Communism	Tina Rosenberg
1996	An American Requiem: God, My Father, and the War That Came Between Us	James Carroll
1997	American Sphinx: The Character of Thomas Jefferson	Joseph J. Ellis
1998	Slaves in the Family	Edward Ball
1999	Embracing Defeat: Japan in the Wake of World War II	John W. Dower
2000	In the Heart of the Sea: The Tragedy of the Whaleship Essex	Nathaniel Philbrick
2001	The Noonday Demon: An Atlas of Depression	Andrew Solomon
2002	Master of the Senate: The Years of Lyndon Johnson	Robert A. Caro
2003	Waiting for Snow in Havana	Carlos Eire
2004	Arc of Justice: A Saga of Race, Civil Rights, and Murder in the Jazz Age	Kevin Boyle
2005	The Year of Magical Thinking	Joan Didion
2006	The Worst Hard Time: The Untold Story of Those Who Survived the Great American Dust Bowl	Timothy Egan

Poetry

YEAR	TITLE	AUTHOR
1950	Paterson: Book III and Selected Poems	William Carlos Williams
1951	The Auroras of Autumn	Wallace Stevens
1952	Collected Poems	Marianne Moore
1953	Collected Poems, 1917–1952	Archibald MacLeish
1954	Collected Poems	Conrad Aiken
1955	The Collected Poems of Wallace Stevens	Wallace Stevens
1956	The Shield of Achilles	W.H. Auden
1957	Things of This World: Poems	Richard Wilbur
1958	Promises: Poems, 1954–1956	Robert Penn Warren
1959	Words for the Wind: The Collected Verse of Theodore Roethke	Theodore Roethke
1960	Life Studies	Robert Lowell
1961	The Woman at the Washington Zoo	Randall Jarrell
1962	Poems	Alan Dugan
1963	Traveling Through the Dark	William Stafford
1964	Selected Poems	John Crowe Ransom
1965	The Far Field	Theodore Roethke
1966	Buckdancer's Choice: Poems	James Dickey
1967	Nights and Days	James Merrill
1968	The Light Around the Body: Poems	Robert Bly
1969	His Toy, His Dream, His Rest: 308 Dream Songs	John Berryman
1970	The Complete Poems	Elizabeth Bishop
1971	To See, To Take: Poems	Mona Van Duyn

National Book Awards (continued)

Poetry (continued)

YEAR	TITLE	AUTHOR
1972	The Collected Poems of Frank O'Hara	Frank O'Hara
	Selected Poems	Howard Moss
1973	Collected Poems, 1951–1971	A.R. Ammons
1974	Diving into the Wreck: Poems, 1971–1972	Adrienne Rich
	The Fall of America: Poems of These States	Allen Ginsberg
1975	Presentation Piece	Marilyn Hacker
1976	Self-Portrait in a Convex Mirror: Poems	John Ashbery
1977	Collected Poems, 1930–1976	Richard Eberhart
1978	The Collected Poems of Howard Nemerov	Howard Nemerov
1979	Mirabell: Books of Number	James Merrill
1980	Ashes: Poems New & Old	Philip Levine
1981	The Need to Hold Still	Lisel Mueller
1982	Life Supports: New and Collected Poems	William Bronk
1983	Country Music: Selected Early Poems	Charles Wright
1984	Selected Poems	Galway Kinnell
1985	Yin	Carolyn Kizer
1986	The Flying Change	Henry Taylor
1987	Thomas and Beulah	Rita Dove
1988	Partial Accounts: New and Selected Poems	William Meredith
1989	New and Collected Poems	Richard Wilbur
1990	The World Doesn't End	Charles Simic
1991	What Work Is: Poems	Philip Levine
1992	New and Selected Poems	Mary Oliver
1993	Garbage	A.R. Ammons
1994	Worshipful Company of Fletchers: Poems	James Tate
1995	Passing Through: The Later Poems, New and Selected	Stanley Kunitz
1996	Scrambled Eggs & Whiskey: Poems, 1991–1995	Hayden Carruth
1997	Effort at Speech: New and Selected Poems	William Meredith
1998	This Time: New and Selected Poems	Gerald Stern
1999	Vice: New and Selected Poems	Ai
2000	Blessing the Boats: New and Selected Poems, 1988–2000	Lucille Clifton
2001	Poems Seven: New and Complete Poetry	Alan Dugan
2002	In the Next Galaxy	Ruth Stone
2003	The Singing	C.K. Williams
2004	Door in the Mountain: New and Collected Poems, 1965–2003	Jean Valentine
2005	Migration: New and Selected Poems	W.S. Merwin
2006	Splay Anthem	Nathaniel Mackey

Young People's Literature

YEAR	TITLE	AUTHOR
1969	Journey from Peppermint Street	Meindert De Jong
1970	A Day of Pleasure: Stories of a Boy Growing Up in Warsaw[7]	Isaac Bashevis Singer
1971	The Marvelous Misadventures of Sebastian[7]	Lloyd Alexander
1972	The Slightly Irregular Fire Engine; or, The Hithering Thithering Djinn[7]	Donald Barthelme
1973	The Farthest Shore[7]	Ursula Le Guin
1974	The Court of the Stone Children[7]	Eleanor Cameron
1975	M.C. Higgins, the Great[7]	Virginia Hamilton
1976	Bert Breen's Barn	Walter D. Edmonds
1977	The Master Puppeteer	Katherine Paterson
1978	The View from the Oak: The Private Worlds of Other Creatures	Judith Kohl & Herbert Kohl
1979	The Great Gilly Hopkins	Katherine Paterson
1980	A Gathering of Days: A New England Girl's Journal, 1830–32[8]	Joan Blos
1981	The Night Swimmers[9]	Betsy Byars
1982	Westmark[9]	Lloyd Alexander
1983	Homesick: My Own Story[9]	Jean Fritz
1996	Parrot in the Oven: Mi Vida	Victor Martinez
1997	Dancing on the Edge	Han Nolan
1998	Holes	Louis Sachar
1999	When Zachary Beaver Came to Town	Kimberly Willis Holt
2000	Homeless Bird	Gloria Whelan
2001	True Believer	Virginia Euwer Wolff
2002	The House of the Scorpion	Nancy Farmer
2003	The Canning Season	Polly Horvath
2004	The Godless	Pete Hautman
2005	The Penderwicks	Jeanne Birdsall

National Book Awards (continued)

Young People's Literature (continued)

YEAR	TITLE	AUTHOR
2006	The Astonishing Life of Octavian Nothing, Traitor to the Nation, Vol. 1: The Pox Party	M.T. Anderson

[1]Fiction (Hardcover).　[2]History and Biography (Nonfiction).　[3]Biography.　[4]History.　[5]Biography and Autobiography.　[6]General Nonfiction (Hardcover).　[7]Children's Books.　[8]Children's Books (Hardcover).　[9]Children's Books, Fiction (Hardcover).

The PEN/Faulkner Award for Fiction

Named for William Faulkner and affiliated with the international writers' organization Poets, Playwrights, Editors, Essayists and Novelists (PEN), the PEN/Faulkner Award was founded by writers in 1980 to honor their peers. A panel of fiction writers selects a winning novel or short-story collection and four runners-up. The winning author receives $15,000, and each of the others receives $5,000.

PEN/Faulkner Web site: <www.penfaulkner.org>.

YEAR	TITLE	AUTHOR	YEAR	TITLE	AUTHOR
1981	How German Is It?	Walter Abish	1993	Postcards	E. Annie Proulx
1982	The Chaneysville Incident	David Bradley	1994	Operation Shylock	Philip Roth
1983	Seaview	Toby Olson	1995	Snow Falling on Cedars	David Guterson
1984	Sent for You Yesterday	John Edgar Wideman	1996	Independence Day	Richard Ford
1985	The Barracks Thief	Tobias Wolff	1997	Women in Their Beds	Gina Berriault
1986	The Old Forest and Other Stories	Peter Taylor	1998	The Bear Comes Home	Rafi Zabor
1987	Soldiers in Hiding	Richard Wiley	1999	The Hours	Michael Cunningham
1988	World's End	T. Coraghessan Boyle	2000	Waiting	Ha Jin
1989	Dusk and Other Stories	James Salter	2001	The Human Stain	Philip Roth
1990	Billy Bathgate	E.L. Doctorow	2002	Bel Canto	Ann Patchett
1991	Philadelphia Fire	John Edgar Wideman	2003	The Caprices	Sabina Murray
1992	Mao II	Don DeLillo	2004	The Early Stories	John Updike
			2005	War Trash	Ha Jin
			2006	The March	E.L. Doctorow
			2007	Everyman	Philip Roth

Newbery Medal Winners, 1922–2007

The American Library Association (ALA) began awarding the John Newbery Medal in 1922 to the author of the most distinguished American children's book of the previous year, as judged by the ALA's Children's Librarians' Section (now called the Association for Library Service to Children). Established at the suggestion of Frederic G. Melcher of the R.R. Bowker Publishing Company, the award is named for John Newbery, the 18th-century English publisher who was among the first to publish books exclusively for children. Prize: inscribed bronze medal.

ALA Newbery Medal Web site: <www.ala.org/alsc/newbery.html>.

YEAR	TITLE	AUTHOR	YEAR	TITLE	AUTHOR
1922	The Story of Mankind	Hendrik Willem van Loon	1935	Dobry	Monica Shannon
1923	The Voyages of Doctor Dolittle	Hugh Lofting	1936	Caddie Woodlawn	Carol Ryrie Brink
1924	The Dark Frigate	Charles Hawes	1937	Roller Skates	Ruth Sawyer
1925	Tales from Silver Lands	Charles Finger	1938	The White Stag	Kate Seredy
1926	Shen of the Sea	Arthur Bowie Chrisman	1939	Thimble Summer	Elizabeth Enright
1927	Smoky, the Cowhorse	Will James	1940	Daniel Boone	James Daugherty
1928	Gay Neck, the Story of a Pigeon	Dhan Gopal Mukerji	1941	Call It Courage	Armstrong Sperry
1929	The Trumpeter of Krakow	Eric P. Kelly	1942	The Matchlock Gun	Walter Edmonds
1930	Hitty, Her First Hundred Years	Rachel Field	1943	Adam of the Road	Elizabeth Janet Gray
1931	The Cat Who Went to Heaven	Elizabeth Coatsworth	1944	Johnny Tremain	Esther Forbes
1932	Waterless Mountain	Laura Adams Armer	1945	Rabbit Hill	Robert Lawson
1933	Young Fu of the Upper Yangtze	Elizabeth Lewis	1946	Strawberry Girl	Lois Lenski
1934	Invincible Louisa: The Story of the Author of Little Women	Cornelia Meigs	1947	Miss Hickory	Carolyn Sherwin Bailey
			1948	The Twenty-One Balloons	William Pène du Bois
			1949	King of the Wind	Marguerite Henry
			1950	The Door in the Wall	Marguerite de Angeli
			1951	Amos Fortune, Free Man	Elizabeth Yates
			1952	Ginger Pye	Eleanor Estes
			1953	Secret of the Andes	Ann Nolan Clark
			1954	...And Now Miguel	Joseph Krumgold

Newbery Medal Winners, 1922–2007 (continued)

YEAR	TITLE	AUTHOR
1955	The Wheel on the School	Meindert DeJong
1956	Carry On, Mr. Bowditch	Jean Lee Latham
1957	Miracles on Maple Hill	Virginia Sorenson
1958	Rifles for Watie	Harold Keith
1959	The Witch of Blackbird Pond	Elizabeth George Speare
1960	Onion John	Joseph Krumgold
1961	Island of the Blue Dolphins	Scott O'Dell
1962	The Bronze Bow	Elizabeth George Speare
1963	A Wrinkle in Time	Madeleine L'Engle
1964	It's Like This, Cat	Emily Neville
1965	Shadow of a Bull	Maia Wojciechowska
1966	I, Juan de Pareja	Elizabeth Borton de Trevino
1967	Up a Road Slowly	Irene Hunt
1968	From the Mixed-Up Files of Mrs. Basil E. Frankweiler	E.L. Konigsburg
1969	The High King	Lloyd Alexander
1970	Sounder	William H. Armstrong
1971	Summer of the Swans	Betsy Byars
1972	Mrs. Frisby and the Rats of NIMH	Robert C. O'Brien
1973	Julie of the Wolves	Jean Craighead George
1974	The Slave Dancer	Paula Fox
1975	M.C. Higgins, the Great	Virginia Hamilton
1976	The Grey King	Susan Cooper
1977	Roll of Thunder, Hear My Cry	Mildred D. Taylor
1978	Bridge to Terabithia	Katherine Paterson
1979	The Westing Game	Ellen Raskin
1980	A Gathering of Days: A New England Girl's Journal, 1830–1832	Joan W. Blos
1981	Jacob Have I Loved	Katherine Paterson
1982	A Visit to William Blake's Inn: Poems for Innocent and Experienced Travelers	Nancy Willard
1983	Dicey's Song	Cynthia Voigt
1984	Dear Mr. Henshaw	Beverly Cleary
1985	The Hero and the Crown	Robin McKinley
1986	Sarah, Plain and Tall	Patricia MacLachlan
1987	The Whipping Boy	Sid Fleischman
1988	Lincoln: A Photobiography	Russell Freedman
1989	Joyful Noise: Poems for Two Voices	Paul Fleischman
1990	Number the Stars	Lois Lowry
1991	Maniac Magee	Jerry Spinelli
1992	Shiloh	Phyllis Reynolds Naylor
1993	Missing May	Cynthia Rylant
1994	The Giver	Lois Lowry
1995	Walk Two Moons	Sharon Creech
1996	The Midwife's Apprentice	Karen Cushman
1997	The View from Saturday	E.L. Konigsburg
1998	Out of the Dust	Karen Hesse
1999	Holes	Louis Sachar
2000	Bud, Not Buddy	Christopher Paul Curtis
2001	A Year Down Yonder	Richard Peck
2002	A Single Shard	Linda Sue Park
2003	Crispin: The Cross of Lead	Avi
2004	The Tale of Despereaux: Being the Story of a Mouse, a Princess, Some Soup, and a Spool of Thread	Kate DiCamillo
2005	Kira-Kira	Cynthia Kadohata
2006	Criss Cross	Lynne Rae Perkins
2007	The Higher Power of Lucky	Susan Patron

Caldecott Medal Winners, 1938–2007

The American Library Association (ALA) awards the Caldecott Medal annually to "the artist of the most distinguished American picture book for children." It was established by the ALA in 1938 on the suggestion of Frederic G. Melcher, chairman of the board of the R.R. Bowker Publishing Company, and named for the 19th-century English illustrator Randolph Caldecott. If the author/reteller/translator/editor is other than the illustrator, that person's name appears in parentheses after that of the illustrator. Prize: inscribed bronze medal.

Web site: <www.ala.org/alsc/caldecott.html>.

YEAR	TITLE	ILLUSTRATOR
1938	Animals of the Bible: A Picture Book	Dorothy P. Lathrop (Helen Dean Fish)
1939	Mei Li	Thomas Handforth
1940	Abraham Lincoln	Ingri and Edgar Parin d'Aulaire
1941	They Were Strong and Good	Robert Lawson
1942	Make Way for Ducklings	Robert McCloskey
1943	The Little House	Virginia Lee Burton
1944	Many Moons	Louis Slobodkin (James Thurber)
1945	Prayer for a Child	Elizabeth Orton Jones (Rachel Field)
1946	The Rooster Crows	Maude and Miska Petersham

Caldecott Medal Winners, 1938–2007 (continued)

YEAR	TITLE	ILLUSTRATOR
1947	The Little Island	Leonard Weisgard (Golden MacDonald, pseud. [Margaret Wise Brown])
1948	White Snow, Bright Snow	Roger Duvoisin (Alvin Tresselt)
1949	The Big Snow	Berta and Elmer Hader
1950	Song of the Swallows	Leo Politi
1951	The Egg Tree	Katherine Milhous
1952	Finders Keepers	Nicolas, pseud. (Nicholas Mordvinoff) (Will, pseud. [William Lipkind])
1953	The Biggest Bear	Lynd Ward
1954	Madeline's Rescue	Ludwig Bemelmans
1955	Cinderella, or the Little Glass Slipper	Marcia Brown (translated from Charles Perrault by Marcia Brown)
1956	Frog Went A-Courtin'	Feodor Rojankovsky (John Langstaff)
1957	A Tree Is Nice	Marc Simont (Janice Udry)
1958	Time of Wonder	Robert McCloskey
1959	Chanticleer and the Fox	Barbara Cooney (adapted from Chaucer's Canterbury Tales by Barbara Cooney)
1960	Nine Days to Christmas	Marie Hall Ets (Marie Hall Ets and Aurora Labastida)
1961	Baboushka and the Three Kings	Nicolas Sidjakov (Ruth Robbins)
1962	Once a Mouse	Marcia Brown
1963	The Snowy Day	Ezra Jack Keats
1964	Where the Wild Things Are	Maurice Sendak
1965	May I Bring a Friend?	Beni Montresor (Beatrice Schenk de Regniers)
1966	Always Room for One More	Nonny Hogrogian (Sorche Nic Leodhas, pseud. [Leclair Alger])
1967	Sam, Bangs & Moonshine	Evaline Ness
1968	Drummer Hoff	Ed Emberley (Barbara Emberley)
1969	The Fool of the World and the Flying Ship	Uri Shulevitz (Arthur Ransome)
1970	Sylvester and the Magic Pebble	William Steig
1971	A Story A Story	Gail E. Haley
1972	One Fine Day	Nonny Hogrogian
1973	The Funny Little Woman	Blair Lent (Arlene Mosel)
1974	Duffy and the Devil	Margot Zemach (Harve Zemach)
1975	Arrow to the Sun	Gerald McDermott
1976	Why Mosquitoes Buzz in People's Ears	Leo and Diane Dillon (Verna Aardema)
1977	Ashanti to Zulu: African Traditions	Leo and Diane Dillon (Margaret Musgrove)
1978	Noah's Ark	Peter Spier
1979	The Girl Who Loved Wild Horses	Paul Goble
1980	Ox-Cart Man	Barbara Cooney (Donald Hall)
1981	Fables	Arnold Lobel
1982	Jumanji	Chris Van Allsburg
1983	Shadow	Marcia Brown (also translator of original French text by Blaise Cendrars)
1984	The Glorious Flight: Across the Channel with Louis Blériot	Alice and Martin Provensen
1985	Saint George and the Dragon	Trina Schart Hyman (Margaret Hodges)
1986	The Polar Express	Chris Van Allsburg
1987	Hey, Al	Richard Egielski (Arthur Yorinks)
1988	Owl Moon	John Schoenherr (Jane Yolen)
1989	Song and Dance Man	Stephen Gammell (Karen Ackerman)
1990	Lon Po Po: A Red-Riding Hood Story from China	Ed Young
1991	Black and White	David Macaulay
1992	Tuesday	David Wiesner
1993	Mirette on the High Wire	Emily Arnold McCully
1994	Grandfather's Journey	Allen Say (Walter Lorraine)
1995	Smoky Night	David Diaz (Eve Bunting)
1996	Officer Buckle and Gloria	Peggy Rathmann
1997	Golem	David Wisniewski
1998	Rapunzel	Paul O. Zelinsky
1999	Snowflake Bentley	Mary Azarian (Jacqueline Briggs Martin)
2000	Joseph Had a Little Overcoat	Simms Taback
2001	So You Want to Be President?	David Small (Judith St. George)
2002	The Three Pigs	David Wiesner
2003	My Friend Rabbit	Eric Rohmann
2004	The Man Who Walked Between the Towers	Mordicai Gerstein
2005	Kitten's First Full Moon	Kevin Henkes
2006	The Hello, Goodbye Window	Chris Raschka (Norton Juster)
2007	Flotsam	David Wiesner

Coretta Scott King Award

Established in 1970, the Coretta Scott King Award honors outstanding African American authors and illustrators of books for young people. The books, which may be fiction or nonfiction, must be original works that portray some aspect of the black experience. In 1982 the award came under the aegis of the American Library Association. Only authors were eligible for the award until 1974, and no illustrator awards were given in 1975–1977 and 1985. Prize: citation, honorarium, and encyclopedia set.

Coretta Scott King Award Web site:
<www.ala.org/ala/emiert/corettascottking bookaward/corettascott.htm>.

1970	Lillie Patterson, *Martin Luther King, Jr.: Man of Peace*
1971	Charlemae Rollins, *Black Troubador: Langston Hughes*
1972	Elton C. Fax, *17 Black Artists*
1973	*I Never Had It Made: The Autobiography of Jackie Robinson,* as told to Alfred Duckett
1974	author: Sharon Bell Mathis, *Ray Charles;* illustrator: George Ford, *Ray Charles*
1975	author: Dorothy Robinson, *The Legend of Africana*
1976	author: Pearl Bailey, *Duey's Tale*
1977	author: James Haskins, *The Story of Stevie Wonder*
1978	author: Eloise Greenfield, *Africa Dream;* illustrator: Carole Byard, *Africa Dream*
1979	author: Ossie Davis, *Escape to Freedom;* illustrator: Tom Feelings, *Something on My Mind*
1980	author: Walter Dean Myers, *The Young Landlords;* illustrator: Carole Byard, *Cornrows*
1981	author: Sidney Poitier, *This Life;* illustrator: Ashley Bryan, *Beat the Story Drum, Pum-Pum*
1982	author: Mildred D. Taylor, *Let the Circle Be Unbroken;* illustrator: John Steptoe, *Mother Crocodile*
1983	author: Virginia Hamilton, *Sweet Whispers, Brother Rush;* illustrator: Peter Mugabane, *Black Child*
1984	author: Lucille Clifton, *Everett Anderson's Good-bye;* illustrator: Pat Cummings, *My Mama Needs Me*
1985	author: Walter Dean Myers, *Motown and Didi*
1986	author: Virginia Hamilton, *The People Could Fly: American Black Folktales;* illustrator: Jerry Pinkney, *The Patchwork Quilt*
1987	author: Mildred Pitts Walter, *Justin and the Best Biscuits in the World;* illustrator: Jerry Pinkney, *Half a Moon and One Whole Star*
1988	author: Mildred L. Taylor, *The Friendship;* illustrator: John Steptoe, *Mufaro's Beautiful Daughters: An African Tale*
1989	author: Walter Dean Myers, *Fallen Angels;* illustrator: Jerry Pinkney, *Mirandy and Brother Wind*
1990	author: Patricia C. & Frederick L. McKissack, *A Long Hard Journey: The Story of the Pullman Porter;* illustrator: Jan Spivey Gilchrist, *Nathaniel Talking*
1991	author: Mildred D. Taylor, *The Road to Memphis;* illustrator: Leo and Diane Dillon, *Aida*
1992	author: Walter Dean Myers, *Now Is Your Time: The African American Struggle for Freedom;* illustrator: Faith Ringgold, *Tar Beach*
1993	author: Patricia A. McKissack, *Dark Thirty: Southern Tales of the Supernatural;* illustrator: Kathleen Atkins Wilson, *The Origin of Life on Earth: An African Creation Myth*
1994	author: Angela Johnson, *Toning the Sweep;* illustrator: Tom Feelings, *Soul Looks Back in Wonder*
1995	author: Patricia C. & Frederick L. McKissack, *Christmas in the Big House, Christmas in the Quarters;* illustrator: James Ransome, *The Creation*
1996	author: Virginia Hamilton, *Her Stories;* illustrator: Tom Feelings, *The Middle Passage: White Ships/Black Cargo*
1997	author: Walter Dean Myers, *Slam;* illustrator: Jerry Pinkney, *Minty: A Story of Young Harriet Tubman*
1998	author: Sharon M. Draper, *Forged by Fire;* illustrator: Javaka Steptoe, *In Daddy's Arms I Am Tall: African Americans Celebrating Fathers*
1999	author: Angela Johnson, *Heaven;* illustrator: Michele Wood, *i See the Rhythm*
2000	author: Christopher Paul Curtis, *Bud, Not Buddy;* illustrator: Brian Pinkney, *In the Time of the Drums*
2001	author: Jacqueline Woodson, *Miracle's Boys;* illustrator: Bryan Collier, *Uptown*
2002	author: Mildred Taylor, *The Land;* illustrator: Jerry Pinkney, *Goin' Someplace Special*
2003	author: Nikki Grimes, *Bronx Masquerade;* illustrator: E.B. Lewis, *Talkin' About Bessie: The Story of Aviator Elizabeth Coleman*
2004	author: Angela Johnson, *The First Part Last;* illustrator: Ashley Bryan, *Beautiful Blackbird*
2005	author: Toni Morrison, *Remember: The Journey to School Integration;* illustrator: Kadir Nelson, *Ellington Was Not a Street*
2006	author: Julius Lester, *Day of Tears: A Novel in Dialogue;* illustrator: Bryan Collier, *Rosa*
2007	author: Sharon Draper, *Copper Sun;* illustrator: Kadir Nelson, *Moses: When Harriet Tubman Led Her People to Freedom*

Did you know? Friends who had searched the Frank family's hiding place after their capture later gave Otto Frank the papers left behind by the Gestapo. Among them he found Anne's diary, which was published as *The Diary of a Young Girl* (originally in Dutch, 1947). Precocious in style and insight, it traces her emotional growth amid adversity. In it she wrote, "In spite of everything I still believe that people are really good at heart." The diary has been translated into more than 50 languages and is the most widely read diary of the Holocaust.

The Man Booker Prize

Awarded to the best full-length novel of the year written by a citizen of the Commonwealth or the Republic of Ireland and published in the UK between 1 October and 30 September. Prize: £50,000 (about $98,000); each shortlisted author receives £1,000 (about $1,950). In 1993, Salman Rushdie was awarded the Booker of Bookers, a special award to mark 25 years of the Booker Prize, for *Midnight's Children*. In 2005,

the Man Booker International Prize was created, to be awarded biennially to a living writer for outstanding lifetime achievement. Prize: £60,000 (about $118,000). Albanian novelist Ismail Kadare won the first Man Booker International Prize in 2005. Nigerian author Chinua Achebe won the second in 2007.

Web site: <www.themanbookerprize.com>.

YEAR	TITLE	AUTHOR
1969	Something to Answer For	P.H. Newby
1970	The Elected Member	Bernice Rubens
1971	In a Free State	V.S. Naipaul
1972	G.	John Berger
1973	The Siege of Krishnapur	J.G. Farrell
1974	The Conservationist	Nadine Gordimer
1974	Holiday	Stanley Middleton
1975	Heat and Dust	Ruth Prawer Jhabvala
1976	Saville	David Storey
1977	Staying On	Paul Scott
1978	The Sea, The Sea	Iris Murdoch
1979	Offshore	Penelope Fitzgerald
1980	Rites of Passage	William Golding
1981	Midnight's Children	Salman Rushdie
1982	Schindler's Ark	Thomas Keneally
1983	Life and Times of Michael K	J.M. Coetzee
1984	Hotel du Lac	Anita Brookner
1985	The Bone People	Keri Hulme
1986	The Old Devils	Kingsley Amis

YEAR	TITLE	AUTHOR
1987	Moon Tiger	Penelope Lively
1988	Oscar and Lucinda	Peter Carey
1989	The Remains of the Day	Kazuo Ishiguro
1990	Possession	A.S. Byatt
1991	The Famished Road	Ben Okri
1992	The English Patient	Michael Ondaatje
1992	Sacred Hunger	Barry Unsworth
1993	Paddy Clarke Ha Ha Ha	Roddy Doyle
1994	How Late It Was, How Late	James Kelman
1995	The Ghost Road	Pat Barker
1996	Last Orders	Graham Swift
1997	The God of Small Things	Arundhati Roy
1998	Amsterdam	Ian McEwan
1999	Disgrace	J.M. Coetzee
2000	The Blind Assassin	Margaret Atwood
2001	True History of the Kelly Gang	Peter Carey
2002	Life of Pi	Yann Martel
2003	Vernon God Little	DBC Pierre
2004	The Line of Beauty	Alan Hollinghurst
2005	The Sea	John Banville
2006	The Inheritance of Loss	Kiran Desai

The Costa Book Awards

The Whitbread Book Awards were inaugurated in 1971, and in 2006 Britain's Costa chain of coffee shops took over the prize. Since 1985, awards have been given in five categories: Novel, First Novel, Biography, Poetry, and Children's. From these a panel of judges chooses one overall winner—the Costa Book of the Year. The total prize fund is £50,000 (about $98,000): each of the category award winners re-

ceives £5,000 (about $9,800), and the Book of the Year winner receives an additional £25,000 (about $49,000).

This list includes Novel award winners from 1971 to 1984 and Book of the Year winners from 1985 to 2006.

Costa Book Awards Web site: <www.costabookawards.com>.

YEAR	TITLE	AUTHOR
1971	The Destiny Waltz	Gerda Charles
1972	The Bird of Night	Susan Hill
1973	The Chip-Chip Gatherers	Shiva Naipaul
1974	The Sacred and Profane Love Machine	Iris Murdoch
1975	Docherty	William McIlvanney
1976	The Children of Dynmouth	William Trevor
1977	Injury Time	Beryl Bainbridge
1978	Picture Palace	Paul Theroux
1979	The Old Jest	Jennifer Johnston
1980	How Far Can You Go?	David Lodge
1981	Silver's City	Maurice Leitch
1982	Young Shoulders	John Wain
1983	Fools of Fortune	William Trevor
1984	Kruger's Alp	Christopher Hope
1985	Elegies	Douglas Dunn
1986	An Artist of the Floating World	Kazuo Ishiguro
1987	Under the Eye of the Clock	Christopher Nolan
1988	The Comforts of Madness	Paul Sayer

YEAR	TITLE	AUTHOR
1989	Coleridge: Early Visions	Richard Holmes
1990	Hopeful Monsters	Nicholas Mosley
1991	A Life of Picasso	John Richardson
1992	Swing Hammer Swing!	Jeff Torrington
1993	Theory of War	Joan Brady
1994	Felicia's Journey	William Trevor
1995	Behind the Scenes at the Museum	Kate Atkinson
1996	The Spirit Level	Seamus Heaney
1997	Tales from Ovid	Ted Hughes
1998	Birthday Letters	Ted Hughes
1999	Beowulf	Seamus Heaney
2000	English Passengers	Matthew Kneale
2001	The Amber Spyglass	Philip Pullman
2002	Samuel Pepys: The Unequalled Self	Claire Tomalin
2003	The Curious Incident of the Dog in the Night-Time	Mark Haddon
2004	Small Island	Andrea Levy
2005	Matisse: The Master	Hilary Spurling
2006	The Tenderness of Wolves	Stef Penney

The Orange Broadband Prize

Awarded to a work of published fiction written in English by a woman and published in the United Kingdom or Ireland. Prize: £30,000 (about $59,500) and a bronze figurine called the "Bessie."
Orange Broadband Prize Web site: <www.orangeprize.co.uk>.

YEAR	TITLE	AUTHOR	YEAR	TITLE	AUTHOR
1996	A Spell of Winter	Helen Dunmore	2003	Property	Valerie Martin
1997	Fugitive Pieces	Anne Michaels	2004	Small Island	Andrea Levy
1998	Larry's Party	Carol Shields	2005	We Need To Talk About Kevin	Lionel Shriver
1999	A Crime in the Neighbourhood	Suzanne Berne	2006	On Beauty	Zadie Smith
2000	When I Lived in Modern Times	Linda Grant	2007	Half of a Yellow Sun	Chimamanda Ngozi Adichie
2001	The Idea of Perfection	Kate Grenville			
2002	Bel Canto	Ann Patchett			

Prix Goncourt

The Prix de l'Académie Goncourt was first awarded in 1903 from the estate of the brothers and French literary figures Edmond Huot de Goncourt (1822–1896) and Jules Huot de Goncourt (1830–1870) for a work of contemporary prose in French. Prize: €10 (about $13.00). An additional prize is awarded for the best work of new fiction.

YEAR	TITLE	AUTHOR	YEAR	TITLE	AUTHOR
1903	Force ennemie	John Antoine Nau	1938	L'Araignée	Henri Troyat
1904	La Maternelle	Léon Frapié	1939	Les Enfants gâtés	Philippe Hériat
1905	Les Civilisés	Claude Farrère	1940	Les Grandes Vacances	Francis Ambrière
1906	Dingley, l'illustre écrivain	Jérôme and Jean Tharaud	1941	Le Vent de mars	Henri Pourrat
1907	Le Rouet d'ivoire	Emile Moselly	1942	Pareil à des enfants	Bernard Marc
1908	Ecrit sur l'eau	Francis de Miomandre	1943	Passage de l'homme	Marius Grout
1909	En France	Marius & Ary Leblond	1944	Le Premier Accroc coûte 200 francs	Elsa Triolet
1910	De Goupil à Margot	Louis Pergaud	1945	Mon village à l'heure allemande	Jean-Louis Bory
1911	Monsieur des Lourdines	Alphonse de Chateaubriant	1946	Histoire d'un fait divers	Jean-Jacques Gautier
1912	Les Filles de la pluie	André Savignon	1947	Les Forêts de la nuit	Jean-Louis Curtis
1913	Le Peuple de la mer	Marc Elder	1948	Les Grandes Familles	Maurice Druon
1914	L'Appel du sol	Adrien Bertrand	1949	Week-end à Zuydcoote	Robert Merle
1915	Gaspard	René Benjamin	1950	Les Jeux sauvages	Paul Colin
1916	Le Feu	Henri Barbusse	1951	Le Rivage des Syrtes	Julien Gracq
1917	La Flamme au poing	Henri Malherbe	1952	Léon Morin, prêtre	Béatrice Beck
1918	Civilisation	Georges Duhamel	1953	Les Bêtes	Pierre Gascar
1919	A l'ombre des jeunes filles en fleur	Marcel Proust	1954	Mandarins	Simone de Beauvoir
1920	Nene	Ernest Perochon	1955	Les Eaux mêlées	Roger Ikor
1921	Batouala	René Maran	1956	Les Racines du ciel	Romain Gary
1922	Le Vitriol de la lune	Henry Béraud	1957	La Loi	Roger Vailland
1922	Le Martyre de l'obèse	Henry Béraud	1958	Saint Germain; ou, la négociation	Francis Walder
1923	Rabevel; ou, le mal des ardents	Lucien Fabré	1959	Le Dernier des justes	André Schwartz-Bart
1924	Le Chèvrefeuille, le Purgatoire, le Chapitre XIII	Thierry Sandre	1960	Dieu est né en exil	Vintila Horia
			1961	La Pitié de Dieu	Jean Cau
1925	Raboliot	Maurice Genevoix	1962	Les Bagages de sable	Anna Langfus
1926	Le Supplice de Phèdre	Henry Deberly	1963	Quand la mer se retire	Armand Lanoux
1927	Latitude nord	Maurice Bedel			
1928	Un Homme se penche sur son passé	Maurice Constantin Weyer	1964	L'État sauvage	Georges Conchon
1929	L'Ordre	Marcel Arland	1965	L'Adoration	Jacques Borel
1930	Malaisie	Henri Fauconnier	1966	Oublier Palerme	Edmonde Charles-Roux
1931	Mal d'amour	Jean Fayard	1967	La Marge	André-Pierre de Mandiargues
1932	Les Loups	Guy Mazeline			
1933	La Condition humaine	André Malraux	1968	Les Fruits de l'hiver	Bernard Clavel
1934	Capitaine Conan	Roger Vercel	1969	Creezy	Félicien Marceau
1935	Sang et lumières	Joseph Peyré	1970	Le Roi des Aulnes	Michel Tournier
1936	L'Empreinte de Dieu	Maxence Van Der Meersch	1971	Les Bêtises	Jacques Laurent
			1972	L'Épervier de Maheux	Jean Carrière
1937	Faux passeports	Charles Plisnier	1973	L'Ogre	Jacques Chessex
			1974	La Dentellière	Pascal Lainé
			1975	La Vie devant soi	Emile Ajar

Prix Goncourt (continued)

YEAR	TITLE	AUTHOR	YEAR	TITLE	AUTHOR
1976	Les Flamboyants	Patrick Grainville	1992	Texaco	Patrick Chamoiseau
1977	John l'enfer	Didier Decoin	1993	La Rocher de Tanios	Amin Maalouf
1978	Rue des boutiques obscures	Patrick Modiano	1994	Un Aller simple	Didier Van Cauwelaert
1979	Pélagie la charrette	Antonine Maillet	1995	Le Testament français	Andreï Makine
1980	Le Jardin d'acclimatation	Yves Navarre	1996	Le Chasseur zéro	Pascale Roze
1981	Anne Marie	Lucien Bodard	1997	La Bataille	Patrick Rambaud
1982	Dans la main de l'ange	Dominique Fernandez	1998	Confidence pour confidence	Paule Constant
1983	Les Égarés	Frédérick Tristan	1999	Je m'en vais	Jean Echenoz
1984	L'Amant	Marguerite Duras	2000	Ingrid Caven	Jean-Jacques Schuhl
1985	Les Noces barbares	Yann Queffélec	2001	Rouge Brésil	Jean-Christophe Rufin
1986	Valet de nuit	Michel Host			
1987	La Nuit sacrée	Tahar Ben Jelloun	2002	Les Ombres errantes	Pascal Quignard
1988	L'Exposition coloniale	Erik Orsenna	2003	La Maîtresse de Brecht	Jacques-Pierre Amette
1989	Un Grand Pas vers le Bon Dieu	Jean Vautrin	2004	Le Soleil des Scorta	Laurent Gaudé
1990	Les Champs d'honneur	Jean Rouaud	2005	Trois jours chez ma mère	François Weyergans
1991	Les Filles du calvaire	Pierre Combescot	2006	Les Bienveillantes	Jonathan Littell

Premio Cervantes, the Cervantes Prize for Hispanic Literature

The Spanish Ministry of Culture sponsors the annual prize, which carries an award of €90,450 (about $125,000). Cervantes Prize Web site: <http://www.mcu.es/premios/CervantesPresentacion.html>.

YEAR	AUTHOR	YEAR	AUTHOR
1976	Jorge Guillén	1992	Dulce María Loynaz
1977	Alejo Carpentier	1993	Miguel Delibes
1978	Dámaso Alonso	1994	Mario Vargas Llosa
1979	Jorge Luis Borges and Gerardo Diego	1995	Camilo José Cela
1980	Juan Carlos Onetti	1996	José García Nieto
1981	Octavio Paz	1997	Guillermo Cabrera Infante
1982	Luis Rosales	1998	José Hierro
1983	Rafael Alberti	1999	Jorge Edwards
1984	Ernesto Sábato	2000	Francisco Umbral
1985	Juan Rulfo	2001	Álvaro Mutis
1986	Antonio Buero Vallejo	2002	José Jiménez Lozano
1987	Carlos Fuentes	2003	Gonzalo Rojas
1988	María Zambrano	2004	Rafael Sánchez Ferlosio
1989	Augusto Roa Bastos	2005	Sergio Pitol
1990	Adolfo Bioy Casares	2006	Antonio Gamoneda
1991	Francisco Ayala		

The Jerusalem Prize

The municipality of Jerusalem awards this prize at the biennial Jerusalem International Book Fair to a writer whose work explores the freedom of the individual in society. Prize: $10,000.
Jerusalem Prize Web site: <www.jerusalembookfair.com>.

YEAR	AUTHOR	COUNTRY	YEAR	AUTHOR	COUNTRY
1963	Bertrand Russell	United Kingdom	1987	J.M. Coetzee	South Africa
1965	Max Frisch	Switzerland	1989	Ernesto Sábato	Argentina
1967	André Schwarz-Bart	France	1991	Zbigniew Herbert	France
1969	Ignazio Silóne	Italy	1993	Stefan Heym	Germany
1971	Jorge Luis Borges	Argentina	1995	Mario Vargas Llosa	Peru
1973	Eugène Ionesco	France	1997	Jorge Semprun	Spain
1975	Simone de Beauvoir	France	1999	Don DeLillo	United States
1977	Octavio Paz	Mexico	2001	Susan Sontag	United States
1979	Sir Isaiah Berlin	United Kingdom	2003	Arthur Miller	United States
1981	Graham Greene	United Kingdom	2005	António Lobo Antunes	Portugal
1983	V.S. Naipaul	United Kingdom	2007	Leszek Kolakowski	Poland
1985	Milan Kundera	France			

T.S. Eliot Prize

Great Britain's Poetry Book Society awards the T.S. Eliot Prize to the best new collection of poetry published in the UK or the Republic of Ireland during the preceding year. The prize is £10,000 (about $19,000).

YEAR	WORK	AUTHOR	COUNTRY
1993	First Language	Ciaran Carson	Ireland
1994	The Annals of Chile	Paul Muldoon	Northern Ireland
1995	My Alexandria	Mark Doty	United States
1996	Sub-Human Redneck Poems	Les Murray	Australia
1997	God's Gift to Women	Don Paterson	United Kingdom
1998	Birthday Letters	Ted Hughes	United Kingdom
1999	Billy's Rain	Hugo Williams	United Kingdom
2000	The Weather in Japan	Michael Longley	Northern Ireland
2001	The Beauty of the Husband	Anne Carson	Canada
2002	Dart	Alice Oswald	United Kingdom
2003	Landing Light	Don Paterson	United Kingdom
2004	Reel	George Szirtes	United Kingdom
2005	Rapture	Carol Ann Duffy	United Kingdom
2006	District and Circle	Seamus Heaney	Ireland

The Bollingen Prize in Poetry

The Bollingen Prize in Poetry is awarded biennially to the American poet whose work represents the highest achievement in the field of American poetry during the preceding two-year period. The committee considers published work, particularly work published during that preceding two-year period. Former winners of the prize are not eligible. Award amount: $100,000.

YEAR	POET	YEAR	POET	YEAR	POET
1948	Ezra Pound	1961	Richard Eberhart	1983	Anthony Hecht
1949	Wallace Stevens		John Hall Wheelock		John Hollander
1950	John Crowe Ransom	1963	Robert Frost	1985	John Ashbery
1951	Marianne Moore	1965	Horace Gregory		Fred Chappell
1952	Archibald MacLeish	1967	Robert Penn Warren	1987	Stanley Kunitz
	William Carlos Williams	1969	John Berryman	1989	Edgar Bowers
1953	W.H. Auden		Karl Shapiro	1991	Laura Riding Jackson
1954	Léonie Adams	1971	Richard Wilbur		Donald Justice
	Louise Bogan		Mona Van Duyn	1993	Mark Strand
1955	Conrad Aiken	1973	James Merrill	1995	Kenneth Koch
1956	Allen Tate	1975	A.R. Ammons	1997	Gary Snyder
1957	E.E. Cummings	1977	David Ignatow	1999	Robert Creeley
1958	Theodore Roethke	1979	W.S. Merwin	2001	Louise Glück
1959	Delmore Schwartz	1981	May Swenson	2003	Adrienne Rich
1960	Yvor Winters		Howard Nemerov	2005	Jay Wright
				2007	Frank Bidart

Architecture

Pritzker Architecture Prize

The Pritzker Prize, awarded by the Hyatt Foundation since 1979, is given to an outstanding living architect for built work. Prize: $100,000 and a bronze medallion. Web site: <www.pritzkerprize.com>.

YEAR	NAME	COUNTRY	YEAR	NAME	COUNTRY
1979	Philip Johnson	United States	1994	Christian de Portzamparc	France
1980	Luis Barragán	Mexico			
1981	James Stirling	Great Britain	1995	Tadao Ando	Japan
1982	Kevin Roche	United States	1996	Rafael Moneo	Spain
1983	Ieoh Ming Pei	United States	1997	Sverre Fehn	Norway
1984	Richard Meier	United States	1998	Renzo Piano	Italy
1985	Hans Hollein	Austria	1999	Sir Norman Foster	Great Britain
1986	Gottfried Boehm	West Germany	2000	Rem Koolhaas	The Netherlands
1987	Kenzo Tange	Japan	2001	Jacques Herzog	Switzerland
1988	Gordon Bunshaft	United States		Pierre de Meuron	Switzerland
	Oscar Niemeyer	Brazil	2002	Glenn Murcutt	Australia
1989	Frank O. Gehry	United States	2003	Jørn Utzon	Denmark
1990	Aldo Rossi	Italy	2004	Zaha Hadid	Great Britain
1991	Robert Venturi	United States	2005	Thom Mayne	United States
1992	Alvaro Siza	Portugal	2006	Paulo Mendes da Rocha	Brazil
1993	Fumihiko Maki	Japan	2007	Richard Rogers	Great Britain

AIA Gold Medal

The American Institute of Architects awards the gold medal for an outstanding body of work.

YEAR	NAME	YEAR	NAME	YEAR	NAME
1907	Sir Aston Webb	1957	Ralph Walker	1983	Nathaniel A. Owings
1909	Charles Follen McKim		Louis Skidmore	1985	William Wayne Caudill[1]
1911	George Browne Post	1958	John Wellborn Root[1]	1986	Arthur Erickson
1914	Jean Louis Pascal	1959	Walter Gropius	1989	Joseph Esherick
1922	Victor Laloux	1960	Ludwig Mies van der Rohe	1990	E. Fay Jones
1923	Henry Bacon	1961	Le Corbusier (Charles-	1991	Charles W. Moore
1925	Sir Edwin L. Lutyens		Édouard Jeanneret)	1992	Benjamin Thompson
	Bertram Grosvenor	1962	Eero Saarinen[1]	1993	Thomas Jefferson[1]
	Goodhue[1]	1963	Alvar Aalto		Kevin Roche
1927	Howard Van Doren Shaw	1964	Pier Luigi Nervi	1994	Sir Norman Foster
1929	Milton Bennett Medary	1966	Kenzo Tange	1995	César Pelli
1933	Ragnar Ostberg	1967	Wallace K. Harrison	1997	Richard Meier
1938	Paul Philippe Cret	1968	Marcel Breuer	1999	Frank O. Gehry
1944	Louis Henry Sullivan[1]	1969	William Wilson Wurster	2000	Ricardo Legorreta
1947	Eliel Saarinen	1970	Richard Buckminster	2001	Michael Graves
1948	Charles Donagh Maginnis		Fuller	2002	Tadao Ando
1949	Frank Lloyd Wright	1971	Louis I. Kahn	2004	Samuel Mockbee[1]
1950	Sir Patrick Abercrombie	1972	Pietro Belluschi	2005	Santiago Calatrava
1951	Bernard Ralph Maybeck	1977	Richard Joseph Neutra[1]	2006	Antoine Predock
1952	Auguste Perret	1978	Philip C. Johnson	2007	Edward Larrabe Barnes[1]
1953	William Adams Delano	1979	Ieoh Ming Pei		
1955	Willem Marinus Dudok	1981	José Luis Sert		
1956	Clarence S. Stein	1982	Romaldo Giurgola		[1]Awarded posthumously.

Special Honors

Hasty Pudding Theatricals Woman of the Year and Man of the Year

The Hasty Pudding Theatricals of Harvard University, an organization of undergraduates, has presented the Woman of the Year award since 1951 and the Man of the Year award since 1967 to performers who have made a "lasting and impressive contribution to the world of entertainment."

YEAR	NAME	YEAR	NAME
1951	Gertrude Lawrence	1980	Meryl Streep and Alan Alda
1952	Barbara Bel Geddes	1981	Mary Tyler Moore and John Travolta
1953	Mamie Eisenhower	1982	Ella Fitzgerald and James Cagney
1954	Shirley Booth	1983	Julie Andrews and Steven Spielberg
1955	Debbie Reynolds	1984	Joan Rivers and Sean Connery
1956	Peggy Ann Garner	1985	Cher and Bill Murray
1957	Carroll Baker	1986	Sally Field and Sylvester Stallone
1958	Katharine Hepburn	1987	Bernadette Peters and Mikhail Baryshnikov
1959	Joanne Woodward	1988	Lucille Ball and Steve Martin
1960	Carol Lawrence	1989	Kathleen Turner and Robin Williams
1961	Jane Fonda	1990	Glenn Close and Kevin Costner
1962	Piper Laurie	1991	Diane Keaton and Clint Eastwood
1963	Shirley MacLaine	1992	Jodie Foster and Michael Douglas
1964	Rosalind Russell	1993	Whoopi Goldberg and Chevy Chase
1965	Lee Remick	1994	Meg Ryan and Tom Cruise
1966	Ethel Merman	1995	Michelle Pfeiffer and Tom Hanks
1967	Lauren Bacall and Bob Hope	1996	Susan Sarandon and Harrison Ford
1968	Angela Lansbury and Paul Newman	1997	Julia Roberts and Mel Gibson
1969	Carol Burnett and Bill Cosby	1998	Sigourney Weaver and Kevin Kline
1970	Dionne Warwick and Robert Redford	1999	Goldie Hawn and Samuel L. Jackson
1971	Carol Channing and James Stewart	2000	Jamie Lee Curtis and Billy Crystal
1972	Ruby Keeler and Dustin Hoffman	2001	Drew Barrymore and Anthony Hopkins
1973	Liza Minnelli and Jack Lemmon	2002	Sarah Jessica Parker and Bruce Willis
1974	Faye Dunaway and Peter Falk	2003	Anjelica Huston and Martin Scorsese
1975	Valerie Harper and Warren Beatty	2004	Sandra Bullock and Robert Downey, Jr.
1976	Bette Midler and Robert Blake	2005	Catherine Zeta-Jones and Tim Robbins
1977	Elizabeth Taylor and Johnny Carson	2006	Halle Berry and Richard Gere
1978	Beverly Sills and Richard Dreyfuss	2007	Scarlett Johansson and Ben Stiller
1979	Candice Bergen and Robert De Niro		

Sport

Golf: Women on the Verge

by Kristina Dell, TIME

Morgan Pressel might have ended up a tennis player. It was in her genes. Her mother was a teaching pro, and her uncle is Aaron Krickstein, the Bollettieri Academy-bred kid who reached number six in the world. But tennis is no longer the only sport affording women a nice living, and Pressel's decision to practice bunker shots over drop shots at age eight is starting to pay off. A leader on the 2007 LPGA money list, she also won the Kraft Nabisco Championship, becoming the youngest woman, at 18, to take a golf major. Uncle Aaron holds the same record in men's pro tennis, except he was 16 at the time. "Aaron was so excited for me, and that was cute to see," says Pressel. With her ranking skyrocketing to fourth in the world, Pressel is on the cusp of greatness.

Her sport would like to claim the same status. Over the past five years, an army of young talent from South Korea to South Florida has invaded the Ladies Professional Golf Association (LPGA), stealing the limelight from overtanned veterans with a splash of color, short skirts, and high-flying ponytails. They've ditched the ice skates for their fathers' drivers, blasting pink balls over greens at Tiger Woods-size distances.

To match this brawn and beauty, the LPGA tour is sharpening its own game, which in 2005 generated about US$67 million in revenue. Commissioner Carolyn Bivens—the first woman to hold the job—hasn't been afraid to take some divots out of the LPGA's old business plan. She's reorganized the tournaments, the staff, even the television production. The goal: close the purse and popularity gap with the men's tour (PGA), as women have done in pro tennis.

She has got the goods: the LPGA field is deep and young. Of the top 10 women on the 2007 LPGA money list, only 2 are older than 27; the remaining 8 have an average age of 22. In addition to Pressel and grand dame Annika Sörenstam, today's talent includes a 21-year-old blonde, blue-eyed beauty who won her second major (Brittany Lincicome); a young Mexican (Lorena Ochoa) on the verge of dethroning longtime number one Sörenstam; a teen phenom, now 20, with a penchant for pink (Paula Creamer); a Japanese rock star trailed by a swarm of photographers (Ai Miyazato); and a swimsuit-calendar model with her own reality-TV show (Natalie Gulbis). "My decision to leave college and turn pro was one of the best decisions I've ever made," says Gulbis. "I'm living my dream and having so much fun."

And let's not forget Michelle Wie, that stylish, 1.8-m (6-ft) Hawaiian palm who fought a wrist injury in 2007. Her US$20 million endorsement contracts rival those of tennis queen Mariya Sharapova, even though she's spent more time trying to qualify (unsuccessfully) for men's tourneys. "These women aren't afraid to exploit their sexuality a little bit," says Rob McNamara, golf professional at Farmington Country Club in Charlottesville VA. "But these pinup girls can play championship-level golf, and that's the key."

Bivens, 54, a former advertising executive at USA Today and president of Initiative Media North America, a press service agency, is poised to make the most of her coterie of cuties. She's promoting a marketing campaign with the tagline "These girls rock" and signed on a personal branding coach, Wendy Newman, who helps players hone their image. "We don't want to cookie-cutter-stamp anyone," says Bivens. "Part of this is to play up their differences."

The allure of pretty women in candy-colored outfits has boosted interest in the sport. While the numbers still pale in comparison with men's golf, attendance at LPGA events rose 5% in 2006, and it's up 10% since 2001. Daily average television viewership for LPGA tournaments broadcast on cable (not including the Golf Channel) reached 417,000 households in 2006, up 59% from 2005, while network viewership that year rose 14%, to 1.7 million households. "The numbers are small, but the percentages are large," says Bivens. Women's golf is one of the few sports that can boast double-digit television growth in the US over the past two years.

With fairways resembling Benetton ads, Bivens must focus on growing the sport internationally as well as capitalizing on impressive American results: of the first six tournaments this year, Americans won five; Ochoa captured the sixth. "What's going on is eerily similar to when women's tennis blew up a decade ago," says John Mascatello, president of SFX Golf. After years of a few players dominating, the arrival of the Williams sisters spawned a Tiger Woods effect, heightening global competition. Today, Asia is the fastest-growing sector in TV, with women's golf in Japan garnering double the ratings of the men. That's one reason Honda is the sponsor of the LPGA's new Thailand tournament.

Taking Charge. To take advantage of the improving climate, the LPGA is trying to get more control of its own destiny. Bivens has upgraded tournament courses and involved the LPGA in the television production of events. In addition to the Solheim Cup, a team competition in which top Europeans take on top Americans, the LPGA owns and operates the year-end ADT Championship. There it can control the fan experience, like having more player interaction, and set broadcast agendas with a focus on player vignettes. By running tournaments, as opposed to licensing them, the LPGA earns money from ticket sales, food, and merchandise. The plan is still a long iron from success. LPGA tournaments have to buy network time, sell their own ads and cover production costs. But the LPGA underwrites half those expenses for ESPN and the Golf Channel, ensuring that all tournaments are televised.

Bivens's approach has not been bogey-free. Since her arrival, seven members of her senior staff have resigned or been fired, including three top executives who walked the same day. Her relationship with the press has been rocky at best. To protect the LPGA's content, Bivens distributed press credentials that tried to limit the use of photos by media organizations. Some refused to sign up. One result: the 2006 Fields Open in Hawaii was virtually blacked out by the media. The differences have since been worked out, but Bivens hasn't really budged. She says she's standing firm to protect how her players and the LPGA are marketed.

Bivens's next controversial move was to push for heftier service fees at LPGA events. She upped the price to tournament owners sevenfold, charging them as much as US$100,000 across a three-year period instead of the US$15,000 they had been paying. She reasoned that the LPGA had substantially increased its value by offering better service and exposure. Besides, tournament fees had not increased in 10 years. The dispute ended with only two tournaments dropping off the LPGA roster—in part because of scheduling conflicts—and new ones quickly filled the void. "It's a difficult job to please everyone," says Mascatello. "She is responsible for the events and the players, and there is an inherent conflict because someone must pay for increased benefits." Next on Bivens's agenda: securing health care for players and boosting LPGA retirement funds.

For the kids on the tour, thoughts of retirement are worth a giggle. Pressel had other issues. The week after her big victory, she played poorly—Lincicome won the Ginn Open. But one bad week isn't going to set her back. "That girl is tougher than a nickel steak," says golf pro McNamara. And so is Boss Bivens.

Golf: Teeing Up a New Game

by Kristina Dell, TIME

The wild beauty of the Chambers Bay Golf Course in Pierce county, Washington, is obvious and abundant. As you begin to walk the course, a second natural element makes its presence known: the wind. It swirls and dips and then slaps you sideways, an "invisible hazard," as the course's architect, Robert Trent Jones, Jr., likes to call it, mimicking the roughness of the stubbly Van Gogh-like landscape.

For Americans used to target golf on manicured greens, this links-style course is a different sport—more blustery St. Andrews than pristine Augusta. It's also a superintendent's dream: tough fescue grass makes up 94% of this Pacific Northwest terrain, requiring half the water and half the work of traditional courses. "I can't get over how few pesticides and fertilizers we need," says David Wienecke, Chambers Bay course superintendent. "We have the same standard of quality for 30% to 40% less cost."

Chambers Bay is not your typical golf course—condos don't line the fairways, carts are forbidden—but in other ways it exemplifies many of the trends in golf architecture: green maintenance practices, natural designs that follow the land, and clever reuse of land. This stunning US$20 million public course was formerly an underproductive mine.

In the oversaturated US golf market, courses have to stand out to survive. The slow but steady decline in golfers over the past six years resulted in a 70% decrease in commissioned courses from 2000 to 2006. The number of core golfers (those playing at least eight rounds a year) fell about 11% from 2000, with a 3% drop in rounds played over the same period, according to the National Golf Foundation. At the same time, more golf courses closed in the US than opened (146 shut down, while only 119 opened), the first such occurrence in six decades. "The game is less attractive to beginners because the courses are too long and hard, take too much time, and are too expensive," says Jones. A top-tier course designer like him earns about US$1 million on a typical commission, so the decrease has made the business tougher.

That's why the designers are teeing up new strategies. They're making the most of every patch of greensward, revamping older courses and shifting their practices to booming markets overseas. With new course construction lagging in the US, the hottest trend in golf architecture is the restoration of classics built by greats like Donald Ross. "We've seen a shift from new construction to remodeling in the past five years, and I think it will continue to grow," says Greg Muirhead, senior designer at Rees Jones, Inc., another leading firm.

To cut costs, they're using hardier grasses like fescue in the Pacific Northwest and paspalum in Hawaii, Florida, and Majorca. These drought-tolerant varieties don't require as much water for irrigation. And designers are working with what the land has to offer—the days of creating a pine forest out of a desert, à la Steven Wynn in Las Vegas, are numbered. "I take advantage of Mother Nature," says designer John Robinson. "At Blue Heron in Medina [OH], I had ravine after ravine, so I positioned the course to hit over those, like a steeplechase."

Big-name designers such as Tom Fazio, Tom Doak, Rees Jones, and Ben Crenshaw have all spent time sprucing up older fairways, updating technology, and incorporating current golfing trends. Rees ("The Open Doctor") Jones, whose nickname refers to his knack for transforming older courses into US Open-worthy playgrounds, says about a third of his projects are fairway refurbishments.

In counterpoint to its stagnation in the US, golf is exploding overseas and attracting PGA stars, including Tiger Woods and Phil Mickelson, to the design game. Courses are popping up in places never before imagined as golfing destinations, such as Ghana, Vietnam, Croatia, and Turkey. In the past five years 1,055 courses were built outside the US, in sunny spots like Majorca as well as in Sweden, where golf among young people is thriving.

Not surprisingly, wealthy, opulent Dubai has some high-profile projects. Woods has signed up to build a course in Dubailand, the region's largest tourism and leisure facility, while Greg Norman is teaming with Sergio García and influential designer Pete Dye to create Dubai's first links-style course. Jack Nicklaus is building a course in the Cape Verde Islands, off the West African coast. Gary Player Design built the first public course in China on an island off Hong Kong and just opened another course near Shanghai. "Seventy percent of the people who live on these courses in Asia don't play golf," says Marc Player, CEO of Gary Player Design. "They just want the lifestyle." Which is easier to achieve than par.

Sport Coverage

T he tables that follow contain the significant information about the top contests of all the major sports that are international in character, as well as some professional and amateur sports that attract a huge national following—such as baseball in the United States and cricket in the United Kingdom, Australia, India, and the other Test Match countries—and some sports, such as rowing, in which national competition overshadows international events. In many sports the Olympic Games held every four years constitute the world championships; they are included in the listings below.

Sporting Codes for Countries

These codes are used to identify countries in the Sport section of the Britannica Almanac.

Codes of the International Olympic Committee (IOC)

AFG	Afghanistan	CYP	Cyprus	KIR	Kiribati
AHO	Netherlands Antilles	CZE	Czech Republic	KOR	Korea, Republic of
		DEN	Denmark	KSA	Saudi Arabia
ALB	Albania	DJI	Djibouti	KUW	Kuwait
ALG	Algeria	DMA	Dominica	LAO	Laos
AND	Andorra	DOM	Dominican Republic	LAT	Latvia
ANG	Angola	ECU	Ecuador	LBA	Libya
ANT	Antigua and Barbuda	EGY	Egypt	LBR	Liberia
ARG	Argentina	ERI	Eritrea	LCA	St. Lucia
ARM	Armenia	ESA	El Salvador	LES	Lesotho
ARU	Aruba	ESP	Spain	LIB	Lebanon
ASA	American Samoa	EST	Estonia	LIE	Liechtenstein
AUS	Australia	ETH	Ethiopia	LTU	Lithuania
AUT	Austria	FIJ	Fiji	LUX	Luxembourg
AZE	Azerbaijan	FIN	Finland	MAD	Madagascar
BAH	Bahamas, The	FRA	France	MAR	Morocco
BAN	Bangladesh	FSM	Micronesia, Federated States of	MAS	Malaysia
BAR	Barbados			MAW	Malawi
BDI	Burundi	GAB	Gabon	MDA	Moldova
BEL	Belgium	GAM	Gambia, The	MDV	Maldives
BEN	Benin	GBR	Great Britain	MEX	Mexico
BER	Bermuda	GBS	Guinea-Bissau	MGL	Mongolia
BHU	Bhutan	GEO	Georgia	MHL	Marshall Islands
BIH	Bosnia and Herzegovina	GEQ	Equatorial Guinea	MKD	Macedonia, Former Yugoslav Republic of
BIZ	Belize	GER	Germany		
BLR	Belarus	GHA	Ghana	MLI	Mali
BOL	Bolivia	GRE	Greece	MLT	Malta
BOT	Botswana	GRN	Grenada	MON	Monaco
BRA	Brazil	GUA	Guatemala	MOZ	Mozambique
BRN	Bahrain	GUI	Guinea	MRI	Mauritius
BRU	Brunei	GUM	Guam	MTN	Mauritania
BUL	Bulgaria	GUY	Guyana	MYA	Myanmar (Burma)
BUR	Burkina Faso	HAI	Haiti	NAM	Namibia
CAF	Central African Republic	HKG	Hong Kong	NCA	Nicaragua
CAM	Cambodia	HON	Honduras	NED	Netherlands, The
CAN	Canada	HUN	Hungary	NEP	Nepal
CAY	Cayman Islands	INA	Indonesia	NGR	Nigeria
CGO	Congo, Republic of the	IND	India	NIG	Niger
CHA	Chad	IRI	Iran	NOR	Norway
CHI	Chile	IRL	Ireland	NRU	Nauru
CHN	China, People's Republic of	IRQ	Iraq	NZL	New Zealand
CIV	Côte d'Ivoire	ISL	Iceland	OMA	Oman
CMR	Cameroon	ISR	Israel	PAK	Pakistan
COD	Congo, Democratic Republic of the	ISV	US Virgin Islands	PAN	Panama
		ITA	Italy	PAR	Paraguay
COK	Cook Islands	IVB	British Virgin Islands	PER	Peru
COL	Colombia	JAM	Jamaica	PHI	Philippines
COM	Comoros	JOR	Jordan	PLE	Palestine
CPV	Cape Verde	JPN	Japan	PLW	Palau
CRC	Costa Rica	KAZ	Kazakhstan	PNG	Papua New Guinea
CRO	Croatia	KEN	Kenya	POL	Poland
CUB	Cuba	KGZ	Kyrgyzstan	POR	Portugal

Sporting Codes for Countries (continued)

Codes of the International Olympic Committee (IOC) (continued)

PRK	Korea, Democratic People's Republic of	SRB	Serbia	TRI	Trinidad and Tobago
PUR	Puerto Rico	SRI	Sri Lanka	TUN	Tunisia
QAT	Qatar	STP	São Tomé and Príncipe	TUR	Turkey
ROU	Romania	SUD	Sudan, The	UAE	United Arab Emirates
RSA	South Africa	SUI	Switzerland	UGA	Uganda
RUS	Russia	SUR	Suriname	UKR	Ukraine
RWA	Rwanda	SVK	Slovakia	URU	Uruguay
SAM	Samoa	SWE	Sweden	USA	United States
SEN	Senegal	SWZ	Swaziland	UZB	Uzbekistan
SEY	Seychelles	SYR	Syria	VAN	Vanuatu
SIN	Singapore	TAN	Tanzania	VEN	Venezuela
SKN	St. Kitts and Nevis	TGA	Tonga	VIE	Vietnam
SLE	Sierra Leone	THA	Thailand	VIN	St. Vincent and the Grenadines
SLO	Slovenia	TJK	Tajikistan		
SMR	San Marino	TKM	Turkmenistan	YEM	Yemen
SOL	Solomon Islands	TLS	East Timor (Timor Leste)	ZAM	Zambia
SOM	Somalia	TOG	Togo	ZIM	Zimbabwe
		TPE	Taiwan		

Continental, Historical, and Other Country Codes

AFR	Africa	DAH	Dahomey	KZK	Kazakhstan	SCO	Scotland
AIA	Anguilla	DMN	Dominica	LIT	Lithuania	SKR	Korea, Rep. of (South Korea)
AME	The Americas	ENG	England	MAC	Macao		
ARS	Saudi Arabia	EUR	Europe	MAU	Mauritius	SPA	Spain
ASI	Asia	FRG	Germany, Federal Republic of	MOL	Moldova	SWZ	Switzerland
BIR	Burma (Myanmar)			MOR	Morocco	TAH	Tahiti
BLS	Belarus	FRO	Faroe Islands	MSR	Montserrat	TAI	Taiwan
BOH	Bohemia	GDR	German Democratic Republic	NIC	Nicaragua	TCA	Turks and Caicos Islands
BOS	Bosnia and Herzegovina			NIR	Northern Ireland		
		HBR	British Honduras	NKO	Korea, Dem. People's Rep. of (North Korea)	TCH	Czechoslovakia
BUR	Burma	HEB	New Hebrides			UAR	United Arab Rep.
BWI	British West Indies	HOL	Holland/The Netherlands			UCS	Union of the Czech Rep. and Slovakia
				OCE	Oceania		
CAM	Cameroon	IOA	International Olympic Athlete	PAL	Palestine		
CEY	Ceylon			PDR	Korea, Dem. People's Rep. of	UNT	Unified Team
CIS	Commonwealth of Indep. States	ICE	Iceland			UPV	Upper Volta
		IHO	Netherlands India			URS	USSR
CKN	Congo-Kinshasa	IRE	Ireland	PNG	Papua New Guinea	UVI	US Virgin Islands
COB	Congo-Brazzaville	IVC	Côte d'Ivoire/Ivory Coast			WAL	Wales
CSV	Czechoslovakia			RHO	Rhodesia	YUG	Yugoslavia
CUR	Curaçao	JAP	Japan	ROC	China, Rep. of	ZAI	Zaire
				SAA	Saarland		

The James E. Sullivan Memorial Trophy

The trophy has been awarded by the Amateur Athletic Union (AAU) since 1930 to honor an athlete who, "by his or her performance, example, and influence as an amateur, has done the most during the year to advance the cause of sportsmanship." The award, named for a past president of the AAU, is usually announced in April. Winners receive a replica in bronze of the original trophy.

Web site: <www.aausports.org>.

YEAR	WINNER	SPORT	YEAR	WINNER	SPORT
1930	Bobby Jones	golf	1941	Leslie MacMitchell	track (middle distance running)
1931	Barney Berlinger	track (decathlon)			
1932	Jim Bausch	track (decathlon)	1942	Cornelius "Dutch" Warmerdam	track (pole vault)
1933	Glenn Cunningham	track (distance running)			
1934	Bill Bonthron	track (middle distance running)	1943	Gilbert Dodds	track (middle distance running)
1935	Lawson Little	golf	1944	Ann Curtis	swimming
1936	Glenn Morris	track (decathlon)	1945	Doc Blanchard	football
1937	Don Budge	tennis	1946	Arnold Tucker	football
1938	Don Lash	track (distance running)	1947	John B. Kelly, Jr.	rowing
1939	Joe Burk	rowing	1948	Bob Mathias	track (decathlon)
1940	Greg Rice	track (distance running)	1949	Dick Button	figure skating
			1950	Fred Wilt	track (distance running)

The James E. Sullivan Memorial Trophy (continued)

YEAR	WINNER	SPORT	YEAR	WINNER	SPORT
1951	Bob Richards	track (pole vault/ decathlon)	1980	Eric Heiden	speed skating
1952	Horace Ashenfelter	track (distance running)	1981	Carl Lewis	track (sprints/long jump)
1953	Sammy Lee	diving	1982	Mary Decker	track (distance running)
1954	Mal Whitfield	track (middle distance running)	1983	Edwin Moses	track (hurdles)
1955	Harrison Dillard	track (sprints/hurdles)	1984	Greg Louganis	diving
1956	Pat McCormick	diving	1985	Joan Benoit Samuelson	track (marathon)
1957	Bobby Morrow	track (sprints)	1986	Jackie Joyner-Kersee	track (heptathlon)
1958	Glenn Davis	track (hurdles)			
1959	Parry O'Brien	track (shot put)	1987	Jim Abbott	baseball
1960	Rafer Johnson	track (decathlon)	1988	Florence Griffith Joyner	track (sprints)
1961	Wilma Rudolph	track (sprints)			
1962	Jim Beatty	track (distance running)	1989	Janet Evans	swimming
1963	John Pennel	track (pole vault)	1990	John Smith	freestyle wrestling
1964	Don Schollander	swimming	1991	Mike Powell	track (long jump)
1965	Bill Bradley	basketball	1992	Bonnie Blair	speed skating
1966	Jim Ryun	track (middle distance running)	1993	Charlie Ward	football
			1994	Dan Jansen	speed skating
1967	Randy Matson	track (shot put/discus)	1995	Bruce Baumgartner	freestyle wrestling
1968	Debbie Meyer	swimming	1996	Michael Johnson	track (middle distance running)
1969	Bill Toomey	track (decathlon)			
1970	John Kinsella	swimming	1997	Peyton Manning	football
1971	Mark Spitz	swimming	1998	Chamique Holdsclaw	basketball
1972	Frank Shorter	track (distance running)			
1973	Bill Walton	basketball	1999	Coco and Kelly Miller	basketball
1974	Rick Wohlhuter	track (middle distance running)			
			2000	Rulon Gardner	Greco-Roman wrestling
1975	Tim Shaw	swimming	2001	Michelle Kwan	figure skating
1976	Bruce Jenner	track (decathlon)	2002	Sarah Hughes	figure skating
1977	John Naber	swimming	2003	Michael Phelps	swimming
1978	Tracy Caulkins	swimming	2004	Paul Hamm	gymnastics
1979	Kurt Thomas	gymnastics	2005	J.J. Redick	basketball
			2006	Jessica Long	swimming

The Olympic Games

By the 6th century BC several sporting festivals had achieved cultural importance in the Greek world. The most prominent among them were the Olympic Games at the city of Olympia, first recorded in 776 BC and held at four-year intervals thereafter. Those games, comprising many of the sports now included in the Summer Games, were abolished in AD 393 by the Roman emperor Theodosius I, probably because of their pagan associations.

In 1887 the 24-year-old French aristocrat and educator Pierre, baron de Coubertin, conceived the idea of reviving the Olympic Games and spent seven years gathering support for his plan. At a international congress in 1894, his plan was accepted and the International Olympic Committee (IOC) was founded. The first modern Olympic Games were held in Athens in April 1896, with some 300 representatives from 13 nations competing. The revival led to the formation of international amateur sports organizations and national Olympic committees throughout the world.

The IOC is responsible for maintaining the regular celebration of the games, seeing that the games are carried out in a spirit of peace and intercultural communication, and promoting amateur sport throughout the world. IOC members may not accept from the government of their country, or from any other entity, instructions that compromise their independence.

The Olympic Games have come to be regarded as the world's foremost sports competition. Before the 1970s the Games were officially limited to amateurs, but since that time many events have been opened to professional athletes. In 1924 the Winter Games were created, and in 1986 the IOC voted to alternate the Winter and Summer Games every two years, beginning in 1994.

The games were canceled during the two world wars (1916, 1940, and 1944) and have frequently served as venues for the expression of political dissent. China refused to participate in the Summer Games from 1956 until 1984 because of Taiwan's participation; 26 nations boycotted the games in 1976 over the participation of New Zealand, some of whose athletes had competed in apartheid-era South Africa; the United States and some 60 other countries boycotted the 1980 games in Moscow to protest the Soviet invasion of Afghanistan, and the Communist bloc and Cuba in turn boycotted the 1984 Los Angeles games.

In light of the IOC's declared independence from political and financial interests, in 1998 the world was shocked by allegations of widespread corruption within the committee. Several committee members, it was found, had accepted bribes to approve the bid of Salt Lake City UT as the site for the 2002 Winter Games. Impropriety was also alleged for several previous bid committees. The IOC responded by expelling six members and in 1999 announced a number of wide-ranging reforms.

IOC Web site: <www.olympic.org>.

Sites of the Modern Olympic Games

Summer Games

YEAR	LOCATION	YEAR	LOCATION	YEAR	LOCATION
1896	Athens, Greece	1948	London, England	1996	Atlanta GA
1900	Paris, France	1952	Helsinki, Finland	2000	Sydney, NSW, Australia
1904	St. Louis MO	1956	Melbourne, VIC, Australia	2004	Athens, Greece
1908	London, England	1960	Rome, Italy	2008	*scheduled to be held*
1912	Stockholm, Sweden	1964	Tokyo, Japan		*8–24 August, Beijing,*
1916	*not held*	1968	Mexico City, Mexico		*China*
1920	Antwerp, Belgium	1972	Munich, West Germany	2012	*scheduled to be held in*
1924	Paris, France	1976	Montreal, QC, Canada		*London, England*
1928	Amsterdam, Netherlands	1980	Moscow, USSR		
1932	Los Angeles CA	1984	Los Angeles CA		
1936	Berlin, Germany	1988	Seoul, South Korea		
1940–44	*not held*	1992	Barcelona, Spain		

Winter Games

YEAR	LOCATION	YEAR	LOCATION	YEAR	LOCATION
1924	Chamonix, France	1960	Squaw Valley CA	1994	Lillehammer, Norway
1928	St. Moritz, Switzerland	1964	Innsbruck, Austria	1998	Nagano, Japan
1932	Lake Placid NY	1968	Grenoble, France	2002	Salt Lake City UT
1936	Garmisch-Partenkirchen,	1972	Sapporo, Japan	2006	Turin, Italy
	Germany	1976	Innsbruck, Austria	2010	*scheduled to be held*
1940–44	*not held*	1980	Lake Placid NY		*12–28 February,*
1948	St. Moritz, Switzerland	1984	Sarajevo, Yugoslavia		*Vancouver, BC, Canada*
1952	Oslo, Norway	1988	Calgary, AB, Canada	2014	*scheduled to be held in*
1956	Cortina d'Ampezzo, Italy	1992	Albertville, France		*Sochi, Russia*

Summer Olympic Games Champions

Gold-medal winners in all Summer Olympic contests since 1896. Note: East and West Germany fielded a joint all-Germany team in 1956, 1960, and 1964, abbreviated here as GER. The Unified Team in 1992 consisted of the Commonwealth of Independent States plus Georgia, and is abbreviated here as UNT.

Archery

MEN'S INDIVIDUAL
1972   John Williams (USA)
1976   Darrell Pace (USA)
1980   Tomi Poikolainen (FIN)
1984   Darrell Pace (USA)
1988   Jay Barrs (USA)
1992   Sebastien Flute (FRA)
1996   Justin Huish (USA)
2000   Simon Fairweather (AUS)
2004   Marco Galiazzo (ITA)

AU CORDON DORE (50 METERS)
1900   Henri Herouin (FRA)

AU CORDON DORE (33 METERS)
1900   Hubert van Innis (BEL)

AU CHAPELET (50 METERS)
1900   Eugène Mougin (FRA)

SUR LA PERCHE A LA HERSE
1900   Emmanuel Foulon (FRA)

AU CHAPELET (33 METERS)
1900   Hubert van Innis (BEL)

SUR LA PERCHE A LA PYRAMIDE
1900   Émile Grumiaux (FRA)

Archery (continued)

DOUBLE AMERICAN ROUND
1904   George Philipp Bryant (USA)

(DOUBLE) YORK ROUND
1904   George Philipp Bryant (USA)
1908   William Dod (GBR)

CONTINENTAL STYLE
1908   Eugène G. Grizot (FRA)

FIXED BIRD TARGET (SMALL)
1920   Edmond van Moer (BEL)

FIXED BIRD TARGET (LARGE)
1920   Édouard Cloetens (BEL)

MOVING BIRD TARGET (28 M)
1920   Hubert van Innis (BEL)

MOVING BIRD TARGET (33 M)
1920   Hubert van Innis (BEL)

MOVING BIRD TARGET (50 M)
1920   Julien Brulé (FRA)

WOMEN'S INDIVIDUAL
1972   Doreen Wilber (USA)
1976   Luann Ryon (USA)
1980   Ketevan Losabenidze (URS)

Summer Olympic Games Champions (continued)

Archery (continued)

WOMEN'S INDIVIDUAL (CONTINUED)
1984 Seo Hyang Soon (KOR)
1988 Kim Soo Nyung (KOR)
1992 Cho Youn Jeong (KOR)
1996 Kim Kyung-Wook (KOR)
2000 Yun Mi-Jin (KOR)
2004 Park Sung Hyun (KOR)

DOUBLE COLUMBIA ROUND
1904 Matilda Scott Howell (USA)

(DOUBLE) NATIONAL ROUND
1904 Matilda Scott Howell (USA)
1908 Sybil Fenton "Queenie" Newall (GBR)

MEN'S TEAM
1904 United States
1988 South Korea
1992 Spain
1996 United States
2000 South Korea
2004 South Korea

WOMEN'S TEAM
1904 United States
1988 South Korea
1992 South Korea
1996 South Korea
2000 South Korea
2004 South Korea

FIXED TARGET (2 EVENTS)
1920 Belgium

MOVING TARGET (28 M)
1920 The Netherlands

MOVING TARGET (33 M)
1920 Belgium

MOVING TARGET (50 M)
1920 Belgium

Association football (soccer)[1]

MEN
1900 Great Britain
1904 Canada
1908 Great Britain
1912 Great Britain
1920 Belgium
1924 Uruguay
1928 Uruguay
1936 Italy
1948 Sweden
1952 Hungary
1956 USSR
1960 Yugoslavia
1964 Hungary
1968 Hungary
1972 Poland
1976 East Germany
1980 Czechoslovakia
1984 France
1988 USSR
1992 Spain
1996 Nigeria

Association football (soccer)[1] (continued)

MEN (CONTINUED)
2000 Cameroon
2004 Argentina

WOMEN
1996 United States
2000 Norway
2004 United States

Athletics (track-and-field) (men)

60 METERS		SEC
1900	Alvin Kraenzlein (USA)	7
1904	Archie Hahn (USA)	7

100 METERS		SEC
1896	Thomas Burke (USA)	12.0
1900	Francis Jarvis (USA)	11.0
1904	Archie Hahn (USA)	11.0
1908	Reginald Walker (RSA)	10.8
1912	Ralph Craig (USA)	10.8
1920	Charles Paddock (USA)	10.8
1924	Harold Abrahams (GBR)	10.6
1928	Percy Williams (CAN)	10.8
1932	Eddie Tolan (USA)	10.3
1936	Jesse Owens (USA)	10.3
1948	Harrison Dillard (USA)	10.3
1952	Lindy Remigino (USA)	10.4
1956	Robert Morrow (USA)	10.5
1960	Armin Hary (GER)	10.2
1964	Robert Hayes (USA)	10.0
1968	James Hines (USA)	9.9
1972	Valery Borzov (URS)	10.14
1976	Hasely Crawford (TRI)	10.06
1980	Allan Wells (GBR)	10.25
1984	Carl Lewis (USA)	9.99
1988	Carl Lewis (USA)	9.92
1992	Linford Christie (GBR)	9.96
1996	Donovan Bailey (CAN)	9.84
2000	Maurice Greene (USA)	9.87
2004	Justin Gatlin (USA)	9.85

200 METERS		SEC
1900	Walter Tewksbury (USA)	22.2
1904	Archie Hahn (USA)	21.6
1908	Robert Kerr (CAN)	22.6
1912	Ralph Craig (USA)	21.7
1920	Allen Woodring (USA)	22.0
1924	Jackson Scholz (USA)	21.6
1928	Percy Williams (CAN)	21.8
1932	Eddie Tolan (USA)	21.2
1936	Jesse Owens (USA)	20.7
1948	Melvin Patton (USA)	21.1
1952	Andy Stanfield (USA)	20.7
1956	Robert Morrow (USA)	20.6
1960	Livio Berruti (ITA)	20.5
1964	Henry Carr (USA)	20.3
1968	Tommie Smith (USA)	19.8
1972	Valery Borzov (URS)	20.00
1976	Donald Quarrie (JAM)	20.23
1980	Pietro Mennea (ITA)	20.19
1984	Carl Lewis (USA)	19.80
1988	Joe DeLoach (USA)	19.75
1992	Mike Marsh (USA)	20.01
1996	Michael Johnson (USA)	19.32
2000	Konstantinos Kenteris (GRE)	20.09
2004	Shawn Crawford (USA)	19.79

Summer Olympic Games Champions (continued)

Athletics (track-and-field) (men) (continued)

400 METERS

		SEC
1896	Thomas Burke (USA)	54.2
1900	Maxwell Long (USA)	49.4
1904	Harry Hillman (USA)	49.2
1908	Wyndham Halswelle (GBR)	50.0
1912	Charles Reidpath (USA)	48.2
1920	Bevil Rudd (RSA)	49.6
1924	Eric Liddell (GBR)	47.6
1928	Raymond Barbuti (USA)	47.8
1932	William Carr (USA)	46.2
1936	Archie Williams (USA)	46.5
1948	Arthur Wint (JAM)	46.2
1952	Vincent George Rhoden (JAM)	45.9
1956	Charles Jenkins (USA)	46.7
1960	Otis Davis (USA)	44.9
1964	Michael Larrabee (USA)	45.1
1968	Lee Evans (USA)	43.8
1972	Vincent Matthews (USA)	44.66
1976	Alberto Juantorena (CUB)	44.26
1980	Viktor Markin (URS)	44.60
1984	Alonzo Babers (USA)	44.27
1988	Steven Lewis (USA)	43.87
1992	Quincy Watts (USA)	43.50
1996	Michael Johnson (USA)	43.49
2000	Michael Johnson (USA)	43.84
2004	Jeremy Wariner (USA)	44.00

800 METERS

		MIN:SEC
1896	Edwin Flack (AUS)	2:11.0
1900	Alfred Tysoe (GBR)	2:01.2
1904	James Lightbody (USA)	1:56.0
1908	Melvin Sheppard (USA)	1:52.8
1912	James Edward Meredith (USA)	1:51.9
1920	Albert Hill (GBR)	1:53.4
1924	Douglas Lowe (GBR)	1:52.4
1928	Douglas Lowe (GBR)	1:51.8
1932	Thomas Hampson (GBR)	1:49.7
1936	John Woodruff (USA)	1:52.9
1948	Malvin Whitfield (USA)	1:49.2
1952	Malvin Whitfield (USA)	1:49.2
1956	Thomas Courtney (USA)	1:47.7
1960	Peter Snell (NZL)	1:46.3
1964	Peter Snell (NZL)	1:45.1
1968	Ralph Doubell (AUS)	1:44.3
1972	David Wottle (USA)	1:45.9
1976	Alberto Juantorena (CUB)	1:43.50
1980	Steven Ovett (GBR)	1:45.40
1984	Joaquim Cruz (BRA)	1:43.00
1988	Paul Ereng (KEN)	1:43.45
1992	William Tanui (KEN)	1:43.66
1996	Vebjoern Rodal (NOR)	1:42.58
2000	Nils Schumann (GER)	1:45.08
2004	Yury Borzakovsky (RUS)	1:44.45

1,500 METERS

		MIN:SEC
1896	Edwin Flack (AUS)	4:33.2
1900	Charles Bennett (GBR)	4:06.2
1904	James Lightbody (USA)	4:05.4
1908	Melvin Sheppard (USA)	4:03.4
1912	Arnold Jackson (GBR)	3:56.8
1920	Albert Hill (GBR)	4:01.8
1924	Paavo Nurmi (FIN)	3:53.6
1928	Harry Larva (FIN)	3:53.2
1932	Luigi Beccali (ITA)	3:51.2
1936	John Lovelock (NZL)	3:47.8
1948	Henry Eriksson (SWE)	3:49.8

1,500 METERS (CONTINUED)

		MIN:SEC
1952	Joseph Barthel (LUX)	3:45.1
1956	Ronald Delany (IRE)	3:41.2
1960	Herbert Elliott (AUS)	3:35.6
1964	Peter Snell (NZL)	3:38.1
1968	Hezekiah Kipchoge ("Kip") Keino (KEN)	3:34.9
1972	Pekka Vasala (FIN)	3:36.3
1976	John Walker (NZL)	3:39.17
1980	Sebastian Coe (GBR)	3:38.40
1984	Sebastian Coe (GBR)	3:32.53
1988	Peter Rono (KEN)	3:35.96
1992	Fermin Cacho Ruiz (ESP)	3:40.12
1996	Noureddine Morceli (ALG)	3:35.78
2000	Noah Ngeny (KEN)	3:32.07
2004	Hicham El Guerrouj (MAR)	3:34.18

5,000 METERS

		MIN:SEC
1912	Hannes Kolehmainen (FIN)	14:36.6
1920	Joseph Guillemot (FRA)	14:55.6
1924	Paavo Nurmi (FIN)	14:31.2
1928	Vilho Ritola (FIN)	14:38.0
1932	Lauri Lehtinen (FIN)	14:30.0
1936	Gunnar Höckert (FIN)	14:22.2
1948	Gaston Reiff (BEL)	14:17.6
1952	Emil Zatopek (TCH)	14:06.6
1956	Vladimir Kuts (URS)	13:39.6
1960	Murray Halberg (NZL)	13:43.4
1964	Robert Keyser Schul (USA)	13:48.8
1968	Mohamed Gammoudi (TUN)	14:05.0
1972	Lasse Viren (FIN)	13:26.4
1976	Lasse Viren (FIN)	13:24.76
1980	Miruts Yifter (ETH)	13:21.00
1984	Said Aouita (MAR)	13:05.59
1988	John Ngugi (KEN)	13:11.70
1992	Dieter Baumann (GER)	13:12.52
1996	Venuste Niyongabo (BDI)	13:07.97
2000	Millon Wolde (ETH)	13:35.49
2004	Hicham El Guerrouj (MAR)	13:14.39

5 MILES

		MIN:SEC
1908	Emil Voigt (GBR)	25:11.2

10,000 METERS

		MIN:SEC
1912	Hannes Kolehmainen (FIN)	31:20.8
1920	Paavo Nurmi (FIN)	31:45.8
1924	Vilho Ritola (FIN)	30:23.2
1928	Paavo Nurmi (FIN)	30:18.8
1932	Janusz Kusocinski (POL)	30:11.4
1936	Ilmari Salminen (FIN)	30:15.4
1948	Emil Zatopek (TCH)	29:59.6
1952	Emil Zatopek (TCH)	29:17.0
1956	Vladimir Kuts (URS)	28:45.6
1960	Pyotr Bolotnikov (URS)	28:32.2
1964	William Mills (USA)	28:24.4
1968	Nabiba Temu (KEN)	29:27.4
1972	Lasse Viren (FIN)	27:38.4
1976	Lasse Viren (FIN)	27:40.38
1980	Miruts Yifter (ETH)	27:42.70
1984	Alberto Cova (ITA)	27:47.54
1988	Brahim Boutaib (MAR)	27:21.46
1992	Khalid Skah (MAR)	27:46.70
1996	Haile Gebrselassie (ETH)	27:07.34
2000	Haile Gebrselassie (ETH)	27:18.20
2004	Kenenisa Bekele (ETH)	27:05.10

Summer Olympic Games Champions (continued)

Athletics (track-and-field) (men) (continued)

MARATHON		HR:MIN:SEC
1896	Spiridon Louis (GRE)	2:58:50.0
1900	Michel Theato (FRA)	2:59:45.0
1904	Thomas Hicks (USA)	3:28:53.0
1908	John Hayes (USA)	2:55:18.4
1912	Kenneth McArthur (RSA)	2:36:54.8
1920	Hannes Kolehmainen (FIN)	2:32:35.8
1924	Albin Stenroos (FIN)	2:41:22.6
1928	Boughèra El Ouafi (FRA)	2:32:57.0
1932	Juan Carlos Zabala (ARG)	2:31:36.0
1936	Kitei Son (JPN)	2:29:19.2
1948	Delfo Cabrera (ARG)	2:34:51.6
1952	Emil Zatopek (TCH)	2:23:03.2
1956	Alain Mimoun-O-Kacha (FRA)	2:25:00.0
1960	Abebe Bikila (ETH)	2:15:16.2
1964	Abebe Bikila (ETH)	2:12:11.2
1968	Mamo Wolde (ETH)	2:20:26.4
1972	Frank Shorter (USA)	2:12:19.8
1976	Waldemar Cierpinski (GDR)	2:09:55.0
1980	Waldemar Cierpinski (GDR)	2:11:03.0
1984	Carlos Lopes (POR)	2:09:21.0
1988	Gelindo Bordin (ITA)	2:10:32.0
1992	Hwang Young-Cho (KOR)	2:13:23.0
1996	Josia Thugwane (RSA)	2:12:36.0
2000	Gezahgne Abera (ETH)	2:10:11.0
2004	Stefano Baldini (ITA)	2:10.55.0

110-METER HURDLES		SEC
1896[2]	Thomas Curtis (USA)	17.6
1900	Alvin Kraenzlein (USA)	15.4
1904	Frederick Schule (USA)	16.0
1908	Forrest Smithson (USA)	15.0
1912	Frederick Kelly (USA)	15.1
1920	Earl Thomson (CAN)	14.8
1924	Daniel Kinsey (USA)	15.0
1928	Sydney Atkinson (RSA)	14.8
1932	George Saling (USA)	14.6
1936	Forrest Towns (USA)	14.2
1948	William Porter (USA)	13.9
1952	Harrison Dillard (USA)	13.7
1956	Lee Calhoun (USA)	13.5
1960	Lee Calhoun (USA)	13.8
1964	Hayes Wendell Jones (USA)	13.6
1968	Willie Davenport (USA)	13.3
1972	Rodney Milburn (USA)	13.24
1976	Guy Drut (FRA)	13.30
1980	Thomas Munkelt (GDR)	13.39
1984	Roger Kingdom (USA)	13.20
1988	Roger Kingdom (USA)	12.98
1992	Mark McKoy (CAN)	13.12
1996	Allen Johnson (USA)	12.95
2000	Anier Garcia (CUB)	13.00
2004	Liu Xiang (CHN)	12.91

200-METER HURDLES		SEC
1900	Alvin Kraenzlein (USA)	25.4
1904	Harry Hillman (USA)	24.6

400-METER HURDLES		SEC
1900	Walter Tewksbury (USA)	57.6
1904[3]	Harry Hillman (USA)	53.0
1908	Charles Bacon (USA)	55.0
1920	Frank Loomis (USA)	54.0
1924	Frederick Morgan Taylor (USA)	52.6
1928	David George Burghley (GBR)	53.4
1932	Robert Tisdall (IRE)	51.7
1936	Glenn Hardin (USA)	52.4
1948	Roy Cochran (USA)	51.1

Athletics (track-and-field) (men) (continued)

400-METER HURDLES (CONTINUED)		SEC
1952	Charles Moore (USA)	50.8
1956	Glenn Davis (USA)	50.1
1960	Glenn Davis (USA)	49.3
1964	Warren Cawley (USA)	49.6
1968	David Hemery (GBR)	48.1
1972	John Akii-Bua (UGA)	47.82
1976	Edwin Moses (USA)	47.64
1980	Volker Beck (GDR)	48.70
1984	Edwin Moses (USA)	47.75
1988	Andre Phillips (USA)	47.19
1992	Kevin Young (USA)	46.78
1996	Derrick Adkins (USA)	47.54
2000	Angelo Taylor (USA)	47.50
2004	Felix Sánchez (DOM)	47.63

2,500-METER STEEPLECHASE		MIN:SEC
1900	George Orton (USA)	7:34.4

2,590-METER STEEPLECHASE		MIN:SEC
1904	James Lightbody (USA)	7:39.6

3,000-METER STEEPLECHASE		MIN:SEC
1920	Percy Hodge (GBR)	10:00.4
1924	Vilho Ritola (FIN)	9:33.6
1928	Toivo Loukola (FIN)	9:21.8
1932	Volmari Iso-Hollo (FIN)	10:33.4[4]
1936	Volmari Iso-Hollo (FIN)	9:03.8
1948	Thore Sjöstrand (SWE)	9:04.6
1952	Horace Ashenfelter (USA)	8:45.4
1956	Christopher Brasher (GBR)	8:41.2
1960	Zdislaw Krzyszkowiak (POL)	8:34.2
1964	Gaston Roelants (BEL)	8:30.8
1968	Amos Biwott (KEN)	8:51.0
1972	Kipchoge Keino (KEN)	8:23.6
1976	Anders Gärderud (SWE)	8:08.02
1980	Bronislaw Malinowski (POL)	8:09.70
1984	Julius Korir (KEN)	8:11.80
1988	Julius Kariuki (KEN)	8:05.51
1992	Mathew Birir (KEN)	8:08.84
1996	Joseph Keter (KEN)	8:07.12
2000	Reuben Kosgei (KEN)	8:21.43
2004	Ezekiel Kemboi (KEN)	8:05.81

3,200-METER STEEPLECHASE		MIN:SEC
1908	Arthur Russell (GBR)	10:47.8

3,000 METERS (TEAM) (TEAM/INDIVIDUAL WINNER)		MIN:SEC
1912	United States/Tell Berna	8:44.6
1920	United States/Horace Brown	8:45.4
1924	Finland/Paavo Nurmi	8:32

3 MILES (TEAM) (TEAM/INDIVIDUAL WINNER)		MIN:SEC
1908	Great Britain/Joseph Deakin	14:39.6

5,000 METERS (TEAM) (TEAM/INDIVIDUAL WINNER)		MIN:SEC
1900	Great Britain-Australia/Charles Bennett	15:20

Summer Olympic Games Champions (continued)

Athletics (track-and-field) (men) (continued)

4 MILES (TEAM) (TEAM/INDIVIDUAL WINNER)	MIN:SEC
1904 United States/Arthur Newton (USA)	21:17.8

4 × 100 METER RELAY	SEC
1912 Great Britain	42.4
1920 United States	42.2
1924 United States	41.0
1928 United States	41.0
1932 United States	40.0
1936 United States	39.8
1948 United States	40.6
1952 United States	40.1
1956 United States	39.5
1960 Germany	39.5
1964 United States	39.0
1968 United States	38.2
1972 United States	38.19
1976 United States	38.33
1980 USSR	38.26
1984 United States	37.83
1988 USSR	38.19
1992 United States	37.40
1996 Canada	37.69
2000 United States	37.61
2004 Great Britain	38.07

4 × 400 METER RELAY	MIN:SEC
1912 United States	3:16.6
1920 Great Britain	3:22.2
1924 United States	3:16.0
1928 United States	3:14.2
1932 United States	3:08.2
1936 Great Britain	3:09.0
1948 United States	3:10.4
1952 Jamaica	3:03.9
1956 United States	3:04.8
1960 United States	3:02.2
1964 United States	3:00.7
1968 United States	2:56.1
1972 Kenya	2:59.8
1976 United States	2:58.65
1980 USSR	3:01.1
1984 United States	2:57.91
1988 United States	2:56.16
1992 United States	2:55.74
1996 United States	2:55.99
2000 United States	2:56.35
2004 United States	2:55.91

1,600-METER RELAY (200 × 200 × 400 × 800 METERS)	MIN:SEC
1908 United States	3:29.4

8,000 M CROSS-COUNTRY	MIN:SEC
1920 Paavo Nurmi (FIN)	27:15

10,000 M CROSS-COUNTRY	MIN:SEC
1924 Paavo Nurmi (FIN)	32:54.8

12,000 M CROSS-COUNTRY	MIN:SEC
1912 Hannes Kolehmainen (FIN)	45:11.6

3,000-METER WALK	MIN:SEC
1920 Ugo Frigerio (ITA)	13:14.2

3,500-METER WALK	MIN:SEC
1908 George Larner (GBR)	14:55

Athletics (track-and-field) (men) (continued)

10,000-METER WALK	MIN:SEC
1912 George Goulding (CAN)	46:28.4
1920 Ugo Frigerio (ITA)	48:06.2
1924 Ugo Frigerio (ITA)	47:49
1948 John Mikaelsson (SWE)	45:13.2
1952 John Mikaelsson (SWE)	45:02.8

10-MILE WALK	HR:MIN:SEC
1908 George Larner (GBR)	1:15:57.4

20,000-METER WALK	HR:MIN:SEC
1956 Leonid Spirin (URS)	1:31:27.4
1960 Vladimir Golubnichy (URS)	1:34:07.2
1964 Kenneth Matthews (GBR)	1:29:34.0
1968 Vladimir Golubnichy (URS)	1:33:58.4
1972 Peter Frenkel (GDR)	1:26:42.6
1976 Daniel Bautista (MEX)	1:24:40.6
1980 Maurizio Damilano (ITA)	1:23:35.5
1984 Ernesto Canto (MEX)	1:23:13.0
1988 Jozef Pribilinec (TCH)	1:19:57.0
1992 Daniel Plaza Montero (ESP)	1:21:45.0
1996 Jefferson Pérez (ECU)	1:20:07.0
2000 Robert Korzeniowski (POL)	1:18:59.0
2004 Ivano Brugnetti (ITA)	1:19.40.0

50,000-METER WALK	HR:MIN:SEC
1932 Thomas Green (GBR)	4:50:10.0
1936 Harold Whitlock (GBR)	4:30:41.4
1948 John Ljunggren (SWE)	4:41:52.0
1952 Giuseppe Dordoni (ITA)	4:28:07.8
1956 Norman Read (NZL)	4:30:42.8
1960 Donald Thompson (GBR)	4:25:30.0
1964 Abdon Pamich (ITA)	4:11:12.4
1968 Christophe Höhne (GDR)	4:20:13.6
1972 Bernd Kannenberg (FRG)	3:56:11.6
1980 Hartwig Gauder (GDR)	3:49:24.0
1984 Raúl Gonzáles (MEX)	3:47:26.0
1988 Vyacheslav Ivanenko (URS)	3:38:29.0
1992 Andrey Perlov (UNT)	3:50:13.0
1996 Robert Korzeniowski (POL)	3:43:03.0
2000 Robert Korzeniowski (POL)	3:42:22.0
2004 Robert Korzeniowski (POL)	3:38:46.0

HIGH JUMP	METERS
1896 Ellery Clark (USA)	1.81
1900 Irving Baxter (USA)	1.90
1904 Samuel Jones (USA)	1.80
1908 Harry Porter (USA)	1.90
1912 Alma Richards (USA)	1.93
1920 Richmond Landon (USA)	1.93
1924 Harold Osborn (USA)	1.98
1928 Robert King (USA)	1.94
1932 Duncan McNaughton (CAN)	1.97
1936 Cornelius Johnson (USA)	2.03
1948 John Winter (AUS)	1.98
1952 Walter Davis (USA)	2.04
1956 Charles Dumas (USA)	2.12
1960 Robert Shavlakadze (URS)	2.16
1964 Valery Brumel (URS)	2.18
1968 Richard Fosbury (USA)	2.24
1972 Yury Tarmak (URS)	2.23
1976 Jacek Wszola (POL)	2.25
1980 Gerd Wessig (GDR)	2.36
1984 Dietmar Mögenburg (FRG)	2.35
1988 Gennady Avdeyenko (URS)	2.38
1992 Javier Sotomayor (CUB)	2.34

Summer Olympic Games Champions (continued)

Athletics (track-and-field) (men) (continued)

HIGH JUMP (CONTINUED)		METERS
1996	Charles Austin (USA)	2.39
2000	Sergey Klyugin (RUS)	2.35
2004	Stefan Holm (SWE)	2.36

STANDING HIGH JUMP		METERS
1900	Ray Ewry (USA)	1.65
1904	Ray Ewry (USA)	1.6
1908	Ray Ewry (USA)	1.57
1912	Platt Adams (USA)	1.63

POLE VAULT		METERS
1896	William Welles Hoyt (USA)	3.30
1900	Irving Baxter (USA)	3.30
1904	Charles Dvorak (USA)	3.50
1908	Edward Cooke (USA); Alfred Gilbert (USA) (tied)	3.71
1912	Harry Babcock (USA)	3.95
1920	Frank Foss (USA)	4.09
1924	Lee Barnes (USA)	3.95
1928	Sabin Carr (USA)	4.20
1932	William Miller (USA)	4.31
1936	Earle Meadows (USA)	4.35
1948	Owen Guinn Smith (USA)	4.30
1952	Robert Richards (USA)	4.55
1956	Robert Richards (USA)	4.56
1960	Donald Bragg (USA)	4.70
1964	Fred Hansen (USA)	5.10
1968	Robert Seagren (USA)	5.40
1972	Wolfgang Nordwig (GDR)	5.50
1976	Tadeusz Slusarski (POL)	5.50
1980	Wladyslaw Kozakiewicz (POL)	5.78
1984	Pierre Quinon (FRA)	5.75
1988	Sergey Bubka (URS)	5.90
1992	Maksim Tarasov (UNT)	5.80
1996	Jean Galfione (FRA)	5.92
2000	Nick Hysong (USA)	5.90
2004	Timothy Mack (USA)	5.95

LONG JUMP		METERS
1896	Ellery Clark (USA)	6.35
1900	Alvin Kraenzlein (USA)	7.18
1904	Meyer Prinstein (USA)	7.34
1908	Francis Irons (USA)	7.48
1912	Albert Gutterson (USA)	7.60
1920	William Pettersson (SWE)	7.15
1924	William de Hart-Hubbard (USA)	7.44
1928	Edward Hamm (USA)	7.73
1932	Edward Gordon (USA)	7.64
1936	Jesse Owens (USA)	8.06
1948	Willie Steele (USA)	7.82
1952	Jerome Biffle (USA)	7.57
1956	Gregory Bell (USA)	7.83
1960	Ralph Boston (USA)	8.12
1964	Lynn Davies (GBR)	8.07
1968	Robert Beamon (USA)	8.90
1972	Randy Williams (USA)	8.24
1976	Arnie Robinson (USA)	8.35
1980	Lutz Dombrowski (GDR)	8.54
1984	Carl Lewis (USA)	8.54
1988	Carl Lewis (USA)	8.72
1992	Carl Lewis (USA)	8.67
1996	Carl Lewis (USA)	8.50
2000	Ivan Pedroso (CUB)	8.55
2004	Dwight Phillips (USA)	8.59

Athletics (track-and-field) (men) (continued)

STANDING LONG JUMP		METERS
1900	Ray Ewry (USA)	3.21
1904	Ray Ewry (USA)	3.47
1908	Ray Ewry (USA)	3.33
1912	Constantinos Tsiklitiras (GRE)	3.37

TRIPLE JUMP		METERS
1896	James Connolly (USA)	13.71
1900	Myer Prinstein (USA)	14.47
1904	Myer Prinstein (USA)	14.35
1908	Timothy Ahearne (GBR)	14.91
1912	Gustaf Lindblom (SWE)	14.76
1920	Vilho Tuulos (FIN)	14.50
1924	Anthony Winter (AUS)	15.53
1928	Mikio Oda (JPN)	15.21
1932	Chuhei Nambu (JPN)	15.72
1936	Naoto Tajima (JPN)	16.00
1948	Arne Åhman (SWE)	15.40
1952	Adhemar Ferreira da Sîlva (BRA)	16.22
1956	Adhemar Ferreira da Silva (BRA)	16.35
1960	Josef Szmidt (POL)	16.81
1964	Josef Szmidt (POL)	16.85
1968	Viktor Saneyev (URS)	17.39
1972	Viktor Saneyev (URS)	17.35
1976	Viktor Saneyev (URS)	17.29
1980	Jaak Uudmae (URS)	17.35
1984	Al Joyner (USA)	17.26
1988	Khristo Markov (BUL)	17.61
1992	Michael Conley (USA)	17.63
1996	Kenny Harrison (USA)	18.09
2000	Jonathan Edwards (GBR)	17.71
2004	Christian Olsson (SWE)	17.79

STANDING TRIPLE JUMP		METERS
1900	Ray Ewry (USA)	10.58
1904	Ray Ewry (USA)	10.54

SHOT PUT		METERS
1896	Robert Garrett (USA)	11.22
1900	Richard Sheldon (USA)	14.10
1904	Ralph Rose (USA)	14.81
1908	Ralph Rose (USA)	14.21
1912	Patrick McDonald (USA)	15.34
1920	Frans Pörhölä (FIN)	14.81
1924	Lemuel Clarence Houser (USA)	14.99
1928	John Kuck (USA)	15.87
1932	Leo Sexton (USA)	16.00
1936	Hans Woellke (GER)	16.20
1948	Wilbur Thompson (USA)	17.12
1952	William Parry O'Brien (USA)	17.41
1956	William Parry O'Brien (USA)	18.57
1960	William Nieder (USA)	19.68
1964	Dallas Long (USA)	20.33
1968	Randy Matson (USA)	20.54
1972	Wladislaw Komar (POL)	21.18
1976	Udo Beyer (GDR)	21.05
1980	Vladimir Kiselyov (URS)	21.35
1984	Alessandro Andrei (ITA)	21.26
1988	Ulf Timmermann (GDR)	22.47
1992	Michael Stulce (USA)	21.70
1996	Randy Barnes (USA)	21.62
2000	Arsi Harju (FIN)	21.29
2004	Yury Bilonog (UKR)	21.16

SHOT PUT (TWO HANDS)		METERS
1912	Ralph Rose (USA)	27.7

Summer Olympic Games Champions (continued)

Athletics (track-and-field) (men) (continued)

DISCUS THROW

		METERS
1896	Robert Garrett (USA)	29.15
1900	Rezso Bauer (HUN)	36.04
1904	Martin Sheridan (USA)	39.28
1908	Martin Sheridan (USA)	40.89
1912	Armas Taipale (FIN)	45.21
1920	Elmer Niklander (FIN)	44.68
1924	Lemuel Clarence Houser (USA)	46.15
1928	Lemuel Clarence Houser (USA)	47.32
1932	John Anderson (USA)	49.49
1936	Kenneth Carpenter (USA)	50.48
1948	Adolfo Consolini (ITA)	52.78
1952	Sim Iness (USA)	55.03
1956	Alfred Oerter (USA)	56.36
1960	Alfred Oerter (USA)	59.18
1964	Alfred Oerter (USA)	61.00
1968	Alfred Oerter (USA)	64.78
1972	Ludvig Danek (TCH)	64.40
1976	Mac Wilkins (USA)	67.50
1980	Viktor Rashchupkin (URS)	66.64
1984	Rolf Danneberg (FRG)	66.60
1988	Jürgen Schult (GDR)	68.82
1992	Romas Ubartas (LTU)	65.12
1996	Lars Riedel (GER)	69.40
2000	Virgilijus Alekna (LTU)	69.30
2004	Virgilijus Alekna (LTU)	69.89

DISCUS (GREEK STYLE)

		METERS
1908	Martin Sheridan (USA)	37.99

DISCUS (TWO HANDS)

		METERS
1912	Armas Taipale (FIN)	82.86

HAMMER THROW

		METERS
1900	John Flanagan (USA)	49.73
1904	John Flanagan (USA)	51.23
1908	John Flanagan (USA)	51.92
1912	Matthew McGrath (USA)	54.74
1920	Patrick Ryan (USA)	52.87
1924	Frederick Tootell (USA)	53.30
1928	Patrick O'Callaghan (IRE)	51.39
1932	Patrick O'Callaghan (IRE)	53.92
1936	Karl Hein (GER)	56.49
1948	Imre Nemeth (HUN)	56.07
1952	Jozsef Csermak (HUN)	60.34
1956	Harold Connolly (USA)	63.19
1960	Vasily Rudenkov (URS)	67.10
1964	Romuald Klim (URS)	69.74
1968	Gyula Zsivotzky (HUN)	73.36
1972	Anatoly Bondarchuk (URS)	75.50
1976	Yury Sedykh (URS)	77.52
1980	Yury Sedykh (URS)	81.80
1984	Juha Tiainen (FIN)	78.08
1988	Sergey Litvinov (URS)	84.80
1992	Andrey Abduvaliyev (UNT)	82.53
1996	Balazs Kiss (HUN)	81.24
2000	Szymon Ziolkowski (POL)	80.02
2004	Koji Murofushi (JPN)	82.91

JAVELIN THROW

		METERS
1908	Eric Lemming (SWE)	54.83
1912	Eric Lemming (SWE)	60.64
1920	Jonni Myyrä (FIN)	65.78
1924	Jonni Myyrä (FIN)	62.96
1928	Erik Lundkvist (SWE)	66.60
1932	Matti Järvinen (FIN)	72.71
1936	Gerhard Stöck (GER)	71.84
1948	Kai Rautavaara (FIN)	69.77

Athletics (track-and-field) (men) (continued)

JAVELIN THROW (CONTINUED)

		METERS
1952	Cy Young (USA)	73.78
1956	Egil Danielson (NOR)	85.71
1960	Viktor Tsybulenko (URS)	84.64
1964	Pauli Nevala (FIN)	82.66
1968	Janis Lusis (URS)	90.10
1972	Klaus Wolfermann (FRG)	90.48
1976	Miklos Nemeth (HUN)	94.58
1980	Dainis Kula (URS)	91.20
1984	Arto Härkönen (FIN)	86.76
1988	Tapio Korjus (FIN)	84.28
1992	Jan Zelezny (TCH)	89.66
1996	Jan Zelezny (CZE)	88.16
2000	Jan Zelezny (CZE)	90.17
2004	Andreas Thorkildsen (NOR)	86.50

JAVELIN (FREESTYLE)

		METERS
1908	Eric Lemming (SWE)	54.45

JAVELIN (TWO HANDS)

		METERS
1912	Juho Saaristo (FIN)	109.42

THROWING THE 56 LB WEIGHT

		METERS
1904	Étienne Desmarteau (CAN)	10.46
1920	Patrick McDonald (USA)	11.26

TUG-OF-WAR

1900	Sweden-Denmark
1904	United States
1908	Great Britain
1912	Sweden
1920	Great Britain

TRIATHLON (LONG JUMP/SHOT PUT/100 YARDS)

1904	Max Emmerich (USA)

PENTATHLON

1912	Jim Thorpe (USA)[5]; Ferdinand Bie (NOR) (cowinners)
1920	Eero Lehtonen (FIN)
1924	Eero Lehtonen (FIN)

DECATHLON

1904	Thomas Kiely (IRL)
1912	Jim Thorpe (USA)[5]; Hugo Wieslander (SWE) (cowinners)
1920	Helge Lövland (NOR)
1924	Harold Osborn (USA)
1928	Paavo Yrjölä (FIN)
1932	James Bausch (USA)
1936	Glenn Morris (USA)
1948	Robert Mathias (USA)
1952	Robert Mathias (USA)
1956	Milton Campbell (USA)
1960	Rafer Johnson (USA)
1964	Willi Holdorf (GER)
1968	William Toomey (USA)
1972	Nikolay Avilov (URS)
1976	Bruce Jenner (USA)
1980	Daley Thompson (GBR)
1984	Daley Thompson (GBR)
1988	Christian Schenk (GDR)
1992	Robert Zmelik (TCH)
1996	Dan O'Brien (USA)
2000	Erki Nool (EST)
2004	Roman Sebrle (CZE)

Summer Olympic Games Champions (continued)

Athletics (track-and-field) (women)

100 METERS		SEC
1928	Elizabeth Robinson (USA)	12.2
1932	Stanislawa Walasiewicz (POL)	11.9
1936	Helen Stephens (USA)	11.5
1948	Francina Blankers-Koen (NED)	11.9
1952	Marjorie Jackson (AUS)	11.5
1956	Elizabeth Cuthbert (AUS)	11.5
1960	Wilma Rudolph (USA)	11.0
1964	Wyomia Tyus (USA)	11.4
1968	Wyomia Tyus (USA)	11.0
1972	Renate Stecher (GDR)	11.07
1976	Annegret Richter (FRG)	11.08
1980	Lyudmila Kondratyeva (URS)	11.06
1984	Evelyn Ashford (USA)	10.97
1988	Florence Griffith Joyner (USA)	10.54
1992	Gail Devers (USA)	10.82
1996	Gail Devers (USA)	10.94
2000	Marion Jones (USA)	10.75
2004	Yuliya Nesterenko (BLR)	10.93

200 METERS		SEC
1948	Francina Blankers-Koen (NED)	24.4
1952	Marjorie Jackson (AUS)	23.7
1956	Elizabeth Cuthbert (AUS)	23.4
1960	Wilma Rudolph (USA)	24.0
1964	Edith Marie McGuire (USA)	23.0
1968	Irena Szewinska (POL)	22.5
1972	Renate Stecher (GDR)	22.40
1976	Bärbel Eckert (GDR)	22.37
1980	Bärbel Eckert-Wöckel (GDR)	22.03
1984	Valerie Brisco-Hooks (USA)	21.81
1988	Florence Griffith Joyner (USA)	21.34
1992	Gwen Torrence (USA)	21.81
1996	Marie-Jose Perec (FRA)	22.12
2000	Marion Jones (USA)	21.84
2004	Veronica Campbell (JAM)	22.05

400 METERS		SEC
1964	Elizabeth Cuthbert (AUS)	52.0
1968	Colette Besson (FRA)	52.0
1972	Monika Zehrt (GDR)	51.08
1976	Irena Szewinska (POL)	49.29
1980	Marita Koch (GDR)	48.88
1984	Valerie Brisco-Hooks (USA)	48.83
1988	Olga Bryzgina (URS)	48.65
1992	Marie-Jose Perec (FRA)	48.83
1996	Marie-Jose Perec (FRA)	48.25
2000	Cathy Freeman (AUS)	49.11
2004	Tonique Williams-Darling (BAH)	49.41

800 METERS		MIN:SEC
1928	Lina Radke-Batschauer (GER)	2:16.8
1960	Lyudmila Lysenko-Shevtsova (URS)	2:04.3
1964	Ann Packer (GBR)	2:01.1
1968	Madeline Manning (USA)	2:00.9
1972	Hildegard Falck (FRG)	1:58.6
1976	Tatyana Kazankina (URS)	1:54.94
1980	Nadezhda Olizarenko (URS)	1:53.50
1984	Doina Melinte (ROM)	1:57.6
1988	Sigrun Wodars (GDR)	1:56.10
1992	Ellen van Langen (NED)	1:55.54
1996	Svetlana Masterkova (RUS)	1:57.73
2000	Maria Mutola (MOZ)	1:56.15
2004	Kelly Holmes (GBR)	1:56.38

Athletics (track-and-field) (women) (continued)

1,500 METERS		MIN:SEC
1972	Lyudmila Bragina (URS)	4:01.4
1976	Tatyana Kazankina (URS)	4:05.48
1980	Tatyana Kazankina (URS)	3:56.6
1984	Gabriella Dorio (ITA)	4:03.25
1988	Paula Ivan (ROM)	3:53.96
1992	Hassiba Boulmerka (ALG)	3:55.30
1996	Svetlana Masterkova (RUS)	4:00.83
2000	Nouria Merah-Benida (ALG)	4:05.10
2004	Kelly Holmes (GBR)	3:57.90

3,000 METERS		MIN:SEC
1984	Maricica Puica (ROM)	8:35.96
1988	Tatyana Samolenko (URS)	8:26.53
1992	Yelena Romanova (UNT)	8:46.04

5,000 METERS		MIN:SEC
1996	Wang Jungxia (CHN)	14:59.88
2000	Gabriela Szabo (ROM)	14:40.79
2004	Meseret Defar (ETH)	14:45.65

10,000 METERS		MIN:SEC
1988	Olga Bondarenko (URS)	31:05.21
1992	Derartu Tulu (ETH)	31:06.02
1996	Fernanda Ribeiro (POR)	31:01.63
2000	Derartu Tulu (ETH)	30:17.49
2004	Xing Huina (CHN)	30:24.36

MARATHON		HR:MIN:SEC
1984	Joan Benoit (USA)	2:24:52
1988	Rosa Mota (POR)	2:25:40
1992	Valentina Yegorova (UNT)	2:32:41
1996	Fatuma Roba (ETH)	2:26:05
2000	Naoko Takahashi (JPN)	2:23:14
2004	Mizuki Noguchi (JPN)	2:26:20

80-METER HURDLES (100 METERS FROM 1972)		SEC
1932	Mildred "Babe" Didrikson (USA)	11.7
1936	Trebisonda Valla (ITA)	11.7
1948	Francina Blankers-Koen (NED)	11.2
1952	Shirley Strickland de La Hunty (AUS)	10.9
1956	Shirley Strickland de La Hunty (AUS)	10.7
1960	Irina Press (URS)	10.8
1964	Karin Balzer (GER)	10.5
1968	Maureen Caird (AUS)	10.3
1972	Annelie Ehrhardt (GDR)	12.59
1976	Johanna Schaller (GDR)	12.77
1980	Vera Komisova (URS)	12.56
1984	Benita Fitzgerald-Brown (USA)	12.84
1988	Iordanka Donkova (BUL)	12.38
1992	Paraskevi Patoulidou (GRE)	12.64
1996	Ludmila Engquist (SWE)	12.58
2000	Olga Shishigina (KAZ)	12.65
2004	Joanna Hayes (USA)	12.37

400-METER HURDLES		SEC
1984	Nawal el Moutawakel (MAR)	54.61
1988	Debra Flintoff-King (AUS)	53.17
1992	Sally Gunnell (GBR)	53.23
1996	Deon Hemmings (JAM)	52.82
2000	Irina Privalova (RUS)	53.02
2004	Fani Halkia (GRE)	52.82

Summer Olympic Games Champions (continued)

Athletics (track-and-field) (women) (continued)

4 × 100-METER RELAY

Year	Team	SEC
1928	Canada	48.4
1932	United States	47.0
1936	United States	46.9
1948	The Netherlands	47.5
1952	United States	45.9
1956	Australia	44.5
1960	United States	44.5
1964	Poland	43.6
1968	United States	42.8
1972	West Germany	42.81
1976	East Germany	42.55
1980	East Germany	41.60
1984	United States	41.65
1988	United States	41.98
1992	United States	42.11
1996	United States	41.95
2000	The Bahamas	41.95
2004	Jamaica	41.73

4 × 400-METER RELAY

Year	Team	MIN:SEC
1972	East Germany	3:23.0
1976	East Germany	3:19.23
1980	USSR	3:20.2
1984	United States	3:18.29
1988	USSR	3:15.18
1992	Unified Team	3:20.20
1996	United States	3:20.91
2000	United States	3:22.62
2004	United States	3:19.01

10,000-METER WALK

Year	Athlete	MIN:SEC
1992	Chen Yueling (CHN)	44:32
1996	Yelena Nikolayeva (RUS)	41:49

20,000-METER WALK

Year	Athlete	MIN:SEC
2000	Wang Liping (CHN)	1:29.05
2004	Athanasia Tsoumeleka (GRE)	1:29:12

HIGH JUMP

Year	Athlete	METERS
1928	Ethel Catherwood (CAN)	1.59
1932	Jean Shiley (USA)	1.66
1936	Ibolya Csak (HUN)	1.60
1948	Alice Coachman (USA)	1.68
1952	Esther Brand (RSA)	1.67
1956	Mildred Louise McDaniel (USA)	1.76
1960	Iolanda Balas (ROM)	1.85
1964	Iolanda Balas (ROM)	1.90
1968	Miloslava Rezkova (TCH)	1.82
1972	Ulrike Meyfarth (FRG)	1.92
1976	Rosemarie Ackermann (GDR)	1.93
1980	Sara Simeoni (ITA)	1.97
1984	Ulrike Meyfarth (FRG)	2.02
1988	Louise Ritter (USA)	2.03
1992	Heike Henkel (GER)	2.02
1996	Stefka Kostadinova (BUL)	2.05
2000	Yelena Yelesina (RUS)	2.01
2004	Yelena Slesarenko (RUS)	2.06

POLE VAULT

Year	Athlete	METERS
2000	Stacy Dragila (USA)	4.60
2004	Yelena Isinbayeva (RUS)	4.91

Athletics (track-and-field) (women) (continued)

LONG JUMP

Year	Athlete	METERS
1948	Olga Gyarmati (HUN)	5.69
1952	Yvette Williams (NZL)	6.24
1956	Elzbieta Krzesinska (POL)	6.35
1960	Vera Krepkina (URS)	6.37
1964	Mary Rand (GBR)	6.76
1968	Viorica Viscopoleanu (ROM)	6.82
1972	Heidemarie Rosendahl (FRG)	6.78
1976	Angela Voigt (GDR)	6.72
1980	Tatyana Kolpakova (URS)	7.06
1984	Anisoara Stanciu (ROM)	6.96
1988	Jackie Joyner-Kersee (USA)	7.40
1992	Heike Drechsler (GER)	7.14
1996	Chioma Ajunwa (NGR)	7.12
2000	Heike Drechsler (GER)	6.99
2004	Tatyana Lebedeva (RUS)	7.07

TRIPLE JUMP

Year	Athlete	METERS
1996	Inessa Kravets (UKR)	15.33
2000	Tereza Marinova (BUL)	15.20
2004	Françoise Mbango Etone (CMR)	15.30

SHOT PUT

Year	Athlete	METERS
1948	Micheline Ostermeyer (FRA)	13.75
1952	Galina Zybina (URS)	15.28
1956	Tamara Tyshkevich (URS)	16.59
1960	Tamara Press (URS)	17.32
1964	Tamara Press (URS)	18.14
1968	Margitta Gummel (GDR)	19.61
1972	Nadezhda Chizhova (URS)	21.03
1976	Ivanka Khristova (BUL)	21.16
1980	Ilona Slupianek (GDR)	22.41
1984	Claudia Losch (FRG)	20.48
1988	Natalya Lisovskaya (URS)	22.24
1992	Svetlana Krivalyova (UNT)	21.06
1996	Astrid Kumbernuss (GER)	20.56
2000	Yanina Korolchik (BLR)	20.56
2004	Yumileidi Cumba (CUB)	19.59

DISCUS THROW

Year	Athlete	METERS
1928	Halina Konopacka (POL)	39.62
1932	Lillian Copeland (USA)	40.58
1936	Gisela Mauermayer (GER)	47.63
1948	Micheline Ostermeyer (FRA)	41.92
1952	Nina Romashkova (URS)	51.42
1956	Olga Fikotova (TCH)	53.69
1960	Nina Ponomaryova-Romashkova (URS)	55.10
1964	Tamara Press (URS)	57.27
1968	Lia Manoliu (ROM)	58.28
1972	Faina Melnik (URS)	66.62
1976	Evelin Schlaak (GDR)	69.00
1980	Evelin Schlaak Jahl (GDR)	69.96
1984	Ria Stalman (NED)	65.36
1988	Martina Hellmann (GDR)	72.30
1992	Maritza Marten (CUB)	70.06
1996	Ilke Wyludda (GER)	69.66
2000	Ellina Zvereva (BLR)	68.40
2004	Natalya Sadova (RUS)	67.02

HAMMER THROW

Year	Athlete	METERS
2000	Kamila Skolimowska (POL)	71.16
2004	Olga Kuzenkova (RUS)	75.02

Summer Olympic Games Champions (continued)

Athletics (track-and-field) (women) (continued)

JAVELIN THROW

		METERS
1932	Mildred "Babe" Didrikson (USA)	43.68
1936	Tilly Fleischer (GER)	45.18
1948	Hermine Bauma (AUT)	45.57
1952	Dana Zatopkova (TCH)	50.47
1956	Inese Jaunzeme (URS)	53.86
1960	Elvira Ozolina (URS)	55.98
1964	Mihaela Penes (ROM)	60.54
1968	Angela Nemeth (HUN)	60.36
1972	Ruth Fuchs (GDR)	63.88
1976	Ruth Fuchs (GDR)	65.94
1980	María Colón (CUB)	68.40
1984	Tessa Sanderson (GBR)	69.56
1988	Petra Felke (GDR)	74.68
1992	Silke Renk (GER)	68.34
1996	Heli Rantanen (FIN)	67.94
2000	Trine Hattestad (NOR)	68.91
2004	Osleidys Menéndez (CUB)	71.53

PENTATHLON (HEPTATHLON FROM 1984)

1964	Irina Press (URS)
1968	Ingrid Becker (FRG)
1972	Mary Peters (GBR)
1976	Siegrun Siegl (GDR)
1980	Nadezhda Tkachenko (URS)
1984	Glynis Nunn (AUS)
1988	Jackie Joyner-Kersee (USA)
1992	Jackie Joyner-Kersee (USA)
1996	Ghada Shouaa (SYR)
2000	Denise Lewis (GBR)
2004	Carolina Klüft (SWE)

Badminton

MEN'S SINGLES

1992	Allan Budi Kusuma (INA)
1996	Poul-Erik Hoyer-Larsen (DEN)
2000	Ji Xinpeng (CHN)
2004	Taufik Hidayat (INA)

MEN'S DOUBLES

1992	South Korea
1996	Indonesia
2000	Indonesia
2004	South Korea

WOMEN'S SINGLES

1992	Susi Susanti (INA)
1996	Bang Soo-Hyun (KOR)
2000	Gong Zhichao (CHN)
2004	Zhang Ning (CHN)

WOMEN'S DOUBLES

1992	South Korea
1996	China
2000	China
2004	China

MIXED DOUBLES

1996	South Korea
2000	China
2004	China

Baseball

1992	Cuba
1996	Cuba
2000	United States
2004	Cuba

Basketball

MEN

1936	United States
1948	United States
1952	United States
1956	United States
1960	United States
1964	United States
1968	United States
1972	USSR
1976	United States
1980	Yugoslavia
1984	United States
1988	USSR
1992	United States
1996	United States
2000	United States
2004	Argentina

WOMEN

1976	USSR
1980	USSR
1984	United States
1988	United States
1992	Unified Team
1996	United States
2000	United States
2004	United States

Boxing

48 KG (105.6 LB)

1968	Francisco Rodríguez (VEN)
1972	Gyorgy Gedo (HUN)
1976	Jorge Hernández (CUB)
1980	Shamil Sabyrov (URS)
1984	Paul Gonzales (USA)
1988	Ivailo Khristov (BUL)
1992	Rogelio Marcelo (CUB)
1996	Daniel Petrov Bojilov (BUL)
2000	Brahim Asloum (FRA)
2004	Yan Bhartelemy Varela (CUB)

51 KG (112 LB)

1904	George Finnegan (USA)
1920	Frank di Genaro (USA)
1924	Fidel La Barba (USA)
1928	Antal Kocsis (HUN)
1932	Istvan Enekes (HUN)
1936	Willi Kaiser (GER)
1948	Pascual Pérez (ARG)
1952	Nate Brooks (USA)
1956	Terence Spinks (GBR)
1960	Gyula Torok (HUN)
1964	Fernando Atzori (ITA)
1968	Ricardo Delgado (MEX)
1972	Georgi Kostadinov (BUL)
1976	Leo Randolph (USA)
1980	Petar Lesov (BUL)
1984	Steven McCrory (USA)
1988	Kim Kwang Sun (KOR)
1992	Chol Choi Su (PRK)
1996	Maikro Romero (CUB)
2000	Wijan Ponlid (THA)
2004	Yuriorkis Gamboa Toledano (CUB)

Summer Olympic Games Champions (continued)

Boxing (continued)

54 KG (118.8 LB)
1904 Oliver Kirk (USA)
1908 Henry Thomas (GBR)
1920 Clarence Walker (RSA)
1924 William Smith (RSA)
1928 Vittorio Tamagnini (ITA)
1932 Horace Gwynne (CAN)
1936 Ulderico Sergo (ITA)
1948 Tibor Csik (HUN)
1952 Pentti Hämäläinen (FIN)
1956 Wolfgang Behrendt (GER)
1960 Oleg Grigoryev (URS)
1964 Takao Sakurai (JPN)
1968 Valery Sokolov (URS)
1972 Orlando Martínez (CUB)
1976 Gu Yong Jo (PRK)
1980 Juan Hernández (CUB)
1984 Maurizio Stecca (ITA)
1988 Kennedy McKinney (USA)
1992 Joel Casamayor (CUB)
1996 Istvan Kovacs (HUN)
2000 Guillermo Rigondeaux Ortiz (CUB)
2004 Guillermo Rigondeaux Ortiz (CUB)

57 KG (125.4 LB)
1904 Oliver Kirk (USA)
1908 Richard Gunn (GBR)
1920 Paul Fritsch (FRA)
1924 John Fields (USA)
1928 Lambertus van Kleveren (NED)
1932 Carmelo Robledo (ARG)
1936 Oscar Casanovas (ARG)
1948 Ernesto Formenti (ITA)
1952 Jan Zachara (TCH)
1956 Vladimir Safronov (URS)
1960 Francesco Musso (ITA)
1964 Stanislav Stepashkin (URS)
1968 Antonio Roldan (MEX)
1972 Boris Kuznetsov (URS)
1976 Angel Herrera (CUB)
1980 Rudi Fink (GDR)
1984 Meldrick Taylor (USA)
1988 Giovanni Parisi (ITA)
1992 Andreas Tews (GER)
1996 Somluck Kamsing (THA)
2000 Bekzat Sattarkhanov (KAZ)
2004 Aleksey Tishchenko (RUS)

60 KG (132 LB)
1904 Harry Spanger (USA)
1908 Frederick Grace (GBR)
1920 Samuel Mosberg (USA)
1924 Hans Nielsen (DEN)
1928 Carlo Orlandi (ITA)
1932 Lawrence Stevens (RSA)
1936 Imre Harangi (HUN)
1948 Gerald Dreyer (RSA)
1952 Aureliano Bolognesi (ITA)
1956 Richard McTaggart (GBR)
1960 Kazimierz Pazdzior (POL)
1964 Jozef Grudzien (POL)
1968 Ronnie Harris (USA)
1972 Jan Szczepanski (POL)
1976 Howard Davis (USA)
1980 Angel Herrera (CUB)
1984 Pernell Whitaker (USA)
1988 Andreas Zuelow (GDR)
1992 Oscar De La Hoya (USA)

Boxing (continued)

60 KG (132 LB) (CONTINUED)
1996 Hocine Soltani (ALG)
2000 Mario Kindelan (CUB)
2004 Mario César Kindelan Mesa (CUB)

64 KG (140.8 LB)
1952 Charles Adkins (USA)
1956 Vladimir Engibaryan (URS)
1960 Bohumil Nemecek (TCH)
1964 Jerzy Kulej (POL)
1968 Jerzy Kulej (POL)
1972 Ray Seales (USA)
1976 Ray Leonard (USA)
1980 Patrizio Oliva (ITA)
1984 Jerry Page (USA)
1988 Vyacheslav Yanovsky (URS)
1992 Héctor Vinent (CUB)
1996 Héctor Vinent (CUB)
2000 Mahamadkadyz Abdullayev (UZB)
2004 Manus Boonjumnong (THA)

69 KG (151.8 LB)
1904 Albert Young (USA)
1920 Julius Schneider (CAN)
1924 Jean Delarge (BEL)
1928 Edward Morgan (NZL)
1932 Edward Flynn (USA)
1936 Sten Suvio (FIN)
1948 Julius Torma (TCH)
1952 Zygmunt Chychla (POL)
1956 Nicolae Linca (ROM)
1960 Giovanni Benvenuti (ITA)
1964 Marian Kasprzyk (POL)
1968 Manfred Wolke (GDR)
1972 Emilio Correa (CUB)
1976 Jochen Bachfeld (GDR)
1980 Andres Aldama (CUB)
1984 Mark Breland (USA)
1988 Robert Wangila (KEN)
1992 Michael Carruth (IRL)
1996 Oleg Saytov (RUS)
2000 Oleg Saytov (RUS)
2004 Bakhtiyar Artayev (KAZ)

71 KG (156.2 LB)
1952 Laszlo Papp (HUN)
1956 Laszlo Papp (HUN)
1960 Wilbert McClure (USA)
1964 Boris Lagutin (URS)
1968 Boris Lagutin (URS)
1972 Dieter Kottysch (FRG)
1976 Jerzy Rybicki (POL)
1980 Armando Martínez (CUB)
1984 Frank Tate (USA)
1988 Park Si Hun (KOR)
1992 Juan Lemus (CUB)
1996 David Reid (USA)
2000 Yermakhan Ibraimov (KAZ)

75 KG (165 LB)
1904 Charles Mayer (USA)
1908 John Douglas (GBR)
1920 Harry Mallin (GBR)
1924 Harry Mallin (GBR)
1928 Piero Toscani (ITA)
1932 Carmen Barth (USA)
1936 Jean Despeaux (FRA)
1948 Laszlo Papp (HUN)

Summer Olympic Games Champions (continued)

Boxing (continued)

75 KG (165 LB) (CONTINUED)

1952	Floyd Patterson (USA)
1956	Gennady Shatkov (URS)
1960	Edward Crook (USA)
1964	Valery Popenchenko (URS)
1968	Christopher Finnegan (GBR)
1972	Vyatcheslav Lemeshev (URS)
1976	Michael Spinks (USA)
1980	Jose Gómez (CUB)
1984	Shin Joon Sup (KOR)
1988	Henry Maske (GDR)
1992	Ariel Hernández (CUB)
1996	Ariel Hernández (CUB)
2000	Jorge Gutiérrez (CUB)
2004	Gaydarbek Gaydarbekov (RUS)

81 KG (178.2 LB)

1920	Edward Eagan (USA)
1924	Harry Mitchell (GBR)
1928	Viktor Avendano (ARG)
1932	David Carstens (RSA)
1936	Roger Michelot (FRA)
1948	George Hunter (RSA)
1952	Norvel Lee (USA)
1956	James Boyd (USA)
1960	Cassius Clay (USA)
1964	Cosimo Pinto (ITA)
1968	Dan Poznyak (URS)
1972	Mate Parlov (YUG)
1976	Leon Spinks (USA)
1980	Slobodan Kacar (YUG)
1984	Anton Josipovic (YUG)
1988	Andrew Maynard (USA)
1992	Torsten May (GER)
1996	Vasily Zhirov (KAZ)
2000	Aleksandr Lebzyak (RUS)
2004	Andre Ward (USA)

OVER 81 KG (178.2 LB) (91 KG; 200.2 LB FROM 1984)

1904	Samuel Berger (USA)
1908	Albert Oldman (GBR)
1920	Ronald Rawson (GBR)
1924	Otto Von Porat (NOR)
1928	Arturo Rodriguez (ARG)
1932	Alberto Santiago Lovell (ARG)
1936	Herbert Runge (GER)
1948	Rafael Iglesias (ARG)
1952	Edward Sanders (USA)
1956	Peter Rademacher (USA)
1960	Franco de Piccoli (ITA)
1964	Joseph Frazier (USA)
1968	George Foreman (USA)
1972	Teofilo Stevenson (CUB)
1976	Teofilo Stevenson (CUB)
1980	Teofilo Stevenson (CUB)
1984	Henry Tillman (USA)
1988	Ray Mercer (USA)
1992	Félix Savon (CUB)
1996	Félix Savon (CUB)
2000	Félix Savon (CUB)
2004	Odlanier Solis Fonte (CUB)

OVER 91 KG (200.2 LB)

1984	Tyrell Biggs (USA)
1988	Lennox Lewis (CAN)
1992	Roberto Balado (CUB)
1996	Vladimir Klichko (UKR)

Boxing (continued)

OVER 91 KG (200.2 LB) (CONTINUED)

2000	Audley Harrison (GBR)
2004	Aleksandr Povetkin (RUS)

Canoeing (men)

KAYAK SINGLES (500 METERS)		MIN:SEC
1976	Vasile Diba (ROM)	1:46.41
1980	Vladimir Parfenovich (URS)	1:43.43
1984	Ian Ferguson (NZL)	1:47.84
1988	Zsolt Gyulay (HUN)	1:44.82
1992	Mikko Kolehmainen (FIN)	1:40.34
1996	Antonio Rossi (ITA)	1:37.423
2000	Knut Holmann (NOR)	1:57.84
2004	Adam van Koeverden (CAN)	1:37.919

KAYAK PAIRS (500 METERS)		MIN:SEC
1976	East Germany	1:35.87
1980	USSR	1:32.38
1984	New Zealand	1:34.21
1988	New Zealand	1:33.98
1992	Germany	1:29.84
1996	Germany	1:28.697
2000	Hungary	1:47.05
2004	Germany	1:27.040

KAYAK SINGLES (1,000 METERS)		MIN:SEC
1936	Gregor Hradetzky (AUT)	4:22.90
1948	Gert Fredriksson (SWE)	4:33.20
1952	Gert Fredriksson (SWE)	4:07.90
1956	Gert Fredriksson (SWE)	4:12.80
1960	Erik Hansen (DEN)	3:53.00
1964	Rolf Peterson (SWE)	3:57.13
1968	Mihaly Hesz (HUN)	4:03.58
1972	Aleksandr Shaparenko (URS)	3:48.06
1976	Rüdiger Helm (GDR)	3:48.20
1980	Rüdiger Helm (GDR)	3:48.77
1984	Alan Thompson (NZL)	3:45.73
1988	Gregory Barton (USA)	3:55.27
1992	Clint Robinson (AUS)	3:37.26
1996	Knut Holmann (NOR)	3:25.785
2000	Knut Holmann (NOR)	3:33.26
2004	Eirik Veraas Larsen (NOR)	3:25.897

KAYAK PAIRS (1,000 METERS)		MIN:SEC
1936	Austria	4:03.80
1948	Sweden	4:07.30
1952	Finland	3:51.10
1956	Germany	3:49.60
1960	Sweden	3:34.70
1964	Sweden	3:38.54
1968	USSR	3:37.54
1972	USSR	3:31.23
1976	USSR	3:29.01
1980	USSR	3:26.72
1984	Canada	3:24.22
1988	United States	3:32.42
1992	Germany	3:16.10
1996	Italy	3:09.190
2000	Italy	3:14.46
2004	Sweden	3:18.420

KAYAK FOURS (1,000 METERS)		MIN:SEC
1964	USSR	3:14.67
1968	Norway	3:14.38
1972	USSR	3:14.02
1976	USSR	3:08.69
1980	East Germany	3:13.76

Summer Olympic Games Champions (continued)

Canoeing (men) (continued)

KAYAK FOURS (1,000 METERS) (CONTINUED)

		MIN:SEC
1984	New Zealand	3:02.28
1988	Hungary	3:00.20
1992	Germany	2:54.18
1996	Germany	2:51.528
2000	Hungary	2:55.18
2004	Hungary	2:56.919

KAYAK SINGLES (10,000 METERS)

		MIN:SEC
1936	Ernst Krebs (GER)	46:01.6
1948	Gert Fredriksson (SWE)	50:47.7
1952	Thorvald Strömberg (FIN)	47:22.8
1956	Gert Fredriksson (SWE)	47:43.4

KAYAK PAIRS (10,000 METERS)

		MIN:SEC
1936	Germany	41:45
1948	Sweden	46:09.4
1952	Finland	44:21.3
1956	Hungary	43:37

COLLAPSIBLE KAYAK SINGLES (10,000 METERS)

		MIN:SEC
1936	Gregor Hradetzky (AUT)	50:01.2

COLLAPSIBLE KAYAK PAIRS (10,000 METERS)

		MIN:SEC
1936	Sweden	45:48.9

KAYAK SINGLES RELAY (1,500 METERS)

		MIN:SEC
1960	Germany	7:39.43

SLALOM KAYAK SINGLES

1972	Siegbert Horn (GDR)
1992	Pierpaolo Ferrazzi (ITA)
1996	Oliver Fix (GER)
2000	Thomas Schmidt (GER)
2004	Benoit Peschier (FRA)

CANADIAN SINGLES (500 METERS)

		MIN:SEC
1976	Aleksandr Rogov (URS)	1:59.23
1980	Sergey Postrekin (URS)	1:53.37
1984	Larry Cain (CAN)	1:57.01
1988	Olaf Heukrodt (GDR)	1:56.42
1992	Nikolay Bukhalov (BUL)	1:51.15
1996	Martin Doktor (CZE)	1:49.934
2000	Gyorgy Kolonics (HUN)	2:24.81
2004	Andreas Dittmer (GER)	1:46.383

CANADIAN PAIRS (500 METERS)

		MIN:SEC
1976	USSR	1:45.81
1980	Hungary	1:43.39
1984	Yugoslavia	1:43.67
1988	USSR	1:41.77
1992	Unified Team	1:41.54
1996	Hungary	1:40.420
2000	Hungary	1:51.28
2004	China	1:40.278

CANADIAN SINGLES (1,000 METERS)

		MIN:SEC
1936	Francis Amyot (CAN)	5:32.10
1948	Josef Holecek (TCH)	5:42.00
1952	Josef Holecek (TCH)	4:56.30
1956	Leon Rottman (ROM)	5:05.30
1960	Janos Parti (HUN)	4:33.03
1964	Jürgen Eschert (GER)	4:35.14
1968	Tibor Tatai (HUN)	4:36.14
1972	Ivan Patzaichin (ROM)	4:08.94
1976	Matija Ljubek (YUG)	4:09.51
1980	Lyubomir Lyubenov (BUL)	4:12.38
1984	Ulrich Eicke (FRG)	4:06.32

Canoeing (men) (continued)

CANADIAN SINGLES (1,000 METERS) (CONTINUED)

		MIN:SEC
1988	Ivans Klementyev (URS)	4:12.78
1992	Nikolay Bukhalov (BUL)	4:05.92
1996	Martin Doktor (CZE)	3:54.418
2000	Andreas Dittmer (GER)	3:54.37
2004	David Cal (ESP)	3:46.201

CANADIAN PAIRS (1,000 METERS)

		MIN:SEC
1936	Czechoslovakia	4:50.10
1948	Czechoslovakia	5:07.10
1952	Denmark	4:38.30
1956	Romania	4:47.40
1960	USSR	4:17.04
1964	USSR	4:04.65
1968	Romania	4:07.18
1972	USSR	3:52.60
1976	USSR	3:52.76
1980	Romania	3:47.65
1984	Romania	3:40.60
1988	USSR	3:48.36
1992	Germany	3:37.42
1996	Germany	3:31.870
2000	Romania	3:37.35
2004	Germany	3:41.802

CANADIAN SINGLES (10,000 METERS)

		MIN:SEC
1948	Frantisek Capek (TCH)	62:05.2
1952	Frank Havens (USA)	57:41.1
1956	Leon Rottman (ROM)	56:41.0

CANADIAN PAIRS (10,000 METERS)

		MIN:SEC
1936	Czechoslovakia	50:35.5
1948	United States	55:55.4
1952	France	54:08.3
1956	USSR	54:02.4

SLALOM CANADIAN SINGLES

1972	Reinhard Eiben (GDR)
1992	Lukas Pollert (TCH)
1996	Michal Martikan (SVK)
2000	Tony Estanguet (FRA)
2004	Tony Estanguet (FRA)

SLALOM CANADIAN PAIRS

1972	East Germany
1992	United States
1996	France
2000	Slovakia
2004	Slovakia

Canoeing (women)

KAYAK SINGLES (500 METERS)

		MIN:SEC
1948	Karen Hoff (DEN)	2:31.90
1952	Sylvi Saimo (FIN)	2:18.40
1956	Yelizaveta Dementyeva (URS)	2:18.90
1960	Antonina Seredina (URS)	2:08.08
1964	Lyudmila Khvedosyuk (URS)	2:12.87
1968	Lyudmila Pinayeva-Khvedosyuk (URS)	2:11.09
1972	Yuliya Ryabchinskaya (URS)	2:03.17
1976	Carola Zirzow (GDR)	2:01.05
1980	Birgit Fischer (GDR)	1:57.96
1984	Agneta Andersson (SWE)	1:58.72
1988	Vanya Gecheva (BUL)	1:55.19
1992	Birgit Fischer Schmidt (GER)	1:51.60
1996	Rita Koban (HUN)	1:47.655
2000	Josefa Idem Guerrini (ITA)	2:13.84
2004	Natasa Janics (HUN)	1:47.741

Summer Olympic Games Champions (continued)

Canoeing (women) (continued)

KAYAK PAIRS (500 METERS)

		MIN:SEC
1960	USSR	1:54.76
1964	Germany	1:56.95
1968	West Germany	1:56.44
1972	USSR	1:53.50
1976	USSR	1:51.15
1980	East Germany	1:43.88
1984	Sweden	1:45.25
1988	East Germany	1:43.46
1992	Germany	1:40.29
1996	Sweden	1:39.329
2000	Germany	1:56.99
2004	Hungary	1:38.101

KAYAK FOURS (500 METERS)

		MIN:SEC
1984	Romania	1:38.34
1988	East Germany	1:40.78
1992	Hungary	1:38.32
1996	Germany	1:31.077
2000	Germany	1:34.53
2004	Germany	1:34.340

SLALOM KAYAK SINGLES

1972	Angelika Bahmann (GDR)
1992	Elisabeth Micheler (GER)
1996	Stepanka Hilgertova (CZE)
2000	Stepanka Hilgertova (CZE)
2004	Elena Kaliska (SVK)

Cricket

1900	Great Britain

Croquet

SINGLES (ONE BALL)

1900	Aumoitte (FRA)

SINGLES (TWO BALLS)

1900	Waydelick (FRA)

DOUBLES

1900	France

Cycling (men)

1,000-METER SPRINT

1896[6]	Paul Masson (FRA)
1900[6]	Georges Taillandier (FRA)
1920	Mauritius Peeters (NED)
1924	Lucien Michard (FRA)
1928	Roger Beaufrand (FRA)
1932	Jacobus Van Egmond (NED)
1936	Toni Merkens (GER)
1948	Mario Ghella (ITA)
1952	Enzo Sacchi (ITA)
1956	Michel Rousseau (FRA)
1960	Sante Gaiardoni (ITA)
1964	Giovanni Pettenella (ITA)
1968	Daniel Morelon (FRA)
1972	Daniel Morelon (FRA)
1976	Anton Tkac (TCH)
1980	Lutz Hesslich (GDR)
1984	Mark Gorski (USA)
1988	Lutz Hesslich (GDR)
1992	Jens Fiedler (GER)
1996	Jens Fiedler (GER)
2000	Marty Nothstein (USA)
2004	Ryan Bayley (AUS)

Cycling (men) (continued)

1,000-METER TIME TRIAL

		MIN:SEC
1896[7]	Paul Masson (FRA)	24.0
1928	Willy Falck-Hansen (DEN)	1:14.4
1932	Edgar Gray (AUS)	1:13.0
1936	Arie van Vliet (NED)	1:12.0
1948	Jacques Dupont (FRA)	1:13.5
1952	Russell Mockridge (AUS)	1:11.1
1956	Leandro Faggin (ITA)	1:09.8
1960	Sante Gaiardoni (ITA)	1:07.27
1964	Patrick Sercu (BEL)	1:09.59
1968	Pierre Trentin (FRA)	1:03.91
1972	Niels Fredborg (DEN)	1:06.44
1976	Klaus-Jürgen Grünke (GDR)	1:05.927
1980	Lothar Thoms (GDR)	1:02.955
1984	Fredy Schmidtke (FRG)	1:06.104
1988	Aleksandr Kirichenko (URS)	1:04.499
1992	José Moreno (ESP)	1:03.342
1996	Florian Rousseau (FRA)	1:02.712
2000	Jason Queally (GBR)	1:01.609
2004	Chris Hoy (GBR)	1:00.711

1,500-METER TEAM PURSUIT

1900	United States

2,000 METERS

1904	Marcus Hurley (USA)

2,000-METER TANDEM

1908	France
1920	Great Britain
1924	France
1928	The Netherlands
1932	France
1936	Germany
1948	Italy
1952	Australia
1956	Australia
1960	Italy
1964	Italy
1968	France
1972	USSR

4,000-METER INDIVIDUAL PURSUIT

1964	Jiri Daler (TCH)
1968	Daniel Rebillard (FRA)
1972	Knut Knudsen (NOR)
1976	Gregor Braun (FRG)
1980	Robert Dill-Bondi (SUI)
1984	Steve Hegg (USA)
1988	Gintautas Umaras (URS)
1992	Christopher Boardman (GBR)
1996	Andrea Collinelli (ITA)
2000	Robert Bartko (GER)
2004	Bradley Wiggins (GBR)

4,000-METER TEAM PURSUIT

1908	Great Britain
1920	Italy
1924	Italy
1928	Italy
1932	Italy
1936	France
1948	France
1952	Italy
1956	Italy
1960	Italy
1964	Germany
1968	Denmark

Summer Olympic Games Champions (continued)

Cycling (men) (continued)

4,000-METER TEAM PURSUIT (CONTINUED)
1972	West Germany
1976	West Germany
1980	USSR
1984	Australia
1988	USSR
1992	Germany
1996	France
2000	Germany
2004	Australia

5,000 METERS   MIN:SEC
1908	Benjamin Jones (GBR)	8:36.2

10,000 METERS   MIN:SEC
1896	Paul Masson (FRA)	17:54.2

20,000 METERS   MIN:SEC
1908	Charles Kingsbury (GBR)	34:13.6

50,000 METERS   HR:MIN:SEC
1920	Henry George (BEL)	1:16:43.2
1924	Jacobus Willems (NED)	1:18:24.0

100,000 METERS   HR:MIN:SEC
1896	Léon Flameng (FRA)	3:08:19.2
1908	Charles Bartlett (GBR)	2:41:48.6

ONE-QUARTER MILE (440 YARDS)   SEC
1904	Marcus Hurley (USA)	31.8

ONE-THIRD MILE (586⅔ YARDS)   SEC
1904	Marcus Hurley (USA)	43.8

ONE-LAP TIME TRIAL (660 YARDS)   SEC
1908	Victor Johnson (GBR)	51.2

ONE-HALF MILE (880 YARDS)   MIN:SEC
1904	Marcus Hurley (USA)	1:09.0

1 MILE   MIN:SEC
1904	Marcus Hurley (USA)	2:41.6

1 MILE 1 FURLONG (1,980 YARDS) TEAM PURSUIT
1908	Great Britain

2 MILES   MIN:SEC
1904	Burton Downing (USA)	4:58.0

5 MILES   MIN:SEC
1904	Charles Schlee (USA)	13:08.2

25 MILES
1904	Burton Downing (USA)

12 HOURS
1896	Adolf Schmal (AUT)

INDIVIDUAL POINTS RACE
1984	Roger Ilegems (BEL)
1988	Dan Frost (DEN)
1992	Giovanni Lombardi (ITA)
1996	Silvio Martinello (ITA)
2000	Juan Llaneras (ESP)
2004	Mikhail Ignatyev (RUS)

Cycling (men) (continued)

KEIRIN   SEC
2000	Florian Rousseau (FRA)	11.020
2004	Ryan Bayley (AUS)	10.601

MADISON
2000	Australia
2004	Australia

TEAM SPRINT   SEC
2000	France	44.233
2004	Germany	43.980

ROAD RACE (INDIVIDUAL)[8]   HR:MIN:SEC
1896	Aristidis Konstantinidis (GRE)	3:22:31.0
1912	Rudolph Lewis (RSA)	10:42:39.0
1920	Harry Stenqvist (SWE)	4:40:01.8
1924	Armand Blanchonnet (FRA)	6:20:48.0
1928	Henry Hansen (DEN)	4:47:18.0
1932	Attilio Pavesi (ITA)	2:28:05.6
1936	Robert Charpentier (FRA)	2:33:05.0
1948	Jose Beyaert (FRA)	5:18:12.6
1952	Andre Noyelle (BEL)	5:06:03.4
1956	Ercole Baldini (ITA)	5:21:17.0
1960	Viktor Kapitonov (URS)	4:20:37.0
1964	Mario Zanin (ITA)	4:39:51.63
1968	Pierfranco Vianelli (ITA)	4:41:25.24
1972	Hennie Kuiper (NED)	4:14:37.0
1976	Bernt Johansson (SWE)	4:46:52.0
1980	Sergey Sukhoruchenkov (URS)	4:48:28.90
1984	Alexei Grewal (USA)	4:59:57.0
1988	Olaf Ludwig (GDR)	4:32:22.0
1992	Fabio Casartelli (ITA)	4:35:21.0
1996	Pascal Richard (SUI)	4:53:56.0
2000	Jan Ullrich (GER)	5:29:08.0
2004	Paolo Bettini (ITA)	5:41:44.0

ROAD RACE (TEAM)   HR:MIN:SEC
1912	Sweden	44:35:33.6
1920	France	19:16:43.2
1924	France	19:30:14
1928	Denmark	15:09:14
1932	Italy	7:27:15.2
1936	France	7:39:16.2
1948	Belgium	15:58:17.4
1952	Belgium	15:20:46.6
1956	France	5:21:17

ROAD TIME TRIAL (INDIVIDUAL)   HR:MIN:SEC
1996	Miguel Indurain (ESP)	1:04:05
2000	Vyacheslav Yekimov (RUS)	57:40.42
2004	Tyler Hamilton (USA)	57.31.74

ROAD TIME TRIAL (TEAM)   HR:MIN:SEC
1960	Italy	2:14:33.53
1964	The Netherlands	2:26:31.19
1968	The Netherlands	2:07:49.06
1972	USSR	2:11:17.8
1976	USSR	2:08:53
1980	USSR	2:01:21.7
1984	Italy	1:58:28
1988	East Germany	1:57:47.7
1992	Germany	2:01:39

CROSS COUNTRY (MOUNTAIN BIKE)   HR:MIN:SEC
1996	Bart Jan Brentjens (NED)	2:17:38
2000	Miguel Martinez (FRA)	2:09:2.50
2004	Julien Absalon (FRA)	2:15.02

Summer Olympic Games Champions (continued)

Cycling (women)

500-METER TIME TRIAL — HR:MIN:SEC

2000	Felicia Ballanger (FRA)	34.140
2004	Anna Meares (AUS)	53.016

INDIVIDUAL SPRINT

1988	Erika Salumae (URS)
1992	Erika Salumae (EST)
1996	Felicia Ballanger (FRA)
2000	Felicia Ballanger (FRA)
2004	Lori-Ann Muenzer (CAN)

3,000-METER INDIVIDUAL PURSUIT

1992	Petra Rossner (GER)
1996	Antonella Bellutti (ITA)
2000	Leontien Zijlaard–van Moorsel (NED)
2004	Sarah Ulmer (NZL)

POINTS RACE

1996	Nathalie Lancien (FRA)
2000	Antonella Bellutti (ITA)
2004	Olga Slyusareva (RUS)

ROAD RACE (INDIVIDUAL) — HR:MIN:SEC

1984	Connie Carpenter-Phinney (USA)	2:11:14.0
1988	Monique Knol (NED)	2:00:52.0
1992	Kathryn Watt (AUS)	2:04:42.0
1996	Jeannie Longo-Ciprelli (FRA)	2:36:13.0
2000	Leontien Zijlaard–van Moorsel (NED)	3:06:31
2004	Sara Carrigan (AUS)	3:24:24

ROAD TIME TRIAL (INDIVIDUAL) — MIN:SEC

1996	Zulfiya Zabirova (RUS)	36:40
2000	Leontien Zijlaard–van Moorsel (NED)	42:00.781
2004	Leontien Zijlaard–van Moorsel (NED)	31:11.53

CROSS COUNTRY (MOUNTAIN BIKE) — HR:MIN:SEC

1996	Paola Pezzo (ITA)	1:50:51
2000	Paola Pezzo (ITA)	1:49:24.38
2004	Gunn-Rita Dahle (NOR)	1:56:51

Diving (men)

3-METER SPRINGBOARD DIVING

1908	Albert Zürner (GER)
1912	Paul Günther (GER)
1920	Louis Kuehn (USA)
1924	Albert White (USA)
1928	Peter Desjardins (USA)
1932	Michael Galitzen (USA)
1936	Richard Degener (USA)
1948	Bruce Harlan (USA)
1952	David Browning (USA)
1956	Robert Clotworthy (USA)
1960	Gary Tobian (USA)
1964	Kenneth Sitzberger (USA)
1968	Bernie Wrightson (USA)
1972	Vladimir Vasin (URS)
1976	Philip Boggs (USA)
1980	Aleksandr Portnov (URS)
1984	Gregory Louganis (USA)
1988	Gregory Louganis (USA)
1992	Mark Edward Lenzi (USA)
1996	Xiong Ni (CHN)
2000	Xiong Ni (CHN)
2004	Peng Bo (CHN)

Diving (men) (continued)

10-METER PLATFORM (HIGH) DIVING

1904	George Sheldon (USA)
1908	Hjalmar Johansson (SWE)
1912	Erik Adlerz (SWE)
1920	Clarence Pinkston (USA)
1924	Albert White (USA)
1928	Peter Desjardins (USA)
1932	Harold Smith (USA)
1936	Marshall Wayne (USA)
1948	Samuel Lee (USA)
1952	Samuel Lee (USA)
1956	Joaquin Capilla Perez (MEX)
1960	Robert Webster (USA)
1964	Robert Webster (USA)
1968	Klaus DiBiasi (ITA)
1972	Klaus DiBiasi (ITA)
1976	Klaus DiBiasi (ITA)
1980	Falk Hoffman (GDR)
1984	Gregory Louganis (USA)
1988	Gregory Louganis (USA)
1992	Sun Shuwei (CHN)
1996	Dmitry Sautin (RUS)
2000	Tian Liang (CHN)
2004	Hu Jia (CHN)

3-METER SYNCHRONIZED SPRINGBOARD DIVING

2000	China
2004	Greece

10-METER SYNCHRONIZED PLATFORM (HIGH) DIVING

2000	Russia
2004	China

PLUNGE FOR DISTANCE

1904	William Paul Dickey (USA)

PLAIN HIGH DIVING

1912	Erik Adlerz (SWE)
1920	Arvid Wallman (SWE)
1924	Richmond Eve (AUS)

Diving (women)

3-METER SPRINGBOARD DIVING

1920	Aileen Riggin (USA)
1924	Elizabeth Becker-Pinkton (USA)
1928	Helen Meany (USA)
1932	Georgia Coleman (USA)
1936	Marjorie Gestring (USA)
1948	Victoria Draves (USA)
1952	Patricia McCormick (USA)
1956	Patricia McCormick (USA)
1960	Ingrid Krämer-Engel-Gulbin (GER)
1964	Ingrid Krämer-Engel-Gulbin (GER)
1968	Sue Gossick (USA)
1972	Micki King (USA)
1976	Jennifer Chandler (USA)
1980	Irina Kalinina (URS)
1984	Sylvie Bernier (CAN)
1988	Gao Min (CHN)
1992	Gao Min (CHN)
1996	Fu Mingxia (CHN)
2000	Fu Mingxia (CHN)
2004	Guo Jingjing (CHN)

10-METER PLATFORM (HIGH) DIVING

1912	Greta Johansson (SWE)

Summer Olympic Games Champions (continued)

Diving (women) (continued)
10-METER PLATFORM (HIGH) DIVING (CONTINUED)

1920	Stefani Fryland Clausen (DEN)
1924	Caroline Smith (USA)
1928	Elizabeth Anna Becker-Pinkston (USA)
1932	Dorothy Poynton (USA)
1936	Dorothy Poynton-Hill (USA)
1948	Victoria Draves (USA)
1952	Patricia McCormick (USA)
1956	Patricia McCormick (USA)
1960	Ingrid Krämer-Engel-Gulbin (GER)
1964	Lesley Leigh Bush (USA)
1968	Milena Duchkova (TCH)
1972	Ulrika Knape (SWE)
1976	Yelena Vaytsekhovskaya (URS)
1980	Martina Jäschke (GDR)
1984	Zhou Ji-Hong (CHN)
1988	Xu Yan-Mei (CHN)
1992	Fu Mingxia (CHN)
1996	Fu Mingxia (CHN)
2000	Laura Wilkinson (USA)
2004	Chantelle Newbery (AUS)

3-METER SYNCHRONIZED SPRINGBOARD DIVING

2000	Russia
2004	China

10-METER SYNCHRONIZED PLATFORM (HIGH) DIVING

2000	China
2004	China

Equestrian sports

GRAND PRIX (DRESSAGE) INDIVIDUAL		MOUNT
1912	Carl Bonde (SWE)	Emperor
1920	Janne Lundblad (SWE)	Uno
1924	Ernst Linder (SWE)	Piccolomini
1928	Carl Friedrich Freiherr von Langen-Parow (GER)	Draufgänger
1932	Xavier Lesage (FRA)	Taine
1936	Heinz Pollay (GER)	Kronos
1948	Hans Moser (SUI)	Hummer
1952	Henri St. Cyr (SWE)	Master Rufus
1956	Henri St. Cyr (SWE)	Juli
1960	Sergey Filatov (URS)	Absent
1964	Henri Chammartin (SUI)	Woermann
1968	Ivan Kizimov (URS)	Ikhor
1972	Liselott Linsenhoff (FRG)	Piaff
1976	Christine Stückelberger (SUI)	Granat
1980	Elisabeth Theurer (AUT)	Mon Cherie
1984	Reiner Klimke (FRG)	Ahlerich
1988	Nicole Uphoff (FRG)	Rembrandt 24
1992	Nicole Uphoff (GER)	Rembrandt 24
1996	Isabell Werth (GER)	Gigolo
2000	Anky van Grunsven (NED)	Bonfire
2004	Anky van Grunsven (NED)	Salinero

GRAND PRIX (DRESSAGE) TEAM

1928	Germany
1932	France
1936	Germany
1948	France
1952	Sweden
1956	Sweden
1964	Germany
1968	West Germany
1972	USSR
1976	West Germany
1980	USSR
1984	West Germany

Equestrian sports (continued)
GRAND PRIX (DRESSAGE) TEAM (CONTINUED)

1988	West Germany
1992	Germany
1996	Germany
2000	Germany
2004	Germany

GRAND PRIX (JUMPING) INDIVIDUAL		MOUNT
1900	Aimé Haegeman (BEL)	Benton II
1912	Jean Cariou (FRA)	Mignon
1920	Tommaso Lequio di Assaba (ITA)	Trebecco
1924	Alphonse Gemuseus (SUI)	Lucette
1928	Frantisek Ventura (TCH)	Eliot
1932	Takeichi Nishi (JPN)	Uranus
1936	Kurt Hasse (GER)	Tora
1948	Humberto Mariles Cortés (MEX)	Arete
1952	Pierre Jonquères d'Oriola (FRA)	Ali Baba
1956	Hans-Günter Winkler (GER)	Halla
1960	Raimondo d'Inzeo (ITA)	Posillipo
1964	Pierre Jonquères d'Oriola (FRA)	Lutteur
1968	William Steinkraus (USA)	Snowbound
1972	Graziano Mancinelli (ITA)	Ambassador
1976	Alwin Schockemöhle (FRG)	Warwick Rex
1980	Jan Kowalczyk (POL)	Artemor
1984	Joe Fargis (USA)	Touch of Class
1988	Pierre Durand (FRA)	Jappeloup
1992	Ludger Beerbaum (GER)	Classic Touch
1996	Ulrich Kirchhoff (GER)	Jus des Pommes
2000	Jeroen Dubbeldam (NED)	Sjiem
2004	Rodrigo Pessoa (BRA)	Baloubet du Rouet

GRAND PRIX (JUMPING) TEAM

1912	Sweden
1920	Sweden
1924	Sweden
1928	Spain
1936	Germany
1948	Mexico
1952	Great Britain
1956	Germany
1960	Germany
1964	Germany
1968	Canada
1972	West Germany
1976	France
1980	USSR
1984	United States
1988	West Germany
1992	The Netherlands
1996	Germany
2000	Germany
2004	Germany

THREE-DAY EVENT (INDIVIDUAL)		MOUNT
1912	Axel Nordlander (SWE)	Lady Artist
1920	Helmer Mörner (SWE)	Germania
1924	Adolph van der Voort van Zijp (NED)	Silver Piece
1928	Charles Pahud de Mortanges (NED)	Marcroix
1932	Charles Pahud de Mortanges (NED)	Marcroix
1936	Ludwig Stubbendorff (GER)	Nurmi
1948	Bernard Chevallier (FRA)	Aiglonne
1952	Hans von Blixen-Finecke, Jr. (SWE)	Jubal
1956	Petrus Kastenman (SWE)	Iluster
1960	Lawrence Morgan (AUS)	Salad Days

Summer Olympic Games Champions (continued)

Equestrian sports (continued)

THREE-DAY EVENT (INDIVIDUAL) (CONTINUED)

		MOUNT
1964	Mauro Checcoli (ITA)	Surbean
1968	Jean-Jacques Goyon (FRA)	Pitou
1972	Richard Meade (GBR)	Laurieston
1976	Edmund Coffin (USA)	Bally-Cor
1980	Federico Euro Roman (ITA)	Rossinan
1984	Mark Todd (NZL)	Charisma
1988	Mark Todd (NZL)	Charisma
1992	Matthew Ryan (AUS)	Kibah Tic Toc
1996	Robert Blyth Tait (NZL)	Ready Teddy
2000	David O'Connor (USA)	Custom Made
2004	Leslie Law (GBR)	Shear L'Eau

THREE-DAY EVENT (TEAM)

1912	Sweden
1920	Sweden
1924	The Netherlands
1928	The Netherlands
1932	United States
1936	Germany
1948	United States
1952	Sweden
1956	Great Britain
1960	Australia
1964	Italy
1968	Great Britain
1972	Great Britain
1976	United States
1980	USSR
1984	United States
1988	West Germany
1992	Australia
1996	Australia
2000	Australia
2004	France

HIGH JUMP

		MOUNT
1900	Dominique Maximien Gardéres (FRA); Gian Giorgio Trissino (ITA) (tied)	Canela; Oreste

LONG JUMP

		MOUNT
1900	Constant van Langhendonck (BEL)	Extra Dry

FIGURE RIDING (INDIVIDUAL)

1920	T. Bouckaert (BEL)

FIGURE RIDING (TEAM)

1920	Belgium

Fencing (men)

FOIL (INDIVIDUAL)

1896	Eugène-Henri Gravelotte (FRA)
1900	Émile Coste (FRA)
1904	Ramón Fonst (CUB)
1912	Nedo Nadi (ITA)
1920	Nedo Nadi (ITA)
1924	Roger Ducret (FRA)
1928	Lucien Gaudin (FRA)
1932	Gustavo Marzi (ITA)
1936	Giulio Gaudini (ITA)
1948	Jehan Buhan (FRA)
1952	Christian d'Oriola (FRA)
1956	Christian d'Oriola (FRA)
1960	Viktor Zhdanovich (URS)
1964	Egon Franke (POL)

Fencing (men) (continued)

FOIL (INDIVIDUAL) (CONTINUED)

1968	Ion Drimba (ROM)
1972	Witold Woyda (POL)
1976	Fabio dal Zotto (ITA)
1980	Vladimir Smirnov (URS)
1984	Mauro Numa (ITA)
1988	Stefano Cerioni (ITA)
1992	Philippe Omnes (FRA)
1996	Alessandro Puccini (ITA)
2000	Kim Young Ho (KOR)
2004	Brice Guyart (FRA)

FOIL (TEAM)

1904	Cuba
1920	Italy
1924	France
1928	Italy
1932	France
1936	Italy
1948	France
1952	France
1956	Italy
1960	USSR
1964	USSR
1968	France
1972	Poland
1976	West Germany
1980	France
1984	Italy
1988	USSR
1992	Germany
1996	Russia
2000	France
2004	Italy

INDIVIDUAL FOIL, PROFESSIONAL (MASTERS)

1896	Leon Pyrgos (GRE)
1900	Lucien Mérignac (FRA)

INDIVIDUAL FOIL, JUNIOR

1904	Arthur Fox (USA)

EPEE (INDIVIDUAL)

1900	Ramón Fonst (CUB)
1904	Ramón Fonst (CUB)
1908	Gaston Alibert (FRA)
1912	Paul Anspach (BEL)
1920	Armand Massard (FRA)
1924	Charles Delporte (BEL)
1928	Lucien Gaudin (FRA)
1932	Giancarlo Cornaggia-Medici (ITA)
1936	Franco Riccardi (ITA)
1948	Luigi Cantone (ITA)
1952	Edoardo Mangiarotti (ITA)
1956	Carlo Pavesi (ITA)
1960	Giuseppe Delfino (ITA)
1964	Grigory Kriss (URS)
1968	Gyoso Kulcsar (HUN)
1972	Csaba Fenyvesi (HUN)
1976	Alexander Pusch (FRG)
1980	Johan Harmenberg (SWE)
1984	Philippe Boisse (FRA)
1988	Arnd Schmitt (FRG)
1992	Eric Srecki (FRA)
1996	Aleksandr Beketov (RUS)
2000	Pavel Kolobkov (RUS)
2004	Marcel Fischer (SUI)

Summer Olympic Games Champions (continued)

Fencing (men) (continued)

EPEE (TEAM)

1908	France
1912	Belgium
1920	Italy
1924	France
1928	Italy
1932	France
1936	Italy
1948	France
1952	Italy
1956	Italy
1960	Italy
1964	Hungary
1968	Hungary
1972	Hungary
1976	Sweden
1980	France
1984	West Germany
1988	France
1992	Germany
1996	Italy
2000	Italy
2004	France

INDIVIDUAL EPEE, PROFESSIONAL (MASTERS)

1900	Albert Ayat (FRA)

INDIVIDUAL EPEE, OPEN (AMATEUR AND MASTERS)

1900	Albert Ayat (FRA)

SABRE (INDIVIDUAL)

1896	Ioannis Georgiadis (GRE)
1900	Georges de la Falaise (FRA)
1904	Manuel Díaz (CUB)
1908	Jeno Fuchs (HUN)
1912	Jeno Fuchs (HUN)
1920	Nedo Nadi (ITA)
1924	Sandor Posta (HUN)
1928	Odon Vitez Tersztyanszky (HUN)
1932	Gyorgy Piller (HUN)
1936	Endre Kabos (HUN)
1948	Aladar Gerevich (HUN)
1952	Pal Kovacs (HUN)
1956	Rudolph Karpati (HUN)
1960	Rudolph Karpati (HUN)
1964	Tibor Pezsa (HUN)
1968	Jerzy Pawlowski (POL)
1972	Viktor Sidyak (URS)
1976	Viktor Krovopuskov (URS)
1980	Viktor Krovopuskov (URS)
1984	Jean-François Lamour (FRA)
1988	Jean-François Lamour (FRA)
1992	Bence Szabo (HUN)
1996	Stanislav Pozdnyakov (RUS)
2000	Mihai Claudiu Covaliu (ROM)
2004	Aldo Montano (ITA)

SABRE (TEAM)

1908	Hungary
1912	Hungary
1920	Italy
1924	Italy
1928	Hungary
1932	Hungary
1936	Hungary
1948	Hungary
1952	Hungary
1956	Hungary

Fencing (men) (continued)

SABRE (TEAM) (CONTINUED)

1960	Hungary
1964	USSR
1968	USSR
1972	Italy
1976	USSR
1980	USSR
1984	Italy
1988	Hungary
1992	Unified Team
1996	Russia
2000	Russia
2004	France

INDIVIDUAL SABRE, PROFESSIONAL (MASTERS)

1900	Antonio Conte (ITA)

THREE-CORNERED SABRE

1906	Gustav Casmir (GER)

SINGLE STICK

1904	Albertson Van Zo Post (CUB)

Fencing (women)

FOIL (INDIVIDUAL)

1924	Ellen Osiier (DEN)
1928	Helene Mayer (GER)
1932	Ellen Preis (AUT)
1936	Ilona Schacherer-Elek (HUN)
1948	Ilona Elek (HUN)
1952	Irene Camber (ITA)
1956	Gillian Sheen (GBR)
1960	Adelheid Schmid (GER)
1964	Ildiko Ujlaki-Rejto (HUN)
1968	Yelena Novikova (URS)
1972	Antonella Ragno Lonzi (ITA)
1976	Ildiko Schwarczenberger (HUN)
1980	Pascale Trinquet (FRA)
1984	Jujie Luan (CHN)
1988	Anja Fichtel (FRG)
1992	Giovanna Trillini (ITA)
1996	Laura Gabriela Badea (ROM)
2000	Valentina Vezzali (ITA)
2004	Valentina Vezzali (ITA)

FOIL (TEAM)

1960	USSR
1964	Hungary
1968	USSR
1972	USSR
1976	USSR
1980	France
1984	West Germany
1988	West Germany
1992	Italy
1996	Italy
2000	Italy

EPEE (INDIVIDUAL)

1996	Laura Flessel (FRA)
2000	Timea Nagy (HUN)
2004	Timea Nagy (HUN)

EPEE (TEAM)

1996	France
2000	Russia
2004	Russia

Summer Olympic Games Champions (continued)

Fencing (women) (continued)

SABRE (INDIVIDUAL)
2004 Mariel Zagunis (USA)

Field hockey

MEN
1908 Great Britain
1920 Great Britain
1928 India
1932 India
1936 India
1948 India
1952 India
1956 India
1960 Pakistan
1964 India
1968 Pakistan
1972 West Germany
1976 New Zealand
1980 India
1984 Pakistan
1988 Great Britain
1992 Germany
1996 The Netherlands
2000 The Netherlands
2004 Australia

WOMEN
1980 Zimbabwe
1984 The Netherlands
1988 Australia
1992 Spain
1996 Australia
2000 Australia
2004 Germany

Golf

MEN, INDIVIDUAL
1900 Charles Sands (USA)
1904 George Lyon (CAN)

MEN, TEAM
1904 United States

WOMEN
1900 Margaret Abbott (USA)

Gymnastics (men)

COMBINED, OR ALL-AROUND (INDIVIDUAL)
1900 Gustave Sandras (FRA)
1904 Julius Lenhardt (USA)
1908 G. Alberto Braglia (ITA)
1912 G. Alberto Braglia (ITA)
1920 Giorgio Zampori (ITA)
1924 Leon Stukelj (YUG)
1928 Georges Miez (SUI)
1932 Romeo Neri (ITA)
1936 Karl-Alfred Schwarzmann (GER)
1948 Veikko Huhtanen (FIN)
1952 Viktor Chukarin (URS)
1956 Viktor Chukarin (URS)
1960 Boris Shakhlin (URS)
1964 Yukio Endo (JPN)
1968 Sawao Kato (JPN)
1972 Sawao Kato (JPN)

Gymnastics (men) (continued)

COMBINED, OR ALL-AROUND (INDIVIDUAL) (CONTINUED)
1976 Nikolay Andrianov (URS)
1980 Aleksandr Dityatin (URS)
1984 Koji Gushiken (JPN)
1988 Vladimir Artyomov (URS)
1992 Vitaly Shcherbo (UNT)
1996 Li Xiaosahuang (CHN)
2000 Aleksey Nemov (RUS)
2004 Paul Hamm (USA)

COMBINED, OR ALL-AROUND (TEAM)
1920 Italy
1924 Italy
1928 Switzerland
1932 Italy
1936 Germany
1948 Finland
1952 USSR
1956 USSR
1960 Japan
1964 Japan
1968 Japan
1972 Japan
1976 Japan
1980 USSR
1984 United States
1988 USSR
1992 Unified Team
1996 Russia
2000 China
2004 Japan

FLOOR EXERCISE
1932 Istvan Pelle (HUN)
1936 Georges Miez (SUI)
1948 Ferenc Pataki (HUN)
1952 William Thoresson (SWE)
1956 Valentin Muratov (URS)
1960 Nobuyuki Aihara (JPN)
1964 Franco Menichelli (ITA)
1968 Sawao Kato (JPN)
1972 Nikolay Andrianov (URS)
1976 Nikolay Andrianov (URS)
1980 Roland Brückner (GDR)
1984 Li Ning (CHN)
1988 Sergey Kharikov (URS)
1992 Li Xiaosahuang (CHN)
1996 Ioannis Melissanidis (GRE)
2000 Igors Vihrovs (LAT)
2004 Kyle Shewfelt (CAN)

HIGH BAR
1896 Hermann Weingärtner (GER)
1904 Anton Heida (USA); Edward Henning (USA)
       (tied)
1924 Leon Stukelj (YUG)
1928 Georges Miez (SUI)
1932 Dallas Bixler (USA)
1936 Aleksanteri Saarvala (FIN)
1948 Josef Stalder (SUI)
1952 Jack Günthard (SUI)
1956 Takashi Ono (JPN)
1960 Takashi Ono (JPN)
1964 Boris Shakhlin (URS)
1968 Mikhail Voronin (URS); Akinori Nakayama
       (JPN) (tied)

Summer Olympic Games Champions (continued)

Gymnastics (men) (continued)

HIGH BAR (CONTINUED)
1972   Mitsuo Tsukahara (JPN)
1976   Mitsuo Tsukahara (JPN)
1980   Stoyan Delchev (BUL)
1984   Shinji Morisue (JPN)
1988   Vladimir Artyomov (URS); Valery Lyukin (URS)
       (tied)
1992   Trent Dimas (USA)
1996   Andreas Wecker (GER)
2000   Aleksey Nemov (RUS)
2004   Igor Cassina (ITA)

PARALLEL BARS
1896   Alfred Flatow (GER)
1904   George Eyser (USA)
1924   August Güttinger (SUI)
1928   Ladislav Vacha (TCH)
1932   Romeo Neri (ITA)
1936   Konrad Frey (GER)
1948   Michael Reusch (SUI)
1952   Hans Eugster (SUI)
1956   Viktor Chukarin (URS)
1960   Boris Shakhlin (URS)
1964   Yukio Endo (JPN)
1968   Akinori Nakayama (JPN)
1972   Sawao Kato (JPN)
1976   Sawao Kato (JPN)
1980   Aleksandr Tkachyov (URS)
1984   Bart Conner (USA)
1988   Vladimir Artyomov (URS)
1992   Vitaly Shcherbo (UNT)
1996   Rustam Sharipov (UKR)
2000   Li Xiaopeng (CHN)
2004   Valery Goncharov (UKR)

SIDE, OR POMMEL, HORSE
1896   Louis Zutter (SUI)
1904   Anton Heida (USA)
1924   Josef Wilhelm (SUI)
1928   Hermann Hänggi (SUI)
1932   Istvan Pelle (HUN)
1936   Konrad Frey (GER)
1948   Paavo Aaltonen (FIN); Veikko Huhtanen (FIN);
       Heikki Savolainen (FIN) (tied)
1952   Viktor Chukarin (URS)
1956   Boris Shakhlin (URS)
1960   Boris Shakhlin (URS); Eugen Ekman (FIN)
       (tied)
1964   Miroslav Cerar (YUG)
1968   Miroslav Cerar (YUG)
1972   Viktor Klimenko (URS)
1976   Zoltan Magyar (HUN)
1980   Zoltan Magyar (HUN)
1984   Li Ning (CHN); Peter Vidmar (USA) (tied)
1988   Lyubomir Geraskov (BUL); Zsolt Borkai (HUN);
       Dmitry Bilozerchev (URS) (tied)
1992   Vitaly Shcherbo (UNT); Pae Gil-su (PRK) (tied)
1996   Li Donghua (SUI)
2000   Marius Urzica (ROM)
2004   Teng Haibin (CHN)

LONG, OR VAULTING, HORSE
1896   Karl Schuhmann (GER)
1904   Anton Heida (USA); George Eyser (USA) (tied)
1924   Frank Kriz (USA)
1928   Eugen Mack (SUI)
1932   Savino Guglielmetti (ITA)
1936   Karl-Alfred Schnorzmann (GER)

Gymnastics (men) (continued)

LONG, OR VAULTING, HORSE (CONTINUED)
1948   Paavo Johannes Aaltonen (FIN)
1952   Viktor Chukarin (URS)
1956   Valentin Muratov (URS); Helmut Bantz (GER)
       (tied)
1960   Takashi Ono (JPN); Boris Shakhlin (URS)
       (tied)
1964   Haruhiro Yamashita (JPN)
1968   Mikhail Voronin (URS)
1972   Klaus Köste (GDR)
1976   Nikolay Andrianov (URS)
1980   Nikolay Andrianov (URS)
1984   Lou Yun (CHN)
1988   Lou Yun (CHN)
1992   Vitaly Shcherbo (UNT)
1996   Aleksey Nemov (RUS)
2000   Gervasio Deferr (ESP)
2004   Gervasio Deferr (ESP)

RINGS
1896   Ioannis Mitropoulos (GRE)
1904   Hermann Glass (USA)
1924   Francesco Martino (ITA)
1928   Leon Stukelj (YUG)
1932   George Gulack (USA)
1936   Alois Hudec (TCH)
1948   Karl Frei (SUI)
1952   Grant Shaginyan (URS)
1956   Albert Azaryan (URS)
1960   Albert Azaryan (URS)
1964   Takuji Hayata (JPN)
1968   Akinori Nakayama (JPN)
1972   Akinori Nakayama (JPN)
1976   Nikolay Andrianov (URS)
1980   Aleksandr Dityatin (URS)
1984   Li Ning (CHN); Koji Gushiken (JPN) (tied)
1988   Holger Behrendt (GDR); Dmitry Bilozerchev
       (URS) (tied)
1992   Vitaly Shcherbo (UNT)
1996   Yury Chechi (ITA)
2000   Szilveszter Csollany (HUN)
2004   Dimosthenis Tampakos (GRE)

TRAMPOLINE
2000   Aleksandr Moskalenko (RUS)
2004   Yury Nikitin (UKR)

ROPE CLIMBING
1896   Nicolaos Andriakopoulos (GRE)
1904   George Eyser (USA)
1924   Bedrich Supcik (TCH)
1932   Raymond Bass (USA)

SWEDISH EXERCISES (TEAM)
1912   Sweden
1920   Sweden

OPTIONAL EXERCISES (TEAM)
1912   Norway
1920   Denmark
1932   United States

PARALLEL BARS (TEAM)
1896   Germany

HORIZONTAL BARS (TEAM)
1896   Germany

Summer Olympic Games Champions (continued)

Gymnastics (men) (continued)

CLUB SWINGING
1904   Edward Hennig (USA)
1932   George Roth (USA)

TUMBLING
1932   Rowland Wolfe (USA)

COMBINED COMPETITION (7 APPARATUS)
1904   Anton Heida (USA)

COMBINED COMPETITION (9 EVENTS)
1904   Adolf Spinnler (SUI)

PRESCRIBED APPARATUS (TEAM)
1904   United States
1908   Sweden
1912   Italy
1952   Sweden
1956   Hungary

MASS EXERCISES (TEAM)
1952   Finland

SIDE HORSE (VAULTS)
1924   Albert Séguin (FRA)

Gymnastics (women)

COMBINED, OR ALL-AROUND (INDIVIDUAL)
1952   Mariya Gorokhovskaya (URS)
1956   Larisa Latynina (URS)
1960   Larisa Latynina (URS)
1964   Vera Caslavska (TCH)
1968   Vera Caslavska (TCH)
1972   Lyudmila Turishcheva (URS)
1976   Nadia Comaneci (ROM)
1980   Yelena Davydova (URS)
1984   Mary-Lou Retton (USA)
1988   Yelena Shushunova (URS)
1992   Tatyana Gutsu (UNT)
1996   Liliya Podkopayeva (UKR)
2000   Simona Amanar (ROM)
2004   Carly Patterson (USA)

COMBINED, OR ALL-AROUND (TEAM)
1928   The Netherlands
1936   Germany
1948   Czechoslovakia
1952   USSR
1956   USSR
1960   USSR
1964   USSR
1968   USSR
1972   USSR
1976   USSR
1980   USSR
1984   Romania
1988   USSR
1992   Unified Team
1996   United States
2000   Romania
2004   Romania

BALANCE BEAM
1952   Nina Bocharova (URS)
1956   Agnes Keleti (HUN)
1960   Eva Bosakova (TCH)

Gymnastics (women) (continued)

BALANCE BEAM (CONTINUED)
1964   Vera Caslavska (TCH)
1968   Natalya Kuchinskaya (URS)
1972   Olga Korbut (URS)
1976   Nadia Comaneci (ROM)
1980   Nadia Comaneci (ROM)
1984   Ecaterina Szabo (ROM); Simona Pauca
         (ROM) (*tied*)
1988   Daniela Silívas (ROM)
1992   Tatyana Lysenko (UNT)
1996   Shannon Miller (USA)
2000   Liu Xuan (CHN)
2004   Catalina Ponor (ROM)

UNEVEN PARALLEL BARS
1952   Margit Korondi (HUN)
1956   Agnes Keleti (HUN)
1960   Polina Astakhova (URS)
1964   Polina Astakhova (URS)
1968   Vera Caslavska (TCH)
1972   Karin Janz (GDR)
1976   Nadia Comaneci (ROM)
1980   Maxi Gnauck (GDR)
1984   Julianne McNamara (USA); Ma Yanhong
         (CHN) (*tied*)
1988   Daniela Silivas (ROM)
1992   Li Lu (CHN)
1996   Svetlana Khorkina (RUS)
2000   Svetlana Khorkina (RUS)
2004   Emilie Lepennec (FRA)

VAULT
1952   Yekaterina Kalinchuk (URS)
1956   Larisa Latynina (URS)
1960   Margarita Nikolayeva (URS)
1964   Vera Caslavska (TCH)
1968   Vera Caslavska (TCH)
1972   Karin Janz (GDR)
1976   Nelli Kim (URS)
1980   Natalya Shaposhnikova (URS)
1984   Ecaterina Szabo (ROM)
1988   Svetlana Boginskaya (URS)
1992   Henrietta Onodi (HUN); Lavinia Milosovici
         (ROM) (*tied*)
1996   Simona Amanar (ROM)
2000   Yelena Zamolodchikova (RUS)
2004   Monica Rosu (ROM)

FLOOR EXERCISE
1952   Agnes Keleti (HUN)
1956   Larisa Latynina (URS); Agnes Keleti (HUN)
         (*tied*)
1960   Larisa Latynina (URS)
1964   Larisa Latynina (URS)
1968   Vera Caslavska (TCH); Larissa Petrik (URS)
         (*tied*)
1972   Olga Korbut (URS)
1976   Nelli Kim (URS)
1980   Nadia Comaneci (ROM); Nelli Kim (URS) (*tied*)
1984   Ecaterina Szabo (ROM)
1988   Daniela Silivas (ROM)
1992   Lavinia Milosovici (ROM)
1996   Liliya Podkopayeva (UKR)
2000   Yelena Zamolodchikova (RUS)
2004   Catalina Ponor (ROM)

Summer Olympic Games Champions (continued)

Gymnastics (women) (continued)

RHYTHMIC GYMNASTICS (INDIVIDUAL)

1984	Lori Fung (CAN)
1988	Marina Lobatch (URS)
1992	Aleksandra Timoshenko (UNT)
1996	Yekaterina Serebryanskaya (UKR)
2000	Yuliya Barsukova (RUS)
2004	Alina Kabayeva (RUS)

RHYTHMIC GYMNASTICS (TEAM)

1996	Spain
2000	Russia
2004	Russia

TRAMPOLINE

2000	Irina Karavayeva (RUS)
2004	Anna Dogonadze (GER)

HAND APPARATUS (TEAM)

1952	Sweden
1956	Hungary

Handball (team) (outdoors to 1972)

MEN

1936	Germany
1952	Sweden (demonstration)
1972	Yugoslavia
1976	USSR
1980	East Germany
1984	Yugoslavia
1988	USSR
1992	Unified Team
1996	Croatia
2000	Russia
2004	Croatia

WOMEN

1976	USSR
1980	USSR
1984	Yugoslavia
1988	South Korea
1992	South Korea
1996	Denmark
2000	Denmark
2004	Denmark

JEU DE PAUME (ROYAL TENNIS)

1908	Jay Gould (USA)

Judo (men)[9]

60 KG (132 LB)

1964	Takehide Nakatani (JPN)
1972	Takao Kawaguchi (JPN)
1976	Héctor Rodríguez (CUB)
1980	Thierry Rey (FRA)
1984	Shinji Hosokawa (JPN)
1988	Kim Jae-Yup (KOR)
1992	Nazim Guseynov (UNT)
1996	Tadahiro Nomura (JPN)
2000	Tadahiro Nomura (JPN)
2004	Tadahiro Nomura (JPN)

66 KG (145.2 LB)

1980	Nikolay Solodukhin (URS)
1984	Yoshiyuki Matsuoka (JPN)
1988	Lee Kyung Ken (KOR)
1992	Rogerio Sampaio Cardoso (BRA)
1996	Udo Quellmalz (GER)
2000	Huseyin Ozkan (TUR)

Judo (men)[9] (continued)

66 KG (145.2 LB) (CONTINUED)

2004	Masato Uchishiba (JPN)

73 KG (160.6 LB)

1972	Takao Kawaguchi (JPN)
1976	Héctor Rodríguez Torres (CUB)
1980	Ezio Gamba (ITA)
1984	Ahn Byeong Keun (KOR)
1988	Marc Alexandre (FRA)
1992	Toshihiko Koga (JPN)
1996	Kenzo Nakamura (JPN)
2000	Giuseppe Maddaloni (ITA)
2004	Lee Won Hee (KOR)

81 KG (178.2 LB)

1972	Toyojazu Nomura (JPN)
1976	Vladimir Nevzorov (URS)
1980	Shota Khabareli (URS)
1984	Frank Wieneke (FRG)
1988	Waldemar Legien (POL)
1992	Hidehiko Yoshida (JPN)
1996	Djamel Bouras (FRA)
2000	Makoto Takimoto (JPN)
2004	Ilias Iliadis (GRE)

90 KG (198 LB)

1964	Isao Okano (JPN)
1972	Shinobu Sekine (JPN)
1976	Isamu Sonoda (JPN)
1980	Jürg Röthlisberger (SUI)
1984	Peter Seisenbacher (AUT)
1988	Peter Seisenbacher (AUT)
1992	Waldemar Legien (POL)
1996	Jeon Ki-Young (KOR)
2000	Mark Huizinga (NED)
2004	Zurab Zviadauri (GEO)

100 KG (220 LB)

1972	Shota Chochoshvili (URS)
1976	Kazuhiro Ninomiya (JPN)
1980	Robert van de Walle (BEL)
1984	Ha Young Zoo (KOR)
1988	Aurelio Miguel (BRA)
1992	Antal Kovacs (HUN)
1996	Pawel Nastula (POL)
2000	Kosei Inoue (JPN)
2004	Ihar Makarau (BLR)

OVER 100 KG (220+ LB)

1964	Isao Inokuma (JPN)
1972	Willem Ruska (NED)
1976	Sergey Novikov (URS)
1980	Angelo Parisi (FRA)
1984	Hitoshi Saito (JPN)
1988	Hitoshi Saito (JPN)
1992	David Khakhaleishvili (UNT)
1996	David Douillet (FRA)
2000	David Douillet (FRA)
2004	Keiji Suzuki (JPN)

OPEN (NO WEIGHT LIMIT)

1964	Antonius Johannes Geesink (NED)
1972	Willem Ruska (NED)
1976	Haruki Uemura (JPN)
1980	Dietmar Lorenz (GDR)
1984	Yasuhiro Yamashita (JPN)

Summer Olympic Games Champions (continued)

Judo (women)[10]

48 KG (105.6 LB)
1992 Cecile Nowak (FRA)
1996 Kye Sun-Hi (PRK)
2000 Ryoko Tamura (JPN)
2004 Ryoko Tani (JPN)

52 KG (114.4 LB)
1992 Almudena Muñoz Martínez (ESP)
1996 Marie-Claire Restoux (FRA)
2000 Legna Verdecia (CUB)
2004 Xian Dongmei (CHN)

57 KG (125.4 LB)
1992 Miriam Blasco Soto (ESP)
1996 Driulis González Morales (CUB)
2000 Isabel Fernández (ESP)
2004 Yvonne Bönisch (GER)

63 KG (138.6 LB)
1992 Catherine Fleury-Vachon (FRA)
1996 Yuko Emoto (JPN)
2000 Severine Vandenhende (FRA)
2004 Ayumi Tanimoto (JPN)

70 KG (154 LB)
1992 Odalis Reve Jiménez (CUB)
1996 Cho Min-Sun (KOR)
2000 Sibelis Veranes (CUB)
2004 Masae Ueno (JPN)

78 KG (171.6 LB)
1992 Kim Mi-Jung (KOR)
1996 Ulla Werbrouck (BEL)
2000 Tang Lin (CHN)
2004 Noriko Anno (JPN)

OVER 78 KG (171.6+ LB)
1992 Zhuang Xiaoyan (CHN)
1996 Sun Fuming (CHN)
2000 Yuan Hua (CHN)
2004 Maki Tsukada (JPN)

Lacrosse

1904 Canada
1908 Canada

Modern pentathlon

INDIVIDUAL (MEN)
1912 Gösta Lilliehöök (SWE)
1920 Gustaf Dyrssen (SWE)
1924 Bo Lindman (SWE)
1928 Sven Thofelt (SWE)
1932 Johan Oxenstierna (SWE)
1936 Gotthardt Handrick (GER)
1948 William Grut (SWE)
1952 Lars-Goran Hall (SWE)
1956 Lars-Goran Hall (SWE)
1960 Ferenc Nemeth (HUN)
1964 Ferenc Torok (HUN)
1968 Björn Ferm (SWE)
1972 Andras Balczo (HUN)
1976 Janusz Pyciak-Peciak (POL)
1980 Anatoly Starostin (URS)
1984 Daniele Masala (ITA)
1988 Janos Martinek (HUN)
1992 Arkadiusz Skrzypaszek (POL)

Modern pentathlon (continued)

INDIVIDUAL (MEN) (CONTINUED)
1996 Aleksandr Parygin (KAZ)
2000 Dmitry Svatkovsky (RUS)
2004 Andrey Moiseyev (RUS)

INDIVIDUAL (WOMEN)
2000 Stephanie Cook (GBR)
2004 Zsuzsanna Voros (HUN)

TEAM (MEN)
1952 Hungary
1956 USSR
1960 Hungary
1964 USSR
1968 Hungary
1972 USSR
1976 Great Britain
1980 USSR
1984 Italy
1988 Hungary
1992 Poland

Motorboat racing

		BOAT
OPEN CLASS, 40 NAUTICAL MILES		
1908	Émile Thubron (FRA)	*Camille*
8-METER CLASS, 40 NAUTICAL MILES		
1908	Thomas Thornycroft, Bernard Redwood (GBR)	*Cyrinus*
UNDER 60-FOOT CLASS, 40 NAUTICAL MILES		
1908	Thomas Thornycroft, Bernard Redwood (GBR)	*Cyrinus*

Polo

1900 team comprising members from Great Britain and the United States
1908 Great Britain
1920 Great Britain
1924 Argentina
1936 Argentina

Rackets

SINGLES
1908 Evan Noel (GBR)

DOUBLES
1908 Vane Pennell, John Jacob Astor (GBR)

Roque

1904 Charles Jacobus (USA)

Rowing (men)[11]

SINGLE SCULLS		MIN:SEC
1900	Henri Barrelet (FRA)	7:35.6
1904	Frank Greer (USA)	10:08.5
1908	Harry Blackstaffe (GBR)	9:26.0
1912	William Kinnear (GBR)	7:47.6
1920	John Kelly, Sr. (USA)	7:35.0
1924	Jack Beresford (GBR)	7:49.2
1928	Henry Pearce (AUS)	7:11.0
1932	Henry Pearce (AUS)	7:44.4
1936	Gustav Schäfer (GER)	8:21.5
1948	Mervyn Wood (AUS)	7:24.4
1952	Yury Tyukalov (URS)	8:12.8
1956	Vyacheslav Ivanov (URS)	8:02.5

Summer Olympic Games Champions (continued)

Rowing (men)[11] (continued)

SINGLE SCULLS (CONTINUED)

		MIN:SEC
1960	Vyacheslav Ivanov (URS)	7:13.96
1964	Vyacheslav Ivanov (URS)	8:22.51
1968	Henri-Jan Wienese (NED)	7:47.80
1972	Yury Malyshev (URS)	7:10.12
1976	Pertti Karppinen (FIN)	7:29.03
1980	Pertti Karppinen (FIN)	7:09.61
1984	Pertti Karppinen (FIN)	7:00.24
1988	Thomas Lange (GDR)	6:49.86
1992	Thomas Lange (GER)	6:51.40
1996	Xeno Mueller (SUI)	6:44.85
2000	Robert Waddell (NZL)	6:48.90
2004	Olaf Tufte (NOR)	6:49.30

DOUBLE SCULLS

		MIN:SEC
1904	United States	10:03.2
1920	United States	7:09.0
1924	United States	6:34.0
1928	United States	6:41.4
1932	United States	7:17.4
1936	Great Britain	7:20.8
1948	Great Britain	6:51.3
1952	Argentina	7:32.2
1956	USSR	7:24.0
1960	Czechoslovakia	6:47.50
1964	USSR	7:10.66
1968	USSR	6:51.82
1972	USSR	7:01.77
1976	Norway	7:13.20
1980	East Germany	6:24.33
1984	United States	6:36.87
1988	The Netherlands	6:21.13
1992	Australia	6:17.32
1996	Italy	6:16.98
2000	Slovenia	6:16.63
2004	France	6:29.00

FOUR SCULLS

		MIN:SEC
1976	East Germany	6:18.65
1980	East Germany	5:49.81
1984	West Germany	5:57.55
1988	Italy	5:53.37
1992	Germany	5:45.17
1996	Germany	5:56.93
2000	Italy	5:45.56
2004	Russia	5:56.85

LIGHTWEIGHT DOUBLE SCULLS

		MIN:SEC
1996	Switzerland	6:23.47
2000	Poland	6:21.75
2004	Poland	6:20.93

PAIRS (WITHOUT COXSWAIN)

		MIN:SEC
1904	United States	10:57.0
1908	Great Britain	9:41.0
1924	The Netherlands	8:19.4
1928	Germany	7:06.4
1932	Great Britain	8:00.0
1936	Germany	8:16.1
1948	Great Britain	7:21.1
1952	United States	8:20.7
1956	United States	7:55.4
1960	USSR	7:02.01
1964	Canada	7:32.94
1968	East Germany	7:26.56
1972	East Germany	6:53.16

Rowing (men)[11] (continued)

PAIRS (WITHOUT COXSWAIN) (CONTINUED)

		MIN:SEC
1976	East Germany	7:23.31
1980	East Germany	6:48.01
1984	Romania	6:45.39
1988	Great Britain	6:36.84
1992	Great Britain	6:27.72
1996	Great Britain	6:20.09
2000	France	6:32.97
2004	Australia	6:30.76

PAIRS (WITH COXSWAIN)

		MIN:SEC
1900	The Netherlands/France	7:34.2
1920	Italy	7:56.0
1924	Switzerland	8:39.0
1928	Switzerland	7:42.6
1932	United States	8:25.8
1936	Germany	8:36.9
1948	Denmark	8:00.5
1952	France	8:28.6
1956	United States	8:26.1
1960	Germany	7:29.14
1964	United States	8:21.23
1968	Italy	8:04.81
1972	East Germany	7:17.25
1976	East Germany	7:58.99
1980	East Germany	7:02.54
1984	Italy	7:05.99
1988	Italy	6:58.79
1992	Great Britain	6:49.83

LIGHTWEIGHT FOURS (WITHOUT COXSWAIN)

		MIN:SEC
1996	Denmark	6:09.58
2000	France	6:01.68
2004	Denmark	6:01.39

FOURS (WITHOUT COXSWAIN)

		MIN:SEC
1900	France	7:11.0
1904	United States	9:53.8
1908	Great Britain	8:34.0
1920	Great Britain	7:08.6
1928	Great Britain	6:36.0
1932	Great Britain	6:58.2
1936	Germany	7:01.8
1948	Italy	6:39.0
1952	Yugoslavia	7:16.0
1956	Canada	7:08.8
1960	United States	6:26.26
1964	Denmark	6:59.30
1968	East Germany	6:39.18
1972	East Germany	6:24.27
1976	East Germany	6:37.42
1980	East Germany	6:08.17
1984	New Zealand	6:03.48
1988	East Germany	6:03.11
1992	Australia	5:55.04
1996	Australia	6:06.37
2000	Great Britain	5:56.24
2004	Great Britain	6:06.98

FOURS (WITH COXSWAIN)

		MIN:SEC
1900	Germany	5:59.0
1912	Germany	6:59.4
1920	Switzerland	6:54.0
1924	Switzerland	7:18.4
1928	Italy	6:47.8
1932	Germany	7:19.0

Summer Olympic Games Champions (continued)

Rowing (men)[11] (continued)

FOURS (WITH COXSWAIN) (CONTINUED)

		MIN:SEC
1936	Germany	7:16.2
1948	United States	6:50.3
1952	Czechoslovakia	7:33.4
1956	Italy	7:19.4
1960	Germany	6:39.12
1964	Germany	7:00.44
1968	New Zealand	6:45.62
1972	West Germany	6:31.85
1976	USSR	6:40.22
1980	East Germany	6:14.51
1984	Great Britain	6:18.64
1988	East Germany	6:10.74
1992	Romania	5:59.37

FOURS, INRIGGERS (WITH COXSWAIN)

		MIN:SEC
1912	Denmark	7:47.0

EIGHTS (WITH COXSWAIN)

		MIN:SEC
1900	United States	6:09.8
1904	United States	7:50.0
1908	Great Britain	7:52.0
1912	Great Britain	6:15.0
1920	United States	6:02.6
1924	United States	6:33.4
1928	United States	6:03.2
1932	United States	6:37.6
1936	United States	6:25.4
1948	United States	5:56.7
1952	United States	6:25.9
1956	United States	6:35.2
1960	Germany	5:57.18
1964	United States	6:18.23
1968	West Germany	6:07.00
1972	New Zealand	6:08.94
1976	East Germany	5:58.29
1980	East Germany	5:49.05
1984	Canada	5:41.32
1988	West Germany	5:46.05
1992	Canada	5:29.53
1996	The Netherlands	5:42.74
2000	Great Britain	5:33.08
2004	United States	5:42.48

SIX-MAN NAVAL ROWING BOATS (2,000 METERS)

		MIN:SEC
1906	Italy	10:45.0

SIXTEEN-MAN NAVAL ROWING BOATS (3,000 METERS)

		MIN:SEC
1906	Greece	16:35.0

Rowing (women)[12]

SINGLE SCULLS

		MIN:SEC
1976	Christine Scheiblich (GDR)	4:05.56
1980	Sanda Toma (ROM)	3:40.69
1984	Valeria Racila (ROM)	3:40.68
1988	Jutta Behrendt (GDR)	7:47.19
1992	Elisabeta Lipa (ROM)	7:25.54
1996	Yekaterina Khodotovich (BLR)	7:32.21
2000	Yekaterina Khodotovich Karsten (BLR)	7:28.14
2004	Katrin Rutschow-Stomporowski (GER)	7:18.12

DOUBLE SCULLS

		MIN:SEC
1976	Bulgaria	3:44.36
1980	USSR	3:16.27

Rowing (women)[12] (continued)

DOUBLE SCULLS (CONTINUED)

		MIN:SEC
1984	Romania	3:26.75
1988	East Germany	7:00.48
1992	Germany	6:49.00
1996	Canada	6:56.84
2000	Germany	6:55.44
2004	New Zealand	7:01.79

LIGHTWEIGHT DOUBLE SCULLS

		MIN:SEC
1996	Romania	7:12.78
2000	Romania	7:02.64
2004	Romania	6:56.05

FOUR SCULLS

		MIN:SEC
1976	East Germany	3:29.99
1980	East Germany	3:15.32
1984	Romania	3:14.11
1988	East Germany	6:21.06
1992	Germany	6:20.18
1996	Germany	6:27.44
2000	Germany	6:19.58
2004	Germany	6:29.29

PAIRS (WITHOUT COXSWAIN)

		MIN:SEC
1976	Bulgaria	4:01.22
1980	East Germany	3:30.49
1984	Romania	3:32.60
1988	Romania	7:28.13
1992	Canada	7:06.22
1996	Australia	7:01.39
2000	Romania	7:11.00
2004	Romania	7:06.55

FOURS (WITH COXSWAIN [WITHOUT IN 1992])

		MIN:SEC
1976	East Germany	3:45.08
1980	East Germany	3:19.27
1984	Romania	3:19.3
1988	East Germany	6:56.0
1992	Canada	6:30.85

EIGHTS (WITH COXSWAIN)

		MIN:SEC
1976	East Germany	3:33.32
1980	East Germany	3:03.32
1984	United States	2:59.80
1988	East Germany	6:15.17
1992	Canada	6:02.62
1996	Romania	6:19.73
2000	Romania	6:06.44
2004	Romania	6:17.70

Rugby football

1900	France
1908	Australia
1920	United States
1924	United States

Sailing (yachting)

BOARDSAILING (WINDGLIDER/DIVISION II) (OPEN)

1984	Stephan van den Berg (NED)
1988	Anthony Bruce Kendall (NZL)

BOARDSAILING (MISTRAL FROM 1996) (MEN)

1992	Franck David (FRA)
1996	Nikolaos Kaklamanakis (GRE)
2000	Christoph Sieber (AUT)
2004	Gal Fridman (ISR)

Summer Olympic Games Champions (continued)

Sailing (yachting) (continued)

BOARDSAILING (MISTRAL FROM 1996) (WOMEN)
1992	Barbara Anne Kendall (NZL)
1996	Lee Lai Shan (HKG)
2000	Alessandra Sensini (ITA)
2004	Faustine Merret (FRA)

SINGLE-HANDED DINGHY (EUROPE) (WOMEN)
1992	Linda Andersen (NOR)
1996	Kristine Roug (DEN)
2000	Shirley Anne Robertson (GBR)
2004	Siren Sundby (NOR)

SINGLE-HANDED DINGHY (LASER) (OPEN)
1996	Robert Scheidt (BRA)
2000	Ben Ainslie (GBR)
2004	Robert Scheidt (BRA)

SINGLE-HANDED DINGHY (FINN FROM 1952)
(MEN; OPEN UNTIL 1992)
1924	Léon Huybrechts (BEL)
1928	Sven Thorell (SWE)
1932	Jacques Lebrun (FRA)
1936	Daniel Kagchelland (NED)
1948	Paul Elvström (DEN)
1952	Paul Elvström (DEN)
1956	Paul Elvström (DEN)
1960	Paul Elvström (DEN)
1964	Wilhelm Kuhweide (GER)
1968	Valentin Mankin (URS)
1972	Serge Maury (FRA)
1976	Jochen Schümann (GDR)
1980	Esko Rechardt (FIN)
1984	Russell Coutts (NZL)
1988	José Luis Doreste (ESP)
1992	José van der Ploeg (ESP)
1996	Mateusz Kusznierewicz (POL)
2000	Iain Percy (GBR)
2004	Ben Ainslie (GBR)

DOUBLE-HANDED DINGHY (470) (MEN)
1976	West Germany
1980	Brazil
1984	Spain
1988	France
1992	Spain
1996	Ukraine
2000	Australia
2004	United States

DOUBLE-HANDED DINGHY (470) (WOMEN)
1988	United States
1992	Spain
1996	Spain
2000	Australia
2004	Greece

YNGLING (WOMEN)
2004	Great Britain

HIGH-PERFORMANCE DINGHY (49ER) (OPEN)
2000	Finland
2004	Spain

MULTIHULL (TORNADO) (OPEN)
1976	Great Britain
1980	Brazil

Sailing (yachting) (continued)

MULTIHULL (TORNADO) (OPEN) (CONTINUED)
1984	New Zealand
1988	France
1992	France
1996	Spain
2000	Austria
2004	Austria

FLEET/MATCH RACE KEELBOAT (SOLING) (OPEN)
1972	United States
1976	Denmark
1980	Denmark
1984	United States
1988	East Germany
1992	Denmark
1996	Germany
2000	Denmark

TWO-PERSON KEELBOAT (STAR) (OPEN)
1932	United States
1936	Germany
1948	United States
1952	Italy
1956	United States
1960	USSR
1964	The Bahamas
1968	United States
1972	Australia
1980	USSR
1984	United States
1988	Great Britain
1992	United States
1996	Brazil
2000	United States
2004	Brazil

40-METER CLASS
1920	Sweden

30-METER CLASS
1920	Sweden

12-METER CLASS
1920 (old)	Norway
1920 (new)	Norway

OVER-10-METER CLASS
1900	France
1908	Great Britain
1912	Norway

10-METER CLASS
1900	Germany
1912	Sweden
1920 (old)	Norway
1920 (new)	Norway

8-METER CLASS
1900	Great Britain
1908	Great Britain
1912	Norway
1920 (old)	Norway
1920 (new)	Norway
1924	Norway
1928	France

Summer Olympic Games Champions (continued)

Sailing (yachting) (continued)

8-METER CLASS (CONTINUED)
1932	United States
1936	Italy

7-METER CLASS
1908	Great Britain
1920 (old)	Great Britain

6.5-METER CLASS
1920 (new)	The Netherlands

6-METER CLASS
1900	Switzerland
1908	Great Britain
1912	France
1920 (old)	Belgium
1920 (new)	Norway
1924	Norway
1928	Norway
1932	Sweden
1936	Great Britain
1948	United States
1952	United States

5.5-METER CLASS
1952	United States
1956	Sweden
1960	United States
1964	Australia
1968	Sweden

18-FOOT CENTERBOARD BOAT
1920	Great Britain

12-FOOT CENTERBOARD BOAT
1920	The Netherlands
1924	Belgium

12-FOOT DINGHY
1928	Sweden

MONOTYPE CLASS
1932	France

MONOTYPE CLASS "NURNBERG"
1936	The Netherlands

SWALLOW
1948	Great Britain

FIREFLY
1948	Denmark

SHARPIE
1956	New Zealand

DRAGON
1948	Norway
1952	Norway
1956	Sweden
1960	Greece
1964	Denmark
1968	United States
1972	Australia

Sailing (yachting) (continued)

TEMPEST
1972	USSR
1976	Sweden

FLYING DUTCHMAN
1960	Norway
1964	New Zealand
1968	Great Britain
1972	Great Britain
1976	West Germany
1980	Spain
1984	United States
1988	Denmark
1992	Spain

Shooting (men)

individual

TRAP (CLAY PIGEON) (OPEN 1968–92)
1900	Roger de Barbarin (FRA)
1908	Walter Ewing (CAN)
1912	James Graham (USA)
1920	Mark Arie (USA)
1924	Gyula Halasy (HUN)
1952	George Généreux (CAN)
1956	Galliano Rossini (ITA)
1960	Ion Dumitrescu (ROM)
1964	Ennio Mattarelli (ITA)
1968	John Braithwaite (GBR)
1972	Angelo Scalzone (ITA)
1976	Donald Haldeman (USA)
1980	Luciano Giovannetti (ITA)
1984	Luciano Giovannetti (ITA)
1988	Donald Monakov (URS)
1992	Petr Hrdlicka (TCH)
1996	Michael Constantine Diamond (AUS)
2000	Michael Constantine Diamond (AUS)
2004	Aleksey Alipov (RUS)

DOUBLE TRAP
1996	Russell Andrew Mark (AUS)
2000	Richard Faulds (GBR)
2004	Ahmed Almaktoum (UAE)

SKEET (OPEN UNTIL 1996)
1968	Yevgeny Petrov (URS)
1972	Konrad Wirnhier (FRG)
1976	Josef Panacek (TCH)
1980	Hans Kjeld Rasmussen (DEN)
1984	Matthew Dryke (USA)
1988	Axel Wegner (GDR)
1992	Zhang Shan (CHN)
1996	Ennio Falco (ITA)
2000	Mykola Milchev (UKR)
2004	Andrea Benelli (ITA)

FREE PISTOL
1896	Sumner Paine (USA)
1900	Karl Konrad Röderer (SUI)
1912	Alfred Lane (USA)
1920	Carl Frederick (USA)
1936	Torsten Ullmann (SWE)
1948	Edwin Vásquez Cam (PER)
1952	Huelet Benner (USA)
1956	Pentti Tapio Linnosvuo (FIN)
1960	Aleksey Gushchin (URS)
1964	Väinö Johannes Markkanen (FIN)
1968	Grigory Kosykh (URS)
1976	Uwe Potteck (GDR)

Summer Olympic Games Champions (continued)

Shooting (men) (continued)
Individual (continued)
FREE PISTOL (CONTINUED)
1980   Aleksandr Melentev (URS)
1984   Xu Haifeng (CHN)
1988   Sorin Babii (ROM)
1992   Konstantin Lukachik (UNT)
1996   Boris Kokorev (RUS)
2000   Tanyu Kiryakov (BUL)
2004   Mikhail Nestruyev (RUS)

RAPID-FIRE PISTOL
1896   Joannis Phrangudis (GRE)
1900   Maurice Larrouy (FRA)
1908   Paul van Asbrock (BEL)
1912   Alfred Lane (USA)
1920   Guilherme Paraense (BRA)
1924   Henry Bailey (USA)
1932   Renzo Morigi (ITA)
1936   Cornelius van Oyen (GER)
1948   Karoly Takacs (HUN)
1952   Karoly Takacs (HUN)
1956   Stefan Petrescu (ROM)
1960   William McMillan (USA)
1964   Pentti Tapio Linnosvuo (FIN)
1968   Jozef Zapedzki (POL)
1972   Jozef Zapedzki (POL)
1976   Norbert Klaar (GDR)
1980   Corneliu Ion (ROM)
1984   Takeo Kamachi (JPN)
1988   Afanasy Kuzmin (URS)
1992   Ralf Schumann (GER)
1996   Ralf Schumann (GER)
2000   Sergey Alifirenko (RUS)
2004   Ralf Schumann (GER)

SMALL-BORE RIFLE (PRONE)
1908   Arthur Ashton Carnell (GBR)
1912   Frederick Hird (USA)
1920   Lawrence Nuesslein (USA)
1924   Pierre Coquelin de Lisle (FRA)
1932   Bertil Rönnmark (SWE)
1936   Willy Røgeberg (NOR)
1948   Arthur Cook (USA)
1952   Iosif Sarbu (ROM)
1956   Gerald Ouellette (CAN)
1960   Peter Kohnke (GER)
1964   Laszlo Hammerl (HUN)
1968   Jan Kurka (TCH)
1972   Ho Jun Li (PRK)
1976   Karlheinz Smieszek (FRG)
1980   Karoly Varga (HUN)
1984   Edward Etzel (USA)
1988   Miroslav Varga (TCH)
1992   Lee Eun Chul (KOR)
1996   Christian Klees (GER)
2000   Jonas Edman (SWE)
2004   Matthew Emmons (USA)

SMALL-BORE RIFLE (3 POSITIONS)
1952   Erling Kongshaug (NOR)
1956   Anatoly Bogdanov (URS)
1960   Viktor Shamburkin (URS)
1964   Lones Wesley Wigger (USA)
1968   Bernd Klingner (FRG)
1972   John Writer (USA)
1976   Lanny Bassham (USA)

Shooting (men) (continued)
Individual (continued)
SMALL-BORE RIFLE (3 POSITIONS) (CONTINUED)
1980   Viktor Vlasov (URS)
1984   Malcolm Cooper (GBR)
1988   Malcolm Cooper (GBR)
1992   Gratchia Petikian (UNT)
1996   Jean-Pierre Amat (FRA)
2000   Rajmond Debevec (SLO)
2004   Jia Zhanbo (CHN)

10-METER RUNNING (GAME) TARGET
1900   Louis Debray (FRA)
1972   Yakov Zheleznyak (URS)
1976   Aleksandr Gazov (URS)
1980   Igor Sokolov (URS)
1984   Li Yuwei (CHN)
1988   Tor Heiestad (NOR)
1992   Michael Jakosits (GER)
1996   Yang Ling (CHN)
2000   Yang Ling (CHN)
2004   Manfred Kurzer (GER)

AIR RIFLE
1984   Philippe Heberle (FRA)
1988   Goran Maksimovic (YUG)
1992   Yury Fedkin (UNT)
1996   Artyom Khadzhibekov (RUS)
2000   Cai Yalin (CHN)
2004   Zhu Quinan (CHN)

AIR PISTOL
1988   Tanyu Kiryakov (BUL)
1992   Wang Yifu (CHN)
1996   Roberto di Donna (ITA)
2000   Franck Dumoulin (FRA)
2004   Wang Yifu (CHN)

FREE RIFLE (300 M, 3 POSITIONS)
1908   Albert Helgerud (NOR)
1912   Paul René Colas (FRA)
1920   Morris Fisher (USA)
1924   Morris Fisher (USA)
1948   Emil Grünig (SUI)
1952   Anatoly Bogdanov (URS)
1956   Vasily Borisov (URS)
1960   Hubert Hammerer (AUT)
1964   Gary Lee Anderson (USA)
1968   Gary Lee Anderson (USA)
1972   Lones Wesley Wigger (USA)

ARMY RIFLE (300 M, 3 POSITIONS)
1896   Georgios Orphanidis (GRE)
1900   Emil Kellenberger (SUI)
1912   Sandor Prokop (HUN)

ARMY RIFLE (200 M)
1896   Pantelis Karasevdas (GRE)

FREE RIFLE (1,000 YD PRONE)
1908   Joshua Millner (GBR)

FULL-BORE RIFLE (300 M STANDING)
1900   Lars Madsen (DEN)

FULL-BORE RIFLE (300 M KNEELING)
1900   Konrad Staeheli (SUI)

Summer Olympic Games Champions (continued)

Shooting (men) (continued)

individual (continued)

FULL-BORE RIFLE (300 M PRONE)
1900   Achille Paroche (FRA)

FULL-BORE RIFLE (300 M)
1900   Emil Kellenberger (SUI)

RIFLE (300 M, 2 POSITIONS)
1920   Morris Fisher (USA)

RIFLE (300 M STANDING)
1920   Carl Osburn (USA)

RIFLE (300 M PRONE)
1920   Otto Olsen (NOR)

RIFLE (600 M PRONE)
1920   Hugo Johansson (SWE)

6-MILLIMETER SMALL GUN (OPEN REAR SIGHT)
1900   C. Grosett (FRA)

SMALL-BORE RIFLE (VANISHING TARGET)
1908   William Styles (GBR)
1912   Wilhelm Carlberg (SWE)

SMALL-BORE RIFLE (MOVING TARGET)
1908   John Francis Fleming (GBR)

RUNNING DEER (100 M SINGLE SHOT)
1908   Oscar Swahn (SWE)
1912   Alfred Swahn (SWE)
1920   Otto Olsen (NOR)
1924   John Boles (USA)

RUNNING DEER (100 M DOUBLE SHOT)
1908   Walter Winans (USA)
1912   Ake Lundeberg (SWE)
1920   Ole Andreas Lilloe-Olsen (NOR)
1924   Ole Andreas Lilloe-Olsen (NOR)

RUNNING DEER (100 M SINGLE AND DOUBLE SHOT)
1952   John Larsen (NOR)
1956   Vitaly Romanenko (URS)

LIVE PIGEON
1900   Léon de Lunden (BEL)

GAME SHOOTING
1900   Donald Mackintosh (AUS)

MILITARY REVOLVER (25 M)
1896   John Paine (USA)

MILITARY REVOLVER (20 M)
1906   Louis Richardet (SUI)
1906   (model 1873–74) Jean Fouconnier (FRA)

REVOLVER AND PISTOL
1900   Paul van Asbrock (BEL)
1908   Paul van Asbrock (BEL)
1912   Alfred Lane (USA)

DUELING PISTOL
1906 (20 m)   Léon Moreaux (FRA)
1906 (25 m)   Konstantinos Skarlatos (GRE)
1912   Alfred Lane (USA)

Shooting (men) (continued)

team

FREE RIFLE (300 M)
1908   Norway
1912   Sweden

ARMY RIFLE (300 M)
1900   Norway

ARMY RIFLE (ALL-AROUND)
1900   United States
1908   United States
1912   United States

FULL-BORE RIFLE (300 M)
1900   Switzerland

SMALL-BORE RIFLE
1900   Great Britain
1908   Great Britain
1920   United States
1924   France

SMALL-BORE RIFLE (VANISHING TARGET)
1912   Sweden

RIFLE (600 M PRONE)
1920   United States

RIFLE (300 M, 2 POSITIONS)
1920   United States

RIFLE (300 M STANDING)
1920   Denmark

RIFLE (300 M PRONE)
1920   United States

RIFLE (ALL-AROUND)
1920   United States
1924   United States

RUNNING DEER (SINGLE SHOT)
1908   Sweden
1912   Sweden
1920   Norway
1924   Norway

RUNNING DEER (DOUBLE SHOT)
1920   Norway
1924   Great Britain

CLAY PIGEON
1900   Great Britain
1908   Great Britain
1912   United States
1920   United States
1924   United States

REVOLVER
1900   Switzerland

PISTOL
1920   United States
1924   United States

REVOLVER AND PISTOL
1900   United States
1908   United States

Summer Olympic Games Champions (continued)

Shooting (men) (continued)

team (continued)

REVOLVER AND PISTOL (CONTINUED)
1912 United States
1920 United States

DUELING PISTOL
1912 Sweden

Shooting (women)

TRAP (CLAY PIGEON)
2000 Daina Gudzineviciute (LTU)
2004 Suzanne Balogh (AUS)

DOUBLE TRAP
1996 Kim Rhode (USA)
2000 Pia Hansen (SWE)
2004 Kimberly Rhode (USA)

SKEET
2000 Zemfira Meftakhetdinova (AZE)
2004 Diana Igaly (HUN)

SPORT PISTOL
1984 Linda Thom (CAN)
1988 Nino Salukvadze (URS)
1992 Marina Logvinenko (UNT)
1996 Li Duihong (CHN)
2000 Mariya Zdravkova Grozdeva (BUL)
2004 Mariya Zdravkova Grozdeva (BUL)

SMALL-BORE RIFLE (3 POSITIONS)
1984 Wu Xiao-Xuan (CHN)
1988 Silvia Sperber (FRG)
1992 Launi Meili (USA)
1996 Aleksandra Ivosev (YUG)
2000 Renata Mauer (POL)
2004 Lyubov Galkina (RUS)

AIR RIFLE
1984 Pat Spurgin (USA)
1988 Irina Chilova (URS)
1992 Yeo Kab Soon (KOR)
1996 Renata Mauer (POL)
2000 Nancy Johnson (USA)
2004 Du Li (CHN)

AIR PISTOL
1988 Jasna Sekaric (YUG)
1992 Marina Logvinenko (UNT)
1996 Olga Klochneva (RUS)
2000 Tao Luna (CHN)
2004 Olena Kostevych (UKR)

Softball
1996 United States
2000 United States
2004 United States

Swimming (men)

50-METER FREESTYLE		SEC
1988	Matthew Biondi (USA)	22.14
1992	Aleksandr Popov (UNT)	21.91
1996	Aleksandr Popov (RUS)	22.13 ·
2000	Anthony Ervin (USA); Gary Hall, Jr. (USA) (tied)	21.98
2004	Gary Hall (USA)	21.93

Swimming (men) (continued)

100-METER FREESTYLE		MIN:SEC
1896	Alfred Hajos (HUN)	1:22.2
1904	Zoltan Halmay (HUN)	1:02.8[13]
1908	Charles Daniels (USA)	1:05.6
1912	Duke Paoa Kahanamoku (USA)	1:03.4
1920	Duke Paoa Kahanamoku (USA)	1:00.4
1924	Johnny Weissmuller (USA)	59.0
1928	Johnny Weissmuller (USA)	58.6
1932	Yasuji Miyazaki (JPN)	58.2
1936	Ferenc Csik (HUN)	57.6
1948	Walter Ris (USA)	57.3
1952	Clark Scholes (USA)	57.4
1956	Jon Henricks (AUS)	55.4
1960	John Devitt (AUS)	55.2
1964	Donald Schollander (USA)	53.4
1968	Michael Wenden (AUS)	52.2
1972	Mark Spitz (USA)	51.22
1976	Jim Montgomery (USA)	49.99
1980	Jörg Wöithe (GDR)	50.40
1984	Ambrose Gaines (USA)	49.80
1988	Matthew Biondi (USA)	48.63
1992	Aleksandr Popov (UNT)	49.02
1996	Aleksandr Popov (RUS)	48.74
2000	Pieter Van den Hoogenband (NED)	48.30
2004	Pieter Van den Hoogenband (NED)	48.17

100 METER FREESTYLE FOR SAILORS		MIN:SEC
1896	Ioannis Malokinis (GRE)	2:20.4

200-METER FREESTYLE		MIN:SEC
1900	Fred Lane (AUS)	2:25.2
1904	Charles Daniels (USA)	2:44.2[14]
1968	Michael Wenden (AUS)	1:55.2
1972	Mark Spitz (USA)	1:52.78
1976	Bruce Furniss (USA)	1:50.29
1980	Sergey Koplyakov (URS)	1:49.81
1984	Michael Gross (FRG)	1:47.44
1988	Duncan Armstrong (AUS)	1:47.25
1992	Yevgeny Sadovy (UNT)	1:46.70
1996	Danyon Loader (NZL)	1:47.63
2000	Pieter Van den Hoogenband (NED)	1:45.35
2004	Ian Thorpe (AUS)	1:44.71

400-METER FREESTYLE		MIN:SEC
1896	Paul Neumann (AUT)	8:12.6[15]
1904	Charles Daniels (USA)	6:16.2[16]
1908	Henry Taylor (GBR)	5:36.8
1912	George Hodgson (CAN)	5:24.4
1920	Norman Ross (USA)	5:26.8
1924	Johnny Weissmuller (USA)	5:04.2
1928	Victoriano Zorilla (ARG)	5:01.6
1932	Clarence Crabbe (USA)	4:48.4
1936	Jack Medica (USA)	4:44.5
1948	William Smith (USA)	4:41.0
1952	Jean Boiteux (FRA)	4:30.7
1956	Murray Rose (AUS)	4:27.3
1960	Murray Rose (AUS)	4:18.3
1964	Donald Schollander (USA)	4:12.2
1968	Michael Burton (USA)	4:09.0
1972	Bradford Cooper (AUS)	4:00.27
1976	Brian Goodell (USA)	3:51.93
1980	Vladimir Salnikov (URS)	3:51.31
1984	George DiCarlo (USA)	3:51.23
1988	Uwe Dassler (GDR)	3:46.95
1992	Yevgeny Sadovy (UNT)	3:45.00

Summer Olympic Games Champions (continued)

Swimming (men) (continued)

400-METER FREESTYLE (CONTINUED)

		MIN:SEC
1996	Danyon Loader (NZL)	3:47.97
2000	Ian Thorpe (AUS)	3:40.59
2004	Ian Thorpe (AUS)	3:43.10

1,500-METER FREESTYLE

		MIN:SEC
1896	Alfred Hajos (HUN)	18:22.2[17]
1900	Johnny Arthur Jarvis (GBR)	13:40.2[18]
1904	Emil Rausch (GER)	27:18.2[19]
1908	Henry Taylor (GBR)	22:48.4
1912	George Hodgson (CAN)	22:00.0
1920	Norman Ross (USA)	23:23.2
1924	Andrew Charlton (AUS)	20:06.6
1928	Arne Borg (SWE)	19:51.8
1932	Kusuo Kitamura (JPN)	19:12.4
1936	Noboru Terada (JPN)	19:13.7
1948	James McLane (USA)	19:18.5
1952	Ford Konno (USA)	18:30.0
1956	Murray Rose (AUS)	17:58.9
1960	John Konrads (AUS)	17:19.6
1964	Robert Windle (AUS)	17:01.7
1968	Michael Burton (USA)	16:38.9
1972	Michael Burton (USA)	15:52.58
1976	Brian Goodell (USA)	15:02.40
1980	Vladimir Salnikov (URS)	14:58.27
1984	Michael O'Brien (USA)	15:05.20
1988	Vladimir Salnikov (URS)	15:00.40
1992	Kieren Perkins (AUS)	14:43.48
1996	Kieren Perkins (AUS)	14:56.40
2000	Grant Hackett (AUS)	14:48.33
2004	Grant Hackett (AUS)	14:43.40

4,000-METER FREESTYLE

		MIN:SEC
1900	Johnny Arthur Jarvis (GBR)	58:24

880-YARD FREESTYLE

		MIN:SEC
1904	Emil Rausch (GER)	13:11.4

1-MILE FREESTYLE

		MIN:SEC
1904	Emil Rausch (GER)	27:18.2

100-METER BUTTERFLY

		SEC
1968	Douglas Russell (USA)	55.9
1972	Mark Spitz (USA)	54.27
1976	Matt Vogel (USA)	54.35
1980	Pär Arvidsson (SWE)	54.92
1984	Michael Gross (FRG)	53.08
1988	Anthony Nesty (SUR)	53.00
1992	Pablo Morales (USA)	53.32
1996	Denis Pankratov (RUS)	52.27
2000	Lars Frölander (SWE)	52.00
2004	Michael Phelps (USA)	51.25

200-METER BUTTERFLY

		MIN
1956	William Yorzyk (USA)	2:19.3
1960	Michael Troy (USA)	2:12.8
1964	Kevin Berry (AUS)	2:06.6
1968	Carl Robie (USA)	2:08.7
1972	Mark Spitz (USA)	2:00.70
1976	Mike Bruner (USA)	1:59.23
1980	Sergey Fesenko (URS)	1:59.76
1984	Jonathan Sieben (AUS)	1:57.04
1988	Michael Gross (FRG)	1:56.94
1992	Mel Stewart (USA)	1:56.26
1996	Denis Pankratov (RUS)	1:56.51
2000	Tom Malchow (USA)	1:55.35
2004	Michael Phelps (USA)	1:54.04

Swimming (men) (continued)

100-METER BACKSTROKE

		MIN:SEC
1904	Walter Brack (GER)	1:16.8[20]
1908	Arno Bieberstein (GER)	1:24.6
1912	Harry Hebner (USA)	1:21.2
1920	Warren Paoa Kealoha (USA)	1:15.2
1924	Warren Paoa Kealoha (USA)	1:13.2
1928	George Kojac (USA)	1:08.2
1932	Masaji Kiyokawa (JPN)	1:08.6
1936	Adolph Kiefer (USA)	1:05.9
1948	Allen Stack (USA)	1:06.4
1952	Yoshinobu Oyakawa (JPN)	1:05.4
1956	David Theile (AUS)	1:02.2
1960	David Theile (AUS)	1:01.9
1968	Roland Matthes (GDR)	58.7
1972	Roland Matthes (GDR)	56.58
1976	John Naber (USA)	55.49
1980	Bengt Baron (SWE)	56.53
1984	Richard Carey (USA)	55.79
1988	Daichi Suzuki (JPN)	55.05
1992	Mark Tewksbury (CAN)	53.98
1996	Jeff Rouse (USA)	54.10
2000	Lenny Krayzelburg (USA)	53.72
2004	Aaron Peirsol (USA)	54.06

200-METER BACKSTROKE

		MIN:SEC
1900	Ernst Hoppenberg (GER)	2:47.0
1964	Jed Graef (USA)	2:10.3
1968	Roland Matthes (GDR)	2:09.6
1972	Roland Matthes (GDR)	2:02.82
1976	John Naber (USA)	1:59.19
1980	Sandor Wladar (HUN)	2:01.93
1984	Richard Carey (USA)	2:00.23
1988	Igor Polyansky (URS)	1:59.37
1992	Martin López-Zubero (ESP)	1:58.47
1996	Brad Bridgewater (USA)	1:58.54
2000	Lenny Krayzelburg (USA)	1:56.76
2004	Aaron Peirsol (USA)	1:54.95

100-METER BREASTSTROKE

		MIN:SEC
1968	Donald McKenzie (USA)	1:07.7
1972	Nobutaka Tagushi (JPN)	1:04.94
1976	John Hencken (USA)	1:03.11
1980	Duncan Goodhew (GBR)	1:03.34
1984	Steve Lundquist (USA)	1:01.65
1988	Adrian Moorhouse (GBR)	1:02.04
1992	Nelson Diebel (USA)	1:01.50
1996	Frederick Deburghgraeve (BEL)	1:00.65
2000	Domenico Fioravanti (ITA)	1:00.46
2004	Kosuke Kitajima (JPN)	1:00.08

200-METER BREASTSTROKE

		MIN:SEC
1908	Frederick Holman (GBR)	3:09.2
1912	Walter Bathe (GER)	3:01.8
1920	Hakan Malmroth (SWE)	3:04.4
1924	Robert Skelton (USA)	2:56.6
1928	Yoshiyuki Tsuruta (JPN)	2:48.8
1932	Yoshiyuki Tsuruta (JPN)	2:45.4
1936	Tetsuo Hamuro (JPN)	2:42.5
1948	Joseph Verdeur (USA)	2:39.3
1952	John Davies (AUS)	2:34.4
1956	Masaru Furukawa (JPN)	2:34.7
1960	William Mulliken (USA)	2:37.4
1964	Ian O'Brien (AUS)	2:27.8
1968	Felipe Muñoz (MEX)	2:28.7
1972	John Hencken (USA)	2:21.55
1976	David Wilkie (GBR)	2:15.11
1980	Robertas Zulpa (URS)	2:15.85
1984	Victor Davis (CAN)	2:13.34

Summer Olympic Games Champions (continued)

Swimming (men) (continued)

200-METER BREASTSTROKE (CONTINUED)		MIN:SEC
1988	Jozsef Szabo (HUN)	2:13.52
1992	Mike Barrowman (USA)	2:10.16
1996	Norbert Rozsa (HUN)	2:12.57
2000	Domenico Fioravanti (ITA)	2:10.87
2004	Kosuke Kitajima (JPN)	2:09.44

400-METER BREASTSTROKE		MIN:SEC
1904	Georg Zacharias (GER)	7:23.6[21]
1912	Walter Bathe (GER)	6:29.6
1920	Hakan Malmroth (SWE)	6:31.8

200-YARD RELAY		MIN:SEC
1904	United States	2:04.6

200-METER MEDLEY		MIN:SEC
1968	Charles Hickcox (USA)	2:12.0
1972	Gunnar Larsson (SWE)	2:07.17
1984	Alex Baumann (CAN)	2:01.42
1988	Tamas Darnyi (HUN)	2:00.17
1992	Tamas Darnyi (HUN)	2:00.76
1996	Attila Czene (HUN)	1:59.91
2000	Massimiliano Rosolino (ITA)	1:58.98
2004	Michael Phelps (USA)	1:57.14

400-METER MEDLEY		MIN:SEC
1964	Richard William Roth (USA)	4:45.4
1968	Charles Hickcox (USA)	4:48.4
1972	Gunnar Larsson (SWE)	4:31.98
1976	Rod Strachan (USA)	4:23.68
1980	Aleksandr Sidorenko (URS)	4:22.89
1984	Alex Baumann (CAN)	4:17.41
1988	Tamas Darnyi (HUN)	4:14.75
1992	Tamas Darnyi (HUN)	4:14.23
1996	Tom Dolan (USA)	4:14.90
2000	Tom Dolan (USA)	4:11.76
2004	Michael Phelps (USA)	4:08.26

4 × 100-METER MEDLEY RELAY		MIN:SEC
1960	United States	4:05.4
1964	United States	3:58.4
1968	United States	3:54.9
1972	United States	3:48.16
1976	United States	3:42.22
1980	Australia	3:45.70
1984	United States	3:39.30
1988	United States	3:36.93
1992	United States	3:36.93
1996	United States	3:34.84
2000	United States	3:33.73
2004	United States	3:30.68

4 × 100-METER FREESTYLE RELAY		MIN:SEC
1964	United States	3:33.2
1968	United States	3:31.7
1972	United States	3:26.42
1984	United States	3:19.03
1988	United States	3:16.53
1992	United States	3:16.74
1996	United States	3:15.41
2000	Australia	3:13.67
2004	South Africa	3:13.17

4 × 200-METER FREESTYLE RELAY		MIN:SEC
1908	Great Britain	10:55.6
1912	Australia	10:11.2
1920	United States	10:04.4
1924	United States	9:53.4

Swimming (men) (continued)

4 × 200-METER FREESTYLE RELAY (CONTINUED)		MIN:SEC
1928	United States	9:36.2
1932	Japan	8:58.4
1936	Japan	8:51.5
1948	United States	8:46.0
1952	United States	8:31.1
1956	Australia	8:23.6
1960	United States	8:10.2
1964	United States	7:52.1
1968	United States	7:52.3
1972	United States	7:35.78
1976	United States	7:23.22
1980	USSR	7:23.50
1984	United States	7:15.69
1988	United States	7:12.51
1992	Unified Team	7:11.95
1996	United States	7:14.84
2000	Australia	7:07.05
2004	United States	7:07.33

60-METER UNDERWATER		MIN:SEC (UNDERWATER)
1900	Charles de Vendeville (FRA)	1:08.4

200-METER OBSTACLE		MIN:SEC
1900	Frederick Lane (AUS)	2:38.4

Swimming (women)

50-METER FREESTYLE		SEC
1988	Kristin Otto (GDR)	25.49
1992	Yang Wenyi (CHN)	24.79
1996	Amy Van Dyken (USA)	24.87
2000	Inge de Bruijn (NED)	24.32
2004	Inge de Bruijn (NED)	24.58

100-METER FREESTYLE		MIN:SEC
1912	Fanny Durack (AUS)	1:22.2
1920	Ethelda Bleibtrey (USA)	1:13.6
1924	Ethel Lackie (USA)	1:12.4
1928	Albina Osipowich (USA)	1:11.0
1932	Helene Madison (USA)	1:06.8
1936	Hendrika Mastenbroek (NED)	1:05.9
1948	Greta Andersen (DEN)	1:06.3
1952	Katalin Szoke (HUN)	1:06.8
1956	Dawn Fraser (AUS)	1:02.0
1960	Dawn Fraser (AUS)	1:01.2
1964	Dawn Fraser (AUS)	59.5
1968	Jan Henne (USA)	1:00.0
1972	Sandra Neilson (USA)	58.59
1976	Kornelia Ender (GDR)	55.65
1980	Barbara Krause (GDR)	54.79
1984	Carrie Steinseifer (USA); Nancy Hogshead (USA) (tied)	55.92
1988	Kristin Otto (GDR)	54.93
1992	Zhuang Yong (CHN)	54.64
1996	Le Jingyi (CHN)	54.50
2000	Inge de Bruijn (NED)	53.83
2004	Jodie Henry (AUS)	53.84

200-METER FREESTYLE		MIN:SEC
1968	Debbie Meyer (USA)	2:10.5
1972	Shane Gould (AUS)	2:03.56
1976	Kornelia Ender (GDR)	1:59.26
1980	Barbara Krause (GDR)	1:58.33
1984	Mary Wayte (USA)	1:59.23
1988	Heike Friedrich (GDR)	1:57.65
1992	Nicole Haislett (USA)	1:57.90
1996	Claudia Poll (CRC)	1:58.16

Summer Olympic Games Champions (continued)

Swimming (women) (continued)

200-METER FREESTYLE (CONTINUED)	MIN:SEC
2000 Susie O'Neill (AUS)	1:58.24
2004 Camelia Potec (ROM)	1:58.03

400-METER FREESTYLE	MIN:SEC
1920 Ethelda Bleibtrey (USA)	4:34.0²²
1924 Martha Norelius (USA)	6:02.2
1928 Martha Norelius (USA)	5:42.8
1932 Helene Madison (USA)	5:28.5
1936 Hendrika Mastenbroek (NED)	5:26.4
1948 Ann Curtis (USA)	5:17.8
1952 Valeria Gyenge (HUN)	5:12.1
1956 Lorraine Crapp (AUS)	4:54.6
1960 Susan Christina von Saltza (USA)	4:50.6
1964 Virginia Duenkel (USA)	4:43.3
1968 Debbie Meyer (USA)	4:31.8
1972 Shane Gould (AUS)	4:19.04
1976 Petra Thümer (GDR)	4:09.89
1980 Ines Diers (GDR)	4:08.76
1984 Tiffany Cohen (USA)	4:07.10
1988 Janet Evans (USA)	4:03.85
1992 Dagmar Hase (GER)	4:07.18
1996 Michelle Smith (IRE)	4:07.25
2000 Brooke Bennett (USA)	4:05.80
2004 Laure Manaudou (FRA)	4:05.34

800-METER FREESTYLE	MIN:SEC
1968 Debbie Meyer (USA)	9:24.0
1972 Keena Rothhammer (USA)	8:53.68
1976 Petra Thümer (GDR)	8:37.14
1980 Michelle Ford (AUS)	8:28.90
1984 Tiffany Cohen (USA)	8:24.95
1988 Janet Evans (USA)	8:20.20
1992 Janet Evans (USA)	8:25.52
1996 Brooke Bennett (USA)	8:27.89
2000 Brooke Bennett (USA)	8:19.67
2004 Ai Shibata (JPN)	8:24.54

100-METER BUTTERFLY	MIN:SEC
1956 Shelley Mann (USA)	1:11.0
1960 Carolyn Schuler (USA)	1:09.5
1964 Sharon Stouder (USA)	1:04.7
1968 Lynette McClements (AUS)	1:05.5
1972 Mayumi Aoki (JPN)	1:03.34
1976 Kornelia Ender (GDR)	1:00.13
1980 Caren Metschuck (GDR)	1:00.42
1984 Mary Meagher (USA)	59.26
1988 Kristin Otto (GDR)	59.00
1992 Qian Hong (CHN)	58.62
1996 Amy Van Dyken (USA)	59.13
2000 Inge de Bruijn (NED)	56.61
2004 Petria Thomas (AUS)	57.72

200-METER BUTTERFLY	MIN:SEC
1968 Aagje Kok (NED)	2:24.7
1972 Karen Moe (USA)	2:15.57
1976 Andrea Pollack (GDR)	2:11.41
1980 Ines Geissler (GDR)	2:10.44
1984 Mary Meagher (USA)	2:06.90
1988 Kathleen Nord (GDR)	2:09.51
1992 Summer Sanders (USA)	2:08.67
1996 Susie O'Neill (AUS)	2:07.76
2000 Misty Hyman (USA)	2:05.88
2004 Otylia Jedrzejczak (POL)	2:06.05

Swimming (women) (continued)

100-METER BACKSTROKE	MIN:SEC
1924 Sybil Bauer (USA)	1:23.2
1928 Maria Braun (NED)	1:22.0
1932 Eleanor Holm (USA)	1:19.4
1936 Dina Senff (NED)	1:18.9
1948 Karen-Margrete Harup (DEN)	1:14.4
1952 Joan Harrison (RSA)	1:14.3
1956 Judith Grinham (GBR)	1:12.9
1960 Lynn Burke (USA)	1:09.3
1964 Cathy Ferguson (USA)	1:07.7
1968 Kaye Hall (USA)	1:06.2
1972 Melissa Belote (USA)	1:05.78
1976 Urike Richter (GDR)	1:01.83
1980 Rica Reinisch (GDR)	1:00.86
1984 Theresa Andrews (USA)	1:02.55
1988 Kristin Otto (GDR)	1:00.89
1992 Krisztina Egerszegi (HUN)	1:00.68
1996 Beth Botsford (USA)	1:01.19
2000 Diana Mocanu (ROM)	1:00.21
2004 Natalie Coughlin (USA)	1:00.37

200-METER BACKSTROKE	MIN:SEC
1968 Pokey Watson (USA)	2:24.8
1972 Melissa Belote (USA)	2:19.19
1976 Ulrike Richter (GDR)	2:13.43
1980 Rica Reinisch (GDR)	2:11.77
1984 Jolanda De Rover (NED)	2:12.38
1988 Krisztina Egerszegi (HUN)	2:09.29
1992 Krisztina Egerszegi (HUN)	2:07.06
1996 Krisztina Egerszegi (HUN)	2:07.83
2000 Diana Mocanu (ROM)	2:08.16
2004 Kirsty Coventry (ZIM)	2:09.19

100-METER BREASTSTROKE	MIN:SEC
1968 Djurdjica Bjedov (YUG)	1:15.8
1972 Cathy Carr (USA)	1:13.58
1976 Hannelore Anke (GDR)	1:11.16
1980 Ute Geweniger (GDR)	1:10.22
1984 Petra van Staveren (NED)	1:09.88
1988 Tanya Dangalakova (BUL)	1:07.95
1992 Yelena Rudkovskaya (UNT)	1:08.00
1996 Penelope Heyns (RSA)	1:07.73
2000 Megan Quann (USA)	1:07.05
2004 Luo Xuejuan (CHN)	1:06.64

200-METER BREASTSTROKE	MIN:SEC
1924 Lucy Morton (GBR)	3:33.2
1928 Hilde Schrader (GER)	3:12.6
1932 Claire Dennis (AUS)	3:06.3
1936 Hideko Maehata (JPN)	3:03.6
1948 Petronella van Vliet (NED)	2:57.2
1952 Eva Szekely (HUN)	2:51.7
1956 Ursula Happe (GER)	2:53.1
1960 Anita Lonsbrough (GBR)	2:49.5
1964 Galina Prozumenshchikova-Stepanova (URS)	2:46.4
1968 Sharon Wichman (USA)	2:44.4
1972 Beverley Whitfield (AUS)	2:41.71
1976 Marina Koshevaya (URS)	2:33.35
1980 Lina Kachushite (URS)	2:29.54
1984 Anne Ottenbrite (CAN)	2:30.38
1988 Silke Hörner (GDR)	2:26.71
1992 Kyoko Iwasaki (JPN)	2:26.65
1996 Penelope Heyns (RSA)	2:25.41
2000 Agnes Kovacs (HUN)	2:24.35
2004 Amanda Beard (USA)	2:23.37

Summer Olympic Games Champions (continued)

Swimming (women) (continued)

200-METER MEDLEY

		MIN:SEC
1968	Claudia Kolb (USA)	2:24.7
1972	Shane Gould (AUS)	2:23.07
1984	Tracy Caulkins (USA)	2:12.64
1988	Daniela Hunger (GDR)	2:12.59
1992	Li Lin (CHN)	2:11.65
1996	Michelle Smith (IRE)	2:13.93
2000	Yana Klochkova (UKR)	2:10.68
2004	Yana Klochkova (UKR)	2:11.14

400-METER MEDLEY

		MIN:SEC
1964	Donna De Varona (USA)	5:18.7
1968	Claudia Kolb (USA)	5:08.5
1972	Gail Neall (AUS)	5:02.97
1976	Ulrike Tauber (GDR)	4:42.77
1980	Petra Schneider (GDR)	4:36.29
1984	Tracy Caulkins (USA)	4:39.24
1988	Janet Evans (USA)	4:37.76
1992	Krisztina Egerszegi (HUN)	4:36.54
1996	Michelle Smith (IRE)	4:39.18
2000	Yana Klochkova (UKR)	4:33.59
2004	Yana Klochkova (UKR)	4:34.83

4 × 100-METER MEDLEY RELAY

		MIN:SEC
1960	United States	4:41.1
1964	United States	4:33.9
1968	United States	4:28.3
1972	United States	4:20.75
1976	East Germany	4:07.95
1980	East Germany	4:06.67
1984	United States	4:08.34
1988	East Germany	4:03.74
1992	United States	4:02.54
1996	United States	4:02.88
2000	United States	3:58.30
2004	Australia	3:57.32

4 × 100-METER FREESTYLE RELAY

		MIN:SEC
1912	Great Britain	5:52.8
1920	United States	5:11.6
1924	United States	4:58.8
1928	United States	4:47.6
1932	United States	4:38.0
1936	The Netherlands	4:36.0
1948	United States	4:29.2
1952	Hungary	4:24.4
1956	Australia	4:17.1
1960	United States	4:08.9
1964	United States	4:03.8
1968	United States	4:02.5
1972	United States	3:55.19
1976	United States	3:44.82
1980	East Germany	3:42.71
1984	United States	3:43.43
1988	East Germany	3:40.63
1992	United States	3:39.46
1996	United States	3:39.29
2000	United States	3:36.61
2004	Australia	3:35.94

4 × 200-METER FREESTYLE RELAY

		MIN:SEC
1996	United States	7:59.87
2000	United States	7:57.80
2004	United States	7:53.42

Swimming (women) (continued)

SYNCHRONIZED SWIMMING (INDIVIDUAL)

1984	Tracie Ruiz (USA)
1988	Carolyn Waldo (CAN)
1992	Kristen Babb-Sprague (USA); Sylvie Fréchette (CAN)[23]

SYNCHRONIZED SWIMMING (DUET)

1984	United States
1988	Canada
1992	United States
2000	Russia
2004	Russia

SYNCHRONIZED SWIMMING (TEAM)

1996	United States
2000	Russia
2004	Russia

Table tennis (men)

SINGLES

1988	Yoo Nam Kyu (KOR)
1992	Jan-Ove Waldner (SWE)
1996	Liu Guoliang (CHN)
2000	Kong Linghui (CHN)
2004	Ryu Seung Min (KOR)

DOUBLES

1988	China
1992	China
1996	China
2000	China
2004	China

Table tennis (women)

SINGLES

1988	Chen Jing (CHN)
1992	Deng Yaping (CHN)
1996	Deng Yaping (CHN)
2000	Wang Nan (CHN)
2004	Zhang Yining (CHN)

DOUBLES

1988	South Korea
1992	China
1996	China
2000	China
2004	China

Taekwondo (men)

58 KG (127.6 LB)

2000	Michail Mouroutsos (GRE)
2004	Chu Mu Yen (TPE)

68 KG (149.6 LB)

2000	Steven Lopez (USA)
2004	Hadi Saei Bonehkohal (IRI)

80 KG (176 LB)

2000	Angel Valodia Matos (CUB)
2004	Steven Lopez (USA)

OVER 80 KG (176+ LB)

2000	Kim Kyong-Hun (KOR)
2004	Moon Sung Dae (KOR)

Summer Olympic Games Champions (continued)

Taekwondo (women)

49 KG (107.8 LB)
2000 Lauren Burns (AUS)
2004 Chen Shih Hsin (TPE)

57 KG (125.4 LB)
2000 Jung Jae-Eun (KOR)
2004 Jang Ji Won (KOR)

67 KG (147.4 LB)
2000 Lee Sun-Hee (KOR)
2004 Luo Wei (CHN)

OVER 67 KG (147.4+ LB)
2000 Chen Zhong (CHN)
2004 Chen Zhong (CHN)

Tennis (men)

SINGLES
1896 John Pius Boland (GBR)
1900 Hugh (Laurie) Doherty (GBR)
1904 Beals Wright (USA)
1908 Josiah Ritchie (GBR)
1912 Charles Winslow (RSA)
1920 Louis Raymond (RSA)
1924 Vincent Richards (USA)
1988 Miloslav Mecir (TCH)
1992 Marc Rosset (SUI)
1996 Andre Agassi (USA)
2000 Yevgeny Kafelnikov (RUS)
2004 Nicolas Massu (CHI)

DOUBLES
1896 John Pius Boland (GBR), Friedrich Thraun (GER)
1900 Hugh (Laurie) Doherty, Reginald Doherty (GBR)
1904 Edgar Leonard, Beals Wright (USA)
1908 George Hillyard, Reginald Doherty (GBR)
1912 Harold Kitson, Charles Winslow (RSA)
1920 Oswald Noel Turnbull, Maxwell Woosnam (GBR)
1924 Francis Hunter, Vincent Richards (USA)
1988 Kenneth Flach, Robert Seguso (USA)
1992 Boris Becker, Michael Stich (GER)
1996 Todd Woodbridge, Mark Woodforde (AUS)
2000 Sebastien Lareau, Daniel Nestor (CAN)
2004 Fernando Gonzalez, Nicolas Massu (CHI)

MIXED DOUBLES
1900 Charlotte Cooper, Reginald Doherty (GBR)
1912 Dora Köring, Heinrich Schomburgk (GER)
1920 Suzanne Lenglen, Max Décugis (FRA)
1924 Hazel Wightman, R. Norris Williams (USA)

Tennis (women)

SINGLES
1900 Charlotte Cooper (GBR)
1908 Dorothy Chambers-Lambert (GBR)
1912 Marguerite Broquedis (FRA)
1920 Suzanne Lenglen (FRA)
1924 Helen Wills-Moody (USA)
1988 Steffi Graf (FRG)
1992 Jennifer Capriati (USA)
1996 Lindsay Davenport (USA)
2000 Venus Williams (USA)
2004 Justine Henin-Hardenne (BEL)

Tennis (women) (continued)

DOUBLES
1920 Winifred Margaret McNair, Kathleen McKane (GBR)
1924 Helen Wills-Moody, Hazel Wightman (USA)
1988 Zina Garrison, Pamela Shriver (USA)
1992 Gigi Fernandez, Mary Joe Fernandez (USA)
1996 Gigi Fernandez, Mary Joe Fernandez (USA)
2000 Serena Williams, Venus Williams (USA)
2004 Li Ting, Sun Tian Tian (CHN)

Tennis—Covered Courts (indoor tennis)

MEN'S SINGLES
1908 Arthur Gore (GBR)
1912 André Gobert (FRA)

MEN'S DOUBLES
1908 Arthur Gore, Herbert Roper-Barrett (GBR)
1912 Maurice Germot, André Gobert (FRA)

WOMEN'S SINGLES
1908 Gladys Eastlake-Smith (GBR)
1912 Edith Hannam (GBR)

MIXED DOUBLES
1912 Edith Hannam, Charles Dixon (GBR)

Triathlon (swim/bike/run) (men)
2000 Simon Whitfield (CAN)
2004 Hamish Carter (NZL)

Triathlon (swim/bike/run) (women)
2000 Brigitte McMahon (SUI)
2004 Kate Allen (AUT)

Volleyball (men)

INDOOR
1964 USSR
1968 USSR
1972 Japan
1976 Poland
1980 USSR
1984 United States
1988 United States
1992 Brazil
1996 The Netherlands
2000 Yugoslavia
2004 Brazil

BEACH
1996 United States
2000 United States
2004 Brazil

Volleyball (women)

INDOOR
1964 Japan
1968 USSR
1972 USSR
1976 Japan
1980 USSR
1984 China
1988 USSR
1992 Cuba
1996 Cuba
2000 Cuba
2004 China

Summer Olympic Games Champions (continued)

Volleyball (women) (continued)

BEACH

1996	Brazil
2000	Australia
2004	United States

Water polo (men)

1900	Great Britain
1904	United States
1908	Great Britain
1912	Great Britain
1920	Great Britain
1924	France
1928	Germany
1932	Hungary
1936	Hungary
1948	Italy
1952	Hungary
1956	Hungary
1960	Italy
1964	Hungary
1968	Yugoslavia
1972	USSR
1976	Hungary
1980	USSR
1984	Yugoslavia
1988	Yugoslavia
1992	Italy
1996	Spain
2000	Hungary
2004	Hungary

Water polo (women)

2000	Australia
2004	Italy

Weight lifting (men)[24, 25]

56 KG (123.2 LB)

		KG
1972	Zygmunt Smalcerz (POL)	337.5
1976	Aleksandr Varonin (URS)	242.5
1980	Kanybek Osmanaliyev (URS)	245.0
1984	Zeng Guoqiang (CHN)	235.0
1988	Sevdalin Marinov (BUL)	270.0
1992	Ivan Ivanov (BUL)	265.0
1996	Halil Mutlu (TUR)	287.5
2000	Halil Mutlu (TUR)	305.0
2004	Halil Mutlu (TUR)	295.0

62 KG (136.4 LB)

		KG
1948	Joseph de Pietro (USA)	307.5
1952	Ivan Udodov (URS)	315.0
1956	Charles Vinci (USA)	342.5
1960	Charles Vinci (USA)	345.0
1964	Aleksey Vakhonin (URS)	357.5
1968	Mohammad Nassiri (IRI)	367.5
1972	Imre Foldi (HUN)	377.5
1976	Norair Nurikian (BUL)	262.5
1980	Daniel Núñez (CUB)	275.0
1984	Wu Shude (CHN)	267.5
1988	Oksen Mirzoyan (URS)	292.5
1992	Chun Byung Kwan (KOR)	287.5
1996	Tang Ningsheng (CHN)	307.5
2000	Nikolay Pechalov (CRO)	325.0
2004	Shi Zhiyong (CHN)	325.0

Weight lifting (men)[24, 25] (continued)

69 KG (151.8 LB)

		KG
1920	Frans de Haes (BEL)	220.0
1924	Pierino Gabetti (ITA)	402.5[26]
1928	Franz Andrysek (AUT)	287.5
1932	Raymond Suvigny (FRA)	287.5
1936	Anthony Terlazzo (USA)	312.5
1948	Mahmoud Fayad (EGY)	332.5
1952	Rafael Chimishkyan (URS)	337.5
1956	Isaac Berger (USA)	352.5
1960	Yevgeny Minayev (URS)	372.5
1964	Yoshinobu Miyake (JPN)	397.5
1968	Yoshinobu Miyake (JPN)	392.5
1972	Norair Nurikian (BUL)	402.5
1976	Nikolay Kolesnikov (URS)	285.0
1980	Viktor Mazin (URS)	290.0
1984	Chen Weiqiang (CHN)	282.5
1988	Naim Suleymanoglu (TUR)	342.5
1992	Naim Suleymanoglu (TUR)	320.0
1996	Naim Suleymanoglu (TUR)	335.0
2000	Galabin Boevski (BUL)	357.5
2004	Zhang Guozheng (CHN)	347.5

70 KG (154 LB)

		KG
1920	Alfred Neyland (EST)	257.5
1924	Edmond Décottignies (FRA)	440.0[26]
1928	Kurt Helbig (GER); Hans Haas (AUT) (tied)	322.5
1932	René Duverger (FRA)	325.0
1936	Mohamed Ahmed Mesbah (EGY); Robert Fein (AUT) (tied)	342.5
1948	Ibrahim Shams (EGY)	360.0
1952	Tommy Kono (USA)	362.5
1956	Igor Rybak (URS)	380.0
1960	Viktor Bushuyev (URS)	397.5
1964	Waldemar Baszanowski (POL)	432.5
1968	Waldemar Baszanowski (POL)	437.5
1972	Mukharbi Kirzhinov (URS)	460.0
1976	Pyotr Korol (URS)	305.0
1980	Yanko Rusev (BUL)	342.5
1984	Yao Jingyuan (CHN)	320.0
1988	Joachim Kunz (GDR)	340.0
1992	Israil Militosyan (UNT)	337.5
1996	Zhan Xugang (CHN)	357.5

77 KG (169.4 LB)

		KG
1920	Henri Gance (FRA)	245.0
1924	Carlo Galimberti (ITA)	492.5[26]
1928	François Roger (FRA)	335.0
1932	Rudolf Ismayr (GER)	345.0
1936	Khadr el Thouni (EGY)	387.5
1948	Frank Spellman (USA)	390.0
1952	Peter George (USA)	400.0
1956	Fyodor Bogdanovsky (URS)	420.0
1960	Aleksandr Kurynov (URS)	437.5
1964	Hans Zdrazila (TCH)	445.0
1968	Viktor Kurentsov (URS)	475.0
1972	Iordan Bikov (BUL)	485.0
1976	Iordan Mitkov (BUL)	335.0
1980	Asen Zlatev (BUL)	360.0
1984	Karl-Heinz Radschinsky (FRG)	340.0
1988	Borislav Gidikov (BUL)	375.0
1992	Fyodor Kassapu (UNT)	357.5
1996	Pablo Lara (CUB)	367.5
2000	Zhan Xugang (CHN)	367.5
2004	Taner Sagir (TUR)	375.0

Summer Olympic Games Champions (continued)

Weight lifting (men)[24, 25] (continued)

85 KG (187 LB)

		KG
1920	Ernest Cadine (FRA)	290.0
1924	Charles Rigoulot (FRA)	502.5[26]
1928	El Sayed Nosseir (EGY)	355.0
1932	Louis Hostin (FRA)	365.0
1936	Louis Hostin (FRA)	372.5
1948	Stanley Stanczyk (USA)	417.5
1952	Trofim Lomakin (URS)	417.5
1956	Tommy Kono (USA)	447.5
1960	Ireneusz Palinski (POL)	442.5
1964	Rudolph Plyukfelder (URS)	475.0
1968	Boris Selitsky (URS)	485.0
1972	Leif Jenssen (NOR)	507.5
1976	Valery Shary (URS)	365.0
1980	Yury Vardanyan (URS)	400.0
1984	Petre Becheru (ROM)	355.0
1988	Israil Arsamakov (URS)	377.5
1992	Pyrros Dimas (GRE)	370.0
1996	Pyrros Dimas (GRE)	392.5
2000	Pyrros Dimas (GRE)	390.0
2004	George Asanidze (GEO)	382.5

94 KG (206.8 LB)

		KG
1952	Norbert Schemansky (USA)	445.0
1956	Arkady Vorobyev (URS)	462.5
1960	Arkady Vorobyev (URS)	472.5
1964	Vladimir Golovanov (URS)	487.5
1968	Kaarlo Kangasniemi (FIN)	517.5
1972	Andon Nikolov (BUL)	525.0
1976	David Rigert (URS)	382.5
1980	Peter Baczako (HUN)	377.5
1984	Nicu Vlad (ROM)	392.5
1988	Anatoly Khrapaty (URS)	412.5
1992	Kakhi Kakhiashvili (UNT)	412.5
1996	Aleksey Petrov (RUS)	402.5
2000	Akakios Kakhiashvilis (GRE)	405.0
2004	Milen Dobrev (BUL)	407.5

99 KG (217.8 LB)

		KG
1980	Ota Zaremba (TCH)	395.0
1984	Rolf Milser (FRG)	385.0
1988	Pavel Kuznetsov (URS)	425.0
1992	Viktor Tregubov (UNT)	410.0
1996	Akakios Kakhiashvilis (GRE)	420.0

105 KG (231 LB)

		KG
1972	Jan Talts (URS)	580.0
1976	Yury Zaytsev (URS)	385.0
1980	Leonid Taranenko (URS)	422.5
1984	Norberto Oberburger (ITA)	390.0
1988	Yury Zakharevitch (URS)	455.0
1992	Ronny Weller (GER)	432.5
1996	Timur Taymazov (UKR)	430.0
2000	Hossein Tavakoli (IRI)	425.0
2004	Dmitry Berestov (RUS)	425.0

OVER 105 KG (231+ LB)

		KG
1920	Filippo Bottino (ITA)	265.5
1924	Giuseppe Tonani (ITA)	517.5[26]
1928	Josef Strassberger (GER)	372.5
1932	Jaroslav Skobia (TCH)	380.0
1936	Josef Manger (GER)	410.0
1948	John Davis (USA)	452.5
1952	John Davis (USA)	460.0
1956	Paul Anderson (USA)	500.0

Weight lifting (men)[24, 25] (continued)

OVER 105 KG (231+ LB) (CONTINUED)

		KG
1960	Yury Vlasov (URS)	537.5
1964	Leonid Zhabotinsky (URS)	572.5
1968	Leonid Zhabotinsky (URS)	572.5
1972	Vasily Alekseyev (URS)	640.0
1976	Vasily Alekseyev (URS)	440.0
1980	Sultan Rakhmanov (URS)	440.0
1984	Dinko Lukin (AUS)	412.5
1988	Aleksandr Kurlovich (URS)	462.5
1992	Aleksandr Kurlovich (UNT)	450.0
1996	Andrey Chemerkin (RUS)	457.5
2000	Hossein Reza Zadeh (IRI)	472.5
2004	Hossein Reza Zadeh (IRI)	472.5

ONE-HAND LIFT (UNLIMITED CLASS)

		KG
1896	Launceston Elliot (GBR)	71.0
1906	Josef Steinbach (AUT)	76.55

TWO-HAND LIFT (UNLIMITED CLASS)

		KG
1896	Viggo Jensen (DEN)	111.5
1904	Perikles Kakousis (GRE)	111.7
1906	Dimitrios Tofalos (GRE)	142.4

ALL-AROUND DUMBBELLS (UNLIMITED CLASS)

1904	Oscar Osthoff (USA)

Weight lifting (women)

48 KG (105.6 LB)

		KG
2000	Tara Nott (USA)	185.0
2004	Nurcan Taylan (TUR)	210.0

53 KG (116.6 LB)

		KG
2000	Yang Xia (CHN)	225.0
2004	Udomporn Polsak (THA)	222.5

58 KG (127.6 LB)

		KG
2000	Soraya Jiménez Mendívil (MEX)	222.5
2004	Chen Yanqing (CHN)	237.5

63 KG (138.6 LB)

		KG
2000	Chen Xiaomin (CHN)	242.5
2004	Natalya Skakun (UKR)	242.5

69 KG (151.8 LB)

		KG
2000	Lin Weining (CHN)	242.5
2004	Liu Chunhong (CHN)	275.0

75 KG (165 LB)

		KG
2000	Maria Isabel Urrutia (COL)	245.0
2004	Pawina Thongsuk (THA)	272.5

OVER 75 KG (165+ LB)

		KG
2000	Ding Meiyuan (CHN)	300.0
2004	Tang Gonghong (CHN)	305.0

Wrestling—Freestyle (men)[24]

48 KG (105.6 LB)

1904	Robert Curry (USA)
1972	Roman Dmitriyev (URS)
1976	Khassan Issaev (BUL)
1980	Claudio Pollio (ITA)
1984	Robert Weaver (USA)
1988	Takashi Kobayashi (JPN)
1992	Kim Il (PRK)
1996	Kim Il (PRK)

Summer Olympic Games Champions (continued)

Wrestling—Freestyle (men)[24] (continued)

55 KG (121 LB)
1904	George Mehnert (USA)
1948	Lennart Viitala (FIN)
1952	Hasan Gemici (TUR)
1956	Mirian Tsalkalamanidze (URS)
1960	Ahmet Bilek (TUR)
1964	Yoshikatsu Yoshida (JPN)
1968	Shigeo Nakata (JPN)
1972	Kiyomi Kato (JPN)
1976	Yuji Takada (JPN)
1980	Anatoly Beloglazov (URS)
1984	Saban Trstena (YUG)
1988	Mitsuru Sato (JPN)
1992	Li Hak-son (PRK)
1996	Valentin Iordanov (BUL)
2000	Namig Amdullayev (AZE)
2004	Mavlet Batirov (RUS)

60 KG (132 LB)
1904	Isidor "Jack" Niflot (USA)
1908	George Mehnert (USA)
1924	Kustaa Pihlajamäki (FIN)
1928	Kaarlo Maakinen (FIN)
1932	Robert Pearce (USA)
1936	Odon Zombory (HUN)
1948	Nasuh Akar (TUR)
1952	Shohachi Ishii (JPN)
1956	Mustafa Dagistanli (TUR)
1960	Terence McCann (USA)
1964	Yojiro Uetake (JPN)
1968	Yojiro Uetake (JPN)
1972	Hideaki Yanagida (JPN)
1976	Vladimir Yumin (URS)
1980	Sergey Beloglazov (URS)
1984	Hideaki Tomiyama (JPN)
1988	Sergey Beloglazov (URS)
1992	Alejandro Puerto Diaz (CUB)
1996	Kendall Cross (USA)
2000	Alireza Dabir (IRI)
2004	Yandro Miguel Quintana (CUB)

63 KG (138.6 LB)
1904	Benjamin Bradshaw (USA)
1908	George Dole (USA)
1920	Charles Ackerly (USA)
1924	Robin Reed (USA)
1928	Allie Morrison (USA)
1932	Hermanni Pihlajamäki (FIN)
1936	Kustaa Pihlajamäki (FIN)
1948	Gazanfer Bilge (TUR)
1952	Bayram Sit (TUR)
1956	Shozo Sasahara (JPN)
1960	Mustafa Dagistanli (TUR)
1964	Osamu Watanabe (JPN)
1968	Masaaki Kaneko (JPN)
1972	Zagalav Abdulbekov (URS)
1976	Yang Jung Mo (KOR)
1980	Magomedgasan Abushev (URS)
1984	Randy Lewis (USA)
1988	John Smith (USA)
1992	John Smith (USA)
1996	Tom Brands (USA)
2000	Murad Umakhanov (RUS)

Wrestling—Freestyle (men)[24] (continued)

66 KG (145.2 LB)
1904	Otto Roehm (USA)
1908	George de Relwyskow (GBR)
1920	Kaarlo "Kalle" Anttila (FIN)
1924	Russell Vis (USA)
1928	Osvald Käpp (EST)
1932	Charles Pacome (FRA)
1936	Karoly Karpati (HUN)
1948	Celal Atik (TUR)
1952	Olle Anderberg (SWE)
1956	Emamali Habibi (IRI)
1960	Shelby Wilson (USA)
1964	Enio Valchev Dimov (BUL)
1968	Abdollah Movahed (IRI)
1972	Dan Gable (USA)
1976	Pavel Pinigin (URS)
1980	Saipulla Absaidov (URS)
1984	You In Tak (KOR)
1988	Arsen Fadzayev (URS)
1992	Arsen Fadzayev (UNT)
1996	Vadim Bogiyev (RUS)
2000	Daniel Igali (CAN)
2004	Elbrus Tedeyev (UKR)

74 KG (162.8 LB)
1904	Charles Eriksen (USA)
1924	Hermann Gehri (SUI)
1928	Arvo Haavisto (FIN)
1932	Jack van Bebber (USA)
1936	Frank Lewis (USA)
1948	Yasar Dogu (TUR)
1952	William Smith (USA)
1956	Mitsuo Ikeda (JPN)
1960	Douglas Blubaugh (USA)
1964	Ismail Ogan (TUR)
1968	Mahmut Atalay (TUR)
1972	Wayne Wells (USA)
1976	Jiichiro Date (JPN)
1980	Valentin Raychev (BUL)
1984	David Schultz (USA)
1988	Kenneth Monday (USA)
1992	Park Jang Soon (KOR)
1996	Buvaysa Saytyev (RUS)
2000	Brandon Slay (USA)
2004	Buvaysa Saytyev (RUS)

84 KG (184.8 LB)
1908	Stanley Bacon (GBR)
1920	Eino Leino (FIN)
1924	Fritz Haggmann (SUI)
1928	Ernst Kyburz (SUI)
1932	Ivar Johansson (SWE)
1936	Émile Poilvé (FRA)
1948	Glen Brand (USA)
1952	David Tsimakurdze (URS)
1956	Nikola Stanchev (BUL)
1960	Hasan Gungor (TUR)
1964	Prodan Stoyanov Gardchev (BUL)
1968	Boris Gurevich (URS)
1972	Levan Tediashvili (URS)
1976	John Peterson (USA)
1980	Ismail Abilov (BUL)
1984	Mark Schultz (USA)
1988	Han Myung Woo (KOR)
1992	Kevin Jackson (USA)
1996	Khadshimurad Magomedov (RUS)

Summer Olympic Games Champions (continued)

Wrestling—Freestyle (men)[24] (continued)

84 KG (184.8 LB) (CONTINUED)
2000   Adam Saytev (RUS)
2004   Cael Sanderson (USA)

90 KG (198.5 LB)
1920   Anders Larsson (SWE)
1924   John Franklin Spellman (USA)
1928   Thure Sjöstedt (SWE)
1932   Peter Mehringer (USA)
1936   Knut Fridell (SWE)
1948   Henry Wittenberg (USA)
1952   Bror Wiking Palm (SWE)
1956   Gholam-Reza Takhti (IRI)
1960   Ismet Atli (TUR)
1964   Aleksandr Medved (URS)
1968   Ahmet Ayuk (TUR)
1972   Ben Peterson (USA)
1976   Levan Tediashvili (URS)
1980   Sanasar Oganesyan (URS)
1984   Ed Banach (USA)
1988   Macharbek Khadartsev (URS)
1992   Macharbek Khadartsev (UNT)
1996   Rasul Khadem Azghadi (IRI)

96 KG (211.2 LB)
1896   Karl Schumann (GER)
1904   Bernhuff Hansen (USA)
1908   George O'Kelly (GBR)
1920   Robert Rothe (SUI)
1924   Harry Steele (USA)
1928   Johan Richthoff (SWE)
1932   Johan Richthoff (SWE)
1936   Kristjan Palusalu (EST)
1948   Gyula Bobis (HUN)
1952   Arsen Mekokishvili (URS)
1956   Hamit Kaplan (TUR)
1960   Wilfried Dietrich (GER)
1964   Aleksandr Ivanitsky (URS)
1968   Aleksandr Medved (URS)
1972   Ivan Yarygin (URS)
1976   Ivan Yarygin (URS)
1980   Ilya Mate (URS)
1984   Lou Banach (USA)
1988   Vasile Puscasu (ROM)
1992   Leri Khabelov (UNT)
1996   Kurt Angle (USA)
2000   Sagid Murtasaliyev (RUS)
2004   Khajimurat Gatsalov (RUS)

120 KG (264 LB)
1972   Aleksandr Medved (URS)
1976   Soslan Andiyev (URS)
1980   Soslan Andiyev (URS)
1984   Bruce Baumgartner (USA)
1988   David Gobedishvili (URS)
1992   Bruce Baumgartner (USA)
1996   Mahmut Demir (TUR)
2000   David Musulbes (RUS)
2004   Artur Taymazov (UZB)

Wrestling—Freestyle (women)

48 KG (105.6 LB)
2004   Irini Merleni (UKR)

55 KG (121 LB)
2004   Saori Yoshida (JPN)

Wrestling—Freestyle (women) (continued)

63 KG (138.6 LB)
2004   Kaori Icho (JPN)

72 KG (158 LB)
2004   Wang Xu (CHN)

Wrestling—Greco-Roman (men)[24]

48 KG (105.6 LB)
1972   Gheorghe Berceanu (ROM)
1976   Aleksey Shumakov (URS)
1980   Zhaksylyk Ushkempirov (URS)
1984   Vincenzo Maenza (ITA)
1988   Vincenzo Maenza (ITA)
1992   Oleg Kucherenko (UNT)
1996   Sim Kwon-Ho (KOR)

55 KG (121 LB)
1948   Pietro Lombardi (ITA)
1952   Boris Gurevich (URS)
1956   Nikolay Solovyev (URS)
1960   Dumitru Pirvulescu (ROM)
1964   Tsutomu Hanahara (JPN)
1968   Petar Kirov (BUL)
1972   Petar Kirov (BUL)
1976   Vitaly Konstantinov (URS)
1980   Vakhtang Blagidze (URS)
1984   Atsuji Miyahara (JPN)
1988   Jon Ronningen (NOR)
1992   Jon Ronningen (NOR)
1996   Armen Nazaryan (ARM)
2000   Sim Kwon-Ho (KOR)
2004   Istvan Majoros (HUN)

60 KG (132 LB)
1924   Eduard Pütsep (EST)
1928   Kurt Leucht (GER)
1932   Jakob Brendel (GER)
1936   Marton Lorincz (HUN)
1948   Kurt Pettersen (SWE)
1952   Imre Hodos (HUN)
1956   Konstantin Vyrupayev (URS)
1960   Oleg Karavayev (URS)
1964   Masamitsu Ichiguchi (JPN)
1968   Janos Varga (HUN)
1972   Rustem Kazakov (URS)
1976   Pertti Ukkola (FIN)
1980   Shamil Serikov (URS)
1984   Pasquale Passarelli (FRG)
1988   Andras Sike (HUN)
1992   An Han Bong (KOR)
1996   Yury Melnichenko (KAZ)
2000   Armen Nazarian (BUL)
2004   Jung Ji Hyun (KOR)

63 KG (138.6 LB)
1912   Kaarlo Koskelo (FIN)
1920   Oskar Friman (FIN)
1924   Kalle Anttila (FIN)
1928   Voldemar Väli (EST)
1932   Giovanni Gozzi (ITA)
1936   Yasar Erkan (TUR)
1948   Mehmet Oktav (TUR)
1952   Yakov Punkin (URS)
1956   Rauno Leonard Mäkinen (FIN)
1960   Muzahir Sille (TUR)
1964   Imre Polyak (HUN)
1968   Roman Rurua (URS)
1972   Georgi Markov (BUL)

Summer Olympic Games Champions (continued)

Wrestling—Greco-Roman (men)[24] (continued)

63 KG (138.6 LB) (CONTINUED)
1976	Kazimierz Lipien (POL)
1980	Stilianos Migiakis (GRE)
1984	Kim Weon Kee (KOR)
1988	Kamandar Madzhidov (URS)
1992	Akif Pirim (TUR)
1996	Wlodzimierz Zawadzki (POL)
2000	Varteres Samurgashev (RUS)

66 KG (145.2 LB)
1908	Enrico Porro (ITA)
1912	Eemil Väre (FIN)
1920	Eemil Väre (FIN)
1924	Oskar Friman (FIN)
1928	Lajos Keresztes (HUN)
1932	Erik Malmberg (SWE)
1936	Lauri Koskela (FIN)
1948	Karl Freij (SWE)
1952	Shazam Safin (URS)
1956	Kyösti Emil Lehtonen (FIN)
1960	Avtandil Koridze (URS)
1964	Kazim Ayvaz (TUR)
1968	Munji Mumemura (JPN)
1972	Shamil Khisamutdinov (URS)
1976	Suren Nalbandyan (URS)
1980	Stefan Rusu (ROM)
1984	Vlado Lisjak (YUG)
1988	Levon Dzhulfalakyan (URS)
1992	Attila Repka (HUN)
1996	Ryszard Wolny (POL)
2000	Filiberto Ascuy Aguilera (CUB)
2004	Farid Mansurov (AZE)

74 KG (162.8 LB)
1932	Ivar Johansson (SWE)
1936	Rudolf Svedberg (SWE)
1948	Erik Gösta Andersson (SWE)
1952	Miklos Szilvasi (HUN)
1956	Mithat Bayrak (TUR)
1960	Mithat Bayrak (TUR)
1964	Anatoly Kolesov (URS)
1968	Rudolf Vesper (GDR)
1972	Viteslav Macha (TCH)
1976	Anatoly Bykov (URS)
1980	Ferenc Kocsis (HUN)
1984	Jouko Salomaki (FIN)
1988	Kim Young Nam (KOR)
1992	Mnatsakan Iskandaryan (UNT)
1996	Filiberto Ascuy Aguilera (CUB)
2000	Murat Kardanov (URS)
2004	Aleksandr Dokturishivili (UZB)

84 KG (184.8 LB)
1908	Frithiof Martenson (SWE)
1912	Claes Johansson (SWE)
1920	Carl Westergren (SWE)
1924	Edward Westerlund (FIN)
1928	Väinö Kokkinen (FIN)
1932	Väinö Kokkinen (FIN)
1936	Ivar Johansson (SWE)
1948	Axel Grönberg (SWE)
1952	Axel Grönberg (SWE)
1956	Givi Kartoziya (URS)
1960	Dimitar Dobrev (BUL)
1964	Branislav Simic (YUG)

Wrestling—Greco-Roman (men)[24] (continued)

84 KG (184.8 LB) (CONTINUED)
1968	Lothar Metz (GDR)
1972	Csaba Hegedus (HUN)
1976	Momir Petkovic (YUG)
1980	Gennady Korban (URS)
1984	Ion Draica (ROM)
1988	Mikhail Mamiashvili (URS)
1992	Peter Farkas (HUN)
1996	Hamza Yerlikaya (TUR)
2000	Hamza Yerlikaya (TUR)
2004	Aleksey Mishin (RUS)

90 KG (198.5 LB)
1908	Verner Weckman (FIN)
1912	Anders Ahlgren (SWE)
1920	Claes Johansson (SWE)
1924	Carl Westergren (SWE)
1928	Ibrahim Moustafa (EGY)
1932	Rudolf Svensson (SWE)
1936	Axel Cadier (SWE)
1948	Karl-Erik Nilsson (SWE)
1952	Kelpo Olavi Gröndahl (FIN)
1956	Valentin Nikolayev (URS)
1960	Tevfik Kis (TUR)
1964	Boyan Radev (BUL)
1968	Boyan Radev (BUL)
1972	Valery Rezantsev (URS)
1976	Valery Rezantsev (URS)
1980	Norbert Nottny (HUN)
1984	Steven Fraser (USA)
1988	Atanas Komchev (BUL)
1992	Maik Bullmann (GER)
1996	Vyacheslav Oleynyk (UKR)

96 KG (211.2 LB)
1896	Karl Schumann (GER)
1908	Richard Weisz (HUN)
1912	Yrjö Saarela (FIN)
1920	Adolf Lindfors (FIN)
1924	Henri Deglane (FRA)
1928	Rudolf Svensson (SWE)
1932	Carl Westergren (SWE)
1936	Kristjan Palusalu (EST)
1948	Ahmet Kirecci (TUR)
1952	Johannes Kotkas (URS)
1956	Anatoly Parfenov (URS)
1960	Ivan Bogdan (URS)
1964	Istvan Kozma (HUN)
1968	Istvan Kozma (HUN)
1972	Nicolae Martinescu (ROM)
1976	Nikolay Balboshin (URS)
1980	Georgi Raikov-Petkov (BUL)
1984	Vasile Andrei (ROM)
1988	Andrzej Wronski (POL)
1992	Héctor Milian (CUB)
1996	Andrzej Wronski (POL)
2000	Mikael Ljungberg (SWE)
2004	Karam Ibrahim (EGY)

120 KG (264 LB)
1972	Anatoly Roshchin (URS)
1976	Aleksandr Kolchinsky (URS)
1980	Aleksandr Kolchinsky (URS)
1984	Jeffrey Blatnick (USA)
1988	Aleksandr Karelin (URS)
1992	Aleksandr Karelin (UNT)

Summer Olympic Games Champions (continued)

Wrestling—Greco-Roman (men)[24] (continued)

120 KG (264 LB) (CONTINUED)
1996 Aleksandr Karelin (RUS)
2000 Rulon Gardner (USA)
2004 Khasan Baroyev (RUS)

[1]The competitions in 1900 and 1904 are said to be unofficial. [2]100-meter event. [3]Hurdles were 2' 6" high, not 3'. [4]An extra lap of 460 meters was run in error. [5]Jim Thorpe was stripped of his gold medals in 1913 when it was discovered he had briefly competed as a professional athlete; in 1982 his gold medals were restored, and he was declared "cowinner" of the events. [6]2,000-meter event. [7]333.3-meter event. [8]Distance varied from 87 to 320 km. [9]Weight classifications were changed in 1980 and 1996. [10]Weight classifications were changed in 2000. [11]The distances in men's rowing events have varied from time to time. In 1904 it was 2 miles; in 1908, 1.5 miles; from 1912 to 1936, 2,000 m; in 1948, 1 mile 350 yards; and since 1952, 2,000 m (1 mile 427 yards). [12]The distance in women's rowing events was 1,000 m until 1988, at which time it became 2,000 m. [13]100 yards. [14]220 yards. [15]500 meters. [16]440 yards. [17]1,200 meters. [18]1,000 meters. [19]One mile. [20]100 yards. [21]440 yards. [22]300 meters. [23]Fréchette's gold medal awarded in 1993 on basis of error in scoring. [24]Weight classifications have been revised numerous times, most recently after the 1996 Games. [25]In 1976 the press lift was removed, weights given thereafter being the total for the clean and jerk and the snatch. [26]Total of five lifts.

Winter Olympic Games Champions

*Gold medalists in all events, 1908–2006 (separate Winter Games were not held until 1924).
Since the 2002 Salt Lake City Games, several athletes have been stripped of medals for having
failed drug tests. New medalists are shown in this table.*

Biathlon (men)

10 KILOMETERS	MIN:SEC
1980 Frank Ullrich (GDR)	32:10.69
1984 Eirik Kvalfoss (NOR)	30:53.8
1988 Frank-Peter Rötsch (GDR)	25:08.1
1992 Mark Kirchner (GER)	26:02.3
1994 Sergey Chepikov (RUS)	28:07.0
1998 Ole Einar Bjørndalen (NOR)	27:16.2
2002 Ole Einar Bjørndalen (NOR)	24:51.3
2006 Sven Fischer (GER)	26:11.6

12.5-KILOMETER PURSUIT	MIN:SEC
2002 Ole Einar Bjørndalen (NOR)	32:34.6
2006 Vincent Defrasne (FRA)	35:20.2

15-KILOMETER MASS START	MIN:SEC
2006 Michael Greis (GER)	47:20.0

20 KILOMETERS	HR:MIN:SEC
1960 Klas Lestander (SWE)	1:33:21.6
1964 Vladimir Melanin (URS)	1:20:26.8
1968 Magnar Solberg (NOR)	1:13:45.9
1972 Magnar Solberg (NOR)	1:15:55.50[1]
1976 Nikolay Kruglov (URS)	1:14:12.26
1980 Anatoly Alyabyev (URS)	1:08:16.31
1984 Peter Angerer (FRG)	1:11:52.70
1988 Frank-Peter Rötsch (GDR)	56:33.3
1992 Yevgeny Redkin (UNT)[2]	57:34.4
1994 Sergey Tarasov (RUS)	57:25.3
1998 Halvard Hanevold (NOR)	56:16.4
2002 Ole Einar Bjørndalen (NOR)	51:03.3
2006 Michael Greis (GER)	54:23.0

4 × 7.5-KILOMETER RELAY	HR:MIN:SEC
1968 USSR	2:13:02.4
1972 USSR	1:51:44.92[1]
1976 USSR	1:57:55.64
1980 USSR	1:34:03.27
1984 USSR	1:38:51.70
1988 USSR	1:22:30.00
1992 Germany	1:24:43.5

Biathlon (men) (continued)

4 × 7.5-KILOMETER RELAY (CONTINUED)	HR:MIN:SEC
1994 Germany	1:30:22.1
1998 Germany	1:19:43.3
2002 Norway	1:23:42.3
2006 Germany	1:21:51.5

MILITARY SKI PATROL
1924 Switzerland
1928 Norway
1936 Italy
1948 Switzerland

DISTANCE SHOOTING
1936 Georg Edenhauser (AUT)

ICE SHOOTING (TEAM)
1936 Austria

TARGET SHOOTING
1936 Ignaz Reiterer (AUT)

Biathlon (women)

7.5 KILOMETERS	MIN:SEC
1992 Anfisa Restsova (UNT)[2]	24:29.2
1994 Myriam Bédard (CAN)	26:08.8
1998 Galina Kukleva (RUS)	23:08.0
2002 Kati Wilhelm (GER)	20:41.4
2006 Florence Baverel-Robert (FRA)	22:31.4

10-KILOMETER PURSUIT	MIN:SEC
2002 Olga Pyleva (RUS)	31:07.7
2006 Kati Wilhelm (GER)	36:43.6

12.5-KILOMETER MASS START	MIN:SEC
2006 Anna Carin Olofsson (SWE)	40:36.5

15 KILOMETERS	MIN:SEC
1992 Antje Misersky (GER)	51:47.2
1994 Myriam Bédard (CAN)	52:06.6
1998 Ekaterina Dafovska (BUL)	54:52.0
2002 Andrea Henkel (GER)	47:29.1

Winter Olympic Games Champions (continued)

Biathlon (women) (continued)

15 KILOMETERS (CONTINUED)		MIN:SEC
2006	Svetlana Ishmuratova (RUS)	49:24.1

4 × 6-KILOMETER RELAY[3]		HR:MIN:SEC
1992	France	1:15:55.6
1994	Russia	1:47:19.5
1998	Germany	1:40:13.6
2002	Germany	1:27:55.0
2006	Russia	1:16:12.5

Bobsled

TWO-MAN BOBSLED		MIN:SEC
1932	United States	8:14.74
1936	United States	5:29.29
1948	Switzerland	5:29.2
1952	West Germany	5:24.54
1956	Italy	5:30.14
1964	Great Britain	4:21.90
1968	Italy	4:41.54
1972	West Germany	4:57.07
1976	East Germany	3:44.42
1980	Switzerland	4:09.36
1984	East Germany	3:25.56
1988	USSR	3:53.48
1992	Switzerland	4:03.26
1994	Switzerland	3:30.81
1998	Canada; Italy (tied)	3:37.24
2002	Germany	3:10.11
2006	Germany	3:43.38

FOUR-MAN BOBSLED		MIN:SEC
1924	Switzerland	5:45.54
1928	United States[4]	3:20.5
1932	United States	7:53.68
1936	Switzerland	5:19.85
1948	United States	5:20.1
1952	West Germany	5:07.84
1956	Switzerland	5:10.44
1964	Canada	4:14.46
1968	Italy	2:17.39
1972	Switzerland	4:43.07
1976	East Germany	3:40.43
1980	East Germany	3:59.92
1984	East Germany	3:20.22
1988	Switzerland	3:47.51
1992	Austria	3:53.90
1994	Germany	3:27.78
1998	Germany	2:39.41
2002	Germany	3:07.51
2006	Germany	3:40.42

TWO-WOMAN BOBSLED		MIN:SEC
2002	United States	1:37.76
2006	Germany	3:49.98

Curling

MEN
1924	Great Britain
1998	Switzerland
2002	Norway
2006	Canada

WOMEN
1998	Canada

Curling (continued)

WOMEN (CONTINUED)
2002	Great Britain
2006	Sweden

Figure Skating

MEN'S SINGLES
1908	Ulrich Salchow (SWE)
1920	Gillis Gräfström (SWE)
1924	Gillis Gräfström (SWE)
1928	Gillis Gräfström (SWE)
1932	Karl Schäfer (AUT)
1936	Karl Schäfer (AUT)
1948	Richard Button (USA)
1952	Richard Button (USA)
1956	Hayes Alan Jenkins (USA)
1960	David Jenkins (USA)
1964	Manfred Schnelldorfer (GER)[5]
1968	Wolfgang Schwarz (AUT)
1972	Ondrej Nepela (TCH)
1976	John Curry (GBR)
1980	Robin Cousins (GBR)
1984	Scott Hamilton (USA)
1988	Brian Boitano (USA)
1992	Viktor Petrenko (UNT)[2]
1994	Aleksey Urmanov (RUS)
1998	Ilia Kulik (RUS)
2002	Aleksey Yagudin (RUS)
2006	Yevgeny Plushchenko (RUS)

WOMEN'S SINGLES
1908	Madge Syers (GBR)
1920	Magda Julin-Mauroy (SWE)
1924	Herma Planck-Szabo (AUT)
1928	Sonja Henie (NOR)
1932	Sonja Henie (NOR)
1936	Sonja Henie (NOR)
1948	Barbara Ann Scott (CAN)
1952	Jeanette Altwegg (GBR)
1956	Tenley Albright (USA)
1964	Sjoukje Dijkstra (NED)
1968	Peggy Fleming (USA)
1972	Beatrix Schuba (AUT)
1976	Dorothy Hamill (USA)
1980	Annett Potzsch (GDR)
1984	Katarina Witt (GDR)
1988	Katarina Witt (GDR)
1992	Kristi Yamaguchi (USA)
1994	Oksana Bayul (UKR)
1998	Tara Lipinski (USA)
2002	Sarah Hughes (USA)
2006	Shizuka Arakawa (JPN)

PAIRS
1908	Anna Hübler, Heinrich Burger (GER)
1920	Ludoviga Jakobsson-Eilers, Walter Jakobsson (FIN)
1924	Helene Engelmann, Alfred Berger (AUT)
1928	Andrée Joly, Pierre Brunet (FRA)
1932	Andrée Brunet-Joly, Pierre Brunet (FRA)
1936	Maxi Herber, Ernst Baier (GER)
1948	Micheline Lannoy, Pierre Baugniet (BEL)
1952	Ria Falk, Paul Falk (FRG)
1956	Elisabeth Schwarz, Kurt Oppelt (AUT)

Winter Olympic Games Champions (continued)

Figure Skating (continued)

PAIRS (CONTINUED)
1960 Barbara Wagner, Robert Paul (CAN)
1964 Lyudmila Belousova, Oleg Protopopov (URS)
1968 Lyudmila Belousova, Oleg Protopopov (URS)
1972 Irina Rodnina, Aleksey Ulanov (URS)
1976 Irina Rodnina, Aleksandr Zaytsev (URS)
1980 Irina Rodnina, Aleksandr Zaytsev (URS)
1984 Yelena Valova, Oleg Vasilyev (URS)
1988 Yekaterina Gordeyeva, Sergey Grinkov (URS)
1992 Natalya Mishkutyonok, Artur Dmitriyev (UNT)[2]
1994 Yekaterina Gordeyeva, Sergey Grinkov (RUS)
1998 Oksana Kazakova, Artur Dmitriyev (RUS)
2002 Yelena Berezhnaya, Anton Sikharulidze (RUS); Jamie Sale, David Pelletier (CAN) (shared)
2006 Tatyana Totmyanin, Maksim Marinin (RUS)

ICE DANCING
1976 Lyudmila Pakhomova, Aleksandr Gorshkov (URS)
1980 Natalya Linichuk, Gennady Karponosov (URS)
1984 Jayne Torvill, Christopher Dean (GBR)
1988 Natalya Bestemyanova, Andrey Bukin (URS)
1992 Marina Klimova, Sergey Ponomarenko (UNT)[2]
1994 Oksana Grishchuk, Yevgeny Platov (RUS)
1998 Oksana Grishchuk, Yevgeny Platov (RUS)
2002 Marina Anissina, Gwendal Peizerat (FRA)
2006 Tatyana Navka, Roman Kostomarov (RUS)

Ice Hockey

MEN
1920 Canada
1924 Canada
1928 Canada
1932 Canada
1936 Great Britain
1948 Canada
1952 Canada
1956 USSR
1960 United States
1964 USSR
1968 USSR
1972 USSR
1976 USSR
1980 United States
1984 USSR
1988 USSR
1992 Unified Team[2]
1994 Sweden
1998 Czech Republic
2002 Canada
2006 Sweden

WOMEN
1998 United States
2002 Canada
2006 Canada

Luge

MEN'S SINGLES
Year	Champion	MIN:SEC
1964	Thomas Köhler (GER)[5]	3:26.77
1968	Manfred Schmid (AUT)	2:52.48
1972	Wolfgang Schneidel (GDR)	3:27.58
1976	Detlef Guenther (GDR)	3:27.688[5]
1980	Bernhard Glass (GDR)	2:54.796
1984	Paul Hildgartner (ITA)	3:04.258
1988	Jens Müller (GDR)	3:05.548
1992	Georg Hackl (GER)	3:02.363

MEN'S SINGLES (CONTINUED)
Year	Champion	MIN:SEC
1994	Georg Hackl (GER)	3:21.571
1998	Georg Hackl (GER)	3:18.436
2002	Armin Zöggeler (ITA)	2:57.941
2006	Armin Zöggeler (ITA)	3:26.088

MEN'S PAIRS
Year	Champion	MIN:SEC
1964	Austria	1:41.62
1968	East Germany	1:35.85
1972	Italy; East Germany (tied)	1:28.35
1976	East Germany	1:25.604[6]
1980	East Germany	1:19.331
1984	West Germany	1:23.620
1988	East Germany	1:31.940
1992	Germany	1:32.053
1994	Italy	1:36.720
1998	Germany	1:41.105
2002	Germany	1:26.082
2006	Austria	1:34.497

WOMEN'S SINGLES
Year	Champion	MIN:SEC
1964	Ortrun Enderlein (GER)[5]	3:24.67
1968	Erica Lechner (ITA)	2:29.37
1972	Anna-Maria Müller (GDR)	2:59.18
1976	Margit Schumann (GDR)	2:50.621[6]
1980	Vera Zozulya (URS)	2:36.537
1984	Steffi Martin (GDR)	2:46.570
1988	Steffi Walter-Martin (GDR)	3:03.973
1992	Doris Neuner (AUT)	3:06.696
1994	Gerda Weissensteiner (ITA)	3:15.517
1998	Silke Kraushaar (GER)	3:23.779
2002	Sylke Otto (GER)	2:52.464
2006	Sylke Otto (GER)	3:07.979

Skeleton

MEN
Year	Champion	MIN:SEC
1928	Jennison Heaton (USA)	3:01.8
1948	Nino Bibbia (ITA)	5:23.2
2002	Jim Shea (USA)	1:41.96
2006	Duff Gibson (CAN)	1:55.88

WOMEN
Year	Champion	MIN:SEC
2002	Tristan Gale (USA)	1:45.11
2006	Maya Pedersen (SUI)	1:59.83

Alpine Skiing (men)

DOWNHILL
Year	Champion	MIN:SEC
1948	Henri Oreiller (FRA)	2:55.0
1952	Zeno Colò (ITA)	2:30.8
1956	Toni Sailer (AUT)	2:52.2
1960	Jean Vuarnet (FRA)	2:06.0
1964	Egon Zimmermann (AUT)	2:18.16[1]
1968	Jean-Claude Killy (FRA)	1:59.85
1972	Bernhard Russi (SUI)	1:51.43
1976	Franz Klammer (AUT)	1:45.73
1980	Leonhard Stock (AUT)	1:45.50
1984	Bill Johnson (USA)	1:45.59
1988	Pirmin Zurbriggen (SUI)	1:59.63
1992	Patrick Ortlieb (AUT)	1:50.37
1994	Tommy Moe (USA)	1:45.75
1998	Jean-Luc Cretier (FRA)	1:50.11
2002	Fritz Strobl (AUT)	1:39.13
2006	Antoine Dénériaz (FRA)	1:48.80

SLALOM
Year	Champion	MIN:SEC
1948	Edy Reinalter (SUI)	2:10.3
1952	Othmar Schneider (AUT)	2:00.0
1956	Toni Sailer (AUT)	3:14.7

Winter Olympic Games Champions (continued)

Alpine Skiing (men) (continued)

SLALOM (CONTINUED)

		MIN:SEC
1960	Ernst Hinterseer (AUT)	2:08.9
1964	Josef Stiegler (AUT)	2:21.13[1]
1968	Jean-Claude Killy (FRA)	1:39.73
1972	Francisco Ochoa (ESP)	1:49.27
1976	Piero Gros (ITA)	2:03.29
1980	Ingemar Stenmark (SWE)	1:44.26
1984	Phil Mahre (USA)	1:39.41
1988	Alberto Tomba (ITA)	1:39.47
1992	Finn Christian Jagge (NOR)	1:44.39
1994	Thomas Stangassinger (AUT)	2:02.02
1998	Hans-Petter Buraas (NOR)	1:49.31
2002	Jean-Pierre Vidal (FRA)	1:41.06
2006	Benjamin Raich (AUT)	1:43.14

GIANT SLALOM

		MIN:SEC
1952	Stein Eriksen (NOR)	2:25.0
1956	Toni Sailer (AUT)	3:00.1
1960	Roger Staub (SUI)	1:48.3
1964	François Bonlieu (FRA)	1:46.71[1]
1968	Jean-Claude Killy (FRA)	3:29.28
1972	Gustavo Thöni (ITA)	3:09.62
1976	Heini Hemmi (SUI)	3:26.97
1980	Ingemar Stenmark (SWE)	2:40.74
1984	Max Julen (SUI)	2:41.18
1988	Alberto Tomba (ITA)	2:06.37
1992	Alberto Tomba (ITA)	2:06.98
1994	Markus Wasmeier (GER)	2:52.46
1998	Hermann Maier (AUT)	2:38.51
2002	Stephan Eberharter (AUT)	2:23.28
2006	Benjamin Raich (AUT)	2:35.00

SUPERGIANT SLALOM

		MIN:SEC
1988	Franck Piccard (FRA)	1:39.66
1992	Kjetil Andre Aamodt (NOR)	1:13.04
1994	Markus Wasmeier (GER)	1:32.53
1998	Hermann Maier (AUT)	1:34.82
2002	Kjetil André Aamodt (NOR)	1:21.58
2006	Kjetil André Aamodt (NOR)	1:30.65

ALPINE COMBINED

		MIN:SEC
1936	Franz Pfnür (GER)	
1948	Henri Oreiller (FRA)	
1972	Gustavo Thoeni (ITA)	
1976	Gustavo Thoeni (ITA)	
1988	Hubert Strolz (AUT)	
1992	Josef Polig (ITA)	
1994	Lasse Kjus (NOR)	3:17.53[7]
1998	Mario Reiter (AUT)	3:08.06
2002	Kjetil André Aamodt (NOR)	3:17.56
2006	Ted Ligety (USA)	3:09.35

Alpine Skiing (women)

DOWNHILL

		MIN:SEC
1948	Hedy Schlunegger (SUI)	2:28.3
1952	Trude Jochom-Beiser (AUT)	1:47.1
1956	Madeleine Berthod (SUI)	1:40.7
1960	Heidi Beibl (GER)[5]	1:37.6
1964	Christl Haas (AUT)	1:55.39[1]
1968	Olga Pall (AUT)	1:40.87
1972	Marie-Therèse Nadig (SUI)	1:36.68
1976	Rosi Mittermaier (FRG)	1:46.16
1980	Annemarie Moser-Pröll (AUT)	1:37.52
1984	Michael Figini (SUI)	1:13.36
1988	Marina Kiehl (FRG)	1:25.86
1992	Kerrin Lee-Gartner (CAN)	1:52.55
1994	Katja Seizinger (GER)	1:35.93
1998	Katja Seizinger (GER)	1:28.29

Alpine Skiing (women) (continued)

DOWNHILL (CONTINUED)

		MIN:SEC
2002	Carole Montillet (FRA)	1:39.56
2006	Michaela Dorfmeister (AUT)	1:32.47

SLALOM

		MIN:SEC
1948	Gretchen Fraser (USA)	1:57.2
1952	Andrea Lawrence-Mead (USA)	2:10.6
1956	Renée Colliard (SUI)	1:52.3
1960	Anne Heggtveit (CAN)	1:49.6
1964	Christine Goitschel (FRA)	1:29.86[1]
1968	Marielle Goitschel (FRA)	1:59.85
1972	Barbara Cochran (USA)	1:31.24
1976	Rosi Mittermaier (FRG)	1:30.54
1980	Hanni Wenzel (LIE)	1:25.09
1984	Paoletta Magoni (ITA)	1:36.47
1988	Vreni Schneider (SUI)	1:36.69
1992	Petra Kronberger (AUT)	1:32.68
1994	Vreni Schneider (SUI)	1:56.01
1998	Hilde Gerg (GER)	1:32.40
2002	Janica Kostelic (CRO)	1:46.10
2006	Anja Pärson (SWE)	1:29.04

GIANT SLALOM

		MIN:SEC
1952	Andrea Lawrence-Mead (USA)	2:06.8
1956	Ossi Reichert (GER)[5]	1:56.5
1960	Yvonne Rüegg (SUI)	1:39.9
1964	Marielle Goitschel (FRA)	1:52.24[1]
1968	Nancy Greene (CAN)	1:51.97
1972	Marie-Thérèse Nadig (SUI)	1:29.90
1976	Kathy Kreiner (CAN)	1:29.13
1980	Hanni Wenzel (LIE)	2:41.66
1984	Debbie Armstrong (USA)	2:20.98
1988	Vreni Schneider (SUI)	2:06.49
1992	Pernilla Wiberg (SWE)	2:12.74
1994	Deborah Compagnoni (ITA)	2:30.97
1998	Deborah Compagnoni (ITA)	2:50.59
2002	Janica Kostelic (CRO)	2:30.01
2006	Julia Mancuso (USA)	2:09.19

SUPERGIANT SLALOM

		MIN:SEC
1988	Sigrid Wolf (AUT)	1:19.03
1992	Deborah Compagnoni (ITA)	1:21.22
1994	Diann Roffe-Steinrotter (USA)	1:22.15
1998	Picabo Street (USA)	1:18.02
2002	Daniela Ceccarelli (ITA)	1:13.59
2006	Michaela Dorfmeister (AUT)	1:32.47

ALPINE COMBINED

		MIN:SEC
1936	Chrislt Cranz (GER)	
1948	Trude Beiser (AUT)	
1972	Annemarie Pröll (AUT)	
1976	Rosi Mittermaier (FRG)	
1988	Anita Wachter (AUT)	
1992	Petra Kronberger (AUT)	
1994	Pernilla Wiberg (SWE)	3:05.16[7]
1998	Katja Seizinger (GER)	2:40.74
2002	Janica Kostelic (CRO)	2:43.28
2006	Janica Kostelic (CRO)	2:51.08

Freestyle Skiing

MEN'S MOGULS

1992	Edgar Grospiron (FRA)
1994	Jean-Luc Brassard (CAN)
1998	Jonny Moseley (USA)
2002	Janne Lahtela (FIN)
2006	Dale Begg-Smith (AUS)

Winter Olympic Games Champions (continued)

Freestyle Skiing (men) (continued)

MEN'S AERIALS

1994	Andreas Schönbächler (SUI)	
1998	Eric Bergoust (USA)	
2002	Ales Valenta (CZE)	
2006	Han Xiaopeng (CHN)	

WOMEN'S MOGULS

1992	Donna Weinbrecht (USA)
1994	Stine Lise Hattestad (NOR)
1998	Tae Satoya (JPN)
2002	Kari Traa (NOR)
2006	Jennifer Heil (CAN)

WOMEN'S AERIALS

1994	Lina Cheryazova (UZB)
1998	Nikki Stone (USA)
2002	Alisa Camplin (AUS)
2006	Evelyne Leu (SUI)

Nordic Skiing (men)

1.5-KILOMETER CROSS-COUNTRY SPRINT		MIN:SEC
2002	Tor Arne Hetland (NOR)	2:56.9
2006	Björn Lind (SWE)	2:26.5

10-KILOMETER CROSS-COUNTRY		MIN:SEC
1992	Vegard Ulvang (NOR)	27:36.0
1994	Bjørn Daehlie (NOR)	24:20.1
1998	Bjørn Daehlie (NOR)	27:24.5

15-KILOMETER CROSS-COUNTRY[8]		HR:MIN:SEC
1924	Thorleif Haug (NOR)	1:14:31.0
1928	Johan Gröttumsbraaten (NOR)	1:37:01.0
1932	Sven Utterström (SWE)	1:23:07.0
1936	Erik-August Larsson (SWE)	1:14:38.0
1948	Martin Lundström (SWE)	1:13:50.0
1952	Hallgeir Brenden (NOR)	1:01:34.0
1956	Hallgeir Brenden (NOR)	49:39.0
1960	Hakkon Brusveen (NOR)	51:55.5
1964	Eero Mäntyranta (FIN)	50:54.1
1968	Harald Grönningen (NOR)	47:54.2
1972	Sven-Ake Lundbäck (SWE)	45:28.24[1]
1976	Nikolay Bazhukov (URS)	43:58.47
1980	Thomas Wassberg (SWE)	41:57.63
1984	Gunde Svan (SWE)	41:25.60
1988	Mikhail Devyatyarov (URS)	41:18.9
1998	Thomas Alsgaard (NOR)	39:13.7
2002	Andrus Veerpalu (EST)	37:07.4
2006	Andrus Veerpalu (EST)	38:01.3

COMBINED PURSUIT[9]		HR:MIN:SEC
1992	Bjørn Daehlie (NOR)	1:05:37.9
1994	Bjørn Daehlie (NOR)	1:00:08.8
1998	Thomas Alsgaard (NOR)	1:07:01.7
2002	Thomas Alsgaard (NOR); Frode Estil (NOR) (tied)[10]	49:48.9
2006	Yevgeny Dementyev (RUS)	1:17:00.8

30-KILOMETER CROSS-COUNTRY		HR:MIN:SEC
1956	Veikko Hakulinen (FIN)	1:44:06.0
1960	Sixten Jernberg (SWE)	1:51:03.9
1964	Eero Mäntyranta (FIN)	1:30:50.7
1968	Franco Nones (ITA)	1:35:39.2
1972	Vyacheslav Vedenin (URS)	1:36:31.15[1]
1976	Sergey Savelyev (URS)	1:30:29.38
1980	Nikolay Zimyatov (URS)	1:27:02.80
1984	Nikolay Zimyatov (URS)	1:28:56.30
1988	Aleksey Prokourorov (URS)	1:24:26.3
1992	Vegard Ulvang (NOR)	1:22:27.8

Nordic Skiing (men) (continued)

30-KILOMETER CROSS-COUNTRY (CONTINUED)		HR:MIN:SEC
1994	Thomas Alsgaard (NOR)	1:12:26.4
1998	Mika Myllylä (FIN)	1:33:56.0
2002	Christian Hoffmann (AUT)[10]	1:11:31.0

50-KILOMETER CROSS-COUNTRY		HR:MIN:SEC
1924	Thorleif Haug (NOR)	3:44:32.0
1928	Per Erik Hedlund (SWE)	4:52:03.3
1932	Veli Saarinen (FIN)	4:28:00.0
1936	Elis Viklund (SWE)	3:30:11.0
1948	Nils Karlsson (SWE)	3:47:48.0
1952	Veikko Hakulinen (FIN)	3:33:33.0
1956	Sixten Jernberg (SWE)	2:50:27.0
1960	Kalevi Hämäläinen (FIN)	2:59:06.3
1964	Sixten Jernberg (SWE)	2:43:52.6
1968	Olle Ellefsäter (NOR)	2:28:45.8
1972	Pål Tyldum (NOR)	2:43:14.75[1]
1976	Ivar Formo (NOR)	2:37:30.05
1980	Nikolay Zimyatov (URS)	2:27:24.60
1984	Thomas Wassberg (SWE)	2:15:55.80
1988	Gunde Svan (SWE)	2:04:30.9
1992	Bjørn Daehlie (NOR)	2:03:41.5
1994	Vladimir Smirnov (KAZ)	2:07:20.3
1998	Bjørn Daehlie (NOR)	2:05:08.2
2002	Mikhail Ivanov (RUS)[10]	2:06:20.8
2006	Giorgio Di Centa (ITA)	2:06:11.8

4 × 10-KILOMETER RELAY		HR:MIN:SEC
1936	Finland	2:41:33.0
1948	Sweden	2:32:08.0
1952	Finland	2:20:16.0
1956	USSR	2:15:30.0
1960	Finland	2:18:45.6
1964	Sweden	2:18:34.6
1968	Norway	2:08:33.5
1972	USSR	2:04:47.94[1]
1976	Finland	2:07:59.72
1980	USSR	1:57:03.46
1984	Sweden	1:55:06.30
1988	Sweden	1:43:58.6
1992	Norway	1:39:26.0
1994	Italy	1:41:15.0
1998	Norway	1:40:55.7
2002	Norway	1:32:45.5
2006	Italy	1:43:45.7

SKI JUMPING (70 METERS)[11]	
1924	Jacob Tullin Thams (NOR)
1928	Alf Andersen (NOR)
1932	Birger Ruud (NOR)
1936	Birger Ruud (NOR)
1948	Petter Hugsted (NOR)
1952	Arnfinn Bergmann (NOR)
1956	Antti Hyvärinen (FIN)
1960	Helmut Recknagel (GER)[5]
1964	Veikko Kankkonen (FIN)
1968	Jiri Raska (TCH)
1972	Yukio Kasaya (JPN)
1976	Hans-Georg Aschenbach (GDR)
1980	Toni Innauer (AUT)
1984	Jens Weissflog (GDR)
1988	Matti Nykänen (FIN)

SKI JUMPING (90 METERS)[11]	
1964	Toralf Engan (NOR)
1968	Vladimir Belousov (URS)
1972	Wojciech Fortuna (POL)
1976	Karl Schnabl (AUT)

Winter Olympic Games Champions (continued)

Nordic Skiing (men) (continued)

SKI JUMPING (90 METERS)[11] (CONTINUED)
1980	Jens Tormanen (FIN)	
1984	Matti Nykänen (FIN)	
1988	Matti Nykänen (FIN)	
1992	Ernst Vettori (AUT)	
1994	Espen Bredesen (NOR)	
1998	Jani Soininen (FIN)	
2002	Simon Ammann (SUI)	
2006	Lars Bystøl (NOR)	

SKI JUMPING (120 METERS)[11]
1992	Toni Nieminen (FIN)
1994	Jens Weissflog (GER)
1998	Kazuyoshi Funaki (JPN)
2002	Simon Ammann (SUI)
2006	Thomas Morganstern (AUT)

NORDIC COMBINED SPRINT (7.5 KILOMETERS)
2002	Samppa Lajunen (FIN)
2006	Felix Gottwald (AUT)

NORDIC COMBINED (15 KILOMETERS)
1924	Thorleif Haug (NOR)
1928	Johan Gröttumsbraaten (NOR)
1932	Johan Gröttumsbraaten (NOR)
1936	Oddbjörn Hagen (NOR)
1948	Heikki Hasu (NOR)
1952	Simon Slåttvik (NOR)
1956	Sverre Stenersen (NOR)
1960	Georg Thoma (GER)[5]
1964	Tormod Knutsen (NOR)
1968	Franz Keller (FRG)
1972	Ulrich Wehling (GDR)
1976	Ulrich Wehling (GDR)
1980	Ulrich Wehling (GDR)
1984	Tom Sandberg (NOR)
1988	Hippolyt Kempf (SUI)
1992	Fabrice Guy (FRA)
1994	Fred Börre Lundberg (NOR)
1998	Bjarte Engen Vik (NOR)
2002	Samppa Lajunen (FIN)
2006	Georg Hettich (GER)

TEAM SKI JUMPING (120 METERS)
1988	Finland (90-m event)
1992	Finland
1994	Germany
1998	Japan
2002	Germany
2006	Austria

NORDIC COMBINED TEAM RELAY
1988	West Germany
1992	Japan
1994	Japan
1998	Norway
2002	Finland
2006	Austria

Nordic Skiing (women)

1.5-KILOMETER CROSS-COUNTRY SPRINT
		MIN:SEC
2002	Yuliya Chepalova (RUS)	3:10.6
2006	Chandra Crawford (CAN)	2:12.3

5-KILOMETER CROSS-COUNTRY
		MIN:SEC
1964	Klavdiya Boyarskikh (URS)	17:50.5
1968	Toini Gustafsson (SWE)	16:45.2
1972	Galina Kulakova (URS)	17:00.50[1]

Nordic Skiing (women) (continued)

5-KILOMETER CROSS-COUNTRY (CONTINUED)
		MIN:SEC
1976	Helena Takalo (FIN)	15:48.69
1980	Raisa Smetanina (URS)	15:06.92
1984	Marja-Liisa Hämäläinen (FIN)	17:04.00
1988	Marjo Matikainen (FIN)	15:04.00
1992	Marjut Lukkarinen (FIN)	14:13.8
1994	Lyubov Yegorova (RUS)	14:08.8
1998	Larisa Lazutina (RUS)	17:39.9

10-KILOMETER CROSS-COUNTRY
		MIN:SEC
1952	Lydia Wideman (FIN)	41:40.0
1956	Lyubov Kozyreva (URS)	38:11.0
1960	Mariya Gusakova (URS)	39:46.6
1964	Klavdiya Boyarskikh (URS)	40:24.3
1968	Toini Gustafsson (SWE)	36:46.5
1972	Galina Kulakova (URS)	34:17.82[1]
1976	Raisa Smetanina (URS)	30:13.41
1980	Barbara Petzold (GDR)	30:31.54
1984	Marja-Liisa Hämäläinen (FIN)	31:44.20
1988	Vida Ventsene (URS)	30:08.30
1998	Larisa Lazutina (RUS)	46:06.9
2002	Bente Skari (NOR)	28:05.6
2006	Kristina Smigun (EST)	27:51.4

COMBINED PURSUIT[12]
		MIN:SEC
1992	Lyubov Yegorova (UNT)[2]	40:08.4
1994	Lyubov Yegorova (RUS)	41:38.1
1998	Larisa Lazutina (RUS)	46:06.9
2002	Beckie Scott (CAN)[10]	25.09:9
2006	Kristina Smigun (EST)	42:48.7

15-KILOMETER CROSS-COUNTRY
		MIN:SEC
1992	Lyubov Yegorova (UNT)[2]	42:20.8
1994	Manuela di Centa (ITA)	39:44.5
1998	Olga Danilova (RUS)	46:55.40
2002	Stefania Belmondo (ITA)	39:54.4

20-KILOMETER CROSS-COUNTRY
		HR:MIN:SEC
1984	Marja-Liisa Hämäläinen (FIN)	1:01:45.0
1988	Tamara Tikhonova (URS)	55:53.6

30-KILOMETER CROSS-COUNTRY
		HR:MIN:SEC
1992	Stefania Belmondo (ITA)	1:22:30.1
1994	Manuela di Centa (ITA)	1:25:41.6
1998	Yuliya Chepalova (RUS)	1:22:01.5
2002	Gabriella Paruzzi (ITA)[10]	1:30:57.1
2006	Katerina Neumannova (CZE)	1:22:25.4

4 × 5-KILOMETER RELAY
		HR:MIN:SEC
2002	Germany	49:30.6
2006	Russia	54:47.7

Sled-dog Race
1932	Emile St. Goddard (CAN)

Snowboarding (men)

GIANT SLALOM
1998	Ross Rebagliati (CAN)
2002	Philipp Schoch (SUI)
2006	Philipp Schoch (SUI)

HALFPIPE
1998	Gian Simmen (SUI)
2002	Ross Powers (USA)
2006	Shaun White (USA)

Winter Olympic Games Champions (continued)

Snowboarding (men) (continued)

SNOWBOARDCROSS
2006 Seth Wescott (USA)

Snowboarding (women)

GIANT SLALOM
1998 Karine Ruby (FRA)
2002 Isabelle Blanc (FRA)
2006 Daniela Meuli (SUI)

HALFPIPE
1998 Nicola Thost (GER)
2002 Kelly Clark (USA)
2006 Hannah Teter (USA)

SNOWBOARDCROSS
2006 Tanja Frieden (SUI)

Speed Skating (men)

4 × 5-KILOMETER RELAY[13]		HR:MIN:SEC
1956	Finland	1:09:01.0
1960	Sweden	1:04:21.4
1964	USSR	59:20.2
1968	Norway	57:30.0
1972	USSR	48:46.15[1]
1976	USSR	1:07:49.75
1980	East Germany	1:02:11.10
1984	Norway	1:06:49.70
1988	USSR	59:51.10
1992	Unified Team[2]	59:34.8
1994	Russia	57:12.5

500 METERS		SEC
1924	Charles Jewtraw (USA)	44.0
1928	Clas Thunberg (FIN); Bernt Evensen (NOR) (tied)	43.4
1932	John Shea (USA)	43.4
1936	Ivar Ballangrud (NOR)	43.4
1948	Finn Helgesen (NOR)	43.1
1952	Kenneth Henry (USA)	43.2
1956	Yevgeny Grishin (URS)	40.2
1960	Yevgeny Grishin (URS)	40.2
1964	Richard McDermott (USA)	40.1
1968	Erhard Keller (FRG)	40.3
1972	Erhard Keller (FRG)	39.44[1]
1976	Yevgeny Kulikov (URS)	39.17
1980	Eric Heiden (USA)	38.03
1984	Sergey Fokichev (URS)	38.19
1988	Uew-Jens Mey (GDR)	36.45
1992	Uew-Jens Mey (GER)	37.14
1994	Aleksandr Golubyov (RUS)	36.33
1998	Hiroyasu Shimizu (JPN)	71.35[14]
2002	Casey Fitzrandolph (USA)	69.23[14]
2006	Joey Cheek (USA)	69.76[14]

1,000 METERS		MIN:SEC
1976	Peter Mueller (USA)	1:19.32[1]
1980	Eric Heiden (USA)	1:15.18
1984	Gaetan Boucher (CAN)	1:15.80
1988	Nikolay Gulyayev (URS)	1:13.03
1992	Olaf Zinke (GER)	1:14.85
1994	Dan Jansen (USA)	1:12.43
1998	Ids Postma (NED)	1:10.71
2002	Gerard van Velde (NED)	1:07.18
2006	Shani Davis (USA)	1:08.89

1,500 METERS		MIN:SEC
1924	Clas Thunberg (FIN)	2:20.8
1928	Clas Thunberg (FIN)	2:21.1

Speed Skating (men) (continued)

1,500 METERS (CONTINUED)		MIN:SEC
1932	John Shea (USA)	2:57.5
1936	Charles Mathisen (NOR)	2:19.2
1948	Sverre Farstad (NOR)	2:17.6
1952	Hjalmar Andersen (NOR)	2:20.4
1956	Yury Mikhaylov (URS); Yevgeny Grishin (URS) (tied)	2:08.6
1960	Yevegeny Grishin (URS); Roald Aas (NOR) (tied)	2:10.4
1964	Ants Antson (URS)	2:10.3
1968	Cornelis Verkerk (NED)	2:03.4
1972	Ard Schenk (NED)	2:02.96[1]
1976	Jan Egil Storholt (NOR)	1:59.38
1980	Eric Heiden (USA)	1:55.44
1984	Gaetan Boucher (CAN)	1:58.36
1988	André Hoffmann (GDR)	1:52.06
1992	Johann Olav Koss (NOR)	1:54.81
1994	Johann Olav Koss (NOR)	1:51.29
1998	Aadne Sondral (NOR)	1:47.87
2002	Derek Parra (USA)	1:43.95
2006	Enrico Fabris (ITA)	1:45.97

5,000 METERS		MIN:SEC
1924	Clas Thunberg (FIN)	8:39.0
1928	Ivar Ballangrud (NOR)	8:50.5
1932	Irving Jaffee (USA)	9:40.8
1936	Ivar Ballangrud (NOR)	8:19.6
1948	Reidar Liaklev (NOR)	8:29.4
1952	Hjalmar Andersen (NOR)	8:10.6
1956	Boris Shilkov (URS)	7:48.7
1960	Viktor Kosichkin (URS)	7:51.3
1964	Knut Johannesen (NOR)	7:38.4
1968	Fred Anton Maier (NOR)	7:22.4
1972	Ard Schenk (NED)	7:23.61[1]
1976	Sten Stensen (NOR)	7:24.48
1980	Eric Heiden (USA)	7:02.29
1984	Thomas Gustafson (SWE)	7:12.28
1988	Thomas Gustafson (SWE)	6:44.63
1992	Geir Karlstad (NOR)	6:59.97
1994	Johann Olav Koss (NOR)	6:34.96
1998	Gianni Romme (NED)	6:22.20
2002	Jochem Uytdehaage (NED)	6:14.66
2006	Chad Hedrick (USA)	6:14.68

10,000 METERS		MIN:SEC
1924	Julius Skutnabb (FIN)	18:04.8
1932	Irving Jaffee (USA)	19:13.6
1936	Ivar Ballangrud (NOR)	17:24.3
1948	Ake Seyffarth (SWE)	17:26.3
1952	Hjalmar Andersen (NOR)	16:45.8
1956	Sigvard Ericsson (SWE)	16:35.9
1960	Knut Johannesen (NOR)	15:46.6
1964	Jonny Nilsson (SWE)	15:50.1
1968	Johnny Höglin (SWE)	15:23.6
1972	Ard Schenk (NED)	15:01.35[1]
1976	Piet Kleine (NED)	14:50.59
1980	Eric Heiden (USA)	14:28.13
1984	Igor Malkov (URS)	14:39.90
1988	Thomas Gustafson (SWE)	13:48.20
1992	Bart Veldkamp (NED)	14:12.12
1994	Johann Olav Koss (NOR)	13:30.55
1998	Gianni Romme (NED)	13:15.33
2002	Jochem Uytdehaage (NED)	12:58.92
2006	Bob de Jong (NED)	13:01.57

COMBINED SPEED SKATING
1924 Clas Thunberg (FIN)

Winter Olympic Games Champions (continued)

Speed Skating (men) (continued)

TEAM PURSUIT

		MIN:SEC
2006	Italy	3:44.46

Speed Skating (women)

500 METERS

		SEC
1960	Helga Haase (GER)[6]	45.9
1964	Lidiya Skoblikova (URS)	45.0
1968	Lyudmila Titova (URS)	46.1
1972	Anne Henning (USA)	43.33[1]
1976	Sheila Young (USA)	42.76
1980	Karin Enke (GDR)	41.78
1984	Christa Rothenburger (GDR)	41.02
1988	Bonnie Blair (USA)	39.10
1992	Bonnie Blair (USA)	40.33
1994	Bonnie Blair (USA)	39.25
1998	Catriona LeMay Doan (CAN)	76.60[14]
2002	Catriona LeMay Doan (CAN)	74.75[14]
2006	Svetlana Zhurova (RUS)	76.57[14]

1,000 METERS

		MIN:SEC
1960	Klara Guseva (URS)	1:34:1
1964	Lidiya Skoblikova (URS)	1:32.6
1968	Carolina Geijssen (NED)	1:32.6
1972	Monika Pflug (FRG)	1:31.40[1]
1976	Tatyana Averina (URS)	1:28.43
1980	Natalya Petruseva (URS)	1:24.10
1984	Karin Enke (GDR)	1:21.61
1988	Christa Rothenburger (GDR)	1:17.65
1992	Bonnie Blair (USA)	1:21.90
1994	Bonnie Blair (USA)	1:18.74
1998	Marianne Timmer (NED)	1:16.51
2002	Chris Witty (USA)	1:13.83
2006	Marianne Timmer (NED)	1:16.05

1,500 METERS

		MIN:SEC
1960	Lidiya Skoblikova (URS)	2:25.2
1964	Lidiya Skoblikova (URS)	2:22.6
1968	Kaija Mustonen (FIN)	2:22.4
1972	Dianne Holum (USA)	2:20.85[1]
1976	Galina Stepanskaya (URS)	2:16.58
1980	Annie Borckink (NED)	2:10.95
1984	Karin Enke (GDR)	2:03.42
1988	Yvonne van Gennip (NED)	2:00.68
1992	Jacqueline Börner (GER)	2:05.87
1994	Emese Hunyady (AUT)	2:02.19
1998	Marianne Timmer (NED)	1:57.58
2002	Anni Friesinger (GER)	1:54.02
2006	Cindy Klassen (CAN)	1:55.27

3,000 METERS

		MIN:SEC
1960	Lidiya Skoblikova (URS)	5:14.3
1964	Lidiya Skoblikova (URS)	5:14.9
1968	Johanna Schut (NED)	4:56.2
1972	Christina Baas-Kaiser (NED)	4:52.14[1]
1976	Tatyana Averina (URS)	4:45.19
1980	Björg Eva Jensen (NOR)	4:32.13
1984	Andrea Schöne (GDR)	4:24.79
1988	Yvonne van Gennip (NED)	4:11.94
1992	Gunda Niemann (GER)	4:19.90
1994	Svetlana Bazhanova (RUS)	4:17.43
1998	Gunda Niemann-Stirnemann (GER)	4:07.29
2002	Claudia Pechstein (GER)	3:57.70
2006	Ireen Wüst (NED)	4:02.43

Speed Skating (women) (continued)

5,000 METERS

		MIN:SEC
1988	Yvonne van Gennip (NED)	7:14.13
1992	Gunda Niemann (GER)	7:31.57
1994	Claudia Pechstein (GER)	7:14.37
1998	Claudia Pechstein (GER)	6:59.61
2002	Claudia Pechstein (GER)	6:46.91
2006	Clara Hughes (CAN)	6:59.07

TEAM PURSUIT

		MIN:SEC
2006	Germany	3:01.25

Short-Track Speed Skating (men)

500 METERS

		SEC
1994	Chae Ji-Hoon (KOR)	43.45
1998	Takafumi Nishitani (JPN)	42.862[6]
2002	Marc Gagnon (CAN)	41.802
2006	Apolo Anton Ohno (USA)	41.935

1,000 METERS

		MIN:SEC
1992	Kim Ki-Hoon (KOR)	1:30.76
1994	Kim Ki-Hoon (KOR)	1:34.57
1998	Kim Dong Sung (KOR)	1:32.428[6]
2002	Steven Bradbury (AUS)	1:29.109
2006	Ahn Hyun Soo (KOR)	1:26.739

1,500 METERS

		MIN:SEC
2002	Apolo Anton Ohno (USA)	2:18.541
2006	Ahn Hyun Soo (KOR)	2:25.341

5000-METER RELAY

		MIN:SEC
1992	South Korea	7:14.02
1994	Italy	7:11.74
1998	Canada	7:06.075[6]
2002	Canada	6:51.579
2006	South Korea	6:43.376

Short-Track Speed Skating (women)

500 METERS

		SEC
1992	Cathy Turner (USA)	47.04
1994	Cathy Turner (USA)	45.98
1998	Annie Perreault (CAN)	46.568[6]
2002	Yang Yang (A) (CHN)	44.187
2006	Wang Meng (CHN)	44.345

1,000 METERS

		MIN:SEC
1994	Chun Lee-Kyung (KOR)	1:36.87
1998	Chun Lee-Kyung (KOR)	1:42.776[6]
2002	Yang Yang (A) (CHN)	1:36.391
2006	Jin Sun Yu (KOR)	1:32.859

1,500 METERS

		MIN:SEC
2002	Ko Gi-Hyun (KOR)	2:31.581
2006	Jin Sun Yu (KOR)	2:23.494

3000-METER RELAY

		MIN:SEC
1992	Canada	4:36.62
1994	South Korea	4:26.64
1998	South Korea	4:16.260[6]
2002	South Korea	4:12.793
2006	South Korea	4:17.040

Winter Pentathlon[15]

1948	Gustav Lindh (SWE)

Winter Olympic Games Champions (continued)

[1]Race first timed in hundredths of a second.   [2]Unified Team, consisting of athletes from the Commonwealth of Independent States plus Georgia.   [3]In 1992 the relay was 3 × 7.5 km; from 1994–2002 it was 4 × 7.5 km.   [4]Five men.   [5]Joint East-West German team.   [6]Race first timed in thousandths of a second.   [7]Competition scored on points until 1994.   [8]1924–52, 18 km.   [9]Results of a 10- or 15-km classical leg determine the starting order of a 10- or 15-km freestyle leg, the first finisher of which is the overall winner; each leg was 15 km in the 2006 Games.   [10]Winner after disqualification of top finisher for drug use.   [11]From 1924 to 1960 the jumping was held on one hill. In 1964 there were two events, one on a 70-m and the other on an 80-m hill; from 1968 to 1988 there were 70-m and 90-m events. From 1992 to 2002 there were 90-m and 120-m events. In 2006 there were 95-m and 125-m events.   [12]Results of a 5- or 7.5-km classical leg determine the starting order of a 5-, 7.5-, or 10-km freestyle leg, the first finisher of which is the overall winner; each leg was 7.5 km in the 2006 Games.   [13]3 × 5-km relay until 1976.   [14]Combined time for two runs.   [15]Includes elements of cross-country skiing, downhill skiing, shooting, fencing, and horse riding.

Olympic Medal Winners—XXVIII Summer Games (2004)

The XXVIII Summer Games were held in Athens, Greece, 13–29 Aug 2004.

EVENT	GOLD MEDALIST	PERFORMANCE	SILVER MEDALIST	BRONZE MEDALIST
Archery				
Men's individual	Marco Galiazzo (ITA)	111–109	Hiroshi Yamamoto (JPN)	Tim Cuddihy (AUS)
Men's team	South Korea	251–245	Taiwan	Ukraine
Women's individual	Park Sung Hyun (KOR)	110–108	Lee Sung Jin (KOR)	Alison Williamson (GBR)
Women's team	South Korea	241–240	China	Taiwan
Badminton				
Men's singles	Taufik Hidayat (INA)	15–8, 15–7	Shon Seung Mo (KOR)	Soni Dwi Kuncoro (INA)
Men's doubles	South Korea	15–11, 15–4	South Korea	Indonesia
Women's singles	Zhang Ning (CHN)	11–8, 6–11, 7–11	Mia Audina (NED)	Zhou Mi (CHN)
Women's doubles	China	7–15, 15–4, 15–8	China	South Korea
Mixed doubles	China	1–15, 15–12, 12–15	Great Britain	Denmark
Baseball				
	Cuba	6–2	Australia	Japan
Basketball				
Men	Argentina	84–69	Italy	United States
Women	United States	74–63	Australia	Russia
Boxing[1]				
48 kg (105.6 lb)	Yan Bhartelemy Varela (CUB)		Atagun Yalcinkaya (TUR)	Zou Shiming (CHN); Sergey Kazakov (RUS)
51 kg (112.2 lb)	Yuriorkis Gamboa Toledano (CUB)		Jerome Thomas (FRA)	Rustamhodza Rahimov (GER); Fuad Aslanov (AZE)
54 kg (118.8 lb)	Guillermo Rigondeaux Ortiz (CUB)		Worapoj Petchkoom (THA)	Bahodirjon Sooltonov (UZB); Aghasi Mammadov (AZE)
57 kg (125.4 lb)	Aleksey Tishchenko (RUS)		Kim Song Guk (PRK)	Jo Seok Hwan (KOR); Vitali Tajbert (GER)
60 kg (132 lb)	Mario César Kindelan Mesa (CUB)		Amir Khan (GBR)	Murat Khrachev (RUS); Serik Yeleuov (KAZ)
64 kg (140.8)	Manus Boonjumnong (THA)		Yudel Johnson Cedeno (CUB)	Ionut Gheorghe (ROM); Boris Georgiev (BUL)
69 kg (151.8 lb)	Bakhtiyar Artayev (KAZ)		Lorenzo Aragon Armenteros (CUB)	Oleg Saytov (RUS); Kim Jung Joo (KOR)
75 kg (165 lb)	Gaydarbek Gaydarbekov (RUS)		Gennady Golovkin (KAZ)	Suriya Prasathinphimai (THA); Andre Dirrell (USA)
81 kg (178.2 lb	Andre Ward (USA)		Magomed Aripgadzhiyev (BLR)	Utkirbek Haydarov (UZB); Ahmed Ismail (EGY)

Olympic Medal Winners—XXVIII Summer Games (2004) (continued)

EVENT	GOLD MEDALIST	PERFORMANCE	SILVER MEDALIST	BRONZE MEDALIST
Boxing (continued)				
91 kg (200.2 lb)	Odlanier Solis Fonte (CUB)		Viktar Zuyev (BLR)	Naser Al-Shami (SYR); Mohamed El-sayed (EGY)
91+ kg (200.2+ lb)	Aleksandr Povetkin (RUS)		Mohamed Aly (EGY)	Roberto Cammarelle (ITA); Michel López Nuñez (CUB)
Canoeing				
Men				
500-m kayak singles	Adam van Koeverden (CAN)	1 min 37.919 sec	Nathan Baggaley (AUS)	Ian Wynne (GBR)
1,000-m kayak singles	Eirik Veraas Larsen (NOR)	3 min 25.897sec	Ben Fouhy (NZL)	Adam van Koeverden (CAN)
500-m kayak pairs	Germany	1 min 27.040 sec	Australia	Belarus
1,000-m kayak pairs	Sweden	3 min 18.420 sec	Italy	Norway
1,000-m kayak fours	Hungary	2 min 56.919 sec	Germany	Slovakia
Slalom kayak singles	Benoit Peschier (FRA)	187.96 pt	Campbell Walsh (GBR)	Fabien Lefevre (FRA)
500-m Canadian singles	Andreas Dittmer (GER)	1 min 46.383 sec	David Cal (ESP)	Maksim Opalev (RUS)
1,000-m Canadian singles	David Cal (ESP)	3 min 46.201 sec	Andreas Dittmer (GER)	Attila Vajda (HUN)
500-m Canadian pairs	China	1 min 40.278 sec	Cuba	Russia
1,000-m Canadian pairs	Germany	3 min 41.802 sec	Russia	Hungary
Slalom Canadian singles	Tony Estanguet (FRA)	189.16 pt	Michal Martikan (SVK)	Stefan Pfannmöller (GER)
Slalom Canadian pairs	Slovakia	207.16 pt	Germany	Czech Rep.
Women				
500-m kayak singles	Natasa Janics (HUN)	1 min 47.741 sec	Josefa Idem (ITA)	Caroline Brunet (CAN)
500-m kayak pairs	Hungary	1 min 38.101 sec	Germany	Poland
500-m kayak fours	Germany	1 min 34.340 sec	Hungary	Ukraine
Slalom kayak singles	Elena Kaliska (SVK)	210.03 pt	Rebecca Giddens (USA)	Helen Reeves (GBR)
Cycling				
Men				
Road race	Paolo Bettini (ITA)	5 hr 41 min 44 sec	Sergio Paulinho (POR)	Axel Merckx (BEL)
Individual road time trial	Tyler Hamilton (USA)	57 min 31.74 sec	Vyacheslav Yekimov (RUS)	Bobby Julich (USA)
1-km time trial	Chris Hoy (GBR)	1 min 0.711 sec	Arnaud Tournant (FRA)	Stefan Nimke (GER)
4,000-m individual pursuit	Bradley Wiggins (GBR)	4 min 16.304 sec	Brad McGee (AUS)	Sergi Escobar (ESP)
4,000-m team pursuit	Australia	3 min 58.223 sec	Great Britain	Spain
Individual sprint	Ryan Bayley (AUS)		Theo Bos (NED)	Rene Wolff (GER)
Team sprint	Germany	43.980 sec	Japan	France
Individual points race	Mikhail Ignatyev (RUS)	93 pt	Joan Llaneras (ESP)	Guido Fulst (GER)
Madison	Australia		Switzerland	Great Britain
Keirin	Ryan Bayley (AUS)		José Escuredo (ESP)	Shane Kelly (AUS)
Mountain bike	Julien Absalon (FRA)	2 hr 15 min 2 sec	José Antonio Hermida (ESP)	Bart Brentjens (NED)
Women				
Road race	Sara Carrigan (AUS)	3 hr 24 min 24 sec	Judith Arndt (GER)	Olga Slyusareva (RUS)
Individual road time trial	Leontien Zijlaard–van Moorsel (NED)	31 min 11.53 sec	Deirdre Demet-Barry (USA)	Karin Thürig (SUI)
500-m time trial	Anna Meares (AUS)	33.952 sec[3]	Jiang Yonghua (CHN)	Natalya Tsylinskaya (BLR)
Individual pursuit	Sarah Ulmer (NZL)	3 min 24.357 sec	Katie Mactier (AUS)	Leontien Zijlaard-van Moorsel (NED)

Olympic Medal Winners—XXVIII Summer Games (2004) (continued)

EVENT	GOLD MEDALIST	PERFORMANCE	SILVER MEDALIST	BRONZE MEDALIST
Cycling (continued)				
Women				
Individual sprint	Lori-Ann Muenzer (CAN)		Tamilla Abasova (RUS)	Anna Meares (AUS)
Individual points race	Olga Slyusareva (RUS)	20 pt	Bélem Guerrero Méndez (MEX)	Maria Luisa Calle Williams (COL)
Mountain bike	Gunn-Rita Dahle (NOR)	1 hr 56 min 51 sec	Marie-Helene Premont (CAN)	Sabine Spitz (GER)
Diving				
Men				
3-m springboard	Peng Bo (CHN)	787.38 pt	Alexandre Despatie (CAN)	Dmitry Sautin (RUS)
10-m platform	Hu Jia (CHN)	748.08 pt	Mathew Helm (AUS)	Tian Liang (CHN)
3-m synchronized springboard	Greece	353.34 pt	Germany	Australia
10-m synchronized platform	China	383.88 pt	Great Britain	Australia
Women				
3-m springboard	Guo Jingjing (CHN)	633.15 pt	Wu Minxia (CHN)	Yuliya Pakhalina (RUS)
10-m platform	Chantelle Newbery (AUS)	590.31 pt	Lao Lishi (CHN)	Loudy Tourky (AUS)
3-m synchronized springboard	China	336.90 pt	Russia	Australia
10-m synchronized platform	China	352.14 pt	Russia	Canada
Equestrian				
Individual 3-day event	Leslie Law (GBR)		Kimberly Severson (USA)	Philippa Funnell (GBR)
Team 3-day event	France		Great Britain	United States
Individual dressage	Anky van Grunsven (NED)		Ulla Salzgeber (GER)	Beatriz Ferrer-Salat (ESP)
Team dressage	Germany		Spain	United States
Individual jumping	Rodrigo Pessoa (BRA)		Chris Kappler (USA)	Marco Kutscher (GER)
Team jumping	Germany		United States	Sweden
Fencing				
Men				
Individual foil	Brice Guyart (FRA)		Salvatore Sanzo (ITA)	Andrea Cassara (ITA)
Team foil	Italy		China	Russia
Individual épée	Marcel Fischer (SUI)		Wang Lei (CHN)	Pavel Kolobkov (RUS)
Team épée	France		Hungary	Germany
Individual sabre	Aldo Montano (ITA)		Zsolt Nemcsik (HUN)	Vladislav Tretiyak (UKR)
Team sabre	France		Italy	Russia
Women				
Individual foil	Valentina Vezzali (ITA)		Giovanna Trillini (ITA)	Sylwia Gruchala (POL)
Individual épée	Timea Nagy (HUN)		Laura Flessel-Colovic (FRA)	Maureen Nisima (FRA)
Team épée	Russia		Germany	France
Individual sabre	Mariel Zagunis (USA)		Tan Xue (CHN)	Sada Jacobson (USA)
Field Hockey				
Men	Australia	2–1	The Netherlands	Germany
Women	Germany	2–1	The Netherlands	Argentina
Gymnastics				
Men				
Team	Japan	173.821 pt	United States	Romania
All-around	Paul Hamm (USA)	57.823 pt	Kim Dae Eun (KOR)	Yang Tae Young (KOR)
Floor exercise	Kyle Shewfelt (CAN)	9.787 pt	Marian Dragulescu (ROM)	Iordan Iovtchev (BUL)

Olympic Medal Winners—XXVIII Summer Games (2004) (continued)

EVENT	GOLD MEDALIST	PERFORMANCE	SILVER MEDALIST	BRONZE MEDALIST
Gymnastics (continued)				
Men				
Vault	Gervasio Deferr (ESP)	9.737 pt	Evkeni Sapronenko (LAT)	Marian Dragulescu (ROM)
Pommel horse	Teng Haibin (CHN)	9.837 pt	Marius Daniel Urzica (ROM)	Takehiro Kashima (JPN)
Rings	Dimosthenis Tampakos (GRE)	9.862 pt	Iordan Iovtchev (BUL)	Yuri Chechi (ITA)
Parallel bars	Valery Goncharov (UKR)	9.787 pt	Hiroyuki Tomita (JPN)	Li Xiaopeng (CHN)
High bar	Igor Cassina (ITA)	9.812 pt	Paul Hamm (USA)	Isao Yoneda (JPN)
Trampoline	Yury Nikitin (UKR)	41.50 pt	Aleksandr Moskalenko (RUS)	Henrik Stehlik (GER)
Women				
Team	Romania	114.283 pt	United States	Russia
All-around	Carly Patterson (USA)	38.387 pt	Svetlana Khorkina (RUS)	Zhang Nan (CHN)
Floor exercise	Catalina Ponor (ROM)	9.750 pt	Nicoleta Daniela Sofronie (ROM)	Patricia Moreno (ESP)
Vault	Monica Rosu (ROM)	9.656 pt	Annia Hatch (USA)	Anna Pavlova (RUS)
Uneven bars	Emilie Lepennec (FRA)	9.687 pt	Terin Humphrey (USA)	Courtney Kupets (USA)
Balance beam	Catalina Ponor (ROM)	9.787 pt	Carly Patterson (USA)	Alexandra Georgiana Eremia (ROM)
Trampoline	Anna Dogonadze (GER)	39.60 pt	Karen Cockburn (CAN)	Huang Shanshan (CHN)
Individual rhythmic	Alina Kabayeva (RUS)	108.400 pt	Irina Chashchina (RUS)	Anna Bessonova (UKR)
Team rhythmic	Russia	51.100 pt	Italy	Bulgaria
Handball (Team)				
Men	Croatia	26–24	Germany	Russia
Women	Denmark	38–36	South Korea	Ukraine
Judo[1,4]				
Men				
60 kg (132 lb)	Tadahiro Nomura (JPN)		Nestor Khergian (GEO)	Khashbaatar Tsagaanbaatar (MGL); Choi Min Ho (KOR)
66 kg (145.2 lb)	Masato Uchishiba (JPN)		Jozef Krnac (SVK)	Georgi Georgiev (BUL); Yordanis Arencibia (CUB)
73 kg (160.6 lb)	Lee Won Hee (KOR)		Vitaly Makarov (RUS)	Leandro Guilheiro (BRA); James Pedro (USA)
81 kg (178.2 lb)	Ilias Iliadis (GRE)		Roman Gontyuk (UKR)	Dmitry Nosov (RUS); Flavio Canto (BRA)
90 kg (198 lb)	Zurab Zviadauri (GEO)		Hiroshi Izumi (JPN)	Khasanbi Taov (RUS); Mark Huizinga (NED)
100 kg (220 lb)	Ihar Makarau (BLR)		Jang Sung Ho (KOR)	Michael Jurack (GER); Ariel Zeevi (ISR)
100+ kg (220+ lb)	Keiji Suzuki (JPN)		Tamerlan Tmenov (RUS)	Dennis van der Geest (NED); Indrek Pertelson (EST)
Women				
48 kg (105.6 lb)	Ryoko Tani (JPN)		Frederique Jossinet (FRA)	Julia Matijass (GER); Gao Feng (CHN)
52 kg (114.4 lb)	Xian Dongmei (CHN)		Yuki Yokosawa (JPN)	Amarilys Savon (CUB); Ilse Heylen (BEL)
57 kg (125.4 lb)	Yvonne Bönisch (GER)		Kye Sun Hui (PRK)	Deborah Gravenstijn (NED); Yurisleidy Lupetey (CUB)
63 kg (138.6 lb)	Ayumi Tanimoto (JPN)		Claudia Heill (AUT)	Urska Zolnir (SLO); (KOR); Driulys Gonzales (CUB)

Olympic Medal Winners—XXVIII Summer Games (2004) (continued)

EVENT	GOLD MEDALIST	PERFORMANCE	SILVER MEDALIST	BRONZE MEDALIST
Judo[1,4] (continued)				
Women				
70 kg (154 lb)	Masae Ueno (JPN)		Edith Bosch (NED)	Qin Dongya (CHN); Annett Böhm (GER)
78 kg (171.6 lb)	Noriko Anno (JPN)		Liu Xia (CHN)	Lucia Morico (ITA); Yurisel Laborde (CUB)
78+ kg (171.6 lb)	Maki Tsukada (JPN)		Dayma Beltran (CUB)	Tea Donguzashvili (RUS); Sun Fuming (CHN)
Modern Pentathlon				
Men	Andrey Moiseyev (RUS)		Andrejus Zadneprovskis (LTU)	Libor Capalini (CZE)
Women	Zsuzsanna Voros (HUN)		Jelena Rublevska (LAT)	Georgina Harland (GBR)
Rowing				
Men				
Single sculls	Olaf Tufte (NOR)	6 min 49.30 sec	Jueri Jaanson (EST)	Ivo Yanakiev (BUL)
Double sculls	France	6 min 29.00 sec	Slovenia	Italy
Quadruple sculls	Russia	5 min 56.85 sec	Czech Rep.	Ukraine
Coxless pairs (oars)	Australia	6 min 30.76 sec	Croatia	South Africa
Coxless fours (oars)	Great Britain	6 min 6.98 sec	Canada	Italy
Eights	United States	5 min 42.48 sec	The Netherlands	Australia
Lightweight double sculls	Poland	6 min 20.93 sec	France	Greece
Lightweight fours	Denmark	6 min 1.39 sec	Australia	Italy
Women				
Single sculls	Katrin Rutschow-Stomporowski (GER)	7 min 18.12 sec	Yekaterina Karsten-Khodotovitch (BLR)	Rumyana Neykova (BUL)
Double sculls	New Zealand	7 min 1.79 sec	Germany	Great Britain
Quadruple sculls	Germany	6 min 29.29 sec	Great Britain	Australia
Coxless pairs (oars)	Romania	7 min 6.55 sec	Great Britain	Belarus
Eights	Romania	6 min 17.70 sec	United States	The Netherlands
Lightweight double sculls	Romania	6 min 56.05 sec	Germany	The Netherlands
Sailing				
Men's 470	United States		Great Britain	Japan
Women's 470	Greece		Spain	Sweden
Men's Mistral	Gal Fridman (ISR)		Nikolaos Kaklamanakis (GRE)	Nick Dempsey (GBR)
Women's Mistral	Faustine Merret (FRA)		Yin Jian (CHN)	Alessandra Sensini (ITA)
Men's Finn	Ben Ainslie (GBR)		Rafael Trujillo (ESP)	Mateusz Kusznierewicz (POL)
Women's Europe	Siren Sundby (NOR)		Lenka Smidova (CZE)	Signe Livbjerg (DEN)
Women's Yngling	Great Britain		Ukraine	Denmark
Mixed 49er	Spain		Ukraine	Great Britain
Mixed Laser	Robert Scheidt (BRA)		Andreas Geritzer (AUT)	Vasilij Zbogar (SLO)
Mixed Star	Brazil		Canada	France
Mixed Tornado	Austria		United States	Argentina
Shooting				
Men				
Rapid-fire pistol	Ralf Schumann (GER)	694.9 pt	Sergey Poliakov (RUS)	Sergey Aliferenko (RUS)
Free pistol	Mikhail Nestruyev (RUS)	663.3 pt	Jin Jong Oh (KOR)	Kim Jong Su (PRK)
Air pistol	Wang Yifu (CHN)	690.0 pt[2]	Mikhail Nestruyev (RUS)	Vladimir Isakov (RUS)
10-m running (game) target	Manfred Kurzer (GER)	682.4 pt[3]	Aleksandr Blinov (RUS)	Dmitry Lykin (RUS)
Small-bore (sport) rifle, 3 positions	Jia Zhanbo (CHN)	1264.5 pt	Michael Anti (USA)	Christian Planer (AUT)
Small-bore (sport) rifle, prone	Matthew Emmons (USA)	599.0 pt	Christian Lusch (GER)	Sergey Martynov (BLR)

Olympic Medal Winners—XXVIII Summer Games (2004) (continued)

EVENT	GOLD MEDALIST	PERFORMANCE	SILVER MEDALIST	BRONZE MEDALIST
Shooting (continued)				
Men				
Air rifle	Zhu Quinan (CHN)	702.7 pt[3]	Li Jie (CHN)	Jozef Gonci (SVK)
Trap	Aleksey Alipov (RUS)	149.0 pt	Giovanni Pellielo (ITA)	Adam Vella (AUS)
Double trap	Ahmed Almaktoum (UAE)	189.0 pt	Rajyavardhan Rathore (IND)	Wang Zheng (CHN)
Skeet	Andrea Benelli (ITA)	149.0 pt	Marko Kemppainen (FIN)	Juan Miguel Rodríguez (CUB)
Women				
Sport pistol	Mariya Grozdeva (BUL)	688.2 pt	Lenka Hykova (CZE)	Irada Ashumova (AZE)
Air pistol	Olena Kostevych (UKR)	483.3 pt	Jasna Sekaric (SCG)	Mariya Grozdeva (BUL)
Small-bore (sport) rifle	Lyubov Galkina (RUS)	688.4 pt	Valentina Turisini (ITA)	Wang Chengyi (CHN)
Air rifle	Du Li (CHN)	502.0 pt[2]	Lyubov Galkina (RUS)	Katerina Kurkova (CZE)
Trap	Suzanne Balogh (AUS)	88.0 pt	Maria Quintanal (ESP)	Lee Bo Na (KOR)
Double trap	Kimberly Rhode (USA)	146.0 pt	Lee Bo Na (KOR)	Gao E (CHN)
Skeet	Diana Igaly (HUN)	97.0	Wei Ning (CHN)	Zemfira Meftakhetdinova (AZE)

Soccer (Association Football)				
Men	Argentina	1–0	Paraguay	Italy
Women	United States	2–1 (overtime)	Brazil	Germany

Softball				
	United States	5–1	Australia	Japan

Swimming				
Men				
50-m freestyle	Gary Hall, Jr. (USA)	21.93 sec	Duje Draganja (CRO)	Roland Mark Schoeman (RSA)
100-m freestyle	Pieter van den Hoogenband (NED)	48.17 sec	Roland Mark Schoeman (RSA)	Ian Thorpe (AUS)
200-m freestyle	Ian Thorpe (AUS)	1 min 44.71 sec[2]	Pieter van den Hoogenband (NED)	Michael Phelps (USA)
400-m freestyle	Ian Thorpe (AUS)	3 min 43.10 sec	Grant Hackett (AUS)	Klete Keller (USA)
1,500-m freestyle	Grant Hackett (AUS)	14 min 43.40 sec[2]	Larsen Jensen (USA)	David Davies (GBR)
100-m backstroke	Aaron Peirsol (USA)	54.06 sec	Markus Rogan (AUT)	Tomomi Morita (JPN)
200-m backstroke	Aaron Peirsol (USA)	1 min 54.95 sec[2]	Markus Rogan (AUT)	Razvan Florea (ROM)
100-m breaststroke	Kosuke Kitajima (JPN)	1 min 0.08 sec	Brendan Hansen (USA)	Hugues Duboscq (FRA)
200-m breaststroke	Kosuke Kitajima (JPN)	2 min 9.44 sec[2]	Daniel Gyurta (HUN)	Brendan Hansen (USA)
100-m butterfly	Michael Phelps (USA)	51.25 sec[2]	Ian Crocker (USA)	Andriy Serdinov (UKR)
200-m butterfly	Michael Phelps (USA)	1 min 54.04 sec[2]	Takashi Yamamoto (JPN)	Stephen Parry (GBR)
200-m individual medley	Michael Phelps (USA)	1 min 57.14 sec[2]	Ryan Lochte (USA)	George Bovell (TRI)
400-m individual medley	Michael Phelps (USA)	4 min 8.26 sec[3]	Erik Vendt (USA)	Laszlo Cseh (HUN)
4 x 100-m freestyle relay	South Africa	3 min 13.17 sec[3]	The Netherlands	United States
4 x 200-m freestyle relay	United States	7 min 7.33 sec	Australia	Italy
4 x 100-m medley relay	United States	3 min 30.68 sec[3]	Germany	Japan
Women				
50-m freestyle	Inge de Bruijn (NED)	24.58 sec	Malia Metella (FRA)	Lisbeth Lenton (AUS)
100-m freestyle	Jodie Henry (AUS)	53.84 sec	Inge de Bruijn (NED)	Natalie Coughlin (USA)
200-m freestyle	Camelia Potec (ROM)	1 min 58.03 sec	Federica Pellegrini (ITA)	Solenne Figues (FRA)
400-m freestyle	Laure Manaudou (FRA)	4 min 05.34 sec	Otylia Jedrzejczak (POL)	Kaitlin Sandeno (USA)
800-m freestyle	Ai Shibata (JPN)	8 min 24.54 sec	Laure Manaudou (FRA)	Diana Munz (USA)

Olympic Medal Winners—XXVIII Summer Games (2004) (continued)

EVENT	GOLD MEDALIST	PERFORMANCE	SILVER MEDALIST	BRONZE MEDALIST
Swimming (continued)				
Women				
100-m backstroke	Natalie Coughlin (USA)	1 min 0.37 sec	Kirsty Coventry (ZIM)	Laure Manaudou (FRA)
200-m backstroke	Kirsty Coventry (ZIM)	2 min 9.19 sec	Stanislava Komarova (RUS)	Reiko Nakamura (JPN)
100-m breaststroke	Luo Xuejuan (CHN)	1 min 6.64 sec[2]	Brooke Hanson (AUS)	Leisel Jones (AUS)
200-m breaststroke	Amanda Beard (USA)	2 min 23.37 sec[2]	Leisel Jones (AUS)	Anne Poleska (GER)
100-m butterfly	Petria Thomas (AUS)	57.72 sec	Otylia Jedrzejczak (POL)	Inge de Bruijn (NED)
200-m butterfly	Otylia Jedrzejczak (POL)	2 min 6.05 sec	Petria Thomas (AUS)	Yuko Nakanishi (JPN)
200-m individual medley	Yana Klochkova (UKR)	2 min 11.14 sec	Amanda Beard (USA)	Kirsty Coventry (ZIM)
400-m individual	Yana Klochkova (UKR)	4 min 34.83 sec	Kaitlin Sandeno (USA)	Georgina Bardach (ARG)
4 x 100-m freestyle relay	Australia	3 min 35.94 sec[3]	United States	The Netherlands
4 x 200-m freestyle relay	United States	7 min 53.42 sec[3]	China	Germany
4 x 100-m medley relay	Australia	3 min 57.32 sec[3]	United States	Germany
Synchronized Swimming				
Duet	Russia	99.833 pt	Japan	United States
Team	Russia	99.667 pt	Japan	United States
Table Tennis				
Men's singles	Ryu Seung Min (KOR)	11-3, 9-11, 11-9, 11-9, 11-13, 11-9	Wang Hao (CHN)	Wang Liqin (CHN)
Men's doubles	China	11-6, 11-9, 7-11, 11-8, 8-11, 11-5	Hong Kong	Denmark
Women's singles	Zhang Yining (CHN)	11-8, 11-7, 11-2, 11-2	Kim Hyang Mi (PRK)	Kim Kyung Ah (KOR)
Women's doubles	China	11-9, 11-7, 11-6, 11-6	South Korea	China
Taekwondo				
Men				
58 kg (127.6 lb)	Chu Mu Yen (TPE)		Oscar Francisco Salazar Blanco (MEX)	Tamer Bayoumi (EGY)
68 kg (149.6 lb)	Hadi Saei Bonehkohal (IRI)		Huang Hsiung Chih (TPE)	Song Seob Myeong (KOR)
80 kg (176 lb)	Steven Lopez (USA)		Bahri Tanrikulu (TUR)	Yossef Karami (IRI)
80+ kg (176+ lb)	Moon Dae Sung (KOR)		Alexandros Nikolaidis (GRE)	Pascal Gentil (FRA)
Women				
49 kg (107.8 lb)	Chen Shih Hsin (TPE)		Yanelis Yuliet Labrada Diaz (CUB)	Yaowapa Boorapolchai (THA)
57 kg (125.4 lb)	Jang Ji Won (KOR)		Nia Abdallah (USA)	Iridia Salazar Blanco (MEX)
67 kg (147.4 lb)	Luo Wei (CHN)		Elisavet Mystakidou (GRE)	Hwang Kyung Sun (KOR)
67+ kg (147.4+ lb)	Chen Zhong (CHN)		Myriam Baverel (FRA)	Adriana Carmona (VEN)
Tennis				
Men's singles	Nicolas Massu (CHI)	6-3, 3-6, 2-6, 6-3, 6-4	Mardy Fish (USA)	Fernando González (CHI)
Men's doubles	Chile	6-2, 4-6 3-6, 7-6, 6-4	Germany	Croatia
Women's singles	Justine Henin-Hardenne (BEL)	6-3, 6-3	Amelie Mauresmo (FRA)	Alicia Molik (AUS)
Women's doubles	China	6-3, 6-3	Spain	Argentina
Track and Field (Athletics)				
Men				
100 m	Justin Gatlin (USA)	9.85 sec	Francis Obikwelu (POR)	Maurice Greene (USA)
200 m	Shawn Crawford (USA)	19.79 sec	Bernard Williams (USA)	Justin Gatlin (USA)

Olympic Medal Winners—XXVIII Summer Games (2004) (continued)

Track and Field (Athletics) (continued)

Men

EVENT	GOLD MEDALIST	PERFORMANCE	SILVER MEDALIST	BRONZE MEDALIST
400 m	Jeremy Wariner (USA)	44.00 sec	Otis Harris (USA)	Derrick Brew (USA)
4 x 100-m relay	Great Britain	38.07 sec	United States	Nigeria
4 x 400-m relay	United States	2 min 55.91 sec	Australia	Nigeria
800 m	Yury Borzakovsky (RUS)	1 min 44.45 sec	Mbulaeni Mulaudzi (RSA)	Wilson Kipketer (DEN)
1,500 m	Hicham El Guerrouj (MAR)	3 min 34.18 sec	Bernard Lagat (KEN)	Rui Silva (POR)
5,000 m	Hicham El Guerrouj (MAR)	13 min 14.39 sec	Kenenisa Bekele (ETH)	Eliud Kipchoge (KEN)
10,000 m	Kenenisa Bekele (ETH)	27 min 05.10 sec[2]	Sileshi Sihine (ETH)	Zersenay Tadesse (ERI)
Marathon	Stefano Baldini (ITA)	2 hr 10 min 55 sec	Mebrahtom Keflezighi (USA)	Vanderlei Lima (BRA)
110-m hurdles	Liu Xiang (CHN)	12.91 sec[2]	Terrence Trammell (USA)	Anier Garcia (CUB)
400-m hurdles	Félix Sánchez (DOM)	47.63 sec	Danny McFarlane (JAM)	Naman Keita (FRA)
3,000-m steeple-chase	Ezekiel Kemboi (KEN)	8 min 5.81sec	Brimin Kipruto (KEN)	Paul Kipsiele Koech (KEN)
20-km walk	Ivano Brugnetti (ITA)	1 hour 19.40 sec	Francisco Javier Fernández (ESP)	Nathan Deakes (AUS)
50-km walk	Robert Korzeniow-ski (POL)	3 hr 38 min 46 sec	Denis Nizhe-gorodov (RUS)	Aleksey Voyevodin (RUS)
High jump	Stefan Holm (SWE)	2.36 m	Matt Hemingway (USA)	Jaroslav Baba (CZE)
Long jump	Dwight Phillips (USA)	8.59 m	John Moffitt (USA)	Joan Lino Martínez (ESP)
Triple jump	Christian Olsson (SWE)	17.79 m	Marian Oprea (ROM)	Danila Burkenya (RUS)
Pole vault	Timothy Mack (USA)	5.95 sec[2]	Toby Stevenson (USA)	Giuseppe Gibilisco (ITA)
Shot put	Yury Bilonog (UKR)	21.16 m	Adam Nelson (USA)	Joachim Olsen (DEN)
Discus throw	Virgilijus Alekna (LTU)	69.89 m[2]	Zoltan Kovago (HUN)	Aleksander Tammert (EST)
Javelin throw	Andreas Thorkildsen (NOR)	86.50 m	Vadims Vasilevskis (LAT)	Sergey Makarov (RUS)
Hammer throw	Adrian Annus (HUN)	83.19 m	Koji Murofushi (JPN)	Ivan Tikhon (BLR)
Decathlon	Roman Sebrele (CZE)		Bryan Clay (USA)	Dmitry Karpov (KAZ)

Women

EVENT	GOLD MEDALIST	PERFORMANCE	SILVER MEDALIST	BRONZE MEDALIST
100 m	Yuliya Nesterenko (BLR)	10.93 sec	Lauryn Williams (USA)	Veronica Campbell (JAM)
200 m	Veronica Campbell (JAM)	22.05 sec	Allyson Felix (USA)	Debbie Ferguson (BAH)
400 m	Tonique Williams-Darling (BAH)	49.41 sec	Ana Guevara (MEX)	Natalya Antyukh (RUS)
4 x 100-m relay	Jamaica	41.73 sec	Russia	France
4 x 400-m relay	United States	3 min 19.01 sec	Russia	Jamaica
800 m	Kelly Holmes (GBR)	1 min 56.38 sec	Hasna Benhassi (MAR)	Jolanda Ceplak (SLO)
1,500 m	Kelly Holmes (GBR)	3 min 57.90 sec	Tatyana Tomashova (RUS)	Maria Cioncan (ROM)
5,000 m	Meseret Defar (ETH)	14 min 45.65 sec	Isabella Ochichi (KEN)	Tirunesh Dibaba (ETH)
10,000 m	Xing Huina (CHN)	30 min 24.36 sec	Ejegayehu Dibaba (ETH)	Derartu Tulu (ETH)
Marathon	Mizuki Noguchi (JPN)	2 hr 26 min 20 sec	Catherine Ndereba (KEN)	Deena Kastor (USA)
100-m hurdles	Joanna Hayes (USA)	12.37 sec[2]	Olena Krasovska (UKR)	Melissa Morrison (USA)
400-m hurdles	Fani Halkia (GRE)	52.82 sec	Ionela Tirlea-Manolache (ROM)	Tetyana Tereshchuk-Antipova (UKR)
20-km walk	Athanasia Tsoumeleka (GRE)	1 hr 29 min 12 sec	Olimpiada Ivanova (RUS)	Jane Saville (AUS)
High jump	Yelena Slesarenko (RUS)	2.06 m[2]	Hestrie Cloete (RSA)	Viktoriya Styopina (UKR)
Long jump	Tatyana Lebedeva (RUS)	7.07 m	Irina Simagina (RUS)	Tatyana Kotova (RUS)
Triple jump	Françoise Mbango Etone (CMR)	15.30 m	Hrysopiyi Devetzi (GRE)	Tatyana Lebedeva (RUS)

Olympic Medal Winners—XXVIII Summer Games (2004) (continued)

EVENT	GOLD MEDALIST	PERFORMANCE	SILVER MEDALIST	BRONZE MEDALIST
Track and Field (Athletics) (continued)				
Women				
Pole vault	Yelena Isinbayeva (RUS)	4.91 m[3]	Svetlana Feofanova (RUS)	Anna Rogowska (POL)
Shot put	Irina Korzhanenko (RUS)	21.06 m	Yumileidi Cumba (CUB)	Nadine Kleinert (GER)
Discus throw	Natalya Sadova (RUS) ·	67.02 m	Anastasia Kelesidou (GRE)	Irina Yachenko (BLR)
Javelin throw	Osleidys Menéndez (CUB)	71.53 m[2]	Steffi Nerius (GER)	Mirela Manjani (GRE)
Hammer throw	Olga Kuzenkova (RUS)	75.02 m[2]	Yipsi Moreno (CUB)	Yunaika Crawford (CUB)
Heptathlon	Carolina Klüft (SWE)		Austra Skujyte (LTU)	Kelly Sotherton (GBR)
Triathlon				
Men	Hamish Carter (NZL)	1 hr 51 min 7.73 sec	Bevan Docherty (NZL)	Sven Reiderer (SUI)
Women	Kate Allen (AUT)	2 hrs 4 min 43.45 sec	Loretta Harrop (AUS)	Susan Williams (USA)
Volleyball				
Men's 12-team tournament	Brazil	25–15, 24–26, 25–20, 25–22	Italy	Russia
Women's 12-team tournament	China	28–30, 25–27, 25–20, 25–23, 15–12	Russia	Cuba
Men's beach	Brazil	21–16, 21–15	Spain	Switzerland
Women's beach	United States	21–17, 21–11	Brazil	United States
Water Polo				
Men	Hungary	8–7	Serbia and Montenegro	Russia
Women	Italy	10–9	Greece	United States
Weightlifting[4]				
Men				
56 kg (123.2 lb)	Halil Mutlu (TUR)	295.0	Wu Meijin (CHN)	Sedat Artuc (TUR)
62 kg (136.4 lb)	Shi Zhiyong (CHN)	325.0 kg	Le Maosheng (CHN)	Israel José Rubio (VEN)
69 kg (151.8 lb)	Zhang Guozheng (CHN)	347.5 kg	Lee Bae Young (KOR)	Nikolay Pechalov (CRO)
77 kg (169.4 lb)	Taner Sagir (TUR)	375.0 kg	Sergey Filimonov (KAZ)	Oleg Perepechenov (RUS)
85 kg (187 lb)	George Asanidze (GEO)	382.5 kg	Andrey Rybakou (BLR)	Pyrros Dimas (GRE)
94 kg (206.8 lb)	Milen Dobrev (BUL)	407.5 kg	Khajimurad Akkayev (RUS)	Eduard Tyukin (RUS)
105 kg (231 lb)	Dimitry Berestov (RUS)	425.0	Igor Razoronov (UKR)	Gleb Pisarevsky (RUS)
105+ kg (231+ lb)	Hossein Reza Zadeh (IRI)	472.5 kg	Viktors Scerbatihs (LAT)	Velichko Cholakov (BUL)
Women				
48 kg (105.6 lb)	Nurcan Taylan (TUR)	210.0 kg	Li Zhuo (CHN)	Aree Wiratthaworn (THA)
53 kg (116.6 lb)	Udomporn Polsak (THA)	222.5 kg	Raema Lisa Rumbewas (INA)	Mabel Mosquera (COL)
58 kg (127.6 lb)	Chen Yanqing (CHN)	237.5 kg	Ri Song Hui (PRK)	Wandee Kameaim (THA)
63 kg (138.6 lb)	Natalya Skakun (UKR)	242.5 kg	Hanna Batsyushka (BLR)	Tatsyana Stukalava (BLR)
69 kg (151.8 lb)	Liu Chunhong (CHN)	275.0	Eszter Krutzler (HUN)	Zarema Kasayeva (RUS)
75 kg (165 lb)	Pawina Thongsuk (THA)	272.5 kg	Nataliya Zabolotnaya (RUS)	Valentina Popova (RUS)
75+ kg (165 lb)	Tang Gonghong (CHN)	305.0 kg	Jang Mi Ran (KOR)	Agata Wrobel (POL)
Wrestling[4]				
Freestyle				
Men				
55 kg (121 lb)	Mavlet Batirov (RUS) ·		Stephen Abas (USA)	Chikara Tanabe (JPN)
60 kg (132 lb)	Yandro Miguel Quintana (CUB)		Masuod Jokar (IRI)	Kenji Inoue (JPN)

Olympic Medal Winners—XXVIII Summer Games (2004) (continued)

EVENT	GOLD MEDALIST	PERFORMANCE	SILVER MEDALIST	BRONZE MEDALIST
Wrestling (continued)				
Freestyle				
Men				
66 kg (145.2 lb)	Elbrus Tedeyev (UKR)		Jamill Kelly (USA)	Makhach Murtazaliyev (RUS)
74 kg (162.8 lb)	Buvaysa Saytyev (RUS)		Gennadiy Laliev (KAZ)	Ivan Fundora (CUB)
84 kg (184.8 lb)	Cael Sanderson (USA)		Moon Eui Jae (KOR)	Sazhid Sazhidov (RUS)
96 kg (211.2 lb)	Khajimurat Gatsalov (RUS)		Magomed Ibragimov (UZB)	Alireza Heidari (IRI)
120+ kg (264 lb)	Artur Taymazov (UZB)		Alireza Rezaei (IRI)	Aydin Polatci (TUR)
Women				
48 kg (105.6 lb)	Irini Merleni (UKR)		Chiharu Icho (JPN)	Patricia Miranda (USA)
55 kg (121 lb)	Saori Yoshida (JPN)		Tonya Verbeek (CAN)	Anna Gomis (FRA)
63 kg (138.6 lb)	Kaori Icho (JPN)		Sara McMann (USA)	Lise Legrand (FRA)
72 kg (158.4 lb)	Wang Xu (CHN)		Guzel Manyurova (RUS)	Kyoko Hamaguchi (JPN)
Greco-Roman				
Men				
55 kg (121 lb)	Istvan Majoros (HUN)		Geidar Mamedaliyev (RUS)	Artiom Kiouregkian (GRE)
60 kg (132 lb)	Jung Ji Hyun (KOR)		Roberto Monzón (CUB)	Armen Nazarian (BUL)
66 kg (145.2 lb)	Farid Mansurov (AZE)		Seref Eroglu (TUR)	Mkkhitar Manukyan (KAZ)
74 kg (162.8 lb)	Aleksandr Dokturishivili (UZB)		Marko Yli-Hannuksela (FIN)	Varteres Samurgachev (RUS)
84 kg (184.8 lb)	Alexey Mishin (RUS)		Ara Abrahamian (SWE)	Vyachaslau Makaranka (BLR)
96 kg (211.2 lb)	Karam Ibrahim (EGY)		Ramaz Nozadze (GEO)	Mehmet Ozal (TUR)
120+ kg (264 lb)	Khasan Baroyev (RUS)		Georgy Tsurtsumiya (KAZ)	Rulon Gardner (USA)

[1]Two bronze medals awarded in each weight division.   [2]Olympic record.   [3]World record.   [4]New weight classes introduced for 2000 games.   [5]Tie.

Olympic Medal Winners—XX Winter Games (2006)

The XX Winter Games were held in Turin, Italy, 10–26 Feb 2006. Since the games, several athletes have been stripped of medals for having failed drug tests. New medalists are shown in this table.

EVENT	GOLD MEDALIST	PERFORMANCE	SILVER MEDALIST	BRONZE MEDALIST
Alpine Skiing				
Men				
Downhill	Antoine Dénériaz (FRA)	1 min 48.80 sec	Michael Walchhofer (AUT)	Bruno Kernen (SUI)
Slalom	Benjamin Raich (AUT)	1 min 43.14 sec	Reinfried Herbst (AUT)	Rainier Schönfelder (AUT)
Giant slalom	Benjamin Raich (AUT)	2 min 35.00 sec	Joël Chenal (FRA)	Hermann Maier (AUT)
Super G	Kjetil André Aamodt (NOR)	1 min 30.65 sec	Hermann Maier (AUT)	Ambrosi Hoffmann (SUI)
Combined event	Ted Ligety (USA)	3 min 09.35 sec	Ivica Kostelic (CRO)	Rainier Schönfelder (AUT)
Women				
Downhill	Michaela Dorfmeister (AUT)	1 min 56.49 sec	Martina Schild (SUI)	Anja Pärson (SWE)
Slalom	Anja Pärson (SWE)	1 min 29.04 sec	Nicole Hosp (AUT)	Marlies Schild (AUT)
Giant slalom	Julia Mancuso (USA)	2 min 09.19 sec	Tanja Poutiainen (FIN)	Anna Ottosson (SWE)
Super G	Michaela Dorfmeister (AUT)	1 min 32.47 sec	Janica Kostelic (CRO)	Alexandra Meissnitzer (AUT)
Combined event	Janica Kostelic (CRO)	2 min 51.08 sec	Marlies Schild (AUT)	Anja Pärson (SWE)

Olympic Medal Winners—XX Winter Games (2006) (continued)

EVENT	GOLD MEDALIST	PERFORMANCE	SILVER MEDALIST	BRONZE MEDALIST
Nordic Skiing				
Men				
1.5-km sprint	Björn Lind (SWE)	2 min 26.5 sec	Roddy Darragon (FRA)	Thobias Fredriksson (SWE)
Team sprint	Thobias Fredriksson, Björn Lind (SWE)	17 min 02.9 sec	Jens Arne Svartedal, Tor Arne Hetland (NOR)	Ivan Alypov, Vasily Rochev (RUS)
15-km classical	Andrus Veerpalu (EST)	38 min 01.3 sec	Lukas Bauer (CZE)	Tobias Angerer (GER)
30-km pursuit	Yevgeny Dementyev (RUS)	1 hr 17 min 0.8 sec	Frode Estil (NOR)	Pietro Piller Cottrer (ITA)
50-km freestyle, mass start	Giorgio Di Centa (ITA)	2 hr 6 min 11.8 sec	Yevgeny Dementyev (RUS)	Mikhail Botwinov (AUT)
4 x 10-km relay	Italy	1 hr 43 min 45.7 sec	Germany	Sweden
95-m ski jump	Lars Bystøl (NOR)	266.5 pt	Matti Hautamäki (FIN)	Roar Ljøkelsøy (NOR)
125-m ski jump	Thomas Morgenstern (AUT)	276.9 pt	Andreas Kofler (AUT)	Lars Bystøl (NOR)
125-m team ski jump	Austria	984.0 pt	Finland	Norway
Nordic combined sprint (7.5-km)	Felix Gottwald (AUT)	17 min 35.0 sec	Magnus Moan (NOR)	Georg Hettich (GER)
Nordic combined 15-km	Georg Hettich (GER)	39 min 44.6 sec	Felix Gottwald (AUT)	Magnus Moan (NOR)
Nordic combined team relay	Austria	49 min 42.6 sec	Germany	Finland
Women				
1.5-km sprint	Chandra Crawford (CAN)	2 min 12.3 sec	Claudia Künzel (GER)	Alena Sidko (RUS)
Team sprint	Anna Dahlberg, Lina Andersson (SWE)	16 min 36.9 sec	Sara Renner, Beckie Scott (CAN)	Aino Kaisa Saarinen, Virpi Kuitunen (FIN)
10-km classical	Kristina Smigun (EST)	27 min 51.4 sec	Marit Bjørgen (NOR)	Hilde G. Pedersen (NOR)
15-km pursuit	Kristina Smigun (EST)	42 min 48.7 sec	Katerina Neumannova (CZE)	Yevgeniya Medvedeva-Abruzova (RUS)
30-freestyle, mass start	Katerina Neumannova (CZE)	1 hr 22 min 25.4 sec	Yuliya Chepalova (RUS)	Justyna Kowalczyk (POL)
4 x 5-km relay	Russia	54 min 47.7 sec	Germany	Italy
Biathlon				
Men				
10-km sprint	Sven Fischer (GER)	26 min 11.6 sec	Halvard Hanevold (NOR)	Frode Andresen (NOR)
12.5-km pursuit	Vincent Defrasne (FRA)	35 min 20.2 sec	Ole Einar Bjørndalen (NOR)	Sven Fischer (GER)
20 km	Michael Greis (GER)	54 min 23.0 sec	Ole Einar Bjørndalen (NOR)	Halvard Hanevold (NOR)
4 x 6-km relay	Germany	1 hr 21 min 51.5 sec	Russia	France
15-km mass start	Michael Greis (GER)	47 min 20.0 sec	Tomasz Sikora (POL)	Ole Einar Bjørndalen (NOR)
Women				
7.5-km sprint	Florence Baverel-Robert (FRA)	22 min 31.4 sec	Anna Carin Olofsson (SWE)	Liliya Yefremova (UKR)
10-km pursuit	Kali Wilhelm (GER)	36 min 43.6 sec	Martina Glagow (GER)	Albina Akhatova (RUS)
15 km	Svetlana Ishmuratova (RUS)	49 min 24.1 sec	Martina Glagow (GER)	Albina Akhatova (RUS)
4 x 6-km relay	Russia	1 hr 16 min 12.5 sec	Germany	France
12.5-km mass start	Anna Carin Olofsson (SWE)	40 min 36.5 sec	Kati Wilhelm (GER)	Uschi Disl (GER)
Freestyle Skiing				
Men				
Moguls	Dale Begg-Smith (AUS)	26.77 pt	Mikko Rönkainen (FIN)	Toby Dawson (USA)
Aerials	Han Xiaopeng (CHN)	250.77 pt	Dmitry Dashinsky (BLR)	Vladimir Lebedev (RUS)

Olympic Medal Winners—XX Winter Games (2006) (continued)

EVENT	GOLD MEDALIST	PERFORMANCE	SILVER MEDALIST	BRONZE MEDALIST
Freestyle Skiing (continued)				
Women				
Moguls	Jennifer Heil (CAN)	26.50 pt	Kari Traa (NOR)	Sandra Laoura (FRA)
Aerials	Evelyne Leu (SUI)	202.55 pt	Li Nina (CHN)	Alisa Camplin (AUS)
Snowboarding				
Men				
Parallel giant slalom	Philipp Schoch (SUI)		Simon Schoch (SUI)	Siegfried Grabner (AUT)
Halfpipe	Shaun White (USA)	46.8 pt	Danny Kass (USA)	Markku Koski (FIN)
Snowboardcross (SBX)	Seth Wescott (USA)		Radoslav Zidek (SVK)	Paul-Henri Delerue (FRA)
Women				
Parallel giant slalom	Daniela Meuli (SUI)		Amelie Kober (GER)	Doris Günther (AUT)
Halfpipe	Hannah Teter (USA)	46.4 pt	Gretchen Bleiler (USA)	Kjersti Buaas (NOR)
Snowboardcross (SBX)	Tanja Frieden (SUI)		Lindsey Jacobellis (USA)	Dominique Maltais (CAN)
Figure Skating				
Men	Yevgeny Plushchenko (RUS)	167.67 pt	Jeffrey Buttle (CAN)	Evan Lysacek (USA)
Women	Shizuka Arakawa (JPN)	191.34 pt	Sasha Cohen (USA)	Irina Slutskaya (RUS)
Pairs	Tatyana Totmyanina, Maksim Marinin (RUS)	135.84 pt	Zhang Dan, Zang Hao (CHN)	Shen Xue, Zhao Hongbo (CHN)
Ice dancing	Tatyana Navka, Roman Kostomarov (RUS)	200.64 pt	Tanith Belbin, Benjamin Agosto (USA)	Yelena Grushina, Ruslan Goncharov (RUS)
Speed Skating				
Men				
500 m	Joey Cheek (USA)	69.76 sec[1]	Dmitry Dorofeyev (RUS)	Lee Kang Seok (KOR)
1,000 m	Shani Davis (USA)	1 min 08.89 sec	Joey Cheek (USA)	Erben Wennemars (NED)
1,500 m	Enrico Fabris (ITA)	1 min 45.97 sec	Shani Davis (USA)	Chad Hedrick (USA)
5,000 m	Chad Hedrick (USA)	6 min 14.68 sec	Sven Kramer (NED)	Enrico Fabris (ITA)
10,000 m	Bob de Jong (NED)	13 min 01.57 sec	Chad Hedrick (USA)	Carl Verheijen (NED)
Team pursuit	Italy	3 min 44.46 sec	Canada	The Netherlands
Women				
500 m	Svetlana Zhurova (RUS)	76.57 sec[1]	Wang Manli (CHN)	Ren Hui (CHN)
1,000 m	Marianne Timmer (NED)	1 min 16.05 sec	Cindy Klassen (CAN)	Anni Friesinger (GER)
1,500 m	Cindy Klassen (CAN)	1 min 55.27 sec	Kristina Groves (CAN)	Ireen Wüst (NED)
3,000 m	Ireen Wüst (NED)	4 min 02.43 sec	Renate Groenewold (NED)	Cindy Klassen (CAN)
5,000 m	Clara Hughes (CAN)	6 min 59.07 sec	Claudia Pechstein (GER)	Cindy Klassen (CAN)
Team pursuit	Germany	3 min 01.25 sec	Canada	Russia
Short-Track Speed Skating				
Men				
500 m	Apolo Anton Ohno (USA)	41.935 sec	François-Louis Tremblay (FRA)	Ahn Hyun Soo (Kor)
1,000 m	Ahn Hyun Soo (KOR)	1 min 26.739 sec[2]	Lee Ho Suk (KOR)	Apolo Anton Ohno (USA)
1,500 m	Ahn Hyun Soo (KOR)	2 min 25.351 sec	Lee Ho Suk (KOR)	Li Jiajun (CHN)
5,000-m relay	South Korea	6 min 43.376 sec[2]	Canada	United States
Women				
500 m	Wang Meng (CHN)	44.345 sec	Evgeniya Radanova (BUL)	Anouk Leblanc-Boucher (CAN)
1,000 m	Jin Sun Yu (KOR)	1 min 32.859 sec	Wang Meng (CHN)	Yang Yang (A) (CHN)

Olympic Medal Winners—XX Winter Games (2006) (continued)

EVENT	GOLD MEDALIST	PERFORMANCE	SILVER MEDALIST	BRONZE MEDALIST
Short-Track Speed Skating (continued)				
Women				
1,500 m	Jin Sun Yu (KOR)	2 min 23.494 sec	Choi Eun Kyung (KOR)	Wang Meng (CHN)
3,000-m relay	South Korea	4 min 17.040 sec	Canada	Italy
Ice Hockey				
Men (winning team)	Sweden	6–2–0	Finland	Czech Republic
Women (winning team)	Canada	5–0–0	Sweden	United States
Curling				
Men (winning team)	Canada	8–3–0	Finland	United States
Women (winning team)	Sweden	9–2–0	Switzerland	Canada
Bobsled				
Two man	André Lange, Kevin Kuske (GER 1)	3 min 43.38 sec	Pierre Lueders, Lascelles Brown (CAN 1)	Martin Annen, Beat Hefti (SUI 1)
Four man	André Lange, Rene Hoppe, Kevin Kuske, Martin Putze (GER 1)	3 min 40.42 sec	Aleksandr Zoubkov, Filipp Yegorov, Aleksey Seliverstov, Aleksey Voyevoda (RUS 1)	Martin Annen, Thomas Lamparter, Beat Hefti, Cedric Grand (SUI 1)
Women	Sandra Kiriasis, Anja Schneiderheinze (GER 1)	3 min 49.98 sec	Shauna Rohbock, Valerie Fleming (USA 1)	Gerda Weissensteiner, Jennifer Isacco (ITA 1)
Luge				
Men (singles)	Armin Zöggeler (ITA)	3 min 26.088 sec	Albert Demchenko (RUS)	Martins Rubenis (LAT)
Men (doubles)	Andreas Linger, Wolfgang Linger (AUT)	1 min 34.497 sec	Andre Florschütz, Torsten Wustlich (GER)	Gerhard Plankensteiner, Oswald Haselrieder
Women (singles)	Sylke Otto (GER)	3 min 07.979 sec	Sylke Kraushaar (GER)	Tatjana Hüfner (GER)
Skeleton				
Men	Duff Gibson (CAN)	1 min 55.88 sec	Jeff Pain (CAN)	Gregor Stähli (SUI)
Women	Maya Pedersen (SUI)	1 min 59.83 sec	Shelley Rudman (GBR)	Mellisa Holllingsworth-Richards (CAN)

[1]Time is combined total of two heats.   [2]Olympic record.

Special Olympics

The Special Olympics is an international program to provide individuals who have intellectual disabilities and are eight years of age or older with year-round sports training and athletic competition in a variety of Olympic-type summer and winter sports. Inaugurated in 1968, the Special Olympics was officially recognized by the International Olympic Committee on 15 Feb 1988. **International headquarters** are in Washington DC.

In June 1963, with support from the Joseph P. Kennedy, Jr., Foundation, **Eunice Kennedy Shriver** (sister of Pres. John F. Kennedy) started a summer day camp at her home in Rockville MD for children with mental retardation. Between 1963 and 1968, the Kennedy Foundation promoted the creation of dozens of similar camps in the United States and Canada. Special awards were developed for physical achievements, and by 1968 Shriver had persuaded the Chicago Park District to join with the Kennedy Foundation in sponsoring a "Special Olympics," held at Soldier Field on 20 July. About 1,000 athletes from 26 US states and Canada participated. The games were such a success that, in December, Special Olympics, Inc. (now **Special Olympics International**), was founded, with chapters in the United States, Canada, and France. The first International Winter Special Olympics Games were held on **5–11 Feb 1977** (in Steamboat Springs CO). The number of participating countries proliferated so that by the early 21st century, there were chapters in some 150 countries. Over 20,000 meets and tournaments are held worldwide each year, culminating in the International Special Olympics Games every two years, alternating between winter and summer sports and each lasting for eight or nine days.

Special Olympics Web site:
<www.specialolympics.org>.

Automobile Racing

Of the various types of automobile races, the closed-circuit, or speedway, course was developed largely in the United States. The Indianapolis 500—now the premier Indy car event—was first run in 1911. A low-slung, fenderless (open-wheel) car—called an Indy car—is essential for this race; its suspension (i.e., its ability to hold the track) is as important to a car's performance as its turbocharged engine. Often the chassis manufacturer is different from the engine manufacturer, resulting in cars identified, for example, as a Brabham/Repco. In such cases the chassis maker is listed first, and the chassis maker receives any money or awards that the car may win.

Indy car racing began in 1909, when the American Automobile Association (AAA) began sponsoring a 24-race championship series, including three races at the newly opened Indianapolis Motor Speedway (IMS). In 1956 the AAA gave up its involvement with auto racing, and the United States Auto Club (**USAC**) was organized as the sport's governing body. In 1978 two race-car owners broke away from USAC to form a new organization, Championship Auto Racing Teams, Inc. (**CART**), which sponsored its own series of races. In 1980 CART and USAC joined to form the Championship Racing League, which dissolved after five races. In 1994 the IMS announced a new Indy Racing League (**IRL**) to oversee the Indianapolis 500 beginning in 1996 and a new series of IRL races (leading to an annual drivers' championship) separate from those sponsored by CART.

The standard cars used for Grand Prix road (i.e., closed highway) racing are known as Formula One (or F-1) cars because they are built according to an evolving formula that was established after World War I by the Fédération Internationale de l'Automobile (**FIA**). Like the Indy car, the Formula One racer is open-wheeled and low-slung, but the F-1 is slightly smaller and more maneuverable.

There are approximately 17 Grand Prix events held worldwide throughout the year. Drivers compete for the **World Championship of Drivers** (inaugurated in 1950), receiving a total number of points based on their placement in each of the official Grand Prix events.

Many Grand Prix drivers participate in various endurance races, the most famous of which is the **Le Mans Grand Prix d'Endurance**, held on the 13.4-km (8.3-mi) Sarthe circuit, Le Mans, France.

Another type of popular racing event is the rally, which was established in 1907. More than 35 such competitions, raced over a specified route on public roads, take place yearly throughout the world. The classic occasion for rally racing is the **Rallye Automobile Monte-Carlo**, now started in various European cities with Monaco as its terminal point.

Stock-car racing, which began in the United States in the first half of the 20th century, involves the racing of commercial cars that have been altered to increase their speed and maneuverability. The National Association for Stock Car Auto Racing (**NASCAR**) was founded in 1947 and awards the Winston Cup to the driver who has achieved the greatest number of points earned in a series of official NASCAR Winston Cup events over the stock-car racing season. The **Daytona 500** is the premiere stock-car event.

Related Web sites: Champ Car: <www.champcar worldseries.com>; USAC: <www.usacracing.com>; IRL: <www.indycar.com>; FIA: <www.fia.com>; Automobile Club de Monaco <www.acm.mc>; NASCAR: <www.nascar.com>.

Formula One Grand Prix Race Results, 2006–07

The season for the Formula One Grand Prix circuit is March–October.
The Turkish Grand Prix, held in Istanbul, was added in 2005.

RACE	DATE	LOCALE	DRIVER (COUNTRY)	WINNER'S TIME (HR:MIN:SEC)
German Grand Prix	30 Jul 2006	Hockenheim	Michael Schumacher (GER)	1:27:51.693
Turkish Grand Prix	27 Aug 2006	Istanbul	Felipe Massa (BRA)	1:28:51.082
Italian Grand Prix	10 Sep 2006	Monza	Michael Schumacher (GER)	1:14:51.975
Chinese Grand Prix	1 Oct 2006	Shanghai	Michael Schumacher (GER)	1:37:32.747
Japanese Grand Prix	8 Oct 2006	Suzuka	Fernando Alonso (ESP)	1:23:53.413
Brazilian Grand Prix	22 Oct 2006	São Paulo	Felipe Massa (BRA)	1:31:53.751
Australian Grand Prix	18 Mar 2007	Melbourne	Kimi Räikkönen (FIN)	1:25:28.770
Malaysian Grand Prix	8 Apr 2007	Kuala Lumpur	Fernando Alonso (ESP)	1:32:14.930
Bahrain Grand Prix	15 Apr 2007	Bahrain	Felipe Massa (BRA)	1:33:27.515
Spanish Grand Prix	13 May 2007	Catalonia	Felipe Massa (BRA)	1:31:36.230
Monaco Grand Prix	27 May 2007	Monte-Carlo	Fernando Alonso (ESP)	1:40:29.329
Canadian Grand Prix	10 Jun 2007	Montreal	Lewis Hamilton (GBR)	1:44:11.292
United States Grand Prix	17 Jun 2007	Indianapolis	Lewis Hamilton (GBR)	1:31:09.965
French Grand Prix	1 Jul 2007	Magny-Cours	Kimi Räikkönen (FIN)	1:30:54.200
British Grand Prix	8 Jul 2007	Silverstone	Kimi Räikkönen (FIN)	1:21:43.074
European Grand Prix	22 Jul 2007	Nürburgring	Fernando Alonso (ESP)	2:06:26.358
Hungarian Grand Prix	5 Aug 2007	Budapest	Lewis Hamilton (GBR)	1:35:52.991

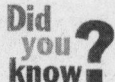 The international space endurance record is held by Russian cosmonaut Valery N. Polyakov. A physician, Polyakov spent over 437 days in Earth orbit in 1994–95. Most of his time in space was aboard the Russian space station Mir.

Indianapolis 500

There was no competition in 1917–18 and 1942–45. An American racer won the race unless otherwise noted.

YEAR	WINNER	AVG. SPEED (MPH)	YEAR	WINNER	AVG. SPEED (MPH)	YEAR	WINNER	AVG. SPEED (MPH)
1911	Ray Harroun	74.602	1952	Troy Ruttman	128.922	1983	Tom Sneva	162.117
1912	Joe Dawson	78.719	1953	Bill Vukovich	128.740	1984	Rick Mears	163.612
1913	Jules Goux (FRA)	75.933	1954	Bill Vukovich	130.840	1985	Danny Sullivan	152.982
1914	René Thomas (FRA)	82.474	1955	Robert Sweikert	128.209	1986	Bobby Rahal	170.722
			1956	Pat Flaherty	128.490	1987	Al Unser	162.175
1915	Ralph DePalma	89.840	1957	Sam Hanks	135.601	1988	Rick Mears	144.809
1916[1]	Dario Resta (FRA)	84.001	1958	Jimmy Bryan	133.791	1989	Emerson Fittipaldi (BRA)	167.581
1919	Howdy Wilcox	88.050	1959	Rodger Ward	135.857			
1920	Gaston Chevrolet	88.618	1960	Jim Rathmann	138.767	1990	Arie Luyendyk (NED)	185.984
1921	Tommy Milton	89.621	1961	A.J. Foyt, Jr.	139.131			
1922	Jimmy Murphy	94.484	1962	Rodger Ward	140.293	1991	Rick Mears	176.457
1923	Tommy Milton	90.954	1963	Parnelli Jones	143.137	1992	Al Unser, Jr.	134.479
1924[2]	L.L. Corum, Joe Boyer	98.234	1964	A.J. Foyt, Jr.	147.350	1993	Emerson Fittipaldi (BRA)	157.207
			1965	Jim Clark (GBR)	150.686			
1925	Peter DePaolo	101.127	1966	Graham Hill (GBR)	144.317	1994	Al Unser, Jr.	160.872
1926[3]	Frank Lockhart	95.904				1995	Jacques Villeneuve (CAN)	153.616
1927	George Souders	97.545	1967	A.J. Foyt, Jr.	151.207			
1928	Louie Meyer	99.482	1968	Bobby Unser	152.882	1996	Buddy Lazier	147.956
1929	Ray Keech	97.585	1969	Mario Andretti	156.867	1997	Arie Luyendyk (NED)	145.827
1930	Billy Arnold	100.448	1970	Al Unser	155.749			
1931	Louis Schneider	96.629	1971	Al Unser	157.735	1998	Eddie Cheever, Jr.	145.155
1932	Fred Frame	104.144	1972	Mark Donohue	162.962			
1933	Louie Meyer	104.162	1973[3]	Gordon Johncock	159.036	1999	Kenny Brack (SWE)	153.176
1934	Bill Cummings	104.863						
1935	Kelly Petillo	106.240	1974	Johnny Rutherford	158.589	2000	Juan Montoya (COL)	167.607
1936	Louie Meyer	109.069	1975[3]	Bobby Unser	149.213	2001	Helio Castroneves (BRA)	153.601
1937	Wilbur Shaw	113.580	1976[3]	Johnny Rutherford	148.725			
1938	Floyd Roberts	117.200				2002	Helio Castroneves (BRA)	166.499
1939	Wilbur Shaw	115.035	1977	A.J. Foyt, Jr.	161.331			
1940	Wilbur Shaw	114.277	1978	Al Unser	161.363	2003	Gil de Ferran (BRA)	156.291
1941[2]	Floyd Davis, Mauri Rose	115.117	1979	Rick Mears	158.899			
			1980	Johnny Rutherford	142.862	2004[3]	Buddy Rice	138.518
1946	George Robson	114.820				2005	Dan Wheldon (GBR)	157.603
1947	Mauri Rose	116.338	1981	Bobby Unser	139.084			
1948	Mauri Rose	119.814	1982	Gordon Johncock	162.029	2006	Sam Hornish, Jr.	157.085
1949	Bill Holland	121.327				2007	Dario Franchitti (GBR)	151.774
1950[3]	Johnnie Parsons	124.002						
1951	Lee Wallard	126.244						

[1]Scheduled 300-mile race.   [2]First driver started the race but was replaced during the race by the second driver named.   [3]Race stopped because of rain (in 1926 after 400 miles, in 1950 after 345 miles, in 1973 after 332.5 miles, in 1975 after 435 miles, in 1976 after 255 miles, and in 2004 after 450 miles).

NASCAR Nextel Cup Champions

YEAR	WINNER	YEAR	WINNER	YEAR	WINNER	YEAR	WINNER
1949	Red Byron	1964	Richard Petty	1979	Richard Petty	1994	Dale Earnhardt
1950	Bill Rexford	1965	Ned Jarrett	1980	Dale Earnhardt	1995	Jeff Gordon
1951	Herb Thomas	1966	David Pearson	1981	Darrell Waltrip	1996	Terry Labonte
1952	Tim Flock	1967	Richard Petty	1982	Darrell Waltrip	1997	Jeff Gordon
1953	Herb Thomas	1968	David Pearson	1983	Bobby Allison	1998	Jeff Gordon
1954	Lee Petty	1969	David Pearson	1984	Terry Labonte	1999	Dale Jarrett
1955	Tim Flock	1970	Bobby Isaac	1985	Darrell Waltrip	2000	Bobby Labonte
1956	Buck Baker	1971	Richard Petty	1986	Dale Earnhardt	2001	Jeff Gordon
1957	Buck Baker	1972	Richard Petty	1987	Dale Earnhardt	2002	Tony Stewart
1958	Lee Petty	1973	Benny Parsons	1988	Bill Elliott	2003	Matt Kenseth
1959	Lee Petty	1974	Richard Petty	1989	Rusty Wallace	2004	Kurt Busch
1960	Rex White	1975	Richard Petty	1990	Dale Earnhardt	2005	Tony Stewart
1961	Ned Jarrett	1976	Cale Yarborough	1991	Dale Earnhardt	2006	Jimmie Johnson
1962	Joe Weatherly	1977	Cale Yarborough	1992	Alan Kulwicki		
1963	Joe Weatherly	1978	Cale Yarborough	1993	Dale Earnhardt		

Baseball

The sport of baseball—given its definitive form in the United States in the late 19th century—is popular throughout the world, though it is not organized internationally except for **Little League** players (children ages 5–18). Little League Baseball was founded in Pennsylvania in 1939. The first Little League World Series was in 1947, and the first Little League outside the US was organized in British Columbia in 1951. Baseball is especially popular in Japan and Latin America; it is also one of the national sports of the US.

On a **professional** level, the premier event of baseball in the US is the **World Series** of **Major League Baseball**, in which the first team to win four games wins the Series. In fact, the Series is not contested on an international level, but rather it is played between the leading team of the **National League** (NL; formed 1876) and the leading team of the **American League** (AL; formed 1900 and including, from 1977, one Canadian team).

Professional baseball began in Japan in 1936. Teams are organized into two leagues of six teams each. The seven-game **Japan Series**, first played in 1950, is contested between the leading team of the Central League (CL) and the leading team of the Pacific League (PL). The modern **Caribbean Series** began in 1970 with the winning team from each league in the Dominican Republic, Mexico, Puerto Rico, and Venezuela.

Related Web sites:
Major League: <http://mlb.mlb.com/index.jsp>;
Little League: <www.littleleague.org>.

Final Major League Standings, 2006

American League

East Division				Central Division				West Division			
CLUB	WON	LOST	GAMES BACK	CLUB	WON	LOST	GAMES BACK	CLUB	WON	LOST	GAMES BACK
New York[1]	97	65	—	Minnesota[1]	96	66	—	Oakland[1]	93	69	—
Toronto	87	75	10	Detroit[1]	95	67	1	Los Angeles	89	73	4
Boston	86	76	11	Chicago	90	72	6	Texas	80	82	13
Baltimore	70	92	27	Cleveland	78	84	18	Seattle	78	84	15
Tampa Bay	61	101	36	Kansas City	62	100	34				

National League

East Division				Central Division				West Division			
CLUB	WON	LOST	GAMES BACK	CLUB	WON	LOST	GAMES BACK	CLUB	WON	LOST	GAMES BACK
New York[1]	97	65	—	St. Louis[1]	83	78	—	San Diego[1]	88	74	—
Philadelphia	85	77	12	Houston	82	80	1½	Los Angeles[1]	88	74	—
Atlanta	79	83	18	Cincinnati	80	82	3½	San Francisco	76	85	11½
Florida	78	84	19	Milwaukee	75	87	8½	Arizona	76	86	12
Washington	71	91	26	Pittsburgh	67	95	16½	Colorado	76	86	12
				Chicago	66	96	17½				

[1]Gained play-off berth.

World Series

AL—American League; NL—National League.

YEAR	WINNING TEAM	LOSING TEAM	RESULTS
1903	Boston Americans (AL)	Pittsburgh Pirates (NL)	5–3
1904	not held		
1905	New York Giants (NL)	Philadelphia Athletics (AL)	4–1
1906	Chicago White Sox (AL)	Chicago Cubs (NL)	4–2
1907[1]	Chicago Cubs (NL)	Detroit Tigers (AL)	4–0
1908	Chicago Cubs (NL)	Detroit Tigers (AL)	4–1
1909	Pittsburgh Pirates (NL)	Detroit Tigers (AL)	4–3
1910	Philadelphia Athletics (AL)	Chicago Cubs (NL)	4–1
1911	Philadelphia Athletics (AL)	New York Giants (NL)	4–2
1912[1]	Boston Red Sox (AL)	New York Giants (NL)	4–3
1913	Philadelphia Athletics (AL)	New York Giants (NL)	4–1
1914	Boston Braves (NL)	Philadelphia Athletics (AL)	4–0
1915	Boston Red Sox (AL)	Philadelphia Phillies (NL)	4–1
1916	Boston Red Sox (AL)	Brooklyn Robins (NL)	4–1
1917	Chicago White Sox (AL)	New York Giants (NL)	4–2
1918	Boston Red Sox (AL)	Chicago Cubs (NL)	4–2
1919	Cincinnati Reds (NL)	Chicago White Sox (AL)	5–3
1920	Cleveland Indians (AL)	Brooklyn Robins (NL)	5–2
1921	New York Giants (NL)	New York Yankees (AL)	5–3
1922[1]	New York Giants (NL)	New York Yankees (AL)	4–0

World Series (continued)

YEAR	WINNING TEAM	LOSING TEAM	RESULTS
1923	New York Yankees (AL)	New York Giants (NL)	4–2
1924	Washington Senators (AL)	New York Giants (NL)	4–3
1925	Pittsburgh Pirates (NL)	Washington Senators (AL)	4–3
1926	St. Louis Cardinals (NL)	New York Yankees (AL)	4–3
1927	New York Yankees (AL)	Pittsburgh Pirates (NL)	4–0
1928	New York Yankees (AL)	St. Louis Cardinals (NL)	4–0
1929	Philadelphia Athletics (AL)	Chicago Cubs (NL)	4–1
1930	Philadelphia Athletics (AL)	St. Louis Cardinals (NL)	4–2
1931	St. Louis Cardinals (NL)	Philadelphia Athletics (AL)	4–3
1932	New York Yankees (AL)	Chicago Cubs (NL)	4–0
1933	New York Giants (NL)	Washington Senators (AL)	4–1
1934	St. Louis Cardinals (NL)	Detroit Tigers (AL)	4–3
1935	Detroit Tigers (AL)	Chicago Cubs (NL)	4–2
1936	New York Yankees (AL)	New York Giants (NL)	4–2
1937	New York Yankees (AL)	New York Giants (NL)	4–1
1938	New York Yankees (AL)	Chicago Cubs (NL)	4–0
1939	New York Yankees (AL)	Cincinnati Reds (NL)	4–0
1940	Cincinnati Reds (NL)	Detroit Tigers (AL)	4–3
1941	New York Yankees (AL)	Brooklyn Dodgers (NL)	4–1
1942	St. Louis Cardinals (NL)	New York Yankees (AL)	4–1
1943	New York Yankees (AL)	St. Louis Cardinals (NL)	4–1
1944	St. Louis Cardinals (NL)	St. Louis Browns (AL)	4–2
1945	Detroit Tigers (AL)	Chicago Cubs (NL)	4–3
1946	St. Louis Cardinals (NL)	Boston Red Sox (AL)	4–3
1947	New York Yankees (AL)	Brooklyn Dodgers (NL)	4–3
1948	Cleveland Indians (AL)	Boston Braves (NL)	4–2
1949	New York Yankees (AL)	Brooklyn Dodgers (NL)	4–1
1950	New York Yankees (AL)	Philadelphia Phillies (NL)	4–0
1951	New York Yankees (AL)	New York Giants (NL)	4–2
1952	New York Yankees (AL)	Brooklyn Dodgers (NL)	4–3
1953	New York Yankees (AL)	Brooklyn Dodgers (NL)	4–2
1954	New York Giants (NL)	Cleveland Indians (AL)	4–0
1955	Brooklyn Dodgers (NL)	New York Yankees (AL)	4–3
1956	New York Yankees (AL)	Brooklyn Dodgers (NL)	4–3
1957	Milwaukee Braves (NL)	New York Yankees (AL)	4–3
1958	New York Yankees (AL)	Milwaukee Braves (NL)	4–3
1959	Los Angeles Dodgers (NL)	Chicago White Sox (AL)	4–2
1960	Pittsburgh Pirates (NL)	New York Yankees (AL)	4–3
1961	New York Yankees (AL)	Cincinnati Reds (NL)	4–1
1962	New York Yankees (AL)	San Francisco Giants (NL)	4–3
1963	Los Angeles Dodgers (NL)	New York Yankees (AL)	4–0
1964	St. Louis Cardinals (NL)	New York Yankees (AL)	4–3
1965	Los Angeles Dodgers (NL)	Minnesota Twins (AL)	4–3
1966	Baltimore Orioles (AL)	Los Angeles Dodgers (NL)	4–0
1967	St. Louis Cardinals (NL)	Boston Red Sox (AL)	4–3
1968	Detroit Tigers (AL)	St. Louis Cardinals (NL)	4–3
1969	New York Mets (NL)	Baltimore Orioles (AL)	4–1
1970	Baltimore Orioles (AL)	Cincinnati Reds (NL)	4–1
1971	Pittsburgh Pirates (NL)	Baltimore Orioles (AL)	4–3
1972	Oakland Athletics (AL)	Cincinnati Reds (NL)	4–3
1973	Oakland Athletics (AL)	New York Mets (NL)	4–3
1974	Oakland Athletics (AL)	Los Angeles Dodgers (NL)	4–1
1975	Cincinnati Reds (NL)	Boston Red Sox (AL)	4–3
1976	Cincinnati Reds (NL)	New York Yankees (AL)	4–0
1977	New York Yankees (AL)	Los Angeles Dodgers (NL)	4–2
1978	New York Yankees (AL)	Los Angeles Dodgers (NL)	4–2
1979	Pittsburgh Pirates (NL)	Baltimore Orioles (AL)	4–3
1980	Philadelphia Phillies (NL)	Kansas City Royals (AL)	4–2
1981	Los Angeles Dodgers (NL)	New York Yankees (AL)	4–2
1982	St. Louis Cardinals (NL)	Milwaukee Brewers (AL)	4–3
1983	Baltimore Orioles (AL)	Philadelphia Phillies (NL)	4–1
1984	Detroit Tigers (AL)	San Diego Padres (NL)	4–1
1985	Kansas City Royals (AL)	St. Louis Cardinals (NL)	4–3
1986	New York Mets (NL)	Boston Red Sox (AL)	4–3
1987	Minnesota Twins (AL)	St. Louis Cardinals (NL)	4–3
1988	Los Angeles Dodgers (NL)	Oakland Athletics (AL)	4–1
1989	Oakland Athletics (AL)	San Francisco Giants (NL)	4–0
1990	Cincinnati Reds (NL)	Oakland Athletics (AL)	4–0

World Series (continued)

YEAR	WINNING TEAM	LOSING TEAM	RESULTS
1991	Minnesota Twins (AL)	Atlanta Braves (NL)	4–3
1992	Toronto Blue Jays (AL)	Atlanta Braves (NL)	4–2
1993	Toronto Blue Jays (AL)	Philadelphia Phillies (NL)	4–2
1994	not held		
1995	Atlanta Braves (NL)	Cleveland Indians (AL)	4–2
1996	New York Yankees (AL)	Atlanta Braves (NL)	4–2
1997	Florida Marlins (NL)	Cleveland Indians (AL)	4–3
1998	New York Yankees (AL)	San Diego Padres (NL)	4–0
1999	New York Yankees (AL)	Atlanta Braves (NL)	4–0
2000	New York Yankees (AL)	New York Mets (NL)	4–1
2001	Arizona Diamondbacks (NL)	New York Yankees (AL)	4–3
2002	Anaheim Angels (AL)	San Francisco Giants (NL)	4–3
2003	Florida Marlins (NL)	New York Yankees (AL)	4–2
2004	Boston Red Sox (AL)	St. Louis Cardinals (NL)	4–0
2005	Chicago White Sox (AL)	Houston Astros (NL)	4–0
2006	St. Louis Cardinals (NL)	Detroit Tigers (AL)	4–1

[1]One tied game.

Major League Baseball All-Time Records[1]

	PLAYERS/TEAMS	NUMBER	SEASON/DATE
Career records for individuals			
Games played	Pete Rose	3,562	1963–86
Consecutive games played	Cal Ripken, Jr.	2,632	1982–98
Batting average[2]	Ty Cobb	.366	1905–28
Hits	Pete Rose	4,256	1963–86
Doubles	Tris Speaker	792	1907–28
Triples	Sam Crawford	309	1899–17
Home runs	Barry Bonds[3, 4]	756[4]	1986–2006
Runs	Rickey Henderson	2,295	1979–2003
Runs batted in	Hank Aaron	2,297	1954–76
Walks (batting)	Barry Bonds[3]	2,426	1986–2006
Stolen bases (batting)	Rickey Henderson	1,406	1979–2003
Wins	Cy Young	511	1890–1911
Earned run average[5]	Ed Walsh	1.82	1904–17
Strikeouts (pitching)	Nolan Ryan	5,714	1966–93
Saves	Trevor Hoffman[3]	482	1993–2006
No-hitters	Nolan Ryan	7	1966–93
Shutouts	Walter Johnson	110	1907–27
Managing, total wins	Connie Mack	3,731	1894–96; 1901–50
Season records for individuals			
Batting average[6]	Hugh Duffy	.440	1894
Hits	Ichiro Suzuki[3]	262	2004
Doubles	Earl Webb	67	1931
Triples	Chief Wilson	36	1912
Home runs	Barry Bonds[3]	73	2001
Runs	Billy Hamilton	198	1894
Runs batted in	Hack Wilson	191	1930
Walks (batting)	Barry Bonds[3]	232	2004
Stolen bases (batting)	Hugh Nicol	138	1887
Wins	Charley Radbourn	59	1884
Earned run average[7]	Tim Keefe	0.86	1880
Strikeouts (pitching)	Matt Kilroy	513	1886
No-hitters	4 players hold record	2	N/A
Saves	Bobby Thigpen	57	1990
Shutouts	George Bradley; Grover Alexander	16	1876; 1916
Game records for individuals[8]			
Hits	Wilbert Robinson; Rennie Stennett	7	10 Jun 1892; 16 Sep 1975
Doubles	too numerous to list	4	N/A
Triples	George Strief; Bill Joyce	4	25 Jun 1885; 18 May 1897
Home runs	too numerous to list	4	N/A

Major League Baseball All-Time Records[1] (continued)

	PLAYERS/TEAMS	NUMBER	SEASON/DATE
Game records for individuals[8] (cont.)			
Runs	Guy Hecker	7	15 Aug 1886
Runs batted in	Jim Bottomley; Mark Whiten	12	16 Sep 1924; 7 Sep 1993
Walks (batting)	Walt Wilmot; Jimmie Foxx	6	22 Aug 1891; 16 Jun 1938
Stolen bases (batting)	George Gore; Billy Hamilton	7	25 Jun 1881; 31 Aug 1894
Strikeouts (pitching)	Roger Clemens[3] (twice); Kerry Wood[3]	20	29 Apr 1986 and 18 Sep 1996; 6 May 1998
Records for teams			
World Series titles	New York Yankees	26	
Consecutive World Series titles	New York Yankees	5	1949–53
Games won in a season	Chicago Cubs; Seattle Mariners	116	1906; 2001
Highest winning percentage in a season	Chicago White Stockings	.798 (67–17)	1880
Batting average in a season	Philadelphia Phillies	.349	1894
Doubles in a season	St. Louis Cardinals; Boston Red Sox	373	1930; 1997
Triples in a season	Baltimore Orioles	153	1894
Home runs in a season	Seattle Mariners	264	1997
Runs in a season	Boston Braves	1,220	1894
Runs batted in in a season	Boston Braves	1,043	1894
Walks (batting) in a season	Boston Red Sox	835	1949
Stolen bases (batting) in a season	New York Giants	347	1911
Strikeouts (pitching) in a season	Chicago Cubs	1,404	2003
Records for games			
Highest total score	Chicago Cubs versus Philadelphia Phillies	26 to 23 (total 49)	25 Aug 1922
Longest nine-inning game	New York Yankees versus Boston Red Sox	4 hr 45 min	18 Aug 2006
Longest extra-inning game (time)	Chicago White Sox versus Milwaukee Brewers	8 hr 6 min	9 May 1984
Longest extra-inning game (innings)	Brooklyn Dodgers versus Boston Braves	26 innings	1 May 1920

[1]Through the 2006 season. [2]Minimum of 5,000 at-bats. [3]Active in 2007. [4]Barry Bonds hit his 756th home run to set the new record for career home runs on 7 Aug 2007. [5]Minimum of 1,500 innings pitched. [6]Minimum of 3.1 plate appearances per game played. [7]Minimum of one inning pitched per game played. [8]Nine-inning games only.

Caribbean Series

YEAR	WINNING TEAM	COUNTRY	YEAR	WINNING TEAM	COUNTRY
1970	Magallanes Navigators	VEN	1989	Zulia Eagles	VEN
1971	Licey Tigers	DOM	1990	Escogido Lions	DOM
1972	Ponce Lions	PUR	1991	Licey Tigers	DOM
1973	Licey Tigers	DOM	1992	Mayagüez Indians	PUR
1974	Caguas Creoles	PUR	1993	Santurce Crabbers	PUR
1975	Bayamon Cowboys	PUR	1994	Licey Tigers	DOM
1976	Hermosillo Orange Growers	MEX	1995	San Juan Senators	PUR
1977	Licey Tigers	DOM	1996	Culiacán Tomato Growers	MEX
1978	Mayagüez Indians	PUR	1997	Northern Eagles	DOM
1979	Magallanes Navigators	VEN	1998	Northern Eagles	DOM
1980	Licey Tigers	DOM	1999	Licey Tigers	DOM
1981	not held		2000	Santurce Crabbers	PUR
1982	Caracas Lions	VEN	2001	Cibao Eagles	DOM
1983	Arecibo Wolves	PUR	2002	Culiacán Tomato Growers	MEX
1984	Zulia Eagles	VEN	2003	Cibao Eagles	DOM
1985	Licey Tigers	DOM	2004	Licey Tigers	DOM
1986	Mexicali Eagles	MEX	2005	Mazatlán Deer	MEX
1987	Caguas Creoles	PUR	2006	Caracas Lions	VEN
1988	Escogido Lions	DOM	2007	Cibao Eagles	DOM

Japan Series

Held since 1950. Table shows results for past 10 years. CL—Central League; PL—Pacific League.

YEAR	WINNING TEAM	LOSING TEAM	RESULTS
1997	Yakult Swallows (CL)	Seibu Lions (PL)	4–1
1998	Yokohama BayStars (CL)	Seibu Lions (PL)	4–2
1999	Fukuoka Daiei Hawks (PL)	Chunichi Dragons (CL)	4–1
2000	Yomiuri Giants (CL)	Fukuoka Daiei Hawks (PL)	4–2
2001	Yakult Swallows (CL)	Osaka Kintetsu Buffaloes (PL)	4–1
2002	Yomiuri Giants (CL)	Seibu Lions (PL)	4–0
2003	Fukuoka Daiei Hawks (PL)	Hanshin Tigers (CL)	4–3
2004	Seibu Lions (PL)	Chunichi Dragons (CL)	4–3
2005	Chiba Lotte Marines (PL)	Hanshin Tigers (CL)	4–0
2006	Nippon Ham Fighters (PL)	Chunichi Dragons (CL)	4–1

Little League World Series

The Little League World Series, first called the National Little League Tournament, was established in 1947. The table shows the Series winners for the past 10 years.

YEAR	WINNING TEAM/HOME	RUNNER-UP	SCORE
1998	Toms River/Toms River NJ	Kashima/Ibaraki (JPN)	12–9
1999	Hirakata/Osaka (JPN)	Phenix City National/Phenix City AL	5–0
2000	Sierra Maestra/Maracaibo (VEN)	Bellaire/Bellaire TX	3–2
2001	Kitasuna/Tokyo (JPN)	Apopka National/Apopka FL	2–1
2002	Valley Sports American/Louisville KY	Sendai Higashi/Sendai (JPN)	1–0
2003	Musashi-Fuchu/Tokyo (JPN)	East Boynton Beach/Boynton Beach FL	10–1
2004	Pabao/Willemstad (AHO)	Conejo Valley/Thousand Oaks CA	5–2
2005	West Oahu/Ewa Beach HI	Pabao/Willemstad (AHO)	7–6
2006	Columbus Northern/Columbus GA	Kawaguchi/Kawaguchi City (JPN)	2–1
2007	Warner Robins American/Warner Robins GA	Tokyo Kitasuna/Tokyo (JPN)	3–2

Basketball

American professional basketball is directed by the **National Basketball Association** (NBA; formed 1949). The NBA is divided into two conferences, the top-ranking teams of which compete yearly for the championship. The NBA began a **women's professional league**, known as the WNBA, in 1997.

As an **amateur** sport, basketball is organized on an international level. Since the inclusion of basketball as an **Olympic sport** in 1936, the winners of the Olympic tournament have been considered the world champions. The **Fédération Internationale de Basketball** (FIBA; founded 1932) instituted separate world championships in 1950 for men and in 1953 for women. (Women's basketball was not admitted to the Olympics until 1976.) Amateur basketball in the United States is most closely followed at the **collegiate** level, where the most important event of the season is the **National Collegiate Athletic Association (NCAA) Championship**. The NCAA tournament was first contested in 1939 (by men's teams only). Women's college basketball was first played on a national level in 1972, under the auspices of the Association for Intercollegiate Athletics for Women (AIAW), which gave way in 1982 to the NCAA's first tournament for women.

Related Web sites: NBA: <www.nba.com>; WNBA: <www.wnba.com>; NCAA: <www.ncaa.org>; FIBA: <www.fiba.com>.

Did you know? In Japan, sumo wrestling was under Imperial patronage between 710 and 1185 and was a popular spectator sport, but during the shogunate, public matches were banned. Professional wrestling in Japan dates from the revival of public matches after 1600. Exceptionally agile men weighing 300 pounds or more are common in this sport. Lengthy rituals and elaborate posturings accompany the bouts, which are, by contrast, quite brief, often lasting only a few seconds.

National Basketball Association Final Standings, 2006—07

EASTERN CONFERENCE

Atlantic Division				Central Division				Southeast Division			
TEAM	WON	LOST	GAMES BACK	TEAM	WON	LOST	GAMES BACK	TEAM	WON	LOST	GAMES BACK
Toronto[1]	47	35	—	Detroit[1]	53	29	—	Miami[1]	44	38	—
New Jersey[1]	41	41	6	Cleveland[1]	50	32	3	Washington[1]	41	41	3
Philadelphia	35	47	12	Chicago[1]	49	33	4	Orlando[1]	40	42	4
New York	33	49	14	Indiana	35	47	18	Charlotte	33	49	11
Boston	24	58	23	Milwaukee	28	54	25	Atlanta	30	52	14

National Basketball Association Final Standings, 2006–07 (continued)

WESTERN CONFERENCE

Northwest Division	WON	LOST	GAMES BACK	Pacific Division	WON	LOST	GAMES BACK	Southwest Division	WON	LOST	GAMES BACK
TEAM				TEAM				TEAM			
Utah[1]	51	31	—	Phoenix[1]	61	21	—	Dallas[1]	67	15	—
Denver[1]	45	37	6	L.A. Lakers[1]	42	40	19	San Antonio[1]	58	24	9
Portland	32	50	19	Golden State[1]	42	40	19	Houston[1]	52	30	15
Minnesota	32	50	19	L.A. Clippers	40	42	21	New Orleans/	39	43	28
Seattle	31	51	20	Sacramento	33	49	28	Oklahoma City			
								Memphis	22	60	45

[1]Gained play-off berth.

National Basketball Association All-Time Records

Source: Sporting News, Official NBA Guide 2006–07.

	PLAYERS/TEAMS	NUMBER	SEASON/DATE
Individual career records			
Games played	Robert Parish	1,611	1976-77—1996-97
Points scored	Kareem Abdul-Jabbar	38,387	1969-70—1988-89
Most games, 50 or more points	Wilt Chamberlain	118	1959-60—1972-73
Most consecutive games, 10 or more points	Michael Jordan	866	25 Mar 1986– 26 Dec 2001
Field goals attempted	Kareem Abdul-Jabbar	28,307	1969-70—1988-89
Field goals made	Kareem Abdul-Jabbar	15,837	1969-70—1988-89
Field-goal percentage[1]	Artis Gilmore	.599	1976-77—1987-88
Three-point field goals attempted	Reggie Miller	6,486	1987-88—2004-05
Three-point field goals made	Reggie Miller	2,560	1987-88—2004-05
Three-point field-goal percentage[2]	Steve Kerr	.454	1988-89—2002-03
Free throws attempted	Karl Malone	13,188	1985-86—2003-04
Free throws made	Karl Malone	9,787	1985-86—2003-04
Free-throw percentage[3]	Mark Price	.904	1986-87—1997-98
Assists	John Stockton	15,806	1984-85—2002-03
Rebounds	Wilt Chamberlain	23,924	1959-60—1972-73
Steals[4]	John Stockton	3,265	1984-85—2002-03
Blocked shots[4]	Hakeem Olajuwon	3,830	1984-85—2001-02
Personal fouls	Kareem Abdul-Jabbar	4,657	1969-70—1988-89
Coaching, total wins	Lenny Wilkens	1,332	1969-70—2004-05, except 1972-1974
Individual season records			
Points scored	Wilt Chamberlain	4,029	1961-62
Field goals attempted	Wilt Chamberlain	3,159	1961-62
Field goals made	Wilt Chamberlain	1,597	1961-62
Field-goal percentage	Wilt Chamberlain	.727	1972-73
Three-point field goals attempted	George McCloud	678	1995-96
Three-point field goals made	Ray Allen	269	2005-06
Three-point field-goal percentage	Steve Kerr	.524	1994-95
Free throws attempted	Wilt Chamberlain	1,363	1961-62
Free throws made	Jerry West	840	1965-66
Free-throw percentage	Calvin Murphy	.958	1980-81
Assists	John Stockton	1,164	1990-91
Rebounds	Wilt Chamberlain	2,149	1960-61
Steals[4]	Alvin Robertson	301	1985-86
Blocked shots[4]	Mark Eaton	456	1984-85
Personal fouls	Darryl Dawkins	386	1983-84
Individual game records			
Points scored	Wilt Chamberlain	100	2 Mar 1962
Field goals attempted	Wilt Chamberlain	63	2 Mar 1962
Field goals made	Wilt Chamberlain	36	2 Mar 1962
Three-point field goals attempted	Damon Stoudamire	21	15 Apr 2005
Three-point field goals made	Kobe Bryant; Donyell Marshall	12	7 Jan 2003 13 Mar 2005
Free throws attempted	Wilt Chamberlain	34	22 Feb 1962
Free throws made	Wilt Chamberlain; Adrian Dantley	28	2 Mar 1962 4 Jan 1984

National Basketball Association All-Time Records (continued)

Individual game records (cont.)	PLAYERS/TEAMS	NUMBER	SEASON/DATE
Assists	Scott Skiles	30	30 Dec 1990
Rebounds	Wilt Chamberlain	55	24 Nov 1960
Steals[4]	Larry Kenon;	11	26 Dec 1976
	Kendall Gill		3 Apr 1999
Blocked shots[4]	Elmore Smith	17	28 Oct 1973
Team records			
Highest winning percentage in a season	Chicago Bulls	.878 (72–10)	1995–96
Consecutive games won	Los Angeles Lakers	33	5 Nov 1971– 7 Jan 1972
Championships	Boston Celtics	16	
Consecutive championships	Boston Celtics	8	1959–66
Game records			
Highest combined score	Detroit Pistons versus Denver Nuggets	370 (186–184)	13 Dec 1983
Longest game (overtime periods)	Indianapolis Olympians versus Rochester Royals	6	6 Jan 1951

[1]Minimum 2,000 made. [2]Minimum 250 made. [3]Minimum 1,200 made. [4]Since 1973–74; before that season steals and blocked shots were not officially recorded by the NBA.

National Basketball Association (NBA) Championship

SEASON	WINNER	RUNNER-UP	RESULTS
1946–47	Philadelphia Warriors	Chicago Stags	4–1
1947–48	Baltimore Bullets	Philadelphia Warriors	4–2
1948–49	Minneapolis Lakers	Washington Capitols	4–2
1949–50	Minneapolis Lakers	Syracuse Nationals	4–2
1950–51	Rochester Royals	New York Knickerbockers	4–3
1951–52	Minneapolis Lakers	New York Knickerbockers	4–3
1952–53	Minneapolis Lakers	New York Knickerbockers	4–1
1953–54	Minneapolis Lakers	Syracuse Nationals	4–3
1954–55	Syracuse Nationals	Fort Wayne Pistons	4–3
1955–56	Philadelphia Warriors	Fort Wayne Pistons	4–1
1956–57	Boston Celtics	St. Louis Hawks	4–3
1957–58	St. Louis Hawks	Boston Celtics	4–2
1958–59	Boston Celtics	Minneapolis Lakers	4–0
1959–60	Boston Celtics	St. Louis Hawks	4–3
1960–61	Boston Celtics	St. Louis Hawks	4–1
1961–62	Boston Celtics	Los Angeles Lakers	4–3
1962–63	Boston Celtics	Los Angeles Lakers	4–2
1963–64	Boston Celtics	San Francisco Warriors	4–1
1964–65	Boston Celtics	Los Angeles Lakers	4–1
1965–66	Boston Celtics	Los Angeles Lakers	4–3
1966–67	Philadelphia 76ers	San Francisco Warriors	4–2
1967–68	Boston Celtics	Los Angeles Lakers	4–2
1968–69	Boston Celtics	Los Angeles Lakers	4–3
1969–70	New York Knickerbockers	Los Angeles Lakers	4–3
1970–71	Milwaukee Bucks	Baltimore Bullets	4–0
1971–72	Los Angeles Lakers	New York Knickerbockers	4–1
1972–73	New York Knickerbockers	Los Angeles Lakers	4–1
1973–74	Boston Celtics	Milwaukee Bucks	4–3
1974–75	Golden State Warriors	Washington Bullets	4–0
1975–76	Boston Celtics	Phoenix Suns	4–2
1976–77	Portland Trail Blazers	Philadelphia 76ers	4–2
1977–78	Washington Bullets	Seattle SuperSonics	4–3
1978–79	Seattle SuperSonics	Washington Bullets	4–1
1979–80	Los Angeles Lakers	Philadelphia 76ers	4–2
1980–81	Boston Celtics	Houston Rockets	4–2
1981–82	Los Angeles Lakers	Philadelphia 76ers	4–2
1982–83	Philadelphia 76ers	Los Angeles Lakers	4–0
1983–84	Boston Celtics	Los Angeles Lakers	4–3
1984–85	Los Angeles Lakers	Boston Celtics	4–2

National Basketball Association (NBA) Championship (continued)

SEASON	WINNER	RUNNER-UP	RESULTS
1985–86	Boston Celtics	Houston Rockets	4–2
1986–87	Los Angeles Lakers	Boston Celtics	4–2
1987–88	Los Angeles Lakers	Detroit Pistons	4–3
1988–89	Detroit Pistons	Los Angeles Lakers	4–0
1989–90	Detroit Pistons	Portland Trail Blazers	4–1
1990–91	Chicago Bulls	Los Angeles Lakers	4–1
1991–92	Chicago Bulls	Portland Trail Blazers	4–2
1992–93	Chicago Bulls	Phoenix Suns	4–2
1993–94	Houston Rockets	New York Knickerbockers	4–3
1994–95	Houston Rockets	Orlando Magic	4–0
1995–96	Chicago Bulls	Seattle SuperSonics	4–2
1996–97	Chicago Bulls	Utah Jazz	4–2
1997–98	Chicago Bulls	Utah Jazz	4–2
1998–99	San Antonio Spurs	New York Knickerbockers	4–1
1999–2000	Los Angeles Lakers	Indiana Pacers	4–2
2000–01	Los Angeles Lakers	Philadelphia 76ers	4–1
2001–02	Los Angeles Lakers	New Jersey Nets	4–0
2002–03	San Antonio Spurs	New Jersey Nets	4–2
2003–04	Detroit Pistons	Los Angeles Lakers	4–1
2004–05	San Antonio Spurs	Detroit Pistons	4–3
2005–06	Miami Heat	Dallas Mavericks	4–2
2006–07	San Antonio Spurs	Cleveland Cavaliers	4–0

Women's National Basketball Association (WNBA) Championship

SEASON	WINNER	RUNNER-UP	RESULTS
1997	Houston Comets	New York Liberty	1–0
1998	Houston Comets	Phoenix Mercury	2–1
1999	Houston Comets	New York Liberty	2–1
2000	Houston Comets	New York Liberty	2–0
2001	Los Angeles Sparks	Charlotte Sting	2–0
2002	Los Angeles Sparks	New York Liberty	2–0
2003	Detroit Shock	Los Angeles Sparks	2–1
2004	Seattle Storm	Connecticut Sun	2–1
2005	Sacramento Monarchs	Connecticut Sun	3–1
2006	Detroit Shock	Sacramento Monarchs	3–2

Division I National Collegiate Athletic Association (NCAA) Championship—Men

YEAR	WINNER	RUNNER-UP	SCORE	YEAR	WINNER	RUNNER-UP	SCORE
1939	Oregon	Ohio State	46–43	1961	Cincinnati	Ohio State	70–65
1940	Indiana	Kansas	60–42	1962	Cincinnati	Ohio State	71–59
1941	Wisconsin	Washington State	39–34	1963	Loyola (IL)	Cincinnati	60–58
1942	Stanford	Dartmouth	53–38	1964	UCLA	Duke	98–83
1943	Wyoming	Georgetown	46–34	1965	UCLA	Michigan	91–80
1944	Utah	Dartmouth	42–40	1966	Texas Western	Kentucky	72–65
1945	Oklahoma A & M	New York	49–45	1967	UCLA	Dayton	79–64
1946	Oklahoma A & M	North Carolina	43–40	1968	UCLA	North Carolina	78–55
1947	Holy Cross	Oklahoma	58–47	1969	UCLA	Purdue	92–72
1948	Kentucky	Baylor	58–42	1970	UCLA	Jacksonville	80–69
1949	Kentucky	Oklahoma State	46–36	1971	UCLA	Villanova	68–62
1950	CCNY	Bradley	71–68	1972	UCLA	Florida State	81–76
1951	Kentucky	Kansas State	68–58	1973	UCLA	Memphis State	87–66
1952	Kansas	St. John's (NY)	80–63	1974	North Carolina State	Marquette	76–64
1953	Indiana	Kansas	69–68				
1954	La Salle	Bradley	92–76	1975	UCLA	Kentucky	92–85
1955	San Francisco	La Salle	77–63	1976	Indiana	Michigan	86–68
1956	San Francisco	Iowa	83–71	1977	Marquette	North Carolina	67–59
1957	North Carolina	Kansas	54–53	1978	Kentucky	Duke	94–88
1958	Kentucky	Seattle	84–72	1979	Michigan State	Indiana State	75–64
1959	California (Berkeley)	West Virginia	71–70	1980	Louisville	UCLA	59–54
				1981	Indiana	North Carolina	63–50
1960	Ohio State	California (Berkeley)	75–55	1982	North Carolina	Georgetown	63–62

Division I National Collegiate Athletic Association (NCAA) Championship—Men (continued)

YEAR	WINNER	RUNNER-UP	SCORE	YEAR	WINNER	RUNNER-UP	SCORE
1983	North Carolina State	Houston	54–52	1996	Kentucky	Syracuse	76–67
1984	Georgetown	Houston	84–75	1997	Arizona	Kentucky	84–79
1985	Villanova	Georgetown	66–64	1998	Kentucky	Utah	78–69
1986	Louisville	Duke	72–69	1999	Connecticut	Duke	77–74
1987	Indiana	Syracuse	74–73	2000	Michigan State	Florida	89–76
1988	Kansas	Oklahoma	83–79	2001	Duke	Arizona	82–72
1989	Michigan	Seton Hall	80–79	2002	Maryland	Indiana	64–52
1990	UNLV	Duke	103–73	2003	Syracuse	Kansas	81–78
1991	Duke	Kansas	72–65	2004	Connecticut	Georgia Tech	82–73
1992	Duke	Michigan	71–51	2005	North Carolina	Illinois	75–70
1993	North Carolina	Michigan	77–71	2006	Florida	UCLA	73–57
1994	Arkansas	Duke	76–72	2007	Florida	Ohio State	84–75
1995	UCLA	Arkansas	89–78				

Division I National Collegiate Athletic Association (NCAA) Championship—Women

YEAR	WINNER	RUNNER-UP	SCORE	YEAR	WINNER	RUNNER-UP	SCORE
1982	Louisiana Tech	Cheyney (PA)	76–62	1995	Connecticut	Tennessee	70–64
1983	USC	Louisiana Tech	69–67	1996	Tennessee	Georgia	83–65
1984	USC	Tennessee	72–61	1997	Tennessee	Old Dominion	68–59
1985	Old Dominion	Georgia	70–65	1998	Tennessee	Louisiana Tech	93–75
1986	Texas	USC	97–81	1999	Purdue	Duke	62–45
1987	Tennessee	Louisiana Tech	67–44	2000	Connecticut	Tennessee	71–52
1988	Louisiana Tech	Auburn	56–54	2001	Notre Dame	Purdue	68–66
1989	Tennessee	Auburn	76–60	2002	Connecticut	Oklahoma	82–70
1990	Stanford	Auburn	88–81	2003	Connecticut	Tennessee	73–68
1991	Tennessee	Virginia	70–67	2004	Connecticut	Tennessee	70–61
1992	Stanford	Western Kentucky	78–62	2005	Baylor	Michigan State	84–62
1993	Texas Tech	Ohio State	84–82	2006	Maryland	Duke	78–75
1994	North Carolina	Louisiana Tech	60–59	2007	Tennessee	Rutgers	59–46

World Amateur Basketball Championship—Men

YEAR	WINNER	RUNNER-UP	YEAR	WINNER	RUNNER-UP
1936[1]	United States	Canada	1978	Yugoslavia	USSR
1948[1]	United States	France	1980[1]	Yugoslavia	Italy
1950	Argentina	United States	1982	USSR	United States
1952[1]	United States	USSR	1984[1]	United States	Spain
1954	United States	Brazil	1986	United States	USSR
1956[1]	United States	USSR	1988[1]	USSR	Yugoslavia
1959	Brazil[2]	United States	1990	Yugoslavia	USSR
1960[1]	United States	USSR	1992[1]	United States	Croatia
1963	Brazil	Yugoslavia	1994	United States	Russia
1964[1]	United States	USSR	1996[1]	United States	Yugoslavia
1967	USSR	Yugoslavia	1998	Yugoslavia	Russia
1968[1]	United States	Yugoslavia	2000[1]	United States	France
1970	Yugoslavia	Brazil	2002	Yugoslavia	Argentina
1972[1]	USSR	United States	2004[1]	Argentina	Italy
1974	USSR	Yugoslavia	2006	Spain	Greece
1976[1]	United States	Yugoslavia			

[1]Olympic championships, recognized as world championships. [2]By default.

The University of Bologna in Italy is the oldest university in Europe. Although the exact date of the university's founding is unknown, there are artifacts showing that masters of rhetoric and logic began to study Roman law there in the 11th century. As well, the first degree of doctor of civil law was awarded by the University of Bologna, in the second half of the 12th century.

World Amateur Basketball Championship—Women

YEAR	WINNER	RUNNER-UP	YEAR	WINNER	RUNNER-UP
1953	United States	Chile	1986	United States	USSR
1957	United States	USSR	1988[1]	United States	Yugoslavia
1959	USSR	Bulgaria	1990	United States	Yugoslavia
1964	USSR	Czechoslovakia	1992[1]	Unified Team[2]	China
1967	USSR	South Korea	1994	Brazil	China
1971	USSR	Czechoslovakia	1996[1]	United States	Brazil
1975	USSR	Japan	1998	United States	Russia
1976[1]	USSR	United States	2000[1]	United States	Australia
1979	United States	South Korea	2002	United States	Russia
1980[1]	USSR	Bulgaria	2004[1]	United States	Australia
1983	USSR	United States	2006	Australia	Russia
1984[1]	United States	South Korea			

[1]Olympic championships, recognized as world championships. [2]Athletes from the Commonwealth of Independent States plus Georgia.

Billiard Games

The game of billiards has a surprising number of **varieties** throughout the world. Factors in that variety include the number and appearance of the billiard balls, the size of the table, the existence of side and corner pockets, and the object of play. The classic form of the game—**three-cushion billiards**—is played on a pocketless table with one red ball and two white balls, one of which is marked with a spot; it is often known as French billiards, carom billiards, or (simply) billiards.

Pocket billiards, which embraces both **snooker** and the game sometimes known (for the sake of clarity) as **English billiards**, is the prevalent form of billiards in the United Kingdom. The world professional snooker championship was first held in 1927; until 1947 it was won every year by Joe Davis (championships were not held during World War II). The championship was discontin-ued during the 1950s, was revived during the 1960s, and became a knockout event in 1969. The results that are given in the table below begin with that year.

The American form of pocket billiards, usually known as **pool**, differs markedly from the British game. Its most popular variations are **eight-ball**, **nine-ball**, and **straight (or 14.1) pool**. Though earlier straight pool tournaments were held with regularity, the game is now not often played in national competition. Since the 1970s nine-ball and eight-ball pool have surpassed straight pool in popularity in the United States, and nine-ball has gained some prominence internationally. In 1990 the **World Pool-Billiard Association** (WPA; founded 1987) inaugurated the nine-ball world championship.

WPA Web site: <www.wpa-pool.com>.

World Three-Cushion Championship

Competition has been held since 1928; table shows champions for the past 10 years.

YEAR	WINNER	YEAR	WINNER	YEAR	WINNER
1997	Dick Jaspers (NED)	2000	Dick Jaspers (NED)	2003	Semih Sayginer (TUR)
1998	Torbjörn Blomdahl (SWE)	2001	Raymond Ceulemans (BEL)	2004	Dick Jaspers (NED)
1999	Dick Jaspers (NED)	2002	Marco Zanetti (ITA)	2005	Daniel Sánchez (ESP)
				2006	Eddy Merckx (BEL)

World Professional Snooker Championship

Competition has been held since 1927; table shows champions for the past 10 years.
Won by a British player unless otherwise noted.

YEAR	WINNER	YEAR	WINNER	YEAR	WINNER
1998	John Higgins	2001	Ronnie O'Sullivan	2004	Ronnie O'Sullivan
1999	Stephen Hendry	2002	Peter Ebdon	2005	Shaun Murphy
2000	Mark Williams	2003	Mark Williams	2006	Graeme Dott
				2007	John Higgins

WPA World Nine-Ball Championships

Competition has been held since 1990; table shows champions for the past 10 years.

YEAR	MEN'S CHAMPION	WOMEN'S CHAMPION	YEAR	MEN'S CHAMPION	WOMEN'S CHAMPION
1998	Kunihiko Takahashi (JPN)	Allison Fisher (GBR)	2003	Thorsten Hohmann (GER)	not held
			2004	Alex Pagulayan (CAN)	Kim Ga Young (KOR)
1999	Nick Varner (USA)	Liu Shin-Mei (TPE)	2005	Wu Chia-Ching (TPE)	not held
2000	Chao Fong-Pang (TPE)	Julie Kelly (IRE)	2006	Ronnie Alcano (PHI)	Kim Ga Young (KOR)
2001	Mika Immonen (FIN)	Allison Fisher (GBR)	2007	to be held 3–11 November	Pan Xiaoting (CHN)
2002	Earl Strickland (USA)	Liu Shin-Mei (TPE)			

Bowling

The world governing body for bowling is the **Fédération Internationale des Quilleurs (FIQ)**. Since 1954 it has sponsored world bowling championships.

In the **United States**, men's bowling is governed by the **American Bowling Congress (ABC)**, which was founded in 1895 but became a constituent of the **United States Bowling Congress (USBC)** in 2004. In 1901 the first national championship was organized; in 1961 the yearly competition was split into two divisions—regular (for those with a combined average score of 851 or higher) and classic (for professionals). The classic division was discontinued in 1980. The **Women's International Bowling Congress**

(WIBC) was organized in 1916 and sponsored an annual women's championship until 2004, when organizational mergers created the USBC. Competition takes place between teams, doubles, and singles. The all-events category is won by the individual who has the best score of nine games—three team, three doubles, and three singles scores. The **Professional Bowlers Association (PBA)** was established in 1958. One of its major tournaments is the annual Tournament of Champions.

Related Web sites: FIQ: <www.fiq.org>; USBC <www.bowl.com>; PBA: <www.pba.com>.

Professional Bowlers Association (PBA) Tournament of Champions

The annual tournament has been held since 1960. This table shows results for the past 40 years.

YEAR	CHAMPION	YEAR	CHAMPION	YEAR	CHAMPION
1967	Jim Stefanich	1981	Steve Cook	1995	Mike Aulby
1968	Dave Davis	1982	Mike Durbin	1996	Dave D'Entremont
1969	Jim Godman	1983	Joe Berardi	1997	John Gant
1970	Don Johnson	1984	Mike Durbin	1998	Bryan Goebel
1971	Johnny Petraglia	1985	Mark Williams	1999	Jason Couch
1972	Mike Durbin	1986	Marshall Holman	2000	Jason Couch
1973	Jim Godman	1987	Pete Weber	2001–02	*not held*
1974	Earl Anthony	1988	Mark Williams	2002–03	Jason Couch
1975	Dave Davis	1989	Del Ballard, Jr.	2003–04	Patrick Healey, Jr.
1976	Marshall Holman	1990	Dave Ferraro	2004–05	Steve Jaros
1977	Mike Berlin	1991	David Ozio	2005–06	Chris Barnes
1978	Earl Anthony	1992	Marc McDowell	2006–07	Tommy Jones
1979	George Pappas	1993	George Branham III		
1980	Wayne Webb	1994	Norm Duke		

United States Bowling Congress (USBC) Bowling Championships—Regular Division

The championships have been held since 1901. This table shows results for the past 20 years.

YEAR	SINGLES	SCORE	ALL-EVENTS	SCORE
1988	Steve Hutkowski	774	Rick Steelsmith	2,053
1989	Paul Tetreault	813	George Hall	2,227
1990	Robert Hochrein	791	Mike Neumann	2,168
1991	Ed Deines	826	Tom Howery	2,216
1992	Gary Blatchford; Bob Youker, Jr. (tied)	801	Mike Tucker	2,158
1993	Dan Bock	798	Jeff Nimke	2,254
1994	John Weltzien	810	Thomas Holt	2,190
1995	Matt Surina	826	Jeff Kwiatkowski	2,191
1996	Don Scudder, Jr.	823	Scott Kurtz	2,224
1997	John Socha	847	Jeff Richgels	2,241
1998	John Gaines	814	Chris Barnes	2,151
1999	Dan Winter	825	Thomas Jones	2,158
2000	Garran Hein	811	Roy Daniels	2,181
2001	Nicholas Hoagland	798	D.J. Archer	2,219
2002	Mark Millsap	823	Stephen A. Hardy	2,279
2003	Ron Bahr	837	Steve Kloempken	2,215
2004[1]	John Janawicz	858	John Janawicz	2,224
2005	David Adam	791	Scott Craddock	2,131
2006	Wendy Macpherson	812	Dave A. Mitchell	2,189
2007	Frederick Aki	814	Mike Rose, Jr.	2,198

[1]*Table shows American Bowling Congress winners through 2004 and USBC winners thereafter.*

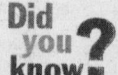
Did you know? Barry Bonds's 73 home runs in 2001 broke the major-league record of 70 hit by the St. Louis Cardinals' Mark McGwire only three years earlier. But the previous record for home runs by a professional ballplayer was 72, hit by Joe Bauman for the minor-league Roswell Rockets in 1954. Bauman hit .400 with 224 RBIs that season, yet he never made it to the major leagues.

United States Bowling Congress (USBC) Women's Bowling Championships—Classic Division

The championships have been held since 1916. The table shows results for the past 20 years.

YEAR	SINGLES	SCORE	ALL-EVENTS	SCORE
1988	Michelle Meyer-Welty	690	Lisa Wagner	1,988
1989	Laura Anderson	683	Nancy Fehr	1,911
1990	Paula Carter; Dana Miller-Mackie (tied)	705	Carol Norman	1,984
1991	Debbie Kuhn	773	Debbie Kuhn	2,036
1992	Patty Ann	680	Mitsuko Tokimoto	1,928
1993	Karen Collura; Kari Murph (tied)	747	Anne Marie Duggan	1,990
1994	Vicki Fifield	716	Wendy Macpherson-Papanos	1,940
1995	Beth Owen	749	Beth Owen	1,983
1996	Cindy Berlanga	723	Lorrie Nichols	1,985
1997	Jan Schmidt	765	Kendra Cameron	2,039
1998	Nellie Glandon	714	Liz Johnson	1,989
1999	Nikki Gianulias	746	Hidemi Mizobuchi	2,065
2000	Cathy Krasner	729	Carolyn Dorin-Ballard	2,147
2001	Lisa Wagner	756	Jonquay Armon	2,044
2002	Theresa Smith	752	Cara Honeychurch	2,150
2003	Michelle Feldman	764	Michelle Feldman	2,048
2004[1]	Sharon Smith	754	Kim Adler	2,133
2005	Leanne Barrette	774	Leanne Barrette	2,231
2006	Karen Stroud	771	Karen Stroud	2,159
2007	Tiffany Stanbrough	745	Wendy Macpherson	2,161

[1]*Table shows Women's International Bowling Congress winners through 2004 and USBC winners thereafter.*

World Tenpin Bowling Championships—Men

In 1979 the singles category was added; previously, the masters had been the only individual event. Also in that year, eights were discontinued and triples were introduced.

YEAR	SINGLES	MASTERS	PAIRS	TRIPLES	FIVES	EIGHTS
1954		Gösta Algeskog (SWE)	FIN		SWE	SWE
1955		Nisse Backstrom (SWE)	SWE		FRG	FIN
1958		Kalle Asukas (FIN)	SWE		FIN	SWE
1960		Tito Reynolds (MEX)	MEX		VEN	MEX
1963		Les Zikes (USA)	USA		USA	USA
1967		David Pond (GBR)	GBR		FIN	USA
1971		Ed Luther (USA)	PUR		USA	USA
1975		Bud Stoudt (USA)	GBR		FIN	FRG
1979	Ollie Ongtawco (PHI)	Gary Bugden (GBR)	AUS	MAS	AUS	
1983	Armando Marino (COL)	Tony Cariello (USA)	AUS	SWE	FIN	
1987	Patrick Rolland (FRA)	Roger Pieters (BEL)	SWE	USA	SWE	
1991	Ying Chieh Ma (TAI)	Mika Koivuniemi (FIN)	USA	USA	TAI	
1995	Marc Doi (CAN)	Chen-Min Yang (TPE)	SWE	NED	NED	
1999	Gery Verbruggen (BEL)	Ahmed Shaheen (QAT)	SWE	FIN	SWE	
2003	Mika Luoto (FIN)	Michael Little (AUS)	SWE	USA	SWE	
2006	Remy Ong (SIN)	Biboy Rivera (PHI)	SWE	KOR	USA	
2008	*to be held 20–31 Aug in Bangkok, Thailand.*					

World Tenpin Bowling Championships—Women

In 1963 fives were played as four-woman teams, European style (either the entire game on one lane or half of the game on one lane, balance on accompanying lane). In 1979 fours were discontinued altogether and triples were introduced. Also in that year, the singles category was added; previously, the masters had been the only individual event.

YEAR	SINGLES	MASTERS	PAIRS	TRIPLES	FOURS	FIVES
1963		Helen Shablis (USA)	USA		MEX	USA
1967		Helen Weston (USA)	MEX		FIN	FIN
1971		Ashie Gonzalez (PUR)	JPN		USA	USA
1975		Anne Haefker (FRG)	SWE		JPN	JPN
1979	Lita de la Rosa (PHI)	Lita de la Rosa (PHI)	PHI	USA		USA
1983	Lena Sulkanen (SWE)	Lena Sulkanen (SWE)	DEN	FRG		SWE
1987	Edda Piccini (MEX)	Annette Hägre (SWE)	USA	USA		USA
1991	Martina Beckel (GER)	Catherine Willis (CAN)	JPN	CAN		KOR
1995	Debby Ship (CAN)	Celia Flores (MEX)	THA	AUS		FIN
1999	Kelly Kulick (USA)	Ann-Maree Putney (AUS)	AUS	KOR		KOR
2003	Zara Glover (GBR)	Diandra Hyman (USA)	GBR	PHI		MAS
2007	*to be held 28 Aug–9 Sep in Monterrey, Mexico.*					

Chess

Wilhelm Steinitz is generally recognized as the first official chess world champion, although dates for his 19th-century reign vary. With a few notable exceptions, each successive champion defeated his predecessor in match play. The first exception followed the death of the incumbent **Alexander Alekhine** in 1946. The **Fédération Internationale des Échecs** (FIDE; founded 1924) stepped in and arranged a tournament among leading contenders to determine a new champion in 1948. FIDE continued to oversee regular tournaments and matches to determine challengers—although another exception occurred in 1975, when **Robert (Bobby) Fischer** refused to defend his crown and retired. In 1993 **Garry Kasparov** pulled out of FIDE to defend his title under rival organizations (Professional Chess Association and later Braingames). Without a universally recognized champion, FIDE struggled to obtain funding for its multiyear system of tournaments and matches leading to a title match. So, in 1999 FIDE began to hold annual **knockout tournaments**, with very fast game play, to determine its champion. In a move to unify the championship, in 2006 a competition was held that pitted the FIDE champion (Veselin Topalov) against the rival classical chess champion (Vladimir Kramnik). Kramnik won the controversial match in an overtime period and was named the undisputed world chess champion.

FIDE began organizing the **women's chess championship** in 1953. Controversy has also afflicted this title, as **Zsuzsa Polgar** refused to accept FIDE's terms for her title defense in 1999. In 2000 FIDE adopted a knockout tournament format for the women's championship similar to that of the open tournament.

Competitions called Olympiads are also held biennially. Competition is open to both men and women, but since 1957 there has been a separate Olympiad that is restricted to women.

FIDE Web site: <www.fide.com>.

World Chess Champions—Men
Generally recognized (see Chess above).

REIGN	NAME	NATIONALITY	REIGN	NAME	NATIONALITY
1866–94	Wilhelm Steinitz	Austrian American	1960–61	Mikhail Tal	Soviet Russian
1894–1921	Emanuel Lasker	German	1961–63	Mikhail Botvinnik	Soviet Russian
1921–27	José Raúl Capablanca	Cuban	1963–69	Tigran Petrosyan	Soviet Georgian-born Armenian
1927–35	Alexander Alekhine	Russian-born French	1969–72	Boris Spassky	Soviet Russian
1935–37	Max Euwe	Dutch	1972–75	Robert (Bobby) Fischer	American
1937–46	Alexander Alekhine	Russian-born French	1975–85	Anatoly Karpov	Soviet Russian
1948–57	Mikhail Botvinnik	Soviet Russian	1985–2000	Garry Kasparov	Azerbaijani-born Russian
1957–58	Vasily Smyslov	Soviet Russian	2000–	Vladimir Kramnik	Russian
1958–60	Mikhail Botvinnik	Soviet Russian			

World Chess Champions—Women

REIGN	NAME	NATIONALITY	REIGN	NAME	NATIONALITY
1927–44	Vera Menchik[1]	Soviet Russian	1978–91	Maya Chiburdanidze	Soviet Georgian
1949–53	Lyudmila Rudenko	Soviet Russian	1991–96	Xie Jun	Chinese
1953–56	Yelizaveta Bykova	Soviet Russian	1996–99	Zsuzsa Polgar	Hungarian
1956–58	Olga Rubtsova	Soviet Russian	1999–2001	Xie Jun	Chinese
1958–62	Yelizaveta Bykova	Soviet Russian	2001–04	Zhu Chen	Chinese
1962–78	Nona Gaprindashvili	Soviet Georgian	2004–06	Antoaneta Stefanova	Bulgarian
			2006–	Xu Yuhua	Chinese

[1]*Killed in an air raid on London in 1944; title left vacant.*

Cricket

Cricket is one of the **national sports** of England, and consequently it is played in nearly all the countries with which England has been associated. The world governing body is the **International Cricket Council** (ICC; founded as the Imperial Cricket Conference in 1909). The most important international cricket matches are the **Test matches**, which have been played since 1877. The Test-playing countries are England, Australia, South Africa (banned from international competition between about 1970 and 1992), West Indies (representing Barbados, Guyana, Jamaica, Trinidad and Tobago, and the Leeward and Windward islands), New Zealand, India, Pakistan, Sri Lanka, Zimbabwe (since 1992), and Bangladesh (since 2000).

The Test table is designed to be read from left to right across the columns. This will indicate, for example, that in Test match play against England, South Africa has won 26 games, has had 50 drawn matches, and has lost 54 games.

The **World Cup** is a quadrennial series of one-day, limited-overs competitions. It was first held in 1975.

Related Web sites: <www.icc-cricket.com>.

All-Time First-Class Test Cricket Standings (as of 30 Sep 2006)

	England			Australia			South Africa			West Indies			New Zealand		
	WINS	DRAWS	LOSSES	W	D	L	W	D	L	W	D	L	W	D	L
England v.	—	—	—	97	88	126	54	50	26	38	44*	52	41	40	7
Australia v.	126	88	97	—	—	—	44	18	15	48	22†	32	22	16	7
South Africa v.	26	50	54	15	18	44	—	—	—	12	5	2	18	11	4
West Indies v.	52	44*	38	32	22†	48	2	5	12	—	—	—	10	16*	9
New Zealand v.	7	40	41	7	16	22	4	11	18	9	16*	10	—	—	—
India v.	17	43	34	15	21†	32	3	6	8	11	41	30	14	22*	9
Pakistan v.	12	36	19‡	11	17	24	2	2	4	13	14	14	21	18	6
Sri Lanka v.	5	5	8	1	6	11	4	5	8	5	3	2	4	10	8
Zimbabwe v.	0	3	3	0	0	3	0	1	6	0	2	4	0	6	7
Bangladesh v.	0	0	4	0	0	4	0	0	4	0	1	3	0	0	4

	India			Pakistan			Sri Lanka			Zimbabwe			Bangladesh		
	WINS	DRAWS	LOSSES	W	D	L	W	D	L	W	D	L	W	D	L
England v.	34	43	17	19‡	36	12	8	5	5	3	3	0	4	0	0
Australia v.	32	21†	15	24	17	11	11	6	1	3	0	0	4	0	0
South Africa v.	8	6	3	2	2	2	8	5	4	6	1	0	4	0	0
West Indies v.	30	41	11	14	14	13	2	3	5	4	2	0	3	1	0
New Zealand v.	9	22*	14	6	18	21	8	10	4	7	6	0	4	0	0
India v.	—	—	—	8	36	12	10	13	3	7	2	2	3	0	0
Pakistan v.	12	36	8	—	—	—	15	10*	7	8	5*	2	6	0	0
Sri Lanka v.	3	13	10	7	10*	15	—	—	—	10	5	0	7	0	0
Zimbabwe v.	2	2	7	2	5*	8	0	5	10	—	—	—	4	3	1
Bangladesh v.	0	0	3	0	0	6	0	0	7	1	3	4	—	—	—

*Including one match abandoned.   †Including one tie.   ‡Including one forfeit.

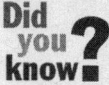 **Did you know?**

Author Ian Fleming desired a simple name, "brief, unromantic, and yet very masculine," when conceiving his secret-agent hero for the novel *Casino Royale* (1953). Fleming, an avid bird-watcher living in Jamaica at the time, discovered the perfect name while reading the book *Birds of the West Indies* (1936) by James Bond, an ornithologist from Philadelphia. In a letter to Bond's wife in 1961, Fleming wrote, "I must confess that your husband has every reason to sue me....In return, I can only offer your James Bond unlimited use of the name Ian Fleming for any purpose he may think fit."

Curling

The game of curling, played on ice and somewhat akin to bowls or shuffleboard, varies little from country to country. The maximum permitted weight of the curling stones is 44 lb (19.96 kg). The top international **men's competition** was instituted in 1959 (called the Scotch Whisky Cup from 1959 to 1967; the Silver Broom from 1968 to 1985; and the World Curling Championship since 1986). Although curling has been played among women of many countries since at least the mid-20th century, the first **women's world curling championship** was not held until 1979.

World Curling Federation Web site: <www.worldcurling.org>.

World Curling Championships—Men

YEAR	WINNER	RUNNER-UP	YEAR	WINNER	RUNNER-UP
1959	Canada	Scotland	1975	Switzerland	Canada
1960	Canada	Scotland	1976	United States	Scotland
1961	Canada	Scotland	1977	Sweden	Canada
1962	Canada	Scotland	1978	United States	Canada
1963	Canada	Scotland	1979	Norway	Switzerland
1964	Canada	Scotland	1980	Canada	Norway
1965	United States	Canada	1981	Switzerland	United States
1966	Canada	Scotland	1982	Canada	Switzerland
1967	Scotland	Canada	1983	Canada	West Germany
1968	Canada	Scotland	1984	Norway	Switzerland
1969	Canada	Scotland	1985	Canada	Sweden
1970	Canada	Scotland	1986	Canada	Scotland
1971	Canada	Scotland	1987	Canada	West Germany
1972	Canada	United States	1988	Norway	Canada
1973	Sweden	Canada	1989	Canada	Switzerland
1974	United States	Canada	1990	Canada	Scotland

World Curling Championships—Men (continued)

YEAR	WINNER	RUNNER-UP	YEAR	WINNER	RUNNER-UP
1991	Scotland	Canada	2001	Sweden	Switzerland
1992	Switzerland	Scotland	2002	Canada	Norway
1993	Canada	Scotland	2003	Canada	Switzerland
1994	Canada	Sweden	2004	Sweden	Germany
1995	Canada	Scotland	2005	Canada	Scotland
1996	Canada	Scotland	2006	Scotland	Canada
1997	Sweden	Germany	2007	Canada	Germany
1998	Canada	Sweden	2008	to be held 5–13 April in Grand Forks ND	
1999	Scotland	Canada			
2000	Canada	Sweden			

World Curling Championships—Women

YEAR	WINNER	RUNNER-UP	YEAR	WINNER	RUNNER-UP
1979	Switzerland	Sweden	1995	Sweden	Canada
1980	Canada	Sweden	1996	Canada	United States
1981	Sweden	Canada	1997	Canada	Norway
1982	Denmark	Sweden	1998	Sweden	Denmark
1983	Switzerland	Norway	1999	Sweden	United States
1984	Canada	Switzerland	2000	Canada	Switzerland
1985	Canada	Scotland	2001	Canada	Sweden
1986	Canada	West Germany	2002	Scotland	Sweden
1987	Canada	West Germany	2003	United States	Canada
1988	West Germany	Canada	2004	Canada	Norway
1989	Canada	Norway	2005	Sweden	United States
1990	Norway	Scotland	2006	Sweden	United States
1991	Norway	Canada	2007	Canada	Denmark
1992	Sweden	United States	2008	to be held 22–30 March in Vernon, BC, Canada	
1993	Canada	Germany			
1994	Canada	Scotland			

Cycling

By all accounts, the greatest cycling event of all is the annual **Tour de France** road race (founded 1903). It is raced in several stages over a distance usually exceeding 3,500 km (2,175 mi). From 1911 to 1929 distances exceeded 5,300 km (3,290 mi). A Tour de France for women was first held in 1984, over an 18-stage course of 991 km (616 mi). In addition to this and a great number of other road races held yearly, there are yearly **road racing world championships.**

Track racing championships are also held. The oldest events of track racing are the **sprint** (in which only the last part of the race can actually be considered sprinting) and the **pursuit** (both a team and an individual event in which contestants start the race on opposite sides of the track and attempt to catch each other). **Mountain bike racing** and **cyclo-cross,** a cross-country bicycle race that requires cyclists to carry their bikes over parts of the course, developed in the latter part of the 20th century. World championships were established for these sports in 1997.

International Cycling Union (Union Cycliste Internationale—UCI) Web site: <www.uci.ch>.

Cycling Champions, 2006–07

In the case of multiday events, the concluding date is given.

EVENT	WINNER (COUNTRY)	DATE
world champions—mountain bikes		27 Aug 2006
men		
Cross-country	Julien Absalon (FRA)	
Downhill	Samuel Hill (AUS)	
women		
Cross-country	Gunn-Rita Dahle Flesjå (NOR)	
Downhill	Sabrina Jonnier (FRA)	
world champions—road		
men		
Individual road race	Paolo Bettini (ITA)	24 Sep 2006
Individual time trial	Fabian Cancellara (SUI)	21 Sep 2006
women		
Individual road race	Marianne Vos (NED)	23 Sep 2006
Individual time trial	Kristin Armstrong (USA)	20 Sep 2006

Cycling Champions, 2006–07 (continued)

EVENT	WINNER (COUNTRY)	DATE
world champions—cyclo-cross		28 Jan 2007
Men	Erwin Vervecken (BEL)	
Women	Maryline Salvetat (FRA)	

	WINNER (COUNTRY)	DATE
world champions—track		1 Apr 2007
men		
Individual pursuit	Bradley Wiggins (GBR)	
Individual sprint	Theo Bos (NED)	
1-km time trial	Chris Hoy (GBR)	
Points	Joan Llaneras (ESP)	
Team pursuit	Great Britain	
Keirin	Chris Hoy (GBR)	
Team sprint	France	
Madison	Bruno Risi, Franco Marvulli (SUI)	
Scratch	Wong Kam-Po (HKG)	
women		
Sprint	Victoria Pendleton (GBR)	
Individual pursuit	Sarah Hammer (USA)	
500-m time trial	Anna Meares (AUS)	
Points	Katherine Bates (AUS)	
Scratch	Yumari González (CUB)	
Keirin	Victoria Pendleton (GBR)	

major elite road-race winners		
Vattenfall Cyclassics	Óscar Freire (ESP)	30 Jul 2006
San Sebastian Classic (Clasica Ciclista San Sebastian)	Xavier Florencio (ESP)	12 Aug 2006
Tour of Spain (Vuelta a España)	Alexandre Vinokourov (KAZ)	17 Sep 2006
Zürich Championship (Züri-Metzgete)	Samuel Sánchez (ESP)	1 Oct 2006
Paris–Tours	Frédéric Guesdon (FRA)	8 Oct 2006
Tour of Lombardy (Giro di Lombardia)	Paolo Bettini (ITA)	14 Oct 2006
Paris–Nice	Alberto Contador (ESP)	18 Mar 2007
Tirreno–Adriatico	Andreas Klöden (GER)	20 Mar 2007
Milan–San Remo	Óscar Freire (ESP)	24 Mar 2007
Tour of Flanders (Ronde van Vlaanderen)	Alessandro Ballan (ITA)	8 Apr 2007
Ghent–Wevelgem	Marcus Burghardt (GER)	11 Apr 2007
Paris–Roubaix	Stuart O'Grady (AUS)	15 Apr 2007
Amstel Gold	Stefan Schumacher (GER)	22 Apr 2007
La Flèche Wallonne	Davide Rebellin (ITA)	25 Apr 2007
Liège–Bastogne–Liège	Danilo Di Luca (ITA)	29 Apr 2007
Tour of Romandie (Tour de Romandie)	Thomas Dekker (NED)	6 May 2007
Tour of Italy (Giro d'Italia)	Danilo Di Luca (ITA)	3 Jun 2007
Critérium du Dauphiné Libéré	Christophe Moreau (FRA)	17 Jun 2007
Tour of Switzerland (Tour de Suisse)	Vladimir Karpets (RUS)	24 Jun 2007
Tour de France	Alberto Contador (ESP)	29 Jul 2007

Tour de France

YEAR	WINNER (COUNTRY)	LENGTH OF ROUTE (KM)	YEAR	WINNER (COUNTRY)	LENGTH OF ROUTE (KM)
1903	Maurice Garin (FRA)	2,428	1922	Firmin Lambot (BEL)	5,375
1904	Henri Cornet (FRA)	2,388	1923	Henri Pélissier (FRA)	5,386
1905	Louis Trousselier (FRA)	2,975	1924	Ottavio Bottecchia (ITA)	5,425
1906	René Pottier (FRA)	4,637	1925	Ottavio Bottecchia (ITA)	5,430
1907	Lucien Petit-Breton (FRA)	4,488	1926	Lucien Buysse (BEL)	5,745
1908	Lucien Petit-Breton (FRA)	4,487	1927	Nicolas Frantz (LUX)	5,341
1909	François Faber (LUX)	4,507	1928	Nicolas Frantz (LUX)	5,377
1910	Octave Lapize (FRA)	4,474	1929	Maurice De Waele (BEL)	5,286
1911	Gustave Garrigou (FRA)	5,344	1930	André Leducq (FRA)	4,818
1912	Odile Defraye (BEL)	5,319	1931	Antonin Magne (FRA)	5,095
1913	Philippe Thys (BEL)	5,387	1932	André Leducq (FRA)	4,520
1914	Philippe Thys (BEL)	5,405	1933	Georges Speicher (FRA)	4,395
1915–18	not held		1934	Antonin Magne (FRA)	4,363
1919	Firmin Lambot (BEL)	5,560	1935	Romain Maes (BEL)	4,338
1920	Philippe Thys (BEL)	5,519	1936	Romain Maes (BEL)	4,442
1921	Léon Scieur (BEL)	5,484	1937	Roger Lapébie (FRA)	4,415

Tour de France (continued)

YEAR	WINNER (COUNTRY)	LENGTH OF ROUTE (KM)	YEAR	WINNER (COUNTRY)	LENGTH OF ROUTE (KM)
1938	Gino Bartali (ITA)	4,694	1976	Lucien Van Impe (BEL)	4,050
1939	Sylvere Maes (BEL)	4,224	1977	Bernard Thévenet (FRA)	4,098
1940–46	*not held*		1978	Bernard Hinault (FRA)	3,920
1947	Jean Robic (FRA)	4,640	1979	Bernard Hinault (FRA)	3,719
1948	Gino Bartali (ITA)	4,922	1980	Joop Zoetemelk (NED)	3,948
1949	Fausto Coppi (ITA)	4,808	1981	Bernard Hinault (FRA)	3,765
1950	Ferdi Kubler (SUI)	4,775	1982	Bernard Hinault (FRA)	3,489
1951	Hugo Koblet (SUI)	4,697	1983	Laurent Fignon (FRA)	3,568
1952	Fausto Coppi (ITA)	4,807	1984	Laurent Fignon (FRA)	3,880
1953	Louison Bobet (FRA)	4,479	1985	Bernard Hinault (FRA)	4,100
1954	Louison Bobet (FRA)	4,469	1986	Greg LeMond (USA)	4,091
1955	Louison Bobet (FRA)	4,855	1987	Stephen Roche (IRL)	4,100
1956	Roger Walkowiak (FRA)	4,496	1988	Pedro Delgado (ESP)	3,300
1957	Jacques Anquetil (FRA)	4,686	1989	Greg LeMond (USA)	3,215
1958	Charly Gaul (LUX)	4,319	1990	Greg LeMond (USA)	3,399
1959	Federico Bahamontes (ESP)	4,355	1991	Miguel Indurain (ESP)	3,935
1960	Gastone Nencini (ITA)	4,173	1992	Miguel Indurain (ESP)	3,983
1961	Jacques Anquetil (FRA)	4,397	1993	Miguel Indurain (ESP)	3,700
1962	Jacques Anquetil (FRA)	4,274	1994	Miguel Indurain (ESP)	3,978
1963	Jacques Anquetil (FRA)	4,137	1995	Miguel Indurain (ESP)	3,635
1964	Jacques Anquetil (FRA)	4,504	1996	*no winner*[1]	3,764
1965	Felice Gimondi (ITA)	4,183	1997	Jan Ullrich (GER)	3,944
1966	Lucien Aimar (FRA)	4,303	1998	Marco Pantani (ITA)	3,831
1967	Roger Pingeon (FRA)	4,780	1999	Lance Armstrong (USA)	3,687
1968	Jan Janssen (NED)	4,662	2000	Lance Armstrong (USA)	3,663
1969	Eddy Merckx (BEL)	4,110	2001	Lance Armstrong (USA)	3,454
1970	Eddy Merckx (BEL)	4,366	2002	Lance Armstrong (USA)	3,272
1971	Eddy Merckx (BEL)	3,689	2003	Lance Armstrong (USA)	3,428
1972	Eddy Merckx (BEL)	3,846	2004	Lance Armstrong (USA)	3,391
1973	Luis Ocaña (ESP)	4,140	2005	Lance Armstrong (USA)	3,608
1974	Eddy Merckx (BEL)	4,098	2006	Floyd Landis (USA)	3,657
1975	Bernard Thévenet (FRA)	4,000	2007	Alberto Contador (ESP)	3,550

[1]*The victory for Bjarne Riis (DEN) was invalidated after he admitted to using illegal performance-enhancing drugs.*

Football

Many types of games are known as football, among them association football (also called soccer), gridiron football (also called American football and known in the United States as, simply, football), Canadian football (also called rugby football), Australian Rules Football (also called footy), and Rugby Union and Rugby League football (also known as rugby, or rugger). Each of these games is unique, though some—such as US football and Canadian football—bear more than a little resemblance, and each has its own distinct following.

American football—professional. The National Football League (NFL) championship play-offs were organized in 1933. The American Football League (founded 1959) was a rival organization until 1970, when it merged with the NFL. The resulting reorganization added a few new teams (1976) and divided the reconstituted NFL into two conferences, the American Football Conference and the National Football Conference. The play-off winner in each conference becomes that conference's representative in the Super Bowl, the final game of the professional football season.

American football—college. Historically the national champion of college football has been informally selected by two rival opinion polls—one based on a survey of collegiate football coaches (currently conducted by *USA Today*) and the other on a survey of

sportswriters (conducted by the Associated Press [AP]). The AP sportswriters' poll began in 1936. The coaches' poll was begun in 1950 by the United Press (now United Press International [UPI]). Where polls designated different teams, both are listed. Desire for a clear-cut national champion led to the creation of the Bowl Championship Series (BCS) in 1999. The BCS uses a formula involving team records, strength of schedule, and rankings to determine the top two teams, who then meet in a national championship game. The site of the game annually shifts between the four major Bowls—Fiesta, Orange, Rose, and Sugar. The first of the Bowl games, the Rose Bowl, had its inaugural game in 1902 during the 12th annual Tournament of Roses festival in Pasadena CA. In 1935 the Sugar Bowl (played in New Orleans LA) and the Orange Bowl (played in Miami FL) were inaugurated. The Fiesta Bowl (played in Phoenix AZ) began play in 1971.

Canadian football—professional. The rules and organization of professional football in Canada have evolved gradually for well over 100 years based on the Canadian Rugby Union (formed in 1891). Until 1936 the game included intercollegiate teams. Since 1959 the Canadian Football League has been divided into two conferences, Eastern and Western. The two teams that win the division championships meet for the championship of the League, the Grey Cup (instituted in 1909). The intercollegiate teams withdrew from the Grey Cup competition in 1936, but the league did not become strictly professional until the mid-1950s.

Australian football—professional. Australian Rules Football, originally called Melbourne Rules Football, emerged in the state of Victoria in the late 1850s as a sporting alternative during the southern winter, when cricket was not played. The Victorian Football Association (formed in 1877) was supplanted by the Victorian Football League (formed in 1896), which was renamed the Australian Football League (AFL) in 1990 after two teams from outside Victoria were admitted in 1987. Currently, the eight AFL teams with the best records at the end of a 22-week season qualify for the play-offs. The first premiership Grand Final was played in 1886.

Association football. The game of association football is governed by the Fédération Internationale de Football Association (FIFA; founded 1904). The quadrennial FIFA World Cup (organized as the World Cup in 1930) was the first official internationally contested association football match. The popularity of the World Cup and, even earlier, the Copa América (1916) in South America led to the development of several regional cup competitions, including the European Champion Clubs' Cup (1955; discontinued after the 1992–93 season and superseded by the UEFA Champions League), the Asian Cup (1956), the African Cup of Nations (1957), and the Libertadores de América Cup (1960). Competition for the FIFA Women's World Cup began in 1991. The Major League Soccer Cup in the US was launched in 1996.

Rugby union football. Rugby union football was open to amateurs only until 1995. The Six Nations Championship was first played in 1882 (as the Four Nations) and is now contested by England, Scotland, Wales, Ireland, France (since 1910), and Italy (since 2000). The international Test matches further include South Africa, New Zealand, and Australia. The International Rugby Football League (FIRA; now FIRA-AER) oversees rugby in 39 other (i.e., non-Test) countries. The chief international competition between Rugby union clubs in the Southern Hemisphere is the tri-nation Super 14 (Super 10 from 1993 to 1995 and Super 12 from 1996 to 2005). Teams from Australia (four), South Africa (five), and New Zealand (five) play in a round-robin tournament; the four teams with the best records qualify for the semifinals. The World Cup, sponsored by the International Rugby Board (founded 1886), was inaugurated in 1987. The competition is held every four years.

Rugby league football. Rugby league World Cup competition began in 1954 between professionals from Australia, France, Great Britain, and New Zealand. In 1975 it was renamed the International Championship. Competition was discontinued after 1977 but revived during the 1980s. The match has been held irregularly every few years.

Related Web sites: National Football League (NFL): <www.nfl.com>; Canadian Football League (CFL): <www.cfl.ca>; Australian Football League (AFL): <www.afl.com.au>; Fédération Internationale de Football Association (FIFA): <www.fifa.com>; Union of European Football Associations (UEFA): <www.uefa.com>; Major League Soccer (MLS): <www.majorleaguesoccer.com>; International Rugby Board (Rugby Union): <www.irb.com>; Rugby League International Federation: <www.rlif.org>; Super 12: <www.super12.rugby.com.au>.

National Football League (NFL) Final Standings, 2006—07

American Football Conference

TEAM	WON	LOST	TIED	TEAM	WON	LOST	TIED
East Division				**South Division**			
New England[1]	12	4	0	Indianapolis[1]	12	4	0
New York Jets[1]	10	6	0	Tennessee	8	8	0
Buffalo	7	9	0	Jacksonville	8	8	0
Miami	6	10	0	Houston	6	10	0
North Division				**West Division**			
Baltimore[1]	13	3	0	San Diego[1]	14	2	0
Cincinnati	8	8	0	Kansas City[1]	9	7	0
Pittsburgh	8	8	0	Denver	9	7	0
Cleveland	4	12	0	Oakland	2	14	0

National Football Conference

TEAM	WON	LOST	TIED	TEAM	WON	LOST	TIED
East Division				**South Division**			
Philadelphia[1]	10	6	0	New Orleans[1]	10	6	0
Dallas[1]	9	7	0	Carolina	8	8	0
New York Giants[1]	8	8	0	Atlanta	7	9	0
Washington	5	11	0	Tampa Bay	4	12	0
North Division				**West Division**			
Chicago[1]	13	3	0	Seattle[1]	9	7	0
Green Bay	8	8	0	St. Louis	8	8	0
Minnesota	6	10	0	San Francisco	7	9	0
Detroit	3	13	0	Arizona	5	11	0

[1]*Gained play-off berth.*

American Pro Football All-Time Records

PLAYERS/TEAMS		NUMBER	SEASON/DATE
Individual career records			
Total games	Morten Andersen	368	1982–2006, except 2005
Total points	Gary Anderson	2,434	1982–2004
Touchdowns, total	Jerry Rice	208	1985–2004
Touchdowns, passing	Dan Marino	420	1983–99
Touchdowns, receiving	Jerry Rice	197	1985–2004
Touchdowns, rushing	Emmitt Smith	164	1990–2004
Field goals made	Gary Anderson	538	1982–2004
Extra points made (kicked)	George Blanda	943	1949–75, except 1959
Passing yardage	Dan Marino	61,361	1983–99
Passing completions	Dan Marino	4,967	1983–99
Receiving yardage	Jerry Rice	22,895	1985–2004
Rushing yardage	Emmitt Smith	18,355	1990–2004
Interceptions (defense)	Paul Krause	81	1964–79
Sacks (defense)[1]	Bruce Smith	200	1985–2003
Coaching, total wins	Don Shula	328	1963–95
Individual season records			
Total points	LaDainian Tomlinson	186	2006
Touchdowns, total	LaDainian Tomlinson	31	2006
Touchdowns, passing	Peyton Manning	49	2004
Touchdowns, receiving	Jerry Rice	22	1987
Touchdowns, rushing	LaDainian Tomlinson	28	2006
Field goals made	Neil Rackers	40	2005
Extra points made (kicked)	Uwe von Schamann	66	1984
Passing yardage	Dan Marino	5,084	1984
Receiving yardage	Jerry Rice	1,848	1995
Rushing yardage	Eric Dickerson	2,105	1984
Interceptions (defense)	Dick Lane	14	1952
Sacks (defense)[1]	Michael Strahan	22.5	2001
Individual game records			
Total points	Ernie Nevers	40	28 Nov 1929
Touchdowns, total	Ernie Nevers; Dub Jones; Gale Sayers	6	28 Nov 1929; 25 Nov 1951; 12 Dec 1965
Touchdowns, passing	Sid Luckman; Adrian Burk; George Blanda; Y.A. Tittle; Joe Kapp	7	14 Nov 1943; 17 Oct 1954; 19 Nov 1961; 28 Oct 1962; 28 Sep 1969
Touchdowns, receiving	Bob Shaw; Kellen Winslow; Jerry Rice	5	2 Oct 1950; 22 Nov 1981; 14 Oct 1990
Touchdowns, rushing	Ernie Nevers	6	28 Nov 1929
Field goals made	Jim Bakken; Rich Karlis; Chris Boniol; Billy Cundiff	7	24 Sep 1967; 5 Nov 1989 (OT); 18 Nov 1996; 15 Sep 2003 (OT)
Longest field goal	Tom Dempsey; Jason Elam	63 yd	8 Nov 1970; 25 Oct 1998
Extra points made (kicked)	Pat Harder; Bob Waterfield; Charlie Gogolak	9	17 Oct 1948; 22 Oct 1950; 27 Nov 1966
Passing yardage	Norm Van Brocklin	554	28 Sep 1951
Receiving yardage	Willie Anderson	336	11 Nov 1989
Rushing yardage	Jamal Lewis	295	14 Sep 2003
Longest run from scrimmage	Tony Dorsett	99 yd	3 Jan 1983
Interceptions (defense)	*too numerous to list*	4	
Sacks (defense)[1]	Derrick Thomas	7	11 Nov 1990
Team season records			
League championships (including Super Bowls)	Green Bay Packers	12	

American Pro Football All-Time Records (continued)

	PLAYERS/TEAMS	NUMBER	SEASON/DATE
Team season records (continued)			
Super Bowl titles	Dallas Cowboys; San Francisco 49ers	5	
Consecutive Super Bowl titles	7 teams hold record	2	
Undefeated season	Miami Dolphins;	14 wins	1972
	Chicago Bears	13 wins	1934
Total points scored	Minnesota Vikings	556	1998
Touchdowns, total	Miami Dolphins	70	1984
Touchdowns, passing	Indianapolis Colts	51	2004
Touchdowns, rushing	Green Bay Packers	36	1962
Field goals made	Arizona Cardinals	43	2005
Passing yardage	St. Louis Rams	5,492	2000
Rushing yardage	New England Patriots	3,165	1978
Game records			
Highest score, one team	Washington Redskins	72	27 Nov 1966
Highest total score	Washington Redskins versus New York Giants	113 (72–41)	27 Nov 1966
Longest game	Miami Dolphins versus Kansas City Chiefs	82:40 (two overtimes)	25 Dec 1971

[1]Since 1982; before that year sacks were not officially recorded by the NFL.

Super Bowl

NFL-AFL championship 1966–70; NFL championship from 1971–72 season.

	SEASON	WINNER	RUNNER-UP	SCORE
I	1966–67	Green Bay Packers (NFL)	Kansas City Chiefs (AFL)	35–10
II	1967–68	Green Bay Packers (NFL)	Oakland Raiders (AFL)	33–14
III	1968–69	New York Jets (AFL)	Baltimore Colts (NFL)	16–7
IV	1969–70	Kansas City Chiefs (AFL)	Minnesota Vikings (NFL)	23–7
V	1970–71	Baltimore Colts (AFC)	Dallas Cowboys (NFC)	16–13
VI	1971–72	Dallas Cowboys (NFC)	Miami Dolphins (AFC)	24–3
VII	1972–73	Miami Dolphins (AFC)	Washington Redskins (NFC)	14–7
VIII	1973–74	Miami Dolphins (AFC)	Minnesota Vikings (NFC)	24–7
IX	1974–75	Pittsburgh Steelers (AFC)	Minnesota Vikings (NFC)	16–6
X	1975–76	Pittsburgh Steelers (AFC)	Dallas Cowboys (NFC)	21–17
XI	1976–77	Oakland Raiders (AFC)	Minnesota Vikings (NFC)	32–14
XII	1977–78	Dallas Cowboys (NFC)	Denver Broncos (AFC)	27–10
XIII	1978–79	Pittsburgh Steelers (AFC)	Dallas Cowboys (NFC)	35–31
XIV	1979–80	Pittsburgh Steelers (AFC)	Los Angeles Rams (NFC)	31–19
XV	1980–81	Oakland Raiders (AFC)	Philadelphia Eagles (NFC)	27–10
XVI	1981–82	San Francisco 49ers (NFC)	Cincinnati Bengals (AFC)	26–21
XVII	1982–83	Washington Redskins (NFC)	Miami Dolphins (AFC)	27–17
XVIII	1983–84	Los Angeles Raiders (AFC)	Washington Redskins (NFC)	38–9
XIX	1984–85	San Francisco 49ers (NFC)	Miami Dolphins (AFC)	38–16
XX	1985–86	Chicago Bears (NFC)	New England Patriots (AFC)	46–10
XXI	1986–87	New York Giants (NFC)	Denver Broncos (AFC)	39–20
XXII	1987–88	Washington Redskins (NFC)	Denver Broncos (AFC)	42–10
XXIII	1988–89	San Francisco 49ers (NFC)	Cincinnati Bengals (AFC)	20–16
XXIV	1989–90	San Francisco 49ers (NFC)	Denver Broncos (AFC)	55–10
XXV	1990–91	New York Giants (NFC)	Buffalo Bills (AFC)	20–19
XXVI	1991–92	Washington Redskins (NFC)	Buffalo Bills (AFC)	37–24
XXVII	1992–93	Dallas Cowboys (NFC)	Buffalo Bills (AFC)	52–17
XXVIII	1993–94	Dallas Cowboys (NFC)	Buffalo Bills (AFC)	30–13
XXIX	1994–95	San Francisco 49ers (NFC)	San Diego Chargers (AFC)	49–26
XXX	1995–96	Dallas Cowboys (NFC)	Pittsburgh Steelers (AFC)	27–17
XXXI	1996–97	Green Bay Packers (NFC)	New England Patriots (AFC)	35–21
XXXII	1997–98	Denver Broncos (AFC)	Green Bay Packers (NFC)	31–24
XXXIII	1998–99	Denver Broncos (AFC)	Atlanta Falcons (NFC)	34–19
XXXIV	1999–2000	St. Louis Rams (NFC)	Tennessee Titans (AFC)	23–16
XXXV	2000–01	Baltimore Ravens (AFC)	New York Giants (NFC)	34–7
XXXVI	2001–02	New England Patriots (AFC)	St. Louis Rams (NFC)	20–17
XXXVII	2002–03	Tampa Bay Buccaneers (NFC)	Oakland Raiders (AFC)	48–21
XXXVIII	2003–04	New England Patriots (AFC)	Carolina Panthers (NFC)	32–29
XXXIX	2004–05	New England Patriots (AFC)	Philadelphia Eagles (NFC)	24–21
XL	2005–06	Pittsburgh Steelers (AFC)	Seattle Seahawks (NFC)	21–10
LXI	2006–07	Indianapolis Colts (AFC)	Chicago Bears (NFC)	29–17

College Football National Champions

SEASON	CHAMPION	SEASON	CHAMPION	SEASON	CHAMPION
1924	Notre Dame	1954	Ohio State (AP),	1981	Clemson
1925	Dartmouth		UCLA (UP)	1982	Penn State
1926	Stanford	1955	Oklahoma	1983	Miami (FL)
1927	Illinois	1956	Oklahoma	1984	Brigham Young
1928	USC	1957	Auburn (AP), Ohio State (UP)	1985	Oklahoma
1929	Notre Dame	1958	Louisiana State	1986	Penn State
1930	Notre Dame	1959	Syracuse	1987	Miami (FL)
1931	USC	1960	Minnesota	1988	Notre Dame
1932	Michigan	1961	Alabama	1989	Miami (FL)
1933	Michigan	1962	USC	1990	Colorado (AP),
1934	Minnesota	1963	Texas		Georgia Tech (UPI)
1935	Southern Methodist	1964	Alabama	1991	Miami (FL; AP),
1936	Minnesota	1965	Alabama (AP), Michigan		Washington (UPI)
1937	Pittsburgh		State (UPI)	1992	Alabama
1938	Texas Christian	1966	Notre Dame	1993	Florida State
1939	Texas A&M	1967	USC	1994	Nebraska
1940	Minnesota	1968	Ohio State	1995	Nebraska
1941	Minnesota	1969	Texas	1996	Florida
1942	Ohio State	1970	Nebraska (AP), Texas (UPI)	1997	Michigan (AP),
1943	Notre Dame	1971	Nebraska		Nebraska (USA
1944	Army	1972	USC		Today/ESPN)
1945	Army	1973	Notre Dame (AP), Alabama	1998	Tennessee
1946	Notre Dame		(UPI)	1999	Florida State
1947	Notre Dame	1974	Oklahoma (AP), USC (UPI)	2000	Oklahoma
1948	Michigan	1975	Oklahoma	2001	Miami (FL)
1949	Notre Dame	1976	Pittsburgh	2002	Ohio State
1950	Oklahoma	1977	Notre Dame	2003	Louisiana State
1951	Tennessee	1978	Alabama (AP), USC (UPI)		(BCS), USC (AP)
1952	Michigan State	1979	Alabama	2004	USC
1953	Maryland	1980	Georgia	2005	Texas
				2006	Florida

Rose Bowl

SEASON	WINNER	RUNNER-UP	SCORE	SEASON	WINNER	RUNNER-UP	SCORE
1901–02	Michigan	Stanford	49–0	1942–43	Georgia	UCLA	9–0
1915–16	Washington State	Brown	14–0	1943–44	USC	Washington	29–0
				1944–45	USC	Tennessee	25–0
1916–17	Oregon	Pennsylvania	14–0	1945–46	Alabama	USC	34–14
1917–18	Mare Island	Camp Lewis	19–7	1946–47	Illinois	UCLA	45–14
1918–19	Great Lakes	Mare Island	17–0	1947–48	Michigan	USC	49–0
1919–20	Harvard	Oregon	7–6	1948–49	Northwestern	California	20–14
1920–21	California	Ohio State	28–0	1949–50	Ohio State	California	17–14
1921–22	California	Washington & Jefferson	0–0	1950–51	Michigan	California	14–6
				1951–52	Illinois	Stanford	40–7
1922–23	USC	Penn State	14–3	1952–53	USC	Wisconsin	7–0
1923–24	Washington	Navy	14–14	1953–54	Michigan State	UCLA	28–20
1924–25	Notre Dame	Stanford	27–10	1954–55	Ohio State	USC	20–7
1925–26	Alabama	Washington	20–19	1955–56	Michigan State	UCLA	17–14
1926–27	Alabama	Stanford	7–7	1956–57	Iowa	Oregon State	35–19
1927–28	Stanford	Pittsburgh	7–6	1957–58	Ohio State	Oregon	10–7
1928–29	Georgia Tech	California	8–7	1958–59	Iowa	California	38–12
1929–30	USC	Pittsburgh	47–14	1959–60	Washington	Wisconsin	44–8
1930–31	Alabama	Washington State	24–0	1960–61	Washington	Minnesota	17–7
				1961–62	Minnesota	UCLA	21–3
1931–32	USC	Tulane	21–12	1962–63	USC	Wisconsin	42–37
1932–33	USC	Pittsburgh	35–0	1963–64	Illinois	Washington	17–7
1933–34	Columbia	Stanford	7–0	1964–65	Michigan	Oregon State	34–7
1934–35	Alabama	Stanford	29–13	1965–66	UCLA	Michigan State	14–12
1935–36	Stanford	Southern Methodist	7–0				
				1966–67	Purdue	USC	14–13
1936–37	Pittsburgh	Washington	21–0	1967–68	USC	Indiana	14–3
1937–38	California	Alabama	13–0	1968–69	Ohio State	USC	27–16
1938–39	USC	Duke	7–3	1969–70	USC	Michigan	10–3
1939–40	USC	Tennessee	14–0	1970–71	Stanford	Ohio State	27–17
1940–41	Stanford	Nebraska	21–13	1971–72	Stanford	Michigan	13–12
1941–42	Oregon State	Duke	20–16	1972–73	USC	Ohio State	42–17

Rose Bowl (continued)

SEASON	WINNER	RUNNER-UP	SCORE	SEASON	WINNER	RUNNER-UP	SCORE
1973–74	Ohio State	USC	42–21	1991–92	Washington	Michigan	34–14
1974–75	USC	Ohio State	18–17	1992–93	Michigan	Washington	38–31
1975–76	UCLA	Ohio State	23–10	1993–94	Wisconsin	UCLA	21–16
1976–77	USC	Michigan	14–6	1994–95	Penn State	Oregon	38–20
1977–78	Washington	Michigan	27–20	1995–96	USC	Northwestern	41–32
1978–79	USC	Michigan	17–10	1996–97	Ohio State	Arizona State	20–17
1979–80	USC	Ohio State	17–16	1997–98	Michigan	Washington State	21–16
1980–81	Michigan	Washington	23–6				
1981–82	Washington	Iowa	28–0	1998–99	Wisconsin	UCLA	38–31
1982–83	UCLA	Michigan	24–14	1999–2000	Wisconsin	Stanford	17–9
1983–84	UCLA	Illinois	45–9	2000–01	Washington	Purdue	34–24
1984–85	USC	Ohio State	20–17	2001–02	Miami (FL)	Nebraska	37–14
1985–86	UCLA	Iowa	45–28	2002–03	Oklahoma	Washington State	34–14
1986–87	Arizona State	Michigan	22–15				
1987–88	Michigan State	USC	20–17	2003–04	USC	Michigan	28–14
				2004–05	Texas	Michigan	38–37
1988–89	Michigan	USC	22–14	2005–06	Texas	USC	41–38
1989–90	USC	Michigan	17–10	2006–07	USC	Michigan	32–18
1990–91	Washington	Iowa	46–34				

Orange Bowl

SEASON	WINNER	RUNNER-UP	SCORE	SEASON	WINNER	RUNNER-UP	SCORE
1934–35	Bucknell	Miami (FL)	26–0	1970–71	Nebraska	Louisiana State	17–12
1935–36	Catholic	Mississippi	20–19	1971–72	Nebraska	Alabama	38–6
1936–37	Duquesne	Mississippi State	13–12	1972–73	Nebraska	Notre Dame	40–6
				1973–74	Penn State	Louisiana State	16–9
1937–38	Auburn	Michigan State	6–0	1974–75	Notre Dame	Alabama	13–11
1938–39	Tennessee	Oklahoma	17–0	1975–76	Oklahoma	Michigan	14–6
1939–40	Georgia Tech	Missouri	21–7	1976–77	Ohio State	Colorado	27–10
1940–41	Mississippi State	Georgetown	14–7	1977–78	Arkansas	Oklahoma	31–6
				1978–79	Oklahoma	Nebraska	31–24
1941–42	Georgia	Texas Christian	40–26	1979–80	Oklahoma	Florida State	24–7
1942–43	Alabama	Boston College	37–21	1980–81	Oklahoma	Florida State	18–17
1943–44	Louisiana State	Texas A&M	19–14	1981–82	Clemson	Nebraska	22–15
1944–45	Tulsa	Georgia Tech	26–12	1982–83	Nebraska	Louisiana State	21–20
1945–46	Miami (FL)	Holy Cross	13–6	1983–84	Miami (FL)	Nebraska	31–30
1946–47	Rice	Tennessee	8–0	1984–85	Washington	Oklahoma	28–17
1947–48	Georgia Tech	Kansas	20–14	1985–86	Oklahoma	Penn State	25–10
1948–49	Texas	Georgia	41–28	1986–87	Oklahoma	Arkansas	42–8
1949–50	Santa Clara	Kentucky	21–13	1987–88	Miami (FL)	Oklahoma	20–14
1950–51	Clemson	Miami (FL)	15–14	1988–89	Miami (FL)	Nebraska	23–3
1951–52	Georgia Tech	Baylor	17–14	1989–90	Notre Dame	Colorado	21–6
1952–53	Alabama	Syracuse	61–6	1990–91	Colorado	Notre Dame	10–9
1953–54	Oklahoma	Maryland	7–0	1991–92	Miami (FL)	Nebraska	22–0
1954–55	Duke	Nebraska	34–7	1992–93	Florida State	Nebraska	27–14
1955–56	Oklahoma	Maryland	20–6	1993–94	Florida State	Nebraska	18–16
1956–57	Colorado	Clemson	27–21	1994–95	Nebraska	Miami	24–17
1957–58	Oklahoma	Duke	48–21	1995–96	Florida State	Notre Dame	31–26
1958–59	Oklahoma	Syracuse	21–6	1996–97	Nebraska	Virginia Tech	41–21
1959–60	Georgia	Missouri	14–0	1997–98	Nebraska	Tennessee	42–17
1960–61	Missouri	Navy	21–14	1998–99	Florida	Syracuse	31–10
1961–62	Louisiana State	Colorado	25–7	1999–2000	Michigan	Alabama	35–34
1962–63	Alabama	Oklahoma	17–0	2000–01	Oklahoma	Florida State	13–2
1963–64	Nebraska	Auburn	13–7	2001–02	Florida	Maryland	56–23
1964–65	Texas	Alabama	21–17	2002–03	USC	Iowa	38–17
1965–66	Alabama	Nebraska	39–28	2003–04	Miami (FL)	Florida State	16–14
1966–67	Florida	Georgia Tech	27–12	2004–05	USC	Oklahoma	55–19
1967–68	Oklahoma	Tennessee	26–24	2005–06	Penn State	Florida State	26–23
1968–69	Penn State	Kansas	15–14	2006–07	Louisville	Wake Forest	24–13
1969–70	Penn State	Missouri	10–3				

Sugar Bowl

SEASON	WINNER	RUNNER-UP	SCORE	SEASON	WINNER	RUNNER-UP	SCORE
1934–35	Tulane	Temple	20–14	1935–36	Texas Christian	Louisiana State	3–2

Sugar Bowl (continued)

SEASON	WINNER	RUNNER-UP	SCORE
1936–37	Santa Clara	Louisiana State	21–14
1937–38	Santa Clara	Louisiana State	6–0
1938–39	Texas Christian	Carnegie Tech	15–7
1939–40	Texas A&M	Tulane	14–13
1940–41	Boston College	Tennessee	19–13
1941–42	Fordham	Missouri	2–0
1942–43	Tennessee	Tulsa	14–7
1943–44	Georgia Tech	Tulsa	20–18
1944–45	Duke	Alabama	29–26
1945–46	Oklahoma A&M	St. Mary's	33–13
1946–47	Georgia	North Carolina	20–10
1947–48	Texas	Alabama	27–7
1948–49	Oklahoma	North Carolina	14–6
1949–50	Oklahoma	Louisiana State	35–0
1950–51	Kentucky	Oklahoma	13–7
1951–52	Maryland	Tennessee	28–13
1952–53	Georgia Tech	Mississippi	24–7
1953–54	Georgia Tech	West Virginia	42–19
1954–55	Navy	Mississippi	21–0
1955–56	Georgia Tech	Pittsburgh	7–0
1956–57	Baylor	Tennessee	13–7
1957–58	Mississippi	Texas	39–7
1958–59	Louisiana State	Clemson	7–0
1959–60	Mississippi	Louisiana State	21–0
1960–61	Mississippi	Rice	14–6
1961–62	Alabama	Arkansas	10–3
1962–63	Mississippi	Arkansas	17–13
1963–64	Alabama	Mississippi	12–7
1964–65	Louisiana State	Syracuse	13–10
1965–66	Missouri	Florida	20–18
1966–67	Alabama	Nebraska	34–7
1967–68	Louisiana State	Wyoming	20–13
1968–69	Arkansas	Georgia	16–2
1969–70	Mississippi	Arkansas	27–22
1970–71	Tennessee	Air Force	34–13
1971–72	Oklahoma	Auburn	40–22
1972–73	Oklahoma	Penn State	14–0
1973–74	Notre Dame	Alabama	24–23
1974–75	Nebraska	Florida	13–10
1975–76	Alabama	Penn State	13–6
1976–77	Pittsburgh	Georgia	27–3
1977–78	Alabama	Ohio State	35–6
1978–79	Alabama	Penn State	14–7
1979–80	Alabama	Arkansas	24–9
1980–81	Georgia	Notre Dame	17–10
1981–82	Pittsburgh	Georgia	24–20
1982–83	Penn State	Georgia	27–23
1983–84	Auburn	Michigan	9–7
1984–85	Nebraska	Louisiana State	28–10
1985–86	Tennessee	Miami (FL)	35–7
1986–87	Nebraska	Louisiana State	30–15
1987–88	Auburn	Syracuse	16–16
1988–89	Florida State	Auburn	13–7
1989–90	Miami (FL)	Alabama	33–25
1990–91	Tennessee	Virginia	23–22
1991–92	Notre Dame	Florida	39–28
1992–93	Alabama	Miami (FL)	34–13
1993–94	Florida	West Virginia	41–7
1994–95	Florida State	Florida	23–17
1995–96	Virginia Tech	Texas	28–10
1996–97	Florida	Florida State	52–20
1997–98	Florida State	Ohio State	31–14
1998–99	Ohio State	Texas A&M	24–14
1999–2000	Florida State	Virginia Tech	46–29
2000–01	Miami (FL)	Florida	37–20
2001–02	Louisiana State	Illinois	47–34
2002–03	Georgia	Florida State	26–13
2003–04	Louisiana State	Oklahoma	21–14
2004–05	Auburn	Virginia Tech	16–13
2005–06	West Virginia	Georgia	38–35
2006–07	Louisiana State	Notre Dame	41–14

Fiesta Bowl

SEASON	WINNER	RUNNER-UP	SCORE
1971–72	Arizona State	Florida State	45–38
1972–73	Arizona State	Missouri	49–35
1973–74	Arizona State	Pittsburgh	28–7
1974–75	Oklahoma State	Brigham Young	16–6
1975–76	Arizona State	Nebraska	17–14
1976–77	Oklahoma	Wyoming	41–7
1977–78	Penn State	Arizona State	42–30
1978–79	Arkansas	UCLA	10–10
1979–80	Pittsburgh	Arizona	16–10
1980–81	Penn State	Ohio State	31–19
1981–82	Penn State	USC	26–10
1982–83	Arizona State	Oklahoma	32–21
1983–84	Ohio State	Pittsburgh	28–23
1984–85	UCLA	Miami (FL)	39–37
1985–86	Michigan	Nebraska	27–23
1986–87	Penn State	Miami (FL)	14–10
1987–88	Florida State	Nebraska	31–28
1988–89	Notre Dame	West Virginia	34–21
1989–90	Florida State	Nebraska	41–17
1990–91	Louisville	Alabama	34–7
1991–92	Penn State	Tennessee	42–17
1992–93	Syracuse	Colorado	26–22
1993–94	Arizona	Miami (FL)	29–0
1994–95	Colorado	Notre Dame	41–24
1995–96	Nebraska	Florida	62–24
1996–97	Penn State	Texas	38–15
1997–98	Kansas State	Syracuse	35–18
1998–99	Tennessee	Florida State	23–16
1999–2000	Nebraska	Tennessee	31–21
2000–01	Oregon State	Notre Dame	41–9
2001–02	Oregon	Colorado	38–16
2002–03	Ohio State	Miami (FL)	31–24
2003–04	Ohio State	Kansas State	35–28
2004–05	Utah	Pittsburgh	35–7
2005–06	Ohio State	Notre Dame	34–20
2006–07	Boise State	Oklahoma	43–42

Did you know? World War II depleted the ranks of many professional sports teams, thereby allowing players into the game who otherwise would not have qualified. Perhaps the two best-known examples of this were Pete Gray, a one-armed outfielder for the St. Louis Browns, and Joe Nuxhall, a 15-year-old pitcher for the Cincinnati Reds.

Heisman Trophy Winners

The Heisman Trophy is named for John Heisman, a director of the Downtown Athletic Club (DAC) in New York City who died in 1936. The trophy goes to an outstanding college football player at the end of the football season each year. A committee comprised of DAC members, members of the media, and representatives from each of the 50 states cast ballots to determine the winner. Web site: <www.heisman.com>.

YEAR	WINNER	COLLEGE	POSITION	YEAR	WINNER	COLLEGE	POSITION
1935	Jay Berwanger	University of Chicago	HB	1971	Pat Sullivan	Auburn	QB
1936	Larry Kelley	Yale	E	1972	Johnny Rodgers	Nebraska	WR
1937	Clint Frank	Yale	HB	1973	John Cappelletti	Penn State	HB
1938	Davey O'Brien	TCU	QB	1974	Archie Griffin	Ohio State	HB
1939	Nile Kinnick	Iowa	HB	1975	Archie Griffin	Ohio State	HB
1940	Tom Harmon	Michigan	HB	1976	Tony Dorsett	Pittsburgh	HB
1941	Bruce Smith	Minnesota	HB	1977	Earl Campbell	Texas	HB
1942	Frank Sinkwich	Georgia	HB	1978	Billy Sims	Oklahoma	HB
1943	Angelo Bertelli	Notre Dame	HB	1979	Charles White	USC	HB
1944	Les Horvath	Ohio State	QB	1980	George Rogers	South Carolina	HB
1945	Felix Blanchard	Army	FB	1981	Marcus Allen	USC	HB
1946	Glenn Davis	Army	HB	1982	Herschel Walker	Georgia	HB
1947	John Lujack	Notre Dame	QB	1983	Mike Rozier	Nebraska	HB
1948	Doak Walker	SMU	HB	1984	Doug Flutie	Boston College	QB
1949	Leon Hart	Notre Dame	DE	1985	Bo Jackson	Auburn	HB
1950	Vic Janowicz	Ohio State	HB	1986	Vinny Testaverde	Miami	QB
1951	Dick Kazmaier	Princeton	HB	1987	Tim Brown	Notre Dame	WR
1952	Billy Vessels	Oklahoma	HB	1988	Barry Sanders	Oklahoma State	RB
1953	John Lattner	Notre Dame	HB	1989	Andre Ware	Houston	QB
1954	Alan Ameche	Wisconsin	FB	1990	Ty Detmer	BYU	QB
1955	Howard Cassady	Ohio State	HB	1991	Desmond Howard	Michigan	WR
1956	Paul Hornung	Notre Dame	QB	1992	Gino Torretta	Miami	QB
1957	John David Crow	Texas A&M	HB	1993	Charlie Ward	Florida State	QB
1958	Pete Dawkins	Army	HB	1994	Rashaan Salaam	Colorado	TB
1959	Billy Cannon	LSU	HB	1995	Eddie George	Ohio State	RB
1960	Joe Bellino	Navy	HB	1996	Danny Wuerffel	Florida	QB
1961	Ernie Davis	Syracuse	HB	1997	Charles Woodson	Michigan	DB
1962	Terry Baker	Oregon State	QB	1998	Ricky Williams	Texas	RB
1963	Roger Staubach	Navy	QB	1999	Ron Dayne	Wisconsin	RB
1964	John Huarte	Notre Dame	QB	2000	Chris Weinke	Florida State	QB
1965	Mike Garrett	USC	HB	2001	Eric Crouch	Nebraska	QB
1966	Steve Spurrier	Florida	QB	2002	Carson Palmer	USC	QB
1967	Gary Beban	UCLA	QB	2003	Jason White	Oklahoma	QB
1968	O.J. Simpson	USC	HB	2004	Matt Leinart	USC	QB
1969	Steve Owens	Oklahoma	HB	2005	Reggie Bush	USC	RB
1970	Jim Plunkett	Stanford	QB	2006	Troy Smith	Ohio State	QB

Canadian Football League Grey Cup

Held since 1909. Table shows results for past 20 years.

YEAR	WINNER	RUNNER-UP	SCORE
1987	Edmonton Eskimos (WFC)	Toronto Argonauts (EFC)	38–36
1988	Winnipeg Blue Bombers (EFC)	British Columbia Lions (WFC)	22–21
1989	Saskatchewan Roughriders (WFC)	Hamilton Tiger-Cats (EFC)	43–40
1990	Winnipeg Blue Bombers (EFC)	Edmonton Eskimos (WFC)	50–11
1991	Toronto Argonauts (EFC)	Calgary Stampeders (WFC)	36–21
1992	Calgary Stampeders (WFC)	Winnipeg Blue Bombers (EFC)	24–10
1993	Edmonton Eskimos (WFC)	Winnipeg Blue Bombers (EFC)	33–23
1994	British Columbia Lions (WFC)	Baltimore Stallions (EFC)	26–23
1995	Baltimore Stallions (SD)	Calgary Stampeders (ND)	37–20
1996	Toronto Argonauts (ED)	Edmonton Eskimos (WD)	43–37
1997	Toronto Argonauts (ED)	Saskatchewan Roughriders (WD)	47–23
1998	Calgary Stampeders (WD)	Hamilton Tiger-Cats (ED)	26–24
1999	Hamilton Tiger-Cats (ED)	Calgary Stampeders (WD)	32–21
2000	British Columbia Lions (WD)	Montreal Alouettes (ED)	28–26
2001	Calgary Stampeders (WD)	Winnipeg Blue Bombers (EFC)	27–19
2002	Montreal Alouettes (ED)	Edmonton Eskimos (WD)	25–16
2003	Edmonton Eskimos (WD)	Montreal Alouettes (ED)	34–22
2004	Toronto Argonauts (ED)	British Columbia Lions (WD)	27–19
2005	Edmonton Eskimos (WD)	Montreal Alouettes (ED)	38–35
2006	British Columbia Lions (WD)	Montreal Alouettes (ED)	25–14

Australian Football League Final Standings, 2006

League ladder after round 22; teams that qualified for play-offs only.

TEAM	WON	LOST	TIED	POINTS	TEAM	WON	LOST	TIED	POINTS
West Coast Eagles	17	5	0	68	Collingwood Magpies	14	8	0	56
Adelaide Crows	16	6	0	64	St. Kilda Saints	14	8	0	56
Fremantle Dockers	15	7	0	60	Melbourne Demons	13	8	1	54
Sydney Swans	14	8	0	56	Western Bulldogs	13	9	0	52

Super 14 Rugby Championship

Four points are awarded for a win and two for a draw; one bonus point is given for a loss by seven points or fewer and one for a team that scores four or more tries. Final match held 19 May 2007, Durban, South Africa.

TEAMS (COUNTRY)	POINTS	W	L	D	BONUS	TEAMS (COUNTRY)	POINTS	W	L	D	BONUS
Sharks (RSA)	45	10	3	0	5	Hurricanes (NZL)	27	6	7	0	3
Bulls (RSA)	42	9	4	0	6	Highlanders (NZL)	27	5	8	0	7
Crusaders (NZL)	42	8	5	0	10	Stormers (RSA)	27	6	7	0	3
Blues (NZL)	42	9	4	0	6	Central Cheetahs (RSA)	22	4	8	1	4
Brumbies (AUS)	40	9	4	0	4	Lions (RSA)	22	5	8	0	2
Chiefs (NZL)	40	7	5	1	10	New South Wales Waratahs (AUS)	21	3	9	1	7
Western Force (AUS)	32	6	6	1	6	Queensland Reds (AUS)	11	2	11	0	3

Six Nations Championship

Five Nations until 2000. Round-robin tournament, usually ending in April.

YEAR	WINNER	YEAR	WINNER	YEAR	WINNER
1947	England, Ireland[1]	1968	France[3]	1989	France
1948	Ireland[2,3]	1969	Wales[2]	1990	Scotland[2,3]
1949	Ireland[2]	1970	France, Wales[1]	1991	England[2,3]
1950	Wales[2,3]	1971	Wales[2,3]	1992	England[2,3]
1951	France, Ireland, Wales	1972	*not completed*	1993	France
1952	Wales[2,3]	1973	*quintuple tie*	1994	Wales
1953	England	1974	Ireland	1995	England[2,3]
1954	England[2], France, Wales[1]	1975	Wales	1996	England[2]
1955	France, Wales[1]	1976	Wales[2,3]	1997	France[3,5]
1956	Wales	1977	France[3,4]	1998	France[3,5]
1957	England[2,3]	1978	Wales[2,3]	1999	Scotland
1958	England	1979	Wales[2]	2000	England
1959	France	1980	England[2,3]	2001	England
1960	England[2], France[1]	1981	France[3]	2002	France[3,5]
1961	France	1982	Ireland[2]	2003	England[2,3]
1962	France	1983	France, Ireland[1]	2004	France[3,6]
1963	England	1984	Scotland[2,3]	2005	Wales[2,3]
1964	Wales	1985	Ireland[2]	2006	France[6]
1965	France, Ireland	1986	France, Scotland[1]	2007	France[6]
1966	France	1987	France[3]		
1967	France	1988	France, Wales[1,2]		

[1]Tied.   [2]Triple Crown (all three matches, excluding France and Italy) winner.   [3]Grand Slam (all matches) winner.   [4]Triple Crown won by Wales.   [5]Triple Crown won by England.   [6]Triple Crown won by Ireland.

Rugby League World Cup

YEAR	WINNER	RUNNER-UP	SCORE	YEAR	WINNER	RUNNER-UP	SCORE
1954	Great Britain	France	16–12	1977[2]	Australia	Great Britain	13–12
1957	Australia	Great Britain	29–21	1988	Australia	New Zealand	25–12
1960	Great Britain	Australia	66–37	1992	Australia	Great Britain	10–6
1968	Australia	France	20–2	1995	Australia	England	16–8
1970	Australia	Great Britain	12–7	2000	Australia	New Zealand	40–12
1972	Great Britain	Australia	10–10[1]	2008	*scheduled to be held in Australia*		
1975[2]	Australia[3]						

[1]Great Britain won on match points.   [2]Called International Championship from 1975 to 1977.   [3]Championships played without a grand final match; England was the runner-up.

Rugby World Cup

YEAR	WINNER	RUNNER-UP	SCORE	YEAR	WINNER	RUNNER-UP	SCORE
1987	New Zealand	France	29–9	1999	Australia	France	35–12
1991	Australia	England	12–6	2003	England	Australia	20–17
1995	South Africa	New Zealand	15–12	2007	to be held 7–9 September in France		

FIFA World Cup——Men

YEAR	WINNER	RUNNER-UP	SCORE	YEAR	WINNER	RUNNER-UP	SCORE
1930	Uruguay	Argentina	4–2	1974	West Germany	The Netherlands	2–1
1934	Italy	Czechoslovakia	2–1	1978	Argentina	The Netherlands	3–1
1938	Italy	Hungary	4–2	1982	Italy	West Germany	3–1
1950	Uruguay	Brazil	2–1	1986	Argentina	West Germany	3–2
1954	West Germany	Hungary	3–2	1990	West Germany	Argentina	1–0
1958	Brazil	Sweden	5–2	1994	Brazil	Italy	0–0 (3–2[1])
1962	Brazil	Czechoslovakia	3–1	1998	France	Brazil	3–0
1966	England	West Germany	4–2	2002	Brazil	Germany	2–0
1970	Brazil	Italy	4–1	2006	Italy	France	1–1 (5–3[1])

[1]Won in a penalty kick shoot-out.

FIFA World Cup——Women

YEAR	WINNER	RUNNER-UP	SCORE	YEAR	WINNER	RUNNER-UP	SCORE
1991	United States	Norway	2–1	1999	United States	China	0–0 (5–4[1])
1995	Norway	Germany	2–0	2003	Germany	Sweden	2–1
				2007	to be held 10–30 Sep in China		

[1]Won in a penalty kick shoot-out.

UEFA Champions League

Known until 1992–93 as the European Champion Clubs' Cup; played on a knockout basis until 1992–93 and as a combination of group and knockout rounds since then.
Table shows results for the past 20 years.

SEASON	WINNING TEAM (COUNTRY)	RUNNER-UP (COUNTRY)	SCORE
1987–88	PSV Eindhoven (NED)	SL Benfica (POR)	0–0 (6–5[1])
1988–89	AC Milan (ITA)	FC Steaua Bucuresti (ROM)	4–0
1989–90	AC Milan (ITA)	SL Benfica (POR)	1–0
1990–91	FK Crvena Zvezda Beograd (YUG)	Olympique de Marseille (FRA)	0–0 (5–3[1])
1991–92	FC Barcelona (ESP)	Sampdoria UC (ITA)	1–0
1992–93	Olympique de Marseille (FRA)	AC Milan (ITA)	1–0
1993–94	AC Milan (ITA)	FC Barcelona (ESP)	4–0
1994–95	AFC Ajax (NED)	AC Milan (ITA)	1–0
1995–96	Juventus FC (ITA)	AFC Ajax (NED)	1–1 (4–2[1])
1996–97	BV Borussia Dortmund (GER)	Juventus FC (ITA)	3–1
1997–98	Real Madrid CF (ESP)	Juventus FC (ITA)	1–0
1998–99	Manchester United (ENG)	Bayern München (GER)	2–1
1999–2000	Real Madrid CF (ESP)	Valencia CF (ESP)	3–0
2000–01	Bayern München (GER)	Valencia CF (ESP)	1–1 (5–4[1])
2001–02	Real Madrid CF (ESP)	Bayer 04 Leverkusen (GER)	2–1
2002–03	AC Milan (ITA)	Juventus FC (ITA)	0–0 (3–2[1])
2003–04	FC Porto (POR)	AS Monaco (FRA)	3–0
2004–05	Liverpool FC (ENG)	AC Milan (ITA)	3–3 (3–2[1])
2005–06	FC Barcelona (ESP)	Arsenal FC (ENG)	2–1
2006–07	AC Milan (ITA)	Liverpool FC (ENG)	2–1

[1]Won in a penalty kick shoot-out.

UEFA European Championship

YEAR	WINNING TEAM	RUNNER-UP	SCORE
1960	Soviet Union	Yugoslavia	2–1
1964	Spain	Soviet Union	2–1
1968	Italy	Yugoslavia	2–0
1972	West Germany	Soviet Union	3–0

UEFA European Championship (continued)

YEAR	WINNING TEAM	RUNNER-UP	SCORE
1976	Czechoslovakia	West Germany	2–2
1980	West Germany	Belgium	2–1
1984	France	Spain	2–0
1988	Holland	Soviet Union	2–0
1992	Denmark	Germany	2–0
1996	Germany	Czech Republic	2–1
2000	France	Italy	2–1
2004	Greece	Portugal	1–0
2008	*to be hosted jointly by Austria and Switzerland*		

Did you know? Organizers claim to have held the world's largest camel race, beating the previous record holder by some 100 camels, in the summer of 2007. The race consisted of 468 camels traveling around a 4-km (2.5-mi) track in Laayoune, Western Sahara. The track was not wide enough for all of the entrants to race at one time, so several heats of 50 camels each, separated into groups by sex and age, were held over three days. A good time for camels, which can attain speeds of about 30 km (18.5 mi) per hour over short stretches, to complete a lap of the "hippocameldrome" is about 10 minutes, and the winning rider in the fastest category—female camels under five years in age—was 14-year-old Zayn Enour.

UEFA Cup

The UEFA Cup is considered Europe's second most important football competition. Established in the 1971–72 season, the Cup was restructured after the UEFA Cup Winners' Cup was abolished in 1998–99. Originally played on an entirely two-legged basis, since 1998 the competition has concluded with a single match. The Cup competition is open to top- and second-ranked teams in each country's league as well as winners of domestic cups.

SEASON	WINNING TEAM (COUNTRY)	RUNNER-UP (COUNTRY)	SCORE
1971–72	Tottenham Hotspur FC (ENG)	Wolverhampton Wanderers FC (ENG)	2–1, 1–1
1972–73	Liverpool FC (ENG)	VfL Borussia Mönchengladbach (FRG)	3–0, 0–2
1973–74	Feyenoord (NED)	Tottenham Hotspur FC (ENG)	2–2, 2–0
1974–75	VfL Borussia Mönchengladbach (FRG)	FC Twente (NED)	0–0, 5–1
1975–76	Liverpool FC (ENG)	Club Brugge KV (BEL)	3–2, 1–1
1976–77	Juventus FC (ITA)	Athletic Club Bilbao (ESP)	1–0, 1–2
1977–78	PSV Eindhoven (NED)	SC Bastia (FRA)	0–0, 3–0
1978–79	VfL Borussia Mönchengladbach (FRG)	FK Crvena Zvezda Beograd (YUG)	1–1, 1–0
1979–80	Eintracht Frankfurt (FRG)	VfL Borussia Mönchengladbach (FRG)	2–3, 1–0
1980–81	Ipswich Town FC (ENG)	AZ Alkmaar (NED)	3–0, 2–4
1981–82	IFK Göteborg (SWE)	Hamburger SV (FRG)	1–0, 3–0
1982–83	RSC Anderlecht (BEL)	SL Benfica (POR)	1–0, 1–1
1983–84	Tottenham Hotspur FC (ENG)	RSC Anderlecht (BEL)	1–1, 1–1 (4–3[1])
1984–85	Real Madrid CF (ESP)	Videoton FCF (HUN)	3–0, 0–1
1985–86	Real Madrid CF (ESP)	1. FC Köln (FRG)	5–1, 0–2
1986–87	IFK Göteborg (SWE)	Dundee United FC (SCO)	1–0, 1–1
1987–88	Bayer 04 Leverkusen (FRG)	RCD Espanyol (ESP)	0–3, 3–0 (3–2[1])
1988–89	SSC Napoli (ITA)	VfB Stuttgart (FRG)	2–1, 3–3
1989–90	Juventus FC (ITA)	AC Fiorentina (ITA)	3–1, 0–0
1990–91	Internazionale FC (ITA)	AS Roma (ITA)	2–0, 0–1
1991–92	AFC Ajax (NED)	Torino Calcio (ITA)	2–2, 0–0
1992–93	Juventus FC (ITA)	BV Borussia Dortmund (FRG)	3–1, 3–0
1993–94	Internazionale FC (ITA)	SV Austria Salzburg (AUT)	1–0, 1–0
1994–95	Parma AC (ITA)	Juventus FC (ITA)	1–0, 1–1
1995–96	FC Bayern München (GER)	FC Girondins de Bordeaux (FRA)	2–0, 3–1
1996–97	FC Schalke 04 (GER)	Internazionale FC (ITA)	1–0, 0–1 (4–1[1])
1997–98	Internazionale FC (ITA)	S.S. Lazio (ITA)	3–0
1998–99	Parma AC (ITA)	Olympique de Marseille (FRA)	3–0
1999–2000	Galatasaray SK (TUR)	Arsenal FC (ENG)	0–0(4–1[1])
2000–01	Liverpool FC (ENG)	Deportivo Alavés (ESP)	5–4
2001–02	Feyenoord (NED)	BV Borussia Dortmund (GER)	3–2

UEFA Cup (continued)

SEASON	WINNING TEAM (COUNTRY)	RUNNER-UP (COUNTRY)	SCORE
2002–03	FC Porto (POR)	Celtic FC (SCO)	3–2[2]
2003–04	Valencia CF (ESP)	Olympique de Marseille (FRA)	2–0
2004–05	CSKA Moscow (RUS)	Sporting (POR)	3–1
2005–06	Sevilla FC (ESP)	Middlesbrough FC (ENG)	4–0
2006–07	Sevilla FC (ESP)	RCD Espanyol (ESP)	2–2 (3–1[1])

[1]Won in a penalty kick shoot-out. [2]Won on "silver goal" in overtime.

Copa Libertadores de América
Contested since 1960. Table shows results for the past 20 years.

YEAR	WINNER (COUNTRY)	RUNNER-UP (COUNTRY)	SCORES
1988	Nacional (URU)	Newell's Old Boys (ARG)	0–1, 3–0
1989	Atlético Nacional (COL)	Olímpia (PAR)	0–2, 2–0 (5–4[1])
1990	Olímpia (PAR)	Barcelona (ECU)	2–0, 1–1
1991	Colo Colo (CHI)	Olímpia (PAR)	0–0, 3–0
1992	São Paulo (BRA)	Newell's Old Boys (ARG)	0–1, 1–0 (3–2[1])
1993	São Paulo (BRA)	Universidad Católica (CHI)	5–1, 0–2
1994	Vélez Sársfield (ARG)	São Paulo (BRA)	1–0, 0–1 (5–4[1])
1995	Grêmio (BRA)	Atlético Nacional (COL)	3–1, 1–1
1996	River Plate (ARG)	América de Cali (COL)	0–1, 2–0
1997	Cruzeiro (BRA)	Sporting Cristal (PER)	0–0, 1–0
1998	Vasco da Gama (BRA)	Barcelona (ECU)	2–0, 2–1
1999	Palmeiras (BRA)	Deportiva Cali (COL)	0–1, 2–1 (4–3[1])
2000	Boca Juniors (ARG)	Palmeiras (BRA)	2–2, 0–0 (4–2[1])
2001	Boca Juniors (ARG)	Cruz Azul (MEX)	1–0, 0–1 (3–1[1])
2002	Olímpia (PAR)	São Caetano (BRA)	0–1, 2–1 (4–2[1])
2003	Boca Juniors (ARG)	Santos (BRA)	2–0, 3–1
2004	Once Caldas (COL)	Boca Juniors (ARG)	0–0, 1–1 (2–0[1])
2005	São Paulo (BRA)	Atlético Paranaense (BRA)	1–1, 4–0
2006	Internacional (BRA)	São Paulo (BRA)	2–1, 2–2
2007	Boca Juniors (ARG)	Grêmio (BRA)	3–0, 2–0

[1]Penalty kick shoot-out.

Copa América

Held since 1916. Table shows results for past 20 years. The cup was contested by rounds in 1989 and 1991 (scores are shown here as winner's wins/losses/draws in final round) and by a final championship match from 1993.

YEAR	WINNER	RUNNER-UP	SCORE	YEAR	WINNER	RUNNER-UP	SCORE
1989	Brazil	Uruguay	3/0/0	1999	Brazil	Uruguay	3–0
1991	Argentina	Brazil	4/0/0	2001	Colombia	Mexico	1–0
1993	Argentina	Mexico	2–1	2003	postponed until 2004		
1995	Uruguay	Brazil	1–1 (4–2[1])	2004	Brazil	Argentina	2–2 (2–0[1])
1997	Brazil	Bolivia	3–1	2007	Brazil	Argentina	3–0

[1]Penalty kick shoot-out.

Asian Cup
Scored on a points (percentage of wins) system until 1972.

YEAR	WINNER	RUNNER-UP	SCORE	YEAR	WINNER	RUNNER-UP	SCORE
1956	South Korea	Israel	83.3	1984	Saudi Arabia	China	2–0
1960	South Korea	Israel	100	1988	Saudi Arabia	South Korea	0–0 (4–3[1])
1964	Israel	India	100	1992	Japan	Saudi Arabia	1–0
1968	Iran	Burma	100	1996	Saudi Arabia	United Arab Emirates	0–0 (4–2[1])
1972	Iran	South Korea	2–1	2000	Japan	Saudi Arabia	1–0
1976	Iran	Kuwait	1–0	2004	Japan	China	3–1
1980	Kuwait	South Korea	3–0	2007	Iraq	Saudi Arabia	1–0

[1]Penalty kick shoot-out.

African Cup of Nations

YEAR	WINNER	RUNNER-UP	SCORE	YEAR	WINNER	RUNNER-UP	SCORE
1957	Egypt	Ethiopia	4–0	1984	Cameroon	Nigeria	3–1
1959	Egypt	The Sudan	2–1	1986	Egypt	Cameroon	0–0 (5–4³)
1962	Ethiopia	Egypt	4–2	1988	Cameroon	Nigeria	1–0
1963	Ghana	The Sudan	3–0	1990	Algeria	Nigeria	1–0
1965	Ghana	Tunisia	3–2	1992	Côte d'Ivoire	Ghana	0–0 (11-10³)
1968	Congo (Kinshasa)	Ghana	1–0	1994	Nigeria	Zambia	2–1
1970	The Sudan	Ghana	1–0	1996	South Africa	Tunisia	2–0
1972	Congo (Brazzaville)	Mali	3–2	1998	Egypt	South Africa	2–0
1974	Zaire	Zambia	2–2, 2–0¹	2000	Cameroon	Nigeria	2–2 (4–3³)
1976	Morocco	Guinea	1–1²	2002	Cameroon	Senegal	0–0 (3–2³)
1978	Ghana	Uganda	2–0	2004	Tunisia	Morocco	2–1
1980	Nigeria	Algeria	3–0	2006	Egypt	Côte d'Ivoire	0–0 (4–2³)
1982	Ghana	Libya	1–1 (7–6³)	2008	to be hosted by Ghana		

¹Game replayed. ²Group format. ³Penalty kick shoot-out.

Major League Soccer Cup

YEAR	WINNER	RUNNER-UP	SCORE	YEAR	WINNER	RUNNER-UP	SCORE
1996	DC United	Los Angeles Galaxy	3–2 (OT)	2002	Los Angeles Galaxy	New England Revolution	1–0
1997	DC United	Colorado Rapids	2–1	2003	San Jose Earthquakes	Chicago Fire	4–2
1998	Chicago Fire	DC United	2–0	2004	DC United	Kansas City Wizards	3–2
1999	DC United	Los Angeles Galaxy	2–0	2005	Los Angeles Galaxy	New England Revolution	1–0 (OT)
2000	Kansas City Wizards	Chicago Fire	1–0	2006	Houston Dynamo	New England Revolution	4–3 (OT)
2001	San Jose Earthquakes	Los Angeles Galaxy	2–1 (OT)				

 **Did you know?** Frank Hayes holds the distinction of being the only deceased jockey ever to have won a horse race. Hayes suffered a heart attack and died while riding in a race at Belmont Park in 1923. Nevertheless, his horse, Sweet Kiss, who went off at 20–1 odds, was the first to cross the finish line.

Golf

In individual events, three of the four major men's golf championships, the **British and US Open tournaments** and the **Professional Golfers' Association Championship**, are played annually at a variety of golf courses in their respective countries. Each is played over 72 holes, and each is preceded by qualifying rounds. The fourth major, the invitational **Masters Tournament**, is held annually at the Augusta [GA] National Golf Course. Events for amateurs include the **US and British Amateur championships**. In 2007 the Professional Golf Association (PGA) inaugurated the **FedExCup**, a season-long competition in which players accumulate points based on their performances in various PGA events (including the major tournaments, which are weighted more heavily), participate in a four-week play-off, and determine the FedExCup champion at a final Tour Championship.

Women's golf has been around nearly as long as men's golf, but until the late 1940s, it was limited to amateurs. Thus, for women, the **British and US Amateur championships** were the major tournaments. The **US Women's Open Championship** was started in 1946, and the **Ladies Professional Golf Association** (LPGA) was formed in 1950. Since that time women's professional golf has flourished. In 1976 the **Women's British Open Championship** was added to the golf calendar.

In team events, the **Ryder Cup** was originally a biennial match between the US and Great Britain, but beginning in 1979 it was expanded into a biennial match between the United States and Europe. The **World Cup**, formerly known as the Canada Cup, is a men's tournament for two-man professional teams. Teams of British and US women golfers compete every two years for the **Curtis Cup**, which since 1964 has involved two days' play of three 18-hole foursomes and six 18-hole singles. The **Solheim Cup**, the women's professional team tournament, had been played in even-numbered years since 1990 but was moved to odd-numbered years (beginning in 2003) following the rescheduling of the Ryder Cup because of the events of 11 Sep 2001.

Related Web sites: United States Golf Association: <www.usga.org>; Professional Golf Association: <www.pgatour.com>; Ladies Professional Golf Association: <www.lpga.com>.

FedExCup

In 2007 the PGA inaugurated the FedExCup, a season-long competition in which players accumulate points based on their performances in various PGA events throughout the year. In a standard (non-major) tournament, for instance, 25,000 points are awarded, with the winner receiving 4,500 points, while a runner-up receives 2,700 points, and so on. The four major tournaments award 27,500 points, with 4,950 going to the winner. The cumulative total of points each player has received during the regular season determines that player's seed going into a four-tournament play-off at the end of the year, for which the top 144 players are eligible. The points are reset for this play-off, with the regular-season leader starting with 100,000 points, the second-place finisher receiving 99,000, and so on. A progressive cut through the first three of these play-off events determines the players who qualify for the final competition, the Tour Championship, which determines the FedExCup champion. The first play-off tournament has a field of 144, the second 120, and the third 70. The winner of each of the first three receives 9,000 points, the second-place finisher 5,400, and so on. The winner of the Tour Championship receives 10,300 points, and each position receives slightly more than corresponding finishes in the other events. The player with the most cumulative play-off points at the end of the Tour Championship becomes the FedExCup champion and is awarded $10 million, the largest single bonus payout in professional sports.

Masters Tournament

Won by an American golfer except as indicated.

YEAR	WINNER	YEAR	WINNER	YEAR	WINNER
1934	Horton Smith	1960	Arnold Palmer	1984	Ben Crenshaw
1935	Gene Sarazen	1961	Gary Player (RSA)	1985	Bernhard Langer (FRG)
1936	Horton Smith	1962	Arnold Palmer	1986	Jack Nicklaus
1937	Byron Nelson	1963	Jack Nicklaus	1987	Larry Mize
1938	Henry Picard	1964	Arnold Palmer	1988	Sandy Lyle (SCO)
1939	Ralph Guldahl	1965	Jack Nicklaus	1989	Nick Faldo (GBR)
1940	Jimmy Demaret	1966	Jack Nicklaus	1990	Nick Faldo (GBR)
1941	Craig Wood	1967	Gay Brewer	1991	Ian Woosnam (GBR)
1942	Byron Nelson	1968	Bob Goalby[1]	1992	Fred Couples
1943–45 *not held*		1969	George Archer	1993	Bernhard Langer (GER)
1946	Herman Keiser	1970	Billy Casper	1994	José María Olazábal (ESP)
1947	Jimmy Demaret	1971	Charles Coody	1995	Ben Crenshaw
1948	Claude Harmon	1972	Jack Nicklaus	1996	Nick Faldo (GBR)
1949	Sam Snead	1973	Tommy Aaron	1997	Tiger Woods
1950	Jimmy Demaret	1974	Gary Player (RSA)	1998	Mark O'Meara
1951	Ben Hogan	1975	Jack Nicklaus	1999	José María Olazábal (ESP)
1952	Sam Snead	1976	Raymond Floyd	2000	Vijay Singh (FIJ)
1953	Ben Hogan	1977	Tom Watson	2001	Tiger Woods
1954	Sam Snead	1978	Gary Player (RSA)	2002	Tiger Woods
1955	Cary Middlecoff	1979	Fuzzy Zoeller[2]	2003	Mike Weir (CAN)
1956	Jack Burke	1980	Seve Ballesteros (ESP)	2004	Phil Mickelson
1957	Doug Ford	1981	Tom Watson	2005	Tiger Woods
1958	Arnold Palmer	1982	Craig Stadler[3]	2006	Phil Mickelson
1959	Art Wall	1983	Seve Ballesteros (ESP)	2007	Zach Johnson

[1]*Play-off averted when Roberto de Vicenzo was penalized for signing an incorrect scorecard.*   [2]*Sudden-death play-off against Tom Watson and Ed Sneed.*   [3]*Won on the first hole of a play-off against Dan Pohl.*

United States Open Championship—Men

Won by an American golfer except as indicated.

YEAR	WINNER	YEAR	WINNER	YEAR	WINNER
1895	Horace Rawlins	1907	Alex Ross	1920	Edward Ray (GBR)
1896	James Foulis	1908	Fred McLeod	1921	James M. Barnes
1897	Joe Lloyd	1909	George Sargent	1922	Gene Sarazen
1898	Fred Herd	1910	Alex Smith	1923	Bobby Jones
1899	Willie Smith	1911	John J. McDermott	1924	Cyril Walker
1900	Harry Vardon (GBR)	1912	John J. McDermott	1925	Willie MacFarlane, Jr.
1901	Willie Anderson	1913	Francis Ouimet	1926	Bobby Jones
1902	Laurence Auchterlonie	1914	Walter Hagen	1927	Tommy Armour
1903	Willie Anderson	1915	Jerome D. Travers	1928	Johnny Farrell
1904	Willie Anderson	1916	Chick Evans	1929	Bobby Jones
1905	Willie Anderson	1917–18 *not held*		1930	Bobby Jones
1906	Alex Smith	1919	Walter Hagen	1931	Billy Burke

United States Open Championship—Men (continued)

YEAR	WINNER	YEAR	WINNER	YEAR	WINNER
1932	Gene Sarazen	1960	Arnold Palmer	1984	Fuzzy Zoeller
1933	John Goodman	1961	Gene Littler	1985	Andy North
1934	Olin Dutra	1962	Jack Nicklaus	1986	Raymond Floyd
1935	Sam Parks, Jr.	1963	Julius Boros	1987	Scott Simpson
1936	Tony Manero	1964	Ken Venturi	1988	Curtis Strange
1937	Ralph Guldahl	1965	Gary Player (RSA)	1989	Curtis Strange
1938	Ralph Guldahl	1966	Billy Casper	1990	Hale Irwin
1939	Byron Nelson	1967	Jack Nicklaus	1991	Payne Stewart
1940	Lawson Little	1968	Lee Trevino	1992	Tom Kite
1941	Craig Wood	1969	Orville Moody	1993	Lee Janzen
1942–45	*not held*	1970	Tony Jacklin (GBR)	1994	Ernie Els (RSA)
1946	Lloyd Mangrum	1971	Lee Trevino	1995	Corey Pavin
1947	Lew Worsham	1972	Jack Nicklaus	1996	Steve Jones
1948	Ben Hogan	1973	Johnny Miller	1997	Ernie Els (RSA)
1949	Cary Middlecoff	1974	Hale Irwin	1998	Lee Janzen
1950	Ben Hogan	1975	Lou Graham	1999	Payne Stewart
1951	Ben Hogan	1976	Jerry Pate	2000	Tiger Woods
1952	Julius Boros	1977	Hubert Green	2001	Retief Goosen (RSA)
1953	Ben Hogan	1978	Andy North	2002	Tiger Woods
1954	Ed Furgol	1979	Hale Irwin	2003	Jim Furyk
1955	Jack Fleck	1980	Jack Nicklaus	2004	Retief Goosen (RSA)
1956	Cary Middlecoff	1981	David Graham (AUS)	2005	Michael Campbell (NZL)
1957	Dick Mayer	1982	Tom Watson	2006	Geoff Ogilvy (AUS)
1958	Tommy Bolt	1983	Larry Nelson	2007	Angel Cabrera (ARG)
1959	Billy Casper				

British Open Tournament—Men

Won by a British golfer unless otherwise indicated.

YEAR	WINNER	YEAR	WINNER	YEAR	WINNER
1860	Willie Park, Sr.	1894	John H. Taylor	1932	Gene Sarazen (USA)
1861	Tom Morris, Sr.	1895	John H. Taylor	1933	Denny Shute (USA)
1862	Tom Morris, Sr.	1896	Harry Vardon	1934	Henry Cotton
1863	Willie Park, Sr.	1897	Harold Hilton	1935	Alfred Perry
1864	Tom Morris, Sr.	1898	Harry Vardon	1936	Alfred Padgham
1865	Andrew Strath	1899	Harry Vardon	1937	Henry Cotton
1866	Willie Park, Sr.	1900	John H. Taylor	1938	Reg A. Whitcombe
1867	Tom Morris, Sr.	1901	James Braid	1939	Richard Burton
1868	Tom Morris, Jr.	1902	Sandy Herd	1940–45	*not held*
1869	Tom Morris, Jr.	1903	Harry Vardon	1946	Sam Snead (USA)
1870	Tom Morris, Jr.	1904	Jack White	1947	Fred Daly (IRE)
1871	*not held*	1905	James Braid	1948	Henry Cotton
1872	Tom Morris, Jr.	1906	James Braid	1949	Bobby Locke (RSA)
1873	Tom Kidd	1907	Arnaud Massy (FRA)	1950	Bobby Locke (RSA)
1874	Mungo Park	1908	James Braid	1951	Max Faulkner
1875	Willie Park, Jr.	1909	John H. Taylor	1952	Bobby Locke (RSA)
1876	Bob Martin	1910	James Braid	1953	Ben Hogan (USA)
1877	Jamie Anderson	1911	Harry Vardon	1954	Peter Thomson (AUS)
1878	Jamie Anderson	1912	Ted Ray	1955	Peter Thomson (AUS)
1879	Jamie Anderson	1913	John H. Taylor	1956	Peter Thomson (AUS)
1880	Robert Ferguson	1914	Harry Vardon	1957	Bobby Locke (RSA)
1881	Robert Ferguson	1915–19	*not held*	1958	Peter Thomson (AUS)
1882	Robert Ferguson	1920	George Duncan	1959	Gary Player (RSA)
1883	Willie Fernie	1921	Jock Hutchison (USA)	1960	Kel Nagle (AUS)
1884	Jack Simpson	1922	Walter Hagen (USA)	1961	Arnold Palmer (USA)
1885	Bob Martin	1923	Arthur Havers	1962	Arnold Palmer (USA)
1886	David Brown	1924	Walter Hagen (USA)	1963	Bob Charles (NZL)
1887	Willie Park, Jr.	1925	James Barnes (USA)	1964	Tony Lema (USA)
1888	Jack Burns	1926	Bobby Jones (USA)	1965	Peter Thomson (AUS)
1889	Willie Park, Jr.	1927	Bobby Jones (USA)	1966	Jack Nicklaus (USA)
1890	John Ball	1928	Walter Hagen (USA)	1967	Roberto de Vicenzo (ARG)
1891	Hugh Kirkaldy	1929	Walter Hagen (USA)	1968	Gary Player (RSA)
1892	Harold Hilton	1930	Bobby Jones (USA)	1969	Tony Jacklin
1893	William Auchterlonie	1931	Tommy Armour (USA)	1970	Jack Nicklaus (USA)

British Open Tournament—Men (continued)

YEAR	WINNER	YEAR	WINNER	YEAR	WINNER
1971	Lee Trevino (USA)	1984	Seve Ballesteros (ESP)	1996	Tom Lehman (USA)
1972	Lee Trevino (USA)	1985	Sandy Lyle (SCO)	1997	Justin Leonard (USA)
1973	Tom Weiskopf (USA)	1986	Greg Norman (AUS)	1998	Mark O'Meara (USA)
1974	Gary Player (RSA)	1987	Nick Faldo	1999	Paul Lawrie (SCO)
1975	Tom Watson (USA)	1988	Seve Ballesteros (ESP)	2000	Tiger Woods (USA)
1976	Johnny Miller (USA)	1989	Mark Calcavecchia (USA)	2001	David Duval (USA)
1977	Tom Watson (USA)	1990	Nick Faldo	2002	Ernie Els (RSA)
1978	Jack Nicklaus (USA)	1991	Ian Baker-Finch (AUS)	2003	Ben Curtis (USA)
1979	Seve Ballesteros (ESP)	1992	Nick Faldo	2004	Todd Hamilton (USA)
1980	Tom Watson (USA)	1993	Greg Norman (AUS)	2005	Tiger Woods (USA)
1981	Bill Rogers (USA)	1994	Nick Price (ZIM)	2006	Tiger Woods (USA)
1982	Tom Watson (USA)	1995	John Daly (USA)	2007	Padraig Harrington (IRL)
1983	Tom Watson (USA)				

US Professional Golfers' Association (PGA) Championship

Won by an American golfer except as indicated.

YEAR	WINNER	YEAR	WINNER	YEAR	WINNER
1916	James M. Barnes	1948	Ben Hogan	1978	John Mahaffey[1]
1917–18	*not held*	1949	Sam Snead	1979	David Graham (AUS)[1]
1919	James M. Barnes	1950	Chandler Harper	1980	Jack Nicklaus
1920	Jock Hutchison	1951	Sam Snead	1981	Larry Nelson
1921	Walter Hagen	1952	Jim Turnesa	1982	Raymond Floyd
1922	Gene Sarazen	1953	Walter Burkemo	1983	Hal Sutton
1923	Gene Sarazen	1954	Chick Harbert	1984	Lee Trevino
1924	Walter Hagen	1955	Doug Ford	1985	Hubert Green
1925	Walter Hagen	1956	Jack Burke	1986	Bob Tway
1926	Walter Hagen	1957	Lionel Hebert	1987	Larry Nelson
1927	Walter Hagen	1958	Dow Finsterwald	1988	Jeff Sluman
1928	Leo Diegel	1959	Bob Rosburg	1989	Payne Stewart
1929	Leo Diegel	1960	Jay Hebert	1990	Wayne Grady (AUS)
1930	Tommy Armour	1961	Jerry Barber[1]	1991	John Daly
1931	Tom Creavy	1962	Gary Player (RSA)	1992	Nick Price (ZIM)
1932	Olin Dutra	1963	Jack Nicklaus	1993	Paul Azinger
1933	Gene Sarazen	1964	Bobby Nichols	1994	Nick Price (ZIM)
1934	Paul Runyan	1965	Dave Marr	1995	Steve Elkington (AUS)
1935	Johnny Revolta	1966	Al Geiberger	1996	Mark Brooks
1936	Denny Shute	1967	Don January[1]	1997	Davis Love III
1937	Denny Shute	1968	Julius Boros	1998	Vijay Singh (FIJ)
1938	Paul Runyan	1969	Raymond Floyd	1999	Tiger Woods
1939	Henry Picard	1970	Dave Stockton	2000	Tiger Woods
1940	Byron Nelson	1971	Jack Nicklaus	2001	David Toms
1941	Vic Ghezzi	1972	Gary Player (RSA)	2002	Rich Beems
1942	Sam Snead	1973	Jack Nicklaus	2003	Shaun Micheel
1943	*not held*	1974	Lee Trevino	2004	Vijay Singh (FIJ)
1944	Bob Hamilton	1975	Jack Nicklaus	2005	Phil Mickelson
1945	Byron Nelson	1976	Dave Stockton	2006	Tiger Woods
1946	Ben Hogan	1977	Lanny Wadkins	2007	Tiger Woods
1947	Jim Ferrier				

[1]*Winner by play-off.*

Ladies Professional Golf Association (LPGA) Championship

Won by an American golfer except as indicated.

YEAR	WINNER	YEAR	WINNER	YEAR	WINNER
1955	Beverly Hanson	1961	Mickey Wright	1967	Kathy Whitworth
1956	Marlene Hagge	1962	Judy Kimball	1968	Sandra Post
1957	Louise Suggs	1963	Mickey Wright	1969	Betsy Rawls
1958	Mickey Wright	1964	Mary Mills	1970	Shirley Englehorn
1959	Betsy Rawls	1965	Sandra Haynie	1971	Kathy Whitworth
1960	Mickey Wright	1966	Gloria Ehret	1972	Kathy Ahern

Ladies Professional Golf Association (LPGA) Championship (continued)

YEAR	WINNER	YEAR	WINNER	YEAR	WINNER
1973	Mary Mills	1985	Nancy Lopez	1997	Chris Johnson
1974	Sandra Haynie	1986	Pat Bradley	1998	Se Ri Pak (KOR)
1975	Kathy Whitworth	1987	Jane Geddes	1999	Juli Inkster
1976	Betty Burfeindt	1988	Sherri Turner	2000	Juli Inkster
1977	Chako Higuchi	1989	Nancy Lopez	2001	Karrie Webb (AUS)
1978	Nancy Lopez	1990	Beth Daniel	2002	Se Ri Pak (KOR)
1979	Donna Caponi	1991	Meg Mallon	2003	Annika Sörenstam (SWE)
1980	Sally Little	1992	Betsy King	2004	Annika Sörenstam (SWE)
1981	Donna Caponi	1993	Patty Sheehan	2005	Annika Sörenstam (SWE)
1982	Jan Stephenson (AUS)	1994	Laura Davies (GBR)	2006	Se Ri Pak (KOR)
1983	Patty Sheehan	1995	Kelly Robbins	2007	Suzann Pettersen (NOR)
1984	Patty Sheehan	1996	Laura Davies (GBR)		

United States Women's Open Championship

Won by an American golfer except as indicated.

YEAR	WINNER	YEAR	WINNER	YEAR	WINNER
1946	Patty Berg	1967	Catherine Lacoste (FRA)[1]	1988	Liselotte Neumann (SWE)
1947	Betty Jameson	1968	Susie Berning	1989	Betsy King
1948	Babe Didrikson Zaharias	1969	Donna Caponi	1990	Betsy King
1949	Louise Suggs	1970	Donna Caponi	1991	Meg Mallon
1950	Babe Didrikson Zaharias	1971	JoAnne Carner	1992	Patty Sheehan
1951	Betsy Rawls	1972	Susie Berning	1993	Lauri Merten
1952	Louise Suggs	1973	Susie Berning	1994	Patty Sheehan
1953	Betsy Rawls	1974	Sandra Haynie	1995	Annika Sörenstam (SWE)
1954	Babe Didrikson Zaharias	1975	Sandra Palmer	1996	Annika Sörenstam (SWE)
1955	Fay Crocker	1976	JoAnne Carner	1997	Alison Nicholas (GBR)
1956	Kathy Cornelius	1977	Hollis Stacy	1998	Se Ri Pak (KOR)
1957	Betsy Rawls	1978	Hollis Stacy	1999	Juli Inkster
1958	Mickey Wright	1979	Jerilyn Britz	2000	Karrie Webb (AUS)
1959	Mickey Wright	1980	Amy Alcott	2001	Karrie Webb (AUS)
1960	Betsy Rawls	1981	Pat Bradley	2002	Juli Inkster
1961	Mickey Wright	1982	Janet Anderson	2003	Hilary Lunke
1962	Murle Breer	1983	Jan Stephenson (AUS)	2004	Meg Mallon
1963	Mary Mills	1984	Hollis Stacy	2005	Birdie Kim (KOR)
1964	Mickey Wright	1985	Kathy Baker	2006	Annika Sörenstam (SWE)
1965	Carol Mann	1986	Jane Geddes	2007	Cristie Kerr
1966	Sandra Spuzich	1987	Laura Davies (GBR)		

[1]*Amateur.*

Ryder Cup

YEAR	RESULT	YEAR	RESULT
1927	United States 9½, Great Britain 2½	1971	United States 18½, Great Britain 13½
1929	Great Britain 7, United States 5	1973	United States 19, Great Britain 13
1931	United States 9, Great Britain 3	1975	United States 21, Great Britain 11
1933	Great Britain 6½, United States 5½	1977	United States 12½, Great Britain 7½
1935	United States 9, Great Britain 3	1979	United States 17, Europe 11
1937	United States 8, Great Britain 4	1981	United States 18½, Europe 9½
1939–45	*not held*	1983	United States 14½, Europe 13½
1947	United States 11, Great Britain 1	1985	Europe 16½, United States 11½
1949	United States 7, Great Britain 5	1987	Europe 15, United States 13
1951	United States 9½, Great Britain 2½	1989	Europe 14, United States 14
1953	United States 6½, Great Britain 5½	1991	United States 14½, Europe 13½
1955	United States 8, Great Britain 4	1993	United States 15, Europe 13
1957	Great Britain 7½, United States 4½	1995	Europe 14½, United States 13½
1959	United States 8½, Great Britain 3½	1997	Europe 14½, United States 13½
1961	United States 14½, Great Britain 9½	1999	United States 14½, Europe 13½
1963	United States 23, Great Britain 9	2001	*postponed until 2002*
1965	United States 19½, Great Britain 12½	2002	Europe 15½, United States 12½
1967	United States 23½, Great Britain 8½	2004	Europe 18½, United States 9½
1969	United States 16, Great Britain 16	2006	Europe 18½, United States 9½

British Amateur Championship—Men

Won by a British golfer except as indicated. Table shows results for the past 20 years.

YEAR	WINNER	YEAR	WINNER	YEAR	WINNER
1988	Christian Hardin (SWE)	1995	Gordon Sherry	2002	Alejandro Larrazábal (ESP)
1989	Stephen Dodd	1996	Warren Bledon		
1990	Rolf Muntz (NED)	1997	Craig Watson	2003	Gary Wolstenholme
1991	Gary Wolstenholme	1998	Sergio García (ESP)	2004	Stuart Wilson
1992	Stephen Dundas	1999	Graeme Storm	2005	Brian McElhinney (IRL)
1993	Ian Pyman	2000	Mikko Ilonen (FIN)	2006	Julien Guerrier (FRA)
1994	Lee James	2001	Michael Hoey (IRL)	2007	Drew Weaver (USA)

United States Amateur Championship—Men

Won by an American golfer except as indicated. Table shows results for the past 20 years.

YEAR	WINNER	YEAR	WINNER	YEAR	WINNER
1988	Eric Meeks	1995	Tiger Woods	2002	Ricky Barnes
1989	Chris Patton	1996	Tiger Woods	2003	Nick Flanagan (AUS)
1990	Phil Mickelson	1997	Matt Kuchar	2004	Ryan Moore
1991	Mitch Voges	1998	Hank Kuehne	2005	Edoardo Molinari (ITA)
1992	Justin Leonard	1999	David Gossett	2006	Richie Ramsay (SCO)
1993	John Harris	2000	Jeff Quinney	2007	Colt Knost
1994	Tiger Woods	2001	Ben Dickerson		

Women's British Open Championship

YEAR	WINNER	YEAR	WINNER	YEAR	WINNER
1976	J. Lee Smith (GBR)	1987	Alison Nicholas (GBR)	1998	Sherri Steinhauer (USA)
1977	Vivien Saunders (GBR)	1988	Corinne Dibnah (AUS)	1999	Sherri Steinhauer (USA)
1978	Janet Melville (GBR)	1989	Jane Geddes (USA)	2000	Sophie Gustafson (SWE)
1979	Alison Sheard (RSA)	1990	Helen Alfredsson (SWE)	2001	Pak Se Ri (KOR)
1980	Debbie Massey (USA)	1991	Penny Grice-Whittaker (GBR)	2002	Karrie Webb (AUS)
1981	Debbie Massey (USA)	1992	Patty Sheehan (USA)	2003	Annika Sörenstam (SWE)
1982	Marta Figueras-Dotti (SPA)	1993	Mardi Lunn (AUS)	2004	Karen Stupples (GBR)
1983	*not held*	1994	Liselotte Neumann (SWE)	2005	Jang Jeong (KOR)
1984	Okamoto Ayako (JAP)	1995	Karrie Webb (AUS)	2006	Sherri Steinhauer (USA)
1985	Betsy King (USA)	1996	Emilee Klein (USA)	2007	Lorena Ochoa (MEX)
1986	Laura Davies (GBR)	1997	Karrie Webb (AUS)		

United States Women's Amateur Championship

Won by an American golfer except as indicated. Table shows results for the past 20 years.

YEAR	WINNER	YEAR	WINNER	YEAR	WINNER
1988	Pearl Sinn	1995	Kelli Kuehne	2002	Becky Lucidi
1989	Vicki Goetze	1996	Kelli Kuehne	2003	Virada Nirapath-pongporn (THA)
1990	Pat Hurst	1997	Silvia Cavalleri (ITA)		
1991	Amy Fruhwirth	1998	Grace Park	2004	Jane Park
1992	Vicki Goetze	1999	Dorothy Delasin	2005	Morgan Pressel
1993	Jill McGill	2000	Marcy Newton	2006	Kimberly Kim
1994	Wendy Ward	2001	Meredith Duncan	2007	María José Uribe (COL)

Ladies' British Amateur Championship

Won by a British golfer except as indicated. Table shows results for the past 20 years.

YEAR	WINNER	YEAR	WINNER	YEAR	WINNER
1988	Joanne Furby	1995	Julie Wade Hall	2002	Rebecca Hudson
1989	Helen Dobson	1996	Kelli Kuehne (USA)	2003	Elisa Serramia (ESP)
1990	Julie Wade Hall	1997	Alison Rose	2004	Louise Stahle (SWE)
1991	Valerie Michaud	1998	Kim Rostron	2005	Louise Stahle (SWE)
1992	Bernille Pedersen (DEN)	1999	Marine Monnet (FRA)	2006	Belén Mozo (ESP)
1993	Catriona Lambert	2000	Rebecca Hudson	2007	Carlota Ciganda (ESP)
1994	Emma Duggleby	2001	Marta Prieto (ESP)		

World Cup

YEAR	WINNER
1953	Argentina (Antonio Cerda and Roberto de Vicenzo)
1954	Australia (Peter Thomson and Kel Nagle)
1955	United States (Chick Harbert and Ed Furgol)
1956	United States (Ben Hogan and Sam Snead)
1957	Japan (Torakichi Nakamura and Koichi Ono)
1958	Ireland (Harry Bradshaw and Christy O'Connor)
1959	Australia (Peter Thomson and Kel Nagle)
1960	United States (Sam Snead and Arnold Palmer)
1961	United States (Sam Snead and Jimmy Demaret)
1962	United States (Sam Snead and Arnold Palmer)
1963	United States (Arnold Palmer and Jack Nicklaus)
1964	United States (Arnold Palmer and Jack Nicklaus)
1965	South Africa (Gary Player and Harold Henning)
1966	United States (Arnold Palmer and Jack Nicklaus)
1967	United States (Arnold Palmer and Jack Nicklaus)
1968	Canada (Al Balding and George Knudson)
1969	United States (Orville Moody and Lee Trevino)
1970	Australia (David Graham and Bruce Devlin)
1971	United States (Jack Nicklaus and Lee Trevino)
1972	Taiwan (Hsieh Min-nan and Lu Liang-huan)
1973	United States (Johnny Miller and Jack Nicklaus)
1974	South Africa (Bobby Cole and Dale Hayes)
1975	United States (Johnny Miller and Lou Graham)

YEAR	WINNER
1976	Spain (Seve Ballesteros and Manuel Piñero)
1977	Spain (Seve Ballesteros and Antonio Garrido)
1978	United States (John Mahaffey and Andy North)
1979	United States (Hale Irwin and John Mahaffey)
1980	Canada (Dan Halldorson and Jim Nelford)
1981	*not held*
1982	Spain (Manuel Piñero and Jose-Maria Cañizares)
1983	United States (Rex Caldwell and John Cook)
1984	Spain (Jose-Maria Cañizares and Jose Rivero)
1985	Canada (Dan Halldorson and Dave Barr)
1986	*not held*
1987	Wales (Ian Woosnam and David Llewellyn)
1988	United States (Ben Crenshaw and Mark McCumber)
1989	Australia (Peter Fowler and Wayne Grady)
1990	Germany (Bernhard Langer and Torsten Giedeon)
1991	Sweden (Anders Forsbrand and Per-Ulrik Johansson)
1992	United States (Fred Couples and Davis Love III)
1993	United States (Fred Couples and Davis Love III)
1994	United States (Fred Couples and Davis Love III)
1995	United States (Fred Couples and Davis Love III)
1996	South Africa (Ernie Els and Wayne Westner)
1997	Ireland (Padraig Harrington and Paul McGinley)
1998	England (Nick Faldo and David Carter)
1999	United States (Tiger Woods and Mark O'Meara)
2000	United States (Tiger Woods and David Duval)
2001	South Africa (Ernie Els and Retief Goosen)
2002	Japan (Shigeki Maruyama and Toshi Izawa)
2003	South Africa (Trevor Immelman and Rory Sabbatini)
2004	England (Paul Casey and Luke Donald)
2005	Wales (Bradley Dredge and Stephen Dodd)
2006	Germany (Marcel Siem and Bernhard Langer)

Curtis Cup

YEAR	RESULT
1932	United States 5½, Britain 3½
1934	United States 6½, Britain and Ireland 2½
1936	United States[1] 4½, Britain and Ireland 4½
1938	United States 5½, Britain and Ireland 3½
1940–46	*not held*
1948	United States 6½, Britain and Ireland 2½
1950	United States 7½, Britain and Ireland 2½
1952	Britain and Ireland 5, United States 4
1954	United States 6, Britain and Ireland 3
1956	Britain and Ireland 5, United States 4
1958	Britain and Ireland[1] 4½, United States 4½
1960	United States 6½, Britain and Ireland 2½
1962	United States 8, Britain and Ireland 1
1964	United States 10½, Britain and Ireland 7½
1966	United States 13, Britain and Ireland 5
1968	United States 10½, Britain and Ireland 7½
1970	United States 11½, Britain and Ireland 6½
1972	United States 10, Britain and Ireland 8

YEAR	RESULT
1974	United States 13, Britain and Ireland 5
1976	United States 11½, Britain and Ireland 6½
1978	United States 12, Britain and Ireland 6
1980	United States 13, Britain and Ireland 5
1982	United States 14½, Britain and Ireland 3½
1984	United States 9½, Britain and Ireland 8½
1986	Britain and Ireland 13, United States 5
1988	Britain and Ireland 11, United States 7
1990	United States 14, Britain and Ireland 4
1992	Britain and Ireland 10, United States 8
1994	Britain and Ireland[1] 9, United States 9
1996	Britain and Ireland 11½, United States 6½
1998	United States 10, Britain and Ireland 8
2000	United States 10, Britain and Ireland 8
2002	United States 11, Britain and Ireland 7
2004	United States 10, Britain and Ireland 8
2006	United States 11½, Britain and Ireland 6½
2008	*to be held 31 May–1 Jun in Scotland*

[1]*In case of a tie the defenders retain the cup.*

Horse Racing

In the **oldest type** of horse racing, the rider sits astride the horse; in the other type of race, best known as **harness racing**, the driver sits in a sulky—a two-wheeled vehicle attached by shafts and traces to the horse. In the former type, a **Thoroughbred** horse is raced over either a track or a course of jumps and turns (**steeplechase**). Harness horses can be trotters or pacers and are Standardbred horses raced on a track.

The English Thoroughbred classics. The races are run by 3-year-old colts and fillies. **The Derby**, first run in 1780, is run at Epsom Downs, Surrey, over 1½ miles. **The Oaks** (for fillies only), also run at Epsom Downs, was first run in 1779; the oldest of the English races, however, is the **St. Leger** (1776). It is run over 1 mile 6½ furlongs at Doncaster, South Yorkshire. The **2,000 Guineas** (1809) is run over 1 mile at Newmarket, Suffolk. A horse that wins the Derby, the St. Leger, and the 2,000 Guineas all in one year is said to have won the **British Triple Crown.**

The American Thoroughbred classics. The **Kentucky Derby**, a **Triple Crown** event first run in 1875 and perhaps the best known of American horse races, is raced at Churchill Downs in Louisville KY, over a 10-furlong (1¼-mile) track. Another of the Triple Crown classics, the **Preakness Stakes**, was instituted in 1873; it is run over 9½ furlongs (1³⁄₁₆ miles) at Pimlico Race Track in Baltimore MD. The third Triple Crown event is the 12-furlong (1½-mile)

Belmont Stakes, established in 1867. It is run at Belmont Park Race Track, Long Island NY. All three events are for 3-year-old horses.

Australian Thoroughbred racing. The Victoria Racing Club's **Melbourne Cup**, first run in 1861, is one of the world's great handicap races. The day on which it is held (the first Tuesday in November) is a public holiday in Melbourne, VIC.

Dubai World Cup, first run in 1996, is the world's richest horse race ($6 million in 2007). The 2,000-m (about 1¼-mi) race is held on the dirt track at the Nad Al Sheba Racecourse in Dubai, United Arab Emirates, and is open to four-year-old and older Thoroughbred horses.

The **Grand National,** the world's most significant and widely followed **steeplechase** race, has been run annually at Aintree Racecourse near Liverpool, England, since 1839. The race, which includes 30 jumps, is run over a traditional distance of 4 miles 4 furlongs.

Harness racing. In the United States, the **Hambletonian Trot** is probably the most prestigious of harness races. It was established in 1926, was raced in New York, Kentucky, and Illinois, and is now run at the Meadowlands in New Jersey.

Related Web sites: US National Thoroughbred Racing Association: <www.ntra.com>; Fédération Equestre Internationale: <www.horsesport.org>; *Thoroughbred Times:* <www.thoroughbredtimes.com>; and *Racing Post:* <www.racingpost.co.uk>.

The oldest stadium in continuous use in professional football is Soldier Field in Chicago. It officially opened in 1924 as Municipal Grant Park Stadium. It was renamed Soldier Field the next year, though construction was not completed until 1928. A section that enclosed the north end of the stadium was completed in 1939, and a controversial upgrade, which added a futuristic shell compared by some to a flying saucer, was added in 2002.

Major Thoroughbred Race Winners 2006—07

United States

DATE	RACE	WINNER	JOCKEY
5 Aug 2006	Test Stakes	Swap Fliparoo	Eibar Coa
6 Aug 2006	Haskell Invitational Handicap	Bluegrass Cat	John Velazquez
12 Aug 2006	Arlington Million Stakes	The Tin Man	Victor Espinoza
12 Aug 2006	Beverly D. Stakes	Gorella	Julien Leparoux
12 Aug 2006	Secretariat Stakes	Showing Up	Cornelio Velasquez
12 Aug 2006	Sword Dancer Invitational Handicap	Go Deputy	Eibar Coa
19 Aug 2006	Alabama Stakes	Pine Island	Javier Castellano
20 Aug 2006	Pacific Classic Stakes	Lava Man	Corey Nakatani
25 Aug 2006	Personal Ensign Handicap	Fleet Indian	José Santos
26 Aug 2006	King's Bishop Stakes	Henny Hughes	John Velazquez
26 Aug 2006	Travers Stakes	Bernardini	Javier Castellano
27 Aug 2006	Ballerina Breeders' Cup Stakes	Dubai Escapade	Edgar Prado
2 Sep 2006	Forego Stakes	Pomeroy	John Velazquez
2 Sep 2006	Woodward Stakes	Premium Tap	Kent Desormeaux
3 Sep 2006	Spinaway Stakes	Appealing Zophie	Shaun Bridgmohan
4 Sep 2006	Del Mar Debutante Stakes	Point Ashley	Victor Espinoza
4 Sep 2006	Hopeful Stakes	Circular Quay	John Velazquez
9 Sep 2006	Gazelle Stakes	Pine Island	Javier Castellano
9 Sep 2006	Man o' War Stakes	Cacique	Edgar Prado
10 Sep 2006	Ruffian Handicap	Pool Land	John Velazquez
23 Sep 2006	Futurity Stakes	King of the Roxy	John Velazquez

Major Thoroughbred Race Winners 2006–07 (continued)

United States (continued)

DATE	RACE	WINNER	JOCKEY
23 Sep 2006	Matron Stakes	Meadow Breeze	Kent Desormeaux
23 Sep 2006	Super Derby XXVII	Strong Contender	Robby Albarado
30 Sep 2006	Clement L. Hirsch Memorial Turf Championship Stakes	The Tin Man	Victor Espinoza
30 Sep 2006	Kentucky Cup Classic Stakes	Ball Four	Willie Martinez
30 Sep 2006	Oak Leaf Stakes	Cash Included	Corey Nakatani
30 Sep 2006	Yellow Ribbon Stakes	Wait a While	Garrett Gomez
7 Oct 2006	Ancient Title Breeders' Cup Handicap	Bordonaro	Patrick Valenzuela
7 Oct 2006	Beldame Stakes	Fleet Indian	José Santos
7 Oct 2006	Flower Bowl Invitational Stakes	Honey Ryder	John Velazquez
7 Oct 2006	Jockey Club Gold Cup Stakes	Bernardini	Javier Castellano
7 Oct 2006	Turf Classic Invitational Stakes	English Channel	John Velazquez
7 Oct 2006	Vosburgh Stakes	Henny Hughes	John Velazquez
8 Oct 2006	Spinster Stakes	Asi Siempre	Julien Leparoux
14 Oct 2006	Champagne Stakes	Scat Daddy	John Velazquez
14 Oct 2006	Frizette Stakes	Sutra	Michael Luzzi
14 Oct 2006	Queen Elizabeth II Challenge Cup Stakes	Vacare	Carlos Marquez, Jr.
4 Nov 2006	Breeders' Cup Classic	Invasor	Fernando Jara
4 Nov 2006	Breeders' Cup Distaff	Round Pond	Edgar Prado
4 Nov 2006	Breeders' Cup Filly and Mare Turf	Ouija Board	Frankie Dettori
4 Nov 2006	Breeders' Cup Juvenile	Street Sense	Calvin Borel
4 Nov 2006	Breeders' Cup Juvenile Fillies	Dreaming of Anna	Rene Douglas
4 Nov 2006	Breeders' Cup Mile	Miesque's Approval	Eddie Castro
4 Nov 2006	Breeders' Cup Sprint	Thor's Echo	Corey Nakatani
4 Nov 2006	Breeders' Cup Turf	Red Rocks	Frankie Dettori
25 Nov 2006	Cigar Mile Handicap	Discreet Cat	Garrett Gomez
25 Nov 2006	Frank J. De Francis Memorial Dash Stakes	Thor's Echo	Corey Nakatani
26 Nov 2006	Hollywood Derby	Showing Up	Cornelio Velasquez
26 Nov 2006	Matriarch Stakes	Price Tag	Edgar Prado
9 Dec 2006	Hollywood Turf Cup Stakes	Boboman	Garrett Gomez
16 Dec 2006	Hollywood Futurity	Stormello	Kent Desormeaux
3 Feb 2007	Donn Handicap	Invasor	Fernando Jara
3 Feb 2007	Strub Stakes	Arson Squad	Garrett Gomez
3 Mar 2007	Fountain of Youth Stakes	Scat Daddy	John Velazquez
3 Mar 2007	Gulfstream Park Handicap	Corinthian	Javier Castellano
3 Mar 2007	Santa Anita Handicap	Lava Man	Corey Nakatani
10 Mar 2007	Louisiana Derby	Circular Quay	John Velazquez
11 Mar 2007	Santa Anita Oaks	Rags to Riches	Garrett Gomez
24 Mar 2007	Lane's End Stakes	Hard Spun	Mario Pino
31 Mar 2007	Florida Derby	Scat Daddy	Edgar Prado
7 Apr 2007	Apple Blossom Handicap	Ermine	Eddie Castro
7 Apr 2007	Ashland Stakes	Christmas Kid	Rene Douglas
7 Apr 2007	Illinois Derby	Cowtown Cat	Fernando Jara
7 Apr 2007	Oaklawn Handicap	Lawyer Ron	Edgar Prado
7 Apr 2007	Santa Anita Derby	Tiago	Mike E. Smith
7 Apr 2007	Wood Memorial Stakes	Nobiz Like Shobiz	Cornelio Velasquez
14 Apr 2007	Arkansas Derby	Curlin	Robby Albarado
14 Apr 2007	Blue Grass Stakes	Dominican	Rafael Bejarano
22 Apr 2007	San Juan Capistrano Invitational Handicap	On the Acorn	Victor Espinoza
4 May 2007	Kentucky Oaks	Rags to Riches	Garrett Gomez
5 May 2007	Kentucky Derby[1]	Street Sense	Calvin Borel
19 May 2007	Preakness Stakes[1]	Curlin	Robby Albarado
28 May 2007	Gamely Breeders' Cup Stakes	Citronnade	David Romero Flores
28 May 2007	Metropolitan Handicap	Corinthian	Kent Desormeaux
28 May 2007	Shoemaker Breeders' Cup Mile Stakes	The Tin Man	Victor Espinosa
2 Jun 2007	Californian Stakes	Buzzards Bay	Jose Valdivia, Jr.
9 Jun 2007	Acorn Stakes	Cotton Blossom	John Velazquez
9 Jun 2007	Belmont Stakes[1]	Rags to Riches	John Velazquez
9 Jun 2007	Charles Whittingham Memorial Handicap	After Market	Alex Solis
30 Jun 2007	Hollywood Gold Cup Stakes	Lava Man	Corey Nakatani
30 Jun 2007	Mother Goose Stakes	Octave	John Velazquez
30 Jun 2007	Suburban Handicap	Political Force	Cornelio Velasquez
7 Jul 2007	United Nations Stakes	English Channel	John Velazquez
21 Jul 2007	Coaching Club American Oaks	Octave	John Velazquez
22 Jul 2007	Eddie Read Handicap	After Market	Alex Solis
28 Jul 2007	Diana Stakes	My Typhoon	Eddie Castro
29 Jul 2007	Jim Dandy Stakes	Street Sense	Calvin Borel

Major Thoroughbred Race Winners 2006–07 (continued)

Canada

DATE	RACE	WINNER	JOCKEY
6 Aug 2006	Breeders' Stakes[2]	Royal Challenger	Patrick Husbands
17 Sep 2006	Woodbine Mile Stakes	Becrux	Patrick Valenzuela
30 Sep 2006	Mazarine Breeders' Cup Stakes	Coy Coyote	Corey Fraser
22 Oct 2006	Canadian International Stakes	Collier Hill	Dean McKeown
24 Jun 2007	Queen's Plate Stakes[2]	Mike Fox	Emma-Jayne Wilson
15 Jul 2007	Prince of Wales Stakes[2]	Alezzandro	Todd Kabel

England

22 Aug 2006	Juddmonte International Stakes	Notnowcato	Ryan Moore
24 Aug 2006	Nunthorpe Stakes	Reverence	Kevin Darley
9 Sep 2006	St. Leger Stakes[3]	Sixties Icon	Frankie Dettori
23 Sep 2006	Queen Elizabeth II Stakes	George Washington	Mick Kinane
5 May 2007	2,000 Guineas[3]	Cockney Rebel	Olivier Peslier
6 May 2007	1,000 Guineas	Finsceal Beo	Kevin Manning
2 Jun 2007	The Derby[3]	Authorized	Frankie Dettori
22 Jun 2007	Ascot Gold Cup	Yeats	Mick Kinane
7 Jul 2007	Coral-Eclipse Stakes	Notnowcato	Ryan Moore
28 Jul 2007	King George VI and Queen Elizabeth Stakes	Dylan Thomas	Johnny Murtagh
1 Aug 2007	Sussex Stakes	Ramonti	Frankie Dettori

Ireland

9 Sep 2006	Irish Champion Stakes	Dylan Thomas	Kieren Fallon
16 Sep 2006	Irish St. Leger	Kastoria	Mick Kinane
26 May 2007	Irish 2,000 Guineas	Cockney Rebel	Olivier Peslier
27 May 2007	Irish 1,000 Guineas	Finsceal Beo	Kevin Manning
1 Jul 2007	Irish Derby	Soldier of Fortune	Seamus Heffernan
15 Jul 2007	Irish Oaks	Peeping Fawn	Johnny Murtagh

France

13 Aug 2006	Prix du Haras de Fresnay-le-Buffard	Librettist	Frankie Dettori
10 Sep 2006	Prix Niel	Rail Link	Christophe Soumillon
1 Oct 2006	Prix de l'Arc de Triomphe	Rail Link	Stéphane Pasquier
1 Oct 2006	Grand Critérium	Holy Roman Emperor	Kieren Fallon
22 Oct 2006	Prix Royal-Oak	Montare	Olivier Peslier
29 Apr 2007	Prix Ganay	Dylan Thomas	Christophe Soumillon
13 May 2007	Poule d'Essai des Poulains	Astronomer Royal	Colm O'Donoghue
13 May 2007	Poule d'Essai des Pouliches	Darjina	Christophe Soumillon
3 Jun 2007	Prix du Jockey Club	Lawman	Frankie Dettori
10 Jun 2007	Prix de Diane	West Wind	Frankie Dettori
24 Jun 2007	Grand Prix de Saint-Cloud	Mountain High	Kieren Fallon
14 Jul 2007	Grand Prix de Paris	Zambezi Sun	Stéphane Pasquier

Germany

3 Sep 2006	Grosser Preis von Baden	Prince Fiori	Filip Minarik
24 Sep 2006	Preis von Europa	Youmzain	Kieren Fallon
1 Jul 2007	Deutsches Derby	Adlerflug	Frederik Johansson

Italy

15 Oct 2006	Gran Premio del Jockey Club	Laverock	David Bonilla
20 May 2007	Derby Italiano	Awelmarduk	Endo Botti

Australia

21 Oct 2006	Caulfield Cup	Tawqeet	Dwayne Dunn
28 Oct 2006	Cox Plate	Fields of Omagh	Craig Williams
7 Nov 2006	Melbourne Cup	Delta Blues	Yasunari Iwata

United Arab Emirates

31 Mar 2007	Dubai Duty Free	Admire Moon	Yutaka Take
31 Mar 2007	Dubai Golden Shaheen	Kelly's Landing	Frankie Dettori
31 Mar 2007	Dubai Sheema Classic	Vengeance of Rain	Anthony Delpech
31 Mar 2007	Dubai World Cup	Invasor	Fernando Jara
31 Mar 2007	Godolphin Mile	Spring at Last	Garrett Gomez
31 Mar 2007	UAE Derby	Asiatic Boy	Weichong Marwing

Major Thoroughbred Race Winners 2006–07 (continued)

Japan

DATE	RACE	WINNER	JOCKEY
26 Nov 2006	Japan Cup	Deep Impact	Yutaka Take

Hong Kong

10 Dec 2006	Hong Kong Cup	Pride	Christophe Lemaire
4 Mar 2007	Hong Kong Gold Cup	Vengeance of Rain	Anthony Delpech
29 Apr 2007	Queen Elizabeth II Cup	Viva Pataca	Mick Kinane

Singapore

20 May 2007	International Cup	Shadow Gate	Katsuharu Tanaka

[1]American Triple Crown race. [2]Canadian Triple Crown race. [3]British Triple Crown race.

Triple Crown Champions—United States

YEAR	HORSE	YEAR	HORSE	YEAR	HORSE	YEAR	HORSE
1919	Sir Barton	1937	War Admiral	1946	Assault	1977	Seattle Slew
1930	Gallant Fox	1941	Whirlaway	1948	Citation	1978	Affirmed
1935	Omaha	1943	Count Fleet	1973	Secretariat		

The Kentucky Derby

YEAR	HORSE	JOCKEY	YEAR	HORSE	JOCKEY
1875	Aristides	Oliver Lewis	1917	Omar Khayyam	Charles Borel
1876	Vagrant	Bobby Swim	1918	Exterminator	William Knapp
1877	Baden-Baden	William Walker	1919	Sir Barton	John Loftus
1878	Day Star	Jimmy Carter	1920	Paul Jones	Ted Rice
1879	Lord Murphy	Charlie Shauer	1921	Behave Yourself	Charles Thompson
1880	Fonso	George Garret Lewis	1922	Morvich	Albert Johnson
1881	Hindoo	James McLaughlin	1923	Zev	Earl Sande
1882	Apollo	Babe Hurd	1924	Black Gold	John D. Mooney
1883	Leonatus	William Donohue	1925	Flying Ebony	Earl Sande
1884	Buchanan	Isaac Murphy	1926	Bubbling Over	Albert Johnson
1885	Joe Cotton	Erskine Henderson	1927	Whiskery	Linus McAtee
1886	Ben Ali	Paul Duffy	1928	Reigh Count	Charles Lang
1887	Montrose	Isaac Lewis	1929	Clyde Van Dusen	Linus McAtee
1888	Macbeth II	George Covington	1930	Gallant Fox	Earl Sande
1889	Spokane	Thomas Kiley	1931	Twenty Grand	Charles Kurtsinger
1890	Riley	Isaac Murphy	1932	Burgoo King	Eugene James
1891	Kingman	Isaac Murphy	1933	Brokers Tip	Don Meade
1892	Azra	Alonzo Clayton	1934	Cavalcade	Mack Garner
1893	Lookout	Eddie Kunze	1935	Omaha	William Saunders
1894	Chant	Frank Goodale	1936	Bold Venture	Ira Hanford
1895	Halma	James Perkins	1937	War Admiral	Charles Kurtsinger
1896	Ben Brush	Willie Simms	1938	Lawrin	Eddie Arcaro
1897	Typhoon II	Fred Garner	1939	Johnstown	James Stout
1898	Plaudit	Willie Simms	1940	Gallahadion	Carroll Bierman
1899	Manuel	Fred Taral	1941	Whirlaway	Eddie Arcaro
1900	Lieut. Gibson	Jimmy Boland	1942	Shut Out	Wayne D. Wright
1901	His Eminence	James Winkfield	1943	Count Fleet	John Longden
1902	Alan-a-Dale	James Winkfield	1944	Pensive	Conn McCreary
1903	Judge Himes	Harold Booker	1945	Hoop Jr.	Eddie Arcaro
1904	Elwood	Frank Prior	1946	Assault	Warren Mehrtens
1905	Agile	Jack Martin	1947	Jet Pilot	Eric Guerin
1906	Sir Huon	Roscoe Troxler	1948	Citation	Eddie Arcaro
1907	Pink Star	Andy Minder	1949	Ponder	Steve Brooks
1908	Stone Street	Arthur Pickens	1950	Middleground	William Boland
1909	Wintergreen	Vincent Powers	1951	Count Turf	Conn McCreary
1910	Donau	Fred Herbert	1952	Hill Gail	Eddie Arcaro
1911	Meridian	George Archibald	1953	Dark Star	Henry Moreno
1912	Worth	Carroll Hugh Shilling	1954	Determine	Raymond York
1913	Donerail	Roscoe Goose	1955	Swaps	William Shoemaker
1914	Old Rosebud	John McCabe	1956	Needles	David Erb
1915	Regret	Joe Notter	1957	Iron Liege	William Hartack
1916	George Smith	John Loftus	1958	Tim Tam	Ismael Valenzuela

The Kentucky Derby (continued)

YEAR	HORSE	JOCKEY	YEAR	HORSE	JOCKEY
1959	Tomy Lee	William Shoemaker	1984	Swale	Laffit Pincay, Jr.
1960	Venetian Way	William Hartack	1985	Spend a Buck	Angel Cordero, Jr.
1961	Carry Back	John Sellers	1986	Ferdinand	William Shoemaker
1962	Decidedly	William Hartack	1987	Alysheba	Chris McCarron
1963	Chateaugay	Braulio Baeza	1988	Winning Colors	Gary Stevens
1964	Northern Dancer	William Hartack	1989	Sunday Silence	Patrick Valenzuela
1965	Lucky Debonair	William Shoemaker	1990	Unbridled	Craig Perret
1966	Kauai King	Don Brumfield	1991	Strike the Gold	Chris Antley
1967	Proud Clarion	Robert Ussery	1992	Lil E. Tee	Pat Day
1968	Forward Pass	Ismael Valenzuela	1993	Sea Hero	Jerry Bailey
1969	Majestic Prince	William Hartack	1994	Go for Gin	Chris McCarron
1970	Dust Commander	Mike Manganello	1995	Thunder Gulch	Gary Stevens
1971	Canonero II	Gustavo Avila	1996	Grindstone	Jerry Bailey
1972	Riva Ridge	Ron Turcotte	1997	Silver Charm	Gary Stevens
1973	Secretariat[1]	Ron Turcotte	1998	Real Quiet	Kent Desormeaux
1974	Cannonade	Angel Cordero, Jr.	1999	Charismatic	Chris Antley
1975	Foolish Pleasure	Jacinto Vasquez	2000	Fusaichi Pegasus	Kent Desormeaux
1976	Bold Forbes	Angel Cordero, Jr.	2001	Monarchos	Jorge Chávez
1977	Seattle Slew	Jean Cruguet	2002	War Emblem	Victor Espinoza
1978	Affirmed	Steve Cauthen	2003	Funny Cide	José Santos
1979	Spectacular Bid	Ronnie Franklin	2004	Smarty Jones	Stewart Elliott
1980	Genuine Risk	Jacinto Vasquez	2005	Giacomo	Mike Smith
1981	Pleasant Colony	Jorge Velasquez	2006	Barbaro	Edgar Prado
1982	Gato del Sol	Eddie Delahoussaye	2007	Street Sense	Calvin Borel
1983	Sunny's Halo	Eddie Delahoussaye			

[1]Fastest time—1 min 59²/₅ sec.

The Preakness Stakes

YEAR	HORSE	JOCKEY	YEAR	HORSE	JOCKEY
1873	Survivor	George Barbee	1911	Watervale	Eddie Dugan
1874	Culpepper	William Donohue	1912	Colonel Holloway	Clarence Turner
1875	Tom Ochiltree	Lloyd Hughes	1913	Buskin	James Butwell
1876	Shirley	George Barbee	1914	Holiday	Andy Schuttinger
1877	Cloverbrook	Cyrus Holloway	1915	Rhine Maiden	Douglas Hoffman
1878	Duke of Magenta	Cyrus Holloway	1916	Damrosch	Linus McAtee
1879	Harold	Lloyd Hughes	1917	Kalitan	Everett Haynes
1880	Grenada	Lloyd Hughes	1918[2]	War Cloud	John Loftus
1881	Saunterer	T. Costello		Jack Hare, Jr.	Charles Peak
1882	Vanguard	T. Costello	1919	Sir Barton	John Loftus
1883	Jacobus	George Barbee	1920	Man o' War	Clarence Kummer
1884	Knight of Ellerslie	S. Fisher	1921	Broomspun	Frank Coltiletti
1885	Tecumseh	James McLaughlin	1922	Pillory	Louis Morris
1886	The Bard	S. Fisher	1923	Vigil	Benny Marinelli
1887	Dunboyne	William Donohue	1924	Nellie Morse	John Merimee
1888	Refund	Fred Littlefield	1925	Coventry	Clarence Kummer
1889	Buddhist	George Anderson	1926	Display	John Maiben
1890	Montague	W. Martin	1927	Bostonian	Alf J. "Whitey" Abel
1894[1]	Assignee	Fred Taral	1928	Victorian	Raymond Workman
1895	Belmar	Fred Taral	1929	Dr. Freeland	Louis Schaefer
1896	Margrave	Henry Griffin	1930	Gallant Fox	Earl Sande
1897	Paul Kauvar	T. Thorpe	1931	Mate	George Ellis
1898	Sly Fox	Willie Simms	1932	Burgoo King	Eugene James
1899	Half Time	R. Clawson	1933	Head Play	Charles Kurtsinger
1900	Hindus	H. Spencer	1934	High Quest	Robert Jones
1901	The Parader	Fred Landry	1935	Omaha	Willie Saunders
1902	Old England	L. Jackson	1936	Bold Venture	George Woolf
1903	Flocarline	W. Gannon	1937	War Admiral	Charles Kurtsinger
1904	Bryn Mawr	Eugene Hildebrand	1938	Dauber	Maurice Peters
1905	Cairngorm	W. Davis	1939	Challedon	George Seabo
1906	Whimsical	Walter Miller	1940	Bimelech	Fred A. Smith
1907	Don Enrique	G. Mountain	1941	Whirlaway	Eddie Arcaro
1908	Royal Tourist	Eddie Dugan	1942	Alsab	Basil James
1909	Effendi	Willie Doyle	1943	Count Fleet	John Longden
1910	Layminster	Roy Estep	1944	Pensive	Conn McCreary

The Preakness Stakes (continued)

YEAR	HORSE	JOCKEY	YEAR	HORSE	JOCKEY
1945	Polynesian	Wayne D. Wright	1977	Seattle Slew	Jean Cruguet
1946	Assault	Warren Mehrtens	1978	Affirmed	Steve Cauthen
1947	Faultless	Doug Dodson	1979	Spectacular Bid	Ron Franklin
1948	Citation	Eddie Arcaro	1980	Codex	Angel Cordero, Jr.
1949	Capot	Ted Atkinson	1981	Pleasant Colony	Jorge Velasquez
1950	Hill Prince	Eddie Arcaro	1982	Aloma's Ruler	Jack Kaenel
1951	Bold	Eddie Arcaro	1983	Deputed Testamony	Donald Miller
1952	Blue Man	Conn McCreary	1984	Gate Dancer	Angel Cordero, Jr.
1953	Native Dancer	Eric Guerin	1985	Tank's Prospect[3]	Pat Day
1954	Hasty Road	Johnny Adams	1986	Snow Chief	Alex Solis
1955	Nashua	Eddie Arcaro	1987	Alysheba	Chris McCarron
1956	Fabius	William Hartack	1988	Risen Star	Eddie Delahoussaye
1957	Bold Ruler	Eddie Arcaro	1989	Sunday Silence	Patrick Valenzuela
1958	Tim Tam	Ismael Valenzuela	1990	Summer Squall	Pat Day
1959	Royal Orbit	William Harmatz	1991	Hansel	Jerry Bailey
1960	Bally Ache	Robert Ussery	1992	Pine Bluff	Chris McCarron
1961	Carry Back	John Sellers	1993	Prairie Bayou	Mike Smith
1962	Greek Money	John L. Rotz	1994	Tabasco Cat	Pat Day
1963	Candy Spots	William Shoemaker	1995	Timber Country	Pat Day
1964	Northern Dancer	William Hartack	1996	Louis Quatorze	Pat Day
1965	Tom Rolfe	Ron Turcotte	1997	Silver Charm	Gary Stevens
1966	Kauai King	Don Brumfield	1998	Real Quiet	Kent Desormeaux
1967	Damascus	William Shoemaker	1999	Charismatic	Chris Antley
1968	Forward Pass	Ismael Valenzuela	2000	Red Bullet	Jerry Bailey
1969	Majestic Prince	William Hartack	2001	Point Given	Gary Stevens
1970	Personality	Eddie Belmonte	2002	War Emblem	Victor Espinoza
1971	Canonero II	Gustavo Avila	2003	Funny Cide	José Santos
1972	Bee Bee Bee	Eldon Nelson	2004	Smarty Jones	Stewart Elliott
1973	Secretariat	Ron Turcotte	2005	Afleet Alex	Jeremy Rose
1974	Little Current	Miguel Rivera	2006	Bernardini	Javier Castellano
1975	Master Derby	Darrel McHague	2007	Curlin	Robby Albarado
1976	Elocutionist	John Lively			

[1]No competition 1891–93.   [2]Run in two divisions in 1918 because of the large number of starters.
[3]Fastest time—1 min 53⅖ sec.

The Belmont Stakes

YEAR	HORSE	JOCKEY	YEAR	HORSE	JOCKEY
1867	Ruthless	Gilbert Patrick	1893	Comanche	Willie Simms
1868	General Duke	Bobby Swim	1894	Henry of Navarre	Willie Simms
1869	Fenian	Charley Miller	1895	Belmar	Fred Taral
1870	Kingfisher	Edward Brown	1896	Hastings	Henry Griffin
1871	Harry Bassett	W. Miller	1897	Scottish Chieftain	J. Scherrer
1872	Joe Daniels	James Rowe	1898	Bowling Brook	Fred Littlefield
1873	Springbok	James Rowe	1899	Jean Bereaud	R. Clawson
1874	Saxon	George Barbee	1900	Ildrim	Nash Turner
1875	Calvin	Bobby Swim	1901	Commando	H. Spencer
1876	Algerine	Billy Donohue	1902	Masterman	John Bullman
1877	Cloverbrook	Cyrus Holloway	1903	Africander	John Bullman
1878	Duke of Magenta	Lloyd Hughes	1904	Delhi	George Odom
1879	Spendthrift	George Evans	1905	Tanya	Eugene Hildebrand
1880	Grenada	Lloyd Hughes	1906	Burgomaster	Lucien Lyne
1881	Saunterer	T. Costello	1907	Peter Pan	G. Mountain
1882	Forester	James McLaughlin	1908	Colin	Joe Notter
1883	George Kinney	James McLaughlin	1909	Joe Madden	Eddie Dugan
1884	Panique	James McLaughlin	1910	Sweep	James Butwell
1885	Tyrant	Paul Duffy	1913[1]	Prince Eugene	Roscoe Troxler
1886	Inspector B	James McLaughlin	1914	Luke McLuke	Merritt Buxton
1887	Hanover	James McLaughlin	1915	The Finn	George Byrne
1888	Sir Dixon	James McLaughlin	1916	Friar Rock	Everett Haynes
1889	Eric	W. Hayward	1917	Hourless	James Butwell
1890	Burlington	Shelby Barnes	1918	Johren	Frank Robinson
1891	Foxford	Edward Garrison	1919	Sir Barton	John Loftus
1892	Patron	W. Hayward	1920	Man o' War	Clarence Kummer

The Belmont Stakes (continued)

YEAR	HORSE	JOCKEY	YEAR	HORSE	JOCKEY
1921	Grey Lag	Earl Sande	1965	Hail to All	John Sellers
1922	Pillory	C.H. Miller	1966	Amberoid	William Boland
1923	Zev	Earl Sande	1967	Damascus	William Shoemaker
1924	Mad Play	Earl Sande	1968	Stage Door Johnny	Heliodoro Gustines
1925	American Flag	Albert Johnson	1969	Arts and Letters	Braulio Baeza
1926	Crusader	Albert Johnson	1970	High Echelon	John Rotz
1927	Chance Shot	Earl Sande	1971	Pass Catcher	Walter Blum
1928	Vito	Clarence Kummer	1972	Riva Ridge	Ron Turcotte
1929	Blue Larkspur	Mack Garner	1973[2]	Secretariat	Ron Turcotte
1930	Gallant Fox	Earl Sande	1974	Little Current	Miguel Rivera
1931	Twenty Grand	Charles Kurtsinger	1975	Avatar	William Shoemaker
1932	Faireno	Tom Malley	1976	Bold Forbes	Angel Cordero, Jr.
1933	Hurryoff	Mack Garner	1977	Seattle Slew	Jean Cruguet
1934	Peace Chance	Wayne D. Wright	1978	Affirmed	Steve Cauthen
1935	Omaha	Willie Saunders	1979	Coastal	Ruben Hernandez
1936	Granville	James Stout	1980	Temperence Hill	Eddie Maple
1937	War Admiral	Charles Kurtsinger	1981	Summing	George Martens
1938	Pasteurized	James Stout	1982	Conquistador Cielo	Laffit Pincay, Jr.
1939	Johnstown	James Stout	1983	Caveat	Laffit Pincay, Jr.
1940	Bimelech	Fred A. Smith	1984	Swale	Laffit Pincay, Jr.
1941	Whirlaway	Eddie Arcaro	1985	Creme Fraiche	Eddie Maple
1942	Shut Out	Eddie Arcaro	1986	Danzig Connection	Chris McCarron
1943	Count Fleet	John Longden	1987	Bet Twice	Craig Perret
1944	Bounding Home	Gayle L. Smith	1988	Risen Star	Eddie Delahoussaye
1945	Pavot	Eddie Arcaro	1989	Easy Goer	Pat Day
1946	Assault	Warren Mehrtens	1990	Go and Go	Michael Kinane
1947	Phalanx	Ruperto Donoso	1991	Hansel	Jerry Bailey
1948	Citation	Eddie Arcaro	1992	A.P. Indy	Eddie Delahoussaye
1949	Capot	Ted Atkinson	1993	Colonial Affair	Julie Krone
1950	Middleground	William Boland	1994	Tabasco Cat	Pat Day
1951	Counterpoint	David Gorman	1995	Thunder Gulch	Gary Stevens
1952	One Count	Eddie Arcaro	1996	Editor's Note	Rene Douglas
1953	Native Dancer	Eric Guerin	1997	Touch Gold	Chris McCarron
1954	High Gun	Eric Guerin	1998	Victory Gallop	Gary Stevens
1955	Nashua	Eddie Arcaro	1999	Lemon Drop Kid	José Santos
1956	Needles	David Erb	2000	Commendable	Pat Day
1957	Gallant Man	William Shoemaker	2001	Point Given	Gary Stevens
1958	Cavan	Pete Anderson	2002	Sarava	Edgar S. Prado
1959	Sword Dancer	William Shoemaker	2003	Empire Maker	Jerry Bailey
1960	Celtic Ash	William Hartack	2004	Birdstone	Edgar Prado
1961	Sherluck	Braulio Baeza	2005	Afleet Alex	Jeremy Rose
1962	Jaipur	William Shoemaker	2006	Jazil	Fernando Jara
1963	Chateaugay	Braulio Baeza	2007	Rags to Riches	John Velazquez
1964	Quadrangle	Manuel Ycaza			

[1]No competition 1911–1912.   [2]Fastest time—2 min 24 sec.

Horse of the Year

A Horse of the Year was selected by the *Daily Racing Form* from 1936 to 1970 and independently by the Thoroughbred Racing Association beginning in 1950. From 1971 these two organizations, plus the National Turf Writers Association, founded the Eclipse Awards, of which the Horse of the Year is the top among the 22 American prizes.

YEAR	HORSE	YEAR	HORSE	YEAR	HORSE	YEAR	HORSE
1936	Granville	1947	Armed	1957	Bold Ruler[1];	1966	Buckpasser
1937	War Admiral	1948	Citation		Dedicate[2]	1967	Damascus
1938	Seabiscuit	1949	Capot[1]; Coaltown[2]	1958	Round Table	1968	Dr. Fager
1939	Challedon	1950	Hill Prince	1959	Sword Dancer	1969	Arts and Letters
1940	Challedon	1951	Counterpoint	1960	Kelso	1970	Fort Marcy[1];
1941	Whirlaway	1952	One Count[1];	1961	Kelso		Personality[2]
1942	Whirlaway		Native Dancer[2]	1962	Kelso	1971	Ack Ack
1943	Count Fleet	1953	Tom Fool	1963	Kelso	1972	Secretariat
1944	Twilight Tear	1954	Native Dancer	1964	Kelso	1973	Secretariat
1945	Busher	1955	Nashua	1965	Roman Brother[1];	1974	Forego
1946	Assault	1956	Swaps		Moccasin[2]	1975	Forego

Horse of the Year (continued)

YEAR	HORSE	YEAR	HORSE	YEAR	HORSE	YEAR	HORSE
1976	Forego	1984	John Henry	1991	Black Tie Affair	2000	Tiznow
1977	Seattle Slew	1985	Spend a Buck	1992	A.P. Indy	2001	Point Given
1978	Affirmed	1986	Lady's Secret	1993	Kotashaan	2002	Azeri
1979	Affirmed	1987	Ferdinand	1994	Holy Bull	2003	Mineshaft
1980	Spectacular Bid	1988	Alysheba	1995	Cigar	2004	Ghostzapper
1981	John Henry	1989	Sunday	1996	Cigar	2005	Saint Liam
1982	Conquistador		Silence	1997	Favorite Trick	2006	Invasor
	Cielo	1990	Criminal	1998	Skip Away		
1983	All Along		Type	1999	Charismatic		

[1]Daily Racing Form.   [2]Thoroughbred Racing Association.

2,000 Guineas

England's 2,000 Guineas race has been run since 1809. The table shows the winners for the past 20 years.

YEAR	HORSE	JOCKEY	YEAR	HORSE	JOCKEY
1988	Doyoun	Walter R. Swinburn	1998	King of Kings	Michael Kinane
1989	Nashwan	Willie Carson	1999	Island Sands	Frankie Dettori
1990	Tirol	Michael Kinane	2000	King's Best	Kieren Fallon
1991	Mystiko	Michael Roberts	2001	Golan	Kieren Fallon
1992	Rodrigo de Triano	Lester Piggott	2002	Rock of Gibraltar	Johnny Murtagh
1993	Zafonic	Pat Eddery	2003	Refuse To Bend	Pat Smullen
1994	Mister Baileys	Jason Weaver	2004	Haafhd	Richard Hills
1995	Pennekamp	Thierry Jarnet	2005	Footstepsinthesand	Kieren Fallon
1996	Mark of Esteem	Frankie Dettori	2006	George Washington	Kieren Fallon
1997	Entrepreneur	Michael Kinane	2007	Cockney Rebel	Olivier Peslier

The Derby

The Derby has been run since 1780. The table shows the winners for the past 20 years.

YEAR	HORSE	JOCKEY	YEAR	HORSE	JOCKEY
1988	Kahyasi	Ray Cochrane	1998	High Rise	Olivier Peslier
1989	Nashwan	Willie Carson	1999	Oath	Kieren Fallon
1990	Quest for Fame	Pat Eddery	2000	Sinndar	Johnny Murtagh
1991	Generous	Alan Munro	2001	Galileo	Mick Kinane
1992	Dr Devious	John Reid	2002	High Chaparral	Johnny Murtagh
1993	Commander in Chief	Mick Kinane	2003	Kris Kin	Kieren Fallon
1994	Erhaab	Willie Carson	2004	North Light	Kieren Fallon
1995	Lammtarra	Walter R. Swinburn	2005	Motivator	Johnny Murtagh
1996	Shaamit	Michael Hills	2006	Sir Percy	Martin Dwyer
1997	Benny the Dip	Willie Ryan	2007	Authorized	Frankie Dettori

The St. Leger

The St. Leger has been run since 1776. The table shows the winners for the past 20 years.

YEAR	HORSE	JOCKEY	YEAR	HORSE	JOCKEY
1987	Reference Point	Steve Cauthen	1997	Silver Patriarch	Pat Eddery
1988	Minster Son	Willie Carson	1998	Nedawi	John Reid
1989	Michelozzo	Steve Cauthen	1999	Mutafaweq	Richard Hills
1990	Snurge	Richard Quinn	2000	Millenary	Richard Quinn
1991	Toulon	Pat Eddery	2001	Milan	Michael Kinane
1992	User Friendly	George Duffield	2002	Bollin Eric	Kevin Darley
1993	Bob's Return	Philip Robinson	2003	Brian Boru	Jamie Spencer
1994	Moonax	Pat Eddery	2004	Rule of Law	Kerrin McEvoy
1995	Classic Cliché	Frankie Dettori	2005	Scorpion	Frankie Dettori
1996	Shantou	Frankie Dettori	2006	Sixties Icon	Frankie Dettori

Triple Crown Champions—British

YEAR	WINNER	YEAR	WINNER	YEAR	WINNER	YEAR	WINNER
1853	West Australian	1891	Common	1900	Diamond Jubilee	1918	Gainsborough
1865	Gladiateur	1893	Isinglass	1903	Rock Sand	1935	Bahram
1866	Lord Lyon	1897	Galtee More	1915	Pommern	1970	Nijinsky
1886	Ormonde	1899	Flying Fox	1917	Gay Crusader		

Melbourne Cup

The Melbourne Cup race has been run since 1861. The table shows the winners for the past 20 years.

YEAR	HORSE	JOCKEY	YEAR	HORSE	JOCKEY
1987	Kensei	Larry Olsen	1997	Might and Power	Jim Cassidy
1988	Empire Rose	Tony Allan	1998	Jezabeel	Chris Munce
1989	Tawrrific	Shane Dye	1999	Rogan Josh	John Marshall
1990	Kingston Rule	Darren Beadman	2000	Brew	Kerrin McEvoy
1991	Let's Elope	Steven King	2001	Ethereal	Scott Seamer
1992	Subzero	Greg Hall	2002	Media Puzzle	Damien Oliver
1993	Vintage Crop	Michael Kinane	2003	Makybe Diva	Glen Boss
1994	Jeune	Wayne Harris	2004	Makybe Diva	Glen Boss
1995	Doriemus	Damien Oliver	2005	Makybe Diva	Glen Boss
1996	Saintly	Darren Beadman	2006	Delta Blues	Yasunari Iwata

The Dubai World Cup

YEAR	HORSE	JOCKEY	YEAR	HORSE	JOCKEY
1996	Cigar	Jerry Bailey	2002	Street Cry	Jerry Bailey
1997	Singspiel	Jerry Bailey	2003	Moon Ballad	Frankie Dettori
1998	Silver Charm	Gary Stevens	2004	Pleasantly Perfect	Alex Solis
1999	Almutawakel	Richard Hills	2005	Roses in May	John Velazquez
2000	Dubai Millennium	Frankie Dettori	2006	Electrocutionist	Frankie Dettori
2001	Captain Steve	Jerry Bailey	2007	Invasor	Fernando Jara

The Hambletonian Trot

YEAR	HORSE	DRIVER	YEAR	HORSE	DRIVER
1926	Guy McKinney	Nat Ray	1967	Speedy Streak	Adelbert Cameron
1927	Iosola's Worthy	Marvin Childs	1968	Nevele Pride	Stanley Dancer
1928	Spencer	William H. Leese	1969	Lindy's Pride	Howard Beissinger
1929	Walter Dear	Walter Cox	1970	Timothy T.	John Simpson, Sr.
1930	Hanover's Bertha	Thomas Berry	1971	Speedy Crown	Howard Beissinger
1931	Calumet Butler	Richard D. McMahon	1972	Super Bowl	Stanley Dancer
1932	The Marchioness	William Caton	1973	Flirth	Ralph Baldwin
1933	Mary Reynolds	Ben White	1974	Christopher T.	William Haughton
1934	Lord Jim	Hugh M. Parshall	1975	Bonefish	Stanley Dancer
1935	Greyhound	Scepter F. Palin	1976	Steve Lobell	William Haughton
1936	Rosalind	Ben White	1977	Green Speed	William Haughton
1937	Shirley Hanover	Henry Thomas	1978	Speedy Somolli	Howard Beissinger
1938	McLin Hanover	Henry Thomas	1979	Legend Hanover	George Sholty
1939	Peter Astra	Hugh M. Parshall	1980	Burgomeister	William Haughton
1940	Spencer Scott	Fred Egan	1981	Shiaway St. Pat	Ray Remmen
1941	Bill Gallon	Lee Smith	1982	Speed Bowl	Tom Haughton
1942	The Ambassador	Ben White	1983	Duenna	Stanley Dancer
1943	Volo Song	Ben White	1984	Historic Freight	Ben Webster
1944	Yankee Maid	Henry Thomas	1985	Prakas	William O'Donnell
1945	Titan Hanover	Harry Pownall, Sr.	1986	Nuclear Kosmos	Ulf Thoresen
1946	Chestertown	Thomas Berry	1987	Mack Lobell	John Campbell
1947	Hoot Mon	Scepter F. Palin	1988	Armbro Goal	John Campbell
1948	Demon Hanover	Harrison Hoyt	1989[1]	Park Avenue Joe	Ronald Waples
1949	Miss Tilly	Fred Egan		Probe	William Fahy
1950	Lusty Song	Delvin Miller	1990	Harmonious	John Campbell
1951	Mainliner	Guy Crippen	1991	Giant Victory	Jack Moiseyev
1952	Sharp Note	Bion Shively	1992	Alf Palema	Mickey McNichol
1953	Helicopter	Harry Harvey	1993	American Winner	Ron Pierce
1954	Newport Dream	Adelbert Cameron	1994	Victory Dream	Michel Lachance
1955	Scott Frost	Joseph O'Brien	1995	Tagliabue	John Campbell
1956	The Intruder	Ned Bower	1996	Continentalvictory	Michel Lachance
1957	Hickory Smoke	John Simpson, Sr.	1997	Malabar Man	Malvern Burroughs
1958	Emily's Pride	Flave Nipe	1998	Muscles Yankee	John Campbell
1959	Diller Hanover	Frank Ervin	1999	Self Possessed	Michel Lachance
1960	Blaze Hanover	Joseph O'Brien	2000	Yankee Paco	Trevor Ritchie
1961	Harlan Dean	James Arthur	2001	Scarlet Knight	Stefan Melander
1962	A.C.'s Viking	Sanders Russell	2002	Chip Chip Hooray	Eric Ledford
1963	Speedy Scot	Ralph Baldwin	2003	Amigo Hall	Michel Lachance
1964	Ayres	John Simpson, Sr.	2004	Windsong's Legacy	Trond Smedsham-mer
1965	Egyptian Candor	Adelbert Cameron			
1966	Kerry Way	Frank Ervin	2005	Vivid Photo	Roger Hammer

The Hambletonian Trot (continued)

YEAR	HORSE	DRIVER	YEAR	HORSE	DRIVER
2006	Glidemaster	John Campbell	2007	Donato Hanover	Ron Pierce

[1]Tied.

Ice Hockey

The **National Hockey League** (NHL), which was organized in Canada in 1917 with five professional teams, welcomed the first US team, the Boston Bruins, in 1924. Since 1926 the symbol of supremacy in professional hockey has been the **Stanley Cup**, which is awarded to the winner of a play-off that concludes the NHL season. The Stanley Cup was presented to amateur champions from 1893 to 1925.

The **World Hockey Championships**, contested by national teams and sponsored by the **International Ice Hockey Federation** (IIHF; founded 1908), have been held since 1930 for men and since 1990 for women.

Related Web sites: National Hockey League: <www.nhl.com>; International Ice Hockey Federation: <www.iihf.com>.

World Hockey Championship—Men

YEAR	WINNER	YEAR	WINNER	YEAR	WINNER	YEAR	WINNER
1930	Canada	1954	USSR	1972[2]	Czechoslovakia	1990	Sweden
1931	Canada	1955	Canada	1973	USSR	1991	Sweden
1932[1]	Canada	1956[1]	USSR	1974	USSR	1992	Sweden
1933	United States	1957	Sweden	1975	USSR	1993	Russia
1934	Canada	1958	Canada	1976	Czechoslovakia	1994	Canada
1935	Canada	1959	Canada	1977	Czechoslovakia	1995	Finland
1936[1]	Great Britain	1960[1]	United States	1978	USSR	1996	Czech Republic
1937	Canada	1961	Canada	1979	USSR	1997	Canada
1938	Canada	1962	Sweden	1980[1]	United States	1998	Sweden
1939	Canada	1963	USSR	1981	USSR	1999	Czech Republic
1940–46 not held		1964[1]	USSR	1982	USSR	2000	Czech Republic
1947	Czechoslovakia	1965	USSR	1983	USSR	2001	Czech Republic
1948[1]	Canada	1966	USSR	1984[1]	USSR	2002	Slovakia
1949	Czechoslovakia	1967	USSR	1985	Czechoslovakia	2003	Canada
1950	Canada	1968[1]	USSR	1986	USSR	2004	Canada
1951	Canada	1969	USSR	1987	Sweden	2005	Czech Republic
1952[1]	Canada	1970	USSR	1988	USSR	2006	Sweden
1953	Sweden	1971	USSR	1989	USSR	2007	Canada

[1]Olympic champions, recognized as world champions (for earlier Olympics, see Olympic Games). [2]In 1972 a separate world championship was held for the first time.

World Hockey Championship—Women

YEAR	WINNER	YEAR	WINNER	YEAR	WINNER
1990	Canada	1999	Canada	2004	Canada
1992	Canada	2000	Canada	2005	United States
1994	Canada	2001	Canada	2006[1]	Canada
1997	Canada	2002[1]	Canada	2007	Canada
1998[1]	United States	2003	canceled		

[1]Olympic champion; separate world championships have not been held in Olympic years. Olympic gold medalists are sometimes considered world champions.

National Hockey League (NHL) Final Standings, 2007

EASTERN CONFERENCE

Northeast Division	WON	LOST	OTL[1]	Atlantic Division	WON	LOST	OTL[1]	Southeast Division	WON	LOST	OTL[1]
Buffalo[2]	53	22	7	New Jersey[2]	49	24	9	Atlanta[2]	43	28	11
Ottawa[2]	48	25	9	Pittsburgh[2]	47	24	11	Tampa Bay[2]	44	33	5
Toronto	40	31	11	New York Rangers[2]	42	30	10	Carolina	40	34	8
Montreal	42	34	6	New York Islanders[2]	40	30	12	Florida	35	31	16
Boston	35	41	6	Philadelphia	22	48	12	Washington	28	40	14

National Hockey League (NHL) Final Standings, 2007 (continued)

WESTERN CONFERENCE

Central Division	WON	LOST	OTL[1]	Northwest Division	WON	LOST	OTL[1]	Pacific Division	WON	LOST	OTL[1]
Detroit[2]	50	19	13	Vancouver[2]	49	26	7	Anaheim[2]	48	20	14
Nashville[2]	51	23	8	Minnesota[2]	48	26	8	San Jose[2]	51	26	5
St. Louis	34	35	13	Calgary[2]	43	29	10	Dallas[2]	50	25	7
Columbus	33	42	7	Colorado	44	31	7	Los Angeles	27	41	14
Chicago	31	42	9	Edmonton	32	43	7	Phoenix	31	46	5

[1]Overtime losses, worth one point.   [2]Qualified for play-offs.

The Stanley Cup

SEASON	WINNER	RUNNER-UP	RESULTS
1892–93	Montreal Amateur Athletic Association	no challengers	
1893–94	Montreal Amateur Athletic Association	Ottawa Generals	2–0
1894–95	Montreal Victorias	no challengers	
1895–96	Winnipeg Victorias (Feb.), Montreal Victorias (Dec.)	Montreal Victorias (Feb.), Winnipeg Victorias (Dec.)	1–0, 1–0
1896–97	Montreal Victorias	Ottawa Capitals	1–0
1897–98	Montreal Victorias	no challengers	
1898–99	Montreal Victorias (Feb.), Montreal Shamrocks (March)	Winnipeg Victorias (Feb.), Queen's University (March)	2–0, 1–0
1899–1900	Montreal Shamrocks	Winnipeg Victorias, Halifax Crescents	2–1, 2–0
1900–01	Winnipeg Victorias	Montreal Shamrocks	2–0
1901–02	Winnipeg Victorias (Jan.), Montreal Amateur Athletic Association (March)	Toronto Wellingtons (Jan.), Winnipeg Victorias (March)	2–0, 2–1
1902–03	Montreal Amateur Athletic Association (Feb.), Ottawa Silver Seven (March)	Winnipeg Victorias (Feb.), Montreal Victorias (March), Rat Portage Thistles (March)	2–1, 1–0, 2–0
1903–04	Ottawa Silver Seven	Winnipeg Rowing Club, Toronto Marlboros, Montreal Wanderers, Brandon Wheat Kings	2–1, 2–0, 0–0 (tie), 2–0
1904–05	Ottawa Silver Seven	Dawson City Nuggets, Rat Portage Thistles	2–0, 2–1
1905–06	Ottawa Silver Seven (Feb., March), Montreal Wanderers (March, Dec.)	Queen's University (Feb.), Smiths Falls (March), Ottawa Silver Seven (March), New Glasgow Cubs (Dec.)	2–0, 2–0, 1–1, 2–0
1906–07	Kenora Thistles (Jan.), Montreal Wanderers (March)	Montreal Wanderers (Jan.), Kenora Thistles (March)	2–0, 1–1
1907–08	Montreal Wanderers	Ottawa Victorias, Winnipeg Maple Leafs, Toronto Trolley Leaguers, Edmonton Eskimos	2–0, 2–0, 1–0, 1–1
1908–09	Ottawa Senators	no challengers	
1909–10	Ottawa Senators (Jan.), Montreal Wanderers (March)	Edmonton Eskimos (Jan.), Galt (Jan.), Berlin Union Jacks (March)	1–0, 2–0, 2–0
1910–11	Ottawa Senators	Port Arthur Bearcats, Galt	1–0, 1–0
1911–12	Quebec Bulldogs	Moncton Victories	2–0
1912–13	Quebec Bulldogs[1]	Sydney Miners	2–0
1913–14	Toronto Blueshirts	Victoria Cougars, Montreal Canadiens	3–0, 1–1
1914–15	Vancouver Millionaires	Ottawa Senators	3–0
1915–16	Montreal Canadiens	Portland Rosebuds	3–2
1916–17	Seattle Metropolitans	Montreal Canadiens	3–1
1917–18	Toronto Arenas	Vancouver Millionaires	3–2
1918–19	no decision[2]		
1919–20	Ottawa Senators	Seattle Metropolitans	3–2
1920–21	Ottawa Senators	Vancouver Millionaires	3–2
1921–22	Toronto St. Pats	Vancouver Millionaires	3–2
1922–23	Ottawa Senators	Edmonton Eskimos, Vancouver Maroons	2–0, 3–1
1923–24	Montreal Canadiens	Calgary Tigers, Vancouver Maroons	2–0, 2–0
1924–25	Victoria Cougars	Montreal Canadiens	3–1
1925–26	Montreal Maroons	Victoria Cougars	3–1
1926–27	Ottawa Senators	Boston Bruins	2–0
1927–28	New York Rangers	Montreal Maroons	3–2
1928–29	Boston Bruins	New York Rangers	2–0
1929–30	Montreal Canadiens	Boston Bruins	2–0
1930–31	Montreal Canadiens	Chicago Black Hawks	3–2
1931–32	Toronto Maple Leafs	New York Rangers	3–0

The Stanley Cup (continued)

SEASON	WINNER	RUNNER-UP	RESULTS
1932–33	New York Rangers	Toronto Maple Leafs	3–1
1933–34	Chicago Black Hawks	Detroit Red Wings	3–1
1934–35	Montreal Maroons	Toronto Maple Leafs	3–0
1935–36	Detroit Red Wings	Toronto Maple Leafs	3–1
1936–37	Detroit Red Wings	New York Rangers	3–2
1937–38	Chicago Black Hawks	Toronto Maple Leafs	3–1
1938–39	Boston Bruins	Toronto Maple Leafs	4–1
1939–40	New York Rangers	Toronto Maple Leafs	4–2
1940–41	Boston Bruins	Detroit Red Wings	4–0
1941–42	Toronto Maple Leafs	Detroit Red Wings	4–3
1942–43	Detroit Red Wings	Boston Bruins	4–0
1943–44	Montreal Canadiens	Chicago Black Hawks	4–0
1944–45	Toronto Maple Leafs	Detroit Red Wings	4–3
1945–46	Montreal Canadiens	Boston Bruins	4–1
1946–47	Toronto Maple Leafs	Montreal Canadiens	4–2
1947–48	Toronto Maple Leafs	Detroit Red Wings	4–0
1948–49	Toronto Maple Leafs	Detroit Red Wings	4–0
1949–50	Detroit Red Wings	New York Rangers	4–3
1950–51	Toronto Maple Leafs	Montreal Canadiens	4–1
1951–52	Detroit Red Wings	Montreal Canadiens	4–0
1952–53	Montreal Canadiens	Boston Bruins	4–1
1953–54	Detroit Red Wings	Montreal Canadiens	4–3
1954–55	Detroit Red Wings	Montreal Canadiens	4–3
1955–56	Montreal Canadiens	Detroit Red Wings	4–1
1956–57	Montreal Canadiens	Boston Bruins	4–1
1957–58	Montreal Canadiens	Boston Bruins	4–2
1958–59	Montreal Canadiens	Toronto Maple Leafs	4–1
1959–60	Montreal Canadiens	Toronto Maple Leafs	4–0
1960–61	Chicago Black Hawks	Detroit Red Wings	4–2
1961–62	Toronto Maple Leafs	Chicago Black Hawks	4–2
1962–63	Toronto Maple Leafs	Detroit Red Wings	4–1
1963–64	Toronto Maple Leafs	Detroit Red Wings	4–3
1964–65	Montreal Canadiens	Chicago Black Hawks	4–3
1965–66	Montreal Canadiens	Detroit Red Wings	4–2
1966–67	Toronto Maple Leafs	Montreal Canadiens	4–2
1967–68	Montreal Canadiens	St. Louis Blues	4–0
1968–69	Montreal Canadiens	St. Louis Blues	4–0
1969–70	Boston Bruins	St. Louis Blues	4–0
1970–71	Montreal Canadiens	Chicago Black Hawks	4–3
1971–72	Boston Bruins	New York Rangers	4–2
1972–73	Montreal Canadiens	Chicago Black Hawks	4–2
1973–74	Philadelphia Flyers	Boston Bruins	4–2
1974–75	Philadelphia Flyers	Buffalo Sabres	4–2
1975–76	Montreal Canadiens	Philadelphia Flyers	4–0
1976–77	Montreal Canadiens	Boston Bruins	4–0
1976–77	Montreal Canadiens	Boston Bruins	4–0
1977–78	Montreal Canadiens	Boston Bruins	4–2
1978–79	Montreal Canadiens	New York Rangers	4–1
1979–80	New York Islanders	Philadelphia Flyers	4–2
1980–81	New York Islanders	Minnesota North Stars	4–1
1981–82	New York Islanders	Vancouver Canucks	4–0
1982–83	New York Islanders	Edmonton Oilers	4–0
1983–84	Edmonton Oilers	New York Islanders	4–1
1984–85	Edmonton Oilers	Philadelphia Flyers	4–1
1985–86	Montreal Canadiens	Calgary Flames	4–1
1986–87	Edmonton Oilers	Philadelphia Flyers	4–3
1987–88	Edmonton Oilers	Boston Bruins	4–0
1988–89	Calgary Flames	Montreal Canadiens	4–2
1989–90	Edmonton Oilers	Boston Bruins	4–1
1990–91	Pittsburgh Penguins	Minnesota North Stars	4–2
1991–92	Pittsburgh Penguins	Chicago Blackhawks	4–0
1992–93	Montreal Canadiens	Los Angeles Kings	4–1
1993–94	New York Rangers	Vancouver Canucks	4–3
1994–95	New Jersey Devils	Detroit Red Wings	4–0
1995–96	Colorado Avalanche	Florida Panthers	4–0
1996–97	Detroit Red Wings	Philadelphia Flyers	4–0
1997–98	Detroit Red Wings	Washington Capitals	4–0
1998–99	Dallas Stars	Buffalo Sabres	4–2

The Stanley Cup (continued)

SEASON	WINNER	RUNNER-UP	RESULTS
1999–2000	New Jersey Devils	Dallas Stars	4–2
2000–01	Colorado Avalanche	New Jersey Devils	4–3
2001–02	Detroit Red Wings	Carolina Hurricanes	4–1
2002–03	New Jersey Devils	Mighty Ducks of Anaheim	4–3
2003–04	Tampa Bay Lightning	Calgary Flames	4–3
2004–05	*not held due to players' strike and season cancellation*		
2005–06	Carolina Hurricanes	Edmonton Oilers	4–3
2006–07	Anaheim Ducks	Ottawa Senators	4–1

[1]*Though Victoria defeated Quebec in challenge games, Victoria's win was not officially recognized.* [2]*Series between Montreal Canadiens and Seattle Metropolitans called off because of flu epidemic.*

Did you know? When Babe Ruth set the single-season home-run record for Major League Baseball in 1927, his 60 home runs accounted for 14 percent of all home runs hit in the major leagues that year. A player in the modern era would need to hit about 300 home runs in a season to attain the same percentage.

Marathon

The marathon is a long-distance footrace first held at the revival of the Olympic Games at Athens in 1896. It commemorates the legendary feat of a Greek soldier who, in 490 BC, is supposed to have run from Marathon to Athens, a distance of about 40 km (25 mi), to bring news of the Athenian victory over the Persians. Appropriately, the first modern marathon winner in 1896 was a Greek, Spyridon Louis. In 1924 the **Olympic marathon distance** was standardized at 42,195 m, or 26 mi 385 yd. This was based on a decision of the British Olympic Committee to start the 1908 Olympic race from Windsor Castle and finish it in front of the royal box in the stadium at London. The marathon was added to the **women's Olympic program** in 1984. Because marathon courses are not of equal difficulty, the **International Association of Athletics Federations** (IAAF) does not list a world record for the event. After the Olympic Games championship, one of the most coveted honors in marathon running is victory in the **Boston Marathon**, held annually since 1897. It draws athletes from all parts of the world and in 1972 became the first marathon officially to allow women to compete. The **New York City Marathon** also attracts participants from many countries. Other popular marathons are held in London, Chicago, Berlin, Dublin, and Rotterdam (The Netherlands).

Related Web sites: Boston Marathon: <www.boston marathon.org>; New York City Marathon: <www.ingnycmarathon.org>.

Boston Marathon

Won by an American runner except as indicated. Times are given in hours:minutes:seconds.

men

YEAR	WINNER	TIME	YEAR	WINNER	TIME
1897	John J. McDermott	2:55:10	1919	Carl W.A. Linder	2:29:13
1898	Ronald J. McDonald (CAN)	2:42:00	1920	Peter Trivoulides (GRE)	2:29:31
1899	Lawrence J. Brignoli	2:54:38	1921	Frank Zuna	2:18:57
1900	John J. Caffrey (CAN)	2:39:44	1922	Clarence H. DeMar	2:18:10
1901	John J. Caffrey (CAN)	2:29:23	1923	Clarence H. DeMar	2:23:47
1902	Sammy A. Mellor	2:43:12	1924	Clarence H. DeMar	2:29:40
1903	John C. Lorden	2:41:29	1925	Charles L. Mellor	2:33:06
1904	Michael Spring	2:39:04	1926	John C. Miles (CAN)	2:25:40
1905	Frederick Lorz	2:38:25	1927	Clarence H. DeMar	2:40:22
1906	Tim Ford	2:45:45	1928	Clarence H. DeMar	2:37:07
1907	Thomas Longboat (CAN)	2:24:24	1929	John C. Miles (CAN)	2:33:08
1908	Thomas P. Morrissey	2:25:43	1930	Clarence H. DeMar	2:34:48
1909	Henri Renaud	2:53:36	1931	James P. Hennigan	2:46:45
1910	Fred L. Cameron (CAN)	2:28:52	1932	Paul deBruyn	2:33:36
1911	Clarence H. DeMar	2:21:39	1933	Leslie S. Pawson	2:31:01
1912	Michael J. Ryan	2:21:18	1934	Dave Komonen (CAN)	2:32:53
1913	Fritz Carlson	2:25:14	1935	John A. Kelley	2:32:07
1914	James Duffy (CAN)	2:25:01	1936	Ellison M. Brown	2:33:40
1915	Edouard Fabre (CAN)	2:31:41	1937	Walter Young (CAN)	2:33:20
1916	Arthur V. Roth	2:27:16	1938	Leslie S. Pawson	2:35:34
1917	William K. Kennedy	2:28:37	1939	Ellison M. Brown	2:28:51
1918	*no regular competition*		1940	Gerard Cote (CAN)	2:28:28

Boston Marathon (continued)

men (continued)

YEAR	WINNER	TIME	YEAR	WINNER	TIME
1941	Leslie S. Pawson	2:30:38	1975	Bill Rodgers	2:09:55
1942	Joe Smith	2:26:51	1976	Jack Fultz	2:20:19
1943	Gerard Cote (CAN)	2:28:25	1977	Jerome Drayton (CAN)	2:14:46
1944	Gerard Cote (CAN)	2:31:50	1978	Bill Rodgers	2:10:13
1945	John A. Kelley	2:30:40	1979	Bill Rodgers	2:09:27
1946	Stylianos Kyriakides (GRE)	2:29:27	1980	Bill Rodgers	2:12:11
1947	Suh Yun Bok (KOR)	2:25:39	1981	Seko Toshihiko (JPN)	2:09:26
1948	Gerard Cote (CAN)	2:31:02	1982	Alberto Salazar	2:08:51
1949	Karl G. Leandersson (SWE)	2:31:50	1983	Greg A. Meyer	2:09:00
1950	Ham Kee Yong (KOR)	2:32:39	1984	Geoff Smith (ENG)	2:10:34
1951	Tanaka Shigeki (JPN)	2:27:45	1985	Geoff Smith (ENG)	2:14:05
1952	Doroteo Flores (GUA)	2:31:53	1986	Robert de Castella (AUS)	2:07:51
1953	Yamada Keizo (JPN)	2:18:51	1987	Seko Toshihiko (JPN)	2:11:50
1954	Veikko L. Karanen (FIN)	2:20:39	1988	Ibrahim Hussein (KEN)	2:08:43
1955	Hamamura Hideo (JPN)	2:18:22	1989	Abebe Mekonnen (ETH)	2:09:06
1956	Antti Viskari (FIN)	2:14:14	1990	Gelindo Bordin (ITA)	2:08:19
1957	John J. Kelley	2:20:05	1991	Ibrahim Hussein (KEN)	2:11:06
1958	Franjo Mihalic (YUG)	2:25:54	1992	Ibrahim Hussein (KEN)	2:08:14
1959	Eino Oksanen (FIN)	2:22:42	1993	Cosmas N'Deti (KEN)	2:09:33
1960	Paavo Kotila (FIN)	2:20:54	1994	Cosmas N'Deti (KEN)	2:07:15
1961	Eino Oksanen (FIN)	2:23:39	1995	Cosmas N'Deti (KEN)	2:09:22
1962	Eino Oksanen (FIN)	2:23:48	1996	Moses Tanui (KEN)	2:09:16
1963	Aurele Vandendriessche (BEL)	2:18:58	1997	Lameck Aguta (KEN)	2:10:34
1964	Aurele Vandendriessche (BEL)	2:19:59	1998	Moses Tanui (KEN)	2:07:34
1965	Shigematsu Morio (JPN)	2:16:33	1999	Joseph Chebet (KEN)	2:09:52
1966	Kimihara Kenji (JPN)	2:17:11	2000	Elijah Lagat (KEN)	2:09:47
1967	David McKenzie (NZL)	2:15:45	2001	Bong-Ju Lee (KOR)	2:09:43
1968	Amby Burfoot	2:22:17	2002	Rodgers Rop (KEN)	2:09:02
1969	Unetani Yoshiaki (JPN)	2:13:49	2003	Robert Kipkoech Cheruiyot (KEN)	2:10:11
1970	Ron Hill (ENG)	2:10:30	2004	Timothy Cherigat (KEN)	2:10:37
1971	Alvaro Mejia (COL)	2:18:45	2005	Hailu Negussie (ETH)	2:11:45
1972	Olavi Suomalainen (FIN)	2:15:30	2006	Robert Kipkoech Cheruiyot (KEN)	2:07:14
1973	Jon Anderson	2:16:03	2007	Robert Kipkoech Cheruiyot (KEN)	2:14:13
1974	Neil Cusack	2:13:39			

women

YEAR	WINNER	TIME	YEAR	WINNER	TIME
1972	Nina Kuscsik	3:10:26	1990	Rosa Mota (POR)	2:25:23
1973	Jacqueline Hansen	3:05:59	1991	Wanda Panfil (POL)	2:24:18
1974	Michiko Gorman	2:47:11	1992	Olga Markova (RUS)	2:23:43
1975	Liane Winter (FRG)	2:42:24	1993	Olga Markova (RUS)	2:25:27
1976	Kim Merritt	2:47:10	1994	Uta Pippig (GER)	2:21:45
1977	Michiko Gorman	2:46:22	1995	Uta Pippig (GER)	2:25:11
1978	Gayle S. Barron	2:44:52	1996	Uta Pippig (GER)	2:27:12
1979	Joan Benoit	2:35:15	1997	Fatuma Roba (ETH)	2:26:23
1980	Jacqueline Gareau (CAN)	2:34:28	1998	Fatuma Roba (ETH)	2:23:21
1981	Allison Roe (NZL)	2:26:46	1999	Fatuma Roba (ETH)	2:23:25
1982	Charlotte Teske (FRG)	2:29:33	2000	Catherine Ndereba (KEN)	2:26:11
1983	Joan Benoit	2:22:42	2001	Catherine Ndereba (KEN)	2:23:53
1984	Lorraine Moller (NZL)	2:29:28	2002	Margaret Okayo (KEN)	2:20:43
1985	Lisa Larsen	2:34:06	2003	Svetlana Zakharova (RUS)	2:25:20
1986	Ingrid Kristiansen (NOR)	2:24:55	2004	Catherine Ndereba (KEN)	2:24:27
1987	Rosa Mota (POR)	2:25:21	2005	Catherine Ndereba (KEN)	2:25:13
1988	Rosa Mota (POR)	2:24:30	2006	Rita Jeptoo (KEN)	2:23:38
1989	Ingrid Kristiansen (NOR)	2:24:33	2007	Lidiya Grigoryeva (RUS)	2:29:18

New York City Marathon

Won by an American runner except as indicated. Times are given in hours:minutes:seconds.

YEAR	MEN	TIME	WOMEN	TIME
1970	Gary Muhrcke	2:31:38	*no finisher*	
1971	Norm Higgins	2:22:54	Beth Bonner	2:55:22
1972	Robert Karlin	2:27:52	Nina Kuscsik	3:08:41
1973	Tom Fleming	2:21:54	Nina Kuscsik	2:57:07

New York City Marathon (continued)

YEAR	MEN	TIME	WOMEN	TIME
1974	Norbert Sander	2:26:30	Katherine Switzer	3:07:29
1975	Tom Fleming	2:19:27	Kim Merritt	2:46:14
1976	Bill Rodgers	2:10:09	Michiko Gorman	2:39:11
1977	Bill Rodgers	2:11:28	Michiko Gorman	2:43:10
1978	Bill Rodgers	2:12:12	Grete Waitz (NOR)	2:32:30
1979	Bill Rodgers	2:11:42	Grete Waitz (NOR)	2:27:33
1980	Alberto Salazar	2:09:41	Grete Waitz (NOR)	2:25:41
1981	Alberto Salazar	2:08:13	Allison Roe (NZL)	2:25:29
1982	Alberto Salazar	2:09:29	Grete Waitz (NOR)	2:27:14
1983	Rod Dixon	2:08:59	Grete Waitz (NOR)	2:27:00
1984	Orlando Pizzolato	2:14:53	Grete Waitz (NOR)	2:29:30
1985	Orlando Pizzolato	2:11:34	Grete Waitz (NOR)	2:28:34
1986	Gianni Poli (ITA)	2:11:06	Grete Waitz (NOR)	2:28:06
1987	Ibrahim Hussein (KEN)	2:11:01	Priscilla Welch (GBR)	2:30:17
1988	Steve Jones (WAL)	2:08:20	Grete Waitz (NOR)	2:28:07
1989	Juma Ikangaa (TAN)	2:08:01	Ingrid Kristiansen (NOR)	2:25:30
1990	Douglas Wakiihuri (KEN)	2:12:39	Wanda Panfil (POL)	2:30:45
1991	Salvador Garcia (MEX)	2:09:28	Liz McColgan (SCO)	2:27:23
1992	Willie Mtolo (RSA)	2:09:29	Lisa Ondieki (AUS)	2:24:40
1993	Andres Espinosa (MEX)	2:10:04	Uta Pippig (GER)	2:26:24
1994	German Silva (MEX)	2:11:21	Tegla Loroupe (KEN)	2:27:37
1995	German Silva (MEX)	2:11:00	Tegla Loroupe (KEN)	2:28:06
1996	Giacomo Leone (ITA)	2:09:54	Anuta Catuna (ROM)	2:28:18
1997	John Kagwe (KEN)	2:08:12	Franziska Rochat-Moser (SUI)	2:28:43
1998	John Kagwe (KEN)	2:08:45	Franca Fiacconi (ITA)	2:25:17
1999	Joseph Chebet (KEN)	2:09:14	Adriana Fernández (MEX)	2:25:06
2000	Abdelkhader El Mouaziz (MAR)	2:10:09	Lyudmila Petrova (RUS)	2:25:45
2001	Tesfaye Jifar (ETH)	2:07:43	Margaret Okayo (KEN)	2:24:21
2002	Rodgers Rop (KEN)	2:08:07	Joyce Chepchumba (KEN)	2:25:56
2003	Martin Lel (KEN)	2:10:30	Margaret Okayo (KEN)	2:22:31
2004	Hendrik Ramaala (RSA)	2:09:28	Paula Radcliffe (GBR)	2:23:10
2005	Paul Tergat (KEN)	2:09:30	Jelena Prokopcuka (LAT)	2:24:41
2006	Marilson Gomes dos Santos (BRA)	2:09:58	Jelena Prokopcuka (LAT)	2:25:05

Chicago Marathon

Won by an American runner except as indicated. Times are given in hours:minutes:seconds.

YEAR	MEN	TIME	WOMEN	TIME
1977	Dan Cloeter	2:17:52	Dorothy Doolittle	2:50:47
1978	Mark Stanforth	2:19:20	Lynae Larson	2:59:25
1979	Dan Cloeter	2:23:20	Laura Michalek	3:15:45
1980	Frank Richardson	2:14:04	Sue Petersen	2:45:03
1981	Philip Coppess	2:16:13	Tina Gandy	2:49:39
1982	Greg Meyer	2:10:59	Nancy Conz	2:33:23
1983	Joseph Nzau (KEN)	2:09:44	Rosa Mota (PRT)	2:31:12
1984	Steve Jones (GBR)	2:08:05	Rosa Mota (PRT)	2:26:01
1985	Steve Jones (GBR)	2:07:13	Joan Benoit Samuelson	2:21:21
1986	Toshihiko Seko (JPN)	2:08:27	Ingrid Kristiansen (NOR)	2:27:08
1987	not held			
1988	Alejandro Cruz (MEX)	2:08:57	Lisa Weidenbach	2:29:17
1989	Paul Davis-Hale (GBR)	2:11:25	Lisa Weidenbach	2:28:15
1990	Martín Pitayo (MEX)	2:09:41	Aurora Cunha (PRT)	2:30:11
1991	Joseildo Rocha (BRA)	2:14:33	Midde Hamrin-Senorski (SWE)	2:36:21
1992	José César De Souza (BRA)	2:16:14	Linda Somers	2:37:41
1993	Luiz Antônio Dos Santos (BRA)	2:13:15	Ritva Lemettinen (FIN)	2:33:18
1994	Luiz Antônio Dos Santos (BRA)	2:11:16	Kristy Johnston	2:31:34
1995	Eamonn Martin (GBR)	2:11:18	Ritva Lemettinen (FIN)	2:28:27
1996	Paul Evans (GBR)	2:08:52	Marian Sutton (GBR)	2:30:41
1997	Khalid Khannouchi (MAR)	2:07:10	Marian Sutton (GBR)	2:29:03
1998	Ondoro Osoro (KEN)	2:06:54	Joyce Chepchumba (KEN)	2:23:57
1999	Khalid Khannouchi (MAR)	2:05:42	Joyce Chepchumba (KEN)	2:25:59
2000	Khalid Khannouchi (USA)	2:07:01	Catherine Ndereba (KEN)	2:21:33
2001	Ben Kimondiu (KEN)	2:08:52	Catherine Ndereba (KEN)	2:18:47
2002	Khalid Khannouchi (USA)	2:05:56	Paula Radcliffe (GBR)	2:17:18
2003	Evans Rutto (KEN)	2:05:50	Svetlana Zakharova (RUS)	2:23:07
2004	Evans Rutto (KEN)	2:06:16	Constantina Tomescu-Dita (ROM)	2:23:45
2005	Felix Limo (KEN)	2:07:02	Deena Kastor	2:21:25
2006	Robert K. Cheruiyot (KEN)	2:07:35	Berhane Adere (ETH)	2:20:42

Rodeo

A uniquely **North American** competition, the rodeo has been held on a more-or-less formal basis since the late 1920s. From 1929 to 1944 the **men's world all-around rodeo champion** was named by the **Rodeo Association of America**. Since 1944 the all-around champion has been the leading money winner of the year—with the exception of the years 1976–78, when the champion was the cowboy who won the most money at the **National Finals Rodeo**. The Rodeo Association of America changed its name several times but has been known as the **Professional** **Rodeo Cowboys Association** (PRCA) since 1975. Among other rodeo sanctioning activities, the PRCA qualifies cowboys for the National Finals Rodeo, currently held in early December in Las Vegas NV. There competitions are held in each of several events, including bronc riding (bareback and saddle), bull riding, calf roping, and steer wrestling (individual and team). Women compete in one event only, barrel racing.

Professional Rodeo Cowboys Association Web site: <www.prorodeo.com>.

Men's World All-Around Rodeo Champions
Awarded since 1929. Table shows champions for the past 20 years.

YEAR	WINNER	YEAR	WINNER	YEAR	WINNER	YEAR	WINNER
1987	Lewis Feild	1992	Ty Murray	1997	Dan Mortensen	2002	Trevor Brazile
1988	Dave Appleton	1993	Ty Murray	1998	Ty Murray	2003	Trevor Brazile
1989	Ty Murray	1994	Ty Murray	1999	Fred Whitfield	2004	Trevor Brazile
1990	Ty Murray	1995	Joe Beaver	2000	Joe Beaver	2005	Ryan Jarrett
1991	Ty Murray	1996	Joe Beaver	2001	Cody Ohl	2006	Trevor Brazile

Did you know? Margaret Waldron, age 74 and legally blind, scored a hole-in-one at Long Point Golf Course on Florida's Amelia Island in 1990. The next day, she did it again on the same hole using the same ball. The longest hole-in-one ever recorded was a 444-yard shot by golfer Robert Mitera, at Miracle Hill Golf Club in Omaha NE in 1965. He was helped by a 50-mph tail wind.

Skiing

A lthough most of the events had been contested at the regional level since the mid-19th century, the first internationally organized **skiing championships** did not take place until 1924. From 1924 to 1931 only **Nordic** competition was involved; **Alpine** championship events were added to world competition in 1931 and to the Olympics in 1936. Except in Olympic years, the Nordic and Alpine championships are held separately and at different locations. **Events** include cross-country races, ski jumping, biathlon, and relay races (Nordic) and downhill and slalom skiing (Alpine). Since 1967, an **Alpine World Cup** has been presented to the competitor with the best combined downhill, slalom, giant slalom, and supergiant slalom (super-G) performance over a series of major contests. A **Nordic World Cup** for cross-country events has been awarded since 1979.

International Ski Federation Web site: <www.fis-ski.com>.

Alpine Skiing World Championships—Men
Results for the past 20 years. The next championships are scheduled to be held in 2009 in Val d'Isère, France.

DOWNHILL		COMBINED		SLALOM	
1988[1]	Permin Zurbriggen (SUI)	1988[1]	Hubert Strolz (AUT)	1989	Rudolf Nierlich (AUT)
1989	Hansjorg Tauscher (FRG)	1989	Marc Girardelli (LUX)	1991	Marc Girardelli (LUX)
1991	Franz Heinzer (SUI)	1991	Stefan Eberharter (AUT)	1992[1]	Finn Christian Jagge (NOR)
1992[1]	Patrick Ortlieb (AUS)	1992[1]	Josef Polig (ITA)		
1993	Urs Lehmann (SUI)	1993	Lasse Kjus (NOR)	1993	Kjetil André Aamodt (NOR)
1994[1]	Tommy Moe (USA)	1994[1]	Lasse Kjus (NOR)	1994[1]	Thomas Stangassinger (AUT)
1995	*not held*	1995	*not held*		
1996	Patrick Ortlieb (AUS)	1996	Marc Girardelli (LUX)	1995	*not held*
1997	Bruno Kernen (SUI)	1997	Kjetil André Aamodt (NOR)	1996	Alberto Tomba (ITA)
1998[1]	Jean-Luc Cretier (FRA)	1998[1]	Mario Reiter (AUT)	1997	Tom Stiansen (NOR)
1999	Hermann Maier (AUT)	1999	Kjetil André Aamodt (NOR)	1998[1]	Hans-Petter Buraas (NOR)
2001	Hannes Trinkl (AUT)	2001	Kjetil André Aamodt (NOR)		
2002[1]	Fritz Strobl (AUT)	2002[1]	Kjetil André Aamodt (NOR)	1999	Kalle Palander (FIN)
2003	Michael Walchhofer (AUT)	2003	Bode Miller (USA)	2001	Mario Matt (AUT)
2005	Bode Miller (USA)	2005	Benjamin Raich (AUT)	2002[1]	Jean-Pierre Vidal (FRA)
2006[1]	Antoine Dénériaz (FRA)	2006[1]	Ted Ligety (USA)	2003	Ivica Kostelic (CRO)
2007	Aksel Lund Svindal (NOR)	2007	Daniel Albrecht (SUI)	2005	Benjamin Raich (AUT)

Alpine Skiing World Championships—Men (continued)

SLALOM (CONT.)
2006[1] Benjamin Raich (AUT)
2007 Mario Matt (AUT)

GIANT SLALOM
1988[1] Alberto Tomba (ITA)
1989 Rudolf Nierlich (AUT)
1991 Rudolf Nierlich (AUT)
1992[1] Alberto Tomba (ITA)
1993 Kjetil André Aamodt (NOR)
1994[1] Markus Wasmeier (GER)
1995 *not held*
1996 Alberto Tomba (ITA)
1997 Michael von Grünigen (SUI)
1998[1] Hermann Maier (AUT)

GIANT SLALOM (CONT.)
1999 Lasse Kjus (NOR)
2001 Michael von Grünigen (SUI)
2002[1] Stephan Eberharter (AUT)
2003 Bode Miller (USA)
2005 Hermann Maier (AUT)
2006[1] Benjamin Raich (AUT)
2007 Aksel Lund Svindal (NOR)

SUPERGIANT SLALOM
1988[1] Franck Piccard (FRA)
1989 Martin Hangl (SUI)
1991 Stephan Eberharter (AUT)
1992[1] Kjetil André Aamodt (NOR)
1993 *not held*
1994[1] Markus Wasmeier (GER)

SUPERGIANT SLALOM (CONT.)
1995 *not held*
1996 Atle Skaardal (NOR)
1997 Atle Skaardal (NOR)
1998[1] Hermann Maier (AUT)
1999 Lasse Kjus (NOR), Hermann Maier (AUT) (tied)
2001 Daron Rahlves (USA)
2002[1] Kjetil André Aamodt (NOR)
2003 Stephan Eberharter (AUT)
2005 Bode Miller (USA)
2006[1] Kjetil André Aamodt (NOR)
2007 Patrick Staudacher (ITA)

[1]*Olympic champions, recognized as world champions.*

Alpine Skiing World Championships—Women

Results for the past 20 years. The next championships are scheduled to be held in 2009 in Val d'Isère, France.

DOWNHILL
1988[1] Marina Kiehl (FRG)
1989 Maria Walliser (SUI)
1991 Petra Kronberger (AUT)
1992[1] Kerrin Lee-Gartner (CAN)
1993 Kate Pace (CAN)
1994[1] Katja Seizinger (GER)
1995 *not held*
1996 Picabo Street (USA)
1997 Hilary Lindh (USA)
1998[1] Katja Seizinger (GER)
1999 Renate Götschl (AUT)
2001 Michaela Dorfmeister (AUT)
2002[1] Carole Montillet (FRA)
2003 Mélanie Turgeon (CAN)
2005 Janica Kostelic (CRO)
2006[1] Michaela Dorfmeister (AUT)
2007 Anja Pärson (SWE)

COMBINED
1988[1] Anita Wachter (AUT)
1989 Tamara McKinney (USA)
1991 Chantal Bournissen (SUI)
1992[1] Petra Kronberger (AUT)
1993 Miriam Vogt (GER)
1994[1] Pernilla Wiberg (SWE)
1995 *not held*
1996 Pernilla Wiberg (SWE)
1997 Renate Götschl (AUT)
1998[1] Katja Seizinger (GER)
1999 Pernilla Wiberg (SWE)
2001 Martina Ertl (GER)
2002[1] Janica Kostelic (CRO)
2003 Janica Kostelic (CRO)

COMBINED (CONT.)
2005 Janica Kostelic (CRO)
2006[1] Janica Kostelic (CRO)
2007 Anja Pärson (SWE)

SLALOM
1988[1] Vreni Schneider (SUI)
1989 Mateja Svet (YUG)
1991 Vreni Schneider (SUI)
1992[1] Petra Kronberger (AUT)
1993 Karin Buder (AUT)
1994[1] Vreni Schneider (SUI)
1995 *not held*
1996 Pernilla Wiberg (SWE)
1997 Deborah Compagnoni (ITA)
1998[1] Hilde Gerg (GER)
1999 Zali Steggall (AUS)
2001 Anja Paerson (SWE)
2002[1] Janica Kostelic (CRO)
2003 Janica Kostelic (CRO)
2005 Janica Kostelic (CRO)
2006[1] Anja Pärson (SWE)
2007 Sarka Zahrobska (CZE)

GIANT SLALOM
1988[1] Vreni Schneider (SUI)
1989 Vreni Schneider (SUI)
1991 Pernilla Wiberg (SWE)
1992[1] Pernilla Wiberg (SWE)
1993 Carole Merle (FRA)
1994[1] Deborah Compagnoni (ITA)
1995 *not held*
1996 Deborah Compagnoni (ITA)

GIANT SLALOM (CONT.)
1997 Deborah Compagnoni (ITA)
1998[1] Deborah Compagnoni (ITA)
1999 Alexandra Meissnitzer (AUT)
2001 Sonja Nef (SUI)
2002[1] Janica Kostelic (CRO)
2003 Anja Pärson (SWE)
2005 Anja Pärson (SWE)
2006[1] Julia Mancuso (USA)
2007 Nicole Hosp (AUT)

SUPERGIANT SLALOM
1988[1] Sigrid Wolf (AUT)
1989 Ulrike Maier (AUT)
1991 Ulrike Maier (AUT)
1992[1] Deborah Compagnoni (ITA)
1993 Katja Seizinger (GER)
1994[1] Diann Roffe-Steinrotter (USA)
1995 *not held*
1996 Isolde Kostner (ITA)
1997 Isolde Kostner (ITA)
1998[1] Picabo Street (USA)
1999 Alexandra Meissnitzer (AUT)
2001 Régine Cavagnoud (FRA)
2002[1] Daniela Ceccarelli (ITA)
2003 Michaela Dorfmeister (AUT)
2005 Anja Pärson (SWE)
2006[1] Michaela Dorfmeister (AUT)
2007 Anja Pärson (SWE)

[1]*Olympic champions, recognized as world champions.*

Alpine World Cup

The winner is determined by the number of points awarded for finishes in various competitions during the season.

YEAR	MEN	WOMEN	YEAR	MEN	WOMEN
1967	Jean-Claude Killy (FRA)	Nancy Greene (CAN)	1990	Pirmin Zurbriggen (SUI)	Petra Kronberger (AUT)
1968	Jean-Claude Killy (FRA)	Nancy Greene (CAN)	1991	Marc Girardelli (LUX)	Petra Kronberger (AUT)
1969	Karl Schranz (AUT)	Gertrude Gabl (AUT)			
1970	Karl Schranz (AUT)	Michele Jacot (FRA)	1992	Paul Accola (SUI)	Petra Kronberger (AUT)
1971	Gustavo Thoeni (ITA)	Annemarie Pröll (AUT)	1993	Marc Girardelli (LUX)	Anita Wachter (AUT)
1972	Gustavo Thoeni (ITA)	Annemarie Pröll (AUT)	1994	Kjetil Andre Aamodt (NOR)	Vreni Schneider (SUI)
1973	Gustavo Thoeni (ITA)	Annemarie Pröll (AUT)	1995	Alberto Tomba (ITA)	Vreni Schneider (SUI)
1974	Piero Gros (ITA)	Annemarie Moser-Pröll (AUT)	1996	Lasse Kjus (NOR)	Katja Seizinger (GER)
1975	Gustavo Thoeni (ITA)	Annemarie Moser-Pröll (AUT)	1997	Luc Alphand (FRA)	Pernilla Wiberg (SWE)
1976	Ingemar Stenmark (SWE)	Rosi Mittermaier (FRG)	1998	Hermann Maier (AUT)	Katja Seizinger (GER)
1977	Ingemar Stenmark (SWE)	Lise-Marie Morerod (SUI)	1999	Lasse Kjus (NOR)	Alexandra Meiss-nitzer (AUT)
1978	Ingemar Stenmark (SWE)	Hanni Wenzel (LIE)	2000	Hermann Maier (AUT)	Renate Götschl (AUT)
1979	Peter Luescher (SUI)	Annemarie Moser-Pröll (AUT)	2001	Hermann Maier (AUT)	Janica Kostelic (CRO)
1980	Andreas Wenzel (LIE)	Hanni Wenzel (LIE)	2002	Stephan Eberharter (AUT)	Michaela Dorf-meister (AUT)
1981	Phil Mahre (USA)	Marie-Therese Nadig (SUI)	2003	Stephan Eberharter (AUT)	Janica Kostelic (CRO)
1982	Phil Mahre (USA)	Erika Hess (SUI)	2004	Hermann Maier (AUT)	Anja Pärson (SWE)
1983	Phil Mahre (USA)	Tamara McKinney (USA)	2005	Bode Miller (USA)	Anja Pärson (SWE)
1984	Pirmin Zurbriggen (SUI)	Erika Hess (SUI)	2006	Benjamin Raich (AUT)	Janica Kostelic (CRO)
1985	Marc Girardelli (LUX)	Michela Figini (SUI)	2007	Aksel Lund Svindal (NOR)	Nicole Hosp (AUT)
1986	Marc Girardelli (LUX)	Maria Walliser (SUI)			
1987	Pirmin Zurbriggen (SUI)	Maria Walliser (SUI)			
1988	Pirmin Zurbriggen (SUI)	Michela Figini (SUI)			
1989	Marc Girardelli (LUX)	Vreni Schneider (SUI)			

Did you know? In the Olympic stadium and its immediate surroundings, the Olympic flag is flown with the flags of the nations taking part in the games. The Olympic flag presented by Baron Coubertin in 1914 is the prototype: it has a white background and in the center are five interlaced rings of blue, yellow, black, green, and red. The blue ring is on the left next to the pole. These rings represent the five continents joined together in the Olympic Movement.

Nordic Skiing World Championships—Men

Championships in some events have been held since 1924. The table shows results for the past 20 years. The next championships are scheduled to be held in January 2008 in Oberstdorf, Germany.

SPRINT

2001	Tor Arne Hetland (NOR)
2002[1]	Tor Arne Hetland (NOR)
2003	Thobias Fredriksson (SWE)
2005	Vassily Rochev (RUS)
2006[1]	Bjørn Lind (SWE)
2007	Jens Arne Svartedal (NOR)

10-KILOMETER CROSS-COUNTRY[2]

1991	Terje Langli (NOR)
1992[1]	Vegard Ulvang (NOR)
1993	Sture Sivertsen (NOR)
1994[1]	Bjørn Daehlie (NOR)
1995	Vladimir Smirnov (KAZ)

10-KM CROSS-COUNTRY[2] (CONT.)

1997	Bjørn Daehlie (NOR)
1998[1]	Bjørn Daehlie (NOR)
1999	Mika Myllyla (FIN)

15-KILOMETER CROSS-COUNTRY[2, 3]

1988[1]	Mikhail Devyatyarov (URS)
1989	Harri Kirvesniemi (FIN–classical), Gunde Svan (SWE–freestyle)
1991	Bjørn Daehlie (NOR)
1992[1]	Bjørn Daehlie (NOR)
1993	Bjørn Daehlie (NOR)
1994[1]	Bjørn Daehlie (NOR)
1995	Vladimir Smirnov (KAZ)

15-KM CROSS-COUNTRY[2, 3] (CONT.)

1997	Bjørn Daehlie (NOR)
1998[1]	Thomas Alsgaard (NOR)
1999	Thomas Alsgaard (NOR)
2001	Per Elofsson (SWE)
2002[1]	Andrus Veerpalu (EST)
2003	Axel Teichmann (GER)
2005	Pietro Piller Cottrer (ITA)
2006[1]	Andrus Veerpalu (EST)
2007	Lars Berger (NOR)

COMBINED PURSUIT[2]

2001	Per Elofsson (SWE)
2002[1]	Thomas Alsgaard (NOR), Frode Estil (NOR) (tied)
2003	Per Elofsson (SWE)

Nordic Skiing World Championships—Men (continued)

COMBINED PURSUIT[2] (CONT.)		30-KM CROSS-COUNTRY (CONT.)		50-KM CROSS-COUNTRY (CONT.)	
2005	Vincent Vittoz (FRA)	2005	*not held*	2006[1]	Giorgio Di Centa (ITA)
2006[1]	Yevgeny Dementyev (RUS)	2006[1]	Yevgeny Dementyev (RUS)	2007	Odd-Bjørn Hjelmeset
		2007	*not held*	**RELAY[4]**	
30-KILOMETER CROSS-COUNTRY				1988[1]	Sweden
1988[1]	Aleksey Prokurorov (URS)	**50-KILOMETER CROSS-COUNTRY**		1989	Sweden
		1988[1]	Gunde Svan (SWE)	1991	Norway
1989	Vladimir Smirnov (URS)	1989	Gunde Svan (SWE)	1992[1]	Norway
1991	Gunde Svan (SWE)	1991	Torgny Mogren (SWE)	1993	Norway
1992[1]	Vegard Ulvang (NOR)	1992[1]	Bjørn Daehlie (NOR)	1994[1]	Italy
1993	Bjørn Daehlie (NOR)	1993	Torgny Mogren (SWE)	1995	Norway
1994[1]	Thomas Alsgaard (NOR)	1994	Vladimir Smirnov (KAZ)	1997	Norway
1995	Vladimir Smirnov (KAZ)	1995	Silvio Fauner (ITA)	1998[1]	Norway
1997	Aleksey Prokurorov (RUS)	1997	Mika Myllyla (FIN)	1999	Austria
		1998[1]	Bjørn Daehlie (NOR)	2001	Norway
1998[1]	Mika Myllyla (FIN)	1999	Mika Myllyla (FIN)	2002[1]	Norway
1999	Mika Myllyla (FIN)	2001	Johann Mühlegg (ESP)	2003	Norway
2001	Andrus Veerpalu (EST)	2002[1]	Mikhail Ivanov (RUS)	2005	Norway
2002[1]	Christian Hoffmann (AUT)	2003	Martin Koukal (CZE)	2006[1]	Italy
2003	Thomas Alsgaard (NOR)	2005	Frode Estil (NOR)	2007	Norway

[1]*Olympic champions, recognized as world champions.* [2]*From 1991 to 1999, the 10-km event was held in tandem with the 15-km event; one event featured classical and the other freestyle technique. Medals were awarded for both races. Beginning in 2001 this pursuit race (skiers competing directly against each other rather than against the clock) led to one medal being awarded upon winning. The 10-km was discontinued, and the 15-km became a stand-alone event featuring classical technique. In 2001–03 the pursuit race featured two 10-km races; since then, two 15-km races.* [3]*18-km cross-country until 1952; 15-km in 1954 and thereafter.* [4]*Military relay until 1939; 40-km relay in 1948 and thereafter.*

Nordic Skiing World Championships—Nordic Combined

The Nordic combined involves a 15-km cross-country race and ski jumping; the combined sprint is a 7.5-km race plus ski jumping. The table shows results for the past 20 years. The next championships are scheduled to be held in January 2008 in Oberstdorf, Germany.

YEAR	COMBINED	YEAR	COMBINED (CONT.)	YEAR	TEAM (CONT.)
1988[1]	Hippolyt Kempf (SUI)	2004	*not held*	1990	*not held*
1989	Trond Einar Elden (NOR)	2005	Ronny Ackermann (GER)	1991	Austria
1990	*not held*	2006[1]	Georg Hettich (GER)	1992[1]	Japan
1991	Fred Børre Lundberg (NOR)	2007	Ronny Ackermann (GER)	1993	Japan
				1994[1]	Japan
1992[1]	Fabrice Guy (FRA)	**YEAR**	**COMBINED SPRINT**	1995	Japan
1993	Kenji Ogiwara (JPN)	1999	Bjarte Engen Vik (NOR)	1996	*not held*
1994[1]	Fred Børre Lundberg (NOR)	2000	*not held*	1997	Norway
		2001	Marco Baacke (GER)	1998[1]	Norway
1995	Fred Børre Lundberg (NOR)	2002[1]	Samppa Lajunen (FIN)	1999	Finland
		2003	Johnny Spillane (USA)	2000	*not held*
1996	*not held*	2004	*not held*	2001	Norway
1997	Kenji Ogiwara (JPN)	2005	Ronny Ackermann (GER)	2002[1]	Finland
1998[1]	Bjarte Engen Vik (NOR)	2006[1]	Felix Gottwald (AUT)	2003	Austria
1999	Bjarte Engen Vik (NOR)	2007	Hannu Manninen (FIN)	2004	*not held*
2000	*not held*			2005	Norway
2001	Bjarte Engen Vik (NOR)	**YEAR**	**TEAM**	2006[1]	Austria
2002[1]	Samppa Lajunen (FIN)	1988[1]	West Germany	2007	Finland
2003	Ronny Ackermann (GER)	1989	Norway		

[1]*Olympic champions, recognized as world champions.*

Nordic Skiing World Championships—Ski Jump

The table shows results for the past 20 years. The next championships are scheduled to be held in January 2008 in Oberstdorf, Germany.

YEAR	NORMAL HILL[1]	YEAR	NORMAL HILL[1] (CONT.)	YEAR	NORMAL HILL[1] (CONT.)
1988[2]	Matti Nykänen (FIN)	1992[2]	Ernst Vettori (AUT)	1995	Takanobu Okabe (JPN)
1989	Jens Weissflog (GDR)	1993	Masahiko Harada (JPN)	1997	Janne Ahonen (FIN)
1991	Heinz Kuttin (AUT)	1994[2]	Espen Bredesen (NOR)	1998[2]	Jani Soininen (FIN)

Nordic Skiing World Championships—Ski Jump (continued)

YEAR	NORMAL HILL[1] (CONT.)	YEAR	LARGE HILL[3] (CONT.)	YEAR	TEAM JUMP (LARGE HILL[3])
1999	Kazuyoshi Funaki (JPN)	1998[2]	Kazuyoshi Funaki (JPN)	1988[2]	Finland
2001	Adam Malysz (POL)	1999	Martin Schmitt (GER)	1989	Finland
2002[2]	Simon Ammann (SUI)	2001	Martin Schmitt (GER)	1991	Austria
2003	Adam Malysz (POL)	2002[2]	Simon Ammann (SUI)	1992[2]	Finland
2005	Rok Benkovic (SLO)	2003	Adam Malysz (POL)	1993	Norway
2006[2]	Lars Bystøl (NOR)	2005	Janne Ahonen (FIN)	1994[2]	Germany
2007	Adam Malysz (POL)	2006[2]	Thomas Morgenstern (AUT)	1995	Finland
		2007	Simon Ammann (SUI)	1997	Finland
YEAR	**LARGE HILL[3]**			1998[2]	Japan
1988[2]	Matti Nykänen (FIN)	**YEAR**	**TEAM JUMP (NORMAL HILL[1])**	1999	Germany
1989	Jari Puikkonen (FIN)	2001	Austria	2001	Germany
1991	Franci Petek (YUG)	2002	not held	2002[2]	Germany
1992[2]	Toni Nieminen (FIN)	2003	not held	2003	Finland
1993	Espen Bredesen (NOR)	2005	Austria	2005	Austria
1994[2]	Jens Weissflog (GER)	2006	not held	2006[2]	Austria
1995	Tommy Ingebrigtsen (NOR)	2007	not held	2007	Austria
1997	Masahiko Harada (JPN)				

[1]The distance of the jump in the normal hill competition has varied over time; since 1992 it has been set at either 90 or 95 meters.   [2]Olympic champions, recognized as world champions.   [3]The distance of the jump in the large hill competition has varied over time; since 1992 it has been set at either 120 or 125 meters.

Nordic Skiing World Championships—Women

Championships in some events have been held since 1952. The table shows results for the past 20 years. The next championships are scheduled to be held in January 2008 in Oberstdorf, Germany.

SPRINT
- 2001   Pirjo Manninen (FIN)
- 2002[1]   Yuliya Chepalova (RUS)
- 2003   Marit Bjørgen (NOR)
- 2005   Emilie Öhrstig (SWE)
- 2006[1]   Chandra Crawford (CAN)
- 2007   Astrid Jacobsen (NOR)

5-KILOMETER CROSS-COUNTRY[2]
- 1988[1]   Marjo Matikainen (FIN)
- 1989   not held
- 1991   Trude Dybendahl (NOR)
- 1992[1]   Marjut Lukkarinen (FIN)
- 1993   Larisa Lazutina (RUS)
- 1994[1]   Lyubov Yegorova (RUS)
- 1995   Larisa Lazutina (RUS)
- 1997   Yelena Vyalbe (RUS)
- 1998[1]   Larisa Lazutina (RUS)
- 1999   Bente Martinsen (NOR)

10-KILOMETER CROSS-COUNTRY[2]
- 1988[1]   Vida Ventsene (URS)
- 1989   Marja-Liisa Kirvesniemi (FIN–classical); Yelena Vyalbe (URS–freestyle)
- 1991   Yelena Vyalbe (URS)
- 1992[1]   Lyubov Yegorova (UNT[3])
- 1993   Stefania Belmondo (ITA)
- 1994[1]   Lyubov Yegorova (RUS)
- 1995   Larisa Lazutina (RUS)
- 1997   Stefania Belmondo (ITA)
- 1998[1]   Larisa Lazutina (RUS)
- 1999   Stefania Belmondo (ITA)
- 2001   Bente Skari-Martinsen (NOR)

10-KM CROSS-COUNTRY[2] (CONT.)
- 2002[1]   Bente Skari (NOR)
- 2003   Bente Skari (NOR)
- 2005   Katerina Neumannova (CZE)
- 2006[1]   Kristina Smigun (EST)
- 2007   Katerina Neumannova (CZE)

COMBINED PURSUIT[2]
- 2001   Virpi Kuitunen (FIN)
- 2002[1]   Beckie Scott (CAN)
- 2003   Kristina Smigun (EST)
- 2005   Yuliya Chepalova (RUS)
- 2006[1]   Kristina Smigun (EST)
- 2007   Olga Zavyalova (RUS)

15-KILOMETER CROSS-COUNTRY
- 1989   Marjo Matikainen (FIN)
- 1991   Yelena Vyalbe (URS)
- 1992[1]   Lyubov Yegorova (URS)
- 1993   Yelena Vyalbe (RUS)
- 1994[1]   Manuela Di Centa (ITA)
- 1995   Larissa Lazutina (RUS)
- 1997   Yelena Vyalbe (RUS)
- 1998[1]   Olga Danilova (RUS)
- 1999   Stefania Belmondo (ITA)
- 2001   Bente Skari-Martinsen (NOR)
- 2002[1]   Stefania Belmondo (ITA)
- 2003   Bente Skari (NOR)

20-KILOMETER CROSS-COUNTRY
- 1988[1]   Tamara Tikhonova (URS)

30-KILOMETER CROSS-COUNTRY
- 1989   Yelena Vyalbe (URS)

30-KM CROSS-COUNTRY (CONT.)
- 1991   Lyubov Yegorova (URS)
- 1992[1]   Stefania Belmondo (ITA)
- 1993   Stefania Belmondo (ITA)
- 1994[1]   Manuela Di Centa (ITA)
- 1995   Yelena Vyalbe (RUS)
- 1997   Yelena Vyalbe (RUS)
- 1998[1]   Yulia Chepalova (RUS)
- 1999   Larisa Lazutina (RUS)
- 2001   canceled
- 2002[1]   Gabriella Paruzzi (ITA)
- 2003   Olga Savyalova (RUS)
- 2005   Marit Bjørgen (NOR)
- 2006[1]   Katerina Neumannova (CZE)
- 2007   Virpi Kuitunen (FIN)

RELAY[4]
- 1988[1]   USSR
- 1989   Finland
- 1991   USSR
- 1992[1]   Unified Team
- 1993   Russia
- 1994[1]   Russia
- 1995   Russia
- 1997   Russia
- 1998[1]   Russia
- 1999   Russia
- 2001   Russia
- 2002[1]   Germany
- 2003   Germany
- 2005   Norway
- 2006[1]   Russia
- 2007   Finland

[1]Olympic champions, recognized as world champions.   [2]From 1991 to 1999, the 5-km event was held in tandem with the 10-km event; one event featured classical and the other freestyle technique. Medals were awarded for both races. Beginning in 2001 this pursuit race (skiers competing directly against each other rather than against the clock) led to one medal being awarded upon winning. The 5-km was discontinued, and

Nordic Skiing World Championships—Women (continued)

the 10-km became a stand-alone event featuring classical technique. In 2001–03 the pursuit race featured two 5-km races; since then, two 7.5-km races. [3]*Unified Team, consisting of athletes from the Commonwealth of Independent States plus Georgia.* [4]*15-km relay until 1974; 20-km in 1976 and thereafter.*

Nordic World Cup

The winner is determined by the number of points awarded for finishes in various competitions during the season.

YEAR	MEN	WOMEN	YEAR	MEN	WOMEN
1979	Oddvar Braa (NOR)	Galina Kulakova (URS)	1994	Vladimir Smirnov (KAZ)	Manuela Di Centa (ITA)
1981	Aleksandr Zavyalov (URS)	Raisa Smetanina (URS)	1995	Bjørn Daehlie (NOR)	Yelena Vyalbe (RUS)
1982	Bill Koch (USA)	Berit Aunli (NOR)	1996	Bjørn Daehlie (NOR)	Manuela Di Centa (ITA)
1983	Aleksandr Zavyalov (URS)	Marja-Liisa Hämä-lainen (FIN)	1997	Bjørn Daehlie (NOR)	Yelena Vyalbe (RUS)
1984	Gunde Svan (SWE)	Marja-Liisa Hämä-lainen (FIN)	1998	Thomas Alsgaard (NOR)	Larisa Lazutina (RUS)
1985	Gunde Svan (SWE)	Anette Boe (NOR)	1999	Bjørn Daehlie (NOR)	Bente Martinsen (NOR)
1986	Gunde Svan (SWE)	Marjo Matikainen (FIN)	2000	Johann Mühlegg (ESP)	Bente Skari-Martinsen (NOR)
1987	Torgny Mogren (SWE)	Marjo Matikainen (FIN)	2001	Per Elofsson (SWE)	Yuliya Chepalova (RUS)
1988	Gunde Svan (SWE)	Marjo Matikainen (FIN)	2002	Per Elofsson (SWE)	Bente Skari (NOR)
1989	Gunde Svan (SWE)	Yelena Vyalbe (URS)	2003	Mathias Fredriksson (SWE)	Bente Skari (NOR)
1990	Vegard Ulvang (NOR)	Larisa Lazutina (URS)	2004	Rene Sommerfeldt (GER)	Gabriella Paruzzi (ITA)
1991	Vladimir Smirnov (URS)	Yelena Vyalbe (URS)	2005	Axel Teichmann (GER)	Marit Bjørgen (NOR)
1992	Bjørn Daehlie (NOR)	Yelena Vyalbe (URS)	2006	Tobias Angerer (GER)	Marit Bjørgen (NOR)
1993	Bjørn Daehlie (NOR)	Lyudmila Yegorova (RUS)	2007	Tobias Angerer (GER)	Virpi Kuitunen (FIN)

Did you know? Before the mid-19th century, golf balls were made of leather and stuffed with feathers. Making a "featherie" was an exacting art, requiring ballmakers to stuff a "top-hat full" of wet feathers into a leather shell. The shell was hammered into a round shape as it dried and hardened. A well-struck featherie could travel some 180–200 yards. The most popular golf balls in the late 19th century were made of gutta-percha, a latex-derived material. The balls would occasionally fragment upon impact, which necessitated a new rule: "If a ball splits into separate pieces, another ball may be laid down where the largest portion lies."

Sled Dog Racing

Sled dog racing (or dogsled racing) is the sport of racing sleds pulled by sled dogs over snow-covered cross-country courses; it was developed from a principal **Eskimo** method of transportation. Dogsleds are still used for transportation and working purposes in some northern areas, although they largely have been replaced by aircraft and snowmobiles. The modern **racing sled** weighs about 30 lb (13.5 kg). Its frame (traditionally of ash) is lashed together with leather and its runners sheathed with steel or aluminum. **Dogs** usually are specially bred and trained Eskimo dogs, Siberian huskies, Samoyeds, or Alaskan Malamutes. The **teams** typically consist of 4–10 dogs, with more being used for longer races. They are driven in pairs in a gang hitch.

Control of the team is by voice, though drivers may carry whips as well. In open country, point-to-point races are held. In more populated areas, back roads form the course, with races usually varying in length from 12–30 mi (19–48 km). A team of dogs can pull the sled and its driver, called a **musher**, at speeds of more than 20 mph (32 km/hr). Teams start at intervals and race for time. Usually, all dogs must finish in the hitch order in which they started, and an injured dog must be carried on the sled.

A dogsled-racing event was included in the 1932 **Winter Olympics** program. The sport is popular in Norway, Canada, Alaska, and the northern states of the contiguous United States. The **Iditarod Trail Sled Dog Race** has been held in Alaska since 1973.

Iditarod Trail Sled Dog Race

Men and women compete together in this annual race held in March between Anchorage and Nome AK. A short race of 56 mi (90 km) organized in 1967 evolved in 1973 into the current race. The course, roughly 1,100 mi (1,770 km) long, partially follows the old Iditarod Trail dogsled mail route blazed from Knik to Nome in 1910. The course length and route vary slightly from year to year, and the middle third takes alternate routes in odd and even years. In 1976 the US Congress designated the original Iditarod Trail as a National Historic Trail.
Iditarod Web site: <www.iditarod.com>.

YEAR	WINNER	TIME	YEAR	WINNER	TIME
1973	Dick Wilmarth	20 days 49 min 41 sec	1991	Rick Swenson	12 days 16 hr 34 min 39 sec
1974	Carl Huntington	20 days 15 hr 2 min 7 sec	1992	Martin Buser	10 days 19 hr 17 min 15 sec
1975	Emmitt Peters	14 days 14 hr 43 min 45 sec	1993	Jeff King	10 days 15 hr 38 min 15 sec
1976	Gerald Riley	18 days 22 hr 58 min 17 sec	1994	Martin Buser	10 days 13 hr 5 min 39 sec
1977	Rick Swenson	16 days 16 hr 27 min 13 sec	1995	Doug Swingley	10 days 13 hr 2 min 39 sec
1978	Dick Mackey	14 days 18 hr 52 min 24 sec	1996	Jeff King	9 days 5 hr 43 min 13 sec
1979	Rick Swenson	15 days 10 hr 37 min 47 sec	1997	Martin Buser	9 days 8 hr 30 min 45 sec
1980	Joe May	14 days 7 hr 11 min 51 sec	1998	Jeff King	9 days 5 hr 52 min 26 sec
1981	Rick Swenson	12 days 8 hr 45 min 2 sec	1999	Doug Swingley	9 days 14 hr 31 min 7 sec
1982	Rick Swenson	16 days 4 hr 40 min 10 sec	2000	Doug Swingley	9 days 58 min 6 sec
1983	Rick Mackey	12 days 14 hr 10 min 44 sec	2001	Doug Swingley	9 days 19 hr 55 min 50 sec
1984	Dean Osmar	12 days 15 hr 7 min 33 sec	2002	Martin Buser	8 days 22 hr 46 min 2 sec
1985	Libby Riddles	18 days 20 hr 17 sec	2003	Robert Sørlie	9 days 15 hr 47 min 36 sec
1986	Susan Butcher	11 days 15 hr 6 min 0 sec	2004	Mitch Seavey	9 days 12 hr 20 min 22 sec
1987	Susan Butcher	11 days 2 hr 5 min 13 sec	2005	Robert Sørlie	9 days 18 hr 39 min 31 sec
1988	Susan Butcher	11 days 11 hr 41 min 40 sec	2006	Jeff King	9 days 11 hr 11 min 36 sec
1989	Joe Runyan	11 days 5 hr 24 min 34 sec	2007	Lance Mackey	9 days 5 hr 8 min 41 sec
1990	Susan Butcher	11 days 1 hr 53 min 23 sec			

Swimming

The **Fédération Internationale de Natation** (International Swimming Federation, FINA, still known by its French acronym that includes an "a" for "Amateur"; founded 1908) is the world governing body for amateur swimming. It held the first world swimming championships in 1973. After 1975 the FINA championships were held in non-Olympic, even-numbered years. (An exception was the 1991 championship that took place in Australia during the summer month of January.) Diving, synchronized (or synchro) swimming, and water polo events are included in the competition.

A distinction is made between **long-course** (50-m) and **short-course** (25-m) pools for purposes of record setting; world championships and other major contests were long held in 50-m pools, but now a separate World Championship and World Cup take place for 25-m pools.
International Swimming Federation Web site: <www.fina.org>.

World Swimming and Diving Championships—Men

The next competition is scheduled to be held in 2009 in Rome, Italy.

swimming

50-M FREESTYLE
1986	Tom Jager (USA)
1991	Tom Jager (USA)
1994	Aleksandr Popov (RUS)
1998	Bill Pilczuk (USA)
2001	Anthony Ervin (USA)
2003	Aleksandr Popov (RUS)
2005	Roland Schoeman (RSA)
2007	Benjamin Wildman-Tobriner (USA)

100-M FREESTYLE
1973	Jim Montgomery (USA)
1975	Andy Coan (USA)
1978	David McCagg (USA)
1982	Jorg Woithe (GDR)
1986	Matt Biondi (USA)
1991	Matt Biondi (USA)
1994	Aleksandr Popov (RUS)
1998	Aleksandr Popov (RUS)

100-M FREESTYLE (CONT.)
2001	Anthony Ervin (USA)
2003	Aleksandr Popov (RUS)
2005	Filippo Magnini (ITA)
2007	Filippo Magnini (ITA)

200-M FREESTYLE
1973	Jim Montgomery (USA)
1975	Tim Shaw (USA)
1978	Bill Forrester (USA)
1982	Michael Gross (FRG)
1986	Michael Gross (FRG)
1991	Giorgio Lamberti (ITA)
1994	Antti Kasvio (FIN)
1998	Michael Klim (AUS)
2001	Ian Thorpe (AUS)
2003	Ian Thorpe (AUS)
2005	Michael Phelps (USA)
2007	Michael Phelps (USA)

400-M FREESTYLE
1973	Rick DeMont (USA)
1975	Tim Shaw (USA)
1978	Vladimir Salnikov (URS)
1982	Vladimir Salnikov (URS)
1986	Rainer Henkel (FRG)
1991	Jörg Hoffmann (GER)
1994	Kieren Perkins (AUS)
1998	Ian Thorpe (AUS)
2001	Ian Thorpe (AUS)
2003	Ian Thorpe (AUS)
2005	Grant Hackett (AUS)
2007	Park Tae Hwan (KOR)

800-M FREESTYLE
2001	Ian Thorpe (AUS)
2003	Grant Hackett (AUS)
2005	Grant Hackett (AUS)
2007	Przemyslaw Stanczyk (POL)

World Swimming and Diving Championships—Men (continued)

swimming

1,500-M FREESTYLE
1973 Steve Holland (AUS)
1975 Tim Shaw (USA)
1978 Vladimir Salnikov (URS)
1982 Vladimir Salnikov (URS)
1986 Rainer Henkel (FRG)
1991 Jörg Hoffmann (GER)
1994 Kieren Perkins (AUS)
1998 Grant Hackett (AUS)
2001 Grant Hackett (AUS)
2003 Grant Hackett (AUS)
2005 Grant Hackett (AUS)
2007 Mateusz Sawrymowicz (POL)

50-M BACKSTROKE
2001 Randall Bal (USA)
2003 Thomas Rupprath (GER)
2005 Aristeidis Grigoriadis (GRE)
2007 Gerhard Zandberg (RSA)

100-M BACKSTROKE
1973 Roland Matthes (GDR)
1975 Roland Matthes (GDR)
1978 Bob Jackson (USA)
1982 Dirk Richter (GDR)
1986 Igor Polyansky (URS)
1991 Jeff Rouse (USA)
1994 Martín Lopez-Zubero (ESP)
1998 Lenny Krayzelburg (USA)
2001 Matt Welsh (AUS)
2003 Aaron Peirsol (USA)
2005 Aaron Peirsol (USA)
2007 Aaron Peirsol (USA)

200-M BACKSTROKE
1973 Roland Matthes (GDR)
1975 Zoltan Verraszto (HUN)
1978 Jesse Vassallo (USA)
1982 Rick Carey (USA)
1986 Igor Polyansky (URS)
1991 Martín Lopez-Zubero (ESP)
1994 Vladimir Selkov (RUS)
1998 Lenny Krayzelburg (USA)
2001 Aaron Peirsol (USA)
2003 Aaron Peirsol (USA)
2005 Aaron Peirsol (USA)
2007 Ryan Lochte (USA)

50-M BREASTSTROKE
2001 Oleg Lisogor (UKR)
2003 James Gibson (GBR)
2005 Mark Warnecke (GER)
2007 Oleg Lisogor (UKR)

100-M BREASTSTROKE
1973 John Hencken (USA)
1975 David Wilkie (GBR)
1978 Walter Kusch (FRG)
1982 Steve Lundquist (USA)
1986 Victor Davis (CAN)
1991 Norbert Rozsa (HUN)

100-M BREASTSTROKE (CONT.)
1994 Norbert Rozsa (HUN)
1998 Fred De Burghgraeve (BEL)
2001 Roman Sloudnov (RUS)
2003 Kosuke Kitajima (JPN)
2005 Brendan Hansen (USA)
2007 Brendan Hansen (USA)

200-M BREASTSTROKE
1973 David Wilkie (GBR)
1975 David Wilkie (GBR)
1978 Nick Nevid (USA)
1982 Victor Davis (CAN)
1986 Joszef Szabo (HUN)
1991 Mike Barrowman (USA)
1994 Norbert Rozsa (HUN)
1998 Kurt Grote (USA)
2001 Brendan Hansen (USA)
2003 Kosuke Kitajima (JPN)
2005 Brendan Hansen (USA)
2007 Kosuke Kitajima (JPN)

50-M BUTTERFLY
2001 Geoff Huegill (AUS)
2003 Matt Welsh (AUS)
2005 Roland Schoeman (RSA)
2007 Roland Schoeman (RSA)

100-M BUTTERFLY
1973 Bruce Robertson (CAN)
1975 Greg Jagenburg (USA)
1978 Joseph Bottom (USA)
1982 Matt Gribble (USA)
1986 Pablo Morales (USA)
1991 Anthony Nesty (SUR)
1994 Rafal Szukala (POL)
1998 Michael Klim (AUS)
2001 Lars Frolander (SWE)
2003 Ian Crocker (USA)
2005 Ian Crocker (USA)
2007 Michael Phelps (USA)

200-M BUTTERFLY
1973 Robin Backhaus (USA)
1975 Bill Forrester (USA)
1978 Mike Bruner (USA)
1982 Michael Gross (FRG)
1986 Michael Gross (FRG)
1991 Melvin Stewart (USA)
1994 Denis Pankratov (RUS)
1998 Denys Silantyev (UKR)
2001 Michael Phelps (USA)
2003 Michael Phelps (USA)
2005 Pawel Korzeniowski (POL)
2007 Michael Phelps (USA)

200-M INDIVIDUAL MEDLEY
1973 Gunnar Larsson (SWE)
1975 Andras Hargitay (HUN)
1978 Graham Smith (CAN)
1982 A. Sidorenko (URS)
1986 Tamas Darnyi (HUN)
1991 Tamas Darnyi (HUN)
1994 Jani Sievinen (FIN)

200-M INDIVIDUAL MEDLEY (CONT.)
1998 Marcel Wouda (NED)
2001 M. Rosolino (ITA)
2003 Michael Phelps (USA)
2005 Michael Phelps (USA)
2007 Michael Phelps (USA)

400-M INDIVIDUAL MEDLEY
1973 Andras Hargitay (HUN)
1975 Andras Hargitay (HUN)
1978 Jesse Vassallo (USA)
1982 Ricardo Prado (BRA)
1986 Tamas Darnyi (HUN)
1991 Tamas Darnyi (HUN)
1994 Tom Dolan (USA)
1998 Tom Dolan (USA)
2001 Alessio Boggiatto (ITA)
2003 Michael Phelps (USA)
2005 Laszlo Cseh (HUN)
2007 Michael Phelps (USA)

4 × 100-M FREESTYLE RELAY
1973 United States
1975 United States
1978 United States
1982 United States
1986 United States
1991 United States
1994 United States
1998 United States
2001 Australia
2003 Russia
2005 United States
2007 United States

4 × 200-M FREESTYLE RELAY
1973 United States
1975 West Germany
1978 United States
1982 United States
1986 East Germany
1991 Germany
1994 Sweden
1998 Australia
2001 Australia
2003 Australia
2005 United States
2007 United States

4 × 100-M MEDLEY RELAY
1973 United States
1975 United States
1978 United States
1982 United States
1986 United States
1991 United States
1994 United States
1998 Australia
2001 United States
2003 United States
2005 United States
2007 Australia

World Swimming and Diving Championships—Men (continued)

diving

1-M SPRINGBOARD
1991	Edwin Jongejans (NED)
1994	Evan Stewart (ZIM)
1998	Yu Zhuocheng (CHN)
2001	Wang Feng (CHN)
2003	Xu Xiang (CHN)
2005	Alexandre Despatie (CAN)
2007	Luo Yutong (CHN)

3-M SPRINGBOARD
1973	Phil Boggs (USA)
1975	Phil Boggs (USA)

3-M SPRINGBOARD (CONT.)
1978	Phil Boggs (USA)
1982	Greg Louganis (USA)
1986	Greg Louganis (USA)
1991	Kent Ferguson (USA)
1994	Yu Zhuocheng (CHN)
1998	Dmitry Sautin (RUS)
2001	Dmitry Sautin (RUS)
2003	Aleksandr Dobrosok (RUS)
2005	Alexandre Despatie (CAN)
2007	Qin Kai (CHN)

PLATFORM
1973	Klaus Dibiasi (ITA)
1975	Klaus Dibiasi (ITA)
1978	Greg Louganis (USA)
1982	Greg Louganis (USA)
1986	Greg Louganis (USA)
1991	Sun Shuwei (CHN)
1994	Dmitry Sautin (RUS)
1998	Dmitry Sautin (RUS)
2001	Tian Liang (CHN)
2003	Alexandre Despatie (CAN)
2005	Hu Jia (CHN)
2007	Gleb Galperin (RUS)

World Swimming and Diving Championships—Women
The next competition is scheduled to be held in 2009 in Rome, Italy.

swimming

50-M FREESTYLE
1986	Tamara Costache (ROM)
1991	Zhuang Yong (CHN)
1994	Le Jingyi (CHN)
1998	Amy Van Dyken (USA)
2001	Inge De Bruijn (NED)
2003	Inge De Bruijn (NED)
2005	Lisbeth Lenton (AUS)
2007	Lisbeth Lenton (AUS)

100-M FREESTYLE
1973	Kornelia Ender (GDR)
1975	Kornelia Ender (GDR)
1978	Barbara Krause (GDR)
1982	Birgit Meineke (GDR)
1986	Kristin Otto (GDR)
1991	Nicole Haislett (USA)
1994	Le Jingyi (CHN)
1998	Jenny Thompson (USA)
2001	Inge De Bruijn (NED)
2003	Hanna-Maria Seppälä (FIN)
2005	Jodie Henry (AUS)
2007	Lisbeth Lenton (AUS)

200-M FREESTYLE
1973	Keena Rothhammer (USA)
1975	Shirley Babashoff (USA)
1978	Cynthia Woodhead (USA)
1982	Annemarie Verstappen (NED)
1986	Heike Friedrich (GDR)
1991	Hayley Lewis (AUS)
1994	Franziska van Almsick (GER)
1998	Claudia Poll (CRC)
2001	Giaan Rooney (AUS)
2003	Alena Popchanka (BLR)
2005	Solenne Figues (FRA)
2007	Laure Manaudou (FRA)

400-M FREESTYLE
1973	Heather Greenwood (USA)
1975	Shirley Babashoff (USA)
1978	Tracey Wickham (AUS)
1982	Carmela Schmidt (GDR)

400-M FREESTYLE (CONT.)
1986	Heike Friedrich (GDR)
1991	Janet Evans (USA)
1994	Yang Aihua (CHN)
1998	Chen Yan (CHN)
2001	Yana Klochkova (UKR)
2003	Hannah Stockbauer (GER)
2005	Laure Manaudou (FRA)
2007	Laure Manaudou (FRA)

800-M FREESTYLE
1973	Novella Calligaris (ITA)
1975	Jenny Turrall (AUS)
1978	Tracey Wickham (AUS)
1982	Kim Linehan (USA)
1986	Astrid Strauss (GDR)
1991	Janet Evans (USA)
1994	Janet Evans (USA)
1998	Brooke Bennett (USA)
2001	Hannah Stockbauer (GER)
2003	Hannah Stockbauer (GER)
2005	Kate Ziegler (USA)
2007	Kate Ziegler (USA)

1,500-M FREESTYLE
2001	Hannah Stockbauer (GER)
2003	Hannah Stockbauer (GER)
2005	Kate Ziegler (USA)
2007	Kate Ziegler (USA)

50-M BREASTSTROKE
2001	Luo Xuejuan (CHN)
2003	Luo Xuejuan (CHN)
2005	Jade Edmistone (AUS)
2007	Jessica Hardy (USA)

100-M BREASTSTROKE
1973	Renate Vogel (GDR)
1975	Hannelore Anke (GDR)
1978	Yuliya Bogdanova (URS)
1982	Ute Geweniger (GDR)
1986	Sylvia Gerasch (GDR)
1991	Linley Frame (AUS)
1994	Samantha Riley (AUS)
1998	Kristy Kowal (USA)

100-M BREASTSTROKE (CONT.)
2001	Luo Xuejuan (CHN)
2003	Luo Xuejuan (CHN)
2005	Leisel Jones (AUS)
2007	Leisel Jones (AUS)

200-M BREASTSTROKE
1973	Renate Vogel (GDR)
1975	Hannelore Anke (GDR)
1978	Lina Kachushite (URS)
1982	Svetlana Varganova (URS)
1986	Silke Hörner (GDR)
1991	Yelena Volkova (URS)
1994	Samantha Riley (AUS)
1998	Agnes Kovacs (HUN)
2001	Agnes Kovacs (HUN)
2003	Amanda Beard (USA)
2005	Leisel Jones (AUS)
2007	Leisel Jones (AUS)

50-M BUTTERFLY
2001	Inge De Bruijn (NED)
2003	Inge De Bruijn (NED)
2005	Danni Miatke (AUS)
2007	Therese Alshammar (SWE)

100-M BUTTERFLY
1973	Kornelia Ender (GDR)
1975	Kornelia Ender (GDR)
1978	Joan Pennington (USA)
1982	Mary T. Meagher (USA)
1986	Kornelia Gressler (GDR)
1991	Qian Hong (CHN)
1994	Liu Limin (CHN)
1998	Jenny Thompson (USA)
2001	Petria Thomas (AUS)
2003	Jenny Thompson (USA)
2005	Jessicah Schipper (AUS)
2007	Lisbeth Lenton (AUS)

200-M BUTTERFLY
1973	Rosemarie Kother (GDR)
1975	Rosemarie Kother (GDR)
1978	Tracy Caulkins (USA)

World Swimming and Diving Championships—Women (continued)

swimming

200-M BUTTERFLY (CONT.)
1982 Ines Geissler (GDR)
1986 Mary T. Meagher (USA)
1991 Summer Sanders (USA)
1994 Liu Limin (CHN)
1998 Susie O'Neill (AUS)
2001 Petria Thomas (AUS)
2003 Otylia Jedrzejczak (POL)
2005 Otylia Jedrzejczak (POL)
2007 Jessicah Schipper (AUS)

50-M BACKSTROKE
2001 Haley Cope (USA)
2003 Nina Zhivanevskaya (ESP)
2005 Giaan Rooney (AUS)
2007 Leila Vaziri (USA)

100-M BACKSTROKE
1973 Ulrike Richter (GDR)
1975 Ulrike Richter (GDR)
1978 Linda Jezek (USA)
1982 Kristin Otto (GDR)
1986 Betsy Mitchell (USA)
1991 Krisztina Egerszegi (HUN)
1994 He Cihong (CHN)
1998 Lea Maurer (USA)
2001 Natalie Coughlin (USA)
2003 Antje Buschschulte (GER)
2005 Kirsty Coventry (ZIM)
2007 Natalie Coughlin (USA)

200-M BACKSTROKE
1973 Melissa Belote (USA)
1975 Birgit Treiber (GDR)
1978 Linda Jezek (USA)
1982 Cornelia Sirch (GDR)
1986 Cornelia Sirch (GDR)

200-M BACKSTROKE (CONT.)
1991 Krisztina Egerszegi (HUN)
1994 He Cihong (CHN)
1998 Roxana Maracineanu (FRA)
2001 Diana Mocanu (ROM)
2003 Katy Sexton (GBR)
2005 Kirsty Coventry (ZIM)
2007 Margaret Hoelzer (USA)

200-M INDIVIDUAL MEDLEY
1973 Andrea Hubner (GDR)
1975 Kathy Heddy (USA)
1978 Tracy Caulkins (USA)
1982 Petra Schneider (GDR)
1986 Kristin Otto (GDR)
1991 Lin Li (CHN)
1994 Lu Bin (CHN)
1998 Wu Yanyan (CHN)
2001 Martha Bowen (USA)
2003 Yana Klochkova (UKR)
2005 Katie Hoff (USA)
2007 Katie Hoff (USA)

400-M INDIVIDUAL MEDLEY
1973 Gudrun Wegner (GDR)
1975 Ulrika Tauber (GDR)
1978 Tracy Caulkins (USA)
1982 Petra Schneider (GDR)
1986 Kathleen Nord (GDR)
1991 Lin Li (CHN)
1994 Dai Guohong (CHN)
1998 Chen Yan (CHN)
2001 Yana Klochkova (UKR)
2003 Yana Klochkova (UKR)
2005 Katie Hoff (USA)
2007 Katie Hoff (USA)

4 × 100-M FREESTYLE RELAY
1973 East Germany
1975 East Germany
1978 United States
1982 East Germany
1986 East Germany
1991 United States
1994 China
1998 United States
2001 Germany
2003 United States
2005 Australia
2007 Australia

4 × 200-M FREESTYLE RELAY
1986 East Germany
1991 Germany
1994 China
1998 Germany
2001 Great Britain
2003 United States
2005 United States
2007 United States

4 × 100-M MEDLEY RELAY
1973 East Germany
1975 East Germany
1978 United States
1982 East Germany
1986 East Germany
1991 United States
1994 China
1998 United States
2001 Australia
2003 China
2005 Australia
2007 Australia

diving

1-M SPRINGBOARD
1991 Gao Min (CHN)
1994 Chen Lixia (CHN)
1998 Irina Lashko (RUS)
2001 Blythe Hartley (CAN)
2003 Irina Lashko (AUS)
2005 Blythe Hartley (CAN)
2007 He Zi (CHN)

3-M SPRINGBOARD
1973 Christa Kohler (GDR)
1975 Irina Kalinina (URS)
1978 Irina Kalinina (URS)

3-M SPRINGBOARD (CONT.)
1982 Megan Neyer (USA)
1986 Gao Min (CHN)
1991 Gao Min (CHN)
1994 Tan Shuping (CHN)
1998 Yulia Pakhalina (RUS)
2001 Guo Jingjing (CHN)
2003 Guo Jingjing (CHN)
2005 Guo Jingjing (CHN)
2007 Guo Jingjing (CHN)

PLATFORM
1973 Ulrika Knape (SWE)

PLATFORM (CONT.)
1975 Janet Ely (USA)
1978 Irina Kalinina (URS)
1982 Wendy Wyland (USA)
1986 Chen Lin (CHN)
1991 Fu Mingxia (CHN)
1994 Fu Mingxia (CHN)
1998 Olena Zhupina (UKR)
2001 Xu Mian (CHN)
2003 Emilie Heymans (CAN)
2005 Laura Wilkinson (USA)
2007 Wang Xin (CHN)

Did you know?

Jim Perry (with the Minnesota Twins in 1970) and Gaylord Perry (with the Cleveland Indians in 1972) are the only brothers in Major League Baseball history to both win Cy Young awards. For all their excellence in pitching the ball, they struggled offensively. Gaylord Perry declared in 1963, "They'll put a man on the moon before I hit a home run." Hours after Neil Armstrong set foot on the moon (20 Jul 1969), Perry hit the only home run of his major league career.

Swimming World Records—Long Course (50-m)

men

EVENT	RECORD HOLDER (NATIONALITY)	PERFORMANCE	DATE
50-m freestyle	Aleksandr Popov (RUS)	21.64 sec	16 Jun 2000
100-m freestyle	Pieter van den Hoogenband (NED)	47.84 sec	19 Sep 2000
200-m freestyle	Michael Phelps (USA)	1 min 43.86 sec	27 Mar 2007
400-m freestyle	Ian Thorpe (AUS)	3 min 40.08 sec	30 Jul 2002
800-m freestyle	Grant Hackett (AUS)	7 min 38.65 sec	27 Jul 2005
1,500-m freestyle	Grant Hackett (AUS)	14 min 34.56 sec	29 Jul 2001
50-m backstroke	Thomas Rupprath (GER)	24.80 sec	27 Jul 2003
100-m backstroke	Aaron Peirsol (USA)	52.98 sec	27 Mar 2007
200-m backstroke	Ryan Lochte (USA)	1 min 54.32 sec	30 Mar 2007
50-m breaststroke	Oleg Lisogor (UKR)	27.18 sec	2 Aug 2002
100-m breaststroke	Brendan Hansen (USA)	59.13 sec	1 Aug 2006
200-m breaststroke	Brendan Hansen (USA)	2 min 08.50 sec	20 Aug 2006
50-m butterfly	Roland Schoeman (RSA)	22.96 sec	25 Jul 2005
100-m butterfly	Ian Crocker (USA)	50.40 sec	30 Jul 2005
200-m butterfly	Michael Phelps (USA)	1 min 52.09 sec	28 Mar 2007
200-m individual medley	Michael Phelps (USA)	1 min 54.98 sec	29 Mar 2007
400-m individual medley	Michael Phelps (USA)	4 min 06.22 sec	1 Apr 2007
4 × 100-m free relay	United States (Michael Phelps, Neil Walker, Cullen Jones, Jason Lezak)	3 min 12.46 sec	19 Aug 2006
4 × 200-m free relay	United States (Michael Phelps, Ryan Lochte, Klete Keller, Peter Vanderkaay)	7 min 03.24 sec	30 Mar 2007
4 × 100-m medley relay	United States (Aaron Peirsol, Brendan Hansen, Ian Crocker, Jason Lezak)	3 min 30.68 sec	21 Aug 2004

women

EVENT	RECORD HOLDER (NATIONALITY)	PERFORMANCE	DATE
50-m freestyle	Inge de Bruijn (NED)	24.13 sec	22 Sep 2000
100-m freestyle	Britta Steffen (GER)	53.30 sec	2 Aug 2006
200-m freestyle	Laure Manaudou (FRA)	1 min 55.52 sec	28 Mar 2007
400-m freestyle	Laure Manaudou (FRA)	4 min 02.13 sec	6 Aug 2006
800-m freestyle	Janet Evans (USA)	8 min 16.22 sec	20 Aug 1989
1,500-m freestyle	Kate Ziegler (USA)	15 min 42.54 sec	17 Jun 2007
50-m backstroke	Leila Vaziri (USA)	28.16 sec	28 Mar 2007
100-m backstroke	Natalie Coughlin (USA)	59.44 sec	27 Mar 2007
200-m backstroke	Kristina Egerszegi (HUN)	2 min 06.62 sec	25 Aug 1991
50-m breaststroke	Jade Edmistone (AUS)	30.31 sec	30 Jan 2006
100-m breaststroke	Leisel Jones (AUS)	1 min 05.09 sec	20 Mar 2006
200-m breaststroke	Leisel Jones (AUS)	2 min 20.54 sec	1 Feb 2006
50-m butterfly	Therese Alshammar (SWE)	25.46 sec	13 Jun 2007
100-m butterfly	Inge de Bruijn (NED)	56.61 sec	17 Sep 2000
200-m butterfly	Jessicah Schipper (AUS)	2 min 05.40 sec	17 Aug 2006
200-m individual medley	Wu Yanyan (CHN)	2 min 09.72 sec	17 Oct 1997
400-m individual medley	Katie Hoff (USA)	4 min 32.89 sec	1 Apr 2007
4 × 100-m free relay	Germany (Petra Dallmann, Daniela Götz, Britta Steffen, Annika Liebs)	3 min 35.22 sec	31 Jul 2006
4 × 200-m free relay	United States (Natalie Coughlin, Dana Vollmer, Lacey Nymeyer, Katie Hoff)	7 min 50.09 sec	29 Mar 2007
4 × 100-m medley relay	Australia (Emily Seebohm, Leisel Jones, Jessicah Schipper, Lisbeth Lenton)	3 min 55.74 sec	31 Mar 2007

Swimming World Records—Short Course (25-m)

men

EVENT	RECORD HOLDER (NATIONALITY)	PERFORMANCE	DATE
50-m freestyle	Roland Schoeman (RSA)	20.98 sec	12 Aug 2006
100-m freestyle	Ian Crocker (USA); Roland Schoeman (RSA)	46.25 sec	27 Mar 2004; 22 Jan 2005
200-m freestyle	Ian Thorpe (AUS)	1 min 41.10 sec	6 Feb 2000
400-m freestyle	Grant Hackett (AUS)	3 min 34.58 sec	18 Jul 2002
800-m freestyle	Grant Hackett (AUS)	7 min 25.28 sec	3 Aug 2001
1,500-m freestyle	Grant Hackett (AUS)	14 min 10.10 sec	7 Aug 2001

Swimming World Records—Short Course (25-m) (continued)

men (continued)

EVENT	RECORD HOLDER (NATIONALITY)	PERFORMANCE	DATE
50-m backstroke	Thomas Rupprath (GER)	23.27 sec	10 Dec 2004
100-m backstroke	Ryan Lochte (USA)	49.99 sec	9 Apr 2006
200-m backstroke	Ryan Lochte (USA)	1 min 49.05 sec	9 Apr 2006
50-m breaststroke	Oleg Lisogor (UKR)	26.17 sec	21 Jan 2006
100-m breaststroke	Ed Moses (USA)	57.47 sec	23 Jan 2002
200-m breaststroke	Ed Moses (USA)	2 min 02.92 sec	17 Jan 2004
50-m butterfly	Kaio Almeida (BRA)	22.60 sec	17 Dec 2005
100-m butterfly	Ian Crocker (USA)	49.07 sec	26 Mar 2004
200-m butterfly	Franck Esposito (FRA)	1 min 50.73 sec	8 Dec 2002
100-m individual medley	Ryk Neethling (RSA)	51.52 sec	11 Feb 2005
200-m individual medley	Ryan Lochte (USA)	1 min 53.31 sec	8 Apr 2006
400-m individual medley	László Cseh (HUN)	4 min 00.37 sec	9 Dec 2005
4 × 100-m free relay	Sweden (Johan Nystrom, Lars Frölander, Mattias Ohlin, Stefan Nystrand)	3 min 09.57 sec	16 Mar 2000
4 × 200-m free relay	Australia (William Kirby, Ian Thorpe, Michael Klim, Grant Hackett)	6 min 56.41 sec	7 Aug 2001
4 × 100-m medley relay	United States (Aaron Peirsol, Brendan Hansen, Ian Crocker, Jason Lezak)	3 min 25.09 sec	11 Oct 2004

women

EVENT	RECORD HOLDER (NATIONALITY)	PERFORMANCE	DATE
50-m freestyle	Therese Alshammar (SWE)	23.59 sec	18 Mar 2000
100-m freestyle	Lisbeth Lenton (AUS)	51.70 sec	9 Aug 2005
200-m freestyle	Lisbeth Lenton (AUS)	1 min 53.29 sec	19 Nov 2005
400-m freestyle	Laure Manaudou (FRA)	3 min 56.09 sec	9 Dec 2006
800-m freestyle	Laure Manaudou (FRA)	8 min 11.25 sec	9 Dec 2005
1,500-m freestyle	Laure Manaudou (FRA)	15 min 42.39 sec	20 Nov 2004
50-m backstroke	Li Hui (CHN)	26.83 sec	2 Dec 2001
100-m backstroke	Natalie Coughlin (USA)	56.71 sec	23 Nov 2002
200-m backstroke	Natalie Coughlin (USA)	2 min 03.62 sec	27 Nov 2001
50-m breaststroke	Jade Edmistone (AUS)	29.90 sec	26 Sep 2004
100-m breaststroke	Leisel Jones (AUS)	1 min 03.86 sec	28 Aug 2006
200-m breaststroke	Liesel Jones (AUS)	2 min 17.75 sec	29 Nov 2003
50-m butterfly	Anna-Karin Kammerling (SWE)	25.33 sec	12 Mar 2005
100-m butterfly	Lisbeth Lenton (AUS)	55.95 sec	28 Aug 2006
200-m butterfly	Yang Yu (CHN)	2 min 04.04 sec	18 Jan 2004
100-m individual medley	Natalie Coughlin (USA)	58.80 sec	23 Nov 2002
200-m individual medley	Allison Wagner (USA)	2 min 07.79 sec	5 Dec 1993
400-m individual medley	Yana Klochkova (UKR)	4 min 27.83 sec	19 Jan 2002
4 × 100-m free relay	The Netherlands (Inge Dekker, Hinkelien Schreuder, Chantal Groot, Marleen Veldhuis)	3 min 33.32 sec	8 Apr 2006
4 × 200-m free relay	China (Xu Yanvei, Zhu Yingven, Tang Jingzhi, Yang Yu)	7 min 46.30 sec	3 Apr 2002
4 × 100-m medley relay	Australia (Tayliah Zimmer, Jade Edmistone, Jessicah Schipper, Lisbeth Lenton)	3 min 51.84 sec	7 Apr 2006

Tennis

Four events dominate world championship tennis. The first of the traditional "Big Four," or "Grand Slam," events was the All-England Lawn Tennis Championships (better known as the Wimbledon Championships), founded in 1877. Its only event the first year was the men's singles championships; women first competed in 1884. Major tennis tournaments also sprang up in the United States (1881 for men; women's singles competition first officially added 1889), France (1891 for men; women's singles competition added 1897), and Australia (1905 for men; women's singles competition added 1922). Open tennis (open, that is, to both professionals and amateurs) became the rule in the Big Four tournaments in 1968. International team tennis was organized in 1900 with the institution of the Davis Cup. Men's teams competing for the Davis Cup play four singles matches and one doubles match in elimination rounds. The Wightman Cup was contested yearly between British and American women's teams from 1923 to 1989. The International Tennis Federation (ITF, formerly the International Lawn Tennis Federation; founded 1913) established the Federation Cup in 1963 (called the Fed Cup since 1994) for international women's team competition. It is decided by elimination rounds of two singles and one doubles contest.

Related Web sites: International Tennis Federation: <www.itftennis.com>; ATP (formerly Association of Tennis Professionals): <www.atptennis.com>; Women's Tennis Association: <www.wtatour.com>.

Australian Open Tennis Championships—Singles

YEAR	MEN	WOMEN
1905	Rodney Heath (AUS)	
1906	Tony Wilding (NZL)	
1907	Horace Rice (AUS)	
1908	Fred Alexander (USA)	
1909	Tony Wilding (NZL)	
1910	Rodney Heath (AUS)	
1911	Norman Brookes (AUS)	
1912	J. Cecil Parke (GBR)	
1913	E.F. Parker (AUS)	
1914	Pat O'Hara Wood (AUS)	
1915	Francis Lowe (GBR)	
1916–18	*not held*	
1919	A.R.F. Kingscote (GBR)	
1920	Pat O'Hara Wood (AUS)	
1921	Rhys Gemmell (AUS)	
1922	James Anderson (AUS)	Margaret Molesworth (AUS)
1923	Pat O'Hara Wood (AUS)	Margaret Molesworth (AUS)
1924	James Anderson (AUS)	Sylvia Lance (AUS)
1925	James Anderson (AUS)	Daphne Akhurst (AUS)
1926	John Hawkes (AUS)	Daphne Akhurst (AUS)
1927	Gerald Patterson (AUS)	Esna Boyd (AUS)
1928	Jean Borotra (FRA)	Daphne Akhurst (AUS)
1929	John Gregory (GBR)	Daphne Akhurst (AUS)
1930	Gar Moon (AUS)	Daphne Akhurst (AUS)
1931	Jack Crawford (AUS)	Coral Buttsworth (AUS)
1932	Jack Crawford (AUS)	Coral Buttsworth (AUS)
1933	Jack Crawford (AUS)	Joan Hartigan (AUS)
1934	Fred Perry (GBR)	Joan Hartigan (AUS)
1935	Jack Crawford (AUS)	Dorothy Round (GBR)
1936	Adrian Quist (AUS)	Joan Hartigan (AUS)
1937	Vivian McGrath (AUS)	Nancye Wynne (AUS)
1938	Don Budge (USA)	Dorothy Bundy (USA)
1939	John Bromwich (AUS)	Emily Westacott (AUS)
1940	Adrian Quist (AUS)	Nancye Wynne (AUS)
1941–45	*not held*	
1946	John Bromwich (AUS)	Nancye Wynne Bolton (AUS)
1947	Dinny Pails (AUS)	Nancye Wynne Bolton (AUS)
1948	Adrian Quist (AUS)	Nancye Wynne Bolton (AUS)
1949	Frank Sedgman (AUS)	Doris Hart (USA)
1950	Frank Sedgman (AUS)	Louise Brough (USA)
1951	Dick Savitt (USA)	Nancye Wynne Bolton (AUS)
1952	Ken McGregor (AUS)	Thelma Long (AUS)
1953	Ken Rosewall (AUS)	Maureen Connolly (USA)
1954	Mervyn Rose (AUS)	Thelma Long (AUS)
1955	Ken Rosewall (AUS)	Beryl Penrose (AUS)
1956	Lew Hoad (AUS)	Mary Carter (AUS)
1957	Ashley Cooper (AUS)	Shirley Fry (USA)
1958	Ashley Cooper (AUS)	Angela Mortimer (GBR)
1959	Alex Olmedo (PER)	Mary Carter-Reitano (AUS)
1960	Rod Laver (AUS)	Margaret Smith (AUS)
1961	Roy Emerson (AUS)	Margaret Smith (AUS)
1962	Rod Laver (AUS)	Margaret Smith (AUS)
1963	Roy Emerson (AUS)	Margaret Smith (AUS)
1964	Roy Emerson (AUS)	Margaret Smith (AUS)
1965	Roy Emerson (AUS)	Margaret Smith (AUS)
1966	Roy Emerson (AUS)	Margaret Smith (AUS)
1967	Roy Emerson (AUS)	Nancy Richey (USA)
1968	Bill Bowrey (AUS)	Billie Jean King (USA)
1969	Rod Laver (AUS)	Margaret Smith Court (AUS)
1970	Arthur Ashe (USA)	Margaret Smith Court (AUS)
1971	Ken Rosewall (AUS)	Margaret Smith Court (AUS)
1972	Ken Rosewall (AUS)	Virginia Wade (GBR)
1973	John Newcombe (AUS)	Margaret Smith Court (AUS)
1974	Jimmy Connors (USA)	Evonne Goolagong (AUS)
1975	John Newcombe (AUS)	Evonne Goolagong (AUS)
1976	Mark Edmondson (AUS)	Evonne Goolagong Cawley (AUS)
1977	Roscoe Tanner (USA)	Kerry Reid (AUS)
1977[1]	Vitas Gerulaitis (USA)	Evonne Goolagong Cawley (AUS)

Australian Open Tennis Championships—Singles (continued)

YEAR	MEN	WOMEN
1978[1]	Guillermo Vilas (ARG)	Chris O'Neill (AUS)
1979[1]	Guillermo Vilas (ARG)	Barbara Jordan (USA)
1980[1]	Brian Teacher (USA)	Håna Mandlikova (TCH)
1981[1]	Johan Kriek (RSA)	Martina Navratilova (USA)
1982[1]	Johan Kriek (RSA)	Chris Evert Lloyd (USA)
1983[1]	Mats Wilander (SWE)	Martina Navratilova (USA)
1984[1]	Mats Wilander (SWE)	Chris Evert Lloyd (USA)
1985[1]	Stefan Edberg (SWE)	Martina Navratilova (USA)
1987[2]	Stefan Edberg (SWE)	Hana Mandlikova (TCH)
1988	Mats Wilander (SWE)	Steffi Graf (FRG)
1989	Ivan Lendl (TCH)	Steffi Graf (FRG)
1990	Ivan Lendl (TCH)	Steffi Graf (FRG)
1991	Boris Becker (GER)	Monica Seles (YUG)
1992	Jim Courier (USA)	Monica Seles (YUG)
1993	Jim Courier (USA)	Monica Seles (YUG)
1994	Pete Sampras (USA)	Steffi Graf (GER)
1995	Andre Agassi (USA)	Mary Pierce (FRA)
1996	Boris Becker (GER)	Monica Seles (YUG)
1997	Pete Sampras (USA)	Martina Hingis (SUI)
1998	Petr Korda (TCH)	Martina Hingis (SUI)
1999	Yevgeny Kafelnikov (RUS)	Martina Hingis (SUI)
2000	Andre Agassi (USA)	Lindsay Davenport (USA)
2001	Andre Agassi (USA)	Jennifer Capriati (USA)
2002	Thomas Johansson (SWE)	Jennifer Capriati (USA)
2003	Andre Agassi (USA)	Serena Williams (USA)
2004	Roger Federer (SUI)	Justine Henin-Hardenne (BEL)
2005	Marat Safin (RUS)	Serena Williams (USA)
2006	Roger Federer (SUI)	Amelie Mauresmo (FRA)
2007	Roger Federer (SUI)	Serena Williams (USA)

[1]Tournament held in December rather than January.   [2]1986 not held.

Australian Open Tennis Championships—Doubles

YEAR	MEN	WOMEN
1905	Tom Tachell, Randolph Lycett	
1906	Tony Wilding, Rodney Heath	
1907	Harry Parker, William Gregg	
1908	Fred Alexander, Alfred Dunlop	
1909	Ernie F. Parker, J.P. Keane	
1910	Horace Rice, Ashley Campbell	
1911	Rodney Heath, Randolph Lycett	
1912	J. Cecil Parke, Charles Dixon	
1913	Ernie F. Parker, Alf Hedemann	
1914	Ashley Campbell, Gerald Patterson	
1915	Horace Rice, Clarrie Todd	
1916–18	not held	
1919	Pat O'Hara Wood, Ron Thomas	
1920	Pat O'Hara Wood, Ron Thomas	
1921	S.H. Eaton-Rice, Rhys Gemmell	
1922	Gerald Patterson, John Hawkes	Esne Boyd, Marjorie Mountain
1923	Pat O'Hara Wood, Bert St. John	Esne Boyd, Sylvia Lance
1924	Norman Brookes, James Anderson	Daphne Akhurst, Sylvia Lance
1925	Gerald Patterson, Pat O'Hara Wood	Daphne Akhurst, Sylvia Lance Harper
1926	Gerald Patterson, John Hawkes	Meryl O'Hara Wood, Esne Boyd
1927	Gerald Patterson, John Hawkes	Meryl O'Hara Wood, Louise Bickerton
1928	Jean Borotra, Jacques Brugnon	Daphne Akhurst, Esne Boyd
1929	Jack Crawford, Harry Hopman	Daphne Akhurst, Louise Bickerton
1930	Jack Crawford, Harry Hopman	Margaret Molesworth, Emily Hood
1931	Charles Donohoe, Ray Dunlop	Daphne Akhurst Cozens, Louise Bickerton
1932	Jack Crawford, Gar Moon	Coral Buttsworth, Marjorie Cox Crawford
1933	Ellsworth Vines, Keith Gledhill	Margaret Molesworth, Emily Hood Westacott
1934	Fred Perry, George Hughes	Margaret Molesworth, Emily Hood Westacott
1935	Jack Crawford, Vivian McGrath	Evelyn Dearman, Nancy Lyle
1936	Adrian Quist, D.P. Turnbull	Thelma Coyne, Nancye Wynne
1937	Adrian Quist, D.P. Turnbull	Thelma Coyne, Nancye Wynne
1938	Adrian Quist, John Bromwich	Thelma Coyne, Nancye Wynne

Australian Open Tennis Championships—Doubles (continued)

YEAR	MEN	WOMEN
1939	Adrian Quist, John Bromwich	Thelma Coyne, Nancye Wynne
1940	Adrian Quist, John Bromwich	Thelma Coyne, Nancye Wynne Bolton
1941–45	*not held*	
1946	Adrian Quist, John Bromwich	Joyce Fitch, Mary Bevis
1947	Adrian Quist, John Bromwich	Thelma Coyne Long, Nancye Wynne Bolton
1948	Adrian Quist, John Bromwich	Thelma Coyne Long, Nancye Wynne Bolton
1949	Adrian Quist, John Bromwich	Thelma Coyne Long, Nancye Wynne Bolton
1950	Adrian Quist, John Bromwich	Louise Brough, Doris Hart
1951	Frank Sedgman, Ken McGregor	Thelma Coyne Long, Nancye Wynne Bolton
1952	Frank Sedgman, Ken McGregor	Thelma Coyne Long, Nancye Wynne Bolton
1953	Lew Hoad, Ken Rosewall	Marueen Connolly, Julia Sampson
1954	Rex Hartwig, Mervyn Rose	Mary Bevis Hawton, Beryl Penrose
1955	Vic Seixas, Tony Trabert	Mary Bevis Hawton, Beryl Penrose
1956	Lew Hoad, Ken Rosewall	Mary Bevis Hawton, Thelma Coyne Long
1957	Lew Hoad, Neale Fraser	Althea Gibson, Shirley Fry
1958	Ashley Cooper, Neale Fraser	Mary Bevis Hawton, Thelma Coyne Long
1959	Rod Laver, Robert Mark	Renee Schuurman, Sandra Reynolds
1960	Rod Laver, Robert Mark	Maria Bueno, Christine Truman
1961	Rod Laver, Robert Mark	Mary Reitano, Margaret Smith
1962	Roy Emerson, Neale Fraser	Margaret Smith, Robyn Ebbern
1963	Bob Hewitt, Fred Stolle	Margaret Smith, Robyn Ebbern
1964	Bob Hewitt, Fred Stolle	Judy Tegart, Lesley Turner
1965	John Newcombe, Tony Roche	Margaret Smith, Lesley Turner
1966	Roy Emerson, Fred Stolle	Carole Graebner, Nancy Richey
1967	John Newcombe, Tony Roche	Judy Tegart, Lesley Turner
1968	Dick Crealy, Allan Stone	Karen Krantzcke, Karrie Melville
1969	Roy Emerson, Rod Laver	Margaret Smith Court, Judy Tegart
1970	Bob Lutz, Stan Smith	Margaret Smith Court, Judy Tegart Dalton
1971	John Newcombe, Tony Roche	Margaret Smith Court, Evonne Goolagong
1972	Owen Davidson, Ken Rosewall	Kerry Harris, Helen Gourlay
1973	Mal Anderson, John Newcombe	Margaret Smith Court, Virginia Wade
1974	Ross Case, Geoff Masters	Evonne Goolagong, Peggy Michel
1975	John Alexander, Phil Dent	Evonne Goolagong, Peggy Michel
1976	John Newcombe, Tony Roche	Evonne Goolagong Cawley, Helen Gourlay
1977	Arthur Ashe, Tony Roche	Dianne Fromholtz, Helen Gourlay
1977[1]	Allan Stone, Ray Ruffels	Evonne Goolagong Cawley, Helen Gourlay Cawley; Mona Guerrant, Kerry Reid[2]
1978[1]	Wojtek Fibak, Kim Warwick	Renata Tomanova, Betsy Nagelsen
1979[1]	Peter McNamara, Paul McNamee	Judy Chaloner, Dianne Evers
1980[1]	Kim Warwick, Mark Edmondson	Martina Navratilova, Betsy Nagelsen
1981[1]	Kim Warwick, Mark Edmondson	Kathy Jordan, Anne Smith
1982[1]	John Alexander, John Fitzgerald	Martina Navratilova, Pam Shriver
1983[1]	Mark Edmondson, Paul McNamee	Martina Navratilova, Pam Shriver
1984[1]	Mark Edmondson, Sherwood Stewart	Martina Navratilova, Pam Shriver
1985[1]	Paul Annacone, Christo van Rensburg	Martina Navratilova, Pam Shriver
1987[3]	Stefan Edberg, Anders Jarryd	Martina Navratilova, Pam Shriver
1988	Rick Leach, Jim Pugh	Martina Navratilova, Pam Shriver
1989	Rick Leach, Jim Pugh	Martina Navratilova, Pam Shriver
1990	Pieter Aldrich, Danie Visser	Jana Novotna, Helena Sukova
1991	Scott Davis, David Pate	Patty Fendick, Mary Joe Fernandez
1992	Todd Woodbridge, Mark Woodforde	Arantxa Sánchez Vicario, Helena Sukova
1993	Danie Visser, Laurie Warder	Gigi Fernandez, Natasha Zvereva
1994	Paul Haarhuis, Jacco Eltingh	Gigi Fernandez, Natasha Zvereva
1995	Jared Palmer, Richey Reneberg	Arantxa Sánchez Vicario, Jana Novotna
1996	Stefan Edberg, Petr Korda	Arantxa Sánchez Vicario, Chanda Rubin
1997	Todd Woodbridge, Mark Woodforde	Martina Hingis, Natasha Zvereva
1998	Jonas Bjorkman, Jacco Eltingh	Martina Hingis, Mirjana Lucic
1999	Jonas Bjorkman, Patrick Rafter	Martina Hingis, Anna Kournikova
2000	Ellis Ferreira, Rick Leach	Lisa Raymond, Rennae Stubbs
2001	Jonas Bjorkman, Todd Woodbridge	Serena Williams, Venus Williams
2002	Mark Knowles, Daniel Nestor	Martina Hingis, Anna Kournikova
2003	Michael Llodra, Fabrice Santoro	Serena Williams, Venus Williams
2004	Michael Llodra, Fabrice Santoro	Virginia Ruano Pascual, Paola Suárez
2005	Wayne Black, Kevin Ullyett	Alicia Molik, Svetlana Kuznetsova
2006	Bob Bryan, Mike Bryan	Yan Zi, Zheng Jie
2007	Bob Bryan, Mike Bryan	Cara Black, Liezel Huber

[1]*Tournament held in December rather than January.*   [2]*Tie; finals rained out.*   [3]*1986 not held.*

French Open Tennis Championships—Singles

From 1891 to 1924, only members of French tennis clubs were eligible to play in the French Open. The table shows the winners only since 1925, when the tournament was opened to international competition.

YEAR	MEN	WOMEN
1925	René Lacoste (FRA)	Suzanne Lenglen (FRA)
1926	Henri Cochet (FRA)	Suzanne Lenglen (FRA)
1927	René Lacoste (FRA)	Kornelia Bouman (NED)
1928	Henri Cochet (FRA)	Helen Wills (USA)
1929	René Lacoste (FRA)	Helen Wills (USA)
1930	Henri Cochet (FRA)	Helen Wills Moody (USA)
1931	Jean Borotra (FRA)	Cilly Aussem (GER)
1932	Henri Cochet (FRA)	Helen Wills Moody (USA)
1933	John Crawford (AUS)	Margaret Scriven (GBR)
1934	Gottfried von Cramm (GER)	Margaret Scriven (GBR)
1935	Fred Perry (GBR)	Hilde Sperling (DEN)
1936	Gottfried von Cramm (GER)	Hilde Sperling (DEN)
1937	Henner Henkel (GER)	Hilde Sperling (DEN)
1938	Don Budge (USA)	Simone Mathieu (FRA)
1939	Don McNeill (USA)	Simone Mathieu (FRA)
1940	*not held*	*not held*
1941	Bernard Destremau (FRA)	*not held*
1942	Bernard Destremau (FRA)	*not held*
1943	Yvon Petra (FRA)	*not held*
1944	Yvon Petra (FRA)	*not held*
1945	Yvon Petra (FRA)	*not held*
1946	Marcel Bernard (FRA)	Margaret Osborne (USA)
1947	Joseph Asboth (HUN)	Patricia Todd (USA)
1948	Frank Parker (USA)	Nelly Landry (BEL)
1949	Frank Parker (USA)	Margaret Osborne du Pont (USA)
1950	Budge Patty (USA)	Doris Hart (USA)
1951	Jaroslav Drobny (TCH)	Shirley Fry (USA)
1952	Jaroslav Drobny (TCH)	Doris Hart (USA)
1953	Ken Rosewall (AUS)	Maureen Connolly (USA)
1954	Tony Trabert (USA)	Maureen Connolly (USA)
1955	Tony Trabert (USA)	Angela Mortimer (GBR)
1956	Lew Hoad (AUS)	Althea Gibson (USA)
1957	Sven Davidson (SWE)	Shirley Bloomer (GBR)
1958	Mervyn Rose (AUS)	Zsuzsi Kormoczi (HUN)
1959	Nicola Pietrangeli (ITA)	Christine Truman (GBR)
1960	Nicola Pietrangeli (ITA)	Darlene Hard (USA)
1961	Manuel Santana (ESP)	Ann Haydon (GBR)
1962	Rod Laver (AUS)	Margaret Smith (AUS)
1963	Roy Emerson (AUS)	Lesley Turner (AUS)
1964	Manuel Santana (ESP)	Margaret Smith (AUS)
1965	Fred Stolle (AUS)	Lesley Turner (AUS)
1966	Tony Roche (AUS)	Ann Haydon Jones (GBR)
1967	Roy Emerson (AUS)	Françoise Durr (FRA)
1968	Ken Rosewall (AUS)	Nancy Richey (USA)
1969	Rod Laver (AUS)	Margaret Smith Court (AUS)
1970	Jan Kodes (TCH)	Margaret Smith Court (AUS)
1971	Jan Kodes (TCH)	Evonne Goolagong (AUS)
1972	Andres Gimeno (ESP)	Billie Jean King (USA)
1973	Ilie Nastase (ROM)	Margaret Smith Court (AUS)
1974	Björn Borg (SWE)	Chris Evert (USA)
1975	Björn Borg (SWE)	Chris Evert (USA)
1976	Adriano Panatta (ITA)	Sue Barker (USA)
1977	Guillermo Vilas (ARG)	Mima Jausovec (YUG)
1978	Björn Borg (SWE)	Virginia Ruzici (ROM)
1979	Björn Borg (SWE)	Chris Evert Lloyd (USA)
1980	Björn Borg (SWE)	Chris Evert Lloyd (USA)
1981	Björn Borg (SWE)	Hana Mandlikova (TCH)
1982	Mats Wilander (SWE)	Martina Navratilova (USA)
1983	Yannick Noah (FRA)	Chris Evert Lloyd (USA)
1984	Ivan Lendl (TCH)	Martina Navratilova (USA)
1985	Mats Wilander (SWE)	Chris Evert Lloyd (USA)
1986	Ivan Lendl (TCH)	Chris Evert Lloyd (USA)
1987	Ivan Lendl (TCH)	Steffi Graf (FRG)
1988	Mats Wilander (SWE)	Steffi Graf (FRG)
1989	Michael Chang (USA)	Arantxa Sánchez Vicario (ESP)
1990	Andres Gómez (ECU)	Monica Seles (YUG)

French Open Tennis Championships—Singles (continued)

YEAR	MEN	WOMEN
1991	Jim Courier (USA)	Monica Seles (YUG)
1992	Jim Courier (USA)	Monica Seles (YUG)
1993	Sergi Bruğuera (ESP)	Steffi Graf (GER)
1994	Sergi Bruğuera (ESP)	Arantxa Sánchez Vicario (ESP)
1995	Thomas Muster (AUT)	Steffi Graf (GER)
1996	Yevgeny Kafelnikov (RUS)	Steffi Graf (GER)
1997	Gustavo Kuerten (BRA)	Iva Majoli (CRO)
1998	Carlos Moya (ESP)	Arantxa Sánchez Vicario (ESP)
1999	Andre Agassi (USA)	Steffi Graf (GER)
2000	Gustavo Kuerten (BRA)	Mary Pierce (FRA)
2001	Gustavo Kuerten (BRA)	Jennifer Capriati (USA)
2002	Albert Costa (ESP)	Serena Williams (USA)
2003	Juan Carlos Ferrero (ESP)	Justine Henin-Hardenne (BEL)
2004	Gastón Gaudio (ARG)	Anastasiya Myskina (RUS)
2005	Rafael Nadal (ESP)	Justine Henin-Hardenne (BEL)
2006	Rafael Nadal (ESP)	Justine Henin-Hardenne (BEL)
2007	Rafael Nadal (ESP)	Justine Henin (BEL)

French Open Tennis Championships—Doubles

YEAR	MEN	WOMEN
1925	Jean Borotra, René Lacoste	Suzanne Lenglen, Didi Vlasto
1926	Vinnie Richards, Howard Kinsey	Suzanne Lenglen, Didi Vlasto
1927	Henri Cochet, Jacques Brugnon	Irene Peacock, Bobby Heine
1928	Jean Borotra, Jacques Brugnon	Phoebe Watson, Eileen Bennett
1929	Jean Borotra, René Lacoste	Lili de Alvarez, Kea Bouman
1930	Henri Cochet, Jacques Brugnon	Helen Wills Moody, Elizabeth Ryan
1931	George Lott, John Van Ryn	Eileen Whittingstall, Betty Nuthall
1932	Henri Cochet, Jacques Brugnon	Helen Wills Moody, Elizabeth Ryan
1933	Pat Hughes, Fred Perry	Simone Mathieu, Elizabeth Ryan
1934	Jean Borotra, Jacques Brugnon	Simone Mathieu, Elizabeth Ryan
1935	Jack Crawford, Adrian Quist	Margaret Scriven, Kay Stammers
1936	Jean Borotra, Marcel Bernard	Simone Mathieu, Billy Yorke
1937	Gottfried von Cramm, Henner Henkel	Simone Mathieu, Billy Yorke
1938	Bernard Destremau, Yvon Petra	Simone Mathieu, Billy Yorke
1939	Don McNeill, Charles Harris	Simone Mathieu, Jadwiga Jedrzejowska
1940–45	not held	
1946	Marcel Bernard, Yvon Petra	Louise Brough, Margaret Osborne
1947	Eustace Fannin, Eric Sturgess	Louise Brough, Margaret Osborne
1948	Lennart Bergelin, Jaroslav Drobny	Doris Hart, Patricia Todd
1949	Pancho Gonzales, Frank Parker	Louise Brough, Margaret Osborne du Pont
1950	Billy Talbert, Tony Trabert	Doris Hart, Shirley Fry
1951	Ken McGregor, Frank Sedgman	Doris Hart, Shirley Fry
1952	Ken McGregor, Frank Sedgman	Doris Hart, Shirley Fry
1953	Lew Hoad, Ken Rosewall	Doris Hart, Shirley Fry
1954	Vic Seixas, Tony Trabert	Maureen Connolly, Nell Hopman
1955	Vic Seixas, Tony Trabert	Beverly Fleitz, Darlene Hard
1956	Don Candy, Robert Perry	Angela Buxton, Althea Gibson
1957	Mal Anderson, Ashley Cooper	Shirley Bloomer, Darlene Hard
1958	Ashley Cooper, Neale Fraser	Rosie Reyes, Yola Ramirez
1959	Nicola Pietrangeli, Orlando Sirola	Sandra Reynolds, Renee Schuurman
1960	Roy Emerson, Neale Fraser	Maria Bueno, Darlene Hard
1961	Roy Emerson, Rod Laver	Sandra Reynolds, Renee Schuurman
1962	Roy Emerson, Neale Fraser	Sandra Reynolds Price, Renee Schuurman
1963	Roy Emerson, Manuel Santana	Ann Haydon Jones, Renee Schuurman
1964	Roy Emerson, Ken Fletcher	Margaret Smith, Leslie Turner
1965	Roy Emerson, Fred Stolle	Margaret Smith, Leslie Turner
1966	Clark Graebner, Dennis Ralston	Margaret Smith, Judy Tegart
1967	John Newcombe, Tony Roche	Françoise Durr, Gail Sheriff
1968	Ken Rosewall, Fred Stolle	Françoise Durr, Ann Haydon Jones
1969	John Newcombe, Tony Roche	Françoise Durr, Ann Haydon Jones
1970	Ilie Nastase, Ion Tiriac	Françoise Durr, Gail Chanfreau
1971	Arthur Ashe, Marty Riessen	Françoise Durr, Gail Chanfreau
1972	Bob Hewitt, Frew McMillan	Billie Jean King, Betty Stove
1973	John Newcombe, Tom Okker	Margaret Smith Court, Virginia Wade
1974	Dick Crealy, Onny Parun	Chris Evert, Olga Morozova
1975	Brian Gottfried, Raul Ramirez	Chris Evert, Martina Navratilova

French Open Tennis Championships—Doubles (continued)

YEAR	MEN	WOMEN
1976	Fred McNair, Sherwood Stewart	Fiorella Bonicelli, Gail Chanfreau Lovera
1977	Brian Gottfried, Raúl Ramírez	Regina Marsikova, Pam Teeguarden
1978	Hank Pfister, Gene Mayer	Mimi Jausovec, Virginia Ruzici
1979	Sandy Mayer, Gene Mayer	Betty Stove, Wendy Turnbull
1980	Victor Amaya, Hank Pfister	Kathy Jordan, Anne Smith
1981	Heinz Gunthardt, Balazs Taroczy	Rosalyn Fairbank, Tanya Harford
1982	Sherwood Stewart, Ferdi Taygan	Martina Navratilova, Anne Smith
1983	Anders Jarryd, Hans Simonsson	Rosalyn Fairbank, Candy Reynolds
1984	Henri Leconte, Yannick Noah	Martina Navratilova, Pam Shriver
1985	Mark Edmondson, Kim Warwick	Martina Navratilova, Pam Shriver
1986	John Fitzgerald, Tomas Smid	Martina Navratilova, Andrea Temesvari
1987	Robert Seguso, Anders Jarryd	Martina Navratilova, Pam Shriver
1988	Emilio Sánchez, Andres Gomez	Martina Navratilova, Pam Shriver
1989	Jim Grabb, Patrick McEnroe	Larisa Savchenko, Natasha Zvereva
1990	Sergio Casal, Emilio Sánchez	Jana Novotna, Helena Sukova
1991	John Fitzgerald, Anders Jarryd	Gigi Fernández, Jana Novotna
1992	Jacob Hlasek, Marc Rosset	Gigi Fernández, Natasha Zvereva
1993	Luke Jensen, Murphy Jensen	Gigi Fernández, Natasha Zvereva
1994	Byron Black, Jonathan Stark	Gigi Fernández, Natasha Zvereva
1995	Jacco Eltingh, Paul Haarhuis	Gigi Fernández, Natasha Zvereva
1996	Yevgeny Kafelnikov, Daniel Vacek	Lindsay Davenport, Mary Joe Fernández
1997	Yevgeny Kafelnikov, Daniel Vacek	Gigi Fernández, Natasha Zvereva
1998	Jacco Eltingh, Paul Haarhuis	Martina Hingis, Jana Novotna
1999	Mahesh Bhupathi, Leander Paes	Serena Williams, Venus Williams
2000	Todd Woodbridge, Mark Woodforde	Martina Hingis, Mary Pierce
2001	Mahesh Bhupathi, Leander Paes	Virginia Ruano Pascual, Paola Suárez
2002	Yevgeny Kafelnikov, Paul Haarhuis	Virginia Ruano Pascual, Paola Suárez
2003	Bob Bryan, Mike Bryan	Kim Clijsters, Ai Sugiyama
2004	Xavier Malisse, Olivier Rochus	Virginia Ruano Pascual, Paola Suárez
2005	Jonas Bjorkman, Max Mirnyi	Virginia Ruano Pascual, Paola Suárez
2006	Jonas Bjorkman, Max Mirnyi	Lisa Raymond, Samantha Stosur
2007	Mark Knowles, Daniel Nestor	Alicia Molik, Mara Santangelo

All-England (Wimbledon) Tennis Championships—Singles

YEAR	MEN	WOMEN
1877	Spencer Gore (GBR)	
1878	Frank Hadow (GBR)	
1879	John Hartley (GBR)	
1880	John Hartley (GBR)	
1881	Willie Renshaw (GBR)	
1882	Willie Renshaw (GBR)	
1883	Willie Renshaw (GBR)	
1884	Willie Renshaw (GBR)	Maud Watson (GBR)
1885	Willie Renshaw (GBR)	Maud Watson (GBR)
1886	Willie Renshaw (GBR)	Blanche Bingley (GBR)
1887	Herbert Lawford (GBR)	Lottie Dod (GBR)
1888	Ernest Renshaw (GBR)	Lottie Dod (GBR)
1889	Willie Renshaw (GBR)	Blanche Bingley Hillyard (GBR)
1890	William Hamilton (GBR)	Lena Rice (GBR)
1891	Wilfred Baddeley (GBR)	Lottie Dod (GBR)
1892	Wilfred Baddeley (GBR)	Lottie Dod (GBR)
1893	Joshua Pim (GBR)	Lottie Dod (GBR)
1894	Joshua Pim (GBR)	Blanche Bingley Hillyard (GBR)
1895	Wilfred Baddeley (GBR)	Charlotte Cooper (GBR)
1896	Harold Mahony (GBR)	Charlotte Cooper (GBR)
1897	Reggie Doherty (GBR)	Blanche Bingley Hillyard (GBR)
1898	Reggie Doherty (GBR)	Charlotte Cooper (GBR)
1899	Reggie Doherty (GBR)	Blanche Bingley Hillyard (GBR)
1900	Reggie Doherty (GBR)	Blanche Bingley Hillyard (GBR)
1901	Arthur Gore (GBR)	Charlotte Cooper Sterry (GBR)
1902	Laurie Doherty (GBR)	Muriel Robb (GBR)
1903	Laurie Doherty (GBR)	Dorothea Douglass (GBR)
1904	Laurie Doherty (GBR)	Dorothea Douglass (GBR)
1905	Laurie Doherty (GBR)	May Sutton (USA)
1906	Laurie Doherty (GBR)	Dorothea Douglass (GBR)
1907	Norman Brookes (AUS)	May Sutton (USA)

All-England (Wimbledon) Tennis Championships—Singles (continued)

YEAR	MEN	WOMEN
1908	Arthur Gore (GBR)	Charlotte Cooper Sterry (GBR)
1909	Arthur Gore (GBR)	Dora Boothby (GBR)
1910	Tony Wilding (NZL)	Dorothea Douglass Lambert Chambers (GBR)
1911	Tony Wilding (NZL)	Dorothea Douglass Lambert Chambers (GBR)
1912	Tony Wilding (NZL)	Ethel Larcombe (GBR)
1913	Tony Wilding (NZL)	Dorothea Douglass Lambert Chambers (GBR)
1914	Norman Brookes (AUS)	Dorothea Douglass Lambert Chambers (GBR)
1915–18	not held	
1919	Gerald Patterson (AUS)	Suzanne Lenglen (FRA)
1920	Bill Tilden (USA)	Suzanne Lenglen (FRA)
1921	Bill Tilden (USA)	Suzanne Lenglen (FRA)
1922	Gerald Patterson (AUS)	Suzanne Lenglen (FRA)
1923	Bill Johnston (USA)	Suzanne Lenglen (FRA)
1924	Jean Borotra (FRA)	Kathleen McKane (GBR)
1925	René Lacoste (FRA)	Suzanne Lenglen (FRA)
1926	Jean Borotra (FRA)	Kathleen McKane Godfree (GBR)
1927	Henri Cochet (FRA)	Helen Wills (USA)
1928	René Lacoste (FRA)	Helen Wills (USA)
1929	Henri Cochet (FRA)	Helen Wills (USA)
1930	Bill Tilden (USA)	Helen Wills Moody (USA)
1931	Sidney Wood (USA)	Cilly Aussem (GER)
1932	Ellsworth Vines (USA)	Helen Wills Moody (USA)
1933	Jack Crawford (AUS)	Helen Wills Moody (USA)
1934	Fred Perry (GBR)	Dorothy Round (GBR)
1935	Fred Perry (GBR)	Helen Wills Moody (USA)
1936	Fred Perry (GBR)	Helen Jacobs (USA)
1937	Don Budge (USA)	Dorothy Round (GBR)
1938	Don Budge (USA)	Helen Wills Moody (USA)
1939	Bobby Riggs (USA)	Alice Marble (USA)
1940–45	not held	
1946	Yvon Petra (FRA)	Pauline Betz (USA)
1947	Jack Kramer (USA)	Margaret Osborne (USA)
1948	Bob Falkenburg (USA)	Louise Brough (USA)
1949	Ted Schroeder (USA)	Louise Brough (USA)
1950	Budge Patty (USA)	Louise Brough (USA)
1951	Dick Savitt (USA)	Doris Hart (USA)
1952	Frank Sedgman (AUS)	Maureen Connolly (USA)
1953	Vic Seixas (USA)	Maureen Connolly (USA)
1954	Jaroslav Drobny (TCH)	Maureen Connolly (USA)
1955	Tony Trabert (USA)	Louise Brough (USA)
1956	Lew Hoad (AUS)	Shirley Fry (USA)
1957	Lew Hoad (AUS)	Althea Gibson (USA)
1958	Ashley Cooper (AUS)	Althea Gibson (USA)
1959	Alex Olmedo (PER)	Maria Bueno (BRA)
1960	Neale Fraser (AUS)	Maria Bueno (BRA)
1961	Rod Laver (AUS)	Angela Mortimer (GBR)
1962	Rod Laver (AUS)	Karen Susman (USA)
1963	Chuck McKinley (USA)	Margaret Smith (AUS)
1964	Roy Emerson (AUS)	Maria Bueno (BRA)
1965	Roy Emerson (AUS)	Margaret Smith (AUS)
1966	Manuel Santana (ESP)	Billie Jean King (USA)
1967	John Newcombe (AUS)	Billie Jean King (USA)
1968[1]	Rod Laver (AUS)	Billie Jean King (USA)
1969	Rod Laver (AUS)	Ann Jones (GBR)
1970	John Newcombe (AUS)	Margaret Smith Court (AUS)
1971	John Newcombe (AUS)	Evonne Goolagong (AUS)
1972	Stan Smith (USA)	Billie Jean King (USA)
1973	Jan Kodes (TCH)	Billie Jean King (USA)
1974	Jimmy Connors (USA)	Chris Evert (USA)
1975	Arthur Ashe (USA)	Billie Jean King (USA)
1976	Björn Borg (SWE)	Chris Evert (USA)
1977	Björn Borg (SWE)	Virginia Wade (GBR)
1978	Björn Borg (SWE)	Martina Navratilova (TCH)
1979	Björn Borg (SWE)	Martina Navratilova (USA)
1980	Björn Borg (SWE)	Evonne Goolagong Cawley (AUS)
1981	John McEnroe (USA)	Chris Evert Lloyd (USA)
1982	Jimmy Connors (USA)	Martina Navratilova (USA)
1983	John McEnroe (USA)	Martina Navratilova (USA)

All-England (Wimbledon) Tennis Championships—Singles (continued)

YEAR	MEN	WOMEN
1984	John McEnroe (USA)	Martina Navratilova (USA)
1985	Boris Becker (FRG)	Martina Navratilova (USA)
1986	Boris Becker (FRG)	Martina Navratilova (USA)
1987	Pat Cash (AUS)	Martina Navratilova (USA)
1988	Stefan Edberg (SWE)	Steffi Graf (GDR)
1989	Boris Becker (FRG)	Steffi Graf (GDR)
1990	Stefan Edberg (SWE)	Martina Navratilova (USA)
1991	Michael Stich (GER)	Steffi Graf (GER)
1992	Andre Agassi (USA)	Steffi Graf (GER)
1993	Pete Sampras (USA)	Steffi Graf (GER)
1994	Pete Sampras (USA)	Conchita Martínez (ESP)
1995	Pete Sampras (USA)	Steffi Graf (GER)
1996	Richard Krajicek (NED)	Steffi Graf (GER)
1997	Pete Sampras (USA)	Martina Hingis (SUI)
1998	Pete Sampras (USA)	Jana Novotna (CZE)
1999	Pete Sampras (USA)	Lindsay Davenport (USA)
2000	Pete Sampras (USA)	Venus Williams (USA)
2001	Goran Ivanisevic (CRO)	Venus Williams (USA)
2002	Lleyton Hewitt (AUS)	Serena Williams (USA)
2003	Roger Federer (SUI)	Serena Williams (USA)
2004	Roger Federer (SUI)	Mariya Sharapova (RUS)
2005	Roger Federer (SUI)	Venus Williams (USA)
2006	Roger Federer (SUI)	Amélie Mauresmo (FRA)
2007	Roger Federer (SUI)	Venus Williams (USA)

[1]Open since 1968.

All-England (Wimbledon) Tennis Championships—Doubles

YEAR	MEN	WOMEN
1879	L.R. Erskine, H. Lawford	
1880	William Renshaw, Ernest Renshaw	
1881	William Renshaw, Ernest Renshaw	
1882	J.T. Hartley, R.T. Richardson	
1883	C.W. Grinstead, C.E. Welldon	
1884	William Renshaw, Ernest Renshaw	
1885	William Renshaw, Ernest Renshaw	
1886	William Renshaw, Ernest Renshaw	
1887	Herbert Wilberforce, P.B. Lyon	
1888	William Renshaw, Ernest Renshaw	
1889	William Renshaw, Ernest Renshaw	
1890	Joshua Pim, F.O. Stoker	
1891	Wilfred Baddeley, Herbert Baddeley	
1892	E.W. Lewis, H.S. Barlow	
1893	Joshua Pim, F.O. Stoker	
1894	Wilfred Baddeley, Herbert Baddeley	
1895	Wilfred Baddeley, Herbert Baddeley	
1896	Wilfred Baddeley, Herbert Baddeley	
1897	Reggie Doherty, Laurie Doherty	
1898	Reggie Doherty, Laurie Doherty	
1899	Reggie Doherty, Laurie Doherty	
1900	Reggie Doherty, Laurie Doherty	
1901	Reggie Doherty, Laurie Doherty	
1902	Sidney Smith, Frank Riseley	
1903	Reggie Doherty, Laurie Doherty	
1904	Reggie Doherty, Laurie Doherty	
1905	Reggie Doherty, Laurie Doherty	
1906	Sidney Smith, Frank Riseley	
1907	Norman Brookes, Anthony Wilding	
1908	Anthony Wilding, M.J.G. Ritchie	
1909	Arthur Gore, H. Roper Barrett	
1910	Anthony Wilding, M.J.G. Ritchie	
1911	Andre Gobert, Max Decugis	
1912	H. Roper Barrett, Charles Dixon	
1913	H. Roper Barrett, Charles Dixon	Winifred McNair, Dora Boothby
1914	Norman Brookes, Anthony Wilding	Elizabeth Ryan, Agatha Morton
1915–18	not held	
1919	R.V. Thomas, Pat O'Hara Wood	Suzanne Lenglen, Elizabeth Ryan

All-England (Wimbledon) Tennis Championships—Doubles (continued)

YEAR	MEN	WOMEN
1920	Richard Williams, Chuck Garland	Suzanne Lenglen, Elizabeth Ryan
1921	Randolph Lycett, Max Woosnam	Suzanne Lenglen, Elizabeth Ryan
1922	James Anderson, Randolph Lycett	Suzanne Lenglen, Elizabeth Ryan
1923	Leslie Godfree, Randolph Lycett	Suzanne Lenglen, Elizabeth Ryan
1924	Frank Hunter, Vincent Richards	Hazel Wightman, Helen Wills
1925	Jean Borotra, René Lacoste	Suzanne Lenglen, Elizabeth Ryan
1926	Jacques Brugnon, Henri Cochet	Mary Browne, Elizabeth Ryan
1927	Bill Tilden, Frank Hunter	Helen Wills, Elizabeth Ryan
1928	Jacques Brugnon, Henri Cochet	Peggy Saunders, Phoebe Watson
1929	Wilmer Allison, John Van Ryn	Peggy Saunders Michell, Phoebe Watson
1930	Wilmer Allison, John Van Ryn	Helen Wills Moody, Elizabeth Ryan
1931	George Lott, John Van Ryn	Phyllis Mudford, Dorothy Barron
1932	Jean Borotra, Jacques Brugnon	Doris Metaxa, Josane Sigart
1933	Jean Borotra, Jacques Brugnon	Elizabeth Ryan, Simone Mathieu
1934	George Lott, Lester Stoefen	Elizabeth Ryan, Simone Mathieu
1935	Jack Crawford, Adrian Quist	Freda James, Kay Stammers
1936	Pat Hughes, Raymond Tuckey	Freda James, Kay Stammers
1937	Don Budge, Gene Mako	Simone Mathieu, Billie Yorke
1938	Don Budge, Gene Mako	Sarah Palfrey Fabyan, Alice Marble
1939	Bobby Riggs, Elwood Cooke	Sarah Palfrey Fabyan, Alice Marble
1940–45	not held	
1946	Jack Kramer, Tom Brown	Louise Brough, Margaret Osborne
1947	Jack Kramer, Bob Falkenburg	Patricia Todd, Doris Hart
1948	John Bromwich, Frank Sedgman	Louise Brough, Margaret Osborne du Pont
1949	Pancho Gonzáles, Frank Parker	Louise Brough, Margaret Osborne du Pont
1950	John Bromwich, Adrian Quist	Louise Brough, Margaret Osborne du Pont
1951	Ken McGregor, Frank Sedgman	Doris Hart, Shirley Fry
1952	Ken McGregor, Frank Sedgman	Doris Hart, Shirley Fry
1953	Ken Rosewall, Lew Hoad	Doris Hart, Shirley Fry
1954	Rex Hartwig, Mervyn Rose	Louise Brough, Margaret Osborne du Pont
1955	Rex Hartwig, Lew Hoad	Angela Mortimer, Anne Shilcock
1956	Ken Rosewall, Lew Hoad	Angela Buxton, Althea Gibson
1957	Budge Patty, Gardnar Mulloy	Althea Gibson, Darlene Hard
1958	Sven Davidson, Ulf Schmidt	Maria Bueno, Althea Gibson
1959	Roy Emerson, Neale Fraser	Jeanne Arth, Darlene Hard
1960	Rafael Osuna, Dennis Ralston	Maria Bueno, Darlene Hard
1961	Roy Emerson, Neale Fraser	Karen Hantze, Billie Jean Moffitt
1962	Bob Hewitt, Fred Stolle	Karen Hantze Susman, Billie Jean Moffitt
1963	Rafael Osuna, Antonio Palafox	Maria Bueno, Darlene Hard
1964	Bob Hewitt, Fred Stolle	Margaret Smith, Leslie Turner
1965	John Newcombe, Tony Roche	Maria Bueno, Billie Jean Moffitt
1966	John Newcombe, Ken Fletcher	Maria Bueno, Nancy Richey
1967	Bob Hewitt, Frew McMillan	Rosemary Casals, Billie Jean Moffitt King
1968[1]	John Newcombe, Tony Roche	Rosemary Casals, Billie Jean King
1969	John Newcombe, Tony Roche	Margaret Smith Court, Judy Tegart
1970	John Newcombe, Tony Roche	Rosemary Casals, Billie Jean King
1971	Rod Laver, Roy Emerson	Rosemary Casals, Billie Jean King
1972	Bob Hewitt, Frew McMillan	Billie Jean King, Betty Stove
1973	Jimmy Connors, Ilie Nastase	Rosemary Casals, Billie Jean King
1974	John Newcombe, Tony Roche	Evonne Goolagong, Peggy Michel
1975	Vitas Gerulaitis, Sandy Mayer	Ann Kiyomura, Kazuko Sawamatsu
1976	Brian Gottfried, Raúl Ramírez	Chris Evert, Martina Navratilova
1977	Ross Case, Geoff Masters	Helen Gourlay Cawley, Joanne Russell
1978	Bob Hewitt, Frew McMillan	Kerry Reid, Wendy Turnbull
1979	John McEnroe, Peter Fleming	Billie Jean King, Martina Navratilova
1980	Peter McNamara, Paul McNamee	Kathy Jordan, Anne Smith
1981	John McEnroe, Peter Fleming	Martina Navratilova, Pam Shriver
1982	Peter McNamara, Paul McNamee	Martina Navratilova, Pam Shriver
1983	John McEnroe, Peter Fleming	Martina Navratilova, Pam Shriver
1984	John McEnroe, Peter Fleming	Martina Navratilova, Pam Shriver
1985	Heinz Günthardt, Balázs Taróczy	Kathy Jordan, Elizabeth Smylie
1986	Joakim Nyström, Mats Wilander	Martina Navratilova, Pam Shriver
1987	Robert Seguso, Ken Flach	Claudia Kohde-Kilsch, Helena Sukova
1988	Robert Seguso, Ken Flach	Steffi Graf, Gabriela Sabatini
1989	John Fitzgerald, Anders Järryd	Jana Novotna, Helena Sukova
1990	Rick Leach, Jim Pugh	Jana Novotna, Helena Sukova
1991	John Fitzgerald, Anders Järryd	Larisa Savchenko, Natasha Zvereva
1992	John McEnroe, Michael Stich	Gigi Fernández, Natasha Zvereva

All-England (Wimbledon) Tennis Championships—Doubles (continued)

YEAR	MEN	WOMEN
1993	Todd Woodbridge, Mark Woodforde	Gigi Fernández, Natasha Zvereva
1994	Todd Woodbridge, Mark Woodforde	Gigi Fernández, Natasha Zvereva
1995	Todd Woodbridge, Mark Woodforde	Arantxa Sánchez Vicario, Jana Novotna
1996	Todd Woodbridge, Mark Woodforde	Helena Sukova, Martina Hingis
1997	Todd Woodbridge, Mark Woodforde	Gigi Fernández, Natasha Zvereva
1998	Jacco Eltingh, Paul Haarhuis	Martina Hingis, Jana Novotna
1999	Mahesh Bhupathi, Leander Paes	Lindsay Davenport, Corina Morariu
2000	Todd Woodbridge, Mark Woodforde	Venus Williams, Serena Williams
2001	Donald Johnson, Jared Palmer	Lisa Raymond, Rennae Stubbs
2002	Todd Woodbridge, Jonas Björkman	Venus Williams, Serena Williams
2003	Todd Woodbridge, Jonas Björkman	Kim Clijsters, Ai Sugiyama
2004	Todd Woodbridge, Jonas Björkman	Cara Black, Rennae Stubbs
2005	Stephen Huss, Wesley Moodie	Cara Black, Liezel Huber
2006	Bob Bryan, Mike Bryan	Yan Zi, Zheng Jie
2007	Arnaud Clément, Michaël Llodra	Cara Black, Liezel Huber

[1]Open since 1968.

United States Open Tennis Championships—Singles

YEAR	MEN	WOMEN
1881	Richard Sears (USA)	
1882	Richard Sears (USA)	
1883	Richard Sears (USA)	
1884	Richard Sears (USA)	
1885	Richard Sears (USA)	
1886	Richard Sears (USA)	
1887	Richard Sears (USA)	Ellen Hansell (USA)
1888	Henry Slocum, Jr. (USA)	Bertha Townsend (USA)
1889	Henry Slocum, Jr. (USA)	Bertha Townsend (USA)
1890	Oliver Campbell (USA)	Ellen Roosevelt (USA)
1891	Oliver Campbell (USA)	Mabel Cahill (USA)
1892	Oliver Campbell (USA)	Mabel Cahill (USA)
1893	Robert Wrenn (USA)	Aline Terry (USA)
1894	Robert Wrenn (USA)	Helen Helwig (USA)
1895	Fred Hovey (USA)	Juliette Atkinson (USA)
1896	Robert Wrenn (USA)	Elisabeth Moore (USA)
1897	Robert Wrenn (USA)	Juliette Atkinson (USA)
1898	Malcom Whitman (USA)	Juliette Atkinson (USA)
1899	Malcom Whitman (USA)	Marion Jones (USA)
1900	Malcom Whitman (USA)	Myrtle McAteer (USA)
1901	William Larned (USA)	Elisabeth Moore (USA)
1902	William Larned (USA)	Marion Jones (USA)
1903	Laurie Doherty (GBR)	Elisabeth Moore (USA)
1904	Holcombe Ward (USA)	May Sutton (USA)
1905	Beals Wright (USA)	Elisabeth Moore (USA)
1906	Bill Clothier (USA)	Helen Homans (USA)
1907	William Larned (USA)	Evelyn Sears (USA)
1908	William Larned (USA)	Maud Barger-Wallach (USA)
1909	William Larned (USA)	Hazel Hotchkiss (USA)
1910	William Larned (USA)	Hazel Hotchkiss (USA)
1911	William Larned (USA)	Hazel Hotchkiss (USA)
1912	Maurice McLoughlin (USA)	Mary Browne (USA)
1913	Maurice McLoughlin (USA)	Mary Browne (USA)
1914	R. Norris Williams (USA)	Mary Browne (USA)
1915	Bill Johnston (USA)	Molla Bjurstedt (NOR)
1916	R. Norris Williams (USA)	Molla Bjurstedt (NOR)
1917	Lindley Murray (USA)	Molla Bjurstedt (NOR)
1918	Lindley Murray (USA)	Molla Bjurstedt (NOR)
1919	Bill Johnston (USA)	Hazel Hotchkiss Wightman (USA)
1920	Bill Tilden (USA)	Molla Bjurstedt Mallory (USA)
1921	Bill Tilden (USA)	Molla Bjurstedt Mallory (USA)
1922	Bill Tilden (USA)	Molla Bjurstedt Mallory (USA)
1923	Bill Tilden (USA)	Helen Wills (USA)
1924	Bill Tilden (USA)	Helen Wills (USA)
1925	Bill Tilden (USA)	Helen Wills (USA)
1926	René Lacoste (FRA)	Molla Bjurstedt Mallory (USA)
1927	René Lacoste (FRA)	Helen Wills (USA)

United States Open Tennis Championships—Singles (continued)

YEAR	MEN	WOMEN
1928	Henri Cochet (FRA)	Helen Wills (USA)
1929	Bill Tilden (USA)	Helen Wills (USA)
1930	John Doeg (USA)	Betty Nuthall (GBR)
1931	Ellsworth Vines (USA)	Helen Wills Moody (USA)
1932	Ellsworth Vines (USA)	Helen Jacobs (USA)
1933	Fred Perry (GBR)	Helen Jacobs (USA)
1934	Fred Perry (GBR)	Helen Jacobs (USA)
1935	Wilmer Allison (USA)	Helen Jacobs (USA)
1936	Fred Perry (GBR)	Alice Marble (USA)
1937	Don Budge (USA)	Anita Lizana (CHI)
1938	Don Budge (USA)	Alice Marble (USA)
1939	Bobby Riggs (USA)	Alice Marble (USA)
1940	Don McNeill (USA)	Alice Marble (USA)
1941	Bobby Riggs (USA)	Sarah Palfrey Cooke (USA)
1942	Ted Schroeder (USA)	Pauline Betz (USA)
1943	Joe Hunt (USA)	Pauline Betz (USA)
1944	Frank Parker (USA)	Pauline Betz (USA)
1945	Frank Parker (USA)	Sarah Palfrey Cooke (USA)
1946	Jack Kramer (USA)	Pauline Betz (USA)
1947	Jack Kramer (USA)	Louise Brough (USA)
1948	Pancho Gonzales (USA)	Margaret du Pont (USA)
1949	Pancho Gonzales (USA)	Margaret du Pont (USA)
1950	Arthur Larsen (USA)	Margaret du Pont (USA)
1951	Frank Sedgman (AUS)	Maureen Connolly (USA)
1952	Frank Sedgman (AUS)	Maureen Connolly (USA)
1953	Tony Trabert (USA)	Maureen Connolly (USA)
1954	Vic Seixas (USA)	Doris Hart (USA)
1955	Tony Trabert (USA)	Doris Hart (USA)
1956	Ken Rosewall (AUS)	Shirley Fry (USA)
1957	Mal Anderson (AUS)	Althea Gibson (USA)
1958	Ashley Cooper (AUS)	Althea Gibson (USA)
1959	Neale Fraser (AUS)	Maria Bueno (BRA)
1960	Neale Fraser (AUS)	Darlene Hard (USA)
1961	Roy Emerson (AUS)	Darlene Hard (USA)
1962	Rod Laver (AUS)	Margaret Smith (AUS)
1963	Rafael Osuna (MEX)	Maria Bueno (BRA)
1964	Roy Emerson (AUS)	Maria Bueno (BRA)
1965	Manuel Santana (SPA)	Margaret Smith (AUS)
1966	Fred Stolle (AUS)	Maria Bueno (BRA)
1967	John Newcombe (AUS)	Billie Jean King (USA)
1968[1]	Arthur Ashe (USA)	Virginia Wade (GBR); Margaret Smith Court (AUS)
1969[1]	Rod Laver (AUS); Stan Smith (USA)	Margaret Smith Court (AUS)
1970	Ken Rosewall (AUS)	Margaret Smith Court (AUS)
1971	Stan Smith (USA)	Billie Jean King (USA)
1972	Ilie Nastase (ROM)	Billie Jean King (USA)
1973	John Newcombe (AUS)	Margaret Smith Court (AUS)
1974	Jimmy Connors (USA)	Billie Jean King (USA)
1975	Manuel Orantes (SPA)	Chris Evert (USA)
1976	Jimmy Connors (USA)	Chris Evert (USA)
1977	Guillermo Vilas (ARG)	Chris Evert (USA)
1978	Jimmy Connors (USA)	Chris Evert (USA)
1979	John McEnroe (USA)	Tracy Austin (USA)
1980	John McEnroe (USA)	Chris Evert Lloyd (USA)
1981	John McEnroe (USA)	Tracy Austin (USA)
1982	Jimmy Connors (USA)	Chris Evert Lloyd (USA)
1983	Jimmy Connors (USA)	Martina Navratilova (USA)
1984	John McEnroe (USA)	Martina Navratilova (USA)
1985	Ivan Lendl (TCH)	Hana Mandlikova (TCH)
1986	Ivan Lendl (TCH)	Martina Navratilova (USA)
1987	Ivan Lendl (TCH)	Martina Navratilova (USA)
1988	Mats Wilander (SWE)	Steffi Graf (FRG)
1989	Boris Becker (FRG)	Steffi Graf (FRG)
1990	Pete Sampras (USA)	Gabriela Sabatini (ARG)
1991	Stefan Edberg (SWE)	Monica Seles (YUG)
1992	Stefan Edberg (SWE)	Monica Seles (YUG)
1993	Pete Sampras (USA)	Steffi Graf (GER)
1994	Andre Agassi (USA)	Arantxa Sánchez Vicario (SPA)
1995	Pete Sampras (USA)	Steffi Graf (GER)

United States Open Tennis Championships—Singles (continued)

YEAR	MEN	WOMEN
1996	Pete Sampras (USA)	Steffi Graf (GER)
1997	Patrick Rafter (AUS)	Martina Hingis (SUI)
1998	Patrick Rafter (AUS)	Lindsay Davenport (USA)
1999	Andre Agassi (USA)	Serena Williams (USA)
2000	Marat Safin (RUS)	Venus Williams (USA)
2001	Lleyton Hewitt (AUS)	Venus Williams (USA)
2002	Pete Sampras (USA)	Serena Williams (USA)
2003	Andy Roddick (USA)	Justine Henin-Hardenne (BEL)
2004	Roger Federer (SUI)	Svetlana Kuznetsova (RUS)
2005	Roger Federer (SUI)	Kim Clijsters (BEL)
2006	Roger Federer (SUI)	Mariya Sharapova (RUS)
2007	Roger Federer (SUI)	Justine Henin (BEL)

[1]In 1968 and 1969 both amateur and open championships were held. Ashe won both men's competitions in 1968; Smith won the amateur championship in 1969. Court won the women's amateur competition in 1968 and both championships in 1969. Thereafter the championships were open.

United States Open Tennis Championships—Doubles

YEAR	MEN	WOMEN
1881	Clarence Clark, Fred Taylor	
1882	Richard Sears, James Dwight	
1883	Richard Sears, James Dwight	
1884	Richard Sears, James Dwight	
1885	Richard Sears, Joseph Clark	
1886	Richard Sears, James Dwight	
1887	Richard Sears, James Dwight	
1888	Oliver Campbell, Valentine Hall	
1889	Henry Slocum, Howard Taylor	Bertha Townsend, Margarette Ballard
1890	Valentine Hall, Clarence Hobart	Ellen Roosevelt, Grace Roosevelt
1891	Oliver Campbell, Robert Huntington	Mabel Cahill, Mrs. W. Fellowes Morgan
1892	Oliver Campbell, Robert Huntington	Mabel Cahill, Adeline McKinley
1893	Clarence Hobart, Fred Hovey	Aline Terry, Hattie Butler
1894	Clarence Hobart, Fred Hovey	Helen Helwig, Juliette Atkinson
1895	Malcom Chace, Robert Wrenn	Helen Helwig, Juliette Atkinson
1896	Carr Neel, Samuel Neel	Elisabeth Moore, Juliette Atkinson
1897	Leo Ware, George Sheldon	Juliette Atkinson, Kathleen Atkinson
1898	Leo Ware, George Sheldon	Juliette Atkinson, Kathleen Atkinson
1899	Holcombe Ward, Dwight Davis	Jane Craven, Myrtle McAteer
1900	Holcombe Ward, Dwight Davis	Edith Parker, Hallie Champlin
1901	Holcombe Ward, Dwight Davis	Juliette Atkinson, Myrtle McAteer
1902	Reginald Doherty, Hugh Doherty	Juliette Atkinson, Marion Jones
1903	Reginald Doherty, Hugh Doherty	Elisabeth Moore, Carrie Neely
1904	Holcombe Ward, Beals Wright	Mary Sutton, Miriam Hall
1905	Holcombe Ward, Beals Wright	Helen Homans, Carrie Neely
1906	Holcombe Ward, Beals Wright	Mrs. L.S. Coe, Mrs. D.S. Platt
1907	Fred Alexander, Harold Hackett	Marie Weimer, Carrie Neely
1908	Fred Alexander, Harold Hackett	Evelyn Sears, Margaret Curtis
1909	Fred Alexander, Harold Hackett	Hazel Hotchkiss, Edith Rotch
1910	Fred Alexander, Harold Hackett	Hazel Hotchkiss, Edith Rotch
1911	Raymond Little, Gustave Touchard	Hazel Hotchkiss, Eleanora Sears
1912	Maurice McLoughlin, Thomas Bundy	Dorothy Green, Mary Browne
1913	Maurice McLoughlin, Thomas Bundy	Mary Browne, Mrs. R.H. Williams
1914	Maurice McLoughlin, Thomas Bundy	Mary Browne, Mrs. R.H. Williams
1915	William Johnston, Clarence Griffin	Hazel Hotchkiss Wightman, Eleanora Sears
1916	William Johnston, Clarence Griffin	Molla Bjurstedt, Eleanora Sears
1917	Fred Alexander, Harold Throckmorton	Molla Bjurstedt, Eleanora Sears
1918	Bill Tilden, Vincent Richards	Marion Zinderstein, Eleanor Goss
1919	Norman Brookes, Gerald Patterson	Marion Zinderstein, Eleanor Goss
1920	William Johnston, Clarence Griffin	Marion Zinderstein, Eleanor Goss
1921	Bill Tilden, Vincent Richards	Mary Browne, Mrs. R.H. Williams
1922	Bill Tilden, Vincent Richards	Marion Zinderstein Jessup, Helen Wills
1923	Bill Tilden, Brian Norton	Kathleen McKane, Phyllis Covell
1924	Howard Kinsey, Robert Kinsey	Hazel Hotchkiss Wightman, Helen Wills
1925	Richard Williams, Vincent Richards	Mary Browne, Helen Wills
1926	Richard Williams, Vincent Richards	Elizabeth Ryan, Eleanor Goss
1927	Bill Tilden, Frank Hunter	Kathleen McKane Godfree, Ermyntrude Harvey
1928	George Lott, John Hennessey	Hazel Hotchkiss Wightman, Helen Wills

United States Open Tennis Championships—Doubles (continued)

YEAR	MEN	WOMEN
1929	George Lott, John Doeg	Phoebe Watson, Peggy Michell
1930	George Lott, John Doeg	Betty Nuthall, Sarah Palfrey
1931	Wilmer Allison, John Van Ryn	Betty Nuthall, Eileen Whittingstall
1932	Ellsworth Vines, Keith Gledhill	Helen Jacobs, Sarah Palfrey
1933	George Lott, Lester Stoefen	Betty Nuthall, Freda James
1934	George Lott, Lester Stoefen	Helen Jacobs, Sarah Palfrey
1935	Wilmer Allison, John Van Ryn	Helen Jacobs, Sarah Palfrey Fabyan
1936	Don Budge, Gene Mako	Marjorie Van Ryn, Carolin Babcock
1937	Gottfried von Cramm, Henner Henkel	Sarah Palfrey Fabyan, Alice Marble
1938	Don Budge, Gene Mako	Sarah Palfrey Fabyan, Alice Marble
1939	Adrian Quist, John Bromwich	Sarah Palfrey Fabyan, Alice Marble
1940	Jack Kramer, Ted Schroeder	Sarah Palfrey Fabyan, Alice Marble
1941	Jack Kramer, Ted Schroeder	Sarah Palfrey Cooke, Margaret Osborne
1942	Gardnar Mulloy, Billy Talbert	Louise Brough, Margaret Osborne
1943	Jack Kramer, Frank Parker	Louise Brough, Margaret Osborne
1944	Don McNeill, Bob Falkenburg	Louise Brough, Margaret Osborne
1945	Gardnar Mulloy, Billy Talbert	Louise Brough, Margaret Osborne
1946	Gardnar Mulloy, Billy Talbert	Louise Brough, Margaret Osborne
1947	Jack Kramer, Ted Schroeder	Louise Brough, Margaret Osborne
1948	Gardnar Mulloy, Billy Talbert	Louise Brough, Margaret Osborne du Pont
1949	John Bromwich, Billy Sidwell	Louise Brough, Margaret Osborne du Pont
1950	John Bromwich, Frank Sedgman	Louise Brough, Margaret Osborne du Pont
1951	Ken McGregor, Frank Sedgman	Shirley Fry, Doris Hart
1952	Mervyn Rose, Vic Seixas	Shirley Fry, Doris Hart
1953	Mervyn Rose, Rex Hartwig	Shirley Fry, Doris Hart
1954	Vic Seixas, Tony Trabert	Shirley Fry, Doris Hart
1955	Kosei Kamo, Atushi Miyagi	Louise Brough, Margaret Osborne du Pont
1956	Lew Hoad, Ken Rosewall	Louise Brough, Margaret Osborne du Pont
1957	Ashley Cooper, Neale Fraser	Louise Brough, Margaret Osborne du Pont
1958	Alex Olmedo, Hamilton Richardson	Jeanne Arth, Darlene Hard
1959	Neale Fraser, Roy Emerson	Jeanne Arth, Darlene Hard
1960	Neale Fraser, Roy Emerson	Darlene Hard, Maria Bueno
1961	Charles McKinley, Dennis Ralston	Darlene Hard, Lesley Turner
1962	Rafael Osuna, Antonio Palafox	Darlene Hard, Maria Bueno
1963	Charles McKinley, Dennis Ralston	Robyn Ebbern, Margaret Smith
1964	Charles McKinley, Dennis Ralston	Billie Jean Moffitt, Karen Susman
1965	Roy Emerson, Fred Stolle	Carole Caldwell Graebner, Nancy Richey
1966	Roy Emerson, Fred Stolle	Maria Bueno, Nancy Richey
1967	John Newcombe, Tony Roche	Billie Jean Moffitt King, Rosemary Casals
1968[1]	Robert Lutz, Stan Smith	Maria Bueno, Margaret Smith Court
1969[1]	Ken Rosewall, Fred Stolle;	Françoise Durr, Darlene Hard;
	Dick Crealy, Allan Stone	Margaret Smith Court, Virginia Wade
1970	Pierre Barthes, Niki Pilic	Margaret Smith Court, Judy Dalton
1971	John Newcombe, Roger Taylor	Rosemary Casals, Judy Dalton
1972	Cliff Drysdale, Roger Taylor	Françoise Durr, Betty Stove
1973	Owen Davidson, John Newcombe	Margaret Smith Court, Virginia Wade
1974	Robert Lutz, Stan Smith	Billie Jean King, Rosemary Casals
1975	Jimmy Connors, Ilie Nastase	Margaret Smith Court, Virginia Wade
1976	Tom Okker, Marty Riessen	Delina Boshoff, Ilana Kloss
1977	Bob Hewitt, Frew McMillan	Martina Navratilova, Betty Stove
1978	Robert Lutz, Stan Smith	Martina Navratilova, Billie Jean King
1979	John McEnroe, Peter Fleming	Wendy Turnbull, Betty Stove
1980	Robert Lutz, Stan Smith	Martina Navratilova, Billie Jean King
1981	John McEnroe, Peter Fleming	Kathy Jordan, Anne Smith
1982	Kevin Curren, Steve Denton	Rosemary Casals, Wendy Turnbull
1983	John McEnroe, Peter Fleming	Martina Navratilova, Pam Shriver
1984	John Fitzgerald, Tomas Smid	Martina Navratilova, Pam Shriver
1985	Ken Flach, Robert Seguso	Claudia Kohde-Kilsch, Helena Sukova
1986	Andres Gómez, Slobodan Zivojinovic	Martina Navratilova, Pam Shriver
1987	Stefan Edberg, Anders Järryd	Martina Navratilova, Pam Shriver
1988	Sergio Casal, Emilio Sánchez	Gigi Fernández, Robin White
1989	John McEnroe, Mark Woodforde	Martina Navratilova, Hana Mandlikova
1990	Pieter Aldrich, Danie Visser	Martina Navratilova, Gigi Fernández
1991	John Fitzgerald, Anders Järryd	Pam Shriver, Natasha Zvereva
1992	Jim Grabb, Richey Reneberg	Gigi Fernández, Natasha Zvereva
1993	Ken Flach, Rick Leach	Arantxa Sánchez Vicario, Helena Sukova
1994	Paul Haarhuis, Jacco Eltingh	Arantxa Sánchez Vicario, Jana Novotna
1995	Todd Woodbridge, Mark Woodforde	Gigi Fernández, Natasha Zvereva

United States Open Tennis Championships—Doubles (continued)

YEAR	MEN	WOMEN
1996	Todd Woodbridge, Mark Woodforde	Gigi Fernández, Natasha Zvereva
1997	Yevgeny Kafelnikov, Daniel Vacek	Lindsay Davenport, Jana Novotna
1998	Sandon Stolle, Cyril Suk	Martina Hingis, Jana Novotna
1999	Sébastien Lareau, Alex O'Brien	Venus Williams, Serena Williams
2000	Lleyton Hewitt, Max Mirnyi	Julie Halard-Decugis, Ai Sugiyama
2001	Wayne Black, Kevin Ullyet	Lisa Raymond, Rennae Stubbs
2002	Mahesh Bhupathi, Max Mirnyi	Virginia Ruano Pascual, Paola Suárez
2003	Jonas Björkman, Todd Woodbridge	Virginia Ruano Pascual, Paola Suárez
2004	Mark Knowles, Daniel Nestor	Virginia Ruano Pascual, Paola Suárez
2005	Bob Bryan, Mike Bryan	Lisa Raymond, Samantha Stosur
2006	Martin Damm, Leander Paes	Nathalie Dechy, Vera Zvonareva
2007	Simon Aspelin, Julian Knowle	Nathalie Dechy, Dinara Safina

[1] *In 1968 and 1969 both amateur and open championships were held. Lutz and Smith won both men's competitions in 1968; Crealy and Stone took the men's amateur championships in 1969. Bueno and Court won both women's competitions in 1968; Court and Wade took the women's amateur championships in 1969. Thereafter the championships were open.*

Davis Cup

YEAR	WINNER	RUNNER-UP	RESULTS	YEAR	WINNER	RUNNER-UP	RESULTS
1900	United States	British Isles	3–0	1955	Australia	United States	5–0
1901	not held			1956	Australia	United States	5–0
1902	United States	British Isles	3–2	1957	Australia	United States	3–2
1903	British Isles[1]	United States	4–1	1958	United States	Australia	3–2
1904	British Isles	Belgium	5–0	1959	Australia	United States	3–2
1905	British Isles	United States	5–0	1960	Australia	Italy	4–1
1906	British Isles	United States	5–0	1961	Australia	Italy	5–0
1907	Australasia[2]	British Isles	3–2	1962	Australia	Mexico	5–0
1908	Australasia	United States	3–2	1963	United States	Australia	3–2
1909	Australasia	United States	5–0	1964	Australia	United States	3–2
1910	not held			1965	Australia	Spain	4–1
1911	Australasia	United States	5–0	1966	Australia	India	4–1
1912	British Isles	Australia	3–2	1967	Australia	Spain	4–1
1913	United States	British Isles	3–2	1968	United States	Australia	4–1
1914	Australasia	United States	3–2	1969	United States	Romania	5–0
1915–18	not held			1970	United States	West Germany	5–0
1919	Australasia	British Isles	4–1	1971	United States	Romania	3–2
1920	United States	Australasia	5–0	1972	United States	Romania	3–2
1921	United States	Japan	5–0	1973	Australia	United States	5–0
1922	United States	Australasia	4–1	1974	South Africa[3]	India	
1923	United States	Australasia	4–1	1975	Sweden	Czechoslovakia	3–2
1924	United States	Australasia	5–0	1976	Italy	Chile	4–1
1925	United States	France	5–0	1977	Australia	Italy	3–1
1926	United States	France	4–1	1978	United States	United Kingdom	4–1
1927	France	United States	3–2	1979	United States	Italy	5–0
1928	France	United States	4–1	1980	Czechoslovakia	Italy	4–1
1929	France	United States	3–2				
1930	France	United States	4–1	1981	United States	Argentina	3–1
1931	France	United Kingdom	3–2	1982	United States	France	4–1
1932	France	United States	3–2	1983	Australia	Sweden	3–2
1933	United Kingdom	France	3–2	1984	Sweden	United States	4–1
1934	United Kingdom	United States	4–1	1985	Sweden	West Germany	3–2
1935	United Kingdom	United States	5–0	1986	Australia	Sweden	3–2
1936	United Kingdom	Australia	3–2	1987	Sweden	India	5–0
1937	United States	United Kingdom	4–1	1988	West Germany	Sweden	4–1
1938	United States	Australia	3–2	1989	West Germany	Sweden	3–2
1939	Australia	United States	3–2	1990	United States	Australia	3–2
1940–45	not held			1991	France	United States	3–1
1946	United States	Australia	5–0	1992	United States	Switzerland	3–1
1947	United States	Australia	4–1	1993	Germany	Australia	4–1
1948	United States	Australia	5–0	1994	Sweden	Russia	4–1
1949	United States	Australia	4–1	1995	United States	Russia	3–2
1950	Australia	United States	4–1	1996	France	Sweden	3–2
1951	Australia	United States	3–2	1997	Sweden	United States	5–0
1952	Australia	United States	4–1	1998	Sweden	Italy	4–1
1953	Australia	United States	3–2	1999	Australia	France	3–2
1954	United States	Australia	3–2	2000	Spain	Australia	3–1

Davis Cup (continued)

YEAR	WINNER	RUNNER-UP	RESULTS	YEAR	WINNER	RUNNER-UP	RESULTS
2001	France	Australia	3–2	2004	Spain	United States	3–2
2002	Russia	France	3–2	2005	Croatia	Slovak Republic	3–2
2003	Australia	Spain	3–1	2006	Russia	Argentina	3–2

[1]Included Ireland up to 1922.   [2]Included Australia and New Zealand up to 1923.   [3]Forfeit; India withdrew from final.

Fed Cup

YEAR	WINNER	RUNNER-UP	RESULTS	YEAR	WINNER	RUNNER-UP	RESULTS
1963	United States	Australia	2–1	1985	Czechoslovakia	United States	2–1
1964	Australia	United States	2–1	1986	United States	Czechoslovakia	3–0
1965	Australia	United States	2–1	1987	West Germany	United States	2–1
1966	United States	West Germany	3–0	1988	Czechoslovakia	USSR	2–1
1967	United States	United Kingdom	2–0	1989	United States	Spain	3–0
1968	Australia	The Netherlands	3–0	1990	United States	USSR	2–1
1969	United States	Australia	2–1	1991	Spain	United States	2–1
1970	Australia	West Germany	3–0	1992	Germany	Spain	2–1
1971	Australia	United Kingdom	3–0	1993	Spain	Australia	3–0
1972	South Africa	United Kingdom	2–1	1994	Spain	United States	3–0
1973	Australia	South Africa	3–0	1995	Spain	United States	3–2
1974	Australia	United States	2–1	1996	United States	Spain	5–0
1975	Czechoslovakia	Australia	3–0	1997	France	The Netherlands	4–1
1976	United States	Australia	2–1	1998	Spain	Switzerland	3–2
1977	United States	Australia	2–1	1999	United States	Russia	4–1
1978	United States	Australia	2–1	2000	United States	Spain	5–0
1979	United States	Australia	3–0	2001	Belgium	Russia	2–1
1980	United States	Australia	3–0	2002	Slovakia	Spain	3–1
1981	United States	United Kingdom	3–0	2003	France	United States	4–1
1982	United States	West Germany	3–0	2004	Russia	France	3–2
1983	Czechoslovakia	West Germany	2–1	2005	Russia	France	3–2
1984	Czechoslovakia	Australia	2–1	2006	Italy	Belgium	3–2

Track & Field

The world governing body for track and field, or athletics, is the **International Association of Athletics Federations** (IAAF), founded in 1912. The sport includes relay running, a number of individual running, jumping, and throwing events, and one event (the decathlon for men and the heptathlon for women) that includes all three activities. The best-known competition for most track-and-field athletics is the **Olympic Games** held every four years. The

World Cup (inaugurated 1977) is a finals-only competition for national, hemispheric, and continental teams. In 1983, however, the first officially recognized non-Olympic world athletics championships were held.

A long-distance event that has special status is the **marathon** race, the standard distance for which is 42,195 m (26 mi 385 yd).

IAAF Web site: <www.iaaf.org>.

Outdoor Track & Field World Records

men

EVENT	RECORD HOLDER (NATIONALITY)	PERFORMANCE	DATE
100 m	Asafa Powell (JAM)[1]	9.74 sec	9 Sep 2007
200 m	Michael Johnson (USA)	19.32 sec	1 Aug 1996
400 m	Michael Johnson (USA)	43.18 sec	26 Aug 1999
800 m	Wilson Kipketer (DEN)	1 min 41.11 sec	24 Aug 1997
1,000 m	Noah Ngeny (KEN)	2 min 11.96 sec	5 Sep 1999
1,500 m	Hicham El Guerrouj (MAR)	3 min 26.00 sec	14 Jul 1998
1 mile	Hicham El Guerrouj (MAR)	3 min 43.13 sec	7 Jul 1999
3,000 m	Daniel Komen (KEN)	7 min 20.67 sec	1 Sep 1996
5,000 m	Kenenisa Bekele (ETH)	12 min 37.35 sec	31 May 2004
10,000 m	Kenenisa Bekele (ETH)	26 min 17.53 sec	26 Aug 2005
marathon[2]	Paul Tergat (KEN)	2 hr 4 min 55 sec	28 Sep 2003
110-m hurdles	Liu Xiang (CHN)	12.88 sec	11 Jul 2006
400-m hurdles	Kevin Young (USA)	46.78 sec	6 Aug 1992
20-km walk	Jefferson Pérez (ECU)	1 hr 17 min 21 sec	23 Aug 2003
50-km walk	Nathan Deakes (AUS)	3 hr 35 min 47 sec	2 Dec 2006

Outdoor Track & Field World Records (continued)

men (continued)

EVENT	RECORD HOLDER (NATIONALITY)	PERFORMANCE	DATE
steeplechase	Saif Saeed Shaheen (QAT)	7 min 53.63 sec	3 Sep 2004
4 × 100-m relay	United States	37.40 sec	8 Aug 1992
4 × 400-m relay	United States	2 min 54.20 sec	22 Jul 1998
high jump	Javier Sotomayor (CUB)	2.45 m (8 ft ½ in)	27 Jul 1993
long jump	Mike Powell (USA)	8.95 m (29 ft 4½ in)	30 Aug 1991
triple jump	Jonathan Edwards (GBR)	18.29 m (60 ft ¼ in)	7 Aug 1995
pole vault	Sergey Bubka (UKR)	6.14 m (20 ft 1¾ in)	31 Jul 1994
shot put	Randy Barnes (USA)	23.12 m (75 ft 10¼ in)	20 May 1990
discus throw	Jürgen Schult (GDR)	74.08 m (243 ft)	6 Jun 1986
hammer throw	Yury Sedykh (URS)	86.74 m (284 ft 7 in)	30 Aug 1986
javelin throw	Jan Zelezny (CZE)	98.48 m (323 ft 1 in)	25 May 1996
decathlon	Roman Sebrle (CZE)	9,026 pt	27 May 2001

women

EVENT	RECORD HOLDER (NATIONALITY)	PERFORMANCE	DATE
100 m	Florence Griffith-Joyner (USA)	10.49 sec	16 Jul 1988
200 m	Florence Griffith-Joyner (USA)	21.34 sec	29 Sep 1988
400 m	Marita Koch (GDR)	47.60 sec	6 Oct 1985
800 m	Jarmila Kratochvilova (TCH)	1 min 53.28 sec	26 Jul 1983
1,000 m	Svetlana Masterkova (RUS)	2 min 28.98 sec	23 Aug 1996
1,500 m	Qu Yunxia (CHN)	3 min 50.46 sec	11 Sep 1993
1 mile	Svetlana Masterkova (RUS)	4 min 12.56 sec	14 Aug 1996
3,000 m	Wang Junxia (CHN)	8 min 6.11 sec	13 Sep 1993
5,000 m	Meseret Defar (ETH)	14 min 16.63 sec	15 Jun 2007
10,000 m	Wang Junxia (CHN)	29 min 31.78 sec	8 Sep 1993
marathon[2]	Paula Radcliffe (GBR)	2 hr 15 min 25 sec	13 Apr 2003
100-m hurdles	Iordanka Donkova (BUL)	12.21 sec	20 Aug 1988
400-m hurdles	Yuliya Pechenkina (RUS)	52.34 sec	8 Aug 2003
20-km walk	Olimpiada Ivanova (RUS)	1 hr 25 min 41 sec	7 Aug 2005
steeplechase	Gulnara Samitova (RUS)	9 min 1.59 sec	4 Jul 2004
4 × 100-m relay	East Germany[1]	41.37 sec	6 Oct 1985
4 × 400-m relay	USSR	3 min 15.17 sec	1 Oct 1988
high jump	Stefka Kostadinova (BUL)	2.09 m (6 ft 10¼ in)	30 Aug 1987
long jump	Galina Chistyakova (URS)	7.52 m (24 ft 8¼ in)	11 Jun 1988
triple jump	Inessa Kravets (UKR)	15.50 m (50 ft 10¼ in)	10 Aug 1995
pole vault	Yelena Isinbayeva (RUS)	5.01 m (16 ft 5¼ in)	12 Aug 2005
shot put	Natalya Lisovskaya (URS)	22.63 m (74 ft 3 in)	7 Jun 1987
discus throw	Gabriele Reinsch (GDR)	76.80 m (252 ft)	9 Jul 1988
hammer throw	Tatyana Lysenko (RUS)[1]	78.61 m (258 ft)	26 May 2007
javelin throw	Osleidys Menéndez (CUB)	71.70 m (235 ft 3 in)	14 Aug 2005
heptathlon	Jackie Joyner-Kersee (USA)	7,291 pt	24 Sep 1988
decathlon	Austra Skujyte (LTU)	8,358 points	15 Apr 2005

[1]Pending ratification.   [2]Not an officially ratified event; best performance on record.

Indoor Track & Field World Records

men

EVENT	RECORD HOLDER (NATIONALITY)	PERFORMANCE	DATE
50 m	Donovan Bailey (CAN)	5.56 sec	9 Feb 1996
60 m	Maurice Greene (USA)	6.39 sec	3 Feb 1998
200 m	Frank Fredericks (NAM)	19.92 sec	18 Feb 1996
400 m	Kerron Clement (USA)	44 min 57 sec	12 Mar 2005
800 m	Wilson Kipketer (DEN)	1 min 42.67 sec	9 Mar 1997
1,000 m	Wilson Kipketer (DEN)	2 min 14.96 sec	20 Feb 2000
1,500 m	Hicham El Guerrouj (MAR)	3 min 31.18 sec	2 Feb 1997
1 mile	Hicham El Guerrouj (MAR)	3 min 48.45 sec	12 Feb 1997
3,000 m	Daniel Komen (KEN)	7 min 24.90 sec	6 Feb 1998
5,000 m	Kenenisa Bekele (ETH)	12 min 49.60 sec	20 Feb 2004
50-m hurdles	Mark McKoy (CAN)	6.25 sec	5 Mar 1986
60-m hurdles	Colin Jackson (GBR)	7.30 sec	6 Mar 1994
5-km walk	Mikhail Shchennikov (RUS)	18 min 07.08 sec	14 Feb 1995
4 × 200-m relay	Great Britain & Northern Ireland	1 min 22.11 sec	3 Mar 1991
4 × 400-m relay	United States	3 min 02.83 sec	7 Mar 1999
4 × 800-m relay	United States	7 min 13.94 sec	6 Feb 2000
High jump	Javier Sotomayor (CUB)	2.43 m (7 ft 11½ in)	4 Mar 1989
Long jump	Carl Lewis (USA)	8.79 m (28 ft 10 in)	27 Jan 1984

Indoor Track & Field World Records (continued)

men (continued)

EVENT	RECORD HOLDER (NATIONALITY)	PERFORMANCE	DATE
Triple jump	Aliecer Urrutia (CUB)	17.83 m (58 ft 6 in)	1 Mar 1997
	Christian Olsson (SWE)		7 Mar 2004
Pole vault	Sergey Bubka (UKR)	6.15 m (20 ft 2¼ in)	21 Feb 1993
Shot put	Randy Barnes (USA)	22.66 m (74 ft 4¼ in)	20 Jan 1989
Heptathlon	Dan O'Brien (USA)	6,476 pt	14 Mar 1993

women

EVENT	RECORD HOLDER (NATIONALITY)	PERFORMANCE	DATE
50 m	Irina Privalova (RUS)	5.96 sec	9 Feb 1995
60 m	Irina Privalova (RUS)	6.92 sec	11 Feb 1993
200 m	Merlene Ottey (JAM)	21.87 sec	13 Feb 1993
400 m	Jarmila Kratochvilova (TCH)	49.59 sec	7 Mar 1982
800 m	Jolanda Ceplak (SLO)	1 min 55.82 sec	3 Mar 2002
1,000 m	Maria Mutola (MOZ)	2 min 30.94 sec	25 Feb 1999
1,500 m	Yelena Soboleva (RUS)	3 min 58.28 sec	18 Feb 2006
1 mile	Doina Melinte (ROM)	4 min 17.14 sec	9 Feb 1990
3,000 m	Meseret Defar (ETH)[1]	8 min 23.72 sec	3 Feb 2007
5,000 m	Tirunesh Dibaba (ETH)	14 min 27.42 sec	27 Jan 2007
50-m hurdles	Cornelia Oschkenat (GDR)	6.58 sec	20 Feb 1988
60-m hurdles	Lyudmila Engquist (URS)	7.69 sec	4 Feb 1990
3-km walk	Claudia Stef (ROM)	11 min 40.33 sec	30 Jan 1999
4 × 200-m relay	Russia	1 min 32.41 sec	29 Jan 2005
4 × 400-m relay	Russia	3 min 23.37 sec	28 Jan 2006
4 × 800-m relay	Russia[1]	8 min 18.54 sec	11 Feb 2007
High jump	Kajsa Bergqvist (SWE)	2.08 m (6 ft 10 in)	4 Feb 2006
Long jump	Heike Drechsler (GDR)	7.37 m (24 ft 2¼ in)	13 Feb 1988
Triple jump	Tatyana Lebedeva (RUS)	15.36 m (50 ft 4¾ in)	6 Mar 2004
Pole vault	Yelena Isinbayeva (RUS)[1]	4.93 m (16 ft 2 in)	10 Feb 2007
Shot put	Helena Fibingerova (TCH)	22.50 m (73 ft 9¾ in)	19 Feb 1977
Pentathlon	Irina Belova (UNT)	4,991 pt	15 Feb 1992

[1]Pending ratification.

World Track & Field Championships—Men

YEAR	WINNER
100 M	
1983	Carl Lewis (USA)
1987	Carl Lewis (USA)
1991	Carl Lewis (USA)
1993	Linford Christie (GBR)
1995	Donovan Bailey (CAN)
1997	Maurice Greene (USA)
1999	Maurice Greene (USA)
2001	Maurice Greene (USA)
2003	Kim Collins (SKN)
2005	Justin Gatlin (USA)
2007	Tyson Gay (USA)
200 M	
1983	Calvin Smith (USA)
1987	Calvin Smith (USA)
1991	Michael Johnson (USA)
1993	Frank Fredericks (NAM)
1995	Michael Johnson (USA)
1997	Ato Boldon (TRI)
1999	Maurice Greene (USA)
2001	Konstadinos Kederis (GRE)
2003	John Capel (USA)
2005	Justin Gatlin (USA)
2007	Tyson Gay (USA)
400 M	
1983	Bert Cameron (JAM)
1987	Thomas Schoenlebe (GDR)
1991	Antonio Pettigrew (USA)
1993	Michael Johnson (USA)

YEAR	WINNER
400 M (CONT.)	
1995	Michael Johnson (USA)
1997	Michael Johnson (USA)
1999	Michael Johnson (USA)
2001	Avard Moncur (BAH)
2003	Jerome Young (USA)
2005	Jeremy Wariner (USA)
2007	Jeremy Wariner (USA)
800 M	
1983	Willi Wülbeck (FRG)
1987	Billy Konchellah (KEN)
1991	Billy Konchellah (KEN)
1993	Paul Ruto (KEN)
1995	Wilson Kipketer (DEN)
1997	Wilson Kipketer (DEN)
1999	Wilson Kipketer (DEN)
2001	André Bucher (SUI)
2003	Djabir Saïd-Guerni (ALG)
2005	Rashid Ramzi (BRN)
2007	Alfred Kirwa Yego (KEN)
1,500 M	
1983	Steve Cram (GBR)
1987	Abdi Bile (SOM)
1991	Noureddine Morceli (ALG)
1993	Noureddine Morceli (ALG)
1995	Noureddine Morceli (ALG)
1997	Hicham El Guerrouj (MAR)
1999	Hicham El Guerrouj (MAR)
2001	Hicham El Guerrouj (MAR)

YEAR	WINNER
1,500 M (CONT.)	
2003	Hicham El Guerrouj (MAR)
2005	Rashid Ramzi (BRN)
2007	Bernard Lagat (USA)
5,000 M	
1983	Eamonn Coghlan (IRL)
1987	Said Aouita (MAR)
1991	Yobes Ondieki (KEN)
1993	Ismael Kirui (KEN)
1995	Ismael Kirui (KEN)
1997	Daniel Komen (KEN)
1999	Salah Hissou (MAR)
2001	Richard Limo (KEN)
2003	Eliud Kipchoge (KEN)
2005	Benjamin Limo (KEN)
2007	Bernard Lagat (USA)
10,000 M	
1983	Alberto Cova (ITA)
1987	Paul Kipkoech (KEN)
1991	Moses Tanui (KEN)
1993	Haile Gebrselassie (ETH)
1995	Haile Gebrselassie (ETH)
1997	Haile Gebrselassie (ETH)
1999	Haile Gebrselassie (ETH)
2001	Charles Kamathi (KEN)
2003	Kenenisa Bekele (ETH)
2005	Kenenisa Bekele (ETH)
2007	Kenenisa Bekele (ETH)

World Track & Field Championships—Men (continued)

YEAR	WINNER
STEEPLECHASE	
1983	Patriz Ilg (FRG)
1987	Francesco Panetta (ITA)
1991	Moses Kiptanui (KEN)
1993	Moses Kiptanui (KEN)
1995	Moses Kiptanui (KEN)
1997	Wilson Boit Kipketer (KEN)
1999	Christopher Koskei (KEN)
2001	Reuben Kosgei (KEN)
2003	Saif Saaeed Shaheen (QAT)
2005	Saif Saaeed Shaheen (QAT)
2007	Brimin Kiprop Kipruto (KEN)
110-M HURDLES	
1983	Greg Foster (USA)
1987	Greg Foster (USA)
1991	Greg Foster (USA)
1993	Colin Jackson (GBR)
1995	Allen Johnson (USA)
1997	Allen Johnson (USA)
1999	Colin Jackson (GBR)
2001	Allen Johnson (USA)
2003	Allen Johnson (USA)
2005	Ladji Doucouré (FRA)
2007	Liu Xiang (CHN)
400-M HURDLES	
1983	Edwin Moses (USA)
1987	Edwin Moses (USA)
1991	Samuel Matete (ZAM)
1993	Kevin Young (USA)
1995	Derrick Adkins (USA)
1997	Stéphane Diagana (FRA)
1999	Fabrizio Mori (ITA)
2001	Felix Sánchez (DOM)
2003	Felix Sánchez (DOM)
2005	Bershawn Jackson (USA)
2007	Kerron Clement (USA)
MARATHON	
1983	Robert de Castella (AUS)
1987	Douglas Wakiihuri (KEN)
1991	Hiromi Taniguchi (JPN)
1993	Mark Plaatjes (USA)
1995	Martín Fiz (ESP)
1997	Abel Antón (ESP)
1999	Abel Antón (ESP)
2001	Gezahegne Abera (ETH)
2003	Jaouad Gharib (MAR)
2005	Jaouad Gharib (MAR)
2007	Luke Kibet (KEN)
20-KM WALK	
1983	Ernesto Canto (MEX)
1987	Maurizio Damilano (ITA)
1991	Maurizio Damilano (ITA)
1993	Valentí Massana (ESP)
1995	Michele Didoni (ITA)
1997	Daniel García (MEX)
1999	Ilya Markov (RUS)
2001	Roman Rasskazov (RUS)
2003	Jefferson Pérez (ECU)
2005	Jefferson Pérez (ECU)
2007	Jefferson Pérez (ECU)
50-KM WALK	
1983	Ronald Weigel (GDR)
1987	Hartwig Gauder (GDR)

YEAR	WINNER
50-KM WALK (CONT.)	
1991	Aleksandr Potashov (URS)
1993	Jesús Angel García (ESP)
1995	Valentin Kononen (FIN)
1997	Robert Korzeniowski (POL)
1999	Ivano Brugnetti (ITA)
2001	Robert Korzeniowski (POL)
2003	Robert Korzeniowski (POL)
2005	Sergey Kirdyapkin (RUS)
2007	Nathan Deakes (AUS)
4 × 100-M RELAY	
1983	United States
1987	United States
1991	United States
1993	United States
1995	Canada
1997	Canada
1999	United States
2001	United States
2003	United States
2005	France
2007	United States
4 × 400-M RELAY	
1983	USSR
1987	United States
1991	United Kingdom
1993	United States
1995	United States
1997	United States
1999	United States
2001	United States
2003	France
2005	United States
2007	United States
HIGH JUMP	
1983	Gennady Avdeyenko (URS)
1987	Patrik Sjöberg (SWE)
1991	Charles Austin (USA)
1993	Javier Sotomayor (CUB)
1995	Troy Kemp (BAH)
1997	Javier Sotomayor (CUB)
1999	Vyacheslav Voronin (RUS)
2001	Martin Buss (GER)
2003	Jacques Freitag (RSA)
2005	Yuri Krymarenko (UKR)
2007	Donald Thomas (BAH)
POLE VAULT	
1983	Sergey Bubka (URS)
1987	Sergey Bubka (URS)
1991	Sergey Bubka (URS)
1993	Sergey Bubka (UKR)
1995	Sergey Bubka (UKR)
1997	Sergey Bubka (UKR)
1999	Maksim Tarasov (RUS)
2001	Dmitri Markov (AUS)
2003	Giuseppe Gibilisco (ITA)
2005	Rens Blom (NED)
2007	Brad Walker (USA)
LONG JUMP	
1983	Carl Lewis (USA)
1987	Carl Lewis (USA)
1991	Mike Powell (USA)
1993	Mike Powell (USA)

YEAR	WINNER
LONG JUMP (CONT.)	
1995	Iván Pedroso (CUB)
1997	Iván Pedroso (CUB)
1999	Iván Pedroso (CUB)
2001	Iván Pedroso (CUB)
2003	Dwight Phillips (USA)
2005	Dwight Phillips (USA)
2007	Irving Saladino (PAN)
TRIPLE JUMP	
1983	Zdzislaw Hoffman (POL)
1987	Khristo Markov (BUL)
1991	Kenny Harrison (USA)
1993	Mike Conley (USA)
1995	Jonathan Edwards (GBR)
1997	Yoelbi Quesada (CUB)
1999	Charles Michael Friedek (GER)
2001	Jonathan Edwards (GBR)
2003	Christian Olsson (SWE)
2005	Walter Davis (USA)
2007	Nelson Évora (POR)
SHOT PUT	
1983	Edward Sarul (POL)
1987	Werner Günthör (SUI)
1991	Werner Günthör (SUI)
1993	Werner Günthör (SUI)
1995	John Godina (USA)
1997	John Godina (USA)
1999	C.J. Hunter (USA)
2001	John Godina (USA)
2003	Andrey Mikhnevich (BLR)
2005	Adam Nelson (USA)
2007	Reese Hoffa (USA)
DISCUS THROW	
1983	Imrich Bugar (TCH)
1987	Jürgen Schult (GDR)
1991	Lars Riedel (GER)
1993	Lars Riedel (GER)
1995	Lars Riedel (GER)
1997	Lars Riedel (GER)
1999	Anthony Washington (USA)
2001	Lars Riedel (GER)
2003	Virgilijus Alekna (LTU)
2005	Virgilijus Alekna (LTU)
2007	Gerd Kanter (EST)
HAMMER THROW	
1983	Sergey Litvinov (URS)
1987	Sergey Litvinov (URS)
1991	Yury Sedykh (URS)
1993	Andrey Abduvaliyev (TJK)
1995	Andrey Abduvaliyev (TJK)
1997	Heinz Weis (GER)
1999	Karsten Kobs (GER)
2001	Szymon Ziolkowski (POL)
2003	Ivan Tikhon (BLR)
2005	Ivan Tikhon (BLR)
2007	Ivan Tikhon (BLR)
JAVELIN THROW	
1983	Detlef Michel (GDR)
1987	Seppo Räty (FIN)
1991	Kimmo Kinnunen (FIN)
1993	Jan Zelezny (CZE)
1995	Jan Zelezny (CZE)

World Track & Field Championships—Men (continued)

JAVELIN THROW (CONT.)
1997	Marius Corbett (RSA)
1999	Aki Parviainen (FIN)
2001	Jan Zelezny (CZE)
2003	Sergey Makarov (RUS)
2005	Andrus Varnik (EST)
2007	Tero Pitkämäki (FIN)

DECATHLON
1983	Daley Thompson (GBR)
1987	Torsten Voss (GDR)
1991	Dan O'Brien (USA)
1993	Dan O'Brien (USA)
1995	Dan O'Brien (USA)
1997	Tomas Dvorak (CZE)

DECATHLON (CONT.)
1999	Tomas Dvorak (CZE)
2001	Tomas Dvorak (CZE)
2003	Tom Pappas (USA)
2005	Bryan Clay (USA)
2007	Roman Sebrle (CZE)

World Track & Field Championships—Women

YEAR	WINNER
100 M	
1983	Marlies Göhr (GDR)
1987	Silke Gladisch (GDR)
1991	Katrin Krabbe (GER)
1993	Gail Devers (USA)
1995	Gwen Torrence (USA)
1997	Marion Jones (USA)
1999	Marion Jones (USA)
2001	Zhanna Pintusevich (UKR)
2003	Torri Edwards (USA)
2005	Lauryn Williams (USA)
2007	Veronica Campbell (JAM)
200 M	
1983	Marita Koch (GDR)
1987	Silke Gladisch (GDR)
1991	Katrin Krabbe (GER)
1993	Merlene Ottey (JAM)
1995	Merlene Ottey (JAM)
1997	Zhanna Pintusevich (UKR)
1999	Inger Miller (USA)
2001	Marion Jones (USA)
2003	Anastasiya Kapachin-skaya (RUS)
2005	Allyson Felix (USA)
2007	Allyson Felix (USA)
400 M	
1983	Jarmila Kratochvilova (TCH)
1987	Olga Bryzgina (URS)
1991	Marie-José Pérec (FRA)
1993	Jearl Miles (USA)
1995	Marie-José Pérec (FRA)
1997	Cathy Freeman (AUS)
1999	Cathy Freeman (AUS)
2001	Amy Mbacke Thiam (SEN)
2003	Ana Guevara (MEX)
2005	Tonique Williams-Darling (BAH)
2007	Christine Ohuruogu (GBR)
800 M	
1983	Jarmila Kratochvilova (TCH)
1987	Sigrun Wodars (GDR)
1991	Liliya Nurutdinova (URS)
1993	Maria Mutola (MOZ)
1995	Ana Quirot (CUB)
1997	Ana Quirot (CUB)
1999	Ludmila Formanova (CZE)
2001	Maria Mutola (MOZ)
2003	Maria Mutola (MOZ)
2005	Zulia Calatayud (CUB)
2007	Janeth Jepkosgei (KEN)
1,500 M	
1983	Mary Decker (USA)
1987	Tatyana Samolenko (URS)
1991	Hassiba Boulmerka (ALG)

YEAR	WINNER
1,500 M (CONT.)	
1993	Liu Dong (CHN)
1995	Hassiba Boulmerka (ALG)
1997	Carla Sacramento (POR)
1999	Svetlana Masterkova (RUS)
2001	Gabriela Szabo (ROM)
2003	Tatyana Tomashova (RUS)
2005	Tatyana Tomashova (RUS)
2007	Maryam Yusuf Jamal (BRN)
3,000 M[1]	
1983	Mary Decker (USA)
1987	Tatyana Samolenko (URS)
1991	Tatyana Dorovskikh (URS)
1993	Qu Yunxia (CHN)
1995	Sonia O'Sullivan (IRL)
1997	Gabriela Szabo (ROM)
1999	Gabriela Szabo (ROM)
2001	Olga Yegorova (RUS)
2003	Tirunesh Dibaba (ETH)
2005	Tirunesh Dibaba (ETH)
2007	Meseret Defar (ETH)
10,000 M[2]	
1987	Ingrid Kristiansen (NOR)
1991	Liz McColgan (GBR)
1993	Wang Junxia (CHN)
1995	Fernanda Ribeiro (POR)
1997	Sally Barsosio (KEN)
1999	Gete Wami (ETH)
2001	Derartu Tulu (ETH)
2003	Berhane Adere (ETH)
2005	Tirunesh Dibaba (ETH)
2007	Tirunesh Dibaba (ETH)
STEEPLECHASE	
2005	Dorcus Inzikuru (UGA)
2007	Yekaterina Volkova (RUS)
100-M HURDLES	
1983	Bettine Jahn (GDR)
1987	Ginka Zagorcheva (BUL)
1991	Ludmila Narozhilenko (URS)
1993	Gail Devers (USA)
1995	Gail Devers (USA)
1997	Ludmila Engquist (SWE)
1999	Gail Devers (USA)
2001	Anjanette Kirkland (USA)
2003	Perdita Felicien (CAN)
2005	Michelle Perry (USA)
2007	Michelle Perry (USA)
400-M HURDLES	
1983	Yekaterina Fesenko (URS)
1987	Sabine Busch (GDR)
1991	Tatyana Ledovskaya (URS)

YEAR	WINNER
400-M HURDLES (CONT.)	
1993	Sally Gunnell (GBR)
1995	Kim Batten (USA)
1997	Nezha Bidouane (MAR)
1999	Daimí Pernía (CUB)
2001	Nezha Bidouane (MAR)
2003	Jana Pittman (AUS)
2005	Yuliya Pechonkina (RUS)
2007	Jana Rawlinson (AUS)
MARATHON	
1983	Grete Waitz (NOR)
1987	Rosa Mota (POR)
1991	Wanda Panfil (POL)
1993	Asari Junko (JPN)
1995	Maria Machado (POR)
1997	Hiromi Suzuki (JPN)
1999	Jong Song Ok (PRK)
2001	Lidia Simon (ROM)
2003	Catherine Ndereba (KEN)
2005	Paula Radcliffe (GBR)
2007	Catherine Ndereba (KEN)
10-KM WALK[2]	
1987	Irina Strakhova (URS)
1991	Alina Ivanova (URS)
1993	Sari Essayeh (FIN)
1995	Irina Stankina (RUS)
1997	Annarita Sidoti (ITA)
20-KM RACE WALK[3]	
1999	Liu Hongyu (CHN)
2001	Olimpiada Ivanova (RUS)
2003	Yelena Nikolayeva (RUS)
2005	Olimpiada Ivanova (RUS)
2007	Olga Kaniskina (RUS)
4 × 100-M RELAY	
1983	East Germany
1987	United States
1991	Jamaica
1993	Russia
1995	United States
1997	United States
1999	Bahamas
2001	Germany
2003	France
2005	United States
2007	United States
4 × 400-M RELAY	
1983	East Germany
1987	East Germany
1991	USSR
1993	United States
1995	United States
1997	Germany

World Track & Field Championships—Women (continued)

YEAR	WINNER	YEAR	WINNER	YEAR	WINNER
4 × 400-M RELAY (CONT.)		**TRIPLE JUMP[4]**		**HAMMER THROW[3] (CONT.)**	
1999	Russia	1993	Anna Biryukova (RUS)	2003	Yipsi Moreno (CUB)
2001	Jamaica	1995	Inessa Kravets (UKR)	2005	Olga Kuzenkova (RUS)
2003	United States	1997	Sarka Kasparkova (CZE)	2007	Betty Heidler (GER)
2005	Russia	1999	Paraskevi Tsiamita (GRE)		
2007	United States	2001	Tatyana Lebedeva (RUS)	**JAVELIN THROW**	
		2003	Tatyana Lebedeva (RUS)	1983	Tiina Lillak (FIN)
HIGH JUMP		2005	Trecia Smith (JAM)	1987	Fatima Whitbread (GBR)
1983	Tamara Bykova (URS)	2007	Yargelis Savigne (CUB)	1991	Xu Demei (CHN)
1987	Stefka Kostadinova (BUL)			1993	Trine Hattestad (NOR)
1991	Heike Henkel (GER)	**SHOT PUT**		1995	Natalya Shikolenko (BLR)
1993	Ioamnet Quintero (CUB)	1983	Helena Fibingerova (TCH)	1997	Trine Hattestad (NOR)
1995	Stefka Kostadinova (BUL)	1987	Natalya Lisovskaya (URS)	1999	Mirela Tzelili (GRE)
1997	Hanne Haugland (NOR)	1991	Huang Zhihong (CHN)	2001	Osleidys Menéndez (CUB)
1999	Inga Babakova (UKR)	1993	Huang Zhihong (CHN)	2003	Mirela Manjani (GRE)
2001	Hestrie Cloete (RSA)	1995	Astrid Kumbernuss (GER)	2005	Osleidys Menéndez (CUB)
2003	Hestrie Cloete (RSA)	1997	Astrid Kumbernuss (GER)	2007	Barbora Spotáková (CZE)
2005	Kajsa Bergqvist (SWE)	1999	Astrid Kumbernuss (GER)		
2007	Blanka Vlasic (CRO)	2001	Yanina Korolchik (BLR)	**HEPTATHLON**	
		2003	Svetlana Krivelyova (RUS)	1983	Ramona Neubert (GDR)
POLE VAULT[3]		2005	Nadezhda Ostapchuk (BLR)	1987	Jackie Joyner-Kersee (USA)
1999	Stacy Dragila (USA)	2007	Valerie Vili (NZL)	1991	Sabine Braun (GER)
2001	Stacy Dragila (USA)			1993	Jackie Joyner-Kersee (USA)
2003	Svetlana Feofanova (RUS)	**DISCUS THROW**		1995	Ghada Shouaa (SYR)
2005	Yelena Isinbayeva (RUS)	1983	Martina Opitz (GDR)	1997	Sabine Braun (GER)
2007	Yelena Isinbayeva (RUS)	1987	Martina Hellmann (GDR)	1999	Eunice Barber (FRA)
		1991	Tsvetanka Khristova (BUL)	2001	Yelena Prokhorova (RUS)
LONG JUMP		1993	Olga Burova (RUS)	2003	Carolina Klüft (SWE)
1983	Heike Daute (GDR)	1995	Ellina Zvereva (BLR)	2005	Carolina Klüft (SWE)
1987	Jackie Joyner-Kersee (USA)	1997	Beatrice Faumuina (NZL)	2007	Carolina Klüft (SWE)
1991	Jackie Joyner-Kersee (USA)	1999	Franka Dietzsch (GER)		
1993	Heike Drechsler (GER)	2001	Ellina Zvereva (BLR)		
1995	Fiona May (ITA)	2003	Irina Yachenko (BLR)		
1997	Ludmila Galkina (RUS)	2005	Franka Dietzsch (GER)		
1999	Niurka Montalvo (ESP)	2007	Franka Dietzsch (GER)		
2001	Fiona May (ITA)				
2003	Eunice Barber (FRA)	**HAMMER THROW[3]**			
2005	Tianna Madison (USA)	1999	Mihaela Melinte (ROM)		
2007	Tatyana Lebedeva (RUS)	2001	Yipsi Moreno (CUB)		

[1]*Became 5,000 m in 1995.*   [2]*Event added in 1987.*   [3]*Event added in 1999.*   [4]*Event added in 1993.*

IAAF World Cup—Men

YEAR	WINNER	YEAR	WINNER	YEAR	WINNER
100 M		**200 M (CONT.)**		**800 M (CONT.)**	
1977	Steve Williams (USA)	1994	John Regis (GBR)	1985	Sammy Koskei (KEN)
1979	James Sanford (USA)	1998	Frank Fredericks (NAM)	1989	Tom McKean (GBR)
1981	Allan Wells (GBR)	2002	Francis Obikwelu (POR)	1992	David Sharpe (GBR)
1985	Ben Johnson (CAN)	2006	Wallace Spearmon (USA)	1994	Mark Everett (USA)
1989	Linford Christie (GBR)			1998	Nils Schumann (GER)
1992	Linford Christie (GBR)	**400 M**		2002	Antonio Manuel Reina (ESP)
1994	Linford Christie (GBR)	1977	Alberto Juantorena (CUB)	2006	Youssef Saad Kamel (BRN)
1998	Obadele Thompson (BAR)	1979	Kashief Hassan (SUD)		
2002	Uchenna Emedolu (NGR)	1981	Cliff Wiley (USA)	**1,500 M**	
2006	Tyson Gay (USA)	1985	Mike Franks (USA)	1977	Steve Ovett (GBR)
		1989	Roberto Hernández (CUB)	1979	Thomas Wessinghage (FRG)
200 M		1992	Sunday Bada (NGR)	1981	Steve Ovett (GBR)
1977	Clancy Edwards (USA)	1994	Antonio Pettigrew (USA)	1985	Omer Khalifa (SUD)
1979	Silvio Leonard (CUB)	1998	Iwan Thomas (GBR)	1989	Abdi Bile (SOM)
1981	Melvin Lattany (USA)	2002	Michael Blackwood (JAM)	1992	Mohammed Suleiman (QAT)
1985	Robson Caetano da Silva (BRA)	2006	LaShawn Merritt (USA)	1994	Noureddine Morceli (ALG)
1989	Robson Caetano da Silva (BRA)	**800 M**		1998	Laban Rotich (KEN)
		1977	Alberto Juantorena (CUB)	2002	Bernard Lagat (KEN)
1992	Robson Caetano da Silva (BRA)	1979	James Maina (KEN)	2006	Alex Kipchirchir (KEN)
		1981	Sebastian Coe (GBR)		

IAAF World Cup—Men (continued)

YEAR	WINNER
3,000 M	
1998	Dieter Baumann (GER)
2002	Craig Mottram (AUS)
2006	Craig Mottram (AUS)
5,000 M	
1977	Miruts Yifter (ETH)
1979	Miruts Yifter (ETH)
1981	Eamonn Coghlan (IRL)
1985	Doug Padilla (USA)
1989	Said Aouita (MAR)
1992	Fita Bayesa (ETH)
1994	Brahim Lahlafi (MAR)
1998	Daniel Komen (KEN)
2002	Alberto García (ESP)
2006	Saif Saaeed Shaheen (QAT)
10,000 M	
1977	Miruts Yifter (ETH)
1979	Miruts Yifter (ETH)
1981	Werner Schildhauer (GDR)
1985	Wodajo Bulti (ETH)
1989	Salvatore Antibo (ITA)
1992	Addis Abebe (ETH)
1994	Khalid Skah (MAR)
STEEPLECHASE	
1977	Michael Karst (FRG)
1979	Henry Rono (KEN)
1981	Boguslaw Maminski (POL)
1985	Julius Kariuki (KEN)
1989	Julius Kariuki (KEN)
1992	Philip Barkutwo (KEN)
1994	Moses Kiptanui (KEN)
1998	Damian Kallabis (GER)
2002	Wilson Boit Kipketer (KEN)
2006	Saif Saaeed Shaheen (QAT)
110-M HURDLES	
1977	Thomas Munkelt (GDR)
1979	Reynaldo Nehemiah (USA)
1981	Greg Foster (USA)
1985	Tony Campbell (USA)
1989	Roger Kingdom (USA)
1992	Colin Jackson (GBR)
1994	Tony Jarrett (GBR)
1998	Falk Balzer (GER)
2002	Anier García (CUB)
2006	Allen Johnson (USA)
400-M HURDLES	
1977	Edwin Moses (USA)
1979	Edwin Moses (USA)
1981	Edwin Moses (USA)
1985	Andre Phillips (USA)
1989	David Patrick (USA)
1992	Samuel Matete (ZAM)
1994	Samuel Matete (ZAM)
1998	Samuel Matete (ZAM)
2002	James Carter (USA)
2006	Kerron Clement (USA)
4 × 100-M RELAYS	
1977	United States
1979	Americas

YEAR	WINNER
4 × 100-M RELAYS (CONT.)	
1981	Europe
1985	United States
1989	United States
1992	United States
1994	Great Britain
1998	Great Britain
2002	United States
2006	United States
4 × 400-M RELAYS	
1977	West Germany
1979	United States
1981	United States
1985	United States
1989	Americas
1992	Africa
1994	Great Britain
1998	United States
2002	Americas
2006	United States
TRIPLE JUMP	
1977	João de Oliveira (BRA)
1979	João de Oliveira (BRA)
1981	João de Oliveira (BRA)
1985	Willie Banks (USA)
1989	Mike Conley (USA)
1992	Jonathan Edwards (GBR)
1994	Yoelbi Quesada (CUB)
1998	Charles Friedek (GER)
2002	Jonathan Edwards (GBR)
2006	Walter Davis (USA)
HIGH JUMP	
1977	Rolf Beilschmidt (GDR)
1979	Franklin Jacobs (USA)
1981	Tyke Peacock (USA)
1985	Patrik Sjöberg (SWE)
1989	Patrik Sjöberg (SWE)
1992	Yury Sergeyenko (UNT[1])
1994	Javier Sotomayor (CUB)
1998	Charles Austin (USA)
2002	Yaroslav Rybakov (RUS)
2006	Tomas Janku (CZE)
POLE VAULT	
1977	Mike Tully (USA)
1979	Mike Tully (USA)
1981	Konstantin Volkov (URS)
1985	Sergey Bubka (URS)
1989	Philippe Collet (FRA)
1992	Igor Potapovich (UNT[1])
1994	Okkert Brits (RSA)
1998	Maksim Tarasov (RUS)
2002	Okkert Brits (RSA)
2006	Steven Hooker (AUS)
LONG JUMP	
1977	Arnie Robinson (USA)
1979	Larry Myricks (USA)
1981	Carl Lewis (USA)
1985	Mike Conley (USA)
1989	Larry Myricks (USA)
1992	Iván Pedroso (CUB)
1994	Fred Salle (GBR)

YEAR	WINNER
LONG JUMP (CONT.)	
1998	Iván Pedroso (CUB)
2002	Savanté Stringfellow (USA)
2006	Irving Saladino (PAN)
SHOT PUT	
1977	Udo Beyer (GDR)
1979	Udo Beyer (GDR)
1981	Udo Beyer (GDR)
1985	Ulf Timmermann (GDR)
1989	Ulf Timmermann (GDR)
1992	Mike Stulce (USA)
1994	C.J. Hunter (USA)
1998	John Godina (USA)
2002	Adam Nelson (USA)
2006	Ralf Bartels (GER)
DISCUS THROW	
1977	Wolfgang Schmidt (GDR)
1979	Wolfgang Schmidt (GDR)
1981	Armin Lemme (GDR)
1985	Georgy Kolnoochenko (URS)
1989	Jürgen Schult (GDR)
1992	Anthony Washington (USA)
1994	Vladimir Dubrovshchik (BLR)
1998	Virgilijus Alekna (LTU)
2002	Róbert Fazekas (HUN)
2006	Virgilijus Alekna (LTU)
JAVELIN THROW	
1977	Michael Wessing (FRG)
1979	Wolfgang Hanisch (GDR)
1981	Dainis Kula (URS)
1985	Uwe Hohn (GDR)
1989	Steve Backley (GBR)
1992	Jan Zelezny (TCH)
1994	Steve Backley (GBR)
1998	Steve Backley (GBR)
2002	Sergey Makarov (RUS)
2006	Andreas Thorkildsen (NOR)
HAMMER THROW	
1977	Karl-Hans Riehm (FRG)
1979	Sergey Litvinov (URS)
1981	Yuriy Sedykh (URS)
1985	Jüri Tamm (URS)
1989	Heinz Weis (FRG)
1992	Tibor Gécsek (HUN)
1994	Andrey Abduvaliyev (TJK)
1998	Tibor Gécsek (HUN)
2002	Adrián Annus (HUN)
2006	Murofushi Koji (JPN)
TEAM	
1977	East Germany
1979	United States
1981	Europe
1985	United States
1989	United States
1992	Africa
1994	Africa
1998	Africa
2002	Africa
2006	Europe

[1]*Unified Team, consisting of athletes from the Commonwealth of Independent States plus Georgia.*

IAAF World Cup—Women

YEAR	WINNER
100 M	
1981	Evelyn Ashford (USA)
1985	Marlies Göhr (GDR)
1977	Marlies Oelsner (GDR)
1979	Evelyn Ashford (USA)
1981	Evelyn Ashford (USA)
1985	Marlies Göhr (GDR)
1989	Sheila Echols (USA)
1992	Natalya Voronova (UNT[1])
1994	Irina Privalova (RUS)
1998	Marion Jones (USA)
2002	Marion Jones (USA)
2006	Sherone Simpson (JAM)
200 M	
1977	Irina Szewinska (POL)
1979	Evelyn Ashford (USA)
1981	Evelyn Ashford (USA)
1985	Marita Koch (GDR)
1989	Silke Möller (GDR)
1992	Marie-José Pérec (FRA)
1994	Merlene Ottey (JAM)
1998	Marion Jones (USA)
2002	Debbie Ferguson (BAH)
2006	Sanya Richards (USA)
400 M	
1977	Irina Szewinska (POL)
1979	Marita Koch (GDR)
1981	Jarmila Kratochvilova (TCH)
1985	Marita Koch (GDR)
1989	Ana Quirot (CUB)
1992	Jearl Miles (USA)
1994	Irina Privalova (RUS)
1998	Falilat Ogunkoya (NGR)
2002	Ana Guevara (MEX)
2006	Sanya Richards (USA)
800 M	
1977	Totka Petrova (BUL)
1979	Nikolina Shtereva (BUL)
1981	Lyudmila Veselkova (URS)
1985	Christine Wachtel (GDR)
1989	Ana Quirot (CUB)
1992	Maria Mutola (MOZ)
1994	Maria Mutola (MOZ)
1998	Maria Mutola (MOZ)
2002	Maria Mutola (MOZ)
2006	Zulia Calatayud (CUB)
1,500 M	
1977	Tatyana Kazankina (URS)
1979	Christiane Wartenburg (GDR)
1981	Tamara Sorokina (URS)
1985	Hildegard Körner (GDR)
1989	Paula Ivan (ROM)
1992	Yekaterina Podkopayeva (UNT[1])
1994	Hassiba Boulmerka (ALG)
1998	Svetlana Masterkova (RUS)
2002	Süreyya Ayhan (TUR)
2006	Maryam Yusuf Jamal (BRN)
3,000 M	
1977	Grete Waitz (NOR)
1979	Svetlana Ulmasova (URS)
1981	Angelika Zauber (GDR)
3,000 M (CONT.)	
1985	Ulrike Bruns (GDR)
1989	Yvonne Murray (GBR)
1992	Derartu Tulu (ETH)
1994	Yvonne Murray (GBR)
1998	Gabriela Szabo (ROM)
2002	Berhane Adere (ETH)
2006	Tirunesh Dibaba (ETH)
5,000 M	
1998	Sonia O'Sullivan (IRL)
2002	Olga Yegorova (RUS)
2006	Meseret Defar (ETH)
10,000 M	
1985	Aurora Cunha (POR)
1989	Kathrin Ullrich (GDR)
1992	Derartu Tulu (ETH)
1994	Elana Meyer (RSA)
STEEPLECHASE	
2006	Alesia Turava (BLR)
100-M HURDLES	
1977	Grazyna Rabsztyn (POL)
1979	Grazyna Rabsztyn (POL)
1981	Tatyana Anisimova (URS)
1985	Cornelia Oschkenat (GDR)
1989	Cornelia Oschkenat (GDR)
1992	Aliuska López (CUB)
1994	Aliuska López (CUB)
1998	Glory Alozie (NGR)
2002	Gail Devers (USA)
2006	Brigitte Foster-Hylton (JAM)
400-M HURDLES	
1979	Bärbel Klepp (GDR)
1981	Ellen Neumann (GDR)
1985	Sabine Busch (GDR)
1989	Sandra Farmer-Patrick (USA)
1992	Sandra Farmer-Patrick (USA)
1994	Sally Gunnell (GBR)
1998	Nezha Bidouane (MAR)
2002	Yuliya Pechonkina (RUS)
2006	Yuliya Pechonkina (RUS)
4 × 100-M RELAYS	
1977	Europe Select
1979	Europe Select
1981	East Germany
1985	East Germany
1989	East Germany
1992	Asia
1994	Africa
1998	United States
2002	Americas
2006	Americas
4 × 400-M RELAYS	
1977	East Germany
1979	East Germany
1981	East Germany
1985	East Germany
1989	Americas
1992	Americas
1994	Great Britain
4 × 400-M RELAYS (CONT.)	
1998	Germany
2002	Americas
2006	Americas
TRIPLE JUMP	
1992	Li Huirong (CHN)
1994	Anna Biryukova (RUS)
1998	Olga Vasdeki (GRE)
2002	Françoise Mbango Etone (CMR)
2006	Tatyana Lebedeva (RUS)
HIGH JUMP	
1977	Rosemarie Ackermann (GDR)
1979	Debbie Brill (CAN)
1981	Ulrike Meyfarth (FRG)
1985	Stefka Kostadinova (BUL)
1989	Silvia Costa (CUB)
1992	Ioamnet Quintero (CUB)
1994	Britta Bilac (SLO)
1998	Monica Iagar-Dinescu (ROM)
2002	Hestrie Cloete (RSA)
2006	Yelena Slesarenko (RUS)
POLE VAULT	
2002	Annika Becker (GER)
2006	Yelena Isinbaeva (RUS)
LONG JUMP	
1977	Lyn Jacenko (AUS)
1979	Anita Stukane (URS)
1981	Sigrid Ulbricht (GDR)
1985	Heike Daute Drechsler (GDR)
1989	Galina Chistyakova (URS)
1992	Heike Drechsler (GER)
1994	Inessa Kravets (UKR)
1998	Heike Drechsler (GER)
2002	Tatyana Kotova (RUS)
2006	Lyudmila Kolchanova (RUS)
SHOT PUT	
1977	Ilona Slupianek (GDR)
1979	Ilona Slupianek (GDR)
1981	Ilona Slupianek (GDR)
1985	Natalya Lisovskaya (URS)
1989	Huang Zhihong (CHN)
1992	Belsis Laza (CUB)
1994	Zhihong Huang (CHN)
1998	Vita Pavlysh (UKR)
2002	Irina Korzhanenko (RUS)
2006	Valerie Vili (NZL)
DISCUS THROW	
1977	Faina Melnik (URS)
1979	Evelin Jahl (GDR)
1981	Evelin Jahl (GDR)
1985	Martina Optiz (GDR)
1989	Ilke Wyludda (GDR)
1992	Maritza Marten (CUB)
1994	Ilke Wyludda (GER)
1998	Franka Dietzsch (GER)
2002	Beatrice Faumuina (NZL)
2006	Franka Dietzsch (GER)

IAAF World Cup—Women (continued)

JAVELIN THROW		HAMMER THROW		TEAM (CONT.)	
1977	Ruth Fuchs (GDR)	2002	Gu Yuan (CHN)	1992	Unified Team[1]
1979	Ruth Fuchs (GDR)	2006	Kamila Skolimowska	1994	Europe
1981	Antoaneta Todorova (BUL)		(POL)	1998	United States
1985	Olga Gavrilova (URS)			2002	Russia
1989	Petra Felke (GDR)	**TEAM**		2006	Russia
1992	Tessa Sanderson (GBR)	1977	Europe Select		
1994	Trine Hattestad (NOR)	1979	East Germany		
1998	Joanna Stone (AUS)	1981	East Germany		
2002	Osleidys Menéndez CUB)	1985	East Germany		
2006	Steffi Nerius (GER)	1989	East Germany		

[1]Unified Team, consisting of athletes from the Commonwealth of Independent States plus Georgia.

World Cross Country Championships

Men's competition held since 1903, women's since 1967. Table shows results from the past 20 years.

men (12,000 meters)

YEAR	INDIVIDUAL (NATIONALITY)	TEAM	YEAR	INDIVIDUAL (NATIONALITY)	TEAM
1988	John Ngugi (KEN)	Kenya	1998	Paul Tergat (KEN)	Kenya
1989	John Ngugi (KEN)	Kenya	1999	Paul Tergat (KEN)	Kenya
1990	Khalid Skah (MAR)	Kenya	2000	Mohammed Mourhit (BEL)	Kenya
1991	Khalid Skah (MAR)	Kenya	2001	Mohammed Mourhit (BEL)	Kenya
1992	John Ngugi (KEN)	Kenya	2002	Kenenisa Bekele (ETH)	Kenya
1993	William Sigei (KEN)	Kenya	2003	Kenenisa Bekele (ETH)	Kenya
1994	William Sigei (KEN)	Kenya	2004	Kenenisa Bekele (ETH)	Ethiopia
1995	Paul Tergat (KEN)	Kenya	2005	Kenenisa Bekele (ETH)	Ethiopia
1996	Paul Tergat (KEN)	Kenya	2006	Kenenisa Bekele (ETH)	Kenya
1997	Paul Tergat (KEN)	Kenya	2007	Zersenay Tadesse (ERI)	Kenya

women (8,000 meters)

YEAR	INDIVIDUAL (NATIONALITY)	TEAM	YEAR	INDIVIDUAL (NATIONALITY)	TEAM
1988	Ingrid Kristiansen (NOR)	USSR	1998	Sonia O'Sullivan (IRE)	Kenya
1989	Annette Sargent (FRA)	USSR	1999	Gete Wami (ETH)	Ethiopia
1990	Lynn Jennings (USA)	USSR	2000	Derartu Tulu (ETH)	Ethiopia
1991	Lynn Jennings (USA)	Kenya	2001	Paula Radcliffe (GBR)	Kenya
1992	Lynn Jennings (USA)	Kenya	2002	Paula Radcliffe (GBR)	Ethiopia
1993	Albertina Dias (POR)	Kenya	2003	Werknesh Kidane (ETH)	Ethiopia
1994	Hellen Chepngeno (KEN)	Portugal	2004	Benita Johnson (AUS)	Ethiopia
1995	Derartu Tulu (ETH)	Kenya	2005	Tirunesh Dibaba (ETH)	Ethiopia
1996	Gete Wami (ETH)	Kenya	2006	Tirunesh Dibaba (ETH)	Ethiopia
1997	Derartu Tulu (ETH)	Ethiopia	2007	Lornah Kiplagat (NED)	Ethiopia

Volleyball

World volleyball championships for men were inaugurated in 1949. Women's competition began in 1952. These biennial championships are organized by the Fédération Internationale de Volleyball (FIVB; founded 1947). Indoor volleyball has been included in the Olympic Games since 1964 and beach volleyball since 1996.

FIVB Web site: <www.fivb.org>.

World Volleyball Championships

YEAR	MEN	WOMEN	YEAR	MEN	WOMEN
1949	USSR		1974	Poland	Japan
1952	USSR	USSR	1976[1]	Poland	Japan
1956	Czechoslovakia	USSR	1978	USSR	Cuba
1960	USSR	USSR	1980[1]	USSR	USSR
1962	USSR	Japan	1982	USSR	China
1964[1]	USSR	Japan	1984[1]	United States	China
1966	Czechoslovakia	Japan	1986	United States	China
1967	not held	Japan	1988[1]	United States	USSR
1968[1]	USSR	USSR	1990	Italy	USSR
1970	East Germany	USSR	1992[1]	Brazil	Cuba
1972[1]	Japan	USSR	1994	Italy	Cuba

World Volleyball Championships (continued)

1996[1]	The Netherlands	Cuba	2002	Brazil	Italy
1998	Italy	Cuba	2004[1]	Brazil	China
2000[1]	Yugoslavia	Cuba	2006	Brazil	Russia

[1]Olympic champions, considered world champions.

Weight Lifting

World weight lifting is overseen by the **International Weightlifting Federation** (IWF; founded 1905). The first **men's international weight lifting competition** was held in London in 1891; the sport was also included in the first modern Olympic Games, in Athens, in 1896. By the 1930s championship events consisted of the snatch, clean and jerk, and press (which was eliminated in 1972).

Women's world championships have been held since 1987, and women's competition was added to the Olympics in 2000. In 1998 the IWF established **new weight classes** (eight for men and seven for women) as well as a new world standard for each class in determining world records.

IWF Web site: <www.iwf.net>.

Weight Lifting World Records

Total weight for snatch and clean-and-jerk lifts. World standards were reset on 1 Jan 1998 and have not been achieved in some men's events.

men

WEIGHT CLASS	WINNER (NATIONALITY)	PERFORMANCE	DATE
56 kg (123 lb)	Halil Mutlu (TUR)	305 kg (672 lb)	16 Sep 2000
62 kg (137 lb)	world standard	325 kg (717 lb)	1 Jan 1998
69 kg (152 lb)	Galabin Boevski (BUL)	357 kg (787 lb)	24 Nov 1999
77 kg (170 lb)	Plamen Zhelyazkov (BUL)	377 kg (831 lb)	27 Mar 2002
85 kg (187 lb)	world standard	395 kg (871 lb)	1 Jan 1998
94 kg (207 lb)	world standard	417 kg (919 lb)	1 Jan 1998
105 kg (231.5 lb)	world standard	440 kg (970 lb)	1 Jan 1998
+105 kg (+231.5 lb)	Hossein Rezazadeh (IRI)	472 kg (1041 lb)	26 Sep 2000

women

WEIGHT CLASS	WINNER (NATIONALITY)	PERFORMANCE	DATE
48kg (106 lb)	Yang Lian (CHN)	217 kg (478 lb)	1 Oct 2006
53 kg (117 lb)	Qiu Hongxia (CHN)	226 kg (498 lb)	2 Oct 2006
58 kg (128 lb)	Chen Yanqing (CHN)	251 kg (553 lb)	3 Dec 2006
63 kg (139 lb)	Pawina Thongsuk (THA)	256 kg (564 lb)	12 Nov 2005
69 kg (152 lb)	Liu Chunhong (CHN)	275 kg (606 lb)	19 Aug 2004
75 kg (165 lb)	Svetlana Podobedova (RUS)	286 kg (631 lb)	2 Jun 2006
+75 kg (+165 lb)	Jang Mi-Ran (KOR)	318 kg (701 lb)	22 May 2006

World Weight Lifting Champions, 2006

Next competition scheduled to be held 14–26 Sep 2007 in Chiang Mai, Thailand.

men

WEIGHT CLASS	WINNER (NATIONALITY)	PERFORMANCE
56 kg (123 lb)	Li Zheng (CHN)	280 kg (617 lb)
62 kg (137 lb)	Qiu Le (CHN)	308 kg (679 lb)
69 kg (152 lb)	Vencelas Dabaya (FRA)	332 kg (732 lb)
77 kg (170 lb)	Taner Sagir (TUR)	361 kg (796 lb)
85 kg (187 lb)	Andrei Rybakou (BUL)	383 kg (844 lb)
94 kg (207 lb)	Ilya Ilin (KAZ)	392 kg (864 lb)
105 kg (231 lb)	Marcin Dolega (POL)	415 kg (915 lb)
105+ kg (231+ lb)	Hossein Rezazadeh (IRI)	448 kg (988 lb)

women

WEIGHT CLASS	WINNER (NATIONALITY)	PERFORMANCE
48 kg (106 lb)	Yang Lian (CHN)	217 kg (478 lb)
53 kg (117 lb)	Qiu Hongxia (CHN)	226 kg (498 lb)
58 kg (128 lb)	Qiu Hongmei (CHN)	237 kg (522 lb)
63 kg (139 lb)	Quyang Xiaofang (CHN)	246 kg (542 lb)
69 kg (152 lb)	Oxana Slivenko (RUS)	263 kg (580 lb)
75 kg (165 lb)	Cao Lei (CHN)	268 kg (591 lb)
75+ kg (165+ lb)	Jang Mi-ran (KOR)	314 kg (692 lb)

INDEX

Page numbers in **boldface** indicate main subject references; references in *italics* indicate illustrations. Photographs are on pages 481 to 496; flags of the world are on pages 497 to 502 and maps of the world are on pages 503 to 512.